TWENTIETH-CENTURY
AUTHOR BIOGRAPHIES
MASTER INDEX

The Gale Biographical Index Series

ISSN 0747-7279

Gale Biographical Index Series
Number 8

TWENTIETH-CENTURY AUTHOR BIOGRAPHIES MASTER INDEX

A consolidated index to
more than 170,000 biographical sketches
concerning modern day authors as they
appear in a selection of the principal
biographical dictionaries devoted to
authors, poets, journalists, and
other literary figures

FIRST EDITION

Edited by Barbara McNeil

Gale Research Company • Book Tower • Detroit, Michigan 48226

Editor: Barbara McNeil
Senior Assistant Editor: Elizabeth Mulligan
Assistant Editor: Amy L. Unterburger
Editorial Assistant: Molly L. Norris

Proofreaders: Marie Devlin, Toni Grow, Mary Jo Todd

Editorial Data Entry Supervisor: Doris D. Goulart
Editorial Data Entry Associate: Jean Portfolio
Senior Data Entry Assistants: Dorothy Cotter, Sue Lynch, Joyce M. Stone
Data Entry Assistants: Ann Bergeron, Pat Greenup, Mariette Legault, William Maher,
Terry Roland, Mildred Sherman, Patti Smith, Ann Stockham, AnnaMarie Woolard

External Production Supervisor: Carol Blanchard
Internal Production Supervisor: Laura Bryant
Senior Internal Production Assistant: Louise Gagne
Internal Production Assistants: Dorothy Kalleberg, Sandy Rock
Art Director: Art Chartow

Publisher: Frederick G. Ruffner
Executive Vice President/Editorial: James M. Ethridge
Editorial Director: Dedria Bryfonski
Director, Literature Division: Christine Nasso
Senior Editor, Biography and Genealogy Master Index: Adele Sarkissian

Library of Congress Cataloging in Publication Data

Main entry under title:

Twentieth-century author biographies master index.

(Gale biographical index series ; no. 8)
1. Authors--20th century--Biography--Indexes.
I. McNeil, Barbara. II. Title: 20th-century author
biographies master index. III. Series.
Z5304.A8T83   1984   809'.04   84-10349
ISBN 0-8103-2095-9
ISBN 0-8103-2096-7 (pbk.)

ISSN 0747-7279

Computerized photocomposition by Computer Composition Corporation
Madison Heights, Michigan

Contents

v

Introduction

Among the books most widely read today are those written by twentieth-century authors. Students from junior high school through college, teachers, librarians, and general readers in all walks of life study and enjoy the wealth of literature that modern writers have produced. And since the writing is inseparable from the writer, there is an equally keen and widespread interest in researching the lives of modern writers.

Twentieth-Century Author Biographies Master Index (TCABMI) is a new research tool that has been prepared especially for those many readers who have a particular interest in modern authors. Concise and easy to use, this index presents only the most pertinent and the most useful information in this special subject area. It provides quick and efficient access to more than 170,000 citations found in over 50 major sources of collective biography that deal with modern writers.

TCABMI is an outgrowth of the more comprehensive index, *Author Biographies Master Index (ABMI)*, which covers writers from all time periods. *TCABMI* aims in particular to make the most useful information on twentieth-century authors affordable for small libraries which may not require the extensive coverage of *ABMI*. Like *ABMI*, *TCABMI* is designed to make biographical research more fruitful and less tedious within its special time frame. *TCABMI* includes citations from *ABMI* (second edition) that pertain to twentieth-century authors. In addition, *TCABMI* includes 30,000 new citations that have been gathered since *ABMI* (second edition) was published in the fall of 1983.

Concept and Scope

As a specialized index, *TCABMI* enables the user to determine, without tedious searching, which edition (or editions) of which publication to consult for biographical information on a twentieth-century author. Almost as helpful, it also reveals if there is no listing for a given individual in the sources indexed. In cases where *TCABMI* shows multiple listings for the same person, the user is able either to choose which source is the most convenient or to locate multiple sketches to compare and expand information furnished by a single listing.

The books cited in *TCABMI* are widely held in most reference collections. While the works covered are of several distinct types (biographical dictionaries, encyclopedias, directories, collected criticisms) all have one common characteristic: each includes at least a moderate amount of biographical, critical, or career-related information on authors.

Sources indexed in *TCABMI* cover authors of many nationalities who write in a wide variety of genres. All the major English-speaking countries are represented, as well as Latin America, Japan, Russia, Spain, Italy, France, and other countries. Among the special subject areas included here are science fiction (*Twentieth-Century Science Fiction Writers*), children's literature (*Something about the Author, Twentieth-Century Children's Writers*), poetry (*Contemporary Poets*), drama (*Contemporary Dramatists*), as well as the western, romance, and mystery categories.

How to Read a Citation

Each citation gives the person's name followed by the years of birth and/or death as found in the source book. If a source has indicated that the dates may not be accurate, the questionable date(s) are followed by a question mark. If there is no year of birth, the death date is preceded by a lower case *d*. The codes for the books indexed follow the dates.

> **Tait,** Dorothy 1902?-1972 *ConAu 33R*
> **Di Grazia,** Thomas d1983 *SmATA 32*

Another feature of *TCABMI* is the portrait indicator. The abbreviation *[port]* indicates that the source cited has a picture of the person.

> **Abe,** Kobo 1924-   *ConLC 8, -22[port]*

A list of the works indexed in *TCABMI*, and the codes used to refer to them, is printed on the endsheets. Complete bibliographic citations to the titles indexed follow this introduction.

Editorial Practices

All names in an indexed work are included in *TCABMI*. This is a time-saver for the researcher as there is no need to consult the source work itself if the desired name is not found, since it is editorial policy to index every name in a particular book.

TCABMI follows standard alphabetizing rules used by the Library of Congress with the exception of those pertaining to *Mac*, *M'*, and *Mc*, which are filed in this work strictly letter by letter. Not all source books use this method of alphabetizing. Therefore, some names may have an alphabetic position in a source book different from their position in this index.

In general, names appear in *TCABMI* as they are listed in the sources indexed. In order to simplify listings, however, some slight editing of citations has been done. When the form of a name or the dates varied slightly among the sources, middle names (or initials), titles, and dates have been added when appropriate. If the spelling or dates for an individual differ substantially from publication to publication, or if there is any reason to believe that more than one person is referred to by the various spellings or dates, *TCABMI* citations have retained those discrepancies:

> **Williams,** Tennessee 1911-   *AuNews 2, CnDr 82, ConLC 5, etc.*
> **Williams,** Tennessee 1911?-1983 *ConAu 108, DcLB DS 4*
> **Williams,** Tennessee 1914?-   *AuNews 1, CnMD, CnMWL, ConAu 5R, etc.*

The above citations refer to the same person. However, since the purpose of *TCABMI* is to lead the user to biographical information in the sources indexed, not to be an authority file, the editor has made no attempt to standardize such entries. These variations can be of importance to anyone attempting to establish biographical details about a person.

In many publications, portions of a name not generally used by the individual are placed in parentheses, e.g.: Hawley, (Edmund) Blair. These parenthetical portions have been omitted except in those cases where the material in parentheses has been considered in alphabetizing by the source publication.

In a very few cases, extremely long names have been shortened because of typesetting limitations. For example: *Northcliffe, Alfred Charles William Harmsworth, Viscount* has been shortened to:

> **Northcliffe,** Alfred Harmsworth, Viscount

It is believed that such editing will not affect the usefulness of individual entries.

Research Aids

Researchers will need to look under all possible listings for a name, especially in the cases of:

1. Names with prefixes or suffixes:

> **DeLaMare,** Walter
> **LaMare,** Walter De
> **Mare,** Walter DeLa

2. Spanish names which may be entered in sources under either part of the surname:

> **Garcia Lorca,** Federico
> **Lorca,** Federico Garcia

3. Chinese names which may be entered in sources in direct or inverted order:

> **Hsun,** Lu
> **Lu Hsun**

Or which may be listed by the Pinyin spelling:

> **Hsiang,** Chung-Hua
> **Xiang,** Zhonghua

4. Names transliterated from non-Roman alphabets:

Yevtushenko, Evgeniy Alexandrovich
Yevtushenko, Yevgeny Alexandrovich

5. Pseudonyms, noms de plume, and stage names:

Christie, Agatha
Westmacott, Mary

Crosby, Bing
Crosby, Harry Lillis

6. Names which may be entered in the sources both under the author's full name and either initials or part of the name:

Eliot, T S
Eliot, Thomas Stearns

Welles, George Orson
Welles, Orson

All cross references appearing in indexed publications have been retained in *TCABMI*, but in the form of regular citations. For example, the entry in *The Writers Directory 1984-1986* reading "Morris, Julian. *See* West, Morris" appears in *TCABMI* as:

Morris, Julian *WrDr 84*

No additional cross references have been added to *TCABMI*.

Suggestions Are Welcome

Future editions of *TCABMI* are planned. Additional sources will be indexed as their availability and usefulness become known. The editor welcomes suggestions for additional works which could be indexed, or any other comments and suggestions.

Bibliographic Key to Publication Codes
for Use in Identifying Sources

Code	Book Indexed
ASpks	*The Author Speaks: Selected "PW" Interviews, 1967-1976.* By *Publishers Weekly* editors and contributors. New York and London: R.R. Bowker Co., 1977.
AuNews	*Authors in the News.* A compilation of news stories and feature articles from American newspapers and magazines covering writers and other members of the communications media. Two volumes. Edited by Barbara Nykoruk. Detroit: Gale Research Co., 1976.

AuNews 1   Volume 1
AuNews 2   Volume 2

Code	Book Indexed
ChlLR	*Children's Literature Review.* Excerpts from reviews, criticism, and commentary on books for children. Detroit: Gale Research Co., 1976-1984.

ChlLR 1   Volume 1, 1976
ChlLR 2   Volume 2, 1976
ChlLR 3   Volume 3, 1978
ChlLR 4   Volume 4, 1982
ChlLR 5   Volume 5, 1983
ChlLR 6   Volume 6, 1984

Code	Book Indexed
CIDMEL 80	*Columbia Dictionary of Modern European Literature.* Second edition. Edited by Jean-Albert Bede and William B. Edgerton. New York: Columbia University Press, 1980.
CnMD	*The Concise Encyclopedia of Modern Drama.* By Siegfried Melchinger. Translated by George Wellwarth. Edited by Henry Popkin. New York: Horizon Press, 1964.

Biographies begin on page 159. "Additional Entries," indicated in this index by the code *SUP*, begin on page 287.

Code	Book Indexed
CnMWL	*The Concise Encyclopedia of Modern World Literature.* Second edition. Edited by Geoffrey Grigson. London: Hutchinson & Co., Ltd., 1970.

Biographies begin on page 29.

Code	Book Indexed
ConAmA	*Contemporary American Authors: A Critical Survey and 219 Bio-Bibliographies.* By Fred B. Millett. New York: Harcourt, Brace & World, Inc., 1940. Reprint. New York: AMS Press, Inc., 1970.

Biographies begin on page 207.

Code	Book Indexed
ConAmTC	*Contemporary American Theater Critics: A Directory and Anthology of Their Works.* Compiled by M.E. Comtois and Lynn F. Miller. Metuchen, New Jersey and London: Scarecrow Press, Inc., 1977.

ConAu	*Contemporary Authors.* A bio-bibliographical guide to current writers in fiction, general nonfiction, poetry, journalism, drama, motion pictures, television, and other fields. Detroit: Gale Research Co., 1967-1984.

ConAu 1R	Volumes 1-4, 1st revision, 1967
ConAu 5R	Volumes 5-8, 1st revision, 1969
ConAu 9R	Volumes 9-12, 1st revision, 1974
ConAu 13R	Volumes 13-16, 1st revision, 1975
ConAu 17R	Volumes 17-20, 1st revision, 1976
ConAu 21R	Volumes 21-24, 1st revision, 1977
ConAu 25R	Volumes 25-28, 1st revision, 1977
ConAu 29R	Volumes 29-32, 1st revision, 1978
ConAu 33R	Volumes 33-36, 1st revision, 1978
ConAu 37R	Volumes 37-40, 1st revision, 1979
ConAu 41R	Volumes 41-44, 1st revision, 1979
ConAu 45	Volumes 45-48, 1974
ConAu 49	Volumes 49-52, 1975
ConAu 53	Volumes 53-56, 1975
ConAu 57	Volumes 57-60, 1976
ConAu 61	Volumes 61-64, 1976
ConAu 65	Volumes 65-68, 1977
ConAu 69	Volumes 69-72, 1978
ConAu 73	Volumes 73-76, 1978
ConAu 77	Volumes 77-80, 1979
ConAu 81	Volumes 81-84, 1979
ConAu 85	Volumes 85-88, 1980
ConAu 89	Volumes 89-92, 1980
ConAu 93	Volumes 93-96, 1980
ConAu 97	Volumes 97-100, 1981
ConAu 101	Volume 101, 1981
ConAu 102	Volume 102, 1981
ConAu 103	Volume 103, 1982
ConAu 104	Volume 104, 1982
ConAu 105	Volume 105, 1982
ConAu 106	Volume 106, 1982
ConAu 107	Volume 107, 1983
ConAu 108	Volume 108, 1983
ConAu 109	Volume 109, 1983
ConAu 110	Volume 110, 1984
ConAu X	This code refers to pseudonym entries which appear only as cross references in the cumulative index to *Contemporary Authors.*

ConAu NR	*Contemporary Authors, New Revision Series.* A bio-bibliographical guide to current writers in fiction, general nonfiction, poetry, journalism, drama, motion pictures, television, and other fields. Detroit: Gale Research Co., 1981-1984.

ConAu 1NR	Volume 1, 1981
ConAu 2NR	Volume 2, 1981
ConAu 3NR	Volume 3, 1981
ConAu 4NR	Volume 4, 1981
ConAu 5NR	Volume 5, 1982
ConAu 6NR	Volume 6, 1982
ConAu 7NR	Volume 7, 1982
ConAu 8NR	Volume 8, 1983
ConAu 9NR	Volume 9, 1983
ConAu 10NR	Volume 10, 1983
ConAu 11NR	Volume 11, 1984

ConAu P-   *Contemporary Authors, Permanent Series.* A bio-bibliographical guide to current authors and their works. Detroit: Gale Research Co., 1975-1978.

ConAu P-1	Volume 1, 1975
ConAu P-2	Volume 2, 1978

ConDr 82   *Contemporary Dramatists.* Third edition. Edited by James Vinson. New York: St. Martin's Press, 1982.

ConDr 82	"Contemporary Dramatists" begin on page 9
ConDr 82A	"Screen Writers" begin on page 887
ConDr 82B	"Radio Writers" begin on page 899
ConDr 82C	"Television Writers" begin on page 911
ConDr 82D	"Musical Librettists" begin on page 921
ConDr 82E	Appendix begins on page 951

ConIsC   *Contemporary Issues Criticism.* Excerpts from criticism of contemporary writings in sociology, economics, politics, psychology, anthropology, education, history, law, theology, and related fields. Detroit: Gale Research Co., 1982-1984.

ConIsC 1	Volume 1, edited by Dedria Bryfonski, 1982
ConIsC 2	Volume 2, edited by Robert L. Brubaker, 1984

ConLC   *Contemporary Literary Criticism.* Excerpts from criticism of the works of today's novelists, poets, playwrights, short story writers, filmmakers, scriptwriters, and other creative writers. Detroit: Gale Research Co., 1973-1984.

ConLC 1	Volume 1, 1973
ConLC 2	Volume 2, 1974
ConLC 3	Volume 3, 1975
ConLC 4	Volume 4, 1975
ConLC 5	Volume 5, 1976
ConLC 6	Volume 6, 1976
ConLC 7	Volume 7, 1977
ConLC 8	Volume 8, 1978
ConLC 9	Volume 9, 1978
ConLC 10	Volume 10, 1979
ConLC 11	Volume 11, 1979
ConLC 12	Volume 12, 1980
ConLC 13	Volume 13, 1980
ConLC 14	Volume 14, 1980
ConLC 15	Volume 15, 1980
ConLC 16	Volume 16, 1981
ConLC 17	Volume 17, 1981
ConLC 18	Volume 18, 1981
ConLC 19	Volume 19, 1981
ConLC 20	Volume 20, 1982
ConLC 21	Volume 21, 1982
ConLC 22	Volume 22, 1982
ConLC 23	Volume 23, 1983
ConLC 24	Volume 24, 1983
ConLC 25	Volume 25, 1983
ConLC 26	Volume 26, 1983
ConLC 27	Volume 27, 1984

ConLCrt 82   *Contemporary Literary Critics.* Second edition. By Elmer Borklund. Detroit: Gale Research Co., 1982.

ConNov 82   *Contemporary Novelists.* Third edition. Edited by James Vinson. New York: St. Martin's Press, 1982.

Deceased novelists are listed in the Appendix, indicated in this index by the code *A*, beginning on page 727.

ConP 80	*Contemporary Poets.* Third edition. Edited by James Vinson. New York: St. Martin's Press, 1980.

Deceased poets are listed in the Appendix, indicated in this index by the code *A*, beginning on page 1723.

ConSFA	*Contemporary Science Fiction Authors.* First edition. Compiled and edited by R. Reginald. New York: Arno Press, 1975. Previously published as *Stella Nova: The Contemporary Science Fiction Authors.* Los Angeles: Unicorn & Son, Publishers, 1970.

Conv	*Conversations.* Conversations series. Detroit: Gale Research Co., 1977-1978.

	Conv 1	Volume 1: *Conversations with Writers*, 1977
	Conv 3	Volume 3: *Conversations with Writers II*, 1978

CreCan	*Creative Canada: A Biographical Dictionary of Twentieth-Century Creative and Performing Artists.* Compiled by the Reference Division, McPherson Library, University of Victoria, British Columbia. Toronto: University of Toronto Press, 1971, 1972.

	CreCan 1	Volume 1, 1971
	CreCan 2	Volume 2, 1972

CroCAP	*Crowell's Handbook of Contemporary American Poetry.* By Karl Malkoff. New York: Thomas Y. Crowell Co., 1973.

Biographies begin on page 43.

CroCD	*Crowell's Handbook of Contemporary Drama.* By Michael Anderson, et al. New York: Thomas Y. Crowell Co., 1971.

DcLB	*Dictionary of Literary Biography.* Detroit: Gale Research Co., 1978-1984.

	DcLB 2	Volume 2: *American Novelists since World War II.* Edited by Jeffrey Helterman and Richard Layman, 1978.
	DcLB 4	Volume 4: *American Writers in Paris, 1920-1939.* Edited by Karen Lane Rood, 1980.
	DcLB 5	Volume 5: *American Poets since World War II.* Two volumes. Edited by Donald J. Greiner, 1980.
	DcLB 6	Volume 6: *American Novelists since World War II.* Second series. Edited by James E. Kibler, Jr., 1980.
	DcLB 7	Volume 7: *Twentieth-Century American Dramatists.* Two volumes. Edited by John MacNicholas, 1981.
	DcLB 8	Volume 8: *Twentieth-Century American Science-Fiction Writers.* Two volumes. Edited by David Cowart and Thomas L. Wymer, 1981.
	DcLB 9	Volume 9: *American Novelists, 1910-1945.* Three volumes. Edited by James J. Martine, 1981.
	DcLB 10	Volume 10: *Modern British Dramatists, 1900-1945.* Two volumes. Edited by Stanley Weintraub, 1982.
	DcLB 13	Volume 13: *British Dramatists since World War II.* Two volumes. Edited by Stanley Weintraub, 1982.
	DcLB 14	Volume 14: *British Novelists since 1960.* Two volumes. Edited by Jay L. Halio, 1983.

DcLB 15	Volume 15: *British Novelists, 1930-1959.* Two volumes. Edited by Bernard Oldsey, 1983.
DcLB 16	Volume 16: *The Beats: Literary Bohemians in Postwar America.* Two volumes. Edited by Ann Charters, 1983.
DcLB 17	Volume 17: *Twentieth-Century American Historians.* Edited by Clyde N. Wilson, 1983.
DcLB 22	Volume 22: *American Writers for Children, 1900-1960.* Edited by John Cech, 1983.
DcLB 25	Volume 25: *American Newspaper Journalists, 1901-1925.* Edited by Perry J. Ashley, 1984.
DcLB 26	Volume 26: *American Screenwriters.* Edited by Robert E. Morsberger, Stephen O. Lesser, and Randall Clark, 1984.

Volumes in the *Dictionary of Literary Biography* series which do not cover twentieth-century authors have not been included in *TCABMI.*

DcLB DS — *Dictionary of Literary Biography Documentary Series: An Illustrated Chronicle.* Detroit, Gale Research Co., 1982-1984.

DcLB DS1	Volume 1, edited by Margaret A. Van Antwerp, 1982
DcLB DS2	Volume 2, edited by Margaret A. Van Antwerp, 1982
DcLB DS3	Volume 3, edited by Mary Bruccoli, 1983
DcLB DS4	Volume 4, edited by Margaret A. Van Antwerp and Sally Johns, 1984

DcLB Y — *Dictionary of Literary Biography Yearbook.* Detroit: Gale Research Co., 1981-1984.

DcLB Y80A	Yearbook: 1980. Edited by Karen L. Rood, Jean W. Ross, and Richard Ziegfeld. "Updated Entries" begin on page 3
DcLB Y80B	Yearbook: 1980. "New Entries" begin on page 127
DcLB Y81A	Yearbook: 1981. Edited by Karen L. Rood, Jean W. Ross, and Richard Ziegfeld. "Updated Entries" begin on page 21
DcLB Y81B	Yearbook: 1981. "New Entries" begin on page 139
DcLB Y82A	Yearbook: 1982. Edited by Richard Ziegfeld. "Updated Entries" begin on page 121
DcLB Y82B	Yearbook: 1982. "New Entries" begin on page 203
DcLB Y83A	Yearbook: 1983. Edited by Mary Bruccoli and Jean W. Ross. "Updated Entries" begin on page 155
DcLB Y83B	Yearbook: 1983. "New Entries" begin on page 175
DcLB Y83N	Yearbook: 1983. "Obituaries" begin on page 103

DcLEL 1940 — *A Dictionary of Literature in the English Language from 1940 to 1970.* Compiled and edited by Robin Myers. Oxford and New York: Pergamon Press, 1978.

DrAP&F 83   *A Directory of American Poets and Fiction Writers.* Names and addresses of 5,533 contemporary poets and fiction writers whose work has been published in the United States. 1983-84 edition. New York: Poets & Writers, Inc. 1983.

    Use the Index to locate listings.

DrmM   *Dream Makers: The Uncommon People Who Write Science Fiction.* By Charles Platt. New York: Berkley Books, 1980.

EncWL 2   *Encyclopedia of World Literature in the 20th Century.* Revised edition. Volume 1: A to D, Volume 2: E to K. Edited by Leonard S. Klein. New York: Frederick Ungar Publishing Co., 1981, 1982.

    Volumes 3 and 4 forthcoming.

FifWWr   *Fifty Western Writers: A Bio-Bibliographical Sourcebook.* Edited by Fred Erisman and Richard W. Etulain. Westport, Connecticut and London: Greenwood Press, 1982.

IntAu&W 82   *The International Authors and Writers Who's Who.* Ninth edition. Edited by Adrian Gaster. Cambridge, England: International Biographical Centre, 1982. Distributed by Gale Research Co., Detroit, Michigan. 1982 edition is combined with *International Who's Who in Poetry* (see below).

IntAu&W 82	Biographical Section
IntAu&W 82X	"Pseudonyms of Included Authors" begin on page 719

IntWWP 82   *International Who's Who in Poetry.* Sixth edition. Edited by Ernest Kay. Cambridge, England: International Biographical Centre, 1982. Distributed by Gale Research Co., Detroit, Michigan. 1982 edition is combined with *International Authors and Writers Who's Who* (see above).

IntWWP 82	Biographical Section begins on page 759
IntWWP 82X	"Pseudonyms of Included Poets" begin on page 1035

LivgBAA   *Living Black American Authors: A Biographical Directory.* By Ann Allen Shockley and Sue P. Chandler. New York and London: R.R. Bowker Co., 1973.

LongCTC   *Longman Companion to Twentieth Century Literature.* By A.C. Ward. London: Longman Group Ltd., 1970.

MichAu 80   *Michigan Authors.* Second edition. By the Michigan Association for Media in Education. Ann Arbor: Michigan Association for Media in Education, 1980.

    The Addendum, indicated in this index by the code *A*, begins on page 339.

ModAL   *Modern American Literature.* Fourth enlarged edition. Four volumes. Compiled and edited by Dorothy Nyren Curley, Maurice Kramer, and Elaine Fialka Kramer. A Library of Literary Criticism. New York: Frederick Ungar Publishing Co., 1969, 1976.

ModAL	Volumes 1-3, 1969
ModAL SUP	Volume 4, Supplement, 1976

ModBlW   *Modern Black Writers.* Compiled and edited by Michael Popkin. A Library of Literary Criticism. New York: Frederick Ungar Publishing Co., 1978.

ModBrL   *Modern British Literature*. Four volumes. A Library of Literary Criticism. New York: Frederick Ungar Publishing Co., 1966, 1975.

ModBrL	Volumes I-III, compiled and edited by Ruth Z. Temple and Martin Tucker, 1966
ModBrL SUP	Volume IV, Supplement, compiled and edited by Martin Tucker and Rita Stein, 1975

ModCmwL   *Modern Commonwealth Literature*. Compiled and edited by John H. Ferres and Martin Tucker. A Library of Literary Criticism. New York: Frederick Ungar Publishing Co., 1977.

ModFrL   *Modern French Literature*. Two volumes. Compiled and edited by Debra Popkin and Michael Popkin. A Library of Literary Criticism. New York: Frederick Ungar Publishing Co., 1977.

ModGL   *Modern German Literature*. Two volumes. Compiled and edited by Agnes Korner Domandi. A Library of Literary Criticism. New York: Frederick Ungar Publishing Co., 1972.

ModLAL   *Modern Latin American Literature*. Two volumes. Compiled and edited by David William Foster and Virginia Ramos Foster. A Library of Literary Criticism. New York: Frederick Ungar Publishing Co., 1975.

ModRL   *Modern Romance Literatures*. Compiled and edited by Dorothy Nyren Curley and Arthur Curley. A Library of Literary Criticism. New York: Frederick Ungar Publishing Co., 1967.

ModSL   *Modern Slavic Literatures*. Two volumes. A Library of Literary Criticism. New York: Frederick Ungar Publishing Co., 1972, 1976.

ModSL 1	Volume I: Russian Literature, compiled and edited by Vasa D. Mihailovich, 1972
ModSL 2	Volume II: Bulgarian, Czechoslovak, Polish, Ukrainian and Yugoslav Literatures, compiled and edited by Vasa D. Mihailovich, et al., 1976

Use the alphabetic listing of authors at the beginning of each volume to locate biographies.

ModWD   *Modern World Drama: An Encyclopedia*. By Myron Matlaw. New York: E.P. Dutton & Co., Inc., 1972.

NatPD 81   *National Playwrights Directory*. Second edition. Edited by Phyllis Johnson Kaye. Waterford, Connecticut: The O'Neill Theater Center, 1981. Distributed by Gale Research Co., Detroit, Michigan.

RGFMBP   *A Reader's Guide to Fifty Modern British Poets*. By Michael Schmidt. London: Heinemann Educational Books Ltd.; New York: Barnes & Noble, 1979.

SmATA   *Something about the Author*. Facts and pictures about authors and illustrators of books for young people. Edited by Anne Commire. Detroit: Gale Research Co., 1971-1984.

SmATA 1	Volume 1, 1971
SmATA 2	Volume 2, 1971
SmATA 3	Volume 3, 1972
SmATA 4	Volume 4, 1973
SmATA 5	Volume 5, 1973

SmATA 6	Volume 6, 1974
SmATA 7	Volume 7, 1975
SmATA 8	Volume 8, 1976
SmATA 9	Volume 9, 1976
SmATA 10	Volume 10, 1976
SmATA 11	Volume 11, 1977
SmATA 12	Volume 12, 1977
SmATA 13	Volume 13, 1978
SmATA 14	Volume 14, 1978
SmATA 15	Volume 15, 1979
SmATA 16	Volume 16, 1979
SmATA 17	Volume 17, 1979
SmATA 18	Volume 18, 1980
SmATA 19	Volume 19, 1980
SmATA 20	Volume 20, 1980
SmATA 20N	Volume 20, Obituary Notices
SmATA 21	Volume 21, 1980
SmATA 21N	Volume 21, Obituary Notices
SmATA 22	Volume 22, 1981
SmATA 22N	Volume 22, Obituary Notices
SmATA 23	Volume 23, 1981
SmATA 23N	Volume 23, Obituary Notices
SmATA 24	Volume 24, 1981
SmATA 24N	Volume 24, Obituary Notices
SmATA 25	Volume 25, 1981
SmATA 25N	Volume 25, Obituary Notices
SmATA 26	Volume 26, 1982
SmATA 26N	Volume 26, Obituary Notices
SmATA 27	Volume 27, 1982
SmATA 27N	Volume 27, Obituary Notices
SmATA 28	Volume 28, 1982
SmATA 28N	Volume 28, Obituary Notices
SmATA 29	Volume 29, 1982
SmATA 29N	Volume 29, Obituary Notices
SmATA 30	Volume 30, 1983
SmATA 30N	Volume 30, Obituary Notices
SmATA 31	Volume 31, 1983
SmATA 31N	Volume 31, Obituary Notices
SmATA 32	Volume 32, 1983
SmATA 32N	Volume 32, Obituary Notices
SmATA 33	Volume 33, 1983
SmATA 33N	Volume 33, Obituary Notices
SmATA 34	Volume 34, 1984
SmATA 34N	Volume 34, Obituary Notices
SmATA X	This code refers to pseudonym entries which appear only as cross references in the cumulative index to *Something about the Author.*

TwCA   *Twentieth Century Authors: A Biographical Dictionary of Modern Literature.* New York: H.W. Wilson Co., 1942, 1955.

TwCA	Original volume, edited by Stanley J. Kunitz and Howard Haycraft, 1942
TwCA SUP	First Supplement, edited by Stanley J. Kunitz, 1955

TwCCW 83   *Twentieth-Century Children's Writers.* Edited by D.L. Kirkpatrick. New York: St. Martin's Press, 1983.

TwCCr&M 80   *Twentieth-Century Crime and Mystery Writers.* Edited by John M. Reilly. New York: St. Martin's Press, 1980.

TwCLC	*Twentieth-Century Literary Criticism.* Excerpts from criticism of the works of novelists, poets, playwrights, short story writers, and other creative writers who died between 1900 and 1960, from the first published critical appraisals to current evaluations. Detroit: Gale Research Co., 1978-1984.

TwCLC 1	Volume 1, 1978
TwCLC 2	Volume 2, 1979
TwCLC 3	Volume 3, 1980
TwCLC 4	Volume 4, 1981
TwCLC 5	Volume 5, 1981
TwCLC 6	Volume 6, 1982
TwCLC 7	Volume 7, 1982
TwCLC 8	Volume 8, 1982
TwCLC 9	Volume 9, 1983
TwCLC 10	Volume 10, 1983
TwCLC 11	Volume 11, 1983
TwCLC 12	Volume 12, 1984

TwCRGW	*Twentieth-Century Romance and Gothic Writers.* Edited by James Vinson. Detroit: Gale Research Co., 1982.

TwCSFW	*Twentieth-Century Science-Fiction Writers.* Edited by Curtis C. Smith. New York: St. Martin's Press, 1981.

TwCSFW	"Twentieth-Century Science-Fiction Writers" begin on page 9
TwCSFW A	"Foreign-Language Writers" begin on page 613
TwCSFW B	"Major Fantasy Writers" begin on page 631

TwCWW	*Twentieth-Century Western Writers.* Edited by James Vinson. Detroit: Gale Research Co., 1982.

TwCWr	*Twentieth Century Writing: A Reader's Guide to Contemporary Literature.* Edited by Kenneth Richardson. Levittown, New York: Transatlantic Arts, Inc., 1971.

WhoTwCL	*Who's Who in Twentieth Century Literature.* By Martin Seymour-Smith. New York: Holt, Rinehart & Winston, 1976.

WorAu	*World Authors.* A volume in the Wilson Authors Series. Edited by John Wakeman. New York: H.W. Wilson Co., 1975, 1980.

WorAu	1950-1970, 1975
WorAu 1970	1970-1975, 1980

WrDr 84	*The Writers Directory 1984-1986.* Chicago: St. James Press, 1983. Distributed by Gale Research Co., Detroit, Michigan.

A

A, F P *ConAmA*
A, Roberto Vargas *DrAP&F 83*
A A *ConAu X, LongCTC*
A Fighter Pilot 1913-1967 *ConAu X*
A M *ConAu X, –49, IntAu&W 82X*
A Riposte *TwCA, TwCA SUP*
A Z *IntWWP 82X*
Aagaard, Bent 1924- *IntAu&W 82*
Aaker, David A 1938- *ConAu 49*
Aakjaer, Jeppe 1866-1930 *ClDMEL 80*
Aal, Katharyn Machan *DrAP&F 83*
Aalben, Patrick *ConAu X*
Aali, Jamiluddin 1926- *IntAu&W 82, IntWWP 82*
Aallyn, Alysse *ConAu X*
Aalto, Alvar 1898-1976 *ConAu 65*
Aaltonen, Annikki 1911- *IntAu&W 82*
Aanrud, Hans 1863-1953 *ClDMEL 80*
Aardema, Verna 1911- *ConAu X, MichAu 80, SmATA 4, WrDr 84*
Aaron, Benjamin 1915- *ConAu 21R*
Aaron, Chester 1923- *ConAu 8NR, –21R, SmATA 9, TwCCW 83*
Aaron, Daniel 1912- *ConAu 7NR, –13R, DcLEL 1940*
Aaron, Hank *ConAu X*
Aaron, Henry Louis 1934- *ConAu 104*
Aaron, Howard *DrAP&F 83*
Aaron, James E 1927- *WrDr 84*
Aaron, James Ethridge 1927- *ConAu 21R*
Aaron, Jonathan *DrAP&F 83*
Aaronovitch, Sam 1919- *ConAu 13R, WrDr 84*
Aarons, Edward S 1916-1975 *ConAu 57, –93, TwCCr&M 80*
Aarons, Slim 1916- *ConAu 106, WrDr 84*
Aaronson, Bernard S 1924- *ConAu 29R*
Aarsleff, Hans 1925- *ConAu 21R*
Aaseng, Nate *ConAu X*
Aaseng, Nathan 1953- *ConAu 106*
Aaseng, Rolf E 1923- *ConAu 49*
Aba/Eclair *IntAu&W 82X*
Abadinsky, Howard 1941- *ConAu 110*
Abajian, James DeTar 1914- *ConAu 65*
Abarbanel, Karin 1950- *ConAu 65*
Abarbanel, Sam X 1914- *ConAu 106*
Abbagnano, Nicola 1901- *ConAu 33R*
Abbas, Ahmad 1914- *ConNov 82, DcLEL 1940, WrDr 84*
Abbas, Khwaja Ahmad 1914- *ConAu 57*
Abbasi, Najam *IntAu&W 82X*
Abbasi, Najmuddin 1927- *IntAu&W 82*
Abbasi, Tanveer 1934- *IntWWP 82*
Abbazia, Patrick 1937- *ConAu 57*
Abbe, Elfriede 1919- *ConAu 13R*
Abbe, George 1911- *ConAu 10NR, –25R*
Abbensetts, Michael 1938- *ConAu 104, ConDr 82, WrDr 84*
Abbett, Robert W 1902- *WrDr 84*
Abbey, Edward *DrAP&F 83*
Abbey, Edward 1927- *ConAu 2NR, –45, FifWWr, TwCWW, WrDr 84*
Abbey, Kieran *TwCCr&M 80*
Abbey, Lloyd Robert 1943- *ConAu 104*
Abbey, Margaret *ConAu X*

Abbey, Merrill R 1905- *ConAu 1R, –3NR, WrDr 84*
Abbington, John *ConAu X*
Abbot, Anthony *ConAu X*
Abbot, Charles Greeley 1872-1973 *ConAu 45, –77*
Abbot, Stephen Eugene 1943- *IntWWP 82*
Abbot, W W 1922- *ConAu 110*
Abbott, Alice *ConAu X, MichAu 80, SmATA X, TwCRGW*
Abbott, Anthony 1893-1952 *TwCCr&M 80*
Abbott, Anthony S 1935- *ConAu 17R*
Abbott, Berenice 1898- *ConAu 106*
Abbott, Carl 1944- *ConAu 11NR, –65*
Abbott, Caroline *LongCTC*
Abbott, Claude Colleer 1889-1971 *ConAu 5R, –89*
Abbott, Eleanor Hallowell 1872-1958 *TwCA, TwCA SUP*
Abbott, Eric Symes 1906-1983 *ConAu 110*
Abbott, Freeland K 1919-1971 *ConAu P-2*
Abbott, George 1887- *ConAu 93, ConDr 82, ModWD, WrDr 84*
Abbott, George 1889- *CnMD*
Abbott, Gertrude Webster 1897- *IntWWP 82*
Abbott, H Porter 1940- *ConAu 45*
Abbott, Jack Henry *ConAu X*
Abbott, Jack Henry 1944- *ConIsC 2[port]*
Abbott, Jacob 1803-1879 *SmATA 22[port]*
Abbott, James H 1924- *ConAu 77*
Abbott, Jerry 1938- *ConAu 45*
Abbott, John J 1930- *ConAu 17R*
Abbott, John Patrick 1930- *WrDr 84*
Abbott, Keith *DrAP&F 83*
Abbott, Lee K, Jr. *DrAP&F 83*
Abbott, Lyman 1835-1922 *TwCA, TwCA SUP*
Abbott, Manager Henry *ConAu X*
Abbott, Margaret Evans 1896-1976 *ConAu 110, MichAu 80*
Abbott, Martin 1922- *WrDr 84*
Abbott, Martin 1922-1977 *ConAu 33R*
Abbott, Mason 1920- *IntWWP 82*
Abbott, May Laura 1916- *ConAu 9R, WrDr 84*
Abbott, O Lawrence 1900- *MichAu 80*
Abbott, Philip R 1944- *ConAu 106*
Abbott, R Tucker 1919- *ConAu 4NR, WrDr 84*
Abbott, Raymond H *DrAP&F 83*
Abbott, Raymond H 1942- *ConAu 57*
Abbott, Richard H 1936- *ConAu 33R*
Abbott, Robert Tucker 1919- *ConAu 9R*
Abbott, Rowland Aubrey Samuel 1909- *ConAu 53*
Abbott, Rufus Henry 1944- *ConAu 107*
Abbott, Sidney 1937- *ConAu 41R*
Abbott, Stephen *DrAP&F 83*
Abbott, Steve *IntWWP 82X*
Abbott, Walter M 1923- *ConAu 9R*
Abbott, Ward *DrAP&F 83*
Abbott, William H *DrAP&F 83*
Abbotts, John 1947- *ConAu 73*
Abboushi, W F 1931- *ConAu 29R*
Abbs, Peter Francis 1942- *ConAu 93, IntWWP 82*
Abcarian, Richard 1929- *ConAu 33R*
Abdallah, Omar *ConAu 49*

Abdel-Malek, Anouar 1924- *ConAu 29R, IntAu&W 82*
Abdelsamad, Moustafa H 1941- *ConAu 53*
Abdul, Raoul 1929- *ConAu 29R, SmATA 12*
Abdul-Rauf, Muhammad 1917- *ConAu 101*
Abdullah, Achmed 1881-1945 *TwCA, TwCA SUP*
Abdullahi, Guda Abdulhamid 1946- *ConAu 93, IntAu&W 82*
Abe, Kobo 1924- *ConAu 65, ConLC 8, –22[port], EncWL 2, TwCSFW A, WorAu*
Abeel, Erica 1937- *ConAu 109*
Abel, Alan 1928- *ConAu 17R*
Abel, Bob *ConAu X*
Abel, Bob 1931-1981 *ConAu X*
Abel, Elie 1920- *ConAu 8NR, –61*
Abel, Ernest Lawrence 1943- *ConAu 41R, IntAu&W 82*
Abel, I W 1908- *ConAu 105*
Abel, Jeanne 1937- *ConAu 17R*
Abel, Lionel 1910- *CnMD, ConAu 61, ModWD, WorAu*
Abel, R Cox *ConSFA*
Abel, Raymond 1911- *SmATA 12*
Abel, Reuben 1911- *ConAu 37R, WrDr 84*
Abel, Robert 1931-1981 *ConAu 105, –11NR*
Abel, Robert H *DrAP&F 83*
Abel, Robert H 1941- *ConAu 102*
Abel, Theodora M 1899- *ConAu 57*
Abel, Theodore 1896- *ConAu 21R*
Abel-Smith, Brian 1926- *ConAu 9NR, –21R, WrDr 84*
Abela, Joseph M 1931- *IntWWP 82*
Abeles, Elvin 1907- *ConAu 104*
Abell, Carol Louise 1940- *IntWWP 82*
Abell, George O 1927- *ConAu 3NR, –9R, WrDr 84*
Abell, Kathleen 1938- *ConAu 49, SmATA 9*
Abell, Kjeld 1901-1961 *ClDMEL 80, CnMD, ConLC 15, EncWL 2, ModWD, WorAu 1970*
Abella, Alex 1950- *ConAu 93*
Abella, Irving Martin 1940- *ConAu 49*
Abella, Rafael 1917- *IntAu&W 82*
Abellan, Jose Luis 1933- *IntAu&W 82*
Abels, Joel M 1926- *ConAmTC*
Abels, Jules 1913- *ConAu 61*
Abelson, Philip Hauge 1913- *ConAu 107*
Abelson, Raziel 1921- *WrDr 84*
Abelson, Raziel A 1921- *ConAu 6NR, –9R*
Abelson, Robert P 1928- *ConAu 41R*
Abend, Norman A 1931- *ConAu 33R*
Aber, William M 1929- *ConAu 57*
Aberbach, Joel D 1940- *ConAu 45*
Abercrombie, Barbara 1939- *ConAu 81, SmATA 16*
Abercrombie, Lascelles 1881-1938 *LongCTC, ModBrL, TwCA, TwCA SUP, TwCWr*
Abercrombie, Nigel James 1908- *ConAu 101, IntAu&W 82, WrDr 84*
Abercrombie, Sir Patrick 1879-1957 *LongCTC*
Abercrombie, Virginia T *DrAP&F 83*
Aberg, Sherrill E 1924- *ConAu 21R*
Aberle, David F 1918- *ConAu 21R*

Adamczewski, Zygmunt 1921- *ConAu 13R*
Adamec, Ludwig W 1924- *ConAu 9NR, –21R, IntAu&W 82, WrDr 84*
Adamic, Alojzij 1899?-1951 *ConAu 109*
Adamic, Louis *ConAu X*
Adamic, Louis 1898-1951 *DcLB 9[port]*
Adamic, Louis 1899-1951 *ConAmA, TwCA, TwCA SUP*
Adamo, Ralph *DrAP&F 83*
Adamov, Arthur 1908-1970 *CIDMEL 80, ConAu 25R, ConAu P-2, ConLC 4, –25[port], CroCD, EncWL 2, ModFrL, ModRL, ModWD, WorAu*
Adamovich, Georgy Viktorovich 1894-1972 *CIDMEL 80*
Adams, A Don *ConAu X*
Adams, A John 1931- *ConAu 33R*
Adams, Adrienne 1906- *ConAu 1NR, –49, SmATA 8*
Adams, Alice *DrAP&F 83*
Adams, Alice 1926- *ConAu 81, ConLC 6, –13, WrDr 84*
Adams, Andy *ConAu X*
Adams, Andy 1859-1935 *FifWWr, TwCWW*
Adams, Angela *MichAu 80*
Adams, Anna *DrAP&F 83, IntWWP 82X*
Adams, Anna Theresa 1926- *IntWWP 82*
Adams, Anne H 1935- *ConAu 41R*
Adams, Annette *ConAu X*
Adams, Ansel 1902- *AuNews 1, ConAu 10NR, –21R, WrDr 84*
Adams, Arthur E 1917- *ConAu 4NR, –5R*
Adams, Arthur Gray 1935- *ConAu 107*
Adams, Arthur Henry 1872-1936 *TwCWr*
Adams, Arthur Merrihew 1908- *ConAu 53*
Adams, Arthur Stanton 1896-1980 *ConAu 102*
Adams, B B *IntWWP 82X*
Adams, Barbara *DrAP&F 83*
Adams, Barbara 1932- *IntWWP 82*
Adams, Bart *ConAu X, TwCWW*
Adams, Betsy *DrAP&F 83*
Adams, Betsy 1942- *ConAu X, MichAu 80*
Adams, Carmen 1915- *IntWWP 82*
Adams, Cedric M 1902-1961 *ConAu 89*
Adams, Charles J 1924- *ConAu 8NR, –17R*
Adams, Charlotte 1899- *ConAu 107*
Adams, Christopher *ConAu X*
Adams, Chuck *ConAu X, WrDr 84*
Adams, Cindy *ConAu 21R*
Adams, Cleve F 1895-1949 *TwCCr&M 80*
Adams, Clifton 1919- *ConAu 13R, TwCWW, WrDr 84*
Adams, Clinton 1918- *ConAu 33R*
Adams, Dale *SmATA X*
Adams, David Charles 1928- *CreCan 1*
Adams, Don 1925- *ConAu 33R, WrDr 84*
Adams, Douglas 1952- *ConLC 27[port], DcLB Y83B[port], WrDr 84*
Adams, Douglas Noel 1952- *ConAu 106, ConDr 82B*
Adams, E M 1919- *ConAu 1R*
Adams, Edith *ConAu X*
Adams, Elsie B 1932- *ConAu 69*
Adams, Ernest 1920- *CreCan 2*
Adams, Ernest Charles 1926- *WrDr 84*
Adams, Florence 1932- *ConAu 49*
Adams, Francis Alexandre 1874-1975 *ConAu 61*
Adams, Frank C 1916- *ConAu 69*
Adams, Frank R 1883-1963 *ConAu 5R*
Adams, Franklin Pierce 1881-1960 *ConAmA, ConAu 93, TwCA SUP*
Adams, Frederick C 1941- *ConAu 105*
Adams, George Matthew 1878-1962 *ConAu 93*
Adams, George Worthington 1905- *ConAu 41R*
Adams, Georgia Sachs 1913- *ConAu 37R*
Adams, Glenda *DrAP&F 83*
Adams, Glenda 1939- *ConAu 104*
Adams, Grace Marie 1926- *WrDr 84*
Adams, Graham, Jr. 1928- *ConAu 17R*
Adams, Harlen Martin 1904- *ConAu P-1, WrDr 84*
Adams, Harriet S *AuNews 2, ConAu 17R, SmATA 1*
Adams, Harriet S 1893?-1982 *SmATA 29N*
Adams, Harriet S 1894-1982 *ConAu 106*
Adams, Harrison *ConAu X*
Adams, Harry Baker 1924- *ConAu 106*
Adams, Hazard 1926- *ConAu 9R, SmATA 6, WrDr 84*
Adams, Henry 1838-1918 *ConAu 104, EncWL 2, TwCLC 4[port]*
Adams, Henry Brooks 1838-1918 *LongCTC,*

ModAL, ModAL SUP, TwCWr, WhoTwCL
Adams, Henry H 1917- *ConAu 21R, MichAu 80*
Adams, Henry Mason 1907- *ConAu P-1*
Adams, Henry T *ConAu X*
Adams, Herbert Mayow 1893- *ConAu P-2*
Adams, Howard 1928- *ConAu 89, IntAu&W 82*
Adams, J Donald 1891-1968 *ConAu 1R, –1NR*
Adams, J Mack 1933- *ConAu 85*
Adams, James E 1941- *ConAu 73*
Adams, James F 1927- *ConAu 17R, WrDr 84*
Adams, James Luther 1901- *ConAu 41R*
Adams, James R 1934- *ConAu 41R*
Adams, James Truslow 1878-1949 *ConAmA, DcLB 17[port], TwCA, TwCA SUP*
Adams, Jay Edward 1929- *ConAu 108*
Adams, Jean Coulthard *CreCan 1*
Adams, Jeanette V *DrAP&F 83*
Adams, Joey 1911- *ConAu 1NR, –49*
Adams, John *ConSFA*
Adams, John Clarke 1910- *ConAu 1R*
Adams, John Cranford 1903-1952 *TwCA SUP*
Adams, John F 1930- *ConAu 33R*
Adams, John M 1905-1981 *ConAu 107*
Adams, John Paul *ConAu X*
Adams, John R 1900- *ConAu 25R*
Adams, Judith *IntAu&W 82X*
Adams, Julia Hubbard 1892-1975 *MichAu 80*
Adams, Julian 1919- *ConAu 11NR, –25R*
Adams, Julian 1920- *WrDr 84*
Adams, Justin *ConAu X, WrDr 84*
Adams, Kenneth Menzies 1922- *ConAu 103, WrDr 84*
Adams, Kramer A 1920- *ConAu 9R*
Adams, L Jerold 1939- *ConAu 49*
Adams, Laura 1943- *ConAu 53*
Adams, Laurie 1941- *ConAu 53, SmATA 33, WrDr 84*
Adams, Lawrence Vaughan 1936- *CreCan 1*
Adams, Leon D 1905- *ConAu 45*
Adams, Leonie *DrAP&F 83*
Adams, Leonie 1899- *CnMWL, ConAmA, ConAu P-1, ConP 80, IntWWP 82X, ModAL, TwCA SUP, TwCWr, WrDr 84*
Adams, Les 1934- *ConAu 97*
Adams, Lillian Loyce 1912- *IntAu&W 82*
Adams, Lois Irene Smith *CreCan 1*
Adams, Lowell *ConAu X*
Adams, Marion 1932- *ConAu 41R*
Adams, Michael C C 1945- *ConAu 89*
Adams, Michael Evelyn 1920- *ConAu 33R, WrDr 84*
Adams, Mildred *ConAu X*
Adams, Nathan Miller 1934- *ConAu 45*
Adams, Paul L 1924- *ConAu 61, IntAu&W 82*
Adams, Percy G 1914- *ConAu 1R, –4NR*
Adams, Perseus 1933- *ConAu 107, ConP 80, WrDr 84*
Adams, Philip R 1908- *ConAu 85*
Adams, Rachel Leona White 1905?-1979 *ConAu 93*
Adams, Ramon Frederick 1889-1976 *ConAu 65*
Adams, Ramona Shepherd 1921- *ConAu 106*
Adams, Richard 1920- *AuNews 1, –2, ConAu 3NR, –49, ConLC 4, –5, –18, SmATA 7, TwCCW 83, WorAu 1970, WrDr 84*
Adams, Richard E W 1931- *ConAu 106*
Adams, Richard N 1924- *ConAu 29R*
Adams, Richard P 1917-1977 *ConAu 69, ConAu P-2*
Adams, Robert 1932- *ConAu 69*
Adams, Robert H 1937- *ConAu 105*
Adams, Robert Martin 1915- *ConAu 4NR, –5R, ConLCrt 82, WrDr 84*
Adams, Robert McCormick 1926- *ConAu 61*
Adams, Robert P 1910- *ConAu 13R*
Adams, Rolland Leroy 1905?-1979 *ConAu 89*
Adams, Russell B, Jr. 1937- *ConAu 69*
Adams, Russell L 1930- *ConAu 53, LivgBAA*
Adams, Ruth Joyce *SmATA 14*
Adams, Sally Pepper *ConAu 41R*
Adams, Sam 1934- *ConAu 57*
Adams, Samuel Hopkins 1871-1958 *TwCA, TwCA SUP*
Adams, Sexton 1936- *ConAu 25R*
Adams, T W 1933- *ConAu 25R, WrDr 84*
Adams, Terrence Dean 1935- *ConAu 33R*
Adams, Theodore Floyd 1898-1980 *ConAu 97, ConAu P-1*

Adams, Thomas F 1927- *ConAu 13R*
Adams, Thomas Randolph 1921- *ConAu 107*
Adams, Val 1917?-1983 *ConAu 109*
Adams, Walter 1922- *ConAu 1R, –3NR, WrDr 84*
Adams, Weld *IntAu&W 82X*
Adams, Willi Paul 1940- *ConAu 105*
Adams, William Howard *ConAu 105*
Adams, William Taylor 1822-1897 *SmATA 28[port]*
Adams, William Yewdale 1927- *ConAu 104*
Adamson, Alan 1919- *ConAu 81*
Adamson, David Grant 1927- *ConAu 13R*
Adamson, Donald 1939- *ConAu 53, IntAu&W 82, WrDr 84*
Adamson, Ed 1915?-1972 *ConAu 37R*
Adamson, Frank *ConAu X*
Adamson, Gareth 1925- *WrDr 84*
Adamson, Gareth 1925-1982? *ConAu 106, –11NR, –13R, SmATA 30N*
Adamson, George Worsley 1913- *ConAu 107, SmATA 30[port]*
Adamson, Graham *ConAu X, SmATA X*
Adamson, Hans Christian 1890-1968 *ConAu 5R*
Adamson, Iain 1928- *IntAu&W 82*
Adamson, Joe *ConAu X*
Adamson, Joseph, III 1945- *ConAu 1NR, –45*
Adamson, Joy 1910-1980 *ConAu 69, –93, ConLC 17, SmATA 11, –22N*
Adamson, Robert 1943- *ConP 80, WrDr 84*
Adamson, Walter L 1946- *ConAu 107*
Adamson, Wendy Wriston 1942- *ConAu 53, SmATA 22[port]*
Adamson, William Robert 1927- *ConAu 21R*
Adas, Michael 1943- *ConAu 53*
Adaskin, Frances James *CreCan 1*
Adaskin, Harry 1901- *CreCan 2*
Adaskin, John 1908-1964 *CreCan 2*
Adaskin, Murray 1906- *CreCan 1*
Adastra *ConAu X*
Adburgham, Alison Haig 1912- *ConAu P-1*
Adcock, Almey St. John 1894- *ConAu 65*
Adcock, Arthur St. John 1864-1930 *LongCTC*
Adcock, Betty *ConAu X, DrAP&F 83*
Adcock, Elizabeth S 1938- *ConAu 57*
Adcock, Fleur 1934- *ConAu 11NR, –25R, ConP 80, DcLEL 1940, IntAu&W 82, IntWWP 82, WorAu 1970, WrDr 84*
Adcock, Frank Ezra 1886-1968 *ConAu 106*
Addams, Charles 1912- *ConAu 61, WrDr 84*
Addanki, Sam 1932- *ConAu 109*
Adde, Leo 1927?-1975 *ConAu 57*
Addeo, Edmond G *ConSFA*
Addeo, Jovita A 1939- *ConAu 103*
Adderholt, Elkhannah *IntAu&W 82X*
Addie, Bob 1911?-1982 *ConAu 105*
Addie, Pauline Betz 1919?- *ConAu 105*
Addington, Arthur Charles 1939- *ConAu 105, IntAu&W 82, WrDr 84*
Addington, Larry Holbrook 1932- *ConAu 33R, WrDr 84*
Addison, Doris Maureen 1926- *WrDr 84*
Addison, Gwen *ConAu X*
Addison, Herbert 1889-1982 *ConAu 108*
Addison, Lloyd *DrAP&F 83, LivgBAA*
Addison, Lloyd 1937- *ConAu 45*
Addison, William 1905- *WrDr 84*
Addison, William Wilkinson 1905- *ConAu 5NR, –13R*
Addleshaw, George William Outram 1907?-1982 *ConAu 107*
Addona, Angelo F 1925- *ConAu 25R, SmATA 14, WrDr 84*
Addy, George M 1927- *ConAu 21R*
Addy, John 1915- *ConAu 69*
Addy, Ted *ConAu X, SmATA X*
Ade, George 1866-1944 *ConAu 110, DcLB 25[port], ModWD, TwCA[port], TwCA SUP, TwCWr*
Ade, Walter Frank Charles 1910- *ConAu 53, IntAu&W 82*
Adedeji, Adebayo 1930- *IntAu&W 82*
Adelberg, Doris *ConAu X, SmATA 7, WrDr 84*
Adelberg, Roy P 1928- *ConAu 17R*
Adelman, Bob 1930- *ConAu 69*
Adelman, Clifford 1942- *ConAu 41R, WrDr 84*
Adelman, Gary 1935- *ConAu 33R*
Adelman, Howard 1938- *ConAu 25R*
Adelman, Irma Glicman *ConAu 3NR, –5R*
Adelman, Irving 1926- *ConAu 21R*

Ahlstrom, G W *ConAu X*
Ahlstrom, Sydney E 1919- *ConAu 21R,
   IntAu&W 82, WrDr 84*
Ahlswede, Ann 1928- *TwCWW, WrDr 84*
Ahmad, Ishtiaq 1937- *ConAu 53*
Ahmad, Nafis 1913- *ConAu 17R*
Ahmad, Suleiman M 1943- *ConAu 110*
Ahmann, Mathew H 1931- *ConAu 9R*
Ahmed, Akbar Salahudin 1943- *IntAu&W 82*
Ahmed, Faiz Faiz *EncWL 2*
Ahmet Hasim 1885-1933 *ClDMEL 80*
Ahnebrink, Lars 1915- *ConAu 5R*
Ahnstrom, D N *IntAu&W 82X*
Ahnstrom, Doris Newell 1915- *ConAu 5R,
   IntAu&W 82*
Aho, James 1942- *ConAu 107*
Aho, Lauri Emil 1901- *IntAu&W 82*
Ahokas, Jaakko 1923- *ConAu 65*
Ahrens, Carl Henry Von 1863-1936 *CreCan 1*
Ahrintzen, Kim 1955- *IntAu&W 82*
Ahsan, Syed Ali 1922- *IntWWP 82*
Ahsen, Akhter 1931- *ConAu 10NR, –61,
   WrDr 84*
Ai *DrAP&F 83*
Ai 1947- *ConAu 85, ConLC 4, –14*
Aichinger, Helga 1937- *ConAu 25R, SmATA 4*
Aichinger, Ilse 1921- *ClDMEL 80, ConAu 85,
   EncWL 2, ModGL*
Aichinger, Peter 1933- *ConAu 11NR, –61*
Aickman, Robert Fordyce 1914- *ConAu 3NR,
   –5R, IntAu&W 82*
Aide, Hamilton 1826-1906 *LongCTC*
Aidenoff, Abraham 1913-1976 *ConAu 37R, –61*
Aidoo, Ama Ata 1942- *ConAu 101, ConDr 82,
   ModBlW, WrDr 84*
Aidoo, Christina Ama Ata 1942- *DcLEL 1940,
   ModCmwL, TwCWr*
Aigner, Alexander 1909- *IntAu&W 82*
Aiguillette *ConAu X*
Aikawa, Jerry K 1921- *WrDr 84*
Aiken, Clarissa Lorenz 1899- *ConAu P-2,
   SmATA 12*
Aiken, Conrad Potter 1889-1973 *CnMD,
   CnMWL, ConAmA, ConAu 4NR, –5R, –45,
   ConLC 1, –3, –5, –10, DcLB 9[port],
   EncWL 2, IntAu&W 82, LongCTC,
   ModAL, ModAL SUP, ModWD,
   SmATA 3, –30[port], TwCA[port],
   TwCA SUP, TwCWr, WhoTwCL*
Aiken, Henry D 1912- *WrDr 84*
Aiken, Henry David 1912-1982 *ConAu 1R, –1NR,
   –106*
Aiken, Irene *ConAu 93*
Aiken, Joan 1924- *ChlLR 1, ConAu 4NR, –9R,
   IntAu&W 82, SmATA 2, –30[port],
   TwCCW 83, TwCCr&M 80, TwCRGW,
   WrDr 84*
Aiken, John 1913- *ConAu 101*
Aiken, John R 1927- *ConAu 33R*
Aiken, Lewis R, Jr. 1931- *ConAu 10NR, –25R,
   WrDr 84*
Aiken, Maurice C 1909?-1983 *ConAu 109*
Aiken, Michael Thomas 1932- *ConAu 9NR,
   –21R*
Aikin, Charles 1901- *ConAu 5R*
Aikman, Ann *ConAu X*
Aikman, David 1944- *ConAu 65*
Aimes, Angelica 1943- *ConAu 81*
Ainger, Alfred 1837-1904 *LongCTC*
Ainsbury, Ray *ConAu X, ConSFA*
Ainsbury, Roy *ConAu X*
Ainslie, Rosalynde 1932- *ConAu 25R*
Ainslie, Tom *ConAu X*
Ainsworth, Charles Harold 1935- *ConAu 49,
   IntAu&W 82*
Ainsworth, Dorothy Sears 1894-1976 *ConAu 69*
Ainsworth, Ed 1902-1968 *ConAu 4NR*
Ainsworth, Edward Maddin 1902-1968 *ConAu 5R*
Ainsworth, G C 1905- *ConAu 73*
Ainsworth, Harriet *ConAu X, TwCRGW,
   WrDr 84*
Ainsworth, Katherine 1908- *ConAu 29R,
   IntAu&W 82*
Ainsworth, Mary D Salter 1913- *ConAu 8NR,
   –21R, WrDr 84*
Ainsworth, Norma *ConAu 5NR, –13R,
   SmATA 9*
Ainsworth, Patricia 1932- *ConAu X,
   IntAu&W 82X, TwCRGW, WrDr 84*
Ainsworth, Ray *ConAu X*
Ainsworth, Roy *ConAu X*
Ainsworth, Ruth 1908- *TwCCW 83, WrDr 84*

Ainsworth, Ruth Gallard 1908- *ConAu X,
   SmATA 7*
Ainsworth, William Harrison 1805-1882
   SmATA 24[port]
Ainsztein, Reuben 1917-1981 *ConAu 108, –110*
Aird, Catherine 1930- *ConAu X,
   IntAu&W 82X, TwCCr&M 80, WrDr 84*
Aird, Eileen M 1945- *ConAu 49*
Airlie, Catherine *ConAu X, IntAu&W 82X,
   TwCRGW, WrDr 84*
Airola, Paavo 1915- *ConAu 81, IntAu&W 82*
Airoy, Gil Carl 1924- *ConAu 41R*
Aisgill, Alice *LongCTC*
Aislin *ConAu X*
Aistis, Jonas 1904-1973 *ClDMEL 80, EncWL 2*
Aistis, Jonas 1908?-1973 *ConAu 41R*
Aistrop, Jack 1916- *ConAu 1R, –3NR,
   SmATA 14*
Aistrup, Allan Bjarne 1948- *IntAu&W 82*
Aitchison, Janet 1962- *ConAu 57*
Aitken, A J 1921- *ConAu 7NR, –13R*
Aitken, Amy 1952- *ConAu 108*
Aitken, Dorothy 1916- *ConAu 2NR, –49,
   SmATA 10*
Aitken, Hugh 1922- *WrDr 84*
Aitken, Hugh George Jeffrey 1922- *ConAu 1R,
   –3NR*
Aitken, Jonathan William Patrick 1942-
   ConAu 21R
Aitken, Thomas, Jr. 1910- *ConAu 1R*
Aitken, W R 1913- *ConAu 41R*
Aitken, William Maxwell *ConAu X*
Aitkin, Don 1937- *ConAu 93*
Aitmatov, Chinghiz *EncWL 2
   TwCCW 83*
Aitmatov, Chingiz 1928- *ConAu 103*
Ajami, Alfred M 1948- *ConAu 110*
Ajar, Emile *ConAu X*
Ajay, Betty 1918- *ConAu 69*
Ajayi, J F Ade 1929- *ConAu 61*
Aka, Aisha Eshe *IntWWP 82X*
Akanji, Sangodare *ConAu X*
Akare, Thomas 1950- *ConAu 109*
Akashi, Yoji 1928- *ConAu 33R*
Akavyahu, Itzhak 1918- *IntWWP 82*
Ake, Claude 1938- *ConAu 21R*
Ake, Claude 1939- *ConAu 10NR*
Akehurst, M B 1940- *ConAu 25R*
Aken, Piet Van 1920- *ClDMEL 80*
Akens, David S 1921- *ConAu 25R*
Akenson, Donald Harman 1941- *ConAu 7NR,
   –57*
Aker, George Frederick 1927- *ConAu 41R*
Akeret, Robert U 1928- *ConAu 45*
Akers, Alan Burt *ConAu X, IntAu&W 82X,
   TwCSFW, WrDr 84*
Akers, Charles Wesley 1920- *ConAu 13R*
Akers, Ellery *DrAP&F 83*
Akers, Floyd *ConAu X, SmATA X,
   TwCCW 83*
Akers, Ronald Louis 1939- *ConAu 1NR, –45*
Akesson, Sonja 1926-1977 *EncWL 2*
Akhmadulina, Bella 1937- *ClDMEL 80,
   ConAu 65, EncWL 2, ModSL 1,
   WhoTwCL, WorAu*
Akhmatova, Anna 1888-1966 *ConAu 25R,
   ConAu P-1, ConLC 25[port], LongCTC,
   TwCWr*
Akhmatova, Anna 1889-1966 *ClDMEL 80,
   ConLC 11, EncWL 2[port], ModSL 1,
   WhoTwCL, WorAu*
Akhnaton, Askia *ConAu X, DrAP&F 83,
   LivgBAA*
Akhurst, Bertram A 1928- *ConAu 45*
Akilandam, Perungalur Vaithialingam 1922-
   IntAu&W 82
Akin, Wallace E 1923- *ConAu 25R*
Akinjogbin, I A 1930- *ConAu 21R*
Akins, Terese *IntWWP 82*
Akins, Zoe 1886-1958 *CnMD, ConAmA,
   DcLB 26[port], ModWD, TwCA,
   TwCA SUP*
Akinsanya, Justus Akinbayo 1936- *IntAu&W 82*
Akita, George 1926- *ConAu 17R*
Akmakjain, Hiag 1926- *ConAu 57*
Akpabot, Samuel Ekpe 1932- *ConAu 101*
Akrigg, G P V 1913- *ConAu 25R*
Akrigg, George Philip Vernon *WrDr 84*
Akrigg, George Philip Vernon 1913-
   IntAu&W 82
Aksenov, Vasily Pavlovich 1932- *ConAu 53,
   ConLC 22[port], WorAu*

Aksionov, Vasily Pavlovich 1932- *TwCWr*
Aksyonov, Vasily Pavlovich 1932- *ClDMEL 80,
   EncWL 2, ModSL 1*
Akutagawa, Ryunosuke 1892-1927 *EncWL 2,
   WorAu*
Al, Ch'ing 1910- *EncWL 2*
Al-Azm, Sadik J *WrDr 84*
Al-Azm, Sadik J 1934- *ConAu 9NR, –21R*
Al-Faruqi, Ismai'il Raji 1921- *ConAu 69*
Al-Issa, Ihsan 1931- *ConAu 109*
Al-Marayati, Abid A 1931- *ConAu 33R,
   IntAu&W 82, WrDr 84*
Al-Shamma, Khalil Mohammed Hassen 1935-
   IntAu&W 82
Al-Van-Gar *ConAu X*
Aladjem, Henrietta H 1917- *ConAu 105*
Alailima, Fay C 1921- *ConAu 33R*
Alain 1868-1951 *ClDMEL 80, EncWL 2,
   ModFrL, WorAu 1970*
Alain-Fournier 1886-1914 *ClDMEL 80,
   CnMWL, ConAu X, EncWL 2, LongCTC,
   ModFrL, ModRL, TwCA, TwCA SUP,
   TwCLC 6[port], TwCWr, WhoTwCL*
Alameen, Stephany Inua *DrAP&F 83*
Alan, A J 1883-1940 *LongCTC*
Alan, Jack *ConAu X*
Alan, Sandy *ConAu X*
Aland, Kurt 1915- *ConAu 25R*
Alander, Rainer 1937- *IntAu&W 82*
Alaoljoy *IntWWP 82X*
Alarie, Pierrette 1921- *CreCan 1*
Alas, Leopoldo 1852-1901 *ClDMEL 80*
Alatri, Paolo 1918- *IntAu&W 82*
Alavi, Buzurg 1907- *EncWL 2*
Alaya, Flavia 1935- *ConAu 33R, WrDr 84*
Alazraki, Jaime 1934- *ConAu 33R, WrDr 84*
Alba, Richard D 1942- *ConAu 109*
Alba, Victor 1916- *ConAu 10NR, –21R,
   WrDr 84*
Alba DeGamez, Cielo Cayetana 1920- *ConAu 93*
Albanese, Catherine L 1940- *ConAu 9NR, –65*
Albanese, Margaret 1911- *IntWWP 82*
Albanesi, Madame 1859-1936 *LongCTC,
   TwCRGW*
Albani, Marie-Louise Emma Cecile 1847-1930
   CreCan 2
Albareda Herrera, Gines 1908- *IntAu&W 82*
Albarella, Joan K *DrAP&F 83*
Albaret, Celeste 1891- *ConAu 73*
Albatross *IntAu&W 82X*
Albaugh, Edwin 1935- *ConAu 89*
Albaugh, Ralph M 1909- *ConAu P-1*
Albaum, Gerald 1933- *ConAu 37R*
Albaum, Melvin 1936- *ConAu 53*
Albee, Edward 1927- *CnMD*
Albee, Edward 1928- *AuNews 1, ConAu 5R,
   –8NR, ConDr 82, ConLC 1, –2, –3, –5, –9,
   –11, –13, –25[port], CroCD, DcLB 7[port],
   DcLEL 1940, EncWL 2[port], LongCTC,
   ModAL, ModAL SUP, ModWD,
   NatPD 81[port], TwCWr, WhoTwCL,
   WorAu, WrDr 84*
Albee, George Sumner 1905-1964 *ConAu 1R*
Alber, Mike 1938- *ConAu 25R*
Albers, Anni 1899- *ConAu 1R, –2NR*
Albers, Henry H 1919- *ConAu 1R, –6NR*
Albers, Josef 1888-1976 *ConAu 1R, –3NR, –65*
Albert, A Adrian 1905-1972 *ConAu 37R*
Albert, Adrien 1907- *WrDr 84*
Albert, Alan *DrAP&F 83*
Albert, Burton, Jr. 1936- *ConAu 8NR, –61,
   IntAu&W 82, SmATA 22[port]*
Albert, Ethel M 1918- *ConAu 21R*
Albert, Gail 1942- *ConAu 108*
Albert, Harold A *ConAu 29R*
Albert, Linda 1939- *ConAu 110*
Albert, Louise 1928- *ConAu 69*
Albert, Marv 1943- *ConAu 101*
Albert, Marvin H *ConAu 73, TwCWW,
   WrDr 84*
Albert, Mimi *DrAP&F 83*
Albert, Mimi 1940- *ConAu 73*
Albert, Samuel L *DrAP&F 83*
Albert, Walter E 1930- *ConAu 21R*
Albert-Birot, Pierre 1876-1967 *ClDMEL 80*
Albertazzie, Ralph 1923- *ConAu 101*
Alberti, Rafael 1902- *ClDMEL 80, CnMD,
   CnMWL, ConAu 85, ConLC 7, EncWL 2,
   ModRL, ModWD, TwCA SUP, TwCWr*
Alberti, Robert E 1938- *ConAu 7NR, –61*
Alberts, David Stephen 1942- *ConAu 29R*
Alberts, Frances Jacobs 1907- *ConAu 5R,*

SmATA 14
Alberts, Krug IntWWP 82X
Alberts, Lily Susanne Krug 1890- IntWWP 82
Alberts, Robert Carman 1907- ConAu 33R,
  IntAu&W 82, WrDr 84
Alberts, Ulrich 1946- IntWWP 82
Alberts, William W 1925- ConAu 21R
Albertson, Chris 1931- ConAu 57
Albertson, Dean 1920- ConAu 1R, -3NR,
  WrDr 84
Albertsson, Kristjan 1897- IntAu&W 82
Albery, Nobuko ConAu 81
Albin, Peter S 1934- ConAu 85
Albini, Joseph L 1930- ConAu 61
Albinski, Henry Stephen 1931- ConAu 8NR,
  -21R, WrDr 84
Albinson, Jack ConAu X
Albinson, James P 1932- ConAu 57
Albion, Lee Smith SmATA 29
Albion, Robert G 1896- WrDr 84
Albion, Robert Greenhalgh 1896- ConAu 1R,
  -3NR
Albion, Robert Greenhalgh 1896-1983 ConAu 110
Albornoz, Aurora De 1926- IntAu&W 82
Albran, Kehlog ConAu X
Albrand, Martha WrDr 84
Albrand, Martha 1913- TwCA SUP
Albrand, Martha 1914- ConAu 13R,
  TwCCr&M 80
Albrand, Martha 1914-1981 ConAu 108, -11NR
Albrecht, C Milton 1904- ConAu 33R
Albrecht, Ernest Jacob 1937- ConAmTC
Albrecht, Lillie 1894- ConAu 5R, SmATA 12
Albrecht, Robert C 1933- ConAu 21R
Albrecht, Ruth E 1910- ConAu 17R
Albrecht, William Price 1907- ConAu 73,
  IntAu&W 82, WrDr 84
Albrecht-Carrie, Rene 1904-1978 ConAu 1R,
  -1NR
Albright, Bets Parker ConAu X
Albright, Bliss 1903- ConAu 33R
Albright, Elizabeth A 1920- ConAu 108
Albright, John Brannon 1930- ConAu 65
Albright, Joseph 1937- ConAu 97
Albright, Peter 1926- ConAu 108
Albright, Raymond W 1901-1965 ConAu P-1
Albright, Roger 1922- ConAu 106
Albright, William Foxwell 1891-1971 ConAu 33R
Albright, William Robert ConAmTC
Albrow, Martin 1937- ConAu 33R, WrDr 84
Alcadevel IntAu&W 82X
Alcalde, E L ConAu X
Alcalde, Miguel ConAu X
Alcantara, Ruben R 1940- ConAu 105
Alcazar DeVelasco Velasco, Angel 1909-
  IntAu&W 82
Alchemy, Jack IntWWP 82X
Alchian, Armen A 1914- ConAu 110
Alcibiade ConAu X
Alcina Franch, Alcina 1922- IntAu&W 82
Alcock, Gudrun SmATA 33
Alcock, Vivien 1924- ConAu 110
Alcock, Vivien 1926- TwCCW 83
Alcorn, John 1935- SmATA 30, -31[port]
Alcorn, Marvin D 1902- ConAu 13R
Alcorn, Pat B 1948- ConAu 107
Alcorn, Robert Hayden 1909- ConAu 5R
Alcosser, Sandra B DrAP&F 83
Alcott, Julia ConAu X
Alcott, Louisa May 1832-1888 ChlLR 1
Alcover I Maspons, Joan 1854-1926 CIDMEL 80
Alcyone ConAu X
Ald, Roy A ConAu 73
Alda, Alan 1936- ConAu 103
Aldan, Daisy DrAP&F 83
Aldan, Daisy 1923- ConAu 8NR, -13R
Aldanov, Mark Aleksandrovich 1886-1957
  CIDMEL 80, TwCWr
Aldanov, Mark Aleksandrovich 1888- TwCA,
  TwCA SUP
Aldcroft, Derek Howard 1936- ConAu 25R,
  WrDr 84
Aldcroft, Karolyn Elizabeth 1947- IntWWP 82
Aldcroft, Kay IntWWP 82X
Aldecoa, Ignacio 1925-1969 CIDMEL 80
Alden, Carella ConAu X
Alden, Dauril 1926- ConAu 105
Alden, Douglas William 1912- ConAu 69
Alden, Isabella Macdonald 1841-1930 LongCTC
Alden, Jack ConAu X
Alden, John D 1921- ConAu 17R
Alden, John R 1908- ConAu 11NR

Alden, John Richard 1903- DcLEL 1940
Alden, John Richard 1908- ConAu 61, WrDr 84
Alden, Michele ConAu X
Alden, Robert L 1937- ConAu 65
Alden, Roberta LongCTC
Alden, Sue WrDr 84
Alder, Francis A 1937- ConAu 61
Alder, Henry 1922- ConAu 49
Alderdice, Eva 1922- IntWWP 82
Alderfer, Clayton P 1940- ConAu 37R
Alderfer, Harold F 1903- ConAu 9R
Alderman, Clifford Lindsey 1902- ConAu 1R,
  -3NR, SmATA 3
Alderman, Geoffrey 1944- ConAu 93
Alderman, Joy 1931- ConAu 61
Alderson, Jo Bartels 1930- ConAu 65
Alderson, Michael R 1931- WrDr 84
Alderson, Stanley 1927- ConAu 5R
Alderson, William T, Jr. 1926- ConAu 9R
Alding, Peter ConAu X, WrDr 84
Alding, Peter 1926- TwCCr&M 80
Aldinger, Wallace S 1905- ConAu 1R
Aldington, Hilda Doolittle 1886- ConAmA
Aldington, Richard 1892-1962 ConAu 85,
  LongCTC, ModBrL, TwCA, TwCA SUP,
  TwCWr
Aldis, Dorothy 1896-1966 ConAu 1R,
  DcLB 22[port], SmATA 2[port]
Aldiss, Brian 1925- WrDr 84
Aldiss, Brian W 1923- DcLEL 1940
Aldiss, Brian W 1925- ConAu 5R, -5NR,
  ConLC 5, -14, ConNov 82, ConSFA,
  DcLB 14[port], DrmM[port], IntAu&W 82,
  SmATA 34[port], TwCSFW, WorAu 1970
Aldon, Adair ConAu X, SmATA 6,
  TwCCW 83
Aldouby, Zwy H 1931- ConAu 33R
Aldous, Allan Charles 1911- SmATA 27
Aldous, Anthony Michael 1935- ConAu 69
Aldous, Tony 1935- ConAu X, IntAu&W 82
Aldred, Cyril 1914- ConAu 6NR, -57
Aldredge, Georgie Redden 1919- IntWWP 82
Aldrich, Ann ConAu X, SmATA X
Aldrich, Bess Streeter 1881-1954 TwCA,
  TwCA SUP
Aldrich, C Knight 1914- ConAu 25R
Aldrich, Frederic DeLong 1899- ConAu P-1
Aldrich, Jonathan DrAP&F 83
Aldrich, Nelson Wilmarth, Jr. 1935- ConAu 110
Aldrich, Ruth I ConAu 105
Aldrich, Thomas Bailey 1836-1907 SmATA 17
Aldridge, A Owen 1915- ConAu 17R,
  IntAu&W 82, WrDr 84
Aldridge, Adele DrAP&F 83
Aldridge, Adele 1934- ConAu 49
Aldridge, Alan 1943?- SmATA 33
Aldridge, Gordon James 1916- WrDr 84
Aldridge, Harold Edward James 1918-
  DcLEL 1940
Aldridge, James 1918- ConAu 61, ConNov 82,
  TwCA SUP, WrDr 84
Aldridge, Jeffrey 1938- ConAu 25R
Aldridge, John W 1922- ConAu 1R, -3NR,
  ConLCrt 82, DcLEL 1940, IntAu&W 82,
  WorAu, WrDr 84
Aldridge, Josephine Haskell ConAu 73,
  SmATA 14
Aldridge, Richard DrAP&F 83
Aldridge, Richard Boughton 1930- ConAu 3NR,
  -9R
Aldriedge, Jean DrAP&F 83
Aldrin, Edwin E, Jr. 1930- ConAu 89
Aldwinckle, Russell 1911- ConAu 69
Aldyne, Nathan ConAu X, WrDr 84
Aleckovic, Mira 1924- IntAu&W 82
Alegria, Ciro 1909-1967 EncWL 2, ModLAL,
  TwCA SUP, TwCWr
Alegria, Fernando 1918- ConAu 5NR, -9R
Alegria, Ricardo E 1921- ConAu 25R,
  SmATA 6
Aleichem, Shalom 1859-1916 LongCTC, TwCA,
  TwCA SUP
Aleichem, Sholom 1859-1916 ConAu X,
  TwCLC 1
Aleixandre, Vicente 1898- CIDMEL 80,
  ConAu 85, ConLC 9, EncWL 2,
  IntAu&W 82, IntWWP 82, WorAu
Aleixandre, Vicente 1900- TwCWr
Aleksandrowicz, Alina 1931- IntAu&W 82
Aleksandrowska, Elzbieta 1928- IntAu&W 82
Aleksin, Anatolii Georgievich 1924- ConAu 109
Aleman, Miguel 1903?-1983 ConAu 110

Alenier, Karren LaLonde DrAP&F 83
Alenier, Karren LaLonde 1947- IntWWP 82
Alent, Rose Marie Bachem ConAu 49
Alepoudelis, Odysseus ConLC 15, WorAu
Aleramo, Sibilla 1876-1960 CIDMEL 80
Aleshire, Joan DrAP&F 83
Alessandra, Anthony J 1947- ConAu 103
Alessandrini, Federico 1906?-1983 ConAu 109
Alexander, Baron 1905- WrDr 84
Alexander, Albert 1914- ConAu 25R
Alexander, Alfred 1908-1983 ConAu 110
Alexander, Anna B Cooke 1913- ConAu 5R, -57,
  SmATA 1
Alexander, Anne 1913- ConAu X
Alexander, Anthony Francis 1920- ConAu 1R
Alexander, Arthur 1927- ConAu 5R
Alexander, Boyd 1913-1980 ConAu 53, -97
Alexander, Boyd 1934- IntAu&W 82
Alexander, Bruce IntAu&W 82X
Alexander, Charles ConAu X
Alexander, Charles C 1935- ConAu 13R
Alexander, Charles Stevenson 1916- ConAu 2NR,
  -5R
Alexander, Charlotte DrAP&F 83
Alexander, Christine 1893-1975 ConAu 61
Alexander, Christopher 1936- WrDr 84
Alexander, Colin James 1920- ConAu 13R,
  DcLEL 1940, IntAu&W 82
Alexander, Conel Hugh O'Donel 1909-1974
  ConAu 73
Alexander, David 1907-1973 ConAu 1R, -41R
Alexander, David M 1945- ConAu 81
Alexander, Denis 1945- ConAu 45
Alexander, Edward 1936- ConAu 13R
Alexander, Edward Porter 1907- ConAu 33R
Alexander, Edwin P 1905- ConAu 29R
Alexander, Eric 1910?-1982 ConAu 106
Alexander, Ernest R 1933- ConAu 103
Alexander, Eugenie 1919- WrDr 84
Alexander, Eugenie Mary 1919- IntAu&W 82
Alexander, Floyce DrAP&F 83
Alexander, Floyce 1938- ConAu 33R, WrDr 84
Alexander, Frances 1888- ConAu 25R,
  IntAu&W 82, SmATA 4
Alexander, Frank 1943- ConAu 65
Alexander, Franklin Osborne 1897- ConAu P-2
Alexander, Franz 1891-1964 ConAu 5R
Alexander, Sir George 1858-1918 LongCTC
Alexander, George Jonathan 1931- ConAu 73
Alexander, George M 1914- ConAu 5R
Alexander, Gil ConAu X
Alexander, Harold Lee 1934- ConAu 69
Alexander, Herbert IntAu&W 82X
Alexander, Herbert E 1927- ConAu 41R
Alexander, Holmes Moss 1906- ConAu 61
Alexander, Hubert G 1909- ConAu 21R
Alexander, I J 1905?-1974 ConAu 53
Alexander, Ian Welsh 1911- ConAu 13R
Alexander, J J G 1935- ConAu 21R
Alexander, James E 1913- ConAu 73
Alexander, Jan ConAu X
Alexander, Janet 1907- ConAu 4NR,
  IntAu&W 82
Alexander, Jean 1926- ConAu 49
Alexander, Joan 1920- ConAu X,
  IntAu&W 82X, WrDr 84
Alexander, Jocelyn Anne Arundel 1930-
  ConAu 1R, -4NR, SmATA 22[port]
Alexander, John Aleck 1912- ConAu 9R
Alexander, John Kurt 1941- ConAu 102
Alexander, John N 1941- ConAu 69
Alexander, John Thorndike 1940- ConAu 33R,
  IntAu&W 82, WrDr 84
Alexander, John W 1918- ConAu 3NR, -5R
Alexander, Jon 1940- ConAu 33R, WrDr 84
Alexander, Josephine 1909- ConAu 104
Alexander, Justin IntAu&W 82X
Alexander, K 1923-1980 ConAu 103
Alexander, Kathryn ConAu X
Alexander, Kenneth John Wilson 1922- ConAu X
Alexander, Kyle ConAu X
Alexander, Lewis M 1921- ConAu 21R
Alexander, Linda 1935- ConAu 21R, SmATA 2,
  WrDr 84
Alexander, Lloyd 1924- ChlLR 5[port],
  TwCCW 83, WrDr 84
Alexander, Lloyd Chudley 1924- ChlLR 1,
  ConAu 1R, -1NR, SmATA 3
Alexander, Louis George 1932- ConAu 102,
  WrDr 84
Alexander, M J 1941- WrDr 84

Alexander, Marc 1929- *ConAu 5R*
Alexander, Marge *ConAu X*
Alexander, Martha 1920- *ConAu 85,*
　SmATA 11[port]
Alexander, Marthann 1907- *ConAu 53*
Alexander, Martin 1930- *ConAu 49*
Alexander, Mary Jean McCutcheon *ConAu 9R*
Alexander, Meena 1951- *IntAu&W 82*
Alexander, Michael J 1941- *ConAu 45*
Alexander, Michael VanCleave 1937- *ConAu 102*
Alexander, Milton 1917- *ConAu 17R*
Alexander, Mrs. 1825-1902 *LongCTC*
Alexander, Patrick James 1926- *WrDr 84*
Alexander, Rae Pace *ConAu X, SmATA X*
Alexander, Raymond Pace 1898-1974 *ConAu 97,*
　SmATA 22[port]
Alexander, Ric *ConAu X*
Alexander, Richard Dale 1929- *ConAu 110*
Alexander, Robert *ConAu X*
Alexander, Robert J 1918- *ConAu 1R, -3NR,*
　IntAu&W 82, WrDr 84
Alexander, Robert Lester 1920- *ConAu 108*
Alexander, Robert McN 1934- *WrDr 84*
Alexander, Robert McNeill 1934- *IntAu&W 82*
Alexander, Robert William 1906?-1980 *ConAu 97*
Alexander, Roy 1899?-1978 *ConAu 81, -85*
Alexander, Samuel 1859-1938 *LongCTC*
Alexander, Shana 1925- *ConAu 61,*
　ConIsC 2[port], WrDr 84
Alexander, Sidney 1912- *ConAu 6NR, -9R*
Alexander, Stanley Walter 1895-1980 *ConAu 97*
Alexander, Stella Tucker 1912- *ConAu 105*
Alexander, Sue 1933- *ConAu 4NR, -53,*
　SmATA 12
Alexander, Taylor Richard 1915- *ConAu 107*
Alexander, Theron 1913- *ConAu 3NR, -5R*
Alexander, Thomas G 1935- *ConAu 65*
Alexander, Thomas W, Jr. 1930- *ConAu 9R*
Alexander, Vincent Arthur 1925-1980 *ConAu 101,*
　SmATA 23N
Alexander, W M 1928- *ConAu 69*
Alexander, William M 1912- *ConAu 33R*
Alexander, Yonah 1931- *ConAu 61*
Alexander, Zane *ConAu X*
Alexandersson, Gunnar V 1922- *ConAu 17R*
Alexandre, Philippe 1932- *ConAu 41R*
Alexandrowicz, Charles Henry 1902- *WrDr 84*
Alexandrowicz, Charles Henry 1902-1975
　ConAu 1R, -1NR
Alexeev, Wassilij 1906- *ConAu 89*
Alexeieff, Alexandre A 1901- *SmATA 14*
Alexeyeva, Lydia *IntWWP 82X*
Alexiadis, George 1911- *IntAu&W 82*
Alexiou, Margaret 1939- *ConAu 69*
Alexis, Jacques-Stephen 1922-1961? *ModBlW,*
　ModFrL
Alexis, Katina *ConAu X*
Alexopoulos, Constantine John 1907- *WrDr 84*
Alfandary-Alexander, Mark 1923- *ConAu 5R*
Alfaro, Juan 1914- *IntAu&W 82*
Alfoldi, Andras 1895- *IntAu&W 82*
Alford, B W E 1937- *WrDr 84*
Alford, Bernard William Ernest 1937-
　ConAu 101
Alford, Neill Herbert, Jr. 1919- *WrDr 84*
Alford, Norman William 1929- *ConAu 37R*
Alford, Robert R 1928- *ConAu 41R*
Alford, Terry 1945- *ConAu 110*
Alfred, Richard 1931- *ConAu X*
Alfred, William 1922- *ConAu 13R, ConDr 82,*
　CroCD, WorAu, WrDr 84
Alfred, William 1923- *ModAL*
Alfsen, John Martin 1902- *CreCan 2*
Alfven, Hannes 1908- *ConAu 29R*
Algarin, Miguel 1941- *ConAu 69*
Algeo, John 1930- *ConAu 7NR, -17R,*
　WrDr 84
Alger, Horatio 1832-1899 *SmATA 16[port]*
　TwCCW 83
Alger, Leclaire 1898-1969 *ConAu 73,*
　SmATA 15
Alger, Philip L 1894- *WrDr 84*
Alger, Philip Langdon 1894-1979 *ConAu 109*
Algery, Andre *ConAu X*
Algren, Nelson 1909-1981 *CnMWL, ConAu 103,*
　-13R, ConLC 4, -10, DcLB Y82A[port],
　-9[port], EncWL 2, ModAL, ModAL SUP,
　TwCA SUP, TwCWr, WhoTwCL
Algulin, Ingemar 1938- *IntAu&W 82*
Alhaique, Claudio 1913- *ConAu 29R*
Ali, Ahmed 1908- *ConAu 25R*
Ali, Ahmed 1910- *ConNov 82, DcLEL 1940,*

IntAu&W 82, WrDr 84
Ali, Chaudhri Mohamad 1905-1980 *ConAu 105*
Ali, Tariq 1943- *ConAu 10NR, -25R*
Aliano, Richard Anthony 1946- *ConAu 10NR,*
　-65
Aliav, Ruth *ConAu X*
Aliber, Robert Z 1930- *ConAu 8NR, -21R,*
　WrDr 84
Alibrandi, Tom 1941- *ConAu 65*
Alice, Princess 1883-1981 *ConAu 103*
Aliesan, Jody *DrAP&F 83*
Aliesan, Jody 1943- *ConAu 7NR, -57*
Aliger, Margarita Iosifovna 1915- *ClDMEL 80,*
　IntWWP 82, TwCWr
Alihan, Milla *ConAu P-2*
Aliki *ConAu X, IntAu&W 82X, SmATA 2,*
　WrDr 84
Alilunas, Leo John 1912- *ConAu 17R*
Alimayo, Chikuyo *ConAu X*
Alington, Adrian Richard 1895-1958 *LongCTC*
Alington, Cyril Argentine 1872-1955 *LongCTC*
Alinsky, Saul 1909-1972 *ConAu 37R*
Alioto, Robert F 1933- *ConAu 45*
Alisky, Marvin 1923- *WrDr 84*
Alisky, Marvin Howard 1923-
　ConAu 5NR, -13R, IntAu&W 82
Alisov, Boris P 1892-1972 *ConAu 37R*
Alitto, Guy S 1942- *ConAu 93*
Alkaaoud, Elizabeth Ann 1945- *IntWWP 82*
Alkema, Chester Jay 1932- *ConAu 53,*
　MichAu 80, SmATA 12
Alker, Hayward R, Jr. 1937- *ConAu 17R*
Alkire, Leland George 1937- *ConAu 101*
Alkire, William Henry 1935- *ConAu 107*
Allaback, Steven Lee 1939- *ConAu 97*
Allaby, Michael 1933- *ConAu 1NR, -45,*
　WrDr 84
Allaire, Joseph L 1929- *ConAu 41R*
Allais, Maurice 1911- *IntAu&W 82*
Allamand, Pascale 1942- *ConAu 69,*
　SmATA 12
Allan, Alfred K 1930- *ConAu 17R*
Allan, Andrew Edward Fairbairn 1907- *CreCan 1*
Allan, D G C 1925- *ConAu 25R*
Allan, Dennis *TwCCr&M 80*
Allan, Elkan 1922- *ConAu 101, WrDr 84*
Allan, Harry T 1928- *ConAu 25R*
Allan, J David 1945- *ConAu 41R*
Allan, John 1950- *WrDr 84*
Allan, Luke d1962 *TwCWW*
Allan, Mabel Esther 1915- *ConAu 2NR, -5R,*
　IntAu&W 82, SmATA 32[port], -5,
　TwCCW 83, WrDr 84
Allan, Maud 1883-1956 *LongCTC*
Allan, Mea 1909-1982 *ConAu 2NR, -5R, -107,*
　IntAu&W 82
Allan, Norman B 1921- *ConAu 105*
Allan, Robert Alexander 1914-1979 *ConAu 106*
Allan, Robin 1934- *ConAu 107, WrDr 84*
Allan, Ted 1916- *ConDr 82, WrDr 84*
Allan, Ted 1918- *ConAu 77*
Allanbrook, Wye J 1943- *ConAu 110*
Alland, Alexander, Jr. 1931- *ConAu 21R*
Alland, Guy 1944- *ConAu 69*
Allard, Dean C 1933- *ConAu 1NR, -45*
Allard, Michel 1924-1976 *ConAu 65*
Allard, Sven 1896-1975 *ConAu P-2*
Allardt, Erik 1925- *ConAu 73*
Allardt, Linda *DrAP&F 83*
Allardt, Linda 1926- *ConAu 104*
Allardt Ekelund, Karin 1895- *IntAu&W 82*
Allardyce, Gilbert Daniel 1932- *ConAu 33R*
Allardyce, Paula *ConAu X, TwCCr&M 80,*
　TwCRGW, WrDr 84
Allaun, Frank Julian 1913- *ConAu 103,*
　IntAu&W 82, WrDr 84
Allbeck, Willard Dow 1898- *ConAu 21R*
Allbeury, Ted 1917- *ConAu X, TwCCr&M 80,*
　WrDr 84
Allbeury, Theodore Edward LeBouthillier 1917-
　ConAu 5NR, -53
Allchin, A M 1930- *ConAu 25R*
Alldridge, James Charles 1910- *ConAu 29R*
Alldritt, Keith 1935- *ConAu 25R,*
　DcLB 14[port]
Allee, Marjorie Hill 1890-1945 *SmATA 17*
Alleger, Daniel E 1903- *ConAu 33R*
Allegro, John 1923- *WrDr 84*
Allegro, John Marco 1923- *ConAu 4NR, -9R,*
　DcLEL 1940, IntAu&W 82
Allen, A B 1903-1975 *ConAu P-2*
Allen, A Dale, Jr. 1935- *ConAu 21R*

Allen, Adam *ConAu X, SmATA X*
Allen, Alex B *ConAu X, SmATA X,*
　TwCCW 83
Allen, Alfred 1925- *IntAu&W 82*
Allen, Allyn *ConAu X, SmATA X*
Allen, Andrew Ralph 1913-1966 *CreCan 1*
Allen, Anita *ConAu X*
Allen, Arthur Augustus 1885-1964 *ConAu 1R*
Allen, Barbara *ConAu X*
Allen, Betsy *ConAu X, SmATA X,*
　TwCCW 83
Allen, C K 1887-1966 *LongCTC*
Allen, Carl 1961- *ConAu 69*
Allen, Catherine Blanche 1883- *ConAu 107*
Allen, Cecil John 1886-1973 *ConAu P-2*
Allen, Charlotte Vale 1941- *ConAu 69*
Allen, Chris 1929- *ConAu 29R*
Allen, Clabon Walter 1904- *WrDr 84*
Allen, Clay *ConAu X*
Allen, Clifford Edward 1902- *ConAu P-1*
Allen, Clifton Judson 1901- *ConAu 108*
Allen, David 1925- *ConAu 33R*
Allen, David Elliston 1932- *ConAu 25R*
Allen, David F 1943- *ConAu 103*
Allen, Dick *DrAP&F 83*
Allen, Dick 1939- *ConAu 33R, IntAu&W 82,*
　WrDr 84
Allen, Diogenes 1932- *ConAu 10NR, -25R,*
　IntAu&W 82, WrDr 84
Allen, Don Cameron 1903- *ConAu 5R*
Allen, Don Cameron 1903-1972 *ConAu 4NR*
Allen, Donald Emerson 1917- *ConAu 45,*
　IntAu&W 82
Allen, Donald M 1912- *ConAu 17R*
Allen, Donald R 1930- *ConAu 45*
Allen, Dorothy Joan 1921- *IntWWP 82*
Allen, Durward L 1910- *ConAu 41R,*
　MichAu 80, WrDr 84
Allen, Dwight W 1931- *ConAu 13R*
Allen, E C *ConAu X*
Allen, Edith Beavers 1920- *ConAu 9R,*
　WrDr 84
Allen, Edith Marion *ConAu P-1*
Allen, Edward D 1923- *ConAu 49*
Allen, Edward J 1907- *ConAu P-1*
Allen, Elisabeth Offutt 1895- *ConAu 57*
Allen, Elizabeth 1914- *MichAu 80*
Allen, Eric 1908-1968 *TwCCW 83*
Allen, Everett S 1916- *ConAu 110*
Allen, Francis A 1919- *ConAu 13R, WrDr 84*
Allen, Francis R 1908- *ConAu 77*
Allen, Frank 1939- *ConAu 109*
Allen, Frederick G 1936- *ConAu 57*
Allen, Frederick Lewis 1890-1954 *TwCA,*
　TwCA SUP
Allen, G C 1900-1982 *ConAu 3NR, -107*
Allen, Garland E 1936- *ConAu 53*
Allen, Gary *ConAu X*
Allen, Gay Wilson 1903- *ConAu 3NR, -5R,*
　WrDr 84
Allen, Geoffrey Francis 1902- *ConAu P-1,*
　WrDr 84
Allen, George 1832-1907 *LongCTC*
Allen, George Cyril 1900- *ConAu 1R,*
　IntAu&W 82
Allen, George Francis 1907- *ConAu P-1*
Allen, Gerald 1942- *ConAu 93*
Allen, Gertrude E 1888- *ConAu 61, SmATA 9*
Allen, Gilbert *DrAP&F 83*
Allen, Gina 1918- *ConAu 1R*
Allen, Grace *WrDr 84*
Allen, Graham 1938- *IntAu&W 82*
Allen, Grant 1848-1899 *TwCSFW*
Allen, Gwenfread Elaine 1904- *ConAu 61*
Allen, H Fredericka *ConAu X*
Allen, H G *ConAu 29R*
Allen, Harold B 1902- *ConAu 10NR, -17R*
Allen, Harold J 1925- *ConAu 45*
Allen, Harry Cranbrook 1917- *ConAu 5R,*
　IntAu&W 82, WrDr 84
Allen, Hazel *ConAu X*
Allen, Henry *ConAu X*
Allen, Henry Wilson 1912- *ConAu 89, TwCWW,*
　WrDr 84
Allen, Herman R 1913?-1979 *ConAu 89*
Allen, Hervey 1889-1949 *ConAu 108,*
　DcLB 9[port], TwCRGW
Allen, Hervey 1899-1949 *ConAmA, LongCTC,*
　TwCA, TwCA SUP, TwCWr
Allen, Heywood 1935- *ConAu 33R*
Allen, Howard W 1931- *ConAu 33R*
Allen, Hubert Raymond 1919- *WrDr 84*

Allen, Hubery Raymond 1919- *IntAu&W 82*
Allen, Ida Bailey 1885-1973 *ConAu 110*
Allen, Ira R 1948- *ConAu 65*
Allen, Irene 1903- *ConAu P-1*
Allen, Irving L, Jr. 1931- *ConAu 110*
Allen, Ivan, Jr. 1911- *ConAu 109*
Allen, Jack 1899- *SmATA 29*
Allen, Jack 1914- *ConAu 4NR, -9R*
Allen, James *ConAu X*
Allen, James B *DrAP&F 83*
Allen, James B 1927- *ConAu 105*
Allen, James B 1931- *ConAu 105, IntWWP 82, MichAu 80*
Allen, James Egert 1896-1980 *ConAu 97, LivgBAA*
Allen, James Lane 1849-1925 *LongCTC*
Allen, James Lovic 1929- *ConAu 33R*
Allen, Jay Presson 1922- *ConAu 73, DcLB 26[port]*
Allen, Jerry 1911- *ConAu 9R*
Allen, Jim *ConAu X, ConDr 82C*
Allen, Johannes 1916- *ConAu 29R*
Allen, John *ConAu X, TwCCr&M 80, WrDr 84*
Allen, John Alexander 1922- *ConAu 25R*
Allen, John D 1898-1972 *ConAu P-2*
Allen, John E 1921- *WrDr 84*
Allen, John Elliston 1921- *IntAu&W 82*
Allen, John Jay 1932- *ConAu 33R, WrDr 84*
Allen, John Logan 1941- *ConAu 85*
Allen, John Stuart 1907-1982 *ConAu 109*
Allen, Jon L 1931- *ConAu 57*
Allen, Judson B 1932- *ConAu 81*
Allen, Kenneth 1941- *ConAu 69*
Allen, Kenneth S 1913- *ConAu 77*
Allen, Laura Jean *ConAu 110*
Allen, Lawrence A 1926- *ConAu 45*
Allen, Layman E 1927- *ConAu 5R*
Allen, Lee 1915-1969 *ConAu 1R, -1NR*
Allen, Leonard 1915?-1981 *ConAu 102*
Allen, Leroy 1912- *ConAu 65, SmATA 11*
Allen, Leslie Christopher 1935- *ConAu 73*
Allen, Leslie H 1887?-1973 *ConAu 49*
Allen, Linda 1925- *ConAu 102, SmATA 33[port]*
Allen, Loring *ConAu X*
Allen, Louis 1922- *ConAu 41R, IntAu&W 82, WrDr 84*
Allen, Louis A 1917- *ConAu 5R*
Allen, M C 1914- *ConAu 9R*
Allen, Marcus *ConAu X*
Allen, Marjorie 1931- *ConAu 69, SmATA 22[port]*
Allen, Marjory 1897- *ConAu P-1*
Allen, Mark *ConAu X*
Allen, Mary *ConAu X*
Allen, Mary 1909- *ConAu 109, WrDr 84*
Allen, Maury 1932- *ConAu 11NR, -17R, SmATA 26[port]*
Allen, Merrill James 1918- *ConAu 69*
Allen, Merritt Parmelee 1892-1954 *SmATA 22*
Allen, Michael 1939- *ConAu 77*
Allen, Michael J B 1941- *ConAu 102*
Allen, Minerva *DrAP&F 83*
Allen, Minerva C 1935- *ConAu 6NR, -57*
Allen, Myron Sheppard 1901- *ConAu P-1*
Allen, Nina 1935- *SmATA 22[port]*
Allen, Paul 1948- *ConAu 81*
Allen, Paula Gunn *DrAP&F 83*
Allen, Peter Christopher 1905- *ConAu 108*
Allen, Phyllis *ConAu 65*
Allen, Phyllis S 1908- *ConAu 65*
Allen, Polly Reynolds 1940- *ConAu 110*
Allen, R Earl 1922- *ConAu 6NR, -9R*
Allen, R L M 1909- *WrDr 84*
Allen, R R 1930- *ConAu 17R*
Allen, Ralph 1913-1966 *CreCan 1, DcLEL 1940*
Allen, Ralph 1926- *CreCan 1*
Allen, Reginald E 1931- *ConAu 33R*
Allen, Richard 1903- *ConAu 25R*
Allen, Richard 1929- *ConAu 11NR, -65*
Allen, Richard C *ConAu X*
Allen, Richard C 1926- *ConAu 25R, IntAu&W 82, WrDr 84*
Allen, Richard Sanders 1917- *ConAu 21R*
Allen, Richard V 1936- *ConAu 21R*
Allen, Roach Van 1917- *ConAu 9R*
Allen, Robert *ConAu X, DrAP&F 83*
Allen, Robert 1946- *ConAu 97*
Allen, Robert Day 1927- *ConAu 107*
Allen, Robert F 1928- *ConAu 33R*
Allen, Robert J 1930- *ConAu 13R*

Allen, Robert L 1942- *ConAu 101, LivgBAA*
Allen, Robert Livingston 1916- *ConAu 17R*
Allen, Robert Loring 1921- *ConAu 1R, -6NR*
Allen, Robert M 1909-1979 *ConAu 1R, -2NR*
Allen, Robert Porter 1905-1963 *ConAu 5R*
Allen, Robert S 1900-1981 *ConAu 6NR, -103, -57*
Allen, Robert Thomas 1911- *ConAu 110, CreCan 1*
Allen, Rodney F 1938- *ConAu 61, SmATA 27[port]*
Allen, Ross R 1928- *ConAu 33R*
Allen, Roy 1906-1983 *ConAu 110*
Allen, Rupert C 1927- *ConAu 65*
Allen, Ruth Finney 1898-1979 *ConAu 85, -93*
Allen, Sam *ConAu X*
Allen, Samuel W *DrAP&F 83*
Allen, Samuel W 1917- *ConAu 49, IntAu&W 82, IntWWP 82, LivgBAA, SmATA 9*
Allen, Sarah Sawyer 1920- *ConAu 89*
Allen, Shirley Seifried 1921- *ConAu 57*
Allen, Shirley Walter 1883- *ConAu P-2*
Allen, Steve 1921- *ConAu 25R, WrDr 84*
Allen, Sue P 1913- *ConAu 25R*
Allen, Sydney, Jr. 1929- *ConAu 29R*
Allen, T D *DrAP&F 83*
Allen, T D 1908- *ConAu X, TwCWW*
Allen, Terril Diener 1908- *ConAu 2NR, -5R*
Allen, Terry D *ConAu X*
Allen, Thomas B 1929- *ConAu 5NR, -13R*
Allen, Tom *ConAu X*
Allen, Tony 1945- *ConAu 77*
Allen, Velta Myrle 1898- *IntWWP 82*
Allen, Vernon L 1933- *ConAu 29R*
Allen, W Sidney 1918- *ConAu 49*
Allen, Walter 1911- *ConAu 61, ConLCrt 82, ConNov 82, LongCTC, ModBrL, TwCWr, WhoTwCL, WorAu, WrDr 84*
Allen, William 1940- *ConAu 65*
Allen, William A 1916- *ConAu 33R*
Allen, William R 1924- *ConAu 17R*
Allen, William Sheridan 1932- *ConAu 13R, WrDr 84*
Allen, William Stannard 1913- *ConAu 101, IntAu&W 82, WrDr 84*
Allen, Woody 1935- *ConAu X, ConDr 82A, ConLC 16, NatPD 81[port], WrDr 84*
Allen Of Hurtwood, Lady Marjory 1897- *ConAu X*
Allendoerfer, Carl 1911-1974 *ConAu P-2*
Allendoerfer, Carl B 1911-1974 *ConAu 11NR*
Allentuch, Harriet Ray 1933- *ConAu 13R*
Allentuck, Marcia Epstein 1928- *ConAu 33R*
Aller, Sussie 1944- *IntAu&W 82*
Allers, Janne 1925- *IntAu&W 82*
Allerton, Mary *ConAu X, SmATA X, WrDr 84*
Alley, Henry Melton *DrAP&F 83*
Alley, Louis Edward 1914- *ConAu 17R*
Alley, Rewi 1897- *ConAu 73, ConP 80, DcLEL 1940, IntAu&W 82, WrDr 84*
Alley, Robert S 1932- *ConAu 33R, WrDr 84*
Alley, Stephen L 1915- *ConAu 110*
Alleyn, Ellen *SmATA X*
Alleyn, George Edmund 1931- *CreCan 2*
Allgire, Mildred J 1910- *ConAu P-2*
Alliluyeva, Svetlana 1926- *ASpks, ConAu 57*
Allin, Clinton Harrop *ConAu X*
Allin, Craig Willard 1946- *ConAu 108*
Allingham, Margery 1904-1966 *ConAu 4NR, -5R, -25R, ConLC 19, LongCTC, TwCA, TwCA SUP, TwCCr&M 80, TwCWr*
Allingham, Michael 1943- *ConAu 97*
Allinsmith, Wesley 1923- *ConAu 85*
Allinson, Beverley 1936- *ConAu 4NR, -49*
Allinson, Gary Dean 1942- *ConAu 77, IntAu&W 82*
Allis, Oswald Thompson 1880-1973 *ConAu 37R*
Allison, A F 1916- *ConAu 106, WrDr 84*
Allison, Alexander Ward 1919- *ConAu 5R*
Allison, Anthony C 1928- *ConAu 29R*
Allison, Bob *SmATA 14*
Allison, C FitzSimons 1927- *ConAu 4NR*
Allison, Christopher Fitzsimons 1927- *ConAu 1R*
Allison, Clay 1914-1978 *ConAu X, TwCWW*
Allison, Dorothy *DrAP&F 83*
Allison, Drummond 1921-1943 *CnMWL*
Allison, Ethel Blanche 1906- *IntWWP 82*
Allison, Graham T, Jr. 1940- *ConAu 2NR, -49*
Allison, Harrison C 1917- *ConAu 49*
Allison, Helen Thomas 1916- *IntWWP 82*

Allison, Henry E 1937- *ConAu 110*
Allison, John Murray 1889- *ConAu 73*
Allison, Kenneth Willway 1894- *IntAu&W 82*
Allison, Marian *ConAu X*
Allison, Michael Frederick Lister 1936- *ConAu 57*
Allison, Mike *ConAu X*
Allison, R Bruce 1949- *ConAu 3NR, -49*
Allison, Ralph B 1931- *ConAu 101*
Allison, Rand *ConAu X*
Allison, Rosemary 1953- *ConAu 93*
Allison, Sam *ConAu X*
Allister, William 1919- *CreCan 2*
Allman, John *DrAP&F 83*
Allman, John 1935- *ConAu 85*
Allman, T D 1944- *ConAu 93*
Allmendinger, David F, Jr. 1938- *ConAu 61*
Allon, Yigal 1918-1980 *ConAu 73, -97*
Allott, Kenneth 1912-1973 *ConAu 89, DcLEL 1940*
Alloway, David N 1927- *ConAu 10NR*
Alloway, David Nelson 1927- *ConAu 21R, IntAu&W 82, WrDr 84*
Alloway, Lawrence 1926- *ConAu 41R*
Allport, Gordon Willard 1897-1967 *ConAu 1R, -3NR, -25R*
Allred, Dorald M 1923- *ConAu 65*
Allred, G Hugh 1932- *ConAu 8NR, -61, IntAu&W 82*
Allred, Gordon T 1930- *ConAu 10NR, -17R, SmATA 10*
Allred, Ruel A 1929- *ConAu 106*
Alls, Kathy *IntAu&W 82*
Allsen, Philip E 1932- *ConAu 4NR, -53*
Allsop, Kenneth 1920-1973 *ConAu 1R, -6NR, DcLEL 1940, SmATA 17, WorAu*
Allsopp, Bruce 1912- *ConAu 2NR, -5R, IntAu&W 82, WrDr 84*
Allswang, John M 1937- *ConAu 41R*
Allum, Nancy 1920- *ConAu P-1*
Allvine, Fred C 1936- *ConAu 61*
Allvine, Glendon 1893?-1977 *ConAu 73*
Allward, Maurice 1923- *WrDr 84*
Allward, Maurice Frank 1923- *ConAu 3NR, -5R, IntAu&W 82*
Allward, Walter Seymour 1876-1955 *CreCan 1*
Allwood, Arthur 1893- *IntWWP 82*
Allwood, Martin Samuel 1916- *ConAu 110, IntAu&W 82, IntWWP 82*
Allworth, Edward 1920- *ConAu 101*
Allyn, Jennifer *ConAu X*
Allyn, Paul *ConAu X*
Allyson, Kym *ConAu X*
Almada-Negreiros, Jose De 1893-1970 *ClDMEL 80*
Alman, David 1919- *ConAu 9R*
Almansi, Guido 1931- *WrDr 84*
Almaraz, Felix D, Jr. 1933- *ConAu 33R*
Almaz, Michael 1921- *ConAu 81*
Almaz, Michael 1927- *IntAu&W 82*
Almedingen, E M 1898-1971 *ConAu X, -1R, ConLC 12, LongCTC, SmATA 3, TwCCW 83, WorAu*
Almedingen, Martha Edith Von 1898-1971 *ConAu 1NR, SmATA 3*
Almon, Bert *DrAP&F 83*
Almon, Bert 1943- *ConAu 110*
Almon, Clopper, Jr. 1934- *ConAu 21R*
Almond, Gabriel A 1911- *WrDr 84*
Almond, Gabriel Abraham 1911- *ConAu 101*
Almond, Genevieve Bujold *CreCan 1*
Almond, Paul 1931- *ConAu 73, CreCan 2*
Almond, Richard 1938- *ConAu 53*
Almonte, Rosa *ConAu X*
Almquist, Don 1929- *SmATA 11*
Almquist, L Arden 1921- *ConAu 29R*
Almy, Millie 1915- *ConAu 85*
Alnaes, Karsten 1938- *IntAu&W 82*
Aloff, Mindy *DrAP&F 83*
Aloian, David 1928- *ConAu 25R*
Alomar, Gabriel 1873-1941 *ClDMEL 80*
Aloni, Nissim 1926- *EncWL 2*
Alonso, Damaso 1898- *ClDMEL 80, ConAu 110, ConLC 14, EncWL 2*
Alonso, Fernando 1941- *IntAu&W 82*
Alonso, J M 1936- *ConAu 102*
Alonso, Ricardo *DrAP&F 83*
Alonso, Rodolfo 1934- *IntWWP 82*
Alonso, William 1933- *ConAu 6NR, -9R*
Alonso Ibarrola, Jose Manuel 1934- *IntAu&W 82*
Alonso Luengo, Luis 1907- *IntAu&W 82*
Alonso Millan, Juan Jose 1936- *CroCD*

Ames, Jennifer *ConAu X, LongCTC, TwCRGW*
Ames, Jocelyn Green *ConAu 5R*
Ames, Lee Judah 1921- *ConAu 1R, –3NR, SmATA 3*
Ames, Leslie *ConAu X,*   *IntAu&W 82X, WrDr 84*
Ames, Lois 1931- *ConAu 101*
Ames, Louise Bates 1908- *ConAu 1R, –3NR*
Ames, Mildred 1919- *ConAu 11NR, –69, SmATA 22[port]*
Ames, Noel *ConAu X*
Ames, Norma 1920- *ConAu 29R*
Ames, Rachel 1922- *ConAu 97*
Ames, Ruth M 1918- *ConAu 29R*
Ames, Sarah Rachel 1922- *WrDr 84*
Ames, Scribner 1908- *ConAu 69*
Ames, Van Meter 1898- *ConAu P-1*
Ames, Walter Lansing 1946- *ConAu 106*
Ames, Winslow 1907- *ConAu P-2*
Ames-Lewis, Francis 1943- *ConAu 108*
Amess, Frederick Arthur 1909- *CreCan 2*
Amey, Lloyd Ronald 1922- *ConAu 45*
Amfitheatrof, Erik 1931- *ConAu 89*
Ami, Ben *ConAu X, –X*
Amica, Jean *IntAu&W 82X*
Amichai, Yehuda 1924- *ConAu 85, ConLC 9, –22[port], WorAu 1970*
Amichai, Yehudah 1924- *EncWL 2*
Amick, Robert G 1933- *WrDr 84*
Amick, Robert Gene 1933- *ConAu 33R*
Amicus *IntWWP 82X*
Amidon, Bill 1935-1979 *ConAu 103, –45*
Amiel, Barbara 1940- *ConAu 101*
Amiel, Denys 1884- *CIDMEL 80*
Amiel, Joseph 1937- *ConAu 101*
Amin, Ali 1913?-1976 *ConAu 65*
Amin, Mohamed 1943- *IntAu&W 82*
Amin, Samir 1931- *ConAu 89*
Amini, Johari M *DrAP&F 83*
Amini, Johari M 1935- *ConAu X, LivgBAA*
Amir, Aharon 1923- *IntWWP 82*
Amir, Menachem 1930- *ConAu 45*
Amis, Breton *ConAu X*
Amis, Kingsley 1922- *AuNews 2, CnMWL, ConAu 8NR, –9R, ConLC 1, –2, –3, –5, –8, –13, ConNov 82, ConP 80, ConSFA, DcLB 15[port], DcLEL 1940, EncWL 2, LongCTC, ModBrL, ModBrL SUP, TwCCr&M 80, TwCSFW, TwCWr, WhoTwCL, WorAu, WrDr 84*
Amis, Lola Elizabeth Jones 1930- *LivgBAA*
Amis, Martin 1949- *ConAu 8NR, –65, ConLC 9, ConNov 82, DcLB 14[port], WrDr 84*
Amis, Martin 1950?- *ConLC 4*
Amishai-Maisels, Ziva *ConAu 49*
Amlund, Curtis Arthur 1927- *ConAu 21R*
Ammar, Abbas 1907?-1974 *ConAu 53*
Amme, Carl H, Jr. 1913- *ConAu 25R*
Ammer, Christine 1931- *ConAu 106, WrDr 84*
Ammer, Dean S 1926- *ConAu 7NR, –17R*
Ammerman, David Leon 1938- *ConAu 57*
Ammerman, Gale Richard 1923- *ConAu 107*
Ammerman, Leila T 1912- *WrDr 84*
Ammerman, Leila Tremaine 1912- *ConAu 33R*
Ammerman, Robert R 1927- *ConAu 13R*
Ammers-Kuller, Jo Van 1884- *TwCA, TwCA SUP*
Ammon, Harry 1917- *ConAu 73*
Ammons, A R *DrAP&F 83*
Ammons, A R 1926- *AuNews 1, ConAu 6NR, –9R, ConLC 2, –3, –5, –8, –9, –25[port], ConP 80, CroCAP, DcLB 5[port], EncWL 2, ModAL SUP, WorAu, WrDr 84*
Ammons, Archie Randolph 1926- *DcLEL 1940, IntAu&W 82, IntWWP 82*
Amo, Tauraatua I *ConAu X*
Amoaku, J K 1936- *ConAu 45*
Amon, Aline 1928- *ConAu 8NR, –61, SmATA 9*
Amor, Amos *ConAu X*
Amore, Roy Clayton 1942- *ConAu 105*
Amorim, Enrique 1900-1960 *EncWL 2, ModLAL*
Amorosi, Ray *DrAP&F 83*
Amory, Anne Reinberg 1931- *ConAu 17R*
Amory, Cleveland 1917- *AuNews 1, ConAu 69, TwCA SUP, WrDr 84*
Amos, William E 1926- *ConAu 17R*
Amos, Winsom 1921- *ConAu 49, MichAu 80*

Amoss, Berthe 1925- *ConAu 21R, SmATA 5*
Amprimoz, Alexandre Laurent Antoine 1948- *ConAu 37R*
Amram, David 1930- *ASpks, ConAu 29R*
Amrine, Michael 1919?-1974 *ConAu 49, –73*
Amstead, B H 1921- *ConAu 21R*
Amster, Linda 1938- *ConAu 45*
Amston, Jerry *IntWWP 82X*
Amstutz, Arnold E 1936- *ConAu 21R*
Amstutz, Mark R 1944- *ConAu 105*
Amter, Joseph A d1982 *ConAu 109*
Amundsen, Kirsten 1932- *ConAu 37R*
Amuzegar, Jahangir 1920- *ConAu 41R*
Amyx, Katherine McClure 1901- *IntWWP 82*
Anand, Mulk Raj 1905- *ConAu 65, ConLC 23[port], ConNov 82, EncWL 2, ModCmwL, WorAu, WrDr 84*
Anand, P A 1931- *IntWWP 82*
Anand, Valerie May Florence 1937- *ConAu 73, IntAu&W 82*
Anania, Michael 1938- *WrDr 84*
Anania, Michael 1939- *ConAu 25R, ConP 80*
Anania, Michael A *DrAP&F 83*
Anastaplo, George 1925- *ConAu 37R*
Anastas, Peter 1937- *ConAu 1NR, –45*
Anastasi, Anne 1908- *ConAu 2NR, –5R, IntAu&W 82*
Anastasio, Dina 1941- *ConAu 107, SmATA 30*
Anastasiou, Clifford 1929- *ConAu 3NR, –49*
Anati, Emmanuel 1930- *WrDr 84*
Anatol *ConAu X*
Anatol, A *ConAu X*
Anaya, Rudolfo *DrAP&F 83*
Anaya, Rudolfo A 1937- *ConAu 1NR, –45, ConLC 23[port]*
Anber, Paul *ConAu X*
Ancel, Marc 1902- *ConAu 69*
Ancel, Martin *IntAu&W 82X*
Ancey, Georges 1860-1917 *ModWD*
Anchell, Melvin 1919- *ConAu 25R*
Anchor, Robert 1937- *ConAu 69*
Anckarsvard, Karin 1915-1969 *ConAu 9R, –103, SmATA 6*
Ancona, George 1929- *ConAu 4NR, –53, SmATA 12*
Ancrom, Nancy *DrAP&F 83*
And, Miekal *DrAP&F 83*
Anday, Melih Cevdet 1915- *CIDMEL 80, EncWL 2*
Andelin, Helen B 1920- *ConAu 89*
Andelman, Eddie 1936- *ConAu 57*
Andelson, Robert V 1931- *ConAu 33R, IntAu&W 82, WrDr 84*
Andereich, Justus *ConAu X*
Anders, Edith Mary 1899- *ConAu P-1, IntAu&W 82*
Anders, Evelyn 1916- *ConAu 29R*
Anders, Gunther S 1902- *IntAu&W 82*
Anders, Leslie 1922- *ConAu 13R, WrDr 84*
Anders, Olaf *IntAu&W 82X*
Anders, Sarah Frances 1927- *ConAu 105*
Anders-Richards, Donald 1928- *ConAu 25R, WrDr 84*
Andersch, Alfred 1914-1980 *CIDMEL 80, ConAu 33R, –93, EncWL 2, ModGL*
Andersch, Elizabeth Genevieve 1913- *ConAu 5R*
Andersdatter, Karla M *DrAP&F 83*
Andersdatter, Karla M 1938- *ConAu 104, SmATA 34[port]*
Andersen, Arlow W 1906- *ConAu P-1*
Andersen, Benny 1929- *CIDMEL 80, ConAu 101, EncWL 2, IntWWP 82X*
Andersen, Benny Allan 1929- *IntWWP 82*
Andersen, Bjorn 1937- *IntAu&W 82*
Andersen, Christopher P 1949- *ConAu 69*
Andersen, D R 1947- *ConAu 108, NatPD 81[port]*
Andersen, Doris 1909- *ConAu 11NR, –21R, TwCCW 83, WrDr 84*
Andersen, Edvard 1916- *IntAu&W 82*
Andersen, Erik B 1933- *IntAu&W 82*
Andersen, Francis Ian 1925- *ConAu 108*
Andersen, Hans 1932- *IntAu&W 82*
Andersen, Hans Christian 1805-1875 *ChlLR 6[port]*
Andersen, Jakob 1936- *IntAu&W 82*
Andersen, Jefferson 1955?-1979 *ConAu 85*
Andersen, Juel 1923- *ConAu 105*
Andersen, Kenneth E 1933- *ConAu 37R*
Andersen, Kurt 1954- *ConAu 106*
Andersen, Marianne S 1934- *ConAu 65*

Andersen, Marion Lineaweaver 1912?-1971 *ConAu 29R*
Andersen, R Clifton 1933- *ConAu 33R*
Andersen, Richard 1931- *ConAu 8NR, –57*
Andersen, Richard 1946- *ConAu 102*
Andersen, Ted *ConAu X, SmATA X*
Andersen, Tryggve 1866-1920 *CIDMEL 80*
Andersen, Uell Stanley 1917- *ConAu 1R*
Andersen, Verner Arne Gerber 1920- *IntWWP 82*
Andersen, Wayne V 1928- *ConAu 9R*
Andersen, Wilhelm 1911- *ConAu 29R*
Andersen, Yvonne 1932- *ConAu 29R, SmATA 27[port]*
Andersen Nexo, Martin 1869-1954 *CIDMEL 80, TwCA, TwCA SUP*
Anderson, A J 1933- *ConAu 106*
Anderson, Alan, Jr. 1943- *WrDr 84*
Anderson, Alan H, Jr. 1943- *ConAu 69*
Anderson, Alan Ross 1925-1973 *ConAu 45, ConAu P-2*
Anderson, Alasdair 1943- *IntAu&W 82*
Anderson, Alex L *IntWWP 82X*
Anderson, Alexander 1845-1909 *LongCTC*
Anderson, Alexander Laurence 1908- *IntWWP 82*
Anderson, Allan 1915- *ConAu 97*
Anderson, Alpha E 1914-1970 *ConAu P-2*
Anderson, Arthur J O 1907- *ConAu 85*
Anderson, Barbara 1948- *ConAu 93*
Anderson, Barry 1935- *ConAu 17R*
Anderson, Bern 1900-1963 *ConAu 1R*
Anderson, Bernard Eric 1936- *ConAu 5NR, –53*
Anderson, Bernhard Word 1916- *ConAu 8NR, –57*
Anderson, Bernice G 1894- *ConAu 101, SmATA 33[port]*
Anderson, Bertha Moore 1892- *ConAu 5R*
Anderson, Beth *DrAP&F 83*
Anderson, Beth 1950- *IntWWP 82*
Anderson, Beverly *ConAu X*
Anderson, Beverly M *ConAu X*
Anderson, Bob 1947- *ConAu 69*
Anderson, Brad 1924- *SmATA 33[port]*
Anderson, Brad Jay 1924- *ConAu 106, SmATA 31*
Anderson, C L 1901- *ConAu 25R*
Anderson, C W 1891-1971 *SmATA 11, TwCCW 83*
Anderson, Camilla M 1904- *ConAu 33R*
Anderson, Carl Dicmann 1912- *ConAu 33R*
Anderson, Carl L 1919- *ConAu 41R*
Anderson, Carla *IntAu&W 82X*
Anderson, Carolyn Hunt 1941- *ConAu 73*
Anderson, Catherine Corley 1909- *ConAu 1R*
Anderson, Charles Burroughs 1905- *ConAu 65*
Anderson, Charles C 1931- *ConAu 29R*
Anderson, Charles Roberts 1902- *ConAu 1R, –3NR*
Anderson, Charles W 1934- *ConAu 9R*
Anderson, Charlotte Maria 1923- *ConAu 81*
Anderson, Chester *ConSFA*
Anderson, Chester 1932- *TwCSFW, WrDr 84*
Anderson, Chester G 1923- *ConAu 25R*
Anderson, Chuck 1933- *ConAu 49*
Anderson, Clarence William 1891-1971 *ConAu 29R, –73*
Anderson, Clifford *ConAu X, –X, SmATA X*
Anderson, Colena M 1891- *ConAu 11NR, –21R*
Anderson, Colin *TwCSFW, WrDr 84*
Anderson, Courtney 1906- *ConAu P-1, WrDr 84*
Anderson, Dave *AuNews 2, ConAu X*
Anderson, David Daniel 1924- *ConAu 5NR, –13R, MichAu 80, WrDr 84*
Anderson, David L 1919- *ConAu 5R*
Anderson, David Poole 1929- *ConAu 89, IntAu&W 82*
Anderson, Dewey 1897- *ConAu 57*
Anderson, Dillon 1906-1973 *ConAu 1R, –45*
Anderson, Donald F 1938- *ConAu 53*
Anderson, Donald K, Jr. 1922- *ConAu 37R, WrDr 84*
Anderson, Doris 1925- *ConAu 89*
Anderson, Douglas *DrAP&F 83*
Anderson, Dwight G 1938- *ConAu 107*
Anderson, E Ruth 1907- *ConAu 93*
Anderson, E W 1901-1981 *ConAu 104*
Anderson, Edgar 1920- *ConAu 33R*
Anderson, Einar 1909- *ConAu 13R*
Anderson, Elbridge Gerry 1907- *ConAu 69*
Anderson, Ella *IntAu&W 82X, SmATA X, WrDr 84*

Anderson, Elliott 1944- *ConAu 93*
Anderson, Eloise Adell 1927- *ConAu 53,*
  SmATA 9
Anderson, Eric 1949- *ConAu 106*
Anderson, Erica 1914- *ConAu 57*
Anderson, Erland *DrAP&F 83*
Anderson, Ethel Louisa 1883-1958 *DcLEL 1940*
Anderson, Eugene N 1900- *ConAu 29R*
Anderson, Ferguson 1914- *ConAu 107,*
  WrDr 84
Anderson, Flavia 1910- *WrDr 84*
Anderson, Frank J 1919- *ConAu 4NR, –9R*
Anderson, Frederick Irving 1877-1947 *TwCA,*
  TwCA SUP, TwCCr&M 80
Anderson, Freeman B 1922- *ConAu 41R*
Anderson, George *ConAu X, SmATA X*
Anderson, George Christian 1907-1976 *ConAu 69,*
  ConAu P-2
Anderson, George K 1901- *ConAu P-2*
Anderson, George L 1905-1971 *ConAu 9NR*
Anderson, George Laverne 1905- *ConAu 5R,*
  –13R
Anderson, George Walter 1932- *ConAmTC*
Anderson, Gerald H 1930- *ConAu 7NR, –17R*
Anderson, Godfrey Tryggve 1909- *ConAu 41R*
Anderson, H Dewey 1897-1975 *ConAu 61, –65*
Anderson, Harold H 1897- *ConAu P-2*
Anderson, Harry V 1903-1983 *ConAu 110*
Anderson, Henry P 1927- *ConAu 33R*
Anderson, Howard Peter 1932- *ConAu 61*
Anderson, Hugh 1920- *ConAu 9R,*
  IntAu&W 82
Anderson, Ian Gibson 1933- *ConAu 85*
Anderson, Irvine H 1928- *ConAu 11NR, –69*
Anderson, J E 1903- *ConAu 37R*
Anderson, J K 1924- *ConAu 10NR, –17R*
Anderson, J Kerby 1951- *ConAu 97*
Anderson, J N *ConAu X*
Anderson, J R L 1911-1981 *ConAu 104, –25R,*
  SmATA 15, –27N
Anderson, Jack *DrAP&F 83*
Anderson, Jack 1922- *AuNews 1, ConAu 6NR,*
  –57, WrDr 84
Anderson, Jack 1935- *ConAu 33R*
Anderson, James *IntAu&W 82, TwCCr&M 80,*
  WrDr 84
Anderson, James 1936- *IntAu&W 82*
Anderson, James D 1933- *ConAu 49*
Anderson, James E 1933- *ConAu 6NR, –9R*
Anderson, James F 1910- *ConAu 41R*
Anderson, James G 1936- *ConAu 25R,*
  WrDr 84
Anderson, James M 1933- *ConAu 33R*
Anderson, James Norman Dalrymple 1908-
  ConAu 9R
Anderson, Jean 1930- *ConAu 41R*
Anderson, Jeanne 1934?-1979 *ConAu 85*
Anderson, Jennifer 1942- *ConAu 57*
Anderson, Jerry M 1933- *ConAu 41R*
Anderson, Jessica *ConAu 4NR, –9R,*
  IntAu&W 82, WrDr 84
Anderson, Joan Wester 1938- *ConAu 9NR, –65*
Anderson, John 1909- *WrDr 84*
Anderson, John B 1922- *ConAu 33R, WrDr 84*
Anderson, John F 1945- *ConAu 53*
Anderson, John K *ConAu X*
Anderson, John L *IntAu&W 82X*
Anderson, John Lonzo 1905- *IntAu&W 82*
Anderson, John M 1914- *ConAu 17R*
Anderson, John Q 1916-1975 *ConAu 1R, –3NR*
Anderson, John Richard Lane 1911-
  IntAu&W 82
Anderson, Jon *DrAP&F 83*
Anderson, Jon 1940- *ConAu 25R, ConLC 9,*
  ConP 80, WrDr 84
Anderson, Joy 1928- *ConAu 25R, SmATA 1*
Anderson, Ken *DrAP&F 83*
Anderson, Ken 1917- *ConAu 25R*
Anderson, Kenneth Norman 1921- *ConAu 102*
Anderson, Kristin *ConAu X*
Anderson, LaVere Francis Shoenfelt 1907-
  ConAu 101, SmATA 27
Anderson, Lee 1896-1972 *ConAu 1R, –37R*
Anderson, Lee Stratton 1925- *ConAu 101*
Anderson, Lester William 1918-1973 *ConAu 5R,*
  –103
Anderson, Lila Pauline Gage 1921- *IntWWP 82*
Anderson, Lindsay 1923- *ConLC 20*
Anderson, Lonzo 1905- *ConAu 25R,*
  IntAu&W 82X, SmATA 2
Anderson, Lucia 1922- *ConAu 41R, SmATA 10*
Anderson, Luther A *ConAu 65, MichAu 80*

Anderson, Madeleine Paltenghi 1899- *ConAu P-1*
Anderson, Madelyn Klein *ConAu 11NR, –69,*
  SmATA 28
Anderson, Maggie *ConAu X, DrAP&F 83*
Anderson, Malcolm 1934- *ConAu 33R,*
  WrDr 84
Anderson, Margaret 1886-1973 *DcLB 4*
Anderson, Margaret 1917- *ConAu 21R*
Anderson, Margaret 1948- *ConAu 101*
Anderson, Margaret Bartlett 1922- *ConAu 9R*
Anderson, Margaret C 1886-1973 *ConAu 108*
Anderson, Margaret C 1891?-1973 *ConAu 45*
Anderson, Margaret J 1931- *ConAu 11NR, –69,*
  SmATA 27[port]
Anderson, Margaret Johnson 1909- *ConAu 1R,*
  –3NR
Anderson, Marjorie Ogilvie 1909- *IntAu&W 82*
Anderson, Marlene *IntWWP 82X*
Anderson, Martin 1936- *ConAu 9NR, –13R*
Anderson, Marvin Walter 1933- *ConAu 41R*
Anderson, Mary 1939- *ConAu 1NR, –49,*
  IntAu&W 82, SmATA 7
Anderson, Mary Desiree 1902- *ConAu 9R*
Anderson, Matthew Smith 1922- *ConAu 13R,*
  IntAu&W 82, WrDr 84
Anderson, Maxwell 1888-1959 *CnMD, ConAmA,*
  ConAu 105, CroCD, DcLB 7[port],
  LongCTC, ModAL, ModWD, TwCA,
  TwCA SUP, TwCLC 2, TwCWr
Anderson, Michael *DrAP&F 83*
Anderson, Mona 1910- *ConAu 6NR, –57,*
  WrDr 84
Anderson, Nathan Ruth 1934- *IntAu&W 82*
Anderson, Norman 1908- *ConAu 4NR,*
  WrDr 84
Anderson, Norman Dean 1928- *ConAu 33R,*
  SmATA 22[port]
Anderson, O Roger 1937- *ConAu 33R*
Anderson, Odie 1943- *LivgBAA*
Anderson, Odin W 1914- *ConAu 25R*
Anderson, Olive M 1915- *ConAu 81*
Anderson, Olive Ruth 1926- *ConAu 107,*
  WrDr 84
Anderson, P Howard 1947- *ConAu 61*
Anderson, Patrick 1936- *ConAu 33R*
Anderson, Paul E 1925- *ConAu 33R*
Anderson, Paul Seward 1913-1975 *ConAu 1R,*
  –6NR
Anderson, Peggy 1938- *ConAu 93, WrDr 84*
Anderson, Poul *DrAP&F 83*
Anderson, Poul 1926- *ConAu 1R, –2NR,*
  ConLC 15, ConSFA, DcLB 8[port],
  DcLEL 1940, IntAu&W 82, TwCSFW,
  WorAu, WrDr 84
Anderson, Quentin 1912- *ConAu 1R, –3NR,*
  ConLCrt 82, WrDr 84
Anderson, R C 1883?-1976 *ConAu 69*
Anderson, Rachel 1943- *ConAu 9NR, –21R,*
  SmATA 34[port], WrDr 84
Anderson, Randall C 1934- *ConAu 41R*
Anderson, Ray Sherman 1925- *ConAu 10NR,*
  –65
Anderson, Raymond L 1927- *ConAu 106*
Anderson, Richard Lloyd 1926- *ConAu 37R,*
  WrDr 84
Anderson, Robert 1917- *ASpks, AuNews 1,*
  CnMD, ConAu 21R, ConDr 82,
  ConLC 23[port], CroCD, DcLB 7[port],
  DcLEL 1940, IntAu&W 82, ModAL,
  ModWD, NatPD 81[port], WorAu,
  WrDr 84
Anderson, Robert A 1944- *ConAu 109*
Anderson, Robert C 1930- *ConAu 85*
Anderson, Robert David 1942- *ConAu 73*
Anderson, Robert H 1918- *ConAu 49*
Anderson, Robert Mapes 1929- *ConAu 108*
Anderson, Robert Newton 1929- *ConAu 49*
Anderson, Robert T 1926- *ConAu 9R*
Anderson, Robert W 1926- *ConAu 17R*
Anderson, Rodney Dean 1938- *ConAu 108*
Anderson, Roy 1936- *ConAu 13R, WrDr 84*
Anderson, Roy Allan 1895- *ConAu 9NR, –13R*
Anderson, Ruth I 1919- *WrDr 84*
Anderson, Ruth Irene 1919- *ConAu 1R*
Anderson, Ruth Nathan 1934- *ConAu 69*
Anderson, Scarvia 1926- *ConAu 41R*
Anderson, Sherwood 1876-1941 *CnMWL,*
  ConAmA, ConAu 104, DcLB DS1[port], –4,
  –9[port], EncWL 2[port], LongCTC,
  ModAL, ModAL SUP, TwCA,

TwCA SUP, TwCLC 1, –10[port], TwCWr,
  WhoTwCL
Anderson, Shirley Lord 1934- *ConAu 11NR, –65*
Anderson, Stanford 1934- *ConAu 25R*
Anderson, Stanley Edwin 1900-1977 *ConAu 1R,*
  –3NR
Anderson, Stanley V 1928- *ConAu 21R*
Anderson, Sydney 1927- *ConAu 106*
Anderson, T W 1918- *ConAu 49*
Anderson, Teresa *DrAP&F 83*
Anderson, Teresa 1944- *ConAu 85*
Anderson, Theodore R 1927- *ConAu 41R*
Anderson, Thomas 1929- *ConAu 1R*
Anderson, Thomas Foxen 1911- *IntAu&W 82*
Anderson, Tom 1910- *ConAu 69*
Anderson, Tommy 1918- *ConAu 45*
Anderson, Totton J 1909- *ConAu 1R*
Anderson, Torsten *IntAu&W 82X*
Anderson, Verily 1915- *ConAu 3NR, –5R,*
  WrDr 84
Anderson, Vernon E 1908- *WrDr 84*
Anderson, Vernon Ellsworth 1908- *ConAu 1R,*
  –5NR, IntAu&W 82
Anderson, Virgila Antris 1899- *ConAu 1R*
Anderson, Virginia 1920- *ConAu 21R*
Anderson, Vivienne *WrDr 84*
Anderson, Vivienne 1916- *ConAu 17R,*
  IntAu&W 82
Anderson, Wallace Ludwig 1917- *ConAu 17R*
Anderson, Walt *ConAu X*
Anderson, Walter 1944- *ConAu 101*
Anderson, Walter Truett 1933- *ConAu 105*
Anderson, Warren DeWitt 1920- *ConAu 17R*
Anderson, Wayne 1946- *ConAu 107*
Anderson, Wayne Jeremy 1908- *ConAu 49*
Anderson, Wendell B 1920- *ConAu 105*
Anderson, William A 1927- *LivgBAA*
Anderson, William C *DrAP&F 83*
Anderson, William C 1920- *ConAu 2NR, –5R,*
  ConSFA
Anderson, William Davis 1938- *ConAu 33R*
Anderson, William H 1905-1972 *ConAu 49*
Anderson, William Henry 1882-1955 *CreCan 2*
Anderson, William Robert 1921- *ConAu 5R*
Anderson, William Scovil 1927- *ConAu 61*
Anderson, Wilton T 1916- *ConAu 17R*
Anderson-Coons, Susan *DrAP&F 83*
Anderson-Imbert, Enrique 1910- *ConAu 10NR,*
  –17R, ModLAL
Andersons, Edgars *ConAu X*
Andersson, Bo E 1934- *IntAu&W 82*
Andersson, Dan 1888-1920 *CIDMEL 80*
Andersson, Erik Stellan 1943- *IntAu&W 82*
Andersson, Ingrid Svea Margareta 1918-
  IntAu&W 82
Andersson, Ingvar 1899?-1974 *ConAu 53*
Andersson, Lars Gunnar 1954- *IntAu&W 82*
Andersson, Theodore 1903- *ConAu 49*
Andersson, Theodore M 1934- *ConAu 25R*
Anderton, David A 1919- *ConAu 9NR, –65*
Anderton, Joanne Gast 1930- *ConAu 61*
Anderton, Johana Gast *ConAu X*
Andervont, Howard Bancroft 1898-1981
  ConAu 103
Andonian, Jeanne 1891?-1976 *ConAu 65*
Andonov-Poljanski, Hristo 1927- *ConAu 9NR,*
  –21R
Andouard *ConAu X*
Andrade, Carlos Drummond De 1902- *ConLC 18,*
  EncWL 2, ModLAL, WorAu 1970
Andrade, Edward Neville DaCosta 1887-1971
  ConAu P-1, LongCTC
Andrade, Eugenio De 1923- *CIDMEL 80*
Andrade, Mario Raul DeMorab 1892-1945
  EncWL 2
Andrade, Mario Raul DeMorab 1893-1945
  ModLAL
Andrade, Oswald De 1890-1954 *EncWL 2,*
  ModLAL, WorAu 1970
Andrade, Victor 1905- *ConAu 69*
Andrain, Charles F 1937- *ConAu 69*
Andre, Evelyn M 1924- *ConAu 11NR, –69,*
  SmATA 27[port]
Andre, Michael *DrAP&F 83*
Andre, Michael 1946- *WrDr 84*
Andre, Robert Paul 1920- *IntAu&W 82*
Andrea, Marianne *DrAP&F 83,*
  IntAu&W 82X
Andreach, Robert J 1930- *ConAu 33R*
Andreano, Ralph L 1929- *ConAu 5R, –6NR*
Andreas, Burton G 1921- *ConAu 81*
Andreas, Thomas *ConAu 49*

Andreas-Salome, Lou 1861-1937 *ClDMEL 80*
Andreasen, Alan R 1934- *ConAu 65*
Andreasen, Nancy C 1938- *ConAu 108*
Andreasen, Uffe 1943- *IntAu&W 82*
Andree, Louise *ConAu X, SmATA X*
Andree, R V 1919- *ConAu 8NR*
Andree, Richard Vernon 1919- *ConAu 57*
Andree, Robert G 1912- *ConAu 29R*
Andreev *TwCA, TwCA SUP*
Andreev, Leonid 1871-1919 *EncWL 2, ModWD*
Andrejcak, Dawna Maydak *DrAP&F 83*
Andreopoulos, Spyros 1929- *ConAu 77*
Andres, Glenn M 1941- *ConAu 73*
Andres, Stefan 1906-1970 *CnMD, ConAu 29R, CroCD, EncWL 2, ModGL, TwCWr, WorAu*
Andres Hernandez, Elena 1929- *IntAu&W 82*
Andresen, Jack *ConAu X*
Andresen, John H, Jr. 1917- *ConAu 57*
Andresen, Sophia DeMello Breyner 1919- *ClDMEL 80*
Andreski, Iris *ConAu X*
Andreski, Stanislav Leonard 1919- *ConAu 61, IntAu&W 82, WrDr 84*
Andrevon, Jean-Pierre 1937- *TwCSFW A*
Andrew, Dr. Robert *IntAu&W 82X*
Andrew, Edward Raymond 1921- *IntAu&W 82, WrDr 84*
Andrew, J Dudley 1945- *ConAu 9NR*
Andrew, James Dudley 1945- *ConAu 65*
Andrew, John 1943- *ConAu 69*
Andrew, Malcolm 1945- *ConAu 105*
Andrew, Mary 1897- *IntAu&W 82*
Andrew, Prudence 1924- *ConAu 1R, -1NR, TwCCW 83, WrDr 84*
Andrew, Warren 1910- *ConAu 21R*
Andrewartha, Herbert George 1907- *WrDr 84*
Andrewes, Christopher Howard 1896- *ConAu 17R*
Andrewes, Patience *ConAu X*
Andrews, A A *ConAu X*
Andrews, Allen 1913- *ConAu 1NR, -49, IntAu&W 82, WrDr 84*
Andrews, Arthur Douglas 1923- *ConAu 69*
Andrews, Barry Geoffrey 1943- *ConAu 2NR, -49*
Andrews, Bart 1945- *ConAu 9NR, -65*
Andrews, Benny 1930- *ConAu 106, SmATA 31[port]*
Andrews, Bruce *DrAP&F 83*
Andrews, Bruce 1948- *ConAu 10NR, -49*
Andrews, Burton 1906- *ConAu P-2*
Andrews, Cecily Fairfield *ConLC 9*
Andrews, Charles McLean 1863-1943 *DcLB 17[port], TwCA, TwCA SUP*
Andrews, Cicily Fairfield *ConAu X, WrDr 84*
Andrews, Claire 1940- *ConAu 33R*
Andrews, Clarence Adelbert 1912- *ConAu 33R, WrDr 84*
Andrews, Donald H 1898-197-? *ConAu P-2*
Andrews, Dorothea Harris 1916-1976 *ConAu 69*
Andrews, E M 1933- *ConAu 93*
Andrews, Eamonn 1922- *IntAu&W 82, WrDr 84*
Andrews, Edgar Harold 1932- *ConAu 105, WrDr 84*
Andrews, Elizabeth 1940- *IntAu&W 82*
Andrews, Elton V *ConAu X*
Andrews, Ernest E 1932- *ConAu 57*
Andrews, F Emerson 1902-1978 *ConAu 1R, -1NR, -81, SmATA 22[port]*
Andrews, F Michael 1916- *ConAu 9R*
Andrews, Frank 1937- *ConAu 61*
Andrews, Frank M 1935- *ConAu 41R*
Andrews, Frederick Cyrus 1902- *IntAu&W 82*
Andrews, George 1926- *ConAu 21R*
Andrews, George F 1918- *ConAu 65*
Andrews, Henry N, Jr. 1910- *ConAu 93*
Andrews, J Cutler 1908-1972 *ConAu 37R*
Andrews, J S 1934- *ConAu 29R*
Andrews, James David 1924- *ConAu 53, IntWWP 82*
Andrews, James Frederick 1936-1980 *ConAu 107*
Andrews, James P 1936?-1980 *ConAu 102*
Andrews, James Sydney 1934- *SmATA 4*
Andrews, Jenne R *DrAP&F 83*
Andrews, John Henry 1939- *ConAu 107, WrDr 84*
Andrews, John Williams 1898-1975 *ConAu 57*
Andrews, Julie 1935- *ConAu 37R, SmATA 7, WrDr 84*
Andrews, Keith 1930- *ConAu 33R*
Andrews, Kenneth R 1916- *ConAu 1R*

Andrews, Laura *ConAu X, SmATA X*
Andrews, Lewis M 1946- *ConAu 65*
Andrews, Lucilla *TwCRGW, WrDr 84*
Andrews, Lyman 1938- *ConAu 49, IntWWP 82, WrDr 84*
Andrews, Marcia *IntWWP 82*
Andrews, Margaret E *ConAu 33R*
Andrews, Mark Edwin 1903- *ConAu P-1*
Andrews, Marshall 1899?-1973 *ConAu 45*
Andrews, Mary Evans *ConAu 5R*
Andrews, Mary Raymond Shipman 1865?-1936 *TwCA*
Andrews, Michael Frank 1916- *ConAu 49*
Andrews, Nancy *DrAP&F 83*
Andrews, Paul Revere 1906-1983 *ConAu 110*
Andrews, Peter 1931- *ConAu 11NR, -17R*
Andrews, Ralph Warren 1897- *ConAu 9R*
Andrews, Raymond *DrAP&F 83*
Andrews, Raymond 1934- *ConAu 81, IntAu&W 82*
Andrews, Robert D *ConAu X*
Andrews, Robert Douglas 1908- *ConAu P-1*
Andrews, Roy Chapman 1884-1960 *SmATA 19, TwCA, TwCA SUP*
Andrews, Stanley 1894- *ConAu 45*
Andrews, V C *ConAu 97*
Andrews, Vicki *MichAu 80*
Andrews, Wayne 1913- *ConAu 3NR, -9R*
Andrews, William G 1930- *ConAu 5R, -7NR*
Andrews, William Linton 1886- *ConAu 9R*
Andrews, William R 1937- *ConAu 53*
Andreyev, Leonid Nikolayevich 1871-1919 *ClDMEL 80, CnMD, ConAu 104, LongCTC, ModSL 1, TwCA, TwCA SUP, TwCLC 3, TwCWr*
Andreyev, Nikolay Efremych 1908-1982 *ConAu 106*
Andrezel, Pierre *ConAu X, LongCTC, TwCA SUP*
Andric, Ivo 1892-1974 *ClDMEL 80*
Andric, Ivo 1892-1975 *ConAu 57, -81, ConLC 8, EncWL 2[port], ModSL 2, TwCWr, WhoTwCL, WorAu*
Andriekus, Leonardas Kazimieras 1914- *ConAu 25R, IntAu&W 82*
Andriessen, Hendrik 1892-1981 *ConAu 108*
Andrieu, Rene Gabriel 1920- *IntAu&W 82*
Andriola, Alfred J 1912-1983 *ConAu 109, SmATA 34N*
Andrist, Ralph K 1914- *ConAu 5NR, -9R*
Androla, Ron *DrAP&F 83*
Andros, Dee G 1924- *ConAu 69*
Andrus, Dyckman 1942- *ConAu 102*
Andrus, Hyrum Leslie 1924- *ConAu 37R, WrDr 84*
Andrus, Paul 1931- *ConAu 65*
Andrus, Vera 1895- *ConAu P-2*
Andrzejewski, Jerzy 1909- *ClDMEL 80, ConAu 25R, EncWL 2, ModSL 2, TwCWr, WhoTwCL*
Andrzejewski, Jerzy 1909-1983 *ConAu 109*
Andrzeyevski, George *ConAu X*
Andrzeyevski, George 1909- *ConAu X, WorAu*
Andujar, Manuel 1913- *ClDMEL 80*
Anduze-Dufy, Raphael 1919- *ConAu X*
Anet, Claude 1868-1931 *TwCA, TwCA SUP*
Angebert, Jean *ConAu X*
Angebert, Jean-Michel *ConAu X*
Angebert, Michel *ConAu X*
Angel, Daniel D 1939- *ConAu 33R*
Angel, Heather 1941- *ConAu 69, WrDr 84*
Angel, J Lawrence 1915- *ConAu 101*
Angel, Marc D 1945- *ConAu 101*
Angel, Marie 1923- *ConAu 29R*
Angel, Mike *IntWWP 82X*
Angelella, Michael 1953- *ConAu 97*
Angeleri, Lucy *DrAP&F 83*
Angeles, Carlos A 1921- *ConP 80, DcLEL 1940*
Angeles, Carlos A Filipino 1921- *WrDr 84*
Angeles, Jose 1930- *ConAu 33R*
Angeles, Peter A 1931- *ConAu 33R*
Angeles, Philip 1909- *ConAu 5R*
Angelilli, Frank Joseph *ConAu X*
Angelique, Pierre *ConAu X*
Angell, Barbara Tanner *DrAP&F 83*
Angell, Ernest 1889-1973 *ConAu 37R*
Angell, Frank Joseph 1919- *ConAu 17R*
Angell, George 1945- *ConAu 101*
Angell, Judie 1937- *ConAu 77, SmATA 22[port]*
Angell, Madeline 1919- *ConAu 10NR, -65, SmATA 18*

Angell, Sir Norman 1872-1967 *ConAu P-1, LongCTC*
Angell, Sir Norman 1874-1967 *TwCA, TwCA SUP*
Angell, Richard B 1918- *ConAu 13R*
Angell, Robert Cooley 1899- *ConAu 101*
Angell, Roger *DrAP&F 83*
Angell, Roger 1920- *ConAu 57, ConLC 26[port]*
Angell, Tony 1940- *ConAu 4NR, -53, MichAu 80*
Angelo, Frank 1914- *ConAu 4NR, -53, MichAu 80*
Angelo, Valenti 1897- *ConAu 73, SmATA 14, TwCCW 83*
Angelocci, Angelo 1926- *ConAu 21R*
Angelou, Maya *DrAP&F 83*
Angelou, Maya 1928- *ConAu 65, ConLC 12, LivgBAA, WrDr 84*
Anger, Kenneth 1930- *ConAu 106*
Angermann, Gerhard O 1904- *ConAu 65*
Angers, Felicite 1845-1924 *CreCan 1*
Angier, Bradford *ConAu 5R, -7NR, SmATA 12*
Angier, Roswell P 1940- *ConAu 101*
Angiolillo, Paul F 1917- *ConAu 105*
Anglade, Jean 1915- *ConAu 103*
Angle, Paul McClelland 1900-1975 *ConAu 57, ConAu P-2, SmATA 20N, TwCA SUP*
Angle, Roger R *DrAP&F 83*
Angle, Roger Roy 1938- *IntWWP 82*
Anglesey, Marquess Of 1922- *DcLEL 1940, WrDr 84*
Anglesey, George C Paget, Marquess Of 1922- *ConAu X*
Anglesey, Henry, Marquess Of 1922- *IntAu&W 82*
Anglesey, Zoe Rita *DrAP&F 83*
Anglin, Douglas G 1923- *ConAu 37R, IntAu&W 82, WrDr 84*
Anglo, Sydney 1934- *ConAu 89*
Anglund, Joan Walsh 1926- *ChlLR 1, ConAu 5R, SmATA 2, WrDr 84*
Ango, Fan D *ConAu X*
Angoff, Allan 1910- *ConAu 45*
Angoff, Charles 1902-1979 *ConAu 4NR, -5R, -85*
Angremy, Jean-Pierre 1937- *ConAu 106, IntAu&W 82*
Angress, R K 1931- *ConAu 37R*
Angress, Ruth K 1931- *WrDr 84*
Angress, Werner T 1920- *ConAu 13R*
Angrist, Shirley S 1933- *ConAu 25R*
Angrist, Stanley W 1933- *ConAu 25R, SmATA 4*
Anguilm, John A 1912- *MichAu 80*
Angus, Douglas Ross 1909- *ConAu 1R, -3NR*
Angus, Fay 1929- *ConAu 89*
Angus, Ian *ConAu X, IntAu&W 82X, WrDr 84*
Angus, J Colin 1907- *WrDr 84*
Angus, John Colin 1907- *ConAu 107, IntAu&W 82*
Angus, Margaret 1908- *ConAu 21R, WrDr 84*
Angus, Sylvia 1921- *ConAu 61, WrDr 84*
Angus, Sylvia 1921-1982 *ConAu 10NR*
Angus, Tom *ConAu X, IntAu&W 82X*
Angus-Butterworth, Lionel 1900- *WrDr 84*
Angus-Butterworth, Lionel Milner 1900- *ConAu 4NR, -53*
Anhalt, Edward *ConAu 85*
Anhalt, Edward 1914- *DcLB 26[port]*
Anhalt, Istvan 1919- *CreCan 1*
Anicar, Tom *ConAu X*
Anita *SmATA X*
Anjaneyulu, Dhulipudi 1924- *IntAu&W 82*
Anka, Paul 1941- *CreCan 2*
Ankenbrand, Frank, Jr. 1905- *ConAu P-2*
Ankenbruck, John 1925- *IntAu&W 82*
Anker, Charlotte 1934- *ConAu 93*
Anker Larsen, Johannes 1874-1957 *TwCA, TwCA SUP*
Ankerdal, Steen 1948- *IntAu&W 82*
Anmar, Frank *ConAu X*
Anna, Timothy E 1944- *ConAu 101*
Annan, Lord 1916- *LongCTC*
Annan, Noel Gilroy 1916- *ConAu 61, DcLEL 1940, IntAu&W 82, WorAu, WrDr 84*
Annand, J K 1908- *ConAu 101, IntAu&W 82X*
Annand, James King 1908- *IntAu&W 82, IntWWP 82, WrDr 84*
Annand, Robert William 1923- *CreCan 1*

Annandale, Barbara *ConAu X*
Annas, George J 1945- *ConAu 77*
Anne-Marie *CreCan 2*
Anne-Mariel *ConAu X*
Annenski, Innokenti F 1856-1909 *ModSL 1*
Annensky, Innokenti F 1856-1909 *EncWL 2*
Annensky, Innokenty F 1856-1909 *CIDMEL 80*
Annensky, Innokenty Fyodorovich 1856-1909 *ConAu 110*
Anness, Milford Edwin 1918- *ConAu 17R*
Annett, Cora *ConAu X, SmATA X*
Annett, John 1930- *ConAu 29R*
Annis, Linda Ferrill 1943- *ConAu 85*
Annixter, Jane *ConAu X, MichAu 80, SmATA 1*
Annixter, Paul *ConAu X, SmATA 1*
Anno, Mitsumasa 1926- *ChlLR 2, ConAu 4NR, −49, SmATA 5[port]*
Annoh, Godfried Kwesi 1944- *IntWWP 82*
Annunzio, Gabriele D' 1863-1938 *LongCTC, ModRL, TwCA[port], TwCA SUP*
Annur, Hanna Abdur *DrAP&F 83*
Anobile, Richard J 1947- *ConAu 5NR, −53*
Anoff, I S 1892- *ConAu 45*
Anona *IntWWP 82X*
Anouilh, Jean 1910- *CIDMEL 80, CnMD, CnMWL, ConAu 17R, ConLC 1, −3, −8, −13, CroCD, EncWL 2[port], LongCTC, ModFrL, ModRL, ModWD, TwCA SUP, TwCWr, WhoTwCL*
Anquillare, John 1942- *ConAu 105*
Anrooy, Frans Van *SmATA 2*
Ansbacher, Heinz L 1904- *ConAu P-1*
Ansbacher, Max G 1935- *ConAu 89*
Ansberry, William F 1926- *ConAu 33R*
Anschel, Eugene 1907- *ConAu 53*
Anschel, Kurt R 1936- *ConAu 41R*
Anscombe, Isabelle 1954- *ConAu 108*
Ansel, Walter 1897-1977 *ConAu 45, −73*
Ansell, Helen 1940- *ConAu 25R*
Ansell, Jack 1925-1976 *ConAu 17R, −69*
Ansell, Michael 1905- *WrDr 84*
Ansell, Sydney Thomas 1907- *IntAu&W 82*
Ansell, Thomas 1907- *IntAu&W 82X*
Anselm, Felix *ConAu X*
Ansen, Alan 1922- *ConAu 1R, −4NR, DcLEL 1940*
Anski, S 1863-1920 *ModWD*
Ansky, S 1863-1920 *CnMD*
Ansle, Dorothy Phoebe *WrDr 84*
Ansley, Gladys Piatt 1906- *ConAu 5R*
Anslinger, Harry Jacob 1892-1975 *ConAu 61, ConAu P-1*
Anson, Bill 1907-1983 *ConAu 110*
Anson, Cyril J 1923- *ConAu 49*
Anson, Jay 1921-1980 *ConAu 97*
Anson, Jay 1924?- *ConAu 81*
Anson, Peter Frederick 1889- *ConAu 9R*
Anspach, Donald F 1942- *ConAu 69*
Anstey, Edgar *ConAu X, IntAu&W 82X*
Anstey, Edgar 1917- *ConAu 3NR, −5R, IntAu&W 82, WrDr 84*
Anstey, F 1856-1934 *LongCTC, ModBrL, TwCA, TwCA SUP, TwCSFW*
Anstey, Roger T 1927- *ConAu 13R*
Anstey, Vera 1889- *ConAu P-1*
Anstruther, James *ConAu X*
Anstruther, Joyce *LongCTC*
Antell, Gerson 1926- *ConAu 53*
Antell, Will D 1935- *ConAu 104, SmATA 31*
Anthes, Richard A 1944- *ConAu 107, WrDr 84*
Anthony *ConAu X*
Anthony, Barbara 1932- *ConAu 103, SmATA 29[port]*
Anthony, C L *ConAu X, IntAu&W 82X, LongCTC, SmATA 4, WrDr 84*
Anthony, Catherine *ConAu 49*
Anthony, David *ConAu 49*
Anthony, Donald Bruce 1936- *IntWWP 82*
Anthony, Earl *LivgBAA*
Anthony, Edward 1895-1971 *ConAu 33R, −73, SmATA 21[port]*
Anthony, Evelyn 1928- *ConAu X, IntAu&W 82, TwCCr&M 80, TwCRGW, WrDr 84*
Anthony, Frank S 1891-1925 *TwCWr*
Anthony, Geraldine C 1919- *ConAu 11NR, −69*
Anthony, Gordon *ConAu X*
Anthony, Inid E 1925- *ConAu 104*
Anthony, J Garner 1899- *ConAu 61*
Anthony, James R 1922- *ConAu 49, WrDr 84*
Anthony, John *ConAu X*

Anthony, Julie 1948- *ConAu 106*
Anthony, Katharine Susan 1877-1965 *ConAu 25R, TwCA, TwCA SUP*
Anthony, Michael 1930- *IntAu&W 82*
Anthony, Michael 1932- *ConAu 10NR, −17R, ConNov 82, DcLEL 1940, LongCTC, ModBlW, WrDr 84*
Anthony, Peter *ConAu X, WrDr 84*
Anthony, Piers 1934- *ConAu X, ConSFA, DcLB 8[port], TwCSFW, WrDr 84*
Anthony, Robert N 1916- *ConAu 5NR, −13R*
Anthony, Susan B 1916- *ConAu 89*
Anthony, William G 1934- *ConAu 17R*
Anthony, William P 1943- *ConAu 77*
Antia, Framroz P 1916- *IntAu&W 82*
Anticaglia, Elizabeth 1939- *ConAu 1NR, −45, SmATA 12*
Antico, John 1924- *ConAu 29R*
Antill, J M 1912- *WrDr 84*
Antill, James Macquarie 1912- *ConAu 33R*
Antin, David *DrAP&F 83*
Antin, David 1932- *ConAu 73, ConP 80*
Antin, Eleanor *DrAP&F 83*
Antin, Mary 1881-1949 *TwCA, TwCA SUP*
Antler 1946- *IntWWP 82*
Antoine, Andre 1858-1943 *CIDMEL 80, LongCTC*
Antoine-Dariaux, Genevieve 1914- *ConAu 57*
Antokolsky, Pavel Grigoryevich 1896-1978 *CIDMEL 80, WorAu 1970*
Anton, Frank Robert 1920- *ConAu 41R, IntAu&W 82*
Anton, Hector R 1919- *ConAu 73*
Anton, John P 1920- *ConAu 9NR, −21R*
Anton, Michael J 1940- *ConAu 57, MichAu 80, SmATA 12*
Anton, Rita 1920- *ConAu 9R*
Antonacci, Robert J 1916- *ConAu 5R, −9NR, MichAu 80*
Antonazzi, Frank J, Jr. *DrAP&F 83*
Antonazzi, Frank Joseph, Jr. 1950- *IntWWP 82*
Antoncich, Betty 1913- *ConAu 13R*
Antoni *ConAu 49*
Antoni, Heller Makary *IntAu&W 82X*
Antoniak, Helen Elizabeth 1947- *ConAu 105*
Antonick, Robert J 1939- *ConAu 37R*
Antoninus, Brother *WrDr 84*
Antoninus, Brother 1912- *ConAu X, ConLC 1, −14, ConP 80, WorAu*
Antonioni, Michelangelo 1912- *ConAu 73, ConLC 20*
Antoniou, Demetrios I 1906- *WorAu 1970*
Antoniutti, Ildebrando 1898-1974 *ConAu 53*
Antonovsky, Aaron 1923- *ConAu 29R*
Antony, Jonquil 1916- *ConAu 13R*
Antony, Peter 1926- *ConAu X, TwCCr&M 80*
Antonych, Bohdan Ihor 1909-1937 *CIDMEL 80, ModSL 2*
Antoun, Richard T 1932- *ConAu 65*
Antreasian, Garo Zareh 1922- *ConAu 81*
Antrim, Harry T 1936- *ConAu 33R*
Antrim, William H 1928- *ConAu 69*
Antrobus, John 1933- *ConAu 11NR, −57, ConDr 82, WrDr 84*
Antschel, Paul 1920-1970 *ConAu 85, ConLC 10, −19, WorAu*
Anttila, Raimo 1935- *ConAu 33R*
Anvic, Frank *ConAu X*
Anvil, Christopher *TwCSFW, WrDr 84*
Anwar, Chairil 1922-1949 *EncWL 2, WorAu 1970*
Anweiler, Oskar 1925- *ConAu 9NR, −65*
Anyon, G Jay 1909- *ConAu 5R*
Anzaldua, Gloria *DrAP&F 83*
Aoki, Haruo 1930- *ConAu 49*
Aoki, Michiko Y *ConAu 107*
Aonyx *IntAu&W 82X*
Aparicio, Vibiana Chamberlin De *DrAP&F 83*
Apel, Karl-Otto 1922- *ConAu 105*
Apel, Willi 1893- *ConAu 1R, −2NR*
Apelqvist, Anders Seved 1929- *IntAu&W 82*
Apeman Mudgeon *IntWWP 82X*
Apfel, Necia H 1930- *ConAu 107*
Apffel, Edmund R, Jr. 1948- *ConAu 107*
Apgar, Virginia 1909-1974 *ConAu 53, −73*
Aphrodite, J *ConAu X*
Apikian, Nevart *ConAmTC*
Apinee, Irene *CreCan 2*
Apitz, Bruno 1900-1979 *ConAu 85*
Apley, John 1908- *IntAu&W 82*
Aplon, Roger *DrAP&F 83*

Apodaca, Rudy S *DrAP&F 83*
Apolinar, Danny 1934- *ConAu 61*
Apollinaire, Guillaume 1880-1918 *CIDMEL 80, CnMD, CnMWL, ConAu X, EncWL 2[port], LongCTC, ModFrL, ModRL, ModWD, TwCA SUP, TwCLC 3, −8[port], TwCWr, WhoTwCL*
Apostle, Chris N 1935- *ConAu 21R*
Apostolon, Billy 1930- *ConAu 97*
App, Austin J 1902- *WrDr 84*
App, Austin Joseph 1902- *ConAu 101*
Appadorai, A 1902- *ConAu 102*
Appel, Allan 1946- *ConAu 77*
Appel, Allen *DrAP&F 83*
Appel, Benjamin 1907-1977 *ConAu 6NR, −13R, −69, SmATA 21N, TwCA, TwCA SUP*
Appel, John J 1921- *ConAu 33R*
Appel, Kenneth Ellmaker 1896-1979 *ConAu 89*
Appel, Martin E 1948- *ConAu 85*
Appel, Marty *ConAu X*
Appelbaum, Judith 1939- *ConAu 77*
Appelbaum, Paul S 1951- *ConAu 108*
Appelbaum, Stephen A 1926- *ConAu 101*
Appelfeld, Aharon 1932- *ConLC 23[port]*
Appell, Don *ConDr 82D*
Appelman, Hyman 1902- *ConAu 5R*
Appiah, Peggy 1921- *ConAu 41R, SmATA 15, TwCCW 83, WrDr 84*
Appignanesi, Lisa 1946- *ConAu 49*
Applbaum, Ronald L 1943- *ConAu 7NR, −57*
Apple, Jacki *DrAP&F 83*
Apple, Max *DrAP&F 83*
Apple, Max 1941- *ConAu 81, ConLC 9*
Apple, Michael W 1942- *ConAu 109*
Apple, R W, Jr. 1934- *ConAu 89*
Applebaum, Louis 1918- *CreCan 1*
Applebaum, Samuel 1904- *ConAu 65*
Applebaum, Stan 1929- *ConAu 85*
Applebaum, William 1906-1979? *ConAu 6NR, −9R*
Applebee, Arthur N 1946- *ConAu 81*
Appleby, Andrew Bell 1929-1980 *ConAu 108*
Appleby, David P 1925- *ConAu 110*
Appleby, John T 1909?-1974 *ConAu 53*
Appleby, Jon 1948- *ConAu 33R*
Appleby, Joyce Oldham 1929- *ConAu 11NR, −69*
Appleby, June *IntAu&W 82X*
Applegarth, Margaret Tyson 1886-1976 *ConAu 69*
Applegate, James 1923- *ConAu 33R, WrDr 84*
Applegate, Richard 1913?-1979 *ConAu 85*
Appleman, Herbert 1933- *NatPD 81[port]*
Appleman, John Alan 1912- *ConAu 2NR, −5R*
Appleman, John Alan 1912-1982 *ConAu 108*
Appleman, M H *NatPD 81[port]*
Appleman, Marjorie *DrAP&F 83*
Appleman, Mark J 1917- *ConAu 29R*
Appleman, Philip *DrAP&F 83*
Appleman, Philip 1926- *ConAu 6NR, −13R, IntAu&W 82, WrDr 84*
Appleman, Roy Edgar 1904- *ConAu P-1*
Appleton, Arthur 1913- *ConAu 93, WrDr 84*
Appleton, George 1902- *IntAu&W 82*
Appleton, James Henry 1919- *ConAu 2NR, −5R*
Appleton, Jane 1934- *ConAu 102*
Appleton, Jay *ConAu X*
Appleton, Joan Hazel 1930- *IntWWP 82*
Appleton, Lawrence *ConAu X*
Appleton, Marion Brymner 1906- *ConAu 105*
Appleton, Sarah *DrAP&F 83*
Appleton, Sarah 1930- *ConAu 37R, ConP 80, IntWWP 82X, WrDr 84*
Appleton, Sheldon Lee 1933- *ConAu 1R, IntAu&W 82, WrDr 84*
Appleton, Victor *ConAu P-2, SmATA 1*
Appleton, Victor, II *ConAu 17R, SmATA X*
Appleton, Victor W, II *ConAu X*
Appleton, William S 1934- *ConAu 101*
Applewhite, Cynthia *ConAu 89*
Applewhite, E J 1919- *ConAu 89*
Applewhite, Harriet Branson 1940- *ConAu 106*
Applewhite, James *DrAP&F 83*
Applewhite, James W 1935- *ConAu 85*
Appley, M H 1921- *ConAu 13R*
Appleyard, Donald S 1928- *ConAu 4NR, −5R, IntAu&W 82*
Appleyard, Reginald Thomas 1927- *ConAu 17R*
Applezweig, M H *ConAu X*
Apps, Jerold W 1934- *ConAu 1NR, −49*
Apps, Jerry *ConAu X*
Aprill, Arnold *DrAP&F 83*
Apsler, Alfred 1907- *ConAu 3NR, −5R,*

SmATA 10, WrDr 84
Apt, Leon 1929- *ConAu 53*
Apted, M R 1919- *ConAu 25R*
Aptekar, Jane 1935- *ConAu 81*
Apter, Andrew William 1947- *ConAmTC*
Apter, David Ernest 1924- *ConAu 1R, –3NR, WrDr 84*
Apter, Michael John 1939- *ConAu 29R, WrDr 84*
Apter, Samson 1910- *ConAu 104*
Aptheker, Bettina 1944- *ConAu 6NR, –29R, IntAu&W 82, WrDr 84*
Aptheker, Herbert 1915- *ConAu 5R, –6NR*
Apthomas, Ifan 1917- *WrDr 84*
Aquarius *IntAu&W 82X, IntWWP 82X*
Aquarius, Qass *ConAu X*
Aquillo, Don *SmATA X*
Aquin, Hubert 1929-1977 *ConAu 105, ConLC 15, CreCan 1*
Aquina, Sister Mary *ConAu X*
Aquinas, Mary *WrDr 84*
Aquino, Benigno S, Jr. 1932-1983 *ConAu 110*
Aquino, Carlos *IntAu&W 82X*
Aquino, Carlos Augusto Tavares De 1940- *IntAu&W 82*
Aquino, Ninoy *ConAu X*
Arab, John 1930- *CreCan 1*
Arafat, Ibtihaj Said 1934- *ConAu 85*
Aragbabalu, Omidiji *ConAu X*
Aragon, Louis 1897- *ClDMEL 80, ConAu 69, ConLC 3, –22[port], EncWL 2[port], LongCTC, ModFrL, ModRL, ModWD, TwCA, TwCA SUP, TwCWr, WhoTwCL*
Aragon, Louis 1897-1982 *ConAu 108*
Aragones, Juan Emilio 1926- *IntAu&W 82*
Araki, James Tomomasa 1925- *ConAu 13R, IntAu&W 82, WrDr 84*
Arana, Helen *DrAP&F 83*
Arango, Jorge Sanin 1916- *ConAu 61*
Aranguren, Jose Luis L 1909- *ClDMEL 80*
Aranha, Jose Pereira DaGraca 1868-1931 *EncWL 2, ModLAL*
Aranha, Ray 1939- *NatPD 81[port]*
Aranow, Edward Ross 1909- *ConAu 41R*
Araoz, Daniel Leon 1930- *ConAu 108*
Arapoff, Nancy 1930- *ConAu 29R*
Arason, Gudlaugur 1950- *IntAu&W 82*
Arasteh, A Reza 1927- *ConAu 105*
Arata, Esther Spring 1918- *ConAu 89*
Arauz DeRobles, Santiago 1936- *IntAu&W 82*
Arbasino, Alberto 1930- *ClDMEL 80, WorAu*
Arbaud, Joseph D' 1871-1950 *ClDMEL 80*
Arbeiter, Jean S 1937- *ConAu 106*
Arber, Edward 1836-1912 *LongCTC*
Arberry, Arthur J 1905-1969 *ConAu 1R, –4NR*
Arbib, Robert 1915- *ConAu 33R*
Arbingast, Stanley A 1910- *ConAu 10NR, –17R*
Arbo, Sebastia Juan 1902- *ClDMEL 80*
Arbogast, William F 1908-1979 *ConAu 89*
Arbor, Jane *TwCRGW, WrDr 84*
Arbor, Lynn Schoettle 1943- *MichAu 80*
Arbuckle, Dorothy Fry 1910-1982 *ConAu 108, SmATA 33N*
Arbuckle, Dugald S 1912- *ConAu 13R*
Arbuckle, Franklin 1909- *CreCan 2*
Arbuckle, George Franklin *CreCan 2*
Arbuckle, Robert D 1940- *ConAu 61*
Arbuckle, Wanda Rector 1910- *ConAu 41R*
Arbus, Loreen Joy *IntAu&W 82*
Arbuthnot, May Hill 1884-1969 *ConAu 9R, SmATA 2*
Arbuzov, Aleksey Nikolayevich 1908- *ClDMEL 80*
Arbuzov, Alexei Nikolaevich 1908- *ConAu 69*
Arbuzov, Alexey Nikolayevich 1908- *ModWD*
Arcana, Judith 1943- *ConAu 103*
Arce, Agustin 1884- *IntAu&W 82*
Arce, Hector 1935-1980 *ConAu 97*
Arceneaux, Thelma Hoffmann Tyler *AuNews 1*
Arcerobledo, Carlos De 1932- *IntAu&W 82*
Arch, E L 1922- *ConAu X, ConSFA, IntAu&W 82X*
Archambault, Gilles 1933- *CreCan 2*
Archambault, Louis DeGonzague Pascal 1915- *CreCan 1*
Archambault, Paul 1937- *ConAu 81*
Archdeacon, Thomas J 1942- *ConAu 65*
Archer, A A *ConAu X, WrDr 84*
Archer, Frank *ConAu X, SmATA X, TwCCr&M 80*
Archer, Fred 1915- *ConAu 7NR, –57, WrDr 84*

Archer, Fred C 1916?-1974 *ConAu 53*
Archer, Gleason Leonard 1916- *ConAu 65, WrDr 84*
Archer, H Richard 1911-1978 *ConAu 6NR, –13R, –89*
Archer, Jeffrey 1940- *ConAu 77, IntAu&W 82, WrDr 84*
Archer, John Hall 1914- *ConAu 101, IntAu&W 82, WrDr 84*
Archer, Jules 1915- *ConAu 6NR, –9R, ConLC 12, SmATA 4, WrDr 84*
Archer, Lee *ConAu X*
Archer, Marion Fuller 1917- *ConAu 5R, SmATA 11*
Archer, Mildred 1911- *ConAu 104, WrDr 84*
Archer, Myrtle 1926- *ConAu 102, IntWWP 82*
Archer, Peter Kingsley 1926- *ConAu 2NR, –5R, IntAu&W 82, WrDr 84*
Archer, Ron *ConAu X, ConSFA, WrDr 84*
Archer, S *IntAu&W 82X*
Archer, S E *ConAu X*
Archer, Sellers G 1908- *ConAu 17R*
Archer, Stephen H 1928- *ConAu 17R*
Archer, Stephen M 1934- *ConAu 105*
Archer, Violet Balestreri 1913- *CreCan 1*
Archer, W G 1907- *ConAu 57*
Archer, William 1856-1924 *CnMD, ConAu 108, DcLB 10[port], LongCTC, ModBrL, ModWD, TwCA*
Archer Houblon, Doreen 1899-1977 *ConAu 106*
Archerd, Armand *ConAu 110*
Archerd, Army *ConAu X*
Archibald, Douglas 1919- *ConAu 101, ConDr 82, WrDr 84*
Archibald, James Montgomery 1920-1983 *ConAu 110*
Archibald, Joe 1898- *ConAu X*
Archibald, John J 1925- *ConAu 5R*
Archibald, Joseph S 1898- *ConAu 5NR, –9R, SmATA 3*
Archibald, William 1924-1970 *ConAu 29R*
Arciniegas, German 1900- *ConAu 10NR, –61, ModLAL*
Arcone, Sonya 1925-1978 *ConAu 21R, –77*
Ard, Ben Neal, Jr. 1922- *ConAu 33R, IntAu&W 82, WrDr 84*
Ard, William 1922-1962? *ConAu 5R*
Ardagh, John 1928- *ConAu 25R*
Ardalan, Nader 1939- *ConAu 69*
Arden, Barbie *ConAu X, SmATA 3*
Arden, Gothard Everett 1905- *ConAu P-1*
Arden, J E M *ConAu X*
Arden, Jane *ConAu 61, ConDr 82, WrDr 84*
Arden, John 1930- *CnMD, ConAu 13R, ConDr 82, ConLC 6, –13, –15, CroCD, DcLB 13[port], DcLEL 1940, EncWL 2, LongCTC, ModBrL SUP, ModWD, TwCWr, WhoTwCL, WorAu, WrDr 84*
Arden, Leon 1932- *ConAu 107*
Arden, Noele *ConAu X*
Arden, William *ConAu X, TwCCr&M 80, WrDr 84*
Ardener, Edwin *ConAu 5R*
Ardies, Tom 1931- *ConAu 33R, TwCCr&M 80, WrDr 84*
Ardizzone, Edward 1900-1979 *ChlLR 3, ConAu 5R, –8NR, –89, LongCTC, SmATA 1, –21N, –28[port], TwCCW 83*
Ardizzone, Tony *DrAP&F 83*
Ardizzone, Tony 1949- *ConAu 85*
Ardley, Neil Richard 1937- *IntAu&W 82*
Ardmore, Jane Kesner 1915- *ConAu 5R, IntAu&W 82*
Ardoin, John 1935- *ConAu 57*
Ardrey, Robert 1908-1980 *CnMD, ConAu 33R, –93, ModWD, TwCA SUP*
Arean, Carlos 1921- *IntAu&W 82*
Arecco, Vera Lustig *ConAu X*
Areeda, Phillip 1930- *WrDr 84*
Areeda, Phillip E 1930- *ConAu 21R*
Arehart-Treichel, Joan 1942- *ConAu 6NR, –57, SmATA 22[port]*
Arellanes, Audrey Spencer 1920- *ConAu 33R*
Arem, Joel E 1943- *ConAu 89*
Arena, Jay M 1909- *ConAu 107*
Arena, John I 1929- *ConAu 45*
Arenander, Britt 1941- *IntAu&W 82*
Arendt, Hannah 1906-1975 *ConAu 17R, –61, ConIsC 1[port], WorAu*
Arenella, Roy 1939- *SmATA 14*
Arens, Richard 1921- *ConAu 73, IntAu&W 82,*

WrDr 84
Arens, William 1940- *ConAu 89*
Arensberg, Ann 1937- *DcLB Y82B[port]*
Arensberg, Conrad Maynadier 1910- *ConAu 61*
Arent, Arthur 1904-1972 *CnMD, ConAu 33R, ConAu P-2, ModWD*
Areopagita *IntAu&W 82X*
Areskoug, Kaj 1933- *ConAu 29R*
Aresty, Esther Bradford *ConAu 9R, WrDr 84*
Areta, Mavis *ConAu X, IntAu&W 82X, WrDr 84*
Arevalo Martinez, Rafael 1884- *ModLAL*
Arey, James A 1936- *ConAu 41R*
Argan, Giulio Carlo 1909- *ConAu 65*
Argenti, Philip 1891?-1974 *ConAu 49*
Argenzio, Victor 1902- *ConAu 53*
Arghezi, Tudor 1880-1967 *ClDMEL 80, EncWL 2, WhoTwCL, WorAu 1970*
Argiro, Larry 1909- *ConAu 5R*
Argo, Ellen *DrAP&F 83*
Argo, Ellen 1933- *ConAu 73*
Argo, Ellen 1933-1983 *ConAu 110*
Argow, Sylvia *DrAP&F 83, IntAu&W 82*
Argow, Waldemar 1916- *ConAu 21R*
Argraves, Hugh Oliver 1922- *IntWWP 82*
Arguedas, Alcides 1879-1946 *EncWL 2, ModLAL*
Arguedas, Jose Maria 1911-1969 *ConAu 89, ConLC 10, –18, EncWL 2, ModLAL, WorAu*
Arguelles, Ivan *DrAP&F 83*
Arguelles, Jose A 1939- *ConAu 45*
Arguelles, Miriam Tarcov 1943- *ConAu 45*
Argus *ConAu X*
Argyle, Aubrey William 1910- *ConAu P-1*
Argyle, Michael 1925- *ConAu 9NR, –21R, WrDr 84*
Argyris, Chris 1923- *ConAu 1R, –5NR*
Argyris, John 1913- *WrDr 84*
Arian, Alan 1938- *ConAu 1NR, –49*
Arian, Edward 1921- *ConAu 33R*
Arias, Ron *DrAP&F 83*
Arias Condeminas, J *IntAu&W 82X*
Arias-Misson, Alain *DrAP&F 83*
Arias-Misson, Alain 1936- *ConAu 77, IntAu&W 82*
Ariel *ConAu X*
Aries, Philippe 1914- *ConAu 89, IntAu&W 82*
Arieti, James Alexander 1948- *ConAu 108*
Arieti, Silvano 1914-1981 *ConAu 10NR, –104, –21R*
Arimond, Carroll 1909-1979 *ConAu 89*
Aring, Charles Dair 1904- *ConAu 49, IntAu&W 82*
Ariss, Bruce 1911- *ConSFA*
Ariton, Kattie *DrAP&F 83*
Ariyoshi, Sawako 1931- *ConAu 105*
Ariyoshi, Shoichiro 1939?-1979 *ConAu 89*
Arjunwadkar, Krishna S 1926- *IntAu&W 82*
Arkell, Anthony John 1898-1980 *ConAu 102, –97*
Arkell, Reginald 1882-1959 *LongCTC, WorAu*
Arkhurst, Frederick S 1920- *ConAu 29R*
Arkhurst, Joyce Cooper 1921- *ConAu 17R, LivgBAA, WrDr 84*
Arkin, Alan 1934- *ConAu 110, SmATA 32*
Arkin, David 1906- *ConAu 21R*
Arkin, Frieda *DrAP&F 83*
Arkin, Frieda 1917- *ConAu 11NR, –65*
Arkin, Herbert 1906- *ConAu 5R*
Arkin, Joseph 1922- *ConAu 5R*
Arkin, Marcus 1926- *ConAu 53, WrDr 84*
Arkin, Richard Lance 1944- *IntAu&W 82*
Arking, Linda *DrAP&F 83*
Arkley, Arthur James 1919- *WrDr 84*
Arkush, Arthur Spencer 1925-1979 *ConAu 85*
Arland, Marcel 1899- *ClDMEL 80, ModFrL*
Arlandson, Leone Ryland 1917- *ConAu 29R*
Arlen, Leslie *TwCRGW*
Arlen, Michael 1895-1956 *LongCTC, ModBrL, TwCA, TwCA SUP, TwCRGW, TwCWr*
Arlen, Michael J 1930- *ASpks, ConAu 61, DcLEL 1940, WrDr 84*
Arleo, Joseph 1933- *ConAu 29R*
Arles, Henri D' 1870-1930 *CreCan 2*
Arlett, Vera Isabel 1896- *IntWWP 82*
Arley, Catherine 1935- *ConAu 2NR, –45*
Arley, Niels Henrik 1911- *IntAu&W 82*
Arlott, John 1914- *ConAu 9R, IntAu&W 82, WrDr 84*
Arlott, Leslie Thomas John 1914- *DcLEL 1940*
Arlotto, Anthony 1939- *ConAu 33R*
Arlow, Jacob A 1912- *ConAu 53*

Arlt, Roberto 1900-1942 *EncWL 2, ModLAL, WhoTwCL*

Armacost, Michael Hayden 1937- *ConAu 101*

Armah, Ayi Kwei 1936- *ConLC 5*

Armah, Ayi Kwei 1938- *ConNov 82, DcLEL 1940*

Armah, Ayi Kwei 1939- *ConAu 61, EncWL 2, ModBlW, ModCmwL, WrDr 84*

Armand, Louis 1905-1971 *ConAu 33R, ConAu P-2*

Armantrout, Rae *DrAP&F 83*

Armas, Jose *DrAP&F 83*

Armas Marcelo, J J 1946- *IntAu&W 82*

Armatas, James P 1931- *ConAu 41R*

Armatrading, Joan 1950- *ConLC 17*

Armbrister, Trevor 1933- *ConAu 89*

Armbruster, Carl J 1929- *ConAu 33R*

Armbruster, F O 1929- *ConAu 49*

Armbruster, Francis E 1923- *ConAu 29R*

Armbruster, Frank *ConAu X*

Armbruster, Maxim Ethan 1902- *ConAu 1R*

Armens, Sven 1921- *ConAu 21R*

Armentrout, William W 1918- *ConAu 33R*

Armer, Alberta Roller 1904- *ConAu 5R, SmATA 9*

Armer, J Michael 1937- *ConAu 106*

Armer, Laura Adams 1874-1963 *ConAmA, ConAu 65, SmATA 13, TwCCW 83*

Armerding, Carl Edwin 1936- *ConAu 104*

Armerding, George D 1899- *ConAu 85*

Armerding, Hudson Taylor 1918- *ConAu 11NR, -21R*

Armes, Roy 1937- *ConAu 73, IntAu&W 82, WrDr 84*

Armfelt, Nicholas 1935- *IntAu&W 82*

Armigo, Theresa R 1948- *IntWWP 82*

Armington, John Calvin 1923- *ConAu 53*

Armistead, Samuel Gordon 1927- *ConAu 53*

Armitage, Angus 1902- *ConAu P-1*

Armitage, E Liddall 1887- *ConAu P-1*

Armitage, Merle 1893-1975 *ConAu 61*

Armitage, Ronda 1943- *TwCCW 83*

Armour, David Arthur 1937- *MichAu 80*

Armour, John *ConAu X*

Armour, Leslie 1931- *ConAu 110*

Armour, Lloyd R 1922- *ConAu 29R*

Armour, Richard 1906- *WrDr 84*

Armour, Richard Willard 1906- *ConAu 1R, -4NR, IntAu&W 82, SmATA 14*

Armour, Rollin Stely 1929- *ConAu 33R, WrDr 84*

Arms, George Warren 1912- *ConAu 5R*

Arms, Johnson *ConAu X*

Arms, Suzanne 1944- *ConAu 57, WrDr 84*

Armstrong, Alan 1936- *ConAu 73*

Armstrong, Alice Catt *IntAu&W 82*

Armstrong, Ann Seidel 1917- *ConAu 9R*

Armstrong, Anne 1924- *ConAu 13R*

Armstrong, Anthony 1897-1976 *ConAu X, LongCTC*

Armstrong, Anthony C *ConAu X*

Armstrong, April 1926- *ConAu 89*

Armstrong, Arthur Hilary 1909- *ConAu 69*

Armstrong, Benjamin Leighton 1923- *ConAu 93*

Armstrong, Brian G 1936- *ConAu 69*

Armstrong, Charlotte 1905-1969 *ConAu 1R, -3NR, -25R, TwCCr&M 80, TwCRGW, WorAu*

Armstrong, Christopher J R 1935- *ConAu 69*

Armstrong, Claude Blakely 1889-1982 *ConAu 108*

Armstrong, D M 1926- *ConAu 11NR, -25R*

Armstrong, David 1945- *ConAu 107*

Armstrong, David M 1944- *ConAu 57*

Armstrong, David Malet 1926- *IntAu&W 82, WrDr 84*

Armstrong, Diana 1943- *ConAu 107*

Armstrong, Douglas Albert 1920- *ConAu 9R, IntAu&W 82, WrDr 84*

Armstrong, Edward Allworthy 1900-1978 *ConAu 4NR, -5R*

Armstrong, Elizabeth 1917- *ConAu 25R*

Armstrong, Frederick H 1926- *ConAu 33R*

Armstrong, George D 1927- *SmATA 10*

Armstrong, Gerry 1929- *ConAu 13R, SmATA 10*

Armstrong, Gregory T 1933- *ConAu 9R*

Armstrong, Hamilton Fish 1893-1973 *ConAu 41R, -93, TwCA, TwCA SUP*

Armstrong, Henry H *ConAu X*

Armstrong, J Scott 1937- *ConAu 1NR, -45*

Armstrong, James 1924- *ConAu 29R*

Armstrong, John Alexander 1922- *ConAu 1R,*

-3NR, WrDr 84

Armstrong, John Borden 1926- *ConAu 33R*

Armstrong, John Byron 1917-1976 *ConAu 5R, -65*

Armstrong, Joseph Gravitt 1943- *ConAu 101*

Armstrong, Judith 1935- *ConAu 102, WrDr 84*

Armstrong, Kathleen Mae 1921- *CreCan 1*

Armstrong, Kay 1921- *CreCan 1*

Armstrong, Keith Francis Whitfield 1950- *ConAu 29R, IntWWP 82*

Armstrong, Louis 1900-1971 *ConAu 29R*

Armstrong, Louise *SmATA 33*

Armstrong, Margaret 1867-1944 *TwCA, TwCA SUP*

Armstrong, Marjorie Moore 1912- *ConAu 89*

Armstrong, Martin Donisthorpe 1882-1974 *ConAu 49, LongCTC, ModBrL, TwCA, TwCA SUP*

Armstrong, Nancy 1924- *WrDr 84*

Armstrong, O K 1893- *ConAu 93*

Armstrong, Patrick Hamilton 1941- *IntAu&W 82*

Armstrong, Paul 1869-1915 *TwCA, TwCA SUP*

Armstrong, Paul 1912- *ConAu 37R*

Armstrong, Raymond *TwCCr&M 80*

Armstrong, Richard 1903- *ConAu 77, SmATA 11, TwCCW 83, WrDr 84*

Armstrong, Richard G 1932- *ConAu 73*

Armstrong, Robert H 1936- *ConAu 108*

Armstrong, Robert Laurence 1926- *ConAu 29R, WrDr 84*

Armstrong, Robert Plant 1919- *ConAu 41R*

Armstrong, Roger D 1939- *ConAu 17R*

Armstrong, Ruth Gallup 1891- *ConAu P-1*

Armstrong, Scott 1945- *ConAu 108*

Armstrong, Terence Ian Fytton 1912-1970 *ConAu 29R, ConAu P-2, LongCTC*

Armstrong, Thomas 1899-1978 *ConAu 5R, -103, LongCTC*

Armstrong, Tilly 1927- *ConAu 107*

Armstrong, Tom 1935- *MichAu 80*

Armstrong, Wallace Edwin 1896-1980 *ConAu 97*

Armstrong, William A 1912- *ConAu 13R*

Armstrong, William A 1915- *ConAu 17R*

Armstrong, William H 1914- *AuNews 1, ChlLR 1, ConAu 9NR, -17R, SmATA 4, TwCCW 83, WrDr 84*

Armstrong, William M 1919- *ConAu 9R, -49*

Armytage, Walter Harry Green 1915- *ConAu 9R, IntAu&W 82*

Arnade, Charles W 1927- *ConAu 33R, IntAu&W 82, WrDr 84*

Arnandez, Richard 1912- *ConAu 6NR*

Arnason, H H 1909- *ConAu 61*

Arnati, Emmanuel 1930- *IntAu&W 82*

Arnaud, Saint Romain *ConAu X*

Arnbak, Birthe Kirstine Paul 1923- *IntWWP 82*

Arndt, Ernst H D 1899- *ConAu P-2, WrDr 84*

Arndt, H W 1915- *ConAu 10NR, -21R*

Arndt, Heinz Wolfgang 1915- *WrDr 84*

Arndt, Karin Jutta 1939- *IntAu&W 82*

Arndt, Karl 1903- *WrDr 84*

Arndt, Karl John Richard 1903- *ConAu 7NR, -17R*

Arndt, Ruth E 1890- *WrDr 84*

Arndt, Walter W 1916- *ConAu 5NR, -13R*

Arnebeck, Bob 1947- *ConAu 108*

Arner, Sivar 1909- *EncWL 2, IntAu&W 82*

Arneson, D J 1935- *ConAu 106*

Arnett, Caroline *ConAu X, SmATA X, TwCRGW*

Arnett, Carroll *DrAP&F 83*

Arnett, Carroll 1927- *ConAu 11NR, -21R*

Arnett, Harold E 1931- *ConAu 8NR, -21R*

Arnett, Ross H, Jr. 1919- *ConAu 2NR, -49*

Arney, William Ray 1950- *ConAu 110*

Arnez, Nancy Levi 1928- *ConAu 29R, LivgBAA*

Arnheim, Daniel D 1930- *ConAu 5NR, -9R*

Arnheim, Rudolf 1904- *ConAu 1R, -3NR, WrDr 84*

Arniches, Carlos 1866-1943 *CnMD*

Arniches Y Barrera, Carlos 1866-1943 *CIDMEL 80*

Arnim, Countess Von *LongCTC*

Arno, Enrico 1913-1981 *SmATA 28N*

Arno, Peter 1904-1968 *ConAu 25R, -73, LongCTC*

Arnold, Adlai F 1914- *ConAu 33R*

Arnold, Alan 1922- *ConAu 5R*

Arnold, Alvin L 1929- *ConAu 93*

Arnold, Armin Herbert 1931- *ConAu 3NR, -9R, IntAu&W 82*

Arnold, Arnold 1921- *ConAu 10NR, -17R*

Arnold, Bob *DrAP&F 83*

Arnold, Bob 1952- *ConAu 105, IntWWP 82*

Arnold, Bruce 1936- *ConAu 93*

Arnold, Carl *ConAu X*

Arnold, Caroline 1944- *ConAu 107, SmATA 34*

Arnold, Charles Harvey 1920- *ConAu 65*

Arnold, Charlotte E Cramer *ConAu 57*

Arnold, Colin *IntWWP 82*

Arnold, Colin Albert Edward 1937- *IntWWP 82*

Arnold, Corliss Richard 1926- *ConAu 49*

Arnold, Denis Midgley 1926- *ConAu 2NR, -5R, IntAu&W 82*

Arnold, Edmund Clarence 1913- *ConAu 1R, -3NR, MichAu 80, WrDr 84*

Arnold, Sir Edwin 1832-1904 *LongCTC*

Arnold, Edwin L 1857?-1935 *ConAu 109*

Arnold, Edwin Lester 1857-1935 *TwCSFW*

Arnold, Elliott 1912-1980 *ConAu 17R, -97, SmATA 22N, -5, TwCA SUP, TwCWW*

Arnold, Emily 1939- *ConAu 109*

Arnold, Emmy 1884- *ConAu 21R*

Arnold, Emmy 1884-1980 *ConAu 9NR*

Arnold, Francena H 1888- *ConAu P-1*

Arnold, G L *ConAu X*

Arnold, Guy 1932- *ConAu 11NR, -25R, IntAu&W 82, WrDr 84*

Arnold, H J P 1932- *ConAu 2NR, WrDr 84*

Arnold, Harry John Philip 1932- *ConAu 5R, IntAu&W 82*

Arnold, Harry L, Jr. 1912- *WrDr 84*

Arnold, Heinz Ludwig 1940- *IntAu&W 82*

Arnold, Herbert 1935- *ConAu 37R*

Arnold, Ida *LongCTC*

Arnold, Janet 1931- *IntAu&W 82*

Arnold, Janet 1932- *ConAu 93, WrDr 84*

Arnold, Joseph H *ConAu X, WrDr 84*

Arnold, June Davis 1926- *ConAu 21R*

Arnold, Kenneth L *DrAP&F 83*

Arnold, Kenneth L 1944- *NatPD 81[port]*

Arnold, L J *ConAu X*

Arnold, Leslie *ConAu X*

Arnold, Lloyd R 1906-1970 *ConAu P-2*

Arnold, Lois B *ConAu 107*

Arnold, M B 1903- *WrDr 84*

Arnold, Magda B 1903- *ConAu 5R*

Arnold, Margot *ConAu X, IntAu&W 82X*

Arnold, Mary Ann 1918- *ConAu 65*

Arnold, Milo Lawrence 1903- *ConAu 57*

Arnold, Olga Moore 1900-1981 *ConAu 102*

Arnold, Oren 1900- *ConAu 2NR, -5R, SmATA 4*

Arnold, Pauline 1894-1974 *ConAu 1R, -2NR*

Arnold, Peter 1943- *ConAu 1NR, -49, WrDr 84*

Arnold, R Douglas 1950- *ConAu 101*

Arnold, Ray Henry 1895- *ConAu 5R*

Arnold, Richard 1912- *ConAu 3NR, -9R*

Arnold, Richard E 1908- *ConAu P-2*

Arnold, Richard K 1923- *ConAu 69*

Arnold, Robert E 1932- *ConAu 49*

Arnold, Robert Thomas *IntWWP 82X*

Arnold, Rollo Davis 1926- *ConAu 21R, WrDr 84*

Arnold, Ron 1937- *ConAu 108*

Arnold, Thurman Wesley 1891-1969 *ConAu P-1, TwCA SUP*

Arnold, William Robert 1933- *ConAu 29R*

Arnold, William Van 1941- *ConAu 110*

Arnold-Baker, Charles 1918- *ConAu 5R*

Arnold-Forster, Mark 1920-1981 *ConAu 105, -65*

Arnoldy, Julie *ConAu X, SmATA X*

Arnosky, Jim 1946- *ConAu 69, SmATA 22[port]*

Arnot, Robin Page 1890- *IntAu&W 82*

Arnothy, Christine 1930- *ConAu 10NR, -65*

Arnott, Anne 1916- *ConAu 73, IntAu&W 82X, WrDr 84*

Arnott, J F 1914-1982 *ConAu 108*

Arnott, Kathleen 1914- *ConAu 57, SmATA 20*

Arnott, Margaret Anne 1916- *IntAu&W 82*

Arnott, Peter Douglas 1931- *ConAu 1R, -3NR, DcLEL 1940, IntAu&W 82, WrDr 84*

Arnoux, Alexandre 1884-1973 *ConAu 37R*

Arnov, Boris, Jr. 1926- *ConAu 1R, -3NR, SmATA 12*

Arnow, Harriette 1908- *WrDr 84*

Arnow, Harriette Louisa Simpson 1908- *ConAu 9R, ConLC 2, -7, -18, ConNov 82, DcLB 6[port], MichAu 80, WorAu*

Arnow, L Earle 1909- *ConAu 69*

Arnstein, Flora J *DrAP&F 83*

Arnstein, Flora J 1885- *ConAu 5R, IntWWP 82*
Arnstein, Helene S 1915- *ConAu 57, SmATA 12*
Arnstein, Walter L 1930- *ConAu 5NR, –13R, SmATA 12*
Arntson, Herbert E 1911- *ConAu 17R, SmATA 12*
Arny, Mary Travis 1909- *ConAu 61*
Arny, Thomas Travis 1940- *ConAu 85*
Aron, Raymond 1905- *WrDr 84*
Aron, Raymond Claude Ferdinand 1905- *CIDMEL 80, ConAu 2NR, –49, IntAu&W 82, WorAu*
Aron, Robert 1898-1975 *ConAu 57, –93*
Aronfreed, Justin 1930- *ConAu 25R*
Aronin, Ben 1904-1980 *ConAu 102, SmATA 25N*
Aronoff, Myron J 1940- *ConAu 107*
Aronpuro, Kari Kalervo 1940- *IntAu&W 82*
Aronson, Alex 1912- *ConAu 45*
Aronson, Alvin 1928- *ConAu 25R*
Aronson, Elliot 1932- *ConAu 33R*
Aronson, Harvey 1929- *ConAu 85*
Aronson, J Richard 1937- *ConAu 81*
Aronson, James 1915- *ConAu 29R*
Aronson, Joseph 1898- *ConAu P-1*
Aronson, Marvin L 1925- *ConAu 41R*
Aronson, Shlomo 1936- *ConAu 73*
Aronson, Theo 1930- *ConAu 4NR, –9R, IntAu&W 82, WrDr 84*
Aronson, Virginia 1954- *ConAu 108*
Arora, Ramesh K 1940- *IntAu&W 82*
Arora, Shirley Lease 1930- *ConAu 1R, SmATA 2*
Aros, Andrew A 1944- *ConAu 97*
Arout, Gabriel 1909-1982 *ConAu 106*
Arp, Hans 1887-1966 *ConAu X, ModGL, WhoTwCL*
Arp, Jean 1887-1966 *ConAu 25R, –81, ConLC 5, ModGL*
Arpad, Joseph J 1937- *ConAu 49*
Arpel, Adrien *ConAu X*
Arpino, Giovanni 1927- *CIDMEL 80*
Arquet, Frank M *IntWWP 82X*
Arquette, Cliff 1905-1974 *ConAu 53*
Arquette, Lois *ConAu X, SmATA 1*
Arrabal, Fernando 1932- *CIDMEL 80, CnMD, ConAu 9R, ConLC 2, –9, –18, CroCD, EncWL 2, ModFrL, ModWD, TwCWr, WorAu*
Arre, Helen *WrDr 84*
Arre, Helen 1912- *ConAu X*
Arre, John *ConAu X*
Arreola, Juan Jose 1918- *EncWL 2, ModLAL*
Arrighi, Mel *DrAP&F 83*
Arrighi, Mel 1933- *ConAu 1NR, –49, IntAu&W 82*
Arrillaga, Maria 1940- *IntWWP 82*
Arrington, Leonard James 1917- *ConAu 9NR, –17R*
Arrow, Kenneth J 1921- *ConAu 13R*
Arrow, William *IntAu&W 82X, WrDr 84*
Arroway, Francis M *ConAu X*
Arrowood, Clinton 1939- *SmATA 19*
Arrowsmith, Judith Mary 1944- *IntWWP 82*
Arrowsmith, Pat 1930- *ConAu 101, IntAu&W 82, WrDr 84*
Arrowsmith, William *DrAP&F 83*
Arrowsmith, William 1924- *WrDr 84*
Arrowsmith, William Ayres 1924- *ConAu 4NR, –9R, IntWWP 82, WorAu*
Arroyo, Stephen J 1946- *ConAu 61*
Arsiennieva, Natalla 1903- *EncWL 2*
Art, Robert 1942- *ConAu 65*
Artaud, Antonin 1895-1948 *EncWL 2[port]*
Artaud, Antonin 1896-1948 *CIDMEL 80, ConAu 104, CroCD, LongCTC, ModFrL, ModRL, ModWD, TwCLC 3, TwCWr, WhoTwCL, WorAu*
Arteaga, Lucio 1924- *ConAu 49*
Artes, Dorothy Beecher 1919- *ConAu 57*
Arther, Richard O 1928- *ConAu 17R*
Athos, John 1908- *ConAu 9R, IntAu&W 82*
Arthur, Alan *ConAu X*
Arthur, Burt *ConAu X, TwCWW, WrDr 84*
Arthur, Don R 1917- *ConAu 29R*
Arthur, Donald Ramsay 1917- *IntAu&W 82, WrDr 84*
Arthur, Elizabeth *DrAP&F 83*
Arthur, Elizabeth 1953- *ConAu 105*
Arthur, Frank 1902- *ConAu X, TwCCr&M 80, WrDr 84*
Arthur, Gladys *ConAu X*

Arthur, Herbert *ConAu X, WrDr 84*
Arthur, Hugh *ConAu X, IntAu&W 82X*
Arthur, Percy E 1910- *ConAu P-1*
Arthur, Robert *ConAu X*
Arthur, Ruth 1905-1979 *TwCCW 83*
Arthur, Ruth Mabel 1905-1979 *ConAu 4NR, –9R, –85, ConLC 12, SmATA 26N, –7*
Arthur, Tiffany *ConAu X*
Arthur, William *ConAu X*
Arthurs, Peter 1933- *ConAu 106*
Artis, Vicki Kimmel 1945- *ConAu 53, SmATA 12*
Artmann, H C 1921- *ConAu 101, EncWL 2*
Artmann, Hans Carl 1921- *CIDMEL 80, ModGL*
Artobolevsky, Ivan I 1905-1977 *ConAu 73*
Artom, Guido 1906- *ConAu 29R*
Artsybashev, Mikhail Petrovich 1878-1927 *CIDMEL 80, CnMD, ModWD, TwCA, TwCA SUP*
Artz, Frederick Binkerd 1894- *ConAu 1R*
Artzybasheff, Boris Mikhailovich 1899-1965 *SmATA 14*
Aruego, Ariane *ConAu 49, SmATA 7*
Aruego, Jose 1932- *ChlLR 5[port], ConAu 37R, SmATA 6[port]*
Aruli, P 1950- *IntWWP 82*
Arundel, Honor 1919-1973 *ConAu 41R, ConAu P-2, ConLC 17, SmATA 24N, –4, TwCCW 83*
Arundel, Jocelyn 1930- *ConAu X, SmATA X*
Arundel, Russell M 1903-1978 *ConAu 77*
Arvay, Harry 1925- *ConAu 8NR, –57*
Arvidsson, Tomas 1941- *IntAu&W 82*
Arvill, Robert *ConAu X*
Arvin, Kay K 1922- *ConAu 65*
Arvin, Newton 1900-1963 *ConLCrt 82, TwCA, TwCA SUP*
Arvio, Raymond Paavo 1930- *ConAu 77*
Arvola, Oiva Vaino 1935- *IntAu&W 82*
ARW *DrAP&F 83*
Arw *IntWWP 82X*
ArW 493 *IntAu&W 82X*
Ary, Donald E 1930- *ConAu 41R*
Ary, Sheila M 1929- *ConAu 13R*
Arya, Usharbudh 1934- *ConAu 105*
Arzak, Nikolay *TwCWr*
Arzt, Max 1897-1975 *ConAu 61*
Asamani, Joseph Owusu 1934- *ConAu 49*
Asante, Molefi K *WrDr 84*
Asante, Molefi K 1942- *ConAu 33R*
Asare, Bediakoi *DcLEL 1940*
Asare, Meshack 1945- *ConAu 11NR, –61*
Asbell, Bernard 1923- *ConAu 1NR, –45*
Asbjornsen, Peter Christen 1812-1885 *SmATA 15*
Asbury, Herbert 1891-1963 *TwCA, TwCA SUP*
Asch, Frank 1946- *ConAu 41R, SmATA 5, WrDr 84*
Asch, Nathan 1902-1964 *ConAu 109, DcLB 4, TwCA, TwCA SUP*
Asch, Sholem 1880-1957 *CIDMEL 80, CnMD, ConAu 105, EncWL 2, LongCTC, ModWD, TwCA, TwCA SUP, TwCLC 3, TwCWr*
Ascheim, Skip 1943- *ConAu 53*
Ascher/Straus *ConAu X*
Ascher *IntAu&W 82X*
Ascher, Abraham 1928- *ConAu 81*
Ascher, Carol *DrAP&F 83*
Ascher, Carol 1941- *ConAu 105*
Ascher, Sheila *DrAP&F 83*
Ascher, Sheila 1944- *ConAu 105, IntAu&W 82*
Ascher-Nash, Franzi 1910- *IntAu&W 82, IntWWP 82*
Ascherson, Neal 1932- *ConAu 13R, ConIsC 2[port]*
Aschmann, Alberta 1921- *ConAu 7NR*
Aschmann, Helen Tann *ConAu 13R*
Ascoli, Max 1898-1978 *ConAu 77*
Asenjo Sedano, Jose 1930- *IntAu&W 82*
Aseyev, Nikolay Nikolayevich 1889-1963 *CIDMEL 80, TwCWr*
Ash, Anthony Lee 1931- *ConAu 3NR, –49*
Ash, Bernard 1910- *ConAu P-1*
Ash, Brian 1936- *WrDr 84*
Ash, Christopher 1914- *ConAu 1R*
Ash, David W 1923- *ConAu 9R*
Ash, Douglas 1914- *ConAu 2NR, –5R, IntAu&W 82, WrDr 84*
Ash, Fenton *TwCSFW*
Ash, John 1948- *IntWWP 82*
Ash, Lee 1917- *ConAu 110*

Ash, Maurice Anthony 1917- *ConAu 101*
Ash, Pauline *WrDr 84*
Ash, Rene Lee 1939- *ConAu 57*
Ash, Roberta *ConAu X*
Ash, Russell 1946- *WrDr 84*
Ash, Russell John 1946- *IntAu&W 82*
Ash, Sarah Leeds 1904- *ConAu P-1, IntAu&W 82, IntWWP 82*
Ash, William Franklin 1917- *ConAu 2NR, –5R*
Ashabranner, Brent 1921- *ConAu 5R, –10NR, SmATA 1*
Ashanti, Baron James *DrAP&F 83*
Ashbaugh, Nancy 1929- *ConAu 73*
Ashbee, Paul 1918- *ConAu 93*
Ashbery, John *DrAP&F 83*
Ashbery, John 1927- *ConAu 5R, –9NR, ConLC 2, –3, –4, –6, –9, –13, –15, –25[port], ConP 80, CroCAP, DcLB Y81A[port], –5[port], DcLEL 1940, IntAu&W 82, ModAL SUP, WorAu, WrDr 84*
Ashbolt, Allan Campbell 1921- *ConAu 104, IntAu&W 82, WrDr 84*
Ashbrook, James Barbour 1925- *ConAu 37R, WrDr 84*
Ashbrook, John *IntWWP 82, WrDr 84*
Ashbrook, William 1922- *ConAu 29R*
Ashburne, Jim G 1912- *ConAu 1R*
Ashby, Cliff 1918- *WrDr 84*
Ashby, Cliff 1919- *ConAu 25R*
Ashby, Eric 1904- *ConAu 61, WrDr 84*
Ashby, Gwynneth Margaret 1922- *ConAu 25R, IntAu&W 82, WrDr 84*
Ashby, LaVerne 1922- *ConAu 21R*
Ashby, LeRoy 1938- *ConAu 33R*
Ashby, Lloyd W 1905- *ConAu 89*
Ashby, Neal 1924- *ConAu 89*
Ashby, Philip H 1916- *WrDr 84*
Ashby, Philip Harrison 1916- *ConAu 17R*
Ashcraft, Allan Coleman 1928- *ConAu 9R*
Ashcraft, Laura 1945- *ConAu 107*
Ashcraft, Laurie *ConAu X*
Ashcraft, Morris 1922- *ConAu 45*
Ashcroft, Nell 1927- *IntWWP 82*
Ashdown, Clifford 1860-1936 *TwCCr&M 80*
Ashdown, Dulcie Margaret 1946- *IntAu&W 82*
Ashe, Arthur 1943- *ConAu 65*
Ashe, Douglas *ConAu X, WrDr 84*
Ashe, Geoffrey Thomas 1923- *ConAu 5R, IntAu&W 82, SmATA 17, WrDr 84*
Ashe, Gordon *ConAu X, LongCTC, TwCCr&M 80, WorAu*
Ashe, John Harold 1907- *IntAu&W 82, IntWWP 82*
Ashe, Mary Ann *ConAu X*
Ashe, Mary Anne *WrDr 84*
Ashe, Penelope 1936- *ConAu X*
Asheim, Lester Eugene 1914- *ConAu 17R*
Ashenfelter, David L 1948- *ConAu 108*
Ashenfelter, Orley C 1942- *ConAu 8NR, –61*
Asher, Don 1926- *ConAu 73*
Asher, Harry 1909- *ConAu 2NR, –5R, WrDr 84*
Asher, John Alexander 1921- *ConAu 21R, IntAu&W 82, WrDr 84*
Asher, Maxine 1930- *ConAu 105*
Asher, Robert Eller 1910- *ConAu 61*
Asher, Sandy 1942- *ConAu 105, DcLB Y83B[port], SmATA 34*
Ashey, Bella *ConAu X, SmATA X*
Ashford, Daisy *ConAu X, SmATA X*
Ashford, Daisy 1881-1972 *LongCTC*
Ashford, Douglas E 1928- *ConAu 73*
Ashford, Gerald 1907- *ConAu 41R*
Ashford, Jeffrey *ConAu X, WrDr 84*
Ashford, Jeffrey 1926- *ConAu 1R, TwCCr&M 80*
Ashford, Margaret Mary 1881-1972 *ConAu 33R, SmATA 10*
Ashford, Ray 1926- *ConAu 65*
Ashlandonian *IntAu&W 82X*
Ashley, Bernard 1935- *ChlLR 4[port], ConAu 93, IntAu&W 82, TwCCW 83, WrDr 84*
Ashley, Elizabeth *ConAu X, SmATA X, WrDr 84*
Ashley, Ernest 1906- *ConAu P-1*
Ashley, Franklin *DrAP&F 83*
Ashley, Franklin 1942- *ConAu 1NR, –45*
Ashley, Gladys *WrDr 84*
Ashley, Graham *ConAu X*
Ashley, Jack 1922- *ConAu 106, IntAu&W 82, WrDr 84*

Ashley, Leonard R N 1928- *ConAu 9NR,*
  IntAu&W 82, WrDr 84
Ashley, Leonard R N 1929- *ConAu 13R*
Ashley, Maurice 1907- *WrDr 84*
Ashley, Maurice Percy 1907- *ConAu 41R,*
  IntAu&W 82
Ashley, Michael 1948- *ConAu 69*
Ashley, Nova Trimble *DrAP&F 83*
Ashley, Nova Trimble 1911- *ConAu 65*
Ashley, Paul P 1896-1979 *ConAu 10NR, -21R,*
  -85
Ashley, Renee A *DrAP&F 83*
Ashley, Robert Paul, Jr. 1915- *ConAu 17R*
Ashley, Rosalind Minor 1923- *ConAu 69*
Ashley, Sally 1935- *ConAu 109*
Ashley, Steven *ConAu X*
Ashley-Montagu, Montague Francis *ConAu X,*
  TwCA SUP
Ashlin, John *ConAu X*
Ashlock, Patrick 1937- *ConAu 61*
Ashlock, Robert B 1930- *ConAu 29R*
Ashmead, John, Jr. 1917- *ConAu 1R*
Ashmole, Bernard 1894- *ConAu 106,*
  IntAu&W 82
Ashmore, Basil 1915- *IntAu&W 82*
Ashmore, Harry Scott 1916- *ConAu 13R*
Ashmore, Jerome 1901- *ConAu P-2*
Ashmore, Lewis *ConAu X*
Ashmore, Owen 1920- *ConAu 106, WrDr 84*
Ashner, Sonie Shapiro 1938- *ConAu 57*
Ashok, Konisha *IntAu&W 82X*
Ashton, Adrian Olsson 1906- *WrDr 84*
Ashton, Ann *ConAu X, TwCRGW*
Ashton, Dore *WrDr 84*
Ashton, Dore 1928- *ConAu 2NR, -5R,*
  IntAu&W 82
Ashton, Elizabeth *TwCRGW, WrDr 84*
Ashton, Helen Rosaline 1891-1958 *LongCTC,*
  TwCA, TwCA SUP
Ashton, Robert 1924- *ConAu 1R, -3NR,*
  IntAu&W 82, WrDr 84
Ashton, Violet 1908- *ConAu 73*
Ashton, Warren T *SmATA X*
Ashton, Winifred *LongCTC, TwCA,*
  TwCA SUP
Ashton, Winifred 1888-1965 *ConAu 93*
Ashton-Warner, Sylvia 1905?- *ModCmwL*
Ashton-Warner, Sylvia 1908- *ConAu 69,*
  ConLC 19, ConNov 82, DcLEL 1940,
  LongCTC, TwCWr, WorAu, WrDr 84
Ashworth, Kenneth H 1932- *ConAu 41R*
Ashworth, Mary Wells Knight 1903- *ConAu 5R*
Ashworth, Wilfred 1912- *ConAu 13R*
Ashworth, William 1920- *ConAu 5R,*
  IntAu&W 82
Asimov, Isaac *DrAP&F 83*
Asimov, Isaac 1920- *ConAu 1R, -2NR,*
  ConLC 1, -3, -9, -19, -26[port], ConNov 82,
  ConSFA, DcLB 8[port], DcLEL 1940,
  DrmM[port], IntAu&W 82, LongCTC,
  SmATA 1, -26[port], TwCCr&M 80,
  TwCSFW, TwCWr, WorAu, WrDr 84
Asinof, Eliot 1919- *ConAu 7NR, -9R,*
  SmATA 6, WrDr 84
Askari, Hussaini Muhammad *ConAu X*
Askenasy, Hans George 1930- *ConAu 77*
Askew, Jack *ConAu X*
Askew, William Clarence 1910- *ConAu 49,*
  IntAu&W 82
Askham, Francis 1910- *ConAu X, WrDr 84*
Askin, A Bradley 1943- *ConAu 73*
Askin, Alma 1911- *ConAu 57*
Askin, I Jayne 1940- *ConAu 109*
Askwith, Betty Ellen 1909- *ConAu 61,*
  LongCTC
Aslanapa, Oktay 1914- *ConAu 37R*
Asman, James 1914- *WrDr 84*
Asmodi, Herbert 1923- *CnMD, CroCD,*
  IntAu&W 82
Asmus, Otto *IntAu&W 82X*
Asna, M Alaeddin 1940- *IntAu&W 82*
Asnyk, Adam Prot 1838-1897 *CIDMEL 80*
Aspaturian, Vernon V 1922- *ConAu 105*
Aspell, Patrick J 1930- *ConAu 25R*
Aspenberg, Gary Alan *DrAP&F 83*
Aspenstrom, Werner 1918- *CIDMEL 80,*
  CroCD, EncWL 2
Aspin, Les 1938- *ConAu 108*
Aspinall, Ruth Alastair 1922- *ConAu 2NR, -5R*
Aspinwall, Dorothy B 1910- *ConAu 49*
Aspiz, Harold 1921- *ConAu 105*
Aspler, Tony 1939- *ConAu 105*

Asprey, Robert Brown 1923- *ConAu 5R, -6NR,*
  IntAu&W 82, WrDr 84
Asprin, Robert 1946- *WrDr 84*
Asprin, Robert Lynn 1946- *ConAu 85,*
  TwCSFW
Aspy, David N 1930- *ConAu 45*
Asquith, Cynthia Mary Evelyn 1887-1960
  ConAu 110
Asquith, Lady Cynthia Mary Evelyn 1887-1960
  LongCTC
Asquith, Elizabeth 1897-1945 *LongCTC*
Asquith, Glenn Hackney 1904- *ConAu 1R, -1NR*
Asquith, Herbert 1881-1947 *LongCTC*
Asquith, Margot 1864-1945 *LongCTC*
Asquith, Nan *TwCRGW, WrDr 84*
Asquith Of Yarnbury, Baroness 1887-1969
  LongCTC
Assael, Henry 1935- *ConAu 41R*
Assagioli, Roberto 1893?-1974 *ConAu 53*
Asselbroke, Archibald Algernon 1923- *ConAu 77*
Asselin, E Donald 1903-1970 *ConAu P-1*
Asselineau, Roger Maurice 1915- *ConAu 97,*
  IntAu&W 82
Assiac *ConAu X, IntAu&W 82X, WrDr 84*
Asta *IntAu&W 82X*
Astells, Juan *IntAu&W 82X*
Aster, Sidney 1942- *ConAu 10NR, -65*
Astier, Pierre A G 1927- *ConAu 45*
Astill, Kenneth N 1923- *ConAu 53*
Astin, Alexander W 1932- *ConAu 7NR, -17R*
Astin, Helen S 1932- *ConAu 29R*
Astiz, Carlos A 1933- *ConAu 25R*
Astl, Jaro Maria 1894- *IntAu&W 82*
Astley, Joan Bright 1910- *ConAu 33R*
Astley, Juliet *ConAu X, -X, WrDr 84*
Astley, Thea 1925- *ConAu 11NR, -65,*
  ConNov 82, DcLEL 1940, WrDr 84
Aston, James *ConAu X, LongCTC,*
  SmATA X
Aston, Margaret 1932- *ConAu 73*
Aston, Michael 1946- *ConAu 61*
Astor, Gerald *WrDr 84*
Astor, Gerald M 1926- *ConAu 107*
Astor, Mary 1906- *ConAu 3NR, -5R,*
  IntAu&W 82
Astor, Michael Langhorne 1916-1980 *ConAu 61,*
  -97
Astor, Susan *DrAP&F 83*
Astor, Susan 1946- *ConAu 105, IntWWP 82*
Astor Family *LongCTC*
Astrachan, Samuel *DrAP&F 83*
Astrachan, Samuel 1934- *ConAu 69*
Astro, Richard 1941- *ConAu 29R*
Astrom, Paul Fredrik Karl 1929- *IntAu&W 82*
Asturias, Miguel Angel 1899-1974 *ConAu 49,*
  ConAu P-2, ConLC 3, -8, -13, EncWL 2,
  ModLAL, TwCWr, WhoTwCL, WorAu
Aswad, Betsy 1939- *ConAu 104*
Aswin *ConAu X*
Asya *IntWWP 82X*
Atallah, Lillian *ConAu X*
Atamian, David 1892?-1978 *ConAu 81*
Atcheson, Richard 1934- *ConAu 29R*
Atchison, Sandra Dallas 1939- *ConAu 10NR,*
  -17R
Atchity, Kenneth John *DrAP&F 83*
Atchity, Kenneth John 1944- *ConAu 1NR, -49,*
  IntWWP 82
Atchley, Bob *ConAu X*
Atchley, Dana W *DrAP&F 83*
Atchley, Dana W 1941- *ConAu 61*
Atchley, Robert C 1939- *ConAu 1NR, -45*
Atene, Ann *SmATA X*
Atene, Anna 1922- *SmATA 12*
Athanas, Verne 1917-1962 *TwCWW*
Athanassiadis, Nikos 1904- *ConAu 33R*
Athans, George 1952- *ConAu 104, WrDr 84*
Athas, Daphne *DrAP&F 83*
Athas, Daphne 1923- *ConAu 1R, -3NR,*
  IntAu&W 82, WrDr 84
Athay, R E 1925- *ConAu 33R*
Athearn, Hope *DrAP&F 83*
Athearn, Robert Greenleaf 1914- *ConAu 1R,*
  -3NR
Atheling, William *ConAu X*
Atheling, William, Jr. *ConAu X, ConLC 14*
Atherton, Alexine 1930- *ConAu 37R*
Atherton, Gertrude Franklin 1857-1948 *ConAmA,*
  ConAu 104, DcLB 9[port], LongCTC,
  TwCA, TwCA SUP, TwCLC 2, TwCWW,
  TwCWr
Atherton, James C 1915- *ConAu 49*

Atherton, James S 1910- *ConAu P-1*
Atherton, Lewis Eldon 1905- *ConAu 1R*
Atherton, Lucius *ConAu X*
Atherton, Maxine *ConAu 5R*
Atherton, Pauline *ConAu X*
Atherton, Pauline 1929- *ConAu 69*
Atherton, Sarah *ConAu X*
Atherton, Wallace N 1927- *ConAu 49*
Athey, Irene J 1919- *ConAu 61*
Athill, Diana 1917- *ConAu 1R, -2NR,*
  DcLEL 1940
Athlone, Countess Of *ConAu X*
Athos *ConAu X*
Athos, Anthony G 1934- *ConAu 25R*
Athos, Mister Olov *IntAu&W 82X*
Atiya, Aziz Suryal 1898- *ConAu 5R,*
  IntAu&W 82
Atiyah, P S 1931- *ConAu 37R*
Atiyeh, George N 1923- *ConAu 57*
Atkeson, Ray A 1907- *ConAu 11NR, -69*
Atkey, Philip 1908- *TwCCr&M 80, WrDr 84*
Atkin, Flora B 1919- *ConAu 93, WrDr 84*
Atkin, J Myron 1927- *ConAu 45*
Atkin, Mary Gage 1929- *ConAu 81*
Atkin, William Wilson 1912?-1976 *ConAu 65*
Atkins, Chester G 1948- *ConAu 45*
Atkins, G Pope 1934- *ConAu 33R*
Atkins, Harold 1910- *ConAu 105*
Atkins, Harry 1933- *ConAu 25R*
Atkins, Jack *ConAu X*
Atkins, James G 1932- *ConAu 17R*
Atkins, Jim *ConAu X*
Atkins, John Alfred 1916- *ConAu 3NR, -9R,*
  IntAu&W 82, TwCSFW, WrDr 84
Atkins, Kenneth R 1920- *ConAu 73, WrDr 84*
Atkins, Meg Elizabeth *ConAu 102, WrDr 84*
Atkins, Oliver F 1916-1977 *ConAu 73*
Atkins, Ollie *ConAu X*
Atkins, Paul Moody 1892-1977 *ConAu 69*
Atkins, Russell *DrAP&F 83*
Atkins, Russell 1926- *ConAu 1NR, -45,*
  IntWWP 82, LivgBAA, WrDr 84
Atkins, Stuart 1914- *ConAu 25R, IntAu&W 82,*
  WrDr 84
Atkins, Thomas *DrAP&F 83*
Atkins, Thomas R 1939- *ConAu 6NR, -8NR,*
  -61
Atkinson, Anthony Barnes 1944- *ConAu 11NR,*
  -69
Atkinson, Basil Ferris Campbell 1895- *ConAu 5R*
Atkinson, Brooks 1894- *ConAu 61, TwCA,*
  TwCA SUP
Atkinson, Carroll 1896- *ConAu P-1*
Atkinson, David J 1943- *ConAu 107*
Atkinson, Eleanor 1863-1942 *TwCA,*
  TwCA SUP
Atkinson, Frank 1922- *ConAu 108, WrDr 84*
Atkinson, Frank 1925- *IntAu&W 82*
Atkinson, Hugh Craig 1933- *ConAu 49*
Atkinson, James 1914- *ConAu 25R,*
  IntAu&W 82, WrDr 84
Atkinson, John W 1923- *ConAu 11NR, -21R*
Atkinson, Justin Brooks 1894- *ConAmTC,*
  IntAu&W 82, TwCA, TwCA SUP
Atkinson, M E 1899-1974 *ConAu X,*
  TwCCW 83
Atkinson, Margaret Fleming *ConAu 73,*
  SmATA 14
Atkinson, Mary *ConAu X*
Atkinson, Mary Evelyn 1899- *SmATA 4*
Atkinson, Nancy 1910- *WrDr 84*
Atkinson, Phillip S 1921- *ConAu 25R*
Atkinson, R C 1929- *ConAu 17R*
Atkinson, R S 1927- *WrDr 84*
Atkinson, Ron *DrAP&F 83*
Atkinson, Ron 1932- *ConAu 57*
Atkinson, Ronald Field 1928- *ConAu 17R,*
  WrDr 84
Atkinson, Walter S 1891-1978 *ConAu 73*
Atkinson, William Christopher 1902- *ConAu 109*
Atkisson, Arthur A 1930- *ConAu 61*
Atkyns, Glenn C 1921- *ConAu 49*
Atlas *ConAmA*
Atlas, Helen Vincent 1931- *ConAu 101*
Atlas, James *DrAP&F 83*
Atlas, Martin 1914- *ConAu 5R*
Atlas, Samuel 1899-1977 *ConAu 73*
Atlee, Philip *WrDr 84*
Atlee, Philip 1915- *TwCCr&M 80*
Atmore, Anthony 1932- *ConAu 25R*
Atomic Alchemist *IntWWP 82X*
Atreya, Shanti Prakash 1917- *IntAu&W 82*

Atsumi, Ikuko 1940- *IntWWP 82*
Attaboy *IntAu&W 82X*
Attaway, Robert J 1942- *ConAu 49*
Attaway, William A 1912- *LivgBAA,*
    –, ModBlW
Attea, Mary *ConAu X*
Atteberry, William L 1939- *ConAu 53*
Attenborough, Bernard George *ConAu 2NR, –49*
Attenborough, David 1926- *WrDr 84*
Attenborough, David Frederick 1926- *ConAu 1R,*
    –6NR
Attenborough, John 1908- *ConAu 101*
Atter, Gordon Francis 1905- *IntAu&W 82,*
    WrDr 84
Atthill, Robert Anthony 1912- *WrDr 84*
Atthill, Robin *WrDr 84*
Atthill, Robin 1912- *ConAu 69, IntAu&W 82*
Attia, Mahmoud Ibrahim 1900- *IntAu&W 82*
Atticus *ConAu X, SmATA X*
Attila *IntAu&W 82X*
Attlee, Clement Richard, Earl 1883-1967
    LongCTC
Attneave, Carolyn L 1920- *ConAu 1NR, –45*
Attridge, Derek 1945- *ConAu 105*
Attwell, Arthur A 1917- *ConAu 49*
Attwell, Mable Lucie 1879-1964 *LongCTC*
Attwood, William 1919- *ConAu 21R*
Atwater, C Elizabeth 1923- *ConAu 13R*
Atwater, Eastwood 1925- *ConAu 110*
Atwater, Florence Hasseltine Carroll *SmATA 16*
Atwater, James David 1928- *ConAu 101*
Atwater, Montgomery Meigs 1904- *ConAu 73,*
    SmATA 15
Atwater, Richard 1892-1938 *TwCCW 83*
Atwater, Richard Tupper 1892-1948 *SmATA 27*
Atwood, Ann 1913- *WrDr 84*
Atwood, Ann Margaret 1913- *ConAu 41R,*
    IntAu&W 82, SmATA 7
Atwood, Drucy *ConAu X*
Atwood, Margaret *DrAP&F 83*
Atwood, Margaret 1939- *ConAu 3NR, –49,*
    ConLC 2, –3, –4, –8, –13, –15, –25[port],
    ConNov 82, ConP 80, DcLEL 1940,
    EncWL 2, IntAu&W 82, IntWWP 82,
    ModCmwL, WorAu 1970, WrDr 84
Atwood, Robert B *AuNews 2*
Atyeo, Don 1950- *ConAu 93*
Atzmon, Zvi 1948- *IntWWP 82*
Aub, Max 1902-1972 *EncWL 2*
Aub, Max 1903-1972 *CIDMEL 80, TwCWr*
Aubanel, Theodore 1829-1886 *CIDMEL 80*
Auberjonois, Fernand 1910- *ConAu 77*
Aubert, Alvin *DrAP&F 83*
Aubert, Alvin 1930- *ConAu 81, ConP 80,*
    WrDr 84
Aubery, Pierre 1920- *ConAu 37R*
Aubey, Robert T 1930- *ConAu 21R*
Aubin, Henry 1942- *ConAu 77*
Aubrey, Frank *TwCSFW*
Aubry, Claude B 1914- *ConAu 106,*
    SmATA 29[port]
Aubry, Octave 1881-1946 *TwCA, TwCA SUP*
Auburn, Mark S 1945- *ConAu 89*
Auchincloss, Louis *DrAP&F 83*
Auchincloss, Louis 1917- *ConAu 1R, –6NR,*
    ConLC 4, –6, –9, –18, ConLCrt 82,
    ConNov 82, DcLB Y80A[port], –2,
    DcLEL 1940, ModAL, ModAL SUP,
    TwCWr, WorAu, WrDr 84
Auchmuty, James Johnston 1909- *ConAu 101,*
    IntAu&W 82, WrDr 84
Auchmuty, James Johnston 1909-1981 *ConAu 109*
Auchterlonie *IntAu&W 82X*
Auchterlonie, Dorothy *WrDr 84*
Auchterlounie, Dorothy 1915- *DcLEL 1940*
Audax *ConAu X*
Audemars, Pierre 1909- *ConAu 7NR, –17R,*
    TwCCr&M 80, WrDr 84
Auden, Renee *ConAu X*
Auden, W H 1907-1973 *CnMD, CnMWL,*
    ConAu 5NR, –9R, –45, ConLC 1, –2, –3, –4,
    –6, –9, –11, –14, ConLCrt 82, ConP 80A,
    DcLB 10[port], EncWL 2[port], LongCTC,
    ModAL, ModAL SUP, ModBrL,
    ModBrL SUP, ModWD, RGFMBP, TwCA,
    TwCA SUP, TwCWr, WhoTwCL
Auderska, Halina 1904- *IntAu&W 82*
Audiberti, Jacques 1899-1965 *CIDMEL 80,*
    CnMD, CroCD, EncWL 2, ModFrL,
    ModWD, WorAu
Audiberti, Jacques 1900-1965 *ConAu 25R*
Audley, Ernest Henry *DcLEL 1940*

Audoux, Marguerite 1863-1937 *LongCTC*
Audus, Leslie John 1911- *IntAu&W 82,*
    WrDr 84
Auel, Jane M 1936- *WrDr 84*
Auel, Jean M 1936- *ConAu 103*
Auer, J Jeffery 1913- *ConAu 6NR, –9R*
Auerbach, Arnold M 1912- *ConAu 17R*
Auerbach, Erich 1892-1957 *EncWL 2, ModGL,*
    WorAu
Auerbach, Erna d1975 *ConAu 61*
Auerbach, George 1905?-1973 *ConAu 45*
Auerbach, Jerold S 1936- *ConAu 21R*
Auerbach, Marjorie 1932- *ConAu 9R*
Auerbach, Nina 1943- *ConAu 85*
Auerbach, Stevanne 1938- *ConAu 8NR, –57*
Auerbach, Stuart C 1935- *ConAu 89*
Auerbach, Sylvia 1921- *ConAu 4NR, –53*
Auezov, Mukhtar Omarkhan-Uli 1897-1961
    EncWL 2
Aufderheide, Lawrence *DrAP&F 83*
Aufricht, Hans 1902- *ConAu 45*
Aug, Ellen *DrAP&F 83*
Aug, Ellen Wendy 1940- *IntWWP 82*
Augarde, Steve 1950- *ConAu 104,*
    SmATA 25[port]
Auge, Bud *ConAu X*
Auge, Henry J, Jr. 1930?-1983 *ConAu 109*
Augelli, John P 1921- *ConAu 17R*
Auger, Hugh A 1917- *IntAu&W 82*
Auger, Pierre Victor 1899- *IntAu&W 82*
Aughtry, Charles Edward 1925- *ConAu 5R*
Augsburger, A Don 1925- *ConAu 21R*
Augsburger, David W 1938- *ConAu 33R*
Augsburger, Myron S 1929- *ConAu 6NR, –13R*
Augstein, Rudolf 1923- *ConAu 110*
Auguet, Roland 1935- *ConAu 105*
August, Eugene R 1935- *ConAu 49*
August, John *LongCTC*
Augustin, Ann Sutherland 1934- *ConAu 57*
Augustin, Elisabeth 1903- *IntAu&W 82,*
    IntWWP 82
Augustin, Pius 1934- *ConAu 17R*
Augustine, Erich *ConAu X*
Augustine, Jane *DrAP&F 83*
Augustson, Ernest *ConAu X*
Augustus, Albert, Jr. *ConAu X*
Aukerman, Robert C 1910- *ConAu 33R,*
    WrDr 84
Aukofer, Frank A 1935- *ConAu 65*
Aukrust, Olav 1883-1929 *CIDMEL 80*
Auld, Rhoda L *ConAu 105*
Auld, William 1924- *IntAu&W 82*
Auleta, Michael S 1909- *ConAu P-2*
Auletta, Ken 1942- *ConAu 69*
Auletta, Richard P 1942- *ConAu 53*
Auletta, Robert 1940- *NatPD 81[port]*
Aulicino, Armand 1920?-1983 *ConAu 109*
Aulick, June L 1906- *ConAu 25R*
Ault, Donald D 1942- *ConAu 81*
Ault, Phil *ConAu X, SmATA X*
Ault, Phillip H 1914- *ConAu 101,*
    SmATA 23[port]
Ault, Rosalie Sain 1942- *ConAu 107*
Ault, Roz *ConAu X*
Aultman, Donald S 1930- *ConAu 17R*
Aultman, Richard E 1933- *ConAu 9NR, –65*
Aumann, Francis Robert 1901- *ConAu 41R,*
    IntAu&W 82
Aumbry, Alan *ConAu X*
Aumonier, Stacy 1887-1928 *LongCTC, TwCA,*
    TwCA SUP
Aumont, Jean-Pierre 1913- *ConAu 29R*
Aune, Bruce 1933- *ConAu 73*
Aung, Htin 1909- *ConAu 3NR, –5R*
Aung, Htin 1910- *SmATA 21[port]*
Aung, U Htin *SmATA X*
Auntie Deb *ConAu X, SmATA X*
Auntie Louise *ConAu X, SmATA X*
Aurand, Harold Wilson 1940- *ConAu 41R*
Aurand, L W 1920- *ConAu 53*
Aurandt, Paul Harvey 1918- *ConAu 102*
Aurelius, Neville *NatPD 81[port]*
Aurell, Tage 1895-1976 *EncWL 2*
Aurner, Robert Ray 1898- *ConAu 5R,*
    IntAu&W 82, WrDr 84
Aurobindo, Sri 1872- *WorAu 1970*
Aurobindo Ghose *EncWL 2*
Aurthur, Robert Alan 1922-1978 *ConAu 81*
Ausala, Margarita 1919- *IntWWP 82*
Ausland, John C 1920- *ConAu 93*
Auslander, Joseph 1897-1965 *TwCA,*
    TwCA SUP

Auslander, Rosalie B 1907- *IntAu&W 82*
Auslander, Rose *IntAu&W 82X*
Austen, George *CreCan 1*
Austen, Michael 1951- *ConAu 109*
Austen, Ralph A 1937- *ConAu 25R*
Auster, Nancy R 1926- *ConAu 65*
Auster, Paul *DrAP&F 83*
Auster, Paul 1947- *ConAu 69, IntWWP 82*
Austgen, Robert Joseph 1932- *ConAu 21R,*
    WrDr 84
Austick, David 1920- *IntAu&W 82*
Austin, Alfred 1835-1913 *LongCTC, TwCWr*
Austin, Allan Edward 1929- *ConAu 73*
Austin, Allen C 1922- *ConAu 33R, WrDr 84*
Austin, Anthony 1919- *ConAu 33R*
Austin, Aurelia *ConAu 53*
Austin, Barbara Leslie *ConAu X*
Austin, Brett *ConAu X, WrDr 84*
Austin, Cedric Ronald Jonah 1912- *IntAu&W 82,*
    WrDr 84
Austin, Charles M 1941- *ConAu 69*
Austin, David Edwards 1926- *ConAu 29R*
Austin, E V *DrAP&F 83*
Austin, Elizabeth S 1907- *ConAu P-2,*
    SmATA 5
Austin, Frank *ConAu X, TwCWW*
Austin, Harry *ConAu X*
Austin, Henry Wilfred 1906- *ConAu 101,*
    WrDr 84
Austin, J L 1911-1960 *WorAu 1970*
Austin, James C 1923- *ConAu 13R, WrDr 84*
Austin, James Henry 1925- *ConAu 81*
Austin, John 1922- *ConAu 61*
Austin, John Langshaw 1911-1960 *LongCTC*
Austin, K A 1911- *ConAu 102*
Austin, Kenneth Ashurst 1911- *IntAu&W 82,*
    WrDr 84
Austin, Lettie J 1925- *ConAu 65, LivgBAA*
Austin, Lewis 1936- *ConAu 73*
Austin, Lloyd James 1915- *ConAu P-1*
Austin, M M 1943- *ConAu 85*
Austin, Margot *ConAu P-1, SmATA 11*
Austin, Mary 1868-1934 *ConAu 109*
Austin, Mary C 1915- *ConAu 5R*
Austin, Mary Hunter 1868-1934 *ConAmA,*
    DcLB 9, FifWWr, TwCA, TwCA SUP,
    TwCWW
Austin, Neal F 1926- *ConAu 25R*
Austin, Norman 1937- *ConAu 89*
Austin, Oliver Luther, Jr. 1903- *ConAu 49,*
    SmATA 7
Austin, Reid 1931- *ConAu 89*
Austin, Richard 1926- *WrDr 84*
Austin, Richard B, Jr. 1930- *ConAu 73*
Austin, Stephen *ConAu X*
Austin, Tom *ConAu X, SmATA X*
Austin, William W 1920- *ConAu 21R,*
    WrDr 84
Austveg, Inger 1915- *IntAu&W 82*
Austwick, John 1904-1965 *ConAu X,*
    TwCCr&M 80
Ausubel, Herman 1920-1977 *ConAu 1R, –69*
Ausubel, Marynn R 1913?-1980 *ConAu 97*
Auten, James H 1938- *ConAu 41R*
Auth, Tony *ConAu X*
Auth, William Anthony, Jr. 1942- *ConAu 108*
Autran Dourado, Waldomiro *ConAu X*
Autrey, C E 1904- *ConAu 1R, –2NR*
Autry, Ewart Arthur 1900- *ConAu 13R*
Autton, Norman 1920- *WrDr 84*
Autton, Norman William James 1920-
    ConAu 101
Auty, Phyllis 1910- *ConAu 2NR, –5R*
Auvert-Eason, Elizabeth 1917- *ConAu 37R*
Auvil, Kenneth W 1925- *ConAu 17R*
Avakian, Arra S 1912- *ConAu 85*
Avakumovic, Ivan 1926- *ConAu 41R*
Avalle-Arce, Juan Bautista 1927- *ConAu 33R,*
    IntWWP 82
Avallone, Michael 1924- *WrDr 84*
Avallone, Michael Angelo, Jr. 1924- *ConAu 4NR,*
    –5R, TwCCr&M 80
Avedon, Richard 1923- *WrDr 84*
Aveline, Claude 1901- *ConAu 5R, –6NR*
Aveling, J C H 1917- *WrDr 84*
Aveni, Anthony F 1938- *ConAu 81*
Averbach, Albert 1902-1975 *ConAu P-2*
Averchenko, Arkady Timofeyevich 1881-1925
    CIDMEL 80
Averill, E W 1906- *ConAu 53*
Averill, Esther 1902- *TwCCW 83, WrDr 84*
Averill, Esther Holden 1902- *ConAu 29R,*

SmATA 1, -28[port]
Averill, H C *TwCWW*
Averill, Lloyd J 1923- *ConAu 10NR*
Averill, Lloyd James 1923- *ConAu 21R*
Averitt, Thomas Fox *DrAP&F 83*
Averitt, Robert T 1931- *ConAu 21R*
Avermaete, Roger 1893- *IntAu&W 82*
Avery, Al *ConAu X, SmATA 3, WrDr 84*
Avery, Burniece Sally 1908- *ConAu 73,
   MichAu 80*
Avery, Catherine B 1909- *ConAu 57*
Avery, David *WrDr 84*
Avery, Edwina Austin 1896-1983 *ConAu 110*
Avery, George C 1926- *ConAu 25R*
Avery, Gillian 1926- *TwCCW 83, WrDr 84*
Avery, Gillian Elise 1926- *ConAu 4NR, -9R,
   IntAu&W 82, SmATA 7*
Avery, Harold 1867-1943 *TwCCW 83*
Avery, Ira 1914- *ConAu 81*
Avery, Kay 1908- *ConAu 1R, SmATA 5*
Avery, Laurence G 1934- *ConAu 33R*
Avery, Lynn *ConAu X, SmATA 5*
Avery, Peter William 1923- *ConAu 13R*
Avery, Richard *ConAu X, IntAu&W 82X,
   TwCSFW*
Avery, Robert J, Jr. 1911?-1983 *ConAu 110*
Avery, Robert Sterling 1917- *ConAu 13R*
Avey, Albert Edwin 1886-1963 *ConAu P-1*
Avey, Ruby Doreen 1927- *ConAu 89,
   IntAu&W 82*
Avi *ConAu X, SmATA X*
Avi-Shaul, Mordechay 1898- *IntWWP 82*
Avi-Yonah, M 1904-1974 *ConAu 5R, -6NR*
Avice, Claude 1925- *ConAu 8NR, -61*
Avila, Lilian Estelle *ConAu 45*
Aviles Fabila, Rene 1940- *IntAu&W 82*
Avineri, Shlomo 1933- *ConAu 25R*
Avison, John 1915- *CreCan 1*
Avison, Margaret 1918- *ConAu 17R, ConLC 2,
   -4, ConP 80, CreCan 1, DcLEL 1940,
   WhoTwCL, WrDr 84*
Avison, N Howard 1934- *ConAu 29R*
Avnery, Uri 1923- *ConAu 105*
Avni, Abraham 1921- *WrDr 84*
Avni, Abraham Albert 1921- *ConAu 33R*
Avramovic, Dragoslav 1919- *ConAu 41R,
   WrDr 84*
Avrelin, M *ConAu X*
Avrett, Robert William 1901- *ConAu 1R*
Avrett, Rosalind Case 1933- *ConAu 110*
Avrett, Roz *ConAu X*
Avrich, Paul Henry 1931- *ConAu 5NR, -49,
   IntAu&W 82*
Avriel, Ehud 1917- *ConAu 69*
Avril, Pierre 1930- *ConAu 29R*
Avriza *IntWWP 82X*
Avrutis, Raymond 1948- *ConAu 69*
Awa, Eme Onuoha 1921- *ConAu 13R*
Awad, Elias M 1934- *ConAu 11NR, -17R*
Awdry, W 1911- *WrDr 84*
Awdry, W V 1911- *TwCCW 83*
Awdry, Wilbert Vere 1911- *ConAu 103,
   IntAu&W 82*
Awe, Chulho 1927- *ConAu 33R*
Awolowo, Obafemi Awo 1909- *ConAu 65*
Awoonor, Kofi *DrAP&F 83*
Awoonor, Kofi 1935- *ConAu 29R, ConP 80,
   DcLEL 1940, EncWL 2, IntAu&W 82,
   ModBlW, ModCmwL, WorAu 1970,
   WrDr 84*
Awoonor-Williams, George 1935- *TwCWr*
Axell, Herbert 1915- *ConAu 81*
Axelos, Celine Tasso 1902- *IntAu&W 82*
Axelrad, Jacob 1899- *ConAu 61*
Axelrad, Sidney 1913-1976 *ConAu 110*
Axelrad, Sylvia Brody 1914- *ConAu 104*
Axelrod, Alan 1952- *ConAu 110*
Axelrod, David B *DrAP&F 83*
Axelrod, David B 1943- *ConAu 1NR, -45*
Axelrod, George 1922- *CnMD, ConAu 65,
   ConDr 82, ModAL, WorAu, WrDr 84*
Axelrod, Herbert Richard 1927- *ConAu 85*
Axelrod, Joseph 1918- *ConAu 33R*
Axelrod, M R *DrAP&F 83*
Axelrod, Paul 1949- *ConAu 110*
Axelrod, Robert 1943- *ConAu 33R*
Axelrod, Steven Gould 1944- *ConAu 81*
Axelrod, Susan *DrAP&F 83*
Axelson, Eric 1913- *ConAu 9NR, -21R,
   IntAu&W 82, WrDr 84*
Axford, H William 1925- *ConAu 37R*
Axford, Joseph Mack 1879-1970 *ConAu P-2*

Axford, Lavonne B 1928- *ConAu 33R*
Axford, Roger W 1920- *ConAu 33R*
Axinn, Donald *DrAP&F 83*
Axinn, June 1923- *ConAu 89*
Axline, W Andrew 1940- *ConAu 25R*
Axtell, James Lewis 1941- *ConAu 108*
Axthelm, Peter M 1943- *ConAu 107*
Axton, David *ConAu X, WrDr 84*
Axton, W F 1926- *ConAu 21R*
Ayal, Igal 1942- *ConAu 37R*
Ayala, Francisco 1906- *ClDMEL 80, EncWL 2,
   TwCWr*
Ayala, Francisco 1934- *ConAu 85*
Ayala, Mitzi 1941- *ConAu 110*
Ayala, Ramon Perez De *CnMWL, ModRL,
   TwCA, TwCA SUP*
Ayandele, E A 1936- *ConAu 21R*
Ayars, Albert Lee 1917- *ConAu 29R, WrDr 84*
Ayars, James Sterling 1898- *ConAu 2NR, -5R,
   IntAu&W 82, MichAu 80, SmATA 4,
   WrDr 84*
Ayatey, Siegfried B Y 1934- *ConAu 25R*
Aybek 1905-1968 *EncWL 2*
Ayckbourn, Alan 1939- *ConAu 21R, ConDr 82,
   ConLC 5, -8, -18, DcLB 13[port],
   DcLEL 1940, IntAu&W 82, WorAu 1970,
   WrDr 84*
Aycock, Don M 1951- *ConAu 106*
Aycock, Shirley *DrAP&F 83*
Aydelotte, William Osgood 1910- *ConAu 57*
Aydy, Catherine *WrDr 84*
Ayearst, Morley 1899- *ConAu P-2*
Ayearst, Morley 1899-1983 *ConAu 109*
Ayer, A J 1910- *WrDr 84*
Ayer, Alfred Jules 1910- *ConAu 5R, -5NR,
   IntAu&W 82, LongCTC, WorAu*
Ayer, Brian *ConAu X*
Ayer, Frederick, Jr. 1917?-1974 *ConAu 45, -73*
Ayer, Hilary *DrAP&F 83*
Ayer, Jacqueline 1932- *WrDr 84*
Ayer, Jacqueline Brandford 1930- *ConAu 69,
   SmATA 13[port]*
Ayer, Margaret *ConAu 65, SmATA 15*
Ayers, Bradley Earl 1935- *ConAu 69*
Ayers, Donald Murray 1923- *ConAu 17R*
Ayers, M R 1935- *ConAu 25R*
Ayers, Mary Alice *DrAP&F 83*
Ayers, Robert H 1918- *ConAu 45*
Ayers, Ronald 1948- *ConAu 61*
Ayers, Rose *ConAu X*
Ayerst, David 1904- *WrDr 84*
Ayerst, David George Ogilvy 1904- *IntAu&W 82*
Ayes, Anthony *IntAu&W 82X*
Ayes, William *IntAu&W 82X*
Aygi, Gennady 1934- *ClDMEL 80*
Ayguesparse, Albert 1900- *ClDMEL 80,
   IntAu&W 82, IntWWP 82*
Aykroyd, Wallace Ruddell 1899-1979 *ConAu 110*
Aylen, Leo *WrDr 84*
Aylen, Leo William 1935- *IntAu&W 82*
Aylen, Leon 1935- *ConAu 102*
Aylesworth, Jim 1943- *ConAu 106*
Aylesworth, John 1938- *ConSFA*
Aylesworth, Thomas G 1927- *ChlLR 6[port],
   ConAu 10NR*
Aylesworth, Thomas Gibbons 1927- *ConAu 25R,
   SmATA 4*
Ayling, Keith 1898-1976 *ConAu 69, -73*
Ayling, Stanley 1909- *WrDr 84*
Ayling, Stanley Edward 1909- *ConAu 45,
   IntAu&W 82*
Aylmer, Sir Felix 1889-1977 *ConAu X,
   DcLEL 1940*
Aylmer, G E 1926- *ConAu 5NR, -13R,
   WrDr 84*
Aylmer, Gerald Edward 1926- *IntAu&W 82*
Aymar, Brandt 1911- *ConAu 1R,
   SmATA 22[port]*
Aymar, Gordon Christian 1893- *ConAu 5R*

Ayme, Marcel 1902-1967 *ClDMEL 80, CnMD,
   ConAu 89, ConLC 11, EncWL 2,
   LongCTC, ModFrL, ModRL, ModWD,
   TwCA SUP, TwCWr*
Aymes, Sister Maria DeLaCruz *ConAu 21R*
Aynes, Edith Annette 1909- *ConAu 45,
   IntAu&W 82*
Aynes, Pat Edith *ConAu X*
Ayni, Sadriddin 1878-1954 *EncWL 2*
Ayraud, Pierre *WorAu*
Ayrault, Evelyn West 1922- *ConAu 9R*
Ayre, Robert Hugh 1900- *ConAu 1R*

Ayre, Thornton *TwCSFW*
Ayres, Alison *ConAu X*
Ayres, Carole Briggs *ConAu X*
Ayres, Elizabeth *DrAP&F 83*
Ayres, James Eyvind 1939- *ConAu 103*
Ayres, Paul *ConAu X*
Ayres, Robert U 1932- *ConAu 93*
Ayres, Ruby Mildred 1883-1955 *LongCTC,
   TwCRGW, TwCWr*
Ayrton, Elisabeth Walshe 1918- *ConAu 3NR,
   -5R*
Ayrton, Elizabeth 1918- *WrDr 84*
Ayrton, Michael 1921-1975 *ConAu 5R, -9NR,
   -61, ConLC 7, DcLEL 1940*
Ayscough, Florence 1878-1942 *LongCTC, TwCA,
   TwCA SUP*
Ayscough, John 1858-1928 *LongCTC, TwCA,
   TwCA SUP*
Aytmatov, Chingiz 1928- *ClDMEL 80,
   EncWL 2*
Ayub Khan, Mohammad 1907-1974 *ConAu P-2*
Ayvazian, L Fred 1919- *ConAu 69*
Ayyildiz, Judy Light *DrAP&F 83*
Azaid *ConAu X, SmATA X*
Azana, Manuel 1880-1940 *ClDMEL 80*
Azar, Edward E 1938- *ConAu 49*
Azarowicz, Marjory 1922- *WrDr 84*
Azbel, Mark Y 1932- *ConAu 105*
Azevedo, Ross E *ConAu 105*
Azkoul, Karim 1915- *IntAu&W 82*
Azneer, J Leonard 1921- *ConAu 33R,
   IntAu&W 82, WrDr 84*
Azorin 1873- *ModRL, TwCA, TwCA SUP,
   TwCWr*
Azorin 1873-1967 *ClDMEL 80, EncWL 2[port]*
Azorin 1873-1969 *ConAu X*
Azorin 1874-1967 *ConLC 11*
Azoy, A C M 1891- *ConAu P-1*
Azrael, Judith Anne *DrAP&F 83*
Azrael, Judith Anne 1938- *ConAu 10NR*
Azrin, Nathan H 1930- *ConAu 1NR, -45*
Azuar, Rafael 1921- *IntAu&W 82*
Azuela, Mariano 1873-1952 *ConAu 104,
   EncWL 2, ModLAL, TwCLC 3, TwCWr,
   WorAu*
Azumi, Atsushi 1907- *ConAu 102*
Azumi, Koya 1930- *ConAu 29R*

B

B B 1905- *LongCTC, SmATA 6*
B-Holm *IntAu&W 82X*
B V *LongCTC*
Baack, Lawrence James 1943- *ConAu 109*
Baal-Teshuva, Jacob 1929- *ConAu 5R*
Baar, James A 1929- *ConAu 102*
Baars, Conrad W 1919-1981 *ConAu 8NR, –57*
Baass, Mildred Vorpahl 1917- *IntWWP 82*
Baastad, Babbis Friis *ConAu X, SmATA 7*
Baatz, Charles A 1916- *ConAu 104*
Baatz, Olga K 1921- *ConAu 104*
Bab *ConAu X*
Baba, Meher 1894-1969 *ConAu 106, –109*
Babaevsky, Semyon Petrovich 1909-
    IntAu&W 82
Babalola, Adeboye 1926- *IntWWP 82*
Babb, Howard S 1924- *ConAu 13R*
Babb, Hugh Webster 1887-1970? *ConAu P-1*
Babb, Lawrence 1902- *ConAu P-2*
Babb, Lawrence Alan 1941- *ConAu 105*
Babb, Sanora 1907- *ConAu 13R, WrDr 84*
Babbage, Stuart Barton 1916- *ConAu 5R, –8NR,
    WrDr 84*
Babbidge, Homer Daniels, Jr. 1925- *ConAu 61*
Babbie, Earl 1938- *ConAu 8NR, –61*
Babbis, Eleanor *ConAu X, SmATA 7*
Babbitt, Bruce E 1938- *ConAu 97*
Babbitt, Irving 1865-1933 *ConAmA, LongCTC,
    ModAL, TwCA, TwCA SUP, WhoTwCL*
Babbitt, Natalie *WrDr 84*
Babbitt, Natalie 1932- *ChlLR 2, ConAu 2NR,
    –49, SmATA 6, TwCCW 83*
Babbitt, Robert *ConAu X, WrDr 84*
Babbler *ConAu X*
Babcock, C Merton 1908- *ConAu 1R, –5R,
    –5NR*
Babcock, Dennis Arthur 1948- *ConAu 61,
    SmATA 22*
Babcock, Dorothy E 1931- *ConAu 65*
Babcock, Frederic 1896- *ConAu 5R*
Babcock, Frederick Morrison 1897?-1983
    ConAu 110
Babcock, Havilah 1898-1964 *ConAu 110*
Babcock, Leland S 1922- *ConAu 106*
Babcock, Nicolas *ConAu X*
Babcock, Robert J 1928- *ConAu 13R*
Babe, Thomas 1941- *ConAu 101, ConDr 82,
    NatPD 81[port], WrDr 84*
Babel, Isaac E 1894-1940? *LongCTC*
Babel, Isaak E 1894- *TwCA, TwCA SUP*
Babel, Isaak E 1894-1935? *CnMD*
Babel, Isaak E 1894-1940? *CnMWL*
Babel, Isaak E 1894-1941 *CIDMEL 80,
    ConAu 104, EncWL 2, ModSL 1,
    ModWD, TwCLC 2, TwCWr, WhoTwCL*
Baber, Asa *DrAP&F 83*
Babiiha, Thaddeo K 1945- *ConAu 110*
Babin, David E 1925- *ConAu 21R*
Babin, Maria Teresa 1910- *ConAu 107*
Babington, Anthony Patrick 1920- *ConAu 61,
    IntAu&W 82, WrDr 84*
Babington Smith, Constance 1912- *IntAu&W 82*
Babits, Mihaly 1883-1941 *CIDMEL 80,
    EncWL 2, WhoTwCL*

Babitz, Eve 1943- *ConAu 81*
Babitz, Sol 1911- *ConAu 41R*
Babladelis, Georgia 1931- *ConAu 8NR, –21R*
Babris, Peter J 1917- *ConAu 10NR, –21R,
    WrDr 84*
Babson, Marian *ConAu 102, TwCCr&M 80,
    WrDr 84*
Babson, Roger Ward 1875-1967 *ConAu 89*
Babula, William 1943- *ConAu 105*
Bacall, Lauren 1924- *ConAu 93, WrDr 84*
Bacchelli, Riccardo 1891- *CIDMEL 80, CnMD,
    ConAu 29R, ConLC 19, EncWL 2,
    ModRL, TwCWr, WorAu*
Bacciocco, Edward J, Jr. 1935- *ConAu 45*
Bach, Alice 1942- *ConAu 101, SmATA 27,
    –30[port]*
Bach, Bert C 1936- *ConAu 21R*
Bach, George Leland 1915- *ConAu 1R, –3NR*
Bach, George Robert 1914- *ConAu 104*
Bach, Kent 1943- *ConAu 85*
Bach, P D Q *ConAu X*
Bach, Richard 1936- *AuNews 1, ConAu 9R,
    ConLC 14, SmATA 13, WrDr 84*
Bach, Wilfrid 1936- *ConAu 10NR, –61*
Bacharach, Alfred L 1891-1966 *ConAu P-1*
Bacharach, Bert 1898-1983 *ConAu 110*
Bachchan, Harbans Rai 1907- *IntAu&W 82*
Bache, William B 1922- *ConAu 25R*
Bachelard, Gaston 1882-1962 *WhoTwCL*
Bachelard, Gaston 1884-1962 *CIDMEL 80,
    ConAu 89, –97, WorAu[port]*
Bacheller, Irving 1859-1950 *TwCA, TwCA SUP*
Bachem Alent, Rose M *ConAu 49*
Bacher, June Masters 1918- *ConAu 108*
Bachler, Wolfgang 1925- *IntAu&W 82*
Bachman, Fred 1949- *ConAu 53, SmATA 12*
Bachman, Ingeborg 1926-1973 *ConAu 45, –93*
Bachman, Jerald G 1936- *ConAu 41R*
Bachman, John W 1916- *WrDr 84*
Bachman, John Walter 1916- *ConAu 5R*
Bachmann, Gideon 1927- *ConAu 104*
Bachmann, Ingeborg 1926-1973 *CIDMEL 80,
    EncWL 2, ModGL, TwCWr, WorAu*
Bachmura, Frank T 1922- *ConAu 45*
Bachrach, Peter 1918- *WrDr 84*
Bacik, James Joseph 1936- *ConAu 105*
Back, Joe W 1899- *ConAu P-2*
Back, Kurt W 1919- *ConAu 13R*
Backer, Dorothy 1925- *ConAu 85*
Backer, John H 1902- *ConAu 33R*
Backer, Morton 1916- *ConAu 17R*
Backgammon, Daisy *ConAu X*
Backhaus, Helmuth Manuel 1920- *IntAu&W 82*
Backhouse, Janet 1938- *ConAu 109*
Backhouse, Sally 1927- *ConAu 21R*
Backlund, Ralph T 1918- *ConAu 73*
Backman, Carl W 1923- *ConAu 17R*
Backman, Jules 1910- *ConAu 1R, –3NR,
    WrDr 84*
Backman, Melvin 1919- *ConAu 21R*
Backman, Milton V, Jr. 1927- *ConAu 33R*
Backstrom, Charles H 1926- *ConAu 13R*
Backstrom, Lars David 1925- *IntAu&W 82,
    IntWWP 82*

Backus, Jean L 1914- *ConAu 33R*
Backus, Oswald P, III 1921-1972 *ConAu 37R,
    ConAu P-2*
Bacmeister, Rhoda W 1893- *ConAu P-1,
    SmATA 11*
Bacon, Ed *ConAmTC*
Bacon, Edmund N 1910- *WrDr 84*
Bacon, Edmund Norwood 1910- *ConAu 41R,
    IntAu&W 82*
Bacon, Edward 1906-1981 *ConAu 102, –29R*
Bacon, Elizabeth 1914- *ConAu 29R, SmATA 3*
Bacon, Elizabeth E 1904- *ConAu P-1*
Bacon, Frances Atchinson 1903- *ConAu 1R,
    MichAu 80*
Bacon, Frank 1864-1922 *ModWD*
Bacon, George Edward 1917- *WrDr 84*
Bacon, Joan Chase *ConAu X*
Bacon, John 1940- *ConAu 53*
Bacon, Josephine Dodge Daskam 1876-1961
    ConAu 97, TwCA, TwCA SUP
Bacon, Lenice Ingram 1895- *ConAu 45*
Bacon, Leonard 1887-1954 *TwCA, TwCA SUP*
Bacon, Margaret *ConAu 106, IntAu&W 82,
    WrDr 84*
Bacon, Margaret Hope 1921- *ConAu 25R,
    SmATA 6[port]*
Bacon, Marion 1901?-1975 *ConAu 57*
Bacon, Martha 1917-1981 *TwCCW 83*
Bacon, Martha Sherman 1917-1981 *ChlLR 3,
    ConAu 104, –85, SmATA 18, –27N*
Bacon, Nancy 1940- *ConAu 93*
Bacon, Peggy 1895- *ConAu P-2, SmATA 2*
Bacon, Phillip 1922- *ConAu 41R*
Bacon, R L 1924- *ConAu 104, SmATA 26,
    TwCCW 83, WrDr 84*
Bacon, Robert *DrAP&F 83*
Bacon, Wallace A 1914- *ConAu 17R*
Bacote, Clarence A 1906- *ConAu P-2*
Bacovia, George 1881-1957 *EncWL 2,
    WhoTwCL*
Bacovia, George 1884-1957 *CIDMEL 80*
Bacque, James 1929- *ConAu 101*
Baczynski, Krzysztof Kamil 1921-1944
    CIDMEL 80
Badanes, Menke *IntAu&W 82X*
Badash, Lawrence 1934- *ConAu 37R*
Badawi, Mohamed Mustafa 1925- *ConAu 1NR,
    –49, WrDr 84*
Badawi, Muhammad Mustafa *ConAu X*
Badcock, Christopher Robert 1946- *ConAu 101,
    WrDr 84*
Baddeley, Alan D 1934- *ConAu 69*
Baddoo, Baldwin Sempy 1930- *IntAu&W 82*
Bade, Jane 1932- *ConAu 89*
Bade, Patrick 1951- *ConAu 89*
Baden, Hans Jurgen 1911- *IntAu&W 82*
Baden-Powell, Dorothy 1920- *ConAu 103*
Baden-Powell, Sir Robert 1857-1941 *LongCTC,
    SmATA 16, –16*
Badeni, June 1925- *WrDr 84*
Bader, Douglas 1910-1982 *ConAu 101, –107*
Bader, Julia 1944- *ConAu 69*
Badger, John D'Arcy 1917- *ConAu 45*
Badger, Ralph E 1890-1978 *ConAu 73,*

Balchin, Nigel Marlin 1908-1970 *ConAu 29R*,
  -97, *ConSFA*, *LongCTC*, *ModBrL*,
  TwCA SUP, *TwCWr*
Balchin, W G V 1916- *ConAu 101*
Balchin, William George Victor 1916- *WrDr 84*
Balcomb, Raymond E 1923- *ConAu 21R*
Balcon, Michael 1896-1977 *ConAu 73*, *-77*
Bald, F Clever 1897-1970 *ConAu P-1*,
  MichAu 80
Bald, R C 1901-1965 *ConAu 5R*, *-6NR*
Bald, Wambly 1902- *DcLB 4*
Baldanza, Frank 1924- *ConAu 1R*
Baldelli, Giovanni 1914- *ConAu 45*
Balderson, Margaret *TwCCW 83*, *WrDr 84*
Balderson, Margaret 1935- *ConAu 25R*
Balderston, Jean *DrAP&F 83*
Balderston, Jean Merrill 1936- *IntWWP 82*
Balderston, John 1889-1954 *DcLB 26[port]*
Balderston, John L 1889-1954 *CnMD*, *LongCTC*,
  ModWD
Balderston, Katharine Canby 1895-1979
  ConAu 93
Baldick, Robert 1927-1972 *ConAu 89*
Baldinger, Kurt 1919- *IntAu&W 82*
Baldinger, Stanley 1932- *ConAu 29R*
Baldini, Antonio 1889-1962 *CIDMEL 80*
Baldree, J Martin, Jr. 1927- *ConAu 53*
Baldridge, Cyrus LeRoy 1889- *SmATA 29*
Baldrige, Letitia *ConAu 25R*
Baldry, Harold Caparne 1907- *ConAu 17R*,
  WrDr 84
Balducci, Carolyn *DrAP&F 83*
Balducci, Carolyn 1946- *ConAu 33R*,
  SmATA 5
Balducci, Ernesto 1922- *ConAu 29R*
Baldwin, Anne Norris 1938- *ConAu 29R*,
  SmATA 5, *WrDr 84*
Baldwin, Arthur W 1904?-1976 *ConAu 69*
Baldwin, Bates *ConAu X*
Baldwin, Bertha Marjorie *IntWWP 82*
Baldwin, Catherine Janet *CreCan 2*
Baldwin, Christina 1946- *ConAu 77*
Baldwin, Clara *ConAu 61*, *SmATA 11*
Baldwin, David Allen 1936- *ConAu 17R*
Baldwin, Dick *ConAu X*
Baldwin, Edward R 1935- *ConAu 45*
Baldwin, Faith 1893-1978 *AuNews 1[port]*,
  ConAu 4NR, *-5R*, *-77*, *LongCTC*,
  TwCA[port], *TwCA SUP*, *TwCRGW*
Baldwin, Gordo *ConAu X*, *SmATA X*
Baldwin, Gordon C 1908- *ConAu 1R*, *-3NR*,
  SmATA 12, *TwCWW*, *WrDr 84*
Baldwin, Hanson Weightman 1903- *ConAu 61*,
  TwCA SUP
Baldwin, James *DrAP&F 83*
Baldwin, James 1841-1925 *SmATA 24[port]*
Baldwin, James 1924- *ConAu 1R*, *-3NR*,
  ConDr 82, *ConLC 1*, *-2*, *-3*, *-4*, *-5*, *-8*, *-13*,
  -15, *-17*, *ConNov 82*, *CroCD*, *DcLB 2*,
  -7[port], *DcLEL 1940*, *EncWL 2*,
  LivgBAA, *LongCTC*, *ModAL*,
  ModAL SUP, *ModBlW*, *ModWD*,
  NatPD 81[port], *SmATA 9*, *TwCWr*,
  WhoTwCL, *WorAu*, *WrDr 84*
Baldwin, Janet 1912- *CreCan 2*
Baldwin, John D 1930- *ConAu 101*
Baldwin, John W 1929- *ConAu 105*
Baldwin, Joyce G 1921- *ConAu 8NR*, *-61*
Baldwin, Leland Dewitt 1897-1981 *ConAu 103*,
  -41R
Baldwin, Marjorie *IntWWP 82X*, *WrDr 84*
Baldwin, Marshall W 1903-1975 *ConAu 57*, *-61*
Baldwin, Mary Hayne 1945- *IntWWP 82*
Baldwin, Michael 1930- *ConAu 3NR*, *-9R*,
  DcLEL 1940, *IntWWP 82*
Baldwin, Monica 1896?-1975 *ConAu 104*
Baldwin, Ned *ConAu X*
Baldwin, Neil *DrAP&F 83*
Baldwin, Rebecca *ConAu X*
Baldwin, Richard S 1910- *ConAu 105*
Baldwin, Robert E 1924- *ConAu 41R*
Baldwin, Roger 1884-1981 *ConAu 105*
Baldwin, Roger E 1929- *ConAu 49*
Baldwin, Stan 1929- *ConAu 2NR*, *-49*,
  SmATA 28
Baldwin, William Lee 1928- *ConAu 1R*, *-3NR*
Bale, Don 1937- *WrDr 84*
Bale, Joy *DrAP&F 83*
Bale, Robert Osborne 1912- *ConAu 1R*
Bales, Carol Ann 1940- *ConAu 45*, *SmATA 29*
Bales, Gerald Albert 1919- *CreCan 2*
Bales, Jack *ConAu X*

Bales, James David 1915- *ConAu 5R*
Bales, James E 1951- *ConAu 107*
Bales, Robert F 1916- *ConAu 93*
Bales, William Alan 1917- *ConAu 5R*
Balestier, Wolcott 1861-1891 *LongCTC*
Balet, Jan B 1913- *ConAu 85*,
  SmATA 11[port]
Baley, James A 1918- *ConAu 5NR*, *-13R*
Balfort, Neil *ConAu X*
Balfour, A J 1848-1930 *LongCTC*
Balfour, Arthur James Balfour, Earl Of 1848-1930
  TwCA[port], *TwCA SUP*
Balfour, Conrad George 1928- *ConAu 53*
Balfour, James 1925- *ConAu 25R*
Balfour, John *ConAu X*
Balfour, Michael 1908- *WrDr 84*
Balfour, Michael Leonard Graham 1908-
  ConAu 6NR, *-9R*
Balfour, Patrick Douglas 1904-1976 *ConAu 6NR*
Balfour-Kinnear, George Purvis Russell 1888-
  ConAu 5R
Balian, Lorna 1929- *ConAu 4NR*, *-53*,
  SmATA 9, *WrDr 84*
Baligh, Helmy H 1931- *ConAu 21R*
Balikci, Asen 1929- *ConAu 29R*
Balinky, Alexander 1919- *ConAu 21R*
Balinski, Stanislaw 1899- *CIDMEL 80*
Balint, Enid *WrDr 84*
Balint, Michael 1896-1970 *ConAu P-1*
Balis, Andrea F 1948- *ConAu 108*
Baljeu, Joost 1925- *ConAu 97*
Balk, Alfred 1930- *ConAu 25R*
Balka, Marie *ConAu X*
Balkany, Marie De 1930- *ConAu 104*
Balke, Willem 1933- *ConAu 107*
Balkin, Richard 1938- *ConAu 77*
Ball, Alan *DrAP&F 83*
Ball, B N 1932- *ConAu X*, *ConSFA*
Ball, Brian N 1932- *ConAu 33R*
Ball, Clive 1941- *WrDr 84*
Ball, David 1937- *ConAu 65*
Ball, Desmond 1947- *ConAu 106*
Ball, Donald W 1934-1976 *ConAu 110*
Ball, Donna 1951- *ConAu 108*
Ball, Doris Bell 1897- *ConAu 1R*, *-2NR*,
  WrDr 84
Ball, Edith L 1905- *ConAu 85*
Ball, F Carlton 1911- *ConAu 17R*
Ball, Frederick Cyril 1905- *IntAu&W 82*
Ball, George W 1909- *ConAu 73*
Ball, Howard 1937- *ConAu 33R*
Ball, Hugo 1886-1927 *CIDMEL 80*, *ModGL*,
  WhoTwCL
Ball, Jane Eklund 1921- *ConAu 33R*
Ball, John 1911- *ConAu 3NR*, *-5R*, *ConSFA*,
  TwCCr&M 80, *WrDr 84*
Ball, John C 1924- *ConAu 5R*, *-8NR*
Ball, John Dudley, Jr. 1911- *IntAu&W 82*
Ball, John M 1923- *ConAu 33R*
Ball, Joseph H 1905- *ConAu P-2*
Ball, M Margaret 1909- *ConAu 25R*
Ball, Marion J 1940- *ConAu 89*
Ball, Michael *IntAu&W 82X*
Ball, Robert Edward 1911- *ConAu 108*
Ball, Robert Hamilton 1902- *ConAu 9R*,
  WrDr 84
Ball, Robert M 1914- *ConAu 97*
Ball, Sir Robert Stawell 1840-1913 *LongCTC*
Ball, Sylvia Patricia 1936- *ConAu 57*
Ball, Zachary *ConAu X*, *SmATA 3*
Ballagas, Emilio 1908-1954 *ModLAL*
Ballantine, Bill *ConAu X*
Ballantine, John *ConAu X*
Ballantine, John 1920- *ConAu 53*
Ballantine, Joseph W 1890?-1973 *ConAu 41R*
Ballantine, Lesley Frost *ConAu X*, *SmATA X*
Ballantine, Richard 1940- *ConAu 1NR*, *-45*
Ballantine, William 1911- *ConAu 106*
Ballantrae, Bernard Edward Fergusson 1911-1980
  ConAu 102
Ballantyne, David 1924- *ConAu 10NR*,
  WrDr 84
Ballantyne, David Watt 1924- *ConAu 65*,
  ConNov 82, *DcLEL 1940*, *LongCTC*,
  TwCWr
Ballantyne, Dorothy Joan 1922- *ConAu 5R*
Ballantyne, John 1917- *WrDr 84*
Ballantyne, R M 1825-1894 *SmATA 24[port]*
Ballantyne, Sheila *DrAP&F 83*
Ballantyne, Sheila 1936- *ConAu 101*
Ballard, Allen B 1930- *ConAu 61*
Ballard, Dean *ConAu X*

Ballard, Edward Goodwin 1910- *ConAu 33R*
Ballard, J G *DrAP&F 83*
Ballard, J G 1930- *ConAu 5R*, *ConLC 3*, *-6*,
  -14, *ConNov 82*, *ConSFA*, *DcLB 14[port]*,
  DrmM[port], *IntAu&W 82*, *TwCSFW*,
  WorAu, *WrDr 84*
Ballard, James Graham 1930- *DcLEL 1940*,
  TwCWr
Ballard, Joan Kadey 1928- *ConAu 5R*,
  MichAu 80
Ballard, Juliet Lyle Brooke 1913- *IntWWP 82*
Ballard, K G *ConAu X*, *TwCCr&M 80*
Ballard, Lowell Clyne 1904- *ConAu P-1*,
  SmATA 12
Ballard, Martin 1929- *ConAu 25R*, *SmATA 1*,
  TwCCW 83, *WrDr 84*
Ballard, P D *ConAu X*, *TwCCr&M 80*
Ballard, Todhunter 1903- *ConAu 13R*
Ballard, W T *ConAu X*
Ballard, Willis Todhunter 1903-1980 *ConAu X*,
  TwCCr&M 80, *TwCWW*
Ballem, John 1925- *ConAu 81*
Ballen, Roger 1950- *ConAu 103*
Baller, Warren Robert 1900- *ConAu 69*
Ballester I Moragues, Alexandre 1934-
  CIDMEL 80
Ballew, Charles *TwCWW*
Balliett, Whitney 1926- *ConAu 17R*,
  DcLEL 1940, *WrDr 84*
Ballin, Caroline *ConAu 17R*
Ballinger, Bill S 1912- *ConAu X*,
  TwCCr&M 80
Ballinger, Harry 1892- *ConAu P-2*
Ballinger, James Lawrence 1919- *ConAu 17R*
Ballinger, Louise Bowen 1909- *ConAu 13R*
Ballinger, Margaret 1894-1980 *ConAu 105*, *-61*
Ballinger, Raymond A 1907- *ConAu 5R*
Ballinger, W A *ConAu X*
Ballinger, William A *ConAu X*
Ballinger, William Sanborn 1912-1980 *ConAu 1R*,
  -1NR, *-97*
Ballon, Robert Jean 1919- *ConAu 45*
Ballon Aguirre, Enrique 1940- *IntAu&W 82*
Ballonoff, Paul A 1943- *ConAu 57*
Ballou, Arthur W 1915- *ConAu 25R*
Ballou, Ellen Elizabeth Bartlett 1905- *ConAu P-2*
Ballowe, James *DrAP&F 83*
Ballowe, James 1933- *ConAu 29R*
Balma, Michael J 1930- *ConAu 17R*
Balmain, Pierre 1914-1982 *ConAu 107*
Balme, Maurice 1925- *ConAu 61*
Balmer, Edwin 1883-1959 *TwCCr&M 80*
Balmer, Heinz 1920- *IntAu&W 82*
Balmont, Konstantin 1867-1943 *ConAu 109*,
  ModSL 1
Balmont, Konstantin Dmitrievich 1867-1943
  EncWL 2
Balmont, Konstantin Dmitriyevich 1867-1942
  CIDMEL 80
Balmont, Konstantin Dmitriyevich 1867-1943
  TwCLC 11[port]
Balog, B E *DrAP&F 83*
Balogh, Baron *WrDr 84*
Balogh, Penelope 1916- *WrDr 84*
Balogh, Penelope 1916-1975 *ConAu P-2*,
  SmATA 1, *-34N*
Balogh, Thomas 1905- *ConAu 57*,
  IntAu&W 82, *WrDr 84*
Baloian, James C *DrAP&F 83*
Balow, Tom 1931- *ConAu 45*, *SmATA 12*
Balsdon, Dacre 1901-1977 *ConAu X*
Balsdon, John Percy Vyvian Dacre 1901-1977
  ConAu 5R, *-73*
Balse, Mayah 1939- *IntAu&W 82*
Balseiro, Jose Agustin 1900- *AuNews 1*,
  ConAu 81, *IntAu&W 82*
Balsiger, David W 1945- *ConAu 11NR*
Balsiger, David Wayne 1945- *ConAu 61*,
  IntAu&W 82
Balsley, Howard L 1913- *ConAu 1R*, *-4NR*
Balsley, Irol Whitmore 1912- *ConAu 13R*
Baltazar, Eulalio *WrDr 84*
Baltazar, Eulalio R 1925- *ConAu 17R*,
  IntAu&W 82
Baltazzi, Evan Serge 1919- *ConAu 65*
Balterman, Marcia Ridlon 1942- *ConAu 25R*
Baltes, Paul B 1939- *ConAu 89*
Balthazar, Earl E 1918- *ConAu 53*
Balthrop, Edward 1919- *IntWWP 82*
Baltz, Howard B 1930- *ConAu 29R*
Baltzell, E Digby 1915- *ConAu 33R*
Balucki, Michael 1837-1901 *ModWD*

Barber, Lucy L 1882?-1974 *ConAu 49*
Barber, Lynn 1944- *ConAu 97*
Barber, Margaret Fairless 1869-1901 *LongCTC,*
TwCA, TwCA SUP
Barber, Mattie Belle 1910- *IntWWP 82*
Barber, Philip W 1903-1981 *ConAu 103*
Barber, Richard 1941- *ConAu 33R,*
IntAu&W 82, WrDr 84
Barber, Richard J 1932- *ConAu 29R*
Barber, Samuel 1910-1981 *ConAu 103*
Barber, Stephen Guy 1921-1980 *ConAu 69, -97*
Barber, T X 1927- *ConAu 41R*
Barber, Theodore Xenophon 1927- *IntAu&W 82*
Barber, Willard Foster 1909- *ConAu P-2*
Barber, William *ConAmTC*
Barber, William Henry 1918- *ConAu 5R*
Barber, William Joseph 1925- *ConAu 8NR, -61*
Barbera, Henry 1929- *ConAu 105*
Barbera, Jack 1945- *ConAu 110*
Barberan, Rafael 1939- *IntAu&W 82*
Barberis *ConAu X*
Barberis, Franco 1905- *ConAu 25R*
Barbero, Yves Regis Francois 1943- *ConAu 57*
Barbet, Pierre 1925- *ConAu X*
Barbette, Jay *ConAu X, TwCCr&M 80,*
WorAu, WrDr 84
Barbini, Ernesto 1909- *CreCan 1*
Barbosa, Jorge 1902-1971 *ClDMEL 80*
Barbosa, Miguel 1925- *IntAu&W 82*
Barbotin, Edmond 1920- *ConAu 57*
Barbour, Arthur Joseph 1926- *ConAu 57*
Barbour, Brian M 1943- *ConAu 49*
Barbour, Douglas 1940- *ConAu 11NR, -69,*
ConP 80, IntAu&W 82, WrDr 84
Barbour, Floyd *LivgBAA*
Barbour, Frances Martha 1895- *ConAu 17R*
Barbour, George Brown 1890-1977 *ConAu 73*
Barbour, Hugh 1921- *ConAu 21R, WrDr 84*
Barbour, Ian G 1923- *ConAu 8NR, -21R*
Barbour, J Murray 1897-1970 *ConAu P-1*
Barbour, John 1937- *ConAmTC*
Barbour, Kenneth Michael 1921- *ConAu 5R,*
-7NR
Barbour, Michael G 1942- *ConAu 2NR, -49*
Barbour, Nevill 1895-1972 *ConAu 5R, -103*
Barbour, Philip L 1898- *ConAu 9R*
Barbour, Ralph Henry 1870-1944 *DcLB 22[port],*
SmATA 16
Barbour, Roger W 1919- *ConAu 61*
Barbour, Russell B 1906- *ConAu P-2*
Barbour, Ruth P 1924- *ConAu 89*
Barbour, Thomas L *ConAu X*
Barbrook, Alec *ConAu X*
Barbrook, Alexander Thomas 1927- *ConAu 45*
Barbu, Ion 1895-1961 *ClDMEL 80, EncWL 2*
Barbusse, Henri 1873-1935 *ClDMEL 80,*
ConAu 105, EncWL 2, ModFrL,
TwCLC 5[port], TwCWr
Barbusse, Henri 1874-1935 *LongCTC,*
TwCA[port], TwCA SUP
Barby, Ralph *IntAu&W 82X*
Barchek, James Robert 1935- *ConAu 41R*
Barchilon, Jacques 1923- *ConAu 5NR, -13R*
Barchus, Agnes J 1893- *ConAu 97*
Barcia, Jose Rubia *ConAu X*
Barck, Oscar Theodore, Jr. 1902- *ConAu 21R*
Barclay, Ann *ConAu X, TwCRGW*
Barclay, Barbara 1938- *ConAu 29R*
Barclay, Cyril Nelson 1896- *ConAu 5R*
Barclay, Florence Louisa 1862-1921 *LongCTC,*
TwCA, TwCA SUP, TwCRGW, TwCWr
Barclay, Glen St. J 1930- *ConAu 77*
Barclay, Harold B 1924- *ConAu 9R*
Barclay, Hartley Wade 1903-1978 *ConAu 81, -85*
Barclay, Isabel *ConAu X, SmATA X*
Barclay, John Bruce 1909- *IntAu&W 82*
Barclay, Oliver R 1919- *ConAu 8NR, -57*
Barclay, Virginia *ConAu X*
Barclay, William *ConAu X*
Barclay, William 1907-1978 *ConAu 73, -77*
Barcus, James E 1938- *ConAu 21R*
Barcynska, Countess 1894-1964 *TwCRGW*
Barcynski, Leon 1949- *ConAu 93*
Barcynski, Leon Roger 1949- *ConAu 10NR*
Barcynski, Vivian G 1917- *ConAu 10NR*
Bard, Bernard 1927- *ConAu 25R*
Bard, Harry 1906-1976 *ConAu 33R*
Bard, James 1925- *ConAu 102*
Bard, Morton 1924- *ConAu 97*
Bard, Patti 1935- *ConAu 21R*
Bard Of Avondale *ConAu X*
Bardach, John E 1915- *ConAu 41R*

Bardacke, Frances Lavender 1919- *ConAmTC*
Bardarson, Hjalmar R 1918- *ConAu 57*
Bardeche, Maurice 1909- *ClDMEL 80*
Barden, Leonard William 1929- *ConAu 1R,*
-2NR
Bardens, Amey E 1894?-1974 *ConAu 53*
Bardens, Dennis Conrad 1911- *ConAu 5R*
Bardi, Pietro Maria 1900- *ConAu 85*
Bardin, John Franklin 1916- *WrDr 84*
Bardin, John Franklin 1916-1981 *ConAu 104, -81,*
TwCCr&M 80
Bardis, Panos D 1924- *ConAu 10NR, -25R,*
IntAu&W 82, IntWWP 82, WrDr 84
Bardolph, Richard 1915- *ConAu P-1*
Bardon, Edward J 1933- *ConAu 81*
Bardon, Jack Irving 1925- *ConAu 101*
Bardos, Marie 1935- *ConAu 13R*
Bardos, Pal 1936- *IntAu&W 82*
Bardot, Louis 1896-1975 *ConAu 61*
Bardsley, Cuthbert K N 1907- *ConAu P-2*
Bardwell, Denver *TwCWW*
Bardwell, George E 1924- *ConAu 1R*
Bardwick, Judith M 1933- *ConAu 103*
Bare, Arnold Edwin 1920- *SmATA 16*
Bare, Colleen Stanley *ConAu 102,*
SmATA 32[port]
Barea, Arturo 1897-1957 *ClDMEL 80,*
LongCTC, TwCA SUP, TwCWr
Bareham, Terence 1937- *ConAu 109, WrDr 84*
Barendrecht, Cor W 1934- *MichAu 80*
Baretski, Charles Allan 1918- *ConAu 77*
Barfield, Arthur Owen 1898- *ConAu 5R*
Barfield, Owen 1898- *ConAu 2NR,*
ConLCrt 82, ConSFA, WrDr 84
Barfod, Gustav 1919- *IntAu&W 82*
Barfoot, Audrey Ilma 1918-1964 *ConAu 5R*
Barfoot, Joan 1946- *ConAu 105, ConLC 18*
Barford, Carol 1931- *ConAu 89, IntAu&W 82*
Barford, Philip 1925- *ConAu 93*
Barg, Barbara *DrAP&F 83*
Barg, Barbara 1941- *IntAu&W 82*
Bargar, B D 1924- *ConAu 17R*
Bargarag, Shibli *ConAu X*
Bargate, Verity 1941?-1981 *ConAu 103*
Bargebuhr, Frederick P 1904- *ConAu P-2*
Bargellini, Piero 1897-1980? *ConAu 97*
Bargen, Walter *DrAP&F 83*
Barger, Harold 1907- *ConAu P-2*
Barger, James 1947- *ConAu 57*
Barghoorn, Frederick C 1911- *WrDr 84*
Barham, Patte *IntAu&W 82*
Baring, Arnulf Martin 1932- *ConAu 41R,*
IntAu&W 82
Baring, Maurice 1874-1945 *ConAu 105,*
LongCTC, ModBrL, TwCA, TwCA SUP,
TwCLC 8[port], TwCWr
Baring-Gould, Sabine 1834-1924 *LongCTC*
Baring-Gould, William Stuart 1913-1967
ConAu 25R
Baringer, William Eldon 1909- *ConAu 1R*
Barish, Jonas A 1922- *ConAu 21R, WrDr 84*
Barish, Matthew 1907- *ConAu 57, SmATA 12*
Baritz, Loren 1928- *ConAu 13R*
Barjavel, Rene 1893- *ConAu 107, TwCSFW A*
Bark, William 1908- *ConAu P-1*
Barka, Vasyl' 1908- *ModSL 2*
Barkalow, Frederick Schenck, Jr. 1914-
ConAu 61
Barkan, Elliot Robert 1940- *IntAu&W 82*
Barkan, Elliott Robert 1940- *ConAu 21R*
Barkan, Stanley H *DrAP&F 83*
Barkas, Janet 1948- *ConAu 57*
Barkee, Asouff *ConAu X*
Barker, A J 1918-1981 *ConAu 7NR, -104, -13R*
Barker, A L 1918- *ConAu 3NR, -9R,*
ConNov 82, DcLB 14[port], IntAu&W 82
Barker, Albert W 1900- *ConAu 73, SmATA 8*
Barker, Arthur E 1911- *WrDr 84*
Barker, Audrey L 1918- *WrDr 84*
Barker, Audrey Lilian 1918- *DcLEL 1940*
Barker, Audrey Lillian 1918- *TwCA SUP*
Barker, Bill *ConAu X*
Barker, C Edward 1908- *IntAu&W 82,*
WrDr 84
Barker, Carol M 1942- *ConAu 45*
Barker, Carol Minturn 1938- *ConAu 107,*
SmATA 31[port]
Barker, Charles Albro 1904- *ConAu 93*
Barker, Charles M, Jr. 1926- *ConAu 13R*
Barker, Chris *IntWWP 82X*
Barker, Christopher Andrew 1952- *IntWWP 82*
Barker, Cicely Mary 1895-1973 *TwCCW 83*

Barker, D R 1930- *ConAu 5R*
Barker, David J P 1938- *WrDr 84*
Barker, Dennis 1929- *ConAu 25R,*
IntAu&W 82, WrDr 84
Barker, Dudley 1910-1980? *ConAu 1R, -1NR,*
-102, IntAu&W 82, TwCCr&M 80
Barker, E M 1906- *ConAu X, WrDr 84*
Barker, Elliott Speer 1886- *ConAu 89*
Barker, Elsa M 1906- *ConAu P-2*
Barker, Elver A 1920- *ConAu 25R*
Barker, Eric 1905-1973 *ConAu 1R, -41R*
Barker, Sir Ernest 1874-1960 *ConAu 103, -93,*
LongCTC, TwCA SUP
Barker, Esther T 1910- *ConAu 2NR, -49*
Barker, Frank Granville 1923- *ConAu P-1*
Barker, George *DrAP&F 83*
Barker, George 1913- *WrDr 84*
Barker, George Granville 1913- *CnMWL,*
ConAu 7NR, -9R, ConLC 8, ConP 80,
EncWL 2, LongCTC, ModBrL,
ModBrL SUP, RGFMBP, TwCA SUP,
TwCWr, WhoTwCL
Barker, Gerard A 1930- *ConAu 69*
Barker, Graham H 1949- *ConAu 106*
Barker, Granville *TwCA, TwCA SUP*
Barker, Harley Granville- 1877-1946
DcLB 10[port], LongCTC
Barker, Howard 1946- *ConAu 102, ConDr 82,*
DcLB 13[port], WrDr 84
Barker, James E 1898- *IntWWP 82*
Barker, Jane Valentine 1930- *ConAu 11NR, -65*
Barker, Jim *IntWWP 82X*
Barker, John W 1933- *ConAu 17R*
Barker, Joseph 1929- *ConAu 103*
Barker, Kenneth S 1932- *ConAu 110*
Barker, Larry L 1941- *ConAu 81*
Barker, Max Samuel 1912- *IntWWP 82*
Barker, Melvern J 1907- *ConAu P-1,*
SmATA 11
Barker, Mildred *DrAP&F 83*
Barker, Myrtie Lillian 1910- *ConAu 5R*
Barker, Nicolas John 1932- *ConAu 102*
Barker, Paul 1935- *IntAu&W 82*
Barker, Philip 1929- *WrDr 84*
Barker, Ralph Hammond 1917- *ConAu 1R,*
-1NR
Barker, Robert L 1937- *ConAu 25R*
Barker, Rodney 1942- *ConAu 45*
Barker, Roger Garlock 1903- *ConAu 11NR,*
ConAu P-1
Barker, Ronald 1921?-1976 *ConAu 65*
Barker, S Omar 1894- *ConAu P-2, IntWWP 82,*
SmATA 10, TwCWW, WrDr 84
Barker, Shirley Frances 1911-1965 *ConAu 5R,*
TwCA SUP
Barker, T 1923- *ConAu 5NR*
Barker, Terence Snarr 1941- *ConAu 45*
Barker, Theodore Cardwell 1923- *ConAu 13R,*
IntAu&W 82, WrDr 84
Barker, Thomas M 1929- *ConAu 21R*
Barker, W Alan 1923- *ConAu 1R, -1NR*
Barker, Wendy 1942- *IntWWP 82*
Barker, Will 1913- *ConAu 9R, SmATA 8*
Barker, Will 1913-1983 *ConAu 110*
Barker, William J *ConAu 65*
Barker, William P 1927- *ConAu 9R*
Barkhouse, Joyce 1913- *ConAu 93*
Barkin, David Peter 1942- *ConAu 37R*
Barkin, Kenneth D 1939- *ConAu 41R*
Barkin, Leo 1905- *CreCan 2*
Barkin, Solomon 1907- *ConAu 29R*
Barkins, Evelyn 1919- *ConAu 29R*
Barkley, James Edward 1941- *SmATA 6*
Barkley, Vada Lee 1919- *ConAu 57*
Barkman, Paul Friesen 1921- *ConAu 17R*
Barkow, Al 1932- *ConAu 4NR, -53, WrDr 84*
Barks, Coleman *DrAP&F 83*
Barks, Coleman Bryan 1937- *ConAu 25R,*
DcLB 5[port], WrDr 84
Barksdale, E C 1944- *ConAu 57*
Barksdale, Hiram C 1921- *ConAu 9R*
Barksdale, Richard K 1915- *ConAu 49,*
LivgBAA
Barkton, S Rush *ConAu X*
Barkworth, Peter 1929- *ConAu 107*
Barlach, Ernst Heinrich 1870-1938 *ClDMEL 80,*
CnMD, EncWL 2[port], ModGL, ModWD
Barlay, Bennett *ConAu X, WrDr 84*
Barlay, Stephen 1930- *ConAu 25R, WrDr 84*
Barlin, Anne L 1916- *ConAu 97*
Barling, Charles *ConAu X*
Barling, Muriel 1904- *ConAu 5R, IntAu&W 82*

Barlough, J Ernest 1953- *ConAu 49*
Barlow, Anna Marie *NatPD 81[port]*
Barlow, Claude W 1907-1976 *ConAu P-2*
Barlow, Derrick 1921- *IntAu&W 82*
Barlow, Frank 1911- *ConAu 3NR, -9R, IntAu&W 82, WrDr 84*
Barlow, Genevieve 1910- *ConAu 21R*
Barlow, George *DrAP&F 83*
Barlow, J Stanley 1924- *ConAu 41R*
Barlow, James 1921-1973 *ConAu 41R, ConAu P-1, DcLEL 1940*
Barlow, Jane 1857-1917 *TwCA[port]*
Barlow, John 1924- *ConAu 21R, WrDr 84*
Barlow, Judith E 1946- *ConAu 107*
Barlow, Nora 1885- *ConAu P-2*
Barlow, Robert O *ConAu 49*
Barlow, Roger *ConAu X*
Barlow, Ruth C *MichAu 80*
Barlow, Samuel L M 1892-1982 *ConAu 107*
Barlow, Sanna Morrison *ConAu X*
Barlow, T Edward 1931- *ConAu 3NR, -45*
Barlow, Wilfred 1915- *ConAu 101, WrDr 84*
Barlowe, Raleigh 1914- *ConAu 17R, WrDr 84*
Barltrop, Robert Arthur Horace 1922- *ConAu 73*
Barman, Alicerose 1919- *ConAu 65*
Barman, Charles R 1945- *ConAu 106*
Barmann, Lawrence 1932- *WrDr 84*
Barmann, Lawrence Francis 1932- *ConAu 9R*
Barmash, Isadore 1921- *ConAu 1NR, -45*
Barn Owl *ConAu X*
Barna, Ed *DrAP&F 83*
Barna, Istvan 1920- *IntAu&W 82*
Barna, Yon 1927- *ConAu 53*
Barnabas *ConAu X, IntAu&W 82X*
Barnaby, Charles Frank 1927- *IntAu&W 82, WrDr 84*
Barnaby, Frank 1927- *ConAu 33R*
Barnaby, Ralph Stanton 1893- *ConAu 61, SmATA 9*
Barnard, Alan 1928- *ConAu 9R*
Barnard, Charles N 1924- *ConAu 1NR, -49*
Barnard, Christiaan 1922- *ConAu 61*
Barnard, Ellsworth 1907- *ConAu 11NR, -21R*
Barnard, F M 1921- *ConAu 25R*
Barnard, Frederick Mechner 1921- *IntAu&W 82, WrDr 84*
Barnard, Harry 1906-1982 *ConAu 3NR, -5R, -107*
Barnard, Howard Clive 1884- *ConAu 85, IntAu&W 82*
Barnard, J Darrell 1906- *ConAu 5R*
Barnard, J Lawrence 1912-1977 *ConAu 77*
Barnard, John 1932- *ConAu 33R*
Barnard, John Lawrence 1912?-1977 *ConAu 73*
Barnard, Leslie Gordon 1890-1961 *CreCan 1*
Barnard, Marjorie Faith 1897- *WrDr 84*
Barnard, Mary *DrAP&F 83*
Barnard, Mary 1909- *ConAu P-2*
Barnard, Robert 1936- *ConAu 77, IntAu&W 82*
Barnard, William Dean 1942- *ConAu 69*
Barnardo, Thomas John 1845-1905 *LongCTC*
Barne, Kitty 1883-1957 *TwCCW 83*
Barner, Bob 1947- *ConAu 93, SmATA 29*
Barnes, Adrienne Martine *ConAu X*
Barnes, Archibald George 1887- *CreCan 1*
Barnes, Arthur K 1911-1969 *TwCSFW*
Barnes, Barry 1943- *ConAu 97*
Barnes, C V *WrDr 84*
Barnes, Chesley Virginia *ConAu X*
Barnes, Clara Ernst 1895- *ConAu 5R*
Barnes, Clive 1927- *AuNews 2, ConAmTC, ConAu 77, WrDr 84*
Barnes, Dick *DrAP&F 83, IntWWP 82X*
Barnes, Djuna 1892-1982 *CnMD, ConAu 9R, -107, ConDr 82, ConLC 3, -4, -8, -11, ConNov 82, DcLB 4, -9[port], EncWL 2, LongCTC, ModAL, ModAL SUP, TwCA, TwCA SUP, TwCWr, WhoTwCL*
Barnes, Douglas 1927- *ConAu 103, WrDr 84*
Barnes, Eric Wollencott 1907-1962 *SmATA 22[port]*
Barnes, Eunice Christine Davis 1914- *IntWWP 82*
Barnes, Gregory Allen 1934- *ConAu 10NR, -25R*
Barnes, Hally 1904- *MichAu 80*
Barnes, Harry Elmer 1889-1968 *ConAu 25R, -89, TwCA, TwCA SUP*
Barnes, Hazel E 1915- *ConAu 3NR, -5R*
Barnes, Henry A 1906-1968 *ConAu P-1*

Barnes, J 1944- *ConAu 85*
Barnes, Jack 1920- *ConAu 89*
Barnes, Jack 1940- *ConAu 9NR, -61*
Barnes, James Anderson 1898- *ConAu 9R*
Barnes, James J 1931- *ConAu 4NR, -9R, WrDr 84*
Barnes, Jane *ConAu X, DrAP&F 83*
Barnes, Jim *DrAP&F 83*
Barnes, Jim 1933- *ConAu 108*
Barnes, Jim Weaver 1933- *IntAu&W 82, IntWWP 82*
Barnes, Joanna 1934- *ConAu 57*
Barnes, John 1908- *ConAu 2NR, -45*
Barnes, John 1917- *ConAu 108*
Barnes, John A G 1909- *IntAu&W 82*
Barnes, John Arundel 1918- *ConAu 101, WrDr 84*
Barnes, John B 1924- *ConAu 33R*
Barnes, Jonathan 1942- *WrDr 84*
Barnes, Joseph Fels 1907-1970 *ConAu 104*
Barnes, Josephine 1912- *WrDr 84*
Barnes, Julian 1946- *ConAu 102, WrDr 84*
Barnes, Kathleen 1950- *IntAu&W 82*
Barnes, Kenneth Charles 1903- *ConAu 106, WrDr 84*
Barnes, Leonard 1895- *ConAu P-2*
Barnes, Margaret Ayer 1886-1967 *ConAmA, ConAu 25R, DcLB 9, TwCA, TwCA SUP*
Barnes, Mary 1923- *ConAu 85*
Barnes, Mary Jane 1913- *IntWWP 82*
Barnes, Patience P 1932- *ConAu 108*
Barnes, Peter 1931- *ConAu 65, ConDr 82, ConLC 5, DcLB 13[port], DcLEL 1940, IntAu&W 82, WrDr 84*
Barnes, Phoebe 1908- *ConAu P-2*
Barnes, R G 1932- *ConAu 33R, IntWWP 82X*
Barnes, Ralph M 1900- *ConAu P-2*
Barnes, Richard Gordon 1932- *IntWWP 82*
Barnes, Robert J 1925- *ConAu 21R*
Barnes, Robert M 1940- *ConAu 45*
Barnes, Sam G 1913- *ConAu 13R*
Barnes, Samuel Henry 1931- *ConAu 21R, IntAu&W 82, WrDr 84*
Barnes, Stephen Emory 1952- *ConAu 105*
Barnes, Steven *ConAu X*
Barnes, Thomas Garden 1930- *ConAu 1R, -1NR*
Barnes, Viola Florence 1885- *ConAu 1R*
Barnes, W D *DrAP&F 83*
Barnes, Wilfred Molson 1882-1955 *CreCan 1*
Barness, Richard 1917- *ConAu 65*
Barnet, Richard J *ConAu 13R, ConIsC 2[port]*
Barnet, Sylvan 1926- *ConAu 1R, -4NR*
Barnetson, William Denholm 1917-1981 *ConAu 103, IntAu&W 82*
Barnett, Adam *ConAu X*
Barnett, Arthur Doak 1921- *ConAu 5R, WrDr 84*
Barnett, Correlli 1927- *WrDr 84*
Barnett, Correlli Douglas 1927- *ConAu 13R, IntAu&W 82*
Barnett, Franklin 1903- *ConAu 69*
Barnett, George Leonard 1915- *ConAu 29R, WrDr 84*
Barnett, Guy 1928- *ConAu 17R*
Barnett, H G 1906- *ConAu 45*
Barnett, Isobel 1918-1980 *ConAu 105*
Barnett, Joe R 1933- *ConAu 106*
Barnett, L David *ConAu X*
Barnett, Leo 1925- *ConAu 29R*
Barnett, Leonard 1919- *WrDr 84*
Barnett, Leonard Palin 1919- *ConAu P-1*
Barnett, Lincoln 1909-1979 *ConAu 102, -89, WorAu*
Barnett, Malcolm Joel 1941- *ConAu 45*
Barnett, Marva T 1913- *ConAu 57*
Barnett, Mary *IntWWP 82*
Barnett, Maurice 1917-1980 *ConAu 97*
Barnett, Michael 1910- *ConAu 57*
Barnett, Moneta 1922-1976 *SmATA 33[port]*
Barnett, Naomi 1927- *ConAu 7NR*
Barnett, Richard B 1941- *ConAu 105*
Barnett, Richard C 1932- *ConAu 33R*
Barnett, S A 1915- *ConAu 6NR*
Barnett, S Anthony 1915- *WrDr 84*
Barnett, Samuel Anthony 1915- *ConAu 13R*
Barnette, Henlee Hulix 1911- *ConAu 49*
Barnette, W Leslie, Jr. 1910- *ConAu P-1*
Barney, Kenneth D 1921- *ConAu 69*
Barney, Laura D 1880?-1974 *ConAu 53*
Barney, LeRoy *WrDr 84*
Barney, LeRoy 1930- *ConAu 33R, IntAu&W 82*

Barney, Maginel Wright 1881-1966 *SmATA 32*
Barney, Natalie 1876-1972 *DcLB 4*
Barney, Natalie Clifford 1878?-1972 *ConAu 33R*
Barney, Stephen A 1942- *ConAu 102*
Barney, William Derald 1916- *IntWWP 82*
Barney, William Lesko 1943- *ConAu 41R*
Barnhart, Clarence L 1900- *ConAu 13R*
Barnhart, Joe Edward 1931- *ConAu 41R*
Barnhill, Myrtle Fait 1896- *ConAu P-1*
Barnhouse, Donald *ConAu 103*
Barnhouse, Ruth Tiffany 1923- *ConAu 85*
Barnick, Johannes Otto Ernst F Karl 1916- *IntAu&W 82*
Barnie, John 1941- *ConAu 57, WrDr 84*
Barnitt, Nedda Lemmon *ConAu 9R*
Barnitz, Harry W 1920-1973 *ConAu P-2*
Barnoon, Shlomo 1940- *ConAu 41R*
Barnouw, Adriaan Jacob 1877-1968 *ConAu 104, SmATA 27N*
Barnouw, Erik 1908- *ConAu 13R, WrDr 84*
Barnouw, Victor 1915- *ConAu 85, SmATA 28*
Barns, John W B 1912-1974 *ConAu 49*
Barnsley, Alan Gabriel 1916- *ConAu 13R, WorAu*
Barnstone, Aliki *DrAP&F 83*
Barnstone, Aliki 1956- *ConAu 105, IntWWP 82*
Barnstone, Willis *DrAP&F 83*
Barnstone, Willis 1927- *ConAu 17R, IntWWP 82, SmATA 20[port]*
Barnum, Jay Hyde 1888?-1962 *SmATA 20[port]*
Barnum, Richard *ConAu X, SmATA 1*
Barnum, W Paul 1933- *ConAu 29R*
Barnwell, D Robinson 1915- *ConAu 17R*
Barnwell, William Curtis 1943- *ConAu 103*
Baro, Gene 1924- *ConP 80, WrDr 84*
Baroff, George Stanley 1924- *ConAu 101*
Baroja, Pio 1872-1956 *CnMWL, ConAu 104, EncWL 2[port], ModRL, TwCLC 8[port], TwCWr, WhoTwCL*
Baroja Y Nessi, Pio 1872-1956 *CIDMEL 80, TwCA, TwCA SUP*
Barolini, Antonio 1910-1971 *CIDMEL 80, ConAu 1R, -1NR*
Barolini, Helen *DrAP&F 83*
Barolini, Helen 1925- *ConAu 73, IntAu&W 82*
Barolsky, Paul 1941- *ConAu 81*
Baron, Alexander 1917- *ConAu 5R, LongCTC, TwCA SUP*
Baron, David *ConAu X*
Baron, Denis Neville 1924- *WrDr 84*
Baron, Dennis E 1944- *ConAu 110*
Baron, Hans 1900- *ConAu 17R*
Baron, Herman 1941- *ConAu 61*
Baron, J W *ConAu X*
Baron, Joseph Alexander 1917- *DcLEL 1940*
Baron, Linda Michelle *DrAP&F 83*
Baron, Mary *DrAP&F 83*
Baron, Mary 1944- *ConAu 2NR, -49*
Baron, Oscar 1908?-1976 *ConAu 65*
Baron, Othello *ConAu X*
Baron, Robert Alex 1920- *ConAu 41R*
Baron, Salo W 1895- *ConAu 69*
Baron, Samuel H 1921- *ConAu 3NR, -9R*
Baron, Virginia Olsen 1931- *ConAu 25R, SmATA 28*
Baron, Wendy 1937- *ConAu 41R, WrDr 84*
Baron Corvo *ConAu X*
Baron Mikan *ConAu X*
Baron Of Remenham *ConAu X*
Barondes, Sue K 1926-1977 *ConAu 1R, -1NR, -69, ConLC 8*
Barone, Dennis *DrAP&F 83*
Barone, Michael 1944- *ConAu 93*
Barone, Patricia *DrAP&F 83*
Baroni, Christophe 1934- *IntAu&W 82*
Baroody, Jamil Murad 1905-1979 *ConAu 85*
Barooshian, Vahan 1932- *ConAu 85*
Barquet, Nicolas 1909- *IntAu&W 82*
Barr, Alfred Hamilton, Jr. 1902-1981 *ConAu 105, -49*
Barr, Alwyn 1938- *ConAu 33R, WrDr 84*
Barr, Anthony 1921- *ConAu 109*
Barr, Betty 1932- *ConAu 97*
Barr, Beverly *ConAu 61*
Barr, Densil *ConAu X, IntAu&W 82, WrDr 84*
Barr, Donald 1921- *ConAu 9R, SmATA 20*
Barr, Donald Roy 1938- *ConAu 69*
Barr, Doris Wilson 1923- *ConAu 33R*
Barr, George 1907- *ConAu 1R, -1NR, SmATA 2*

Barr, Gladys Hutchison 1904-1976 *ConAu 1R,*
-6NR
Barr, James 1924- *ConAu 1R, -4NR,*
IntAu&W 82, WrDr 84
Barr, Jeff 1941- *ConAu 69*
Barr, Jene 1900- *ConAu 3NR, -5R*
Barr, Jennifer 1945- *ConAu 102*
Barr, John J 1942- *ConAu 61*
Barr, O Sydney 1919- *ConAu 13R*
Barr, Pat 1934- *ConAu 21R*
Barr, Patricia Miriam 1934- *IntAu&W 82*
Barr, Robert 1850-1912 *TwCA[port]*
Barr, Robert R 1931- *ConAu 110*
Barr, Stephen 1904- *ConAu P-1*
Barr, Stringfellow 1897-1982 *ConAu 1R, -1NR,*
-106, TwCA SUP[port]
Barr, Tony *ConAu X*
Barraclough, Geoffrey 1908- *ConAu 101,*
WorAu, WrDr 84
Barraclough, Solon L 1922- *ConAu 41R*
Barraga, Natalie Carter 1915- *ConAu 41R*
Barral, Mary-Rose 1925- *ConAu 33R,*
WrDr 84
Barranger, M S 1937- *ConAu 29R, WrDr 84*
Barras, Jonetta Rose 1950- *IntWWP 82*
Barras-Abney, Jonetta *DrAP&F 83*
Barratt, G R V *ConAu X*
Barratt, Glynn 1944- *ConAu 110*
Barratt, Ken *IntWWP 82X*
Barratt, Kenneth Samuel 1906- *IntWWP 82*
Barratt Brown, Michael 1918- *ConAu 97,*
WrDr 84
Barrault, Jean-Louis 1910- *CIDMEL 80,*
ConAu 105
Barrax, Gerald W *DrAP&F 83*
Barrax, Gerald William 1933- *ConAu 10NR, -65,*
LivgBAA
Barreau, Jean-Claude 1933- *IntAu&W 82*
Barrell, G R 1917- *WrDr 84*
Barrell, Geoffrey Richard 1917- *IntAu&W 82*
Barrell, Sarah Webb 1946?-1979 *ConAu 89*
Barren, Charles 1913- *ConAu 4NR, -9R,*
ConSFA
Barreno, Maria Isabel 1939- *AuNews 1[port],*
ConAu X
Barrer, Gertrude *SmATA X*
Barrer-Russell, Gertrude 1921- *SmATA 27[port]*
Barrera, Mario 1939- *ConAu 97*
Barres, Maurice 1862-1923 *CIDMEL 80,*
LongCTC, ModFrL, TwCA, TwCA SUP
Barres, Oliver 1921- *ConAu 13R*
Barrett, Anne Mainwaring 1911- *ConAu P-2,*
TwCCW 83, WrDr 84
Barrett, Bob 1925- *ConAu 73*
Barrett, C Kingsley 1917- *ConAu 10NR, -21R*
Barrett, Charles Kingsley 1917- *WrDr 84*
Barrett, Clifford Leslie 1894-1971 *ConAu 33R*
Barrett, Clifton Waller 1901- *ConAu 41R*
Barrett, Dean 1942- *ConAu 69*
Barrett, Donald N 1920- *ConAu 13R*
Barrett, Edward L, Jr. 1917- *ConAu 25R*
Barrett, Edward W 1910- *WrDr 84*
Barrett, Eugene F 1921- *ConAu 57*
Barrett, George W 1908- *ConAu 17R*
Barrett, Gerald Van 1936- *ConAu 37R*
Barrett, Harold 1925- *ConAu 81*
Barrett, Harry Bemister 1922- *ConAu 85,*
IntAu&W 82
Barrett, Henry Charles 1923- *ConAu 53*
Barrett, Ivan J 1910- *ConAu 49*
Barrett, J Edward 1932- *ConAu 37R*
Barrett, James H 1906- *ConAu 33R*
Barrett, James Lee 1929- *ConAu 81*
Barrett, John G 1921- *WrDr 84*
Barrett, John Gilchrist 1921- *ConAu 2NR, -5R,*
IntAu&W 82
Barrett, John Henry 1913- *ConAu 101,*
WrDr 84
Barrett, Judi 1941- *ConAu X, WrDr 84*
Barrett, Judith 1941- *ConAu 103, SmATA 26*
Barrett, Laurence I 1935- *ConAu 17R, -69*
Barrett, Leonard E 1920- *ConAu 65*
Barrett, Linton Lomas 1904- *ConAu 5R*
Barrett, Lynne *DrAP&F 83*
Barrett, Marvin *DrAP&F 83*
Barrett, Marvin 1920- *ConAu 11NR, -69*
Barrett, Mary Ellin 1927- *ConAu 17R*
Barrett, Max 1930- *ConAu 81, IntAu&W 82*
Barrett, Maye *ConAu X, IntAu&W 82X*
Barrett, Michael Dennis 1947- *ConAu 85*
Barrett, Nancy Smith 1942- *ConAu 37R,*
WrDr 84

Barrett, Nathan Noble 1933- *ConAu 17R,*
NatPD 81[port]
Barrett, Neal, Jr. *TwCSFW, WrDr 84*
Barrett, Norman 1935- *ConAu 107*
Barrett, Patricia 1914- *ConAu 5R*
Barrett, Raina *ConAu X*
Barrett, Ron 1937- *SmATA 14*
Barrett, Rona 1936- *AuNews 1, ConAu 103*
Barrett, Russell Hunter 1919- *ConAu 17R*
Barrett, Susan 1938- *ConAu 109*
Barrett, Sylvia 1914- *ConAu 25R*
Barrett, Ward J 1927- *ConAu 29R*
Barrett, William *IntAu&W 82X*
Barrett, William 1913- *ConAu 11NR, -13R,*
ConLC 27[port]
Barrett, William Edmund 1900- *ConAu 5R,*
ConSFA
Barrett, William R 1922?-1977 *ConAu 73*
Barrett, Wilson 1846-1904 *LongCTC*
Barretto, Larry 1890- *ConAu X, TwCA,*
TwCA SUP
Barretto, Laurence Brevoort 1890-1971
ConAu 33R
Barriault, Arthur 1915?-1976 *ConAu 65*
Barricelli, Jean-Pierre 1924- *ConAu 105*
Barrick, Mac E 1933- *ConAu 33R*
Barrie, Alexander 1923- *ConAu 1R, -5NR,*
IntAu&W 82, WrDr 84
Barrie, Donald C 1905- *ConAu 17R*
Barrie, J M 1860-1937 *TwCCW 83*
Barrie, J M 1860-1937 *ConAu 104,*
TwCLC 2
Barrie, Sir James Matthew 1860-1937 *CnMD,*
DcLB 10[port], EncWL 2, LongCTC,
ModBrL, ModWD, TwCA, TwCA SUP,
TwCWr, WhoTwCL
Barrie, Jane *ConAu X, IntAu&W 82X,*
WrDr 84
Barrie, Susan *TwCRGW, WrDr 84*
Barrier, Michael 1940- *ConAu 109*
Barrier, Norman G 1940- *ConAu 4NR, -53*
Barriger, John Walker 1899-1976 *ConAu 69*
Barrington, E *LongCTC, TwCA, TwCA SUP,*
TwCRGW
Barrington, Ernest James William 1909-
WrDr 84
Barrington, H W *ConAu X*
Barrington, John *ConAu X*
Barrington, Josephine 1910- *CreCan 2*
Barrington, Maurice *ConAu X, LongCTC*
Barrington, Michael *ConAu X*
Barrington, Nicholas *IntAu&W 82X*
Barrington, P V *ConAu X*
Barrington, Pamela *ConAu X*
Barrington, Thomas Joseph 1916- *ConAu 104,*
WrDr 84
Barrington-Ward, Robert McGowan 1891-1948
LongCTC
Barrio, Raymond *DrAP&F 83*
Barrio, Raymond 1921- *ConAu 11NR, -25R,*
WrDr 84
Barrio-Garay, Jose Luis 1932- *ConAu 81*
Barrios, Eduardo 1884-1963 *EncWL 2,*
ModLAL, TwCWr
Barris, Alex 1922- *ConAu 61*
Barris, Chuck *WrDr 84*
Barris, Chuck 1929- *ConAu 109*
Barritt, Denis P 1914- *ConAu 21R*
Barro, Robert Joseph 1944- *ConAu 97*
Barrol, Grady *ConAu X, SmATA X*
Barroll, John Leeds, III 1928- *ConAu 101*
Barron, Ann Forman *ConAu 69*
Barron, Arthur *ConDr 82C*
Barron, Charlie Nelms 1922-1977 *ConAu 69*
Barron, Frank 1922- *ConAu 5R, -8NR*
Barron, Gayle 1945- *ConAu 109*
Barron, Gloria Joan 1934- *ConAu 81*
Barron, Greg 1952- *ConAu 110*
Barron, Jerome A 1933- *ConAu 45*
Barron, Milton L 1918- *WrDr 84*
Barron, Milton Leon 1918- *ConAu 1R*
Barron, Neil 1934- *ConAu 102*
Barron, Oswald 1868-1939 *LongCTC*
Barros Pardo, Tomas 1922- *IntAu&W 82*
Barrosse, Thomas 1926- *ConAu 9R*
Barrow, Andrew 1945- *ConAu 97*
Barrow, Geoffrey W S 1924- *ConAu 7NR, -17R*
Barrow, Harold M 1909- *ConAu 106*
Barrow, Joseph Louis 1914-1981 *ConAu 103*
Barrow, Leo 1925- *ConAu 110*
Barrow, Pamela *ConAu X, WrDr 84*
Barrow, Rhoda Catharine 1910- *ConAu X*

Barrow, Robin 1944- *ConAu 10NR, -65,*
IntAu&W 82, WrDr 84
Barrow, Terence 1923- *ConAu 41R*
Barrow, Thomas C 1929- *ConAu 21R*
Barrow, William 1927- *ConAu X*
Barrow, William Rowell 1922- *IntWWP 82*
Barrows, Anita *DrAP&F 83*
Barrows, Anita 1947- *ConAu 49*
Barrows, Chester L 1892?-1975 *ConAu 104*
Barrows, Marjorie *ConAu P-2*
Barrows, Marjorie 1892?-1983 *ConAu 109*
Barrows, R M *ConAu X*
Barrows, Ruth *ConAu X, ConAu X*
Barrows, Susanna Isabel 1944- *ConAu 108*
Barry, Anne 1940- *ConAu 85*
Barry, Bob 1930- *NatPD 81*
Barry, Clive 1922- *ConNov 82, DcLEL 1940,*
WrDr 84
Barry, Colman J 1921- *ConAu 13R*
Barry, Sir Gerald R 1898-1968 *LongCTC*
Barry, Herbert, III 1930- *ConAu 37R*
Barry, Hugh Collis 1912- *WrDr 84*
Barry, Iris 1895-1969 *ConAu 104*
Barry, Jack *DrAP&F 83*
Barry, Jack 1939- *ConAu 69*
Barry, Jackson G 1926- *ConAu 29R*
Barry, James Donald 1926- *ConAu 33R*
Barry, James P 1918- *ConAu 37R,*
IntAu&W 82, SmATA 14, WrDr 84
Barry, Jan *DrAP&F 83, IntWWP 82X*
Barry, Jane 1925- *ConAu 5R, IntAu&W 82,*
TwCWW, WrDr 84
Barry, Jerome B 1894-1975 *ConAu 1R, -61*
Barry, Jocelyn *ConAu X*
Barry, John Vincent William 1903-1969
ConAu 1R, -103
Barry, Joseph 1917- *ConAu 57*
Barry, Katharina Watjen 1936- *ConAu 9R,*
SmATA 4
Barry, Kevin *ConAu X*
Barry, Lucy 1934- *ConAu 17R*
Barry, Margaret Stuart 1927- *ConAu 106,*
TwCCW 83
Barry, Mary J 1928- *ConAu 49*
Barry, Mike *WrDr 84*
Barry, Noeline 1915- *IntWWP 82X*
Barry, Philip 1896-1949 *CnMD, ConAmA,*
ConAu 109, DcLB 7[port], LongCTC,
ModAL, ModWD, TwCA, TwCA SUP,
TwCLC 11[port], TwCWr
Barry, Raymond Walker 1894- *ConAu P-1*
Barry, Richard Hugh 1908- *IntAu&W 82*
Barry, Robert Everett 1931- *ConAu 2NR, -5R,*
IntAu&W 82, SmATA 6, WrDr 84
Barry, Roger Graham 1935- *ConAu 102*
Barry, Scott 1952- *ConAu 89,*
SmATA 32[port]
Barry, Spranger *ConAu X*
Barrymore, John 1882-1942 *LongCTC*
Barrymore, Lionel 1878-1954 *LongCTC*
Barrymore, Maurice 1847-1905 *LongCTC*
Barsac, Louis *LongCTC*
Barsacq, Andre 1909-1973 *ConAu 41R*
Barsh, Russel Lawrence 1950- *ConAu 105*
Barsis, Max 1894?-1973 *ConAu 41R*
Barsky, Arthur 1900?-1982? *ConAu 106*
Barson, John 1936- *ConAu 85*
Barsotti, C 1933- *ConAu 65*
Barstow, Stan 1928- *ConAu 1R, -1NR,*
ConNov 82, DcLB 14[port], IntAu&W 82,
ModBrL SUP, TwCWr, WrDr 84
Barstow, Stanley 1928- *DcLEL 1940*
Bart, Andre Schwarz *ConAu X*
Bart, Benjamin F 1917- *ConAu 25R,*
IntAu&W 82
Bart, Gunther *IntWWP 82X*
Bart, Lionel 1930- *ConAu 65, ConDr 82D,*
WrDr 84
Bart, Pauline B 1930- *ConAu 53*
Bart, Peter 1932- *ConAu 93*
Bartee, Darrell H *DrAP&F 83*
Bartek, E J 1921- *ConAu 37R*
Bartek, Edward J 1921- *WrDr 84*
Bartel, Pauline C 1952- *ConAu 81*
Bartel, Roland 1919- *ConAu 17R*
Bartell, Ernest 1932- *ConAu 33R*
Bartels, Charles Kwamina 1927- *IntAu&W 82*
Bartels, Robert 1913- *ConAu 13R, WrDr 84*
Bartels, Robert A 1923- *ConAu 1R*
Bartels, Susan Ludvigson *ConAu X*
Bartels, Susan Ludvigson 1942- *ConAu 57*
Bartelski, Leslaw 1920- *IntAu&W 82*

Basterra, Ramon De 1888-1928 *ClDMEL 80*
Bastia VanBuylaere, France 1936- *IntAu&W 82*
Bastiaensen, Michel 1944- *IntAu&W 82*
Bastias, Constantine 1901?-1972 *ConAu 37R*
Bastico, Ettore 1876-1972 *ConAu 37R*
Bastien, Hermas 1896- *CreCan 2*
Bastin, J S 1927- *ConAu 11NR*
Bastin, John Sturgus 1927- *ConAu 21R*
Bastlund, Knud 1925- *ConAu 21R*
Bastos, Augusto Roa 1917- *TwCWr*
Basu, Arindam 1948- *ConAu 61*
Basu, Asoke 1940- *ConAu 106*
Basu, Buddhadev *WorAu 1970*
Basu, Romen 1923- *ConAu 77, IntAu&W 82*
Bataille, Georges 1897-1962 *ClDMEL 80,*
  ConAu 101, –89, EncWL 2, ModFrL,
  WorAu
Bataille, Gretchen M 1944- *ConAu 102*
Bataille, Henry 1872-1922 *ClDMEL 80, CnMD,*
  ModWD
Batarde, Edwarde 1953- *IntWWP 82*
Batbedat, Jean 1926- *ConAu 37R*
Batchelder, Alan Bruce 1931- *ConAu 21R*
Batchelder, Howard T 1909- *ConAu P-2*
Batcheller, John M 1918- *ConAu 45*
Batchelor, C D 1888-1977 *ConAu 73*
Batchelor, David 1943- *ConAu 101, WrDr 84*
Batchelor, Edward, Jr. 1930- *ConAu 110*
Batchelor, George Keith 1920- *WrDr 84*
Batchelor, John 1942- *ConAu 93, IntAu&W 82,*
  WrDr 84
Batchelor, John 1947- *ConAu 109*
Batchelor, John Calvin 1948- *ConAu 105*
Batchelor, Joy 1914- *SmATA 29*
Batchelor, Julie F E 1947- *ConAu 109*
Batchelor, Reg *ConAu X*
Batcher, Elaine Kotler 1944- *ConAu 109*
Bate, Lucy 1939- *ConAu 69, SmATA 18*
Bate, Norman Arthur 1916- *ConAu 1R,*
  SmATA 5, WrDr 84
Bate, Sam 1907- *ConAu 102*
Bate, Sam 1909- *IntAu&W 82*
Bate, Walter Jackson 1918- *ConAu 5R,*
  ConLCrt 82, IntAu&W 82, WorAu,
  WrDr 84
Bateman, Barbara Dee 1933- *ConAu 41R*
Bateman, Robert 1922-1973 *ConAu 5R, –7NR,*
  ConSFA
Bateman, Walter L 1916- *ConAu 29R*
Bates, Alan Lawrence 1923- *ConAu 17R*
Bates, Arthenia J 1920- *ConAu 57*
Bates, Barbara S 1919- *ConAu 17R,*
  SmATA 12
Bates, Betty 1921- *ConAu X, SmATA 19*
Bates, Caroline 1932- *ConAu 103*
Bates, Daisey *LivgBAA*
Bates, Darrell 1913- *ConAu P-1, IntAu&W 82,*
  WrDr 84
Bates, David Robert 1916- *IntAu&W 82*
Bates, David Vincent 1922- *ConAu 110*
Bates, Elizabeth 1921- *ConAu 77*
Bates, Ernest Sutherland 1879-1939 *TwCA*
Bates, H E 1905-1974 *ConAu 45, –93, LongCTC,*
  ModBrL, TwCWr, WhoTwCL
Bates, Harry *WrDr 84*
Bates, Harry 1900- *TwCSFW*
Bates, Herbert Ernest 1905- *TwCA,*
  TwCA SUP
Bates, J Leonard 1919- *ConAu 13R*
Bates, James 1926- *WrDr 84*
Bates, Jefferson D 1920- *ConAu 81*
Bates, Jerome E 1917- *ConAu 17R*
Bates, Katharine Lee 1859-1929 *TwCA,*
  TwCA SUP, TwCWr
Bates, Kenneth Francis 1904- *ConAu P-1*
Bates, Lucius Christopher 1901?-1980
  ConAu 101
Bates, Margaret J 1918- *ConAu 17R*
Bates, Marston 1906-1974 *ConAu 5R, –7NR, –49*
Bates, Maxwell Bennett 1906- *CreCan 2*
Bates, Paul Allen 1920- *ConAu 37R,*
  IntAu&W 82
Bates, Peter Watson 1920- *ConAu 102,*
  WrDr 84
Bates, Ralph 1899- *LongCTC, ModBrL, TwCA,*
  TwCA SUP, TwCWr
Bates, Ralph Samuel 1906- *ConAu 1R,*
  WrDr 84
Bates, Robert H 1942- *ConAu 11NR, –69*
Bates, Ronald Gordon Nudell 1924- *ConAu 25R,*
  CreCan 1, DcLEL 1940, IntAu&W 82,

WrDr 84
Bates, Scott *DrAP&F 83*
Bates, Scott 1923- *ConAu 49*
Bates, Timothy M 1946- *ConAu 53*
Bateson, Charles Henry 1903- *ConAu 69*
Bateson, Frederick Wilse 1901-1978 *ConAu 5R,*
  –6NR, ConLCrt 82, ModBrL, WorAu
Bateson, Gregory 1904-1980 *ConAu 101, –41R*
Batey, Richard 1933- *ConAu 33R*
Batey, Tom 1946- *ConAu 107*
Bath, Philip Ernest 1898- *ConAu P-1*
Batherman, Muriel *ConAu X*
Bathke, Edwin A 1936- *ConAu 57*
Bathke, Nancy E 1938- *ConAu 57*
Batho, Edith Clara 1895- *ConAu P-1,*
  IntAu&W 82, WrDr 84
Bathurst, Bill *DrAP&F 83*
Bathurst, Sheila *ConAu X*
Batiuk, Thomas M 1947- *ConAu 69*
Batki, John *DrAP&F 83*
Batki, John 1942- *ConAu 45*
Batllori I Munne, Miquel 1909- *IntAu&W 82*
Batra, Raveendra N 1943- *ConAu 89*
Batson, Edward 1906- *WrDr 84*
Batson, George 1918-1977 *ConAu 33R, –73*
Batson, Larry 1930- *ConAu 57*
Battaglia, Anthony 1939- *ConAu 108*
Battaglia, Aurelius *SmATA 33*
Battaglia, Elio Lee 1928- *ConAu 1R, –1NR*
Battaglia, Elizabeth Louise 1925- *MichAu 80*
Battalia, O William 1928- *ConAu 45*
Battan, Louis J 1923- *ConAu 13R*
Battcock, Gregory 1938-1980 *ConAu 105,*
  –11NR, –21R
Battelle, Phyllis 1922- *ConAu 77*
Batten, Charles Linwood, Jr. 1942- *ConAu 85*
Batten, Harry Mortimer 1888-1958 *SmATA 25*
Batten, Jack 1932- *ConAu 49*
Batten, James Knox 1936- *ConAu 102*
Batten, James William 1919- *ConAu 33R,*
  WrDr 84
Batten, Jean Gardner 1909- *ConAu 106,*
  IntAu&W 82, WrDr 84
Batten, Joyce Mortimer *ConAu X*
Batten, Mary 1937- *ConAu 41R, SmATA 5*
Batten, Peter 1916- *ConAu 97*
Batten, S Archer *IntAu&W 82X*
Batten, T R 1904- *WrDr 84*
Batten, Thomas Reginald 1904- *ConAu 13R*
Battenhouse, Roy W 1912- *WrDr 84*
Battenhouse, Roy Wesley 1912- *ConAu 13R,*
  IntAu&W 82
Batterberry, Ariane Ruskin 1935- *ConAu 69,*
  SmATA 13
Batterberry, Michael 1932- *SmATA 32*
Batterberry, Michael Carver 1932- *ConAu 77*
Battersby, James L 1936- *ConAu 41R*
Battersby, Martin 1914?-1982 *ConAu 106*
Battersby, William John 1904-1976 *ConAu 4NR,*
  –5R
Battestin, Martin Carey 1930- *ConAu 13R,*
  IntAu&W 82, WrDr 84
Battin, M Pabst *DrAP&F 83*
Battin, R Ray 1925- *ConAu 6NR, –9R*
Battis, Emery John 1915- *ConAu 1R*
Battiscombe, Esther Georgina 1905- *ConAu P-1*
Battiscombe, Georgina 1905- *IntAu&W 82,*
  WrDr 84
Battista, Miriam 1912?-1980 *ConAu 103*
Battista, O A 1917- *ConAu 7NR, –13R*
Battisti, Eugenio 1924- *ConAu 37R*
Battle, Allen Overton 1927- *ConAu 41R,*
  IntAu&W 82
Battle, Gerald N 1914- *ConAu 57*
Battle, Jean Allen 1914- *ConAu 25R*
Battle, Lois 1942- *ConAu 106*
Battle, Richard John Vulliamy 1907-1982
  ConAu 106
Battle, Sol 1934- *ConAu 25R*
Battles, Edith 1921- *ConAu 41R, IntAu&W 82*
Battles, Ford Lewis 1915- *ConAu 13R*
Battles, Roxy Edith 1921- *SmATA 7*
Batto, Bernard Frank 1941- *ConAu 57*
Batts, Michael S 1929- *ConAu 41R,*
  IntAu&W 82
Batty, Charles David 1932- *ConAu 17R*
Batty, Joyce D 1919- *ConAu 17R*
Batty, Linda Schmidt 1940- *ConAu 61*
Battye, Louis Neville 1923- *ConAu 5R*
Batuk *IntWWP 82X*
Baty, Gaston 1885?-1952 *ClDMEL 80*
Baty, Gordon B 1938- *ConAu 57*

Baty, Roger M 1937- *ConAu 77*
Baty, Wayne 1925- *ConAu 5NR, –13R*
Bauby, Cathrina 1927- *ConAu 49*
Bauchart *ConAu X*
Baudelaire, Charles Pierre 1821-1867
  ClDMEL 80
Baudouy, Michel-Aime 1909- *ConAu P-2,*
  IntAu&W 82, SmATA 7
Bauduc, R *ConAu X*
Baudy, Nicolas 1904?-1971 *ConAu 33R*
Bauer, Caroline Feller 1935- *ConAu 77*
Bauer, Douglas *DrAP&F 83*
Bauer, E Charles 1916- *ConAu 9R*
Bauer, Erwin A 1919- *ConAu 6NR, –9R*
Bauer, Florence Marvyne *ConAu P-2*
Bauer, Fred 1934- *ConAu 29R*
Bauer, Friedhold 1934- *CroCD*
Bauer, George C 1942- *ConAu 73*
Bauer, George Howard 1933- *ConAu 29R*
Bauer, Grace *DrAP&F 83*
Bauer, Hanna R 1918- *ConAu 57*
Bauer, Harry C 1902-1979 *ConAu 85,*
  ConAu P-1
Bauer, Helen 1900- *ConAu 5R, SmATA 2*
Bauer, Josef Martin 1901- *ConAu 5R, –5NR,*
  ModGL
Bauer, K Jack 1926- *ConAu 10NR, –25R*
Bauer, Karl Jack 1926- *WrDr 84*
Bauer, Malcolm Clair 1914- *ConAu 102*
Bauer, Marion Dane 1938- *ConAu 11NR, –69,*
  SmATA 20
Bauer, Peter Thomas 1915- *ConAu 103,*
  WrDr 84
Bauer, Raymond A 1916-1977 *ConAu 11NR*
Bauer, Raymond Augustine 1916-1977 *ConAu 61,*
  –73
Bauer, Robert A 1910- *ConAu 69*
Bauer, Royal D M 1889- *ConAu 33R*
Bauer, Steven *DrAP&F 83*
Bauer, Walter 1904-1976 *ConAu 101, EncWL 2,*
  ModGL
Bauer, William Waldo 1892-1967 *ConAu 5R,*
  –7NR
Bauer, Wolfgang 1941- *ClDMEL 80, CroCD*
Bauer, Wolfgang L 1930- *ConAu 13R*
Bauer, Yehuda 1926- *ConAu 29R,*
  IntAu&W 82, WrDr 84
Bauer-Patitz, Dolores *IntWWP 82X*
Bauernfeind, Harry B 1904- *ConAu P-2*
Bauernschmidt, Marjorie 1926- *SmATA 15*
Baugh, Albert C 1891-1981 *ConAu 103, –107*
Baugh, Daniel A 1931- *ConAu 69*
Baughan, Peter Edward 1934- *ConAu 107,*
  IntAu&W 82, WrDr 84
Baughman, Dorothy 1940- *ConAu 65*
Baughman, Ernest W 1916- *ConAu 33R*
Baughman, James P 1936- *ConAu 25R*
Baughman, John Lee 1913- *ConAu 97*
Baughman, M Dale 1919- *ConAu 41R*
Baughman, Ray Edward 1925- *ConAu 4NR, –9R*
Baughman, Urbanus E, Jr. 1905?-1978 *ConAu 81*
Baughman, William Charles 1921- *IntAu&W 82*
Baughn, William Hubert 1918- *ConAu 1R*
Baukhage, Hilmar Robert 1889-1976 *AuNews 2,*
  ConAu 65
Bauland, Peter 1932- *ConAu 25R*
Baulch, Jerry T 1913- *ConAu 77*
Baulch, Lawrence 1926- *ConAu 25R*
Baum, Allyn Z 1924- *ConAu 17R, SmATA 20*
Baum, Bernard H 1926- *ConAu 37R, WrDr 84*
Baum, Daniel 1934- *ConAu 6NR, –13R*
Baum, David William 1940- *ConAu 53*
Baum, Gregory *ConAu 25R*
Baum, L Frank 1856-1919 *ConAu 108,*
  DcLB 22[port], SmATA 18, TwCCW 83,
  TwCLC 7[port], TwCSFW
Baum, Louis F *ConAu X*
Baum, Lyman Frank 1856-1919 *LongCTC,*
  TwCA
Baum, Paull Franklin 1886-1964 *ConAu 5R, –103*
Baum, Rainer C 1934- *ConAu 107*
Baum, Richard 1940- *ConAu 57*
Baum, Richard Fitzgerald 1913- *ConAu 5R*
Baum, Robert J 1941- *ConAu 85*
Baum, Thomas 1940- *ConAu 65*
Baum, Vicki 1888?-1960 *ConAu 93, LongCTC,*
  TwCA, TwCA SUP, TwCWr
Baum, Willi 1931- *ConAu 29R, SmATA 4*
Bauman, Clarence 1928- *ConAu 45*
Bauman, Edward Walter 1927- *ConAu 106*
Bauman, H Carl 1913- *ConAu 9R*
Baumann, Amy Beeching 1922- *ConAu 21R,*

SmATA 10

Baumann, Carol Edler 1932- *ConAu 33R,*
IntAu&W 82, WrDr 84
Baumann, Charles Henry 1926- *ConAu 73*
Baumann, Charly 1928- *ConAu 89*
Baumann, Edward 1925- *ConAu 109*
Baumann, Elwood D *SmATA 33*

Baumann, Hans 1914- *ConAu 3NR, –5R,*
IntAu&W 82, SmATA 2
Baumann, Kurt 1935- *ConAu 77,*
SmATA 21[port]
Baumann, Susan *DrAP&F 83*
Baumann, Walter 1935- *ConAu 29R*
Baumbach, Jonathan *DrAP&F 83*
Baumbach, Jonathan 1933- *ConAu 13R,*
ConLC 6, –23[port], ConNov 82,
DcLB Y80B[port], IntAu&W 82, WrDr 84
Baumback, Clifford M 1915- *ConAu 6NR, –57*
Baume, Michael 1930- *ConAu 25R*
Baumer, Franklin L 1913- *ConAu 110*
Baumer, William H, Jr. 1909- *ConAu 1R, –1NR*
Baumgaertel, Walter 1902- *ConAu 69*
Baumgard, Herbert Mark 1920- *ConAu 13R*
Baumgardt, David 1890-1963 *ConAu 1R, –103*
Baumgart, Reinhard 1929- *ModGL*
Baumgartner, Frederic J 1945- *ConAu 110*
Baumgartner, John Stanley 1924- *ConAu 9R*
Bauml, Franz H *ConAu 49*
Baumol, William J 1922- *ConAu 7NR, –13R,*
WrDr 84
Baumrin, Bernard H 1934- *ConAu 9R*
Baumrin, Stefan *ConAu X*
Baur, Jean *DrAP&F 83*
Baur, John Edward 1922- *ConAu 9R, WrDr 84*
Baus, Herbert M 1914- *ConAu 11NR*
Baus, Herbert Michael 1914- *ConAu 25R,*
WrDr 84
Bausani, Alessandro 1921- *ConAu 45*
Bausch, Richard *DrAP&F 83*
Bausch, Richard 1945- *ConAu 101*
Bausch, Robert 1945- *ConAu 109*
Bausch, William J 1929- *ConAu 11NR, –29R*
Bausenwein, Hans 1924- *IntAu&W 82*
Bavin, Bill 1919- *ConAu 73*
Bavngaard, Knud 1915- *IntAu&W 82*
Bawden, Nina 1925- *ChlLR 2, ConAu X,*
ConNov 82, DcLB 14[port], DcLEL 1940,
IntAu&W 82, SmATA 4, TwCCW 83,
TwCCr&M 80, WrDr 84
Bawn, Mary *ConAu X*
Bax *ConAu X*
Bax, Arnold 1883-1953 *LongCTC*
Bax, Clifford 1886-1962 *DcLB 10, LongCTC,*
ModBrL
Bax, Ernest Belfort 1854-1926 *LongCTC*
Bax, Martin 1933- *ConAu 65, WrDr 84*
Bax, Roger *ConAu X, TwCCr&M 80, WorAu,*
WrDr 84
Baxandall, Rosalyn Fraad 1939- *ConAu 81*
Baxt, George 1923- *ConAu 21R,*
TwCCr&M 80, WrDr 84
Baxter, Annette Kar 1926- *ConAu 1R, –4NR*
Baxter, Batsell Barrett 1916- *ConAu 33R*
Baxter, Sir Beverley 1891-1964 *LongCTC*
Baxter, Brian *WrDr 84*
Baxter, Caroline 1956- *WrDr 84*
Baxter, Carolyn *DrAP&F 83*
Baxter, Charles *DrAP&F 83*
Baxter, Charles 1947- *ConAu 57*
Baxter, Craig 1929- *ConAu 11NR, –25R,*
WrDr 84
Baxter, Douglas Clark 1942- *ConAu 85*
Baxter, Edna M 1890- *WrDr 84*
Baxter, Edna May 1890- *ConAu P-1*
Baxter, Eric George 1918- *ConAu 17R*
Baxter, Eric Peter 1913- *ConAu 9R*
Baxter, George Owen *ConAu X, TwCWW*
Baxter, Glen 1944- *ConAu 109*
Baxter, Gordon F, Jr. 1923- *ConAu 1NR, –45*
Baxter, Hazel *ConAu X*
Baxter, Ian F G *ConAu 11NR, –21R*
Baxter, James Finney, III 1893-1975 *ConAu 65*
Baxter, James Keir 1926-1972 *ConAu 77,*
ConLC 14, ConP 80A, DcLEL 1940,
EncWL 2, LongCTC, ModCmwL, TwCWr,
WorAu
Baxter, James Phinney, III 1893-1975 *ConAu 57,*
TwCA SUP
Baxter, James Sidlow 1903- *ConAu 73*
Baxter, John *ConAu X*
Baxter, John 1939- *ConAu 29R, ConSFA,*

DcLEL 1940, TwCSFW, WrDr 84
Baxter, Maurice Glen 1920- *ConAu 13R*
Baxter, Michael John 1944- *ConAu 103*
Baxter, Mike *ConAu X*
Baxter, Patricia Edith Wilson *ConAu 107,*
IntAu&W 82
Baxter, Phyllis *ConAu X*
Baxter, Raymond Frederic 1922- *IntAu&W 82*
Baxter, Shane V *ConAu X, WrDr 84*
Baxter, Stephen B 1929- *ConAu 17R*
Baxter, Valerie *ConAu X, TwCCW 83,*
WrDr 84
Baxter, William F 1929- *ConAu 89*
Baxter, William T 1906- *ConAu 107, WrDr 84*
Baxter, Zenobia L 1907- *LivgBAA*
Bay, Christian 1921- *ConAu 33R*
Bay, Howard 1912- *ConAu 81*
Bayar, Maris 1937- *IntWWP 82*
Baybars, Taner 1936- *ConAu 4NR, –53,*
ConP 80, DcLEL 1940, IntAu&W 82,
IntWWP 82, WrDr 84
Bayefsky, Aba 1923- *CreCan 1*
Bayer, Hans 1914- *IntAu&W 82*
Bayer, Ingeborg 1927- *IntAu&W 82*
Bayer, Konrad 1932-1964 *CroCD*
Bayer, Oliver Weld *ConAu X*
Bayer, Ronald 1943- *ConAu 106*
Bayer, William 1939- *ConAu 33R, WrDr 84*
Bayer-Berenbaum, Linda 1948- *ConAu 107*
Bayerl, Elizabeth 1950- *WrDr 84*
Bayerle, Gustav 1931- *ConAu 53*
Bayes, Ronald H *DrAP&F 83*
Bayes, Ronald H 1932- *ConAu 10NR, –25R*
Bayh, Birch E, Jr. 1928- *ConAu 41R*
Baylen, Joseph O 1920- *ConAu 10NR, –25R,*
IntAu&W 82, WrDr 84
Bayles, Ernest E 1897- *ConAu 73*
Bayles, Michael D 1941- *ConAu 1NR, –49*
Bayless, John 1913?-1983 *ConAu 109*
Bayless, Kenneth 1913?-1972 *ConAu 104*
Bayless, Raymond 1920- *ConAu 85*
Bayley, Barrington John 1937- *ConAu 37R,*
IntAu&W 82, TwCSFW, WrDr 84
Bayley, Charles Calvert 1907- *ConAu 33R,*
WrDr 84
Bayley, David H 1933- *ConAu 13R*
Bayley, Edwin Richard 1918- *ConAu 108*
Bayley, John 1925- *ConAu 85, ConLCrt 82,*
WrDr 84
Bayley, Peter 1921- *ConAu 101, WrDr 84*
Bayley, Stephen 1951- *ConAu 106, WrDr 84*
Bayley, Viola Powles 1911- *ConAu 5R, –5NR*
Baylis, John 1946- *ConAu 101, WrDr 84*
Baylis, Lilian 1874-1937 *LongCTC*
Bayliss, John Clifford 1915- *DcLEL 1940*
Bayliss, John Clifford 1919- *ConAu 13R*
Bayliss, Timothy *WrDr 84*
Bayliss, Timothy 1936- *ConAu X,*
IntAu&W 82X, IntWWP 82X
Baylor, Byrd 1924- *ChlLR 3, ConAu 81,*
SmATA 16
Baylor, Robert Arthur 1925- *ConAu 13R*
Bayly, Ada Ellen 1857-1903 *LongCTC*
Bayly, Joseph 1920- *ConAu 17R, WrDr 84*
Baym, Max I 1895- *ConAu 41R*
Bayne, David C 1918- *ConAu 41R*
Bayne, Stephen Fielding, Jr. 1908-1974 *ConAu 45*
Bayne-Jardine, C C 1932- *ConAu 25R*
Baynes, Cary F 1873?-1977 *ConAu 104*
Baynes, John 1928- *WrDr 84*
Baynes, John Christopher Malcolm 1928-
ConAu 21R, IntAu&W 82
Baynes, Ken 1934- *ConAu 110*
Baynes, Norman Hepburn 1877-1961 *LongCTC*
Baynes, Pauline Diana 1922- *SmATA 19[port]*
Baynham, Henry Wellesley Forster 1933-
ConAu 29R, IntAu&W 82, WrDr 84
Bayr, Rudolf 1919- *CnMD, CroCD*
Bayrd, Edwin 1944- *ConAu 97*
Bays, Gwendolyn McKee *ConAu 13R*
Bayton, James A 1912- *LivgBAA*
Bayyati, Abd Al-Wahhab, Al- 1926- *EncWL 2*
Bazan, Emilia Pardo 1852- *ModRL*
Bazelon, David Thomas 1923- *ConAu 17R*
Bazelon, Irwin Allen 1922- *ConAu 102*
Bazhan, Mykola 1904- *CIDMEL 80, ModSL 2*
Bazin, Andre 1918-1958 *WorAu 1970*
Bazin, Germain 1907- *ConAu 5R*
Bazin, Germain Rene Michel *IntAu&W 82*
Bazin, Herve 1911- *CIDMEL 80, ConAu X,*
ModFrL, TwCWr, WorAu

Bazin, Nancy Topping 1934- *ConAu 41R*
Bazin, Rene 1853-1932 *CIDMEL 80, LongCTC,*
TwCA, TwCA SUP
Bazley, Margaret C 1938- *ConAu 106*
Bazley, Rosemary 1900- *IntWWP 82*
BB *TwCCW 83*
BB 1905- *ConAu X, SmATA 6*
Beach, Bert Beverly 1928- *ConAu 57*
Beach, Charles 1818-1883 *SmATA X*
Beach, Charles Amory *ConAu X, SmATA 1*
Beach, Dale S 1923- *ConAu 13R*
Beach, Earl F 1912- *ConAu 13R*
Beach, Edward L *DrAP&F 83*
Beach, Edward L 1918- *WrDr 84*
Beach, Edward Latimer 1918- *ConAu 5R, –6NR,*
SmATA 12
Beach, Frank Ambrose 1911- *ConAu 110,*
WrDr 84
Beach, Joseph Warren 1880-1957 *TwCA SUP*
Beach, Mark B 1937- *ConAu 69*
Beach, Mary *DrAP&F 83*
Beach, Rex Ellingwood 1877-1949 *LongCTC,*
MichAu 80, TwCA, TwCA SUP, TwCWW,
TwCWr
Beach, Stewart Taft 1899-1979 *ConAu 85, –93,*
SmATA 23[port]
Beach, Sylvia 1887-1962 *ConAu 108, DcLB 4,*
LongCTC
Beach, Vincent W 1917- *ConAu 33R*
Beach, Waldo 1916- *ConAu 61*
Beachcomber *ConAu X, WorAu*
Beachcroft, Nina 1931- *ConAu 97, SmATA 18,*
TwCCW 83, WrDr 84
Beachcroft, Thomas Owen 1902- *ConAu P-1,*
IntAu&W 82, WrDr 84
Beachy, Lucille 1935- *ConAu 77*
Beadell, Len 1923- *ConAu 102, WrDr 84*
Beadle, Leigh P 1941- *ConAu 65*
Beadle, Muriel McClure Barnett 1915-
ConAu 21R
Beadles, William T 1902- *ConAu 17R*
Beagle, Peter S *DrAP&F 83*
Beagle, Peter S 1939- *ConAu 4NR, –9R,*
ConLC 7, ConSFA, DcLB Y80B[port],
WrDr 84
Beaglehole, J C 1901-1971 *ConAu 33R,*
ConAu P-2
Beaglehole, John Cante 1901-1971 *LongCTC*
Beakley, George Carroll, Jr. 1922- *ConAu 1NR,*
–45
Beal, Anthony Ridley 1925- *ConAu 9R*
Beal, George M 1917- *ConAu 21R*
Beal, Gwyneth 1943- *ConAu 69*
Beal, J David 1921- *WrDr 84*
Beal, M F *DrAP&F 83*
Beal, M F 1937- *ConAu 73, DcLB Y81B[port]*
Beal, Merrill D 1898- *ConAu 1R, –5NR*
Beale, Betty *ConAu 73*
Beale, Calvin L 1923- *ConAu 1R*
Beale, Dorothea 1831-1906 *LongCTC*
Beale, Howard 1898- *ConAu 109*
Beale, Howard Kennedy 1899-1959
DcLB 17[port]
Bealer, Alex W 1921-1980 *ConAu 2NR, –45, –97,*
SmATA 22N, –8
Beales, Derek 1931- *ConAu 73*
Bealey, Frank 1922- *WrDr 84*
Bealey, Frank William 1922- *IntAu&W 82*
Bealey, William 1922- *ConAu 2NR, –5R*
Beall, J H *IntWWP 82X*
Beall, James Howard 1945- *IntWWP 82*
Beall, James Lee 1924- *ConAu 11NR, –65*
Beall, Karen F 1938- *ConAu 106*
Beals, Alan R 1928- *ConAu 37R*
Beals, Carleton 1893-1979 *ConAu 1R, –3NR,*
SmATA 12, TwCA, TwCA SUP
Beals, Frank Lee 1881-1972 *ConAu 5R, –103,*
SmATA 26N
Beals, Kathie Stahl *ConAmTC*
Beals, Ralph Leon 1901- *ConAu 21R*
Beam, Alvin Wesley 1912-1982 *ConAu 107*
Beam, C Richard *ConAu 45*
Beam, George D 1934- *ConAu 69*
Beam, Jeffery *DrAP&F 83*
Beam, Philip C 1910- *ConAu 97*
Beaman, Joyce Proctor 1931- *ConAu 29R,*
WrDr 84
Beaman, S G Hulme 1886-1932 *TwCCW 83*
Beame, Rona 1934- *ConAu 45, SmATA 12*
Beament, Harold 1898- *CreCan 2*
Beament, Thomas Harold *CreCan 2*

Beamish, Annie O'Meara DeVic 1883-
    ConAu 13R
Beamish, Anthony Hamilton d1983 *ConAu 109*
Beamish, Huldine V 1904- *ConAu P-1*
Beamish, Noel DeVic 1883- *ConAu X*
Beamish, Sir Tufton Victor Hamilton 1917-
    ConAu X
Bean, Amelia *TwCWW*
Bean, Constance A *ConAu 41R*
Bean, David 1932- *WrDr 84*
Bean, George Ewart 1903- *ConAu 25R*
Bean, Henry 1945- *ConAu 109*
Bean, Keith Fenwick 1911- *ConAu P-1*
Bean, Lowell John 1931- *ConAu 41R,*
    IntAu&W 82
Bean, Mabel Greene 1898?-1977 *ConAu 73*
Bean, Normal *ConAu X*
Bean, Orson 1928- *ConAu 77*
Bean, Walton 1914- *ConAu 25R*
Beaney, Jan *ConAu X,   SmATA X*
Beanlands, Sophia Theresa Pemberton *CreCan 1*
Bear, David 1949- *ConAu 106*
Bear, Greg 1951- *TwCSFW, WrDr 84*
Bear, James A, Jr. 1919- *ConAu 21R*
Bear, Joan 1918- *ConAu 57*
Bear, John 1938- *ConAu 73*
Bear, Roberta Meyer 1942- *ConAu 21R*
Bearce, George D 1922- *ConAu 9R*
Bearchell, Charles 1925- *ConAu 93*
Beard, Charles Austin 1874-1948 *ConAmA,*
    DcLB 17[port], LongCTC, SmATA 18,
    TwCA, TwCA SUP
Beard, Dan 1850-1941 *SmATA 22[port]*
Beard, Daniel Carter 1850-1941 *TwCA,*
    TwCA SUP
Beard, Geoffrey 1929- *WrDr 84*
Beard, James 1903- *ConAu 81, WrDr 84*
Beard, James F 1919- *ConAu 1R*
Beard, Mary Ritter 1876-1958 *TwCA,*
    TwCA SUP
Beard, Peter H 1938- *ConAu 13R*
Bearden, James Hudson 1933- *ConAu 21R*
Bearden, Romare 1914- *ConAu 102,*
    SmATA 22
Beardmore, Cedric *ConAu X, SmATA X*
Beardmore, George 1908-1979 *ConAu 69,*
    SmATA 20
Beardslee, John W, III 1914- *ConAu 37R*
Beardsley, Charles Noel 1914- *ConAu 1R, –2NR*
Beardsley, Elizabeth Lane *ConAu 29R*
Beardsley, John 1952- *ConAu 109*
Beardsley, Monroe Curtis 1915- *ConAu 17R*
Beardsley, Richard K 1918-1978 *ConAu 11NR,*
    –17R, –77
Beardsley, Theodore S, Jr. 1930- *ConAu 33R,*
    WrDr 84
Beardsworth, Millicent Monica 1915- *ConAu 103,*
    WrDr 84
Beardwood, Roger 1932- *ConAu 89*
Beardwood, Valerie Fairfield *ConAu 5R*
Beare, Francis Wright 1902- *ConAu 1R*
Beare, Muriel Anita Nikki 1928- *MichAu 80*
Beare, Nikki 1928- *ConAu 37R*
Bearman, Jane 1917- *ConAu 105, SmATA 29*
Bearn, Pierre 1902- *IntWWP 82*
Bearne, C G 1939- *ConAu 97*
Bearss, Edwin C 1923- *ConAu 10NR, –25R*
Beaser, Herbert W 1913?-1979 *ConAu 85*
Beasley, Edward, Jr. 1932- *LivgBAA*
Beasley, Jerry C 1940- *ConAu 37R*
Beasley, M Robert 1918- *ConAu 9R*
Beasley, Maurine 1936- *ConAu 104*
Beasley, Rex 1925- *ConAu 9R*
Beasley, W Conger, Jr. 1940- *ConAu 4NR, –53*
Beasley, William Gerald 1919- *ConAu 53,*
    WrDr 84
Beasley-Murray, George Raymond 1916-
    ConAu 65, IntAu&W 82, WrDr 84
Beath, Paul Robert 1905- *ConAu 5R*
Beaton, Anne *ConAu X*
Beaton, Cecil 1904-1980 *ConAu 81, –93,*
    LongCTC
Beaton, Chris *IntAu&W 82X*
Beaton, George 1894- *ConAu X*
Beaton, Leonard 1929-1971 *ConAu 4NR, –5R,*
    –29R
Beaton-Jones, Cynon 1921- *ConAu 5R*
Beattie, Ann *DrAP&F 83*
Beattie, Ann 1947- *ConAu 81, ConLC 8, –13,*
    –18, DcLB Y82B[port]
Beattie, Carol 1918- *ConAu 29R*
Beattie, Edward J, Jr. 1918- *ConAu 106*

Beattie, Jessie Louise 1896- *ConAu 2NR, –5R,*
    CreCan 2, IntAu&W 82, WrDr 84
Beattie, John Hugh Marshall 1915- *ConAu 37R,*
    WrDr 84
Beatts, Anne Patricia 1947- *ConAu 102*
Beatty, Bill *ConAu X*
Beatty, Elizabeth *ConAu X, SmATA X*
Beatty, Hetty Burlingame 1907-1971 *ConAu 1R,*
    –103, SmATA 5
Beatty, Jerome, Jr. 1918- *ConAu 3NR, –9R,*
    SmATA 5
Beatty, John 1922-1975 *ConAu 4NR, –5R, –57,*
    SmATA 25N, –6, TwCCW 83
Beatty, John William 1869-1941 *CreCan 1*
Beatty, Morgan 1902-1975 *ConAu 61*
Beatty, Patricia 1922- *TwCCW 83, WrDr 84*
Beatty, Patricia Robbins 1922- *ConAu 1R, –3NR,*
    SmATA 1, –30[port]
Beatty, Rita Gray 1930- *ConAu 45*
Beatty, Robert Owen 1924-1976 *ConAu 69*
Beatty, Warren *ConAu X*
Beatty, William Alfred 1912- *ConAu P-1*
Beatty, William K 1926- *ConAu 41R*
Beaty, Betty *WrDr 84*
Beaty, Betty 1922- *ConAu 73, TwCRGW*
Beaty, David 1919- *ConAu 1R, –2NR,*
    ConNov 82, IntAu&W 82, WrDr 84
Beaty, Janice J 1930- *ConAu 13R*
Beaty, Jerome 1924- *ConAu 85*
Beaty, John Richard 1932- *CreCan 1*
Beaty, Richard 1932- *CreCan 1*
Beaty, Shirley MacLean 1934- *ConAu 103*
Beaty, Warren 1937?- *ConAu 109*
Beaubien, Jeanine *CreCan 1*
Beauchamp, Edward R 1933- *ConAu 61*
Beauchamp, Kathleen Mansfield 1888-1923
    ConAu 104, LongCTC, TwCA,
    TwCA SUP
Beauchamp, Kenneth 1939- *WrDr 84*
Beauchamp, Kenneth L 1939- *ConAu 29R, –29R*
Beauchamp, Mary Annette *LongCTC, TwCA,*
    TwCA SUP
Beauchamp, Pat *ConAu X*
Beauchamp, Tom L 1939- *ConAu 73*
Beauchemin, Neree 1850-1931 *CreCan 2*
Beauclerk, Helen DeVere 1892-1969 *LongCTC,*
    TwCA, TwCA SUP, TwCRGW
Beaude, Henri 1870-1930 *CreCan 2*
Beaudet, Henri *CreCan 2*
Beaudet, Jean-Marie 1908- *CreCan 1*
Beaudet, Liliane Vien 1912- *IntAu&W 82*
Beaudoin, Kenneth L *DrAP&F 83*
Beaudoin, Kenneth Lawrence 1913- *ConAu 29R,*
    WrDr 84
Beaudouin, David *DrAP&F 83*
Beaufitz, William *ConAu X*
Beaufort, John 1912- *ConAmTC, ConAu 104,*
    IntAu&W 82
Beaufre, Andre 1902-1975 *ConAu 57, –65*
Beaulac, Willard L 1899- *ConAu 9R*
Beaulieu, Maurice 1924- *CreCan 1*
Beaulne, Guy 1921- *CreCan 2*
Beauman, Eric Bentley *ConAu 9R,*
    IntAu&W 82
Beauman, Katharine Bentley *WrDr 84*
Beauman, Katharine Burgoyne Bentley 1902-
    ConAu 102
Beauman, Katharine Burgoyne Bentley 1903-
    IntAu&W 82
Beaumont, Beverly *ConAu X*
Beaumont, C Estelle 1937- *IntAu&W 82*
Beaumont, Charles 1929-1967 *ConAu 5R, –103,*
    TwCSFW
Beaumont, Charles Allen 1926- *ConAu 1R*
Beaumont, Cyril William 1891-1976 *ConAu 13R,*
    –65
Beaumont, George Ernest 1888-1974 *ConAu 49*
Beaumont, Roger A 1935- *ConAu 65*
Beaurline, L A 1927- *ConAu 21R*
Beausang, Michael F, Jr. 1936- *ConAu 57*
Beausay, Florence E 1911- *ConAu 21R,*
    WrDr 84
Beausoleil, Beau *DrAP&F 83*
Beausoleil, Beau 1941- *ConAu 81*
Beausoleil, Laura *DrAP&F 83*
Beauvais, Robert 1911- *ConAu 104*
Beauvoir, Simone De 1908- *CIDMEL 80,*
    CnMWL, ConAu 9R, ConLC 1, –2, –4, –8,
    –14, EncWL 2, LongCTC, ModFrL,
    ModRL, TwCA SUP, TwCWr, WhoTwCL
Beaver, Bruce 1928- *ConAu 97, ConP 80,*
    DcLEL 1940, IntAu&W 82, WrDr 84

Beaver, Harold 1929- *ConAu 21R*
Beaver, Patrick 1923- *ConAu 33R, WrDr 84*
Beaver, Paul E 1953- *WrDr 84*
Beaver, Robert Pierce 1906- *ConAu 5R, –7NR*
Beaverbrook, Lord 1879-1964 *LongCTC*
Beaverbrook, Baron William M Aitken 1879-1964
    ConAu 103, –89
Beazley, Sir John Davidson 1885-1970 *LongCTC*
Bebb, Russ, Jr. 1930- *ConAu 49*
Bebell, Mildred Hoyt 1909- *ConAu P-1*
Bebey, Francis 1929- *ConAu 69*
Bebler, A Anton 1937- *ConAu 2NR, –49*
Bebler, Anton A 1937- *IntAu&W 82*
Bec, Pierre 1921- *IntWWP 82*
Bechczyc-Rudnicka, Maria 1888- *IntAu&W 82*
Bechdolt, Frederick Ritchie 1874-1950 *TwCWW*
Becher, Johannes Robert 1891-1958 *CIDMEL 80,*
    CnMD, ModGL, ModWD
Becher, Ulrich 1910- *CnMD, ConAu 101,*
    CroCD
Bechervaise, John Mayston 1910- *ConAu 5NR,*
    –13R, IntAu&W 82, WrDr 84
Bechko, P A 1950- *WrDr 84*
Bechko, Peggy Anne 1950- *ConAu 2NR, –49,*
    MichAu 80, TwCWW
Bechoefer, Bernhard G 1904- *ConAu 1R*
Becht, J Edwin 1918- *ConAu 29R*
Bechtel, Helmut 1929- *IntAu&W 82*
Bechtel, Louise Seaman 1894- *ConAu P-2,*
    SmATA 4
Bechtol, William M 1931- *ConAu 49*
Beck, Aaron T 1921- *ConAu 11NR, –21R*
Beck, Alan M 1942- *ConAu 45*
Beck, Arnold Hugh William 1916- *IntAu&W 82*
Beck, Art *DrAP&F 83, IntWWP 82X*
Beck, Barbara L 1927- *ConAu 17R,*
    SmATA 12
Beck, Beatrix 1914- *CIDMEL 80*
Beck, Calvin Thomas 1937- *ConAu 97*
Beck, Carl 1930- *ConAu 1R, –1NR*
Beck, Clive 1939- *ConAu 49*
Beck, David *ConAmTC*
Beck, Doc *ConAu X*
Beck, Dorothy *DrAP&F 83*
Beck, Dorothy Amelia 1928- *IntWWP 82*
Beck, Earl Clifton 1891-1977 *ConAu 110,*
    MichAu 80
Beck, Earl Ray 1916- *ConAu 33R,*
    IntAu&W 82, WrDr 84
Beck, Eliza Louisa Moresby *LongCTC*
Beck, Evelyn Torton 1933- *ConAu 33R,*
    WrDr 84
Beck, Frank Gene 1949- *IntWWP 82*
Beck, Harry *ConAu X*
Beck, Helen L 1908- *ConAu 73*
Beck, Henry G J 1914- *ConAu 9R*
Beck, Horace P 1920- *ConAu 77*
Beck, Hubert Frederick 1931- *ConAu 29R,*
    WrDr 84
Beck, James 1930- *ConAu 85*
Beck, James Murray 1914- *ConAu 101*
Beck, John Jacob, Jr. 1941- *ConAu 53*
Beck, Julian 1925- *ConAu 102*
Beck, L Adams d1931 *TwCRGW*
Beck, Leslie 1907?-1978 *ConAu 104*
Beck, Lewis White 1913- *ConAu 2NR, –5R,*
    WrDr 84
Beck, Lily Adams d1931 *LongCTC, TwCA,*
    TwCA SUP
Beck, Marilyn 1928- *ConAu 65*
Beck, Phineas *ConAu X*
Beck, Regina *DrAP&F 83*
Beck, Robert *LivgBAA*
Beck, Robert Edward 1941- *ConAu 104*
Beck, Robert H 1918- *ConAu 29R*
Beck, Robert Nelson 1924-1980 *ConAu 1R,*
    –4NR
Beck, Thomas D 1943- *ConAu 57*
Beck, Toni 1925- *ConAu 57*
Beck, Victor Emanuel 1894-1963 *ConAu 5R*
Beck, Warren *ConAu 1R, –3NR, DcLEL 1940,*
    DrAP&F 83, IntAu&W 82, WrDr 84
Beck, Warren Albert 1918- *ConAu 5R, –6NR,*
    WrDr 84
Beckel, Graham 1913- *ConAu 1R*
Beckelhymer, Hunter 1919- *ConAu 3NR,*
    WrDr 84
Beckelhymer, Paul Hunter 1919- *ConAu 1R*
Becker, A C, Jr. 1920- *ConAu 65*
Becker, Abraham S 1927- *ConAu 33R*
Becker, Albert B 1903-1972 *ConAu P-2*
Becker, Arthur P 1918- *ConAu 29R*

Becker, B Jay 1904- *ConAu 65*
Becker, Beril 1901- *ConAu P-1, SmATA 11*
Becker, Bill *ConAu X*
Becker, Bruce *ConAu 57*
Becker, Carl Lotus 1873-1945 *DcLB 17[port], TwCA SUP*
Becker, Carol *DrAP&F 83*
Becker, Ernest 1925-1974 *ConAu 97*
Becker, Florence *ConAu X*
Becker, Gary S 1930- *ConAu 11NR, -61, WrDr 84*
Becker, George Joseph 1908- *ConAu 5R, -7NR, IntAu&W 82, WrDr 84*
Becker, Harold K 1933- *ConAu 29R*
Becker, Hellmut 1913- *IntAu&W 82*
Becker, Jillian 1932- *ConAu 77, IntAu&W 82, WrDr 84*
Becker, John E 1930- *ConAu 49*
Becker, John Leonard 1901- *ConAu P-1, SmATA 12*
Becker, Joseph M 1908- *ConAu 7NR, -17R*
Becker, Jurek 1937- *ClDMEL 80, ConAu 85, ConLC 7, -19, EncWL 2, IntAu&W 82*
Becker, Jurgen 1932- *ClDMEL 80*
Becker, Klaus *ConAu X*
Becker, Knuth 1891-1974 *ClDMEL 80*
Becker, Lawrence C 1939- *ConAu 85*
Becker, Lucille Frackman 1929- *ConAu 29R, WrDr 84*
Becker, Manning H 1922- *ConAu 13R*
Becker, Marion Rombauer 1903-1976 *ConAu 37R, -69*
Becker, Marvin Burton 1922- *ConAu 107*
Becker, May Lamberton 1873-1958 *SmATA 33[port], TwCA, TwCA SUP*
Becker, Paula Lee 1941- *ConAu 17R*
Becker, Peter 1921- *ConAu 53, IntAu&W 82, WrDr 84*
Becker, Robin 1951- *ConAu 110*
Becker, Ruby Wirt 1915- *ConAu 33R*
Becker, Russell J 1923- *ConAu 37R*
Becker, Samuel L 1923- *ConAu 7NR, -13R*
Becker, Seymour 1934- *ConAu 25R*
Becker, Stephen *DrAP&F 83*
Becker, Stephen 1927- *ConAu 3NR, -5R, ConNov 82, DcLEL 1940, IntAu&W 82, WrDr 84*
Becker, Thomas W 1933- *ConAu 5R*
Becker, Walter 1950- *ConLC 26[port]*
Becker, Wesley C 1928- *ConAu 33R*
Becker, William 1903?-1983 *ConAu 110*
Beckerman, Bernard 1921- *ConAu 1R, IntAu&W 82, WrDr 84*
Beckerman, Wilfred 1925- *ConAu 7NR, -17R, WrDr 84*
Becket, Michael Ivan 1942- *IntAu&W 82*
Beckett, Gillian 1935- *IntAu&W 82*
Beckett, John A 1916- *ConAu 33R*
Beckett, Kenneth A 1929- *ConAu 10NR*
Beckett, Kenneth Albert 1929- *ConAu 65, IntAu&W 82*
Beckett, Lucy 1942- *ConAu 49*
Beckett, Ralph L 1923- *ConAu 5R*
Beckett, Ronald Brymer 1891- *ConAu 5R*
Beckett, Samuel 1906- *ClDMEL 80, CnMD, CnMWL, ConAu 5R, ConDr 82, ConLC 1, -2, -3, -4, -6, -9, -10, -11, -14, -18, ConNov 82, ConP 80, CroCD, DcLB 13[port], -15[port], EncWL 2[port], LongCTC, ModBrL, ModBrL SUP, ModFrL, ModRL, ModWD, TwCA SUP, TwCWr, WhoTwCL, WrDr 84*
Beckett, Sheilah 1913- *SmATA 33[port]*
Beckey, Fred W 1923- *ConAu 109*
Beckford, George L 1934- *ConAu 97*
Beckham, Barry 1944- *ConAu 29R, ConNov 82, LivgBAA, WrDr 84*
Beckham, Stephen Dow 1941- *ConAu 61*
Beckhart, Benjamin Haggott 1897-1975 *ConAu 57*
Beckingham, Charles Fraser 1914- *ConAu 61, WrDr 84*
Beckinsale, Monica 1914- *ConAu 69*
Beckinsale, Robert Percy 1908- *ConAu 2NR, -5R, WrDr 84*
Beckler, Marion Floyd 1889- *ConAu P-1*
Beckles Willson, Robina Elizabeth 1930- *WrDr 84*
Beckman, Aldo Bruce 1934- *ConAu 73*
Beckman, Erik 1935- *IntAu&W 82, IntWWP 82*
Beckman, Gail M 1938- *WrDr 84*

Beckman, Gail McKnight 1938- *ConAu 53*

Beckman, Gunnel 1910- *ConAu 33R, ConLC 26[port], SmATA 6*
Beckman, Patti *ConAu X*
Beckmann, David M 1948- *ConAu 8NR, -61*
Beckmann, George Michael 1926- *ConAu 5R*
Beckmann, Martin J 1924- *ConAu 37R*
Beckmann, Petr 1924- *ConAu 69, IntAu&W 82*
Beckner, Weldon 1933- *ConAu 33R*
Beckovic, Matija 1939- *ConAu 33R, EncWL 2*
Beckson, Karl 1926- *ConAu 2NR, -5R*
Beckwith, B K 1902- *ConAu 73*
Beckwith, Burnham Putnam 1904- *ConAu 33R, WrDr 84*
Beckwith, Charles E 1917- *ConAu 37R*
Beckwith, John 1927- *CreCan 1*
Beckwith, John Gordon 1918- *ConAu 9R, WrDr 84*
Beckwith, Lillian 1916- *ConAu X, IntAu&W 82, WrDr 84*
Beckwith, Yvonne *ConAu 106*
Becleanu-Lancu, Adela 1935- *IntAu&W 82*
Becquart, Betty Louise 1945- *IntWWP 82*
Becque, Henry Francois 1837-1899 *CnMD, ModWD*
Becquer, Gustavo Adolfo 1836-1870 *ClDMEL 80*
Becsi, Kurt 1920- *IntAu&W 82*
Bedau, Hugo Adam 1926- *ConAu 4NR, -9R*
Beddall, Barbara G 1919- *ConAu 33R*
Beddall-Smith, Charles John 1916- *ConAu 13R*
Beddington, Roy 1910- *WrDr 84*
Beddoe, Ellaruth *ConAu X*
Beddoes, Richard H 1926- *ConAu 37R*
Bede, Andrew *ConAu X*
Bede, Jean-Albert 1903-1977 *ConAu 69*
Bedeian, Arthur G 1946- *ConAu 110*
Bedel, Maurice 1884-1954 *TwCA, TwCA SUP*
Bedell, George C 1928- *ConAu 41R*
Bedell, L Frank 1888- *ConAu P-1*
Bedford, A N *ConAu X, SmATA 3*
Bedford, Annie North *ConAu X, SmATA 3*
Bedford, Charles Harold 1929- *ConAu 57*
Bedford, Donald F *ConAu X*
Bedford, Emmett G 1922- *ConAu 45*
Bedford, Henry Frederick 1931- *ConAu 9R, WrDr 84*
Bedford, John *ConAu X, WrDr 84*
Bedford, Kenneth *ConAu X*
Bedford, Norton M 1916- *ConAu 5R*
Bedford, Sybille 1911- *ASpks, ConAu 9R, ConNov 82, DcLEL 1940, IntAu&W 82, ModBrL, WorAu, WrDr 84*
Bedford-Jones, Henry James O'Brien 1887-1949 *TwCA, TwCA SUP*
Bediako, K A *ConAu X*
Bedier, Joseph 1864-1938 *TwCA SUP*
Bedikian, Antriganik A 1886?-1980 *ConAu 93*
Bedinger, Margery 1891- *ConAu 57*
Bedinger, Singleton Berry 1907- *ConAu 49*
Bedini, Silvio A 1917- *ConAu 33R, WrDr 84*
Bednar, Alfonz 1914- *ModSL 2*
Bednarik, Charles 1925- *ConAu 77*
Bednarik, Chuck *ConAu X*
Bedoukian, Kerop 1907- *ConAu 93*
Bedrij, Orest 1933- *ConAu 85*
Bedsole, Adolph 1914- *ConAu 13R*
Bee, Clair 1900-1983 *ConAu 109*
Bee, Clair Francis 1900- *ConAu 1R*
Bee, David 1931- *ConAu 17R*
Bee, Helen L 1939- *ConAu 89*
Bee, Jay *ConAu X*
Beebe, Ann 1919- *ConAu 41R*
Beebe, B F 1920- *ConAu 1R, IntAu&W 82X, SmATA 1, WrDr 84*
Beebe, Frank L 1914- *ConAu 89*
Beebe, Frederick S 1914-1973 *ConAu 41R*
Beebe, H Keith 1921- *ConAu 29R*
Beebe, Lucius Morris 1902-1966 *ConAu 25R*
Beebe, Maurice 1926- *ConAu 1R, -1NR, IntAu&W 82, WrDr 84*
Beebe, Ralph K 1932- *ConAu 33R, WrDr 84*
Beebe, William 1877-1962 *ConAmA, ConAu 73, SmATA 19, TwCA, TwCA SUP*
Beeby, Betty 1923- *SmATA 25[port]*
Beeby, C E 1902- *ConAu 109*
Beeby, Clarence Edward 1902- *WrDr 84*
Beech, George T 1931- *ConAu 9R*
Beech, H R 1925- *WrDr 84*
Beech, Harold Reginald 1925- *ConAu 25R*
Beech, Keyes 1913- *ConAu 33R*
Beech, Robert 1940- *ConAu 33R*

Beech, Webb *ConAu X, SmATA 5*
Beecham, Justin *ConAu X*
Beecham, Sir Thomas 1879-1961 *LongCTC*
Beechcroft, T O 1902- *LongCTC*
Beechcroft, William *ConAu X*
Beecher, Johannes R 1891-1958 *CroCD*
Beecher, John 1904- *WrDr 84*
Beecher, John 1904-1980 *AuNews 1, ConAu 5R, -8NR, -105, ConLC 6, ConP 80*
Beecher, William 1933- *ConAu 65*
Beechhold, Henry F 1928- *ConAu 33R*
Beechick, Ruth 1925- *ConAu 108*
Beeching, Henry Charles 1859-1919 *LongCTC*
Beeching, Jack 1922- *ConAu 21R, ConSFA, SmATA 14*
Beecroft, John William Richard 1902-1966 *ConAu 5R*
Beedell, Suzanne 1921- *ConAu 69*
Beedham, Brian James 1928- *IntAu&W 82*
Beeding, Francis *LongCTC, TwCA, TwCA SUP, TwCCr&M 80, TwCWr*
Beef, B F *IntAu&W 82X*
Beegle, Charles William 1928- *ConAu 106*
Beegle, Dewey Maurice 1919- *ConAu 5R*
Beek, Martin A 1909- *ConAu 13R*
Beekman, Allan 1913- *ConAu 33R, WrDr 84*
Beekman, E M 1939- *ConAu 33R*
Beekman, John 1918- *ConAu 61*
Beeks, Graydon 1919- *ConAu 65*
Beeler, Nelson Frederick 1910- *ConAu 69, SmATA 13*
Beeman, Richard R 1942- *ConAu 77*
Beene, Greg *DrAP&F 83*
Beer, Barrett Lynn 1936- *ConAu 49*
Beer, Doris 1924- *IntWWP 82*
Beer, Edith Lynn 1930- *ConAu 11NR*
Beer, Eloise C S 1903- *ConAu 13R*
Beer, Ethel S 1897-1975 *ConAu 57, ConAu P-2*
Beer, Francis Anthony 1939- *ConAu 10NR, -25R*
Beer, Fritz 1911- *IntAu&W 82*
Beer, John B 1926- *ConAu 5R, -7NR*
Beer, Kathleen Costello 1926- *ConAu 25R*
Beer, Lawrence W 1932- *ConAu 37R*
Beer, Lisl *ConAu X*
Beer, Patricia 1924- *ConAu 61, ConP 80, DcLEL 1940, WrDr 84*
Beer, Samuel 1911- *WrDr 84*
Beer, Samuel Hutchison 1911- *ConAu 61*
Beer, Stafford 1926- *WrDr 84*
Beer, Thomas 1889-1940 *TwCA, TwCA SUP*
Beer, Vic *ConAu X*
Beer-Hofmann, Richard 1866-1945 *ClDMEL 80, CnMD, EncWL 2, ModGL, ModWD*
Beerbohm, Henry Maximilian 1872-1956 *ConAu 104*
Beerbohm, Sir Max 1872-1956 *CnMD, CnMWL, LongCTC, ModBrL, ModBrL SUP, ModWD, TwCA, TwCA SUP, TwCLC 1, -1, TwCWr*
Beers, Burton Floyd 1927- *ConAu 1R, WrDr 84*
Beers, Dorothy Sands 1917- *ConAu 49, SmATA 9*
Beers, Henry Putney 1907- *ConAu 13R*
Beers, Lorna 1897- *ConAu 49, SmATA 14*
Beers, Paul Benjamin 1931- *ConAu 102*
Beers, V Gilbert 1928- *ConAu 1NR, -49, SmATA 9*
Beery, Mary *WrDr 84*
Beery, Mary 1907- *ConAu 5R*
Beesly, Patrick 1913- *ConAu 85, IntAu&W 82*
Beeson, Trevor Randall 1926- *ConAu 93, WrDr 84*
Beeton, Max *IntAu&W 82X*
Beeton, Ridley 1929- *ConAu 93*
Beevers, John 1911-1975 *ConAu 61*
Beezley, P C 1895- *ConAu 5R*
Beezley, William H 1942- *ConAu 49*
Befu, Harumi 1930- *ConAu 53*
Beg, Toran *ConAu X*
Begbie, Harold 1871-1929 *LongCTC*
Begg, A Charles 1912- *ConAu 102*
Begg, Alexander Charles 1912- *WrDr 84*
Begg, Howard Bolton 1896- *ConAu 5R*
Begg, Neil Colquhoun 1915- *ConAu 102, IntAu&W 82, WrDr 84*
Beggs, David 1909- *WrDr 84*
Beggs, David, III 1931-1966 *ConAu P-1*
Beggs, Donald L 1941- *ConAu 33R*
Beggs, Edward Larry 1933- *ConAu 89*
Begin, Catherine Agnes Marie 1939- *CreCan 2*
Begin, Menachem 1913- *ConAu 109*

Begin, Mireille *CreCan 1*
Begley, James 1929- *ConAu 25R*
Begley, Kathleen A 1948- *ConAu 77, SmATA 21*
Begnal, Michael H 1939- *ConAu 73*
Begner, Edith P *ConAu 1R, –3NR*
Begovic, Milan 1876-1948 *ClDMEL 80, EncWL 2, ModSL 2*
Beguelin, Jean Charles Henry 1945- *IntAu&W 82*
Beguin, Albert 1901-1957 *ClDMEL 80*
Beha, Ernest Andrew 1908- *ConAu P-1*
Beha, Sister Helen Marie 1926- *ConAu 21R*
Behan, Brendan 1923-1964 *CnMD, ConAu 73, ConDr 82E, ConLC 1, –8, –11, –15, CroCD, DcLB 13[port], DcLEL 1940, EncWL 2, LongCTC, ModBrL, ModBrL SUP, ModWD, TwCWr, WhoTwCL, WorAu*
Behan, Leslie *ConAu X*
Behara, Devendra Nath 1940- *ConAu 41R*
Behbudiy, Mahmud Khoja 1874-1919 *EncWL 2*
Behee, John 1933- *MichAu 80*
Behle, William Harroun 1909- *ConAu 5R, WrDr 84*
Behlen, Charles *DrAP&F 83*
Behlen, Charles 1949- *IntWWP 82*
Behler, Ernst 1928- *ConAu 41R*
Behler, Gebhard Maria 1908- *IntAu&W 82*
Behlmer, Rudy 1926- *ConAu 8NR, –57*
Behm, Marc 1925- *ConAu 101*
Behm, William H, Jr. 1922- *ConAu 13R*
Behme, Robert Lee 1924- *ConAu 57*
Behn, Harry 1898-1973 *ConAu 5R, –5NR, –53, SmATA 2, –34N, TwCCW 83*
Behn, Noel 1928- *TwCCr&M 80, WrDr 84*
Behney, John Bruce 1905- *ConAu 101*
Behnke, Charles A 1891- *ConAu P-2*
Behnke, Frances L *ConAu 33R, SmATA 8*
Behnke, John 1945- *ConAu 69*
Behr, Edward 1926- *ConAu 1R, –3NR, WrDr 84*
Behr, Hans-Georg 1937- *CroCD*
Behr, Joyce 1929- *SmATA 15*
Behr, Marion 1939- *ConAu 105*
Behrend, George 1922- *IntAu&W 82, WrDr 84*
Behrend, Jeanne 1911- *ConAu 17R*
Behrens, Erna 1917- *IntAu&W 82*
Behrens, Helen Kindler 1922- *ConAu 61*
Behrens, Herman D 1901- *ConAu 33R*
Behrens, John C 1933- *ConAu 37R, WrDr 84*
Behrens, June York 1925- *ConAu 8NR, –17R, SmATA 19*
Behrens, Roy R 1946- *ConAu 110*
Behrens-Giegl, Erna *IntAu&W 82X*
Behrman, Carol H 1925- *ConAu 7NR, –61, SmATA 14*
Behrman, Daniel 1923- *ConAu 65*
Behrman, Jack Newton 1922- *ConAu 29R, WrDr 84*
Behrman, Lucy Creevey *ConAu X*
Behrman, S N 1893-1973 *CnMD, ConAmA, ConAu 45, ConAu P-1, CroCD, DcLB 7[port], LongCTC, ModAL, ModWD, TwCA, TwCA SUP*
Behrndt, Anne 1942- *IntWWP 82*
Behrstock, Barry 1948- *ConAu 106*
Beichman, Arnold 1913- *ConAu 49*
Beichner, Paul Edward 1912- *ConAu 33R*
Beier, Ernst G 1916- *ConAu 21R*
Beier, Ulli 1922- *ConAu 4NR, –9R, TwCWr, WrDr 84*
Beigel, Allan 1940- *ConAu 101*
Beigel, Herbert 1944- *ConAu 97*
Beigel, Hugo George 1897- *ConAu 37R*
Beik, Paul H 1915- *ConAu 13R, WrDr 84*
Beilenson, Edna 1909-1981 *ConAu 103, –85*
Beilenson, Laurence W 1899- *ConAu 29R*
Beiler, Edna 1923- *ConAu 1R, –1NR*
Beilharz, Edwin Alanson 1907- *ConAu 33R*
Beim, Norman 1923- *ConAu 85, NatPD 81[port]*
Beimiller, Carl 1913?-1979 *ConAu 89*
Bein, Albert 1902- *CnMD, ModWD*
Beine, George Holmes 1893- *ConAu 93*
Beining, Guy R *DrAP&F 83*
Beirne, Joseph Anthony 1911-1974 *ConAu 45, –53*
Beirne, Brother Kilian 1896- *ConAu 21R*
Beiser, Arthur 1931- *ConAu 93, SmATA 22*
Beiser, Germaine 1931- *SmATA 11*
Beisner, Robert L 1936- *ConAu 25R, WrDr 84*
Beissel, Henry 1929- *ConAu 65, ConP 80,*

WrDr 84
Beissel, Henry Eric 1929- *ConAu 10NR*
Beisser, Arnold R 1925- *ConAu 25R*
Beistle, Shirley *ConAu X*
Beit-Hallahmi, Benjamin 1943- *ConAu 105*
Beith, Sir John Hay 1876-1952 *LongCTC, TwCA, TwCA SUP*
Beitler, Ethel Jane 1906- *ConAu 2NR, –5R*
Beitler, Stanley 1924- *ConAu 5R*
Beitz, Charles R 1949- *ConAu 1NR, –49*
Beitzinger, A J 1918- *ConAu 45*
Beizer, Boris 1934- *ConAu 105*
Beja, Morris 1935- *ConAu 29R, IntAu&W 82, WrDr 84*
Bejerot, Nils Johan Artur 1921- *ConAu 29R*
Bekessy, Jean *ConAu X, TwCA SUP*
Bekh, Wolfgang Johannes 1925- *IntAu&W 82*
Bekker, Hugo 1925- *ConAu 41R*
Bekker-Nielsen, Hans 1933- *ConAu 25R*
Bel Geddes, Joan *ConAu X*
Belair, Felix, Jr. 1907-1978 *ConAu 77*
Belair, Richard L 1934- *ConAu 13R*
Belaney, Archibald Stansfeld 1888-1938 *CreCan 1, LongCTC, SmATA 24[port]*
Belanger, Jerome D 1938- *ConAu 69*
Belasco, David 1853-1931 *ConAu 104, DcLB 7[port]*
Belasco, David 1859-1931 *LongCTC, ModAL, ModWD, TwCA[port], TwCLC 3, TwCWr*
Belcastro, Joseph 1910- *ConAu P-2*
Belch, Caroline Jean 1916- *ConAu 45*
Belchem, David *ConAu X*
Belchem, R F K 1911-1981 *ConAu 108*
Belcheva, Elisaveta *ConLC 10*
Belden, Gail *ConAu X*
Belden, Louise Conway 1910- *ConAu 104*
Belden, Wilanne Schneider 1925- *ConAu 106*
Belding, Robert E 1911- *ConAu 33R*
Beldone, Phil *ConAu X*
Belehradek, Jan 1896-1980 *ConAu 97*
Beleno *ConAu X*
Belew, M Wendell 1922- *ConAu 33R*
Belfer, Nancy 1930- *ConAu 85*
Belfield, Eversley 1918- *ConAu 11NR*
Belfield, Eversley Michael Gallimore 1918- *ConAu 25R, IntAu&W 82, WrDr 84*
Belford, Lee A 1913- *ConAu 17R*
Belfrage, Cedric 1904- *ASpks, ConAu 3NR, –9R, TwCA, TwCA SUP, WrDr 84*
Belfrage, Sally 1936- *ConAu 105*
Belgion, Montgomery 1892-1973 *ConAu P-1*
Belgum, David 1922- *ConAu 6NR, –13R*
Belin, David W 1928- *ConAu 85*
Beling, Willard A 1919- *ConAu 53*
Belinkov, Arkady Viktorovich 1922?-1970 *ConAu 29R*
Belitsky, A Harvey 1929- *ConAu 33R*
Belitt, Ben *DrAP&F 83*
Belitt, Ben 1911- *ConAu 7NR, –13R, ConLC 22[port], ConP 80, DcLB 5[port], TwCA SUP, WrDr 84*
Beljon, Johannes Jacobus 1922- *IntAu&W 82*
Belkin, Samuel 1911-1976 *ConAu 1R, –6NR, –65*
Belkind, Allen 1927- *ConAu 29R*
Belknap, Ivan 1916- *ConAu 5R*
Belknap, Robert H 1917- *ConAu 45*
Belknap, Robert L 1929- *ConAu 33R, WrDr 84*
Belknap, S Yancey 1895- *ConAu P-1*
Bell, A Donald 1920- *ConAu 25R*
Bell, Adrian Hanbury 1901-1980 *ConAu 102, –97, LongCTC, TwCA, TwCA SUP*
Bell, Alan P 1932- *ConAu 33R*
Bell, Alexander Graham 1847-1922 *LongCTC*
Bell, Alistair Macready 1913- *CreCan 2*
Bell, Arthur 1939- *ConAu 85*
Bell, Barbara H 1920- *IntWWP 82*
Bell, Bernard Iddings 1886-1958 *TwCA SUP*
Bell, C F Moberly 1847-1911 *LongCTC*
Bell, Carol *ConAu X*
Bell, Carolyn *ConAu X, IntAu&W 82X, WrDr 84*
Bell, Carolyn Shaw 1920- *ConAu 29R*
Bell, Catherine *WrDr 84*
Bell, Charles G *DrAP&F 83*
Bell, Charles G 1916- *WrDr 84*
Bell, Charles G 1929- *ConAu 37R*
Bell, Charles Greenleaf 1916- *ConAu 1R, –2NR, ConP 80, IntAu&W 82*
Bell, Clive 1881-1964 *ConAu 89, –97, LongCTC, ModBrL, TwCA[port], TwCA SUP*
Bell, Colin John 1938- *ConAu 29R*

Bell, Corydon Whitten 1894- *ConAu 5R, SmATA 3*
Bell, Cyrus *IntAu&W 82X*
Bell, Daniel 1919- *ConAu 1R, –4NR, ConIsC 2[port], DcLEL 1940, WorAu 1970, WrDr 84*
Bell, David R 1932- *ConAu 93*
Bell, David S 1945- *ConAu 61*
Bell, David Victor John 1944- *ConAu 1NR, –45*
Bell, Derrick Albert, Jr. 1930- *ConAu 104*
Bell, Donald 1934- *CreCan 2*
Bell, Earl H 1903-1963 *ConAu 1R*
Bell, Eileen 1907- *ConAu 33R*
Bell, Elizabeth Rose 1912- *ConAu 106*
Bell, Elliot V 1902-1983 *ConAu 108*
Bell, Emily Mary *ConAu X, SmATA X*
Bell, Eric Temple 1883-1960 *TwCA SUP*
Bell, Forest Stirling *DrAP&F 83*
Bell, Gail Winther 1936- *ConAu 41R*
Bell, Gerald D 1937- *ConAu 49*
Bell, Gertrude 1911- *ConAu 13R, SmATA 12*
Bell, Gertrude Margaret Lowthian 1868-1926 *LongCTC*
Bell, Gina *ConAu X, SmATA 7*
Bell, Gordon Bennett 1934- *ConAu 104*
Bell, Harold Idris 1879-1967 *ConAu P-1*
Bell, Harry 1899- *WrDr 84*
Bell, Harry McAra 1899- *ConAu P-1*
Bell, Irene Wood 1944- *ConAu 89*
Bell, J Bowyer 1931- *ConAu 17R*
Bell, Jack L 1904-1975 *ConAu 1R, –6NR, –61*
Bell, James 1917- *ConAu 73*
Bell, James B 1932- *ConAu 101*
Bell, James Edward 1941- *ConAu 33R, IntAu&W 82, WrDr 84*
Bell, James Kenton 1937- *ConAu 25R, WrDr 84*
Bell, Janet *ConAu X, SmATA X*
Bell, John *ConAu X*
Bell, John 1944- *ConAu 97*
Bell, John C 1902?-1981 *ConAu 103*
Bell, John Elderkin 1913- *ConAu 81*
Bell, John Joy 1871-1934 *LongCTC*
Bell, John Patrick 1935- *ConAu 101*
Bell, Joseph 1837-1911 *LongCTC*
Bell, Joseph N 1921- *ConAu 5R*
Bell, Josephine *WrDr 84*
Bell, Josephine 1897- *ConAu X, TwCCr&M 80*
Bell, Joyce *WrDr 84*
Bell, Joyce 1920- *ConAu 8NR, –57*
Bell, Joyce Denebrink 1936- *ConAu 17R*
Bell, L Nelson 1894-1973 *ConAu 45, ConAu P-1*
Bell, Leland V 1934- *ConAu 49*
Bell, Leslie Richard 1906-1962 *CreCan 2*
Bell, Louise Price *ConAu P-1*
Bell, Mackenzie 1856-1930 *TwCA[port]*
Bell, Margaret Elizabeth 1898- *ConAu 1R, –1NR, SmATA 2*
Bell, Martin 1918- *DcLEL 1940*
Bell, Marvin *DrAP&F 83*
Bell, Marvin 1937- *ConAu 21R, ConLC 8, ConP 80, CroCAP, DcLB 5[port], IntWWP 82, WorAu 1970, WrDr 84*
Bell, Mary Hayley *ConAu X*
Bell, Michael Davitt 1941- *ConAu 81*
Bell, Michael Steven *DrAP&F 83*
Bell, Neil 1887-1964 *LongCTC, TwCA, TwCA SUP*
Bell, Norman 1899- *ConAu 61, SmATA 11*
Bell, Norman W 1928- *ConAu 1R, –1NR*
Bell, Oliver 1913- *ConAu 53*
Bell, Philip W 1924- *ConAu 29R*
Bell, Quentin 1910- *ConAu 57, WorAu 1970, WrDr 84*
Bell, R C 1917- *ConAu 7NR, –17R*
Bell, Raymond M 1907- *WrDr 84*
Bell, Raymond Martin 1907- *ConAu 29R, SmATA 13*
Bell, Robert 1942- *ConAu 101*
Bell, Robert Charles 1917- *IntAu&W 82, WrDr 84*
Bell, Robert Eugene 1914- *ConAu 37R, IntAu&W 82, WrDr 84*
Bell, Robert Roy 1924- *ConAu 1R, –1NR*
Bell, Robert Stanley Warren 1871-1921 *SmATA 27*
Bell, Robert Vaughn 1924- *ConAu 110*
Bell, Rose 1939- *ConAu 29R*
Bell, Rudolph M 1942- *ConAu 45*
Bell, Sallie Lee Riley *ConAu 1R, –1NR*
Bell, Sarah Fore 1920- *ConAu 53*

Bell, Sidney 1929- *ConAu 41R*
Bell, Stephen 1935- *ConAu 65*
Bell, Steve *MichAu 80*
Bell, Thelma Harrington 1896- *ConAu 1R,
   SmATA 3*
Bell, Thornton *ConAu X, ConSFA*
Bell, Vanessa 1879-1961 *LongCTC*
Bell, Vicars Walker 1904- *ConAu P-1,
   IntAu&W 82, LongCTC*
Bell, Wendell 1924- *ConAu 1R, –4NR*
Bell, Whitfield Jenks, Jr. 1914- *ConAu 105*
Bell, William 1924-1948 *DcLEL 1940*
Bell, William J *AuNews 1*
Bell, William Stewart 1921- *ConAu 1R*
Bell, Winifred 1914- *ConAu 9NR, –17R*
Bell-Smith, Frederick Martlett 1846-1923
   CreCan 2
Bell-Villada, Gene Harold 1941- *ConAu 105*
Bell-Zano, Gina *ConAu X, SmATA 7*
Bellah, James Warner 1899-1976 *ConAu 5R, –69,
   TwCA, TwCA SUP, TwCWW*
Bellah, Robert N 1927- *ConAu 21R*
Bellairs, Angus D'Albini 1918- *WrDr 84*
Bellairs, George 1902- *ConAu X,
   TwCCr&M 80*
Bellairs, John 1938- *ConAu 8NR, –21R,
   IntAu&W 82, SmATA 2, WrDr 84*
Bellak, Leopold 1916- *ConAu 85*
Bellam, Ruben Carl 1918- *IntAu&W 82*
Bellamann, Henry 1882-1945 *TwCA,
   TwCA SUP*
Bellamy, Edward 1850-1898 *TwCSFW*
Bellamy, Francis Rufus 1886-1972 *ConAu 33R*
Bellamy, Guy 1935- *ConAu 9NR, –65*
Bellamy, Harmon *ConAu X*
Bellamy, James A 1925- *ConAu 49*
Bellamy, Joe David *DrAP&F 83*
Bellamy, Joe David 1941- *ConAu 41R*
Bellamy, Ralph 1904- *ConAu 101*
Bellan, Ruben Carl 1918- *ConAu 13R,
   WrDr 84*
Bellancourt, Max Edmond Henri 1920-
   IntAu&W 82
Bellefleur, Leon 1910- *CreCan 1*
Bellegarde, Ida Rowland 1904- *IntWWP 82*
Bellem, Robert Leslie 1902-1968 *TwCCr&M 80*
Beller, Anne Scott *ConAu 77*
Beller, Elmer Adolph 1894-1980 *ConAu 97*
Beller, Jacob 1896- *ConAu P-2*
Beller, William Stern 1919- *ConAu 5R*
Bellerby, Frances 1899-1975 *ConAu 101*
Bellhouse, Alan Robert 1914- *IntAu&W 82*
Bellhouse, Alan Robert 1914-1980 *ConAu 108*
Belli, Angela 1935- *ConAu 37R*
Belli, Carlos German 1927- *IntWWP 82*
Belli, Melvin M 1907- *ConAu 104*
Bellido, Jose Maria 1922- *CIDMEL 80,
   ModWD*
Bellin, Edward J *ConAu X*
Bellinger, Cindy *DrAP&F 83*
Bellis, David James 1944- *ConAu 108*
Bellman, Richard 1920- *ConAu 69*
Bellman, Samuel I 1926- *WrDr 84*
Bellman, Samuel Irving 1926- *ConAu 7NR, –17R*
Belloc, Hilaire 1870-1953 *CnMWL, ConAu 106,
   EncWL 2, LongCTC, ModBrL,
   ModBrL SUP, TwCA, TwCA SUP,
   TwCCW 83, TwCLC 7[port], TwCWr*
Belloc, M A *ConAu X*
Belloc Lowndes *TwCA, TwCA SUP*
Bellochio, Marco 1939- *ConAu 110*
Bellocq, Louise *ConAu X*
Bellone, Enrico 1938- *ConAu 106*
Bellow, Saul *DrAP&F 83*
Bellow, Saul 1915- *AuNews 2, CnMWL,
   ConAu 5R, ConDr 82, ConLC 1, –2, –3, –6,
   –8, –10, –13, –15, –25[port], ConNov 82,
   CroCD, DcLB DS3[port], –Y82A[port], –2,
   DcLEL 1940, EncWL 2[port], LongCTC,
   ModAL, ModAL SUP, TwCA SUP,
   TwCWr, WhoTwCL, WrDr 84*
Bellows, James G 1922- *ConAu 102*
Bellows, Roger Marion 1905- *ConAu 1R*
Bellows, Thomas J 1935- *ConAu 45*
Belmont, Eleanor Robson 1879-1979 *ConAu 97*
Belmont, Georges 1909- *ConAu 29R*
Belmont, Herman S 1920- *ConAu 41R*
Belmonte, Thomas 1946- *ConAu 93*
Beloff, Lord 1913- *WrDr 84*
Beloff, Max 1913- *ConAu 5R, IntAu&W 82,
   LongCTC*
Beloff, Michael 1942- *ConAu 21R*

Beloff, Nora *WrDr 84*
Beloff, Nora 1919- *ConAu 106, IntAu&W 82*
Belok, Michael Victor 1923- *ConAu 33R*
Beloof, Robert *IntWWP 82X*
Beloof, Robert Lawrence 1923- *ConAu 21R,
   IntWWP 82, WrDr 84*
Belote, James H 1922- *ConAu 33R*
Belote, Julianne 1929- *ConAu 61*
Belote, William Milton 1922- *ConAu 49*
Belous, Russell E 1925- *ConAu 25R*
Belov, Vasily Ivanovich 1932- *CIDMEL 80*
Belozersky, Andrei 1905-1972 *ConAu 37R*
Belpre, Pura 1899-1982 *ConAu 109, –73,
   SmATA 16, –30N*
Belsen, Patricia *IntAu&W 82X, IntWWP 82X*
Belser, Lee 1925- *ConAu 73*
Belser, Reimond Karel Maria De *ConLC 14*
Belshaw, Cyril S 1921- *ConAu 9R*
Belshaw, Michael 1928- *ConAu 21R*
Belshaw, Sheila Margaret 1925- *IntAu&W 82*
Belsley, David A 1939- *ConAu 29R*
Belting, Natalia Maree 1915- *ConAu 1R, –3NR,
   SmATA 6*
Belton, John Raynor 1931- *ConAu 69,
   SmATA 22[port]*
Beltrametti, Franco 1937- *IntWWP 82*
Beltran, Miriam 1914- *ConAu 33R*
Beltran, Pedro 1897-1979 *ConAu 85, –93*
Belushi, John 1949-1982 *ConAu 106*
Belveal, L Dee 1918- *ConAu 21R*
Belvedere, Lee *ConAu X, IntAu&W 82X,
   SmATA 7, WrDr 84*
Belville, Cheryl Walsh 1944- *ConAu 109*
Bely, Andrey 1880-1934 *CIDMEL 80, CnMWL,
   ConAu X, EncWL 2, ModSL 1,
   TwCLC 7[port], WhoTwCL, WorAu*
Bely, Jeanette L 1916- *ConAu 33R*
Belyaev, Aleksandr 1884-1942 *TwCSFW A*
Belz, Carl 1937- *ConAu 11NR, –29R*
Belz, Herman Julius 1937- *ConAu 65*
Bemberg, George 1915- *IntAu&W 82*
Bemelmans, Ludwig 1898-1962 *ChlLR 6[port],
   ConAu 73, DcLB 22[port], LongCTC,
   SmATA 15, TwCA, TwCA SUP,
   TwCCW 83, TwCWr*
Bemis, Samuel Flagg 1891-1973 *ConAu 9R, –45,
   DcLB 17[port], TwCA, TwCA SUP*
Bemister, Henry *ConAu X, IntAu&W 82X*
Ben, Ilke *ConAu X*
Ben-Amos, Dan 1934- *ConAu 11NR, –69*
Ben-Avraham, Chofetz Chaim *ConAu X*
Ben-Dov, Meir *ConAu X*
Ben-Ephraim *IntWWP 82X*
Ben-Ezer, Ehud 1936- *ConAu 8NR, –61,
   IntWWP 82*
Ben-Gurion, David 1886-1973 *ConAu 101, –45*
Ben-Horav, Naphthali *ConAu 49*
Ben-Horin, Meir 1918- *ConAu 29R, WrDr 84*
Ben-Israel-Kidron, Hedva *ConAu 33R*
Ben-Jochannan, Yosef 1918- *ConAu 69*
Ben Shimon Halevi, Zev *WrDr 84*
Ben-Yosef, Avraham Chaim *WrDr 84*
Ben-Yosef, Avraham Chaim 1917- *ConAu X*
Benagh, Jim 1937- *ConAu 9NR, –57,
   MichAu 80*
Benamou, Michel J 1929-1978 *ConAu 3NR, –5R*
Benante, Joseph P 1936- *ConAu 33R*
Benarde, Melvin A 1923- *ConAu 25R*
Benarde, Melvin Albert 1924- *WrDr 84*
Benardete, Jane Johnson 1930- *ConAu 45*
Benario, Herbert W 1929- *ConAu 25R*
Benarria, Allan *ConAu X*
Benary, Margot *ConAu X, SmATA X*
Benary-Isbert, Margot 1889-1979 *ConAu 4NR,
   –5R, –89, ConLC 12, SmATA 2, –21N*
Benasutti, Marion 1908- *ConAu 21R,
   SmATA 6, WrDr 84*
Benatar, Stephen 1937- *ConAu 110*
Benavente, Jacinto 1866-1954 *CIDMEL 80,
   CnMD, ConAu 106, EncWL 2, ModRL,
   ModWD, TwCLC 3, TwCWr*
Benavente Y Martinez, Jacinto 1866-1954
   LongCTC, TwCA, TwCA SUP
Bence, Evelyn *ConAu 110*
Bence-Jones, Mark 1930- *ConAu 5NR, –13R,
   WrDr 84*
Benchley, Nathaniel 1915-1981 *TwCCW 83*
Benchley, Nathaniel Goddard 1915-1981
   *ConAu 1R, –2NR, –105, IntAu&W 82,
   SmATA 25[port], –28N, –3, WorAu*
Benchley, Peter 1940- *WrDr 84*
Benchley, Peter B 1940- *AuNews 2,*

ConAu 17R, ConLC 4, –8, SmATA 3
Benchley, Robert Charles 1889-1945 *ConAmA,
   ConAu 105, LongCTC, ModAL, TwCA,
   TwCA SUP, TwCLC 1, TwCWr*
Benda, Harry J 1919- *ConAu 9R*
Benda, Julien 1867-1956 *CIDMEL 80,
   LongCTC, ModFrL, TwCA, TwCA SUP*
Bendavid, Avrom 1942- *ConAu 41R*
Bendelac, Alegria 1928- *IntWWP 82*
Bender, Coleman 1921- *WrDr 84*
Bender, Coleman C 1921- *ConAu 33R*
Bender, David R 1942- *ConAu 102*
Bender, Frederic L 1943- *ConAu 69*
Bender, Hans 1919- *CIDMEL 80, ModGL*
Bender, Henry E, Jr. 1937- *ConAu 33R*
Bender, James F 1905- *ConAu 17R*
Bender, Jan O 1909- *IntAu&W 82*
Bender, Jay *ConAu X*
Bender, John B 1940- *ConAu 65*
Bender, Louis W 1927- *ConAu 33R*
Bender, Lucy Ellen 1942- *ConAu 25R,
   SmATA 22[port]*
Bender, Marylin 1925- *ConAu 21R*
Bender, Richard 1930- *ConAu 45*
Bender, Robert M 1936- *ConAu 33R*
Bender, Ross Thomas 1929- *ConAu 61*
Bender, Stephen 1942- *ConAu 61*
Bender, Thomas 1944- *ConAu 73*
Bender, Todd K 1936- *ConAu 9NR, –21R,
   WrDr 84*
Benderly, Beryl Lieff 1943- *ConAu 108*
Bendick, Jeanne 1919- *ChlLR 5[port],
   ConAu 2NR, –5R, SmATA 2*
Bendick, Robert L 1917- *ConAu 61,
   SmATA 11*
Bendiner, Elmer 1916- *ConAu 7NR, –57*
Bendiner, Robert 1909- *ConAu 9R,
   IntAu&W 82, WrDr 84*
Bendit, Gladys Williams 1889?- *ConAu P-1*
Bendit, Laurence John 1898-1974 *ConAu P-2*
Bendix, Frances *DrAP&F 83*
Bendix, Reinhard 1916- *ConAu 1R, –4NR,
   WrDr 84*
Bendixson, Terence 1934- *ConAu 93, WrDr 84*
Benedek, Istvan 1915- *IntAu&W 82*
Benedek, Therese 1892-1977 *ConAu 41R*
Benedetti, David *DrAP&F 83*
Benedetti, David T 1948- *IntWWP 82*
Benedetti, Mario 1920- *EncWL 2, IntWWP 82,
   ModLAL*
Benedetti, Robert L 1939- *ConAu 29R*
Benedetto, Antonio Di 1922- *ModLAL*
Benedetto, Arnold J 1916-1966 *ConAu 5R*
Benedict, Bertram 1892-1978 *ConAu 77*
Benedict, Burton 1923- *ConAu 109*
Benedict, Dianne 1941- *ConAu 110*
Benedict, Dorothy Potter 1889-1979 *ConAu 93,
   ConAu P-1, SmATA 11, –23N*
Benedict, Elinor *DrAP&F 83*
Benedict, Joseph *ConAu X*
Benedict, Lois Trimble 1902-1967 *ConAu P-2,
   SmATA 12*
Benedict, Marion 1923- *ConAu 109*
Benedict, Michael Les 1945- *ConAu 45*
Benedict, Rex 1920- *TwCCW 83, WrDr 84*
Benedict, Rex Arthur 1920- *ConAu 17R,
   SmATA 8*
Benedict, Robert P 1924- *ConAu 41R*
Benedict, Ruth Fulton 1887-1948 *TwCA SUP*
Benedict, Stewart H 1924- *ConAu 13R,
   SmATA 26[port]*
Benedictus, David 1938- *WrDr 84*
Benedictus, David Henry 1938- *ConAu 73,
   ConNov 82, DcLB 14[port], DcLEL 1940*
Benedikt, Michael *DrAP&F 83*
Benedikt, Michael 1935- *ConAu 7NR, –13R,
   ConLC 4, –14, ConP 80, CroCAP,
   DcLB 5[port], DcLEL 1940, IntAu&W 82,
   IntWWP 82, WrDr 84*
Benediktsson, Einar 1864-1940 *CIDMEL 80*
Benediktsson, Jakob 1907- *IntAu&W 82*
Benefield, Barry 1877- *TwCA, TwCA SUP*
Benefield, June 1921- *ConAu 45*
Benell, Julie 1906?-1982 *ConAu 105*
Benelli, Sem 1877-1949 *CIDMEL 80, CnMD,
   ModWD*
Benello, C George 1926- *ConAu 33R*
Benes, Jan 1936- *ASpks, ConAu 29R*
Benesch, Kurt 1926- *CroCD*
Benesova, Bozena 1873-1936 *ModSL 2*
Benet, Edouard *ConAu X*
Benet, James 1914- *ConAu 8NR, –61*

Benet, Juan 1927- *ClDMEL 80*
Benet, Laura 1884-1979 *ConAu 6NR, -9R, -85, SmATA 23N, -3*
Benet, Mary Kathleen 1943- *ConAu 57, WrDr 84*
Benet, Stephen Vincent 1898-1943 *CnMWL, ConAmA, ConAu 104, DcLB 4, EncWL 2, LongCTC, ModAL, TwCA, TwCA SUP, TwCLC 7[port], TwCSFW, TwCWr, WhoTwCL*
Benet, Sula 1903- *ConAu 89, SmATA 21[port]*
Benet, Sula 1903?-1982 *SmATA 33N*
Benet, Sula 1906-1982 *ConAu 108*
Benet, William Rose 1886-1950 *ConAmA, LongCTC, TwCA, TwCA SUP*
Benetar, Judith 1941- *ConAu 53, WrDr 84*
Benevolo, Leonardo 1923- *ConAu 89*
Benezra, Barbara 1921- *ConAu 13R, SmATA 10*
Benfield, Derek 1926- *ConAu 10NR, -21R, IntAu&W 82*
Benfield, Richard E 1940- *ConAu 77*
Benford, Gregory 1941- *ConAu 69, DcLB Y82B[port], DrmM[port], IntAu&W 82, TwCSFW, WrDr 84*
Benford, Harry 1917- *ConAu 89, IntAu&W 82*
Benford, Timothy B 1941- *ConAu 11NR, -69*
Benge, Eugene J 1896- *ConAu 9NR, -57*
Bengelsdorf, Irving S 1922- *ConAu 57*
Bengengruen, Werner 1892-1964 *ModGL*
Bengis, Ingrid *DrAP&F 83*
Bengtson, John Erik Robert 1938- *IntAu&W 82*
Bengtson, Vern L 1941- *ConAu 4NR, -49, WrDr 84*
Bengtsson, Arvid 1916- *ConAu 33R*
Bengtsson, Frans Gunnar 1894-1954 *EncWL 2*
Benguerel I Llobet, Xavier 1905- *ClDMEL 80*
Benham, Leslie 1922- *ConAu 9R*
Benham, Lois 1924- *ConAu 9R*
Benham, Mary Lile 1914- *ConAu 102*
Benichou, Paul 1908- *ConAu 57*
Benington, John 1921- *ConAu 5R*
Beniuc, Mihai 1907- *IntAu&W 82*
Benjamin, Alice *ConAu X*
Benjamin, Anna Shaw 1925- *ConAu 41R*
Benjamin, Annette Francis 1928- *ConAu 17R*
Benjamin, Bry 1924- *ConAu 17R*
Benjamin, Burton Richard 1917- *ConAu 101*
Benjamin, Claude 1911- *ConAu 9R*
Benjamin, David *IntWWP 82X*
Benjamin, Edward Bernard 1897- *ConAu 69*
Benjamin, Gerald 1945- *ConAu 49*
Benjamin, Harry 1885- *ConAu P-1*
Benjamin, Herbert S 1922- *ConAu 5R*
Benjamin, Joseph 1921- *ConAu 57*
Benjamin, Laszlo 1915- *EncWL 2*
Benjamin, Lewis Saul 1874-1932 *LongCTC*
Benjamin, Nora *ConAu X*
Benjamin, Philip 1922-1966 *ConAu 5R, -25R*
Benjamin, Ralph *WrDr 84*
Benjamin, Robert 1949- *ConAu 109*
Benjamin, Roger W 1942- *ConAu 37R*
Benjamin, Ruth *DrAP&F 83*
Benjamin, Stanley L 1895- *MichAu 80*
Benjamin, Walter 1892-1940 *ClDMEL 80, EncWL 2[port], ModGL, WorAu 1970*
Benjamin, William Evarts 1942- *ConAu 25R*
Benjaminson, Peter 1945- *ConAu 73*
Benji, Thomas *ConAu 49*
Benko, Nancy *WrDr 84*
Benko, Stephen 1924- *ConAu 9R, IntAu&W 82*
Benkovitz, Miriam J 1911- *ConAu 4NR, -9R, IntAu&W 82, WrDr 84*
Benn, Anthony Wedgwood 1925- *WrDr 84*
Benn, Caroline DeCamp Wedgwood 1926- *ConAu 1R*
Benn, Gottfried 1886-1956 *ClDMEL 80, CnMWL, ConAu 106, EncWL 2[port], ModGL, TwCLC 3, WhoTwCL, WorAu*
Benn, Matthew *ConAu X, WrDr 84*
Bennani, B M 1946- *ConAu 61*
Bennani, Ben *DrAP&F 83*
Benne, Kenneth Dean 1908- *ConAu 33R, WrDr 84*
Bennell, Florence B 1912- *ConAu 33R*
Benner, Ralph Eugene 1932- *ConAu 33R*
Bennett, A E 1898- *ConAu 65, WrDr 84*
Bennett, Addison C 1918- *ConAu 5R, -7NR*
Bennett, Adrian A 1941- *ConAu 53*
Bennett, Alan 1934- *ConAu 103, ConDr 82, DcLEL 1940, WrDr 84*

Bennett, Alice *ConAu X*
Bennett, Amy Foley 1939- *IntWWP 82*
Bennett, Anna Elizabeth 1914- *ConAu 17R*
Bennett, Archibald F 1896- *ConAu P-1*
Bennett, Arnold 1867-1931 *CnMD, CnMWL, ConAu 106, DcLB 10[port], EncWL 2, LongCTC, ModBrL, ModBrL SUP, ModWD, TwCA, TwCA SUP, TwCLC 5[port], TwCWr, WhoTwCL*
Bennett, Bruce *DrAP&F 83*
Bennett, Bruce 1952- *ConAu 110*
Bennett, Bruce Lanyon 1917- *ConAu 25R*
Bennett, Charles 1901- *ConAu P-1*
Bennett, Charles 1932- *ConAu 25R*
Bennett, Charles Edward 1910- *ConAu 9R, IntAu&W 82*
Bennett, Christine *ConAu X*
Bennett, Daniel *ConAu X*
Bennett, Daphne Nicholson *ConAu 41R*
Bennett, David H 1935- *ConAu 25R*
Bennett, Dennis J 1917- *ConAu 49*
Bennett, Dorothea *ConAu X, SmATA X*
Bennett, Dwight *ConAu X, TwCWW, WrDr 84*
Bennett, Edward 1924- *ConAu 5R*
Bennett, Edward M 1927- *ConAu 33R, IntAu&W 82, WrDr 84*
Bennett, Elizabeth Deare *WrDr 84*
Bennett, Ernest Walter 1921- *WrDr 84*
Bennett, Ethel Mary Granger 1891- *ConAu P-1*
Bennett, Frances Grant 1899- *ConAu P-2*
Bennett, Fredna W 1906- *ConAu P-1*
Bennett, Gary L *DrAP&F 83*
Bennett, Geoffrey 1909-1983 *ConAu 110*
Bennett, Geoffrey Martin 1909- *ConAu 13R, IntAu&W 82, WrDr 84*
Bennett, George 1920- *ConAu 5R*
Bennett, George Harold 1930- *ConAu 97*
Bennett, Gertrude Ryder *ConAu 53, IntAu&W 82, IntWWP 82, WrDr 84*
Bennett, Gordon A 1940- *ConAu 29R*
Bennett, Gordon C *DrAP&F 83*
Bennett, Gordon C 1935- *ConAu 33R*
Bennett, Gwendolyn B 1902- *LivgBAA*
Bennett, H O *IntAu&W 82X, WrDr 84*
Bennett, H S 1889- *LongCTC*
Bennett, Hal *ConAu X, DrAP&F 83*
Bennett, Hal 1930- *LivgBAA*
Bennett, Hal 1936- *ConLC 5, WrDr 84*
Bennett, Hall *ConAu X*
Bennett, Harold 1936- *ConAu 41R*
Bennett, Howard Franklin 1911- *ConAu 1R*
Bennett, Isadora 1900-1980 *ConAu 93*
Bennett, Jack Arthur Walter 1911-1981 *ConAu 6NR, -9R, -103*
Bennett, James D 1926- *ConAu 61*
Bennett, James Richard 1932- *ConAu 33R, WrDr 84*
Bennett, James Thomas 1942- *ConAu 106*
Bennett, Jay 1912- *ConAu 11NR, -69, SmATA 27*
Bennett, Jean Frances *ConAu X*
Bennett, Jeremy *ConAu X*
Bennett, Jill 1947- *ConAu 106*
Bennett, Joan 1896- *LongCTC, WrDr 84*
Bennett, John *DrAP&F 83*
Bennett, John 1920- *ConAu 29R, IntWWP 82, WrDr 84*
Bennett, John Jerome Nelson 1939- *ConAu 21R*
Bennett, John M *DrAP&F 83*
Bennett, John Michael 1942- *ConAu 2NR, -49, IntAu&W 82, IntWWP 82*
Bennett, John W 1918- *ConAu 69*
Bennett, John William 1915- *ConAu 1R, -4NR*
Bennett, Jonathan 1930- *ConAu 1NR, -45*
Bennett, Joseph D 1922-1972 *ConAu 1R, -33R*
Bennett, Josephine Waters 1899-1975 *ConAu 1R, -103, DcLEL 1940*
Bennett, Judith d1979 *ConAu 85*
Bennett, Kay Curley 1922- *ConAu 17R*
Bennett, Lerone, Jr. 1928- *ConAu 2NR, -45, LivgBAA*
Bennett, Louise *WrDr 84*
Bennett, Louise 1919- *ConP 80*
Bennett, Margaret E 1893- *ConAu 5R*
Bennett, Margot *ConSFA*
Bennett, Margot 1912-1980 *ConAu 105, TwCCr&M 80*
Bennett, Marion T 1914- *ConAu 9R*
Bennett, Melba Berry 1901-1968 *ConAu P-2*
Bennett, Meridan 1927- *ConAu 25R*
Bennett, Michael 1943- *ConAu 101,*

Bennett, Mildred R 1909- *ConAu P-2*
Bennett, Neville 1937- *ConAu 102, WrDr 84*
Bennett, Noel 1939- *ConAu 45*
Bennett, Norman Robert 1932- *ConAu 3NR, -9R*
Bennett, Paul *DrAP&F 83*
Bennett, Paul Lewis 1921- *ConAu 1R, -4NR, IntWWP 82*
Bennett, Penelope Agnes 1938- *ConAu 13R*
Bennett, Rachel *ConAu X*
Bennett, Rainey 1907- *SmATA 15*
Bennett, Richard 1899- *SmATA 21*
Bennett, Rita 1934- *ConAu 69*
Bennett, Robert A 1927- *ConAu 5NR, -13R*
Bennett, Robert L 1931- *ConAu 41R*
Bennett, Robert Russell 1894-1981 *ConAu 105*
Bennett, Russell H 1896- *SmATA 25*
Bennett, Scott 1939- *ConAu 33R*
Bennett, Thomas L 1942- *ConAu 85*
Bennett, Victor 1919- *ConAu 5R, -7NR*
Bennett, Will *DrAP&F 83*
Bennett, William 1941- *ConAu 107*
Bennett, William L 1924- *ConAu 17R*
Bennett, William Robert 1921- *ConAu 13R*
Bennett-Coverley, Louise 1919- *ConAu 97*
Bennett-England, Rodney 1936- *WrDr 84*
Bennett-England, Rodney Charles 1936- *ConAu 61*
Bennetts, Pamela 1922- *ConAu 37R, IntAu&W 82, TwCRGW, WrDr 84*
Bennie, William Andrew 1921- *ConAu 69*
Benning, Lee Edwards 1934- *ConAu 53*
Bennion, Barbara Elisabeth 1930- *ConAu 110*
Bennion, Elisabeth 1930- *WrDr 84*
Bennis, Warren 1925- *WrDr 84*
Bennis, Warren G 1925- *ConAu 5NR, -53*
Benoff, Mac 1915?-1972 *ConAu 37R*
Benoist-Mechin, Jacques 1901- *ConAu 105*
Benoist-Mechin, Jacques 1901-1983 *ConAu 109*
Benoit, Emile 1909- *WrDr 84*
Benoit, Emile 1910-1978 *ConAu 3NR, -5R, -77*
Benoit, Leroy James 1913- *ConAu 33R*
Benoit, Pierre 1886-1962 *ClDMEL 80, ConAu 93, TwCA, TwCA SUP*
Benoit, Pierre Maurice 1906- *ConAu 41R, CreCan 1*
Benoit, Real 1916- *CreCan 2*
Benoit, Richard 1899?-1969 *ConAu 104*
Benoliel, Jeanne Quint 1919- *ConAu 49*
Bense, Walter F 1932- *ConAu 1NR, -45*
Bensen, Alice R 1911- *ConAu 69, WrDr 84*
Bensen, Donald R 1927- *ConAu 5NR, -9R, ConSFA*
Bensen, Robert *DrAP&F 83*
Bensheimer, Virginia *DrAP&F 83*
Bensko, John 1949- *ConAu 105*
Bensman, Joseph 1922- *ConAu 10NR, -21R*
Bensol, Oscar *ConAu X, IntAu&W 82X*
Benson, A George 1924- *ConAu 69*
Benson, Arthur Christopher 1862-1925 *LongCTC, TwCA*
Benson, B A *ConAu X*
Benson, Ben 1915-1959 *TwCCr&M 80*
Benson, C Randolph 1923- *ConAu 29R*
Benson, Carmen 1921- *ConAu 57*
Benson, Charles S 1922- *ConAu 8NR, -17R*
Benson, Constantine Walter 1909-1982 *ConAu 108*
Benson, Daniel *ConAu X, WrDr 84*
Benson, Dennis C 1936- *ConAu 37R*
Benson, E F 1867-1940 *TwCCr&M 80*
Benson, Edward Frederic 1867-1940 *LongCTC, ModBrL, TwCA, TwCWr*
Benson, Elizabeth P 1924- *ConAu 93*
Benson, Eugene 1928- *ConAu 89*
Benson, Frank Atkinson 1921- *WrDr 84*
Benson, Frederick R 1934- *ConAu 33R, WrDr 84*
Benson, Frederick William 1948- *ConAu 101*
Benson, Gigi 1941- *ConAu 108*
Benson, Ginny *ConAu X*
Benson, Godfrey Rathbone 1864-1945 *TwCA, TwCA SUP*
Benson, Harry 1929- *ConAu 108*
Benson, Herbert 1935- *ConAu 85*
Benson, J L 1920- *ConAu 105*
Benson, Jackson J 1930- *ConAu 25R, WrDr 84*
Benson, Joyce Lorentzson *DrAP&F 83*
Benson, Kathleen 1947- *ConAu 85, IntAu&W 82*
Benson, Larry D 1929- *ConAu 37R*

Benson, Lyman 1909- *ConAu 49, IntAu&W 82, WrDr 84*
Benson, Margaret H Benson 1899- *ConAu 5R*
Benson, Mary 1919- *ConAu 1NR, -49, IntAu&W 82*
Benson, Maxine 1939- *ConAu 65*
Benson, Nathaniel Anketell 1903-1966 *CreCan 2*
Benson, Rachel *ConAu X*
Benson, Randolph 1923- *WrDr 84*
Benson, Richard *ConAu X*
Benson, Robert G 1930- *ConAu 29R*
Benson, Robert Hugh 1871-1914 *LongCTC, TwCA, TwCA SUP*
Benson, Robert Slater 1942- *ConAu 33R*
Benson, Rolf Eric 1951- *ConAu 102*
Benson, Ruth Crego 1937- *ConAu 41R*
Benson, Sally 1900-1972 *ConAu 37R, ConAu P-1, ConLC 17, SmATA 1, -27N, TwCA SUP*
Benson, Stella 1892-1933 *LongCTC, ModBrL, TwCA, TwCA SUP, TwCWr, WhoTwCL*
Benson, Stephana Vere 1909- *ConAu 13R*
Benson, Steve *DrAP&F 83*
Benson, Ted *ConAu X*
Benson, Theodora 1906-1968 *LongCTC*
Benson, Thomas Godfrey 1899- *ConAu P-1*
Benson, Thomas W 1937- *ConAu 29R*
Benson, Virginia 1923- *ConAu 57*
Benson, William Howard 1902- *ConAu 1R*
Bensted-Smith, Richard Brian 1929- *ConAu 13R*
Benstock, Bernard 1930- *ConAu 7NR, -17R, IntAu&W 82, WrDr 84*
Benstock, Shari 1944- *ConAu 97*
Bent, Alan Edward 1939- *ConAu 4NR, -49*
Bent, Charles N 1935- *ConAu 21R*
Bent, Rudyard K 1901- *ConAu 1R*
Bent, Silas 1882-1945 *TwCA, TwCA SUP*
Bent, Ted *DrAP&F 83*
Benteen, John *ConAu X*
Bentel, Pearl Bucklen 1901- *ConAu P-2*
Benthall, Jonathan Charles Mackenzie 1941- *ConAu 41R, IntAu&W 82*
Bentham, Frederick 1911- *ConAu 105*
Bentham, Jay *ConAu X*
Benthic, Arch E *ConAu X*
Benthul, Herman F 1911- *ConAu 33R*
Bentine, Michael *WrDr 84*
Bentley, Beth *DrAP&F 83*
Bentley, Beth 1928- *ConAu 101, IntWWP 82, WrDr 84*
Bentley, E C 1875-1956 *ConAu 108, TwCCr&M 80, TwCLC 12[port]*
Bentley, Edmund Clerihew 1875-1956 *LongCTC, TwCA, TwCA SUP, TwCWr*
Bentley, Eric 1916- *ConAu 5R, -6NR, ConDr 82, ConLC 24[port], ConLCrt 82, DcLEL 1940, TwCA SUP, WrDr 84*
Bentley, G E, Jr. 1930- *ConAu 1R, -4NR*
Bentley, Gerald Eades 1901- *ConAu 41R, WrDr 84*
Bentley, Gerald Eades, Jr. 1930- *IntAu&W 82*
Bentley, Howard Beebe 1925- *ConAu 9R*
Bentley, Mrs. James C *ConAu X*
Bentley, Janice Babb 1933- *ConAu 13R*
Bentley, Judith 1945- *ConAu 107*
Bentley, Margaret *WrDr 84*
Bentley, Margaret 1926- *ConAu 108*
Bentley, Nicolas Clerihew 1907-1978 *ConAu 11NR, -65, -81, LongCTC, SmATA 24N, TwCCr&M 80*
Bentley, Olive *IntWWP 82*
Bentley, Phyllis Eleanor 1894-1977 *ConAu 1R, -3NR, LongCTC, ModBrL, SmATA 25N, -6[port], TwCA[port], TwCA SUP, TwCCr&M 80, TwCWr*
Bentley, Sarah 1946- *ConAu 29R*
Bentley, Virginia W 1908- *ConAu 57*
Bentley-Taylor, David 1915- *ConAu 77*
Benton, Dorothy Gilchrist 1919- *ConAu 57*
Benton, Helen Hemingway 1902?-1974 *ConAu 104*
Benton, John Frederic 1931- *ConAu 69*
Benton, John W 1933- *ConAu 29R*
Benton, Josephine Moffett 1905- *ConAu 5R*
Benton, Kenneth 1909- *WrDr 84*
Benton, Kenneth Carter 1909- *ConAu 1NR, -49, IntAu&W 82, TwCCr&M 80*
Benton, Lewis R 1920- *ConAu 17R*
Benton, Nelson 1924- *ConAu 110*
Benton, Patricia 1907- *ConAu 5R, IntAu&W 82, WrDr 84*
Benton, Peggie 1906- *ConAu 49*

Benton, Peggie 1909- *WrDr 84*
Benton, Richard G 1938- *ConAu 81*
Benton, Robert *ConAu X*
Benton, Robert 1932- *ConAu 1R, -2NR, ConDr 82A*
Benton, Thomas Hart 1889-1975 *ConAu 53, -93*
Benton, Wilbourn Eugene 1917- *ConAu 1R*
Benton, Will *ConAu X*
Benton, William 1900-1973 *ConAu 41R, ConAu P-1*
Bentov, Itzhak 1923?-1979 *ConAu 85*
Bentov, Mordechai 1900- *IntAu&W 82*
Bentz, William F 1940- *ConAu 53*
Benveniste, Asa 1925- *ConAu 69, ConP 80, IntWWP 82, WrDr 84*
Benveniste, Guy 1927- *ConAu 8NR, -61*
Benveniste, Rachelle *DrAP&F 83*
Benvenisti, Meron 1934- *ConAu 65*
Benward, Bruce 1921- *ConAu 9NR*
Benward, Bruce Charles 1921- *ConAu 9R*
Beny, Roloff 1924- *ConAu X, CreCan 2, WrDr 84*
Beny, Wilfred Roy 1924- *ConAu 21R, CreCan 2*
Benyo, Richard 1946- *ConAu 77*
Benz, Ernst Wilhelm 1907- *ConAu 13R*
Benz, Frank L 1930- *ConAu 41R*
Benzie, William 1930- *ConAu 37R, WrDr 84*
Benziger, James 1914- *ConAu 13R*
Benzo-Mestre, Miguel 1922- *IntAu&W 82*
Benzoni, Juliette 1920- *ConAu 101*
Beorse, Bryn 1896- *ConAu 45*
Bequaert, Lucia H *ConAu 65*
Ber, Alice *CreCan 1*
Bera, Sudhir 1933- *IntWWP 82*
Beranek, Leo L 1914- *ConAu 5R*
Beranek, William 1922- *ConAu 5R*
Beranova, Jana 1932- *IntWWP 82*
Berard, J Aram 1933- *ConAu 17R*
Berardo, Felix M 1934- *ConAu 8NR, -57*
Berberova, Nina 1901- *ConAu 33R*
Berbrich, Joan D 1925- *ConAu 29R, WrDr 84*
Berbusse, Edward J 1912- *ConAu 21R*
Berch, William O *ConAu X*
Berchen, Ursula 1919- *ConAu 65*
Berchen, William 1920- *ConAu 65*
Berck, Martin G 1928- *ConAu 65*
Berckman, Evelyn Domenica 1900-1978 *ConAu 1R, -1NR, TwCCr&M 80, TwCRGW*
Bercovici, Konrad 1882-1961 *TwCA, TwCA SUP*
Bercovici, Rion 1903?-1976 *ConAu 69*
Bercovitch, Reuben 1923- *ConAu 104, IntAu&W 82*
Bercovitch, Sacvan 1933- *ConAu 41R*
Berczeller, Richard 1902- *ConAu 9R*
Berd, Francoise *CreCan 1*
Berdes, George R 1931- *ConAu 29R*
Berdie, Douglas R 1946- *ConAu 53*
Berdie, Ralph F 1916- *ConAu 17R*
Berdie, Ralph F 1916-1974 *ConAu 11NR*
Berding, Andrew H 1902- *ConAu X*
Berdyayev, Nikolay Aleksandrovich 1874-1948 *CIDMEL 80, LongCTC, TwCA, TwCA SUP*
Bere, Rennie Montague 1907- *ConAu 65, WrDr 84*
Bereday, George Z F 1920- *ConAu 1R, -4NR, IntAu&W 82*
Bereg, Eli *IntWWP 82X*
Berelson, Bernard R 1912-1979 *ConAu 3NR, -5R, -89*
Berelson, David 1943- *ConAu 25R*
Berelson, Howard 1940- *SmATA 5*
Berenbaum, Linda Bayer *ConAu X*
Berends, Hans Engel 1908- *CreCan 2*
Berends, Polly Berrien 1939- *ConAu 108*
Berendsohn, Walter A 1884- *ConAu 33R*
Berendt, Joachim Ernst 1922- *ConAu 69*
Berendzen, Richard 1938- *ConAu 85*
Berenson, Bernard 1865-1959 *LongCTC, TwCA SUP*
Berenson, Bernhard 1865-1959 *TwCA*
Berenson, Conrad 1930- *ConAu 9R*
Berenstain, Jan *SmATA 12*
Berenstain, Janice 1923- *ConAu 25R*
Berenstain, Michael 1951- *ConAu 97*
Berenstain, Stan 1923- *SmATA 12*
Berenstain, Stanley 1923- *ConAu 25R*
Berent, Waclaw 1873-1940 *CIDMEL 80, ModSL 2*

Bereny, Gail Rubin 1942- *ConAu 85*
Beresford, Anne 1929- *ConAu 97, ConP 80, IntWWP 82X, WrDr 84*
Beresford, Elisabeth *ConAu 102, IntAu&W 82, SmATA 25[port], TwCCW 83, TwCRGW, WrDr 84*
Beresford, J D 1873-1947 *TwCSFW*
Beresford, John Davys 1873-1947 *LongCTC, ModBrL, TwCA, TwCA SUP, TwCWr*
Beresford, Marcus 1919- *ConAu 108*
Beresford, Maurice 1920- *WrDr 84*
Beresford, Maurice Warwick 1920- *ConAu 13R*
Beresford-Howe, Constance 1922- *WrDr 84*
Beresford-Howe, Constance Elizabeth 1922- *AuNews 2, ConAu 53, CreCan 2, DcLEL 1940, IntAu&W 82*
Beresiner, Yasha 1940- *ConAu 69*
Beretta, Lia 1934- *ConAu 17R*
Berg, A Scott 1949- *ConAu 81, WrDr 84*
Berg, Alan D 1932- *ConAu 45*
Berg, Barry 1942- *NatPD 81[port]*
Berg, Bengt 1946- *IntAu&W 82*
Berg, Darrel E 1920- *ConAu 17R*
Berg, Dave *ConAu X*
Berg, Dave 1920- *ConAu X, SmATA X, WrDr 84*
Berg, David 1920- *ConAu 10NR, -21R, SmATA 27[port]*
Berg, Fred Anderson 1948- *ConAu 37R*
Berg, Frederick S 1928- *ConAu 53*
Berg, Friedrich Kantor *ConAu X*
Berg, Goesta 1903- *ConAu 69*
Berg, Hans Walter 1916- *IntAu&W 82*
Berg, Irwin August 1913- *ConAu 13R*
Berg, Ivar E, Jr. 1929- *ConAu 21R*
Berg, Jean Horton 1913- *ConAu 1R, -4NR, -53, SmATA 6*
Berg, Joan *ConAu X, SmATA X*
Berg, Keg *IntAu&W 82X*
Berg, Larry L 1939- *ConAu 41R*
Berg, Lasse 1943- *ConAu 73*
Berg, Leila 1917- *TwCCW 83, WrDr 84*
Berg, Leila Rita 1917- *ConAu 101, IntAu&W 82*
Berg, Louis 1901-1972 *ConAu 37R*
Berg, Maryleona 1922- *IntWWP 82*
Berg, Orley M 1918- *ConAu 17R*
Berg, Paul Conrad 1921- *ConAu 33R*
Berg, Rick 1951- *ConAu 93*
Berg, Rilla *IntAu&W 82X*
Berg, Stephen *DrAP&F 83*
Berg, Stephen 1934- *ConAu 8NR, -13R, ConP 80, DcLB 5[port], WrDr 84*
Berg, Thomas L 1930- *ConAu 69*
Berg, Viola Jacobson 1918- *ConAu 5NR, -53, IntAu&W 82*
Berg, William 1938- *ConAu 97*
Bergamin, Jose 1897- *CIDMEL 80*
Bergamini, David H 1928- *ConAu 1R*
Bergamini, David H 1928-1983 *ConAu 110*
Bergamini, John D 1925?-1982 *ConAu 108*
Bergaust, Erik 1925-1978 *ConAu 73, -77, SmATA 20*
Berge, Carol *DrAP&F 83, WrDr 84*
Berge, Carol 1928- *ConAu 7NR, -13R, ConP 80*
Berge, H C Ten *IntWWP 82X*
Berge, Hans Cornelis Ten 1938- *IntWWP 82*
Bergel, Egon Ernst 1894-1969 *ConAu P-2*
Bergel, Hans 1925- *IntAu&W 82*
Bergelson, Dovid 1884-1952 *EncWL 2*
Bergen, Polly 1930- *ConAu 69*
Bergendoff, Conrad John Immanuel 1895- *ConAu 33R*
Bergengruen, Werner 1892-1964? *CIDMEL 80, TwCWr, WorAu*
Berger, Andrew John 1915- *ConAu 41R*
Berger, Arthur A 1933- *ConAu 25R, WrDr 84*
Berger, Arthur Asa 1933- *ConAu 10NR*
Berger, Bennett Maurice 1926- *ConAu 1R, -4NR*
Berger, Carl 1925- *ConAu 9R*
Berger, Colonel *ConAu X*
Berger, Elmer 1908- *ConAu 61*
Berger, Evelyn Miller 1896- *ConAu 37R, WrDr 84*
Berger, H Jean 1924- *ConAu 13R*
Berger, Hans 1914- *IntAu&W 82*
Berger, Harry, Jr. 1924- *ConAu 110*
Berger, Hilbert J 1920- *ConAu 57*
Berger, Ivan 1939- *ConAu 97*
Berger, John 1926- *ConAu 81, ConLC 2, -19,*

ConNov 82, DcLB 14[port], DcLEL 1940,
ModBrL SUP, WorAu 1970, WrDr 84
Berger, John J 1945- ConAu 69
Berger, Josef 1903-1971 ConAu 5R, –33R
Berger, Joseph 1924- ConAu 41R
Berger, Klaus 1901- ConAu P-1
Berger, Marilyn 1935- ConAu 101
Berger, Marjorie Sue 1916- ConAu 13R
Berger, Mark L 1942- ConAu 109
Berger, Melvin H 1927- ConAu 4NR, –5R,
ConLC 12, SmATA 5
Berger, Michael Louis 1943- ConAu 77,
IntAu&W 82
Berger, Mogens 1933- IntAu&W 82
Berger, Morroe 1917-1981 ConAu 1R, –4NR,
–103
Berger, Nan 1914- WrDr 84
Berger, Peter Ludwig 1929- ConAu 1R, –1NR
Berger, Phil 1942- ConAu 61
Berger, Raimund 1917-1954 CroCD
Berger, Rainer 1930- ConAu 37R
Berger, Raoul 1901- ConAu 93
Berger, Raymond M 1950- ConAu 109
Berger, Rene Edgar Marcel 1915- IntAu&W 82
Berger, Robert W 1936- ConAu 49
Berger, Suzanne E DrAP&F 83
Berger, Suzanne E 1944- ConAu 105
Berger, Terry 1933- ConAu 37R, SmATA 8,
WrDr 84
Berger, Thomas 1924- ConAu 1R, –5NR,
ConLC 3, –5, –8, –11, –18, ConNov 82,
DcLB Y80A[port], –2, DcLEL 1940,
IntAu&W 82, ModAL SUP, TwCWW,
WorAu, WrDr 84
Berger, Yves 1933- TwCWr
Berger, Yves 1934- ConAu 85
Bergeret, Hugues CreCan 1
Bergeret, Ida Treat 1889?-1978 ConAu 77
Bergeron, David M 1938- ConAu 2NR, –45
Bergeron, Paul H 1938- ConAu 101
Bergeron, Suzanne 1930- CreCan 1
Bergeron, Victor 1902- ConAu 89
Bergeson, John B 1935- ConAu 69
Bergevin, Paul Emile 1906- ConAu 2NR, –5R
Bergey, Alyce 1934- ConAu 5R, –7NR
Bergfeld, Annabelle Wagner 1903- IntWWP 82
Berggolts, Olga Fyodorovna 1910-1975
CIDMEL 80
Bergh, Herman VanDen 1897-1967 CIDMEL 80
Berghahn, Volker R 1938- ConAu 103,
IntAu&W 82, WrDr 84
Bergie, Sigrid DrAP&F 83
Bergier, Jacques 1912-1978 ConAu 81, –85
Bergin, Allen E 1934- ConAu 45
Bergin, Kenneth Glenny 1911-1981 ConAu 103
Bergin, Thomas Goddard 1904- ConAu 3NR,
–9R
Bergman, Andrew TwCCr&M 80, WrDr 84
Bergman, Arlene Eisen 1942- ConAu 61
Bergman, Bernard Aaron 1894-1980 ConAu 102,
–97
Bergman, Bo Hjalmar 1869-1967 ConAu 25R
Bergman, David DrAP&F 83
Bergman, David 1950- ConAu 106
Bergman, Ernst Ingmar 1918- CIDMEL 80
Bergman, Floyd L 1927- ConAu 2NR, –49
Bergman, Hannah E 1925- ConAu 69
Bergman, Henry Eric 1893-1958 CreCan 2
Bergman, Hjalmar 1883-1931 CIDMEL 80,
EncWL 2
Bergman, Hjalmar Frederik 1883-1931 CnMD,
ModWD, WorAu
Bergman, Ingmar 1918- ConAu 81, ConLC 16
Bergman, Ingrid 1915-1982 ConAu 107
Bergman, Jay Asa 1948- ConAu 110
Bergman, Jules 1929- ConAu 108
Bergman, Samuel Hugo 1883-1975 ConAu 57
Bergman Sucksdorff, Astrid 1927- IntAu&W 82
Bergmann, A IntWWP 82X
Bergmann, Ernst W 1896?-1977 ConAu 69
Bergmann, Fred Louis 1916- ConAu 61
Bergmann, Frithjof H 1930- ConAu 101
Bergmann, Peter G 1915- ConAu 21R
Bergonzi, Bernard 1929- ConAu 8NR, –17R,
DcLEL 1940, IntAu&W 82, WrDr 84
Bergonzo, Jean Louis 1939- ConAu P-2
Bergquist, Laura 1918-1982 ConAu 108
Bergreen, Laurence R 1950- ConAu 104
Bergson, Abram 1914- ConAu 13R, WrDr 84
Bergson, Deirdre Levinson DrAP&F 83
Bergson, Henri 1859-1942 CIDMEL 80
Bergson, Henri Louis 1859-1941 EncWL 2,

LongCTC, ModFrL, TwCA, TwCA SUP,
TwCWr, WhoTwCL
Bergson, Leo ConAu X
Bergsson, Guobergur 1932- EncWL 2
Bergstein, Eleanor 1938- ConAu 5NR, –53,
ConLC 4
Bergsten, Gunilla Ulander 1933- IntAu&W 82
Bergsten, Staffan 1932- ConAu 6NR, –57,
IntAu&W 82
Bergstrom, Berit 1942- IntAu&W 82
Bergstrom, Louise 1914- ConAu 29R
Bergstrom, Vera IntWWP 82X
Bergstrom, Vera Ramona 1909- IntWWP 82
Beringause, Arthur F 1919- ConAu 33R
Beringer, Richard E 1933- ConAu 81
Berisal IntAu&W 82X
Beristain, Antonio 1924- IntAu&W 82
Berk, Fred 1911?-1980 ConAu 97
Berke, Joel S 1936-1981 ConAu 110
Berke, Joel Sommers 1936-1981 ConAu 105
Berke, Joseph H 1939- ConAu 57
Berke, Judie 1938- IntAu&W 82
Berke, Judith A DrAP&F 83
Berke, Nancy L DrAP&F 83
Berke, Roberta 1943- ConAu 106
Berkebile, Don H 1926- ConAu 8NR, –61
Berkebile, Fred D 1900-1978 ConAu 5R, –103,
SmATA 26N
Berkelaar, Willy IntWWP 82X
Berkeley, Anthony 1893-1970 ConAu X,
LongCTC, TwCA, TwCA SUP
Berkeley, Anthony 1893-1971 TwCCr&M 80
Berkeley, David S 1917- ConAu 41R
Berkeley, Ellen Perry 1931- ConAu 110
Berkemeyer, William C 1908- ConAu P-2
Berkey, Barry Robert 1935- ConAu 69,
SmATA 24[port]
Berkey, Helen 1898- ConAu P-2
Berkhof, Aster 1920- IntAu&W 82
Berkhofer, Robert Frederick, Jr. 1931-
ConAu 13R
Berkin, Carol Ruth 1942- ConAu 11NR, –69
Berkley, Constance E DrAP&F 83
Berkley, Constance Elaine 1931- LivgBAA
Berkman, Edward O 1914- ConAu 9NR, –61
Berkman, Harold W 1926- ConAu 5NR, –53
Berkman, Richard Lyle 1946- ConAu 1NR, –45
Berkman, Sue 1936- ConAu 45
Berkman, Sylvia DrAP&F 83
Berkman, Sylvia 1907- WrDr 84
Berkman, Ted ConAu X
Berkoff, Steven 1937- ConAu 104
Berkoff, Steven 1939?- ConDr 82, WrDr 84
Berkove, Lawrence Ivan 1930- ConAu 106
Berkovits, Eliezer 1908- ConAu 1R, –2NR
Berkovitz, Irving H 1924- ConAu 57
Berkow, Ira 1940- ConAu 97, IntAu&W 82
Berkowitz, Bernard 1909- AuNews 1
Berkowitz, David Sandler 1913- ConAu 33R,
IntAu&W 82, WrDr 84
Berkowitz, Freda Pastor 1910- ConAu P-1,
SmATA 12
Berkowitz, Gerald M 1942- ConAu 110
Berkowitz, Luci 1938- ConAu 33R
Berkowitz, Marvin 1938- ConAu 29R
Berkowitz, Morris Ira 1931- ConAu 53
Berkowitz, Pearl H 1921- ConAu 21R
Berkowitz, Sol 1922- ConAu 1NR, –45
Berkshire, Castleton IntAu&W 82X
Berkson, Bill DrAP&F 83
Berkson, Bill 1939- ConAu 9NR, –21R,
ConP 80, IntAu&W 82, IntWWP 82,
WrDr 84
Berkson, William Koller 1944- ConAu 102,
WrDr 84
Berl, Emmanuel 1892-1976 CIDMEL 80
Berl-Lee, Maria ConAu X, IntAu&W 82X,
IntWWP 82X
Berlak, Harold 1932- ConAu 33R
Berland, Howard DrAP&F 83
Berland, Jayne 1922- IntWWP 82
Berland, Theodore 1929- ConAu 2NR, –5R
Berlanstein, Lenard R 1947- ConAu 69
Berle, Adolf A, Jr. 1895-1971 ConAu 29R,
ConAu P-2
Berle, Milton 1908- AuNews 1, ConAu 77
Berleant, Arnold 1932- ConAu 29R
Berlin, Ellin 1904- ConAu 65
Berlin, Ira 1941- ConAu 101
Berlin, Irving 1888- ConAu 108
Berlin, Irving N 1917- ConAu 21R
Berlin, Isaiah 1909- WrDr 84

Berlin, Sir Isaiah 1909- ConAu 85,
DcLEL 1940, LongCTC, WorAu
Berlin, Michael J 1938- ConAu 69
Berlin, Normand 1931- ConAu 57
Berlin, Sven Paul 1911- ConAu 85,
IntAu&W 82
Berlind, Bruce DrAP&F 83
Berlind, Bruce 1926- ConAu 33R, IntWWP 82
Berliner, Don 1930- ConAu 105, SmATA 33
Berliner, Franz 1930- ConAu 29R, SmATA 13
Berliner, Herman A 1944- ConAu 77
Berliner, Joseph S 1921- ConAu 69
Berlitz, Charles 1914- ConAu 9NR
Berlitz, Charles L 1913- SmATA 32[port]
Berlitz, Charles L Frambach 1913- ConAu 5R
Berloni, William 1956- ConAu 77
Berlye, Milton K 1915- ConAu 49
Berlyne, Daniel Ellis 1924- ConAu 13R
Berman, Arthur I 1925- WrDr 84
Berman, Arthur Irwin 1925- ConAu 97
Berman, Bennett H 1927- ConAu 105
Berman, Bruce David 1944- ConAu 41R
Berman, Cassia DrAP&F 83
Berman, Cassia 1949- IntWWP 82
Berman, Claire 1936- ConAu 10NR, –25R,
WrDr 84
Berman, Connie 1949- ConAu 93
Berman, Daniel M 1928-1967 ConAu 1R, –1NR
Berman, Ed 1941- ConAu 106
Berman, Edgar F 1924- ConAu 97
Berman, Eleanor 1934- ConAu 85
Berman, Emile Zola 1902-1981 ConAu 104
Berman, Harold Joseph 1918- ConAu 89
Berman, Larry 1951- ConAu 93
Berman, Louise M 1928- ConAu 21R
Berman, Mark NatPD 81[port]
Berman, Mark L DrAP&F 83
Berman, Marshall 1940- ConAu 29R
Berman, Milton 1924- ConAu 1R
Berman, Morton 1924- ConAu 2NR, –5R,
IntAu&W 82
Berman, Paul 1949- ConAu 110
Berman, Rhoda Gelfond DrAP&F 83
Berman, Ronald 1930- ConAu 13R
Berman, Sanford 1933- ConAu 37R, WrDr 84
Berman, Simeon M 1935- ConAu 49
Berman, Susan 1945- ConAu 65
Berman, William C 1932- ConAu 41R
Bermange, Barry 1933- ConAu 57, ConDr 82,
IntAu&W 82, WrDr 84
Bermant, Chaim 1929- ConAu 6NR, –57,
ConNov 82, IntAu&W 82, WrDr 84
Bermel, Albert 1927- ConAmTC, ConAu 11NR,
–69, NatPD 81[port]
Bermont, Hubert Ingram 1924- ConAu 5NR,
–9R
Bermosk, Loretta Sue 1918- ConAu 3NR, –9R
Bern, Maria Rasputin Soloviev 1900?-1977
ConAu 73

Berna, Paul 1910- ConAu 73, SmATA 15
Bernabei, Alfio 1941- ConAu 77
Bernabei, Alfio 1947- IntAu&W 82
Bernadette ConAu X, IntAu&W 82X,
SmATA 4
Bernal, Ignacio 1910- ConAu 97
Bernal, John Desmond 1901-1971 ConAu 33R,
–97, LongCTC, WorAu
Bernal, Judith F 1939- ConAu 57
Bernal, Martin Gardiner 1937- ConAu 104
Bernal Y Garcia Y Pimentel, Ignacio 1910-
ConAu 5NR, –9R
Bernanos, Georges 1888-1948 CIDMEL 80,
CnMD, ConAu 104, EncWL 2[port],
LongCTC, ModFrL, ModRL, ModWD,
TwCA, TwCA SUP, TwCLC 3, TwCWr,
WhoTwCL
Bernard IntAu&W 82X
Bernard, George 1939- ConAu 73
Bernard, Guy ConAu X
Bernard, H Russell 1940- ConAu 41R
Bernard, Harold W 1908- ConAu 1R, –4NR
Bernard, Harry 1898?- CreCan 2
Bernard, Hugh Y, Jr. 1919- ConAu 21R
Bernard, Jack F 1930- ConAu 21R
Bernard, Jacqueline 1921- ConAu 21R,
SmATA 8
Bernard, Jay ConAu X
Bernard, Jean-Jacques 1888-1972 CIDMEL 80,
CnMD, ConAu 37R, LongCTC, ModFrL,
ModWD
Bernard, Jean-Marc 1881-1915 CIDMEL 80

Bernard, Kenneth *DrAP&F 83*
Bernard, Kenneth 1930- *ConAu 41R, ConDr 82, NatPD 81[port], WrDr 84*
Bernard, Kenneth A 1906- *ConAu 29R*
Bernard, Laureat J 1922- *ConAu 25R*
Bernard, Marley *ConAu X*
Bernard, Oliver 1925- *ConAu 13R, DcLEL 1940, IntWWP 82, WrDr 84*
Bernard, Paul Peter 1929- *ConAu 89*
Bernard, Rafe *ConSFA*
Bernard, Richard Marion 1948- *ConAu 105*
Bernard, Robert *ConAu X, IntAu&W 82X, WrDr 84*
Bernard, Sidney *DrAP&F 83*
Bernard, Sidney 1918- *ConAu 29R, WrDr 84*
Bernard, Stefan *ConAu X*
Bernard, Thelma Rene 1940- *ConAu 57*
Bernard, Tristan 1866-1947 *CnMD, LongCTC, ModWD*
Bernard, Will 1915- *ConAu 93*
Bernardi, Mario 1930- *CreCan 1*
Bernardo, Aldo S 1920- *ConAu 1R, -4NR*
Bernardo, James V 1913- *ConAu 17R*
Bernari, Carlo 1909- *ClDMEL 80, EncWL 2*
Bernarn, Terrave *ConAu X*
Bernauer, George F 1941- *ConAu 29R*
Bernays, Anne *DrAP&F 83, SmATA X*
Bernays, Anne 1930- *ConAu X, IntAu&W 82*
Bernays, Edward L 1891- *ConAu 17R, WrDr 84*
Bernazza, Ann Marie *ConAu X*
Bernbach, William 1911-1982 *ConAu 108*
Bernd, Joseph Laurence 1923- *ConAu 17R*
Berndt, Ronald Murray 1916- *ConAu 3NR, -5R*
Berndt, Walter 1900?-1979 *ConAu 89*
Berndtson, Arthur 1913- *ConAu 108*
Berne, Arlene *ConAu X*
Berne, Eric Lennard 1910-1970 *ConAu 4NR, -5R, -25R*
Berne, Leo *ConAu X, -X*
Berne, Patricia H 1934- *ConAu 110*
Berne, Stanley *DrAP&F 83*
Berne, Stanley 1923- *ConAu 1NR, -45, IntAu&W 82, IntWWP 82*
Berner, Carl Walter 1902- *ConAu 49*
Berner, Jeff *DrAP&F 83*
Berner, Jeff 1940- *ConAu 89, IntWWP 82*
Berner, Robert *DrAP&F 83*
Berner, Robert B 1940- *ConAu 41R*
Berners, Lord 1883-1950 *LongCTC*
Bernert, Eleanor H *ConAu X*
Bernet, Michael M 1930- *ConAu 25R*
Bernhard, Thomas 1931- *ClDMEL 80, ConAu 85, ConLC 3, CroCD, EncWL 2, ModGL*
Bernhardsen, Bris *ConAu X*
Bernhardsen, Christian 1923- *ConAu 29R*
Bernhardt, Alphonse *IntAu&W 82X*
Bernhardt, Debra E 1953- *MichAu 80*
Bernhardt, Frances Simonsen 1932- *ConAu 103*
Bernhardt, Karl S 1901-1967 *ConAu P-1*
Bernhardt, Marcia A 1926- *MichAu 80*
Bernhardt, Sarah 1844-1923 *LongCTC*
Bernheim, Evelyne 1935- *ConAu 21R*
Bernheim, Kayla F 1946- *ConAu 108*
Bernheim, Marc 1924- *ConAu 21R*
Bernheimer, Alan *DrAP&F 83, IntWWP 82X*
Bernheimer, Alan Weyl, Jr. 1948- *IntWWP 82*
Bernheimer, Martin 1936- *ConAu 69*
Bernier, Francoys 1927- *CreCan 1*
Bernier, Olivier 1941- *ConAu 105*
Bernikow, Louise *DrAP&F 83*
Berns, Walter Fred 1919- *ConAu 101, ConIsC 1[port]*
Bernstein, Alec *TwCA SUP*
Bernstein, Alvin H 1939- *ConAu 89*
Bernstein, Anne C 1944- *ConAu 105*
Bernstein, Arnold 1920- *ConAu 29R*
Bernstein, Barton Jannen 1936- *ConAu 37R, IntAu&W 82, WrDr 84*
Bernstein, Blanche 1912- *ConAu 110*
Bernstein, Burton *DrAP&F 83*
Bernstein, Burton 1932- *ConAu 1R, -4NR, IntAu&W 82, WrDr 84*
Bernstein, Carl 1944- *AuNews 1, ConAu 81, WrDr 84*
Bernstein, Charles *DrAP&F 83*
Bernstein, Charles 1950- *IntWWP 82*
Bernstein, David 1915?-1974 *ConAu 53*
Bernstein, Douglas A 1942- *ConAu 45*
Bernstein, Gerry 1927- *ConAu 105*
Bernstein, Harry 1909- *ConAu 1R, -1NR*

Bernstein, Henry Leon Gustave Charles 1876-1953 *ClDMEL 80, CnMD, ModWD, TwCA, TwCA SUP*
Bernstein, Hillel 1892?-1977 *ConAu 69*
Bernstein, J S 1936- *ConAu 25R*
Bernstein, Jacob 1946- *ConAu 104*
Bernstein, Jane *DrAP&F 83*
Bernstein, Jane 1949- *ConAu 104*
Bernstein, Jeremy 1929- *ConAu 13R*
Bernstein, Jerry Marx 1908-1969 *ConAu P-2*
Bernstein, Joanne E 1943- *ConAu 77, SmATA 15*
Bernstein, Joseph M 1908?-1975 *ConAu 57*
Bernstein, Leonard 1918- *ConAu 1R, -2NR, IntAu&W 82, WrDr 84*
Bernstein, Lewis 1915- *ConAu 33R*
Bernstein, Margery 1933- *ConAu 57*
Bernstein, Marilyn 1929- *ConAu 21R*
Bernstein, Marver H 1919- *ConAu 1R, -2NR*
Bernstein, Marvin David 1923- *ConAu 45*
Bernstein, Merton C 1923- *ConAu 17R*
Bernstein, Mordechai 1893-1983 *ConAu 109*
Bernstein, Morey 1919- *ConAu 21R*
Bernstein, Norman R 1927- *ConAu 33R*
Bernstein, Philip S 1901- *ConAu 49*
Bernstein, Richard K 1934- *ConAu 105*
Bernstein, Seymour *ConAu 109*
Bernstein, Theodore M 1904-1979 *ConAu 1R, -3NR, SmATA 12, -27N*
Bernstein, Walter 1919- *ConAu 106*
Bernzweig, Eli P 1927- *ConAu 29R*
Berofsky, Bernard 1935- *ConAu 89*
Berque, Jacques Augustin 1910- *ConAu 85*
Berquist, Goodwin F 1930- *ConAu 21R*
Berrett, LaMar C 1926- *ConAu 53*
Berrian, Albert H 1925- *ConAu 37R*
Berriault, Gina 1926- *WorAu*
Berridge, Celia 1943- *ConAu 110*
Berridge, Elizabeth Eileen 1921- *ConAu 6NR, -57, IntAu&W 82*
Berridge, Percy Stuart Attwood 1901- *ConAu 29R, IntAu&W 82*
Berrien, Edith Heal *ConAu X, SmATA 7*
Berrien, F Kenneth 1909-1971 *ConAu 1R, -1NR, -29R*
Berrigan, Daniel *DrAP&F 83*
Berrigan, Daniel 1921- *ConAu 11NR*
Berrigan, Daniel J 1921- *ASpks, ConAu 33R, ConLC 4, ConP 80, DcLB 5[port], WrDr 84*
Berrigan, Edmund J, Jr. 1934- *ConAu 61*
Berrigan, Edmund Joseph Michael, Jr. 1934-1983 *ConAu 110*
Berrigan, Philip 1923- *ConAu 11NR*
Berrigan, Philip Francis 1923- *ConAu 13R*
Berrigan, Ted *ConAu X, DrAP&F 83*
Berrigan, Ted 1934- *ConAu X, ConP 80, DcLB 5[port], WrDr 84*
Berrill, Jacquelyn 1905- *ConAu 17R, SmATA 12*
Berrill, Norman John 1903- *ConAu 17R, IntAu&W 82, WrDr 84*
Berrington, Hugh Bayard 1928- *ConAu 49, IntAu&W 82, WrDr 84*
Berrington, John *ConAu X, SmATA 6, WorAu 1970, WrDr 84*
Berrisford, Judith *WrDr 84*
Berrisford, Judith Mary 1912- *ConAu X*
Berry, Adrian M 1937- *ConAu 9NR, -57, WrDr 84*
Berry, B J *ConAu X*
Berry, Barbara 1937- *WrDr 84*
Berry, Barbara J 1937- *ConAu 33R, SmATA 7*
Berry, Boyd M 1939- *ConAu 69*
Berry, Brewton 1901- *ConAu 1R, -3NR, WrDr 84*
Berry, Brian J L 1934- *ConAu 5NR, -13R*
Berry, Bryan 1930-1955 *TwCSFW*
Berry, Burton Yost 1901- *ConAu 85*
Berry, Charles H 1930- *ConAu 69*
Berry, Chuck 1926- *ConLC 17*
Berry, Cicely 1926- *ConAu 93, WrDr 84*
Berry, D C *DrAP&F 83*
Berry, D C 1942- *ConAu 45*
Berry, David 1942- *ConAu 29R*
Berry, David 1943- *ConAu 108*
Berry, David Adams 1943- *NatPD 81[port]*
Berry, Don 1932- *ConAu 106, TwCWW, WrDr 84*
Berry, Edmund G 1915- *ConAu 1R*
Berry, Edward I 1940- *ConAu 57*
Berry, Elizabeth 1920- *ConAu 21R*

Berry, Erick 1892-1974 *ConAu X, SmATA X*
Berry, Francis 1915- *ConAu 5R, -5NR, ConP 80, IntAu&W 82, IntWWP 82, WrDr 84*
Berry, Frederic Aroyce, Jr. 1906-1978 *ConAu 77*
Berry, Helen *ConAu X*
Berry, Henry 1926- *ConAu 85*
Berry, I William 1934- *ConAu 105, IntAu&W 82*
Berry, Ila F 1922- *IntWWP 82*
Berry, Jack 1918- *ConAu 37R*
Berry, James 1932- *ConAu 21R*
Berry, James Gomer 1883-1968 *ConAu 89*
Berry, Jane Cobb 1915?-1979 *ConAu 85, SmATA 22N*
Berry, Jas Gomer *ConAu X*
Berry, Jason 1949- *ConAu 45*
Berry, Jim 1946- *ConAu X, -107*
Berry, Jo 1933- *ConAu 102*
Berry, John *DrAP&F 83*
Berry, Jonas *ConAu X*
Berry, Katherine F 1877- *ConAu P-2*
Berry, Lloyd E 1935- *ConAu 13R*
Berry, Lynn 1948- *ConAu 61*
Berry, Mary Frances 1938- *ConAu 33R*
Berry, Nicholas O 1936- *ConAu 93*
Berry, Paul 1919- *ConAu 102, IntAu&W 82, WrDr 84*
Berry, Roland 1951- *ConAu 93*
Berry, Ron 1920- *ConAu 25R, IntAu&W 82, WrDr 84*
Berry, Thomas 1914- *ConAu 21R, WrDr 84*
Berry, Thomas Edwin 1930- *ConAu 102*
Berry, Thomas Elliott 1917- *ConAu 33R*
Berry, Wallace Taft 1928- *ConAu 8NR, -17R, WrDr 84*
Berry, Wendell 1934- *AuNews 1, ConAu 73, ConLC 4, -6, -8, -27[port], ConP 80, DcLB 5[port], -6[port], IntWWP 82, WrDr 84*
Berry, Wendell E *DrAP&F 83*
Berry, William D 1926- *ConAu 73, SmATA 14*
Berry, William Turner 1888- *ConAu P-2*
Berryhill, Michael *DrAP&F 83*
Berryman, James Thomas 1902-1971 *ConAu 93*
Berryman, Jim *ConAu X*
Berryman, John 1914-1972 *ConAu 33R, ConAu P-1, ConLC 1, -2, -3, -4, -6, -8, -10, -13, -25[port], ConP 80A, CroCAP, DcLEL 1940, EncWL 2, ModAL, ModAL SUP, TwCA SUP, WhoTwCL*
Bersani, Leo 1931- *ConAu 5NR, -53*
Berscheid, Ellen 1936- *ConAu 25R*
Berson, Harold 1926- *ConAu 33R, SmATA 4*
Berson, Lenora E 1926- *ConAu 93*
Berssenbrugge, Mei-Mei *DrAP&F 83*
Berssenbrugge, Mei-Mei 1947- *ConAu 104*
Berst, Charles A 1932- *ConAu 41R*
Bertagnolli, Leslie *DrAP&F 83*
Bertcher, Harvey 1929- *ConAu 85*
Berteaut, Simone 1923- *ASpks*
Bertelson, David 1934- *ConAu 21R*
Berthelot, Joseph A 1927- *ConAu 21R, MichAu 80*
Berthoff, Rowland 1921- *ConAu 33R*
Berthoff, Warner 1925- *ConAu 2NR, -5R*
Berthold, Margot 1922- *ConAu 73, IntAu&W 82*
Berthold, Mary Paddock 1909- *ConAu 53*
Berthoud, Jacques 1935- *ConAu 10NR, -17R*
Berthrong, Donald J 1922- *ConAu 81*
Bertillon, Alphonse 1853-1914 *LongCTC*
Bertin, Charles 1919- *ClDMEL 80, CnMD, ModWD*
Bertin, Charles-Francois *ConAu X*
Bertin, Jack *WrDr 84*
Bertin, Leonard M 1918- *ConAu 13R*
Bertman, Stephen 1937- *ConAu 45*
Berto, Giuseppe 1912-1978 *EncWL 2*
Berto, Giuseppe 1914-1978 *ClDMEL 80, ModRL, TwCA SUP*
Bertocci, Peter A 1910- *ConAu 17R*
Bertolino, James *DrAP&F 83*
Bertolino, James 1942- *ConAu 1NR, -45, ConP 80, WrDr 84*
Bertolucci, Bernardo 1940- *ConAu 106, ConLC 16*
Berton, Peter 1922- *ConAu 77*
Berton, Pierre 1920- *ConAu 1R, -2NR, CreCan 1, DcLEL 1940, WrDr 84*
Berton, Ralph 1910- *ConAu 49*
Bertonasco, Marc F 1934- *ConAu 89*

Bertram, Anthony 1897-1978 ConAu 104
Bertram, George Colin Lawder 1911-
ConAu 13R
Bertram, James 1910- WrDr 84
Bertram, James Munro 1910- ConAu 65,
IntWWP 82
Bertram, Jean DeSales ConAu 45
Bertram, Noel ConAu X
Bertram-Cox, Jean DeSales ConAu X
Bertrana, Prudenci 1867-1942 CIDMEL 80
Bertrand, Alvin L 1918- ConAu 45
Bertrand, Charles ConAu X
Bertrand, Lewis 1897?-1974 ConAu 53
Bertrand, Michel 1944- ConAu 73
Bertrand, Sandra 1943- NatPD 81[port]
Berval, Paul CreCan 1
Berwanger, Eugene H ConAu 21R
Berwick, Jean Shepherd 1929- ConAu 9R,
SmATA X
Berwick, Keith 1928- ConAu 33R
Besanceney, Paul H 1924- ConAu 45
Besant, Annie 1847-1933 ConAu 105, LongCTC,
TwCA, TwCA SUP, TwCLC 9[port]
Besas, Peter 1933- ConAu 77
Besaw, Victor John 1916- IntAu&W 82
Besch, Lutz 1918- CnMD
Beschloss, Michael R 1955- ConAu 101
Besci, Kurt 1920- CroCD
Beshers, James M 1931- ConAu 1R
Beshoar, Barron B 1907- ConAu 69
Besier, Rudolf 1878-1942 LongCTC, ModWD,
TwCA
Beskow, Bo 1906- ConAu 11NR, –61,
IntAu&W 82
Beskow, Elsa 1874-1953 SmATA 20
Besoyan, Rick 1924?-1970 ConAu 25R
Besre, Jean 1938- CreCan 2
Bessa-Luis, Agustina 1922- CIDMEL 80
Bessborough, Earl Of 1913- ConAu X
Bessborough, Frederick Ponsonby, Earl Of 1913-
IntAu&W 82
Besser, Gretchen Rous 1928- ConAu 41R,
IntAu&W 82
Besser, Milton 1911-1976 ConAu 65, –69
Bessette, Gerard 1920- ConAu 37R, CreCan 1
Bessie, Alvah DrAP&F 83
Bessie, Alvah 1904- ConAmA, ConAu 2NR,
–5R, ConLC 23[port], DcLB 26[port],
TwCA, TwCA SUP, WrDr 84
Bessinger, Jess B, Jr. 1921- ConAu 13R
Bessom, Malcolm E 1940- ConAu 57
Bessy, Maurice 1910- ConAu 10NR, –65
Best, Adam ConAu X
Best, Allena Champlin 1892-1974 ConAu P-2,
SmATA 2, –25N
Best, Charles Herbert 1899-1978 ConAu 103, –45
Best, Gary A 1939- ConAu 33R
Best, Herbert 1894- ConAu P-2, SmATA 2,
TwCSFW, WrDr 84
Best, Herbert 1894-1981 TwCCW 83
Best, James J 1938- ConAu 37R
Best, John 1929- IntWWP 82
Best, John Wesley 1909- ConAu 17R
Best, Judith A 1938- ConAu 69
Best, Marc ConAu X
Best, Marshall A 1901?-1982 ConAu 106
Best, Michael R 1939- ConAu 37R
Best, Otto F 1929- ConAu 69
Best, Rayleigh Breton Amis 1905- ConAu P-1
Best, Thomas W 1939- ConAu 29R
Bestall, Alfred 1892- TwCCW 83
Beste, R Vernon 1908- ConAu 1R, –4NR
Bester, Alfred 1913- ConAu 13R, ConSFA,
DcLB 8[port], DcLEL 1940, DrmM[port],
TwCSFW, WrDr 84
Besterman, Theodore 1904-1976 ConAu 105,
LongCTC
Bestic, Alan Kent 1922- ConAu 13R
Beston, Henry 1888-1968 ConAu 25R, TwCA,
TwCA SUP
Bestor, Arthur, Jr. 1908- ConAu 1R, –6NR
Bestor, Arthur E 1908- WrDr 84
Bestul, Thomas H 1942- ConAu 53
Betancourt, Jeanne 1941- ConAu 49
Betancourt, Romulo 1908-1981 ConAu 104
Betenson, Lula Parker 1884- ConAu 61
Beth ConAu X
Beth, Loren Peter 1920- ConAu 1R, –3NR
Beth, Mary ConAu X, SmATA X
Betham-Edwards, Matilda Barbara 1836-1919
LongCTC
Bethancourt, T Ernesto 1932- ChlLR 3,

ConAu X, SmATA 11
Bethel, Dell 1929- ConAu 29R
Bethel, Elizabeth Rauh 1942- ConAu 106
Bethel, Gar DrAP&F 83
Bethel, Paul Duane 1919- ConAu 25R
Bethell, Jean 1922- ConAu 3NR, –9R,
SmATA 8
Bethell, Mary Ursula 1874-1945 CnMWL,
LongCTC, TwCWr, WhoTwCL
Bethell, Nicholas 1938- WrDr 84
Bethell, Nicholas William 1938- ConAu 1NR,
–45
Bethell, Tom 1940- ConAu 77
Bethers, Ray 1902- ConAu P-1, SmATA 6
Bethge, Eberhard 1909- ConAu 85
Bethmann, Erich 1909- WrDr 84
Bethmann, Erich Waldemar 1904- ConAu P-2
Bethune, Lebert DrAP&F 83
Bethurum, F Dorothy 1897- ConAu P-2
Beti, Mongo 1932- ConLC 27[port], EncWL 2,
ModBlW, ModFrL, TwCWr
Betis, Willard Emory ConAu X
Betjeman, John 1906- WrDr 84
Betjeman, Sir John 1906- CnMWL, ConAu 9R,
ConLC 2, –6, –10, –10, ConP 80, LongCTC,
ModBrL, ModBrL SUP, RGFMBP,
TwCA SUP, TwCWr, WhoTwCL
Betocchi, Carlo 1899- CIDMEL 80,
ConAu 4NR, –9R, EncWL 2, IntWWP 82,
WorAu
Betsko, Kathleen 1939- NatPD 81[port]
Bett, Walter Reginald 1903- ConAu P-1
Bettelheim, Bruno 1903- ConAu 81,
WorAu 1970, WrDr 84
Bettelheim, Charles 1913- ConAu 73
Bettelheim, Frederick A 1923- ConAu 49
Betten, Neil B 1939- ConAu 105
Bettenson, Henry 1908- ConAu 13R
Betteridge, Anne WrDr 84
Betteridge, Anne 1926- ConAu X,
IntAu&W 82X, SmATA X, TwCRGW
Betteridge, Don ConAu X, LongCTC,
TwCCr&M 80
Betteridge, H T 1910- ConAu 5R
Bettersworth, John Knox 1909- ConAu 2NR,
–5R
Betti, Liliana 1939- ConAu 101
Betti, Ugo 1892-1953 CIDMEL 80, CnMD,
CnMWL, ConAu 104, EncWL 2,
LongCTC, ModRL, ModWD,
TwCLC 5[port], TwCWr, WorAu
Bettina 1903- ConAu X, SmATA 1,
TwCCW 83
Bettis, Joseph Dabney 1936- ConAu 33R
Bettmann, Otto Ludwig 1903- ConAu 17R
Betts, Charles L 1908- ConAu 101, WrDr 84
Betts, Donni 1948- ConAu 5NR, –53
Betts, Doris DrAP&F 83
Betts, Doris 1932- ConAu 9NR,
DcLB Y82B[port]
Betts, Doris June Waugh 1932- ConAu 13R,
ConLC 6
Betts, Emmett Albert 1903- ConAu 33R
Betts, George 1944- ConAu 2NR, –45
Betts, Glynne Robinson 1934- ConAu 105
Betts, James ConAu X
Betts, John 1939- ConAu 106, WrDr 84
Betts, Lorne 1918- CreCan 2
Betts, Raymond Frederick 1925- ConAu 1R,
–3NR, WrDr 84
Betts, Richard Kevin 1947- ConAu 85,
IntAu&W 82
Betts, Victoria Bedford 1913- WrDr 84
Betts, William Wilson, Jr. 1926- ConAu 33R,
IntAu&W 82, WrDr 84
Betz, Betty 1920- ConAu 1R
Betz, Eva Kelly 1897-1968 ConAu P-1,
SmATA 10
Betz, Hans Dieter 1931- ConAu 4NR, –53
Beuf, Ann H 1939- ConAu 85
Beukes, Gerhard Johannes 1913- IntAu&W 82
Beum, Robert DrAP&F 83
Beum, Robert Lawrence 1929- ConAu 9R
Beurdeley, Michel 1911- ConAu 49
Beutel, William Charles 1930- ConAu 101
Beuttler, Edward ConAu 73
Bevan, Alistair ConAu X
Bevan, Aneurin 1897-1960 ConAu 106
Bevan, Bryan 1913- ConAu 13R, IntAu&W 82
Bevan, E Dean 1938- ConAu 33R
Bevan, Edwyn Robert 1870-1943 LongCTC
Bevan, Gloria TwCRGW, WrDr 84

Bevan, Jack 1920- ConAu 13R, DcLEL 1940
Bevan, James 1930- ConAu 106, WrDr 84
Bevenot, Maurice 1897-1980 ConAu 105
Beveridge, Lord 1879-1963 LongCTC
Beveridge, Albert Jeremiah 1862-1927
DcLB 17[port], TwCA, TwCA SUP
Beveridge, Andrew A 1945- ConAu 93
Beveridge, George David, Jr. 1922- ConAu 102
Beveridge, Meryle Secrest 1930- ConAu 81
Beveridge, Oscar Maltman 1913- ConAu 9R
Beveridge, William 1908- WrDr 84
Beveridge, William Ian Beardmore 1908-
ConAu 106, IntAu&W 82
BeVier, Michael Judson ConAu 97
Bevilacqua, Alberto 1934- ConAu 29R
Bevington, David M 1931- ConAu 1R, –3NR
Bevington, Helen Smith 1906- ConAu 13R,
WorAu
Bevis, Em Olivia 1932- ConAu 1NR, –49
Bevis, Herbert Urlin 1902- ConAu P-2
Bevis, James ConAu X
Bevlin, Marjorie Elliott 1917- ConAu 9R
Bew, Pauline 1938- IntWWP 82
Bewes, Richard 1934- ConAu 102, WrDr 84
Bewick, Thomas 1753-1828 SmATA 16
Bewkes, Eugene Garrett 1895- ConAu 5R
Bewley, Charles Henry 1888- ConAu 5R
Bewley, Marius 1918-1973 ConAu 3NR, –5R,
–41R, ConLCrt 82
Bewley, Mary IntWWP 82X
Bexar, Phil TwCWW
Bey, Doktor IntAu&W 82X
Bey, Isabelle ConAu X, WrDr 84
Beyath, Yahya Kemal 1884-1958 CIDMEL 80
Beye, Charles Rowan 1930- ConAu 93
Beyea, Basil 1910- ConAu 61
Beyer, Andrew 1943- ConAu 11NR, –69
Beyer, Audrey White 1916- ConAu 13R,
SmATA 9
Beyer, Evelyn M 1907- ConAu P-2
Beyer, Glenn H 1913-1969 ConAu 1R, –2NR
Beyer, Robert 1913?-1978 ConAu 77
Beyer, Werner W 1911- WrDr 84
Beyer, Werner William 1911- ConAu 9R,
IntAu&W 82
Beyerchen, Alan 1945- ConAu 81
Beyerhaus, Peter 1929- ConAu 93
Beyerholm, Jorgen 1936- IntAu&W 82
Beyers, Charlotte Kempner 1931- ConAu 85,
IntAu&W 82
Beyfus, Drusilla WrDr 84
Beyfus, Drusilla 1927- ConAu 107,
IntAu&W 82
Beyle, Thad L 1934- ConAu 37R
Beynon, D Islwyn 1920- IntAu&W 82
Beynon, Huw 1942- ConAu 107, WrDr 84
Beynon, John ConAu X, TwCSFW, WorAu
Beytagh, Gonville Ffrench ConAu X
Beyz, Alexis IntWWP 82X
Bez IntAu&W 82X
Bezio, May Rowland d1977 ConAu 69
Bezroundoff, Jean Basile CreCan 1
Bezruc, Petr 1867-1958 CIDMEL 80, EncWL 2,
ModSL 2
Bezruchka, Stephen 1943- ConAu 107
Bh IntAu&W 82X
Bhagat, Goberdhan 1928- ConAu 29R,
WrDr 84
Bhagat, O P 1929- DcLEL 1940
Bhagavatula, Murty S 1921- ConAu 29R
Bhagwati, Jagdish N 1934- ConAu 17R
Bhajan, Yogi ConAu X
Bhaktivedanta, A C ConAu X
Bhaktivedanta Swami, A C ConAu X
Bhana, Surendra 1939- ConAu 57
Bharati, Agehananda 1923- ConAu 1R, –4NR,
IntAu&W 82, WrDr 84
Bharati, Subramania 1882-1921 EncWL 2
Bhardwaj, Surinder Mohan 1934- ConAu 45
Bharti, Ma Satya 1942- ConAu 102
Bhaskaran, M P 1920- IntWWP 82
Bhaskaran, M P 1921- DcLEL 1940
Bhasker IntAu&W 82X
Bhatia, Hans Raj 1904- ConAu 53
Bhatia, Jamunadevi 1919- ConAu 101,
WrDr 84
Bhatia, Jamundevi 1919- IntAu&W 82
Bhatia, June WrDr 84
Bhatia, June 1919- ConAu X
Bhatia, Krishan 1926?-1974 ConAu 53
Bhatia, Prem Narain 1911- DcLEL 1940

IntAu&W 82, WrDr 84
Billington, Monroe Lee 1928- *ConAu 21R*
Billington, Rachel 1942- *AuNews 2,*
  ConAu 33R, ConDr 82B, WrDr 84
Billington, Ray Allen 1903- *WrDr 84*
Billington, Ray Allen 1903-1981 *ConAu 1R,*
  -5NR, -103, IntAu&W 82
Billington, Raymond John 1930- *ConAu 110,*
  IntAu&W 82, WrDr 84
Billmeyer, Fred W, Jr. 1919- *ConAu 85,*
  WrDr 84
Billout, Guy Rene 1941- *ConAu 85,*
  IntAu&W 82, SmATA 10
Bills, Robert E 1916- *ConAu 107*
Billy, Andre 1882-1971 *ConAu 29R*
Bilow, Pat 1941- *ConAu 106*
Bilsland, Bilko *ConAu X*
Bilsland, E C 1931- *ConAu 69*
Bimler, Richard William 1940- *ConAu 41R*
Binder, Aaron 1927- *ConAu 57*
Binder, David 1931- *ConAu 65*
Binder, Eando 1911-1974 *ConAu X, TwCSFW*
Binder, Frederick M 1931- *ConAu 29R*
Binder, Frederick Moore 1920- *ConAu 41R*
Binder, Leonard 1927- *ConAu 61*
Binder, Otto Oscar 1911-1974 *ConAu 1R, -3NR,*
  -53, ConSFA
Binder, Pearl 1904- *ConAu X*
Binding, Rudolf Georg 1867-1938 *ClDMEL 80,*
  ModGL
Bindloss, Harold 1866-1945 *LongCTC, TwCA,*
  TwCA SUP, TwCWW
Bindman, Arthur J 1925- *ConAu 45*
Bindoff, Stanley Thomas 1908-1980 *ConAu 102,*
  -73
Binford, Jesse S, Jr. 1928- *WrDr 84*
Binford, Laurence C 1935- *WrDr 84*
Bing, Elisabeth D 1914- *ConAu 11NR, -69*
Bing, Rudolf 1902- *ConAu 89*
Bingaman, Ron 1936- *ConAu 61*
Binger, Carl A L 1889-1976 *ConAu 65, -73*
Binger, Norman H 1914- *ConAu 33R*
Binger, Walter 1888?-1979 *ConAu 85*
Bingham, Alfred Mitchell 1905- *TwCA,*
  TwCA SUP
Bingham, Barry, Jr. 1933- *ConAu 106*
Bingham, Caroline 1938- *ConAu 10NR, -57,*
  IntAu&W 82, WrDr 84
Bingham, Carson 1920- *ConAu X*
Bingham, Charlotte 1942- *ConAu 11NR,*
  WrDr 84
Bingham, Charlotte Mary Therese 1942-
  ConAu 105, DcLEL 1940
Bingham, David A 1926- *ConAu 53*
Bingham, Edwin R 1920- *ConAu 2NR, -5R*
Bingham, Evangeline M L 1899- *ConAu 65*
Bingham, Jane Marie 1941- *ConAu 104*
Bingham, John 1908- *ConAu 11NR, WrDr 84*
Bingham, John Michael Ward 1908-1960
  ConAu 21R, DcLEL 1940, LongCTC,
  TwCCr&M 80
Bingham, Jonathan B 1914- *ConAu 33R,*
  WrDr 84
Bingham, June Rossbach 1919- *ConAu 1R,*
  WrDr 84
Bingham, M P 1918- *ConAu 49*
Bingham, Madeleine 1912- *ConAu 11NR, -13R,*
  DcLEL 1940
Bingham, Robert C 1927- *ConAu 21R*
Bingham, Robert E 1925- *ConAu 29R*
Bingham, Robert Kamerer 1925?-1982
  ConAu 107
Bingham, Sallie *DrAP&F 83*
Bingham, Sallie 1937- *ConAu X,*
  NatPD 81[port]
Bingley, Clive 1936- *WrDr 84*
Bingley, Clive Hamilton 1936- *ConAu 17R*
Bingley, David Ernest 1920- *ConAu 2NR, -45,*
  IntAu&W 82, TwCWW
Binham, Philip Frank 1924- *ConAu 107,*
  WrDr 84
Binion, Rudolph 1927- *ConAu 1R, -4NR,*
  WrDr 84
Binkley, Anne *ConAu X, SmATA X*
Binkley, Luther John 1925- *ConAu 5R,*
  WrDr 84
Binkley, Olin T 1908- *ConAu 45*
Binkley, William Campbell 1889-1970
  ConAu 104, -107
Binnemans, Charles-Louis 1922- *IntAu&W 82*
Binney, Judith Mary Caroline 1940-
  IntAu&W 82

Binning, Bertram Charles 1909- *CreCan 1*
Binns, Archie 1899- *ConAu 73, TwCA,*
  TwCA SUP
Binns, J W 1940- *ConAu 53*
Binsfeld, Edmund Louis 1909- *IntWWP 82*
Binswanger, Ludwig 1881-1966 *ConAu 107*
Binyon, Claude 1905-1978 *ConAu 77*
Binyon, Laurence 1869-1943 *LongCTC, ModBrL,*
  TwCA, TwCA SUP, TwCWr
Binzen, Bill *ConAu X, SmATA 24[port]*
Binzen, William *ConAu 89, SmATA X*
Biossat, Bruce 1910?-1974 *ConAu 104*
Biot, Francois 1923- *ConAu 13R*
Biow, Milton H 1882?-1976 *ConAu 65*
Bioy Casares, Adolfo 1914- *ConAu 29R,*
  ConLC 4, -8, -13, EncWL 2, IntAu&W 82,
  ModLAL
Birabeau, Andre 1890- *CnMD, ModWD*
Birch, Alison Wyrley 1922- *ConAu 85*
Birch, Anthony Harold 1924- *ConAu 5NR, -13R,*
  IntAu&W 82, WrDr 84
Birch, Bruce C 1941- *ConAu 10NR, -65*
Birch, Charles Allan 1903- *WrDr 84*
Birch, Clive Francis William 1931- *IntAu&W 82*
Birch, Cyril 1925- *ConAu 85*
Birch, Daniel R 1937- *ConAu 101*
Birch, David L 1937- *ConAu 25R*
Birch, Edith *IntWWP 82*
Birch, Herbert G 1918-1973 *ConAu 41R*
Birch, Leo Bedrich 1902- *ConAu 33R,*
  IntWWP 82
Birch, Lionel d1982? *ConAu 106*
Birch, Michele Anne *DrAP&F 83*
Birch, Nigel 1906-1981 *ConAu 108*
Birch, Reginald Bathurst 1856-1943 *SmATA 19*
Birch, William G 1909- *ConAu 53*
Birchall, Ian H 1939- *ConAu 97*
Bircham, Deric 1934- *WrDr 84*
Bircham, Deric Neale 1934- *ConAu 89,*
  IntAu&W 82
Bird, Anthony Cole 1917- *ConAu 13R*
Bird, Brandon *ConAu X*
Bird, C *ConAu X*
Bird, Caroline 1915- *ConAu 11NR, -17R,*
  WrDr 84
Bird, Cordwainer *ConAu X*
Bird, Cyril Kenneth 1887-1965 *ConAu P-1,*
  LongCTC
Bird, Dennis Leslie 1930- *WrDr 84*
Bird, Dorothy Maywood 1899- *ConAu P-1,*
  WrDr 84
Bird, Florence 1908- *ConAu 97*
Bird, George Lloyd 1900- *ConAu 2NR, -5R*
Bird, Harrison K 1910- *ConAu 85*
Bird, James Harold 1923- *ConAu 102,*
  IntAu&W 82, WrDr 84
Bird, Junius Bouton 1907-1982 *ConAu 106*
Bird, Lewis P 1933- *ConAu 97*
Bird, Patricia Amy 1941- *ConAu 7NR, -61*
Bird, Richard 1938- *ConAu 4NR, -9R*
Bird, Vivian 1910- *ConAu 102, WrDr 84*
Bird, W Ernest 1890- *ConAu P-1*
Bird, Will R 1891- *ConAu 13R*
Bird, William 1888-1963 *DcLB 4*
Bird, William Richard 1891- *CreCan 2*
Birdsall, Steve 1944- *ConAu 7NR, -53*
Birdwell, Russell 1903-1977 *ConAu 107*
Birdwhistell, Ray L 1918- *ConAu 45*
Birdwood, George F B 1929- *WrDr 84*
Birenbaum, Arnold 1939- *ConAu 108*
Birenbaum, Halina 1929- *ConAu 45*
Birenbaum, Harvey 1936- *ConAu 109*
Birenbaum, William M 1923- *ConAu 29R,*
  WrDr 84
Birimisa, George 1924- *ConAu 89, ConDr 82,*
  IntAu&W 82
Birkby, Carel 1910- *IntAu&W 82*
Birkenhead, Earl Of 1872-1930 *LongCTC*
Birkenhead, Lord *ConAu X*
Birkenmayer, Sigmund Stanley 1923-
  ConAu 21R
Birket-Smith, Kaj 1893- *ConAu P-1*
Birkett, Lord 1883-1962 *LongCTC*
Birkin, Andrew 1945- *ConAu 97*
Birkin, Charles 1907- *ConAu 69*
Birkley, Marilyn 1916- *ConAu 41R*
Birkos, Alexander S 1936- *ConAu 25R*
Birks, Tony 1937- *ConAu 69*
Birksted-Breen, Dana 1946- *ConAu 102*
Birla, Ghanshyamdas 1894-1983 *ConAu 110*
Birla, Lakshminiwas N 1909- *ConAu P-1*
Birladeanu, Victor 1928- *IntAu&W 82*

Birley, Julia 1928- *ConAu 13R, DcLEL 1940*
Birley, Robert 1903-1982 *ConAu 110*
Birmingham, David 1938- *ConAu 17R*
Birmingham, F A 1911-1982 *ConAu 107, -11NR*
Birmingham, Frances A 1920- *ConAu 17R*
Birmingham, Frederic Alexander 1911-1982
  ConAu 17R
Birmingham, George A 1865-1950 *LongCTC,*
  TwCA, TwCA SUP, TwCWr
Birmingham, John 1951- *ConAu 45*
Birmingham, Lloyd 1924- *SmATA 12*
Birmingham, Maisie *WrDr 84*
Birmingham, Maisie 1914- *ConAu 101*
Birmingham, Stephen 1931- *WrDr 84*
Birmingham, Stephen 1932- *AuNews 1,*
  ConAu 2NR, -49
Birmingham, Walter 1913- *ConAu 17R,*
  WrDr 84
Birn, Randi 1935- *ConAu 73*
Birn, Raymond Francis 1935- *ConAu 102,*
  WrDr 84
Birnbach, Martin 1929- *ConAu 1R, WrDr 84*
Birnbaum, Eleazar 1929- *ConAu 37R,*
  IntAu&W 82
Birnbaum, Milton 1919- *ConAu 33R*
Birnbaum, Norman 1926- *ConAu 5NR, -53*
Birnbaum, Philip 1904- *ConAu 1NR, -49,*
  IntAu&W 82
Birnbaum, Phyllis 1945- *ConAu 102*
Birne, Henry 1921- *ConAu 17R*
Birney, Alfred Earle 1904- *CreCan 1,*
  IntWWP 82
Birney, Alice Lotvin 1938- *ConAu 33R,*
  WrDr 84
Birney, Earle *DrAP&F 83*
Birney, Earle 1904- *ConAu 1R, -5NR,*
  ConLC 1, -4, -6, -11, ConNov 82, ConP 80,
  CreCan 1, IntAu&W 82, LongCTC,
  ModCmwL, TwCWr, WorAu 1970,
  WrDr 84
Birney, Hoffman 1891-1958 *TwCWW*
Birnie, Whittlesey 1945- *ConAu 97*
Birnkrant, Arthur 1906?-1983 *ConAu 108*
Biro, B S 1921- *ConAu 11NR, -25R*
Biro, Charlotte Slovak 1904- *ConAu 57*
Biro, Val *ConAu X*
Biro, Val 1921- *ConAu X, SmATA 1,*
  TwCCW 83, WrDr 84
Birrell, Augustine 1850-1933 *LongCTC, TwCA,*
  TwCA SUP, TwCWr
Birrell, James Peter 1928- *WrDr 84*
Birrell, Verla Leone 1903- *IntWWP 82*
Birren, Faber 1900- *ConAu 7NR, -13R*
Birren, James E 1918- *ConAu 17R*
Birse, A H 1889- *ConAu P-2*
Birstein, Ann *DrAP&F 83*
Birstein, Ann 1927- *ConAu 17R, WrDr 84*
Birt, David 1936- *ConAu 73*
Birtha, Becky *DrAP&F 83*
Bis *IntWWP 82X*
Bischof, Ledford Julius 1914- *ConAu 9R*
Bischof, David F 1951- *ConAu 81, TwCSFW,*
  WrDr 84
Bischoff, F A 1928- *ConAu 89*
Bischoff, Julia Bristol 1909-1970 *ConAu P-2,*
  SmATA 12
Bischoff, Paul 1921- *IntAu&W 82*
Bish, Robert L 1942- *ConAu 53*
Bishai, Wilson B 1923- *ConAu 33R*
Bisher, James F 1918- *ConAu 2NR, -5R*
Bishin, William R 1939- *ConAu 61*
Bishir, John 1933- *ConAu 41R*
Bishoff, Donald Brian, Jr. 1936- *ConAmTC*
Bishop, Bonnie 1943- *ConAu 103*
Bishop, Claire Huchet *ConAu 73, SmATA 14,*
  TwCCW 83, WrDr 84
Bishop, Conrad 1941- *NatPD 81[port]*
Bishop, Crawford M 1885- *ConAu P-2*
Bishop, Curtis Kent 1912-1967 *ConAu P-1,*
  SmATA 6
Bishop, Donald G 1907- *ConAu 1R, -3NR,*
  IntAu&W 82, WrDr 84
Bishop, Donald H 1920- *ConAu 105*
Bishop, E Morchard *ConAu X*
Bishop, Elizabeth 1911-1979 *ConAu 5R, -89,*
  ConLC 1, -4, -9, -13, -15, ConP 80,
  CroCAP, DcLB 5[port], DcLEL 1940,
  EncWL 2, ModAL, ModAL SUP,
  SmATA 24N, TwCA SUP, TwCWr
Bishop, Eugene C 1909-1983 *ConAu 109*
Bishop, Evelyn Morchard *ConAu X*
Bishop, Ferman 1922- *ConAu 21R, WrDr 84*

Blackman, Sheldon 1935- *ConAu 33R*
Blackman, Victor 1922- *ConAu 103, WrDr 84*
Blackmer, Donald L M 1929- *ConAu 33R, WrDr 84*
Blackmon, C Robert 1925- *ConAu 33R*
Blackmore, Dorothy S 1914- *ConAu 41R*
Blackmore, Howard Loftus 1917- *IntAu&W 82*
Blackmore, Jane *TwCRGW*
Blackmore, John T 1931- *ConAu 41R*
Blackmore, Peter 1909- *ConAu 9R*
Blackmur, R P 1904-1965 *ConAu 25R, ConLC 24[port], ConLCrt 82, EncWL 2*
Blackmur, Richard Palmer 1904-1965 *ConAu P-1, ConLC 2, LongCTC, ModAL, ModAL SUP, TwCA, TwCA SUP, TwCWr*
Blackoff, Edward M 1934- *ConAu 9R*
Blackshear, Helen F 1911- *ConAu 10NR*
Blackshear, Helen Friedman 1911- *ConAu 25R, IntWWP 82*
Blackstock, Charity *ConAu X, TwCCr&M 80, TwCRGW, TwCWr, WrDr 84*
Blackstock, Lee *ConAu X, WrDr 84*
Blackstock, Nelson 1944- *ConAu 97*
Blackstock, Paul W 1913- *ConAu 13R*
Blackstock, Walter 1917- *ConAu 5R, -9NR*
Blackstone, Bernard 1911- *ConAu 69*
Blackstone, Geoffrey Vaughan 1910- *ConAu P-1*
Blackstone, Tessa 1942- *ConAu 102, WrDr 84*
Blackstone, William T 1931- *ConAu 11NR, -17R*
Blackton, Peter *ConAu X, SmATA X*
Blackwelder, Bernice Fowler 1902- *ConAu 1R*
Blackwelder, Boyce Watson 1913-1976 *ConAu 17R*
Blackwell, Alice Stone 1857-1950 *TwCA, TwCA SUP*
Blackwell, David 1919- *LivgBAA*
Blackwell, Earl 1913- *ConAu 81*
Blackwell, John 1913- *WrDr 84*
Blackwell, Leslie 1885- *ConAu 9R*
Blackwell, Lois S 1943- *ConAu 85*
Blackwell, Louise 1919-1977 *ConAu 37R*
Blackwell, Muriel F 1929- *ConAu 108*
Blackwell, Richard J 1929- *WrDr 84*
Blackwell, Richard Joseph 1929- *ConAu 33R*
Blackwell, Roger D 1940- *ConAu 93*
Blackwell, William L 1929- *ConAu 21R*
Blackwood, Alan 1932- *ConAu 110*
Blackwood, Algernon 1869-1951 *ConAu 105, LongCTC, TwCA, TwCA SUP, TwCCr&M 80, TwCLC 5[port], TwCWr*
Blackwood, Andrew W 1915- *WrDr 84*
Blackwood, Andrew W, Jr. 1915- *ConAu 1R, -5NR*
Blackwood, Andrew Watterson 1882-1966 *ConAu 5R, -103*
Blackwood, Caroline 1931- *ConAu 85, ConLC 6, -9, ConNov 82, DcLB 14[port], WrDr 84*
Blackwood, Cheryl Prewitt 1957- *ConAu 108*
Blackwood, George D 1919- *ConAu 13R*
Blackwood, James R 1918- *ConAu 21R*
Blackwood, Paul Everett 1913- *ConAu 102*
Blade, Alexander *TwCSFW*
Bladel, Roderick L *ConAu 97*
Bladen, Ashby 1929- *ConAu 106*
Bladen, V W 1900- *ConAu 61*
Blades, Ann 1947- *ConAu 77, SmATA 16, TwCCW 83, WrDr 84*
Blades, Brian Brewer 1906-1977 *ConAu 73*
Blades, James 1901- *ConAu 65, IntAu&W 82, WrDr 84*
Bladow, Suzanne Wilson 1937- *ConAu 61, SmATA 14*
Blaffer, Sarah C *ConAu X*
Blaffer-Hrdy, Sarah C 1946- *ConAu 41R*
Blaga, Lucian 1895-1961 *ClDMEL 80, EncWL 2*
Blagden, Cyprian 1906-1962 *ConAu 1R*
Blagden, David 1944- *ConAu 53*
Blagowidow, George *DrAP&F 83*
Blagowidow, George 1923- *ConAu 77*
Blaher, Damian J 1913- *ConAu 21R*
Blaich, Theodore Paul 1902- *ConAu P-1*
Blaike, Avona *ConAu X*
Blaikie, Robert Jackson 1923- *ConAu 33R*
Blaiklock, Edward Musgrave 1903- *ConAu 7NR, -17R*
Blaine, James *ConAu X, WrDr 84*
Blaine, James Cyril Dickson 1904- *IntAu&W 82*
Blaine, John 1914- *ConAu X, SmATA X*

Blaine, Marge 1937- *SmATA X*
Blaine, Margery Kay 1937- *ConAu 61, SmATA 11*
Blaine, Thomas R 1895- *ConAu 106*
Blaine, Tom R *ConAu X*
Blaine, William L 1931- *ConAu 65*
Blainey, Ann 1935- *ConAu 25R*
Blainey, Geoffrey Norman 1930- *ConAu 25R, IntAu&W 82, WrDr 84*
Blair *ConAu X*
Blair, Alan 1915- *IntAu&W 82*
Blair, Anne Denton 1914- *ConAu 110*
Blair, Calvin Patton 1924- *ConAu 13R*
Blair, Carvel Hall 1924- *ConAu 49*
Blair, Charles E 1920- *ConAu 25R*
Blair, Claude 1922- *ConAu 5R, -11NR, IntAu&W 82, WrDr 84*
Blair, Clay Drewry, Jr. 1925- *AuNews 2, ConAu 77*
Blair, Dike 1919- *ConAu 9R*
Blair, Don 1933- *ConAu 65*
Blair, Dorothy S 1913- *WrDr 84*
Blair, Edward H 1938- *ConAu 7NR, -17R*
Blair, Edward P 1910- *ConAu 11NR*
Blair, Edward Payson 1910- *ConAu P-1*
Blair, Eric *IntAu&W 82X*
Blair, Eric Arthur 1903-1950 *LongCTC, SmATA 29[port]*
Blair, Eric Hugh 1903-1950 *ConAu 104*
Blair, Everetta Love 1907- *ConAu P-2*
Blair, Frank 1915- *ConAu 93*
Blair, George S 1924- *ConAu 17R, WrDr 84*
Blair, Glenn Myers 1908- *ConAu 5R, WrDr 84*
Blair, Harold Arthur 1902- *IntAu&W 82*
Blair, Harry Wallace 1938- *ConAu 109*
Blair, Helen 1910- *SmATA 29*
Blair, J Allen 1913- *ConAu 89*
Blair, Jane N 1911- *ConAu 57*
Blair, John George 1934- *ConAu 13R, IntAu&W 82*
Blair, John M 1914-1976 *ConAu 69, -73*
Blair, Kathryn *TwCRGW, WrDr 84*
Blair, Kay Kimery Reynolds 1942- *ConAu 33R, WrDr 84*
Blair, Leon Borden 1917- *ConAu 29R*
Blair, Lucile *ConAu X*
Blair, Norma Baker *DrAP&F 83*
Blair, Olive Tinker 1892- *MichAu 80*
Blair, Paxton 1892-1974 *ConAu 53*
Blair, Peter Hunter *ConAu X*
Blair, Philip M 1928- *ConAu 41R*
Blair, Ruth VanNess 1912- *ConAu 21R, SmATA 12, WrDr 84*
Blair, Sam 1932- *ConAu 53*
Blair, Thomas 1926- *ConAu 106, IntAu&W 82, WrDr 84*
Blair, Walter 1900- *ConAu 3NR, -5R, SmATA 12, WrDr 84*
Blair, Wilfrid *ConAu X*
Blair-Fish, Wallace Wilfrid 1889-1968 *ConAu P-2*
Blairman, Jacqueline *WrDr 84*
Blais, Madeleine 1947- *ConAu 104*
Blais, Marie-Claire 1939- *ConAu 21R, ConLC 2, -4, -6, -13, -22[port], CreCan 1, EncWL 2, ModCmwL, ModFrL, WorAu*
Blaisdell, Anne *ConAu X, TwCCr&M 80, WrDr 84*
Blaisdell, Donald Christy 1899- *ConAu 37R*
Blaisdell, Foster W 1927- *ConAu 69*
Blaisdell, Harold F 1914- *ConAu 65*
Blaisdell, Paul H 1908- *ConAu 61*
Blaise, Clark *DrAP&F 83*
Blaise, Clark 1940- *AuNews 2, ConAu 5NR, -53, WrDr 84*
Blake, Baron *WrDr 84*
Blake, Alfred *ConAu X, WrDr 84*
Blake, Andrew *ConAu X, WrDr 84*
Blake, Brian 1918- *ConAu 109, WrDr 84*
Blake, Bud *ConAu X*
Blake, David H 1940- *ConAu 41R*
Blake, Eubie *ConAu X*
Blake, Fay M 1920- *ConAu 53*
Blake, Forrester 1912- *TwCWW*
Blake, Gary 1944- *ConAu 85*
Blake, George 1893-1961 *LongCTC, TwCA, TwCA SUP, TwCWr*
Blake, Harlan Morse 1923- *ConAu 25R*
Blake, Israel George 1902- *ConAu 21R*
Blake, James 1922-1979 *ConAu 85, -93*
Blake, James Hubert 1883-1983 *ConAu 109*

Blake, James Washington *DrAP&F 83*
Blake, Jennifer *ConAu X, IntAu&W 82X, WrDr 84*
Blake, Jonas *ConAu X*
Blake, Judith 1926- *ConAu 1R*
Blake, Julian Watson 1918- *ConAu 65*
Blake, Justin *ConAu X, IntAu&W 82X, WrDr 84*
Blake, Katherine *ConAu X, DrAP&F 83*
Blake, Kathleen 1944- *ConAu 57*
Blake, Kay *ConAu X*
Blake, Ken *ConAu X, WrDr 84*
Blake, L J 1913- *ConAu 11NR*
Blake, Leslie *IntAu&W 82X*
Blake, Leslie James 1913- *ConAu 25R, IntAu&W 82, WrDr 84*
Blake, Minden V 1913- *ConAu 69*
Blake, Mindy *ConAu X*
Blake, Monica *ConAu X, IntAu&W 82X*
Blake, Nelson Manfred 1908- *ConAu 1R, -3NR*
Blake, Nicholas 1904-1972 *ConAu X, ConLC 1, LongCTC, TwCA, TwCA SUP, TwCCr&M 80, TwCWr, WhoTwCL*
Blake, Nicola *IntAu&W 82X*
Blake, Norman Francis 1934- *ConAu 93, WrDr 84*
Blake, Olive *SmATA X*
Blake, Patricia 1933- *ConAu 49*
Blake, Patrick *ConAu X, WrDr 84*
Blake, Paul C 1916- *ConAu 25R*
Blake, Peter 1920- *WrDr 84*
Blake, Peter Jost 1920- *ConAu 65*
Blake, Quentin 1932- *ConAu 11NR, -25R, SmATA 9*
Blake, Reed H 1933- *ConAu 57*
Blake, Richard A 1939- *ConAu 93*
Blake, Robert *ConAu X*
Blake, Robert 1916- *WrDr 84*
Blake, Robert Norman William 1916- *ConAu 9R, DcLEL 1940, WorAu*
Blake, Robert R 1918- *ConAu 21R*
Blake, Robert W 1930- *ConAu 33R*
Blake, Sally *ConAu X, IntAu&W 82X, WrDr 84*
Blake, Sally 1925- *WrDr 84*
Blake, Sally Mirliss *DrAP&F 83*
Blake, Sally Mirliss 1925- *ConAu 17R, IntAu&W 82*
Blake, Sexton *TwCCr&M 80*
Blake, Stephanie *TwCRGW, WrDr 84*
Blake, Thomas *ConSFA*
Blake, Walker E *ConAu X, SmATA 5*
Blake, Wendon *ConAu X*
Blake, William 1757-1827 *SmATA 30[port]*
Blake, William J 1894-1968 *ConAu 5R, -25R*
Blakeley, Phyllis 1922- *ConAu 61*
Blakeley, Thomas J 1931- *ConAu 3NR, -9R*
Blakely, R J 1915- *ConAu 37R*
Blakely, William Paul 1924- *IntWWP 82*
Blakeman, Beth R *DrAP&F 83*
Blakeman, Beth Renee 1951- *IntWWP 82*
Blakemore, Colin 1944- *ConAu 85*
Blakemore, Harold 1930- *IntAu&W 82*
Blaker, Alfred A 1928- *ConAu 65*
Blaker, Richard 1893-1940 *TwCA*
Blakeslee, Alton 1913- *ConAu 105*
Blakeslee, Thomas R 1937- *ConAu 101*
Blakey, Scott 1936- *ConAu 85*
Blakey, Walker Jameson 1940- *ConAu 69*
Blakiston, Georgiana 1903- *ConAu 69*
Blakiston, Hugh Noel 1905- *IntAu&W 82*
Blakney, Raymond D 1897?-1970 *ConAu 104*
Blalock, Hubert Morse, Jr. 1926- *ConAu 5NR, -13R*
Blaman, Anna 1905-1960 *ClDMEL 80, EncWL 2*
Blamires, David 1936- *ConAu 65, WrDr 84*
Blamires, Harry 1916- *ConAu 5NR, -9R, IntAu&W 82, WrDr 84*
Blanc, Suzanne *TwCCr&M 80, WrDr 84*
Blance, Ellen 1931- *ConAu 7NR, -57*
Blanch, Lesley 1907- *ConAu 102, WrDr 84*
Blanch, Robert J 1938- *ConAu 21R*
Blanch, Stuart Yarworth 1918- *ConAu 106*
Blanchard, Allan E 1929- *ConAu 69*
Blanchard, B Everard 1909- *ConAu 41R*
Blanchard, Carroll Henry, Jr. 1928- *ConAu 13R*
Blanchard, Fessenden Seaver 1888-1963 *ConAu 5R*
Blanchard, Howard L 1909- *ConAu 5R*
Blanchard, J Richard 1912- *ConAu 89, IntAu&W 82*

Blanchard, Kendall A 1942- *ConAu 11NR, –69*
Blanchard, Nina *ConAu 101*
Blanchard, Paula 1936- *ConAu 81*
Blanchard, Ralph Harrub 1890-1973 *ConAu P-1*
Blanchard, William 1922- *WrDr 84*
Blanchard, William Henry 1922- *ConAu 8NR, –21R*
Blanche, Pierre 1927- *ConAu 25R*
Blanchet, Eileen 1924- *ConAu 57*
Blanchette, Oliva 1929- *ConAu 53*
Blanchette, Olivia 1929- *IntAu&W 82*
Blanchot, Maurice 1907- *ClDMEL 80, EncWL 2, ModFrL, WorAu*
Blanck, Gertrude 1914- *ConAu 85*
Blanck, Jacob Nathaniel 1906-1974 *ConAu 53, ConAu P-1*
Blanck, Rubin 1914- *ConAu 25R*
Blanco, Luis Anado 1903?-1975 *ConAu 104*
Blanco, Richard L 1926- *ConAu 57*
Blanco Pinan, Salvador 1911- *IntAu&W 82*
Blanco Tobio, Manuel 1919- *IntAu&W 82*
Blanco White, Amber 1887-1981 *ConAu 105*
Bland, Alexander *ConAu X*
Bland, Edith Nesbit 1858-1924 *ChlLR 3, TwCA, TwCA SUP*
Bland, Fabian *LongCTC*
Bland, Hester Beth 1906- *ConAu 57*
Bland, Hubert 1856-1914 *LongCTC*
Bland, Mrs. Hubert *LongCTC*
Bland, Jeffrey 1946- *ConAu 106*
Bland, Jennifer *ConAu X, WrDr 84*
Bland, Larry I 1940- *ConAu 109*
Bland, Randall Walton 1942- *ConAu 5NR, –53*
Blandford, Percy 1912- *WrDr 84*
Blandford, Percy William 1912- *ConAu 9R, IntAu&W 82*
Blandino, Giovanni 1923- *ConAu 21R, IntAu&W 82*
Blane, Gertrude *ConAu X, SmATA X*
Blane, Howard T 1926- *ConAu 10NR, –25R*
Blanford, James T 1917- *ConAu 33R*
Blank, Blanche D *ConAu 41R*
Blank, Edward L 1943- *ConAmTC*
Blank, Franklin 1921- *IntAu&W 82*
Blank, George 1945- *ConAu 110*
Blank, Joseph P 1919- *ConAu 93*
Blank, Leonard 1927- *ConAu 33R*
Blank, Sheldon Haas 1896- *ConAu 1R*
Blanke, Huldrych 1931- *IntAu&W 82*
Blankenship, A B 1914- *ConAu 7NR, –13R, WrDr 84*
Blankenship, Edward Gary 1943- *ConAu 45*
Blankenship, Lela 1886- *ConAu 5R*
Blankenship, William D 1934- *ConAu 33R*
Blankenstein, Marc *IntAu&W 82X*
Blankfort, Michael 1907-1982 *ConAu 1R, –2NR, –107, NatPD 81[port]*
Blankner, Frederika *DrAP&F 83*
Blankoff, Jean Desire 1931- *IntAu&W 82*
Blanksten, George I 1917- *ConAu 1R, –1NR*
Blanpied, Pamela Wharton *DrAP&F 83*
Blanpied, Pamela Wharton 1937- *ConAu 102*
Blanshard, Brand 1892- *ConAu 1R*
Blanshard, Paul 1892-1980 *ConAu 93, TwCA SUP*
Blanton, Catherine 1907- *ConAu 1R*
Blanton, Jeremy 1939- *CreCan 2*
Blanzaco, Andre C 1934- *ConAu 29R*
Blasco Ibanez, Vicente 1867-1928 *ClDMEL 80, ConAu 110, EncWL 2, ModRL, TwCA, TwCA SUP, TwCLC 12[port], TwCWr*
Blase, Melvin G 1933- *ConAu 33R, WrDr 84*
Blaser, Robin 1925- *ConAu 8NR, –57, ConP 80, DcLEL 1940, WrDr 84*
Blashford-Snell, John Nicholas 1936- *ConAu 102, IntAu&W 82, WrDr 84*
Blasier, Cole 1925- *ConAu 21R*
Blasing, Mutlu Konuk 1944- *ConAu 89*
Blasing, Randy *DrAP&F 83*
Blass, Birgit A 1940- *ConAu 29R*
Blassen, Sal *IntAu&W 82X*
Blassingame, John W 1940- *ConAu 49, ConIsC 1[port], LivgBAA*
Blassingame, Wyatt 1909- *SmATA 34[port]*
Blassingame, Wyatt R 1909- *WrDr 84*
Blassingame, Wyatt Rainey 1909- *ConAu 1R, –3NR, IntAu&W 82, SmATA 1*
Blatchford, Christie 1951- *ConAu 73*
Blatchford, Robert 1851-1943 *LongCTC*
Blathwayt, Jean 1910- *ConAu 106, WrDr 84*
Blatt, Burton 1927- *ConAu 41R*
Blatt, John Markus 1921- *WrDr 84*

Blatt, Sidney J 1928- *ConAu 37R*
Blatter, Dorothy 1901- *ConAu P-1*
Blattner, H W *DrAP&F 83*
Blatty, William 1928- *WrDr 84*
Blatty, William Peter 1928- *ConAu 5R, –9NR, ConLC 2*
Blau, Abram 1907-1979 *ConAu 85*
Blau, Eric 1921- *ConAu 85*
Blau, Francine D 1946- *ConAu 106, WrDr 84*
Blau, Joseph L 1909- *ConAu 9R*
Blau, Joshua 1919- *ConAu 7NR, –13R*
Blau, Milton *ConAu X*
Blau, Peter M 1918- *ConAu 1R, –1NR, IntAu&W 82, WrDr 84*
Blau, Sheldon Paul 1935- *ConAu 57*
Blau, Yehoshua *ConAu X*
Blau, Zena Smith 1922- *ConAu 1NR, –45*
Blaufarb, Douglas S 1918- *ConAu 85*
Blaug, Mark 1927- *ConAu 1R, –1NR*
Blauner, Laurie *DrAP&F 83*
Blauner, Laurie 1953- *IntWWP 82*
Blauner, Robert 1929- *ConAu 17R*
Blaushild, Babette 1927- *ConAu 29R*
Blaustein, Albert P 1921- *ConAu 1R, –1NR, WrDr 84*
Blaustein, Arthur I 1933- *ConAu 10NR, –25R*
Blaustein, Elliott H 1915- *ConAu 41R*
Blaustein, Esther 1935- *ConAu 45*
Blauw, Johannes 1912- *ConAu 9R*
Blaxland, Gregory 1918- *ConAu 9R, IntAu&W 82, WrDr 84*
Blaxland, John 1917- *ConAu 5R*
Blaxland, W Gregory 1918- *ConAu 3NR*
Blaylock, James P 1950- *ConAu 110*
Blayney, Margaret S 1926- *ConAu 53*
Blayre, Christopher 1861-1943 *TwCSFW*
Blaze, Wayne 1951- *ConAu 61*
Blazek, Douglas *DrAP&F 83*
Blazek, Douglas 1941- *ConAu 25R, IntWWP 82*
Blazer, Dan G, II 1944- *ConAu 110*
Blazer, J S *ConAu X*
Blazier, Kenneth D 1933- *ConAu 11NR, –69*
Blazquez, Feliciano 1937- *IntAu&W 82*
Blazynski, Tadeusz 1924- *WrDr 84*
Bleakley, David Wylie 1925- *ConAu 102, IntAu&W 82, WrDr 84*
Blecher, George M *DrAP&F 83*
Blecher, M 1909-1938 *EncWL 2*
Blechman, Barry M 1943- *ConAu 97*
Blechman, Burt 1927- *ConNov 82, WrDr 84*
Blechman, Robert 1932- *ConAu 21R, DcLEL 1940*
Bledlow, John *ConAu X*
Bledsoe, Jerry 1941- *ConAu 85*
Bledsoe, Joseph C 1918- *ConAu 33R*
Bledsoe, Thomas 1914- *ConAu 9NR, –13R*
Bledsoe, William Ambrose 1906-1981 *ConAu 104*
Bleeck, Oliver *ConAu X, TwCCr&M 80, WrDr 84*
Bleeker, Mordecia *ConAu X*
Bleeker, Sonia 1909-1971 *ConAu X, SmATA 2, –26N*
Blees, Robert A 1922- *ConAu 17R*
Blegen, Carl 1887-1971 *ConAu 33R*
Blegen, Theodore Christian 1891-1969 *ConAu 3NR, –5R*
Blegvad, Erik 1923- *ConAu 97, SmATA 14*
Blegvad, Lenore 1926- *ConAu 69, SmATA 14*
Blehl, Vincent Ferrer 1921- *ConAu 9R*
Blei, Franz 1871-1942 *ModGL*
Blei, Norbert *DrAP&F 83*
Bleiberg, German 1915- *ClDMEL 80*
Bleiberg, Robert Marvin 1924- *ConAu 103*
Bleich, Alan R 1913- *ConAu 13R*
Bleich, Harold 1930?-1980 *ConAu 93*
Bleicher, Michael N 1935- *ConAu 37R*
Bleier, Robert Patrick 1946- *ConAu 85*
Bleier, Rockey *ConAu X*
Blench, John Wheatley 1926- *ConAu 13R*
Blend, Charles Daniels 1918- *ConAu 21R*
Blenkinsopp, Joseph 1927- *ConAu 37R, WrDr 84*
Bleser, Carol K 1935- *ConAu 107*
Blesh, Rudi 1899- *ConAu X, IntAu&W 82, WrDr 84*
Blesh, Rudolph Pickett 1899- *ConAu 17R*
Blessing, Richard Allen 1939- *ConAu 53*
Bletschacher, Richard 1936- *IntAu&W 82*
Bletter, Robert 1933?-1976 *ConAu 61*
Bletter, Rosemarie Haag 1939- *ConAu 57*
Blevins, James Lowell 1936- *ConAu 106*

Blevins, Leon W 1937- *ConAu 57*
Blevins, William L 1937- *ConAu 33R*
Blevins, Winfred 1938- *ConAu 1NR, –45*
Bleything, Dennis H 1946- *ConAu 61*
Bleznick, Donald W 1924- *ConAu 21R*
Blicker, Seymour 1940- *ConAu 77*
Blicq, Anthony 1926- *ConAu 33R*
Bligh, Aurora *DrAP&F 83*
Bligh, Norman *ConAu X*
Blight, John 1913- *ConAu 69, ConP 80, WrDr 84*
Blinder, Elliot 1949- *ConAu 106*
Blinderman, Abraham 1916- *ConAu 53, –61*
Blinn, Johna *ConAu X*
Blinn, Walter Craig 1930- *ConAu 61*
Blish, James 1921-1975 *ConAu 1R, –3NR, –57, ConLC 14, ConSFA, DcLB 8[port], DcLEL 1940, TwCSFW, WorAu*
Blishen, Bernard Russell 1919- *ConAu 1R, –3NR*
Blishen, Edward 1920- *ConAu 11NR, –17R, SmATA 8, WrDr 84*
Bliss, Carey Stillman 1914- *ConAu 41R, IntAu&W 82*
Bliss, Corinne Demas *DrAP&F 83*
Bliss, Corinne Demas 1947- *ConAu 104*
Bliss, Edward, Jr. 1912- *ConAu 41R*
Bliss, George William 1918-1978 *ConAu 81, –85*
Bliss, Michael 1941- *ConAu 103*
Bliss, Reginald *SmATA X*
Bliss, Ronald G 1942- *ConAu 53, SmATA 12*
Bliss, S W *DrAP&F 83*
Bliss, Sally Brayley *CreCan 2*
Blissett, Marlan 1938- *ConAu 41R*
Blistein, Elmer M 1920- *ConAu 9R*
Blitch, Fleming Lee *ConAu X*
Blits, Jan H 1943- *ConAu 110*
Blitzstein, Marc 1905-1964 *CnMD, ConAu 110, ModWD*
Bliven, Bruce 1889-1977 *ConAu 37R, –69, TwCA, TwCA SUP*
Bliven, Bruce, Jr. 1916- *ConAu 7NR, –17R, SmATA 2*
Bliven, Naomi 1925- *ConAu 33R*
Blixen, Baroness Karen 1885-1962 *ClDMEL 80, ConAu P-2, ConLC 10, LongCTC, TwCA, TwCA SUP, WhoTwCL*
Blixen-Finecke, Karen 1885-1962 *TwCWr*
Blizzard, S W 1914?-1976 *ConAu 65*
Bloch, Alice *DrAP&F 83*
Bloch, Ariel A 1933- *ConAu 41R*
Bloch, Barbara 1925- *ConAu 106*
Bloch, Blanche 1890-1980 *ConAu 97*
Bloch, Chana *DrAP&F 83*
Bloch, Chana 1940- *ConAu 105, IntWWP 82X*
Bloch, Dorothy 1912- *ConAu 93*
Bloch, E Maurice *ConAu 25R*
Bloch, Ernst 1885-1977 *ConAu 29R, –73*
Bloch, Florence Chana 1940- *IntWWP 82*
Bloch, Gorm Arne 1923- *IntAu&W 82*
Bloch, Herbert Aaron 1904-1965 *ConAu 1R*
Bloch, Herman D 1914- *ConAu 29R*
Bloch, Jean-Richard 1884-1947 *TwCA, TwCA SUP*
Bloch, Jean-Richard 1886-1947 *ClDMEL 80*
Bloch, Lucienne 1909- *SmATA 10*
Bloch, Lucienne S 1937- *ConAu 93, IntAu&W 82*
Bloch, Marie Halun 1910- *ConAu 1R, –4NR, SmATA 6, WrDr 84*
Bloch, Robert *DrAP&F 83*
Bloch, Robert 1917- *ConAu 5R, –5NR, ConSFA, IntAu&W 82, SmATA 12, TwCCr&M 80, TwCSFW, WrDr 84*
Bloch-Hoell, Nils Egede 1915- *IntAu&W 82*
Bloch-Michel, Jean 1912- *WorAu*
Blocher, Henri 1937- *ConAu 10NR, –65*
Blochman, Lawrence G 1900- *WrDr 84*
Blochman, Lawrence G 1900-1975 *ConAu 53, ConAu P-2, SmATA 22, TwCCr&M 80*
Block, Allan *DrAP&F 83*
Block, Allan 1923- *ConAu 49, IntWWP 82*
Block, Arthur John 1916?-1981 *ConAu 105*
Block, Eugene B 1890- *ConAu 2NR, –5R*
Block, Hal 1914?-1981 *ConAu 104*
Block, Irvin 1917- *ConAu 17R, SmATA 12*
Block, Jack 1921- *ConAu 33R*
Block, Jack 1931- *ConAu 53*
Block, Jean Libman *ConAu 5R*
Block, Joel D 1943- *ConAu 89*
Block, Lawrence *DrAP&F 83*
Block, Lawrence 1938- *ConAu 1R, –6NR, TwCCr&M 80, WrDr 84*

Block, Libbie 1910?-1972 *ConAu 33R*
Block, Marvin Avram 1903- *ConAu 106*
Block, Michael 1942- *ConAu 101*
Block, Ralph 1889-1974 *ConAu 45*
Block, Seymour Stanton 1918- *ConAu 89*
Block, Stanley Byron 1939- *ConAu 85*
Block, Thomas H 1945- *ConAu 101*
Block, Walter 1941- *ConAu 6NR, –57*
Block, Zenas 1916- *ConAu 107*
Blockcolski, Lewis *DrAP&F 83*
Blocker, Clyde Edward 1918- *ConAu 33R*
Blockinger, Betty *ConAu X*
Blocklinger, Peggy O'More 1895- *ConAu 5R*
Blodgett, Beverley 1926- *ConAu 57*
Blodgett, Geoffrey Thomas 1931- *ConAu 17R*
Blodgett, Harold William 1900- *ConAu 13R*
Blodgett, Harriet Eleanor 1919- *ConAu 33R*
Blodgett, Richard 1940- *ConAu 1NR, –49*
Bloem, Diane Brummel 1935- *ConAu 85*
Bloem, Jakobus Cornelis 1887-1966 *ClDMEL 80*
Bloembergen, Nicolaas 1920- *WrDr 84*
Bloemertz, Gunther Friedrich Werner 1923-
IntAu&W 82
Bloesch, Donald George 1928- *ConAu 13R,*
IntAu&W 82, WrDr 84
Bloesser, Robert 1930- *ConAu 37R*
Blofeld, John E C 1913- *WrDr 84*
Blofeld, John Eaton Calthorpe 1913-
ConAu 4NR, –53, IntAu&W 82
Blok, Aleksander 1880-1921 *ClDMEL 80,*
CnMWL, LongCTC, ModSL 1, ModWD,
TwCA, TwCA SUP, TwCLC 5[port],
TwCWr, WhoTwCL
Blok, Alexander 1880-1921 *CnMD, ConAu 104*
Blok, Alexandr 1880-1921 *EncWL 2*
Blok, Anton 1935- *ConAu 97*
Blom, Eric Walter 1888-1959 *LongCTC*
Blom, Gaston E 1920- *ConAu 25R*
Blom, Karl Arne 1946- *ConAu 11NR, –69*
Blom-Cooper, Louis Jacques 1926- *ConAu 5R*
Blomerus, Helene Marie 1931- *IntAu&W 82*
Blomfield, Adelaide *DrAP&F 83*
Blond, Anthony 1928- *ConAu 106, WrDr 84*
Blondal, Patricia Anne Jenkins 1926- *CreCan 1*
Blondel, Jean DelFernand DelPierre 1929-
WrDr 84
Blondel, Jean Fernand Pierre 1929- *ConAu 101*
Blondel, Maurice 1861-1949 *ClDMEL 80*
Blondell, Joan 1906?-1979 *ConAu 93*
Blondin, Antoine 1922- *IntAu&W 82*
Blood, Charles Lewis 1929- *ConAu 73,*
SmATA 28
Blood, Jerome W 1926- *ConAu 9R*
Blood, Marie Louise 1931- *IntWWP 82*
Blood, Marje *ConAu 41R, WrDr 84*
Blood, Matthew *ConAu X*
Blood, Robert O, Jr. 1921- *ConAu 1R, –3NR*
Bloodstone, John *ConAu X*
Bloom, Alan Herbert 1906- *ConAu 3NR, –9R*
Bloom, Edward A 1914- *WrDr 84*
Bloom, Edward Alan 1914- *ConAu 1R, –2NR*
Bloom, Erick Franklin 1944- *ConAu 57*
Bloom, Freddy 1914- *ConAu 101*
Bloom, Mrs. Freddy 1914- *WrDr 84*
Bloom, Gordon F 1918- *ConAu 13R*
Bloom, Harold 1930- *ConAu 13R,*
ConLC 24[port], ConLCrt 82, DcLEL 1940,
IntAu&W 82, WorAu 1970, WrDr 84
Bloom, Harry 1913-1981 *ConAu 104, TwCWr*
Bloom, Harry 1921- *WrDr 84*
Bloom, Herman Irving 1908- *ConAu 102*
Bloom, Janet *DrAP&F 83*
Bloom, John Ernest George 1921- *ConAu 5R*
Bloom, John Porter 1924- *ConAu 49*
Bloom, Lillian D 1920- *ConAu 11NR, –17R*
Bloom, Lynn 1934- *WrDr 84*
Bloom, Lynn Marie Zimmerman 1934-
ConAu 6NR, –13R
Bloom, Melvyn H 1938- *ConAu 45*
Bloom, Murray Teigh 1916- *ASpks, ConAu 17R,*
NatPD 81[port], WrDr 84
Bloom, Pauline *ConAu 41R*
Bloom, Robert 1930- *ConAu 17R*
Bloom, Samuel W 1921- *WrDr 84*
Bloom, Samuel William 1921- *ConAu 3NR, –9R*
Bloom, Ursula *ConAu 25R, IntAu&W 82,*
TwCRGW, WrDr 84
Bloom, William 1948- *WrDr 84*
Blooman, Percy A 1906- *ConAu P-1,*
IntAu&W 82
Bloomberg, Edward 1937- *ConAu 41R*
Bloomberg, Marty *ConAu X*

Bloomberg, Max Arthur 1938- *ConAu 101*
Bloomberg, Morton 1936- *ConAu 53*
Bloome, Enid P 1925- *ConAu 85*
Bloomfield, Anthony John Westgate 1922-
ConAu 1R, DcLEL 1940, IntAu&W 82,
WorAu, WrDr 84
Bloomfield, Arthur 1931- *ConAu 65*
Bloomfield, Arthur Irving 1914- *ConAu 41R*
Bloomfield, B C 1931- *ConAu 5NR, –9R*
Bloomfield, Barry 1931- *WrDr 84*
Bloomfield, Harold H 1944- *ConAu 9NR, –57*
Bloomfield, Lincoln P 1920- *WrDr 84*
Bloomfield, Lincoln Palmer 1920- *ConAu 1R,*
–5NR, IntAu&W 82
Bloomfield, Masse 1923- *ConAu 8NR, –61*
Bloomfield, Maureen *DrAP&F 83*
Bloomfield, Morton W 1913- *ConAu 2NR, –5R*
Bloomingdale, Teresa 1930- *ConAu 105*
Bloomquist, Edward R 1924- *ConAu 29R*
Bloomstein, Morris J 1928- *ConAu 25R*
Bloore, Ronald L 1925- *CreCan 2*
Blos, Joan 1928- *WrDr 84*
Blos, Joan W 1928- *ConAu 101,*
SmATA 33[port], TwCCW 83
Blos, Joan W 1929?- *SmATA 27*
Blos, Peter 1904- *ConAu 89*
Bloss, F Donald 1920- *ConAu 53*
Bloss, Meredith 1908-1982 *ConAu 107*
Blossom, Frederick A 1878?-1974 *ConAu 49*
Blossom, Laurel *DrAP&F 83*
Blossom, Thomas 1912- *ConAu 21R*
Blotner, Joseph 1923- *ASpks, AuNews 1,*
ConAu 1R, WrDr 84
Blotnick, Elihu 1939- *ConAu 106*
Blouet, Brian Walter 1936- *ConAu 93*
Blouet, Leon Paul *LongCTC*
Blough, Glenn O 1904- *MichAu 80*
Blough, Glenn Orlando 1907- *ConAu P-1,*
SmATA 1
Blount, Charles 1913- *ConAu 17R*
Blount, Margaret 1924- *ConAu 69*
Blount, Roy, Jr. 1941- *ConAu 10NR*
Blount, Roy Alton 1941- *ConAu 53*
Bloustein, Edward J 1925- *ConAu 41R*
Blow, Ernest J *ConSFA*
Blow, Suzanne 1932- *ConAu 45*
Bloy, Leon Marie 1846-1917 *ClDMEL 80,*
ModFrL
Blue, Betty 1922- *ConAu 1NR, –45*
Blue, Frederick Judd 1937- *ConAu 53*
Blue, Martha Ward 1942- *ConAu 104*
Blue, Rose 1931- *ConAu 41R, SmATA 5*
Blue, Wallace *ConAu X*
Blue Cloud, Peter *DrAP&F 83, IntWWP 82X*
Blue Cloud, Peter Avoniawenvate 1933-
IntWWP 82
Bluebond-Langner, Myra 1948- *ConAu 81*
Bluefarb, Samuel 1919- *ConAu 37R*
Bluemle, Andrew 1929- *ConAu 1R*
Bluestein, Daniel Thomas 1943- *ConAu 65*
Bluestein, Gene 1928- *ConAu 81*
Bluestone, George 1928- *ConAu 1R, –1NR*
Bluestone, Max 1926- *ConAu 13R*
Bluh, Bonnie *DrAP&F 83*
Bluh, Bonnie 1926- *ConAu 97*
Bluhm, Heinz 1907- *ConAu P-1, IntAu&W 82,*
WrDr 84
Bluhm, William T 1923- *ConAu 13R*
Blum, Albert A 1924- *ConAu 5R, –11NR,*
WrDr 84
Blum, Carol Kathlyn 1934- *ConAu 101*
Blum, David 1935- *ConAu 107*
Blum, Eleanor 1914- *ConAu 1R*
Blum, Etta *DrAP&F 83*
Blum, Fred 1932- *ConAu 13R*
Blum, Harold P 1929- *ConAu 103*
Blum, Henrik L 1915- *ConAu 6NR, –9R*
Blum, Jerome 1913- *ConAu 1R, WrDr 84*
Blum, John Morton 1921- *ConAu 2NR, –5R,*
DcLEL 1940
Blum, Judy *AuNews 1[port]*
Blum, Leon 1872-1950 *ClDMEL 80*
Blum, Lucille Hollander 1904- *ConAu 101*
Blum, Ralph 1932- *AuNews 1[port]*
Blum, Richard A 1943- *IntAu&W 82*
Blum, Richard Hosmer 1927- *ConAu 13R*
Blum, Rick *IntAu&W 82X*
Blum, Shirley Neilsen 1932- *ConAu 33R*
Blum, Stella 1916- *ConAu 97*
Blum, Virgil Clarence 1913- *ConAu 13R*
Blumberg, Arnold 1925- *ConAu 33R,*
IntAu&W 82, WrDr 84

Blumberg, Dorothy Rose 1904- *ConAu P-2*
Blumberg, Gary 1938- *ConAu 2NR, –45*
Blumberg, Harry 1903- *ConAu 73*
Blumberg, Leonard U 1920- *ConAu 101*
Blumberg, Myrna 1932- *ConAu 21R*
Blumberg, Nathan Bernard 1922- *ConAu 41R*
Blumberg, Philip Irvin 1919- *WrDr 84*
Blumberg, Phillip Irvin 1919- *ConAu 101*
Blumberg, Rena J 1934- *ConAu 109*
Blumberg, Rhoda 1917- *ConAu 9NR, –65*
Blumberg, Rhoda L 1926- *ConAu 6NR*
Blumberg, Robert S 1945- *ConAu 57*
Blume, Bernhard 1901- *CnMD, ModWD*
Blume, Friedrich 1893-1975 *ConAu 73*
Blume, Helmut 1914- *CreCan 2*
Blume, Judy 1938- *ChlLR 2, ConAu 29R,*
ConLC 12, SmATA 2, –31[port],
TwCCW 83, WrDr 84
Blumenfeld, Frank Yorick 1932- *WrDr 84*
Blumenfeld, Gerry 1906- *ConAu 21R*
Blumenfeld, Hans 1892- *ConAu P-2, WrDr 84*
Blumenfeld, Harold 1905- *ConAu 97*
Blumenfeld, Meyer 1905-1980 *ConAu 97*
Blumenfeld, Ralph David 1864-1948 *LongCTC*
Blumenfeld, Samuel Leon 1926- *ConAu 41R*
Blumenfeld, Yorick 1932- *ConAu 25R*
Blumenkron, Carmen *IntWWP 82X*
Blumenkron Bernard, Carmen Virginia
IntWWP 82
Blumensaadt Pedersen, Pelle 1929- *IntAu&W 82*
Blumenson, Martin 1918- *ConAu 1R, –4NR,*
WrDr 84
Blumenthal, Arthur L 1936- *ConAu 29R*
Blumenthal, Gerda Renee 1923- *ConAu 1R,*
WrDr 84
Blumenthal, Gertrude 1907-1971 *ConAu 104,*
SmATA 27N
Blumenthal, Henry 1911- *ConAu 29R,*
IntAu&W 82
Blumenthal, L Roy 1908-1975 *ConAu 61*
Blumenthal, Lassor Agoos 1926- *ConAu 25R*
Blumenthal, Marcia *DrAP&F 83*
Blumenthal, Michael C *DrAP&F 83*
Blumenthal, Michael C 1949- *ConAu 110*
Blumenthal, Michael Charles 1949- *IntWWP 82*
Blumenthal, Monica David 1930-1981 *ConAu 103,*
–73
Blumenthal, Norm *ConAu 97*
Blumenthal, Shirley 1943- *ConAu 108*
Blumenthal, Sidney 1909- *ConAu 106*
Blumenthal, Walter Hart 1883-1969 *ConAu P-1*
Blumin, Stuart M 1940- *ConAu 65*
Bluming, Mildred G 1919- *ConAu 106*
Blumrich, Josef F 1913- *ConAu 93*
Blumrosen, Alfred W 1928- *ConAu 53*
Blundel, Anne *ConAu X*
Blundell, Harold 1902- *ConAu 101*
Blundell, Mary E *LongCTC*
Blunden, Edmund Charles 1896-1974 *ConAu 45,*
ConAu P-2, ConLC 2, LongCTC, ModBrL,
ModBrL SUP, RGFMBP, TwCA,
TwCA SUP, TwCWr, WhoTwCL
Blunden, Margaret 1939- *ConAu 21R*
Blunk, Frank M 1897?-1976 *CónAu 69*
Blunn, Oswald Maurice 1926- *IntAu&W 82*
Blunsden, John 1930- *ConAu 57*
Blunsdon, Norman 1915-1968 *ConAu P-1*
Blunt, Anthony 1907- *WrDr 84*
Blunt, Anthony 1907-1983 *ConAu 109*
Blunt, Anthony Frederick 1907- *IntAu&W 82*
Blunt, Don *ConAu X, WrDr 84*
Blunt, J K *LongCTC*
Blunt, Wilfred Scawen 1840-1922 *LongCTC*
Blunt, Wilfrid 1901- *ConAu 5NR, –13R,*
IntAu&W 82, WrDr 84
Blunt, Wilfrid Scawen 1840-1922 *ModBrL*
Bluphocks, Lucien *ConAu X*
Bluth, B J 1934- *ConAu 106*
Blutig, Eduard *ConAu X, SmATA X*
Bly, Carol *DrAP&F 83*
Bly, Carol 1930- *ConAu 108*
Bly, Robert *DrAP&F 83*
Bly, Robert 1926- *ConAu 5R, ConLC 1, –2, –5,*
–10, –15, ConP 80, CroCAP, DcLB 5[port],
DcLEL 1940, EncWL 2, ModAL SUP,
WhoTwCL, WorAu, WrDr 84
Bly, Thomas J 1918?-1979 *ConAu 85*
Bly, William J *DrAP&F 83*
Blyn, George 1919- *ConAu 37R*
Blyth, Alan Geoffrey 1929- *ConAu 1NR, –49,*
WrDr 84
Blyth, Chay 1940- *ConAu 110, WrDr 84*

Blyth, Estelle 1882?-1983 *ConAu 109*
Blyth, Henry 1910- *WrDr 84*
Blyth, Henry 1910-1983 *ConAu 110*
Blyth, Henry Edward 1910- *ConAu 21R,*
  IntAu&W 82
Blyth, Jeffrey 1926- *ConAu 65*
Blyth, John *ConAu X, IntAu&W 82X,*
  WrDr 84
Blyth, Myrna 1939- *ConAu 10NR*
Blyth, Myrna 1940- *ConAu 65*
Blythe, Anne Susan 1956- *IntAu&W 82*
Blythe, Herbert 1847-1905 *LongCTC*
Blythe, LeGette 1900- *ConAu 1R, -1NR*
Blythe, Ronald 1922- *WrDr 84*
Blythe, Ronald George 1922- *ConAu 5R,*
  IntAu&W 82
Blyton, Carey 1932- *ConAu 49, SmATA 9*
Blyton, Enid 1897-1968 *TwCCW 83*
Blyton, Enid Mary d1968 *LongCTC*
Blyton, Enid Mary 1897-1968 *ConAu 77,*
  SmATA 25[port]
Blyton, Enid Mary 1898?-1968 *ConAu 25R*
Boa, Kenneth 1945- *ConAu 8NR, -61*
Boadella, David 1931- *ConAu 53, IntWWP 82*
Boahen, Albert Adu 1932- *IntAu&W 82*
Boak, Arthur Edward Romilly 1888-1962
  ConAu 5R
Boak, Denis 1932- *ConAu 13R*
Boalch, Donald Howard 1914- *ConAu 9R,*
  WrDr 84
Boalt, Gunnar 1910- *ConAu 7NR, -57*
Board, C Stephen 1942- *ConAu 57*
Board, Joan *IntWWP 82*
Board, Joseph Breckinridge 1931- *ConAu 29R*
Boardman, Arthur 1927- *ConAu 61, WrDr 84*
Boardman, Charles *WrDr 84*
Boardman, Charles C 1932- *ConAu 29R*
Boardman, Eunice *ConAu X*
Boardman, Fon W, Jr. 1911- *WrDr 84*
Boardman, Fon Wyman, Jr. 1911- *ConAu 1R,*
  -3NR, IntAu&W 82, SmATA 6
Boardman, Francis 1915-1976 *ConAu 69*
Boardman, Gwenn R 1924- *ConAu X,*
  SmATA 12
Boardman, John 1927- *ConAu 101, WrDr 84*
Boardman, Neil S 1907- *ConAu P-1*
Boardman, Peter 1950- *ConAu 97*
Boardman, Peter 1950-1982 *ConAu 108*
Boardman, Tom 1930- *ConSFA*
Boardwell, Robert Lee 1926- *ConAu 103*
Boarino, Gerald L 1931- *ConAu 21R*
Boarman, Patrick M 1922- *ConAu 9NR, -13R*
Boas, F S 1862-1957 *LongCTC*
Boas, Franz 1858-1942 *TwCA SUP*
Boas, Guy 1896-1966 *ConAu P-1*
Boas, Louise Schutz 1885- *ConAu 5R*
Boas, Marie *ConAu X*
Boas, Maurits Ignatius 1892- *ConAu 1R, -5NR*
Boase, Alan Martin 1902- *ConAu 5R,*
  IntAu&W 82
Boase, Alan Martin 1902-1982 *ConAu 10NR,*
  -108
Boase, Paul Henshaw 1915- *ConAu 37R*
Boase, Roger 1946- *IntAu&W 82*
Boase, Thomas Sherrer Ross 1898-1974
  ConAu P-2
Boase, Wendy 1944- *ConAu 106,*
  SmATA 28[port]
Boateng, E A 1920- *ConAu 11NR*
Boateng, Ernest Amano 1920- *ConAu 21R,*
  IntAu&W 82
Boateng, Yaw Maurice *ConAu X*
Boatman, Don Earl 1913- *ConAu 1R*
Boatner, Mark Mayo, III 1921- *ConAu 21R,*
  SmATA 29[port]
Boatright, Mody Coggin 1896-1970 *ConAu 3NR,*
  -5R, -89
Boatright, Philip 1934- *IntWWP 82*
Boatwright, Howard Leake 1918- *ConAu 53*
Boaz, Martha *ConAu 3NR, -9R*
Bob, Brother *ConAu X*
Boba, Imre 1919- *ConAu 69*
Bobak, Bronislav Joseph 1923- *CreCan 1*
Bobak, Bruno 1923- *CreCan 1*
Bobak, Molly 1922- *CreCan 2*
Bobb, Bernard Earl 1917- *ConAu 5R*
Bobbe, Dorothie DeBear 1905-1975 *ConAu 57,*
  ConAu P-2, SmATA 1, -25N
Bobbitt, Philip 1948- *ConAu 108*
Bober, Stanley 1932- *ConAu 11NR, -21R*
Bobette *ConAu X*
Bobinski, George S 1929- *ConAu 29R,*

WrDr 84
Bobker, Lee R 1925- *ConAu 9NR, -53*
Boboc, Alexandru 1930- *IntAu&W 82*
Bobri *SmATA X*
Bobri, Vladimir *SmATA X*
Bobri, Vladimir V 1898- *ConAu 105*
Bobrick, Sam 1932- *NatPD 81*
Bobritsky, Vladimir 1898- *SmATA 32*
Bobrow, Davis Bernard 1936- *ConAu 7NR, -57*
Bobrow, Edwin E 1928- *ConAu 8NR, -21R*
Bobrowski, Johannes 1917-1965 *ClDMEL 80,*
  ConAu 77, EncWL 2, ModGL, TwCWr,
  WorAu 1970
Bocca, Al *ConAu X*
Bocca, Geoffrey 1923-1983 *ConAu 110*
Boccio, Karen Corinne *DrAP&F 83*
Bochenski, Innocentius M *ConAu X*
Bochenski, Joseph M 1902- *ConAu 5R, -7NR*
Bochner, Salomon 1899- *ConAu 41R, WrDr 84*
Bociany, Kosy I *IntAu&W 82X*
Bock, Alan W 1943- *ConAu 41R*
Bock, Carl H 1930- *ConAu P-2*
Bock, Ernst G W 1928- *IntAu&W 82*
Bock, Fred 1939- *ConAu 10NR, -25R*
Bock, Frederick *DrAP&F 83*
Bock, Frederick 1916- *ConAu 9R*
Bock, Hal *ConAu X, SmATA X*
Bock, Harold I 1939- *ConAu 29R, SmATA 10*
Bock, Joanne 1940- *ConAu 57*
Bock, Layeh A *DrAP&F 83*
Bock, Paul J 1922- *ConAu 53*
Bock, Philip K 1934- *ConAu 11NR*
Bock, Philip Karl 1934- *ConAu 25R, WrDr 84*
Bock, William Sauts 1939- *SmATA 14*
Bockelman, Wilfred 1920- *ConAu 37R*
Bockius, William Lawrence 1924- *IntWWP 82*
Bockl, George 1909- *ConAu 61*
Bockle, Franz *ConAu X*
Bockmon, Guy Alan 1926- *ConAu 5R*
Bockris, Victor *DrAP&F 83*
Bockus, H William 1915- *ConAu 53*
Bocock, Robert James 1940- *ConAu 69,*
  WrDr 84
Boczek, Boleslaw Adam 1922- *ConAu 1R, -4NR*
Bod, Peter 1911- *ConAu X*
Bodansky, Oscar 1901-1977 *ConAu 73*
Bodart, Joni 1947- *ConAu 106*
Bodden, Ilona 1940- *IntAu&W 82*
Boddewyn, J 1929- *ConAu 25R*
Boddie, Charles Emerson 1911- *ConAu 65,*
  LivgBAA
Boddy, Frederick Arthur 1914- *ConAu 61,*
  IntAu&W 82, WrDr 84
Boddy, William Charles 1913- *ConAu 101*
Bode, Carl *DrAP&F 83*
Bode, Carl 1911- *ConAu 1R, -3NR,*
  IntAu&W 82, IntWWP 82, WrDr 84
Bode, Elroy 1931- *ConAu 10NR, -25R*
Bode, Janet 1943- *ConAu 69*
Bode, Roy E 1948- *ConAu 77*
Bodecker, N M 1922- *ConAu 4NR,*
  TwCCW 83, WrDr 84
Bodecker, Nils Mogens 1922- *ConAu 49,*
  SmATA 8
Bodeen, DeWitt 1908- *ConAu 10NR, -25R*
Bodell, Mary *ConAu X*
Bodelsen, Anders 1937- *ClDMEL 80, EncWL 2*
Bodelsen, Merete 1907- *IntAu&W 82*
Boden, Hilda *ConAu X, SmATA X*
Boden, Margaret A 1936- *ConAu 93, WrDr 84*
Bodenham, Hilda 1901- *ConAu 6NR, -9R,*
  SmATA 13
Bodenheim, Maxwell 1892-1954 *ConAu 110,*
  DcLB 9[port]
Bodenheim, Maxwell 1893-1954 *ModAL,*
  TwCA[port], TwCA SUP
Bodenheimer, Edgar 1908- *ConAu 33R*
Bodet, Jaime Torres *ConAu X*
Bodey, Hugh 1939- *ConAu 61, WrDr 84*
Bodger, Joan *ConAu X*
Bodian, Nat G 1921- *ConAu 103*
Bodie, Idella F 1925- *ConAu 41R, SmATA 12*
Bodin, Paul 1909- *ConAu 65*
Bodington, Nancy H 1912- *ConAu 53*
Bodington, Nancy Hermione *IntAu&W 82,*
  WrDr 84
Bodker, Cecil 1927- *ConAu 73,*
  ConLC 21[port], IntAu&W 82, SmATA 14
Bodkin, Cora 1944- *ConAu 69*
Bodkin, M M'Donnell 1850-1933 *TwCCr&M 80*
Bodkin, Maud 1875-1967 *ConAu P-1,*
  ConLCrt 82, TwCA SUP

Bodkin, Ronald G 1936- *ConAu 33R, WrDr 84*
Bodkin, Thomas 1887-1961 *LongCTC*
Bodle, Yvonne Gallegos 1939- *ConAu 33R,*
  WrDr 84
Bodmer, Walter Fred 1936- *ConAu 102,*
  WrDr 84
Bodmershof, Imma Von 1895- *IntAu&W 82*
Bodnar, John Edward 1944- *ConAu 110*
Bodo, Murray 1937- *ConAu 7NR, -57*
Bodo, Peter T 1949- *ConAu 85*
Bodoh, John J 1931- *ConAu 45*
Bodsworth, Charles Fred 1918- *IntAu&W 82*
Bodsworth, Charles Frederick *CreCan 2*
Bodsworth, Fred 1918- *ConAu 1R, -3NR,*
  ConNov 82, CreCan 2, SmATA 27[port],
  WrDr 84
Bodtke, Richard *DrAP&F 83*
Bodwell, Richard *ConAu X*
Body, Geoffrey 1929- *WrDr 84*
Boe, Deborah *DrAP&F 83*
Boe, Deborah Lynn 1951- *IntWWP 82*
Boeck, Johann A 1917- *CroCD*
Boeckle, Franz 1921- *ConAu 101*
Boeckman, Charles 1920- *ConAu 13R,*
  SmATA 12
Boeckman, Patti *ConAu 109*
Boege, Ulrich Gustav 1940- *ConAu 97,*
  IntAu&W 82
Boegehold, Betty 1913- *ConAu 69*
Boegner, Marc 1881-1970 *ConAu 29R*
Boehlke, Frederick J, Jr. 1926- *ConAu 21R*
Boehlke, Robert R 1925- *ConAu 5R*
Boehlow, Robert H 1925- *ConAu 53*
Boehm, Eric H 1918- *ConAu 13R*
Boehm, Herb *ConAu X*
Boehm, Karl 1894-1981 *ConAu 105*
Boehm, William D 1946- *ConAu 61*
Boehme, Lillian R *ConAu X*
Boehringer, Robert 1885?-1974 *ConAu 53*
Boelcke, Willi A 1929- *ConAu 107*
Boelen, Bernard J 1916- *ConAu 41R*
Boell, Heinrich 1917- *ConAu 21R*
Boeman, John 1923- *ConAu 108*
Boer, Charles 1939- *ConAu 69, ConP 80,*
  DcLB 5, WrDr 84
Boer, Harry R 1913- *ConAu 1R, -4NR*
Boesch, Mark Joseph 1917- *ConAu 21R,*
  SmATA 12
Boesel, David 1938- *ConAu 41R*
Boesen, Victor 1908- *ConAu 37R, SmATA 16*
Boesiger, Willi 1904- *ConAu 102*
Boestamam, Ahmad 1920- *IntAu&W 82*
Boeth, Richard 1933-1982 *ConAu 107*
Boetie, Dugmore 1920?-1966 *ConAu 109*
Boettcher, Henry J 1893- *ConAu P-1*
Boettinger, Henry M 1924- *ConAu 73*
Boeve, Edgar G 1929- *ConAu 21R*
Boewe, Charles 1924- *ConAu 9R*
Boff, Vic 1915- *ConAu 103*
Boffa, Giovanni 1922- *IntWWP 82*
Boffey, David Barnes 1945- *ConAu 110*
Bogaduck *ConAu X*
Bogan, James 1945- *ConAu 103*
Bogan, James J *DrAP&F 83*
Bogan, Louise 1897-1970 *ConAmA, ConAu 25R,*
  -73, ConLC 4, EncWL 2, ModAL,
  ModAL SUP, TwCA, TwCA SUP,
  TwCWr
Bogard, Travis 1918- *ConAu 69*
Bogarde, Dirk 1921- *ConAu X, ConLC 19,*
  DcLB 14[port], WrDr 84
Bogart, Carlotta 1929- *ConAu 61*
Bogart, Leo 1921- *ConAu 41R*
Bogat, Shatan *ConAu X*
Bogatyryov, Konstantin 1924?-1976 *ConAu 65*
Bogdanor, Vernon 1943- *ConAu 81, WrDr 84*
Bogdanovich, Peter 1939- *ConAu 5R,*
  IntAu&W 82
Bogdanovitch, Peter 1939- *WrDr 84*
Boge, Kari 1950- *IntAu&W 82*
Bogen, Don *DrAP&F 83*
Bogen, James Benjamin 1935- *ConAu 89*
Bogen, Karen Iris *DrAP&F 83*
Bogen, Laurel Ann *DrAP&F 83*
Bogen, Nancy *DrAP&F 83*
Bogen, Nancy R 1932- *ConAu 97*
Bogert, L Jean 1888-1970 *ConAu P-1*
Boggan, E Carrington 1943- *ConAu 101*
Boggess, Louise Bradford 1912- *ConAu 7NR,*
  -13R
Boggs, Bill *ConAu X*
Boggs, James 1919- *ConAu 77, LivgBAA*

TwCCW 83

Bond, Nancy 1945- *ConAu 9NR, –65, SmATA 22[port], TwCCW 83*
Bond, Nelson S 1908- *ConAu P-1, TwCSFW, WrDr 84*
Bond, Otto F 1885- *ConAu 1R*
Bond, Pearl *DrAP&F 83*
Bond, Ray *ConAu X*
Bond, Raymond T 1893?-1981 *ConAu 104*
Bond, Richmond Pugh 1899- *ConAu P-2*
Bond, Ruskin 1934- *ConAu 29R, DcLEL 1940, IntAu&W 82, SmATA 14, TwCCW 83*
Bond, Rusking 1934- *WrDr 84*
Bond, Simon 1947- *ConAu 104*
Bond, William J 1941- *ConAu 108*
Bondanella, Peter Eugene 1943- *ConAu 10NR, –65*
Bondarev, Yury Vasilyevich 1924- *CIDMEL 80*
Bonderoff, Jason 1946- *ConAu 97*
Bondi, Hermann 1919- *IntAu&W 82*
Bondi, Joseph C 1936- *ConAu 11NR, –29R*
Bondurant, Joan V 1918- *ConAu 41R*
Bondy, Francois 1915- *IntAu&W 82*
Bone, Sir David William 1874-1959 *LongCTC, TwCA, TwCA SUP*
Bone, Edith 1889?-1975 *ConAu 57*
Bone, Lady Gertrude Helena 1876- *LongCTC*
Bone, Harold MacPherson 1896- *ConAmTC*
Bone, Hugh A 1909- *WrDr 84*
Bone, Hugh Alvin, Jr. 1909- *ConAu 1R, –3NR*
Bone, J F 1916- *ConSFA, TwCSFW, WrDr 84*
Bone, James 1872-1962 *LongCTC*
Bone, Jesse F 1916- *ConAu 57*
Bone, Sir Muirhead 1876-1953 *LongCTC*
Bone, Quentin 1918- *ConAu 85*
Bone, Robert 1924- *ConAu 69*
Bone, Robert C 1917- *ConAu 37R*
Bone, Stephen 1904-1958 *LongCTC*
Bonehill, Ralph *ConAu X*
Bonellie, Helen-Janet 1937- *ConAu 41R*
Boness, A James 1928- *ConAu 37R*
Bonett, Emery *WrDr 84*
Bonett, Emery 1906- *ConAu X, TwCCr&M 80*
Bonett, John 1906- *ConAu X, TwCCr&M 80*
Bonett, John And Emery *TwCCr&M 80*
Bonetti, Edward 1928- *ConAu 93*
Bonewits, Isaac *ConAu X*
Bonewits, P E I 1949- *ConAu 93*
Boney, Elaine E 1921- *ConAu 110*
Boney, F N 1929- *ConAu 41R*
Boney, William Jerry 1930- *ConAu 21R*
Bonfante, Larissa *ConAu 11NR, –69*
Bongar, Emmet W 1919- *ConAu 33R*
Bongartz, Heinz *ConAu X*
Bongartz, Roy 1924- *ConAu 13R*
Bongie, Laurence L 1929- *ConAu 61*
Bonham, Barbara 1926- *WrDr 84*
Bonham, Barbara Thomas 1926- *ConAu 7NR, –17R, SmATA 7*
Bonham, Frank 1914- *ConAu 4NR, –9R, ConLC 12, SmATA 1, TwCCW 83, TwCWW, WrDr 84*
Bonham-Carter, Helen Violet 1887-1969 *DcLEL 1940*
Bonham-Carter, Victor 1913- *ConAu 9R, DcLEL 1940, WrDr 84*
Bonham Carter, Violet 1887-1965 *LongCTC*
Bonham Carter, Violet 1887-1969 *ConAu P-2*
Bonheddy, Goronwy *IntWWP 82X*
Bonheim, Helmut 1930- *ConAu 1R, –4NR*
Bonhoeffer, Dietrich 1906-1945 *WorAu*
Bonhomme, Denise 1926- *ConAu 104*
Bonhomme, Jean 1936- *CreCan 1*
Boni, Albert 1892-1981 *ConAu 104, –65*
Boni, Margaret Bradford 1893?-1974 *ConAu 53*
Bonica, John Joseph 1917- *WrDr 84*
Bonime, Florence *DrAP&F 83*
Bonime, Florence 1907- *ConAu 49*
Bonime, Walter 1909- *ConAu X*
Bonine, Gladys Nichols 1907- *ConAu P-1*
Bonine, Vivian Small *IntWWP 82X*
Bonine, Vivian Way 1912- *IntWWP 82*
Bonington, Chris 1934- *WrDr 84*
Bonington, Christian 1934- *ConAu 1NR, –45, IntAu&W 82*
Bonini, Charles P 1933- *ConAu 13R*
Bonis, Ferenc 1932- *IntAu&W 82*
Bonjean, Charles M 1935- *ConAu 41R*
Bonk, James *DrAP&F 83*
Bonk, Wallace J 1923- *ConAu 9R*
Bonn, Thomas L 1939- *ConAu 109*
Bonnamy, Francis *ConAu X*

Bonnar, Alphonsus 1895-1968 *ConAu P-1*
Bonnefoy, Yves 1923- *CIDMEL 80, ConAu 85, ConLC 9, –15, EncWL 2, IntAu&W 82, ModFrL, WhoTwCL, WorAu*
Bonnekamp, Sonja Maria 1930- *IntAu&W 82*
Bonnell, Dorothy Haworth 1914- *ConAu 1R, –3NR*
Bonnell, John Sutherland 1893- *ConAu 5R*
Bonnell, Paula *DrAP&F 83*
Bonner, Brian 1917- *ConAu 104, WrDr 84*
Bonner, Gerald 1926- *ConAu 5NR, –9R*
Bonner, James 1910- *WrDr 84*
Bonner, James Calvin 1904- *ConAu 9R, –9NR, WrDr 84*
Bonner, John Tyler 1920- *ConAu 49*
Bonner, Mary Graham 1890-1974 *ConAu 49, –73, SmATA 19*
Bonner, Michael 1924- *ConAu X, TwCWW, WrDr 84*
Bonner, Parker *ConAu X, TwCWW*
Bonner, Paul Hyde 1893-1968 *ConAu 1R, –103*
Bonner, Thomas, Jr. 1942- *ConAu 110*
Bonner, Thomas N 1923- *ConAu 9R*
Bonner, William H 1924- *ConAu 53*
Bonnett, John *WrDr 84*
Bonnette, Jeanne DeLamarter 1907- *ConAu 41R, IntWWP 82*
Bonnette, Victor *ConAu X*
Bonneville, Douglas A 1931- *ConAu 21R*
Bonney, Bill *ConAu X*
Bonney, H Orrin 1903-1979 *ConAu 9R, –103*
Bonney, Lorraine G 1922- *ConAu 1NR, –45*
Bonney, Merl Edwin 1902- *ConAu P-2, WrDr 84*
Bonney, Therese 1897-1978 *ConAu 73*
Bonnice, Joseph G 1930- *ConAu 49*
Bonnie, Richard J 1945- *ConAu 4NR, –53*
Bonnielizabethoag *DrAP&F 83*
Bonniere, Rene 1928- *CreCan 2*
Bonnifield, Paul 1937- *ConAu 104*
Bonnor, William Bowen 1920- *ConAu 9R, IntAu&W 82, WrDr 84*
Bonny, Helen L 1921- *ConAu 2NR, –49*
Bono, Philip 1921- *ConAu 101*
Bonoma, T V 1946- *ConAu 85*
Bonomi, Patricia U 1928- *ConAu 85*
Bonsal, Philip Wilson 1903- *ConAu 85*
Bonsal, Stephen 1865?-1951 *TwCA SUP*
Bonsall, Crosby 1921- *TwCCW 83, WrDr 84*
Bonsall, Crosby Barbara Newell 1921- *ConAu 73, SmATA 23[port]*
Bonsels, Waldemar 1881-1952 *CIDMEL 80, TwCA, TwCA SUP*
Bontecou, Eleanor 1890?-1976 *ConAu 65*
Bontempelli, Massimo 1878-1960 *CIDMEL 80, CnMD, EncWL 2, ModWD*
Bontempo, Charles J 1931- *ConAu 61*
Bontemps, Arna 1902-1973 *ChlLR 6[port]*
Bontemps, Arna Wendell 1902-1973 *ConAu 1R, –4NR, –41R, ConLC 1, –18, ModBlW, SmATA 2, –24N, WorAu 1970*
Bontly, Thomas *DrAP&F 83*
Bontly, Thomas 1939- *ConAu 57*
Bontrager, John K 1923- *ConAu 65*
Bony, Jean 1908- *ConAu 101*
Bonython, Hugh 1920- *WrDr 84*
Bonzon, Paul-Jacques 1908-1978 *ConAu 93, SmATA 22[port]*
Boodman, David M 1923- *ConAu 21R*
Boody, Shirley Bright 1919- *ConAu 89*
Boog Watson, Elspeth Janet 1900- *ConAu P-1*
Booher, Dianna Daniels 1948- *ConAu 103, SmATA 33[port]*
Book-Senninger, Claude 1928- *ConAu 45*
Bookbinder, David J 1951- *ConAu 101*
Bookbinder, Robert 1950- *ConAu 110*
Bookchin, Murray 1921- *ConAu 1NR, ConIsC 1[port]*
Booker, Anton S *ConAu X*
Booker, Betty *DrAP&F 83*
Booker, Malcolm 1915- *ConAu 108*
Booker, Simeon Saunders 1918- *ConAu 9R, LivgBAA*
Booklover *IntWWP 82X*
Bookspan, Martin 1926- *ConAu 41R*
Bookstein, Abraham 1940- *ConAu 53*
Boom, Alfred B 1928- *ConAu 25R*
Boon, Francis *ConAu X*
Boon, Louis Paul 1912-1979 *CIDMEL 80, ConAu 73, EncWL 2, WhoTwCL*
Boone, Buford 1909?-1983 *ConAu 109*
Boone, Charles Eugene 1934- *ConAu X*

Boone, Daniel R 1927- *ConAu 33R, WrDr 84*
Boone, Debby *ConAu X*
Boone, Deborah Ann 1956- *ConAu 110*
Boone, Gray Davis 1938- *ConAu 93*
Boone, Joy Bale *DrAP&F 83*
Boone, Louis Eugene 1941- *ConAu 41R*
Boone, Muriel 1893- *ConAu 69*
Boone, Pat 1934- *ConAu 1R, –2NR, SmATA 7, WrDr 84*
Boontje *ConAu X*
Boore, W H 1904- *ConAu 5NR*
Boore, Walter Hugh 1904- *ConAu 5R, IntAu&W 82, WrDr 84*
Boorer, Wendy 1931- *ConAu 6NR, –57*
Boorman, Howard L 1920- *ConAu 41R*
Boorman, Scott A 1949- *ConAu 29R*
Boorstein, Edward 1915- *ConAu 73*
Boorstin, Daniel J 1914- *AuNews 2, ConAu 1R, –1NR, DcLB 17[port], DcLEL 1940, IntAu&W 82, WorAu, WrDr 84*
Boorstin, Paul 1944- *ConAu 103*
Boos, Frank Holgate 1893-1968 *ConAu P-2*
Boot, John C G 1936- *ConAu 17R, WrDr 84*
Boote, Robert Edward 1920- *ConAu 65*
Booth, Alan R 1934- *ConAu 107*
Booth, Charles 1840-1916 *LongCTC*
Booth, Charles Orrell 1918- *ConAu 13R*
Booth, Edwin *ConAu 7NR, –17R, TwCWW, WrDr 84*
Booth, Ernest Sheldon 1915- *ConAu 53*
Booth, Geoffrey *ConAu X, WrDr 84*
Booth, George C 1901- *ConAu P-1*
Booth, Irwin *ConAu X*
Booth, John Bennion 1880-1961 *LongCTC*
Booth, John E 1919- *ConAu 9R*
Booth, Ken 1943- *ConAu 102, IntAu&W 82, WrDr 84*
Booth, Mark Warren 1943- *ConAu 107*
Booth, Martin 1944- *ConAu 93, ConLC 13, ConP 80, WrDr 84*
Booth, Patrick John 1929- *ConAu P-1*
Booth, Philip *DrAP&F 83*
Booth, Philip 1907-1981 *ConAu 106*
Booth, Philip 1925- *ConAu 5R, –5NR, ConLC 23[port], ConP 80, DcLB Y82B[port], IntWWP 82, WorAu, WrDr 84*
Booth, Philip E 1923- *DcLEL 1940*
Booth, Rosemary Frances 1928- *ConAu 53*
Booth, Stephen 1933- *ConAu 69*
Booth, Taylor L 1933- *ConAu 53*
Booth, Wayne Clayson 1921- *ConAu 1R, –3NR, ConLC 24[port], ConLCrt 82, DcLEL 1940, WrDr 84*
Booth, William 1829-1912 *LongCTC*
Boothby, Guy Newell 1867-1905 *LongCTC*
Boothe, Clare 1903- *LongCTC, ModWD, TwCA, TwCA SUP*
Boothroyd, Basil 1910- *ConAu 33R, IntAu&W 82, WrDr 84*
Boothroyd, Christine 1934- *IntWWP 82*
Boothroyd, John Basil 1910- *DcLEL 1940*
Bootle, Stan Kelly *ConAu X*
Booton, Catherine Kage 1919- *ConAu 61*
Booton, Harold 1932- *WrDr 84*
Booton, Harold Williams 1932- *IntAu&W 82*
Booty, John Everitt 1925- *ConAu 85*
Boovarsson, Guomundur 1904-1974 *CIDMEL 80*
Bopp, Karl Richard 1906-1979 *ConAu 107*
Bor, Matej 1913- *ModSL 2*
Bor, Norman 1893?-1973 *ConAu 104*
Bor, Vane *IntWWP 82X*
Boraas, Roger S 1926- *ConAu 33R*
Borah, Woodrow Wilson 1912- *ConAu 3NR, –5R*
Borak, Jeffrey *ConAmTC*
Borberg, Svend 1888-1947 *CnMD*
Borch, Ted *ConAu X*
Borchard, Ruth 1910- *ConAu 13R*
Borchardt, Dietrich Hans 1916- *ConAu 9NR, –21R, IntAu&W 82*
Borchardt, Frank L 1938- *ConAu 33R, WrDr 84*
Borchardt, Rudolf 1877-1945 *CIDMEL 80, ModGL*
Borchers, Gladys L 1891- *ConAu P-1*
Borchert, Gerald Leo 1932- *ConAu 37R*
Borchert, James 1941- *ConAu 104*
Borchert, Wolfgang 1921-1947 *CIDMEL 80, CnMD, ConAu 104, CroCD, EncWL 2, ModGL, ModWD, TwCLC 5[port], WorAu*
Bordeaux, Henry 1870-1963 *CIDMEL 80, LongCTC, TwCA[port], TwCA SUP*

MichAu 80
Bottome, Edgar M 1937- *ConAu 33R*
Bottome, Phyllis 1884-1963 *ConAu X,
LongCTC, ModBrL, TwCA, TwCA SUP,
TwCWr*
Bottomley, Gordon 1874-1948 *DcLB 10,
LongCTC, ModBrL, TwCA, TwCA SUP,
TwCWr*
Bottomley, Horatio William 1860-1933 *LongCTC*
Bottomly, Heath 1919- *ConAu 105*
Bottomore, T B 1920- *ConAu 4NR*
Bottomore, Thomas 1920- *WrDr 84*
Bottomore, Thomas Burton 1920- *ConAu 9R*
Bottoms, A E 1939- *ConAu 73*
Bottoms, David *DrAP&F 83*
Bottoms, David 1949- *ConAu 105,
DcLB Y83B[port]*
Bottoms, Lawrence W 1908- *ConAu 89*
Bottrall, Margaret 1909- *ConAu 104,
DcLEL 1940, IntAu&W 82, WrDr 84*
Bottrall, Ronald 1906- *ConAu 53, ConP 80,
ModBrL, WhoTwCL, WorAu 1970,
WrDr 84*
Botwinick, Jack 1923- *ConAu 41R*
Bouber, Herman 1880- *CnMD*
Bouce, Paul-Gabriel 1936- *ConAu 73*
Bouchard, Lois Kalb 1938- *ConAu 25R*
Bouchard, Marie Cecile 1926- *CreCan 1*
Bouchard, Mary 1912-1945 *CreCan 1*
Bouchard, Robert H 1923- *ConAu 17R*
Bouchard, Simonne Mary 1912-1945 *CreCan 1*
Bouchard, Victor 1926- *CreCan 2*
Boucher, Alan 1918- *ConAu 9NR*
Boucher, Alan Estcourt 1918- *ConAu 5R*
Boucher, Andre-Pierre 1936- *CreCan 2*
Boucher, Anthony 1911-1968 *ConAu X, DcLB 8,
TwCA SUP, TwCCr&M 80, TwCSFW*
Boucher, Frank 1901-1977 *ConAu 110*
Boucher, John G 1930- *ConAu 37R*
Boucher, Paul Edward 1893- *ConAu P-1*
Boucher, Pierre 1921- *CreCan 1*
Boucher, Sandy 1936- *ConAu 110*
Boucher, Wayne I 1934- *ConAu 53*
Bouchey, Myrna *DrAP&F 83*
Boucolon, Maryse 1937- *ConAu 110*
Boudat, Marie-Louise 1909- *ConAu P-1*
Boudin, Jean *DrAP&F 83*
Boudon, Raymond 1934- *ConAu 49*
Boudreau, Eugene H 1934- *ConAu 45*
Boudreaux, Patricia Duncan 1941- *ConAu 33R*
Bough, Lee *ConAu X*
Bough McTreve *IntWWP 82X*
Boughner, Daniel C 1909-1974 *ConAu 49,
ConAu P-2*
Boughton, James Murray 1940- *ConAu 41R*
Boughton, Willis Arnold 1885-1977 *ConAu 73*
Boughtwood, Alice Marian 1897- *IntWWP 82*
Bouhier, Jean Georges Alfred Leon 1912-
IntWWP 82
Bouillon, Georges 1915- *IntWWP 82*
Bouissac, Paul 1934- *ConAu 65*
Boularan, Jacques 1890-1972 *ConAu 37R*
Boulby, Mark 1929- *ConAu 37R*
Boulding, Elise 1920- *ConAu 8NR, -21R*
Boulding, Kenneth Ewart 1910- *ConAu 5R,
-7NR*
Boulger, James Denis 1931-1979 *ConAu 109*
Boulle, Pierre Francois Marie-Louis 1912-
*ConAu 9R, SmATA 22[port], TwCSFW A,
TwCWr, WorAu*
Boulogne, Jean 1942- *ConAu 93*
Boult, Adrian 1889-1983 *ConAu 109*
Boult, Adrian Cedric 1889- *IntAu&W 82*
Boult, S Kye *ConAu X*
Boulting *ConAu X*
Boulton, David 1935- *ConAu 25R,
IntAu&W 82*
Boulton, James T 1924- *WrDr 84*
Boulton, James Thompson 1924- *ConAu 29R,
IntAu&W 82*
Boulton, Jane Balch 1921- *ConAu 65*
Boulton, Laura Theresa Craytor 1899?-1980
ConAu 110
Boulton, Marjorie 1924- *ConAu 9NR, -65,
IntWWP 82*
Boulware, Marcus Hanna 1907- *ConAu 1NR,
-45, LivgBAA*
Bouma, Donald H 1918- *ConAu 41R,
MichAu 80*
Bouma, J L *TwCWW, WrDr 84*
Bouma, Mary LaGrand *ConAu 93*
Bouman, Pieter M 1938- *ConAu 29R*

Bouman, Walter Richard 1929- *ConAu 29R*
Boumelha, Penelope Ann 1950- *ConAu 110*
Boumelha, Penny *ConAu X*
Bounds, Sydney J 1920- *TwCSFW, WrDr 84*
Bouraoui, H A 1932- *ConAu 9NR, -65*
Bouraoui, Hedi 1932- *IntWWP 82*
Bourbon, Ken *ConAu X*
Bourdeaux, Michael Alan 1934- *ConAu 33R,
IntAu&W 82, WrDr 84*
Bourdet, Edouard 1887-1945 *CIDMEL 80,
CnMD, ModWD*
Bourdon, David 1934- *ConAu 37R*
Bourdon, Sylvia Diane Eve 1949- *ConAu 85*
Bouregy, Thomas 1909?-1978 *ConAu 104*
Bouret, Jean 1914- *ConAu 85*
Bourges, Elemir 1852-1925 *CIDMEL 80*
Bourget, Paul 1852-1935 *CIDMEL 80,
ConAu 107, LongCTC, TwCA,
TwCA SUP, TwCLC 12[port]*
Bourgholtzer, Frank 1919- *ConAu 25R*
Bourguignon, Erika 1924- *ConAu 85*
Bourinot, Arthur Stanley 1893- *CreCan 2*
Bourjaily, Monte Ferris 1894-1979 *ConAu 85,
-97*
Bourjaily, Vance *DrAP&F 83*
Bourjaily, Vance 1922- *ASpks, ConAu 1R,
-2NR, ConLC 8, ConNov 82, Conv 1,
DcLB 2, DcLEL 1940, ModAL, WorAu,
WrDr 84*
Bourke, Patrick Albert 1915- *WrDr 84*
Bourke, Vernon J 1907- *ConAu 3NR, -9R,
IntAu&W 82, WrDr 84*
Bourke-White, Margaret 1904-1971 *ConAu 29R,
ConAu P-1*
Bourliaguet, Leonce 1895-1965 *ConAu 102*
Bourne, Aleck William 1885?-1974 *ConAu 53*
Bourne, Charles P 1931- *ConAu 9R*
Bourne, Dorothy D 1893- *ConAu P-2*
Bourne, Eulalia *ConAu 97*
Bourne, Frank C 1914- *WrDr 84*
Bourne, Frank Card 1914- *ConAu 17R*
Bourne, Geoffrey Howard 1909- *ConAu 33R,
IntAu&W 82, WrDr 84*
Bourne, George 1863-1927 *CnMWL, LongCTC,
WhoTwCL, WorAu*
Bourne, James R 1897- *ConAu P-2*
Bourne, Kenneth 1930- *ConAu 11NR, -25R,
IntAu&W 82, WrDr 84*
Bourne, L S 1939- *ConAu 33R*
Bourne, Larry Stuart 1939- *WrDr 84*
Bourne, Lesley *ConAu X, SmATA X,
WrDr 84*
Bourne, Lyle E, Jr. 1932- *ConAu 53*
Bourne, Miriam Anne 1931- *ConAu 10NR, -21R,
SmATA 16*
Bourne, Peter *ConAu X*
Bourne, Peter Geoffrey 1939- *ConAu 7NR, -57*
Bourne, Randolph Silliman 1886-1918 *ModAL,
TwCA, TwCA SUP*
Bourne, Ruth M *ConAu 33R*
Bourneuf, Alice E 1912-1980 *ConAu 102*
Bourquin, Paul Henry James 1916- *IntAu&W 82,
WrDr 84*
Bourricaud, Francois 1922- *ConAu 29R*
Bouscaren, Anthony Trawick 1920- *ConAu 1R,
-5NR, IntAu&W 82*
Bouscaren, T Lincoln 1884- *ConAu P-1*
Bousono, Carlos 1923- *CIDMEL 80, WorAu*
Bousquet, Joe 1897-1950 *CIDMEL 80*
Bousquet, Marie-Louis Valentin 1887?-1975
ConAu 104
Boussard, Jacques Marie 1910- *ConAu 29R*
Boustead, John Edmund Hugh 1895-1980
ConAu 97
Boutell, Clarence Burley 1908-1981 *ConAu 104*
Boutell, Clip *ConAu X*
Boutens, Peter Cornelis 1870-1943 *WorAu 1970*
Boutens, Pieter Cornelis 1870-1943 *CIDMEL 80,
EncWL 2*
Boutet DeMonvel, M 1850?-1913
SmATA 30[port]
Boutilier, Mary A 1943- *ConAu 105*
Bouton, James Alan 1939- *ConAu 89*
Bouton, Jim *ConAu X*
Bouvard, Marguerite Anne 1937- *ConAu 37R*
Bouvard, Marguerite Guzman *DrAP&F 83*
Bouvier, Emile 1906- *ConAu 37R*
Bouvier, Leon F 1922- *ConAu 105*
Bova, Ben 1932- *ChlLR 3, ConAu 1R, -5R,
-11NR, ConSFA, DcLB Y81B[port],
SmATA 6, TwCSFW, WrDr 84*
Bovard, Oliver K 1872-1945 *DcLB 25[port]*

Bovasso, Julie 1930- *ConAu 25R, ConDr 82,
WrDr 84*
Bovee, Courtland Lowell 1944- *ConAu 49*
Bovee, Ruth *ConAu X*
Boven, William 1887?-1970 *ConAu 104*
Bovey, John *DrAP&F 83*
Bovey, John 1913- *ConAu 107*
Bovis, H Eugene 1928- *ConAu 29R*
Bovoso, Carole *DrAP&F 83*
Bovoso, Carole 1937- *IntAu&W 82*
Bow, Russell 1925- *ConAu 21R*
Bowd, Douglas Gordon 1918- *WrDr 84*
Bowden, Betsy 1948- *ConAu 107*
Bowden, Edwin T, Jr. 1924- *ConAu 8NR, -13R*
Bowden, Elbert Victor 1924- *ConAu 41R*
Bowden, Etta *ConSFA*
Bowden, Gregory Houston 1948- *ConAu 41R*
Bowden, Henry Warner 1939- *ConAu 49*
Bowden, J J 1927- *ConAu 29R*
Bowden, James H *DrAP&F 83*
Bowden, James Henry 1934- *IntWWP 82*
Bowden, Jean 1925- *ConAu 7NR, -53*
Bowden, Jean 1928- *WrDr 84*
Bowden, Jim *ConAu X, TwCWW, WrDr 84*
Bowden, Joan Chase 1925- *ConAu 89*
Bowden, Leonard 1933- *ConAu 17R*
Bowden, Mary W 1941- *WrDr 84*
Bowden, Mary Weatherspoon 1941- *ConAu 110*
Bowden, Michael *IntWWP 82X*
Bowden, Michael Todd 1950- *IntWWP 82*
Bowden, Phil *ConSFA*
Bowden, Roland Heywood 1916- *ConAu 106,
IntWWP 82, WrDr 84*
Bowder, Diana 1942- *ConAu 109*
Bowditch, James L 1939- *ConAu 89*
Bowdle, Donald N 1935- *ConAu 49*
Bowdler, Roger 1934- *ConAu 97*
Bowe, Frank 1947- *ConAu 104*
Bowe, Gabriel P 1923- *ConAu 21R*
Bowe, Kate *ConAu X*
Bowe, Patrick 1945- *ConAu 106*
Bowen, Barbara C 1937- *ConAu 37R, WrDr 84*
Bowen, Betty Morgan 1921- *ConAu X,
SmATA X*
Bowen, Catherine Drinker 1897-1973 *ConAu 5R,
-45, SmATA 7, TwCA SUP*
Bowen, Croswell 1905-1971 *ConAu 33R*
Bowen, David *SmATA X*
Bowen, Desmond 1921- *ConAu 33R,
IntAu&W 82, WrDr 84*
Bowen, Earl Kenneth 1918- *ConAu 5R*
Bowen, Edmund 1898-1980 *ConAu 105*
Bowen, Elbert Russell 1918- *ConAu 13R*
Bowen, Elizabeth 1899-1973 *ConAu 41R,
ConAu P-2, ConLC 1, -3, -6, -11, -15,
-22[port], DcLB 15[port], EncWL 2[port],
LongCTC, ModBrL, ModBrL SUP, TwCA,
TwCA SUP, TwCWr, WhoTwCL*
Bowen, Euros 1904- *IntAu&W 82*
Bowen, Ezra 1927- *ConAu 85*
Bowen, Geraint 1915- *IntAu&W 82*
Bowen, Haskell L 1929- *ConAu 41R*
Bowen, Howard R 1908- *ConAu 8NR, -21R,
WrDr 84*
Bowen, Humphry J M 1929- *WrDr 84*
Bowen, Ian 1908- *ConAu 105, WrDr 84*
Bowen, J Donald 1922- *ConAu 8NR, -17R*
Bowen, James Keith 1932- *ConAu 37R*
Bowen, John 1916- *ConAu 103*
Bowen, John 1924- *ConAu 1R, -2NR,
ConDr 82, ConNov 82, CroCD,
DcLB 13[port], TwCWr, WorAu, WrDr 84*
Bowen, John Griffith 1924- *DcLEL 1940,
IntAu&W 82*
Bowen, Joshua David 1930- *ConAu 105,
SmATA 22[port]*
Bowen, Marjorie *TwCCr&M 80*
Bowen, Marjorie 1886-1952 *LongCTC, TwCA,
TwCA SUP, TwCRGW, TwCWr*
Bowen, Peter 1939- *ConAu 57*
Bowen, Ralph H 1919- *ConAu 69*
Bowen, Richard M 1928- *ConAu 21R,
WrDr 84*
Bowen, Robert O 1920- *ConAu 9R,
DcLEL 1940, WrDr 84*
Bowen, Robert Sidney 1900-1977 *SmATA 21N*
Bowen, Robert Sidney 1901?-1977 *ConAu 69*
Bowen, Robert Sydney 1900-1977 *ConAu 73*
Bowen, William 1933- *WrDr 84*
Bowen, Zack 1934- *ConAu 29R, WrDr 84*
Bowen-Judd, Sara *WrDr 84*
Bowen-Judd, Sara 1922- *ConAu 5NR, -9R*

Bower, Alison *IntAu&W 82X*
Bower, B M 1871-1940 *LongCTC, TwCA[port], TwCWW*
Bower, Barbara Euphan *ConAu X*
Bower, David A 1945- *ConAu 37R*
Bower, Donald E 1920- *ConAu 77*
Bower, Eli M 1917- *ConAu 89*
Bower, Fay Louise 1929- *ConAu 53*
Bower, Gordon H 1932- *ConAu 17R*
Bower, Julia Wells 1903- *ConAu 41R*
Bower, Keith *ConAu X, -X, IntAu&W 82X*
Bower, Louise 1900- *ConAu P-2*
Bower, Muriel 1921- *ConAu 49*
Bower, Robert T 1919- *ConAu 49*
Bower, Roger *DrAP&F 83*
Bower, Sharon Anthony 1932- *ConAu 65*
Bower, William Clayton 1878- *ConAu 5R*
Bowering, George 1935- *ConAu 10NR, -21R, ConLC 15, CreCan 1, DcLEL 1940, ModCmwL*
Bowering, George 1937- *IntAu&W 82*
Bowering, George 1938- *ConP 80, WrDr 84*
Bowering, Marilyn R 1949- *ConAu 101*
Bowering, Peter Edwin 1926- *IntAu&W 82*
Bowers, C A 1935- *ConAu 29R*
Bowers, Claude Gernade 1878-1958 *DcLB 17[port], TwCA, TwCA SUP*
Bowers, Edgar 1924- *ConAu 5R, ConLC 9, ConP 80, DcLB 5[port], DcLEL 1940, IntWWP 82, WorAu, WrDr 84*
Bowers, Faubion 1917- *ConAu 5R, IntAu&W 82, WrDr 84*
Bowers, Fredson 1905- *WrDr 84*
Bowers, Fredson Thayer 1905- *ConAu 2NR, -5R, IntAu&W 82*
Bowers, George K 1916- *ConAu 1R, -2NR*
Bowers, Greg *DrAP&F 83*
Bowers, John *DrAP&F 83*
Bowers, John 1928- *ConAu 33R, WrDr 84*
Bowers, John Waite 1935- *ConAu 41R*
Bowers, Kenneth S 1937- *ConAu 97*
Bowers, Margaretta Keller 1908- *ConAu 5R, WrDr 84*
Bowers, Mary Beacom 1932- *ConAu 105*
Bowers, Neal 1948- *ConAu 110*
Bowers, Q David 1938- *ConAu 41R*
Bowers, Ronald 1941- *ConAu 41R*
Bowers, Santha Rama Rau 1923- *ConAu 1R*
Bowers, Warner Fremont 1906- *ConAu 61*
Bowers, William 1916- *ConAu 102*
Bowers, William J 1935- *ConAu 97*
Bowersock, G W 1936- *ConAu 81*
Bowes, Anne LaBastille *ConAu X*
Bowes, Karen Laila 1948- *CreCan 1*
Bowett, Derek William 1927- *ConAu 6NR, -9R*
Bowett, Derek Williams 1927- *IntAu&W 82*
Bowick, Dorothy Mueller *ConAu X*
Bowie, David 1947- *ConAu X, ConLC 17*
Bowie, Janetta 1907- *ConAu 102, WrDr 84*
Bowie, Jim *ConAu X, IntAu&W 82X, WrDr 84*
Bowie, Malcolm McNaughton 1943- *IntAu&W 82*
Bowie, Norman E 1942- *ConAu 33R, WrDr 84*
Bowie, Robert R 1909- *ConAu P-1*
Bowie, Sam *ConAu X*
Bowie, Walter Russell 1882-1969 *ConAu 3NR, -5R*
Bowker, Francis E 1917- *ConAu 41R*
Bowker, John Westerdale 1935- *ConAu 25R, WrDr 84*
Bowker, Lee Harrington 1940- *ConAu 108*
Bowker, Margaret 1936- *ConAu 25R, WrDr 84*
Bowker, Robin Marsland *WrDr 84*
Bowker, Robin Marsland 1920- *ConAu 65*
Bowlby, John 1907- *ConAu 49, IntAu&W 82, WrDr 84*
Bowle, John 1905- *WrDr 84*
Bowle, John Edward 1905- *ConAu 1R, -1NR, IntAu&W 82*
Bowler, R Arthur 1930- *ConAu 57*
Bowles, Chester 1901- *ConAu 69*
Bowles, D Richard 1910- *ConAu 33R*
Bowles, Edmund A 1925- *ConAu 33R*
Bowles, Ella Shannon 1886-1975 *ConAu 57*
Bowles, Frank H 1907-1975 *ConAu 13R, -57*
Bowles, Gordon Townsend 1904- *ConAu P-1*
Bowles, Jane 1917-1973 *ConAu 41R, ConAu P-2, ConLC 3, DcLEL 1940, ModAL, WhoTwCL, WorAu*
Bowles, John 1938- *ConAu 106*
Bowles, Kerwin *ConAu X*

Bowles, Norma L *ConAu 77*
Bowles, Paul *DrAP&F 83*
Bowles, Paul 1910- *ConAu 1R, -1NR, ConLC 1, -2, -19, ConNov 82, DcLB 5[port], -6[port], EncWL 2, IntAu&W 82, ModAL, ModAL SUP, TwCA SUP[port], TwCWr, WhoTwCL, WrDr 84*
Bowles, Paul Frederick 1911- *DcLEL 1940*
Bowley, Marian E A 1911- *WrDr 84*
Bowley, Rex Lyon 1925- *ConAu 103, IntAu&W 82, WrDr 84*
Bowling, Jackson M 1934- *ConAu 5R*
Bowman, Albert Hall 1921- *ConAu 41R*
Bowman, Ann L *DrAP&F 83*
Bowman, Bob *ConAu X*
Bowman, Bruce 1938- *ConAu 65*
Bowman, Clell Edgar 1904- *ConAu 105*
Bowman, David J 1919- *ConAu 9R*
Bowman, Derek 1931- *ConAu 102, IntAu&W 82, IntWWP 82, WrDr 84*
Bowman, Frank Paul 1927- *ConAu 33R*
Bowman, Henry A 1903- *ConAu P-1*
Bowman, Herbert Eugene 1917- *IntAu&W 82*
Bowman, James Cloyd 1880-1961 *ConAu 97, SmATA 23[port]*
Bowman, Jeanne *ConAu X*
Bowman, John S 1931- *ConAu 5NR, -9R, SmATA 16*
Bowman, John Wick 1894- *ConAu 1R, -6NR*
Bowman, Karl M 1888-1973 *ConAu 41R*
Bowman, Kathleen 1942- *ConAu 69*
Bowman, LeRoy 1887-1971 *ConAu 33R*
Bowman, Locke E, Jr. 1927- *ConAu 2NR, -5R*
Bowman, Marcelle 1914- *ConAu 25R*
Bowman, Mary D 1924- *ConAu 25R*
Bowman, Mary Jean 1908- *ConAu 33R*
Bowman, Ned Alan 1932- *ConAu 41R*
Bowman, Paul Hoover 1914- *ConAu 33R*
Bowman, Pierre L 1944- *ConAmTC*
Bowman, Raymond Albert 1903-1979 *ConAu 89*
Bowman, Robert Mackenzie 1928- *ConAu 25R, WrDr 84*
Bowman, Robert T 1910- *ConAu 73*
Bowman, Roberta Pipes 1915- *IntWWP 82*
Bowman, Sylvia E 1914- *WrDr 84*
Bowman, Sylvia Edmonia 1914- *ConAu 1R*
Bowman, Ward S, Jr. 1911- *ConAu 49*
Bowmer, Angus L 1904-1979 *ConAu 85*
Bowne, Ford *ConAu 49*
Bowood, Richard *ConAu X*
Bowra, Sir Cecil Maurice 1898-1970 *ConAu 1R, LongCTC, ModBrL, TwCA SUP*
Bowra, Sir Cecil Maurice 1898-1971 *ConAu 2NR, -29R*
Bowser, Eileen 1928- *ConAu 11NR, -69*
Bowser, Frederick P 1937- *ConAu 49*
Bowser, Joan *ConAu X*
Bowser, Pearl 1931- *ConAu 33R*
Bowskill, Derek 1928- *ConAu 77*
Bowyer, Chaz 1926- *ConAu 93*
Bowyer, John W 1921- *ConAu 37R*
Bowyer, Mathew Justice 1926- *ConAu 37R, WrDr 84*
Box, Edgar *WrDr 84*
Box, Edgar 1925- *ConAu X, TwCCr&M 80*
Box, Muriel 1905- *WrDr 84*
Box, Muriel Violette 1905- *IntAu&W 82*
Box, Sydney 1907-1983 *ConAu 109*
Boxer, Arabella *WrDr 84*
Boxer, Charles Ralph 1904- *ConAu 102*
Boxerman, David Samuel 1945- *ConAu 61*
Boy, Angelo V 1929- *ConAu 69*
Boyajian, Aram *DrAP&F 83*
Boyajian, Cecile *ConAu X*
Boyars, Arthur 1925- *DcLEL 1940*
Boyarsky, Bill 1936- *ConAu 25R*
Boyce, Chris 1943- *ConAu 73*
Boyce, David George 1942- *ConAu 103*
Boyce, George A 1898- *ConAu 53, SmATA 19*
Boyce, Gray Cowan 1899- *ConAu 5R, WrDr 84*
Boyce, Joseph Nelson 1937- *ConAu 102*
Boyce, Richard Fyfe 1896- *ConAu 69*
Boyce, Ronald R 1931- *ConAu 3NR, -9R*
Boychuk, Bohdan 1927- *ModSL 2*
Boycott, Desmond Morse *ConAu X*
Boyd, Alamo *ConAu X, WrDr 84*
Boyd, Andrew 1920- *ConAu 1R*
Boyd, Ann S *ConAu X*
Boyd, Beverly M 1925- *ConAu 69*
Boyd, Blanche McCrary *DrAP&F 83*
Boyd, Bob *ConAu X*

Boyd, Carse *ConAu X*
Boyd, Dean *ConAu 5R*
Boyd, E 1904?-1974 *ConAu 53*
Boyd, Elizabeth French 1905- *IntAu&W 82, WrDr 84*
Boyd, Ernest Augustus 1887-1946 *LongCTC, TwCA, TwCA SUP*
Boyd, Frank *ConAu X*
Boyd, Harper W, Jr. 1917- *ConAu 13R*
Boyd, Herb 1938- *ConAu 110*
Boyd, Hugh Alexander 1907- *IntAu&W 82, WrDr 84*
Boyd, Jack 1932- *ConAu 49*
Boyd, James 1888-1944 *ConAmA, DcLB 9[port], LongCTC, TwCA, TwCA SUP*
Boyd, James M 1919- *ConAu 33R, WrDr 84*
Boyd, James Sterling 1917- *ConAu 49*
Boyd, John 1919- *ConAu X, ConSFA, DcLB 8[port], TwCSFW, WrDr 84*
Boyd, John D 1916- *ConAu 25R*
Boyd, John Francis 1910- *ConAu 5R*
Boyd, Julian P 1903-1980 *ConAu 65, -97*
Boyd, K T *IntAu&W 82X*
Boyd, Katy 1918- *IntAu&W 82*
Boyd, Malcolm 1923- *ASpks, ConAu 4NR, -5R, IntAu&W 82, WrDr 84*
Boyd, Margaret 1913- *WrDr 84*
Boyd, Martin A'Beckett 1893-1972 *ConAu P-1, LongCTC, ModCmwL, TwCWr*
Boyd, Maurice 1921- *ConAu 9R*
Boyd, Mildred Worthy 1921- *ConAu 17R*
Boyd, Myron F 1909-1978 *ConAu 41R*
Boyd, Nancy *ConAmA, ConAu X, LongCTC*
Boyd, Neil *ConAu X*
Boyd, R L F 1922- *ConAu 57*
Boyd, Robert H 1912- *ConAu 53*
Boyd, Robert S 1928- *ConAu 13R*
Boyd, Robert T 1914- *ConAu 108*
Boyd, Robin 1919- *ConAu 17R, DcLEL 1940*
Boyd, Rosabel White 1900- *IntWWP 82*
Boyd, Shyla *DrAP&F 83*
Boyd, Shylah 1945- *ConAu 61*
Boyd, Sue Abbott *DrAP&F 83*
Boyd, Sue Abbott 1921- *ConAu 65, IntAu&W 82*
Boyd, Thomas Alexander 1898-1935 *ConAmA, DcLB 9, LongCTC, TwCA*
Boyd, Waldo T 1918- *ConAu 29R, SmATA 18, WrDr 84*
Boyd, William 1885- *ConAu 41R*
Boyd, William C 1903-1983 *ConAu 109*
Boyd, William Harland 1912- *ConAu 11NR, -69*
Boydston, Jo Ann 1924- *ConAu 29R, IntAu&W 82*
Boye, I B 1935- *IntAu&W 82*
Boye, Karin 1900-1941 *CIDMEL 80, EncWL 2, TwCSFW A, WhoTwCL, WorAu 1970*
Boyer, Brian D 1939- *ConAu 45*
Boyer, Bruce Hatton 1946- *ConAu 101*
Boyer, Carl B 1906-1976 *ConAu 65*
Boyer, Dwight 1912- *ConAu 65*
Boyer, Elizabeth 1913- *ConAu 81*
Boyer, Ernest LeRoy 1928- *ConAu 110*
Boyer, Harold W 1908- *ConAu 1R*
Boyer, John 1946- *ConAu 103*
Boyer, Paul Samuel 1935- *ConAu 1NR, -49*
Boyer, Richard Edwin 1932- *ConAu 21R*
Boyer, Richard Lewis 1943- *ConAu 11NR, -69*
Boyer, Richard O 1903-1973 *ConAu 45*
Boyer, Robert *ConAu X, WrDr 84*
Boyer, Robert E 1929- *ConAu 41R, SmATA 22[port]*
Boyer, Sophia Ames 1907?-1972 *ConAu 37R*
Boyer, William H 1924- *ConAu 106*
Boyer, William W, Jr. 1923- *ConAu 13R*
Boyers, Robert 1942- *ConAu 4NR, -53, WrDr 84*
Boyes, Megan 1923- *WrDr 84*
Boyes, Roger 1952- *IntAu&W 82*
Boykin, James H 1914- *ConAu 2NR, -5R*
Boykin, Randon C *DrAP&F 83*
Boylan, Boyd *ConAu X*
Boylan, Brian Richard 1936- *ConAu 81*
Boylan, James 1927- *ConAu 1R, -1NR*
Boylan, Leona Davis 1910- *ConAu 61*
Boylan, Lucile 1906- *ConAu P-1*
Boyland, Eric 1905- *WrDr 84*
Boyle, Andrew 1919- *WrDr 84*
Boyle, Andrew 1923- *ConAu 5R*
Boyle, Andrew Philip More 1919- *ConAu 102, IntAu&W 82*
Boyle, Andrew Philip More 1922- *DcLEL 1940*

Boyle, Ann 1916- *ConAu 29R*, *SmATA 10*, *WrDr 84*
Boyle, Deirdre 1949- *ConAu 110*
Boyle, Edward Charles Gurney 1923-1981 *ConAu 108*
Boyle, Eleanor Vere 1825-1916 *SmATA 28*
Boyle, Hal *ConAu X*
Boyle, Harold V 1911-1974 *ConAu 101*, *-89*
Boyle, Harry Joseph 1915- *ConAu 7NR*, *-13R*, *CreCan 2*
Boyle, J A 1916-1979 *ConAu 9NR*, *-61*, *-85*
Boyle, Jack *TwCCr&M 80*
Boyle, John Hunter 1930- *ConAu 41R*
Boyle, Joyce 1901- *ConAu P-1*
Boyle, Kay *DrAP&F 83*
Boyle, Kay 1902- *ConNov 82*, *ConP 80*, *DcLB 4*, *-9[port]*, *WrDr 84*
Boyle, Kay 1903- *ConAmA*, *ConAu 13R*, *ConLC 1*, *-5*, *-19*, *EncWL 2*, *IntWWP 82*, *LongCTC*, *ModAL*, *TwCA*, *TwCA SUP*, *WhoTwCL*
Boyle, Mark *ConAu X*
Boyle, Mary 1882?-1975 *ConAu 53*
Boyle, Patrick 1905- *ConLC 19*
Boyle, Robert 1915- *ConAu 13R*
Boyle, Robert H 1928- *ConAu 17R*
Boyle, Sarah Patton 1906- *ConAu P-1*
Boyle, Stanley E 1927- *ConAu 41R*
Boyle, T Coraghessan *DrAP&F 83*
Boyle, Ted Eugene 1933- *ConAu 21R*
Boylen, Margaret Currier 1921-1967 *ConAu 1R*, *-103*
Boyles, C S, Jr. 1905- *ConAu 1R*
Boylesve, Rene 1867-1926 *CIDMEL 80*, *TwCA*, *TwCA SUP*
Boylston, Helen Dore 1895- *ConAu 73*, *SmATA 23[port]*, *TwCCW 83*, *WrDr 84*
Boyne, Walter J 1929- *ConAu 107*
Boynton, Lewis Delano 1909- *ConAu 5R*, *-6NR*, *WrDr 84*
Boynton, Percy Holmes 1875-1946 *TwCA*, *TwCA SUP*
Boynton, Peter S 1920?-1971 *ConAu 104*
Boynton, Searles Roland 1926- *ConAu 77*
Boyson, Emil 1897- *CIDMEL 80*
Boyum, Joy Gould 1934- *ConAu 33R*
Boyum, Keith O 1945- *ConAu 102*
Boz 1812-1870 *SmATA X*
Bozarslan, Mehmet Emin 1934- *IntAu&W 82*
Bozarth-Campbell, Alla 1947- *ConAu 105*
Boze, Arthur Phillip 1945- *ConAu 57*
Bozeman, Adda 1908- *WrDr 84*
Bozeman, Adda VonBruemmer 1908- *ConAu 3NR*, *-5R*, *IntAu&W 82*
Bozeman, Theodore Dwight 1942- *ConAu 85*
Bozic, Mirko 1919- *ModSL 2*
Bozzone, Bill 1947- *NatPD 81[port]*
Braak, Menno Ter 1902-1940 *CIDMEL 80*, *EncWL 2*
Braasch, William Frederick 1878- *ConAu P-2*
Braat, Leendert Pieter Johan 1908- *IntAu&W 82*
Braaten, Oskar Alexander 1881-1939 *CIDMEL 80*
Brabazon, James *ConAu X*
Brabazon, James 1923- *WrDr 84*
Brabb, George J 1925- *ConAu 41R*
Brabec, Barbara 1937- *ConAu 93*
Brablec, Carl 1908- *MichAu 80*
Brabson, George Dana 1900- *ConAu P-1*
Bracco, Roberto 1861-1943 *ModWD*
Bracco, Roberto 1862-1943 *CIDMEL 80*
Brace, Edward Roy 1936- *ConAu 102*
Brace, Geoffrey 1930- *ConAu 11NR*, *-69*
Brace, Gerald Warner 1901-1978 *ConAu 13R*, *-81*, *TwCA SUP*
Brace, Richard Munthe 1915-1977 *ConAu 1R*, *-69*
Brace, Timothy *ConAu X*
Bracegirdle, Brian 1933- *ConAu 101*, *WrDr 84*
Bracegirdle, Cyril 1920- *ConAu 45*
Bracewell, Ronald N 1921- *ConAu 57*
Bracewell-Milnes, Barry 1931- *ConAu 33R*, *WrDr 84*
Bracewell-Milnes, John Barry 1931- *IntAu&W 82*
Bracey, Howard E 1905- *ConAu 13R*
Bracey, John H, Jr. 1941- *ConAu 29R*, *LivgBAA*
Bracher, Karl Dietrich 1922- *ConAu 1NR*, *-45*, *IntAu&W 82*
Bracher, Marjory Louise Scholl 1906- *ConAu P-1*
Bracher, Ulrich 1927- *IntAu&W 82*

Brack, Harold Arthur *WrDr 84*
Brack, Harold Arthur 1923- *ConAu 17R*
Brack, O M, Jr. 1938- *ConAu 41R*
Brack, Vektris *ConAu X*
Brackbill, Yvonne 1928- *ConAu 21R*
Bracken, Dorothy Kendall 1910- *ConAu 21R*
Bracken, Joseph Andrew 1930- *ConAu 37R*
Bracken, Peg 1920- *ConAu 1R*, *-6NR*
Brackenridge, R Douglas 1932- *ConAu 101*
Bracker, Jon *DrAP&F 83*
Bracker, Jon 1936- *ConAu 17R*
Brackett, Charles 1892-1969 *DcLB 26[port]*
Brackett, Leigh 1915-1978 *ConAu 1R*, *-1NR*, *-77*, *ConSFA*, *DcLB 8[port]*, *-26[port]*, *TwCSFW*
Brackman, Arnold C 1923- *AuNews 1*, *ConAu 2NR*, *-5R*, *IntAu&W 82*, *WrDr 84*
Bracy, William 1915- *ConAu 61*
Bradbrook, Muriel Clara 1909- *ConAu 7NR*, *-13R*, *WrDr 84*
Bradburn, Norman M 1933- *ConAu 37R*
Bradburne, E S 1915- *ConAu 25R*
Bradbury, Bianca 1908- *ConAu 5NR*, *-13R*, *SmATA 3*
Bradbury, E P *TwCSFW*
Bradbury, Edward P *ConAu X*
Bradbury, Elaine Magdalene Arouette 1947- *IntAu&W 82*
Bradbury, John M 1908-1969 *ConAu P-1*
Bradbury, Malcolm 1932- *ConAu 1R*, *-1NR*, *ConLCrt 82*, *ConNov 82*, *DcLB 14[port]*, *DcLEL 1940*, *IntAu&W 82*, *IntWWP 82*, *ModBrL*, *ModBrL SUP*, *TwCWr*, *WorAu 1970*, *WrDr 84*
Bradbury, Parnell 1904- *ConAu 13R*
Bradbury, Peggy 1930- *ConAu 65*
Bradbury, Ray *DrAP&F 83*
Bradbury, Ray 1920- *AuNews 1*, *-2*, *CnMWL*, *ConAu 1R*, *-2NR*, *ConLC 1*, *-3*, *-10*, *-15*, *ConNov 82*, *ConSFA*, *DcLB 2*, *-8[port]*, *DcLEL 1940*, *DrmM[port]*, *LongCTC*, *SmATA 11*, *TwCA SUP*, *TwCCr&M 80*, *TwCSFW*, *TwCWr*, *WrDr 84*
Bradby, Anne Barbara 1912- *LongCTC*
Bradby, Godfrey Fox 1863-1947 *LongCTC*
Braddock, Richard R 1920-1974 *ConAu 1R*, *-103*
Braddon, Miss 1837-1915 *LongCTC*
Braddon, George *ConAu X*
Braddon, Mary Elizabeth 1837?-1915 *ConAu 108*
Braddon, Russell 1921- *ConAu 1R*, *-2NR*, *ConSFA*, *DcLEL 1940*, *IntAu&W 82*, *WrDr 84*
Braddy, Haldeen 1908-1980 *ConAu 101*, *-17R*
Brade-Birks, Stanley Graham 1887- *ConAu P-1*
Braden, Bernard 1916- *CreCan 2*
Braden, Charles Samuel 1887- *ConAu 5R*
Braden, Dennis *DrAP&F 83*
Braden, Irene A *ConAu X*
Braden, Waldo W 1911- *ConAu 5R*, *-5NR*, *WrDr 84*
Braden, William 1930- *ConAu 21R*
Bradfield, James McComb 1917- *ConAu 5R*
Bradfield, Jolly Roger *ConAu X*
Bradfield, Nancy 1913- *ConAu 29R*, *IntAu&W 82*, *WrDr 84*
Bradfield, Richard 1896- *ConAu P-2*
Bradfield, Roger 1924- *ConAu 17R*
Bradford, Adam *ConAu X*
Bradford, Barbara Taylor 1933- *ConAu 89*
Bradford, Benjamin 1925- *ConAu 85*, *IntAu&W 82*, *NatPD 81[port]*
Bradford, Ernle 1922- *ConAu 101*, *DcLEL 1940*, *WorAu*
Bradford, Gamaliel 1863-1932 *ConAmA*, *DcLB 17[port]*, *TwCA*, *TwCA SUP*
Bradford, Jason *IntAu&W 82X*
Bradford, Leland P 1905- *ConAu 9NR*
Bradford, Leland Powers 1905- *ConAu 13R*, *WrDr 84*
Bradford, Leroy 1922- *ConAu 105*
Bradford, Lois J 1936- *ConAu 104*
Bradford, M E 1934- *ConAu 77*, *WrDr 84*
Bradford, Patience Andrewes 1918- *ConAu 33R*
Bradford, Peter Amory 1942- *ConAu 61*, *WrDr 84*
Bradford, Reed H 1912- *ConAu 49*
Bradford, Richard 1932- *ConAu 2NR*, *-49*, *TwCWW*, *WrDr 84*
Bradford, Richard H 1938- *ConAu 89*
Bradford, Roark 1896-1948 *LongCTC*, *TwCA*, *TwCA SUP*
Bradford, Robert W 1918- *ConAu 77*

Bradford, Roy Hamilton 1920- *ConAu 109*
Bradford, Sax 1907-1966 *ConAu 1R*
Bradford, Walter L *DrAP&F 83*
Bradford, Walter L 1937- *LivgBAA*
Bradford, Will *ConAu X*
Bradford, William Castle 1910- *ConAu 9R*
Bradlee, Ben 1921- *WrDr 84*
Bradlee, Benjamin C 1921- *AuNews 2*, *ConAu 61*
Bradlee, Frederic 1920- *ConAu 21R*
Bradley, Alfred 1925- *ConAu 105*
Bradley, Andrew Cecil 1851-1935 *LongCTC*, *TwCA*, *TwCA SUP*
Bradley, Ardyth *DrAP&F 83*
Bradley, Bert E 1926- *ConAu 41R*
Bradley, Bill *ConAu X*
Bradley, Brigitte L 1924- *ConAu 37R*
Bradley, C Paul 1918- *ConAu 106*
Bradley, Concho *ConAu X*
Bradley, David *DrAP&F 83*
Bradley, David 1950- *ConAu 104*, *ConLC 23[port]*
Bradley, David G 1916- *ConAu 13R*
Bradley, Duane 1914- *ConAu X*
Bradley, Ed 1911?-1983 *ConAu 110*
Bradley, Ed 1941- *ConAu 108*
Bradley, Erwin S 1906- *ConAu P-2*
Bradley, Francis Herbert 1846-1924 *LongCTC*
Bradley, Gladys 1910- *IntWWP 82*
Bradley, Gladys Lilian 1900- *WrDr 84*
Bradley, Harold Frank 1904- *IntWWP 82*
Bradley, Harold Whitman 1903- *ConAu 33R*
Bradley, Hassell 1930- *ConAu 65*
Bradley, Henry 1845-1923 *LongCTC*
Bradley, Ian 1900- *WrDr 84*
Bradley, Ian Campbell 1950- *ConAu 103*, *IntAu&W 82*
Bradley, James Vandiver 1924- *ConAu 37R*, *WrDr 84*
Bradley, John 1930- *ConAu 10NR*, *-25R*
Bradley, John Hodgdon, Jr. 1898-1962 *TwCA*, *TwCA SUP*
Bradley, John Lewis 1917- *ConAu 29R*, *WrDr 84*
Bradley, Joseph F 1917- *ConAu 21R*
Bradley, Julia 1911- *IntAu&W 82*
Bradley, Katharine Harris 1848-1914 *LongCTC*
Bradley, Sir Kenneth Granville 1904- *ConAu P-1*
Bradley, Marion *DrAP&F 83*
Bradley, Marion Zimmer 1930- *ConAu 7NR*, *-57*, *ConSFA*, *DcLB 8[port]*, *TwCSFW*, *WrDr 84*
Bradley, Marjorie D 1931- *ConAu 25R*
Bradley, Matt 1947- *ConAu 105*
Bradley, Michael *ConAu X*
Bradley, Omar Nelson 1893-1981 *ConAu 103*
Bradley, Preston 1888-1983 *ConAu 110*
Bradley, R C 1929- *ConAu 33R*, *WrDr 84*
Bradley, Ramona K 1909- *WrDr 84*
Bradley, Ritamary 1916- *ConAu 49*
Bradley, Robert A 1917- *ConAu 21R*
Bradley, Sam *DrAP&F 83*
Bradley, Sam 1917- *ConAu 21R*, *IntWWP 82X*, *WrDr 84*
Bradley, Samuel McKee 1917- *IntWWP 82*
Bradley, Sculley 1897- *ConAu 89*
Bradley, Van Allen 1913- *ConAu 37R*
Bradley, Virginia 1912- *ConAu 8NR*, *-61*, *SmATA 23[port]*
Bradley, William 1934- *ConAu 45*
Bradley, William Aspenwall 1878-1939 *ConAu 107*, *DcLB 4*
Bradley, William L 1918- *ConAu 21R*
Bradley, William Warren 1943- *ConAu 101*
Bradlow, Edna Rom *ConAu P-1*
Bradlow, Frank Rosslyn 1913- *ConAu P-1*, *WrDr 84*
Bradner, Enos 1892- *ConAu 57*
Bradnum, Frederick *ConDr 82B*
Bradshaw, Brendan 1937- *ConAu 73*
Bradshaw, George 1909?-1973 *ConAu 45*
Bradshaw, Gillian 1956- *ConAu 103*
Bradshaw, Thornton F 1917- *ConAu 108*
Bradstreet, Vallerie *ConAu X*
Bradt, A Gordon 1896- *ConAu 57*
Bradt, A Gordon 1896-1983 *ConAu 110*
Bradway, John S 1890- *ConAu P-2*
Bradwell, James *ConAu X*, *WrDr 84*
Brady, Charles Andrew 1912- *ConAu 5R*
Brady, Darlene A 1951- *ConAu 102*

Brady, Esther Wood 1905- *ConAu 93,*
SmATA 31
Brady, Frank 1924- *ConAu 13R*
Brady, Frank 1934- *ConAu 9NR, –61*
Brady, Gene P 1927- *ConAu 107*
Brady, George Stuart 1887-1977 *ConAu 73*
Brady, Gerald Peter 1929- *ConAu 5R*
Brady, Irene 1943- *ConAu 33R, SmATA 4*
Brady, James Winston 1928- *ConAu 101*
Brady, John 1942- *ConAu 10NR, –65*
Brady, John Paul 1928- *ConAu 5NR, –13R*
Brady, Kathleen *DrAP&F 83*
Brady, Kristin 1949- *ConAu 109*
Brady, Leo 1917- *ConAu 69*
Brady, Lillian 1902- *ConAu 105,*
SmATA 28[port]
Brady, Mary Lou 1937- *ConAu 106*
Brady, Maureen *DrAP&F 83*
Brady, Maxine L 1941- *ConAu 69*
Brady, Michael 1928- *ConAu 93*
Brady, Peter *ConAu X*
Brady, Ryder *DrAP&F 83*
Brady, Sally Ryder 1939- *ConAu 103*
Brady, Terence 1939- *ConAu 106,*
IntAu&W 82
Brady, William S *TwCWW, WrDr 84*
Braenne, Berit 1918- *ConAu 21R*
Braestrup, Carl Bjorn 1897-1982 *ConAu 107*
Braestrup, Peter 1929- *ConAu 97*
Braff, Allan James 1930- *ConAu 108*
Bragdon, Clifford R 1940- *ConAu 57*
Bragdon, Elspeth MacDuffie 1897- *ConAu 5R,*
–5NR, SmATA 6
Bragdon, Henry Wilkinson 1906-1980
ConAu 3NR, –5R, –97
Bragdon, Lillian Jacot *ConAu 73, SmATA 24*
Bragg, Arthur N 1897- *ConAu P-1*
Bragg, Bill *ConAu X*
Bragg, Dobby *ConAu X*
Bragg, Mabel Caroline 1870-1945 *SmATA 24*
Bragg, Melvyn 1939- *ConAu 10NR, –57,*
ConLC 10, ConNov 82, DcLB 14[port],
DcLEL 1940, IntAu&W 82, WorAu 1970,
WrDr 84
Bragg, W F 1892-1967 *TwCWW*
Bragg, William Fredrick, Jr. 1922- *ConAu 109*
Braham, Allan 1937- *WrDr 84*
Braham, Allan John Witney 1937- *ConAu 105,*
IntAu&W 82
Braham, Randolph Lewis 1922- *ConAu 1R,*
–5NR
Brahm, Lila *IntAu&W 82X*
Brahms, Caryl *ConAu X*
Brahms, Caryl 1901- *ConDr 82D, LongCTC,*
TwCCr&M 80, TwCWr, WrDr 84
Brahs, Stuart J 1940- *ConAu 57*
Braht, Josef Anton 1910- *IntAu&W 82*
Braht-Wladsee, J *IntAu&W 82X*
Brahtz, John F Peel 1918- *ConAu 73*
Braider, Donald 1923-1976 *ConAu 65,*
ConAu P-2
Braidwood, Robert John 1907- *ConAu 108*
Brailsford, Frances *ConAu X*
Brailsford, Frances Wosmek 1917- *ConAu X*
Brailsford, Henry Noel 1873-1958 *LongCTC,*
TwCA, TwCA SUP
Braimah, Joseph Adam 1916- *ConAu 61*
Braiman, Susan 1943- *ConAu 97*
Brain, George B 1920- *ConAu 41R*
Brain, James Lewton *ConAu X*
Brain, Joseph J 1920- *ConAu 13R*
Brain, Robert 1933- *ConAu 73*
Brainard, Harry Gray 1907- *ConAu 1R*
Brainard, Joe *DrAP&F 83*
Brainard, Joe 1942- *ConAu 65*
Braine, John 1922- *ConAu 1R, –1NR,*
ConLC 1, –3, ConNov 82, DcLB 15[port],
DcLEL 1940, EncWL 2, LongCTC,
ModBrL, ModBrL SUP, TwCWr, WorAu,
WrDr 84
Brainerd, Barron 1928- *ConAu 33R*
Brainerd, Charles Jon 1944- *ConAu 103*
Brainerd, John W 1918- *ConAu 57*
Braithwaite, Althea 1940- *ConAu 97,*
IntAu&W 82, SmATA 23[port]
Braithwaite, E R 1920- *ConAu 106*
Braithwaite, E R 1920- *WrDr 84*
Braithwaite, Edward 1930- *DcLEL 1940*
Braithwaite, Eustace Adolph 1912- *DcLEL 1940*
Braithwaite, Eustace Edward Ricardo 1920-
LongCTC, TwCWr
Braithwaite, John Victor Maxwell *CreCan 2*

Braithwaite, Max 1911- *ConAu 93, CreCan 2*
Braithwaite, William Stanley Beaumont 1878-1962
TwCA, TwCA SUP
Braitstein, Marcel 1935- *CreCan 2*
Brake, Mike 1936- *ConAu 93*
Brakel, Samuel J 1943- *ConAu 33R*
Brakhage, Stan 1933- *ConAu 41R, WrDr 84*
Bralver, Eleanor 1913- *ConAu 97*
Braly, Malcolm 1925-1980 *ASpks, ConAu 17R,*
–97
Bram *IntAu&W 82X*
Bram, Elizabeth 1948- *ConAu 9NR, –65,*
SmATA 30[port]
Bram, Joseph 1904-1974 *ConAu 110*
Bramah, Ernest 1868-1942 *LongCTC, TwCA,*
TwCA SUP, TwCCr&M 80, TwCWr
Bramall, Eric 1927- *ConAu 9R*
Braman, Karen Jill 1943- *MichAu 80*
Braman, Kitte *MichAu 80*
Braman, Sandra *DrAP&F 83*
Brambach, Rainer 1917- *IntAu&W 82*
Bramble, Forbes 1939- *ConAu 89,*
IntAu&W 82, WrDr 84
Bramble, Mark *ConDr 82D*
Brameld, Theodore 1904- *ConAu 17R,*
WrDr 84
Bramer, Jennie 1900- *ConAu P-1*
Bramer, John C, Jr. 1924- *ConAu 1R*
Bramesco, Norton J 1924- *ConAu 106*
Bramlett, John *ConAu X*
Brammell, P Roy 1900- *ConAu 65*
Brammer, Lawrence M 1922- *ConAu 13R*
Brammer, William 1930?-1978 *ConAu 77*
Brams, Stanley Howard 1910- *ConAu 9R,*
MichAu 80
Brams, Steven J 1940- *ConAu 10NR*
Brams, Steven John 1940- *ConAu 61,*
IntAu&W 82
Bramsen, Mikael 1940- *IntAu&W 82*
Bramson, Leon 1930- *ConAu 1R, –4NR,*
WrDr 84
Bramson, Robert M 1925- *ConAu 108*
Bramwell, Charlotte *ConAu X, TwCRGW*
Bramwell, Dana G 1948- *ConAu 57*
Bramwell, James Guy 1911- *ConAu 9R*
Branca, Albert A 1916- *ConAu 13R*
Branca, Stella Usque 1931- *IntAu&W 82*
Brancaforte, Benito 1934- *ConAu 37R*
Brancati, Vitaliano 1907-1954 *CIDMEL 80,*
ConAu 109, EncWL 2, ModRL,
TwCLC 12[port], WorAu
Brancato, Gilda 1949- *ConAu 107*
Brancato, Robin F 1936- *ConAu 11NR, –69,*
SmATA 23[port]
Branch, Alan E 1933- *ConAu 105*
Branch, Anna Hempstead 1875-1937 *TwCA,*
TwCA SUP
Branch, Beatrice *IntWWP 82X*
Branch, Beatrice Estella 1903- *IntWWP 82*
Branch, Daniel Paulk 1931- *ConAu 17R*
Branch, Edgar Marquess 1913- *ConAu 13R,*
IntAu&W 82, WrDr 84
Branch, Harold Francis 1894-1966 *ConAu 5R*
Branch, Kip 1947- *ConAu 108*
Branch, Mary 1910- *ConAu 10NR, –25R*
Branch, Melville C 1913- *ConAu 41R*
Branch, William B 1929- *LivgBAA*
Branch, William Blackwell 1927- *ConAu 81*
Branche, Lewis W 1927- *ConAmTC*
Brand, Alice Glarden *DrAP&F 83*
Brand, C E 1895- *ConAu P-2*
Brand, Carl Fremont 1892- *ConAu 13R*
Brand, Charles M 1932- *ConAu 21R*
Brand, Charles Peter 1923- *ConAu 13R*
Brand, Christianna *ConAu X*
Brand, Christianna 1907- *TwCCW 83*
Brand, Christianna 1909- *TwCCr&M 80,*
WrDr 84
Brand, Clay *ConAu X, WrDr 84*
Brand, Eugene L 1931- *ConAu 8NR, –61*
Brand, Garrison *ConAu X*
Brand, Jeanne L 1919- *ConAu 13R*
Brand, Max *ConAu X*
Brand, Max 1892-1944 *FifWWr, LongCTC,*
TwCA, TwCA SUP, TwCCr&M 80,
TwCWW
Brand, Millen 1906-1980 *ConAu 21R, –97,*
ConLC 7, TwCA, TwCA SUP
Brand, Mona 1915- *IntAu&W 82, WrDr 84*
Brand, Myles 1942- *ConAu 37R*
Brand, Oscar 1920- *ConAu 1R, –4NR,*
NatPD 81[port], WrDr 84

Brand, Peter *ConAu X*
Brand, Sandra 1918- *ConAu 85, IntAu&W 82*
Brand, Stewart 1938- *AuNews 1, ConAu 81*
Brand, Susan *ConAu X*
Brand, Victor *WrDr 84*
Brandabur, Edward 1930- *ConAu 41R*
Brandao, Raul Germano 1867-1930 *CIDMEL 80,*
EncWL 2
Brande, Dorothea 1893-1948 *TwCA,*
TwCA SUP
Brande, Ralph T 1921- *ConAu 25R*
Brandel, Arthur Meyer 1913?-1980 *ConAu 102*
Brandel, Marc *ConAu X*
Brandel, Marc Beresford 1919- *IntAu&W 82*
Brandell, Gunnar 1916- *ConAu 103*
Branden, Nathaniel 1930- *ConAu 33R,*
WrDr 84
Branden, Victoria *ConAu 101*
Brandenberg, Aliki 1929- *WrDr 84*
Brandenberg, Aliki Liacouras 1929- *ConAu 1R,*
–4NR, IntAu&W 82, SmATA 2
Brandenberg, Franz 1932- *ConAu 29R,*
SmATA 8, WrDr 84
Brandenburg, Frank R 1926- *ConAu 13R*
Brander, Michael 1924- *ConAu 7NR, –53*
Brandes, Georg 1842-1927 *TwCLC 10[port]*
Brandes, Georg Morris Cohen 1842-1927
CIDMEL 80, ConAu 105, LongCTC,
TwCA, TwCA SUP, TwCWr
Brandes, Joseph 1928- *ConAu 5R, WrDr 84*
Brandes, Norman Scott 1923- *ConAu 57*
Brandes, Paul D 1919- *ConAu 45*
Brandes, Paul D 1920- *ConAu 2NR*
Brandewyne, Rebecca 1955- *ConAu 107*
Brandhorst, Carl T 1898- *ConAu P-2,*
SmATA 23[port]
Brandi, John *DrAP&F 83*
Brandi, John 1943- *ConAu 73, ConP 80,*
IntAu&W 82, IntWWP 82, WrDr 84
Brandmuller, Johannes *IntAu&W 82X*
Brandner, Gary 1933- *ConAu 1NR, –45*
Brandon, Beatrice *ConAu X*
Brandon, Brumsic, Jr. 1927- *ConAu 61,*
SmATA 9
Brandon, Curt *ConAu X, SmATA 6*
Brandon, Dick H 1934- *ConAu 17R*
Brandon, Dick H 1934-1981 *ConAu 10NR*
Brandon, Donald 1926- *ConAu 69*
Brandon, Dorothy 1899?-1977 *ConAu 69*
Brandon, Frances Sweeney 1916- *ConAu 9R*
Brandon, Frank *ConAu X*
Brandon, Henry 1916- *ConAu 49, WrDr 84*
Brandon, James Rodger 1927- *ConAu 11NR, –69*
Brandon, Joe *ConAu X, WrDr 84*
Brandon, John Gordon 1879-1941 *TwCCr&M 80*
Brandon, Johnny *ConAu 105, NatPD 81[port]*
Brandon, Robert Joseph 1918- *ConAu 105*
Brandon, Robin *ConAu X*
Brandon, Samuel George Frederick 1907-1971
ConAu 102
Brandon, Sheila *ConAu X, TwCRGW,*
WrDr 84
Brandon, William 1914- *ConAu 77*
Brandon-Cox, Hugh 1917- *ConAu 93,*
IntAu&W 82, WrDr 84
Brandreth, Gyles 1948- *ConAu 65,*
IntAu&W 82, SmATA 28[port], WrDr 84
Brandstaetter, Roman 1906- *ModWD*
Brandstatter, A F 1914- *ConAu 107*
Brandstatter, Roman 1906- *CnMD*
Brandstrom, Maud 1928- *IntAu&W 82*
Brandt, Alvin G 1922- *ConAu 13R*
Brandt, Anthony 1936- *ConAu 69*
Brandt, Catharine 1905- *ConAu 106*
Brandt, Edward R 1931- *IntWWP 82*
Brandt, Floyd S 1930- *ConAu 21R*
Brandt, Harvey *ConAu X*
Brandt, Jane Lewis 1915- *ConAu 97*
Brandt, Joergen Gustava 1929- *IntWWP 82*
Brandt, Jorgen Gustava 1929- *CIDMEL 80,*
EncWL 2
Brandt, Keith *ConAu X, SmATA X*
Brandt, Leslie F 1919- *ConAu 8NR, –21R,*
IntAu&W 82, WrDr 84
Brandt, Lucile 1900- *ConAu 61*
Brandt, Nat *ConAu X*
Brandt, Nathan Henry, Jr. 1929- *ConAu 102*
Brandt, Rex 1914- *ConAu 5NR, –13R*
Brandt, Richard M 1922- *ConAu 33R,*
WrDr 84
Brandt, Roger *ConAu X*
Brandt, Sue R 1916- *ConAu 25R*

Breger, Brian David 1951- *IntWWP 82*
Breger, Louis 1935- *ConAu 69*
Breggin, Peter Roger 1936- *ConAu 81*
Bregman, Jacob I 1923- *ConAu 41R*
Bregman, Jay 1940- *ConAu 109*
Brehm, Shirley A 1926- *ConAu 69*
Breig, Joseph Anthony 1905- *ConAu 5R*
Breighner, Harry Daniel, Sr. 1909- *IntWWP 82*
Breihan, Carl William 1916- *ConAu 1R, –1NR*
Breillat, Catherine 1950- *ConAu 33R*
Breimyer, Harold F 1914- *ConAu 17R, WrDr 84*
Breinburg, Petronella 1927- *WrDr 84*
Breinburg, Petronella Alexandrina 1927- *ConAu 4NR, –53, SmATA 11*
Breines, Paul 1941- *ConAu 61*
Breisach, Ernst Adolf 1923- *ConAu 1R*
Breisky, William J 1928- *ConAu 53, SmATA 22*
Breit, Harvey 1909-1968 *ConAu 6NR*
Breit, Harvey 1913?-1968 *ConAu 5R, –25R, WorAu*
Breit, Marquita E 1942- *ConAu 57*
Breit, William 1933- *ConAu 33R*
Breitbart, Vicki 1942- *ConAu 93*
Breitenkamp, Edward C 1913- *ConAu 10NR*
Breitenkamp, Edward Carlton 1913- *ConAu 25R*
Breitman, George 1916- *ConAu 7NR, –61*
Breitman, Richard D 1947- *ConAu 105*
Breitmeyer, Lois Fromm 1923- *MichAu 80*
Breitner, I Emery 1929- *ConAu 57*
Brekke, Paal 1923- *CIDMEL 80*
Breland, Osmond Philip 1910- *ConAu 9R, IntAu&W 82, WrDr 84*
Brelis, Dean 1924- *ConAu 9R*
Brelis, Nancy 1929- *ConAu 21R*
Brelsford, William 1907- *WrDr 84*
Brelsford, William Vernon 1907- *ConAu P-1*
Breman, Paul 1931- *ConAu 21R*
Bremer, Francis J 1947- *ConAu 93*
Bremner, Robert H 1917- *ConAu 9NR, –21R*
Bremond, Henri 1865-1933 *CIDMEL 80*
Brems, Hans 1915- *ConAu 10NR*
Brems, Hans J 1915- *ConAu 25R, WrDr 84*
Bremser, Bonnie 1939- *DcLB 16[port]*
Bremser, Ray *DrAP&F 83*
Bremser, Ray 1934- *ConAu 17R, ConP 80, DcLB 16[port], WrDr 84*
Bremyer, Jayne Dickey 1924- *ConAu 61*
Brenan, Gerald 1894- *ConAu 1R, –3NR, LongCTC, TwCA SUP, WrDr 84*
Brend, Ruth M 1927- *ConAu 105*
Brendel, Otto Johannes 1901-1973 *ConAu 97*
Brendon, Piers 1940- *ConAu 101, IntAu&W 82, WrDr 84*
Brendtro, Larry K 1940- *ConAu 29R, MichAu 80*
Brener, Milton E 1930- *ConAu 29R*
Brengelmann, Johannes Clemens 1920- *ConAu 5R*
Brennan, Anne 1936- *ConAu 109*
Brennan, Bernard P 1918- *ConAu 5R*
Brennan, Christopher *WrDr 84*
Brennan, Christopher 1917- *ConAu X*
Brennan, Christopher John 1870-1932 *EncWL 2, ModCmwL, TwCWr, WorAu*
Brennan, Donald 1926-1980 *ConAu 97*
Brennan, John 1914- *WrDr 84*
Brennan, John N H 1914- *ConAu 1R, –4NR, IntAu&W 82*
Brennan, Joseph Gerard 1910- *ConAu 1R, –3NR*
Brennan, Joseph Lomas 1903- *ConAu 2NR, –5R, SmATA 6*
Brennan, Joseph Payne *DrAP&F 83*
Brennan, Joseph Payne 1918- *ConAu 1R, –4NR, IntAu&W 82, IntWWP 82, WrDr 84*
Brennan, Lawrence D 1915- *ConAu 5R*
Brennan, Louis A 1911- *ConAu 17R*
Brennan, Louis A 1911-1983 *ConAu 109*
Brennan, Maeve *DrAP&F 83*
Brennan, Maeve 1917- *ConAu 81, ConLC 5*
Brennan, Matthew J 1917- *ConAu 106*
Brennan, Maynard J 1921- *ConAu 13R*
Brennan, Michael Joseph, Jr. 1928- *ConAu 13R*
Brennan, Neil F 1923- *ConAu 37R, WrDr 84*
Brennan, Niall 1918- *ConAu 13R*
Brennan, Nicholas 1948- *ConAu 106*
Brennan, Ray 1908?-1972 *ConAu 37R*
Brennan, Richard O 1916- *ConAu 89*
Brennan, Tim *ConAu X, IntAu&W 82X, SmATA X*
Brennan, Will *ConAu X*

Brennand, Frank *ConAu X*
Brennecke, John H 1934- *ConAu 37R*
Brenneman, Helen Good 1925- *ConAu 21R, WrDr 84*
Brennen, Anna *NatPD 81[port]*
Brenner, Anita 1905-1974 *ConAu 49, –53*
Brenner, Barbara Johnes 1925- *ConAu 9R, SmATA 4*
Brenner, Erma 1911- *ConAu 69*
Brenner, Fred 1920- *SmATA 34*
Brenner, Gerry 1937- *ConAu 110*
Brenner, Hildegard 1927- *IntAu&W 82*
Brenner, Isabel *ConAu X, IntAu&W 82X*
Brenner, Marie 1949- *ConAu 73*
Brenner, Rebecca Summer *DrAP&F 83*
Brenner, Rebecca Summer 1945- *ConAu 10NR*
Brenner, Summer *DrAP&F 83*
Brenner, Summer 1945- *ConAu 61*
Brenner, Yehojachin Simon 1926- *ConAu 11NR, –21R, WrDr 84*
Brenni, Vito J 1923- *ConAu 49*
Brent, Arthur *IntWWP 82X*
Brent, Beryl *ConAu X*
Brent, Harold Patrick 1943- *ConAu 33R*
Brent, Harry *ConAu X*
Brent, Madeleine *TwCRGW, WrDr 84*
Brent, Peter 1931- *ConAu 65, IntAu&W 82, WrDr 84*
Brent, Stuart *ConAu 73, SmATA 14*
Brent-Dyer, Elinor M 1894-1969 *TwCCW 83*
Brent-Dyer, Elinor Mary 1895-1969 *ConAu 101*
Brent Of Bin Bin *ConAu X, TwCWr*
Brentano, Robert 1926- *ConAu 21R*
Brenton, Howard 1942- *ConAu 69, ConDr 82, DcLB 13[port], IntAu&W 82, WrDr 84*
Brereton, Geoffrey 1906- *ConAu 25R*
Bresky, Dushan 1920- *ConAu 53, IntAu&W 82*
Breslau, Alan Jeffry 1926- *ConAu 69*
Breslauer, George W 1946- *ConAu 29R*
Breslauer, Samuel Daniel 1942- *ConAu 102*
Breslin, Catherine 1936- *ConAu 93*
Breslin, Herbert H 1924- *ConAu 53*
Breslin, James 1930- *ConAu 73*
Breslin, James E 1935- *ConAu 33R*
Breslin, Jimmy 1930- *AuNews 1, ConAu X, ConLC 4, WrDr 84*
Breslove, David 1891- *ConAu 9R*
Breslow, Michael *DrAP&F 83*
Bress, Hyman 1931- *CreCan 2*
Bressett, Kenneth E 1928- *ConAu 93*
Bressi, Betty *DrAP&F 83*
Bressler, Henri Lucien 1901- *IntAu&W 82*
Bressler, Leo A 1911- *ConAu 57*
Bressler, Marion Ann 1921- *ConAu 57*
Bresson, Robert 1907- *ConAu 110, ConLC 16*
Bretall, Robert Walter 1913-1980 *ConAu 110*
Bretnor, R 1911- *ConSFA*
Bretnor, Reginald 1911- *ConAu 10NR, –65, TwCSFW, WrDr 84*
Breton, Albert 1929- *ConAu 61, WrDr 84*
Breton, Andre 1896-1966 *CIDMEL 80, ConAu 25R, ConAu P-2, ConLC 2, –9, –15, EncWL 2[port], LongCTC, ModFrL, ModRL, ModWD, TwCA SUP, TwCWr, WhoTwCL*
Bretscher, Paul G 1921- *ConAu 8NR, –17R*
Brett, Bernard 1925- *ConAu 97, SmATA 22[port]*
Brett, David *ConAu X*
Brett, Dorothy 1883-1977 *ConAu 73*
Brett, Grace Neff 1900-1975 *ConAu 9R, SmATA 23*
Brett, Hawksley *SmATA X*
Brett, Leo *ConAu X, ConSFA, IntAu&W 82X*
Brett, Mary Elizabeth *ConAu 9R, WrDr 84*
Brett, Michael *ConAu X, TwCCr&M 80, WrDr 84*
Brett, Molly *ConAu X, WrDr 84*
Brett, Peter *DrAP&F 83*
Brett, Peter David 1943- *ConAu 77, IntAu&W 82*
Brett, Raymond Laurence 1917- *ConAu 1R, –3NR, IntAu&W 82, WrDr 84*
Brett, Rosalind *TwCRGW, WrDr 84*
Brett, Simon 1945- *ConAu 69, TwCCr&M 80, WrDr 84*
Brett-James, Antony 1920- *ConAu 5R, –7NR, IntAu&W 82, WrDr 84*
Brett-Smith, Richard 1923- *ConAu 21R*
Brett Young, Francis 1884-1954 *LongCTC, TwCA, TwCA SUP, TwCWr*

Brett-Young, Jessica 1883-1970 *ConAu P-1*
Brettell, Noel Harry 1908- *DcLEL 1940, IntWWP 82*
Bretton, Henry L 1916- *ConAu 2NR, –5R*
Brettschneider, Bertram D 1924- *ConAu 33R*
Breuer, Bessie 1893-1975 *ConAu 61, ConAu P-2*
Breuer, Elizabeth 1892- *TwCA, TwCA SUP*
Breuer, Ernest Henry 1902-1972 *ConAu P-2*
Breuer, Georg 1919- *ConAu 105*
Breuer, Lee 1937- *ConAu 110*
Breuer, Marcel 1902-1981 *ConAu 5R, –5NR, –104*
Breuer, Miles J 1888-1947 *TwCSFW*
Breugelmans, Rene 1925- *ConAu 103*
Breuil, Henri 1877-1961 *LongCTC*
Breunig, Jerome Edward 1917- *ConAu 13R*
Breunig, Leroy Clinton 1915- *ConAu 61*
Brevis, Carl August *IntWWP 82X*
Brew, J O 1906- *ConAu 61*
Brew, Kwesi 1928- *DcLEL 1940, IntWWP 82*
Brew, O H Kwesi 1928- *ConP 80, WrDr 84*
Breward, Ian 1934- *WrDr 84*
Brewer, Annie M 1925- *ConAu 107*
Brewer, Derek Stanley 1923- *ConAu 1R, –4NR, IntAu&W 82*
Brewer, Edward S 1933- *ConAu 33R*
Brewer, Frances Joan 1913-1965 *ConAu P-1*
Brewer, Fredric Aldwyn 1921- *ConAu 17R*
Brewer, Garry D 1941- *WrDr 84*
Brewer, Garry Dwight 1941- *ConAu 33R, IntAu&W 82*
Brewer, Gil *TwCCr&M 80*
Brewer, Gil 1922- *WrDr 84*
Brewer, J Mason 1896-1975 *ConAu P-2*
Brewer, Jack A 1933- *ConAu 21R*
Brewer, James H Fitzgerald 1916- *ConAu 9R*
Brewer, Jeutonne 1939- *ConAu 77*
Brewer, John Mason 1896- *LivgBAA*
Brewer, Kenneth *DrAP&F 83*
Brewer, Kenneth W 1941- *ConAu 110*
Brewer, Kenneth Wayne 1941- *IntWWP 82*
Brewer, Margaret L 1929- *ConAu 29R*
Brewer, Sally King 1947- *SmATA 33*
Brewer, Sam Pope 1909?-1976 *ConAu 65*
Brewer, Thomas B 1932- *ConAu 21R*
Brewer, William C 1897?-1974 *ConAu 53*
Brewer, Wilmon 1895- *ConAu 5R, IntAu&W 82, IntWWP 82, WrDr 84*
Brewi, Janice 1933- *ConAu 110*
Brewington, Marion Vernon 1902-1974 *ConAu 3NR, –5R, –53*
Brewster, Benjamin *ConAu X, IntAu&W 82X, SmATA 2, –5, WrDr 84*
Brewster, David *DrAP&F 83*
Brewster, Dorothy 1883-1979 *ConAu 1R, –3NR, –85*
Brewster, Elizabeth 1922- *ConAu 10NR, –25R, ConP 80, CreCan 1, DcLEL 1940, IntAu&W 82, IntWWP 82, WrDr 84*
Brewster, Townsend 1924- *ConAu 105, NatPD 81[port]*
Brewton, John Edmund 1898- *ConAu 3NR, –5R, SmATA 5*
Breycha-Vauthier, Arthur 1903- *IntAu&W 82*
Breyer, N L 1942- *ConAu 49*
Breyer, Stephen Gerald 1938- *ConAu 107*
Breyfogle, Valorie *DrAP&F 83*
Breytenbach, Breyten 1939- *ConLC 23[port]*
Breza, Tadeusz 1905-1970 *CIDMEL 80, ConAu 29R*
Brezan, Inrij 1916- *IntAu&W 82*
Brezhnev, Leonid I 1906-1982 *ConAu 108*
Brezina, Otokar 1868-1929 *CIDMEL 80, EncWL 2, ModSL 2, WorAu*
Brian *ConAu X*
Brian, Alan B *ConAu X*
Brian, Denis 1923- *ConAu 25R*
Brian, James *LongCTC*
Briand, Paul L, Jr. 1920- *ConAu 1R, –4NR*
Briand, Rena 1935- *ConAu 29R, WrDr 84*
Briao, Fernandes De *WorAu 1970*
Briarton, Grendel *ConAu X, WrDr 84*
Brice, Douglas 1916- *ConAu 21R, WrDr 84*
Brice, Marshall Moore 1898- *ConAu 17R*
Brichant, Colette Dubois 1926- *ConAu 13R*
Brick, John 1922-1973 *ConAu 45, ConAu P-1, SmATA 10*
Brick, Michael 1922- *ConAu 13R*
Brick, Michael 1922-1974 *ConAu 9NR*
Bricker, Victoria Reifler 1940- *ConAu 53*
Brickhill, Paul Chester Jerome 1916- *ConAu 9R, DcLEL 1940, TwCWr*

Brickman, Marshall 1941- *ConAu 81*
Brickman, William Wolfgang 1913- *ConAu 1R, -1NR, IntAu&W 82, WrDr 84*
Brickner, Richard P *DrAP&F 83*
Brickner, Richard P 1933- *ConAu 2NR, -5R*
Bricuth, John 1940- *ConAu X*
Bridenbaugh, Carl 1903- *ConAu 4NR, -9R*
Bridge, Ann *TwCA[port]*
Bridge, Ann 1889-1974 *ConAu X, TwCA SUP, TwCCr&M 80, TwCRGW*
Bridge, Ann 1891-1974 *LongCTC*
Bridge, Raymond 1943- *ConAu 69*
Bridgecross, Peter *ConAu X*
Bridgeman, Harriet 1942- *ConAu 85, IntAu&W 82*
Bridgeman, Richard *ConAu X*
Bridgeman, William Barton 1916- *ConAu 9R*
Bridger, Adam *ConAu X, TwCWW*
Bridger, Gordon 1932- *ConAu 65*
Bridgers, Sue Ellen *DrAP&F 83*
Bridgers, Sue Ellen 1942- *ConAu 11NR, -65, ConLC 26[port], SmATA 22[port]*
Bridges, Hal 1918- *ConAu 1R*
Bridges, Herb 1929- *ConAu 110*
Bridges, Howard *ConAu X*
Bridges, Lee *DrAP&F 83*
Bridges, Lee 1927- *IntWWP 82*
Bridges, Robert Seymour 1844-1930 *ConAu 104, LongCTC, ModBrL, TwCA, TwCA SUP, TwCLC 1, TwCWr, WhoTwCL*
Bridges, Victor 1878-1972 *TwCCr&M 80*
Bridges, William 1901- *WrDr 84*
Bridges, William 1933- *ConAu 33R*
Bridges, William Andrew 1901- *ConAu 33R, IntAu&W 82, SmATA 5*
Bridges-Adams, William 1889-1965 *ConAu P-1*
Bridgman, Elizabeth 1921- *ConAu 73*
Bridgman, Sarah Atherton 1889?-1975 *ConAu 57*
Bridgwater, Patrick 1931- *ConAu 5R*
Bridie, James 1888-1951 *CnMD, ConAu X, CroCD, DcLB 10[port], EncWL 2, LongCTC, ModBrL, ModWD, TwCLC 3, TwCWr, WhoTwCL, WorAu*
Bridson, Douglas Geoffrey 1910- *DcLEL 1940*
Bridson, Gavin 1936- *ConAu 105*
Bridwell, Norman Ray 1928- *ConAu 5NR, -13R, SmATA 4, WrDr 84*
Briedis, Ilmars *IntWWP 82X*
Briefs, Goetz Antony 1889-1974 *ConAu 49, ConAu P-2*
Briegel, Ann C 1915- *ConAu 33R*
Brien, Alan 1925- *IntAu&W 82*
Brien, Roger 1910- *CreCan 1*
Brier, Bob 1943- *ConAu 102*
Brier, Howard Maxwell 1903-1969 *ConAu P-1, SmATA 8*
Brier, Peter A 1935- *ConAu 105*
Brier, Royce 1894-1975 *ConAu 93*
Brier, Warren Judson 1931- *ConAu 25R*
Brierley, David 1936- *ConAu 107*
Brieux, Eugene 1858-1932 *CIDMEL 80, CnMD, LongCTC, ModFrL, ModWD, TwCA, TwCA SUP*
Briffault, Herma Hoyt 1898-1981 *ConAu 104*
Briffault, Robert Stephen 1876-1948 *LongCTC, TwCA, TwCA SUP*
Brigadere, Anna 1861-1933 *EncWL 2*
Brigden, Frederick Henry 1871-1956 *CreCan 1*
Briggs, Asa 1921- *ConAu 5R, -7NR, DcLEL 1940, IntAu&W 82, LongCTC, WrDr 84*
Briggs, Austin, Jr. 1931- *ConAu 29R*
Briggs, Berta N 1884?-1976 *ConAu 69*
Briggs, Carole S 1950- *ConAu 110*
Briggs, Charlie 1927- *ConAu 1NR, -49*
Briggs, Desmond Lawther 1931- *ConAu 108*
Briggs, Dorothy Corkille 1924- *ConAu 29R*
Briggs, Ellis O 1899-1976 *ConAu 65, -73*
Briggs, F Allen 1916- *ConAu 33R*
Briggs, Fred 1932- *ConAu 73*
Briggs, G A 1891?-1978 *ConAu 104*
Briggs, George McSpadden 1919- *ConAu 33R*
Briggs, Jean 1925- *ConAu 93, WrDr 84*
Briggs, K M 1898-1980 *TwCCW 83*
Briggs, Katharine Mary 1898-1980 *ConAu 9R, -102, IntAu&W 82, SmATA 25N*
Briggs, Kenneth 1934- *WrDr 84*
Briggs, Kenneth Arthur 1941- *ConAu 101*
Briggs, Kenneth R 1934- *ConAu 33R*
Briggs, L Cabot 1909-1975 *ConAu 3NR, -5R, -57*
Briggs, Olin Dewitt 1934- *IntAu&W 82*

Briggs, Peter 1921-1975 *ConAu 57, ConAu P-2, SmATA 31N*
Briggs, R C 1915- *ConAu 37R*
Briggs, Raymond 1934- *TwCCW 83, WrDr 84*
Briggs, Raymond Redvers 1934- *ConAu 73, SmATA 23[port]*
Briggs, Shirley Ann 1918- *ConAu 106*
Briggs, Vernon M, Jr. 1937- *ConAu 73*
Briggs, Victor William 1935- *IntAu&W 82*
Briggs, Walter Ladd 1919- *ConAu 69*
Brigham, Besmilr *DrAP&F 83*
Brigham, Besmilr 1923- *ConAu 29R*
Brigham, John C 1942- *ConAu 41R*
Brighouse, Harold 1882-1958 *CnMD, ConAu 110, DcLB 10[port], LongCTC, ModWD, TwCA, TwCA SUP, TwCWr*
Bright, Deborah 1949- *ConAu 97*
Bright, Greg 1951- *ConAu 93*
Bright, John 1908- *ConAu 5R*
Bright, Lee C 1931- *IntAu&W 82*
Bright, Mary Chavelita 1860-1945 *LongCTC, TwCA, TwCA SUP*
Bright, Pamela 1914- *WrDr 84*
Bright, Pamela Mia 1914- *ConAu 109*
Bright, Richard 1902- *ConAu 69*
Bright, Robert 1902- *ConAu 73, SmATA 24[port], TwCCW 83, WrDr 84*
Bright, Sarah *ConAu X*
Bright, William 1928- *ConAu 33R*
Brightbill, Charles K 1910-1966 *ConAu 1R, -103*
Brightman, Robert 1920- *ConAu 105*
Brighton, Howard 1925- *ConAu 57*
Brighton, Wesley, Jr. *ConAu X*
Brightwell, L R 1889- *SmATA 29*
Brignano, Russell C 1935- *ConAu 57*
Brignetti, Raffaelio 1922?-1978 *ConAu 104*
Brigola, Alfredo L 1923- *ConAu 41R*
Briles, Judith 1946- *ConAu 106*
Briley, John 1925- *WrDr 84*
Briley, John Richard 1925- *ConAu 101, IntAu&W 82*
Brilhart, John K 1929- *ConAu 21R*
Brill, Abraham Arden 1874-1948 *TwCA SUP*
Brill, Earl H 1925- *ConAu 17R*
Brill, Ernie *DrAP&F 83*
Brill, Leon 1915- *ConAu 110*
Brill, Steven *ConAu 85*
Brilliant, Alan 1936- *WrDr 84*
Brilliant, Ashleigh 1933- *ConAu 11NR, -65*
Brilliant, Richard 1929- *ConAu 33R, WrDr 84*
Briloff, Abraham J 1917- *ConAu 61*
Brim, Orville G, Jr. 1923- *ConAu 2NR, -5R*
Brimberg, Stanlee 1947- *ConAu 49, SmATA 9, WrDr 84*
Brin, David 1950- *ConAu 102*
Brin, Herb 1915- *ConAu 49*
Brin, Ruth Firestone 1921- *ConAu 8NR, -17R, SmATA 22[port]*
Brincken, Gertrud VonDen 1892- *IntAu&W 82*
Brinckloe, Julie 1950- *ConAu 65, SmATA 13*
Brind'Amour, Yvette 1918- *CreCan 1*
Brindel, June Rachuy *DrAP&F 83*
Brindel, June Rachuy 1919- *ConAu 49, IntWWP 82, SmATA 7*
Brindle, Reginald Smith 1917- *ConAu X, IntAu&W 82, WrDr 84*
Brindze, Ruth 1903- *ConAu 73, SmATA 23[port]*
Brinegar, David F 1910- *ConAu 77*
Brines, Francisco 1932- *CIDMEL 80*
Brines, Russell Dean 1911- *ConAu 69*
Briney, Robert E 1933- *ConAu 4NR, -53*
Bring, Mitchell 1951- *ConAu 106*
Bringhurst, Robert *DrAP&F 83*
Bringhurst, Robert 1946- *ConAu 6NR, -57*
Brinig, Myron 1900- *TwCA, TwCA SUP*
Brinitzer, Carl 1907-1974 *ConAu 3NR, -5R, -53*
Brink, Alijda 1911- *IntWWP 82*
Brink, Andre 1935- *ConAu 104, ConLC 18, WrDr 84*
Brink, Andre Philippus 1935- *IntAu&W 82*
Brink, Carol Ryrie 1895-1981 *ConAu 1R, -3NR, -104, IntAu&W 82, SmATA 1, -27N, -31[port], TwCCW 83*
Brink, T L 1949- *ConAu 89*
Brink, Wellington 1895-1979 *ConAu 85*
Brinker, Paul A 1919- *ConAu 25R*
Brinkerhoff, Dericksen Morgan 1921- *ConAu 85*
Brinkley, Alan 1949- *ConAu 107*
Brinkley, David 1920- *ConAu 97*
Brinkley, George A 1931- *ConAu 17R*
Brinkley, Joel 1952- *ConAu 102*

Brinkley, William 1917- *ConAu 11NR, -21R*
Brinkman, George L 1942- *ConAu 53*
Brinkman, Grover 1903- *ConAu 73*
Brinkman, Michael W 1943- *MichAu 80*
Brinkmann, Rolf Dieter 1940-1975 *CIDMEL 80, ModGL*
Brinks, Herbert J 1935- *ConAu 29R, MichAu 80*
Brinley, Bertrand R 1917- *ConAu 29R*
Brinnin, John Malcolm *DrAP&F 83*
Brinnin, John Malcolm 1916- *ConAu 1R, -1NR, ConP 80, DcLEL 1940, TwCA SUP, WhoTwCL, WrDr 84*
Brinsmead, H F 1922- *ConAu 10NR, -21R, ConLC 21[port], SmATA 18, WrDr 84*
Brinsmead, Hesba 1922- *TwCCW 83*
Brinsmead, Hungerford 1922- *IntAu&W 82*
Brint, Armand Ian 1952- *ConAu 105*
Brinton, Clarence Crane 1898- *TwCA, TwCA SUP*
Brinton, Crane 1898-1968 *ConAu 5R, -25R*
Brinton, Henry 1901-1977 *ConAu 1R, -4NR*
Brinton, Howard Haines 1884-1973 *ConAu 3NR, -5R*
Brion, Guy *ConAu X*
Brion, John M 1922- *ConAu 21R*
Brion, Marcel 1895- *CIDMEL 80*
Briones Gonzalez, Jose Manuel 1930- *IntAu&W 82*
Briquebec, John *ConAu X, SmATA X*
Brisbane, Arthur 1864-1936 *DcLB 25[port], TwCA*
Brisbane, Holly E 1927- *ConAu 33R*
Brisbane, Katharine Elizabeth 1932- *ConAu 107*
Brisbane, Katherine Elizabeth 1932- *IntAu&W 82*
Brisbane, Robert Hughes 1913- *ConAu 77, LivgBAA*
Brisby, Stewart *DrAP&F 83*
Brisby, Stewart 1945- *IntWWP 82*
Brisco, P A *WrDr 84*
Brisco, Pat A 1927- *ConAu X, SmATA X*
Brisco, Patty *ConAu X, SmATA X, TwCRGW, WrDr 84*
Briscoe, D Stuart 1930- *ConAu 9NR, -17R*
Briscoe, Jill 1935- *ConAu 8NR, -61*
Briscoe, Mary Louise 1937- *ConAu 109*
Brisk, Melvin J 1924-1981 *ConAu 104*
Brisk, Rita 1925- *IntWWP 82*
Briskin, Jacqueline 1927- *ConAu 29R, WrDr 84*
Briskin, Mae Seidman *DrAP&F 83*
Brisley, Joyce Lankester 1896- *ConAu 97, SmATA 22*
Brisley, Joyce Lankester 1896-1978 *TwCCW 83*
Brisman, Leslie 1944- *ConAu 61*
Brissenden, Paul Frederick 1885-1974 *ConAu 53, ConAu P-2*
Brissenden, R F 1928- *ConAu 10NR, -21R*
Brissenden, Robert Francis 1928- *DcLEL 1940*
Brister, C W, Jr. 1926- *ConAu 7NR, -13R*
Brister, Richard 1915- *ConAu 13R, WrDr 84*
Bristol, David *DrAP&F 83*
Bristol, Julius *ConAu X*
Bristol, Lee Hastings, Jr. 1923-1979 *ConAu 4NR, -5R, -89*
Bristow, Allen P 1929- *ConAu 8NR, -21R*
Bristow, Gwen 1903- *WrDr 84*
Bristow, Gwen 1903-1980 *ConAu 102, -17R, TwCA, TwCA SUP*
Bristow, Robert O'Neil 1926- *ConAu 25R, IntAu&W 82, WrDr 84*
Bristowe, Anthony 1921- *ConAu P-1*
Britain, Dan *ConAu X, WrDr 84*
Britannicus *CreCan 2*
Britchky, Seymour 1930- *ConAu 102*
Britindian *ConAu X, IntAu&W 82X, WrDr 84*
Britsch, Ralph A 1912- *ConAu 101*
Britsch, Todd A 1937- *ConAu 101*
Britt, Alan *DrAP&F 83*
Britt, Albert 1874-1969 *ConAu 5R, -103, SmATA 28N*
Britt, Dell 1934- *ConAu 25R, SmATA 1*
Britt, Katrina *TwCRGW, WrDr 84*
Britt, Steuart Henderson 1907-1979 *ConAu 1R, -2NR, -85*
Brittain, Bill *DrAP&F 83*
Brittain, Donald Code 1928- *CreCan 2*
Brittain, Frederick d1969 *ConAu 3NR, -5R*
Brittain, Joan Tucker 1928- *ConAu 37R*
Brittain, John A 1923- *ConAu 73*

Broner, E M *DrAP&F 83, WrDr 84*
Broner, E M 1930- *ConAu 8NR, −17R,
ConLC 19, MichAu 80*
Bronfeld, Stewart 1929- *ConAu 109*
Bronfenbrenner, Martin 1914- *ConAu 13R*
Bronfenbrenner, Urie 1917- *ConAu 97*
Broniewski, Wladyslaw 1897-1962 *ClDMEL 80,
EncWL 2, ModSL 2*
Bronin, Andrew 1947- *ConAu 45*
Bronk, William *DrAP&F 83*
Bronk, William 1918- *ConAu 89, ConLC 10,
ConP 80, WrDr 84*
Bronne, Carlo 1901- *ClDMEL 80*
Bronnen, Arnolt 1895-1959 *ClDMEL 80, CnMD,
CroCD, ModWD*
Bronner, Edwin Blaine 1920- *ConAu 5R, −7NR,
WrDr 84*
Bronnum, Karsten H 1949- *IntAu&W 82*
Bronowski, Jacob 1908-1974 *ConAu 1R, −3NR,
−53, WorAu*
Bronsen, David 1926- *ConAu 37R*
Bronson, Bertrand Harris 1902- *ConAu 61*
Bronson, Lita *ConAu X*
Bronson, Lynn *ConAu X,   SmATA X,
TwCCW 83*
Bronson, Oliver *ConAu X*
Bronson, Wilfrid Swancourt 1894- *ConAu 73*
Bronson, William 1926-1976 *ConAu 41R, −65*
Bronson, Wolfe *ConAu X*
Bronstein, Arthur J 1914- *ConAu 9R, WrDr 84*
Bronstein, Leo 1903?-1976 *ConAu 65*
Bronstein, Lynne *DrAP&F 83*
Bronstein, Lynne 1950- *ConAu 77*
Bronstein, Yetta *ConAu X*
Bronte, Louisa *ConAu X, IntAu&W 82X,
TwCRGW, WrDr 84*
Bronte Family *LongCTC*
Bronwell, Arthur *WrDr 84*
Bronwell, Arthur B 1909- *ConAu 33R,
IntAu&W 82*
Brook, Barry S 1918- *ConAu 25R*
Brook, David 1932- *ConAu 13R, IntAu&W 82,
WrDr 84*
Brook, Donna *DrAP&F 83*
Brook, George Leslie 1910- *WrDr 84*
Brook, Leslie 1910- *ConAu 5NR, −9R*
Brook, Peter 1925- *ConAu 105, CroCD*
Brook, Victor John Knight 1887-1974 *ConAu 1R,
−103*
Brook-Shepherd, Gordon 1918- *ConAu 3NR,
−9R*
Brooke, A B *ConAu X*
Brooke, Avery 1923- *ConAu 6NR, −57*
Brooke, Bernard Jocelyn 1909- *DcLEL 1940*
Brooke, Brian 1911- *ConAu 85*
Brooke, Bryan Nicholas 1915- *ConAu 1NR, −45,
WrDr 84*
Brooke, Carol *ConAu X*
Brooke, Charles Frederick Tucker 1883-1946
TwCA SUP
Brooke, Christopher N L 1927- *WrDr 84*
Brooke, Christopher Nugent Lawrence 1927-
ConAu 2NR, −5R, IntAu&W 82
Brooke, Dinah 1936- *ConAu 4NR, −49,
WrDr 84*
Brooke, Jocelyn 1908-1966 *ConAu 5R,
LongCTC, ModBrL, TwCA SUP*
Brooke, John 1920- *IntAu&W 82, WrDr 84*
Brooke, John Balmain 1907- *WrDr 84*
Brooke, Joshua *ConAu X*
Brooke, L Leslie 1862-1940 *TwCCW 83*
Brooke, Leonard Leslie 1862-1940 *SmATA 17*
Brooke, Maxey 1913- *ConAu 9R*
Brooke, Nicholas Stanton 1924- *ConAu 25R*
Brooke, Robert Taliaferro 1945- *IntAu&W 82*
Brooke, Rupert 1887-1915 *CnMWL,
ConAu 104, LongCTC, ModBrL,
ModBrL SUP, TwCA, TwCA SUP,
TwCLC 2, −7[port], TwCWr, WhoTwCL*
Brooke, Stopford Augustus 1832-1916 *LongCTC*
Brooke, Tal 1945- *ConAu 93, IntAu&W 82X*
Brooke, Tucker 1883-1946 *LongCTC*
Brooke-Haven, P *ConAu X, SmATA X*
Brooke-Little, John 1927- *ConAu 10NR*
Brooke-Little, John Philip Brooke 1927-
ConAu 21R, IntAu&W 82, WrDr 84
Brooke-Rose, Christine *ConNov 82,
IntAu&W 82, WrDr 84*
Brooke-Rose, Christine 1923- *EncWL 2,
ModBrL, ModBrL SUP*
Brooke-Rose, Christine 1926- *ConAu 13R,
DcLB 14[port], DcLEL 1940, TwCWr,*

WorAu
Brooker, Bertram 1888-1955 *CreCan 1*
Brooker, Clark *ConAu X, WrDr 84*
Brookes, Edgar Harry 1897- *ConAu 1R, −3NR*
Brookes, Murray 1926- *WrDr 84*
Brookes, Pamela 1920- *IntAu&W 82*
Brookes, Pamela 1922- *ConAu 25R, WrDr 84*
Brookes, Reuben Solomon 1914- *ConAu P-1*
Brookes, Stella Brewer *LivgBAA*
Brookfield, Charles 1857-1913 *LongCTC*
Brookhouse, Christopher *DrAP&F 83*
Brookhouse, Christopher 1938- *ConAu 29R*
Brookhouser, Frank 1912?-1975 *ConAu 1R, −61*
Brookins, Dana 1931- *ConAu 69,
SmATA 28[port]*
Brookins, Dewey C 1904- *ConSFA*
Brookman, Denise Cass 1921- *ConAu 1R*
Brookman, Rosina Francesca 1932- *ConAu 61*
Brookover, Wilbur 1911- *WrDr 84*
Brookover, Wilbur Bone 1911- *ConAu 33R*
Brooks, A Russell 1906- *ConAu P-2, WrDr 84*
Brooks, Albert *ConAu X*
Brooks, Albert Ellison 1908- *WrDr 84*
Brooks, Anita 1914- *ConAu X, −17R,
SmATA 5*
Brooks, Anne Tedlock 1905- *ConAu 1R, −1NR*
Brooks, C Carlyle 1888- *ConAu P-1*
Brooks, Charles Benton 1921- *ConAu 1R*
Brooks, Charles E 1921- *ConAu 53*
Brooks, Charles Stephen 1878-1934 *TwCA,
TwCA SUP*
Brooks, Charles V W 1912- *ConAu 77*
Brooks, Charlotte K *ConAu 89, LivgBAA,
SmATA 24*
Brooks, Cleanth 1906- *ConAu 17R,
ConLC 24[port], ConLCrt 82, EncWL 2,
IntAu&W 82, LongCTC, ModAL,
TwCA SUP, WhoTwCL, WrDr 84*
Brooks, D P 1915- *ConAu 11NR, −25R*
Brooks, David H 1929- *ConAu 61*
Brooks, Deems M 1934- *ConAu 69*
Brooks, Douglas *ConAu X*
Brooks, Edwin 1929- *WrDr 84*
Brooks, Elston *ConAmTC*
Brooks, Emerson M 1905?-1982 *ConAu 108*
Brooks, Fredric *IntWWP 82*
Brooks, Gary D 1942- *ConAu 41R*
Brooks, George E, Jr. 1933- *ConAu 33R,
IntAu&W 82, WrDr 84*
Brooks, Glenn E, Jr. 1931- *ConAu 1R*
Brooks, Gregory 1961- *ConAu 102*
Brooks, Gwendolyn *DrAP&F 83*
Brooks, Gwendolyn 1917- *AuNews 1,
ConAu 1R, −1NR, ConLC 1, −2, −4, −5, −15,
ConP 80, CroCAP, DcLB 5[port],
DcLEL 1940, EncWL 2, LivgBAA,
ModAL, ModAL SUP, ModBlW,
SmATA 6, TwCA SUP, WrDr 84*
Brooks, H Allen 1925- *ConAu 81,
IntAu&W 82, WrDr 84*
Brooks, Harvey 1915- *ConAu 25R*
Brooks, Hugh C 1922- *ConAu 29R*
Brooks, Hunter O 1929- *ConAu 77*
Brooks, James L 1940- *ConAu 73*
Brooks, Janice Young 1943- *ConAu 9NR, −65*
Brooks, Jeremy 1926- *ConAu 5R, −7NR,
DcLB 14[port], DcLEL 1940, IntAu&W 82,
WrDr 84*
Brooks, Jerome 1931- *ConAu 2NR, −49,
SmATA 23[port]*
Brooks, Jerome E 1895?-1983 *ConAu 109*
Brooks, John *ConAu X*
Brooks, John 1920- *ConAu 6NR, −13R,
DcLEL 1940*
Brooks, Karen 1949- *ConAu 57*
Brooks, Keith 1923- *ConAu 17R*
Brooks, Leonard 1911- *ConAu 13R*
Brooks, Lester 1924- *ConAu 33R, SmATA 7*
Brooks, Maria 1933- *ConAu 41R*
Brooks, Marshall 1953- *IntWWP 82*
Brooks, Mel 1926- *ConAu 65, ConLC 12,
DcLB 26[port]*
Brooks, Nelson Herbert 1902-1978 *ConAu 77*
Brooks, Pat 1931- *ConAu 7NR, −57*
Brooks, Patricia 1926- *ConAu 11NR, −25R,
IntAu&W 82*
Brooks, Paul 1909- *ConAu 7NR, −13R,
WrDr 84*
Brooks, Peter 1938- *ConAu 1NR, −45*
Brooks, Peter Wright 1920- *ConAu 9R,
WrDr 84*
Brooks, Philip 1899?-1975 *ConAu 104*

Brooks, Polly Schoyer 1912- *ConAu 1R,
SmATA 12*
Brooks, Richard 1912- *ConAu 73, ConDr 82A*
Brooks, Robert A 1920-1976 *ConAu 65*
Brooks, Robert Emanuel 1941- *ConAu 57*
Brooks, Ron 1948- *SmATA 33*
Brooks, Steve *DrAP&F 83*
Brooks, Stewart M 1923- *ConAu 9NR, −17R*
Brooks, Terry *DrAP&F 83*
Brooks, Terry 1944- *ConAu 77, IntAu&W 82*
Brooks, Thomas R 1925- *ConAu 73*
Brooks, Tim 1942- *ConAu 102*
Brooks, VanWyck 1886-1963 *ConAmA,
ConAu 1R, −6NR, ConLCrt 82, LongCTC,
ModAL, TwCA, TwCA SUP, TwCWr*
Brooks, W Hal 1933- *ConAu 57*
Brooks, Walter R 1886-1958 *TwCCW 83*
Brooks, Walter Rollin 1886-1958 *SmATA 17*
Brooks, William D 1929- *ConAu 33R*
Brooks-Davies, Douglas 1942- *ConAu 73*
Brookshier, Frank *ConAu 93*
Brookter, Marie 1934?- *AuNews 1*
Broom, Leonard 1911- *ConAu 5NR, −13R*
Broome, Charles L 1925- *ConAu 41R*
Broome, Harvey 1902-1968 *ConAu 110*
Broomell, Myron H 1906-1970 *ConAu P-1*
Broomfield, Gerald Webb 1895-1976 *ConAu 5R,
−103*
Broomfield, J H 1935- *ConAu 25R*
Broomsnodder, B MacKinley 1940- *ConAu 8NR,
−13R*
Brophy, Ann 1931- *ConAu 106*
Brophy, Brigid 1929- *ConAu 5R, ConLC 6, −11,
ConNov 82, DcLB 14[port], DcLEL 1940,
EncWL 2, IntAu&W 82, LongCTC,
ModBrL, ModBrL SUP, TwCWr,
WhoTwCL, WorAu, WrDr 84*
Brophy, Donald F 1934- *ConAu 10NR, −21R*
Brophy, Elizabeth Bergen 1929- *ConAu 61,
IntAu&W 82*
Brophy, James David, Jr. 1926- *ConAu 1R,
−3NR, IntAu&W 82*
Brophy, James Joseph 1912- *ConAu 65*
Brophy, Jere E 1940- *ConAu 2NR, −45*
Brophy, Jim *ConAu X*
Brophy, John 1899-1965 *ConAu P-1, LongCTC,
TwCA, TwCA SUP, TwCWr*
Brophy, Liam 1910- *ConAu 9R*
Brophy, Robert Henry, III 1948- *IntWWP 82*
Brophy, Robert J 1928- *ConAu 5NR, −53*
Brophy, W Michael 1953- *IntAu&W 82*
Brose, Olive J 1919- *ConAu 41R*
Brosman, Catharine 1934- *IntWWP 82*
Brosman, Catharine Savage *DrAP&F 83*
Brosman, Catharine Savage 1934- *ConAu 61,
ConLC 9, IntWWP 82X*
Brosnahan, L F 1922- *WrDr 84*
Brosnahan, Leonard Francis 1922- *ConAu 102*
Brosnan, James Patrick 1929- *ConAu 1R, −3NR,
SmATA 14*
Brosnan, Jim *ConAu X, SmATA X*
Bross, Irwin D J 1921- *ConAu 37R, WrDr 84*
Brossard, Chandler *DrAP&F 83*
Brossard, Chandler 1922- *ConAu 8NR, −61,
ConNov 82, DcLB 16[port], DcLEL 1940,
WrDr 84*
Broster, D K 1877-1950 *TwCRGW*
Broster, Dorothy Kathleen 1878?-1950 *TwCWr*
Brostowin, P R *DrAP&F 83*
Brostowin, Patrick Ronald 1931- *ConAu 13R*
Broszkiewicz, Jerzy 1922- *CroCD, ModWD*
Brother Dimitrios *IntWWP 82X*
Brother Joe El-The Moor *DrAP&F 83*
Brothers, Jay 1931- *ConAu 103*
Brothers, Joyce *WrDr 84*
Brothers, Joyce 1927- *AuNews 1*
Brothers, Joyce 1929- *ConAu 21R*
Brotherston, Gordon 1939- *ConAu 25R,
WrDr 84*
Brotherston, James Gordon 1939- *ConAu 11NR*
Brotherton, Manfred 1900?-1981 *ConAu 102*
Brott, Alexander 1915- *CreCan 2*
Brott, Boris 1944- *CreCan 1*
Brott, Charlotte *CreCan 2*
Brott, Lotte *CreCan 2*
Broudy, Harry S 1905- *ConAu 1R, −3NR*
Broue, Pierre 1926- *ConAu 69*
Brough, George *CreCan 1*
Brough, John 1917- *IntAu&W 82, WrDr 84*
Brough, R Clayton 1950- *ConAu 7NR, −57*
Broughton, Bradford B 1926- *ConAu 21R*
Broughton, Diane 1943- *ConAu 81,*

Brown, L J *ConAu X*
Brown, Ladbroke *LongCTC*
Brown, Laurel 1911- *IntWWP 82X*
Brown, Lee Dolph 1890-1971 *ConAu 29R*
Brown, Leigh *ConAu 65*
Brown, Leland 1914- *ConAu 1R, WrDr 84*
Brown, Lennox *NatPD 81[port]*
Brown, Lennox John 1934- *ConAu 93*
Brown, LeRoy Chester 1908- *ConAu P-1*
Brown, Leslie Hilton 1917-1980 *ConAu 7NR,
  -9R, IntAu&W 82*
Brown, Leslie Wilfrid 1912- *ConAu 17R*
Brown, Lester Louis 1928- *ConAu 33R*
Brown, Letitia Woods 1915-1976 *ConAu 69, -73*
Brown, Linda A *DrAP&F 83*
Brown, Lindajean *DrAP&F 83*
Brown, Lionel 1888-1964 *LongCTC*
Brown, Lloyd Arnold 1907-1966 *ConAu P-1*
Brown, Louis M 1909- *ConAu 49*
Brown, Loverne W *DrAP&F 83*
Brown, Lyle C 1926- *ConAu 41R*
Brown, Lyn Ingoldsby 1918- *IntWWP 82*
Brown, M L T *ConAu 13R*
Brown, Macalister 1924- *ConAu 89*
Brown, Marc Tolon 1946- *ConAu 69,
  SmATA 10*
Brown, Marcia 1918- *ConAu 41R, SmATA 7*
Brown, Marel 1899- *ConAu 102, IntAu&W 82,
  IntWWP 82, WrDr 84*
Brown, Margaret Wise 1910-1952 *ConAu 108,
  DcLB 22[port], TwCCW 83*
Brown, Margery *ConAu 25R, SmATA 5*
Brown, Marian A 1911- *ConAu 73*
Brown, Marilyn McMeen Miller 1938-
  ConAu 6NR
Brown, Marion Marsh 1908- *ConAu 1R, -3NR,
  SmATA 6*
Brown, Mark 1900- *WrDr 84*
Brown, Mark Herbert 1900- *ConAu P-2*
Brown, Marshall L 1924- *ConAu 21R*
Brown, Marvin L, Jr. 1920- *ConAu 53*
Brown, Maurice 1881-1955 *LongCTC*
Brown, Maurice F 1928- *ConAu 41R*
Brown, Melvin Edward *DrAP&F 83*
Brown, Merle Elliott 1925-1978 *ConAu 108*
Brown, Michael 1931- *ConAu 33R*
Brown, Michael Barratt *ConAu X*
Brown, Michael John 1932- *ConAu 29R*
Brown, Michele 1947- *IntAu&W 82*
Brown, Milton Perry, Jr. 1928- *ConAu 9R*
Brown, Morna Doris 1907- *ConAu 5R, -5NR*
Brown, Morris Cecil 1943- *ConAu 37R*
Brown, Moses *ConAu X*
Brown, Muriel 1938- *ConAu 107, WrDr 84*
Brown, Muriel W 1892- *ConAu P-2*
Brown, Murray 1929- *ConAu 37R, WrDr 84*
Brown, Myra Berry 1918- *ConAu 1R, -3NR,
  SmATA 6*
Brown, Nathaniel Hapgood 1929- *ConAu 101*
Brown, Ned 1882?-1976 *ConAu 65*
Brown, Neville 1932- *ConAu 9R*
Brown, Newell 1917- *ConAu 97*
Brown, Norman Donald 1935- *ConAu 53*
Brown, Norman O 1913- *ConAu 21R, WorAu*
Brown, Otis *DrAP&F 83*
Brown, Palmer 1919- *ConAu 107, TwCCW 83*
Brown, Pamela 1924- *TwCCW 83, WrDr 84*
Brown, Pamela Beatrice 1924- *ConAu 13R,
  SmATA 5*
Brown, Parker B 1928- *ConAu 53*
Brown, Patricia L *LivgBAA*
Brown, Paula 1925- *ConAu 110*
Brown, Peter 1935- *ConAu 21R*
Brown, Peter Douglas 1925- *ConAu 25R,
  WrDr 84*
Brown, Peter Lancaster 1927- *ConAu 4NR, -53*
Brown, R Allen 1924- *ConAu 5R, -11NR*
Brown, R G S 1929- *ConAu 29R*
Brown, Rae *ConAu 49*
Brown, Ralph Adams 1908- *ConAu 33R,
  WrDr 84*
Brown, Raymond Bryan 1923- *ConAu 17R*
Brown, Raymond E 1928- *ConAu 97*
Brown, Raymond George 1924- *ConAu 109,
  WrDr 84*
Brown, Raymond Kay 1936- *ConAu 102*
Brown, Raymond Lamont 1939- *ConAu 73,
  IntAu&W 82*
Brown, Re Mona 1917- *ConAu 41R*
Brown, Rebecca *DrAP&F 83*
Brown, Rex Vandestene 1933- *ConAu 53*
Brown, Richard C 1917- *ConAu 2NR, -5R*

Brown, Richard D 1939- *ConAu 53*
Brown, Richard E 1937- *ConAu 73*
Brown, Richard H 1927- *ConAu 9R*
Brown, Richard H 1940- *ConAu 109, WrDr 84*
Brown, Richard Howard 1929- *ConAu 57*
Brown, Richard Maxwell 1927- *ConAu 11NR,
  -17R*
Brown, Rita Mae *DrAP&F 83*
Brown, Rita Mae 1944- *ConAu 2NR, -11NR,
  -45*
Brown, Robert Carlton 1886-1959 *ConAu 107*
Brown, Robert Craig 1935- *ConAu 101*
Brown, Robert D 1924- *ConAu 104*
Brown, Robert E 1907- *ConAu 5R*
Brown, Robert Edward *DrAP&F 83*
Brown, Robert Edward 1945- *ConAu 65*
Brown, Robert G 1923- *WrDr 84*
Brown, Robert Goodell 1923- *ConAu 33R*
Brown, Robert Joseph 1907- *ConAu P-1,
  SmATA 14*
Brown, Robert L 1921- *ConAu 21R, WrDr 84*
Brown, Robert McAfee 1920- *ConAu 7NR, -13R,
  WrDr 84*
Brown, Robin 1937- *ConAu 97, IntAu&W 82*
Brown, Robyn Elizabeth 1951- *IntWWP 82*
Brown, Roderick Haig- *ConAu X*
Brown, Roderick Langmere Haig Haig- *CreCan 1*
Brown, Roger Glenn 1941- *ConAu 77*
Brown, Roger H 1931- *ConAu 9R*
Brown, Roger William 1925- *ConAu 13R,
  WrDr 84*
Brown, Rollo Walter 1880-1956 *TwCA,
  TwCA SUP*
Brown, Ronald 1900- *ConAu 81*
Brown, Rosalie Moore *WrDr 84*
Brown, Rosalie Moore 1910- *ConAu X, -5R,
  IntAu&W 82X, SmATA 9*
Brown, Rosel George 1926-1967 *ConAu 102,
  TwCSFW*
Brown, Rosellen *DrAP&F 83*
Brown, Rosellen 1939- *ConAu 77*
Brown, Roy 1921- *ConAu 65, IntAu&W 82,
  WrDr 84*
Brown, Roy 1921-1982 *TwCCW 83*
Brown, Sanborn C 1913-1981 *ConAu 106, -11NR,
  -17R*
Brown, Sevellon, III 1913-1983 *ConAu 110*
Brown, Seyom 1933- *ConAu 65*
Brown, Sheldon S 1937- *ConAu 7NR, -53*
Brown, Sidney DeVere 1925- *ConAu 33R*
Brown, Spencer *DrAP&F 83*
Brown, Stanley 1924- *ConAu 49*
Brown, Stanley C 1928- *ConAu 77*
Brown, Stanley H 1927- *ConAu 45*
Brown, Stephen W 1940- *ConAu 33R*
Brown, Sterling 1901- *ConAu 85, ConLC 1,
  -23[port], ConP 80, LivgBAA, ModBlW,
  WorAu 1970, WrDr 84*
Brown, Sterling A *DrAP&F 83*
Brown, Steven Ford *DrAP&F 83*
Brown, Steven R 1939- *ConAu 49*
Brown, Stuart C 1938- *ConAu 29R*
Brown, Stuart Gerry 1912- *ConAu 21R*
Brown, Susan Jenkins 1896- *ConAu 85*
Brown, T Merritt 1913- *ConAu 41R*
Brown, Terence 1944- *ConAu 102, WrDr 84*
Brown, Theo W 1934- *ConAu 8NR, -61*
Brown, Theodore L 1928- *ConAu 33R*
Brown, Theodore M 1925- *ConAu 33R,
  WrDr 84*
Brown, Thomas H 1930- *ConAu 57*
Brown, Tony *ConAu X*
Brown, Truesdell S 1906- *ConAu 13R*
Brown, Turner, Jr. *ConAu X*
Brown, Velma Darbo 1921- *ConAu 97*
Brown, Vinson 1912- *ConAu 1R, -1NR,
  SmATA 19, WrDr 84*
Brown, Virginia Sharpe 1916- *ConAu 13R*
Brown, Virginia Suggs 1924- *ConAu 69,
  LivgBAA*
Brown, W Anthony 1933- *ConAu 110*
Brown, W Norman 1892-1975 *ConAu 57, -61*
Brown, Wallace 1933- *ConAu 17R*
Brown, Walter Lee 1924- *ConAu 33R*
Brown, Walter R 1929- *ConAu 2NR, -45,
  SmATA 19*
Brown, Warner *ConAu X*
Brown, Warren 1894-1978 *ConAu 81, -85*
Brown, Wayne 1944- *ConAu 101, ConP 80,
  WrDr 84*
Brown, Weldon A 1911- *ConAu 65*
Brown, Wenzell 1912- *ConAu 1R, -5NR*

Brown, Wesley *DrAP&F 83*
Brown, Wilfred 1908- *ConAu 9R, IntAu&W 82,
  WrDr 84*
Brown, Will *SmATA X*
Brown, Will C *ConAu X*
Brown, William Campbell 1928- *ConAu 57*
Brown, William E 1907-1975 *ConAu P-2*
Brown, William F 1920- *ConAu 33R*
Brown, William F 1928- *ConAu 33R,
  ConDr 82D, NatPD 81[port]*
Brown, William J *ConAu 97*
Brown, William James 1889- *ConAu 5R*
Brown, William L 1910-1964 *ConAu 1R,
  SmATA 5*
Brown, Zenith Jones 1898- *ConAu 9R, TwCA,
  TwCA SUP*
Brown, Zenith Jones 1898-1983 *ConAu 110*
Brown-Azarowicz, Marjory F 1922- *ConAu 33R*
Browne, Anthony 1946- *ConAu 97*
Browne, Courtney 1915- *ConAu 21R*
Browne, Dik 1917- *AuNews 1*
Browne, E Martin 1900-1980 *ConAu 97,
  ConAu P-2, IntAu&W 82, LongCTC*
Browne, G Peter 1930- *ConAu 21R,
  IntAu&W 82, WrDr 84*
Browne, Gary Lawson 1939- *ConAu 101*
Browne, George Stephenson 1890-1970
  ConAu P-2
Browne, Hablot Knight 1815-1882
  SmATA 21[port]
Browne, Harry *WrDr 84*
Browne, Harry 1918- *ConAu X*
Browne, Harry 1933- *ConAu 3NR, -49,
  WrDr 84*
Browne, Henry 1918- *ConAu 102,
  IntAu&W 82, WrDr 84*
Browne, Howard 1908- *ConAu 73*
Browne, Jackson 1950- *ConLC 21[port]*
Browne, Joseph William 1914- *ConAu 105*
Browne, Joy 1944- *ConAu 97*
Browne, Laurence Edward 1887- *WrDr 84*
Browne, Lewis 1897-1949 *TwCA, TwCA SUP*
Browne, Malcolm W 1931- *ConAu 17R*
Browne, Margaret 1936- *IntWWP 82*
Browne, Maria 1938- *WrDr 84*
Browne, Matthew *SmATA X*
Browne, Maurice 1881-1955 *ModWD*
Browne, Michael Dennis *DrAP&F 83*
Browne, Michael Dennis 1940- *ConAu 29R,
  ConP 80, WrDr 84*
Browne, Ray B 1922- *ConAu 11NR, -17R,
  IntAu&W 82*
Browne, Raymond 1897- *ConAu 73*
Browne, Robert S 1924- *ConAu 37R*
Browne, Roland Andrew 1910- *ConAu 65*
Browne, Sam *ConAu X*
Browne, Stanley George 1907- *WrDr 84*
Browne, Theodore R 1911?-1979 *ConAu 81*
Browne, Thomas Alexander 1826-1915 *LongCTC*
Browne, Walter A 1895- *ConAu 37R*
Browne, William P 1945- *ConAu 109*
Browne, Wynyard Barry 1911-1964 *DcLB 13,
  LongCTC*
Brownell, Baker 1887-1965 *TwCA SUP*
Brownell, Blaine Allison 1942- *ConAu 65*
Brownell, John Arnold 1924- *ConAu 21R*
Brownell, Peleg Franklin 1856-1946 *CreCan 2*
Brownell, William Crary 1851-1928 *TwCA,
  TwCA SUP*
Browning, David 1938- *ConAu 37R*
Browning, Dixie Burrus 1930- *ConAu 110*
Browning, Don 1934- *ConAu 2NR, -49,
  WrDr 84*
Browning, Douglas 1929- *ConAu 13R*
Browning, Elizabeth 1924- *ConAu 57*
Browning, Frank 1946- *ConAu 107*
Browning, Gordon 1938- *ConAu 37R*
Browning, John S *ConAu X*
Browning, L J *ConAu X*
Browning, Mary 1887- *ConAu P-1*
Browning, Norma Lee 1914- *ConAu 8NR, -61*
Browning, Oscar 1837-1923 *LongCTC*
Browning, Peter 1928- *ConAu 104*
Browning, Preston M, Jr. 1929- *ConAu 57*
Browning, Reed 1938- *ConAu 57*
Browning, Robert 1914- *ConAu 33R,
  IntAu&W 82, WrDr 84*
Browning, Robert L 1924- *ConAu 85*
Browning, Shelia *IntWWP 82X*
Browning, Stella Daniel 1917- *IntWWP 82*
Browning, Sterry *WrDr 84*
Browning, Tod 1882-1962 *ConLC 16*

Bryan, Martin 1908- *ConAu 1R*
Bryan, Mavis *ConAu X*
Bryan, Roy *DrAP&F 83*
Bryan, Wright 1905- *ConAu 77*
Bryans, Robert Harbinson 1928- *ConAu 5R, –11NR*
Bryans, Robin *ConAu X*
Bryans, Robin 1928- *ConAu X, WrDr 84*
Bryant, Anita 1940- *ConAu X*
Bryant, Arthur 1899- *WrDr 84*
Bryant, Sir Arthur Wynne Morgan 1899- *ConAu 105, LongCTC, TwCA, TwCA SUP*
Bryant, Bear *ConAu X*
Bryant, Bernice 1908- *ConAu P-1, SmATA 11*
Bryant, Beth Elaine 1936- *ConAu 13R*
Bryant, Cyril E 1917- *ConAu 61*
Bryant, Donald 1905- *ConAu 13R, WrDr 84*
Bryant, Dorothy 1930- *ConAu 4NR, –53, WrDr 84*
Bryant, Edward *DrAP&F 83*
Bryant, Edward 1928- *ConAu 9R, –11NR*
Bryant, Edward 1945- *ConAu 1NR, –45, DrmM[port], TwCSFW, WrDr 84*
Bryant, F J, Jr. *DrAP&F 83*
Bryant, Gay 1945- *ConAu 73*
Bryant, Helen *DrAP&F 83*
Bryant, Helen 1906- *IntWWP 82*
Bryant, Henry A, Jr. 1943- *ConAu 4NR, –53*
Bryant, James Cecil, Jr. 1931- *ConAu 49, IntAu&W 82*
Bryant, Jerry H 1928- *ConAu 33R, WrDr 84*
Bryant, Joseph Allen, Jr. 1919- *ConAu 5R, WrDr 84*
Bryant, Katherine Cliffton 1912- *ConAu 13R*
Bryant, Keith L, Jr. 1937- *ConAu 49*
Bryant, L A 1927- *LivgBAA*
Bryant, Margaret M 1900- *ConAu 1R, –4NR*
Bryant, Paul 1913-1983 *ConAu 108*
Bryant, Robert Harry 1925- *ConAu 21R, WrDr 84*
Bryant, Shasta M 1924- *ConAu 41R*
Bryant, Sylvia Leigh 1947- *IntWWP 82*
Bryant, T Alton 1926- *ConAu 10NR, –25R*
Bryant, Traphes L 1914- *ConAu 77*
Bryant, Verda E 1910- *ConAu P-2*
Bryant, Willis Rooks 1892-1965 *ConAu 5R, –103*
Bryce, James 1838-1922 *LongCTC*
Bryce, Murray D 1917- *ConAu 13R*
Brychta, Alex 1956- *ConAu 103, SmATA 21[port]*
Bryde, John F 1920- *ConAu 33R, WrDr 84*
Bryden, Bill 1942- *ConAu X, IntAu&W 82*
Bryden, John Marshall 1941- *ConAu 1NR, –49*
Bryden, John R 1913- *ConAu 33R*
Bryden, Ronald 1927- *WrDr 84*
Bryden, William Campbell Rough 1942- *ConAu 105*
Bryer, Jackson R 1937- *ConAu 3NR, –9R*
Bryers, Paul 1945- *ConAu 73*
Bryfonski, Dedria 1947- *ConAu 101*
Bryher *ConAu X*
Bryher 1894- *ConAu X, ConNov 82, LongCTC, ModBrL*
Bryher, Winifred 1894- *TwCA SUP*
Bryks, Rachmil 1912-1974 *ConAu 97*
Bryll, Ernest 1935- *ClDMEL 80*
Brymer, Jack 1915- *ConAu 110*
Brymner, William 1855-1925 *CreCan 2*
Bryne, Edward *DrAP&F 83*
Brynes, Edward 1944- *IntWWP 82*
Brynildsen, Ken *DrAP&F 83*
Brynildsen, Ken 1944- *ConAu 110*
Bryning, Frank 1907- *TwCSFW*
Brynjulfsdottir, Anna Kristin 1938- *IntAu&W 82*
Bryson, Bernarda 1905- *ConAu 49, SmATA 9*
Bryson, Conrey 1905- *ConAu 93*
Bryson, Lyman 1888-1959 *TwCA SUP*
Bryson, Phillip J 1939- *ConAu 69*
Bryson, Reid Allen 1920- *ConAu 101*
Bryusov, Valery 1873-1924 *TwCLC 10[port]*
Bryusov, Valery Yakovlevich 1873-1924 *ClDMEL 80, ConAu 107, EncWL 2, ModSL 1, TwCA, TwCA SUP, TwCSFW A, TwCWr*
Brzekowski, Jan 1903- *ClDMEL 80*
Brzezinski, Zbigniew 1928- *WrDr 84*
Brzezinski, Zbigniew K 1928- *ConAu 1R, –5NR*
Brzozowski, Leopold Stanislaw Leon 1878-1911 *ModSL 2*
Brzozowski, Stanislaw 1878-1911 *ClDMEL 80*
Bubar, Margaret Weber 1920?-1978 *ConAu 77*

Bubb, Mel *ConAu X*
Bube, Richard H 1927- *ConAu 8NR, –21R, WrDr 84*
Bubeck, Mark I 1928- *ConAu 61*
Buber, Martin 1878-1965 *ConAu 25R, ConIsC 2[port], EncWL 2[port], ModGL, TwCA SUP, WhoTwCL*
Buccellati, Giorgio 1937- *ConAu 41R*
Bucchieri, Theresa F 1908- *ConAu 73*
Bucco, Martin 1929- *ConAu 29R*
Buch, Hans Christoph 1944- *IntAu&W 82*
Buchan, Alastair 1918-1976 *ConAu 65, –73*
Buchan, Bryan 1945- *ConAu 107*
Buchan, David 1933- *ConAu X*
Buchan, John 1875-1940 *ConAu 108, TwCCr&M 80*
Buchan, Baron John Tweedsmuir 1875-1940 *CnMWL, LongCTC, ModBrL, TwCA, TwCA SUP, TwCWr*
Buchan, Norman Findlay 1922- *ConAu 109*
Buchan, Perdita 1940- *ConAu 21R*
Buchan, Stuart 1942- *ConAu 57*
Buchan, Thomas Buchanan 1931- *ConAu 25R*
Buchan, Tom 1931- *ConAu X, ConP 80, WrDr 84*
Buchanan, A Russell 1906- *ConAu 13R*
Buchanan, Betty 1923- *ConAu 101*
Buchanan, Chuck *ConAu X*
Buchanan, Colin 1934- *WrDr 84*
Buchanan, Colin Ogilvie 1934- *ConAu 25R*
Buchanan, Cynthia *DrAP&F 83*
Buchanan, Cynthia 1942- *ConAu 1NR, –45, NatPD 81[port]*
Buchanan, Cynthia D 1937- *ConAu 5R*
Buchanan, Daniel C 1892- *ConAu 17R*
Buchanan, David 1933- *ConAu 57*
Buchanan, Donald W 1908- *ConAu P-1*
Buchanan, George 1904- *ConAu 3NR, –9R, ConNov 82, ConP 80, IntAu&W 82, IntWWP 82, WrDr 84*
Buchanan, George Wesley 1921- *ConAu 37R*
Buchanan, James J 1925- *ConAu 33R, WrDr 84*
Buchanan, James M 1919- *WrDr 84*
Buchanan, James McGill 1919- *ConAu 3NR, –5R*
Buchanan, Joan 1936- *IntAu&W 82*
Buchanan, Keith 1919- *ConAu 10NR, –21R*
Buchanan, Laura *ConAu X*
Buchanan, Marie *ConAu 10NR*
Buchanan, Marie 1922- *ConAu 65, WrDr 84*
Buchanan, Patrick *ConAu X*
Buchanan, Pegasus 1920- *ConAu 9R*
Buchanan, R A 1930- *ConAu 7NR*
Buchanan, Robert Angus 1930- *ConAu 17R, IntAu&W 82, WrDr 84*
Buchanan, Robert Williams 1841-1901 *LongCTC*
Buchanan, Thomas G 1919- *ConAu 1R*
Buchanan, William 1930- *ConAu X, WrDr 84*
Buchanan, William J 1926- *ConAu 73*
Buchanan-Brown, John 1929- *ConAu 102*
Buchard, Robert 1931- *ConAu 33R*
Buchdahl, Gerd 1914- *ConAu 57, IntAu&W 82, WrDr 84*
Buchele, William Martin 1895- *ConAu 57*
Buchen, Irving H 1930- *ConAu 25R*
Bucher, Bradley 1932- *ConAu 37R*
Bucher, Charles A 1912- *ConAu 3NR, –9R*
Bucher, Francois 1927- *ConAu 3NR, –5R, WrDr 84*
Bucher, Glenn R 1940- *ConAu 57*
Bucher, Magnus Eugen 1927- *ConAu 41R, IntAu&W 82*
Bucher, Marcel 1929- *IntAu&W 82*
Buchheim, Lothar-Guenther 1918- *ConAu 85*
Buchheim, Lothar-Gunther 1918- *ConLC 6*
Buchheimer, Naomi Barnett *ConAu X*
Buchheit, Lee C 1950- *ConAu 81*
Buchholtz, Johannes 1882-1940 *TwCA, TwCA SUP*
Buchler, Justus 1914- *ConAu 5R*
Buchman, Dian Dincin 1917- *ConAu 8NR, –61*
Buchman, Frank N D 1878-1961 *LongCTC*
Buchman, Herman 1920- *ConAu 41R*
Buchman, Randall L 1929- *ConAu 1NR, –45*
Buchman, Sidney 1902-1975 *ConAu 61, –93, DcLB 26[port]*
Buchwald, Art 1925- *AuNews 1, ConAu 5R, IntAu&W 82, SmATA 10, WorAu, WrDr 84*
Buchwald, Arthur 1925- *DcLEL 1940*
Buchwald, Emilie *DrAP&F 83*

Buchwald, Emilie 1935- *ConAu 2NR, –49, SmATA 7*
Buchwald-Pelc, Paulina Maria 1934- *IntAu&W 82*
Buck, Ashley d1980 *ConAu 97*
Buck, Charles 1915- *ConAu 33R*
Buck, Doris P 1898?-1980 *ConAu 102*
Buck, Frederick Silas *ConAu 5R*
Buck, George C 1918- *ConAu 69*
Buck, Harry M 1921- *ConAu 33R, WrDr 84*
Buck, James H 1924- *ConAu 104*
Buck, Joan Juliet 1948- *ConAu 108*
Buck, John Lossing 1890-1975 *ConAu 2NR, –45, –61*
Buck, John N 1906- *ConAu P-2*
Buck, Lewis 1925- *ConAu 73, SmATA 18*
Buck, Margaret Waring 1910- *ConAu 5R, IntAu&W 82, SmATA 3, WrDr 84*
Buck, Marion A 1909- *ConAu P-1*
Buck, Paul Herman 1899-1978 *ConAu 81, TwCA, TwCA SUP*
Buck, Pearl S 1892-1973 *AuNews 1, ConAmA, ConAu 1R, –1NR, –41R, ConLC 7, –11, –18, DcLB 9[port], LongCTC, ModAL, SmATA 1, –25[port], TwCA, TwCA SUP, TwCWr*
Buck, Peggy S 1930- *ConAu 65*
Buck, Philip W 1900- *ConAu 65*
Buck, Robert N 1914- *ConAu 103*
Buck, Stratton 1906- *ConAu P-2*
Buck, Vernon Ellis 1934- *ConAu 37R, WrDr 84*
Buck, William Ray *WrDr 84*
Buck, William Ray 1930- *ConAu 1R*
Buckeridge, Anthony 1912- *TwCCW 83, WrDr 84*
Buckeridge, Anthony Malcolm 1912- *ConAu 2NR, –49, SmATA 6*
Buckeye, Donald A 1930- *ConAu 49*
Buckholdt, David R 1942- *ConAu 101*
Buckholts, Claudia *DrAP&F 83*
Buckholts, Claudia 1944- *IntWWP 82*
Buckhout, Robert 1935- *ConAu 45*
Buckingham, Burdette H 1907?-1977 *ConAu 73*
Buckingham, Clyde E 1907- *ConAu P-1*
Buckingham, James 1932- *ConAu 29R*
Buckingham, Jamie 1932- *ConAu X*
Buckingham, Nancy *WrDr 84*
Buckingham, Nancy 1924- *TwCRGW*
Buckingham, Peter Allan 1938- *IntWWP 82*
Buckingham, Walter S, Jr. 1924-1967 *ConAu 1R, –103*
Buckingham, Willis J 1938- *ConAu 29R*
Buckingham-White, Mary Ellen *IntWWP 82*
Buckland, Karen 1961- *IntWWP 82*
Buckland, Michael K 1941- *ConAu 97*
Buckland, Raymond Brian 1934- *ConAu 73*
Buckle, George Earle 1854-1935 *LongCTC*
Buckle, Richard 1916- *ConAu 97, IntAu&W 82, WrDr 84*
Buckler, Ernest 1908- *ConAu P-1, ConLC 13, ConNov 82, CreCan 2, DcLEL 1940, TwCWr*
Buckler, Ernest Redmond 1908- *WrDr 84*
Buckler, William Earl 1924- *ConAu 1R, –5NR*
Buckley, Christopher *DrAP&F 83*
Buckley, Christopher 1948- *IntWWP 82*
Buckley, Doris Heather *ConAu X*
Buckley, Fergus Reid 1930- *ConAu 21R*
Buckley, Fiona *ConAu X, IntAu&W 82X*
Buckley, Francis Joseph 1928- *ConAu 33R, WrDr 84*
Buckley, Helen E 1918- *ConAu 3NR, –5R, SmATA 2*
Buckley, J Q *DrAP&F 83*
Buckley, James Lane 1923- *ConAu 61*
Buckley, Jerome Hamilton 1917- *ConAu 1R, –3NR*
Buckley, Julian Gerard 1905- *ConAu 41R*
Buckley, Mary L *ConAu 53*
Buckley, Michael F 1880?-1977 *ConAu 69*
Buckley, Michael J 1931- *ConAu 73*
Buckley, Priscilla 1921- *ConAu 81*
Buckley, Roger N 1937- *ConAu 97*
Buckley, Ruth 1924- *WrDr 84*
Buckley, Shawn 1943- *ConAu 93*
Buckley, Suzanne Shelton 1946- *ConAu 108*
Buckley, Thomas 1932- *WrDr 84*
Buckley, Thomas H 1932- *ConAu 29R*
Buckley, Vincent 1925- *ConAu 101, ConP 80, DcLEL 1940, WrDr 84*
Buckley, William F, Jr. 1925- *AuNews 1, ConAu 1R, –1NR, ConIsC 1[port],*

ConLC 7, –18, DcLB Y80B[port],
DcLEL 1940, IntAu&W 82, WorAu,
WrDr 84
Buckley Neville, Heather 1910- *ConAu 103*
Bucklin, Louis P 1928- *ConAu 97*
Buckman, Peter 1941- *ConAu 11NR, WrDr 84*
Buckman, Peter Michael Amiel 1941- *ConAu 65,*
IntAu&W 82
Buckmaster, Henrietta *ConAu X*
SmATA 6, WorAu
Bucknall, Barbara Jane 1933- *ConAu 33R,*
WrDr 84
Buckner, Gloria 1926- *IntWWP 82*
Buckner, Robert 1906- *ConAu 1R,*
DcLB 26[port]
Buckner, Sally *DrAP&F 83*
Buckner, Sally Beaver 1931- *ConAu 61,*
IntWWP 82
Buckstead, Richard C 1929- *ConAu 49*
Buckvar, Felice *DrAP&F 83*
Buckvar, Felice 1938- *ConAu 107*
Buczkowski, Leopold 1905- *CIDMEL 80,*
ConAu 41R, ModSL 2
Buday, George 1907- *ConAu X, WrDr 84*
Buday, Gyorgy 1907- *ConAu 107*
Budberg, Moura 1892-1974 *ConAu 53*
Budbill, David *DrAP&F 83*
Budbill, David 1940- *ConAu 73, IntWWP 82*
Budd, Edward C 1920- *ConAu 21R*
Budd, Elaine Rounds 1925- *ConAu 101,*
IntAu&W 82
Budd, Kenneth George 1904-1972 *ConAu P-1*
Budd, Lillian 1897- *WrDr 84*
Budd, Lillian Peterson 1897- *ConAu 1R, –4NR,*
IntAu&W 82, SmATA 7
Budd, Louis J 1921- *ConAu 1R, –3NR*
Budd, Mavis *ConAu 102, WrDr 84*
Budd, Richard W 1934- *ConAu 21R*
Budd, William C 1923- *ConAu 49*
Buddee, Paul Edgar 1913- *ConAu 103,*
IntAu&W 82, WrDr 84
Budden, Laura Madeline 1894- *ConAu 5R*
Bude, John 1901-1957 *TwCCr&M 80*
Budenz, Julia *DrAP&F 83*
Budenz, Louis Francis 1891-1972 *ConAu 89*
Budge, Ian 1936- *ConAu 29R, WrDr 84*
Budge, Sir Wallis 1857-1934 *LongCTC*
Budgen, Frank Spencer Curtis 1882-1971
ConAu 29R
Budick, Sanford 1942- *ConAu 33R*
Budimir, Velimir 1926- *ConAu 65*
Budoff, Penny Wise 1939- *ConAu 110*
Budrys, A J 1931- *DcLB 8[port]*
Budrys, Algirdas Jonas 1931- *ConAu 1R, –4NR*
Budrys, Algis 1931- *ConAu X, ConSFA,*
DrmM[port], TwCSFW, WrDr 84
Budurowycz, Bohdan B 1921- *ConAu 3NR, –5R*
Budy, Andrea Hollander *DrAP&F 83*
Budzik, Janet K Sims 1942- *ConAu 37R*
Budzinski, Klaus 1921- *IntAu&W 82*
Bueche, Frederick J 1923- *WrDr 84*
Buechner, Carl Frederick 1926- *DcLEL 1940*
Buechner, Frederick *DrAP&F 83*
Buechner, Frederick 1926- *ConAu 11NR, –13R,*
ConLC 2, –4, –6, –9, ConNov 82,
DcLB Y80B[port], IntAu&W 82, ModAL,
ModAL SUP, TwCWr, WorAu, WrDr 84
Buechner, John C 1934- *ConAu 21R*
Buechner, Thomas S 1926- *ConAu 49*
Buehnau, Ludwig *ConAu X*
Buehner, Andrew J 1905- *ConAu 17R*
Buehr, Walter Franklin 1897-1971 *ConAu 3NR,*
–5R, –33R, SmATA 3
Buehrig, Edward Henry 1910- *ConAu 37R*
Buehrig, Gordon Miller 1904- *ConAu 101*
Buel, Richard, Jr. 1933- *ConAu 73*
Bueler, Lois E 1940- *ConAu 57*
Bueler, William Merwin 1934- *ConAu 37R,*
WrDr 84
Buell, Frederick 1942- *WrDr 84*
Buell, Frederick Henderson *DrAP&F 83*
Buell, Frederick Henderson 1942- *ConAu 33R,*
IntWWP 82
Buell, John 1927- *ConAu 1R, ConLC 10,*
CreCan 1
Buell, Jon A 1939- *ConAu 102*
Buell, Lawrence 1939- *ConAu 49*
Buell, Robert Kingery 1908-1971 *ConAu P-2*
Buell, Victor P 1914- *ConAu 8NR, –21R,*
WrDr 84
Buelow, George J 1929- *ConAu 21R*

Buenker, John D 1937- *ConAu 1NR, –45*
Bueno, Jose DeLaTorre 1905?-1980 *ConAu 93*
Bueno DeMesquita, Bruce James 1946-
ConAu 108
Buergenthal, Thomas 1934- *ConAu 37R*
Buerger, Martin Julian 1903- *WrDr 84*
Buerkle, Jack Vincent 1923- *ConAu 41R*
Buero Vallejo, Antonio 1916- *CIDMEL 80,*
CnMD, ConAu 106, ConLC 15, CroCD,
EncWL 2, IntAu&W 82, ModWD,
TwCWr
Bueschel, Richard 1926- *WrDr 84*
Bueschel, Richard M 1926- *ConAu 11NR*
Bueschel, Richard Martin 1926- *ConAu 25R*
Buetow, Harold A 1919- *ConAu 53*
Buettner, Ludwig 1909- *IntAu&W 82*
Buettner-Janusch, John 1924- *ConAu 49*
Bufalari, Giuseppe 1927- *ConAu 25R*
Buferd, Norma Bradley 1937- *ConAu 69*
Buff, Conrad 1886-1975 *SmATA 19*
Buff, Mary Marsh 1890-1970 *SmATA 19*
Buffalo Bill *LongCTC*
Buffalo Chuck *ConAu X*
Buffaloe, Neal D 1924- *ConAu 53*
Buffington, Albert F 1905- *ConAu 33R*
Buffington, Robert 1933- *ConAu 21R, WrDr 84*
Bufis, Paul *DrAP&F 83*
Bufkin, Ernest Claude, Jr. 1929- *ConAu 101*
Buford, Thomas O 1932- *ConAu 29R*
Bugaev, Boris Nikolayevich 1880-1934 *WorAu*
Bugayev, Boris Nikolayevich 1880-1934
ConAu 104
Bugbee, Emma 1888?-1981 *ConAu 105,*
SmATA 29N
Bugbee, Ruth Carson 1903- *ConAu 1R, –1NR*
Bugental, James F T 1915- *ConAu 10NR, –21R,*
WrDr 84
Bugg, James L, Jr. 1920- *ConAu 5R*
Bugg, Ralph 1922- *ConAu 73*
Buggie, Frederick D 1929- *ConAu 97,*
IntAu&W 82
Buggs, George *DrAP&F 83*
Buglass, Leslie J 1917- *ConAu 13R*
Bugliarello, George 1927- *ConAu 41R,*
IntAu&W 82
Bugliosi, Vincent T 1934- *ConAu 73*
Bugnet, Georges-Charles-Jules 1879- *CreCan 2*
Buhite, Russell D 1938- *ConAu 101*
Buhle, Mari Jo 1943- *ConAu 108*
Buhler, Charlotte B 1893- *ConAu P-2*
Buhler, Curt Ferdinand 1905- *ConAu 1R*
Buhs, Martha *CreCan 1*
Buissonneau, Paul 1926- *CreCan 2*
Buist, Charlotte *ConAu X*
Buist, Vincent 1919?-1979 *ConAu 89*
Buitenhuis, Peter M 1925- *ConAu 25R,*
IntAu&W 82, WrDr 84
Buitrago, Ann Mari 1929- *ConAu 105*
Bujold, Genevieve 1943- *CreCan 1*
Bukalski, Peter J 1941- *ConAu 41R*
Buker, George E 1923- *ConAu 53*
Bukovsky, Vladimir 1942- *IntAu&W 82*
Bukowski, Charles *DrAP&F 83*
Bukowski, Charles 1920- *ConAu 17R, ConLC 2,*
–5, –9, ConP 80, DcLB 5[port],
DcLEL 1940, IntAu&W 82, ModAL SUP,
WhoTwCL, WorAu 1970, WrDr 84
Buktenica, Norman A 1930- *ConAu 33R*
Bulatkin, Eleanor Webster 1913- *ConAu 33R*
Bulatovic, Miodrag 1930- *ConAu 5R, EncWL 2,*
ModSL 2, TwCWr, WorAu 1970
Buley, R Carlyle 1893-1968 *ConAu 25R,*
ConAu P-2, TwCA SUP
Bulgakov, Mikhail 1891-1940 *CnMD,*
ConAu 105, ModWD, TwCLC 2,
TwCSFW A
Bulgakov, Mikhail Afanasievich 1891-1940
EncWL 2
Bulgakov, Mikhail Afanasyevich 1891-1940
CIDMEL 80, ModSL 1, TwCWr,
WhoTwCL, WorAu
Bulgaroff, Akakij Mokiewitsch *IntWWP 82X*
Bulger, William T 1927- *ConAu 69*
Bulkeley, Christy C *AuNews 2*
Bulkley, Dwight H 1919- *ConAu 105*
Bull, Angela 1936- *ConAu 9NR, –21R,*
IntAu&W 82, TwCCW 83, WrDr 84
Bull, Geoffrey Taylor 1921- *ConAu 3NR, –9R,*
IntAu&W 82
Bull, Guyon Boys Garrett 1912- *ConAu 5R,*
–5NR
Bull, Hedley 1932- *WrDr 84*

Bull, Hedley Norman 1932- *ConAu 5R*
Bull, John 1914- *ConAu 69*
Bull, Norman John 1916- *ConAu 93, WrDr 84*
Bull, Odd 1907- *ConAu 81*
Bull, Olaf Jacob Martin Luther 1883-1933
CIDMEL 80, EncWL 2
Bull, Peter 1912- *ConAu 11NR, WrDr 84*
Bull, Peter Cecil 1912- *ConAu 25R,*
IntAu&W 82
Bull, Robert J 1920- *ConAu 97*
Bull, Storm 1913- *ConAu 9R*
Bull, William E 1909-1972 *ConAu P-1*
Bull-Hansen, Haakon 1951- *IntAu&W 82*
Bulla, Clyde Robert 1914- *ConAu 3NR, –5R,*
SmATA 2, TwCCW 83, WrDr 84
Bullard, E John, III 1942- *ConAu 33R*
Bullard, Fred Mason 1901- *ConAu 25R*
Bullard, Helen 1902- *ConAu 7NR, –17R,*
WrDr 84
Bullard, Oral 1922- *ConAu 8NR, –61*
Bullard, Pamela 1948- *ConAu 106*
Bullard, Roger A 1937- *ConAu 33R*
Bulle, Florence 1925- *ConAu 93*
Bulleid, Henry A V 1912- *ConAu P-1, WrDr 84*
Bullen, Arthur Henry 1857-1920 *LongCTC*
Bullen, Dana R 1931- *ConAu 73*
Bullen, Donald G 1946- *IntWWP 82*
Bullen, Frank Thomas 1857-1915 *LongCTC,*
TwCA
Bullen, Keith Edward 1906-1976 *ConAu 106*
Bullen, Leonard *CreCan 1*
Bullen, Robert 1926?-1976 *ConAu 69*
Bullen Bear *WrDr 84*
Buller, Herman 1923- *ConAu 61, IntAu&W 82*
Buller, Herman 1927- *WrDr 84*
Bullett, Gerald William 1893-1958 *LongCTC,*
TwCA, TwCA SUP, TwCWr
Bulliet, Richard W 1940- *ConAu 7NR, –57*
Bullingham, Rodney *ConAu X*
Bullins, Ed *CroCD*
Bullins, Ed 1935- *ConAu 49, ConDr 82,*
ConLC 5, –7, DcLB 7[port], DcLEL 1940,
EncWL 2, IntAu&W 82, LivgBAA,
ModBlW, NatPD 81[port], WorAu 1970,
WrDr 84
Bullins, Ed 1936?- *ConLC 1, ModAL SUP*
Bullis, Harry Amos 1890-1963 *ConAu P-2*
Bullis, Jerald *DrAP&F 83*
Bullis, Jerald 1944- *ConAu 1NR, –49*
Bullitt, Orville H 1894-1979 *ConAu 33R, –89*
Bullitt, William C 1891-1967 *ConAu 89*
Bullock, Baron 1914- *WrDr 84*
Bullock, Alan Louis Charles 1914- *ConAu 1R,*
DcLEL 1940, IntAu&W 82, LongCTC
Bullock, Alice Lowe 1904- *ConAu 89*
Bullock, Barbara *ConAu X*
Bullock, C Hassell 1939- *ConAu 89*
Bullock, Charles S, III 1942- *ConAu 33R*
Bullock, Frederick William Bagshawe 1903-
ConAu 4NR, –5R, IntAu&W 82
Bullock, Henry 1907?-1973 *ConAu 41R*
Bullock, Henry Allen 1906- *LivgBAA*
Bullock, Michael 1918- *WrDr 84*
Bullock, Michael Hale 1918- *ConAu 7NR, –17R,*
ConP 80, DcLEL 1940, IntAu&W 82
Bullock, Paul 1924- *ConAu 11NR, –29R*
Bullock-Wilson, Barbara 1945- *ConAu 65*
Bullough, Bonnie 1927- *ConAu 11NR, –69*
Bullough, Donald Auberon 1928- *ConAu 107,*
IntAu&W 82
Bullough, Geoffrey 1901-1982 *ConAu 1R, –5NR,*
–106, IntAu&W 82
Bullough, Vern 1928- *ConAu 11NR*
Bullough, Vern L 1928- *ConAu 4NR, –9R,*
WrDr 84
Bullough, William A 1933- *ConAu 101*
Bullus, Eric 1906- *WrDr 84*
Bulman, Joan Carroll Boone 1904- *ConAu 103*
Bulman, Oliver Meredith Boone 1902-1974
ConAu 49
Bulmer, Henry Kenneth *WrDr 84*
Bulmer, Henry Kenneth 1921- *ConAu 13R,*
DcLEL 1940, IntAu&W 82
Bulmer, Kenneth 1921- *ConAu 9NR, ConSFA,*
TwCSFW
Bulmer-Thomas, Ivor 1905- *ConAu P-1,*
IntAu&W 82, WrDr 84
Bulosan, Carlos 1914-1956 *TwCA SUP*
Bulpin, Thomas Victor 1918- *ConAu 4NR, –9R,*
IntAu&W 82, WrDr 84
Bulthuis, Rico Johannes 1911- *IntAu&W 82*
Bultmann, Rudolf Karl 1884-1976 *ConAu 5R, –65,*

WorAu
Bumagin, Victoria Edith Werosub 1923-
    ConAu 89, IntAu&W 82
Bump, Jerome 1943- *ConAu 109*
Bumppo, Nathaniel John Balthazar 1940-
    ConAu 97
Bumppo, Natty *ConAu X*
Bumpus, Jerry *DrAP&F 83*
Bumpus, Jerry 1937- *ConAu 10NR, –65,*
    DcLB Y81B[port]
Bumsted, J M 1938- *ConAu 41R, WrDr 84*
Bunce, Alan 1939- *ConAu 77*
Bunce, Frank David 1907- *ConAu P-1*
Bunce, Linda Susan 1956- *ConAu 107*
Bunch, Clarence *ConAu 53*
Bunch, David R *ConAu 29R, IntWWP 82,*
    TwCSFW, WrDr 84
Bunche, Ralph Johnson 1904-1971 *ConAu 33R*
Bundukhari, El *ConAu X*
Bundy, Clarence E 1906- *ConAu 85*
Bundy, William P 1917- *ConAu 104*
Bunge, Mario A 1919- *ConAu 9R*
Bunge, Walter R 1911- *ConAu 25R*
Bungert, Keswick Alfons 1929- *IntAu&W 82*
Bungey, John Henry 1944- *WrDr 84*
Buni, Andrew 1931- *ConAu 21R*
Bunim, Irving M 1901?-1980 *ConAu 103*
Bunin, Catherine 1967- *ConAu 93,*
    SmATA 30[port]
Bunin, Ivan 1870-1953 *EncWL 2,*
    TwCLC 6[port]
Bunin, Ivan Alekseyevich 1870-1953 *CIDMEL 80,*
    CnMWL, LongCTC, ModSL 1, TwCA,
    TwCA SUP, TwCWr, WhoTwCL
Bunin, Ivan Alexeyevich 1870-1953 *ConAu 104*
Bunin, Sherry 1925- *ConAu 93,*
    SmATA 30[port]
Buning, Sietze *ConAu X*
Bunje *CreCan 2*
Bunke, H Charles 1922- *ConAu 9R*
Bunke, Joan Elizabeth 1934- *ConAmTC*
Bunker, Capt. Moss *IntAu&W 82X*
Bunker, Captain Moss *WrDr 84*
Bunker, Edward 1933- *ConAu 41R*
Bunker, Gerald Edward 1938- *ConAu 37R*
Bunn, John T 1924- *ConAu 37R*
Bunn, John W 1898- *ConAu P-2*
Bunn, Ronald F 1929- *ConAu 21R*
Bunn, Thomas 1944- *ConAu 69*
Bunnell, Peter C 1937- *ConAu 33R*
Bunnell, William S 1925- *ConAu P-1*
Bunt, Lucas N H 1905- *ConAu 69*
Bunting, A E *ConAu X, SmATA X,*
    TwCCW 83
Bunting, Anne Evelyn 1928- *ConAu 5NR, –53,*
    SmATA 18
Bunting, Bainbridge 1913-1981 *ConAu 8NR, –61*
Bunting, Basil 1900- *ConAu 7NR, –53,*
    ConLC 10, ConP 80, EncWL 2,
    ModBrL SUP, RGFMBP, WhoTwCL,
    WorAu, WrDr 84
Bunting, Brian Percy 1920- *IntAu&W 82*
Bunting, Daniel George *LongCTC*
Bunting, Eve *ConAu X, SmATA X*
Bunting, Eve 1928- *TwCCW 83*
Bunting, Glenn 1957- *SmATA 22*
Bunting, John Reginald 1916- *IntAu&W 82*
Bunting, Josiah, III 1939- *ConAu 45*
Bunuan, Josefina S 1935- *ConAu 33R*
Bunuel, Luis 1900- *ConAu 101, ConLC 16*
Bunuel, Luis 1900-1983 *ConAu 110*
Bunzel, John H 1924- *ConAu 17R*
Buol, S W 1934- *ConAu 49*
Buonocore, Michaelina *IntWWP 82*
Buor, Joy Olney 1918- *MichAu 80*
Bupp, Walter *TwCSFW*
Burack, Abraham Saul 1908-1978 *ConAu 4NR,*
    –9R, –77
Burack, Elmer H 1927- *ConAu 37R, WrDr 84*
Burack, Sylvia 1916- *ConAu 21R*
Burack, Sylvia K 1916- *ConAu 9NR*
Buranelli, Vincent 1919- *ConAu 5NR, –9R,*
    WrDr 84
Burbank, Garin 1940- *ConAu 69*
Burbank, Jim *DrAP&F 83*
Burbank, Natt B 1903- *ConAu P-2*
Burbank, Nelson L 1898- *ConAu P-1*
Burbank, Rex James 1925- *ConAu 1R*
Burbridge, Branse 1921- *ConAu 97*
Burby, Raymond J, III 1942- *ConAu 11NR, –69*
Burby, William E 1893- *ConAu P-1*
Burch, Claire *DrAP&F 83*

Burch, Claire R 1925- *ConAu 101*
Burch, Francis Floyd 1932- *ConAu 29R,*
    IntAu&W 82
Burch, George Bosworth 1902-1973 *ConAu 109*
Burch, Mary Lou 1914- *ConAu 104*
Burch, Monte G 1943- *ConAu 103*
Burch, Pat 1944- *ConAu 57*
Burch, Philip H 1930- *ConAu 106*
Burch, Preston M 1884-1978 *ConAu 77*
Burch, Robert 1925- *TwCCW 83, WrDr 84*
Burch, Robert Joseph 1925- *ConAu 2NR, –5R,*
    IntAu&W 82, SmATA 1
Burcham, Nancy A 1942- *ConAu 89*
Burcham, William Ernest 1913- *WrDr 84*
Burchard, John Ely 1898-1975 *ConAu 1R, –6NR,*
    –61
Burchard, Max N 1925- *ConAu 21R*
Burchard, Peter Duncan 1921- *ConAu 3NR, –5R,*
    SmATA 5
Burchard, Rachael C 1921- *ConAu 33R*
Burchard, S H *ConAu X*
Burchard, Sue 1937- *ConAu 4NR, –53,*
    SmATA 22
Burchardt, Bill 1917- *ConAu X, IntAu&W 82,*
    TwCWW, WrDr 84
Burchardt, Nellie 1921- *ConAu 21R, SmATA 7,*
    WrDr 84
Burchardt, William Robert 1917- *ConAu 89*
Burchell, Mary *TwCRGW, WrDr 84*
Burchell, R A 1941- *ConAu 106, WrDr 84*
Burchett, Randall E d1971 *ConAu 1R, –103*
Burchett, Wilfred 1911-1983 *ConAu 110*
Burchett, Wilfred G 1911- *WrDr 84*
Burchett, Wilfred Graham 1911- *ConAu 2NR,*
    –49
Burchfield, Joe D 1937- *ConAu 85*
Burchfield, Robert William 1923- *ConAu 41R,*
    IntAu&W 82
Burchwood, Katharine T *ConAu 57*
Burciaga, Jose Antonio *DrAP&F 83*
Burck, Jacob 1907-1982 *ConAu 106*
Burckel, Nicholas C 1943- *ConAu 103*
Burckhardt, Carl Jacob 1891-1974 *ConAu 49, –93*
Burd, Laurence Hull 1915-1983 *ConAu 109*
Burd, VanAkin 1914- *ConAu 41R*
Burda, R W 1932- *ConAu 73*
Burden, Jean *DrAP&F 83*
Burden, Jean 1914- *ConAu 3NR, –9R,*
    IntAu&W 82, IntWWP 82, WrDr 84
Burden, William Douglas 1898-1978 *ConAu 81*
Burder, John 1940- *ConAu 110, WrDr 84*
Burdett, Winston 1913- *ConAu 29R*
Burdette, Franklin L 1911-1975 *ConAu 61, –65*
Burdge, Rabel J 1937- *ConAu 69*
Burdick, Donald W 1917- *ConAu 53*
Burdick, Eric 1934- *ConAu 29R*
Burdick, Eugene 1918-1965 *ConAu 5R, –25R,*
    SmATA 22[port], TwCSFW, TwCWr,
    WorAu
Burdick, Loraine 1929- *ConAu 57*
Burdon, Randal Mathews 1896- *ConAu P-1*
Bureau, William H 1913- *ConAu 102*
Buren, Martha 1910- *ConAu P-1, IntAu&W 82*
Burfield, Eva *ConAu X, IntAu&W 82X*
Burford, Eleanor *ConAu X, SmATA 2,*
    TwCRGW, WorAu, WrDr 84
Burford, Lolah 1931- *ConAu 41R, TwCRGW,*
    WrDr 84
Burford, Roger Lewis 1930- *ConAu 41R*
Burford, William *DrAP&F 83*
Burford, William 1927- *ConAu 5R, –7NR,*
    ConP 80, DcLEL 1940, IntWWP 82,
    WrDr 84
Burg, Dale R 1942- *ConAu 106*
Burg, David 1933- *ConAu X*
Burg, Marie *IntAu&W 82*
Burge, Ethel 1916- *ConAu 65*
Burgeon, G A L *ConAu X*
Burger, Albert E 1941- *ConAu 37R*
Burger, Angela Sutherland 1936- *ConAu 81*
Burger, Carl Victor 1888-1967 *ConAu P-2,*
    SmATA 9
Burger, Chester 1921- *ConAu 9R*
Burger, Edward J, Jr. 1933- *ConAu 110*
Burger, George V 1927- *ConAu 57*
Burger, Henry G 1923- *ConAu 41R*
Burger, Hermann 1942- *IntAu&W 82*
Burger, Jack *ConAu X*
Burger, John *ConAu X*
Burger, John R 1942- *ConAu 81*
Burger, Nash Kerr 1908- *ConAu P-2*
Burger, Robert E 1931- *ConAu 85,*

IntAu&W 82
Burger, Robert S 1913- *ConAu 29R*
Burger, Ruth 1917- *ConAu 17R*
Burger, Sarah Greene 1935- *ConAu 69*
Burges, Norman Alan 1911- *WrDr 84*
Burgess, Ann Marie *ConAu X, SmATA X*
Burgess, Anthony *DrAP&F 83*
Burgess, Anthony 1917- *AuNews 1, ConAu X,*
    –1R, ConLC 1, –2, –4, –5, –8, –10, –13, –15,
    –22[port], ConNov 82, ConSFA,
    DcLB 14[port], DcLEL 1940, EncWL 2,
    LongCTC, ModBrL, ModBrL SUP,
    TwCSFW, TwCWr, WhoTwCL, WorAu,
    WrDr 84
Burgess, C F 1922- *ConAu 21R*
Burgess, Charles 1932- *ConAu 33R, WrDr 84*
Burgess, Chester F 1922- *WrDr 84*
Burgess, Chester Francis 1922- *IntAu&W 82*
Burgess, Christopher Victor 1921- *ConAu 9R*
Burgess, Em *ConAu X, SmATA X*
Burgess, Eric 1912- *ConAu 101*
Burgess, Eric 1920- *ConAu 3NR, –5R*
Burgess, Gelett 1866-1951 *LongCTC,*
    SmATA 30, –32[port], TwCA, TwCA SUP,
    TwCCr&M 80, TwCWr
Burgess, Jackson 1927- *ConAu 9R*
Burgess, John H 1923- *ConAu 33R*
Burgess, Linda Cannon 1911- *ConAu 73*
Burgess, Lorraine Marshall 1913- *ConAu 106*
Burgess, M Elaine *ConAu 13R*
Burgess, M R 1948- *ConAu 6NR*
Burgess, Mary Wyche 1916- *ConAu 61,*
    SmATA 18
Burgess, Michael *ConAu X, SmATA X*
Burgess, Norman 1923- *ConAu 25R, WrDr 84*
Burgess, Perry 1886-1962 *TwCA SUP*
Burgess, Philip Mark 1939- *ConAu 25R*
Burgess, Robert F 1927- *ConAu 11NR*
Burgess, Robert Forrest 1927- *ConAu 25R,*
    SmATA 4
Burgess, Robert Herrmann 1913- *ConAu 5NR,*
    –9R, WrDr 84
Burgess, Robert L 1938- *ConAu 29R*
Burgess, Thornton W 1874-1965 *DcLB 22[port]*
Burgess, Thornton Waldo 1874-1965 *ConAu 73,*
    SmATA 17, TwCCW 83
Burgess, Trevor *ConAu X, SmATA X*
Burgess, W Randolph 1889-1978 *ConAu 81,*
    ConAu P-2
Burgess, Warren E 1932- *WrDr 84*
Burgess-Kohn, Jane 1928- *ConAu 73*
Burgett, Donald Robert 1925- *ConAu 21R,*
    MichAu 80
Burghard, August 1901- *AuNews 2,*
    ConAu 7NR, –17R
Burghardt, Andrew Frank 1924- *ConAu 5R*
Burghardt, Walter J 1914- *ConAu 1R, –4NR,*
    IntAu&W 82
Burghley, Rose *TwCRGW, WrDr 84*
Burgin, C David 1939- *ConAu 73*
Burgin, G B 1856-1944 *TwCRGW*
Burgin, George Brown 1856-1944 *LongCTC*
Burgin, Richard *DrAP&F 83*
Burgin, Richard 1947- *ConAu 25R*
Burgos, Joseph A, Jr. 1945- *ConAu 106*
Burgoyne, Elizabeth 1902- *ConAu X, WrDr 84*
Burgoyne, Leon E 1916- *MichAu 80*
Burgstaller, Heimo Peter 1932- *IntAu&W 82*
Burgtorf, Frances D 1916- *MichAu 80*
Burgwyn, Diana 1937- *ConAu 108*
Burgwyn, Mebane Holoman 1914- *ConAu 49,*
    SmATA 7
Burhoe, Ralph Wendell 1911- *ConAu 17R*
Buri, Fritz 1907- *ConAu 8NR, –17R*
Burian, Jarka M 1927- *ConAu 33R, WrDr 84*
Burich, Nancy J 1943- *ConAu 29R*
Burick, Si 1909- *ConAu 85*
Burk, Bill E 1932- *ConAu 65*
Burk, Bruce 1917- *ConAu 61*
Burk, Ronnie *DrAP&F 83*
Burkard, Michael *DrAP&F 83*
Burke, Alan Dennis 1949- *ConAu 106*
Burke, Arvid James 1906- *ConAu 21R,*
    WrDr 84
Burke, C J 1917-1973 *ConAu 45*
Burke, Carl F 1917- *ConAu 25R*
Burke, Carol *DrAP&F 83*
Burke, Carol 1950- *ConAu 65*
Burke, David 1927- *ConAu 105*
Burke, Edmund M 1928- *ConAu 9R*
Burke, Fielding *TwCA, TwCA SUP*
Burke, France *DrAP&F 83*

Burke, Fred George 1926- *ConAu 13R*
Burke, Gerald 1914- *ConAu 1NR, –45*
Burke, J Bruce 1933- *ConAu 37R*
Burke, J F 1915- *ConAu 65*
Burke, James 1917- *WrDr 84*
Burke, James 1936- *ConAu 102, IntAu&W 82, WrDr 84*
Burke, James Lee 1936- *ConAu 7NR, –13R*
Burke, James Wakefield 1916- *ConAu 1NR, –45*
Burke, John *ConAu X, SmATA X*
Burke, John 1922- *ConAu 9NR, WrDr 84*
Burke, John Emmett 1908- *ConAu 37R*
Burke, John Frederick 1922- *ConAu 5R, IntAu&W 82, TwCCr&M 80*
Burke, John Garrett 1917- *ConAu 77*
Burke, Jonathan *ConAu X, WrDr 84*
Burke, Joseph 1913- *ConAu 103*
Burke, Kenneth 1897- *ConAmA, ConAu 5R, ConLC 2, –24[port], ConLCrt 82, ConP 80, ModAL, ModAL SUP, TwCA, TwCA SUP, WhoTwCL, WrDr 84*
Burke, Leda *ConAu X*
Burke, Michael 1927- *ConAu 73*
Burke, Owen *ConAu X, WrDr 84*
Burke, Peter 1937- *ConAu 25R*
Burke, Ralph *TwCSFW*
Burke, Richard C 1932- *ConAu 53*
Burke, Robert E 1921- *ConAu 21R*
Burke, Russell 1946- *ConAu 33R*
Burke, S M 1906- *ConAu 49*
Burke, Shifty *ConAu 49, WrDr 84*
Burke, Stanley 1923- *ConAu 101*
Burke, Ted 1934?-1978 *ConAu 77*
Burke, Theta 1926- *MichAu 80*
Burke, Thomas 1886-1945 *LongCTC, TwCA[port], TwCA SUP, TwCCr&M 80*
Burke, Tom *ConAu 73*
Burke, Ulick Peter 1937- *WrDr 84*
Burke, Vee *ConAu X*
Burke, Velma Whitgrove 1921- *ConAu 4NR, –53*
Burke, Virginia M 1916- *ConAu 45*
Burke, W Warner 1935- *ConAu 37R*
Burkert, Nancy Ekholm 1933- *SmATA 24[port]*
Burkert, Walter 1931- *ConAu 103*
Burket, Harriet 1908- *ConAu 37R*
Burkett, David 1934- *ConAu 9NR, –65*
Burkett, Eva M 1903- *ConAu 33R*
Burkett, Jack 1914- *ConAu 101, WrDr 84*
Burkett, Molly 1932- *ConAu 9NR, –53*
Burkett, William R, Jr. 1943- *ConSFA*
Burkey, Richard M 1930- *ConAu 93*
Burkhalter, Barton R 1938- *ConAu 11NR, –25R*
Burkhardt, Richard Wellington 1918- *ConAu 1R*
Burkhart, Charles 1924- *ConAu 13R*
Burkhart, Erika 1922- *CIDMEL 80*
Burkhart, James Austin 1918- *ConAu 9R*
Burkhart, Kathryn Watterson 1942- *ConAu 45*
Burkhart, Kitsi *ConAu X*
Burkhart, Robert E 1937- *ConAu 29R*
Burkhead, Jesse 1916- *ConAu 1R, –3NR*
Burkholder, Esther York 1911- *IntWWP 82*
Burkholz, Herbert *DrAP&F 83*
Burkholz, Herbert 1932- *ConAu 11NR, –25R*
Burki, Roland 1906- *IntAu&W 82*
Burkill, Tom Alec 1912- *ConAu 33R, WrDr 84*
Burkin, Ivan 1919- *IntWWP 82*
Burkle, Howard R 1925- *ConAu 107*
Burkman, Katherine H 1934- *ConAu 29R*
Burkowsky, Mitchell R 1931- *ConAu 29R*
Burks, Ardath Walter 1915- *ConAu 107*
Burks, Arthur W 1915- *ConAu 69*
Burks, David D 1924- *ConAu 33R*
Burks, Gordon Engledow 1904- *ConAu 1R*
Burkunk, Willem F 1925- *IntAu&W 82*
Burl, Aubrey 1926- *ConAu 97*
Burland, Brian *DrAP&F 83, WrDr 84*
Burland, Brian 1931- *SmATA 34[port]*
Burland, Brian Berkeley 1931- *ConAu 7NR, –13R*
Burland, C A *ConAu X*
Burland, Cottie Arthur 1905- *ConAu 5R, –5NR, IntAu&W 82, SmATA 5*
Burleigh, Anne Husted 1941- *ConAu 29R*
Burleigh, David Robert 1907- *ConAu 1R*
Burley, George Joseph 1939- *ConAmTC, ConAu 107*
Burley, W J 1914- *ConAu 33R, TwCCr&M 80, WrDr 84*
Burley, William John 1914- *IntAu&W 82*
Burling, Robbins 1926- *ConAu 17R*
Burlingame, Roger 1889-1967 *ConAu 5R, SmATA 2, TwCA, TwCA SUP*

Burlingame, Virginia 1900- *ConAu P-2*
Burlingham, Dorothy 1891-1979 *ConAu 109*
Burlingham, Dorothy Tiffany 1891-1979 *ConAu 93*
Burlyuk, David Davidovich 1882-1967 *CIDMEL 80*
Burma, John H 1913- *ConAu 1R, –5NR*
Burman, Alice Caddy 1896?-1977 *SmATA 24N*
Burman, Ben Lucien 1895- *ConAu 5R, SmATA 6, TwCA, TwCA SUP, WrDr 84*
Burman, Ben Lucien 1896- *ConAu 8NR, IntAu&W 82, TwCCW 83*
Burman, Jose Lionel 1917- *ConAu 109, WrDr 84*
Burmeister, Edwin 1939- *ConAu 29R*
Burmeister, Eva 1899- *ConAu P-1*
Burmeister, Jon 1932- *DcLEL 1940*
Burmeister, Jon 1933- *ConAu 29R, WrDr 84*
Burmeister, Lou E 1928- *ConAu 45*
Burmike *IntAu&W 82X*
Burn, Andrew Robert 1902- *ConAu 1R, –1NR, IntAu&W 82, WrDr 84*
Burn, Barbara 1940- *ConAu 85*
Burn, Doris 1923- *ConAu 29R, SmATA 1*
Burn, J Harold 1892- *ConAu P-1*
Burn, J Harold 1892-1982 *ConAu 108*
Burn, Joshua Harold 1892- *IntAu&W 82*
Burn, Michael Clive 1912- *IntAu&W 82, IntWWP 82*
Burnaby, John 1891-1978 *ConAu 104, ConAu P-1*
Burnam, Tom 1913- *ConAu 61*
Burnand, Sir Francis Cowley 1836-1917 *LongCTC*
Burne, Glen *ConAu X*
Burne, Glenn S 1921- *ConAu 21R*
Burne, Kevin G 1925- *ConAu 13R*
Burne, Ralph *ConAu X*
Burnell, Richard Desborough 1917- *IntAu&W 82*
Burner, David 1937- *ConAu 10NR, –25R*
Burnes, Carol *DrAP&F 83*
Burness, Sheil *IntAu&W 82X*
Burness, Tad *ConAu X*
Burness, Wallace B 1933- *ConAu 69*
Burnet, F Macfarlane 1899- *WrDr 84*
Burnet, George Bain 1894- *ConAu P-2*
Burnet, MacFarlane 1899- *ConAu 73, IntAu&W 82*
Burnet, Mary E 1911- *ConAu 53*
Burnett, Alfred David 1937- *ConAu 102, IntWWP 82, WrDr 84*
Burnett, Avis 1937- *ConAu 41R*
Burnett, Ben George 1924-1975 *ConAu 1R, –3NR*
Burnett, Calvin 1921- *ConAu 33R*
Burnett, Collins W 1914- *ConAu 3NR, –9R*
Burnett, Constance Buel 1893- *ConAu 5R*
Burnett, David 1931-1971 *ConAu 9R, –33R*
Burnett, David 1937- *IntAu&W 82*
Burnett, Dorothy Kirk 1924- *ConAu 5R*
Burnett, Frances Eliza Hodgson 1849-1924 *LongCTC, TwCA, TwCA SUP*
Burnett, Frances Hodgson 1849-1924 *ConAu 108, TwCCW 83*
Burnett, George 1918- *WrDr 84*
Burnett, Hallie *DrAP&F 83, WrDr 84*
Burnett, Hallie Southgate *ConAu 6NR, –13R, IntAu&W 82, TwCA SUP*
Burnett, Ivy Compton *LongCTC*
Burnett, Janet 1915- *ConAu 49*
Burnett, Joe Ray 1928- *ConAu 17R*
Burnett, John 1925- *ConAu 57, IntAu&W 82, WrDr 84*
Burnett, Laurence 1907- *ConAu 49*
Burnett, Leon R 1925?-1983 *ConAu 109*
Burnett, W R 1899-1982 *ConAu 106, DcLB 9[port], TwCCr&M 80, TwCWW*
Burnett, Whit 1899-1973 *ConAu 41R, ConAu P-2, TwCA, TwCA SUP*
Burnett, William Riley 1899- *ConAmA, ConAu 5R, LongCTC, TwCA, TwCA SUP, TwCWr*
Burnette, O Lawrence, Jr. 1927- *ConAu 33R, WrDr 84*
Burney, Anton *ConAu X*
Burney, Elizabeth 1934- *ConAu 21R*
Burney, Eugenia 1913- *ConAu 29R*
Burnford, S D *ConAu X, SmATA 3*
Burnford, Sheila 1918- *ChlLR 2, ConAu 1R, –1NR, CreCan 2, SmATA 3, TwCCW 83, WrDr 84*
Burnham, Alan 1913- *ConAu 13R*
Burnham, Clara Louise 1854-1927 *TwCA*

Burnham, Deborah *DrAP&F 83*
Burnham, Dorothy E 1921- *ConAu 65*
Burnham, James 1905- *TwCA SUP*
Burnham, John *ConAu X*
Burnham, John C 1929- *ConAu 33R*
Burnham, Robert Ward, Jr. 1913- *ConAu 17R*
Burnham, Sophy 1936- *AuNews 1, ConAu 41R, IntAu&W 82*
Burnham, Walter Dean 1930- *ConAu 101*
Burniaux, Constant 1892-1975 *CIDMEL 80*
Burnier, Andreas *IntAu&W 82X*
Burnim, Kalman A 1928- *ConAu 1R*
Burningham, John 1936- *TwCCW 83, WrDr 84*
Burningham, John Mackintosh 1936- *ConAu 73, SmATA 16*
Burnley, Judith *ConAu 97*
Burns, Alan 1929- *ConAu 5NR, –9R, ConNov 82, DcLB 14[port], IntAu&W 82, WrDr 84*
Burns, Alan Cuthbert 1887- *WrDr 84*
Burns, Alan Cuthbert 1887-1980 *ConAu 102*
Burns, Alma 1919- *ConAu 81*
Burns, Arthur F 1904- *ConAu 13R, IntAu&W 82, WrDr 84*
Burns, Betty 1909- *ConAu P-2*
Burns, Bobby *ConAu X*
Burns, Carol 1934- *ConAu 29R, IntAu&W 82, WrDr 84*
Burns, Chester R 1937- *ConAu 103*
Burns, E Bradford 1932- *ConAu 17R*
Burns, Edward McNall 1897-1972 *ConAu 1R, –103*
Burns, Eedson Louis Millard 1897- *ConAu 5R, –5NR*
Burns, Gerald P 1918- *ConAu 17R*
Burns, Helen M 1922- *ConAu 110*
Burns, Hobert Warren 1925- *ConAu 1R*
Burns, James MacGregor 1918- *ConAu 5R, DcLEL 1940, WorAu, WrDr 84*
Burns, James W 1937- *ConAu 33R*
Burns, Jean 1934- *ConAu 103*
Burns, Jim 1936- *ConAu 101, ConP 80, DcLEL 1940, IntAu&W 82, IntWWP 82, WrDr 84*
Burns, Joan Simpson 1927- *ConAu 65, IntAu&W 82, WrDr 84*
Burns, John Horne 1916-1953 *ModAL, TwCA SUP, TwCWr*
Burns, John McLauren 1932- *ConAu 109*
Burns, John V 1907- *ConAu P-2*
Burns, Marilyn *SmATA 33*
Burns, Norman T 1930- *ConAu 69*
Burns, Paul C *ConAu 1R, –4NR, SmATA 5*
Burns, Ralph *DrAP&F 83*
Burns, Ralph J 1901- *ConAu P-2*
Burns, Ray *SmATA X*
Burns, Raymond 1924- *SmATA 9*
Burns, Rex 1935- *ConAu 77, TwCCr&M 80, WrDr 84*
Burns, Richard Dean 1929- *ConAu 8NR, –17R*
Burns, Richard Stephen 1943- *IntWWP 82*
Burns, Richard W 1920- *ConAu 69*
Burns, Robert A *DrAP&F 83*
Burns, Robert Grant *DrAP&F 83*
Burns, Robert Grant 1938- *ConAu 25R*
Burns, Robert Ignatius 1921- *ConAu 7NR, –17R, IntAu&W 82*
Burns, Robert M C, Jr. 1940- *ConAu 102*
Burns, Robert Whitehall *WrDr 84*
Burns, Ruby V 1901- *ConAu 106*
Burns, Scott *ConAu X*
Burns, Sheila *ConAu X, TwCRGW, WrDr 84*
Burns, Stanley *DrAP&F 83*
Burns, Tex *ConAu X, TwCWW, WrDr 84*
Burns, Thomas 1928- *ConAu 41R*
Burns, Thomas LaBorie 1942- *IntWWP 82*
Burns, Thomas Stephen 1927- *ConAu 49*
Burns, Tom 1913- *ConAu 5R, –5NR*
Burns, Vincent Godfrey 1893-1979 *AuNews 2, ConAu 41R, –85*
Burns, Walter Noble 1872-1932 *TwCWW*
Burns, Wayne 1918- *ConAu 1R, –1NR*
Burns, William *DrAP&F 83*
Burns, William A 1909- *ConAu 11NR, ConAu P-1, SmATA 5*
Burns, Zed H 1903- *ConAu 33R*
Burns-Bisogno, Louisa 1936- *NatPD 81[port]*
Burnshaw, Stanley *DrAP&F 83*
Burnshaw, Stanley 1906- *ConAu 9R, ConLC 3, –13, ConP 80, WorAu, WrDr 84*
Burnside, Wesley M 1918- *ConAu 65*
Burnstein, George *CreCan 1*

Byers, David 1941- *ConAu 53*
Byers, Edward E 1921- *ConAu 1R, –3NR*
Byers, Horace 1906- *WrDr 84*
Byers, Irene 1906- *ConAu 3NR, –9R, WrDr 84*
Byers, R McCulloch 1913- *ConAu 69*
Byers Brown, Betty 1927- *WrDr 84*
Byfield, Barbara Ninde 1930- *ConAu 1R, –4NR, SmATA 8*
Byham, William C 1936- *ConAu 25R*
Bykaw, Vasil 1924- *EncWL 2*
Bykov, Vasil Vladimirovich 1924- *CIDMEL 80*
Bykov, Vasily Vladimirovich 1924- *ConAu 102*
Bylinsky, Gene 1930- *ConAu 77*
Bynner, Witter 1881-1968 *ConAmA, ConAu 1R, –4NR, –25R, TwCA, TwCA SUP*
Bynum, David E 1936- *ConAu 37R*
Bynum, Terrell Ward 1941- *ConAu 101*
Byock, Jesse L 1945- *ConAu 110*
Byola, DaUgo *IntAu&W 82X*
Byola, Ugo Da *IntWWP 82X*
Byrd, Bobby *DrAP&F 83*
Byrd, Bobby 1942- *ConAu X*
Byrd, C L *ConAu X*
Byrd, Cecil Kash 1913- *ConAu 17R*
Byrd, Don *DrAP&F 83*
Byrd, Eldon Arthur 1939- *ConAu 45*
Byrd, Elizabeth 1912- *ConAu 5R, –5NR, SmATA 34[port]*
Byrd, Emmett *ConAu X*

Byrd, John Crowe *ConAu X*
Byrd, Martha 1930- *ConAu 29R*
Byrd, Richard E 1931- *ConAu 7NR*
Byrd, Richard Evelyn 1888-1957 *ConAu 57, TwCA, TwCA SUP*
Byrd, Richard Odell 1943- *IntWWP 82*
Byrd, Robert 1942- *SmATA 33*
Byrd, Robert James 1942- *ConAu 65*
Byrne, David 1953?- *ConLC 26[port]*
Byrne, Donald E, Jr. 1942- *ConAu 73*
Byrne, Donn 1889-1928 *LongCTC, TwCA, TwCA SUP, TwCWr*
Byrne, Donn 1931- *ConAu 5NR, –9R, IntAu&W 82*
Byrne, Donn E *WrDr 84*
Byrne, Edmund F 1933- *ConAu 29R*
Byrne, Edward M 1935- *ConAu 29R*
Byrne, Frank Loyola 1928- *ConAu 21R, –53*
Byrne, Gary C 1942- *ConAu 49*
Byrne, Herbert Winston 1917- *ConAu 1R*
Byrne, James *LongCTC*
Byrne, James E 1945- *ConAu 81*
Byrne, John 1940- *ConAu 104, ConDr 82, WrDr 84*
Byrne, John Keyes 1926- *ConAu 102, ConLC 19, IntAu&W 82, WorAu 1970, WrDr 84*
Byrne, Muriel St. Clare 1895- *ConAu P-1, IntAu&W 82*

Byrne, Peter 1925- *ConAu 65*
Byrne, Ralph 1901- *ConAu X*
Byrne, Richard Hill 1915- *ConAu 21R*
Byrne, Robert 1928- *ConAu 110*
Byrne, Robert 1930- *ConAu 73, WrDr 84*
Byrne, Stuart J 1913- *ConAu 102*
Byrnes, Edward T 1929- *ConAu 53*
Byrnes, Eugene F 1890?-1974 *ConAu 49*
Byrnes, Robert F 1917- *ConAu 10NR*
Byrnes, Robert Francis 1917- *ConAu 25R*
Byrnes, Thomas Edmund 1911- *ConAu 13R*
Byrom, James 1911- *ConAu X, WrDr 84*
Byrom, Michael 1925- *ConAu 5R*
Byron, Carl R 1948- *ConAu 97*
Byron, Cheryl *DrAP&F 83*
Byron, Christopher M 1944- *ConAu 77*
Byron, Gilbert *DrAP&F 83*
Byron, Gilbert 1903- *ConAu 17R*
Byron, John *ConAu X*
Byron, Robert 1905-1941 *LongCTC*
Byron, Stuart *DrAP&F 83*
Byron, William J 1927- *ConAu 81*
Byrt, Edwin Andrew 1932- *WrDr 84*
Bystrzycki, Przemyslaw 1923- *IntAu&W 82*
Bytwerk, Randall Lee 1950- *ConAu 109*
Bywater, Ingram 1840-1914 *LongCTC*
Bywater, William G, Jr. 1940- *ConAu 61*

C

C 3 3 *SmATA X*
Cab-Addae, Kwesi 1946- *IntAu&W 82*
Caballero, Ann Mallory 1928- *ConAu 17R*
Caballero, Oscar 1942- *IntAu&W 82*
Caballero Bonald, Jose Manuel 1926-
 ClDMEL 80
Caballero Calderon, Eduardo 1910- *ModLAL*
Cabalquinto, Luis *DrAP&F 83*
Cabalquinto, Luis 1935- *IntWWP 82*
Cabanis, Jose 1922- *ClDMEL 80*
Cabaniss, Alice *DrAP&F 83*
Cabaniss, James Allen 1911- *ConAu 1R, -5NR*
Cabarga, Leslie 1954- *ConAu 77*
Cabassa, Victoria 1912- *ConAu 49*
Cabbell, Paul 1942- *ConAu 53*
Cabeceiras, James 1930- *WrDr 84*
Cabeen, David Clark 1886- *ConAu P-1*
Cabell, Branch *ConAmA*
Cabell, James Branch 1879-1958 *CnMWL,*
 ConAmA, ConAu 105, DcLB 9[port],
 LongCTC, ModAL, TwCA, TwCA SUP,
 TwCLC 6[port], TwCWr
Cabibi, John F J 1912- *ConAu 53*
Cable, George Washington 1844-1925 *ConAu 104,*
 TwCLC 3, -4[port]
Cable, Howard Reid 1920- *CreCan 1*
Cable, James 1920- *ConAu 85, IntAu&W 82*
Cable, John L 1934- *ConAu 69*
Cable, Mary *DrAP&F 83*
Cable, Mary 1920- *ConAu 11NR, -25R,*
 SmATA 9
Cable, Thomas Monroe 1942- *ConAu 106*
Cabot, Blake 1905?-1974 *ConAu 53*
Cabot, John Moors 1901-1981 *ConAu 103*
Cabot, Robert Moors 1924- *ConAu 29R,*
 WrDr 84
Cabot, Thomas Dudley 1897- *ConAu 93*
Cabot, Tracy 1941- *ConAu 81*
Cabral, Alberto *ConAu X*
Cabral, Alexandre 1917- *ClDMEL 80*
Cabral, O M *ConAu X*
Cabral, Olga *DrAP&F 83*
Cabral, Olga 1909- *ConAu 10NR, -25R*
Cabral DeMelo Neto, Joao 1920- *WorAu 1970*
Cabrera, James C 1935- *ConAu 109*
Cabrera Infante, G 1929- *ConLC 25[port]*
Cabrera Infante, Guillermo 1929- *ConAu 85,*
 ConLC 5, EncWL 2, ModLAL,
 WorAu 1970
Caccia-Dominioni, Paolo 1896- *ConAu 21R*
Cacciatore, Edoardo 1912- *IntWWP 82*
Cacciatore, Vera 1911- *ConAu 5R, -5NR,*
 IntAu&W 82, IntWWP 82, WrDr 84
Cachapero, Emilya *DrAP&F 83*
Cachia, Pierre 1921- *WrDr 84*
Cachia, Pierre J E 1921- *ConAu 11NR*
Cachia, Pierre Jacques Elie 1921- *ConAu 25R,*
 IntAu&W 82
Cacoyannis, Michael 1922- *ConAu 101*
Cadbury, Henry Joel 1883-1974 *ConAu 53,*
 ConAu P-1
Cadden, Joseph E 1911?-1980 *ConAu 101*
Caddoe, Sean *DrAP&F 83*
Caddy, Alice *SmATA X*

Caddy, John *DrAP&F 83*
Cade, Jack *IntAu&W 82X*
Cade, Robin *ConNov 82, WrDr 84*
Cade, Steven *WrDr 84*
Cade, Toni *ConAu X*
Cadell, Elizabeth 1903- *ConAu 11NR, -57,*
 TwCRGW, WrDr 84
Cadenhead, Ivie Edward, Jr. 1923- *ConAu 41R*
Cadet, John 1935- *ConAu 77*
Cadieux, Charles L 1919- *ConAu 57*
Cadieux, Lorenzo 1903-1976 *ConAu 103, -49*
Cadieux, Marcel 1915-1981 *ConAu 108*
Cadle, David Dean *DrAP&F 83*
Cadle, Dean 1920- *ConAu 25R, IntAu&W 82*
Cadmus *ConAu X*
Cadnum, Michael *DrAP&F 83*
Cadogan, Alexander 1884-1968 *ConAu 106*
Cadogan, Mary 1928- *ConAu 106,*
 IntAu&W 82, WrDr 84
Cadou, Rene Guy 1920-1951 *ClDMEL 80,*
 WorAu
Cadwaladr *IntAu&W 82X*
Cadwallader, Clyde T 1898- *ConAu 5R*
Cadwallader, Sharon 1936- *ConAu 1NR, -49,*
 SmATA 7
Cady, Arthur 1920-1983 *ConAu 109*
Cady, Edwin H 1917- *WrDr 84*
Cady, Edwin Harrison 1917- *ConAu 1R, -4NR*
Cady, Frank *DrAP&F 83*
Cady, Harrison 1877-1970 *SmATA 19*
Cady, Jack *DrAP&F 83*
Cady, Jack A 1932- *ConAu 9NR, -65*
Cady, John Frank 1901- *ConAu 1R, -4NR,*
 WrDr 84
Cady, Steve 1927- *ConAu 45*
Caedmon, Father *ConAu X*
Caefer, Raymond J 1926- *ConAu 17R*
Caeiro, Alberto *WorAu 1970*
Caemmerer, Richard R 1904- *ConAu 1R, -5NR*
Caen, Herb 1916- *AuNews 1, ConAu 1R,*
 -1NR
Caesar, Eugene Lee 1927- *MichAu 80*
Caesar, Gene 1927- *ConAu 1R, -1NR*
Caetani, Princess Marguerite 1880-1963
 LongCTC
Cafferty, Bernard 1934- *ConAu 41R*
Caffey, David L 1947- *ConAu 45*
Caffrey, John G 1922- *ConAu 17R*
Caffrey, Kate *ConAu 1NR, -49, IntAu&W 82,*
 WrDr 84
Cagan, Phillip 1927- *WrDr 84*
Cagan, Phillip D 1927- *ConAu 17R*
Cage, John *DrAP&F 83*
Cage, John 1912- *ConAu 9NR, -13R,*
 DcLEL 1940, WorAu 1970, WrDr 84
Cagle, Malcolm W 1918- *ConAu 108,*
 SmATA 32
Cagle, William R 1933- *ConAu 65*
Cagney, Peter 1918- *ConAu X*
Cahalan, Don 1912- *ConAu 102*
Cahalane, Victor H 1901- *ConAu P-2,*
 IntAu&W 82
Cahan, Abraham 1860-1951 *ConAu 108,*
 DcLB 9[port], -25[port], ModAL, TwCA,

 TwCA SUP
Cahen, Alfred B 1932- *ConAu 17R*
Cahen, Oscar 1916-1956 *CreCan 2*
Cahill, Audrey Fawcett 1929- *ConAu 21R,*
 WrDr 84
Cahill, Daniel J 1929- *ConAu 69*
Cahill, Gilbert A 1912- *ConAu 107*
Cahill, James F 1926- *ConAu 1R, -6NR*
Cahill, Jane 1901- *ConAu P-2*
Cahill, Kevin Michael 1936- *ConAu 102*
Cahill, Robert S 1933- *ConAu 13R*
Cahill, Susan Neunzig 1940- *ConAu 37R*
Cahill, Thomas 1940- *ConAu 49*
Cahill, Tom *ConAu X*
Cahn, Edgar S 1935- *ConAu 29R*
Cahn, Irving W 1903- *ConAmTC*
Cahn, Rhoda 1922- *ConAu 81*
Cahn, Robert 1917- *ConAu 108*
Cahn, Sammy 1913- *ASpks, ConAu 85*
Cahn, Steven M 1942- *ConAu 21R*
Cahn, William 1912-1976 *ConAu 21R, -69*
Cahn, Zvi 1896- *ConAu P-2*
Cahnman, Werner J 1902- *ConAu 49*
Caiden, Gerald E 1936- *ConAu 29R*
Caidin, Martin 1927- *AuNews 2, ConAu 1R,*
 -2NR, ConSFA, TwCSFW, WrDr 84
Caiger-Smith, Alan 1930- *ConAu 13R*
Caillavet, Gaston Arman De 1870-1915
 ClDMEL 80
Caillois, Roger 1913-1978 *ConAu 25R, -85*
Caillou, Alan 1914- *ConAu X, TwCCr&M 80,*
 WrDr 84
Cailloux, Andre 1920- *CreCan 2*
Cain, Arthur H 1913- *ConAu 1R, -4NR,*
 SmATA 3
Cain, Bob *ConAu X*
Cain, Christopher *ConAu X, SmATA 8*
Cain, G *WorAu 1970*
Cain, George 1943- *LivgBAA*
Cain, Glen G 1933- *ConAu 21R*
Cain, Guillermo *ConAu X*
Cain, James Mallahan 1892-1977 *AuNews 1,*
 CnMWL, ConAu 8NR, -17R, -73,
 ConLC 3, -11, LongCTC, ModAL, TwCA,
 TwCA SUP, TwCCr&M 80, TwCWr
Cain, Maureen Elizabeth 1938- *ConAu 73*
Cain, Michael Peter 1941- *ConAu 93*
Cain, Michael Scott *DrAP&F 83*
Cain, Robert Owen 1934- *ConAu 65*
Cain, Thomas H 1931- *ConAu 93*
Caine, Sir Hall 1853-1931 *LongCTC, ModBrL,*
 TwCA, TwCA SUP, TwCWr
Caine, Sir Hall 1858-1931 *TwCRGW*
Caine, Jeffrey 1944- *ConAu 85*
Caine, Lynn *ASpks*
Caine, Mark *ConAu X*
Caine, Mitchell *ConAu X*
Caine, Stanley P 1940- *ConAu 41R*
Caine, Sydney 1902- *ConAu P-2*
Caird, George Bradford 1917- *ConAu 61,*
 IntAu&W 82, WrDr 84
Caird, Janet 1913- *WrDr 84*
Caird, Janet Hinshaw 1913- *ConAu 2NR, -49,*
 IntAu&W 82, TwCCr&M 80, TwCRGW

Cairncross, Alec *ConAu X*
Cairncross, Alexander 1911- *WrDr 84*
Cairncross, Sir Alexander Kirkland 1911-
  ConAu 8NR, -61
Cairncross, Frances 1944- *ConAu 57*
Cairncross, John 1913- *IntAu&W 82*
Cairney, John 1930- *ConAu 105*
Cairns, David *IntAu&W 82X*
Cairns, David 1904- *ConAu 11NR, -61,
  IntAu&W 82, WrDr 84*
Cairns, Dorian 1901-1973 *ConAu 37R*
Cairns, Earle E 1910- *ConAu 1R, IntAu&W 82,
  WrDr 84*
Cairns, Grace Edith 1907- *ConAu 1R*
Cairns, Huntington 1904- *ConAu 5NR, -53*
Cairns, James Ford 1914- *ConAu 105, WrDr 84*
Cairns, Jennifer *IntAu&W 82X*
Cairns, John C 1924- *ConAu 5NR, -13R*
Cairns, Patrick *IntAu&W 82X*
Cairns, Thomas W 1931- *ConAu 21R*
Cairns, Trevor 1922- *ConAu 33R,
  IntAu&W 82, SmATA 14, WrDr 84*
Cairo, Jon *ConAu X, IntAu&W 82X*
Caiserman, Ghitta 1923- *CreCan 1*
Caiserman-Roth, Ghitta 1923- *CreCan 1*
Caissa *ConAu X*
Cake, Patrick *ConAu X*
Caks, Aleksandrs 1901-1950 *ClDMEL 80,
  EncWL 2*
Calabrese, Alphonse F X 1923- *ConAu 69*
Calabrese, Anthony 1938- *ConAu 89*
Calabresi, Guido 1932- *ConAu 41R*
Calaferte, Louis 1928- *ConAu 1NR, -45*
Calais, Jean *ConAu X, IntWWP 82X*
Calamandrei, Mauro 1925- *ConAu 69*
Calamari, John D 1921- *ConAu 37R*
Calandrelli Sola, Elsa 1935- *IntWWP 82*
Calasibetta, Charlotte M 1917- *ConAu 103*
Calde, Mark A 1945- *ConAu 69*
Caldecott, Moyra 1927- *ConAu 77, SmATA 22*
Caldecott, Randolph 1846-1886 *SmATA 17*
Calder, Angus 1942- *ConAu 29R, DcLEL 1940,
  IntAu&W 82, WrDr 84*
Calder, C R, Jr. 1928- *ConAu 81*
Calder, Daniel Gillmore 1939- *ConAu 103*
Calder, David Lewis Scott 1946- *IntWWP 82*
Calder, Ethan 1922- *ConAmTC*
Calder, Jason *ConAu X*
Calder, Jenni 1941- *ConAu 1NR, -45*
Calder, Kent E 1948- *ConAu 107*
Calder, Matthew Lewis 1919- *IntAu&W 82,
  WrDr 84*
Calder, Nigel 1931- *ConAu 11NR, WrDr 84*
Calder, Nigel David Ritchie 1931- *ConAu 21R,
  DcLEL 1940*
Calder, Ritchie 1906- *ConAu X, -1R, LongCTC,
  WorAu*
Calder, Robert *ConAu X*
Calder, Robert 1941- *ConAu 69*
Calder, Robert Lorin 1941- *ConAu 65*
Calder-Marshall, Arthur 1908- *ConAu 61,
  ConNov 82, WorAu, WrDr 84*
Calderon, George 1868-1915 *LongCTC*
Calderon, Roberto R *DrAP&F 83*
Calderone, Mary Steichen 1904- *AuNews 1,
  ConAu 104*
Calderwood, Ivan E 1899- *ConAu 57*
Calderwood, James Dixon 1917- *ConAu 3NR,
  -5R*
Calderwood, James Lee 1930- *ConAu 21R,
  WrDr 84*
Caldicott, Helen 1939?- *ConIsC 2[port]*
Caldiero, A F *DrAP&F 83*
Caldwell, Bettye 1924- *ConAu 104*
Caldwell, C Edson 1906-1974 *ConAu P-2*
Caldwell, Edward S 1928- *ConAu 65*
Caldwell, Erskine *DrAP&F 83*
Caldwell, Erskine 1903- *AuNews 1, ConAmA,
  ConAu 1R, -2NR, ConLC 1, -8, -14,
  ConNov 82, DcLB 9[port], EncWL 2,
  IntAu&W 82, LongCTC, ModAL,
  ModAL SUP, TwCA, TwCA SUP,
  TwCWr, WhoTwCL, WrDr 84*
Caldwell, Gaylon L 1920- *ConAu 33R*
Caldwell, Grant 1947- *IntWWP 82*
Caldwell, Harry B 1935- *ConAu 37R*
Caldwell, Helen F 1904- *ConAu 77*
Caldwell, Inga Gilson 1897- *ConAu 61*
Caldwell, Irene Catherine 1908-1979 *ConAu 9R,
  -103*
Caldwell, James *ConAu X*
Caldwell, Janet Taylor 1900- *TwCA,*

Caldwell, John 1928- *ConAu 73*
Caldwell, John Cope 1913- *ConAu 21R,
  SmATA 7*
Caldwell, John Edward 1927- *IntWWP 82*
Caldwell, Joseph H 1934- *ConAu 21R*
Caldwell, Justin *DrAP&F 83*
Caldwell, Kathryn 1942- *ConAu 69*
Caldwell, Louis O 1935- *ConAu 69*
Caldwell, Lynton Keith 1913- *ConAu 29R*
Caldwell, Malcolm 1931- *ConAu 25R*
Caldwell, Marge 1914- *ConAu 97*
Caldwell, Oliver Johnson 1904- *ConAu 37R*
Caldwell, Robert Graham 1904- *ConAu 17R,
  WrDr 84*
Caldwell, Robert Granville 1882-1976 *ConAu 65*
Caldwell, Stratton Franklin 1925- *IntWWP 82*
Caldwell, Taylor 1900- *ConAu 5R, -5NR,
  ConLC 2, LongCTC, TwCRGW, WrDr 84*
Calef, Wesley 1914- *ConAu 13R*
Calender, June 1938- *NatPD 81[port]*
Caley, Rod *ConAu X*
Calhoon, Richard P 1909- *ConAu 57*
Calhoon, Robert M 1935- *ConAu 4NR, -53*
Calhoun, Calfrey C 1928- *ConAu 37R*
Calhoun, Chad *ConAu X*
Calhoun, Daniel F 1929- *ConAu 65*
Calhoun, Don Gilmore 1914- *ConAu 85*
Calhoun, Donald W 1917- *ConAu 104*
Calhoun, Eric *ConAu X*
Calhoun, James Frank 1941- *ConAu 109*
Calhoun, Mary Huiskamp 1926- *ConAu X, -5R,
  SmATA 2*
Calhoun, Richard J 1926- *WrDr 84*
Calhoun, Richard James 1926- *ConAu 33R*
Calhoun, Robert L 1896-1983 *ConAu 110*
Calhoun, Thomas 1940- *ConAu 89*
Calia, Vincent F 1926- *ConAu 53*
Calian, Carnegie Samuel 1933- *ConAu 25R,
  IntAu&W 82, WrDr 84*
Caliban *ConAu X*
Califano, Joseph A, Jr. 1931- *ConAu 2NR, -45,
  WrDr 84*
Calin, William 1936- *ConAu 11NR, -21R*
Calinescu, George 1899-1965 *ClDMEL 80,
  EncWL 2*
Calisher, Hortense *DrAP&F 83*
Calisher, Hortense 1911- *ASpks, ConAu 1R,
  -1NR, ConLC 2, -4, -8, ConNov 82,
  DcLB 2, DcLEL 1940, ModAL SUP,
  TwCWr, WorAu, WrDr 84*
Calitri, Charles *DrAP&F 83*
Calitri, Charles 1916- *WrDr 84*
Calitri, Charles J 1916- *ConAu 5R*
Calitri, Princine *ConAu 33R*
Calkin, Homer Leonard 1912- *ConAu 41R*
Calkin, Ruth Harms 1918- *ConAu 102*
Calkins, A Jean 1933- *IntWWP 82*
Calkins, Fay *ConAu X*
Calkins, Franklin *ConAu X*
Calkins, Jean *DrAP&F 83*
Calkins, Rodello 1920- *ConAu 105*
Call, Alice E LaPlant 1914- *ConAu 13R*
Call, Frank Oliver 1878-1956 *CreCan 1*
Call, Hughie Florence 1890-1969 *ConAu 5R,
  SmATA 1*
Calladine, Andrew G 1941- *ConAu 102*
Calladine, Carole E 1942- *ConAu 102*
Callaghan, Barry 1937- *ConAu 101*
Callaghan, Catherine A 1931- *ConAu 33R*
Callaghan, Morley 1903- *WrDr 84*
Callaghan, Morley Edward 1903- *ConAu 9R,
  ConLC 3, -14, ConNov 82, CreCan 2,
  EncWL 2, LongCTC, ModCmwL, TwCA,
  TwCA SUP, TwCWr, WhoTwCL*
Callahan, Charles C 1910- *ConAu P-2*
Callahan, Claire Wallis 1890- *ConAu 5R*
Callahan, Daniel 1930- *ConAu 21R*
Callahan, John *ConAu X*
Callahan, John F 1912- *ConAu 33R, WrDr 84*
Callahan, Nelson J *WrDr 84*
Callahan, Nelson J 1927- *ConAu 33R*
Callahan, North 1908- *ConAu 1R, -2NR,
  WrDr 84*
Callahan, Philip Serna 1923- *ConAu 102,
  SmATA 25[port]*
Callahan, Raymond 1938- *ConAu 69*
Callahan, Roy 1904- *WrDr 84*
Callahan, Sidney Cornelia 1933- *ConAu 17R*
Callahan, Sterling G 1916- *ConAu 21R*
Callahan, William *WrDr 84*
Callan, Edward T 1917- *ConAu 17R*

Callan, Jamie *DrAP&F 83*
Callan, Jamie 1954- *ConAu 109*
Callan, Michael Feeney 1951- *IntAu&W 82*
Callan, Richard J 1932- *ConAu 53*
Callan, Selma *IntAu&W 82X*
Callander, R N 1933- *IntAu&W 82*
Callard, Maurice 1912- *WrDr 84*
Callard, Maurice Frederic Thomas 1912-
  ConAu 1R, -3NR
Callard, Thomas Henry 1912- *ConAu 9R*
Callas, Theo *ConAu X, WrDr 84*
Callaway, Joseph A 1920- *ConAu 65*
Callaway, Kathy *DrAP&F 83*
Callaway, Kathy 1943- *ConAu 107*
Callcott, George H 1929- *ConAu 29R*
Callcott, Margaret Law 1929- *ConAu 61*
Callen, Larry *ConAu X, SmATA X*
Callen, Lawrence Willard, Jr. 1927- *ConAu 73,
  SmATA 19*
Callen, William B 1930- *ConAu 21R*
Callenbach, Ernest 1929- *ConAu 6NR, -57*
Callender, Charles 1928- *ConAu 41R*
Callender, Julian 1904- *ConAu X*
Callender, Wesley P, Jr. 1923- *ConAu 17R*
Calleo, David P 1934- *ConAu 10NR, -17R*
Callihan, E L 1903- *ConAu P-2*
Callihan, E Lee 1903- *WrDr 84*
Callinan, Bernard J 1913- *WrDr 84*
Callinan, Bernard James 1913- *ConAu 110*
Callis, Helmut G 1906- *ConAu 5NR, -53*
Callis, Robert 1920- *ConAu 37R*
Callison, Brian 1934- *WrDr 84*
Callison, Brian Richard 1934- *ConAu 29R*
Callister, Frank 1916- *ConAu 13R, WrDr 84*
Callmann, Rudolf 1892-1976 *ConAu 65, -69*
Callow, Alexander B, Jr. 1925- *ConAu 21R*
Callow, James T 1928- *ConAu 41R*
Callow, Philip 1924- *WrDr 84*
Callow, Philip Kenneth 1924- *ConAu 6NR, -13R,
  ConNov 82, DcLEL 1940*
Calloway, Doris Howes 1923- *ConAu 21R*
Callum, Myles 1934- *ConAu 9R*
Callwood, June 1924- *ConAu X, IntAu&W 82*
Calman, Alvin R 1895-1983 *ConAu 110*
Calmann, John 1935-1980 *ConAu 21R, -97*
Calmann-Levy, Robert 1899-1982 *ConAu 108*
Calmenson, Stephanie 1952- *ConAu 107*
Calmer, Edgar 1907- *DcLB 4*
Calmer, Ned 1907- *ConAu 69*
Calnan, Thomas Daniel 1915- *ConAu 29R*
Calne, Roy Yorke 1930- *ConAu 61*
Calter, Paul 1934- *ConAu 41R*
Caltofen, Rodolfo 1895- *IntAu&W 82*
Calvert, Barry 1930- *WrDr 84*
Calvert, Elinor H 1929- *ConAu 5R*
Calvert, John *ConAu X, SmATA X,
  TwCA SUP*
Calvert, Laura D 1922- *ConAu 37R*
Calvert, Mary *WrDr 84*
Calvert, Mary 1941- *ConAu 93*
Calvert, Monte A 1938- *ConAu 21R*
Calvert, Patricia 1931- *ConAu 105*
Calvert, Peter 1936- *ConAu 11NR, -25R,
  WrDr 84*
Calvert, Robert, Jr. 1922- *ConAu 25R*
Calverton, Victor Francis 1900-1940 *TwCA*
Calvez, Jean-Yves 1927- *ConAu 57*
Calvin, Henry *ConAu X, IntAu&W 82X,
  WrDr 84*
Calvin, Melvin 1911- *WrDr 84*
Calvin, Ross 1890?-1970 *ConAu 104*
Calvino, Italo 1923- *ClDMEL 80, ConAu 85,
  ConLC 5, -8, -11, -22[port], EncWL 2[port],
  IntAu&W 82, ModRL, TwCSFW A,
  TwCWr, WhoTwCL, WorAu*
Calvo Sotelo, Joaquin 1905- *ClDMEL 80,
  CroCD, IntAu&W 82, ModWD*
Calvocoressi, Peter 1912- *ConAu 65,
  IntAu&W 82, WrDr 84*
Cam, Helen Maud 1885-1968 *ConAu P-1*
Camara, Helder Pessoa 1909- *ConAu 61*
Camara, Laye 1928-1980 *EncWL 2, ModBlW,
  ModFrL*
Camba, Julio 1884-1962 *ClDMEL 80*
Camber, Andrew *ConAu X*
Cambier, Guy 1934- *IntAu&W 82*
Cambon, Glauco 1921- *ConAu 7NR, -17R*
Cambridge, Elizabeth 1893-1949 *LongCTC,
  TwCA, TwCA SUP*
Camejo, Peter Miguel 1939- *ConAu 105*
Camenzind, Jsef Maria 1904- *IntAu&W 82*
Camerini, Mario 1895-1981 *ConAu 103*

Cameron, A J 1920- *ConAu 73*
Cameron, Alan 1938- *ConAu 8NR, -61*
Cameron, Alexander Durand 1924- *IntAu&W 82*
Cameron, Allan Gillies 1930- *ConAu 102, WrDr 84*
Cameron, Allan W 1938- *ConAu 33R*
Cameron, Angus DeMille 1913- *ConAu 102*
Cameron, Angus Fraser 1941-1983 *ConAu 109*
Cameron, Ann 1943- *ConAu 101, SmATA 27[port]*
Cameron, Bella 1918- *IntWWP 82*
Cameron, Betsy 1949- *ConAu 101*
Cameron, Bruce 1913- *ConAu 1R*
Cameron, Constance Carpenter 1937- *ConAu 49*
Cameron, D A *ConAu X*
Cameron, D Y *ConAu X, WrDr 84*
Cameron, David R 1941- *ConAu 73*
Cameron, Donald *ConAu X, WrDr 84*
Cameron, Donald Allan 1937- *ConAu 8NR, -21R*
Cameron, Edna M 1905- *ConAu P-1, SmATA 3*
Cameron, Eleanor 1912- *ChLR 1, ConAu 1R, -2NR, IntAu&W 82, SmATA 1, -25[port], TwCCW 83, WrDr 84*
Cameron, Eleanor Elford 1910- *ConAu 77*
Cameron, Elizabeth *ConAu X, SmATA X*
Cameron, Elizabeth Jane 1910-1976 *ConAu 1R, -1NR, -69, SmATA 30N, -32[port]*
Cameron, Frank T 1909- *ConAu P-1*
Cameron, George Glenn 1905-1979 *ConAu 89*
Cameron, Harold W 1905- *ConAu 81*
Cameron, Helen Graham 1907- *IntAu&W 82*
Cameron, Ian *ConAu X, WrDr 84*
Cameron, Ian 1924- *ConAu X, ConSFA, IntAu&W 82X*
Cameron, J M 1910- *ConAu 2NR, -5R*
Cameron, James 1911- *ConAu 21R, IntAu&W 82, WrDr 84*
Cameron, James Munro 1910- *DcLEL 1940, WrDr 84*
Cameron, James R 1929- *ConAu 33R*
Cameron, James Walter 1911- *DcLEL 1940*
Cameron, Jane *IntAu&W 82X*
Cameron, John *LongCTC*
Cameron, John 1914- *ConAu 29R*
Cameron, Julie *ConAu X*
Cameron, Kate *ConAu X*
Cameron, Kenneth 1922- *ConAu 103, IntAu&W 82*
Cameron, Kenneth Neill 1908- *ConAu 3NR, -9R*
Cameron, Kenneth Walter 1908- *ConAu 8NR, -21R*
Cameron, Kim S 1946- *ConAu 109*
Cameron, Lorna *ConAu X*
Cameron, Lou 1924- *ConAu 1R, -4NR, TwCWW, WrDr 84*
Cameron, Mary Owen 1915- *ConAu 13R*
Cameron, Meribeth E 1905- *ConAu 1R*
Cameron, Norman 1905-1953 *CnMWL, TwCWr, WhoTwCL, WorAu*
Cameron, Polly 1928- *ConAu 17R, SmATA 2*
Cameron, Roderick 1913- *WrDr 84*
Cameron, Rondo 1925- *WrDr 84*
Cameron, Rondo E 1925- *ConAu 1R, -5NR*
Cameron, Silver Donald 1937- *ConAu X, WrDr 84*
Cameron, William Bruce 1920- *ConAu 37R*
Cameron Watt, Donald 1928- *IntAu&W 82*
Camilo, Don *ConAu X*
Cammack, Floyd M 1933- *ConAu 6NR, -9R*
Cammaerts, Emile Leon 1878-1953 *LongCTC, TwCA SUP*
Cammann, Schuyler VanRensselaer 1912- *ConAu 9R*
Cammarata, Jerry F 1947- *ConAu 81, IntAu&W 82*
Cammer, Leonard 1913- *ConAu 65*
Camner, James 1950- *ConAu 108*
Camoin, Francois Andre 1939- *ConAu 61*
Camp, Candace P 1949- *ConAu 102*
Camp, Charles Lewis 1893-1975 *ConAu 61, SmATA 31N*
Camp, Dalton Kingsley 1920- *ConAu 61*
Camp, Fred V 1911- *ConAu 49*
Camp, James *DrAP&F 83*
Camp, James 1923- *ConAu 33R*
Camp, John 1915- *ConAu 93, WrDr 84*
Camp, Roderic 1945- *ConAu 102*
Camp, T Edward 1929- *ConAu 13R*
Camp, Wesley D 1915- *ConAu 17R*
Camp, William Newton Alexander 1926- *ConAu 61*

Campa, Arthur L 1905- *ConAu 73*
Campaigne, Jameson Gilbert 1914- *ConAu 1R*
Campana, Dino 1885-1932 *ClDMEL 80, CnMWL, EncWL 2, ModRL, WhoTwCL, WorAu*
Campanella, Francis B 1936- *ConAu 53*
Campanile, Achille 1899-1976 *CIDMEL 80*
Campanile, Archille 1900?-1977 *ConAu 69*
Campbell, Alan K 1923- *ConAu 3NR, -5R*
Campbell, Albert Angus 1919-1980 *ConAu 105*
Campbell, Alexander 1912-1977 *ConAu 61, -69*
Campbell, Alistair 1907-1974 *ConAu P-1*
Campbell, Alistair 1925- *ConP 80, DcLEL 1940, IntWWP 82, WrDr 84*
Campbell, Angus 1910- *ConAu X, IntAu&W 82X*
Campbell, Ann R 1925- *ConAu 21R, SmATA 11*
Campbell, Anne 1888- *MichAu 80*
Campbell, Archibald Bruce 1881- *ConAu P-1*
Campbell, Arnold Everitt 1906-1980 *ConAu 108*
Campbell, Arthur A 1924- *ConAu 1R*
Campbell, Ballard Crooker, Jr. 1940- *ConAu 104*
Campbell, Beatrice Murphy *ConAu X*
Campbell, Beatrice Murphy 1908- *ConAu X*
Campbell, Bernard G 1930- *ConAu 21R*
Campbell, Blanche 1902- *ConAu 5R*
Campbell, Bridget *WrDr 84*
Campbell, Bruce *ConAu X, SmATA X, -1*
Campbell, Camilla 1905- *ConAu P-2, SmATA 26[port]*
Campbell, Carlos Cardozo 1937- *ConAu 102*
Campbell, Charles Arthur 1897-1974 *ConAu 49*
Campbell, Charles S 1911- *ConAu 69*
Campbell, Clive *ConAu X*
Campbell, Clyde Crane *IntAu&W 82X*
Campbell, Colin Dearborn 1917- *ConAu 33R*
Campbell, Cy 1925- *ConAu 97*
Campbell, David 1915-1979 *ConAu 97, ConP 80, DcLEL 1940, WorAu*
Campbell, David A 1927- *ConAu 11NR, -25R*
Campbell, David P 1934- *ConAu 21R*
Campbell, Dennis M 1945- *ConAu 73*
Campbell, Donald 1940- *ConAu 69, ConP 80, WrDr 84*
Campbell, Donald Guy 1922- *ConAu 17R*
Campbell, Douglas 1922- *CreCan 1*
Campbell, Douglas G *DrAP&F 83*
Campbell, E G 1923- *ConAu 107*
Campbell, E Simms 1906-1971 *ConAu 93*
Campbell, Edward D C, Jr. 1946- *ConAu 106*
Campbell, Edward F, Jr. 1932- *ConAu 13R*
Campbell, Elizabeth McClure 1891- *ConAu 37R, WrDr 84*
Campbell, Enid 1932- *ConAu 109*
Campbell, Ernest Q 1926- *ConAu 37R*
Campbell, Eugene Edward 1915- *ConAu 21R*
Campbell, Ewing *DrAP&F 83*
Campbell, Ewing 1940- *ConAu 73*
Campbell, F Gregory, Jr. 1939- *ConAu 69*
Campbell, Francis Stuart *ConAu X, IntAu&W 82X, WrDr 84*
Campbell, G S 1940- *ConAu 107, WrDr 84*
Campbell, Gabrielle Margaret Vere 1886-1952 *LongCTC*
Campbell, George 1916- *ConP 80, WrDr 84*
Campbell, George F 1915- *WrDr 84*
Campbell, George Frederick 1915- *ConAu 65*
Campbell, Grace 1895-1963 *CreCan 1*
Campbell, Graeme 1931- *ConAu 77*
Campbell, Hannah *ConAu 9R*
Campbell, Herbert James 1925- *ConAu 97, WrDr 84*
Campbell, Hope *ConAu 61, SmATA 20*
Campbell, Hope 1925- *ConAu 10NR*
Campbell, Howard E 1925- *ConAu 7NR, -57*
Campbell, Ian 1899-1978 *ConAu 103, -53*
Campbell, Ian 1942- *ConAu 9NR, -65, IntAu&W 82, WrDr 84*
Campbell, Ian Barclay 1916- *WrDr 84*
Campbell, J Arthur 1916- *ConAu 53*
Campbell, J Ramsey 1946- *ConAu 9R, WrDr 84*
Campbell, Jack K 1927- *ConAu 21R*
Campbell, James 1920- *ConAu 57*
Campbell, James E 1945- *ConAu 107*
Campbell, James Marshall 1895-1977 *ConAu 69, -73*
Campbell, Jane *ConAu X, SmATA X*
Campbell, Jane 1934- *ConAu 41R*
Campbell, Jeff H 1931- *ConAu 41R*
Campbell, Jeffrey *ConAu X*

Campbell, Jeremy 1931- *ConAu 109*
Campbell, Joan 1929- *ConAu 109*
Campbell, Joanna *ConAu X*
Campbell, John Coert 1911- *ConAu 1R, -3NR*
Campbell, John Franklin 1940?-1971 *ConAu 33R*
Campbell, John Lorne 1906- *ConAu 29R*
Campbell, John R 1933- *ConAu 53*
Campbell, John W, Jr. 1910-1971 *ConAu 29R, ConAu P-2, ConSFA, DcLB 8[port], TwCSFW, WorAu*
Campbell, Joseph 1904- *ConAu 1R, -3NR, TwCA SUP*
Campbell, Judith 1914- *ConAu X, IntAu&W 82X, WrDr 84*
Campbell, Karen *ConAu X, TwCRGW, WrDr 84*
Campbell, Karlyn Kohrs 1937- *ConAu 4NR, -53*
Campbell, Keith 1938- *ConAu 106*
Campbell, Keith Oliver 1920- *ConAu 110*
Campbell, Mrs. Kemper *ConAu X*
Campbell, Ken 1941- *ConAu 77*
Campbell, Kenneth 1901?-1979 *ConAu 85*
Campbell, Lawrence James 1931- *ConAu 106, WrDr 84*
Campbell, Litta Belle 1886-1980 *ConAu 5R, -5NR*
Campbell, Luke *ConAu X*
Campbell, Malcolm J 1930- *ConAu 6NR, -57*
Campbell, Margaret *ConAu 69*
Campbell, Margaret 1916- *ConAu 106, WrDr 84*
Campbell, Maria 1940- *ConAu 102*
Campbell, Marjorie Wilkins 1901- *ConAu 97*
Campbell, Michael Mussen 1924- *ConAu 102*
Campbell, Nancy A 1930- *MichAu 80*
Campbell, Oscar James 1879-1970 *ConAu 29R*
Campbell, Patricia J 1930- *ConAu 103*
Campbell, Patricia Piatt 1901- *ConAu 25R*
Campbell, Patrick 1913- *DcLEL 1940*
Campbell, Mrs. Patrick 1865-1940 *LongCTC*
Campbell, Patrick Gordon 1913-1980 *ConAu 102*
Campbell, Patty *ConAu X*
Campbell, Paul Newell 1923- *ConAu 21R, WrDr 84*
Campbell, Penelope 1935- *ConAu 33R*
Campbell, Peter 1926- *ConAu 11NR, ConAu P-1*
Campbell, Peter Anthony 1935- *ConAu 21R*
Campbell, Peter Walter 1926- *WrDr 84*
Campbell, R J 1867-1956 *LongCTC*
Campbell, R T *ConAu X*
Campbell, R W *ConAu X, SmATA 1*
Campbell, R Wright 1927- *ConAu 6NR, -57*
Campbell, Ramsey 1946- *ConAu 7NR, -57, IntAu&W 82*
Campbell, Randolph B 1940- *ConAu 41R*
Campbell, Rex R 1931- *ConAu 41R*
Campbell, Rita Ricardo 1920- *ConAu 57*
Campbell, Robert 1922-1977 *ConAu 8NR, -53, -73*
Campbell, Robert 1926- *WrDr 84*
Campbell, Robert B 1923- *ConAu 69*
Campbell, Robert C 1924- *ConAu 49*
Campbell, Robert Dale 1914- *ConAu 9R*
Campbell, Robert Wellington 1926- *ConAu 1R, -3NR*
Campbell, Rosemae Wells 1909- *ConAu 13R, SmATA 1*
Campbell, Roy 1901?-1957 *CnMWL, ConAu 104, EncWL 2, LongCTC, ModBrL, ModBrL SUP, ModCmwL, TwCA, TwCA SUP, TwCLC 5[port], TwCWr, WhoTwCL*
Campbell, Sheldon 1919- *ConAu 41R*
Campbell, Stanley W 1926- *ConAu 49*
Campbell, Stephen K 1935- *ConAu 49*
Campbell, Thomas F 1924- *ConAu 21R*
Campbell, Thomas M 1936- *ConAu 49*
Campbell, Walter Stanley 1887-1957 *TwCA, TwCA SUP*
Campbell, Wilfred 1858-1918 *ConAu X, CreCan 2*
Campbell, Wilfred 1861?-1918? *TwCLC 9[port]*
Campbell, Will D 1924- *ConAu 5R, -7NR*
Campbell, William 1858?-1918 *ConAu 106*
Campbell, William Edward March 1893-1954 *ConAmA, ConAu 108, TwCA SUP*
Campbell, William Wilfred 1861?-1918? *CreCan 2*
Campbell-Johnson, Alan 1913- *ConAu 65*
Campbell-Purdie, Wendy 1925- *ConAu 21R*
Campen, Richard N 1912- *ConAu 69*

Carmi, T 1925- *ConAu X, WorAu 1970*
Carmichael, Ann *ConAu X*
Carmichael, Calum M 1938- *ConAu 53*
Carmichael, D R 1941- *ConAu 33R*
Carmichael, Franklin 1890-1945 *CreCan 2*
Carmichael, Fred 1924- *ConAu 10NR*
Carmichael, Fred Walker 1924- *ConAu 17R, WrDr 84*
Carmichael, Harry 1908-1979 *ConAu X, TwCCr&M 80*
Carmichael, Hoagland Howard 1899-1981 *ConAu 108*
Carmichael, Hoagy *ConAu X*
Carmichael, Joel 1915- *ConAu 1R, -2NR*
Carmichael, Leonard 1898-1973 *ConAu 41R, -45*
Carmichael, Oliver Cromwell 1891-1966 *ConAu P-1*
Carmichael, Peter A 1897- *ConAu P-2*
Carmichael, Stokely 1941- *ConAu 57*
Carmichael, Thomas N 1919-1972 *ConAu P-2*
Carmichael, William Edward 1922- *ConAu 37R, WrDr 84*
Carmilly, Moshe 1908- *ConAu 41R*
Carmines, Al 1936- *ConAu 103, ConDr 82D*
Carmody, Denise Lardner 1935- *ConAu 93*
Carmody, Jay 1900?-1973 *ConAu 41R*
Carmoy, Guy De 1907- *ConAu 89*
Carnac, Carol *ConAu X*
Carnac, Carol 1894-1958 *TwCCr&M 80*
Carnahan, Walter Hervey 1891- *ConAu P-1*
Carnall, Geoffrey Douglas 1927- *ConAu 13R, WrDr 84*
Carnap, Rudolf P 1891-1970 *ConAu 29R, ConAu P-1, WorAu*
Carnegie, Andrew 1835-1919 *LongCTC*
Carnegie, Dale 1888-1955 *LongCTC*
Carnegie, Dorothy Vanderpool *AuNews 1*
Carnegie, Raymond Alexander 1920- *ConAu 11NR, -21R*
Carnegie, Sacha *ConAu X*
Carnegy, Patrick 1940- *ConAu 81*
Carnell, Corbin Scott 1929- *ConAu 10NR, -65*
Carnell, E J 1912-1972 *ConAu X*
Carnell, Edward John 1919-1967 *ConAu P-1*
Carnell, John 1912-1972 *ConAu 104, -25R, ConSFA*
Carner, Josep 1884-1970 *CIDMEL 80*
Carner, Mosco 1904- *ConAu P-1, IntAu&W 82, WrDr 84*
Carnero, Guillermo 1947- *IntAu&W 82*
Carnes, Conrad D 1936- *ConAu 85*
Carnes, Paul N 1921-1979 *ConAu 85*
Carnes, Ralph L 1931- *ConAu 33R*
Carnes, Valerie Folts-Bohanan 1945- *ConAu 33R*
Carnevali, Doris L *ConAu 69*
Carney, James 1914- *ConAu 21R*
Carney, John J, Jr. 1932- *ConAu 69*
Carney, John Otis 1922- *ConAu 1R, -3NR*
Carney, Matthew 1922- *ConAu 108*
Carney, Richard E 1929- *WrDr 84*
Carney, Richard Edward 1929- *ConAu 37R*
Carney, T F 1931- *ConAu 1NR, -49*
Carney, W Alderman 1922- *ConAu 25R*
Carnicelli, D D 1931- *ConAu 61*
Carnochan, W B 1930- *ConAu 33R, WrDr 84*
Carnot, Joseph B 1941- *ConAu 45*
Carnoy, Martin 1938- *ConAu 10NR, -65*
Carnwath, Joan Gertrude 1920- *IntAu&W 82*
Caro, Francis G 1936- *ConAu 11NR, -69*
Caro, Robert A *ConAu 101, WrDr 84*
Caro Baroja, Julio 1914- *CIDMEL 80*
Caroe, Olaf Kirkpatrick 1892-1981 *ConAu 105, IntAu&W 82*
Caroe, Olaf Kirkpatrick 1892-1982 *ConAu 109*
Carol, Bill J *ConAu X, SmATA X, WrDr 84*
Carol, Jacqueline *ConAu X*
Caroll, Nonie 1926- *ConAu 103*
Caron, Paul 1874-1941 *CreCan 1*
Caron, Roger 1938- *ConAu 89*
Carona, Philip Ben 1925- *ConAu 1R, -4NR*
Caronia, Guiseppe 1884?-1977 *ConAu 69*
Caroselli, Remus F 1916- *ConAu 97*
Carossa, Hans 1878-1956 *CIDMEL 80, EncWL 2[port], ModGL, TwCA, TwCA SUP, TwCWr*
Carosso, Vincent Phillip 1922- *ConAu 3NR, -9R*
Carothers, J Edward 1907- *ConAu 41R*
Carothers, Robert L *DrAP&F 83*
Carothers, Robert Lee 1942- *ConAu 45*
Carousso, Georges 1909- *ConAu 89*
Carozzi, Albert Victor 1925- *ConAu 53*
Carp, Frances Merchant 1918- *ConAu 21R*

Carpelan, Bo 1926- *ConAu 2NR, -49, EncWL 2, IntAu&W 82, IntWWP 82, SmATA 8*
Carpenter, Allan 1917- *ConAu 3NR, -9R, SmATA 3, WrDr 84*
Carpenter, Andrew 1943- *ConAu 93*
Carpenter, Charles A 1929- *ConAu 33R*
Carpenter, Clarence Ray 1905-1975 *ConAu 57*
Carpenter, Don *DrAP&F 83*
Carpenter, Don 1931- *ConAu 1NR, -45*
Carpenter, Duffy *ConAu X, TwCCr&M 80*
Carpenter, Edward 1844-1929 *LongCTC, ModBrL, WhoTwCL*
Carpenter, Elizabeth Sutherland 1920- *ConAu 41R*
Carpenter, Elmer J *ConSFA*
Carpenter, Frances 1890-1972 *ConAu 4NR, -5R, -37R, SmATA 27N, -3*
Carpenter, Francis Ross 1925- *ConAu 101*
Carpenter, Fred *ConAu X, -X*
Carpenter, Frederic I 1903- *WrDr 84*
Carpenter, Frederic Ives 1903- *ConAu 5R*
Carpenter, Humphrey 1946- *ConAu 89, WrDr 84*
Carpenter, James A 1928- *ConAu 37R*
Carpenter, John 1936- *ConAu 65*
Carpenter, John A 1921-1978 *ConAu 9R, -77*
Carpenter, John Jo *ConAu X, TwCWW*
Carpenter, John R 1936- *ConAu 9NR*
Carpenter, John Randell *DrAP&F 83*
Carpenter, John Randell 1936- *IntWWP 82*
Carpenter, Joyce Frances 1926- *ConAu 33R*
Carpenter, L P 1940- *WrDr 84*
Carpenter, Liz *ConAu X*
Carpenter, Margaret Haley *ConAu 5R, IntAu&W 82, IntWWP 82*
Carpenter, Marjorie 1896- *ConAu 45*
Carpenter, Nan Cooke 1912- *ConAu 25R, WrDr 84*
Carpenter, Patricia 1920- *ConAu 29R, SmATA 11*
Carpenter, Peter 1922- *ConAu 13R*
Carpenter, Rhys 1889-1980 *ConAu 57, -93*
Carpenter, Richard C 1916- *ConAu 13R*
Carpenter, William *DrAP&F 83*
Carpenter, William 1940- *ConAu 106, IntWWP 82*
Carpentier, Alejo 1904-1980 *ConAu 11NR, -65, -97, ConLC 8, -11, EncWL 2, ModLAL, TwCWr, WorAu*
Carper, Jean Elinor 1932- *ConAu 7NR, -17R*
Carper, L Dean 1931- *ConAu 49*
Carpozi, George, Jr. 1920- *ConAu 11NR, -13R*
Carr, A H Z 1902-1971 *ConAu X, TwCCr&M 80*
Carr, Albert H Z 1902-1971 *ConAu 1R, -1NR, -33R*
Carr, Archie F 1909- *ConAu 13R*
Carr, Arthur C 1918- *ConAu 37R*
Carr, Arthur Japheth 1914- *ConAu 57*
Carr, Catharine *ConAu X, WrDr 84*
Carr, Dan *DrAP&F 83, IntWWP 82X*
Carr, Daniel Paul 1951- *IntWWP 82*
Carr, David William 1911- *ConAu 37R*
Carr, Donald Eaton 1903- *ConAu 13R*
Carr, Dorothy Stevenson Laird 1912- *ConAu 9R*
Carr, E H 1892- *LongCTC, WrDr 84*
Carr, Edward Hallet 1892- *ConAu 61*
Carr, Edward Hallet 1892-1982 *ConAu 108*
Carr, Edward Hallett 1892- *TwCA SUP*
Carr, Edwin George 1937- *ConAu 61*
Carr, Emily 1871-1945 *CreCan 1, DcLEL 1940, LongCTC*
Carr, Eugenie Waddell 1946- *ConAmTC*
Carr, Francis 1924- *WrDr 84*
Carr, Glyn 1908- *ConAu X, SmATA X, TwCCr&M 80, WrDr 84*
Carr, Gwen B 1924- *ConAu 41R*
Carr, Harriett Helen 1899- *ConAu P-1, MichAu 80, SmATA 3*
Carr, Ian 1933- *ConAu 110*
Carr, J L 1912- *ConAu 102, WrDr 84*
Carr, Janet Baker *ConAu X*
Carr, Jay Phillip 1936- *ConAmTC, ConAu 89*
Carr, Jess 1930- *ConAu 29R, WrDr 84*
Carr, Jo Crisler 1926- *ConAu 21R, WrDr 84*
Carr, John C 1929- *ConAu 53*
Carr, John Dickson 1905- *ConLC 3, LongCTC, TwCA, TwCA SUP*
Carr, John Dickson 1906-1977 *ConAu 3NR, -49, -69, TwCCr&M 80, TwCWr*
Carr, John Geoffrey 1927- *WrDr 84*

Carr, John Laurence 1916- *ConAu 49*
Carr, Lois Green 1922- *ConAu 61*
Carr, Margaret 1935- *ConAu 105, TwCCr&M 80, WrDr 84*
Carr, Mary Jane 1899- *ConAu P-1, SmATA 2*
Carr, Michael Harold 1935- *ConAu 109*
Carr, Pat *DrAP&F 83*
Carr, Pat M 1932- *ConAu 65*
Carr, Philippa *ConAu X, TwCRGW, WrDr 84*
Carr, Raymond 1919- *ConAu 8NR, -17R, WrDr 84*
Carr, Robert Kenneth 1908-1979 *ConAu 85, -93*
Carr, Roberta *ConAu X, TwCRGW, WrDr 84*
Carr, Robyn *TwCRGW, WrDr 84*
Carr, Stephen L *ConAu 57*
Carr, Terry 1937- *ConAu 81, ConSFA, TwCSFW, WrDr 84*
Carr, Virginia Mason *ConAu X*
Carr, Virginia Spencer 1929- *ConAu 61*
Carr, Warren Tyree 1917- *ConAu 5R*
Carr, William 1921- *ConAu 73*
Carr, William George 1901- *ConAu 53, WrDr 84*
Carr, William H A 1924- *ConAu 7NR, -13R*
Carr-Saunders, Alexander Morris 1886-1966 *ConAu 1R, -103*
Carraco, Carol Crowe *ConAu X*
Carranco, Lynwood 1921- *ConAu 6NR*
Carranco, Lynwood 1922- *ConAu 57*
Carras, Mary C *ConAu 85*
Carrasquer, F 1915- *IntAu&W 82*
Carre Sanchez, Maria DelPilar 1921- *IntAu&W 82*
Carrel, Alexis 1873-1944 *TwCA SUP*
Carrel, Mark 1916- *ConAu X*
Carrell, Alexis 1873-1944 *TwCA*
Carrell, Norman Gerald 1905- *ConAu P-2, IntAu&W 82, WrDr 84*
Carrera Andrade, Jorge 1902-1978 *ModLAL*
Carrera Andrade, Jorge 1903-1978 *ConAu 85, EncWL 2, TwCA SUP[port]*
Carrere, Helene Marie 1912- *IntWWP 82*
Carrick, A B *ConAu X*
Carrick, Carol 1935- *ConAu 1NR, -45, SmATA 7*
Carrick, Donald 1929- *ConAu 5NR, -53, MichAu 80, SmATA 7*
Carrick, Edward *ConAu X, WrDr 84*
Carrick, John *ConAu X, IntAu&W 82X*
Carrick, Malcolm 1945- *ConAu 77, IntAu&W 82, SmATA 28[port], WrDr 84*
Carrie, Jacques *DrAP&F 83*
Carrier, Constance *DrAP&F 83*
Carrier, Constance 1908- *ConAu 33R, IntWWP 82, WrDr 84*
Carrier, Esther Jane 1925- *ConAu 17R*
Carrier, Jean-Guy 1945- *ConAu 101*
Carrier, Louis-Georges 1927- *CreCan 2*
Carrier, Roch 1937- *ConLC 13, ModCmwL*
Carrier, Roch 1938- *CreCan 2*
Carrier, Warren *DrAP&F 83*
Carrier, Warren 1918- *ConAu 3NR, -9R, IntWWP 82, WrDr 84*
Carrigan, Andrew G *DrAP&F 83*
Carrigan, Andrew G 1935- *ConAu 1NR, -45, IntWWP 82, MichAu 80*
Carrigan, D Owen 1933- *ConAu 25R*
Carrighar, Sally 1905?- *ConAu 93, SmATA 24[port]*
Carriker, Robert C 1940- *ConAu 69*
Carrillo, Lawrence W 1920- *ConAu 13R, WrDr 84*
Carringer, Robert L 1941- *ConAu 97*
Carrington, Charles Edmund 1897- *ConAu 5R, IntAu&W 82, WrDr 84*
Carrington, Frank G 1936- *ConAu 57*
Carrington, Glenda *DrAP&F 83*
Carrington, Grant *DrAP&F 83*
Carrington, Grant 1938- *ConAu 104*
Carrington, Harold 1938-1964 *LivgBAA*
Carrington, Molly 1908- *ConAu X*
Carrington, Noel Lewis 1894- *IntAu&W 82*
Carrington, Paul Dewitt 1931- *ConAu 29R, WrDr 84*
Carrington, Richard 1921- *ConAu 9R*
Carrington, William Langley 1900-1970 *ConAu P-1*
Carris, Joan Davenport 1938- *ConAu 106*
Carrison, Daniel J 1917- *ConAu 37R*
Carrithers, David W 1943- *ConAu 110*
Carrithers, Gale H, Jr. 1932- *ConAu 41R*

Cartmill, Cleve 1908-1964 *TwCSFW*
Cartnal, Alan 1950- *ConAu 105*
Cartner, William Carruthers 1910- *ConAu 73,*
SmATA 11
Carton, R C 1856-1928 *LongCTC*
Cartosio, Emma De *IntWWP 82*
Cartter, Allan Murray 1922-1976 *ConAu 5R,*
-8NR
Cartwright, Desmond S 1924- *ConAu 89*
Cartwright, Gary 1934- *ConAu 89*
Cartwright, James McGregor *ConAu X*
Cartwright, Joseph H 1939- *ConAu 73*
Cartwright, N *ConAu X*
Cartwright, Rosalind Dymond 1922- *ConAu 81*
Cartwright, Sally 1923- *ConAu 2NR, -49,*
SmATA 9
Cartwright, William H 1915- *ConAu 9R*
Carty, James William, Jr. 1925- *ConAu 53*
Caruba, Alan 1937- *ConAu 65*
Carus, Paul 1852-1919 *TwCA*
Carus-Wilson, Eleanora Mary 1897- *ConAu 5R*
Caruso, John Anthony 1907- *ConAu 33R,*
WrDr 84
Caruth, Donald L 1935- *ConAu 29R*
Carvajal, Ricardo *ConAu X*
Carvalho, Maria Judite De 1921- *ClDMEL 80*
Carvalho, Raul Maria De 1920- *IntWWP 82*
Carvalho, Ronald De 1893-1935 *ModLAL*
Carvalho-Neto, Paulo De 1923- *ConAu 4NR, -53,*
IntAu&W 82
Carvel, Shane *IntWWP 82X*
Carvell, Fred J 1934- *ConAu 29R*
Carver, Dave *ConAu X, TwCWW*
Carver, Frank G 1928- *ConAu 49*
Carver, Fred D 1936- *ConAu 29R*
Carver, Jeffrey A *DrAP&F 83*
Carver, Jeffrey A 1949- *ConAu 101*
Carver, John *ConAu X, -X, SmATA X*
Carver, Michael 1915- *ConAu 69,*
IntAu&W 82, WrDr 84
Carver, Norman Francis, Jr. 1928- *ConAu 41R,*
WrDr 84
Carver, Raymond *DrAP&F 83*
Carver, Raymond 1938- *ConAu 33R,*
ConLC 22[port], IntAu&W 82
Carver, Saxon Rowe 1905- *ConAu P-1*
Carvic, Heron d1980 *ConAu 103, -53,*
TwCCr&M 80
Cary *SmATA X*
Cary, Barbara Knapp 1912?-1975 *ConAu 61,*
SmATA 31N
Cary, Bob 1921- *ConAu 105*
Cary, Carl *DrAP&F 83*
Cary, Diana Serra *ConAu 57*
Cary, Harold Whiting 1903- *ConAu P-1*
Cary, James Donald 1919- *ConAu 5R*
Cary, John H 1926- *ConAu 9R*
Cary, Joyce 1888-1957 *CnMWL, ConAu 104,*
DcLB 15[port], EncWL 2[port], LongCTC,
ModBrL, ModBrL SUP, TwCA SUP,
TwCLC 1, TwCWr, WhoTwCL
Cary, Jud *ConAu X, WrDr 84*
Cary, Lee J 1925- *ConAu 29R*
Cary, Louis F 1915- *SmATA 9*
Cary, Lucian 1886-1971 *ConAu 33R*
Cary, Otis 1921- *ConAu 61, IntAu&W 82*
Cary, Peggy-Jean Montgomery 1918- *ConAu 57*
Cary, Richard 1909- *ConAu 21R, WrDr 84*
Cary, William L 1910-1983 *ConAu 109*
Cary, Zenja Saft 1932?-1983 *ConAu 110*
Caryl, Jean *ConAu X, SmATA X*
Caryl, Warren 1920- *ConAu 21R*
Cas-Ka-B *IntAu&W 82X*
Casaccia, Gabriel 1907- *ModLAL*
Casada, James A 1942- *ConAu 109*
Casado, Demetrio 1923- *IntAu&W 82*
Casado, Pablo Gil 1931- *ConAu 49*
Casady, Cort 1947- *ConAu 105*
Casady, Donald Rex 1926- *ConAu 13R*
Casalandra, Estelle *ConAu X*
Casale, Joan T 1935- *ConAu 61*
Casale, Ottavio M 1934- *ConAu 104*
Casals, Pablo 1876-1973 *ConAu X*
Casals, Pau Carlos Salvador Defillo De 1876-1973
ConAu 45, -93
Casanova Villar, Francisco 1923- *IntAu&W 82*
Casberg, Melvin Augustus 1909- *ConAu 104*
Casciani, Eda Maria 1932- *IntWWP 82*
Cascio, Chuck 1946- *ConAu 93*
Casdorph, Herman Richard 1928- *ConAu 101*
Casdorph, Paul D 1932- *ConAu 106*
Case, Brian David 1937- *ConAu 25R*

Case, David *WrDr 84*
Case, David 1937- *ConAu 107, TwCRGW*
Case, Elinor Rutt 1914- *ConAu 1R*
Case, Fred E 1918- *ConAu 4NR, -5R*
Case, Geoffrey *ConAu 77*
Case, Jack Gaylord 1918?-1970 *ConAu 104*
Case, John *DrAP&F 83*
Case, Josephine Young 1907- *ConAu P-2*
Case, Justin *ConAu X*
Case, L L *ConAu X*
Case, Leland Davidson 1900- *ConAu 17R*
Case, Leonard L 1900- *MichAu 80*
Case, Lynn M 1903- *ConAu 13R*
Case, Marshal T 1941- *ConAu 57, SmATA 9*
Case, Maurice 1910-1968 *ConAu P-2*
Case, Michael *ConAu X, SmATA 5*
Case, Patricia J 1952- *ConAu 110*
Case, Robert Ormond 1895- *TwCWW*
Case, Victoria 1897- *ConAu 5R*
Case, Walter 1900?-1983 *ConAu 110*
Casebier, Allan 1934- *ConAu 65*
Casebier, Virginia 1918- *ConAu 41R*
Caseleyr, Camille Auguste Marie 1909-
ConAu P-1
Casement, Richard 1942-1982 *ConAu 108*
Casemore, Robert 1915- *ConAu 73*
Casewit, Curtis W 1922- *ConAu 6NR, -13R,*
ConSFA, SmATA 4
Casey Jones d1900 *LongCTC*
Casey, Bill H 1930- *ConAu 1R*
Casey, Brigid 1950- *ConAu 49, SmATA 9*
Casey, Daniel J 1937- *ConAu 6NR, -57*
Casey, Deb *DrAP&F 83*
Casey, Edward Scott 1939- *ConAu 102*
Casey, Gavin S 1907- *TwCWr*
Casey, Gladys *ConAu X*
Casey, Jane Barnes 1942- *ConAu 104*
Casey, John *ConLC 15*
Casey, John Dudley *DrAP&F 83*
Casey, John Dudley 1939- *ConAu 69*
Casey, Juanita 1925- *ConAu 49,*
DcLB 14[port]
Casey, Kevin 1940- *ConAu 25R, WrDr 84*
Casey, Lawrence B 1905-1977 *ConAu 69, -73*
Casey, Mart *ConAu X*
Casey, Michael *DrAP&F 83*
Casey, Michael 1947- *ConAu 65, ConLC 2,*
ConP 80, DcLB 5[port], IntAu&W 82,
WrDr 84
Casey, Michael T 1922- *ConAu 21R*
Casey, Patrick *ConAu X*
Casey, Richard Gardiner 1890-1976 *ConAu 61,*
-65
Casey, Robert Joseph 1890-1962 *ConAu 89*
Casey, Rosemary 1904-1976 *ConAu 65*
Casey, Rosemary Alice 1922- *ConAu 5R*
Casey, Thomas Francis 1923- *ConAu 13R*
Casey, W Wilson 1954- *ConAu 107*
Casey, Warren 1935- *ConAu 101, ConDr 82D*
Casey, William VanEtten 1914- *ConAu 57*
Casgrain, Therese 1896?-1981 *ConAu 108*
Casgrain, Therese F 1896?-1981 *ConAu 110*
Cash, Anthony 1933- *ConAu 102, WrDr 84*
Cash, Arthur H 1922- *ConAu 110*
Cash, Grace 1915- *ConAu 21R, WrDr 84*
Cash, Grady *ConAu X*
Cash, James Allan 1901- *ConAu 4NR, -5R*
Cash, John R *ConAu X*
Cash, Johnny 1932- *ConAu 110*
Cash, Joseph Harper 1927- *ConAu 41R*
Cash, Kevin 1926- *ConAu 77*
Cash, Peter Maurice 1949- *IntWWP 82*
Cash, Philip 1931- *ConAu 106*
Cash, Sebastian *ConAu X*
Cash, Wilbur Joseph 1901-1941 *WorAu*
Cashin, Edward J 1927- *ConAu 9NR*
Cashin, Edward L *ConAu X*
Cashin, Edward L 1927- *ConAu 21R*
Cashin, James A 1911- *ConAu 17R, WrDr 84*
Cashin, James A 1911-1982 *ConAu 10NR*
Cashman, John *ConAu X*
Cashman, Paul Harrison 1924- *ConAu 13R*
Cashman, Sean Dennis 1943- *ConAu X*
Cashorali, Peter *DrAP&F 83*
Casiano, Americo *DrAP&F 83*
Caskey, John Langdon 1908- *ConAu 13R,*
IntAu&W 82
Casler, Lawrence 1932- *ConAu 49*
Casmier, Adam A 1934- *ConAu 33R*
Casmir, Fred L 1928- *ConAu 37R*
Casner, A James 1907- *ConAu 4NR, -5R*
Caso, Adolph 1934- *ConAu 7NR, -57*

Cason, Mabel Earp 1892-1965 *ConAu P-1,*
SmATA 10
Casona, Alejandro 1903-1965 *ClDMEL 80,*
CnMD, ConAu X, CroCD, EncWL 2,
ModWD, TwCWr
Casotti, Fred 1923- *ConAu 93*
Caspari, Ernest W 1909- *ConAu 41R*
Caspary, Vera 1899- *ConAu 9NR,*
IntAu&W 82, WrDr 84
Caspary, Vera 1904- *ConAu 13R, LongCTC,*
TwCA SUP, TwCCr&M 80
Casper, Barry M 1939- *ConAu 69*
Casper, Henry W 1909- *ConAu 37R*
Casper, Jonathan D 1942- *ConAu 53*
Casper, Joseph Andrew 1941- *ConAu 65*
Casper, Leonard 1923- *WrDr 84*
Casper, Leonard Ralph 1923- *ConAu 1R*
Casper, Linda Ty *ConAu X*
Casque, Sammy *ConAu X*
Casriel, H Daniel 1924- *ConAu 13R*
Casriel, H Daniel 1924-1983 *ConAu 110*
Cass, Carl Bartholomew 1901- *ConAu P-1*
Cass, James 1915- *ConAu 101*
Cass, Joan Evelyn *ConAu 1R, -5NR,*
SmATA 1, WrDr 84
Cass, Ronald A 1949- *ConAu 106*
Cass, Thomas 1931- *WrDr 84*
Cass, Zoe *TwCRGW, WrDr 84*
Cassady, Carolyn 1923- *DcLB 16[port]*
Cassady, Neal 1926-1968 *DcLB 16[port]*
Cassady, Ralph, Jr. 1900-1978 *ConAu 1R, -4NR,*
-77
Cassandra 1909-1967 *ConAu X, LongCTC*
Cassara, Ernest 1925- *ConAu 41R*
Cassavetes, John 1929- *ConAu 85, ConDr 82A,*
ConLC 20
Cassedy, James H 1919- *ConAu 1R, WrDr 84*
Cassedy, Sylvia 1930- *ConAu 105,*
SmATA 27[port]
Cassel, Don 1942- *ConAu 110*
Cassel, Lili 1924- *SmATA X*
Cassel, Mana-Zucca 1891-1981 *ConAu 103*
Cassel, Russell N 1911- *ConAu 37R,*
IntAu&W 82, WrDr 84
Cassel, Virginia Cunningham *ConAu 105*
Cassell, Frank Allan 1941- *ConAu 33R*
Cassell, Frank Hyde 1916- *ConAu 37R*
Cassell, Richard Allan 1921- *ConAu 21R*
Cassell, Sylvia 1924- *ConAu 5R*
Cassells, John *ConAu X*
Casselman, Karen Leigh 1942- *ConAu 107*
Cassels, Alan 1929- *ConAu 33R, WrDr 84*
Cassels, John *TwCCr&M 80*
Cassels, Louis 1922-1974 *ConAu 4NR, -9R, -45*
Casseres *TwCA, TwCA SUP*
Casserley, H C 1903- *ConAu 9NR, -65*
Casserley, Julian Victor Langmead 1909-
ConAu 9R
Cassiday, Bruce 1920- *ConAu 1R, -4NR*
Cassidy, Charles 1936- *WrDr 84*
Cassidy, Charles Michael Ardagh 1936-
IntAu&W 82
Cassidy, Claude *ConAu X*
Cassidy, Claudia *ConAmTC*
Cassidy, Frederic Gomes 1907- *ConAu 1R,*
WrDr 84
Cassidy, George *WrDr 84*
Cassidy, Harold G 1906- *ConAu 25R*
Cassidy, John A 1908- *ConAu 33R*
Cassidy, John R 1922- *ConAu 89*
Cassidy, Michael 1936- *ConAu 105, -97*
Cassidy, Vincent H 1923- *ConAu 21R*
Cassidy, William L *ConAu 103*
Cassie, William Fisher 1905- *WrDr 84*
Cassilis, Robert *ConAu X*
Cassill, Kay *ConAu 89, DrAP&F 83*
Cassill, R V *DrAP&F 83*
Cassill, R V 1919- *ConAu 7NR, -9R, ConLC 4,*
-23[port], ConNov 82, DcLB 6,
IntAu&W 82, WorAu, WrDr 84
Cassill, Ronald Verlin 1919- *DcLEL 1940*
Cassils, Peter *ConAu X*
Cassin, Rene Samuel 1887-1976 *ConAu 65*
Cassinelli, C W 1925- *ConAu 1R*
Cassirer, Ernst 1874-1945 *TwCA SUP*
Cassity, Turner *DrAP&F 83*
Cassity, Turner 1929- *ConAu 11NR, -17R,*
ConLC 6, WrDr 84
Casso, Evans J 1914- *ConAu 57*
Cassola, Albert Maria 1915-1974 *ConAu P-1*
Cassola, Carlo 1917- *ClDMEL 80, ConAu 101,*
EncWL 2, ModRL, TwCWr, WorAu

Chamberlain, Marisha *DrAP&F 83*
Chamberlain, Mary 1947- *WrDr 84*
Chamberlain, Muriel Evelyn 1932- *ConAu 93*
Chamberlain, Narcisse 1924- *ConAu 13R*
Chamberlain, Neil Wolverton 1915- *ConAu 6NR,*
    -13R
Chamberlain, Robert Lyall 1923- *ConAu 13R*
Chamberlain, Samuel 1895-1975 *ConAu 53,*
    ConAu P-2
Chamberlain, Samuel S 1851-1916 *DcLB 25[port]*
Chamberlain, Wilson *ConAu X*
Chamberlain, Wilt 1936- *ConAu 103*
Chamberland, Paul 1939- *CreCan 2*
Chamberland, Pierre E 1931- *IntAu&W 82*
Chamberlin, Enid C S 1900?-1982? *ConAu 106*
Chamberlin, Eric Russell 1926- *ConAu 97*
Chamberlin, J E 1943- *ConAu 85*
Chamberlin, J Gordon 1914- *ConAu 1R, -4NR*
Chamberlin, Judi 1944- *ConAu 81*
Chamberlin, Leslie J 1926- *ConAu 53*
Chamberlin, M Hope 1920-1974 *ConAu 45, -49*
Chamberlin, Mary 1914- *ConAu 45, WrDr 84*
Chamberlin, Waldo 1905- *ConAu 65*
Chamberlin, William Henry 1897-1969
    ConAu 5R, TwCA, TwCA SUP
Chambers, Aidan 1934- *ConAu 25R,*
    IntAu&W 82, SmATA 1, TwCCW 83,
    WrDr 84
Chambers, Anthony H 1943- *ConAu 108*
Chambers, Catherine E *SmATA X*
Chambers, Charles Hadden 1860-1921
    ConAu 110
Chambers, Charles Hadden 1860-1921
    DcLB 10[port], LongCTC, TwCA,
    TwCA SUP
Chambers, Clarke A 1921- *ConAu 41R*
Chambers, Dewey W 1929- *ConAu 29R*
Chambers, E K *ModBrL*
Chambers, Sir Edmund Kerchever 1866-1954
    LongCTC, TwCA, TwCA SUP
Chambers, Edward J 1925- *ConAu 17R*
Chambers, Frank P 1900- *ConAu P-1*
Chambers, George *DrAP&F 83*
Chambers, Howard V *ConAu X*
Chambers, Jack *CreCan 2*
Chambers, Jane 1937- *ConAu 85,*
    NatPD 81[port]
Chambers, Jane 1937-1983 *ConAu 109*
Chambers, Jim Bernard 1919- *WrDr 84*
Chambers, John 1931- *CreCan 2*
Chambers, Jonathan David 1898-1970 *ConAu 1R,*
    -3NR
Chambers, Lenoir 1891-1970 *ConAu 104*
Chambers, M M 1899- *ConAu 5NR, -9R*
Chambers, Margaret Ada Eastwood 1911-
    ConAu 9R, SmATA 2
Chambers, Merritt Madison 1899- *WrDr 84*
Chambers, Mortimer Hardin, Jr. 1927-
    ConAu 6NR, -9R
Chambers, Peggy 1911- *ConAu X, SmATA 2*
Chambers, Peter *ConAu X*
Chambers, R W 1865-1933 *LongCTC*
Chambers, R W 1874-1942 *LongCTC*
Chambers, Raymond John 1917- *ConAu 17R,*
    WrDr 84
Chambers, Robert William 1865-1933 *TwCA*
Chambers, Robin 1942- *ConAu 103, WrDr 84*
Chambers, Whittaker 1901-1961 *ConAu 89,*
    LongCTC, WorAu
Chambers, William E 1943- *ConAu 73*
Chambers, William Nisbet 1916- *ConAu 5R,*
    -8NR
Chambers, William Trout 1896- *ConAu P-1*
Chambers, William Walker 1913- *ConAu 29R,*
    IntAu&W 82, WrDr 84
Chambert, Christian 1940- *IntAu&W 82*
Chambertin, Ilya 1931- *ConAu X*
Chambliss, William C 1908?-1975 *ConAu 57*
Chambliss, William J 1923- *ConAu 13R*
Chambliss, William J 1933- *ConAu 77*
Chamelin, Neil Charles 1942- *ConAu 69*
Chametzky, Jules 1928- *ConAu 33R*
Chamiel, Haim Itzchak 1917- *IntWWP 82*
Chamlee, Ruth Miller 1893?-1983 *ConAu 110*
Chamorro, Victor 1939- *IntAu&W 82*
Champagne, Claude 1891-1965 *CreCan 2*
Champagne, Marian 1915- *ConAu 5R*
Champernowne, David 1912- *ConAu 104,*
    WrDr 84
Champigny, Robert J 1922- *ConAu 33R*
Champion, Dick *ConAu X*
Champion, John C 1923- *ConAu 8NR, -17R*

Champion, John E 1922- *ConAu 13R*
Champion, Larry S 1932- *ConAu 9NR, -21R,*
    IntAu&W 82, WrDr 84
Champion, R A 1925- *ConAu 29R*
Champion, Richard Gordon 1931- *ConAu 77*
Champkin, Peter 1918- *ConAu 5R,*
    DcLEL 1940, WrDr 84
Champlin, Charles 1926- *ConAu 69*
Champlin, James R 1928- *ConAu 21R*
Champlin, John Michael 1937- *ConAu 110*
Champlin, Joseph M 1930- *ConAu 1NR, -49*
Champlin, Tim *ConAu X*
Champney, Freeman 1911- *ConAu 25R*
Chamson, Andre 1900- *ClDMEL 80,*
    ConAu 2NR, -5R, IntAu&W 82, TwCA,
    TwCA SUP
Ch'an, Chu 1913- *ConAu X*
Chan, Jeffrey Paul *DrAP&F 83*
Chan, Loren Briggs 1943- *ConAu 8NR, -57*
Chan, Stephen 1949- *IntWWP 82*
Chanaidh, Fear *ConAu X*
Chanakya *ConAu X*
Chanan, Ben *ConAu X*
Chanan, Gabriel 1942- *ConAu 7NR, -57*
Chanan, Michael 1946- *ConAu 106, WrDr 84*
Chance, John Newton 1911- *ConAu 102,*
    TwCCr&M 80, WrDr 84
Chance, John Newton 1911-1983 *ConAu 110*
Chance, Jonathan *ConAu X, -X, ConSFA*
Chance, Michael R A 1911- *ConAu 85*
Chance, Stephen *ConAu X, IntAu&W 82X,*
    TwCCW 83, WrDr 84
Chancellor, John *AuNews 1*
Chancellor, John 1900-1971 *ConAu P-2*
Chancellor, John 1927- *ConAu 109*
Chancellor, Paul 1900-1975 *ConAu 57*
Chancellor, Valerie Edith 1936- *IntAu&W 82*
Chand, Meira 1942- *ConAu 106*
Chand, Tan *IntWWP 82X*
Chanda, Asok Kumar 1902- *ConAu 17R*
Chandler, A Bertram 1912- *ConAu 21R,*
    ConSFA, IntAu&W 82, TwCSFW,
    WrDr 84
Chandler, Alfred D, Jr. 1918- *ConAu 4NR, -9R*
Chandler, Alice 1931- *ConAu 53*
Chandler, Alice 1939- *IntAu&W 82*
Chandler, Allison 1906- *ConAu P-1*
Chandler, B J 1921- *ConAu 1R*
Chandler, Caroline A 1906-1979 *ConAu 17R, -93,*
    SmATA 22N, -24
Chandler, David 1934- *ConAu 11NR, WrDr 84*
Chandler, David Geoffrey 1934- *ConAu 25R,*
    IntAu&W 82
Chandler, David Leon *ConAu 1NR, -49*
Chandler, David Porter 1933- *ConAu 45,*
    SmATA 28
Chandler, E Russell, Jr. 1932- *ConAu 77*
Chandler, Edna Walker 1908-1982 *ConAu 1R,*
    -4NR, -108, SmATA 11, -31N
Chandler, Frank *ConAu X, WrDr 84*
Chandler, George 1915- *ConAu 5NR, -9R,*
    IntAu&W 82, WrDr 84
Chandler, Howard 1915?-1981 *ConAu 104*
Chandler, Janet Carncross *DrAP&F 83*
Chandler, Jennifer 1940- *ConAu 9NR*
Chandler, Joyce A *DrAP&F 83*
Chandler, Linda S 1929- *ConAu 106*
Chandler, Margaret Kueffner 1922- *ConAu 17R*
Chandler, Norman 1899-1973 *ConAu 89*
Chandler, Raymond 1888-1959 *CnMWL,*
    ConAu 104, LongCTC, ModAL,
    ModAL SUP, TwCA SUP, TwCCr&M 80,
    TwCLC 1, -7[port], TwCWr, WhoTwCL
Chandler, Richard Eugene 1916- *ConAu 5R*
Chandler, Robert Wilbur 1921- *ConAu 102*
Chandler, Rose Wiley 1921- *IntWWP 82*
Chandler, Ruth Forbes 1894-1978 *ConAu 1R,*
    -103, SmATA 2, -26N
Chandler, S Bernard 1921- *ConAu 21R,*
    IntAu&W 82, WrDr 84
Chandler, Sue P *LivgBAA*
Chandler, T J 1928- *ConAu 107*
Chandler, Tertius 1915- *ConAu 102, WrDr 84*
Chandola, Anoop C 1937- *ConAu 37R*
Chandonnet, Ann 1943- *ConAu 8NR, -61*
Chandonnet, Ann Fox *DrAP&F 83*
Chandor, Anthony 1932- *ConAu 29R*
Chandos, Fay *ConAu X, TwCRGW, WrDr 84*
Chandos, John 1918- *ConAu X*
Chandra, G S *DrAP&F 83*
Chandra, Pramod 1930- *ConAu 77*
Chandrasekhar, Sripati 1918- *ConAu 89*

Chandrasekhar, Subrahmanyan 1910- *WrDr 84*
Chaneles, Sol 1926- *ConAu 41R*
Chaney, Jill 1932- *ConAu 11NR, -25R,*
    TwCCW 83, WrDr 84
Chaney, Norman 1935- *ConAu 110*
Chaney, Otto Preston, Jr. 1931- *ConAu 33R*
Chaney, William A 1922- *ConAu 33R*
Chang, Ai-ling 1921- *EncWL 2*
Chang, Constance D 1917- *ConAu 61*
Chang, Dae H 1928- *ConAu 6NR, -57*
Chang, Diana *DrAP&F 83*
Chang, Eileen 1920- *WorAu*
Chang, Hsin-Hai 1900- *ConAu 5R*
Chang, Isabelle C 1924- *ConAu 21R,*
    IntAu&W 82
Chang, Isabelle C 1925- *WrDr 84*
Chang, Jen-Chi 1903- *ConAu P-1*
Chang, Kia-Ngau 1889- *ConAu 5R*
Chang, Kwang-Chih 1931- *ConAu 41R*
Chang, Parris 1936- *ConAu 6NR, -57*
Chang, Richard T 1933- *ConAu 61*
Chang-Rodriguez, Eugenio *ConAu 6NR*
Chang-Rodriguez, Eugenio 1924- *ConAu 9R*
Chanin, Abraham 1921- *ConAu 89*
Chankin, Donald O 1934- *ConAu 57*
Channel, A R *ConAu X, SmATA 3,*
    TwCCW 83
Channels, Vera G 1915- *ConAu 69*
Channing, Edward 1856-1931 *DcLB 17[port],*
    TwCA, TwCA SUP
Channing, Steven A 1940- *ConAu 33R,*
    WrDr 84
Chanover, E Pierre 1932- *ConAu 29R*
Chanover, Hyman 1920- *ConAu 2NR, -49*
Chanover, Pierre E *DrAP&F 83*
Chansky, Norman M 1929- *ConAu 21R*
Chant, Barry 1938- *ConAu 11NR, -65*
Chant, Donald 1928- *ConAu 101*
Chant, Eileen Joyce 1945- *ConAu 61*
Chant, Joy *ConAu X*
Chant, Joy 1945- *ConAu X*
Chant, Ken 1933- *ConAu 89*
Chantier, P *IntAu&W 82X*
Chantikian, Kosrof *DrAP&F 83*
Chantiles, Vilma Liacouras 1925- *ConAu 6NR,*
    -57
Chantler, David T 1925- *ConAu 93, WrDr 84*
Chao, Buwei Yang 1889- *ConAu 61*
Chao, Kang 1929- *ConAu 33R*
Chao, Shu-Li 1906-1970 *EncWL 2*
Chao, Yuen Ren 1892-1982 *ConAu 106,*
    ConAu P-2, IntAu&W 82
Chapel, Paul 1926- *ConAu 25R*
Chapelle, Howard I 1901-1975 *ConAu 57,*
    ConAu P-2
Chapian, Marie 1938- *ConAu 106,*
    SmATA 29[port]
Chapin, Dwight Allan 1938- *ConAu 41R*
Chapin, F Stuart, Jr. 1916- *ConAu 2NR, -5R,*
    WrDr 84
Chapin, Harold 1886-1915 *CnMD, LongCTC,*
    ModWD
Chapin, Harry 1942-1981 *ConAu 104, -105*
Chapin, Henry 1893- *ConAu 93*
Chapin, Henry 1893-1983 *ConAu 110*
Chapin, June Roediger 1931- *ConAu 37R*
Chapin, Katherine Garrison 1890-1977 *ConAu X,*
    WorAu
Chapin, Kim 1942- *ConAu 9NR, -53,*
    MichAu 80
Chapin, Louis LeBourgeois, Jr. 1918-1981
    ConAmTC, ConAu 103
Chapin, Ned 1927- *ConAu 13R*
Chapin, Schuyler G 1923- *ConAu 77*
Chapin, Victor 1919?-1983 *ConAu 109*
Chapin, William 1918- *ConAu 37R*
Chaplin, Bill *ConAu X*
Chaplin, Charles Spencer 1889-1977 *ConAu 73,*
    -81, ConLC 16
Chaplin, Charlie 1889-1977 *ConAu X*
Chaplin, George 1914- *AuNews 2, ConAu 69*
Chaplin, James Patrick 1919- *ConAu 1R, -1NR,*
    WrDr 84
Chaplin, Sid 1916- *ConAu P-1, ConNov 82,*
    WrDr 84
Chaplin, Sidney 1916- *DcLEL 1940,*
    IntAu&W 82
Chaplin, W W 1895?-1978 *ConAu 81*
Chapman, A H 1924- *ConAu 25R*
Chapman, Abraham 1915- *ConAu 45*
Chapman, Allen *ConAu P-2, -X, SmATA 1*
Chapman, Alvah H, Jr. *AuNews 2*

Chapman, Brian 1923- *ConAu 9R,*
IntAu&W 82
Chapman, Carleton B 1915- *ConAu 69*
Chapman, Charles F 1881-1976 *ConAu 65*
Chapman, Christine 1933- *ConAu 73*
Chapman, Christopher 1927- *CreCan 1*
Chapman, Clark Russell 1945- *ConAu 110*
Chapman, Colin 1929- *ConAu 29R*
Chapman, Constance Elizabeth 1919-
IntAu&W 82
Chapman, Donald 1923- *ConAu 109*
Chapman, Dorothy Hilton 1934- *ConAu 57*
Chapman, Edmund H 1906- *ConAu P-1*
Chapman, Elizabeth 1919- *ConAu P-1,*
SmATA 10, WrDr 84
Chapman, Elwood N 1916- *ConAu 37R*
Chapman, Frank Michler 1864-1945 *TwCA,*
TwCA SUP
Chapman, G W Vernon 1925- *ConAu 29R*
Chapman, Gaynor 1935- *SmATA 32[port]*
Chapman, Graham 1941?- *ConLC 21[port]*
Chapman, Guy Patterson 1889-1972 *ConAu 101,*
-89, WorAu
Chapman, Hester W 1899-1976 *ConAu 9R, -9NR,*
-65, TwCRGW
Chapman, J Dudley 1928- *ConAu 8NR, -21R,*
WrDr 84
Chapman, James 1919- *ConAu 41R*
Chapman, Jean *ConAu 97, SmATA 34*
Chapman, John 1900-1972 *ConAu 33R*
Chapman, John Jay 1862-1933 *ConAu 104,*
TwCA, TwCA SUP, TwCLC 7[port]
Chapman, John L 1920- *ConAu 1R*
Chapman, John Roy 1927- *ConAu 77*
Chapman, John Stanton Higham 1891-1972
ConAu 107, SmATA 27N, TwCA,
TwCA SUP
Chapman, Joseph Irvine 1912- *ConAu 61*
Chapman, June R 1918- *ConAu 5R*
Chapman, Karen C 1942- *ConAu 65*
Chapman, Kenneth Francis 1910- *ConAu P-1,*
IntAu&W 82
Chapman, Kenneth G 1927- *ConAu 13R*
Chapman, Laura *DrAP&F 83*
Chapman, Laura 1935- *ConAu 105*
Chapman, Lee *WrDr 84*
Chapman, Loren James 1927- *ConAu 53*
Chapman, M Winslow 1903- *ConAu 93*
Chapman, Marie M 1917- *ConAu 11NR, -61*
Chapman, Maristan *ConAu X, SmATA X,*
TwCA, TwCA SUP
Chapman, R W 1881-1960 *LongCTC*
Chapman, Raymond 1924- *ConAu 2NR, -5R,*
IntAu&W 82
Chapman, Richard Arnold 1937- *ConAu 105,*
IntAu&W 82
Chapman, Rick M 1943- *ConAu 49*
Chapman, Robert 1937- *ConAu 107, WrDr 84*
Chapman, Roger E 1916- *ConAu 21R*
Chapman, Ronald 1917- *WrDr 84*
Chapman, Ronald George 1917- *ConAu 5R,*
IntAu&W 82
Chapman, Ruth 1912?-1979 *ConAu 104*
Chapman, Samuel Greeley 1929- *ConAu 9NR,*
-17R, WrDr 84
Chapman, Stanley D 1935- *ConAu 9NR*
Chapman, Stanley David 1935- *ConAu 21R,*
IntAu&W 82, WrDr 84
Chapman, Stepan *ConAu 41R*
Chapman, Steven *ConAu X*
Chapman, Sydney 1888-1970 *ConAu 106*
Chapman, Vera 1898- *ConAu 81,*
SmATA 33[port]
Chapman, Victoria L 1944- *ConAu 57*
Chapman, Walker *ConAu X, SmATA X,*
WorAu 1970
Chapman, Walter *WrDr 84*
Chapman, William 1850-1917 *CreCan 2*
Chapman-Mortimer, William Charles 1907-
ConAu 13R, IntAu&W 82, WrDr 84
Chapnick, Howard 1922- *ConAu 65*
Chappel, Bernice M 1910- *ConAu 89*
Chappell, Clovis G 1882-1972 *ConAu 65*
Chappell, Fred *DrAP&F 83*
Chappell, Fred 1936- *ConAu 5R, -8NR,*
DcLB 6[port], IntWWP 82
Chappell, Gordon 1939- *ConAu 57*
Chappell, Helen 1947- *ConAu 104*
Chappell, Jeannette *ConAu X*
Chappell, Mollie *ConAu 102, TwCRGW,*
WrDr 84
Chappell, Vere Claiborne 1930- *ConAu 5R*

Chappell, Warren 1904- *ConAu 8NR, -17R,*
SmATA 6
Chappell, William 1908- *ConAu 106*
Chappelow, Allan *ConAu 53, IntAu&W 82,*
WrDr 84
Chapple, Eliot Dismore 1909- *ConAu 41R*
Chapple, John Alfred Victor 1928- *ConAu 21R,*
WrDr 84
Chapple, Steve *DrAP&F 83*
Chapple, Steve 1949- *ConAu 77*
Chappuis, Pierre 1930- *IntWWP 82*
Chaput, Donald Charles 1933- *MichAu 80*
Chapygin, Aleksey Pavlovich 1870-1937
ClDMEL 80
Char, Rene 1907- *ClDMEL 80, CnMWL,*
ConAu 13R, ConLC 9, -11, -14, EncWL 2,
ModFrL, ModRL, TwCWr, WhoTwCL,
WorAu
Char, Tin-Yuke 1905- *ConAu 57*
Char, Yum *ConAu X*
Charanis, Peter 1908- *ConAu 37R*
Charbonneau, Christine 1944- *CreCan 1*
Charbonneau, Helene 1894- *CreCan 2*
Charbonneau, Jean 1875-1960 *CreCan 1*
Charbonneau, Louis 1924- *ConAu 85, ConSFA,*
TwCSFW, WrDr 84
Charbonneau, Robert 1911-1967 *CreCan 2*
Charby, Jay *ConAu X*
Chard, Brigid 1934- *ConAu 105*
Chard, Judy 1916- *ConAu 77, IntAu&W 82,*
WrDr 84
Chard, Leslie Frank, II 1934- *ConAu 33R,*
WrDr 84
Chardiet, Bernice 1927?- *ConAu 103,*
SmATA 27
Chardonne, Jacques 1884-1968 *ClDMEL 80,*
TwCA, TwCA SUP
Charents, Eghishe 1897-1937 *EncWL 2*
Chargaff, Erwin 1905- *ConAu 101*
Charhadi, Driss Ben Hamed *ConAu 13R*
Chari, V Krishna 1924- *ConAu 17R*
Charkin, Paul 1907- *ConSFA*
Charland, William, Jr. 1937- *ConAu 97*
Charle, Will *WrDr 84*
Charles, Anita *TwCRGW, WrDr 84*
Charles, C M 1931- *ConAu 1NR, -49*
Charles, David *ConAu X*
Charles, Don C 1918- *ConAu 9R*
Charles, Donald *ConAu X, SmATA X*
Charles, Gerda *WrDr 84*
Charles, Gerda 1914- *ConAu 1R, -1NR,*
ConNov 82, DcLB 14[port], DcLEL 1940,
WorAu
Charles, Gordon H 1920- *ConAu 104*
Charles, Henry *WrDr 84*
Charles, Louis *ConAu X*
Charles, Maggi *IntAu&W 82X*
Charles, Mark *ConAu X*
Charles, Nicholas *WrDr 84*
Charles, Richard *WrDr 84*
Charles, Robert *ConAu X*
Charles, Sascha 1896?-1972 *ConAu 37R*
Charles, Searle F 1923- *ConAu 9R, WrDr 84*
Charles, Theresa *ConAu X, TwCRGW,*
WrDr 84
Charles, Will *ConAu X*
Charles-Roux, Edmonde 1920- *ConAu 85*
Charles-Roux, Edmonde 1922- *IntAu&W 82*
Charleston, Robert Jesse 1916- *ConAu 102,*
IntAu&W 82, WrDr 84
Charlesworth, Arthur Riggs 1911- *ConAu 53*
Charlesworth, Grace 1906- *WrDr 84*
Charlesworth, James Clyde 1900-1974 *ConAu 9R,*
-45
Charlesworth, John Kaye 1889- *ConAu P-1*
Charlesworth, Marigold 1926- *CreCan 1*
Charlesworth, Maxwell John 1925- *ConAu 1R,*
-2NR
Charlier, Patricia Simonet 1923- *ConAu 37R*
Charlier, Roger Henri 1921- *ConAu 37R,*
IntAu&W 82, WrDr 84
Charlip, Remy 1929- *ConAu 33R, SmATA 4,*
WrDr 84
Charlot, Jean 1898-1979 *ConAu 4NR, -5R,*
SmATA 31N, -8
Charlotte *IntAu&W 82X*
Charlotte, Susan 1954- *ConAu 109,*
NatPD 81[port]
Charlson, David *ConAu X*
Charlton, Bobby 1937- *WrDr 84*
Charlton, Donald Geoffrey 1925- *ConAu 1R,*
-1NR, IntAu&W 82
Charlton, Evan 1912-1983 *ConAu 110*

Charlton, Geoffrey Norman 1943- *IntWWP 82*
Charlton, H B 1890-1961 *LongCTC*
Charlton, Jack *ConAu X*
Charlton, James 1939- *ConAu 81*
Charlton, John *ConAu X, WrDr 84*
Charlton, John 1935- *ConAu 109*
Charlton, Michael 1923- *SmATA 34*
Charlton, Robert F 1911- *WrDr 84*
Charlwood, D E 1915- *ConAu 9NR, WrDr 84*
Charlwood, Don *ConAu X*
Charlwood, Donald Ernest Cameron 1915-
ConAu 21R, IntAu&W 82
Charmatz, Bill 1925- *ConAu 29R. SmATA 7*
Charnance, L P *ConAu X*
Charnas, Suzy McKee *DrAP&F 83*
Charnas, Suzy McKee 1939- *ConAu 93,*
TwCSFW, WrDr 84
Charney, Ann *ConAu 102*
Charney, David H 1923- *ConAu 81*
Charney, George 1905?-1975 *ConAu 61*
Charney, Hanna K 1931- *ConAu 49*
Charney, Maurice 1929- *ConAu 3NR, -9R*
Charnin, Martin 1934- *ConAu 103*
Charnley, John 1911-1982 *ConAu 107*
Charnley, Mitchell Vaughn 1898- *ConAu 69*
Charnock, Joan Paget 1903- *ConAu P-2,*
IntAu&W 82, WrDr 84
Charnwood, Baron Godfrey Rathbone Benson
1864-1945 *LongCTC, TwCA, TwCA SUP*
Charny, Carmi 1925- *ConAu 7NR, -13R,*
WorAu 1970
Charny, Israel 1931- *WrDr 84*
Charny, Israel W 1931- *ConAu 57*
Charosh, Mannis 1906- *ConAu 29R, SmATA 5*
Charpentier, Gabriel 1925- *CreCan 2*
Charques, Dorothy 1899-1976 *ConAu 65, -73*
Charriere, Henri 1906-1973 *ConAu 101*
Charriere, Henri 1907?-1973 *ASpks, ConAu 45*
Charron, Shirley 1935- *ConAu 69*
Charry, Elias 1906- *ConAu 69*
Charteris, Hugo 1922-1970 *ConAu 105, -89,*
WorAu
Charteris, Leslie 1907- *ConAu 5R, -10NR,*
IntAu&W 82, LongCTC, TwCA,
TwCA SUP, TwCCr&M 80, TwCWr,
WrDr 84
Charters, Ann *WrDr 84*
Charters, Ann 1936- *ConAu 9NR, -17R*
Charters, Samuel 1929- *ConAu 9R, -9NR*
Chartham, Robert *ConAu X*
Chartier, Emile 1868-1951 *ClDMEL 80*
Chartier, Emile-Auguste *WorAu 1970*
Chartier, Emilio *ConAu X*
Charvat, Frank John 1918- *ConAu 1R*
Charvet, John 1938- *ConAu 85*
Charvet, Patrice Edouard 1903- *IntAu&W 82*
Chary, Frederick B 1939- *ConAu 49*
Charyn, Jerome *DrAP&F 83*
Charyn, Jerome 1937- *ConAu 5R, -7NR,*
ConLC 5, -8, -18, ConNov 82,
DcLB Y83B[port], DcLEL 1940,
IntAu&W 82, WrDr 84
Chasan, Daniel Jack 1943- *ConAu 29R*
Chase, Adam *ConAu X*
Chase, Alan L 1929- *ConAu 1R*
Chase, Alice *SmATA 4*
Chase, Alice Elizabeth 1906- *ConAu P-1*
Chase, Alston Hurd 1906- *ConAu 5R, WrDr 84*
Chase, Borden d1971 *TwCWW*
Chase, Borden 1900-1971 *DcLB 26[port]*
Chase, Charity *IntWWP 82X*
Chase, Chris *AuNews 1*
Chase, Cleveland Bruce 1904?-1975 *ConAu 53*
Chase, Clinton I 1927- *ConAu 106*
Chase, Cora G 1898- *ConAu 7NR, -61,*
IntAu&W 82
Chase, Donald 1943- *ConAu 53*
Chase, Elaine Raco *DrAP&F 83*
Chase, Gilbert 1906- *ConAu 17R*
Chase, Harold W 1922- *ConAu 4NR, -9R*
Chase, Ilka 1905-1978 *ConAu 9NR, -61, -77*
Chase, James Hadley *WrDr 84*
Chase, James Hadley 1906- *TwCCr&M 80,*
TwCWr
Chase, James S 1932- *ConAu 85*
Chase, Judith Wragg 1907- *ConAu 41R*
Chase, Larry *ConAu X*
Chase, Lawrence 1943- *ConAu 97*
Chase, Loriene Eck *ConAu 102*
Chase, Loring D 1916- *ConAu 25R*
Chase, Mary Coyle 1907-1981 *CnMD,*
ConAu 105, -77, LongCTC, ModWD,

Chesbro, George C 1940- *ConAu 77*
Chesebro, James William 1944- *ConAu 108*
Chesen, Eli S 1944- *ConAu 37R, WrDr 84*
Chesham, Henry *ConAu X, IntAu&W 82X*
Chesham, Sallie *WrDr 84*
Chesham, Sallie 1917- *ConAu 29R, MichAu 80*
Chesher, Kim 1955- *ConAu 102, WrDr 84*
Chesher, Richard 1940- *ConAu 106*
Cheshire, David 1944- *ConAu 97*
Cheshire, Geoffrey Leonard 1917- *ConAu P-1*
Cheshire, Maxine 1930- *ConAu 108*
Cheskin, Louis 1909- *WrDr 84*
Cheskin, Louis 1909-1981 *ConAu 5R, -5NR, -105*
Chesler, Bernice 1932- *ConAu 25R*
Chesler, Phyllis 1940- *ConAu 4NR, -49*
Cheslock, Louis 1898- *ConAu P-1, WrDr 84*
Chesney, Inga L 1928- *ConAu 45*
Chesney, Kellow 1914- *ConAu 29R*
Chesnoff, Richard Z 1937- *ConAu 10NR, -25R*
Chesnut, J Stanley 1926- *ConAu 21R*
Chesnutt, Charles Waddell 1858-1932 *ConAu 106, EncWL 2, ModBlW, TwCA, TwCA SUP, TwCLC 5[port]*
Chess, Stella 1914- *ConAu 85*
Chess, Victoria 1939- *ConAu 107, SmATA 33*
Chesser, Eustace 1902-1973 *ConAu 4NR, -9R, -45*
Chessex, Jacques 1934- *CIDMEL 80, ConAu 65*
Chessman, Caryl 1921-1960 *ConAu 73*
Chessman, G Wallace 1919- *ConAu 13R*
Chessman, Ruth 1910- *ConAu P-2*
Chester, Alfred 1929?-1971 *ConAu 33R*
Chester, Deborah 1957- *ConAu 102*
Chester, Edward W 1935- *ConAu 21R*
Chester, George Randolph 1869-1924 *TwCA*
Chester, Laura *DrAP&F 83*
Chester, Laura 1949- *ConAu 9NR, -65*
Chester, Michael 1928- *ConAu 1R, -1NR*
Chester, Norman 1907- *ConAu 109, IntAu&W 82, WrDr 84*
Chester, Peter *ConAu X*
Chesterman, Charles W 1913- *ConAu 107, WrDr 84*
Chesterman, Clement 1894-1983 *ConAu 110*
Chesterman, Jean *WrDr 84*
Chesterman, Jean 1920- *IntWWP 82*
Chesters, Graham 1944- *WrDr 84*
Chesterton, Arthur Kenneth 1899- *ConAu P-1*
Chesterton, Mrs. Cecil 1870-1962 *LongCTC*
Chesterton, Denise *TwCRGW, WrDr 84*
Chesterton, G K 1874-1936 *CnMWL, ConAu 104, DcLB 10[port], EncWL 2, LongCTC, ModBrL, ModBrL SUP, SmATA 27[port], TwCCr&M 80, TwCLC 1, -6[port], TwCSFW, WhoTwCL*
Chesterton, Gilbert Keith 1874-1936 *TwCA, TwCA SUP, TwCWr*
Chestor, Rui *ConAu X*
Chetham-Strode, Warren 1896- *ConAu P-1*
Chetham-Strode, Warren 1897- *LongCTC*
Chethimattam, John B 1922- *ConAu 25R*
Chetin, Helen 1922- *ConAu 29R, SmATA 6*
Chetwode, Penelope 1910- *ConAu 102, WrDr 84*
Chetwynd, Berry *ConAu X*
Chetwynd, Tom 1938- *ConAu 45*
Chetwynd-Hayes, Ronald Henry Glynn 1919- *ConAu 61, IntAu&W 82*
Cheung, Steven N S 1935- *ConAu 25R*
Cheuse, Alan 1940- *ConAu 49*
Chevalier, Christa 1937- *ConAu 107*
Chevalier, Elizabeth Pickett 1896- *IntAu&W 82*
Chevalier, Haakon 1901- *IntAu&W 82, WrDr 84*
Chevalier, Haakon 1902- *ConAu 61*
Chevalier, Louis 1911- *ConAu 85*
Chevalier, Maurice 1888-1972 *ConAu 33R*
Chevalier, Paul Eugene George 1925- *ConAu 106*
Chevalley, Alexis 1899- *IntAu&W 82*
Chevallier, Gabriel 1895-1969 *TwCWr*
Chevallier, Raymond 1929- *ConAu 103*
Chevigny, Bell Gale 1936- *ConAu 57*
Chevigny, Hector 1904-1965 *TwCA SUP*
Chevigny, Paul G 1935- *ConAu 97*
Chevigny, Pierre *ASpks*
Cheville, Roy A 1897- *ConAu 97*
Chew, Allen F 1924- *ConAu 33R, WrDr 84*
Chew, Peter 1924- *ConAu 57*
Chew, Ruth 1920- *ConAu 41R, IntAu&W 82, SmATA 7*

Cheyette, Irving 1904- *ConAu 69*
Cheyfitz, Eric *DrAP&F 83*
Cheyney, Arnold B 1926- *ConAu 8NR, -21R*
Cheyney, Peter 1896-1951 *TwCCr&M 80, TwCWr*
Cheyney-Coker, Syl 1945- *ConP 80, WrDr 84*
Chi, Madeleine 1930- *ConAu 11NR, -69*
Chi, Richard Hu See-Yee 1918- *ConAu 37R*
Chi, Richard See Yee 1918- *IntAu&W 82, WrDr 84*
Chi, Wen-Shun 1910- *ConAu 13R*
Chi-Wei *ConAu X*
Chiang, Fay *DrAP&F 83*
Chiang, Yee 1903-1977 *ConAu 65, -73, LongCTC, TwCA SUP*
Chiapelli, Fredi 1921- *IntAu&W 82*
Chiara, Piero 1913- *ConAu 8NR, -53*
Chiarelli, Luigi 1880-1947 *CIDMEL 80, ModWD*
Chiarelli, Luigi 1886-1947 *CnMD*
Chiarenza, Carl 1935- *ConAu 109*
Chiari, Joseph 1911- *ConAu 4NR, -5R, IntAu&W 82*
Chiaromonte, Nicola 1905-1972 *CIDMEL 80, ConAu 104*
Chibeau, Edmond *DrAP&F 83, IntWWP 82X*
Chibeau, Edmond Victor Peter 1947- *IntWWP 82*
Chibnall, Marjorie McCallum 1915- *ConAu 29R, WrDr 84*
Chicago, Judy 1939- *ConAu 85*
Chichester, Sir Francis 1901-1972 *ConAu 37R, ConAu P-1*
Chichester, George Forrest 1915- *IntAu&W 82*
Chichester, Jane *ConAu X*
Chichetto, James William *DrAP&F 83*
Chick, Edson M 1929- *ConAu 21R*
Chickering, Arthur W 1927- *ConAu 29R*
Chickering, Roger 1942- *ConAu 73*
Chickos, James Speros 1941- *ConAu 49*
Chicorel, Marietta *ConAu 85, IntAu&W 82*
Chidester, Ann 1919- *TwCA SUP*
Chidsey, Donald Barr 1902-1981 *ConAu 2NR, -5R, -103, SmATA 27N, -3, TwCA SUP*
Chidzero, Bernard Thomas Gibson 1927- *ConAu 1R*
Chielens, Edward E 1943- *ConAu 53*
Ch'ien, Ts'un-Hsun *ConAu X*
Chiesa, Francesco 1871-1973 *CIDMEL 80, ConAu 104*
Chifamba, Jane Eugenia 1937- *IntAu&W 82*
Chignon, Niles *ConAu X*
Chigounis, Evans *DrAP&F 83*
Chigounis, Evans 1931- *ConAu 45*
Chilcote, Ronald H 1935- *ConAu 8NR, -21R*
Chilcott, Barbara *CreCan 1*
Chilcott, John H 1924- *ConAu 41R*
Child, Harold Hannyngton 1869-1945 *LongCTC*
Child, Heather 1912- *ConAu 9R*
Child, Irvin L 1915- *ConAu 41R*
Child, John 1922- *ConAu 93, WrDr 84*
Child, Julia 1912- *ConAu 41R, WrDr 84*
Child, Philip Albert 1898-1978 *ConAu P-1, ConLC 19, CreCan 2*
Child, Robin Anne 1939- *IntWWP 82*
Child, Roderick 1949- *ConAu 25R, WrDr 84*
Childe, Vere Gordon 1892-1957 *TwCA SUP*
Childers, David C *DrAP&F 83*
Childers, Erskine 1870-1922 *LongCTC, TwCA, TwCCr&M 80, TwCWr*
Childers, Joanne *DrAP&F 83*
Childers, Thomas 1940- *ConAu 37R*
Childress, Alice *DrAP&F 83*
Childress, Alice 1920- *ConAu 3NR, -45, ConDr 82, ConLC 12, -15, DcLB 7[port], LivgBAA, SmATA 7, WrDr 84*
Childress, James Franklin 1940- *ConAu 11NR, -65*
Childress, William 1933- *ConAu 41R*
Childs, Barney 1926- *ConAu 21R*
Childs, C Sand *ConAu X*
Childs, David 1933- *WrDr 84*
Childs, David Haslam 1933- *ConAu 37R, IntAu&W 82*
Childs, Fay 1890-1971 *SmATA 1, -25N*
Childs, H Fay 1890-1971 *ConAu P-1*
Childs, Harwood Lawrence 1898-1972 *ConAu 37R, ConAu P-2*
Childs, James 1939- *NatPD 81[port]*
Childs, James Bennett 1896-1977 *ConAu 73*
Childs, Marilyn Grace Carlson 1923- *ConAu 9R*
Childs, Marquis 1903- *WrDr 84*
Childs, Marquis William 1903- *ConAu 61,*

TwCA SUP
Childs, Maryanna 1910- *ConAu 9R*
Childs, Timothy 1941- *ConAu 97*
Childs, W H J 1905?-1983 *ConAu 109*
Chiles, Robert E 1923- *ConAu 17R*
Chiles, Webb 1941- *ConAu 108*
Chill, Dan S 1945- *ConAu 69*
Chilson, Richard William 1943- *ConAu 6NR, -57*
Chilson, Robert 1945- *ConAu 69, TwCSFW, WrDr 84*
Chilton, Charles *ConSFA*
Chilton, Charles 1917- *TwCSFW, WrDr 84*
Chilton, Eleanor Carroll 1898-1949 *TwCA, TwCA SUP*
Chilton, Irma 1930- *ConAu 103*
Chilton, John 1932- *ConAu 8NR, -61*
Chilton, Shirley R 1923- *ConAu 77*
Chilver, Guy 1910-1982 *ConAu 107, -109*
Chilver, Peter 1933- *ConAu 25R, WrDr 84*
Chimaera *ConAu X, SmATA 2*
Chimet, Iordan 1924- *IntAu&W 82*
Chimhashu, Zinana *IntAu&W 82X*
Chin, Chuan *ConAu X*
Chin, Frank *DrAP&F 83*
Chin, Frank 1940- *ConAu 33R*
Chin, Robert 1918- *ConAu 61*
Chin, Yang Li *WorAu*
Chinard, Gilbert 1882?-1972 *ConAu 104*
Chinas, Beverly N 1924- *ConAu 89*
Chinery, Michael 1938- *ConAu 103, SmATA 26, WrDr 84*
Ching, James C 1926- *ConAu 37R*
Ching, Julia 1934- *ConAu 101*
Ching, Laureen *DrAP&F 83*
Ching-Hsiung, Wu *ConAu X*
Ching-P'Ei *IntAu&W 82X*
Chinitz, Benjamin 1924- *ConAu 9R*
Chinmoy *ConAu 49*
Chinmoy, Sri 1931- *ConAu 2NR*
Chinn, Laurene Chambers 1902-1978 *ConAu 1R, -103*
Chinn, Robert 1928- *ConAu 69*
Chinn, William G 1919- *ConAu 33R*
Chinnov, Igor Vladimirovich 1909- *CIDMEL 80*
Chinoy, Ely 1921-1975 *ConAu 1R, -1NR, -57*
Chinoy, Helen Krich 1922- *ConAu 17R*
Chinweizu 1943- *ConAu 103*
Chioatto, Ulysses 1962- *IntWWP 82*
Chiocchio, Fernande *CreCan 2*
Chiplin, Brian 1945- *WrDr 84*
Chipman, Bruce Lewis 1946- *ConAu 37R, WrDr 84*
Chipman, Donald 1928- *WrDr 84*
Chipman, Donald E 1928- *ConAu 29R*
Chipman, John S 1926- *ConAu 104*
Chipp, D L 1925- *ConAu 108*
Chipp, Herschel B 1913- *ConAu 25R*
Chippendale, George McCartney 1921- *WrDr 84*
Chipperfield, Joseph E 1912-1976 *TwCCW 83*
Chipperfield, Joseph Eugene 1912-1980? *ConAu 6NR, -9R, SmATA 2*
Chirenje, J Mutero 1935- *ConAu 65*
Chiriaeff, Ludmilla 1924- *CreCan 1*
Chirol, Sir Valentine 1852-1929 *LongCTC*
Chirovsky, Nicholas L 1919- *ConAu 4NR, -53*
Chisholm, A M 1872-1960 *TwCWW*
Chisholm, A R 1888- *ConAu 5R*
Chisholm, Anne *ConAu 109*
Chisholm, Hugh 1866-1924 *LongCTC*
Chisholm, Hugh J, Jr. 1913-1972 *ConAu 37R*
Chisholm, K Lomneth 1919- *ConAu 61*
Chisholm, Mary K *WrDr 84*
Chisholm, Mary K 1924- *ConAu 37R*
Chisholm, Matt 1919- *ConAu X, IntAu&W 82X, TwCWW, WrDr 84*
Chisholm, Michael 1931- *ConAu 37R, WrDr 84*
Chisholm, R F 1904- *ConAu P-2*
Chisholm, Roderick Milton 1916- *ConAu 102*
Chisholm, Roger K 1937- *ConAu 33R*
Chisholm, Sam Whitten 1919- *ConAu 5R*
Chisholm, Shirley 1924- *ConAu 29R, ConIsC 2[port], LivgBAA, WrDr 84*
Chisholm, William S, Jr. 1931- *ConAu 49*
Chism Peace, Yvonne *DrAP&F 83*
Chisolm, Lawrence 1929- *ConAu 9R*
Chissell, Joan Olive *WrDr 84*
Chissell, Joan Olive 1919- *ConAu 61*
Chitham, Edward 1932- *ConAu 103, WrDr 84*
Chitrabhanu, Gurudev Shree 1922- *ConAu 89*
Chitre, Dilip 1938- *DcLEL 1940*
Chittenden, Elizabeth F 1903- *ConAu 61,*

SmATA 9
Chittenden, Margaret 1933- SmATA 28[port]
Chittenden, Margaret 1935- ConAu 4NR, –53
Chittick, William O 1937- ConAu 41R
Chittock, John Dudley 1928- IntAu&W 82
Chittum, Ida 1918- ConAu 37R, SmATA 7, WrDr 84
Chitty, Arthur Benjamin 1914- ConAu 4NR, –53
Chitty, Letitia 1897-1982 ConAu 108
Chitty, Susan 1929- WrDr 84
Chitty, Susan Elspeth 1929- ConAu P-1
Chitty, Sir Thomas Willes 1926- ConAu 5R, ConLC 11, WorAu
Chitwood, B J 1931- ConAu 97
Chitwood, Marie Downs 1918- ConAu 9R
Chitwood, Oliver Perry 1874-1971 ConAu P-1
Chiu, Hong-Yee 1932- ConAu 53
Chiu, Hungdah 1936- ConAu 37R, IntAu&W 82, WrDr 84
Chlamyda, Jehudil ConAu X
Chloros, A G 1926-1982 ConAu 108
Chloros, Aleck George ConAu X
Chlumberg, Hans 1897-1930 CnMD, ModWD
Chmaj, Betty E 1930- ConAu 97
Chmielewski, Edward 1928- ConAu 13R
Ch'o, Chou ConAu X
Cho, Yong Hyo 1934- ConAu 105
Cho, Yong Sam 1925- ConAu 5R
Choat, Ernest George 1924- IntAu&W 82
Choate, Alec Herbert 1915- IntWWP 82
Choate, Ernest A 1900- ConAu 49
Choate, Gwen Peterson 1922- ConAu 1R
Choate, J E 1916- ConAu 33R
Choate, Judith 1940- ConAu 105, SmATA 30
Choate, R G ConAu X
Chobanian, Aram V 1929- ConAu 108
Chobot, Manfred 1947- IntAu&W 82
Chocano, Jose Santos 1875-1934 EncWL 2, ModLAL
Chochlik ConAu X
Chodes, John 1939- ConAu 9NR, –61, IntAu&W 82, NatPD 81[port]
Chodor, Kathleen DrAP&F 83
Chodorov, Edward 1904- CnMD, ConAu 102, ModWD
Chodorov, Jerome 1911- ConAu 65, ConDr 82D, ModWD, NatPD 81[port], WrDr 84
Chodorov, Stephan 1934- ConAu 17R
Chodorow, Nancy 1944- ConAu 105
Choi, Won-Kyu 1933- IntWWP 82
Choldin, Marianna Tax 1942- ConAu 109
Choleric, Brother ConAu X
Cholmondeley, Alice LongCTC
Cholmondeley, Mary 1859-1925 LongCTC, TwCA
Chomette, Rene Lucien 1898-1981 ConAu 103
Chommie, John C 1914-1974 ConAu P-2
Chomsky, Avram Noam 1928- DcLEL 1940
Chomsky, Noam 1928- ConAu 17R, ConIsC 1[port], WorAu 1970, WrDr 84
Chomsky, William 1896-1977 ConAu 73, –77
Chonel, Charlotte ConAu X
Chong, Kyong-Jo ConAu X
Chong, Peng-Khuan ConAu 25R
Chong, Ping DrAP&F 83
Choper, Jesse H 1935- ConAu 5NR, –13R
Chopin, Kate 1851-1904 ConAu 104, ModAL, ModAL SUP, TwCLC 5[port]
Chopin, Rene 1885-1953 CreCan 2
Chopourian, Giragos H 1914- IntAu&W 82
Choquette, Adrienne 1915- CreCan 1
Choquette, Ernest 1862-1941 CreCan 2
Choquette, Robert 1905- CreCan 1
Chorafas, Dimitris N 1926- ConAu 4NR, –5R, WrDr 84
Chorao, Kay 1936- ConAu 1NR, –49, SmATA 8
Chorell, Walentin 1912- CroCD, EncWL 2
Chorley, Desmond Mason 1924- IntAu&W 82
Chorlton, David DrAP&F 83
Chorlton, David 1948- IntWWP 82
Chorny, Merron 1922- ConAu 41R
Chorny, Sasha 1880-1932 ClDMEL 80
Choromanski, Michal 1904-1972 ModSL 2, TwCWr
Choron, Jacques 1904-1972 ConAu 33R, ConAu P-1
Chorpenning, Charlotte 1872-1955 TwCCW 83
Chothia, Jean 1944- ConAu 105
Chotjewitz, Peter 1934- ModGL
Chotzinoff, Samuel 1889-1964 ConAu 93
Chou, Eric 1916- IntAu&W 82

Chou, Li-Po 1908-1979 EncWL 2
Chou, Shu-Jen 1881-1936 TwCLC 3, WorAu 1970
Chou, Ya-Luu 1924- ConAu 41R
Chou, Yu-Jui IntAu&W 82X
Choucri, Nazli 1943- ConAu 81
Choudhury, G W 1926- ConAu 25R
Choukas, Michael 1901- ConAu P-2
Chouraqui, Andre 1917- ConAu 10NR
Chouraqui, Andre Nathan 1917- ConAu 65, IntAu&W 82
Chow, Gregory C 1929- ConAu 13R
Chow, Yung-Teh 1916- ConAu 37R
Chowder, Ken 1950- ConAu 102
Chowdhary, Savitri Devi 1907- ConAu P-1
Choy, Bong-Youn 1914- ConAu 69
Choy, Ruby Leong 1919- IntWWP 82
Chrimes, Stanley Bertram 1907- IntAu&W 82, WrDr 84
Chrislock, Carl H 1917- ConAu 45
Chrisman, Arthur Bowie 1889-1953 TwCCW 83
Chrisman, Harry E 1906- ConAu 1R
Christ, Carl F 1923- ConAu 21R
Christ, Carol T 1944- ConAu 93
Christ, Henry I 1915- ConAu 2NR, –5R, WrDr 84
Christ, John M 1934- ConAu 106
Christ, Richard 1931- IntAu&W 82
Christ, Robert Balthasar 1904- IntAu&W 82
Christ, Ronald 1936- ConAu 10NR, –25R, WrDr 84
Christ-Janer, Albert William 1910-1973 ConAu 4NR, –45
Christen, Robert J 1928- ConAu 107
Christen, Robert J 1928-1981 ConAu 108
Christen, Yves 1948- IntAu&W 82
Christensen, Ann 1946- ConAu 108
Christensen, Anna ConAu X
Christensen, Clyde M 1905- ConAu 53
Christensen, David E 1921- ConAu 13R
Christensen, Edward L 1913- ConAu 25R
Christensen, Eleanor Ingalls 1913- ConAu 53
Christensen, Erwin Ottomar 1890- ConAu P-1
Christensen, Francis 1902- ConAu P-2
Christensen, Gardell Dano 1907- ConAu 9R, SmATA 1
Christensen, Harold T 1909- ConAu 45
Christensen, Inger 1935- ClDMEL 80
Christensen, J A 1927- WrDr 84
Christensen, Jack Arden 1927- ConAu 53, IntAu&W 82
Christensen, James L 1922- ConAu 97
Christensen, Jerome 1948- ConAu 110
Christensen, Jo Ippolito ConAu X
Christensen, Nadia DrAP&F 83
Christensen, Otto Henry 1898- ConAu 33R
Christensen, Paul DrAP&F 83
Christensen, Paul 1943- ConAu 77, WrDr 84
Christensen, Sandra 1944- ConAu 110
Christensen, Yolanda Maria Ippolito 1943- ConAu 7NR, –57
Christenson, Cornelia V 1903- ConAu P-2, WrDr 84
Christenson, Larry 1928- ConAu 8NR, –57
Christenson, Nordis 1929- ConAu 108
Christenson, Reo M 1918- ConAu 37R
Christesen, Barbara 1940- ConAu 107
Christesen, C B 1911- WrDr 84
Christesen, Clement Byrne 1911- ConAu 102, IntAu&W 82
Christgau, Alice Erickson 1902- ConAu P-2, SmATA 13
Christgau, John DrAP&F 83
Christgau, John 1934- ConAu 103
Christgau, Robert 1942- ConAu 65
Christiaens, Andre 1905- IntWWP 82
Christian, A B ConAu X
Christian, Barbara T 1943- ConAu 110
Christian, C W 1927- ConAu 21R
Christian, Carol Cathay 1923- ConAu 53, WrDr 84
Christian, Frederick ConAu X
Christian, Frederick H TwCWW, WrDr 84
Christian, Garth Hood 1921-1967 ConAu P-1
Christian, George 1927- ConAu 65
Christian, Henry A 1931- ConAu 33R
Christian, James L 1927- ConAu 57
Christian, Jill ConAu X, IntAu&W 82X, WrDr 84
Christian, John ConAu X, WrDr 84
Christian, John Wyrill 1926- WrDr 84
Christian, Louise ConAu X

Christian, Marcus Bruce 1900- ConAu 73, LivgBAA
Christian, Mary Blount 1933- ConAu 1NR, –45, SmATA 9, WrDr 84
Christian, Peter ConAu X
Christian, Portia Frances 1908- ConAu 103
Christian, Rebecca 1952- ConAu 107
Christian, Reginald Frank 1924- ConAu 3NR, –5R, IntAu&W 82
Christian, Roy Cloberry 1914- ConAu 93, IntAu&W 82, WrDr 84
Christian, William A, Jr. 1944- ConAu 107
Christiani, Dounia Bunis 1913- ConAu 13R
Christians, Clifford Glenn 1939- ConAu 104
Christiansen, Arthur 1904-1963 ConAu 1R, LongCTC
Christiansen, Harley Duane 1930- ConAu 4NR, –53
Christiansen, Richard Dean 1931- ConAmTC
Christiansen, Sigurd Wesley 1891-1947 ClDMEL 80, TwCA, TwCA SUP
Christianson, Gale E 1942- ConAu 81
Christianson, John Robert 1934- ConAu 21R
Christiansson, Hans 1916- IntAu&W 82
Christie, A B 1909- WrDr 84
Christie, Agatha TwCRGW
Christie, Agatha 1890-1976 AuNews 1[port], –2[port], ConAu 10NR, –17R, –61, ConLC 1, –8, –12, DcLB 13[port], TwCCr&M 80
Christie, Agatha 1891-1976 ConLC 6, LongCTC, TwCA[port], TwCA SUP, TwCWr
Christie, Ann Philippa IntAu&W 82
Christie, Campbell 1893-1963 LongCTC
Christie, Dorothy LongCTC
Christie, George C 1934- ConAu 37R
Christie, Hugh ConAu X, IntAu&W 82X
Christie, Ian 1919- WrDr 84
Christie, Ian Ralph 1919- ConAu 2NR, –5R, IntAu&W 82
Christie, Jean 1912- ConAu 101
Christie, John 1882-1962 LongCTC
Christie, John Aldrich 1920- ConAu 65
Christie, Keith ConAu X
Christie, Lindsay H 1906?-1976 ConAu 61
Christie, Milton 1921- ConAu 17R
Christie, Philippa ConAu 4NR
Christie, Treavor L 1905-1969 MichAu 80
Christie, Trevor L 1905-1969 ConAu P-2
Christie-Murray, David 1913- ConAu 4NR, –53, IntAu&W 82, WrDr 84
Christina, Martha DrAP&F 83
Christina-Marie DrAP&F 83, IntWWP 82X, MichAu 80
Christine, Charles T 1936- ConAu 33R
Christine, Dorothy Weaver 1934- ConAu 33R
Christman, Don R 1919- ConAu 17R
Christman, Elizabeth 1914- ConAu 89
Christman, Henry 1906-1980 ConAu 103
Christman, Henry Max 1932- ConAu 65
Christman, R J 1919- ConAu 89
Christmann, Helmut 1924- IntAu&W 82
Christmas, R A DrAP&F 83
Christol, Carl Quimby 1914- ConAu 4NR, –5R
Christoph, James B 1928- WrDr 84
Christoph, James Bernard 1928- ConAu 4NR, –5R, IntAu&W 82
Christopher, Joe R 1935- ConAu 4NR, –53
Christopher, John 1922- ChlLR 2, ConAu X, ConSFA, DcLEL 1940, SmATA X, TwCCW 83, TwCSFW, WorAu, WrDr 84
Christopher, John B 1914- ConAu 13R
Christopher, Kenneth ConAu X
Christopher, Louise ConAu X
Christopher, Matt IntAu&W 82X
Christopher, Matt F 1917- WrDr 84
Christopher, Matthew F 1917- ConAu 1R, –5NR, IntAu&W 82, SmATA 2
Christopher, Maurine ConAu 65
Christopher, Milbourne ConAu 105
Christopher, Nicholas DrAP&F 83
Christopher, Nicholas 1951- ConAu 108
Christopher, Robert Collins 1924- ConAu 102
Christophersen, Merrill Gaerdon 1904- IntWWP 82
Christophersen, Paul 1911- WrDr 84
Christophersen, Paul Hans 1911- ConAu 57
Christov, Solveig 1918- EncWL 2
Christowe, Stoyan 1898- ConAu 65
Christy, Betty 1924- ConAu 57
Christy, Dama IntWWP 82X
Christy, George ConAu 9R

Christy, Howard Chandler 1873?-1952
  SmATA 21[port]
Christy, Joe ConAu X
Christy, Joseph M 1919- ConAu 29R
Christy, Marian 1932- ConAu 65
Christy, Teresa E 1927- ConAu 73
Chroman, Eleanor 1937- ConAu 45
Chroman, Nathan 1929- ConAu 77
Chroust, Anton-Hermann C 1907- ConAu P-1
Chruden, Herbert J 1918- ConAu 5R
Chrysler, C Donald 1925- MichAu 80
Chu, Arthur 1916- ConAu 81
Chu, Daniel 1933- ConAu 13R, SmATA 11
Chu, Grace Zia 1899- ConAu 4NR, -5R
Chu, Kong 1926- ConAu 49
Chu, Louis H 1915- ConAu 13R
Chu, Samuel C 1929- ConAu 69
Ch'u, Tung-Tsu 1910- ConAu 1R, -2NR
Chu, Valentin Yuan-Ling 1919- ConAu 9R
Chu, W R ConAu X
Chuan-Chin ConAu X
Chubak, Sadeq 1916- EncWL 2
Chubb, Elmer ConAu X
Chubb, Mary Alford 1903- IntAu&W 82
Chubb, Thomas Caldecot 1899-1972 ConAu 1R,
  -6NR, -33R
Chudacoff, Howard P 1943- ConAu 45
Chudley, Ron 1937- ConAu 110
Chuikov, Vasili Ivanovich 1900-1982 ConAu 106
Chukovskaya, Lidiya Korneyevna 1907-
  CIDMEL 80, WorAu

Chukovsky, Kornei 1882-1969 ConAu 4NR, -25R,
  SmATA 34[port]
Chukovsky, Korney Ivanovich 1882-1969
  CIDMEL 80, ConAu 5R, SmATA 5,
  WorAu
Chuks-Adophy 1920- IntAu&W 82
Chulak, Armando d1975 ConAu 109
Chuman, Frank Fujio 1917- ConAu 69
Chun, Jinsie K S 1902- ConAu 49
Chun, Richard 1935- ConAu 65
Chung, Edward K 1931- ConAu 107
Chung, Hyung C 1931- ConAu 57
Chung, Joseph Sang-Hoon 1929- ConAu 49
Chung, Kyung Cho 1921- ConAu 33R
Chung-Shu, Ch'ien 1910- ConLC 22[port]
Chung-Yu, Chu ConAu X
Chupack, Henry 1915- ConAu 49
Church, Avery Grenfell 1937- IntWWP 82
Church, Jeffrey ConAu X
Church, Joseph 1918- ConAu 1R
Church, Margaret 1920- ConAu 13R, WrDr 84
Church, Peter ConAu X
Church, Ralph 1927- ConAu 37R
Church, Richard 1893-1972 ConAu 1R, -3NR,
  -33R, LongCTC, ModBrL, SmATA 3,
  TwCA, TwCA SUP, TwCCW 83, TwCWr
Church, Robert L 1938- ConAu 61
Church, Ronald James Harrison 1915- ConAu 1R
Church, Ruth Ellen ConAu 5R, -7NR
Church, William Farr 1912- ConAu 105
Churchill, Allen 1911- ConAu 97
Churchill, Caryl 1938- ConAu 102, ConDr 82,
  DcLB 13[port], IntAu&W 82, WrDr 84
Churchill, Creighton 1912- ConAu 69
Churchill, David 1935- ConAu 106
Churchill, Donald 1930- ConDr 82C
Churchill, E Richard 1937- ConAu 11NR, -17R,
  SmATA 11, WrDr 84
Churchill, Edward Delos 1895-1972 ConAu 37R
Churchill, Elizabeth WrDr 84
Churchill, Guy E 1926- ConAu 29R
Churchill, Joyce ConAu X
Churchill, Linda R 1938- ConAu 11NR, -21R
Churchill, R C 1916- ConAu 9R
Churchill, Randolph 1911-1968 ConAu 89,
  LongCTC
Churchill, Reginald Charles 1916- IntAu&W 82
Churchill, Rhona Adelaide 1913- ConAu 5R
Churchill, Samuel 1911- ConAu 17R
Churchill, Sarah 1914-1982 ConAu 107
Churchill, Thomas DrAP&F 83
Churchill, Winston 1871-1947 ConAmA,
  LongCTC, TwCA SUP, TwCWr
Churchill, Sir Winston Leonard Spencer 1874-1965
  ConAu 97, LongCTC, TwCA, TwCA SUP,
  TwCWr
Churchman, C West 1913- ConAu 9NR, -21R
Churchman, Michael 1929- ConAu 37R
Churchward, L G 1919- WrDr 84
Chute, B J DrAP&F 83

Chute, B J 1913- ConAu 1R, IntAu&W 82X,
  SmATA 2, WrDr 84
Chute, Beatrice Joy 1913- IntAu&W 82
Chute, Marchette 1909- TwCCW 83, WrDr 84
Chute, Marchette Gaylord 1909- ConAu 1R,
  -5NR, IntAu&W 82, SmATA 1,
  TwCA SUP
Chute, Robert M 1926- ConAu 109
Chute, Rupert ConAu X
Chute, William J 1914- ConAu 9R
Chwalek, Henryka C 1918- ConAu 17R
Chwast, Jacqueline 1932- ConAu 5NR, -49,
  SmATA 6
Chwast, Seymour 1931- SmATA 18
Chyet, Stanley F 1931- ConAu 33R
Ciabattari, Jane DrAP&F 83
Cialente, Fausta 1900- ConAu X, TwCWr
Cianciolo, Patricia Jean 1929- ConAu 37R,
  MichAu 80
Ciaramitaro, Andrew James 1955- ConAu 110
Ciaramitaro, Barbara 1946- ConAu 107
Ciarcia, Steve 1947- ConAu 110
Ciardi, John DrAP&F 83
Ciardi, John 1916- ConAu 5R, -5NR,
  ConLC 10, ConP 80, DcLB 5[port],
  DcLEL 1940, ModAL, SmATA 1,
  TwCA SUP, TwCCW 83, WrDr 84
Ciccorella, Aubra Dair ConAu 65
Cicellis, Catherine-Mathilda 1926- ConAu 1R,
  DcLEL 1940
Cicellis, Kay 1926- ConAu 3NR, WrDr 84
Cicero IntAu&W 82X
Cicognani, Cardinal Amleto Giovanni 1883-1973
  ConAu 45
Cicognani, Bruno 1879-1972 CIDMEL 80
Cicourel, Aaron V 1928- ConAu 53
Cid Perez, Jose 1906- ConAu 4NR, -53
Ciechanowski, Jan 1888?-1973 ConAu 41R
Cienciala, Anna M 1929- ConAu 89
Cieplak, Tadeusz N 1918- ConAu 11NR, -69
Ciletti, James DrAP&F 83
Cilffriw, Gwynfor ConAu X
Cilliers, Charl Jean Francois 1941- IntWWP 82
Cimbollek, Robert 1937- ConAu 57
Ciment, Michel 1938- ConAu 97, IntAu&W 82
Cimino, Michael 1943?- ConAu 105, ConLC 16
Cinberg, Bernard L 1905-1979 ConAu 85
Cinderalla IntAu&W 82X
Cingo, Zivko 1936- CIDMEL 80, ModSL 2
Cinna ConAu X
Ciocchini, Hector Eduardo 1922- IntWWP 82
Cioffari, Vincenzo 1905- ConAu 17R
Cioffi, Lou 1926- ConAu 109
Cioran, E M 1911- ConAu 25R, WorAu
Cioran, Emile-Marcel 1911- CIDMEL 80
Cipes, Robert M 1930- ConAu 21R
Ciplijauskaite, Birute 1929- ConAu 37R,
  IntAu&W 82
Cipolla, Carlo M 1922- ConAu 2NR, -5R,
  WrDr 84
Cipolla, Joan Bagnel ConAu 49
Cipriano, Anthony 1941- ConAu 102
Circus, Anthony ConAu X
Circus, Jim ConAu X
Cire ConAu X
Ciria, Alberto 1934- ConAu 73
Cirino, Leonard John DrAP&F 83
Cirino, Leonard John 1943- IntWWP 82
Cirino, Linda D 1941- ConAu 65
Cirino, Robert 1937- ConAu 61
Cismaru, Alfred 1933- ConAu 61
Cisneros, Sandra DrAP&F 83
Ciszek, Walter 1904- ConAu P-1
Citati, Pietro 1930- ConAu 4NR, -53
Citino, David DrAP&F 83
Citino, David 1947- ConAu 104
Citrine, Walter McLennan 1887-1983 ConAu 109
Cittafino, Ricardo ConAu X
Cituentes IntWWP 82X
Ciuba, Edward J 1935- ConAu 61
Civasaqui, Jose 1916- IntWWP 82, -82X
Civille, John R 1940- ConAu 11NR, -69
Cixous, Helene 1937- CIDMEL 80
Claassen, Harold 1905- ConAu P-2
Clabaugh, Gary K 1940- ConAu 69
Clabby, John 1911- ConAu 104, WrDr 84
Clack, Robert Wood 1886-1964 ConAu 110,
  MichAu 80
Claerbaut, David 1946- ConAu 1NR, -45
Claes, Ernest Andre Jozef 1885-1968 EncWL 2
Claffey, William J 1925- ConAu 21R
Clafin, Lola White DrAP&F 83

Claflin, Edward 1949- ConAu 97
Clagett, John 1916- ConAu 5R, -6NR
Clagett, Marshall 1916- ConAu 1R, -5NR
Claghorn, Charles Eugene 1911- ConAu 57
Clague, Ewan 1896- ConAu 29R
Clague, Maryhelen 1930- ConAu 81
Claiborne, Craig 1920- ConAu 1R, -5NR
Claiborne, Robert 1919- ConAu 29R
Claiborne, Sybil DrAP&F 83
Clain-Stefanelli, Vladimir 1914-1982 ConAu 108
Clair, Andree ConAu 29R, SmATA 19
Clair, Bernard 1951- ConAu 102
Clair, Rene 1898-1981 ConAu X, ConLC 20,
  IntAu&W 82
Claire, Ames IntWWP 82X
Claire, Keith ConAu X
Claire, William DrAP&F 83
Claire, William Francis 1935- ConAu 7NR, -57,
  IntWWP 82
Clammer, David 1943- ConAu 69
Clampett, Bob AuNews 1
Clampitt, Amy ConAu 110, DrAP&F 83
Clancy, John Gregory 1922- ConAu 13R
Clancy, Joseph P 1928- ConAu 101
Clancy, Laurence James 1942- ConAu 108
Clancy, Laurie ConAu X
Clancy, Laurie 1942- WrDr 84
Clancy, Thomas H 1923- ConAu 7NR, -13R,
  WrDr 84
Clancy, William 1922-1982 ConAu 106
Clanton, Gene 1934- ConAu 41R
Clanton, Gordon 1942- ConAu 57
Clapham, Arthur Roy 1904- ConAu 109
Clapham, Christopher 1941- WrDr 84
Clapham, John 1908- ConAu 10NR, -25R,
  IntAu&W 82, WrDr 84
Clapham, Sidney Walter 1912- WrDr 84
Clapp, James Gordon 1909-1970 ConAu P-1
Clapp, Margaret Antoinette 1910-1974 ConAu 49,
  TwCA SUP
Clapp, Patricia 1912- ConAu 10NR, -25R,
  IntAu&W 82, SmATA 4, TwCCW 83,
  WrDr 84
Clapp, Verner W 1901-1972 ConAu 37R
Clapperton, Richard 1934- ConAu 25R
Clar, C Raymond 1903- ConAu 37R
Clardy, Andrea 1943- ConAu 97
Clardy, J V 1929- ConAu 33R
Clare, Elizabeth ConAu X, WrDr 84
Clare, Ellen ConAu X, WrDr 84
Clare, Francis D ConAu X
Clare, George 1920- WrDr 84
Clare, Helen ConAu X, IntAu&W 82X,
  SmATA 3, TwCCW 83, WrDr 84
Clare, Josephine DrAP&F 83
Clare, Josephine 1933- ConAu 73
Clare, Margaret ConAu X
Clare, William 1935- WrDr 84
Claremon, Neil DrAP&F 83
Clarens, Carlos 1936- ConAu 21R
Clareson, Thomas D 1926- ConAu 1R, -2NR
Clarfield, Gerard Howard 1936- ConAu 103
Claridge, Gordon S 1932- ConAu 21R
Clarie, Thomas C 1943- ConAu 93
Clarin 1852-1901 CIDMEL 80
Clarizio, Harvey F 1934- ConAu 33R
Clark IntAu&W 82X
Clark, Baron 1903- WrDr 84
Clark, Admont Gulick 1919- ConAu 53
Clark, Alan 1928- ConAu 13R
Clark, Alfred Alexander Gordon 1900- LongCTC
Clark, Alice S 1922- ConAu 41R
Clark, Andrew H 1911- WrDr 84
Clark, Andrew Hill 1911-1975 ConAu P-2
Clark, Ann L 1913- ConAu 7NR, -17R
Clark, Ann Nolan 1896- ConAu 2NR,
  TwCCW 83, WrDr 84
Clark, Ann Nolan 1898- ConAu 5R, SmATA 4
Clark, Anne 1909- ConAu 29R
Clark, Arthur Melville 1895- ConAu 9R
Clark, Badger ConAu X
Clark, Barrett Harper 1890-1953 TwCA,
  TwCA SUP
Clark, Ben T 1928- ConAu 53
Clark, Bill ConAu X
Clark, Billy C 1928- ConAu 1R
Clark, Brian 1932- ConAu 41R, ConDr 82,
  WrDr 84
Clark, Bruce 1918- ConAu 69, WrDr 84
Clark, Burton R 1921- ConAu 110
Clark, C E Frazer, Jr. 1925- ConAu 33R
Clark, C H Douglas 1890- ConAu P-2

Clark, C M H 1915- *ConAu 97*
Clark, Carol 1948- *ConAu 57*
Clark, Catherine Anthony 1892-1977 *ConAu P-1, CreCan 1, TwCCW 83*
Clark, Champ 1923- *ConAu 108*
Clark, Charles E 1929- *WrDr 84*
Clark, Charles Edwin 1929- *ConAu 29R*
Clark, Charles Manning Hope 1915- *DcLEL 1940*
Clark, Charles Tallifero 1917- *ConAu 13R*
Clark, China Debra 1950- *ConAu 45*
Clark, Christopher Stuart *ConAu X*
Clark, Clifford E, Jr. 1941- *ConAu 81*
Clark, Colin 1905- *ConAu 8NR, -61*
Clark, Curt *ConSFA, WrDr 84*
Clark, David *ConAu X, TwCCW 83, WrDr 84*
Clark, David Allen *ConAu X*
Clark, David Gillis 1933- *ConAu 53*
Clark, David Ridgley 1920- *ConAu 9NR, -17R, IntAu&W 82, WrDr 84*
Clark, Dennis E 1916- *ConAu 29R*
Clark, Dennis J 1927- *ConAu 1R, -1NR*
Clark, Don 1925- *ConAu 57*
Clark, Don 1930- *ConAu 29R*
Clark, Donald E 1933- *ConAu 8NR, -21R*
Clark, Dora Mae 1893- *ConAu 41R*
Clark, Dorothy Park 1899- *ConAu 5R*
Clark, Eleanor *DrAP&F 83*
Clark, Eleanor 1913- *ConAu 9R, ConLC 5, -19, ConNov 82, DcLB 6[port], DcLEL 1940, IntAu&W 82, TwCA SUP, WrDr 84*
Clark, Electa 1910- *ConAu 69*
Clark, Eliot Candee 1883-1980 *ConAu 97*
Clark, Ella Elizabeth 1896- *ConAu 105*
Clark, Ellery Harding, Jr. 1909- *ConAu 10NR, -65*
Clark, Elmer Talmage 1886-1966 *ConAu 5R*
Clark, Eric 1911- *ConAu 9NR, -13R, WrDr 84*
Clark, Eric 1937- *ConAu 102, WrDr 84*
Clark, Eugenie 1922- *ConAu 49*
Clark, Evans 1888-1970 *ConAu 104*
Clark, Francis 1919- *ConAu 17R*
Clark, Frank J 1922- *ConAu 13R, SmATA 18*
Clark, Fred George 1890-1972 *ConAu 37R*
Clark, Frederick Stephen 1908- *ConAu 21R*
Clark, G N 1890- *LongCTC*
Clark, Gail 1944- *ConAu 97*
Clark, Garel *ConAu X, SmATA X*
Clark, Geoffrey D *DrAP&F 83*
Clark, George Norman 1890-1979 *ConAu 65, -85*
Clark, George Sidney Roberts Kitson *ConAu X*
Clark, Gerald 1918- *ConAu 13R*
Clark, Gordon H 1902- *ConAu 1R, -1NR*
Clark, Grahame 1907- *ConAu 5R, -10NR*
Clark, Gregory 1892-1977 *ConAu 89, CreCan 1*
Clark, Harry 1917- *ConAu 61*
Clark, Harry Hayden 1901-1971 *ConAu P-2*
Clark, Henry B, II 1930- *ConAu 5R, -8NR*
Clark, Howard *ConAu X, WrDr 84*
Clark, J Desmond 1916- *IntAu&W 82, WrDr 84*
Clark, J H 1929- *ConAu 106*
Clark, J P 1935- *IntAu&W 82*
Clark, J R 1947- *ConAu 106*
Clark, James Anthony 1907- *ConAu 65*
Clark, James M 1930- *ConAu 21R*
Clark, James Stanford 1906- *MichAu 80*
Clark, James V 1927- *ConAu 13R*
Clark, Jean *DrAP&F 83*
Clark, Jean C 1920- *ConAu 93*
Clark, Jere Walton 1922- *ConAu 21R*
Clark, Jerome L 1928- *ConAu 37R*
Clark, Jerry E 1942- *ConAu 73*
Clark, Joan 1934- *ConAu 93*
Clark, John Desmond 1916- *ConAu 61*
Clark, John Drury 1907- *ConAu 37R*
Clark, John G 1932- *ConAu 17R*
Clark, John Grahame Douglas 1907- *ConAu 65, IntAu&W 82, WrDr 84*
Clark, John Maurice 1884-1963 *ConAu 5R*
Clark, John Pepper 1935- *ConAu 65, ConDr 82, ConP 80, DcLEL 1940, EncWL 2, LongCTC, ModBlW, ModCmwL, ModWD, TwCWr, WorAu 1970, WrDr 84*
Clark, John R 1930- *ConAu 37R, WrDr 84*
Clark, John R K 1946- *ConAu 101*
Clark, John Williams 1907- *ConAu 13R*
Clark, Joseph D 1893- *ConAu P-2*
Clark, Joseph James 1893-1971 *ConAu 29R, ConAu P-2*
Clark, Joseph L 1881- *ConAu P-2*

Clark, Katerina 1941- *ConAu 110*
Clark, Kenneth *WrDr 84*
Clark, Kenneth 1903-1983 *ConAu 109*
Clark, Sir Kenneth 1903- *ConAu 93, LongCTC, TwCA SUP*
Clark, Kenneth Bancroft 1914- *ConAu 33R, LivgBAA, WrDr 84*
Clark, L D *DrAP&F 83*
Clark, L D 1922- *ConAu 1R, -1NR, IntAu&W 82*
Clark, Laurence 1914- *ConAu 13R, WrDr 84*
Clark, Laverne Harrell *DrAP&F 83*
Clark, LaVerne Harrell 1929- *ConAu 11NR, -13R, IntAu&W 82, IntWWP 82, WrDr 84*
Clark, Leonard 1905-1981 *ConAu 7NR, -105, -13R, ConP 80, DcLEL 1940, IntAu&W 82, IntWWP 82, SmATA 29N, -30[port], TwCCW 83*
Clark, Leonard H 1915- *ConAu 4NR, -53*
Clark, Leroy D *ConAu 11NR, -61*
Clark, Lindley Hoag 1920- *ConAu 65*
Clark, Lydia Benson *ConAu X*
Clark, Mabel Margaret 1903-1975 *ConAu 101*
Clark, Malcolm, Jr. 1917- *ConAu 106*
Clark, Manning 1915- *ConAu 9R*
Clark, Marden J 1916- *ConAu 61*
Clark, Margaret Goff 1913- *ConAu 1R, -5NR, SmATA 8*
Clark, Marguerite Sheridan 1892?-1982 *ConAu 107*
Clark, Maria Louisa 1926- *ConAu 5R, IntAu&W 82*
Clark, Marion L 1942?-1977 *ConAu 73*
Clark, Marion L 1943-1977 *ConAu 77*
Clark, Marjorie A 1911- *ConAu 33R, WrDr 84*
Clark, Mary Higgins 1929- *IntAu&W 82*
Clark, Mary Higgins 1930- *WrDr 84*
Clark, Mary Higgins 1931- *ConAu 81*
Clark, Mary Jane 1915- *ConAu 57*
Clark, Mary Lou *ConAu X, IntAu&W 82X*
Clark, Mary T *ConAu 102, -37R, WrDr 84*
Clark, Mavis Thorpe *ConAu 8NR, -57, ConLC 12, SmATA 8, TwCCW 83, WrDr 84*
Clark, Melissa 1949- *ConAu 104*
Clark, Merle *ConAu X, SmATA X, WrDr 84*
Clark, Michael *DrAP&F 83*
Clark, Miles 1920- *ConAu 21R*
Clark, Naomi *DrAP&F 83*
Clark, Naomi 1932- *ConAu 77*
Clark, Neil McCullough 1890- *ConAu 5R*
Clark, Norman H 1925- *ConAu 69*
Clark, Paraskeva 1898- *CreCan 1*
Clark, Parlin *ConAu X*
Clark, Patricia Denise Robins *WrDr 84*
Clark, Patricia Finrow 1929- *ConAu 17R, SmATA 11*
Clark, Ramsey 1927- *ConAu 29R*
Clark, Robert 1911- *WrDr 84*
Clark, Robert Alfred 1908- *ConAu 101*
Clark, Robert E 1912- *ConAu 41R*
Clark, Robert E D 1906- *ConAu 5R*
Clark, Robert John 1911- *IntWWP 82*
Clark, Robert L, Jr. 1945- *ConAu 103*
Clark, Romane Lewis 1925- *ConAu 17R*
Clark, Ron 1933- *NatPD 81[port]*
Clark, Ronald Harry 1904- *ConAu 110, WrDr 84*
Clark, Ronald William 1916- *ConAu 25R, ConSFA, SmATA 2*
Clark, Ruth C 1920- *ConAu 69*
Clark, Samuel 1945- *ConAu 89*
Clark, Samuel Delbert 1910- *ConAu 11NR, ConAu P-1*
Clark, Septima Poinsette 1898- *ConAu 5R*
Clark, Stephen R L 1945- *ConAu 77*
Clark, Sue C 1935- *ConAu 41R*
Clark, Sydney Aylmer 1890-1975 *ConAu 4NR, -5R, -57*
Clark, Terry Nichols 1940- *ConAu 25R, IntAu&W 82, WrDr 84*
Clark, Thomas Dionysius 1903- *ConAu 4NR, -5R*
Clark, Thomas Willard 1941- *ConAu 81*
Clark, Tom *DrAP&F 83*
Clark, Tom 1941- *ConAu X, ConP 80, WrDr 84*
Clark, Truman R 1935- *ConAu 61*
Clark, Van D 1909- *ConAu P-1, SmATA 2*
Clark, Virginia *ConAu X, SmATA X*

Clark, Walter H, Jr. *MichAu 80*
Clark, Walter Houston *WrDr 84*
Clark, Walter Houston 1902- *ConAu 37R*
Clark, Walter VanTilburg 1909- *DcLEL 1940*
Clark, Walter VanTilburg 1909-1971 *ConAu 9R, -33R, ConNov 82A, DcLB 9[port], FifWWr, ModAL, SmATA 8, TwCA SUP, TwCWW*
Clark, William A 1931- *ConAu 33R*
Clark, William Bedford 1947- *ConAu 109*
Clark, William Donaldson 1916- *ConAu 29R, WrDr 84*
Clark, William Smith, II 1900-1969 *ConAu P-2*
Clark Of Herriotshall, Arthur Melville 1895- *IntWWP 82, WrDr 84*
Clarke, Alfred McDonald 1912- *IntWWP 82*
Clarke, Amy Key 1892- *IntAu&W 82*
Clarke, Anna 1919- *ConAu 102, IntAu&W 82, TwCCr&M 80, WrDr 84*
Clarke, Arthur C 1917- *ConAu 1R, -2NR, ConLC 1, -4, -13, -18, ConNov 82, ConSFA, DcLEL 1940, IntAu&W 82, LongCTC, SmATA 13, TwCA SUP, TwCSFW, TwCWr, WrDr 84*
Clarke, Arthur G 1887- *ConAu P-2*
Clarke, Austin 1896-1974 *CnMD SUP, ConAu 49, ConAu P-2, ConLC 6, -9, DcLB 10[port], EncWL 2, LongCTC, ModBrL, ModBrL SUP, RGFMBP, TwCA SUP, TwCWr*
Clarke, Austin C 1934- *WrDr 84*
Clarke, Austin Chesterfield 1934- *ConAu 25R, ConLC 8, ConNov 82, DcLEL 1940, IntAu&W 82*
Clarke, Basil Fulford Lowther 1908-1978 *ConAu 4NR, -5R, -89*
Clarke, Boden *ConAu X, IntAu&W 82X*
Clarke, Brenda 1926- *ConAu 9NR, WrDr 84*
Clarke, Brenda Margaret Lilian 1926- *ConAu 65, IntAu&W 82*
Clarke, Captain Jafar *ConAu X*
Clarke, Charles Galloway 1899-1983 *ConAu 110*
Clarke, Cheryl *DrAP&F 83*
Clarke, Clorinda 1917- *ConAu 25R, SmATA 7, WrDr 84*
Clarke, Cyril 1907- *WrDr 84*
Clarke, David E 1920- *ConAu 17R*
Clarke, David Ulysses 1908- *NatPD 81[port]*
Clarke, David Waldo 1907- *ConAu 9R, IntAu&W 82*
Clarke, Derrick Harry 1919- *ConAu 103, WrDr 84*
Clarke, Dorothy Clotelle 1908- *WrDr 84*
Clarke, Dudley Wrangel 1899-1974 *ConAu P-1*
Clarke, Duncan L 1941- *ConAu 97*
Clarke, Dwight Lancelot 1885-1971 *ConAu 1R, -103*
Clarke, Ernest George 1927- *ConAu 102*
Clarke, Garry E 1943- *ConAu 77*
Clarke, George Frederick 1883- *CreCan 2*
Clarke, George Timothy *ConAu 1R, -1NR*
Clarke, Gillian 1937- *ConAu 106, ConP 80, WrDr 84*
Clarke, H Harrison 1902- *ConAu 1R, -5NR*
Clarke, Hans Thacher 1887-1972 *ConAu 37R*
Clarke, Harry Eugene, Jr. 1921- *ConAu 5R*
Clarke, Henry Charles 1899- *ConAu 102, WrDr 84*
Clarke, Henry Harrison 1902- *WrDr 84*
Clarke, Hockley *WrDr 84*
Clarke, Hockley 1899- *ConAu X*
Clarke, Howard William 1929- *ConAu 37R*
Clarke, Hugh Vincent 1919- *ConAu 102, WrDr 84*
Clarke, I F 1918- *ConSFA*
Clarke, Ian Robert 1954- *IntWWP 82*
Clarke, J F Gates 1905- *ConAu P-1*
Clarke, Jack Alden *WrDr 84*
Clarke, Jack Alden 1924- *ConAu 29R*
Clarke, James F 1906- *ConAu 69*
Clarke, James Hall *ConAu X*
Clarke, James W 1937- *ConAu 110*
Clarke, Joan *WrDr 84*
Clarke, Joan B 1920- *ConAu 104*
Clarke, Joan B 1921- *SmATA 27*
Clarke, Joan Dorn 1924- *ConAu 9R*
Clarke, Joan L 1920- *WrDr 84*
Clarke, John *ConAu X, DrAP&F 83, SmATA 5*
Clarke, John 1913- *ConAu P-1*
Clarke, John Henrik 1915- *AuNews 1, ConAu 53, LivgBAA*

Clarke, John Joseph 1879- *ConAu 5R, –5NR*
Clarke, Kenneth W 1917- *ConAu 17R*
Clarke, Lige 1942- *ConAu 41R*
Clarke, Martin Lowther 1909- *ConAu 2NR, –5R, WrDr 84*
Clarke, Mary 1923- *ConAu 104, WrDr 84*
Clarke, Mary Stetson 1911- *ConAu 8NR, –21R, SmATA 5, WrDr 84*
Clarke, Mary Washington 1913- *ConAu 11NR, –25R*
Clarke, Mary Whatley 1899- *ConAu 2NR, –5R, WrDr 84*
Clarke, Michael *ConAu X,   –49, SmATA X, –6*
Clarke, Pauline 1921- *ConAu X, IntAu&W 82, SmATA 3, TwCCW 83, WrDr 84*
Clarke, Peter 1936- *ConAu 104*
Clarke, Peter Edward 1929- *IntWWP 82*
Clarke, Peter Frederick 1942- *ConAu 73, WrDr 84*
Clarke, Peter Hugh 1933- *IntAu&W 82*
Clarke, Richard *ConAu X*
Clarke, Robert *ConAu X*
Clarke, Robin Harwood 1937- *ConAu 9NR, –13R*
Clarke, Ron 1937- *ConAu 107*
Clarke, Ronald Francis 1933- *ConAu 21R*
Clarke, Shirley 1925- *ConLC 16*
Clarke, Stephan P 1945- *ConAu 69*
Clarke, T E B 1907- *ConDr 82A*
Clarke, Thomas E 1918- *ConAu 53*
Clarke, Thomas Ernest Bennett 1907- *ConAu 103, IntAu&W 82*
Clarke, Thurston 1946- *ConAu 77*
Clarke, Tom 1918- *ConDr 82C*
Clarke, Tom E 1915- *ConAu 5R*
Clarke, William Dixon 1927- *ConAu 5R*
Clarke, William Kendall 1911?-1981 *ConAu 104*
Clarke, William Malpas 1922- *ConAu 41R*
Clarke, William Thomas 1932- *ConAu 57*
Clarke McKenna, Neva Yvonne 1920- *IntAu&W 82*
Clarkson, Adrienne 1939- *ConAu 49*
Clarkson, E Margaret 1915- *ConAu 1R, –5NR, WrDr 84*
Clarkson, Ewan 1929- *ConAu 25R, SmATA 9, WrDr 84*
Clarkson, G P 1934- *WrDr 84*
Clarkson, Geoffrey P E 1934- *ConAu 2NR, –5R*
Clarkson, Gerald William Wensley 1938- *IntAu&W 82*
Clarkson, Helen *WrDr 84*
Clarkson, J F *ConAu X, WrDr 84*
Clarkson, Jan Nagel 1943- *ConAu 93*
Clarkson, Jesse Dunsmore 1897-1973 *ConAu 5R, –45*
Clarkson, L A 1933- *ConAu 73*
Clarkson, Paul S 1905- *ConAu 29R*
Clarkson, Stephen 1937- *ConAu 41R, IntAu&W 82*
Clarkson, Tom 1913- *ConAu 103, WrDr 84*
Clary, Jack 1932- *ConAu 57*
Clasen, Claus-Peter 1931- *ConAu 41R*
Clasper, Paul Dudley 1923- *ConAu 1R*
Claspy, Everett M 1907?-1973 *ConAu 41R*
Claster, Daniel S 1932- *ConAu 21R*
Claude, Richard Pierre 1934- *ConAu 29R, WrDr 84*
Claudel, Alice Moser *DrAP&F 83*
Claudel, Alice Moser 1918- *ConAu 2NR, –49*
Claudel, Paul 1868-1955 *ClDMEL 80, CnMD, CnMWL, ConAu 104, EncWL 2[port], LongCTC, ModFrL, ModRL, ModWD, TwCA, TwCA SUP, TwCLC 2, –10[port], TwCWr, WhoTwCL*
Claudia, Sister Mary 1906- *ConAu P-1*
Claudia, Susan *ConAu X*
Claudius, I *IntWWP 82X*
Claus, Hugo 1929- *ClDMEL 80, CnMD, EncWL 2, ModWD, WorAu 1970*
Claus, Marshall R 1936-1970 *ConAu P-2*
Clausen, Aage R 1932- *ConAu 49*
Clausen, Andy 1943- *DcLB 16[port]*
Clausen, Connie 1923- *ConAu 1R*
Clausen, Dennis M 1943- *ConAu 106*
Clausen, Hans C 1914- *IntAu&W 82*
Clausen, Jan *DrAP&F 83*
Clausen, Svend 1893-1961 *CnMD*
Clauser, Suzanne 1929- *ConAu 37R*
Claussen, Karen *DrAP&F 83*
Claussen, Sophus 1865-1932 *ClDMEL 80*
Clavel, Bernard 1923- *ConAu 2NR, –45,*

Clavel, Maurice 1918- *CnMD*
Clavel, Maurice 1920-1979 *ClDMEL 80, ConAu 85*
Clavell, James 1924- *ConAu 25R, ConLC 6, –25[port], WrDr 84*
Clawson, Marion 1905- *ConAu 10NR, –65*
Clawson, Robert W 1939- *ConAu 108*
Clay, Carolyn Elizabeth 1948- *ConAmTC*
Clay, Charles 1906- *CreCan 1*
Clay, Charles Travis 1885-1978 *ConAu 77*
Clay, Comer 1910- *ConAu 45*
Clay, Duncan *ConAu X*
Clay, Floyd Martin 1927- *ConAu 45*
Clay, George R *DrAP&F 83*
Clay, Grady E 1916- *ConAu 93*
Clay, James 1924- *ConAu 17R*
Clay, Jim *ConAu X*
Clay, Lucius D 1897-1978 *ConAu 77, –81*
Clay, Marie M 1926- *ConAu 8NR, –61*
Clay, Patrice 1947- *ConAu 106*
Clay, Roberta L 1900- *ConAu P-2*
Claybaugh, Amos L 1917- *ConAu 69*
Claydon, Leslie Francis 1923- *ConAu 53*
Clayes, Stanley A 1922- *ConAu 29R*
Claypool, Jane *ConAu X*
Clayre, Alasdair 1935- *ConAu 102, IntAu&W 82, IntWWP 82, WrDr 84*
Clayton, Barbara *ConAu X*
Clayton, Bruce 1939- *ConAu 69*
Clayton, Charles Curtis 1902- *ConAu 73*
Clayton, Donald D 1935- *ConAu 65*
Clayton, Fay Marie 1925- *IntWWP 82*
Clayton, Howard 1918- *ConAu 29R*
Clayton, Howard 1929- *ConAu 65*
Clayton, Ina *IntWWP 82X*
Clayton, James E 1929- *ConAu 9R*
Clayton, James L 1931- *ConAu 29R*
Clayton, Jo 1939- *ConAu 81*
Clayton, John *ConAu X*
Clayton, John 1892-1979 *ConAu 33R, –89*
Clayton, John J *DrAP&F 83*
Clayton, John J 1935- *ConAu 11NR*
Clayton, John Jacob 1935- *ConAu 25R*
Clayton, Keith 1928- *ConAu 11NR, –21R*
Clayton, Paul C 1932- *ConAu 61*
Clayton, Peter Arthur 1937- *IntAu&W 82*
Clayton, Richard Henry Michael 1907- *ConAu 4NR, –5R*
Clayton, Stanley 1911- *WrDr 84*
Clayton, Susan *ConAu X*
Clayton, Sylvia *WrDr 84*
Clayton, Sylvia Ruth *ConAu 103, IntAu&W 82*
Clayton, Thomas 1932- *ConAu 41R*
Clayton, Thompson B 1904- *ConAu 57*
Claytor, Gertrude Boatwright 1890?-1973 *ConAu 45*
Cleage, Albert B, Jr. 1911- *ConAu 65, LivgBAA*
Cleall, Charles 1927- *ConAu 5R, IntAu&W 82, WrDr 84*
Cleare, John S 1936- *ConAu 65, WrDr 84*
Clearman, Mary *DrAP&F 83*
Cleary, Beverly 1916- *ChlLR 2, ConAu 1R, –2NR, IntAu&W 82, SmATA 2, TwCCW 83*
Cleary, Beverly Atlee 1916- *WrDr 84*
Cleary, David Powers 1915- *ConAu 106*
Cleary, Florence Damon 1896- *ConAu 81*
Cleary, James William 1927- *ConAu 17R*
Cleary, Jon 1917- *ConAu 1R, –3NR, ConNov 82, DcLEL 1940, IntAu&W 82, TwCCr&M 80, WorAu, WrDr 84*
Cleary, Marion E 1935- *IntWWP 82*
Cleary, Polly Chase *DrAP&F 83*
Cleary, Robert E 1932- *ConAu 41R*
Cleator, Philip Ellaby 1908- *ConAu 102*
Cleaver, Bill 1920-1981 *ChlLR 6[port], ConAu 73, SmATA 22[port], –27N, TwCCW 83*
Cleaver, Carole 1934- *ConAu 49, SmATA 6*
Cleaver, Dale G 1928- *ConAu 17R*
Cleaver, Eldridge 1935- *ConAu 21R, DcLEL 1940, LivgBAA, WrDr 84*
Cleaver, Elizabeth 1939- *ConAu 97, SmATA 23[port]*
Cleaver, Hylton Reginald 1891-1961 *ConAu 73, LongCTC*
Cleaver, Nancy *ConAu X*
Cleaver, Vera 1919- *ChlLR 6[port], ConAu 73, SmATA 22[port], TwCCW 83, WrDr 84*
Cleaver, William J 1920-1981 *ConAu 104*
Cleaves, Emery N 1902- *ConAu 33R*

Cleaves, Freeman 1904- *ConAu 1R*
Cleaves, Peter S 1943- *ConAu 69*
Clebsch, William Anthony 1923- *ConAu 13R*
Clecak, Peter 1938- *ConAu 41R, WrDr 84*
Cleese, John 1939- *ConLC 21[port]*
Cleeve, Brian 1921- *WrDr 84*
Cleeve, Brian Talbot 1921- *ConAu 1NR, –49, TwCCr&M 80, TwCRGW*
Clegg, Alec *ConAu X*
Clegg, Alexander Bradshaw 1909- *ConAu 85*
Clegg, Charles Myron, Jr. 1916- *ConAu 25R*
Clegg, Jerry S 1933- *ConAu 77*
Clegg, John 1909- *WrDr 84*
Clegg, Reed K 1907- *ConAu P-1*
Clegg, Stewart 1947- *ConAu 11NR, –69*
Clegg, William Paul 1936- *WrDr 84*
Cleghorn, Reese 1930- *ConAu 25R*
Cleghorn, Sarah Norcliffe 1876-1959 *TwCA, TwCA SUP*
Cleland, Charles C 1924- *ConAu 41R*
Cleland, Charles E 1936- *MichAu 80*
Cleland, David I 1926- *ConAu 10NR, –25R*
Cleland, Hugh *ConAu X*
Cleland, Mabel *ConAu X, SmATA 5*
Cleland, Marie Immaculee 1905- *IntAu&W 82*
Cleland, Morton *ConAu X*
Cleland, W Wendell 1888-1972 *ConAu 37R*
Clelland, Catherine *ConAu X*
Clelland, Richard C 1921- *ConAu 17R*
Clem, Alan L 1929- *ConAu 3NR, –9R, WrDr 84*
Clemeau, Carol *ConAu X, DrAP&F 83*
Clemen, Wolfgang H 1909- *WrDr 84*
Clemen, Wolfgang Hermann 1909- *ConAu 1R, –2NR, IntAu&W 82*
Clemence, Richard Vernon 1910- *ConAu 1R*
Clemens, Alphonse H 1905-1977 *ConAu 73*
Clemens, Bryan T 1934- *ConAu 97*
Clemens, Cyril 1902- *AuNews 2*
Clemens, Diane S 1936- *ConAu 29R*
Clemens, Rodgers *ConAu X*
Clemens, Samuel Langhorne 1835-1910 *ConAu 104, LongCTC, TwCA, TwCSFW*
Clemens, Virginia Phelps 1941- *ConAu 85*
Clemens, Walter C, Jr. 1933- *ConAu 7NR, –17R, WrDr 84*
Clement, Alfred John 1915- *ConAu 25R, WrDr 84*
Clement, Charles Baxter 1940- *ConAu 105*
Clement, Evelyn Geer 1926- *ConAu 53*
Clement, George H 1909- *ConAu 29R, WrDr 84*
Clement, Hal 1922- *ConAu X, ConSFA, DcLB 8[port], TwCSFW, WrDr 84*
Clement, Herbert F 1927- *ConAu 81*
Clement, Jane Tyson 1917- *ConAu 25R*
Clement, Roland C 1912- *ConAu 49*
Clemente, Vince *DrAP&F 83*
Clements, A L 1932- *ConAu 29R*
Clements, Arthur L 1932- *WrDr 84*
Clements, Barbara Evans 1945- *ConAu 89*
Clements, Bruce 1931- *ConAu 5NR, –53, SmATA 27[port], TwCCW 83*
Clements, Colleen D 1936- *ConAu 110*
Clements, Eileen Helen 1905- *ConAu P-1*
Clements, Ellen Catherine 1920- *ConAu 13R, WrDr 84*
Clements, Frank Alexander 1942- *ConAu 93, IntAu&W 82*
Clements, Harold M, Sr. 1907- *ConAu 69*
Clements, John 1916- *ConAu 11NR, –69*
Clements, Julia *IntAu&W 82X*
Clements, Julia 1906- *ConAu P-1*
Clements, Kendrick Alling 1939- *ConAu 110*
Clements, Robert 1912- *WrDr 84*
Clements, Robert John 1912- *ConAu 1R, –5NR*
Clements, Robert W 1939- *ConAu 110*
Clements, Ronald Ernest 1929- *ConAu 13R*
Clements, Tad S 1922- *ConAu 25R*
Clements, Traverse 1900?-1977 *ConAu 69*
Clements, William 1933?-1983 *ConAu 110*
Clements, William M 1943- *ConAu 106*
Clements, Wilma H 1906- *IntWWP 82*
Clemhout, Simone 1934- *ConAu 73*
Cleminshaw, Clarence Higbee 1902- *ConAu 106*
Clemmons, Francois *DrAP&F 83*
Clemmons, Francois 1945- *ConAu 41R*
Clemmons, Robert Starr 1910- *ConAu P-2, WrDr 84*
Clemmons, Vincent Burton 1938- *IntWWP 82*
Clemmons, William 1932- *ConAu 57*
Clemo, Jack 1916- *ConAu X, ConP 80,*

Clune, Henry W *DrAP&F 83*
Clune, Henry W 1890- *ConAu 1R, −5NR*
Clunies Ross, Anthony 1932- *ConAu 53*
Clurman, Harold 1901-1980 *ConAmTC,*
  ConAu 1R, −2NR, −101, DcLEL 1940,
  IntAu&W 82
Cluster, Dick 1947- *ConAu 97*
Clute, Morrel J 1912- *ConAu 13R*
Clute, Robert Eugene 1924- *ConAu 41R*
Clutha, Janet Paterson Frame 1924- *ConAu 1R,*
  −2NR
Cluthe, E *DrAP&F 83*
Clutterbuck, Richard 1917- *ConAu 9NR, −21R,*
  IntAu&W 82, WrDr 84
Clutton, Cecil 1909- *IntAu&W 82, WrDr 84*
Clutton-Brock, Arthur 1868-1924 *LongCTC,*
  TwCA
Clutton-Brock, Arthur Guy 1906- *ConAu 110*
Cluver, Eustace Henry 1894- *ConAu P-1*
Cluysenaar, Anne 1936- *WrDr 84*
Cluysenaar, Anne Alice Andrea *IntWWP 82*
Cluysenaar, Anne Alice Andree 1936- *ConAu 102,*
  ConP 80, IntAu&W 82
Clyde, Norman Asa 1885-1972 *ConAu 41R*
Clyde Cool *ConAu X*
Clymer, Eleanor 1906- *ConAu 9NR, −61,*
  IntAu&W 82, SmATA 9, TwCCW 83,
  WrDr 84
Clymer, Floyd 1895-1970 *ConAu 104*
Clymer, Kenton James 1943- *ConAu 109*
Clymer, Reuben Swinburne 1878- *ConAu P-1*
Clynder, Monica *ConAu X*
Clyne, Douglas 1912- *WrDr 84*
Clyne, James F 1898?-1977 *ConAu 69*
Clyne, Patricia Edwards *ConAu 101,*
  SmATA 31[port]
Clyne, Terence *ConAu X, −X*
Clytus, John 1929- *ConAu 29R*
Cnudde, Charles F 1938- *ConAu 29R*
Coad, Frederick Roy 1925- *ConAu 103,*
  WrDr 84
Coad, Kermit *DrAP&F 83*
Coad, Oral Sumner 1887- *ConAu 45*
Coakley, Lakme 1912- *ConAu 69*
Coakley, Mary Lewis 1907- *ConAu P-1,*
  IntAu&W 82, WrDr 84
Coakley, William Leo *DrAP&F 83*
Coale, Samuel Chase 1943- *ConAu 11NR, −65*
Coalhart, Testus *IntAu&W 82X*
Coalson, Glo 1946- *ConAu 103,*
  SmATA 26[port]
Coan, Eugene V 1943- *ConAu 110*
Coan, Otis W 1895- *ConAu P-2*
Coan, Richard W 1928- *WrDr 84*
Coan, Richard Welton 1928- *ConAu 69,*
  IntAu&W 82
Coates, Austin 1922- *ConAu 102, WrDr 84*
Coates, Belle 1896- *ConAu 5R, SmATA 2*
Coates, Charles R 1915- *ConAu 106*
Coates, Donald Robert 1922- *ConAu 2NR, −49*
Coates, Doreen Frances 1912- *ConAu 107,*
  WrDr 84
Coates, Gary J 1947- *ConAu 110*
Coates, Geoffrey Edward 1917- *ConAu 37R*
Coates, Ken 1930- *IntAu&W 82*
Coates, Robert Myron 1897-1973 *ConAu 5R,*
  −41R, DcLB 4, −9[port], TwCA,
  TwCA SUP
Coates, Ruth Allison 1915- *ConAu 57,*
  SmATA 11
Coates, Sheila *TwCRGW*
Coates, William Ames 1916-1973 *ConAu 37R*
Coates, Willson H 1899-1976 *ConAu 37R, −69*
Coats, Alice M 1905- *ConAu 53, SmATA 11*
Coats, George Wesley 1936- *ConAu 21R,*
  WrDr 84
Coats, Peter 1910- *ConAu 1NR, −49*
Coatsworth, Elizabeth 1893- *DcLB 22[port],*
  TwCCW 83, WrDr 84
Coatsworth, Elizabeth Jane 1893- *ChlLR 2,*
  ConAu 4NR, −5R, SmATA 2, TwCA,
  TwCA SUP
Cobaugh, Stephen Marcus 1955- *IntAu&W 82*
Cobb, Alice 1909- *ConAu 5R*
Cobb, Carl Wesley 1926- *ConAu 21R*
Cobb, Charlie 1944- *LivgBAA*
Cobb, Faye Davis 1932- *ConAu 9R*
Cobb, Frank I 1869-1923 *DcLB 25[port]*
Cobb, G Belton 1892-1971 *ConAu 104,*
  TwCCr&M 80
Cobb, Humphrey 1899-1944 *LongCTC, TwCA,*
  TwCA SUP

Cobb, Irvin S 1876-1944 *DcLB 25[port],*
  LongCTC, TwCA, TwCA SUP
Cobb, Irwin 1876-1944 *TwCWr*
Cobb, Jane *ConAu X, SmATA X*
Cobb, John 1938- *WrDr 84*
Cobb, John Boswell, Jr. 1925- *ConAu 1R, −2NR,*
  IntAu&W 82
Cobb, Jonathan 1946- *ConAu 93*
Cobb, Nathan 1943- *ConAu 105*
Cobb, Richard 1917- *WrDr 84*
Cobb, Robert A 1941- *ConAu 69*
Cobb, Roger W 1941- *ConAu 104*
Cobb, Thomas *DrAP&F 83*
Cobb, Vicki 1938- *ChlLR 2, ConAu 33R,*
  SmATA 8, WrDr 84
Cobb, William *DrAP&F 83*
Cobbett *ConAu X*
Cobbett, Richard *ConAu X, IntAu&W 82X,*
  SmATA X, WrDr 84
Cobbing, Bob 1920- *ConAu 101, ConP 80,*
  DcLEL 1940, WrDr 84
Cobbledick, James R 1935- *ConAu 97*
Cobbs, Price M 1928- *ConAu 21R, LivgBAA*
Cobden-Sanderson, T J 1840-1922 *LongCTC*
Cobean, Charles Scott 1952- *IntWWP 82*
Cober, Alan Edwin 1935- *SmATA 7*
Coberly, Lenore McComas 1925- *IntWWP 82*
Cobham, Sir Alan *ConAu X, SmATA X*
Coble, John 1924- *ConAu 9R*
Cobleigh, Ira U 1903- *ConAu 81*
Coblentz, Stanton A *DrAP&F 83*
Coblentz, Stanton A 1896- *WrDr 84*
Coblentz, Stanton Arthur 1896- *ConAu 5R,*
  ConSFA, IntAu&W 82, TwCSFW
Cobley, John 1914- *ConAu 13R*
Cobrin, Harry Aaron 1902- *ConAu P-2*
Coburn, Andrew *DrAP&F 83*
Coburn, Andrew 1932- *ConAu 4NR, −53*
Coburn, D L 1938- *ConAu 89, ConLC 10,*
  NatPD 81[port]
Coburn, Frederick Simpson 1871-1960 *CreCan 2*
Coburn, John Bowen 1914- *ConAu 1R, −2NR*
Coburn, Karen Levin 1941- *ConAu 65*
Coburn, Kathleen 1905- *ConAu 93, CreCan 2,*
  DcLEL 1940
Coburn, L J *TwCWW, WrDr 84*
Coburn, Louis 1915- *ConAu 104*
Coburn, Thomas B 1944- *ConAu 110*
Coburn, Walt 1889-1971 *ConAu P-1, TwCWW*
Cocagnac, Augustin Maurice Jean 1924-
  ConAu 25R, SmATA 7
Coccioli, Carlo 1920- *ClDMEL 80,*
  ConAu 9NR, −13R, ModRL, TwCWr
Coch-Y-Bonddhu *ConAu X*
Cochard, Thomas Sylvester 1893- *ConAu 57*
Cochet, Gabriel 1888-1973 *ConAu 45*
Cochran, Bert 1917- *ConAu 45*
Cochran, Bobbye A 1949- *SmATA 11*
Cochran, Charles L 1940- *ConAu 57*
Cochran, Clarke E 1945- *ConAu 107*
Cochran, Hamilton 1898-1977 *ConAu 1R, −6NR,*
  −73
Cochran, Jacqueline 1910?-1980 *ConAu 101*
Cochran, Jeff *ConAu X, IntAu&W 82X,*
  WrDr 84
Cochran, John R 1937- *ConAu 41R*
Cochran, Leonard *DrAP&F 83*
Cochran, Leslie H 1939- *ConAu 2NR, −49*
Cochran, Marsha Rabe 1948- *ConAmTC*
Cochran, Rice E *ConAu X*
Cochran, Thomas 1902- *WrDr 84*
Cochran, Thomas C 1902- *ConAu 8NR, −61,*
  DcLB 17[port]
Cochrane, Arthur C 1909- *ConAu 4NR, −5R*
Cochrane, Elizabeth 1867-1922 *DcLB 25[port]*
Cochrane, Eric 1928- *ConAu 49*
Cochrane, Glynn 1940- *ConAu 53*
Cochrane, Hugh 1923- *ConAu 103*
Cochrane, James D 1938- *ConAu 29R*
Cochrane, James L 1942- *ConAu 33R*
Cochrane, Jennifer 1936- *ConAu 102*
Cochrane, Louise Morley 1918- *ConAu 9R*
Cochrane, Pauline A 1929- *ConAu 11NR, −110*
Cochrane, Peggy 1926- *WrDr 84*
Cochrane, Shirley Graves *DrAP&F 83*
Cochrane, Willard W 1914- *ConAu 11NR*
Cochrane, Willard Wesley 1914- *ConAu 21R*
Cochrane, William E 1926- *ConAu 97*
Cochrane DeAlencar, Gertrude E Luise 1906-
  ConAu 5R
Cockburn, Claud 1904-1981 *ConAu 102, −105,*
  WorAu

Cockburn, Thomas Aiden 1912- *ConAu 9R*
Cockcroft, James D 1935- *ConAu 10NR, −25R*
Cockcroft, John 1897-1967 *ConAu P-2*
Cockerell, Douglas Bennett 1870-1945 *LongCTC*
Cockerell, Hugh Anthony Lewis 1909-
  ConAu P-1
Cockerell, Sir Sydney Carlyle 1867-1962
  LongCTC
Cockett, Mary 1915- *ConAu 4NR, −9R,*
  IntAu&W 82, SmATA 3, TwCCW 83,
  WrDr 84
Cocking, Clive 1938- *ConAu 105*
Cocking, John Martin 1914- *ConAu 53,*
  WrDr 84
Cockrell, Amanda *ConAu X*
Cockrell, Cathy *DrAP&F 83*
Cockrell, Marian 1909- *ConAu P-2, TwCRGW,*
  WrDr 84
Cockrell, Pearl Hand 1921- *IntWWP 82*
Cockshut, A O J 1927- *ConAu 10NR, WrDr 84*
Cockshut, Anthony Oliver John 1927-
  ConAu 17R
Cocozzella, Peter 1937- *ConAu 37R*
Cocteau, Jean 1889-1963 *CnMD, CnMWL,*
  ConAu P-2, ConLC 1, −8, −15, −16,
  LongCTC, ModFrL, ModRL, ModWD,
  TwCA, TwCA SUP, TwCWr, WhoTwCL
Cocteau, Jean 1889-1964 *EncWL 2[port]*
Cocteau, Jean 1891-1963 *ClDMEL 80*
Codding, George A, Jr. 1923- *ConAu 33R,*
  WrDr 84
Code, Grant Hyde 1896-1974 *ConAu 49*
Codel, Martin 1903?-1973 *ConAu 41R*
Codel, Michael R 1939- *ConAu 73*
Coder, S Maxwell 1902- *WrDr 84*
Coder, Samuel Maxwell 1902- *ConAu 37R*
Codere, Helen 1917- *ConAu 69*
Coderre, Emile 1893-1970 *CreCan 2*
Codevilla, Angelo 1943- *ConAu 61*
Codrescu, Andrei *DrAP&F 83*
Codrescu, Andrei 1946- *ConAu 33R,*
  IntWWP 82, WrDr 84
Cody, Captain 1846-1917 *LongCTC*
Cody, Al *ConAu X, TwCWW, WrDr 84*
Cody, C S 1923- *ConAu X*
Cody, D Thane R 1932- *ConAu 57*
Cody, Fred 1916- *ConAu 107*
Cody, Hiram Alfred 1872-1948 *CreCan 2*
Cody, James P *ConAu X*
Cody, James R *WrDr 84*
Cody, John 1925- *ConAu 101*
Cody, John J 1930- *ConAu 29R*
Cody, Judith *DrAP&F 83*
Cody, Judith Ann 1946- *IntWWP 82*
Cody, Martin L 1941- *ConAu 53*
Cody, S F 1862-1913 *LongCTC*
Cody, Stetson *TwCWW*
Cody, Walt *ConAu X,   WrDr 84*
Coe, C Norton 1915- *ConAu 1R*
Coe, Christine Sadler *ConAu X*
Coe, Douglas *ConAu X, SmATA X*
Coe, Fred 1914-1979 *ConAu 85*
Coe, Lloyd 1899-1976 *ConAu 69, SmATA 30N*
Coe, Michael Douglas 1929- *ConAu 1R, −4NR,*
  WrDr 84
Coe, Michelle E 1917- *ConAu 106*
Coe, Miriam 1902- *IntWWP 82, WrDr 84*
Coe, Ralph T 1929- *ConAu 1R, −1NR*
Coe, Richard Livingston 1916- *ConAmTC,*
  ConAu 65
Coe, Richard N 1923- *WrDr 84*
Coe, Richard Nelson 1923- *ConAu 25R*
Coe, Rodney Michael 1933- *ConAu 41R*
Coe, Tucker *TwCCr&M 80, WrDr 84*
Coe, William C 1930- *ConAu 37R, WrDr 84*
Coel, Margaret 1937- *ConAu 106*
Coelho, George Victor 1918- *ConAu 1NR, −45*
Coelho Neto, Henrique Maximiano 1864-1934
  ModLAL
Coen, Rena Neumann 1925- *ConAu 13R,*
  SmATA 20, WrDr 84
Coens, Sister Mary Xavier 1918- *ConAu 21R*
Coerr, Eleanor 1922- *ConAu 11NR*
Coerr, Eleanor Beatrice 1922- *ConAu 25R,*
  SmATA 1, WrDr 84
Coetzee, J M 1940- *ConAu 77, ConLC 23[port]*
Cofer, Charles N 1916- *ConAu 37R*
Cofer, Judith Ortiz *DrAP&F 83*
Coffee, Arthur B 1897- *MichAu 80*
Coffey, Alan R 1931- *ConAu 33R*
Coffey, Brian *ConAu X, WrDr 84*
Coffey, Dairine 1933- *ConAu 21R*

Collier, Eugenia W 1928- *ConAu 49, LivgBAA*
Collier, Gaydell M 1935- *ConAu 93*
Collier, Gaylan Jane 1924- *ConAu 37R*
Collier, Graham 1923- *ConAu 17R*
Collier, Graham 1937- *ConAu 105, IntAu&W 82, WrDr 84*
Collier, Herbert L 1933- *ConAu 103*
Collier, James Lincoln 1928- *ChlLR 3, ConAu 4NR, -9R, SmATA 8*
Collier, Jane *ConAu X, IntAu&W 82X, SmATA X, WrDr 84*
Collier, John 1901-1980 *ConAu 10NR, -65, -97, LongCTC, ModBrL, TwCA, TwCA SUP, TwCCr&M 80*
Collier, Johnnie Lucille *ConAu X*
Collier, Joy *ConAu X*
Collier, Kenneth 1910- *WrDr 84*
Collier, Kenneth Gerald 1910- *ConAu 85*
Collier, Leonard Dawson 1908- *ConAu 5R*
Collier, Louise Wilbourn 1925- *ConAu 109*
Collier, Lucille Ann 1919?- *ConAu 109*
Collier, Lucy Ann *ConAu X*
Collier, Margaret *ConAu X, IntAu&W 82X, WrDr 84*
Collier, Peter 1939- *ConAu 65, WrDr 84*
Collier, Phyllis K 1939- *ConAu 110*
Collier, Richard 1924- *ConAu 1R, -5NR, IntAu&W 82, WrDr 84*
Collier, Ron 1930- *CreCan 2*
Collier, Simon 1938- *ConAu 21R*
Collier, Zena *DrAP&F 83*
Collier, Zena 1926- *ConAu 3NR, IntAu&W 82X, SmATA 23[port], WrDr 84*
Colligan, Elsa *DrAP&F 83*
Colligan, Francis J 1908- *ConAu P-2*
Collignon, Jean Henri 1918- *ConAu 1R*
Collignon, Joseph 1930- *ConAu 89*
Collin, Marion 1928- *ConAu 5NR, -9R, TwCRGW, WrDr 84*
Collin, Richard Oliver 1940- *ConAu 105*
Collin, W E 1893- *LongCTC*
Collings, Edwin Geoffrey *WrDr 84*
Collings, Ellsworth 1887- *ConAu 73*
Collings, I J *WrDr 84*
Collings, Jillie *WrDr 84*
Collings, Michael R *DrAP&F 83*
Collingswood, Frederick *WrDr 84*
Collingwood, Charles 1917- *ConAu 29R*
Collingwood, Robin George 1889-1943 *CnMWL, LongCTC, TwCA SUP*
Collingwood, William Gershom 1854-1932 *LongCTC*
Collins, Alice H 1907- *ConAu 65*
Collins, Arnold Quint 1935- *ConAu 73*
Collins, Barbara J 1929- *ConAu 6NR, -57, WrDr 84*
Collins, Barry 1941- *ConAu 102, ConDr 82, WrDr 84*
Collins, Barry E 1937- *ConAu 7NR, -13R*
Collins, Beulah Stowe 1923-1983 *ConAu 110*
Collins, Billy *DrAP&F 83*
Collins, Billy 1941- *IntWWP 82*
Collins, Carvel 1912- *ConAu 8NR, -17R, IntAu&W 82, WrDr 84*
Collins, Charles C 1919- *ConAu 25R*
Collins, Charles William 1880-1964 *ConAu 89*
Collins, Christopher 1936- *ConAu 49*
Collins, Churton 1848-1908 *LongCTC*
Collins, Cindy *ConAu X*
Collins, Clark *ConAu X*
Collins, D *ConAu X*
Collins, Dale 1897- *TwCA, TwCA SUP*
Collins, David A 1931- *ConAu 21R*
Collins, David R 1940- *ConAu 11NR, WrDr 84*
Collins, David Raymond 1940- *ConAu 29R, SmATA 7*
Collins, Desmond 1940- *ConAu 73*
Collins, Douglas 1912-1972 *ConAu 33R*
Collins, Elsie M 1904- *MichAu 80*
Collins, F Herbert 1890- *ConAu P-1*
Collins, Fletcher, Jr. 1906- *ConAu 53*
Collins, Freda 1904- *ConAu X, WrDr 84*
Collins, Frederica Joan Hale 1904- *ConAu P-1*
Collins, Gary 1934- *ConAu 7NR, -57*
Collins, Geoffrey Morison 1923- *WrDr 84*
Collins, George R 1917- *ConAu 1R, -1NR*
Collins, Harold Reeves 1915- *ConAu 25R, WrDr 84*
Collins, Harry C *ConAu X*
Collins, Henry 1917- *ConAu 17R*
Collins, Hunt *ConAu X, SmATA X, WorAu, WrDr 84*

Collins, Jackie *WrDr 84*
Collins, Jackie 1939- *ConAu 102*
Collins, James Daniel 1917- *ConAu 1R, -5NR*
Collins, Jean E 1948- *ConAu 110*
Collins, Jeffrey *ConAu X*
Collins, John H 1893- *ConAu 1R*
Collins, John Martin 1921- *ConAu 49*
Collins, Joseph B 1898?-1975 *ConAu 53*
Collins, Judy 1939- *ConAu 103*
Collins, June Irene 1935- *ConAu 37R*
Collins, L John 1905- *ConAu P-1*
Collins, L John 1905-1982 *ConAu 108*
Collins, Larry 1929- *ConAu 65, WrDr 84*
Collins, Lewis John 1905- *WrDr 84*
Collins, Lorraine 1931- *ConAu 57*
Collins, Margaret 1909- *ConAu 89*
Collins, Marie 1935- *ConAu 53*
Collins, Marjorie A 1930- *ConAu 11NR, -65*
Collins, Martha *DrAP&F 83*
Collins, Max, Jr. 1948- *ConAu 103*
Collins, Meghan 1926- *ConAu 101*
Collins, Michael *WrDr 84*
Collins, Michael 1905- *WrDr 84*
Collins, Michael 1924- *ConAu X, TwCCr&M 80*
Collins, Michael 1930- *ASpks, ConAu 5NR, -53*
Collins, Myron D 1901- *ConAu P-1*
Collins, Myrtle T 1915- *ConAu 101*
Collins, Norman Richard 1907-1982 *ConAu 105, -107, IntAu&W 82, LongCTC, TwCA SUP*
Collins, Orvis F 1918- *ConAu 69*
Collins, Pat Lowery 1932- *ConAu 107, SmATA 31[port]*
Collins, Peter 1942- *ConAu 77*
Collins, Philip Arthur William 1923- *ConAu 5R, -8NR, IntAu&W 82, WrDr 84*
Collins, Robert 1924- *ConAu 89*
Collins, Robert E 1927- *ConAu 69*
Collins, Robert M 1943- *ConAu 110*
Collins, Robert Oakley 1933- *ConAu 1R, -4NR, -9R*
Collins, Rowland Lee 1934- *ConAu 9R*
Collins, Ruth Philpott 1890-1975 *ConAu 1R, -4NR, -53, SmATA 30N*
Collins, Thomas Hightower 1910- *ConAu 102*
Collins, Trish 1927- *ConAu 106*
Collins, W E 1893- *LongCTC*
Collins, Will *ConAu X*
Collins, William Alexander Roy 1900-1976 *ConAu 69*
Collins, William B *ConAmTC*
Collins, William Bernard 1913- *ConAu 5R*
Collins Persse, Michael 1931- *WrDr 84*
Collinson, Laurence 1925- *WrDr 84*
Collinson, Laurence Henry 1925- *ConAu 103, ConP 80*
Collinson, Patrick 1929- *IntAu&W 82*
Collinson, Roger 1936- *ConAu 110, WrDr 84*
Collis, John Stewart 1900- *ConAu 61, IntAu&W 82*
Collis, Kevin F 1930- *ConAu 107*
Collis, Louise 1925- *ConAu 21R, IntAu&W 82, WrDr 84*
Collis, Maurice 1889-1973 *ConAu 4NR, -5R, -89, LongCTC, TwCA SUP*
Collis, Robert *WrDr 84*
Collis, William Robert Fitzgerald 1900- *ConAu P-1*
Collison, David 1937- *ConAu 105*
Collison, Koder M 1910- *ConAu 53*
Collison, Robert Lewis Wright 1914- *ConAu 2NR, -5R*
Colliss, Gertrude Florence Mary 1908- *ConAu 5R*
Collodi, Carlo 1826-1890 *ChlLR 5[port], SmATA X*
Collom, Jack *DrAP&F 83*
Collom, Jack 1931- *ConAu 77*
Colloms, Brenda 1919- *ConAu 7NR, -61, IntAu&W 82, WrDr 84*
Collymore, Frank 1893- *WrDr 84*
Collymore, Frank Appleton 1893- *ConP 80, DcLEL 1940*
Collyns, Robin 1940- *ConAu 69*
Colm, Gerhard 1897-1968 *ConAu 5R, -103*
Colman, Arthur D 1937- *ConAu 33R*
Colman, E Adrian M 1930- *ConAu 57, WrDr 84*
Colman, George, The Younger *CreCan 2*

Colman, Hila *ConAu 7NR, -13R, SmATA 1*
Colman, John Edward 1923- *ConAu 21R, WrDr 84*
Colman, Juliet Benita 1944- *ConAu 61*
Colman, Libby Lee 1940- *ConAu 33R*
Colman, Morris 1899?-1981 *SmATA 25N*
Colmer, John Anthony 1921- *ConAu 85, IntAu&W 82, WrDr 84*
Colmer, Michael 1942- *ConAu 69*
Colodny, Robert G 1915- *ConAu 37R*
Colombo, Dale *ConAu X*
Colombo, John Robert 1936- *ConAu 11NR, -25R, ConP 80, CreCan 2, IntAu&W 82, IntWWP 82, WrDr 84*
Colonius, Lillian 1911- *ConAu 21R, SmATA 3*
Colony, Horatio 1900-1977 *ConAu 37R*
Colorado, Antonio J 1903- *ConAu X, SmATA 23[port]*
Colorado Capella, Antonio Julio 1903- *ConAu 17R*
Colquhoun, Archibald 1912-1964 *ConAu 89, WorAu*
Colquhoun, Frank 1909- *ConAu 106, WrDr 84*
Colquhoun, Ithell 1906- *ConAu 13R, IntWWP 82, WrDr 84*
Colquhoun, Keith 1927- *ConAu 102, WrDr 84*
Colquitt, Betsy Feagan 1926- *ConAu 53, IntAu&W 82*
Colson, Bill *TwCWW*
Colson, Charles W 1931- *ConAu 102*
Colson, Elizabeth 1917- *WrDr 84*
Colson, Elizabeth Florence 1917- *ConAu 1R, -53*
Colson, Frederick *ConAu X*
Colson, Greta 1913- *ConAu P-1*
Colson, Howard P 1910- *ConAu 29R*
Colson, John 1918- *WrDr 84*
Colson-Haig, S *CreCan 2*
Colston, Lowell Gwen 1919- *ConAu 53*
Colston-Baynes, Dorothy 1881?-1973 *ConAu 104, LongCTC*
Colt, Clem *ConAu X, IntAu&W 82X, TwCWW, WrDr 84*
Colt, Martin *ConAu X, SmATA X, -1*
Colt, Zandra *WrDr 84*
Colter, Cyrus 1910- *ConAu 10NR, -65, ConNov 82, IntAu&W 82, LivgBAA, WrDr 84*
Colter, Shayne *ConAu X, WrDr 84*
Coltharp, Lurline H 1913- *ConAu 17R, WrDr 84*
Coltman, Ernest Vivian *ConAu X*
Coltman, Will *ConAu X, TwCWW*
Colton, C E 1914- *ConAu 2NR, -5R*
Colton, Clarence Eugene 1914- *WrDr 84*
Colton, Harold S 1881-1970 *ConAu 1R, -3NR*
Colton, Helen 1918- *ConAu 57*
Colton, James *ConAu X, WrDr 84*
Colton, James B, II 1908- *ConAu 37R*
Colton, Joel 1918- *ConAu 1R, -2NR, IntAu&W 82, WrDr 84*
Coltrane, James *ConAu X*
Colum, Mary 1887?-1957 *LongCTC, TwCA, TwCA SUP*
Colum, Padraic 1881-1972 *CnMD, ConAu 33R, -73, LongCTC, ModBrL, ModBrL SUP, ModWD, SmATA 15, TwCA, TwCA SUP, TwCCW 83, TwCWr*
Columella *SmATA X*
Colver, A Wayne 1923- *ConAu 93*
Colver, Alice Mary 1892- *ConAu 69*
Colver, Anne 1908- *ConAu 2NR, -45, SmATA 7*
Colvett, Latayne *ConAu X*
Colville, Alex 1920- *CreCan 1*
Colville, David Alexander 1920- *CreCan 1*
Colville, Derek Kent 1923- *ConAu 105*
Colville, John 1915- *ConAu 61, WrDr 84*
Colville, John Rupert 1915- *ConAu 10NR*
Colvin, Brenda 1897-1981 *ConAu 108*
Colvin, Elaine Wright 1942- *ConAu 106*
Colvin, Howard Montagu 1919- *ConAu 61*
Colvin, Ian G 1912-1975 *ConAu 57, ConAu P-2*
Colvin, James *ConAu X*
Colvin, Ralph Whitmore 1920-1981 *ConAu 104, -107*
Colvin, Sir Sidney 1845-1927 *LongCTC, TwCA, TwCA SUP*
Colwell, C Carter 1932- *ConAu 41R*
Colwell, Eileen 1904- *ConAu 29R, SmATA 2*
Colwell, Ernest Cadman 1901-1974 *ConAu 4NR, -5R, -53*
Colwell, Richard J 1930- *ConAu 69*

Colwell, Robert 1931- *ConAu 33R*
Colwin, Laurie 1944- *DcLB Y80B[port]*
Colwin, Laurie 1945- *ConAu 89, ConLC 5, –13, –23*
Colyer, Penrose 1940- *ConAu 65*
Comaish, Peter William 1958- *IntWWP 82*
Coman, Dale Rex 1906- *ConAu 81*
Coman, Edwin Truman, Jr. 1903- *ConAu 9R*
Comay, Joan *ConAu 103, IntAu&W 82, WrDr 84*
Combe, Gordon Desmond 1917- *WrDr 84*
Combe, Marion *WrDr 84*
Comber, Elizabeth *WorAu*
Comber, Lillian 1916- *ConAu 3NR, –9R*
Combs, A W 1912- *ConAu 10NR, –17R*
Combs, David 1934- *ConAu 108*
Combs, Elisha Trammell, Jr. 1924- *DcLEL 1940*
Combs, James E 1941- *ConAu 101*
Combs, Jerald A 1937- *ConAu 110*
Combs, Richard Earl 1934- *ConAu 33R*
Combs, Robert *ConAu X*
Combs, Tram *DrAP&F 83*
Combs, Tram 1924- *ConAu 13R*
Comden, Betty 1919- *ConAu 2NR, –49, ConDr 82D*
Comeau, Arthur M 1938- *ConAu 61*
Comer, James Pierpont 1934- *ConAu 61*
Comerford, Pat *IntAu&W 82X*
Comey, James H *DrAP&F 83*
Comey, James Hugh 1947- *ConAu 65, IntAu&W 82*
Comfort, Alex 1920- *ConAu 1NR, ConLC 7, ConNov 82, ConP 80, IntWWP 82, WrDr 84*
Comfort, Alexander 1920- *ConAu 1R, DcLEL 1940, IntAu&W 82, LongCTC, ModBrL, TwCA SUP*
Comfort, Charles Fraser 1900- *CreCan 2*
Comfort, Howard 1904- *ConAu 37R*
Comfort, Iris Tracy 1917- *ConAu 6NR, –13R, IntAu&W 82, WrDr 84*
Comfort, Jane Levington 1903- *ConAu X, SmATA 1*
Comfort, Mildred Houghton 1886- *ConAu 9R, SmATA 3*
Comfort, Montgomery *ConAu X, IntAu&W 82X*
Comfort, Richard A 1933- *ConAu 21R*
Comfort, Will Levington 1878-1932 *MichAu 80, TwCA, TwCA SUP, TwCWW*
Comidas, Chinas *ConAu X*
Comini, Alessandra 1934- *ConAu 93, WrDr 84*
Comins, Ethel M 1901- *ConAu 8NR, –61, SmATA 11*
Comins, Jeremy 1933- *ConAu 65, SmATA 28[port]*
Comito, Terry Allen 1935- *ConAu 109*
Commager, Henry Steele 1902- *ConAu 21R, DcLB 17[port], SmATA 23[port], TwCA SUP, WrDr 84*
Commentator *IntAu&W 82X*
Commins, William Dollard, Sr. 1899-1983 *ConAu 109*
Commire, Anne *ConAu 69, NatPD 81[port]*
Committe, Thomas C 1922- *ConAu 65*
Commoner, Barry 1917- *ConAu 65, ConIsC 1[port], WrDr 84*
Como, William 1925- *ConAu 69*
Comparetti, Alice Creed Pattee 1907- *ConAu 37R*
Compere, Mickie *ConAu X*
Compfort, Marjorie Lenore *DrAP&F 83*
Complo, Sister Jannita Marie 1935- *ConAu 57*
Comprone, Joseph J 1943- *ConAu 5NR, –53*
Compton, Ann *ConAu X*
Compton, Anne Elizabeth 1949- *IntAu&W 82*
Compton, D G 1930- *ConAu 25R, ConSFA, TwCSFW, WrDr 84*
Compton, Guy *ConAu X*
Compton, Henry *IntWWP 82X*
Compton, Henry 1909- *WrDr 84*
Compton, Henry Pasfield 1909- *ConAu 9R, IntWWP 82*
Compton, James Vincent 1928- *ConAu 29R, WrDr 84*
Compton, Joseph 1891-1964 *LongCTC*
Compton-Burnett, Ivy 1884-1969 *EncWL 2*
Compton-Burnett, Ivy 1892?-1969 *CnMWL, ConAu 1R, –4NR, –25R, ConLC 1, –3, –10, –15, LongCTC, ModBrL, ModBrL SUP, TwCA SUP, TwCWr, WhoTwCL*
Compton-Hall, Richard 1929- *ConAu 107*

Comrey, Andrew Laurence 1923- *ConAu 106*
Comstock, Anthony 1844-1915 *ConAu 110, LongCTC*
Comstock, Helen 1893-1970 *ConAu 4NR, –5R, –89*
Comstock, Henry B 1908- *ConAu P-2*
Comstock, Mary Bryce 1934- *ConAu 105*
Comstock, W Richard 1928- *ConAu 73*
Comte, The Great *ConAu X, SmATA X*
Comtois, Ulysse 1931- *CreCan 1*
Comus *SmATA X*
Comyns, Barbara 1912- *ConAu X*
Comyns-Carr, Barbara Irene Veronica 1912- *ConAu 5R*
Conacher, D J 1918- *ConAu 25R*
Conacher, J B 1916- *ConAu 25R*
Conan, Laure 1845-1924 *CreCan 1*
Conan Doyle *LongCTC, TwCA, TwCA SUP*
Conan Doyle, Adrian Malcolm 1910-1970 *ConAu 5R, –29R*
Conan Doyle, Sir Arthur 1859-1930 *SmATA X*
Conant, Eaton H 1930- *ConAu 53*
Conant, Howard 1921- *ConAu 8NR, –17R*
Conant, James Bryant 1893-1978 *ConAu 13R, –77*
Conant, Kenneth John 1894- *ConAu 1R, WrDr 84*
Conant, Ralph W 1926- *ConAu 29R, WrDr 84*
Conant, Roger 1909- *ConAu 107*
Conard, Alfred Fletcher 1911- *ConAu 13R*
Conard, Joseph W 1911- *ConAu 13R*
Conarroe, Joel 1934- *ConAu 29R*
Conarroe, Richard R 1928- *ConAu 69*
Conaway, James 1941- *ConAu 33R*
Concha, Joseph L *DrAP&F 83*
Conchon, Georges 1925- *IntAu&W 82*
Conconi, Charles N 1938- *ConAu 77*
Conde, Carmen 1907- *ClDMEL 80*
Conde, Jesse C 1912- *ConAu 57*
Conde, Maryse *ConAu X*
Conde Abellan, Carmen 1907- *IntAu&W 82*
Condee, Ralph Waterbury 1916- *ConAu 17R*
Condit, Carl W 1914- *WrDr 84*
Condit, Carl Wilbur 1914- *ConAu 1R, –4NR, IntAu&W 82*
Condit, Martha Olson 1913- *ConAu 73, SmATA 28*
Condliffe, John Bell 1891-1981 *ConAu 106, ConAu P-1*
Condon, Eddie 1905-1973 *ConAu 45*
Condon, George Edward 1916- *ConAu 1NR, –45*
Condon, Jack *ConAu X*
Condon, John C 1938- *ConAu 21R*
Condon, John C, Jr. 1938- *ConAu 10NR*
Condon, Margaret Jean *DrAP&F 83*
Condon, Richard 1915- *ConAu 1R, –2NR, ConLC 4, –6, –8, –10, ConNov 82, ModAL, ModAL SUP, TwCCr&M 80, TwCSFW, WorAu, WrDr 84*
Condon, Robert 1921?-1972 *ConAu 37R*
Condor, Gladyn *ConAu X*
Condray, Bruno *ConAu X, WrDr 84*
Condry, Dorothea June Douglass 1935- *IntWWP 82*
Condry, William 1918- *WrDr 84*
Condry, William Moreton 1918- *ConAu 103, IntAu&W 82*
Cone, Carl B 1916- *ConAu 9R, WrDr 84*
Cone, Edward Toner 1917- *ConAu 110*
Cone, Fairfax Mastick 1903-1977 *ConAu 69, –73*
Cone, Ferne Geller 1921- *ConAu 107*
Cone, James H 1938- *ConAu 33R, LivgBAA*
Cone, John F 1926- *ConAu 17R*
Cone, Molly 1918- *WrDr 84*
Cone, Molly Lamken 1918- *ConAu 1R, –1NR, SmATA 1, –28[port]*
Cone, William F 1919- *ConAu 57*
Conerly, Perian Collier 1926- *ConAu 5R*
Coney, Michael G 1932- *ConAu 97, TwCSFW, WrDr 84*
Confer, Vincent 1913- *ConAu 21R*
Conford, Ellen 1942- *ConAu 33R, SmATA 6, TwCCW 83, WrDr 84*
Confucius *ConAu X*
Congdon, Herbert Wheaton 1876-1965 *ConAu 5R*
Congdon, Kirby *DrAP&F 83*
Congdon, Kirby 1924- *ConAu 7NR, –13R*
Congdon, William Grosvenor 1912- *ConAu 7NR, –17R*
Conger, John 1921- *ConAu 6NR, –13R, WrDr 84*
Conger, Lesley *ConAu X, SmATA X*

Congrat-Butler, Stefan 1914?-1979 *ConAu 103, –89*
Congreve, Willard J 1921- *ConAu 57*
Conil, Jean 1917- *ConAu 13R*
Conine, Ernest 1925- *ConAu 69*
Coniston, Ed *ConAu X, TwCWW*
Conkey, Virginia 1939- *IntWWP 82*
Conkin, Paul K 1929- *ConAu 33R*
Conkle, D Steven *DrAP&F 83*
Conkle, E P 1899- *CnMD, ConAu 65, ModWD*
Conklin, Barbara P 1927- *ConAu 109*
Conklin, Gladys Plemon 1903- *ConAu 1R, –4NR, SmATA 2*
Conklin, Groff 1904-1968 *ConAu 1R, –3NR*
Conklin, John E 1943- *ConAu 37R, WrDr 84*
Conklin, Paul S *SmATA 33*
Conkling, Grace Walcott Hazard 1878-1958 *TwCA, TwCA SUP*
Conkling, Hilda 1910- *SmATA 23[port], TwCA, TwCA SUP*
Conlay, Iris 1910- *ConAu P-1*
Conley, Ellen Alexander 1938- *ConAu 103*
Conley, Enid Mary 1917- *ConAu 10NR, –65*
Conley, Everett Nathaniel 1949- *LivgBAA*
Conley, John 1912- *ConAu 61*
Conley, Phillip Mallory 1887- *ConAu 69*
Conley, Robert J *DrAP&F 83*
Conley, Robert J 1940- *ConAu 41R, IntWWP 82*
Conlin, David A 1897- *ConAu 17R*
Conlin, Joseph R 1940- *ConAu 49*
Conlon, Denis J 1932- *ConAu 37R, IntAu&W 82*
Conly, Robert Leslie 1918?-1973 *ConAu 41R, –73, SmATA 23[port]*
Conn, Canary Denise 1949- *ConAu 57*
Conn, Charles Paul 1945- *ConAu 6NR, –57*
Conn, Charles William 1920- *ConAu 10NR, –21R*
Conn, Frances G 1925- *ConAu 33R*
Conn, Jan E 1952- *ConAu 110*
Conn, Martha Orr 1935- *ConAu 93*
Conn, Peter J 1942- *ConAu 33R*
Conn, Stetson 1908- *ConAu P-1*
Conn, Stewart 1936- *ConDr 82, ConP 80, WrDr 84*
Conn, Walter E 1940- *ConAu 110*
Connable, Alfred 1931- *ConAu 81*
Connah, Margaret Heywood 1912- *IntWWP 82*
Connally, Eugenia Horstman 1931- *ConAu 103*
Connell, Brian Reginald 1916- *ConAu 1R, –4NR, WrDr 84*
Connell, Evan S *DrAP&F 83*
Connell, Evan S, Jr. 1924- *ConAu 1R, –2NR, ConLC 4, –6, ConNov 82, DcLB Y81A[port], –2, DcLEL 1940, ModAL SUP, WhoTwCL, WorAu, WrDr 84*
Connell, F Norreys 1874-1948 *LongCTC*
Connell, Francis J 1888-1967 *ConAu P-1*
Connell, John 1909-1965 *LongCTC*
Connell, Jon 1952- *ConAu 97*
Connell, K H 1917-1973 *ConAu P-2*
Connell, Kirk *ConAu X, SmATA X*
Connell, Maureen 1931- *ConAu 104*
Connell, Norreys 1874-1948 *TwCA, TwCA SUP*
Connell, Richard Edward 1893-1949 *TwCA, TwCA SUP*
Connell, William 1916- *WrDr 84*
Connell, William Fraser 1916- *ConAu 104, IntAu&W 82*
Connellan, Leo *DrAP&F 83*
Connellan, Leo 1928- *ConAu 81*
Connelly, Marc 1890- *CnMD, ConAmA, ConAu 85, ConLC 7, DcLB 7[port], LongCTC, ModAL, ModWD*
Connelly, Marc 1890-1980 *ConAu 102, DcLB Y80A[port], SmATA 25N*
Connelly, Marcus Cook 1890- *TwCA, TwCA SUP*
Connelly, Merval Hannah 1914- *IntWWP 82X*
Connelly, Michele *DrAP&F 83*
Connelly, Owen 1924- *ConAu 17R*
Connelly, Philip M 1904?-1981 *ConAu 104*
Connelly, Thomas L 1938- *ConAu 11NR, –17R*
Connely, Willard 1888-1967 *ConAu P-2*
Conner, Berenice Gillete 1908- *ConAu 65*
Conner, Patrick 1947- *ConAu 106, WrDr 84*
Conner, Patrick Rearden 1907- *IntAu&W 82*
Conner, Patrick Rearden 1907- *ConAu 5R*
Conner, Paul Willard 1937- *ConAu 17R*
Conner, Rearden 1907- *ConAu X, WrDr 84*

Conner, Reardon 1907- *LongCTC*
Conners, Bernard F 1926- *ConAu 41R*
Conners, Kenneth Wray 1909- *ConAu 29R,*
    WrDr 84
Connery, Robert Howe 1907- *ConAu 41R*
Connett, Eugene Virginius, III 1891-1969
    ConAu P-1
Connette, Earle 1910- *ConAu P-1*
Connick, C Milo *WrDr 84*
Connick, C Milo 1917- *ConAu 1R*
Conniff, Frank 1914-1971 *ConAu 93*
Conniff, James C G 1920- *ConAu 21R*
Connington, J J 1880-1947 *LongCTC, TwCA,*
    TwCA SUP, TwCCr&M 80
Connolly, Cyril Vernon 1903-1974 *CnMWL,*
    ConAu 53, ConAu P-2, ConLCrt 82,
    LongCTC, ModBrL, TwCA SUP, TwCWr
Connolly, Francis X 1909-1965 *ConAu P-1*
Connolly, Geraldine *DrAP&F 83*
Connolly, James Brendan 1868-1957 *TwCA,*
    TwCA SUP
Connolly, Jerome Patrick 1931- *SmATA 8*
Connolly, Paul *ConAu X, WrDr 84*
Connolly, Peter 1935- *ConAu 103, WrDr 84*
Connolly, Ray *WrDr 84*
Connolly, Ray 1940- *ConAu 101, IntAu&W 82*
Connolly, Robert D 1917- *ConAu 69*
Connolly, Thomas Edmund 1918- *ConAu 1R,*
    -4NR
Connolly, Vivian 1925- *ConAu 1NR, -49*
Connor, Jim 1935- *ConAu 107*
Connor, John Andrew 1957- *IntWWP 82*
Connor, John Anthony 1930- *ConAu 13R*
Connor, Joyce Mary *WrDr 84*
Connor, Joyce Mary 1929- *ConAu X, -10NR*
Connor, Kevin *WrDr 84*
Connor, Lawrence S 1925- *ConAu 89*
Connor, Patricia 1943- *ConAu 25R*
Connor, Patrick Reardon *IntAu&W 82X*
Connor, Ralph *ConAu X*
Connor, Ralph 1860-1937 *CreCan 1, LongCTC,*
    TwCA, TwCA SUP, TwCWW, TwCWr
Connor, Seymour V 1923- *ConAu 53*
Connor, Susanna Pflaum *ConAu X*
Connor, Tony 1930- *ConAu X, ConP 80,*
    DcLEL 1940, WrDr 84
Connor, W Robert 1934- *ConAu 41R*
Connor, Walter Downing 1942- *ConAu 106*
Connor, William 1909?-1967 *ConAu 25R*
Connor, Sir William Neil *LongCTC*
Connor-Bey, Brenda *DrAP&F 83*
Connors, Andree *DrAP&F 83*
Connors, Bruton 1931- *ConAu X,*
    IntWWP 82X, WrDr 84
Connors, Dorsey *ConAu 45*
Connors, Joseph 1945- *ConAu 106*
Conolly, L W 1941- *ConAu 106*
Conor, Glen *ConAu X*
Conot, Robert E 1929- *ConAu 2NR, -45,*
    WrDr 84
Conover, C Eugene 1903- *ConAu 5R*
Conover, Carole 1941- *ConAu 89*
Conover, Chris 1950- *SmATA 31[port]*
Conover, Hobart H 1914- *ConAu 13R*
Conover, Jessica Arline Wilcox *ConAu X*
Conover, Roger L *DrAP&F 83*
Conquest, Edwin Parker, Jr. 1931- *ConAu 29R*
Conquest, George Robert Acworth 1917-
    DcLEL 1940
Conquest, Ned 1931- *ConAu X, WrDr 84*
Conquest, Owen 1875-1961 *ConAu X, LongCTC,*
    SmATA X
Conquest, Robert 1917- *ConAu 9NR, -13R,*
    ConP 80, ConSFA, IntAu&W 82,
    IntWWP 82, LongCTC, TwCSFW,
    TwCWr, WorAu, WrDr 84
Conra, Fredwa 1921- *IntAu&W 82*
Conrad, Alfred Borys 1899?-1979 *ConAu 104*
Conrad, Andree 1945- *ConAu 29R*
Conrad, Barnaby 1922- *ConAu 6NR, -9R,*
    WorAu
Conrad, Brad *DrAP&F 83*
Conrad, Brenda *ConAu X, TwCCr&M 80*
Conrad, C *WorAu 1970*
Conrad, David Eugene 1928- *ConAu 17R*
Conrad, Earl 1912- *ConAu 1R, -10NR*
Conrad, Edna 1893- *ConAu P-2*
Conrad, Jack 1923- *ConAu 9R*
Conrad, John W 1935- *ConAu 4NR, -53*
Conrad, Joseph 1857-1924 *CnMD, CnMWL,*
    ConAu 104, DcLB 10[port],
    EncWL 2[port], LongCTC, ModBrL,

ModBrL SUP, ModWD, SmATA 27[port],
    TwCA, TwCA SUP, TwCLC 1, -6[port],
    TwCWr, WhoTwCL
Conrad, Kenneth *ConAu X, IntAu&W 82X*
Conrad, L K *ConAu X*
Conrad, Nancy Lu 1927- *IntAu&W 82*
Conrad, Robert 1928- *ConAu 41R*
Conrad, Robert Arnold *ConAu X*
Conrad, Susan 1941- *WrDr 84*
Conrad, Sybil 1921- *ConAu 21R*
Conrad, Tod *ConAu X*
Conrad, William Chester 1882- *ConAu P-1*
Conradi *IntAu&W 82X*
Conradi-Bleibtreu, Ellen 1929- *IntAu&W 82*
Conradis, Heinz 1907- *ConAu P-1*
Conrads, Ulrich 1923- *ConAu 9R*
Conran, Anthony 1931- *ConAu 65, ConP 80,*
    DcLEL 1940, WrDr 84
Conran, Shirley 1932- *ConAu 103, WrDr 84*
Conran, Terence Orby 1931- *ConAu 85*
Conron, Brandon 1919- *ConAu 17R,*
    DcLEL 1940
Conrow, Robert W 1942- *ConAu 57, WrDr 84*
Conroy, Charles W 1922- *ConAu 13R*
Conroy, F Hilary 1919- *IntAu&W 82*
Conroy, Frank 1936- *ConAu 77*
Conroy, Jack 1899- *ConAu X, ConNov 82,*
    DcLB Y81B[port], IntAu&W 82,
    SmATA 19, WrDr 84
Conroy, John Wesley 1899- *ConAu 3NR, -5R,*
    SmATA X
Conroy, Mary 1941- *ConAu 110*
Conroy, Michael R 1945- *ConAu 9NR, -53*
Conroy, Pat 1945- *AuNews 1, ConAu 85,*
    DcLB 6[port]
Conroy, Patricia 1941- *ConAu 93*
Conroy, Peter V, Jr. 1944- *ConAu 53*
Conscience, Hendrik 1812-1883 *ClDMEL 80*
Considine, Bob 1906- *AuNews 2, ConAu X*
Considine, Douglas M 1915- *ConAu 11NR, -69*
Considine, John Joseph 1897- *ConAu 1R*
Considine, Robert Bernard 1906-1975 *ConAu 61,*
    -93
Consilvio, Thomas 1947- *ConAu 57*
Consolo, Dominick P 1923- *ConAu 33R*
Constable, Anthony 1929- *WrDr 84*
Constable, John W 1922- *ConAu 81*
Constable, Patricia Ann 1934- *IntWWP 82*
Constable, Patricia Anna *IntWWP 82X*
Constable, Trevor James 1925- *ConAu 89*
Constable, William George 1887-1976 *ConAu 5R,*
    -65
Constain, Thomas B 1885-1965 *ConAu 25R*
Constandur S, Denis 1910- *IntAu&W 82*
Constant, Alberta Wilson 1908-1981 *ConAu 1R,*
    -4NR, -109, SmATA 22[port], -28N
Constant, Clinton 1912- *IntAu&W 82*
Constant, Stephen 1931- *WrDr 84*
Constant, Yvonne *ConAmTC*
Constantelos, Demetrios J 1927- *ConAu 8NR,*
    -21R, WrDr 84
Constantin, James A 1922- *ConAu 13R*
Constantin, Robert W 1937- *ConAu 25R*
Constantin-Weyer, Maurice 1881-1964 *CreCan 2,*
    TwCA, TwCA SUP
Constantine, Larry L 1943- *ConAu 81*
Constantine, Mildred 1914- *ConAu 105*
Constantineau, Gilles 1933- *CreCan 2*
Constiner, Merle *TwCWW, WrDr 84*
Contant, Alexis 1858-1918 *CreCan 2*
Conte, Arthur 1920- *IntAu&W 82*
Conte, Michel 1932- *CreCan 2*
Conti, Haroldo 1925- *ModLAL*
Conton, William 1925- *ConAu 1R, WrDr 84*
Contoski, Victor *DrAP&F 83*
Contoski, Victor 1936- *ConAu 25R*
Contosta, David R 1945- *ConAu 104*
Contreras, Heles 1933- *ConAu 37R*
Contreras Pazo, Francisco 1913- *IntAu&W 82*
Converse, John Marquis 1909-1980 *ConAu 102*
Converse, Paul D 1889-1968 *ConAu P-2*
Converse, Philip E 1928- *ConAu 6NR, -13R*
Convict Writer, The *ConAu X*
Conway, Alan 1920- *ConAu 1R, -2NR,*
    WrDr 84
Conway, Arlington B *ConAu X*
Conway, Celine *TwCRGW, WrDr 84*
Conway, David 1939- *ConAu 106, WrDr 84*
Conway, Denise *ConAu X*
Conway, E Carolyn 1927- *WrDr 84*
Conway, Freda 1911- *ConAu 25R, WrDr 84*
Conway, Gordon *ConAu X, SmATA X*

Conway, Harry Donald 1917- *WrDr 84*
Conway, J D 1905-1967 *ConAu 1R, -2NR*
Conway, Joan Ditzel 1933- *ConAu 97*
Conway, John Seymour 1929- *ConAu 25R*
Conway, Laura *TwCRGW, WrDr 84*
Conway, Margaret 1935- *ConAu 37R*
Conway, Peter *ConAu X*
Conway, Theresa 1951- *ConAu 103*
Conway, Thomas D 1934- *ConAu 21R*
Conway, Troy *ConAu X, TwCCr&M 80,*
    WrDr 84
Conway, Veronica Delphine DeWeld Silmon- 1920-
    IntAu&W 82
Conway, Ward *ConAu X*
Conway, William J 1904-1983 *ConAu 110*
Conybeare, Charles Augustus *ConAu X*
Conyers, James E 1932- *ConAu 41R*
Conyngham, William Joseph 1924- *ConAu 53*
Conze, Edward J D 1904- *ConAu 13R*
Conzelman, James Gleason 1898-1970 *ConAu 104*
Conzelman, Jimmy *ConAu X*
Coogan, Daniel 1915- *ConAu 21R*
Coogan, John W 1947- *ConAu 107*
Coogan, Joseph Patrick 1925- *ConAu 1R, -4NR*
Cook, Adrian 1940- *ConAu 49*
Cook, Alan Hugh 1922- *ConAu 106,*
    IntAu&W 82, WrDr 84
Cook, Albert *DrAP&F 83*
Cook, Albert 1925- *WrDr 84*
Cook, Albert Spaulding 1925- *ConAu 1R, -1NR,*
    WorAu
Cook, Alice Rice 1899-1973 *ConAu 41R*
Cook, Ann Jennalie 1934- *ConAu 105*
Cook, Arlene Ethel 1936- *ConAu 65*
Cook, Bernadine F 1924- *MichAu 80,*
    SmATA 11
Cook, Beverly Blair 1926- *ConAu 37R*
Cook, Blanche Wiesen 1941- *ConAu 4NR, -53*
Cook, Bruce 1932- *ConAu 33R*
Cook, Chris 1945- *ConAu 6NR, -57, WrDr 84*
Cook, Daniel 1914- *ConAu 33R*
Cook, Daniel J 1938- *ConAu 53*
Cook, David 1929- *ConAu 107*
Cook, David 1940- *ConAu 103, IntAu&W 82,*
    WrDr 84
Cook, David A 1945- *ConAu X*
Cook, David C, III 1912- *ConAu 57*
Cook, David T 1946- *ConAu 65*
Cook, Don 1920- *ConAu 13R, WrDr 84*
Cook, Don Lewis 1928- *ConAu 69*
Cook, Dorothy Mary *WrDr 84*
Cook, Dorothy Mary 1907- *ConAu 103*
Cook, F P 1937- *ConAu 93*
Cook, Fred James 1911- *ConAu 3NR, -9R*
Cook, Geoffrey *DrAP&F 83, IntWWP 82X*
Cook, Geoffrey Arthur 1946- *ConAu 77,*
    IntAu&W 82, IntWWP 82
Cook, George Allan 1916- *ConAu 21R*
Cook, George Cram 1873-1924 *CnMD,*
    LongCTC, ModWD, TwCA, TwCA SUP
Cook, George S 1920- *ConAu 49*
Cook, Gladys Emerson 1899- *ConAu 5R*
Cook, Gladys Moon 1907- *ConAu 33R*
Cook, Glenn J 1913- *ConAu 25R*
Cook, Harold Lewis 1897- *IntWWP 82*
Cook, Harold Reed 1902- *ConAu 13R*
Cook, Hugh C B 1910- *ConAu 57*
Cook, Ida *WrDr 84*
Cook, J David 1927- *ConAmTC*
Cook, J Gordon 1916- *ConAu 9R*
Cook, Jack *ConAu X*
Cook, James 1926- *ConAu 73*
Cook, James Graham 1925-1966 *ConAu 1R, -103*
Cook, James W 1932- *ConAu 69*
Cook, Jeffrey 1934- *ConAu 97, WrDr 84*
Cook, Joan Marble 1920- *ConAu 57*
Cook, John Augustine 1940- *ConAu 45*
Cook, John Lennox 1923- *ConAu 106*
Cook, Joseph Jay 1924- *ConAu 1R, -2NR,*
    SmATA 8
Cook, Karmen *DrAP&F 83*
Cook, Kenneth Bernard 1929- *DcLEL 1940*
Cook, Lennox 1923- *ConAu X, WrDr 84*
Cook, Luther T 1901- *ConAu 89*
Cook, Lyn *WrDr 84*
Cook, Lyn 1918- *ConAu X, IntAu&W 82X,*
    SmATA X
Cook, Margaret G 1903- *ConAu 5R*
Cook, Marjorie 1920- *ConAu 81*
Cook, Mark 1942- *ConAu 37R, WrDr 84*
Cook, Mary Jane 1929- *ConAu 93*

Cook, Melva Janice 1919- *ConAu 9NR, -21R*
Cook, Melvin A 1911- *ConAu 2NR, -49, WrDr 84*
Cook, Mercer 1903- *ConAu 77, LivgBAA*
Cook, Michael 1933- *ConAu 93, ConDr 82, WrDr 84*
Cook, Michael 1950- *IntWWP 82*
Cook, Myra B 1933- *ConAu 21R*
Cook, Nilla Cram 1908-1982 *ConAu 108*
Cook, Olive 1916- *ConAu 3NR, -5R*
Cook, Olive Rambo 1892- *ConAu 13R*
Cook, P Lesley 1922- *ConAu 13R*
Cook, Paul H *DrAP&F 83*
Cook, Paul H 1950- *ConAu 106, IntWWP 82*
Cook, Petronelle Marguerite Mary 1925- *ConAu 81, IntAu&W 82*
Cook, R L 1921- *IntAu&W 82*
Cook, Ramona Graham *ConAu 5R*
Cook, Ramsay 1931- *ConAu 102*
Cook, Raymond Allen 1919- *ConAu 45*
Cook, Reginald Lansing 1903- *ConAu 65*
Cook, Richard I 1927- *ConAu 21R*
Cook, Robert I 1920- *ConAu 33R*
Cook, Robert William Arthur 1931- *ConAu 25R*
Cook, Robin 1931- *ConAu X, DcLEL 1940, WrDr 84*
Cook, Robin 1940- *ConAu 108, ConLC 14*
Cook, Roderick 1932- *ConAu 9R*
Cook, Stanley 1922- *ConAu 93, ConP 80, IntAu&W 82, IntWWP 82, WrDr 84*
Cook, Stephani 1944- *ConAu 106*
Cook, Stuart W 1913- *ConAu 1R, -1NR*
Cook, Sylvia 1938- *ConAu 49*
Cook, Terry 1942- *ConAu 73*
Cook, Warren Lawrence 1925- *ConAu 37R, WrDr 84*
Cook, Whitfield 1909- *ConAu 107*
Cook, Will 1921-1964 *TwCWW*
Cook, William H 1931- *ConAu 104*
Cook, William J, Jr. 1938- *ConAu 29R*
Cook, William Wallace 1867-1933 *MichAu 80, TwCWW*
Cooke, Alfred Alistair 1908- *DcLEL 1940*
Cooke, Alistair 1908- *AuNews 1, ConAu 9NR, -57, LongCTC, TwCA SUP, WrDr 84*
Cooke, Barbara *ConAu 57*
Cooke, Barclay 1912-1981 *ConAu 105, -97*
Cooke, Bernard 1922- *WrDr 84*
Cooke, Bernard J 1922- *ConAu 9NR, -13R*
Cooke, Charles Harris 1904?-1977 *ConAu 73*
Cooke, Croft- *TwCA, TwCA SUP*
Cooke, David Coxe 1917- *ConAu 1R, -2NR, SmATA 2*
Cooke, Donald Ewin 1916- *ConAu 1R, -4NR, SmATA 2*
Cooke, Edward F 1923- *ConAu 41R*
Cooke, Gerald 1925- *ConAu 13R*
Cooke, Gilbert William 1899- *ConAu P-1*
Cooke, Greville 1894- *ConAu 13R*
Cooke, Hereward Lester 1916-1973 *ConAu 1R, -1NR, -45*
Cooke, Hope 1940- *ConAu 108, WrDr 84*
Cooke, Jacob Ernest *WrDr 84*
Cooke, Jacob Ernest 1924- *ConAu 1R*
Cooke, John D 1892-1972 *ConAu 106*
Cooke, John Estes *ConAu X*
Cooke, Joseph R 1926- *ConAu 65*
Cooke, M E *ConAu X, TwCCr&M 80*
Cooke, Margaret *ConAu X*
Cooke, Michael G 1934- *ConAu 110*
Cooke, Robert 1930- *ConAu 101*
Cooke, Terence James 1921-1983 *ConAu 110*
Cooke, William 1942- *ConAu 33R, IntWWP 82, WrDr 84*
Cookman, A V 1894-1962 *LongCTC*
Cookson, Catherine 1906- *ConAu 9NR, -13R, SmATA 9, TwCRGW, WrDr 84*
Cookson, Frank Barton 1912-1977 *ConAu 69*
Cookson, Peter W 1913- *ConAu 49*
Cookson, William George 1939- *ConAu 49, IntWWP 82*
Cool, Ola C 1890?-1977 *ConAu 69*
Coole, W W *ConAu X*
Cooley, John Kent 1927- *ConAu 13R, WrDr 84*
Cooley, Lee Morrison 1919- *ConAu 3NR, -9R*
Cooley, Leland Frederick 1909- *ConAu 4NR, -5R*
Cooley, Peter *DrAP&F 83*
Cooley, Peter John 1940- *ConAu 69, IntWWP 82*
Cooley, Richard A 1925- *ConAu 21R*
Coolidge, Archibald C, Jr. 1928- *ConAu 37R*

Coolidge, Clark *DrAP&F 83*
Coolidge, Clark 1939- *ConAu 33R, ConP 80, WrDr 84*
Coolidge, Dane 1873-1940 *TwCWW*
Coolidge, Olivia 1908- *WrDr 84*
Coolidge, Olivia Ensor 1908- *ConAu 2NR, -5R, SmATA 1, -26[port]*
Cooling, Benjamin Franklin 1938- *ConAu 53*
Coolwater, John *ConAu X*
Coombes, B L 1894?-1974 *ConAu 53*
Coombs, Charles Anthony 1918-1981 *ConAu 105, -109*
Coombs, Charles Ira 1914- *ConAu 4NR, -5R, SmATA 3*
Coombs, Chick *ConAu X, SmATA 3*
Coombs, David John 1937- *IntAu&W 82*
Coombs, Derek Michael 1937- *IntAu&W 82*
Coombs, Douglas 1924- *ConAu 13R*
Coombs, Edith Grace 1890- *CreCan 1*
Coombs, H Samm 1928- *ConAu 93*
Coombs, Herbert Cole 1906- *ConAu 93*
Coombs, Joyce 1906- *WrDr 84*
Coombs, Orde M *ConAu 73, LivgBAA*
Coombs, Patricia *WrDr 84*
Coombs, Patricia 1926- *ConAu 1R, -1NR, IntAu&W 82, SmATA 3*
Coombs, Philip 1915- *WrDr 84*
Coombs, Philip H 1915- *ConAu 8NR, -17R*
Coombs, Robert H 1934- *ConAu 41R, IntAu&W 82*
Coon, Betty *DrAP&F 83*
Coon, Carleton Stevens 1904-1981 *ConAu 2NR, -5R, -104, IntAu&W 82, WorAu*
Coon, Gene L 1924-1973 *ConAu 1R, -103*
Coon, Martha Sutherland 1884- *ConAu P-2*
Coon, Nelson 1895- *ConAu 69*
Coon, Stephen 1948- *ConAu 57*
Cooney, Barbara 1917- *ConAu 3NR, -5R, SmATA 6*
Cooney, Caroline B 1947- *ConAu 97*
Cooney, David M 1930- *ConAu 17R*
Cooney, Ellen *DrAP&F 83*
Cooney, Eugene J 1931- *ConAu 45*
Cooney, Michael 1921- *ConAu 25R*
Cooney, Nancy Evans 1932- *ConAu 105*
Cooney, Seamus 1933- *ConAu 53*
Cooney, Timothy J 1929- *ConAu 107*
Coons, Frederica Bertha 1910- *ConAu 17R*
Coons, William R 1934- *ConAu 41R*
Coontz, Otto 1946- *ConAu 105, SmATA 33[port]*
Coop, Howard 1928- *ConAu 25R*
Coope, Rosalys 1921- *ConAu 45*
Cooper, Alfred Morton 1890- *ConAu P-1*
Cooper, Alice 1948- *ConAu 106*
Cooper, Arnold Cook 1933- *ConAu 17R*
Cooper, Barbara Ann 1929- *ConAu 9R, IntAu&W 82*
Cooper, Bernarr 1912- *ConAu 41R, IntAu&W 82*
Cooper, Brian 1919- *WrDr 84*
Cooper, Brian Newman 1919- *ConAu 1R, IntAu&W 82, TwCCr&M 80*
Cooper, Bruce M 1925- *ConAu 9NR, -13R*
Cooper, Bryan 1932- *ConAu 25R, WrDr 84*
Cooper, C Everett *IntAu&W 82X*
Cooper, Carl *ConAu X*
Cooper, Charles Arthur 1906-1972 *MichAu 80*
Cooper, Charles M 1909- *ConAu 41R*
Cooper, Charles W 1904- *ConAu P-2*
Cooper, Chester L 1917- *ConAu 29R*
Cooper, Christopher 1941- *ConAu 107*
Cooper, Christopher Donald H 1942- *WrDr 84*
Cooper, Christopher Donald Huntington 1942- *ConAu 29R*
Cooper, Christopher John 1941- *WrDr 84*
Cooper, Clarence L, Jr. *LivgBAA*
Cooper, Colin Symons 1926- *ConAu 102, ConSFA, WrDr 84*
Cooper, Courtney Ryley 1886-1940 *TwCA, TwCA SUP, TwCWW*
Cooper, Darien B 1937- *ConAu 1NR, -49*
Cooper, David Edward 1942- *ConAu 49*
Cooper, David Graham 1931- *ConAu 97, IntAu&W 82*
Cooper, Derek 1925- *WrDr 84*
Cooper, Derek Macdonald 1925- *ConAu 102*
Cooper, Lady Diana 1901- *DcLEL 1940*
Cooper, Lady Diana Duff 1892- *LongCTC*
Cooper, Dominic 1944- *ConAu 65, WrDr 84*
Cooper, Doris Louise 1902- *IntWWP 82*

Cooper, Duff 1890-1954 *LongCTC*
Cooper, Edith Emma 1862-1913 *LongCTC*
Cooper, Edmund 1926- *ConAu 33R, ConSFA, IntAu&W 82, TwCSFW, WrDr 84*
Cooper, Elizabeth Ann 1927- *ConAu 1R*
Cooper, Elizabeth Keyser 1910- *ConAu 1R, -1NR*
Cooper, Emmanuel 1938- *ConAu 3NR*
Cooper, Emmanuel 1940- *ConAu 49*
Cooper, Esther *ConAu X*
Cooper, Everett *ConAu X*
Cooper, Frank E 1910-1968 *ConAu P-2*
Cooper, Giles 1918-1966 *ConDr 82E, CroCD, DcLB 13[port], LongCTC*
Cooper, Giles 1918-1971 *DcLEL 1940*
Cooper, Gladys 1888-1971 *ConAu 33R*
Cooper, Gordon 1932- *TwCCW 83, WrDr 84*
Cooper, Gordon John Llewellyn 1932- *ConAu 61, SmATA 23[port]*
Cooper, Grace Rogers 1924- *ConAu 41R, IntAu&W 82*
Cooper, Harold E 1928- *ConAu 45*
Cooper, Harold H 1911?-1976 *ConAu 69*
Cooper, Harold R 1911?-1978 *ConAu 77*
Cooper, Helen *DrAP&F 83*
Cooper, Henry Spotswood Fenimore, Jr. 1933- *ConAu 69*
Cooper, Henry St. John *ConAu X, TwCRGW*
Cooper, I S 1922- *ConAu 69*
Cooper, Jacqueline 1924- *ConAu 107*
Cooper, James A *ConAu X*
Cooper, James Fenimore 1789-1851 *SmATA 19*
Cooper, James L 1934- *ConAu 53*
Cooper, James M 1939- *ConAu 45*
Cooper, James R *ConAu X*
Cooper, Jamie Lee *ConAu 9R*
Cooper, Jane *DrAP&F 83*
Cooper, Jane 1924- *ConAu 25R, ConP 80, IntWWP 82, WrDr 84*
Cooper, Jane Todd *DrAP&F 83*
Cooper, Jeff 1920- *ConAu 41R*
Cooper, Jefferson *ConAu X, WrDr 84*
Cooper, Jeremy 1946- *ConAu 93, WrDr 84*
Cooper, Jilly 1937- *ConAu 105, TwCRGW, WrDr 84*
Cooper, John C 1933- *ConAu 9NR*
Cooper, John Charles *DrAP&F 83*
Cooper, John Charles 1933- *ConAu 21R*
Cooper, John Cobb 1887- *ConAu 5R*
Cooper, John Dean *ConAu X*
Cooper, John E 1922- *ConAu 25R, WrDr 84*
Cooper, John Irwin 1905- *ConAu 41R*
Cooper, John L 1936- *ConAu 21R*
Cooper, John M 1912- *ConAu 21R*
Cooper, John Milton, Jr. 1940- *ConAu 105*
Cooper, John Owen 1938- *ConAu 89*
Cooper, John R *ConAu P-2, SmATA 1*
Cooper, Joseph Bonar 1912- *ConAu 17R, WrDr 84*
Cooper, Joseph D 1917-1975 *ConAu 4NR, -5R, -57*
Cooper, Kay 1941- *ConAu 1NR, -45, SmATA 11*
Cooper, Kenneth C 1948- *ConAu 110*
Cooper, Kenneth Schaaf 1918- *ConAu 9R*
Cooper, Kent *DrAP&F 83*
Cooper, Kent 1880-1965 *ConAu 89*
Cooper, Lee Pelham 1926- *ConAu 4NR, -5R, SmATA 5, WrDr 84*
Cooper, Leslie M 1930- *ConAu 41R*
Cooper, Lester 1919- *ConAu 108, SmATA 32*
Cooper, Lettice 1897- *ConAu 5NR, -9R, ConNov 82, IntAu&W 82, TwCCW 83, WrDr 84*
Cooper, Louise 1952- *ConAu 107*
Cooper, Louise Field 1905- *ConAu 1R, -4NR, TwCA SUP*
Cooper, Lynna *ConAu X*
Cooper, M Truman *DrAP&F 83*
Cooper, Mae 1923- *ConAu 17R, IntAu&W 82*
Cooper, Mario 1905- *ConAu 21R*
Cooper, Martin DuPre 1910- *ConAu 103, IntAu&W 82, WrDr 84*
Cooper, Sister Mary Ursula 1925- *ConAu 5R*
Cooper, Matthew 1952- *ConAu 85*
Cooper, Mattie Lula *ConAu X*
Cooper, Michael *DrAP&F 83*
Cooper, Michael 1930- *ConAu 13R*
Cooper, Michael Scott 1952- *IntWWP 82*
Cooper, Michele F 1941- *ConAu 85*
Cooper, Morley *ConAu X*
Cooper, Parley J 1937- *ConAu 10NR, -65*

Cooper, Patricia J 1936- *ConAu 97*
Cooper, Paul 1926- *ConAu 49*
Cooper, Paul F 1900?-1970 *ConAu 104*
Cooper, Paulette 1944- *ConAu 37R, WrDr 84*
Cooper, Philip 1926- *ConAu 33R*
Cooper, Phyllis 1939- *ConAu 53*
Cooper, Richard N 1934- *ConAu 10NR*
Cooper, Richard Newell 1934- *ConAu 25R, IntAu&W 82, WrDr 84*
Cooper, Robert Andrew 1926- *IntAu&W 82*
Cooper, Robert G 1943- *ConAu 110*
Cooper, Sandi E 1936- *ConAu 49*
Cooper, Saul 1934- *ConAu 1R*
Cooper, Signe Skott 1921- *ConAu 4NR, –53*
Cooper, Susan 1935- *TwCCW 83*
Cooper, Susan Mary 1935- *ChlLR 4[port], ConAu 29R, IntAu&W 82, SmATA 4, WrDr 84*
Cooper, Sylvia 1903- *ConAu P-2, MichAu 80*
Cooper, Wayne 1938- *ConAu 93*
Cooper, Wendy 1919- *ConAu 6NR, –13R, IntAu&W 82, WrDr 84*
Cooper, Wilhelmina 1939?-1980 *ConAu 97*
Cooper, Will 1929- *ConAu 69*
Cooper, William 1910- *ConAu X, ConNov 82, DcLEL 1940, LongCTC, ModBrL, TwCWr, WorAu, WrDr 84*
Cooper, William F 1932- *ConAu 69*
Cooper, William Hurlbert 1924- *ConAu 49*
Cooper, William J, Jr. 1940- *ConAu 69*
Cooper, William Mansfield 1903- *WrDr 84*
Cooper, Sir William Mansfield 1903- *IntAu&W 82*
Cooper, William W 1914- *ConAu 13R*
Cooper, Wyatt 1927-1978 *AuNews 2, ConAu 73, –77*
Cooper-Clark, Diana 1945- *ConAu 109*
Cooper-Klein, Nina *ConAu X, IntAu&W 82X*
Cooperman, Hasye *WrDr 84*
Cooperman, Hasye 1909- *ConAu 37R, IntAu&W 82, IntWWP 82*
Cooperman, Stanley *DrAP&F 83*
Cooperman, Stanley 1929-1976 *ConAu P-2*
Coopersmith, Harry 1903- *ConAu P-2*
Coopersmith, Jerome 1925- *ConAu 73*
Coopersmith, Stanley 1926- *ConAu 21R*
Cooperstein, Claire 1923- *IntWWP 82*
Coote, Brian 1929- *WrDr 84*
Cootner, Paul Harold 1930- *ConAu 9R*
Coover, James B 1925- *ConAu 6NR, –57*
Coover, Robert *DrAP&F 83*
Coover, Robert 1932- *ConAu 3NR, –45, ConLC 3, –7, –15, ConNov 82, DcLB Y81A[port], –2, DcLEL 1940, IntAu&W 82, ModAL SUP, WorAu 1970, WrDr 84*
Coox, Alvin D 1924- *WrDr 84*
Coox, Alvin David 1924- *ConAu 29R, IntAu&W 82*
Copani, Peter 1942- *ConAu 89, NatPD 81[port]*
Cope, David *DrAP&F 83*
Cope, David Edge 1948- *MichAu 80*
Cope, David Howell 1941- *ConAu 33R*
Cope, Jack 1913- *ConAu X, ConNov 82, DcLEL 1940, IntAu&W 82, ModCmwL, TwCWr, WrDr 84*
Cope, Jackson I 1925- *WrDr 84*
Cope, Jackson Irving 1925- *ConAu 103*
Cope, Myron 1929- *ConAu 57*
Cope, Oliver 1902- *ConAu 109*
Cope, Robert Knox 1913- *ConAu 9R*
Cope, Sir Zachary 1881- *ConAu P-1*
Copeau, Jacques 1877-1949 *CIDMEL 80*
Copeau, Jacques 1879-1949 *CnMD, ModWD*
Copel, Sidney L 1930- *ConAu 21R*
Copeland, Ann *DrAP&F 83*
Copeland, Bill *ConAu X*
Copeland, Bonnie Chapman 1919- *ConAu 101*
Copeland, Carolyn Faunce 1930- *ConAu 65*
Copeland, E Luther 1916- *ConAu 3NR, –9R*
Copeland, Edwin 1916- *WrDr 84*
Copeland, Helen 1920- *ConAu 25R, SmATA 4*
Copeland, Helen M *DrAP&F 83*
Copeland, James Isaac 1910- *ConAu 106*
Copeland, Melvin T 1884-1975 *ConAu 57, ConAu P-2*
Copeland, Miles 1916- *ConAu 29R, WrDr 84*
Copeland, Morris A 1895- *ConAu P-1*
Copeland, Paul William 1917- *ConAu 25R*
Copeland, Paul Worthington *ConAu 105, SmATA 23*

Copeland, Ross H 1930- *ConAu 25R*
Copeland, Thomas Wellsted 1907-1979 *ConAu 5R, –85*
Copeman, George Henry 1922- *ConAu 5R, –8NR, WrDr 84*
Copenhaver, Charles L 1915-1982 *ConAu 107*
Coper, Rudolf 1904- *ConAu P-1*
Copi, Irving M 1917- *ConAu 1R, –5NR, WrDr 84*
Copic, Branko 1915- *EncWL 2, ModSL 2*
Coplan, Kate M 1901- *ConAu 5R*
Copland, Aaron 1900- *ConAu 5R*
Copleston, Frederick Charles 1907- *ConAu 7NR, –13R, WrDr 84*
Coplin, William D 1939- *ConAu 21R*
Copman, Louis 1934- *ConAu 57*
Copp, Andrew James, III 1916- *ConAu 25R*
Copp, E Anthony 1945- *ConAu 102*
Copp, Jim *WrDr 84*
Coppa, Frank John 1937- *ConAu 33R, WrDr 84*
Coppage, George Herman 1922- *IntWWP 82*
Coppard, A E 1878-1957 *EncWL 2, TwCCr&M 80, TwCLC 5[port]*
Coppard, Alfred Edgar 1878-1957 *LongCTC, ModBrL, TwCA, TwCA SUP, TwCWr, WhoTwCL*
Coppard, Audrey 1931- *ConAu 29R*
Coppe, Abiezer *ConAu X*
Coppee, Francois Edouard Joachim 1842-1908 *CnMD, ModWD*
Coppel, Alec 1909?-1972 *ConAu 33R, TwCCr&M 80*
Coppel, Alfred *DrAP&F 83*
Coppel, Alfred 1921- *ConAu 10NR, –17R, ConSFA, DcLB Y83B[port], TwCSFW, WrDr 84*
Copper, Arnold 1934- *ConAu 97*
Copper, Basil 1924- *TwCCr&M 80, WrDr 84*
Copper, John Franklin 1940- *ConAu 11NR, –69*
Copper, Lynna *WrDr 84*
Copper, Marcia S 1934- *ConAu 53*
Copperman, Paul 1947- *ConAu 101*
Copperud, Roy H 1915- *ConAu 9R, WrDr 84*
Coppock, John Oates 1914- *ConAu 13R*
Coppock, John Terence 1921- *ConAu 102*
Coppock, Joseph David 1909- *ConAu 49*
Coppola, Francis Ford 1933- *ConLC 16*
Coppola, Francis Ford 1939- *ConAu 77*
Coppola, Raymond T 1947- *ConAu 102*
Coppone, Filadelfio 1934- *IntWWP 82*
Coram, Christopher *ConAu X*
Corazon, Maria *IntAu&W 82X*
Corazon DeLosReyes, Maria *IntWWP 82X*
Corbally, John Edward, Jr. 1924- *ConAu 5R*
Corbeil, Claude 1940- *CreCan 1*
Corbett, Chan *TwCSFW*
Corbett, Edmund V *WrDr 84*
Corbett, Edmund Victor *IntAu&W 82*
Corbett, Edward P J 1919- *ConAu 9NR, –17R, WrDr 84*
Corbett, Elizabeth Frances 1887-1981 *ConAu 2NR, –5R, –102, TwCA, TwCA SUP*
Corbett, J Elliott 1920- *ConAu 29R*
Corbett, James Arthur 1908- *ConAu 65*
Corbett, Janice M 1935- *ConAu 37R*
Corbett, Jim 1875-1955 *LongCTC*
Corbett, John Ambrose 1908- *WrDr 84*
Corbett, Patrick 1916- *ConAu 17R*
Corbett, Pearson H 1900- *ConAu P-1*
Corbett, Richmond McLain 1902- *ConAu P-1*
Corbett, Ruth 1912- *ConAu 29R, MichAu 80*
Corbett, Scott 1913- *ChlLR 1, ConAu 1R, –1NR, IntAu&W 82, SmATA 2, TwCCW 83, WrDr 84*
Corbett, Thomas H 1938- *ConAu 77*
Corbett, William *DrAP&F 83*
Corbin, Arnold 1911- *ConAu 9R*
Corbin, Charles B 1940- *ConAu 29R*
Corbin, Claire 1913- *ConAu 41R, WrDr 84*
Corbin, Donald A 1920- *ConAu 33R*
Corbin, H Dan 1912- *ConAu 41R*
Corbin, Iris *ConAu X*
Corbin, John B 1935- *ConAu 105*
Corbin, Richard 1911- *ConAu 3NR, –5R*
Corbin, Sabra Lee *ConAu X, SmATA X*
Corbin, William 1916- *ConAu X, SmATA 3*
Corbishley, Thomas 1903-1976 *ConAu 7NR, –13R, –65*
Corbitt, Helen Lucy 1906-1978 *ConAu 4NR, –5R, –89*

Corbluth, Elsa 1928- *IntWWP 82*
Corbusier *TwCA SUP*
Corbusier, Le 1887-1965 *LongCTC*
Corby, Dan *ConAu X, SmATA 3, TwCCW 83, WrDr 84*
Corcoran, Barbara *DrAP&F 83*
Corcoran, Barbara 1911- *ConAu 11NR, –21R, ConLC 17, IntAu&W 82, SmATA 3, WrDr 84*
Corcoran, Gertrude B 1922- *ConAu 29R*
Corcoran, Gertrude B 1923- *WrDr 84*
Corcoran, Jean Kennedy 1926- *ConAu 1R*
Corcos, Lucille 1908-1973 *ConAu 21R, SmATA 10*
Cord, Barry 1913- *TwCWW, WrDr 84*
Cord, Robert L 1935- *ConAu 33R*
Cord, Steven Benson 1928- *ConAu 21R*
Cord, William O 1921- *ConAu 37R*
Cordasco, Francesco 1920- *ConAu 6NR, –13R*
Cordelier, Maurice *ConAu X*
Cordell, Alexander 1914- *ConAu X, DcLEL 1940, SmATA 7, TwCCW 83, WrDr 84*
Cordell, Paul *DrAP&F 83*
Cordell, Richard Albert 1896- *ConAu 1R*
Corden, W M 1927- *ConAu 33R*
Corden, Warner Max 1927- *WrDr 84*
Corder, Brice W 1936- *ConAu 53*
Corder, Eric *ConAu X*
Corder, George Edward 1904- *ConAu 110*
Corder, Jim 1929- *ConAu 17R*
Cordes, Margarethe 1898- *IntAu&W 82*
Cordier, Andrew W 1901-1975 *ConAu 106*
Cordier, Charles 1911- *CnMD*
Cordier, Gilbert *ConAu X*
Cordier, Ralph Waldo 1902- *ConAu 37R*
Cordingly, David 1938- *ConAu 93, WrDr 84*
Cordis, Lonny *ConAu X*
Cords, Nicholas J 1929- *ConAu 105*
Cordtz, Dan 1927- *ConAu 73*
Cordwell, Miriam 1908- *ConAu 89*
Corea, Gena *ConAu X*
Corea, Genoveffa 1946- *ConAu 81*
Corelli, Marie 1855-1924 *LongCTC, ModBrL, TwCA, TwCA SUP, TwCRGW, TwCWr*
Coren, Alan 1938- *ConAu 69, SmATA 32[port], WrDr 84*
Corenanda, A L A *IntAu&W 82X*
Corey, Dorothy *ConAu 11NR, –69, SmATA 23[port]*
Corey, Lewis 1894-1953 *TwCA, TwCA SUP*
Corey, Paul 1903- *ConAu 2NR, –5R, ConSFA, TwCA, TwCA SUP, WrDr 84*
Corey, Stephen *DrAP&F 83*
Corey, Stephen 1948- *IntWWP 82*
Corfe, Thomas Howell 1928- *ConAu 103, SmATA 27*
Corfe, Tom 1928- *ConAu X, SmATA X*
Corfield, Conrad Laurence 1893-1980 *ConAu 105*
Corfman, Eunice 1928-1980 *ConAu 97*
Corina, Maurice 1936- *ConAu 57*
Coriolanus *IntAu&W 82X, WrDr 84*
Cork, Patrick *ConAu X*
Cork, Richard 1947- *WrDr 84*
Cork, Richard Graham 1947- *ConAu 107, IntAu&W 82*
Corke, Helen 1882- *ConAu P-1*
Corke, Hilary 1921- *ConAu 97, ConP 80, IntAu&W 82, WrDr 84*
Corkery, Christopher Jane *DrAP&F 83*
Corkery, Daniel 1878-1964 *TwCA SUP*
Corkey, Robert 1881-1966 *ConAu P-1*
Corkran, David Hudson, Jr. 1902- *ConAu 5R*
Corkran, Herbert, Jr. 1924- *ConAu 29R*
Corle, Edwin 1906-1956 *TwCA SUP, TwCWW*
Corless, Roger 1938- *ConAu 108*
Corlett, William 1938- *ConAu 103, TwCCW 83, WrDr 84*
Corlew, Robert Ewing 1922- *ConAu 110*
Corley, Anthony 1923- *ConAu 1R*
Corley, Edwin 1931-1981 *ConAu 105, –25R*
Corley, Ernest *ConAu X, WrDr 84*
Corley, Ray *ConAu X*
Corley, Robert N 1930- *ConAu 3NR, –9R*
Corley, Thomas Anthony Buchanan 1923- *WrDr 84*
Corliss, Charlotte N 1932- *ConAu 53*
Corliss, William R 1926- *ConAu 1NR, –45*
Cormack, Alexander James Ross 1942- *ConAu 106*
Cormack, Barbara Villy 1903- *CreCan 2*
Cormack, James Maxwell Ross 1909- *ConAu P-1*

Cormack, Margaret Grant 1913- *ConAu 1R, SmATA 11*
Cormack, Margaret Lawson 1912- *ConAu 1R*
Cormack, Patrick 1939- *WrDr 84*
Cormack, Sandy *ConAu X*
Corman, Avery 1935- *ConAu 85*
Corman, Cid 1924- *ConAu X, ConLC 9, ConP 80, DcLB 5, WrDr 84*
Corman, Sidney 1924- *ConAu 85*
Cormier, Frank 1927- *ConAu 21R*
Cormier, Ramona 1923- *ConAu 49*
Cormier, Raymond J 1938- *ConAu 4NR, -53, IntAu&W 82*
Cormier, Robert 1925- *TwCCW 83, WrDr 84*
Cormier, Robert Edmund 1925- *ConAu 1R, -5NR, ConLC 12, SmATA 10*
Cormillot, Albert E J 1938- *ConAu 69*
Corn, Alfred *DrAP&F 83*
Corn, Alfred 1943- *ConAu 104, ConP 80, DcLB Y80B[port], WrDr 84*
Corn, Ira George, Jr. 1921-1982 *ConAu 106, -85*
Cornea, Carol *ConAu X*
Cornehls, James V 1936- *ConAu 93*
Cornelisen, Ann 1926- *ConAu 25R*
Cornelius, Temple H 1891-1964 *ConAu P-1*
Cornelius, Wanda Pyle 1936- *ConAu 105*
Cornell, Douglas B 1906?-1982 *ConAu 106*
Cornell, Felix M 1896?-1970 *ConAu 104*
Cornell, Francis Griffith 1906-1979 *ConAu 89*
Cornell, George W 1920- *ConAu 9R*
Cornell, J *SmATA X*
Cornell, James 1938- *ConAu 11NR, -69, SmATA 27[port]*
Cornell, Jean Gay 1920- *ConAu 1NR, -45, SmATA 23*
Cornell, Jeffrey 1945- *SmATA 11*
Cornell, Katharine 1898-1974 *ConAu 49*
Corner, George W 1889-1981 *ConAu 102, -104*
Corner, Philip Lionel 1933- *ConAu 21R*
Cornett, Joe D 1935- *ConAu 53*
Cornett, R Orin 1913- *WrDr 84*
Cornevin, Robert 1919- *IntAu&W 82*
Cornfeld, Gaalyahu 1902- *ConAu 73*
Cornford, Frances Crofts 1886-1960 *LongCTC, TwCWr*
Cornford, Francis Macdonald 1874-1943 *LongCTC, TwCA SUP*
Cornforth, Maurice 1909-1980 *ConAu 4NR, -5R, -102*
Corngold, Stanley 1934- *WrDr 84*
Corngold, Stanley Alan 1934- *ConAu 37R*
Cornillon, John Raymond Koppleman 1941- *ConAu 17R*
Cornish, Dudley T 1915- *ConAu 17R*
Cornish, Edward 1927- *ConAu 108*
Cornish, F *TwCSFW*
Cornish, John Buckley 1914- *ConAu 25R, CreCan 1, DcLEL 1940*
Cornish, Sam 1935- *ConAu 41R, ConP 80, WrDr 84*
Cornish, Samuel James 1935- *DcLEL 1940, SmATA 23[port]*
Cornish, Samuel James 1938- *LivgBAA*
Cornish, W R 1937- *ConAu 29R*
Cornman, James W 1929- *ConAu 69*
Cornman, James W 1929-1978 *ConAu 11NR*
Corno DiBassetto *LongCTC*
Cornock, Stroud 1938- *ConAu 25R*
Cornuelle, Richard C 1927- *ConAu 17R*
Cornwall, E Judson 1924- *ConAu 6NR, -57*
Cornwall, Ian Wolfran 1909- *ConAu 9R*
Cornwall, J Spencer 1888?-1983 *ConAu 109*
Cornwall, James Marshall *ConAu X*
Cornwall, Jim *ConAu X*
Cornwall, Martin *ConAu X*
Cornwell, Anita R *DrAP&F 83*
Cornwell, Bernard 1944- *ConAu 104*
Cornwell, David John Moore *WrDr 84*
Cornwell, David John Moore 1931- *ConAu 5R, ConLC 9, -15, WorAu*
Cornwell, Smith *ConAu X*
Coromines, Pere 1870-1939 *CIDMEL 80*
Coronel, Jorge Icaza *ConAu X*
Corpman, Izora *DrAP&F 83*
Corporal Trim *ConAu X*
Corr, Michael William 1940- *IntWWP 82*
Corradi, Gemma 1939- *ConAu 21R*
Corrall, Alice Enid 1916- *ConAu 5R*
Corre, Alan D 1931- *ConAu 37R*
Correa, Gustavo 1914- *ConAu 49, IntAu&W 82*
Correa, Joao 1943- *IntAu&W 82*

Correa, Judith Green *ConAu X*
Corredor-Matheos, Jose 1929- *IntAu&W 82*
Correia-Afonso, John 1924- *ConAu 33R*
Correia DaRocha, Adolfo *WorAu 1970*
Corren, Grace *ConAu X, WrDr 84*
Correy, Lee *ConAu X, WrDr 84*
Correy, Lee 1928- *ConAu X, SmATA X, TwCSFW*
Corrigan, Adeline 1909- *ConAu 69, SmATA 23[port]*
Corrigan, Barbara 1922- *ConAu 57, SmATA 8*
Corrigan, Francis Joseph 1919- *ConAu 5R*
Corrigan, John D 1900- *ConAu 41R*
Corrigan, John Thomas 1936- *ConAu 10NR, -65*
Corrigan, Mark 1905-1962 *TwCCr&M 80*
Corrigan, Paul G, Jr. *DrAP&F 83*
Corrigan, Paul George 1951- *IntWWP 82*
Corrigan, Ralph L, Jr. 1937- *ConAu 33R*
Corrigan, Robert A 1935- *ConAu 9R*
Corrigan, Robert W 1927- *WrDr 84*
Corrigan, Robert Willoughby 1927- *ConAu 5R, -6NR*
Corrington, John William *DrAP&F 83*
Corrington, John William 1932- *ConAu 8NR, -13R, ConP 80, DcLB 6[port], DcLEL 1940, WrDr 84*
Corriveau, Monique 1927- *ConAu 61*
Corriveau, Verna Cutter 1952- *IntAu&W 82*
Corsa, Helen Storm 1915- *ConAu 17R*
Corsaro, Francesco Andrea 1924- *ConAu 85*
Corsaro, Frank *ConAu X*
Corsaro, Maria C 1949- *ConAu 107*
Corsel, Ralph 1920- *ConAu 25R*
Corseri, Gary Steven *DrAP&F 83*
Corsi, Jerome R 1946- *ConAu 89*
Corsini, Raymond J 1914- *ConAu 1R, -3NR*
Corso, Gregory *DrAP&F 83*
Corso, Gregory 1930- *ConAu 5R, ConLC 1, -11, ConP 80, CroCAP, DcLB 5[port], -16[port], TwCWr, WorAu 1970, WrDr 84*
Corso, Nunzio Gregory 1930- *DcLEL 1940*
Corson, Fred Pierce 1896- *ConAu P-2*
Corson, Hazel W 1906- *ConAu 1R, -2NR*
Corson, John J 1905- *ConAu 1R, -5NR*
Corson, Richard *ConAu 41R, WrDr 84*
Corstanje, Auspicius Van *ConAu 107*
Corstanje, Charles Van *ConAu X*
Corston, George 1932- *ConSFA*
Cort, David 1904- *ConAu 9R*
Cort, M C *ConAu X, SmATA 1*
Cort, Van *TwCWW*
Cortazar, Julio 1914- *ConAu 21R, ConLC 2, -3, -5, -10, -13, -15, EncWL 2[port], ModLAL, TwCWr, WhoTwCL, WorAu*
Cortazzo, Carman 1936- *ConAu 109*
Corteen, Wes *ConAu X, -X, WrDr 84*
Cortes, Carlos E 1934- *ConAu 8NR, -61, IntAu&W 82*
Cortes, Juan B 1925- *ConAu 37R*
Cortesao, Jaime 1884-1960 *CIDMEL 80*
Cortese, A James 1917- *ConAu 65*
Cortesi, Lawrence *ConAu X*
Cortez, Alfredo 1880-1946 *CIDMEL 80*
Cortez, Jayne *DrAP&F 83*
Cortez, Jayne 1936?- *ConAu 73, LivgBAA*
Cortezon Álvarez, Daniel 1927- *IntAu&W 82*
Corti *IntWWP 82X*
Corti, Doris Joyce 1928- *IntWWP 82*
Cortissoz, Royal 1869-1948 *TwCA, TwCA SUP*
Cortner, Richard C 1935- *ConAu 104*
Cortright, David 1946- *ConAu 57*
Corty, Floyd L 1916- *ConAu 13R*
Corvo, Baron 1860-1913 *LongCTC, ModBrL, TwCA, TwCA SUP, TwCWr*
Corwen, Leonard 1921- *ConAu 93*
Corwin, Cecil *ConAu X*
Corwin, Judith Hoffman 1946- *SmATA 10*
Corwin, Norman 1910- *AuNews 2, ConAu 1R, -1NR, TwCA SUP, WrDr 84*
Corwin, Ronald Gary 1932- *ConAu 8NR, -17R*
Cory, Adela Florence *LongCTC*
Cory, Corrine *ConAu 49*
Cory, Daniel 1904-1972 *ConAu 37R*
Cory, David 1872-1966 *ConAu 25R*
Cory, Desmond *WrDr 84*
Cory, Desmond 1928- *ConAu X, TwCCr&M 80*
Cory, Howard L 1931- *ConAu X*
Cory, Irene E Cravens 1910- *ConAu 49*
Cory, Jean-Jacques 1947- *ConAu 57*
Cory, Ray *ConAu X, IntAu&W 82X*
Corya, I E *ConAu 49*

Cosbuc, George 1866-1918 *CIDMEL 80*
Cosby, Bill *ConAu X*
Cosby, William Henry, Jr. 1937- *ConAu 81*
Cosby, Yvonne Shepard 1886?-1980 *ConAu 97*
Cosell, Howard 1920- *ConAu 108*
Cosem, Michael 1939- *IntWWP 82*
Cosentino, Donald J 1941- *ConAu 108*
Coser, Lewis A 1913- *ConAu 1R, -4NR, WrDr 84*
Coser, Rose Laub 1916- *ConAu 13R*
Cosgrave, John O'Hara, II 1908-1968 *ConAu 1R, -1NR, SmATA 21N*
Cosgrave, Patrick 1941- *ConAu 33R, WrDr 84*
Cosgrove, Carol Ann 1943- *ConAu 29R*
Cosgrove, Margaret Leota 1926- *ConAu 6NR, -9R*
Cosgrove, Mark P 1947- *ConAu 85*
Cosgrove, Maynard Giles 1895- *ConAu 57*
Cosgrove, Rachel *ConAu X, IntAu&W 82X*
Cosgrove, Richard A 1941- *ConAu 104*
Cosgrove, Stanley 1911- *CreCan 2*
Cosgrove, Stephen E 1945- *AuNews 1, ConAu 69*
Cosh, Mary *WrDr 84*
Cosh, Mary 1921- *ConAu 5R*
Cosic, Dobrica 1921- *CIDMEL 80, ConLC 14, EncWL 2, ModSL 2*
Coskey, Evelyn 1932- *ConAu 41R, SmATA 7*
Coslow, Sam 1905-1982 *ConAu 106, -77*
Cosman, Carol *ConAu 104*
Cosman, Madeleine Pelner 1937- *ConAu 105*
Cosmos, Eddie *IntWWP 82X*
Cosneck, Bernard Joseph 1912- *ConAu 49*
Coss, Thurman L 1926- *ConAu 13R*
Cosseboom, Kathy Groehn *ConAu X*
Cosser, Phyllis *IntAu&W 82X*
Cossi, Olga 1921- *ConAu 81*
Cossman, E Joseph 1918- *ConAu 17R*
Cost, March d1973 *ConAu X*
Costa, Albert Bernard 1929- *ConAu 13R*
Costa, Gustavo 1930- *ConAu 37R*
Costa, Joaquin 1846-1911 *CIDMEL 80*
Costa, Richard Hauer 1921- *ConAu 21R*
Costa I Llobera, Miquel 1854-1922 *CIDMEL 80*
Costa-Pinto, Luiz DeAguiar 1920- *IntAu&W 82*
Costain, Thomas Bertram 1885-1965 *ConAu 5R, CreCan 2, DcLB 9[port], DcLEL 1940, LongCTC, TwCA SUP, TwCRGW, TwCWr*
Costantin, M M 1935- *ConAu 45*
Costanzo, Gerald *DrAP&F 83*
Costas, Orlando E 1942- *ConAu 101*
Costas, Procope 1900?-1974 *ConAu 53*
Costello, Anne 1937- *ConAu 102*
Costello, Chris 1947- *ConAu 107*
Costello, David F 1904- *ConAu 33R, SmATA 23[port], WrDr 84*
Costello, Donald P 1931- *ConAu 17R*
Costello, Elvis 1955- *ConLC 21[port]*
Costello, Grace Seymour 1883-1983 *ConAu 110*
Costello, John E 1943- *ConAu 85*
Costello, Mark *DrAP&F 83*
Costello, Michael *ConAu X*
Costello, Peter 1946- *ConAu 93*
Costello, William Aloysious 1904-1969 *ConAu 1R, -103*
Costelloe, M Joseph 1914- *ConAu 41R*
Coster, Robert *ConAu X*
Costigan, Daniel M 1929- *ConAu 33R, WrDr 84*
Costigan, Giovanni 1905- *ConAu P-1, IntAu&W 82*
Costigan, James 1928- *ConAu 73*
Costikyan, Edward N 1924- *ConAu 17R*
Costinescu, Tristan *ConAu X*
Costis, Harry G 1928- *ConAu 45*
Costley, Bill *DrAP&F 83*
Costley, Bill 1942- *ConAu X, IntWWP 82, WrDr 84*
Costley, William K, Jr. 1942- *ConAu 81*
Costonis, John J 1937- *ConAu 4NR, -49*
Cote, Aurele DeFoy Suzor *CreCan 1*
Cote, Richard G 1934- *ConAu 69*
Cotes, Mrs. Everard 1861-1922 *CreCan 1*
Cotes, Peter *WrDr 84*
Cotes, Peter 1912- *ConAu 4NR, -5R, IntAu&W 82*
Cotes, Sara Jeannette Duncan 1861-1922 *CreCan 1*
Cothern, Fayly H 1926- *ConAu 1R, WrDr 84*
Cothran, J Guy 1897- *ConAu P-2*
Cothran, Jean 1910- *ConAu 93*

Cotler, Gordon 1923- *ConAu 1R*
Cotler, Sherwin B 1941- *ConAu 65*
Cotlow, Lewis N 1898- *ConAu 65*
Cotner, Robert Crawford 1906- *ConAu 37R*
Cotner, Thomas E 1916- *ConAu 37R*
Cott, Hugh B 1900- *WrDr 84*
Cott, Jonathan *DrAP&F 83*
Cott, Jonathan 1942- *ConAu 53, IntAu&W 82, IntWWP 82, SmATA 23[port]*
Cott, Nancy F 1945- *ConAu 81*
Cottam, Clarence 1899-1974 *ConAu 97, SmATA 25*
Cottam, Keith M 1941- *ConAu 81*
Cottam, Walter P 1894- *ConAu P-1*
Cotten, Nell Wyllie 1908- *ConAu 1R*
Cotter, Charles H 1919- *WrDr 84*
Cotter, Charles Henry 1919- *ConAu 13R*
Cotter, Cornelius Philip 1924- *ConAu 1R, -1NR*
Cotter, Edward F 1917- *ConAu 5R, -6NR*
Cotter, James Finn 1929- *ConAu 33R, WrDr 84*
Cotter, Janet M 1914- *ConAu 61*
Cotter, Richard V 1924- *ConAu 41R*
Cotterell, Geoffrey 1919- *DcLEL 1940, IntAu&W 82, WorAu, WrDr 84*
Cotterell, Peter 1930- *ConAu 1NR, -49*
Cotterill, Sarah *DrAP&F 83*
Cottle, Charles *ConAu X*
Cottle, Thomas J 1937- *ConAu 33R, WrDr 84*
Cottle, William C 1913- *ConAu 41R*
Cottler, Joseph 1899- *ConAu P-2, SmATA 22[port]*
Cotton, Billy *WrDr 84*
Cotton, John *TwCSFW*
Cotton, John 1925- *ConAu 11NR, -33R, -65, ConP 80, DcLEL 1940, IntWWP 82, WrDr 84*
Cotton, Norris 1900- *ConAu 103*
Cotton, Phebe E 1911- *MichAu 80*
Cottrell, Alan 1919- *ConAu 10NR, -65, IntAu&W 82, WrDr 84*
Cottrell, Fred 1903- *ConAu 1R*
Cottrell, Geoffrey 1919- *ConAu 5R*
Cottrell, Jack 1938- *ConAu 107*
Cottrell, June 1927- *IntAu&W 82*
Cottrell, Leonard 1913-1974 *ConAu 4NR, -5R, DcLEL 1940, SmATA 24[port], TwCWr, WorAu*
Cottrell, Leonard S, Jr. 1899- *ConAu 107*
Cottrell, Richard 1936- *IntAu&W 82*
Cottrell, Robert D 1930- *ConAu 53*
Cottrell, Sue *IntAu&W 82X*
Cottrell, Susan Lynne 1949- *IntAu&W 82*
Couani, Anna 1948- *IntWWP 82*
Coubier, Heinz 1905- *CnMD, IntAu&W 82*
Couch *TwCA, TwCA SUP*
Couch, Helen F 1907- *ConAu P-2*
Couch, Osma Palmer *ConAu X*
Couch, William, Jr. *LivgBAA*
Coudenhove-Kalergi, Richard 1894-1972 *ConAu 37R*
Coudert, Allison P 1941- *ConAu 110*
Coudert, Jo 1923- *ConAu 17R*
Couffer, Jack C 1924- *ConAu 1R, -1NR*
Couger, J Daniel 1929- *ConAu 8NR, -53*
Coughlan, John W 1927- *ConAu 21R*
Coughlan, Margaret N 1925- *ConAu 107*
Coughlan, Robert 1914- *ConAu 65, WrDr 84*
Coughlin, Bernard J 1922- *ConAu 13R*
Coughlin, Charles E 1891-1979 *ConAu 97*
Coughlin, George G 1900- *ConAu 107*
Coughlin, Joseph Welter 1919- *ConAu 1R*
Coughlin, Violet L *ConAu 73*
Coughran, Larry C 1925- *ConAu 21R*
Coughtry, John Graham 1931- *CreCan 1*
Couldery, Fred A J 1928- *ConAu 9R*
Coulet DuGard, Rene 1919- *ConAu 4NR, -53, IntAu&W 82, IntWWP 82*
Coulette, Henri *DrAP&F 83*
Coulette, Henri 1927- *ConAu 65, ConP 80, WrDr 84*
Coulling, Sidney Baxter 1924- *ConAu 102*
Couloumbis, Theodore A 1935- *ConAu 7NR, -17R*
Coulson, Charles Alfred 1910-1974 *ConAu 4NR, -5R*
Coulson, Felicity Carter 1906- *ConAu 9R*
Coulson, John H A 1906- *WrDr 84*
Coulson, John Hubert Arthur 1906- *ConAu 9R*
Coulson, Juanita 1933- *ConAu 9NR, -25R, ConSFA, IntAu&W 82, TwCRGW,*

TwCSFW, WrDr 84
Coulson, Robert 1924- *ConAu 49*
Coulson, Robert 1928- *WrDr 84*
Coulson, Robert S 1928- *ConAu 9NR, -21R, IntAu&W 82, TwCSFW*
Coulson, William D E 1942- *ConAu 89*
Coulter, E Merton 1890-1981 *ConAu 3NR, -104*
Coulter, Edwin M 1937- *ConAu 104*
Coulter, Ellis Merton 1890- *ConAu 9R, TwCA SUP*
Coulter, John William 1888- *ConAu 3NR, -5R, CreCan 1, IntAu&W 82*
Coulter, N Arthur, Jr. 1920- *ConAu 65*
Coulter, Stephen 1914- *ConAu 109, TwCCr&M 80, WrDr 84*
Coulthard, Jean 1908- *CreCan 1*
Coulton, George Gordon 1858-1947 *LongCTC, TwCA SUP*
Coulton, James *ConAu X*
Council, Norman Briggs 1936- *ConAu 102*
Cound, John J 1928- *ConAu 37R*
Counsell, John 1905- *WrDr 84*
Counsell, John William 1905- *ConAu 57*
Counselman, Mary Elizabeth *DrAP&F 83*
Counselman, Mary Elizabeth 1911- *ConAu 106*
Count, Earl W 1899- *ConAu 37R, IntAu&W 82, WrDr 84*
Counter, Kenneth 1930- *ConAu 25R*
Countryman, The *ConAu X*
Countryman, Vern 1917- *ConAu 13R, WrDr 84*
Counts, Charles Richard 1934- *ConAu 49*
Counts, George Sylvester 1889-1974 *ConAu 5R, -53, TwCA SUP*
Couper, J M 1914- *WrDr 84*
Couper, John Mill 1914- *ConAu 45*
Couperus, Louis Marie Anne 1863-1923 *CIDMEL 80, EncWL 2, LongCTC, TwCA, TwCA SUP, TwCWr, WhoTwCL*
Coupey, Philippe 1937- *ConAu 104*
Coupling, J J *ConAu X*
Courage, James Francis 1903-1963 *ConAu 77, LongCTC, TwCWr*
Courant, Richard 1888-1972 *ConAu 33R*
Courian, Ruppen-Joseph 1908- *IntAu&W 82*
Courlander, Harold 1908- *ConAu 3NR, -9R, IntAu&W 82, MichAu 80, SmATA 6*
Cournos, John 1881-1966 *ConAu P-2, LongCTC, TwCA, TwCA SUP*
Couroucli, Jennifer 1922- *ConAu 29R*
Course, Alfred George 1895- *ConAu 9R*
Course, Edwin 1922- *ConAu 77*
Coursen, H R *DrAP&F 83*
Coursen, Herbert R, Jr. 1932- *ConAu 4NR, -53*
Court, Margaret Smith 1942- *ConAu 106*
Court, W H B 1905?-1971 *ConAu 104*
Court, Wesli *DrAP&F 83*
Court, Wesli 1940- *ConAu 11NR, -69, IntWWP 82, MichAu 80*
Courteline, Georges 1858?-1929 *CIDMEL 80, CnMD, ModFrL, ModWD*
Courtenay, William J 1935- *ConAu 9R*
Courter, Gay 1944- *ConAu 7NR, -57, WrDr 84*
Courthion, Pierre-Barthelemy 1902- *ConAu 81, IntAu&W 82*
Courthope, William John 1842-1917 *LongCTC, TwCA, TwCA SUP*
Courtier, S H 1904-1974 *ConAu P-2, TwCCr&M 80*
Courtine, Robert 1910- *ConAu 81*
Courtis, Stuart Appleton 1874-1969 *ConAu 105, SmATA 29N*
Courtland, Roberta *ConAu X*
Courtneidge, Cicely 1893-1980 *ConAu 105*
Courtney, Anthony Tosswill 1908- *WrDr 84*
Courtney, C C *ConDr 82D*
Courtney, Caroline *TwCRGW, WrDr 84*
Courtney, Gwendoline *ConAu P-1, WrDr 84*
Courtney, John *ConAu X*
Courtney, Ragan 1941- *ConAu 97*
Courtney, Richard 1927- *ConAu 105*
Courtney, Robert *ConAu X*
Courtney, William J 1921- *ConAu 102*
Courtney, Winifred F 1918- *ConAu 109*
Courtois, Helene *IntWWP 82*
Courtot, Martha *DrAP&F 83*
Courtwright, David T 1952- *ConAu 110*
Courville, Donovan A 1901- *ConAu 45*
Coury, Louise Andree 1895?-1983 *ConAu 109, SmATA 34N*
Couse, Harold C 1925- *ConAu 17R*
Couser, G Thomas 1946- *ConAu 89*
Cousineau, Yves *CreCan 1*

Cousins, Albert Newton 1919- *ConAu 41R*
Cousins, Geoffrey Esmond 1900- *ConAu 25R, WrDr 84*
Cousins, Linda S *DrAP&F 83*
Cousins, Margaret 1905- *ConAu 1R, -1NR, IntAu&W 82, SmATA 2, WrDr 84*
Cousins, Norman 1912- *ConAu 17R, DcLEL 1940, TwCA SUP*
Cousins, Norman 1915- *WrDr 84*
Cousins, Peter Edward 1928- *ConAu 104, WrDr 84*
Cousse, Raymond 1942- *ConAu 101*
Cousteau, Jacques-Yves 1910- *ConAu 65, IntAu&W 82*
Cousteau, Philippe Pierre 1940-1979 *ConAu 33R, -89*
Coustillas, Pierre 1930- *ConAu 73*
Coutard, Wanda Lundy Hale 1902?-1982 *ConAu 106*
Coutinho, Joaquim 1886?-1978 *ConAu 77*
Couto, Richard A 1941- *ConAu 89*
Coutts, Frederick 1899- *WrDr 84*
Coutts, Frederick Lee 1899- *ConAu 109*
Coutu, Jean 1925- *CreCan 1*
Couture, Andrea 1943- *ConAu 85*
Couture, Guillaume 1851-1915 *CreCan 1*
Couture, Severe *CreCan 1*
Couturier, Louis 1910- *ConAu 101*
Couzyn, Jeni 1942- *ConAu 85, ConP 80, TwCSFW, WrDr 84*
Covatta, Anthony Gallo 1944- *ConAu 53*
Covell, Jon Carter 1910- *ConAu 97*
Coven, Brenda *ConAu 110*
Coveney, James 1920- *ConAu 41R, IntAu&W 82*
Coventry, John Seton 1915- *ConAu 93*
Cover, Arthur Byron 1950- *ConAu 107*
Cover, Robert M 1943- *ConAu 57*
Coverdale, John F 1940- *ConAu 73*
Coverley, Louise Bennett *ConAu X*
Covert, James Thayne 1932- *ConAu 37R*
Covert, Paul 1941- *ConAu 103*
Covey, Cyclone 1922- *ConAu 21R*
Covey, Stephen R 1932- *ConAu 33R*
Covici, Pascal, Jr. 1930- *ConAu 1R*
Coville, Bruce 1950- *ConAu 97, SmATA 32[port]*
Coville, Walter J 1914- *ConAu 1R, -5R, -5NR*
Covin, Theron Michael 1947- *ConAu 57*
Covina, Gina 1952- *ConAu 101*
Covington, James W 1917- *ConAu 33R, WrDr 84*
Covington, Martin Vaden 1936- *ConAu 37R*
Covino, Frank 1931- *ConAu 57*
Covino, Michael *DrAP&F 83*
Covvey, H Dominic J 1944- *ConAu 110*
Cowan, Alan *ConAu X*
Cowan, Charles Donald 1923- *ConAu 102*
Cowan, Don F 1919- *WrDr 84*
Cowan, Edward 1944- *ConAu 103, WrDr 84*
Cowan, Evelyn 1924- *IntAu&W 82*
Cowan, G 1933- *ConAu 25R*
Cowan, G H 1917- *ConAu 17R*
Cowan, Geoffrey 1942- *ConAu 97*
Cowan, George McKillop 1916- *ConAu 102*
Cowan, Gordon 1933- *WrDr 84*
Cowan, Gregory M 1935- *ConAu 65*
Cowan, Gregory M 1935-1979 *ConAu 9NR*
Cowan, Henry 1919- *WrDr 84*
Cowan, Henry Jacob 1919- *ConAu 4NR, -53, IntAu&W 82*
Cowan, Ian B 1932- *WrDr 84*
Cowan, Ian Borthwick 1932- *ConAu 8NR, -61, IntAu&W 82*
Cowan, J L 1929- *ConAu 25R*
Cowan, James C 1927- *ConAu 29R, WrDr 84*
Cowan, Janice 1941- *ConAu 97*
Cowan, Joseph Lloyd 1929- *WrDr 84*
Cowan, Louise Shillingburg 1916- *ConAu 1R*
Cowan, Michael H 1937- *ConAu 21R*
Cowan, Peter 1914- *ConAu 9NR, -21R, ConNov 82, DcLEL 1940, WrDr 84*
Cowan, Richard O 1934- *ConAu 53*
Cowan, Stuart DuBois 1917- *ConAu 104*
Cowan, Tom Keith 1916- *WrDr 84*
Cowan, Wood 1896-1977 *ConAu 69*
Coward, Noel 1899-1973 *AuNews 1, CnMD, ConAu 41R, ConAu P-2, ConLC 1, -9, CroCD, DcLB 10[port], EncWL 2, LongCTC, ModBrL, ModBrL SUP, ModWD, TwCA, TwCA SUP, TwCWr*
Coward, Roger Vilven 1916- *WrDr 84*

TwCA SUP
Craig, Gordon Alexander 1913- ConAu 25R
Craig, H A L 1921-1978 ConAu 81, –85
Craig, Hardin 1875-1968 LongCTC,
TwCA SUP
Craig, Hazel Thompson 1904- ConAu 1R
Craig, James 1930- ConAu 73
Craig, Jasmine ConAu X
Craig, Jean Teresa 1936- ConAu 5R
Craig, John 1921- WrDr 84
Craig, John 1921-1982 TwCCW 83
Craig, John David 1903- ConAu P-2
Craig, John Dixon d1946 CreCan 1
Craig, John Eland ConAu X, SmATA 2
Craig, John Ernest 1921- ConAu 101,
SmATA 23[port]
Craig, John H 1885- ConAu P-1
Craig, Larry ConAu X
Craig, Lee ConAu X
Craig, M Jean 1915- ConAu 73, SmATA 17
Craig, Margaret Maze 1911-1964 ConAu 1R,
SmATA 9
Craig, Mary 1923- WrDr 84
Craig, Mary Francis 1923- ConAu 1R, –4NR,
SmATA 6, TwCRGW
Craig, Mary Francis Shura 1927- IntAu&W 82
Craig, May 1889?-1975 ConAu 101, –89
Craig, Nancy ConAu X
Craig, Patricia 1943- WrDr 84
Craig, Peggy ConAu X
Craig, Philip R 1933- ConAu 25R
Craig, Richard B 1935- ConAu 53
Craig, Robert 1917- IntAu&W 82
Craig, Robert B 1944- ConAu 49
Craig, Robert Charles 1921- ConAu 17R,
WrDr 84
Craig, Robert D 1934- ConAu 81
Craig, Webster ConAu X
Craighead, Frank C, Jr. 1916- ConAu 97
Craigie, Mrs. 1867-1906 LongCTC
Craigie, Edward Horne 1894- ConAu P-2
Craigie, Sir William Alexander 1867-1957
LongCTC
Craik, Arthur ConAu X
Craik, Dinah Maria 1826-1887 SmATA 34[port]
Craik, Kenneth H 1936- ConAu 1NR, –45
Craik, T W 1927- WrDr 84
Craik, Thomas Wallace 1927- ConAu 106
Craik, Wendy Ann 1934- ConAu 25R,
IntAu&W 82, WrDr 84
Craille, Wesley ConAu X
Crain, Jeff ConAu X
Crain, John 1926?-1979 ConAu 89
Crain, Robert L 1934- ConAu 21R
Crain, Sharie 1942- ConAu 77
Craine, Eugene R 1917-1977 ConAu 33R
Cram, Mildred 1889- ConAu 49
Cramer, Alice Carver DrAP&F 83
Cramer, Clarence H 1905-1982 ConAu 9NR
Cramer, Clarence Henley 1905- ConAu 13R
Cramer, George H 1913- ConAu 21R
Cramer, Harold 1927- ConAu 29R
Cramer, J S 1928- ConAu 29R
Cramer, James 1915- ConAu 21R
Cramer, John Francis 1899-1967 ConAu P-1
Cramer, Kathryn 1943- ConAu 25R
Cramer, Richard Louis 1947- ConAu 102,
IntAu&W 82
Cramer, Richard S 1928- ConAu 29R
Cramer, Stanley H 1933- ConAu 29R,
WrDr 84
Crampton, Bryan Carlos IntAu&W 82X
Crampton, Charles Gregory 1911- ConAu 21R
Crampton, Georgia Ronan 1925- ConAu 57
Cramton, Roger C 1929- ConAu 33R
Cran, Marion 1875-1942 LongCTC
Cranbrook, James L ConAu X
Crandall, James E 1930- ConAu 41R
Crandall, Joy ConAu X
Crandall, Norma WrDr 84
Crandall, Norma 1907- ConAu 69,
IntAu&W 82, IntWWP 82, –82X
Crandell, Richard F 1901-1974 ConAu 53
Crane, Alex ConAu X
Crane, Barbara J 1934- ConAu 107,
SmATA 31[port]
Crane, Bill ConAu X
Crane, Burton DrAP&F 83
Crane, Caroline 1930- ConAu 3NR, –9R,
SmATA 11, WrDr 84
Crane, Catherine C 1940- ConAu 101
Crane, Diana 1933- ConAu 89

Crane, Donald P 1933- ConAu 61
Crane, Edgar 1917- ConAu 17R
Crane, Edna Temple ConAu X
Crane, Frances 1896- TwCCr&M 80, WrDr 84
Crane, Frank H 1912- ConAu 89
Crane, Hart 1899-1932 CnMWL, ConAmA,
ConAu 104, DcLB 4, EncWL 2, LongCTC,
ModAL, ModAL SUP, TwCA,
TwCA SUP, TwCLC 2, –5[port], TwCWr,
WhoTwCL
Crane, James G 1927- ConAu 13R
Crane, Jim ConAu X
Crane, Joan St. C 1927- ConAu 73
Crane, Julia G 1925- ConAu 41R
Crane, M A ConAu X
Crane, Morley Benjamin 1890-1983 ConAu 110
Crane, Philip Miller 1930- ConAu 9R
Crane, R S 1886-1967 ConAu 85,
ConLC 27[port], ConLCrt 82
Crane, Richard 1944- ConAu 77, ConDr 82,
IntAu&W 82, WrDr 84
Crane, Robert ConAu X, TwCWW
Crane, Robert Dickson 1929- ConAu 81
Crane, Roy SmATA X
Crane, Royston Campbell 1901-1977 ConAu 89,
SmATA 22N
Crane, Stephen 1871-1900 ConAu 109,
LongCTC, ModAL, TwCLC 11[port]
Crane, Sylvia E 1918- ConAu 33R,
IntAu&W 82, WrDr 84
Crane, Theodore Rawson 1929- ConAu 97
Crane, Walter 1845-1915 SmATA 18
Crane, Wilder 1928- ConAu 45
Crane, William B 1904-1981 ConAu 107
Crane, William D 1892- ConAu 5R, SmATA 1
Crane, William Earl 1899- ConAu 103
Craner, Hedda 1946- IntAu&W 82
Cranfield, Charles E B 1915- ConAu 2NR, –5R
Cranfield, Geoffrey Alan 1920- ConAu 5R
Cranford, Clarence William 1906- ConAu 1R
Cranford, Robert J 1908- ConAu P-2
Cranin, A Norman 1927- ConAu 73
Cranko, John 1927-1973 ConAu 45
Crankshaw, Edward 1909- ConAu 25R,
LongCTC, TwCA SUP
Cranny, Titus Francis 1921- ConAu 25R
Cranston, Edward ConAu X
Cranston, Maurice 1920- ConAu 3NR, –5R,
DcLEL 1940, IntAu&W 82, WrDr 84
Cranston, Mechthild ConAu 53
Cranwell, John Philips 1904- ConAu 61
Crapanzano, Vincent 1939- ConAu 5NR, –53
Crapol, Edward P 1936- ConAu 45
Crapps, Robert W 1925- ConAu 53
Crapsey, Adelaide 1878-1914 TwCA
Crary, Catherine S 1909- ConAu P-1
Crary, Margaret Coleman 1906- ConAu 5R,
SmATA 9
Crase, Douglas DrAP&F 83
Crase, Douglas 1944- ConAu 106
Crassweller, Robert D 1915- ConAu 21R
Craster, John Montagu 1901-1975 ConAu 108
Crathern, Alice Tarbell 1894-1973 ConAu 110,
MichAu 80
Craton, Michael John 1931- ConAu 41R
Cratty, Bryant J 1929- ConAu 11NR, –25R,
WrDr 84
Craveirinha, Jose 1922- ClDMEL 80
Craven, Avery 1885-1980 DcLB 17[port]
Craven, George M 1929- ConAu 61
Craven, Margaret 1901-1980 ConAu 103,
ConLC 17
Craven, Roy C, Jr. 1924- ConAu 69
Craven, Thomas 1889-1969 ConAu 97,
SmATA 22[port], TwCA, TwCA SUP
Craven, Wesley Frank 1905-1981 ConAu 103, –61
Cravens, Gwen DrAP&F 83
Cravens, Gwyneth ConAu 85
Cravens, Hamilton 1938- ConAu 103
Craveri, Marcello 1914- ConAu 21R
Crawells, Carl ConAu X
Crawford, Alan Pell 1953- ConAu 101
Crawford, Ann Fears 1932- ConAu 9NR, –21R
Crawford, Bill ConAu X
Crawford, C Merle 1924- ConAu 45
Crawford, Char 1935- ConAu 57
Crawford, Charles F d1983 ConAu 109
Crawford, Charles O 1934- ConAu 37R
Crawford, Charles P 1945- ConAu 45,
SmATA 28
Crawford, Charles W 1931- ConAu 8NR, –61
Crawford, Christina 1939- ConAu 85, WrDr 84

Crawford, Clan, Jr. 1927- ConAu 57
Crawford, David L 1890?-1974 ConAu 45
Crawford, Deborah 1922- ConAu 49, SmATA 6
Crawford, Donald W 1938- ConAu 45
Crawford, F Marion 1854-1909 ConAu 107,
TwCLC 10[port]
Crawford, Francis Marion 1854-1909 LongCTC
Crawford, Fred Roberts 1924- ConAu 2NR, –45
Crawford, Iain 1922- ConAu 1R
Crawford, James M 1925- ConAu 89
Crawford, Jean 1907?-1976 ConAu 104
Crawford, Jerry L 1934- ConAu 106
Crawford, Joanna 1941- ConAu 9R
Crawford, John E 1904-1971 ConAu P-2,
SmATA 3
Crawford, John R 1915?-1976 ConAu 65
Crawford, John Richard 1932- ConAu 106,
WrDr 84
Crawford, John S 1928- ConAu 106
Crawford, John W 1914- ConAu 1R
Crawford, John William 1936- ConAu 4NR, –53,
IntAu&W 82
Crawford, Joyce 1931- ConAu 25R
Crawford, Kenneth G 1902-1983 ConAu 108
Crawford, Kenneth Gale 1902- ConAu 81
Crawford, Linda DrAP&F 83
Crawford, Linda 1938- ConAu 65, MichAu 80
Crawford, Matsu W 1902- ConAu P-2
Crawford, Max DrAP&F 83
Crawford, Max 1938- ConAu 77
Crawford, Mel 1925- SmATA 33
Crawford, Oliver 1917- ConAu 85
Crawford, Patricia ConAu 103
Crawford, Phyllis 1899- SmATA 3
Crawford, Richard 1935- ConAu 9NR, –57
Crawford, Robert ConAu X, TwCCr&M 80,
WrDr 84
Crawford, Robert Platt 1893- ConAu P-2
Crawford, Stanley DrAP&F 83
Crawford, Stanley Gottlieb 1937- ConAu 69
Crawford, T S 1945- ConAu 29R
Crawford, Tad DrAP&F 83
Crawford, Thelmar Wyche 1905- ConAu 1R
Crawford, Theresa 1956- ConAu 110
Crawford, Tom DrAP&F 83
Crawford, Vaughn Emerson 1917?-1981
ConAu 104
Crawford, William 1929- ConAu 1R, –4NR
Crawford, William H 1907?-1973 ConAu 104
Crawford, William Hulfish 1913-1982 ConAu 105
Crawford, William P 1922- ConAu 106,
WrDr 84
Crawley, Aidan Merivale 1908- ConAu 61,
WrDr 84
Crawley, Budge 1911- CreCan 1
Crawley, C W 1899- ConAu 109
Crawley, Frank Radford 1911- CreCan 1
Crawley, Gerard M 1938- ConAu 106
Crawley, Judith 1914- CreCan 2
Crawshaw, Nancy 1914- IntAu&W 82
Cray, Ed 1933- ConAu 81
Cray, Edward 1933- IntAu&W 82, WrDr 84
Crayder, Dorothy 1906- ConAu 33R,
SmATA 7
Crayder, Teresa ConAu X, SmATA X
Crayencour, Marguerite De ConLC 19
Craynecour, Marguerite De WorAu
Craz, Albert G 1926- ConAu 8NR, –17R,
SmATA 24[port]
Creager, Alfred L 1910- ConAu 17R
Creager, Clara 1930- WrDr 84
Creagh, Patrick 1930- ConAu 25R
Creagh-Osborne, Richard 1928- ConAu 7NR,
–9R
Creamer, Robert W 1922- ConAu 21R,
WrDr 84
Crean, John Edward, Jr. 1939- ConAu 41R
Creasey, John 1908-1973 ConAu 5R, –8NR,
–41R, ConLC 11, LongCTC,
TwCCr&M 80, TwCWr, WorAu
Creasy, Rosalind R ConAu 110
Crechales, Anthony George 1926- ConAu 29R
Crechales, Tony ConAu X
Crecine, John Patrick 1939- ConAu 7NR, –57
Crecy, Jeanne ConAu X, SmATA X,
WrDr 84
Credland, Peter 1946- ConAu 69
Credle, Ellis 1902- ConAu 9NR, –13R,
SmATA 1
Credo ConAu X
Creed, David ConAu X
Creekmore, Betsey B 1915- ConAu 69

Creekmore, Hubert 1907-1966 *TwCA SUP*
Creel, George 1876-1953 *DcLB 25[port]*
Creel, Herrlee G 1905- *ConAu 85*
Creel, Stephen Melville 1938- *ConAu 69*
Creeley, Bobbie *DrAP&F 83*
Creeley, Robert *DrAP&F 83*
Creeley, Robert 1926- *ConAu 1R, ConLC 1, -2, -4, -8, -11, -15, ConP 80, CroCAP, DcLB 5[port], -16[port], EncWL 2, IntAu&W 82, ModAL, ModAL SUP, WhoTwCL, WorAu, WrDr 84*
Creeley, Robert White 1922- *DcLEL 1940*
Creelman, Marjorie B 1908- *ConAu P-2*
Creer, Thomas L 1934- *ConAu 69*
Creese, Bethea *ConAu 5NR, -9R, WrDr 84*
Creeth, Edmund Homer 1928- *ConAu 102*
Creevey, Lucy E 1940- *ConAu 29R*
Cregan, David 1931- *ConAu 1NR, -45, ConDr 82, DcLB 13[port], DcLEL 1940, WrDr 84*
Creger, Ralph 1914- *ConAu 13R*
Cregier, Don M 1930- *ConAu 69*
Crehan, Joseph Hugh 1906- *IntAu&W 82, WrDr 84*
Crehan, Thomas 1919- *ConAu 2NR, -5R*
Creigh, Dorothy 1921- *ConAu 105*
Creighton, Don *ConAu X, WrDr 84*
Creighton, Donald Grant 1902-1979 *ConAu 101, -93, WorAu*
Creighton, Helen 1899- *ConAu 41R*
Creighton, Helen 1914- *ConAu 33R*
Creighton, Jane *DrAP&F 83*
Creighton, Joanne V 1942- *ConAu 69*
Creighton, John *DrAP&F 83*
Creighton, Luella 1901- *ConAu P-1, CreCan 2*
Creighton, Thomas H 1904- *ConAu 5R, -6NR*
Crellin, John 1916- *ConAu 69*
Cremeans, Charles D 1915- *ConAu 5R*
Cremer, Jan 1940- *ConAu 13R, IntAu&W 82*
Cremer, Robert Roger 1947- *ConAu 61*
Cremieux, Benjamin 1888-1944 *CIDMEL 80*
Cremin, Lawrence Arthur 1925- *ConAu 33R*
Crena DeIongh, Daniel 1888-1970 *ConAu 29R, ConAu P-2*
Crenner, James *DrAP&F 83*
Crenner, James 1938- *ConAu 13R*
Crenshaw, James L 1934- *ConAu 37R, IntAu&W 82, WrDr 84*
Crenshaw, Mary Ann *ConAu 8NR, -57*
Crepeau, Richard C 1941- *ConAu 105*
Cressey, Donald 1919- *WrDr 84*
Cressey, Donald R 1919- *ConAu 6NR, -13R, IntAu&W 82*
Cressey, William W 1939- *ConAu 33R*
Cresson, Bruce Collins 1930- *ConAu 45*
Cresswell, Helen *ConAu 8NR*
Cresswell, Helen 1934- *SmATA 1, TwCCW 83*
Cresswell, Helen 1936- *ConAu 17R, IntAu&W 82, WrDr 84*
Cresswell, Jasmine 1941- *ConAu 110*
Creston, Dormer *ConAu X, LongCTC*
Creswell, H B 1869-1960 *LongCTC*
Creswell, K A C 1879- *ConAu P-1*
Cretan, Gladys 1921- *ConAu 29R, SmATA 2*
Cretzmeyer, F X, Jr. 1913- *ConAu 13R*
Creutzer, Christian *IntAu&W 82X*
Crevel, Rene 1900-1935 *CIDMEL 80*
Crew, Francis Albert Eley 1888-1973 *ConAu P-2*
Crew, Louie *DrAP&F 83*
Crew, Louie 1936- *ConAu 81, WrDr 84*
Crewe, Jennifer *DrAP&F 83*
Crews, Donald *ConAu 108, SmATA 30*
Crews, Donald 1938- *SmATA 32[port]*
Crews, Frederick C 1933- *ConAu 1R, -1NR, ConLCrt 82, IntAu&W 82, WrDr 84*
Crews, Harry *DrAP&F 83*
Crews, Harry 1935- *AuNews 1, ConAu 25R, ConLC 6, -23[port], ConNov 82, DcLB 6[port], WorAu 1970, WrDr 84*
Crews, Judson *DrAP&F 83*
Crews, Judson 1917- *ConAu 7NR, -13R, ConP 80, WrDr 84*
Crews, William J 1931- *ConAu 25R*
Cribb, Larry 1934- *ConAu 109*
Cribbet, John E 1918- *ConAu 17R*
Crichton, Douglas *WrDr 84*
Crichton, James 1907- *WrDr 84*
Crichton, James Dunlop 1907- *ConAu 5NR, -13R*
Crichton, John 1916- *ConAu 17R*
Crichton, John Michael 1942- *IntAu&W 82*
Crichton, Kyle Samuel 1896-1960 *ConAu 89,*

TwCA, TwCA SUP
Crichton, Michael *WrDr 84*
Crichton, Michael 1942- *AuNews 2, ConAu 25R, ConLC 2, -6, ConNov 82, DcLB Y81B[port], SmATA 9, TwCCr&M 80, TwCSFW, WorAu 1970*
Crichton, Robert 1925- *AuNews 1, ConAu 17R, WrDr 84*
Crichton Smith, Iain *WorAu 1970*
Crick, Bernard 1929- *ConAu 1R, -5NR, IntAu&W 82*
Crick, Bernard R 1929- *WrDr 84*
Crick, Donald Herbert 1916- *ConAu 102, WrDr 84*
Crickillon, Jacques 1940- *IntAu&W 82*
Criden, Joseph 1916- *ConAu 77*
Criden, Yosef *ConAu X*
Crighton, John Clark 1903- *ConAu 33R, WrDr 84*
Crighton, Richard E 1921- *ConAu 109*
Crile, Barney *ConAu X*
Crile, George, Jr. 1907- *ConAu 89, WrDr 84*
Crim, Evelyn R 1927- *IntWWP 82*
Crim, Keith R 1924- *ConAu 29R*
Crim, Mort 1935- *ConAu 41R*
Crimmins, James Custis 1935- *ConAu 5R, -11NR*
Crinkley, Richmond Dillard 1940- *ConAu 29R, WrDr 84*
Cripe, Helen 1932- *ConAu 8NR, -61*
Cripps, Anthony 1913- *ConAu 13R*
Cripps, Joy *IntWWP 82*
Cripps, Joy Beaudette *IntWWP 82X*
Cripps, Joyce 1923- *IntWWP 82*
Cripps, L L 1914- *ConAu 97*
Cripps, Thomas 1932- *ConAu 97*
Crisler, Fritz *ConAu X*
Crisler, Herbert Orin 1899-1982 *ConAu 107*
Crisler, Lois d1971 *ConAu 104*
Crisp, Anthony Thomas 1937- *ConAu 101, WrDr 84*
Crisp, C G 1936- *ConAu 37R*
Crisp, Frank R 1915- *ConAu 9R*
Crisp, Norman James 1923- *ConAu 93*
Crisp, Quentin 1908?- *ConAu 109*
Crisp, Robert *ConAu 1R*
Crisp, Tony *ConAu X, WrDr 84*
Crispin, Edmund 1921-1978 *ConAu X, ConLC 22[port], ConSFA, TwCCr&M 80, WorAu*
Crispin, John 1936- *ConAu 53*
Crispin, Ruth Helen Katz 1940- *ConAu 93*
Crispo, John 1933- *ConAu 37R, WrDr 84*
Crissey, Elwell 1899- *ConAu P-2*
Crist, Judith 1922- *AuNews 1, ConAu 81, WrDr 84*
Crist, Lyle M 1924- *ConAu 53*
Crist, Raymond E 1904- *ConAu 73*
Crist, Steven G 1956- *ConAu 101*
Cristabel 1916- *ConAu X*
Cristofer, Michael 1945?- *ConAu 110, NatPD 81[port]*
Cristofer, Michael 1946- *ConDr 82, DcLB 7[port], WrDr 84*
Cristol, Vivian *ConAu 17R*
Cristy, R J *ConAu X*
Criswell, Cloyd M 1908- *ConAu P-1*
Criswell, W A 1909- *ConAu 17R*
Critchfield, Howard J 1920- *ConAu 53*
Critchfield, Richard 1931- *ConAu 41R, IntAu&W 82, WrDr 84*
Critchley, Edmund M R 1931- *ConAu 21R*
Critchley, Julian 1930- *ConAu 85*
Critchley, Lynne *ConAu X*
Critchley, Thomas Alan 1919- *ConAu 29R, WrDr 84*
Crites, Ronald W 1945- *ConAu 102*
Crites, Stephen D 1931- *ConAu 41R*
Critic *ConAu X*
Criticus *ConAu X*
Crittenden, Mabel 1917- *ConAu 103*
Crnjanski, Milos 1893- *CIDMEL 80, ConAu P-1, EncWL 2, ModSL 2, WorAu 1970*
Crobaugh, Emma 1903- *AuNews 2, IntWWP 82*
Croce, Arlene 1934- *ConAu 104*
Croce, Benedetto 1866-1952 *CIDMEL 80, EncWL 2[port], LongCTC, TwCA, TwCA SUP, TwCWr*
Crocetti, Guido M 1920-1979 *ConAu 85*
Crocker, Helen Bartter 1929- *ConAu 69*

Crocker, Lester G 1912- *ConAu 5R, -5NR, WrDr 84*
Crocker, Lionel George 1897- *ConAu P-2*
Crocker, Mary Wallace 1941- *ConAu 93*
Crocker, Thomas Dunstan 1936- *ConAu 108*
Crocker, Walter 1902- *WrDr 84*
Crocker, Walter Russell 1902- *ConAu 17R*
Crockett, Albert Stevens 1873-1969 *ConAu 89*
Crockett, Christina *ConAu X*
Crockett, George Ronald 1906- *ConAu P-1*
Crockett, James Underwood 1915-1979 *ConAu 33R, -89*
Crockett, Samuel Rutherford 1860-1914 *LongCTC, TwCA, TwCA SUP, TwCCW 83*
Crocombe, Ronald Gordon 1929- *ConAu 13R, WrDr 84*
Crofford, Emily 1927- *ConAu 107*
Crofford, Lena H 1908- *ConAu P-1*
Croft, Andrew 1906- *WrDr 84*
Croft, Noel Andrew Cotton 1906- *IntAu&W 82*
Croft, Sutton *ConAu X*
Croft-Cooke, Rupert 1903-1979 *ConAu 4NR, -9R, -89, TwCA[port], TwCA SUP, TwCCr&M 80*
Croft-Cooke, Rupert 1904- *LongCTC*
Croft-Murray, Edward 1907-1980 *ConAu 102*
Crofton, Denis Hayes 1908- *ConAu 109*
Crofts, Freeman Wills 1879-1957 *LongCTC, TwCA, TwCA SUP, TwCCr&M 80, TwCWr*
Crofts, John E V 1887-1972 *ConAu P-2*
Crofut, Bill *SmATA X*
Crofut, William E, III 1934- *ConAu 25R, SmATA 23[port]*
Crohn, Burrill B 1884-1983 *ConAu 110*
Croise, Jacques *ConAu X*
Croitoru *IntAu&W 82X*
Croizier, Ralph 1935- *ConAu 61*
Croly, Herbert David 1869-1930 *TwCA, TwCA SUP*
Croman, Dorothy Young *ConAu X*
Crombie, Alistair Cameron 1915- *IntAu&W 82, WrDr 84*
Cromie, Alice Hamilton 1914- *ConAu 3NR, -9R, SmATA 24*
Cromie, Robert 1856-1907 *TwCSFW*
Cromie, Robert 1909- *ConAu 1R, -1NR*
Cromie, William J 1930- *ConAu 13R, SmATA 4*
Crommelynck, Fernand 1885-1970 *CnMD, ConAu 89, ModWD, WorAu[port]*
Crommelynck, Fernand 1886-1970 *CIDMEL 80, EncWL 2*
Crommelynck, Fernand 1888-1970 *ModFrL*
Cromptom, Margaret 1901- *ConAu P-1*
Crompton, Anne Eliot 1930- *ConAu 33R, SmATA 23[port]*
Crompton, John *ConAu X*
Crompton, Louis 1925- *ConAu 33R, WrDr 84*
Crompton, Margaret 1901- *WrDr 84*
Crompton, Margaret Norah 1901- *IntAu&W 82*
Crompton, Richmal 1890-1969 *ConAu X, LongCTC, SmATA 5, TwCCW 83*
Cromwell, Chester R 1925- *ConAu 89*
Cromwell, Elsie *ConAu X*
Cromwell, Harvey 1907- *ConAu 17R*
Cromwell, John 1887-1979 *ConAu 89*
Cromwell, John 1914?-1979 *ConAu 89*
Cromwell, Otelia *LivgBAA*
Cromwell, Richard Sidney 1925- *ConAu 53*
Cronbach, Abraham 1882-1965 *ConAu 1R, SmATA 11*
Crone, Bonnie Warren 1934- *IntAu&W 82*
Crone, Rainer 1942- *ConAu 33R*
Crone, Ruth 1919- *ConAu 9R, SmATA 4*
Croner, Helga 1914- *ConAu 107*
Cronin, A J 1896-1981 *ConAu 1R, -5NR, -102, LongCTC, ModBrL, SmATA 25N, TwCA, TwCA SUP, TwCWr*
Cronin, Anthony 1926- *DcLEL 1940, WrDr 84*
Cronin, Anthony 1928- *IntAu&W 82*
Cronin, Archibald Joseph 1896- *IntAu&W 82*
Cronin, George 1933- *ConAu 101*
Cronin, James E 1908- *ConAu 45*
Cronin, John F 1908- *ConAu 37R*
Cronin, Joseph M 1935- *ConAu 49*
Cronin, Sylvia 1929- *ConAu 89*
Cronin, Thomas E 1940- *ConAu 85*
Cronin, Vincent Archibald Patrick 1924- *ConAu 5NR, -9R, LongCTC*

Cronkhite, Bernice Brown 1893-1983 *ConAu 110*
Cronkite, Walter 1916- *ASpks, AuNews 1, -2, ConAu 69, WrDr 84*
Cronley, Jay 1943- *ConAu 81*
Cronne, Henry Alfred 1904- *ConAu 65*
Cronon, E David 1924- *ConAu 1R, -1NR*
Cronstatter, Gerch *IntWWP 82X*
Cronus, Diodorus *ConAu X*
Crook, Bette 1921- *ConAu 73*
Crook, Compton Newby *WrDr 84*
Crook, David 1910- *ConAu 97*
Crook, Howard 1937- *ConAu 107*
Crook, Isabel 1915- *ConAu 97*
Crook, J A 1921- *ConAu 21R*
Crook, Joseph 1937- *WrDr 84*
Crook, Joseph Mordaunt 1937- *ConAu 41R, IntAu&W 82*
Crook, Margaret Brackenbury 1886- *ConAu P-1*
Crook, Roger H 1921- *ConAu 1R, -4NR*
Crook, William 1933- *ConAu 102*
Crookall, Robert 1890- *ConAu 33R*
Crookenden, Napier 1915- *ConAu 11NR, -69*
Crooker, Barbara *DrAP&F 83*
Crooks, James B 1933- *ConAu 25R*
Croome, Pamela Elizabeth 1917- *IntWWP 82*
Cropp, Ben 1936- *ConAu 33R, WrDr 84*
Cropper, Margaret 1886-1980 *ConAu 102*
Cros, Earl *SmATA X*
Crosbie, Hugh Provan 1912- *IntAu&W 82*
Crosbie, John S 1920- *ConAu 73*
Crosbie, Provan 1912- *ConAu 9R, IntAu&W 82X*
Crosbie, Sylvia Kowitt 1938- *ConAu 73*
Crosby, Alexander L 1906-1980 *ConAu 29R, -93, SmATA 2, -23N*
Crosby, Alfred W, Jr. 1931- *ConAu 17R, WrDr 84*
Crosby, Bing 1904-1977 *ConAu X*
Crosby, Caresse 1892-1970 *ConAu 25R*
Crosby, Donald A 1932- *ConAu 53*
Crosby, Donald F 1933- *ConAu 77*
Crosby, Harry 1898-1929 *ConAu 107, DcLB 4*
Crosby, Harry C *WrDr 84*
Crosby, Harry H 1919- *ConAu 5NR, -13R*
Crosby, Harry Lillis 1904-1977 *ConAu 73*
Crosby, Henry Grew 1898-1929 *ConAu X*
Crosby, Henry Sturgis *ConAu X*
Crosby, James O 1924- *ConAu 89*
Crosby, Jeremiah *ConAu X*
Crosby, John 1912- *WrDr 84*
Crosby, John Campbell 1912- *ConAu 1R, -4NR*
Crosby, John F 1931- *ConAu 7NR, -17R*
Crosby, Michael 1940- *ConAu 11NR, -17R*
Crosby, Muriel 1908- *ConAu 17R*
Crosby, Philip B 1926- *ConAu 73*
Crosby, Ruth 1897- *ConAu 49*
Crosby, Sumner McK 1909- *ConAu 13R*
Crosby, Sumner McK 1909-1982 *ConAu 108*
Crosby, Tempe Fenn *IntWWP 82*
Crosher, G R 1911- *ConAu 69, SmATA 14*
Crosland, Andrew T 1944- *ConAu 53*
Crosland, Anthony 1918-1977 *ConAu 69, -73*
Crosland, Margaret *WrDr 84*
Crosland, Margaret 1920- *ConAu 1NR, -49, IntAu&W 82*
Cross, Aleene Ann 1922- *ConAu 29R*
Cross, Alfred Rupert 1912- *IntAu&W 82*
Cross, Amanda *WrDr 84*
Cross, Amanda 1926- *ConAu X, TwCCr&M 80*
Cross, Anthony Glenn 1936- *ConAu 37R, WrDr 84*
Cross, Beverley 1931- *ConAu 102, ConDr 82, WrDr 84*
Cross, Beverly 1931- *DcLEL 1940*
Cross, Brenda *WrDr 84*
Cross, Claire 1932- *ConAu 21R, IntAu&W 82, WrDr 84*
Cross, Colin 1928- *WrDr 84*
Cross, Colin John 1928- *ConAu 7NR, -9R*
Cross, Donna Woolfolk 1947- *ConAu 97*
Cross, Frank Moore, Jr. 1921- *ConAu 65*
Cross, Gilbert B *ConAu 105*
Cross, Gillian 1945- *TwCCW 83*
Cross, Helen Reeder *ConAu X, SmATA X*
Cross, Herbert James 1934- *ConAu 45*
Cross, Ian 1925- *ConNov 82, DcLEL 1940, TwCWr, WrDr 84*
Cross, Ira Brown 1880-1977 *ConAu 106*
Cross, James *ConAu X, DrAP&F 83, WrDr 84*
Cross, Jennifer 1932- *ConAu 29R*

Cross, John Keir 1914-1967 *ConAu 73, TwCSFW*
Cross, K G W 1927-1967 *ConAu P-1*
Cross, K Patricia 1926- *ConAu 33R, WrDr 84*
Cross, Leslie 1909-1977 *ConAu 65, -89*
Cross, M Claire *ConAu X*
Cross, Milton 1897-1975 *ConAu 53*
Cross, Polton *TwCSFW*
Cross, Ralph D 1931- *ConAu 93*
Cross, Richard 1950?-1983 *ConAu 110*
Cross, Richard K 1940- *ConAu 33R, IntAu&W 82, WrDr 84*
Cross, Robert 1925- *WrDr 84*
Cross, Robert Brandt 1914- *ConAu 37R*
Cross, Robert Dougherty 1924- *ConAu 1R*
Cross, Robert Singlehurst 1925- *ConAu 5R*
Cross, Rupert 1912-1980 *ConAu 102, -105*
Cross, Samuel S 1919- *ConAu 45*
Cross, T T *ConAu X*
Cross, Theodore Lamont 1924- *ConAu 45, IntAu&W 82*
Cross, Victor *ConAu X, WrDr 84*
Cross, Wilbur L 1918- *WrDr 84*
Cross, Wilbur Lucius 1862-1948 *TwCA, TwCA SUP*
Cross, Wilbur Lucius, III 1918- *ConAu 1R, -2NR, SmATA 2*
Crossan, Darryl *ConAu X*
Crossan, G D 1950- *WrDr 84*
Crosscountry *ConAu X*
Crossen, Ken 1910- *ConAu X, TwCCr&M 80, WrDr 84*
Crossen, Kendell Foster 1910- *ConAu 1R, -4NR*
Crosser, Paul K 1902-1976 *ConAu 1R, -3NR*
Crossett, David Allen 1941- *ConAmTC*
Crossley-Holland, Kevin 1941- *TwCCW 83, WrDr 84*
Crossley-Holland, Kevin John William 1941- *ConAu 41R, ConP 80, DcLEL 1940, IntAu&W 82, IntWWP 82, SmATA 5*
Crossman, Richard 1907-1974 *ConAu 49, -61, WorAu*
Crosson, Robert *DrAP&F 83*
Croteau, John Tougas 1910- *ConAu 9R*
Crothers, George D 1909- *ConAu P-1*
Crothers, J Frances 1913- *ConAu 33R, WrDr 84*
Crothers, Jessie F *ConAu X*
Crothers, Rachel 1878-1958 *CnMD, ConAmA, DcLB 7[port], LongCTC, ModWD, TwCA[port], TwCA SUP*
Crothers, Samuel McChord 1857-1927 *TwCA, TwCA SUP*
Crotty, William J 1936- *ConAu 21R*
Crouch, Harold 1940- *ConAu 89*
Crouch, Marcus 1913- *ConAu 5NR, -9R, SmATA 4*
Crouch, Marcus S 1913- *WrDr 84*
Crouch, Stanley *DrAP&F 83*
Crouch, Stanley 1945- *LivgBAA*
Crouch, Steve 1915- *ConAu 9NR, -53*
Crouch, Steve 1915-1983 *ConAu 109*
Crouch, Thomas W 1932- *ConAu 73*
Crouch, Tom D 1944- *ConAu 106*
Crouch, W George 1903-1970 *ConAu 5R, -89*
Crouch, Winston Winford 1907- *ConAu 106*
Croudace, Glynn 1917- *ConAu 29R*
Crouse, Russel 1893-1966 *ConAu 25R, ModWD, TwCA SUP*
Crouse, Russell M 1893-1966 *ConAu 77*
Crouse, Timothy 1947- *ConAu 77*
Crouse, William H 1911- *WrDr 84*
Crouse, William Harry 1907- *ConAu 5R, -6NR*
Crout, George C 1917- *ConAu 11NR, -29R, SmATA 11*
Crouzet, Francois Marie-Joseph 1922- *ConAu 3NR, -9R*
Croves, Hal *ConAu X*
Crovitz, Herbert F 1932- *ConAu 29R*
Crow, Alice 1894-1966 *ConAu P-1*
Crow, C P 1938- *ConAu 102*
Crow, Carl 1883-1945 *TwCA, TwCA SUP*
Crow, Donna Fletcher 1941- *ConAu 108*
Crow, Duncan 1920- *ConAu 85, IntAu&W 82, WrDr 84*
Crow, Elizabeth Smith 1946- *ConAu 103*
Crow, Jeffrey J 1947- *ConAu 85, IntAu&W 82*
Crow, John Armstrong 1906- *ConAu 13R*
Crow, Lester D 1897-1983 *ConAu 110*
Crow, Lester Donald 1897- *ConAu P-1*
Crow, Mark 1948- *ConAu 57*
Crow, Martin M 1901- *ConAu P-2*

Crow, Mary *DrAP&F 83*
Crow, William Bernard 1895-1976 *ConAu 65, ConAu P-1*
Crowbate, Ophelia Mae *ConAu X*
Crowcroft, Andrew 1923- *ConAu 21R*
Crowcroft, Jane *ConAu X*
Crowcroft, Peter 1923- *ConAu 101*
Crowder, Christopher M D 1922- *ConAu 103*
Crowder, Michael 1934- *ConAu 1R, -1NR, IntAu&W 82, WrDr 84*
Crowder, Richard H 1909- *WrDr 84*
Crowder, Richard Henry 1909- *ConAu P-1*
Crowe, Amanda Cockrell 1948- *ConAu 101*
Crowe, Bettina 1911- *WrDr 84*
Crowe, Bettina Lum 1911- *ConAu 9R, IntAu&W 82, SmATA 6*
Crowe, C B *ConAu X*
Crowe, Cecily *TwCRGW, WrDr 84*
Crowe, Charles 1928- *ConAu 17R*
Crowe, Charles Monroe 1902-1978 *ConAu 1R, -103*
Crowe, E Odell 1925?-1983 *ConAu 110*
Crowe, F J 1929- *ConAu X*
Crowe, John *ConAu X, TwCCr&M 80, WrDr 84*
Crowe, John 1906- *ConAu P-1*
Crowe, Kenneth C 1934- *ConAu 103*
Crowe, Philip Kingsland 1908-1976 *ConAu 65, -69*
Crowe, Robert L 1937- *ConAu 69*
Crowe, Sylvia 1901- *ConAu P-1*
Crowe-Carraco, Carol 1943- *ConAu 93*
Crowell, George H 1931- *ConAu 25R*
Crowell, Grace Noll 1877-1969 *ConAu 107, SmATA 34[port]*
Crowell, Joan 1921- *ConAu 57*
Crowell, Muriel Beyea 1916- *ConAu 57*
Crowell, Norton B 1914- *ConAu 9R, WrDr 84*
Crowell, Pers 1910- *ConAu 29R, SmATA 2*
Crowell, Robert Leland 1909- *ConAu 109*
Crowl, Philip A 1914- *ConAu 110*
Crowley, Aleister 1875-1947 *ConAu X, LongCTC, TwCLC 7[port]*
Crowley, Arthur McBlair 1945- *ConAu 107*
Crowley, Daniel J 1921- *ConAu 9NR, -21R*
Crowley, Edward Alexander 1875-1947 *ConAu 104*
Crowley, Ellen T 1943- *ConAu 97*
Crowley, Frances G 1921- *ConAu 105*
Crowley, James B 1929- *ConAu 21R*
Crowley, John 1942- *ConAu 61, DcLB Y82B[port], TwCSFW, WrDr 84*
Crowley, John Edward 1943- *ConAu 53*
Crowley, John W 1945- *ConAu 69*
Crowley, Mart 1935- *ConAu 73, ConDr 82, DcLB 7[port], NatPD 81[port], WrDr 84*
Crowley, Mary C 1915- *ConAu 97*
Crowley, Raymond 1895-1982 *ConAu 106*
Crown, David A 1928- *ConAu 10NR*
Crown, David Allan 1928- *ConAu 25R, WrDr 84*
Crown, Paul 1928- *ConAu 17R*
Crowson, P S 1913- *ConAu 53, WrDr 84*
Crowther, Betty 1939- *ConAu 61*
Crowther, Bosley 1905-1981 *ConAu 103, -65*
Crowther, Duane S 1934- *ConAu 25R*
Crowther, Geoffrey 1907-1972 *ConAu 33R*
Crowther, George 1927- *WrDr 84*
Crowther, Harold Francis 1920- *WrDr 84*
Crowther, James Gerald 1899- *ConAu 73, SmATA 14, WrDr 84*
Crowther, Wilma 1918- *ConAu 5R*
Croxford, Leslie 1944- *ConAu 81*
Croxton, Anthony H 1902- *ConAu 61*
Croxton, C A 1945- *WrDr 84*
Croxton, Frederick E 1899- *ConAu P-2*
Croy, Homer 1883-1965 *ConAu 110, -89, DcLB 4, TwCA, TwCA SUP*
Crozet, Charlotte 1926- *ConAu 25R, IntAu&W 82*
Crozetti, Lora *IntAu&W 82X*
Crozetti, R Warner *ConAu X*
Crozetti, Ruth G Warner 1915- *IntAu&W 82*
Crozier, Brian 1918- *ConAu 3NR, -9R, IntAu&W 82, WrDr 84*
Crozier, Eric John 1914- *DcLEL 1940, LongCTC*
Crozier, John Beattie 1849-1921 *TwCA, TwCA SUP*
Crud *ConAu X*
Cruden, Robert 1910- *ConAu 33R*
Cruickshank, Allan D 1907-1974 *ConAu 53*

Cruickshank, C G 1914- *ConAu 9NR, -21R*
Cruickshank, Charles Greig 1914- *IntAu&W 82, WrDr 84*
Cruickshank, Helen Gere 1907- *ConAu P-1*
Cruickshank, John 1924- *ConAu 1R, -4NR, IntAu&W 82, WrDr 84*
Cruickshank, William M 1915- *ConAu 89*
Cruikshank, George 1792-1878 *SmATA 22[port]*
Crum, Howard Alvin 1928- *MichAu 80*
Crum The Bum *ConAu X*
Crumarums *ConAu X*
Crumb, Jan Barry 1943- *IntWWP 82*
Crumb, Robert 1943- *ConAu 106, ConLC 17*
Crumbaker, Alice 1911- *ConAu 81*
Crumbaugh, James Charles 1912- *ConAu 37R*
Crumbley, D Larry 1941- *ConAu 29R*
Crumbum *ConAu X*
Crumley, James *DrAP&F 83*
Crumley, James 1909- *ConAu 69*
Crumm, Lloyd C, Jr. 1927- *ConAu 10NR, -65*
Crummey, Robert O 1936- *ConAu 25R*
Crump, Barry 1935- *WrDr 84*
Crump, Barry John 1935- *ConAu 8NR, -13R, DcLEL 1940*
Crump, Fred H, Jr. 1931- *ConAu 3NR, -9R, SmATA 11*
Crump, Galbraith Miller 1929- *ConAu 57*
Crump, Geoffrey Herbert 1891- *ConAu P-1*
Crump, Irving 1887- *ConAu 73*
Crump, James Irving 1887-1979 *ConAu 89, SmATA 21N*
Crump, Kenneth G, Jr. 1931- *ConAu 21R*
Crump, Spencer *WrDr 84*
Crump, Spencer 1923- *ConAu 21R, IntAu&W 82*
Crump, Spencer 1933- *ConAu 9NR*
Crump, Thomas 1929- *ConAu 49*
Crumpet, Peter *ConAu X*
Crumpler, Frank H 1935- *ConAu 77*
Crumpler, Gus H 1911- *ConAu 69*
Crumrine, N Ross, II 1934- *ConAu 8NR, -13R*
Crumski *ConAu X*
Crunden, Reginald *ConAu X*
Crunden, Robert M 1940- *ConAu 29R*
Crunk *ConAu X*
Cruse, David C *DrAP&F 83*
Cruse, Harold 1919- *ConAu 77, LivgBAA, MichAu 80*
Cruso, Thalassa 1909- *ConAu 65*
Crusoe, Edwin, IV *DrAP&F 83*
Crustt *ConAu X*
Crux, June Roper *CreCan 1*
Cruz, Joan Carroll 1931- *ConAu 73*
Cruz, Ray 1933- *SmATA 6*
Cruz, Victor Hernandez 1949- *ConAu 65, ConP 80, CroCAP, WrDr 84*
Cryer, Gretchen *ConDr 82D*
Cryer, Gretchen 1936?- *ConLC 21[port]*
Crying Wind *ConAu X*
Crystal, David 1941- *ConAu 7NR, -17R, WrDr 84*
Crystal, John C 1920- *ConAu 102*
Crystal Gazer *MichAu 80*
Csak, Gyula 1930- *IntAu&W 82*
Cselenyi, Jozsef 1928- *CreCan 2*
Csicsery-Ronay, Istvan 1917- *ConAu 21R*
Csikos-Nagy, Bela 1915- *ConAu 73*
Csokor, Franz Theodor 1885-1969 *CnMD, CroCD, EncWL 2, ModGL, ModWD*
Csorba, Gyozo 1916- *IntWWP 82*

Ctvrtek, Vaclav 1911-1976 *ConAu 107, SmATA 27N*
Cua, Antonio S 1932- *ConAu 7NR, -17R, IntAu&W 82, WrDr 84*
Cuba, Ivan 1920- *IntAu&W 82, IntWWP 82*
Cuban, Larry 1934- *ConAu 29R*
Cubas, Braz *ConAu X*
Cubeiro, Emilio *DrAP&F 83*
Cubeiro, Emilio 1947- *IntWWP 82*
Cuber, John F 1911- *ConAu 9R*
Cubeta, Paul 1925- *ConAu 5R, WrDr 84*
Cudahy, Brian J 1936- *ConAu 41R*
Cuddihy, John Murray 1922- *ConAu 85*
Cuddon, J A 1928- *WrDr 84*
Cuddon, John Anthony 1928- *ConAu 3NR, -5R*
Cuddy, Don 1925- *ConAu 69*
Cude, Jean Ring 1906- *IntWWP 82*
Cudlipp, Edythe 1929- *ConAu 33R*
Cuelho, Art 1943- *ConAu 61*
Cuelho, Art, Jr. *DrAP&F 83*
Cuevas, Clara 1933- *ConAu 57*

Cuff, Barry *ConAu X*
Cuff, Robert Dennis 1941- *ConAu 109*
Cuffari, Richard 1925-1978 *SmATA 25N, -6*
Cuisenaire, Emile-Georges 1891?-1976 *ConAu 61*
Cuisenier, Jean 1927- *ConAu 73*
Culbert, Samuel Alan 1938- *ConAu 69*
Culbert, T Patrick 1930- *ConAu 107*
Culbertson, Don S 1927- *ConAu 9R*
Culbertson, Hugh M *ConAu 77*
Culbertson, John M 1921- *ConAu 9R, MichAu 80*
Culbertson, Judi 1941- *ConAu 85*
Culbertson, Manie 1927- *ConAu 49*
Culbertson, Paul T 1905- *ConAu 37R*
Culex *ConAu X*
Culkin, Ann Marie 1918- *ConAu 9R*
Cull, John Guinn, Jr. 1934- *ConAu 41R, IntAu&W 82*
Cullen, Charles T 1940- *ConAu 53*
Cullen, Countee 1903-1946 *ConAmA, ConAu 108, DcLB 4, EncWL 2, ModAL, ModAL SUP, ModBlW, SmATA 18, TwCA, TwCA SUP, TwCLC 4[port]*
Cullen, E J *DrAP&F 83*
Cullen, George Francis 1901-1980 *ConAu 102*
Cullen, Joseph P 1920- *ConAu 49*
Cullen, Lee Stowell 1922- *ConAu 103*
Cullen, Maurice Galbraith 1866-1934 *CreCan 2*
Cullen, Maurice R, Jr. 1927- *ConAu 73*
Cullen, Patrick 1940- *ConAu 29R*
Cullen, Paula Bramsen *DrAP&F 83*
Cullen, Peta *ConAu X*
Culler, A Dwight 1917- *ConAu 17R*
Culler, Annette Lorena *ConAu X*
Culler, Jonathan 1944- *ConAu 104*
Culley, Thomas R 1931- *ConAu 33R*
Culliford, Stanley George 1920- *ConAu 65*
Culligan, Joe *ConAu X*
Culligan, Matthew J 1918- *ConAu 81*
Cullinan, Bernice Ellinger 1926- *ConAu 104*
Cullinan, Elizabeth 1933- *ConAu 11NR, -25R*
Cullinan, Gerald 1916- *ConAu 21R*
Cullinan, Patrick Roland 1932- *IntWWP 82*
Cullinane, Leo Patrick 1907?-1978 *ConAu 77*
Culliney, John L 1942- *ConAu 65*
Cullingford, Ada Sophia 1908- *IntWWP 82*
Cullingford, Cecil Howard Dunstan 1904- *ConAu 5R, -7NR, IntAu&W 82*
Cullingford, Guy 1907- *ConAu X, TwCCr&M 80, WrDr 84*
Cullingworth, J Barry 1929- *ConAu 1R, -1NR, IntAu&W 82, WrDr 84*
Cullman, Marguerite Wagner 1908- *ConAu 1R*
Cullmann, Oscar 1902- *ConAu 106*
Cullop, Charles P 1927- *ConAu 25R*
Cullum, Ridgewell 1867-1943 *TwCWW*
Cullum, Ridgwell 1867-1943 *LongCTC, TwCA, TwCA SUP*
Cully, Iris V 1914- *ConAu 1R, -1NR*
Cully, Kendig Brubaker *WrDr 84*
Cully, Kendig Brubaker 1913- *ConAu 1R, -1NR*
Culotta, Nino *ConAu X*
Culp, Delos Poe 1911- *ConAu 17R*
Culp, John H 1907- *WrDr 84*
Culp, John Hewett, Jr. 1907- *ConAu 29R, TwCWW*
Culp, Louanna McNary 1901-1965 *ConAu P-1, SmATA 2*
Culp, Paula 1941- *ConAu 57*
Culpepper, Robert H 1924- *ConAu 77*
Culross, Michael 1942- *ConAu 33R*
Culshaw, John 1924-1980 *ConAu 11NR, -21R, -97*
Culshaw, Olive 1916- *IntWWP 82*
Culver, Dwight W 1921- *ConAu 9R*
Culver, Elsie Thomas 1898- *ConAu P-2*
Culver, Kathryn *ConAu X*
Culver, Kenneth Leon 1903- *ConAu 103*
Culver, Marjorie *DrAP&F 83*
Culver, Roger B 1940- *ConAu 104*
Culver, Timothy J *WrDr 84*
Cum, R *ConAu X*
Cumberland, Charles C 1914-1970 *ConAu 1R, -2NR*
Cumberland, John Hammett 1924- *ConAu 106*
Cumberland, Kenneth B 1913- *WrDr 84*
Cumberland, Kenneth Brailey 1913- *ConAu 53, IntAu&W 82*
Cumberland, Marten 1892-1972 *ConAu P-1, TwCCr&M 80*
Cumberland, William Henry 1929- *ConAu 17R*
Cumberlege, Marcus 1938- *WrDr 84*

Cumberlege, Marcus Crossley 1938- *ConAu 97, ConP 80, IntAu&W 82*
Cumberlege, Vera 1908- *ConAu 81*
Cumbler, John T 1946- *ConAu 89*
Cumbo, Kattie M 1938- *LivgBAA*
Cumes, J W C 1922- *ConAu 73*
Cuming, Geoffrey John 1917- *ConAu 3NR, -5R*
Cuming, Pamela 1944- *ConAu 107*
Cumings, Bruce Glenn 1943- *ConAu 107*
Cumming, Patricia *DrAP&F 83*
Cumming, Patricia 1932- *ConAu 11NR*
Cumming, Patricia Arens 1932- *ConAu 61, IntAu&W 82, IntWWP 82*
Cumming, Primrose 1915- *TwCCW 83*
Cumming, Primrose Amy 1915- *ConAu 33R, SmATA 24, WrDr 84*
Cumming, Robert *DrAP&F 83*
Cumming, Robert 1945- *ConAu 106*
Cumming, Robert Denoon 1916- *ConAu 107*
Cumming, William P 1900- *WrDr 84*
Cumming, William Patterson 1900- *ConAu 33R, IntAu&W 82*
Cummings, Ann *ConAu X*
Cummings, Arthur J 1920?-1979 *ConAu 89*
Cummings, Betty Sue 1918- *ConAu 73, SmATA 15*
Cummings, Bruce Frederick 1889-1919 *LongCTC, TwCA, TwCA SUP*
Cummings, Charles 1940- *ConAu 107*
Cummings, D W 1935- *ConAu 101*
Cummings, E E 1894-1962 *CnMD, CnMWL, ConAmA, ConAu 73, ConLC 1, -3, -8, -12, -15, DcLB 4, EncWL 2, LongCTC, ModAL, ModAL SUP, ModWD, TwCA, TwCA SUP, TwCWr, WhoTwCL*
Cummings, Florence *ConAu 49*
Cummings, Jean 1930- *ConAu 33R, MichAu 80*
Cummings, Larry Lee 1937- *ConAu 53*
Cummings, M A *ConSFA*
Cummings, Milton C, Jr. 1933- *WrDr 84*
Cummings, Milton Curtis, Jr. 1933- *ConAu 13R*
Cummings, Parke 1902- *ConAu P-1, SmATA 2*
Cummings, Paul 1933- *ConAu 8NR, -21R*
Cummings, Ray 1887-1957 *DcLB 8[port], TwCSFW*
Cummings, Richard *ConAu X, SmATA X*
Cummings, Richard LeRoy 1933- *ConAu 45*
Cummings, Thomas G 1944- *ConAu 97*
Cummings, Violet M 1905- *ConAu 57*
Cummings, W T 1933- *ConAu 1R*
Cummins, D Duane 1935- *ConAu 37R, IntAu&W 82*
Cummins, Geraldine Dorothy 1890-1969 *ConAu P-1*
Cummins, James *DrAP&F 83*
Cummins, James Vernon 1948- *IntWWP 82*
Cummins, Paul F 1937- *ConAu 33R*
Cummins, Walter *DrAP&F 83*
Cummins, Walter 1936- *ConAu 41R*
Cumpian, Carlos G *DrAP&F 83*
Cundari, Emilia 1933- *CreCan 2*
Cundiff, Edward William 1919- *ConAu 1R, -4NR*
Cundy, Henry Martyn 1913- *ConAu 5R*
Cuneo, Gilbert Anthony 1913-1978 *ConAu 77*
Cuneo, John R 1911- *ConAu 53*
Cunha, Euclydes Da 1866-1909 *ModLAL*
Cunha, George Martin 1911- *ConAu 25R*
Cuninggim, Merrimon 1911- *ConAu 41R*
Cunliffe, Barrington Windsor 1939- *ConAu 9NR, -53, IntAu&W 82*
Cunliffe, Barry *ConAu X*
Cunliffe, Barry 1939- *ConAu X, WrDr 84*
Cunliffe, Elaine 1922- *ConAu 33R, WrDr 84*
Cunliffe, John 1933- *TwCCW 83*
Cunliffe, John Arthur 1933- *ConAu 11NR, -61, SmATA 11*
Cunliffe, John William 1865-1946 *TwCA, TwCA SUP*
Cunliffe, Marcus 1922- *ConAu 10NR, WrDr 84*
Cunliffe, Marcus Falkner 1922- *ConAu 21R, IntAu&W 82*
Cunliffe, William Gordon 1929- *ConAu 25R*
Cunning, Alfred *IntWWP 82X*
Cunningham, Aline *ConAu 9NR, -57*
Cunningham, Barry 1940- *ConAu 73*
Cunningham, Bob *ConAu X*
Cunningham, Captain Frank *ConAu X, SmATA X*
Cunningham, Cathy *ConAu X, SmATA X*
Cunningham, Chet 1928- *ConAu 4NR, -49,*

SmATA 23, TwCWW, WrDr 84
Cunningham, Dale S 1932- *ConAu 8NR, -13R,*
SmATA 11
Cunningham, Donald H 1935- *ConAu 103*
Cunningham, E V *WrDr 84*
Cunningham, E V 1914- *ConAu X, ConNov 82,*
SmATA 7, TwCCr&M 80
Cunningham, Eugene 1896-1957 *TwCWW*
Cunningham, Floyd F 1899- *ConAu P-1,*
WrDr 84
Cunningham, Frank *ConAu X*
Cunningham, H H 1913-1969 *ConAu P-1*
Cunningham, Imogen 1883-1976 *ConAu 65*
Cunningham, J V *DrAP&F 83*
Cunningham, J V 1911- *ConAu 1R, -1NR,*
ConLC 3, ConLCrt 82, ConP 80,
DcLB 5[port], WorAu, WrDr 84
Cunningham, James F 1901- *ConAu P-2*
Cunningham, James Vincent 1911- *DcLEL 1940,*
IntWWP 82
Cunningham, Joseph F X 1925- *ConAu 69*
Cunningham, Joseph Sandy 1928- *ConAu 61*
Cunningham, Julia 1916- *TwCCW 83*
Cunningham, Julia W 1916- *WrDr 84*
Cunningham, Julia Woolfolk 1916- *ConAu 4NR,*
-9R, ConLC 12, SmATA 1, -26[port]
Cunningham, Laura *DrAP&F 83*
Cunningham, Laura 1947- *ConAu 85*
Cunningham, Lawrence 1935- *ConAu 85*
Cunningham, Louis Arthur 1900-1954 *CreCan 2*
Cunningham, Lyda Sue Martin 1938- *ConAu 17R*
Cunningham, Merce *WrDr 84*
Cunningham, Michael A 1945- *ConAu 41R*
Cunningham, Noble E, Jr. 1926- *ConAu 81*
Cunningham, Paul James, Jr. 1917- *ConAu 73*
Cunningham, R Walter 1932- *ConAu 103*
Cunningham, Richard 1939- *ConAu 101*
Cunningham, Robert Louis 1926- *ConAu 41R*
Cunningham, Robert M, Jr. 1909- *ConAu 1NR,*
-49
Cunningham, Robert Stanley 1907- *ConAu 53*
Cunningham, Rosemary 1916- *ConAu 9R*
Cunningham, Virginia 1909- *ConAu X,*
SmATA X
Cunninghame Graham, Robert Bontine 1852-1936
LongCTC, ModBrL, TwCA, TwCA SUP
Cunnington, Phillis 1887- *WrDr 84*
Cunnington, Phillis 1887-1974 *ConAu 53*
Cunqueiro, Alvaro 1911- *CIDMEL 80,*
EncWL 2
Cunz, Dieter 1910-1969 *ConAu P-2*
Cuomo, George *DrAP&F 83*
Cuomo, George 1929- *ConAu 5R, -7NR,*
DcLB Y80B[port]
Cuomo, Mario Matthew 1932- *ConAu 103,*
WrDr 84
Cupitt, Don 1934- *ConAu 41R, IntAu&W 82*
Cuppy, Will 1884-1949 *ConAu 108*
Cuppy, William Jacob 1884-1949 *TwCA,*
TwCA SUP
Cure, Karen 1949- *ConAu 9NR, -65*
Curel, Francois De 1854-1928 *CIDMEL 80,*
CnMD, ModFrL, ModWD
Curiae, Amicus *ConAu X, SmATA X*
Curie, Eve 1904- *ConAu P-1, SmATA 1*
Curl, David H 1932- *ConAu 93*
Curl, Donald Walter 1935- *ConAu 33R*
Curl, James Stevens 1937- *ConAu 37R,*
IntAu&W 82, WrDr 84
Curlah, Curt *IntWWP 82X*
Curle, Adam *ConAu X*
Curle, Charles T W 1916- *ConAu 33R*
Curle, Richard Henry Parnell 1883-1968
LongCTC
Curler, Bernice 1915- *ConAu 85*
Curley, Arthur 1938- *ConAu 9NR, -21R*
Curley, Charles 1949- *ConAu 57*
Curley, Daniel *DrAP&F 83*
Curley, Daniel 1918- *ConAu 3NR, -9R,*
IntAu&W 82, SmATA 23[port], WrDr 84
Curley, Dorothy Nyren 1927- *ConAu X, -1R*
Curley, Michael J 1900-1972 *ConAu 37R*
Curley, Thomas *DrAP&F 83*
Curley, Walter J P 1922- *ConAu 53*
Curling, Audrey *ConAu 61, IntAu&W 82*
Curling, Bill *ConAu X*
Curling, Bryan 1911- *WrDr 84*
Curling, Bryan William Richard 1911-
ConAu 102
Curnoe, Gregory Richard 1936- *CreCan 1*
Curnow, Allen 1911- *ConAu 69, ConDr 82,*
ConP 80, IntAu&W 82, IntWWP 82,

LongCTC, ModCmwL, TwCWr, WorAu,
WrDr 84
Curnow, Frank *ConAu X*
Curran, Bob *ConAu X*
Curran, Charles A 1913- *ConAu 33R*
Curran, Charles E 1934- *ConAu 21R,*
IntAu&W 82, WrDr 84
Curran, Charles John 1921-1980 *ConAu 105*
Curran, Dolores 1932- *ConAu 6NR, -57*
Curran, Donald J 1926- *ConAu 45*
Curran, Francis X 1914- *ConAu 17R,*
IntAu&W 82, WrDr 84
Curran, Jan Goldberg 1937- *ConAu 101*
Curran, Joseph M 1932- *ConAu 103*
Curran, Mona *ConAu 5R*
Curran, Peter Malcolm 1922- *ConAu 103,*
WrDr 84
Curran, Phil R 1911- *ConAu 73*
Curran, Robert 1923- *ConAu 89*
Curran, Samuel 1912- *ConAu 109*
Curran, Samuel Crowe 1912- *IntAu&W 82*
Curran, Stuart 1940- *ConAu 29R*
Curran, Thomas J 1929- *ConAu 45*
Curran, Ward S 1935- *ConAu 41R*
Curran, William John 1925- *ConAu 108*
Currelley, Lorraine Rainie *DrAP&F 83*
Curren, Polly 1917- *ConAu 1R, -4NR*
Current, Richard N 1912- *ConAu 1R, -5NR*
Current-Garcia, Eugene 1908- *ConAu 17R*
Currer-Briggs, Noel 1919- *ConAu 73*
Currey, Cecil B 1932- *ConAu 25R*
Currey, R F 1894- *ConAu P-1*
Currey, R F 1894-1983 *ConAu 109*
Currey, R N *IntAu&W 82X*
Currey, R N 1907- *WrDr 84*
Currey, Ralph Nixon 1907- *ConAu 93, ConP 80,*
IntAu&W 82
Currey, Richard *DrAP&F 83*
Currie, Ann 1922?-1980 *ConAu 102*
Currie, David *ConAu X*
Currie, David P 1936- *ConAu 106*
Currie, Glenne 1926- *ConAmTC*
Currie, Lauchlin 1902- *ConAu 73*
Currier, Alvin C 1932- *ConAu 21R*
Currier, Frederick P 1923- *ConAu 85*
Currier, Richard L 1940- *ConAu 57*
Currier And Ives *LongCTC*
Curro, Evelyn Malone 1907- *ConAu 5R*
Curros Enriquez, Manuel 1851-1908 *CIDMEL 80*
Curry, Andrew 1931- *ConAu 57*
Curry, Avon *ConAu X, WrDr 84*
Curry, David *ConAu X*
Curry, David 1942- *ConAu 69*
Curry, Estell H 1907- *ConAu P-2*
Curry, F Hayden 1940- *ConAu 108*
Curry, George E 1947- *ConAu 69*
Curry, Gladys J *ConAu X*
Curry, Jane 1932- *TwCCW 83, WrDr 84*
Curry, Jane Louise 1932- *ConAu 7NR, -17R,*
IntAu&W 82, SmATA 1
Curry, Jennifer 1934- *ConAu 77*
Curry, Kenneth 1910- *ConAu 8NR, -17R*
Curry, Leonard Preston 1929- *ConAu 29R*
Curry, Lerond 1938- *ConAu 33R, WrDr 84*
Curry, Martha Mulroy 1926- *ConAu 61*
Curry, Mary Earle Lowry 1917- *IntWWP 82*
Curry, Paul 1917- *ConAu 69*
Curry, Peggy Simson *DrAP&F 83*
Curry, Peggy Simson 1911- *ConAu 33R,*
SmATA 8, TwCWW, WrDr 84
Curry, Richard O 1931- *WrDr 84*
Curry, Richard Orr 1931- *ConAu 13R,*
IntAu&W 82
Curry, Thomas A 1901?-1976 *ConAu 69*
Curry, Windell *ConAu X*
Curry-Lindahl, Kai 1917- *ConAu 2NR, -49,*
IntAu&W 82
Curtayne, Alice 1898- *ConAu 53*
Curteis, Ian 1935- *ConAu 103, IntAu&W 82,*
WrDr 84
Curti, Merle 1897- *ConAu 4NR, -5R,*
DcLB 17[port], TwCA SUP
Curtin, James R 1922- *ConAu 17R*
Curtin, Mary Ellen 1922- *ConAu 57*
Curtin, Philip *ConAu X*
Curtin, Phillip D 1922- *ConAu 7NR, -13R*
Curtin, William M 1927- *ConAu 53*
Curtis, Alan R 1936- *ConAu 105*
Curtis, Anthony 1926- *ConAu 101,*
IntAu&W 82, WrDr 84
Curtis, Arnold 1917- *ConAu 29R*
Curtis, Bruce 1944- *SmATA 30[port]*

Curtis, Carol Edwards 1943- *ConAu 77*
Curtis, Charles J 1921- *ConAu 21R*
Curtis, Charles Ralph 1899- *ConAu 5R*
Curtis, Charlotte *AuNews 2, ConAu 9R*
Curtis, David 1942- *ConAu 21R*
Curtis, Donald 1915- *ConAu 103*
Curtis, Douglas 1936- *WrDr 84*
Curtis, Edith Roelker 1893-1977 *ConAu 1R, -103*
Curtis, Gerald 1904-1983 *ConAu 109*
Curtis, Howard J 1906-1972 *ConAu 37R*
Curtis, J Montgomery 1905-1982 *ConAu 108*
Curtis, Jack 1922- *ConAu 103*
Curtis, Jackie 1947- *ConAu 103, ConDr 82,*
WrDr 84
Curtis, James 1953- *ConAu 108*
Curtis, James C 1938- *ConAu 105*
Curtis, Jared Ralph 1936- *ConAu 101*
Curtis, John *ConAu X*
Curtis, Lewis Perry 1900-1976 *ConAu 65,*
ConAu P-2
Curtis, Linda Lee *DrAP&F 83*
Curtis, Lindsay R 1916- *ConAu 41R*
Curtis, Lynn A 1943- *ConAu 61*
Curtis, Margaret James 1897- *ConAu 1R*
Curtis, Marjorie *ConAu X*
Curtis, Mark H 1920- *ConAu 5R*
Curtis, Michael Raymond 1923- *ConAu 103*
Curtis, Norman 1917- *ConAu 45*
Curtis, Patricia 1921- *SmATA 23[port]*
Curtis, Patricia 1924- *ConAu 69*
Curtis, Paul *ConAu X*
Curtis, Peter *ConAu X,   LongCTC,*
SmATA 8, TwCCr&M 80, TwCRGW,
WrDr 84
Curtis, Philip 1920- *ConAu 109*
Curtis, Price *ConAu X*
Curtis, Richard A 1937- *ConAu 106, ConSFA,*
SmATA 29
Curtis, Richard Hale *ConAu X*
Curtis, Richard Kenneth 1924- *ConAu 1R*
Curtis, Rosemary Ann 1935- *ConAu 9R*
Curtis, Sharon 1951- *WrDr 84*
Curtis, Thomas Bradford 1911- *ConAu 61*
Curtis, Thomas Dale 1952- *WrDr 84*
Curtis, Tom *ConAu X, IntAu&W 82X*
Curtis, Tony 1925- *ConAu 73*
Curtis, Tony 1946- *ConAu 106, IntAu&W 82,*
WrDr 84
Curtis, Wade *ConAu X, SmATA X, WrDr 84*
Curtis, Will *ConAu X, IntAu&W 82X,*
WrDr 84
Curtis, William J R 1948- *ConAu 110,*
WrDr 84
Curtis Brown, Beatrice 1901-1974 *ConAu P-2*
Curtiss, John S 1899- *ConAu P-2*
Curtiss, Ursula 1923- *WrDr 84*
Curtiss, Ursula Reilly 1923- *ConAu 1R, -5NR,*
TwCCr&M 80
Curtiss, Vienna Ione 1909- *WrDr 84*
Curtius, Ernst Robert 1886-1956 *EncWL 2,*
WorAu
Curtler, Hugh Mercer 1937- *ConAu 89*
Curto, Josephine 1929- *WrDr 84*
Curto, Josephine J 1927- *ConAu 17R*
Curvers, Alexis-Theophile 1906- *CIDMEL 80*
Curwin, Richard L 1944- *ConAu 77*
Curwood, James Oliver 1878-1927 *CreCan 1,*
LongCTC, MichAu 80, TwCA,
TwCA SUP, TwCWW
Curzon, Charles *IntAu&W 82X*
Curzon, Clare *ConAu X*
Curzon, Daniel *ConAu 73, DrAP&F 83*
Curzon, Gordon Anthony Peter L 1919-
IntWWP 82
Curzon, Lady *ConAu X, WrDr 84*
Curzon, Lucia *ConAu X, WrDr 84*
Curzon, Sam *ConAu X*
Curzon, Virginia *ConAu X*
Curzon Of Kedleston, G N Curzon, Marquis
1859-1925 *LongCTC, TwCA, TwCA SUP*
Cusac, Marian H 1932- *ConAu 33R*
Cusack, Anne E *DrAP&F 83*
Cusack, Cyril 1910- *WrDr 84*
Cusack, Dymphna 1902- *ConAu 9R, TwCWr,*
WrDr 84
Cusack, Dymphna 1902-198-? *ConAu 11NR*
Cusack, Ellen Dymphna 1902- *IntAu&W 82*
Cusack, Lawrence X 1919- *ConAu 5R*
Cusack, Michael J 1928- *ConAu 69*
Cushing, Barry E 1945- *ConAu 4NR, -53*
Cushing, Harvey Williams 1869-1939 *LongCTC*
Cushing, Jane 1922- *ConAu 29R*

Cushing, Mary W 189-?-1974 *ConAu 53*
Cushion, John Patrick 1915- *ConAu 93, IntAu&W 82*
Cushman, Clarissa White Fairchild 1889-1980 *ConAu 93*
Cushman, Dan 1909- *ConAu 3NR, -5R, MichAu 80, TwCWW, WrDr 84*
Cushman, Jerome 1914- *ConAu 1R, SmATA 2, WrDr 84*
Cushman, Robert F 1918- *ConAu 77*
Cusick, Bart Charles, III 1944- *IntAu&W 82*
Cusick, Philip A 1937- *ConAu 69*
Cuskelly, Eugene James 1924- *ConAu 5R*
Cuskey, Walter 1934- *ConAu 41R*
Cuss, Camerer 1909?-1970 *ConAu 104*
Cussler, Clive 1931- *ConAu 1NR, -45, WrDr 84*
Custer, Chester Eugene 1920- *ConAu 41R*
Custer, Clint *ConAu X*
Cusumano, Michele *DrAP&F 83*
Cutbush, Andrew Stuart Banks 1947- *IntWWP 82*
Cutchen, Billye Walker 1930- *ConAu 77, SmATA 15*
Cutcliffe Hyne *LongCTC*
Cutforth, John Ashlin 1911- *ConAu 9R*
Cuthbert, David *ConAmTC*
Cuthbert, Diana Daphne Holman-Hunt 1913- *ConAu 1R*
Cuthbert, Eleonora Isabel 1902- *ConAu P-1*
Cuthbert, Mary *ConAu X*
Cuthbert, Neil 1951- *NatPD 81[port]*
Cuthbertson, Gilbert Morris 1937- *ConAu 57*
Cuthbertson, Tom 1945- *ConAu 1NR, -45*
Cutler, Bruce *DrAP&F 83*
Cutler, Bruce 1930- *ConAu 1R, -2NR, IntWWP 82*
Cutler, Carl C 1878-1966 *ConAu 1R, -103*
Cutler, Carol 1926- *ConAu 103*
Cutler, Charles L 1930- *ConAu 65*
Cutler, Donald R 1930- *ConAu 21R*
Cutler, Ebbitt 1923- *ConAu 4NR, -49, IntAu&W 82, SmATA 9*
Cutler, Irving H 1923- *ConAu 9NR, -21R*
Cutler, Ivor 1923- *ConAu 5R, -9NR, IntAu&W 82, IntWWP 82, SmATA 24[port], WrDr 84*
Cutler, Katherine Noble 1905- *ConAu 4NR, -5R*
Cutler, Roland *DrAP&F 83*
Cutler, Roland 1938- *ConAu 102*
Cutler, Samuel *ConAu X, SmATA 5*
Cutler, William Worcester, III 1941- *ConAu 103*
Cutliffe, Stephen H 1947- *ConAu 102*
Cutliffe Hyne *TwCA, TwCA SUP*
Cutlip, Scott Munson 1915- *ConAu 5R*
Cutright, Paul Russell 1897- *ConAu 65*
Cutright, Phillips 1930- *ConAu 5R*
Cutshall, Alden 1911- *ConAu 3NR, -9R*
Cutsumbis, Michael N 1935- *ConAu 45*
Cutt, Margaret Nancy 1913- *WrDr 84*
Cutt, W Towrie 1898- *ConAu 81, SmATA 16*
Cutt, W Towrie 1898-1981 *TwCCW 83*
Cutter, Donald C 1922- *ConAu 33R*
Cutter, Fred 1924- *ConAu 57*
Cutter, Robert Arthur 1930- *ConAu 8NR, -57*
Cutting, Edith E 1918- *ConAu 106*
Cuttino, G P 1914- *ConAu 21R*
Cuttle, Evelyn Roeding *ConAu 57*
Cuttler, Charles D 1913- *ConAu 29R*
Cutts, John P 1927- *ConAu 45*
Cutts, Richard 1923- *ConAu 33R*
Cutts, William M 1857-1943 *CreCan 1*
Cutul, Ann-Marie 1945- *ConAu 103*
Cuyler, Louise E 1908- *ConAu 21R*
Cuyler, Stephen *ConAu X, SmATA X*
Cuyler, Susanna 1946- *ConAu 61*
Cwojdzinski, Antoni 1896- *ModWD*
Cykler, Edmund A 1903- *ConAu 9R*
Cynan *ConAu X*
Cynthia *AuNews 1, ConAu X*
Cyr, Don 1935- *ConAu 103*
Cyr, John Edwin 1915- *ConAu 103*
Cyriax, James Henry 1904- *WrDr 84*
Cysarz, Herbert 1896- *IntAu&W 82*
Czaczkes, Shmuel Yosef *ConAu X*
Czaja, Michael 1911- *ConAu 57*
Czaplinski, Suzanne 1943- *ConAu 61*
Czaykowski, Bogdan 1932- *ClDMEL 80*
Czcibor, Stanislaw *IntAu&W 82X*
Czechowicz, Jozef 1903-1939 *ClDMEL 80, EncWL 2, ModSL 2*
Czeike, Felix 1926- *IntAu&W 82*

Czerminska, Malgorzata 1940- *IntAu&W 82*
Czerniawski, Adam 1934- *ClDMEL 80, ConAu 37R*
Czerny, Peter G 1941- *ConAu 65*
Czobor, Agnes 1920- *ConAu 37R*
Czuchnowski, Marian 1909- *ClDMEL 80*
Czura, Roman Peter 1913- *ConAu 89*
Czyzewski, Tytus 1885-1945 *ModSL 2*

D

Daane, Calvin J 1925- *ConAu 41R*
Daane, James 1914- *ConAu 21R*
Dabberdt, Walter F 1942- *ConAu 107*
Dabbs, Jack Autrey 1914- *ConAu 17R*
Dabbs, James McBride 1896-1970 *ConAu P-1*
Dabit, Eugene 1898-1936 *ClDMEL 80*
Dabkin, Edwin Franden 1898?-1976 *ConAu 65*
Dabney, Dick *DrAP&F 83*
Dabney, Dick 1933-1981 *ConAu 105, –69*
Dabney, Joseph Earl 1929- *ConAu 49, WrDr 84*
Dabney, Ross H 1934- *ConAu 21R*
Dabney, Virginius 1901- *ConAu 1NR, –45, IntAu&W 82, TwCA SUP, WrDr 84*
Dabney, William M 1919- *ConAu 9R*
D'Abreu, Gerald Joseph 1916- *ConAu P-2*
Dabrowska, Maria 1889-1965 *ClDMEL 80, ConAu 106, ConLC 15, EncWL 2, ModSL 2*
DaCal, Ernesto Guerra 1911- *ConAu 4NR, –5R*
Dace, Letitia 1941- *ConAu 106*
Dace, Tish 1941- *ConAu X, WrDr 84*
Dace, Wallace 1920- *ConAu 61, NatPD 81[port]*
Dacey, Florence *DrAP&F 83*
Dacey, Norman F 1908- *ConAu 2NR, –5R*
Dacey, Philip *DrAP&F 83*
Dacey, Philip 1939- *ConAu 37R, IntWWP 82*
Dachman, Ken 1958- *ConAu 110*
Dachs, David 1922- *ConAu 69*
Dachs, David 1922-1980 *ConAu 11NR*
DaCosta, Maria Fatima Velho *AuNews 1*
Dacre Of Glanton, Baron *WrDr 84*
DaCruz, Daniel 1921- *ConAu 3NR, –5R, WrDr 84*
Dacy, Douglas Calvin 1927- *ConAu 104*
Dadie, Bernard Binlin 1916- *ConAu 25R, EncWL 2, ModBlW, ModFrL*
Daedalus *ConAu X*
Daehlin, Reidar A 1910- *ConAu P-1*
Daem, Thelma Bannerman 1914- *ConAu 5R*
Daemer, Will *ConAu X, WrDr 84*
Daemmrich, Horst S 1930- *ConAu 1NR, –45, IntAu&W 82*
Daenzer, Bernard J 1916- *WrDr 84*
Daenzer, Bernard John 1916- *ConAu 53*
Dafoe, Christopher Grannis 1936- *ConAmTC*
Dagan, Avigdor 1912- *ConAu 33R*
Dagbjartsdottir, Vilborg 1930- *IntAu&W 82*
Dagenais, James J 1928- *ConAu 41R*
Dagenais, John *DrAP&F 83*
Dagenais, Pierre *CreCan 1*
Dager, Edward Z 1921- *ConAu 61*
Dagerman, Stig 1923-1954 *ClDMEL 80, CnMD, CroCD, EncWL 2, ModWD, WhoTwCL, WorAu 1970*
Dagg, Anne Innis 1933- *ConAu 11NR, –69*
Daglarca, Fazil Husnu 1914- *ClDMEL 80, EncWL 2*
Daglish, Eric Fitch 1892-1966 *ConAu 102, LongCTC, TwCA, TwCA SUP*
Dagmar, Peter *ConSFA*
Dagnol, Jules N *IntAu&W 82X*
D'Agostino, Angelo 1926- *ConAu 17R*
D'Agostino, Dennis John 1957- *ConAu 106*

D'Agostino, Giovanna P 1914- *ConAu 57*
D'Agostino, Joseph D 1929- *ConAu 69*
Dagover, Lil 1897-1980 *ConAu 105*
Dagrin, Bengt Gosta 1940- *IntAu&W 82*
Dahari, A *IntWWP 82X*
Daheim, Mary 1937- *ConAu 110*
Dahinden, Justus 1925- *ConAu 81*
Dahl, Arlene 1928- *ConAu 105*
Dahl, Borghild 1890- *ConAu 1R, –2NR, IntAu&W 82, SmATA 7, WrDr 84*
Dahl, Curtis 1920- *ConAu 1R, –2NR, IntAu&W 82, WrDr 84*
Dahl, Georg 1905- *ConAu 85*
Dahl, Gordon J 1932- *ConAu 49*
Dahl, John *IntAu&W 82X*
Dahl, Lennart 1922- *IntWWP 82*
Dahl, Murdoch 1914- *WrDr 84*
Dahl, Murdoch Edgcumbe 1914- *ConAu P-1*
Dahl, Nils A 1911- *ConAu 65*
Dahl, Roald *DrAP&F 83*
Dahl, Roald 1916- *ChlLR 1, ConAu 1R, –6NR, ConLC 1, –6, –18, ConNov 82, DcLEL 1940, IntAu&W 82, SmATA 1, –26[port], TwCCW 83, TwCCr&M 80, WorAu, WrDr 84*
Dahl, Robert 1915- *WrDr 84*
Dahl, Robert Alan 1915- *ConAu 65, ConIsC 1[port]*
Dahlbeck, Eva 1920- *IntAu&W 82*
Dahlberg, Edward 1900-1977 *ConAu 9R, –69, ConLC 1, –7, –14, ModAL, ModAL SUP, TwCA SUP, TwCWr*
Dahlberg, Edwin T 1892- *ConAu P-2*
Dahlberg, Jane S 1923- *ConAu 21R*
Dahlen, Beverly *DrAP&F 83*
Dahlie, Hallvard 1925- *WrDr 84*
Dahllof, Tell Gunnar 1912- *IntAu&W 82*
Dahlstedt, Marden 1921- *ConAu 1NR, –45, SmATA 8, WrDr 84*
Dahlstrom, Earl C 1914- *ConAu 17R*
Dahm, Charles W 1937- *ConAu 107*
Dahms, Alan M 1937- *ConAu 49*
Dahmus, Joseph Henry 1909- *ConAu 21R*
Dahood, Mitchell 1922-1982 *ConAu 106, –25R*
Dahrendorf, Ralf 1929- *ConAu 1R, –3NR, IntAu&W 82, WrDr 84*
Daiches, David 1912- *ConAu 5R, –7NR, ConLCrt 82, LongCTC, ModBrL, TwCA SUP, WrDr 84*
Daigon, Arthur 1928- *ConAu 33R*
Daigon, Ruth *DrAP&F 83*
Daiken, Leslie Herbert 1912-1964 *ConAu 1R*
Dailey, Charles A 1923- *ConAu 89*
Dailey, Janet 1944- *ConAu 89, TwCRGW, TwCWW, WrDr 84*
Dailey, Joel George *DrAP&F 83*
Daily, Jay E 1923- *ConAu 33R*
Daily, Susan *DrAP&F 83*
Daily, Susan Elaine 1950- *IntWWP 82*
Dain, Floyd Russell 1910- *MichAu 80*
Dain, Martin J 1924- *ConAu 13R*
Dain, Norman 1925- *ConAu 9R*
Dain, Phyllis 1929- *ConAu 69*
Dainton, Courtney 1920- *ConAu 9R*

Dainton, Frederick 1914- *WrDr 84*
Daisne, Johan 1912-1978 *ClDMEL 80, EncWL 2, ModWD*
Daiute, Robert James 1926- *ConAu 9R, –13R*
Dakers, Elaine Kidner 1905-1978 *ConAu 85, LongCTC*
Dakin, Arthur Hazard 1905- *ConAu 106*
Dakin, David Martin 1908- *ConAu 73*
Dakin, Edwin Franden 1898-1976 *ConAu 104*
Dakin, Julian 1939-1971 *ConAu P-2*
Dakshinamurthy, Madhava 1944- *IntWWP 82*
Dal, Ayaz Ali 1959- *IntWWP 82*
Dal, Erik 1922- *IntAu&W 82*
Dalal, Mrs. Nergis 1920- *DcLEL 1940*
Dalal, Suresh Purushottamdas 1932- *IntWWP 82*
Daland, Robert T 1919- *ConAu 21R*
Dalbor, John B 1929- *ConAu 17R*
Dalcourt, Gerard Joseph 1927- *ConAu 33R, WrDr 84*
Dalcroze, Emile Jaques 1865-1951 *LongCTC*
Dale, Antony 1912- *ConAu 107, IntAu&W 82, WrDr 84*
Dale, Celia Marjorie 1912- *ConAu 3NR, –5R, IntAu&W 82*
Dale, D M C 1930- *ConAu 21R*
Dale, Edward Everett 1879-1972 *ConAu 4NR, –5R*
Dale, Edwin L, Jr. 1923- *ConAu 69*
Dale, Ernest 1917- *ConAu 13R*
Dale, Jack *ConAu X, SmATA X*
Dale, James 1886- *ConAu P-2*
Dale, John B 1905- *ConAu 13R*
Dale, Magdalene L 1904- *ConAu 13R*
Dale, Margaret Jessy 1911- *ConAu 3NR, –5R, IntAu&W 82*
Dale, Norman *ConAu X*
Dale, Paul Worthen 1923- *ConAu 25R, WrDr 84*
Dale, Peter 1938- *ConAu 1NR, –45, ConP 80, IntAu&W 82, IntWWP 82, WrDr 84*
Dale, Reginald Rowland 1907- *ConAu 21R, WrDr 84*
Dale, Richard 1932- *ConAu 33R, WrDr 84*
Dale, Robin *IntAu&W 82X*
Dale, Roman *ConAu X*
Dale, Suzanne *DrAP&F 83*
D'Alelio, Ellen F 1938- *ConAu 17R*
Dales, Richard C 1926- *ConAu 45*
Daleski, H M 1926- *ConAu 33R, IntAu&W 82, WrDr 84*
D'Alessandro, Robert 1942- *ConAu 61*
Dalet, Roger 1927- *ConAu 107*
Daley, Arthur 1904-1974 *ConAu 45, ConAu P-2*
Daley, Bill *ConAu X*
Daley, Eliot A 1936- *ConAu 97*
Daley, Joseph A 1927- *ConAu 53*
Daley, Robert 1930- *ConAu 1R, –2NR, WrDr 84*
Dalfiume, Richard Myron 1936- *ConAu 25R*
D'Alfonso, John 1918- *ConAu 29R*
Dalgliesh, Alice 1893-1979 *ConAu 73, –89, SmATA 17, –21N, TwCCW 83*
Dalglish, Edward Russell 1913- *ConAu 37R, WrDr 84*

Dali, Salvador 1904- *ConAu 104*
Dalitz, Richard Henry 1925- *WrDr 84*
Dallaire, Jean-Philippe 1916-1965 *CreCan 2*
D'Allard, Hunter *ConAu X*
Dallas, Athena Gianakas *ConAu X*
Dallas, Eneas Sweetland 1828-1879 *LongCTC*
Dallas, John *ConAu X*
Dallas, Philip 1921- *ConAu 61*
Dallas, Ruth 1919- *ConAu 10NR, –65,*
ConP 80, DcLEL 1940, IntAu&W 82,
IntWWP 82, LongCTC, TwCCW 83,
WrDr 84
Dallas, Sandra *ConAu X*
Dallas, Vincent *ConAu X, WrDr 84*
Dallas-Damis, Athena G 1925- *ConAu 81*
Dallek, Robert 1934- *ConAu 25R, WrDr 84*
D'Allenger, Hugh *ConAu X, –73*
Dallin, Alexander 1924- *ConAu 1R, –5NR*
Dallin, David Julievich 1889-1962 *TwCA SUP*
Dallin, Leon 1918- *ConAu 1R, –1NR,*
IntAu&W 82
Dallman, Elaine *DrAP&F 83*
Dallmann, Martha Elsie 1904- *ConAu 1R*
Dallmayr, Fred R 1928- *ConAu 1NR, –49*
Dally, Ann 1926- *ConAu 3NR, –5R, WrDr 84*
Dalmain, Jean *CreCan 2*
Dalmain, Monique Tremblay *CreCan 2*
Dalmas, John *ConAu X*
D'Alonzo, C Anthony 1912-1972 *ConAu 37R*
DalPoggetto, Newton Francis 1922- *ConAu 61*
Dalrymple, Byron W 1910- *ConAu 6NR, –57*
Dalrymple, Dorothy 1910- *MichAu 80*
Dalrymple, Douglas J 1934- *ConAu 73*
Dalrymple, Jean 1910- *ConAu 5R, –5NR,*
WrDr 84
Dalrymple, Willard 1921- *ConAu 21R,*
WrDr 84
Dalsass, Diana 1947- *ConAu 106*
Dalton, Brian James 1924- *WrDr 84*
Dalton, Claire *ConAu X*
Dalton, Clive *ConAu X*
Dalton, David 1944- *ConAu 97*
Dalton, Dorothy *DrAP&F 83*
Dalton, Dorothy 1915- *ConAu 21R,*
IntAu&W 82, IntWWP 82
Dalton, Elizabeth 1936- *ConAu 85*
Dalton, Gene W 1928- *ConAu 25R*
Dalton, George 1926- *ConAu 106*
D'Alton, Louis 1900-1951 *ConAu 110, DcLB 10*
Dalton, Priscilla *ConAu X, TwCCr&M 80,*
WrDr 84
Dalton, Richard 1930- *ConAu 57*
Dalton, Stephen 1937- *ConAu 85*
Dalven, Rae 1904- *ConAu 33R, IntWWP 82*
Daly, Anne 1896- *ConAu P-2*
Daly, Augustin 1838-1899 *ModWD*
Daly, Cahal Brendan 1917- *ConAu 104,*
IntAu&W 82, WrDr 84
Daly, Carroll John 1889-1958 *TwCCr&M 80*
Daly, Donald F *ConAu 69*
Daly, Elizabeth 1878-1967 *ConAu 25R,*
ConAu P-2, DcLEL 1940, TwCA SUP,
TwCCr&M 80
Daly, Emily Joseph 1913- *ConAu 9R*
Daly, Faye Kennedy 1936- *ConAu 97*
Daly, Herman E 1938- *ConAu 89*
Daly, Jim *ConAu X*
Daly, John Jay 1888?-1976 *ConAu 69*
Daly, Leo 1920- *ConAu 105, WrDr 84*
Daly, Lowrie J 1914- *WrDr 84*
Daly, Lowrie John 1914- *ConAu 13R*
Daly, Mary 1928- *ConAu 25R, ConIsC 1[port],*
WrDr 84
Daly, Mary Tinley 1904?-1979 *ConAu 85*
Daly, Sister Mary Virginia 1925- *ConAu 17R*
Daly, Maureen *ConAu X, ConLC 17,*
SmATA 2, TwCCW 83, WrDr 84
Daly, Robert 1943- *ConAu 104*
Daly, Robert Welter 1916-1975 *ConAu 9R, –103*
Daly, Saralyn R *DrAP&F 83*
Daly, Saralyn R 1924- *ConAu 57*
Daly, Thomas Augustine 1871-1948 *TwCA,*
TwCA SUP
Daly, Thomas Cullen 1918- *CreCan 1*
Daly, Tom 1918- *CreCan 1*
Dalzel, Peter *ConAu X*
Dalzel Job, P 1913- *ConAu 13R*
Dalzell, Kathleen Elizabeth 1919- *WrDr 84*
Dalzell, Robert, Jr. 1937- *ConAu 81*
Dam, Hari N 1921- *ConAu 57*
Dam, Kenneth W 1932- *ConAu 69*
Dam, Niels Albert 1880-1972 *CIDMEL 80*

Damachi, Ukandi 1942- *ConAu 2NR, –45*
Damas, Leon-Gontran 1912-1978 *ConAu 73,*
EncWL 2, ModBlW, ModFrL
D'Amato, Alex 1919- *ConAu 41, SmATA 20*
Damato, Anthony 1927- *NatPD 81[port]*
D'Amato, Anthony A 1937- *ConAu 29R,*
IntAu&W 82, WrDr 84
D'Amato, Barbara 1938- *ConAu 69*
D'Amato, Janet 1925- *ConAu 1NR, –49,*
SmATA 9
Damaz, Paul F 1917- *ConAu 5R, WrDr 84*
Dambrauskas, Joan Arden 1933- *ConAu 104*
D'Ambrosio, Charles A 1932- *ConAu 21R*
D'Ambrosio, Richard A 1927- *ConAu 102*
D'Ambrosio, Vinnie-Marie *DrAP&F 83*
D'Ambrosio, Vinnie-Marie 1928- *ConAu 45,*
IntAu&W 82, IntWWP 82
Dame, Enid *DrAP&F 83*
Dame, Enid 1943- *IntWWP 82*
Dame, Lawrence 1898- *ConAu P-1*
D'Amelio, Dan 1927- *ConAu 33R*
Dameron, Chip *DrAP&F 83*
Dameron, J Lasley 1925- *ConAu 53*
Damerst, William A 1923- *ConAu 17R,*
IntAu&W 82, WrDr 84
Dames, Michael 1938- *WrDr 84*
Damgaard, Joern 1935- *IntAu&W 82*
Damiani, Bruno Mario 1942- *ConAu 57*
Damiano, Laila *ConAu X*
Damien, Christine *DrAP&F 83*
Damm, John S 1926- *ConAu 37R*
Damon, Gene *ConAu X*
Damon, S Foster 1893-1971 *ConAu 101*
Damon, Samuel Foster 1893-1971 *TwCA,*
TwCA SUP
Damon, Virgil Green 1895-1972 *ConAu 37R,*
ConAu P-1
Damor, Hakji *ConAu X*
Damore, Leo 1929- *ConAu 81*
D'Amour, Rolland 1913- *CreCan 2*
Dampier, Sir William Cecil 1867-1952*
TwCA SUP
Damrosch, Helen Therese *SmATA X*
Damrosch, Leopold, Jr. 1941- *ConAu 45*
Damsker, Matt 1951- *ConAu 108*
Damtoft, Walter A 1922- *ConAu 57*
Dan, R *IntAu&W 82X*
Dana, Amber *ConAu X*
Dana, Barbara 1940- *ConAu 8NR, –17R,*
SmATA 22[port]
Dana, E H *ConAu X*
Dana, Richard *ConAu X*
Dana, Richard H 1927- *ConAu 85*
Dana, Richard Henry, Jr. 1815-1882*
SmATA 26[port]
Dana, Robert *DrAP&F 83*
Dana, Robert 1929- *ConAu 33R, ConP 80,*
WrDr 84
Dana, Rose *ConAu X*
Danachair, Caoimhin O *SmATA X*
Danagher, Edward F 1919- *ConAu 9R*
Danaher, Kevin 1913- *ConAu 33R,*
SmATA 22[port], WrDr 84
Danan, Alexis 1889?-1979 *ConAu 89*
Danbury, Iris *TwCRGW, WrDr 84*
Danby, Frank 1864-1916 *LongCTC*
Danby, Hope 1899- *ConAu P-1*
Danby, John B 1905-1983 *ConAu 109*
Danby, Kenneth Edison 1940- *CreCan 2*
Danby, Mary 1941- *ConAu X, WrDr 84*
Danby, Miles William 1925- *ConAu 13R*
Dance, E H 1894- *ConAu 37R*
Dance, Edward Herbert 1894- *IntAu&W 82,*
WrDr 84
Dance, F E X 1929- *ConAu 1R, –1NR*
Dance, Frank E X *ConAu X*
Dance, Jim 1924?-1983 *ConAu 110*
Dance, S Peter 1932- *ConAu 69*
Dance, Stanley 1910- *WrDr 84*
Dance, Stanley Frank 1910- *ConAu 8NR, –17R,*
IntAu&W 82
Dancer, J B *TwCWW, WrDr 84*
D'Ancona, Mirella Levi 1919- *ConAu 6NR, –53*
Dancy, John Christopher 1920- *ConAu 107,*
WrDr 84
Dandrea, Carmine 1929- *IntWWP 82*
D'Andrea, Kate *ConAu X, SmATA X*
Dandy, James Edgar 1903-1976 *ConAu 104*
Dane, Carl *ConAu X*
Dane, Clemence *ConAu X*
Dane, Clemence 1887-1965 *DcLB 10[port],*
TwCCr&M 80

Dane, Clemence 1888-1965 *CnMD, LongCTC,*
ModBrL, ModWD, TwCA, TwCA SUP,
TwCWr
Dane, Les 1925- *ConAu 89*
Dane, Mark *ConAu X, WrDr 84*
Dane, Mary *ConAu X, WrDr 84*
Dane, Nathan 1916-1980 *ConAu 97*
Dane, II 1916-1980 *ConAu 108*
Daneff, Stephen Constantine 1931- *ConAu 106*
Danelski, David J 1930- *ConAu 13R*
Danenberg, Leigh 1893-1976 *ConAu 69*
Danford, Howard G 1904- *ConAu P-1*
Danforth, Mildred E *ConSFA*
Danforth, Paul M *IntAu&W 82X, WrDr 84*
Dangaard, Colin 1942- *ConAu 85*
D'Angelo, Edward 1932- *ConAu 37R*
D'Angelo, Lou *ConAu X*
D'Angelo, Luciano 1932- *ConAu 33R*
Dangerfield, Balfour *ConAu X, SmATA 2*
Dangerfield, Clint *ConAu X, WrDr 84*
Dangerfield, George Bubb 1904- *ConAu 9R,*
IntAu&W 82, WorAu, WrDr 84
Dangerfield, Rodney 1922?- *ConAu 102*
Danhof, Clarence H 1911- *ConAu 37R*
Dani, Ahmad Hasan 1920- *ConAu 13R*
Daniel, Anita 1893?-1978 *ConAu 77,*
SmATA 23, –24N
Daniel, Anne *ConAu X, SmATA X*
Daniel, Cletus E 1943- *ConAu 107*
Daniel, Daniel 1890?-1981 *ConAu 104*
Daniel, Elna Worrell Burchfield *ConAu X*
Daniel, Emmett Randolph 1935- *ConAu 102*
Daniel, George Bernard, Jr. 1927- *ConAu 13R*
Daniel, Glyn 1914- *WrDr 84*
Daniel, Glyn E 1914- *ConAu 57, DcLEL 1940,*
TwCCr&M 80, TwCWr
Daniel, Hawthorne 1890- *ConAu 5R,*
IntAu&W 82, SmATA 8
Daniel, James 1916- *ConAu 69*
Daniel, Jerry C 1937- *ConAu 33R*
Daniel, John T *DrAP&F 83*
Daniel, Laurent *WorAu 1970*
Daniel, Norman 1919- *ConAu 6NR, –57*
Daniel, Pete 1938- *ConAu 37R, WrDr 84*
Daniel, Pierre *CreCan 1*
Daniel, Price, Jr. 1941-1981 *ConAu 103*
Daniel, Ralph Thomas 1921- *ConAu 53*
Daniel, Robert L 1923- *ConAu 33R*
Daniel, Robert W 1915- *ConAu 25R*
Daniel, Roland 1880-1969 *TwCCr&M 80*
Daniel, Walter C 1922- *ConAu 110*
Daniel, Yuly 1925- *CIDMEL 80*
Daniel, Yuri 1926- *TwCWr*
Daniel-Rops 1901-1965 *CIDMEL 80*
Daniela *IntAu&W 82X*
Daniele, Joseph William 1927- *ConAu 89*
Daniell, Albert Scott 1906-1965 *ConAu 3NR,*
–5R
Daniell, David Scott 1906-1965 *ConAu X,*
TwCCW 83
Daniell, Jere Rogers 1932- *ConAu 11NR, –29R*
Daniell, Rosemary *DrAP&F 83*
Daniells, James Roy 1902- *CreCan 1*
Daniells, Lorna M 1918- *ConAu 89*
Daniells, Roy 1902- *ConAu 57, ConP 80,*
CreCan 1, DcLEL 1940, WrDr 84
Danielou, Alain 1907- *ConAu 73*
Danielou, Jean 1905-1974 *ConAu 49,*
ConAu P-2
Daniels, Anna Kleegman 1893-1970 *ConAu 29R*
Daniels, Arlene Kaplan 1930- *ConAu 29R*
Daniels, David 1933- *ConAu 53*
Daniels, Dorothy 1915- *ConAu 89, TwCRGW,*
WrDr 84
Daniels, Draper 1913- *ConAu 53*
Daniels, Draper 1913-1983 *ConAu 109*
Daniels, Elizabeth Adams 1920- *ConAu 37R,*
WrDr 84
Daniels, Farrington 1889-1972 *ConAu 5R, –37R*
Daniels, Frank James 1900?-1983 *ConAu 110*
Daniels, George F 1935- *ConAu 10NR, –25R*
Daniels, George M 1927- *ConAu 29R*
Daniels, Guy 1919- *ConAu 21R, SmATA 11,*
–7
Daniels, Harold R 1919- *ConAu 17R*
Daniels, Jim *DrAP&F 83*
Daniels, John Clifford 1915- *ConAu 13R*
Daniels, John S *ConAu X, TwCWW,*
WrDr 84

Daniels, Jonathan 1902-1981 *ConAu 105, -49, TwCA, TwCA SUP*
Daniels, Les 1943- *ConAu 9NR, -65*
Daniels, Marie-Therese 1906- *IntWWP 82*
Daniels, Mary 1937- *ConAu 93, WrDr 84*
Daniels, Max *WrDr 84*
Daniels, Norman *ConAu 89*
Daniels, Norman 1942- *ConAu 106*
Daniels, Pamela 1937- *ConAu 101*
Daniels, Peter *IntWWP 82X*
Daniels, R Balfour 1900- *ConAu 49*
Daniels, Randy 1949- *ConAu 81*
Daniels, Robert 1926- *WrDr 84*
Daniels, Robert Laurence 1933- *ConAmTC*
Daniels, Robert V 1926- *ConAu 1R, -2NR*
Daniels, Roger 1927- *ConAu 5R, -8NR*
Daniels, Sally 1931- *ConAu 1R*
Daniels, Shouri *ConAu X*
Daniels, Steven Lloyd 1945-1973 *ConAu 33R*
Daniels, Velma Seawell 1931- *ConAu 108*
Danielson, J D *ConAu X*
Danielson, Michael N 1934- *ConAu 33R*
Danielson, Wayne Allen 1929- *ConAu 77*
Danielsson, Bengt Emmerik 1921- *ConAu 107, IntAu&W 82*
Danielsson, Gudmundur 1910- *IntAu&W 82*
Daniere, Andre L 1926- *ConAu 9R*
Daniken, Erich Von 1935- *IntAu&W 82*
Danilo *IntWWP 82X*
Daniloff, Nicholas 1934- *ConAu 85*
Danilov, Victor J 1924- *ConAu 6NR, -13R*
Daninos, Pierre 1913- *ConAu 77, IntAu&W 82, TwCWr, WorAu*
Danio *IntAu&W 82X*
Danish, Barbara *DrAP&F 83*
Danish, Barbara 1948- *ConAu 57*
Dank, Milton 1920- *ConAu 11NR, -69, SmATA 31[port]*
Danker, Frederick William 1920- *ConAu 5NR, -13R*
Danker, William J 1914- *WrDr 84*
Danker, William John 1914- *ConAu 13R*
Danky, James Philip 1947- *ConAu 69*
Danly, Robert Lyons 1947- *ConAu 108*
Dann, Colin 1943- *ConAu 108, WrDr 84*
Dann, Jack *DrAP&F 83*
Dann, Jack 1945- *ConAu 2NR, -49, IntAu&W 82, TwCSFW, WrDr 84*
Dann, Uriel 1922- *ConAu 25R*
Dannay, Frederic 1905-1982 *ASpks, ConAu 1R, -1NR, -107, ConLC 11, LongCTC, TwCA, TwCA SUP, TwCCr&M 82*
Dannemiller, Lawrence 1925- *ConAu 1R*
Dannenfeldt, Karl H 1916- *ConAu 25R*
Danner, Margaret *DrAP&F 83*
Danner, Margaret 1915- *ConAu 29R, LivgBAA, MichAu 80*
Dannett, Sylvia G L 1909- *ConAu 1R, -4NR*
D'Annunzio, Gabriele 1863-1938 *CIDMEL 80, CnMD, ConAu 104, EncWL 2, LongCTC, ModRL, ModWD, TwCA[port], TwCA SUP, TwCLC 6[port], TwCWr, WhoTwCL*
Danoff, I Michael 1940- *ConAu 97*
Danojlic, Milovan 1937- *IntAu&W 82*
Danon, Ruth *DrAP&F 83*
Danowski, T S 1914- *ConAu 9R*
Dansereau, Fernand 1928- *CreCan 2*
Danska, Herbert 1928- *ConAu 29R*
Danson, Lawrence Neil 1942- *ConAu 85*
Dante, Robert *DrAP&F 83*
Dantes, Edmund *IntWWP 82X*
D'Antibes, Germain *ConAu X*
Danto, Arthur C 1924- *ConAu 17R, WrDr 84*
Danto, Bruce L 1927- *ConAu 7NR, -53*
Danton, J Periam 1908- *ConAu 9R, IntAu&W 82*
Danton, Rebecca *ConAu X, IntAu&W 82X, TwCRGW, WrDr 84*
Dantzic, Cynthia Maris 1933- *ConAu 101*
Dantzig, George Bernard 1914- *ConAu 106*
Danvers, Jack 1909- *ConAu X*
Danzig, Allan 1931- *ConAu 45*
Danzig, Allison 1898- *ConAu 37R, WrDr 84*
Danzig, Fred P 1925- *ConAu 65*
Danziger, Edmund J, Jr. 1938- *ConAu 102*
Danziger, Kurt 1926- *ConAu 41R*
Danziger, Marlies K 1926- *ConAu 25R*
Danziger, Paula 1944- *ConLC 21[port], SmATA 30*
Dapper, Gloria 1922- *ConAu 17R*
D'Aprix, Roger M 1932- *ConAu 33R*

Darashaw, F *IntAu&W 82X*
Darbelnet, Jean 1904- *ConAu 10NR, -25R*
Darben, Althea Gibson 1927- *LivgBAA*
Darby, Catherine *ConAu X, TwCRGW, WrDr 84*
Darby, Edith M 1906- *IntWWP 82*
Darby, Gene Kegley 1921- *ConAu 2NR, -5R*
Darby, Henry Clifford 1909- *ConAu 5R, IntAu&W 82, WrDr 84*
Darby, J N *ConAu X, SmATA X, WrDr 84*
Darby, John 1940- *ConAu 105, WrDr 84*
Darby, N J *ConAu X*
Darby, Patricia *ConAu 73, SmATA 14*
Darby, Ray 1912- *ConAu 17R, SmATA 7*
D'Arch Smith, Timothy 1936- *ConAu 13R, IntAu&W 82*
Darcy, Clare *ConAu 102, TwCRGW, WrDr 84*
D'Arcy, G Minot 1930- *ConAu 9R*
Darcy, Jean *ConAu X*
D'Arcy, Jean 1913-1983 *ConAu 109*
D'Arcy, Margaretta *WrDr 84*
D'Arcy, Margaretta 1934- *ConAu 104*
D'Arcy, Martin Cyril 1888-1976 *ConAu 3NR, -5R, -69*
D'Arcy, Pamela *ConAu X, TwCRGW, WrDr 84*
D'Arcy, Paul F 1921- *ConAu 17R*
D'Arcy-Orga, Ates *WrDr 84*
Darden, William R 1936- *ConAu 77*
Dardess, John W 1937- *ConAu 45*
Dardig, Jill C 1935- *ConAu 69*
Dardis, Thomas 1926- *WrDr 84*
Dardis, Tom 1926- *ConAu 9NR, -65*
Dare, Simon 1897- *LongCTC*
Dareff, Hal 1920- *ConAu 65*
Darga, Bert 1931- *ConAu 110*
Dargan, Olive Tilford 1869-1968 *TwCA, TwCA SUP*
D'Argyre, Gilles *ConAu 49*
Darien, Peter *ConAu X*
Daring, Hope *MichAu 80*
Daringer, Helen Fern 1892- *ConAu P-2, SmATA 1*
Dario, Ruben 1867-1916 *ConAu X, EncWL 2[port], ModLAL, TwCA, TwCA SUP, TwCLC 4[port], TwCWr, WhoTwCL*
Darity, William A, Jr. 1953- *LivgBAA*
Dark, Alvin Ralph 1922- *ConAu 105*
Dark, Eleanor 1901- *ModCmwL, TwCA SUP, TwCWr*
Dark, Harris Edward 1922- *ConAu 57*
Dark, Johnny *ConAu X   IntAu&W 82X, WrDr 84*
Dark, Philip John Crosskey 1918- *ConAu 2NR, -49*
Dark, Sidney 1874-1947 *LongCTC*
Darke, Marjorie 1929- *ConAu 81, IntAu&W 82, SmATA 16, TwCCW 83, WrDr 84*
Darley, John 1948- *IntWWP 82*
Darley, John M 1938- *ConAu 93*
Darling, Justice 1849-1936 *LongCTC*
Darling, Arthur Burr 1892-1971 *ConAu 5R, -33R*
Darling, Edward 1907-1974 *ConAu 3NR, -49, -53*
Darling, Frank Clayton 1925- *ConAu 17R*
Darling, Fraser 1903- *LongCTC*
Darling, Jay Norwood 1876-1962 *ConAu 93*
Darling, John R 1937- *ConAu 93, IntAu&W 82*
Darling, Kathy *ConAu X, SmATA X*
Darling, Lois 1917- *WrDr 84*
Darling, Lois MacIntyre 1917- *ConAu 3NR, -5R, SmATA 3*
Darling, Louis 1916-1970 *ConAu 3NR, -5R, -89, SmATA 23N, -3*
Darling, Mary Kathleen 1943- *ConAu 4NR, -53, SmATA 9*
Darling, Richard L 1925- *ConAu 21R*
Darlington, Alice B 1906-1973 *ConAu 41R, ConAu P-2*
Darlington, Andrew John 1947- *IntWWP 82*
Darlington, C D 1903-1981 *ConAu 10NR*
Darlington, Charles F 1904- *ConAu P-2*
Darlington, Cyril Dean 1903- *ConAu 9R, IntAu&W 82*
Darlington, Cyril Dean 1903-1981 *ConAu 108*
Darlington, Joy 1947- *ConAu 89*
Darlington, Sandy *DrAP&F 83*
Darlington, W A 1890- *LongCTC*
Darlington, William Aubrey 1890- *ConAu P-1*

Darlon, Christopher *IntWWP 82X*
Darlow, Michael 1934- *ConAu 104*
Darlton, Clark 1920- *ConAu X*
Darnay, Arsen *TwCSFW, WrDr 84*
Darr, Ann *DrAP&F 83*
Darr, Ann 1920- *ConAu 7NR, -57*
Darracott, Joseph C 1934- *ConAu 106*
Darrah, William C 1909- *ConAu 57*
Darroch, Maurice A 1903- *ConAu P-2*
Darroch, Sandra Jobson 1942- *ConAu 89*
Darrow, Clarence Seward 1857-1938 *TwCA, TwCA SUP*
Darrow, Ralph C 1918- *ConAu 61*
Darrow, Richard W 1915- *ConAu 21R*
Darrow, Whitney, Jr. 1909- *ConAu 61, SmATA 13*
Dart, John 1936- *ConAu 65*
Dart, Raymond Arthur 1893- *ConAu P-1*
Daruwalla, Keki Nasserwanji 1937- *DcLEL 1940*
Darvas, Jozsef 1912- *CroCD*
Darvas, Nicholas 1920- *ConAu 61*
Darveaux, Terry A 1943- *ConAu 65*
Darvill, Fred T, Jr. 1927- *ConAu 6NR, -57*
Darwin, Bernard Richard M 1876-1961 *LongCTC*
Darwin, Len *SmATA X*
Darwin, Leonard 1916- *SmATA 24*
Darwin, M B *ConAu X*
Dary, David Archie 1934- *ConAu 29R, WrDr 84*
Daryush, Elizabeth 1887-1977 *ConAu 3NR, -49, ConLC 6, -19, RGFMBP*
Das, D K 1935- *ConP 80, WrDr 84*
Das, Deb Kumar 1935- *ConAu 102, DcLEL 1940*
Das, Durga 1900-1974 *ConAu 49, ConAu P-2*
Das, Gurcharan 1943- *ConAu 33R*
Das, Jagannath Prasad 1931- *ConAu 6NR, -57*
Das, Jivananda 1899-1954 *ModCmwL*
Das, Kamala 1934- *ConAu 101, ConP 80, DcLEL 1940, WrDr 84*
Das, Manmath Nath 1926- *ConAu 8NR, -13R*
Das, Salilendar Nath 1931- *IntWWP 82*
Dasent, Sir George Webbe 1817-1896 *SmATA 29*
Dasgupta, Ajit Kumar 1930- *IntAu&W 82*
Dasgupta, Gautam 1949- *ConAmTC*
DasGupta, Jyotirindra 1933- *ConAu 53*
Dash, Jack Brien 1907- *IntWWP 82*
Dash, Joan 1925- *ConAu 49*
Dash, Samuel 1925- *ConAu 105*
Dash, Tony 1945- *ConAu 33R*
Dashiell, Alfred Sheppard 1901-1970 *ConAu 89*
Dashti, Ali 1894- *ConAu 85*
Dashwood, Edmee Elizabeth Monica 1890-1943 *LongCTC*
Dashwood, Robert Julian 1899- *ConAu P-1*
DaSilva, Leon *ConAu X*
DaSilva Nunes, Armando *CreCan 1*
Daskam, Josephine Dodge 1876- *ConAu X*
Dasmann, Raymond 1919- *ConAu 2NR, -5R*
Dass, Ram *ConAu X*
Dassin, Jules *ConDr 82A*
Dassonville, Michel A 1927- *ConAu 73*
Dassylva, Martial 1936- *ConAmTC*
Dater, Henry M 1909?-1974 *ConAu 49*
Datesh, John Nicholas 1950- *ConAu 97*
Dathorne, O R 1934- *WrDr 84*
Dathorne, Oscar Ronald 1934- *ConAu 57, ConNov 82, DcLEL 1940*
Daube, David 1909- *ConAu 1R, -1NR, IntAu&W 82, WrDr 84*
Daubeny, Peter 1921-1975 *ConAu 61*
Daubler, Theodor 1876-1934 *CIDMEL 80, ModGL*
Daudet, Leon 1867?-1942 *CIDMEL 80*
Dauenhauer, Richard *DrAP&F 83*
Dauenhauer, Richard L 1942- *ConAu 11NR, -61*
Dauer, Dorothea W 1917- *ConAu 37R*
Dauer, Manning J 1909- *ConAu 89*
Dauer, Rosamond 1934- *ConAu 10NR, -65, SmATA 23[port]*
Dauer, Victor Paul 1909- *ConAu 17R*
Daugert, Stanley M 1918- *ConAu 17R*
Daughdrill, James H, Jr. 1934- *ConAu 41R*
Daughen, Joseph R 1935- *ConAu 33R*
Daugherty, Charles Michael 1914- *ConAu 73, SmATA 16*
Daugherty, James 1889-1974 *TwCCW 83*
Daugherty, James Henry 1889-1974 *ConAu 49, -73, SmATA 13*
Daugherty, Richard D 1922- *ConAu 108*
Daugherty, Sarah Bowyer 1949- *ConAu 106*
Daugherty, Sonia Medwedeff d1971 *ConAu 104,*

SmATA 27N
Daughtrey, Anne Scott 1920- ConAu 17R,
  WrDr 84
D'Aulaire, Edgar Parin 1898- ConAu 49,
  DcLB 22[port], SmATA 5, TwCCW 83,
  WrDr 84
D'Aulaire, Ingri 1904- DcLB 22[port]
D'Aulaire, Ingri 1904-1980 ConAu 102, -49,
  SmATA 24N, -5
D'Aulaire, Ingri Parin 1904-1980 TwCCW 83
Daumal, Rene 1908-1944 ClDMEL 80,
  EncWL 2
Daunt, Jon DrAP&F 83
Daunt, Jon 1951- IntWWP 82
Dauphin, Susan Helfrich 1928- ConAmTC
Dauster, Frank 1925- ConAu 53
Dauten, Carl Anton 1913-1976 ConAu 3NR, -5R
Dauthendey, Max 1867-1918 ModGL
Dauw, Dean C 1933- ConAu 6NR, -53
D'Avanzo, Mario Louis 1931- ConAu 41R
Davar, Ashok ConAu 69
Dave IntAu&W 82X
Dave, Shyam ConAu X
Daveluy, Marie CreCan 1
Daveluy, Marie-Claire 1880-1968 CreCan 1
Daveluy, Paule Cloutier 1919- ConAu 9R,
  SmATA 11
Daveluy, Raymond 1926- CreCan 1
Davenport, Diana DrAP&F 83
Davenport, Doris DrAP&F 83
Davenport, Elaine 1946- ConAu 102, WrDr 84
Davenport, Francine ConAu X
Davenport, Gene L 1935- ConAu 33R
Davenport, Guy DrAP&F 83
Davenport, Guy, Jr. 1927- ConAu 33R,
  ConLC 6, -14, ConNov 82
Davenport, Gwen 1910- ConAu 9R
Davenport, John 1938- WrDr 84
Davenport, Marcia 1903- ConAu 9R, LongCTC,
  TwCA SUP, TwCRGW, WrDr 84
Davenport, Spencer ConAu X
Davenport, T R H 1926- ConAu 77
Davenport, Thomas Rodney Hope 1926-
  IntAu&W 82
Davenport, Walter 1889-1971 ConAu 104
Davenport, William H 1908- WrDr 84
Davenport, William Henry 1908- ConAu 1R,
  -4NR, IntAu&W 82
Daventry, Leonard 1915- ConAu 17R, ConSFA
Daves, Delmer 1904-1977 DcLB 26[port]
Daves, Delmer Lawrence 1904?-1977 ConAu 73
Daves, Francis Marion 1903- ConAu 45
Daves, Jessica 1898?-1974 ConAu 53
Daves, Michael 1938- ConAu 9R
Davey, Cyril James 1911- ConAu 2NR, -5R
Davey, Frank 1907?-1983 ConAu 109
Davey, Frank 1940- ConAu X, ConP 80,
  CreCan 2, WrDr 84
Davey, Frankland Wilmot 1940- ConAu 65
Davey, Gilbert 1913- ConAu P-1, WrDr 84
Davey, Jocelyn 1908- ConAu X, TwCCr&M 80
Davey, John ConAu X
Davey, John 1939- ConAu X, MichAu 80
Davi, Hans Leopold 1928- IntWWP 82
Daviau, Donald George 1927- ConAu 81,
  IntAu&W 82
Davico, Oskar 1909- ClDMEL 80, EncWL 2,
  IntWWP 82, ModSL 2
David, Alfred 1929- ConAu 85
David, Almitra DrAP&F 83
David, Anne 1924- ConAu 29R
David, B IntWWP 82X
David, Carl 1949- ConAu 108
David, Elizabeth WrDr 84
David, Emily ConAu X
David, Heather M 1937- ConAu 37R, WrDr 84
David, Henry P 1923- ConAu 6NR, -13R
David, Irene 1921- ConAu 110
David, Jack 1946- ConAu 110
David, Jay ConAu X
David, Jonathan SmATA 3
David, Lester 1914- ConAu 37R
David, Martin H 1935- ConAu 37R
David, Michael Robert 1932- ConAu 53
David, Nellie Maillard 1917- CreCan 2
David, Nicholas ConAu X
David, Paul A 1935- ConAu 97
David, Paul T 1906- ConAu 2NR, -5R
David, Stephen M 1934- ConAu 33R
David, William ConAu X
David-Neel, Alexandra 1868-1969 ConAu 25R
Davidow, Mike 1913- ConAu 57

Davidow-Goodman, Ann ConAu X
Davids, Anthony 1923- ConAu 41R
Davids, Lewis Edmund 1917- ConAu 37R
Davids, Richard Carlyle 1913- ConAu 97
Davidson, Aarno 1905- IntWWP 82
Davidson, Abraham A 1935- ConAu 53
Davidson, Alan Eaton 1924- ConAu 103,
  WrDr 84
Davidson, Alastair 1939- ConAu 29R
Davidson, Angus Henry Gordon 1898-1980
  ConAu 25R, -97
Davidson, Avram 1923- ConAu 101, ConSFA,
  DcLB 8[port], TwCSFW, WrDr 84
Davidson, Basil 1914- ConAu 1R, -1NR,
  IntAu&W 82, SmATA 13, WorAu,
  WrDr 84
Davidson, Bill ConAu X
Davidson, Cathy Notari 1949- ConAu 106
Davidson, Chalmers Gaston 1907- ConAu 29R,
  WrDr 84
Davidson, Chandler 1936- ConAu 45
Davidson, Clarissa Start ConAu X
Davidson, Clifford Oscar 1932- ConAu 45,
  IntWWP 82
Davidson, David 1908- ConAu 49, -57,
  TwCA SUP, WrDr 84
Davidson, Diane 1924- ConAu 29R
Davidson, Donald 1893-1968 ConAmA,
  ConAu 4NR, -5R, -25R, ConLC 2, -13, -19,
  TwCA, TwCA SUP
Davidson, Donald H 1917- ConAu 2NR, -45
Davidson, E E 1923- ConAu 33R
Davidson, Ellen Prescott ConAu 49
Davidson, Emily DrAP&F 83
Davidson, Eugene 1902- ConAu 1R, -3NR,
  IntAu&W 82, WrDr 84
Davidson, Eva Rucker 1894?-1974 ConAu 53
Davidson, Frank Geoffrey 1920- ConAu 29R,
  WrDr 84
Davidson, Glen W 1936- ConAu 9NR, -61,
  IntAu&W 82
Davidson, Gustav 1895-1971 ConAu 29R
Davidson, H R Ellis 1914- ConAu 11NR, -17R
Davidson, Harold G 1912- ConAu 65
Davidson, Henry A 1905-1973 ConAu 45
Davidson, Herbert A 1932- ConAu 17R
Davidson, Hugh 1930- CreCan 2
Davidson, Hugh H 1911- ConAu 102
Davidson, Irwin Delmore 1906-1981 ConAu 105
Davidson, James Dale 1947- ConAu 107
Davidson, James Norris Goddard 1908- CreCan 1
Davidson, James West 1946- ConAu 85
Davidson, Jessica 1915- ConAu 41R, SmATA 5
Davidson, John 1857-1909 LongCTC, ModBrL
Davidson, John 1900- ConAu X
Davidson, Julian M 1931- ConAu 102
Davidson, Lawrence H LongCTC
Davidson, Lionel 1922- ConAu 1R, -1NR,
  DcLB 14[port], DcLEL 1940, IntAu&W 82,
  TwCCr&M 80, TwCSFW, WrDr 84
Davidson, Margaret 1936- ConAu 25R,
  SmATA 5
Davidson, Marion ConAu X, SmATA X
Davidson, Marshall B 1907- ConAu 33R
Davidson, Mary R 1885-1973 ConAu 5R,
  SmATA 9
Davidson, Mary S 1940- ConAu 107
Davidson, Max D 1899?-1977 ConAu 73
Davidson, Michael ConAu X, DrAP&F 83,
  IntAu&W 82X
Davidson, Michael 1944- ConAu 106, ConP 80,
  WrDr 84
Davidson, Michael Childers 1897- ConAu 29R
Davidson, Mickie 1936- ConAu 9R
Davidson, Mildred 1935- ConAu 93, WrDr 84
Davidson, Morris 1898-1979 ConAu 85
Davidson, Muriel 1924?-1983 ConAu 110
Davidson, Paul 1930- ConAu 6NR, -13R
Davidson, Peter CreCan 1
Davidson, Philip 1902- ConAu 73
Davidson, R SmATA X
Davidson, Raymond 1926- SmATA 32[port]
Davidson, Richard DrAP&F 83
Davidson, Robert F 1902- ConAu 49
Davidson, Roger H 1936- ConAu 9NR, -21R,
  WrDr 84
Davidson, Rosalie 1921- ConAu 69,
  SmATA 23[port]
Davidson, Sandra Calder 1935- ConAu 41R
Davidson, Sara 1943- ConAu 81, ConLC 9
Davidson, Sol M 1924- ConAu 17R, WrDr 84
Davidson, William 1918- ConAu 93

Davidson, William Robert 1919- ConAu 17R
Davidson-Houston, J Vivian 1901-1965 ConAu 5R
Davie, Alan 1920- IntWWP 82
Davie, Donald 1922- ConAu 1R, -1NR,
  ConLCrt 82, ConP 80,
  IntWWP 82, LongCTC, ModBrL,
  ModBrL SUP, RGFMBP, TwCWr,
  WhoTwCL, WorAu, WrDr 84
Davie, Donald Alfred 1922- DcLEL 1940
Davie, Elspeth IntAu&W 82
Davie, Ian 1924- ConAu 102, WrDr 84
Davie, Maurice Rea 1893-1964 ConAu 5R
Davie, Michael 1924- ConAu 57
Davie, Owen H 1916- WrDr 84
Davie-Martin, Hugh ConAu X, IntAu&W 82X,
  WrDr 84
Davied, Camille ConAu X
Davies, A Mervyn 1899-1976 ConAu 17R, -69
Davies, Ada Hilton 1893- ConAu P-2
Davies, Alan 1951- IntWWP 82
Davies, Alan T 1933- ConAu 33R
Davies, Alfred T 1930- ConAu 13R
Davies, Andrew 1936- ConAu 105,
  IntAu&W 82, SmATA 27, TwCCW 83
Davies, Bettilu D 1942- ConAu 101,
  SmATA 33[port]
Davies, Christie 1941- ConAu X,
  IntAu&W 82X, WrDr 84
Davies, Colin ConAu X
Davies, Colliss 1912- ConAu P-1
Davies, D Jacob 1916-1974 ConAu 5R, -103
Davies, Daniel R 1911- ConAu 37R,
  IntAu&W 82, WrDr 84
Davies, David 1893-1951 LongCTC
Davies, David Margerison 1923- ConAu 5R,
  IntAu&W 82, WrDr 84
Davies, David Michael 1929- ConAu 109
Davies, David W 1908- ConAu 3NR, -9R
Davies, E T 1903- WrDr 84
Davies, Ebenezer Thomas 1903- ConAu P-1
Davies, Eileen Winifred 1910- ConAu P-1
Davies, Ernest Albert John 1902- IntAu&W 82
Davies, Evelyn 1924- ConAu 8NR, -61
Davies, Evelyn A 1915- ConAu 61
Davies, Frederick Herbert 1916- IntAu&W 82
Davies, Gareth Alban 1926- IntAu&W 82
Davies, George Colliss Boardman 1912-
  IntAu&W 82
Davies, Gwendoline Elizabeth 1880-1951
  LongCTC
Davies, Harriet Vaughn 1879?-1978 ConAu 77
Davies, Horton Marlais 1916- ConAu 5R, -7NR,
  WrDr 84
Davies, Hugh Sykes 1909- TwCSFW, WorAu,
  WrDr 84
Davies, Hunter WrDr 84
Davies, Hunter 1936- ConAu 57
Davies, Ioan 1936- ConAu 21R
Davies, Ivor K 1930- ConAu 53
Davies, J Clarence, III 1937- ConAu 29R
Davies, J Kenneth 1925- ConAu 57
Davies, James Chowning 1918- ConAu 45
Davies, Jasper WrDr 84
Davies, Joan WrDr 84
Davies, John Christopher Hughes WrDr 84
Davies, John Christopher Hughes 1941-
  ConAu 93, IntAu&W 82
Davies, John Gordon 1919- ConAu 5R, -69,
  IntAu&W 82, WrDr 84
Davies, John Paton, Jr. 1908- ConAu 9R
Davies, John Tasman 1924- IntAu&W 82,
  WrDr 84
Davies, L P 1914- ConAu 9NR, -21R, ConSFA,
  TwCCr&M 80, TwCSFW, WrDr 84
Davies, Laurence 1926- ConAu 57
Davies, Mansel Morris 1913- ConAu 9R,
  WrDr 84
Davies, Margaret 1923- WrDr 84
Davies, Margaret Constance 1923- ConAu 9R,
  IntAu&W 82
Davies, Margaret Lloyd 1935- ConAu 106
Davies, Margaret Sidney 1885-1963 LongCTC
Davies, Martin 1936- WrDr 84
Davies, Martin Brett 1936- ConAu 102
Davies, Merton E 1917- ConAu 85
Davies, Morton 1939- ConAu 37R
Davies, Nancy DrAP&F 83
Davies, Nigel 1920- ConAu 102, WrDr 84
Davies, Norman 1939- ConAu 41R
Davies, Oliver 1905- ConAu P-2, IntAu&W 82,
  WrDr 84
Davies, P C W 1946- ConAu X, WrDr 84

Davies, Paul 1946- *ConAu 106*
Davies, Pennar 1911- *ConAu 13R*
Davies, Peter 1937- *ConAu 53*
Davies, Piers Anthony David 1941- *ConAu 103,
   IntAu&W 82, IntWWP 82, WrDr 84*
Davies, R E G 1921- *ConAu 17R*
Davies, R T 1923- *ConAu 9R*
Davies, R W 1925- *ConAu 33R*
Davies, Ray 1944- *ConLC 21[port]*
Davies, Rhys 1903-1978 *ConAu 4NR, -9R, -81,
   ConLC 23[port], LongCTC, ModBrL,
   TwCA SUP*
Davies, Richard O 1937- *ConAu 17R*
Davies, Robert William 1925- *IntAu&W 82,
   WrDr 84*
Davies, Robertson 1913- *ConAu 33R,
   ConDr 82, ConLC 2, -7, -13, -25[port],
   ConNov 82, CreCan 1, DcLEL 1940,
   IntAu&W 82, LongCTC, ModCmwL,
   TwCWr, WorAu, WrDr 84*
Davies, Rod 1941- *ConAu 61*
Davies, Rosemary Reeves 1925- *ConAu 49*
Davies, Rupert E 1909- *WrDr 84*
Davies, Rupert Eric 1909- *ConAu 3NR, -5R,
   IntAu&W 82*
Davies, Ruth A 1915- *ConAu 29R*
Davies, Stan Gebler 1943- *ConAu 65*
Davies, Stephen *ConDr 82B*
Davies, Stevan L 1948- *ConAu 107*
Davies, Thomas M, Jr. 1940- *ConAu 6NR, -57*
Davies, Trefor Rendall 1913- *ConAu P-1*
Davies, W H 1871-1940 *CnMWL, ConAu 104,
   EncWL 2, LongCTC, ModBrL,
   TwCLC 5[port], TwCWr, WhoTwCL*
Davies, Walford 1940- *IntAu&W 82*
Davies, Walter C *ConAu X*
Davies, Walter Merlin 1913- *WrDr 84*
Davies, William David 1911- *ConAu 1R, -1NR,
   IntAu&W 82*
Davies, William Henry 1871-1940 *TwCA,
   TwCA SUP*
Davies, William Robertson 1913- *CreCan 1*
Davies, William Thomas Pennar 1911-
   IntAu&W 82
Davies, Wyndham 1926- *ConAu 25R*
Davies-Shiel, Michael 1929- *IntAu&W 82*
Davignon, Grace *CreCan 2*
Davin, Dan 1913- *ConNov 82, LongCTC,
   TwCWr, WorAu, WrDr 84*
Davin, Daniel Marcus 1913- *ConAu 3NR, -9R,
   DcLEL 1940, IntAu&W 82*
DaVinci, Mona *DrAP&F 83*
Davinson, Donald 1932- *WrDr 84*
Davinson, Donald E 1932- *ConAu 3NR, -5R*
Daviot, Gordon *ConAu X, TwCCr&M 80*
Daviot, Gordon 1896-1952 *DcLB 10[port]*
Daviot, Gordon 1897-1952 *LongCTC,
   TwCA SUP, TwCWr*
Davis, Adelle 1904-1974 *ConAu 37R, -49*
Davis, Allen, III 1929- *ConAu 108,
   NatPD 81[port]*
Davis, Allen F 1931- *ConAu 10NR, -21R,
   WrDr 84*
Davis, Allison 1902- *ConAu 106, LivgBAA*
Davis, Angela 1944- *ConAu 10NR*
Davis, Angela Y 1944- *ConAu 57,
   ConIsC 1[port]*
Davis, Ann E 1932- *ConAu 69*
Davis, Arthur G 1915- *ConAu 13R, WrDr 84*
Davis, Arthur Kennard 1910- *ConAu P-1*
Davis, Arthur Kyle, Jr. 1897- *ConAu P-2*
Davis, Arthur P 1904- *ConAu 61, LivgBAA*
Davis, Audrey *ConAu X*
Davis, Barbara 1955- *ConAu 108*
Davis, Barbara Chilcott *CreCan 1*
Davis, Barbara Kerr 1946- *ConAu 104*
Davis, Ben Reeves 1927- *ConAu 77*
Davis, Berrie 1922- *ConAu 101*
Davis, Bertram Hylton 1918- *ConAu 1R, -1NR,
   IntAu&W 82*
Davis, Bette 1908- *ConAu 61*
Davis, Bette J 1923- *ConAu 93, SmATA 15*
Davis, Bill C 1951- *ConAu 110*
Davis, Bradley B *DrAP&F 83*
Davis, Burke *DrAP&F 83*
Davis, Burke 1913- *ConAu 1R, -4NR,
   SmATA 4, WrDr 84*
Davis, Calvin DeArmond 1927- *ConAu 5R*
Davis, Chan 1926- *TwCSFW*
Davis, Charles Alfred 1923- *ConAu 5R*
Davis, Charles Till 1929- *ConAu 37R*
Davis, Charlie *DrAP&F 83*

Davis, Christopher *DrAP&F 83*
Davis, Christopher 1928- *ConAu 3NR, -9R,
   SmATA 6, WrDr 84*
Davis, Cliff *ConAu X*
Davis, Clive Edward 1914- *ConAu 17R*
Davis, Clyde Brion 1894-1962 *ConAu 5R,
   DcLB 9, TwCA, TwCA SUP*
Davis, Creath 1939- *ConAu 6NR, -57*
Davis, Curtis Carroll 1916- *ConAu 6NR, -9R,
   IntAu&W 82, WrDr 84*
Davis, Curtis Harrison 1949- *ConAmTC*
Davis, D Dwight 1908-1965 *SmATA 33*
Davis, D Evan 1923- *ConAu 17R*
Davis, Daniel S 1936- *ConAu 45, SmATA 12*
Davis, Daphne *ConAu 65*
Davis, David Brion 1927- *ConAu 9NR, -17R,
   WrDr 84*
Davis, David C L 1928- *ConAu 33R*
Davis, David Howard 1941- *ConAu 53,
   WrDr 84*
Davis, Deane C 1900- *ConAu 108*
Davis, Don *ConAu X, TwCWW*
Davis, Donald George 1928- *CreCan 2*
Davis, Donald Gordon, Jr. 1939- *ConAu 6NR,
   -53*
Davis, Dorothy Salisbury 1916- *ConAu 37R,
   IntAu&W 82, TwCCr&M 80, TwCRGW,
   WorAu, WrDr 84*
Davis, Douglas F 1935- *ConAu 105*
Davis, E Adams *ConAu X*
Davis, Earle 1905- *ConAu 65*
Davis, Edwin Adams 1904- *ConAu P-2*
Davis, Eleanor Harmon 1909- *ConAu 106*
Davis, Elise Miller 1915- *ConAu 69*
Davis, Elizabeth 1936- *ConAu X*
Davis, Elizabeth Gould 1910-1974 *ConAu 53*
Davis, Elmer Holmes 1890-1958 *TwCA,
   TwCA SUP*
Davis, Elwood Craig 1896- *ConAu 1R, -3NR*
Davis, F James 1920- *ConAu 1R, -4NR*
Davis, Fitzroy 1912-1980 *ConAu 102, -49,
   IntAu&W 82*
Davis, Flora 1934- *ConAu 10NR, -65*
Davis, Forest K 1918- *ConAu 41R*
Davis, Frank G 1915- *ConAu 85*
Davis, Franklin M, Jr. 1918-1981 *ConAu 1R,
   -4NR*
Davis, Fred 1925- *ConAu 13R*
Davis, Frederick Barton 1909- *ConAu 1R*
Davis, Frederick Clyde 1902-1977 *TwCCr&M 80*
Davis, Garold N 1932- *ConAu 41R*
Davis, Gary A 1938- *ConAu 106*
Davis, Genevieve 1928- *ConAu 65*
Davis, Genny Wright 1948- *ConAu 105*
Davis, George *DrAP&F 83*
Davis, George 1939- *ConAu 9NR*
Davis, George B 1939- *ConAu 65, LivgBAA*
Davis, George L, Sr. 1921- *ConAu 57*
Davis, Gerry *WrDr 84*
Davis, Gerry 1930- *TwCSFW*
Davis, Gil *ConAu X*
Davis, Gilbert 1899-1983 *ConAu 109*
Davis, Gita *WrDr 84*
Davis, Gordon *ConAu X*
Davis, Gordon B 1930- *ConAu 4NR, -53*
Davis, Grania 1943- *ConAu 85*
Davis, Grant Miller 1937- *ConAu 11NR, -29R*
Davis, Gwen 1936- *AuNews 1, ConAu 1R,
   -2NR*
Davis, H Grady 1890- *ConAu P-2*
Davis, H L 1894-1960 *DcLB 9[port], FifWWr,
   TwCWW*
Davis, Harold Eugene 1902- *ConAu 1R, -1NR,
   IntAu&W 82, WrDr 84*
Davis, Harold Lenoir 1896-1960 *ConAu 89,
   TwCA, TwCA SUP*
Davis, Harold S 1919- *ConAu 57*
Davis, Harriet Eager 1892?-1974 *ConAu 49*
Davis, Harry Rex 1921- *ConAu 1R*
Davis, Helene *DrAP&F 83*
Davis, Henry P 1894?-1970 *ConAu 104*
Davis, Herbert John 1893-1967 *ConAu 1R, -1NR*
Davis, Hope Hale *ConAu 25R, DrAP&F 83,
   WrDr 84*
Davis, Hope Harding 1915?-1976 *ConAu 69*
Davis, Horace Bancroft 1898- *ConAu 21R,
   WrDr 84*
Davis, Horance G, Jr. 1924- *ConAu 65*
Davis, Howard V 1915- *ConAu 25R*
Davis, Hubert J 1904- *ConAu 107,
   SmATA 31[port]*
Davis, I M 1926- *ConAu 61*

Davis, Irene Mary 1926- *IntAu&W 82*
Davis, J Cary 1905- *ConAu 41R*
Davis, J Madison *DrAP&F 83*
Davis, J William 1908- *ConAu 102*
Davis, Jack Leonard 1917- *ConAu 106*
Davis, James *ConAmTC*
Davis, James Allan 1929- *ConAu 1R, -1NR*
Davis, James C 1895-1981 *ConAu 108*
Davis, James H 1932- *ConAu 89*
Davis, James Richard 1936- *ConAu 65*
Davis, James Robert 1945- *ConAu 85,
   SmATA 32[port]*
Davis, James W 1935- *ConAu 29R*
Davis, Jan Haddle 1950- *ConAu 93*
Davis, Jean Reynolds 1927- *ConAu 61*
Davis, Jed H 1921- *ConAu 17R*
Davis, Jerome 1891-1979 *ConAu 3NR, -5R, -89*
Davis, Jim *ConAu X, SmATA X*
Davis, Jinnie Y 1945- *ConAu 107*
Davis, Joe Lee 1906-1974 *ConAu 5R, -103*
Davis, Johanna 1937-1974 *ConAu 41R, -53*
Davis, John 1917- *WrDr 84*
Davis, John David 1937- *ConAu 29R, WrDr 84*
Davis, John Gilbert *WrDr 84*
Davis, John H 1904- *ConAu 29R*
Davis, John H 1929- *ConAu 25R*
Davis, John J 1936- *ConAu 33R*
Davis, John King 1884-1967 *ConAu P-1*
Davis, Joseph C 1908- *ConAu 97*
Davis, Joseph Stancliffe 1885-1975 *ConAu 101,
   -57*
Davis, Judith 1925- *ConAu 106*
Davis, Julia 1900- *ConAu 1R, -1NR,
   IntAu&W 82, SmATA 6, WrDr 84*
Davis, Julian 1902?-1974 *ConAu 53*
Davis, Keith 1918- *ConAu 1R, -5NR, WrDr 84*
Davis, Ken 1906- *ConAu 49*
Davis, Kenneth R 1921- *ConAu 17R*
Davis, Kenneth S 1912- *ConAu 13R*
Davis, Kingsley 1908- *ConAu 8NR, -13R*
Davis, L J *DrAP&F 83*
Davis, L J 1940- *ConAu 11NR, -25R*
Davis, Lance Edwin 1928- *ConAu 53,
   IntAu&W 82*
Davis, Lanny J 1945- *ConAu 57*
Davis, Lawrence B 1939- *ConAu 45*
Davis, Lenwood G 1939- *ConAu 25R, LivgBAA*
Davis, Lew A 1930- *ConAu 21R*
Davis, Lloyd *DrAP&F 83*
Davis, Lloyd 1931- *ConAu 69*
Davis, Lois Carlile 1921- *ConAu 13R*
Davis, Lou Ellen 1936- *ConAu 81*
Davis, Louis E 1918- *ConAu 53*
Davis, Louise Littleton 1921- *ConAu 103,
   SmATA 25[port]*
Davis, Loyal Edward 1896-1982 *ConAu 107*
Davis, Luther 1921- *ConAu 105*
Davis, Luther 1938- *NatPD 81[port]*
Davis, Lydia *DrAP&F 83*
Davis, M Edward 1899- *ConAu 5R*
Davis, Maggie *ConAu 9NR, -13R*
Davis, Maralee 1924- *ConAu X*
Davis, Marc 1934- *ConAu 29R*
Davis, Margaret Banfield 1903- *ConAu P-1*
Davis, Margaret Thomson *WrDr 84*
Davis, Margaret Thomson 1926- *ConAu 102,
   DcLB 14[port]*
Davis, Marguerite 1889- *SmATA 34*
Davis, Marilyn K 1928- *ConAu 5R*
Davis, Martha 1942- *ConAu 4NR, -49*
Davis, Martyn P 1929- *WrDr 84*
Davis, Mary Lee 1935- *ConAu 4NR, -49,
   SmATA 9*
Davis, Mary Octavia 1901- *ConAu P-2,
   SmATA 6*
Davis, Maxine *ConAu X*
Davis, Melton S 1910- *ConAu 41R*
Davis, Michael 1925- *WrDr 84*
Davis, Michael 1940- *ConAu 33R*
Davis, Michael Justin 1925- *ConAu 102,
   IntAu&W 82*
Davis, Mildred *ConAu 77*
Davis, Mildred Ann 1916- *ConAu 5R*
Davis, Millard C 1930- *ConAu 69*
Davis, Monte 1949- *ConAu 103*
Davis, Morris 1933- *ConAu 11NR, -61*
Davis, Morton D 1930- *ConAu 65*
Davis, Moshe 1916- *ConAu 4NR, -9R,
   IntAu&W 82*
Davis, Murray *CreCan 1*
Davis, Murray S 1940- *ConAu 53*
Davis, Myrna 1936- *ConAu 69*

Davis, Natalie Zemon 1928- *ConAu 53*
Davis, Nolan 1942- *ConAu 49*
Davis, Norman 1913- *ConAu 106*,
 IntAu&W 82
Davis, Norman Maurice 1936- *ConAu 69*
Davis, Nuel Pharr 1915- *ConAu 29R*
Davis, Olivia 1922- *ConAu 81*
Davis, Ossie 1917- *ConDr 82*, *DcLB 7[port]*,
 LivgBAA, *NatPD 81[port]*, *WorAu 1970*,
 WrDr 84
Davis, Owen 1874-1956 *CnMD*, *ModWD*,
 TwCA, *TwCA SUP*
Davis, Patrick 1925- *ConAu 93*, *WrDr 84*
Davis, Paxton 1925- *ConAu 3NR*, *-9R*,
 SmATA 16
Davis, Peter 1937- *ConAu 107*
Davis, Philip E 1927- *ConAu 49*
Davis, Polly Ann 1931- *ConAu 102*
Davis, Proxade 1906- *IntWWP 82*
Davis, R G 1933- *ConAu 57*
Davis, Raecile Gwaltney 1910- *IntWWP 82*
Davis, Ralph C 1894- *ConAu 33R*
Davis, Ralph Henry Carless 1918- *ConAu 5R*,
 -6NR, *IntAu&W 82*, *WrDr 84*
Davis, Rebecca Blaine Harding 1831-1910
 ConAu 104, *TwCLC 6[port]*
Davis, Rex D 1924- *ConAu 9R*
Davis, Richard *WrDr 84*
Davis, Richard 1945- *ConAu 7NR*, *-53*
Davis, Richard Beale 1907- *ConAu 2NR*, *-5R*
Davis, Richard Harding 1864-1916 *LongCTC*,
 TwCA, *TwCA SUP*
Davis, Richard Perceval 1935- *IntAu&W 82*
Davis, Richard Whitlock 1935- *ConAu 33R*,
 WrDr 84
Davis, Robert Con 1948- *ConAu 104*
Davis, Robert Murray 1934- *ConAu 33R*
Davis, Robert Prunier 1929- *ConAu 3NR*, *-5R*,
 WrDr 84
Davis, Robert Ralph, Jr. 1941- *ConAu 37R*
Davis, Rocky 1927- *ConAu 61*
Davis, Ronald L 1936- *ConAu 37R*
Davis, Rosemary *ConAu 5R*
Davis, Rosemary L *ConAu X*
Davis, Roy Eugene 1931- *ConAu 6NR*, *-9R*
Davis, Russell Gerard 1922- *ConAu 5R*,
 SmATA 3
Davis, Sammy, Jr. 1925- *ConAu 108*
Davis, Samuel 1930- *ConAu 29R*
Davis, Stanley Nelson 1924- *ConAu 108*
Davis, Stratford 1915- *ConAu X*
Davis, Suzanne *ConAu X*
Davis, Sydney Charles Houghton 1887-
 ConAu 5R
Davis, Terence 1924- *ConAu 21R*
Davis, Thadious M *DrAP&F 83*
Davis, Thomas J 1946- *ConAu 4NR*, *-53*
Davis, Thulani *DrAP&F 83*
Davis, Timothy Francis Tothill 1941- *ConAu 81*
Davis, Tom Edward 1929- *ConAu 85*
Davis, Verne Theodore 1889-1973 *ConAu 1R*,
 MichAu 80, *SmATA 6*
Davis, Vincent 1930- *ConAu 7NR*, *-17R*,
 WrDr 84
Davis, Violet Amy 1918- *IntWWP 82*
Davis, W Jackson 1942- *ConAu 107*
Davis, W Jefferson 1885-1973 *ConAu P-2*
Davis, W N, Jr. 1915- *ConAu 81*
Davis, Walter Richardson 1928- *ConAu 102*
Davis, Wayne Harry 1930- *ConAu 33R*,
 WrDr 84
Davis, Wiley H 1913- *ConAu 25R*
Davis, William 1933- *ConAu 10NR*, *-65*
Davis, William C 1946- *ConAu 8NR*, *-61*
Davis, William H 1939- *ConAu 33R*
Davis, William Jackson 1942- *WrDr 84*
Davis, William Stearns 1877-1930 *TwCA*
Davis, William Virgil *DrAP&F 83*
Davis, William Virgil 1940- *ConAu 106*,
 IntWWP 82
Davis, Winston 1939- *ConAu 104*
Davis-Gardner, Angela *DrAP&F 83*
Davis-Gardner, Angela 1942- *ConAu 110*
Davis-Goff, Annabel *DrAP&F 83*
Davis-Goff, Annabel 1942- *ConAu 85*
Davis-Weyer, Caecilia 1929- *ConAu 41R*
Davison, Dennis 1923- *WrDr 84*
Davison, Edward Lewis 1898-1970 *ConAu 29R*
Davison, Frank Dalby 1893-1970 *ConLC 15*,
 TwCWr
Davison, Geoffrey 1927- *ConAu 110*, *WrDr 84*

Davison, Gladys Patton 1905- *ConAu P-1*
Davison, Jane 1932?-1981 *ConAu 104*
Davison, Jean 1937- *ConAu 10NR*, *-65*
Davison, Kenneth E 1924- *ConAu 9R*
Davison, Ned J 1926- *ConAu 45*
Davison, Peter *DrAP&F 83*
Davison, Peter 1928- *ConAu 3NR*, *-9R*,
 ConP 80, *DcLB 5[port]*, *DcLEL 1940*,
 IntAu&W 82, *WorAu 1970*, *WrDr 84*
Davison, Roderic H 1916- *ConAu 37R*
Davison, Verne E 1904- *ConAu 69*
Davisson, Charles Nelson 1917- *ConAu 25R*
Davisson, William I 1929- *ConAu 11NR*, *-17R*
Davitt, Thomas Edward 1904- *ConAu 25R*
D'Avrigny, France *IntWWP 82X*
Davy, Francis X 1916- *ConAu 29R*
Davy, George Mark Oswald 1898-1983
 ConAu 110
Davys, Sarah *IntAu&W 82X*
Dawdy, Doris Ostrander *ConAu 53*
Dawe, Bruce 1930- *ConAu 11NR*, *-69*,
 ConP 80, *IntWWP 82X*, *WrDr 84*
Dawe, Donald Bruce 1930- *IntAu&W 82*,
 IntWWP 82
Dawe, Donald G 1926- *ConAu 33R*
Dawe, Roger David 1934- *ConAu 3NR*, *-9R*
Dawes, Dorothy *ConAu X*
Dawes, Edward Naasson 1914- *WrDr 84*
Dawes, Frank 1933- *ConAu 69*
Dawes, Nathaniel Thomas, Jr. 1937- *ConAu 49*
Dawes, Neville Augustus 1926- *ConAu 13R*,
 DcLEL 1940
Dawes, Robyn M 1936- *ConAu 37R*
Dawidowicz, Lucy S 1915- *ConAu 25R*,
 WrDr 84
Dawis, Rene V 1928- *ConAu 45*
Dawisha, Adeed Isam 1944- *ConAu 102*
Dawisha, Adhid 1944- *WrDr 84*
Dawkins, Cecil *DrAP&F 83*
Dawkins, Cecil 1927- *ConAu 5R*
Dawkins, Richard 1941- *ConAu 69*
Dawley, David 1941- *ConAu 45*
Dawley, Powel Mills 1907- *ConAu 57*
Dawlish, Peter 1899-1963 *ConAu X*,
 TwCCW 83
Dawn, C Ernest 1918- *ConAu 61*
Dawood, N J 1927- *ConAu 49*
Dawson, Alan David 1942- *ConAu 77*
Dawson, Carl 1938- *ConAu 1NR*, *-45*
Dawson, Christopher Henry 1889-1970
 ConAu 1R, *-6NR*, *-29R*, *TwCA SUP*
Dawson, Coningsby William 1883-1959 *TwCA*,
 TwCA SUP
Dawson, Elizabeth *ConAu X*, *WrDr 84*
Dawson, Elizabeth 1930- *ConAu X*,
 IntAu&W 82X
Dawson, Elmer A *ConAu P-2*, *SmATA 1*
Dawson, Fielding *DrAP&F 83*
Dawson, Fielding 1930- *ConAu 85*, *ConLC 6*
Dawson, Frank G 1925- *ConAu 69*
Dawson, Geoffrey 1874-1944 *LongCTC*
Dawson, George Glenn 1925- *ConAu 37R*,
 WrDr 84
Dawson, Giles E 1903- *ConAu P-2*
Dawson, Grace Strickler 1891- *ConAu 17R*
Dawson, Guy Fielding Lewis 1930- *IntAu&W 82*
Dawson, Howard A 1895?-1979 *ConAu 89*
Dawson, Jan 1939?-1980 *ConAu 101*
Dawson, Jennifer *ConAu 10NR*, *-57*,
 ConNov 82, *DcLEL 1940*, *WrDr 84*
Dawson, Jerry F 1933- *ConAu 33R*
Dawson, Jonathan Dean 1941- *IntAu&W 82*
Dawson, Joseph G, III 1945- *ConAu 110*
Dawson, Linda 1949- *WrDr 84*
Dawson, Mary 1919- *ConAu 21R*, *SmATA 11*
Dawson, Mary Martha 1908- *IntWWP 82*
Dawson, Mildred A 1897- *ConAu 17R*
Dawson, Minnie E 1906-1978 *ConAu 85*
Dawson, Peter *ConAu X*
Dawson, Peter 1907- *TwCWW*
Dawson, Philip 1928- *ConAu 21R*
Dawson, Richard E 1939- *ConAu 73*
Dawson, Robert 1941- *ConAu 21R*
Dawson, Robert L 1943- *ConAu 105*
Dawson, Sea-Flower White *DrAP&F 83*
Dawson, Walter *IntAu&W 82X*
Day, A Grove 1904- *ConAu 8NR*, *-21R*
Day, Alan Charles Lynn 1924- *ConAu 1R*
Day, Alan J 1942- *ConAu 105*
Day, Albert Edward 1884-1973 *ConAu 45*,
 ConAu P-2
Day, Albert M 1897-1979 *ConAu 85*, *-93*

Day, Alice Taylor 1928- *ConAu 17R*
Day, Ann *IntWWP 82X*
Day, Ann Elizabeth 1927- *IntWWP 82*
Day, Beth 1924- *ConAu 3NR*, *-9R*,
 SmATA 33[port]
Day, Bradford M 1916- *ConAu 104*, *ConSFA*
Day, Clarence 1874-1935 *ConAu 108*
Day, Clarence Shepard, Jr. 1874-1935 *ConAmA*,
 LongCTC, *TwCA*, *TwCA SUP*, *TwCWr*
Day, David 1944- *ConAu 93*
Day, Donald *ConAu X*, *IntWWP 82X*
Day, Dorothy 1897-1980 *ConAu 102*, *-65*
Day, Douglas 1932- *ConAu 8NR*, *-9R*
Day, Gardiner Mumford 1900-1981 *ConAu 104*
Day, George Harold 1900- *ConAu P-1*
Day, Gwynn McLendon 1908- *ConAu P-1*
Day, Holman Francis 1865-1935 *TwCA*,
 TwCA SUP
Day, J Edward 1914- *ConAu 17R*
Day, J Laurence 1934- *ConAu 65*
Day, James F 1917- *WrDr 84*
Day, James Francis 1917- *ConAu 33R*
Day, James Wentworth 1899- *ConAu 13R*
Day, James Wentworth 1899-1983?
 ConAu 10NR
Day, James Wentworth 1899-1983 *ConAu 108*
Day, Jean-Luc *IntAu&W 82X*
Day, John A 1913- *ConAu 17R*
Day, John Patrick 1919- *ConAu 5R*
Day, John R 1917- *ConAu 9NR*
Day, John Robert 1917- *ConAu 5R*,
 IntAu&W 82, *WrDr 84*
Day, Kenneth 1912- *ConAu 9R*
Day, LeRoy Judson 1917- *ConAu 21R*
Day, Lila *IntWWP 82X*
Day, Lincoln H 1928- *ConAu 17R*
Day, Lucille *DrAP&F 83*
Day, Lucille 1947- *ConAu 110*
Day, M H 1927- *ConAu 102*
Day, Martin Steele 1917- *ConAu 5R*, *-7NR*
Day, Maurice 1892- *SmATA 30*
Day, Max *ConAu X*
Day, Melvin Norman 1923- *ConAu 109*
Day, Michael *ConAu X*
Day, Michael Herbert 1927- *IntAu&W 82*,
 WrDr 84
Day, Owen 1890- *ConAu 69*
Day, Paul Woodford 1916- *ConAu 25R*
Day, Peter Morton 1914- *ConAu 1R*
Day, Price 1907-1978 *ConAu 81*, *-85*
Day, R H 1927- *ConAu 29R*
Day, Ralph Lewis 1926- *ConAu 5R*, *-7NR*
Day, Richard B 1942- *ConAu 49*
Day, Richard E 1929- *ConAu 33R*
Day, Richard Wrisley *ConAmTC*
Day, Robert *DrAP&F 83*
Day, Robert Adams 1924- *ConAu 53*
Day, Robert S 1941- *TwCWW*, *WrDr 84*
Day, Robin 1923- *WrDr 84*
Day, Stacey B 1927- *WrDr 84*
Day, Stacey Biswas 1927- *ConAu 33R*,
 IntAu&W 82
Day Lewis, C 1904-1972 *ConAu 33R*,
 ConLC 10, *ConLCrt 82*, *DcLB 15[port]*,
 EncWL 2, *TwCCW 83*, *TwCCr&M 80*
Day-Lewis, Cecil 1904-1972 *CnMWL*,
 ConAu P-1, *ConLC 1*, *-6*, *LongCTC*,
 ModBrL, *ModBrL SUP*, *TwCA*,
 TwCA SUP, *TwCWr*, *WhoTwCL*
Day-Lewis, Sean Francis 1931- *IntAu&W 82*
Dayan, Moshe 1915-1981 *ConAu 105*, *-21R*
Dayan, Yael 1939- *AuNews 1*, *ConAu 89*,
 WorAu
Dayananda, James Yesupriya 1934- *ConAu 81*
Dayaratnam, Pasala 1932- *IntAu&W 82*
Daynes, Byron W 1937- *ConAu 110*
Dayton, David *DrAP&F 83*
Dayton, Donald W 1942- *ConAu 69*
Dayton, Edward R 1924- *ConAu 85*
Dayton, Irene *DrAP&F 83*
Dayton, Irene Catherine Glossenger 1922-
 ConAu 6NR, *-57*, *IntAu&W 82*,
 IntWWP 82
Dazai, Osamu 1909-1948 *CnMWL*, *ConAu X*,
 EncWL 2, *TwCLC 11[port]*, *WhoTwCL*,
 WorAu
D'Azevedo, Warren L 1920- *ConAu 93*
Dazey, Agnes J *ConAu P-2*, *SmATA 2*
Dazey, Frank M *ConAu P-2*, *SmATA 2*
Dck *IntAu&W 82X*
Deacon, Eileen *ConAu X*, *SmATA X*
Deacon, Joseph John 1920- *ConAu 69*

Deacon, Lois 1899- *IntAu&W 82, WrDr 84*
Deacon, Richard *ConAu X, IntAu&W 82X,*
　SmATA X, WrDr 84
Deacon, Ruth E 1923- *ConAu 102*
Deacon, William Arthur 1890-1964 *ConAu 89*
Deagon, Ann *DrAP&F 83*
Deagon, Ann 1930- *ConAu 57*
Deahl, James 1945- *IntWWP 82*
Deak, Edward Joseph, Jr. 1943- *ConAu 53*
Deak, Francis 1899-1972 *ConAu 33R*
Deak, Istvan 1926- *ConAu 11NR, -25R,*
　WrDr 84
Deakin, Frederick William Dampier 1913-
　ConAu 5R, -5NR
Deakin, James 1929- *ConAu 8NR, -21R*
Deakin, Rose 1937- *ConAu 109*
Deakin, William 1913- *IntAu&W 82, WrDr 84*
Deakins, Roger Lee 1933- *ConAu 61*
Deal, Babs H 1929- *ConAu 1R, -1NR*
Deal, Borden *DrAP&F 83*
Deal, Borden 1922- *ConAu 1R, -2NR, DcLB 6,*
　IntAu&W 82, WrDr 84
Deal, Susan Strayer *DrAP&F 83*
Deal, William Sanford 1910- *ConAu 3NR, -5R,*
　IntAu&W 82
Deale, Kenneth Edwin Lee 1907- *ConAu 4NR,*
　-5R
Dealey, E M 1892-1969 *ConAu P-2*
Dealey, Ted *ConAu X*
Dean, Abner 1910-1982 *ConAu 107*
Dean, Amber 1902- *ConAu 2NR, -5R,*
　TwCCr&M 80, WrDr 84
Dean, Anabel 1915- *ConAu 37R, SmATA 12,*
　WrDr 84
Dean, Basil 1888- *ConAu 69, ModWD*
Dean, Beryl 1911- *ConAu 9R, WrDr 84*
Dean, Burton V 1924- *ConAu 1NR, -45*
Dean, Dudley *TwCWW*
Dean, Dwight G 1918- *ConAu 17R, WrDr 84*
Dean, E Douglas 1916- *ConAu 97*
Dean, Edwin Robinson 1933- *ConAu 17R*
Dean, Frances Mary 1905?-1983 *ConAu 110*
Dean, Herbert Morris 1938- *ConAu 105*
Dean, Howard E 1916- *ConAu 41R*
Dean, Ida *ConAu X*
Dean, Jeffrey S 1939- *ConAu 37R*
Dean, Joan 1925- *ConAu 101*
Dean, Joel 1906- *ConAu 33R*
Dean, John *ConAu X*
Dean, John Aurie 1921- *ConAu 53*
Dean, John Wesley, III 1938- *ConAu 105*
Dean, Karen Strickler 1923- *ConAu 109*
Dean, Leonard Fellows 1909- *ConAu 105*
Dean, Luella Jo 1908?-1977 *ConAu 69*
Dean, Malcolm 1948- *ConAu 105*
Dean, Morton 1935- *ConAu 69*
Dean, Nancy 1930- *ConAu 65*
Dean, Nell Marr 1910- *ConAu 21R*
Dean, Roy 1925- *ConAu 6NR, -57*
Dean, Shelley *WrDr 84*
Dean, Stanley 1908- *ConAu 73*
Dean, Vera Micheles 1903-1972 *ConAu 37R,*
　TwCA SUP
Dean, Warren 1932- *ConAu 29R*
Dean, William Denard 1937- *ConAu 37R,*
　IntAu&W 82, WrDr 84
Dean, William F 1899-1981 *ConAu 105*
Dean, Winton Basil 1916- *ConAu 10NR, -65,*
　IntAu&W 82
Dean, Yetive H 1909- *ConAu P-1*
DeAndrea, William L 1952- *ConAu 81*
Deane, Dee Shirley 1928- *ConAu 81*
Deane, Elisabeth *ConAu X*
Deane, Herbert Andrew 1921- *ConAu 1R*
Deane, James G 1923- *ConAu 89*
Deane, Lorna 1909- *ConAu X*
Deane, Nancy H 1939- *ConAu 29R*
Deane, Norman *ConAu X, LongCTC,*
　TwCCr&M 80
Deane, Seamus Francis 1940- *IntAu&W 82*
Deane, Shirley Joan 1920- *ConAu 1R, -2NR*
Deane-Drummond, Anthony 1917- *WrDr 84*
Deane-Drummond, Sophia T Pemberton
　CreCan 1
DeAngeli, Marguerite 1889- *DcLB 22[port],*
　TwCCW 83, WrDr 84
DeAngeli, Marguerite Lofft 1889- *AuNews 2,*
　ChlLR 1, ConAu 3NR, -5R, MichAu 80,
　SmATA 1, -27[port]
DeAngelis, Jacqueline *DrAP&F 83*
Dearden, Harold 1883-1962 *LongCTC*
Dearden, James A 1924-1976 *ConAu 33R*

Dearden, James Shackley 1931- *ConAu 25R,*
　IntAu&W 82, WrDr 84
Dearden, John 1919- *ConAu 33R*
Deardorff, Robert 1912- *ConAu 61*
Deardorff, Tom 1940- *ConAu 89*
Dearing, Vinton Adams 1920- *ConAu 110*
Dearlove, John 1944- *ConAu 97*
DeArmand, Frances Ullmann *ConAu 5R,*
　SmATA 10
DeArmas, Frederick A 1945- *ConAu 37R,*
　IntAu&W 82
DeArment, Robert K 1925- *ConAu 93*
Dearmer, Geoffrey 1893- *ConAu P-2,*
　IntAu&W 82
Dearmin, Jennie Tarascou 1924- *ConAu 5R*
Dearstyne, Howard B 1903-1979 *ConAu 85*
Deary, Terry 1946- *ConAu 110*
Deason, Hilary J 1903- *ConAu 73*
D'Easum, Cedric 1907- *ConAu 73*
D'Easum, Dick *ConAu X*
Deasy, C M 1918- *ConAu 93*
Deasy, Mary Margaret 1914- *ConAu 5R,*
　WrDr 84
Deaton, Charles W 1942- *ConAu 93*
Deaton, John 1939- *ConAu 11NR, -61*
Deats, Paul, Jr. 1918- *ConAu 13R*
Deats, Randy 1954- *ConAu 93*
Deats, Richard 1932- *WrDr 84*
Deats, Richard Louis 1932- *ConAu 21R*
Deaux, George *DrAP&F 83*
Deaux, George 1931- *ConAu 5R, WrDr 84*
DeAyala, *TwCA, TwCA SUP*
DeAyala, Ramon Perez *ModRL*
DeBakey, Michael Ellies 1908- *IntAu&W 82*
DeBakey, Michael Ellis 1908- *ConAu 73,*
　WrDr 84
DeBanke, Cecile 1889-1965 *ConAu P-1,*
　LongCTC, SmATA 11
DeBary, Brett *ConAu X*
DeBary, William Theodore 1919- *ConAu 57*
DeBeaubien, Philip Francis 1913-1979 *ConAu 85*
DeBeaufort, Agathe Henriette Marie
　IntAu&W 82X
DeBeaufort, Henriette L T *IntAu&W 82X*
DeBeausobre, Julia Mikhailovna *ConAu X*
DeBeauvoir, Simone *ConAu X, ModRL*
DeBedts, Ralph F 1914- *ConAu 9R*
DeBeer, Esmond Samuel 1895- *ConAu P-1*
DeBeer, Sir Gavin Rylands 1899-1972 *ConAu P-1*
DeBelder, J L 1912- *IntWWP 82*
DeBenedetti, Charles Louis 1943- *ConAu 102*
DeBerard, Ella 1900- *ConAu X*
Deberdt-Malaquais, Elisabeth 1937- *ConAu 57*
Deberitz, Jan 1950- *IntAu&W 82*
DeBeus, Jacobus Gysbertus 1909- *ConAu 102*
Debevec Henning, Sylvie Marie 1948- *ConAu 109*
Debicki, Andrew P 1934- *ConAu 37R*
Debicki, Roman 1896- *ConAu 1R*
DeBlank, Joost 1908-1968 *ConAu P-1*
DeBlasis, Celeste 1946- *ConAu 4NR, -53,*
　WrDr 84
DeBlij, Harm J 1935- *ConAu 8NR, -13R,*
　WrDr 84
Debo, Angie 1890- *ConAu 69, ConIsC 1[port]*
DeBoer, John C 1923- *ConAu 29R, WrDr 84*
DeBoer, John James 1903-1969 *ConAu 1R, -3NR*
DeBois, Helma *ConAu X*
DeBois, Wilhelmina J E 1923- *ConAu 17R*
DeBoissiere, Ralph 1907- *ConAu 106*
DeBold, Richard C 1927- *ConAu 21R*
DeBolt, William Walter *IntWWP 82*
DeBona, Maurice, Jr. 1926- *ConAu 65*
DeBono, Edward 1933- *ConAu 10NR, -21R,*
　IntAu&W 82, WrDr 84
DeBonville, Bob 1926- *ConAu 69*
DeBorchgrave, Arnaud 1926- *ConAu 73*
DeBorhegyi, Suzanne Catherine Sims 1926-
　ConAu 5R
DeBorn, Edith *WrDr 84*
DeBorn, Edith 1901- *ConAu 25R*
Debray, Regis 1942- *ConAu 21R*
Debre, Michel 1912- *IntAu&W 82*
Debreczeny, Paul 1932- *ConAu 33R, WrDr 84*
DeBreffny, Brian 1931- *ConAu 77*
DeBreffny, Brian O'Rorke 1929- *IntAu&W 82*
Debrett, Hal *ConAu X*
Debreu, Gerard 1921- *ConAu 37R, WrDr 84*
DeBrissac, Malcolm *ConAu X*
Debrot, Cola 1902- *IntAu&W 82X*
Debrot, Nicolaas 1902- *IntAu&W 82*
DeBrunhoff, Laurent 1925- *ConAu X*
DeBruyn, Monica G 1952- *ConAu 65,*

　SmATA 13
Debu-Bridel, Jacques 1902- *IntAu&W 82*
Debus, Allen George 1926- *ConAu 37R,*
　IntAu&W 82, WrDr 84
DeCamp, Catherine C 1907- *ConAu 9NR*
DeCamp, Catherine Crook 1907- *ConAu 21R,*
　IntAu&W 82, SmATA 12, WrDr 84
DeCamp, Dot 1920- *NatPD 81[port]*
DeCamp, Graydon 1934- *ConAu 97*
DeCamp, L Sprague 1907- *ConAu 1R, -1NR,*
　-9NR, ConSFA, DcLB 8[port],
　IntAu&W 82, SmATA 9, TwCSFW,
　WorAu, WrDr 84
DeCampi, John Webb 1939- *ConAu 69*
DeCanio, Stephen J 1942- *ConAu 57*
DeCapite, Raymond Anthony 1924- *ConAu 1R*
Decarie, Therese Gouin 1923- *ConAu 41R*
DeCarl, Lennard 1940- *ConAu 81*
DeCasseres, Benjamin 1873-1945 *TwCA,*
　TwCA SUP
DeCastro, Fernando J 1937- *ConAu 53*
DeCastro, Jose Maria Ferreira *ModRL*
DeCastro, Josue 1908-1973 *ConAu 33R*
Decaudin, Michel H F 1919- *IntAu&W 82*
Decaunes, Luc *IntWWP 82*
DeCaux, Len 1899- *ConAu X, WrDr 84*
DeCaux, Leonard Howard 1899- *ConAu 29R*
Decaux, Lucile *ConAu X*
Decebal *IntAu&W 82X*
DeCecco, John Paul 1925- *ConAu 17R*
DeCervera, Alejo 1919- *ConAu 21R*
DeCespedes, Alba 1911- *ModRL*
DeChair, Somerset 1911- *ConAu 1NR, -45,*
　IntAu&W 82, IntWWP 82, LongCTC,
　WrDr 84
Dechant, Emerald V 1926- *ConAu 9R*
DeChant, John A 1917-1974 *ConAu 53,*
　ConAu P-2
DeCharms, Richard, IV 1927- *ConAu 41R*
DeChatellerault, Victor *ConAu X*
Dechert, Charles R 1927- *ConAu 10NR, -21R*
DeChirico, Giorgio 1888-1978 *ConAu 81, -89*
DeChristoforo, Ron 1951- *ConAu 81*
Deci, Edward L 1942- *ConAu 53*
Decker, Beatrice 1919- *ConAu 61*
Decker, Donald M 1923- *ConAu 37R*
Decker, Duane Walter 1910-1964 *ConAu 5R,*
　SmATA 5
Decker, Esther Bailey 1913- *IntWWP 82*
Decker, Hannah S 1937- *ConAu 85*
Decker, Leslie E 1930- *ConAu 9R*
Decker, Robert Owen 1927- *ConAu 65*
Decker, William *DrAP&F 83, WrDr 84*
Decker, William B 1926- *ASpks, TwCWW*
Deckert, Alice Mae *ConAu 13R*
Declan, Peter *IntAu&W 82X*
DeClements, Barthe 1920- *ConAu 105*
DeCock, Liliane 1939- *ConAu 2NR, -45*
Decolta, Ramon *ConAu X, TwCCr&M 80*
DeConde, Alexander 1920- *ConAu 5R, -6NR*
DeCormier-Shekerjian, Regina *DrAP&F 83*
DeCosta, Rene 1939- *ConAu 102*
DeCoste, Fredrik 1910- *ConAu P-2*
DeCoster, Cyrus C 1914- *ConAu 49*
DeCoy, Robert H, Jr. 1920- *ConAu 25R,*
　LivgBAA
DeCrespigny, Rafe 1936- *ConAu 57, WrDr 84*
DeCristoforo, Romeo John 1917- *ConAu 3NR,*
　-9R, WrDr 84
DeCrow, Karen 1937- *ConAu 33R, WrDr 84*
Decter, Midge 1927- *ConAu 2NR, -45,*
　WrDr 84
Dedecius, Karl 1921- *IntAu&W 82*
DeDecker, Jacques 1945- *IntAu&W 82*
Dedek, John F 1929- *ConAu 33R*
Deden, Claus Jorgen 1943- *IntAu&W 82*
Dederick, Robert 1919- *ConP 80, WrDr 84*
Dedeyan, Charles 1910- *IntAu&W 82*
DeDienes, Andre 1913- *ConAu 41R*
Dedijer, Vladimir 1914- *ConAu 1R, -4NR*
Dedina, Michel Jean Bernard 1933- *ConAu 33R*
Dedini, Eldon 1921- *ConAu 65*
Dedmon, Emmett 1918- *ConAu 5NR, -9R,*
　WrDr 84
Dedmon, Emmett 1918-1983 *ConAu 110*
Dee, Henry *ConAu X*
Dee, Peter 1939- *NatPD 81[port]*
Dee Jay Gee *IntWWP 82X*
Deeble, Russell John 1944- *IntWWP 82*
Deedy, John 1923- *ConAu 33R,*
　SmATA 24[port]
Deegan, Paul Joseph 1937- *ConAu 102*

SmATA 28[port]

Delaney, Norman Conrad 1932- *ConAu 37R,
WrDr 84*

Delaney, Robert Finley 1925- *ConAu 1R, –6NR*

Delaney, Shelagh 1930- *WrDr 84*

Delaney, Shelagh 1939- *CnMD, ConAu 17R,
ConDr 82, CroCD, DcLB 13[port],
DcLEL 1940, LongCTC, ModWD, TwCWr,
WorAu*

Delaney, Steve 1938- *ConAu 110*

Delaney, Thomas Nicholas, III 1951-
ConAu 10NR

Delaney, William A 1926- *ConAu 106*

DeLange, Nicholas 1944- *ConAu 89*

Delano, Anthony 1930- *ConAu 102,
IntAu&W 82, WrDr 84*

Delano, Hugh 1933- *ConAu 65, SmATA 20*

Delano, Isaac O 1904- *ConAu 25R*

Delano, Kenneth J 1934- *ConAu 57*

DeLantagne, Cecile *ConAu X*

Delany, Kevin F X 1927- *ConAu 73*

Delany, Paul 1937- *ConAu 29R*

Delany, Samuel R *DrAP&F 83*

Delany, Samuel R 1942- *ConAu 81, ConLC 8,
–14, ConNov 82, ConSFA, DcLB 8[port],
DrmM[port], LivgBAA, TwCSFW,
WorAu 1970, WrDr 84*

DeLaPasture *TwCA, TwCA SUP*

DeLaPasture, Mrs. Henry 1866-1945 *LongCTC*

Delaplane, Stanton Hill 1907- *ConAu 25R*

Delaporte, Ernest P 1924- *ConAu 97*

Delaporte, Theophile *ConAu X*

DeLaPortilla, Marta 1927- *ConAu 61*

DeLapp, Ardyce Lucile 1903- *ConAu 97*

DeLapp, George Leslie 1895- *ConAu 102*

DeLaRamee, Louise 1839-1908 *SmATA 20*

DeLaRenta, Francoise DeLangiade 1921?-1983
ConAu 110

DeLaRoche, Mazo 1879-1961 *CreCan 2,
TwCRGW*

DeLaRoche, Mazo 1885-1961 *ConAu 85,
ConLC 14, LongCTC, TwCA, TwCWr*

DeLaSagesse, Marie *CreCan 1*

DeLasCuevas, Ramon *ConAu X*

DeLaSerna *TwCA, TwCA SUP*

DeLaSerna, Ramon Gomez *ModRL*

DeLaTorre, Lillian 1902- *ConAu X,
TwCA SUP, TwCCr&M 80, WrDr 84*

DeLaTorre, Victor Raul Haya *ConAu X*

DeLaTousche D'Avrigny, Francoise Anne 1907-
IntWWP 82

Delattre, Pierre 1930- *ConAu 105*

DeLaubenfels, David J 1925- *ConAu 53*

DeLaunay, Jacques Forment 1924- *ConAu 3NR,
–9R, IntAu&W 82*

Delaune, Jewel Lynn DeGrummond *SmATA 7*

Delaune, Lynn *ConAu 1R*

Delaunoy, Didier 1937- *ConAmTC*

DeLaura, David Joseph 1930- *ConAu 21R,
WrDr 84*

Delaurentis, Louise Budde *DrAP&F 83*

DeLaurentis, Louise Budde 1920- *ConAu 5R,
SmATA 12*

DeLaVentoliere, Michel *IntWWP 82X*

DeLaWarr, George Walter 1904-1969 *ConAu P-1*

Delay, Claude *ConAu X*

Delay-Baillen, Claude 1934- *ConAu 53*

Delay-Tubiana, Claude 1934- *ConAu 4NR*

Delbanco, Nicholas *DrAP&F 83*

Delbanco, Nicholas F 1942- *ConAu 17R,
ConLC 6, –13, DcLB 6[port], WrDr 84*

DelBarco, Lucy Salamanca *ConAu 17R*

Delblanc, Sven 1931- *CIDMEL 80, EncWL 2*

DelBoca, Angelo 1925- *ConAu 25R*

Delbridge, Rosemary 1949?-1981 *ConAu 105*

Delcarte, Francoise 1936- *IntWWP 82*

DelCastillo, Michel 1933- *ConAu 109, ModRL,
WorAu*

DelCastillo, Richard Griswold *ConAu X*

Delcroix, Carlo 1896-1977 *ConAu 73*

Delderfield, Eric R 1909- *WrDr 84*

Delderfield, Eric Raymond 1909- *ConAu 4NR,
–53, IntAu&W 82, SmATA 14*

Delderfield, R F 1912-1972 *ASpks, SmATA 20,
TwCRGW*

Delderfield, Ronald Frederick 1912-1972
ConAu 37R, –73, DcLEL 1940

Delear, Frank J 1914- *ConAu 9NR, –21R,
WrDr 84*

Deledda, Grazia 1871-1936 *CIDMEL 80,
EncWL 2, ModRL, TwCA, TwCA SUP,*

TwCWr, WhoTwCL

DeLeeuw, Adele 1899- *WrDr 84*

DeLeeuw, Adele Louise 1899- *ConAu 1R, –1NR,
SmATA 1, –30[port]*

DeLeeuw, Cateau Wilhelmina 1903-1975
ConAu 1R, –3NR

DeLeeuw, Hendrik 1891-1977 *ConAu 73*

Delehanty, Randolph 1944- *ConAu 106*

DeLeiris, Alain 1922- *ConAu 73*

DeLeon, Luis *IntAu&W 82X*

Deleon, Nephtali *DrAP&F 83*

DeLeon, Nephtali 1945- *IntWWP 82*

DeLerma, Dominique-Rene 1928- *ConAu 1NR,
–45*

Delessert, Etienne 1941- *ConAu 21R,
SmATA 27*

DeLey, Herbert 1936- *ConAu 21R*

Delfgaauw, Bernard 1912- *ConAu 21R,
IntAu&W 82*

Delfosse, Georges 1869-1939 *CreCan 2*

Delgado, Alan 1910- *WrDr 84*

Delgado, Alan George 1909- *ConAu 5NR, –9R,
IntAu&W 82*

Delgado, Jose Manuel R 1915- *ConAu 29R*

Delgado, Ramon Louis 1937- *ConAu 85,
IntAu&W 82, NatPD 81[port]*

D'Elia, Donald John 1933- *ConAu 57*

DeLiancourt, Raoul *ConAu X*

Delibes, Miguel 1920- *CIDMEL 80, ConAu X,
ConLC 8, –18, EncWL 2, TwCWr,
WorAu 1970*

Delibes Setien, Miguel 1920- *ConAu 1NR, –45*

Delicado, Pepe *IntAu&W 82X*

Deligiorgis, Stavros 1933- *ConAu 61*

DeLillo, Don *DrAP&F 83*

DeLillo, Don 1936- *ConAu 81, ConLC 8, –10,
–13, –27[port], ConNov 82, DcLB 6,
WrDr 84*

DeLima, Agnes 1887?-1974 *ConAu 53*

DeLima, Clara Rosa 1922- *ConAu 6NR, –57*

DeLima, Sigrid *DrAP&F 83*

DeLima, Sigrid 1921- *ConAu 25R,
IntAu&W 82, WorAu, WrDr 84*

Delin, Bertil 1922- *IntAu&W 82*

Delisle, Francoise 1886?-1974 *ConAu 53*

DeLisser, H G 1878-1944 *TwCLC 12[port]*

DeLisser, Herbert George 1878-1944 *ConAu 109*

Delius, Anthony 1916- *WrDr 84*

Delius, Anthony Ronald St. Martin 1916-
*ConAu 17R, ConP 80, DcLEL 1940,
TwCWr*

Delk, Robert Carlton 1920- *ConAu 45*

Dell, Belinda *WrDr 84*

Dell, Belinda 1925- *ConAu X*

Dell, Christopher 1927- *ConAu 65*

Dell, Dudley *IntAu&W 82X*

Dell, E T, Jr. 1923- *ConAu 13R*

Dell, Edmund 1921- *ConAu 103, IntAu&W 82,
WrDr 84*

Dell, Ethel Mary 1881-1939 *TwCRGW, TwCWr*

Dell, Floyd 1887-1969 *ConAmA, ConAu 89,
DcLB 9[port], LongCTC, ModAL, TwCA,
TwCA SUP*

Dell, Roberta E 1946- *ConAu 81*

Dell, Sidney 1918- *ConAu 2NR, –5R, WrDr 84*

Della-Piana, Gabriel M 1926- *ConAu 73*

DellaPergola, Edith 1918- *CreCan 1*

DellaPergola, Luciano 1910- *CreCan 1*

Dellin, Lubomir, A D 1920- *ConAu 45*

Delling, Gerhard 1905- *IntAu&W 82*

Dellinger, David 1915- *ConAu 65*

Delloff, Irving Arthur 1920- *ConAu 13R*

DelMar, Florentina *IntAu&W 82X*

DelMar, Marcia 1950- *ConAu 105*

DelMar, Norman 1919- *WrDr 84*

Delmar, Roy *ConAu X, SmATA X*

Delmar, Vina 1905- *ConAu 65, TwCA,
TwCA SUP, TwCRGW, WrDr 84*

Delmer, Denis Sefton 1904- *ConAu 5R*

Delmonico, Andrea *ConAu X*

DelNorte, Scott *IntAu&W 82X*

DeLoach, Allen *DrAP&F 83*

DeLoach, Allen 1939- *ConAu 85*

DeLoach, Charles F 1927- *ConAu 37R,
WrDr 84*

DeLoach, Clarence, Jr. 1936- *ConAu 57*

Delon, Floyd Gurney 1929- *ConAu 69*

DeLone, Richard H 1940- *ConAu 101*

DeLone, Ruth *ConAu X*

DeLong, Thomas A 1935- *ConAu 106*

DeLongchamps, Joanne *DrAP&F 83*

DeLongchamps, Joanne 1923- *ConAu 3NR, –9R,*

IntWWP 82, WrDr 84

DeLora, Joann S 1935- *ConAu X, –53*

Deloria, Vine, Jr. 1933- *ASpks, ConAu 5NR,
–53, ConLC 21[port], SmATA 21[port]*

Delorko, Olinko 1910- *IntWWP 82*

Delorme, Andre *ConAu X*

Delorme, Michele *ConAu X*

Delort, Robert 1932- *ConAu 102*

DeLosReyes, Gabriel *ConAu 45*

DeLosReyes, Maria Corazon 1919- *IntWWP 82*

Deloughery, Grace L 1933- *ConAu 33R,
WrDr 84*

Delp, Michael *DrAP&F 83*

Delp, Michael W 1948- *ConAu 77, MichAu 80*

Delpar, Helen 1936- *ConAu 53*

DelRey, Lester 1915- *ConAu 65, ConSFA,
DcLB 8[port], SmATA 22[port], TwCSFW,
–, WrDr 84*

Delta *ConAu X*

Delton, Jina 1961- *ConAu 106*

Delton, Judy 1931- *ConAu 8NR, –57,
SmATA 14*

Delton, Julie 1959- *ConAu 108*

DeLuca, A Michael 1912- *ConAu 21R*

DeLuca, Charles J 1927- *ConAu 73*

DeLucca, John 1920- *ConAu 41R*

Delulio, John 1938- *SmATA 15*

Delumeau, Jean 1923- *ConAu 97*

DeLuna, Frederick Adolph 1928- *ConAu 65*

Delupis, Ingrid 1939- *ConAu 103*

DelValle, Irma *DrAP&F 83*

DelValle, Irma 1944- *IntWWP 82*

DelValle Inclan, Ramon *ModRL, TwCA,
TwCA SUP*

DelVecchio, John M 1947- *ConAu 110*

Delving, Michael 1914-1978 *ConAu X,
SmATA X, TwCCr&M 80, WorAu*

DeLynn, Eileen 1920- *WrDr 84*

Delynn, Jane *DrAP&F 83*

DeLynn, Jane 1946- *ConAu 77*

DeLys, Paul *IntAu&W 82X*

DeLyser, Femmy 1935- *ConAu 110*

Delzell, Charles F 1920- *ConAu 1R, –2NR,
IntAu&W 82, WrDr 84*

DeMadariaga *LongCTC, TwCA, TwCA SUP*

DeMadariaga, Isabel 1919- *ConAu 107*

Demaine, Don *ConAu X*

DeMandiargues, Andre Pieyre *ConAu X*

DeManio, Jack 1914- *ConAu 61*

Demant, Vigo Auguste 1893-1983 *ConAu 109*

DeMar, Esmeralda *ConAu X*

Demaray, Donald E 1926- *ConAu 1R, –1NR,
IntAu&W 82, WrDr 84*

DeMarco, Angelus A 1916- *ConAu 9R*

DeMarco, Arlene *AuNews 1*

DeMarco, Donald 1937- *ConAu 7NR, –61*

DeMare, Eric Samuel 1910- *ConAu 6NR, –9R*

DeMare, George 1912- *ConAu 21R*

Demarest, Chris L 1951- *ConAu 109*

Demarest, Doug *ConAu X, SmATA X*

Demarest, Phyllis Gordon 1911-1969 *ConAu 104*

Demaret, Pierre 1943- *ConAu 61*

Demaria, Robert *DrAP&F 83*

DeMaria, Robert 1928- *ConAu 5NR*

DeMarinis, Rick 1934- *ConAu 9NR, –57*

Demaris, Ovid 1919- *ConAu X, TwCCr&M 80,
WrDr 84*

DeMaris, Ron *DrAP&F 83*

Demas, Vida 1927- *ConAu 49, SmATA 9*

DeMatteo, Donna 1941- *ConAu 25R,
NatPD 81[port]*

DeMauny, Erik 1920- *ConAu 33R,
DcLEL 1940*

DeMause, Lloyd 1931- *ConAu 65*

Dember, Jean Wilkins 1930- *LivgBAA*

Dembo, L S 1929- *ConAu 2NR*

Dembo, Lawrence Sanford 1929- *ConAu 1R*

Demby, William 1922- *ConAu 81, LivgBAA,
ModBlW*

DeMedici, Marino 1933- *ConAu 89*

Demedts, Andre 1906- *IntWWP 82*

DeMello, Agustin *DrAP&F 83*

Dement, William Charles 1928- *ConAu 105*

DeMente, Boye 1928- *ConAu 8NR, –21R*

DeMenton, Francisco *ConAu X*

Demers, James 1942- *ConAu X*

DeMesne, Eugene Frederick P C *ConAu 41R,
IntAu&W 82, IntWWP 82*

DeMessieres, Nicole 1930- *ConAu 107*

Demetillo, Ricardo D 1920- *DcLEL 1940*

Demetillo, Ricaredo 1920- *ConAu 102,
ConP 80, IntAu&W 82, WrDr 84*

Demetrius, James Kleon 1924- *ConAu 21R*
Demetrius, Lucia 1910- *IntAu&W 82*
Demetz, Peter 1922- *ConAu 65, IntAu&W 82*
Demeuse, Pierre-J 1909- *IntAu&W 82*
Demi *ConAu X*
DeMichael, Don 1928-1982 *ConAu 106*
Demijohn, Thom *ConAu X, WrDr 84*
DeMilan, Sister Jean *ConAu X*
DeMille, Agnes 1905- *ConAu X*
DeMille, Alexandria *ConAu X*
Demille, Darcy 1929- *LivgBAA*
DeMille, Nelson 1943- *ConAu 6NR, –57*
DeMille, Richard *DrAP&F 83*
DeMille, Richard 1922- *ConAu 21R, WrDr 84*
Deming, Barbara 1917- *ConAu 85*
Deming, Louise Macpherson 1916-1976
  ConAu 61
Deming, Richard 1915- *ConAu 3NR, –9R,*
  IntAu&W 82, SmATA 24[port],
  TwCCr&M 80, WrDr 84
Deming, Robert H 1937- *ConAu 21R, WrDr 84*
DeMirjian, Arto, Jr. 1931- *ConAu 57*
Demise, Phil *DrAP&F 83, IntWWP 82X*
DeMolen, Richard Lee 1938- *ConAu 45*
Demone, Harold W, Jr. 1924- *ConAu 5R, –9NR*
DeMonfried, Henri 1879?-1974 *ConAu 53*
Demong, Phyllis 1920- *ConAu 106*
DeMontaigne, Joy 1935- *IntAu&W 82*
DeMontalvo, Luis Galvez *ConAu X*
DeMontebello, Guy-Philippe Lannes 1936-
  ConAu 45
DeMontfort, Guy *ConAu X*
DeMontherlant *TwCA, TwCA SUP*
DeMontherlant, Henry 1896- *ModRL*
DeMontreville Polak, Doris 1904?-1974
  ConAu 49
DeMordaunt, Walter Julius 1925- *ConAu 33R,*
  WrDr 84
Demorest, Jean-Jacques 1920- *ConAu 5R*
Demorest, Stephen 1949- *ConAu 101*
DeMorgan, William Frend 1839-1917 *LongCTC,*
  ModBrL, TwCA, TwCA SUP, TwCWr
DeMorny, Peter *ConAu X*
Demos, Paul 1888-1983 *ConAu 109*
Demotes, Michael *ConAu X*
Demott, Benjamin *DrAP&F 83*
DeMott, Benjamin 1924- *ConAu 5R, WorAu*
DeMott, Donald W 1928- *ConAu 61*
DeMourgues, Odette 1914- *ConAu 5R*
Dempewolff, Richard F 1914- *ConAu 1R, –1NR*
Dempsey, David 1914- *WrDr 84*
Dempsey, David Knapp 1914- *ConAu 2NR, –5R*
Dempsey, Hugh Aylmer 1929- *ConAu 11NR,*
  –69
Dempsey, Jack *ConAu X*
Dempsey, Lotta *ConAu 101*
Dempsey, Paul K 1935- *ConAu 25R*
Dempsey, Richard A 1932- *ConAu 61*
Dempsey, William Harrison 1895- *ConAu 89*
Dempsey, William Harrison 1895-1983
  ConAu 109
Dempster, Chris 1943- *ConAu 106*
Dempster, Derek David 1924- *ConAu 13R*
Dempster, Ronald Tomberai *DcLEL 1940*
Dempster, Stuart 1936- *ConAu 104*
Demske, James Michael 1922- *ConAu 29R*
Demura, Fumio 1940- *ConAu 61*
Demuth, Norman 1898-1968 *ConAu P-1*
Den, Petr *ConAu X*
Den-Boer, James *DrAP&F 83*
Denali, Peter *ConAu X*
DeNatale, Francine *WrDr 84*
DeNauroy, Rene *IntAu&W 82X*
Denbeaux, Fred J 1914- *ConAu 5R*
Denbie, Roger *ConAu X*
Denbigh, Kenneth George 1911- *ConAu 106,*
  WrDr 84
DenBoer, James 1937- *ConAu 10NR*
DenBoer, James D 1937- *ConAu 21R, ConP 80,*
  WrDr 84
Denby, Edwin 1903-1983 *ConAu 110*
Denby, Edwin Orr 1903- *DcLEL 1940*
Dendel, Esther 1910- *ConAu 102*
Dender, Jay *ConAu X, IntAu&W 82X*
Dendy, Marshall C 1902- *ConAu P-2*
DeNeef, Arthur Leigh 1942- *ConAu 102*
Deneen, James R 1928- *ConAu 45*
Denenberg, Herbert S 1929- *ConAu 37R*
DeNeufville, Richard 1939- *ConAu 53,*
  WrDr 84
Denevan, William M 1931- *ConAu 41R*
DeNevers, Noel 1932- *ConAu 37R*

DeNevi, Donald P 1937- *ConAu 37R*
Denfeld, Duane 1939- *ConAu 41R*
Deng, William 1929- *ConAu 13R*
Dengler, Dieter 1938- *ConAu 102*
Dengler, Marianna 1935- *ConAu 102*
Denham, Alice *DrAP&F 83*
Denham, Alice 1933- *ConAu 21R*
Denham, Avery Strakosch d1970 *ConAu 104*
Denham, Bertie 1927- *ConAu 93*
Denham, H M 1897- *ConAu 61*
Denham, Henry Mangles 1897- *IntAu&W 82*
Denham, Mary Orr 1918- *ConAu 1R, –2NR*
Denham, Reginald 1894- *ConAu P-1*
Denham, Reginald 1894-1983 *ConAu 109*
Denham, Robert D 1938- *ConAu 53*
Denham, Sully *ConAu X*
Denhardt, Robert Moorman 1912- *ConAu 101*
DenHartog, Jacob P 1901- *WrDr 84*
DenHollander, Arie Nicolaas Jan 1906-1976
  ConAu P-2
Denholm, David 1924- *WrDr 84*
Denholm, Therese Mary Zita White 1933-
  ConAu 9R
Denholtz, Elaine *DrAP&F 83*
Denholtz, Elaine 1932- *ConAu 73,*
  NatPD 81[port]
Dening, Greg 1931- *ConAu 107*
Denis, Armand 1896?-1971 *ConAu 104*
Denis, Barbara J 1940- *ConAu 81*
Denis, Charlotte *ConAu X*
Denis, Guy 1942- *IntAu&W 82*
Denis, Laura *IntAu&W 82X*
Denis, Michaela Holdsworth *ConAu 13R*
Denis, Paul 1909- *ConAu 21R*
Denise, Patricia 1922- *CreCan 1*
Denisoff, R Serge 1939- *ConAu 33R, WrDr 84*
Denison, Barbara 1926- *ConAu 13R*
Denison, Corrie *ConAu X*
Denison, Dulcie Winifred Catherine 1920-
  IntAu&W 82
Denison, Edward Fulton 1915- *ConAu 21R,*
  IntAu&W 82, WrDr 84
Denison, Merrill 1893- *CreCan 1*
Denison, Michael 1915- *ConAu 109, WrDr 84*
Denison, Muriel Goggin 1885-1954 *CreCan 1*
Denison, Norman 1925- *ConAu 65*
Denisova, Alexandra *CreCan 1*
DeNiverville, Louis *CreCan 1*
Denker, Henry 1912- *AuNews 1, CnMD SUP,*
  ConAu 33R, WrDr 84
Denkler, Horst 1935- *ConAu 4NR, –53,*
  IntAu&W 82
Denkstein, Vladimir 1906- *ConAu 103*
Denman, Donald Robert 1911- *ConAu 8NR, –61,*
  WrDr 84
Denmark, Florence L 1932- *ConAu 85*
Denmark, Harrison *ConAu X*
Dennehy, Raymond L 1934- *ConAu 109*
Dennenberg, Herbert 1929- *WrDr 84*
Dennes, William Ray 1898- *ConAu 73*
Dennett, Daniel C 1942- *ConAu 97*
Dennett, Herbert Victor 1893- *ConAu 5R, –5NR*
Dennett, Tyler 1883-1949 *TwCA, TwCA SUP*
Denney, Diana 1910- *ConAu 104, SmATA 25*
Denney, Myron Keith 1930- *ConAu 102*
Denney, Reuel Nicholas 1913- *ConAu 1R, –2NR,*
  IntWWP 82
Denney, Ruell *DrAP&F 83*
Denning, Baron 1899- *WrDr 84*
Denning, Basil W 1928- *ConAu 33R*
Denning, Melita *ConAu X*
Denning, Patricia *ConAu X*
Dennis, Arthur *ConAu X*
Dennis, Benjamin Gumbu 1929- *ConAu 45*
Dennis, C J 1876-1938 *LongCTC, TwCWr*
Dennis, Carl *DrAP&F 83*
Dennis, Carl 1939- *ConAu 77*
Dennis, Charles 1946- *ConAu 65*
Dennis, Everette Eugene 1942- *ConAu 41R,*
  IntAu&W 82
Dennis, Geoffrey Pomeroy 1892-1963 *LongCTC,*
  TwCA, TwCA SUP
Dennis, Henry C 1918- *ConAu 41R*
Dennis, James M 1932- *ConAu 102*
Dennis, John V 1916- *ConAu 107*
Dennis, Landt 1937- *ConAu 65*
Dennis, Lane T 1943- *ConAu 93*
Dennis, Lawrence 1893-1977 *ConAu 73*
Dennis, Morgan 1891?-1960 *SmATA 18*
Dennis, Nigel 1912- *CnMD, CnMWL,*
  ConAu 25R, ConDr 82, ConLC 8,
  ConNov 82, CroCD, DcLB 13[port],

–15[port], *DcLEL 1940, EncWL 2,*
  ModBrL, ModWD SUP, ModWD, TwCWr,
  WorAu, WrDr 84
Dennis, Patrick *ConAu X, WorAu*
Dennis, Peggy 1909- *ConAu 77*
Dennis, Peter 1945- *ConAu 41R*
Dennis, Ralph *AuNews 1*
Dennis, Robert C 1920- *ConAu 101,*
  IntAu&W 82
Dennis, Robert C 1920-1983 *ConAu 110*
Dennis, Suzanne Easton 1922- *ConAu 25R*
Dennis, Wayne 1905-1976 *ConAu 17R, –65, –69*
Dennis, Wesley 1903-1966 *SmATA 18*
Dennis-Jones, Harold 1915- *ConAu 8NR, –57,*
  WrDr 84
Dennison, A Dudley, Jr. 1914- *ConAu 9NR, –57*
Dennison, George 1925- *ConAu 101*
Dennison, George M 1935- *ConAu 53*
Dennison, Laura *DrAP&F 83*
Dennison, Sam 1926- *ConAu 109*
Dennison, Shane 1933- *ConAu 73*
Denniston, Denise 1946- *ConAu 69*
Denniston, Elinore 1900-1978 *ConAu 81,*
  SmATA 24N
Denniston, Lyle 1931- *ConAu 65*
Denny, Alma 1912- *ConAu 89*
Denny, Brian *ConAu X*
Denny, John Howard 1920- *ConAu P-1*
Denny, Ludwell 1894-1970 *ConAu 29R*
Denny, M Ray 1918- *ConAu 41R*
Denny, Norman George 1901- *ConAu 107*
Denny-Brown, Derek Ernest 1901-1981
  ConAu 103
Dennys, Rodney Onslow 1911- *ConAu 85*
Denoeu, Francois 1898-1975 *ConAu 53*
Denomme, Robert Thomas 1930- *ConAu 25R,*
  IntWWP 82
Denoon, Donald 1940- *ConAu 73*
DeNorby, Irene Jellinek *CreCan 1*
DeNovo, John A 1916- *ConAu 9R*
Densen-Gerber, Judianne 1934- *ConAu 37R,*
  WrDr 84
Densford, Edna 1920- *IntWWP 82*
Denslow, W W 1856-1915 *SmATA 16*
Denson, Alan *IntWWP 82*
Denson, John Lee 1903-1982 *ConAu 108*
Dent, Alan Holmes 1905-1978 *ConAu 5NR, –9R,*
  DcLEL 1940, LongCTC
Dent, Anthony Austen 1915- *ConAu 25R*
Dent, Barbara Patricia 1919- *WrDr 84*
Dent, Colin 1921- *ConAu 13R, WrDr 84*
Dent, Harold Collett 1894- *ConAu 5R, –5NR,*
  IntAu&W 82, WrDr 84
Dent, Harry 1930- *ConAu 81*
Dent, J M 1849-1926 *LongCTC*
Dent, Lester 1904-1959 *TwCCr&M 80,*
  TwCSFW
Dent, Robert William 1917- *ConAu 105*
Dent, Tom *DrAP&F 83, LivgBAA*
Dentan, Michel 1926- *IntAu&W 82*
Dentan, Robert Claude 1907- *ConAu 1R, –2NR*
Dentay, Elizabeth Benson Guy *CreCan 2*
Dentinger, Stephen *ConAu X,*
  IntAu&W 82X, TwCCr&M 80
Dentler, Robert A 1928- *ConAu 1R, –1NR*
Denton, Charles Frederick 1941- *WrDr 84*
Denton, Charles Frederick 1942- *ConAu 37R*
Denton, H M 1882- *ConAu P-1*
Denton, J H 1939- *ConAu 41R*
Denton, Jeremiah A, Jr. 1924- *ConAu 69*
Denton, Jon *ConAmTC*
Denton, Wallace 1928- *ConAu 1R*
Dentry, Robert *ConAu X*
Denues, Celia 1915- *ConAu 41R*
Denver, Boone *ConAu X*
Denver, Drake C *ConAu X, TwCWW,*
  WrDr 84
Denver, Lee *TwCWW*
Denver, Rod *ConAu X*
Denver, Walt *ConAu X*
Denys, Teresa 1947- *ConAu 105*
Denzel, Justin F 1917- *ConAu 4NR, –53*
Denzer, Ann *ConAu X*
Denzer, Ann Wiseman *ConAu X, SmATA X*
Denzer, Peter W 1921- *ConAu 5R*
Denzin, Norman K 1941- *ConAu 29R*
DeOliveira Campos, Roberto 1917- *IntAu&W 82*
Deon, Michel 1919- *ConAu 37R*
Deotale, Chandrakant 1936- *IntWWP 82*
DeOtero, Blas *ModRL*
DePalma, Brian 1940- *ConAu 109, ConLC 20*

Diener, Mary Eleanor 1929- *IntWWP 82*
Diener, Royce 1918- *ConAu 110*
Dienes, C Thomas 1940- *ConAu 11NR, –69*
Dienstag, Eleanor 1938- *ConAu 65*
Dienstein, William 1909- *ConAu P-1*
Dienstfrey, Patricia 1939- *IntWWP 82*
Dierenfield, Richard Bruce 1922- *ConAu 17R, IntAu&W 82, WrDr 84*
Dierickx, C W 1921- *ConAu 61*
Dierks, Jack C 1930- *WrDr 84*
Dierks, Jack Cameron 1930- *ConAu 29R*
Diers, Carol Jean 1933- *ConAu 33R*
Diesendorf, Margaret 1912- *IntWWP 82*
Diesing, Paul R 1922- *ConAu 1R, –2NR*
Dieska, L Joseph 1913- *ConAu 37R*
Dieskau, Dietrich Fischer *ConAu X*
Dietl, Ulla 1940- *ConAu 33R*
Dietrich, John E 1913- *ConAu 17R*
Dietrich, Margret 1920- *IntAu&W 82*
Dietrich, Noah 1889-1982 *ConAu 106, –45*
Dietrich, R F 1936- *ConAu 21R*
Dietrich, Richard V 1924- *ConAu 4NR, –53*
Dietrich, Robert *ConAu X*
Dietrich, Robert S 1928- *ConAu 1R*
Dietrich, Wilson G 1916- *ConAu 25R*
Dietz, Betty Warner *ConAu X*
Dietz, David Henry 1897- *ConAu 1R, –2NR, IntAu&W 82, SmATA 10*
Dietz, Elisabeth H 1908- *ConAu 29R*
Dietz, Howard 1896- *ConAu 53, ConDr 82D, ModWD*
Dietz, Howard 1896-1983 *ConAu 110*
Dietz, Lew 1906- *WrDr 84*
Dietz, Lew 1907- *ConAu 3NR, –5R, SmATA 11*
Dietz, Marjorie J 1918- *ConAu 65*
Dietz, Norman D 1930- *ConAu 10NR, –21R*
Dietz, Peter O 1935- *ConAu 33R*
Dietze, Charles Edgar 1919- *ConAu 69*
Dietze, Gottfried 1922- *ConAu 21R*
Dietzel, Paul 1924- *ConAu 21R*
Dietzenschmidt, Anton 1893-1955 *CnMD*
Dieudonne, Jean Alexandre 1906- *IntAu&W 82*
Diez-Canedo, Enrique 1879-1944 *CIDMEL 80*
Diez DelCorral, Luis 1911- *ConAu 13R*
DiFiore, Anthony G *DrAP&F 83*
DiFranco, Fiorenza 1932- *ConAu 1NR, –45*
Digennaro, Joseph 1939- *ConAu 53*
Digges, Jeremiah *ConAu X*
Digges, Sister Mary Laurentia 1910- *ConAu P-2*
Diggins, John P 1935- *ConAu 37R*
Diggle, James 1944- *ConAu 61*
Diggory, James C 1920- *ConAu 9NR, –21R*
Diggs, Bernard James 1916- *ConAu 106*
Diggs, Elizabeth 1939- *ConAu 109, NatPD 81[port]*
DiGiacomo, Salvatore 1860-1934 *CIDMEL 80, EncWL 2*
DiGiovanni, Edoardo *CreCan 2*
DiGirolamo, Vittorio 1928- *ConAu 45*
D'Ignazio, Fred 1949- *ConAu 110*
DiGrazia, Thomas d1983 *SmATA 32[port]*
DiGuisa, Giano *ConAu X*
Dihoff, Gretchen 1942- *ConAu 41R*
Dijkstra, Bram 1938- *ConAu 37R*
Dikeman, May *DrAP&F 83*
Diklay, M *IntWWP 82X*
Diko *IntWWP 82X*
Dikshit, R D 1939- *ConAu 10NR, –65*
Diktonius, Elmer Rafael 1896-1961 *CIDMEL 80, EncWL 2*
Dikty, Julian May *ConAu X*
Dikty, T E 1920- *ConSFA*
Dil, Zakhmi *ConAu X*
DiLampedusa, Giuseppe *ModRL*
Dilcock, Noreen 1907- *ConAu 103, IntAu&W 82, WrDr 84*
DiLella, Alexander Anthony 1929- *ConAu 21R, WrDr 84*
DiLello, Richard 1945- *ConAu 41R*
DiLeo, Joseph H 1902- *ConAu 33R, WrDr 84*
Diles, Dave 1931- *ConAu 8NR, –57*
Diles, David L 1931- *MichAu 80*
Dilke, Annabel 1942- *ConAu P-1*
Dilke, Caroline 1940- *ConAu 102, WrDr 84*
Dilke, Oswald Ashton Wentworth 1915- *ConAu 69, IntAu&W 82, WrDr 84*
Dilks, David Neville 1938- *ConAu 8NR, –61, IntAu&W 82*
Dilks, Elizabeth-Thomas S 1918- *IntWWP 82*
Dill, Alonzo T 1914- *ConAu 37R*
Dill, Marshall, Jr. 1916- *ConAu 1R*

Dillard, Annie *DrAP&F 83*
Dillard, Annie 1945- *ConAu 3NR, –49, ConLC 9, DcLB Y80B[port], IntAu&W 82, SmATA 10, WrDr 84*
Dillard, Dudley 1913- *ConAu 25R*
Dillard, Emil *DrAP&F 83*
Dillard, Emil Lee 1921- *ConAu 57, IntWWP 82*
Dillard, Hardy Cross 1902- *WrDr 84*
Dillard, J L 1924- *ConAu 41R*
Dillard, James *TwCWW*
Dillard, Polly Hargis 1916- *ConAu 5NR, –9R, SmATA 24[port]*
Dillard, R H W *DrAP&F 83*
Dillard, R H W 1937- *ConAu 10NR, –21R, ConLC 5, ConP 80, DcLB 5[port], WrDr 84*
Dille, Denijs 1904- *IntAu&W 82*
Dille, John M 1921?-1971 *ConAu 33R*
Dille, Robert Crabtree 1924?-1983 *ConAu 109*
Dillehay, Ronald C 1935- *ConAu 21R*
Dillenbeck, Marsden V *ConAu P-2*
Dillenberger, Jane 1916- *ConAu 7NR, –17R*
Dillenberger, John 1918- *ConAu 1R, –2NR, WrDr 84*
Diller, Edward 1925- *ConAu 85*
Diller, Phyllis 1917- *ConAu 81*
Dilles, James 1923- *ConAu 1R*
Dilley, Frank B 1931- *ConAu 13R*
Dilliard, Irving 1904- *ConAu 21R*
Dilligan, Robert J 1940- *ConAu 108*
Dilling, Judith *ConAu X*
Dillingham, Beth 1927- *ConAu 53*
Dillingham, William B 1930- *ConAu 13R, WrDr 84*
Dillistone, Frederick William 1903- *ConAu 1R, –5NR*
Dillman, David D 1900?-1983 *ConAu 110*
Dillon, Barbara 1927- *ConAu 110*
Dillon, Bert 1937- *ConAu 77*
Dillon, Conley Hall 1906- *ConAu 1R*
Dillon, David 1941- *ConAu 69*
Dillon, Diane C 1933- *SmATA 15[port]*
Dillon, Eilis 1920- *ConAu 4NR, –9R, ConLC 17, SmATA 2, TwCCW 83, WrDr 84*
Dillon, George 1906-1968 *ConAmA, ConAu 89, TwCA, TwCA SUP*
Dillon, George Lewis 1944- *ConAu 102*
Dillon, J T 1940- *ConAu 33R*
Dillon, John M 1939- *ConAu 77*
Dillon, Lawrence S 1910- *ConAu 45, IntAu&W 82*
Dillon, Leo 1933- *SmATA 15[port]*
Dillon, Martin 1949- *ConAu 61*
Dillon, Merton L 1924- *ConAu 13R*
Dillon, Millicent G *DrAP&F 83*
Dillon, Millicent G 1925- *ConAu 65*
Dillon, Norma Louise 1948- *IntAu&W 82*
Dillon, Richard Hugh 1924- *ConAu 8NR, –17R*
Dillon, Wallace Neil 1922- *ConAu 1R*
Dillon, Wilton Sterling 1923- *ConAu 37R, WrDr 84*
Dilly Tante *ConAu X*
Dilman, Ilham 1930- *WrDr 84*
Dilmen, Gungor 1930- *CIDMEL 80*
Dilorenzo, Ronald Eugene 1931- *ConAu 110*
Dilsaver, Paul *DrAP&F 83*
Dilson, Jesse 1914- *ConAu 25R, SmATA 24, WrDr 84*
Diltz, Bert Case 1894- *ConAu 9NR, –65*
DiMarco, Gino *ConAu X*
DiMarco, Luis Eugenio 1937- *ConAu 2NR, –45*
Dimberg, Ronald G 1938- *ConAu 61*
Dimbleby, Jonathan 1944- *ConAu 108, WrDr 84*
DiMeglio, Clara 1933- *ConAu 97*
DiMeglio, John E 1934- *ConAu 77*
Diment, Adam *ASpks, TwCCr&M 80, WrDr 84*
DiMento, Joseph F 1947- *ConAu 69*
Dimeo, Steven *DrAP&F 83*
Dimer, Eugenia *IntWWP 82X*
DiMichele, Mary 1949- *ConAu 97*
Dimick, Kenneth M 1937- *ConAu 29R*
Dimmette, Celia Puhr 1896- *ConAu P-2, IntWWP 82*
Dimmitt, Richard Bertrand 1925- *ConAu 17R*
Dimnet, Ernest 1866-1954 *TwCA[port], TwCA SUP*
Dimock, Edward Cameron, Jr. 1929- *ConAu 102*
Dimock, Gladys Ogden 1908- *ConAu 5R*
Dimock, Hedley G 1928- *ConAu 5R*

Dimock, Marshall Edward 1903- *ConAu 1R, –2NR, WrDr 84*
DiMona, Joseph *ConAu 104*
Dimond, E Grey 1918- *ConAu 85*
Dimond, Mary Clark *ConAu 93*
Dimond, Stanley E 1905- *ConAu 13R*
Dimond, Stuart John 1938- *ConAu 33R*
Dimondstein, Geraldine 1926- *ConAu 33R*
Dimont, Madelon 1938- *ConAu 41R*
Dimont, Max I 1912- *ConAu 17R*
Dimont, Penelope *ConAu X, WrDr 84*
Dimson, Wendy *ConAu X*
Dine, Carol *DrAP&F 83*
Dine, S S Van *LongCTC, TwCA, TwCA SUP*
Dineley, David Lawrence 1927- *ConAu 101*
Diner, Hasia R 1946- *ConAu 9NR, –61*
Diner, Steven J 1944- *ConAu 110*
Dinerman, Beatrice 1933- *ConAu 13R, WrDr 84*
Dinerman, Helen Schneider 1921?-1974 *ConAu 53*
Dinerstein, Herbert S 1919- *ConAu 108*
Dines, Glen 1925- *ConAu 9R*
Dines, Harry Glen 1925- *SmATA 7*
Dines, Michael 1916- *ConAu 103, IntAu&W 82*
Dinesen, Isak 1885-1962 *CIDMEL 80, ConAu X, ConLC 10, EncWL 2, LongCTC, TwCA, TwCA SUP, TwCWr*
Ding, J N *ConAu X*
Dinger, Aagot 1910- *IntAu&W 82*
Dinges, John 1941- *ConAu 101*
Dingle, Herbert 1890- *ConAu 13R*
Dingman, Roger 1938- *ConAu 93*
Dings, John 1939- *ConAu 41R*
Dingwall, Eric John *ConAu 89*
Dingwall, W Orr 1934- *ConAu 21R*
Dingwall, Joyce *TwCRGW, WrDr 84*
Dingwell, Joyce *TwCRGW, WrDr 84*
Dinhofer, Alfred D 1929- *ConAu 25R*
Dinhofer, Alfred D 1930- *WrDr 84*
Dinitz, Simon 1926- *ConAu 37R*
Dinkin, Robert J 1940- *ConAu 107*
Dinkmeyer, Don C 1924- *ConAu 41R*
Dinman, Bertram David 1925- *ConAu 109*
Dinnan, James A 1929- *ConAu 69*
Dinneen, Betty 1929- *ConAu 8NR, –57*
Dinnerstein, Leonard 1934- *ConAu 9NR, –21R, WrDr 84*
Dino *ConAu X*
Dino, Isidoro M I-D 1910- *IntWWP 82*
Dinsdale, Patricia Joudry *CreCan 2*
Dinsdale, Tim 1924- *ConAu 1R, –2NR, SmATA 11, WrDr 84*
Dinsky, Lazar 1891?-1976 *ConAu 69*
Dinsmore, Herman H 1900?-1980 *ConAu 97*
Dintenfass, Mark *DrAP&F 83*
Dintenfass, Mark 1941- *ConAu 11NR, –25R, WrDr 84*
Dintiman, George B 1936- *ConAu 5NR, –53*
Dinwiddie, Elza Teresa *ConAu 110*
Dinwiddie, Faye Love 1908- *IntAu&W 82*
Diogenes *IntAu&W 82X*
Diole, Philippe Victor 1908- *ConAu 53*
Diomede, Matthew *DrAP&F 83*
Diomede, Matthew 1940- *IntWWP 82*
Dion, Sister Anita 1918- *ConAu 2NR*
Dion, Gerard 1912- *ConAu 41R*
Dion, Sister Raymond DeJesus 1918- *ConAu 5R*
Dione, Robert L 1922- *ConAu 57*
Dionisopoulos, P Allan 1921- *ConAu 29R*
Dionne, Claire Gagnier *CreCan 1*
Dionne, Rene 1929- *IntAu&W 82*
Dionysus *IntAu&W 82X*
Diop, Birago 1906- *CIDMEL 80, EncWL 2, ModBlW, ModFrL*
Diop, Cheikh Anta 1923- *ConAu 110*
Diop, David Mandessi 1927-1960 *ModBlW, ModFrL*
Dioramananda *DrAP&F 83, IntWWP 82X*
DiOrio, Al 1950- *ConAu 9NR, –57*
Diorio, Margaret *IntWWP 82*
Diorio, Margaret Toarello *DrAP&F 83*
Diotima *ConAu X*
Dipalma, Ray *DrAP&F 83*
DiPalma, Ray 1943- *ConAu 29R*
DiPasquale, Dominic 1932- *ConAu 57*
DiPasquale, Emanual *DrAP&F 83*
DiPego, Gerald F 1941- *ConAu 85*
DiPersio, Michael S 1934- *ConAu 110*
DiPeso, Charles C 1920- *ConAu 57*
DiPietro, Robert Joseph 1932- *ConAu 7NR, –17R, WrDr 84*

Dodd, Donald B 1940- *ConAu 6NR, -57*
Dodd, Ed Benton 1902- *ConAu 73, SmATA 4*
Dodd, Edward *ConAu 49*
Dodd, Edward Howard, Jr. 1905- *ConAu 49*
Dodd, James Harvey 1892-1969 *ConAu 1R, -103*
Dodd, Lynley 1941- *ConAu 107*
Dodd, Marguerite 1911- *ConAu 5R*
Dodd, Philip W 1904?-1983 *ConAu 110*
Dodd, Stuart C 1900-1975 *ConAu 41R*
Dodd, Thomas J 1907-1971 *ConAu 29R*
Dodd, Wayne *DrAP&F 83*
Dodd, Wayne D 1930- *ConAu 33R, IntAu&W 82, IntWWP 82, WrDr 84*
Dodd, William Edward 1869-1940 *DcLB 17[port]*
Dodderidge, Esme 1916- *ConAu 97*
Dodds, E R 1893-1979 *ConAu 101*
Dodds, Gordon Barlow 1932- *ConAu 5R*
Dodds, John Wendell 1902- *ConAu 5R, IntAu&W 82, WrDr 84*
Dodds, Robert Clyde 1918- *ConAu 5R*
Dodds, Robert H 1914-1976 *ConAu P-2*
Dodds, Tracy Ann 1952- *ConAu 85*
Doder, Dusko 1937- *ConAu 102*
Doderer, Heimito Von 1896-1966 *CIDMEL 80, ConAu X, EncWL 2, ModGL, TwCWr, WhoTwCL, WorAu*
Dodge, Bertha Sanford 1902- *ConAu 2NR, -5R, SmATA 8, WrDr 84*
Dodge, Calvert R 1931- *ConAu 61*
Dodge, Daniel *ConAu X*
Dodge, David 1910- *ConAu 65, TwCCr&M 80, WorAu, WrDr 84*
Dodge, Dick 1918?-1974 *ConAu 49*
Dodge, Dorothy R 1927- *ConAu 45*
Dodge, Ernest Stanley 1913-1980 *ConAu 1R, -2NR, -97, IntAu&W 82*
Dodge, Fremont *ConAu X*
Dodge, Gil *ConAu X*
Dodge, H Robert 1929- *ConAu 29R*
Dodge, Langdon *ConAu X*
Dodge, Lon *DrAP&F 83*
Dodge, Lowell 1940- *ConAu 33R*
Dodge, Mabel *ConAmA*
Dodge, Marshall 1935- *ConAu 89*
Dodge, Mary Elizabeth Mapes 1831?-1905 *SmATA 21[port]*
Dodge, Mary Mapes 1831?-1905 *ConAu 109*
Dodge, Nicholas A 1933- *ConAu 65*
Dodge, Norton T 1927- *ConAu 25R*
Dodge, Peter 1926- *ConAu 37R, WrDr 84*
Dodge, Richard Holmes 1926- *ConAu 8NR, -13R*
Dodge, Steve *ConAu X*
Dodge, Wendell Phillips 1883-1976 *ConAu 65*
Dodgshon, Robert A 1941- *WrDr 84*
Dodson, Daniel B 1918- *ConAu 3NR, -9R, WrDr 84*
Dodson, Fitzhugh James 1923- *ConAu 29R*
Dodson, James L 1910- *ConAu 53*
Dodson, Kenneth 1907- *WrDr 84*
Dodson, Kenneth MacKenzie 1907- *ConAu 1R, SmATA 11*
Dodson, Oscar H 1905- *ConAu 5R*
Dodson, Owen *DrAP&F 83*
Dodson, Owen 1914-1983 *ConAu 110*
Dodson, Owen Vincent 1914- *ConAu 65, LivgBAA*
Dodson, Richard S, Jr. 1896- *ConAu P-1*
Dodson, Susan 1941- *ConAu 97*
Dodson, Tom 1914- *ConAu 29R*
Dodwell, Peter C 1930- *ConAu 29R, IntAu&W 82, WrDr 84*
Doebler, Charles H 1925- *ConAu 21R*
Doebler, John 1932- *ConAu 89*
Doeblin, Alfred 1878-1957 *ConAu 110*
Doehring, Donald G 1927- *ConAu 29R*
Doell, Charles E 1894- *ConAu P-1*
Doely, Sarah Bentley *ConAu X*
Doenecke, Justus Drew 1938- *ConAu 104*
Doenitz, Karl 1891-1980 *ConAu 103*
Doerffler, Alfred 1884- *ConAu 1R*
Doeringer, Peter B 1941- *ConAu 61*
Doerkson, Margaret 1921- *ConAu 105*
Doermann, Humphrey 1930- *ConAu 25R*
Doerr, Arthur H 1924- *ConAu 41R*
Doerschuk, Anna Beatrice 1880?-1974 *ConAu 49*
Doeser, Linda 1950- *ConAu 81*
Doezema, Linda Pegman 1948- *ConAu 102*
Dogan, Mattei 1920- *ConAu 25R, IntAu&W 82*
Dogg, Professor R L *ConAu X*
Doggett, Frank 1906- *ConAu P-2*

Dogyear, Drew *ConAu X*
Dohan, Mary Helen 1914- *ConAu 85, WrDr 84*
Dohanyi Lajos, Lajos *CreCan 1*
Doherty, Catherine DeHueck 1900- *ConAu 65*
Doherty, Charles Hugh 1913- *ConAu 9R, SmATA 6*
Doherty, Dennis J 1932- *ConAu 102*
Doherty, Eddie *ConAu X*
Doherty, Edward J 1890-1975 *ConAu 57, -65*
Doherty, Felix 1908- *NatPD 81[port]*
Doherty, Geoffrey 1927- *ConSFA*
Doherty, Herbert J, Jr. 1926- *ConAu 1R*
Doherty, Ivy Duffy *ConAu X*
Doherty, Ivy R Duffy 1922- *ConAu 5NR, -9R*
Doherty, Robert W 1935- *ConAu 21R*
Doherty, William Thomas, Jr. 1923- *ConAu 53*
Dohme, Alvin R L 1910- *ConAu 110*
Dohrenwend, Barbara Snell 1927- *ConAu 25R*
Dohrenwend, Barbara Snell 1927-1982 *ConAu 11NR*
Doig, Desmond 1921- *ConAu 69*
Doig, Ivan 1939- *ConAu 81*
Doig, Jameson W 1933- *ConAu 37R*
Doimi DiDelupis, Ingrid *ConAu X*
Doinas, Stefan Augustin 1922- *EncWL 2*
Dokey, Richard *DrAP&F 83*
Dokmai Sot 1905-1963 *EncWL 2*
Dolan, Anthony *DrAP&F 83*
Dolan, Anthony R 1948- *ConAu 73*
Dolan, Edward F, Jr. 1924- *ConAu 33R, SmATA 31*
Dolan, Jay P 1936- *ConAu 81*
Dolan, John Patrick 1923-1982? *ConAu 2NR, -5R, -106*
Dolan, John Richard 1893- *ConAu 9R*
Dolan, Josephine Aloyse 1913- *ConAu 49*
Dolan, Paul 1910- *ConAu 9R*
Dolan, Winthrop W 1909- *ConAu 57*
Dolberg, Alexander 1933- *ConAu 33R*
Dolbier, Maurice 1912- *ConAu 65*
Dolby, James Louis 1926- *ConAu 45*
Dolce, Philip C 1941- *ConAu 57*
Dolci, Danilo 1924- *TwCWr, WorAu*
Dolden, A Stuart 1893- *ConAu 105*
Dole, Gertrude E 1915- *ConAu 41R*
Dole, Jeremy H 1932- *ConAu 17R*
Dole, Nathan Haskell 1852-1935 *TwCA, TwCA SUP*
Dolega, Christine *DrAP&F 83*
Dolezel, Lubomir 1922- *ConAu 45*
Dolgoff, Ralph L 1932- *ConAu 33R*
Dolgoff, Sam 1902- *ConAu 102*
Dolgun, Alexander Michael 1926- *ConAu 104*
Doliber, Earl L 1947- *ConAu 49*
Dolim, Mary Nuzum 1925- *ConAu 17R*
Dolin, Edwin 1928- *ConAu 45*
Dolin, Samuel Joseph 1917- *CreCan 2*
Doliner, Roy 1932- *ConAu 1R, -1NR*
Dolinger, Jane 1932- *AuNews 2*
Dolinsky, Meyer 1923- *ConAu 57*
Dolinsky, Mike 1923- *ConAu X*
Dolit, Alan 1934- *ConAu 61*
Doll, Richard 1912- *ConAu 108, WrDr 84*
Doll, Ronald C 1913- *ConAu 8NR, -13R, IntAu&W 82, WrDr 84*
Dollar, Jimmy *ConAu X*
Dollar, Truman E 1937- *ConAu 97*
Dollard, John 1900-1980 *ConAu 102*
Dollen, Charles Joseph 1926- *ConAu 5R, -6NR*
Dolley, Michael 1925-1983 *ConAu 109*
Dolliver, Barbara Babcock 1927- *ConAu 5R*
Dolloff, Eugene Dinsmore 1890-1972 *ConAu 1R, -103*
Dolmatch, Theodore B 1924- *ConAu 41R*
Dolmetsch, Carl Frederick 1911- *IntAu&W 82, WrDr 84*
Dolmetsch, Carl R 1924- *ConAu 21R*
Dolores, Sister Marian *ConAu X*
Dolphin *DrAP&F 83*
Dolphin, Robert, Jr. 1935- *ConAu 29R*
Dols, Michael W 1942- *ConAu 69*
Dolson, Hildegarde 1908- *ConAu X, -5R, SmATA 5, TwCCr&M 80, WrDr 84*
Doman, Glenn 1919- *WrDr 84*
Doman, Glenn J 1919- *ConAu 61*
Doman, June *ConAu X*
Domanovic, Radoje 1873-1908 *ModSL 2*
Domanska, Janina *AuNews 1, ConAu 11NR, -17R, SmATA 6*
Domar, Evsey D 1914- *WrDr 84*
Domaradzki, Theodore Felix 1910- *ConAu 1NR, -45*

Domb, Cyril 1920- *ConAu 109*
D'Ombrain, Nicholas 1944- *WrDr 84*
Dombrovsky, Yury Osipovich 1909-1978 *CIDMEL 80*
Dombrowski, Gerard *DrAP&F 83*
Dombrowski, James A 1897-1983 *ConAu 109*
Domecq, Bustos *IntAu&W 82X*
Domecq, H Bustos *ConAu X*
Domenchina, Juan Jose 1898-1959 *CIDMEL 80*
Domencich, Thomas A *ConAu 29R*
Domergue, Maurice 1907- *ConAu 25R*
Domhoff, G William 1936- *ConAu 45, ConIsC 1[port]*
Domin, Hilde 1912- *CIDMEL 80, EncWL 2, IntAu&W 82, IntWWP 82, ModGL*
Domingo, Jorge Ignacio 1945- *ConAu 102*
Dominguez, Richard H 1941- *ConAu 102*
Dominguez Martin, Joaquin 1925- *IntAu&W 82*
Domini, John *DrAP&F 83*
Domini, Jon *ConAu X*
Domini, Rey *ConAu X*
Dominian, Jack 1929- *ConAu 104, WrDr 84*
Dominic, Magie *DrAP&F 83*
Dominic, Sister Mary *ConAu X, IntAu&W 82X*
Dominic, R B *ConAu X, TwCCr&M 80, WorAu 1970*
Dominick, Raymond Hunter, III 1945- *ConAu 110*
Dominique, Francois *CreCan 2*
Domino, John *SmATA X*
Dominowski, Roger L 1939- *ConAu 1NR, -45*
Dominy, Eric Norman 1918- *ConAu 9R, WrDr 84*
Domjan, Joseph 1907- *ConAu 3NR, -9R, SmATA 25[port]*
Domke, Helmut George 1914-1974 *ConAu P-1*
Domke, Martin 1892- *ConAu P-1*
Dommen, Arthur J 1934- *ConAu 9R*
Dommermuth, William P 1925- *ConAu 17R, WrDr 84*
Dommeyer, Frederick Charles 1909- *ConAu 37R*
Doms, Andre 1932- *IntWWP 82*
Domville, Eric 1929- *ConAu 41R*
Domville, James DeBeaujeu 1933- *CreCan 2*
Don Tomasito *ConAu X*
Donabedian, Avedis 1919- *ConAu 73*
Donagan, Alan 1925- *ConAu 5R*
Donagan, Barbara 1927- *ConAu 17R*
Donaghy, Henry J 1930- *ConAu 53*
Donaghy, William A 1910?-1975 *ConAu 53*
Donahoe, Bernard Francis 1932- *ConAu 17R*
Donahoe, Jim *DrAP&F 83*
Donahue, Don 1942- *ConAu 69*
Donahue, Francis James 1917- *ConAu 17R, IntAu&W 82, WrDr 84*
Donahue, George T 1911- *ConAu 17R*
Donahue, Jack Clifford 1917- *ConAu 97*
Donahue, Kenneth 1915- *ConAu 102*
Donahue, Phil 1935- *ConAu 107*
Donahue, Roy L 1908- *ConAu 89*
Donald, Aida DiPace 1930- *ConAu 21R*
Donald, David Herbert 1920- *ConAu 4NR, -9R, DcLB 17[port], WorAu*
Donald, Ian 1910- *WrDr 84*
Donald, Larry W 1945- *ConAu 93*
Donald, Maxwell Bruce 1897-1978 *ConAu 89*
Donald, R V *ConAu X*
Donald, Vivian *ConAu X*
Donald, William 1910- *WrDr 84*
Donalda, Pauline 1882- *CreCan 1*
Donalds, Gordon *ConAu X, SmATA X, WrDr 84*
Donaldson, Betty 1923- *ConAu 103*
Donaldson, E Talbot 1910- *ConAu 2NR, -49*
Donaldson, Elvin F 1903-1972 *ConAu 1R, -103*
Donaldson, Frances 1907- *ConAu 61, WrDr 84*
Donaldson, Gordon 1913- *ConAu 5NR, -13R, IntAu&W 82, WrDr 84*
Donaldson, Ian 1935- *ConAu 69*
Donaldson, John W 1893?-1979 *ConAu 85*
Donaldson, Kenneth 1908- *ConAu 73*
Donaldson, Malcolm 1884- *ConAu P-1*
Donaldson, Margaret 1926- *ConAu 103*
Donaldson, Norman 1922- *ConAu 33R, WrDr 84*
Donaldson, Robert Herschel 1943- *ConAu 85*
Donaldson, Sam 1934- *ConAu 109*
Donaldson, Scott 1928- *ConAu 11NR, -25R, WrDr 84*
Donaldson, Stephen R 1947- *ConAu 89, WrDr 84*

Dorsonville, Max 1943- *ConAu 65*
Dorst, Jean 1924- *WrDr 84*
Dorst, Jean Pierre 1924- *ConAu 3NR, –5R*
Dorst, Tankred 1925- *CnMD SUP, ConAu 41R, CroCD, ModWD*
Dorwart, J M 1944- *ConAu 97*
Dorwart, Reinhold August 1911- *ConAu 65*
Dorworth, Alice Grey 1907- *ConAu 5R*
Dosa, Marta Leszlei *ConAu 45*
Doskocilova *IntAu&W 82X*
Doskocilova, Haná 1936- *ConAu 8NR, –61*
Doskocilova-Sekyrkova, Hana 1936-
IntAu&W 82
DosPassos, John 1896-1970 *CnMD, ConAmA, ConAu 3NR, –29R, ConLC 1, –4, –8, –11, –15, –25[port], DcLB DS1[port], –4, –9[port], EncWL 2[port], LongCTC, ModAL, ModAL SUP, ModWD, TwCA, TwCA SUP, TwCWr, WhoTwCL*
Doss, Helen 1918- *ConAu 6NR, –9R, SmATA 20*
Doss, Margot P 1922- *WrDr 84*
Doss, Margot Patterson 1922- *ConAu 29R, SmATA 6*
Dossage, Jean *ConAu X*
Dossi, Carlo 1849-1910 *CIDMEL 80*
Dossick, Philip 1941- *ConAu 81, IntAu&W 82*
Dostal, Cyril A *DrAP&F 83*
Doster, William C 1921- *ConAu 13R*
Dostoyevsky, Fyodor Mikhaylovich 1821-1881
CIDMEL 80
Dothard, Robert Loos 1909?-1979 *ConAu 85*
Dotson, Floyd 1917- *ConAu 25R*
Dotson, John L, Jr. 1937- *ConAu 105*
Dotson, Lillian O 1921- *ConAu 25R*
Dott, R H, Jr. 1929- *ConAu 53*
Dottig *SmATA X*
Dotts, M Franklin 1929- *ConAu 57*
Dotts, Maryann J 1933- *ConAu 33R, IntAu&W 82, WrDr 84*
Doty, Brant Lee 1921- *ConAu 17R*
Doty, C Stewart 1928- *ConAu 65*
Doty, Carolyn 1941- *ConAu 105*
Doty, Carolyn House *DrAP&F 83*
Doty, Gladys 1908- *ConAu 53*
Doty, Gresdna Ann 1931- *ConAu 41R*
Doty, James Edward 1922- *ConAu 37R*
Doty, Jean Slaughter 1929- *ConAu 2NR, –45, SmATA 28[port]*
Doty, M R *DrAP&F 83*
Doty, Richard 1942- *ConAu 109*
Doty, Robert McIntyre 1933- *ConAu 102*
Doty, Roy 1922- *ConAu 8NR, –53, SmATA 28[port]*
Doty, William G 1939- *ConAu 5NR, –53*
Doty, William Lodewick 1919-1979 *ConAu 1R, –1NR*
Doubiago, Sharon *DrAP&F 83*
Doubleday, Neal Frank 1905-1976 *ConAu 41R*
Doubrovsky, Serge 1928- *ConAu 110*
Doubtfire, Dianne 1918- *WrDr 84*
Doubtfire, Dianne Joan 1918- *ConAu 1R, –1NR, IntAu&W 82, SmATA 29[port]*
Doucet, Louis-Joseph 1874-1959 *CreCan 1*
Doucette, Leonard E 1936- *ConAu 33R*
Douds, Charles Tucker 1898-1982 *ConAu 106*
Dougall, Donald 1920- *IntAu&W 82*
Dougall, Herbert E 1902- *ConAu P-1*
Dougall, Ian *ConDr 82B*
Dougall, Robert 1913- *IntAu&W 82*
Dougan, Michael B 1944- *ConAu 69*
Dougherty, Betty Joyce 1922- *ConAu 61, WrDr 84*
Dougherty, Charles 1922- *SmATA 18*
Dougherty, Ching-Yi 1915- *ConAu 5R*
Dougherty, James 1937- *ConAu 106*
Dougherty, Joanna Foster *ConAu X*
Dougherty, Jude Patrick 1930- *ConAu 45*
Dougherty, Richard 1921- *ConAu 1R, –2NR, WrDr 84*
Dougherty, Richard Martin 1935- *ConAu 33R*
Doughtie, Edward 1935- *ConAu 45*
Doughty, Bradford 1921- *ConAu 65*
Doughty, Charles Montagu 1843-1926 *LongCTC, ModBrL*
Doughty, Nigel *IntAu&W 82X*
Doughty, Nina Beckett 1911- *ConAu 53*
Doughty, Oswald 1889- *ConAu P-1*
Doughty, Paul L 1930- *ConAu 85*
Douglas, Albert *ConAu X, IntAu&W 82X, WrDr 84*
Douglas, Lord Alfred Bruce 1870-1945 *LongCTC*

Douglas, Ann *IntAu&W 82X*
Douglas, Ann C *ConAu X*
Douglas, Arthur 1928- *WrDr 84*
Douglas, Carole Nelson 1944- *ConAu 107*
Douglas, Charles H 1926- *ConAu 109*
Douglas, Clifford Hugh 1879- *LongCTC*
Douglas, David Charles 1898-1982 *ConAu 107, –73*
Douglas, Ellen *ConAu X, DrAP&F 83*
Douglas, Emily 1899- *ConAu X*
Douglas, George 1869-1902 *LongCTC*
Douglas, George H 1934- *ConAu 81*
Douglas, Glenn *ConAu X*
Douglas, Gregory A *DrAP&F 83, IntAu&W 82X*
Douglas, Helen Bee *ConAu X*
Douglas, Helen Gahagan 1900-1980 *ConAu 101*
Douglas, J D 1922- *ConAu 6NR, –13R*
Douglas, James Dixon 1922- *WrDr 84*
Douglas, James McM *ConAu X, SmATA 5*
Douglas, James William Bruce 1914- *WrDr 84*
Douglas, John 1929- *WrDr 84*
Douglas, Kathryn *ConAu X, SmATA X*
Douglas, Keith 1920-1944 *DcLEL 1940, EncWL 2, LongCTC, ModBrL SUP, RGFMBP, WhoTwCL, WorAu*
Douglas, Kim *IntAu&W 82X*
Douglas, Leonard M 1910- *ConAu P-2*
Douglas, Lloyd Cassel 1877-1951 *LongCTC, MichAu 80, TwCA, TwCA SUP, TwCWr*
Douglas, Louis H 1907- *ConAu 21R*
Douglas, Mack R 1922- *ConAu 21R*
Douglas, Marjory Stoneman 1890- *AuNews 2, ConAu 1R, –2NR, SmATA 10*
Douglas, Mary 1921- *ConAu 97*
Douglas, Michael *WorAu 1970, WrDr 84*
Douglas, Mike 1925- *ConAu 89*
Douglas, Norman 1868-1952 *CnMWL, LongCTC, ModBrL, TwCA, TwCA SUP, TwCWr, WhoTwCL*
Douglas, Paul Howard 1892-1976 *ConAu 69*
Douglas, R M *ConAu X*
Douglas, Robert *ConAu X*
Douglas, Rodney K 1922- *IntWWP 82*
Douglas, Roy 1924- *ConAu 73*
Douglas, Shane *ConAu X*
Douglas, Thorne 1926-1977 *ConAu X, TwCWW*
Douglas, William A 1934- *ConAu 45*
Douglas, William Orville 1898-1980 *ConAu 9R, –93, ConIsC 1[port], DcLEL 1940, TwCA SUP*
Douglas-Hamilton, James Alexander 1942-
ConAu 33R, WrDr 84
Douglas-Home, Alec *ConAu X, WrDr 84*
Douglas-Home, Henry 1907-1980 *ConAu 101, –103*
Douglas-Home, Robin 1932-1968 *ConAu P-2*
Douglas Home, William 1912- *IntAu&W 82, WorAu 1970*
Douglas-Scott-Montagu, Edward *ConAu X*
Douglass, Amanda Hart *ConAu X*
Douglass, Donald McNutt 1899-1975 *ConAu 1R, –103*
Douglass, Elisha Peairs 1915- *ConAu 81*
Douglass, Frederick 1817-1895 *SmATA 29[port]*
Douglass, Harl Roy 1892?- *ConAu 5R*
Douglass, Herbert Edgar 1927- *ConAu 73*
Douglass, James W 1937- *ConAu 10NR, –25R*
Douglass, Malcolm P 1923- *ConAu 73*
Douglass, Marcia Kent *ConAu X*
Douglass, Paul F 1904- *ConAu 3NR, –5R*
Douglass, Robert W 1934- *ConAu 57*
Douglass, William A 1939- *ConAu 69*
Doulis, Thomas *DrAP&F 83*
Doulis, Thomas 1931- *ConAu 5R, –11NR*
Doulos, Jay *ConAu X*
Doumato, Lamia 1947- *ConAu 103*
Dourado, Autran 1926- *ConAu 25R, ConLC 23[port]*
Douskey, Franz *DrAP&F 83*
Doutremont, Henri *CreCan 2*
Douty, Esther M 1909-1978 *ConAu 3NR*
Douty, Esther M 1911-1978 *ConAu 5R, –85, SmATA 23N, –8*
Douty, Norman F 1899- *ConAu 49*
Douvan, Elizabeth Ann Malcolm 1926-
ConAu 106
Dove, Rita *DrAP&F 83*
Dove, Rita 1952- *ConAu 109, IntWWP 82*
Doveglion *ConAu X*
Dover, Sir 1920- *IntAu&W 82*

Dover, C J 1919- *ConAu 13R*
Dover, K J 1920- *ConAu 25R, WrDr 84*
Dover Wilson, John 1881-1969 *ConAu 25R, LongCTC*
Dovery, Margaret 1903- *IntAu&W 82*
Dovey, Irma *DrAP&F 83*
Dovlos, Jay *ConAu X*
Dow, Blanche H 1893-1973 *ConAu 41R*
Dow, Emily R 1904- *ConAu P-1, SmATA 10*
Dow, J Kamal 1936- *ConAu 29R*
Dow, Marguerite 1926- *WrDr 84*
Dow, Neal 1906- *ConAu 17R*
Dow, Philip *DrAP&F 83*
Dow, Sterling 1903- *ConAu P-2*
Dowd, Douglas F 1919- *ConAu 5R*
Dowd, Laurence P 1914- *ConAu 17R*
Dowd, Maxine *ConAu X*
Dowd, Merle E 1918- *ConAu 85*
Dowdell, Dorothy Karns 1910- *ConAu 5NR, –9R, SmATA 12*
Dowden, Anne Ophelia Todd 1907- *ConAu 3NR, –9R, SmATA 7, WrDr 84*
Dowden, George D, Jr. *DrAP&F 83*
Dowden, George Duncan 1932- *ConAu 4NR, –53, IntAu&W 82, IntWWP 82, WrDr 84*
Dowdeswell, Wilfrid Hogarth 1914- *WrDr 84*
Dowdey, Clifford 1904- *ConAu 9R, TwCA, TwCA SUP*
Dowdey, Landon Gerald 1923- *ConAu 89, SmATA 11*
Dowdy, Andrew 1936- *ConAu 49*
Dowdy, Homer E 1922- *ConAu 5R, MichAu 80*
Dowdy, Mrs. Regera *ConAu X, SmATA X, WrDr 84*
Dowell, Coleman 1925- *ConAu 10NR, –25R, WrDr 84*
Dowell, Jack 1908- *ConAu 57*
Dower, Penn *ConAu X*
Dowie, James Iverne 1911- *ConAu 41R*
Dowie, Mark 1939- *ConAu 85*
Dowler, James R 1925- *ConAu 29R, TwCWW, WrDr 84*
Dowley, D M *ConAu X*
Dowley, Timothy Edward 1946- *ConAu 101*
Dowling, Allen 1900- *ConAu 29R*
Dowling, Basil 1910- *ConAu 97, ConP 80, DcLEL 1940, IntWWP 82, WrDr 84*
Dowling, Dorothea *WrDr 84*
Dowling, Dorothea Helena *IntAu&W 82, IntWWP 82*
Dowling, Eddie 1894-1976 *ConAu 65*
Dowling, Harry Filmore 1904- *ConAu 102*
Dowling, Joseph A 1926- *ConAu 37R*
Dowling, Mavis Annette *IntWWP 82*
Dowling, Thomas, Jr. 1921- *ConAu 85*
Dowling, Tom *ConAu X*
Dowling, Vivyan 1915- *IntAu&W 82*
Down, Goldie 1918- *ConAu 11NR, –25R*
Downar, Joan *IntWWP 82X*
Downard, William L 1940- *ConAu 49*
Downer, Alan Seymour 1912-1970 *ConAu 33R, ConAu P-1*
Downer, Marion 1892?-1971 *ConAu 33R, SmATA 25[port]*
Downes *TwCA, TwCA SUP*
Downes, Bryan 1939- *WrDr 84*
Downes, Bryan Trevor 1939- *ConAu 33R*
Downes, David Anthony 1927- *ConAu 33R, WrDr 84*
Downes, Edward 1911- *ConAu 105*
Downes, Gwladys Violet 1915- *CreCan 2*
Downes, Mollie Patricia Panter *ConAu X*
Downes, Quentin *ConAu X, TwCCr&M 80, WrDr 84*
Downes, Randolph Chandler 1901-1975
ConAu 49, –61
Downey, Bill *ConAu X*
Downey, Fairfax Davis 1893- *ConAu 1R, –1NR, IntAu&W 82, SmATA 3, WrDr 84*
Downey, Glanville 1908- *ConAu 1R, –1NR*
Downey, Harris 1907- *ConAu 13R*
Downey, James 1939- *ConAu 101*
Downey, Lawrence William 1921- *ConAu 17R*
Downey, Murray William 1910- *ConAu 1R, –1NR*
Downey, Roger Bayard 1937- *ConAmTC*
Downey, William L 1922- *ConAu 110*
Downie, Freda 1929- *ConAu 106, ConP 80, WrDr 84*
Downie, Jill 1938- *ConAu 108*
Downie, John 1931- *ConAu 108*
Downie, Leonard, Jr. 1942- *ConAu 1NR, –49,*

DuBruck, Alfred J 1922- *ConAu 37R*
DuBruck, Edelgard E 1925- *ConAu 17R, WrDr 84*
Dubs, Homer H 1892-1969 *ConAu P-1*
Dubus, Andre 1936- *ConAu 21R, ConLC 13*
Dubus, Elizabeth Nell 1933- *ConAu 110*
Duby, Georges 1919- *ConAu 104*
DuCann, Charles Garfield Lott 1889?-1983 *ConAu 109*
Ducas, Dorothy 1905- *ConAu 5R*
Ducasse, Curt John 1881-1969 *ConAu 1R, -6NR*
Duce, Robert 1908- *ConAu 5R, WrDr 84*
Duceppe, Jean 1924- *CreCan 1*
Duchacek, Ivo D 1913- *ConAu 1R, -1NR, WrDr 84*
DuChaillu, Paul 1831?-1903 *SmATA 26[port]*
Duchamp, Marcel 1887-1968 *ConAu 110*
Duche, Jean 1915- *ConAu 9R, -9NR, IntAu&W 82*
Duchene, Louis-Francois 1927- *ConAu 105, WrDr 84*
Duchesne, Antoinette *ConAu X*
Duchesne, Jacques 1897-1971 *ConAu X*
Duchesne, Janet 1930- *SmATA 32*
Ducic, Jovan 1871?-1943 *EncWL 2, ModSL 2*
Ducic, Jovan 1874-1943 *ClDMEL 80*
DuCille, Ann *DrAP&F 83*
Duckat, Walter Benjamin 1911- *ConAu 29R*
Ducker, Bruce 1938- *ConAu 65*
Duckert, Mary 1929- *ConAu 53*
Duckett, Alfred 1917?- *ConAu 45*
Duckett, Eleanor Shipley 1880?-1976 *ConAu 69*
Duckham, A N 1903- *WrDr 84*
Duckham, Alec Narraway 1903- *ConAu 73*
Duckham, Baron Frederick 1933- *ConAu 103, IntAu&W 82, WrDr 84*
Duckworth, Alistair M 1936- *ConAu 41R*
Duckworth, George E 1903-1972 *ConAu 1R, -1NR, -33R*
Duckworth, Leslie Blakey 1904- *ConAu 105, IntAu&W 82, WrDr 84*
Duckworth, Renee 1928- *IntWWP 82*
Duclos, Paul Charles *IntAu&W 82X*
Ducornet, Erica 1943- *ConAu 37R, -77, IntAu&W 82, SmATA 7*
Ducreux, Louis Raymond 1911- *IntAu&W 82*
Duda, Margaret B 1941- *ConAu 65*
Dudden, Arthur P 1921- *ConAu 3NR, -5R*
Dudek, Louis 1918- *ConAu 1NR, -45, ConLC 11, -19, ConP 80, CreCan 2, ModCmwL, WrDr 84*
Dudintsev, Vladimir Dmitrievich 1918- *ClDMEL 80*
Dudintsev, Vladimir Dmitriyevich 1918- *ModSL 1, TwCWr, WorAu*
Dudley, Austin Edison 1931- *IntWWP 82*
Dudley, B J 1931- *ConAu 25R*
Dudley, Barbara Hudson 1921- *ConAu 65*
Dudley, Donald Reynolds 1910-1972 *ConAu 4NR, -5R*
Dudley, Edward 1926- *ConAu 45*
Dudley, Ernest 1908- *ConAu 13R*
Dudley, Frank *TwCA SUP*
Dudley, Geoffrey A 1917- *WrDr 84*
Dudley, Geoffrey Arthur 1917- *ConAu 6NR, -13R, IntAu&W 82*
Dudley, Guilford, Jr. 1907- *ConAu P-2*
Dudley, Guilford A 1921-1972 *ConAu 41R*
Dudley, Helen *ConAu X, IntAu&W 82X*
Dudley, Jay *ConAu X*
Dudley, Louise 1884- *ConAu 73*
Dudley, Nancy *ConAu X, SmATA X*
Dudley, Robert *SmATA X*
Dudley, Ruth H 1905- *ConAu 61, SmATA 11*
Dudley Edwards, Ruth 1944- *ConAu 107*
Dudley-Smith, T *TwCCr&M 80*
Dudley-Smith, Timothy 1926- *ConAu 103, WrDr 84*
Dudman, Richard 1918- *ConAu 45*
Due, Linnea A 1948- *ConAu 105*
Dueker, Christopher W 1939- *ConAu 57*
Dueker, Joyce S 1942- *ConAu 57*
Dueland, Joy V *ConAu 66, SmATA 27*
Duell, Charles Halliwell 1905-1970 *ConAu 104*
Duemer, Joseph *DrAP&F 83*
Duerr, Edwin 1904- *ConAu 73*
Duerrenmatt, Friedrich 1921- *ConAu 17R*
Duerrson, Werner 1932- *IntAu&W 82*
Dufault, Peter Kane *DrAP&F 83*
Dufault, Peter Kane 1923- *ConAu 33R, WrDr 84*
Duff, Charles St. Lawrence 1894-1966 *ConAu 1R,*

—*2NR*
Duff, David Skene 1912- *WrDr 84*
Duff, Ernest A 1929- *ConAu 25R*
Duff, Gerald 1938- *ConAu 45*
Duff, John B 1931- *ConAu 1NR, -45*
Duff, Maggie *ConAu X*
Duff, Margaret K *ConAu 37R*
Duff, Raymond S 1923- *ConAu 21R*
Duffany, Brett P *DrAP&F 83*
Duffee, David E 1946- *ConAu 104*
Duffey, Margery 1926- *ConAu 73*
Duffield, Anne 1893- *ConAu P-1, IntAu&W 82, TwCRGW*
Duffield, Gervase E 1935- *WrDr 84*
Duffin, Henry Charles 1884- *ConAu P-1*
Duffus, Robert Luther 1888-1972 *ConAu 101, -37R, TwCA, TwCA SUP*
Duffy, Antonia Susan 1936- *IntAu&W 82*
Duffy, Ben *ConAu X*
Duffy, Bernard C 1902-1972 *ConAu 37R*
Duffy, Charles 1940- *ConAu 104*
Duffy, Clinton T 1898-1982 *ConAu 108*
Duffy, Edmund 1899-1962 *ConAu 93*
Duffy, Elizabeth 1904- *ConAu P-2*
Duffy, Francis R 1915- *ConAu 49*
Duffy, Helene 1926- *ConAu 17R*
Duffy, John 1915- *ConAu 8NR, -17R*
Duffy, John J 1934- *ConAu 57*
Duffy, Maureen 1933- *ConAu 25R, ConDr 82, ConNov 82, DcLB 14[port], DcLEL 1940, IntAu&W 82, IntWWP 82, TwCWr, WhoTwCL, WrDr 84*
Duffy, Regis Anthony 1934- *ConAu 110*
Dufour, Yvon 1930- *CreCan 1*
Dufrechou, Carole *ConAu X*
Dufty, William 1916- *ConAu 65*
Dugan, Alan *DrAP&F 83*
Dugan, Alan 1923- *ConAu 81, ConLC 2, -6, ConP 80, CroCAP, DcLB 5[port], DcLEL 1940, ModAL, ModAL SUP, WorAu, WrDr 84*
Dugan, George 1909-1982 *ConAu 107*
Dugan, James 1912-1967 *ConAu 4NR, -5R*
Dugan, James Michael 1929- *DcLEL 1940*
Dugan, Michael 1947- *ConAu 77, SmATA 15*
DuGard *TwCA, TwCA SUP*
Dugard, C J R 1936- *ConAu 85*
DuGard, Roger Martin *ModRL*
Dugas, Jean-Paul *CreCan 2*
Dugas, Marcel-Henri 1883-1947? *CreCan 1*
Dugdale, Norman 1921- *WrDr 84*
Duggal, Kartar Singh 1917- *IntAu&W 82*
Duggan, Alfred Leo 1903-1964 *ConAu 73, LongCTC, ModBrL, SmATA 25[port], TwCA SUP, TwCWr*
Duggan, George Henry 1912- *ConAu 17R, WrDr 84*
Duggan, Joseph J 1938- *ConAu 29R*
Duggan, Mary M 1921- *ConAu 25R*
Duggan, Maurice 1922-1974 *TwCCW 83*
Duggan, Maurice Noel 1922-1975 *ConAu 53, -73, DcLEL 1940, SmATA 30N*
Duggan, William Redman 1915- *ConAu 69*
Duggans, Pat *ConAu X*
Dugger, Ronnie 1930- *ConAu 21R*
Duggins, James, Jr. 1933- *ConAu 37R*
Dughi, Nancy *ConAu 1R*
Dugmore, Clifford William 1909- *ConAu 13R, IntAu&W 82*
Duguid, Charles 1884- *ConAu 109, IntAu&W 82*
Duguid, John Bright 1895-1980 *ConAu 102*
Duguid, Julian 1902- *TwCA, TwCA SUP*
Duguid, Robert *ConAu X*
Duguid, Sandra R *DrAP&F 83*
Duhamel, Georges 1884-1966 *ClDMEL 80, ConAu 25R, -81, ConLC 8, EncWL 2, LongCTC, ModFrL, ModRL, ModWD, TwCA, TwCA SUP, TwCWr, WhoTwCL*
Duhamel, Marcel 1900?-1977 *ConAu 104*
Duhamel, P Albert 1920- *ConAu 5R*
Duhamel, Roger 1916- *CreCan 1*
Duhamel, Vaughn L *DrAP&F 83*
DuHault, Jean *ConAu X*
Duhl, Leonard J 1926- *ConAu 13R, WrDr 84*
Duignan, Peter 1926- *ConAu 11NR, -13R*
Duiker, William J 1932- *ConAu 81*
Dujardin, Edouard 1861-1949 *ClDMEL 80, ConAu 109, LongCTC*
DuJardin, Rosamond Neal 1902-1963 *ConAu 1R, -103, SmATA 2*
Duka, Ivo *WrDr 84*

Duke, Alvah 1908- *ConAu 45*
Duke, Benjamin 1931- *ConAu 49*
Duke, Charles 1940- *ConAu 11NR, -69*
Duke, Donald 1929- *WrDr 84*
Duke, Donald Norman 1929- *ConAu 7NR, -17R, IntAu&W 82*
Duke, Forrest R 1918- *ConAu 77*
Duke, James T 1933- *ConAu 65*
Duke, John *ConAu X*
Duke, Madelaine *WrDr 84*
Duke, Madelaine 1925- *ConAu 9NR, -57, ConSFA, IntAu&W 82*
Duke, Raoul *IntAu&W 82X*
Duke, Richard DeLaBarre 1930- *ConAu 57*
Duke, Vernon 1903-1969 *ConAu P-2*
Duke, Will *ConAu X, WrDr 84*
Duke-Elder, Stewart 1896-1978 *ConAu 77*
Dukelsky, Vladimir 1903-1969 *ConAu X*
Duker, Abraham G 1907- *ConAu 53*
Duker, Sam 1905-1978 *ConAu 13R, -77*
Dukert, Joseph Michael 1929- *ConAu 3NR, -5R, WrDr 84*
Dukes, Ashley 1885-1959 *ConAu 110, DcLB 10[port]*
Dukes, Paul 1934- *ConAu 9NR, -21R, WrDr 84*
Dukes, Philip *ConAu X*
Dukes, Tyrone 1946?-1983 *ConAu 110*
Dukore, Bernard F 1931- *ConAu 25R, WrDr 84*
Dukore, Margaret Mitchell *DrAP&F 83*
Dukore, Margaret Mitchell 1950- *ConAu 106*
Dulac, Edmund 1882-1953 *SmATA 19*
Dulack, Thomas 1935- *ConAu 25R*
Dulany, Don E, Jr. 1928- *ConAu 69*
Dulany, Harris *DrAP&F 83*
Dulany, Harris 1940- *ConAu 33R*
Dulieu, Jean *ConAu X*
Duling, Paul 1916- *IntWWP 82*
Dull, Jonathan R 1942- *ConAu 69*
Dulles, Allen 1893-1969 *ConAu P-2*
Dulles, Avery 1918- *WrDr 84*
Dulles, Avery Robert 1918- *ConAu 3NR, -9R, IntAu&W 82*
Dulles, Eleanor Lansing 1895- *ConAu 9R*
Dulles, Foster Rhea 1900-1970 *ConAu 29R, ConAu P-1, TwCA SUP*
Dulles, John W F 1913- *ConAu 1R, -1NR*
Dullin, Charles 1865-1949 *ClDMEL 80*
Duloup, Victor *ConAu X*
Dulsey, Bernard M 1914- *ConAu 9R*
Dulzer, Marie Ann 1935- *ConAmTC*
Dumarchais, Pierre 1882-1970 *ConAu 29R, TwCA, TwCA SUP*
Dumarchey, Pierre *ConAu X*
Dumas, Alexandre 1802-1870 *SmATA 18*
Dumas, Andre 1918- *ConAu 73*
Dumas, Claire *ConAu X*
Dumas, Claudine *WrDr 84*
DuMas, Frank 1918- *ConAu 106*
Dumas, Frederic 1913- *ConAu 69*
Dumas, Gerald *DrAP&F 83*
Dumas, Gerald J 1930- *ConAu 25R*
Dumas, Henry L 1934-1968 *ConAu 85, ConLC 6*
Dumas, Philippe 1940- *ConAu 107*
DuMaurier, Daphne 1907- *ConAu 5R, -6NR, ConLC 6, -11, ConNov 82, IntAu&W 82, LongCTC, ModBrL, SmATA 27[port], TwCA, TwCA SUP, TwCCr&M 80, TwCRGW, TwCWr, WrDr 84*
Dumbleton, William A 1927- *ConAu 37R*
Dumbrille, Dorothy Martha 1897- *CreCan 2, WrDr 84*
Dumery, Henry 1920- *ConAu 101*
Dumitriu, Petru 1924- *IntAu&W 82, ModRL, TwCWr, WorAu*
Dummett, Michael Anthony Eardley 1925- *ConAu 102*
Dumon *IntAu&W 82X*
Dumond, Dwight Lowell 1895-1976 *ConAu 65, -69*
Dumont, Jean-Paul 1940- *ConAu 73*
Dumouchel, Albert 1916- *CreCan 1*
Dumoulin, Heinrich 1905- *ConAu 4NR, -5R*
Dumpleton, John LeFevre 1924- *ConAu 13R*
Dumpty, Humpty S *ConAu X*
Dun, Angus 1892-1971 *ConAu 33R*
Dun, Mao *ConAu X*
Dunas, Joseph C 1900- *ConAu 17R*
Dunathan, Arni T 1936- *ConAu 53*
Dunaway, David King 1948- *ConAu 107*

Dunaway, John M 1945- *ConAu 89*
Dunbabin, J P D 1938- *ConAu 69*
Dunbar, Charles Stuart 1900- *ConAu 107,
WrDr 84*
Dunbar, David *ConAu X*
Dunbar, Dorothy 1923- *ConAu 9R*
Dunbar, Edward *ConAu X*
Dunbar, Ernest 1927- *ConAu 25R*
Dunbar, Janet 1901- *ConAu 6NR, -9R,
IntAu&W 82*
Dunbar, John Greenwell 1930- *ConAu 21R*
Dunbar, Maxwell 1914- *WrDr 84*
Dunbar, Maxwell John 1914- *ConAu 103*
Dunbar, Paul Laurence 1872-1906 *ConAu 104,
ModBlW, SmATA 34[port], TwCLC 2,
-12[port]*
Dunbar, Robert E 1926- *ConAu 85,
SmATA 32[port]*
Dunbar, Tony 1949- *ConAu 33R*
Dunbar, Willis F 1902-1970 *ConAu 4NR, -5R,
MichAu 80*
Dunbaugh, Frank Montgomery 1895- *ConAu 45*
Dunboyne, Lord 1917- *IntAu&W 82, WrDr 84*
Duncan, A D 1930- *ConAu 33R*
Duncan, A R C 1915- *WrDr 84*
Duncan, Alex *ConAu X,   IntAu&W 82X,
WrDr 84*
Duncan, Alistair 1927- *ConAu 61*
Duncan, Anthony Douglas 1930- *WrDr 84*
Duncan, Archibald A M 1926- *WrDr 84*
Duncan, Archibald Alexander McBeth 1926-
ConAu 81, IntAu&W 82
Duncan, Ardinelle Bean 1913- *ConAu 1R*
Duncan, Ben 1927- *WrDr 84*
Duncan, Bingham 1911- *ConAu 85*
Duncan, Bowie 1941- *ConAu 33R*
Duncan, Bruce *ConSFA*
Duncan, C J 1916- *ConAu 25R*
Duncan, Charles T 1914- *ConAu 17R*
Duncan, Chester 1913- *ConAu 93*
Duncan, Clyde H 1903- *ConAu 17R*
Duncan, David 1913- *ConAu 5R, TwCSFW,
WrDr 84*
Duncan, David Douglas 1916- *AuNews 1*
Duncan, Delbert J 1895- *ConAu 41R*
Duncan, Denis 1920- *ConAu 107*
Duncan, Dougal 1921- *ConAu 102*
Duncan, Elmer H 1933- *ConAu 69*
Duncan, Erika *DrAP&F 83*
Duncan, Florence Belle 1917?-1980 *ConAu 97*
Duncan, Frances 1942- *ConAu 97*
Duncan, George *ConAu X*
Duncan, Gregory *ConAu X, SmATA 3*
Duncan, Hugh Dalziel 1909-1970 *ConAu P-2*
Duncan, Irma 1897-1977 *ConAu 49, -73*
Duncan, Jane *ConAu X, SmATA X*
Duncan, Jane 1910-1976 *TwCCW 83*
Duncan, Joseph E 1921- *ConAu 5R*
Duncan, Julia Coley *ConAu X*
Duncan, Julia K *ConAu P-2, SmATA 1*
Duncan, Kenneth Sandilands 1912- *ConAu 9R*
Duncan, Kunigunde 1886- *ConAu 5R*
Duncan, Lois 1934- *ConAu X, -2NR,
ConLC 26[port], IntAu&W 82, SmATA 1,
TwCCW 83, WrDr 84*
Duncan, Marion Moncure 1913-1978 *ConAu 77*
Duncan, Norman 1871-1916 *CreCan 2,
TwCCW 83*
Duncan, Otis Dudley 1921- *ConAu 6NR, -13R*
Duncan, Pam 1938- *ConAu 37R*
Duncan, Pope A 1920- *ConAu 13R*
Duncan, Robert *DrAP&F 83*
Duncan, Robert 1919- *ConAu 9R, ConLC 1, -2,
-4, -7, -15, ConP 80, CroCAP,
DcLB 5[port], DcLEL 1940, -16[port],
EncWL 2, ModAL, ModAL SUP, WorAu,
WrDr 84*
Duncan, Robert F 1890?-1974 *ConAu 53*
Duncan, Robert L 1927- *WrDr 84*
Duncan, Robert Lipscomb 1927- *ConAu 106,
TwCCr&M 80*
Duncan, Ronald 1914-1982 *CnMD, ConAu 4NR,
-5R, -107, ConDr 82, ConP 80, CroCD,
DcLB 13[port], DcLEL 1940, IntAu&W 82,
IntWWP 82, ModBrL, ModWD, TwCWr*
Duncan, Sara Jeannette 1862-1922 *CreCan 1*
Duncan, T Bentley 1929- *ConAu 77*
Duncan, Thomas 1905- *ConAu 1NR*
Duncan, Thomas William 1905- *ConAu 1R*
Duncan, W Murdoch 1909-1976 *ConAu 6NR,
-13R, TwCCr&M 80*
Duncan, W R *ConAu X*

Duncan, W Raymond 1936- *ConAu 41R*
Duncan, William 1944- *WrDr 84*
Duncanson, Michael E 1948- *ConAu 57*
Duncker, Frede 1929- *IntAu&W 82*
Duncombe, David C 1928- *ConAu 29R*
Duncombe, Frances 1900- *ConAu 25R,
SmATA 25*
Dundee, Robert *ConAu X*
Dundes, Alan 1934- *ConAu 9NR, -21R*
Dundy, Elaine 1927- *ConNov 82, WrDr 84*
Dundy, Elaine 1937?- *ConAu 97, TwCWr*
Dunetz, Lora *DrAP&F 83, IntWWP 82*
Dunford, Judith 1933- *ConAu 107*
Dunham, Arthur 1893- *ConAu 33R*
Dunham, Barrows 1905- *ConAu 5R*
Dunham, Bertha Mabel 1881- *CreCan 2*
Dunham, Bob *ConAu X*
Dunham, Donald Carl 1908- *ConAu 1R*
Dunham, H Warren 1906- *ConAu 8NR, -13R,
WrDr 84*
Dunham, John L 1939- *ConAu 29R*
Dunham, Katherine 1910- *ConAu 65, LivgBAA*
Dunham, Kingsley 1910- *WrDr 84*
Dunham, Lowell 1910- *ConAu 37R*
Dunham, Mabel 1881-1957 *CreCan 2*
Dunham, Montrew Goetz 1919- *ConAu 17R*
Dunham, Robert 1931- *ConAu 69*
Dunham, William Huse, Jr. 1901- *ConAu 49*
Dunhill, Alfred H 1896?-1971 *ConAu 104*
Dunilac, Julien *IntAu&W 82X*
Dunkel, Harold Baker 1912- *ConAu 5R*
Dunkel, Richard H 1933- *ConAu 73*
Dunkerley, Roderic 1884- *ConAu P-1*
Dunkerley, William Arthur 1852-1941 *TwCA,
TwCA SUP*
Dunkin, Paul S 1905- *WrDr 84*
Dunkin, Paul Shaner 1905-1975 *ConAu P-2*
Dunkle, William F, Jr. 1911- *ConAu 53*
Dunkling, Leslie Alan 1935- *ConAu 81*
Dunkman, William E 1903- *ConAu P-2,
WrDr 84*
Dunlap, Aurie N 1907-1977 *ConAu 37R*
Dunlap, G D 1923- *ConAu 49*
Dunlap, Jan *ConAu 65*
Dunlap, Jane *ConAu X*
Dunlap, Joseph R 1913- *ConAu 85*
Dunlap, Leslie W 1911- *ConAu 37R, WrDr 84*
Dunlap, Lon *ConAu X*
Dunlap, Orrin Elmer, Jr. 1896-1970 *ConAu P-1*
Dunleavy, Gareth Winthrop 1923- *ConAu 33R*
Dunleavy, Janet Egleson 1928- *ConAu 6NR, -57*
Dunlop, Agnes M R d1982 *ConAu 9NR*
Dunlop, Agnes Mary Robinson *ConAu 13R*
Dunlop, Derrick Melville 1902-1980 *ConAu 101*
Dunlop, Eileen 1938- *ConAu 73,
SmATA 24[port], WrDr 84*
Dunlop, Ian Geoffrey David 1925- *ConAu 5NR,
-9R, IntAu&W 82, WrDr 84*
Dunlop, John B 1942- *ConAu 57*
Dunlop, John T 1914- *WrDr 84*
Dunlop, John Thomas 1914- *ConAu 5NR, -13R*
Dunlop, Richard 1921- *ConAu 7NR, -17R,
WrDr 84*
Dunmore, John 1923- *ConAu 106,
IntAu&W 82, WrDr 84*
Dunmore, Spencer S 1928- *ConAu 33R,
WrDr 84*
Dunn, Alan 1900-1974 *ConAu 49, ConAu P-2*
Dunn, Catherine M 1930- *ConAu 37R*
Dunn, Charles W 1915- *ConAu 49,
IntAu&W 82, WrDr 84*
Dunn, Delmer D 1941- *ConAu 25R*
Dunn, Donald H 1929- *ConAu 33R*
Dunn, Douglas 1942- *ConAu 2NR, -45,
ConLC 6, ConP 80, IntAu&W 82,
IntWWP 82, WorAu 1970, WrDr 84*
Dunn, Edgar S, Jr. 1921- *ConAu 9R*
Dunn, Edward D 1883?-1978 *ConAu 77*
Dunn, Eleanor *ConAu X*
Dunn, Esther Cloudman 1891-1977 *ConAu 73*
Dunn, Ethel 1932- *ConAu 21R*
Dunn, Halbert Louis 1896-1975 *ConAu 61*
Dunn, Hampton 1916- *ConAu 57*
Dunn, Harold 1929- *ConAu 9R*
Dunn, Harris *ConAu X*
Dunn, Harvey T 1884-1952 *SmATA 34[port]*
Dunn, Hugh Patrick 1916- *WrDr 84*
Dunn, James *ConAu X*
Dunn, James D 1939- *ConAu 73*
Dunn, James Taylor 1912- *ConAu 4NR, -5R*
Dunn, Jean 1921- *ConAu 109*
Dunn, Jerry G 1916- *ConAu 11NR, -21R*

Dunn, John 1940- *ConAu 11NR, -69*
Dunn, Judith F *ConAu X*
Dunn, Judy *ConAu X, SmATA 5*
Dunn, Katherine 1945- *ConAu 33R*
Dunn, Kaye *ConAu X*
Dunn, Lloyd W 1906- *ConAu 57*
Dunn, Marion Herndon 1920- *ConAu 29R*
Dunn, Mary Lois 1930- *ConAu 61, SmATA 6*
Dunn, Nell 1936- *ConAu X, ConNov 82,
DcLEL 1940, WrDr 84*
Dunn, Patience Louise 1922- *ConAu 5R*
Dunn, Peter Norman 1926- *IntAu&W 82,
WrDr 84*
Dunn, Robert *DrAP&F 83*
Dunn, Samuel Watson 1918- *ConAu 1R, -5NR,
WrDr 84*
Dunn, Si 1944- *ConAu 77*
Dunn, Stephen *DrAP&F 83*
Dunn, Stephen 1939- *ConAu 33R, ConP 80,
WrDr 84*
Dunn, Stuart 1900- *ConAu 57*
Dunn, Thomas G 1950- *NatPD 81[port]*
Dunn, Thomas Tinsley 1901- *ConAu 107*
Dunn, Waldo Hilary 1882-1969 *ConAu P-2*
Dunn, Walter Scott, Jr. 1928- *ConAu 101*
Dunn, William J 1906- *ConAu 33R*
Dunn, William L 1924- *ConAu 37R*
Dunnahoo, Terry 1927- *ConAu 41R,
IntAu&W 82, SmATA 7*
Dunnam, Maxie D 1934- *ConAu 73*
Dunne, Carol *DrAP&F 83*
Dunne, Finley Peter 1867-1936 *ConAu 108,
LongCTC, TwCA, TwCA SUP*
Dunne, George H 1905- *ConAu 1R, -5NR,
WrDr 84*
Dunne, Gerald T 1919- *ConAu 1NR, -45*
Dunne, J W 1875-1949 *LongCTC*
Dunne, John Gregory 1932- *AuNews 1,
ConAu 25R, DcLB Y80B[port],
TwCCr&M 80, WrDr 84*
Dunne, John S 1929- *ConAu 13R, WrDr 84*
Dunne, Mary Chavelita *LongCTC*
Dunne, Mary Collins 1914- *ConAu 41R,
SmATA 11*
Dunne, Peter Finlay 1867-1936 *TwCWr*
Dunne, Philip 1908- *ConAu 11NR, ConAu P-1,
DcLB 26[port]*
Dunne, Robert Williams 1895-1977 *ConAu 69*
Dunnell, Robert C 1942- *ConAu 89*
Dunner, Joseph 1908- *ConAu 21R*
Dunnett, Alastair MacTavish 1908- *ConAu 65,
IntAu&W 82*
Dunnett, Dorothy 1923- *ConAu 1R, -3NR,
IntAu&W 82, TwCCr&M 80, TwCRGW,
WrDr 84*
Dunnett, Margaret 1909- *ConAu 108*
Dunnigan, Alice Allison 1906-1983 *ConAu 109*
Dunning, Barbara Renkens *DrAP&F 83*
Dunning, Brad 1957- *ConAu 102*
Dunning, Bruce 1940- *ConAu 77*
Dunning, John 1942- *ConAu 93*
Dunning, John H 1927- *WrDr 84*
Dunning, John Harry 1927- *ConAu 104,
IntAu&W 82*
Dunning, Lawrence *DrAP&F 83*
Dunning, Lawrence 1931- *ConAu 77,
IntAu&W 82*
Dunning, Philip Hart 1890- *CnMD*
Dunning, Philip Hart 1890-1968 *ModWD*
Dunning, Ralph Cheever 1878-1930 *ConAu 107,
DcLB 4*
Dunning, Robert William 1938- *ConAu 5NR,
-53*
Dunning, Stephen *DrAP&F 83*
Dunning, Stephen 1924- *ConAu 25R,
MichAu 80*
Dunning, William Archibald 1857?-1922
DcLB 17[port]
Dunnington, Hazel Brain 1912- *ConAu 21R*
Dunoyer, Maurice *ConAu X*
Dunoyer DeSegonzac, Andre 1884-1974
ConAu 53
Dunphy, Jack 1914- *ConAu 25R*
Dunsany, Lord 1878-1957 *TwCLC 2,
TwCSFW B*
Dunsany, Baron Edward J M Drax Plunkett
1878-1957 *CnMD, ConAu 104,
DcLB 10[port], LongCTC, ModBrL,
ModWD, TwCA, TwCA SUP, TwCWr*
Dunsheath, Joyce 1902- *ConAu 5R*
Dunsheath, Percy 1886- *ConAu 107*
Dunsmore, Roger 1938- *ConAu 110*

Dye, Harold E 1907- *ConAu 29R*
Dye, James W 1934- *ConAu 21R*
Dye, Margaret 1932- *ConAu 81*
Dye, Rex J 1899- *MichAu 80*
Dye, Thomas R 1935- *ConAu 33R*
Dyen, Isidore 1913- *ConAu 53, WrDr 84*
Dyer, Beverly 1921- *ConAu 61*
Dyer, Braven 1900?-1983 *ConAu 110*
Dyer, Brian *ConAu X, WrDr 84*
Dyer, C Raymond *ConAu X*
Dyer, Charles 1928- *ConAu 21R, ConDr 82,*
    CroCD, DcLB 13[port], DcLEL 1940,
    IntAu&W 82, WrDr 84
Dyer, Christopher 1935- *WrDr 84*
Dyer, Elinor Mary Brent *ConAu X*
Dyer, Esther R 1950- *ConAu 102*
Dyer, Frederick C *IntAu&W 82*
Dyer, Frederick C 1918- *ConAu 17R, WrDr 84*
Dyer, George Bell 1903-1978 *ConAu 81, –85*
Dyer, George E 1928-1974 *ConAu 37R*
Dyer, George J 1927- *ConAu 13R*
Dyer, James 1934- *ConAu 102, IntAu&W 82,*
    WrDr 84
Dyer, John M 1920- *WrDr 84*
Dyer, John Martin 1920- *ConAu 13R*
Dyer, John Percy 1902-1975 *ConAu 1R, –103*
Dyer, John Thomas 1918- *WrDr 84*
Dyer, Lucinda 1947- *ConAu 105*
Dyer, Raymond *ConAu X*
Dyer, Roberta Coldren 1914- *IntWWP 82*
Dyer, T A 1947- *ConAu 101*
Dyer, Thomas A *DrAP&F 83*
Dyer, Thomas G 1943- *ConAu 107*
Dyer, Wayne W 1940- *ConAu 69, MichAu 80,*
    WrDr 84
Dyer, William G 1925- *ConAu 41R*
Dygard, Thomas J 1931- *ConAu 85,*
    SmATA 24[port]
Dygasinski, Adolf 1839-1902 *ClDMEL 80*
Dygat, Stanislaw 1914-1978 *ClDMEL 80,*
    EncWL 2
Dygert, James H 1934- *ConAu 10NR, –65*
Dyk, Viktor 1877-1931 *ClDMEL 80, ModSL 2*
Dyk, Walter 1899-1972 *ConAu 37R*
Dyke *TwCA, TwCA SUP*
Dyke, Henry Van *DrAP&F 83*
Dyke, John 1935- *ConAu 25R*
Dykema, Karl W 1906-1970 *ConAu P-2*
Dykeman, Richard M 1943- *ConAu 93*
Dykeman, Wilma *WrDr 84*
Dykeman, Wilma 1920- *ConAu X, –1NR*
Dykes, Archie R 1931- *ConAu 7NR, –17R*
Dykes, Jack 1929- *ConAu X, WrDr 84*
Dykes, Jeff C 1900- *ConAu 2NR, –5R*
Dykhuizen, George 1899- *ConAu 49*
Dykstra, Gerald 1922- *ConAu 45*
Dykstra, Robert R 1930- *ConAu 25R*
Dylan, Bob 1941- *ConAu 41R, ConLC 3, –4, –6,*
    –12, ConP 80, DcLB 16[port],
    DcLEL 1940, IntAu&W 82, IntWWP 82,
    WrDr 84
Dymally, Mervyn Malcolm 1926- *ConAu 41R*
Dyment, Clifford 1914-1971 *ConAu 33R,*
    ConAu P-1
Dymoke, Juliet 1919- *ConAu X,*
    IntAu&W 82X, TwCRGW, WrDr 84
Dymond, Rosalind *ConAu X*
Dymov, Ossip 1878-1959 *CnMD, ModWD*
Dymsza, William A 1920- *ConAu 2NR*
Dymsza, William A 1922- *ConAu 49*
Dynes, Russell R 1923- *ConAu 6NR, –9R*
Dyonnet, Edmond 1859-1954 *CreCan 2*
Dyott, George M 1883-1972 *ConAu 37R*
Dyregrov, Michael *IntWWP 82X*
Dyrkjob, Aage 1904- *IntWWP 82*
Dyrness, William A 1943- *ConAu 33R,*
    WrDr 84
Dyroff, Jan Michael 1942- *ConAu 61*
Dyson, A E 1928- *WrDr 84*
Dyson, Anne Jane 1912- *ConAu 21R*
Dyson, Anthony Edward 1928- *ConAu 57,*
    IntAu&W 82
Dyson, Edward George 1865-1931 *TwCWr*
Dyson, Freeman 1923- *WrDr 84*
Dyson, Freeman John 1923- *ConAu 89*
Dyson, Lowell Keith 1929- *ConAu 107*
Dywasuk, Colette Taube 1941- *ConAu 45*
Dzierzbicki, Stanislaw 1910- *IntAu&W 82*
Dziewanowski, M Kamil 1913- *ConAu 29R*
Dzyuba, Ivan 1931- *ClDMEL 80*

E

E M *IntWWP 82X*
E P *ConAmA*
E R *CreCan 1*
E T *IntAu&W 82X*
E V B *SmATA X*
Ea *IntAu&W 82X*
Eaborn, Colin 1923- *WrDr 84*
Eades, Joan *DrAP&F 83*
Eadie, Donald 1919- *ConAu 33R, WrDr 84*
Eadie, John W 1935- *ConAu 104*
Eady, Cornelius Robert *DrAP&F 83*
Eady, W P R *CreCan 2*
Eagan, Andrea Boroff 1943- *ConAu 73*
Eagar, Frances 1940- *ConAu 61, SmATA 11*
Eager, Edward d1964 *TwCCW 83*
Eager, Edward 1911-1964 *ConAu 73, DcLB 22[port], SmATA 17*
Eagle, Chester 1933- *ConAu 57*
Eagle, Dorothy 1912- *ConAu 9NR, −21R*
Eagle, Joanna 1934- *ConAu 25R*
Eagle, Mike 1942- *SmATA 11*
Eagle, Robert H 1921-1969 *ConAu P-2*
Eagle, Solomon *LongCTC*
Eagles, Douglas Alan 1943- *ConAu 110*
Eaglesfield, Francis *ConAu X, WrDr 84*
Eagleson, John 1941- *ConAu 53*
Eagleton, Terence 1943- *WrDr 84*
Eagleton, Terence Francis 1943- *ConAu 7NR, −57*
Eagleton, Terry 1943- *ConAu X, ConLCrt 82*
Eagleton, Thomas Francis 1929- *ConAu 105*
Eagly, Robert V 1933- *ConAu 49*
Eakin, Frank Edwin, Jr. 1936- *ConAu 53*
Eakin, Mary K 1917- *ConAu 1R, −1NR*
Eakin, Mary Mulford 1914- *ConAu 106*
Eakin, Richard M 1910- *ConAu 61*
Eakin, Sue 1918- *ConAu 69*
Eakins, David W 1923- *ConAu 49*
Eakins, Patricia *DrAP&F 83*
Eales, John R 1910- *ConAu 9R*
Ealy, Lawrence Orr 1915- *ConAu 33R*
Eames, Alexandra 1942- *ConAu 105*
Eames, David *DrAP&F 83*
Eames, David 1934- *ConAu 77*
Eames, Edwin 1930- *ConAu 41R*
Eames, Hugh 1917- *ConAu 45*
Eames, John Douglas 1915- *ConAu 69*
Eames, S Morris 1916- *ConAu 57*
Eardley, George C 1926- *ConAu 57*
Earhart, H Byron 1935- *ConAu 37R, IntAu&W 82, WrDr 84*
Earl, David M 1911- *ConAu 13R*
Earl, Donald 1931- *ConAu 57*
Earl, Johnrae 1919?-1978 *ConAu 77*
Earl, Lawrence 1915- *ConAu 9R*
Earl, Paul Hunter 1945- *ConAu 2NR, −49*
Earl, Robert Arthur William 1954- *IntWWP 82*
Earl Of Arran *ConAu X*
Earle, Garet W *IntAu&W 82X*
Earle, Marilee *ConAu X*
Earle, Olive Lydia 1888- *ConAu 21R, SmATA 7*
Earle, Peter G 1923- *ConAu 17R*
Earle, Ralph 1907- *ConAu 1R, −4NR*

Earle, William *ConAu X*
Earle, William Alexander 1919- *ConAu 85*
Earley, George W 1927- *ConSFA*
Earley, Martha *ConAu X*
Earley, Thomas Powell 1911- *IntWWP 82*
Earley, Tom 1911- *ConAu P-2, IntWWP 82X, WrDr 84*
Earling, Shell *IntAu&W 82X*
Earll, Tony *ConAu X*
Earlson, Ian Malcolm *ConAu X*
Early, Eleanor d1969 *TwCA SUP*
Early, James 1923- *ConAu 45*
Early, Richard E 1908- *ConAu 102*
Early, Robert Bruce 1940- *ConAu 49*
Earnest, Ernest Penney 1901- *ConAu 33R, WrDr 84*
Earney, Fillmore C F 1931- *ConAu 57*
Earnshaw, A 1924- *ConSFA*
Earnshaw, Anthony 1924- *ConAu 53, WrDr 84*
Earnshaw, Brian 1929- *ConAu 11NR, −25R, SmATA 17*
Earp, Virgil *ConAu X*
Easmon, R Sarif *ConDr 82, WrDr 84*
Easmon, R Sarif 1930?- *ModCmwL*
Easmon, Raymond Sarif 1925- *DcLEL 1940*
Easmon, Sarif *LongCTC*
Eason, Ruth P 1898?-1978 *ConAu 81*
Easson, James 1895-1979 *ConAu 5R, −103*
Easson, Robert 1941- *ConSFA*
Easson, William M 1931- *ConAu 65*
East, Ben 1898- *ConAu 33R, MichAu 80*
East, Charles *DrAP&F 83*
East, Charles 1924- *ConAu 17R*
East, John 1937- *WrDr 84*
East, John Marlborough 1936- *ConAu 21R*
East, John Porter 1931- *ConAu 17R, WrDr 84*
East, Michael *ConAu X, WorAu, WrDr 84*
East, P D 1921-1971 *ConAu 1R, −103*
East, W Gordon 1902- *ConAu 69*
East, William Gordon 1902- *WrDr 84*
Eastaugh, Kenneth 1929- *ConAu 106, WrDr 84*
Eastaway, Edward *ConAu X, LongCTC*
Easterlin, Richard 1926- *ConAu 109*
Easterman, Alexander Levvey 1890-1983 *ConAu 110*
Eastham, Thomas 1923- *ConAu 77*
Easthope, Gary 1945- *ConAu 69*
Eastin, Roy B 1917- *ConAu 41R*
Eastlake, William *DrAP&F 83*
Eastlake, William 1917- *ConAu 5R, −5NR, ConLC 8, ConNov 82, DcLB 6[port], FifWWr, IntAu&W 82, ModAL SUP, TwCWW, WorAu, WrDr 84*
Eastland, Terry 1950- *ConAu 97*
Eastlick, John Taylor 1912- *ConAu 106*
Eastman, Addison J 1918- *ConAu 85*
Eastman, Ann Heidbreder 1933- *ConAu 37R*
Eastman, Arthur M 1918- *ConAu 21R*
Eastman, Charles *NatPD 81[port]*
Eastman, Edward Roe 1885- *ConAu P-1*
Eastman, Frances Whittier 1915- *ConAu 1R*
Eastman, G Don *ConAu 49*
Eastman, Harry Claude MacColl 1923- *ConAu 105*

Eastman, Joel Webb 1939- *ConAu 13R*
Eastman, Max 1883-1969 *ConAmA, ConAu 9R, −25R, LongCTC, TwCA, TwCA SUP*
Eastman, P D 1909- *ConAu 107, SmATA 33[port]*
Eastman, Richard M 1916- *ConAu 17R*
Eastman, Robert E 1913- *ConAu 93*
Eastman, Roger 1931- *ConAu 53*
Eastment, Winifred V 1899- *WrDr 84*
Easton, Allan 1916- *ConAu 2NR, −49*
Easton, Carol 1933- *ConAu 65*
Easton, David 1917- *ConAu 33R, IntAu&W 82, WrDr 84*
Easton, Edward *ConAu X*
Easton, Edward 1940- *WrDr 84*
Easton, Loyd D 1915- *ConAu 21R, WrDr 84*
Easton, Robert 1915- *ConAu 7NR, −13R, TwCWW, WrDr 84*
Easton, Stewart Copinger 1907- *ConAu 1R, −2NR*
Eastwick, Ivy Olive 1905- *ConAu 2NR, −5R, SmATA 3, WrDr 84*
Eastwood, C Cyril 1916- *ConAu 5R*
Eatock, Marjorie 1927- *ConAu 89*
Eaton, Anne T 1881-1971 *SmATA 32[port]*
Eaton, Burnham *IntWWP 82X*
Eaton, Charles Edward *DrAP&F 83*
Eaton, Charles Edward 1916- *ConAu 2NR, −5R, ConP 80, WrDr 84*
Eaton, Clement 1898- *ConAu 1R, −4NR, WrDr 84*
Eaton, Dorothy Burnham 1901- *IntWWP 82*
Eaton, Evelyn *DrAP&F 83*
Eaton, Evelyn Sybil Mary 1902- *ConAu 53, IntWWP 82, TwCA SUP*
Eaton, Faith 1927- *ConAu 103*
Eaton, George L *ConAu X, SmATA X, WrDr 84*
Eaton, J H 1927- *ConAu 1R, −4NR*
Eaton, Jeanette 1886-1968 *ConAu 73, SmATA 24[port]*
Eaton, John Herbert 1927- *WrDr 84*
Eaton, Joseph W 1919- *ConAu 1R, −4NR, IntAu&W 82*
Eaton, Leonard K 1922- *ConAu 21R*
Eaton, Lucy Ellen 1905- *IntAu&W 82, IntWWP 82*
Eaton, Richard Behrens 1914- *WrDr 84*
Eaton, Theodore H, Jr. 1907- *ConAu 53*
Eaton, Tom 1940- *ConAu 41R, SmATA 22[port]*
Eaton, Trevor 1934- *ConAu 21R, IntAu&W 82, WrDr 84*
Eaton, Walter Prichard 1878-1957 *TwCA, TwCA SUP*
Eaton, William Edward 1943- *ConAu 69*
Eaves, James Clifton 1912- *ConAu 13R*
Eaves, T C Duncan 1918- *ConAu 77*
Eavey, Charles B 1889- *ConAu 5R*
Eavey, Louise Bone 1900- *ConAu 5R*
Eayrs, James 1926- *ConAu 106*
Eba, Andy *IntAu&W 82X*
Eban, Abba 1915- *ConAu 57*
Eban, Aubrey *ConAu X*

Ebb, Fred 1935- *ConAu 69, ConDr 82D*
Ebbesen, Ebbe B 1944- *ConAu 2NR, –49*
Ebbett, Eva 1925- *ConAu 103*
Ebbett, Eve 1925- *ConAu X, IntAu&W 82X, WrDr 84*
Ebbett, Frances Eva 1925- *IntAu&W 82*
Ebejer, Francis 1925- *ConAu 29R*
Ebel, Alex 1927- *SmATA 11*
Ebel, Henry 1938- *ConAu 53*
Ebel, Robert L 1910- *ConAu 89*
Ebel, Suzanne *ConAu X, TwCRGW, WrDr 84*
Ebeling, Gerhard 1912- *ConAu 5NR, –9R*
Ebelt, Alfred 1904- *MichAu 80*
Ebener, Dietrich 1920- *IntAu&W 82*
Ebenstein, Ronnie Sue 1946- *ConAu 103*
Ebenstein, William 1910-1976 *ConAu 1R, –6NR, –65*
Eber, Dorothy Margaret Harley 1930- *ConAu 41R, SmATA 27*
Eber, Irene 1929- *ConAu 102*
Eberhard, Wolfram 1909- *ConAu 2NR, –49*
Eberhardt, Newman Charles 1912- *ConAu 1R*
Eberhardt, Peter *ConAu X*
Eberhart, Dikkon 1946- *ConAu 93*
Eberhart, George M 1950- *ConAu 105*
Eberhart, Mignon G 1899- *WrDr 84*
Eberhart, Mignon Good 1899- *ASpks, AuNews 2, ConAu 73, LongCTC, TwCA, TwCA SUP, TwCCr&M 80, TwCRGW*
Eberhart, Perry 1924- *ConAu 17R*
Eberhart, Richard *DrAP&F 83*
Eberhart, Richard 1904- *ConAu 1R, –2NR, ConLC 3, –11, –19, ConP 80, IntAu&W 82, LongCTC, ModAL, ModAL SUP, TwCA SUP, TwCWr, WhoTwCL, WrDr 84*
Eberle, Irmengarde 1898-1979 *ConAu 1R, –2NR, –85, SmATA 2, –23N*
Eberle, Paul 1928- *ConAu 101*
Eberly, Carole 1943- *MichAu 80*
Eberman, Willis Gilbert 1917- *ConAu 9R*
Ebershoff-Coles, Susan Vaughan 1941- *ConAu 102*
Ebersohn, Wessel 1940- *ConAu 97*
Ebersole, A V, Jr. 1919- *ConAu 37R*
Eberstadt, Charles F 1914?-1974 *ConAu 53*
Ebert, Alan 1935- *ConAu 85*
Ebert, Arthur Frank *WrDr 84*
Ebert, Arthur Frank 1902- *ConAu 5R*
Ebert, James D 1921- *WrDr 84*
Ebert, John E 1922- *ConAu 106*
Ebert, Katherine 1921- *ConAu 107*
Ebert, Peter 1918- *CreCan 2*
Ebert, Roger 1942- *ConAu 69, WrDr 84*
Eblana, Sister 1907- *ConAu P-1*
Eble, Kenneth Eugene 1923- *ConAu 1R, –4NR, WrDr 84*
Eblen, Jack Ericson 1936- *ConAu 33R*
Eblis, J Philip *ConAu X*
Ebner, Hans, Jr. 1944- *MichAu 80*
Ebner, Jeannie 1918- *IntAu&W 82X, IntWWP 82*
Ebner-Allinger, Jeannie 1918- *IntAu&W 82*
Ebon, Martin 1917- *ConAu 10NR, –21R, WrDr 84*
Ebsen, Buddy 1908- *ConAu X*
Ebsen, Christian, Jr. 1908- *ConAu 103*
Ebsworth, Raymond 1911- *ConAu 1R*
Eby, Cecil DeGrotte *WrDr 84*
Eby, Cecil DeGrotte 1927- *ConAu 4NR, IntAu&W 82*
Eccles *SmATA X*
Eccles, David 1904- *ConAu 53*
Eccles, Frank 1923- *ConAu 103, WrDr 84*
Eccles, Henry E 1898- *ConAu P-1, WrDr 84*
Eccles, John 1903- *ConAu 65, WrDr 84*
Eccles, John Carew 1903- *ConAu 9NR*
Eccles, William 1917- *WrDr 84*
Eccles, William J 1917- *ConAu 9R*
Eccli, Sandra Fulton 1936- *ConAu 102*
Echegaray, Jose 1832-1916 *ClDMEL 80, CnMD, ConAu 104, ModRL, ModWD, TwCLC 4[port], TwCWr*
Echenique Posse, Maria Elisa DelRosario 1929- *IntWWP 82*
Echeruo, Michael 1937- *WrDr 84*
Echeruo, Michael J C 1937- *ConAu 8NR, –57, ConP 80*
Echeverria, Durand 1913- *ConAu 9R, WrDr 84*
Echewa, T Obinkaram 1940- *ConAu 73*
Echlin, Edward Patrick 1930- *ConAu 21R,*

WrDr 84
Echols, Barbara E 1934- *ConAu 106*
Echols, John M 1913-1982 *ConAu 2NR, –5R, –107*
Echols, Margit 1944- *ConAu 97*
Eck, Diana L 1945- *ConAu 107*
Eckardt, A Roy 1918- *ConAu 37R, WrDr 84*
Eckardt, Alice L 1923- *ConAu 37R*
Eckardt, Arthur Roy 1918- *IntAu&W 82*
Eckaus, Richard S 1926- *ConAu 45*
Eckblad, Edith G 1923- *WrDr 84*
Eckblad, Edith Gwendolyn 1923- *ConAu 17R, IntAu&W 82, SmATA 23[port]*
Eckbo, Garrett 1910- *ConAu 25R, IntAu&W 82, WrDr 84*
Ecke, Betty Tseng Yu-Ho 1923- *ConAu 5R*
Ecke, Betty Tseng Yu-Ho 1924- *ConAu 6NR*
Eckel, Malcolm W 1912- *ConAu 61*
Eckelberry, Grace Kathryn 1902- *ConAu P-2*
Eckels, Jon *ConAu 3NR, –49, DrAP&F 83, LivgBAA, WrDr 84*
Ecker, H Paul 1922-1976 *ConAu P-2*
Ecker-Racz, L Laszlo 1906- *ConAu 49*
Eckerson, Olive Taylor 1901- *ConAu 1R*
Eckert, Allan W 1931- *ConAu 13R, ConLC 17, SmATA 27, –29[port]*
Eckert, Edward K 1943- *ConAu 77*
Eckert, Horst 1931- *ConAu 37R, SmATA 8*
Eckert, Ruth E 1905- *ConAu 13R*
Eckert, Thor, Jr. 1949- *ConAmTC*
Eckes, Alfred Edward, Jr. 1942- *ConAu 9NR, –61*
Eckhardt, Bob *ConAu X*
Eckhardt, Robert Christian 1913- *ConAu 85*
Eckhardt, Tibor 1888-1972 *ConAu 37R*
Eckhardt-Gramatte, Sonia *CreCan 1*
Eckhardt-Gramatte, Sophie-Carmen *CreCan 1*
Eckholm, Erik P 1949- *ConAu 6NR, –57*
Eckley, Grace 1932- *ConAu 45*
Eckley, Mary M *ConAu 102*
Eckley, Wilton Earl, Jr. 1929- *ConAu 49*
Eckman, Frederick *DrAP&F 83*
Eckman, Frederick 1924- *ConAu 33R*
Eckman, Lester S 1937- *ConAu 2NR, –49*
Eckmar, F R *ConAu X*
Eckstein, Alexander 1915-1976 *ConAu 1R, –6NR, –69*
Eckstein, Gustav 1890-1981 *ConAu 104, –57, TwCA SUP*
Eckstein, Harry 1924- *ConAu 1R, –1NR*
Eckstein, Otto 1927- *ConAu 13R*
Eckstrom, Jack Dennis *ConSFA*
Eclov, Shirley *ConAu X*
Eco, Umberto 1932- *ConAu 77*
Economou, George *DrAP&F 83*
Economou, George 1934- *ConAu 25R, ConP 80, IntAu&W 82, WrDr 84*
Economu, George 1934- *IntWWP 82*
Ecroyd, Donald H 1923- *ConAu 1R, –4NR*
Edari, Ronald S 1943- *ConAu 65*
Edberg, Rolf 1912- *ConAu 11NR*
Edberg, Rolf Filip 1912- *ConAu 69, IntAu&W 82*
Edd, Karl 1926- *IntWWP 82*
Eddings, David 1931- *ConAu 110*
Eddington, Sir Arthur Stanley 1882-1944 *LongCTC, TwCA, TwCA SUP*
Eddins, Dwight 1939- *WrDr 84*
Eddins, Dwight L 1939- *ConAu 33R*
Eddison, E R 1882-1945 *ConAu 109, TwCSFW B*
Eddison, Eric Rucker 1882-1945 *WorAu*
Eddison, John 1916- *ConAu 8NR, –61*
Eddison, Roger 1916- *ConAu P-1*
Eddleman, H Leo 1911- *ConAu 9NR, –13R*
Eddy, Albert *CreCan 2*
Eddy, Edward D 1921- *ConAu 73*
Eddy, Elizabeth *DrAP&F 83*
Eddy, Elizabeth M 1926- *ConAu 21R*
Eddy, George Sherwood 1871-1963 *TwCA, TwCA SUP*
Eddy, John J 1933- *ConAu 73*
Eddy, John P 1932- *ConAu 9NR*
Eddy, John Paul 1932- *ConAu 61*
Eddy, John Percy 1881-1975 *ConAu 61*
Eddy, Mary Baker 1821-1910 *LongCTC*
Eddy, Paul 1944- *ConAu 73*
Eddy, Roger Whittlesey 1920- *ConAu 17R*
Eddy, Samuel K 1926- *ConAu 1R*
Ede, Janina 1937- *SmATA 33[port]*
Edel, Abraham 1908- *ConAu 1R, IntAu&W 82, WrDr 84*

Edel, Gottfried 1929- *IntAu&W 82*
Edel, Joseph Leon 1907- *DcLEL 1940, IntAu&W 82*
Edel, Leon 1907- *ConAu 1R, –1NR, ConLCrt 82, WorAu, WrDr 84*
Edel, Matthew 1941- *ConAu 29R*
Edelberg, Cynthia Dubin 1940- *ConAu 89, IntAu&W 82*
Edelen, Georges 1924- *ConAu 93*
Edell, Celeste *ConAu 1R, SmATA 12*
Edelman, Elaine *DrAP&F 83, IntWWP 82*
Edelman, Lily 1915-1981 *ConAu 102, –61, SmATA 22[port]*
Edelman, Maurice 1911-1975 *ConAu 61, –65, DcLEL 1940, LongCTC, TwCWr, WorAu*
Edelman, Murray J 1919- *ConAu 33R, WrDr 84*
Edelman, Paul S 1926- *ConAu 9R*
Edelman, Richard *DrAP&F 83*
Edelson, Edward 1932- *ConAu 17R*
Edelstein, Arthur *ConAu 9NR*
Edelstein, Arthur 1923- *ConAu 65*
Edelstein, David S 1913- *ConAu 61*
Edelstein, J M 1924- *ConAu 53*
Edelstein, Morton A 1925- *ConAu 69*
Eden, Alvin N 1926- *ConAu 9NR, –61*
Eden, Anthony 1897-1977 *ConAu 69, –77*
Eden, Dorothy 1912-1982 *ConAu 106, –81, TwCCr&M 80, TwCRGW*
Edens, David 1926- *ConAu 108*
Eder, George Jackson 1900- *ConAu 85, WrDr 84*
Edey, Maitland A 1910- *ConAu 6NR, –57, ConISC 1[port], SmATA 25[port]*
Edfelt, Bo Johannes 1904- *ClDMEL 80, IntAu&W 82*
Edgar, David 1948- *ConAu 57, ConDr 82, DcLB 13[port], WrDr 84*
Edgar, Frank Terrell 1932- *ConAu 69*
Edgar, Josephine *ConAu X, TwCRGW, WrDr 84*
Edgar, Ken 1925- *ConAu 49*
Edgar, Neal Lowndes 1927- *ConAu 69*
Edgar, Neal Lowndes 1927-1983 *ConAu 110*
Edgar, Peter 1918- *ConSFA*
Edge, David O 1932- *ConAu 73*
Edge, Findley B 1916- *ConAu 5R, WrDr 84*
Edge, Terry *IntWWP 82X*
Edgerton, Angie Rose 1891- *IntWWP 82*
Edgerton, Franklin 1885-1963 *ConAu 110*
Edgerton, Harold E 1903- *WrDr 84*
Edgerton, Harold Eugene 1903- *ConAu 5NR, –53*
Edgerton, Joseph S 1900?-1983 *ConAu 109*
Edgerton, Robert B 1931- *ConAu 53*
Edgerton, William B 1914- *ConAu 29R, IntAu&W 82*
Edgeworth, Maria 1767-1849 *SmATA 21[port]*
Edgington, Eugene Sinclair 1924- *ConAu 25R, WrDr 84*
Edginton, May 1883-1957 *TwCRGW*
Edgley, Charles K 1943- *ConAu 57*
Edgley, Roy 1925- *ConAu 29R, WrDr 84*
Edgren, Harry D 1899- *ConAu P-2*
Edgy, Wardore *ConAu X*
Edie, James M 1927- *ConAu 9R*
Ediger, Peter J 1926- *ConAu 33R*
Edilog *IntAu&W 82X*
Edinborough, Arnold 1922- *ConAu 73*
Edinger, Edward F 1922- *ConAu 69*
Edington, Andrew 1914- *ConAu 73*
Edison, Judith *ConAu X*
Edison, Michael 1937- *ConAu 110*
Edison, Thomas Alva 1847?-1931 *LongCTC*
Edkins, Anthony 1927- *ConAu 97*
Edkins, Diana M 1947- *ConAu 41R*
Edler, Peter 1934- *ConAu 107*
Edlin, Herbert 1904?-1976 *ConAu 69*
Edlin, Herbert Leeson 1913- *ConAu 61*
Edlin, Herbert Leeson 1913-1976 *ConAu 9NR*
Edlin, John Bruce 1945- *IntAu&W 82*
Edlin, Rosabelle Alpern 1914- *ConAu 9R*
Edman, David 1930- *ConAu 37R*
Edman, Irwin 1896-1954 *TwCA, TwCA SUP*
Edman, Marion 1901- *ConAu P-1*
Edman, Victor Raymond 1900-1967 *ConAu 1R, –6NR*
Edmiston, Jean 1913- *ConAu 13R*
Edmiston, Susan 1940- *ConAu 65*
Edmond, Jay *ConAu X*
Edmonds, Alan *ConAu X*
Edmonds, Ann *ConAu X, IntAu&W 82X*

Edmonds, Arthur Denis 1932- *ConAu 73*
Edmonds, Cecil John 1889- *ConAu P-1*
Edmonds, Charles *ConAu X, IntAu&W 82X, WrDr 84*
Edmonds, Helen 1904-1968 *ConAu 5R, -25R*
Edmonds, Helen G 1911- *ConAu 65, LivgBAA*
Edmonds, I G 1917- *ConAu 33R, SmATA 8*
Edmonds, Margaret Hammett *ConAu 101*
Edmonds, Margot *ConAu X*
Edmonds, Paul *ConAu X*
Edmonds, R H G 1920- *ConAu 69*
Edmonds, Robert 1920- *WrDr 84*
Edmonds, Robin *ConAu X*
Edmonds, Ronald R 1935-1983 *ConAu 110*
Edmonds, Vernon H 1927- *ConAu 37R, IntAu&W 82*
Edmonds, Walter D 1903- *TwCCW 83*
Edmonds, Walter Dumaux 1903- *ConAmA, ConAu 2NR, -5R, DcLB 9[port], IntAu&W 82, ModAL, SmATA 1, -27[port], TwCA, TwCA SUP, WrDr 84*
Edmondson, Clifton Earl 1937- *ConAu 102*
Edmondson, G C 1922- *ConAu 11NR, -57, ConSFA, TwCSFW, WrDr 84*
Edmondson, Wallace *ConAu X*
Edmonson, Harold A 1937- *ConAu 41R*
Edmonson, Munro S 1924- *WrDr 84*
Edmonson, Munro Sterling 1924- *ConAu 33R, IntAu&W 82*
Edmund, Sean *ConAu X, SmATA 4*
Edmunds, H Tudor 1897- *ConAu 106*
Edmunds, Malcolm 1938- *ConAu 73*
Edmunds, Murrell 1898- *ConAu 1R, -4NR*
Edmunds, Simeon 1917- *ConAu 17R*
Edmunds, Stahrl W 1917- *ConAu 69*
Edmundson, Garry C *ConAu X*
Edom, Clifton C 1907- *ConAu 105*
Edridge, Michaela 1934- *IntWWP 82*
Edsall, Howard Linn *DrAP&F 83*
Edsall, Marian S 1920- *ConAu 49, SmATA 8*
Edschmid, Kasimir 1890-1966 *ClDMEL 80, ModGL*
Edson, Harold *ConAu X*
Edson, J T 1928- *ConAu 29R, TwCWW, WrDr 84*
Edson, Peter 1896-1977 *ConAu 73*
Edson, Russell *ConAu 33R, DrAP&F 83*
Edson, Russell 1935- *ConLC 13, ConP 80, WrDr 84*
Edstrom, Mauritz Natanael 1927- *IntAu&W 82*
Eduardi, Guillermo *ConAu X*
Edward VIII 1894-1972 *ConAu 33R*
Edwardes, Allen *ConAu X*
Edwardes, Michael 1923- *ConAu 10NR*
Edwardes, Michael F H 1923- *ConAu 57*
Edwardes, Peter Ivan *IntWWP 82*
Edwards, A W F 1935- *ConAu 73*
Edwards, Al *ConAu X*
Edwards, Alexander *ConAu X*
Edwards, Allen Jack 1926- *ConAu 33R, WrDr 84*
Edwards, Allen L 1914- *ConAu 10NR, -25R*
Edwards, Anne 1927- *ConAu 61, TwCRGW, WrDr 84*
Edwards, Anne-Marie 1932- *ConAu 85*
Edwards, Anthony David 1936- *ConAu 13R*
Edwards, Aubrey Carroll 1909- *IntAu&W 82*
Edwards, Audrey 1947- *ConAu 81, SmATA 31*
Edwards, Bertram *ConAu X, SmATA X*
Edwards, Betty 1926- *ConAu 105, WrDr 84*
Edwards, Blake 1922- *ConAu 81*
Edwards, Bronwen Elizabeth 1948- *ConAu X, SmATA X*
Edwards, Carl N 1943- *ConAu 57*
Edwards, Cassie 1936- *IntWWP 82*
Edwards, Cecile Pepin 1916- *ConAu 5R, SmATA 25[port]*
Edwards, Charles Edward 1930- *ConAu 17R*
Edwards, Charles Mundy, Jr. 1903- *ConAu 45*
Edwards, Charleszime Spears 1907- *LivgBAA*
Edwards, Charlotte *ConAu 29R*
Edwards, Christine 1902- *ConAu P-1*
Edwards, Clifford D 1934- *ConAu 61*
Edwards, Corwin D 1901-1979 *ConAu 10NR, -17R, -85*
Edwards, David 1945?- *ConSFA*
Edwards, David C 1937- *ConAu 41R*
Edwards, David Lawrence 1929- *ConAu 5R*
Edwards, David Vandeusen 1941- *ConAu 105*
Edwards, Donald 1904- *ConAu 65, WrDr 84*
Edwards, Donald Earl 1916- *ConAu X*
Edwards, Dorothy 1914-1982 *ConAu 107, -25R,*

SmATA 31N, -4, TwCCW 83
Edwards, Douglas 1917- *ConAu 110*
Edwards, Edgar O 1919- *ConAu 1R, -6NR*
Edwards, Eli *ConAu X*
Edwards, Elizabeth *ConAu 49*
Edwards, Elwyn Hartley 1927- *ConAu 8NR, -61*
Edwards, F E *ConAu X*
Edwards, Francis *ConAu X*
Edwards, Francis Oborn 1922- *IntAu&W 82*
Edwards, Frank Allyn 1908-1967 *ConAu 1R, -1NR*
Edwards, G B 1899-1976 *ConAu 110, ConLC 25*
Edwards, George 1914- *ConAu 53*
Edwards, George Charles, III 1947- *ConAu 107*
Edwards, Gillian Mary 1918- *ConAu 25R, IntAu&W 82, WrDr 84*
Edwards, Gunvor *SmATA 32*
Edwards, Gunvor 193-?- *ConAu 107*
Edwards, Gus 1939- *ConAu 108, NatPD 81[port]*
Edwards, Harry *LivgBAA*
Edwards, Harry 1942- *ConAu 109*
Edwards, Harvey 1929- *ConAu 25R, SmATA 5, WrDr 84*
Edwards, Henry James 1893- *ConAu 13R*
Edwards, Herbert Charles 1912- *ConAu 9R, SmATA 12*
Edwards, Hilton 1903- *ConAu 65*
Edwards, Hugh 1878-1952 *WhoTwCL*
Edwards, I E S 1909- *ConAu 7NR*
Edwards, Iorwerth 1909- *WrDr 84*
Edwards, Iorwerth Eiddon Stephen 1909- *ConAu 13R, IntAu&W 82*
Edwards, James Don 1926- *ConAu 4NR, -9R*
Edwards, Jane Campbell 1932- *ConAu 13R, SmATA 10*
Edwards, Jaroldeen 1932- *ConAu 102*
Edwards, Jerome E 1937- *ConAu 37R*
Edwards, Joseph Castro 1909- *WrDr 84*
Edwards, Josephine Cunnington 1904- *ConAu 13R*
Edwards, Julia Spalding 1920- *ConAu 37R*
Edwards, Julie *ConAu X*
Edwards, Julie 1935- *ConAu X, SmATA 7*
Edwards, June *ConAu X, IntAu&W 82X, WrDr 84*
Edwards, K Morgan 1912- *ConAu 5R*
Edwards, Kate F 1877-1980 *ConAu 107*
Edwards, Kenneth Charles 1904- *IntAu&W 82*
Edwards, Lee 1932- *ConAu 10NR, -25R*
Edwards, Leo d1944 *AuNews 1*
Edwards, Lynne 1943- *ConAu 73*
Edwards, Margaret *DrAP&F 83*
Edwards, Margaret 1902- *ConAu P-2*
Edwards, Marie Babare *ConAu 57*
Edwards, Mark R 1945- *NatPD 81[port]*
Edwards, Mark U, Jr. 1946- *ConAu 10NR, -65*
Edwards, Marvin L 1915- *ConAu 13R*
Edwards, Max *ConAu X*
Edwards, Michael 1932- *ConAu 85*
Edwards, Michael 1938- *ConAu 106, IntWWP 82, WrDr 84*
Edwards, Monica 1912- *TwCCW 83, WrDr 84*
Edwards, Monica LeDoux Newton 1912- *ConAu 9R, SmATA 12*
Edwards, Norman *ConAu X, WrDr 84*
Edwards, O C, Jr. 1928- *ConAu 53*
Edwards, Owen Dudley 1938- *ConAu 7NR, -57*
Edwards, Sir Owen Morgan 1858-1920 *TwCA, TwCA SUP*
Edwards, P Max H 1914- *ConAu 37R*
Edwards, Page *DrAP&F 83*
Edwards, Page, Jr. 1941- *WrDr 84*
Edwards, Page L, Jr. 1941- *ConAu 1NR, -45*
Edwards, Paul 1923- *ConAu 85*
Edwards, Paul Geoffrey 1926- *ConAu 57*
Edwards, Paul M 1933- *ConAu 41R*
Edwards, Peter 1934- *ConAu 109*
Edwards, Philip 1923- *WrDr 84*
Edwards, Philip Walter 1923- *ConAu 25R, IntAu&W 82*
Edwards, Phoebe *ConAu X*
Edwards, R M *ConAu X*
Edwards, Ralph 1894- *ConAu P-1*
Edwards, Rem Blanchard 1934- *ConAu 37R, IntAu&W 82*
Edwards, Richard Alan 1934- *ConAu 69*
Edwards, Richard C 1944- *ConAu 2NR, -45*
Edwards, Ron 1930- *ConAu 105*
Edwards, Ronald George 1930- *WrDr 84*

Edwards, Roselyn 1929- *ConAu 25R*
Edwards, Ruth Dudley *ConAu X*
Edwards, S W *IntWWP 82X*
Edwards, Sally Cary 1929- *ConAu 25R, SmATA 7*
Edwards, Samuel *ConAu X, SmATA X, WrDr 84*
Edwards, Stephen *ConAu X*
Edwards, T Bentley 1906- *ConAu P-2*
Edwards, Thomas R 1928- *ConAu 5R, WrDr 84*
Edwards, Tilden Hampton, Jr. 1935- *ConAu 102*
Edwards, Verne E, Jr. 1924- *ConAu 33R*
Edwards, Ward 1927- *ConAu 21R*
Edwards, William 1896- *ConAu P-1*
Edwards, William B 1927- *ConAu 5R*
Edwards, William J 1930- *ConAmTC*
Edwards Bello, Joaquin 1887-1967 *ModLAL*
Edwin, Brother B *ConAu X*
Edwin-Scott, Geoffrey Norman 1948- *IntWWP 82*
Eeden, Frederik Willem Van 1860-1932 *ClDMEL 80, EncWL 2*
Eeg-Olofsson, Richard Georg 1898- *IntAu&W 82*
Eekman, Thomas 1923- *ConAu 81, IntAu&W 82*
Eells, George 1922- *ConAu 21R*
Eells, Robert J 1944- *ConAu 102*
Efemey, Raymond 1928- *ConAu 21R*
Effinger, Geo Alec 1947- *ConAu 37R, TwCSFW*
Effinger, George Alec 1947- *DcLB 8[port], WrDr 84*
Efird, James M 1932- *ConAu 37R*
Efron, Alexander 1897- *ConAu P-2*
Efron, Arthur 1931- *ConAu 69*
Efron, Benjamin 1908- *ConAu 5R, -5NR*
Efron, Edith Carol 1922- *ConAu 102*
Efros, Israel 1891-1981 *ConAu 102, -21R*
Efros, Susan *DrAP&F 83*
Efros, Susan Elyse 1947- *ConAu 104*
Efrot *ConAu X*
Egami, Tomi 1899- *ConAu 61*
Egan, Alvie Mary 1918- *IntWWP 82*
Egan, David R 1943- *ConAu 102*
Egan, Desmond 1940?- *IntAu&W 82*
Egan, E W 1922- *ConAu 9NR, -21R*
Egan, Ferol 1923- *ConAu 29R, IntAu&W 82, WrDr 84*
Egan, Gerard 1930- *ConAu 29R*
Egan, John P 1934- *ConAu 110*
Egan, Lesley *ConAu X, WrDr 84*
Egan, Leslie *TwCCr&M 80*
Egan, Melinda A 1950- *ConAu 102*
Egan, Michael 1941- *ConAu 45*
Egan, Philip S 1920- *ConAu 1R*
Egan, Robert 1945- *ConAu 77*
Egbert, Donald Drew 1902-1973 *ConAu 37R, ConAu P-2, DcLEL 1940*
Egbuna, Obi 1938- *WrDr 84*
Egbuna, Obi B 1938- *DcLEL 1940*
Egbuna, Obi Benedict 1938- *ConDr 82*
Egbuna, Obi Benue 1938- *ConAu 102, TwCWr*
Egea, Julio Alfredo 1926- *IntWWP 82*
Egejuru, Phanuel Akubueze *ConAu 106*
Egelhof, Joseph 1919?-1980 *ConAu 97*
Egermeier, Elsie E 1890- *ConAu 5R*
Egerton, Frank N, III 1936- *ConAu 110*
Egerton, George 1860-1945 *LongCTC, TwCA, TwCA SUP*
Egerton, George W 1942- *ConAu 85*
Egerton, John 1935- *ConAu 85*
Egerton, Lucy *ConAu X*
Egg, Maria 1910- *ConAu 29R*
Egg-Benes, Maria *ConAu X*
Egge, Peter 1869-1959 *ClDMEL 80, CnMD, TwCA, TwCA SUP*
Eggebrecht, Jurgen 1898- *IntWWP 82*
Eggeling, Hans Friedrich 1878-1977 *ConAu 1R, -73*
Eggen, Arnljot 1923- *IntWWP 82*
Eggenberger, David 1918- *ConAu 9R, SmATA 6*
Eggenschwiler, David 1936- *ConAu 37R*
Egger, Ellen *IntAu&W 82X*
Egger, M David 1936- *ConAu 57*
Egger, Rowland Andrews 1908-1979 *ConAu 4NR, -5R*
Eggers, J Philip 1940- *ConAu 33R*
Eggers, William T 1912- *ConAu 29R*
Eggert, Gerald G 1926- *ConAu 21R*

Eggert, James Edward 1943- *ConAu 107*
Eggert, Jim *ConAu X*
Eggleston, Edward 1837-1902 *SmATA 27[port]*
Eggleston, Jessie 1906- *IntWWP 82*
Eggleston, Wilfrid 1901- *ConAu 8NR, -21R, IntAu&W 82, WrDr 84*
Egielski, Richard 1952- *SmATA 11*
Egler, Frank E 1911- *ConAu 29R, WrDr 84*
Egleson, Janet F *ConAu X*
Egleton, Clive 1927- *ConAu 103, TwCCr&M 80, WrDr 84*
Eglinton, John 1868-1961 *LongCTC, ModBrL*
Eglite, Karina *IntWWP 82X*
Eglite-Berzina, Karina 1911- *IntWWP 82*
Eglitis, Anslavs Leo 1906- *IntAu&W 82*
Egner, Thorbjorn 1912- *IntAu&W 82*
Egremont, Max 1948- *ConAu 93*
Eguchi, Shinichi 1914-1979 *ConAu 85*
Egyedi, Bela 1913- *IntAu&W 82*
Egypt, Ophelia Settle 1903- *ConAu 81, LivgBAA, SmATA 16*
Ehle, John *DrAP&F 83*
Ehle, John 1925- *ConAu 1R, -9R, ConLC 27[port], IntAu&W 82, WrDr 84*
Ehlers, Henry James 1907- *ConAu 13R, WrDr 84*
Ehmann, James 1948- *ConAu 109*
Ehmke, Horst Paul August 1927- *IntAu&W 82*
Ehninger, Douglas Wagner 1913-1979 *ConAu 4NR, -5R*
Ehre, Edward 1905- *ConAu 9R*
Ehre, Milton 1933- *ConAu 53*
Ehrenberg, Victor Leopold 1891-1976 *ConAu 4NR, -5R, -65*
Ehrenbourg, Ilya 1891-1967 *TwCA, TwCA SUP*
Ehrenburg, Ilya 1891-1967 *ConAu 102, -25R, ConLC 18*
Ehrenburg, Ilya Grigorevich 1891-1967 *EncWL 2*
Ehrenburg, Ilya Grigoryevich 1891-1967 *LongCTC, ModSL 1, TwCWr*
Ehrendorfer, Friedrich 1927- *IntAu&W 82*
Ehrenfeld, David W 1938- *ConAu 81*
Ehrenpreis, Anne Henry 1927- *ConAu 53*
Ehrenpreis, Irvin 1920- *ConAu 110*
Ehrenreich, Barbara 1941- *ConAu 73*
Ehrenreich, Herman 1900?-1970 *ConAu 104*
Ehrenstein, Albert 1886-1950 *ModGL*
Ehrensvaerd, Goesta 1910- *ConAu 2NR, -49*
Ehrenwald, Jan 1900- *ConAu 2NR, -49*
Ehrenzweig, Albert A 1906- *WrDr 84*
Ehrenzweig, Albert A 1906-1974 *ConAu P-2*
Ehresman, Donald L 1937- *ConAu 69*
Ehresmann, Julia M 1939- *ConAu 33R*
Ehret, Christopher 1941- *ConAu 37R, WrDr 84*
Ehrhardt, Reinhold 1900- *ConAu 29R*
Ehrhart, W D *DrAP&F 83*
Ehrhart, W D 1948- *ConAu 7NR, -61*
Ehrhart, William Daniel 1948- *IntAu&W 82, IntWWP 82*
Ehrlich, Amy 1942- *ConAu 37R, SmATA 25*
Ehrlich, Anne Howland 1933- *ConAu 8NR, -61, IntAu&W 82*
Ehrlich, Arnold 1923- *ConAu 33R*
Ehrlich, Bettina *TwCCW 83*
Ehrlich, Bettina Bauer 1903- *ConAu P-1, SmATA 1*
Ehrlich, Cyril 1925- *ConAu 103, WrDr 84*
Ehrlich, Eugene 1922- *WrDr 84*
Ehrlich, Eugene H 1922- *ConAu 1R, -5NR*
Ehrlich, Gretel *DrAP&F 83*
Ehrlich, Howard J 1932- *ConAu 17R*
Ehrlich, Jack 1930- *ConAu X, TwCWW, WrDr 84*
Ehrlich, Jacob Wilburn 1900-1971 *ConAu 33R*
Ehrlich, Jake *ConAu X*
Ehrlich, John Gunther 1930- *ConAu 1R, -4NR*
Ehrlich, Leonard 1905- *TwCA*
Ehrlich, Leonard Harry 1924- *ConAu 102*
Ehrlich, Max 1909- *ConAu 1R, -1NR, IntAu&W 82, TwCSFW, WrDr 84*
Ehrlich, Nathaniel J 1940- *ConAu 53*
Ehrlich, Otto Hild 1892-1979 *ConAu 85*
Ehrlich, Paul 1932- *ConAu 8NR, -65, WrDr 84*
Ehrlich, Robert S 1935- *ConAu 21R*
Ehrlich, Shelley *DrAP&F 83*
Ehrlich, Walter 1921- *ConAu 53*
Ehrlichman, John *DrAP&F 83*
Ehrlichman, John Daniel 1925- *ConAu 65*
Ehrman, John 1920- *WrDr 84*
Ehrman, John Patrick William 1920- *ConAu 4NR, -5R, IntAu&W 82*
Ehrman, Lee 1935- *ConAu 69*

Ehrmann, Herbert B 1891-1970 *ConAu P-2*
Ehrsam, Theodore George 1909- *ConAu 45*
Ehsan, Mohsin 1932- *IntWWP 82*
Eibl-Eibesfeldt, Irenaeus 1928- *ConAu 3NR*
Eibl-Eibesfeldt, Irenaus 1928- *ConAu 9R*
Eibling, Harold Henry 1905- *ConAu 37R*
Eiby, George 1918- *ConAu 53*
Eich, Guenter 1907-1971 *ConAu 93*
Eich, Gunter 1907- *ConLC 15*
Eich, Gunter 1907-1972 *CIDMEL 80, EncWL 2, ModGL, TwCWr, WhoTwCL, WorAu*
Eichelbaum, Samuel 1894-1967 *ModWD*
Eichelbaum, Stanley 1926- *ConAmTC, ConAu 73*
Eichelberger, Clark M 1896-1980 *ConAu 93*
Eichelberger, Clayton L 1925- *ConAu 41R*
Eichelberger, Rosa Kohler 1896- *ConAu 102*
Eichenberg, Fritz 1901- *ConAu 6NR, -57, SmATA 9*
Eichenlaub, John Ellis 1922- *ConAu 1R, -4NR*
Eicher, Elizabeth *ConAu 17R*
Eicher, Joanne B 1930- *ConAu 49*
Eichhorn, David Max 1906- *ConAu P-1*
Eichhorn, Douglas *DrAP&F 83*
Eichhorn, Werner 1899- *ConAu 29R*
Eichhorw, Werner 1899- *IntAu&W 82*
Eichler, Margrit 1942- *ConAu 107*
Eichler, Richard W 1921- *IntAu&W 82*
Eichman, Mark 1949- *ConAu 109, NatPD 81[port]*
Eichner, Alfred S 1937- *ConAu 5NR, -13R*
Eichner, Hans 1921- *ConAu 4NR, -5R, WrDr 84*
Eichner, James A 1927- *ConAu 13R, SmATA 4*
Eichner, Maura *DrAP&F 83*
Eichner, Maura 1915- *ConAu X, -37R*
Eichorn, Dorothy H 1924- *ConAu 49*
Eickhoff, Andrew R 1924- *ConAu 21R, WrDr 84*
Eid, Leif 1908?-1976 *ConAu 65*
Eidelberg, Ludwig 1898-1970 *ConAu 29R, ConAu P-1*
Eidelberg, Paul 1928- *ConAu 21R*
Eidem, Odd 1913- *EncWL 2*
Eidenberg, Eugene 1939- *ConAu 81*
Eidesheim, Julie 1884-1972 *ConAu 104*
Eidlitz, Marilla 1945- *IntAu&W 82*
Eidsvik, Charles Vernon 1943- *ConAu 101*
Eidt, Robert C 1923- *ConAu 33R*
Eidus, Janice *DrAP&F 83*
Eiduson, Bernice Tabackman 1921- *ConAu 1R*
Eifert, Virginia Snider 1911-1966 *ConAu 1R, SmATA 2*
Eigeldinger, Marc 1917- *IntAu&W 82, IntWWP 82*
Eigen, Manfred 1927- *ConAu 108*
Eigner, Edwin M 1931- *ConAu 21R*
Eigner, Larry 1927- *ConAu X, ConLC 9, ConP 80, DcLB 5[port], WrDr 84*
Eigner, Laurence 1927- *ConAu 6NR, -9R*
Eigra *IntAu&W 82X*
Eiker, Mathilde 1893- *TwCA, TwCA SUP*
Eiland, Murray L 1936- *ConAu 85*
Eilers, Angelika 1943- *IntAu&W 82*
Eilers, Hazel Kraft 1910- *WrDr 84*
Eilon, Samuel 1923- *ConAu 4NR, -5R, WrDr 84*
Eimer, D Robert 1927- *ConAu 13R*
Eimerl, Sarel 1925- *ConAu 21R*
Einarsdottir, Malfridur 1899- *IntAu&W 82*
Einbond, Bernard Lionel *DrAP&F 83*
Einbond, Bernard Lionel 1937- *ConAu 37R, IntWWP 82, WrDr 84*
Einhorn, Virginia Hilu *ConAu X*
Einhorn, Wendy *DrAP&F 83*
Einsel, Mary 1929- *WrDr 84*
Einsel, Mary E 1929- *ConAu 29R*
Einsel, Naiad *SmATA 10*
Einsel, Walter 1926- *SmATA 10*
Einstein, Albert 1879-1955 *LongCTC*
Einstein, Albert 1947- *ConAu 109*
Einstein, Alfred 1880-1952 *LongCTC, TwCA SUP*
Einstein, Charles 1926- *ConAu 65, ConSFA*
Einstein, Elizabeth 1939- *ConAu 109*
Einstein, Stanley 1934- *ConAu 4NR, -53*
Einstoss, Ron 1930?-1977 *ConAu 69*
Einzig, Barbara *DrAP&F 83*
Einzig, Paul 1897-1973 *ConAu 5NR, -9R, -89*
Eirelin, Glenn *ConAu X, IntAu&W 82X*
Eiriksson, Eyvindur Petur 1935- *IntAu&W 82*
Eis, Ruth Beate 1909- *IntAu&W 82*

Eisdorfer, Carl 1930- *ConAu 41R*
Eisele, Albert A 1936- *ConAu 41R*
Eisele, Robert H 1948- *ConAu 108, IntAu&W 82, NatPD 81[port]*
Eiseley, Loren Corey 1907-1977 *ASpks, ConAu 1R, -6NR, -73, ConLC 7, DcLEL 1940, WorAu*
Eiseman, Alberta 1925- *ConAu 77, SmATA 15*
Eisen, Carol G *ConAu 49*
Eisen, Jack 1925- *ConAu 73*
Eisenach, Eldon J 1938- *ConAu 106*
Eisenberg, Azriel 1903- *ConAu 10NR*
Eisenberg, Azriel Louis 1903- *ConAu 49, SmATA 12*
Eisenberg, Daniel Bruce 1946- *ConAu 6NR, -57*
Eisenberg, Dennis 1929- *WrDr 84*
Eisenberg, Dennis Harold 1929- *ConAu 25R*
Eisenberg, Gerson G 1909- *ConAu 81, IntAu&W 82*
Eisenberg, Hershey H 1927- *ConAu 104*
Eisenberg, Howard 1946- *ConAu 101*
Eisenberg, Larry 1919- *ConAu 33R, TwCSFW, WrDr 84*
Eisenberg, Lawrence B *ConAu 77*
Eisenberg, Lee 1946- *ConAu 9NR, -61*
Eisenberg, Lisa 1949- *ConAu 110*
Eisenberg, Maurice 1902-1972 *ConAu 37R*
Eisenberg, Ralph 1930-1973 *ConAu 3NR, -5R, -45*
Eisenberg, Ronald L 1945- *ConAu 73*
Eisenberg, Ruth F *DrAP&F 83*
Eisenberger, Kenneth 1948- *ConAu 81*
Eisenbud, Jule 1908- *ConAu 49*
Eisendle, Helmut Otto Johannes 1939- *IntAu&W 82*
Eisendrath, Craig R 1936- *ConAu 49*
Eisenhower, Dwight David 1890-1969 *ConAu 65*
Eisenhower, John S D 1922- *ConAu 33R*
Eisenhower, Milton S 1899- *ConAu 73*
Eisenman, Peter D 1932- *ConAu 108, WrDr 84*
Eisenmenger, Robert Waltz 1926- *ConAu 37R*
Eisenreich, Herbert 1925- *IntAu&W 82, ModGL*
Eisenschiml, Otto 1880-1963 *ConAu 1R*
Eisenson, Jon 1907- *ConAu 17R, WrDr 84*
Eisenstadt, A S 1920- *ConAu 4NR, -9R*
Eisenstadt, Shmuel N 1923- *ConAu 25R, IntAu&W 82*
Eisenstadt, Shmuel Noah *WrDr 84*
Eisenstaedt, Alfred 1898- *ConAu 108*
Eisenstat, Jane Sperry 1920- *ConAu 1R*
Eisenstein, Elizabeth L 1923- *ConAu 89*
Eisenstein, Ira 1906- *ConAu 21R*
Eisenstein, Phyllis 1946- *ConAu 85, TwCSFW, WrDr 84*
Eisenstein, Sam A 1932- *ConAu 61, NatPD 81[port]*
Eisenstein, Samuel A *DrAP&F 83*
Eisenthaler, Hans *IntWWP 82X*
Eiserer, Leonard Arnold 1948- *ConAu 73*
Eisinger, Chester Emanuel 1915- *ConAu 21R*
Eisinger, Peter K 1942- *ConAu 69*
Eisler, Colin 1931- *ConAu 85*
Eisler, Georg 1928- *ConAu 106*
Eisler, Paul 1922- *ConAu 61*
Eisler, Riane Tennenhaus 1931- *ConAu 73*
Eisman, Hy 1927- *ConAu 65*
Eisman, Mark 1948- *ConAu 108, NatPD 81[port]*
Eismann, Bernard N 1933- *ConAu 1R*
Eisner, Betty Grover 1915- *ConAu 29R, WrDr 84*
Eisner, Gisela 1925- *ConAu P-1, WrDr 84*
Eisner, Lotte Henriette *ConAu 45*
Eisner, Robert 1922- *ConAu 107, WrDr 84*
Eisner, Simon *ConAu X*
Eisner, Victor 1921- *ConAu 53*
Eisner, Will 1917- *ConAu 108, SmATA 31[port]*
Eissenstat, Bernard W 1927- *ConAu 45*
Eister, Allan W 1915-1979 *ConAu 2NR, -45*
Eiteman, David 1930- *ConAu 45*
Eiteman, Wilford J 1902- *ConAu 1R, -4NR*
Eitinger, Leo 1912- *ConAu 89*
Eitner, Lorenz E A 1919- *ConAu 1R, -5NR, WrDr 84*
Eitzen, Allan 1928- *SmATA 9*
Eitzen, D Stanley 1934- *ConAu 4NR, -53*
Eitzen, Ruth 1924- *ConAu 41R, SmATA 9*
Ekblaw, Sidney E 1903- *ConAu 37R*
Ekeblad, Frederick A 1917- *ConAu 5R*
Ekeh, Peter P 1937- *ConAu 102*

Ekeloef, Gunnar 1907-1968 *ConAu 25R*
Ekelof, Gunnar 1907-1968 *CIDMEL 80,*
  ConAu X, ConLC 27[port], EncWL 2,
  WhoTwCL, WorAu
Ekelund, Vilhelm 1880-1949 *CIDMEL 80,*
  EncWL 2
Ekerwald, Carl-Goran 1923- *IntAu&W 82*
Ekirch, A Roger 1950- *ConAu 109*
Ekirch, Arthur A, Jr. 1915- *ConAu 2NR, –5R,*
  IntAu&W 82, WrDr 84
Ekker, Charles 1930- *ConAu 37R*
Eklund, Gordon 1945- *ConAu 33R,*
  DcLB Y83B[port], TwCSFW, WrDr 84
Eklund, Jane Mary *ConAu X*
Eklund, John M 1909- *WrDr 84*
Ekman, Paul 1934- *ConAu 37R*
Ekman, Rosalind 1933- *ConAu 33R*
Ekner, Reidar 1929- *IntWWP 82*
Ekola, Giles C 1927- *ConAu 17R*
Ekstein, Rudolf 1912- *ConAu 4NR, –5R*
Eksteins, Modris 1943- *ConAu 77*
Ekstrom, Arthur Hugo Fredrik 1899-
  IntAu&W 82
Ekstrom, Jan Olof 1923- *IntAu&W 82*
Ekstrom, Margareta 1930- *IntAu&W 82*
Ekvall, Robert Brainerd 1898- *ConAu 1R, –5NR,*
  WrDr 84
Ekwall, Eldon E 1933- *ConAu 29R*
Ekwell, Eilert 1877-1964 *LongCTC*
Ekwensi, C O D *ConAu X*
Ekwensi, Cyprian 1921- *ConAu 29R, ConLC 4,*
  ConNov 82, DcLEL 1940, EncWL 2,
  LongCTC, ModBlW, ModCmwL,
  TwCCW 83, TwCWr, WhoTwCL, WorAu,
  WrDr 84
El-Aref, Aref d1973 *ConAu 41R*
El-Ayouty, Yassin 1928- *ConAu 29R*
El-Baz, Farouk 1938- *ConAu 10NR, –25R*
El Bi *IntAu&W 82X*
El Crummo *ConAu X*
El-Erian, Abdullah Ali 1920-1981 *ConAu 108*
El-Meligi, A Moneim 1923- *ConAu 17R*
El-Messidi, Kathy Groehn 1946- *ConAu 57,*
  MichAu 80
El-Nil, Ebn *ConAu X*
El Ruisenor DeLaVera *IntAu&W 82X*
El Saffar, Ruth 1941- *ConAu 69*
El-Said, Sadek M 1924- *IntAu&W 82*
El Uqsor *ConAu X*
Ela, Jonathan P 1945- *ConAu 81*
Elagin, Ivan 1918- *IntWWP 82*
Elam, Dorothy Allen Conley 1904- *LivgBAA*
Elam, Richard M 1920- *ConAu 61, SmATA 9*
Elashoff, Janet Dixon 1942- *ConAu 61*
Elath, Eliahu 1903- *ConAu 13R, WrDr 84*
Elazar, Daniel J 1934- *ConAu 21R*
Elbert, Edmund J 1923- *ConAu 37R*
Elbert, George A 1911- *ConAu 61*
Elbert, Joyce *WrDr 84*
Elbert, Samuel Hoyt 1907- *ConAu 1R, –5NR,*
  IntAu&W 82
Elbert, Virginie Fowler 1912- *ConAu 8NR, –61*
Elbin, Paul Nowell 1905- *ConAu 69*
Elbing, Alvar O, Jr. 1928- *ConAu 21R*
Elbing, Carol J 1930- *ConAu 21R*
Elbogen, Paul 1894- *ConAu 5R, IntAu&W 82*
Elborn, Geoffrey 1950- *ConAu 109*
Elbow, Peter 1935- *ConAu 65*
Elbrecht, Paul G 1921- *ConAu 17R*
Elcock, Howard James 1942- *ConAu 29R,*
  WrDr 84
Eldefonso, Edward 1933- *ConAu 21R*
Elder, Art *WrDr 84*
Elder, Gary *DrAP&F 83*
Elder, Gary 1939- *ConAu 73, IntWWP 82*
Elder, Glen H, Jr. 1934- *ConAu 3NR, –49*
Elder, John 1933- *WrDr 84*
Elder, Joseph *ConSFA*
Elder, Karl *DrAP&F 83*
Elder, Karl 1948- *ConAu 77, IntAu&W 82*
Elder, Leon *ConAu X*
Elder, Lonne, III 1931- *ConAu 81, ConDr 82,*
  DcLB 7[port], DcLEL 1940, LivgBAA,
  WrDr 84
Elder, Mark Lee 1935- *ConAu 2NR, –49,*
  IntAu&W 82
Elder, Michael Aiken 1931- *ConAu 33R,*
  WrDr 84
Elder, Robert Ellsworth 1915- *ConAu 1R*
Eldershaw, Barnard M *TwCWr*
Eldershaw, M Barnard *TwCSFW, WrDr 84*
Eldjarn, Kristjan 1916-1982 *ConAu 110*

Eldred, Vince 1924- *ConAu 69*
Eldredge, H Wentworth 1909- *ConAu 41R*
Eldredge, Laurence H 1902- *ConAu P-2*
Eldridge, Colin Clifford 1942- *ConAu 107,*
  WrDr 84
Eldridge, Frank R 1889?-1976 *ConAu 69*
Eldridge, J E T 1936- *ConAu 11NR, –25R*
Eldridge, John E T 1936- *WrDr 84*
Eldridge, Paul 1888- *ConAu 9R*
Eldridge, Retha Hazel 1910- *ConAu P-1*
Eleanor, Sister Joseph *ConAu 25R*
Elegant, Robert Sampson 1928- *ConAu 1R,*
  –1NR, IntAu&W 82, WrDr 84
Elek, Paul 1906?-1976 *ConAu 69*
Elektorowicz, Leszek 1924- *IntAu&W 82*
Elethea, Abba *ConAu X, DrAP&F 83*
Elevitch, M D *DrAP&F 83*
Elevitch, M D 1925- *ConAu 2NR, –49*
Eley, Lynn W 1925- *ConAu 25R*
Elfenbein, Julien 1897- *ConAu 1R, –5NR,*
  IntAu&W 82, WrDr 84
Elfenbein, Julien 1897-1983 *ConAu 109*
Elfman, Blossom 1925- *ConAu 2NR, –45,*
  SmATA 8
Elford, Homer J R 1912- *ConAu 9NR, –21R*
Elgar, Frank 1899- *ConAu 102*
Elgarresta Ramirez DeHaro, Jose 1945-
  IntAu&W 82
Elgin, Kathleen 1923- *ConAu 25R*
Elgin, Mary 1917-1965 *ConAu X, TwCRGW*
Elgin, Suzette Haden 1936- *ConAu 8NR, –61,*
  TwCSFW, WrDr 84
Elia 1775-1834 *SmATA X*
Eliach, Yaffa 1935- *ConAu 110*
Eliade, Mircea 1907- *ConAu 65, ConLC 19,*
  EncWL 2, WorAu
Elias, Albert J 1920- *ConAu 81*
Elias, C E, Jr. 1924- *ConAu 13R*
Elias, Christopher 1925- *ConAu 33R*
Elias, Eileen 1910- *ConAu X*
Elias, Horace J 1910- *ConAu 89*
Elias, John L 1933- *ConAu 69*
Elias, Robert Henry 1914- *ConAu 61*
Elias, Taslim Olawale 1914- *ConAu 6NR, –13R*
Eliason, Joyce 1934- *ConAu 77*
Eliav, Arie L 1921- *ConAu 11NR, –69*
Elie, Robert 1915- *CreCan 1*
Elin Pelin 1877-1949 *EncWL 2*
Elin Pelin 1878-1949 *ModSL 2*
Elinson, Jack 1917- *ConAu 2NR, –45*
Elioseff, Lee Andrew 1933- *ConAu 17R*
Eliot, Alexander 1919- *ConAu 1NR, –49,*
  IntAu&W 82
Eliot, Anne 1903-1979 *ConAu X, SmATA X,*
  TwCRGW
Eliot, George Fielding 1894-1971 *ConAu 29R,*
  TwCA, TwCA SUP
Eliot, Sonny 1926- *ConAu 81*
Eliot, T S 1888-1965 *CnMWL, ConAu 5R,*
  –25R, ConLC 1, –2, –3, –6, –9, –10, –13, –15,
  –24[port], ConLCrt 82, CroCD,
  DcLB 7[port], –10[port], EncWL 2[port],
  LongCTC, ModAL, ModAL SUP, ModBrL,
  ModBrL SUP, ModWD, RGFMBP, TwCA,
  TwCA SUP, TwCWr, WhoTwCL
Eliot, Thomas H 1907- *ConAu 89*
Eliot, Thomas Stearns 1888-1965 *CnMD*
Eliot Hurst, M E 1938- *ConAu 57*
Eliovson, Sima Benveniste 1919- *ConAu 5NR,*
  –13R, IntAu&W 82
Elis, Islwyn Ffowc 1924- *ConAu 93*
Eliscu, Frank 1912- *ConAu 57*
Elisofon, Eliot 1911-1973 *ConAu 41R,*
  SmATA 21N
Elison, George 1937- *ConAu 53*
Elizabeth 1866-1941 *LongCTC, TwCA,*
  TwCA SUP, TwCRGW
Elizabeth Marie, Sister 1914- *ConAu 9R*
Elizabeth, Queen Of Roumania *LongCTC*
Elizondo, Salvador 1932- *EncWL 2, ModLAL*
Elizondo, Sergio D *DrAP&F 83*
Elkholy, Abdo A 1925- *ConAu 21R*
Elkin, Benjamin 1911- *ConAu 1R, –4NR,*
  SmATA 3, WrDr 84
Elkin, Frederick 1918- *ConAu 41R*
Elkin, H V *ConAu X*
Elkin, Judith Laikin 1928- *ConAu 4NR, –53*
Elkin, Michael 1949- *ConAmTC*
Elkin, Stanley *DrAP&F 83*
Elkin, Stanley 1930- *ConAu 8NR, –9R,*
  ConLC 4, –6, –9, –14, –27[port], ConNov 82,

  DcLB Y80A[port], –2, WorAu 1970,
  WrDr 84
Elkin, Stephen L 1941- *ConAu 93*
Elkind, David 1931- *ConAu 1NR, –45*
Elkind, Sue Saniel *DrAP&F 83*
Elkins, Dov Peretz 1937- *ConAu 29R,*
  SmATA 5, WrDr 84
Elkins, Ella Ruth 1929- *ConAu 25R*
Elkins, Stanley Maurice 1925- *ConAu 102*
Elkins, William R 1926- *ConAu 33R*
Elkon, Juliette *ConAu X*
Elkon-Hamelecourt, Juliette 1912- *ConAu 57*
Elkouri, Frank 1921- *ConAu 69*
Ellacott, S E 1911- *ConAu 3NR, SmATA 19,*
  WrDr 84
Ellacott, Samuel Ernest 1911- *ConAu 5R,*
  IntAu&W 82
Elledge, Jim *DrAP&F 83*
Elledge, Jim 1950- *ConAu 102*
Elledge, W Paul 1938- *ConAu 25R*
Ellen, Barbara 1938- *ConAu 5R*
Ellenberger, Henri F 1905- *ConAu P-2*
Ellenbogen, Eileen 1917- *ConAu 104*
Ellender, Raphael 1906-1972 *ConAu 37R*
Ellens, J Harold 1932- *ConAu 7NR, –57*
Ellenson, Gene 1921- *ConAu 57*
Eller, John 1935- *ConAu 105*
Eller, Ronald D 1948- *ConAu 110*
Eller, Vernard 1927- *ConAu 9NR, –21R,*
  WrDr 84
Eller, William 1921- *ConAu 77*
Ellerbeck, Anna-Marie *CreCan 1*
Ellerbeck, Rosemary *ConAu 106, TwCRGW,*
  WrDr 84
Ellerbee, Linda 1944- *ConAu 110*
Ellerman, Annie Winifred *WrDr 84*
Ellerman, Annie Winifred 1894- *ConAu 104,*
  LongCTC
Ellerman, Annie Winifred 1894-1983 *ConAu 108*
Ellerre *IntAu&W 82X*
Ellery, John Blaise 1920- *ConAu 9R*
Ellett, Marcella Howard 1931- *ConAu 21R*
Ellfeldt, Lois 1910- *ConAu 33R*
Ellicott, V L *ConAu X*
Ellicott, Valcoulon MeMoyne 1893-1983
  ConAu 109
Ellin, E M 1905- *ConAu P-2, TwCCW 83,*
  WrDr 84
Ellin, Stanley 1916- *ConAu 1R, –4NR, Conv 3,*
  IntAu&W 82, TwCCr&M 80, WorAu,
  WrDr 84
Elling, Karl A 1935- *ConAu 25R*
Elling, Ray H 1929- *ConAu 33R*
Ellinger, John Henry 1919- *WrDr 84*
Ellingsworth, Huber W 1928- *ConAu 10NR,*
  –21R
Ellington, Duke 1899-1974 *ConAu X*
Ellington, Edward Kennedy 1899-1974 *ConAu 49,*
  –97
Ellington, James W 1927- *ConAu 37R*
Ellington, Richard 1915?-1980 *ConAu 102*
Ellinwood, Leonard 1905- *ConAu 1R*
Elliot, Alistair 1932- *IntAu&W 82,*
  IntWWP 82
Elliot, Asa *ConAu X*
Elliot, Daniel *ConAu X*
Elliot, Edith M 1912- *ConAu 21R*
Elliot, Elisabeth 1926- *ConAu 5R, –6NR*
Elliot, Geraldine *ConAu X*
Elliot, Ian 1925- *ConAu 69*
Elliot, Jeffrey M 1947- *ConAu 106*
Elliot, John 1918- *ConSFA, WrDr 84*
Elliott, Alan C 1952- *ConAu 102*
Elliott, Allan *ConAu X*
Elliott, Andrew Jackson 1899-1965 *CreCan 1*
Elliott, Aubrey 1917- *ConAu 93, IntAu&W 82*
Elliott, Bob 1923- *ConAu 109*
Elliott, Brian Robinson 1910- *ConAu 25R,*
  IntAu&W 82, WrDr 84
Elliott, Bruce *ConSFA*
Elliott, Bruce 1915?-1973 *ConAu 41R*
Elliott, C Orville 1913- *ConAu 33R, WrDr 84*
Elliott, Chip *ConAu X*
Elliott, Christopher 1929- *WrDr 84*
Elliott, Christopher Robin 1929- *IntAu&W 82*
Elliott, Corinne 1917- *IntAu&W 82*
Elliott, David W 1939- *ConAu 45*
Elliott, Donald 1928- *ConAu 69*
Elliott, E E, III 1945- *ConAu 29R*
Elliott, Emory 1942- *ConAu 69*
Elliott, Errol Thomas 1894- *ConAu 69*
Elliott, George P 1918-1980 *ConAu 1R, –2NR,*

-97, ConLC 2, ConP 80, DcLEL 1940,
IntAu&W 82, ModAL, ModAL SUP,
WorAu
Elliott, Harley DrAP&F 83
Elliott, Harley 1940- ConAu 4NR, -49
Elliott, James Francis 1914-1981 ConAu 110
Elliott, Jan Walter 1939- ConAu 37R, WrDr 84
Elliott, Janice 1931- ConAu 8NR, -13R,
DcLB 14[port], IntAu&W 82, WrDr 84
Elliott, John 1938- ConAu 25R
Elliott, John E 1931- ConAu 1R, -5NR
Elliott, John Huxtable 1930- ConAu 3NR, -5R,
IntAu&W 82, WrDr 84
Elliott, John R, Jr. 1937- ConAu 25R
Elliott, Jumbo ConAu X
Elliott, K A C 1903- ConAu 108
Elliott, Kit 1936- ConAu 29R
Elliott, Lawrence 1924- ConAu 3NR, -5R
Elliott, Leonard M 1902- ConAu P-1
Elliott, Lesley 1905- ConAu 77
Elliott, M Margaret Drake 1904- IntWWP 82
Elliott, Malissa Childs 1929?-1979 ConAu 101,
-85
Elliott, Margaret 1904- IntWWP 82X
Elliott, Margaret Drake 1904- IntWWP 82X,
MichAu 80
Elliott, Mark Rowe 1947- ConAu 107
Elliott, Neil 1939- ConAu 25R
Elliott, Osborn 1924- ConAu 1R, -69
Elliott, P R C 1943?-1983 ConAu 110
Elliott, Ralph H 1925- ConAu 1R, -2NR
Elliott, Raymond Pruitt 1904- ConAu 17R
Elliott, Richard V 1934- ConAu 33R
Elliott, Robert ConAu X, CreCan 1
Elliott, Robert B ConAu X
Elliott, Robert Carl 1914- ConAu 1R
Elliott, Roberta ConAu 97, WrDr 84
Elliott, Russell Richard 1912- ConAu 69
Elliott, Sarah M 1930- ConAu 41R,
SmATA 14
Elliott, Sheldon D 1906-1972 ConAu 33R
Elliott, Spencer Hayward 1883-1967 ConAu P-1
Elliott, Sumner Locke 1917- ConAu 2NR, -5R,
TwCSFW, WrDr 84
Elliott, Susan 1947- ConAu 104
Elliott, Thomas Joseph 1941- ConAu 49
Elliott, Ward E Y 1937- ConAu 85
Elliott, William Douglas DrAP&F 83
Elliott, William Douglas 1938- ConAu 9NR, -65
Elliott, William Isaac DrAP&F 83
Elliott, William Marion 1903- ConAu P-1
Elliott, William Rowcliffe 1910- WrDr 84
Elliott, William Yandell 1896-1979 ConAu 85
Elliott-Binns, Michael Ferrers 1923- WrDr 84
Elliott-Cannon, Arthur Elliott 1919-
IntAu&W 82
Ellis, A E ConLC 7
Ellis, Albert 1913- ConAu 1R, -2NR, WrDr 84
Ellis, Alec 1932- ConAu 1NR, -45, WrDr 84
Ellis, Amanda M 1898-1969 ConAu P-2
Ellis, Anne Weir 1931- WrDr 84
Ellis, Anyon ConAu X, SmATA X
Ellis, Audrey ConAu 10NR, -65, IntAu&W 82,
WrDr 84
Ellis, B Robert 1940- ConAu 53
Ellis, Brooks 1897-1976 ConAu 65
Ellis, Charles Drummond 1895-1980 ConAu 105
Ellis, Charles Howard 1895- ConAu P-1
Ellis, Clyde T 1908- ConAu P-2
Ellis, Craig DrAP&F 83
Ellis, Craig 1946- IntWWP 82
Ellis, Cuthbert Hamilton 1909- ConAu 13R
Ellis, D E ConSFA
Ellis, David Maldwyn 1914- ConAu 9R
Ellis, Edward Robb 1911- ConAu 25R,
WrDr 84
Ellis, Ella T WrDr 84
Ellis, Ella Thorp DrAP&F 83
Ellis, Ella Thorp 1928- ConAu 2NR, -49,
IntAu&W 82, SmATA 7
Ellis, Elmo I 1918- ConAu 33R
Ellis, Florence Hawley 1906- ConAu 61
Ellis, Frank 1904?-1976 ConAu 65
Ellis, Frank Hale 1916- ConAu 73
Ellis, Frank K 1933- ConAu 25R
Ellis, Gene DrAP&F 83
Ellis, Gwynn Pennant WrDr 84
Ellis, Harold 1926- WrDr 84
Ellis, Harry Bearse 1921- ConAu 1R, -2NR,
IntAu&W 82, SmATA 9, WrDr 84
Ellis, Havelock 1859-1939 ConAu 109,
LongCTC, ModBrL, TwCA, TwCA SUP

Ellis, Henry C 1927- ConAu 97
Ellis, Herbert ConAu X, SmATA X
Ellis, Hilda Roderick ConAu X
Ellis, Howard S 1898- ConAu 49
Ellis, Howard Woodrow 1914- ConAu 1R
Ellis, Humphrey Francis 1907- ConAu 5R,
WrDr 84
Ellis, J R 1938- ConAu 85
Ellis, Jack C 1922- ConAu 89
Ellis, James 1935- ConAu 37R
Ellis, James Hervey Stewart 1893- ConAu P-2
Ellis, Jody 1925- ConAu 57
Ellis, John M 1936- ConAu 3NR, -49
Ellis, John Marion 1917- ConAu 49
Ellis, John O 1917- ConAu 85
Ellis, John Tracy 1905- ConAu 1R, -5NR
Ellis, Joseph J 1943- ConAu 53
Ellis, Kate Ferguson DrAP&F 83
Ellis, Kathy ConAu X
Ellis, Keith 1927- WrDr 84
Ellis, Keith Stanley 1927- ConAu 102
Ellis, Kenneth John 1945- IntWWP 82
Ellis, L Ethan 1898-1977 ConAu 4NR
Ellis, Landon ConAu X
Ellis, Leigh 1959- ConAu 105
Ellis, Leo R 1909- ConAu 9R
Ellis, Lewis Ethan 1898- ConAu 5R
Ellis, Louise WrDr 84
Ellis, M B 1915- ConAu 69
Ellis, M LeRoy 1928- ConAu 37R
Ellis, Marc H 1952- ConAu 107
Ellis, Mark 1945- WrDr 84
Ellis, Mark Karl 1945- ConAu 103
Ellis, Mary Jackson 1916- ConAu 1R
Ellis, Mary Leith 1921- ConAu 21R, WrDr 84
Ellis, Melvin Richard 1912- ConAu 13R,
SmATA 7
Ellis, Neal DrAP&F 83
Ellis, Norman R 1924- ConAu 13R
Ellis, Olivia ConAu X, WrDr 84
Ellis, Peter Berresford 1943- ConAu 81,
IntAu&W 82
Ellis, Ray C 1898- ConAu P-2
Ellis, Richard 1938- ConAu 104
Ellis, Richard E 1937- ConAu 61
Ellis, Richard N 1939- ConAu 33R,
IntAu&W 82, WrDr 84
Ellis, Richard White Bernard 1902- ConAu P-1
Ellis, Ron 1941- ConAu 77
Ellis, Royston 1941- ConAu 5R, DcLEL 1940,
IntAu&W 82, WrDr 84
Ellis, Ulrich 1904- WrDr 84
Ellis, Ulrich Ruegg 1904- IntAu&W 82
Ellis, Ulrich Ruegg 1904-1981 ConAu 108
Ellis, William 1918- ConAu 49
Ellis, William Donohue 1918- ConAu 49,
IntAu&W 82
Ellison, Alfred 1916- ConAu 1R
Ellison, Craig W 1944- ConAu 6NR, -57
Ellison, George W 1907?-1983 ConAu 110
Ellison, Gerald Alexander 1910- ConAu P-1
Ellison, Glenn 1911- ConAu 89
Ellison, H L 1903- ConAu 6NR
Ellison, Harlan DrAP&F 83
Ellison, Harlan 1934- ConAu 5R, -5NR,
ConLC 1, -13, ConSFA, DcLB 8[port],
DrmM[port], TwCSFW, WorAu 1970,
WrDr 84
Ellison, Henry 1931-1965 ConAu 5R
Ellison, Henry Leopold 1903- ConAu 5R,
WrDr 84
Ellison, Herbert J 1929- ConAu 13R
Ellison, James E 1927- ConAu 13R
Ellison, James Whitfield DrAP&F 83
Ellison, James Whitfield 1929- ASpks,
ConAu 1R, -1NR
Ellison, James Whitfield 1930- MichAu 80
Ellison, Jerome 1907-1981 ConAu 104, -29R
Ellison, Jessie T DrAP&F 83
Ellison, Joan Audrey 1928- IntAu&W 82,
WrDr 84
Ellison, John Malcus 1889- ConAu 1R
Ellison, Katherine 1941- ConAu 101
Ellison, Kay 1922- IntWWP 82
Ellison, Lucile Watkins 1907?-1979 ConAu 109,
-93, SmATA 22N
Ellison, Max 1914- AuNews 1, ConAu 57,
MichAu 80
Ellison, Ralph DrAP&F 83
Ellison, Ralph 1914- WrDr 84
Ellison, Ralph Waldo 1914- ConAu 9R,
ConLC 1, -3, -11, ConNov 82, DcLB 2,

DcLEL 1940, EncWL 2, LivgBAA,
ModAL, ModAL SUP, ModBlW, TwCWr,
WhoTwCL, WorAu
Ellison, Reuben Young 1907- ConAu 13R
Ellison, Tiger ConAu X
Ellison, Virginia Howell 1910- ConAu 33R,
SmATA 4, WrDr 84
Ellison, William McLaren 1919?-1978 ConAu 81
Elliston, Frederick Allen 1944- ConAu 105
Elliston, Thomas R 1919-1977 ConAu 73
Elliston, Valerie Mae 1929- ConAu 9R
Ellithorpe, Harold 1925- ConAu 77
Ellman, Michael 1942- ConAu 45
Ellmann, Richard 1918- ConAu 1R, -2NR,
ConLCrt 82, DcLEL 1940, IntAu&W 82,
WorAu, WrDr 84
Ellsberg, Daniel 1931- ConAu 69
Ellsberg, Edward 1891- ConAu 5R, SmATA 7,
TwCA, TwCA SUP
Ellsworth, P T 1897- ConAu 17R
Ellsworth, Ralph E 1907- WrDr 84
Ellsworth, Ralph Eugene 1907- ConAu 1R,
-2NR
Ellsworth, S George 1916- ConAu 45
Ellsworth, Sallie Bingham 1937- ConAu 1R
Ellsworth, Scott 1954- ConAu 109
Ellul, Jacques 1912- ConAu 81
Ellwood, Gracia Fay 1938- ConAu 29R, -29R,
WrDr 84
Ellwood, Robert Scott, Jr. 1933- ConAu 41R,
IntAu&W 82
Ellwood, Scott IntAu&W 82X
Elman, Richard DrAP&F 83
Elman, Richard 1934- ConAu 17R, ConLC 19
Elman, Robert 1930- ConAu 3NR, -45
Elmandjra, Mahdi 1933- ConAu 89
Elmblad, Mary 1927- ConAu 108
Elmen, Paul H 1913- ConAu 89
Elmendorf, Mary Lindsay 1917- ConAu 57
Elmer, Carlos Hall 1920- ConAu 102
Elmer, Irene 1937- ConAu 1R
Elmore, Patricia DrAP&F 83
Elms, Alan C 1938- ConAu 69
Elmslie, Kenward DrAP&F 83
Elmslie, Kenward 1929- ConAu 9NR, -21R,
ConP 80, DcLEL 1940, IntWWP 82,
WrDr 84
Elmslie, William Alexander Leslie 1885-1965
ConAu P-1
Elmstrom, George P 1925- ConAu 5R
Elon, Florence DrAP&F 83
Elon, Florence 1946- IntAu&W 82
Eloul, Rita Letendre CreCan 2
Elovic, Barbara DrAP&F 83
Elovitz, Mark H 1938- ConAu 69
Elphinstone, Francis ConAu X, WrDr 84
Elphinstone, Murgatroyd ConAu X
Elsasser, Albert B 1918- ConAu 69
Elsasser, Glen Robert 1935- ConAu 65
Elsberg, John DrAP&F 83
Elsberg, John 1945- IntWWP 82
Elsberry, Terence 1943- ConAu 45
Elsbree, Langdon 1929- ConAu 33R
Else, Gerald Frank 1908-1982 ConAu 107, -61
Elsen, Albert E 1927- ConAu 11NR
Elsen, Albert Edward 1927- ConAu 5R,
IntAu&W 82, WrDr 84
Elsey, David DrAP&F 83
Elshtain, Jean Bethke 1941- ConAu 106
Elskamp, Max 1862-1931 CIDMEL 80
Elsmere, Jane Shaffer 1932- ConAu 37R,
WrDr 84
Elsna, Hebe TwCRGW, WrDr 84
Elsner, Gisela 1937- CIDMEL 80, ConAu 9R,
TwCWr
Elsner, Henry, Jr. 1930- ConAu 21R
Elsom, John WrDr 84
Elsom, John Edward 1934- ConAu 65,
IntAu&W 82
Elson, Edward L R 1906- ConAu 3NR, -5R,
WrDr 84
Elson, Lawrence M 1935- ConAu 53
Elson, R N ConAu X, WrDr 84
Elson, Robert T 1906- ConAu 77
Elson, Ruth Miller 1917- ConAu 13R
Elson, Virginia DrAP&F 83
Elspeth ConAu X, SmATA 6
Elsschot, Willem 1882-1960 EncWL 2,
WhoTwCL
Elstar, Dow ConAu X, -X, IntAu&W 82X
Elstob, Peter 1915- ConAu 1R, -1NR,
IntAu&W 82, WrDr 84

IntAu&W 82
Engle, Paul *DrAP&F 83*
Engle, Paul 1908- *ConAmA, ConAu 1R, -5NR, ConP 80, IntWWP 82, WorAu, WrDr 84*
Engle, Thelburn L 1901- *WrDr 84*
Engle, Thelburn LaRoy 1901- *ConAu 13R*
Engle Paananen, Eloise 1923- *IntAu&W 82*
Englebardt, Stanley L 1925- *IntAu&W 82*
Englebert, Victor 1933- *ConAu 57, SmATA 8*
Englefield, Ronald 1891-1975 *ConAu 105*
Engleman, Finis E 1895- *ConAu 9R*
Engler, Larry 1949- *ConAu 53*
Engler, Richard E, Jr. 1925- *ConAu 37R*
Engler, Robert 1922- *ConAu 1R, -2NR*
Englert, Clement Cyril 1910- *ConAu 1R, -5NR*
English, Arnold *ConAu X*
English, Barbara 1933- *ConAu 33R, WrDr 84*
English, Brenda H *IntAu&W 82X, WrDr 84*
English, Charles *ConAu X*
English, David 1931- *ConAu 69*
English, Deirdre 1948- *ConAu 85*
English, E Schuyler 1899-1981 *ConAu 103, -107*
English, Earl 1905- *ConAu 37R*
English, Edward d1973 *ConAu 41R*
English, Elizabeth Lois *IntAu&W 82*
English, Fenwick Walter 1939- *ConAu 1NR, -45*
English, Isobel 1923- *ConNov 82*
English, Isobel 1925- *ConAu 53, WrDr 84*
English, James W 1915- *ConAu 21R*
English, Jean M 1937- *ConAu 29R*
English, John W 1940- *ConAu 69*
English, Maurice 1909- *ConAu 9R, ConP 80, WrDr 84*
English, O Spurgeon 1901- *ConAu P-2*
English, Ronald 1913- *ConAu P-1, WrDr 84*
English, Thomas Hopkins 1895- *ConAu 2NR, -5R*
English, Thomas Saunders 1928- *ConAu 105*
Englizian, H Crosby 1923- *ConAu 21R*
Engquist, Richard 1933- *ConAu 29R*
Engren, Edith *ConAu X*
Engs, Robert Francis 1943- *ConAu 101*
Engstrand, Iris Wilson 1935- *ConAu 107*
Engstrand, Stuart David 1905-1955 *TwCA SUP*
Engstrom, Clas Erik 1927- *IntAu&W 82*
Engstrom, Ted W *ConAu X*
Engstrom, Ted W 1916- *ConAu 65*
Engstrom, Theodore W 1916- *ConAu 9NR*
Engstrom, W A 1925- *ConAu 57*
Enis, Ben M 1942- *ConAu 7NR, -57*
Enke, Stephen 1916?-1974 *ConAu 53, -65*
Enloe, Cynthia H 1938- *ConAu 37R*
Enlow, David R 1916- *ConAu 5R, -10NR*
Ennes, James Marquis, Jr. 1933- *ConAu 102*
Ennis, Bruce J 1940- *ConAu 110*
Ennis, John 1944- *IntAu&W 82*
Ennis, Robert H 1927- *ConAu 10NR, -25R*
Eno, Susan *ConAu 101*
Enoch, Kurt 1895-1982 *ConAu 106*
Enockson, Paul G 1938- *ConAu 110*
Enomiya-Lassalle, Hugo M 1898- *ConAu 21R*
Enquist, Per Olov 1934- *ClDMEL 80, ConAu 109, EncWL 2*
Enrick, Norbert Lloyd 1920- *ConAu 6NR, -13R*
Enright, D J 1920- *ConAu 1NR, ConLC 8, ConLCrt 82, ConP 80, IntWWP 82, SmATA 25[port], WrDr 84*
Enright, Dennis Joseph 1920- *ConAu 1R, ConLC 4, DcLEL 1940, EncWL 2, IntAu&W 82, LongCTC, ModBrL, ModBrL SUP, TwCWr, WhoTwCL, WorAu*
Enright, Elizabeth 1909-1968 *ChlLR 4, ConAu 25R, -61, DcLB 22[port], SmATA 9, TwCCW 83*
Enroth, Clyde A 1926- *ConAu 37R*
Ensana, Joel 1935- *NatPD 81[port]*
Enscoe, Gerald 1926- *ConAu 5R, -10NR*
Ensign, Thomas 1940- *ConAu 101*
Ensign, Tod *ConAu X*
Ensing, Riemke 1939- *IntWWP 82*
Ensley, Francis Gerald 1907- *ConAu P-1*
Enslin, Morton Scott 1897- *ConAu 17R*
Enslin, Theodore *DrAP&F 83*
Enslin, Theodore 1925- *ConAu 4NR, -53, ConP 80, IntWWP 82, WrDr 84*
Ensminger, Marion Eugene 1908- *ConAu 1NR, -49*
Ensor, Alick Charles Davidson 1906- *IntAu&W 82*
Ensor, Allison 1935- *ConAu 25R*
Ensor, David 1906- *IntAu&W 82X, WrDr 84*

Ensor, Sir Robert Charles Kirkwood 1877-1950? *LongCTC*
Enstrom, Robert 1946- *ConAu 104*
Enteman, Willard F 1936- *ConAu 33R*
Enterline, James Robert 1932- *ConAu 41R*
Enthoven, Alain C 1930- *ConAu 49*
Entine, Alan D 1936- *ConAu 21R*
Entrekin, Charles *DrAP&F 83*
Entrekin, Charles E 1941- *IntWWP 82*
Entwisle, Doris R 1924- *ConAu 5R*
Entwisle, Eric Arthur 1900- *WrDr 84*
Entwistle, Florence Vivienne 1889?-1982 *ConAu 105*
Entwistle, Harold 1923- *ConAu 29R*
Entwistle, Noel 1936- *ConAu 93*
Entwistle, Theodore Rowland *ConAu X*
Enz, Jacob John 1919- *ConAu 41R*
Enzensberger, Hans Magnus 1929- *ClDMEL 80, EncWL 2, ModGL, TwCWr, WorAu*
Enzinck, Willem 1920- *IntAu&W 82*
Enzler, Clarence J 1910?-1976 *ConAu 69*
Eorsi, Istvan 1931- *CroCD, IntAu&W 82*
Epafrodito *ConAu X*
Epand, Len 1950- *ConAu 85*
Epernay, Mark *ConAu X*
Ephesian 1894-1949 *LongCTC*
Ephron, Delia 1944- *ConAu 97*
Ephron, Henry 1911- *ConAu 73*
Ephron, Nora 1941- *AuNews 2, ConAu 65, ConLC 17*
Ephron, Phoebe 1916-1971 *ConAu 33R*
Epler, Percy H 1872-1975 *ConAu 57*
Epp, Eldon Jay 1930- *ConAu 7NR, -17R, WrDr 84*
Epp, Frank H 1929- *ConAu 29R*
Epp, Margaret Agnes 1913- *ConAu 3NR, -9R, IntAu&W 82, SmATA 20, WrDr 84*
Epperly, Elizabeth Rollins 1951- *ConAu 106*
Epperson, Gordon 1921- *ConAu 25R*
Eppie *ConAu X*
Eppinga, Jacob D 1917- *ConAu 33R*
Eppinger, Josh 1940- *ConAu 89*
Eppink, Norman R 1906- *ConAu 53*
Epple, Anne Orth 1927- *ConAu 33R, SmATA 20, WrDr 84*
Epps, Edgar G 1929- *ConAu 49*
Epps, Garrett 1950- *ConAu 69*
Epps, Preston H 1888- *ConAu 37R*
Epps, Robert L 1932- *ConAu 17R*
Epsilon *ConAu X*
Epstein, Anne Merrick 1931- *ConAu 69, SmATA 20*
Epstein, Arnold Leonard 1924- *IntAu&W 82*
Epstein, Barbara 1928- *ConAu 110*
Epstein, Benjamin Robert 1912- *ConAu 45*
Epstein, Benjamin Robert 1912-1983 *ConAu 109*
Epstein, Beryl Williams 1910- *ConAu 2NR, -5R, SmATA 1, -31[port]*
Epstein, Charlotte 1921- *ConAu 8NR, -61*
Epstein, Cy 1942- *ConAu 108*
Epstein, Cynthia Fuchs 1933- *ConAu 29R, WrDr 84*
Epstein, Daniel Mark *DrAP&F 83*
Epstein, Daniel Mark 1948- *ConAu 2NR, -49, ConLC 7, IntWWP 82*
Epstein, David G 1943- *ConAu 69*
Epstein, Dena J 1916- *ConAu 41R*
Epstein, Edward Jay 1935- *ConAu 17R*
Epstein, Edwin M 1937- *ConAu 25R*
Epstein, Elaine *DrAP&F 83*
Epstein, Erwin H 1939- *ConAu 29R, WrDr 84*
Epstein, Eugene 1944- *ConAu 69*
Epstein, Fritz T 1898- *ConAu 69*
Epstein, Helen 1947- *ConAu 89, WrDr 84*
Epstein, Howard M 1927- *ConAu 21R*
Epstein, Jacob 1956- *ConLC 19*
Epstein, Sir Jacob 1880-1959 *LongCTC*
Epstein, Jason 1928- *ConAu 57*
Epstein, Judith Sue *DrAP&F 83*
Epstein, Judith Sue 1947- *ConAu 69*
Epstein, Julius 1901-1975 *ConAu 57*
Epstein, Julius 1909- *DcLB 26[port]*
Epstein, June 1918- *WrDr 84*
Epstein, June Sadie 1918- *ConAu 73*
Epstein, Leon David 1919- *ConAu 13R, IntAu&W 82*
Epstein, Leslie *DrAP&F 83*
Epstein, Leslie 1938- *ConAu 73, ConLC 27[port]*
Epstein, Melech 1889?-1979 *ConAu 89*
Epstein, Morris 1921-1973 *ConAu 45, ConAu P-1*

Epstein, Perle S 1938- *ConAu 9NR, -65, SmATA 27[port]*
Epstein, Philip 1909-1952 *DcLB 26[port]*
Epstein, Samuel 1909- *ConAu 4NR, -9R, SmATA 1, -31[port]*
Epstein, Seymour *DrAP&F 83*
Epstein, Seymour 1917- *ConAu 1R, -5NR, IntAu&W 82, WrDr 84*
Epstein, William 1912- *ConAu 11NR, -69*
Epstein, William H 1944- *ConAu 61*
Epton, Nina C *ConAu 11NR*
Epton, Nina Consuelo *ConAu 5R*
Equi, Elaine *DrAP&F 83*
Eramus, M Nott *ConAu X*
Erasmus, Charles J 1921- *ConAu 1R*
Erasmus, K G *IntAu&W 82X*
Erasmus, Edward T 1920- *ConAu 106*
Erb, Alta Mae 1891- *ConAu P-1*
Erb, Paul 1894- *ConAu 9R, WrDr 84*
Erbe, Pamela *DrAP&F 83*
Erbsen, Claude E 1938- *ConAu 89*
Erdahl, Carol Syvertsen 1932- *ConAu 108*
Erdahl, Lowell O 1931- *ConAu 109*
Erdman, David V 1911- *ConAu 1R, -1NR*
Erdman, Howard Loyd 1935- *ConAu 21R*
Erdman, Loula Grace d1976 *ConAu 5R, -10NR, SmATA 1, TwCWW*
Erdman, Nikolai Robertovich 1902?-1970 *ConAu 29R, ModWD*
Erdman, Nikolay Robertovich 1902?-1970 *ClDMEL 80*
Erdman, Paul E 1932- *AuNews 1, ConAu 61, ConLC 25[port], TwCCr&M 80, WrDr 84*
Erdmann, Nikolai 1902-1936 *CnMD*
Erdoes, Richard 1912- *ConAu 77, SmATA 28, -33[port]*
Erdos, Paul L 1914- *ConAu 29R*
Erdt, Terrence 1942- *ConAu 106*
Erenburg, Ilya Grigoriyevich 1891-1967 *TwCA, TwCA SUP*
Erenburg, Ilya Grigoryevich 1891-1967 *ClDMEL 80*
Erens, Patricia 1938- *ConAu 93*
Erford, Esther *DrAP&F 83*
Erhard *IntAu&W 82X*
Erhard, Thomas A 1923- *ConAu 33R*
Erhard, Tom 1923- *WrDr 84*
Erhard, Walter 1920- *SmATA 30*
Eric, Kenneth *ConAu X*
Erichsen, Eli Store 1894- *IntAu&W 82*
Erichsen, Heino R 1924- *ConAu 110*
Erichsen-Brown, Gwethalyn Graham *CreCan 1*
Erichsen-Nelson, Jean 1934- *ConAu 109*
Ericksen, Ephraim Gordon 1917- *ConAu 5R*
Ericksen, Gerald L 1931- *ConAu 29R*
Ericksen, Kenneth J 1939- *ConAu 37R*
Ericksen, Stanford Clark 1911- *ConAu 108*
Erickson, Arthur 1924- *ConAu 89*
Erickson, Arvel Benjamin 1905-1974 *ConAu P-2*
Erickson, Carolly 1943- *ConAu 11NR, -69*
Erickson, Catherine *DrAP&F 83*
Erickson, Charlotte Joanne 1923- *IntAu&W 82*
Erickson, Don 1932- *ConAu 110*
Erickson, Donald A 1925- *ConAu 29R*
Erickson, E Walfred 1911- *ConAu 5R, -5NR*
Erickson, Edsel L 1928- *ConAu 53*
Erickson, Erling Arthur 1934- *ConAu 33R, WrDr 84*
Erickson, John 1929- *ConAu 101*
Erickson, Keith V 1943- *ConAu 29R*
Erickson, Lorene 1938- *IntWWP 82*
Erickson, M E 1918- *ConAu 9R*
Erickson, Marilyn T 1936- *ConAu 73*
Erickson, Marion J 1913- *ConAu 17R*
Erickson, Millard J 1932- *ConAu 93*
Erickson, Milton H 1901-1980 *ConAu 106, -97*
Erickson, Phoebe 1907- *ConAu 1R, -3NR*
Erickson, Robert 1917- *ConAu 109*
Erickson, Russell E 1932- *ConAu 93, SmATA 27[port]*
Erickson, Sabra Rollins 1912- *ConAu 5R, -5NR*
Erickson, Stephen A 1940- *ConAu 85*
Erickson, W Bruce 1938- *ConAu 49*
Erickson, Walter *WrDr 84*
Ericson, Edward E 1939- *ConAu 69*
Ericson, Joe Ellis 1925- *ConAu 41R*
Ericson, Walter *ConAu X, SmATA 7, TwCA SUP*
Ericsson, Emily 1904-1976 *ConAu 65*
Ericsson, Mary Kentra 1910- *ConAu 1R, -5NR*
Ericsson, Ronald James 1935- *ConAu 110*
Eriksen, Peter 1930- *IntAu&W 82*

IntAu&W 82, WrDr 84
Everett, Arthur 1914- *ConAu 103*
Everett, Donald E 1920- *ConAu 9R*
Everett, Douglas Hugh 1916- *WrDr 84*
Everett, Gail *ConAu X*
Everett, Glenn D 1921- *ConAu 69*
Everett, Graham *DrAP&F 83*
Everett, Graham L 1947- *IntWWP 82*
Everett, Joann Marie *DrAP&F 83*
Everett, Peter 1931- *ConAu 69, ConDr 82B, ConNov 82, WrDr 84*
Everett, Peter W 1924- *ConAu 13R*
Everett, Wade *TwCWW, WrDr 84*
Everett, Walter 1936- *ConAu 93*
Evergood, Philip 1901-1973 *ConAu 41R*
Everhart, James W, Jr. 1924- *ConAu 89*
Everhart, Jim *ConAu X*
Everingham, Barry Mitchell 1940- *IntAu&W 82*
Everingham, Douglas 1923- *WrDr 84*
Everitt, Alan 1926- *ConAu 11NR*
Everitt, Alan Milner 1926- *ConAu 21R, WrDr 84*
Everitt, Arva Graham Johnson 1916?-1982 *ConAu 107*
Everitt, Bridget Mary 1924- *ConAu 45*
Everitt, C W F 1934- *ConAu 65*
Everitt, David Samuel 1952- *ConAu 110*
Everman, Welch D *DrAP&F 83*
Everman, Welch D 1946- *ConAu 57*
Evermay, March *TwCA SUP*
Evernden, Margery 1916- *ConAu 5R, IntAu&W 82, SmATA 5, WrDr 84*
Eversdyk-Smulders, Emilie Caroline H 1903- *IntAu&W 82*
Eversdyk-Smulders, Lily *IntAu&W 82X*
Eversley, David Edward Charles 1921- *ConAu 1R, -1NR*
Eversole, Finley T 1933- *ConAu 9R*
Everson, Dale Millar 1928- *ConAu 17R*
Everson, Ida Gertrude 1898- *ConAu 37R*
Everson, Ronald 1903- *WrDr 84*
Everson, Ronald G 1903- *ConLC 27[port]*
Everson, Ronald Gilmour 1903- *ConAu 17R, ConP 80, CreCan 1*
Everson, William *DrAP&F 83*
Everson, William 1912- *WrDr 84*
Everson, William Keith 1929- *ConAu 1R, -2NR*
Everson, William Oliver 1912- *ConAu 9R, ConLC 1, -5, -14, ConP 80, DcLB 5[port], -16[port], WorAu*
Everton, Macduff 1947- *ConAu 104*
Evertts, Eldonna Louise Becker 1917- *ConAu 21R*
Everwine, Peter *DrAP&F 83*
Everwine, Peter 1930- *ConAu 73, ConP 80, WrDr 84*
Everwyn, Klas Ewert 1930- *IntAu&W 82*

Every, George 1909- *ConAu 6NR, -13R, IntAu&W 82, WrDr 84*
Evetts, Julia Ann 1944- *ConAu 69, WrDr 84*
Evins, Joseph Landon 1910- *ConAu 61*
Evoe *ConAu X, LongCTC, TwCA, TwCA SUP*
Evoy, John J 1911- *ConAu 5R*
Evreinov, Nikolai Nikolaivich 1879-1953 *CnMD*
Evslin, Bernard 1922- *ConAu 9NR, -21R, SmATA 28*
Evslin, Dorothy 1923- *ConAu 57*
Evtushenko, Evgeniy Alexandrovich 1933- *ConLC 1, WhoTwCL, WorAu*
Evtushenko, Evgeny Alexandrovich 1933- *EncWL 2*
Ewald, William Bragg, Jr. 1925- *ConAu 107*
Ewart, Andrew 1911- *ConAu 17R*
Ewart, Charles *ConAu X*
Ewart, Gavin 1916- *WrDr 84*
Ewart, Gavin B 1916- *ConAu 89, ConLC 13, ConP 80, WorAu*
Ewbank, Henry L, Jr. 1924- *ConAu 73*
Ewbank, Walter F 1918- *ConAu 25R*
Ewell, Judith 1943- *ConAu 107*
Ewen, David 1907- *ConAu 1R, -2NR, SmATA 4, WrDr 84*
Ewen, Frederic 1899- *ConAu 73, IntAu&W 82, WrDr 84*
Ewen, Paterson 1925- *CreCan 2*
Ewen, Robert B 1940- *ConAu 37R*
Ewen, Stuart 1945- *ConAu 69*
Ewens, Gwendoline Wilson *WrDr 84*
Ewer, Monica 1889-1964 *LongCTC*
Ewers, Hanns Heinz 1871-1943 *ConAu 109, TwCLC 12[port]*
Ewers, John C 1909- *ConAu 7NR, -17R, IntAu&W 82*
Ewert, David 1922- *ConAu 105*
Ewing, Alfred Cyril 1899-1973 *ConAu 4NR, -5R*
Ewing, David Walkley 1923- *ConAu 1R, -5NR, WrDr 84*
Ewing, Donald M 1895?-1978 *ConAu 81*
Ewing, Elizabeth 1904- *ConAu 41R*
Ewing, Elizabeth Cameron 1906- *WrDr 84*
Ewing, Frederick R *ConAu X, WrDr 84*
Ewing, George W 1923- *ConAu 45*
Ewing, John Alexander 1923- *ConAu 105*
Ewing, John Melvin 1925- *ConAu 53*
Ewing, John S 1916- *ConAu 13R*
Ewing, Juliana Horatia 1841-1885 *SmATA 16*
Ewing, Kathryn 1921- *ConAu 7NR, -61, SmATA 20*
Ewing, Pebles *ConAu X*
Ewing, Sherman 1901-1975 *ConAu 57*
Ewton, Ralph W, Jr. 1938- *ConAu 81*
Ewy, Donna 1934- *ConAu 33R*
Ewy, Rodger 1931- *ConAu 33R*

Ex-R S M *ConAu X*
Exall, Barry *ConAu X*
Excellent, Matilda *ConAu X, IntAu&W 82X, WrDr 84*
Exell, Frank Kingsley 1902- *ConAu 5R*
Exley, Frederick *DrAP&F 83*
Exley, Frederick 1929- *ConAu 81, DcLB Y81B[port]*
Exley, Frederick 1930- *AuNews 2, ConLC 6, -11*
Exman, Eugene 1900-1975 *ConAu 61, ConAu P-1*
Exton, Clive 1930- *ConAu 61, ConDr 82C, DcLEL 1940, WrDr 84*
Exton, William, Jr. 1907- *ConAu 45, WrDr 84*
Exupery, Antoine DeSaint *ModRL*
Eyck, Frank 1921- *ConAu 11NR, -25R, IntAu&W 82, WrDr 84*
Eyck, Pieter Nicolaas Van 1887-1954 *CIDMEL 80*
Eye, Glen G 1904- *ConAu 2NR, -49*
Eyen, Tom *ConAu 25R, NatPD 81[port]*
Eyen, Tom 1941- *ConDr 82, WrDr 84*
Eyerly, Jeannette Hyde 1908- *ConAu 1R, -4NR, SmATA 4*
Eyestone, Robert 1942- *ConAu 41R*
Eykman, Christoph 1937- *ConAu 41R*
Eyles, Leonora 1889-1960 *LongCTC*
Eyles, Wilfred Charles 1891- *ConAu P-2*
Eyre, Annette *ConAu X, IntAu&W 82X, TwCRGW, WrDr 84*
Eyre, Dorothy *ConAu X*
Eyre, Katherine Wigmore 1901-1970 *ConAu 104, SmATA 26[port]*
Eyre, Richard M 1944- *ConAu 61*
Eyre, Ronald 1929- *ConAu 104, IntAu&W 82*
Eyre, S Robert 1922- *ConAu 21R, WrDr 84*
Eysenck, H J 1916- *ConAu 4NR, WrDr 84*
Eysenck, Hans Jurgen 1916- *ConAu 9R, IntAu&W 82*
Eysman, Harvey 1939- *ConAu 104*
Eyster, C William 1917- *ConAu 29R*
Eyvindur *IntAu&W 82X*
Ezekiel, Mordecai J B 1899?-1974 *ConAu 53, -53, -65*
Ezekiel, Nissim 1924- *ConAu 61, ConP 80, DcLEL 1940, IntAu&W 82, IntWWP 82, ModCmwL, WrDr 84*
Ezekiel, Raphael S 1931- *ConAu 53*
Ezell, Harry E 1918-1974 *ConAu 1R, -103*
Ezell, John Samuel 1917- *ConAu 1R*
Ezell, Macel D 1934- *ConAu 77*
Ezera, Kalu 1925- *ConAu 13R*
Ezergailis, Andrew 1930- *ConAu 89*
Ezorsky, Gertrude *ConAu 89*
Ezzell, Marilyn 1937- *ConAu 109*

F

F P A *ConAmA, ConAu X, TwCA, TwCA SUP*
Faas, Larry A 1936- *ConAu 29R*
Fabbri, Diego 1911-1980 *ClDMEL 80, CnMD, ConAu 105, ModWD*
Fabbri, Nancy Rash 1940- *ConAu 103*
Fabe, Maxene 1943- *ConAu 77, SmATA 15*
Faber, Adele 1928- *ConAu 77*
Faber, Charles F 1926- *ConAu 29R*
Faber, Doris 1924- *ConAu 8NR, –17R, SmATA 3*
Faber, Harold 1919- *ConAu 8NR, –13R, SmATA 5*
Faber, John 1918- *ConAu 13R, WrDr 84*
Faber, Nancy W 1909-1976 *ConAu 5R, –65*
Faber, Richard 1924- *ConAu 61, IntAu&W 82*
Faber, Robertoh *DrAP&F 83*
Faber-Kaiser, Andreas 1944- *ConAu 73*
Faber-Perathoner, Hans 1907- *IntAu&W 82*
Fabian, Donald L 1919- *ConAu 21R*
Fabian, Josephine C 1903- *ConAu P-1*
Fabian, Robert 1901-1978 *ConAu 77, –81*
Fabian, Ruth *ConAu X*
Fabian, Walter 1902- *IntAu&W 82*
Fabilli, Mary *DrAP&F 83*
Fabinyi, Andrew 1908-1978 *ConAu 108*
Fabio, Sarah Webster *DrAP&F 83*
Fabio, Sarah Webster 1928- *ConAu 69, LivgBAA*
Fabisch, Judith Patricia 1938- *ConAu 103*
Fabos, Julius Gy 1932- *ConAu 97*
Fabra I Poc, Pompeu 1868-1948 *ClDMEL 80*
Fabre, Genevieve E 1936- *ConAu 109*
Fabre, Jean Henri 1823-1915 *LongCTC, SmATA 22[port]*
Fabre, Michel J 1933- *ConAu 1NR, –45*
Fabrega, Horacio, Jr. 1934- *ConAu 73*
Fabri, Ralph 1894-1975 *ConAu 57, ConAu P-2*
Fabricand, Burton Paul 1923- *ConAu 93*
Fabricant, Noah D 1904-1964 *ConSFA*
Fabricius, Johan Wigmore 1899- *ConAu 5NR, –53, IntAu&W 82, TwCA, TwCA SUP*
Fabrizio, Ray 1930- *ConAu 33R*
Fabrizius, Peter *ConAu X, IntAu&W 82X, WrDr 84*
Fabry, Joseph B 1909- *ConAu 25R, IntAu&W 82, WrDr 84*
Fabrycky, Wolter Joseph 1932- *ConAu 21R*
Fabun, Don 1920- *ConAu 45*
Fac, Boleslaw 1929- *IntAu&W 82*
Fackenheim, Emil L 1916- *ConAu 21R, IntAu&W 82, WrDr 84*
Facklam, Margery Metz 1927- *ConAu 5R, –6NR, SmATA 20*
Fackre, Gabriel Joseph 1926- *ConAu 7NR, –17R*
Facos, James *DrAP&F 83*
Facos, James F 1924- *ConAu 41R*
Fadeev, Alexandr Alexandrovich 1901-1956 *EncWL 2*
Fader, Daniel 1930- *ConAu 33R*
Fader, Shirley Sloan 1931- *ConAu 77*
Faderman, Lillian 1940- *ConAu 33R*
Fadeyev, Aleksandr Aleksandrovich 1901-1956 *ClDMEL 80, ModSL 1, TwCWr*

Fadiman, Clifton 1904- *ConAu 9NR, –61, SmATA 11, TwCA, TwCA SUP*
Fadiman, Edwin, Jr. 1925- *ConAu 29R*
Fadiman, James 1939- *ConAu 33R*
Fadner, Frank 1910- *ConAu 9R*
Faegre, Torvald 1941- *ConAu 89*
Faelten, Sharon 1950- *ConAu 106*
Faerystone, Elizabeth-Jane *IntWWP 82X*
Faesi, Robert 1883-1972 *CnMD*
Faessler, Shirley 1921?- *ConAu 106*
Fagan, Brian Murray 1936- *ConAu 41R, WrDr 84*
Fagan, Edward R 1924- *ConAu 5NR, –9R*
Fage, John Donnelly 1921- *ConAu 5R, –7NR, WrDr 84*
Fagen, Donald 1948- *ConLC 26[port]*
Fagen, Richard R 1933- *ConAu 7NR, –17R*
Fagen, Stanley Alan 1936- *ConAu 102*
Fager, Charles E 1942- *ConAu 21R*
Fagerstrom, Stan 1923- *ConAu 57*
Fagg, John 1916- *ConAu 81*
Fagg, S V 1918- *WrDr 84*
Fagg, William Buller 1914- *ConAu 102*
Fagin, Larry *DrAP&F 83*
Fagles, Robert 1933- *ConAu 104*
Fagley, Richard M 1910- *ConAu 1R*
Fagothey, Austin 1901- *ConAu P-1*
Fague, William Robert 1927- *ConAu 109*
Fagundo, Ana Maria 1938- *ConAu 37R*
Fagunwa, Daniel O 1910?-1963 *TwCWr, WhoTwCL*
Fagus 1872-1933 *ClDMEL 80*
Fagyas, Maria *ConAu 33R*
Faherty, William B 1914- *ConAu 5R, –5NR*
Fahey, Frank M 1917- *ConAu 101*
Fahey, James C 1903-1974 *ConAu 53*
Fahkhanel, Heidewig 1942- *IntAu&W 82*
Fahlstrom, Oyvind Axel Christian 1928-1976 *ConAu 69*
Fahn, Abraham 1916- *WrDr 84*
Fahnestock, Beatrice Beck 1899?-1980 *ConAu 97*
Fahrmann, Willi 1929- *IntAu&W 82*
Fahs, Ivan J 1932- *ConAu 45*
Fahs, Sophia Blanche Lyon 1876-1978 *ConAu 77*
Fahy, Christopher *DrAP&F 83*
Fahy, Christopher 1937- *ConAu 11NR, –69*
Fain, Haskell 1926- *ConAu 33R*
Fain, James Gerard 1933- *ConAu 104*
Fainlight, Ruth *DrAP&F 83, WrDr 84*
Fainlight, Ruth 1931- *ConAu 8NR, –17R, ConP 80, IntAu&W 82, IntWWP 82*
Fainsod, Merle 1907-1972 *ConAu 33R, ConAu P-1*
Fainstein, Norman Ira 1944- *ConAu 102*
Fainstein, Susan S 1938- *ConAu 93*
Fair, A A *ConAu X, LongCTC, TwCA SUP, TwCCr&M 80*
Fair, Charles M 1916- *ConAu 10NR, –13R*
Fair, Harold L 1924- *ConAu 89*
Fair, James R, Jr. 1920- *ConAu 29R*
Fair, Marvin L 1897?-1983 *ConAu 110*
Fair, Ray C 1942- *ConAu 29R*
Fair, Ronald *DrAP&F 83*
Fair, Ronald L 1932- *ConAu 69, ConLC 18,*

Fair, Sylvia 1933- *ConAu 69, SmATA 13*
Fairbairn, Ann 1902?-1972 *ConAu X*
Fairbairn, Arthur Rex Dugard 1904-1957 *TwCWr*
Fairbairn, Douglas 1926- *ConAu 33R, IntAu&W 82, WrDr 84*
Fairbairn, Garry L 1947- *ConAu 77*
Fairbairn, Helen *ConAu X*
Fairbairn, Ian John 1933- *ConAu 53, IntAu&W 82*
Fairbairns, Zoe 1948- *ConAu 103, WrDr 84*
Fairbank, Alfred John 1895-1982 *ConAu 5R, –6NR, –106*
Fairbank, Janet Ayer 1878?-1951 *TwCA, TwCA SUP*
Fairbank, John King 1907- *ConAu 1R, –3NR, ConIsC 2[port], DcLEL 1940*
Fairbanks, Carol 1935- *ConAu 69*
Fairbrother, Nan 1913-1971 *ConAu 3NR, –5R, –33R*
Fairburn, Arthur Rex Dugard 1904-1957 *LongCTC, WorAu*
Fairburn, Eleanor 1928- *ConAu 8NR, –61, IntAu&W 82, WrDr 84*
Fairchild, Henry Pratt 1880-1956 *TwCA SUP*
Fairchild, Hoxie Neale 1894-1973 *ConAu 5R, –45*
Fairchild, Louis W 1901-1981 *ConAu 105*
Fairchild, William *ConAu 73*
Faire, Zabrina *ConAu X, TwCRGW, WrDr 84*
Fairfax, Beatrice *ConAu X*
Fairfax, Felix *ConAu X*
Fairfax, John 1930- *ConAu 97, ConP 80, IntAu&W 82, IntWWP 82, WrDr 84*
Fairfax, John 1937- *ConAu 49*
Fairfax-Blakeborough, Jack *ConAu X*
Fairfax-Blakeborough, John 1883-1978? *ConAu 102*
Fairfax-Lucy, Brian 1898-1974 *ConAu P-2, SmATA 26N, –6*
Fairfield, Cicily Isabel 1892- *LongCTC*
Fairfield, Darrell *WrDr 84*
Fairfield, John *ConAu X*
Fairfield, Leslie P 1941- *ConAu 107*
Fairfield, Richard Ivan 1937- *ConAu 41R*
Fairfield, Roy P 1918- *ConAu 33R*
Fairhall, David Keir 1934- *ConAu 103*
Fairholme, Elizabeth Carola 1910- *ConAu 97*
Fairless, Caroline S 1947- *ConAu 105*
Fairless, Michael 1869-1901 *LongCTC, TwCA, TwCA SUP*
Fairley, Barker 1887- *ConAu 1R*
Fairley, Irene R 1940- *ConAu 73*
Fairley, James S 1940- *ConAu 102, WrDr 84*
Fairley, M C 1937- *WrDr 84*
Fairley, Michael Charles 1937- *ConAu 37R*
Fairley, Peter 1930- *ConAu 29R*
Fairlie, Gerard 1899- *TwCCr&M 80, WrDr 84*
Fairlie, Gerard 1899-1983 *ConAu 109, SmATA 34N*
Fairlie, Henry 1924- *ConAu 104*
Fairman, Charles 1897- *ConAu 45*
Fairman, Herbert Walter 1907-1982 *ConAu 108*
Fairman, Honora C 1927?-1978 *ConAu 81*

Fairman, Joan Alexandra 1935- *ConAu 33R, SmATA 10, WrDr 84*
Fairman, Paul W 1916-1977 *ConSFA, TwCSFW*
Fairn, Duncan 1906- *WrDr 84*
Fairweather, Eugene Rathbone 1920- *ConAu 108*
Fairweather, George W 1921- *ConAu 13R*
Fairweather, Virginia 1922- *ConAu 29R*
Faison, S Lane, Jr. 1907- *ConAu 89*
Faissler, Margareta 1902- *ConAu 5R*
Fait, Hollis F 1918- *ConAu 1R, –5NR, IntAu&W 82*
Faith, Percy 1908-1976 *CreCan 1*
Faith, William Robert *ConAu X*
Faithfull, Gail 1936- *ConAu 57, SmATA 8*
Faiz, Faiz Ahmed 1911- *ModCmwL*
Faiz, Faiz Ahmed 1912?- *EncWL 2*
Fakhry, Majid 1923- *ConAu 29R*
Fakinos, Aris 1935- *ConAu 81*
Falassi, Alessandro 1945- *ConAu 105*
Falb, Lewis W 1935- *ConAu 102*
Falck, Colin 1934- *ConAu 65, ConP 80, IntAu&W 82, WrDr 84*
Falco, Edward *DrAP&F 83*
Falco, Maria J 1932- *ConAu 61*
Falcoff, Mark 1941- *ConAu 65*
Falcon *ConAu X*
Falcon, Jack *IntAu&W 82X*
Falcon, Richard *ConAu X*
Falcon, Walter Phillip 1936- *ConAu 109*
Falcon, William D 1932- *ConAu 17R*
Falcon-Barker, Ted 1923- *ConAu 25R*
Falconer, Alun d1973 *ConAu 104*
Falconer, James *ConAu X, SmATA X*
Falconer, Kenneth *ConAu X*
Falconer, Lee N *ConAu X*
Falero, Frank, Jr. 1937- *ConAu 37R*
Fales, Dean Abner, Jr. 1925- *ConAu 110*
Fales, Edward 1906- *ConAu 97*
Falk, Charles John 1899-1971 *ConAu P-2*
Falk, Elsa *ConAu X*
Falk, Irving A 1921- *ConAu 21R*
Falk, Kathryn 1940- *ConAu 97*
Falk, Lee Harrison 1915- *ConAu 97, IntAu&W 82, NatPD 81[port]*
Falk, Leslie A 1915- *ConAu 9R*
Falk, Louis A 1896?-1979 *ConAu 85*
Falk, Marcia *DrAP&F 83*
Falk, Minna Regina 1900-1983 *ConAu 109*
Falk, Richard A 1930- *ConAu 5R, ConIsC 1[port]*
Falk, Robert 1914- *ConAu 89*
Falk, Roger 1910- *ConAu 65*
Falk, Signi Lenea 1906- *ConAu 5R, WrDr 84*
Falk, Stanley Lawrence 1927- *ConAu 1R, –2NR, WrDr 84*
Falk, Ze'ev W 1923- *ConAu 21R, WrDr 84*
Falk-Roenne, Arne 1920- *ConAu 21R*
Falkberget, Johan Petter 1879-1967 *CIDMEL 80, EncWL 2*
Falke, H *IntAu&W 82X*
Falkirk, Richard *WrDr 84*
Falkland Cary, Thomas Litton 1897- *IntAu&W 82*
Falkner, John Meade 1858-1932 *CnMWL, LongCTC, WorAu*
Falkner, Leonard 1900- *ConAu 21R, SmATA 12*
Falkner, Murry Charles 1899-1975 *ConAu P-2*
Falkner, William *ConAmA*
Fall, Bernard B 1926-1967 *ASpks, ConAu 1R, –6NR, –25R, WorAu*
Fall, Frieda Kay 1913- *ConAu 41R*
Fall, Thomas 1917- *ConAu X, SmATA X*
Fallaci, Oriana 1930- *ConAu 77, ConLC 11, IntAu&W 82*
Fallada, Hans 1893-1947 *CIDMEL 80, LongCTC, ModGL, TwCA, TwCA SUP, WhoTwCL*
Fallaw, Wesner 1907- *ConAu 1R*
Faller, Kevin 1920- *ConAu 4NR, –53, WrDr 84*
Fallere, Felicia *ConAu X*
Fallers, Lloyd A 1925-1974 *ConAu 4NR, –9R, –49*
Falley, Margaret Dickson 1898-1983 *ConAu 110*
Fallis, Laurence S *DrAP&F 83*
Fallon, Carlos 1909- *ConAu 41R*
Fallon, Frederic 1944-1970 *ConAu 41R*
Fallon, George *ConAu X*
Fallon, Jack *ConAu X*
Fallon, John W 1924- *ConAu 77*
Fallon, Martin *ConAu X, TwCCr&M 80, WrDr 84*

Fallon, Padraic 1905-1974 *ConAu 103, –89*
Fallon, Peter 1951- *ConAu 106, IntAu&W 82, IntWWP 82*
Fallon, Tom *DrAP&F 83*
Fallows, James M 1949- *ConAu 2NR, –45*
Falls, Charles Buckles 1874-1960 *SmATA 27*
Falls, Cyril Bentham 1888- *ConAu P-1*
Falls, Joe 1928- *ConAu 77*
Fallwell, Marshall Leigh, Jr. 1943- *ConAu 69*
Falorp, Nelson P *ConAu X*
Falstein, Louis 1909- *ConAu 97*
Faludy, George 1913- *ConAu 21R*
Falwell, Jerry 1933- *ConAu 102*
Famiglietti, Eugene Paul 1931?-1980 *ConAu 97*
Family Doctor *IntAu&W 82X, WrDr 84*
Famodulan, Ermino Y Falqueza 1938- *IntWWP*
Famularo, Joseph John 1922- *ConAu 1R, –4NR*
Fan, Kuang Huan 1932- *ConAu 21R*
Fancher, Betsy 1928- *DcLB Y83B[port]*
Fancher, Ewilda 1928- *ConAu 61*
Fancher, Raymond E, Jr. 1940- *ConAu 69*
Fanchon, Lisa *ConAu X*
Fancutt, Walter 1911- *ConAu P-1, IntAu&W 82, WrDr 84*
Fandel, John *DrAP&F 83*
Fandel, John 1925- *ConAu 69*
Fane, Bron *ConAu X, ConSFA, IntAu&W 82X*
Fane, Julian 1927- *WrDr 84*
Fane, Julian Charles 1927- *ConAu 6NR, –13R, DcLEL 1940, IntAu&W 82*
Fang, Irving E 1929- *ConAu 49*
Fang, Josephine Riss 1922- *ConAu 69*
Fangen, Ronald August 1895-1946 *EncWL 2*
Fanger, Donald 1929- *ConAu 13R*
Fann, K T 1937- *ConAu 61*
Fann, William E 1930- *ConAu 2NR, –49*
Fannin, Allen 1939- *ConAu 69*
Fanning, Buckner 1926- *ConAu 69*
Fanning, Charles 1942- *ConAu 81*
Fanning, Leonard M 1888-1967 *ConAu 5R, SmATA 5*
Fanning, Louis A 1927- *ConAu 69*
Fanning, Michael 1942- *ConAu 89*
Fanning, Odom 1920- *ConAu 53, WrDr 84*
Fanning, Robbie 1947- *ConAu 77*
Fanon, Frantz 1925-1961 *ConAu 89, ConIsC 1[port], WorAu*
Fanshawe, David 1942- *ConAu 97*
Fant, Joseph Lewis, III 1928- *ConAu 13R*
Fant, Louis J, Jr. 1931- *ConAu 37R*
Fanta, J Julius 1907- *ConAu 33R*
Fante, John 1909-1983 *DcLB Y83N[port]*
Fante, John 1911- *ConAu 69, TwCA, TwCA SUP*
Fante, John 1911-1983 *ConAu 109*
Fantel, Hans 1922- *ConAu 49*
Fanthorpe, Patricia Alice 1938- *ConAu 89*
Fanthorpe, R Lionel 1935- *ConAu 73, ConSFA, IntAu&W 82*
Fanthorpe, U A *IntWWP 82X*
Fanthorpe, Ursula Askham 1929- *IntWWP 82*
Fantini, Mario D *ConAu 77*
Fantl, Susan *DrAP&F 83*
Fantoni, Barry 1940- *WrDr 84*
Farabee, Barbara 1944- *ConAu 57*
Faraday, Ann 1935- *ConAu 77*
Faragher, E S *IntWWP 82X*
Faragher, Eric Steven 1957- *IntWWP 82*
Farago, Ladislas 1906-1980 *ConAu 10NR, –102, –65*
Farah, Caesar Elie 1929- *ConAu 41R*
Farah, Madelain 1934- *ConAu 73*
Farah, Nuruddin 1945- *ConAu 106, EncWL 2*
Faralla, Dana 1909- *ConAu 49, IntAu&W 82X, SmATA 9*
Faralla, Dorothy 1909- *ConAu 49, IntAu&W 82, SmATA X*
Farallon, Cerise *ConAu X*
Faramelli, Norman Joseph 1932- *ConAu 109*
Farau, Alfred 1904-1972 *ConAu 37R*
Farb, Peter 1929-1980 *ConAu 13R, –97, SmATA 12, –22N, WorAu 1970*
Farber, Bernard 1922- *ConAu 21R*
Farber, Donald C 1923- *ConAu 29R*
Farber, Edward 1914-1982 *ConAu 110*
Farber, Joseph C 1903- *ConAu 33R*
Farber, Leslie Hillel 1912-1981 *ConAu 103, –110*
Farber, Marvin 1901- *ConAu 49*
Farber, Norma 1909- *ConAu 102, SmATA 25[port], TwCCW 83*

Farber, Seymour M 1912- *ConAu 57*
Farber, Stephen E 1943- *ConAu 103*
Farber, Susan L 1945- *ConAu 106*
Farber, Thomas *DrAP&F 83*
Farber, Thomas 1944- *ConAu 103*
Farberman, Harvey A 1939- *ConAu 45*
Farberow, Norman L 1918- *ConAu 7NR, –17R, IntAu&W 82*
Farca, Marie C 1935- *ConAu 37R*
Farel, Conrad *ConAu X*
Farely, Alison *ConAu X, IntAu&W 82X, WrDr 84*
Farer, Tom J 1935- *ConAu 8NR, –17R*
Farewell, Nina *ConAu X, IntAu&W 82X*
Farewell, Patricia *DrAP&F 83*
Farge *TwCA, TwCA SUP*
Farge, Monique *SmATA X*
Fargis, Paul 1939- *ConAu 21R*
Fargo, Doone *ConAu X,   WrDr 84*
Fargo, Joe *ConAu X*
Fargue, Leon-Paul 1876-1947 *CIDMEL 80, ConAu 109, EncWL 2, ModFrL, TwCLC 11[port], WhoTwCL, WorAu*
Farhi, Moris 1935- *ConAu 77*
Farhi, Musa Moris 1935- *IntAu&W 82*
Faria, A J 1944- *ConAu 102*
Farias, James *DrAP&F 83*
Farias Diaz-Noriega, Juan 1935- *IntAu&W 82*
Faricy, Robert L 1926- *ConAu 37R, WrDr 84*
Faridi, Nasiruddin Mohammad 1929- *ConAu 29R, IntAu&W 82*
Faridi, S N *ConAu X, IntAu&W 82X*
Faridi, Shah Nasir 1929- *WrDr 84*
Faries, Clyde J 1928- *ConAu 37R*
Farigoule, Louis 1885-1972 *ConAu X, –37R, LongCTC*
Farina, Richard 1936?-1966 *ConAu 25R, –81*
Farina, Richard 1937?-1966 *ConLC 9*
Farinella, Salvatore *DrAP&F 83*
Faris, Robert E L 1907- *ConAu 17R*
Farish, Donald J 1942- *ConAu 106, WrDr 84*
Farish, Margaret Kennedy 1918- *ConAu 5R*
Farjeon, Annabel 1919- *ConAu 53, SmATA 11*
Farjeon, Eleanor 1881-1965 *ConAu P-1, LongCTC, SmATA 2, TwCA, TwCA SUP, TwCCW 83, TwCWr*
Farjeon, Herbert 1887-1946 *TwCWr*
Farjeon, Joseph Jefferson 1883-1955 *TwCA, TwCA SUP*
Farkas, Emil 1946- *ConAu 69*
Farkas, Philip 1914- *ConAu 49*
Farleigh, John 1900-1965 *LongCTC*
Farley, Blanche *DrAP&F 83*
Farley, Carol 1936- *ConAu X, –10NR, MichAu 80, SmATA 4, WrDr 84*
Farley, Edward 1929- *ConAu 61*
Farley, Eugene J 1916- *ConAu 33R*
Farley, James Aloysius 1888-1976 *ConAu 65*
Farley, Jean 1928- *ConAu 21R*
Farley, Miriam Southwell 1907?-1975 *ConAu 57*
Farley, Ralph Milne 1887-1963 *TwCSFW, WorAu*
Farley, Rawle 1922- *ConAu 45, WrDr 84*
Farley, Walter *ConAu 8NR*
Farley, Walter 1915- *ConAu 17R, ConLC 17, SmATA 2*
Farley, Walter 1920- *DcLB 22[port], WrDr 84*
Farley, Walter 1922- *TwCCW 83*
Farley-Hills, David 1931- *ConAu 73*
Farlie, Barbara L 1936- *ConAu 65*
Farmacevten *ConAu X*
Farmer, Albert J 1894- *ConAu 21R*
Farmer, Bernard James 1902- *ConAu 5R*
Farmer, Bertram Hughes 1916- *ConAu 104, WrDr 84*
Farmer, Charles J 1943- *ConAu 10NR, –57*
Farmer, Don 1938- *ConAu 65*
Farmer, Gary R 1923- *ConAu 57*
Farmer, Gene 1919-1972 *ConAu 37R*
Farmer, Herbert Henry 1892-1981? *ConAu 102*
Farmer, Kathleen 1946- *ConAu 10NR, –65*
Farmer, Laurence 1895?-1976 *ConAu 65*
Farmer, Martha L 1912- *ConAu 21R*
Farmer, Penelope 1939- *ConAu 9NR, –13R, TwCCW 83, WrDr 84*
Farmer, Peter *ConAu X*
Farmer, Philip Jose *DrAP&F 83*
Farmer, Philip Jose 1918- *ConAu 1R, –4NR, ConLC 1, –19, ConSFA, DcLB 8[port], DrmM[port], TwCSFW, WorAu 1970, WrDr 84*
Farmer, R L *ConAu X*

Farmer, Richard Neil 1928- *ConAu 8NR, -17R, WrDr 84*
Farmer, Robert Allen 1938- *ConAu 21R*
Farmer, William R 1921- *ConAu 109*
Farmer Jones *ConAu X*
Farmiloe, Dorothy 1920- *WrDr 84*
Farmiloe, Dorothy Alicia 1920- *ConAu 8NR, -61*
Farnash, Hugh *ConAu X*
Farnborough, B *IntAu&W 82X*
Farndale, James *WrDr 84*
Farndale, James 1916- *ConAu 25R*
Farndale, W A J 1916- *ConAu 11NR, WrDr 84*
Farner, Donald S 1915- *ConAu 53*
Farnes, Eleanor *TwCRGW, WrDr 84*
Farnham, Burt *ConAu X, SmATA X*
Farnham, Emily 1912- *ConAu 69*
Farnham, Marynia F 1900?-1979 *ConAu 85*
Farnham, Thomas J 1938- *ConAu 4NR, -53*
Farnie, D A 1926- *ConAu 73*
Farnill, Barrie 1923- *WrDr 84*
Farnol, Jeffery 1878-1952 *TwCA, TwCA SUP, TwCRGW*
Farnol, Jeffrey 1878-1952 *LongCTC, TwCWr*
Farnsworth, Dana 1905- *ConAu 61*
Farnsworth, E Allan 1928- *ConAu 13R*
Farnsworth, James *ConAu X, IntAu&W 82X*
Farnsworth, Jerry 1895- *ConAu P-1*
Farnsworth, Lee W 1932- *ConAu 33R*
Farnsworth, Paul Randolph 1899- *ConAu P-2*
Farnsworth, Robert M 1929- *ConAu 53*
Farnum, K T *ConAu X*
Farnworth, Warren 1935- *ConAu 93*
Farny, Michael H 1934- *ConAu 65*
Faron, Boleslaw 1937- *IntAu&W 82*
Faron, Louis C 1923- *ConAu 9R*
Farquhar, Betty Murphy 1924- *IntWWP 82*
Farquhar, Francis P 1887-1975 *ConAu 57, ConAu P-1*
Farquhar, Margaret C 1905- *ConAu 69, SmATA 13*
Farquharson, Charlie *ConAu X*
Farr, Alfred Derek 1930- *IntAu&W 82, WrDr 84*
Farr, David M L 1922- *ConAu 37R*
Farr, Diana Pullein-Thompson *ConAu 7NR, -13R, IntAu&W 82*
Farr, Dorothy M 1905- *ConAu 77*
Farr, Douglas *ConAu X*
Farr, Finis 1904-1982 *ConAu 1R, -1NR, -105, SmATA 10*
Farr, John *ConAu X, TwCCr&M 80, WrDr 84*
Farr, Judith 1937- *ConAu 29R*
Farr, Kenneth R 1942- *ConAu 73*
Farr, Michael Bryant 1924- *ConAu 29R*
Farr, Roger C *ConAu 33R*
Farr, Walter Greene, Jr. 1925- *ConAu 106*
Farra, Madame E *ConAu X*
Farragher, Shaun *DrAP&F 83*
Farrally, Betty 1915- *CreCan 2*
Farran, Don Wilson 1902- *IntAu&W 82, IntWWP 82X*
Farran, Donald Wilson 1902- *IntWWP 82*
Farran, Roy Alexander 1921- *WrDr 84*
Farrant, Elizabeth *DrAP&F 83*
Farrant, Leda 1927- *ConAu 21R*
Farrar, John Chipman 1896-1974 *ConAu 53, -65*
Farrar, Lancelot Leighton, Jr. 1932- *ConAu 4NR, -53*
Farrar, Larston Dawn 1915-1970 *ConAu 1R, -29R*
Farrar, Richard B, Jr. 1939- *ConAu 65*
Farrar, Ronald T 1935- *WrDr 84*
Farrar, Ronald Truman 1935- *ConAu 33R*
Farrar, Rowena Rutherford 1903- *ConAu 108*
Farrar, Susan Clement 1917- *ConAu 101, SmATA 33[port]*
Farrar-Hockley, Anthony Heritage 1924- *ConAu 69*
Farrd, H R 1955- *IntAu&W 82*
Farrell, Alan 1920- *ConAu 13R*
Farrell, Anne A 1916- *ConAu 25R*
Farrell, Ben *ConAu X, SmATA X, WrDr 84*
Farrell, Bernard 1939- *IntAu&W 82*
Farrell, Bryan Henry 1923- *ConAu 2NR, -49, IntAu&W 82*
Farrell, Catharine *ConAu X*
Farrell, Cliff 1899- *ConAu 65, TwCWW, WrDr 84*
Farrell, David *ConAu X, WrDr 84*
Farrell, Desmond *ConAu X*

Farrell, Francis 1912-1983 *ConAu 109*
Farrell, Frank *ConAu X*
Farrell, J G 1935-1979 *ConAu 73, -89, ConLC 6, ConNov 82A, DcLB 14[port]*
Farrell, James Gordon 1935- *DcLEL 1940*
Farrell, James T 1904-1979 *ASpks, ConAmA, ConAu 5R, -9NR, -89, ConLC 1, -4, -8, -11, Conv 3, DcLB DS2[port], -4, -9[port], EncWL 2, LongCTC, ModAL, TwCA, TwCA SUP, TwCWr, WhoTwCL*
Farrell, John J 1934- *ConAu 110*
Farrell, John Philip 1939- *ConAu 102*
Farrell, John Wade *ConAu X*
Farrell, Kathleen Amy 1912- *ConAu 5R*
Farrell, Kirby 1942- *ConAu 33R*
Farrell, M J *ConAu X, WrDr 84*
Farrell, M J 1905- *IntAu&W 82X*
Farrell, Matthew Charles 1921- *ConAu 49*
Farrell, Melvin L 1930- *ConAu 5NR, -13R*
Farrell, Michael 1944- *ConAu 69*
Farrell, Patricia *ConAu X*
Farrell, Robert T 1938- *ConAu 93*
Farrelly, M John 1927- *ConAu 13R*
Farren, David *ConAu X*
Farren, Mick 1943- *TwCSFW, WrDr 84*
Farren, Richard J *ConAu X*
Farrer, Claire R 1936- *ConAu 10NR, -65*
Farrer, David 1906- *ConAu 25R*
Farrer, David 1906-1983 *ConAu 109*
Farrer, Katharine 1911- *WrDr 84*
Farrer, Katharine Dorothy 1911- *ConAu 5R, TwCCr&M 80*
Farrer, Keith Thomas Henry 1916- *ConAu 110*
Farrimond, John 1913- *ConAu 102, WrDr 84*
Farrington, Benjamin 1891-1974 *ConAu 53, -65, SmATA 20N*
Farrington, Ian S 1947- *WrDr 84*
Farrington, Margot *DrAP&F 83*
Farrington, S Kip, Jr. 1904-1983 *ConAu 109*
Farrington, Selwyn Kip, Jr. 1904- *ConAu 73, SmATA 20*
Farris, Christine *DrAP&F 83*
Farris, John *ConAu 101, DrAP&F 83*
Farris, Martin T 1925- *ConAu 11NR*
Farris, Martin Theodore 1925- *ConAu 21R*
Farris, Paul Leonard 1919- *ConAu 9R*
Farrison, William Edward 1902- *ConAu 29R*
Farriss, N M 1938- *ConAu 25R*
Farrokhzad, Forugh 1935-1967 *EncWL 2*
Farrow, G E 1862-1920? *TwCCW 83*
Farrow, J *ConAu X*
Farrow, James S *ConAu X, WrDr 84*
Farson, Daniel 1927- *WrDr 84*
Farson, Daniel Negley 1927- *ConAu 93, IntAu&W 82*
Farson, Negley 1890-1960 *ConAu 93, LongCTC, TwCA, TwCA SUP*
Farstad, Arthur L 1935- *ConAu 109*
Farthing, Alberta 1920- *IntWWP 82*
Farthing, Alison 1936- *WrDr 84*
Farthing Owens, Alberta *IntWWP 82X*
Farwell, Byron E 1921- *ConAu 9NR, -13R*
Farwell, George Michell 1911-1976 *ConAu 21R, -69*
Farzan, Massud 1936- *ConAu 53*
Fasana, Paul James 1933- *ConAu 37R*
Faschon, Susanne 1925- *IntAu&W 82*
Fasel, George W 1938- *ConAu 21R*
Fasel, Ida *DrAP&F 83*
Fasold, Ralph W 1940- *ConAu 29R*
Fassbinder, Rainer Werner 1946-1982 *ConAu 106, -93, ConLC 20*
Fassett, James 1904- *ConAu 49*
Fassler, Joan 1931- *ConAu 61, SmATA 11*
Fast, Barbara 1924- *ConAu 104*
Fast, Howard 1914- *ConAu 1R, -1NR, ConLC 23[port], ConNov 82, ConSFA, DcLB 9[port], ModAL, SmATA 7, TwCA SUP, TwCCr&M 80, TwCSFW, TwCWW, TwCWr, WrDr 84*
Fast, Jonathan 1948- *WrDr 84*
Fast, Jonathan David 1948- *ConAu 77, TwCSFW*
Fast, Julius 1919- *ConAu 11NR*
Fast, Julius 1919- *ConAu 25R*
Fastlife *ConAu X*
Fatchen, Max 1920- *ConAu 11NR, -25R, SmATA 20, TwCCW 83, WrDr 84*
Fatemi, Nasrollah S 1910- *ConAu 77*
Father Xavier *SmATA X*
Fatigati, Evelyn DeBuhr 1948- *ConAu 77, SmATA 24*

Fatio *IntAu&W 82X*
Fatio, Louise 1904- *ConAu 37R, IntAu&W 82, SmATA 6, TwCCW 83, WrDr 84*
Fatisha *DrAP&F 83, IntWWP 82X*
Fatjo, Thomas Joseph, Jr. 1940- *ConAu 107*
Fatouros, Arghyrios A 1932- *ConAu 13R, WrDr 84*
Fatout, Paul 1897- *ConAu 21R*
Faucette, John M 1943- *ConSFA*
Faucher, Jean 1924- *CreCan 2*
Faucher, Real *DrAP&F 83*
Faucher, Real 1940- *ConAu 101*
Faucher, W Thomas 1945- *ConAu 57*
Fauchois, Rene 1882-1962 *ModWD*
Fauconnier, Henri *TwCA, TwCA SUP*
Faulconer, Mary Goodnow 1905- *IntWWP 82*
Faulhaber, Charles Bailey 1941- *ConAu 53*
Faulhaber, Martha 1926- *ConAu 33R, SmATA 7*
Faulk, John Henry 1913- *ConAu 102*
Faulk, Odie B 1933- *ConAu 25R, WrDr 84*
Faulkner, Alex 1905?-1983 *ConAu 109*
Faulkner, Anne Irvin 1906- *ConAu 1R, -2NR, SmATA 23[port]*
Faulkner, Charles Herman 1937- *ConAu 25R, WrDr 84*
Faulkner, Elsie 1905- *ConAu 65*
Faulkner, Harold Underwood 1890-1968 *ConAu 1R, -103*
Faulkner, John Wesley Thompson, III 1901-1963 *ConAu 1R, -1NR*
Faulkner, Joseph E 1928- *ConAu 45*
Faulkner, Nancy 1906- *ConAu X, SmATA X*
Faulkner, Pete *IntWWP 82X*
Faulkner, Peter 1933- *ConAu 3NR, -5R, IntAu&W 82*
Faulkner, Peter William 1953- *IntWWP 82*
Faulkner, Ray 1906- *ConAu 5R*
Faulkner, Trader 1930- *ConAu 102*
Faulkner, Virginia 1913-1980 *ConAu 11NR*
Faulkner, Virginia Louise 1913- *ConAu 65*
Faulkner, Waldron 1898-1979 *ConAu 85, -93*
Faulkner, William 1897-1962 *AuNews 1, CnMD, CnMWL, ConAmA, ConAu 81, ConLC 1, -3, -6, -8, -9, -11, -14, -18, CroCD, DcLB DS2[port], -9[port], EncWL 2[port], LongCTC, ModAL, ModAL SUP, ModWD, TwCA, TwCA SUP, TwCCr&M 80, TwCWr, WhoTwCL*
Faulknor, Chauncy Clifford Vernon 1913- *IntAu&W 82*
Faulknor, Cliff 1913- *IntAu&W 82X, TwCCW 83, WrDr 84*
Faulknor, Clifford Vernon 1913- *ConAu 8NR, -17R*
Faull, Lesley *WrDr 84*
Faunce, Roland Cleo 1905- *ConAu 1R*
Faunce, William A 1928- *WrDr 84*
Faunce, William Alden 1928- *ConAu 25R*
Faupel, John F 1906- *ConAu 5R*
Faure, Elie 1873-1937 *ClDMEL 80, TwCA, TwCA SUP*
Faure, Lucie 1908-1977 *ConAu 73*
Faure, Raoul Cohen 1909- *TwCA SUP*
Faure, William C, Jr. 1949- *ConAu 109*
Faure, William Caldwell *WrDr 84*
Faurot, Albert 1914- *ConAu 77*
Faurot, Jean H 1911- *ConAu 29R*
Faurot, Jeannette 1943- *ConAu 106*
Faurot, Ruth Marie 1916- *ConAu 85*
Fauset, Arthur Huff 1899- *ConAu 25R, LivgBAA*
Fauset, Jessie Redmon 1884?-1961 *ConAu 109, ConLC 19, TwCA SUP*
Fausold, Martin L 1921- *ConAu 21R*
Fausset, Hugh I'Anson 1895-1965 *ConAu 93, LongCTC, ModBrL, TwCA, TwCA SUP*
Faust, Clarence H 1901-1975 *ConAu 57*
Faust, Drew Gilpin 1947- *ConAu 110*
Faust, Frederick 1892-1944? *ConAu 108*
Faust, Frederick 1892-1944 *LongCTC, TwCA, TwCA SUP*
Faust, Irvin *DrAP&F 83*
Faust, Irvin 1924- *ConAu 33R, ConLC 8, ConNov 82, Conv 3, DcLB Y80A[port], -2, IntAu&W 82, WrDr 84*
Faust, Naomi F *ConAu 61, IntAu&W 82, IntWWP 82*
Faust-Kubler, Erika 1926- *IntAu&W 82*
Fausti, Remo P 1917- *ConAu 41R*
Fauth, Robert T 1916- *ConAu 1R*
Fautsko, Timothy F 1945- *ConAu 85*

Ferguson, Ted 1936- *ConAu 65*
Ferguson, Tom 1943- *ConAu 107*
Ferguson, Walter 1930- *SmATA 34[port]*
Ferguson, Walter W 1930- *ConAu 107*
Ferguson, William *DrAP&F 83*
Ferguson, William 1943- *ConAu 49*
Fergusson, Adam 1932- *IntAu&W 82*
Fergusson, Bernard Edward 1911-1980
 ConAu 7NR, –9R, –102, –105, IntAu&W 82
Fergusson, Erna 1888-1964 *ConAu P-1,*
 SmATA 5
Fergusson, Francis 1904- *ConAu 3NR, –9R,*
 ConLCrt 82, IntAu&W 82, TwCA SUP,
 WrDr 84
Fergusson, Harvey 1890-1971 *ConAu 33R,*
 FifWWr, TwCA, TwCA SUP, TwCWW
Fergusson, James 1904-1973 *ConAu 104*
Fergusson Hannay, Lady *ConAu 9R*
Fergusson Hannay, Doris 1902?-1982
 ConAu 6NR, –107
Fericano, Paul *DrAP&F 83*
Fericano, Paul F 1951- *ConAu 69, IntWWP 82*
Ferkiss, Victor C 1925- *ConAu 21R*
Ferland, Albert 1872-1943 *CreCan 2*
Ferland, Carol 1936- *ConAu 102*
Ferlin, Nils 1898-1961 *EncWL 2*
Ferling, Lawrence *ConAu X*
Ferlinghetti, Lawrence *DrAP&F 83*
Ferlinghetti, Lawrence 1919?- *ConAu 3NR, –5R,*
 ConDr 82, ConLC 2, –6, –10, –27[port],
 ConP 80, CroCAP, CroCD, DcLB 16[port],
 DcLEL 1940, ModAL, TwCWr,
 WhoTwCL, WorAu
Ferlinghetti, Lawrence 1920- *DcLB 5*
Ferlita, Ernest 1927- *ConAu 11NR, –29R,*
 IntAu&W 82, NatPD 81[port], WrDr 84
Ferm, Betty 1926- *ConAu 21R*
Ferm, Deane William 1927- *ConAu 33R,*
 WrDr 84
Ferm, Robert Livingston 1931- *ConAu 13R*
Ferm, Vergilius Ture Anselm 1896-1974
 ConAu 9R, –49
Ferman, Edward L 1937- *ConAu 106, ConSFA*
Ferman, Joseph W 1906- *ConSFA*
Ferman, Joseph W 1906-1975 *ConAu 104*
Fermi, Laura 1907- *WrDr 84*
Fermi, Laura 1907-1977 *ConAu 1R, –6NR,*
 SmATA 28N, –6
Fermor, Patrick Leigh 1915- *ConAu 81,*
 DcLEL 1940, LongCTC, TwCWr, WorAu
Fern, Alan M 1930- *ConAu 33R*
Fern, Eugene A 1919- *ConAu 1R, SmATA 10*
Fernald, John 1905- *ConAu P-2*
Fernand, Daniel *ConAu X*
Fernandez, Benedict J 1936- *ConAu 85*
Fernandez, Daniel *DrAP&F 83*
Fernandez, Daniel 1938- *IntWWP 82*
Fernandez, Gladys Craven 1939- *ConAu 106*
Fernandez, Happy Craven *ConAu X*
Fernandez, James William 1930- *ConAu 107*
Fernandez, John P 1941- *ConAu 10NR, –65*
Fernandez, Joseph A 1921- *ConAu 37R*
Fernandez, Julio A 1936- *ConAu 33R*
Fernandez, Lily Netto 1944- *IntWWP 82*
Fernandez, Miguel 1931- *IntAu&W 82*
Fernandez Almagro, Melchor 1893-1966
 CIDMEL 80
Fernandez DeLamora, Gonzalo 1924-
 IntAu&W 82
Fernandez DeLaReguera, Ricardo 1914-
 ConAu 3NR, –5R
Fernandez DeLaReguera, Ricardo 1916-
 CIDMEL 80
Fernandez DeLaReguera Ugarte, Ricardo 1914-
 IntAu&W 82
Fernandez Florez, Wenceslao 1885?-1964
 CIDMEL 80
Fernandez-Marina, R 1909- *ConAu 41R*
Fernandez Santos, Jesus 1926- *CIDMEL 80*
Fernando, Lloyd 1926- *ConAu 77,*
 IntAu&W 82
Fernea, Elizabeth Warnock 1927- *ConAu 13R*
Fernea, Robert Alan 1932- *ConAu 33R*
Fernett, Gene 1924- *ConAu 49*
Ferneyhough, Frank 1911- *IntAu&W 82*
Ferneyhough, Roger Edmund 1941- *IntAu&W 82*
Ferns, Henry Stanley 1913- *ConAu 4NR, –5R*
Fernsworth, Lawrence 1893?-1977? *ConAu 89*
Ferracuti, Franco 1927- *ConAu 11NR, –25R*
Ferrante, Don *ConAu X*
Ferrante, Joan M 1936- *ConAu 85,*
 IntAu&W 82

Ferrar, Harold 1935- *WrDr 84*
Ferrarelli, Rina *DrAP&F 83*
Ferrari, Mary Selby *DrAP&F 83*
Ferraris, Fred *DrAP&F 83*
Ferraro, Gary P 1940- *ConAu 89*
Ferrars, E X 1907- *ConAu X*
Ferrars, Elizabeth 1907- *ConAu X,*
 IntAu&W 82, TwCCr&M 80, WrDr 84
Ferrat, Jacques Jean *TwCSFW*
Ferrater Mora, Jose 1912- *CIDMEL 80,*
 ConAu 1R
Ferre, Frederick 1933- *ConAu 13R, WrDr 84*
Ferre, Gustave A 1918- *ConAu 1R*
Ferre, Nels F S 1908-1971 *ConAu P-2*
Ferreira, Jose Gomes 1900- *CIDMEL 80*
Ferreira, Vergilio 1916- *CIDMEL 80*
Ferreira DeCastro, Jose Maria 1898-1974
 CIDMEL 80, ConAu 102, –49, EncWL 2,
 ModRL, TwCWr, WhoTwCL
Ferreiro Alemparte, Jaime 1918- *IntAu&W 82*
Ferrell, Mallory Hope 1935- *ConAu 33R*
Ferrell, Robert Hugh 1921- *ConAu 5R, –6NR*
Ferrell, Robert W 1913- *ConAu 13R*
Ferreol, Marcel Auguste 1899-1974 *ConAu 53,*
 –97, WorAu 1970
Ferrer, Aldo 1927- *ConAu 11NR, –25R*
Ferrero, Guglielmo 1871-1942 *TwCA,*
 TwCA SUP
Ferrero, Leo 1903-1933 *CnMD*
Ferres, Antonio 1924- *IntAu&W 82*
Ferres, Antonio 1925- *CIDMEL 80*
Ferres, John Howard 1932- *ConAu 41R*
Ferrett, Mabel 1917- *IntWWP 82*
Ferrier, Janet Mackay 1919- *ConAu 9R*
Ferrier, Lucy *ConAu X*
Ferril, Thomas Hornsby 1896- *ConAu 65,*
 ConP 80, TwCA SUP, WrDr 84
Ferrini, Vincent *DrAP&F 83*
Ferrini, Vincent 1913- *IntWWP 82*
Ferris, Helen Josephine 1890-1969 *ConAu 77,*
 SmATA 21[port]
Ferris, James Cody *ConAu P-2, SmATA X*
Ferris, Norman 1931- *ConAu 81*
Ferris, Paul 1929- *WrDr 84*
Ferris, Paul Frederick 1929- *ConAu 3NR, –5R,*
 DcLEL 1940
Ferris, Theodore Parker 1908-1972 *ConAu 37R*
Ferris, Timothy 1944- *ConAu 11NR, –69*
Ferris, Tom *ConAu X*
Ferriss, Abbott Lamoyne 1915- *ConAu 29R,*
 WrDr 84
Ferritor, Daniel Edward 1939- *ConAu 49*
Ferro, Marc 1924- *ConAu 77*
Ferro, Robert *DrAP&F 83*
Ferro, Robert 1941- *WrDr 84*
Ferro, Robert Michael 1941- *ConAu 29R*
Ferron, Jacques 1921- *CreCan 1*
Ferron, Marcelle 1924- *CreCan 1*
Ferry, Anne Davidson 1930- *ConAu 17R*
Ferry, Charles 1927- *ConAu 97*
Ferry, David *DrAP&F 83*
Ferry, David Russell 1924- *ConAu 13R*
Ferry, John Douglass 1912- *WrDr 84*
Ferry, W Hawkins 1914- *ConAu 61*
Fersh, Seymour H 1926- *ConAu 37R*
Ferster, C B 1922-1981 *ConAu 102, –97*
Ferster, Marilyn B *ConAu X*
Fertig, Nelle 1919- *IntWWP 82*
Ferullo, Dan 1948- *ConAu 106*
Feshbach, Norma Deitch 1926- *ConAu 8NR, –61*
Feshbach, Seymour 1925- *ConAu 8NR, –37R*
Fesler, James W 1911- *ConAu 21R*
Fesperman, John T 1925- *ConAu 2NR, –5R,*
 WrDr 84
Fess, Philip E 1931- *ConAu 33R*
Fessel, Murray 1927- *ConAu 21R*
Fessenden, Anne Lathrop *DrAP&F 83*
Fessenden, Katherine 1896?-1974 *ConAu 53*
Fessenden, Seth A 1903- *ConAu 17R*
Fessenden, Seth A 1903-1976 *ConAu 10NR*
Fessenko, Tatiana 1915- *ConAu 13R,*
 IntAu&W 82, IntWWP 82
Fessler, Loren W 1923- *ConAu 9R*
Fest, Joachim C 1926- *ConAu 49*
Fest, Thorrel B 1910- *ConAu P-1*
Festa, Gail *DrAP&F 83*
Fester, Richard 1910- *IntAu&W 82*
Festinger, Leon 1919- *ConAu 1R*
Fetherling, Dale 1941- *ConAu 77*
Fetherling, Doug 1947- *ConP 80, WrDr 84*
Fetler, Andrew *DrAP&F 83*
Fetler, Andrew 1925- *ConAu 13R*

Fetridge, William Harrison 1906- *ConAu 73*
Fetros, John G 1932- *ConAu 57*
Fetscher, Iring 1922- *ConAu 69*
Fettamen, Ann *ConAu X*
Fetter, Elizabeth Head 1904-1973 *ConAu 5R,*
 –41R
Fetter, Frank Whitson 1899- *ConAu 106*
Fetter, Richard Leland 1943- *ConAu 89,*
 IntAu&W 82
Fetterman, Elsie 1927- *ConAu 97*
Fetterman, John 1920-1975 *ConAu 61, –93*
Fettig, Art 1929- *ConAu 73*
Fetz, Ingrid 1915- *SmATA 30[port]*
Fetze, Georg Otto *IntAu&W 82X*
Fetzer, John F 1931- *ConAu 61*
Feucht, Oscar E 1895- *ConAu 103*
Feuchtwanger, E J 1924- *ConAu 11NR, –69*
Feuchtwanger, Lion 1884-1958 *CIDMEL 80,*
 CnMD, ConAu 104, EncWL 2, LongCTC,
 ModGL, ModWD, TwCA, TwCA SUP,
 TwCLC 3
Feuer, Kathryn Beliveau 1926- *ConAu 102*
Feuer, Lewis S 1912- *ConAu 3NR, –5R*
Feuerlicht, Ignace *ConAu P-2*
Feuerlicht, Roberta Strauss 1931- *ConAu 17R*
Feuerstein, Phyllis A 1930- *ConAu 105*
Feuerwerger, Marvin C 1950- *ConAu 104*
Feuerwerker, Albert 1927- *ConAu 8NR, –21R,*
 WrDr 84
Feulner, Patricia N 1946- *ConAu 105*
Feur, D C *ConAu X*
Feustel, Gunther 1924- *IntAu&W 82*
Feustel, Ingeborg 1926- *IntAu&W 82*
Feval, Paul 1860-1933 *TwCA, TwCA SUP*
Fey, Harold Edward 1898- *ConAu 17R*
Feydeau, Georges 1862-1921 *CIDMEL 80,*
 CnMD, EncWL 2, ModFrL, ModWD,
 TwCWr, WorAu
Feydy, Anne Lindbergh 1940- *SmATA 32*
Ffolliott, Rosemary 1934- *ConAu 97*
Ffrench-Beytagh, Gonville 1912- *ConAu 103*
Ffrench Blake, Neil 1940- *ConAu 69*
Ffrench Blake, R L V 1913- *ConAu 61*
Fiacc, Padraic 1924- *ConAu X, WrDr 84*
Fialka, Ladislav 1931- *CroCD*
Fialkowski, Barbara *DrAP&F 83*
Fialkowski, Barbara 1946- *ConAu 77*
Fiammenghi, Gioia 1929- *SmATA 9*
Fiandt, Mary K 1914- *ConAu 89*
Fiarotta, Noel *ConAu X*
Fiarotta, Noel 1944- *ConAu 69, SmATA 15*
Fiarotta, Phyllis *ConAu X*
Fiarotta, Phyllis 1942- *ConAu 69, SmATA 15*
Fiber, Alan *ConAu 102, WrDr 84*
Ficarotta, Noel 1944- *ConAu 11NR*
Ficarotta, Phyllis 1942- *ConAu 11NR*
Fichte, Hubert 1935- *CIDMEL 80*
Fichtelius, Karl-Erik 1924- *ConAu 53*
Fichter, George S 1922- *ConAu 7NR, –17R,*
 IntAu&W 82, SmATA 7, WrDr 84
Fichter, Joseph H 1908- *ConAu 1R, –4NR*
Ficke, Arthur Davison 1883-1945 *TwCA,*
 TwCA SUP
Ficken, Frederick A 1910-1978 *ConAu 81*
Ficker, Victor B 1937- *ConAu 33R*
Fickert, Kurt J 1920- *ConAu 37R,*
 IntAu&W 82, WrDr 84
Fickett, Harold L, Jr. 1918- *ConAu 13R*
Fickett, Lewis P, Jr. 1926- *ConAu 21R*
Fickle, James Edward 1939- *ConAu 106*
Fickling, G G *ConAu X*
Fickling, Skip Forrest 1925- *ConAu 5R*
Fidelio *ConAu X*
Fidelsberger, Heinz 1920- *IntAu&W 82*
Fidler, Kathleen 1899- *ConAu 25R, SmATA 3*
Fidler, Kathleen 1899-1980 *TwCCW 83*
Fie, Jacquelyn Joyce 1937- *ConAu 57*
Fiedler, Fred E 1922- *ConAu 21R, WrDr 84*
Fiedler, Jean *ConAu 11NR, –29R, DrAP&F 83,*
 SmATA 4
Fiedler, Leslie A *DrAP&F 83*
Fiedler, Leslie A 1917- *ConAu 7NR, –9R,*
 ConLC 13, –24[port], ConLCrt 82,
 ConNov 82, DcLEL 1940, EncWL 2,
 IntAu&W 82, IntWWP 82, ModAL SUP,
 WhoTwCL, WorAu, WrDr 84
Fiedler, Lois 1928- *ConAu 17R*
Fiedler, Sally A *DrAP&F 83*
Fieg, Victor P 1924- *ConAu 106*
Field, Adelaide 1916- *ConAu 106*
Field, Andrew 1938- *ConAu 97*
Field, Arthur J 1927-1975 *ConAu 33R*

Field, Barbara *NatPD 81[port]*
Field, Barbara 1935- *ConAu 110*
Field, Charles *ConAu X, TwCWW*
Field, Daniel 1938- *ConAu 65*
Field, David D 1918- *ConAu 73*
Field, Dawn Stewart 1940- *ConAu 57, WrDr 84*
Field, Dick 1912- *ConAu 57*
Field, Edward *DrAP&F 83*
Field, Edward 1924- *ConAu 10NR, –13R, ConP 80, CroCAP, DcLEL 1940, SmATA 8, WorAu 1970, WrDr 84*
Field, Elinor Whitney 1889-1980 *ConAu 109, SmATA 28N*
Field, Ernest R 1925- *ConAu 5R*
Field, Eugene 1850-1895 *SmATA 16*
Field, Frances Fox 1913?-1977 *ConAu 69*
Field, Frank 1936- *ConAu 21R*
Field, Frank Chester *ConAu X*
Field, Frank McCoy 1887-1978 *ConAu 103, –45*
Field, G W 1914- *ConAu 37R*
Field, Gans T *IntAu&W 82X, WrDr 84*
Field, George B 1929- *ConAu 101*
Field, Gordon Lawrence 1939- *ConAu 17R*
Field, Hazel E 1891- *ConAu P-1*
Field, Henry 1902- *ConAu 69*
Field, Irving M 1934- *ConAu 25R*
Field, James Alfred, Jr. 1916- *ConAu 25R*
Field, Joanna *ConAu X, IntAu&W 82X, WrDr 84*
Field, John 1910- *ConAu 33R, WrDr 84*
Field, John 1928- *WrDr 84*
Field, John P 1936- *ConAu 37R*
Field, Joyce W 1932- *ConAu 29R*
Field, Leslie A 1926- *ConAu 29R*
Field, Mark G 1923- *ConAu 37R, IntAu&W 82, WrDr 84*
Field, Michael *LongCTC, ModBrL*
Field, Michael 1915-1971 *ConAu 29R*
Field, Minna *ConAu 25R*
Field, Penelope *ConAu X*
Field, Peter *WrDr 84*
Field, Phyllis Frances 1946- *ConAu 107*
Field, Rachel 1894-1942 *ConAmA, ConAu 109, DcLB 9, –22[port], LongCTC, SmATA 15, TwCA, TwCA SUP, TwCCW 83, TwCRGW, TwCWr*
Field, Sara Bard 1882- *TwCA, TwCA SUP*
Field, Stanley *DrAP&F 83*
Field, Stanley 1911- *ConAu 9NR, –21R*
Field, Thomas P 1914- *ConAu 9R*
Field, Walter S 1899- *ConAu 49*
Fielden, Charlotte 1934- *ConAu 93*
Fielden, John 1939- *IntAu&W 82*
Fielden, Thomas Perceval 1882- *ConAu 5R*
Fielder, Mildred 1913- *ConAu 10NR, –13R, WrDr 84*
Fielding, A 1884- *LongCTC, TwCCr&M 80*
Fielding, A E *TwCA*
Fielding, A W 1918- *ConAu X, WrDr 84*
Fielding, Alan Gabriel Barnsley 1916- *DcLEL 1940*
Fielding, Daphne Winifred Louise 1904- *ConAu 9R*
Fielding, G J 1934- *ConAu 97*
Fielding, Gabriel 1916- *ConAu X, ConNov 82, ModBrL, ModBrL SUP, WorAu, WrDr 84*
Fielding, Hubert *WrDr 84*
Fielding, Joy 1945- *ConAu 2NR, –49*
Fielding, Nancy 1913- *ConAu 108*
Fielding, Raymond 1931- *WrDr 84*
Fielding, Raymond E 1931- *ConAu 8NR, –17R, IntAu&W 82*
Fielding, Temple 1913-1983 *ConAu 109*
Fielding, Temple Hornaday 1913- *ConAu 21R*
Fielding, Waldo L 1921- *ConAu 45*
Fielding, William J 1886- *ConAu 13R*
Fielding, Xan *ConAu X*
Fieldler, Leslie A 1917- *ConLC 4, ModAL*
Fields, Alan *ConAu X*
Fields, Ann 1926- *IntWWP 82*
Fields, Arthur C 1926?-1974 *ConAu 49*
Fields, Beverly 1917- *ConAu 49*
Fields, Dorothy 1905-1974 *ConAu 49, –93*
Fields, Howard K 1938- *ConAu 81*
Fields, Jeff *AuNews 2*
Fields, Jennie *DrAP&F 83*
Fields, Joseph 1895-1966 *CnMD, ConAu 25R, ModWD*
Fields, Julia *DrAP&F 83*
Fields, Julia 1938- *ConAu 73, LivgBAA*
Fields, Kenneth 1939- *ConAu 110*
Fields, Nora *ConAu 49*

Fields, Rick *DrAP&F 83*
Fields, Rick 1942- *ConAu 9NR, –65*
Fields, Rona M 1934- *ConAu 69*
Fields, Totie *ConAu X*
Fields, Victor Alexander 1901- *ConAu 5R, WrDr 84*
Fields, Wilbert J 1917- *ConAu 13R*
Fields, Wilmer Clemont 1922- *ConAu 106*
Fieler, Frank B 1933- *ConAu 41R*
Fiene, Donald M 1930- *ConAu 69*
Fiene, Ernest 1894-1965 *ConAu P-1*
Fiennes, Ranulph 1944- *ConAu 3NR, –45, IntAu&W 82, WrDr 84*
Fiennes, Richard *ConAu X*
Fiennes, Richard 1909- *WrDr 84*
Fiennes, Richard N 1909- *ConAu 21R*
Fiering, Norman Sanford 1935- *ConAu 105*
Fierro, Robert Daniel 1945- *ConAu 109*
Fieser, Louis F 1899-1977 *ConAu 73*
Fieser, Max 1930- *ConAu 13R*
Fiester, Mark 1907- *ConAu 65*
Fieve, Ronald R 1930- *ConAu 107*
Fife, Austin E 1909- *ConAu 53*
Fife, Dale 1910- *ConAu 85, SmATA 18*
Fife, Robert Oldham 1918- *ConAu 37R*
Fifer, Ken *DrAP&F 83*
Fifer, Ken 1947- *ConAu 104*
Fifield, William 1916- *ConAu 9NR, –13R, IntAu&W 82, WrDr 84*
Fifoot, Cecil Herbert Stuart 1899-1975 *ConAu 107*
Figes, Eva 1932- *ConAu 4NR, –53, ConNov 82, DcLB 14[port], DcLEL 1940, IntAu&W 82, WrDr 84*
Figgins, Ross 1936- *ConAu 11NR, –69*
Figh, Margaret Gillis 1896- *ConAu P-2*
Fighter Pilot, A *ConAu X*
Figler, Howard Elliot 1939- *ConAu 109*
Figueira, Gaston *IntWWP 82X*
Figueira Moran, Jose Gaston 1905- *IntWWP 82*
Figueiredo, Fidelino DeSousa 1888-1967 *CIDMEL 80*
Figueiredo, Tomaz De 1920- *CIDMEL 80*
Figueroa, John 1920- *ConP 80, DcLEL 1940, WrDr 84*
Figueroa, John Joseph Maria 1920- *ConAu 108*
Figueroa, John L *DrAP&F 83*
Figueroa, John L 1936- *ConAu 65*
Figueroa, Jose-Angel *DrAP&F 83*
Figueroa, Loida *ConAu X*
Figueroa, Pablo 1938- *ConAu 61, SmATA 9*
Figueroa Chapel, Ramon *DrAP&F 83*
Figueroa-Chapel, Ramon Antonio 1935- *ConAu 45*
Figueroa-Mercado, Loida 1917- *ConAu 9NR, –57*
Figurito, Joseph 1922- *ConAu 29R*
Fijan, Carol 1918- *ConAu 53, SmATA 12*
Fikso, Eunice Cleland 1927- *ConAu 5R*
Filas, Francis Lad 1915- *ConAu 2NR, –5R*
Filby, P William 1911- *ConAu 3NR, –9R, IntAu&W 82, WrDr 84*
Filene, Peter G 1940- *ConAu 21R*
Filep, Robert Thomas 1931- *ConAu 1NR, –45*
Filiatrault, Jean 1919- *CreCan 1*
Filicchia, Ralph 1935- *ConAu 103*
Filion, Jean-Paul 1927- *CreCan 2*
Filipovitch, Anthony J 1947- *ConAu 102*
Filippo, Eduardo De 1900- *WorAu 1970*
Filler, Louis 1912- *ConAu 1R, –2NR*
Fillingham, Ann *IntWWP 82X*
Fillingham, Ann Beatrice 1946- *IntWWP 82*
Fillingham, Patricia *DrAP&F 83*
Fillmer, Henry Thompson 1932- *ConAu 21R*
Fillmore, Lowell 1882- *ConAu P-1*
Fillmore, Roscoe Alfred 1887- *ConAu 5R*
Filosa, Gary 1931- *ConAu 65, WrDr 84*
Filson, Brent *DrAP&F 83*
Filson, Floyd Vivian 1896- *ConAu 61*
Filstrup, Jane 1946- *ConAu 110*
Filstrup, Janie *ConAu X*
Finale, Frank Louis *DrAP&F 83*
Finale, Frank Louis 1942- *IntWWP 82*
Finberg, Herbert Patrick Reginald 1900-1974 *ConAu 53, ConAu P-1*
Finch, Brian 1936- *IntAu&W 82*
Finch, Christopher 1939- *WrDr 84*
Finch, Donald George 1937- *ConAu 53*
Finch, Henry LeRoy 1918- *ConAu 41R*
Finch, J F 1951- *IntWWP 82*
Finch, John *ConDr 82C*
Finch, John 1911- *NatPD 81[port]*

Finch, Matthew *ConAu X, IntAu&W 82X, WrDr 84*
Finch, Merton *ConAu X, IntAu&W 82X, WrDr 84*
Finch, Peter 1947- *IntAu&W 82, WrDr 84*
Finch, Robert 1900- *ConAu 9NR, WrDr 84*
Finch, Robert Duer Claydon 1900- *ConAu 57, ConLC 18, ConP 80, CreCan 2, LongCTC*
Fincher, Cameron Lane 1926- *ConAu 41R*
Fincher, Ernest B 1910- *ConAu 9NR, –53*
Finck, Furman J 1900- *ConAu P-2*
Fincke, Gary *DrAP&F 83*
Fincke, Gary 1945- *ConAu 57*
Finckenauer, James O 1939- *ConAu 108*
Finder, Martin *ConAu X, SmATA X*
Findlater, Jane Helen 1866-1946 *LongCTC*
Findlater, Mary 1865-1964 *LongCTC*
Findlater, Richard 1921- *ConAu X, IntAu&W 82, WrDr 84*
Findlay, Bruce Allyn 1895-1972 *ConAu P-1*
Findlay, David Kilpatrick 1901- *ConAu P-1*
Findlay, James F, Jr. 1930- *ConAu 49*
Findlay, John Niemeyer 1903- *ConAu 5R, –5NR, IntAu&W 82*
Findlay, Norman Edward 1920- *IntWWP 82*
Findlay, Robert R 1932- *ConAu 45*
Findley, Carter Vaughn 1941- *ConAu 102*
Findley, Paul 1921- *ConAu 29R*
Findley, Timothy 1930- *ConAu 25R, ConLC 27[port]*
Findling, John Ellis 1941- *ConAu 102*
Fine, Anne 1947- *ConAu 105, SmATA 29, TwCCW 82*
Fine, Benjamin 1905-1975 *ConAu 4NR, –5R, –57*
Fine, Elsa Honig 1930- *ConAu 49*
Fine, Estelle *ConAu X*
Fine, I V 1918- *ConAu 17R*
Fine, Marlene Rosen *DrAP&F 83*
Fine, Nathan 1893?-1979 *ConAu 89*
Fine, Ralph Adam 1941- *ConAu 29R*
Fine, Reuben 1914- *ConAu 17R*
Fine, S Morton 1930- *ConAu 104*
Fine, Sidney 1920- *ConAu 1R, –1NR, IntAu&W 82, WrDr 84*
Fine, Warren 1943- *ConAu 21R*
Fine, William Michael 1924- *ConAu 13R*
Fineberg, Robert Gene 1940- *ConAu 107*
Finegan, Jack 1908- *ConAu 1R, –1NR, IntAu&W 82, WrDr 84*
Finegan, T Aldrich 1929- *ConAu 108*
Fineman, Irving 1893- *ConAu 1R, –5R, TwCA, TwCA SUP*
Finer, Leslie 1921- *ConAu 13R*
Finer, Samuel 1915- *WrDr 84*
Finer, Samuel Edward 1915- *ConAu 41R, IntAu&W 82*
Finestone, Harold 1920- *ConAu 110*
Finestone, Harry 1920- *ConAu 45*
Fingarette, Herbert 1921- *ConAu 77*
Finger, Charles J 1869-1941 *TwCCW 83*
Finger, Charles Joseph 1869?-1941 *TwCA*
Finger, Seymour Maxwell 1915- *ConAu 104*
Fingesten, Peter 1916- *ConAu 13R*
Finifter, Ada W 1938- *ConAu 104*
Finisterre, Alejandro *IntAu&W 82X*
Fink, Arthur Emil 1903- *ConAu 1R*
Fink, Augusta 1916- *ConAu 33R, IntAu&W 82, WrDr 84*
Fink, Brat *ConAu X*
Fink, Edith 1918- *ConAu 61*
Fink, Eli E 1908?-1979 *ConAu 85*
Fink, Gary M 1936- *ConAu 53*
Fink, Josef 1912- *IntAu&W 82*
Fink, Joseph 1915- *ConAu 57*
Fink, Lawrence Alfred 1930- *ConAu 97*
Fink, Merton 1921- *ConAu 9R, IntAu&W 82, WrDr 84*
Fink, Paul Jay 1933- *ConAu 53*
Fink, Stevanne Auerbach *ConAu X*
Fink, William B 1916- *ConAu 41R, SmATA 22*
Fink, Z S 1902- *ConAu P-1*
Finke, Blythe Foote 1922- *ConAu 65, IntAu&W 82, SmATA 26[port]*
Finke, Jack A 1918?-1979 *ConAu 89*
Finkel, Donald *DrAP&F 83*
Finkel, Donald 1929- *ConAu 9NR, –21R, ConP 80, DcLEL 1940, IntWWP 82, WorAu 1970, WrDr 84*
Finkel, George 1909-1975 *ConAu P-2, SmATA 8, TwCCW 83*
Finkel, Lawrence S 1925- *ConAu 13R*
Finkel, LeRoy 1939- *ConAu 105*

Finkelhor, Dorothy Cimberg 1902- *ConAu 110*
Finkell, Max *ConAu X*
Finkelman, Paul 1949- *ConAu 105*
Finkelstein, Bonnie B 1946- *ConAu 85*
Finkelstein, Caroline *DrAP&F 83*
Finkelstein, Jacob Joel 1922-1974 *ConAu 53*
Finkelstein, Leonid Vladimirovitch 1924-
    ConAu 21R
Finkelstein, Louis 1895- *ConAu 13R*
Finkelstein, Marina S 1921?-1972 *ConAu 33R*
Finkelstein, Milton 1920- *ConAu 89*
Finkelstein, Miriam *DrAP&F 83*
Finkelstein, Miriam 1928- *ConAu 108*
Finkelstein, Norman *DrAP&F 83*
Finkelstein, Norman 1954- *IntWWP 82*
Finkelstein, Sidney 1910?-1974 *ConAu 45*
Finkle, Jason L 1926- *ConAu 21R*
Finklehoffe, Fred F 1910-1977 *ConAu 73*
Finlator, John Haywood 1911- *ConAu 102*
Finlay, Campbell K 1909- *ConAu 5R*
Finlay, David J 1934- *ConAu 25R*
Finlay, Finona *ConAu X*
Finlay, Ian 1906- *IntAu&W 82, WrDr 84*
Finlay, Ian Hamilton 1925- *ConAu 81, ConP 80,
    DcLEL 1940, WorAu, WrDr 84*
Finlay, Matthew Henderson 1916- *ConAu 13R*
Finlay, William *ConAu X, IntAu&W 82X,
    WrDr 84*
Finlay, Winifred 1910- *TwCCW 83, WrDr 84*
Finlay, Winifred Lindsay Crawford 1910-
    *ConAu 9R, IntAu&W 82,
    SmATA 23[port]*
Finlayson, Ann 1925- *ConAu 29R, SmATA 8*
Finlayson, Roderick 1904- *ConAu X*
Finlayson, Roderick David 1904- *ConAu 81,
    ConNov 82, LongCTC*
Finler, Joel W 1938- *ConAu 77*
Finletter, Thomas K 1893-1980 *ConAu 101*
Finletter, Gerald Eric 1931- *ConAu 105*
Finley, Glenna *ConAu X*
Finley, Glenna 1925- *AuNews 1, ConAu X,
    IntAu&W 82, TwCRGW, WrDr 84*
Finley, Harold M 1916- *ConAu 17R*
Finley, James 1943- *ConAu 97*
Finley, Jeanne *DrAP&F 83*
Finley, Jeanne 1951- *IntWWP 82*
Finley, Joseph E 1919- *ConAu 69*
Finley, Lewis M 1929- *ConAu 61*
Finley, M I 1912- *ConAu 10NR*
Finley, Mike *DrAP&F 83*
Finley, Moses 1912- *WrDr 84*
Finley, Moses I 1912- *ConAu 5R*
Finman, Ted 1931- *ConAu 110*
Finn, David 1921- *ConAu 73*
Finn, James 1924- *ConAu 108*
Finn, Jonathan 1884?-1971 *ConAu 29R*
Finn, Mary B *IntWWP 82X*
Finn, Mary Beavers 1907- *IntWWP 82*
Finn, Mike *DrAP&F 83*
Finn, R Welldon *ConAu X*
Finn, Ralph L 1912- *ConAu 9NR*
Finn, Ralph Leslie 1912- *ConAu 5R*
Finn, Ralph Leslie 1922- *IntAu&W 82,
    WrDr 84*
Finn, Reginald Patrick Arthur Welldon 1900-
    ConAu 13R
Finn, Reginald Patrick Arthur Welldon 1900-1971
    ConAu 10NR
Finn, Rex Welldon *ConAu X*
Finnegan, Brenda Brown 1942- *IntWWP 82*
Finnegan, Frances 1941- *WrDr 84*
Finnegan, James *DrAP&F 83*
Finnegan, Robert 1906-1947 *TwCCr&M 80*
Finnegan, Ruth H *ConAu X*
Finneran, Richard J 1943- *ConAu 29R,
    WrDr 84*
Finnerty, Adam Daniel 1944- *ConAu 81*
Finney, Ben R 1933- *ConAu 1NR, -45*
Finney, Charles G 1905- *ConAu P-2, ConSFA,
    TwCA, TwCA SUP*
Finney, Gertrude Elva 1892- *ConAu P-1*
Finney, Gretchen Ludke 1901- *ConAu 9R*
Finney, Humphrey S 1902- *ConAu 97*
Finney, Jack *ConAu X*
Finney, Jack 1911- *ConSFA, DcLB 8,
    TwCCr&M 80, TwCSFW, WrDr 84*
Finney, Jim *DrAP&F 83*
Finney, Mark *ConAu X, IntAu&W 82X*
Finney, Nathaniel Solon 1903-1982 *ConAu 108*
Finney, Patricia 1958- *ConAu 97, WrDr 84*
Finney, Paul B 1929- *ConAu 73*

Finney, Theodore Mitchell 1902- *ConAu 61*
Finney, Walter Braden 1911- *ConAu 110*
Finnigan, Joan 1925- *ConAu 17R, ConP 80,
    DcLEL 1940, WrDr 84*
Finnin, Mary *ConAu 106, IntWWP 82,
    WrDr 84*
Finocchiaro, Mary 1913- *ConAu 29R*
Finow, Hans-Achim *IntAu&W 82X*
Fins, Alice 1944- *ConAu 110*
Fiore, Edith 1930- *ConAu 85*
Fiore, Michael V 1934- *ConAu 45*
Fiore, Peter A 1927- *WrDr 84*
Fiore, Peter Amadeus 1927- *ConAu 33R*
Fiore, Robert Louis 1935- *ConAu 73*
Fiore, Silvestro 1921- *ConAu 17R*
Fiorentino, Luigi 1913- *IntWWP 82*
Fiorenza, Elisabeth Schuessler 1938- *ConAu 106*
Fiori, Pamela A 1944- *ConAu 89*
Fiorina, Morris Paul, Jr. 1946- *ConAu 85*
Fiorino, A John 1926- *ConAu 29R, WrDr 84*
Fiorio, Franco Emilio 1912-1975 *ConAu 61*
Firbank, Arthur Annesley Ronald 1886-1926
    TwCA, TwCA SUP
Firbank, Ronald 1886-1926 *CnMWL,
    ConAu 104, EncWL 2, LongCTC, ModBrL,
    ModBrL SUP, TwCLC 1, TwCWr,
    WhoTwCL*
Firchow, Evelyn Scherabon 1932- *ConAu 11NR,
    -21R*
Firchow, Peter 1937- *ConAu 37R,
    IntAu&W 82, WrDr 84*
Firebrace, Sir Aylmer Newton George 1886-
    ConAu 5R
Fireman, A *IntAu&W 82X*
Fireside, Harvey F 1929- *ConAu 29R,
    IntAu&W 82, WrDr 84*
Firestone, Harvey Samuel, Jr. 1898-1973
    ConAu 41R
Firestone, O J 1913- *ConAu 41R, WrDr 84*
Firestone, Shulamith 1945- *WrDr 84*
Firestone, Tom *ConAu X*
Firestone, Willard David 1909- *IntAu&W 82*
Firey, Walter Irving 1916- *ConAu 1R,
    WrDr 84*
Firkins, Oscar W 1864-1932 *TwCA*
Firkins, Peter Charles 1926- *ConAu 107,
    WrDr 84*
Firmage, George J 1928- *ConAu 9R*
Firmin, Angela *CreCan 2*
Firmin, Charlotte 1954- *ConAu 106,
    SmATA 29[port]*
Firmin, Peter 1928- *ConAu 81, SmATA 15*
Firooze, Frank *IntAu&W 82X*
Firsoff, V Axel 1910- *ConAu 93*
First, Ruth 1925-1982 *ConAu 10NR, -107, -53,
    IntAu&W 82*
Firth, Grace 1922- *ConAu 73*
Firth, Maureen 1935- *IntWWP 82*
Firth, Mike *NatPD 81[port]*
Firth, Raymond William 1901- *ConAu 65*
Firth, Robert E 1921- *ConAu 77*
Firth, Tony 1937?-1980 *ConAu 97*
Firth Goddard, Hazel *IntWWP 82X*
Fis, Teodor 1912- *IntAu&W 82*
Fisch, Edith L 1923- *ConAu 77*
Fisch, Gerald G 1922- *ConAu 13R*
Fisch, Harold 1923- *ConAu 37R, IntAu&W 82,
    WrDr 84*
Fisch, Martin L 1924- *ConAu 109*
Fisch, Max H 1900- *ConAu 33R*
Fisch, Richard 1926- *ConAu 106*
Fischbach, Julius 1894- *ConAu 2NR, -5R,
    SmATA 10*
Fischel, Walter J 1902-1973 *ConAu 41R,
    ConAu P-2*
Fischer, Alfred 1920- *ConAu 73*
Fischer, Ann 1919-1971 *ConAu P-2*
Fischer, Bermann Gottfried 1897- *IntAu&W 82*
Fischer, Bobby *ConAu X*
Fischer, Bruno 1908- *ConAu 77,
    TwCCr&M 80, WrDr 84*
Fischer, Carl H 1903- *ConAu 17R*
Fischer, Claude S 1948- *ConAu 107*
Fischer, David Hackett 1935- *ConAu 17R*
Fischer, Donald E 1935- *ConAu 41R*
Fischer, Edward A 1914- *WrDr 84*
Fischer, Edward Adam 1914- *ConAu 1R, -1NR,
    IntAu&W 82*
Fischer, Ernst 1899-1972 *ConAu 37R*
Fischer, F Johs *IntAu&W 82X*
Fischer, Friedrich Johann 1911- *IntAu&W 82*

Fischer, Friedrich Johs *IntAu&W 82X*
Fischer, Fritz 1908- *ConAu 9NR, -65*
Fischer, George 1923- *ConAu 9NR, -53*
Fischer, George 1932- *ConAu 25R*
Fischer, Gerald C 1928- *ConAu 9NR, -21R*
Fischer, Gerhard 1930- *IntAu&W 82*
Fischer, J L 1923- *ConAu 17R*
Fischer, Joel 1939- *ConAu 4NR, -53*
Fischer, John 1910-1978 *ConAu 4NR, -9R, -81*
Fischer, Leck 1904-1956 *CnMD*
Fischer, LeRoy Henry 1917- *ConAu 8NR, -17R*
Fischer, Louis 1896-1970 *ConAu 25R,
    ConAu P-1, TwCA SUP*
Fischer, Otokar 1883-1938 *CIDMEL 80*
Fischer, Robert H 1918- *ConAu 37R, WrDr 84*
Fischer, Robert James 1943- *ConAu 103*
Fischer, Roger Adrian 1939- *ConAu 109*
Fischer, Victor 1924- *ConAu 110*
Fischer, Wolfgang Georg 1933- *ConAu 33R*
Fischer-Dieskau, Dietrich 1925- *ConAu 97*
Fischetti, John 1916-1980 *ConAu 102*
Fischl, Viktor 1912- *ConAu X*
Fischman, Leonard L 1919- *ConAu 10NR, -13R*
Fischtrom, Harvey 1933-1974 *ConAu 53,
    ConAu P-2*
Fish, Byron Morris 1908- *ConAu 45*
Fish, J *IntAu&W 82X*
Fish, Julian *ConAu X*
Fish, Kenneth L 1926- *ConAu 29R*
Fish, Margery 1892-1969 *ConAu 4NR, -5R*
Fish, Peter Graham 1937- *ConAu 69*
Fish, Robert L *DrAP&F 83*
Fish, Robert L 1912-1981 *ConAu 103, -13R,
    TwCCr&M 80*
Fish, Stanley Eugene 1938- *ConLCrt 82*
Fishbein, Harold Dennis 1938- *ConAu 105*
Fishbein, Meyer H 1916- *ConAu 41R*
Fishbein, Morris 1889-1976 *ConAu 4NR, -5R,
    -69*
Fishburn, Angela Mary 1933- *WrDr 84*
Fishburn, Hummel 1901- *ConAu P-1*
Fishburn, Janet Forsythe 1937- *ConAu 108*
Fishburn, Peter C 1936- *ConAu 45*
Fishel, Elizabeth 1950- *ConAu 103*
Fishel, Leslie H, Jr. 1921- *ConAu 21R*
Fishel, Wesley R 1919-1977 *ConAu 69, -73*
Fisher, A E *WrDr 84*
Fisher, A Garth 1933- *ConAu 104*
Fisher, A Stanley T 1906- *ConAu 93,
    IntAu&W 82, WrDr 84*
Fisher, Aileen 1906- *TwCCW 83, WrDr 84*
Fisher, Aileen Lucia 1906- *ConAu 2NR, -5R,
    SmATA 1, -25[port]*
Fisher, Alan W 1939- *ConAu 53, WrDr 84*
Fisher, Alden L 1928-1970 *ConAu P-2*
Fisher, Allan G B 1895-1976 *ConAu 33R*
Fisher, Allen J 1907?-1980 *ConAu 102*
Fisher, Ameel J 1909- *ConAu 104*
Fisher, Arthur 1931- *ConAu 110*
Fisher, Barbara 1940- *ConAu 104,
    NatPD 81[port], SmATA 34*
Fisher, Bart 1943- *ConAu 45*
Fisher, Bob *ConAu X*
Fisher, Brian 1939- *CreCan 2*
Fisher, Brian Lawrence 1929- *IntWWP 82*
Fisher, C William 1916- *ConAu 5R, -6NR*
Fisher, Charles Alfred 1916-1982? *ConAu 105*
Fisher, Charles Harold *WrDr 84*
Fisher, Clavin C 1912- *ConAu 65,
    SmATA 24[port]*
Fisher, Clay *ConAu X, TwCWW, WrDr 84*
Fisher, David 1946- *WrDr 84*
Fisher, David E 1932- *ConAu 4NR, -53,
    WrDr 84*
Fisher, David L *DrAP&F 83*
Fisher, David Lincoln 1947- *IntWWP 82*
Fisher, Dorothy Canfield 1879-1958 *ConAmA,
    DcLB 9, LongCTC, ModAL, TwCA,
    TwCA SUP, TwCCW 83*
Fisher, Douglas 1934- *ConAu 102*
Fisher, Douglas Mason 1919- *ConAu 89*
Fisher, Edward 1902- *ConAu 1R, IntAu&W 82,
    WrDr 84*
Fisher, Edward A 1920- *ConAmTC*
Fisher, Ernest Arthur 1887- *ConAu 13R*
Fisher, Esther Oshiver 1910- *ConAu 85*
Fisher, Eugene J 1943- *ConAu 105*
Fisher, Franklin M 1934- *ConAu 17R,
    WrDr 84*
Fisher, Fred L 1911- *ConAu 1R, -5NR*
Fisher, Gary 1938- *ConAu 103*
Fisher, Gene Harvey 1922- *ConAu 41R*

Fisher, Gene L 1947- *ConAu 81*
Fisher, George *IntAu&W 82X*
Fisher, George William *DrAP&F 83*
Fisher, Glenn W 1924- *ConAu 53*
Fisher, Graham 1920- *IntAu&W 82*
Fisher, Harold Henry 1890-1975 *ConAu 61*
Fisher, Harrison 1954- *IntWWP 82*
Fisher, Harvey Irvin 1916- *ConAu 69*
Fisher, Helen E 1945- *ConAu 108*
Fisher, Herbert Albert Laurens 1865-1940
  LongCTC, TwCA, TwCA SUP
Fisher, Humphrey J 1933- *ConAu 33R*
Fisher, J R 1943- *ConAu 1NR, –45*
Fisher, J Thomas 1936- *ConAu 33R*
Fisher, James 1912-1970 *ConAu 89*
Fisher, James R, Jr. 1937- *ConAu 81*
Fisher, Joe 1947- *ConAu 103*
Fisher, Johanna 1922- *ConAu 93*
Fisher, John 1909- *ConAu 81, SmATA 15*
Fisher, John C 1927- *ConAu 41R*
Fisher, John H 1919- *ConAu 11NR*
Fisher, John Hurt 1919- *ConAu 21R*
Fisher, Laine *ConAu X*
Fisher, Laura Harrison 1934- *ConAu 13R,*
  SmATA 5
Fisher, Lawrence V 1923- *ConAu 17R,*
  WrDr 84
Fisher, Lee 1908- *ConAu 33R*
Fisher, Leonard Everett 1924- *ConAu 1R, –2NR,*
  IntAu&W 82, SmATA 34[port], –4,
  WrDr 84
Fisher, Lillian Estelle 1891- *ConAu P-1,*
  WrDr 84
Fisher, Lois Jeannette 1909- *ConAu 5R*
Fisher, Louis 1934- *ConAu 37R, IntAu&W 82,*
  WrDr 84
Fisher, M F *DrAP&F 83*
Fisher, M F K 1908- *ConAu 77*
Fisher, Malcolm R 1923- *ConAu 110*
Fisher, Margaret S 1918- *ConAu 17R*
Fisher, Margery 1913- *ConAu 73,*
  IntAu&W 82, SmATA 20
Fisher, Margot *ConAu X*
Fisher, Marvin 1927- *ConAu 21R, WrDr 84*
Fisher, Mary Hannah 1910- *IntWWP 82*
Fisher, Mary L 1928- *ConAu 33R*
Fisher, Michael John 1933- *ConAu 1R, –3NR,*
  IntAu&W 82
Fisher, Miles Mark 1899-1970 *ConAu P-1*
Fisher, Miriam Louise Scharfe 1939- *ConAu 13R*
Fisher, Morris 1922- *ConAu 21R*
Fisher, Neal F 1936- *ConAu 106*
Fisher, Nigel 1913- *ConAu 102, IntAu&W 82,*
  WrDr 84
Fisher, Norman George 1910-1972 *ConAu 107*
Fisher, Peter Jack 1930- *ConAu 69*
Fisher, Philip A 1907- *ConAu 61*
Fisher, Ralph Talcott, Jr. 1920- *ConAu 41R,*
  WrDr 84
Fisher, Rhoda Lee 1924- *ConAu 65*
Fisher, Richard 1936- *ConAu 17R*
Fisher, Richard B 1919- *ConAu 77,*
  IntAu&W 82
Fisher, Robert 1943- *ConAu 109*
Fisher, Robert Charles 1930- *ConAu 53*
Fisher, Robert Emerson 1946- *IntWWP 82*
Fisher, Robert J 1924- *ConAu 61*
Fisher, Robert Percival 1935- *ConAu 93*
Fisher, Roger 1922- *ConAu 37R, WrDr 84*
Fisher, Roy 1930- *ConAu 81, ConLC 25[port],*
  ConP 80, DcLEL 1940, IntAu&W 82,
  IntWWP 82, WrDr 84
Fisher, Rudolph 1897-1934 *ConAu 107,*
  TwCLC 11[port]
Fisher, Seymour 1922- *ConAu 33R*
Fisher, Sterling Wesley 1899?-1978 *ConAu 81,*
  –85
Fisher, Steve 1912- *TwCCr&M 80*
Fisher, Vardis 1895-1968 *ConAmA, ConAu 5R,*
  –25R, ConLC 7, DcLB 9[port], FifWWr,
  LongCTC, ModAL, TwCA, TwCA SUP,
  TwCWW
Fisher, Wade *ConAu X, WrDr 84*
Fisher, Wallace E 1918- *ConAu 10NR, –21R*
Fisher, Walter R 1931- *ConAu 13R*
Fisher, Welthy Honsinger 1879-1980
  ConAu 2NR, –102, IntAu&W 82
Fisher, Welthy Honsinger 1880- *ConAu 1R*
Fisher, Wesley Andrew 1944- *ConAu 104*
Fisher, William Bayne 1916- *ConAu 65,*
  IntAu&W 82, WrDr 84
Fishler, Mary Shiverick 1920- *ConAu 5R*

Fishlock, David Jocelyn 1932- *WrDr 84*
Fishman, Betty G 1918- *ConAu 5R*
Fishman, Burton J 1942- *ConAu 45*
Fishman, Charles *DrAP&F 83*
Fishman, Charles 1942- *ConAu 7NR, –57,*
  IntWWP 82
Fishman, George Samuel 1937- *ConAu 25R*
Fishman, Jack 1920- *ConAu 7NR, –9R*
Fishman, Joshua A 1926- *ConAu 41R*
Fishman, Ken 1950- *ConAu 105*
Fishman, Leo 1914- *ConAu 17R*
Fishman, Lew 1939- *ConAu 11NR, –61*
Fishman, Sterling 1932- *ConAu 45*
Fishman, William Jack 1921- *IntAu&W 82*
Fishta, Gjergj 1871-1940 *ClDMEL 80*
Fishwick, Marshall William 1923- *ConAu 5R,*
  –6NR
Fisk, E K 1917- *ConAu 17R*
Fisk, McKee 1900- *ConAu P-2*
Fisk, Nicholas 1923- *ConAu 11NR, –65,*
  ConSFA, SmATA 25[port], TwCCW 83,
  TwCSFW, WrDr 84
Fisk, Samuel 1907- *ConAu 57*
Fiske, Edward B 1937- *ConAu 85*
Fiske, Marjorie *ConAu 1NR, IntAu&W 82*
Fiske, Roger 1910- *WrDr 84*
Fiske, Roger Elwyn 1910- *ConAu 13R*
Fiske, Sharon *WrDr 84*
Fiske, Tarleton *ConAu X, IntAu&W 82X*
Fiskin, A M I 1916-1975 *ConAu P-2*
Fison, David Charles 1908- *WrDr 84*
Fiss, Owen M 1938- *WrDr 84*
Fiszel, Henryk 1910- *ConAu 29R,*
  IntAu&W 82
Fiszman, Joseph R 1921- *ConAu 41R*
Fitch, Alger Morton, Jr. 1919- *ConAu 53*
Fitch, Clarke *ConAmA, ConAu X, SmATA X*
Fitch, Clyde 1865-1909 *CnMD, ConAu 110,*
  ModAL, ModWD
Fitch, Donald S 1949- *ConAu 106*
Fitch, Edwin M 1902- *ConAu P-2*
Fitch, George Ashmore 1883-1979 *ConAu 85*
Fitch, Geraldine T 1892?-1976 *ConAu 69*
Fitch, James Marston, Jr. 1909- *ConAu 89*
Fitch, John, IV *ConAu X, SmATA X*
Fitch, Kenneth 1929- *ConAu 49*
Fitch, Lyle C 1913- *ConAu 13R*
Fitch, Raymond E 1930- *ConAu 110*
Fitch, Robert Beck 1938- *ConAu 21R*
Fitch, Stanley K 1920- *ConAu 29R*
Fitch, William Clyde 1865-1909 *DcLB 7[port]*
Fitch, Willis Stetson 1896?-1978 *ConAu 81*
Fite, Gilbert C 1918- *ConAu 33R*
Fite, James David 1933- *ConAu 107*
Fite, Mack *ConAu X,*
Fitler, Mary Biddle 1878?-1966 *ConAu 25R*
Fitrat, Abdalrauf 1886-1937 *EncWL 2*
Fitschen, Dale 1937- *ConAu 77, SmATA 20*
Fitt, Mary 1897-1959 *LongCTC, TwCCr&M 80*
Fitter, Richard 1913- *WrDr 84*
Fitter, Richard Sidney Richmond 1913-
  ConAu 11NR, –65, IntAu&W 82
Fitting, Greer A 1943- *ConAu 81*
Fitting, James E 1939- *ConAu 45, MichAu 80*
Fitting, Melvin 1942- *ConAu 11NR, –29R*
Fitton, James 1899-1982 *ConAu 106*
Fitts, Dudley 1903-1968 *ConAu 25R, –93,*
  ModAL, TwCA, TwCA SUP
Fitts, William Howard 1918- *ConAu 21R*
Fitz, Jean DeWitt 1912- *ConAu 29R*
Fitz-Gerald, Carolyn 1932- *ConAu 41R*
Fitz-Randolph, Jane 1915- *ConAu 103*
Fitzalan, Roger *ConAu X, SmATA X,*
  WrDr 84
Fitzbauer, Erich 1927- *IntAu&W 82*
Fitzell, John 1922- *ConAu 13R*
Fitzgeorge-Parker, Tim 1920- *WrDr 84*
Fitzgerald, Arlene J *ConAu 8NR, –21R*
FitzGerald, C P 1902- *ConAu 11NR*
Fitzgerald, C P 1902- *ConAu 17R*
Fitzgerald, Captain Hugh *ConAu X,*
  SmATA X
FitzGerald, Cathleen 1932- *ConAu 33R*
Fitzgerald, Charles Patrick 1902- *WrDr 84*
Fitzgerald, E V K 1947- *ConAu 73*
Fitzgerald, Edward 1898?-1982 *ConAu 108*
Fitzgerald, Edward Earl 1919- *ConAu 73,*
  SmATA 20
Fitzgerald, Ernest Abner 1925- *ConAu 29R,*

WrDr 84
Fitzgerald, F A 1940- *SmATA 15*
Fitzgerald, F Scott 1896-1940 *AuNews 1,*
  CnMD, CnMWL, ConAmA, ConAu 110,
  DcLB DS1[port], –Y81A[port], –4, –9[port],
  EncWL 2[port], LongCTC, ModAL,
  ModAL SUP, TwCA, TwCA SUP,
  TwCLC 1, –6[port], TwCWr, WhoTwCL
FitzGerald, Frances 1940- *ASpks, ConAu 41R*
FitzGerald, Garret 1926- *ConAu 109*
Fitzgerald, Garret 1926- *WrDr 84*
Fitzgerald, George R 1932- *ConAu 97*
Fitzgerald, Gerald 1930- *ConAu 37R*
Fitzgerald, Gerald E 1920- *ConAu 25R*
FitzGerald, Gregory *DrAP&F 83*
FitzGerald, Gregory 1923- *ConAu 1NR, –49*
Fitzgerald, Hal *ConAu X*
Fitzgerald, Hiram E 1940- *ConAu 77*
Fitzgerald, Jack *ConAu X*
Fitzgerald, James A 1892- *ConAu 1R, –1NR*
Fitzgerald, James V 1889?-1976 *ConAu 69*
Fitzgerald, John *ConAu X*
Fitzgerald, John D 1907- *ChlLR 1, ConAu 93,*
  SmATA 20, TwCCW 83
Fitzgerald, John Joseph 1928- *ConAu 37R*
Fitzgerald, Julia *WrDr 84*
Fitzgerald, Julia 1943- *ConAu X,*
  IntAu&W 82X, TwCRGW
FitzGerald, Kathleen Whalen 1938- *ConAu 109*
Fitzgerald, Laurine Elisabeth 1930- *ConAu 37R*
Fitzgerald, Lawrence P 1906-1976 *ConAu 1R,*
  –2NR
Fitzgerald, Lionel LeMoine 1890-1956 *CreCan 1*
Fitzgerald, Michael G 1950- *ConAu 77*
Fitzgerald, Nancy 1951- *ConAu 85*
Fitzgerald, Nigel 1906- *TwCCr&M 80,*
  WrDr 84
Fitzgerald, Patrick 1928- *ConAu 9R*
Fitzgerald, Penelope 1916- *ConAu 85,*
  ConLC 19, ConNov 82, DcLB 14[port],
  WrDr 84
FitzGerald, R D 1902- *ModCmwL*
Fitzgerald, Richard 1938- *ConAu 45*
Fitzgerald, Robert *DrAP&F 83*
Fitzgerald, Robert 1910- *DcLB Y80B[port]*
FitzGerald, Robert D 1902- *WrDr 84*
FitzGerald, Robert David 1902- *ConAu 17R,*
  ConLC 19, ConP 80, IntAu&W 82,
  IntWWP 82, TwCWr, WorAu
Fitzgerald, Robert Stuart 1910- *ConAu 1R,*
  –1NR, ConP 80, IntAu&W 82,
  IntWWP 82, ModAL, TwCA SUP,
  WrDr 84
Fitzgerald, Stephen 1938- *ConAu 97, WrDr 84*
Fitzgerald, Tamsin 1950- *ConAu 77*
Fitzgerald, Valerie *TwCRGW, WrDr 84*
Fitzgerald, Zelda Sayre 1900-1948 *AuNews 1*
Fitzgerald-Bush, Frank *IntWWP 82X*
Fitzgerald-Bush, Frank Shepard 1925-
  IntWWP 82
Fitzgibbon, Constantine 1919- *ConAu 1R, –2NR,*
  IntAu&W 82, TwCSFW, WorAu,
  WrDr 84
FitzGibbon, Constantine 1919-1983 *ConAu 109*
Fitzgibbon, Joanne Eileen Theodora 1916-
  ConAu 5R
Fitzgibbon, Robert Louis Constantine 1919-
  DcLEL 1940
Fitzgibbon, Russell Humke 1902- *ConAu 65*
FitzGibbon, Theodora 1916- *ConAu 3NR,*
  WrDr 84
Fitzgibbons, James P 1912?-1983 *ConAu 110*
Fitzhardinge, Joan Margaret 1912- *ConAu 6NR,*
  –13R, IntAu&W 82, SmATA 2
Fitzhenry, Robert Irvine 1918- *ConAu 110*
Fitzhugh, Jewell Burnice Kirby 1904-
  IntWWP 82
Fitzhugh, Jewell Kirby *IntWWP 82X*
Fitzhugh, Louise 1928-1974 *ChlLR 1,*
  ConAu 53, ConAu P-2, SmATA 1, –24N,
  TwCCW 83
Fitzhugh, Robert Tyson 1906-1981 *ConAu 104*
Fitzlyon, Cecily April Mead 1920- *ConAu 5R,*
  IntAu&W 82
Fitzlyon, Kyril 1910- *ConAu 93*
Fitzmaurice, George 1877-1963 *ConAu 93,*
  ModWD
Fitzmaurice-Kelly, James 1857?-1923 *TwCA,*
  TwCA SUP
Fitzmyer, Joseph A 1920- *ConAu 5NR, –9R*
Fitzomer, Stephen *IntWWP 82X*

Fletcher, Robert Henry 1885?-1972 *ConAu 37R*
Fletcher, Ronald 1921- *ConAu 33R*,
IntAu&W 82, *WrDr 84*
Fletcher, William C 1932- *ConAu 21R*
Fletcher, William Whigham 1918- *ConAu 81*,
WrDr 84
Fletcher-Cooke, John 1911- *ConAu 102*,
IntAu&W 82, *WrDr 84*
Fleur, Anne 1901- *SmATA 31*
Fleur, Paul *ConAu X*
Fleur, William *WrDr 84*
Fleuridas, Ellie Rae *ConAu X*
Fleury, Delphine 1904- *ConAu X*
Flew, Antony 1923- *WrDr 84*
Flew, Antony G N 1923- *ConAu 3NR, –5R*,
IntAu&W 82
Flexner, Abraham 1866-1959 *TwCA*,
TwCA SUP
Flexner, Eleanor 1908- *ConAu 45*
Flexner, James Thomas 1908- *ConAu 1R, –2NR*,
SmATA 9, *WorAu 1970*, *WrDr 84*
Flexner, Stuart B 1928- *WrDr 84*
Flexner, Stuart Berg 1928- *ConAu 11NR, –13R*
Flick, Carlos Thomas 1927- *ConAu 89*
Fliegel, Frederick C 1925- *ConAu 49*
Flieger, Wilhelm 1931- *ConAu 25R*
Flier, Michael Stephen 1941- *ConAu 37R*,
WrDr 84
Fliess, Peter Joachim 1915- *ConAu 21R*,
IntAu&W 82, *WrDr 84*
Flinders, Neil J 1934- *ConAu 21R*, *WrDr 84*
Flink, Salomon J 1906- *ConAu 1R*
Flinn, M W 1917- *ConAu 17R*
Flinn, M W 1917-1983 *ConAu 110*
Flint, Betty Margaret 1920- *ConAu 21R*,
WrDr 84
Flint, Cort Ray 1915- *ConAu 49*, *WrDr 84*
Flint, E DeP *ConAu X*
Flint, Frank Stewart 1885-1960 *LongCTC*,
ModBrL, *TwCA*, *TwCA SUP*
Flint, Homer Eon 1892-1924 *TwCSFW*
Flint, John Edgar 1930- *ConAu 37R*,
IntAu&W 82, *WrDr 84*
Flint, Roland *DrAP&F 83*
Flintoff, Eddie 1933- *IntWWP 82*
Flippo, Chet 1943- *ConAu 89*
Flippo, Edwin B 1925- *ConAu 33R*
Flitner, Andreas 1922- *IntAu&W 82*
Flitner, David P, Jr. 1949- *ConAu 1NR, –45*,
SmATA 7
Floan, Howard R 1918- *ConAu 17R*
Floethe, Louise Lee 1913- *ConAu 1R, –2NR*,
SmATA 4
Floethe, Richard 1901- *ConAu 33R*, *SmATA 4*
Floherty, John Joseph 1882-1964
SmATA 25[port]
Flood, Charles Bracelen 1929- *ConAu 41R*,
WrDr 84
Flood, E Thadeus 1932- *ConAu 49*
Flood, John 1902- *IntWWP 82*
Flood, Kenneth Urban 1925- *ConAu 9R*
Flood, Robert 1935- *ConAu 106*
Flook, Maria 1952- *ConAu 110*
Flora, Fletcher 1914- *ConAu 1R*
Flora, Fletcher 1914-1968 *TwCCr&M 80*
Flora, Fletcher 1914-1969 *ConAu 3NR*
Flora, James 1914- *ConAu 3NR, –5R*,
SmATA 1, –30[port], *TwCCW 83*,
WrDr 84
Flora, Joseph M 1934- *WrDr 84*
Flora, Joseph Martin 1934- *ConAu 5NR, –13R*
Floren, Lee 1910- *ConAu 3NR, –5R*, *WrDr 84*
Florence, Philip Sargant 1890-1982 *ConAu 106*
Florence, Ronald 1942- *ConAu 33R*, *WrDr 84*
Florentin, Eddy 1923- *ConAu 49*
Flores, Angel 1900- *ConAu 103*
Flores, Ivan 1923- *ConAu 7NR, –17R*,
WrDr 84
Flores, Janis 1946- *ConAu 10NR, –65*
Flores, John 1943- *ConAu 77*
Florescu, Radu R 1925- *ConAu 41R*
Florian, Douglas 1950- *SmATA 19*
Florian, Miroslav 1931- *ModSL 2*
Florian, Tibor 1908- *ConAu 73*, *IntAu&W 82*,
IntWWP 82
Florin, Lambert F 1905- *ConAu 7NR, –17R*
Florinsky, Michael T 1894- *WrDr 84*
Florinsky, Michael T 1894-1981 *ConAu 1R, –105*,
IntAu&W 82
Floriot, Rene 1902-1975 *ConAu 61*
Florit, Eugenio 1903- *ConAu 104*
Florman, Samuel C 1925- *ConAu 102*

Florsheim, Stewart *DrAP&F 83*
Florsheim, Stewart 1952- *IntWWP 82*
Flory, Charles D 1902- *ConAu 41R*
Flory, Harry R 1899-1976 *ConAu 69*
Flory, Jane Trescott 1917- *ConAu 3NR, –9R*,
SmATA 22[port]
Flory, Julia McCune 1882-1971 *ConAu 29R*,
ConAu P-2
Flory, Sheldon *DrAP&F 83*
Flott, Phil, Jr. 1944- *IntWWP 82*
Floud, Roderick 1942- *ConAu 1NR, –45*
Flower, Dean S 1938- *ConAu 21R*
Flower, Desmond John Newman 1907-
ConAu 9R, *IntAu&W 82*
Flower, Elizabeth Farquhar 1914- *ConAu 103*
Flower, Harry Alfred 1901- *ConAu P-1*
Flower, Jake *WrDr 84*
Flower, John 1936- *ConAu 37R*
Flower, John Matthew 1929- *WrDr 84*
Flower, Margaret 1907- *ConAu 61*, *WrDr 84*
Flower, Newman 1879-1964 *ConAu 9R*
Flower, Sir Newman 1879-1964 *LongCTC*
Flower, Pat 1914-1978 *TwCCr&M 80*
Flower, Raymond 1921- *ConAu 108*
Flower, Robin Ernest William 1881-1946
LongCTC
Flowerdew, Phyllis *ConAu 103*, *SmATA 33*,
WrDr 84
Flowers, Ann Moore 1923- *ConAu 9R*
Flowers, Betty S 1947- *ConAu 65*
Flowers, Charles 1942- *ConAu 29R*
Flowers, Charles E 1920- *ConAu 93*
Flowers, John V 1938- *ConAu 106*
Floyd, Barry Neil 1925- *ConAu 33R*
Floyd, Gareth 1940- *SmATA 31*
Floyd, Harriet 1925- *ConAu 69*
Floyd, Lois Gray 1910?-1978 *ConAu 81, –85*
Floyd, Troy S 1920- *ConAu 37R*
Floyd, W E G 1939- *ConAu 33R*
Floyd, William Anderson 1928- *ConAu 29R*
Fluchere, Henri 1914- *ConAu 77*
Fluck, Reginald Alan Paul 1928- *ConAu 9R*
Flugel, Heinz 1907- *IntAu&W 82*
Flumiani, Carlo M 1911- *ConAu 9NR, –13R*
Fluno, Robert Y 1916- *ConAu 33R*
Flusser, Martin 1947- *ConAu 73*
Fly, Claude L 1905- *ConAu 97*
Flygt, Sten G 1911- *ConAu 9R*
Flying Officer X *ConAu X*
Flynn, Barbara 1928- *SmATA 9*
Flynn, Charles F 1949- *ConAu 57*
Flynn, Don 1928- *NatPD 81[port]*
Flynn, Donald R 1928- *ConAu 29R*
Flynn, Fahey 1916-1983 *ConAu 110*
Flynn, Frank 1906- *IntAu&W 82*, *WrDr 84*
Flynn, George *DrAP&F 83*
Flynn, George L 1931- *ConAu 9NR, –65*
Flynn, George Q 1937- *ConAu 25R*
Flynn, Gerard 1924- *ConAu 41R*
Flynn, Jackson *ConAu X*, *SmATA X*,
WrDr 84
Flynn, James Joseph 1911- *ConAu 21R*
Flynn, James Robert 1934- *ConAu 21R*,
IntAu&W 82, *WrDr 84*
Flynn, John *IntWWP 82X*
Flynn, John Joseph 1936- *ConAu 17R*
Flynn, John Joseph 1947- *IntWWP 82*
Flynn, John Thomas 1882-1964 *ConAu 89*,
TwCA, *TwCA SUP*
Flynn, Leslie Bruce 1918- *ConAu 1R, –2NR*,
WrDr 84
Flynn, Paul P 1942- *ConAu 37R*
Flynn, Robert *DrAP&F 83*
Flynn, Robert 1932- *ConAu 29R*, *TwCWW*,
WrDr 84
Flynn, T T 1902- *TwCWW*
Flynn, Tony 1951- *IntWWP 82*
Flynt, Candace *DrAP&F 83*
Flynt, Candace 1947- *ConAu 102*
Flynt, J Wayne 1940- *IntAu&W 82*
Flynt, Josiah 1869-1907 *TwCA*, *TwCA SUP*
Flynt, Larry *AuNews 2*
Flynt, Wayne 1940- *ConAu 37R*
Flythe, Starkey S, Jr. 1935- *ConAu 69*
Fo, Dario 1926- *CroCD*, *EncWL 2*
Foat Tugay, Emine 1897- *ConAu P-1*
Focillon, Henri 1881-1943 *CIDMEL 80*
Foda, Aun *ConAu X, –X*
Fodaski-Black, Martha 1929- *ConAu 73*
Fodor, Andras 1929- *IntWWP 82*
Fodor, Eugene 1905- *ConAu 21R*
Fodor, Ladislaus 1898- *CnMD*

Fodor, M W 1890?-1977 *ConAu 69*
Fodor, Ronald V 1944- *ConAu 65*,
SmATA 25[port]
Foell, Earl W 1929- *ConAu 69*
Foelsch, Rolli V T 1944- *IntAu&W 82*
Foerster, Leona M 1930- *ConAu 89*
Foerster, Lotte B 1910- *ConAu 77*
Foerster, Norman 1887- *ConAmA*, *ConAu 5R*,
TwCA, *TwCA SUP*
Foerster, Richard *DrAP&F 83*
Foerster, Rolf Hellmut 1927- *IntAu&W 82*
Foff, Arthur R 1925-1973 *ConAu P-2*
Fogarty, Jonathan Titulescu, Esq. *ConAu X*
Fogarty, Michael P 1916- *ConAu 9NR*
Fogarty, Michael Patrick 1916- *ConAu 21R*,
IntAu&W 82, *WrDr 84*
Fogarty, Robert S 1938- *ConAu 9NR, –65*
Fogazzaro, Antonio 1842-1911 *CIDMEL 80*,
LongCTC, *ModRL*, *TwCA*, *TwCA SUP*
Fogdall, Alberta Brooks 1912- *IntAu&W 82*
Fogel, Aaron *DrAP&F 83*
Fogel, Daniel *ConAu X*
Fogel, Daniel Khan *ConAu X*
Fogel, Daniel Mark *DrAP&F 83*
Fogel, Robert W 1926- *ConAu 77*
Fogel, Ruby *ConAu 17R*
Fogelquist, Donald Frederick 1906- *ConAu 69*
Fogels, Ingrida 1920- *IntWWP 82*
Fogelson, Robert M 1937- *ConAu 81*
Fogerty, Elsie 1865-1945 *LongCTC*
Fogg, Gordon Elliott 1919- *IntAu&W 82*,
WrDr 84
Foghammar, Stig Sverker *IntAu&W 82*
Fogle, Bruce 1944- *ConAu 106*
Fogle, French R 1912- *ConAu 37R*
Fogle, Richard Harter 1911- *ConAu 5R, –5NR*
Foglio, Frank 1921- *ConAu 57*
Foiles, Keith Andrew 1926-1983 *ConAu 109*
Foin, Theodore C 1940- *ConAu 93*
Foisie, Jack 1919- *ConAu 104*
Foix, J V 1893- *EncWL 2*
Foix, Josep Vicenc 1894- *CIDMEL 80*
Fokkema, D W 1931- *ConAu 7NR, –17R*
Foladare, Joseph 1909- *ConAu 102*
Folb, Edith A 1938- *ConAu 102*
Folch-Ribas, Jacques 1928- *ConAu 69*
Foldes, Jolan 1903- *TwCA*, *TwCA SUP*
Foldes, Peter 1916- *IntAu&W 82*
Folds, Thomas M *ConAu 93*
Folejewski, Zbigniew 1910- *ConAu 7NR, –17R*
Foley, Allen Richard 1898-1978 *ConAu 45, –77*
Foley, Bernice Williams 1902- *ConAu 29R*,
SmATA 28[port]
Foley, Charles 1908- *ConAu P-1*
Foley, Daniel Joseph 1913- *ConAu 5R, –5NR*
Foley, Doug 1942- *ConAu 57*
Foley, Duncan K 1942- *ConAu 93*
Foley, Gerald 1936- *ConAu 11NR, –69*
Foley, Helen *ConAu X*
Foley, John 1917-1974 *ConAu 4NR, –9R, –53*
Foley, June 1944- *ConAu 109*
Foley, Leonard 1913- *ConAu 89*
Foley, Louise Munro 1933- *ConAu 37R*,
WrDr 84
Foley, Martha 1897?-1977 *ConAu 73*
Foley, Mary Mix 1918- *ConAu 102*
Foley, Rae 1900-1978 *ConAu X*, *SmATA X*,
TwCCr&M 80
Foley, Richard N 1910?-1980 *ConAu 102*
Foley, Scott *ConAu X*
Foley, Vincent D 1919- *ConAu 57*
Foley, William E 1938- *ConAu 33R*
Foley, Winifred 1914- *ConAu 102*
Folkard, Charles James 1878-1963 *ConAu 109*,
SmATA 28
Folke, Will *ConAu X*
Folkers, George Fulton 1929- *ConAu 49*
Folkerts, George W 1938- *ConAu 53*
Folkman, Jerome Daniel 1907- *ConAu P-2*,
WrDr 84
Follain, Jean 1903-1971 *CIDMEL 80*,
WorAu 1970
Folland, H F 1906- *ConAu 49*
Follett, Helen 1884?-1970 *ConAu 107*,
SmATA 27N
Follett, Ken 1949- *ConAu 81*, *ConLC 18*,
DcLB Y81B[port]
Follett, Robert J R 1928- *ConAu 8NR, –21R*
Folley, Terence T 1931- *ConAu 21R*
Folley, Vern L 1936- *ConAu 69*
Folliard, Edward T 1899-1976 *ConAu 69*
Follis, Anne Bowen 1947- *ConAu 106*

Follmann, J F, Jr. 1908- *ConAu 7NR, −17R*
Folmsbee, Stanley J 1899-1974 *ConAu P-2*
Folsom, Alan Lynn 1942- *IntAu&W 82*
Folsom, Franklin 1907- *ConAu 1R, −2NR, IntAu&W 82, SmATA 5*
Folsom, Franklin Brewster 1907- *WrDr 84*
Folsom, Jack *ConAu X*
Folsom, John B 1931- *ConAu 45*
Folsom, Kenneth E 1921- *ConAu 21R*
Folsom, Marion Bayard 1893- *ConAu P-2*
Folsom, Marvin Hugh 1929- *ConAu 57*
Folsom, Robert S 1915- *ConAu 77*
Folta, Jeannette R 1934- *ConAu 25R*
Foltin, Lore Barbara 1913- *ConAu P-2*
Foltz, William J 1936- *ConAu 9R*
Foltz-Gray, Dorothy *DrAP&F 83*
Foltz-Gray, Dorothy J 1949- *IntWWP 82*
Fomon, Samuel J 1923- *ConAu 53*
Fon Eisen, Anthony T 1917- *ConAu 13R*
Fonarow, Jerry 1935- *ConAu 4NR, −53*
Fonda, Henry 1905-1982 *ConAu 107*
Foner, Eric 1943- *ConAu 29R, WrDr 84*
Foner, Jack D 1910- *ConAu 77*
Foner, Nancy 1945- *ConAu 53*
Foner, Philip S 1910- *WrDr 84*
Foner, Philip Sheldon 1910- *ConAu 3NR, −9R*
Fonfrias, Ernesto Juan 1909- *IntAu&W 82*
Fong, Wen Chih 1930- *ConAu 103*
Fong-Torres, Ben 1945- *ConAu 93*
Fonseca, Aloysius 1915- *WrDr 84*
Fonseca, Aloysius Joseph 1915- *ConAu 9NR, −13R*
Fonseca, Antonio Jose Branquinho Da 1905- *CIDMEL 80*
Fonseca, John DosReis 1925- *ConAu 17R, WrDr 84*
Fonseca, John R 1925- *ConAu 8NR*
Fonseca, Manuel Da 1911- *CIDMEL 80*
Fonstad, Karen Wynn 1945- *ConAu 104*
Fontain, Gregory *IntWWP 82*
Fontaine, Andre 1910- *ConAu 65*
Fontaine, Andre Lucien Georges 1921- *ConAu 25R, IntAu&W 82*
Fontaine, Joan 1917- *ConAu 81*
Fontaine, Teri *DrAP&F 83*
Fontana, Bernard L 1931- *ConAu 7NR, −17R*
Fontana, Thomas M 1951- *NatPD 81[port]*
Fontana, Vincent James 1923- *ConAu 13R*
Fontane, Theodor 1819-1898 *CIDMEL 80*
Fontanet, Jean-Claude 1925- *IntAu&W 82*
Fontanet, Joseph 1921-1980 *ConAu 105*
Fontenay, Charles L 1917- *ConAu 25R, ConSFA, TwCSFW*
Fontenay, Charles Louis 1917- *WrDr 84*
Fontenelle, Don H 1946- *ConAu 106*
Fontenot, Ken *DrAP&F 83, IntWWP 82X*
Fontenot, Kenneth Michael 1948- *IntWWP 82*
Fontenot, Mary Alice 1910- *ConAu 37R, SmATA 34[port], WrDr 84*
Fontenrose, Joseph 1903- *ConAu 5R, WrDr 84*
Fonteyn, Margot *ConAu X*
Fonteyn DeArias, Margot 1919- *ConAu 110*
Fonzi, Bruno 1913?-1976 *ConAu 65*
Foo-Canto, Lourdes-Lai 1922- *IntAu&W 82*
Fooks, Ernest Leslie 1906- *IntAu&W 82*
Fooner, Michael *ConAu 81, SmATA 22[port]*
Foord, Archibald Smith 1914-1969 *ConAu P-1*
Foot, Hugh Mackintosh 1907- *ConAu 9R*
Foot, M R D 1919- *ConAu 3NR*
Foot, Michael 1913- *ConAu 108, WrDr 84*
Foot, Michael Mackintosh 1913- *DcLEL 1940*
Foot, Michael Richard Daniell 1919- *ConAu 5R, WrDr 84*
Foot, Paul Mackintosh 1937- *ConAu 17R*
Foot, Philippa Ruth 1920- *ConAu 101*
Foote, A Edward 1937- *ConAu 73*
Foote, Darby Mozelle 1942- *ConAu 61*
Foote, Dorothy Norris 1908- *ConAu P-2*
Foote, Horton 1916- *ConAu 73, ConDr 82C, DcLB 26, WorAu*
Foote, Mary Hallock 1847-1938 *FifWWr*
Foote, Shelby *DrAP&F 83*
Foote, Shelby 1916- *ConAu 3NR, −5R, ConNov 82, DcLB 2, −17[port], DcLEL 1940, IntAu&W 82, TwCA SUP, WrDr 84*
Foote, Timothy 1926- *ConAu 93*
Foote, Wilder 1905-1975 *ConAu 57*
Foote-Smith, Elizabeth *DrAP&F 83*
Foote-Smith, Elizabeth 1913- *ConAu 69*
Footman, David John 1895- *ConAu 97, IntAu&W 82*

Footner, Hulbert 1879-1944 *TwCCr&M 80*
Foran, Donald J 1943- *ConAu 33R*
Forberg, Ati 1925- *ConAu X, SmATA 22[port]*
Forberg, Beate Gropius 1925- *ConAu 105*
Forbes, Bryan 1926- *ConAu 69, ConDr 82A, IntAu&W 82, WrDr 84*
Forbes, Cabot L *ConAu X, SmATA X*
Forbes, Calvin *DrAP&F 83*
Forbes, Calvin 1945- *ConAu 49*
Forbes, Clarence A 1901- *ConAu 77*
Forbes, Colin *WrDr 84*
Forbes, Colin 1923- *ConAu X*
Forbes, Daniel *WrDr 84*
Forbes, DeLoris Stanton 1923- *ConAu 5NR, −9R*
Forbes, Elliot 1917- *ConAu 9R*
Forbes, Eric Gray 1933- *ConAu 10NR, −65*
Forbes, Esther 1891-1967 *ConAu 25R, ConAu P-1, ConLC 12, DcLB 22[port], SmATA 2, TwCCW 83*
Forbes, Esther 1894?-1967 *TwCA, TwCA SUP*
Forbes, Graham B *ConAu P-2, SmATA 1*
Forbes, Henry W 1918- *ConAu 1R*
Forbes, J V G 1916- *ConAu 9R*
Forbes, Jack D 1934- *ConAu 1R, −4NR*
Forbes, James 1871-1938 *ModWD*
Forbes, Joanne R 1930- *ConAu 37R*
Forbes, John Douglas 1910- *ConAu 53*
Forbes, Kathryn 1909-1966 *ConAu X, SmATA X*
Forbes, Kenneth Keith 1892- *CreCan 2*
Forbes, Malcolm S 1919- *ConAu 69*
Forbes, Patrick 1925- *ConAu 25R*
Forbes, Rosita 1893-1967 *LongCTC, TwCA, TwCA SUP*
Forbes, Stanton 1923- *ConAu X, TwCCr&M 80, WrDr 84*
Forbes, Thomas Rogers 1911- *ConAu 41R, IntAu&W 82*
Forbes-Boyd, Eric 1897- *ConAu 13R, IntAu&W 82*
Forbes-Dennis, Phyllis 1884-1963 *ConAu 93*
Forbes-Robertson, Sir Johnston 1853-1937 *LongCTC*
Forbis, Judith 1934- *ConAu 101*
Forbis, William H 1918- *ConAu 37R*
Forbus, Ina B *ConAu 1R, WrDr 84*
Force, Roland W 1924- *ConAu 41R*
Force, William M 1916- *ConAu 21R*
Forcey, Charles B 1925- *ConAu 1R, −1NR*
Forche, Carolyn *DrAP&F 83*
Forche, Carolyn 1950- *ConAu 109, ConLC 25[port], DcLB 5[port]*
Forchheimer, Paul 1913- *ConAu 53*
Forcione, Alban Keith 1938- *ConAu 33R, WrDr 84*
Ford, Agnes Gibbs 1902- *ConAu P-2*
Ford, Albert Lee *ConAu X*
Ford, Alec George 1926- *ConAu 5R, WrDr 84*
Ford, Alice 1906- *ConAu P-1*
Ford, Amasa B 1922- *ConAu 21R*
Ford, Arthur L 1937- *ConAu 57*
Ford, Barbara *SmATA 34*
Ford, Betty *ConAu X*
Ford, Boris 1917- *IntAu&W 82, WrDr 84*
Ford, Brian J 1939- *ConAu 41R, IntAu&W 82*
Ford, Brian John 1939- *WrDr 84*
Ford, Cathy Diane 1952- *ConAu 105*
Ford, Charles Henri *DrAP&F 83*
Ford, Charles Henri 1913- *ConAu 25R, ConP 80, DcLB 4, IntAu&W 82, IntWWP 82, WrDr 84*
Ford, Colin John 1934- *ConAu 85, IntAu&W 82*
Ford, Collier *ConAu X*
Ford, Connie May 1912- *IntWWP 82*
Ford, Corey 1902-1969 *ConAu 25R*
Ford, D W Cleverley 1914- *ConAu 9NR*
Ford, Daniel 1931- *ConAu 11NR, −17R, IntAu&W 82, WrDr 84*
Ford, David *ConAu X, WrDr 84*
Ford, Donald Frank Williams 1924- *ConAu 5R*
Ford, Donald H 1926- *ConAu 41R*
Ford, Douglas 1914- *WrDr 84*
Ford, Douglas William Cleverley 1914- *ConAu 61*
Ford, Edmund Brisco 1901- *ConAu 85*
Ford, Edsel 1928-1970 *ConAu 29R, ConAu P-1*
Ford, Edward 1928- *ConAu 102*
Ford, Elaine 1938- *ConAu 102*
Ford, Elbur *ConAu X, SmATA 2, TwCRGW, WrDr 84*

Ford, Elizabeth *ConAu X, TwCRGW, WrDr 84*
Ford, Elizabeth Bloomer 1918- *ConAu 105*
Ford, Ford Madox 1873-1939 *CnMWL, ConAu 104, EncWL 2[port], LongCTC, ModBrL, ModBrL SUP, TwCA, TwCA SUP, TwCLC 1, TwCWr, WhoTwCL*
Ford, Frank B 1932- *ConAu 85, NatPD 81[port]*
Ford, Franklin L 1920- *ConAu 17R*
Ford, Fred *ConAu X*
Ford, George *ConAu 107, SmATA 31[port]*
Ford, George Barry 1885-1978 *ConAu 81*
Ford, George D 1880?-1974 *ConAu 53*
Ford, George H 1914- *ConAu 1R, −2NR, IntAu&W 82, WrDr 84*
Ford, George L 1914- *ConAu 5R*
Ford, Gerald R 1913- *ConAu 110*
Ford, Gertrude *DrAP&F 83*
Ford, Gordon Buell, Jr. 1937- *ConAu 21R, IntAu&W 82, WrDr 84*
Ford, Guy B 1922- *ConAu 5R*
Ford, Harvey Seabury 1905?-1978 *ConAu 73*
Ford, Herbert 1927- *WrDr 84*
Ford, Herbert Paul 1927- *ConAu 17R, IntAu&W 82*
Ford, Hilary *ConAu X, SmATA X, WorAu, WrDr 84*
Ford, Hildegarde *ConAu X, SmATA X*
Ford, J Massingberd *ConAu X*
Ford, James Allan 1920- *ConAu P-1, IntAu&W 82, WrDr 84*
Ford, James L C 1907- *ConAu 29R*
Ford, Jesse Hill 1928- *ConAu 1R, −1NR, ConNov 82, DcLB 6[port], DcLEL 1940, WrDr 84*
Ford, Joan Elizabeth *DrAP&F 83*
Ford, Joe Taylor 1940- *NatPD 81*
Ford, John 1895-1973 *ConAu 45, ConLC 16*
Ford, Josephine Massyngbaerde *ConAu 41R*
Ford, Kathleen 1932- *ConAu 25R*
Ford, Kirk *ConAu X, WrDr 84*
Ford, Lee 1936- *ConAu 25R*
Ford, Lee Ellen 1917- *WrDr 84*
Ford, Leighton F S 1931- *ConAu 17R*
Ford, LeRoy 1922- *ConAu 9R*
Ford, Leslie *ConAu X*
Ford, Leslie 1898- *ConAu X, TwCA, TwCA SUP, TwCCr&M 80*
Ford, Lewis *ConAu X, TwCWW*
Ford, Marcia *ConAu X, SmATA 6*
Ford, Marcus Peter 1950- *ConAu 108*
Ford, Margaret Patricia 1925- *ConAu 9R*
Ford, Mary Forker 1905- *ConAu 9R*
Ford, Michael C *DrAP&F 83*
Ford, Murray J S 1923- *ConAu 93*
Ford, Nancy K 1906-1961 *ConAu 109, SmATA 29N*
Ford, Nick Aaron 1904- *ConAu 25R*
Ford, Nick Aaron 1904-1982 *ConAu 11NR*
Ford, Norman D 1921- *ConAu 10NR*
Ford, Norman Dennis 1921- *ConAu 21R*
Ford, Norrey *ConAu X, IntAu&W 82X, WrDr 84*
Ford, Patrick 1914- *ConAu 21R*
Ford, Paul F 1947- *ConAu 105*
Ford, Percy 1894- *IntAu&W 82, WrDr 84*
Ford, Percy 1894-1983 *ConAu 110*
Ford, Phyllis M 1928- *ConAu 33R*
Ford, R A D 1915- *ConAu 97, ConP 80*
Ford, Richard *DrAP&F 83*
Ford, Richard 1944- *ConAu 11NR, −69, WrDr 84*
Ford, Richard Brice 1935- *ConAu 37R*
Ford, Richard Clyde 1870-1951 *MichAu 80*
Ford, Robert A D 1915- *DcLEL 1940, IntWWP 82, WrDr 84*
Ford, Robert E 1913-1975 *ConAu P-2*
Ford, Robert N 1909- *ConAu 33R, WrDr 84*
Ford, Stephen 1949- *ConAu 77*
Ford, Thomas R 1923- *ConAu 49*
Ford, Thomas W 1924- *ConAu 21R*
Ford, W Clay 1946- *ConAu 93*
Ford, W Herschel 1900- *ConAu 5NR, −9R*
Ford, Webster *ConAu AmA, ConAu X*
Ford, Whitey *ConAu X*
Ford, William *DrAP&F 83*
Ford, Worthington Chauncey 1858-1941 *TwCA, TwCA SUP*
Forde, Gerhard O 1927- *ConAu 89*
Forde, Nicholas *IntAu&W 82X*

Forde-Johnston, James 1927- *ConAu 3NR, -9R,*
  IntAu&W 82, WrDr 84
Forder, Anthony 1925- *WrDr 84*
Forder, Charles Robert 1907- *WrDr 84*
Fordham, Peta *WrDr 84*
Fordham, Peta 1905- *ConAu 106, IntAu&W 82*
Fordin, Hugh 1935- *ConAu 57, WrDr 84*
Fore, William Frank 1928- *ConAu 5R*
Forell, George W 1919- *ConAu 1R, -1NR*
Foreman, Carl 1914- *ConAu 41R, ConDr 82A,*
  DcLB 26[port], IntAu&W 82, WrDr 84
Foreman, Clark H 1902-1977 *ConAu 69*
Foreman, Gene 1934- *ConAu 77*
Foreman, Harry 1915- *ConAu 33R*
Foreman, Kenneth Joseph 1891- *ConAu P-2*
Foreman, L L 1901- *ConAu 5R, -5NR,*
  TwCWW
Foreman, Lawton Durant 1913- *ConAu 9R*
Foreman, Michael 1938- *ConAu 10NR, -21R,*
  SmATA 2, TwCCW 83, WrDr 84
Foreman, Paul *DrAP&F 83*
Foreman, Richard 1937- *ConAu 65, ConDr 82,*
  NatPD 81[port], WrDr 84
Foreman, Russell Ralph 1921- *ConAu 77*
Foreman, Thomas Elton 1918- *ConAmTC*
Forer, Lois G 1914- *ConAu 29R*
Forer, Lucille K *ConAu 37R*
Forer, Mort 1922- *ConAu 97*
Fores, John 1914- *ConAu 25R*
Forest, Antonia *TwCCW 83, WrDr 84*
Forest, Antonia 1915?- *ConAu 103,*
  SmATA 29[port]
Forest, Felix C *ConAu X*
Forest, Ilse 1896- *ConAu P-2*
Forest, Lee *ConAu X*
Forester, Bruce Michael 1939- *ConAu 107*
Forester, C S 1899-1966 *ConAu 25R, -73,*
  SmATA 13
Forester, Cecil Scott 1899-1966 *LongCTC,*
  ModBrL, TwCA, TwCA SUP, TwCWr
Forez *ConAu X*
Forfang, Asmund 1952- *IntAu&W 82*
Forget, Florent 1918- *CreCan 1*
Forgie, George B 1941- *ConAu 89*
Forgus, Ronald 1928- *ConAu 41R*
Forio, Robert *ConAu X*
Forisha, Barbara L *ConAu X*
Forisha-Kovach, Barbara L 1941- *ConAu 107*
Forkosch, Morris D 1908- *ConAu 41R*
Form, William H 1917- *ConAu 65*
Forma, Warren 1923- *ConAu 45*
Forman, Brenda 1936- *ConAu 6NR, -9R,*
  SmATA 4
Forman, Celia Adler 1890?-1979 *ConAu 85*
Forman, Charles William 1916- *ConAu 13R,*
  WrDr 84
Forman, Harrison 1904-1978 *ConAu 5R, -77*
Forman, Harry Buxton 1842-1917 *LongCTC*
Forman, Henry James 1879-1966 *ConAu 5R*
Forman, James Douglas 1932- *ConAu 4NR, -9R,*
  ConLC 21[port], IntAu&W 82, SmATA 8
Forman, Joan *ConAu 102, IntAu&W 82,*
  WrDr 84
Forman, Jonathan 1887-1974 *ConAu P-2*
Forman, Leona S 1940- *ConAu 25R*
Forman, Marc A 1935- *ConAu 57*
Forman, Milos 1932- *ConAu 109*
Forman, Robert Edgar 1924- *ConAu 9R*
Forman, Sholto 1915- *ConAu 25R*
Formby, William A 1943- *ConAu 109*
Formhals, Robert W Y S 1919- *ConAu 53*
Formica, Mercedes 1918- *IntAu&W 82*
Fornari, Franco 1921- *ConAu 29R*
Fornari, Harry D 1919- *ConAu 69*
Fornell, Earl Wesley 1915-1969 *ConAu 1R, -103*
Fornes, Maria Irene 1930- *ConAu 25R,*
  ConDr 82, DcLB 7, IntWWP 82,
  NatPD 81, WrDr 84
Forno, Lawrence J 1943- *ConAu 37R*
Forrest, Alfred Clinton 1916-1978 *ConAu 103,*
  -49
Forrest, Allen *TwCWW*
Forrest, Caleb *ConAu X*
Forrest, David *ConAu X, IntAu&W 82X,*
  WrDr 84
Forrest, Derek W 1926- *ConAu 77, WrDr 84*
Forrest, Earle Robert 1883-1969 *ConAu 1R, -103*
Forrest, Felix C 1913- *ConAu X*
Forrest, George 1915- *IntAu&W 82X*
Forrest, John Galbraith 1898-1982 *ConAu 107*
Forrest, Julian *ConAu X*
Forrest, Leon 1937- *ConAu 89, ConLC 4*

Forrest, Norman *WrDr 84*
Forrest, Norman 1905- *ConAu X*
Forrest, Richard S 1932- *ConAu 9NR, -57*
Forrest, Sybil *ConAu X, SmATA X*
Forrest, W G 1925- *ConAu 25R*
Forrest, Wilbur S 1887-1977 *ConAu 69*
Forrest, William George Grieve 1925-
  IntAu&W 82, WrDr 84
Forrest-Webb, Robert 1929- *ConAu 4NR, -49,*
  IntAu&W 82
Forrestal, Dan J, Jr. 1912- *ConAu 77*
Forrestal, Parker *IntWWP 82X*
Forrestall, Thomas DeVany 1936- *CreCan 1*
Forrester, Helen *ConAu X, IntAu&W 82X,*
  WrDr 84
Forrester, Jay Wright 1918- *ConAu 1NR, -45,*
  IntAu&W 82
Forrester, Larry 1924- *ConAu 25R*
Forrester, Leland S 1905?-1978 *ConAu 81*
Forrester, Marian *ConAu X*
Forrester, Mary 1905- *ConAu X, WrDr 84*
Forrester, Maureen 1931- *CreCan 2*
Forrester, Ray 1911- *ConAu 21R*
Forrester, Rex 1928- *WrDr 84*
Forrester, Rex Desmond 1928- *ConAu 103*
Forrester, Victoria 1940- *ConAu 108*
Forrester, William Ray 1911- *WrDr 84*
Forsberg, Gerald 1912- *ConAu 102,*
  IntAu&W 82, WrDr 84
Forsberg, Helen *ConAmTC*
Forsberg, Malcolm I 1908- *ConAu 21R*
Forsberg, Roberta J 1914- *WrDr 84*
Forsberg, Roberta Jean 1914- *ConAu 105*
Forsee, Aylesa *ConAu 1R, -1NR,*
  IntAu&W 82, SmATA 1, WrDr 84
Forsh, Olga Dmitriyevna 1873-1961 *CIDMEL 80*
Forssell, Lars 1928- *CIDMEL 80, CnMD,*
  CroCD, EncWL 2, WorAu 1970
Forster, Arnold 1912- *ConAu 13R*
Forster, E M 1879-1970 *CnMWL, ConAu 25R,*
  ConAu P-1, ConLC 1, -2, -3, -4, -9, -10, -13,
  -15, -22[port], ConLCrt 82, EncWL 2[port],
  LongCTC, ModBrL, ModBrL SUP, TwCA,
  TwCA SUP, TwCSFW, TwCWr,
  WhoTwCL
Forster, Francis Michael 1907- *CreCan 2*
Forster, Friedrich 1895-1958 *CnMD*
Forster, John Wycliffe Lowes 1850-1938
  CreCan 1
Forster, Kent 1916- *ConAu 21R, WrDr 84*
Forster, Leonard Wilson 1913- *IntAu&W 82*
Forster, Margaret 1938- *WrDr 84*
Forster, Merlin H 1928- *ConAu 41R*
Forster, Michael *CreCan 2, IntAu&W 82X*
Forster, Peter 1926?-1982 *ConAu 107*
Forster, Robert 1926- *ConAu 41R,*
  IntAu&W 82
Forstman, H Jackson 1929- *ConAu 13R*
Forsyth, Anne 1933- *ConAu 29R*
Forsyth, David J C 1940- *ConAu 41R*
Forsyth, David P 1930- *ConAu 9R*
Forsyth, Frederick 1938- *ConAu 85, ConLC 2,*
  -5, ConNov 82, TwCCr&M 80, WrDr 84
Forsyth, George H, Jr. 1901- *ConAu 37R*
Forsyth, Ilene 1928- *ConAu 37R*
Forsyth, James 1913- *CnMD, ConAu 73,*
  ConDr 82, DcLEL 1940, ModWD,
  WrDr 84
Forsyth, Shelia Constance 1938- *IntWWP 82*
Forsythe, Elizabeth 1927- *ConAu 93*
Forsythe, Irene *ConAu 49*
Forsythe, Robert 1896-1960 *ConAu X, TwCA,*
  TwCA SUP
Forsythe, Sidney A 1920- *ConAu 41R*
Fort, Charles 1874-1932 *TwCA*
Fort, John 1942- *ConAu 77*
Fort, Paul 1872-1960 *CIDMEL 80, WorAu*
Fort, Williams Edwards, Jr. 1905- *ConAu 37R*
Fortas, Abe 1910-1982 *ConAu 106*
Forte, Allen 1926- *ConAu 41R*
Forte, Dan 1935- *ConAu 65*
Forte, David F 1941- *ConAu 53*
Fortebraccia, Donato *ConAu X*
Fortes, Meyer 1906-1983 *ConAu 109*
Fortin, Marc-Aurele 1888-1970 *CreCan 2*
Fortini, Franco 1917- *CIDMEL 80*
Fortman, Edmund J 1901- *ConAu 11NR, -21R*
Fortner, Ethel N *DrAP&F 83*
Fortner, Ethel Nestell 1907- *IntWWP 82*
Fortnum, Peggy 1919- *ConAu X,*
  SmATA 26[port]
Fortunato, Peter *DrAP&F 83*

Forty, George 1927- *ConAu 89*
Forward, Luke *ConAu X*
Forward, Robert L 1932- *ConAu 103*
Forzano, Giovacchino 1884-1970 *CIDMEL 80,*
  CnMD, ConAu 104, ModWD
Fosburgh, Hugh 1916-1976 *ConAu 69*
Fosburgh, Lacey 1942- *ConAu 85*
Fosburgh, Pieter Whitney 1914?-1978 *ConAu 77*
Foscue, Edwin Jay 1899-1972 *ConAu 1R, -103*
Fosdick, Harry Emerson 1878-1969 *ConAu 25R,*
  TwCA SUP
Fosdick, Raymond Blaine 1883-1972 *ConAu 37R*
Foshee, John 1931- *ConAu 69*
Foskett, D J 1918- *ConAu 5NR*
Foskett, Daphne 1911- *ConAu 102, WrDr 84*
Foskett, Douglas John 1918- *ConAu 1R,*
  IntAu&W 82, WrDr 84
Foskett, Reginald 1909-1973 *ConAu P-2*
Foss, Christopher F 1946- *ConAu 93*
Foss, Dennis C 1947- *ConAu 104*
Foss, Phillip Oliver *ConAu 13R*
Foss, William Otto 1918- *ConAu 17R*
Fosse, Alfred *ConAu X, WrDr 84*
Fosse, Bob *ConAu X*
Fosse, Bob 1925- *ConDr 82D, ConLC 20*
Fosse, Robert Louis 1927- *ConAu 110*
Fossum, Robert H 1923- *ConAu 25R,*
  IntAu&W 82, WrDr 84
Foster, Alan Dean 1946- *ConAu 5NR, -53,*
  IntAu&W 82, TwCSFW, WrDr 84
Foster, Brad W 1955- *SmATA 34*
Foster, Carno A 1916- *ConAu 41R*
Foster, Catharine Osgood 1907- *ConAu 65*
Foster, Cedric 1900-1975 *ConAu 89*
Foster, Charles Howell 1913- *ConAu 17R*
Foster, Charles Irving 1898- *ConAu 1R*
Foster, Charles R 1927- *ConAu 110*
Foster, Charles William 1939- *ConAu 57*
Foster, Craig Curtis 1947- *LivgBAA*
Foster, Daniel W 1930- *ConAu 108*
Foster, David 1908- *ConAu 97*
Foster, David Manning 1944- *ConAu 97,*
  ConNov 82, WrDr 84
Foster, David William 1940- *ConAu 8NR, -21R,*
  WrDr 84
Foster, Don 1948- *ConAu 33R, IntWWP 82,*
  WrDr 84
Foster, Donald 1928- *ConAu 53*
Foster, Doris VanLiew 1899- *ConAu 1R, -102,*
  SmATA 10
Foster, Dorothy 1936- *ConAu 93*
Foster, E C 1902- *ConAu 53, SmATA 9*
Foster, Earl M 1940- *ConAu 57*
Foster, Edward Halsey 1942- *ConAu 2NR, -49,*
  WrDr 84
Foster, Elizabeth 1905-1963 *ConAu 1R,*
  SmATA 10
Foster, Elizabeth Read 1912- *ConAu 106,*
  WrDr 84
Foster, Elizabeth Vincent 1902- *ConAu 85,*
  SmATA 12
Foster, F Blanche 1919- *ConAu 61, SmATA 11*
Foster, Francis *ConAu X*
Foster, Francis 1896-1975 *ConAu 109*
Foster, Frederick *ConAu X*
Foster, G Allen 1907-1969 *SmATA 26*
Foster, Genevieve 1893-1979 *ConAu 4NR, -5R,*
  -89, SmATA 2, -23N
Foster, Genevieve W 1902- *ConAu 69*
Foster, George *ConAu X, IntAu&W 82X,*
  WrDr 84
Foster, George Allen 1927- *ConAu 9R*
Foster, George Cecil 1893- *ConSFA*
Foster, H Lincoln 1906- *ConAu P-1*
Foster, Hal *AuNews 2, ConAu X, SmATA X*
Foster, Harold 1892-1982 *ConAu 107,*
  SmATA 31N
Foster, Henry Hubbard, Jr. 1911- *ConAu 1R,*
  -2NR
Foster, Herbert L 1928- *ConAu 57*
Foster, Herbert W 1920?-1979 *ConAu 89*
Foster, Iris *WrDr 84*
Foster, Iris 1944- *ConAu X*
Foster, Jack Donald 1930- *ConAu 29R*
Foster, James C 1943- *ConAu 7NR, -57*
Foster, Jeanne 1930- *TwCWW*
Foster, Jeanne Robert 1884-1970 *ConAu 104*
Foster, Joanna 1928- *ConAu 5R, -8NR*
Foster, John 1648?-1681 *DcLB 24*
Foster, John 1915- *ConAu 5R*
Foster, John 1925- *ConAu 33R*
Foster, John Burt, Jr. 1945- *ConAu 106*

Foster, John Lawrence 1930- *ConAu 53*
Foster, John Thomas 1925- *SmATA 8*
Foster, John Wilson 1942- *WrDr 84*
Foster, Joseph O'Kane 1898- *ConAu 49,*
 IntAu&W 82
Foster, Joseph Reginald 1920- *IntAu&W 82*
Foster, Julian F S 1926- *ConAu 29R*
Foster, K Neill 1935- *ConAu 4NR, -53*
Foster, Laura Louise 1918- *ConAu 17R,*
 SmATA 6
Foster, Lee 1923?-1977 *ConAu 69*
Foster, Lee Edwin 1943- *ConAu 33R*
Foster, Linda Nemec *DrAP&F 83*
Foster, M A 1939- *ConAu 9NR, -57*
Foster, Malcolm 1931- *ConAu 109*
Foster, Malcolm Burton 1931- *WrDr 84*
Foster, Margaret Lesser 1899?-1979 *ConAu 89,*
 SmATA 21N
Foster, Margery S 1914- *ConAu 5R*
Foster, Marguerite H 1909- *ConAu P-2*
Foster, Marian Curtis 1909-1978 *ConAu 73, -85,*
 SmATA 23[port]
Foster, Mark Stewart 1939- *ConAu 106*
Foster, Martha S *ConAu 5R*
Foster, Michael 1904-1956 *ConAu 110, DcLB 9*
Foster, O'Kane *ConAu 49*
Foster, Paul 1931- *ConAu 9NR, -21R,*
 ConDr 82, IntAu&W 82, NatPD 81[port],
 WrDr 84
Foster, Peter 1947- *ConAu 108*
Foster, Philip 1927- *ConAu 69*
Foster, Reginald Francis 1896-1975 *ConAu 107*
Foster, Richard *ConAu X, TwCCr&M 80,*
 WrDr 84
Foster, Richard J 1942- *ConAu 85*
Foster, Robert A 1949- *ConAu 81*
Foster, Ruel E 1916- *WrDr 84*
Foster, Ruel Elton 1916- *ConAu 33R*
Foster, Simon *WrDr 84*
Foster, Virginia Ramos *ConAu 29R*
Foster, W Bert 1869-1929 *TwCWW*
Foster-Harris, William 1903?-1978 *ConAu 104*
Foster VanLiew, Doris 1899- *WrDr 84*
Fothergill, Brian 1921- *ConAu 17R,*
 IntAu&W 82, WrDr 84
Fothergill, Philip G 1908- *ConAu 5R*
Fottler, Myron David 1941- *ConAu 37R*
Foucault, Michel 1926- *CIDMEL 80,*
 ConAu 105, WorAu 1970
Fougasse *ConAu X, LongCTC*
Fougere, Jean 1914- *IntAu&W 82*
Fouhy, Ed 1934- *ConAu 69*
Foulds, Elfrida Vipont 1902- *ConAu 4NR, -53,*
 IntAu&W 82, WrDr 84
Foulke, Adrienne 1915- *ConAu 65*
Foulke, Robert 1930- *ConAu 45*
Foulke, Roy Anderson 1896- *ConAu 1R, -1NR*
Foulkes, A Peter 1936- *ConAu 37R*
Foulkes, Albert Peter 1936- *IntAu&W 82*
Foulkes, David 1935- *ConAu 107*
Foulkes, Fred K 1941- *ConAu 33R*
Foulkes, Peter 1936- *WrDr 84*
Foulon, Roger 1923- *CIDMEL 80*
Fountain, Helen VanAlstyne 1906- *IntWWP 82*
Fountain, Leatrice 1924- *ConAu 21R*
Fouraker, Lawrence Edward 1923- *ConAu 1R*
Fourest, Henri-Pierre 1911- *ConAu 109*
Fourest, Michel *ConAu X*
Fournier, Alain 1886-1914 *LongCTC, ModRL,*
 TwCA, TwCA SUP
Fournier, Claude 1931- *CreCan 1*
Fournier, Henri Alban 1886-1914 *ConAu 104*
Fournier, Pierre 1916- *ConAu 89, ConLC 11,*
 WorAu
Fourth, Clifton *ConAu X*
Fourth Brother, The *ConAu X, SmATA X*
Fourtouni, Eleni *DrAP&F 83*
Foust, Paul J 1920- *ConAu 49*
Fouste, E Bonita Rutledge 1926- *ConAu 13R*
Fout, John C 1937- *ConAu 57*
Fowke, Edith Margaret 1913- *ConAu 37R,*
 IntAu&W 82, SmATA 14, WrDr 84
Fowkes, Robert Allen 1913- *ConAu 106*
Fowler, Alastair David Shaw 1930- *ConAu 13R,*
 IntAu&W 82, WrDr 84
Fowler, Austin 1928- *ConAu 21R*
Fowler, Charles B 1931- *ConAu 8NR, -57,*
 IntAu&W 82
Fowler, David Covington 1921- *ConAu 1R*
Fowler, Don D 1936- *ConAu 33R, WrDr 84*
Fowler, Douglas 1940- *ConAu 57*
Fowler, Elaine W 1914- *ConAu 93*

Fowler, Elizabeth Millspaugh 1921- *ConAu 102*
Fowler, Eugene Devlan 1890-1960 *ConAu 89, -97*
Fowler, Francis George 1870-1918 *LongCTC,*
 TwCA, TwCA SUP
Fowler, Gene 1890-1960 *ConAu X, TwCA,*
 TwCA SUP
Fowler, Gene 1931- *ConAu 5NR, -53, ConP 80,*
 WrDr 84
Fowler, George P 1909- *ConAu 41R*
Fowler, Giles Merrill 1934- *ConAmTC*
Fowler, Guy 1893?-1966 *ConAu 25R*
Fowler, H W 1858-1933 *LongCTC*
Fowler, Harry 1934- *ConAu 1NR, -45*
Fowler, Helen Rosa Huxley 1917- *ConAu P-1*
Fowler, Henry Watson 1858-1933 *TwCA,*
 TwCA SUP
Fowler, James W, III 1940- *ConAu 104*
Fowler, Jim *ConAu X*
Fowler, John M 1926- *ConAu 103*
Fowler, Kenneth Abrams 1900- *ConAu 5R,*
 TwCWW
Fowler, Mark 1949- *ConAu 65*
Fowler, Mary Elizabeth 1911- *ConAu P-2*
Fowler, Mary Jane *ConAu X*
Fowler, Michael 1929- *ConAu 109*
Fowler, Raymond Dalton, Jr. 1930- *ConAu 110*
Fowler, Raymond E 1933- *ConAu 85*
Fowler, Robert H 1926- *ConAu 73*
Fowler, Roger 1938- *ConAu 65*
Fowler, Sandra 1937- *ConAu 106, IntWWP 82,*
 WrDr 84
Fowler, Sydney 1874-1965 *LongCTC,*
 TwCCr&M 80
Fowler, Truth Mary 1907- *IntWWP 82*
Fowler, Virginie *ConAu X*
Fowler, Wilfred 1907- *ConAu P-1*
Fowler, Will 1922- *ConAu 5R*
Fowler, William Morgan, Jr. 1944- *ConAu 1NR,*
 -45
Fowler, Wilton B 1936- *ConAu 53*
Fowles, Jib 1940- *ConAu 69*
Fowles, John 1926- *ASpks, ConAu 5R,*
 ConLC 1, -2, -3, -4, -6, -9, -10, -15,
 ConNov 82, DcLB 14[port], DcLEL 1940,
 EncWL 2, ModBrL SUP, SmATA 22[port],
 TwCWr, WorAu, WrDr 84
Fowlie, Wallace 1908- *ConAu 5R, -5NR,*
 ModAL, TwCA SUP
Fowller, Kenneth Abrams 1900- *WrDr 84*
Fox, Adam 1883- *ConAu P-1*
Fox, Adam 1883-1977 *ConAu 10NR*
Fox, Aileen 1907- *ConAu 5R, -5NR, WrDr 84*
Fox, Alan 1920- *WrDr 84*
Fox, Alan John *ConAu 13R*
Fox, Allan M 1948- *ConAu 41R*
Fox, Annette Baker 1912- *ConAu 109*
Fox, Anthony *ConAu X, WrDr 84*
Fox, Beryl 1931- *CreCan 2*
Fox, C Lynn 1948- *ConAu 110*
Fox, Charles Elliot 1878- *ConAu P-1*
Fox, Charles Philip 1913- *ConAu 1R, -1NR,*
 SmATA 12
Fox, Connie *ConAu X, DrAP&F 83,*
 MichAu 80
Fox, David J 1927- *ConAu 13R*
Fox, Dickie Lee 1944- *IntWWP 82*
Fox, Dorothea Warren 1914- *ConAu 61*
Fox, Douglas A 1927- *ConAu 41R*
Fox, Douglas McMurray 1940- *ConAu 33R*
Fox, E Inman 1933- *ConAu 17R*
Fox, Edward J 1913- *ConAu 1R*
Fox, Edward L 1938- *ConAu 110*
Fox, Edward Whiting 1911- *ConAu 106*
Fox, Eleanor *ConAu X, SmATA X*
Fox, Fontaine Talbot, Jr. 1884-1964 *ConAu 89,*
 SmATA 23N
Fox, Frances Margaret *ConAu X*
Fox, Frances Margaret 1870-1959 *MichAu 80*
Fox, Frank W 1940- *ConAu 109*
Fox, Fred 1903?-1981 *ConAu 104,*
 SmATA 27N
Fox, Frederic Ewing 1917-1981 *ConAu 1R, -103*
Fox, Freeman *ConAu X, SmATA X*
Fox, G F 1911- *ConAu 5R, -5NR*
Fox, G P 1938- *ConAu 11NR, -21R*
Fox, Gail 1942- *ConAu 103*
Fox, Gardner F 1911- *ConSFA, TwCSFW,*
 WrDr 84
Fox, George 1934- *ConAu 37R*
Fox, Gilbert T 1915- *ConAu 69*
Fox, Gill *ConAu X*
Fox, Grace 1899- *ConAu 37R*

Fox, Grace Imogene 1907- *ConAu 1R*
Fox, H B 1910- *ConAu 57*
Fox, Hanna *DrAP&F 83*
Fox, Helen Morgenthau 1885?-1974 *ConAu 45*
Fox, Hugh 1932- *ConAu 11NR, WrDr 84*
Fox, Hugh Bernard 1932- *ConAu 25R,*
 MichAu 80
Fox, Jack C 1925- *ConAu 21R*
Fox, Jack Vernon 1918-1982 *ConAu 106*
Fox, James M *ConAu 102, DrAP&F 83*
Fox, Jean M *MichAu 80*
Fox, John *ConAu X*
Fox, John, Jr. 1862?-1919 *ConAu 108,*
 DcLB 9[port]
Fox, John, Jr. 1863?-1919 *TwCA, TwCA SUP,*
 TwCWr
Fox, John H 1925- *ConAu 5R, -8NR*
Fox, John Richard 1927- *CreCan 1*
Fox, Joseph M 1934- *ConAu 106*
Fox, Karl A 1917- *ConAu 7NR, -17R,*
 WrDr 84
Fox, Larry *ConAu 106, SmATA 30*
Fox, Len 1905- *WrDr 84*
Fox, Leonard Phillips 1905- *IntAu&W 82*
Fox, Levi 1914- *ConAu 77, IntAu&W 82,*
 WrDr 84
Fox, Logan J 1922- *ConAu 53*
Fox, Lorraine 1922-1976 *SmATA 11, -27N*
Fox, Lucia *DrAP&F 83*
Fox, Lucia Ugara De *ConAu X*
Fox, M W 1937- *WrDr 84*
Fox, Marcia R 1942- *ConAu 105*
Fox, Mary Virginia 1919- *ConAu 29R*
Fox, Matthew 1940- *ConAu 109*
Fox, Michael A 1940- *ConAu 103*
Fox, Michael Wilson 1937- *ConAu 73,*
 SmATA 15
Fox, Milton S 1904-1971 *ConAu 33R*
Fox, Mona Alexis *WrDr 84*
Fox, Norman Arnold 1911-1960 *TwCWW*
Fox, Owen *ConAu X*
Fox, Paula *DrAP&F 83*
Fox, Paula 1923- *ChlLR 1, ConAu 73,*
 ConLC 2, SmATA 17, TwCCW 83,
 WrDr 84
Fox, Paula 1932- *ConLC 8*
Fox, Petronella *SmATA X, WrDr 84*
Fox, Ralph H 1913-1973 *ConAu 49*
Fox, Ralph Winston 1900-1937 *TwCA[port],*
 TwCA SUP
Fox, Ray Errol 1941- *ConAu 85, IntAu&W 82,*
 NatPD 81[port]
Fox, Renee Claire 1928- *ConAu 49*
Fox, Richard G 1939- *ConAu 41R*
Fox, Richard Wightman 1945- *ConAu 93*
Fox, Robert Barlow 1930- *ConAu 13R*
Fox, Robert J 1927- *ConAu 1NR, -45,*
 SmATA 33[port]
Fox, Robert R *DrAP&F 83*
Fox, Robert R 1943- *ConAu 77*
Fox, Ruth 1895- *ConAu 73*
Fox, Samuel 1905- *ConAu P-2*
Fox, Samuel 1908- *WrDr 84*
Fox, Samuel J 1919- *ConAu 53*
Fox, Sharon E 1938- *ConAu 45*
Fox, Siv Cedering 1939- *ConAu 41R*
Fox, Sonny 1925- *ConAu 41R*
Fox, Stephen R 1945- *ConAu 29R*
Fox, Susan *DrAP&F 83*
Fox, Ted *ConAu X*
Fox, Terry Curtis 1948- *NatPD 81[port]*
Fox, Uffa 1898-1972 *ConAu 37R*
Fox, V Helen *ConAu X*
Fox, Vernon 1916- *ConAu 37R*
Fox, Victor J *ConAu X*
Fox, Willard 1919- *ConAu 21R*
Fox, William L *DrAP&F 83*
Fox, William Lloyd 1921- *ConAu 17R*
Fox, William McNair 1924- *ConAu 5R*
Fox, William Price 1926- *ConAu 11NR, -17R,*
 ConLC 22[port], Conv 1,
 DcLB Y81A[port], -2
Fox, William Thornton Rickert 1912- *ConAu 108*
Fox, William Wellington 1909- *ConAu 1R*
Fox-Genovese, Elizabeth 1941- *ConAu 10NR,*
 -65
Fox-Lockert, Lucia 1928- *MichAu 80*
Fox-Martin, Milton 1914?-1977 *ConAu 69*
Fox-Sheinwold, Patricia *ConAu 102*
Foxall, Raymond 1916- *ConAu 5NR, -9R,*
 IntAu&W 82, WrDr 84
Foxe, Arthur N 1902-1982 *ConAu 108*

WrDr 84
Frankenstein, Alfred Victor 1906-1981 *ConAu 1R,*
  -2NR, -104
Frankenstein, Carl 1905- *ConAu 9R*
Frankenthal, Kate 1889-1976 *ConAu 65*
Frankes, George Edward 1932- *ConAu 29R*
Frankfort, Ellen 1936- *ConAu 29R*
Frankforter, A Daniel 1939- *ConAu 81*
Frankfurt, Harry Gordon 1929- *ConAu 41R*
Frankhouser, Floyd Richard 1944- *WrDr 84*
Frankl, Viktor E 1905- *ConAu 65*
Frankland, Mark 1934- *ConAu 69*
Frankland, Noble 1922- *ConAu 65, WrDr 84*
Franklin, A *ConAu X*
Franklin, Adele 1887?-1977 *ConAu 69*
Franklin, Alexander John 1921- *ConAu 13R,*
  IntAu&W 82, WrDr 84
Franklin, Alfred White 1905- *ConAu 7NR, -57*
Franklin, Ben A 1927- *ConAu 89*
Franklin, Benjamin *ConAu X*
Franklin, Billy J 1940- *ConAu 33R*
Franklin, Burt 1903-1972 *ConAu P-1*
Franklin, Charles 1909- *ConAu X*
Franklin, Colin 1923- *ConAu 77, IntAu&W 82*
Franklin, Denson Nauls 1914- *ConAu 1R*
Franklin, Edward Herbert 1930- *ConAu 13R*
Franklin, Elizabeth *ConAu X*
Franklin, Eugene *ConAu X*
Franklin, George E 1890-1971 *ConAu P-1*
Franklin, H Bruce 1934- *ConAu 5R, -9NR,*
  ConSFA, IntAu&W 82
Franklin, Harold 1920- *SmATA 13*
Franklin, Harold 1926- *ConAu 29R*
Franklin, Harold L 1934- *ConAu 57*
Franklin, Harry 1906- *ConAu P-1, WrDr 84*
Franklin, J *IntAu&W 82X*
Franklin, J E *DrAP&F 83*
Franklin, J E 1937- *ConAu 61, NatPD 81[port]*
Franklin, Jay 1897-1967 *ConAu X, TwCA,*
  TwCA SUP
Franklin, Jennie 1937- *IntAu&W 82*
Franklin, Jerome L 1943- *ConAu 102*
Franklin, Jimmie Lewis 1939- *ConAu 106*
Franklin, Joe 1926- *ConAu 108*
Franklin, John H 1915- *WrDr 84*
Franklin, John Hope 1915- *ConAu 1R, -1NR,*
  -3NR, -5R, DcLEL 1940, IntAu&W 82,
  LivgBAA
Franklin, Jon Daniel 1942- *ConAu 104*
Franklin, Keith *ConAu X*
Franklin, Linda Campbell 1941- *ConAu 105,*
  WrDr 84
Franklin, Marc A 1932- *ConAu 29R*
Franklin, Marshall 1929- *ConAu 53*
Franklin, Max *ConAu X, IntAu&W 82X,*
  SmATA X, TwCCr&M 80, WrDr 84
Franklin, Miles 1879-1954 *ConAu 104,*
  ModCmwL, TwCLC 7[port], TwCWr
Franklin, Nat *ConAu X*
Franklin, Olga 1912- *ConAu 102, WrDr 84*
Franklin, R W 1937- *ConAu 9NR, -21R*
Franklin, Richard 1918- *ConAu 21R*
Franklin, Richard Langdon 1925- *WrDr 84*
Franklin, S Harvey 1928- *ConAu 105*
Franklin, Samuel Harvey 1928- *WrDr 84*
Franklin, Sidney 1903-1976 *ConAu 65*
Franklin, Staines *CreCan 1*
Franklin, Steve *ConAu X, SmATA X*
Franklyn, Charles Aubrey Hamilton 1896-
  ConAu 9R, IntAu&W 82
Franklyn, Robert Alan 1918- *ConAu 89*
Franko, Ivan 1856-1916 *ClDMEL 80, EncWL 2,*
  ModSL 2
Franko, Lawrence G 1942- *ConAu 37R*
Franks, C E S 1936- *ConAu 77*
Franks, Celia *CreCan 1*
Franks, Cyril Maurice 1923- *ConAu 13R*
Franks, Ed *ConAu X*
Franks, Lucinda 1946- *ConAu 53*
Franks, Robert Sleightholme 1871-1963
  ConAu 5R
Fransella, Fay *ConAu 25R*
Fransen, Piet Frans 1913- *IntAu&W 82*
Frantz, Charles 1925- *ConAu 3NR, -5R*
Frantz, Harry Warner 1891-1982 *ConAu 106*
Frantz, Joe B 1917- *ConAu 1R, -1NR,*
  WrDr 84
Frantz, Ralph Jules 1902-1979 *ConAu 77, -89,*
  DcLB 4
Franz, Barbara E 1946- *ConAu 110*
Franz, Carl 1944- *ConAu 107*

Franz, Gunther 1902- *IntAu&W 82*
Franz, William S 1945- *ConAu 110*
Franzblau, Abraham N 1901- *ConAu 29R*
Franzblau, Abraham N 1901-1982 *ConAu 108*
Franzblau, Rose N 1905-1979 *ConAu 29R, -89*
Franzen, Gosta 1906- *ConAu 41R,*
  IntAu&W 82
Franzen, Lavern G 1926- *ConAu 7NR, -61*
Franzen, Nils-Olof 1916- *ConAu 29R,*
  SmATA 10
Franzero, Carlo Maria 1892- *ConAu 1R, -5NR*
Franzero, Charles Marie *ConAu X*
Franzius, Enno 1901- *ConAu 25R*
Franzmann, Martin Hans 1907-1976 *ConAu 1R,*
  -3NR
Franzwa, Gregory M 1926- *ConAu 9NR, -21R*
Frary, Michael 1918- *ConAu 77*
Frasca, John 1916-1979 *ConAu 3NR, -49, -93*
Frascatoro, Gerald *ConAu X*
Frascino, Edward 193-?- *SmATA 33*
Frascona, Joseph Lohengrin 1910- *ConAu 17R*
Frasconi, Antonio 1919- *ConAu 1R, -1NR,*
  SmATA 6
Frase, Larry E 1945- *ConAu 41R*
Frase, Robert W 1912- *ConAu 33R*
Fraser, Alex *ConAu X*
Fraser, Allan 1900- *ConAu 57*
Fraser, Amy Stewart 1892- *ConAu 9NR, -49,*
  WrDr 84
Fraser, Anthea *ConAu 10NR*
Fraser, Anthea 1930- *ConAu 65, IntAu&W 82,*
  WrDr 84
Fraser, Antonia 1932- *ConAu 85, DcLEL 1940,*
  SmATA 32, TwCCr&M 80, -80,
  WorAu 1970, WrDr 84
Fraser, Arthur Ronald 1888-1974 *ConAu 53*
Fraser, Arvonne S 1925- *ConAu 33R*
Fraser, B Kay 1941- *ConAu 69*
Fraser, Betty *SmATA X*
Fraser, Blair 1909-1968 *ConAu P-2*
Fraser, Bruce 1910- *ConAu 109*
Fraser, Carol Lucille 1930- *CreCan 2*
Fraser, Colin 1935- *ConAu 21R*
Fraser, Conon 1930- *ConAu P-1, WrDr 84*
Fraser, Dean 1916- *ConAu 45*
Fraser, Dorothy May 1903?-1980 *ConAu 102*
Fraser, Douglas 1910- *WrDr 84*
Fraser, Douglas Ferrar 1929- *ConAu 1R, -4NR*
Fraser, Douglas Jamieson 1910- *ConAu 102,*
  IntAu&W 82, IntWWP 82
Fraser, Edith Emily Rose Oram 1903-
  ConAu P-1
Fraser, Elise Parker 1903- *ConAu 1R*
Fraser, Elizabeth Marr 1928- *SmATA 31*
Fraser, G S 1915-1980 *ConAu 105, -85,*
  ConLCrt 2, ConP 80, ModBrL, WorAu
Fraser, George MacDonald 1925- *ConAu 2NR,*
  -45, ConLC 7, DcLEL 1940,
  IntAu&W 82, WorAu 1970, WrDr 84
Fraser, Gordon Holmes 1898- *ConAu P-1*
Fraser, Harry 1937- *WrDr 84*
Fraser, Ian 1897-1974 *ConAu 53*
Fraser, Ian Watson 1907- *WrDr 84*
Fraser, J T 1923- *ConAu 8NR, -61*
Fraser, James *ConAu X, WrDr 84*
Fraser, Jane *ConAu X, IntAu&W 82X,*
  TwCRGW, WrDr 84
Fraser, Janet Hobhouse *ConAu X*
Fraser, John 1931- *ConAu 29R*
Fraser, Kathleen *DrAP&F 83*
Fraser, Kathleen 1937- *ConAu 106, ConP 80,*
  WrDr 84
Fraser, Maxwell *ConAu X*
Fraser, Morris 1941- *ConAu 102, WrDr 84*
Fraser, Neil McCormick 1902- *ConAu 5R*
Fraser, Peter 1928- *ConAu 107, WrDr 84*
Fraser, Peter 1932- *ConAu 33R*
Fraser, Raymond 1941- *ConAu 107*
Fraser, Ronald 1888-1974 *ConAu X, LongCTC*
Fraser, Ronald 1901- *ConAu X*
Fraser, Russell A 1927- *WrDr 84*
Fraser, Russell Alfred 1927- *ConAu 37R*
Fraser, Shelagh *IntAu&W 82*
Fraser, Stewart Erskine 1929- *ConAu 10NR,*
  -13R
Fraser, Sylvia 1935- *ConAu 1NR, -45*
Fraser, W B 1905- *ConAu P-2*
Fraser, W Hamish 1941- *ConAu 103, WrDr 84*
Fraser, W Lionel d1965 *ConAu P-1*
Fraser, Walter Ian Reid 1911- *WrDr 84*
Fraser Darling, Frank 1903-1979 *ConAu 61, -89*
Fraser Harrison, Brian 1918- *ConAu P-1*

Fraser Of Tullybelton, Baron *WrDr 84*
Frasier, James E 1923- *ConAu 17R*
Frassanito, William A 1946- *ConAu 9NR, -57*
Fratcher, William Franklin 1913- *ConAu 3NR,*
  -5R, WrDr 84
Fratti, Mario 1927- *ClDMEL 80, ConAmTC,*
  ConAu 77, ConDr 82, CroCD, ModWD,
  NatPD 81[port], WrDr 84
Frautschi, R L 1926- *ConAu 17R*
Fray *IntWWP 82X*
Fray Angelus *IntAu&W 82X*
Fraydas, Stan 1918- *ConAu 57*
Frayling, Christopher 1946- *ConAu 110*
Frayn, Michael 1933- *ConAu 5R, ConDr 82,*
  ConLC 7, ConNov 82, ConSFA,
  DcLB 13[port], -14[port], DcLEL 1940,
  IntAu&W 82, ModBrL SUP, TwCSFW,
  WorAu, WrDr 84
Frayne, June 1924- *ConAu 101*
Frazee, Charles A 1929- *ConAu 37R, WrDr 84*
Frazee, Steve 1909- *ConAu 5R, -5NR,*
  TwCSFW, TwCWW, WrDr 84
Frazer, Andrew *ConAu X*
Frazer, Fred *ConAu X*
Frazer, Sir James George 1854-1941 *LongCTC,*
  TwCA, TwCA SUP
Frazer, Mark Petrovich *ConAu X*
Frazer, Robert Caine *ConAu X, TwCCr&M 80*
Frazer, Robert W 1911- *ConAu 17R*
Frazer, William J, Jr. 1924- *ConAu 17R*
Frazer, Winifred Loesch Dusenbury 1916-
  ConAu 13R, -25R
Frazer-Hurst, Douglas 1883- *ConAu P-1*
Frazetta, Frank 1928- *ConAu 104*
Frazier, Allie M 1932- *ConAu 110*
Frazier, Arthur *ConAu X, WrDr 84*
Frazier, Claude Albee 1920- *ConAu 29R*
Frazier, Cliff 1934- *ConAu 109*
Frazier, Edward Franklin 1894-1962 *ConAu 108*
Frazier, Evelyn McD *IntAu&W 82X*
Frazier, George 1911-1974 *ConAu 49,*
  ConAu P-2
Frazier, Kendrick 1942- *ConAu 101*
Frazier, Neta Lohnes 1890- *ConAu 1R, -1NR,*
  SmATA 7, WrDr 84
Frazier, Sarah *ConAu X*
Frazier, Shervert Hughes 1921- *ConAu 85*
Frazier, Thomas R 1931- *ConAu 33R*
Frazier, Walt 1945- *ConAu 103*
Frears, J R 1936- *ConAu 107*
Freas, Frank Kelly 1922- *ConAu 102*
Frech, Frances 1923- *ConAu 97*
Freddi, Cris 1955- *ConAu 106*
Frede, Richard *DrAP&F 83*
Frede, Richard 1934- *ConAu 69*
Fredeman, William E 1928- *ConAu 33R*
Fredenburgh, Franz A 1906- *ConAu 33R*
Frederic, Harold 1856-1898 *ModAL,*
  ModAL SUP
Frederic, Sister M Catherine *ConAu X*
Frederic, Mike *WrDr 84*
Frederick, Carl Louis 1942- *ConAu 65*
Frederick, Dick *ConAu X*
Frederick, Gersami Karen *DrAP&F 83*
Frederick, John *ConAu X, TwCWW*
Frederick, John Hutchinson 1896- *ConAu 1R*
Frederick, K C *DrAP&F 83*
Frederick, Lee *ConAu X, IntAu&W 82X*
Frederick, Lorraine H *IntWWP 82X*
Frederick, Oswald *ConAu X*
Frederick, Pauline 1908- *ConAu 102*
Frederick, Robert Allen 1928- *ConAu 3NR, -45*
Fredericks, Carlton 1910- *AuNews 1,*
  ConAu 7NR, -53
Fredericks, Dr. Frank *WrDr 84*
Fredericks, Frank *ConAu X*
Fredericks, Frohm *ConAu X*
Fredericks, Leo Brook *IntWWP 82X*
Fredericks, P C *WrDr 84*
Fredericks, Pierce Griffin 1920- *ConAu 13R*
Fredericks, Vic *ConAu X*
Frederika, Queen 1917-1981 *ConAu 108*
Frederiksen, Martin W 1930-1980 *ConAu 101*
Frederikson, Edna 1904- *ConAu 49*
Fredge, Frederique 1906- *ConAu P-2*
Fredman, Alice G 1924- *ConAu 102*
Fredman, Henry John 1927- *ConAu 29R*
Fredman, John *ConAu X*
Fredman, Ruth Gruber 1934- *ConAu 106*
Fredman, Stephen *DrAP&F 83*
Fredricks, Edgar J 1942- *ConAu 25R,*
  MichAu 80

Fredrickson, George M 1934- *ConAu 8NR, -17R*
Fredrickson, Olive A 1901- *ConAu 49*
Fredriksson, Don 1926- *ConAu 110*
Free *ConAu X*
Free, Ann Cottrell *ConAu 9R*
Free, Colin *ConDr 82B*
Free, James S 1908- *ConAu 77*
Free, Lloyd A 1908- *ConAu 13R*
Free, William Joseph 1933- *ConAu 9R*
Free, William Norris 1933- *ConAu 25R*
Freeborn, Brian 1939- *ConAu 65*
Freeborn, Richard 1926- *WrDr 84*
Freeborn, Richard H 1926- *ConAu 1R, -1NR,*
  IntAu&W 82
Freed, Alvyn M 1913- *ConAu 8NR, -61,*
  SmATA 22[port]
Freed, Arthur 1894-1973 *ConAu 41R*
Freed, Barry *ConAu X*
Freed, Donald 1932- *ConAu 85*
Freed, Louis Franklin 1903- *ConAu 5R,*
  IntAu&W 82
Freed, Lynn *DrAP&F 83*
Freed, Lynn 1945- *ConAu 108*
Freed, Margaret DeHaan 1917- *ConAu 73*
Freed, Ray *DrAP&F 83*
Freedberg, Sydney Joseph 1914- *ConAu 1R,*
  -1NR, IntAu&W 82, WrDr 84
Freedeman, Charles E 1926- *ConAu 102*
Freedgood, Lillian 1911- *ConAu 13R*
Freedgood, Morton 1912?- *AuNews 1,*
  ConAu 108, WrDr 84
Freedland, Michael 1934- *ConAu 11NR, -65,*
  IntAu&W 82, WrDr 84
Freedland, Nat 1936- *ConAu 65*
Freedley, George Reynolds 1904-1967
  ConAu 4NR, -5R
Freedman, Alfred M 1917- *ConAu 4NR, -49*
Freedman, Arthur M 1916- *ConAu 41R*
Freedman, Benedict 1919- *ConAu 69,*
  SmATA 27[port]
Freedman, Daniel X 1921- *ConAu 41R*
Freedman, David Noel 1922- *ConAu 1R, -1NR*
Freedman, Harry 1922- *CreCan 2*
Freedman, Hy 1914- *ConAu 85*
Freedman, Leonard 1924- *ConAu 1R, -1NR*
Freedman, M David 1938- *ConAu 41R*
Freedman, Marcia K 1922- *ConAu 10NR, -25R*
Freedman, Mary Morrison *CreCan 2*
Freedman, Maurice 1920-1975 *ConAu 61,*
  ConAu P-2
Freedman, Mervin Burton 1920- *ConAu 29R,*
  WrDr 84
Freedman, Monroe H 1928- *ConAu 107*
Freedman, Morris 1920- *ConAu 3NR, -5R*
Freedman, Nancy 1920- *ConAu 1NR, -45,*
  SmATA 27[port], TwCSFW, WrDr 84
Freedman, Richard 1932- *ConAu 77*
Freedman, Robert Owen 1941- *ConAu 33R*
Freedman, Ronald 1917- *ConAu 6NR, -9R,*
  WrDr 84
Freedman, Russell 1929- *ConAu 7NR, -17R,*
  SmATA 16
Freedman, Warren 1921- *ConAu 17R*
Freefield, Lois *DrAP&F 83*
Freehill, Maurice F 1915- *ConAu 5R*
Freehof, Solomon B 1892- *ConAu 93*
Freek, George 1945- *NatPD 81[port]*
Freeland, Jay *ConAu X*
Freeland, John Maxwell 1920- *ConAu 13R,*
  WrDr 84
Freeland, Richard M 1941- *ConAu 81*
Freeland, Stephen L 1911?-1977 *ConAu 69*
Freeley, Austin J 1922- *ConAu 5R*
Freeling, Nicolas 1927- *ASpks, ConAu 1NR,*
  -49, ConNov 82, IntAu&W 82,
  TwCCr&M 80, TwCWr, WorAu, WrDr 84
Freely, Maureen 1952- *ConAu 97*
Freeman, A Myrick, III 1936- *ConAu 85*
Freeman, Anne Frances 1936- *ConAu 1R*
Freeman, Anne Hobson *DrAP&F 83*
Freeman, Arthur 1938- *ConAu 1R, -1NR*
Freeman, Austin 1862-1943 *LongCTC, TwCA,*
  TwCA SUP
Freeman, Barbara C 1906- *ConAu 73,*
  SmATA 28, TwCCW 83, WrDr 84
Freeman, C Wade 1906- *ConAu 5R*
Freeman, Charles K 1900-1980 *ConAmTC,*
  ConAu 97
Freeman, Cynthia *ConAu X, TwCRGW,*
  WrDr 84
Freeman, Darlene 1934- *ConAu 29R*
Freeman, Dave *ConAu X*

Freeman, David 1922- *ConAu 102,*
  IntAu&W 82
Freeman, David 1945- *ConAu 108, ConDr 82,*
  NatPD 81[port], WrDr 84
Freeman, David Hugh 1924- *ConAu 1R*
Freeman, Devery *DrAP&F 83*
Freeman, Don 1908-1978 *ConAu 77,*
  SmATA 17, TwCCW 83
Freeman, Donald Cary 1938- *ConAu 53*
Freeman, Donald McKinley 1931- *ConAu 37R*
Freeman, Douglas Southall 1886-1953 *ConAu 109,*
  DcLB 17[port], TwCA, TwCA SUP,
  TwCLC 11[port]
Freeman, Eugene 1906- *ConAu 41R*
Freeman, G L 1904- *ConAu 13R*
Freeman, Gary 1945- *ConAu 93*
Freeman, Gillian 1929- *ConAu 3NR, -5R,*
  ConNov 82, DcLEL 1940, IntAu&W 82,
  WrDr 84
Freeman, Harold Webber 1899- *LongCTC,*
  TwCA, TwCA SUP
Freeman, Harrop A 1907- *ConAu 13R*
Freeman, Harry 1906-1978 *ConAu 77*
Freeman, Howard E 1929- *ConAu 5R, -6NR*
Freeman, Ira Henry 1906- *ConAu P-1*
Freeman, Ira Maximilian 1905- *ConAu 73,*
  SmATA 21[port]
Freeman, James Dillet 1912- *ConAu 17R*
Freeman, James Montague 1936- *ConAu 102*
Freeman, Jayne Stewart 1933- *ConAmTC*
Freeman, Jean Todd 1929- *ConAu 25R*
Freeman, Jo 1945- *ConAu 8NR, -61,*
  ConIsC 1[port], IntAu&W 82, WrDr 84
Freeman, John 1880-1929 *LongCTC, ModBrL,*
  TwCA
Freeman, John Crosby 1941- *ConAu 13R*
Freeman, Joseph 1897-1965 *ConAu 89, TwCA,*
  TwCA SUP
Freeman, Kathleen 1897-1959 *LongCTC,*
  TwCCr&M 80
Freeman, Larry *ConAu X*
Freeman, Lea David 1887?-1976 *ConAu 69*
Freeman, Leslie J 1944- *ConAu 106*
Freeman, Linton C 1927- *ConAu 69*
Freeman, Lucy 1916- *ConAu 3NR, -5R,*
  SmATA 24[port], WrDr 84
Freeman, Mae 1907- *ConAu 73,*
  SmATA 25[port]
Freeman, Margaret B 1899-1980 *ConAu 109*
Freeman, Margaret B 1900?-1980 *ConAu 97*
Freeman, Margaret C 1913- *ConAu 57*
Freeman, Margaret N 1915- *ConAu 9R*
Freeman, Mary E Wilkins 1852-1930 *ConAu 106,*
  LongCTC, TwCA, TwCLC 9[port]
Freeman, Max Herbert 1907- *ConAu 109*
Freeman, Paul 1929?-1980 *ConAu 101*
Freeman, Peter J *ConAu X*
Freeman, R Austin 1862-1943 *TwCCr&M 80*
Freeman, Richard Austin 1862-1943 *TwCA,*
  TwCA SUP
Freeman, Richard B 1944- *ConAu 85*
Freeman, Richard Borden 1908- *ConAu 1R,*
  WrDr 84
Freeman, Roger A 1904- *ConAu 25R, WrDr 84*
Freeman, Roger A 1928- *ConAu 65*
Freeman, Roger Anthony 1928- *ConAu 10NR*
Freeman, Roger L 1928- *ConAu 69*
Freeman, Ruth B 1906- *ConAu 41R*
Freeman, Ruth Lazear Sunderlin 1907-
  ConAu P-1
Freeman, Spencer 1892- *IntAu&W 82,*
  WrDr 84
Freeman, Susan Tax 1938- *ConAu 85*
Freeman, Thomas *WrDr 84*
Freeman, Thomas 1919- *ConAu 93*
Freeman, Thomas Walter 1908- *ConAu 5R,*
  WrDr 84
Freeman, Walter 1895-1972 *ConAu 33R,*
  ConAu P-1
Freeman, Warren S 1911- *ConAu 5R*
Freeman, William T *DrAP&F 83*
Freeman, Winifred Edith 1918- *WrDr 84*
Freeman Allen, Geoffrey 1922- *WrDr 84*
Freeman-Grenville, Greville S Parker 1918-
  ConAu 3NR, -5R, IntAu&W 82, WrDr 84
Freeman-Ishill, Rose 1895- *ConAu P-1*
Freemantle, Brian 1936- *ConAu 65,*
  TwCCr&M 80, WrDr 84
Freemon, Frank R 1938- *ConAu 45*
Freer, Coburn 1939- *ConAu 105*
Freer, Harold Wiley 1906- *ConAu P-2*
Freer, Maureen 1933- *IntWWP 82*

Freericks, Mary *DrAP&F 83*
Freericks, Mary Avakian 1935- *IntWWP 82*
Freese, Arthur S 1917- *ConAu 77*
Freese, Mathias Balogh *DrAP&F 83*
Freestrom, Hubert J 1928- *ConAu 37R*
Fregault, Guy 1918-1977 *ConAu 101*
Fregly, Bert 1922- *ConAu 8NR, -57*
Fregosi, Claudia 1946- *ConAu 69,*
  SmATA 24[port]
Frei, Bruno 1897- *IntAu&W 82*
Frei, Eduardo *ConAu X*
Frei Montalva, Eduardo 1911-1982 *ConAu 110*
Freiburger, Walter *IntAu&W 82X*
Freid, Jacob 1913- *ConAu 1R*
Freidel, Frank Burt, Jr. 1916- *ConAu 1R, -5NR*
Freides, Thelma K 1930- *ConAu 49*
Freidin, Seymour Kenneth 1917- *ConAu 1R,*
  -2NR
Freidson, Eliot 1923- *ConAu 5R, -8NR*
Freifeld, Lois Unger 1934- *IntWWP 82*
Freihofer, Lois Diane 1933- *ConAu 13R*
Freilich, Joan S 1941- *ConAu 57*
Freilich, Morris 1928- *ConAu 37R*
Freilicher, Melvyn *DrAP&F 83*
Freilicher, Melvyn 1946- *IntAu&W 82*
Freiman, Lillian 1908- *CreCan 1*
Freire-Maia, Newton 1918- *ConAu 29R,*
  IntAu&W 82
Freistadt, Benedikt 1897- *IntAu&W 82*
Freitas, Margarete Elisabeth 1927- *ConAu 45*
Freivalds, John 1944- *ConAu 69*
Freixedo, Salvador 1923- *ConAu 29R*
Fremantle, Anne 1910- *ConAu 13R, LongCTC,*
  TwCA SUP, WrDr 84
Fremgen, James Morgan 1933- *ConAu 17R,*
  WrDr 84
Fremlin, Celia 1914- *ConAu X, TwCCr&M 80,*
  WrDr 84
Fremont, W B *ConAu X*
Fremont-Smith, Eliot 1929- *ConAu 105*
Frenaud, Andre 1907- *CIDMEL 80, WorAu*
French, Alfred 1916- *ConAu 102, IntAu&W 82,*
  WrDr 84
French, Alice 1850-1934 *LongCTC*
French, Ashley *ConAu X,   TwCRGW,*
  WrDr 84
French, Bevan M 1937- *ConAu 97*
French, Brandon 1944- *ConAu 89*
French, Calvin L 1934- *ConAu 53*
French, Charles E 1923- *ConAu 1NR, -45*
French, David *DrAP&F 83*
French, David 1939- *ConAu 101, ConDr 82,*
  WrDr 84
French, Don *IntAu&W 82X*
French, Doris *ConAu X*
French, Dorothy Kayser 1926- *ConAu 3NR, -9R,*
  IntAu&W 82, SmATA 5
French, Edward L 1916-1969 *ConAu P-2*
French, Fiona 1944- *ConAu 29R, IntAu&W 82,*
  SmATA 6, TwCCW 83, WrDr 84
French, Herbert E 1912- *ConAu 45*
French, Joan *DrAP&F 83*
French, Kathryn *ConAu X, SmATA X*
French, Maida Parlow 1901- *CreCan 1*
French, Marilyn 1929- *ConAu 3NR, -69,*
  ConLC 10, -18, WrDr 84
French, Michael Raymond 1944- *ConAu 89,*
  IntAu&W 82
French, Paul *ConAu X, LongCTC, SmATA X,*
  TwCSFW
French, Peter 1918- *ConAu 1R*
French, Peter A 1942- *ConAu 1NR, -45,*
  IntAu&W 82
French, Philip 1933- *ConAu 103*
French, R B D 1904- *WrDr 84*
French, R B D 1904-1981 *ConAu 104,*
  ConAu P-2
French, Richard 1947- *ConAu 11NR, -69*
French, Scott Robert 1948- *ConAu 57*
French, Simon 1957- *ConAu 105*
French, Warren G 1922- *ConAu 1R, -1NR,*
  WrDr 84
French, Will 1890?-1979 *ConAu 89*
French, William 1926- *ConAu 69*
French, William Marshall 1907- *ConAu P-1*
Frend, A *ConAu X*
Frend, W H C 1916- *ConAu 9NR, -21R*
Frend, William 1916- *WrDr 84*
Frend, William Hugh Clifford 1916-
  IntAu&W 82
Frenk-Westheim, Mariana *IntAu&W 82*
Frenkel, Jacob A 1943- *ConAu 89*

Frenkel, Richard E 1924- *ConAu 21R*
Frenkiel, Zygmunt 1902- *IntAu&W 82*
Frenssen, Gustav 1863-1945 *TwCA, TwCA SUP*
Frentzen, Jeffrey 1956- *ConAu 109*
Frenz, Horst 1912- *ConAu 29R*
Frere, Emile 1917-1974 *ConAu 41R*
Frere, James Arnold 1920- *ConAu 5R*
Frere, Maud 1923- *CIDMEL 80*
Frere, Paul 1917- *ConAu 5R*
Frere, Sheppard 1916- *ConAu 21R*
Frerichs, A C 1910- *ConAu P-2*
Freschet, Berniece 1927- *ConAu 11NR, -17R*
Frese, Dolores Warwick 1936- *ConAu 5R, -9NR*
Fretheim, Terence E 1936- *ConAu 11NR, -25R*
Fretwell, Stephen DeWitt 1942- *ConAu 53*
Freuchen, Peter 1886-1957 *TwCA, TwCA SUP*
Freud, Anna 1895- *IntAu&W 82*
Freud, Anna 1895-1982 *ConAu 108*
Freud, Clement 1924- *ConAu 102*
Freud, Sigmund 1856-1939 *EncWL 2[port],
    LongCTC, TwCA, TwCA SUP, TwCWr,
    WhoTwCL*
Freudenberger, Herman 1922- *ConAu 13R,
    WrDr 84*
Freudenheim, Leslie Ann Mandelson 1941-
    ConAu 69
Freudenheim, Yehoshua 1894-1975 *ConAu P-2*
Freudenthal, Hans 1905- *ConAu 11NR, -25R*
Freund, E Hans 1905- *ConAu 1R*
Freund, Gerald 1930- *ConAu 1R, -1NR*
Freund, Gisele 1912- *ConAu 49*
Freund, John E 1921- *ConAu 13R*
Freund, Paul A 1908- *ConAu 1R*
Freund, Philip 1909- *ConAu 13R, WrDr 84*
Freund, Rudolf 1915-1969 *SmATA 28*
Freundlich, August L 1924- *ConAu 49*
Freundlich, Eisabeth 1906- *IntAu&W 82*
Frevert, Peter 1938- *ConAu 81*
Frew, David R 1943- *ConAu 77*
Frewer, Glyn 1931- *ConAu 10NR, WrDr 84*
Frewer, Glyn Mervyn Louis 1931- *ConAu 13R,
    IntAu&W 82, SmATA 11*
Frewin, Leslie 1917- *ConAu 5R*
Frewin, Leslie 1920- *WrDr 84*
Frewin, Leslie Ronald 1917- *ConAu 11NR*
Frey, Andrew 1905?-1983 *ConAu 109*
Frey, Erich A 1931- *ConAu 45*
Frey, Frederick Ward 1929- *ConAu 53*
Frey, Henry A 1923- *ConAu 33R*
Frey, John Andrew 1929- *ConAu 89*
Frey, Leonard H 1927- *ConAu 29R*
Frey, Marlys 1931- *ConAu 10NR, -25R*
Frey, Richard L 1905- *ConAu 89*
Freybe, Heidi Huberta 1914- *WrDr 84*
Freydorf, Roswith Von *IntAu&W 82*
Freyer, Frederic *ConAu X*
Freyre, Gilberto DeMello 1900- *EncWL 2,
    ModLAL, TwCWr, WorAu*
Freytag, Joseph *ConAu X*
Freytag, Josephine *ConAu X*
Friar, Kimon 1911- *ConAu 85, IntAu&W 82,
    IntWWP 82, WorAu*
Friar, Will *IntWWP 82X*
Friar Tuck *ConAu X*
Fribourg, Marjorie G 1920- *ConAu 1R, -4NR*
Frick, C H *ConAu X, IntAu&W 82X,
    SmATA 6, WrDr 84*
Frick, Constance *ConAu X, SmATA 6*
Frick, Elizabeth 1913- *IntWWP 82*
Frick, Ford Christopher 1894-1978 *ConAu 89*
Frick, George F 1925- *ConAu 13R*
Fricke, Cedric V 1928- *ConAu 13R*
Fricks, Richard *DrAP&F 83*
Friday, Nancy *WrDr 84*
Friday, Nancy 1937- *ConAu 77*
Friday, Peter *ConAu X, IntAu&W 82X*
Fridegard, Jan 1897-1968 *CIDMEL 80*
Fridfinnsson, Gudmundur L 1905- *IntAu&W 82*
Fridolin *IntAu&W 82X*
Fridy, Wallace 1910- *ConAu 1R*
Friebert, Stuart *DrAP&F 83*
Friebert, Stuart 1931- *ConAu 65*
Fried, Barbara Ruth 1924- *ConAu 45*
Fried, Charles 1935- *ConAu 29R*
Fried, Eleanor L 1913- *ConAu 29R*
Fried, Emanuel *DrAP&F 83*
Fried, Emanuel 1913- *ConAu 73*
Fried, Erich 1921- *CIDMEL 80, ModGL,
    WorAu*
Fried, Frederick 1908- *ConAu 77,
    IntAu&W 82*
Fried, John J 1940- *ConAu 33R*

Fried, Joseph P *WrDr 84*
Fried, Joseph P 1939- *ConAu 37R*
Fried, Lawrence 1926-1983 *ConAu 110*
Fried, Marc 1922- *ConAu 77*
Fried, Marc B 1944- *ConAu 77*
Fried, Mary McKenzie Hill 1914- *ConAu 93*
Fried, Morton H 1923- *ConAu 21R*
Fried, Peter A 1943- *ConAu 108*
Fried, Philip *DrAP&F 83*
Fried, Philip Henry 1945- *IntWWP 82*
Fried, Richard M 1941- *ConAu 73*
Fried, William 1945- *ConAu 57*
Friedan, Betty 1921- *ConAu 65,
    ConIsC 2[port], WrDr 84*
Friedberg, Ardy 1935- *ConAu 108*
Friedberg, Gertrude *WrDr 84*
Friedberg, Gertrude 1908- *ConAu 21R,
    ConSFA, TwCSFW*
Friedberg, Martha Asher *DrAP&F 83*
Friedberg, Maurice 1929- *ConAu 1R, -5NR,
    WrDr 84*
Friede, Eleanor Kask 1920- *ConAu 101*
Friedelbaum, Stanley H 1927- *ConAu 37R*
Friedell, Egon 1878-1938 *EncWL 2*
Frieden, Bernard J 1930- *ConAu 10NR, -13R,
    IntAu&W 82, WrDr 84*
Friedenberg, Edgar Z 1921- *ConAu 65,
    ConIsC 1[port]*
Friedenberg, Walter Drew 1928- *ConAu 89*
Friedenthal, Richard 1896-1979 *ConAu 103, -89*
Frieder, Emma 1891- *ConAu P-2*
Friederich, Werner Paul 1905- *ConAu 13R*
Friederichsen, Kathleen 1910- *ConAu 17R*
Friedgut, Theodore H 1931- *ConAu 89*
Friedheim, Robert L 1934- *ConAu 21R*
Friedkin, William 1939- *ConAu 107*
Friedl, Ernestine 1920- *ConAu 37R*
Friedl, John 1945- *ConAu 4NR, -53*
Friedland, Klaus 1920- *IntAu&W 82*
Friedland, Ronald Lloyd 1937-1975 *ConAu 57,
    ConAu P-2*
Friedland, Ronnie 1945- *ConAu 106*
Friedland, Seymour 1928- *ConAu 25R*
Friedland, William H 1923- *ConAu 13R,
    WrDr 84*
Friedlander, Albert H 1927- *ConAu 9NR,
    WrDr 84*
Friedlander, Albert Hoschander 1927-
    ConAu 21R
Friedlander, Ernst Peter 1906-1966 *CreCan 1*
Friedlander, Howard 1941- *ConAu 105*
Friedlander, Joanne K 1930- *ConAu 61,
    SmATA 9*
Friedlander, Stanley Lawrence 1938- *ConAu 17R*
Friedlander, Walter A 1891- *ConAu 37R,
    WrDr 84*
Friedman, Alan Warren 1939- *ConAu 25R,
    WrDr 84*
Friedman, Albert B 1920- *ConAu 1R*
Friedman, Alice R 1900- *ConAu 41R*
Friedman, Arnold D'Arcy 1900-1981 *ConAu 109*
Friedman, Arnold P 1909- *ConAu 1NR, -45*
Friedman, Arthur 1935- *ConAmTC*
Friedman, Avner 1932- *ConAu 53*
Friedman, B H *DrAP&F 83*
Friedman, B H 1926- *ConAu 1R, -3NR,
    ConLC 7, WrDr 84*
Friedman, Barton R 1935- *IntWWP 82*
Friedman, Bernard 1896-1983 *ConAu 110*
Friedman, Bruce Jay *DrAP&F 83*
Friedman, Bruce Jay 1930- *ConAu 9R,
    ConDr 82, ConLC 3, -5, ConNov 82,
    DcLB 2, DcLEL 1940, ModAL,
    ModAL SUP, NatPD 81[port], WorAu,
    WrDr 84*
Friedman, David 1945- *ConAu 89*
Friedman, Debbie *DrAP&F 83*
Friedman, Ed *DrAP&F 83*
Friedman, Edward Ludwig 1903- *ConAu 1R*
Friedman, Elias *WrDr 84*
Friedman, Elizabeth 1893?-1980 *ConAu 102*
Friedman, Estelle Ehrenwald 1920- *ConAu 5R,
    SmATA 7*
Friedman, Eve Rosemary Tibber 1929-
    ConAu 5R
Friedman, Hal *ConAu X*
Friedman, Harold 1942- *ConAu 89*
Friedman, Ina R 1926- *ConAu 53*
Friedman, Irving S 1915- *ConAu 3NR, -45*
Friedman, Isaiah 1921- *ConAu 53*
Friedman, Jacob Horace 1916- *IntAu&W 82,
    IntWWP 82, WrDr 84*

Friedman, Jerrold David *ConAu X*
Friedman, John *WrDr 84*
Friedman, Josephine Troth 1928- *ConAu 77*
Friedman, Joy Troth *ConAu X*
Friedman, Judi 1935- *AuNews 2, ConAu 65*
Friedman, Ken *ConAu 65, DrAP&F 83*
Friedman, Kenneth 1939- *ConAu 25R*
Friedman, Kenneth S 1949- *IntWWP 82*
Friedman, Lawrence J 1940- *ConAu 53*
Friedman, Lawrence M 1930- *WrDr 84*
Friedman, Lawrence Meir 1930- *ConAu 5NR,
    -13R*
Friedman, Lenemaja 1924- *ConAu 61*
Friedman, Leon 1933- *ConAu 81*
Friedman, Lester David 1945- *ConAu 108*
Friedman, Maralyn *DrAP&F 83*
Friedman, Marcia 1925- *ConAu 57*
Friedman, Marvin 1930- *SmATA 33*
Friedman, Maurice Stanley 1921- *ConAu 13R*
Friedman, Melvin J 1928- *ConAu 21R,
    IntAu&W 82, WrDr 84*
Friedman, Michael H 1945- *ConAu 101*
Friedman, Milton 1912- *ConAu 1R, -1NR,
    ConIsC 1[port], IntAu&W 82, WrDr 84*
Friedman, Murray 1926- *ConAu 57*
Friedman, Myles I 1924- *ConAu 6NR, -57*
Friedman, Nancy 1950- *ConAu 107*
Friedman, Norman *DrAP&F 83*
Friedman, Norman 1925- *ConAu 1R, -1NR,
    IntAu&W 82, WrDr 84*
Friedman, Paul *DrAP&F 83*
Friedman, Paul 1899-1972 *ConAu 37R*
Friedman, Paul Belais 1953- *ConAu 110*
Friedman, Ralph 1916- *ConAu 69*
Friedman, Richard *DrAP&F 83*
Friedman, Rose D *ConAu 101*
Friedman, Rosemary 1929- *ConAu 3NR,
    IntAu&W 82, WrDr 84*
Friedman, Roslyn Berger 1924- *ConAu 17R*
Friedman, Roy *DrAP&F 83*
Friedman, Roy 1934- *ConAu 25R*
Friedman, S L *DrAP&F 83, IntWWP 82X*
Friedman, Samuel L 1908- *IntWWP 82*
Friedman, Sanford *DrAP&F 83*
Friedman, Sanford 1928- *ConAu 73*
Friedman, Sara Ann 1935- *ConAu 77*
Friedman, Saul S 1937- *ConAu 57*
Friedman, Sonia *CreCan 1*
Friedman, Stuart 1913- *ConAu 1R*
Friedman, Susan Stanford 1943- *ConAu 109*
Friedman, Thomas L 1953- *ConAu 109*
Friedman, Warner G 1934- *ConAu 97*
Friedman, Winifred 1923?-1975 *ConAu 61*
Friedman-August, Dorothy *DrAP&F 83*
Friedman-Gramatte, Sonia *CreCan 1*
Friedmann, Arnold 1925- *ConAu 41R*
Friedmann, Georges Philippe 1902-1977
    ConAu 104
Friedmann, Herbert 1900- *ConAu 106*
Friedmann, John 1926- *ConAu 85,
    IntAu&W 82*
Friedmann, Thomas *DrAP&F 83*
Friedmann, Wolfgang Gaston 1907-1972
    ConAu 6NR
Friedmann, Yohanan 1936- *ConAu 33R,
    WrDr 84*
Friedrich, Anton *ConAu X*
Friedrich, Carl J 1901- *WrDr 84*
Friedrich, Carl Joachim 1901- *ConAu 69*
Friedrich, Dick *ConAu X*
Friedrich, Heinz 1922- *IntAu&W 82*
Friedrich, Otto 1929- *SmATA 33[port]*
Friedrich, Otto Alva 1929- *ConAu 3NR, -5R*
Friedrich, Paul 1927- *ConAu 29R, WrDr 84*
Friedrich, Richard 1936- *ConAu 103*
Friedrichs, Christopher R 1947- *ConAu 89*
Friedrichs, Robert W 1923- *ConAu 49*
Friedrichs, Yvonne *IntAu&W 82*
Friedson, Anthony M 1924- *ConAu 108*
Friel, Brian 1929- *ConAu 21R, ConDr 82,
    ConLC 5, DcLB 13[port], DcLEL 1940,
    IntAu&W 82, ModBrL SUP, ModWD,
    WorAu, WrDr 84*
Frielink, A Barend 1917- *ConAu 21R*
Friend, Barbara *DrAP&F 83*
Friend, Joseph H 1909-1972 *ConAu P-2*
Friend, Krebs 1895?-1967? *DcLB 4*
Friend, Robert *DrAP&F 83*
Friend, Robert 1913- *ConAu 7NR, -13R,
    WrDr 84*
Friendlich, Dick 1909- *ConAu X, SmATA X*
Friendlich, Richard J 1909- *ConAu P-1,*

SmATA 11
Friendly, Alfred 1911- *ConAu 101,*
IntAu&W 82
Friendly, Fred W 1915- *ConAu 21R*
Friendly, Henry Jacob 1903- *ConAu 103*
Friermood, Elisabeth H 1903- *WrDr 84*
Friermood, Elisabeth Hamilton 1903- *ConAu 1R,*
-1NR, SmATA 5
Fries, Albert Charles 1908- *ConAu 1R, -4NR*
Fries, Erik Olof Elias 1900- *IntAu&W 82*
Fries, Fritz Rudolf 1935- *ConAu 11NR, -25R*
Fries, James Franklin 1938- *ConAu 89*
Fries, Robert Francis 1911- *ConAu 106*
Frieseke, Frances 1914- *IntWWP 82*
Friesel, Uwe 1939- *IntAu&W 82*
Friess, Horace Leland 1900-1975 *ConAu 61, -65*
Friggens, Arthur 1920- *ConAu 103*
Friggieri, Oliver 1937- *IntWWP 82*
Friis, Babbis *ConAu X, SmATA 7*
Friis, Erik J 1913- *WrDr 84*
Friis, Erik Johan 1913- *ConAu 69,*
IntAu&W 82
Friis, Harald T 1893-1976 *ConAu 65*
Friis-Baastad, Babbis Ellinor 1921-1970
ConAu 17R, ConLC 12, SmATA 7
Frijling-Schreuder, E C M 1908- *ConAu 61*
Frillmann, Paul W 1911-1972 *ConAu 37R,*
ConAu P-2
Friman, Alice *DrAP&F 83*
Friman, Alice R 1933- *IntWWP 82*
Frimbo, E M *ConAu X*
Friml, Rudolph 1879-1972 *ConAu 37R*
Frimmer, Steven 1928- *ConAu 33R,*
SmATA 31
Frimoth, Lenore B 1927- *ConAu 5R*
Fringeli, Albin 1899- *IntAu&W 82*
Fringeli, Dieter 1942- *IntAu&W 82*
Frings, Ketti 1915-1981 *ConAu 101, -103*
Frings, Manfred S 1925- *ConAu 8NR, -17R*
Frink, Charles 1928- *NatPD 81[port]*
Frink, Maurice 1895-1972 *ConAu P-2*
Frinta, Mojmir S 1922- *ConAu 25R, WrDr 84*
Fripp, Patricia 1945- *ConAu 93*
Fripp, Thomas William 1864-1931 *CreCan 2*
Frisbee, Lee *DrAP&F 83*
Frisbie, Louise Kelley 1913- *ConAu 61,*
IntAu&W 82
Frisbie, Margery 1923- *ConAu 5R*
Frisbie, Richard P 1926- *ConAu 2NR, -5R*
Frisby, Terence 1932- *ConAu 65, ConDr 82,*
DcLEL 1940, IntAu&W 82, WrDr 84
Frisch, Karl Von 1886- *ConAu 85*
Frisch, Max 1911- *ClDMEL 80, CnMD,*
ConAu 85, ConLC 3, -9, -14, -18, CroCD,
EncWL 2[port], IntWWP 82, ModGL,
ModWD, TwCWr, WhoTwCL, WorAu
Frisch, Morton J 1923- *ConAu 33R*
Frisch, Otto Robert 1904- *ConAu 9R*
Frisch, Paul Z 1926?-1977 *ConAu 73*
Frischauer, Willi 1906- *ConAu 5R, -7NR*
Frischwasser-Ra'anan, H F *ConAu X*
Frise, Adolf 1910- *IntAu&W 82*
Friskey, Margaret Richards 1901- *ConAu 2NR,*
-5R, SmATA 5
Frison, George C 1924- *ConAu 93*
Fritchman, Stephen Hole 1902- *ConAu 105*
Frith, H J 1921- *ConAu 102*
Frith, Harold James *WrDr 84*
Frith, Nigel 1941- *ConAu 69*
Fritko, Dieter 1931- *IntAu&W 82*
Fritsch, Albert J 1933- *WrDr 84*
Fritsch, Albert Joseph 1933- *ConAu 102*
Fritsch, Bruno 1926- *ConAu 11NR, -69*
Fritsch, Charles T 1912- *WrDr 84*
Fritschler, A Lee 1937- *ConAu 33R*
Fritz *ConAu X, IntAu&W 82X*
Fritz, Henry E 1927- *ConAu 17R*
Fritz, Jean 1915- *TwCCW 83, WrDr 84*
Fritz, Jean Guttery 1915- *ChlLR 2, ConAu 1R,*
-5NR, SmATA 1, -29[port]
Fritz, Leah 1931- *ConAu 93*
Fritz, Walter Helmut 1929- *IntWWP 82*
Fritze, Julius Arnold 1918- *ConAu 103*
Frobert, Knud Aage 1927- *IntAu&W 82*
Frobish, Nestle J 1930- *ConAu 101*
Froboess, Harry 1899- *ConAu P-2*
Froding, Gustaf 1860-1911 *ClDMEL 80*
Froebel, Friedrich Wilhelm August 1782-1852
LongCTC
Froelich, Robert Earl 1929- *ConAu 3NR, -45*
Froggy *IntWWP 82X*
Frohlich, Norman 1941- *ConAu 77*

Frohman, Charles E 1901-1976 *ConAu P-2*
Frohock, W M 1908- *ConAu 73*
Froissart, Jean 1338?-1410? *SmATA 28*
Froman, Elizabeth Hull 1920-1975 *ConAu 53,*
ConAu P-1, SmATA 10
Froman, Lewis A, Jr. 1935- *ConAu 5R*
Froman, Nanny Ingeborg 1922- *IntAu&W 82*
Froman, Per Olof 1926- *IntAu&W 82*
Froman, Robert 1917- *ConAu 1R, -1NR,*
SmATA 8
Fromberg, Robert *DrAP&F 83*
Frome, David *ConAu X, TwCA,*
TwCA SUP, TwCCr&M 80
Frome, Michael 1920- *ConAu 1R, -1NR,*
IntAu&W 82, WrDr 84
Fromer, Margot J 1939- *ConAu 110*
Fromkin, David 1932- *ConAu 109*
Fromkin, Victoria A 1923- *ConAu 89*
Fromm, Erich 1900-1980 *ConAu 73, -97,*
IntAu&W 82, TwCA SUP, WhoTwCL
Fromm, Erika 1910- *ConAu 9R, IntAu&W 82*
Fromm, Gary 1933- *ConAu 7NR, -17R*
Fromm, Harold 1933- *ConAu 21R*
Fromm, Herbert 1905- *ConAu 1NR, -49*
Fromm, Lilo 1928- *ConAu 81, IntAu&W 82,*
SmATA 29[port]
Fromme, Babbette Brandt 1925- *ConAu 106*
Frommel, Wolfgang 1902- *IntAu&W 82*
Frommer, Harvey 1937- *ConAu 103*
Froncek, Thomas 1942- *ConAu 81*
Frondizi, Risieri 1910- *ConAu 41R*
Frontier, Tex *ConAu X*
Frooks, Dorothy 1899- *ConAu 57*
Froomkin, Joseph 1927- *ConAu 21R*
Frosch, Thomas Richard 1943- *ConAu 69*
Froscher, Wingate 1918- *ConAu 1R*
Frost, A B 1851-1928 *SmATA 19*
Frost, Carol *DrAP&F 83*
Frost, Carol 1948- *ConAu 11NR, -69*
Frost, Celestine *DrAP&F 83*
Frost, David 1939- *WrDr 84*
Frost, David Paradine 1939- *ConAu 69,*
DcLEL 1940
Frost, Deana *IntWWP 82X*
Frost, Dianna *IntWWP 82X*
Frost, Erica *ConAu X, SmATA X*
Frost, Ernest 1918- *ConAu 9R, IntAu&W 82,*
WrDr 84
Frost, Everett L 1942- *ConAu 65*
Frost, Frank 1929- *ConAu 89*
Frost, Frederick *ConAu X, TwCCr&M 80*
Frost, Gavin 1930- *ConAu 1NR, -45*
Frost, Gerhard Emanuel 1909- *ConAu P-1*
Frost, Helen 1898- *ConAu P-1*
Frost, James A 1918- *ConAu 37R*
Frost, Joe L 1933- *ConAu 25R*
Frost, Joni *ConAu X*
Frost, Lawrence A 1907- *ConAu 11NR, -69*
Frost, Lesley 1899- *ConAu 21R, SmATA 14*
Frost, Lesley 1899-1983 *ConAu 110,*
SmATA 34N
Frost, Leslie Miscampbell 1895-1973 *ConAu 41R*
Frost, Marjorie 1914- *ConAu 25R*
Frost, Max Gilbert 1908- *ConAu P-1*
Frost, Peter Kip 1936- *ConAu 33R, WrDr 84*
Frost, Richard *DrAP&F 83*
Frost, Richard 1929- *ConAu 33R, IntWWP 82,*
WrDr 84
Frost, Richard H 1930- *ConAu 25R*
Frost, Richard T 1926-1972 *ConAu 37R,*
ConAu P-1
Frost, Robert 1874?-1963 *CnMWL, ConAmA,*
ConAu 89, ConLC 1, -3, -4, -9, -10, -13, -15,
-26[port], EncWL 2[port], LongCTC,
ModAL, ModAL SUP, SmATA 14, TwCA,
TwCA SUP, TwCWr, WhoTwCL
Frost, Robert Carlton 1926- *ConAu 53*
Frost, S E, Jr. 1899- *ConAu P-2*
Frost, Stanley Brice 1913- *ConAu 61, WrDr 84*
Frost, William 1917- *ConAu 41R*
Frostic, Gwen 1906- *ConAu 17R, MichAu 80*
Frostick, Michael 1917- *ConAu 9R*
Froy, Herald *ConAu X, WrDr 84*
Froydarlund, Jan Anker 1911- *IntWWP 82*
Frucht, Phyllis 1936- *ConAu 57*
Fruchtenbaum, Arnold G 1943- *ConAu 11NR,*
-61
Fruchter, Benjamin 1914- *ConAu 1R, WrDr 84*
Fruchter, Norman 1937- *ConAu 81*
Fruehling, Rosemary T 1933- *ConAu 33R*
Frugoni, Cesare 1881-1978 *ConAu 73*

Fruhan, William E, Jr. 1943- *ConAu 41R*
Fruits, Wanda Fae 1930- *IntWWP 82*
Frum, Barbara 1937- *ConAu 101*
Fruman, Norman 1923- *ConAu 37R*
Frumkes, Lewis Burke 1939- *IntAu&W 82*
Frumkin, Gene *DrAP&F 83*
Frumkin, Gene 1928- *ConAu 4NR, -9R,*
WrDr 84
Frumkin, Robert M 1928- *ConAu 9NR, -21R*
Fruton, Joseph S 1912- *ConAu 49, WrDr 84*
Fry, Alan 1931- *ConAu 1NR, -45*
Fry, Barbara 1932- *ConAu 25R*
Fry, C George 1936- *ConAu 37R*
Fry, Christine 1943- *ConAu 107*
Fry, Christopher 1907- *CnMD, CnMWL,*
ConAu 9NR, -17R, ConDr 82, ConLC 2,
-10, -14, ConP 80, CroCD, DcLB 13[port],
EncWL 2, LongCTC, ModBrL,
ModBrL SUP, ModWD, TwCA SUP,
TwCWr, WrDr 84
Fry, David *ConAu X*
Fry, Dennis Butler 1907- *ConAu 109*
Fry, Dennis Butler 1907-1983 *ConAu 110*
Fry, Donald K 1937- *ConAu 25R*
Fry, E Maxwell 1899- *ConAu 65*
Fry, Earl H 1947- *ConAu 102*
Fry, Edward 1925- *WrDr 84*
Fry, Edward Bernard 1925- *ConAu 5NR, -9R*
Fry, Hilary G 1922- *ConAu 17R*
Fry, Howard T 1919- *ConAu 37R*
Fry, John 1930- *ConAu 93*
Fry, Lynette *CreCan 2*
Fry, Maggie Culver 1900- *AuNews 1*
Fry, Maxwell *ConAu X*
Fry, Michael G 1934- *ConAu 69*
Fry, P Eileen 1947- *ConAu 104*
Fry, Roger Elliot 1866-1934 *LongCTC, ModBrL,*
TwCA, TwCA SUP
Fry, Ronald W 1949- *ConAu 57, WrDr 84*
Fry, Rosalie K 1911- *TwCCW 83, WrDr 84*
Fry, Rosalie Kingsmill 1911- *ConAu 9R,*
SmATA 3
Fry, Ruth 1878-1962 *LongCTC*
Fry, William Finley, Jr. 1924- *ConAu 5R,*
WrDr 84
Fryatt, Norma R *ConAu 57*
Fryburger, Vernon R, Jr. 1918- *ConAu 1R*
Fryd, Norbert 1913-1976 *ConAu 65*
Frydman, Szajko 1911- *ConAu 25R*
Frye, Alton 1936- *ConAu 21R, WrDr 84*
Frye, Ellen 1940- *ConAu 49*
Frye, Herman Northrup 1912- *DcLEL 1940*
Frye, John 1910- *ConAu 49*
Frye, Keith 1935- *ConAu 53*
Frye, Northrop 1912- *ConAu 5R, -8NR,*
ConLC 24[port], ConLCrt 82, EncWL 2,
IntAu&W 82, WorAu, WrDr 84
Frye, Richard Nelson 1920- *ConAu 3NR, -5R,*
IntAu&W 82, WrDr 84
Frye, Roland 1921- *WrDr 84*
Frye, Roland Mushat 1921- *ConAu 9R,*
IntAu&W 82
Frye, William R 1918- *ConAu 73*
Fryer, Colin Bernard 1933- *WrDr 84*
Fryer, Donald S *ConAu X*
Fryer, Holly C 1908- *ConAu P-1*
Fryer, Jonathan 1950- *ConAu 85, IntAu&W 82*
Fryer, Judith 1939- *ConAu 69*
Fryer, Mary Beacock 1929- *ConAu 97*
Fryer, William T 1900?-1980 *ConAu 93*
Frykenberg, Robert E 1930- *WrDr 84*
Frykenberg, Robert Eric 1930- *ConAu 25R,*
IntAu&W 82
Fryklund, Verne C 1896- *ConAu 13R*
Frykman, John H 1932- *ConAu 33R*
Frym, Gloria *DrAP&F 83*
Frym, Gloria 1947- *ConAu 105, IntWWP 82*
Frymier, Jack Rimmel 1925- *ConAu 17R*
Fryscak, Milan 1932- *ConAu 53*
Fryttkow, Graf Von *IntAu&W 82X*
Fuchida, Mitsuo 1902?-1976 *ConAu 65*
Fuchs, Anton 1920- *IntAu&W 82*
Fuchs, Bruno Gunter 1928- *ModGL*
Fuchs, Daniel *DrAP&F 83*
Fuchs, Daniel 1909- *ConAu 81, ConLC 8,*
-22[port], ConNov 82, DcLB 9, -26[port],
ModAL, ModAL SUP, WhoTwCL,
WorAu 1970, WrDr 84
Fuchs, Daniel 1934- *ConAu 37R*
Fuchs, Elinor 1933- *ConAu 105*
Fuchs, Erich 1916- *ConAu 29R, SmATA 6*
Fuchs, Estelle *ConAu 57*

Fuchs, Jacob 1939- *ConAu 21R*
Fuchs, Jerome H 1922- *ConAu 69*
Fuchs, Josef 1912- *ConAu 21R*
Fuchs, Lawrence Howard 1927- *ConAu 1R, -5NR*
Fuchs, Lucy 1935- *ConAu 73*
Fuchs, Roland J 1933- *ConAu 81*
Fuchs, Victor Robert 1924- *ConAu 1R, -2NR*
Fuchs, Vivian 1908- *ConAu 104, WrDr 84*
Fucilla, Joseph G 1897- *ConAu 89*
Fucini, Renato 1843-1921 *ClDMEL 80*
Fuegi, John 1936- *ConAu 37R, WrDr 84*
Fuehrer, Mark Edwin *DrAP&F 83*
Fueloep-Miller, Rene 1891-1963 *ConAu 110*
Fuentes, Carlos 1928- *AuNews 2, ConAu 10NR, -69, ConLC 3, -8, -10, -13, -22[port], EncWL 2[port], IntAu&W 82, WorAu*
Fuentes, Carlos 1929- *ModLAL, TwCWr, WhoTwCL*
Fuentes, Martha Ayers 1923- *ConAu 73, IntAu&W 82, NatPD 81[port]*
Fuentes, Roberto 1934- *ConAu 57*
Fuentes Blanco, Maria DeLosReyes 1927- *IntAu&W 82, IntWWP 82*
Fuentes Labrador, Juan Luis 1944- *IntAu&W 82*
Fuentes Mohr, Alberto 1928?-1979 *ConAu 85*
Fuerer-Haimendorf, Christoph Von 1909- *ConAu 13R, ConAu P-1*
Fuermann, George Melvin 1918- *ConAu 103*
Fuess, Claude Moore 1885-1963 *TwCA, TwCA SUP*
Fufuka, Karama *ConAu X*
Fugard, Athol 1932- *ConAu 85, ConDr 82, ConLC 5, -9, -14, -25[port], DcLEL 1940, EncWL 2, ModCmwL, TwCWr, WhoTwCL, WorAu 1970, WrDr 84*
Fugate, Francis L 1915- *ConAu 25R*
Fugate, Joe K 1931- *ConAu 21R*
Fugate, Terence 1930- *ConAu 5R*
Fugere, Jean-Paul 1921- *CreCan 2*
Fugitt, Eva D 1929- *ConAu 109*
Fuhmann, Franz 1922- *ModGL*
Fuhrman, Lee 1903?-1977 *ConAu 73*
Fuhrmann, Joseph T 1940- *ConAu 73*
Fuhro, Wilbur J 1914- *ConAu 9R*
Fujikawa, Gyo *SmATA 30*
Fujita, Tamao 1905- *ConAu 37R, SmATA 7*
Fujiwara, Michiko 1946- *ConAu 77, SmATA 15*
Fujiwara, Yoichi 1909- *ConAu 105*
Fuka, Vladimir 1926-1977 *ConAu 104, SmATA 27N*
Fukei, Gladys Arlene 1920- *ConAu 13R*
Fuks, Ladislav 1923- *ClDMEL 80, EncWL 2, ModSL 2*
Fukuda, Haruko 1946- *ConAu 109, IntAu&W 82, WrDr 84*
Fukuda, Tsuneari 1912- *CnMD, ModWD*
Fukuda, Tsutomu 1905- *ConAu 103, DcLEL 1940, WrDr 84*
Fukui, Haruhiro 1935- *ConAu 29R*
Fukutake, Tadashi 1917- *ConAu 5NR, -13R, IntAu&W 82, WrDr 84*
Fukuyama, Yoshio 1921- *ConAu 41R*
Fulani, Richard *DrAP&F 83*
Fulbright, J William 1905- *ConAu 9R, WrDr 84*
Fulbright, James L 1941- *IntAu&W 82*
Fulco, William J 1936- *ConAu 49*
Fuld, James J 1916- *ConAu 21R, IntAu&W 82, WrDr 84*
Fulda, Carl H 1909-1975 *ConAu P-2*
Fulda, Ludwig 1862-1932 *ClDMEL 80*
Fulda, Ludwig 1862-1939 *ModWD*
Fuldauer, Ivan 1927- *ConAu 69*
Fuldheim, Dorothy 1893- *ConAu 49*
Fulford, Robert 1932- *ConAu 89*
Fulford, Roger 1902-1983 *ConAu 109*
Fulford, Roger Thomas Baldwin 1902- *ConAu 65, IntAu&W 82, LongCTC*
Fulker, Tina 1954- *IntWWP 82*
Fulks, Bryan 1897- *ConAu 97*
Full, Harold 1919- *ConAu 17R*
Fullarton, Geraldine *IntWWP 82X*
Fuller, Alfred C 1885-1973 *ConAu 45*
Fuller, Beverley 1927- *ConAu 69*
Fuller, Blair *DrAP&F 83*
Fuller, Blair 1927- *ConAu 9R*
Fuller, Buckminster 1895- *WrDr 84*
Fuller, Catherine Leuthold 1916- *ConAu 29R, SmATA 9*
Fuller, Charles 1939- *ConAu 108,*

ConLC 25[port], NatPD 81[port]
Fuller, David O 1903- *ConAu 53*
Fuller, Dorothy Mason 1898- *ConAu 101*
Fuller, Edgar 1904-1973 *ConAu 45*
Fuller, Edmund 1914- *ConAu 77, DcLEL 1940, SmATA 21[port], WorAu, WrDr 84*
Fuller, Edward C 1907- *ConAu 53*
Fuller, George Newman 1873-1957 *MichAu 80*
Fuller, Harold 1940- *ConAu 65*
Fuller, Helen 1914?-1972 *ConAu 37R*
Fuller, Henry Blake 1857-1929 *ConAu 108, TwCA, TwCA SUP*
Fuller, Hoyt W 1927-1981 *ConAu 103, -53, LivgBAA*
Fuller, Hoyt W 1928- *ConAmTC*
Fuller, Iola 1906- *ConAu X, MichAu 80, SmATA 3*
Fuller, Jean Overton 1915- *ConAu 4NR, -5R, IntAu&W 82, WrDr 84*
Fuller, John 1916- *WrDr 84*
Fuller, John 1937- *ConAu 9NR, WrDr 84*
Fuller, John Frederick Charles 1878-1966 *ConAu P-1, WorAu*
Fuller, John Grant, Jr. 1913- *ConAu 1R, -2NR*
Fuller, John Harold 1916- *ConAu P-1*
Fuller, John Leopold 1937- *ConAu 21R, ConP 80, DcLEL 1940, IntAu&W 82, IntWWP 82, WorAu 1970*
Fuller, Lois Hamilton 1915- *ConAu 1R, SmATA 11*
Fuller, Lon 1902-1978 *ConAu 77, ConAu P-2*
Fuller, Margaret 1810-1850 *SmATA X*
Fuller, Miriam Morris 1933- *ConAu 37R*
Fuller, Paul E 1932- *ConAu 73*
Fuller, Peter 1947- *ConAu 97*
Fuller, R Buckminster 1895- *ConAu 9R, ModAL SUP, WorAu 1970*
Fuller, R Buckminster 1895-1983 *ConAu 109*
Fuller, Reginald Horace 1915- *ConAu 3NR, -5R, WrDr 84*
Fuller, Roger *ConAu X*
Fuller, Roy 1912- *EncWL 2, TwCCW 83, WrDr 84*
Fuller, Roy Broadbent 1912- *ConAu 5R, ConLC 4, ConNov 82, ConP 80, DcLB 15[port], LongCTC, ModBrL, ModBrL SUP, RGFMBP, TwCA SUP, TwCCr&M 80, TwCWr, WhoTwCL*
Fuller, Samuel 1911- *TwCCr&M 80, WrDr 84*
Fuller, Samuel 1912- *DcLB 26[port]*
Fuller, Wayne E 1919- *ConAu 13R*
Fuller, William A 1924- *ConAu 41R*
Fullerton, Alexander 1924- *WrDr 84*
Fullerton, Alexander Fergus 1924- *ConAu 7NR, -17R*
Fullerton, Gail 1927- *ConAu X, WrDr 84*
Fullerton, Gail Jackson 1927- *ConAu 37R*
Fullinwider, Robert King 1942- *ConAu 108*
Fullinwider, S 1933- *ConAu 109*
Fullmer, Daniel W 1922- *ConAu 33R*
Fullmer, J Z 1920- *WrDr 84*
Fullmer, June Z 1920- *ConAu 25R*
Fulmer, Robert M 1939- *ConAu 10NR, -57*
Fulop-Miller, Rene *ConAu X*
Fulop-Miller, Rene 1891-1963 *TwCA, TwCA SUP*
Fulton, Albert Rondthaler 1902- *ConAu 1R*
Fulton, Alice *DrAP&F 83*
Fulton, Gere 1939- *ConAu 53*
Fulton, Len *DrAP&F 83*
Fulton, Len 1934- *ConAu 57*
Fulton, Norman 1927- *ConAu 37R*
Fulton, Paul C 1901- *ConAu P-1*
Fulton, Robert Lester 1926- *ConAu 105*
Fulton, Robin 1937- *ConAu 33R, ConP 80, WrDr 84*
Fults, John Lee 1932- *ConAu 53, SmATA 33*
Fultz, Walter J 1924?-1971 *ConAu 104*
Fulweiler, Howard Wells 1932- *ConAu 77*
Fumento, Rocco *DrAP&F 83*
Fumento, Rocco 1923- *ConAu 1R, WrDr 84*
Funabashi, Seiichi 1904?-1976 *ConAu 65*
Fundaburk, Emma Lila 1922- *ConAu 41R*
Funderburk, Guy B 1902- *ConAu 45*
Funderburk, Thomas Ray 1928- *ConAu 17R*
Fune, Jonathan *IntAu&W 82X*
Funigiello, Philip J 1939- *ConAu 65*
Funk, Arthur Layton 1914- *ConAu 21R*
Funk, Nancy Melich 1942- *ConAmTC*
Funk, Peter V K 1921- *ConAu 21R*
Funk, Rainer 1943- *ConAu 109*
Funk, Robert Walter 1926- *ConAu 33R*

Funk, Thompson 1911- *ConAu 2NR, -49, SmATA 7*
Funk, Tom *ConAu X, SmATA 7*
Funk, Wilfred John 1883-1965 *ConAu 89*
Funke, Lewis 1912- *ConAu 49, SmATA 11*
Funkhouser, Erica *DrAP&F 83*
Funt, Julian 1907?-1980 *ConAu 97*
Funt, Marilyn 1937- *ConAu 102*
Fuoss, Robert Martin 1912-1980 *ConAu 93*
Furbank, P N 1920- *ConAu 21R*
Furbee, Leonard J 1896?-1975 *ConAu 61*
Furch, Janne *IntAu&W 82X*
Furchgott, Terry 1948- *ConAu 105, SmATA 29*
Furer, Howard B 1934- *ConAu 33R*
Furey, Michael *ConAu X*
Furfey, Paul Hanly 1896- *ConAu P-2*
Furgurson, Ernest B 1929- *ConAu 73*
Furgurson, Pat *ConAu X*
Furley, David John 1922- *ConAu 108*
Furman, Laura *ConAu 104, DrAP&F 83*
Furmanov, Dmitri Andreyevich 1891-1926 *TwCWr*
Furmanov, Dmitriy Andreyevich 1891-1926 *ClDMEL 80*
Furnas, J C 1905- *ConAu 77*
Furnas, Joseph Chamberlain 1905- *WorAu*
Furnberg, Louis 1909-1957 *CnMD*
Furneaux, Rupert 1908- *ConAu 1R, -1NR*
Furness, Edna 1916- *WrDr 84*
Furness, Edna L 1906- *ConAu 37R*
Furness, Edna Lue *IntAu&W 82*
Furnish, Dorothy Jean 1921- *ConAu 106*
Furnish, Victor Paul 1931- *ConAu 10NR, -21R, WrDr 84*
Furniss, Edgar Stephenson 1890-1972 *ConAu 37R*
Furniss, Norman Francis 1922- *ConAu 1R*
Furniss, Tim 1948- *ConAu 109*
Furniss, W Todd 1921- *ConAu 57*
Furnivall, Frederick James 1825-1910 *LongCTC*
Furphy, Joseph 1843-1912 *EncWL 2, ModCmwL, TwCWr*
Furrer, Juerg 1939- *ConAu 69*
Furse, John 1932- *ConAu 109, WrDr 84*
Furst, Alan 1941- *ConAu 69*
Furst, Lilian R 1931- *WrDr 84*
Furst, Lilian Renee 1931- *ConAu 102*
Furtado, Celso 1920- *ConAu 9NR, -17R, IntAu&W 82*
Furtado, R DeL 1917- *IntAu&W 82*
Furth, Alex *ConAu X*
Furth, George 1932- *ConAu 73, ConDr 82D, NatPD 81[port]*
Furth, Hans G 1920- *ConAu 45*
Furthman, Jules 1888-1966 *DcLB 26[port]*
Furtney, Diane *DrAP&F 83*
Furtwangler, Virginia *DrAP&F 83*
Furukawa, Toshi 1924- *ConAu 2NR, -45, SmATA 24[port]*
Fusco, Margie 1949- *ConAu 85*
Fusero, Clemente 1913-1975 *ConAu 81*
Fusfeld, Daniel R 1922- *ConAu 45*
Fuson, Ben W 1911- *WrDr 84*
Fuson, Benjamin Willis 1911- *ConAu 37R, IntAu&W 82*
Fuson, Robert Henderson 1927- *ConAu 89*
Fuss, Peter 1932- *ConAu 9NR, -21R*
Fussell, Edwin 1922- *ConAu 53*
Fussell, G E 1889- *ConAu 3NR*
Fussell, George Edwin 1889- *ConAu 5R, IntAu&W 82, WrDr 84*
Fussell, Paul 1924- *ConAu 8NR, -17R*
Fussenegger, Gertrud 1912- *IntAu&W 82*
Fussner, F Smith 1920- *ConAu 5NR*
Fussner, Frank Smith 1920- *ConAu 1R, WrDr 84*
Fust, Milan 1888-1967 *ClDMEL 80*
Futrell, Gene Allen 1928- *ConAu 107*
Futrelle, Jacques 1875-1912 *TwCA, TwCCr&M 80*
Futuyma, Douglas Joel 1942- *ConAu 108*
Fyfe, H B 1918- *ConSFA, TwCSFW, WrDr 84*
Fyffe, Don 1925- *ConAu 25R*
Fyleman, Rose 1877-1957 *LongCTC, SmATA 21[port], TwCA, TwCA SUP, TwCCW 83*
Fyler, John M 1943- *ConAu 89*
Fyodorov, Yevgeny Konstantinovich *ConAu X*
Fysh, Wilmot Hudson 1895- *ConAu 17R*
Fyson, J G 1904- *ConAu P-2, IntAu&W 82X, TwCCW 83, WrDr 84*

Fyson, Jenny Grace 1904-   *IntAu&W 82*
Fyzee, Asaf Ali Asghar 1899-   *DcLEL 1940*

Fyson, Jenny Grace 1904-   *IntAu&W 82*
Fyzee, Asaf Ali Asghar 1899-   *DcLEL 1940*

G

G B *ConAu X*
G B S *LongCTC*
G K C *LongCTC*
Gaa, Charles J 1911- *ConAu 17R*
Gaan, Margaret 1914- *ConAu 81*
Gaard, David 1945- *ConAu 25R*
Gaathon, A L 1898- *ConAu 49*
Gabbard, G N *DrAP&F 83*
Gabbard, Lucina P 1922- *ConAu 110*
Gabel, Creighton 1931- *ConAu 106*
Gabel, Joseph 1912- *ConAu 101*
Gabel, Margaret 1938- *ConAu 33R*
Gabel, Medard 1946- *ConAu 11NR, –65*
Gaberman, Judith *DrAP&F 83*
Gable, Tom 1944- *ConAu 93*
Gablehouse, Charles John 1928- *ConAu 21R,*
  IntAu&W 82
Gablik, Suzi 1934- *ConAu 33R, WrDr 84*
Gabo, Naum 1890-1977 *ConAu 73, ConAu P-2*
Gabor, Dennis 1900- *ConAu 17R*
Gabor, Georgia M 1930- *ConAu 108*
Gabor, Mark 1939- *ConAu 81*
Gaboury, Antonio 1919- *ConAu 2NR, –45*
Gabre-Medhin, Tsegaye 1936- *ConAu 101*
Gabriel, A L 1907- *ConAu 5R, –6NR*
Gabriel, Astrik L 1907- *IntAu&W 82*
Gabriel, Daniel *DrAP&F 83*
Gabriel, H 1922- *ConAu 77*
Gabriel, Joyce 1949- *ConAu 97*
Gabriel, Jueri 1940- *ConAu 93*
Gabriel, Juri 1940- *WrDr 84*
Gabriel, Juri Evald 1940- *IntAu&W 82*
Gabriel, Mabel McAfee 1884?-1976 *ConAu 65*
Gabriel, Margot *IntAu&W 82X*
Gabriel, Philip Louis 1918- *ConAu 93,*
  IntAu&W 82
Gabriel, Phyllis 1949- *IntAu&W 82*
Gabriel, Ralph Henry 1890- *ConAu 13R,*
  WrDr 84
Gabriel, Richard Alan 1942- *ConAu 104*
Gabriel, Roman 1940- *ConAu 107*
Gabriel-Robinet, Louis 1909-1975 *ConAu 61*
Gabriel Y Galan, Jose Maria 1870-1905
  ClDMEL 80
Gabriella, Katharyn Rosa 1943- *IntWWP 82*
Gabrielson, Frank 1911?-1980 *ConAu 93*
Gabrielson, Ira N 1889-1977 *ConAu 73,*
  ConAu P-1
Gabrielson, James 1917- *ConAu 29R*
Gach, Gary 1947- *ConAu 77, IntWWP 82*
Gach, Gary J *DrAP&F 83*
Gach, Michael Reed 1952- *ConAu 110*
Gackenbach, Dick *SmATA 30*
Gadamer, Hans-Georg 1900- *ConAu 85*
Gadd, David 1912- *ConAu 57*
Gadda, Carlo Emilio 1893-1973 *ClDMEL 80,*
  ConAu 89, ConLC 11, EncWL 2, ModRL,
  TwCWr, WhoTwCL, WorAu
Gadda-Conti, Piero 1902- *IntAu&W 82*
Gaddes, Peter *ConAu X*
Gaddis, J Wilson 1910?-1975 *ConAu 57*
Gaddis, John Lewis 1941- *ConAu 45*
Gaddis, Peggy 1895-1966 *ConAu X*
Gaddis, Thomas Eugene 1908- *ConAu 29R*

Gaddis, Vincent Hayes 1913- *ConAu 13R,*
  WrDr 84
Gaddis, William *DrAP&F 83*
Gaddis, William 1922- *ConAu 17R, ConLC 1,*
  –3, –6, –8, –10, –19, ConNov 82, DcLB 2,
  DcLEL 1940, EncWL 2, ModAL SUP,
  WorAu, WrDr 84
Gaddy, C Welton 1941- *ConAu 61*
Gadler, Steve J 1905- *ConAu 97*
Gadney, Reg 1941- *ConAu 3NR, –49,*
  TwCCr&M 80, WrDr 84
Gado, Frank 1936- *ConAu 49*
Gadouas, Robert *CreCan 2*
Gadpaille, Warren J 1924- *ConAu 61*
Gaebelein, Frank Ely 1899- *ConAu 1R, –2NR,*
  –13R
Gaeddert, Lou Ann 1931- *ConAu 73,*
  SmATA 20
Gaedeke, Ralph M 1941- *ConAu 9NR, –65*
Gaeng, Paul A 1924- *ConAu 37R*
Gaer, Joseph 1897- *ConAu 9R*
Gaer, Yossef *ConAu X*
Gaertner, Ken *DrAP&F 83*
Gaess, Roger *DrAP&F 83*
Gaess, Roger 1934- *ConAu 104*
Gaff, Jerry Gene 1936- *ConAu 85*
Gaffney, Elizabeth *DrAP&F 83*
Gaffney, James 1931- *ConAu 6NR, –57*
Gaffney, Mason 1923- *ConAu 3NR, –49*
Gafford, Charlotte *DrAP&F 83*
Gag, Flavia 1907-1979 *ConAu 5R, –104,*
  SmATA 24N
Gag, Wanda 1893-1946 *ChlLR 4[port],*
  DcLB 22[port], TwCA, TwCA SUP,
  TwCCW 83
Gagarin, Michael 1942- *ConAu 89*
Gage, Edwin 1943- *ConAu 85*
Gage, Mary 1940- *IntAu&W 82*
Gage, Nathaniel Lees 1917- *ConAu 69*
Gage, Nicholas *ConAu 49*
Gage, Paul *IntWWP 82X*
Gage, William 1915-1973 *ConAu P-2*
Gage, William W 1925- *ConAu 13R*
Gage, Wilson *WrDr 84*
Gage, Wilson 1922- *ConAu X, SmATA 3*
Gagen, Robert Ford 1847-1926 *CreCan 1*
Gager, John Goodrich, Jr. 1937- *ConAu 104*
Gager, Nancy Land 1932?-1980 *ConAu 93*
Gagliano, Frank 1931- *ConAu 1NR, –45,*
  ConDr 82, NatPD 81[port], WrDr 84
Gagliardo, John G 1933- *ConAu 21R, WrDr 84*
Gagliardo, Ruth Garver 1895?-1980 *ConAu 104,*
  SmATA 22N
Gagnard, Frank Lewis 1929- *ConAmTC*
Gagnier, Claire 1924- *CreCan 1*
Gagnier, Ed 1936- *ConAu 65*
Gagnier, Gerald Ray D'Iese 1926-1951? *CreCan 2*
Gagnier, Josephat Jean 1885-1949 *CreCan 2*
Gagnon, Charles 1934- *CreCan 2*
Gagnon, Clarence Alphonse 1881-1942 *CreCan 1*
Gagnon, Jean-Louis 1913- *ConAu 21R,*
  CreCan 1
Gagnon, John H 1931- *ConAu 33R*
Gagnon, Maurice 1912- *CreCan 2*

Gagnon, Paul Adelard 1925- *ConAu 104*
Gahagan, Helen *ConAu X*
Gahagan, Jayne D 1929?-1983 *ConAu 110*
Gaherty, Sherry 1951- *ConAu 57*
Gahl, Christoph Martin 1947- *IntAu&W 82*
Gaida-Gaidamavicius, Pranas 1914- *IntAu&W 82*
Gail, Marzieh *ConAu 11NR, –69*
Gailey, Harry A 1926- *ConAu 1NR, –45*
Gailey, James Herbert, Jr. 1916- *ConAu 5R*
Gailmor, William S 1910?-1970 *ConAu 104*
Gainer, Bernard 1944- *ConAu 109*
Gaines, Bill *ConAu X*
Gaines, Diana 1912- *ConAu 1R*
Gaines, Ernest J *DrAP&F 83*
Gaines, Ernest J 1933- *AuNews 1, ConAu 6NR,*
  –9R, ConLC 3, –11, –18, ConNov 82,
  DcLB Y80A[port], –2, IntAu&W 82,
  LivgBAA, ModBlW, WorAu 1970,
  WrDr 84
Gaines, Frederick *DrAP&F 83*
Gaines, Jack *ConAu X*
Gaines, Jacob 1918- *ConAu 101*
Gaines, Pierce Welch 1905- *ConAu 13R*
Gaines, Richard L 1925- *ConAu 49*
Gaines, William Maxwell 1922- *ConAu 108*
Gainham, Sarah *WrDr 84*
Gainham, Sarah 1922- *ConAu X, DcLEL 1940,*
  TwCCr&M 80
Gains, Larry 1900-1983 *ConAu 110*
Gainsbrugh, Glen M 1949- *ConAu 25R*
Gainsbrugh, Martin R 1907-1977 *ConAu 69*
Gainsburg, Joseph 1894- *ConAu 5R*
Gainza Paz, Alberto 1899-1977 *ConAu 73, –77*
Gaiser, Gerd 1908-1976 *ClDMEL 80, ModGL,*
  TwCWr, WorAu
Gaite, Francis *ConAu X, TwCCr&M 80*
Gaither, Frances Ormond Jones 1889-1955
  TwCA SUP
Gaither, Gant 1917- *ConAu 9R*
Gaitskell, Charles D 1908- *ConAu 29R*
Gajdusek, D Carleton 1923- *WrDr 84*
Gajdusek, Robert Elemer 1925- *ConAu 102*
Gajdusek, Robin *ConAu X*
Gal, Allon 1934- *ConAu 1NR, –45*
Gal, Hans 1890- *ConAu 5R, IntAu&W 82,*
  WrDr 84
Gal, Istvan 1912-1982 *ConAu 107*
Gal, Laszlo 1933- *SmATA 32*
Gala, Antonio 1936- *ClDMEL 80*
Galaction, Gala 1879-1961 *ClDMEL 80*
Galai, Schmuel 1933- *WrDr 84*
Galai, Shmuel 1933- *ConAu 107*
Galambos, Louis 1931- *ConAu 81*
Galamian, Ivan 1903-1981 *ConAu 108*
Galand, Rene 1923- *ConAu 45, IntAu&W 82*
Galanoy, Terry 1927- *ConAu 4NR, –45*
Galanskov, Yuri 1939?-1972 *ConAu 37R*
Galantay, Ervin Yvan 1930- *ConAu 101*
Galante, Pierre 1909- *ConAu 13R, WrDr 84*
Galanter, Eugene 1924- *ConAu 1R*
Galassi, Jonathan 1949- *ConAu 101*
Galatopoulos, Stelios 1932- *ConAu 110,*
  WrDr 84
Galbraith, Clare K 1919- *ConAu 33R*

Galbraith, Georgie Starbuck 1909-1980 *ConAu 97,*
  ConAu P-1
Galbraith, Jean 1906- *ConAu 37R, WrDr 84*
Galbraith, John Kenneth 1908- *ConAu 21R,*
  ConIsC 1[port], LongCTC, WorAu,
  WrDr 84
Galbraith, John S 1916- *ConAu 5R, -6NR*
Galbraith, Madelyn 1897-1976 *ConAu P-2*
Galbraith, Vivian Hunter 1889-1976 *ConAu 73*
Galbraith, Vivian Hunter 1891?-1976 *ConAu 69*
Galbreath, Robert 1938- *ConAu 41R*
Galczynski, Konstanty Ildefons 1905-1953
  CIDMEL 80, EncWL 2, ModSL 2
Galdone, Paul 1914- *ConAu 73, SmATA 17*
Galdos *TwCA, TwCA SUP*
Galdos, Benito Perez 1845-1920 *ModRL*
Gale, Barry 1935- *ConAu 110*
Gale, Bill *ConAu X*
Gale, Elliot N 1938- *ConAu 110*
Gale, Herbert M 1907- *ConAu P-1*
Gale, John *ConAu X*
Gale, Raymond Floyd 1918- *ConAu 25R*
Gale, Richard M 1932- *ConAu 25R*
Gale, Richard Nelson 1896-1982 *ConAu 107*
Gale, Robert Lee 1919- *ConAu 3NR, -9R,*
  IntAu&W 82
Gale, Vi *ConAu 33R, ConP 80, DrAP&F 83,*
  IntWWP 82, WrDr 84
Gale, Wade R 1925- *IntAu&W 82*
Gale, William 1925- *ConAu 97*
Gale, William C *ConAu X*
Gale, William Daniel 1906- *ConAu 107,*
  WrDr 84
Gale, William Keene 1940- *ConAmTC*
Gale, Zona *DrAP&F 83*
Gale, Zona 1874-1938 *CnMD, ConAmA,*
  ConAu 105, DcLB 9[port], LongCTC,
  ModWD, TwCA, TwCA SUP,
  TwCLC 7[port], TwCWr
Galeano, Eduardo H 1940- *ConAu 29R*
Galella, Ron 1931- *AuNews 1, ConAu 53,*
  WrDr 84
Galenson, Walter 1914- *ConAu 11NR, -25R,*
  WrDr 84
Galewitz, Herb 1928- *ConAu 41R*
Galfo, Armand J 1924- *ConAu 17R*
Galich, Aleksandr Arkadyevich 1919-1977
  CIDMEL 80
Galich, Alexander 1918?-1977 *ConAu 73*
Galilea, Segundo 1928- *ConAu 105*
Galinsky, Ellen 1942- *ConAu 9NR, -65,*
  SmATA 23[port]
Galinsky, G Karl 1942- *ConAu 33R, WrDr 84*
Galipault, John Burton 1930- *IntAu&W 82*
Galipeau, Jacques 1924- *CreCan 1*
Gall, Istvan 1931- *IntAu&W 82*
Gall, Meredith D 1942- *ConAu 6NR, -53*
Gall, Morris 1907- *ConAu 45*
Gall, Sally M *DrAP&F 83*
Gall, Sally M 1941- *ConAu 110*
Gallacher, Tom 1934- *ConDr 82, IntAu&W 82,*
  WrDr 84
Gallager, Gale *ConAu X*
Gallagher, Buell Gordon 1904- *ConAu 65*
Gallagher, Charles A 1927- *ConAu 9NR, -61*
Gallagher, David P 1944- *ConAu 45*
Gallagher, Dorothy 1935- *ConAu 65*
Gallagher, Edward J 1892?-1978 *ConAu 81*
Gallagher, Idella J 1917- *ConAu 108*
Gallagher, James Roswell 1903- *ConAu 57,*
  WrDr 84
Gallagher, John F 1936- *ConAu 17R*
Gallagher, Katherine 1935- *IntWWP 82*
Gallagher, Kent G 1933- *ConAu 33R*
Gallagher, Louis Joseph 1885-1972 *ConAu 37R*
Gallagher, Mary 1947- *ConAu 97, NatPD 81*
Gallagher, Sister Mary Dominic 1917-
  ConAu 17R
Gallagher, Matthew P 1919- *ConAu 5R*
Gallagher, Patricia *ConAu 11NR, -65,*
  TwCRGW, WrDr 84
Gallagher, Patrick 1930- *ConAu 45*
Gallagher, Rachel *ConAu 89*
Gallagher, Richard Farrington 1926- *ConAu 1R,*
  -6NR
Gallagher, Robert E 1922- *ConAu 13R*
Gallagher, Tess *ConP 80, DrAP&F 83,*
  WrDr 84
Gallagher, Tess 1943- *ConAu 106*
Gallagher, Tess 1944- *ConLC 18*
Gallagher, Thomas *ConAu 1R, -5NR*
Gallagher, William M 1923-1975 *ConAu 89*

Gallaher, Art, Jr. 1925- *ConAu 1R, -3NR,*
  WrDr 84
Gallahue, David L 1943- *ConAu 77*
Gallahue, John 1930- *ConAu 110*
Gallant, Christine C 1940- *ConAu 106*
Gallant, James *DrAP&F 83*
Gallant, Mavis *DrAP&F 83*
Gallant, Mavis 1922- *ConAu 69, ConLC 7, -18,*
  ConNov 82, CreCan 2, DcLEL 1940,
  WorAu, WrDr 84
Gallant, Roy Arthur 1924- *ConAu 4NR, -5R,*
  ConLC 17, SmATA 4, WrDr 84
Gallant, T Grady 1920- *ConAu 5R, WrDr 84*
Gallardo, Jose Luis 1927- *IntAu&W 82*
Gallati, Mary Ernestine *ConAu 5R*
Gallati, Robert R J 1913- *ConAu 1R, -1NR*
Galle, F C 1919- *ConAu 61*
Galle, William 1938- *ConAu 93*
Gallegly, J S 1898- *ConAu 5R*
Gallegos, Romulo 1884-1968? *TwCWr*
Gallegos, Romulo 1884-1969 *EncWL 2,*
  ModLAL
Galler, David 1929- *ConAu 25R*
Galler, Meyer 1914- *ConAu 89*
Gallerite, The *ConAu X*
Gallery, Dan *ConAu X*
Gallery, Daniel V 1901-1977 *ConAu 13R, -69*
Galleymore, Frances 1946- *WrDr 84*
Gallico, Paul 1897-1976 *ASpks, AuNews 1,*
  ConAu 5R, -65, -69, ConLC 2,
  DcLB 9[port], SmATA 13, TwCA SUP,
  TwCWr
Gallie, Menna Humphreys 1920- *ConAu 1R,*
  -1NR
Gallie, W B 1912- *ConAu 85*
Gallienne *TwCA, TwCA SUP*
Gallienne, Margaret *IntWWP 82X*
Gallienne, Margaret Ellen 1913- *IntWWP 82*
Gallimard, Gaston 1881-1975 *ConAu 61*
Gallimore, Ronald 1938- *ConAu 65*
Gallin, Sister Mary Alice 1921- *ConAu 13R*
Galliner, Peter 1920- *IntAu&W 82*
Gallix, Francois 1939- *ConAu 109*
Gallman, Waldemar J 1899-1980 *ConAu 101,*
  ConAu P-1
Gallner, Sheldon M 1949- *ConAu 53*
Gallo, Louis *DrAP&F 83*
Gallo, Louis Jacob 1945- *IntWWP 82*
Gallo, Max 1932- *ConAu 85*
Gallo, Rose Adrienne 1938- *ConAu 107*
Gallois, Claire 1938- *ConAu 85, IntAu&W 82*
Gallon, Arthur J 1915- *ConAu 57*
Gallop, David 1928- *ConAu 65*
Gallop, Jane 1952- *ConAu 107*
Galloping Gourmet *ConAu X*
Galloway, A D 1920- *ConAu 25R*
Galloway, Allan Douglas 1920- *WrDr 84*
Galloway, David D 1937- *ConAu 21R*
Galloway, George Barnes 1898-1967 *ConAu 1R,*
  -103
Galloway, John C 1915-1970 *ConAu P-2*
Galloway, Jonathan F 1939- *ConAu 77*
Galloway, Joseph S 1941- *ConAu 73*
Galloway, Margaret Cecilia 1915- *ConAu 13R*
Gallu, Samuel *AuNews 2, ConAu 85*
Gallucci, Robert L 1946- *ConAu 61*
Gallun, Raymond Z 1910- *ConSFA*
Gallun, Raymond Z 1911- *ConAu 9NR, -65,*
  IntAu&W 82, TwCSFW, WrDr 84
Gallup, Dick *DrAP&F 83*
Gallup, Dick 1941- *ConAu 33R*
Gallup, Donald 1913- *ConAu 11NR*
Gallup, Donald Clifford 1913- *ConAu 25R*
Gallup, George 1901- *WrDr 84*
Gallup, George Horace 1901- *ConAu 13R,*
  LongCTC
Gallup, Lucy 1911- *MichAu 80*
Gallwey, W Timothy 1938- *ConAu 4NR, -53,*
  WrDr 84
Gallwitz, Klaus 1930- *ConAu 109*
Galouye, Daniel F 1911- *TwCSFW, WrDr 84*
Galouye, Daniel F 1920-1976 *ConAu 9R,*
  ConSFA
Galston, Arthur William 1920- *ConAu 102*
Galsworthy, John 1867-1933 *CnMD, CnMWL,*
  ConAu 104, DcLB 10[port], EncWL 2,
  LongCTC, ModBrL, ModBrL SUP,
  ModWD, TwCA, TwCA SUP, TwCLC 1,
  TwCWr, WhoTwCL
Galt, Thomas Franklin, Jr. 1908- *ConAu 5R,*
  MichAu 80, SmATA 5

Galt, Tom *DrAP&F 83*
Galt, Tom 1908- *ConAu X, MichAu 80,*
  SmATA 5
Galton, Sir Francis 1822-1911 *LongCTC*
Galton, Lawrence 1913- *ConAu 6NR, -57*
Galub, Jack 1915- *ConAu 85*
Galus, Henry S 1923- *ConAu 5R*
Galvan, Roberto A *DrAP&F 83*
Galvao, Henrique 1895- *TwCWr*
Galvez, Manuel 1882-1962 *EncWL 2, ModLAL,*
  TwCWr
Galvez DeMontalvo, Luis 1927- *ConAu X*
Galvin, Brendan *DrAP&F 83*
Galvin, Brendan 1938- *ConAu 1NR, -45,*
  DcLB 5[port]
Galvin, James 1951- *ConAu 108*
Galvin, John R 1929- *ConAu 21R*
Galvin, Patrick 1927- *ConAu 102, IntAu&W 82*
Galvin, Thomas J 1932- *ConAu 10NR, -13R*
Galway, James 1939- *ConAu 105*
Galway, Norman *ConAu X*
Galway, Robert Conington *TwCCr&M 80*
Galwey, Geoffrey 1912- *WrDr 84*
Gam, Rita 1927- *ConAu 45*
Gambaccini, Peter 1950- *ConAu 105*
Gambaro, Griselda 1928- *ModLAL*
Gambino, Thomas D 1942- *ConAu 101*
Gamble, Andrew Michael 1947- *ConAu 69,*
  WrDr 84
Gamble, Frederick John 1904- *ConAu P-1*
Gamble, Mary *ConAu X*
Gamble, Michael 1943- *ConAu 110*
Gamble, Quo Vadis Gex 1950- *LivgBAA*
Gamble, Sidney David 1890-1968 *ConAu P-1*
Gamble, Teri Kwal 1947- *ConAu 110*
Gamboa, Manuel Manazar *DrAP&F 83*
Gamboa, Reymundo *DrAP&F 83*
Gambrell, Herbert Pickens 1898- *ConAu 1R*
Gambrill, Eileen 1934- *ConAu 89*
Gambs, John S 1899- *ConAu 13R*
Gamer, Robert E 1938- *ConAu 65*
Gamerdinger, Senta 1925- *IntAu&W 82*
Gamerman, Martha 1941- *ConAu 77,*
  SmATA 15
Gamillscheg, Felix 1921- *IntAu&W 82*
Gamm, David B 1948- *ConAu 69*
Gammage, Allen Z 1917- *ConAu 5R, -11NR*
Gammage, Bill *ConAu X*
Gammage, William Leonard 1942- *ConAu 10NR,*
  -57
Gammelgaard, Knud 1939- *IntAu&W 82*
Gammelgaard, Per 1948- *IntWWP 82*
Gammell, Susanna Valentine Mitchell 1897?-1979
  ConAu 85
Gammon, Roland I 1920-1981 *ConAu 103, -49*
Gammond, Peter 1925- *ConAu 81*
Gamoran, Mamie G 1900- *ConAu 3NR, -5R,*
  IntAu&W 82
Gamow, George 1904-1968 *ConAu 102, -93,*
  TwCA SUP
Gamsakhurdia, Konstantine 1891-1975 *EncWL 2*
Gamson, F D 1963- *IntWWP 82*
Gamson, Leland Pablo *DrAP&F 83*
Gamson, Leland Pablo 1950- *IntWWP 82*
Gamson, William A 1934- *WrDr 84*
Gamson, William Anthony 1934- *ConAu 33R*
Gamst, Frederick C 1936- *ConAu 11NR*
Gamst, Frederick Charles 1936- *ConAu 29R,*
  WrDr 84
Gance, Abel 1889-1981 *ConAu 108*
Gandalac, Lennard *ConAu X*
Gandee, Lee R 1917- *ConAu 33R*
Gandevia, Bryan Harle 1925- *ConAu 106,*
  WrDr 84
Gandley, Kenneth Royce *WrDr 84*
Gandley, Kenneth Royce 1920- *ConAu 69,*
  IntAu&W 82
Gandolfo, Joe M 1936- *ConAu 105*
Gangel, Kenneth O 1935- *ConAu 25R*
Gangemi, Kenneth *DrAP&F 83*
Gangemi, Kenneth 1937- *ConAu 29R*
Gangewere, Robert J 1936- *ConAu 89*
Ganivet, Angel 1865-1898 *CIDMEL 80*
Ganley, Albert Charles 1918- *ConAu 13R*
Gann, Ernest K 1910- *WrDr 84*
Gann, Ernest Kellogg 1910- *DcLEL 1940*
Gann, Ernest Kellogg 1910- *AuNews 1,*
  ConAu 1R, -1NR, ConLC 23[port],
  TwCWr, WorAu
Gann, L H 1924- *ConAu 3NR*
Gann, Lewis Henry 1924- *ConAu 5R,*
  IntAu&W 82, WrDr 84

Gann, Walter *TwCWW*
Gannello, Alfreda Mavis 1926- *IntWWP 82*
Gannello, Mavis *IntWWP 82X*
Gannett, Lewis Stiles 1891-1966 *ConAu 89,*
  TwCA, TwCA SUP
Gannett, Ruth Chrisman 1896-1979 *SmATA 33*
Gannett, Ruth Stiles 1923- *ConAu 21R,*
  SmATA 3, TwCCW 83, WrDr 84
Gannold, John *IntAu&W 82X*
Gannon, Robert Haines 1931- *ConAu 4NR, –9R,*
  SmATA 8
Gannon, Robert Ignatius 1893-1978 *ConAu 77,*
  ConAu P-1
Gannon, Thomas M 1936- *ConAu 109*
Gans, Bruce Michael *DrAP&F 83*
Gans, Bruce Michael 1951- *ConAu 81*
Gans, Eric L 1941- *ConAu 33R, WrDr 84*
Gans, Herbert J 1927- *ConAu 1R, –6NR,*
  WrDr 84
Gans, Roma 1894- *ConAu 77*
Gans-Ruedin, E 1915- *ConAu 65*
Gansberg, Judith M 1947- *ConAu 85*
Ganshof, Francois-Louis 1895- *ConAu P-2*
Ganss, George Edward 1905- *ConAu 49*
Gant, Chuck *ConAu X*
Gant, Jonathan *ConAu X, WrDr 84*
Gant, Lisbeth A 1948- *LivgBAA*
Gant, Matthew *ConAu X*
Gant, Phyllis 1922- *ConAu 57*
Gant, Richard *WrDr 84*
Gantner, Neilma *WrDr 84*
Gantner, Neilma Baillieu 1922- *ConAu 104*
Gantos, Jack *ConAu X, SmATA X*
Gantos, John, Jr. 1951- *ConAu 65, SmATA 20*
Gantry, Susan Nadler 1947- *ConAu 61*
Gantt, Fred, Jr. 1922-197-? *ConAu 3NR, –9R*
Gantt, William Andrew Horsley 1893-1980
  ConAu 102, –97
Gantz, Charlotte Orr 1909- *ConAu 49*
Gantzer, Colleen *ConAu X*
Gantzer, Hugh 1931- *ConAu 61*
Ganz, Arthur 1928- *ConAu 49*
Ganz, David L 1951- *ConAu 105*
Ganz, Margaret Leonore 1927- *ConAu 45*
Ganzel, Dewey Alvin, Jr. 1927- *ConAu 25R*
Ganzglass, Martin Richard 1941- *ConAu 33R*
Ganzo, Robert 1898- *WorAu*
Gaos, Vicente 1919- *ClDMEL 80*
Gapanov, Boris 1934?-1972 *ConAu 37R*
Gara, Larry 1922- *ConAu 53*
Garab, Arra M 1930- *ConAu 81*
Garant, Albert Antonio Serge *CreCan 2*
Garant, Serge 1929- *CreCan 2*
Garard, Ira D 1888- *ConAu 73*
Garaudy, Roger 1913- *ClDMEL 80*
Garb, Solomon 1920- *ConAu 9NR, –13R,*
  WrDr 84
Garbarino, Joseph William 1919- *ConAu 53*
Garbarino, Merwyn S *ConAu 77*
Garber, Eugene K *DrAP&F 83*
Garber, Eugene K 1932- *ConAu 6NR, –57*
Garber, Frederick 1929- *ConAu 53*
Garber, Lee O 1900- *ConAu 37R*
Garbett, Sir Colin Campbell 1881- *ConAu P-1*
Garbini, Giovanni 1931- *ConAu 9NR, –21R*
Garbo, Norman 1919- *ConAu 9NR, –17R*
Garborg, Arne 1851-1924 *ClDMEL 80, CnMD*
Garbutt, Bernard 1900- *ConAu 110,*
  SmATA 31
Garbutt, Douglas 1922- *WrDr 84*
Garceau, Oliver 1911- *ConAu P-2, WrDr 84*
Garceau, Raymond 1919- *CreCan 1*
Garcia, Ann O'Neal 1939- *ConAu 108*
Garcia, F Chris 1940- *ConAu 4NR, –53*
Garcia, George Haddad *ConAu X*
Garcia, Mario R 1947- *ConAu 77*
Garcia Castaneda, Salvador 1932- *ConAu 61*
Garcia DeCastro, Ramon 1931- *IntAu&W 82*
Garcia Hortelano, Juan 1928- *ClDMEL 80,*
  TwCWr
Garcia Lopez, Angel 1935- *IntAu&W 82*
Garcia Lorca, Federico 1898?-1936 *ClDMEL 80,*
  CnMWL, ConAu 104, EncWL 2[port],
  ModRL, ModWD, TwCA, TwCA SUP,
  TwCLC 7[port], TwCWr
Garcia Lorca, Federico 1899-1936 *TwCLC 1*
Garcia Marquez, Gabriel 1928- *ConAu 10NR,*
  –33R, ConLC 2, –3, –8, –10, –15, –27[port],
  EncWL 2[port], ModLAL, WhoTwCL,
  WorAu
Garcia Marquina, Francisco 1937- *IntAu&W 82*
Garcia Nieto, Jose 1914- *ClDMEL 80*

Garcia Pavon, Francisco 1919- *ClDMEL 80,*
  IntAu&W 82
Garcia Perez, Alfonso 1945- *IntAu&W 82*
Garcia Ruescas, Francisco 1914- *IntAu&W 82*
Garcia Serrano, Rafael 1917- *ClDMEL 80*
Garcitoral, Alicio 1902- *IntAu&W 82*
Gard *TwCA, TwCA SUP*
Gard, H M *IntWWP 82X*
Gard, Janice *ConAu X, WrDr 84*
Gard, Joyce 1911- *ConAu 73, IntAu&W 82,*
  SmATA X, TwCCW 83, WrDr 84
Gard, Richard A 1914- *ConAu 1R, –1NR*
Gard, Robert Edward 1910- *ConAu 85,*
  SmATA 18
Gard, Roger Martin Du *ModRL*
Gard, Wayne 1899- *ConAu 1R*
Gardam, Jane 1928- *ConAu 2NR, –49,*
  DcLB 14[port], SmATA 28, TwCCW 83,
  WrDr 84
Garden, Bruce *WrDr 84*
Garden, Bruce 1936- *ConAu X, IntAu&W 82X*
Garden, Edward 1930- *WrDr 84*
Garden, Edward James Clarke 1930- *ConAu 25R,*
  IntAu&W 82
Garden, Graeme 1943- *ConAu 107*
Garden, John *ConAu X*
Garden, Nancy *DrAP&F 83*
Garden, Nancy 1938- *ConAu 33R, SmATA 12,*
  WrDr 84
Garden, Robert Hal 1937- *ConAu 69*
Gardiner, Alfred George 1865-1946 *LongCTC*
Gardiner, C Harvey 1913- *ConAu 1R, –1NR*
Gardiner, Charles Wrey 1901-1981 *ConAu 103*
Gardiner, Dorothy 1894-1979 *ConAu 93,*
  TwCCr&M 80, TwCWW
Gardiner, Glenn Lion 1896-1962 *ConAu 1R*
Gardiner, Judy 1922- *ConAu 9NR, –21R*
Gardiner, Lora Jean *DrAP&F 83*
Gardiner, Lora Jean 1954- *IntWWP 82*
Gardiner, Mary Summerfield 1896-1982
  ConAu 106
Gardiner, Muriel 1901- *ConAu 77*
Gardiner, Patrick 1922- *WrDr 84*
Gardiner, Patrick Lancaster 1922- *ConAu 1R,*
  –5NR, IntAu&W 82
Gardiner, Robert K A 1914- *ConAu 21R*
Gardiner, Robert W 1932- *ConAu 53, WrDr 84*
Gardiner, Stephen 1925- *ConAu 97,*
  IntAu&W 82
Gardiol, Rita M *ConAu 81*
Gardner, Alan 1925- *ConAu 21R*
Gardner, Angela Davis *ConAu X*
Gardner, Anne *ConAu 49*
Gardner, Brian 1931- *ConAu 13R,*
  IntAu&W 82, WrDr 84
Gardner, Carl 1931- *ConAu 107*
Gardner, Charles J 1912- *WrDr 84*
Gardner, D Bruce 1924- *ConAu 49*
Gardner, David Emmett 1928- *CreCan 2*
Gardner, David Pierpont 1933- *ConAu 21R*
Gardner, Dic *ConAu X,   SmATA X*
Gardner, Dorothy E M 1900-1972 *ConAu P-2*
Gardner, E Clinton 1920- *ConAu 13R*
Gardner, Edward Clinton 1920- *WrDr 84*
Gardner, Eldon J 1909- *ConAu 41R*
Gardner, Erle Stanley 1889-1970 *ConAu 5R,*
  –25R, LongCTC, TwCA, TwCA SUP,
  TwCCr&M 80, TwCWr
Gardner, Frank M 1908- *WrDr 84*
Gardner, Frank Matthias 1908-1980 *ConAu 109*
Gardner, Geoffrey *DrAP&F 83*
Gardner, Geoffrey 1943- *IntWWP 82*
Gardner, Gerald 1929- *ConAu 1R, –5NR*
Gardner, Helen 1908- *WrDr 84*
Gardner, Helen Louise 1908- *ConAu 97,*
  ConLCrt 82, IntAu&W 82, WorAu
Gardner, Herb 1934- *NatPD 81[port]*
Gardner, Howard 1943- *ConAu 9NR, –65*
Gardner, Hy 1908- *ConAu 101*
Gardner, Isabella Stewart 1915-1981 *ConAu 104,*
  –97, ConP 80, CroCAP, DcLEL 1940,
  WorAu
Gardner, Jack Irving 1934- *ConAu 102*
Gardner, Jani 1943- *ConAu 25R*
Gardner, Jeanne LeMonnier 1925- *ConAu 17R,*
  SmATA 5
Gardner, Jeffrey *ConAu X, WrDr 84*
Gardner, John 1912- *IntAu&W 82*
Gardner, John 1926- *DcLEL 1940,*
  TwCCr&M 80, WrDr 84
Gardner, John 1933-1982 *DcLB Y82A[port]*

Gardner, John Champlin, Jr. 1933-1982
  AuNews 1, ConAu 107, –65, ConLC 2, –3,
  –5, –7, –8, –10, –18, ConNov 82, Conv 1,
  DcLB 2, DcLEL 1940, ModAL SUP,
  SmATA 31N, WorAu 1970
Gardner, John E 1917- *ConAu 17R*
Gardner, John Edmund 1926- *ConAu 103,*
  IntAu&W 82
Gardner, John William 1912- *ConAu 1R, –4NR,*
  –5R, DcLEL 1940
Gardner, Joseph L 1933- *ConAu 29R*
Gardner, Lawrence *ConAu X*
Gardner, Leonard *DrAP&F 83*
Gardner, Lewis *DrAP&F 83*
Gardner, Lewis 1943- *ConAu 65*
Gardner, Lloyd C 1934- *ConAu 3NR, –9R*
Gardner, Lucille 1913- *ConAu 69*
Gardner, Marilyn *ConAu 101*
Gardner, Martin 1914- *ConAu 73, SmATA 16*
Gardner, Mary Adelaide 1920- *ConAu 21R,*
  IntAu&W 82, WrDr 84
Gardner, Miriam *WrDr 84*
Gardner, Nancy Bruff *WrDr 84*
Gardner, Nancy Bruff 1915- *ConAu 13R*
Gardner, Noel *ConAu X*
Gardner, Paul *ConAu 69*
Gardner, Paul 1930- *WrDr 84*
Gardner, R H 1918- *ConAmTC, ConAu 33R*
Gardner, Ralph D 1923- *ConAu 6NR, –13R,*
  WrDr 84
Gardner, Richard *DrAP&F 83*
Gardner, Richard 1931- *ConAu 10NR, –21R,*
  SmATA 24[port]
Gardner, Richard A 1931- *ConAu 33R,*
  SmATA 13, WrDr 84
Gardner, Richard Kent 1928- *ConAu 69*
Gardner, Richard Newton 1927- *ConAu 89*
Gardner, Riley W 1921- *ConAu 13R*
Gardner, Robert 1911- *ConAu 61*
Gardner, Sandra *DrAP&F 83*
Gardner, Sheldon 1934- *ConAu 104,*
  SmATA 33[port]
Gardner, Stephen *DrAP&F 83*
Gardner, Wanda Kirby *ConAu 73*
Gardner, Wayland Downing 1928- *ConAu 73*
Gardner, William Earl 1928- *ConAu 3NR, –5R*
Gardner, William Henry 1902-1969 *ConAu P-1*
Gardner, Wynelle B 1918- *ConAu 65*
Gardner-Smith, Percival 1888- *ConAu P-2*
Gardons, S S *ConAu X, IntWWP 82X,*
  WrDr 84
Gardonyi, Geza 1863-1922 *ClDMEL 80*
Gardonyi, Zoltan 1906- *IntAu&W 82*
Gare, Nene 1919- *IntAu&W 82*
Gareau, Etienne 1915- *ConAu 45*
Gareau, Frederick H 1923- *ConAu 5R*
Garelick, May 1910- *ConAu 73, SmATA 19*
Garey, Terry A *DrAP&F 83*
Garey, Terry A 1948- *IntWWP 82*
Garfield, Brian 1939- *ConAu 1R, –6NR,*
  IntAu&W 82, TwCCr&M 80, TwCWW,
  WrDr 84
Garfield, Evelyn Picon 1940- *ConAu 9NR, –57*
Garfield, James B 1881- *SmATA 6*
Garfield, Leon 1921- *ConAu 17R, ConLC 12,*
  SmATA 1, –32[port], TwCCW 83,
  WrDr 84
Garfield, Patricia L 1934- *ConAu 85*
Garfield, Sol L 1918- *ConAu 29R*
Garfinkel, Alan 1941- *ConAu 105*
Garfinkel, Bernard 1929- *ConAu 25R*
Garfinkel, Herbert 1920- *ConAu 1R*
Garfinkel, Louis 1928- *NatPD 81[port]*
Garfinkel, Patricia *DrAP&F 83*
Garfinkel, Patricia 1938- *IntWWP 82*
Garfinkle, Louis Alan 1928- *IntAu&W 82*
Garfitt, Roger 1944- *ConAu 33R, ConP 80,*
  IntWWP 82, WrDr 84
Garforth, Francis William 1917- *ConAu 9R,*
  WrDr 84
Garfunkel, Louis X 1897?-1972 *ConAu 37R*
Gargan, William Dennis 1905-1979 *ConAu 106*
Gargi, Balwant 1916- *DcLEL 1940*
Garibaldi, Gerald 1951- *ConAu 108*
Gariepy, Henry 1930- *ConAu 2NR, –49*
Garin, Marita *DrAP&F 83*
Garioch, Robert 1909-1981 *ConAu 103,*
  ConP 80
Garis, Howard R 1873-1962 *DcLB 22[port]*
Garis, Howard Roger 1873-1962 *ConAu 73,*
  SmATA 13
Garis, Robert 1925- *ConAu 17R*

Garitano, Rita *DrAP&F 83*
Garland, Bennett *ConAu X, IntAu&W 82X,
TwCWW, WrDr 84*
Garland, Charles T 1910?-1976 *ConAu 69*
Garland, George *ConAu X, WrDr 84*
Garland, George 1904- *TwCWW*
Garland, Hamlin 1860-1940 *ConAmA,
ConAu 104, FifWWr, LongCTC, ModAL,
TwCA, TwCA SUP, TwCLC 3, TwCWW*
Garland, Madge 1900- *ConAu 25R*
Garland, Mary 1922- *ConAu 89*
Garland, Patrick *DcLEL 1940*
Garland, Phyl 1935- *ConAu 69, LivgBAA*
Garlick, Peter C 1923- *ConAu 41R*
Garlick, Raymond 1926- *ConAu 4NR, -53,
ConP 80, IntAu&W 82, WrDr 84*
Garlington, Phil 1943- *ConAu 81*
Garlington, Warren K 1923- *ConAu 9R*
Garlinski, Jozef 1913- *IntAu&W 82, WrDr 84*
Garlinski, Jozef 1914- *ConAu 108*
Garment, Grace R 1927?-1976 *ConAu 104*
Garmon, William S 1926- *ConAu 21R*
Garn, Edwin Jacob 1932- *ConAu 107*
Garn, Jake *ConAu X*
Garneau, Hector DeSaint-Denys 1912-1943
CreCan 1, WorAu 1970
Garneau, Henri DeSaint-Denys 1912-1943
CreCan 1
Garneau, Joseph Rene Sylvain *CreCan 2*
Garneau, St.-Denys 1912-1943 *CreCan 1*
Garneau, Sylvain 1930-1953 *CreCan 2*
Garner, Alan *ConSFA*
Garner, Alan 1934- *IntAu&W 82, SmATA 18,
TwCCW 83, WrDr 84*
Garner, Alan 1935- *ConAu 73, ConLC 17*
Garner, Claud Wilton 1891- *ConAu 9R*
Garner, Dwight L 1913- *ConAu 25R*
Garner, H F 1926- *ConAu 73*
Garner, Harry Hyman 1910- *ConAu 17R*
Garner, Hugh 1913-1979 *ConAu 69, ConLC 13,
CreCan 1, DcLEL 1940, ModCmwL,
TwCWr*
Garner, Patrick C *DrAP&F 83*
Garner, Paul 1910- *ConAu 37R*
Garner, Roberta 1943- *ConAu 85*
Garner, Rolf *TwCSFW*
Garner, Ross 1914- *ConAu 33R*
Garner, Wendell 1921- *WrDr 84*
Garner, Wendell R 1921- *ConAu 5R, -11NR*
Garner, William 1920- *ConAu 29R, WrDr 84*
Garner, William R 1936- *ConAu 21R*
Garnet, Eldon 1946- *ConAu 9NR, -61*
Garnett, A Campbell 1894-1970 *ConAu 2NR*
Garnett, Arthur Campbell 1894- *ConAu 1R*
Garnett, Bill *ConAu X*
Garnett, Christopher Browne 1906-1975
ConAu 61
Garnett, Constance 1861-1946 *LongCTC*
Garnett, David 1892-1981 *ConAu 5R, -103,
ConLC 3, LongCTC, ModBrL, TwCA,
TwCA SUP, TwCWr*
Garnett, Edward 1868-1937 *LongCTC, TwCA,
TwCA SUP*
Garnett, Eve *TwCCW 83*
Garnett, Eve C R *WrDr 84*
Garnett, Eve C R 1910?- *ConAu 1R, -2NR,
IntAu&W 82, SmATA 3*
Garnett, Richard 1835-1906 *LongCTC*
Garnett, Richard 1923- *WrDr 84*
Garnett, Richard Duncan Carey 1923- *ConAu 5R*
Garnett, Roger *ConAu X, TwCCr&M 80,
WrDr 84*
Garnett, Tay 1894?-1977 *ConAu 73*
Garnett, William John 1941- *ConAu 102*
Garnham, Nicholas 1937- *ConAu 33R*
Garnham, Percy Cyril Claude 1901- *WrDr 84*
Garofalo, Reebee *ConAu X*
Garofalo, Robert L 1944- *ConAu 77*
Garoian, Leon 1925- *ConAu 1R*
Garoogian, Rhoda 1933- *ConAu 102*
Garoyan, Leon 1925- *ConAu 5NR*
Garrad, Larch S 1936- *ConAu 61*
Garrard, Christopher *IntAu&W 82X*
Garrard, Gene *ConAu X*
Garrard, Jeanne Sue *ConAu 81*
Garrard, Lancelot Austin 1904- *ConAu P-1,
WrDr 84*
Garratt, Arthur John 1916- *IntAu&W 82*
Garraty, John A 1920- *ConAu 1R, -2NR,
DcLB 17[port], SmATA 23*
Garreau, Joel 1948- *ConAu 101*
Garrels, Robert M 1916- *WrDr 84*

Garrels, Robert Minard 1916- *MichAu 80*
Garret, Maxwell R 1917- *ConAu 106*
Garretson, Lucy Reed 1936- *ConAu 97*
Garretson, Robert L 1920- *ConAu 17R*
Garretson, Victoria Diane 1945- *ConAu 108*
Garrett, Albert Charles 1915-1983 *ConAu 109*
Garrett, Alfred B 1906- *ConAu 5R*
Garrett, Charles 1925-1977 *ConAu 73*
Garrett, Charlotte *DrAP&F 83*
Garrett, Clarke 1935- *ConAu 73*
Garrett, Eileen Jeanette 1893-1970 *ConAu P-2*
Garrett, Florence Rome 1912- *IntWWP 82,
WrDr 84*
Garrett, Franklin M 1906- *ConAu 57*
Garrett, Garet 1878-1954 *TwCA, TwCA SUP*
Garrett, George *DrAP&F 83*
Garrett, George 1929- *DcLB Y83A[port],
WrDr 84*
Garrett, George Palmer 1929- *ConAu 1R, -1NR,
ConLC 3, -11, ConNov 82, ConP 80,
DcLB 2, -5[port], DcLEL 1940, WorAu*
Garrett, Gerald R 1940- *ConAu 73*
Garrett, Gerard 1928- *ConAu 73*
Garrett, Helen 1895- *SmATA 21[port]*
Garrett, Howard 1931- *ConAu 61*
Garrett, James Leo, Jr. 1925- *ConAu 33R*
Garrett, Jane 1914- *ConAu 105*
Garrett, John 1920- *ConAu 33R*
Garrett, Leonard J 1926- *ConAu 17R*
Garrett, Leslie *DrAP&F 83*
Garrett, Leslie 1931- *ConAu 17R*
Garrett, Lillian *WrDr 84*
Garrett, Lillian 1914- *ConAu 29R*
Garrett, Peter K 1940- *ConAu 25R*
Garrett, Randall 1927- *ConSFA, TwCSFW,
WrDr 84*
Garrett, Richard 1920- *ConAu 81,
IntAu&W 82, WrDr 84*
Garrett, Romeo Benjamin 1910- *ConAu 37R*
Garrett, Thomas M 1924- *ConAu 1R, -5NR*
Garrett, Thomas Samuel 1913-1980 *ConAu 1R,
-3NR*
Garrett, Tom *ConAu X*
Garrett, Truman *ConAu X*
Garrett, Wendell D 1929- *ConAu 9R*
Garrett, William 1890-1967 *ConAu P-1*
Garrido, Raul Guerra 1935- *IntAu&W 82*
Garrido Chamorro, Manuel 1923- *IntAu&W 82*
Garrido Lopera, Jose Maria 1919- *IntAu&W 82*
Garrigan, Owen 1928- *ConAu 21R*
Garrigan, Sean *IntWWP 82X*
Garrigue, Jean 1914-1972 *ConAu 5R, -37R,
ConLC 2, -8, ConP 80A, DcLEL 1940,
ModAL, ModAL SUP, TwCA SUP*
Garrigue, Sheila 1931- *ConAu 69,
SmATA 21[port]*
Garrison, Barbara 1931- *SmATA 19*
Garrison, Christian 1942- *ConAu 65*
Garrison, Frederick *ConAmA, ConAu X,
SmATA X*
Garrison, James 1943- *ConAu 61*
Garrison, Joan *ConAu X*
Garrison, Joseph *DrAP&F 83*
Garrison, Karl C 1900- *ConAu 37R*
Garrison, Lisa *DrAP&F 83*
Garrison, Omar V 1913- *ConAu 33R, WrDr 84*
Garrison, Peggy *DrAP&F 83*
Garrison, R Benjamin 1926- *ConAu 5NR, -13R*
Garrison, Webb B 1919- *ConAu 1R, -2NR,
SmATA 25[port]*
Garrison, Winfred Ernest 1874-1969 *ConAu 1R,
-6NR*
Garrity *ConAu X*
Garrity, Dave *ConAu X*
Garrity, Devin Adair 1905-1981 *ConAu 107*
Garrity, Devin Adair 1906-1981 *ConAu 103*
Garrity, Joan Terry 1940- *ConAu 69*
Garrity, Joan Theresa *AuNews 1*
Garrity, Richard 1903- *ConAu 77*
Garrity, Terry *ConAu X*
Garrone, Filippo 1925- *IntAu&W 82*
Garrone, Cardinal Gabriel Marie 1901-
IntAu&W 82
Garrow, David J 1953- *ConAu 93*
Garroway, Dave *ConAu X*
Garroway, David Cunningham 1913-1982
ConAu 107
Garry, Charles R 1909- *ConAu 73*
Garside, Roger R 1938- *ConAu 107*
Garskof, Michele Hoffnung *ConAu X*
Garson, Barbara *ConAu 33R*
Garson, Barbara 1941- *NatPD 81[port]*

Garson, G David 1943- *ConAu 4NR, -53*
Garson, Helen Sylvia 1925- *ConAu 107*
Garson, Noel George 1931- *ConAu 29R*
Garson, Paul 1946- *ConAu 49*
Garst, Doris Shannon 1894- *ConAu 1R,
SmATA 1*
Garst, John Fredric 1932- *ConAu 45*
Garst, Robert E 1900-1980 *ConAu 108, -97*
Garst, Shannon *ConAu X, SmATA X*
Garstang, Jack *ConAu X*
Garstang, James Gordon 1927- *ConAu 13R*
Garstein, Oskar Bernhard 1924- *ConAu 13R*
Gart, Murray Joseph 1924- *ConAu 103*
Garten, Hugh F 1904-1975 *ConAu 3NR, -5R*
Gartenberg, Egon 1911- *ConAu 57*
Gartenberg, Leo 1906- *ConAu 9R*
Garth, Jackson *IntAu&W 82X*
Garth, Will *ConAu X*
Garthoff, Raymond L 1929- *WrDr 84*
Garthoff, Raymond Leonard 1929- *ConAu 5R*
Garthwaite, Malaby *ConAu X*
Garthwaite, Marion Hook 1893- *ConAu 5R,
IntAu&W 82, SmATA 7*
Gartland, Robert Aldrich 1927- *ConAu 17R*
Gartman, Louise 1920- *ConAu 17R*
Gartner, Alan 1935- *ConAu 33R*
Gartner, Chloe Maria 1916- *ConAu 1R, -5NR,
IntAu&W 82, WrDr 84*
Gartner, Lloyd P 1927- *ConAu 1R, -2NR*
Gartner, Michael G 1938- *ConAu 77*
Garton, Charles 1926- *ConAu 45*
Garton, Malinda Dean d1976 *ConAu 1R, -103,
SmATA 26N*
Garton, Nancy Wells 1908- *ConAu 5R*
Garton, Nina R 1905- *ConAu P-2*
Garve, Andrew 1908- *ConAu X, TwCCr&M 80,
WorAu, WrDr 84*
Garver, Richard B 1934- *ConAu 33R*
Garvey, Amy Jacques 1896?-1973 *ConAu 45*
Garvey, Edward B 1914- *ConAu 41R*
Garvey, John 1944- *ConAu 65*
Garvey, Mona 1934- *ConAu 29R*
Garvey, Robert 1908- *ConAu 107*
Garvey, Robert 1908-1983 *ConAu 109*
Garvey, Terence Willcocks 1915- *ConAu 103*
Garvice, Charles 1833-1920 *TwCRGW*
Garvie, A F 1934- *ConAu 73*
Garvin, Amelia Beers 1878-1956 *CreCan 1*
Garvin, Charles D 1929- *ConAu 6NR, -57*
Garvin, James Louis 1868-1947 *LongCTC*
Garvin, Katharine 1904- *ConAu 5R*
Garvin, Lawrence 1945- *ConAu 53*
Garvin, Paul L 1919- *ConAu 5NR, -13R*
Garvin, Philip 1947- *ConAu 73*
Garvin, Richard M 1934- *ConAu 49, ConSFA*
Garvin, William 1922- *ConAu 25R*
Garwood, Darrell Nelson 1909- *ConAu 29R*
Gary, Madeleine 1923- *WrDr 84*
Gary, Madeleine Sophie 1923- *LivgBAA*
Gary, Romain *ConAu X*
Gary, Romain 1914- *CIDMEL 80, ConAu X,
ModFrL, ModRL, TwCWr, WorAu*
Gary, Romain 1914-1980 *ConLC 25[port]*
Garza, Daniel *DrAP&F 83*
Garza, Roberto Jesus 1934- *ConAu 104*
Garzilli, Enrico 1937- *ConAu 41R*
Garzya, Antonio 1927- *IntAu&W 82*
Gascar, Pierre 1916- *CIDMEL 80, ConAu X,
ConLC 11, EncWL 2, IntAu&W 82,
ModFrL, ModRL, WorAu*
Gascoigne, Arthur Bamber 1935- *DcLEL 1940*
Gascoigne, Bamber 1935- *ConAu 10NR, -25R,
IntAu&W 82, WrDr 84*
Gascoigne, Marguerite *ConAu X*
Gascon, The *ConAu X*
Gascon, Jean 1921- *CreCan 1*
Gascoyne, David 1916- *ConAu 10NR, -65,
ConP 80, IntAu&W 82, IntWWP 82,
LongCTC, ModBrL, RGFMBP, TwCWr,
WhoTwCL, WorAu, WrDr 84*
Gaselee, John Stephen 1933- *WrDr 84*
Gash, Jonathan 1933- *ConAu X*
Gash, Norman 1912- *ConAu 1R, -1NR,
IntAu&W 82, WrDr 84*
Gaskell, Jane 1941- *ConAu 5R, -11NR,
ConSFA, DcLEL 1940, WrDr 84*
Gaskell, Philip 1926- *ConAu 3NR, -5R,
IntAu&W 82, WrDr 84*
Gaskell, Thomas Frohock 1916- *ConAu 17R*
Gaskill, Harold V 1905-1975 *ConAu 57*
Gaskin, Catherine 1929- *ConAu 10NR, -65,
DcLEL 1940, IntAu&W 82, TwCCr&M 80,*

Gega, Peter C 1924- *ConAu 73*
Geherin, David J 1943- *ConAu 101*
Gehlbach, Frederick Renner 1935- *ConAu 106*
Gehlen, Reinhard 1902-1979 *ConAu 89*
Gehman, Betsy Holland 1932- *ConAu 17R*
Gehman, Henry Snyder 1888- *ConAu 13R*
Gehman, Henry Snyder 1918- *WrDr 84*
Gehman, Richard Boyd 1921-1972 *ConAu 1R*,
 –33R
Gehr, Mary *SmATA 32[port]*
Gehrels, Franz 1922- *ConAu 101*
Gehri, Alfred 1896?-1972 *ConAu 33R*
Gehris, Paul 1934- *ConAu 45*
Gehrts, Barbara 1930- *IntAu&W 82*
Geier, Arnold 1926- *ConAu 1R*
Geier, Joan Austin *DrAP&F 83*
Geier, Woodrow A 1914- *ConAu 21R*
Geigel Polanco, Vicente 1904-1979 *ConAu 85*
Geiger, Don Jesse 1923- *ConAu 5R, WrDr 84*
Geiger, H Kent 1922- *ConAu 5NR*
Geiger, Homer Kent 1922- *ConAu 1R*,
 WrDr 84
Geiger, Louis G 1913- *ConAu 13R*
Geiger, Raymond Aloysius *AuNews 1*
Geiger-Torel, Herman 1907- *CreCan 1*
Geigley, Vance A 1907- *ConSFA*
Geijerstam, Carl-Erik Af 1914- *IntAu&W 82*,
 IntWWP 82
Geijerstam, Gosta Af 1888- *TwCA, TwCA SUP*
Geil, Georg Seeberg 1930- *IntAu&W 82*
Geipel, Eileen 1932- *ConAu 107*,
 SmATA 30[port]
Geipel, John 1937- *ConAu 73*
Geiringer, Karl 1899- *ConAu 13R*
Geis, Darlene Stern *ConAu 1R, –5NR*,
 SmATA 7
Geis, Florence L 1933- *ConAu 8NR, –57*
Geis, Gilbert 1925- *ConAu 6NR, –9R*
Geis, Richard E 1927- *ConAu 101, ConSFA*
Geisel, Eva *IntWWP 82X*
Geisel, Helen 1898-1967 *ConAu 107*,
 SmATA 26[port]
Geisel, Theodor Seuss *TwCCW 83*
Geisel, Theodor Seuss 1904- *ChlLR 1*,
 ConAu 13R, SmATA 1, –28[port], TwCA,
 TwCA SUP
Geiser, Robert L 1931- *ConAu 97*
Geisinger, David L 1938- *ConAu 110*
Geisler, Norman 1932- *WrDr 84*
Geisler, Norman L 1932- *ConAu 10NR*
Geisler, Norman Leo 1932- *ConAu 25R*
Geismar, L L 1921- *ConAu 11NR, –25R*
Geismar, Ludwig Leo 1921- *WrDr 84*
Geismar, Maxwell 1909-1979 *ConAu 1R, –104*,
 ConLCrt 82, TwCA SUP
Geissler, Christian 1928- *IntAu&W 82*
Geissman, Erwin William 1920-1980 *ConAu 101*
Geist, Harold 1916- *ConAu 7NR, –17R*,
 WrDr 84
Geist, Kenneth L 1936- *ConAu 81*
Geist, Robert John 1912- *ConAu 41R*
Geist, Roland C 1896- *ConAu 89*
Geist, Valerius 1938- *ConAu 8NR, –61*
Geitgey, Doris A 1920- *ConAu 53*
Geiwitz, P James 1938- *ConAu 11NR, –29R*
Gelatt, Roland 1920- *ConAu 13R*
Gelb, Arthur 1924- *ConAu 1R*
Gelb, Barbara Stone 1926- *ConAu 1R*
Gelb, Ignace Jay 1907- *ConAu 9R*
Gelb, Joyce 1940- *ConAu 61*
Gelb, Leslie H 1937- *ConAu 103*
Gelb, Norman 1929- *ConAu 108*
Gelbart, Larry 1923- *ConAu 73*,
 ConLC 21[port]
Gelbart, Larry 1928- *WrDr 84*
Gelber, Harry Gregor 1926- *ConAu 25R*,
 IntAu&W 82
Gelber, Jack 1926- *CnMD*
Gelber, Jack 1932- *ConAu 1R, –2NR*,
 ConDr 82, ConLC 1, –6, –14, CroCD,
 DcLB 7[port], DcLEL 1940, ModAL,
 ModWD, NatPD 81[port], TwCWr,
 WorAu, WrDr 84
Gelber, Lionel 1907- *WrDr 84*
Gelber, Lionel Morris 1907- *ConAu 13R*,
 IntAu&W 82
Gelber, Steven M 1943- *ConAu 53*
Geld, Ellen Bromfield 1932- *ConAu 37R*
Geldard, Frank Arthur 1904- *ConAu 41R*,
 IntAu&W 82
Geldart, William 1936- *SmATA 15*
Gelderman, Carol Wettlaufer 1935- *ConAu 105*

Gelernt, Jules 1928- *ConAu 21R*
Gelfand, Lawrence Emerson 1926- *ConAu 3NR*,
 –5R, IntAu&W 82
Gelfand, Morris Arthur 1908- *ConAu 49*
Gelfman, Judith S 1937- *ConAu 65*
Gelfond, Rhoda *DrAP&F 83*
Gelfond, Rhoda 1946- *ConAu 49*
Gelhorn, Martha *DrAP&F 83*
Gelinas, Gratien 1909- *CreCan 2*
Gelinas, Paul J 1911- *ConAu 41R, SmATA 10*
Gelinas, Pierre 1925- *CreCan 2*
Gell, Frank *ConAu X*
Geller, Allen 1941- *ConAu 25R*
Geller, Bruce 1930-1978 *ConAu 77*
Geller, Evelyn *ConAu X*
Geller, Ruth *DrAP&F 83*
Geller, Uri 1946- *ConAu 69, IntAu&W 82*
Gellerman, Saul W 1929- *ConAu 5R, –8NR*
Gellert, Gyorgy 1922- *IntAu&W 82*
Gellert, Judith 1925- *ConAu 33R*
Gellert, Lew *ConAu X*
Gelles, Richard J 1946- *ConAu 8NR, –61*
Gelley, Alexander 1933- *ConAu 108*
Gellhorn, Ernst 1893-1973 *ConAu P-2*
Gellhorn, Martha 1908- *ConAu 77, ConLC 14*,
 ConNov 82, DcLB Y82B[port], TwCA,
 TwCA SUP, WrDr 84
Gellhorn, Walter 1906- *ASpks, ConAu 13R*
Gellinek, Christian 1930- *ConAu 9NR, –21R*
Gellinek, Janis Little *ConAu X*
Gellis, Roberta 1927- *WrDr 84*
Gellis, Roberta L 1927- *ConAu 3NR, –5R*,
 TwCRGW
Gellman, Estelle Sheila 1941- *ConAu 53*
Gellman, Irwin F 1942- *ConAu 1NR, –45*
Gellner, Ernest Andre 1925- *ConAu 4NR, –5R*,
 WrDr 84
Gellner, John 1907- *ConAu 29R*
Gelman, David Graham 1926- *ConAu 103*
Gelman, Rita Golden 1937- *ConAu 81*
Gelman, Steve 1934- *ConAu 25R, SmATA 3*
Gelman, Woodrow 1915?-1978 *ConAu 104*
Gelman, Woody *ConAu X*
Gelmis, Joseph S 1935- *ConAu 45*
Gelpi, Albert 1931- *ConAu 33R, WrDr 84*
Gelpi, Donald L 1934- *ConAu 7NR, –17R*
Gelsted, Otto 1888-1968 *ClDMEL 80*
Gelven, Michael 1937- *ConAu 29R, WrDr 84*
Gelzer, Matthias 1886-1974 *ConAu P-2*
Gemier, Firmin 1869-1933 *ClDMEL 80*
Gemme, Francis Robert 1934- *ConAu 21R*
Gemme, Leila Boyle 1942- *ConAu 81*
Gemmell, Alan Robertson 1913- *WrDr 84*
Gemmett, Robert J 1936- *ConAu 33R*
Gemmill, Jane Brown 1898- *ConAu 1R*
Gemmill, Paul F 1890?-1976 *ConAu 69*
Gemming, Elizabeth 1932- *ConAu 9NR, –65*,
 SmATA 11
Gems, Pam 1925- *ConAu 107, ConDr 82*,
 DcLB 13[port], WrDr 84
Genauer, Emily *WrDr 84*
Genauer, Emily 1911- *ConAu 106*
Genberg, Kjell E 1940- *IntAu&W 82*
Gencsy, Eva Von *CreCan 2*
Gendel, Evelyn W 1916?-1977 *ConAu 104*,
 SmATA 27N
Gendell, Murray 1924- *ConAu 5NR, –9R*
Gendlin, Eugene T 1926- *ConAu 1R*
Gendron, George M 1949- *ConAu 93*
Gendron, Pierre 1934- *CreCan 1*
Gendzier, Irene Lefel 1936- *ConAu 21R*
Gendzier, Stephen J 1930- *ConAu 33R*
Genega, Paul *DrAP&F 83*
Genega, Paul 1949- *IntWWP 82*
Generoso, Marc-Antonie *IntAu&W 82X*
Genest, Emile *CreCan 1*
Genet *ConAu X, WorAu*
Genet, Jean 1907- *IntAu&W 82*
Genet, Jean 1910- *ClDMEL 80, CnMD*,
 CnMWL, ConAu 17R, ConLC 1, –2, –5,
 –10, –14, CroCD, EncWL 2[port],
 LongCTC, ModFrL, ModRL, ModWD,
 TwCWr, WhoTwCL, WorAu
Genette, Gerard 1930- *ClDMEL 80*
Geneve, Pierre *IntAu&W 82X*
Genevoix, Maurice 1890-1980 *ClDMEL 80*,
 ConAu 102, IntAu&W 82
Genn, Calder *ConAu X*
Gennaro, Joseph F, Jr. 1924- *ConAu 101*
Genne, Elizabeth Steel 1911- *ConAu 108*
Genne, William H 1910- *ConAu 17R*
Genoves Tarazaga, Santiago 1923- *ConAu 107*

Genovese, Eugene D 1930- *ConAu 10NR*
Genovese, Eugene Dominick 1930- *ConAu 69*,
 DcLB 17[port], WorAu 1970[port]
Gensemer, Robert Eugene 1936- *ConAu 110*
Genser, Cynthia 1950- *ConAu 69, IntWWP 82*
Genser, Cynthia Kraman *DrAP&F 83*
Gensler, Kinereth *DrAP&F 83*
Gensler, Kinereth 1922- *IntWWP 82*
Genszler, G William, II 1915- *ConAu 65*
Gent, Peter 1942- *AuNews 1, ConAu 89*,
 DcLB Y82B[port]
Genthe, Charles V 1937- *ConAu 29R, WrDr 84*
Gentil, Richard 1917- *ConAu 102, WrDr 84*
Gentile, Giovanni 1875-1944 *ClDMEL 80*
Gentle, Mary 1956- *ConAu 106*
Gentleman, David 1930- *WrDr 84*
Gentleman, David William 1930- *ConAu 25R*,
 SmATA 7
Gentleman, Dorothy Corbett 1911- *IntWWP 82*
Gentles, Frederick 1912- *ConAu 29R*
Gentry, Byron B 1913- *ConAu 13R*
Gentry, Curt *WrDr 84*
Gentry, Curt 1931- *ConAu 5NR, –9R*,
 TwCSFW
Gentry, Dwight L 1919- *ConAu 1R*
Gentry, Jane *DrAP&F 83*
Gentry, Peter *ConAu X, –X, –X*
Gentz, William Howard 1918- *ConAu 107*
Gentzler, J Mason 1930- *ConAu 93*
Genzler, G William, II 1915- *ConAu 9NR*
Geoffrey, Charles *ConAu X*
Geoffrey, Theodate *ConAu X*
Geoghegan, Sister Barbara 1902- *ConAu P-1*
Georgakas, Dan *DrAP&F 83*
Georgakas, Dan 1938- *ConAu 1NR, –45*,
 IntWWP 82, MichAu 80
George, Alexander Lawrence 1920- *ConAu 13R*
George, Alfred Raymond 1912- *ConAu 108*
George, Charles H 1922- *ConAu 9R*
George, Chief Dan 1899-1981 *ConAu 108, –110*
George, Claude Swanson, Jr. 1920- *ConAu 13R*,
 WrDr 84
George, Collins Crusor 1909- *ConAu 77*
George, Dan *ConAu X*
George, Daniel 1890-1967 *LongCTC*
George, David *ConAu X*
George, E Madison 1907-1975 *ConAu 103*
George, Edgar Madison 1907- *ConAu 1R*
George, Eliot *WrDr 84*
George, Emery *DrAP&F 83*
George, Emery Edward 1933- *ConAu 41R*,
 IntAu&W 82, IntWWP 82
George, Eugene *ConAu X*
George, Graham Elias 1912- *CreCan 2*,
 WrDr 84
George, Jay *ConAu X*
George, Jean Craighead 1919- *ChlLR 1*,
 ConAu 5R, SmATA 2, TwCCW 83,
 WrDr 84
George, John E 1936- *ConAu 53*
George, John L 1916- *ConAu 5R, SmATA 2*
George, Jonathan *ConAu X, –X*,
 IntAu&W 82X, WrDr 84
George, Kathleen E *DrAP&F 83*
George, M Dorothy *ConAu P-1*
George, Malcom F 1930- *ConAu 57*
George, Marion E *ConAu X*
George, Mary Yanaga 1940- *ConAu 29R*,
 WrDr 84
George, N L 1902- *ConAu P-2*
George, Peter 1924-1966 *ConAu 25R, TwCSFW*
George, Phil *DrAP&F 83*
George, Richard R 1943- *ConAu 104*
George, Robert Esmonde Gordon 1890-1969
 ConAu P-1
George, Rolf 1930- *ConAu 110*
George, Roy E 1923- *ConAu 37R*
George, S C 1898- *SmATA 11*
George, Sally *DrAP&F 83*
George, Sally 1945- *ConAu 105*
George, Sara 1947- *ConAu 65*
George, Sidney Charles 1898- *ConAu 53*
George, Stefan Anton 1868-1933 *ClDMEL 80*,
 CnMWL, ConAu 104, EncWL 2[port],
 LongCTC, ModGL, TwCA, TwCA SUP,
 TwCLC 2, TwCWr, WhoTwCL
George, Susan Akers 1934- *ConAu 77*
George, W Lloyd 1900?-1975 *ConAu 53*,
 SmATA 30N
George, W R P 1912- *ConAu 69*
George, Walter Lionel 1882-1926 *LongCTC*,
 TwCA

Ghiotto, Renato 1923- *ConAu 49*
Ghirshman, Roman 1895- *IntAu&W 82*
Ghiselin, Brewster *DrAP&F 83*
Ghiselin, Brewster 1903- *ConAu 13R,*
ConLC 23[port], ConP 80, WrDr 84
Ghiselin, Brewster 1906- *DcLEL 1940*
Ghiselin, Michael Tenant 1939- *ConAu 49*
Ghiselli, Edwin E 1907- *ConAu 37R*
Ghnassia, Maurice Jean-Henri 1920- *ConAu 49*
Ghose, Amal 1929- *ConAu 106*
Ghose, Aurobindo 1872-1950 *EncWL 2,*
WorAu 1970
Ghose, Chinmoy Kumar *ConAu X*
Ghose, Sudhin N 1899- *ConAu 5R*
Ghose, Zulfikar *DrAP&F 83*
Ghose, Zulfikar 1935- *ConAu 65, ConNov 82,*
ConP 80, ModCmwL, WrDr 84
Ghose, Zulifikar 1935- *DcLEL 1940*
Ghosh, Arun Kumar 1930- *ConAu 10NR, –21R,*
IntAu&W 82, WrDr 84
Ghosh, Jyotis Chandra 1904?-1975 *ConAu 57*
Ghosh, Tapan 1928- *ConAu 53*
Ghougassian, Joseph P 1944- *ConAu 49*
Ghurye, G S 1893- *ConAu 3NR, –5R*
Giacosa, Giuseppe 1847-1906 *ConAu 104,*
ModWD, TwCLC 7[port]
Giallombardo, Rose 1925- *ConAu 61*
Giamatti, A Bartlett 1938- *ConAu 97*
Giamatti, Valentine 1911-1982 *ConAu 106*
Giammarino, Jaye *IntWWP 82, WrDr 84*
Giammatteo, Hollis *DrAP&F 83*
Gianakaris, C J 1934- *ConAu 25R, MichAu 80*
Gianakaris, Constantine John 1934-
IntAu&W 82, WrDr 84
Giannaris, George 1936- *ConAu 2NR, –45,*
WrDr 84
Giannestras, Nicholas J 1909- *WrDr 84*
Giannestras, Nicholas J 1909-1978 *ConAu 105*
Giannetti, Louis D 1937- *ConAu 33R*
Giannini, David *DrAP&F 83*
Giannini, David 1948- *IntWWP 82*
Giannone, Richard 1934- *ConAu 21R*
Giannoni, Carlo Borromeo 1939- *ConAu 41R*
Gianoli, Paul *DrAP&F 83*
Giauque, William Francis 1895-1982 *ConAu 106*
Gibaldi, Joseph 1942- *ConAu 89*
Gibb, Hamilton 1895-1971 *ConAu 1R, –6NR,*
–33R
Gibb, Jack R 1914- *ConAu 17R*
Gibb, Lee *ConAu X, WorAu, WrDr 84*
Gibbard, Graham S 1942- *ConAu 53*
Gibberd, Frederick 1908- *WrDr 84*
Gibberd, Kathleen 1897- *IntAu&W 82,*
WrDr 84
Gibbings, Robert 1889-1958 *LongCTC,*
TwCA SUP
Gibbon, John Murray 1875-1952 *CreCan 1*
Gibbon, Lewis Grassic 1901-1935 *CnMWL,*
ConAu X, LongCTC, TwCA, TwCA SUP,
TwCLC 4[port]
Gibbon, Monk 1896- *ConAu 69, ConP 80,*
WrDr 84
Gibbon, Vivian 1917- *ConAu 103*
Gibbons, Barbara 1934- *ConAu 10NR, –61*
Gibbons, Brian 1938- *ConAu 11NR, –25R*
Gibbons, Don C 1926- *ConAu 110*
Gibbons, Euell 1911-1975 *ASpks, AuNews 1,*
ConAu 61, ConAu P-2
Gibbons, Faye 1938- *ConAu 109*
Gibbons, Floyd 1887-1939 *DcLB 25[port]*
Gibbons, Floyd Phillips 1887-1939 *TwCA,*
TwCA SUP
Gibbons, Gail 1944- *ConAu 69,*
SmATA 23[port]
Gibbons, Helen Bay 1921- *ConAu 17R*
Gibbons, John William 1907-1983 *ConAu 109*
Gibbons, Maurice 1931- *ConAu 89*
Gibbons, Reginald *DrAP&F 83*
Gibbons, Reginald 1947- *ConAu 97,*
IntWWP 82
Gibbons, Stella 1902- *WrDr 84*
Gibbons, Stella Dorothea 1902- *ConAu 13R,*
ConNov 82, IntAu&W 82, IntWWP 82,
LongCTC, ModBrL, TwCA, TwCA SUP,
TwCWr
Gibbs, A James 1922- *ConAu 17R*
Gibbs, A M 1933- *ConAu 33R*
Gibbs, Alonzo 1915- *ConAu 5R, –5NR,*
IntAu&W 82, SmATA 5, WrDr 84
Gibbs, Anthony 1902-1975 *ConAu X*
Gibbs, Anthony Matthews 1933- *WrDr 84*
Gibbs, Arthur Hamilton 1888-1964 *TwCA,*

Gibbs, Barbara *DrAP&F 83*
Gibbs, Barbara 1912- *ConAu 25R, IntWWP 82*
Gibbs, C Earl 1935- *ConAu 69*
Gibbs, Cosmo Hamilton *LongCTC*
Gibbs, Esther 1904- *ConAu 57*
Gibbs, Henry *TwCCr&M 80*
Gibbs, Henry St. John Clair *ConAu 1R*
Gibbs, James A *ConAu X*
Gibbs, James A 1922- *ConAu 69*
Gibbs, James Atwood 1922- *ConAu 11NR*
Gibbs, Jeanne Osborne 1920- *IntWWP 82*
Gibbs, Jim *ConAu X*
Gibbs, Joanifer 1947- *ConAu 57*
Gibbs, John G 1930- *ConAu 41R*
Gibbs, Mark 1920- *ConAu 5R*
Gibbs, Mary Ann *ConAu X, TwCRGW,*
WrDr 84
Gibbs, May 1877-1969 *ConAu 104,*
SmATA 27N, TwCCW 83
Gibbs, Paul T 1897- *ConAu 9R*
Gibbs, Peter 1903- *WrDr 84*
Gibbs, Peter Bawtree 1903- *ConAu 1R,*
IntAu&W 82
Gibbs, Sir Philip Hamilton 1877-1962 *ConAu 89,*
LongCTC, ModBrL, TwCA, TwCA SUP,
TwCWr
Gibbs, R Darnley 1904- *WrDr 84*
Gibbs, Rafe *ConAu X, IntAu&W 82X*
Gibbs, Raphael Sanford 1912- *ConAu 5R,*
IntAu&W 82
Gibbs, Tony *ConAu X*
Gibbs, William E 1936- *ConAu P-2*
Gibbs, Wolcott, Jr. 1935- *ConAu 85*
Gibbs-Smith, Charles Harvard 1909-
ConAu 4NR, –9R, IntAu&W 82, WrDr 84
Gibbs-Smith, Charles Harvard 1909-1981
ConAu 108
Gibbs-Wilson, Kathryn 1930- *ConAu 10NR*
Gibby, Robert Gwyn 1916- *ConAu 13R*
Giberson, Dorothy *ConAu 1R, –2NR*
Gibian, George 1924- *ConAu 1R, –5NR*
Giblin, Charles Homer 1928- *ConAu 41R*
Giblin, James Cross 1933- *ConAu 106,*
SmATA 33[port]
Gibney, Frank 1924- *ConAu 11NR, –69*
Gibney, Harriet *ConAu X*
Gibran, Jean 1933- *ConAu 69*
Gibran, Kahlil 1883-1931 *ConAu 104, TwCA,*
TwCA SUP, TwCLC 1, –9[port]
Gibson, Alexander Dunnett 1901-1978 *ConAu 77*
Gibson, Arrell Morgan 1921- *ConAu 41R*
Gibson, Charles 1920- *ConAu 21R*
Gibson, Charles E 1916- *WrDr 84*
Gibson, Charles Edmund 1916- *ConAu 5R*
Gibson, Charline 1937- *ConAu 69, LivgBAA*
Gibson, D Parke 1930-1979 *ConAu 85, –93*
Gibson, Derlyne 1936- *ConAu 21R*
Gibson, Donald B 1933- *ConAu X*
Gibson, Douglas 1910- *IntWWP 82*
Gibson, E Dana 1906- *ConAu 29R*
Gibson, E Lawrence 1935- *ConAu 93*
Gibson, Elsie 1907- *ConAu 61*
Gibson, Ernest Dana 1906- *WrDr 84*
Gibson, Evan K 1909- *ConAu 105*
Gibson, Frank K 1924- *ConAu 37R*
Gibson, Gerald Don 1938- *ConAu 104*
Gibson, Gertrude Hevener 1906- *ConAu 5R*
Gibson, Gifford Guy 1943- *ConAu 77*
Gibson, H B 1914- *ConAu 102*
Gibson, Harry Clark *ConAu X*
Gibson, Ian Wallace 1919- *CreCan 1*
Gibson, James Charles 1919- *IntAu&W 82*
Gibson, James J 1904- *ConAu 85*
Gibson, James L 1935- *ConAu 5R, –8NR*
Gibson, James W 1932- *ConAu 41R*
Gibson, Janice T 1934- *ConAu 41R*
Gibson, John 1907- *ConAu 33R*
Gibson, John 1941- *IntAu&W 82*
Gibson, John M 1899- *ConAu 1R*
Gibson, Josephine *ConAu X, SmATA 2,*
WrDr 84
Gibson, Karon Rose 1946- *ConAu 105*
Gibson, M Munro *IntWWP 82X*
Gibson, Maralee G 1924- *ConAu 17R*
Gibson, Margaret *DrAP&F 83*
Gibson, Margaret 1944- *ConAu 77*
Gibson, Margaret 1948- *ConAu 103*
Gibson, Miles 1947- *ConAu 102, WrDr 84*
Gibson, Morgan *DrAP&F 83*
Gibson, Morgan 1929- *ConAu 25R,*
IntAu&W 82, IntWWP 82

Gibson, Nevin H 1915- *ConAu 49*
Gibson, P J *DrAP&F 83*
Gibson, Paul *DrAP&F 83*
Gibson, Quentin 1913- *WrDr 84*
Gibson, Quentin Boyce 1913- *IntAu&W 82*
Gibson, Raymond E 1924- *ConAu 21R*
Gibson, Reginald Walter 1901- *ConAu P-1*
Gibson, Richard 1931- *ConAu 41R*
Gibson, Robert 1927- *WrDr 84*
Gibson, Robert Donald Davidson 1927-
ConAu 65, IntAu&W 82
Gibson, Robert William, Jr. 1923- *ConAu 107*
Gibson, Ronald George 1909- *ConAu 109*
Gibson, Rosemary *ConAu 49*
Gibson, Shirley 1927- *ConAu 103*
Gibson, Stephen M *DrAP&F 83*
Gibson, Walker 1919- *ConAu 1R, –1NR*
Gibson, Walter B 1897- *ConAu 108, –110,*
WrDr 84
Gibson, Walter Brown 1897- *TwCCr&M 80*
Gibson, Walter Samuel 1932- *ConAu 102,*
WrDr 84
Gibson, Wilfrid Wilson 1878-1962 *LongCTC,*
ModBrL, TwCA, TwCA SUP
Gibson, William 1914- *CnMD, ConAu 9R,*
–9NR, ConDr 82, ConLC 23[port],
DcLB 7[port], DcLEL 1940, ModAL,
ModWD, NatPD 81[port], WorAu,
WrDr 84
Gibson, William Carleton 1913- *ConAu 17R*
Gibson, William E 1944- *ConAu 33R*
Gibson-Jarvie, Clodagh 1923- *ConAu 105*
Gichon, Mordechai 1922- *ConAu 89*
Gicovate, Bernard 1922- *ConAu 37R*
Gidal, Peter 1946- *ConAu 103*
Gidal, Sonia 1922- *ConAu 5R, SmATA 2*
Gidal, Tim N 1909- *ConAu 5R, SmATA 2*
Giddings, James Louis 1909-1964 *ConAu P-1*
Giddings, John Calvin 1930- *ConAu 109,*
WrDr 84
Giddings, Robert 1935- *ConAu 9NR*
Giddings, Robert Lindsay 1935- *ConAu 21R*
Giddins, Gary 1948- *ConAu 77*
Gide, Andre 1869-1951 *CIDMEL 80, CnMD,*
CnMWL, ConAu 104, EncWL 2[port],
LongCTC, ModFrL, ModRL, ModWD,
TwCA, TwCA SUP, TwCLC 5[port],
–12[port], TwCWr, WhoTwCL
Gidley, Charles *ConAu X*
Gidley, M 1941- *ConAu 102*
Gidlow, Elsa *DrAP&F 83*
Gidlow, Elsa 1898- *ConAu 77*
Gidlund, Aili Estrid Ingrid 1905- *IntAu&W 82*
Gidney, James B 1914- *ConAu 45*
Giedion, Siegfried 1893- *TwCA SUP*
Giegling, John A 1935- *ConAu 29R,*
SmATA 17, WrDr 84
Gielgud, Gwen Bagni *ConAu X*
Gielgud, John 1904- *WrDr 84*
Gielgud, Val 1900- *WrDr 84*
Gielgud, Val Henry 1900- *ConAu 5NR, –9R,*
TwCCr&M 80
Giere, Ronald N 1938- *ConAu 4NR, –49*
Giergielewicz, Mieczyslaw 1901- *ConAu P-2*
Gierow, Karl Ragnar 1904-1982 *ConAu 108*
Gierow, Karl Ragnar Kunt 1904- *CnMD,*
ModWD
Giersch, Julius *ConAu X*
Giertz, Bo H 1905- *ConAu 9NR, –21R*
Gies, Frances 1915- *ConAu 9NR, –25R*
Gies, Joseph 1916- *ConAu 9NR*
Gies, Joseph Cornelius 1916- *ConAu 5R*
Gies, Thomas G 1921- *ConAu 33R*
Giesbrecht, Martin Gerhard 1933- *ConAu 4NR,*
–53
Giesey, Ralph E 1923- *ConAu 25R, WrDr 84*
Giessler, Phillip Bruce 1938- *ConAu 8NR, –61*
Giesy, J U 1877-1947 *TwCSFW*
Giff, Patricia Reilly 1935- *ConAu 101,*
SmATA 33[port]
Giffen, Daniel H 1938- *ConAu 107*
Giffin, Frederick Charles 1938- *ConAu 41R*
Giffin, James Manning 1935- *ConAu 105*
Giffin, Sidney F 1907-1977 *ConAu 73*
Gifford, Barry *DrAP&F 83*
Gifford, Barry 1946- *ConAu 9NR, –65*
Gifford, Denis 1927- *ConAu 101, IntAu&W 82,*
WrDr 84
Gifford, Don 1919- *ConAu 53*
Gifford, Edward Stewart, Jr. 1907- *ConAu P-2,*
WrDr 84
Gifford, Francis Newton *ConAu X*

Gifford, Frank 1930- *ConAu 109*
Gifford, Griselda 1931- *ConAu 107*
Gifford, Henry 1913- *ConAu 17R*
Gifford, James Fergus, Jr. 1940- *ConAu 57*
Gifford, Prosser 1929- *ConAu 101*
Gifford, Terry 1946- *ConAu 106*
Gifford, Thomas 1937- *ConAu 77,*
  TwCCr&M 80, WrDr 84
Gifford, William *DrAP&F 83*
Gifford-Jones, W *ConAu X*
Gigeroff, Alex K 1931- *WrDr 84*
Giggal, Kenneth 1927- *ConAu 104,*
  IntAu&W 82, WrDr 84
Giglio, Ernest D 1931- *ConAu 33R*
Gigon, Fernand 1908- *IntAu&W 82*
Giguere, Diane 1937- *ConAu 25R, CreCan 1,*
  IntAu&W 82
Giguere, Roland 1929- *CreCan 2*
Gih, Andrew 1901- *ConAu 21R*
Gijsen, Marnix 1899- *CIDMEL 80,*
  EncWL 2[port]
Gil, David G 1924- *ConAu 29R*
Gil, David Georg 1924- *WrDr 84*
Gil, Federico Guillermo 1915- *ConAu 1R, –2NR,*
  WrDr 84
Gil, Ildefonso Manuel 1912- *CIDMEL 80*
Gil-Albert, Juan 1906- *CIDMEL 80*
Gil DeBiedma, Jaime 1929- *CIDMEL 80*
Gilb, Corinne Lathrop 1925- *ConAu 17R*
Gilbar, Steven 1941- *ConAu 106*
Gilbert, Alan 1944- *WrDr 84*
Gilbert, Allan H 1888- *ConAu 9R*
Gilbert, Amy M 1895- *ConAu 49*
Gilbert, Anna 1916- *ConAu X, TwCRGW,*
  WrDr 84
Gilbert, Anne 1927- *ConAu 7NR, –57*
Gilbert, Anthony 1899-1973 *ConAu X,*
  LongCTC, TwCCr&M 80, WorAu
Gilbert, Arlene E 1934- *ConAu 49*
Gilbert, Arthur 1926- *ConAu 17R*
Gilbert, Arthur 1926-1976 *ConAu 9NR*
Gilbert, Ben W 1918- *ConAu 45*
Gilbert, Benjamin Franklin 1918- *ConAu 7NR,*
  –17R, IntAu&W 82, WrDr 84
Gilbert, Bentley Brinkerhoff 1924- *ConAu 25R,*
  WrDr 84
Gilbert, Bill 1931- *ConAu 105*
Gilbert, Celia *DrAP&F 83*
Gilbert, Charles 1913- *ConAu 41R*
Gilbert, Chris *DrAP&F 83*
Gilbert, Christine B 1909- *ConAu 103*
Gilbert, Creighton Eddy 1924- *ConAu 33R,*
  WrDr 84
Gilbert, David T 1953- *ConAu 106*
Gilbert, Doris Wilcox *ConAu 17R*
Gilbert, Dorothy *DrAP&F 83*
Gilbert, Dorothy 1936- *IntWWP 82*
Gilbert, Doug 1938-1979 *ConAu 104*
Gilbert, Douglas 1942- *ConAu 53*
Gilbert, Douglas L 1925- *ConAu 13R, WrDr 84*
Gilbert, Edith 1917- *MichAu 80*
Gilbert, Edmund William 1900-1973 *ConAu 65*
Gilbert, Edwin 1907-1976 *ConAu 69, –77*
Gilbert, Felix 1905- *ConAu 106*
Gilbert, Florence Ruth 1917- *DcLEL 1940*
Gilbert, George 1922- *ConAu 69*
Gilbert, Glen A 1913- *IntAu&W 82*
Gilbert, Glenn G 1936- *WrDr 84*
Gilbert, Glenn Gordon 1936- *ConAu 33R*
Gilbert, Gordon Allan 1942- *ConAu 103*
Gilbert, Gustave M 1911-1977 *ConAu 69*
Gilbert, Harriett 1948- *ConAu 9NR, –57,*
  SmATA 30[port], WrDr 84
Gilbert, Harry 1946- *ConAu 106*
Gilbert, Herbert 1926- *CreCan 2*
Gilbert, Herman Cromwell 1923- *ConAu 29R*
Gilbert, Jack *DrAP&F 83*
Gilbert, Jack G 1934- *ConAu 25R*
Gilbert, James 1935- *ConAu 69*
Gilbert, Jarvey 1917- *ConAu 33R*
Gilbert, Joan 1931- *ConAu 21R, SmATA 10*
Gilbert, John Raphael 1926- *ConAu 107,*
  IntAu&W 82, WrDr 84
Gilbert, Julie Goldsmith 1949- *ConAu 77*
Gilbert, Kenneth 1931- *CreCan 2*
Gilbert, Kittie Bruneau *CreCan 1*
Gilbert, Manu *ConAu X, WrDr 84*
Gilbert, Marilyn B 1926- *ConAu 1NR*
Gilbert, Martin 1936- *ConAu 9R, DcLEL 1940,*
  IntAu&W 82, WrDr 84
Gilbert, Mary *WrDr 84*
Gilbert, Michael 1912- *WrDr 84*

Gilbert, Michael Francis 1912- *ConAu 1R, –1NR,*
  DcLEL 1940, TwCCr&M 80, WorAu
Gilbert, Milton 1909?-1979 *ConAu 93*
Gilbert, Miriam 1919- *ConAu X*
Gilbert, Nan *ConAu X, IntAu&W 82X,*
  SmATA 2, WrDr 84
Gilbert, Neil 1940- *ConAu 77*
Gilbert, Robert E 1939- *ConAu 53*
Gilbert, Rod 1941- *ConAu 109*
Gilbert, Russell Wieder 1905- *ConAu 45*
Gilbert, Ruth 1917- *ConP 80, WrDr 84*
Gilbert, Ruth Gallard Ainsworth 1908-
  ConAu 4NR, –9R
Gilbert, S R 1948- *ConAu 101*
Gilbert, Sandra M *DrAP&F 83*
Gilbert, Sandra M 1936- *ConAu 41R*
Gilbert, Sara 1943- *ConAu 6NR, –57,*
  SmATA 11
Gilbert, Stephen 1912- *ConAu 25R, TwCSFW*
Gilbert, Susan Marie 1962- *IntWWP 82*
Gilbert, Virginia *DrAP&F 83, IntWWP 82X*
Gilbert, Virginia Lee 1946- *IntWWP 82*
Gilbert, Sir W S 1836-1911 *ConAu 104*
Gilbert, William Herbert *CreCan 2*
Gilbert, Sir William Schwenck 1836-1911
  ModWD, TwCLC 3
Gilbert, Willie 1916- *ConAu 45, IntAu&W 82*
Gilbert, Zack 1925- *ConAu 65*
Gilberts, Helen Ilene 1909- *ConAu 29R,*
  IntAu&W 82, WrDr 84
Gilbertson, Merril Thomas 1911- *ConAu 9R*
Gilbertson, Mildred *WrDr 84*
Gilbertson, Mildred Geiger 1908- *ConAu 2NR,*
  –5R, IntAu&W 82, SmATA 2
Gilbo, Patrick F 1937- *ConAu 107*
Gilboa, Amir 1917- *WorAu*
Gilboa, Yehoshua A 1918- *ConAu 29R,*
  IntAu&W 82
Gilborn, Alice 1936- *ConAu 69*
Gilbreath, Alice 1921- *ConAu 10NR, –25R,*
  SmATA 12
Gilbreath, Kent 1945- *ConAu 45*
Gilbreth, Frank B, Jr. 1911- *ConAu 9R,*
  ConLC 17, SmATA 2
Gilbreth, Lillian Evelyn Moller 1878-1972
  ConAu 33R
Gilburt, Samuel G 1910- *IntWWP 82*
Gilcher, Edwin L 1909- *ConAu 29R*
Gilchrist, Agnes A 1907-1976 *ConAu 65*
Gilchrist, Alan William 1913- *ConAu 21R*
Gilchrist, Andrew 1910- *ConAu 109*
Gilchrist, Elizabeth *DrAP&F 83*
Gilchrist, Ellen *DrAP&F 83*
Gilchrist, J 1927- *ConAu 25R*
Gilday, Robert M 1925?-1980 *ConAu 101*
Gilden, Bert 1915?-1971 *ConAu 29R,*
  ConAu P-1
Gilden, K B *ConAu X*
Gilden, Katya *ConAu 9R*
Gilder, Eric 1911- *ConAu 89*
Gilder, George F 1939- *AuNews 1, ConAu 9NR,*
  –17R, ConIsC 1[port]
Gilder, Rosamond *ConAu 1R*
Gilder, Rosamond 1891- *ConAmTC*
Gildersleeve, Thomas 1927- *WrDr 84*
Gildersleeve, Thomas R 1927- *ConAu 29R*
Gildner, Gary *DrAP&F 83*
Gildner, Gary 1938- *ConAu 33R, IntWWP 82,*
  WrDr 84
Gildner, Judith 1943- *ConAu 89*
Gildrie, Richard P 1945- *ConAu 73*
Gildzen, Alex 1943- *ConAu 41R*
Giles, Carl H 1935- *ConAu 29R*
Giles, Elizabeth *ConAu X*
Giles, Frederick John 1928- *ConAu 93*
Giles, Gordon A *ConAu X*
Giles, James R 1937- *ConAu 73*
Giles, Janice Holt d1979 *ConAu 1R, TwCRGW*
Giles, Janice Holt 1909-1979 *ConAu 3NR*
Giles, John 1921- *ConAu 104, WrDr 84*
Giles, John Richard 1921- *IntAu&W 82*
Giles, Kenneth *TwCCr&M 80*
Giles, Kris *ConAu X*
Giles, Mary E 1934- *ConAu 108*
Giles, Raymond *ConAu X*
Giles, Raymond 1926- *ConAu X*
Gilfillan, Edward S, Jr. 1906- *ConAu 57*
Gilfillan, Merrill *DrAP&F 83*
Gilfond, Henry *ConAu 9NR, –21R,*
  NatPD 81[port], SmATA 2
Gilford, C B 1920- *ConAu 17R*
Gilford, Madeline Lee 1923- *ConAu 85*

Gilge, Jeanette 1924- *ConAu 61,*
  SmATA 22[port]
Gilgen, Albert R 1930- *ConAu 37R*
Gilgoff, Alice 1946- *ConAu 85*
Gilgun, John F *DrAP&F 83*
Gilhooley, Jack 1940- *ConAu X, IntAu&W 82,*
  NatPD 81[port]
Gilhooley, John 1940- *ConAu 85*
Gilhooley, Leonard 1921- *ConAu 37R*
Gili, Elizabeth Helen 1913- *WrDr 84*
Gilien, Sasha 1925?-1971 *ConAu 33R*
Giliomee, Hermann 1938- *ConAu 102*
Gilison, Jerome Martin 1935- *ConAu 103*
Gilkes, A N 1900- *ConAu 5R*
Gilkey, Langdon 1919- *ConAu 7NR, –17R*
Gilkin, Iwan 1858-1924 *CIDMEL 80*
Gilkyson, Bernice Kenyon 1898?-1982 *ConAu 106*
Gill, Alan *ConAu X*
Gill, Bartholomew *ConAu X*
Gill, Bob 1931- *ConAu 1R*
Gill, Brendan *DrAP&F 83*
Gill, Brendan 1914- *ConAmTC, ConAu 73,*
  ConNov 82, Conv 1, TwCA SUP,
  WrDr 84
Gill, Charles Ignace Adelard 1871-1918 *CreCan 1*
Gill, Crispin 1916- *ConAu 21R*
Gill, David 1934- *WrDr 84*
Gill, David Lawrence William 1934- *ConAu 29R,*
  ConP 80, IntWWP 82
Gill, Derek L T 1919- *ConAu 4NR, –49,*
  SmATA 9
Gill, Dominic 1941- *ConAu 106*
Gill, Eric 1882-1940 *LongCTC, TwCA SUP*
Gill, Evan Robertson 1892- *ConAu 9R*
Gill, Frederick Cyril 1898- *ConAu 5R*
Gill, I K 1924- *ConAu 61*
Gill, Jerry H 1933- *ConAu 33R, WrDr 84*
Gill, John *DrAP&F 83*
Gill, John Edward 1938- *ConAu 106*
Gill, Joseph 1901- *ConAu 3NR, –9R,*
  IntAu&W 82, WrDr 84
Gill, M Lakshmi 1943- *DcLEL 1940*
Gill, Margery Jean 1925- *SmATA 22[port]*
Gill, Myrna Lakshmi 1943- *WrDr 84*
Gill, Patrick *ConAu X*
Gill, Peter 1939- *ConAu 103, ConDr 82,*
  IntAu&W 82, WrDr 84
Gill, Richard 1922- *ConAu 41R*
Gill, Richard T 1927- *ConAu 21R*
Gill, Robert S 1911- *CreCan 1*
Gill, Ronald Crispin 1916- *ConAu 102,*
  IntAu&W 82, WrDr 84
Gill, Traviss 1891- *ConAu P-1*
Gill, William Henry 1910- *WrDr 84*
Gillan, Garth J 1939- *ConAu 102*
Gillan, Maria *DrAP&F 83*
Gillan, Patricia Wagstaff 1936- *ConAu 102*
Gillchrest, Muriel Noyes 1905- *ConAu 25R*
Gille, Hans-Werner 1928- *IntAu&W 82*
Gillelan, G Howard 1917- *ConAu 6NR*
Gillelan, George Howard 1917- *ConAu 1R*
Gillen, Lucy *TwCRGW, WrDr 84*
Gillen, Mollie 1908- *ConAu 41R, IntAu&W 82*
Gillenson, Lewis William 1918- *ConAu 5R*
Gilles, Albert S, Sr. 1888- *ConAu 57*
Gilles, Daniel 1917- *CIDMEL 80, ConAu 103,*
  IntAu&W 82
Gillese, John Patrick 1920- *ConAu 13R*
Gillespie, A Lincoln, Jr. 1895-1950 *DcLB 4*
Gillespie, Alfred 1924- *ConAu 77*
Gillespie, Dizzy *ConAu X*
Gillespie, Gerald 1933- *ConAu 10NR, WrDr 84*
Gillespie, Gerald Ernest Paul 1933- *ConAu 25R,*
  IntAu&W 82
Gillespie, I S 1923- *ConAu 65*
Gillespie, James E, Jr. 1940- *ConAu 53*
Gillespie, Janet Wicks 1913- *ConAu 5R*
Gillespie, John Birks 1917- *ConAu 104*
Gillespie, John E 1921- *ConAu 17R*
Gillespie, John T 1928- *ConAu 73*
Gillespie, Marcia Ann 1944- *AuNews 2,*
  LivgBAA
Gillespie, Neal C 1933- *ConAu 33R*
Gillespie, Netta *DrAP&F 83*
Gillespie, Netta 1930- *IntWWP 82*
Gillespie, Robert B 1917- *ConAu 49*
Gillespie, Robert W 1922?-1983 *ConAu 110*
Gillespie, Susan 1904- *ConAu X*
Gillet, Lev 1892?-1980 *ConAu 97*
Gillet, Philippe 1923- *IntWWP 82*
Gillett, Charlie 1942- *ConAu 33R, WrDr 84*
Gillett, Eric Walkey 1893-1978 *ConAu 3NR, –5R*

Gillett, J D 1913- *ConAu 49*
Gillett, Margaret 1930- *ConAu 1R, –2NR,*
   IntAu&W 82, WrDr 84
Gillett, Mary Bledsoe *ConAu P-2, SmATA 7*
Gillette, Arnold S 1904- *ConAu 1R, –2NR*
Gillette, Bob *IntAu&W 82X, WrDr 84*
Gillette, Henry 1915- *WrDr 84*
Gillette, Henry Sampson 1915- *ConAu 5R,*
   SmATA 14
Gillette, Kathleen *DrAP&F 83*
Gillette, Kathleen Ann 1947- *IntAu&W 82*
Gillette, Paul 1938- *ConAu 53*
Gillette, Virginia M 1920- *ConAu 57,*
   MichAu 80
Gillette, William 1855-1937 *ModWD*
Gillette, William 1933- *ConAu 108*
Gillham, D G 1921- *ConAu 21R*
Gilliam, Dorothy B 1936- *ConAu 97*
Gilliam, Elizabeth M 1930- *IntWWP 82*
Gilliam, Florence *DcLB 4*
Gilliam, Terry 1940- *ConAu 108*
Gilliam, Terry 1941?- *ConLC 21[port]*
Gillian, Jerry *ConAu X*
Gillian, Kay *ConAu X*
Gilliatt, Penelope *DrAP&F 83, WrDr 84*
Gilliatt, Penelope 1932- *AuNews 2, ConAu 13R,*
   ConLC 2, –10, –13, ConNov 82,
   DcLB 14[port], DcLEL 1940, WorAu 1970
Gillie, Christopher 1914- *ConAu 102,*
   IntAu&W 82, WrDr 84
Gillie, Oliver 1937- *ConAu 65*
Gillies, Don 1926- *CreCan 1*
Gillies, John 1925- *ConAu 73*
Gillies, Mary Davis 1900- *ConAu P-2*
Gillies, Valerie 1948- *ConP 80, WrDr 84*
Gilligan, Edmund 1899-1973 *ConAu 45,*
   TwCA SUP
Gilligan, Sonja Carl 1936- *ConAu 57*
Gilliland, Alexis A 1931- *ConAu 108*
Gilliland, Charles *ConAu X*
Gilliland, Charles Edward, Jr. 1916-1975
   ConAu 110
Gilliland, Hap 1918- *ConAu 5NR, –53*
Gilliland, Mary *DrAP&F 83*
Gillin, Caroline J 1932- *ConAu 45*
Gillin, Donald George 1930- *ConAu 33R*
Gillin, John P 1907-1973 *ConAu 41R, –45*
Gillingham, John 1940- *ConAu 97*
Gillings, Richard John 1902- *ConAu 77*
Gillinson, Stanley 1920- *WrDr 84*
Gillion, Kenneth Lowell 1929- *ConAu 93*
Gillis, Daniel 1935- *ConAu 106*
Gillis, Everett Alden 1914- *ConAu 41R*
Gillis, John R 1939- *ConAu 33R*
Gillis, Patricia Ingle 1932- *ConAu 108*
Gillispie, Charles C 1918- *ConAu 13R*
Gillman, Olga Marjorie 1894- *ConAu 5R*
Gillman, Richard *DrAP&F 83*
Gillman, Richard 1929- *ConAu 17R*
Gillmer, Thomas C 1911- *ConAu 6NR, –57*
Gillmer, Tom *ConAu X*
Gillmor, C Stewart *ConAu 45*
Gillmor, Daniel S 1917?-1975 *ConAu 61*
Gillmor, Donald M 1926- *ConAu 41R*
Gillmor, Frances 1903- *ConAu P-2, WrDr 84*
Gillmore, David 1934- *ConAu 21R*
Gillon, Adam 1921- *ConAu 5R, –8NR,*
   IntAu&W 82, WrDr 84
Gillon, Diana 1915- *ConAu 13R, ConSFA*
Gillon, Meir 1907- *ConAu 13R, ConSFA*
Gillott, Jacky 1939-1980 *ConAu 102,*
   DcLB 14[port]
Gillquist, Peter E 1938- *ConAu 29R*
Gilluly, James 1896-1980 *ConAu 102*
Gillum, Helen L 1909- *ConAu 69*
Gilman, C Malcolm B 1898-1981 *ConAu 107*
Gilman, Charlotte Perkins 1860-1935 *ConAu 106,*
   TwCLC 9[port]
Gilman, Dorothy 1923- *ConAu X, SmATA 5,*
   TwCCr&M 80, WrDr 84
Gilman, Dugan *DrAP&F 83*
Gilman, Esther 1925- *SmATA 15*
Gilman, George G 1936- *ConAu X, TwCWW,*
   WrDr 84
Gilman, J D *ConAu X*
Gilman, James *ConAu X*
Gilman, Lawrence 1878-1939 *TwCA,*
   TwCA SUP
Gilman, Richard 1925- *ConAmTC, ConAu 5NR,*
   –53, DcLEL 1940
Gilman, Robert Cham *ConAu X, TwCSFW,*
   WrDr 84

Gilman, Sander L 1944- *ConAu 5NR, –53*
Gilman, Stephen 1917- *ConAu 107*
Gilman, William 1909- *ConAu 1R*
Gilman, William H 1911-1976 *ConAu 17R, –65*
Gilmer, Ann *ConAu X*
Gilmer, Beverly VonHaller 1909- *ConAu 5R,*
   –5NR
Gilmer, Walker 1935- *ConAu 33R*
Gilmore, Al-Tony 1946- *ConAu 7NR, –57*
Gilmore, Alec 1928- *ConAu 93*
Gilmore, Anthony 1900- *WrDr 84*
Gilmore, Charles L *ConAu 33R*
Gilmore, Christopher Cook 1940- *ConAu 101*
Gilmore, Daniel F 1922- *ConAu 65*
Gilmore, Don 1930- *ConAu 29R*
Gilmore, Eddy Lanier King 1907- *ConAu 5R*
Gilmore, Edith Spacil 1920- *ConAu 1R*
Gilmore, Gene 1920- *ConAu 33R*
Gilmore, Harold L 1931- *ConAu 53*
Gilmore, Haydn 1928- *ConAu 85*
Gilmore, Iris 1900- *ConAu 97,*
   SmATA 22[port]
Gilmore, J Herbert, Jr. 1925- *ConAu 33R*
Gilmore, James Malcolm 1930- *IntAu&W 82*
Gilmore, Jene Carlton 1933- *ConAu 33R*
Gilmore, John *DrAP&F 83*
Gilmore, John 1935- *ConAu 25R*
Gilmore, Joseph L 1929- *ConAu 81*
Gilmore, Maeve *ConAu 102, IntAu&W 82,*
   WrDr 84
Gilmore, Maeve d1983 *ConAu 110*
Gilmore, Mary 1865-1962 *LongCTC, ModCmwL,*
   TwCWr
Gilmore, Richard 1943- *ConAu 107*
Gilmore, Thomas B 1932- *ConAu 73*
Gilmore, Virginia Alma 1912- *IntWWP 82*
Gilmour, Garth Hamilton 1925- *ConAu P-1*
Gilmour, Glenn Harvey 1939- *CreCan 2*
Gilmour, H B 1939- *ConAu 81*
Gilmour, Robert S 1940- *ConAu 69*
Gilner, Elias 1888?-1976 *ConAu 65*
Gilot, Francoise 1921- *ConAu 108*
Gilpatric, Guy 1896-1950 *TwCA, TwCA SUP*
Gilpatrick, Eleanor G 1930- *ConAu 9NR, –21R*
Gilpin, Alan 1924- *ConAu 11NR, –25R,*
   WrDr 84
Gilpin, Alec Richard 1920- *ConAu 45,*
   MichAu 80
Gilpin, Laura *DrAP&F 83*
Gilpin, Robert G, Jr. 1930- *ConAu 5R*
Gilroy, Frank D *DrAP&F 83*
Gilroy, Frank D 1925- *ConAu 81, ConDr 82,*
   ConLC 2, CroCD, DcLB 7[port],
   DcLEL 1940, IntAu&W 82, ModWD,
   NatPD 81[port], WrDr 84
Gilroy, Harry 1908?-1981 *ConAu 104*
Gilroy, Thomas Laurence 1951- *ConAu 103*
Gilroy, Tom *ConAu X*
Gilsenbach, Reimar 1925- *IntAu&W 82*
Gilson, Etienne 1884-1978 *ClDMEL 80*
Gilson, Etienne Henri 1884-1978 *ConAu 81*
Gilson, Etienne Henry 1884-1978 *ConAu 102,*
   TwCA, TwCA SUP
Gilson, Goodwin Woodrow 1918- *ConAu 17R*
Gilson, Jamie 1933- *SmATA 34*
Gilson, Thomas Q 1916- *ConAu 5R*
Gilstrap, Robert L 1933- *ConAu 9R*
Gilzean, Elizabeth Houghton Blanchet 1913-
   ConAu 9R
Gimbel, John 1922- *ConAu 1R, –2NR,*
   WrDr 84
Gimbutas, Marija 1921- *ConAu 13R*
Gimferrer, Pere 1945- *ClDMEL 80*
Gimmestad, Victor E 1912- *ConAu 57*
Gimmestad, Victor E 1912-1982 *ConAu 109*
Gimpel, Herbert J 1915- *ConAu 17R*
Gimpel, Jean 1918- *ConAu 69*
Gimson, Alfred Charles 1917- *ConAu 5R,*
   WrDr 84
Ginandes, Shepard 1928- *ConAu 41R*
Ginder, Richard 1914- *ConAu 65*
Gindin, James 1926- *ConAu 2NR, –5R,*
   IntAu&W 82, WrDr 84
Giner DeGrado, Carlos 1930- *IntAu&W 82*
Giner DeLosRios, Francisco 1839-1915
   ClDMEL 80, ConAu 105
Gines DeAlbareda *IntAu&W 82X*
Gingell, Benjamin Broughton 1924- *ConAu 104,*
   IntAu&W 82, IntWWP 82, WrDr 84
Ginger *IntWWP 82X*
Ginger, Ann F 1925- *WrDr 84*
Ginger, Ann Fagan 1925- *ConAu 4NR, –53*

Ginger, Helen 1916- *ConAu 17R*
Ginger, John 1933- *ConAu 25R, IntAu&W 82,*
   WrDr 84
Gingerich, Melvin 1902-1975 *ConAu P-2*
Gingerich, Owen 1930- *ConAu 5NR, –53*
Gingher, Marianne *DrAP&F 83*
Ginglend, David R 1913- *ConAu 17R*
Gingold, Hermione *ConAu 5R*
Gingrich, Arnold 1903-1976 *ConAu 13R, –65,*
   –69
Gingrich, F Wilbur 1901- *ConAu P-2*
Giniger, Kenneth Seeman 1919- *ConAu 3NR,*
   –5R, IntAu&W 82
Ginn, Robert Jay, Jr. 1946- *ConAu 107*
Ginnes, Judith Segel *ConAu 85*
Ginnings, Harriett W *ConAu X*
Ginns, Patsy M 1937- *ConAu 69*
Ginns, Ronald 1896- *ConAu P-1*
Ginott, Haim G 1922-1973 *ConAu 45*
Ginsberg, Allen *DrAP&F 83*
Ginsberg, Allen 1926- *AuNews 1, ConAu 1R,*
   –2NR, ConLC 1, –2, –3, –4, –6, –13,
   ConP 80, CroCAP, DcLB 5[port], –16[port],
   DcLEL 1940, EncWL 2, IntAu&W 82,
   IntWWP 82, LongCTC, ModAL,
   ModAL SUP, TwCWr, WhoTwCL, WorAu,
   WrDr 84
Ginsberg, Earl *IntAu&W 82X*
Ginsberg, Leon H 1936- *ConAu 105*
Ginsberg, Louis 1895-1976 *ConAu 13R, –65*
Ginsberg, Robert 1937- *ConAu 25R*
Ginsberg, Ruta *CreCan 2*
Ginsburg, Carl *DrAP&F 83*
Ginsburg, Herbert 1939- *ConAu 73*
Ginsburg, Mirra *ConAu 11NR, –17R, ConSFA,*
   IntAu&W 82, SmATA 6
Ginsburg, Ruth Bader 1933- *ConAu 53*
Ginsburg, Seymour 1927- *ConAu 21R*
Ginsburgh, Robert N 1923- *ConAu 13R*
Ginsburgs, George 1932- *ConAu 4NR, –53,*
   WrDr 84
Ginsbury, Norman 1902- *ConAu 5R, WrDr 84*
Ginsbury, Norman 1903- *IntAu&W 82*
Ginter, Maria 1922- *ConAu 105, WrDr 84*
Ginther, John R 1922- *ConAu 107*
Gintis, Herbert 1940- *ConAu 57*
Ginzberg, Eli 1911- *ConAu 5R, –8NR,*
   WrDr 84
Ginzberg, Yevgeniya 1906?-1977 *ConAu 69*
Ginzburg, Natalia Levi 1916- *ClDMEL 80,*
   ConAu 85, ConLC 5, –11, EncWL 2,
   ModRL, WorAu
Ginzburg, Ralph 1929- *ConAu 21R*
Gioia, Dana *DrAP&F 83*
Giono, Jean 1895-1970 *ClDMEL 80, CnMD,*
   CnMWL, ConAu 2NR, –29R, –45,
   ConLC 4, –11, EncWL 2, ModFrL,
   ModRL, ModWD, TwCA, TwCA SUP,
   TwCWr, WhoTwCL
Giordan, Alma Roberts 1917- *ConAu 57*
Giordan, Marion d1983 *ConAu 110*
Giorno, John *DrAP&F 83*
Giorno, John 1936- *ConAu 33R*
Gioseffi, Daniela *DrAP&F 83*
Gioseffi, Daniela 1941- *ConAu 3NR, –45,*
   IntWWP 82X
Gioseffi, Dorothy Daniela 1941- *IntAu&W 82,*
   IntWWP 82
Giovacchini, Peter L 1922- *ConAu 101*
Giovannetti, Alberto 1913- *ConAu 9R*
Giovanni, Edoardo Di *CreCan 2*
Giovanni, Nikki *DrAP&F 83*
Giovanni, Nikki 1943- *AuNews 1,*
   ChlLR 6[port], ConAu 29R, ConLC 2, –4,
   –19, ConP 80, DcLB 5[port], DcLEL 1940,
   LivgBAA, SmATA 24[port], WorAu 1970,
   WrDr 84
Giovannitti, Arturo 1884-1959 *TwCA*
Giovannitti, Len *DrAP&F 83*
Giovannitti, Len 1920- *ConAu 13R*
Giovanopoulos, Paul Arthur 1939- *SmATA 7*
Giovene, Andrea 1904- *ConAu 85, ConLC 7*
Gipe, George 1933- *ConAu 77*
Gippius, Zinaida Nikolayevna 1869-1945
   ClDMEL 80, ConAu 106, EncWL 2,
   WhoTwCL, WorAu 1970
Gips, James E 1946- *IntAu&W 82*
Gipson, Fred 1908-1973 *ConAu 3NR,*
   TwCCW 83, TwCWW
Gipson, Frederick Benjamin 1908-1973
   ConAu 1R, –45, SmATA 2, –24N
Gipson, John 1932- *ConAu 61*

Gipson, Lawrence Henry 1880-1971 *ConAu 3NR,*
−5R, −33R, DcLB 17[port], WorAu
Giragosian, Newman H 1922- *ConAu 93*
Girard, Benoit 1932- *CreCan 2*
Girard, Hazel Batten 1901- *MichAu 80*
Girard, James P *DrAP&F 83*
Girard, James P 1944- *ConAu 69*
Girard, Joe 1928- *ConAu 9NR, −77*
Girard, Marvin Eugene 1924- *MichAu 80*
Girard, Rene N 1923- *ConAu 4NR, −9R*
Girard, Robert C 1932- *ConAu 101*
Girardi, Joe *ConAu X*
Girardot, Norman J 1943- *ConAu 110*
Giraud, Albert 1860-1929 *ClDMEL 80*
Giraud, Marcel 1900- *ConAu 77*
Giraudier, Antonio 1926- *IntWWP 82*
Giraudoux, Jean 1882-1944 *ClDMEL 80, CnMD,*
CnMWL, ConAu 104, EncWL 2[port],
LongCTC, ModFrL, ModRL, ModWD,
TwCA, TwCA SUP, TwCLC 2, −7[port],
TwCWr, WhoTwCL
Girchop *IntAu&W 82X*
Girdlestone, Cuthbert Morton 1895-1975
ConAu 3NR, −5R, −65
Girion, Barbara 1937- *ConAu 85,*
SmATA 26[port]
Girling, John 1926- *WrDr 84*
Girling, John L S 1926- *ConAu 106*
Girling, Richard 1945- *ConAu 108*
Girod, Gerald R 1939- *ConAu 53*
Girod, Gordon H 1920- *ConAu 1R*
Girodo, Michel 1945- *ConAu 81*
Gironella, Jose Maria 1917- *ClDMEL 80,*
ConAu 101, ConLC 11, EncWL 2,
ModRL, TwCA SUP, TwCWr
Giroud, Francoise 1916- *AuNews 1, ConAu 81,*
IntAu&W 82
Giroux, Andre 1916- *CreCan 1*
Giroux, Antoinette *CreCan 2*
Giroux, Colette Mary Elizabeth *CreCan 2*
Giroux, Germaine *CreCan 2*
Giroux, Joan 1922- *ConAu 93*
Giroux, Joye S 1930- *IntWWP 82, MichAu 80*
Giroux, Robert 1914- *ConAu 107*
Girri, Alberto 1919- *ModLAL*
Girson, Rochelle *ConAu 21R*
Girtin, Thomas 1913- *ConAu 9R*
Girvan, Helen 1891- *ConAu 73*
Girzaitis, Loretta 1920- *ConAu 2NR, −49*
Giscombe, C S *DrAP&F 83*
Gish, Arthur G 1939- *ConAu 29R, WrDr 84*
Gish, Lillian 1906- *WrDr 84*
Gishford, Anthony 1908-1975 *ConAu 53*
Gisolfi, Anthony M 1909- *ConAu P-2*
Gissing, George Robert 1857-1903 *ConAu 105,*
LongCTC, ModBrL, TwCLC 3
Gist, Noel Pitts 1899- *ConAu 1R, −1NR*
Gist, Ronald R 1932- *ConAu 21R*
Gitchoff, G Thomas 1938- *ConAu 53*
Gitchoff, Tom 1938- *ConAu X*
Gitin, David *DrAP&F 83*
Gitin, David 1941- *ConAu 2NR, −49,*
IntWWP 82
Gitin, Maria *DrAP&F 83*
Gitin, Maria 1946- *ConAu 8NR, −61*
Gitlin, Murray 1903- *ConAu 1R*
Gitlin, Todd *DrAP&F 83*
Gitlin, Todd 1943- *ConAu 29R*
Gitlow, A Leo 1918- *ConAu 1R*
Gitlow, Benjamin 1891-1965 *ConAu 89*
Gitell, Marilyn 1931- *ConAu 9NR, −21R*
Gittelsohn, Roland B 1910- *ConAu 2NR, −5R,*
WrDr 84
Gittelson, Celia *ConAu 105*
Gitter, A George 1926- *ConAu 102*
Gittinger, J Price *ConAu 41R*
Gittings, Christine *WrDr 84*
Gittings, Jo Manton 1919- *ConAu 3NR, −5R,*
SmATA 3
Gittings, John 1938- *ConAu 9NR, −21R*
Gittings, Robert 1911- *WrDr 84*
Gittings, Robert William Victor 1911-
ConAu 25R, ConP 80, IntAu&W 82,
IntWWP 82, SmATA 6, WorAu 1970
Gittins, Jean 1908- *IntAu&W 82*
Gittleman, Edwin 1929- *ConAu 21R*
Gittleman, Sol 1934- *ConAu 65*
Gittler, Joseph B 1912- *ConAu 37R, WrDr 84*
Giudici, Ann Couper 1929- *ConAu 73*
Giudici, Giovanni 1924- *ClDMEL 80*
Giunti, Renato 1905-1983 *ConAu 109*
Giurlani, Aldo *ConAu X, WorAu 1970*

Giuseppi, Charles Stephen Neville 1909-
IntWWP 82
Giuseppi, John 1900- *ConAu P-2*
Giuttari, Theodore Richard 1931- *ConAu 29R*
Givens, John 1943- *ConAu 77*
Givner, Abraham 1944- *ConAu 89*
Givner, Joan Mary 1936- *ConAu 108*
Gizzi, Michael *DrAP&F 83*
Gizzi, Michael 1949- *IntWWP 82*
Gjedsig, Lars F B 1944- *IntAu&W 82*
Gjellerup, Karl Adolph 1857-1919 *ClDMEL 80,*
TwCWr
Gjelsness, Barent *DrAP&F 83*
Gjessing, Ketil 1934- *IntWWP 82*
Gjuzel, Bogomil 1939- *IntAu&W 82*
Glaab, Charles N 1927- *ConAu 5R, −8NR*
Glackin, William Charles 1917- *ConAmTC*
Glacumakis, George, Jr. 1937- *ConAu 41R*
Glad, Betty 1929- *ConAu 21R*
Glad, Donald 1915- *ConAu 13R*
Glad, Paul W 1926- *ConAu 73*
Gladden, E Norman 1897- *ConAu 21R*
Gladden, Edgar Norman 1897- *WrDr 84*
Gladden, Vivianne Cervantes 1927- *ConAu 102*
Glade, William Patton, Jr. 1929- *ConAu 41R,*
IntAu&W 82
Gladilin, Anatoly Tikhonovich 1935- *ClDMEL 80,*
ConAu 101
Glading, Jan *DrAP&F 83*
Gladish, David F 1928- *ConAu 41R*
Gladkov, Fyodor Vasilievich 1883-1958 *EncWL 2*
Gladkov, Fyodor Vasilyevich 1883-1958
ClDMEL 80, ModSL 1, TwCA,
TwCA SUP, TwCWr
Gladstone, Arthur M 1921- *ConAu 97*
Gladstone, Gary 1935- *ConAu 29R, SmATA 12*
Gladstone, Gerald 1929- *CreCan 2*
Gladstone, Josephine 1938- *ConAu 21R*
Gladstone, M J 1923- *ConAu 53*
Gladstone, Maggie *ConAu X*
Gladstone, Meredith 1939- *ConAu 69*
Gladwell, Derek Channon 1925- *WrDr 84*
Gladwin, David Daniel 1937- *IntAu&W 82*
Gladwin, William Zachary *ConAu X,*
SmATA X
Gladwyn, Edward *IntAu&W 82X*
Gladwyn, Hubert Miles 1900- *WrDr 84*
Gladych, B Michael 1910- *ConAu 5R*
Glaeser, Ernst 1902-1962 *TwCA, TwCA SUP*
Glaessner, Verina 1942- *WrDr 84*
Glaettli, Walter E 1920- *ConAu 21R*
Glahe, Fred R 1934- *ConAu 37R, WrDr 84*
Glaister, John 1892-1971 *ConAu 104*
Glang, Gabrielle *DrAP&F 83*
Glanville, Brian 1931- *WrDr 84*
Glanville, Brian Lester 1931- *ConAu 3NR, −5R,*
ConLC 6, ConNov 82, DcLB 15[port],
DcLEL 1940, IntAu&W 82, WorAu
Glanville, Maxwell 1918- *ConAu 85,*
NatPD 81[port]
Glanz, Edward C 1924- *ConAu 1R*
Glanz, Rudolf 1892-1978 *ConAu 3NR, −49*
Glaser, Comstock *WrDr 84*
Glaser, Daniel 1918- *ConAu 61*
Glaser, Dianne E 1937- *ConAu 77, SmATA 31*
Glaser, E M 1913- *ConAu 21R*
Glaser, Edward 1918-1972 *ConAu 37R*
Glaser, Eleanor Dorothy 1918- *ConAu X,*
WrDr 84
Glaser, Elton *DrAP&F 83*
Glaser, Elton Albert, II 1945- *IntWWP 82*
Glaser, Eva Schocken 1918-1982 *ConAu 105*
Glaser, Isabel *DrAP&F 83*
Glaser, Isabel Joshlin 1929- *ConAu 77*
Glaser, Karl Georg Hermann 1928- *IntAu&W 82*
Glaser, Kurt 1914- *ConAu 1R, −5NR, WrDr 84*
Glaser, Lynn 1943- *ConAu 21R*
Glaser, Michael S *DrAP&F 83*
Glaser, Michael S 1943- *IntWWP 82*
Glaser, Milton 1929- *ConAu 11NR, −17R,*
SmATA 11
Glaser, Robert 1921- *ConAu 7NR, −17R*
Glaser, Rollin Oliver 1932- *ConAu 10NR, −25R*
Glaser, William Arnold 1925- *ConAu 1R, −6NR,*
WrDr 84
Glasgow, Douglas G *ConAu 108*
Glasgow, Ellen 1873-1945 *ConAu 104,*
DcLB 9[port], TwCLC 2
Glasgow, Ellen Anderson Gholson 1874-1945
ConAmA, LongCTC, ModAL, TwCA,
TwCA SUP, TwCLC 7[port], TwCWr
Glasgow, Eric 1924- *ConAu 69, IntWWP 82*

Glasgow, Gordon H H 1926- *ConAu 29R*
Glasheen, Adaline 1920- *ConAu 101*
Glasheen, Patrick 1897- *ConAu P-1*
Glaskin, G M 1923- *ConAu 5NR,*
IntAu&W 82, WrDr 84
Glaskin, Gerald Marcus 1923- *ConAu 53,*
DcLEL 1940
Glaskowsky, Nicholas A, Jr. 1928- *ConAu 3NR,*
−5R
Glasner, Ann K *DrAP&F 83*
Glason, Catherine Mara 1946- *IntWWP 82*
Glaspell, Susan 1876-1948 *DcLB 9[port]*
Glaspell, Susan 1882-1948 *CnMD, ConAmA,*
ConAu 110, DcLB 7[port], LongCTC,
ModWD, TwCA, TwCA SUP
Glasrud, Bruce 1940- *ConAu 41R*
Glasrud, Clarence A 1911- *WrDr 84*
Glass, Albert J 1908-1983 *ConAu 109*
Glass, Andrew J 1935- *ConAu 65*
Glass, Bill 1935- *ConAu 73*
Glass, David Victor 1911-1978 *ConAu 81, −85*
Glass, Ian Cameron 1926- *ConAu 77*
Glass, Joanna *DrAP&F 83*
Glass, Joanna 1936- *ConAu 81,*
NatPD 81[port]
Glass, John F 1936- *ConAu 53*
Glass, Justine Claire *ConAu X*
Glass, Laurie 1965- *IntWWP 82*
Glass, Malcolm 1936- *ConAu 104*
Glass, Montague Marsden 1877-1934 *TwCA*
Glass, Ruth *IntAu&W 82, WrDr 84*
Glass, Sandra *ConAu X*
Glass, Stanley Thomas 1932- *ConAu 21R,*
WrDr 84
Glassberg, B Y 1902- *ConAu P-1*
Glassburner, Bruce 1920- *ConAu 33R*
Glassco, John 1909-1981 *ConAu 102, −13R,*
ConLC 9, ConP 80, CreCan 2
Glasscock, Amnesia *ConAu X*
Glasscock, Anne Bonner 1924- *ConAu 1R*
Glasse, Robert Marshall 1929- *ConAu 29R*
Glasser, Allen 1918- *ConAu 9R*
Glasser, Carole *DrAP&F 83*
Glasser, Carole 1952- *IntWWP 82*
Glasser, Paul H 1929- *ConAu 29R*
Glasser, Perry *DrAP&F 83*
Glasser, Selma 1910- *ConAu 110*
Glasser, Stephen A 1943- *ConAu 53*
Glasser, William 1925- *ConAu 73*
Glassford, Wilfred *ConAu X*
Glassgold, Peter 1939- *ConAu 103*
Glassman, Jon David 1944- *ConAu 69*
Glassman, Michael 1899- *ConAu 13R,*
WrDr 84
Glassman, Seth 1947- *NatPD 81[port]*
Glassner, Lester 1939- *ConAu 107*
Glassner, Martin Ira 1932- *ConAu 41R*
Glasson, T Francis 1906- *WrDr 84*
Glasson, Thomas Francis 1906- *ConAu P-1*
Glassop, Lawson 1913-1966 *ConAu P-1*
Glasstone, Victor 1924- *ConAu 10NR, −65*
Glatstein, Jacob 1896-1971 *ConAu 33R,*
EncWL 2[port]
Glatthorn, Allan A 1924- *ConAu 13R*
Glatzer, Hal 1946- *ConAu 57*
Glatzer, Nahum Norbert 1903- *ConAu 7NR,*
−13R
Glauber, Uta 1936- *ConAu 29R, SmATA 17*
Glaus, Marlene A 1933- *ConAu 21R*
Glavin, Anthony *DrAP&F 83*
Glavin, John P 1933- *ConAu 57*
Glazarova, Jarmila 1901- *TwCWr*
Glaze, Andrew *DrAP&F 83*
Glaze, Andrew Louis 1920- *ConAu 8NR, −17R,*
IntWWP 82, WrDr 84
Glaze, Eleanor *DrAP&F 83*
Glaze, Eleanor 1930- *AuNews 1, ConAu 49*
Glaze, Thomas E 1914- *ConAu 1R*
Glazebrook, Christopher John 1948- *IntWWP 82*
Glazebrook, G P DeT 1899- *ConAu 102*
Glazebrook, Philip 1937- *ConAu 29R, WrDr 84*
Glazener, Mary U 1921- *ConAu 17R*
Glazer, Nathan 1923- *ConAu 5R, DcLEL 1940,*
IntAu&W 82, WrDr 84
Glazer, Nona Y *ConAu X*
Glazer, Sidney 1905- *ConAu 1R, MichAu 80,*
WrDr 84
Glazer, Tom 1914- *ConAu 8NR, −61,*
SmATA 9
Glazer-Malbin, Nona 1932- *ConAu 33R*
Glazier, Kenneth MacLean 1912- *ConAu 9R*
Glazier, Lyle *DrAP&F 83*

Godsey, John Drew 1922- *ConAu 13R,*
  IntAu&W 82, WrDr 84
Godshalk, William Leigh 1937- *ConAu 41R*
Godsiff, Patricia Mary 1915- *WrDr 84*
Godson, John 1937- *ConAu 77*
Godwin, Anthony Richard James Wylie
  1920?-1976 *ConAu 104*
Godwin, Edward William 1933- *CreCan 1*
Godwin, Eric 1913- *WrDr 84*
Godwin, Gail *DrAP&F 83*
Godwin, Gail 1937- *ConAu 29R, ConLC 5, -8,*
  -22[port], ConNov 82, DcLB 6[port],
  WrDr 84
Godwin, Gaylord 1906?-1979 *ConAu 85*
Godwin, George 1889- *ConAu 5R*
Godwin, Harry 1901- *ConAu 109*
Godwin, John 1922- *WrDr 84*
Godwin, John 1928- *ConAu 1R*
Godwin, John 1929- *ConAu 1NR*
Godwin, John Frederick 1922- *ConAu 102,*
  IntAu&W 82
Godwin, Joscelyn 1945- *ConAu 69*
Godwin, Ted 1933- *CreCan 1*
Godwin, Tom 1915- *ConSFA, TwCSFW,*
  WrDr 84
Godwin, Tony *ConAu X*
Goebel, Dorothy 1898-1976 *ConAu 65, -69*
Goebel, Gerhard 1932- *IntAu&W 82*
Goebel, Julius, Jr. 1893?-1973 *ConAu 45*
Goebel, Ulf *DrAP&F 83*
Goedecke, W Robert 1928- *ConAu 29R*
Goedel, Kurt 1906-1978 *ConAu 108*
Goedertier, Joseph M 1907- *ConAu P-2*
Goedicke, Hans 1926- *ConAu 1NR, -45*
Goedicke, Patricia *DrAP&F 83*
Goedicke, Patricia 1931- *ConAu 11NR,*
  WrDr 84
Goedicke, Patricia McKenna 1931- *ConAu 25R,*
  ConP 80, IntAu&W 82
Goedicke, Victor 1912- *ConAu 17R*
Goel, M Lal 1936- *ConAu 53*
Goeller, Carl 1930- *ConAu 21R*
Goelz, Paul Cornelius 1914- *ConAu 109*
Goen, Clarence C 1924- *ConAu 1R, WrDr 84*
Goen, Rayburne Wyndham, Jr. 1942- *ConAu 107*
Goen, Tex, Jr. *ConAu X*
Goeney, William M 1914- *ConAu 5R*
Goerdt, Arthur L 1912- *ConAu 41R*
Goergen, Donald 1943- *ConAu 61*
Goering, Helga *ConAu X*
Goering, Reinhard 1887-1936 *ClDMEL 80,*
  CnMD, ModWD
Goerling, Lars 1931-1966 *ConAu P-2*
Goerner, E A 1929- *ConAu 49*
Goertz, Donald C 1939- *ConAu 53*
Goertzel, Ted George 1942- *ConAu 69*
Goes, Albrecht 1908- *EncWL 2, ModGL*
Goetel, Ferdynand 1890-1960 *ClDMEL 80,*
  EncWL 2, ModSL 2, TwCA, TwCA SUP,
  TwCWr
Goethals, George W 1920- *ConAu 13R*
Goetsch-Trevelyan, Katharine *ConAu X*
Goettel, Elinor 1930- *ConAu 29R, SmATA 12,*
  WrDr 84
Goetz, Billy E 1904- *ConAu P-1*
Goetz, Curt 1888-1960 *CnMD, CroCD*
Goetz, Delia 1898- *ConAu 73, SmATA 22*
Goetz, George *TwCA, TwCA SUP*
Goetz, Ignacio L 1933- *ConAu 37R*
Goetz, Lee Garrett 1932- *ConAu 25R*
Goetz, Ruth Goodman 1912- *IntAu&W 82,*
  NatPD 81[port]
Goetz, Wolfgang 1885-1955 *CnMD, ModWD*
Goetze, Albrecht E R 1897-1971 *ConAu 33R*
Goetzel, Charlotte *CreCan 2*
Goetzmann, William H 1930- *ConAu 21R*
Goff, Frederick Richmond 1916- *ConAu 7NR,*
  -17R
Goff, Frederick Richmond 1916-1982 *ConAu 108*
Goff, Martyn 1923- *ConAu 2NR, -5R,*
  IntAu&W 82, WrDr 84
Goffart, Walter 1934- *ConAu 37R*
Goffin, Raymond C 1890?-1976 *ConAu 65*
Goffin, Robert 1898- *ClDMEL 80*
Goffman, Erving 1922- *ConAu 21R,*
  IntAu&W 82, WrDr 84
Goffman, Erving 1922-1982 *ConAu 9NR, -108*
Goffstein, M B 1940- *ChlLR 3, ConAu 9NR,*
  -21R, SmATA 8
Gofman, John W 1918- *ConAu 65*
Goforth, Ellen *ConAu X, WrDr 84*
Goga, Octavian 1881-1938 *ClDMEL 80*

Gogarty, Oliver St. John 1878-1957 *ConAu 109,*
  DcLB 15[port], LongCTC, ModBrL,
  TwCA, TwCA SUP, TwCWr
Goggin, Muriel *CreCan 1*
Goggin, Terrence P 1941- *ConAu 103*
Gogh, Lucy Van *CreCan 1*
Gogisgi *ConAu X, DrAP&F 83*
Goh, Cheng-Taik 1943- *IntAu&W 82*
Goh, Cheng-Teik 1943- *ConAu 41R*
Gohdes, Clarence Louis Frank 1901- *ConAu 13R*
Goheen, Robert 1919- *WrDr 84*
Gohil, Pratap 1950- *IntAu&W 82*
Gohil, Pratapsinh *IntAu&W 82X*
Gohman, Fred Joseph 1918- *ConAu 5R*
Goines, Donald 1935?-1974 *AuNews 1*
Goins, Ellen H 1927- *ConAu 33R*
Goist, Park Dixon 1936- *ConAu 37R*
Goitein, S D 1900- *ConAu 8NR, -61*
Goitein, Solomon Dob Fritz *ConAu X*
Gojawiczynska, Pola 1896-1963 *ClDMEL 80*
Gokak, Vinayak Krishna *WrDr 84*
Gokak, Vinayak Krishna 1909- *ConAu 69,*
  IntAu&W 82, IntWWP 82
Gokceli, Yasa Kemal *WorAu*
Gokhale, Balkrishna Govind 1919- *ConAu 1R,*
  -4NR
Golan, Aviezer 1922- *ConAu 104*
Golan, Martin *DrAP&F 83*
Golan, Matti 1936- *ConAu 101*
Golann, Cecil Paige 1921- *ConAu 33R,*
  SmATA 11
Golann, Stuart E 1936- *ConAu 57*
Golant, William 1937- *ConAu 65, WrDr 84*
Golay, Alice *IntAu&W 82*
Golay, Frank H 1915- *ConAu 1R, -1NR*
Golbin, Andree 1923- *SmATA 15*
Golburgh, Stephen J 1935- *ConAu 21R*
Gold, Aaron 1937- *ConAu 101*
Gold, Aaron 1937-1983 *ConAu 109*
Gold, Alan R 1948- *ConAu 45*
Gold, Barbara K 1945- *ConAu 110*
Gold, Don 1931- *ConAu 9NR, -61*
Gold, Doris B 1919- *ConAu 9NR, -21R*
Gold, Douglas 1894- *ConAu P-1*
Gold, Edward *DrAP&F 83*
Gold, Edwin Richard 1905- *WrDr 84*
Gold, H L 1914- *ConSFA, TwCSFW*
Gold, Herbert *DrAP&F 83*
Gold, Herbert 1924- *ConAu 9R, ConLC 4, -7,*
  -14, ConNov 82, DcLB Y81A[port], -2,
  DcLEL 1940, MichAu 80, ModAL,
  TwCWr, WorAu, WrDr 84
Gold, Herman *DrAP&F 83*
Gold, Horace L 1914- *WrDr 84*
Gold, Horace Leonard 1914- *IntAu&W 82,*
  WorAu
Gold, Ivan *DrAP&F 83*
Gold, Ivan 1932- *ConAu 3NR, -5R, WrDr 84*
Gold, Joseph 1933- *ConAu 21R*
Gold, Lloyd *NatPD 81[port]*
Gold, Martin 1931- *ConAu 29R*
Gold, Michael 1893-1967 *DcLB 9*
Gold, Michael 1894-1967 *CnMD, ConAu X,*
  ModWD, TwCA, TwCA SUP
Gold, Milton J 1917- *ConAu 17R*
Gold, Phyllis 1941- *ConAu 57, SmATA 21*
Gold, Robert S 1924- *ConAu 53, IntAu&W 82*
Gold, Seymour M 1933- *ConAu 41R*
Gold, Sharlya *ConAu 8NR, -61, SmATA 9*
Gold, Sylviane 1948- *ConAmTC*
Gold, Thomas 1920- *IntAu&W 82*
Gold, Victor 1922- *WrDr 84*
Gold, Victor Roland 1924- *ConAu 53*
Gold, William E 1912- *ConAu 69*
Goldbarth, Albert *DrAP&F 83*
Goldbarth, Albert 1948- *ConAu 6NR, -53,*
  ConLC 5, ConP 80, WrDr 84
Goldbeck, David M 1942- *ConAu 49*
Goldbeck, Frederick E 1902- *ConAu 102*
Goldbeck, Nikki 1947- *ConAu 49*
Goldbeck, Willis 1899?-1979 *ConAu 89*
Goldberg, Alvin Arnold 1931- *ConAu 41R*
Goldberg, Arnold I 1929- *ConAu 103*
Goldberg, Arthur J 1908- *ConAu 65, WrDr 84*
Goldberg, Barbara *DrAP&F 83*
Goldberg, Barney 1918- *ConAu 21R*
Goldberg, Carl 1938- *ConAu 3NR, -49,*
  IntAu&W 82
Goldberg, Dick 1947- *ConAu 97, DcLB 7[port]*
Goldberg, Dorothy K *ConAu 103*
Goldberg, E Marshall 1930- *ConAu 11NR, -69*
Goldberg, E Marshall 1931- *MichAu 80*

Goldberg, Edward M 1931- *ConAu 53*
Goldberg, Eric 1890- *CreCan 2*
Goldberg, George 1935- *ConAu 69*
Goldberg, Gerald Jay *DrAP&F 83*
Goldberg, Gerald Jay 1929- *ConAu 49*
Goldberg, Harvey E 1939- *ConAu 45*
Goldberg, Herb 1937- *ConAu 9NR, -61*
Goldberg, Herbert S 1926- *SmATA 25[port]*
Goldberg, Herman Raphael 1915- *ConAu 5NR,*
  -9R
Goldberg, Hyman 1908?-1970 *ConAu 104*
Goldberg, Isaac 1887-1938 *TwCA*
Goldberg, Jan *ConAu X*
Goldberg, Joan Rachel 1955- *ConAu 110*
Goldberg, Joseph P 1918- *ConAu 37R*
Goldberg, Leah 1911-1970 *ConAu 25R*
Goldberg, Lester *DrAP&F 83*
Goldberg, Louis *ConAu X*
Goldberg, Louis 1908- *ConAu 13R, WrDr 84*
Goldberg, Lucianne Cummings 1935- *ConAu 85*
Goldberg, M A 1919-1970 *ConAu P-2*
Goldberg, M Hirsh 1942- *ConAu 73*
Goldberg, Maxwell Henry 1907- *ConAu 103*
Goldberg, Miriam Levin 1914- *ConAu 41R*
Goldberg, Moses H 1940- *ConAu 93*
Goldberg, Myra *DrAP&F 83*
Goldberg, Nathan 1903?-1979 *ConAu 85*
Goldberg, Norman L 1906- *ConAu 81*
Goldberg, P Selvin 1917- *ConAu 5R*
Goldberg, Philip 1944- *ConAu 85*
Goldberg, Phyllis 1941- *ConAu 57*
Goldberg, Ray A 1926- *ConAu 49*
Goldberg, Reuben L 1883-1970 *ConAu 9NR*
Goldberg, Reuben Lucius 1883-1970 *ConAu 5R*
Goldberg, Robert Alan 1949- *ConAu 105*
Goldberg, Rube *ConAu X*
Goldberg, Samuel Louis 1926- *WrDr 84*
Goldberg, Sidney 1931- *ConAu 77*
Goldberg, Stan J 1939- *ConAu 49,*
  SmATA 26[port]
Goldberg, Steven 1941- *ConAu 53*
Goldberger, Arthur Stanley 1930- *ConAu 9R*
Golde, Peggy 1930- *ConAu 37R*
Golde, Roger A 1934- *ConAu 69*
Goldemberg, Isaac 1945- *ConAu 11NR, -69*
Goldemberg, Rose Leiman 1928- *ConAu 2NR,*
  -49, NatPD 81[port]
Golden, Arthur 1924- *ConAu 33R*
Golden, Gail Kadison *DrAP&F 83*
Golden, Harry 1902-1981 *ConAu 2NR, -104,*
  WorAu
Golden, Harry 1903- *ConAu 1R*
Golden, James L 1919- *ConAu 109*
Golden, Jeffrey S 1950- *ConAu 33R*
Golden, L L L *ConAu 21R*
Golden, Leon 1930- *ConAu 17R, WrDr 84*
Golden, Morris 1926- *ConAu 1R*
Golden, Rima *DrAP&F 83, IntWWP 82X*
Golden, Robert Edward 1945- *ConAu 65*
Golden, Ruth I 1910- *ConAu P-2*
Golden, Samuel A 1909- *ConAu 110*
Golden, Sean V 1948- *ConAu 107*
Golden, Virginia *IntWWP 82X*
Golden, Virginia Preston 1913- *IntWWP 82*
Golden Silver *ConAu X*
Goldenberg, Edie N 1945- *ConAu 69*
Goldenberg, Herbert 1926- *ConAu 41R*
Goldenberg, I Ira 1936- *ConAu 110*
Goldenberg, Marion Heather 1934- *IntWWP 82*
Goldenberg, Robert 1942- *ConAu 109*
Goldensohn, Barry *DrAP&F 83*
Goldensohn, Barry 1937- *ConAu 77*
Goldensohn, Lorrie *DrAP&F 83*
Goldenson, Daniel R 1944- *ConAu 25R*
Goldenson, Robert M 1908- *ConAu 29R,*
  WrDr 84
Goldenthal, Allan Benarria 1920- *ConAu 17R*
Goldenthal, Jolene *NatPD 81[port]*
Goldfaden, Abraham 1840-1908 *ModWD*
Goldfader, Edward H 1930- *ConAu 29R*
Goldfarb, Nathan 1913- *ConAu 13R, WrDr 84*
Goldfarb, Ronald 1933- *WrDr 84*
Goldfarb, Ronald L 1933- *ConAu 9NR, -21R*
Goldfarb, Russell M 1934- *ConAu 37R,*
  WrDr 84
Goldfarb, Sally F 1957- *ConAu 104*
Goldfarb, Sidney *DrAP&F 83*
Goldfeder, Cheryl *ConAu X, MichAu 80,*
  SmATA X
Goldfeder, James 1943- *ConAu X*
Goldfeder, Jim *ConAu X, SmATA X*
Goldfein, Alan *DrAP&F 83*

Goold-Adams, Richard John Moreton 1916-
 ConAu 13R, IntAu&W 82
Gooneratne, Malini Yasmine 1935- IntWWP 82
Gooneratne, Yasmine 1935- ConAu 29R
Goor, Nancy 1944- SmATA 34
Goor, Ron 1940- SmATA 34
Goossen, Agnes ConAu X, SmATA X
Goossen, Eugene 1920- WrDr 84
Goossen, Irvy W 1924- ConAu 37R
Gopal, Honnalgere 1944- IntWWP 82
Gopal, Sarvepalli 1923- ConAu 104,
 DcLEL 1940, WrDr 84
Gopaleen, Myles Na LongCTC, WorAu
Goralski, Robert 1928- ConAu 105
Goran, Call ConAu X
Goran, Lester 1928- ConAu 45
Goran, Morris 1916- WrDr 84
Goran, Morris 1918- ConAu 1R, -2NR
Gorbanevskaya, Natalya Yevgenevna 1936-
 CIDMEL 80, WorAu 1970
Gorbatov, Alexander V 1891?-1973 ConAu 45
Gorbatov, Boris Leontievich 1908-1954 TwCWr
Gorden, Raymond L 1919- ConAu 53
Gordenker, Leon 1923- ConAu 21R
Gordh, George 1912- ConAu 13R
Gordimer, Nadine 1923- ConAu 3NR, -5R,
 ConLC 3, -5, -7, -10, -18, ConNov 82,
 DcLEL 1940, EncWL 2, IntAu&W 82,
 ModCmwL, TwCWr, WhoTwCL, WorAu,
 WrDr 84
Gordin, Jacob 1853-1909 ModWD
Gordin, Richard Davis 1928- ConAu 53
Gordis, Robert 1908- ConAu 9NR, -13R,
 IntAu&W 82, WrDr 84
Gordon IntWWP 82X
Gordon, Ad ConAu X
Gordon, Alan F 1947- ConAu 102
Gordon, Albert I 1903-1968 ConAu P-1
Gordon, Alex ConAu X
Gordon, Alvin J 1912- ConAu 33R
Gordon, Ambrose, Jr. 1920- ConAu 33R
Gordon, Angela ConAu X
Gordon, Anne Wolrige ConAu X
Gordon, Anthony IntWWP 82X
Gordon, Antoinette K 1892?-1975 ConAu 57
Gordon, Arthur 1912- ConAu 5R
Gordon, Barbara 1913- ConAu 89
Gordon, Barry 1934- ConAu 102, WrDr 84
Gordon, Bernard K 1932- ConAu 85
Gordon, Bernard Ludwig 1931- ConAu 29R,
 SmATA 27[port]
Gordon, Bertram M 1943- ConAu 101
Gordon, Beverly 1948- ConAu 93
Gordon, Bonnie DrAP&F 83
Gordon, Caroline 1895-1981 ConAu 103,
 ConAu P-1, ConLC 6, -13,
 DcLB Y81A[port], -4, -9[port], EncWL 2,
 ModAL SUP, TwCA, TwCA SUP
Gordon, Charles F DrAP&F 83
Gordon, Charles William 1860-1937 ConAu 109,
 CreCan 1, LongCTC, TwCA, TwCA SUP
Gordon, Coco DrAP&F 83
Gordon, Coco 1938- IntWWP 82
Gordon, Cyrus Herzl 1908- ConAu 1R, -5NR,
 IntAu&W 82, WrDr 84
Gordon, Dane R 1925- ConAu 33R
Gordon, David TwCSFW
Gordon, David Cole 1922- ConAu 25R
Gordon, David J 1929- ConAu 105
Gordon, Diana WrDr 84
Gordon, Diana R 1938- ConAu 49
Gordon, Donald ConAu X, WrDr 84
Gordon, Donald Craigie 1911- ConAu 17R,
 WrDr 84
Gordon, Donald Ramsay 1929- ConAu 37R,
 WrDr 84
Gordon, Doreen ConAu X
Gordon, Dorothy 1893-1970 ConAu 73,
 SmATA 20[port]
Gordon, Edmund Wyatt 1921- ConAu 37R,
 LivgBAA
Gordon, Edwin 1927- ConAu 10NR, -17R
Gordon, Ernest 1916- ConAu 1R, -2NR,
 WrDr 84
Gordon, Esme 1910- ConAu 108
Gordon, Esther Saranga 1935- ConAu 7NR, -53,
 SmATA 10
Gordon, Ethel E 1915- WrDr 84
Gordon, Ethel Edison 1915- ConAu 53,
 TwCRGW
Gordon, Felice 1939- ConAu 97
Gordon, Fred DrAP&F 83

Gordon, Frederick ConAu P-2, SmATA 1
Gordon, Fritz ConAu X, IntAu&W 82X,
 WrDr 84
Gordon, Gary ConAu X
Gordon, George ConAu X
Gordon, George Byron 1911- ConAu 33R
Gordon, George N 1926- ConAu 1R, -5NR,
 WrDr 84
Gordon, Gerald 1909- ConAu P-1
Gordon, Gerald Timothy DrAP&F 83
Gordon, Giles 1940- WrDr 84
Gordon, Giles Alexander Esme 1940- ConAu 41R,
 ConNov 82, ConP 80, DcLB 14[port],
 IntAu&W 82, IntWWP 82
Gordon, Gordon 1906- TwCCr&M 80,
 WrDr 84
Gordon, Gordon 1912- ConAu 5R, -7NR
Gordon, Guanetta Stewart ConAu 37R
Gordon, Hal ConAu X, SmATA X
Gordon, Harold J, Jr. 1919- ConAu 33R
Gordon, Harry ConAu X
Gordon, Helen IntAu&W 82X
Gordon, Henry Alfred 1925- ConAu 5NR, -53
Gordon, Hortense 1887-1961 CreCan 2
Gordon, I R F 1939- ConAu 69
Gordon, Ian ConAu X
Gordon, Ian A 1908- ConAu 11NR
Gordon, Ian Alistair 1908- ConAu 25R,
 IntAu&W 82, WrDr 84
Gordon, Ida 1907- WrDr 84
Gordon, Ida L 1907- ConAu P-2
Gordon, Ira J 1923- ConAu 69
Gordon, Jaimy DrAP&F 83
Gordon, James 1918- ConAu 61
Gordon, Jane ConAu X
Gordon, Janet ConAu X, LongCTC,
 TwCA SUP
Gordon, Joanne J 1956- ConAu 108
Gordon, John ConAu X
Gordon, John 1925- ConAu 11NR, -25R,
 SmATA 6, TwCCW 83
Gordon, John Fraser 1916- ConAu 105,
 IntAu&W 82, WrDr 84
Gordon, John Rutherford 1890-1974 ConAu 104
Gordon, John Steele 1944- ConAu 57
Gordon, John William 1925- ConAu 103,
 WrDr 84
Gordon, Katharine WrDr 84
Gordon, Kermit 1916-1976 ConAu 65
Gordon, Kirpal DrAP&F 83
Gordon, Kurtz ConAu X
Gordon, Leland James 1897- ConAu 41R
Gordon, Leonard 1935- ConAu 53
Gordon, Leonard A 1938- ConAu 37R
Gordon, Leonard H D 1928- ConAu 29R
Gordon, Lesley ConAu X
Gordon, Lew ConAu X, SmATA X, WrDr 84
Gordon, Lillian L 1925-1977 ConAu 29R
Gordon, Lincoln 1913- IntAu&W 82
Gordon, Linda 1940- ConAu 10NR, -65
Gordon, Lois G 1938- ConAu 33R, WrDr 84
Gordon, Lou 1917?-1977 ConAu 69
Gordon, Marek Henryk 1918- IntWWP 82
Gordon, Margaret Anna 1939- SmATA 9
Gordon, Margaret T 1939- ConAu 81
Gordon, Mary DrAP&F 83
Gordon, Mary 1949- ConAu 102, ConLC 13,
 -22[port], DcLB Y81A[port], -6
Gordon, Michael 1940- ConAu 41R
Gordon, Mildred 1905-1979 TwCCr&M 80
Gordon, Mildred 1912-1979 ConAu 5R, -7NR,
 -85, SmATA 24N
Gordon, Mitchell 1925- ConAu 5R
Gordon, Myron J 1920- ConAu 5R, -6NR
Gordon, Nancy ConAu X
Gordon, Nancy Doris 1918- IntWWP 82
Gordon, Neil 1895-1941 LongCTC, TwCA,
 TwCA SUP
Gordon, Noah 1926- ConAu 17R
Gordon, Oliver ConAu X
Gordon, Patricia 1909- ConAu 21R
Gordon, Percival Hector 1884-1975 ConAu 41R
Gordon, Peter ConAu X
Gordon, Ray WrDr 84
Gordon, Rex WrDr 84
Gordon, Rex 1917- ConAu X, ConSFA,
 TwCSFW
Gordon, Richard WrDr 84
Gordon, Richard 1921- ConAu X, DcLEL 1940,
 TwCWr, WrDr 84
Gordon, Richard L 1934- ConAu 29R
Gordon, Robert DrAP&F 83, NatPD 81[port]

Gordon, Robert A 1908-1978 ConAu 4NR, -5R,
 -77
Gordon, Robert C 1921- ConAu 5R
Gordon, Ruth 1896- ASpks, ConAu 81,
 NatPD 81[port], WrDr 84
Gordon, Sanford D 1924- ConAu 33R
Gordon, Selma ConAu X, SmATA 3
Gordon, Shirley 1921- ConAu 97
Gordon, Sol 1923- ConAu 4NR, -53,
 ConLC 26[port], SmATA 11
Gordon, Steve 1938?-1982 ConAu 108
Gordon, Stewart ConAu X, SmATA X,
 WrDr 84
Gordon, Strathearn 1902-1983 ConAu 109
Gordon, Stuart 1947- TwCSFW, WrDr 84
Gordon, Suzanne 1945- ConAu 4NR, -49
Gordon, Sydney 1914- ConAu 29R,
 IntAu&W 82, WrDr 84
Gordon, Theodore J 1930- ConAu 17R
Gordon, Thomas 1918- ConAu 29R, WrDr 84
Gordon, Tom ConAu X
Gordon, Walter Kelly 1930- ConAu 33R
Gordon, Walter L 1906- ConAu 97
Gordon, Wendell 1916- ConAu 17R
Gordon Clark, A A LongCTC
Gordon Walker, Patrick 1907- ConAu 29R
Gordone, Charles 1925- ConAu 93, ConDr 82,
 ConLC 1, -4, DcLB 7[port], LivgBAA,
 NatPD 81[port], WrDr 84
Gordons, The ConAu X, SmATA X, WrDr 84
Gordy, Berry, Sr. 1888-1978 ConAu 102
Gore, Arthur Kattendyke S D A 1910-1983
 ConAu 109
Gore, Charles 1853-1932 LongCTC
Gore, John Francis 1885- IntAu&W 82
Gore, John Francis 1885?-1983 ConAu 110
Gore, Robert Hayes 1886-1972 ConAu 89
Gore, William Jay 1924- ConAu 9R
Gore-Booth, Lord 1909- WrDr 84
Gore-Booth, Constance LongCTC
Gore-Booth, Eva Selena 1870-1926 LongCTC
Goreau, Angeline 1951- ConAu 102
Gorecki, Jan 1926- ConAu 57
Gorelick, Molly C 1920- ConAu 21R,
 SmATA 9
Gorelik, Mordecai 1899- ConAu P-2, WrDr 84
Gorell Barnes, William 1909- WrDr 84
Goren, Charles H 1901- ConAu 69, WrDr 84
Goren, Judith DrAP&F 83
Goren, Judith 1933- ConAu 61, IntWWP 82,
 MichAu 80
Gorenko, Anna Andreyevna 1888- ConAu X,
 ConLC 11, WorAu
Gorenstein, Shirley 1928- ConAu 73
Gorer, Geoffrey Edgar 1905- ConAu 69,
 TwCA SUP
Gores, Joe ConAu X
Gores, Joe 1931- ConAu X, TwCCr&M 80,
 WrDr 84
Gores, Joseph N 1931- ConAu 10NR, -25R
Gorey, Edward 1925- ConAu 9NR, WrDr 84
Gorey, Edward St. John 1925- ConAu 5R,
 Conv 1, SmATA 27, -29[port]
Gorey, Hays ConAu 57
Gorgey, Gabor 1929- CroCD, IntAu&W 82
Gorham, Charles Orson 1911-1975 ConAu 1R,
 -6NR, -61
Gorham, J U 1920- ConAu 53
Gorham, Maurice Anthony Coneys 1902-
 ConAu 9R
Gorham, Michael ConAu X, IntAu&W 82X,
 SmATA 5, WrDr 84
Gorki, Maxim 1868-1936 CnMD
Gorky, Maksim 1868-1936 CIDMEL 80
Gorky, Maxim 1868-1936 CnMWL, ConAu X,
 EncWL 2[port], ModSL 1, ModWD,
 TwCA, TwCA SUP, TwCLC 8[port],
 TwCWr, WhoTwCL
Gorling, Lars 1931-1966 ConAu 25R
Gorman, Beth ConAu X
Gorman, Burton William 1907- ConAu 29R
Gorman, George H 1916-1982 ConAu 106
Gorman, Ginny ConAu X, WrDr 84
Gorman, Herbert Sherman 1893-1954 TwCA,
 TwCA SUP
Gorman, John Andrew 1938- ConAu 41R
Gorman, Katherine 1899-1972 ConAu P-2
Gorman, LeRoy 1949- IntAu&W 82
Gorman, Ralph 1897-1972 ConAu 37R
Gorman, Santina 1903- MichAu 80
Gorman, T Walter 1916?-1972 ConAu 37R
Gormley, Gerard 1931- ConAu 81

Gormley, Mike 1945- *ConAu 69*
Gorn, Janice L 1915- *ConAu 53*
Gorney, Roderic 1924- *ConAu 73*
Gorney, Sondra 1918- *ConAu 45*
Gornick, Vivian 1935- *ConAu 101, WrDr 84*
Gorodetsky, Gabriel 1945- *ConAu 69*
Gorodetsky, Sergey Mitrofanovich 1884-1967 *CIDMEL 80*
Gorostiza, Jose 1901-1973 *ModLAL*
Gorrell, Robert 1914- *WrDr 84*
Gorrell, Robert Mark 1914- *ConAu 1R, -5NR*
Gorsline, Douglas 1913- *ConAu 9NR*
Gorsline, Douglas Warner 1913- *ConAu 61, SmATA 11*
Gorsline, Marie 1928- *ConAu 106, SmATA 28[port]*
Gorsline, S M *ConAu X, SmATA X*
Gorst, Elliot Marcet 1885-1973 *ConAu 104*
Gorst-Williams, Jessica Anthea 1948- *IntWWP 82*
Gorter, Herman 1864-1927 *CIDMEL 80, WorAu*
Gortner, Ross A, Jr. 1912- *ConAu 5R*
Gortner, Willis Alway 1913- *ConAu 108*
Gorton, Richard A 1932- *ConAu 7NR, -57*
Goryan, Sirak *ConAu X, LongCTC, SmATA X*
Gosden, Freeman F 1899-1982 *ConAu 108*
Gosden, Peter Henry John Heather 1927- *ConAu 93*
Gosdin, Rex 1938?-1983 *ConAu 109*
Gose, Elliott B, Jr. 1926- *ConAu 33R*
Goshay, Robert C 1931- *ConAu 13R*
Goshen, Charles E 1916- *ConAu 21R*
Goshorn, Elizabeth 1953- *ConAu 61*
Goslin, David A 1936- *ConAu 9R*
Gosling, J C B 1930- *ConAu 77, WrDr 84*
Gosling, John Neville 1905- *ConAu 5R*
Gosling, Nigel 1909-1982 *ConAu 106*
Gosling, William Flower 1901- *ConAu 5R, WrDr 84*
Goslovich, Marianne *ConAu X*
Gosnell, Betty 1921- *ConAu X, IntAu&W 82*
Gosnell, David Foote 1932- *IntWWP 82*
Gosnell, Elizabeth Duke Tucker 1921- *ConAu 29R*
Gosnell, Harold F 1896- *WrDr 84*
Gosnell, Harold Foote 1896- *ConAu 41R, IntAu&W 82*
Goss, Clay 1946- *ConAu 57*
Gosse, Sir Edmund William 1849-1928 *CnMWL, LongCTC, ModBrL, TwCA, TwCA SUP, TwCW*
Gosselin, Chris 1929- *ConAu 110*
Gossett, Philip 1941- *ConAu 89*
Gossett, Thomas F 1916- *ConAu 13R*
Gossman, Lionel 1929- *ConAu 7NR, -17R*
Gostelow, Mary 1943- *ConAu 8NR, -61*
Gotama *IntAu&W 82X*
Gotanda, Philip Kan 1949- *NatPD 81[port]*
Gotesky, Rubin 1906- *ConAu 45*
Gotfurt, Frederick 1902?-1973 *ConAu 104*
Gothe, Jurgen R 1944- *IntAu&W 82*
Gotlieb, Allan 1928- *WrDr 84*
Gotlieb, Phyllis 1926- *ConAu 7NR, -13R, ConLC 18, ConP 80, ConSFA, CreCan 2, DcLEL 1940, IntAu&W 82, IntWWP 82, TwCSFW, WrDr 84*
Gots, Ronald E 1943- *ConAu 65*
Gotschalk, Felix C 1929- *TwCSFW, WrDr 84*
Gotshalk, D W 1901-1973 *ConAu 1R, -6NR*
Gotshalks, Irene Apinee *CreCan 2*
Gotshalks, Juris 1924- *CreCan 1*
Gotshalks, Jury 1924- *CreCan 1*
Gotshalks, Yury 1924- *CreCan 1*
Gott, George *DrAP&F 83*
Gott, K D 1923- *ConAu 81*
Gott, Richard *WrDr 84*
Gott, Richard 1938- *ConAu 81*
Gotta, Salvator 1887- *IntAu&W 82*
Gottchalk, Laura Riding *ConAmA*
Gottehrer, Barry H 1935- *ConAu 13R*
Gotterer, Malcolm H 1924- *ConAu 37R*
Gottesfeld, Evelyn 1948- *ConAu 104*
Gottesman, Irving I 1930- *ConAu 37R*
Gottesman, Ronald 1933- *ConAu 33R*
Gottesman, S D *ConAu X*
Gottfried, Alex 1919- *ConAu 1R*
Gottfried, Chet *DrAP&F 83*
Gottfried, Joseph Gath 1935- *NatPD 81[port]*
Gottfried, Martin 1933- *ConAmTC, ConAu 21R, DcLEL 1940*

Gottfried, Theodore Mark 1928- *ConAu 33R*
Gottlieb, Adolph 1903-1974 *ConAu 49*
Gottlieb, Beatrice M 1889?-1979 *ConAu 89*
Gottlieb, Bernhardt Stanley 1898- *ConAu 1R*
Gottlieb, Bill *SmATA X*
Gottlieb, Darcy *DrAP&F 83*
Gottlieb, Darcy 1922- *ConAu 77*
Gottlieb, Elaine *ConAu 61, DrAP&F 83*
Gottlieb, Gerald 1923- *ConAu 5R, SmATA 7*
Gottlieb, Lois Davidson 1926- *ConAu 17R*
Gottlieb, Naomi R 1925- *ConAu 57*
Gottlieb, Paul 1936- *ConAu 93*
Gottlieb, Robin 1928- *ConAu 1R, -2NR*
Gottlieb, William P 1917- *ConAu 101, SmATA 24*
Gottman, John M 1942- *ConAu 69*
Gottschalk, Elin Toona 1937- *ConAu 81*
Gottschalk, Laura Riding *ConAmA, ConAu X, WrDr 84*
Gottschalk, Louis 1899-1975 *ConAu 9NR, -13R, -57, TwCA SUP*
Gottschalk, Louis A 1916- *ConAu 5NR, -53*
Gottschalk, Paul A 1939- *ConAu 61*
Gottschalk, Shimon S 1929- *ConAu 89*
Gottschalk, Stephen 1940- *ConAu 77*
Gottsegen, Abby J 1956- *ConAu 105*
Gottsegen, Gloria Behar 1930- *ConAu 77*
Gottshall, Franklin H 1902- *WrDr 84*
Gottshall, Franklin Henry 1902- *ConAu 2NR, -5R, IntAu&W 82*
Gottwald, Norman Karol 1926- *ConAu 108*
Gotwals, Vernon 1924- *ConAu 5R*
Gotz, Ignacio L 1933- *ConAu X, WrDr 84*
Gotzsche, Anne-Lise 1939- *ConAu 97*
Goud, Anne 1917- *ConAu 61*
Goudeket, Maurice 1889-1977 *ConAu 69*
Goudey, Alice E 1898- *ConAu 73, SmATA 20[port]*
Goudge, Elizabeth 1900- *ConAu 5R, -5NR, LongCTC, SmATA 2, TwCA, TwCA SUP, TwCCW 83, TwCRGW, TwCWr, WrDr 84*
Goudie, Andrew Shaw 1945- *ConAu 1NR, -49*
Goudsmit, Samuel Abraham 1902-1978 *ConAu 81*
Gouge, Orson *ConAu X*
Gough, Barry Morton 1938- *ConAu 11NR, -61*
Gough, Catherine *ConAu X*
Gough, Catherine 1931- *ConAu 25R, SmATA 24[port]*
Gough, John Wiedhofft 1900- *ConAu 13R*
Gough, Kathleen *ConAu X*
Gough, Vera *ConAu 25R*
Gougov, Nikola Delchev 1914- *ConAu 45*
Gouhier, Henri 1898- *IntAu&W 82*
Gouin, Jacques R J 1919- *IntAu&W 82*
Goul, Roman Borisovich 1896- *CIDMEL 80*
Goulart, Frances Sheridan 1938- *ConAu 7NR, -57, MichAu 80*
Goulart, Ron 1933- *ConAu 7NR, -25R, ConSFA, IntAu&W 82, SmATA 6, TwCCr&M 80, TwCSFW, WrDr 84*
Gould, Alan *ConAu X, WorAu*
Gould, Alfred Ernest 1909- *ConAu 5R*
Gould, Beatrice Blackmar 1898- *ConAu P-2*
Gould, Bernard *LongCTC*
Gould, Bruce Grant 1942- *ConAu 45*
Gould, Carol C 1946- *ConAu 103*
Gould, Cecil 1918- *ConAu 9NR, -21R*
Gould, Chester 1900- *ConAu 77*
Gould, Douglas Parsons 1919- *ConAu 1R*
Gould, Ed 1936- *ConAu 93*
Gould, Felix *ConAu P-1*
Gould, Gerald 1885-1936 *ModBrL*
Gould, Glenn 1932- *CreCan 2*
Gould, Henry Hale 1952- *IntWWP 82*
Gould, James A 1922- *ConAu 33R, WrDr 84*
Gould, James Warren 1924- *ConAu 2NR, -5R*
Gould, Jay R 1906- *ConAu 45*
Gould, Jean R 1919- *ConAu 3NR, -5R, IntAu&W 82, SmATA 11, WrDr 84*
Gould, Joan 1927- *ConAu 107*
Gould, John A 1944- *ConAu 57*
Gould, John Thomas 1908- *ConAu 65, TwCA SUP*
Gould, Joseph E 1912- *ConAu 9R*
Gould, Josiah B 1928- *ConAu 45*
Gould, Joy *ConAu X*
Gould, Leroy C 1937- *ConAu 93*
Gould, Leslie 1902-1977 *ConAu 73*
Gould, Lettie *ConAu X*
Gould, Lewis L 1939- *ConAu 41R*
Gould, Lilian 1920- *ConAu 2NR, -49,*

SmATA 6
Gould, Lois *DrAP&F 83, WrDr 84*
Gould, Lois 1938?- *ConAu 77, ConLC 4, -10*
Gould, Marilyn 1928- *SmATA 15*
Gould, Mary Earle 1885- *ConAu 5R*
Gould, Maurice 1909- *WrDr 84*
Gould, Maurice M 1909- *ConAu 5R, -5NR*
Gould, Michael *ConAu X*
Gould, Milton Samuel 1909- *ConAu 93*
Gould, Peter 1932- *WrDr 84*
Gould, Peter Robin 1932- *ConAu 1R*
Gould, Randall 1898?-1979 *ConAu 89*
Gould, Richard A 1939- *ConAu 7NR, -53*
Gould, Roberta *DrAP&F 83*
Gould, Roger L 1935- *ConAu 110*
Gould, Ronald 1904- *ConAu 102, WrDr 84*
Gould, Shirley *ConAu 81*
Gould, Stephen Jay 1941- *ConAu 10NR, -77*
Gould, Warwick 1947- *ConAu 110*
Gould, Wesley Larson 1917- *ConAu 1R, -2NR*
Goulden, Joseph C 1934- *ConAu 8NR, -17R, WrDr 84*
Goulden, Mark 1896?-1980 *ConAu 101*
Goulder, Grace *ConAu X*
Goulding, Brian 1933- *ConAu 103*
Goulding, Dorothy 1898- *CreCan 2*
Goulding, Dorothy Jane 1923- *ConAu 65*
Goulding, Peter G 1920- *ConAu 106, WrDr 84*
Goulding, Ray 1922- *ConAu 85*
Gouldner, Alvin Ward 1920-1980 *ConAu 102, -13R*
Gouled, Vivian G 1911- *ConAu 41R*
Goulet, Denis A 1931- *ConAu 41R, IntAu&W 82*
Goulet, John 1942- *ConAu 85*
Goulet, Robert 1924- *ConAu 1R*
Goulett, Harlan M 1927-1969 *ConAu P-2*
Goulianos, Joan Rodman 1939- *ConAu 49*
Goullart, Peter 1902- *ConAu P-1*
Goulyashki, Andrei 1914- *ConAu 101*
Gourdie, Thomas 1913- *ConAu 1R, -1NR*
Gourdie, Tom 1913- *WrDr 84*
Gourdine, Delcie Southall *DrAP&F 83*
Gourevitch, Doris-Jeanne *ConAu 17R*
Gouri, Haim 1923- *ConAu 103*
Gouriadec, Yvette Brind'Amour Le *CreCan 1*
Gourlay, David 1922- *WrDr 84*
Gourley, G Douglas 1911- *ConAu 1R*
Gourley, Jay 1947- *ConAu 73*
Gourlie, Norah Dundas *ConAu P-1*
Gourmont, Remy De 1858-1915 *CIDMEL 80, ConAu 109, LongCTC, ModRL, TwCA, TwCA SUP*
Gouzenko, Igor 1919-1982 *ConAu 107*
Govan, Christine Noble 1897- *WrDr 84*
Govan, Christine Noble 1898- *ConAu 1R, -2NR, SmATA 9*
Govan, Thomas P 1907-1979 *ConAu 2NR, -45*
Gove, Philip Babcock 1902-1972 *ConAu 37R, ConAu P-1*
Gove, Samuel K 1923- *ConAu 33R*
Goveia, Elsa Vesta 1925- *ConAu 21R, DcLEL 1940, WrDr 84*
Govenar, Alan B 1952- *ConAu 109*
Goveneche, Gabriel *ConAu X*
Gover, John Robert 1929- *DcLEL 1940*
Gover, Robert *DrAP&F 83*
Gover, Robert 1929- *ConAu 9R, ConNov 82, WhoTwCL, WorAu, WrDr 84*
Govern, Elaine 1939- *ConAu 53, SmATA 26*
Govier, Katherine 1948- *ConAu 101*
Govinda, Anagarika 1898- *ConAu 21R, IntAu&W 82*
Govoni, Albert P 1914- *ConAu 53, IntAu&W 82*
Govoni, Albert P 1914-1982 *ConAu 108*
Govoni, Corrado 1884-1965 *WhoTwCL*
Govoni, Laura E 1914- *ConAu 33R*
Govorchin, Gerald Gilbert 1912- *ConAu 13R*
Gow, Donald John 1920-1973 *ConAu 41R*
Gow, Ronald 1897- *ConAu P-2, ConDr 82, IntAu&W 82, WrDr 84*
Gowan, Donald E 1929- *ConAu 69*
Gowan, Elsie Park Young 1905- *CreCan 1*
Gowan, John C 1912- *WrDr 84*
Gowan, John Curtis 1912- *ConAu 5NR, -13R*
Gowans, Alan 1923- *ConAu 1R, -2NR, WrDr 84*
Gowar, Antonia *ConAu X*
Gowen, Emmett 1902- *ConAu P-1*
Gowen, James A 1928- *ConAu 17R*
Gower, Herschel 1919- *ConAu 5R*

Gowers, Sir Ernest Arthur 1880-1966 *ConAu 89,*
DcLEL 1940, LongCTC, WorAu
Gowin, D Bob 1925- *ConAu 108*
Gowing, Lawrence 1918- *ConAu 9R, WrDr 84*
Gowing, Margaret Mary 1921- *ConAu 81,*
IntAu&W 82, WrDr 84
Gowing, Peter Gordon 1930- *ConAu 53*
Gowland, Mariano E 1933- *ConAu 5R*
Goy, Erwin 1905- *IntWWP 82*
Goyder, George Armin 1908- *ConAu 105,*
WrDr 84
Goyen, William *DrAP&F 83*
Goyen, William 1915- *AuNews 2, ConAu 5R,*
-6NR, ConLC 5, -8, -14, ConNov 82,
DcLB 2, DcLEL 1940, WorAu, WrDr 84
Goyen, William 1915-1983 *ConAu 110,*
DcLB Y83N[port]
Goyen, William 1918- *ModAL*
Goyeneche, Gabriel *ConAu X*
Goyer, Robert Stanton 1923- *ConAu 41R*
Goytisolo, Juan 1931- *CIDMEL 80, ConAu 85,*
ConLC 5, -10, -23[port], EncWL 2[port],
ModRL, TwCWr, WorAu
Goytisolo, Luis 1937- *CIDMEL 80*
Gozzano, Guido 1883-1916 *CIDMEL 80,*
EncWL 2, WhoTwCL
Graaf, Peter *ConAu X, WorAu*
Grabar, Pierre 1898- *IntAu&W 82*
Grabato Dias, Joao Pedro *CIDMEL 80*
Grabbe, Paul 1902- *ConAu 93*
Graber, Alexander 1914- *ConAu 1R, -1NR,*
SmATA 7
Graber, Doris A 1923- *ConAu 33R*
Graber, Gerry S 1928- *ConAu 81*
Graber, Richard 1927- *ConAu 85,*
SmATA 26[port]
Grabianski, Janusz 1928-1976 *ConAu 2NR, -45*
Grabianski, Janusz 1929-1976 *SmATA 30N*
Grabill, James, Jr. 1949- *IntWWP 82*
Grabill, Jim *DrAP&F 83, IntWWP 82X*
Grabill, Joseph L 1931- *ConAu 29R*
Grabill, Paul E *DrAP&F 83*
Grabman, Richard *DrAP&F 83*
Grabner-Haider, Anton 1940- *ConAu 73*
Grabo, Norman Stanley 1930- *ConAu 1R*
Graboff, Abner 1919- *ConAu 107*
Grabois, Aryeh 1930- *ConAu 105*
Grabosky, Peter Nils 1945- *ConAu 85*
Grabowski, Z Anthony 1903- *ConAu 5R*
Graburn, Nelson 1936- *ConAu 1NR, -45*
Gracchus, Sidney J 1930- *ConAu 97*
Grace, Betty *MichAu 80*
Grace, Dorman John 1904- *IntWWP 82*
Grace, Gerald R 1936- *ConAu 45*
Grace, Helen K 1935- *ConAu 53*
Grace, Joan C 1921- *ConAu 61*
Grace, Joseph *ConAu X*
Grace, Sherrill E 1944- *ConAu 110*
Grace, William Joseph 1910- *ConAu P-1*
Gracey, Harry L 1933- *ConAu 41R*
Gracia, Jorge J E 1942- *ConAu 109*
Gracq, Julien 1909- *ModFrL, ModRL*
Gracq, Julien 1910- *CIDMEL 80, CnMD,*
ConLC 11, EncWL 2, TwCA SUP
Gracy, David B, II 1941- *WrDr 84*
Gracy, David Bergen, II 1941- *ConAu 25R*
Gracza, Margaret Young 1928- *ConAu 13R*
Grad, Frank P 1924- *ConAu 33R*
Grade, Arnold 1928- *ConAu 29R*
Grade, Chaim 1910-1982 *ConAu 107, -93,*
ConLC 10, EncWL 2
Gradnik, Alojz 1882-1967 *CIDMEL 80,*
ModSL 2
Gradon, Pamela Olive Elizabeth 1915- *ConAu 97*
Gradons, S S *IntAu&W 82X*
Grady, Jack *DrAP&F 83*
Grady, James 1949- *ConAu 104*
Grady, Ronan Calistus, Jr. 1921- *ConAu 49*
Grady, Tex *ConAu X, WrDr 84*
Grae, Ida 1918- *ConAu 89, -97*
Graebner, Alan 1938- *ConAu 61*
Graebner, Norman Arthur 1915- *ConAu 7NR,*
-13R, WrDr 84
Graebner, Walter A 1909- *ConAu P-1*
Graebner, William Sievers 1943- *ConAu 104*
Graedon, Joe 1945- *ConAu 77*
Graef, Hilda C 1907- *ConAu 5R*
Graefe *TwCA, TwCA SUP*
Graeff, Grace Marie 1918- *ConAu 21R*
Graeme, Bruce 1900- *ConAu X, IntAu&W 82,*
TwCCr&M 80
Graeme, David *ConAu X, TwCCr&M 80*

Graeme, Roderic *ConAu X, WrDr 84*
Graeme, Roderic 1926- *TwCCr&M 80*
Graeme, Sheila 1944- *ConAu 25R*
Graey, Julian *IntAu&W 82X*
Graf, Jess *DrAP&F 83*
Graf, LeRoy Philip 1915- *ConAu 41R*
Graf, Oskar Maria 1894-1967 *CIDMEL 80,*
EncWL 2, ModGL, TwCA, TwCA SUP
Graf, Rudolf F 1926- *ConAu 9R*
Graf, Walter 1903- *IntAu&W 82*
Graf Willibald *IntWWP 82X*
Grafe, Felix *ConAu X*
Graff, George 1886-1973 *ConAu 41R*
Graff, Gerald 1937- *ConAu 29R*
Graff, Henry Franklin 1921- *ConAu 1R, -1NR,*
IntAu&W 82, WrDr 84
Graff, Polly Anne Colver *ConAu X, SmATA X*
Graff, S Stewart 1908- *ConAu 49, SmATA 9*
Graff, Sigmund 1898- *ModWD*
Grafton, Ann *ConAu X*
Grafton, Carl 1942- *ConAu 53*
Grafton, Garth *CreCan 1*
Grafton, Sue 1940- *ConAu 108*
Graglia, Lino A 1930- *ConAu 69*
Graham, Brother *WrDr 84*
Graham, A John 1930- *ConAu 8NR, -13R*
Graham, A S 1917- *ConAu 104*
Graham, Ada 1931- *ConAu 4NR, -29R,*
IntAu&W 82, SmATA 11, WrDr 84
Graham, Aelred 1907- *ConAu 5R, -5NR*
Graham, Alexander John 1930- *WrDr 84*
Graham, Alice Walworth 1905- *ConAu 1R,*
-5NR
Graham, Alistair Dundas 1938- *ConAu 49*
Graham, Andrew Guillemard 1913-1981
ConAu 103
Graham, Angus 1919- *ConAu 17R*
Graham, Barbara 1947- *NatPD 81[port]*
Graham, Billy 1918- *ConAu X, WrDr 84*
Graham, Brenda Knight 1942- *ConAu 103,*
SmATA 32[port]
Graham, Carlotta *ConAu X*
Graham, Charles S *ConAu X, WrDr 84*
Graham, Charlotte *ConAu X*
Graham, Clarence H 1906-1971 *ConAu 33R*
Graham, Courtenay *DrAP&F 83*
Graham, Cunninghame *TwCA, TwCA SUP*
Graham, David Duane 1927- *ConAu 69*
Graham, David Victor 1948- *ConAmTC*
Graham, Desmond 1940- *ConAu 73, WrDr 84*
Graham, Don 1940- *ConAu 102*
Graham, Donald 1931- *ConAu P-2*
Graham, Dorothy 1893-1959 *TwCA,*
TwCA SUP
Graham, Eleanor 1896- *ConAu 73, SmATA 18,*
TwCCW 83, WrDr 84
Graham, Elizabeth *ConAu X*
Graham, Ennis 1839-1920 *LongCTC*
Graham, Frank, Jr. 1925- *ConAu 4NR, -9R,*
SmATA 11, WrDr 84
Graham, Fred P 1931- *ConAu 37R*
Graham, Gene S 1924- *ConAu 41R*
Graham, George Jackson, Jr. 1938- *ConAu 45*
Graham, Gerald 1903- *WrDr 84*
Graham, Gerald Sandford 1903- *ConAu 102*
Graham, Grace 1910- *ConAu P-1*
Graham, Gwethalyn 1913-1965 *CreCan 1*
Graham, Harry 1874-1936 *TwCCW 83*
Graham, Harry Edward 1940- *ConAu 29R*
Graham, Harry Jocelyn Clive 1874-1936 *CnMWL,*
LongCTC
Graham, Henry 1930- *ConAu 103, ConP 80,*
WrDr 84
Graham, Howard Jay 1905- *ConAu P-2*
Graham, Hugh *ConAu X*
Graham, Hugh 1936- *WrDr 84*
Graham, Hugh Davis 1936- *ConAu 21R,*
IntAu&W 82
Graham, Ian 1923- *ConAu 2NR, -45*
Graham, Ilse 1914- *ConAu 8NR, -57*
Graham, Irvin 1909- *IntAu&W 82*
Graham, J W 1925- *ConAu 93*
Graham, J Walter 1906- *ConAu 1R*
Graham, Jack *TwCCr&M 80*
Graham, James *ConAu X, WrDr 84*
Graham, John *ConAu X*
Graham, John 1926- *ConAu 33R, SmATA 11,*
WrDr 84
Graham, John Alexander 1941- *ConAu 25R*
Graham, John Charles Edward 1931-
IntAu&W 82
Graham, John Remington 1940- *ConAu 33R*

Graham, John Thomas 1928- *ConAu 53*
Graham, Jorie *DrAP&F 83*
Graham, Jory 1925- *ConAu 29R*
Graham, Jory 1925-1983 *ConAu 109*
Graham, Joseph M 1911?-1971 *ConAu 104*
Graham, Katharine 1917- *AuNews 1,*
ConAu 105
Graham, Kenneth 1936- *ConAu 77*
Graham, Kennon *ConAu X, SmATA X*
Graham, Lawrence Sherman 1936- *ConAu 45,*
IntAu&W 82
Graham, Le *LivgBAA*
Graham, Lee E 1913?-1977 *ConAu 73*
Graham, Lloyd M 1889- *ConAu 97*
Graham, Lola Amanda 1896- *IntWWP 82*
Graham, Lola Beall *IntWWP 82X*
Graham, Loren R 1933- *ConAu 21R*
Graham, Lorenz 1902- *TwCCW 83, WrDr 84*
Graham, Lorenz B 1902- *ConAu 9R, LivgBAA,*
SmATA 2
Graham, Malcolm 1923- *ConAu 53*
Graham, Margaret Althea 1924- *ConAu 9R*
Graham, Margaret Bloy 1920- *ConAu 77,*
SmATA 11
Graham, Michael 1898-1972 *ConAu 104*
Graham, Milton D 1916- *ConAu 45*
Graham, Neill *ConAu X, TwCCr&M 80*
Graham, Neill 1941- *ConAu 109*
Graham, Otis L, Jr. 1935- *ConAu 11NR, -21R*
Graham, Patricia Albjerg 1935- *ConAu 25R*
Graham, Philip *DrAP&F 83*
Graham, Philip Leslie 1915-1963 *ConAu 89*
Graham, Rachel 1895- *ConAu P-1*
Graham, Ramona *ConAu X*
Graham, Richard 1934- *ConAu 29R*
Graham, Robert *WrDr 84*
Graham, Robert 1943- *ConAu X*
Graham, Robert Bontine Cunninghame 1852-1936
LongCTC
Graham, Robert G 1925- *ConAu 25R*
Graham, Robin Lee 1949- *ConAu 49,*
SmATA 7
Graham, Ruth *ConAu X*
Graham, Sean 1920- *ConAu 21R*
Graham, Sheilah *WrDr 84*
Graham, Sheilah 1908?- *AuNews 1, ConAu 108*
Graham, Shirley Lola 1906-1977 *LivgBAA*
Graham, Shirley Lola 1907-1977 *ConAu X,*
SmATA X, TwCA SUP
Graham, Stephen 1884-1975 *ConAu 93,*
LongCTC, TwCA, TwCA SUP
Graham, Susan 1912- *ConAu 17R*
Graham, Taylor *DrAP&F 83*
Graham, Thomas F 1923- *ConAu 21R*
Graham, Tom *ConAmA, ConAu X*
Graham, Vanessa *ConAu X*
IntAu&W 82X
Graham, Victor Ernest 1920- *ConAu 93,*
WrDr 84
Graham, Virginia *ConAu X*
Graham, W Fred 1930- *ConAu 33R, WrDr 84*
Graham, W S 1918- *ConAu 73, ConP 80,*
RGFMBP
Graham, William Franklin 1918- *ConAu 9R*
Graham, William Fred 1930- *IntAu&W 82*
Graham, William Hugh 1912- *WrDr 84*
Graham, William S 1918- *WrDr 84*
Graham, William Sydney 1918- *DcLEL 1940,*
IntAu&W 82, ModBrL, WorAu
Graham, Winston *WrDr 84*
Graham, Winston 1909- *ConNov 82,*
TwCCr&M 80
Graham, Winston 1910- *ConAu 2NR, -49,*
ConLC 23[port]
Graham, Winston Mawdsley 1911?- *TwCWr*
Graham Scott, Peter 1923- *ConAu 108*
Graham-White, Anthony 1940- *ConAu 61*
Graham-Yooll, Andrew M 1944- *ConAu 108*
Grahame, Kenneth 1859-1932 *ChlLR 5[port],*
CnMWL, ConAu 108, LongCTC, ModBrL,
TwCA, TwCA SUP, TwCCW 83, TwCWr
Grahn, Judy *DrAP&F 83*
Grainger, A J 1929- *ConAu 33R*
Grainger, J H 1917- *ConAu 77*
Grainger, Muriel Arnott 1905- *IntWWP 82*
Gralapp, Leland Wilson 1921- *ConAu 13R*
Gram, Harold A 1927- *ConAu 25R*
Gram, Moltke 1938- *ConAu 69*
Gramatky, Hardie 1907-1979 *AuNews 1,*
ConAu 1R, -3NR, -85, DcLB 22[port],
SmATA 1, -23N, -30[port], TwCCW 83
Gramatte, Sophie-Carmen Eckhardt- *CreCan 1*

Grambs, Jean D 1919- *ConAu 7NR, −17R*
Gramet, Charles *ConAu 1R*
Grammaticus *ConAu X*
Grampp, William D 1914- *ConAu 33R,*
 IntAu&W 82, WrDr 84
Grams, Armin 1924- *ConAu 45, IntAu&W 82*
Grams Wehdeking, Alma Luise *IntAu&W 82*
Gramsch, Werner 1907- *IntAu&W 82*
Gramsci, Antonio 1891-1937 *ClDMEL 80*
Granados, Paul *ConAu X, WrDr 84*
Granados, Vicente 1943- *IntAu&W 82*
Granasztoi, Pal 1908- *IntAu&W 82*
Granat, Robert *DrAP&F 83*
Granat, Robert 1925- *ConAu 1R, −2NR,*
 WrDr 84
Granato, Carol *DrAP&F 83*
Granatstein, J L 1939- *ConAu 10NR, −25R*
Granbeck, Marilyn 1927- *ConAu 77*
Granberg, Wilbur J 1906- *ConAu 5R*
Granberry, Edwin Phillips 1897- *ConAu P-2,*
 TwCA, TwCA SUP
Granby, Milton *ConAu X*
Grand, Samuel 1912- *ConAu 107*
Grand, Sarah Frances Elizabeth 1862-1943
 LongCTC, TwCA, TwCA SUP
Granda, Chabuca *ConAu X*
Grandbois, Alain 1900- *CreCan 1*
Grande, Felix 1937- *ClDMEL 80*
Grande, Luke M 1922- *ConAu 2NR, −5R*
Grandfield, Raymond J 1931- *ConAu 53*
Grandower, Elissa *ConAu X, TwCCr&M 80,*
 WrDr 84
Grandy, Richard 1942- *ConAu 77*
Grange, Chris *ConAu X*
Grange, Cyril 1900- *ConAu P-1*
Grange, Peter *ConNov 82, SmATA 5,*
 TwCRGW, WrDr 84
Granger, Bruce Ingham 1920- *ConAu 1R,*
 IntAu&W 82, WrDr 84
Granger, Byrd Howell 1912- *ConAu 107*
Granger, Clive W J 1934- *ConAu 8NR, −9R*
Granger, Darius John *ConAu X*
Granger, Margaret Jane 1925?-1977 *ConAu 104,*
 SmATA 27N
Granger, Peggy *ConAu X, SmATA X*
Granger, Percy 1945- *NatPD 81[port]*
Granich, Irving 1894-1967 *ConAu 97*
Granich, Irwin 1893-1967 *ConAu 45*
Granick, David 1926- *ConAu 1R, WrDr 84*
Granick, Harry 1898- *ConAu 85,*
 NatPD 81[port]
Granik, Theodore 1906-1970 *ConAu 89*
Granin, Daniel 1918- *WorAu 1970*
Granin, Daniil Aleksandrovich 1918-
 ClDMEL 80
Granite, Harvey R 1927- *ConAu 33R*
Granite, Tony *ConAu X, WrDr 84*
Granovetter, Mark S 1943- *ConAu 85, WrDr 84*
Granovsky, Anatoli 1922-1974 *ConAu 53*
Granowsky, Alvin 1936- *ConAu 21R*
Gransden, Antonia 1928- *ConAu 77,*
 IntAu&W 82
Granstaff, Bill 1925- *SmATA 10*
Grant, Alexander T K 1906- *WrDr 84*
Grant, Alexander Thomas Kingdom 1906-
 ConAu 53
Grant, Ambrose *WrDr 84*
Grant, Anthony *IntAu&W 82X, WrDr 84*
Grant, Barbara M 1932- *ConAu 53*
Grant, Ben *ConAu X*
Grant, Brian W 1939- *ConAu 7NR, −57*
Grant, Bruce 1893-1977 *ConAu 1R, −6NR, −69,*
 SmATA 25N, −5
Grant, Bruce 1925- *WrDr 84*
Grant, Bruce Alexander 1925- *ConAu 107*
Grant, C D *DrAP&F 83*
Grant, Charles *IntAu&W 82X*
Grant, Charles L 1942- *ConAu 85, TwCSFW,*
 WrDr 84
Grant, Cynthia D *DrAP&F 83*
Grant, Cynthia D 1950- *ConAu 104,*
 SmATA 33[port]
Grant, Darryl Clarence 1953- *ConAmTC*
Grant, David *ConAu X, WrDr 84*
Grant, Don *ConAu X*
Grant, Dorothy Fremont 1900- *ConAu P-2*
Grant, Edward 1926- *IntAu&W 82*
Grant, Elliott Mansfield 1895-1969 *ConAu 5R,*
 −5NR
Grant, Ellsworth Strong 1917- *ConAu 57*
Grant, Eva 1907- *ConAu 49, SmATA 7*
Grant, Evva H 1913-1977 *ConAu 104, −107,*
 SmATA 27N
Grant, Frederick Clifton 1891-1974 *ConAu 1R,*
 −49
Grant, Gerald 1938- *ConAu 81*
Grant, Gordon H 1875-1962 *ConAu 102,*
 SmATA 25[port]
Grant, Gwen 1940- *ConAu 106*
Grant, Gwendoline Ellen 1940- *IntWWP 82*
Grant, H Roger 1943- *ConAu 89*
Grant, Hilda Kay *ConAu 1R, CreCan 1*
Grant, Isabel F 1887-1983 *ConAu 110*
Grant, J B 1940- *ConAu 6NR, −57*
Grant, Jack *ConAu X*
Grant, James Edward 1905-1966 *DcLB 26*
Grant, James G 1926?-1979 *ConAu 89*
Grant, James Russell 1924- *ConAu 101,*
 IntWWP 82, WrDr 84
Grant, Jane *ConAu X, IntAu&W 82X*
Grant, Jane 1895-1972 *ConAu 33R, ConAu P-2*
Grant, Joan 1907- *ConAu X, TwCWr*
Grant, Joanne B 1940- *ConAu 106*
Grant, John 1933- *ConAu 77*
Grant, John Douglas 1932- *IntAu&W 82*
Grant, John E 1925- *ConAu 41R*
Grant, John J 1932- *ConAu 53*
Grant, John Webster 1919- *ConAu 5R, −6NR,*
 WrDr 84
Grant, Judith 1929- *ConAu 21R*
Grant, Julius 1901- *IntAu&W 82, WrDr 84*
Grant, Kay *ConAu 21R, CreCan 1*
Grant, Landon *ConAu X, WrDr 84*
Grant, Leigh 1947- *SmATA 10*
Grant, Louis T 1943- *ConAu 53*
Grant, Madeleine Parker 1895- *ConAu 73*
Grant, Margaret *WrDr 84*
Grant, Mary *IntWWP 82X*
Grant, Mary Amelia 1890- *ConAu P-2*
Grant, Mary Kathryn 1941- *ConAu 81*
Grant, Matthew *ConSFA*
Grant, Matthew G *ConAu X, SmATA X*
Grant, Maxwell *ConAu X,*
 TwCCr&M 80, WrDr 84
Grant, Michael 1914- *ConAu 1R, −4NR,*
 WrDr 84
Grant, Myrna 1934- *ConAu 4NR, −53,*
 SmATA 21[port]
Grant, Neil 1938- *ConAu 33R, SmATA 14,*
 WrDr 84
Grant, Nigel 1932- *WrDr 84*
Grant, Nigel Duncan Cameron 1932-
 ConAu 7NR, −17R, IntAu&W 82
Grant, Ozro F 1908- *ConAu P-2*
Grant, Richard *WrDr 84*
Grant, Richard B 1925- *ConAu 1R, −4NR*
Grant, Robert 1852-1940 *TwCA, TwCA SUP*
Grant, Robert B 1934- *ConAu 45*
Grant, Robert M 1917- *ConAu 65*
Grant, Roderick 1941- *IntAu&W 82, WrDr 84*
Grant, Ronald A 1927- *IntAu&W 82*
Grant, Venzo *ConAu X*
Grant, Verne 1917- *ConAu 53, IntAu&W 82,*
 WrDr 84
Grant, Vernon W 1904- *ConAu 17R*
Grant, W Leonard 1914- *ConAu 17R*
Grant, Wilson Wayne 1941- *ConAu 97*
Grant, Zalin 1941- *ConAu 73*
Grant Wallace, Lewis *ConAu X*
Grantham, Alexander 1899- *ConAu P-2*
Grantham, Dewey Wesley, Jr. 1921- *ConAu 1R,*
 −1NR
Grantland, Keith *ConAu X*
Granton, Ester Fannie 1914?-1980 *ConAu 101*
Granvik, Erik Alexander 1917- *IntAu&W 82*
Granville, Joseph E 1923- *ConAu 65*
Granville, Wilfred 1905- *ConAu P-1*
Granville-Barker, Harley Granville 1877-1946
 CnMD, ConAu 104, LongCTC, ModBrL,
 ModWD, TwCA, TwCA SUP, TwCLC 2,
 TwCWr, WhoTwCL
Grape, Oliver *ConAu X*
Grapho *ConAu X*
Gras, Felix 1844-1901 *ClDMEL 80*
Grass, Guenter 1927- *ConAu 13R*
Grass, Gunter 1927- *ClDMEL 80, ConLC 1, −2,*
 −4, −6, −11, −15, −22[port], CroCD,
 EncWL 2[port], ModGL, ModWD,
 TwCWr, WorAu
Grass, Gunter 1928- *CnMD*
Grass, Gunther 1927- *WhoTwCL*
Grasse, Pierre-Paul 1895- *IntAu&W 82*
Grassi, Joseph A 1922- *ConAu 103*
Grasso, Domenico 1917- *ConAu 73*

Grasten, Peter *IntAu&W 82X*
Grasty, Charles H 1863-1924 *DcLB 25*
Grathwohl, Larry D 1947- *ConAu 65*
Grathwohl, Susan *DrAP&F 83*
Graton, Francoise 1930- *CreCan 1*
Grattan, C Hartley 1902-1980 *ConAu 1NR, −101*
Grattan, Clinton Hartley 1902- *ConAu 1R,*
 TwCA, TwCA SUP
Grattan-Guinness, I 1941- *ConAu 73*
Gratus, Jack 1935- *ConAu 93, IntAu&W 82,*
 WrDr 84
Grau, Jacinto 1877-1958 *ClDMEL 80, ModWD*
Grau, Joseph A 1921- *ConAu 65*
Grau, Shirley Ann *DrAP&F 83*
Grau, Shirley Ann 1929- *AuNews 2, ConAu 1R,*
 −89, ConLC 4, −9, ConNov 82, DcLB 2,
 DcLEL 1940, ModAL, WorAu, WrDr 84
Graubard, Mark 1904- *WrDr 84*
Graubard, Mark A 1904- *ConAu 1R, −5NR,*
 IntAu&W 82
Graubard, Paul S 1932- *ConAu 103*
Grauer, Ben 1908-1977 *ConAu 69*
Grauman, Lawrence, Jr. 1935- *ConAu 33R,*
 WrDr 84
Graupe, Daniel 1934- *ConAu 41R*
Graupera, Carlos M 1915- *ConAu 49*
Graur, Alexandru 1900- *IntAu&W 82*
Grava, Sigurd 1934- *ConAu 77*
Grave, Elsa Margareta 1918- *IntAu&W 82*
Grave, S A 1916- *ConAu 5R*
Gravel, Fern *SmATA X*
Gravel, Mike 1930- *ConAu 41R, WrDr 84*
Gravely, William B 1939- *ConAu 49*
Graven, Jack *DrAP&F 83*
Graver, Lawrence Stanley 1931- *ConAu 25R,*
 WrDr 84
Graversen, Pat 1935- *ConAu 109*
Graves, Alfred Perceval 1846-1931 *LongCTC*
Graves, Allen W 1915- *ConAu 17R*
Graves, Barbara Farris 1938- *ConAu 41R*
Graves, Charles Parlin 1911-1972 *ConAu 4NR,*
 −5R, −37R, SmATA 4
Graves, Clotilde Inez Augusta Mary 1863?-1932
 LongCTC
Graves, Edgar B 1898-1983 *ConAu 109*
Graves, Eleanor MacKenzie 1926- *ConAu 102*
Graves, Jocelyn *IntAu&W 82X*
Graves, John 1920- *ConAu 9NR,*
 DcLB Y83B[port]
Graves, John Alexander 1920- *ConAu 1R, −13R,*
 FifWWr
Graves, Leon B 1946- *ConAu 29R*
Graves, Neil *DrAP&F 83*
Graves, Nora Calhoun 1914- *ConAu 73*
Graves, Richard L 1928- *ConAu 57*
Graves, Richard L 1931- *ConAu 61*
Graves, Richard Perceval 1945- *ConAu 9NR, −65*
Graves, Robert 1895- *CnMWL, ConAu 5R,*
 −5NR, ConLC 1, −2, −6, −11, ConLCrt 82,
 ConNov 82, ConP 80, EncWL 2[port],
 IntAu&W 82, LongCTC, ModBrL,
 ModBrL SUP, RGFMBP, TwCA,
 TwCA SUP, TwCSFW, TwCWr,
 WhoTwCL, WrDr 84
Graves, Susan B 1933- *ConAu 41R*
Graves, Tricia *ConAu X*
Graves, Valerie *WrDr 84*
Graves, W Brooke 1899- *ConAu P-1*
Graves, Wallace *DrAP&F 83*
Graves, Wallace 1922- *ConAu 33R, WrDr 84*
Graveyard, Aloysius *IntAu&W 82X*
Gravley, Ernestine Hudlow 1918- *IntAu&W 82,*
 IntWWP 82
Grawoig, Sheila *ConAu X*
Gray, Alexander 1929- *CreCan 1*
Gray, Sir Alexander 1882-1968 *ConAu 5R*
Gray, Alfred Orren 1914- *WrDr 84*
Gray, Alfred Orrin 1914- *ConAu 7NR, −17R*
Gray, Alice Wirth *DrAP&F 83*
Gray, Amlin 1946- *NatPD 81[port]*
Gray, Angela *ConAu X, TwCRGW, WrDr 84*
Gray, Anne 1931- *ConAu 9NR, −65*
Gray, Barry 1916- *ConAu 61*
Gray, Basil 1904- *ConAu P-1*
Gray, Berkeley 1889-1965 *TwCCr&M 80*
Gray, Betsy *ConAu X*
Gray, Bettyanne 1934- *ConAu 81*
Gray, Bill *ConAu X*
Gray, Bradford H 1942- *ConAu 57*
Gray, Captain Bill *ConAu X*
Gray, Carla *IntWWP 82X*
Gray, Charles Augustus 1938- *ConAu 17R*

Gray, Clayton 1918- *IntAu&W 82, WrDr 84*
Gray, Cleve 1918- *WrDr 84*
Gray, Clifford F 1930- *ConAu 25R*
Gray, Curme *TwCSFW*
Gray, Darrell 1945- *ConAu 65*
Gray, David 1927-1983 *ConAu 110*
Gray, Dorothea Helen Forbes d1983 *ConAu 110*
Gray, Dorothy *MichAu 80*
Gray, Dorothy 1936- *ConAu 69*
Gray, Dorothy Kate *WrDr 84*
Gray, Dorothy Kate 1918- *ConAu 102*
Gray, Dulcie *WrDr 84*
Gray, Dulcie 1920- *ConAu 3NR, -5R, IntAu&W 82X, TwCCr&M 80*
Gray, Dwight E 1903- *ConAu P-2*
Gray, Eden 1907- *ConAu 93*
Gray, Edna Redmond 1905?-1983 *ConAu 110*
Gray, Edwyn 1927- *ConAu 41R, IntAu&W 82*
Gray, Elizabeth Janet *TwCCW 83, WrDr 84*
Gray, Elizabeth Janet 1902- *ConAu X, SmATA 6*
Gray, Farnum Moore 1940- *ConAmTC, ConAu 49*
Gray, Floyd 1926- *ConAu 10NR, -25R*
Gray, Francine DuPlessix *DrAP&F 83*
Gray, Francine DuPlessix 1930- *ASpks, ConAu 11NR, -61, ConLC 22[port], WrDr 84*
Gray, Genevieve S 1920- *ConAu 33R, SmATA 4*
Gray, George Hugh 1922- *ConAu 7NR, -17R*
Gray, Gibson 1922- *ConAu 33R*
Gray, Giles Wilkeson 1889- *ConAu 5R*
Gray, Gordon 1909-1982 *ConAu 109*
Gray, Harold 1894-1968 *ConAu 107, SmATA 32, -33[port]*
Gray, Harold James 1907- *ConAu 107, WrDr 84*
Gray, Harriet *ConAu X,   TwCRGW, WrDr 84*
Gray, J Glenn 1913-1977 *ConAu 37R, -73*
Gray, J M 1930- *ConAu 53*
Gray, J Richard 1929- *ConAu 1R, -5NR*
Gray, J Stanley 1894- *ConAu P-2*
Gray, Jack 1927- *ConAu 103, ConDr 82, WrDr 84*
Gray, James 1899- *ConAu 13R, TwCA, TwCA SUP*
Gray, James H 1906- *ConAu 97*
Gray, James R 1921- *ConAu 33R*
Gray, Jane *ConAu X, IntAu&W 82X*
Gray, Jeffrey 1934- *WrDr 84*
Gray, Jeffrey A 1934- *ConAu 104*
Gray, Jenny *ConAu X, SmATA 4*
Gray, John 1866-1934 *CnMWL*
Gray, John 1913- *ConAu 9R*
Gray, John 1915- *IntAu&W 82*
Gray, John 1927- *CreCan 1*
Gray, John E 1922- *ConAu 65*
Gray, John Milner 1889-1970 *ConAu 29R*
Gray, John Morgan 1907- *ConAu 103*
Gray, John S 1910- *ConAu 73*
Gray, John W 1935- *ConAu 17R*
Gray, Juanita R 1918- *ConAu 61*
Gray, Lee Learner 1924- *ConAu 73*
Gray, Linda Crockett 1943- *ConAu 109*
Gray, Marian *ConAu X*
Gray, Marianne 1947- *ConAu 110*
Gray, Martin *ASpks*
Gray, Martin 1925- *AuNews 1*
Gray, Martin 1926- *ConAu 77, IntAu&W 82*
Gray, Mayo Loiseau *DrAP&F 83*
Gray, Mayo Loiseau 1938- *ConAu 104*
Gray, Michael H 1946- *ConAu 103*
Gray, Nicholas Stuart 1922-1981 *ConAu 103, -11NR, -21R, SmATA 27N, -4, TwCCW 83*
Gray, Nicolete 1911- *WrDr 84*
Gray, Nicolete Mary 1911- *ConAu 103, IntAu&W 82*
Gray, Nigel 1941- *ConAu 85, SmATA 33[port]*
Gray, Noel 1898- *ConAu 65*
Gray, Oscar S 1926- *ConAu 29R*
Gray, Pat *DrAP&F 83*
Gray, Patricia Clark *ConAu 29R, SmATA 7*
Gray, Patricia Violet 1928- *IntAu&W 82*
Gray, Patrick W *DrAP&F 83*
Gray, Patrick Worth 1937- *IntWWP 82*
Gray, Patsey *ConAu X, SmATA 7*
Gray, Peter 1908- *ConAu 41R*
Gray, Philip *ConAu X, IntWWP 82X*
Gray, Ralph D 1933- *ConAu 8NR, -21R*

Gray, Richard 1929- *ConAu X, WrDr 84*
Gray, Richard Butler 1922- *ConAu 1R, -2NR, WrDr 84*
Gray, Robert F 1912- *ConAu 17R*
Gray, Robert Keith 1923- *ConAu 1R*
Gray, Robert Mack 1922- *ConAu 13R*
Gray, Ronald Douglas 1919- *ConAu 7NR, -17R*
Gray, Ronald Francis 1918- *ConAu 5R*
Gray, Russell *ConAu X, WrDr 84*
Gray, Simon 1936- *AuNews 1, ConAu 21R, ConDr 82, ConLC 9, -14, ConNov 82, CreCan 2, DcLB 13[port], DcLEL 1940, WrDr 84*
Gray, Stephen E 1925- *ConAu 73*
Gray, Tony 1922- *WrDr 84*
Gray, Tony George Hugh 1922- *ConAu X*
Gray, Vanessa *ConAu X*
Gray, Wellington Burbank 1919-1977 *ConAu 1R, -103*
Gray, William Bittle 1891- *ConAu 13R*
Gray, William Bittle 1891-1974 *ConAu 11NR*
Gray, William R 1946- *ConAu 97, IntAu&W 82*
Gray, Wood 1905?-1977 *ConAu 69*
Graybar, Lloyd J 1938- *ConAu 57*
Graybeal, David M 1921- *ConAu 17R*
Graybill, Florence Curtis 1898- *ConAu 97*
Graybill, Ron 1944- *ConAu 33R*
Graydon, Ruth *DrAP&F 83*
Grayeff, Felix 1906- *ConAu 77, IntAu&W 82*
Grayland, Eugene C 1916-1976 *ConAu 11NR*
Grayland, Eugene Charles *ConAu P-1*
Grayland, V Merle *ConAu X*
Grayland, Valerie *ConAu 11NR, WrDr 84*
Grayland, Valerie Merle *ConAu 9R, IntAu&W 82, SmATA 7*
Graymont, Barbara *ConAu 81*
Grayson, A K 1935- *ConAu 41R*
Grayson, Alice Barr *ConAu X*
Grayson, Benson Lee 1932- *ConAu 93*
Grayson, C Jackson, Jr. 1923- *ConAu 106, WrDr 84*
Grayson, Cary Travers, Jr. 1919- *ConAu 10NR, -17R*
Grayson, Cecil 1920- *ConAu 13R, IntAu&W 82*
Grayson, Charles 1905-1973 *ConAu 41R*
Grayson, David 1870-1946 *LongCTC, MichAu 80, TwCA, TwCA SUP*
Grayson, Ethel Kirk 1890- *CreCan 1*
Grayson, Henry Wesley 1910- *ConAu 41R, IntAu&W 82*
Grayson, Janet 1934- *ConAu 53*
Grayson, L M 1947- *ConAu 89*
Grayson, Laura *IntAu&W 82X*
Grayson, Marion F 1906-1976 *ConAu 4NR, -5R, -69*
Grayson, Melvin J 1924- *ConAu 45*
Grayson, Richard *DrAP&F 83*
Grayson, Richard 1951- *ConAu 85, IntAu&W 82*
Grayson, Robert A 1927- *ConAu 33R*
Grayson, Ruth 1926- *ConAu 73*
Grayston, Kenneth 1914- *IntAu&W 82*
Graystone, Lynn *ConAu X*
Grayzel, Solomon 1896-1980 *ConAu 1R, -4NR*
Grazhdanin, Misha *ConAu X*
Graziano, Anthony M 1932- *ConAu 93*
Graziano, Frank *DrAP&F 83*
Grealey, Thomas Louis 1916- *ConAu 81*
Grealis, Walt 1929- *ConAu 77*
Greally, John 1934- *WrDr 84*
Grealy, Desmond 1923?-1979 *ConAu 85*
Grean, Stanley 1920- *ConAu 29R, WrDr 84*
Great Comte, The *ConAu X, SmATA X*
Great Merlini, The *ConAu X*
Greatorex, Susan Marian 1948- *ConAmTC*
Greatorex, Wilfred 1921- *ConAu 103, ConDr 82C*
Greaves, H R G 1907- *ConAu 5R*
Greaves, Harold Richard Goring *IntAu&W 82*
Greaves, John 1898- *ConAu 103*
Greaves, John Howard 1947- *IntWWP 82*
Greaves, Margaret 1914- *ConAu 25R, SmATA 7, TwCCW 83, WrDr 84*
Greaves, Percy Laurie, Jr. 1906- *ConAu 49, IntAu&W 82*
Greaves, Richard L 1938- *ConAu 33R*
Grebanier, Bernard 1903- *ConAu 21R*
Grebanier, Bernard 1903-1977 *ConAu 10NR*
Grebe, Maria Ester 1928- *ConAu 25R*
Grebstein, Lawrence C 1937- *ConAu 29R*

Grebstein, Sheldon Norman 1928- *ConAu 1R, -5NR, IntAu&W 82, WrDr 84*
Greco, Jose 1918- *ConAu 85*
Greco, Margaret *ConAu X*
Greco, Stephen *DrAP&F 83*
Gree, Alain 1936- *ConAu 89, SmATA 28[port]*
Greeff, Adele *IntWWP 82X*
Greeff, Adele Montgomery Burcher 1911- *IntWWP 82*
Greeley, Andrew 1928- *WrDr 84*
Greeley, Andrew M 1928- *ConAu 5R, -7NR*
Green, A S 1880-1932 *TwCWr*
Green, A Wingfall 1900-1971? *ConAu P-1*
Green, Abel 1900-1973 *ConAu 41R*
Green, Adam *ConAu X, SmATA X*
Green, Adolph 1915- *ConAu 110, ConDr 82D*
Green, Alan 1906-1975 *ConAu 53, -57*
Green, Alan Singer 1907- *ConAu 85*
Green, Andrew M 1927- *WrDr 84*
Green, Andrew Malcolm 1927- *ConAu 73, IntAu&W 82*
Green, Anita Jane 1940- *ConAu 85*
Green, Anna Katharine 1846-1935 *LongCTC, TwCA, TwCCr&M 80*
Green, Anne 1899- *ConAmA, LongCTC, TwCA, TwCA SUP*
Green, Anne M 1922- *ConAu 1R*
Green, Arnold W 1914- *ConAu 5R*
Green, Arthur S 1927- *ConAu 5R*
Green, Ben K 1911-1974 *AuNews 1*
Green, Benny 1927- *ConAu X, WrDr 84*
Green, Bernard 1927- *ConAu 25R*
Green, Bryan Stuart Westmacott 1901- *ConAu P-1*
Green, Celia Elizabeth 1935- *ConAu 65, WrDr 84*
Green, Clifford 1934- *IntAu&W 82*
Green, Constance McLaughlin 1897-1975 *ConAu 9R, -61*
Green, D *ConAu X, SmATA 4*
Green, David 1910- *WrDr 84*
Green, David Bronte 1910- *ConAu 13R, IntAu&W 82*
Green, David E 1942- *ConAu 33R, -77, WrDr 84*
Green, David M 1932- *ConAu 41R*
Green, Deborah 1948- *ConAu 104*
Green, Dennis Howard 1922- *ConAu 110*
Green, Donald E 1936- *ConAu 1NR, -45*
Green, Donald Ross 1924- *ConAu 37R, WrDr 84*
Green, Dorothy 1915- *IntAu&W 82, IntWWP 82, WrDr 84*
Green, Edith Pinero 1929- *ConAu 77*
Green, Edward 1920- *ConAu 13R*
Green, Elisabeth Sara 1940- *WrDr 84*
Green, Elizabeth A H 1906- *ConAu 21R, WrDr 84*
Green, Elmer Ellsworth 1917- *ConAu 103*
Green, Ernestene L 1939- *ConAu 57*
Green, F C 1891-1964 *ConAu 89, WorAu*
Green, Fitzhugh 1917- *ConAu 77*
Green, Fletcher Melvin 1895-1978 *ConAu 1R, -6NR*
Green, Frederick Lawrence 1902-1953 *LongCTC, TwCA SUP*
Green, Frederick Pratt 1903- *ConAu 102, IntWWP 82, WrDr 84*
Green, Galen *DrAP&F 83*
Green, Galen 1949- *ConAu 57*
Green, Geoffrey *DrAP&F 83*
Green, George MacEwan 1931- *ConAu 81*
Green, George S 1930- *ConAu 97*
Green, Georgia M 1944- *ConAu 93*
Green, Gerald 1922- *ASpks, ConAu 8NR, -13R, WorAu, WrDr 84*
Green, Gil 1906- *ConAu 73*
Green, H Gordon 1912- *ConAu 110*
Green, Hannah *ConAu 49, -73, ConLC 3, DrAP&F 83, SmATA X*
Green, Harold P 1922- *ConAu 13R*
Green, Henry 1905-1973 *DcLB 15[port], EncWL 2*
Green, Henry 1905-1974 *CnMWL, ConAu X, -49, ConLC 2, -13, LongCTC, ModBrL, ModBrL SUP, TwCA SUP, TwCWr, WhoTwCL*
Green, Hollis Lynn 1933- *ConAu 103*
Green, J C *IntWWP 82X*
Green, J C R 1949- *ConAu 104, WrDr 84*
Green, James J 1902- *MichAu 80*
Green, James L 1919- *ConAu 17R, WrDr 84*

Gressitt, J Linsley 1914- *IntAu&W 82*
Gressley, Gene M 1931- *ConAu 10NR*
Gressley, Gene Maurice 1931- *ConAu 17R*
Greth, Roma *NatPD 81[port]*
Gretz, Susanna 1937- *ConAu 29R*, *SmATA 7*
Gretzer, John *SmATA 18*
Greulach, Victor A 1906- *ConAu 49*, *WrDr 84*
Greve, Elsa *ConAu X*
Greve, Felix Paul 1879-1948 *ConAu 104*
Grevenius, Herbert 1901- *ModWD*
Grew, James Hooper 1906- *ConAu 103*
Grew, Raymond 1930- *ConAu 13R*
Grewdead, Roy *ConAu X*
Grewer, Eira M 1931- *ConAu 21R*
Grex, Leo *ConAu X*, *TwCCr&M 80*,
  WrDr 84
Grey, Abby Weed 1903?-1983 *ConAu 110*
Grey, Anthony 1938- *ConAu 29R*, *WrDr 84*
Grey, Belinda *TwCRGW*
Grey, Beryl 1927- *ConAu 109*, *WrDr 84*
Grey, Beryl Elizabeth 1927- *IntAu&W 82*
Grey, Brenda *ConAu X*, *TwCRGW*, *WrDr 84*
Grey, Charles *ConAu X*, *TwCSFW*, *WrDr 84*
Grey, David Lennox 1935- *ConAu 93*
Grey, Sir Edward 1862-1933 *TwCA*,
  TwCA SUP
Grey, Elizabeth *ConAu X*
Grey, Georgina *ConAu X*, *TwCRGW*,
  WrDr 84
Grey, Ian *WrDr 84*
Grey, Ian 1918- *ConAu 2NR*, *-5R*,
  IntAu&W 82
Grey, Jerry 1926- *ConAu 5NR*, *-53*,
  SmATA 11, *WrDr 84*
Grey, Louis *WrDr 84*
Grey, Marian Powys 1883?-1972 *ConAu 104*
Grey, Robert Waters *DrAP&F 83*
Grey, Robert Waters 1943- *ConAu 49*
Grey, Robin *ConAu X*
Grey, Vivian *ConAu 17R*
Grey, Zane 1872-1939 *ConAu 104*,
  DcLB 9[port], *FifWWr*, *TwCLC 6[port]*,
  TwCWW
Grey, Zane 1875?-1939 *LongCTC*, *TwCA*,
  TwCA SUP, *TwCWr*
Grey Of Fallodon, Edward Grey, Viscount
  1862-1933 *LongCTC*, *TwCA*, *TwCA SUP*
Grey Owl 1888-1938 *CreCan 1*, *SmATA X*,
  TwCW 83
Grey-Wilson, Christopher 1944- *WrDr 84*
Greyser, Stephen A 1935- *ConAu 33R*
Greysmith, David 1942- *WrDr 84*
Gri *ConAu X*, *SmATA X*
Gribbin, Lenore S 1922- *ConAu 33R*
Gribbin, William James 1943- *ConAu 1NR*, *-45*
Gribble, Charles E 1936- *ConAu 41R*
Gribble, Dorothy Rose Jessie *IntWWP 82*
Gribble, Harry Wagstaff 1891?-1981 *ConAu 102*
Gribble, James 1938- *ConAu 29R*
Gribble, Leonard 1908- *WrDr 84*
Gribble, Leonard Reginald 1908- *ConAu 7NR*,
  -53, *LongCTC*, *TwCCr&M 80*
Gribbons, Warren D 1921- *ConAu 29R*
Grice, Frederick 1910- *ConAu 3NR*, *-9R*,
  IntAu&W 82, *SmATA 6*, *TwCCW 83*,
  WrDr 84
Grice, Julia A 1940- *ConAu 77*, *MichAu 80*
Gridban, Bolsted *ConAu X*
Gridban, Volsted *TwCSFW*, *WrDr 84*
Grider, Dorothy 1915- *SmATA 31[port]*
Gridley, Marion E 1906-1974 *ConAu 103*, *-45*,
  SmATA 26N
Gridley, Roy E 1935- *ConAu 109*
Gridzewski, Mieczylawski 1895?-1970
  ConAu 104
Grieb, Kenneth J 1939- *ConAu 29R*, *WrDr 84*
Grieb, Lyndal 1940- *ConAu 61*
Grieder, Josephine 1939- *ConAu 53*
Grieder, Theodore 1926- *ConAu 45*
Grieder, Walter 1924- *ConAu 41R*, *SmATA 9*
Grieg, Michael 1922- *ConAu 17R*
Grieg, Nordahl 1902-1943 *TwCLC 10[port]*
Grieg, Nordahl Brun 1902-1943 *CIDMEL 80*,
  CnMD, *EncWL 2*, *ModWD*, *TwCWr*,
  WhoTwCL
Grieg, Nordhal 1902-1943 *ConAu 107*
Grier, B R 1913- *ConAu 25R*
Grier, Barbara G 1933- *ConAu 107*
Grier, Sir Edmund Wyly *CreCan 2*
Grier, Eldon 1917- *CreCan 2*
Grier, Frances Belle Powner 1886?-1980?
  ConAu 104

Grier, William H *LivgBAA*
Grier, Sir Wyly 1862-1957 *CreCan 2*
Grierson, Edward 1914- *ConAu 1R*, *-4NR*,
  WrDr 84
Grierson, Edward 1914-1975 *TwCCr&M 80*
Grierson, Francis 1848-1927 *TwCA*, *TwCA SUP*
Grierson, Francis Durham 1888-1972 *ConAu 104*
Grierson, Herbert John Clifford 1886-1960
  ConAu 93
Grierson, Sir Herbert John Clifford 1866-1960
  LongCTC, *ModBrL*, *TwCA*, *TwCA SUP*
Grierson, John 1909-1977 *ConAu 69*,
  ConAu P-2
Grierson, Linden 1914- *ConAu P-1*
Grierson, Patricia *DrAP&F 83*
Grierson, Philip 1910- *IntAu&W 82*
Gries, Tom 1923?-1977 *ConAu 69*
Griese, Arnold A 1921- *ConAu 1NR*, *-49*,
  SmATA 9
Griese, Friedrich 1890-1975 *CnMD*, *ModWD*
Grieson, Ronald Edward 1943- *ConAu 1NR*, *-49*
Griesse, Carolyn 1941- *ConAu 107*
Griessman, Benjamin Eugene 1934- *ConAu 41R*
Griest, Guinevere L 1924- *ConAu 65*
Grieve, Andrew W 1925- *ConAu 9R*
Grieve, C M 1892-1978 *ConAu 85*
Grieve, Christopher Murray 1892- *ConAu 5R*,
  ConLC 11, *-19*, *LongCTC*, *TwCA*,
  TwCA SUP
Grieves, Forest Leslie 1938- *ConAu 53*,
  IntAu&W 82
Grifalconi, Ann 1929- *ConAu 5R*, *-9NR*,
  SmATA 2
Griff *ConAu X*
Griff, Alan 1900-1964 *LongCTC*
Griffen, Edmund *ConAu X*
Griffen, Jeff 1923- *ConAu 13R*
Griffin, A H 1911- *ConAu 9NR*, *-21R*
Griffin, Al 1919- *ConAu 33R*
Griffin, Anne J *ConAu X*
Griffin, Arthur Harry 1911- *IntAu&W 82*
Griffin, Arthur J 1921- *ConAu 1NR*, *-49*
Griffin, Barbara C 1945- *ConAu 53*
Griffin, C F *ConAu X*
Griffin, C W 1925- *ConAu 53*
Griffin, Charles C 1902-1976 *ConAu 65*
Griffin, Charles Henry 1922- *ConAu 17R*
Griffin, David *WorAu 1970*
Griffin, David Ray 1939- *ConAu 77*
Griffin, Donald R 1915- *ConAu 37R*,
  IntAu&W 82, *WrDr 84*
Griffin, Edward M 1937- *ConAu 89*
Griffin, Emilie Russell Dietrich 1936- *ConAu 103*
Griffin, Ernest G 1916- *ConAu 25R*
Griffin, Gerald G 1933- *ConAu 9NR*, *-57*
Griffin, Gillett Good 1928- *SmATA 26*
Griffin, Glen C 1934- *ConAu 29R*
Griffin, Gwyn 1922?-1967 *ConAu 89*, *WorAu*
Griffin, Harry 1911- *WrDr 84*
Griffin, Henry William 1935- *ConAmTC*
Griffin, Jacqueline P 1927- *ConAu 33R*
Griffin, James A 1934- *ConAu 29R*
Griffin, John Howard 1902- *WhoTwCL*
Griffin, John Howard 1920-1980 *AuNews 1*,
  ConAu 1R, *-2NR*, *-101*, *WorAu*
Griffin, John Q 1948- *ConAu 77*
Griffin, Jonathan *WrDr 84*
Griffin, Jonathan 1906- *ConP 80*, *IntWWP 82X*
Griffin, Judith Berry *ConAu 108*,
  SmATA 34[port]
Griffin, Keith B 1938- *ConAu 7NR*, *-57*,
  WrDr 84
Griffin, Marvin 1907-1982 *ConAu 108*
Griffin, Mary 1916- *ConAu 61*
Griffin, Mary Claire 1924- *ConAu 17R*
Griffin, Robert 1936- *ConAu 53*
Griffin, Robert John Thurlow 1906- *IntWWP 82*,
  WrDr 84
Griffin, Stuart 1917- *ConAu 5R*
Griffin, Susan *DrAP&F 83*
Griffin, Susan 1943- *ConAu 3NR*, *-49*,
  IntAu&W 82, *IntWWP 82*,
  NatPD 81[port]
Griffin, T F 1949- *IntWWP 82*
Griffin, Tom 1946- *NatPD 81[port]*
Griffin, Viele *TwCA*, *TwCA SUP*
Griffin, Walter *DrAP&F 83*
Griffin, Walter 1937- *ConAu 73*
Griffin, William 1935- *ConAu 93*,
  NatPD 81[port]
Griffin, William Lloyd 1938- *ConAu 21R*
Griffith, A Kinney 1897- *ConAu 1R*

Griffith, A Leonard 1920- *ConAu 5NR*
Griffith, Albert J 1932- *ConAu 37R*
Griffith, Arthur Leonard 1920- *ConAu 9R*,
  WrDr 84
Griffith, Benjamin Woodward, Jr. 1922-
  ConAu 1R, *-5NR*
Griffith, Corinne 1898?-1979 *ConAu 89*
Griffith, Ernest S 1896- *WrDr 84*
Griffith, Ernest Stacey 1896- *ConAu 13R*,
  IntAu&W 82
Griffith, Francis 1906- *ConAu 106*
Griffith, George 1857-1906 *TwCSFW*
Griffith, Helen V 1934- *ConAu 105*
Griffith, Hubert Freeling 1896-1953 *LongCTC*
Griffith, Jeannette *ConAu X*, *SmATA 4*
Griffith, Jerry 1932- *ConAu 53*
Griffith, Kathryn 1923- *ConAu 73*
Griffith, Kenneth 1921- *ConAu 69*
Griffith, Leon Odell, Sr. 1921- *ConAu 1R*, *-2NR*,
  WrDr 84
Griffith, Lucille B 1905- *ConAu 17R*, *WrDr 84*
Griffith, Patricia Browning *DrAP&F 83*
Griffith, Patricia Browning 1935- *ConAu 77*
Griffith, Paul *DrAP&F 83*
Griffith, Paul 1921- *ConAu 21R*
Griffith, Paul 1921-1983 *ConAu 109*
Griffith, Richard 1912-1969 *ConAu 1R*, *-6NR*
Griffith, Robert William 1940- *ConAu 45*
Griffith, Samuel Blair, II 1906-1983 *ConAu 109*
Griffith, Thomas 1915- *ConAu 21R*,
  IntAu&W 82, *WrDr 84*
Griffith, Thomas Gwynfor 1926- *ConAu 103*,
  IntAu&W 82, *WrDr 84*
Griffith, William E 1920- *ConAu 61*, *WrDr 84*
Griffith, Winthrop 1931- *ConAu 9R*
Griffiths, A Bede 1906- *ConAu 7NR*, *-13R*
Griffiths, Bruce 1938- *IntAu&W 82*
Griffiths, Bryn David *WrDr 84*
Griffiths, Bryn David 1933- *ConAu 101*,
  ConP 80, *IntWWP 82X*
Griffiths, Bryn Lyn David *IntWWP 82*
Griffiths, Charles 1919- *WrDr 84*
Griffiths, Daniel E 1917- *ConAu 25R*
Griffiths, G D 1910-1973 *ConAu P-2*,
  SmATA 20N, *TwCCW 83*
Griffiths, Grace 1921- *ConAu 106*
Griffiths, Helen 1939- *ConAu 7NR*, *-17R*,
  IntAu&W 82, *SmATA 5*, *TwCCW 83*,
  WrDr 84
Griffiths, John C 1934- *ConAu 108*
Griffiths, John Gwyn 1911- *ConAu 106*,
  IntAu&W 82, *WrDr 84*
Griffiths, Kitty Anna *ConAu 105*
Griffiths, Louise Benckenstein 1907- *ConAu 1R*
Griffiths, Mel 1910- *ConAu 85*
Griffiths, Michael Compton 1928- *ConAu 37R*,
  IntAu&W 82
Griffiths, Naomi 1934- *ConAu 101*
Griffiths, Paul 1947- *ConAu 107*
Griffiths, Sir Percival Joseph 1899- *ConAu 103*
Griffiths, Ralph A 1937- *ConAu 105*
Griffiths, Reginald William Hargreaves 1912-
  DcLEL
Griffiths, Richard 1935- *WrDr 84*
Griffiths, Richard Mathias 1935- *ConAu 8NR*,
  -17R
Griffiths, Sally 1934- *ConAu 25R*, *WrDr 84*
Griffiths, Trevor 1935- *ConAu 97*, *ConDr 82*,
  ConLC 13, *DcLB 13[port]*, *DcLEL 1940*,
  WrDr 84
Griffiths, Vivian Lawrence 1935- *IntWWP 82*
Griffiths Ormhaug, Ella 1926- *IntAu&W 82*
Grigg, Charles M 1918- *ConAu 13R*
Grigg, John 1924- *WrDr 84*
Grigg, John Edward Poynder 1924- *ConAu 104*,
  IntAu&W 82
Griggs, Charles Irwin 1902- *ConAu 1R*
Griggs, Earl Leslie 1899- *ConAu 73*
Griggs, Lee 1928- *ConAu 69*
Griggs, Tamar 1941- *ConAu 77*
Grignon, Claude-Henri 1894- *CreCan 2*
Grignon, Germaine Guevremont *CreCan 1*
Grigorescu, Ioan 1930- *IntAu&W 82*
Grigsby, Gordon *DrAP&F 83*
Grigsby, Gordon 1927- *ConAu 97*
Grigson, Geoffrey 1905- *ConAu 25R*, *ConLC 7*,
  ConP 80, *IntWWP 82*, *WrDr 84*
Grigson, Geoffrey Edward Harvey 1902-
  LongCTC, *ModBrL*, *ModBrL SUP*,
  TwCA SUP, *WhoTwCL*
Grigson, Jane 1928- *ConAu 1NR*, *-49*,
  IntAu&W 82, *WrDr 84*

Grile, Dod *LongCTC*
Grilikhes, Alexandra B *DrAP&F 83*
Grill, Nannette L 1935- *ConAu 65*
Grill, Sebastian *IntAu&W 82X*
Grillet, Alain Robbe- *ModRL*
Grilliot, Harold J 1937- *ConAu 107, WrDr 84*
Grillo, John 1942- *ConDr 82*
Grillo, Ralph David 1940- *ConAu 49*
Grillo, Virgil 1938- *ConAu 53*
Grimal, Pierre Antoine 1912- *ConAu 7NR, –13R*
Grimaldi, J V 1916- *ConAu 3NR, –5R*
Grimault, Berthe 1940- *ConAu 13R*
Grimble, Sir Arthur Francis 1888-1956
    DcLEL 1940, LongCTC
Grimble, Charles James *ConAu X*
Grimble, Ian 1921- *ConAu 2NR, –5R,
    IntAu&W 82, WrDr 84*
Grime, Harold 1896- *WrDr 84*
Grimes, Alan P 1919- *ConAu 1R, –1NR,
    WrDr 84*
Grimes, Howard 1915- *ConAu 25R*
Grimes, Johnnie Marie *ConAu 103*
Grimes, Joseph E 1928- *ConAu 37R*
Grimes, Lee 1920- *ConAu 61*
Grimes, Naomi 1950- *IntWWP 82*
Grimes, Nikki *DrAP&F 83*
Grimes, Nikki 1950- *ConAu 77, IntWWP 82X*
Grimes, Orville F, Jr. 1943- *ConAu 106,
    WrDr 84*
Grimes, Paul 1924- *ConAu 77*
Grimes, Ronald L 1943- *ConAu 1NR, –45*
Grimes, W H 1892-1972 *ConAu 33R*
Grimley, Mildred H 1919- *ConAu 5R*
Grimm, Cherry Barbara 1930- *ConAu 101*
Grimm, Cherry Barbara Lockett *WrDr 84*
Grimm, Hans 1875-1959 *ClDMEL 80*
Grimm, Harold John 1901- *ConAu 13R*
Grimm, Jacob Ludwig Karl 1785-1863
    SmATA 22[port]
Grimm, Reinhold 1931- *ConAu 8NR, –61*
Grimm, Wilhelm Karl 1786-1859
    SmATA 22[port]
Grimm, William C 1907- *ConAu 49,
    SmATA 14*
Grimond, Jo 1913- *WrDr 84*
Grimond, Joseph 1913- *ConAu 108,
    IntAu&W 82*
Grimsditch, Herbert Borthwick 1898-1971
    ConAu 104
Grimshaw, Allen Day 1929- *ConAu 9NR, –65*
Grimshaw, Beatrice Ethel 1871-1953 *LongCTC*
Grimshaw, James A, Jr. 1940- *ConAu 109*
Grimshaw, Mark *ConAu X*
Grimshaw, Nigel 1925- *ConAu 101,
    SmATA 23[port]*
Grimsley, Gordon *ConAu X, SmATA X*
Grimsley, Linda 1940- *ConAu 81*
Grimsley, Ronald 1915- *ConAu 3NR, –5R*
Grimsley, Will 1914- *ConAu 33R*
Grimsson, Stefan Hordur 1919- *EncWL 2*
Grimstead, Hettie *WrDr 84*
Grimstead, Hettie 1903- *TwCRGW*
Grimsted, David Allen 1935- *ConAu 25R*
Grimsted, Patricia Kennedy 1935- *ConAu 77*
Grimwade, Andrew 1930- *WrDr 84*
Grimwade, Arthur Girling 1913- *WrDr 84*
Grin, Aleksandr 1880-1932 *ClDMEL 80*
Grinberg, Miguel 1937- *IntWWP 82*
Grindal, Bruce T 1940- *ConAu 41R*
Grindea, Miron 1909- *ConAu 5R, –5NR*
Grindel, Carl W 1905- *ConAu 85*
Grindel, Eugene 1895-1952 *ConAu 104*
Grindel, John Anthony 1937- *ConAu 65*
Grindell, Robert M 1933- *ConAu 13R*
Grinder, Michael 1942- *ConAu 61*
Grindle, Carleton *ConAu X*
Grindley, John 1926- *ConAu 25R*
Grindrod, Muriel 1902- *WrDr 84*
Grindrod, Muriel Kathleen 1902- *ConAu 5R,
    IntAu&W 82*
Gringhuis, Dirk *ConAu X, MichAu 80,
    SmATA X*
Gringhuis, Richard H 1918-1974 *ConAu 1R,
    –5NR, MichAu 80, SmATA 25N, –6*
Grinker, Morton *DrAP&F 83*
Grinnell, David *ConAu X, TwCSFW*
Grinnell, George Bird 1849-1938 *SmATA 16*
Grinsell, Leslie Valentine 1907- *ConAu 3NR,
    –9R*
Grinspoon, Lester 1928- *ConAu 81*
Grinstead, David 1939- *ConAu 105*
Grinstein, Alexander 1918- *ConAu 5NR, –13R*

Gripari, Pierre 1925- *ConAu 29R*

Gripe, Maria 1923- *ChlLR 5[port], ConAu 29R,
    IntAu&W 82, SmATA 2*
Grise, Jeannette *ConAu X*
Grisewood, Harman 1906- *ConAu P-2*
Grisez, Germain G 1929- *ConAu 6NR, –13R*
Grisham, Noel 1916- *ConAu 10NR, –25R,
    WrDr 84*
Grispino, Joseph Aloysius 1922- *ConAu 17R*
Griswold, Erwin N 1904- *ConAu P-1*
Griswold, Francis 1902- *TwCA, TwCA SUP*
Griswold, Wesley S 1909- *ConAu 1R*
Griswold DelCastillo, Richard Allan 1942-
    ConAu 101
Gritsch, Eric W 1931- *ConAu 10NR, –21R,
    IntAu&W 82, WrDr 84*
Grivas, Theodore 1922- *ConAu 9R*
Grob, Gerald N 1931- *ConAu 1R, –5NR,
    WrDr 84*
Groch, Judith 1929- *ConAu 9R,
    SmATA 25[port]*
Grochowiak, Stanislaw 1934-1976 *ClDMEL 80*
Grode, Redway *ConAu X, SmATA X*
Groenbjerg, Kirsten A 1946- *ConAu 85*
Groene, Bertram Hawthorne 1923- *ConAu 45*
Groene, Janet 1936- *ConAu 37R*
Groenhoff, Edwin L 1924- *ConAu 57*
Groennings, Sven O 1934- *ConAu 45*
Groenoset, Dagfinn 1920- *ConAu 93*
Grof, Stanislav 1931- *ConAu 73*
Groff, Patrick J 1924- *ConAu 41R*
Groff, Warren F 1924- *ConAu 53*
Grogan, Emmett 1942-1978 *ConAu 41R*
Grogger, Paula 1892- *IntAu&W 82*
Groh, Ed 1910- *ConAu 49*
Groh, George W 1922- *ConAu 85*
Grohler, Harald O 1938- *IntAu&W 82*
Grohman, Joann Sills 1928- *ConAu 107*
Grohn, Hans Werner 1929- *IntAu&W 82*
Grohskopf, Bernice *DrAP&F 83*
Grohskopf, Bernice 1921- *ConAu 3NR, –5R,
    IntAu&W 82, SmATA 7, WrDr 84*
Groia, Phil 1941- *ConAu 53*
Grol, Lini R 1913- *ConAu 8NR, –61,
    SmATA 9*
Groll, Gunter 1914- *IntAu&W 82*
Grollman, Earl A 1925- *ConAu 21R,
    SmATA 22[port]*
Grollman, Sharon Hya 1954- *ConAu 81*
Grollmes, Eugene E 1931- *ConAu 29R*
Gromacki, Robert Glenn 1933- *ConAu 4NR, –53*
Gromada, Thaddeus V 1929- *ConAu 45*
Groman, George L 1928- *ConAu 21R*
Grombach, John V 1901- *ConAu 103*
Grondal, Gylfi 1936- *IntAu&W 82*
Grondona, L St. Clare 1890- *ConAu 103*
Grondona, L St. Clare 1890-1982 *ConAu 108*
Grondona, Leo St Clare 1890- *WrDr 84*
Groneman, Chris Harold 1906- *ConAu 1R, –1NR*
Groningen, Bernhard A Van 1894- *IntAu&W 82*
Gronowicz, Antoni *DrAP&F 83*
Gronowicz, Antoni 1913- *ConAu 25R,
    IntWWP 82, NatPD 81[port]*
Groocock, J M 1929- *ConAu 57*
Groom, Arthur William 1898-1964 *ConAu 1R,
    –1NR, SmATA 10*
Groom, Bernard 1892- *ConAu P-2*
Groom, Winston 1943- *ConAu 85*
Groome, Thomas H 1945- *ConAu 110*
Gropius, Walter Adolf 1883-1969 *ConAu 25R*
Gropman, Donald S 1936- *ConAu 101*
Gropper, William 1897-1977 *ConAu 102, –89*
Gros, Andre 1908- *IntAu&W 82*
Gros, Bernard 1917- *IntAu&W 82*
Grosbard, Ulu 1929- *ConAu 25R*
Grose, B Donald 1943- *ConAu 45*
Groseclose, Elgin 1899- *ConAu P-2,
    IntAu&W 82, WrDr 84*
Groseclose, Elgin E 1899-1983 *ConAu 109*
Grosjean, Jean 1912- *ClDMEL 80*
Grosman, Brian A 1935- *ConAu 73*
Grosman, Ladislav 1921- *ConAu 102*
Grosman, Tatyana 1904-1982 *ConAu 107*
Grosofsky, Leslie *ConAu X*
Gross, Alan 1947- *ConAu 89*
Gross, Beatrice 1933- *ConAu 77*
Gross, Ben Samuel 1891-1979 *ConAu 89, –97*
Gross, Bertram M 1912- *ConAu 9NR*
Gross, Bertram Myron 1912- *ConAu 13R*
Gross, Beverly 1938- *ConAu 29R*
Gross, Carl 1911- *ConAu 13R, WrDr 84*

Gross, Dan S *IntAu&W 82X, IntWWP 82X*
Gross, Daniel R 1942- *ConAu 53*
Gross, David C 1923- *ConAu 102*
Gross, Ernest A 1906- *ConAu 5R*
Gross, Feliks 1906- *ConAu 29R*
Gross, Franz B 1919- *ConAu 29R*
Gross, Gerald 1932- *ConAu 9R*
Gross, Hanna 1928- *ConAu 41R*
Gross, Harvey S 1922- *ConAu 8NR, –13R*
Gross, Helen Shimota 1931- *ConAu 9R*
Gross, Irma H 1892- *ConAu P-1*
Gross, James A 1933- *ConAu 57*
Gross, Joel 1949- *ConAu 29R*
Gross, Joel 1951- *WrDr 84*
Gross, Johannes Heinrich 1916- *ConAu 29R*
Gross, John 1935- *ConAu 29R, WrDr 84*
Gross, John J 1912-1970 *ConAu P-2*
Gross, John Owen 1894-1971 *ConAu P-2*
Gross, Kenneth G 1939- *ConAu 25R*
Gross, Leslie 1927- *ConAu 5R*
Gross, Llewellyn 1914- *ConAu 25R*
Gross, Ludwik 1904- *IntAu&W 82, WrDr 84*
Gross, Marjorie P 1924- *ConAmTC*
Gross, Martin 1934- *ConAu 11NR, –13R*
Gross, Martin L 1925- *ConAu 7NR, –9R*
Gross, Mary Anne 1943- *ConAu 49*
Gross, Michael 1891?-1979 *ConAu 97*
Gross, Michael 1952- *ConAu 93*
Gross, Milton *AuNews 1*
Gross, Milton 1912?-1973 *ConAu 41R*
Gross, Natan 1919- *IntAu&W 82*
Gross, Neal 1920-1981 *ConAu 108*
Gross, Phyllis P 1915- *ConAu 93*
Gross, Richard 1920- *WrDr 84*
Gross, Richard Edmund 1920- *ConAu 1R, –1NR*
Gross, Ronald *DrAP&F 83*
Gross, Ronald 1935- *ConAu 5R, –5NR*
Gross, Ruth Belov 1929- *SmATA 33[port]*
Gross, S 1933- *ConAu 45*
Gross, Sarah Chokla 1906-1976 *ConAu 61, –65,
    SmATA 26N, –9*
Gross, Seymour L 1926- *ConAu 1R, –3NR*
Gross, Sheldon H 1921- *ConAu 81*
Gross, Shelley 1938- *ConAu 21R*
Gross, Shelly *ConAu X*
Gross, Stuart D 1914- *ConAu 57, MichAu 80*
Gross, Suzanne 1933- *ConAu 17R*
Gross, Terence 1947- *ConAu 101*
Gross, Theodore Faro 1949- *NatPD 81[port]*
Gross, Theodore L 1930- *ConAu 41R*
Gross, Walter 1923- *ConAu 21R*
Gross, Walter 1924- *IntAu&W 82*
Gross, William Joseph 1894- *ConAu P-1*
Grossack, Irvin Millman 1927- *ConAu 97*
Grossack, Martin Myer 1928- *ConAu 6NR, –9R*
Grossbach, Robert 1941- *ConAu 33R*
Grossberg, Mimi 1905- *IntAu&W 82*
Grossen, Neal E 1943- *ConAu 93*
Grosser, Alfred 1925- *ConAu 2NR, –45,
    IntAu&W 82*
Grosser, Morton 1931- *ConAu 97*
Grosshans, Henry 1921- *ConAu 29R*
Grossholtz, Jean 1929- *ConAu 13R*
Grossinger, Richard *DrAP&F 83*
Grossinger, Richard 1944- *ConAu 103*
Grossinger, Tania 1937- *ConAu 4NR, –53,
    WrDr 84*
Grosskurth, Phyllis 1924- *ConAu 9NR, –13R*
Grossman, Alfred 1927- *ConAu 5R, ConNov 82,
    DcLEL 1940, WrDr 84*
Grossman, Allen R 1932- *ConAu 1R, –1NR*
Grossman, Edith Marian 1936- *ConAu 108*
Grossman, Edith Searle 1863-1931 *TwCWr*
Grossman, Ellie *ConAu 110*
Grossman, Florence *DrAP&F 83*
Grossman, Frances Kaplan 1939- *ConAu 57*
Grossman, Gary H 1948- *ConAu 69*
Grossman, Herbert 1934- *ConAu 17R,
    WrDr 84*
Grossman, Jean Schick 1894-1972 *ConAu 37R*
Grossman, Julian 1931- *ConAu 53*
Grossman, Kurt R 1897-1972 *ConAu 33R*
Grossman, Lawrence 1945- *ConAu 65*
Grossman, Lee 1931- *ConAu 69*
Grossman, Manuel Lester 1939- *ConAu 106*
Grossman, Martin *DrAP&F 83*
Grossman, Martin A 1951- *ConAu 102*
Grossman, Martin Allen 1943- *ConAu 77,
    IntWWP 82, MichAu 80*
Grossman, Mary Louise 1930- *ConAu 77*
Grossman, Morton Charles 1919- *ConAu 1R,
    –2NR*

Grossman, Nancy S 1940- *SmATA 29[port]*
Grossman, Reinhardt 1931- *WrDr 84*
Grossman, Richard *DrAP&F 83*
Grossman, Richard L 1921- *ConAu 97*
Grossman, Robert 1940- *SmATA 11*
Grossman, Ron *DrAP&F 83*
Grossman, Ronald P 1934- *ConAu 21R*
Grossman, Ronald W 1950- *IntWWP 82*
Grossman, Samuel 1897- *ConAu 53,
    IntAu&W 82*
Grossman, Sebastian P 1934- *ConAu 21R,
    WrDr 84*
Grossman, Shelly 1928?-1975 *ConAu 57*
Grossman, Vasily Semyonovich 1905-1964
    ClDMEL 80
Grossman, William L 1906-1980 *ConAu 97,
    ConAu P-2*
Grossmann, Reinhardt S 1931- *ConAu 33R*
Grosso, Alfonso 1928- *ClDMEL 80,
    IntAu&W 82X*
Grosso Ramos, Alfonso 1928- *IntAu&W 82*
Grossu, Sergiu 1920- *ConAu 8NR, –57*
Grossvogel, David I 1925- *ConAu 1R, –4NR,
    IntAu&W 82*
Grosswirth, Marvin 1931- *ConAu 33R*
Grosvenor, Donna K 1938- *ConAu 109*
Grosvenor, Gilbert Hovey 1875-1966 *ConAu 93*
Grosvenor, Kali Diana 1960- *ConAu 69,
    LivgBAA*
Grosvenor, Melville Bell 1901-1982 *ConAu 106,
    –69*
Grosvenor, Verta Mae 1938- *ConAu 69,
    LivgBAA*
Grosvenor, Verta Mae 1939- *ASpks*
Grosvenor, Vertamae *DrAP&F 83*
Groth, Alexander J 1932- *ConAu 41R*
Groth, John 1908- *ConAu 101,
    SmATA 21[port]*
Grotjahn, Martin 1904- *ConAu 41R*
Grotowski, Jerzy 1933- *ConAu 105*
Groueff, Stephane *ASpks*
Grouling, Thomas E 1940- *ConSFA*
Groult, Benoite Marie Rose 1920- *IntAu&W 82*
Groulx, Georges 1922- *CreCan 1*
Groulx, Gilles 1931- *CreCan 2*
Grounds, Roger 1938- *ConAu 97, WrDr 84*
Groundwater, William 1906?-1982 *ConAu 106*
Groupe, Darryl R *ConAu X, IntWWP 82X*
Groussard, Serge 1921- *ConAu 108*
Grout, Donald Jay 1902- *ConAu 102*
Grout, Jack 1910- *ConAu 69*
Grout, Patricia Bulkeley 1942- *IntAu&W 82*
Grout, Ruth E 1901- *ConAu P-2*
Grove, Fred 1913- *WrDr 84*
Grove, Fred H 1913- *ConAu 1R, –2NR,
    IntAu&W 82, TwCWW*
Grove, Frederick Philip 1871?-1948 *ConAu X,
    CreCan 1, LongCTC, ModCmwL, TwCWr*
Grove, Frederick Philip 1879-1948
    TwCLC 4[port], TwCSFW, TwCWW
Grove, Jack William 1920- *ConAu 5R*
Grove, Lee E d1971 *ConAu 104*
Grove, Pearce S 1930- *ConAu 73*
Grove, Will O *ConAu X*
Grover, Betty Oliphant *CreCan 1*
Grover, David H 1925- *ConAu 13R*
Grover, David S 1939- *ConAu 89*
Grover, John W 1927- *ConAu 77*
Grover, Linda 1934- *ConAu 29R, WrDr 84*
Grover, Marshall *TwCWW*
Grover, Philip 1929- *ConAu 104, WrDr 84*
Grover, Raymond Frank 1931- *IntAu&W 82*
Grover-Rogof, Jay *DrAP&F 83*
Groves, Colin Peter 1942- *ConAu 61*
Groves, Don George *ConAu 106*
Groves, Edythe Muriel 1923- *IntWWP 82*
Groves, Francis Richard 1889- *ConAu P-1*
Groves, Georgina *ConAu X, SmATA X,
    WrDr 84*
Groves, H E 1921- *ConAu 5R*
Groves, Harold M 1897- *ConAu 5R*
Groves, J W 1910- *ConSFA*
Groves, Jay 1922- *ConSFA*
Groves, Paul 1930- *ConAu 93*
Groves, Reg 1908- *ConAu 13R*
Groves, Reginald 1908- *IntAu&W 82*
Groves, Ruth Clouse 1902- *ConAu P-2*
Groves, Sheila 1945- *WrDr 84*
Grow, Lawrence 1939- *ConAu 10NR, –73*
Grub, Phillip D 1932- *ConAu 25R*
Grubar, Francis S 1924- *ConAu 33R*
Grubb *ConAu X*

Grubb, David Herbert Watkins 1941-
    IntWWP 82
Grubb, Davis Alexander 1919-1980 *ConAu 1R,
    –4NR, –101, DcLB 6*
Grubb, Frederick 1930- *ConAu 101, ConP 80,
    WrDr 84*
Grubb, Kenneth George 1900-1980 *ConAu 97,
    ConAu P-1, IntAu&W 82*
Grubb, Norman Percy 1895- *ConAu P-1,
    WrDr 84*
Grubb, W Norton 1948- *ConAu 110*
Grubbs, Donald H 1936- *ConAu 81*
Grubbs, Frank Leslie, Jr. 1931- *ConAu 29R*
Grubbs, Robert L 1919- *ConAu 1R, –2NR*
Grube, Georges M A 1899- *ConAu P-1*
Grubel, Herbert G 1934- *ConAu 5NR, –9R*
Gruber, Frank 1904-1969 *ConAu 25R,
    ConAu P-1, TwCCr&M, TwCWW*
Gruber, Frederick C 1903- *ConAu 49*
Gruber, Gary R 1940- *ConAu 9NR, –53*
Gruber, Helmut 1928- *ConAu 103*
Gruber, Ira D 1934- *ConAu 110*
Gruber, Jacob W 1921- *ConAu 1R*
Gruber, Joseph John 1930- *ConAu 5R, –6NR*
Gruber, Karl J 1909- *IntAu&W 82*
Gruber, Martin Jay 1937- *ConAu 8NR, –53*
Gruber, Ruth *ConAu 25R*
Gruber, Terry 1953- *ConAu 97*
Gruber, Martin 1931- *ConAu 33R, WrDr 84*
Grubian, Motel 1909?-1972 *ConAu 104*
Grubinski, Waclaw 1883-1973 *ClDMEL 80*
Gruder, Galina Maria 1924- *IntAu&W 82*
Grudin, Louis 1898- *ConAu 1R, IntWWP 82*
Grue, Lee Meitzen *DrAP&F 83*
Gruelle, John 1880-1938 *SmATA 32*
Gruelle, Johnny *SmATA X*
Gruelle, Johnny 1880-1938 *DcLB 22,
    TwCCW 83*
Gruelle, Worth *AuNews 2*
Gruen, John 1926- *ConAu 8NR, –17R*
Gruen, Victor 1903-1980 *ConAu 10NR*
Gruen, Victor D 1903-1980 *ConAu 13R, –97,
    IntAu&W 82*
Gruenbaum, Adolf 1923- *ConAu 5NR, –9R*
Gruenbaum, Ludwig *ConAu 49*
Gruenberg, Benjamin Charles 1875-1965
    ConAu P-1
Gruenberg, Sidonie Matsner 1881-1974 *ConAu 49,
    ConAu P-1, SmATA 2, –27N*
Grueneberg, Hans 1907-1982 *ConAu 108*
Gruenhagen, Robert W 1932- *ConAu 29R*
Gruening, Ernest Henry 1887-1974 *ConAu 49,
    TwCA, TwCA SUP*
Gruenstein, Peter 1947- *ConAu 77*
Gruenther, Alfred M 1899-1983 *ConAu 109*
Gruffydd, Peter 1935- *ConAu 104, ConP 80,
    WrDr 84*
Gruhier, Fabien 1945- *IntAu&W 82*
Gruhn, Carrie E 1907- *ConAu P-1*
Gruits, Patricia Beall 1923- *ConAu 105*
Gruliow, Leo 1913- *ConAu 5R, –73*
Grumbach, Doris *DrAP&F 83*
Grumbach, Doris 1918- *ConAu 5R, –9NR,
    ConLC 13, –22[port], WrDr 84*
Grumelli, Antonio 1928- *ConAu 37R*
Grumet, Robert Steven 1949- *ConAu 102*
Grumich, Charles A 1905?-1981 *ConAu 104*
Grumley, Michael 1941- *ConAu 29R, WrDr 84*
Grumme, Marguerite *ConAu 5R*
Grummer, Arnold E 1923- *ConAu 106*
Grun, Bernard 1901-1972 *ConAu 37R*
Grun, Max VonDer 1926- *ClDMEL 80*
Grunbaum, Adolf 1923- *ConAu X,
    IntAu&W 82, WrDr 84*
Grunberg, Karl 1891- *CnMD*
Grund, Josef Carl 1920- *ConAu 73*
Grundberg, Andy *ConAu X, DrAP&F 83*
Grundberg, John Andrew 1947- *ConAu 103*
Grundgens, Gustaf 1899-1963 *CroCD*
Grundstein, Nathan 1913- *ConAu 37R,
    WrDr 84*
Grundt, Leonard 1936- *ConAu 57*
Grundy, Bill 1923- *IntAu&W 82*
Grundy, Joan 1920- *ConAu 109, WrDr 84*
Grundy, John Brownsdon Clowes 1902-
    IntAu&W 82
Grundy, Kenneth W 1936- *ConAu 73*
Grundy, Mabel Barnes *TwCRGW*
Grundy, R F Brooks 1903- *WrDr 84*
Grundy, Rupert Francis Brooks 1903-
    IntAu&W 82
Gruneau, Richard S 1948- *ConAu 110*

Gruneberg, Hans 1907- *IntAu&W 82, WrDr 84*
Grunfeld, Frederic V 1929- *ConAu 73,
    IntAu&W 82, WrDr 84*
Grunge *ConAu X*
Grunlan, Stephen Arthur 1942- *ConAu 101*
Grunwald, Henry Anatole 1922- *ConAu 107*
Grunwald, Stefan *DrAP&F 83*
Grunwald, Stefan 1933- *ConAu 29R*
Grupp, Stanley E 1927- *ConAu 53*
Grusas, Juozas 1901- *EncWL 2*
Grusd, Edward Elihu 1904- *ConAu P-2*
Gruskin, Alan D 1904-1970 *ConAu 29R,
    ConAu P-1*
Gruson, Edward S 1929- *ConAu 45*
Gruss, Edmond C 1933- *ConAu 53*
Grutz, Mariellen Procopio 1946- *ConAu 93*
Grutzmacher, Harold M, Jr. 1930- *ConAu 29R*
Gruver, Rebecca *ConAu X*
Gruver, William R, II 1929- *ConAu 45*
Grylls, David 1947- *ConAu 85*
Grylls, Rosalie Glynn *ConAu 65*
Grymer, Claus Torben 1946- *IntAu&W 82*
Grynberg, Henryk 1936- *ConAu 29R*
Gryst, Edward 1911- *ConAu 1R*
Grzesczak, Marian 1934- *IntWWP 82*
Gsteiger, Manfred 1930- *IntAu&W 82*
Gstrein, Heinz 1941- *IntAu&W 82*
Guadagna, Ingeborg 1914- *IntAu&W 82*
Guadagnolo, Joseph F 1912- *ConAu 5R*
Guadaloupe, Brother Jose De 1896-1974 *ConAu X*
Guado, Sergio *ConAu X*
Guandolo, John 1919- *ConAu 21R, WrDr 84*
Guaragna, Salvatore 1893-1981 *ConAu 105*
Guard, Dave *ConAu X*
Guard, David 1934- *ConAu 77*
Guardo, Carol Joan 1939- *ConAu 103*
Guare, John 1938- *ConAu 73, ConDr 82,
    ConLC 8, –14, DcLB 7[port], IntAu&W 82,
    NatPD 81[port], WorAu 1970, WrDr 84*
Guareschi, Giovanni 1908-1968 *ClDMEL 80,
    ConAu 105, –25R, ModRL, TwCA SUP,
    TwCW*
Guarino, M Vincent 1939- *ConAu 41R*
Guback, Thomas H 1937- *ConAu 25R*
Gubar, Susan 1944- *ConAu 108*
Gubern, Santiago 1933- *ConAu 2NR, –45*
Gubernat, Susan Anne *DrAP&F 83*
Gubina, Indra 1927- *IntAu&W 82, IntWWP 82*
Gubrium, Jaber F 1943- *ConAu 4NR, –53,
    WrDr 84*
Gubser, Nicholas J 1938- *ConAu 17R*
Guccione, Robert, Jr. *AuNews 2*
Guck, Dorothy 1913- *ConAu 49, MichAu 80,
    SmATA 27[port]*
Gudanowska, B *DrAP&F 83*
Gudde, Erwin Gustav 1889-1969 *ConAu 4NR,
    –5R*
Guder, Eileen 1919- *ConAu 17R*
Gudiol, Jose *ConAu X*
Gudiol I Ricart, Josep 1904- *ConAu 81*
Gudiol Ricart, Jose M *ConAu X*
Gudiol Ricart, Josep *ConAu X*
Gudjonsson, Halldor Kiljan 1902- *ConAu 103*
Gudmundsson, Thoroddur 1904- *IntAu&W 82*
Gudmundsson, Tomas 1901- *EncWL 2*
Gudschinsky, Sarah Caroline 1919-1975
    ConAu P-2
Guedalla, Philip 1889-1944 *LongCTC, ModBrL,
    TwCA, TwCA SUP, TwCWr*
Guede, Norina Lami 1913- *ConAu 9R*
Guedeja-Marron Perez, Justo 1919-
    IntAu&W 82
Guedroitz, Prince Alexis 1923- *IntAu&W 82*
Guehenne, Jean 1890-1978 *ConAu X*
Guehenno, Jean 1890-1978 *ClDMEL 80,
    ConAu 104, IntAu&W 82, WorAu 1970*
Guehenno, Marcel 1890- *IntAu&W 82X*
Guelbenzu, Jose Maria 1944- *ClDMEL 80*
Guelich, Robert A 1939- *ConAu 2NR, –45*
Guemple, Lee 1930- *ConAu 41R, IntAu&W 82*
Guenette, Robert 1935- *ConAu 25R*
Guenter, Erich *ConAu X*
Guenther, Charles *DrAP&F 83*
Guenther, Charles 1920- *ConAu 29R,
    IntAu&W 82, IntWWP 82, WrDr 84*
Guenther, Herbert 1947- *IntAu&W 82*
Guenther, Herbert V 1917- *ConAu 73*
Guenther, John *ConAu 5R, –9NR*
Guenther, Wallace 1929- *ConAu 65*
Guerard, Albert J *DrAP&F 83*
Guerard, Albert Joseph 1914- *ConAu 1R, –2NR,
    ConNov 82, IntAu&W 82, TwCA SUP,*

Gupta, Brijen Kishore 1929- *ConAu 1NR, –45*
Gupta, Dharam C 1924- *IntAu&W 82*
Gupta, Marie 1946- *ConAu 57*
Gupta, Ram Chandra 1927- *ConAu 21R*
Gupta, S 1927- *ConAu 57*
Gupta, Shiv K 1930- *ConAu 57*
Gupta, Sulekh Chandra 1928- *ConAu 13R*
Guptara, Prabhu Siddhartha 1949- *ConAu 81, IntWWP 82*
Guptill, Nathanael M 1917- *ConAu 45*
Gurdjieff, George Ivanovitch 1868-1949 *LongCTC*
Gurganus, Allan *DrAP&F 83*
Gurin, Joel 1953- *ConAu 108*
Gurko, Leo 1914- *ConAu 5R, –5NR, SmATA 9*
Gurko, Miriam *SmATA 9, WrDr 84*
Gurman, Alan S 1945- *ConAu 5NR, –53*
Gurnee, Jeanne 1926- *ConAu 93*
Gurnee, Russell H 1922- *ConAu 107*
Gurney, A R, Jr. *DrAP&F 83*
Gurney, A R, Jr. 1930- *ConAu 77, ConDr 82, NatPD 81[port], WrDr 84*
Gurney, Gene 1924- *ConAu 5R, –9NR*
Gurney, J Eric 1910- *ConAu 1R, –2NR*
Gurney, Lawrence Stuart 1921- *IntWWP 82*
Gurney, Nancy Jack 1915?-1973 *ConAu 45*
Gurney, Peter *ConAu X*
Guro, Yelena Genrikhovna 1877-1913 *ClDMEL 80*
Gurr, A J 1936- *WrDr 84*
Gurr, Andrew 1936- *ConAu 33R*
Gurr, Edward 1905- *WrDr 84*
Gurr, Ted Robert 1936- *ConAu 41R*
Gurrey, Percival 1890-1980 *ConAu 97*
Gurster, Eugen 1895- *IntAu&W 82*
Gurwitsch, Aron 1901-1973 *ConAu 41R, ConAu P-1*
Gusev, Sergey Ivanovich 1867-1963 *TwCA, TwCA SUP*
Gusewelle, C W *DrAP&F 83*
Gusfield, Joseph R 1923- *ConAu 53*
Guss, Donald L 1929- *ConAu 17R*
Guss, Jack Raphael 1919- *NatPD 81[port]*
Guss, Leonard M 1926- *ConAu 21R*
Gussman, Boris 1914- *ConAu 5R*
Gussow, Joan Dye 1928- *ConAu 29R*
Gussow, Mel 1933- *ConAmTC, ConAu 107*
Gustaf VI, Adolf, King Of Sweden 1882-1973 *ConAu 45*
Gustafson, Alrik 1903-1970 *ConAu 1R, –103*
Gustafson, Donald F 1934- *ConAu 9R*
Gustafson, James M 1925- *ConAu 25R*
Gustafson, Jim *DrAP&F 83*
Gustafson, Paula Catherine 1941- *ConAu 106*
Gustafson, Ralph 1909- *ConAu 8NR, –21R, ConP 80, CreCan 2, IntAu&W 82, IntWWP 82, TwCA SUP, WrDr 84*
Gustafson, Richard Clarence 1933- *IntWWP 82*
Gustafson, Richard F 1934- *ConAu 17R*
Gustafson, Sarah R *ConAu X, SmATA 1*
Gustafson, Scott 1956- *SmATA 34[port]*
Gustafson, W Eric 1933- *ConAu 57*
Gustafsson, Lars 1936- *ClDMEL 80, ConAu 85, EncWL 2*
Gustaitis, Rasa 1934- *ConAu 25R*
Gustas, Aldona *IntAu&W 82X*
Gustavson, Carl G 1915- *ConAu 17R*
Gustin, Lawrence R 1937- *ConAu 57, MichAu 80*
Gustkey, Earl 1940- *ConAu 57*
Gut, Gom *ConAu X*
Gutcheon, Beth R 1945- *ConAu 2NR, –49*
Gutek, Gerald L 1935- *ConAu 81*
Gutenberg, Arthur W 1920- *ConAu 37R*
Guterman, Simeon L 1907- *ConAu 41R*
Guterman, Stanley S 1934- *ConAu 29R*
Gutersloh, Albert Paris 1887-1973 *EncWL 2, ModGL*
Gutheim, Frederick 1908- *ConAu 9NR, –21R*
Guthke, Karl S 1933- *ConAu 41R, IntAu&W 82*
Guthman, Edwin 1919- *ConAu 33R*
Guthman, William H 1924- *ConAu 57*
Guthmann, Harry George 1896- *ConAu 1R*
Guthrie, A B *DrAP&F 83*
Guthrie, A B, Jr. 1901- *ConLC 23[port], ConNov 82, DcLB 6, FifWWr, TwCWW, WrDr 84*
Guthrie, Alfred Bertram, Jr. 1901- *ConAu 57, DcLEL 1940, ModAL, TwCA SUP*
Guthrie, Anne 1890-1979 *ConAu 5R, SmATA 28*
Guthrie, Donald 1916- *ConAu 7NR, –13R*

Guthrie, Harvey Henry, Jr. 1924- *ConAu 13R*
Guthrie, Hugh *ConAu X*
Guthrie, Hunter 1901-1974 *ConAu 53*
Guthrie, Isobel *ConAu X*
Guthrie, James Shields 1931- *ConAu 33R*
Guthrie, James W 1936- *ConAu 41R*
Guthrie, John 1908- *ConAu 106, WrDr 84*
Guthrie, John A 1907- *ConAu 1R*
Guthrie, Judith Bretherton 1905?-1972 *ConAu 37R*
Guthrie, Ramon 1896-1973 *ConAu 5R, –45, DcLB 4, WorAu 1970*
Guthrie, Robert V 1930- *ConAu 53*
Guthrie, Russell Dale 1936- *ConAu 106*
Guthrie, Thomas Anstey 1856-1934 *LongCTC, TwCA, TwCA SUP*
Guthrie, Sir Tyrone 1900-1971 *ConAu 29R, –29R, CreCan 1*
Guthrie, William Keith Chambers 1906-1981 *ConAu 103, –11NR, –65, IntAu&W 82*
Guthrie, Sir William Tyrone 1900-1971 *CreCan 1*
Guthrie, Woodrow Wilson 1912-1967 *ConAu 93*
Guthrie, Woody 1912-1967 *ConAu X*
Guthrie-Smith, William Herbert 1861-1940 *TwCWr*
Gutierrez, Donald 1932- *ConAu 109*
Gutierrez-Vega, Zenaida 1924- *ConAu 41R*
Gutkelch, Walter 1901- *CnMD*
Gutkin, Harry 1915- *ConAu 101*
Gutkind, Erwin A 1886-1968 *ConAu 5R, –8NR*
Gutkind, Lee 1943- *ConAu 5NR, –53*
Gutman, Herbert G 1928- *ConAu 65*
Gutman, Judith Mara 1928- *ConAu 21R, WrDr 84*
Gutman, Naham 1899?-1981 *ConAu 102, SmATA 25N*
Gutman, Richard J S 1949- *ConAu 101*
Gutman, Robert 1926- *ConAu 45*
Gutman, Robert W 1925- *ConAu 25R, IntAu&W 82, WrDr 84*
Gutmann, James 1897- *ConAu P-2*
Gutmann, Joseph 1923- *ConAu 1NR, –49*
Gutmann, Myron P 1949- *ConAu 105*
Gutnik, Martin J 1942- *ConAu 3NR, –49*
Gutsche, Thelma 1915- *ConAu 21R*
Gutt, Dieter 1924- *ConAu X*
Guttenberg, Barnett *ConAu 89*
Guttenberg, Virginia 1914- *ConAu 81*
Guttentag, Marcia 1932-1977 *ConAu 8NR, –57*
Gutteridge, Anne C 1943- *ConAu 108*
Gutteridge, Bernard 1916- *DcLEL 1940*
Gutteridge, Don 1937- *ConAu 9NR, –65, ConP 80, WrDr 84*
Gutteridge, Donald George 1937- *IntAu&W 82*
Gutteridge, Lindsay 1923- *ConAu 49, TwCSFW, WrDr 84*
Gutteridge, Richard 1911- *WrDr 84*
Gutteridge, William Frank 1919- *ConAu 13R, IntAu&W 82, WrDr 84*
Gutterson, Herbert 1915- *ConAu 9R*
Gutting, Gary 1942- *ConAu 103*
Gutting, Harald 1928- *IntAu&W 82*
Guttmacher, Alan F 1898-1974 *ConAu 1R, –6NR, –49*
Guttmacher, Manfred S 1898-1966 *ConAu P-1*
Guttman, Dena 1934- *WrDr 84*
Guttman, Irving 1928- *CreCan 1*
Guttmann, Alexander *ConAu 29R*
Guttmann, Allen 1932- *ConAu 1R, –1NR, WrDr 84*
Gutton, Andre Henry Georges 1904- *IntAu&W 82*
Guttridge, Leonard F 1918- *ConAu 85*
Guttsman, Wilhelm Leo 1920- *ConAu 9R*
Guttsman, William Leo 1920- *IntAu&W 82*
Gutzke, Manford G 1896- *ConAu 17R*
Guy, Anne W *ConAu 5R*
Guy, David 1948- *ConAu 105*
Guy, Elizabeth Benson 1928- *CreCan 2*
Guy, Harold A 1904- *ConAu 17R*
Guy, Helen *IntWWP 82*
Guy, Rosa 1928- *ConAu 17R, ConLC 26[port], SmATA 14, TwCCW 83, WrDr 84*
Guyard, Marius-Francois 1921- *IntAu&W 82*
Guyer, Paul 1948- *ConAu 105*
Guyot, James F 1932- *ConAu 53*
Guyotat, Pierre 1940- *ClDMEL 80*
Guyton, Arthur C 1919- *ConAu 7NR, –17R*
Guzie, Tad W 1934- *ConAu 5NR, –13R*
Guzikowski, Robert *DrAP&F 83*
Guzman, Martin Luis 1887-1976 *EncWL 2*
Guzzwell, John 1930- *ConAu 13R*

Gwaitney, John Langston 1928- *LivgBAA*
Gwaltney, Francis Irby 1921- *ConAu 1R, –2NR*
Gwaltney, John Langston 1928- *ConAu 33R, –77, ConIsC 1[port], WrDr 84*
Gwendolyn *ConAu X*
Gwilliam, Kenneth M 1937- *ConAu 17R*
Gwin, Lucy 1943- *ConAu 109*
Gwinn, Christine Margaret 1900- *WrDr 84*
Gwinup, Thomas 1932- *ConAu 73*
Gwirtzman, Milton S 1933- *ConAu 29R*
Gwyn, Julian 1937- *ConAu 57*
Gwyn, Richard 1934- *ConAu 25R, WrDr 84*
Gwyn, W B 1927- *ConAu 5NR, –13R*
Gwyn, William Brent *WrDr 84*
Gwynn, Denis Rolleston 1893- *ConAu P-1*
Gwynn, Frances 1923- *IntAu&W 82*
Gwynn, Harri 1913- *IntAu&W 82*
Gwynn, Mary *DrAP&F 83*
Gwynn, Stephen Lucius 1864-1950 *LongCTC, ModBrL, TwCA, TwCA SUP*
Gwynne, Erskine 1898?-1948 *ConAu 107, DcLB 4*
Gwynne, Fred 1926- *SmATA 27*
Gwynne, Peter 1941- *ConAu 89*
Gwynne-Jones, Allan 1892-1982 *ConAu 107*
Gwyther, Michaela 1920- *IntAu&W 82*
Gwythr, Michaela 1920- *IntWWP 82*
Gyarfas, Endre 1936- *IntAu&W 82*
Gyarfas, Miklos 1915- *CroCD*
Gye, Marie-Louise Emma Cecile Lajeunesse *CreCan 2*
Gyftopoulos, Elias Panayiotis 1927- *ConAu 104*
Gyldenspjaet *IntAu&W 82X*
Gyldenvand, Lily M 1917- *ConAu 6NR, –13R, WrDr 84*
Gyles, Sheila *IntAu&W 82X*
Gyllenhammar, Pehr G 1935- *ConAu 73*
Gyllensten, Lars Johan Wictor 1921- *ClDMEL 80, EncWL 2, IntAu&W 82*
Gyorgyey, Clara 1936- *ConAu 77, IntAu&W 82*
Gysbers, Norman C 1932- *ConAu 61*
Gysin, Brion *DrAP&F 83*
Gysin, Brion 1916- *DcLB 16[port]*
Gyurkovics, Tibor 1931- *IntAu&W 82*
Gzowski, Peter 1934- *ConAu 106*

H

H D 1886-1961 *ConAmA, ConAu X, ConLC 3, -8, -14, LongCTC, TwCA, TwCA SUP, TwCWr, WhoTwCL*
H G *IntAu&W 82X*
H M S *ConAu X*
H M W *ConAu X*
Haaby, Lawrence O 1915- *ConAu 33R*
Haac, Oscar A 1918- *ConAu 33R, IntAu&W 82, WrDr 84*
Haack, Susan 1945- *ConAu 61*
Haaf, Beverly T 1936- *ConAu 97*
Haag, Jessie Helen 1917- *ConAu 5NR, -13R*
Haage, Peter 1940- *IntAu&W 82*
Haagensen, Erling 1945- *IntAu&W 82*
Haake, Katharine Koss *DrAP&F 83*
Haaker, Ann M *ConAu 25R*
Haan, Aubrey Edwin 1908- *ConAu 1R*
Haanpaa, Pentti 1905-1955 *EncWL 2*
Haar, Charles M 1920- *ConAu 33R, WrDr 84*
Haar, Francis 1908- *ConAu 53*
Haar, Franklin B 1906- *ConAu P-1*
Haar, James 1929- *ConAu 21R, WrDr 84*
Haarer, Alec Ernest 1894-1970 *ConAu 4NR, -5R*
Haarhoff, Theodore Johannes 1892-1971 *ConAu P-1*
Haas, Albert E 1917- *ConAu 21R*
Haas, Ben L 1926-1977 *ConAu 8NR, -9R, -73*
Haas, Carolyn Buhai 1926- *ConAu 9NR, -65*
Haas, Charlie 1952- *ConAu 73*
Haas, Darla Lawayne 1950- *IntWWP 82*
Haas, Dorothy F *ConAu 3NR, -5R*
Haas, Ernst B 1924- *ConAu 81*
Haas, Gerda 1922- *ConAu 110*
Haas, Harold I 1925- *ConAu 29R*
Haas, Irene 1929- *ConAu 97, SmATA 17*
Haas, Irvin 1916- *ConAu 41R*
Haas, J Eugene 1926- *ConAu 41R*
Haas, James E 1943- *ConAu 7NR, -61*
Haas, Kenneth B, Sr. 1898- *ConAu 6NR, -57*
Haas, Kurt *ConAu 53*
Haas, LaVerne 1942- *ConAu 49*
Haas, Lynne 1939- *ConAu 65*
Haas, Mary Odin 1910- *ConAu P-1*
Haas, Mary Rosamond 1910- *ConAu 9R*
Haas, Michael 1938- *ConAu 37R, -53*
Haas, Raymond Michael 1935- *ConAu 37R*
Haas, Robert Bartlett 1916- *ConAu 108*
Haas, Robert Lewis 1936- *ConAu 101*
Haase, Ann Marie Bernazza 1942- *ConAu 33R*
Haase, John 1923- *ConAu 5R*
Haavikko, Paavo Juhani 1930- *IntAu&W 82*
Haavikko, Paavo Juhani 1931- *ConAu 106, ConLC 18, CroCD, EncWL 2, IntWWP 82*
Habakkuk, John Hrothgar 1915- *IntAu&W 82, WrDr 84*
Habe, Hans 1911-1977 *ConAu 2NR, -45, -73, IntAu&W 82, TwCA SUP*
Habel, Norman C 1932- *ConAu 17R*
Habenstreit, Barbara 1937- *ConAu 29R, SmATA 5*
Haber, Audrey 1940- *ConAu 33R*
Haber, Eitan 1940- *ConAu 104*
Haber, Heinz 1913- *ConAu 73*

Haber, Jack 1939- *ConAu 69*
Haber, Joyce 1932- *ConAu 65*
Haber, Louis 1910- *ConAu 29R, SmATA 12*
Haber, Ralph Norman 1932- *ConAu 33R*
Haber, Samuel 1928- *ConAu 9R*
Haber, Tom Burns 1900- *ConAu P-2*
Haber, William 1899- *ConAu P-2*
Haberer, Joseph 1929- *ConAu 65*
Haberland, Guenther Walter 1931- *IntAu&W 82*
Haberler, Gottfried 1900- *ConAu 103, WrDr 84*
Haberly, David T 1942- *ConAu 106*
Haberly, Loyd 1896-1981 *ConAu 103, -105*
Haberman, Daniel *DrAP&F 83*
Haberman, Daniel 1933- *ConAu 110, IntWWP 82*
Haberman, Donald 1933- *ConAu 21R*
Haberman, Martin 1932- *ConAu 57*
Haberman, Richard 1945- *WrDr 84*
Haberman, Shelby J 1947- *ConAu 103*
Habermann, Helen M 1927- *ConAu 53*
Habermas, Juergen 1929- *ConAu 109*
Habermas, Jurgen 1929- *ConIsC 1[port]*
Habernig, Christine *WorAu 1970*
Haberstroh, Chadwick John 1927- *ConAu 41R*
Habetin, Rudolf 1902- *IntAu&W 82*
Habgood, John Stapylton 1927- *ConAu 5NR, -13R, IntAu&W 82, WrDr 84*
Habig, Marion Alphonse 1901- *ConAu 5R, -5NR, WrDr 84*
Hablutzel, Philip 1935- *ConAu 37R*
Hach, Clarence Woodrow 1917- *ConAu 13R*
Hache, Marie-Jeanne 1913- *IntAu&W 82*
Hache, Yannik *IntAu&W 82X*
Hachey, Thomas E 1938- *ConAu 37R*
Hachten, Harva *ConAu 108*
Hachten, William Andrews 1924- *ConAu 107*
Hacikyan, A J 1931- *ConAu 33R*
Hacikyan, Agop Jack 1931- *WrDr 84*
Hack, Walter G 1925- *ConAu 29R*
Hackady, Hal *ConAu 105*
Hacker, Andrew 1929- *ConAu 1R, -1NR, WrDr 84*
Hacker, Frederick J 1914- *ConAu 104*
Hacker, Leonard *ConAu X*
Hacker, Louis Morton 1899- *ConAu 17R, TwCA, TwCA SUP, WrDr 84*
Hacker, Marilyn *DrAP&F 83*
Hacker, Marilyn 1942- *ConAu 77, ConLC 5, -9, -23[port], ConP 80, IntWWP 82, WrDr 84*
Hacker, Mary Louise 1908- *ConAu P-2*
Hacker, Rose 1906- *ConAu 13R, WrDr 84*
Hacker, Shyrle 1910- *ConAu 101*
Hackes, Peter Sidney 1924- *ConAu 102*
Hackett, Albert 1900- *DcLB 26[port], ModWD*
Hackett, Blanche Ann 1924- *ConAu 73*
Hackett, Brian 1911- *IntAu&W 82*
Hackett, Buddy 1924- *ConAu 108*
Hackett, Cecil Arthur 1908- *ConAu 13R, IntAu&W 82, WrDr 84*
Hackett, Charles J 1915- *ConAu 73*
Hackett, Donald F 1918- *ConAu 29R*
Hackett, Francis 1883-1962 *ConAu 108, -89,*

LongCTC, TwCA, TwCA SUP
Hackett, Herbert L 1917-1964 *ConAu 1R*
Hackett, Jan Michele 1952- *ConAu 105*
Hackett, John 1910- *WrDr 84*
Hackett, John W 1924- *ConAu 17R*
Hackett, John Winthrop 1910- *ConAu 89*
Hackett, Laura Lyman 1916- *ConAu 17R*
Hackett, Marie G 1923- *ConAu 37R*
Hackett, Pat *ConAu 105*
Hackett, Paul 1920- *ConAu 29R*
Hackett, Peter 1940- *ConAu 108*
Hackett, Philip *DrAP&F 83*
Hackett, Philip 1941- *ConAu 77*
Hackett, Roger F 1922- *ConAu 77*
Hackforth-Jones, Gilbert 1900- *ConAu 13R*
Hacking, Ian 1936- *ConAu 69*
Hackleman, Michael A 1946- *ConAu 106*
Hackman, J Richard 1940- *ConAu 1NR, -49*
Hackman, Martha L 1912- *ConAu 29R*
Hackman, Neil *DrAP&F 83*
Hackney, Alan Charles Langley 1924- *ConAu 5R*
Hackney, F Sheldon 1933- *IntAu&W 82*
Hackney, Sheldon 1933- *ConAu 41R*
Hackney, Vivian 1914- *ConAu 21R*
Hacks, Peter 1928- *ClDMEL 80, CnMD, CroCD, EncWL 2, ModGL, ModWD*
Hadas, Moses 1900-1966 *ConAu 1R, -6NR, -25R, WorAu*
Hadas, Pamela White *DrAP&F 83*
Hadas, Pamela White 1946- *ConAu 93*
Hadas, Rachel *DrAP&F 83*
Hadassah *IntWWP 82X*
Hadawi, Sami 1904- *ConAu 21R*
Hadda, David 1923- *IntWWP 82*
Haddad, George M 1910- *ConAu 17R*
Haddad, Qassim *IntWWP 82X*
Haddad, Qassim Moh'd Hamad 1948- *IntWWP 82*
Haddad, Robert M 1930- *ConAu 69*
Haddad, William Frederick 1928- *ConAu 108*
Haddad, Yvonne Y 1935- *ConAu 108*
Haddad-Garcia, George 1954- *ConAu 107*
Haddan, Eugene E 1918- *ConAu 108*
Hadden, Jeffrey K 1936- *ConAu 106*
Hadden, Maude Miner 1880-1967 *ConAu P-2*
Haddix, Cecille *ConAu X*
Haddix-Kontos, Cecille P 1937- *ConAu 69*
Haddo, Oliver *ConAu X*
Haddon, Christopher *LongCTC, TwCA, TwCA SUP*
Haddon, Sarah *IntAu&W 82X*
Haddox, John Herbert 1929- *ConAu 45*
Hader, Berta 1890?-1976 *ConAu 65, -73*
Hader, Berta 1891?-1976 *SmATA 16, TwCCW 83*
Hader, Elmer 1889-1973 *TwCCW 83*
Hader, Elmer Stanley 1889-1973 *ConAu 73, SmATA 16*
Hadfield, Alan 1904- *IntAu&W 82*
Hadfield, Alice M 1908- *ConAu 108*
Hadfield, Alice Mary 1908- *IntAu&W 82*
Hadfield, Charles 1909- *ConAu 7NR*
Hadfield, E C R *ConAu X*

Halasz, Nicholas 1895- *ConAu 17R, WrDr 84*
Halbach, Edward C, Jr. 1931- *ConAu 93*
Halban, Peter 1946- *IntAu&W 82*
Halbe, Max 1865-1944 *CnMD, ModWD*
Halbe, Max 1865-1945 *ClDMEL 80*
Halberg, Arvo Kusta *ConAu X*
Halberstadt, John 1941- *ConAu 49*
Halberstadt, William Harold 1930- *ConAu 1R*
Halberstam, David 1934- *ConAu 10NR, –69,
DcLEL 1940, WorAu 1970, WrDr 84*
Halberstam, Michael J 1932-1980 *ConAu 10NR,
–102, –65*
Halcomb, Ruth 1936- *ConAu 97*
Halcon Villalon-Daoiz, Manuel 1903-
IntAu&W 82
Halcrow, Harold Graham 1911- *ConAu 17R*
Haldane, A R B 1900-1982 *ConAu 108*
Haldane, Don 1914- *CreCan 1*
Haldane, J B S 1892-1964 *ConAu 101,
TwCCW 83, TwCSFW*
Haldane, John Burdon Sanderson 1892-1964
LongCTC, TwCA, TwCA SUP
Haldane, R A 1907- *ConAu 69*
Haldane, Roger John 1945- *SmATA 13*
Haldane-Stevenson, James Patrick *WrDr 84*
Haldane-Stevenson, James Patrick 1910-
ConAu 45, IntWWP 82
Haldar, Gopal 1902- *IntAu&W 82*
Haldeman, Charles 1931- *ConAu 5R*
Haldeman, H R 1926- *ConAu 81*
Haldeman, Jack C 1941- *TwCSFW, WrDr 84*
Haldeman, Joe *DrAP&F 83*
Haldeman, Joe 1943- *ConAu 6NR, –53,
DcLB 8[port], IntAu&W 82, TwCSFW,
WrDr 84*
Haldeman, Linda 1935- *ConAu 85*
Hale, Agnes Burke 1890-1981 *ConAu 103*
Hale, Allean Lemmon 1914- *ConAu 33R,
WrDr 84*
Hale, Arlene 1924- *ConAu 1R, –1NR*
Hale, Charles A 1930- *ConAu 25R*
Hale, Clarence B 1905- *ConAu 69*
Hale, David G 1938- *ConAu 45*
Hale, Dennis 1944- *ConAu 25R*
Hale, Edward Everett 1822-1909 *SmATA 16*
Hale, Francis Joseph 1922- *ConAu 53*
Hale, Frank W, Jr. 1927- *ConAu 65, LivgBAA*
Hale, Helen *ConAu X, SmATA X*
Hale, Irina 1932- *ConAu 105,
SmATA 26[port]*
Hale, J Russell 1918- *ConAu 101*
Hale, Janet Campbell 1947- *ConAu 49*
Hale, John 1926- *ConAu 102, ConDr 82,
DcLEL 1940, IntAu&W 82, WrDr 84*
Hale, John Rigby 1923- *ConAu 102*
Hale, Judson 1933- *ConAu 69*
Hale, Julian Anthony Stuart 1940- *ConAu 41R*
Hale, K Miss *IntAu&W 82X*
Hale, Katherine 1878-1956 *CreCan 1*
Hale, Kathleen 1898- *ConAu 73, IntAu&W 82,
SmATA 17, TwCCW 83, WrDr 84*
Hale, Leon 1921- *ConAu 10NR, –17R*
Hale, Leslie 1902- *ConAu P-1*
Hale, Lewis David 1930- *ConAmTC*
Hale, Linda 1929- *ConAu 5R, SmATA 6*
Hale, Lionel Ramsay 1909-1977 *ConAu 107*
Hale, Lucretia Peabody 1820-1900
SmATA 26[port]
Hale, Margaret *ConAu X*
Hale, Michael *ConAu X, WrDr 84*
Hale, Nancy *DrAP&F 83*
Hale, Nancy 1908- *ConAu 5R, ConNov 82,
DcLB Y80B[port], IntAu&W 82,
SmATA 31[port], TwCA SUP, WrDr 84*
Hale, Nathan Cabot 1925- *ConAu 53*
Hale, Oron James 1902- *ConAu 13R*
Hale, Patricia Whitaker 1922- *ConAu 53*
Hale, Philip 1916- *ConAu X*
Hale, Richard W 1909-1976 *ConAu 65*
Hale, Tenny 1924- *IntAu&W 82*
Hale, Wanda *ConAu X*
Hale, William Harlan 1910-1974 *ConAu 49, –93*
Hales, E E Y 1908- *ConAu 85*
Hales, Edward John 1927- *ConAu 106*
Hales, Jonathan 1937- *IntAu&W 82*
Hales, Loyde 1933- *ConAu 89*
Hales-Tooke, Ann Mary Margaret 1926-
WrDr 84
Halevi, Z'ev Ben Shimon *ConAu X*
Halevy, Daniel 1872-1962 *ClDMEL 80*
Halevy, Elie 1870-1937 *LongCTC*

Halevy, Ludovic 1834-1908 *ModWD*
Haley, Alex 1921- *ASpks, ConAu 77,
ConLC 8, –12, LivgBAA, WrDr 84*
Haley, Andrew G 1904- *ConAu P-1*
Haley, Bruce Everts 1933- *ConAu 108*
Haley, Gail E 1939- *ConAu 21R, SmATA 28,
WrDr 84*
Haley, James L 1951- *ConAu 77*
Haley, Jay 1923- *ConAu 9NR, –21R*
Haley, Joseph Edmund 1915- *ConAu 13R,
WrDr 84*
Haley, K H D 1920- *ConAu 25R*
Haley, Kenneth 1920- *WrDr 84*
Haley, Kenneth Harold Dobson 1920-
IntAu&W 82
Haley, Michael 1952- *ConAu 109*
Haley, Neale *ConAu 41R*
Haley, Richard 1934- *IntAu&W 82*
Half, Robert 1918- *ConAu 107*
Hali 1837-1914 *ModCmwL*
Halide Edib Adivar 1884-1964 *ClDMEL 80*
Halifax, Joan 1942- *ConAu 85*
Halikarnas Balikcisi 1886-1973 *ClDMEL 80*
Halio, Jay L 1928- *ConAu 10NR, –25R*
Halkett, John G 1933- *ConAu 57*
Halkin, Shimon 1899- *ConAu 53, IntAu&W 82*
Halkin, Simon 1899- *WrDr 84*
Hall, Adam *WrDr 84*
Hall, Adam 1920- *ConAu X, SmATA X,
TwCCr&M 80*
Hall, Adele 1910- *ConAu 1R, SmATA 7*
Hall, Adrian 1927- *ConAu 106*
Hall, Alfred Rupert 1920- *ConAu 9R,
IntAu&W 82*
Hall, Alice Clay 1900- *ConAu 73,
IntWWP 82X*
Hall, Alice Elizabeth *IntWWP 82*
Hall, Andrew 1935- *ConAu 21R*
Hall, Angus 1932- *ConAu 21R, WrDr 84*
Hall, Ann 1929- *ConAu X*
Hall, Anna Gertrude 1882-1967 *ConAu P-1,
SmATA 8*
Hall, Anthony Stewart 1945- *ConAu 102,
WrDr 84*
Hall, Ariel Perry 1906- *ConAu 69*
Hall, Arlene Stevens 1923- *ConAu 17R*
Hall, Asa Zadel 1875-1965 *ConAu 1R, –4NR*
Hall, Austin 1882?-1933 *TwCSFW*
Hall, Aylmer 1914- *ConAu X, TwCCW 83,
WrDr 84*
Hall, B C 1936- *ConAu 9NR*
Hall, B Clarence, Jr. 1936- *ConAu 57, WrDr 84*
Hall, B K 1932- *ConAu 106*
Hall, Bennie Caroline *ConAu 1R*
Hall, Borden *ConAu X, SmATA X*
Hall, Brian P 1935- *ConAu 9NR, –61,
SmATA 31[port]*
Hall, C Margaret 1937- *ConAu 73*
Hall, Calvin Springer, Jr. 1909- *ConAu 13R*
Hall, Cameron P 1898- *ConAu 49*
Hall, Carolyn Vosburg 1927- *ConAu 61,
MichAu 80*
Hall, Caryl *ConAu X*
Hall, Challis A, Jr. 1917-1968 *ConAu 1R, –103*
Hall, Charles A M 1924- *ConAu 107*
Hall, Claudia *ConAu X, WrDr 84*
Hall, Clifton L 1898- *ConAu P-1*
Hall, D J 1903- *ConAu 13R*
Hall, Daniel George Edward 1891-1979
ConAu 103, IntAu&W 82
Hall, David *DrAP&F 83*
Hall, David D 1936- *ConAu 108*
Hall, Don 1929- *ConAu 110*
Hall, Don Alan 1938- *ConAu 108*
Hall, Donald *DrAP&F 83*
Hall, Donald 1928- *WrDr 84*
Hall, Donald Andrew 1928- *ConAu 2NR, –5R,
ConLC 1, –13, ConP 80, DcLB 5[port],
DcLEL 1940, SmATA 23[port], WorAu*
Hall, Donald John 1903- *IntAu&W 82*
Hall, Donald Ray 1933- *ConAu 33R*
Hall, Douglas John 1928- *ConAu 69*
Hall, Douglas Kent 1938- *ConAu 33R*
Hall, Edward Twitchell 1914- *ConAu 65*
Hall, Elizabeth 1929- *ConAu 65*
Hall, Elizabeth Cornelia 1898- *ConAu 37R*
Hall, Elizabeth Wason 1912- *ConAu 1R*
Hall, Elsie Irene 1914- *IntWWP 82*
Hall, Elvajean 1910- *ConAu 8NR, –13R,
SmATA 6*
Hall, Eric J 1933- *ConAu 97*
Hall, Evan *ConAu X, WrDr 84*

Hall, F H 1926- *ConAu 77*
Hall, Fernau *ConAu 102, IntAu&W 82,
WrDr 84*
Hall, Frederic Sauser *ConAu X*
Hall, Gene E 1941- *ConAu 93*
Hall, Geoffrey Fowler 1888-1970 *ConAu P-1*
Hall, George 1941- *ConAu 85*
Hall, George F 1908- *ConAu 45*
Hall, Georgette Brockman 1915- *ConAu 57*
Hall, Gerald L 1936- *IntWWP 82*
Hall, Geraldine M 1935- *ConAu 33R*
Hall, Gimone 1940- *ConAu 29R, WrDr 84*
Hall, Gladys 1891?-1977 *ConAu 73*
Hall, Gordon Langley 1924- *ConAu X, –1R*
Hall, Granville Stanley 1844?-1924 *TwCA,
TwCA SUP*
Hall, Gus 1910- *ConAu 108*
Hall, Gwendolyn Midlo 1929- *ConAu 41R*
Hall, H Douglas *DrAP&F 83*
Hall, H Duncan 1891-1976 *ConAu 65,
ConAu P-2*
Hall, Halbert Weldon 1941- *ConAu 53*
Hall, Harold Fielding- *TwCA SUP*
Hall, Haywood 1898- *ConAu 77*
Hall, Helen 1892- *ConAu 104*
Hall, Henry Marion 1877- *ConAu 5R*
Hall, Holworthy *TwCA, TwCA SUP*
Hall, J C 1920- *ConAu 101, ConP 80*
Hall, J Curtis 1926- *ConAu 53*
Hall, J DeP *ConAu X*
Hall, J Tillman 1916- *ConAu 1R, –6NR*
Hall, Jacquelyn 1943- *ConAu 97*
Hall, James *ConAu X*
Hall, James 1918- *ConAu 102, WrDr 84*
Hall, James 1933- *ConAu 53*
Hall, James B *DrAP&F 83*
Hall, James B 1918- *ConAu 1R, –1NR,
ConNov 82, DcLEL 1940, IntAu&W 82,
IntWWP 82, WrDr 84*
Hall, James C, Jr. 1932- *LivgBAA*
Hall, James Norman 1887-1951 *SmATA 21[port],
TwCA, TwCA SUP*
Hall, James W 1937- *ConAu 45*
Hall, Jay C *ConAu X*
Hall, Jean R 1941- *ConAu 105*
Hall, Jeni 1939- *WrDr 84*
Hall, Jerome 1901- *ConAu P-1, IntAu&W 82,
WrDr 84*
Hall, Jesse *ConAu X, SmATA X*
Hall, Jim *DrAP&F 83*
Hall, Joan Joffe *DrAP&F 83*
Hall, John 1937- *ConAu 93*
Hall, John C 1915- *ConAu 57*
Hall, John C 1920- *WrDr 84*
Hall, John Clive 1920- *DcLEL 1940,
IntWWP 82*
Hall, John F 1919- *ConAu 1R*
Hall, John O P 1911- *ConAu 9R*
Hall, John Ryder *IntAu&W 82X, WrDr 84*
Hall, John Whitney 1916- *ConAu 25R*
Hall, Josef Washington 1894-1960 *ConAu 89,
TwCA, TwCA SUP*
Hall, Joseph 1906- *ConAu 41R*
Hall, Julie 1943- *ConAu 110*
Hall, Kathleen 1924- *WrDr 84*
Hall, Kathleen Mary 1924- *ConAu 3NR, –5R*
Hall, Kendall *ConAu X*
Hall, Kenneth Franklin 1926- *ConAu 17R*
Hall, Kermit L 1944- *ConAu 101*
Hall, Laurence James 1940- *ConAu 97*
Hall, Lawrence Sargent *DrAP&F 83*
Hall, Lawrence Sargent 1915- *ConAu 1R*
Hall, Leland 1883-1957 *TwCA, TwCA SUP*
Hall, Leonard 1899- *ConAu 65*
Hall, Linda B 1939- *ConAu 106*
Hall, Livingston 1903- *ConAu P-2*
Hall, Louis Brewer 1920- *ConAu 110*
Hall, Luella J 1890-1973 *ConAu 103, –45*
Hall, Lynn 1937- *ConAu 9NR, –21R,
SmATA 2, TwCCW 83, WrDr 84*
Hall, Malcolm 1945- *ConAu 4NR, –49,
SmATA 7*
Hall, Manly Palmer 1901- *ConAu 93*
Hall, Marie Boas 1919- *ConAu 1R, –9R,
WrDr 84*
Hall, Marjory 1908- *ConAu X, IntAu&W 82X,
SmATA X, WrDr 84*
Hall, Mark W 1943- *ConAu 33R*
Hall, Martin Hardwick 1925- *ConAu 33R*
Hall, Mary Anne 1934- *ConAu 29R*
Hall, Mary Bowen 1932- *ConAu 21R*
Hall, Michael Garibaldi 1926- *ConAu 13R*

Hall, Monty 1924- *ConAu 108*
Hall, N John 1933- *ConAu 61, IntAu&W 82*
Hall, Nancy Lee 1923- *ConAu 57*
Hall, Natalie Watson 1923- *ConAu 5R*
Hall, Nathaniel B 1916- *LivgBAA*
Hall, Noel 1902-1983 *ConAu 109*
Hall, Norah E L *WrDr 84*
Hall, Norah E L 1914- *ConAu 97*
Hall, O M *ConAu X*
Hall, Oakley 1920- *ConAu 3NR, -9R, TwCWW, WrDr 84*
Hall, Patrick 1932- *ConAu 21R*
Hall, Penelope C 1933- *ConAu 17R*
Hall, Peter 1930- *CroCD*
Hall, Peter 1932- *WrDr 84*
Hall, Peter Geoffrey 1932- *ConAu 8NR, -17R, IntAu&W 82*
Hall, Phil 1953- *ConAu 102*
Hall, Pierre Edward Arthur 1920- *IntAu&W 82*
Hall, R Cargill 1937- *ConAu 1NR, -49*
Hall, Radclyffe 1886?-1943 *ConAu 110, LongCTC, ModBrL, TwCA, TwCA SUP, TwCLC 12[port], TwCWr*
Hall, Richard 1925- *ConAu 9NR, -17R, WrDr 84*
Hall, Richard Compton *ConAu X*
Hall, Richard H 1934- *ConAu 77*
Hall, Robert A, Jr. 1911- *ConAu 5NR, -13R*
Hall, Robert Benjamin 1918- *ConAu 57*
Hall, Robert Burnett, Jr. 1923- *ConAu 109*
Hall, Robert E 1924- *ConAu 17R*
Hall, Robert King 1912- *WrDr 84*
Hall, Robert Lee 1941- *ConAu 73*
Hall, Robert T 1938- *ConAu 110*
Hall, Rodney 1935- *ConAu 109, ConP 80, DcLEL 1940, WrDr 84*
Hall, Roger 1939- *WrDr 84*
Hall, Roger Leighton 1939- *ConDr 82*
Hall, Roger Wolcott 1919- *ConAu 29R*
Hall, Rosalys Haskell 1914- *ConAu 9R, SmATA 7*
Hall, Ross H 1926- *ConAu 61*
Hall, Rubylea 1910- *ConAu P-2*
Hall, Ruth 1933?-1981 *ConAu 104*
Hall, Steven 1960- *ConAu 93*
Hall, Susan 1940- *ConAu 57*
Hall, Ted Byron 1902- *ConAu P-2*
Hall, Theodore *DrAP&F 83*
Hall, Thor 1927- *ConAu 37R, WrDr 84*
Hall, Tom T 1936- *ConAu 102*
Hall, Tony *ConAu X*
Hall, Tord Erik Martin 1910- *ConAu 29R*
Hall, Trevor Henry 1910- *ConAu 29R, WrDr 84*
Hall, Van Beck 1934- *ConAu 45*
Hall, Vernon, Jr. 1913- *ConAu 3NR, -5R*
Hall, W Douglas 1926- *IntAu&W 82*
Hall, Wade *DrAP&F 83*
Hall, Wade H 1934- *ConAu 5R, -6NR*
Hall, Walter *DrAP&F 83*
Hall, Walter 1940- *ConAu 21R, IntWWP 82*
Hall, Wayne E 1947- *ConAu 105*
Hall, William Norman 1915-1974 *ConAu 53*
Hall, Willis 1929- *CnMD, ConAu 101, ConDr 82, CroCD, DcLEL 1940, LongCTC, ModWD, WrDr 84*
Hall, Wilson 1922- *ConAu 69*
Hall, Wilton Earle, Jr. 1930- *IntAu&W 82*
Hall-Clarke, James *ConAu X, SmATA X*
Hall-Jones, Frederick George 1891-1982 *ConAu 108*
Hall-Quest, Olga Wilbourne 1899- *ConAu 5R, SmATA 11*
Halla, Chris *DrAP&F 83*
Halla, Robert Christian 1949- *ConAu 77*
Halladay, Geneva Rose 1926- *IntWWP 82*
Hallahan, William H *ConAu 109*
Hallam, Atlantis 1915- *ConAu 5R*
Hallam, H E 1923- *ConAu 21R*
Hallam, John Harvey 1917- *ConAu 13R*
Hallard, Peter *TwCCW 83*
Hallard, Peter J *SmATA 3*
Hallas, Richard *SmATA X*
Hallberg, Charles William 1899- *ConAu P-1*
Hallberg, Peter 1916- *ConAu 4NR, -53, IntAu&W 82*
Halle, Jean-Claude 1939- *ConAu 93*
Halle, Katherine Murphy *ConAu 41R*
Halle, Kay *ConAu X*
Halle, Louis J 1910- *ConAu 1R, -2NR*
Halleck, Seymour L 1929- *ConAu 21R*
Haller, Archibald O, Jr. 1926- *ConAu 45*

Haller, Bill *ConAu X, WrDr 84*
Haller, Ellis M 1915-1981 *ConAu 103*
Haller, John S, Jr. 1940- *ConAu 61, IntAu&W 82*
Haller, Mark H 1928- *ConAu 5NR, -9R*
Haller, Mike 1945- *ConAu 110*
Haller, Robert S 1933- *ConAu 1R, -2NR*
Haller, Robin Meredith 1944- *ConAu 65*
Haller, Scot *DrAP&F 83*
Haller, William 1885-1974 *ConAu 49*
Halleran, E E 1905- *WrDr 84*
Halleran, Eugene E 1905- *ConAu 1R, TwCWW*
Hallet, Jean-Pierre 1927- *ConAu 17R*
Hallett, Ellen Kathleen 1899- *ConAu P-1*
Hallett, Garth L 1927- *ConAu 69*
Hallett, Graham 1929- *ConAu 25R, WrDr 84*
Hallett, Hugh Victor Dudley 1919- *IntAu&W 82*
Hallett, Kathryn J 1937- *ConAu 57*
Hallett, Robin 1926- *ConAu 103, WrDr 84*
Hallgarten, George W F 1901-1975 *ConAu 57, -65*
Hallgarten, Peter A 1931- *ConAu 97*
Hallgarten, S F 1902- *IntAu&W 82X, WrDr 84*
Hallgarten, Siegfried Fritz 1902- *ConAu 3NR, -5R, IntAu&W 82*
Hallgren, Mauritz Alfred 1899-1956 *TwCA, TwCA SUP*
Halliburton, Richard 1900-1939 *TwCA, TwCA SUP*
Halliburton, Rudia, Jr. 1929- *ConAu 81*
Halliburton, Warren J 1924- *ConAu 33R, LivgBAA, SmATA 19*
Halliday, Brett *ConAu X, TwCCr&M 80, WorAu*
Halliday, Dorothy *IntAu&W 82X, TwCCr&M 80, TwCRGW, WrDr 84*
Halliday, E M 1913- *ConAu 1R*
Halliday, Frank Ernest 1903-1982 *ConAu 1R, -2NR, -106, IntAu&W 82*
Halliday, Fred 1937- *ConAu 53*
Halliday, James *ConAu X*
Halliday, Jerry 1949- *ConAu 69*
Halliday, Jon 1939- *ConAu 97*
Halliday, Michael *ConAu X, LongCTC, TwCCr&M 80*
Halliday, Miriam *DrAP&F 83*
Halliday, Richard 1905-1973 *ConAu 41R*
Halliday, William Ross 1926- *ConAu 49, IntAu&W 82*
Hallie, Philip P 1922- *ConAu 9NR, -13R*
Hallier, Amedee 1913- *ConAu 73*
Halligan, Nicholas 1917- *ConAu 5NR, -13R*
Hallin, Emily Watson *ConAu 10NR*
Hallin, Emily Watson 1919- *ConAu 25R, SmATA 6, WrDr 84*
Hallinan, Hazel Hunkins 1891?-1982 *ConAu 106*
Hallinan, Nancy *DrAP&F 83*
Hallinan, Nancy 1921- *ConAu 3NR, -9R*
Hallinan, P K 1944- *ConAu 11NR, -69*
Hallinan, Vincent 1896- *ConAu 1R*
Hallion, Richard Paul, Jr. 1948- *ConAu 41R*
Halliwell, David 1936- *ConAu 11NR, -65, ConDr 82, DcLEL 1940, IntAu&W 82, WrDr 84*
Halliwell, David 1937- *CroCD*
Halliwell, Leslie 1929- *ConAu 1NR, -49, WrDr 84*
Hallman, Frank Curtis 1943?-1975 *ConAu 104*
Hallman, G Victor, III 1930- *ConAu 101*
Hallman, Ralph J 1911- *ConAu 13R*
Hallman, Ruth 1929- *ConAu 85, SmATA 28*
Hallo, William W 1928- *ConAu 37R, WrDr 84*
Hallock, Brook *DrAP&F 83*
Halloran, Richard 1930- *ConAu 29R*
Halloway, Vance 1916- *ConAu 53*
Hallowell, A Irving 1892-1974 *ConAu 5R, -53*
Hallowell, Christopher L 1945- *ConAu 93*
Hallowell, John H 1913- *ConAu 5NR, -13R*
Hallpike, C R 1938- *ConAu 41R*
Halls, Christopher Peter John 1930- *IntAu&W 82*
Halls, Geraldine *WrDr 84*
Halls, Geraldine 1919- *ConAu 103*
Halls, W D 1918- *ConAu 5NR*
Halls, Wilfred Douglas 1918- *ConAu 1R, WrDr 84*
Hallstead, William F, III 1924- *ConAu 5R, -6NR, SmATA 11*
Hallstein, Walter 1901-1982 *ConAu 106*
Hallstrom, Per August Leonard 1866-1960 *ModWD*

Hallums, James R *ConSFA*
Hallus, Tak *ConAu X*
Hallward, Michael 1889- *ConAu 49, SmATA 12*
Halm, George N 1901- *ConAu 21R*
Halman, Talat Sait 1931- *ConAu 4NR, -53, IntAu&W 82, IntWWP 82*
Halmos, Paul 1911-1977 *ConAu 8NR, -17R*
Halpe, Ashley 1933- *IntWWP 82*
Halper, Albert 1904- *ConAmA, ConAu 3NR, -5R, DcLB 9[port], TwCA, TwCA SUP*
Halper, Nathan 1908?-1983 *ConAu 110*
Halper, Thomas 1942- *ConAu 41R*
Halperin, Don A 1925- *ConAu 57*
Halperin, Irving *DrAP&F 83*
Halperin, Irving 1922- *ConAu 29R*
Halperin, John 1941- *ConAu 6NR, -53*
Halperin, Mark 1940- *ConAu 9NR, -65*
Halperin, Maurice 1906- *ConAu 73*
Halperin, Morton H 1938- *ConAu 3NR, -9R*
Halperin, S William 1905-1979 *ConAu 85, -97*
Halperin, Samuel 1930- *ConAu 1R, -1NR*
Halpern, A M 1914- *ConAu 17R*
Halpern, Barbara Strachey 1912- *ConAu 106*
Halpern, Daniel *DrAP&F 83*
Halpern, Daniel 1945- *ConAu 33R, ConLC 14, ConP 80, IntAu&W 82, IntWWP 82, WrDr 84*
Halpern, Howard Marvin 1929- *ConAu 93*
Halpern, Joel M 1929- *ConAu 3NR, -5R*
Halpern, Manfred 1924- *ConAu 9R*
Halpern, Martin 1929- *ConAu 5R, -7NR, NatPD 81[port]*
Halpern, Moyshe Leyb 1886-1932 *EncWL 2*
Halpern, Oscar Saul 1912- *ConAu 97*
Halpern, Paul G 1937- *ConAu 45*
Halpern, Paul J 1942- *ConAu 7NR, -57*
Halpern, Stephen Mark 1940- *ConAu 57*
Halpert, Inge D 1926- *ConAu 21R*
Halpert, Stephen 1941- *ConAu 37R*
Halpin, Andrew Williams 1911- *ConAu 17R, WrDr 84*
Halprin, Anna Schuman 1920- *ConAu 85, IntAu&W 82*
Halprin, Lawrence 1916- *ConAu 41R, IntAu&W 82*
Hals, Ronald M 1926- *ConAu 33R*
Halsall, Elizabeth 1916- *ConAu 33R, WrDr 84*
Halsall, Eric 1920- *ConAu 107, WrDr 84*
Halsband, Robert 1914- *ConAu 8NR, -17R*
Halsell, Grace 1923- *AuNews 1, ConAu 21R, SmATA 13*
Halsey, A H 1923- *ConAu 7NR, -17R, WrDr 84*
Halsey, Albert Henry 1923- *IntAu&W 82*
Halsey, Elizabeth 1890- *ConAu P-2*
Halsey, Elizabeth Tower 1903?-1976 *ConAu 65*
Halsey, George Dawson 1889-1970 *ConAu 1R, -103*
Halsey, Margaret 1910- *ConAu 81*
Halsey, Martha T 1932- *ConAu 37R*
Halsman, Philippe 1906-1979 *ConAu 10NR, -21R, -89*
Halstead, William Perdue 1906-1982 *ConAu 109*
Halsted, Anna Roosevelt 1906-1975 *ConAu 61, SmATA 30N*
Halter, Carl Frederick 1915- *ConAu 17R*
Halter, Jon C 1941- *ConAu 61, SmATA 22[port]*
Halton, David 1940- *ConAu 73*
Haltrecht, Montague 1932- *ConAu 29R, IntAu&W 82, WrDr 84*
Halverson, Alton C O 1922- *ConAu 61*
Halverson, Richard C 1916- *ConAu 1R, -3NR*
Halverson, Richard P 1941- *ConAu 109*
Halverson, William H 1930- *ConAu 37R*
Halvorson, Arndt L 1915- *ConAu 3NR, -5R*
Halvtand *IntAu&W 82X*
Halward, Leslie G 1904?-1976 *ConAu 65*
Ham, Olive Mary 1918- *WrDr 84*
Ham, Wayne 1938- *ConAu 11NR*
Ham, Wayne Albert 1938- *ConAu 21R, WrDr 84*
Hamachek, Don E 1933- *ConAu 17R*
Hamada, Hirosuke 1893- *ConAu 45*
Hamady, Walter *AuNews 1*
Hamalainen, Helvi Helena 1907- *IntAu&W 82*
Hamalainen, Pekka Kalevi 1938- *ConAu 97*
Hamalian, Leo 1920- *ConAu 2NR, -5R*
Hamaoui, Ernest 1916- *IntAu&W 82*
Hamasaki, Richard 1952- *IntWWP 82*
Hamberg, Daniel 1924- *ConAu 1R*

Hamberg, Lars 1922- *IntAu&W 82*
Hamberger, John F 1934- *ConAu 69,*
  SmATA 14
Hambleton, Jack *CreCan 2*
Hambleton, John 1901-1961 *CreCan 2*
Hambleton, Ronald 1917- *CreCan 2,*
  DcLEL 1940
Hambletonian *ConAu X*
Hamblett, Theora 1895?-1977 *ConAu 69*
Hamblin, C L 1922- *ConAu 25R*
Hamblin, Dora Jane 1920- *ConAu 37R*
Hamblin, Robert L 1927- *ConAu 97*
Hamblin, W K 1928- *ConAu 53*
Hambourg, Boris 1884-1954 *CreCan 2*
Hambro, Carl 1914- *IntAu&W 82*
Hamburg, Carl H 1915- *ConAu 37R, WrDr 84*
Hamburg, David A 1925- *ConAu 109*
Hamburger, Anne Ellen 1929- *IntWWP 82*
Hamburger, Ernest 1891?-1980 *ConAu 97*
Hamburger, Estelle 1898?-1983 *ConAu 110*
Hamburger, Jean 1909- *IntAu&W 82*
Hamburger, Kaete 1896- *ConAu 29R*
Hamburger, Kate 1896- *IntAu&W 82*
Hamburger, Max 1897-1970 *ConAu P-2*
Hamburger, Michael 1924- *WrDr 84*
Hamburger, Michael J 1924- *ConAu 3NR, -45*
Hamburger, Michael Peter Leopold 1924-
  ConAu 2NR, -5R, ConLC 5, -14, ConP 80,
  DcLEL 1940, IntWWP 82, RGFMBP,
  WorAu
Hamburger, Philip 1914- *ConAu 5R,*
  IntAu&W 82, WrDr 84
Hamburger, Robert 1943- *ConAu 8NR, -61*
Hamburgh, Max 1922- *ConAu 61*
Hamby, Alonzo L 1940- *WrDr 84*
Hamby, Alonzo Lee 1940- *ConAu 37R*
Hamby, James A *DrAP&F 83*
Hamby, James A 1943- *IntWWP 82*
Hamby, Wallace Bernard 1903- *WrDr 84*
Hamel, Guy F Claude 1935- *IntWWP 82*
Hamel, Martine Van *CreCan 2*
Hamel, Peter Michael 1947- *ConAu 97*
Hamel, Suzanne Paradis *CreCan 1*
Hamel Dobkin, Kathleen 1945- *ConAu 110*
Hamelin, Louis-Edmond 1923- *ConAu 110*
Hamelink, Jacques 1939- *IntAu&W 82*
Hamell, Patrick Joseph 1910- *ConAu P-1,*
  IntAu&W 82, WrDr 84
Hamelman, Paul William 1930-1976 *ConAu 41R*
Hamer, David Allan 1938- *ConAu 45*
Hamer, Frank 1929- *ConAu 105*
Hamer, Martin J 1931- *LivgBAA*
Hamer, Mick 1946- *ConAu 109*
Hamer, Philip 1891-1971 *ConAu 104*
Hamermesh, Daniel S 1943- *ConAu 110*
Hamermesh, Morton 1915- *ConAu 5R*
Hamerow, Theodore S 1920- *ConAu 49*
Hamerstrom, Frances 1907- *ConAu 69,*
  SmATA 24[port]
Hames, Inez 1892- *ConAu 29R*
Hamey, J A 1956- *ConAu 109*
Hamey, L A 1918- *ConAu 109*
Hamil, Thomas Arthur 1928- *ConAu 73,*
  SmATA 14
Hamil, Tom *SmATA X*
Hamill, Denis 1951- *ConAu 110*
Hamill, Ethel *ConAu X, TwCRGW, WrDr 84*
Hamill, Janet *DrAP&F 83*
Hamill, Pete 1935- *ConAu 25R, ConLC 10*
Hamill, Robert H 1912- *WrDr 84*
Hamill, Robert H 1912-1975 *ConAu P-2*
Hamill, Sam *DrAP&F 83*
Hamilton, Adam *ConAu X*
Hamilton, Alex John 1939- *ConAu 103*
Hamilton, Alfred Starr *DrAP&F 83*
Hamilton, Alfred Starr 1914- *ConAu 53*
Hamilton, Alice *ConAu X, SmATA X*
Hamilton, B L St. John 1914- *ConAu 13R*
Hamilton, Bernard 1932- *WrDr 84*
Hamilton, Beth Alleman 1927- *ConAu 110*
Hamilton, Bruce 1900-1974 *ConAu 109*
Hamilton, Buzz *ConAu X*
Hamilton, Carl 1914- *ConAu 53*
Hamilton, Carlos D 1908- *ConAu 69*
Hamilton, Carol Jean Barber 1935- *IntWWP 82*
Hamilton, Charles *TwCCW 83*
Hamilton, Charles 1913- *ConAu 3NR, -5R,*
  WrDr 84
Hamilton, Charles F 1915- *ConAu 89*
Hamilton, Charles Granville 1905- *ConAu 41R,*
  IntWWP 82

Hamilton, Charles Harold St. John 1875-1961
  ConAu 73, LongCTC, SmATA 13
Hamilton, Charles Vernon 1929- *ConAu 77,*
  LivgBAA
Hamilton, Charles W 1890- *ConAu 5R*
Hamilton, Cicely 1872-1952 *DcLB 10[port],*
  LongCTC
Hamilton, Clare *ConAu X*
Hamilton, Clayton 1881-1946 *TwCA,*
  TwCA SUP
Hamilton, Clive *ConAu X, LongCTC,*
  SmATA X, TwCA SUP
Hamilton, Cosmo 1872?-1942 *LongCTC, TwCA,*
  TwCA SUP
Hamilton, Dave *ConAu X*
Hamilton, David 1918- *ConAu 29R, WrDr 84*
Hamilton, Denis 1918- *ConAu 109,*
  IntAu&W 82
Hamilton, Donald 1916- *ConAu 1R, -2NR,*
  TwCCr&M 80, TwCWW, WrDr 84
Hamilton, Dorothy 1906- *ConAu 33R,*
  SmATA 12
Hamilton, Dorothy 1906-1983 *ConAu 110*
Hamilton, Earl J 1899- *ConAu P-1*
Hamilton, Edith 1867-1963 *ConAu 77,*
  SmATA 20[port], TwCA, TwCA SUP
Hamilton, Edmond 1904-1977 *ConAu 1R, -3NR,*
  ConLC 1, ConSFA, DcLB 8[port],
  TwCSFW
Hamilton, Edward G 1897- *ConAu P-1*
Hamilton, Eleanor Poorman 1909- *ConAu 1R,*
  -2NR
Hamilton, Elissa L A *DrAP&F 83*
Hamilton, Elizabeth 1906- *ConAu P-1,*
  IntAu&W 82, SmATA 23[port], WrDr 84
Hamilton, Elizabeth 1928- *ConAu 97*
Hamilton, Ernest *ConAu X*
Hamilton, Franklin W 1923- *WrDr 84*
Hamilton, Franklin Willard 1923- *ConAu 33R*
Hamilton, Franklin Williard 1923- *MichAu 80*
Hamilton, Gail *ConAu X, DrAP&F 83,*
  IntAu&W 82X
Hamilton, George Ronald 1909- *IntAu&W 82*
Hamilton, Sir George Rostrevor 1888-1967
  ConAu 93, LongCTC, ModBrL
Hamilton, Henry W 1898- *ConAu 33R*
Hamilton, Hervey *WrDr 84*
Hamilton, Holman 1910-1980 *ConAu 10NR,*
  -13R, -97
Hamilton, Horace Ernst 1911- *ConAu 21R*
Hamilton, Howard Devon 1920- *ConAu 13R*
Hamilton, Ian 1938- *ConAu 106, ConP 80,*
  DcLEL 1940, WorAu 1970, WrDr 84
Hamilton, J Wallace 1900-1968 *ConAu P-1*
Hamilton, Jack *ConAu X*
Hamilton, James Robertson 1921- *ConAu 103,*
  WrDr 84
Hamilton, Jean Tyree 1909- *ConAu 33R*
Hamilton, Joan Lesley 1942- *ConAu 102*
Hamilton, Julia *ConAu X, IntAu&W 82X,*
  TwCRGW, WrDr 84
Hamilton, Kay *ConAu X*
Hamilton, Kelly *NatPD 81[port]*
Hamilton, Kenneth 1917- *ConAu 17R,*
  WrDr 84
Hamilton, Leona 1915- *IntWWP 82*
Hamilton, Marshall Lee 1937- *ConAu 37R*
Hamilton, Mary Agnes 1884-1966 *LongCTC,*
  TwCA, TwCA SUP
Hamilton, Max 1912- *WrDr 84*
Hamilton, Michael *ConAu X*
Hamilton, Michael 1927- *ConAu 29R*
Hamilton, Milton W 1901- *ConAu P-1*
Hamilton, Mollie *ConAu X*
Hamilton, Morse 1943- *ConAu 108*
Hamilton, Neill G 1925- *ConAu 61*
Hamilton, Nigel 1944- *ConAu 101*
Hamilton, Patrick 1904-1962 *CnMD,*
  DcLB 10[port], LongCTC, ModWD,
  TwCA SUP, TwCCr&M 80, TwCWr,
  WhoTwCL
Hamilton, Patrick Macfarlan 1892-1977
  ConAu 108
Hamilton, Paul *ConAu X, WrDr 84*
Hamilton, Peter 1947- *ConAu 73, WrDr 84*
Hamilton, Priscilla *WrDr 84*
Hamilton, Prudence Harvey 1917- *IntAu&W 82*
Hamilton, Raphael N 1892- *ConAu P-2*
Hamilton, Richard F 1930- *ConAu 108*
Hamilton, Robert 1928- *LivgBAA*
Hamilton, Robert W *ConAu X*
Hamilton, Ronald 1909- *ConAu 13R, WrDr 84*

Hamilton, Rosemary Deveson *CreCan 2*
Hamilton, Russell G 1934- *ConAu 61*
Hamilton, Seena M 1926- *ConAu 17R*
Hamilton, Steve *DrAP&F 83*
Hamilton, Virginia 1936- *AuNews 1, ChlLR 1,*
  ConAu 25R, ConLC 26[port], SmATA 4,
  TwCCW 83, WrDr 84
Hamilton, W B 1908-1972 *ConAu 37R*
Hamilton, W D 1936- *ConAu 105*
Hamilton, Wade *ConAu X, WrDr 84*
Hamilton, Wallace 1919- *ConAu 85,*
  IntAu&W 82, NatPD 81[port]
Hamilton, Wallace 1919-1983 *ConAu 110*
Hamilton, Walter 1908- *ConAu 109*
Hamilton, William *WrDr 84*
Hamilton, William 1939- *ConAu 69*
Hamilton, William, Jr. 1924- *ConAu 53*
Hamilton, William B 1930- *ConAu 102,*
  WrDr 84
Hamilton, William Baskerville 1908-1972
  ConAu P-1
Hamilton-Edwards, Gerald 1906- *WrDr 84*
Hamilton-Edwards, Gerald Kenneth Savery 1906-
  ConAu 21R, IntAu&W 82
Hamizrachi, Yoram 1942- *ConAu 107*
Hamlet, Ova *ConAu X*
Hamley, Dennis 1935- *ConAu 11NR, -57*
Hamlin, Charles Hughes 1907- *ConAu 69*
Hamlin, Gladys E *ConAu 37R*
Hamlin, Griffith Askew 1919- *ConAu 37R,*
  IntAu&W 82
Hamlin, Marjorie 1921- *ConAu 105*
Hamlin, Wilfrid G 1918- *ConAu 93*
Hamlyn, David Walter 1924- *IntAu&W 82*
Hamm, Charles Edward 1925- *ConAu 103*
Hamm, Glenn Bruce 1936- *ConAu 53*
Hamm, Jack 1916- *ConAu 5R, -9NR*
Hamm, Marie Roberson 1917- *ConAu 65*
Hamm, Michael Franklin 1943- *ConAu 89*
Hamm, Russell Leroy 1926- *ConAu 2NR, -5R*
Hammack, James W, Jr. 1937- *ConAu 81*
Hamman, Ray T 1945- *ConAu 69*
Hammar, Russell A 1920- *ConAu 104*
Hammarberg-Akesson, Jarl 1940- *IntWWP 82*
Hammarskjoeld, Dag 1905-1961 *ConAu 77*
Hammarskjold, Dag 1905-1961 *ConAu X*
Hammel, Claus 1932- *CroCD*
Hammel, Eric M 1946- *ConAu 107*
Hammel, Faye 1929- *ConAu 1R, -5NR*
Hammen, Carl Schlee 1923- *ConAu 53*
Hammen, Oscar J 1907- *ConAu P-2*
Hammer, Carl, Jr. 1910- *ConAu 53*
Hammer, David Harry 1893?-1978 *ConAu 81*
Hammer, Emanuel F 1926- *ConAu 29R,*
  IntAu&W 82, WrDr 84
Hammer, George *NatPD 81[port]*
Hammer, Jeanne-Ruth 1912- *ConAu 9R*
Hammer, Jefferson J 1933- *ConAu 41R*
Hammer, Kenneth M 1918- *ConAu 85*
Hammer, Lillian *IntWWP 82*
Hammer, Louis *DrAP&F 83*
Hammer, Louis 1931- *IntWWP 82*
Hammer, Patrick, Jr. *DrAP&F 83*
Hammer, Richard 1928- *ConAu 11NR, -25R,*
  SmATA 6
Hammer, Signe *ConAu 102*
Hammerich, Dick *ConAmTC*
Hammerman, Donald R 1925- *ConAu 13R*
Hammerman, Gay M 1926- *ConAu 33R,*
  SmATA 9
Hammershaimb, Erling 1904- *IntAu&W 82*
Hammerstein, Oscar, II 1895-1960 *ConAu 101,*
  ModWD
Hammes, John A 1924- *ConAu 13R, WrDr 84*
Hammett, Dashiell 1894-1961 *AuNews 1,*
  CnMWL, ConAu 81, ConLC 3, -5, -10, -19,
  LongCTC, ModAL, ModAL SUP, TwCA,
  TwCA SUP, TwCCr&M 80, TwCWr,
  WhoTwCL
Hammett, Samuel Dashiell 1894-1961 *AuNews 1*
Hamming, Richard W 1915- *ConAu 57*
Hammond, Albert L 1892-1970 *ConAu 1R, -103*
Hammond, Barbara 1873-1961 *LongCTC*
Hammond, Charles Montgomery, Jr. 1922-
  ConAu 106
Hammond, Dorothy 1924- *ConAu 69*
Hammond, Dorothy Lee 1934- *WrDr 84*
Hammond, Edwin Hughes 1919- *ConAu 13R*
Hammond, Gerald 1926- *ConAu 107*
Hammond, Guyton B 1930- *ConAu 17R*
Hammond, J D 1933- *ConAu 45*
Hammond, J L 1872-1949 *LongCTC*

Hammond, Jane *ConAu X, IntAu&W 82X, WrDr 84*
Hammond, John 1910- *ConAu 106*
Hammond, Karla M 1949- *IntWWP 82*
Hammond, Keith *ConAu X*
Hammond, Laurence *ConAu 104*
Hammond, Lawrence Victor Francis 1925- *ConAu 81*
Hammond, Mac *DrAP&F 83*
Hammond, Mac 1926- *ConAu 17R, IntWWP 82, WrDr 84*
Hammond, Mason 1903- *ConAu 65*
Hammond, N G L 1907- *ConAu 5NR, -13R*
Hammond, Nicholas 1907- *WrDr 84*
Hammond, Nicholas Geoffrey Lempriere 1907- *IntAu&W 82*
Hammond, Norman 1944- *ConAu 3NR, -49*
Hammond, Paul 1947- *ConAu 57*
Hammond, Paul Y 1929- *ConAu 1R, -2NR*
Hammond, Percy Hunter 1873-1936 *TwCA, TwCA SUP*
Hammond, Peter 1942- *IntWWP 82*
Hammond, Peter B 1928- *ConAu 69*
Hammond, Philip C 1924- *ConAu 5R*
Hammond, Phillip E 1931- *ConAu 7NR, -17R*
Hammond, Ralph *WrDr 84*
Hammond, Ralph 1913- *ConAu X*
Hammond, Richard J 1911- *ConAu 61*
Hammond, Ross W 1918- *ConAu 33R*
Hammond, Thomas Taylor 1920- *ConAu 9R*
Hammond, W Rogers 1920- *ConAu 45*
Hammond, Winifred G 1899- *ConAu 107, SmATA 29[port]*
Hammond Innes, Ralph 1913- *ConAu 4NR, -5R, IntAu&W 82, LongCTC, WrDr 84*
Hammonds, Michael 1942- *ConAu 45*
Hammontree, Marie 1913- *WrDr 84*
Hammontree, Marie Gertrude 1913- *ConAu 5R, SmATA 13*
Hamner, Earl, Jr. 1923- *AuNews 2, ConAu 73, ConLC 12, DcLB 6[port]*
Hamner, Robert Daniel 1941- *ConAu 106*
Hamod, Sam *DrAP&F 83*
Hamod, Sam 1936- *ConAu 45, MichAu 80*
Hamori, Laszlo Dezso 1911- *ConAu 9R*
Hamp, Eric P 1920- *ConAu 17R*
Hamp, Pierre 1876-1962 *CIDMEL 80*
Hampden, John 1898- *ConAu 109*
Hampden-Turner, Charles M 1934- *ConAu 33R*
Hampl, Patricia *DrAP&F 83*
Hampl, Patricia 1946- *ConAu 104, IntWWP 82*
Hample, Stuart 1926- *ConAu 108*
Hampsch, George 1927- *ConAu 13R, WrDr 84*
Hampshire, Stuart 1914- *IntAu&W 82, WorAu, WrDr 84*
Hampson, Anne *TwCRGW, WrDr 84*
Hampson, Denman 1929- *SmATA 15*
Hampson, Norman 1922- *ConAu 25R, IntAu&W 82, WrDr 84*
Hampson, Zena 1926- *IntAu&W 82*
Hampton, Christopher *WrDr 84*
Hampton, Christopher 1946- *ConAu 25R, ConDr 82, ConLC 4, DcLB 13[port], DcLEL 1940, WrDr 84*
Hampton, Christopher 1948- *CroCD*
Hampton, Christopher Martin 1929- *ConAu 4NR, -53, ConP 80, DcLEL 1940, IntAu&W 82*
Hampton, David R 1933- *ConAu 81*
Hampton, H Duane 1932- *ConAu 33R*
Hampton, Jack Fitz-Gerald 1909- *WrDr 84*
Hampton, Kathleen 1923- *ConAu 1R*
Hampton, Mark *ConAu X, IntAu&W 82X, WrDr 84*
Hampton, Robert E 1924- *ConAu 33R*
Hampton, Trevor Arthur 1912- *WrDr 84*
Hampton, William 1929- *ConAu 33R, WrDr 84*
Hamre, Leif 1914- *ConAu 4NR, -5R, IntAu&W 82, SmATA 5, WrDr 84*
Hamsa, Bobbie 1944- *ConAu 106*
Hamscher, Albert N 1946- *ConAu 73*
Hamsher, J Herbert 1938- *ConAu 57*
Hamshere, Cyril 1912- *ConAu 41R*
Hamsun, Knut Pederson 1859-1952 *CIDMEL 80, CnMD, ConAu X, EncWL 2[port], LongCTC, TwCA, TwCA SUP, TwCLC 2, TwCWr, WhoTwCL*
Han, Seung Soo 1936- *ConAu 2NR, -45*
Han, Sungjoo 1940- *ConAu 53*
Han, Suyin 1917- *ConAu 17R, DcLEL 1940,*

TwCWr, WorAu, WrDr 84
Hanagan, Eva 1923- *ConAu 101*
Hanagan, Michael Patrick 1947- *ConAu 109*
Hanaghan, Jonathan 1887-1967 *ConAu 65*
Hanami, Tadashi A 1930- *ConAu 89*
Hanan, Patrick Dewes 1927- *ConAu 106*
Hanani, Joseph 1908- *IntWWP 82*
Hanau, Laia 1916- *ConAu 89*
Hanawalt, Barbara A 1941- *ConAu 101*
Hanbury, Harold Grenville 1898- *WrDr 84*
Hanbury-Tenison, A Robin 1936- *WrDr 84*
Hanbury-Tenison, Airling Robin 1936- *ConAu 57, IntAu&W 82*
Hanbury-Tenison, Marika 1938- *ConAu 104*
Hanbury-Tenison, Marika 1938-1982 *ConAu 108*
Hance, Kenneth G 1903- *ConAu 85*
Hance, William A 1916- *ConAu 9R, WrDr 84*
Hanchett, William 1922- *ConAu 33R*
Hancock, Alice VanFossen 1890- *ConAu 1R*
Hancock, Carla *ConAu 89*
Hancock, Carol Helen Brooks *ConAu X*
Hancock, Edward L 1930- *ConAu 1NR, -45*
Hancock, Geoffrey White 1946- *ConAu 101, IntAu&W 82*
Hancock, Harold B 1913- *ConAu 53*
Hancock, Keith *ConAu X*
Hancock, Leslie 1941- *ConAu 21R*
Hancock, Lyn 1938- *ConAu 77*
Hancock, M Donald 1939- *ConAu 33R*
Hancock, Malcolm 1936- *ConAu 25R*
Hancock, Mary A 1923- *ConAu 37R, SmATA 31*
Hancock, Maxine 1942- *ConAu 8NR, -61*
Hancock, Morgan 1941- *ConAu 103*
Hancock, Niel Anderson 1941- *ConAu 97*
Hancock, Ralph Lowell 1903- *ConAu P-1*
Hancock, Roger Nelson 1929- *ConAu 97*
Hancock, Sheila 1942- *ConAu 49*
Hancock, Sibyl 1940- *ConAu 1NR, -49, SmATA 9*
Hancock, Taylor 1920- *ConAu 97*
Hancock, W K 1898- *ConAu 5R, -5NR*
Hand, G J 1931- *ConAu 25R*
Hand, Geoffrey Joseph Philip 1931- *WrDr 84*
Hand, Jack *DrAP&F 83*
Hand, Jackson 1913- *ConAu 10NR, -61*
Hand, Joan Carole *DrAP&F 83*
Hand, Joan Carole 1943- *ConAu 57*
Hand, John *ConAu X*
Hand, Thomas A 1915- *ConAu 13R*
Hand, Wayland D 1907- *ConAu 41R*
Handel, Gerald 1924- *ConAu 11NR, -21R, IntAu&W 82*
Handel-Mazzetti, Enrica Von 1871-1955 *ModGL*
Handelman, Howard 1943- *ConAu 57*
Handelman, John R 1948- *ConAu 77*
Handelsman, Judith Florence 1948- *ConAu 61*
Handford, Michael Anthony 1944- *WrDr 84*
Handke, Peter *DrAP&F 83*
Handke, Peter 1942- *CIDMEL 80, ConAu 77, ConLC 5, -8, -10, -15, CroCD, EncWL 2[port], ModGL, WorAu 1970*
Handl, Irene 1902- *ConAu 103, IntAu&W 82*
Handl, Irene 1912- *WrDr 84*
Handler, Frances Clark *IntWWP 82*
Handler, Jerome S 1933- *ConAu 53*
Handler, Julian Harris 1922- *ConAu 21R*
Handler, Meyer Srednick 1905-1978 *ConAu 77*
Handler, Milton 1903- *ConAu 61*
Handler, Philip 1917-1981 *ConAu 105, -33R*
Handley, Eric Walter 1926- *WrDr 84*
Handley, Graham Roderick 1926- *ConAu 105, WrDr 84*
Handley-Taylor, Geoffrey 1920- *ConAu 5R, -7NR, IntAu&W 82, WrDr 84*
Handlin, Jim *DrAP&F 83*
Handlin, Mary 1913-1976 *ConAu 65, ConAu P-2*
Handlin, Oscar 1915- *ConAu 1R, -5NR, DcLB 17[port], DcLEL 1940, TwCA SUP, WrDr 84*
Handman, Herbert Ira 1932- *ConAu 89*
Handover, P M 1923-1974 *ConAu 9R, -53*
Handscombe, Richard 1935- *ConAu 37R*
Handy, Edward Smith Craighill 1893?-1980 *ConAu 102*
Handy, Mary Nixeon Civille 1909- *IntWWP 82*
Handy, Nixeon Civille *DrAP&F 83, IntWWP 82X*
Handy, Robert T 1918- *ConAu 2NR, -5R*
Handy, Rollo 1927- *ConAu 9R, IntAu&W 82, WrDr 84*

Handy, Toni 1930- *ConAu 97*
Handy, William J 1918- *ConAu 45*
Hane, Mikiso 1922- *ConAu 81*
Hane, Roger 1940-1974 *SmATA 20N*
Hanenkrat, Frank 1939- *ConAu 93*
Haner, F T 1929- *ConAu 53*
Hanes, Bailey C 1915- *ConAu 77*
Hanes, Elizabeth Sill *ConAu 1R*
Hanes, Frank Borden *DrAP&F 83*
Hanes, Frank Borden 1920- *ConAu 1R, WrDr 84*
Haney, David P 1938- *ConAu 6NR, -57*
Haney, John B 1931- *ConAu 29R*
Haney, Lynn 1941- *ConAu 1NR, -49, SmATA 23[port]*
Haney, Thomas K 1936- *ConAu 13R*
Haney, Thomas R *ConAu 45*
Haney, William Valentine Patrick 1925- *ConAu 17R, WrDr 84*
Hanf, James A 1923- *IntWWP 82*
Hanff, Helene *ConAu 3NR, -5R, SmATA 11*
Hanford, Lloyd D 1901- *ConAu 13R*
Hanford, Lloyd D 1901-1979 *ConAu 11NR*
Hanford, S A 1898-1978 *ConAu 81*
Hangen, Welles 1930- *ConAu 9R*
Hanifi, M Jamil 1935- *ConAu 61*
Haning, Bob *ConAu X*
Haning, James R 1928- *ConAu 2NR, -45*
Hank *IntWWP 82X*
Hanke, Howard August 1911- *ConAu 1R*
Hanke, Lewis Ulysses 1905- *ConAu 65*
Hanke-Maiwald, Gertrud 1918- *IntAu&W 82*
Hankey, Cyril Patrick 1886-1973 *ConAu 1R, -103*
Hankey, Donald William Alers 1884-1916 *LongCTC*
Hankey, Rosalie A *ConAu X*
Hankey, Roy 1932- *ConAu 108*
Hankin, St. John 1869-1909 *CnMD, ConAu 110, DcLB 10, ModWD*
Hankins, Clabe *ConAu X*
Hankins, Frank Hamilton 1877-1970 *ConAu 104*
Hankins, John Erskine 1905- *ConAu 49, IntAu&W 82*
Hankins, Norman E 1935- *ConAu 11NR, -61*
Hankins, Thomas Leroy 1933- *ConAu 108*
Hankinson, Cyril Francis James 1895- *ConAu P-1*
Hankla, Bonnie Susan 1951- *IntWWP 82*
Hankla, Cathryn *DrAP&F 83*
Hankla, Susan *IntWWP 82X*
Hanks, Lucien M 1910- *ConAu 37R*
Hanks, Stedman Shumway 1889-1979 *ConAu 85*
Hanle, Dorothea Zack 1917- *ConAu 13R*
Hanley, Boniface Francis 1924- *ConAu 9R*
Hanley, Clifford 1922- *ConAu 3NR, -9R, ConNov 82, DcLB 14[port], IntAu&W 82, WrDr 84*
Hanley, Elizabeth *ConAu X*
Hanley, Evelyn A 1916-1980 *ConAu 41R, -97*
Hanley, Gerald 1916- *WrDr 84*
Hanley, Gerald Anthony 1916- *ConAu 1R, -6NR, ConNov 82, DcLEL 1940, LongCTC, TwCA SUP, TwCWr*
Hanley, Hope Anthony 1926- *ConAu 5NR, -9R*
Hanley, James 1901- *CnMD SUP, ConAu 73, ConDr 82, ConLC 3, -5, -8, -13, ConNov 82, EncWL 2, LongCTC, ModBrL, ModBrL SUP, TwCA, TwCA SUP, TwCWr, WhoTwCL, WrDr 84*
Hanley, Katharine Rose 1932- *ConAu 37R*
Hanley, Michael F, IV 1941- *ConAu 65*
Hanley, Mike *ConAu X*
Hanley, Theodore Dean 1917- *ConAu 5R*
Hanley, Thomas O'Brien 1918- *ConAu 1R, -1NR*
Hanley, William *DrAP&F 83*
Hanley, William 1931- *CnMD SUP, ConAu 41R, ConDr 82, CroCD, DcLEL 1940, ModWD, WrDr 84*
Hanlon, Emily *DrAP&F 83*
Hanlon, Emily 1945- *ConAu 77, SmATA 15*
Hanlon, John 1912- *ConAu 57*
Hann, Jacquie 1951- *ConAu 73, SmATA 19*
Hanna, Alfred Jackson 1893-1978 *ConAu 2NR, -45*
Hanna, David 1917- *ConAu 6NR, -57*
Hanna, J Marshall 1907- *ConAu 1R*
Hanna, John Paul 1932- *ConAu 1NR, -45*
Hanna, Lavone Agnes 1896- *ConAu 13R*
Hanna, Mary Carr *DrAP&F 83*
Hanna, Mary Carr 1905- *ConAu 45*

Hanna, Mary T 1935- *ConAu 97*
Hanna, Paul R 1902- *ConAu 45, SmATA 9*
Hanna, Span Dionysus 1953- *IntWWP 82*
Hanna, Thomas 1928- *ConAu 1R, -1NR*
Hanna, Tom *DrAP&F 83*
Hanna, W C *ConSFA*
Hanna, William John 1931- *ConAu 8NR, -61*
Hannaford, John W 1918- *ConAu 45*
Hannah, Barbara 1891- *ConAu 97*
Hannah, Barry *DrAP&F 83*
Hannah, Barry 1942- *ConAu 108, -110, ConLC 23[port], DcLB 6*
Hannak, Johann Jacques 1892- *ConAu P-1*
Hannam, Charles 1925- *ConAu 11NR*
Hannam, Charles Lewis *WrDr 84*
Hannam, Charles Lewis 1925- *ConAu 61*
Hannan, Edward James 1921- *WrDr 84*
Hannan, Greg *DrAP&F 83*
Hannan, Joseph F 1923- *ConAu 3NR, -9R*
Hannau, Hans W 1904- *ConAu 10NR*
Hannau, Hans Walter 1904- *ConAu 21R, IntAu&W 82*
Hannavy, John Michael 1946- *ConAu 11NR, -69*
Hannaway, Patricia H 1929- *ConAu 61*
Hannaway, Patti 1929- *ConAu X*
Hannay, Allen 1946- *ConAu 109*
Hannay, Doris Fergusson *ConAu X*
Hannay, James Owen 1865-1950 *LongCTC, TwCA, TwCA SUP*
Hannay, Margaret Patterson 1944- *ConAu 104*
Hanneman, Audre 1926- *ConAu 21R*
Hanners, LaVerne 1921- *IntWWP 82*
Hanney, Peter 1930-1976 *ConAu 105*
Hannibal *ConAu X*
Hannibal, Edward *DrAP&F 83*
Hannibal, Edward L 1936- *ConAu 29R, WrDr 84*
Hannifin, Jerry 1917- *ConAu 77*
Hannigan, Paul *DrAP&F 83*
Hanning, Hugh Peter James 1925- *ConAu 25R, WrDr 84*
Hanning, Robert William 1938- *ConAu 93*
Hannon, Ezra *WrDr 84*
Hannula, Reino 1919- *ConAu 105*
Hannum, Alberta Pierson 1906- *ConAu 65*
Hano, Arnold 1922- *ConAu 5NR, -9R, SmATA 12*
Hanrahan, John David 1938- *ConAu 77, IntAu&W 82*
Hanrieder, Wolfram F 1931- *ConAu 8NR, -21R*
Hansberry, Lorraine 1930-1965 *AuNews 2, CnMD SUP, ConAu 109, -25R, ConDr 82E, ConLC 17, CroCD, DcLB 7[port], DcLEL 1940, EncWL 2, ModAL SUP, ModBlW, ModWD, WorAu*
Hansbrough, Vivian Pearl 1908- *IntWWP 82*
Hansel, Robert R 1936- *ConAu 110*
Hansell, Antonina *ConAu X*
Hansen, Al 1927- *ConAu 17R*
Hansen, Alvin Harvey 1887-1975 *ConAu 57, ConAu P-1*
Hansen, Ann Natalie 1927- *WrDr 84*
Hansen, Axel 1916- *IntWWP 82*
Hansen, Barbara Joan *WrDr 84*
Hansen, Bertrand Lyle 1922- *ConAu 9R*
Hansen, Carl 1906- *ConAu 2NR, -5R*
Hansen, Carl 1906-1983 *ConAu 110*
Hansen, Caryl 1929- *ConAu 108*
Hansen, Chadwick 1926- *ConAu 29R, WrDr 84*
Hansen, Donald A 1933- *ConAu 73*
Hansen, Donald Charles 1935- *ConAu 33R*
Hansen, Emmanuel 1937- *ConAu 104*
Hansen, Flemming 1938- *ConAu 93*
Hansen, Forest Warnyr 1931- *ConAu 45*
Hansen, Gary B 1935- *ConAu 3NR, -9R*
Hansen, Gunnar *DrAP&F 83*
Hansen, Harry 1884-1977 *ConAu 69, -73, TwCA, TwCA SUP*
Hansen, Ib 1923- *IntAu&W 82*
Hansen, Jon *DrAP&F 83*
Hansen, Joseph *DrAP&F 83*
Hansen, Joseph 1923- *ConAu 29R, IntAu&W 82, TwCCr&M 80, WrDr 84*
Hansen, Joyce 1942- *ConAu 105*
Hansen, Kenneth H 1917- *ConAu 13R*
Hansen, Klaus J 1931- *ConAu 21R*
Hansen, Linda *ConAmTC*
Hansen, Marcus Lee 1892-1938 *TwCA, TwCA SUP*
Hansen, Martin Alfred 1909-1955 *CIDMEL 80, EncWL 2*
Hansen, Mary Lewis 1933- *ConAu 17R*

Hansen, Michael 1922- *WrDr 84*
Hansen, Niles M 1937- *ConAu 25R*
Hansen, Norman J 1918- *ConAu 29R*
Hansen, Richard H 1929- *ConAu 1R*
Hansen, Rodney Thor 1940- *ConAu 53*
Hansen, Roger D 1935- *ConAu 105*
Hansen, Ron 1947- *ConAu 89*
Hansen, Rosanna 1947- *ConAu 105*
Hansen, Terrence Leslie 1920-1974 *ConAu 37R*
Hansen, Thorkild 1927- *CIDMEL 80, EncWL 2*
Hansen, Tom *DrAP&F 83*
Hansen, Vern *ConSFA*
Hansen, W Lee 1928- *ConAu 29R*
Hansen, William F 1941- *ConAu 49*
Hansen, Willy Blok 1916- *CreCan 1*
Hanser, Richard 1909-1981 *ConAu 5R, -8NR, -105, SmATA 13*
Hanshew, Thomas W 1857-1914 *TwCCr&M 80*
Hansi 1873- *ConAu X*
Hansman, William 1913- *ConSFA*
Hanson, A H 1913-1971 *ConAu 4NR, -89*
Hanson, Agnes O 1905- *ConAu 107*
Hanson, Albert Henry 1913- *ConAu 5R*
Hanson, Anne Coffin 1921- *ConAu 21R*
Hanson, Anthony Tyrrell 1916- *ConAu 9NR, -21R*
Hanson, E Kenneth 1930- *ConAu 5R, -13R*
Hanson, Earl D 1927- *ConAu 73, WrDr 84*
Hanson, Earl Parker 1899-1978 *ConAu 41R*
Hanson, F Allan 1939- *ConAu 41R*
Hanson, Harvey 1941- *ConAu 65*
Hanson, Howard 1896-1981 *ConAu 103*
Hanson, Howard Gordon 1931- *ConAu 21R*
Hanson, Irene 1898- *ConAu 49*
Hanson, Isabel 1929- *ConAu 106*
Hanson, James Arthur 1940- *ConAu 49*
Hanson, Jim *DrAP&F 83*
Hanson, Jim 1953- *ConAu 97, IntWWP 82*
Hanson, Joan 1938- *ConAu 33R, SmATA 8, WrDr 84*
Hanson, Joseph E 1894?-1971 *ConAu 104, SmATA 27N*
Hanson, June Andrea 1941- *ConAu 97*
Hanson, Kenneth *DrAP&F 83*
Hanson, Kenneth O 1922- *ConAu 7NR, -53, ConLC 13, ConP 80, IntWWP 82, WrDr 84*
Hanson, Michael James 1942- *ConAu 61, WrDr 84*
Hanson, Michael Peter James 1936- *WrDr 84*
Hanson, Norwood Russell 1924-1967 *ConAu 5R, -8NR*
Hanson, Paul D 1939- *ConAu 61*
Hanson, Pauline *ConAu 45, ConP 80, WrDr 84*
Hanson, Peggy L 1934- *ConAu 29R*
Hanson, Peggy Lee 1934- *WrDr 84*
Hanson, Philip 1936- *ConAu 103, WrDr 84*
Hanson, R P C 1916- *ConAu 9NR, -21R*
Hanson, Richard Patrick Crosland 1916- *IntAu&W 82*
Hanson, Richard S 1931- *ConAu 37R*
Hanson, Robert Carl 1926- *ConAu 37R*
Hanson, Robert P 1918- *ConAu 9R*
Hanson, Ruth Katie 1900- *ConAu 5R*
Hanson, Simon *ConAu X*
Hanson, Willy Blok 1916- *CreCan 1*
Hansten, Philip D 1943- *ConAu 33R*
Hanushek, Eric Alan 1943- *ConAu 41R*
Hany, Arthur 1924- *IntWWP 82*
Hanzlicek, C G *DrAP&F 83*
Hanzlicek, C G 1942- *ConAu 73*
Hao, Yen-Ping 1934- *ConAu 53*
Hapgood, Charles Hutchins 1904- *ConAu 17R*
Hapgood, David 1926- *ConAu 13R, WrDr 84*
Hapgood, Fred 1942- *ConAu 93*
Hapgood, Hutchins 1869-1944 *TwCA, TwCA SUP*
Hapgood, Norman 1868-1937 *TwCA*
Hapgood, Ruth K 1920- *ConAu 49*
Happe, Peter 1932- *ConAu 45*
Happel, Robert A 1916- *ConAu 1R*
Happold, F C 1893- *ConAu 101*
Haq, Mahbub Ul 1934- *ConAu 13R*
Haqqee, Shanul Haq 1917- *IntWWP 82*
Harada, Wayne *ConAmTC*
Harald, Eric *ConAu X, SmATA X*
Haraldsson, Erlendur 1931- *ConAu 101*
Harap, Henry 1893-1981 *ConAu 104*
Harap, Louis 1904- *ConAu 57*
Harari, Ehud 1935- *ConAu 65*
Harasymowicz, Jerzy 1933- *CIDMEL 80*

Haraway, Donna Jeanne 1944- *ConAu 73*
Harbage, Alfred Bennett 1901-1976 *ConAu 5R, -5NR, -65, TwCA SUP, TwCCr&M 80*
Harbaugh, John W 1926- *ConAu 49*
Harbaugh, William Henry 1920- *ConAu 1R*
Harberger, Arnold C 1924- *ConAu 6NR, -13R, WrDr 84*
Harbert, Earl N 1934- *ConAu 33R*
Harbert, Mary Ann 1945- *ConAu 61*
Harbeson, Georgiana Brown 1894?-1980 *ConAu 101*
Harbeson, Gladys Evans 1899- *ConAu 21R, WrDr 84*
Harbeson, John Willis 1938- *ConAu 57*
Harbin, Calvin E 1916- *ConAu 21R*
Harbinson, Robert *ConAu X, WrDr 84*
Harbinson, W A 1941- *ConAu 9NR, -61*
Harbison, Frederick Harris 1912-1976 *ConAu 65*
Harbison, Peter 1939- *ConAu 65*
Harbison, Robert 1940- *ConAu 102*
Harbottle, Michael Neale 1917- *ConAu 29R, WrDr 84*
Harbottle, Phil 1941- *ConSFA*
Harbron, John Davison 1924- *ConAu 9R*
Harburg, E Y 1896-1981 *ConAu 103, -85*
Harburg, Yip *ConAu X*
Harbury, Colin Desmond 1922- *ConAu 102, WrDr 84*
Harcave, Sidney S 1916- *ConAu 17R*
Harcleroad, Fred F 1918- *ConAu 8NR, -17R*
Harcourt, G C 1931- *ConAu 25R*
Harcourt, Geoffrey Colin 1931- *WrDr 84*
Harcourt, Melville 1909- *ConAu 5R*
Harcourt, Palma *ConAu 77, WrDr 84*
Harcourt, Peter 1931- *ConAu 81*
Harcourt, Peter Millais 1923- *IntAu&W 82*
Hard, Edward W, Jr. 1939- *ConAu 85*
Hard, Frederick 1897- *ConAu P-2*
Hard, Margaret 1888?-1974 *ConAu 49*
Hard, T W *ConAu X*
Hard Af Segerstad, Birgit 1911- *IntAu&W 82*
Hardach, Gerd 1941- *ConAu 105*
Hardaway, Francine 1941- *ConAu 81*
Hardcastle, Michael 1933- *ConAu 25R, TwCCW 83, WrDr 84*
Harden, Donald B 1901- *ConAu 5R, IntAu&W 82, WrDr 84*
Harden, O Elizabeth 1935- *WrDr 84*
Harden, Oleta Elizabeth 1935- *ConAu 37R*
Harden, William 1903- *ConAu 93*
Harder, Eleanor 1925- *ConAu 37R*
Harder, Geraldine Gross 1926- *ConAu 53*
Harder, Raymond Wymbs, Jr. 1920- *ConAu 85*
Harder, Uffe 1930- *IntWWP 82*
Hardesty, Nancy A 1941- *ConAu 8NR, -57*
Hardgrave, Robert L, Jr. 1939- *ConAu 11NR, -25R*
Hardie, Charles Dunn 1911- *WrDr 84*
Hardie, David *IntAu&W 82X*
Hardie, Frank 1911- *ConAu 33R, IntAu&W 82, WrDr 84*
Hardiman, James W 1919- *ConAu 33R*
Hardin, Charles M 1908- *ConAu 49*
Hardin, Clement *ConAu X, TwCWW, WrDr 84*
Hardin, Clifford M 1915- *WrDr 84*
Hardin, Dave *WrDr 84*
Hardin, Garrett 1915- *ConAu 17R*
Hardin, Garrett James 1915- *ConAu 9NR*
Hardin, J D *ConAu X*
Hardin, Mitch *ConAu X*
Hardin, Paul, III 1931- *ConAu 25R*
Hardin, Peter *ConAu X*
Hardin, Richard F 1937- *ConAu 45*
Hardin, Robert 1934- *ConAu 77*
Hardin, Tim 1941?-1981 *ConAu 102*
Hardin, Tom *ConAu X*
Hardin, Wes *ConAu X*
Harding, A F 1946- *ConAu 77*
Harding, Barbara 1926- *ConAu 41R*
Harding, Bertita 1902- *ConAu 5R*
Harding, Bertita 1907- *TwCA, TwCA SUP*
Harding, Carl B *ConAu X*
Harding, D W 1906- *ConAu P-1, ConLCrt 82, WrDr 84*
Harding, D W 1940- *ConAu 41R*
Harding, Davis P 1915?-1970 *ConAu 104*
Harding, Donald Edward 1916- *ConAu 4NR, -53*
Harding, Donald Edwards 1916- *IntAu&W 82, IntWWP 82*
Harding, George 1923- *IntAu&W 82X, WrDr 84*

Harding, Gunnar 1940- *ClDMEL 80*
Harding, Harold F 1903- *ConAu 37R*
Harding, Harry 1946- *ConAu 109*
Harding, Jack 1914- *ConAu 29R*
Harding, James 1929- *ConAu 33R, WrDr 84*
Harding, John 1948- *ConAu 97, ConDr 82, WrDr 84*
Harding, Karl Gunnar 1940- *IntWWP 82*
Harding, Lee 1937- *ConAu 106, IntAu&W 82, SmATA 31, -32, TwCSFW, WrDr 84*
Harding, Matt *ConAu X*
Harding, Matthew Whitman *ConAu X, WrDr 84*
Harding, Patrick *IntWWP 82X*
Harding, Peter *ConAu X*
Harding, T D 1948- *ConAu 85*
Harding, Thomas G 1937- *ConAu 21R*
Harding, Todd *WrDr 84*
Harding, Vincent 1931- *LivgBAA*
Harding, Virginia Hamlet 1909- *ConAu 45*
Harding, Walter 1917- *WrDr 84*
Harding, Walter Roy 1917- *ConAu 1R, -1NR*
Harding, Wes *TwCWW*
Harding, William Harry 1945- *ConAu 93*
Hardinge, George *LongCTC*
Hardinge, Helen Mary 1901- *ConAu P-2, IntAu&W 82*
Hardingham, John 1916- *WrDr 84*
Hardingham, John Frederick Watson 1916- *ConAu P-1*
Hardison, O B *DrAP&F 83*
Hardison, O B, Jr. 1928- *ConAu 6NR*
Hardison, Osborne B 1928- *ConAu 5R, IntAu&W 82, WrDr 84*
Hardisty, M W 1909- *WrDr 84*
Hardman, David Rennie *WrDr 84*
Hardman, David Rennie 1901- *IntWWP 82*
Hardman, John 1944- *ConAu 45*
Hardman, Richards Lynden 1924- *ConAu 13R*
Hardon, John A 1914- *WrDr 84*
Hardon, John Anthony 1914- *ConAu 1R, -2NR*
Hardoy, Jorge Enrique 1926- *ConAu 33R*
Hardt, Ernst 1876-1947 *ModWD*
Hardt, J Pearce 1922- *ConAu 3NR, -5R*
Hardwick, Adam *ConAu X*
Hardwick, Clyde T 1915- *ConAu 5R*
Hardwick, Elizabeth 1916- *ConAu 3NR, -5R, ConLC 13, ConNov 82, DcLB 6[port], WorAu, WrDr 84*
Hardwick, Homer *ConAu X, IntAu&W 82X*
Hardwick, Michael 1924- *ConAu 2NR, -49, IntAu&W 82, WrDr 84*
Hardwick, Mollie *ConAu 2NR, -49, IntAu&W 82, TwCRGW, WrDr 84*
Hardwick, Richard H 1923- *WrDr 84*
Hardwick, Richard Holmes, Jr. 1923- *ConAu 5R, -9NR, SmATA 12*
Hardwick, Sylvia *ConAu X*
Hardwicke, Sir Cedric 1893-1964 *LongCTC*
Hardwig, Ferdinand *IntAu&W 82X*
Hardy, Adam *ConAu X, IntAu&W 82X, WrDr 84*
Hardy, Alan 1932- *ConAu 73*
Hardy, Alexander Gray 1920-1973 *ConAu 45*
Hardy, Alice Dale *ConAu P-2, SmATA 1*
Hardy, Sir Alister Clavering 1896- *ConAu 85*
Hardy, Arthur Sherburne 1847-1930 *TwCA*
Hardy, Barbara *WrDr 84*
Hardy, Barbara 1924- *ConAu 85, ConLCrt 82, IntAu&W 82*
Hardy, Bobbie 1913- *WrDr 84*
Hardy, C Colburn 1910- *ConAu 6NR, -53*
Hardy, Clarence 1935- *IntWWP 82*
Hardy, Clarence H *IntWWP 82X*
Hardy, David A 1936- *ConAu 8NR, -61, IntAu&W 82, SmATA 9*
Hardy, Douglas *ConAu X*
Hardy, Edward R 1908- *ConAu P-1*
Hardy, Eric *ConAu 61*
Hardy, Evelyn 1902- *ConAu 21R, IntAu&W 82*
Hardy, Frank 1917- *TwCWr*
Hardy, J P 1933- *ConAu 25R*
Hardy, Jason *ConAu X*
Hardy, John Edward 1922- *ConAu 13R*
Hardy, John Philips 1933- *WrDr 84*
Hardy, Laura *TwCRGW*
Hardy, Leroy C 1927- *ConAu 29R*
Hardy, Melissa Arnold 1952- *ConAu 102*
Hardy, Michael 1933- *ConAu 25R*
Hardy, Peter 1931- *ConAu 65*
Hardy, Richard Earl 1938- *ConAu 37R,*

Hardy, Robert 1917- *WrDr 84*
Hardy, Ronald Harold 1919- *ConAu 5R, DcLEL 1940, IntAu&W 82*
Hardy, Russ *TwCWW*
Hardy, Stuart *ConAu X, SmATA X*
Hardy, Thomas 1840-1928 *CnMWL, ConAu 104, EncWL 2[port], LongCTC, ModBrL, ModBrL SUP, ModWD, RGFMBP, SmATA 25[port], TwCLC 4[port], -10[port], TwCWr, WhoTwCL*
Hardy, W G 1895-1979 *ConAu 5NR, TwCRGW*
Hardy, William George 1895- *ConAu 5R, CreCan 1, IntAu&W 82*
Hardy, William Marion 1922- *ConAu 1R, -2NR*
Hardyck, Curtis D 1929- *ConAu 29R*
Hare, A Paul 1923- *ConAu 1R, -2NR*
Hare, Bill *ConAu X*
Hare, Cyril 1900-1958 *LongCTC, TwCCr&M 80*
Hare, David 1947- *ConAu 97, ConDr 82, DcLB 13[port], DcLEL 1940, IntAu&W 82, WrDr 84*
Hare, Douglas Robert Adams 1929- *ConAu 45*
Hare, Eric B 1894- *ConAu P-1*
Hare, F Kenneth 1919- *ConAu 37R*
Hare, John 1935- *ConAu 21R, WrDr 84*
Hare, Nathan 1934- *ConAu 41R, LivgBAA*
Hare, Norma Q 1924- *ConAu 101*
Hare, Peter H 1935- *ConAu 33R*
Hare, R M 1919- *ConAu 2NR, WrDr 84*
Hare, Richard 1907-1966 *ConAu P-1*
Hare, Richard Mervyn 1919- *ConAu 5R, WorAu 1970*
Hare, Ronald 1899- *ConAu 77*
Hare, VanCourt, Jr. 1929- *ConAu 25R*
Hare, William Moorman 1934- *ConAu 101*
Hare Duke, Michael 1925- *WrDr 84*
Harel, Isser 1912- *ConAu 10NR, -65*
Haresnape, Geoffrey Laurence 1939- *IntWWP 82*
Hareven, Tamara K 1937- *ConAu 25R, IntAu&W 82, WrDr 84*
Harewood 1923- *IntAu&W 82*
Harford, David K 1947- *ConAu 49*
Harger, William Henderson 1936- *ConAu 57*
Hargrave, John Gordon 1894-1982 *ConAu 110*
Hargrave, Leonie *WrDr 84*
Hargrave, O T 1936- *ConAu 33R*
Hargrave, Rowena Hullett 1906- *ConAu 33R*
Hargreaves, Harry 1922- *ConAu 5R*
Hargreaves, John D 1924- *ConAu 9R, WrDr 84*
Hargreaves, Mary W M 1914- *ConAu 37R*
Hargreaves, Reginald Charles 1888- *ConAu P-1*
Hargreaves-Mawdsley, W Norman 1921-1980 *ConAu 7NR, -9R*
Hargroder, Charles M 1926- *ConAu 73*
Hargrove, Barbara *WrDr 84*
Hargrove, Barbara Watts 1924- *ConAu 33R*
Hargrove, Erwin C 1930- *WrDr 84*
Hargrove, Katharine T *ConAu 33R*
Hargrove, Marion 1919- *TwCA SUP*
Hargrove, Merwin Matthew 1910- *ConAu 9R, WrDr 84*
Hargrove, Nancy Duvall 1941- *ConAu 97*
Hariharan, V 1952- *IntWWP 82*
Harik, Iliya F 1934- *ConAu 25R*
Haring, Bernard 1912- *ConAu X, WrDr 84*
Haring, Firth *DrAP&F 83*
Haring, Firth 1937- *ConAu 25R*
Haring, Joseph E 1931- *ConAu 33R, WrDr 84*
Haring, Norris G 1923- *ConAu 1R, -2NR*
Haring, Philip S 1915- *ConAu 37R, WrDr 84*
Harington, Donald *DrAP&F 83*
Harington, Donald 1935- *ConAu 7NR, -13R*
Harington, Joy 1914- *WrDr 84*
Haris, Petros *EncWL 2*
Harjo, Joy *DrAP&F 83*
Harjo, Joy 1951- *IntWWP 82*
Harjo, Patty Leah *DrAP&F 83*
Harjo, Suzan Shown *DrAP&F 83*
Hark, Mildred *ConAu X, SmATA X*
Harkabi, Yehoshafat 1921- *ConAu 73*
Harkaway, Hal *ConAu X*
Harker, Kenneth 1927- *ConAu 97, ConSFA*
Harker, Lizzie Allen 1863-1933 *TwCA*
Harker, Ronald 1909- *ConAu 77*
Harkey, Ira Brown, Jr. 1918- *ConAu 57, WrDr 84*
Harkey, William G 1914- *ConAu 25R*

Harkins, Arthur M 1936- *ConAu 97*
Harkins, Philip 1912- *ConAu 29R, SmATA 6*
Harkins, William E 1921- *ConAu 33R*
Harkness, Bruce 1923- *ConAu 13R*
Harkness, D W 1937- *ConAu 29R*
Harkness, David J 1913- *ConAu 3NR, -9R*
Harkness, David W 1937- *IntAu&W 82, WrDr 84*
Harkness, Edward *DrAP&F 83*
Harkness, Edward 1947- *ConAu 77*
Harkness, Georgia Elma 1891-1974 *ConAu 1R, -6NR, -53*
Harkness, Gladys Estelle Suiter 1908?-1973 *ConAu 41R*
Harkness, Marjory Gane 1880- *ConAu P-2*
Harknett, Terry 1936- *ConAu 6NR, -57*
Harknett, Terry Williams *WrDr 84*
Harlan *ConAu X*
Harlan, Glen *ConAu X, SmATA X, WrDr 84*
Harlan, John Marshall 1899-1971 *ConAu 33R*
Harlan, Louis Rudolph 1922- *ConAu 21R*
Harlan, William K 1938- *ConAu 45*
Harland, Henry 1861-1905 *LongCTC*
Harle, Elizabeth *ConAu X, TwCRGW, WrDr 84*
Harlequin *ConAu X*
Harley, John *ConAu X, IntAu&W 82X*
Harling, Robert 1910- *DcLEL 1940, TwCCr&M 80, WrDr 84*
Harling, Thomas *ConAu X*
Harlow, Enid 1939- *ConAu 102*
Harlow, Francis H 1928- *ConAu 57*
Harlow, Harry F 1905- *ConAu 97*
Harlow, Joan Hiatt 1932- *ConAu 89*
Harlow, John *TwCWW*
Harlow, LeRoy F 1913- *ConAu 85*
Harlow, Lewis A 1901- *ConAu P-1*
Harlow, Neal 1908- *ConAu 109*
Harlow, Robert 1923- *CreCan 2*
Harlow, Samuel Ralph 1885-1972 *ConAu 1R, -37R*
Harlow, W M 1900- *ConAu 13R*
Harman, Alec *ConAu X*
Harman, Claire *ConAu X*
Harman, David 1944- *ConAu 105*
Harman, Fred 1902?-1982 *ConAu 106, SmATA 30N*
Harman, Gilbert H 1938- *ConAu 73*
Harman, Hugh 1903-1982 *ConAu 108, SmATA 33N*
Harman, Jane *ConAu X, WrDr 84*
Harman, Jeanne Perkins 1919- *ConAu 11NR, -69, IntAu&W 82*
Harman, Nicholas 1933- *ConAu 101*
Harman, P M 1943- *ConAu 110*
Harman, R Alec *ConAu X*
Harman, Richard Alexander 1917- *ConAu 5NR, -9R*
Harman, Willis W 1918- *ConAu 5R*
Harmel, Robert 1950- *ConAu 110*
Harmelink, Barbara *ConAu 61, SmATA 9*
Harmer, Daniel Jevon 1911- *CreCan 1*
Harmer, Mabel 1894- *ConAu 9R*
Harmer, Ruth Mulvey 1919- *ConAu 9R*
Harmer, Shirley 1930- *CreCan 2*
Harmin, Merrill 1928- *ConAu 89*
Harmon, A J 1926- *ConAu 21R*
Harmon, Gary L 1935- *ConAu 37R*
Harmon, Glynn 1933- *ConAu 45*
Harmon, H H *ConAu X*
Harmon, James Judson 1933- *ConAu 21R*
Harmon, Jim 1933- *ConAu X*
Harmon, Lily 1912- *ConAu 105*
Harmon, Lyn S 1930- *ConAu 21R*
Harmon, Margaret 1906- *ConAu 69, SmATA 20[port]*
Harmon, Maurice 1930- *ConAu 9NR, -21R, WrDr 84*
Harmon, Nolan Bailey 1892- *ConAu 89*
Harmon, R Bartlett 1932- *ConAu 17R*
Harmon, Robert Bartlett 1932- *ConAu 8NR*
Harmon, Susanna M 1940- *ConAu 57*
Harmon, William *DrAP&F 83*
Harmon, William Ruth 1938- *ConAu 33R, IntWWP 82*
Harms, Ernest 1895-1974 *ConAu 49, ConAu P-1*
Harms, John 1900- *ConAu 17R*
Harms, Leroy Stanley 1928- *ConAu 8NR, -53*
Harms, Robert T 1932- *ConAu 37R*
Harms, Valerie *DrAP&F 83*
Harms, Valerie 1940- *ConAu 2NR, -49*

Harmsen, Dorothy B Bahneman *ConAu 103*
Harmsen, Frieda 1931- *ConAu 107*
Harmston, Olivia *ConAu X, WrDr 84*
Harmsworth, Alfred Charles William 1865-1922
 LongCTC
Harmsworth, E C *ConAu X*
Harmsworth, Esmond Cecil 1898-1978 *ConAu 89*
Harmsworth, Harold Sidney 1868-1940 *LongCTC*
Harnack, Curtis *DrAP&F 83*
Harnack, Curtis 1927- *ConAu 1R, -2NR,
 IntAu&W 82, WrDr 84*
Harnack, R Victor 1927- *ConAu 13R*
Harnan, Edna Terry 1919- *IntAu&W 82*
Harnan, Terry *IntAu&W 82X*
Harnan, Terry 1920- *ConAu 45, SmATA 12*
Harnden, Ruth Peabody *ConAu 73*
Harner, James L 1946- *ConAu 110*
Harness, Charles L 1915- *ConSFA, DcLB 8,
 TwCSFW, WrDr 84*
Harnett, Cynthia 1893-1981 *SmATA 32N,
 TwCCW 83*
Harnett, Cynthia Mary 1893- *ConAu P-1,
 SmATA 5*
Harnetty, Peter 1927- *ConAu 37R*
Harnik, Bernard 1910- *ConAu 93*
Harnsberger, Caroline Thomas 1902- *ConAu 61*
Harnwell, Gaylord Probasco 1903-1982
 ConAu 106
Haro, Robert P 1936- *ConAu 33R*
Haro Tecglen, Eduardo 1924- *IntAu&W 82*
Haroldson, William *ConAu X*
Harper, Bill *ConAu X*
Harper, Carol Ely *ConAu 61, IntWWP 82*
Harper, Daniel *ConAu X, WrDr 84*
Harper, David *ConAu X*
Harper, Elaine *ConAu X*
Harper, Floyd H 1899-1978 *ConAu 77*
Harper, George McLean 1863-1947 *TwCA,
 TwCA SUP*
Harper, George Mills 1914- *WrDr 84*
Harper, George W *DrAP&F 83*
Harper, Harold W *ConAu 89*
Harper, Harry H, Jr. 1910-1983 *ConAu 110*
Harper, Howard 1904- *ConAu 1R*
Harper, Howard M, Jr. 1930- *ConAu 21R*
Harper, J Russell 1914- *ConAu 33R*
Harper, James E 1927- *ConAu 41R*
Harper, Joan 1932- *ConAu 101*
Harper, John C 1924- *ConAu 103*
Harper, John Dickson 1910- *ConAu 103*
Harper, John Russell 1914- *WrDr 84*
Harper, Kate *ConAu X*
Harper, Katherine E 1946- *ConAu 103*
Harper, Marvin Henry 1901- *ConAu 49*
Harper, Mary Wood *ConAu X, SmATA X*
Harper, Michael *DrAP&F 83*
Harper, Michael Claude 1931- *ConAu 65*
Harper, Michael S 1938- *ConAu 33R, ConLC 7,
 -22[port], ConP 80, IntAu&W 82,
 LivgBAA, WrDr 84*
Harper, Paula 1938- *ConAu 105*
Harper, Robert A 1924- *ConAu 17R*
Harper, Robert J C 1927- *ConAu 13R*
Harper, Stephen 1924- *ConAu 97,
 IntAu&W 82*
Harper, Tom 1923?-1983 *ConAu 110*
Harper, Vincent *TwCSFW*
Harper, Wilhelmina 1884-1973 *ConAu P-1,
 SmATA 26N, -4*
Harper, William A 1944- *ConAu 77*
Harper-Nelson, John 1922- *IntAu&W 82*
Harpole, Patricia Chayne 1933- *ConAu 37R*
Harr, Barbara *DrAP&F 83*
Harr, Lorraine Ellis 1912- *IntWWP 82*
Harr, Wilber C 1908-1971 *ConAu 1R, -103*
Harraden, Beatrice 1864-1936 *LongCTC, TwCA,
 TwCA SUP, TwCWr*
Harragan, Betty Lehan 1921- *ConAu 77*
Harrah, Barbara K 1938- *ConAu 107*
Harrah, David 1926- *ConAu 5R, WrDr 84*
Harrah, David Fletcher 1949- *ConAu 65*
Harral, Stewart 1906-1964 *ConAu 5R*
Harrar, E S 1905- *ConAu P-1*
Harrar, J George 1906-1982 *ConAu 110*
Harre, John 1931- *ConAu 21R*
Harre, Rom 1927- *ConAu 2NR, -5R, WrDr 84*
Harrell, Allen W 1922- *ConAu 29R*
Harrell, Costen J 1885- *ConAu 5R*
Harrell, David Edwin, Jr. 1930- *ConAu 37R,
 IntAu&W 82, WrDr 84*
Harrell, Irene B 1927- *ConAu 9NR*
Harrell, Irene Burk 1927- *ConAu 21R,

IntWWP 82, WrDr 84
Harrell, John G 1922- *ConAu 3NR, -9R*
Harrell, Sara Gordon 1940- *ConAu 105,
 SmATA X*
Harrell, Stevan 1947- *ConAu 106*
Harrell, Thomas Willard 1911- *ConAu 1R*
Harrelson, Walter Joseph 1919- *ConAu 9R,
 WrDr 84*
Harrer, Heinrich 1912- *ConAu 7NR, -17R,
 IntAu&W 82*
Harries, Joan 1922- *ConAu 107*
Harries, Karsten 1937- *ConAu 25R*
Harriett 1905- *ConAu 77*
Harriford, Daphne *WrDr 84*
Harrigan, Anthony 1925- *ConAu 21R*
Harrigan, Edward 1845-1911 *ModWD*
Harrigan, Kathryn Rudie 1951- *ConAu 109*
Harriman, John 1904-1960 *TwCA, TwCA SUP*
Harriman, Margaret 1928- *ConAu 21R*
Harriman, Richard L 1944- *ConAu 33R*
Harriman, Sarah 1942- *ConAu 57*
Harrington, Alan *DrAP&F 83*
Harrington, Alan 1919- *ConAu 73*
Harrington, Ann *IntWWP 82X*
Harrington, Charles 1942- *ConAu 9NR, -65*
Harrington, Curtis 1928- *ConAu 103*
Harrington, Denis J 1932- *ConAu 69*
Harrington, Donald Szantho 1914- *ConAu 21R*
Harrington, Elbert W 1901- *WrDr 84*
Harrington, Elbert Wellington 1901- *ConAu 37R*
Harrington, Evelyn Davis 1911- *ConAu 4NR*
Harrington, Geri *ConAu 6NR, -57*
Harrington, Harold David 1903- *ConAu 25R*
Harrington, Harold David 1903-1981
 ConAu 11NR
Harrington, Jack 1918- *ConAu 57*
Harrington, Jeremy 1932- *ConAu 41R*
Harrington, Joseph 1903- *TwCCr&M 80*
Harrington, Joseph Daniel 1923- *ConAu 89*
Harrington, Joyce 1930?- *TwCCr&M 80*
Harrington, K *ConAu X*
Harrington, Lyn Davis 1911- *ConAu X, -5R,
 SmATA X*
Harrington, Mark Raymond 1882-1971
 ConAu P-2
Harrington, Michael 1928- *ConAu 17R,
 ConIsC 1[port], WrDr 84*
Harrington, Ty 1951- *ConAu 102*
Harrington, William 1931- *ConAu 4NR, -9R*
Harris, Alan 1928- *ConAu 5R*
Harris, Albert J 1908- *ConAu 1R, -5NR,
 WrDr 84*
Harris, Alf 1928- *ConAu 53*
Harris, Alfred *DrAP&F 83*
Harris, Alice Kessler 1941- *ConAu 37R*
Harris, Andrea *ConAu X*
Harris, Andrew *ConAu X*
Harris, Aurand 1915- *ConAu 93, IntAu&W 82,
 TwCCW 83, WrDr 84*
Harris, Barbara S 1927- *ConAu 49*
Harris, Ben Charles 1907-1978 *ConAu 57, -89*
Harris, Ben M 1923- *ConAu 2NR, -5R*
Harris, Bernice Kelly 1894?-1973 *ConAu 5R, -45*
Harris, Bertha *DrAP&F 83*
Harris, Bertha 1937- *ConAu 29R*
Harris, Beulah d1970 *ConAu 104*
Harris, Bill 1933- *ConAu 109*
Harris, Blanche *CreCan 1*
Harris, Brian *ConAu X*
Harris, Brownie 1949- *ConAu 107*
Harris, Bruce Fairgray 1921- *WrDr 84*
Harris, Carl V 1937- *ConAu 97*
Harris, Charlaine 1951- *ConAu 105*
Harris, Charles 1923- *ConAu 102*
Harris, Charles B 1940- *ConAu 53*
Harris, Charles H, III 1937- *ConAu 13R*
Harris, Chauncy D 1914- *ConAu 29R,
 WrDr 84*
Harris, Chester W 1910- *ConAu P-1*
Harris, Christie 1907- *ConAu 5R, -6NR,
 ConLC 12, SmATA 6, TwCCW 83,
 WrDr 84*
Harris, Christopher *LongCTC*
Harris, Clyde E, Jr. *ConAu 21R*
Harris, Colver *ConAu X, SmATA 7*
Harris, Curtis C, Jr. 1930- *ConAu 53*
Harris, Cyril 1891- *ConAu P-1*
Harris, Dale Benner 1914- *ConAu 13R*
Harris, Daniel A 1942- *ConAu 89*
Harris, David 1946- *ConAu 69*
Harris, David W 1948- *ConAu 107*
Harris, Del 1937- *ConAu 8NR*

Harris, Delmer William 1937- *ConAu 61*
Harris, Dorothy Joan 1931- *ConAu 1NR, -45,
 SmATA 13*
Harris, Douglas Hershel 1930- *ConAu 25R*
Harris, Dudley Arthur 1925- *WrDr 84*
Harris, Edward Arnold 1910-1976 *ConAu 65*
Harris, Emily Katharine *DrAP&F 83*
Harris, Ernest E 1914- *ConAu 33R, WrDr 84*
Harris, Errol E 1908- *ConAu 2NR, -49*
Harris, F Brayton 1932- *ConAu 21R*
Harris, Frank 1856-1931 *CnMD, ConAu 109,
 LongCTC, ModBrL, TwCA, TwCA SUP,
 TwCWr, WhoTwCL*
Harris, Fred R 1930- *ConAu 77, WrDr 84*
Harris, Frederick John 1943- *ConAu 57*
Harris, Gene Gray 1929- *ConAu 17R*
Harris, Gertrude 1916- *ConAu 57*
Harris, H A 1902- *ConAu 49*
Harris, H K *DrAP&F 83*
Harris, Helen 1927- *ConAu 61, WrDr 84*
Harris, Herbert 1911- *ConAu 102,
 IntAu&W 82, TwCCr&M 80, WrDr 84*
Harris, Herbert 1914?-1974 *ConAu 49*
Harris, Hyde *ConAu X*
Harris, Ian 1937- *ConAu 107*
Harris, Irving David 1914- *ConAu 13R*
Harris, James E 1928- *ConAu 110*
Harris, Jana *DrAP&F 83*
Harris, Jana 1947- *ConAu 105, IntWWP 82,
 WrDr 84*
Harris, Jane Allen 1918- *ConAu 1R*
Harris, Janet 1932-1979 *ConAu 33R, -93,
 SmATA 23N, -4*
Harris, Janette Hoston 1939- *LivgBAA*
Harris, Jay S 1938- *ConAu 85*
Harris, Jed *ConAu X*
Harris, Jessica B 1948- *ConAmTC*
Harris, Jessica L 1939- *ConAu 33R*
Harris, Joel Chandler 1848-1908 *ConAu 104,
 TwCLC 2*
Harris, John 1915- *ConAu 2NR, -5R*
Harris, John 1916- *ConAu 93, IntAu&W 82,
 WrDr 84*
Harris, John 1931- *IntAu&W 82*
Harris, John Beynon 1903-1969 *ConAu 102, -89,
 ConLC 19, ConSFA, LongCTC*
Harris, John S 1917- *ConAu 29R, WrDr 84*
Harris, John S 1929- *ConAu 65*
Harris, John Wyndham Parkes Lucas Beynon
 WorAu
Harris, Joseph Pratt 1896- *ConAu 1R*
Harris, Julian 1896- *ConAu 1R*
Harris, Julie 1925- *ConAu 103*
Harris, Karen H 1934- *ConAu 103*
Harris, Kathleen *ConAu X*
Harris, Kathryn Gibbs *ConAu X*
Harris, Kathryn Gibbs 1930- *ConAu 65*
Harris, Kenneth 1904-1983 *ConAu 109*
Harris, Larry M *ConAu X*
Harris, Larry Mark *WrDr 84*
Harris, Laurence Mark *WrDr 84*
Harris, Lavinia *ConAu X, SmATA X*
Harris, Lawren Phillips 1910- *CreCan 1*
Harris, Lawren Stewart 1885-1970 *CreCan 2*
Harris, Leon A, Jr. 1926- *ConAu 3NR, -9R,
 SmATA 4*
Harris, Leonard 1929- *ConAu 9NR, -65,
 WrDr 84*
Harris, Lloyd J 1947- *ConAu 61*
Harris, Lorle K 1912- *ConAu 97,
 SmATA 22[port]*
Harris, Louis 1921- *ConAu 13R*
Harris, Louise 1903- *ConAu 7NR, -17R,
 IntAu&W 82, WrDr 84*
Harris, MacDonald 1921- *ConAu X, ConLC 9,
 WrDr 84*
Harris, Madalene 1925- *ConAu 105*
Harris, Marcia Lee 1951- *ConAu 109*
Harris, Marie *DrAP&F 83*
Harris, Marie 1943- *ConAu 104*
Harris, Marilyn *ConAu X*
Harris, Marilyn 1931- *ConAu X, TwCRGW,
 WrDr 84*
Harris, Marion Rose 1925- *ConAu P-1,
 WrDr 84*
Harris, Marjorie 1919- *WrDr 84*
Harris, Marjorie Silliman 1890- *ConAu P-1*
Harris, Mark *DrAP&F 83*
Harris, Mark 1922- *ConAu 2NR, -5R,
 ConLC 19, ConNov 82, DcLB Y80A[port],
 -2, DcLEL 1940, IntAu&W 82,

WorAu 1970, WrDr 84
Harris, Mark Jonathan 1941- *ConAu 104,
SmATA 32[port]*
Harris, Marshall D 1903- *ConAu 1R, –1NR*
Harris, Marvin 1927- *ConAu 110,
ConIsC 2[port]*
Harris, Mary B 1943- *ConAu 53*
Harris, Mary Imogene *WrDr 84*
Harris, Mary Imogene 1926- *ConAu 49,
IntWWP 82*
Harris, Mary K 1905-1966 *ConAu P-1,
TwCCW 83*
Harris, Mary Law 1892?-1980 *ConAu 102*
Harris, Max 1921- *DcLEL 1940, TwCWr*
Harris, Michael H 1941- *ConAu 57*
Harris, Michael R 1936- *ConAu 29R, WrDr 84*
Harris, Middleton 1908- *LivgBAA*
Harris, Miles F 1913- *ConAu 5R, –6NR*
Harris, Nancy C *DrAP&F 83*
Harris, P B 1929- *ConAu 104*
Harris, Patricia *ConAu 57*
Harris, Paul Anthony 1948- *IntAu&W 82*
Harris, Peter 1923- *WrDr 84*
Harris, Peter Bernard 1929- *IntAu&W 82,
WrDr 84*
Harris, Philip Robert 1926- *ConAu 8NR, –17R,
WrDr 84*
Harris, R Baine 1927- *ConAu 73*
Harris, R J C 1922- *ConAu 65*
Harris, R Laird 1911- *ConAu 1R, –1NR*
Harris, Radie *ConAu 65*
Harris, Richard 1934- *ConAu 107*
Harris, Richard Colebrook 1936- *ConAu 97*
Harris, Richard H 1942- *ConAu 103*
Harris, Richard N 1942- *ConAu 77*
Harris, Ricky 1922- *ConAu 103*
Harris, Robert *DrAP&F 83*
Harris, Robert 1849-1919 *CreCan 1*
Harris, Robert 1907- *ConAu 5R*
Harris, Robert Dalton 1921- *ConAu 93*
Harris, Robert Harry 1941- *ConAu 108*
Harris, Robert T 1912- *ConAu 5R*
Harris, Robin *ConAu X*
Harris, Robin S 1919- *ConAu 21R*
Harris, Roger *ConAu X*
Harris, Ronald Walter 1916- *ConAu 5R,
IntAu&W 82, WrDr 84*
Harris, Rosemary 1923- *TwCCW 83, WrDr 84*
Harris, Rosemary Jeanne 1923- *ConAu 33R,
IntAu&W 82, SmATA 4, TwCCr&M 80,
TwCRGW*
Harris, Roy J 1903?-1980 *ConAu 93*
Harris, S E 1897-1974 *ConAu 65*
Harris, Sara Lee *ConAu X*
Harris, Seymour Edwin 1897-1974 *ConAu 53,
TwCA SUP*
Harris, Sheldon H 1928- *ConAu 37R, WrDr 84*
Harris, Sherwood 1932- *ConAu 97, SmATA 25*
Harris, Stephen L 1937- *ConAu 29R*
Harris, Sydney J *ConAmTC*
Harris, Sydney J 1917- *ConAu 11NR*
Harris, Sydney Justin 1917- *ConAu 61*
Harris, T George 1924- *ConAu 69*
Harris, Theodore Findley 1931- *AuNews 1*
Harris, Theodore Wailson 1921- *IntAu&W 82*
Harris, Theodore Wilson 1921- *DcLEL 1940*
Harris, Thistle Y *WrDr 84*
Harris, Thistle Y 1902- *ConAu X*
Harris, Thomas A 1913?- *ConAu 93*
Harris, Thomas J 1892?-1983 *ConAu 109*
Harris, Thomas O 1935- *ConAu 73*
Harris, Timothy Hyde 1946- *ConAu 101*
Harris, Valerie 1952- *NatPD 81[port]*
Harris, Walter A 1929- *ConAu 29R, WrDr 84*
Harris, Warren G 1936- *ConAu 77*
Harris, William Bliss 1901?-1981 *ConAu 104*
Harris, William C 1933- *ConAu 21R*
Harris, William J *DrAP&F 83*
Harris, William J 1942- *ConAu 5NR, –53*
Harris, Wilson 1883-1955 *LongCTC*
Harris, Wilson 1921- *ConAu 11NR, –65,
ConLC 25[port], ConNov 82, ConP 80,
EncWL 2, LongCTC, ModBlW,
ModCmwL, WhoTwCL, WorAu 1970,
WrDr 84*
Harrison, Allan E 1925- *ConAu 6NR, –57*
Harrison, Barbara 1941- *ConAu 29R*
Harrison, Barbara Grizzuti 1934- *ConAu 77*
Harrison, Bennett 1942- *ConAu 53*
Harrison, Bernard 1933- *ConAu 93,
IntAu&W 82, WrDr 84*
Harrison, Bill *ConAu X*

Harrison, Brian Fraser 1918- *ConAu 102,
WrDr 84*
Harrison, C William 1913- *ConAu 107*
Harrison, Carey 1944- *ConAu 61, ConDr 82B*
Harrison, Chip *WrDr 84*
Harrison, Chip 1952- *ConAu 29R*
Harrison, Cynthia Ellen 1946- *ConAu 57*
Harrison, David Lakin 1926- *WrDr 84*
Harrison, David Lee 1937- *ConAu 93,
SmATA 26[port]*
Harrison, Deloris 1938- *ConAu 61, SmATA 9*
Harrison, Elizabeth *WrDr 84*
Harrison, Elizabeth Cavanna *WrDr 84*
Harrison, Elizabeth Fancourt 1921-
IntAu&W 82, TwCRGW
Harrison, Everett F 1902- *ConAu P-1,
IntAu&W 82, WrDr 84*
Harrison, Francis Llewelyn 1905- *IntAu&W 82*
Harrison, Frank R, III 1935- *ConAu 53*
Harrison, Fred 1917- *ConAu 29R*
Harrison, Frederic 1831-1923 *LongCTC*
Harrison, G B 1894- *ConAu 3NR*
Harrison, George Bagshawe 1894- *ConAu 1R,
LongCTC, TwCA SUP*
Harrison, George Russell 1898- *ConAu P-2*
Harrison, Hank 1940- *ConAu 41R*
Harrison, Harry 1925- *ConAu 1R, –5NR,
ConSFA, DcLB 8[port], SmATA 4,
TwCSFW, WrDr 84*
Harrison, Helen P 1935- *ConAu 102*
Harrison, Helga 1924- *WrDr 84*
Harrison, Henry Sydnor 1880-1930 *LongCTC,
TwCA*
Harrison, Howard 1930- *ConAu 5R,
IntAu&W 82, WrDr 84*
Harrison, J F C 1921- *ConAu 10NR, –25R*
Harrison, J P *ConAu 77*
Harrison, James Thomas 1937- *ConAu 8NR,
–13R*
Harrison, Jan Emma 1946- *IntWWP 82*
Harrison, Jay S 1927-1974 *ConAu 53*
Harrison, Jim *DrAP&F 83*
Harrison, Jim 1937- *ConAu X, ConLC 6, –14,
ConP 80, DcLB Y82B[port], MichAu 80,
WorAu 1970, WrDr 84*
Harrison, Joan 1909- *ConAu 104*
Harrison, John Baughman 1907- *ConAu 1R*
Harrison, John F C 1921- *WrDr 84*
Harrison, John M 1914- *ConAu 25R*
Harrison, John Raymond 1933- *AuNews 2,
ConAu 101*
Harrison, K C 1915- *ConAu 3NR*
Harrison, Keith 1932- *WrDr 84*
Harrison, Keith Edward 1932- *ConAu 73,
ConP 80*
Harrison, Kenneth 1915- *WrDr 84*
Harrison, Kenneth Cecil 1915- *ConAu 9R,
IntAu&W 82*
Harrison, Louise C 1908- *ConAu P-1*
Harrison, Lowell H 1922- *ConAu 37R,
WrDr 84*
Harrison, M John 1945- *ConAu 53, TwCSFW*
Harrison, Marcus 1924- *ConAu 102*
Harrison, Martin 1930- *ConAu 49*
Harrison, Mary *ConAu X*
Harrison, Mary St. Leger 1852-1931 *LongCTC,
TwCA, TwCA SUP*
Harrison, Max *ConAu 69, IntAu&W 82*
Harrison, Michael 1907- *ConAu 97,
TwCCr&M 80, WrDr 84*
Harrison, Michael John 1945- *WrDr 84*
Harrison, Michelle Jessica 1942- *ConAu 109*
Harrison, Molly 1909- *ConAu 108*
Harrison, Paul M 1923- *ConAu 53*
Harrison, Randall P 1929- *ConAu 11NR, –69*
Harrison, Raymond H 1911- *ConAu 17R*
Harrison, Rebecca *MichAu 80*
Harrison, Rex 1908- *WrDr 84*
Harrison, Richard A 1945- *ConAu 107*
Harrison, Richard John 1920- *ConAu 109,
IntAu&W 82, WrDr 84*
Harrison, Robert 1932- *ConAu 25R*
Harrison, Roger 1938- *WrDr 84*
Harrison, Roland Kenneth 1920- *ConAu 49*
Harrison, Ronald George 1921- *WrDr 84*
Harrison, Rosina 1899- *ConAu 102,
IntAu&W 82, WrDr 84*
Harrison, Ross 1943- *ConAu 9NR, –61*
Harrison, Royden John 1927- *ConAu 17R,
IntAu&W 82, WrDr 84*
Harrison, S Gerald 1924- *ConAu 13R*
Harrison, Sarah 1946- *ConAu 102, WrDr 84*

Harrison, Saul I 1925- *ConAu 10NR, –21R*
Harrison, Selig S 1927- *ConAu 85*
Harrison, Sidney 1903- *IntAu&W 82, WrDr 84*
Harrison, Stanley 1913- *WrDr 84*
Harrison, Stanley R 1927- *ConAu 41R*
Harrison, Sydney Gerald 1924- *IntAu&W 82,
WrDr 84*
Harrison, Tony 1937- *ConAu 65, ConP 80,
IntAu&W 82, IntWWP 82, WrDr 84*
Harrison, Wallace 1895-1981 *ConAu 108*
Harrison, Whit *ConAu X*
Harrison, Wilfrid 1909- *ConAu P-1,
IntAu&W 82*
Harrison, William *DrAP&F 83*
Harrison, William 1933- *ConAu 9NR, –17R*
Harrison, William Clinton 1919- *ConAu 25R*
Harrison-Church, Ronald James 1915-
ConAu 13R
Harrison Church, Ronald James 1915- *WrDr 84*
Harrison Matthews, Leonard 1901- *IntAu&W 82*
Harriss, C Lowell 1912- *ConAu 1R, –2NR,
WrDr 84*
Harriss, Joseph 1936- *ConAu 57*
Harriss, R P 1902- *ConAu 73*
Harriss, Robert Preston 1902- *ConAmTC*
Harrity, Richard 1907-1973 *ConAu 41R*
Harrod, Elizabeth 1920- *IntWWP 82*
Harrod, Leonard Montague 1905- *ConAu 13R*
Harrod, Sir Roy Forbes 1900-1978 *ConAu 9R,
–103, WorAu*
Harrold, William *DrAP&F 83*
Harrold, William 1936- *ConAu 41R,
IntAu&W 82, IntWWP 82*
Harron, Don 1924- *ConAu 104, WrDr 84*
Harrop-Allin, Clinton 1936- *ConAu 107,
WrDr 84*
Harroun, Catherine 1907- *ConAu 109*
Harrow, Benjamin 1888-1970 *ConAu 104*
Harrowe, Fiona *ConAu X*
Harrower, Elizabeth 1928- *ConAu 101,
ConNov 82, DcLEL 1940, WrDr 84*
Harrower, Molly 1906- *ConAu 5R*
Harsch, Ernest 1951- *ConAu 69*
Harsch, Hilya *ConAu X, WrDr 84*
Harsch, Joseph Close 1905- *ConAu 102*
Harsent, David 1942- *ConAu 93, ConP 80,
IntAu&W 82, WrDr 84*
Harsh, George 1908?-1980 *ConAu 93*
Harsh, Wayne C 1924- *ConAu 29R*
Harshaw, Ruth H 1890-1968 *ConAu 107,
SmATA 27*
Harshbarger, David Dwight 1938- *ConAu 53*
Harshman, Marc *DrAP&F 83*
Harson, Sley *ConAu X*
Harss, Luis 1936- *ConAu 17R*
Harstad, Peter Tjernagel 1935- *ConAu 37R*
Harston, Ruth 1944- *ConAu 41R*
Hart, Albert Bushnell 1854-1943 *DcLB 17[port],
TwCA, TwCA SUP*
Hart, Albert Gailord 1909- *ConAu P-2*
Hart, Alexandra 1939- *ConAu 6NR*
Hart, Allan H 1935- *ConAu 106*
Hart, Archibald D 1932- *ConAu 93*
Hart, Arthur Tindal 1908- *ConAu 9R*
Hart, B H Liddell *LongCTC*
Hart, Barry *ConAu X*
Hart, Sir Basil Henry Liddell 1895-1970
ConAu X
Hart, Bruce 1938- *ConAu 107*
Hart, Carol 1944- *ConAu 65*
Hart, Carole 1943- *ConAu 107*
Hart, Caroline *TwCRGW*
Hart, Carolyn Gimpel 1936- *ConAu 13R*
Hart, Donald J 1917- *ConAu 9R*
Hart, Douglas J 1950- *ConAu 101*
Hart, Edward J 1941- *ConAu 53*
Hart, Edward L *DrAP&F 83*
Hart, Edward L 1916- *ConAu 37R*
Hart, Ellis *ConAu X*
Hart, Ernest H 1910- *ConAu 102*
Hart, Frances N 1890-1943 *LongCTC, TwCA,
TwCA SUP, TwCCr&M 80*
Hart, Francis *ConAu X*
Hart, Francis Dudley 1909- *ConAu 108*
Hart, Freck 1939- *IntAu&W 82X*
Hart, Gavin 1939- *ConAu 106*
Hart, George L, III 1942- *ConAu 93*
Hart, H L A 1907- *ConAu 1R, –2NR*
Hart, Henry C 1916- *ConAu 41R*
Hart, Henry Hersch 1886-1968 *ConAu P-1*
Hart, Herbert Michael 1928- *ConAu 9R*
Hart, James David 1911- *ConAu 1R, –1NR*

IntAu&W 82
Haseloff, Charles *DrAP&F 83*
Hasenclever, Herbert Frederick 1924-1978
  ConAu 81
Hasenclever, Walter 1890-1940 *ClDMEL 80,*
  CnMD, ModGL, ModWD
Hasenhuttl, Gotthold 1933- *IntAu&W 82*
Hasford, Gustav *DrAP&F 83*
Hasford, Gustav 1947- *ConAu 85*
Hashim, Jawad M 1938- *IntAu&W 82*
Hashmi, Alamgir *DrAP&F 83*
Hashmi, Alamgir 1951- *ConAu 77,*
  IntAu&W 82, IntWWP 82
Haskale, Hadassah *DrAP&F 83*
Haskale, Hadassah 1934- *IntWWP 82*
Haskell, Arnold Lionel 1903-1981? *ConAu 5R,*
  -7NR, -102, SmATA 6
Haskell, Douglas 1899-1979 *ConAu 89*
Haskell, Edward Froehlich 1906- *ConAu 105*
Haskell, Francis 1928- *WrDr 84*
Haskell, Francis James Herbert 1928-
  ConAu 6NR, -9R, IntAu&W 82
Haskell, John Duncan, Jr. 1941- *ConAu 107*
Haskell, Martin R 1912- *ConAu 41R*
Haskett, Edythe Rance 1915- *ConAu 21R,*
  LivgBAA
Haskin, Dorothy C 1905- *ConAu 5R, WrDr 84*
Haskin, Gretchen 1936- *ConAu 103*
Haskins, Anne *DrAP&F 83*
Haskins, Barbara *ConAu X*
Haskins, George Lee 1915- *ConAu 1R, -1NR,*
  WrDr 84
Haskins, Ilma 1919- *ConAu 45*
Haskins, James 1941- *ChlLR 3, ConAu 33R,*
  SmATA 9
Haskins, Jim 1941- *ChlLR 3, ConAu X,*
  LivgBAA, SmATA X, WrDr 84
Haskins, Lola *DrAP&F 83*
Haskins, Sam 1926- *ConAu 103*
Haslam, Gerald *DrAP&F 83*
Haslam, Gerald W 1937- *ConAu 11NR*
Haslam, Gerald William 1937- *ConAu 29R,*
  IntAu&W 82, WrDr 84
Haslegrave, Herbert Leslie 1902- *WrDr 84*
Hasler, Eveline 1937- *ConAu 106*
Hasler, Joan 1931- *ConAu 29R, SmATA 28*
Haslerud, George M 1906- *ConAu 45*
Hasley, Louis 1906- *ConAu 37R, IntWWP 82*
Hasley, Lucile 1909- *ConAu P-1*
Hasling, John 1928- *ConAu 33R*
Haslip, Joan *ASpks*
Haslip, Joan 1912- *ConAu 107*
Hasluck, Paul 1905- *ConAu 109, WrDr 84*
Haslund, Ebba 1917- *IntAu&W 82*
Haspel, Eleanor C 1944- *ConAu 69*
Hass, C Glen 1915- *ConAu 17R*
Hass, Eric 1905?-1980 *ConAu 102*
Hass, Hans 1919- *ConAu 108*
Hass, Robert *DrAP&F 83*
Hass, Robert 1941- *ConLC 18, ConP 80,*
  WrDr 84
Hassall, Christopher Vernon 1912-1963
  ConAu 89, LongCTC, ModBrL, TwCWr,
  WorAu
Hassall, John 1868-1948 *LongCTC*
Hassall, Mark 1940- *ConAu 73*
Hassall, William Owen 1912- *ConAu 13R,*
  IntAu&W 82, WrDr 84
Hassan, Ihab 1925- *ConAu 1R, -3NR, -5R,*
  ConLCrt 82, DcLEL 1940, IntAu&W 82,
  WrDr 84
Hassan, William Ephraim, Jr. 1923- *ConAu 33R*
Hasse, Henry L d1977 *ConSFA*
Hasse, Margaret M *DrAP&F 83*
Hassel, Odd 1897-1981 *ConAu 108*
Hassel, Sven 1917- *ConAu 93, IntAu&W 82*
Hasselblatt, Dieter Reinhold 1926- *IntAu&W 82*
Hassenger, Robert 1937- *ConAu 21R*
Hassin, Jamiel Daud *DrAP&F 83*
Hassing, Per 1916- *ConAu 37R*
Hassler, Donald M *DrAP&F 83*
Hassler, Donald M 1937- *ConAu 41R,*
  WrDr 84
Hassler, Jon 1933- *ConAu 73, SmATA 19*
Hassler, Warren W, Jr. 1926- *ConAu 9R,*
  IntAu&W 82
Hassler, William T 1954- *ConAu 104*
Hasso, Signe Eleonora Cecilia 1915-
  IntAu&W 82
Hassrick, Peter H 1941- *ConAu 1NR, -49*
Hastings, Adrian Christopher 1929- *ConAu 7NR,*
  -17R, IntAu&W 82

Hastings, Alan *ConAu X*
Hastings, Arthur Claude 1935- *ConAu 37R*
Hastings, Cecily Mary Eleanor 1924- *ConAu 5R*
Hastings, Graham *ConAu X, WrDr 84*
Hastings, Harrington *ConAu X*
Hastings, Hubert DeCronin 1902- *ConAu 109*
Hastings, Hudson *ConAu X*
Hastings, Ian 1912- *ConAu 45*
Hastings, Macdonald 1909- *ConAu 53,*
  IntAu&W 82, TwCCr&M 80
Hastings, Macdonald 1909-1982 *ConAu 9NR*
Hastings, Margaret 1910- *ConAu 41R*
Hastings, Max 1945- *ConAu 81, IntAu&W 82*
Hastings, Michael 1938- *ConAu 97, ConDr 82,*
  WrDr 84
Hastings, Paul Guiler 1914- *ConAu 1R*
Hastings, Philip Kay 1922- *ConAu 102*
Hastings, Phyllis 1904- *ConAu 8NR, -9R,*
  TwCRGW, WrDr 84
Hastings, Robert Paul 1933- *ConAu 73,*
  IntAu&W 82, WrDr 84
Hastings, William T 1881- *ConAu 5R*
Haston, Dougal 1940-1977 *ConAu 105*
Hastorf, Albert H 1920- *ConAu 97*
Hasty, Ronald W 1941- *ConAu 4NR, -53*
Haswell, Chetwynd John Drake 1919-
  ConAu 41R, IntAu&W 82, WrDr 84
Haswell, Harold Alanson, Jr. 1912- *ConAu 45*
Haswell, Jock *WrDr 84*
Haswell, Jock 1919- *ConAu X, IntAu&W 82X*
Hatch, Alden 1898-1975 *ConAu 57, -65*
Hatch, Denison 1935- *ConAu 33R, WrDr 84*
Hatch, Elizabeth A 1897- *ConAmTC*
Hatch, Elvin 1937- *ConAu 45*
Hatch, Eric S 1902?-1973 *ConAu 41R*
Hatch, Eric Stow 1901-1973 *TwCA, TwCA SUP*
Hatch, Gerald *ConSFA*
Hatch, James V 1928- *ConAu 41R*
Hatch, John 1917- *WrDr 84*
Hatch, John Charles 1917- *ConAu 9R,*
  IntAu&W 82
Hatch, Mary Cottam 1912-1970 *ConAu 109,*
  SmATA 28
Hatch, Nathan O 1946- *ConAu 109*
Hatch, Preble D K 1898- *ConAu P-2*
Hatch, Raymond N 1911- *ConAu 21R*
Hatch, Richard A 1940- *ConAu 9NR*
Hatch, Richard Allen 1940- *ConAu 21R*
Hatch, Robert McConnell 1910- *ConAu 93*
Hatch, William Henry Paine 1875-1972
  ConAu 37R
Hatcher, George W 1906?-1983 *ConAu 110*
Hatcher, Harlan Henthorne 1898- *ConAu P-2,*
  MichAu 80, TwCA, TwCA SUP
Hatcher, John 1942- *ConAu 33R, IntAu&W 82,*
  WrDr 84
Hatcher, John S 1940- *ConAu 97*
Hatcher, Nat B 1897- *ConAu 1R*
Hatcher, Robert Anthony 1937- *ConAu 93*
Hatem, Mohamed Abdel-Kader *ConAu X*
Hatfield, Antoinette Kuzmanich 1929- *ConAu 85*
Hatfield, Dorothy B 1921- *ConAu 53*
Hatfield, Elaine 1937- *ConAu 10NR*
Hatfield, Henry Caraway 1912- *ConAu 65*
Hatfield, Mark O 1922- *ConAu 77*
Hathaway, Baxter L 1909- *ConAu 1R, -5NR,*
  MichAu 80
Hathaway, Bo 1942- *ConAu 106*
Hathaway, Dale E 1925- *ConAu 9R*
Hathaway, Jan *ConAu X*
Hathaway, Jeanine *DrAP&F 83*
Hathaway, Lulu 1903- *ConAu 13R*
Hathaway, Mavis *ConAu X*
Hathaway, Nancy 1946- *ConAu 108*
Hathaway, Sibyl Collings 1884- *ConAu 1R*
Hathaway, Starke R 1903- *ConAu 5R*
Hathaway, Stephen *DrAP&F 83*
Hathaway, William *DrAP&F 83*
Hathaway, William Kitchen 1944- *ConAu 73,*
  IntWWP 82
Hathcock, Louise *ConAu 1R*
Hathorn, Richard Y 1917- *ConAu 1NR*
Hathorn, Richmond 1917- *ConAu 1R*
Hatim, Muhammad 'Abd Al-Qadir 1918-
  ConAu 89
Hatlen, Burton 1936- *ConAu 109*
Hatley, George B 1924- *ConAu 106*
Hatlo, Jimmy 1898-1963 *ConAu 93,*
  SmATA 23N
Hatmon, Paul W 1921- *ConAu 106*
Hatt, Harold Ernest 1932- *ConAu 21R,*
  WrDr 84

Hatta, Mohammed 1902-1980 *ConAu 97*
Hattaway, Herman 1938- *ConAu 65*
Hatteras, Owen *ConAmA*
Hatteras, Owen, III *ConAu X*
Hattersley, Ralph 1921- *ConAu 103*
Hattersley, Roy 1932- *ConAu 103, WrDr 84*
Hattery, Lowell H 1916- *ConAu 17R*
Hatton, Ragnhild 1913- *WrDr 84*
Hatton, Ragnhild Marie 1913- *ConAu 25R,*
  IntAu&W 82
Hatton, Robert Wayland 1934- *ConAu 37R*
Hattwick, Richard E 1938- *ConAu 73*
Hatvany, George Egon *ConAu 53, DrAP&F 83*
Hatzfeld, Helmut A 1892-1979 *ConAu 85, -97*
Haubenstein, Edith 1930- *IntAu&W 82*
Hauberg, Clifford A 1906- *ConAu 37R*
Hauck, Allan 1925- *ConAu 1R*
Hauck, Paul A 1924- *ConAu 41R*
Hauck, Richard Boyd 1936- *ConAu 53*
Hauerwas, Stanley Martin 1940- *ConAu 57*
Haug, James *DrAP&F 83*
Haug, James 1954- *IntWWP 82*
Haugaard, Erik 1923- *TwCCW 83, WrDr 84*
Haugaard, Erik Christian 1923- *ConAu 3NR,*
  -5R, IntAu&W 82, SmATA 4
Haugaard, William P 1929- *WrDr 84*
Haugaard, William Paul 1929- *ConAu 25R*
Hauge, Alfred 1915- *ClDMEL 80*
Hauge, Olav H 1905- *ClDMEL 80*
Hauge, Olav H 1908- *IntWWP 82*
Haugen, Edmund Bennett 1913- *ConAu 17R*
Haugen, Einar 1906- *ConAu 9NR, -21R,*
  WrDr 84
Haugen, Paal-Helge 1945- *IntAu&W 82,*
  IntWWP 82
Haugh, Richard 1942- *ConAu 9NR, -57*
Haugh, Robert F 1910- *ConAu 61*
Haughey, John C 1930- *ConAu 77*
Haught, John F 1942- *ConAu 85*
Haughton, Claire Shaver 1901- *ConAu 85*
Haughton, Rosemary 1927- *ConAu 5R,*
  IntAu&W 82, WrDr 84
Haughton, Sidney Henry 1888-1982 *ConAu 107*
Haughton-James, Jean Rosemary 1924-1981
  ConAu 105
Haugland, Vern 1908- *ConAu 93*
Hauk, Barbara *DrAP&F 83*
Hauk, Maung *ConAu X*
Haukeness, Helen *DrAP&F 83*
Haule, James M 1945- *ConAu 109*
Hauman, Doris 1898- *SmATA 32*
Hauman, George 1890-1961 *SmATA 32*
Haun, Harry *ConAmTC*
Haun, Paul 1906-1969 *ConAu P-2*
Haupt, Zygmunt 1907?-1975 *ConAu 61*
Hauptmann, Carl 1858-1921 *ClDMEL 80,*
  CnMD, ModGL, ModWD
Hauptmann, Gerhart 1862-1946 *ClDMEL 80,*
  CnMD, ConAu 104, EncWL 2[port],
  LongCTC, ModGL, ModWD, TwCA,
  TwCA SUP, TwCLC 4[port], TwCWr,
  WhoTwCL
Hauptmann, Helmut 1928- *IntAu&W 82*
Haury, Emil W 1904- *ConAu 65*
Hausdorff, Don 1927- *ConAu 45*
Hauser, Arnold 1892- *TwCA SUP*
Hauser, Arnold Rudolf 1929- *IntAu&W 82*
Hauser, Charles McCorkle 1929- *ConAu 69*
Hauser, Harald 1912- *CnMD, CroCD,*
  IntAu&W 82
Hauser, Heinrich 1901- *TwCA, TwCA SUP*
Hauser, Hillary 1944- *ConAu 11NR, -69*
Hauser, Margaret L 1909- *ConAu P-1,*
  SmATA 10
Hauser, Marianne *DrAP&F 83*
Hauser, Marianne 1910- *ConAu P-1,*
  DcLB Y83B[port], WrDr 84
Hauser, Philip M 1909- *WrDr 84*
Hauser, Phillip M 1909- *ConAu 17R*
Hauser, Robert Mason 1942- *ConAu 109*
Hauser, Susan *DrAP&F 83*
Hauser, Thomas 1946- *ConAu 85*
Hauser, William B 1939- *ConAu 69*
Haushalter, Fred L 1893- *MichAu 80*
Haushofer, Albrecht 1903-1945 *ClDMEL 80,*
  ModGL
Hausknecht, Murray 1925- *ConAu 37R*
Hausman, Gerald *DrAP&F 83*
Hausman, Gerald 1945- *ConAu 2NR, -45,*
  IntWWP 82, SmATA 13
Hausman, Gerry *ConAu X, SmATA X*
Hausman, Patricia 1953- *ConAu 107*

Hausman, Warren H 1939- *ConAu 17R*

Hausmann, Bernard A 1899- *ConAu P-2*

Hausmann, Manfred 1898- *CnMD, ModGL*

Hausmann, Winifred 1922- *ConAu 11NR*

Hausmann, Winifred Wilkinson 1922- *WrDr 84*

Hausrath, Alfred Hartmann 1901- *ConAu 41R*

Haussig, Hans Wilhelm 1916- *ConAu 29R*

Hautzig, Deborah 1956- *ConAu 89, SmATA 31[port]*

Hautzig, Esther 1930- *WrDr 84*

Hautzig, Esther Rudomin 1930- *ConAu 1R, –5NR, IntAu&W 82, SmATA 4*

Havard, Cyril 1925- *WrDr 84*

Havard, Lezley 1944- *NatPD 81[port]*

Havard, William C, Jr. 1923- *ConAu 1R, –5NR*

Havel, J E 1928- *ConAu 41R, IntAu&W 82*

Havel, Vaclav 1936- *CIDMEL 80, ConAu 104, ConLC 25[port], CroCD, EncWL 2, ModSL 2, ModWD, WorAu 1970*

Havelock, Christine Mitchell 1924- *ConAu 85*

Havelock, Eric Alfred 1903- *ConAu P-1*

Havelock, Ronald G 1935- *ConAu 85*

Haveman, Lotte 1936- *IntAu&W 82*

Haveman, Robert Henry 1936- *ConAu 17R, WrDr 84*

Havemann, Ernest 1912- *ConAu 1R*

Havemann, Joel 1943- *ConAu 85*

Havemann, Robert 1910-1982 *ConAu 110*

Havemeyer, Loomis 1886-1971 *ConAu 33R*

Haven, Richard 1924- *ConAu 25R*

Havenhand, John *ConAu X, SmATA X*

Havens, Daniel F 1931- *ConAu 69*

Havens, George R 1890-1977 *ConAu 4NR, –5R, –73*

Havens, Murray Clark 1932- *ConAu 41R, IntAu&W 82*

Havens, Sam 1936- *NatPD 81[port]*

Havens, Shirley 1925- *ConAu 89*

Havens, Stewart *IntAu&W 82X*

Havens, Thomas R H 1939- *ConAu 41R*

Haver, Ronald D 1939- *ConAu 109*

Haverkamp-Begemann, Egbert 1923- *ConAu 11NR, –17R*

Haverstick, John 1919- *ConAu 25R*

Haverstock, Mary Sayre 1932- *ConAu 81*

Haverstock, Nathan Alfred 1931- *ConAu 53*

Haviaras, Stratis *DrAP&F 83*

Haviaras, Stratis 1935- *ConAu X, WrDr 84*

Havighurst, Alfred 1904- *WrDr 84*

Havighurst, Alfred F 1904- *ConAu 33R, IntAu&W 82*

Havighurst, Marion Boyd d1974 *ConAu 49, ConAu P-1*

Havighurst, Robert James 1900- *ConAu 21R*

Havighurst, Walter 1901- *WrDr 84*

Havighurst, Walter Edwin 1901- *ConAu 1R, –1NR, MichAu 80, SmATA 1, TwCA SUP*

Havil, Anthony *WrDr 84*

Haviland, Virginia 1911- *ConAu 17R, SmATA 6*

Havill, Juanita *DrAP&F 83*

Havill, Steven 1945- *ConAu 108*

Havis, Allan 1951- *ConAu 108, NatPD 81[port]*

Havlice, Patricia Pate 1943- *ConAu 29R*

Havlik, John F 1917- *ConAu 45*

Havoc, June 1916- *ConAu 107*

Havran, Martin Joseph 1929- *ConAu 1R, –1NR, IntAu&W 82, WrDr 84*

Havrevold, Finn 1905- *ConAu 109*

Havrilesky, Thomas M 1939- *ConAu 4NR, –53*

Haw, Richard Claude 1913- *ConAu P-1*

Haw Haw, Lord *LongCTC*

Hawes, Charles Boardman 1889-1923 *TwCA, TwCCW 83*

Hawes, Evelyn J *AuNews 1, ConAu 13R, IntAu&W 82*

Hawes, Frances Cooper 1897- *ConAu P-1*

Hawes, Gene R 1922- *ConAu 3NR, –5R*

Hawes, Grace M 1926- *ConAu 69*

Hawes, Hampton 1929?-1977 *ConAu 69*

Hawes, John T 1906?-1983 *ConAu 109*

Hawes, Joseph M 1938- *ConAu 53*

Hawes, Judy 1913- *ConAu 33R, SmATA 4, WrDr 84*

Hawes, Lynne Salop 1931- *ConAu 106*

Hawes, William 1931- *ConAu 77*

Hawgood, John Arkas 1905-1971 *ConAu 104*

Hawi, Khalil 1925- *EncWL 2*

Hawk, Affable *LongCTC*

Hawk, Alex *ConAu X, IntAu&W 82X,*

WrDr 84

Hawk, Grace E 1905-1983 *ConAu 110*

Hawk, Virginia Driving *SmATA 8*

Hawke, David Freeman 1923- *ConAu 102*

Hawke, Gary Richard 1942- *ConAu 102, WrDr 84*

Hawke, Nancy *ConAu X*

Hawken, William R 1917- *ConAu 5NR, –9R*

Hawkes, Christopher 1905- *ConAu 105, IntAu&W 82*

Hawkes, Glenn R 1919- *ConAu 17R*

Hawkes, Jacquetta 1910- *ConAu 69, IntAu&W 82, LongCTC, TwCA SUP, TwCSFW, WrDr 84*

Hawkes, John *DrAP&F 83*

Hawkes, John 1925- *ConAu 1R, –2NR, ConDr 82, ConLC 1, –2, –3, –4, –7, –9, –14, –15, –27[port], ConNov 82, CroCD, DcLB Y80A[port], –2, –7[port], DcLEL 1940, EncWL 2, IntAu&W 82, ModAL, ModAL SUP, WhoTwCL, WorAu, WrDr 84*

Hawkes, Terence 1932- *ConAu 17R*

Hawkesworth, Eric 1921- *ConAu 29R, SmATA 13, WrDr 84*

Hawkesworth, John 1920- *IntAu&W 82*

Hawking, Stephen William 1942- *WrDr 84*

Hawkins, A Desmond *ConAu X*

Hawkins, Sir Anthony Hope 1863-1933 *LongCTC, TwCA, TwCA SUP*

Hawkins, Arthur 1903- *ConAu 8NR, –21R, SmATA 19*

Hawkins, Bobbie Louise *DrAP&F 83*

Hawkins, Brett W 1937- *ConAu 11NR, –21R*

Hawkins, Desmond 1908- *ConAu 9NR, –65*

Hawkins, Edward H 1934- *ConAu 85*

Hawkins, Frances P 1913- *ConAu 105*

Hawkins, Gerald Stanley 1928- *ConAu 17R, WrDr 84*

Hawkins, Gordon 1919- *ConAu 41R*

Hawkins, Hugh 1929- *ConAu 1R*

Hawkins, Hunt *DrAP&F 83*

Hawkins, Jim 1944- *ConAu 73*

Hawkins, John C 1948- *ConAu 106*

Hawkins, John Noel 1944- *ConAu 8NR, –61*

Hawkins, Odie 1937- *ConAu 57, LivgBAA*

Hawkins, Peter S 1945- *ConAu 110*

Hawkins, Quail 1905- *ConAu 17R, SmATA 6*

Hawkins, Robert 1923- *ConAu 21R*

Hawkins, Tom *DrAP&F 83*

Hawkins, William 1912- *ConAu 1R*

Hawkinson, John Samuel 1912- *ConAu 5R, –21R, SmATA 4*

Hawkinson, Lucy 1924-1971 *ConAu 103, SmATA 21[port]*

Hawks, Howard 1896-1977 *ConAu 73*

Hawksworth, David Leslie 1946- *IntAu&W 82*

Hawksworth, Henry D 1933- *ConAu 73*

Hawksworth, Marjorie *DrAP&F 83*

Hawley, Amos H 1910- *ConAu 37R*

Hawley, Blair 1924- *WrDr 84*

Hawley, Cameron 1905-1969 *ConAu 1R, –25R*

Hawley, Donald Frederick 1921- *ConAu 108*

Hawley, Donald Thomas 1923- *ConAu 11NR, –65*

Hawley, Ellis W 1929- *ConAu 7NR, –17R*

Hawley, Florence M *ConAu X*

Hawley, Gessner G 1906?-1983 *ConAu 110*

Hawley, Henrietta Ripperger 1890?-1974 *ConAu 49*

Hawley, Isabel Lockwood 1935- *ConAu 7NR, –57*

Hawley, Jane Stouder 1936- *ConAu 21R*

Hawley, John Stratton 1941- *ConAu 110*

Hawley, Mabel C *ConAu P-2, SmATA 1*

Hawley, Michael James 1953- *ConAmTC*

Hawley, Robert Coit 1933- *ConAu 7NR, –57*

Haworth, Bobs Cogill 1904- *CreCan 1*

Haworth, Don *ConDr 82B*

Haworth, Frieda Mary *WrDr 84*

Haworth, Lawrence 1926- *ConAu 5R*

Haworth, Mary *ConAu X*

Haworth, Peter 1889- *CreCan 2*

Haworth, Zema Barbara Cogill 1904- *CreCan 1*

Haworth-Booth, Michael 1896- *ConAu 5R, IntAu&W 82*

Haws, Duncan 1921- *ConAu 97*

Hawthorn, Jeremy 1942- *ConAu 97*

Hawthorn, John Raymond 1911- *WrDr 84*

Hawthorn, Maggie 1929- *ConAmTC*

Hawthorne, Jennie 1916- *ConAu P-1, WrDr 84*

Hawthorne, Julian 1846-1934 *TwCA*

Hawton, Hector 1901- *ConAu 13R, WrDr 84*

Haxton, Brooks *DrAP&F 83*

Hay, David M 1935- *ConAu 53*

Hay, Dennis 1952- *ConAu 105*

Hay, Denys 1915- *ConAu 13R, IntAu&W 82, WrDr 84*

Hay, Eloise K 1926- *ConAu 9R*

Hay, Gyula 1900-1975 *CIDMEL 80, CroCD, ModWD, WorAu 1970*

Hay, Ian 1876-1952 *LongCTC, TwCA, TwCA SUP, TwCWr*

Hay, Jacob 1920- *ConAu 25R*

Hay, James G 1936- *ConAu 4NR, –53*

Hay, John 1838-1905 *ConAu 108*

Hay, John 1915- *ConAu 9NR, –65, IntWWP 82, SmATA 13*

Hay, John 1928- *ConSFA*

Hay, Julius 1900-1975 *CnMD*

Hay, Leon Edwards *ConAu 25R*

Hay, Nigel *IntAu&W 82X*

Hay, Peter 1935- *ConAu 21R*

Hay, Robert Dean 1921- *ConAu 8NR, –61*

Hay, Sara Henderson 1906- *ConAu P-1*

Hay, Stephen 1925- *WrDr 84*

Hay, Stephen N 1925- *ConAu 5R*

Hay, Thomas Robson 1888-1974 *ConAu 49*

Hay, Timothy *ConAu X*

Hay, Walter S 1904- *IntWWP 82*

Haya DeLaTorre, Victor Raul 1895-1979 *ConAu 89*

Hayakawa, S I 1906- *ConAu 13R, WrDr 84*

Hayakawa, Samuel Ichiye 1906- *TwCA SUP*

Hayami, Yujiro 1932- *ConAu 77*

Hayaseca Y Eizaguirre, Jorge *ConAu X*

Hayashi, Fumiko 1904-1951 *EncWL 2*

Hayashi, Shuseki *ConAu X*

Hayashi, Tetsumaro 1929- *ConAu 37R, IntAu&W 82, WrDr 84*

Hayat, Ruhi *IntAu&W 82X*

Haycock, Ken Roy 1948- *ConAu 104*

Haycox, Ernest 1899-1950 *FifWWr, TwCA SUP, TwCWW*

Haycraft, Howard 1905- *ConAu 21R, SmATA 6*

Haycraft, Molly Costain 1911- *ConAu 13R, SmATA 6*

Hayden, Albert A 1923- *ConAu 33R, WrDr 84*

Hayden, C Gervin *ConAu X*

Hayden, Carl T 1877-1972 *ConAu 33R*

Hayden, Dolores 1945- *ConAu 9NR, –65*

Hayden, Donald E 1915- *ConAu 10NR, –25R, WrDr 84*

Hayden, Eric William 1919- *ConAu 2NR, –5R, WrDr 84*

Hayden, Howard K 1930- *ConAu 17R*

Hayden, Jay *ConAu X*

Hayden, Jay G 1884-1971 *ConAu 89*

Hayden, John O 1932- *ConAu 10NR, –25R*

Hayden, Julia Elizabeth 1939?-1981 *ConAu 104*

Hayden, Julie *ConAu X*

Hayden, Martin S 1912- *ConAu 69*

Hayden, Naura 1942- *ConAu 73*

Hayden, Robert C 1937- *ConAu 69, SmATA 28, WrDr 84*

Hayden, Robert E 1913-1980 *ConAu 69, –97, ConLC 5, –9, –14, ConP 80, Conv 1, CroCAP, DcLB 5[port], DcLEL 1940, LivgBAA, ModBlW, SmATA 19, –26N, WorAu 1970*

Hayden, Thomas E 1939- *ConAu 107*

Hayden, Tom *ConAu X*

Hayden, Torey L 1951- *ConAu 103*

Haydn, Hiram Collins 1907-1973 *ConAu 45, ConAu P-1, DcLEL 1940, TwCA SUP*

Haydon, A Eustace 1880-1975 *ConAu 61*

Haydon, Glen 1896-1966 *ConAu P-1*

Haydon, June 1932- *ConAu 109*

Hayek, Friedrich August Von 1899- *ConAu 93, LongCTC, TwCA SUP, WrDr 84*

Hayes, Alden C 1916- *ConAu 57*

Hayes, Alfred 1911- *ConAu 106, ModAL, TwCA SUP*

Hayes, Ann *DrAP&F 83*

Hayes, Ann Louise 1924- *ConAu 25R, IntWWP 82*

Hayes, Anna Hansen 1886- *ConAu 1R*

Hayes, Bartlett H 1904- *ConAu 77*

Hayes, Billy *ConAu 97*

Hayes, Carlton Joseph Huntley 1882-1964 *ConAu 1R, –3NR, LongCTC, SmATA 11, TwCA SUP*

Hayes, Charles L *DrAP&F 83*

Hayes, Dorsha *ConAu 77, DrAP&F 83*
Hayes, Douglas A 1918- *ConAu 1R*
Hayes, E Nelson 1920- *ConAu 29R*
Hayes, Edward C 1937- *ConAu 45*
Hayes, Edward L 1931- *ConAu 29R*
Hayes, Francis Clement 1904- *ConAu P-2*
Hayes, Geoffrey 1947- *ConAu 9NR, –65,
SmATA 26[port]*
Hayes, Grace Person 1919- *ConAu 33R*
Hayes, Harold T P 1926- *ConAu 69*
Hayes, James T 1923- *ConAu 29R*
Hayes, John F 1904- *ConAu P-1, CreCan 1,
SmATA 11, WrDr 84*
Hayes, John F 1904-1980 *TwCCW 83*
Hayes, John Haralson 1934- *ConAu 69*
Hayes, John Michael 1919- *ConAu 108,
DcLB 26*
Hayes, John P 1949- *ConAu 93*
Hayes, John R 1929- *ConAu 108*
Hayes, John S 1910-1981 *ConAu 108*
Hayes, Joseph 1918- *ConAu 7NR, –17R,
DcLEL 1940, TwCCr&M 80, WrDr 84*
Hayes, Louis D 1940- *ConAu 29R, WrDr 84*
Hayes, Margaret 1925- *ConAu 21R*
Hayes, Mary Anne 1956- *ConAu 105*
Hayes, Mary-Rose 1939- *ConAu 102*
Hayes, Nelson Taylor 1903-1971 *ConAu 1R,
–33R*
Hayes, Paul J 1922- *ConAu 57*
Hayes, Paul Martin 1942- *ConAu 77,
IntAu&W 82, WrDr 84*
Hayes, Ralph 1927- *ConAu 21R*
Hayes, Robert M 1926- *ConAu 9R*
Hayes, Samuel Perkins 1910- *ConAu 3NR, –5R,
WrDr 84*
Hayes, Sheila 1937- *ConAu 106*
Hayes, Timothy *TwCWW*
Hayes, Wayland Jackson 1893-1972 *ConAu P-1*
Hayes, Will *ConAu 5R, SmATA 7*
Hayes, William Dimitt 1913- *ConAu 5R,
SmATA 8*
Hayes, Wilson *ConAu X*
Hayford, Fred Kwesi 1937- *ConAu 45*
Hayford, Taria *ConAu X*
Hayley Bell, Mary *ConAu 25R*
Hayman *ConAu X*
Hayman, Carol Bessent 1927- *ConAu 53,
WrDr 84*
Hayman, David 1927- *ConAu 7NR, –17R,
WrDr 84*
Hayman, Jane *DrAP&F 83*
Hayman, John L, Jr. 1929- *ConAu 25R*
Hayman, LeRoy 1916- *ConAu 85*
Hayman, Max 1908- *ConAu 17R*
Hayman, Ronald 1932- *ConAu 25R,
IntAu&W 82, WrDr 84*
Hayman, Walter Kurt 1926- *IntAu&W 82,
WrDr 84*
Haymes, Robert C 1931- *ConAu 33R*
Hayn, Annette *DrAP&F 83*
Hayn, Annette 1922- *ConAu 65*
Hayna, Lois Beebe *DrAP&F 83*
Haynes, Alfred H 1910- *ConAu 5R*
Haynes, Anna *ConAu X*
Haynes, Anne *ConAu X*
Haynes, Betsy 1937- *ConAu 8NR, –57*
Haynes, Dorothy K 1918- *WrDr 84*
Haynes, Elizabeth Sterling d1957 *CreCan 2*
Haynes, Glynn W 1936- *ConAu 65*
Haynes, James 1932- *ConAu 110*
Haynes, Linda *ConAu X*
Haynes, Maria S 1912- *ConAu 25R*
Haynes, Mary *DrAP&F 83*
Haynes, Pat *ConAu X*
Haynes, Renee Oriana *WrDr 84*
Haynes, Renee Oriana 1906- *ConAu 49,
IntAu&W 82X*
Haynes, Richard F 1935- *ConAu 49*
Haynes, Robert Talmadge, Jr. 1926- *ConAu 1R*
Haynes, Robert Vaughn 1929- *ConAu 41R,
IntAu&W 82*
Haynes, Sybille 1926- *WrDr 84*
Haynes, Sybille Edith 1926- *ConAu 57*
Haynes, William Warren 1921- *ConAu 5R,
–8NR*
Haynes Dixon, Margaret Rumer 1907-
IntWWP 82
Hays, Brooks 1898- *WrDr 84*
Hays, Brooks 1898-1981 *ConAu 105,
ConAu P-1*
Hays, David G 1928- *ConAu 21R*
Hays, Elinor Rice *ConAu 1R*

Hays, H R 1904-1980 *ConAu 105, –81,
ConP 80, SmATA 26[port]*
Hays, Helen Ireland 1903- *ConAu 61*
Hays, Hoffman Reynolds 1904- *TwCA SUP*
Hays, Janice Nicholson 1929- *WrDr 84*
Hays, Paul R 1903-1980 *ConAu 93, ConAu P-2*
Hays, Peter L 1938- *ConAu 33R, WrDr 84*
Hays, R Vernon 1902- *ConAu 89*
Hays, Richard D 1942- *ConAu 37R*
Hays, Robert Glenn 1935- *ConAu 53*
Hays, Samuel Pfrimmer 1921- *ConAu 103*
Hays, Terence E 1942- *ConAu 69*
Hays, Wilma Pitchford 1909- *ConAu 1R, –5NR,
SmATA 1, –28[port], WrDr 84*
Haystead, Wesley 1942- *ConAu 6NR, –57*
Hayter, Alethea 1911- *ConAu 29R,
IntAu&W 82, WrDr 84*
Hayter, Earl W 1901- *ConAu 41R*
Hayter, Teresa *WrDr 84*
Hayter, William 1906- *WrDr 84*
Hayter, William Goodenough 1906- *ConAu 9NR*
Hayter, Sir William Goodenough 1906-
ConAu 21R
Haythorne, George Vickers 1909- *WrDr 84*
Haythornthwaite, Philip John 1951- *ConAu 103,
IntAu&W 82, WrDr 84*
Hayton, Richard Neil 1916- *ConAu 57*
Haytov, Nicolay 1919- *IntAu&W 82*
Hayward, Brooke 1937- *ConAu 81*
Hayward, Charles Harold 1898- *ConAu 7NR,
–9R*
Hayward, Jack 1931- *ConAu 6NR, –57*
Hayward, John 1905-1965 *LongCTC*
Hayward, John F 1916-1983 *ConAu 109*
Hayward, John F 1918- *ConAu 5R*
Hayward, John Forest 1916- *WrDr 84*
Hayward, John Forrest 1916- *ConAu 9R*
Hayward, Max 1925?-1979 *ConAu 85, –93*
Hayward, Richard *ConAu X*
Hayward, Richard 1893- *ConAu P-1*
Haywood, Carolyn 1898- *ConAu 5R, –5NR,
SmATA 1, –29[port], TwCCW 83,
WrDr 84*
Haywood, Charles 1904- *ConAu 1R, WrDr 84*
Haywood, Dixie 1933- *ConAu 105*
Haywood, H Carl 1931- *ConAu 3NR, –49*
Haywood, Harry *ConAu X*
Haywood, John Alfred 1913- *ConAu 17R*
Haywood, Richard Mansfield 1905-1977
ConAu 69, ConAu P-2
Haywood, Richard Mowbray 1933- *ConAu 25R,
IntAu&W 82, WrDr 84*
Hazak, Yehiel 1936- *IntWWP 82*
Hazam, Louis J 1911-1983 *ConAu 110*
Hazard, Geoffrey Edward 1934- *IntWWP 82*
Hazard, Jack *ConAu X, WrDr 84*
Hazard, John Newbold 1909- *ConAu 1R,
WrDr 84*
Hazard, Laurence *ConAu X*
Hazard, Leland 1893- *ConAu 17R*
Hazard, Patrick D 1927- *ConAu 13R*
Hazard, Paul 1878-1944 *CIDMEL 80*
Hazel, Robert *DrAP&F 83*
Hazelrigg, Meredith K 1942- *ConAu 33R*
Hazelton, Alexander *ConAu X*
Hazelton, Roger 1909- *ConAu 1R, –1NR*
Hazelwood-Brady, Anne *DrAP&F 83*
Hazen, Allen Tracy 1904- *ConAu P-1*
Hazen, Barbara Shook 1930- *ConAu 105,
SmATA 27[port]*
Hazlehurst, Cameron 1941- *ConAu 103,
IntAu&W 82, WrDr 84*
Hazlett, Bill *ConAu X*
Hazlett, William Scott 1931-1983 *ConAu 110*
Hazlitt, Henry 1894- *ConAu 3NR, –5R,
IntAu&W 82, WrDr 84*
Hazlitt, Joseph *ConAu X*
Hazo, Robert G 1931- *ConAu 21R*
Hazo, Samuel *DrAP&F 83*
Hazo, Samuel 1928- *ConAu 5R, –8NR,
ConP 80, IntWWP 82, WrDr 84*
Hazzard, Lowell B 1898-1978 *ConAu 77*
Hazzard, Mary *DrAP&F 83*
Hazzard, Mary 1928- *ConAu 105*
Hazzard, Shirley *DrAP&F 83*
Hazzard, Shirley 1931- *ConAu 4NR, –9R,
ConLC 18, ConNov 82, DcLB Y82B[port],
DcLEL 1940, IntAu&W 82, WorAu 1970,
WrDr 84*
Hc *IntAu&W 82X*
Heacox, Cecil E 1903- *ConAu 101*
Head, Ann *ConAu X*

Head, Bessie 1937- *ConAu 29R,
ConLC 25[port], ConNov 82, DcLEL 1940,
IntAu&W 82, WrDr 84*
Head, Bruce 1931- *CreCan 1*
Head, Constance 1939- *ConAu 37R,
IntAu&W 82, WrDr 84*
Head, Edith 1898?-1981 *ConAu 105*
Head, Gay *ConAu X, SmATA X*
Head, George Bruce 1931- *CreCan 1*
Head, Gwen *DrAP&F 83*
Head, Gwen Tandy 1940- *ConAu 89,
IntWWP 82*
Head, K Maynard 1938- *ConAu 110*
Head, Lee 1931- *ConAu 65*
Head, Lee 1931-1983 *ConAu 110*
Head, Matthew *WrDr 84*
Head, Matthew 1907- *ConAu X,
TwCCr&M 80, WorAu*
Head, Richard G 1938- *ConAu 53*
Head, Robert V 1929- *ConAu 41R*
Head, Sydney W 1913- *ConAu 9NR, –65*
Head, Timothy E 1934- *ConAu 13R*
Heading, Roger 1930- *WrDr 84*
Headings, Mildred J 1908- *ConAu 37R*
Headington, Christopher 1930- *WrDr 84*
Headington, Christopher John Magenis 1930-
ConAu 106
Headlam, Walter George 1866-1908 *TwCA*
Headley, Elizabeth *TwCCW 83*
Headley, Elizabeth 1909- *ConAu X, SmATA X*
Headstrom, Richard 1902- *ConAu 1R, –2NR,
–77, SmATA 8, WrDr 84*
Heady, Earl O 1916- *ConAu 8NR, –17R*
Heady, Eleanor B 1917- *WrDr 84*
Heady, Eleanor Butler 1917- *ConAu 41R,
SmATA 7, –8*
Heady, Harold F 1916- *WrDr 84*
Heady, Harold Franklin 1916- *ConAu 53*
Heafford, Michael R 1938- *WrDr 84*
Heagney, Anne 1901- *ConAu 5R*
Heal, Edith 1903- *ConAu 1R, –2NR,
SmATA 7*
Heal, Jeanne 1917- *ConAu P-1, IntAu&W 82*
Heald, Charles Brehmer 1882-1974 *ConAu 49*
Heald, Edward Thornton 1885- *ConAu 17R*
Heald, Tim 1944- *TwCCr&M 80, WrDr 84*
Heald, Timothy Villiers 1944- *ConAu 2NR, –49,
IntAu&W 82*
Healey, B J *ConAu X*
Healey, Ben 1908- *WrDr 84*
Healey, Ben J 1908- *ConAu 77*
Healey, Benjamin James 1908- *IntAu&W 82*
Healey, Brooks *ConAu X, IntAu&W 82X,
SmATA X*
Healey, Denis 1917- *WrDr 84*
Healey, Denis Winston 1917- *ConAu 110*
Healey, F G 1903- *ConAu P-2*
Healey, James 1936- *ConAu 53*
Healey, James Stewart 1931- *ConAu 57*
Healey, Larry 1927- *ConAu 101*
Healey, Robert 1921- *ConAu 61*
Healy, David Frank 1926- *ConAu 17R,
WrDr 84*
Healy, Eloise Klein *DrAP&F 83*
Healy, Fleming 1911- *ConAu 5R*
Healy, George Robert 1923- *ConAu 17R*
Healy, George W, Jr. 1905- *ConAu 69*
Healy, James N 1916- *IntAu&W 82*
Healy, John D 1921- *ConAu 93*
Healy, Sister Kathleen *ConAu 61*
Healy, Patrick, III 1910- *ConAu 110*
Healy, Paul Francis 1915- *ConAu 17R*
Healy, Richard J 1916- *ConAu 25R, WrDr 84*
Healy, Sean D 1927- *ConAu 11NR, –25R*
Healy, Timothy S 1923- *ConAu 41R*
Heaney, John J 1925- *ConAu 5NR, –9R*
Heaney, Seamus 1939- *ConAu 85, ConLC 5, –7,
–14, –25[port], ConP 80, DcLEL 1940,
EncWL 2, ModBrL SUP, WorAu 1970,
WrDr 84*
Heap, Desmond 1907- *ConAu P-1,
IntAu&W 82, WrDr 84*
Heaps, Willard A 1908- *ConAu 85*
Heaps, Willard Allison 1909- *SmATA 26[port]*
Heard, Alexander 1917- *ConAu 17R*
Heard, Gerald 1889-1971 *ConAu 29R,
ConAu P-2, LongCTC, TwCA,
TwCA SUP, TwCCr&M 80, TwCSFW*
Heard, H F 1889-1971 *ConAu X, LongCTC,
TwCCr&M 80, TwCSFW*
Heard, Henry FitzGerald 1889-1971 *TwCA,
TwCA SUP*

Heard, J Norman 1922- *ConAu 9R*
Heard, Nathan Cliff 1936- *ConAu 53, LivgBAA*
Hearder, Harry 1924- *ConAu 5R*
Hearn, Charles R 1937- *ConAu 77*
Hearn, Janice W 1938- *ConAu 65*
Hearn, John 1920- *ConAu 97*
Hearn, Lafcadio 1850-1904 *ConAu 105, ModAL, TwCLC 9[port]*
Hearn, Sneed *ConAu X*
Hearnden, Arthur 1931- *ConAu 65*
Hearne, John 1926- *ConNov 82, DcLEL 1940, LongCTC, WorAu, WrDr 84*
Hearne, Reginald 1919- *WrDr 84*
Hearnshaw, Leslie Spencer 1907- *ConAu 89*
Hearon, Shelby *DrAP&F 83*
Hearon, Shelby 1931- *AuNews 2, ConAu 25R*
Hearsey, John Edward Nicholl 1928- *ConAu 5R, -8NR, IntAu&W 82, WrDr 84*
Hearst, George Randolph 1904-1972 *ConAu 89*
Hearst, James *DrAP&F 83*
Hearst, James 1900- *ConAu 85*
Hearst, William Randolph 1863-1951 *DcLB 25[port], LongCTC*
Heartman, Harold *ConAu X*
Heasman, Kathleen Joan 1913- *ConAu P-1, WrDr 84*
Heater, Derek Benjamin 1931- *ConAu 6NR, -57, IntAu&W 82, WrDr 84*
Heath, Beth LaPointe 1906- *IntWWP 82*
Heath, Catherine 1924- *ConAu 93, DcLB 14[port], IntAu&W 82, WrDr 84*
Heath, Charles Chastain 1921- *ConAu 69*
Heath, Douglas H 1925- *ConAu 17R*
Heath, Dwight B 1930- *ConAu 7NR, -17R, WrDr 84*
Heath, Edward 1916- *ConAu 33R, IntAu&W 82, WrDr 84*
Heath, G Louis 1944- *ConAu 37R, WrDr 84*
Heath, Harry E, Jr. 1919- *ConAu 85*
Heath, James 1920- *ConAu 17R*
Heath, Jim F 1931- *ConAu 29R*
Heath, Monica *ConAu X*
Heath, Monroe 1899-1966 *ConAu P-1*
Heath, Nita *IntAu&W 82X*
Heath, Peter *ConSFA*
Heath, Peter 1922- *ConAu 41R*
Heath, Robert William 1931- *ConAu 13R*
Heath, Roy 1917- *ConAu 9R*
Heath, Roy A K 1926- *ConAu 106, ConNov 82, WrDr 84*
Heath, Royton Edward 1907- *ConAu 9R*
Heath, Sandra *ConAu X, WrDr 84*
Heath, Sharon *TwCRGW, WrDr 84*
Heath, Terrence 1936- *ConAu 97*
Heath, Veronica 1927- *ConAu X, SmATA X, WrDr 84*
Heath, William *DrAP&F 83*
Heath, William W 1929- *WrDr 84*
Heath, William Webster 1929- *ConAu 1R, IntAu&W 82*
Heath-Stubbs, John 1918- *WrDr 84*
Heath-Stubbs, John Francis Alexander 1918- *ConAu 13R, ConP 80, DcLEL 1940, IntWWP 82, LongCTC, ModBrL, TwCA SUP, TwCWr*
Heathcott, Mary *WrDr 84*
Heathcott, Mary 1914- *ConAu X*
Heather, George *IntAu&W 82X*
Heaton, Charles Huddleston 1928- *ConAu 1R, WrDr 84*
Heaton, Eric William 1920- *ConAu 61, IntAu&W 82*
Heaton, Herbert 1890-1973 *ConAu 5R, -41R*
Heaton, Peter 1919- *ConAu 104*
Heaton, Rose Henniker 1884-1975 *ConAu 61*
Heaton-Ward, William Alan 1919- *ConAu 102, WrDr 84*
Heatter, Gabriel 1890-1972 *ConAu 89*
Heaven, Constance 1911- *ConAu 2NR, -49, SmATA 7, TwCRGW, WrDr 84*
Hebald, Carol *DrAP&F 83*
Hebard, Edna L 1913- *ConAu 9R*
Hebb, D O 1904- *ConAu 1R, -2NR, WrDr 84*
Hebblethwaite, Brian Leslie 1939- *ConAu 109*
Hebblethwaite, Peter 1930- *ConAu 69, WrDr 84*
Hebden, Mark *ConAu X, IntAu&W 82X, WrDr 84*
Hebert, Adrien 1890- *CreCan 2*
Hebert, Anne 1916- *ConAu 85, ConLC 4, -13, CreCan 1, EncWL 2, ModCmwL, ModFrL, WorAu*

Hebert, Ernest 1941- *ConAu 102*
Hebert, F Edward 1901-1979 *ConAu 106, -110*
Hebert, Gabriel 1886-1963 *ConAu 1R*
Hebert, Henri 1884-1950 *CreCan 2*
Hebert, Jacques 1923- *ConAu 11NR, -25R*
Hebert, Louis Phillippe 1850-1917 *CreCan 1*
Hebert, Marjolaine *CreCan 2*
Hebert, Paul 1924- *CreCan 2*
Hebert, Pierre 1944- *CreCan 2*
Hebert, Tom 1938- *ConAu 69*
Hebron, Chris *IntWWP 82X*
Hebson, Ann Porter 1925- *ConAu 17R*
Hechinger, Fred M 1920- *ConAu 77, WrDr 84*
Hechler, Ken 1914- *ConAu 109*
Hecht, Anthony *DrAP&F 83*
Hecht, Anthony 1923- *CnMWL, ConAu 6NR, -9R, ConLC 8, -13, -19, ConP 80, CroCAP, DcLB 5[port], DcLEL 1940, WhoTwCL, WorAu, WrDr 84*
Hecht, Ben 1893?-1964 *CnMD, ConAmA, LongCTC, TwCA, TwCA SUP*
Hecht, Ben 1894-1964 *ConAu 85, ConLC 8, DcLB 7[port], -9[port], -25[port], -26[port], ModWD*
Hecht, George J 1895-1980 *ConAu 97, SmATA 22N*
Hecht, Henri Joseph 1922- *ConAu 29R, SmATA 9*
Hecht, James L 1926- *ConAu 33R*
Hecht, Joseph C 1924- *ConAu 29R*
Hecht, Marie B 1918- *ConAu 21R*
Hecht, Roger *DrAP&F 83*
Hecht, Roger 1926- *ConAu 17R*
Hecht, Warren Jay 1946- *ConAu 103, MichAu 80*
Hechter, Michael 1943- *ConAu 69, WrDr 84*
Hechtkopf, Henryk 1910- *SmATA 17*
Hechtlinger, Adelaide 1914- *ConAu 29R*
Heck, Bessie Holland 1911- *ConAu 5R, SmATA 26[port]*
Heck, Frank H 1904- *ConAu 69*
Heck, Harold J 1906- *ConAu 41R*
Heck, Peter M 1937- *ConAu 53*
Heck, Suzanne Wright 1939- *ConAu 53*
Heckart, Beverly Anne 1938- *ConAu 103*
Heckel, Robert V 1925- *ConAu 9R*
Heckelmann, Charles N 1913- *ConAu 49, TwCWW, WrDr 84*
Heckert, J Brooks 1893- *ConAu 5R*
Heckler, Jonellen 1943- *ConAu 109*
Heckman, Hazel Melissa 1904- *ConAu 21R*
Heckman, William O 1921- *ConAu 21R*
Hecko, Frantisek 1905-1960 *ModSL 2*
Heckscher, August 1913- *ASpks, ConAu 1R*
Heckscher, William 1904- *WrDr 84*
Hed *IntAu&W 82X*
Hedayat, Sadeq 1903-1951 *EncWL 2*
Hedayat, Sadiq *WorAu 1970*
Hedberg, Tor Harald 1862-1931 *CnMD*
Hedde, Wilhelmina Genevava 1895- *ConAu 5R*
Hedden, Walter Page 1898?-1976 *ConAu 65*
Hedden, Worth Tuttle 1896- *ConAu P-2*
Hedderwick, Mairi 1939- *SmATA 30[port]*
Hedge, Leslie 1922- *ConAu 9R*
Hedgeman, Anna Arnold 1899- *ConAu P-1*
Hedges, Bob A 1919- *ConAu 45*
Hedges, David 1930- *ConAu 45*
Hedges, Doris Ryde 1900- *CreCan 1*
Hedges, Elaine R 1927- *ConAu 7NR, -57*
Hedges, Joseph *WrDr 84*
Hedges, Joseph 1936- *ConAu X*
Hedges, Sid G 1897-1974 *ConAu 4NR, SmATA 28[port]*
Hedges, Sidney George 1897- *ConAu 9R*
Hedges, Trimble 1906- *ConAu P-2*
Hedges, Ursula M 1940- *ConAu 29R*
Hedges, William L 1923- *ConAu 37R*
Hedin, Mary *ConAu 103, DrAP&F 83*
Hedin, Robert *DrAP&F 83*
Hedin, Sven Anders Von 1865-1952 *TwCA, TwCA SUP*
Hedley, Ann *DrAP&F 83*
Hedley, George 1899- *ConAu P-2*
Hedley, Leslie Woolf *DrAP&F 83*
Hedley, Olwen 1912- *ConAu 9NR, -61, IntAu&W 82, WrDr 84*
Hedlund, Ronald D 1941- *ConAu 33R*
Hedman Iwan *IntAu&W 82X*
Hedman-Morelius, Iwan 1931- *IntAu&W 82*
Hedore, Win *CreCan 2*
Hedrick, Addie M 1903- *ConAu P-2*
Hedrick, Basil C 1932- *ConAu 33R*

Hedrick, Floyd 1927- *WrDr 84*
Hedrick, Floyd Dudley 1927- *ConAu 33R*
Hedrick, Joan Doran 1944- *ConAu 107*
Hedrick, Travis K 1904?-1977 *ConAu 69*
Hedrick, Ulysses Prentiss 1870-1951 *MichAu 80*
Heefner, David Kerry 1945- *NatPD 81[port]*
Heeley, Desmond 1931- *CreCan 1*
Heeney, Brian 1933- *ConAu 89*
Heer, David MacAlpine 1930- *ConAu 13R, WrDr 84*
Heer, Nancy Whittier *ConAu 33R*
Heeresma, Heere 1932- *ConAu 25R*
Heermance, J Noel 1939- *ConAu 25R*
Heerwagen, Paul K 1895- *ConAu 29R, WrDr 84*
Heese, Marie 1942- *IntAu&W 82*
Heezen, Bruce C 1924-1977 *ConAu 49, -69*
Heffer, Eric Samuel 1922- *IntAu&W 82*
Hefferman, Thomas 1939- *IntAu&W 82*
Heffern, Richard 1950- *ConAu 61*
Heffernan, James A W 1939- *ConAu 25R*
Heffernan, Michael *DrAP&F 83*
Heffernan, Michael 1942- *ConAu 77*
Heffernan, Paul 1905?-1983 *ConAu 110*
Heffernan, Thomas *DrAP&F 83*
Heffernan, Thomas Farel 1933- *ConAu 107*
Heffernan, Thomas Patrick Carroll 1939- *ConAu 81*
Heffernan, William A 1937- *ConAu 25R*
Heffley, Wayne 1927- *ConAu 9R*
Heffner, Richard D 1925- *ConAu 69*
Heffron, Dorris 1944- *ConAu 49, WrDr 84*
Hefley, James C 1930- *ConAu 7NR, -13R*
Heflin, Donald *ConAu X*
Hefner, Hugh 1926- *AuNews 1, ConAu 110*
Hefner, Paul *ConAu X*
Hefter, Richard 1942- *ConAu 107, SmATA 31[port]*
Hefti, Flora McKinney 1907- *IntWWP 82*
Hegarty, Edward J 1891- *ConAu 1R, -5NR*
Hegarty, Ellen 1918- *ConAu 37R*
Hegarty, Sister M Loyola *ConAu X*
Hegarty, Reginald Beaton 1906-1973 *ConAu 41R, ConAu P-1, SmATA 10*
Hegarty, Walter 1922- *ConAu 65, WrDr 84*
Hegedus, Geza 1912- *IntAu&W 82*
Hegel, Richard 1927- *ConAu 6NR, -57*
Hegel, Robert Earl 1943- *ConAu 108*
Hegeler, Sten 1923- *ConAu 107, IntAu&W 82, WrDr 84*
Hegeman, Elizabeth Blair 1942- *ConAu 61*
Hegeman, Mary Theodore 1907- *IntAu&W 82, WrDr 84*
Heger, Theodore Ernest 1907- *ConAu 33R*
Hegesippus *ConAu X, WrDr 84*
Heggelbacher, Othmar 1912- *IntAu&W 82*
Heggelund, Kjell 1932- *IntWWP 82*
Heggen, Thomas O 1919-1949 *TwCA SUP*
Heggoy, Alf Andrew 1938- *ConAu 37R*
Hegi, Ursula *DrAP&F 83*
Hegi, Ursula 1946- *ConAu 104*
Heginbotham, Stanley J 1938- *ConAu 106*
Heglar, Mary Schnall 1934- *ConAu 49*
Hegner, William Edward 1928- *ConAu 93, IntAu&W 82*
Hegstad, Roland R 1926- *ConAu 57*
Hegyi, Erzsebet 1927- *IntAu&W 82*
Heiber, Helmut 1924- *ConAu 49*
Heiberg, Gunnar Edvard Rode 1857-1929 *CIDMEL 80, CnMD, ModWD, WorAu*
Heiby, Walter A 1918- *ConAu 21R*
Heichberger, Robert Lee 1930- *ConAu 53*
Heicher, Merlo K W 1882-1967 *ConAu P-1*
Heidbreder, Margaret Ann *ConAu X*
Heide, Florence Parry 1919- *ConAu 93, SmATA 32[port], TwCCW 83*
Heide, Robert 1939- *ConAu 103*
Heidegger, Martin 1889-1976 *CIDMEL 80, ConAu 65, -81, ConLC 24[port], LongCTC, TwCA SUP, TwCWr*
Heideman, Eugene P 1929- *ConAu 69*
Heiden, Carol A Wilhelm 1939- *ConAu 57*
Heiden, Heino 1923- *CreCan 2*
Heidenheim, Hanns H 1922- *IntAu&W 82*
Heidenreich, Charles Albert 1917- *ConAu 25R*
Heidenstam, Verner Von 1859-1940 *CIDMEL 80, ConAu 104, TwCA, TwCA SUP, TwCLC 5[port]*
Heiderstadt, Dorothy 1907- *ConAu 1R, -1NR, SmATA 6*
Heidi, Gloria *ConAu 69*
Heidingsfield, Myron S 1914-1969 *ConAu 1R,*

–103
Heidish, Marcy 1947- *DcLB Y82B[port]*
Heidish, Marcy Moran 1947- *ConAu 101*
Heie, Sigbjorn Helge 1945- *IntWWP 82*
Heiferman, Ronald Ian 1941- *ConAu 61*
Heifetz, Hank *DrAP&F 83*
Heifetz, Harold 1919- *ConAu 10NR, –25R, NatPD 81[port], WrDr 84*
Heifetz, Milton D 1921- *ConAu 57*
Heifner, Jack 1946- *ConAu 105, ConLC 11, NatPD 81[port]*
Heiges, P Myers 1887-1968 *ConAu P-1*
Heijermans, Herman 1864-1924 *CIDMEL 80, CnMD, EncWL 2, ModWD*
Heijke, John 1927- *ConAu 21R*
Heilbron, J L 1934- *ConAu 4NR, –53*
Heilbroner, Joan Knapp 1922- *ConAu 1R*
Heilbroner, Robert L *WrDr 84*
Heilbroner, Robert Louis 1919- *ConAu 1R, –4NR*
Heilbronner, Walter L 1924- *ConAu 25R*
Heilbrun, Carolyn G 1926- *ConAu 1NR, –45, ConLC 25, TwCCr&M 80, WrDr 84*
Heilbrunn, Otto 1906-1969 *ConAu P-1*
Heilesen, Eileen DeLynn *WrDr 84*
Heilig, Matthias R 1881- *ConAu P-2*
Heiliger, Edward Martin 1909- *ConAu 13R*
Heilman, Arthur 1914- *ConAu 5R, –5NR*
Heilman, Grant 1919- *ConAu 53*
Heilman, Joan Rattner *ConAu 6NR, –57*
Heilman, Robert B 1906- *WrDr 84*
Heilman, Robert Bechtold 1906- *ConAu 9NR, –13R, ConLCrt 82, IntAu&W 82*
Heilman, Samuel C 1946- *ConAu 69*
Heilner, VanCampen 1899-1970 *ConAu 29R*
Heim, Alice W 1913- *WrDr 84*
Heim, Alice Winifred 1913- *ConAu 33R*
Heim, Bruno Bernard 1911- *ConAu 89*
Heim, Emmy 1885-1954 *CreCan 2*
Heim, Ralph D 1895- *WrDr 84*
Heim, Ralph Daniel 1895- *ConAu 73*
Heiman, Ernest J 1930- *ConAu 4NR, –53*
Heiman, Grover George, Jr. 1920- *ConAu 5R, –6NR*
Heiman, Judith 1935- *ConAu 1R*
Heiman, Marcel 1909-1976 *ConAu 65*
Heimann, Susan 1940- *ConAu 33R*
Heimarck, Theodore 1906- *ConAu 5R*
Heimbeck, Raeburne S 1930- *ConAu 29R*
Heimberg, Marilyn Markham *ConAu X*
Heimdahl, Ralph 1909- *ConAu 69*
Heimer, Mel 1915-1971 *ConAu 4NR*
Heimer, Melvin Lytton 1915-1971 *ConAu 1R, –29R*
Heimert, Alan 1928- *ConAu 5R*
Heimler, Eugene 1922- *ConAu 8NR, –13R*
Heimlich, Henry Jay 1920- *ConAu 102*
Heimsath, Charles H 1928- *ConAu 17R*
Hein, Eleanor C 1933- *ConAu 61*
Hein, John 1921- *ConAu 1NR, –45*
Hein, Leonard William 1916- *ConAu 53*
Hein, Lucille Eleanor 1915- *ConAu 2NR, –5R, SmATA 20, WrDr 84*
Hein, Norvin 1914- *ConAu 61*
Hein, Piet 1905- *CIDMEL 80, ConAu 4NR, –49*
Heinberg, Paul 1924- *ConAu 45, IntWWP 82*
Heindel, Richard Heathcote 1912-1979 *ConAu 89*
Heine, Carl 1936- *ConAu 57*

Heine, Ralph W 1914- *ConAu 41R*
Heine, William C 1919- *ConAu 97*
Heineman, Benjamin Walter, Jr. 1944- *ConAu 105*
Heinemann, George Alfred 1918- *SmATA 31*
Heinemann, Katherine *DrAP&F 83*
Heinemann, Katherine 1918- *ConAu 77, IntWWP 82*
Heinemann, Larry *DrAP&F 83*
Heinemann, Larry C 1944- *ConAu 110*
Heinemann, William 1863-1920 *LongCTC*
Heinen, Hubert 1937- *ConAu 41R*
Heinesen, William 1900- *CIDMEL 80*
Heiney, Donald 1921- *ConAu 1R, –3NR, ConLC 9*
Heinke, Clarence H 1912- *ConAu 53*
Heinl, Nancy G 1916- *ConAu 81*
Heinl, Robert Debs, Jr. 1916-1979 *ConAu 4NR, –5R, –85*
Heinlein, Robert *DrAP&F 83*
Heinlein, Robert 1907- *WrDr 84*
Heinlein, Robert A 1907- *ConAu 1R, –1NR,*

ConLC 1, –3, –8, –14, –26[port], ConNov 82, ConSFA, DcLB 8[port], SmATA 9, TwCA SUP, TwCCW 83, TwCSFW, TwCWr
Heinrich, Bernd 1940- *ConAu 109*
Heinrich, Peggy *DrAP&F 83*
Heinrich, Willi 1920- *ConAu 93, IntAu&W 82, WorAu*
Heins, A James 1931- *ConAu 5R*
Heins, Ethel L 1918- *ConAu 102*
Heins, Henry Hardy 1923- *ConSFA*
Heins, Marjorie 1946- *ConAu 69*
Heins, Paul 1909- *ConAu 69, SmATA 13*
Heinsohn, A G, Jr. 1896- *ConAu P-1*
Heinsohn, George Edwin 1933- *WrDr 84*
Heintz, Ann Christine 1930- *ConAu 8NR, –61*
Heintz, Bonnie L 1924- *ConAu 69*
Heintz, John 1936- *ConAu 45*
Heintze, Carl 1922- *ConAu 57, SmATA 26[port]*
Heintzelman, Donald S 1938- *ConAu 93*
Heinz, G *ConAu X*
Heinz, W C 1915- *ConAu 4NR, –5R, SmATA 26[port], WrDr 84*
Heinz, William Frederick 1899- *ConAu 61*
Heinzelman, Kurt 1947- *ConAu 101*
Heinzelmann, Josef 1936- *IntAu&W 82*
Heinzen, Mildred *ConAu X*
Heinzerling, Larry E 1945- *ConAu 73*
Heinzman, George Melville 1916- *ConAu 1R*
Heiremans, Luis Alberto 1928-1964 *CroCD*
Heirich, Max 1931- *ConAu 29R*
Heise, David R 1937- *ConAu 89*
Heise, Edward Tyler 1912- *ConAu 1R*
Heise, Hans-Jurgen 1930- *IntAu&W 82, IntWWP 82*
Heise, Kenan 1933- *ConAu 57*
Heiseler, Bernt Von 1907- *CnMD, ModWD*
Heiseler, Henry Von 1875-1928 *ModWD*
Heisenberg, Werner 1901-1976 *ConAu 65*
Heiser, Charles B, Jr. 1920- *ConAu 45, WrDr 84*
Heiser, Victor George 1873-1972 *ConAu 33R*
Heiserman, Arthur Ray 1929-1975 *ConAu 1R, –103*
Heiserman, David L 1940- *ConAu 8NR, –61*
Heisey, Alan Milliken 1928- *ConAu 57*
Heiskell, John Netherland 1872-1972 *ConAu 89*
Heisler, Martin O 1938- *ConAu 45*
Heissenbuettel, Helmut 1921- *ConAu 81*
Heissenbuttel, Helmut 1921- *CIDMEL 80, EncWL 2, ModGL, WorAu 1970*
Heitler, Walter 1904-1981 *ConAu 8NR, –13R*
Heitman, Sidney 1924- *ConAu 9R*
Heitner, Robert R 1920- *ConAu 5R, WrDr 84*
Heitzmann, William Ray 1948- *ConAu 97, IntAu&W 82*
Heizer, Robert Fleming 1915-1979 *ConAu 102*
Hejinian, John Paull 1941- *WrDr 84*
Hejinian, Lyn *DrAP&F 83*
Hejmadi, Padma *DcLEL 1940*
Hejzlar, Zdenek 1921- *IntAu&W 82*
Hekker, Terry 1932- *ConAu 97*
Helbig, Alethea 1928- *ConAu 97*
Helbing, Lothar *IntAu&W 82X*
Helbing, Terry 1951- *ConAu 89*
Helbling, Hanno 1930- *IntAu&W 82*
Helbling, Robert E 1923- *ConAu 49*
Helbo, Andre 1947- *IntAu&W 82*
Helck, C Peter 1893- *ConAu 1R, –1NR*
Held, Claude 1936- *IntWWP 82*
Held, David 1951- *ConAu 110*
Held, Jack Preston 1926- *ConAu 33R*
Held, Jacqueline 1936- *ConAu 73*
Held, Joseph 1930- *ConAu 45*
Held, Julius Samuel 1905- *ConAu 103*
Held, Peter *WrDr 84*
Held, R Burnell 1921- *ConAu 33R*
Held, Ray E 1918- *ConAu 45*
Held, Richard Marx 1922- *ConAu 41R*
Held, Virginia P 1929- *ConAu 1R, –1NR, WrDr 84*
Helder, Dom *ConAu X*
Helder, Herberto 1930- *CIDMEL 80*
Heldman, Dan C 1943- *ConAu 110*
Heleniak, Kathryn Moore *ConAu 110*
Helfert, Erich A 1931- *ConAu 9R*
Helfert, Roy Rudolph 1936- *IntAu&W 82*
Helfgott, Daniel 1952- *ConAu 106*
Helfgott, Roy B 1925- *ConAu 81*
Helfman, Elizabeth S 1911- *ConAu 5R, –5NR, SmATA 3, WrDr 84*

Helfman, Harry Carmozin 1910- *ConAu 25R, SmATA 3, WrDr 84*
Helforth, John *ConAu X*
Helfritz, Hans 1902- *ConAu 41R*
Helgadottir, Gudrun 1935- *IntAu&W 82*
Helgason, Jon 1914- *IntAu&W 82*
Helgi, Johannes 1926- *IntAu&W 82*
Heliczer, Piero 1937- *IntWWP 82*
Helitzer, Florence 1928- *ConAu 17R*
Helka, Leena 1924- *IntAu&W 82*
Hellberg, Hans-Eric 1927- *ConAu 101, IntAu&W 82*
Hellegers, Andre E 1926-1979 *ConAu 85*
Hellen, J A 1935- *ConAu 61*
Hellenhofferu, Vojtech Kapristian Z *ConAu X*
Hellens, Franz 1881-1972 *CIDMEL 80*
Heller *ConAu X*
Heller, Abraham M 1898-1975 *ConAu 57*
Heller, Bernard 1896-1976 *ConAu 65*
Heller, Celia S 1927- *ConAu 37R, IntAu&W 82*
Heller, David 1922-1968 *ConAu P-1*
Heller, Deane 1924- *ConAu 9R*
Heller, Erich 1911- *ConAu 8NR, –13R, IntAu&W 82, WrDr 84*
Heller, Francis H 1917- *ConAu 1R*
Heller, Friedrich 1932- *IntAu&W 82*
Heller, H Robert 1940- *ConAu 69*
Heller, Herbert Lynn 1908- *ConAu 21R*
Heller, Janet Ruth *DrAP&F 83*
Heller, Janet Ruth 1949- *IntWWP 82*
Heller, Jean 1942- *ConAu 73*
Heller, Joseph *DrAP&F 83*
Heller, Joseph 1923- *AuNews 1, ConAu 5R, –8NR, ConDr 82, ConLC 1, –3, –5, –8, –11, ConNov 82, DcLB Y80A[port], –2, DcLEL 1940, EncWL 2, ModAL, ModAL SUP, TwCWr, WhoTwCL, WorAu, WrDr 84*
Heller, Linda 1944- *ConAu 108*
Heller, Mark 1914- *ConAu 10NR, –61, WrDr 84*
Heller, Michael *DrAP&F 83*
Heller, Michael D 1937- *ConAu 45, ConP 80, IntWWP 82, WrDr 84*
Heller, Mike *ConAu X*
Heller, Peter 1920- *ConAu 41R*
Heller, Reinhold 1940- *ConAu 77*
Heller, Robert 1899?-1973 *ConAu 41R*
Heller, Robert W 1933- *ConAu 25R*
Heller, Sipa 1897?-1980 *ConAu 97*
Heller, Steve F *DrAP&F 83*
Heller, Walter W 1915- *ConAu 21R, IntAu&W 82, WrDr 84*
Heller, Wilson Battin 1893-1983 *ConAu 110*
Hellerman, Herbert 1927- *ConAu 53*
Hellerstein, Jerome R 1907- *ConAu P-1*
Hellie, Ann 1925- *ConAu 77, MichAu 80*
Hellie, Richard 1937- *ConAu 33R, IntAu&W 82, WrDr 84*
Hellinger, Douglas A 1948- *ConAu 69*
Hellinger, Stephen H 1948- *ConAu 69*
Hellison, Donald R 1938- *ConAu 53*
Hellman, Arthur D 1942- *ConAu 69*
Hellman, C Doris 1910-1973 *ConAu 41R*
Hellman, Geoffrey T 1907-1977 *ConAu 69, –73*
Hellman, Hal *ConAu X*
Hellman, Hal 1927- *ConAu X, IntAu&W 82X, SmATA 4, WrDr 84*
Hellman, Harold 1927- *ConAu 10NR, –25R, IntAu&W 82, SmATA 4*
Hellman, Hugo E 1908- *ConAu P-2*
Hellman, Lillian 1905- *AuNews 1, –2, CnMD, ConDr 82, ConLC 2, –4, CroCD, EncWL 2, ModAL, ModAL SUP, ModWD, TwCA, TwCA SUP, WhoTwCL*
Hellman, Lillian 1906- *ConAu 13R, ConLC 8, –14, –18, DcLB 7[port]*
Hellman, Lillian 1907- *LongCTC, NatPD 81[port], WrDr 84*
Hellman, Robert 1919- *ConAu 17R*
Hellmann, Anna 1902?-1972 *ConAu 33R*
Hellmann, Donald C 1933- *ConAu 45*
Hellmann, Ellen 1908- *ConAu 106, WrDr 84*
Hellmann, John 1948- *ConAu 105*
Hellmuth, Jerome 1911- *ConAu 13R*
Hellmuth, William Frederick, Jr. 1920- *ConAu 1R, –4NR*
Hellstrom, Ward 1930- *ConAu 33R, WrDr 84*
Hellwig, Monika Konrad 1929- *ConAu 37R*
Hellyer, A G L 1902- *ConAu 4NR, IntAu&W 82*

Hellyer, Arthur *ConAu X*
Hellyer, Arthur George Lee 1902- *ConAu 9R, WrDr 84*
Hellyer, David Tirrell 1913- *ConAu 17R*
Hellyer, Jill 1925- *IntWWP 82, WrDr 84*
Hellyer, Paul T 1923- *ConAu 69, IntAu&W 82, WrDr 84*
Helm, Bertrand P 1929- *ConAu 37R*
Helm, E Eugene 1928- *ConAu 1R*
Helm, Ernest Eugene 1928- *ConAu 2NR*
Helm, Everett 1913- *ConAu 49*
Helm, P J 1916- *ConAu 3NR*
Helm, Peter James 1916- *ConAu 9R, IntAu&W 82*
Helm, Robert Meredith 1917- *ConAu 17R*
Helm, Thomas 1919- *ConAu 5R*
Helm-Pirgo, Marian 1897- *ConAu 77, IntAu&W 82*
Helmer, John 1946- *ConAu 41R*
Helmer, William F 1926- *ConAu 33R*
Helmer, William J 1936- *ConAu 73*
Helmericks, Bud *ConAu X*
Helmericks, Constance Chittenden 1918- *ConAu 9R*
Helmericks, Harmon Robert 1917- *ConAu 29R*
Helmering, Doris Wild 1942- *ConAu 65*
Helmers, Dow 1906- *ConAu 61*
Helmes, Scott *DrAP&F 83*
Helmholz, R H 1940- *ConAu 61*
Helmi, Jack *ConAu X*
Helming, Ann 1924- *ConAu 1R, -2NR*
Helmker, Judith A 1940- *WrDr 84*
Helmker, Judith Anne 1940- *ConAu 33R*
Helmlinger, Trudy 1942- *IntAu&W 82*
Helmlinger, Trudy 1943- *ConAu 69*
Helmore, G A 1922- *ConAu 29R*
Helmore, Geoffrey Anthony 1922- *WrDr 84*
Helmreich, Ernst Christian 1902- *ConAu 1R, WrDr 84*
Helmreich, Jonathan Ernst 1936- *ConAu 105*
Helmreich, Paul C 1933- *ConAu 53*
Helmreich, Robert Louis 1937- *ConAu 65*
Helmreich, William B 1945- *ConAu 105*
Helms, Randel 1942- *ConAu 49, WrDr 84*
Helms, Roland Thomas, Jr. 1940- *ConAu 102*
Helms, Tom *ConAu X*
Helmstadter, Gerald C 1925- *ConAu 13R*
Heloise *ConAu X*
Helper, Rose *ConAu 77*
Helperin, Mark W *DrAP&F 83*
Helpern, Milton 1902-1977 *ConAu 69, -73*
Helpmann, Barbara Chilcott Davis *CreCan 1*
Helprin, Mark 1947- *ConAu 81, ConLC 7, -10, -22[port]*
Helps, Racey 1913-1971 *ConAu 29R, ConAu P-2, SmATA 2, -25N*
Helson, Harry 1898- *ConAu P-1*
Helterman, Jeffrey A 1942- *ConAu 103*
Helton, David 1940- *ConAu 25R*
Helton, Tinsley 1915- *ConAu 1R*
Helvick, James 1904- *ConAu X, WorAu*
Helweg, Hans H 1917- *SmATA 33*
Helwig, David 1938- *ConAu 33R, ConP 80, DcLEL 1940, WrDr 84*
Heman, Bob *DrAP&F 83*
Hemant *IntWWP 82X*
Hembree, Charles R 1938- *ConAu 33R*
Hemdahl, Reuel Gustaf 1903-1977 *ConAu 37R*
Hemenway, Robert *DrAP&F 83*
Hemenway, Robert 1921- *ConAu 33R*
Hemesath, Caroline 1899- *ConAu 61*
Heming, Arthur 1870-1940 *CreCan 2*
Hemingway, Emmett *IntWWP 82X*
Hemingway, Ernest 1899?-1961 *AuNews 2, CnMD, CnMWL, ConAu 77, ConAmA, ConLC 1, -3, -6, -8, -10, -13, -19, DcLB DS1[port], -Y81A[port], -4, -9[port], EncWL 2[port], LongCTC, MichAu 80, ModAL, ModAL SUP, ModWD, TwCA, TwCA SUP, TwCWr, WhoTwCL*
Hemingway, Leicester C 1915-1982 *ConAu 107*
Hemingway, Mary Welsh 1908- *ConAu 73, Conv 1, WrDr 84*
Hemingway, Patricia Drake 1926-1978 *ConAu 69, -69, -73*
Hemingway, Taylor *ConAu X*
Heminway, John Hylan, Jr. 1944- *ConAu 25R, WrDr 84*
Hemleben, Sylvester John 1902- *ConAu P-2*
Hemley, Cecil Herbert 1914-1966 *ConAu 1R, -1NR, -25R*
Hemley, Elaine Gottlieb *ConAu X*

Hemlow, Joyce 1906- *ConAu 5R, IntAu&W 82, WrDr 84*
Hemming, John Henry 1935- *ConAu 29R, IntAu&W 82, WrDr 84*
Hemming, Roy 1928- *ConAu 61, SmATA 11*
Hemmings, F W J 1920- *ConAu 97*
Hemmings, Frederic William John 1920- *IntAu&W 82*
Hemon, Louis 1880-1913 *ClDMEL 80, LongCTC, TwCA, TwCA SUP*
Hemphill, Charles F, Jr. 1917- *ConAu 101*
Hemphill, George 1922- *ConAu 13R, WrDr 84*
Hemphill, John K 1919- *ConAu 53*
Hemphill, Martha Locke 1904-1973 *ConAu 37R*
Hemphill, Paul 1938- *WrDr 84*
Hemphill, Paul James 1936?- *AuNews 2, ConAu 49*
Hemphill, W Edwin 1912- *ConAu 21R*
Hempstone, Smith 1929- *ConAu 1R, -1NR*
Hemschemeyer, Judith *DrAP&F 83*
Hemschemeyer, Judith 1935- *ConAu 49*
Hen, Jozef 1923- *IntAu&W 82*
Henaghan, Jim 1919- *ConAu 102*
Henault, Gilles 1920- *CreCan 2*
Henault, Marie 1921- *ConAu 33R, IntAu&W 82, WrDr 84*
Hencken, Hugh O'Neill 1902-1981 *ConAu 104, IntAu&W 82*
Hendee, John C 1938- *ConAu 93*
Hendel, Charles William 1890- *ConAu P-1*
Hendel, Charles William 1890-1982 *ConAu 108*
Hendel, Samuel 1909- *ConAu 1R, -1NR*
Hendelson, William H 1904-1975 *ConAu 104*
Henderley, Brooks *ConAu P-2, SmATA 1*
Henderlite, Rachel 1905- *ConAu 1R*
Hendershot, Carl H *WrDr 84*
Hendershot, Ralph 1896?-1979 *ConAu 89*
Henderson, Alexander Ernest 1916- *WrDr 84*
Henderson, Alexander John 1910- *ConAu P-1*
Henderson, Algo Donmyer 1897- *ConAu 1R, -1NR*
Henderson, Archibald 1877-1963 *ConAu 93, LongCTC, TwCA, TwCA SUP*
Henderson, Archibald 1916- *ConAu 53*
Henderson, Arn *DrAP&F 83*
Henderson, Bert C 1904- *ConAu P-1*
Henderson, Bill *DrAP&F 83*
Henderson, Bill 1941- *ConAu 33R*
Henderson, C William 1925- *ConAu 65*
Henderson, Charles, Jr. 1923- *ConAu 45*
Henderson, Charles P, Jr. 1941- *ConAu 41R*
Henderson, Dan Fenno 1921- *ConAu 17R, IntAu&W 82, WrDr 84*
Henderson, David *DrAP&F 83*
Henderson, David 1942- *ConAu 10NR, -25R, DcLEL 1940*
Henderson, Dion 1921- *ConAu 5NR, -9R*
Henderson, Dwight F 1937- *ConAu 41R*
Henderson, F M 1921- *WrDr 84*
Henderson, G P 1915- *ConAu 29R*
Henderson, G P 1920- *ConAu 37R*
Henderson, George *CreCan 2*
Henderson, George 1931- *ConAu 25R*
Henderson, George L 1925- *ConAu 69*
Henderson, George Patrick 1915- *WrDr 84*
Henderson, Hamish 1919- *ConP 80, WrDr 84*
Henderson, Harold Gould 1889-1974 *ConAu 53*
Henderson, Harry B, Jr. 1914- *ConAu 109*
Henderson, Ian 1910-1969 *ConAu P-2*
Henderson, Ian Thomson 1908- *WrDr 84*
Henderson, Isabel 1933- *ConAu 25R*
Henderson, James 1871-1951 *CreCan 2*
Henderson, James 1934- *ConAu 33R, WrDr 84*
Henderson, James Youngblood 1944- *ConAu 110*
Henderson, Jean Carolyn Glidden 1916- *ConAu 102*
Henderson, Jennifer 1929- *ConAu 107*
Henderson, John 1906?-1982 *ConAu 108*
Henderson, John 1915- *ConAu 5R*
Henderson, John S 1919- *ConAu 5R*
Henderson, John W 1910- *ConAu 25R*
Henderson, Keith 1883-1982 *ConAu 106, -107*
Henderson, Keith M 1934- *ConAu 21R*
Henderson, Kenneth David Druitt 1903- *ConAu P-1, WrDr 84*
Henderson, Laurance G 1924?-1977 *ConAu 73*
Henderson, Laurence 1928- *ConAu 53, WrDr 84*
Henderson, Lawrence Austin 1915- *IntAu&W 82*
Henderson, Lawrence W 1921- *ConAu 103*
Henderson, LeGrand 1901-1965 *ConAu 5R,*

SmATA 9
Henderson, Lois T *DrAP&F 83*
Henderson, Lois T 1918- *ConAu 81*
Henderson, Mary *ConAu X, LongCTC*
Henderson, Mary C 1928- *ConAu 77*
Henderson, Michael 1932- *ConAu 110*
Henderson, Nancy 1943- *ConAu 41R*
Henderson, Nancy Wallace 1916- *ConAu 97, IntAu&W 82, NatPD 81[port], SmATA 22[port]*
Henderson, Patrick 1927- *WrDr 84*
Henderson, Paul *DcLEL 1940, LongCTC*
Henderson, Peter 1904- *ConAu 108*
Henderson, Philip Prichard 1906-1977 *ConAu 104, ConAu P-1*
Henderson, Randall 1888- *ConAu P-1*
Henderson, Richard 1924- *ConAu 5NR, -13R, WrDr 84*
Henderson, Richard B 1921- *ConAu 77*
Henderson, Richard I 1926- *ConAu 11NR, -69*
Henderson, Robert 1906- *ConAu 106*
Henderson, Robert M 1926- *ConAu 33R*
Henderson, Robert W 1920- *ConAu 1R*
Henderson, S P A 1929- *ConAu 37R*
Henderson, Stephen E 1925- *ConAu 29R*
Henderson, Sylvia *ConAu X, LongCTC*
Henderson, Thomas W 1949- *ConAu 73*
Henderson, Vivian Wilson 1923-1976 *ConAu 61, -65*
Henderson, W O 1904- *ConAu 4NR*
Henderson, William, III 1922- *ConAu 17R*
Henderson, William James 1855-1937 *TwCA*
Henderson, William L 1927- *ConAu 33R, WrDr 84*
Henderson, William Otto 1904- *ConAu 1R, IntAu&W 82, WrDr 84*
Henderson, Zenna 1917- *ConAu 1R, -1NR, ConSFA, DcLB 8[port], SmATA 5, TwCSFW, WrDr 84*
Henderson-Howat, Gerald *WrDr 84*
Henderson Smith, Stephen Lane 1919- *IntWWP 82, WrDr 84*
Hendi, Peter 1943- *IntAu&W 82*
Hendin, David 1945- *ConAu 41R*
Hendin, Josephine 1946- *ConAu 102*
Hendler, Earl *DrAP&F 83*
Hendon, William S 1933- *ConAu 45*
Hendra, Tony *ConAu 102*
Hendren, Ron 1945- *ConAu 77*
Hendrich, Paula Griffith 1928- *ConAu 1R, -1NR*
Hendrick, Burton Jesse 1870?-1949 *TwCA, TwCA SUP*
Hendrick, George 1929- *ConAu 8NR, -13R*
Hendrick, Irving G 1936- *ConAu 81*
Hendrick, Ives 1898-1972 *ConAu 33R, ConAu P-1*
Hendrick, T W 1909- *ConAu 108*
Hendrick, Thomas William 1909- *WrDr 84*
Hendricks, Faye N 1913- *ConAu 69*
Hendricks, Frances Wade Kellam 1900- *ConAu 37R*
Hendricks, Gay 1945- *ConAu 73*
Hendricks, Geoffrey *DrAP&F 83*
Hendricks, George David, Sr. 1913- *ConAu 5R, WrDr 84*
Hendricks, Glenn Leonard 1928- *ConAu 57*
Hendricks, J Edwin 1935- *ConAu 41R*
Hendricks, Robert J 1944- *ConAu 45*
Hendricks, Walter 1892-1979 *ConAu 103*
Hendricks, William Lawrence 1929- *ConAu 2NR, -49*
Hendrickson, Carol Follmuth 1920- *IntWWP 82*
Hendrickson, Donald Eugene 1941- *ConAu 93*
Hendrickson, James E 1932- *ConAu 21R, WrDr 84*
Hendrickson, Paul 1944- *ConAu 108*
Hendrickson, Robert 1933- *ConAu 1NR, -49*
Hendrickson, Robert A 1923- *ConAu 29R, WrDr 84*
Hendrickson, Walter Brookfield, Jr. 1936- *ConAu 1R, -1NR, SmATA 9*
Hendrie, Don, Jr. *DrAP&F 83*
Hendrie, Don, Jr. 1942- *ConAu 3NR, -49*
Hendriks, A L 1922- *ConAu 97, ConP 80, WrDr 84*
Hendriks, P G *IntAu&W 82X*
Hendriksen, Eldon Sende 1917- *ConAu 13R*
Hendry, Allan 1950- *ConAu 106*
Hendry, J F 1912- *ConAu 29R*
Hendry, James Findlay 1912- *IntAu&W 82, WrDr 84*
Hendry, Thomas 1929- *ConAu 69, ConDr 82,*

CreCan 2, WrDr 84
Hendry, Tom 1929- *ConAu X*
Hendryx, James Beardsley 1880-1963 *TwCWW*
Hendy, Philip 1900-1980 *ConAu 102*
Henegan, Lucius Herbert, Jr. 1902?-1979
ConAu 85
Heneman, Herbert Gerhard, Jr. 1916- *ConAu 1R,
-1NR*
Henes, Donna *DrAP&F 83*
Henfrey, Colin 1941- *ConAu 13R*
Henfrey, Norman 1929- *ConAu 25R*
Henig, Gerald S 1942- *ConAu 57*
Henig, Robin Marantz 1953- *ConAu 108*
Henig, Ruth B 1943- *ConAu 49*
Henig, Suzanne 1936- *ConAu 2NR, -45*
Henige, David 1938- *ConAu 103*
Heninger, S K, Jr. 1922- *ConAu 1R, -1NR*
Henisch, Heinz K 1922- *ConAu 73*
Henissart, Paul 1923- *ConAu 29R, WrDr 84*
Henke, Dan 1924- *ConAu 53*
Henke, Emerson Overbeck 1916- *ConAu 17R*
Henkel, Barbara Osborn 1921- *ConAu 9R*
Henkel, Stephen Charles 1933- *ConAu 37R,
WrDr 84*
Henkels, Robert M, Jr. 1939- *ConAu 57*
Henkels, Walter 1906- *IntAu&W 82*
Henkes, Paul 1898- *IntWWP 82*
Henkes, Robert 1922- *ConAu 33R, WrDr 84*
Henkin, Harmon 1940?-1980 *ConAu 101*
Henkin, Louis 1917- *ConAu 33R, WrDr 84*
Henkle, Henrietta 1909- *ConAu 69*
Henle, Faye d1972 *ConAu 37R*
Henle, Fritz 1909- *ConAu 73*
Henle, James 1891?-1973 *ConAu 37R*
Henle, Jane 1913- *ConAu 77*
Henle, Mary 1913- *ConAu 33R*
Henle, Robert John 1909- *ConAu 110*
Henle, Theda O 1918- *ConAu 33R*
Henler, Benni 1926- *IntAu&W 82*
Henley, Arthur 1921- *ConAu 21R, WrDr 84*
Henley, Beth 1952- *ConAu X, ConLC 23[port],
NatPD 81[port]*
Henley, Charles *DrAP&F 83*
Henley, Elizabeth Becker 1952- *ConAu 107*
Henley, Gail 1952- *ConAu 89, IntAu&W 82*
Henley, Karyn 1952- *ConAu 102*
Henley, Nancy Eloise Main 1934- *ConAu 106*
Henley, Norman 1915- *ConAu 17R*
Henley, Patricia *DrAP&F 83*
Henley, Virginia 1935- *ConAu 109*
Henley, W Ballentine 1905- *ConAu 61*
Henley, Wallace 1941- *ConAu 65*
Henley, William Ernest 1849-1903 *ConAu 105,
LongCTC, TwCLC 8[port]*
Henmark, Kai 1932- *IntAu&W 82*
Henn, Harry George 1919- *ConAu 45*
Henn, Mary Ann *DrAP&F 83*
Henn, Thomas Rice 1901-1974 *ConAu 4NR, -5R*
Hennacy, Ammon 1893-1970 *ConAu 104*
Hennedy, Hugh L 1929- *ConAu 41R*
Henneman, John Bell, Jr. 1935- *ConAu 45*
Hennen, Tom *DrAP&F 83*
Hennesey, James J 1926- *ConAu 33R*
Hennessey, Caroline *ConAu X*
Hennessey, David James George 1932-
ConAu 106
Hennessey, Frank Charles 1894-1941 *CreCan 1*
Hennessey, R A S 1937- *ConAu 29R*
Hennessy, Bernard C 1924- *ConAu 13R*
Hennessy, James Pope 1916-1973 *ConAu X*
Hennessy, Josslyn 1903- *ConAu 9R*
Hennessy, Madeleine *DrAP&F 83,
IntWWP 82X*
Hennessy, Mary L 1927- *ConAu 21R*
Hennessy, Max *ConAu X, IntAu&W 82X,
WrDr 84*
Hennicke, Karl August 1927- *IntWWP 82*
Hennig, Margaret 1940- *ConAu 81*
Hennig, Rolf 1928- *IntAu&W 82*
Henning, Charles N 1915- *ConAu 1R*
Henning, Daniel Howard 1931- *ConAu 2NR, -45*
Henning, Edward B 1922- *ConAu 17R*
Henning, Jean Maxine Oliver 1918- *IntWWP 82*
Henning, Standish 1932- *ConAu 107*
Hennings, Dorothy Grant 1935- *ConAu 4NR,
-53*
Henningsen, Sven 1910- *IntAu&W 82*
Hennissart, Martha *ConAu 85, WorAu 1970*
Henrey, Madeleine 1906- *ConAu 6NR, -13R,
IntAu&W 82, WrDr 84*
Henrey, Robert *ConAu X*
Henrey, Mrs. Robert *ConAu X*

Henri, Adrian 1932- *ConAu 25R, ConP 80,
DcLEL 1940, IntWWP 82, WrDr 84*
Henri, Florette 1908- *ConAu 73*
Henri, G *ConAu X*
Henri, Raymond *DrAP&F 83*
Henrichsen, Walt, Jr. 1934- *ConAu 89*
Henricks, Kaw *ConAu X*
Henrickson, Richard 1948- *NatPD 81[port]*
Henries, A Doris Banks 1913?-1981 *ConAu 103*
Henrietta *IntWWP 82X*
Henriod, Lorraine 1925- *ConAu 45,
SmATA 26[port]*
Henriques, Robert David Quixano 1905-1967
LongCTC, TwCA SUP
Henriques, Veronica 1931- *ConAu 102,
WrDr 84*
Henriquez Urena, Pedro 1884-1946 *ModLAL*
Henry, Bessie Walker 1921- *ConAu 9R*
Henry, Bill *ConAu X*
Henry, Buck 1930- *ConAu 77, ConDr 82A,
DcLB 26[port]*
Henry, Carl F H 1913- *ConAu 6NR, -13R,
IntAu&W 82*
Henry, Carol *DrAP&F 83*
Henry, Claud 1914- *ConAu 45*
Henry, Daniel *ConAu X*
Henry, David Dodds 1905- *ConAu 106*
Henry, David Lee *ConAu X*
Henry, Dewitt *DrAP&F 83*
Henry, Eric P 1943- *ConAu 108*
Henry, Frances 1931- *ConAu 77*
Henry, Francoise 1902-1982 *ConAu 106*
Henry, Gerrit *DrAP&F 83*
Henry, Harold Wilkinson 1926- *ConAu 37R*
Henry, Harriet *ConAu 49*
Henry, James P 1914- *ConAu 104*
Henry, James S 1950- *ConAu 49*
Henry, Jeanne Heffernan 1940- *ConAu 105*
Henry, Jeff 1922- *CreCan 2*
Henry, Joanne Landers 1927- *ConAu 17R,
SmATA 6*
Henry, Joseph B *WrDr 84*
Henry, Joseph B 1901- *ConAu P-2*
Henry, Jules 1904-1969 *ConAu 109*
Henry, Kenneth 1920- *ConAu 57*
Henry, Laurin L 1921- *ConAu 1R*
Henry, Marguerite *ConAu 9NR, TwCCW 83,
WrDr 84*
Henry, Marguerite 1902- *ChlLR 4[port],
ConAu 17R, DcLB 22[port], IntAu&W 82,
SmATA 11*
Henry, Martha 1939- *CreCan 1*
Henry, Mick *IntWWP 82X*
Henry, O 1862-1909? *TwCLC 1*
Henry, O 1862-1910 *ConAu X, LongCTC,
ModAL, TwCA, TwCA SUP, TwCWW,
TwCWr, WhoTwCL*
Henry, Oliver *ConAu X*
Henry, Peter 1926- *ConAu 109*
Henry, Robert *ConAu X*
Henry, Robert Selph 1889-1970 *ConAu 1R, -103,
DcLB 17[port]*
Henry, Shirley 1925?-1972 *ConAu 33R*
Henry, T E *ConAu X, SmATA X*
Henry, Vera *ConAu P-2, MichAu 80,
WrDr 84*
Henry, W P 1929- *ConAu 17R*
Henry, Will *ConAu X, TwCWW, WrDr 84*
Henry, William Earl 1917- *ConAu 108*
Henry, William Mellors 1890-1970 *ConAu 89*
Henschel, Elizabeth Georgie *ConAu 107,
IntAu&W 82, WrDr 84*
Hensen, Herwig 1917- *CnMD, ModWD*
Hensey, Frederick G 1931- *ConAu 89*
Hensey, Fritz *ConAu X*
Henshall, Audrey Shore 1927- *ConAu 9R,
WrDr 84*
Henshaw, James Ene 1924- *ConAu 101,
ConDr 82, DcLEL 1940, TwCWr,
WrDr 84*
Henshaw, Richard 1945- *ConAu 101*
Henshaw, Tom 1924- *ConAu 103*
Henshel, Richard L 1939- *ConAu 57*
Hensley, Charles S 1919- *ConAu 41R*
Hensley, Joe L *DrAP&F 83*
Hensley, Joe L 1926- *ConAu 33R, TwCSFW,
WrDr 84*
Hensley, Stewart 1914?-1976 *ConAu 65*
Henslin, James Marvin 1937- *ConAu 41R*
Henson, Clyde E 1914- *ConAu 5R*
Henson, David *DrAP&F 83*
Henson, Herbert Hensley 1863-1947 *CnMWL,*

LongCTC, WorAu
Henson, James Maury 1936- *ConAu 106*
Henson, Jim *ConAu X*
Henson, Lance *DrAP&F 83*
Henstra, Friso 1928- *SmATA 8*
Henthorn, William E 1928- *ConAu 41R*
Hentoff, Nat *WrDr 84*
Hentoff, Nat 1925- *ChlLR 1, ConAu 1R,
-5NR, ConLC 26[port], SmATA 27,
TwCCW 83*
Henty, George Alfred 1832-1902 *LongCTC*
Henwood, James N J 1932- *ConAu 29R*
Henz, Rudolf 1897- *IntAu&W 82*
Henze, Donald F 1928- *ConAu 21R*
Hepburn, Andrew H 1899?-1975 *ConAu 57*
Hepburn, James Gordon 1922- *ConAu 85*
Hepburn, Ronald William 1927- *ConAu 13R,
WrDr 84*
Hepner, Harry W 1893- *ConAu 29R*
Hepner, James O 1933- *ConAu 57*
Heppenheimer, T A 1947- *ConAu 93*
Heppenheimer, Thomas A 1947- *WrDr 84*
Heppenstall, Margit Strom 1913- *ConAu 21R*
Heppenstall, Rayner 1911-1981 *ConAu 1R, -103,
ConLC 10, ConP 80, EncWL 2,
IntWWP 82, LongCTC, ModBrL,
ModBrL SUP, WorAu*
Hepple, Bob Alexander 1934- *ConAu 29R,
IntAu&W 82*
Hepple, Peter 1927- *ConAu 81*
Heppner, Sam 1913- *ConAu 25R, WrDr 84*
Heppner, Sam 1913-1983 *ConAu 109*
Hepting, George Henry 1907- *IntAu&W 82*
Hepworth, James B 1910- *ConAu 1R*
Hepworth, James Michael *WrDr 84*
Hepworth, James Michael 1938- *ConAu 73*
Hepworth, James R 1948- *IntWWP 82*
Hepworth, Mike 1938- *WrDr 84*
Hepworth, Philip 1912- *ConAu 17R*
Hepwroth, Noel P 1934- *WrDr 84*
Herald *SmATA X*
Herald, George William 1911- *ConAu 73*
Herald, Kathleen *ConAu X, TwCCW 83*
Heraud, Brian J 1934- *ConAu 73*
Heravi, Mehdi 1940- *ConAu 29R*
Herber, Bernard P 1929- *ConAu 21R*
Herber, Harold L 1929- *ConAu 108*
Herber, Lewis *ConAu X*
Herberg, Will 1909-1977 *ConAu 69, -73*
Herberger, Charles Frederick 1920- *ConAu 41R,
IntAu&W 82*
Herbers, John N 1923- *ConAu 33R*
Herbert, Sir A P 1890-1971 *ConAu 33R, -33R,
-97*
Herbert, Sir Alan Patrick 1890-1971
*DcLB 10[port], LongCTC, ModBrL,
TwCA, TwCA SUP, TwCWr*
Herbert, Anthony B 1930- *ConAu 77*
Herbert, Arthur *ConAu X, TwCWW,
WrDr 84*
Herbert, Cecil *ConAu X, SmATA X*
Herbert, David Thomas 1935- *ConAu 2NR, -49*
Herbert, Don 1917- *ConAu 29R, SmATA 2*
Herbert, Eugenia W 1929- *ConAu 93*
Herbert, Frank 1920- *ConAu 5NR, -53,
ConLC 12, -23[port], ConSFA,
DcLB 8[port], DrmM[port], SmATA 9,
TwCSFW, WorAu 1970, WrDr 84*
Herbert, Frederick Hugh 1897-1958 *TwCA SUP*
Herbert, George *IntAu&W 82X*
Herbert, Gilbert 1924- *ConAu 107, WrDr 84*
Herbert, Ivor 1925- *ConAu 4NR, -53,
IntAu&W 82, WrDr 84*
Herbert, James 1943- *ConAu 81, TwCSFW,
WrDr 84*
Herbert, Jean 1897-1980 *ConAu 9NR*
Herbert, Jean Daniel Fernand 1897- *ConAu 17R*
Herbert, John 1924- *ConAu 21R*
Herbert, John 1926- *ConAu X, ConDr 82,
IntAu&W 82X, WrDr 84*
Herbert, Kevin 1921- *ConAu 17R*
Herbert, Marie 1941- *ConAu 69*
Herbert, Martin 1933- *ConAu 103*
Herbert, Miranda C 1950- *ConAu 97*
Herbert, Moss 1914- *IntAu&W 82*
Herbert, Robert L 1929- *ConAu 5NR, -9R*
Herbert, Theodore T 1942- *ConAu 65*
Herbert, Thomas Walter, Jr. 1938- *ConAu 104*
Herbert, Wally *ConAu X, SmATA X*
Herbert, Walter William 1934- *ConAu 69,
SmATA 23*

Hertz, Peter Donald 1933- *ConAu 37R*
Hertz, Richard C 1916- *ConAu 21R*
Hertz, Solange 1920- *ConAu 5R*
Hertzberg, Arthur 1921- *ConAu 17R*
Hertzberg, Hazel W 1918- *ConAu 73*
Hertzell, Eric *CreCan 1*
Hertzler, Joyce O 1895-1975 *ConAu 1R, –103*
Hertzler, Lois Shank 1927- *ConAu 57*
Hertzman, Lewis 1927- *ConAu 9R, IntAu&W 82, WrDr 84*
Herum, John 1931- *ConAu 61*
Herve, Jean-Luc *ConAu 49*
Herve-Bazin, Jean Pierre Marie 1911- *ConAu 81, WorAu*
Hervent, Maurice *ConAu X*
Hervey, Jane *ConAu X*
Hervey, Michael 1920- *ConAu 9R*
Hervieu, Paul Ernest 1857-1915 *CIDMEL 80, ModWD*
Herwig, Holger H 1941- *ConAu 7NR, –61*
Herwig, Rob 1935- *WrDr 84*
Herz, Irene 1948- *ConAu 93*
Herz, Jerome Spencer *ConAu 45*
Herz, Jerry *ConAu X*
Herz, John H 1908- *ConAu 41R*
Herz, Martin F 1917- *ConAu 9NR, –21R, WrDr 84*
Herz, Peggy 1936- *ConAu 37R*
Herz, Stephanie M 1900- *ConAu 101*
Herzberg, Abel J 1898- *CnMD*
Herzberg, Donald Gabriel 1925-1980 *ConAu 101*
Herzberg, Gerhard 1904- *IntAu&W 82, WrDr 84*
Herzberg, Joseph Gabriel 1907-1976 *ConAu 65*
Herzberg, Lily *WrDr 84*
Herzberger, Maximillian Jacob 1899-1982 *ConAu 106*
Herzel, Catherine 1908- *ConAu 5R*
Herzfeld, Thomas J 1945- *ConAu 107*
Herzka, Heinz-Stefan 1935- *ConAu 37R*
Herzog, Arthur 1927- *ConAu 9NR, –17R, WrDr 84*
Herzog, Chaim 1918- *ConAu 103*
Herzog, E *ConAu X*
Herzog, Emile Salomon Wilhelm 1885- *LongCTC, TwCA, TwCA SUP*
Herzog, Gerard 1920- *ConAu 104*
Herzog, Haim 1918- *IntAu&W 82*
Herzog, John P 1931- *ConAu 29R*
Herzog, Stephen J 1938- *ConAu 33R*
Herzog, Werner 1942- *ConAu 89, ConLC 16*
Herzstein, Robert Edwin 1940- *ConAu 7NR, –57*
Hesburgh, Theodore M 1917- *ConAu 13R*
Heschel, Abraham Joshua 1907-1972 *ConAu 4NR, –5R, –37R*
Heseltine, George Coulehan 1895-1980 *ConAu 97*
Heseltine, Nigel 1916- *ConAu 9R*
Heskes, Irene 1928- *ConAu 93*
Hesketh, Phoebe 1909- *ConAu P-1, ConP 80, IntAu&W 82, IntWWP 82, WrDr 84*
Heskett, J L 1933- *ConAu 8NR, –13R*
Hesky, Olga d1974 *ConAu 53, ConAu P-2*
Hesla, David 1929- *ConAu 33R, WrDr 84*
Heslep, Robert Durham 1930- *ConAu 37R, WrDr 84*
Heslin, Jo-Ann 1946- *ConAu 93*
Heslin, Richard 1936- *ConAu 37R*
Heslop, J Malan 1923- *ConAu 37R*
Hespro, Herbert *ConAu X*
Hess, Albert Gunter 1909- *ConAu P-1*
Hess, Alexander 1898?-1981 *ConAu 105*
Hess, Bartlett L 1910- *ConAu 61*
Hess, Beth B *ConAu 9NR, –65*
Hess, Eckhard H 1916- *ConAu 57*
Hess, Gary R 1937- *ConAu 21R, WrDr 84*
Hess, Hannah S 1934- *ConAu 45*
Hess, Hans 1908-1975 *ConAu 53*
Hess, Harvey *DrAP&F 83*
Hess, Harvey 1939- *IntAu&W 82*
Hess, John L 1917- *ConAu 102*
Hess, John M 1929- *ConAu 21R*
Hess, Kamelle *DrAP&F 83*
Hess, Karen 1918- *ConAu 105*
Hess, Karl 1923- *ConAu 81*
Hess, Lilo 1916- *ConAu 33R, SmATA 4*
Hess, Lynn *DrAP&F 83*
Hess, Margaret Johnston 1915- *ConAu 6NR, –57*
Hess, Robert D 1920- *ConAu 21R*
Hess, Robert L 1932- *ConAu 29R, IntAu&W 82, WrDr 84*
Hess, Stephen 1933- *ConAu 10NR, –17R*
Hess, Thomas B 1920-1978 *ConAu 77, –81*

Hess, William N 1925- *ConAu 29R*
Hesse, Hermann 1877-1962 *CIDMEL 80, ConAu P-2, ConLC 1, –2, –3, –6, –17, –25[port], EncWL 2[port], ModGL, TwCA, TwCA SUP, TwCWr, WhoTwCL*
Hesse, Hermann 1887-1962 *ConLC 11*
Hesse, Mary Brenda 1924- *ConAu 17R, WrDr 84*
Hesse-Avotina, Zeltite 1925- *IntAu&W 82*
Hesselgesser, Debra 1939- *ConAu 69*
Hesselgrave, David J 1924- *ConAu 81*
Hesseltine, William Best 1902-1963 *ConAu 1R*
Hessert, Paul 1925- *ConAu 33R, WrDr 84*
Hessing, Dennis *ConAu X*
Hession, Charles H 1911- *ConAu 33R*
Hession, Roy 1908- *ConAu 81*
Hessler, Gene 1928- *ConAu 73*
Hesslink, George K 1940- *ConAu 21R*
Hester, Hubert Inman 1895- *ConAu 5R, –5NR*
Hester, James J 1931- *ConAu 37R*
Hester, Kathleen B 1905- *ConAu P-2*
Hester, M L *DrAP&F 83*
Hester, Marcus B 1937- *ConAu 33R*
Hester, Martin L 1947- *IntWWP 82*
Heston, Alan 1934- *ConAu 97*
Heston, Charlton 1924- *ConAu 108, –110*
Heston, Edward 1908?-1973 *ConAu 45*
Heston, Leonard L 1930- *ConAu 101*
Heth, Meir 1932- *ConAu 21R*
Hetherington, Alastair 1919- *ConAu 109*
Hetherington, Hector Alastair 1919- *IntAu&W 82*
Hetherington, Hugh W 1903- *ConAu 5R*
Hetherington, John Aikman 1907-1974 *ConAu 53, –93, DcLEL 1940*
Hetherington, John Rowland 1899- *IntAu&W 82*
Hetherington, Thomas Baines 1919- *IntAu&W 82, WrDr 84*
Hetherington, Tom *IntAu&W 82X*
Hethmon, Robert H 1925- *ConAu 13R*
Heton, Eric William 1920- *WrDr 84*
Hettich, David William 1932- *ConAu 21R*
Hettich, Michael *DrAP&F 83*
Hettinger, Herman Strecker 1902-1972 *ConAu 37R*
Hettlinger, Richard F 1920- *ConAu 7NR, –17R*
Hetu, Jacques 1938- *CreCan 1*
Hetzell, Margaret Carol 1917-1978 *ConAu 81, –85*
Hetzler, Florence M 1926- *ConAu 107*
Hetzler, Stanley Arthur 1919- *ConAu 37R*
Hetzron, Robert 1937- *ConAu 33R, WrDr 84*
Heuer, John 1941- *ConAu 69*
Heuer, Kenneth John 1927- *ConAu 110*
Heuman, William 1912- *WrDr 84*
Heuman, William 1912-1971 *ConAu 5R, –7NR, SmATA 21[port], TwCWW*
Heumann, Milton 1947- *ConAu 110*
Heuscher, Julius E 1918- *ConAu 9R*
Heuser, Franz 1931- *IntAu&W 82*
Heuss, John 1908-1966 *ConAu P-1*
Heussler, Robert 1924- *ConAu 5R, –8NR, WrDr 84*
Heuterman, Thomas H 1934- *ConAu 101*
Heuvelmans, Bernard 1916- *ConAu 97*
Heuvelmans, Martin 1903- *ConAu 49*
Heuyer, Georges 1884-1977 *ConAu 73*
Hevener, John W 1933- *ConAu 103*
Heward, Constance 1884-1968 *TwCCW 83*
Heward, Edmund 1912- *ConAu 93*
Heward, Efa Prudence 1896-1947 *CreCan 1*
Heward, Prudence 1896-1947 *CreCan 1*
Heward, William L 1949- *ConAu 4NR, –53, MichAu 80*
Hewat, Alan V *DrAP&F 83*
Hewens, Frank Edgar 1912- *ConAu 45*
Hewer, Humphrey Robert 1903-1974 *ConAu 105*
Hewes, Dorothy W 1922- *ConAu 37R*
Hewes, Hayden 1943- *ConAu 85*
Hewes, Henry 1917- *ConAmTC, ConAu 13R*
Hewes, Jeremy Joan 1944- *ConAu 77*
Hewes, Laurence 1902- *ConAu 105*
Hewes, Leslie 1906- *ConAu 41R*
Hewett, Anita 1918- *ConAu 21R, IntAu&W 82, SmATA 13, TwCCW 83, WrDr 84*
Hewett, Dorothy 1923- *ConAu 97, ConDr 82, ConP 80, IntAu&W 82, WrDr 84*
Hewett, William S 1924- *ConAu 21R*
Hewins, Geoffrey Shaw 1889- *ConAu P-1*
Hewins, Ralph Anthony 1909- *ConAu P-1, IntAu&W 82*
Hewish, Antony 1924- *IntAu&W 82*

Hewison, Robert 1943- *ConAu 81, IntAu&W 82*
Hewitson, John Nelson 1917- *ConAu 29R*
Hewitt, Alison Hope 1915- *WrDr 84*
Hewitt, Arthur Wentworth 1883- *ConAu 69*
Hewitt, Barnard 1906- *ConAu 13R*
Hewitt, Ben *IntAu&W 82X, IntWWP 82X*
Hewitt, Cecil Rolph 1901- *ConAu 102*
Hewitt, Emily Clark 1944- *ConAu 2NR, –45*
Hewitt, Garnet 1939- *ConAu 110*
Hewitt, Geof *DrAP&F 83*
Hewitt, Geof 1943- *ConAu 33R, ConP 80, WrDr 84*
Hewitt, H J 1890- *ConAu 13R*
Hewitt, James 1928- *ConAu 6NR, –57*
Hewitt, Jean D 1925- *ConAu 77*
Hewitt, John 1907- *ConAu 97, ConP 80, DcLEL 1940, IntAu&W 82, WrDr 84*
Hewitt, John P 1941- *ConAu 53*
Hewitt, Philip Nigel 1945- *ConAu 81*
Hewitt, William Henry 1936- *ConAu 17R*
Hewlett, Dorothy d1979 *ConAu 85*
Hewlett, Frank West 1909?-1983 *ConAu 110*
Hewlett, Maurice Henry 1861-1923 *LongCTC, ModBrL, TwCA, TwCA SUP, TwCWr*
Hewlett, Richard Greening 1923- *ConAu 9R*
Hewlett, Roger S 1911?-1977 *ConAu 73*
Hewlett, Virginia B 1912?-1979 *ConAu 85*
Hewson, John 1930- *ConAu 37R, WrDr 84*
Hewton, Randolph Stanley 1888-1960 *CreCan 1*
Hexner, Ervin Paul 1893-1968 *ConAu 5R, –103*
Hext, Harrington *ConAu X, LongCTC, SmATA X, TwCA, TwCA SUP, TwCCr&M 80*
Hextall, David *ConAu X*
Hexter, J H 1910- *ConAu 13R*
Hey, Betty *CreCan 2*
Hey, John D 1944- *ConAu 106*
Hey, Nigel 1936- *WrDr 84*
Hey, Nigel S 1936- *ConAu 33R, SmATA 20*
Hey, Phillip H *DrAP&F 83*
Hey, Richard 1926- *CnMD, CroCD*
Hey, Baron Victor Alexander Sereld K 1876-1928 *CnMWL*
Heydenburg, Harry E 1891?-1979 *ConAu 89*
Heydenreich, Ludwig Heinrich 1903- *ConAu 105*
Heydon, Sir Peter Richard 1913-1971 *ConAu P-1*
Heydron, Vicki Ann 1945- *WrDr 84*
Heyduck-Huth, Hilde 1929- *ConAu 57, SmATA 8*
Heyel, Carl 1908- *ConAu 7NR, –17R*
Heyen, William *DrAP&F 83*
Heyen, William 1940- *ConAu 33R, ConLC 13, –18, ConP 80, DcLB 5[port], WrDr 84*
Heyer, Georgette 1902-1974 *ConAu 49, –93, LongCTC, TwCA, TwCA SUP, TwCCr&M 80, TwCRGW, TwCWr*
Heyer, Paul 1936- *WrDr 84*
Heyerdahl, Thor 1914- *ConAu 5R, –5NR, ConLC 26[port], IntAu&W 82, LongCTC, SmATA 2, TwCA SUP, TwCWr, WrDr 84*
Heyler, David B, Sr. 1905?-1983 *ConAu 110*
Heym, Georg 1887-1912 *CIDMEL 80, ConAu 106, ModGL, TwCLC 9[port], WhoTwCL*
Heym, Stefan 1913- *ConAu 4NR, –9R, IntAu&W 82, ModGL, TwCA SUP*
Heyman, Abigail 1942- *ConAu 57, WrDr 84*
Heyman, Ken 1930- *SmATA 34[port]*
Heymanns, Betty 1932- *ConAu 85*
Heyne, Paul 1931- *ConAu 89*
Heynen, James Alvin 1940- *IntAu&W 82, IntWWP 82*
Heynen, Jim *DrAP&F 83*
Heynen, Jim 1940- *ConAu 77, IntAu&W 82X*
Heynicke, Kurt 1891- *ModWD*
Heyns, Barbara 1943- *ConAu 85*
Heyse, Paul Johann Ludwig Von 1830-1914 *CIDMEL 80, ConAu 104, TwCLC 8[port]*
Heyst, Axel 1903- *ConAu X*
Heyward, Carter 1945- *ConAu 65*
Heyward, Dorothy Kuhns 1890-1961 *DcLB 7[port], ModWD*
Heyward, DuBose 1885-1940 *CnMD, ConAmA, ConAu 108, DcLB 7[port], –9[port], LongCTC, ModAL, ModWD, SmATA 21[port], TwCA, TwCA SUP, TwCWr*
Heywood, Christopher 1928- *ConAu 41R*
Heywood, Lorimer D 1899-1977 *ConAu 73*
Heywood, Philip 1938- *ConAu 69*

Heywood, Rosalind 1895- *ConAu 89,*
   IntAu&W 82
Heywood, Terence *ConAu P-1, DcLEL 1940*
Heywood Thomas, John 1926- *WrDr 84*
Heyworth, Peter Lawrence Frederick 1921-
   ConAu 65, IntAu&W 82
Heyworth-Dunne, James d1974 *ConAu 53*
Hiaasen, Carl 1953- *ConAu 105*
Hiat, Elchik *ConAu X*
Hibbard, George Richard 1915- *ConAu 85*
Hibbard, Howard 1928- *ConAu 9NR, –53*
Hibben, Frank Cummings 1910- *ConAu 1R,*
   –2NR, IntAu&W 82
Hibberd, Jack 1940- *ConAu 103, ConDr 82,*
   IntAu&W 82, WrDr 84
Hibbert, Christopher 1924- *ConAu 1R, –2NR,*
   IntAu&W 82, LongCTC, SmATA 4,
   WrDr 84
Hibbert, Eleanor 1906- *ConAu 17R, ConLC 7,*
   SmATA 2, WorAu
Hibbert, Eleanor Alice Burford *WrDr 84*
Hibbert, Eleanor Burford 1906- *ConAu 9NR*
Hibbett, Howard 1920- *ConAu 106, WrDr 84*
Hibbs, Ben 1901-1975 *ConAu 104, –65*
Hibbs, Douglas A, Jr. 1944- *ConAu 3NR, –49*
Hibbs, John 1925- *WrDr 84*
Hibbs, John Alfred Blyth 1925- *ConAu 103,*
   IntAu&W 82
Hibbs, Paul 1906- *ConAu P-1*
Hibdon, James E 1924- *ConAu 25R, WrDr 84*
Hichens, Robert Smythe 1864-1950 *LongCTC,*
   ModBrL, TwCA, TwCA SUP, TwCRGW,
   TwCWr
Hick, John 1922- *WrDr 84*
Hick, John Harwood 1922- *ConAu 6NR, –9R*
Hickel, Walter J 1919- *ConAu 41R*
Hicken, Victor 1921- *ConAu 21R, WrDr 84*
Hickerson, J Mel 1897- *ConAu 25R*
Hickey, Edward Shelby 1928?-1978 *ConAu 81,*
   –85
Hickey, Joseph J 1907- *ConAu 41R*
Hickey, Michael 1929- *ConAu 102*
Hickey, Neil 1931- *ConAu 1R*
Hickey, T Earl *ConSFA*
Hickey, William *ConAu X*
Hickford, Jessie 1911- *ConAu 53*
Hickin, Norman 1910- *ConAu 85,*
   IntAu&W 82, WrDr 84
Hickinbotham, James 1914- *WrDr 84*
Hickman, Bert G, Jr. 1924- *ConAu 108,*
   WrDr 84
Hickman, C Addison 1916- *ConAu 103*
Hickman, Charles 1905-1983 *ConAu 109*
Hickman, Janet 1940- *ConAu 10NR, –65,*
   SmATA 12
Hickman, Martha Whitmore 1925- *ConAu 10NR,*
   –25R, SmATA 26[port]
Hickman, Martin B 1925- *ConAu 65*
Hickman, Peggy 1906- *ConAu 73*
Hickok, Dorothy Jane 1912- *ConAu 73*
Hickok, Lorena A 1892?-1968 *ConAu 73,*
   SmATA 20[port]
Hickok, Robert 1927- *ConAu 61*
Hickok, Will *ConAu X*
Hicks, Alice Louise 1914- *IntWWP 82*
Hicks, Betty Brown *IntWWP 82X*
Hicks, Charles 1916- *ConAu 5R*
Hicks, Clifford B 1920- *ConAu 9NR*
Hicks, Clifford Byron 1920- *ConAu 5R*
Hicks, David E 1931- *ConAu 7NR, –9R*
Hicks, Eleanor *ConAu X, SmATA 1,*
   WrDr 84
Hicks, Eleanor B *ConAu X*
Hicks, George L 1935- *ConAu 65*
Hicks, Granville 1901-1982 *ConAmA,*
   ConAu 9R, –107, ConLCrt 82, ConNov 82,
   TwCA, TwCA SUP
Hicks, Harvey *ConAu X*
Hicks, J L *ConAu X*
Hicks, Jack 1942- *ConAu 97*
Hicks, Jim 1937- *ConAu 107*
Hicks, John 1904- *ConAu 65, WrDr 84*
Hicks, John 1918- *ConAu 25R*
Hicks, John Donald 1890-1972 *ConAu 1R, –2NR*
Hicks, John Edward 1890?-1971 *ConAu 104*
Hicks, John H 1919- *ConAu 45*
Hicks, John Richard 1904- *IntAu&W 82*
Hicks, John V 1907- *ConAu 110*
Hicks, Raymond L 1926- *ConAu 61*
Hicks, Robert E 1920- *ConAu 109*
Hicks, Ronald G 1934- *ConAu 73*
Hicks, Tyler Gregory 1921- *ConAu 103*

Hicks, Ursula Kathleen 1896- *ConAu 103*
Hicks, Valerie *IntWWP 82X*
Hicks, Warren B 1921- *ConAu 33R*
Hicks, Wilson 1897-1970 *ConAu 29R*
Hicky, Daniel Whitehead 1902- *AuNews 1*
Hidaka, Yoshki 1936- *IntAu&W 82*
Hidalgo, Jose Luis 1919-1947 *CIDMEL 80*
Hidayat, Sadik 1903-1951 *WorAu 1970*
Hidayat, Sadiq 1903-1951 *WhoTwCL*
Hidayatullah, Mohammad 1905- *IntAu&W 82*
Hidden, Norman 1913- *WrDr 84*
Hidden, Norman Frederick 1913- *ConAu 77*
Hidien, Norman *IntWWP 82*
Hidore, John J 1932- *ConAu 6NR, –57*
Hidy, Muriel E 1906- *ConAu 97*
Hidy, Ralph Willard 1905- *ConAu 5R*
Hieatt, A Kent 1921- *ConAu 21R*
Hieatt, Constance B 1928- *WrDr 84*
Hieatt, Constance Bartlett 1928- *ConAu 5R,*
   –8NR, IntAu&W 82, SmATA 4
Hiebel, Friedrich 1903- *ConAu 11NR, –65*
Hiebert, Clarence 1927- *ConAu 61*
Hiebert, D Edmond 1910- *ConAu 17R,*
   IntAu&W 82, WrDr 84
Hiebert, Paul Gerhardt 1892- *ConAu P-2,*
   CreCan 2, TwCWr
Hiebert, Ray Eldon 1932- *ConAu 7NR, –17R,*
   SmATA 13
Hieng, Andrej 1925- *ModSL 2*
Hiernaux, Jean-Robert-Laurent 1921- *ConAu 57*
Hieronymus, Clara Booth Wiggins 1913-
   ConAmTC, ConAu 73
Hierro, Jose 1922- *CIDMEL 80*
Hierro, Nicolas Del 1934- *IntAu&W 82*
Hiers, John Turner 1945- *ConAu 102*
Hiers, Richard H 1932- *ConAu 53*
Hiesberger, Jean Marie 1941- *ConAu 41R*
Hiestand, Dale L 1925- *ConAu 41R*
Hiester, Mary Augusta *CreCan 2*
Hifler, Joyce 1925- *ConAu 21R*
Higbee, Edward 1910- *ConAu 13R, WrDr 84*
Higbee, Kenneth Leo 1941- *ConAu 101*
Higby, Mary Jane *ConAu 25R*
Higden, Cato *IntAu&W 82X*
Higdon, David Leon 1939- *ConAu 77*
Higdon, Hal 1931- *ConAu 3NR, –9R,*
   SmATA 4, WrDr 84
Higelin, J M 1924- *IntAu&W 82*
Higenbottam, Frank 1910- *ConAu 25R*
Higgie, Lincoln William 1938- *ConAu 5R*
Higginbotham, A Leon, Jr. 1928- *ConAu 110*
Higginbotham, Jay 1937- *ConAu 93, WrDr 84*
Higginbotham, John E 1933- *ConAu 29R*
Higginbotham, Prieur Jay 1937- *IntAu&W 82*
Higginbotham, R Don 1931- *ConAu 17R*
Higginbotham, Sanford Wilson 1913- *ConAu 105*
Higginbotham, Virginia 1935- *ConAu 110*
Higginbottom, J Winslow 1945-
   SmATA 29[port]
Higgins, A C 1930- *ConAu 37R*
Higgins, A J B 1911- *ConAu 13R*
Higgins, Aidan 1927- *ConAu 9R, ConNov 82,*
   DcLB 14[port], DcLEL 1940,
   ModBrL SUP, WrDr 84
Higgins, Alice 1924?-1974 *ConAu 53*
Higgins, Angus 1911- *WrDr 84*
Higgins, Chester 1946- *ConAu 73, LivgBAA*
Higgins, Colin 1941- *ConAu 33R,*
   DcLB 26[port]
Higgins, Dick *DrAP&F 83*
Higgins, Dick 1938- *ConAu X, IntWWP 82X,*
   WrDr 84
Higgins, Don 1928- *ConAu 25R*
Higgins, Frank *DrAP&F 83*
Higgins, George P *DrAP&F 83*
Higgins, George V 1939- *ConAu 77, ConLC 4,*
   –10, –18, ConNov 82, DcLB Y81A[port], –2,
   TwCCr&M 80, WrDr 84
Higgins, George V 1940?- *ConLC 7*
Higgins, Ink *ConAu X*
Higgins, Jack *TwCCr&M 80, WrDr 84*
Higgins, James E 1926- *ConAu 73*
Higgins, Jean C 1932- *ConAu 29R*
Higgins, John A 1931- *ConAu 77*
Higgins, John J 1935- *ConAu 45*
Higgins, Judith *DrAP&F 83*
Higgins, Judith Holden 1930- *ConAu 102*
Higgins, Marguerite 1920-1966 *ConAu 5R, –25R*
Higgins, Paul C 1950- *ConAu 106*
Higgins, Paul Lambourne 1916- *ConAu 1R,*
   –2NR
Higgins, Reynold Alleyne 1916- *ConAu 25R,*

   WrDr 84
Higgins, Richard C 1938- *ConAu 8NR, –13R,*
   IntAu&W 82, IntWWP 82
Higgins, Ronald 1929- *ConAu 81*
Higgins, Rosaline 1937- *IntAu&W 82*
Higgins, Rosalyn 1937- *ConAu 3NR, –9R,*
   WrDr 84
Higgins, Thomas Joseph 1899- *ConAu 1R, –5NR,*
   WrDr 84
Higgins, Trumbull 1919- *ConAu 17R*
Higgins, W Robert 1938- *ConAu 37R,*
   WrDr 84
Higginson, Fred H 1921- *ConAu 1R*
Higginson, Margaret V 1923- *ConAu 105*
Higginson, William J *DrAP&F 83*
Higginson, William J 1938- *IntAu&W 82*
Higgs, David 1939- *ConAu 61*
Higgs, E S 1908-1976 *ConAu 69*
Higgs, Eric Sidney 1908- *ConAu 9R*
Higgs, Gerald B 1921- *ConAu 106*
High, Dallas M 1931- *ConAu 21R*
High, Graham John 1948- *IntWWP 82*
High, Monique Raphel 1949- *ConAu 102*
High, Philip E 1914- *ConAu 97, ConSFA,*
   TwCSFW, WrDr 84
High, Stanley 1895-1961 *ConAu 89*
Higham, Charles 1931- *ConAu 33R, ConP 80,*
   DcLEL 1940, WrDr 84
Higham, David 1895-1978 *ConAu 1R, –2NR*
Higham, Florence May Grier 1896-1980
   ConAu 97
Higham, John 1920- *ConAu 1R, –6NR*
Higham, Robert R A 1935- *WrDr 84*
Higham, Robin 1925- *ConAu 1R, –1NR,*
   IntAu&W 82, WrDr 84
Higham, Roger Stephen *WrDr 84*
Higham, Roger Stephen 1935- *ConAu 33R*
Highberger, Ruth 1917- *ConAu 65*
Highet, Gilbert Arthur 1906-1978 *ASpks,*
   ConAu 1R, –6NR, –73, DcLEL 1940,
   LongCTC, TwCA SUP
Highet, Helen *SmATA X*
Highet, John 1918- *WrDr 84*
Highland, Dora *ConAu X, WrDr 84*
Highland, Monica *WrDr 84*
Highsmith, Mary Patricia 1921- *DcLEL 1940*
Highsmith, Patricia 1921- *ConAu 1R, –1NR,*
   ConLC 2, –4, –14, ConNov 82,
   IntAu&W 82, TwCCr&M 80, WhoTwCL,
   WorAu, WrDr 84
Highsmith, Richard Morgan, Jr. 1920-
   ConAu 37R
Hightower, Florence 1916-1981 *TwCCW 83*
Hightower, Florence Cole 1916-1981 *ConAu 1R,*
   –103, SmATA 27N, –4
Hightower, Paul *ConAu X*
Highwater, Jamake *DrAP&F 83*
Highwater, Jamake 1942- *ConAu 10NR, –65,*
   ConLC 12, SmATA 30, –32[port],
   TwCCW 83, WrDr 84
Higman, B W 1943- *ConAu 81*
Higman, Francis M 1935- *ConAu 25R*
Hignett, Sean 1934- *ConAu 49, WrDr 84*
Higonnet, Margaret Randolph 1941- *ConAu 61*
Higonnet, Patrice Louis-Rene 1938- *ConAu 65*
Higson, James D 1925- *ConAu 49*
Higson, P J W *IntAu&W 82X*
Higson, Philip 1933- *IntAu&W 82X, WrDr 84*
Hikmet, Nazim 1902-1963 *CIDMEL 80, CnMD,*
   ConAu 93, EncWL 2, TwCWr, WhoTwCL,
   WorAu 1970
Hilary, Christopher 1927?-1979 *ConAu 89*
Hilberg, Raul 1926- *ConAu 33R, WrDr 84*
Hilberry, Conrad *DrAP&F 83*
Hilberry, Conrad 1928- *ConAu 10NR*
Hilberry, Conrad Arthur 1928- *ConAu 25R,*
   IntAu&W 82, IntWWP 82, MichAu 80,
   WrDr 84
Hilborn, Ann 1942- *ConAu 109*
Hilborn, Harry 1900- *ConAu P-2*
Hildebrand, George H 1913- *ConAu 8NR, –17R*
Hildebrand, Grant 1934- *ConAu 57*
Hildebrand, Joel H 1881-1983 *ConAu 109*
Hildebrand, Joel Henry 1881- *ConAu P-1*
Hildebrand, Verna 1924- *ConAu 33R, WrDr 84*
Hildebrandt, Greg 1939- *ConAu 104,*
   SmATA 33
Hildebrandt, Tim 1939- *SmATA 33*
Hilderbrand, Robert Clinton 1947- *ConAu 105*
Hildesheimer, Wolfgang 1916- *CIDMEL 80,*
   CnMD, ConAu 101, CroCD, EncWL 2,
   IntAu&W 82, ModGL, ModWD

Hildick, E W 1925- *ConAu X, SmATA 2, TwCCW 83, WrDr 84*
Hildick, Edmund Wallace 1925- *SmATA 2*
Hildick, Wallace 1925- *ConAu 25R, TwCCr&M 80*
Hildreth, Margaret Holbrook 1927- *ConAu 89*
Hildum, Donald C 1930- *ConAu 21R*
Hilfer, Anthony Channell 1936- *ConAu 73*
Hilger, Sister Mary Inez 1891-1977 *ConAu 21R, -73*
Hilken, Glen A 1936- *ConAu 61*
Hill, Adelaide Cromwell *LivgBAA*
Hill, Adrian Keith Graham 1895-1977 *ConAu 73, -77*
Hill, Alexis *WrDr 84*
Hill, Alfred T 1908- *ConAu 21R*
Hill, Archibald Anderson 1902- *ConAu 49*
Hill, Barrington 1915- *WrDr 84*
Hill, Barrington Julian Warren 1915- *ConAu 5R, IntAu&W 82*
Hill, Brian 1896- *ConAu P-1*
Hill, Brian Merrikin 1917- *IntWWP 82*
Hill, Carol *DrAP&F 83*
Hill, Carol 1942- *ConAu 77, ConNov 82, WrDr 84*
Hill, Christopher 1912- *ConAu 4NR, -9R, WorAu 1970, WrDr 84*
Hill, Claude 1911- *ConAu 21R*
Hill, Clifford S 1927- *ConAu 7NR, -13R*
Hill, Daniel G, Jr. 1896?-1979 *ConAu 89*
Hill, Dave *ConAu X*
Hill, David Charles 1936- *ConAu 11NR, -17R*
Hill, Deborah 1936- *ConAu 108*
Hill, Dee *ConAu X*
Hill, Denise 1919- *ConAu 106*
Hill, Desmond 1920- *ConAu 5R*
Hill, Devra Z *ConAu X*
Hill, Dilys M 1935- *ConAu 61*
Hill, Donna *ConAu 7NR, -13R, DrAP&F 83, SmATA 24[port]*
Hill, Dorothy 1907- *WrDr 84*
Hill, Douglas 1935- *ConAu 4NR, -53, ConSFA, WrDr 84*
Hill, Earle 1941- *ConAu 33R*
Hill, Elizabeth Starr 1925- *ConAu 17R, SmATA 24[port], WrDr 84*
Hill, Ellen Wise 1942- *ConAu 77*
Hill, Ernest 1915- *ConAu 53, ConSFA*
Hill, Errol 1921- *WrDr 84*
Hill, Errol Gaston 1921- *ConAu 45, ConDr 82*
Hill, Evan 1919- *ConAu 5NR, -9R*
Hill, Fiona *ConAu X*
Hill, Fowler 1901?-1973 *ConAu 37R*
Hill, Francis 1899-1980 *ConAu 108*
Hill, Frank Ernest 1888-1969 *ConAu 73*
Hill, Frank Ernest 1888-1970? *TwCA, TwCA SUP*
Hill, Gene 1928- *ConAu 97*
Hill, Geoffrey 1932- *ConAu 81, ConLC 5, –8, –18, ConP 80, DcLEL 1940, EncWL 2, IntAu&W 82, ModBrL SUP, RGFMBP, WorAu 1970, WrDr 84*
Hill, George E 1907- *ConAu P-1*
Hill, George Roy 1922- *ConLC 26[port]*
Hill, George Roy 1923?- *ConAu 110*
Hill, George William 1861-1934 *CreCan 2*
Hill, Gladwin 1914- *ConAu 25R*
Hill, Grace Brooks *ConAu P-2, SmATA 1*
Hill, Grace Livingston 1865-1947 *TwCA, TwCA SUP, TwCRGW*
Hill, Graham 1929-1975 *ConAu 108*
Hill, H D N *ConAu X*
Hill, Hamlin 1931- *ConAu 3NR, –9R, IntAu&W 82*
Hill, Harold E 1905- *ConAu 11NR, –69*
Hill, Helen *ConAu X*
Hill, Helen M 1915- *ConAu 57, SmATA 27*
Hill, Henry Bertram 1907- *ConAu 1R*
Hill, Herbert 1924- *ConAu 65*
Hill, Howard Edward 1897- *IntAu&W 82*
Hill, Hyacinthe *ConAu X*
Hill, I William 1908- *ConAu 65*
Hill, J C 1888- *ConAu 37R*
Hill, Jack 1896- *MichAu 80*
Hill, James *ConAu X, WrDr 84*
Hill, James N 1934- *ConAu 33R*
Hill, James William Francis 1899- *IntAu&W 82*
Hill, Jeanne Foster *DrAP&F 83*
Hill, Jim Dan 1897- *ConAu P-1*
Hill, John Campbell 1888- *WrDr 84*
Hill, John Edward Christopher 1912- *IntAu&W 82*

Hill, John Hugh 1905- *ConAu 1R, –5NR*
Hill, John P 1936- *ConAu 29R*
Hill, John S 1929- *ConAu 37R*
Hill, John Wiley 1890-1977 *ConAu 69*
Hill, Kathleen Louise 1917- *ConAu 3NR, –9R, SmATA 4*
Hill, Kay *ConAu X, SmATA X*
Hill, Ken 1937- *ConAu 108*
Hill, King *ConAu X*
Hill, Knox C 1910- *ConAu P-1*
Hill, L A 1918- *ConAu 21R*
Hill, L Draper 1935- *ConAu 17R, WrDr 84*
Hill, Larry D 1935- *ConAu 73*
Hill, Lee H 1899-1974 *ConAu 37R, –45*
Hill, Lew *ConAu X*
Hill, Lorna *WrDr 84*
Hill, Lorna 1902- *ConAu P-1, SmATA 12, TwCCW 83*
Hill, Margaret 1915- *ConAu 1R, –1NR*
Hill, Marnesba D 1913- *ConAu 101*
Hill, Mars 1927- *NatPD 81[port]*
Hill, Marvin S 1928- *ConAu 61*
Hill, Mary A 1939- *ConAu 102*
Hill, Mary Raymond 1923- *ConAu 6NR, –57*
Hill, Mary V 1941- *ConAu 102*
Hill, Meg *ConAu X*
Hill, Michael 1943- *WrDr 84*
Hill, Monica *ConAu X, SmATA 3*
Hill, Nancy Klenk 1936- *ConAu 108*
Hill, Napoleon 1883?-1970 *ConAu 104*
Hill, Nellie *ConAu X, DrAP&F 83*
Hill, Norman Llewellyn 1895- *ConAu 5R*
Hill, Pamela 1920- *ConAu 1NR, –49, TwCRGW, WrDr 84*
Hill, Pati *ConAu 69, DrAP&F 83*
Hill, Peter Proal 1926- *ConAu 33R*
Hill, Philip G 1934- *ConAu 33R*
Hill, Polly 1914- *ConAu X*
Hill, R Carter 1945- *ConAu 110*
Hill, R Lance 1943- *ConAu 11NR, –65*
Hill, Ralph Nading 1917- *ConAu 1R, –1NR*
Hill, Reginald 1936- *WrDr 84*
Hill, Reginald Charles 1936- *ConAu 73, TwCCr&M 80*
Hill, Richard 1901- *ConAu 1R, –1NR*
Hill, Richard 1941- *ConAu 33R, WrDr 84*
Hill, Richard E 1920- *ConAu 33R*
Hill, Richard F *DrAP&F 83*
Hill, Richard Johnson 1925- *ConAu 4NR, –9R*
Hill, Robert 1948- *IntWWP 82*
Hill, Robert W *DrAP&F 83*
Hill, Robert W 1919-1982 *ConAu 9R, –107, SmATA 12, –31N*
Hill, Roberta J *DrAP&F 83*
Hill, Rosalind Mary Theodosia 1908- *ConAu P-1, WrDr 84*
Hill, Roscoe E 1936- *ConAu 37R*
Hill, Ruth A *ConAu X, SmATA 6*
Hill, Ruth Beebe 1913- *ConAu 89, WrDr 84*
Hill, Ruth Livingston *ConAu X, SmATA X*
Hill, Samuel E 1913- *ConAu 17R*
Hill, Samuel S, Jr. 1927- *ConAu 5NR, –9R*
Hill, Susan 1942- *ConAu 33R, ConDr 82B, ConLC 4, ConNov 82, DcLB 14[port], DcLEL 1940, WorAu 1970, WrDr 84*
Hill, Thomas English 1909- *ConAu 13R*
Hill, Tom *IntAu&W 82X*
Hill, W M *ConAu 49*
Hill, W Speed 1935- *ConAu 41R*
Hill, Walter 1942- *ConAu 109*
Hill, Weldon *ConAu X*
Hill, West T, Jr. 1915- *ConAu 37R*
Hill, Wilhelmina 1902- *ConAu 57*
Hill, William Joseph 1924- *ConAu 37R, WrDr 84*
Hill, Winfred F 1929- *ConAu 29R*
Hill-Reid, William Scott 1890- *ConAu 5R*
Hillaby, John 1917- *ConAu 109, WrDr 84*
Hillam, Ray C 1928- *ConAu 107*
Hillard, James M 1920- *ConAu 73*
Hillary, Edmund 1919- *WrDr 84*
Hillary, Sir Edmund 1919- *ASpks, LongCTC*
Hillary, Richard Hope 1919-1943 *LongCTC, TwCA SUP*
Hillas, Julian *ConAu X*
Hillbruner, Anthony 1914- *ConAu 41R*
Hillcourt, William 1900- *ConAu 93, SmATA 27*
Hillebrand, Bruno 1935- *IntAu&W 82*
Hillebrand, Werner F 1931- *IntWWP 82*
Hillegas, Mark R 1926- *ConAu 33R*
Hillenbrand, Barry R 1941- *ConAu 73*

Hillenbrand, Martin Joseph 1915- *ConAu 108*
Hiller, Catherine *DrAP&F 83*
Hiller, Catherine 1946- *ConAu 106*
Hiller, Doris *ConAu X*
Hiller, Eric *DrAP&F 83*
Hiller, Flora *ConAu X*
Hiller, Lejaren 1924- *WrDr 84*
Hiller, Lejaren A, Jr. 1924- *ConAu 1R*
Hillerman, Tony 1925- *ConAu 29R, SmATA 6, TwCCr&M 80, WrDr 84*
Hillers, Delbert R 1932- *ConAu 77*
Hillers, H W 1925- *ConAu 73*
Hillert, Margaret 1920- *AuNews 1, ConAu 1NR, –49, IntWWP 82, MichAu 80, SmATA 8*
Hillery, George A, Jr. 1927- *ConAu 25R*
Hilles, Frederick Whiley 1900-1975 *ConAu 5R, –61*
Hillgarth, J N 1929- *ConAu 37R, WrDr 84*
Hillgarth, Jocelyn Nigel 1929- *IntAu&W 82*
Hillgruber, Andreas 1925- *ConAu 106, IntAu&W 82*
Hilliard, Jan 1911- *ConAu X, CreCan 1*
Hilliard, Noel 1929- *ConAu 7NR, –9R, ConLC 15, ConNov 82, DcLEL 1940, IntAu&W 82, WrDr 84*
Hilliard, Robert L 1925- *ConAu 107*
Hilliard, Sam B 1930- *ConAu 61*
Hillier, Bevis 1940- *ConAu 29R, WrDr 84*
Hillier, Caroline 1931- *WrDr 84*
Hillier, Jack Ronald 1912- *ConAu 3NR, –5R, IntAu&W 82, WrDr 84*
Hillier, Jim 1941- *WrDr 84*
Hilliker, Grant 1921- *ConAu 33R*
Hilling, David 1935- *ConAu 29R*
Hilling, John Bryan 1934- *IntAu&W 82*
Hillinger, Brad 1952- *ConAu 73*
Hillis, Charles Richard 1913- *ConAu 13R*
Hillis, Dave 1945- *ConAu 57*
Hillis, Dick 1913- *ConAu X, WrDr 84*
Hillix, W A 1927- *ConAu 89*
Hillman, Barry 1942- *ConAu 102, WrDr 84*
Hillman, Barry Leslie 1944- *IntAu&W 82*
Hillman, Brenda *DrAP&F 83*
Hillman, Howard 1934- *ConAu 41R*
Hillman, James 1926- *ConAu 89*
Hillman, Martin *ConAu X*
Hillman, Priscilla 1940- *ConAu 108*
Hillman, Ruth Estelyn Ryder 1925- *ConAu 53*
Hillmann, Dr. Heinz *IntAu&W 82X*
Hillocks, George, Jr. 1934- *ConAu 53*
Hills, C A R 1955- *ConAu 106*
Hills, Denis 1913- *ConAu 10NR, –65, WrDr 84*
Hills, Edwin Sherbon 1906- *WrDr 84*
Hills, Francis Elizabeth *WrDr 84*
Hills, George 1918- *ConAu 25R, WrDr 84*
Hills, L Rust 1924- *ConAu 25R*
Hills, Lee 1906- *ConAu 101*
Hills, Lee And Tina *AuNews 2*
Hills, Patricia Gorton Schulze 1936- *ConAu 103*
Hills, Philip James 1933- *WrDr 84*
Hills, Stuart Lee 1932- *ConAu 33R*
Hills, Theodore Lewis 1925- *ConAu 5R*
Hillson, Maurie 1925- *ConAu 17R*
Hillstrom, Tom 1943- *ConAu 102*
Hillus, Wilhelm *ConAu X*
Hillway, Tyrus 1912- *ConAu 1R, –4NR*
Hillyer, Robert Silliman 1895-1961 *ConAmA, ConAu 89, TwCA, TwCA SUP*
Hilscher, Gottfried H 1938- *IntAu&W 82*
Hilsdale, Paul 1922- *ConAu 9R*
Hilsenrath, Edgar 1926- *ConAu 49*
Hilsman, Roger 1919- *ConAu 5R, WrDr 84*
Hilt, Douglas Richard 1932- *ConAu 65*
Hiltebeital, Alf 1942- *ConAu 103*
Hiltner, Seward 1909- *ConAu 1R, –1NR, WrDr 84*
Hilton, Alec *ConAu X*
Hilton, Alice Mary 1924- *ConAu 29R*
Hilton, Bruce 1930- *ConAu 5R, –8NR*
Hilton, Conrad N 1887-1979 *ConAu 81*
Hilton, David *DrAP&F 83*
Hilton, Della 1934- *ConAu 69*
Hilton, Earl 1914- *ConAu 21R*
Hilton, George Woodman 1925- *ConAu 1R, –4NR, WrDr 84*
Hilton, Howard H 1926- *ConAu 105*
Hilton, Irene Pothus 1912- *ConAu 1R, SmATA 7*
Hilton, James 1900-1954 *ConAu 108, LongCTC, ModBrL, SmATA 34[port], TwCA, TwCA SUP, TwCCr&M 80, TwCSFW,*

SmATA 4
Hiskett, Mervyn 1920- *ConAu 61*
Hislop, Codman 1906- *ConAu P-2*
Hiss, Alger 1904- *ConAu 33R*
Hiss, Tony 1941- *ConAu 77*
Hitchcock, Alfred 1899-1980 *ConAu 97,*
ConLC 16, SmATA 24N, −27[port]
Hitchcock, Alma Reville 1899-1982 *ConAu 107*
Hitchcock, Donald R 1930- *IntAu&W 82*
Hitchcock, George *DrAP&F 83*
Hitchcock, George 1914- *ConAu 33R, ConP 80,*
IntWWP 82, WrDr 84
Hitchcock, H Wiley 1923- *ConAu 1NR, −45*
Hitchcock, Henry-Russell 1903- *IntAu&W 82,*
WrDr 84
Hitchcock, James 1938- *ConAu 33R*
Hitchcock, Raymond John 1922- *ConAu 85,*
WrDr 84
Hitchcock, Susan Tyler 1950- *ConAu 102*
Hitchens, Bert *TwCCr&M 80*
Hitchens, Dolores 1908?-1973 *ConAu 45,*
TwCCr&M 80
Hitchin, Martin Mewburn 1917- *ConAu 13R*
Hitching, Francis 1933- *ConAu 103*
Hitchman, James H 1932- *ConAu 37R,*
WrDr 84
Hitchman, Janet 1916-1980 *ConAu 21R, −97*
Hite, James 1941- *ConAu 53*
Hite, Shere D 1942- *ConAu 81*
Hitiris, Theodore 1938- *ConAu 41R*
Hitrec, Joseph George 1912-1972 *ConAu P-2*
Hitsman, J Mackay 1917-1970 *ConAu P-1*
Hitt, Russell T 1905- *ConAu 1R*
Hitt, William D 1929- *ConAu 49*
Hitte, Kathryn 1919- *ConAu 21R, SmATA 16*
Hitti, Philip K 1886-1978 *ConAu 1R, −6NR, −81*
Hitz, Demi 1942- *ConAu 8NR, −61,*
SmATA 11
Hively, Pete 1934- *ConAu 69*
Hivnor, Robert 1916- *ConAu 65, ConDr 82,*
CroCD, WrDr 84
Hix, Charles 1942- *ConAu 102*
Hix, Hubert E *DrAP&F 83*
Hixon, Don L 1942- *ConAu 73*
Hixson, Joseph R 1927- *ConAu 65*
Hixson, Richard F 1932- *ConAu 21R*
Hixson, William B, Jr. 1940- *ConAu 37R,*
WrDr 84
Hjalmarsson, Johann 1939- *IntWWP 82*
Hjartarson, Snorri 1906- *ClDMEL 80,*
EncWL 2
Hjelm, Magnus Benedikt 1904- *IntAu&W 82*
Hjelte, George 1893- *ConAu 29R*
Hjortsberg, William *DrAP&F 83*
Hjortsberg, William 1941- *ConAu 33R,*
IntAu&W 82, WrDr 84
Hlasko, Marek 1933?-1969 *ConAu 25R*
Hlasko, Marek 1934?-1969 *ClDMEL 80,*
EncWL 2, ModSL 2, TwCWr, WorAu
Hlt *IntAu&W 82X*
Hlybinny, Vladimir *ConAu X, IntAu&W 82X*
Hnizdovsky, Jacques 1915- *SmATA 32[port]*
Ho, Alfred K 1919- *ConAu 25R*
Ho, Ch'i-Fang 1912-1977 *EncWL 2*
Ho, Minfong 1951- *ConAu 77, IntAu&W 82,*
SmATA 15
Ho, Ping-Ti 1917- *ConAu 5R, −11NR*
Ho Chu Tai *IntWWP 82X*
Hoa, Nguyen-Dinh *ConAu X*
Hoadley, Irene B 1938- *WrDr 84*
Hoadley, Irene Braden 1938- *ConAu 29R*
Hoadley, Walter E 1916- *ConAu 102*
Hoag, Bonnie Elizabeth *DrAP&F 83*
Hoag, David *DrAP&F 83*
Hoag, Edwin 1926- *ConAu 13R, WrDr 84*
Hoagland, Edward *DrAP&F 83*
Hoagland, Edward 1932- *ConAu 1R, −2NR,*
ConNov 82, DcLB 6[port], WorAu 1970,
WrDr 84
Hoagland, Eric *LivgBAA*
Hoagland, Everett 1942- *ConAu 33R*
Hoagland, Jimmie Lee 1940- *ConAu 101*
Hoagland, Kathleen M Dooher *ConAu 5R*
Hoagland, Mahlon B 1921- *ConAu 85*
Hoang Van Chi 1915- *ConAu 7NR, −13R*
Hoar, Peter 1912- *ConAu 84*
Hoare, Merval Hannah 1914- *ConAu 103,*
IntWWP 82, WrDr 84
Hoare, Robert John 1921-1975 *ConAu 6NR, −9R*
Hoare, Wilber W, Jr. 1921-1976 *ConAu 65*
Hoban, Lillian 1925- *ConAu 69,*
SmATA 22[port]

Hoban, Russell 1925- *TwCCW 83, WrDr 84*
Hoban, Russell C 1925- *ChlLR 3, ConAu 5R,*
ConLC 7, −25[port], SmATA 1
Hoban, Tana *ConAu 93, SmATA 22[port]*
Hobana, Ion 1931- *IntAu&W 82*
Hobart, Alice Tisdale 1882-1967 *ConAu X, −5R,*
−25R, TwCA, TwCA SUP
Hobart, Billie 1935- *ConAu 49*
Hobart, Donald Bayne *TwCWW*
Hobart, Lois *WrDr 84*
Hobart, Lois Elaine *ConAu 5R, SmATA 7*
Hobart, Robertson *TwCCr&M 80*
Hobbes, John Oliver 1867-1906 *LongCTC*
Hobbing, Enno 1920- *ConAu 89*
Hobbs, Cecil 1907- *ConAu 21R, WrDr 84*
Hobbs, Charles R 1931- *ConAu 13R, WrDr 84*
Hobbs, Fredric 1931- *ConAu 81*
Hobbs, Herschel H 1907- *WrDr 84*
Hobbs, Herschel Harold 1907- *ConAu 2NR, −5R*
Hobbs, J Kline *DrAP&F 83*
Hobbs, J Kline 1920- *ConAu 108, MichAu 80A*
Hobbs, J Kline 1938- *NatPD 81[port]*
Hobbs, John Leslie 1916-1964 *ConAu 5R*
Hobbs, Perry *ConAu X*
Hobbs, Peter V 1936- *ConAu 53*
Hobbs, Robert 1946- *ConAu 106*
Hobbs, Suzanne Marie *DrAP&F 83*
Hobbs, William 1939- *ConAu 21R*
Hobbs, Williston C 1925?-1978 *ConAu 81*
Hobby, Bertram Maurice 1905-1983 *ConAu 110*
Hobby, Oveta Culp 1905- *ConAu 81*
Hobby, William P 1932- *ConAu 85*
Hobday, Charles Henry 1917- *IntWWP 82*
Hobday, Victor C 1914- *ConAu 97*
Hobden, Andree Maillet *CreCan 2*
Hobel, Phil *ConAu X*
Hoben, John B 1908- *ConAu 37R*
Hoben, Sandra *DrAP&F 83*
Hoberecht, Earnest 1918- *ConAu 21R*
Hoberman, Mary Ann 1930- *ConAu 41R,*
SmATA 5
Hobgood, Burnet M 1922- *ConAu 101*
Hobhouse, Christina 1941- *ConAu 25R,*
WrDr 84
Hobhouse, Hermione 1934- *ConAu 41R,*
WrDr 84
Hobhouse, Janet 1948- *ConAu 57*
Hobley, Leonard Frank 1903- *ConAu 5NR, −13R,*
WrDr 84
Hobsbaum, Hannah 1937- *IntWWP 82*
Hobsbaum, Philip 1932- *ConAu 3NR, −9R,*
ConP 80, DcLEL 1940, IntAu&W 82,
IntWWP 82, WrDr 84
Hobsbawm, E J 1917- *WorAu 1970*
Hobsbawm, Eric 1941- *WrDr 84*
Hobsbawm, Eric John Ernest 1917- *ConAu 3NR,*
−5R
Hobson, Anthony Robert Alwyn 1921-
ConAu 13R, IntAu&W 82, WrDr 84
Hobson, Burton 1933- *ConAu 2NR, −5R,*
SmATA 28
Hobson, Edmund Schofield, Jr. 1931- *ConAu 45*
Hobson, Fred Colby 1943- *WrDr 84*
Hobson, Fred Colby, Jr. 1943- *ConAu 5NR, −53*
Hobson, Geary *DrAP&F 83*
Hobson, Hank *ConAu X*
Hobson, Harold 1904- *ConAu 81, CroCD,*
DcLEL 1940, IntAu&W 82, LongCTC,
WrDr 84
Hobson, Harry 1908- *ConAu P-1*
Hobson, Julius W 1922?-1977 *ConAu 102,*
LivgBAA
Hobson, Laura Z 1900- *ConAu 17R, ConLC 7,*
−25[port], ConNov 82, DcLEL 1940,
TwCA SUP, WrDr 84
Hobson, Mary 1926- *ConAu 106, WrDr 84*
Hobson, Polly *WrDr 84*
Hobson, Polly 1913- *ConAu X, IntAu&W 82X*
Hobson, William 1911- *ConAu 103, WrDr 84*
Hobzek, Mildred J 1919- *ConAu 101*
Hoch, Edward D *DrAP&F 83*
Hoch, Edward D 1930- *ConAu 11NR, −29R,*
IntAu&W 82, TwCCr&M 80, TwCSFW,
WrDr 84
Hoch, Paul L 1942- *ConAu 65*
Hochbaum, H Albert 1911- *ConAu 103*
Hochfield, George 1926- *ConAu 1R*
Hochhuth, Rolf 1931- *ClDMEL 80, CnMD,*
ConAu 5R, ConLC 4, −11, −18, CroCD,
EncWL 2[port], ModGL, ModWD,
TwCWr, WorAu
Hochman, Harold M 1936- *ConAu 108*

Hochman, Sandra *DrAP&F 83*
Hochman, Sandra 1936- *ConAu 5R, ConLC 3,*
−8, ConP 80, DcLB 5[port], WorAu 1970,
WrDr 84
Hochman, Shel 1944- *ConAu 69*
Hochman, Shirley D 1917- *ConAu 61*
Hochman, Stanley Richard 1928- *ConAu 103*
Hochmuth, Karl 1919- *IntAu&W 82*
Hochschild, Arlie Russell 1940- *ConAu 57,*
SmATA 11
Hochschild, Harold K 1892-1981 *ConAu 103*
Hochstein, Rolaine *ConAu 45, DrAP&F 83*
Hochwaelder, Fritz 1911- *ConAu 29R*
Hochwald, Werner 1910- *ConAu 17R,*
WrDr 84
Hochwalder, Fritz 1911- *CnMD, ConAu X,*
CroCD, EncWL 2, IntAu&W 82, ModGL,
ModWD, TwCWr, WorAu
Hockaby, Stephen *ConAu X, WrDr 84*
Hockaby, Stephen 1901- *ConAu X, LongCTC*
Hocke, Gustav Rene 1908- *IntAu&W 82*
Hockenberry, Hope *ConAu X, SmATA X*
Hocker, Karla *ConAu 49*
Hockett, Charles F 1916- *ConAu 17R,*
WrDr 84
Hockey, Lawrence William 1904- *IntWWP 82*
Hocking, Anne 1890- *TwCCr&M 80*
Hocking, Anthony 1938- *ConAu 102, WrDr 84*
Hocking, Brian 1914-1974 *ConAu P-2*
Hocking, Joseph 1860-1937 *LongCTC, TwCA,*
TwCA SUP
Hocking, Mary 1921- *ConAu 101, ConLC 13,*
IntAu&W 82, WrDr 84
Hocking, Silas Kitto 1850-1935 *LongCTC*
Hocking, William Ernest 1873-1966 *ConAu P-1,*
TwCA SUP
Hockley, G C 1931- *ConAu 29R*
Hockney, David 1937- *WrDr 84*
Hocks, Richard A 1936- *ConAu 81*
Hodder-Williams, Christopher 1926- *ConAu 1R,*
−1NR, ConSFA, TwCSFW, WrDr 84
Hodder-Williams, John C Glazebrook 1927-
DcLEL 1940
Hoddinott, R F 1913- *WrDr 84*
Hoddis, Jakob Van 1887-1942 *WhoTwCL*
Hodeir, Andre 1921- *ConAu 85*
Hodemart, Peter *WrDr 84*
Hodenfield, Jan *ConAmTC*
Hodes, Aubrey 1927- *ConAu 33R*
Hodes, Scott 1937- *ConAu 49*
Hodgart, Matthew 1916- *ConAu 9NR,*
WrDr 84
Hodgart, Matthew John Caldwell 1916-
ConAu 5R, IntAu&W 82
Hodge, Alan 1915-1979 *ConAu 89*
Hodge, David W 1935- *ConAu 61*
Hodge, E Chatterton *ConAu X*
Hodge, Francis 1915- *ConAu 33R, WrDr 84*
Hodge, Gene 1898- *ConAu 45*
Hodge, James L 1935- *ConAu 41R*
Hodge, Jane Aiken 1917- *ConAu 3NR, −5R,*
IntAu&W 82, TwCRGW, WrDr 84
Hodge, Marshall Bryant 1925- *ConAu P-2*
Hodge, Merle 1944- *DcLEL 1940*
Hodge, P W 1934- *ConAu 33R, SmATA 12*
Hodge, Paul William 1934- *IntAu&W 82,*
WrDr 84
Hodge, William H 1932- *ConAu 65*
Hodgell, P C 1951- *ConAu 109*
Hodges, Barbara K 1893-1949 *LongCTC, TwCA,*
TwCA SUP
Hodges, C Walter 1909- *ConAu 5NR, −13R,*
IntAu&W 82, TwCCW 83, WrDr 84
Hodges, Carl G 1902-1964 *ConAu 5R,*
SmATA 10
Hodges, Cyril Walter 1909- *SmATA 2*
Hodges, Donald Clark 1923- *ConAu 6NR, −53,*
IntAu&W 82, WrDr 84
Hodges, Doris M 1915- *ConAu 11NR,*
WrDr 84
Hodges, Doris Marjorie 1915- *ConAu 25R*
Hodges, Elizabeth *DrAP&F 83*
Hodges, Elizabeth Jamison *ConAu 9R,*
SmATA 1
Hodges, Elma J 1910- *MichAu 80*
Hodges, Gil 1924-1972 *ConAu 109*
Hodges, Graham Rushing 1915- *ConAu 5R*
Hodges, Harold Mellor, Jr. 1922- *ConAu 17R,*
IntAu&W 82
Hodges, Henry 1920- *ConAu 37R*
Hodges, Henry G 1888- *ConAu 5R*
Hodges, Herbert Arthur 1905-1976 *ConAu 69,*

WrDr 84
Holley, Frederick S 1924- *ConAu 109*
Holley, I B, Jr. 1919- *ConAu 37R*
Holley, Irving Brinton, Jr. 1919- *WrDr 84*
Holli, Melvin G 1933- *ConAu 11NR*
Holli, Melvin George 1933- *ConAu 25R,*
MichAu 80, WrDr 84
Hollick, Ann L 1941- *ConAu 57*
Holliday, Barbara Gregg 1917- *ConAu 73*
Holliday, David 1931- *IntWWP 82*
Holliday, James *ConAu X*
Holliday, Joe 1910- *ConAu X, SmATA X*
Holliday, Joseph 1910- *ConAu P-2, SmATA 11*
Holliday, Robert Cortes 1880-1946 *TwCA,*
TwCA SUP
Hollindale, Peter 1936- *ConAu 103, WrDr 84*
Holling, Holling C 1900-1973 *TwCCW 83*
Holling, Holling Clancy 1900-1973 *ConAu 106,*
SmATA 15, -26N
Hollingdale, R J 1930- *ConAu 102*
Hollingdale, Reginald John 1930- *WrDr 84*
Hollingdrake, Sybil 1926- *IntAu&W 82*
Hollinger, Verna R 1908- *IntWWP 82*
Hollings, Michael 1921- *ConAu 81*
Hollingshead, August DeBelmont 1907-
ConAu 13R
Hollingshead, Kyle 1941- *ConAu 11NR, -21R,*
WrDr 84
Hollingsworth, Dorothy Frances 1916- *ConAu 85*
Hollingsworth, Harold M 1932- *ConAu 53*
Hollingsworth, J Rogers 1932- *ConAu 7NR,*
-13R
Hollingsworth, Kent 1929- *ConAu 81*
Hollingsworth, Lyman B 1919- *ConAu 45*
Hollingsworth, Mary H 1910- *ConAu 69*
Hollingsworth, Paul M 1932- *ConAu 29R,*
WrDr 84
Hollingworth, Brian Charles 1935- *IntAu&W 82*
Hollis, Barbara Coonley 1922- *IntWWP 82,*
WrDr 84
Hollis, Christopher 1902-1977 *ConAu 69, -73*
Hollis, Daniel W 1922- *ConAu 5R*
Hollis, H H 1921-1977 *TwCSFW*
Hollis, Harry Newcombe, Jr. 1938- *ConAu 57*
Hollis, Helen Rice *WrDr 84*
Hollis, Helen Rice 1908- *ConAu 61*
Hollis, James R 1940- *ConAu 41R*
Hollis, Jim *ConAu X, IntWWP 82X,*
WrDr 84
Hollis, Jocelyn *DrAP&F 83*
Hollis, Jocelyn 1927- *IntWWP 82*
Hollis, Joseph William 1922- *ConAu 25R*
Hollis, Lucile Ussery 1921- *ConAu 25R,*
WrDr 84
Hollister, Bernard C 1938- *ConAu 3NR, -49*
Hollister, C Warren 1930- *ConAu 1R, -1NR,*
IntAu&W 82
Hollister, Charles A 1918- *ConAu 17R*
Hollister, George E 1905- *ConAu P-2*
Hollister, Herbert A 1933- *ConAu 104*
Hollister, James P 1949- *IntAu&W 82*
Hollister, Leo E 1920- *ConAu 21R*
Hollmann, Clide John 1896-1966 *ConAu 5R*
Hollo, Anselm *DrAP&F 83*
Hollo, Anselm 1934- *ConAu 9NR, -21R,*
ConP 80, DcLEL 1940, IntWWP 82,
WrDr 84
Hollom, Philip Arthur Dominic 1912-
ConAu 13R
Hollon, W Eugene 1913- *ConAu 2NR*
Hollon, William Eugene 1913- *AuNews 1,*
ConAu 1R
Holloway, Anthony 1922- *ConAmTC*
Holloway, Brenda Wilmar 1908- *ConAu P-1*
Holloway, David 1924- *ConAu 107, WrDr 84*
Holloway, Emory 1885-1977 *ConAu 49, -73,*
TwCA, TwCA SUP
Holloway, Geoffrey 1918- *ConAu 49, ConP 80,*
WrDr 84
Holloway, George 1921- *ConAu 25R*
Holloway, Glenna R 1928- *IntWWP 82*
Holloway, Harry 1925- *ConAu 9R,*
IntAu&W 82, WrDr 84
Holloway, James Y 1927- *ConAu 53*
Holloway, John 1919- *DcLEL 1940*
Holloway, John 1920- *ConAu 3NR, -5R,*
ConLCrt 82, ConP 80, IntAu&W 82,
IntWWP 82, ModBrL, WorAu, WrDr 84
Holloway, Marcella M 1913- *ConAu 89*
Holloway, Mark 1917- *ConAu 21R,*
IntAu&W 82, WrDr 84
Holloway, Maurice 1920- *ConAu 9R*

Holloway, Robert J 1921- *ConAu 13R*
Holloway, Stanley 1890-1982 *ConAu 106*
Holloway, Teresa 1906- *ConAu 17R,*
SmATA 26[port]
Holloway, Thomas H 1944- *ConAu 106*
Holloway, W V 1903- *ConAu 1R, -2NR*
Hollowell, John 1945- *ConAu 102*
Hollowood, A Bernard 1910- *WrDr 84*
Hollowood, Albert Bernard 1910-1981 *ConAu 9R,*
-103
Hollweg, Arnd 1927- *IntAu&W 82*
Holly, Harry *IntAu&W 82X*
Holly, J Fred 1915- *ConAu 5R, -6NR*
Holly, J Hunter 1932- *ConAu X, ConSFA*
Holly, Joan Carol 1932- *ConAu 1R, -1NR*
Holly, Joan Hunter 1932- *ConAu X*
Hollyday, Frederic B M 1928- *ConAu 45*

Holm, Anne 1922- *ConAu 17R, SmATA 1*
Holm, Bjorn 1946- *IntAu&W 82*
Holm, Hans Henrik 1896- *IntWWP 82*
Holm, John Cecil 1904- *ModWD*
Holm, John Cecil 1906- *CnMD*
Holm, Marilyn D 1944- *ConAu 17R*
Holm, Peter Rowde 1931- *IntAu&W 82*
Holm, Sven 1902- *ConAu P-1*
Holm, Sven 1940- *ClDMEL 80*
Holman, Bob *DrAP&F 83*
Holman, C Hugh 1914- *ConAu 5R,*
TwCCr&M 80, WrDr 84
Holman, Dennis 1915- *ConAu 9R*
Holman, Edward Lee 1894- *WrDr 84*
Holman, Felice 1919- *ConAu 3NR, -5R,*
IntAu&W 82, SmATA 7, TwCCW 83,
WrDr 84
Holman, Harriet R 1912- *ConAu 37R*
Holman, L Bruce 1939- *ConAu 61*
Holman, Mary A 1933- *ConAu 93*
Holman, Ottilie Ann 1949- *IntWWP 82*
Holman, Portia Grenfell 1903-1983 *ConAu 109*
Holman, Robert 1936- *WrDr 84*
Holman, William R 1926- *ConAu 49*
Holmans, Alan Edward 1934- *ConAu 1R*
Holmas, Stig 1946- *IntWWP 82*
Holmberg, Margit 1912- *IntWWP 82*
Holme, Bryan 1913- *ConAu 103,*
SmATA 26[port]
Holme, Constance 1881?-1955 *LongCTC, TwCA,*
TwCA SUP
Holme, K E *ConAu X, WorAu 1970,*
WrDr 84
Holme, Thea 1903- *ConAu 41R*
Holmelund, Paul 1890- *ConAu 5R*
Holmer, Paul L 1916- *WrDr 84*
Holmer, Paul Leroy 1916- *ConAu 37R,*
IntAu&W 82
Holmes, Ann Hitchcock 1922- *ConAmTC*
Holmes, Anna-Marie Ellerbeck 1943- *CreCan 1*
Holmes, Arthur Frank 1924- *ConAu 33R,*
WrDr 84
Holmes, Burnham 1942- *ConAu 97*
Holmes, C Raymond 1929- *ConAu 57*
Holmes, Charles M 1923- *ConAu 29R*
Holmes, Charles S 1916-1976 *ConAu 41R, -61*
Holmes, Charlotte *DrAP&F 83*
Holmes, Clyde 1940- *IntWWP 82*
Holmes, Colin 1938- *ConAu 11NR, -25R*
Holmes, David Charles 1919- *ConAu 9R*
Holmes, David Leonard 1936- *CreCan 2*
Holmes, David Morton 1929- *ConAu 33R,*
WrDr 84
Holmes, Doloris *DrAP&F 83*
Holmes, Douglas 1933- *ConAu 41R*
Holmes, Edward M 1910- *ConAu 37R,*
WrDr 84
Holmes, Efner Tudor 1949- *ConAu 65*
Holmes, Frank Wakefield 1924- *ConAu 109*
Holmes, Frederic L 1932- *ConAu 93*
Holmes, Geoffrey Shorter 1928- *ConAu 25R,*
WrDr 84
Holmes, Grant *ConAu X*
Holmes, H H *ConAu X, TwCCr&M 80*
Holmes, Jack David Lazarus 1930- *ConAu 41R,*
IntAu&W 82
Holmes, Jay 1922- *ConAu X, WrDr 84*
Holmes, John *IntAu&W 82X, IntWWP 82X,*
WrDr 84
Holmes, John 1913- *ConAu 104, WrDr 84*
Holmes, John Albert 1904-1962 *WorAu*
Holmes, John Clellon *DrAP&F 83*
Holmes, John Clellon 1926- *ConAu 4NR, -9R,*

ConNov 82, DcLB 16[port], DcLEL 1940,
IntAu&W 82, WrDr 84
Holmes, John Haynes 1879-1964 *ConAu 89,*
TwCA SUP
Holmes, John W 1910- *ConAu 109*
Holmes, Joseph Everett 1922- *ConAu 1R, -1NR*
Holmes, Joseph R 1928?-1983 *ConAu 109*
Holmes, Kenneth Lloyd 1915- *ConAu 37R*
Holmes, L P 1895- *WrDr 84*
Holmes, Lowell D 1925- *ConAu 33R,*
IntAu&W 82, WrDr 84
Holmes, Marjorie 1910- *WrDr 84*
Holmes, Marjorie Rose 1910- *AuNews 1,*
ConAu 1R, -5NR
Holmes, Martin 1905- *ConAu 1NR, -49,*
WrDr 84
Holmes, Michael 1931- *ConAu 25R*
Holmes, Michael Stephan 1942- *ConAu 77*
Holmes, Nancy 1921- *ConAu 69*
Holmes, Oliver Wendell 1809-1894
SmATA 34[port]
Holmes, Parker Manfred 1895- *ConAu P-1*
Holmes, Paul Allen 1901- *ConAu P-2*
Holmes, Paul Anthony 1956- *IntAu&W 82*
Holmes, Paul Carter 1926- *ConAu 11NR, -21R*
Holmes, Raymond *CreCan 1, IntAu&W 82X,*
IntWWP 82X, WrDr 84
Holmes, Richard 1946- *ConAu 106*
Holmes, Rick *ConAu X, SmATA X*
Holmes, Robert 1862-1930 *CreCan 2*
Holmes, Robert A 1943- *ConAu 57*
Holmes, Robert L 1935- *ConAu 41R*
Holmes, Robert Lewis 1926- *WrDr 84*
Holmes, Robert Merrill 1925- *ConAu 89*
Holmes, Tiffany 1944- *ConAu 97*
Holmes, Tommy 1903-1975 *ConAu 57*
Holmes, Urban Tigner, Jr. 1900-1972 *ConAu P-2*
Holmes, W J 1900- *ConAu 29R*
Holmes, William Kersley 1882- *ConAu P-1*
Holmgren, Sister George Ellen *ConAu X*
Holmgren, Helen Jean 1930- *ConAu 97*
Holmgren, Mark *DrAP&F 83*
Holmgren, Norah 1939- *ConAu 102*
Holmgren, Virginia C 1909- *ConAu 107,*
SmATA 26[port]
Holmquist, Anders 1933- *ConAu 29R*
Holmquist, Eve 1921- *ConAu 53, SmATA 11*
Holmqvist, Lasse 1930- *IntAu&W 82*
Holmqvist, Nils 1925- *IntAu&W 82*
Holmsten, Aldona 1932- *IntAu&W 82*
Holmsten, Georg 1913- *IntAu&W 82*
Holmstrand, Marie Juline 1908- *ConAu 5R*
Holmstrom, Edwin 1898- *ConAu P-1*
Holmstrom, Lynda Lytle 1939- *ConAu 33R,*
WrDr 84
Holmvik, Oyvind 1914- *ConAu 17R*
Holquist, Michael 1935- *ConAu 2NR, -45*
Holroyd, Michael 1935- *WrDr 84*
Holroyd, Michael DeCourcy Fraser 1935-
ConAu 4NR, -53, DcLEL 1940,
IntAu&W 82, WorAu 1970
Holroyd, Sam *ConAu X*
Holroyd, Stuart 1933- *ConAu 93*
Holsaert, Eunice d1974 *ConAu 53*
Holsinger, Jane Lumley *ConAu 17R*
Holske, Katherine d1973 *ConAu 104*
Holsopple, Barbara 1943- *ConAu 73*
Holst, Johan J 1937- *ConAu 11NR, -25R*
Holst, Lawrence E 1929- *ConAu 61*
Holst, Spencer *DrAP&F 83*
Holstein, Count Ludvig 1864-1943 *ClDMEL 80*
Holsti, Kalevi J 1935- *ConAu 21R, WrDr 84*
Holsti, Ole R 1933- *ConAu 11NR*
Holsti, Ole Rudolf 1933- *ConAu 25R, WrDr 84*
Holt, Andrew *ConAu X*
Holt, Edgar Crawshaw 1900-1975 *ConAu 1R,*
-6NR, -61
Holt, Gavin 1891- *ConAu X*
Holt, Hans 1909- *CnMD*
Holt, Helen *ConAu X*
Holt, James 1939- *ConAu 25R*
Holt, John 1923- *ConAu 69, ConIsC 2[port]*
Holt, John 1926- *ConAu 11NR, -25R*
Holt, John Agee 1920- *ConAu 1R*
Holt, Kare 1917- *ClDMEL 80, EncWL 2*
Holt, Lee E 1912- *ConAu 13R*
Holt, Len *LivgBAA*
Holt, Luther Emmett, Jr. 1895-1974 *ConAu 53*
Holt, Margaret 1937- *ConAu 17R, SmATA 4*
Holt, Margaret VanVechten 1899-1963
SmATA 32
Holt, Michael 1929- *ConAu 5NR, -53,*

SmATA 13, WrDr 84
Holt, Michael F 1940- ConAu 81
Holt, Rackham SmATA X
Holt, Robert Rutherford 1917- ConAu 41R,
IntAu&W 82
Holt, Robert T 1928- ConAu 37R
Holt, Rochelle DrAP&F 83
Holt, Rochelle L 1946- ConAu X, -57
Holt, Stephen ConAu X, SmATA X
Holt, Tex ConAu X, TwCWW, WrDr 84
Holt, Thelma Jewett 1913- ConAu 29R
Holt, Thomas J 1928- ConAu 102
Holt, Victoria ConAu X
Holt, Victoria 1906- ConAu X, SmATA 2,
TwCRGW, WorAu, WrDr 84
Holt, Virginia ConLC 7
Holt, Will 1929- ConAu 105
Holt, William 1897-1977 ConAu 69, ConAu P-1
Holtan, Orley I 1933- ConAu 33R
Holtby, Robert Tinsley 1921- ConAu 108,
WrDr 84
Holtby, Winifred 1898-1935 LongCTC, ModBrL,
TwCA, TwCA SUP, TwCWr
Holter, Don W 1905- ConAu 37R
Holthusen, Hans Egon 1913- ConAu 45,
ModGL, TwCWr, WorAu
Holtje, Herbert F 1931- ConAu 8NR, -61
Holtom, Jenifer Jane 1932- IntWWP 82
Holton, Felicia Antonelli 1921- ConAu 69
Holton, Gerald 1922- ConAu 13R
Holton, Leonard WrDr 84
Holton, Leonard 1915- ConAu X,
IntAu&W 82X, SmATA 2, TwCCr&M 80,
WorAu
Holton, Milne 1931- ConAu 41R
Holton, Richard H 1926- ConAu 107
Holtrop, William Frans 1908- ConAu 57
Holttum, Richard Eric 1895- WrDr 84
Holtz, Avraham 1934- ConAu 29R
Holtz, Barry W 1947- ConAu 109
Holtz, Herman R 1919- ConAu 105
Holtzman, Abraham 1921- ConAu 1R, -2NR,
WrDr 84
Holtzman, Jerome 1926- ConAu 4NR, -53
Holtzman, Paul D 1918- ConAu 33R
Holtzman, Wayne Harold 1923- ConAu 37R,
WrDr 84
Holtzman, Will 1951- ConAu 102
Holub, Miroslav 1923- ConAu 10NR, -21R,
ConLC 4, ModSL 2, WhoTwCL, WorAu
Holway, John 1929- ConAu 57
Holyer, Erna Maria 1925- ConAu 29R,
IntAu&W 82, SmATA 22[port]
Holyer, Ernie ConAu X, IntAu&W 82X,
SmATA X
Holyer, Ernie 1925- WrDr 84
Holz, Arno 1863-1929 CIDMEL 80, CnMD,
ModGL, ModWD
Holz, Detlev WorAu 1970
Holz, Loretta 1943- ConAu 65, SmATA 17
Holz, Lorretta 1943- ConAu 10NR
Holz, Robert K 1930- ConAu 53
Holzapfel, Rudi 1938- DcLEL 1940
Holzapfel, Rudolf Patrick 1938- ConAu P-1
Holzberger, William George 1932- ConAu 53
Holzer, Hans 1920- ConAu 7NR, -13R
Holzman, Dennis Tilden DrAP&F 83
Holzman, Franklyn D 1918- WrDr 84
Holzman, Franklyn Dunn 1918- ConAu 61
Holzman, Lew DrAP&F 83
Holzman, Philip Seidman 1922- ConAu 37R
Holzman, Red ConAu X
Holzman, Robert Stuart 1907- ConAu 1R, -2NR
Holzman, William 1920- ConAu 101
Holzner, Burkart 1931- ConAu 93
Hom, Ken 1949- ConAu 109
Homan, Robert Anthony 1929- ConAu 5R,
WrDr 84
Homans, Abigail Adams 1879-1974 ConAu 104
Homans, George Caspar 1910- ConAu 107
Homans, Peter 1930- ConAu 11NR, -21R,
WrDr 84
Homberg, Hans 1903- CnMD
Homberger, Conrad P 1900- ConAu 13R
Homberger, Eric 1942- ConAu 106, WrDr 84
Homburger, Erik ConAu X
Home, Alex Douglas 1903- WrDr 84
Home, Alexander Frederick 1903- ConAu 102
Home, Henry Douglas ConAu X
Home, Michael ConAu X, TwCCr&M 80
Home, William Douglas 1912- CnMD,
ConAu 102, ConDr 82, CroCD,

DcLB 13[port], DcLEL 1940, ModWD,
WorAu 1970, WrDr 84
Home Of The Hirsel, Baron 1903- IntAu&W 82
Homer, Art DrAP&F 83
Homer, Frederic D 1939- ConAu 65
Homer, Sidney 1902-1983 ConAu 110
Homer, William Innes 1929- ConAu 13R,
WrDr 84
Homes, Geoffrey 1902-1978 TwCCr&M 80
Homokbodogei IntAu&W 82X
Homola, Samuel 1929- ConAu 97,
IntAu&W 82
Homoras ConAu X
Homrighausen, Elmer George 1900- ConAu 45,
IntAu&W 82
Homsher, Lola Mae 1913- ConAu 1R
Homze, Alma C 1932- ConAu 29R, SmATA 17
Homze, Edward L 1930- ConAu 33R
Hon Member For X IntAu&W 82X
Honan, Park 1928- ConAu 77, IntAu&W 82,
WrDr 84
Honce, Charles E 1895-1975 ConAu 61
Honchar, Oles 1918- CIDMEL 80, EncWL 2,
ModSL 2
Honderich, Ted 1933- ConAu 33R,
IntAu&W 82, WrDr 84
Hone, Joseph 1937- ConAu 65, WrDr 84
Hone, Ralph E 1913- ConAu 9NR, -21R
Honecker, George J DrAP&F 83
Honey, P J 1922- ConAu 13R
Honey, William 1910- ConAu 33R
Honeycombe, Gordon 1936- ConAu 77,
IntAu&W 82, WrDr 84
Honeycutt, Benjamin L 1938- ConAu 57
Honeycutt, Roy Lee, Jr. 1926- ConAu 41R
Honeyman, Brenda ConAu X, -X,
IntAu&W 82X, WrDr 84
Hong, Edna H 1913- ConAu 9NR, -21R
Hong, Howard V 1912- ConAu 9NR, -21R,
WrDr 84
Hong, Jane Fay 1954- ConAu 93
Hong, Sara 1927- IntWWP 82
Hong, Yong Ki 1929?-1979 ConAu 85
Hongo, Garrett Kaoru DrAP&F 83
Honig, Donald DrAP&F 83
Honig, Donald 1931- ConAu 9NR, -17R,
SmATA 18
Honig, Edwin DrAP&F 83
Honig, Edwin 1919- ConAu 4NR, -5R,
ConP 80, DcLB 5[port], IntAu&W 82,
IntWWP 82, WorAu, WrDr 84
Honig, Louis 1911-1977 ConAu 73, -77
Honig, Lucy DrAP&F 83
Honigfeld, Gilbert ConAu 49
Honigmann, E A J 1927- ConAu 9NR, -21R
Honigmann, John J 1914-1977 ConAu 1R, -2NR
Honnalgere, Gopal 1944- ConAu 73
Honness, Elizabeth H 1904- ConAu 25R,
SmATA 2
Honnold, John Otis, Jr. 1915- ConAu 8NR, -13R
Honold, Rolf 1919- CnMD
Honore, Antony Maurice 1921- ConAu 1R,
-1NR
Honour, Hugh 1927- ConAu 103, IntAu&W 82
Honourable Member For X ConAu X
Honri, Peter 1929- ConAu 103, WrDr 84
Honton, Margaret DrAP&F 83
Hoobler, Dorothy ConAu 11NR, -69,
SmATA 28[port]
Hoobler, Thomas ConAu 11NR, -69,
SmATA 28[port]
Hood, Buck 1907?-1983 ConAu 110
Hood, Christopher 1943- WrDr 84
Hood, David Crockett 1937- ConAu 37R
Hood, Donald W 1918- ConAu 37R
Hood, Dora 1885- ConAu P-2
Hood, F C 1895-1971 ConAu P-1
Hood, Flora M 1898- ConAu 5R
Hood, Graham Stanley 1936- ConAu 77,
IntAu&W 82
Hood, Hugh 1928- ConAu 1NR, -49,
ConLC 15, ConNov 82, CreCan 1,
DcLEL 1940, IntAu&W 82, WrDr 84
Hood, Joseph F 1925- ConAu 33R, SmATA 4
Hood, Margaret Page 1892- ConAu 1R
Hood, Martin Sinclair Frankland 1917- WrDr 84
Hood, Peter DrAP&F 83
Hood, Robert Allison 1880-1958 CreCan 2
Hood, Robert E 1926- ConAu 21R,
SmATA 21[port]
Hood, Sarah ConAu X
Hood, Sinclair 1917- ConAu 9NR, -21R

Hood, William 1920- ConAu 109
Hood Phillips, Owen 1907- WrDr 84
Hoofnagle, Keith Lundy 1941- ConAu 13R
Hoogasian-Villa, Susie 1921- ConAu 17R
Hoogenboom, Ari 1927- ConAu 45
Hoogenboom, Olive 1927- ConAu 21R
Hoogestraat, Wayne E ConAu 5R
Hoogland, Marianne IntAu&W 82X
Hook, Andrew 1932- ConAu 53
Hook, Diana Ffarington 1918- ConAu 61
Hook, Donald D 1928- ConAu 4NR, -53
Hook, Frances 1912- ConAu 105,
SmATA 27[port]
Hook, Frank S 1922- ConAu 21R
Hook, J N 1913- ConAu 2NR, -5R
Hook, Martha 1936- ConAu 105, SmATA 27
Hook, Sidney 1902- ConAu 7NR, -9R,
IntAu&W 82, TwCA SUP, WrDr 84
Hooke, Nina Warner 1907- ConAu 73
Hooker, C A 1942- ConAu 4NR
Hooker, Clifford Alan 1942- ConAu 49
Hooker, Craig Michael 1951- ConAu 57
Hooker, J R 1929- WrDr 84
Hooker, James Ralph 1929- ConAu 21R
Hooker, Jeremy 1941- ConAu 77, ConP 80,
IntAu&W 82, WrDr 84
Hooker, Richard ConAu X
Hooker, Ruth 1920- ConAu 69,
SmATA 21[port]
Hooker, William DrAP&F 83
Hookham, Hilda Henriette 1915- ConAu 9R
Hooks, G Eugene 1927- ConAu 1R
Hooks, Gene ConAu X
Hooks, William H 1921- ConAu 81,
SmATA 16
Hoole, Daryl VanDam 1934- ConAu 21R
Hoole, Margaret Mary 1921- IntWWP 82
Hoole, W Stanley 1903- ConAu 7NR, -17R
Hooper, Byrd ConAu X, SmATA X
Hooper, David 1915- ConAu 85
Hooper, Douglas 1927- ConAu 25R
Hooper, Hedley Colwill 1919- IntWWP 82
Hooper, John W 1926- ConAu 29R
Hooper, Meredith Jean 1939- ConAu 106,
SmATA 28[port], WrDr 84
Hooper, Patricia DrAP&F 83
Hooper, Paul F 1938- ConAu 101
Hooper, Peter IntWWP 82X
Hooper, Reginald Smythe 1909- WrDr 84
Hooper, Walter 1931- ConAu 7NR, -17R
Hooper, William Loyd 1931- ConAu 3NR, -5R
Hoopes, Clement R 1906-1979 ConAu 73, -89
Hoopes, Donelson F 1932- ConAu 33R
Hoopes, James 1944- ConAu 10NR, -65
Hoopes, Ned 1932- WrDr 84
Hoopes, Ned E 1932- ConAu 17R,
SmATA 21[port]
Hoopes, Robert Griffith 1920- ConAu 1R, -1NR
Hoopes, Roy 1922- ConAu 21R, SmATA 11
Hoopes, Townsend Walter 1922- ConAu 97
Hoople, Cheryl G SmATA 32
Hoops, Richard A 1933- ConAu 41R
Hoorn, Carol Lucille CreCan 2
Hoornik, Ed 1910-1970 CnMD, ConAu 104
Hoos, Ida Russakoff 1912- ConAu 17R
Hooson, David John Mahler 1926- ConAu 17R
Hooten, William J 1900- ConAu 61
Hooton, Charles ConAu X
Hooton, Earnest Albert 1887-1954 TwCA,
TwCA SUP
Hoover, Calvin Bryce 1897-1974 ConAu 49,
ConAu P-1
Hoover, Dorothy Estheryne McFadden 1918-
ConAu 49, LivgBAA
Hoover, Dwight Wesley 1926- ConAu 33R,
IntAu&W 82, WrDr 84
Hoover, Edgar M 1907- ConAu 13R
Hoover, F Louis 1913- ConAu 41R
Hoover, H M 1935- ConAu 105, SmATA 33
Hoover, Hardy 1902- ConAu 29R
Hoover, Helen 1910- ConAu 21R,
IntAu&W 82, SmATA 12, WrDr 84
Hoover, Herbert 1874-1964 ConAu 108
Hoover, Herbert Clark 1874-1964 ConAu 89
Hoover, Herbert Theodore 1930- ConAu 106
Hoover, J Edgar 1895-1972 ConAu 1R, -2NR,
-33R
Hoover, John P 1910- ConAu 53
Hoover, Kenneth H 1920- ConAu 7NR, -57
Hoover, Marjorie L 1910- ConAu 41R
Hoover, Mary B 1917- ConAu 93

Hornstein, Lillian Herlands 1909- *ConAu 45*
Hornstein, Patricia 1928- *IntWWP 82*
Hornstein, Reuben Aaron 1912- *ConAu 106*
Hornung, Clarence Pearson 1899- *ConAu 9NR,*
–17R
Hornung, E W 1866-1921 *ConAu 108,*
TwCCr&M 80
Hornung, Ernest William 1866-1921 *LongCTC,*
TwCA, TwCA SUP, TwCWr
Hornung, Maximilian 1942- *ConAu 107*
Horobin, Ian M 1899-1976 *ConAu 69*
Horovitz, Frances 1938- *WrDr 84*
Horovitz, Frances Margaret 1938- *ConP 80,*
DcLEL 1940, IntAu&W 82, IntWWP 82
Horovitz, Israel *DrAP&F 83*
Horovitz, Israel 1939- *ConAu 33R, ConDr 82,*
CroCD, DcLB 7[port], DcLEL 1940,
IntWWP 82, ModAL SUP,
NatPD 81[port], WorAu 1970, WrDr 84
Horovitz, Michael 1935- *ConAu 81, ConP 80,*
DcLEL 1940, IntWWP 82, WrDr 84
Horowitz, Al *ConAu X*
Horowitz, David 1903- *ConAu 69*
Horowitz, David 1939- *ConAu 13R*
Horowitz, David A 1941- *ConAu 89*
Horowitz, David Charles 1937- *ConAu 89*
Horowitz, Edward 1904- *ConAu 1R, –4NR*
Horowitz, Elinor Lander *ConAu 77*
Horowitz, Esther 1920- *ConAu 49*
Horowitz, Gene 1930- *ConAu 77*
Horowitz, I A 1907-1973 *ConAu 41R*
Horowitz, Ira 1934- *ConAu 41R*
Horowitz, Irving Louis 1929- *ConAu 41R*
Horowitz, Jacob 1900-1979 *ConAu 89*
Horowitz, Joseph 1948- *ConAu 109*
Horowitz, Laura 1943-1983 *ConAu 110*
Horowitz, Leonard M 1937- *ConAu 37R*
Horowitz, Mardi J 1934- *ConAu 33R*
Horowitz, Michael M 1933- *ConAu 41R*
Horowitz, Mikhail *DrAP&F 83*
Horowitz, Mikhail 1950- *IntWWP 82*
Horowitz, Morris A 1919- *ConAu 9NR, –65*
Horowitz, Robert S 1924- *ConAu 9R*
Horowitz, Shel *DrAP&F 83*
Horrell, C William 1918- *ConAu 61*
Horrock, Berta Crone 1896?-1983 *ConAu 110*
Horrock, Nicholas 1936- *ConAu 49*
Horrocks, Brian 1895- *WrDr 84*
Horrocks, Brian Gwynne 1895- *IntAu&W 82*
Horrocks, Edna M 1908- *ConAu P-2*
Horrocks, John E 1913- *ConAu 5R*
Horsburgh, H J N 1918- *ConAu 25R*
Horsefield, John Keith 1901- *ConAu 5R,*
WrDr 84
Horsely, David *ConAu X*
Horsely, Ramsbottom *ConAu X*
Horseman, Elaine 1925- *ConAu 13R*
Horsley, David *ConAu X, IntAu&W 82X,*
TwCWW
Horsley, James Allen 1938- *ConAu 45*
Horsman, Reginald 1931- *ConAu 1R, –2NR,*
WrDr 84
Horst, Eberhard 1924- *IntAu&W 82*
Horst, Irvin B 1915- *ConAu 41R*
Horst, Samuel 1919- *ConAu 21R*
Horta, Maria Teresa 1937- *AuNews 1*
Horton, Felix Lee *ConAu X, WrDr 84*
Horton, Frank E 1939- *ConAu 29R, WrDr 84*
Horton, John 1905- *ConAu 3NR, –9R*
Horton, Louise *DrAP&F 83*
Horton, Louise 1916- *ConAu 2NR, –49*
Horton, Lowell 1936- *ConAu 53*
Horton, Patricia Campbell 1943- *ConAu 89*
Horton, Paul B 1916- *WrDr 84*
Horton, Paul Burleigh 1916- *ConAu 1R*
Horton, Paul Chester 1942- *ConAu 106*
Horton, Rod W 1910- *ConAu 49*
Horton, Russell M 1946- *ConAu 97*
Horton, Stanley M 1916- *ConAu 6NR, –57*
Horton, Susan R 1941- *ConAu 109*
Horton, Theresa Annette *IntWWP 82X*
Horvat, Branko 1928- *ConAu 53*
Horvath, Betty 1927- *ConAu 17R,*
IntAu&W 82, MichAu 80, SmATA 4,
WrDr 84
Horvath, Janos 1921- *ConAu 41R*
Horvath, Joan 1944- *ConAu 81*
Horvath, John, Jr. *DrAP&F 83*
Horvath, Odon Von 1901-1938 *ClDMEL 80,*
CnMD, EncWL 2[port], ModGL, ModWD,
TwCA
Horvath, Violet Mary 1924- *ConAu 29R,*

WrDr 84
Horwich, Frances R 1908- *ConAu P-1,*
SmATA 11
Horwitz, Elinor Lander *SmATA 33*
Horwitz, Julius *DrAP&F 83*
Horwitz, Julius 1920- *ConAu 9R, ConLC 14,*
WrDr 84
Horwitz, Simi L 1949- *ConAu 103*
Horwitz, Sylvia L 1911- *ConAu 61*
Horwood, Harold 1923- *ConAu 9NR, –21R,*
IntAu&W 82
Hosain, Attia 1913- *DcLEL 1940*
Hoselitz, Bert F 1913- *ConAu 1R, –1NR*
Hosford, Bowen I 1916- *ConAu 107*
Hosford, Dorothy 1900-1952 *SmATA 22[port]*
Hosford, Jessie 1892- *ConAu 41R, SmATA 5*
Hosford, Philip L 1926- *ConAu 57*
Hosford, Ray E 1933- *ConAu 85*
Hoshiarpuri, Abdus S Akhtar 1918- *IntWWP 82*
Hoshiarpuri, Akhtar *IntWWP 82X*
Hosie, Stanley W 1922- *ConAu 25R*
Hosier, Helen Kooiman 1928- *ConAu 8NR, –61*
Hosken, Clifford 1882-1950 *TwCCr&M 80*
Hosken, Fran P 1919- *ConAu 6NR, –57*
Hoskin, Cyril Henry 1911?-1981 *ConAu 102*
Hosking, Eric 1909- *ConAu 101, IntAu&W 82*
Hosking, Geoffrey A 1942- *ConAu 85*
Hoskins, Katharine Bail 1924- *ConAu 65*
Hoskins, Katherine *IntWWP 82X*
Hoskins, Katherine DeMontalant 1909-
ConAu P-2, ConP 80, IntAu&W 82,
WrDr 84
Hoskins, Katherine DeMontalent Lackey 1909-
IntWWP 82
Hoskins, Robert 1933- *ConAu 29R, TwCSFW,*
WrDr 84
Hoskins, William George 1908- *ConAu 13R*
Hoskyns-Abrahall, Clare *ConAu 29R,*
SmATA 13
Hosley, Richard 1921- *ConAu 5R, –8NR*
Hosmer, Charles B, Jr. 1932- *ConAu 13R*
Hosmon, Robert Stahr 1943- *ConAu 45*
Hosokawa, Bill *ConAu X*
Hosokawa, William K 1915- *ConAu 11NR,*
–29R
Hospers, John 1918- *ConAu 1R, –2NR*
Hospital, Janette Turner 1942- *ConAu 108*
Hoss, Marvin Allen 1929- *ConAu 29R*
Hossent, Harry 1916- *ConAu P-1, WrDr 84*
Hostetler, Marian 1932- *ConAu 9NR, –65*
Hostetter, B Charles 1916- *ConAu 1R, –1NR*
Hostler, Charles W 1919- *ConAu 21R*
Hostovsky, Egon 1908-1973 *ClDMEL 80,*
ConAu 89, EncWL 2, ModSL 2, TwCWr,
WorAu
Hostrop, Richard W 1925- *WrDr 84*
Hostrop, Richard Winfred 1925- *ConAu 25R*
Hotaling, Edward 1937- *ConAu 77*
Hotchkiss, Bill *DrAP&F 83*
Hotchkiss, Bill 1936- *ConAu 104, IntAu&W 82,*
IntWWP 82
Hotchkiss, Jeanette 1901- *ConAu 21R*
Hotchkiss, Ralf D 1947- *ConAu 33R*
Hotchner, A E 1920- *ConAu 69, WrDr 84*
Hotchner, Tracy 1950- *ConAu 102*
Hotham, Gary 1950- *IntAu&W 82*
Hothem, Lar 1938- *ConAu 106*
Hotson, John Hargrove 1930- *ConAu 25R,*
WrDr 84
Hotson, John Leslie 1897- *TwCA SUP*
Hotson, Leslie 1897- *LongCTC*
Hotspur *ConAu X*
Hottois, James W 1943- *ConAu 77*
Hotz, Robert B 1914- *ConAu 101*
Hou, Chi-Ming 1924- *ConAu 21R*
Houchen, Marianne Andrea 1922- *IntAu&W 82*
Houchin, Thomas D 1925- *ConAu 77*
Houck, Carter 1924- *ConAu 77, SmATA 22*
Houck, John W 1931- *ConAu 11NR, –29R*
Houdini *ConAu X*
Houedard, Dom Sylvester 1924- *WrDr 84*
Houedard, Pierre-Sylvester 1924- *ConAu 103*
Houedard, Sylvester 1924- *ConP 80*
Houfe, Simon 1942- *ConAu 103*
Hougan, James Richard 1942- *ConAu 77*
Hougan, Jim *ConAu X*
Hough, Charlotte 1924- *ConAu 5NR, –9R,*
SmATA 9, TwCCW 83, WrDr 84
Hough, Emerson 1857-1923 *DcLB 9, FifWWr,*
TwCA, TwCA SUP, TwCWW
Hough, Graham 1908- *WrDr 84*
Hough, Graham Goulder 1908- *ConAu 69,*

ConLCrt 82, DcLEL 1940, WorAu
Hough, Henry 1896- *WrDr 84*
Hough, Henry Beetle 1896- *ConAu 1R, –2NR,*
TwCA SUP
Hough, Henry W 1906- *ConAu 25R*
Hough, Hugh 1924- *ConAu 73*
Hough, John T, Jr. 1946- *ConAu 33R*
Hough, Joseph C, Jr. 1933- *ConAu 21R*
Hough, Lindy *DrAP&F 83*
Hough, Lindy Downer 1944- *ConAu 8NR, –61,*
IntWWP 82
Hough, Louis 1914- *ConAu 37R*
Hough, Richard *TwCCW 83*
Hough, Richard Alexander *WrDr 84*
Hough, Richard Alexander 1922- *ConAu 3NR,*
–5R, IntAu&W 82, SmATA 17
Hough, S B 1917- *ConAu 3NR, TwCCr&M 80,*
WrDr 84
Hough, Stanley Bennett 1917- *ConAu 5R*
Houghteling, James L, Jr. 1920- *ConAu 5R*
Houghton, Alfred Thomas 1896- *WrDr 84*
Houghton, Barbara Flora 1932- *IntWWP 82*
Houghton, Bernard 1935- *ConAu 77*
Houghton, Claude 1889-1961 *LongCTC, TwCA,*
TwCA SUP
Houghton, Elizabeth *ConAu X*
Houghton, Eric 1930- *ConAu 1R, –2NR,*
IntAu&W 82, SmATA 7, WrDr 84
Houghton, George William 1905- *ConAu 13R*
Houghton, Neal D 1895- *ConAu P-2, WrDr 84*
Houghton, Norris 1909- *ConAu 21R, –65*
Houghton, Samuel G 1902-1975 *ConAu 65*
Houghton, Stanley 1881-1913 *CnMD,*
ConAu 110, DcLB 10[port], LongCTC,
ModWD
Houghton, Tim *DrAP&F 83*
Houghton, Walter E, Jr. 1904- *ConAu P-1*
Houghton, Walter Edwards 1904-1983
ConAu 109
Houghton, William Stanley 1881-1913 *TwCA,*
TwCWr
Houlden, J L 1929- *ConAu 77*
Houle, Cyril O 1913- *ConAu 3NR, –5R,*
WrDr 84
Houlehen, Robert J 1918- *ConAu 49,*
SmATA 18
Houlgate, Deke 1930- *ConAu 61*
Hoult, Norah 1898- *LongCTC, TwCA,*
TwCA SUP, WhoTwCL
Houn *IntAu&W 82X*
Houn, Franklin W 1920- *ConAu 21R,*
IntAu&W 82, WrDr 84
Hounsome, Terry 1944- *ConAu 109*
Houpt, Katherine Albro 1939- *ConAu 105*
Hourani, George F 1913- *ConAu 45*
Hours, Madeleine 1915- *ConAu 49*
Hours-Miedan, Madeleine *ConAu X*
Hours-Miedan, Magdeleine *ConAu X*
House, Anne W *ConAu X*
House, Charles Albert 1916- *ConAu 25R*
House, Ernest Robert 1937- *ConAu 45*
House, Humphry 1908-1955 *WorAu*
House, Jay Elmer 1872-1936 *TwCA*
House, John William 1919- *ConAu 106,*
WrDr 84
House, Kurt D 1947- *ConAu 104*
House, Robert Burton 1892- *ConAu P-1*
House, Robert J 1932- *ConAu 101*
House, Robert W 1920- *ConAu 53*
House, Victor 1893-1983 *ConAu 109*
Household, Geoffrey 1900- *ConAu 77,*
ConLC 11, ConNov 82, DcLEL 1940,
IntAu&W 82, LongCTC, SmATA 14,
TwCA, TwCA SUP, TwCCr&M 80,
WrDr 84
Household, Humphrey 1906- *WrDr 84*
Houselander, Caryll 1900-1954 *SmATA 31*
Houselander, Caryll 1901-1954 *ConAu 110*
Houseman, Barton L 1933- *ConAu 61*
Houseman, Gerald L 1935- *ConAu 108*
Houseman, John 1902- *ConAu 110*
Houseman, Lorna 1924- *WrDr 84*
Housen, Sevrin *DrAP&F 83*
Housepian, Marjorie 1923- *ConAu 33R*
Houser, Dave G 1941- *IntAu&W 82*
Housley, Norman 1952- *ConAu 108*
Housman, A E 1859-1936 *CnMWL, ConAu 104,*
EncWL 2, LongCTC, ModBrL,
ModBrL SUP, RGFMBP, TwCLC 1,
–10[port], TwCWr, WhoTwCL
Housman, Alfred Edward 1859-1936 *TwCA,*
TwCA SUP

Housman, Laurence 1865-1959 *CnMD,*
ConAu 106, DcLB 10[port], LongCTC,
ModBrL, ModWD, SmATA 25[port],
TwCA, TwCA SUP, TwCLC 7[port]
Housser, Muriel Yvonne McKague *CreCan 2*
Housser, Yvonne McKague 1898- *CreCan 2*
Houston, Beverle 1936- *ConAu 89*
Houston, James A 1921- *ChlLR 3, ConAu 65,*
SmATA 13, TwCCW 83, WrDr 84
Houston, James D *DrAP&F 83*
Houston, James D 1933- *ConAu 25R, WrDr 84*
Houston, James Mackintosh 1922- *ConAu 13R*
Houston, Jeanne Wakatsuki 1934- *ConAu 103*
Houston, Joan 1928- *ConAu 17R*
Houston, John Porter 1933- *ConAu 3NR, –9R*
Houston, Neal B 1928- *ConAu 41R*
Houston, Peyton *DrAP&F 83*
Houston, Peyton 1910- *ConAu 1NR, –49,*
IntWWP 82
Houston, R B *ConAu X, WrDr 84*
Houston, Robert *DrAP&F 83*
Houston, Robert 1935- *ConAu 37R*
Houston, Tex *TwCWW*
Houston, W Robert 1928- *ConAu 3NR, –5R,*
WrDr 84
Houston, Will *ConAu X*
Houtart, Francois 1925- *ConAu 13R*
Houthakker, Hendrik S 1924- *ConAu 17R*
Houton, Kathleen *ConAu X*
Houts, Marshall 1919- *ConAu 21R*
Houts, Peter S 1933- *ConAu 49*
Hovannisian, Richard G 1932- *ConAu 21R,*
IntAu&W 82, WrDr 84
Hovda, Robert W 1920- *ConAu 3NR, –9R*
Hovde, A J *DrAP&F 83*
Hovde, Christian A 1922- *ConAu 5R*
Hovde, Howard 1928- *ConAu 25R*
Hovell, Lucille A 1916- *ConAu 5R*
Hovell, Lucy A 1916- *ConAu X*
Hoverland, H Arthur 1928- *ConAu 45*
Hoverstad, Torstein Bugge 1944- *IntAu&W 82*
Hoversten, Chester E 1922- *ConAu 5R*
Hovet, Svein *IntAu&W 82*
Hovey, E Paul 1908- *ConAu 1R, –1NR,*
WrDr 84
Hovey, Richard Bennett 1917- *ConAu 25R*
Hoveyda, Fereydoun 1924- *ConAu 101*
Hoving, Thomas 1931- *ConAu 101*
Howald, Reed Anderson 1930- *ConAu 57*
Howar, Barbara *WrDr 84*
Howar, Barbara 1934- *ConAu 89*
Howar, Barbara 1935?- *AuNews 1, –2*
Howard, A E Dick 1933- *ConAu 13R, WrDr 84*
Howard, Alan 1934- *ConAu 37R*
Howard, Alvin Wendell 1922-1975 *ConAu 33R*
Howard, Anthony 1934- *ConAu 109*
Howard, Anthony Michell 1934- *IntAu&W 82*
Howard, Barbara 1930- *ConAu 53*
Howard, Ben *DrAP&F 83*
Howard, Ben 1944- *ConAu 73*
Howard, Bion B 1912- *ConAu 13R*
Howard, Blanche 1923- *ConAu 101*
Howard, Bronson Crocker 1842-1908 *ModWD*
Howard, C Jeriel 1939- *ConAu 29R*
Howard, Carleton 1912- *ConAu X*
Howard, Cecil *ConAu X*
Howard, Charles Frederick 1904- *ConAu 17R*
Howard, Christopher 1913- *ConAu 21R*
Howard, Clark *DrAP&F 83*
Howard, Clive d1974 *ConAu 53*
Howard, Constance 1910- *ConAu 11NR,*
WrDr 84
Howard, Constance Mildred 1910- *ConAu 69*
Howard, Coralie *ConAu X*
Howard, D L 1930- *ConAu 8NR*
Howard, Daniel F 1928- *ConAu 41R*
Howard, David M 1928- *ConAu 10NR, –25R,*
IntAu&W 82, WrDr 84
Howard, Derek Lionel 1930- *ConAu 5R*
Howard, Dick 1943- *ConAu 77*
Howard, Don 1940- *ConAu 106*
Howard, Donald Roy 1927- *ConAu 1R, –1NR,*
WrDr 84
Howard, Dorothy 1912- *ConAu 65*
Howard, Dorothy Gray 1902- *ConAu 93,*
IntAu&W 82
Howard, Edmund 1909- *ConAu 85*
Howard, Edward G 1918?-1972 *ConAu 104*
Howard, Edwin 1924- *ConAmTC, ConAu 65*
Howard, Elbert J 1901- *ConAu P-1*
Howard, Elizabeth *ConAu X, SmATA X*
Howard, Elizabeth 1907- *IntAu&W 82X,*

MichAu 80
Howard, Elizabeth Jane 1923- *ConAu 5R, –8NR,*
ConLC 7, ConNov 82, DcLEL 1940,
IntAu&W 82, ModBrL, ModBrL SUP,
TwCWr, WorAu, WrDr 84
Howard, Frances Minturn *DrAP&F 83,*
IntWWP 82
Howard, Fred D 1919- *ConAu 1R, –4NR*
Howard, Frederick James 1904- *ConAu 109*
Howard, Gerald J 1950- *ConAu 108*
Howard, Gilbert 1934- *ConAu 49*
Howard, Harold P 1905- *ConAu P-2*
Howard, Harry N 1902- *WrDr 84*
Howard, Harry Nicholas 1902- *ConAu 49*
Howard, Hartley *ConAu X, TwCCr&M 80*
Howard, Hayden *ConSFA*
Howard, Helen Addison 1904- *ConAu 3NR, –5R,*
IntAu&W 82, WrDr 84
Howard, Ian P 1927- *ConAu 21R*
Howard, Ivan *ConSFA*
Howard, J Woodford, Jr. 1931- *ConAu 33R,*
WrDr 84
Howard, James A 1922- *ConAu 8NR, –13R*
Howard, James H 1925- *ConAu 41R*
Howard, James K 1943- *ConAu 85*
Howard, James T 1934- *ConAu 101*
Howard, Jane R *DrAP&F 83*
Howard, Jane Temple 1935- *ConAu 29R,*
WrDr 84
Howard, Jean 1913- *ConAu X*
Howard, Jessica *ConAu X*
Howard, John 1916- *ConAu 41R*
Howard, John Nelson 1921- *IntAu&W 82*
Howard, John R 1933- *ConAu 53*
Howard, John Tasker 1890-1964 *ConAu 89,*
TwCA SUP
Howard, Joseph Kinsey 1906-1951 *TwCA SUP*
Howard, Joseph Leon 1917- *ConAu 1R, –1NR*
Howard, Joyce 1922- *ConAu 5R*
Howard, Katherine *IntAu&W 82X*
Howard, Kenneth Samuel 1882-1972 *ConAu 9R,*
–103
Howard, Lee M 1922- *ConAu 108*
Howard, Leigh *ConAu X*
Howard, Leon 1903- *DcLEL 1940*
Howard, Leon 1903-1982 *ConAu 109*
Howard, Linden *TwCRGW, WrDr 84*
Howard, Lowell Bennett 1925- *ConAu 13R,*
WrDr 84
Howard, Mary 1907- *ConAu X, TwCRGW,*
WrDr 84
Howard, Maureen 1930- *ConAu 53, ConLC 5,*
–14, DcLB Y83B[port]
Howard, Michael 1922- *WrDr 84*
Howard, Michael Eliot 1922- *ConAu 1R, –2NR,*
IntAu&W 82
Howard, Michael S 1922-1974 *ConAu 53*
Howard, Moses L 1928- *ConAu 109*
Howard, Munroe 1913-1974 *ConAu P-2*
Howard, Nona *ConAu X*
Howard, Noni *DrAP&F 83*
Howard, Oliver Otis 1830-1909 *ConAu 109*
Howard, Patricia 1937- *ConAu 7NR, –17R,*
IntAu&W 82, WrDr 84
Howard, Peter D 1908-1965 *ConAu P-1*
Howard, Philip 1933- *WrDr 84*
Howard, Philip Nicholas Charles 1933-
ConAu 65, IntAu&W 82
Howard, Prosper *ConAu X, SmATA X*
Howard, Richard *DrAP&F 83*
Howard, Richard 1929- *AuNews 1, ConAu 53,*
–85, ConLC 7, –10, ConP 80, CroCAP,
DcLB 5[port], DcLEL 1940, ModAL SUP,
WorAu, WrDr 84
Howard, Robert 1926- *ConAu 41R*
Howard, Robert E 1906-1936 *ConAu 105,*
TwCLC 8[port], TwCWW
Howard, Robert West 1908- *ConAu 1R, –1NR,*
SmATA 5
Howard, Roger 1938- *ConAu 93, ConDr 82,*
WrDr 84
Howard, Ronnalie Roper *ConAu X*
Howard, Roy Wilson 1883-1964 *ConAu 89*
Howard, Sidney 1891-1939 *DcLB 26[port]*
Howard, Sidney Coe 1891-1939 *CnMD,*
ConAmA, DcLB 7[port], LongCTC,
ModAL, ModWD, TwCA, TwCA SUP
Howard, Stanley E 1888?-1980 *ConAu 102*
Howard, Ted *ConAu X*
Howard, Theodore Korner 1915- *ConAu 103*
Howard, Thomas 1930- *ConAu 37R*
Howard, Troy *ConAu X*

Howard, Vechel *ConAu X, TwCWW*
Howard, Vernon 1918- *ConAu 108*
Howard, Warren F *ConAu X*
Howard, Warren Starkie 1930- *ConAu 5R*
Howard-Hill, Trevor Howard 1933- *ConAu 85,*
IntAu&W 82
Howard-Williams, Jeremy 1922- *ConAu 106,*
WrDr 84
Howarth, David 1912- *ConAu 9NR, –13R,*
SmATA 6, WrDr 84
Howarth, Donald 1931- *ConAu 25R, ConDr 82,*
DcLEL 1940, WrDr 84
Howarth, John *ConAu X*
Howarth, Pamela 1954- *ConAu 102, WrDr 84*
Howarth, Patrick 1916- *WrDr 84*
Howarth, Patrick John Fielding 1916- *ConAu 77*
Howarth, Stephen 1953- *ConAu 107*
Howarth, Thomas Edward Brodie 1914-
IntAu&W 82
Howarth, W D 1922- *ConAu 45*
Howarth, William 1940- *WrDr 84*
Howarth, William Louis 1940- *ConAu 37R,*
IntAu&W 82
Howat, Gerald 1928- *WrDr 84*
Howat, Gerald Malcolm David 1928- *ConAu 93*
Howat, John K 1937- *ConAu 49*
Howatch, Joseph 1935- *ConAu 65, WrDr 84*
Howatch, Susan 1940- *AuNews 1, ConAu 45,*
TwCRGW, WrDr 84
Howden, Molly *IntWWP 82X*
Howe, Charles Horace 1912- *ConAu 53*
Howe, Charles L 1932- *ConAu 17R*
Howe, Daniel Walker 1937- *ConAu 29R*
Howe, Deborah 1946-1978 *ConAu 105,*
SmATA 29
Howe, Doris *WrDr 84*
Howe, Doris Kathleen *ConAu 3NR, –49*
Howe, E W 1853-1937 *DcLB 25[port]*
Howe, Edgar Watson 1853-1937 *TwCA,*
TwCA SUP
Howe, Ellic Paul 1910- *ConAu 25R*
Howe, Fanny *DrAP&F 83*
Howe, Florence 1929- *ConAu 109*
Howe, G Melvyn 1920- *ConAu 101*
Howe, George Locke 1898-1977 *ConAu 69*
Howe, Helen Huntington 1905-1975 *ConAu 57,*
ConAu P-2, DcLEL 1940, TwCA SUP
Howe, Hubert S, Jr. 1942- *ConAu 57*
Howe, Irving 1920- *ConAu 9R, ConLCrt 82,*
DcLEL 1940, EncWL 2, ModAL,
TwCA SUP, WrDr 84
Howe, James 1946- *ConAu 105,*
SmATA 29[port]
Howe, James Robinson 1935- *ConAu 69*
Howe, Jonathan Trumbull 1935- *ConAu 29R*
Howe, Mark Anthony DeWolfe 1864-1960
ConAu 89
Howe, Mark Antony DeWolfe 1864-1960 *TwCA,*
TwCA SUP
Howe, Muriel *IntAu&W 82X, WrDr 84*
Howe, Nelson S 1935- *ConAu 33R, WrDr 84*
Howe, Quincy 1900-1977 *ConAu 49, –69*
Howe, Reuel L 1905- *ConAu 1R, –21R*
Howe, Richard J 1937- *ConAu 77*
Howe, Robin 1908- *WrDr 84*
Howe, Russell Warren 1925- *ConAu 49*
Howe, Susan *DrAP&F 83*
Howe, Tina *ConAu 109, NatPD 81[port]*
Howe, W Asquith 1910- *ConAu 29R*
Howe, William Hugh 1928- *ConAu 65*
Howell, Anthony 1945- *ConP 80, WrDr 84*
Howell, Barbara *DrAP&F 83*
Howell, Barbara 1937- *ConAu 49*
Howell, Benjamin Franklin 1890-1976 *ConAu 65*
Howell, Chauncey *ConAmTC*
Howell, Christopher *DrAP&F 83*
Howell, Christopher 1945- *IntWWP 82*
Howell, Clark, Sr. 1863-1936 *DcLB 25[port]*
Howell, Clinton T 1913- *ConAu 29R*
Howell, David 1936- *WrDr 84*
Howell, David Arthur Russell 1936- *ConAu 109*
Howell, F Clark 1925- *WrDr 84*
Howell, Freda 1912- *IntWWP 82*
Howell, Helen 1934- *ConAu 57*
Howell, James Edwin 1928- *ConAu 1R*
Howell, John *ConAu X*
Howell, John C 1924- *ConAu 9NR*
Howell, John Christian 1924- *ConAu 21R,*
WrDr 84
Howell, John M 1933- *ConAu 33R*
Howell, Joseph T 1942- *ConAu 45*
Howell, Leon 1936- *ConAu 25R*

Howell, Pat 1947- *SmATA 15*
Howell, Patricia Hagan *DrAP&F 83*
Howell, Patricia Hagan 1939- *ConAu 81*
Howell, Reet 1945- *ConAu 110*
Howell, Richard W 1926- *ConAu 57*
Howell, Robert Lee 1928- *ConAu 25R*
Howell, Roger 1936- *ConAu 11NR*
Howell, Roger, Jr. 1936- *ConAu 21R,
IntAu&W 82, WrDr 84*
Howell, S *ConAu X, SmATA X*
Howell, Thomas 1944- *ConAu 73*
Howell, Virginia Tier *ConAu X, SmATA 4,
WrDr 84*
Howell, Wilbur Samuel 1904- *ConAu 33R*
Howell, William C 1932- *ConAu 93*
Howells, J Harvey 1912- *ConAu 97*
Howells, John G 1918- *ConAu 9NR*
Howells, John Gwilym 1918- *ConAu 21R,
IntAu&W 82, WrDr 84*
Howells, Roscoe 1919- *ConAu 104*
Howells, William Dean 1837-1920 *ConAu 104,
ModAL, ModAL SUP, ModWD,
TwCLC 7[port], TwCSFW*
Howells, William White 1908- *ConAu 1R, -2NR,
WrDr 84*
Hower, Edward *DrAP&F 83*
Hower, Edward 1941- *ConAu 106*
Hower, Ralph M 1903-1973 *ConAu 1R, -45*
Howes, Barbara *DrAP&F 83*
Howes, Barbara 1914- *ConAu 9R, ConLC 15,
ConP 80, DcLEL 1940, IntAu&W 82,
IntWWP 82, SmATA 5, WorAu, WrDr 84*
Howes, Connie B 1933- *ConAu 89*
Howes, Edith 1874?-1954 *TwCCW 83*
Howes, Jane *WrDr 84*
Howes, Michael 1904- *ConAu 61*
Howes, Paul Griswold 1892- *ConAu 29R*
Howes, Raymond Floyd 1903- *ConAu P-1,
WrDr 84*
Howes, Robert Gerard 1919- *ConAu 1R, -4NR*
Howes, Royce 1901-1973 *ConAu 41R,
ConAu P-2*
Howes, Wright 1882-1978 *ConAu 104*
Howick, William Henry 1924- *ConAu 33R*
Howie, Carl G 1920- *ConAu 13R*
Howith, Harry 1934- *ConAu 25R, ConP 80,
WrDr 84*
Howitzer, Bronson *ConAu X*
Howkins, John 1945- *ConAu 65*
Howland, Bette 1937- *ConAu 85*
Howland, Harold Edward 1913-1980 *ConAu 102*
Howlett, Duncan 1906- *ConAu 107, WrDr 84*
Howlett, John 1940- *ConAu 69, WrDr 84*
Howorth, M K *ConAu X*
Howorth, Margaret *IntAu&W 82X*
Howorth, Muriel K *ConAu P-1*
Howse, Ernest Marshall 1902- *ConAu 49,
WrDr 84*
Howson, Charles Gordon 1948- *IntWWP 82*
Howton, F William 1925- *ConAu 29R*
Hoxie, R Gordon 1919- *ConAu 103*
Hoy, Cyrus H 1926- *ConAu 21R*
Hoy, David 1930- *ConAu 17R*
Hoy, Elizabeth *TwCRGW*
Hoy, James F 1939- *ConAu 57*
Hoy, John C 1933- *ConAu 9NR, -21R*
Hoy, Nina *ConAu X*
Hoye, Anna Scott 1915- *ConAu 13R*
Hoyem, Andrew *DrAP&F 83*
Hoyem, Andrew 1935- *ConAu 9R, ConP 80,
DcLB 5[port], WrDr 84*
Hoyer, Alexander 1914- *IntAu&W 82*
Hoyer, George W 1919- *ConAu 1R, -4NR*
Hoyer, H Conrad 1907- *ConAu 33R*
Hoyer, Mildred N *ConAu 57, IntAu&W 82,
IntWWP 82*
Hoyland, Michael 1925- *WrDr 84*
Hoyland, Michael David 1925- *ConAu 21R,
IntWWP 82*
Hoyle, Fred 1915- *ConAu 3NR, -5R, ConSFA,
DcLEL 1940, TwCSFW, TwCWr, WorAu,
WrDr 84*
Hoyle, Geoffrey 1941- *ConSFA*
Hoyle, Geoffrey 1942- *ConAu 6NR, -53,
IntAu&W 82, SmATA 18, TwCSFW,
WrDr 84*
Hoyle, Martha Byrd *ConAu X*
Hoyle Daccache, Ruth 1946- *IntAu&W 82*
Hoyles, J Arthur 1908- *ConAu 5R, WrDr 84*
Hoyo, Arturo Del 1917- *IntAu&W 82*
Hoyt, Charles Alva 1931- *ConAu 33R*
Hoyt, Charles Hale 1860-1900 *ModWD*

Hoyt, Charles K 1938- *ConAu 110*
Hoyt, Clark 1942- *ConAu 69*
Hoyt, Don A *DrAP&F 83*
Hoyt, Don Allen 1944- *IntWWP 82*
Hoyt, Edwin P *DrAP&F 83*
Hoyt, Edwin Palmer 1923- *ConAu 1R, -1NR,
SmATA 28*
Hoyt, Elizabeth Ellis 1893- *ConAu 37R*
Hoyt, Erich 1950- *ConAu 106*
Hoyt, Herman Arthur 1909- *ConAu 29R*
Hoyt, Homer 1896- *ConAu 1R, -1NR,
IntAu&W 82*
Hoyt, Jo Wasson 1927- *ConAu 21R*
Hoyt, Joseph B 1913- *ConAu 5R, WrDr 84*
Hoyt, Kenneth B 1924- *ConAu 1NR, -45*
Hoyt, Mary Finch 1924?- *ConAu 107*
Hoyt, Murray 1904- *ConAu 9R, IntAu&W 82*
Hoyt, Olga 1922- *ConAu 25R, SmATA 16*
Hoyt, Palmer 1897-1979 *ConAu 89*
Hozeny, Tony 1946- *ConAu 61*
Hozjusz *ConAu X*
Hqt, N *IntAu&W 82X*
Hrabal, Bohumil 1914- *ClDMEL 80,
ConAu 106, ConLC 13, EncWL 2,
ModSL 2, WhoTwCL*
Hrastnik, Franz 1904- *CnMD*
Hrdy, Sarah Blaffer 1946- *ConAu 107*
Hrishko, Wasyl 1914- *IntAu&W 82*
Hromadka, Josef L 1889-1971 *ConAu P-1*
Hrubin, Frantisek 1910-1971 *ModSL 2*
Hruska-Cortes, Elias *DrAP&F 83*
Hruska-Cortes, Elias 1943- *ConAu 45*
Hruza, Zdenek 1926- *ConAu 61*
Hrynko, Victor *IntAu&W 82X*
Hsia, Adrian 1938- *ConAu 77*
Hsia, C-T 1921- *ConAu 1R, -2NR*
Hsia, Chih-Tsing 1921- *IntAu&W 82*
Hsia, David Yi-Yung 1925-1972 *ConAu 33R*
Hsia, Hsiao *ConAu X, -X*
Hsia, Tsi-An 1916-1965 *ConAu P-2*
Hsiang, Yeh *ConAu X*
Hsiao, Hsia *WrDr 84*
Hsiao, Katharine H 1923- *ConAu 77*
Hsiao, Kung-Chuan 1897- *ConAu 1R,
IntAu&W 82*
Hsiao, Tso-Liang 1910- *ConAu 1R*
Hsin-Hai, Chang 1898?-1972 *ConAu 37R*
Hsiung, James Chieh 1935- *ConAu 37R*
HSS *IntAu&W 82X*
Hsu, Benedict 1933- *ConAu 69*
Hsu, Chih-Mo 1897-1931 *EncWL 2*
Hsu, Cho-Yun 1930- *ConAu 9NR, -17R*
Hsu, Francis Lang Kwang 1909- *ConAu 1R,
-1NR*
Hsu, Immanuel C Y 1923- *ConAu 1R*
Hsu, Kai-Yu 1922- *ConAu 21R, WrDr 84*
Hsueh, Chun-Tu 1922- *ConAu 41R*
Hsun, Lu *ConAu X, WorAu 1970*
Htin Aung, U *ConAu X*
Hu, Shi Ming *ConAu X*
Hu, Shih 1891-1962 *EncWL 2*
Hu, Shu Ming 1927- *ConAu 85*
Hu, Sze-Tsen 1914- *ConAu 41R*
Huaco, George A 1927- *ConAu 17R*
Huang, David S 1930- *ConAu 9R*
Huang, Parker 1914- *ConAu 2NR, -45*
Huang, Philip Chung-Chih 1940- *ConAu 105*
Huang, Po-Fei *ConAu X*
Huang, Ray 1918- *ConAu 8NR, -61*
Huang, Stanley S C 1923- *ConAu 77*
Huant, Ernest Albin Camille 1909- *IntAu&W 82*
Hubach, Robert R 1916- *ConAu 1R*
Hubalek, Claus 1926- *CnMD, ModWD*
Hubartt, Paul Leroy 1919- *ConAu 5R*
Hubbard, Barbara Marx 1929- *ConAu 103*
Hubbard, D L 1929- *ConAu 21R*
Hubbard, David Allan 1928- *ConAu 33R*
Hubbard, David G 1920- *ConAu 33R*
Hubbard, Don 1926- *ConAu 109*
Hubbard, Elbert 1856-1915 *TwCA, TwCA SUP*
Hubbard, Frank McKinney 1868-1930 *TwCA,
TwCA SUP*
Hubbard, Frank T 1921?-1976 *ConAu 65*
Hubbard, Freeman 1894- *ConAu 5R*
Hubbard, L Ron 1911- *ConAu 77, TwCSFW,
WrDr 84*
Hubbard, Lucien 1889?-1971 *ConAu 33R*
Hubbard, Margaret Ann 1909- *ConAu X*
Hubbard, P M 1910-1980 *ConAu 85, -97,
TwCCr&M 80*
Hubbard, Paul H 1900?-1983 *ConAu 109*
Hubbard, Preston John 1918- *ConAu 5R*

Hubbard, Ray 1924- *ConAu 103*
Hubbard, Robert Hamilton 1916- *ConAu 1R,
WrDr 84*
Hubbard, Thomas Leslie Wallan 1905-
ConAu P-1
Hubbell, Harriet Weed 1909- *ConAu 5R*
Hubbell, Harry M 1881-1971 *ConAu 29R*
Hubbell, Jay Broadus 1885-1979 *ConAu 1R*
Hubbell, John G 1927- *ConAu 65*
Hubbell, Lindley Williams 1901- *ConAu P-1*
Hubbell, Patricia 1928- *ConAu 17R,
IntWWP 82X, SmATA 8*
Hubbell, Richard Whittaker 1914- *ConAu 13R,
WrDr 84*
Hubbert, M King 1903- *WrDr 84*
Hubbs, Carl Leavitt 1894-1979 *ConAu 89*
Hubenka, Lloyd John 1931- *ConAu 49*
Huber, Jack T *WrDr 84*
Huber, Jack T 1918- *ConAu 21R*
Huber, Joan 1925- *ConAu 77*
Huber, Leonard Victor 1903- *ConAu 6NR, -57*
Huber, Morton Wesley 1923- *ConAu 17R*
Huber, Richard Miller 1922- *ConAu 33R,
WrDr 84*
Huber, Thomas 1937- *ConAu 29R*
Huberman, Barbara *CreCan 1*
Huberman, Edward 1910- *ConAu 13R*
Huberman, Elizabeth Duncan Lyle 1915-
ConAu 13R
Huberman, Leo 1903-1968 *ConAu 1R, -4NR*
Hubert, James Lee 1947- *ConAu 73*
Hubert, Jim *ConAu X*
Hubert, Manon *IntAu&W 82X*
Hubert, Marianne 1940- *IntAu&W 82*
Hubert, Renee Riese 1916- *ConAu 61*
Hubin, Allen J 1936- *ConAu 33R*
Hubka, Betty 1924- *ConAu 13R*
Hublay, Miklos 1918- *CroCD*
Hubler, David 1941- *ConAu 110*
Hubler, Edward L 1902-1965 *ConAu P-1*
Hubler, Herbert Clark 1910- *ConAu 85*
Hubler, Richard G *DrAP&F 83*
Hubler, Richard G 1912- *ConAu 1R, -2NR,
IntAu&W 82, WrDr 84*
Hubley, Faith Elliot 1924- *ConAu 81*
Hubley, John 1914-1977 *SmATA 24N*
Hubschman, Thomas *DrAP&F 83*
Huby, Pamela Margaret 1922- *ConAu 21R,
WrDr 84*
Huch, Ricarda Octavia 1864-1947 *ClDMEL 80,
EncWL 2[port], ModGL, TwCA,
TwCA SUP*
Huchel, Peter 1903-1981 *ClDMEL 80, CnMD,
ConAu 81, EncWL 2, ModGL,
WorAu 1970*
Huck, Arthur 1926- *WrDr 84*
Huckaby, Elizabeth 1905- *ConAu 106*
Huckaby, Gerald 1933- *ConAu 33R*
Hucker, Charles O 1919- *ConAu 69*
Huckins, Wesley C 1918- *ConAu 21R*
Huckleberry, E R 1894- *ConAu 11NR, -61*
Huckshorn, Robert J 1928- *ConAu 97*
Hudd, John *IntAu&W 82X*
Hudd, Roy 1936- *ConAu 105*
Huddle, David *DrAP&F 83*
Huddle, David 1942- *ConAu 57*
Huddle, Frank, Jr. 1943- *ConAu 37R*
Huddleston, Eugene L 1931- *ConAu 102*
Huddleston, Lee Eldridge 1935- *ConAu 21R*
Huddleston, Rodney D 1937- *ConAu 33R*
Huddleston, Trevor 1913- *WrDr 84*
Huddy, Delia 1934- *ConAu 25R*
Hudgens, A Gayle 1941- *ConAu 37R*
Hudgins, Andrew *DrAP&F 83*
Hudgins, H C, Jr. 1932- *ConAu 33R*
Hudnut, Robert K 1934- *ConAu 25R, WrDr 84*
Hudon, Edward Gerard 1915- *ConAu 5R*
Hudson, Alec *ConAu X*
Hudson, Charles 1932- *WrDr 84*
Hudson, Charles M 1932- *ConAu 33R*
Hudson, Darril 1931- *ConAu 45*
Hudson, Derek 1911- *ConAu 9R, IntAu&W 82,
WrDr 84*
Hudson, Geoffrey Francis 1903-1974 *ConAu 49*
Hudson, Gladys W 1926- *ConAu 33R,
WrDr 84*
Hudson, Gossie Harold 1930- *ConAu 93*
Hudson, Herman 1923- *ConAu 97*
Hudson, Hosea *LivgBAA*
Hudson, James A 1924- *ConAu 33R, WrDr 84*
Hudson, James Jackson 1919- *ConAu 25R,*

Hunter, Archibald MacBride 1906- *ConAu 9R, WrDr 84*
Hunter, Beatrice Trum 1918- *ConAu 7NR, −17R*
Hunter, C Bruce 1917- *ConAu 61*
Hunter, Christine 1910- *ConAu X, WrDr 84*
Hunter, Clingham *SmATA X*
Hunter, Dard 1883-1966 *ConAu 25R, ConAu P-1*
Hunter, David *IntAu&W 82X*
Hunter, Dawe *SmATA X*
Hunter, Doris 1929- *WrDr 84*
Hunter, Doris Ann Leenhouts 1929- *ConAu 37R, IntAu&W 82*
Hunter, Edith Fisher 1919- *ConAu 107, SmATA 31[port]*
Hunter, Edward 1902-1978 *ConAu 5R, −77*
Hunter, Elizabeth *TwCRGW, WrDr 84*
Hunter, Eric J 1930- *WrDr 84*
Hunter, Evan *DrAP&F 83*
Hunter, Evan 1926- *ConAu 5R, −5NR, ConLC 11, ConNov 82, DcLB Y82B[port], DcLEL 1940, SmATA 25[port], TwCCr&M 80, TwCSFW, WhoTwCL, WorAu, WrDr 84*
Hunter, Frank *ConAmTC*
Hunter, Frederic *NatPD 81[port]*
Hunter, Frederick J 1916- *ConAu 33R*
Hunter, Geoffrey Basil Bailey 1925- *ConAu 33R, WrDr 84*
Hunter, Gordon C 1924- *ConAu 106*
Hunter, Hall *ConAu X*
Hunter, Henry MacGregor 1929- *ConAu 109*
Hunter, Hilda 1921- *ConAu 49, SmATA 7*
Hunter, Howard Eugene 1929- *ConAu 41R*
Hunter, J A H 1902- *ConAu P-1*
Hunter, J F M 1924- *ConAu 37R*
Hunter, J Paul 1934- *ConAu 9NR, −21R*
Hunter, Jack D 1921- *ConAu 5R, −6NR, WrDr 84*
Hunter, James H 1890- *ConAu 85, IntAu&W 82*
Hunter, James Paul 1934- *IntAu&W 82, WrDr 84*
Hunter, Jim 1939- *ConAu 7NR, −9R, DcLB 14[port], DcLEL 1940, WrDr 84*
Hunter, Joan *ConAu X*
Hunter, Joe *ConAu X*
Hunter, John *ConAu X, TwCWW, WrDr 84*
Hunter, John M 1921- *ConAu 13R*
Hunter, Kermit 1910- *ModWD*
Hunter, Kim 1922- *ConAu 61*
Hunter, Kristin *DrAP&F 83*
Hunter, Kristin 1931- *AuNews 1, ChlLR 3, ConAu 13R, ConNov 82, LivgBAA, SmATA 12, TwCCW 83, WrDr 84*
Hunter, Leigh *ConAu X*
Hunter, Leslie S 1890-1983 *ConAu 110*
Hunter, Leslie Stannard 1890- *ConAu P-1*
Hunter, Louise H *ConAu 41R*
Hunter, Mac *ConAu X*
Hunter, Marjorie 1922- *ConAu 69*
Hunter, Mary Vann 1937- *ConAu 107*
Hunter, Maud Lily 1910- *ConAu 4NR, −9R*
Hunter, Mel 1927- *ConAu 93*
Hunter, Michael 1949- *ConAu 104, WrDr 84*
Hunter, Milton R 1902-1975 *ConAu 104*
Hunter, Mollie 1922- *ConAu X, ConLC 21[port], SmATA 2, TwCCW 83, WrDr 84*
Hunter, N C 1908-1971 *DcLB 10*
Hunter, Norman 1899- *TwCCW 83, WrDr 84*
Hunter, Norman Charles 1908-1971 *CnMD, ConAu 29R, CroCD*
Hunter, Norman George Lorimer 1899- *ConAu 93, IntAu&W 82, SmATA 26[port]*
Hunter, Paul *ConAu X, DrAP&F 83, NatPD 81[port]*
Hunter, Richard 1923-1981 *ConAu 105*
Hunter, Robert E 1940- *ConAu 41R*
Hunter, Robert Grams 1927- *ConAu 93*
Hunter, Rodello 1920- *ConAu X*
Hunter, Sam 1923- *ConAu 8NR, −13R*
Hunter, Sarah Ann 1911- *IntWWP 82*
Hunter, Stephen 1946- *ConAu 102*
Hunter, Terryl *DrAP&F 83*
Hunter, Thomas 1932- *ConAu 108*
Hunter, Tim 1947- *ConAu 85*
Hunter, Valancy *ConAu X*
Hunter, Vickie *ConAu X*
Hunter, Victoria Alberta 1929- *ConAu 5R*
Hunter, William A 1908- *ConAu 13R*
Hunter, William B, Jr. 1915- *ConAu 77*

Hunter Blair, Pauline 1921- *ConAu 29R, SmATA 3*
Hunter Blair, Peter 1912- *ConAu 107*
Hunter Blair, Peter 1912-1982 *ConAu 108*
Hunting, Constance 1925- *ConAu 45, IntWWP 82*
Huntington, Anna Hyatt 1876-1973 *ConAu 45*
Huntington, Cynthia *DrAP&F 83*
Huntington, Gale 1902- *ConAu 9R*
Huntington, Harriet Elizabeth 1909- *ConAu 5R, −5NR, SmATA 1, WrDr 84*
Huntington, Henry S, Jr. 1892-1981 *ConAu 103*
Huntington, Samuel Phillips 1927- *ConAu 1R, −1NR, WrDr 84*
Huntington, Thomas Waterman 1893-1973 *ConAu 45*
Huntington, Virginia 1889- *ConAu 21R*
Huntley, Chester Robert 1911-1974 *AuNews 1, ConAu 49, −97*
Huntley, Chet 1911-1974 *ASpks, AuNews 1, ConAu X*
Huntley, Daniel *DrAP&F 83*
Huntley, Frank Livingstone 1902- *ConAu 33R*
Huntley, Herbert Edwin 1892- *ConAu P-1*
Huntley, James L 1911- *ConAu 101*
Huntley, James Robert 1923- *ConAu 29R, WrDr 84*
Huntley, Timothy Wade 1939- *ConAu 102*
Huntly, Frances E *LongCTC*
Hunton, Mary *ConAu X*
Hunton, Richard Edwin 1924- *ConAu 21R, WrDr 84*
Huntress, Keith G 1913- *ConAu 5R*
Huntsberger, John 1931- *ConAu 5R*
Huntsberry, William E 1916- *ConAu 1R, −2NR, SmATA 5*
Hunzicker, Beatrice Plumb 1886- *ConAu 5R*
Huot, Charles Edouard Masson 1855-1930 *CreCan 1*
Huot, Juliette *CreCan 1*
Hupka, Robert 1919- *ConAu 61*
Huppe, Bernard F 1911- *ConAu 3NR, −5R, WrDr 84*
Huppert, George 1934- *ConAu 29R*
Hurd, Charles 1903-1968 *ConAu P-1*
Hurd, Clement 1908- *ConAu 9NR, −29R, SmATA 2*
Hurd, Douglas 1930- *ConAu 10NR, −25R*
Hurd, Edith 1910- *ConAu 9NR*
Hurd, Edith Thacher *WrDr 84*
Hurd, Edith Thacher 1910- *ConAu 13R, SmATA 2*
Hurd, Florence 1918- *ConAu 103*
Hurd, John C, Jr. 1928- *ConAu 17R*
Hurd, Michael John 1928- *ConAu 65, IntAu&W 82, WrDr 84*
Hurd, Thacher 1949- *ConAu 106*
Hure, Anne 1918- *ConAu 9R*
Hureau, Jean 1915- *ConAu 110*
Hureau, Jean Emile Pierre 1915- *IntAu&W 82*
Hurewitz, J C 1914- *ConAu 1R, −2NR*
Hurford-Janes, Henry 1909- *IntAu&W 82*
Hurkey, Rooan *ConAu X*
Hurlbut, Allen F 1910-1983 *ConAu 110*
Hurlbut, Cornelius S, Jr. 1906- *ConAu 11NR*
Hurlbut, Cornelius Searle, Jr. 1906- *ConAu 25R, WrDr 84*
Hurlbut, Jesse Lyman 1843-1930 *TwCA*
Hurlbutt, Robert H, III 1924- *ConAu 13R*
Hurley, Alfred F 1928- *ConAu 97*
Hurley, Doran 1900-1964 *ConAu 5R*
Hurley, F Jack 1940- *ConAu 45*
Hurley, Jane 1928- *ConAu 13R*
Hurley, John 1928- *ConAu 33R, WrDr 84*
Hurley, John J *WrDr 84*
Hurley, John J 1930- *ConAu 104*
Hurley, Kathy 1947- *ConAu 109, NatPD 81[port]*
Hurley, Leslie J 1911- *ConAu 49*
Hurley, Mark J 1919- *ConAu 53*
Hurley, Neil 1925- *ConAu 29R*
Hurley, Vic 1898-1978 *ConAu 1R, −103*
Hurley, W Maurice 1916- *ConAu 37R*
Hurley, Wilfred G 1895-1973 *ConAu 45, ConAu P-2*
Hurley, William James, Jr. 1924- *ConAu 9R*
Hurley, William Maurice 1916- *IntAu&W 82*
Hurlimann, Bettina *ConAu X*
Hurlimann, Bettina 1909-1983 *SmATA 34N*
Hurlimann, Ruth 1939- *ConAu X, SmATA 31, −32[port]*
Hurlock, Elizabeth Bergner 1898- *ConAu 41R*

Hurm, Ken 1934- *ConAu 106*
Hurne, Ralph 1932- *ConAu 21R*
Hurok, Sol 1888-1974 *ConAu 49*
Hurren, Bernard John 1907- *IntAu&W 82*
Hurry, Leslie 1909- *CreCan 2*
Hursch, Carolyn J *ConAu 41R*
Hurst, Alexander Anthony 1917- *ConAu 5R*
Hurst, C J *IntWWP 82X*
Hurst, Charles G, Jr. 1928- *ConAu 37R, LivgBAA*
Hurst, Charles John 1946- *IntWWP 82*
Hurst, Fannie 1889-1968 *ConAmA, ConAu 25R, ConAu P-1, LongCTC, TwCA, TwCA SUP, TwCRGW, TwCWr*
Hurst, G Cameron, III 1941- *ConAu 85*
Hurst, James M 1924- *ConAu 29R, WrDr 84*
Hurst, James Richard 1925- *IntWWP 82*
Hurst, M E Eliot *ConAu X*
Hurst, Michael 1931- *ConAu 21R*
Hurst, Norman 1944- *ConAu 53*
Hurst, Richard Maurice 1938- *ConAu 101*
Hurst, Virginia Radcliffe 1914?-1976 *ConAu 69*
Hurstfield, Joel 1911-1980 *ConAu 6NR, −102, −53*
Hurston, Zora Neale 1901-1960 *ConLC 7*
Hurston, Zora Neale 1903-1960 *ConAu 85, ModBlW, TwCA, TwCA SUP*
Hurt, Freda Mary Elizabeth 1911- *ConAu 103, WrDr 84*
Hurt, Henry 1942- *ConAu 106*
Hurt, James 1934- *ConAu 45*
Hurtgen, Andre O 1932- *ConAu 81*
Hurtubise, Jacques 1939- *CreCan 2*
Hurvitz, Leon Nahum 1923- *ConAu 106*
Hurwitz, Abraham B 1905- *ConAu 29R*
Hurwitz, Edith F 1941- *ConAu 108, WrDr 84*
Hurwitz, Howard L 1916- *ConAu 37R*
Hurwitz, Johanna *DrAP&F 83*
Hurwitz, Johanna 1937- *ConAu 10NR, −65, SmATA 20[port]*
Hurwitz, Ken 1948- *ConAu 33R*
Hurwitz, Moshe 1844-1910 *ModWD*
Hurwitz, Samuel J 1912-1972 *ConAu P-2*
Hurwitz, Stephan 1901-1981 *ConAu 103*
Hurwood, Bernhardt J 1926- *ConAu 25R, SmATA 12*
Husain, Syed Mumtaz 1918- *IntAu&W 82*
Husar, John 1937- *ConAu 81*
Husayn, Taha 1889-1973 *EncWL 2*
Husband, William Hollow 1899?-1978 *ConAu 81*
Huseman, Richard C 1939- *ConAu 109*
Husen, Torsten 1916- *ConAu 9NR, −21R*
Huser, Verne 1931- *ConAu 106*
Huson, Paul 1942- *ConAu 29R, WrDr 84*
Huss, Roy 1927- *ConAu 25R*
Hussein, Taha 1889-1973 *ConAu 45*
Husserl, Edmund 1859-1938 *WorAu*
Hussey, David Edward 1934- *ConAu 9NR, −57*
Hussey, John A 1913- *ConAu 61, IntAu&W 82*
Hussey, Leonard *IntAu&W 82X*
Hussey, Maurice Percival 1925- *ConAu 9R*
Huste, Annemarie 1943- *ConAu 57*
Husted, Darrell 1931- *ConAu 81*
Husten, Bruce H 1948- *ConAmTC*
Huston, Fran 1936- *ConAu X, WrDr 84*
Huston, James Alvin 1918- *ConAu 41R*
Huston, John 1906- *ConAu 73, ConDr 82A, ConLC 20, DcLB 26[port]*
Huston, Luther A 1888- *ConAu P-2*
Huston, Mervyn J 1912- *WrDr 84*
Huston, Mervyn James 1912- *ConAu 8NR, −61*
Hustvedt, Lloyd 1922- *ConAu 21R*
Huszar, George B De 1919- *ConAu P-2*
Hutchcroft, Vera 1923- *ConAu 102*
Hutchens, Eleanor Newman 1919- *ConAu 13R*
Hutchens, John Kennedy 1905- *ConAu 65*
Hutchens, Paul 1902-1977 *ConAu 61, SmATA 31[port]*
Hutcheson, Richard G, Jr. 1921- *ConAu 107*
Hutchin, Kenneth Charles 1908- *ConAu 110, IntAu&W 82, WrDr 84*
Hutchings, Alan Eric 1910- *ConAu 1R*
Hutchings, Arthur 1906- *WrDr 84*
Hutchings, Arthur James Bramwell 1905- *IntAu&W 82*
Hutchings, Arthur James Bramwell 1906- *ConAu 5R, −6NR*
Hutchings, Margaret Joscelyne 1918- *ConAu 3NR, −9R*
Hutchings, Monica Mary 1917- *ConAu 9R*
Hutchings, Patrick A 1929- *ConAu 4NR, −53*
Hutchings, Raymond 1924- *ConAu 33R*

Hutchins, Carleen Maley 1911- *ConAu 17R,*
SmATA 9
Hutchins, Francis Gilman 1939- *ConAu 21R,*
IntAu&W 82, WrDr 84
Hutchins, Maude *ConNov 82, DrAP&F 83,*
WrDr 84
Hutchins, Maude 1889?- *ConAu 61, WorAu*
Hutchins, Pat 1942- *ConAu 81, SmATA 15,*
TwCCW 83, WrDr 84
Hutchins, Robert Maynard 1899-1977 *ConAu 69*
Hutchins, Ross Elliott 1906- *ConAu 5NR, -9R,*
SmATA 4
Hutchinson, Alfred 1924-1972 *DcLEL 1940,*
TwCWr
Hutchinson, Arthur Stuart Menteth 1879-1971
ConAu 29R, LongCTC, TwCA,
TwCA SUP, TwCWr
Hutchinson, C Alan 1914- *ConAu 29R*
Hutchinson, Eliot Dole 1900- *ConAu 61*
Hutchinson, G Evelyn 1903- *ConAu P-1*
Hutchinson, George 1920-1980 *ConAu 97*
Hutchinson, H Lester 1904- *ConAu 17R*
Hutchinson, John 1921- *ConAu 45*
Hutchinson, Joseph 1902- *ConAu 109*
Hutchinson, Joseph Burtt 1902- *IntAu&W 82*
Hutchinson, Margaret Massey 1904- *ConAu P-1*
Hutchinson, Mary Jane 1924- *ConAu 106*
Hutchinson, Michael E 1925- *ConAu 17R*
Hutchinson, Pearse 1927- *ConAu 103, ConP 80,*
WrDr 84
Hutchinson, Peter 1943- *ConAu 8NR, -61*
Hutchinson, Ray Coryton 1907-1975 *ConAu 1R,*
-3NR, -61, LongCTC, ModBrL, TwCA,
TwCA SUP, TwCWr
Hutchinson, Richard Wyatt 1894-1970 *ConAu 5R,*
-89
Hutchinson, Robert *DrAP&F 83*
Hutchinson, Robert 1924- *ConAu 13R,*
WrDr 84
Hutchinson, Vernal 1922- *ConAu 49*
Hutchinson, Warner Alton, Jr. 1929- *ConAu 110*
Hutchinson, William K 1945- *ConAu 102*
Hutchison, Bruce 1901- *ConAu 103, CreCan 1,*
LongCTC
Hutchison, Chester Smith 1902- *ConAu P-2*
Hutchison, Dwight 1890?-1975 *ConAu 57*
Hutchison, E R 1926- *ConAu 10NR, -25R*
Hutchison, Harold Frederick 1900- *ConAu 1R,*
-4NR
Hutchison, Henry 1923- *WrDr 84*
Hutchison, Jane Campbell 1932- *ConAu 37R*
Hutchison, Joe *DrAP&F 83*
Hutchison, John Alexander 1912- *ConAu 69*
Hutchison, Joseph Gerald, Jr. 1950- *IntWWP 82*
Hutchison, Margaret *CreCan 2, DcLEL 1940*
Hutchison, Sidney Charles 1912- *ConAu 25R,*
WrDr 84
Hutchison, William Bruce 1901- *CreCan 1,*
DcLEL 1940
Hutchison, William Robert 1930- *ConAu 21R*
Huth, Angela 1938- *ConAu 85, IntAu&W 82*
Huth, Marta 1898- *ConAu 106*
Huth, Mary Jo 1929- *ConAu 103*
Huth, Tom 1941- *ConAu 97*
Huthmacher, J Joseph 1929- *ConAu 21R,*
SmATA 5, WrDr 84
Huthmacher, Jacob Joseph 1929- *IntAu&W 82*
Hutman, Norma Louise 1935- *ConAu 25R*
Hutschnecker, Arnold A 1898- *ConAu 81,*
IntAu&W 82
Hutson, Anthony 1934- *WrDr 84*
Hutson, Anthony Brian Austen 1934- *ConAu 93*
Hutson, Fatisha 1940- *IntWWP 82*
Hutson, James H 1937- *ConAu 85*
Hutson, Jan 1932- *ConAu 106*
Hutson, Joan 1929- *ConAu 89*
Hutt, Maurice George 1928- *ConAu 13R*
Hutt, Max L 1908- *ConAu 57*
Hutt, W H 1899- *ConAu 57*
Hutt, William 1920- *CreCan 1*
Hutt, Wolfgang 1925- *IntAu&W 82*
Hutten, Baroness Von 1874-1957 *TwCRGW*
Huttenback, Robert A 1928- *ConAu 25R*
Hutterli, Kurt 1944- *IntAu&W 82*
Huttig, Jack W 1919- *ConAu 53*
Huttner, Matthew 1915-1975 *ConAu 104*
Hutto, Nelson 1904- *ConAu P-1, SmATA 20*
Hutton, Ann 1929- *ConAu 108*
Hutton, Clarke 1898- *ConAu 107*
Hutton, Edward 1875-1969 *LongCTC*
Hutton, Geoffrey 1928- *ConAu 41R*
Hutton, Ginger *ConAu X*

Hutton, Harold 1912- *ConAu 102*
Hutton, J Bernard 1911- *ConAu 21R*
Hutton, James 1902- *ConAu 77*
Hutton, John 1928- *ConAu 107, WrDr 84*
Hutton, John Henry 1885-1968 *ConAu P-1*
Hutton, Joseph Bernard 1911- *WrDr 84*
Hutton, Malcolm 1921- *ConAu 107*
Hutton, Richard 1949- *ConAu 109*
Hutton, Virginia Carol 1940- *ConAu 77*
Hutton, Warwick 1939- *ConAu 9NR, -61,*
SmATA 20[port], WrDr 84
Huus, Helen 1913- *ConAu 1R, -1NR*
Huvos, Kornel 1913- *ConAu 49*
Huws, Daniel 1932- *ConAu 81, ConP 80,*
WrDr 84
Huxhold, Harry N 1922- *ConAu 61*
Huxley, Aldous 1894-1963 *CnMD, CnMWL,*
ConAu 85, ConLC 1, -3, -4, -5, -8, -11, -18,
EncWL 2[port], LongCTC, ModBrL,
ModBrL SUP, ModWD, TwCA,
TwCA SUP, TwCSFW, TwCWr,
WhoTwCL
Huxley, Anthony Julian 1920- *ConAu 7NR, -9R,*
IntAu&W 82, WrDr 84
Huxley, Elspeth 1907- *ConAu 77, IntAu&W 82,*
LongCTC, TwCCr&M 80, TwCWr,
WorAu, WrDr 84
Huxley, George Leonard 1932- *ConAu 21R,*
IntAu&W 82, WrDr 84
Huxley, Herbert Henry 1916- *ConAu 5R,*
IntWWP 82
Huxley, Sir Julian Sorrell 1887-1975 *ConAu 7NR,*
-9R, -57, LongCTC, TwCA, TwCA SUP,
TwCWr
Huxley, Laura Archera *ConAu 13R*
Huxley-Blythe, Peter J 1925- *ConAu 17R*
Huxtable, Ada Louise *WrDr 84*
Huxtable, John 1912- *ConAu 13R, WrDr 84*
Huxtable, Marjorie 1897- *LongCTC*
Huyck, Dorothy Boyle 1925?-1979 *ConAu 89*
Huyck, Margaret Hellie 1939- *ConAu 49*
Huyck, Peter H 1940- *ConAu 107*
Huygen, Wil 1922- *ConAu 81*
Huygen, Willibrod Joseph 1922- *IntAu&W 82*
Huyghe, Rene 1906- *ConAu 81*
Huyler, Jean Wiley 1935- *ConAu 69*
Huynh, Quang Nhuong 1946- *ConAu 107*
Huysmans, Charles Marie Georges 1848-1907
ConAu 104
Huysmans, Joris Karl 1848-1907 *CIDMEL 80,*
ConAu X, ModFrL, ModRL,
TwCLC 7[port], WhoTwCL
Huzar, Eleanor G 1922- *ConAu 85*
Hwang, David Henry 1957- *NatPD 81[port]*
Hyam, Ronald 1936- *ConAu 97, IntAu&W 82,*
WrDr 84
Hyams, Barry 1911- *ConAu 13R*
Hyams, Edward 1910-1975 *ConAu 5R, -8NR,*
-61, LongCTC, TwCWr, WorAu
Hyams, Joe 1923- *ConAu X, WrDr 84*
Hyams, Joseph 1923- *ConAu 7NR, -17R*
Hyatt, Carole S 1935- *ConAu 93*
Hyatt, James Philip 1909- *ConAu 9R*
Hyatt, Richard Herschel 1944- *ConAu 101*
Hybels, Saundra 1938- *ConAu 57*
Hyde, Dayton O 1925- *ConAu 25R,*
IntAu&W 82, MichAu 80, SmATA 9,
WrDr 84
Hyde, Douglas 1860-1949 *LongCTC, ModWD,*
TwCA, TwCA SUP
Hyde, Douglas 1911- *ConAu 109*
Hyde, Eleanor *DrAP&F 83, TwCRGW*
Hyde, Fillmore 1896?-1970 *ConAu 104*
Hyde, George E 1882- *ConAu 5R*
Hyde, H Montgomery 1907- *WrDr 84*
Hyde, Harford Montgomery 1907- *ConAu 5R,*
LongCTC
Hyde, Hawk 1925- *ConAu X, SmATA X*
Hyde, Janet S 1948- *WrDr 84*
Hyde, Janet Shibley 1948- *ConAu 10NR, -65*
Hyde, L K 1901- *ConAu P-1*
Hyde, Laurence Evelyn 1914- *ConAu 17R,*
WrDr 84
Hyde, Lewis *DrAP&F 83*
Hyde, Lewis 1945- *IntWWP 82*
Hyde, Margaret Oldroyd 1917- *ConAu 1R,*
-1NR, ConLC 21[port], SmATA 1
Hyde, Mary Morley Crapo 1912- *ConAu 49*
Hyde, Michael 1908- *WrDr 84*
Hyde, Robin 1906-1939 *LongCTC, TwCWr,*
WhoTwCL
Hyde, Shelley *SmATA X*

Hyde, Simeon, Jr. 1919- *ConAu 21R*
Hyde, Stuart W 1923- *ConAu 61*
Hyde, Tracy Elliot *ConAu 49*
Hyde, W Lewis 1945- *ConAu 104*
Hyde, Wayne Frederick 1922- *ConAu 1R,*
SmATA 7
Hyden, Goeran 1938- *ConAu 103*
Hyder, Clyde Kenneth 1902- *ConAu 33R,*
IntAu&W 82, WrDr 84
Hyder, O Quentin 1930- *ConAu 105*
Hydler, Glenda *DrAP&F 83*
Hyer, James Edgar 1923- *ConAu 77*
Hyer, Paul Van 1926- *ConAu 104*
Hyers, M Conrad 1933- *ConAu 33R, WrDr 84*
Hyett, Barbara Helfgott *DrAP&F 83*
Hygen, Johan B 1911- *ConAu 21R*
Hyink, Bernard L 1913- *ConAu 45*
Hyland, Ann 1936- *WrDr 84*
Hyland, Drew A 1939- *ConAu 89*
Hyland, Frances 1927- *CreCan 2*
Hyland, Jean Scammon 1926- *ConAu 49*
Hyland, Stanley 1914- *ConAu 9R,*
TwCCr&M 80, WrDr 84
Hylander, Clarence John 1897-1964 *ConAu 5R,*
SmATA 7
Hyldbakk, Hans 1898- *IntAu&W 82*
Hylton, Delmer Paul 1920- *ConAu 17R,*
WrDr 84
Hyma, Albert 1893- *ConAu 17R*
Hyman, Alan 1910- *ConAu 102, WrDr 84*
Hyman, Ann 1936- *ConAu 53*
Hyman, David N 1943- *ConAu 7NR, -57*
Hyman, Dick 1904- *ConAu 7NR, -17R*
Hyman, Frieda Clark 1913- *ConAu 5R*
Hyman, Harold M 1924- *ConAu 5R,*
IntAu&W 82, WrDr 84
Hyman, Helen Kandel 1920- *ConAu 105*
Hyman, Herbert H 1918- *ConAu 21R,*
WrDr 84
Hyman, Irwin A 1935- *ConAu 93*
Hyman, Jackie Diamond 1949- *ConAu 108*
Hyman, Lawrence W 1919- *ConAu 41R,*
IntAu&W 82
Hyman, Paula 1946- *ConAu 89*
Hyman, Richard J 1921- *ConAu 1NR, -45*
Hyman, Robin Philip 1931- *ConAu 41R,*
SmATA 12
Hyman, Ronald T 1933- *ConAu 9NR, -21R,*
IntAu&W 82, WrDr 84
Hyman, Sidney 1917- *ConAu 102*
Hyman, Stanley Edgar 1919-1970 *ConAu 25R,*
-85, ConLCrt 82, WorAu
Hyman, Trina Schart 1939- *ConAu 2NR, -49,*
SmATA 7
Hymans, Jacques Louis 1937- *ConAu 57*
Hymes, Dell Hathaway 1927- *ConAu 13R,*
IntAu&W 82
Hymes, Lucia Manley 1907- *ConAu 5R,*
SmATA 7
Hymmen, Friedrich Wilhelm 1913- *IntAu&W 82*
Hymoff, Edward 1924- *ConAu 17R*
Hynd, Alan 1904?-1974 *ConAu 45*
Hyndman, Donald W 1936- *ConAu 57*
Hyndman, Jane Andrews Lee 1912-1978
ConAu 5NR, -89, SmATA 1, -23N
Hyndman, Robert Utley 1906?-1973 *ConAu 97,*
SmATA 18
Hynds, Frances Jane 1929- *ConAu 77*
Hyne, C J Cutcliffe 1865-1944 *TwCSFW*
Hyne, Charles John Cutcliffe Wright 1865?-1944
LongCTC, TwCA, TwCA SUP
Hyne, Cutcliffe *TwCA, TwCA SUP*
Hynek, J Allen 1910- *ConAu 81*
Hyneman, Charles Shang 1900- *ConAu P-1*
Hynes, Samuel 1924- *ConAu 105, WrDr 84*
Hyrst, Eric 1927- *CreCan 1*
Hyslop, Beatrice F 1900?-1973 *ConAu 45*
Hyslop, Lois Boe 1908- *ConAu 41R,*
IntAu&W 82
Hytier, Jean 1899-1983 *ConAu 109*
Hytten, Ella *IntAu&W 82X*

I

I, S *ConAmA*
I S *TwCA, TwCA SUP*
I-To, Wen *WorAu 1970*
Iacoban, Mircea Radu 1940- *IntAu&W 82*
Iacone, Salvatore J 1945- *ConAu 85,*
IntAu&W 82
Iacuzzi, Alfred 1896-1977 *ConAu 73*
Iams, Jack 1910- *TwCCr&M 80, WrDr 84*
Iams, Thomas M, Jr. 1928- *ConAu 9R*
Ian *IntAu&W 82X*
Ian, Janis 1951- *ConAu 105, ConLC 21[port]*
Ianni, Francis A J 1926- *ConAu 45,*
IntAu&W 82
Ianniello, Lynne Young 1925- *ConAu 17R*
Iannone, Jeanne Koppel *SmATA 7*
Iannone, Ron 1940- *ConAu 53*
Iannuzzi, John N 1935- *ConAu 93,*
TwCCr&M 80, WrDr 84
Iatrides, John O 1932- *ConAu 10NR, -25R*
Ibanez, Vicente Blasco *ConAu X*
Ibanez, Vicente Blasco 1867-1928 *LongCTC,*
ModRL, TwCA, TwCA SUP
Ibarbourou, Juana De 1895- *ModLAL*
Ibarra, Crisostomo *ConAu X*
Ibbotson, Eva 1925- *ConAu 81, SmATA 13*
Ibbotson, M C 1930- *ConAu 25R, SmATA 5*
Ibele, Oscar Herman 1917- *ConAu 106*
Ibingira, G S K 1932- *ConAu 103*
Ibrahim, Abdel-Sattar 1939- *ConAu 69*
Ibrahim, Ibrahim Abdelkader 1923- *ConAu 13R*
Ibraileanu, Garabet 1871-1936 *CIDMEL 80*
Ibsen, Henrik 1828-1906 *CIDMEL 80, CnMD,*
ConAu 104, LongCTC, ModWD,
TwCLC 2, -8[port]
Ibuka, Masaru 1908- *ConAu 102*
Ibuse, Masuji 1898- *ConLC 22[port], EncWL 2,*
WhoTwCL
Icaza, Jorge 1906-1978 *EncWL 2, ModLAL*
Icaza Coronel, Jorge 1906-1978 *ConAu 85, -89*
Ice, Jackson Lee 1925- *ConAu 25R, WrDr 84*
Ice, Ruth *DrAP&F 83*
Icenhower, Joseph Bryan 1913- *ConAu 5R,*
-5NR
Ichikawa, Kon 1915- *ConLC 20*
Icks, Robert J 1900- *ConAu 41R*
Icolari, Daniel Leonardo 1942- *ConAu 17R*
Iconoclast 1833- *TwCA, TwCA SUP*
Iddon, Don 1913?-1979 *ConAu 89*
Iddow, Josephine 1926- *IntWWP 82*
Idell, Albert Edward 1901-1958 *TwCA SUP*
Idelsohn, Abraham Zevi 1882-1938 *ConAu 109*
Iden, William *ConAu X*
Idle, Eric *ConLC 21[port]*
Idriess, Ion 1890- *TwCWr*
Idriess, Ion L 1891?-1979 *ConAu 89*
Idris, Yusuf 1927- *EncWL 2*
Iduarte, Andres 1907- *ConAu 33R*
Idyll, C P 1916- *ConAu 8NR*
Idyll, Clarence Purvis 1916- *ConAu 9R*
Ierardi, Francis B 1886-1970 *ConAu 104*
Ifetayo, Femi Funmi 1954- *LivgBAA*
Ifft, James B 1935- *ConAu 53*
Ifkovic, Edward 1943- *ConAu 8NR, -61*
Iggers, Georg G 1926- *ConAu 25R, WrDr 84*

Iggers, Wilma Abeles 1921- *ConAu 25R,*
WrDr 84
Iggulden, John Manners 1917- *ConAu 9R,*
ConSFA, DcLEL 1940, WrDr 84
Iglauer, Edith 1917- *ConAu 77*
Iglehart, Alfreda P 1950- *ConAu 109*
Iglehart, Louis Tillman 1915-1981 *ConAu 104*
Iglesias, Mario 1924- *ConAu 45*
Iglesies, Ignasi 1871-1928 *CIDMEL 80*
Iglitzin, Lynne 1931- *ConAu 41R*
Igloo, Spiro *ConAu X*
Ignacio, Joselyn *DrAP&F 83*
Ignatow, David *DrAP&F 83*
Ignatow, David 1914- *ConAu 9R, ConLC 4, -7,*
-14, ConP 80, CroCAP, DcLB 5[port],
DcLEL 1940, IntAu&W 82, IntWWP 82,
WorAu, WrDr 84
Ignatow, Rose Graubart *DrAP&F 83*
Ignotus, Paul 1901-1978 *ConAu 5R, -8NR, -77*
Igo, John 1927- *WrDr 84*
Igo, John N, Jr. 1927- *ConAu 13R,*
IntAu&W 82, IntWWP 82
Igoe, James 1935- *ConAu 108*
Igoe, Lynn Moody 1937- *ConAu 108*
Ihde, Don 1934- *ConAu 33R, WrDr 84*
Ihimaera, Witi 1944- *ConAu 77, ConNov 82,*
WrDr 84
Ihnat, Steve 1935?-1972 *ConAu 33R*
Iino, Norimoto 1918- *ConAu 61*
Ijzer, Meta Van *IntAu&W 82*
Ik, Kim Yong *DrAP&F 83*
Ikan, Ron 1941- *IntWWP 82*
Ike, Nobutaka 1916- *ConAu 21R*
Ikeda, Daisaku 1928- *ConAu 85, IntAu&W 82*
Ikeda, Kiyoshi 1928- *ConAu 104*
Ikejiani, Okechukwu 1917- *ConAu 17R*
Ikenberry, Oliver Samuel 1908- *ConAu 53*
Ikerman, Ruth C 1910- *ConAu 13R, WrDr 84*
Ikle, Fred C 1924- *WrDr 84*
Ikle, Fred Charles 1924- *ConAu 45*
Iko, Momoko *DrAP&F 83*
Iko, Momoko 1940- *ConAu 77*
Ikor, Roger 1912- *IntAu&W 82*
Ilanjian, Zenas 1922- *IntAu&W 82*
Ilardi, Vincent 1925- *ConAu 29R*
Ilardo, Joseph A 1944- *ConAu 89*
Ilchman, Warren Frederick 1934- *ConAu 1R,*
-1NR
Ilenkov, Vasili Pavlovich 1897- *ModWD*
Ilersic, Alfred Roman 1920- *WrDr 84*
Iles, Bert *WrDr 84*
Iles, Bert 1912- *ConAu X*
Iles, Francis *ConAu X, LongCTC, TwCA,*
TwCA SUP, TwCCr&M 80
Il'f, Ilya And Petrov, Yevgeniy *CnMWL*
Il'f, Ilya Arnoldovich 1897-1937 *CIDMEL 80,*
EncWL 2, ModSL 1, TwCA, TwCA SUP,
TwCWr
Ilg, Frances L 1902-1981 *ConAu 104, -107*
Ilial, Leo *CreCan 2*
Ilich, John 1933- *ConAu 106*
Ilie, Paul 1932- *ConAu 10NR, -25R, WrDr 84*
Illakowiczowna, Kazimiera 1892- *CIDMEL 80*
Illan, Jose M 1924- *ConAu 45*

Illes, Endre 1902- *CroCD*
Illes, Robert E 1914- *ConAu 103*
Illiano, Antonio 1934- *ConAu 41R*
Illich, Ivan 1926- *WrDr 84*
Illich, Ivan D 1926- *AuNews 2, ConAu 10NR,*
-53
Illick, Joseph E 1934- *ConAu 17R*
Illingworth, Frank 1908- *ConAu 5R, -5NR*
Illingworth, John 1904?-1980 *ConAu 97*
Illingworth, Neil 1934- *ConAu 13R*
Illingworth, Ronald Stanley 1909- *ConAu 3NR,*
-9R, IntAu&W 82, WrDr 84
Illwitzer, Elinor G 1934- *ConAu 29R*
Illyes, Gyula 1902- *CIDMEL 80, CnMD,*
CroCD, EncWL 2, IntAu&W 82, TwCWr,
WorAu
Illyes, Gyula 1902-1983 *ConAu 109*
Ilmer, Walter 1926- *IntAu&W 82*
Ilogu, Edmund Christopher Onyedum 1920-*
IntAu&W 82
Ilowite, Sheldon A 1931- *ConAu 106,*
SmATA 27[port]
Ilsley, Dent *ConAu X, SmATA X*
Ilsley, Velma E 1918- *WrDr 84*
Ilsley, Velma Elizabeth 1918- *ConAu 3NR, -9R,*
SmATA 12
Ilyenkov, Vassily 1897- *CnMD*
Imamura, Shigeo 1922- *ConAu 77*
Imber, Gerald 1941- *ConAu 89*
Imbrie, John 1925- *ConAu 107*
Imbrie, Katherine P 1952- *ConAu 104*
Imbrie, McCrea 1918- *NatPD 81[port]*
Imbs, Bravig 1904-1946 *ConAu 107, DcLB 4,*
TwCA, TwCA SUP
Imerti, Arthur D 1915- *ConAu 37R*
Imfeld, Al 1935- *ConAu 69*
Imhoff, Maurice Lee 1930- *ConAu 108*
Immel, Mary Blair 1930- *ConAu 6NR, -13R,*
SmATA 28[port], WrDr 84
Immerman, Leon Andrew 1952- *ConAu 103*
Immerwahr, Sara Anderson 1914- *ConAu 108*
Immoos, Thomas 1918- *ConAu 85*
Immroth, John Phillip 1936- *WrDr 84*
Immroth, John Phillip 1936-1976 *ConAu P-2*
Imo, Nell *IntWWP 82X*
Imperato, Pascal James 1937- *ConAu 106*
Impey, Oliver 1936- *ConAu 108*
Imrie, Richard *ConAu X*
Inada, Lawson Fusao *DrAP&F 83*
Inada, Lawson Fusao 1938- *ConAu 33R*
Inalcik, Halil 1916- *ConAu 49*
Inayat-Khan, Pir Vilayat 1916- *ConAu 93*
Inbau, Fred E 1909- *ConAu 1R, -1NR,*
WrDr 84
Inber, Vera Mikhailovna 1890?-1972 *TwCWr*
Inber, Vera Mikhailovna 1893-1972 *ConAu 37R*
Inber, Vera Mikhaylovna 1890-1972 *CIDMEL 80*
Ince, Basil A 1933- *ConAu 57*
Ince, Martin 1952- *ConAu 110*
Inch, Morris Alton 1925- *ConAu 11NR, -29R,*
IntAu&W 82, WrDr 84
Inchfawn, Fay 1881- *LongCTC*
Inciardi, James A 1939- *ConAu 8NR, -61,*
IntAu&W 82

Inclan, Ramon DelValle- 1866-1936 *ModRL,*
TwCA, TwCA SUP
Incledon, Philip *IntWWP 82X, WrDr 84*
Incogniteau, Jean-Louis *ConAu X*
Ind, Allison 1903-1974 *ConAu P-1*
Indelman, Elchanan Chonon 1908?-1983
ConAu 109
Indelman-Yinnon, Moshe 1895?-1977 *ConAu 73*
Inderlied, Mary Elizabeth 1945- *ConAu 49*
Indian, G Ivan Di *IntWWP 82X*
Indik, Bernard P 1932- *ConAu 33R*
Inez, Colette *DrAP&F 83*
Inez, Colette 1931- *ConAu 37R, WrDr 84*
Infante, Guillermo Cabrera *WorAu 1970*
Infield, Glenn B 1920-1981 *ConAu 5R, –5NR,
–103*
Ing, Dean 1931- *ConAu 106*
Ingalls, Daniel H H 1916- *ConAu 17R*
Ingalls, Jeremy *DrAP&F 83*
Ingalls, Jeremy 1911- *ConAu 1R, IntAu&W 82,
IntWWP 82, WrDr 84*
Ingalls, Robert P 1941- *ConAu 107*
Ingalls, Robert Paul 1941- *ConAu 110*
Ingamells, Rex 1913-1955 *TwCWr*
Ingard, K Uno 1921- *ConAu 33R*
Ingate, Mary 1912- *ConAu 73, WrDr 84*
Ingbar, Mary Lee 1926- *ConAu 41R*
Inge, M Thomas 1936- *ConAu 9NR, –17R,
WrDr 84*
Inge, William 1913-1973 *CnMD, ConAu 9R,
ConDr 82E, ConLC 1, –8, –19, CroCD,
DcLB 7[port], DcLEL 1940, ModAL,
ModWD, TwCA SUP, TwCWr*
Inge, William Ralph 1860-1954 *LongCTC,
TwCA, TwCA SUP*
Ingelfinger, Franz Joseph 1910-1980 *ConAu 97*
Ingelow, Jean 1820-1897 *SmATA 33[port]*
Ingersol, Jared *ConAu X*
Ingersoll, David E 1939- *ConAu 41R*
Ingersoll, John H 1925- *ConAu 73*
Ingersoll, Ralph 1900- *WrDr 84*
Ingersoll, Ralph McAllister 1900- *ConAu P-1,
TwCA SUP*
Ingersoll, Robert Franklin 1933- *ConAu 104*
Ingham, Colonel Frederic *SmATA X*
Ingham, Daniel *ConAu X, IntAu&W 82X,
WrDr 84*
Ingham, Jennie 1944- *ConAu 108*
Ingham, Kenneth 1921- *ConAu 108, –110,
WrDr 84*
Ingham, Richard Arnison 1935- *ConAu 104,
WrDr 84*
Ingham, Robert E 1934- *ConAu 108,
NatPD 81[port]*
Ingilby, Joan Alicia 1911- *ConAu 9R, WrDr 84*
Ingimarsson, Oskar 1928- *IntAu&W 82*
Ingle, Clifford 1915- *ConAu 29R*
Ingle, Dwight Joyce 1907- *ConAu P-1*
Ingleby, Terry 1901- *ConAu 106*
Ingles, G Lloyd 1901- *ConAu P-1*
Inglin, Meinrad 1893-1971 *CIDMEL 80*
Inglis, Brian 1916- *ConAu 7NR, –17R,
IntAu&W 82, WrDr 84*
Inglis, David Rittenhouse 1905- *ConAu 5R,
–5NR*
Inglis, James 1927- *ConAu 21R*
Inglis, John K 1933- *ConAu 106*
Inglis, R M G 1910-1975 *ConAu 8NR*
Inglis, Robert Morton Gall 1910- *ConAu 13R*
Inglis, Ruth Langdon 1927- *ConAu 1NR, –49*
Inglis, Stuart J 1923- *ConAu 41R*
Inglis, Susan *TwCRGW*
Inglis-Jones, Elisabeth 1900- *IntAu&W 82,
WrDr 84*
Inglot, Mieczyslaw 1931- *IntAu&W 82*
Ingold, Gerard 1922- *ConAu 106*
Ingold, Klara 1913- *ConAu 61*
Ingraham, Leonard W 1913- *ConAu 25R,
SmATA 4*
Ingraham, Mark H 1896- *ConAu 61*
Ingraham, Mark H 1896-1982 *ConAu 109*
Ingraham, Vernon L 1924- *ConAu 33R*
Ingram, Alyce *DrAP&F 83*
Ingram, Anne Bower 1937- *ConAu 102*
Ingram, Bowen *ConAu 37R*
Ingram, Sir Bruce 1877-1963 *LongCTC*
Ingram, Collingwood 1880-1981 *ConAu 103, –61*
Ingram, Derek Thynne 1925- *ConAu 9R,
WrDr 84*
Ingram, Forrest L 1938- *ConAu 53*
Ingram, Gregory Keith 1944- *ConAu 77*
Ingram, Helen Moyer 1937- *ConAu 105*

Ingram, Hunter *TwCWW, WrDr 84*
Ingram, James C 1922- *ConAu 5R*
Ingram, Kenneth 1882-1965 *ConAu P-1*
Ingram, Maria *DrAP&F 83*
Ingram, Thomas Henry 1924- *ConAu 2NR, –49*
Ingram, Thomas Theodore Scott 1927-
IntAu&W 82
Ingram, Tom 1924- *ConAu X*
Ingram, Vernon Martin 1924- *WrDr 84*
Ingram, William 1930- *ConAu 41R*
Ingram, Willis J *ConAu X*
Ingrams, Doreen 1906- *WrDr 84*
Ingrams, Doreen Constance 1906- *ConAu 33R,
SmATA 20*
Ingrams, Richard 1937- *ConAu 103, WrDr 84*
Ingrao, Charles W 1948- *ConAu 101*
Ingstad, Helge Marcus 1899- *ConAu 65,
IntAu&W 82*
Ingwersen, Faith 1934- *ConAu 69*
Ingwersen, Niels 1935- *ConAu 69*
Inkeles, Alex 1920- *ConAu 1R, –1NR*
Inkiow, Dimiter 1932- *ConAu 101*
Inlow, Gail M 1910- *ConAu 4NR, –5R*
Inman, Billie Andrew 1929- *ConAu 29R*
Inman, Edna Perla 1914- *IntWWP 82*
Inman, Jack 1919- *ConAu 25R*
Inman, Loretta L 1893- *IntWWP 82*
Inman, P *DrAP&F 83*
Inman, Robert 1931- *ConAu 17R, WrDr 84*
Inman, Will *DrAP&F 83*
Inman, Will 1923- *ConAu 25R, IntWWP 82*
Inmerito *ConAu X*
Inmon, W H 1945- *ConAu 110*
Innaurato, Albert 1948- *ConDr 82,
ConLC 21[port], NatPD 81[port], WrDr 84*
Inneo, Anthony *NatPD 81[port]*
Innerhofer, Franz 1944- *ConAu 101*
Innes, Brian 1928- *ConAu 21R, IntAu&W 82*
Innes, Christopher David 1941- *ConAu 107*
Innes, Frank C 1934- *ConAu 45*
Innes, Hammond *WrDr 84*
Innes, Hammond 1913- *ConAu X, ConNov 82,
LongCTC, TwCCr&M 80, TwCWr,
WorAu*
Innes, Jean *ConAu X, IntAu&W 82X,
WrDr 84*
Innes, John 1863-1941 *CreCan 1*
Innes, Michael *WrDr 84*
Innes, Michael 1906- *ConAu X, ConLC 14,
ConNov 82, LongCTC, TwCA,
TwCA SUP, TwCCr&M 80, TwCWr*
Innes, Ralph Hammond *ConAu X*
Innes, Rosemary Elizabeth 1917- *ConAu 25R,
IntAu&W 82*
Inness-Brown, Elizabeth *DrAP&F 83*
Innis, Donald Quayle 1924- *ConAu 41R*
Innis, Mary Quayle 1899- *CreCan 1*
Innis, Pauline B 1918- *ConAu 1R, –4NR*
Inoue, Yukitoshi 1945- *ConAu 25R*
Inouye, Daniel K 1924- *ConAu 25R*
Inouye, Jon 1955- *IntAu&W 82*
Insall, Donald W 1926- *ConAu 61,
IntAu&W 82*
Insel, Deborah 1949- *ConAu 110*
Insight, James *ConAu X*
Insingel, Mark 1935- *ConAu 110, IntWWP 82*
Insipidus *IntAu&W 82X*
Intriligator, Michael D 1938- *ConAu 53*
Inverarity, Robert Bruce 1909- *IntAu&W 82,
WrDr 84*
Inyart, Gene 1927- *ConAu X, SmATA 6*
Iodice, Ruth G *DrAP&F 83*
Iodice, Ruth Genevieve 1925- *IntAu&W 82*
Iokepa, Kaipo *IntAu&W 82X*
Ionesco, Eugene 1912- *CIDMEL 80, CnMD,
CnMWL, ConAu 9R, ConLC 1, –4, –6, –9,
–11, –15, CroCD, EncWL 2[port],
IntAu&W 82, LongCTC, ModFrL, ModRL,
ModWD, SmATA 7, TwCWr, WhoTwCL,
WorAu*
Ionescu, Ghita 1913- *ConAu 103, WrDr 84*
Iorga, Nicolae 1871-1940 *CIDMEL 80, CnMD*
Iorio, James 1921- *ConAu 61, IntWWP 82*
Iorio, John 1925- *ConAu 49*
Iorizzo, Luciano J 1930- *ConAu 73*
Ipcar, Dahlov 1917- *ConAu 9NR, –17R,
IntAu&W 82, SmATA 1*
Ippolito, Donna *DrAP&F 83*
Ippolito, Donna 1945- *ConAu 104*
Ipsen, D C 1921- *ConAu 33R, IntAu&W 82,
WrDr 84*
Iqbal, Afzal 1919- *ConAu 10NR, –61*

Iqbal, Muhammad 1877-1938 *EncWL 2,
WorAu 1970*
Iqbal, Sir Muhammad 1873-1938 *ModCmwL*
Iqua *ConAu X*
Irai *IntWWP 82X*
Iraikkuruvanaar 1942- *IntWWP 82*
Iranek-Osmecki, Kazimierz Wincenty 1897-
ConAu 49, IntAu&W 82
Irani, Merwan S *ConAu X*
Irbe, A G *IntAu&W 82X*
Irbe, Andrejs *IntAu&W 82X*
Irbe, Gunars 1924- *IntAu&W 82*
Irby, Kenneth *DrAP&F 83*
Irby, Kenneth 1936- *ConAu 69, ConP 80,
IntWWP 82, WrDr 84*
Ireland, David 1927- *ConAu 25R, ConNov 82,
WrDr 84*
Ireland, Doreen *IntAu&W 82X, WrDr 84*
Ireland, Earl 1928- *ConAu 5R*
Ireland, Joe C 1936- *ConAu 73, IntWWP 82*
Ireland, Kevin 1933- *ConAu 73, ConP 80,
IntWWP 82, WrDr 84*
Ireland, Norma Olin 1907- *ConAu 3NR, –9R*
Ireland, Patrick *ConAu X*
Ireland, Robert M 1937- *ConAu 45*
Ireland, Thelma Brown 1899- *IntWWP 82*
Iremonger, Lucille *WrDr 84*
Iremonger, Lucille 1921?- *ConAu 6NR, –9R,
IntAu&W 82*
Iremonger, Valentin 1918- *ConAu 101,
ConP 80, WrDr 84*
Ireson, Barbara 1927- *ConAu 5R*
Irgang, Jacob 1930- *ConAu 85*
Irion, Mary Jean 1922- *ConAu 21R, WrDr 84*
Irion, Paul E 1922- *ConAu 21R*
Irion, Ruth 1921- *ConAu 65*
Irish, Donald P 1919- *ConAu 49*
Irish, Marian D 1909- *ConAu 9R*
Irish, Richard K 1932- *ConAu 65*
Irish, William *ConAu X, TwCA SUP,
TwCCr&M 80*
Iriye, Akira 1934- *ConAu 11NR, –25R*
Irland, David *ConAu X*
Iron, Ralph *ConAu X, LongCTC*
Ironmaster, Maximus *ConAu X*
Irsfeld, John Henry *DrAP&F 83*
Irsfeld, John Henry 1937- *ConAu 65*
Irvin, Bob *ConAu X*
Irvin, Fred 1914- *SmATA 15*
Irvin, Rea 1881-1972 *ConAu 93*
Irvin, Robert W 1933-1980 *ConAu 103*
Irvine, Betty Jo Kish 1943- *ConAu 77*
Irvine, Demar 1908- *ConAu 33R*
Irvine, Keith 1924- *ConAu 29R, IntAu&W 82,
WrDr 84*
Irvine, R R 1936- *ConAu 81*
Irvine, Sidney H 1931- *ConAu 106*
Irvine, William 1906-1964 *ConAu 106,
TwCA SUP*
Irving, Alexander *SmATA X*
Irving, Blanche M *IntWWP 82*
Irving, Brian William 1932- *ConAu 53*
Irving, Clifford 1930- *WrDr 84*
Irving, Clifford Michael 1930- *AuNews 1,
ConAu 1R, –2NR*
Irving, Clive 1933- *ConAu 85*
Irving, David John Cawdell 1938- *ConAu 13R*
Irving, Gordon 1918- *ConAu 25R*
Irving, Henry *ConAu X*
Irving, John *DrAP&F 83*
Irving, John 1942- *ConAu 25R, ConLC 13,
–23[port], ConNov 82, DcLB Y82A[port],
–6[port], WrDr 84*
Irving, Nancy *ConAu X*
Irving, R L Graham 1877-1969 *ConAu P-1*
Irving, Robert 1913- *ConAu X, SmATA X*
Irving, T B 1914- *ConAu 37R*
Irving, William *ConAu X*
Irving-James, Thomas 1914- *IntAu&W 82*
Irwin, Ann 1915- *ConAu 101*
Irwin, Constance 1913- *WrDr 84*
Irwin, Constance Frick 1913- *ConAu 1R, –5NR,
IntAu&W 82, SmATA 6*
Irwin, Cynthia C *ConAu X*
Irwin, David George 1933- *ConAu 53,
IntAu&W 82, WrDr 84*
Irwin, Francis William 1905- *ConAu 105*
Irwin, George 1910-1971 *ConAu 41R*
Irwin, Grace Lilian 1907- *ConAu 17R,
CreCan 2, WrDr 84*
Irwin, Hadley *ConAu X*
Irwin, Inez Haynes 1873-1970 *ConAu 102,*

TwCA, TwCA SUP

Irwin, James W 1891?-1977 ConAu 73
Irwin, John Conran 1917- WrDr 84
Irwin, John T 1940- ConAu 53
Irwin, John V 1915- ConAu 1NR
Irwin, John V 1917- ConAu 45
Irwin, Keith Gordon 1885-1964 ConAu 5R,
SmATA 11
Irwin, Margaret 1889-1967 ConAu 93,
LongCTC, TwCA SUP, TwCRGW,
TwCWr
Irwin, P K ConAu X, CreCan 1
Irwin, Paul 1940- ConAu 107
Irwin, Peter George 1925- WrDr 84
Irwin, Raymond 1902- ConAu P-1
Irwin, Ruth Beckey 1906- ConAu 29R
Irwin, Theodore 1907- ConAu 65
Irwin, Vera Rushforth 1913- ConAu 33R
Irwin, W R 1915- ConAu 65
Irwin, Wallace Admah 1875-1959 TwCA,
TwCA SUP
Irwin, Will 1873-1948 DcLB 25[port]
Irwin, William Arthur 1898- IntAu&W 82
Irwin, William Henry 1873-1948 TwCA,
TwCA SUP
Irwin-Williams, Cynthia 1936- ConAu 1NR, –45
Irzykowski, Karol 1873-1944 ClDMEL 80,
ModSL 2
Isaac, Erich 1928- ConAu 45
Isaac, Joanne 1934- ConAu 25R,
SmATA 21[port]
Isaac, Joseph 1922- WrDr 84
Isaac, Paul Edward 1926- ConAu 17R,
WrDr 84
Isaac, Peter 1921- WrDr 84
Isaac, Peter Charles Gerald 1921- IntAu&W 82
Isaac, Rael Jean 1933- ConAu 17R
Isaac, Stephen 1925- ConAu 33R
Isaacs, Alan 1925- ConAu 3NR, –9R,
IntAu&W 82, WrDr 84
Isaacs, Bernard 1924- ConAu 107, WrDr 84
Isaacs, E Elizabeth 1917- ConAu 5R
Isaacs, Edith Somborn 1884-1978 ConAu 77
Isaacs, Harold Robert 1910- ConAu 1R, –2NR,
IntAu&W 82
Isaacs, Jacob ConAu X, SmATA X
Isaacs, Neil D 1931- ConAu 5R, –9NR,
ConSFA
Isaacs, Norman Ellis 1908- ConAu 81
Isaacs, Stan 1929- ConAu 13R
Isaacs, Stephen David 1937- ConAu 81
Isaacs, Susan 1943- ConAu 89, WrDr 84
Isaacson, Robert L 1928- ConAu 7NR, –17R
Isaak, Robert A 1945- ConAu 61
Isadora, Rachel SmATA 32
Isais, Juan M 1926- ConAu 29R
Isakovsky, Mikhail Vasilyevich 1900-1973
ConAu 41R
Isaksson, Roy U S 1948- IntAu&W 82
Isaksson, Ulla 1916- ConAu 109
Isaksson, Ulla Margareta 1916- ClDMEL 80
Isban, Samuel 1905- ConAu 2NR, –49
Isbister, Clair ConAu X
Isbister, Jean Sinclair 1915- ConAu 1NR,
IntAu&W 82
Ise, John 1885-1960? ConAu P-1
Iseler, Elmer Walter 1927- CreCan 1
Isely, Flora Kunigunde Duncan ConAu X
Isely, Helen Sue 1917- ConAu 5R
Iseminger, Gary 1937- ConAu 37R
Isenberg, Irwin M 1931- ConAu 17R
Isenberg, Irwin M 1931-1979 ConAu 11NR
Isenberg, Seymour 1930- ConAu 33R, WrDr 84
Isenhour, Thomas Lee 1939- ConAu 57
Iser, Wolfgang 1926- ConAu 57
Ish-Kishor, Judith 1892-1972 ConAu 103,
SmATA 11
Ish-Kishor, Sulamith 1896-1977 ConAu 69, –73,
SmATA 17, TwCCW 83
Ish-Koshor, Judith 1892- ConAu 1R
Ishak, Fayek Matta 1922- ConAu 41R,
IntAu&W 82
Ishak, Yusof Bin 1910?-1970 ConAu 104
Isham, Charlotte H 1912- ConAu 73,
SmATA 21[port]
Isham, Linda 1938- ConAu 107
Ishee, John A 1934- ConAu 25R
Isherwood, Christopher DrAP&F 83
Isherwood, Christopher 1904- CnMD, CnMWL,
ConAu 13R, ConDr 82, ConLC 1, –9, –11,
–14, ConNov 82, DcLB 15[port],
EncWL 2, LongCTC, ModBrL,

ModBrL SUP, ModWD, TwCA,
TwCA SUP, TwCWr, WhoTwCL,
WrDr 84
Ishida, Takeshi 1923- ConAu 97
Ishigo, Estelle 1899- ConAu 61
Ishiguro, Hide 1934- WrDr 84
Ishiguro, Kazuo 1954?- ConLC 27[port],
WrDr 84
Ishikawa, Takuboku 1886-1912 EncWL 2
Ishino, Iwao 1921- ConAu 17R
Ishlinsky, Aleksandr Yulevich 1913-
IntAu&W 82
Ishlon, Deborah 1925- ConAu 1R
Ishmael, Woodi 1914- SmATA 31
Ishmole, Jack 1924- ConAu 49
Ishwaran, K 1922- ConAu 49, WrDr 84
Isichei, Elizabeth Mary 1939- ConAu 5NR, –53,
WrDr 84
Isichel, Elizabeth Mary 1939- IntAu&W 82
Isis ConAu X
Iskander, Fazil 1929- ClDMEL 80, ConAu 102
Isla, Moran, Francisco 1946- IntAu&W 82
Islam, A K M Aminul 1933- ConAu 41R
Islam, Kazi Nazrul 1899?-1976 ConAu 69
Island IntAu&W 82X, IntWWP 82X
Islas, Maya DrAP&F 83
Islas, Maya 1947- IntAu&W 82, IntWWP 82X
Isle, Walter 1933- ConAu 25R
Isler, Ursula 1923- IntAu&W 82
Ismach, Arnold H 1930- ConAu 85
Ismail, A H 1923- ConAu 25R
Isogai, Hiroshi 1940- ConAu 102
Ispahani, Mirza Abol Hassan 1902-1981
ConAu 108
Israel, Abby 1942- ConAu 107
Israel, Charles DrAP&F 83
Israel, Charles 1920- WrDr 84
Israel, Charles Edward 1920- ConAu 1R,
ConNov 82, CreCan 1, DcLEL 1940
Israel, Elaine 1945- ConAu 9NR, –53,
SmATA 12
Israel, Fred L 1934- ConAu 17R
Israel, Gerard 1928- ConAu 81
Israel, Jerry 1941- ConAu 29R, WrDr 84
Israel, John 1935- ConAu 21R, WrDr 84
Israel, Jonathan I 1946- ConAu 109
Israel, Marion Louise 1882-1973 ConAu 1R, –103,
SmATA 26N
Israel, Martin 1927- ConAu 109
Israel, Peter DrAP&F 83
Israel, Saul 1910- ConAu P-1
Issachar ConAu X
Issawi, Charles Philip 1916- ConAu 4NR, –5R
Isser, Natalie 1927- ConAu 53
Issler, Anne Roller 1892- ConAu 49
Istrati, Panait 1881-1938 ClDMEL 80
Istrati, Panait 1884-1935 TwCA, TwCA SUP,
TwCWr
Isvaran, Manjeri d1967 ModCmwL
Iswolsky, Helen 1896-1975 ConAu 5R, –61
Italiaander, Rolf 1913- ConAu 5R, –6NR,
IntAu&W 82, IntWWP 82
Itamar, Yaos-Kest 1934- IntWWP 82
Itse, Elizabeth M 1930- ConAu 1NR, –49
Itzin, Catherine 1944- ConAu 77, IntAu&W 82
Itzin, Charles F DrAP&F 83
Itzkoff, Seymour William WrDr 84
Itzkoff, Seymour William 1928- ConAu 33R
Ivamy, Edward 1920- WrDr 84
Ivan, Martha Miller Pfaff 1909- ConAu P-2
Ivancevich, John M 1939- ConAu 29R
Ivannikoff, Lydia 1909- IntWWP 82
Ivanov, Georgy Vladimirovich 1894-1958
ClDMEL 80
Ivanov, Georgyi Vladimirovich 1894-1958 WorAu
Ivanov, Miroslav 1929- ConAu 81
Ivanov, Vsevolod Vyacheslavovich 1895-1963
ClDMEL 80, CnMD, CnMWL, ConAu 93,
ModSL 1, ModWD, TwCWr, WorAu
Ivanov, Vyacheslav Ivanovich 1866-1949
ClDMEL 80, EncWL 2, ModSL 1
Ivask, George 1910- IntWWP 82
Ivask, Ivar 1927- ConAu 37R, ConLC 14
Ivask, Yury Pavlovich 1910- ClDMEL 80
Ivens, Michael William 1924- ConAu 5R,
WrDr 84
Ivens, Virginia R 1922- ConAu 105
Ivers, Larry Edward 1936- ConAu 77
Iversen, Gudmund R 1934- ConAu 4NR, –53
Iversen, Nick 1951- ConAu 73
Iverson, Genie 1942- ConAu 9NR, –65
Iverson, Jeffrey 1934- ConAu 105, WrDr 84

Iverson, Lucille DrAP&F 83
Iverson, Lucille K 1925- ConAu 61
Iverson, Peter James 1944- ConAu 106
Ives, Burl 1909- ConAu 103
Ives, Edward D 1925- ConAu 25R
Ives, Lawrence ConAu X
Ives, Morgan ConAu X, WrDr 84
Ives, Rich IntWWP 82X
Ives, Richard Lee 1951- IntWWP 82
Ives, Sandy ConAu X
Ives, Sumner 1911- ConAu 9R
Ivey, Allen E 1933- ConAu 2NR, –49
Ivey, Donald 1918- ConAu 89
Ivie, Robert M 1930- ConAu 9R
Ivimy IntWWP 82X
Ivings, Jacqueline Margaret 1935- CreCan 1
Ivnev, Riurik ConAu X
Ivo, Ledo 1924- TwCWr
Ivory, James 1928- ConAu 109
Ivry, Alfred Lyon 1935- ConAu 1NR, –45
Iwamatsu, Jun Atsushi 1908- ConAu 73,
SmATA 14

Iwaszkiewicz, Jaroslaw 1894-1980 ClDMEL 80,
CnMD, ConAu 97, EncWL 2, ModSL 2,
ModWD
Iwata, Masakazu 1917- ConAu 17R, WrDr 84
Iyengar, B K Sundararaja 1918- ConAu 97,
IntAu&W 82
Iyengar, K R Srinivasa 1908- ConAu 5R, –8NR,
IntWWP 82
Iyengar, S Kesava 1894- ConAu 17R
Iyer, Baghavan Narashimhan 1930- ConAu 57
Iyer, Raghavan 1930- ConAu 6NR
Izant, Grace Goulder 1893- ConAu P-1
Izard, Barbara 1926- ConAu 29R
Izard, Carroll E 1923- ConAu 4NR, –49
Izban, Samuel 1905- ConAu X, IntAu&W 82
Izenberg, Gerald N 1939- ConAu 105
Izenour, George Charles 1912- ConAu 93
Izumi, Kyoka 1873-1939 EncWL 2
Izzard, Ralph William Burdick 1910-
IntAu&W 82
Izzo, Herbert J 1928- ConAu 41R

J

J *AuNews 1, ConAu X*
J R L *IntAu&W 82X*
J S P *IntAu&W 82X*
Jaastad, Birger 1904- *IntAu&W 82*
Jabavu, Noni *DcLEL 1940*
Jabavu, Noni Helen Nontando 1921- *TwCWr*
Jabay, Earl 1925- *ConAu 21R*
Jabber, Fuad 1943- *ConAu 49*
Jabes, Edmond 1912- *EncWL 2*
Jabez *ConAu X, CreCan 2, IntAu&W 82X*
Jablonski, Edward 1922- *ConAu 1R, –2NR*
Jablonski, Ronald E 1929- *ConAu 104*
Jabs, Carolyn 1950- *ConAu 110*
Jac, Lee *SmATA X*
Jacaway, Taffy Marie 1928- *ConAmTC*
Jaccard, Roland 1941- *IntAu&W 82*
Jaccottet, Philippe 1925- *WorAu 1970*
Jacek, Lukasiewicz 1934- *IntAu&W 82*
Jack *IntAu&W 82X*
Jack Crawford, Jr. *DrAP&F 83*
Jack, Donald Lamont 1924- *ConAu 1R, –3NR, CreCan 1*
Jack, Homer A 1916- *ConAu 41R, IntAu&W 82*
Jack, Ian 1923- *WrDr 84*
Jack, Ian Robert James 1923- *ConAu 57*
Jack, R Ian 1935- *ConAu 3NR, –49*
Jack, Sheila Beryl 1918- *IntWWP 82*
Jackendoff, Ray S 1945- *ConAu 6NR, –53*
Jacker, Corinne 1933- *ConAu 17R, NatPD 81[port], WrDr 84*
Jackins, Harvey 1916- *ConAu 1NR, –49*
Jacklin, Anthony 1944- *ConAu 85*
Jacklin, Tony 1944- *ConAu X, IntAu&W 82*
Jackman, Edwin Russell 1894-1967 *ConAu P-1*
Jackman, Leslie A J 1919- *ConAu 29R*
Jackman, Stuart 1922- *ConAu 101, TwCCr&M 80, WrDr 84*
Jackman, Sydney Wayne 1925- *ConAu 1R, –1NR, IntAu&W 82, WrDr 84*
Jackmon, Marvin X 1944- *ConAu 49*
Jackowska, Nicki 1942- *IntWWP 82*
Jacks, Lawrence Pearsall 1860-1955 *LongCTC, TwCA, TwCA SUP, TwCWr*
Jacks, M L 1894-1964 *LongCTC*
Jacks, Oliver *ConAu X, IntAu&W 82X, TwCCr&M 80, WrDr 84*
Jackson, A B 1925- *ConAu 104*
Jackson, Alan 1938- *ConAu 101, ConP 80, DcLEL 1940, WrDr 84*
Jackson, Alan Arthur 1922- *IntAu&W 82*
Jackson, Albert 1943- *ConAu 93*
Jackson, Albina *ConAu X*
Jackson, Alexander Young 1882- *CreCan 2*
Jackson, Allan 1905?-1976 *ConAu 65*
Jackson, Anna J 1926- *ConAu 103*
Jackson, Anne *ConAu X*
Jackson, Anthony 1926- *ConAu 11NR, –69, WrDr 84*
Jackson, Archibald Stewart 1922- *ConAu 61*
Jackson, Arthur 1921- *ConAu 104, IntAu&W 82*
Jackson, Aubrey Joseph 1911- *IntAu&W 82*
Jackson, B R 1937- *ConAu 25R*

Jackson, Barbara 1914-1981 *ConAu 6NR, –103*
Jackson, Barbara Ann Garvey Seagrave 1929- *ConAu 21R, WrDr 84*
Jackson, Sir Barry Vincent 1879-1961 *LongCTC*
Jackson, Basil 1920- *ConAu 8NR, –57*
Jackson, Blyden 1910- *ConAu 57*
Jackson, Brian 1933?-1983 *ConAu 110*
Jackson, Brian Henry 1926- *CreCan 1*
Jackson, Brooks 1941- *ConAu 97*
Jackson, Bruce 1936- *ConAu 89*
Jackson, C O 1901- *ConAu P-1*
Jackson, C Paul 1902- *ConAu 5R, –6NR, MichAu 80*
Jackson, Caary Paul 1902- *ConAu X, SmATA 6*
Jackson, Carlton 1933- *ConAu 21R*
Jackson, Carole *ConAu 104*
Jackson, Charles 1903-1968 *ConAu 101, –25R, LongCTC, TwCA SUP*
Jackson, Clarence J-L *ConAu X*
Jackson, Clyde Owen 1928- *LivgBAA, WrDr 84*
Jackson, Dave 1944- *ConAu 81*
Jackson, David Cooper 1931- *ConAu 109, WrDr 84*
Jackson, Derrick 1939- *ConAu 77*
Jackson, Don D 1920-1968 *ConAu P-1*
Jackson, Donald 1919- *ConAu 17R*
Jackson, Donald Dale 1935- *ConAu 1NR, –49*
Jackson, Dorothy Virginia Steinhauer 1924- *ConAu 13R*
Jackson, Douglas Northrop 1929- *ConAu 37R, IntAu&W 82*
Jackson, E F *ConAu X, WrDr 84*
Jackson, Edgar 1910- *ConAu 77*
Jackson, Ellen B 1943- *ConAu 110*
Jackson, Esther Merle 1922- *ConAu 13R*
Jackson, Everatt *ConAu X, IntAu&W 82X, WrDr 84*
Jackson, Franklin Jefferson *ConAu X*
Jackson, Gabriel 1921- *ConAu 21R*
Jackson, Gabriele Johanna Bernhard 1934- *ConAu 29R*
Jackson, Gainor W 1926- *WrDr 84*
Jackson, Geoffrey 1915- *ConAu 61, IntAu&W 82, WrDr 84*
Jackson, George D 1929- *ConAu 81*
Jackson, George S 1906-1976 *ConAu 61, ConAu P-1*
Jackson, Gordon 1934- *ConAu 104*
Jackson, Gordon Noel 1913- *WrDr 84*
Jackson, Graham 1949- *IntAu&W 82*
Jackson, Guida *DrAP&F 83*
Jackson, Guida 1930- *ConAu 93, IntAu&W 82*
Jackson, H C L 1894-1954 *MichAu 80*
Jackson, Haywood *DrAP&F 83, IntWWP 82X*
Jackson, Henry Martin 1912-1983 *ConAu 110*
Jackson, Herbert C 1917- *ConAu 9R, WrDr 84*
Jackson, Herbert G 1928- *WrDr 84*
Jackson, Herbert G, Jr. 1928- *ConAu 37R*
Jackson, Holbrook 1874-1948 *LongCTC, TwCA, TwCA SUP*
Jackson, J P *ConAu X*
Jackson, Jacqueline 1928- *ConAu 45*
Jackson, Jacquelyne Johnson 1932- *ConAu 37R*

Jackson, James P 1925- *ConAu 77*
Jackson, Jesse 1908- *ConAu 25R, ConLC 12, LivgBAA, SmATA 2, –29[port], TwCCW 83, WrDr 84*
Jackson, Jesse 1908-1983 *ConAu 109*
Jackson, John Archer 1929- *ConAu 13R*
Jackson, John E 1942- *ConAu 101*
Jackson, John Glover 1907- *LivgBAA*
Jackson, John Howard 1932- *ConAu 41R*
Jackson, John N 1925- *ConAu 37R, IntAu&W 82, WrDr 84*
Jackson, Jon A 1938- *ConAu 81*
Jackson, Joseph 1924- *ConAu 11NR, ConAu P-1*
Jackson, Joseph Henry 1894-1955 *TwCA, TwCA SUP*
Jackson, Joy J 1928- *ConAu 29R*
Jackson, Karl 1942- *ConAu 102*
Jackson, Katherine Gauss 1904-1975 *ConAu 57*
Jackson, Keith 1928- *ConAu 8NR, –61*
Jackson, Kenneth Terry 1939- *ConAu 21R, WrDr 84*
Jackson, Laura *WrDr 84*
Jackson, Laura Riding 1901- *ConAu 65, ConLC 7, TwCA SUP*
Jackson, Louise A 1937- *ConAu 93*
Jackson, Lucille *ConAu X*
Jackson, Lydia 1900?-1983 *ConAu 110*
Jackson, Lydia Octavia 1902- *IntWWP 82*
Jackson, Mae *DrAP&F 83*
Jackson, Mae 1946- *ConAu 81*
Jackson, Mahalia 1901-1972 *ConAu 33R*
Jackson, Margaret Weymouth 1895- *AuNews 1*
Jackson, Martin A 1941- *ConAu 89*
Jackson, Mary 1924- *ConAu 61*
Jackson, Miles Merrill, Jr. 1929- *ConAu 41R, LivgBAA*
Jackson, Nell C 1929- *LivgBAA*
Jackson, Neta 1944- *ConAu 89*
Jackson, Neville *ConAu X, WrDr 84*
Jackson, Nora 1915- *ConAu X, WrDr 84*
Jackson, Norman 1932- *ConAu 25R, IntWWP 82*
Jackson, O B *ConAu X, SmATA 6*
Jackson, Paul R 1905- *ConAu P-1*
Jackson, Percival Ephrates 1891-1970 *ConAu 1R, –3NR*
Jackson, Peter 1926- *WrDr 84*
Jackson, Philip W 1928- *ConAu 21R*
Jackson, R E *ConAu X, IntAu&W 82X*
Jackson, R Eugene 1941- *ConAu 109, NatPD 81[port]*
Jackson, Richard *DrAP&F 83*
Jackson, Richard 1946- *ConAu 110, IntWWP 82*
Jackson, Robert 1911- *ConAu 9R*
Jackson, Robert Blake 1926- *ConAu 5R, –6NR, SmATA 8*
Jackson, Robert J 1936- *ConAu 25R, WrDr 84*
Jackson, Robert L 1935- *ConAu 73*
Jackson, Robert Louis 1923- *ConAu 109*
Jackson, Robert S 1926- *ConAu 29R*
Jackson, Rosemary Elizabeth 1917- *WrDr 84*
Jackson, Ruth A *ConAu 45*

Jackson, S Wesley 1936- *ConAu 33R*
Jackson, Sally *ConAu X, SmATA X*
Jackson, Sam *ConAu X*
Jackson, Sara *ConAu X*
Jackson, Scoop *ConAu X*
Jackson, Sheila *DrAP&F 83*
Jackson, Shirley 1919-1965 *ConAu 1R, –4NR,
–25R, ConLC 11, ConNov 82A,
DcLB 6[port], DcLEL 1940, LongCTC,
ModAL, SmATA 2, TwCA SUP,
TwCCr&M 80, TwCRGW*
Jackson, Stephanie *ConAu X*
Jackson, Teague 1938- *ConAu 93*
Jackson, W A Douglas 1923- *ConAu 45*
Jackson, W G F 1917- *ConAu 25R*
Jackson, W T H 1915- *ConAu 1R, –1NR*
Jackson, W Turrentine 1915- *ConAu 13R*
Jackson, Wes 1936- *ConAu 3NR, –49*
Jackson, William 1917- *WrDr 84*
Jackson, William Arthur Douglas 1923-
IntAu&W 82
Jackson, William Godfrey Fothergill 1917-
IntAu&W 82
Jackson, William Haywood 1930- *IntWWP 82*
Jackson, William Keith 1928- *IntAu&W 82,
WrDr 84*
Jackson, William Peter Uprichard 1918-
WrDr 84
Jackson, William Vernon 1926- *ConAu 21R*
Jackson, Wilma 1931- *ConAu 73*
Jackson-Haight, Mabel V 1912- *ConAu 25R*
Jaco, E Gartly 1923- *ConAu 1R, –1NR,
WrDr 84*
Jacob, Alaric 1909- *ConAu 5R, IntAu&W 82*
Jacob, Anthony Dillingham *WrDr 84*
Jacob, Charles E 1931- *ConAu 5NR, –13R*
Jacob, Ernest Fraser 1894-1971 *ConAu 1R,
–3NR*
Jacob, Evariste C *IntAu&W 82X*
Jacob, Francois 1920- *ConAu 102*
Jacob, Fred E 1899- *ConAu 105*
Jacob, Helen Pierce 1927- *ConAu 69,
SmATA 21[port]*
Jacob, Herbert 1933- *ConAu 77*
Jacob, Jean-Noel 1915- *IntAu&W 82*
Jacob, John *DrAP&F 83*
Jacob, Margaret Candee 1943- *ConAu 65*
Jacob, Max 1876-1944 *CIDMEL 80, CnMWL,
ConAu 104, EncWL 2, ModFrL, ModRL,
TwCLC 6[port], WhoTwCL, WorAu*
Jacob, Nancy L 1943- *ConAu 29R*
Jacob, Naomi 1884-1964 *TwCRGW*
Jacob, Naomi Ellington 1889?-1964 *LongCTC,
TwCA, TwCA SUP, TwCWr*
Jacob, Paul 1940- *ConAu 103, ConP 80,
DcLEL 1940, WrDr 84*
Jacob, Philip E 1914- *ConAu 4NR, –53*
Jacob, Piers Anthony Dillingham 1934-
ConAu 21R
Jacobi, Carl 1908- *ConAu P-1*
Jacobi, Jolande Szekacs 1890- *ConAu 9R*
Jacobi, Peter Paul 1930- *ConAmTC*
Jacobik, Gray *DrAP&F 83*
Jacobs, Arthur David 1922- *ConAu 4NR, –5R,
IntAu&W 82, WrDr 84*
Jacobs, Barry 1932- *ConAu 101*
Jacobs, Charles Juan Stephen Richard 1902-
IntWWP 82
Jacobs, Clyde 1925- *ConAu 37R, WrDr 84*
Jacobs, Dan N 1924- *ConAu 4NR,
IntAu&W 82, WrDr 84*
Jacobs, Dan N 1925- *ConAu 5R*
Jacobs, David Michael 1942- *ConAu 57*
Jacobs, Diane 1948- *ConAu 73*
Jacobs, Donald M 1937- *ConAu 110*
Jacobs, Flora Gill 1918- *ConAu 1R, SmATA 5*
Jacobs, Francine 1935- *ConAu 1NR, –49*
Jacobs, Francis G 1939- *WrDr 84*
Jacobs, Frank 1929- *ConAu 6NR, –13R,
SmATA 30[port], WrDr 84*
Jacobs, G Walker 1948- *ConAu 49*
Jacobs, Glenn 1940- *ConAu 29R*
Jacobs, Harold 1941- *ConAu 45*
Jacobs, Harvey 1915- *ConAu 21R*
Jacobs, Harvey 1930- *ConAu 29R*
Jacobs, Hayes B 1919- *ConAu 9R*
Jacobs, Helen Hull 1908- *ConAu 9R,
IntAu&W 82, SmATA 12, WrDr 84*
Jacobs, Herbert A 1903- *ConAu 13R*
Jacobs, Howard 1908- *ConAu 65*
Jacobs, James B 1947- *ConAu 101*
Jacobs, Jane 1916- *ConAu 21R, DcLEL 1940*

Jacobs, Jerome L 1931- *ConAu 89*
Jacobs, Jerry 1932- *ConAu 11NR, –29R,
IntAu&W 82*
Jacobs, Jill *ConAu X*
Jacobs, Jim 1942- *ConAu 97, ConDr 82D,
ConLC 12, NatPD 81[port]*
Jacobs, John 1916- *WrDr 84*
Jacobs, John 1918- *ConAu 21R*
Jacobs, Joseph 1854-1916 *SmATA 25[port]*
Jacobs, Leah *ConAu X, WrDr 84*
Jacobs, Leland Blair 1907- *ConAu 73,
SmATA 20*
Jacobs, Lewis 1906- *ConAu 77*
Jacobs, Linda C 1943- *ConAu 29R,
SmATA 21[port]*
Jacobs, Lou, Jr. 1921- *ConAu 9NR, –21R,
SmATA 2*
Jacobs, Louis 1920- *ConAu 1R, –1NR,
IntAu&W 82, WrDr 84*
Jacobs, Lucky *DrAP&F 83*
Jacobs, Melville 1902-1971 *ConAu 1R, –103*
Jacobs, Michael 1955- *NatPD 81[port]*
Jacobs, Milton 1920- *ConAu 37R*
Jacobs, Norman 1924- *ConAu 77*
Jacobs, Paul 1918-1978 *ConAu 13R, –73*
Jacobs, Pepita Jimenez 1932- *ConAu 17R*
Jacobs, Robert Durene 1918- *ConAu 41R*
Jacobs, Robert L 1904- *IntAu&W 82*
Jacobs, Roderick A 1934- *ConAu 21R*
Jacobs, Ruth Harriet 1924- *ConAu 89*
Jacobs, Sheldon 1931- *ConAu 106*
Jacobs, Sophia Yarnall 1902- *ConAu 106*
Jacobs, Susan 1940- *ConAu X, SmATA 30*
Jacobs, T C H 1899-1976 *ConAu X,
TwCCr&M 80*
Jacobs, Vivian 1916?-1981 *ConAu 103*
Jacobs, Walter Darnell 1922- *ConAu 17R,
WrDr 84*
Jacobs, Wilbur R 1918- *WrDr 84*
Jacobs, Wilbur Ripley 1918- *ConAu 13R*
Jacobs, William Jay 1933- *ConAu 7NR, –57,
SmATA 28[port]*
Jacobs, William Wymark 1863-1943 *LongCTC,
ModBrL, TwCA, TwCA SUP, TwCWr*
Jacobs And Casey *ConLC 12*
Jacobsen, Claus 1940- *IntAu&W 82*
Jacobsen, Jens Peter 1847-1885 *CIDMEL 80*
Jacobsen, Josephine 1908- *ConAu 33R,
ConP 80, WorAu 1970, WrDr 84*
Jacobsen, Lydik S 1897?-1976 *ConAu 69*
Jacobsen, Lyle E 1929- *ConAu 13R*
Jacobsen, Marion Leach 1908- *ConAu 61*
Jacobsen, O Irving 1896- *ConAu P-2*
Jacobsen, Phebe R 1922- *ConAu 73*
Jacobsen, Rolf 1907- *CIDMEL 80, IntWWP 82*
Jacobsen, Thorkild 1904- *ConAu 105*
Jacobsohn, Gary J 1946- *ConAu 89*
Jacobson, Bernard Isaac 1936- *ConAu 109*
Jacobson, Cliff 1940- *ConAu 85*
Jacobson, Dale *DrAP&F 83*
Jacobson, Dale 1949- *IntWWP 82*
Jacobson, Dan 1929- *ConAu 1R, –2NR,
ConLC 4, –14, ConNov 82, DcLB 14[port],
DcLEL 1940, IntAu&W 82, ModBrL SUP,
ModCmwL, TwCWr, WorAu, WrDr 84*
Jacobson, Daniel 1923- *ConAu 53, MichAu 80,
SmATA 12*
Jacobson, David B 1928- *ConAu 53*
Jacobson, Edith 1897?-1978 *ConAu 85*
Jacobson, Edmund 1888- *ConAu 9R*
Jacobson, Ethel *ConAu 37R, WrDr 84*
Jacobson, Frederick L 1938- *ConAu 49*
Jacobson, Gary Charles 1944- *ConAu 109*
Jacobson, Harold Karan 1929- *ConAu 3NR, –9R*
Jacobson, Helen Saltz 1921- *ConAu 6NR, –57*
Jacobson, Howard Boone 1925- *ConAu 1R*
Jacobson, Jon 1938- *ConAu 61, WrDr 84*
Jacobson, Julius 1922- *ConAu 45*
Jacobson, Michael F 1943- *ConAu 77*
Jacobson, Morris K 1906- *ConAu 3NR, –45,
SmATA 21[port]*
Jacobson, Nils Olof 1937- *ConAu 110*
Jacobson, Nolan Pliny 1909- *ConAu 8NR, –21R,
IntAu&W 82*
Jacobson, Robert 1940- *ConAu 89*
Jacobson, Rodolfo 1915- *ConAu 41R*
Jacobson, Sheldon Albert 1903- *ConAu 37R,
WrDr 84*
Jacobson, Sibyl C 1942- *ConAu 65*
Jacobson, Stephen A 1934- *ConAu 97*
Jacobson, Steve *ConAu X*
Jacobstein, J Myron 1920- *ConAu 53*

Jacobus, Donald Lines 1887-1970 *ConAu 4NR,
–5R*
Jacobus, Elaine Wegener 1908- *ConAu 33R*
Jacobus, Lee A 1935- *ConAu 33R, WrDr 84*
Jacobus, Mary 1944- *ConAu 105, WrDr 84*
Jacoby, Arnold 1913- *IntAu&W 82*
Jacoby, Henry 1905- *ConAu 77*
Jacoby, Joseph E 1944- *ConAu 97*
Jacoby, Neil H 1909-1979 *ConAu 10NR, –21R,
–89*
Jacoby, Oswald 1902- *ConAu 107*
Jacoby, Russell 1945- *ConAu 77*
Jacoby, Stephen M 1940- *ConAu 57*
Jacoby, Susan *ConAu 108*
Jacopetti, Alexandra 1939- *ConAu X, –57,
SmATA 14*
Jacot, B L *ConAu X*
Jacot, Michael 1924- *ConAu 104*
Jacot DeBoinod, Bernard Louis 1898-1977
ConAu 9R, –77
Jacoway, Elizabeth 1944- *ConAu 110*
Jacquelin *CreCan 2*
Jacqueline *ConAu X*
Jacquemin, Jean *IntWWP 82X*
Jacqueney, Mona G 1914- *ConAu 41R,
IntAu&W 82*
Jacqueney, Theodore 1943?-1979 *ConAu 89*
Jacques, Robin 1920- *SmATA 30, –32[port]*
Jacquet, Constant Herbert, Jr. 1925- *ConAu 106*
Jade, Matt *IntAu&W 82X*
Jaded Observer *ConAu X*
Jados, Stanley S 1912-1977 *ConAu 33R*
Jaeckle, Erwin 1909- *IntWWP 82*
Jaeger, Cyril Karel Stuart 1912- *ConAu 1R*
Jaeger, Donna Michelle 1948- *IntWWP 82*
Jaeger, Edmund C 1887- *ConAu P-2*
Jaeger, Edmund C 1887-1983 *ConAu 110*
Jaeger, Frank 1926-1977 *CIDMEL 80,
EncWL 2*
Jaeger, Gerard A 1952- *IntAu&W 82*
Jaeger, Harry 1922- *WrDr 84*
Jaeger, Harry J, Jr. 1919?-1979 *ConAu 85*
Jaeger, Cardinal Lorenz 1892-1975 *ConAu 57*
Jaeger, Marigold *IntWWP 82X*
Jaeger, Michele Anne 1958- *IntWWP 82*
Jaeger, Sharon Ann *DrAP&F 83*
Jaeger, Sharon Ann 1945- *IntWWP 82*
Jaeger, Walter H E 1902?-1982 *ConAu 108*
Jaeggi, Urs 1931- *IntAu&W 82*
Jaen, Didier Tisdel 1933- *ConAu 29R*
Jaenen, Cornelius John 1927- *ConAu 85*
Jaffa, Aileen Raby 1900- *IntWWP 82*
Jaffa, George 1916- *IntAu&W 82X, WrDr 84*
Jaffa, Harry V 1918- *ConAu 33R*
Jaffe, A J 1912- *ConAu 5R*
Jaffe, Aniela 1903- *IntAu&W 82*
Jaffe, Annette Williams *DrAP&F 83*
Jaffe, Bernard 1896- *ConAu 5R*
Jaffe, Dan *DrAP&F 83*
Jaffe, Dan 1933- *ConAu 25R*
Jaffe, Dennis T 1946- *ConAu 89*
Jaffe, Elsa *ConAu X*
Jaffe, Eugene D 1937- *ConAu 37R*
Jaffe, Frederick S 1925-1978 *ConAu 5NR, –9R*
Jaffe, Gabriel Vivian 1923- *ConAu 13R,
WrDr 84*
Jaffe, Harold *DrAP&F 83*
Jaffe, Harold 1938- *ConAu 29R*
Jaffe, Hilde 1927- *ConAu 105*
Jaffe, Hosea 1921- *IntAu&W 82*
Jaffe, Irma B 1917- *ConAu 1NR, –45*
Jaffe, Louis Leventhal 1905- *ConAu 21R*
Jaffe, Louise *DrAP&F 83*
Jaffe, Michael 1923- *ConAu 21R*
Jaffe, Nora Crow 1944- *ConAu 106*
Jaffe, Rona *WrDr 84*
Jaffe, Rona 1932?- *AuNews 1, ConAu 73*
Jaffe, Sandra Sohn 1943- *ConAu 101*
Jaffe, Sherril 1945- *ConAu 103*
Jaffe, Susan *DrAP&F 83*
Jaffe, William 1898- *ConAu 57*
Jaffee, Dwight M 1943- *ConAu 57*
Jaffee, Mary L *ConAu X*
Jaffer, Frances *DrAP&F 83, IntWWP 82X*
Jaffin, David 1937- *ConAu 65, ConP 80,
WrDr 84*
Jaffri, Khairunnissa 1947- *IntAu&W 82*
Jagan, Cheddi 1918- *IntAu&W 82*
Jagasirpian, Ponnappa Baliah 1925-
IntAu&W 82
Jagendorf, Moritz Adolf 1888-1981 *ConAu 5R,
–102, SmATA 2, –24N*

Jagendorf, Moritz Adolph 1888- IntAu&W 82
Jager, Martin Otto 1925- WrDr 84
Jager, Okke 1928- ConAu 8NR, -61
Jager, Ronald 1932- ConAu 41R
Jaggard, Geoffrey 1902-1970 ConAu P-2
Jagger, John Hubert 1880- ConAu P-1
Jagger, Mick 1944- ConLC 17
Jagger, Peter 1938- ConAu 103, IntAu&W 82,
   WrDr 84
Jagoda, Robert Eugene DrAP&F 83
Jagoda, Robert Eugene 1923- ConAu 73,
   IntAu&W 82
Jahan, Rounaq 1944- ConAu 49, IntAu&W 82
Jaher, Frederic Cople 1934- ConAu 9R
Jahier, Piero 1884-1966 WhoTwCL
Jahn, Ernst A 1929- ConAu 69
Jahn, Hans Henny 1894-1959 CroCD
Jahn, Joseph Michael 1943- ConAu 5NR, -49
Jahn, Melvin E 1938- ConAu 9R
Jahn, Michael 1943- ConAu X,
   SmATA 28[port]
Jahn, Mike ConAu X, SmATA X
Jahnn, Hans Henny 1894-1959 CIDMEL 80,
   CnMD, EncWL 2, ModGL, ModWD
Jahns, T R DrAP&F 83
Jahoda, Gloria Adelaide Love 1926-1980
   AuNews 1, ConAu 1R, -4NR, -104
Jahsmann, Allan Hart 1916- ConAu 106,
   SmATA 28[port]
Jaime & Rene IntWWP 82X
Jaimes Freyre, Ricardo 1868-1933 ModLAL
Jain, Girilal 1922- ConAu 9R
Jain, Jagdishchandra 1909- IntAu&W 82
Jain, Ravindra Kumar 1937- ConAu 29R
Jain, Sagar C 1930- ConAu 10NR, -25R
Jain, Sharad Chandra 1933- ConAu 25R
Jaini, Padmanabh S 1923- ConAu 103
Jakes, John 1932- ConAu 10NR, -57, ConSFA,
   DcLB Y83B[port], IntAu&W 82, TwCSFW,
   TwCWW, WrDr 84
Jakle, John Allais 1939- ConAu 107
Jakob IntAu&W 82X
Jakob Jonsson, Fra Hrauni IntAu&W 82X
Jakobovits, Immanuel 1921- ConAu 108
Jakobovits, Leon Alex 1938- ConAu 25R
Jakobsdottir, Svava 1930- IntAu&W 82
Jakobsen, Bent 1942- IntAu&W 82
Jakobsen, Ulf IntWWP 82X
Jakobson, Roman 1896-1982 ConAu 107, -77,
   WorAu 1970
Jakobsson, Jokull 1933- CIDMEL 80
Jaksch, Wenzel 1896-1966 ConAu P-1
Jakubauskas, Edward B 1930- ConAu 57
Jakubowski, Patricia 1941- ConAu 65
Jaloux, Edmond 1878-1949 CIDMEL 80
James, Adam IntWWP 82X
James, Alan 1943- ConAu 104, IntAu&W 82,
   WrDr 84
James, Allen ConAu X
James, Andrew ConAu X, IntAu&W 82X,
   SmATA X
James, Anthony ConAu X
James, Bernard 1922- ConAu 110
James, Bessie Rowland 1895-1974 ConAu 107
James, Bill ConAu X
James, Brian ConAu X
James, Brian 1892-1972 ConAu X,
   DcLEL 1940
James, Bruno S 1906- ConAu 5R
James, Burnett 1919- ConAu 5R
James, C B ConAu X
James, C L R 1901- ConNov 82
James, C W ConAu X
James, Cary A 1935- ConAu 29R
James, Charles J 1944- ConAu 5NR, -53
James, Charles Lyman 1934- ConAu 29R,
   LivgBAA
James, Cliff IntWWP 82X
James, Clifford Thomas 1943- IntWWP 82
James, Clive 1939- ConAu 105, IntAu&W 82,
   WrDr 84
James, Coy Hilton 1915- ConAu 103
James, Cy ConAu X, IntAu&W 82X,
   TwCWW, WrDr 84
James, Cynthia ConAu X
James, Cyril L R 1901- IntAu&W 82, WrDr 84
James, D Clayton 1931- ConAu 29R
James, D G 1905-1968 ConAu 1R, -4NR
James, Dan TwCWW
James, David ConAu X, DrAP&F 83
James, David Edward 1937- WrDr 84
James, David Geraint 1922- IntAu&W 82,

WrDr 84
James, Denise ConAu 29R
James, Don 1905- ConAu 1R, -2NR
James, Dorothy Buckton 1937- ConAu 109
James, Dorris Clayton 1931- IntAu&W 82
James, Dynely ConAu X, SmATA 6,
   WrDr 84
James, Edgar C 1933- ConAu 5NR, -13R
James, Edward ConAu X
James, Edward T 1917- ConAu 33R
James, Edwin ConAu X
James, Edwin Oliver 1888-1972 ConAu P-1
James, Eleanor 1912- ConAu 41R
James, Eric Arthur 1925- ConAu P-1
James, Estelle 1935- ConAu 37R
James, Fleming, Jr. 1904- ConAu P-1
James, Frances 1903- CreCan 1
James, George W 1949- ConAu 109
James, H Thomas 1915- ConAu 25R
James, Harry Clebourne 1896-1978 ConAu 4NR,
   -5R, SmATA 11
James, Heather 1914- ConAu 45
James, Henry 1843-1916 CnMD, CnMWL,
   ConAu 104, EncWL 2[port], LongCTC,
   ModAL, ModAL SUP, ModBrL,
   ModBrL SUP, ModWD, TwCLC 2,
   -11[port], TwCWr, WhoTwCL
James, Henry 1879-1947 TwCA, TwCA SUP
James, John ConAu 45
James, John Ivor Pulsford 1913- WrDr 84
James, Josef C 1916?-1973 ConAu 45
James, Joseph B 1912- ConAu 17R
James, Josephine ConAu X, SmATA 6
James, Judith ConAu X
James, Kristin ConAu X
James, Laurie 1930- IntAu&W 82
James, Leonard Frank 1904- ConAu 49,
   IntAu&W 82
James, Louis 1933- ConAu 6NR, -13R,
   IntAu&W 82X, WrDr 84
James, M R 1862-1936 TwCLC 6[port]
James, M R 1940- ConAu 57
James, Margaret TwCRGW, WrDr 84
James, Marlise Ann 1945- ConAu 57
James, Marquis 1891-1955 TwCA, TwCA SUP
James, Matthew ConAu X, WrDr 84
James, Merlin IntWWP 82X
James, Michael 1922?-1981 ConAu 104
James, Montague Rhodes 1862-1936 ConAu 104,
   LongCTC, TwCA, TwCA SUP, TwCWr
James, Muriel ConAu 85
James, Nancy Esther DrAP&F 83
James, Naomi 1949- ConAu 102
James, Noel David Glaves 1911- ConAu 107,
   IntAu&W 82, WrDr 84
James, Norah Cordner 1900- ConAu 29R,
   LongCTC, TwCA, TwCA SUP
James, P D 1920- ASpks, ConAu 21R,
   ConLC 18, TwCCr&M 80
James, Paul ConAu X
James, Peter N 1940- ConAu 57
James, Philip ConAu X
James, Philip Seaforth 1914- ConAu P-1,
   WrDr 84
James, Phyllis D 1920- WrDr 84
James, Preston Everett 1899- ConAu 45
James, R ConAu X
James, R V Rhodes 1933- WrDr 84
James, Robert A 1946-1983 ConAu 109
James, Robert Clarke 1918- ConAu 5R
James, Robert Rhodes 1933- ConAu 17R
James, Robert Vidal Rhodes 1933- ConAu X,
   DcLEL 1940, IntAu&W 82
James, Ronald ConAu X
James, Sibyl DrAP&F 83
James, Simon ConAu X
James, Stanton ConAu X
James, Susan ConAu X
James, Sydney V 1929- ConAu 1R, WrDr 84
James, T F ConAu X, SmATA 8
James, Thelma Gray 1899- ConAu 5R
James, Theodore, Jr. 1934- ConAu 33R,
   WrDr 84
James, Theodore E 1913- ConAu 57
James, Thomas N ConAu X
James, Trevor ConAu X
James, Walter 1912- ConAu 5R
James, Walter S ConAu X
James, Warren E 1922- ConAu 45
James, Weldon 1912- ConAu 1R
James, Will 1892-1942 SmATA 19, TwCA,

TwCA SUP, TwCCW 83, TwCWW
James, William ConAu X
James, William 1842-1910 ConAu 109,
   LongCTC, ModAL, ModAL SUP,
   WhoTwCL
James, William Louis Gabriel 1933-
   IntAu&W 82
James, William M ConAu X, TwCWW,
   WrDr 84
James, Sir William Milbourne 1881- ConAu P-1
James, Wilma Roberts 1905- ConAu 105
James Hoggard IntWWP 82X
Jameson, Eric ConAu X, WrDr 84
Jameson, J Franklin 1859-1937 DcLB 17[port]
Jameson, Judith ConAu X
Jameson, Kenneth 1913- ConAu 77
Jameson, Margaret Storm 1891- IntAu&W 82
Jameson, Samuel H 1896- ConAu 45
Jameson, Storm 1891- ConAu 81, ConNov 82,
   WrDr 84
Jameson, Storm 1897- LongCTC, ModBrL,
   TwCA, TwCA SUP, TwCWr
Jameson, Vic 1924- ConAu 17R
Jamia IntWWP 82X
Jamiaque, Yves 1922- CnMD
Jamieson, Bob ConAu X
Jamieson, Edna Jaques CreCan 2
Jamieson, Paul F 1903- ConAu P-1
Jamieson, Robert John 1943- ConAu 110
Jamison, A Leland 1911- ConAu 89
Jamison, Andrew 1948- ConAu 29R
Jamme, Albert 1916- ConAu 5R, WrDr 84
Jammes, Francis 1868-1938 CIDMEL 80,
   EncWL 2, ModFrL, ModRL, TwCA,
   TwCA SUP, WhoTwCL
Jamus, Hortensio IntAu&W 82X
Jan ConAu X
Jan, George P 1925- ConAu 21R
Janac, Lou DrAP&F 83
Janas, Frankie-Lee 1908- ConAu 106
Janda, Kenneth 1935- ConAu 13R
Jandl, Ernst 1925- CIDMEL 80, IntAu&W 82,
   IntWWP 82
Jandt, Fred E 1944- ConAu 53
Jandy, Edward Clarence 1899-1980 ConAu 97
Jane IntWWP 82X
Jane, Mary Childs 1909- ConAu 1R, -4NR,
   SmATA 6
Jane, Nancy 1946- ConAu 89
Jane Chance DrAP&F 83
Janeczko, Paul B 1945- ConAu 104
Janes, Clara 1940- IntAu&W 82
Janes, Edward C 1908- ConAu 93,
   SmATA 25[port]
Janet, Lillian WrDr 84
Janevski, Slavko 1920- CIDMEL 80, ModSL 2
Janeway, Eliot 1913- WrDr 84
Janeway, Elizabeth DrAP&F 83
Janeway, Elizabeth 1913- AuNews 1,
   ConAu 2NR, -45, DcLEL 1940,
   SmATA 19, TwCA SUP
Janger, Allen R 1932- ConAu 29R, WrDr 84
Janice ConAu X
Janifer, Laurence M 1933- ConAu 5NR, -9R,
   ConSFA, TwCSFW, WrDr 84
Janik, Allan 1941- ConAu 53
Janik, Carolyn 1940- ConAu 89
Janik, Phyllis DrAP&F 83
Janis, Irving L 1918- ConAu 8NR, -17R
Janis, J Harold 1910- ConAu 13R
Janiw, Wolodymyr 1908- IntAu&W 82
Janker, Josef W 1922- IntAu&W 82
Jankowsky, Kurt Robert 1928- ConAu 37R
Jankuhn, Herbert 1905- IntAu&W 82
Janner, Greville Ewan 1928- ConAu 8NR, -13R,
   IntAu&W 82
Janoff, Ronald Wiley DrAP&F 83
Janos, Andrew C 1934- ConAu 106

Janosch 1931- ConAu X, SmATA 8
Janovy, John, Jr. 1937- ConAu 97
Janowitz, Abraham DrAP&F 83
Janowitz, Morris 1919- ConAu 13R
Janowitz, Phyllis DrAP&F 83
Janowitz, Phyllis 1940- ConAu 93, IntWWP 82
Janowitz, Tama DrAP&F 83
Janowitz, Tama 1957- ConAu 106
Janowski, Tadeus Marian 1923- ConAu 53
Janowski, Thaddeus-Marian 1923- WrDr 84
Janowsky, Oscar I 1900- WrDr 84
Janowsky, Oscar Isaiah 1900- ConAu 1R, -5R,
   -5NR

Janrup, Birgit 1931- *ConAu 97*
Jans, Adrien 1905-1973 *ClDMEL 80*
Jans, Emerson *ConAu X*
Jans, Zephyr *ConAu X*
Jansen, Clifford J 1935- *ConAu 33R*
Jansen, G H 1919- *ConIsC 1[port]*
Jansen, Hank *IntAu&W 82X*
Jansen, Jared *ConAu X, SmATA X, WrDr 84*
Jansen, John Frederick 1918- *ConAu 21R,
IntAu&W 82, WrDr 84*
Jansen, Leonhard 1906- *IntAu&W 82*
Jansen, Oliver 1914- *ConAu 10NR*
Jansen, Robert B 1922- *ConAu 81*
Janson, Donald 1921- *ConAu 5R*
Janson, Dora Jane 1916- *ConAu 106,
SmATA 31[port]*
Janson, H W 1913-1982 *ConAu 4NR, -107*
Janson, Hank *ConAu X, WrDr 84*
Janson, Horst Woldemar 1913- *ConAu 1R,
SmATA 9*
Janson, Jacques Jean Simon Marie 1944-
IntAu&W 82
Janson, Marguerite 1904- *IntAu&W 82*
Janssen, Lawrence H 1921- *ConAu 13R*
Janssens, Paul Mary *ConAu 53*
Jansson, Tove 1914- *ChlLR 2, ConAu 17R,
EncWL 2, IntAu&W 82, SmATA 3*
Janta, Alexander 1908-1974 *ConAu 101, -53*
Jantsch, Erich 1929- *ConAu 65*
Jantsch, Erich 1929-1980 *ConAu 10NR*
Jantzen, Steven L 1941- *ConAu 77*
Janus *ConAu X, IntAu&W 82X*
Janus, Grete *ConAu X, SmATA X*
Januz, Lauren Robert 1939- *ConAu 108*
Janzen, John M 1937- *ConAu 81*
Jaques, Edna 1891- *CreCan 2*
Jaques, Elliott 1917- *ConAu 6NR, -13R,
WrDr 84*
Jaques, Faith 1923- *ConAu 103,
SmATA 21[port]*
Jaques, Florence Page 1890-1972 *ConAu 103,
-104*
Jaques, Francis Lee 1887-1969 *SmATA 28*
Jaques, Louis Barker 1911- *WrDr 84*
Jaquette, Jane Stallmann 1942- *ConAu 105*
Jaramillo, Samuel 1925- *ConAu 41R*
Jarchow, Merrill Earl 1910- *ConAu 41R*
Jardiel Poncela, Enrique 1901-1952 *ClDMEL 80,
CnMD, CroCD, ModWD*
Jardim, Anne 1936- *ConAu 107*
Jardine, Jack 1931- *ConAu 21R*
Jardine, Julie Ann 1926- *ConSFA*
Jareed *ConAu X*
Jares, Joe 1937- *ConAu 33R, WrDr 84*
Jarmain, W Edwin 1938- *ConAu 13R*
Jarman, Cosette C 1909- *ConAu P-2*
Jarman, Rosemary Hawley 1935- *ConAu 2NR,
-49, SmATA 7*
Jarman, Thomas Leckie 1907- *ConAu 4NR, -5R,
IntAu&W 82, WrDr 84*
Jarman, Walton Maxey 1904-1980 *ConAu 108*
Jarmuth, Sylvia L 1912- *ConAu 25R*
Jarnes, Benjamin 1888-1949 *EncWL 2*
Jarnes Millan, Benjamin 1888-1949 *ClDMEL 80*
Jarnow, Jeannette 1909- *ConAu 53*
Jaroch, F A Randy 1947- *ConAu 89*
Jaroch, Randy *ConAu X*
Jaron, Elishewa *IntAu&W 82X*
Jarrell, John W 1908?-1978 *ConAu 81*
Jarrell, Mary VonSchrader 1914- *ConAu 77*
Jarrell, Randall 1914-1965 *ChlLR 6[port],
ConAu 6NR, -6NR, -25R, ConLC 1, -2, -6,
-9, -13, ConLCrt 82, ConP 80A, CroCAP,
DcLEL 1940, EncWL 2, ModAL,
ModAL SUP, SmATA 7, TwCA SUP,
TwCCW 83, TwCWr, WhoTwCL*
Jarrett, Cora Hardy 1877- *TwCA, TwCA SUP,
TwCCr&M 80*
Jarrett, Derek 1928- *ConAu 57, IntAu&W 82,
WrDr 84*
Jarrett, Emmett *DrAP&F 83*
Jarrett, H Reginald 1916- *ConAu 3NR*
Jarrett, Harold Reginald 1916- *ConAu 9R*
Jarrett, James Louis 1917- *ConAu 53*
Jarrett, Marjorie 1923- *ConAu 105*
Jarriel, Thomas Edwin 1934- *ConAu 109*
Jarriel, Tom *ConAu X*
Jarrott, Mattie L 1881?-1973 *ConAu 41R*
Jarry, Alfred 1873-1907 *ClDMEL 80, CnMD,
ConAu 104, EncWL 2, LongCTC, ModFrL,
ModRL, ModWD, TwCLC 2, WhoTwCL*

Jarv, Harry Johannes 1921- *IntAu&W 82*
Jarvie, I C 1937- *ConAu 53*
Jarvis, Ana C 1936- *ConAu 65*
Jarvis, Donald 1923- *CreCan 1*
Jarvis, E K *ConAu X*
Jarvis, F Washington 1939- *ConAu 37R*
Jarvis, Fred G 1930- *ConAu 33R*
Jarvis, Frederick G H 1930- *IntAu&W 82,
WrDr 84*
Jarvis, Jennifer M 1935- *ConAu 13R*
Jarvis, Lilian 1931- *CreCan 2*
Jarvis, Martin 1941- *ConAu 105*
Jarvis, Rupert Charles 1899- *ConAu 103,
WrDr 84*
Jarvis, William Don 1913- *ConAu P-1*
Jasen, David A 1937- *ConAu 29R*
Jashemski, Wilhelmina Feemster 1910-
ConAu P-1
Jasienczyk, Janusz *IntAu&W 82X*
Jasik, Rudolf 1919-1960 *ModSL 2*
Jasmin, Andre 1922- *CreCan 2*
Jasmin, Claude 1930- *CreCan 2*
Jasner, W K *ConAu X*
Jasny, Naum 1883- *ConAu P-1*
Jason *ConAu X*
Jason, Jerry *WrDr 84*
Jason, Johnny *ConAu X, WrDr 84*
Jason, Philip K *DrAP&F 83*
Jason, Philip K 1941- *IntWWP 82*
Jason, Stuart *ConAu X, WrDr 84*
Jaspan, Norman *ConAu 103*
Jasper, Catherine 1907- *IntWWP 82*
Jaspers, Karl 1883-1969 *ConAu 25R,
TwCA SUP, TwCWr*
Jaspersohn, William 1947- *ConAu 102*
Jaspert, Werner Pincus 1926- *IntAu&W 82*
Jasspe, Arthur *IntAu&W 82, NatPD 81[port]*
Jassy, Marie-France Perrin *ConAu X*
Jastak, Joseph Florian 1901-1979 *ConAu 4NR,
-5R, -85*
Jastrow, Joseph 1863-1944 *TwCA, TwCA SUP*
Jastrow, Robert 1925- *ConAu 21R,
IntAu&W 82, WrDr 84*
Jastrun, Mieczyslaw 1903- *ClDMEL 80,
EncWL 2, ModSL 2*
Jauncey, James H 1916- *ConAu 1R, -5NR*
Jaurand, Yvonne 1912- *ConAu 9R*
Jaures, Jean-Leon 1859-1914 *ClDMEL 80*
Jauss, Anne Marie 1907- *ConAu 1R, -4NR,
SmATA 10, WrDr 84*
Jauss, David *DrAP&F 83*
Jaussi, Laureen Richardson 1934- *ConAu 73*
Javier, Miranda *ConAu X, IntAu&W 82X*
Javitch, Daniel Gilbert 1941- *ConAu 103*
Javits, Benjamin A 1894-1973 *ConAu 41R*
Javits, Eric Moses 1931- *ConAu 1R*
Javits, Jacob Koppel 1904- *ConAu 1R, -1NR*
Javor, F A *ConSFA*
Javor, Otto 1925- *IntAu&W 82*
Jawien, Andrzej *ConAu X*
Jaworska, Wladyslawa Jadwiga 1910- *ConAu 53*
Jaworski, Leon 1905- *ConAu P-1*
Jaworski, Leon 1905-1982 *ConAu 108*
Jaworskyj, Michael 1921- *ConAu 61*
Jax Kerlerec Et Alii *IntWWP 82X*
Jaxon, Milt *ConAu X*
Jay, Antony 1930- *WrDr 84*
Jay, Antony Rupert 1930- *ConAu 25R,
IntAu&W 82*
Jay, Charlotte *WrDr 84*
Jay, Charlotte 1919- *ConAu X, TwCCr&M 80*
Jay, Donald *ConAu X*
Jay, Douglas Patrick Thomas 1907- *ConAu 65,
IntAu&W 82*
Jay, Eric George 1907- *ConAu 5R,
IntAu&W 82, WrDr 84*
Jay, G S *ConAu X*
Jay, Geraldine Mary 1919- *WrDr 84*
Jay, James M 1927- *ConAu 53*
Jay, Karla 1947- *ConAu 85*
Jay, Marion *ConAu X, WrDr 84*
Jay, Martin 1944- *ConAu 53*
Jay, Mel *ConAu X*
Jay, Neva *IntWWP 82X*
Jay, Peter 1937- *ConAu 109*
Jay, Peter 1945- *WrDr 84*
Jay, Peter A 1940- *ConAu 101*
Jay, Peter Antony Charles 1945- *ConAu 97,
ConP 80, IntAu&W 82*
Jay, Robert Ravenelle 1925- *ConAu 106*
Jay, Ruth I 1920- *ConAu 93*
Jay, Ruth Johnson *ConAu X*

Jay, Simon *ConAu X*
Jayawardena, Visakha Kumari 1931- *ConAu 45*
Jayme, William North 1925- *ConAu 9R*
Jayne, Sears 1920- *ConAu 13R, WrDr 84*
Jaynes, Clare *ConAu X*
Jaynes, Julian 1923- *ConAu 41R*
Jaynes, Richard A 1935- *ConAu 65*
Jaynes, Roger W 1946- *ConAu 85*
Jaynes, Ruth 1899- *ConAu P-2*
Jazayery, M Ali 1924- *ConAu 9NR, -21R*
Jd-Dam *IntAu&W 82X*
Jeake, Samuel, Jr. *ConAu X, SmATA X*
Jeal, Tim 1945- *ConAu 9NR, -21R,
IntAu&W 82, WrDr 84*
Jean, Gabrielle Lucille 1924- *ConAu 37R,
IntAu&W 82*
Jean, Marcel 1900- *ConAu 25R*
Jean-Louis *ConAu X*
Jeannerat, Pierre Gabriel 1902- *ConAu 5R*
Jeanneret-Gris, C-E *TwCA SUP*
Jeanniere, Abel 1921- *ConAu 49*
Jeans, Barbara *IntAu&W 82X*
Jeans, Sir James Hopwood 1877-1946 *LongCTC,
TwCA, TwCA SUP*
Jeans, Marylu Terral 1914- *ConAu 89*
Jebavy, Vaclav *WorAu*
Jebb, Gladwyn 1900- *ConAu 21R*
Jedamus, Paul 1923- *ConAu 37R*
Jedlitzka, Maria *ConAu X*
Jedrey, Christopher M 1949- *ConAu 101*
Jedrzejewicz, Waclaw 1893- *ConAu 25R,
IntAu&W 82*
Jeef, Kalle *ConAu X*
Jeeves, Malcolm 1926- *WrDr 84*
Jeeves, Malcolm A 1926- *ConAu 29R*
Jeffares, A Norman 1920- *ConAu 85, WrDr 84*
Jeffares, Alexander Norman 1920- *IntAu&W 82,
IntWWP 82*
Jeffcoate, Norman 1907- *WrDr 84*
Jeffer, Marsha 1940- *ConAu 41R*
Jefferies, Richard 1848-1887 *SmATA 16*
Jefferies, Susan Herring 1903- *ConAu P-1*
Jefferis, Barbara 1917- *ConAu 81*
Jefferis, Florice Stripling *IntWWP 82*
Jeffers, H Paul 1934- *ConAu 93*
Jeffers, Jo *ConAu X*
Jeffers, Lance *DrAP&F 83*
Jeffers, Lance 1919- *ConAu 65, LivgBAA*
Jeffers, Paul Edward, Jr. 1925- *IntWWP 82*
Jeffers, Robinson 1887-1962 *CnMD, CnMWL,
ConAmA, ConAu 85, ConLC 2, -3, -11, -15,
EncWL 2, FifWWr, LongCTC, ModAL,
ModAL SUP, ModWD, TwCA,
TwCA SUP, TwCWr, WhoTwCL*
Jeffers, Susan 1942- *ConAu 97, SmATA 17*
Jefferson, Alan 1921- *ConAu 33R,
IntAu&W 82, WrDr 84*
Jefferson, Blanche Waugaman 1909- *ConAu 5R*
Jefferson, Carter 1927- *ConAu 17R*
Jefferson, Ian *ConAu X*
Jefferson, Omar Xavier *ConAu X*
Jefferson, Sarah *ConAu X, SmATA X*
Jefferson, Xavier T 1952- *ConAu 73*
Jeffery, Graham 1935- *WrDr 84*
Jeffery, Grant 1924- *ConAu 1R*
Jeffery, L H 1915- *ConAu 1R*
Jeffery, Ransom 1943- *ConAu 21R*
Jeffery, William P, Jr. 1919- *ConAu 57*
Jefferys, Allan *ConAu 93*
Jefferys, Charles William 1869-1951 *CreCan 2*
Jefford, Bat *ConAu X, TwCWW*
Jeffrey, Adi-Kent Thomas *WrDr 84*
Jeffrey, Adi-Kent Thomas 1916- *ConAu 37R*
Jeffrey, Christopher *ConAu X*
Jeffrey, David Lyle 1941- *ConAu 7NR, -57*
Jeffrey, Julie Roy 1941- *ConAu 93*
Jeffrey, Lloyd Nicholas 1918- *ConAu 37R,
IntAu&W 82, WrDr 84*
Jeffrey, Mildred M *ConAu 5R, DrAP&F 83*
Jeffrey, Richard Carl 1926- *ConAu 103*
Jeffrey, Ruth *ConAu X*
Jeffrey, William *TwCCr&M 80*
Jeffreys, Harold 1891- *ConAu 109*
Jeffreys, J G *ConAu X, IntAu&W 82X,
TwCCr&M 80, WrDr 84*
Jeffreys, Montagu 1900- *WrDr 84*
Jeffreys, Montagu Vaughan Castelman 1900-
ConAu 4NR, -5R, IntAu&W 82
Jeffreys-Jones, Rhodri 1942- *ConAu 77*
Jeffries, Sir Charles Joseph 1896-1972
ConAu 4NR, -5R
Jeffries, Derwin J 1915- *ConAu 57*

Jeffries, Graham Montague 1900- *ConAu 77, IntAu&W 82X*
Jeffries, John Worthington 1942- *ConAu 103*
Jeffries, Lewis I 1942- *ConAu 103*
Jeffries, Ona 1893?-1973 *ConAu 41R*
Jeffries, Roderic 1926- *ConAu 9NR, -17R, SmATA 4, TwCCr&M 80, WrDr 84*
Jeffries, Virginia M 1911- *ConAu 5R*
Jeffs, Julian 1931- *ConAu 37R, IntAu&W 82, WrDr 84*
Jeffs, Rae 1921- *ConAu 25R, WrDr 84*
Jefkins, Frank William 1920- *ConAu 9NR, -13R, WrDr 84*
Jehlen, Myra 1940- *ConAu 101*
Jekyll, Gertrude 1843-1932 *LongCTC*
Jelaurin *IntWWP 82X*
Jelavich, Barbara 1923- *ConAu 53*
Jelenski, Constantin 1922- *ConAu 101*
Jelinek, Estelle C 1935- *ConAu 102*
Jelinek, Hena Maes *ConAu X*
Jellema, Rod *DrAP&F 83*
Jellema, Roderick 1927- *ConAu 41R*
Jellicoe, Ann 1927- *ConAu 85, ConDr 82, ConLC 27[port], CroCD, DcLB 13[port], ModWD, TwCCW 83, TwCWr, WorAu, WrDr 84*
Jellicoe, Geoffrey 1900- *WrDr 84*
Jellicoe, Geoffrey Alan 1900- *ConAu 13R, IntAu&W 82*
Jellicoe, Patricia Ann 1927- *DcLEL 1940*
Jellicoe, Sidney 1906-1973 *ConAu P-2*
Jellicoe, Susan 1907- *IntAu&W 82*
Jellinek, George 1919- *ConAu 89*
Jellinek, Irene 1910- *CreCan 1*
Jellinek, J Stephan 1930- *ConAu 81*
Jellinek, Paul 1897- *ConAu 13R*
Jellison, Charles Albert, Jr. 1924- *ConAu 1R*
Jelly, George Oliver 1909- *ConAu 103, WrDr 84*
Jemie, Onwuchekwa 1940- *ConAu 89*
Jencks, Charles 1939- *ConAu 2NR, -49, IntAu&W 82, WrDr 84*
Jencks, Christopher 1936- *ConAu 2NR, -49*
Jenison, Don P 1897- *ConAu 7NR, -17R*
Jenkin, A K Hamilton 1900-1980 *ConAu 102*
Jenkins, Alan 1914- *ConAu 6NR, -57, IntAu&W 82, WrDr 84*
Jenkins, Alan C 1912- *IntAu&W 82*
Jenkins, Cecil 1927- *ConAu 107*
Jenkins, Clarke 1917- *LivgBAA*
Jenkins, Clive 1926- *ConAu 5NR, -13R*
Jenkins, David 1928- *ConAu 97*
Jenkins, David Clive *IntAu&W 82*
Jenkins, Dorothy Helen 1907-1972 *ConAu 37R*
Jenkins, Elizabeth *WrDr 84*
Jenkins, Elizabeth 1905- *ConAu 73*
Jenkins, Elizabeth 1907- *WorAu*
Jenkins, Ferrell 1936- *ConAu 6NR, -57*
Jenkins, Frances Briggs 1905- *ConAu P-2*
Jenkins, Gilmour 1894-1981 *ConAu 108*
Jenkins, Gladys Gardner 1901- *ConAu 1R, -4NR*
Jenkins, Goeffrey 1920- *ConAu 5R*
Jenkins, Gwyn 1919- *ConAu 1R*
Jenkins, Harold 1909- *ConAu 9R, IntAu&W 82, WrDr 84*
Jenkins, Holt M 1920- *ConAu 17R*
Jenkins, Hugh 1908- *ConAu 104*
Jenkins, Iredell 1909- *ConAu 106*
Jenkins, James J 1923- *ConAu 13R*
Jenkins, Jean R 1926- *IntWWP 82*
Jenkins, Jerry B 1949- *ConAu 5NR, -49*
Jenkins, John 1928- *ConAu 45*
Jenkins, John Geraint 1929- *ConAu 21R, WrDr 84*
Jenkins, John H 1940- *ConAu 10NR, -65*
Jenkins, John Robin 1912- *ConAu 1R, DcLEL 1940, WorAu*
Jenkins, Kenneth V 1930- *ConAu 53*
Jenkins, Louis *DrAP&F 83*
Jenkins, Louis 1942- *ConAu 4NR, -53*
Jenkins, Margaret Ezizabeth 1905- *WorAu*
Jenkins, Marie Magdalen 1909- *ConAu 41R, SmATA 7*
Jenkins, Michael 1936- *ConAu 25R, WrDr 84*
Jenkins, Nancy 1937- *ConAu 109*
Jenkins, Patricia 1927-1982 *ConAu 106*
Jenkins, Patricia Anne *CreCan 1*
Jenkins, Paul *DrAP&F 83*
Jenkins, Peter 1951- *ConAu 89*
Jenkins, Phyllis *ConAu X*
Jenkins, Ray 1935- *ConAu 103, WrDr 84*
Jenkins, Reese Valmer 1938- *ConAu 65*

Jenkins, Robin 1912- *ConAu 1NR, ConNov 82, DcLB 14[port], WorAu, WrDr 84*
Jenkins, Romilly James Heald 1907-1969 *ConAu 5R, -5NR*
Jenkins, Roy 1920- *WrDr 84*
Jenkins, Roy Harris 1920- *ConAu 9R, DcLEL 1940, IntAu&W 82, WorAu*
Jenkins, Simon 1943- *WrDr 84*
Jenkins, Simon David 1943- *ConAu 81, IntAu&W 82*
Jenkins, Speight 1937- *IntAu&W 82*
Jenkins, Will F 1896-1975 *ConAu 4NR, -9R, -57, ConSFA, TwCWW*
Jenkins, William A 1922- *ConAu 61, SmATA 9*
Jenkins, William Marshall, Jr. 1918- *ConAu 105*
Jenkinson, Edward Bernard 1930- *ConAu 21R*
Jenkinson, Michael 1938- *ConAu 25R*
Jenks, Almet 1892-1966 *ConAu P-1*
Jenks, C Wilfred 1909-1973 *ConAu 4NR*
Jenks, Clarence Wilfred 1909- *ConAu 9R*
Jenks, George Charles 1850-1929 *TwCWW*
Jenks, Randolph 1912- *ConAu 9R*
Jenks, William Howard, Jr. 1938- *ConAu 41R*
Jenkyns, Richard 1949- *ConAu 108*
Jenner, Bruce 1949- *ConAu 110*
Jenner, Chrystie 1950- *ConAu 77*
Jenner, Delia 1944- *ConAu 21R*
Jenner, Heather *ConAu X*
Jenner, Philip Norman 1921- *ConAu 89*
Jenner, W J F 1940- *ConAu 29R*
Jenness, Aylette 1934- *ConAu 25R*
Jenni, Adolfo 1911- *IntAu&W 82, IntWWP 82*
Jennifer, Susan *ConAu X, WrDr 84*
Jennings, Dana Close 1923- *ConAu 53*
Jennings, Dean *WrDr 84*
Jennings, Dean Southern 1905-1969 *ConAu 89*
Jennings, Edward M 1936- *ConAu 29R*
Jennings, Elizabeth 1926- *ConAu 8NR, -61, ConLC 5, -14, ConP 80, DcLEL 1940, EncWL 2, IntWWP 82, LongCTC, ModBrL, ModBrL SUP, RGFMBP, TwCWr, WhoTwCL, WorAu, WrDr 84*
Jennings, Gary 1928- *ConAu 9NR*
Jennings, Gary Gayne 1928- *ConAu 5R, IntAu&W 82, SmATA 9*
Jennings, Ivor 1903-1965 *ConAu 5R*
Jennings, James M 1924- *ConAu 37R*
Jennings, Jerry 1935- *ConAu 7NR, -53*
Jennings, Jesse David 1909- *ConAu 33R*
Jennings, John Edward, Jr. 1906-1973 *ConAu 45, ConAu P-1, TwCA SUP*
Jennings, Kate *DrAP&F 83*
Jennings, Kate 1946- *IntWWP 82*
Jennings, Lane 1944- *ConAu 102*
Jennings, Leslie Nelson 1890-1972 *ConAu P-1*
Jennings, Michael 1931- *ConAu 69*
Jennings, Patrick *ConAu X*
Jennings, Paul 1918- *WrDr 84*
Jennings, Paul Francis 1918- *ConAu 4NR, -9R, DcLEL 1940, IntAu&W 82*
Jennings, Raymond P 1924- *ConAu 110*
Jennings, Richard 1907- *ConAu 17R*
Jennings, Robert *ConAu X, SmATA X*
Jennings, Robert E 1931- *ConAu 11NR, -61*
Jennings, Robert Maurice 1924- *ConAmTC*
Jennings, S M *ConAu X, SmATA X*
Jennings, Ted C 1949- *ConAu 81*
Jennings, Terry John 1938- *IntAu&W 82*
Jennings, Vivien *ConAu 61*
Jennings, Waylon 1937- *ConLC 21[port]*
Jennings, William Dale 1917- *ConAu 25R*
Jennison, C S *ConAu X, SmATA 6*
Jennison, Christopher 1938- *ConAu 53*
Jennison, Keith Warren 1911- *ConAu 73, SmATA 14*
Jennison, Peter S 1922- *ConAu 4NR, -9R*
Jenny, Hans H 1922- *ConAu 103*
Jenny, Hans Robert 1912- *IntAu&W 82*
Jens, Walter 1923- *ConAu 89, IntAu&W 82, ModGL*
Jensen, Ad E 1899-1965 *ConAu P-2*
Jensen, Alan F 1938- *ConAu 53*
Jensen, Albert C 1924- *ConAu 85*
Jensen, Andrew F, Jr. 1929- *ConAu 57*
Jensen, Ann 1902- *ConAu 21R*
Jensen, Arthur Robert 1923- *ConAu 1R, -2NR, WrDr 84*
Jensen, Clayne 1930- *WrDr 84*
Jensen, Clayne R 1930- *ConAu 8NR, -17R*
Jensen, DeLamar 1925- *ConAu 7NR, -9R, WrDr 84*
Jensen, Dwight 1934- *ConAu 85*

Jensen, Frede 1926- *ConAu 57*
Jensen, Gordon Duff 1926- *ConAu 106*
Jensen, Gwendolyn Evans 1936- *ConAu 57*
Jensen, H James 1933- *ConAu 25R*
Jensen, Irene K 1925- *ConAu 69*
Jensen, Irving L 1920- *ConAu 7NR, -17R*
Jensen, J Vernon 1922- *ConAu 49*
Jensen, Jo *ConAu 49*
Jensen, Johannes Vilhelm 1873-1950 *ClDMEL 80, EncWL 2, TwCA, TwCA SUP, TwCWr*
Jensen, John H 1929- *ConAu 21R*
Jensen, John Martin 1893- *ConAu P-1*
Jensen, Julie *ConAu X*
Jensen, Larry Cyril 1938- *ConAu 106*
Jensen, Laura *DrAP&F 83*
Jensen, Laura 1948- *ConAu 103*
Jensen, Lawrence N 1924- *ConAu 17R*
Jensen, Lloyd 1936- *ConAu 61*
Jensen, Magny Landstad 1903- *IntWWP 82*
Jensen, Marlene 1947- *ConAu 81*
Jensen, Mary TenEyck Bard 1904-1970 *ConAu 5R, -29R*
Jensen, Maxine Dowd 1919- *ConAu 65*
Jensen, Merrill 1905-1980 *ConAu 77, DcLB 17[port]*
Jensen, Michael C 1939- *ConAu 49*
Jensen, Niels 1927- *ConAu 49, SmATA 25[port]*
Jensen, Ole Klindt *ConAu X*
Jensen, Oliver 1914- *ConAu 25R*
Jensen, Paul K 1916- *ConAu 17R*
Jensen, Paul M 1944- *ConAu 53*
Jensen, Pauline Marie 1900- *ConAu P-2*
Jensen, Peter *ConAu X*
Jensen, Richard 1941- *WrDr 84*
Jensen, Richard C 1936- *ConAu 49*
Jensen, Richard J 1941- *ConAu 33R*
Jensen, Rolf 1912- *ConAu 21R*
Jensen, Rosalie 1938- *ConAu 57*
Jensen, Vernon H 1907- *ConAu 106*
Jensen, Virginia Allen 1927- *ConAu 1NR, -45, SmATA 8*
Jensi, Muganwa Nsiku *ConAu X*
Jenson, Robert W 1930- *ConAu 5R, -9NR*
Jenson, William R 1946- *ConAu 101*
Jentes, Martin 1938- *IntWWP 82*
Jentz, Gaylord Adair 1931- *ConAu 25R*
Jenyns, R Soame 1904-1976 *ConAu 73*
Jenyns, Roger Soame d1976 *ConAu 69*
Jenyns, Soame *ConAu X*
Jephcott, Agnes Pearl 1900- *IntAu&W 82*
Jeppson, J O 1926- *WrDr 84*
Jeppson, Janet O 1926- *ConAu 49*
Jepsen, Stanley M 1912- *ConAu 77*
Jepson, Selwyn 1899- *TwCCr&M 80, WrDr 84*
Jeremias, Joachim 1900- *ConAu 5R, -11NR*
Jeremy, Sister Mary *ConAu 5R*
Jeritza, Maria 1887-1982 *ConAu 107*
Jerman, Sylvia Paul *ConAu X, MichAu 80*
Jernick, Ruth 1948- *ConAu 107*
Jerome, Jerome Klapka 1859-1927 *DcLB 10[port], LongCTC, ModBrL, ModWD, TwCA, TwCWr*
Jerome, John 1932- *ConAu 2NR, -45*
Jerome, Joseph *ConAu X, WrDr 84*
Jerome, Judson *DrAP&F 83*
Jerome, Judson 1927- *WrDr 84*
Jerome, Judson Blair 1927- *ConAu 4NR, -9R, ConP 80, IntAu&W 82*
Jerome, Lawrence E 1944- *ConAu 77*
Jerome, Mark *ConAu X*
Jerome, Roman *IntAu&W 82X*
Jerrold, Douglas 1893-1964 *LongCTC*
Jerrybilt *ConAu X*
Jersild, Arthur T 1902- *ConAu 1R*
Jersild, Devon 1958- *IntWWP 82*
Jersild, P C 1935- *EncWL 2*
Jersild, Paul T 1931- *ConAu 37R*
Jersild, Per Christian 1935- *ClDMEL 80*
Jervell, Jacob 1925- *ConAu 8NR, -61*
Jervis, Frank Robert Joseph 1906- *WrDr 84*
Jeschke, Marlin 1929- *ConAu 45*
Jeschke, Susan 1942- *ConAu 77, SmATA 27*
Jeschke, Wolfgang 1936- *IntAu&W 82*
Jesensky, Janko 1874-1945 *ClDMEL 80, ModSL 2, TwCWr*
Jesmer, Elaine 1939- *AuNews 1, ConAu 49, WrDr 84*
Jespersen, James 1934- *ConAu 103*
Jesse, F Tennyson 1889-1958 *TwCCr&M 80*
Jesse, Friniwyd Tennyson 1895?-1958 *LongCTC, TwCA, TwCA SUP*

Jesse, Michael *ConAu X*
Jessel, Camilla Ruth 1937- *ConAu 104,*
SmATA 29[port]
Jessel, George 1898-1981 *ConAu 103, –89*
Jessel, John *ConAu X, WorAu*
Jessen, Carl A 1887?-1978 *ConAu 77*
Jessner, Irene 1910- *CreCan 1*
Jessner, Lucie Ney 1896-1979 *ConAu 93*
Jessop, Thomas Edmund 1896- *ConAu 9R,*
IntAu&W 82
Jessor, Richard 1924- *ConAu 41R*
Jessup, Frances *ConAu X*
Jessup, Frank W 1909- *WrDr 84*
Jessup, John Knox 1907-1979 *ConAu 101, –89*
Jessup, Michael H 1937- *ConAu 109*
Jessup, Philip C 1897- *ConAu 77*
Jessup, Richard 1925- *TwCWW, WrDr 84*
Jessup, Richard 1925?-1982 *ConAu 108*
Jesus, Carolina Maria De 1921- *TwCWr*
Jeter, Jacky *ConAu X*
Jeter, Jacquelyn I 1935- *ConAu 25R*
Jett, Stephen C 1938- *ConAu 10NR*
Jett, Stephen Clinton 1938- *ConAu 25R,*
IntAu&W 82, WrDr 84
Jette, Fernand 1921- *ConAu 5R*
Jeune, Paul 1950- *ConAu 101*
Jeury, Michel 1934- *TwCSFW A*
Jevons, Frederic Raphael 1929- *ConAu 61,*
IntAu&W 82
Jevons, Marshall *ConAu X*
Jewell, Derek 1927- *ConAu 33R, WrDr 84*
Jewell, Edmund F 1896?-1978 *ConAu 81*
Jewell, Edward Alden 1888-1947 *TwCA,*
TwCA SUP
Jewell, Malcolm E 1928- *ConAu 1R, –5NR*
Jewell, Nancy 1940- *ConAu 7NR, –61*
Jewell, Richard Edward Coxhead 1920-
IntAu&W 82
Jewett, Alyce Lowrie 1908- *ConAu P-1*
Jewett, Ann E 1921- *ConAu 93*
Jewett, Eleanore Myers 1890-1967 *ConAu 5R,*
SmATA 5
Jewett, Paul King 1919- *ConAu 53*
Jewett, Robert 1933- *ConAu 2NR, –45*
Jewett, Sarah Orne 1849-1909 *ConAu 108,*
ModAL, SmATA 15, TwCLC 1
Jewkes, John 1902- *IntAu&W 82*
Jezard, Alison 1919- *ConAu 29R, SmATA 34*
Jezer, Marty 1940- *ConAu 109*
Jezewski, Bohdan O 1900-1980 *ConAu 5R, –103,*
IntAu&W 82
Jezierski, Eugeniusz 1902- *IntAu&W 82*
Jha, Akhileshwar 1932- *ConAu 107, WrDr 84*
Jhabvala, R Prawer 1927- *WrDr 84*
Jhabvala, Ruth Prawer *DrAP&F 83*
Jhabvala, Ruth Prawer 1927- *ConAu 1R, –2NR,*
ConLC 4, –8, ConNov 82, DcLEL 1940,
EncWL 2, IntAu&W 82, ModCmwL,
TwCWr, WorAu
Jianou, Ionel 1905- *ConAu 9NR, –21R*
Jidejian, Nina 1921- *ConAu 29R*
Jilemnicky, Peter 1901-1949 *CIDMEL 80,*
EncWL 2, ModSL 2
Jiler, John 1946- *NatPD 81[port]*
Jiles, Paulette 1943- *ConAu 101, ConLC 13*
Jimenez, Francisco *DrAP&F 83*
Jimenez, Francisco 1943- *IntAu&W 82*
Jimenez, Janey 1953- *ConAu 77*
Jimenez, Juan Ramon 1881-1958 *CIDMEL 80,*
CnMWL, ConAu 104, EncWL 2[port],
ModRL, TwCLC 4[port], TwCWr,
WhoTwCL, WorAu
Jimenez DeCisneros Y Baudin, Consuelo 1956-
IntAu&W 82
Jimenez Vasco, Felipe 1908- *IntAu&W 82*
Jipson, Wayne R 1931- *ConAu 45*
Jirasek, Alois 1851-1930 *EncWL 2*
Jiskogo *ConAu X*
Jo, Yung-Hwan 1932- *ConAu 45*
Jo-Hsi, Chen *ConAu X*
Jo Mish *IntWWP 82X*
Jo-Mo, Dr. *DrAP&F 83*
Joachim *DrAP&F 83*
Joachim, Otto 1910- *CreCan 1*
Joachim, Walter 1912- *CreCan 2*
Joad, Cyril Edwin Mitchinson 1891-1953
LongCTC, TwCA, TwCA SUP
Joan, Polly *DrAP&F 83*
Joan, Polly 1933- *ConAu 101*
Joans, Ted *DrAP&F 83*
Joans, Ted 1928- *ConAu 2NR, –45,*
DcLB 16[port], LivgBAA

Joaquin, Nick 1917- *EncWL 2*
Jobb, Jamie 1945- *ConAu 85, SmATA 29*
Jobes, Gertrude Blumenthal 1907- *ConAu 5R,*
ConAu P-1
Jobin, Louis 1845-1928 *CreCan 2*
Jobin, Raoul 1906- *CreCan 1*
Jobson, Gary Alan 1950- *ConAu 93*
Jobson, Hamilton 1914- *ConAu 73,*
TwCCr&M 80, WrDr 84
Jobson, Sandra *ConAu X*
Jobst, Herbert 1915- *IntAu&W 82*
Jocelyn, Richard *ConAu X,   WrDr 84*
Jocer, Jean *IntAu&W 82X*
Jochnowitz, George 1937- *ConAu 49*
Jodoin, Rachel 1937- *IntAu&W 82*
Jodorowsky, Raquel *IntWWP 82X*
Jodorowsky Prullansky, Raquel 1927-
IntWWP 82
Joe *IntAu&W 82X*
Joedicke, Juergen 1925- *ConAu 17R*
Joel, Asher Alexander 1912- *ConAu 108*
Joel, Billy *ConAu X*
Joel, Billy 1949- *ConLC 26[port]*
Joel, William Martin 1949- *ConAu 108*
Joels, Merrill E 1915- *ConAu 25R*
Joelson, Annette 1903-1971 *ConAu 29R*
Joen, John *IntWWP 82X*
Joerns, Consuelo *SmATA 33*
Joers, Lawrence E C 1900- *ConAu 41R*
Joesting, Edward Henry 1925- *ConAu 103*
Jofen, Jean 1922- *ConAu 37R*
Joffe, Joyce 1940- *ConAu 77*
Johannes, R *ConAu 49*
Johannes Ur Kotlum 1899-1972 *CIDMEL 80,*
EncWL 2
Johannesen, Richard L 1937- *ConAu 17R*
Johannessen, Matthias 1930- *IntWWP 82*
Johannesson, Olof 1908- *ConAu X*
Johanningmeier, E V 1937- *ConAu 104*
Johannis, Theodore B, Jr. 1914- *ConAu 33R*
Johannsen, Christa 1914- *IntAu&W 82*
Johannsen, Hano D 1933- *ConAu 29R*
Johannsen, Klaus *IntAu&W 82X*
Johannsen, Robert Walter 1925- *ConAu 1R*
Johannsson, Kristjan Tryggvi 1929- *IntAu&W 82*
Johansen, Bruce Elliott 1950- *ConAu 110*
Johansen, Dorothy O 1904- *ConAu P-1*
Johanson, Donald C 1943- *ConAu 107,*
ConIsC 1[port]
Johanson, Stanley Morris 1933- *ConAu 45*
Johansson, Thomas B 1943- *ConAu 102*
John *IntAu&W 82X*
John Paul I, Pope 1912-1978 *ConAu 81*
John Paul II, Pope 1920- *ConAu 106*
John, B *ConAu X*
John, Betty 1907- *ConAu X, IntAu&W 82,*
WrDr 84
John, Colin *ConAu X*
John, Dane *ConAu X*
John, Donas *DrAP&F 83*
John, Donas 1937- *IntWWP 82*
John, Elizabeth Beaman 1907- *ConAu 5R, –8NR*
John, Eloise *IntWWP 82X*
John, Errol *ConDr 82, WrDr 84*
John, Errol 1925?- *CnMD, ModWD*
John, Helen James 1930- *ConAu 61*
John, June 1925- *WrDr 84*
John, M P 1911- *IntWWP 82*
John, Miriam *IntAu&W 82X*
John, Nancy *TwCRGW, WrDr 84*
John, Robert *ConAu 29R, WrDr 84*
Johnn, David *ConAu X, IntAu&W 82X*
Johnn-Saint Johnn, Allison Nichols *IntWWP 82*
Johnpoll, Bernard K 1918- *ConAu 9NR, –21R*
Johns, Albert Cameron 1914- *ConAu 6NR, –49*
Johns, Avery *WrDr 84*
Johns, Avery 1905- *ConAu X, SmATA 2*
Johns, Claude J, Jr. 1930- *ConAu 77*
Johns, Edward Alistair 1936- *ConAu 45,*
WrDr 84
Johns, Foster *ConAu X*
Johns, Geoffrey *ConAu X*
Johns, Geoffrey 1923- *WrDr 84*
Johns, Glover S, Jr. 1911?-1976 *ConAu 65*
Johns, John E 1921- *ConAu 9R*
Johns, June 1925- *ConAu 57, IntAu&W 82X*
Johns, Kenneth *ConAu X*
Johns, Marston *ConAu X*
Johns, Orrick 1887-1946 *TwCA, TwCA SUP*
Johns, Ray E 1900- *ConAu 41R*
Johns, Richard A 1929- *ConAu 17R, WrDr 84*
Johns, Robert Clyde 1919- *WrDr 84*

Johns, W E 1893-1968 *LongCTC, TwCCW 83,*
TwCSFW
Johns, Warren L 1929- *ConAu 21R*
Johns, Whitey *ConAu X*
Johns, William Earle 1893-1968 *ConAu 73*
Johns Smith, June 1925- *IntAu&W 82*
Johnsen, Trevor Bernard Meldal *ConAu X*
Johnsgard, Paul A 1931- *ConAu 1NR, –49,*
IntAu&W 82, WrDr 84
Johnson *IntWWP 82X*
Johnson, A *ConAu X*
Johnson, A E *ConAu X, SmATA 2, WrDr 84*
Johnson, A Ross 1939- *WrDr 84*
Johnson, Alan P 1929- *ConAu 17R*
Johnson, Albert 1904- *ConAu 6NR, –9R*
Johnson, Alden Porter 1914-1972 *ConAu 104*
Johnson, Alicia L 1944- *LivgBAA*
Johnson, Allen 1941- *ConAu 85*
Johnson, Allison H 1910- *ConAu 41R*
Johnson, Alvin Saunders 1874-1971 *ConAu 29R,*
TwCA SUP
Johnson, Amandus 1877-1974 *ConAu 49*
Johnson, Amil John 1896- *IntAu&W 82*
Johnson, Andrew N 1887- *ConAu 61*
Johnson, Ann Cox *ConAu X*
Johnson, Anna M 1860-1943 *MichAu 80*
Johnson, Annabel 1921- *TwCCW 83*
Johnson, Annabel Jones 1921- *ConAu 9R,*
SmATA 2
Johnson, Annabell 1921- *WrDr 84*
Johnson, Anthony Leonard 1939- *IntWWP 82*
Johnson, Arnold W 1900- *ConAu P-1*
Johnson, Arthur Menzies 1921- *ConAu 21R*
Johnson, Aubrey Rodway 1901- *IntAu&W 82,*
WrDr 84
Johnson, Audrey P 1915- *ConAu 93*
Johnson, Avah 1925- *IntWWP 82*
Johnson, B C 1945- *ConAu 107*
Johnson, B F 1920- *ConAu 3NR*
Johnson, B S 1933-1973 *ConAu 9NR, ConLC 9,*
DcLB 14[port], WorAu 1970
Johnson, Barbara Ferry 1923- *ConAu 73,*
Conv 3, TwCRGW
Johnson, Barry L 1934- *ConAu 33R*
Johnson, Barry L 1943- *ConAu 61*
Johnson, Bea d1976 *ConAu 65*
Johnson, Ben E 1940- *ConAu 8NR, –61*
Johnson, Benjamin A 1937- *ConAu 9NR, –21R*
Johnson, Benton 1928- *ConAu 81*
Johnson, Bernard 1933- *ConAu 33R*
Johnson, Bernard H, Jr. 1920- *LivgBAA*
Johnson, Bertha French 1906- *ConAu 41R*
Johnson, Bobby *DrAP&F 83*
Johnson, Bradford 1937- *ConAu 57*
Johnson, Brian 1925- *ConAu 106*
Johnson, Brian Stanley 1933-1974 *TwCWr*
Johnson, Bruce 1933- *ConAu 33R*
Johnson, Bryan Stanley 1933-1973 *ConAu 9R,*
–49, –53, ConLC 6, DcLEL 1940,
ModBrL SUP
Johnson, Burdetta Faye 1920- *IntAu&W 82*
Johnson, Burges 1877-1963 *ConAu 89*
Johnson, Byron Lindberg 1917- *ConAu 21R*
Johnson, C Edward *ConAu X*
Johnson, C F *ConAu X*
Johnson, Carl E 1937- *ConAu 25R*
Johnson, Carl G 1915- *ConAu 101*
Johnson, Carol Virginia 1928- *ConAu 6NR, –9R*
Johnson, Carroll B 1938- *ConAu 73*
Johnson, Cecil Edward 1927- *ConAu 33R*
Johnson, Chalmers A 1931- *ConAu 5R, –6NR*
Johnson, Charlene *ConAu X*
Johnson, Charles *DrAP&F 83*
Johnson, Charles Benjamin 1928-1980
ConAu 4NR, –5R
Johnson, Charles Ellicott 1920-1969 *ConAu 1R,*
–103
Johnson, Charles R 1925- *ConAu 65,*
SmATA 11
Johnson, Charles Richard 1948- *ConLC 7*
Johnson, Charles S *ConAu X*
Johnson, Charles W 1934- *ConAu 107*
Johnson, Christopher Howard 1937- *ConAu 106*
Johnson, Christopher Louis McIntosh 1931-
ConAu 8NR, –13R
Johnson, Chuck *ConAu X, SmATA X*
Johnson, Clair 1915?-1980 *ConAu 97*
Johnson, Claudia Alta 1912- *ConAu 89*
Johnson, Clive 1930- *ConAu 29R*
Johnson, Crockett 1906-1975 *ConAu X,*
SmATA X, TwCCW 83
Johnson, Curt *DrAP&F 83*

Johnson, Curt 1928- *ConAu 33R*
Johnson, Curtiss Sherman 1899- *ConAu 45*
Johnson, D Barton 1933- *ConAu 33R*
Johnson, D Bruce 1942- *ConAu 61*
Johnson, D Gale 1916- *ConAu 17R, WrDr 84*
Johnson, D William 1945- *ConAu 97, SmATA 23[port]*
Johnson, Dale A 1936- *ConAu 37R*
Johnson, Dave W 1931- *ConAu 93*
Johnson, David *DrAP&F 83*
Johnson, David 1927- *ConAu 8NR, –13R, IntAu&W 82*
Johnson, David George 1906- *ConAu 9R*
Johnson, David Lawrence 1943- *WrDr 84*
Johnson, Denis *DrAP&F 83*
Johnson, Diane *DrAP&F 83*
Johnson, Diane 1934- *ConAu 41R, ConLC 5, –13, DcLB Y80B[port], WrDr 84*
Johnson, Donald Bruce 1921- *ConAu 1R, WrDr 84*
Johnson, Donald M 1909- *ConAu 1R*
Johnson, Donald McIntosh 1903- *ConAu 5R, –8NR*
Johnson, Donna Kay 1935- *ConAu 106*
Johnson, Donovan A 1910- *ConAu 1R, –5R, –5NR*
Johnson, Dorothy Biddle 1887?-1974 *ConAu 53*
Johnson, Dorothy E 1920- *ConAu 53*
Johnson, Dorothy M 1905- *WrDr 84*
Johnson, Dorothy Marie 1905- *ConAu 5R, –6NR, FifWWr, SmATA 6, TwCWW*
Johnson, Dorris 1914- *ConAu 109*
Johnson, Douglas W 1934- *ConAu 6NR, –57*
Johnson, E A J 1900-1972 *ConAu P-1*
Johnson, E Ashby 1917- *ConAu 33R*
Johnson, E Ned *ConAu X*
Johnson, E Richard 1937- *ConAu 104, TwCCr&M 80*
Johnson, E W 1941- *ConAu 29R*
Johnson, Earl, Jr. 1933- *ConAu 10NR, –61*
Johnson, Edgar 1901- *ConAu 9R, TwCA SUP*
Johnson, Edgar 1912- *TwCCW 83*
Johnson, Edgar Raymond 1912- *ConAu 9R, SmATA 2*
Johnson, Edwin Clark 1945- *ConAu 107*
Johnson, El *IntWWP 82X*
Johnson, Electa Search 1909- *ConAu 1R*
Johnson, Elizabeth 1911- *ConAu 1R, –4NR, SmATA 7*
Johnson, Ellen Argo *ConAu X*
Johnson, Elmer Douglas 1915- *ConAu 3NR, –9R*
Johnson, Elmer Hubert 1917- *ConAu 13R, WrDr 84*
Johnson, Elvira Hildergarde Thompson 1908- *IntWWP 82*
Johnson, Emil Richard 1937- *WrDr 84*
Johnson, Enid 1892- *ConAu 73*
Johnson, Eola 1909- *ConAu 49*
Johnson, Eric W 1918- *ConAu 4NR, –5R, SmATA 8, WrDr 84*
Johnson, Evelyne 1932- *ConAu 69, SmATA 20*
Johnson, Eyvind 1900-1976 *ClDMEL 80, ConAu 69, –73, ConLC 14, EncWL 2, WorAu 1970*
Johnson, Falk S 1913- *ConAu 17R, WrDr 84*
Johnson, Ferd 1905- *ConAu 69*
Johnson, Forrest B 1935- *ConAu 106*
Johnson, Franklyn A 1921- *ConAu 1R, –4NR*
Johnson, Frederick 1932- *ConAu 73*
Johnson, Fridolf 1905- *ConAu 103*
Johnson, Frosty 1935- *ConAu X*
Johnson, G Orville 1915- *ConAu 1R, –4NR*
Johnson, Gaylord 1884- *ConAu P-1, SmATA 7*
Johnson, Geoffrey 1893-1966 *ConAu P-1*
Johnson, George 1917- *ConAu 5R*
Johnson, George Clayton *ConSFA*
Johnson, Gerald White 1890-1980 *ConAu 85, –97, SmATA 19, –28N, TwCA SUP*
Johnson, Gertrude F 1929- *ConAu 57*
Johnson, Greer 1920?-1974 *ConAu 53*
Johnson, Greg *DrAP&F 83*
Johnson, H B, Jr. 1931- *ConAu 29R*
Johnson, H Webster 1906- *ConAu 4NR, WrDr 84*
Johnson, Halvard *DrAP&F 83*
Johnson, Harland 1936- *ConAu 33R, WrDr 84*
Johnson, Harold L 1924- *ConAu 13R*
Johnson, Harold Leland *DrAP&F 83*
Johnson, Harold Leland 1908- *IntWWP 82*
Johnson, Harold Scholl 1929- *ConAu 37R*
Johnson, Harold V 1897- *ConAu 1R, –5NR*

Johnson, Harry Alleyn 1920- *LivgBAA*
Johnson, Harry Alleyn 1921- *ConAu 45*
Johnson, Harry G 1923-1977 *ConAu 5R, –69*
Johnson, Harry L 1929- *ConAu 29R*
Johnson, Harry Morton 1917- *ConAu 9R*
Johnson, Harvey Leroy 1904- *ConAu 37R*
Johnson, Haynes Bonner 1931- *ConAu 5R*
Johnson, Henry *ConAu X*
Johnson, Herbert A 1934- *ConAu 4NR, –5R*
Johnson, Herbert J 1933- *ConAu 29R*
Johnson, Herbert Webster 1906- *ConAu 5R*
Johnson, Hewlett 1874-1966 *DcLEL 1940, LongCTC*
Johnson, Hildegard Binder 1908- *ConAu 3NR, –9R*
Johnson, Howard Albert 1915-1974 *ConAu 1R, –49*
Johnson, Hugh E A 1939- *ConAu 93, IntAu&W 82*
Johnson, Humphrey Wynne 1925-1976 *ConAu 61*
Johnson, Irma Bolan 1903- *ConAu 1R, –1NR*
Johnson, Irving McClure 1905- *ConAu 1R*
Johnson, Jalmar Edwin 1905- *ConAu 5R*
Johnson, James A 1932- *ConAu 110*
Johnson, James Craig 1944- *ConAu 53*
Johnson, James E 1927- *ConAu 77*
Johnson, James H 1930- *ConAu 11NR*
Johnson, James Henry 1930- *ConAu 25R, IntAu&W 82, WrDr 84*
Johnson, James J 1939- *ConAu 33R*
Johnson, James L 1927- *ConAu 9NR, –21R*
Johnson, James P 1937- *ConAu 81*
Johnson, James Ralph 1922- *ConAu 1R, –2NR, IntAu&W 82, SmATA 1, WrDr 84*
Johnson, James Rosser 1916- *ConAu 9R*
Johnson, James Turner 1938- *ConAu 61*
Johnson, James Weldon 1871-1938 *ConAmA, ConAu 104, EncWL 2, ModAL SUP, ModBlW, SmATA X, TwCA, TwCA SUP, TwCLC 3*
Johnson, James William 1871-1938 *SmATA 31[port]*
Johnson, James William 1927- *ConAu 53*
Johnson, Jane 1951- *ConAu 110*
Johnson, Jane M 1914- *ConAu 49*
Johnson, Jann *ConAu X*
Johnson, Jean Dye 1920- *ConAu 21R*
Johnson, Jennifer Hilary 1945- *IntWWP 82*
Johnson, Jenny *IntWWP 82X*
Johnson, Jerry Mack 1927- *ConAu 4NR, –53*
Johnson, Jesse J 1914- *LivgBAA, WrDr 84*
Johnson, Jim *ConAu X*
Johnson, Jinna *ConAu X*
Johnson, Joan D 1929- *ConAu 106*
Johnson, Joan Helen 1931- *ConAu 61*
Johnson, Joe *DrAP&F 83*
Johnson, Joe 1940- *LivgBAA*
Johnson, Joe Donald 1943- *ConAu 57*
Johnson, John Bockover, Jr. 1912-1972 *ConAu 106*
Johnson, John E 1929- *ConAu 110, SmATA 34*
Johnson, John J 1912- *ConAu 9R*
Johnson, John Myrton 1941- *ConAu 93*
Johnson, Johnni 1922- *ConAu 13R*
Johnson, Joseph A, Jr. 1914?-1979 *ConAu 89*
Johnson, Joseph E 1946- *ConAu 37R, WrDr 84*
Johnson, Joseph M 1883?-1973 *ConAu 45*
Johnson, Josephine *DrAP&F 83*
Johnson, Josephine 1910- *WrDr 84*
Johnson, Josephine Winslow 1910- *ConAmA, ConAu 25R, ConNov 82, TwCA, TwCA SUP*
Johnson, Joy Duvall 1932- *ConAu 110*
Johnson, Karen 1951- *ConAu 69*
Johnson, Kathryn 1929- *ConAu 33R*
Johnson, Keith B 1933- *ConAu 29R*
Johnson, Kendall 1928- *ConAu 69*
Johnson, Kenneth G 1922- *ConAu 41R*
Johnson, Kenneth M 1903- *ConAu 5R*
Johnson, Kristi Planck 1944- *ConAu 57*
Johnson, L D 1916- *ConAu 33R*
Johnson, Lady Bird *ConAu X*
Johnson, LaVerne B 1925- *ConAu 65, SmATA 13*
Johnson, Lemuel A 1941- *ConAu 53*
Johnson, Lewis Kerr 1904- *ConAu 1R*
Johnson, Lincoln F, Jr. 1920- *ConAu 81*
Johnson, Lionel Pigot 1867-1902 *LongCTC*
Johnson, Lois Smith 1894- *ConAu P-1, SmATA 6*
Johnson, Lois Walfrid 1936- *ConAu 6NR, –57, SmATA 22[port]*

Johnson, Louis 1924- *ConAu 101, ConP 80, DcLEL 1940, LongCTC, TwCWr, WrDr 84*
Johnson, Luke Timothy 1943- *ConAu 107*
Johnson, Lyndon Baines 1908-1973 *ConAu 41R, –53*
Johnson, Lynn Eric 1932- *ConAu 108*
Johnson, M Glen 1936- *ConAu 41R*
Johnson, Malcolm 1904-1976 *ConAu 65, –69*
Johnson, Malcolm L 1937- *ConAu 69*
Johnson, Manly 1920- *ConAu 89*
Johnson, Margaret 1926- *ConAu 37R*
Johnson, Marilue Carolyn 1931- *ConAu 1NR, –45*
Johnson, Marion Georgina Wikeley 1912-1980 *ConAu 9R, –97*
Johnson, Marshall D 1935- *ConAu 33R*
Johnson, Mary Anne 1943- *ConAu 53*
Johnson, Mary Frances K 1929?-1979 *ConAu 104, SmATA 27N*
Johnson, Mary Kitz 1904- *ConAu P-1*
Johnson, Mary Louise *ConAu X*
Johnson, Maryanna 1925- *ConAu 33R*
Johnson, Maurice 1913- *ConAu 1R*
Johnson, Mauritz 1922- *ConAu 41R*
Johnson, Mel *WrDr 84*
Johnson, Mendal W 1928-1976 *ConAu 101*
Johnson, Merle Allison 1934- *ConAu 37R*
Johnson, Michael Henderson Flowers 1928- *IntWWP 82*
Johnson, Michael L *DrAP&F 83*
Johnson, Michael L 1943- *ConAu 4NR, –53, IntWWP 82*
Johnson, Mike *WrDr 84*
Johnson, Milton 1932- *SmATA 31*
Johnson, Natalie *SmATA X*
Johnson, Nicholas 1934- *ConAu 29R, WrDr 84*
Johnson, Nick *DrAP&F 83*
Johnson, Nick 1944- *IntWWP 82*
Johnson, Niel M 1931- *ConAu 41R*
Johnson, Nora 1933- *ConAu 106*
Johnson, Nunnally 1897-1977 *ConAu 69, –81, DcLB 26[port]*
Johnson, Olga Weydemeyer 1901- *ConAu P-2*
Johnson, Oliver A 1923- *ConAu 29R*
Johnson, Owen McMahon 1878-1952 *TwCA, TwCA SUP*
Johnson, Pal Espolin 1940- *IntAu&W 82*
Johnson, Pamela Hansford 1912-1981 *ConAu 1R, –2NR, –104, ConLC 1, –7, –27[port], ConNov 82, DcLB 15[port], IntAu&W 82, LongCTC, ModBrL, ModBrL SUP, TwCA SUP, TwCWr*
Johnson, Patricia M 1937- *IntAu&W 82*
Johnson, Patrick Spencer 1938- *ConAu 9R*
Johnson, Paul 1928- *WrDr 84*
Johnson, Paul Bede 1928- *ConAu 17R*
Johnson, Paul C 1904- *ConAu 81*
Johnson, Paul Emanuel 1898- *ConAu 13R*
Johnson, Paul Victor 1920- *ConAu 1R, WrDr 84*
Johnson, Paula Janice 1946- *ConAu 106*
Johnson, Pauline 1862?-1913 *CreCan 2*
Johnson, Pauline B *ConAu 1R*
Johnson, Peter 1930- *ConAu 65*
Johnson, Philip 1900- *IntAu&W 82*
Johnson, Philip A 1915- *ConAu 13R*
Johnson, Philip Cortelyou 1906- *ConAu 106*
Johnson, Phyllis Anne 1937- *ConAu 108*
Johnson, Pierce 1921- *ConAu 41R*
Johnson, Quentin G 1930- *ConAu 9R*
Johnson, R S 1946- *ConAu 29R*
Johnson, Rachel H 1887-1983 *ConAu 110*
Johnson, Ralph W 1923- *ConAu 77*
Johnson, Ray 1927- *ConAu 17R*
Johnson, Ray DeForest 1926- *ConAu 65*
Johnson, Ray W 1900- *ConSFA*
Johnson, Richard *ConAu X, MichAu 80*
Johnson, Richard A *WrDr 84*
Johnson, Richard A 1937- *ConAu 37R*
Johnson, Richard B 1914-1977 *ConAu 41R*
Johnson, Richard C 1919- *ConAu 33R*
Johnson, Richard D 1927- *ConAu 109*
Johnson, Richard N 1900-1971 *ConAu 104*
Johnson, Richard T 1938- *ConAu 53*
Johnson, Richard Tanner *WrDr 84*
Johnson, Rita *DrAP&F 83*
Johnson, Robert A 1921- *ConAu 61*
Johnson, Robert Clyde 1919- *ConAu 5R*
Johnson, Robert E 1923- *WrDr 84*
Johnson, Robert Erwin 1923- *ConAu 37R*
Johnson, Robert Ivar 1933- *ConAu 53*

Jones, Betty Millsaps 1940- *ConAu 109*
Jones, Bill *IntWWP 82X*
Jones, Billy M 1925- *ConAu 10NR, –21R*
Jones, Bob *ConAu X*
Jones, Bob 1911- *ConAu 25R*
Jones, Bob, Jr. 1911- *WrDr 84*
Jones, Bobi *IntAu&W 82X*
Jones, Brian 1938- *ConP 80, WrDr 84*
Jones, Bruce *ConAmTC*
Jones, Bryan L 1945- *ConAu 110*
Jones, C Clyde 1922- *ConAu 109*
Jones, C Robert *NatPD 81[port]*
Jones, Candy 1925- *ConAu 107*
Jones, Carolyn 1932- *ConAu 29R*
Jones, Carolyn 1933-1983 *ConAu 110*
Jones, Charles 1910- *ConAu P-1*
Jones, Charles Alfred 1921-1982 *ConAu 107*
Jones, Charles Edwin 1932- *ConAu 49*
Jones, Charles O 1931- *ConAu 7NR, –17R*
Jones, Charles W 1905- *ConAu 13R,*
 IntAu&W 82, WrDr 84
Jones, Christina Hendry 1896- *ConAu 73*
Jones, Christine 1937- *ConAu 61*
Jones, Christopher William 1937- *ConAu 21R,*
 WrDr 84
Jones, Clifford M 1902- *ConAu 17R, WrDr 84*
Jones, Craig 1945- *ConAu 81*
Jones, Cranston E 1918- *ConAu 1R*
Jones, Curran L 1919- *IntAu&W 82*
Jones, Cyril Meredith 1904- *ConAu P-2,*
 WrDr 84
Jones, D F *ConSFA, TwCSFW, WrDr 84*
Jones, D G 1929- *ConAu 29R, ConLC 10,*
 ConP 80
Jones, D Gareth 1940- *ConAu 106*
Jones, D L 1925- *ConAu 25R*
Jones, D Mervyn 1922- *ConAu 21R*
Jones, Daisy Marvel 1906- *ConAu 17R*
Jones, Dan Burne 1908- *ConAu 65*
Jones, Daniel 1881-1967 *ConAu 5R, –6NR*
Jones, David *IntWWP 82X*
Jones, David 1895-1974 *CnMWL, ConAu 9R,*
 –53, ConLC 2, –4, –7, –13, EncWL 2,
 LongCTC, ModBrL, ModBrL SUP,
 RGFMBP, TwCWr, WhoTwCL, WorAu
Jones, David Arthur 1946- *ConAu 73*
Jones, David Rhodes 1932- *ConAu 101*
Jones, David Robert 1947- *ConAu 103*
Jones, Dennis 1932- *CreCan 1*
Jones, Diana Wynne 1934- *ConAu 4NR, –49,*
 ConLC 26[port], SmATA 9, TwCCW 83,
 WrDr 84
Jones, Don *DrAP&F 83*
Jones, Don 1938- *IntWWP 82, WrDr 84*
Jones, Donald 1931- *ConAu 85*
Jones, Donald 1938- *ConAu 17R*
Jones, Dorothy Holder *ConAu 9R*
Jones, Douglas C 1924- *ConAu 21R,*
 IntAu&W 82, TwCWW, WrDr 84
Jones, Douglas G 1929- *WrDr 84*
Jones, Douglas Gordon 1929- *CreCan 1,*
 DcLEL 1940, IntWWP 82
Jones, Duane *ConAu X*
Jones, DuPre Anderson 1937- *ConAu 21R*
Jones, E B C 1893-1966 *LongCTC*
Jones, E H 1925- *LongCTC*
Jones, E Stanley 1884-1973 *ConAu 41R, –93*
Jones, E Terrence 1941- *ConAu 33R, WrDr 84*
Jones, E Winston 1911- *ConAu 13R*
Jones, Edgar A, Jr. 1921- *ConAu 89*
Jones, Edna *IntWWP 82X*
Jones, Edward Allen 1903- *ConAu 25R*
Jones, Edward E 1926- *ConAu 17R*
Jones, Edward H, Jr. 1922- *ConAu 13R*
Jones, Eldred Durosimi 1925- *ConAu 45*
Jones, Eli Stanley 1884- *TwCA SUP*
Jones, Elizabeth Anne 1934- *IntWWP 82*
Jones, Elizabeth B 1907- *ConAu 61*
Jones, Elizabeth Orton 1910- *ConAu 77,*
 SmATA 18
Jones, Elwyn 1923-1982 *ConAu 106, –69*
Jones, Emlyn 1912-1975 *ConAu P-2*
Jones, Emrys 1920- *ConAu 17R, IntAu&W 82,*
 WrDr 84
Jones, Enid Huws 1911- *ConAu 49*
Jones, Eric Lionel 1936- *ConAu 104, WrDr 84*
Jones, Ernest 1879-1958 *WorAu*
Jones, Evan 1915- *ConAu 6NR, –9R,*
 SmATA 3
Jones, Evan 1931- *WrDr 84*
Jones, Evan David 1903- *IntAu&W 82*
Jones, Evan Lloyd 1931- *ConP 80, IntWWP 82*

Jones, Eve 1924- *ConAu 1R*
Jones, Everett L 1915- *ConAu 13R*
Jones, Everett LeRoi 1934- *WorAu*
Jones, Ezra Earl 1939- *ConAu 57*
Jones, Faustine Childress 1927- *ConAu 77*
Jones, Felix Edward Aylmer 1889- *ConAu P-1*
Jones, Frances P 1890- *ConAu 9R*
Jones, Frank E 1917- *ConAu 13R*
Jones, Frank Lancaster 1937- *ConAu 29R,*
 WrDr 84
Jones, Frank Pierce 1905-1975 *ConAu 110*
Jones, Franklin Ross 1921- *ConAu 53*
Jones, Frieda K 1905- *IntWWP 82*
Jones, G Curtis 1911- *ConAu 3NR, –5R*
Jones, G O 1917- *ConAu 25R*
Jones, G William 1931- *ConAu 11NR, –21R*
Jones, Gareth 1939- *ConAu 102*
Jones, Garth N 1925- *ConAu 81*
Jones, Gary M 1925- *ConAu 17R*
Jones, Gayl *DrAP&F 83*
Jones, Gayl 1949- *ConAu 77, ConLC 6, –9,*
 IntAu&W 82
Jones, Gene 1928- *ConAu 21R*
Jones, George Fenwick 1916- *ConAu 7NR, –13R*
Jones, George Hilton 1924- *ConAu 33R,*
 WrDr 84
Jones, George Thaddeus 1917- *ConAu 53*
Jones, Gillingham *ConAu X, SmATA X*
Jones, Glyn 1905- *CnMWL, ConAu 3NR, –9R,*
 ConNov 82, ConP 80, DcLB 15[port],
 IntAu&W 82, ModBrL, WorAu, WrDr 84
Jones, Gonner *ConSFA*
Jones, Gordon W 1915- *ConAu 45*
Jones, Goronwy John 1915- *ConAu 9R,*
 IntAu&W 82
Jones, Gwendolyn *ConAu 33R*
Jones, Gwilym Peredur 1892-1975 *ConAu 57*
Jones, Gwyn 1907- *ConNov 82, DcLB 15[port],*
 IntAu&W 82, LongCTC, ModBrL,
 WrDr 84
Jones, Gwyn Owain 1917- *IntAu&W 82,*
 WrDr 84
Jones, Gwyneth A 1952- *ConAu 107*
Jones, H G 1924- *ConAu 33R*
Jones, H John F 1924- *ConAu 9R*
Jones, Hardin Blair 1914-1978 *ConAu 77*
Jones, Harold *ConAu X*
Jones, Harold 1904- *ConAu 85, SmATA 14*
Jones, Harriet *ConAu X*
Jones, Harry Lee 1921?-1983 *ConAu 110*
Jones, Helen *WrDr 84*
Jones, Helen 1917- *ConAu 105*
Jones, Helen Hinckley 1903- *ConAu 5R, –5NR,*
 IntAu&W 82, SmATA 26[port]
Jones, Helen L 1903-1973 *ConAu 104*
Jones, Helen L 1904?-1973 *SmATA 22N*
Jones, Henri 1921- *ConAu 41R*
Jones, Henry Albert 1889-1981 *ConAu 103*
Jones, Henry Arthur 1851-1929 *ConAu 110,*
 DcLB 10[port], LongCTC, ModBrL,
 ModWD
Jones, Herbert Kelsey 1922- *CreCan 1*
Jones, Hettie *DrAP&F 83*
Jones, Hettie 1934- *ConAu 81, SmATA 27*
Jones, Hilda Mary 1921- *IntWWP 82*
Jones, Hortense P 1918- *ConAu 61, SmATA 9*
Jones, Howard 1940- *ConAu 65*
Jones, Howard Mumford 1892-1980 *ConAu 85,*
 –97, IntAu&W 82, TwCA SUP
Jones, Ina *DrAP&F 83*
Jones, Iris Eileen 1932- *MichAu 80*
Jones, Iris Sanderson 1932- *ConAu 73,*
 MichAu 80
Jones, J *IntAu&W 82X*
Jones, J Faragut *ConAu X*
Jones, J Ithel 1911- *ConAu P-2*
Jones, Jack *ConAu X*
Jones, Jack 1884-1970 *LongCTC, WorAu*
Jones, Jack 1913- *ConAu 109*
Jones, Jack 1924- *ConAu 85*
Jones, James 1921-1977 *AuNews 1, –2,*
 ConAu 1R, –6NR, –69, ConLC 1, –3, –10,
 ConNov 82A, DcLB 2, DcLEL 1940,
 EncWL 2, ModAL, ModAL SUP,
 TwCA SUP, TwCWr
Jones, James C 1922- *ConAu 69*
Jones, James Henry 1907?-1977 *ConAu 73*
Jones, James Larkin 1913- *ConAu 109*
Jones, Jeanne 1937- *ConAu 61*
Jones, Jeannette 1944- *ConAu 110*
Jones, Jenkin Lloyd 1911- *ConAu 9R*

Jones, Jo *ConAu 33R*
Jones, Joanna *ConAu X, IntAu&W 82X,*
 WrDr 84
Jones, John 1924- *IntAu&W 82*
Jones, John Bush 1940- *ConAmTC, ConAu 33R*
Jones, John Idris 1938- *IntWWP 82*
Jones, John J *ConAu X*
Jones, John Paul, Jr. 1912- *ConAu 11NR, –69*
Jones, Joseph Jay 1908- *ConAu 1R, –1NR*
Jones, Joseph L 1897-1980 *ConAu 102*
Jones, Juanita B 1921- *IntWWP 82*
Jones, Judith Paterson 1938- *ConAu 106*
Jones, Julia 1923- *ConDr 82C, IntAu&W 82,*
 WrDr 84
Jones, K Westcott *ConAu X*
Jones, Karen Midkiff 1948- *ConAu 104*
Jones, Katharine M 1900- *ConAu 5R*
Jones, Kathleen 1922- *ConAu 81, IntAu&W 82*
Jones, Kathleen Eve 1944- *ConAu 102*
Jones, Kelsey 1922- *CreCan 1*
Jones, Ken D 1930- *ConAu 49*
Jones, Kenley 1935- *ConAu 69*
Jones, Kenneth E 1920- *ConAu 57*
Jones, Kenneth LaMar 1931- *ConAu 53*
Jones, Kenneth S 1919- *ConAu 21R*
Jones, L H *IntAu&W 82*
Jones, Landon Y 1943- *ConAu 105, WrDr 84*
Jones, Langdon 1942- *TwCSFW, WrDr 84*
Jones, Lawrence Elmore 1906- *IntAu&W 82*
Jones, Leon 1936- *ConAu 101*
Jones, Leonidas M, Sr. 1923- *ConAu 45*
Jones, Leroi *DrAP&F 83*
Jones, LeRoi 1934- *ConAu 21R, ConDr 82,*
 ConLC 1, –2, –10, –14, ConNov 82,
 ConP 80, CroCAP, CroCD, DcLEL 1940,
 LivgBAA, ModAL, ModAL SUP, ModWD,
 WhoTwCL, WorAu, WrDr 84
Jones, Leslie 1929- *WrDr 84*
Jones, Lewis 1897-1939 *DcLB 15*
Jones, Lewis Pinckney 1916- *ConAu 61*
Jones, Lloyd S 1931- *ConAu 1R, –4NR*
Jones, Louis C 1908- *ConAu 5R*
Jones, Luke *WrDr 84*
Jones, Lyndon Hamer 1927- *ConAu 103,*
 WrDr 84
Jones, Lynn Berta Springbett *CreCan 2*
Jones, Madeline Adams 1913- *ConAu 21R*
Jones, Madison 1925- *WrDr 84*
Jones, Madison Percy 1925- *ConAu 7NR, –13R,*
 ConLC 4, ConNov 82, DcLEL 1940,
 IntAu&W 82
Jones, Major J 1919- *ConAu 33R, LivgBAA*
Jones, Malcolm V 1940- *ConAu 103,*
 IntAu&W 82, WrDr 84
Jones, Maldwyn Allen 1922- *ConAu 1R, –4NR*
Jones, Marc Edmund 1888- *ConAu 33R*
Jones, Margaret Alice Bartlett 1906- *IntWWP 82*
Jones, Margaret Boone *ConAu 25R, SmATA X*
Jones, Margaret E W 1938- *ConAu 37R,*
 WrDr 84
Jones, Marion *WrDr 84*
Jones, Marion Patrick 1943?- *ConNov 82*
Jones, Marvin 1886-1976 *ConAu 65*
Jones, Mary Alice 1898- *ConAu 17R,*
 SmATA 6
Jones, Mary Brush 1925- *ConAu 25R*
Jones, Mary Voell 1933- *ConAu 21R, WrDr 84*
Jones, Maxwell 1907- *ConAu 25R*
Jones, Maynard Benedict 1904-1972 *ConAu 93*
Jones, McClure *SmATA 34[port]*
Jones, Mervyn 1922- *ConAu 1NR, –45,*
 ConLC 10, ConNov 82, DcLEL 1940,
 WrDr 84
Jones, Michael 1940- *ConAu 104*
Jones, Michael Owen 1942- *ConAu 101*
Jones, Miriam *ConAu X, IntAu&W 82X*
Jones, Morgan Glyn 1905- *IntWWP 82*
Jones, Morris Val 1914- *ConAu 5R*
Jones, Nard 1904-1972 *ConAu X, TwCWW*
Jones, Neil R 1909- *ConSFA, TwCSFW,*
 WrDr 84
Jones, Nita Adrian *IntWWP 82X*
Jones, Noel 1939- *ConAu 81*
Jones, Oakah L, Jr. 1930- *ConAu 8NR, –17R*
Jones, Orlando *ConAu X*
Jones, Owen Rogers *WrDr 84*
Jones, Owen Rogers 1922- *ConAu 1R*
Jones, Pat *ConAu X*
Jones, Patricia *DrAP&F 83*
Jones, Paul *DrAP&F 83*
Jones, Paul Davis 1940- *ConAu 49*
Jones, Paul J 1897?-1974 *ConAu 53*

K

K, R ConAmA

K C-L IntAu&W 82X

K J IntWWP 82X

K-Turkel, Judi 1934- ConAu 8NR

K V S, Murti IntWWP 82X

Ka-Tzetnik 135633 ConAu 29R

Kaba, Lansine 1941- ConAu 61

Kabadi, Dwarakanath H 1936- IntWWP 82

Kabasele, Joseph ConAu X

Kabat, Elvin Abraham 1914- IntAu&W 82,
    WrDr 84

Kabdebo, Lorant 1936- IntAu&W 82

Kabdebo, Tamas ConAu X, SmATA X

Kabdebo, Thomas George 1934- ConAu 7NR,
    –53, SmATA 10, WrDr 84

Kabibble, Osh ConAu X, SmATA X

Kabo Arntsen, Irene K IntAu&W 82X

Kabo Kristine 1924- IntAu&W 82

Kabraji, Fredoon 1897- ConAu P-1

Kac, Mark 1914- IntAu&W 82

Kacew, Romain 1914-1980 ConAu 102, –108,
    WorAu

Kacew, Roman ConAu X

Kachel, Zew 1912- IntWWP 82

Kachmar, Jessie DrAP&F 83

Kachmar, Jessie 1913- IntWWP 82

Kachol, Kew IntWWP 82X

Kachru, Braj Behari 1932- ConAu 8NR, –61

Kacsur, Ann DrAP&F 83

Kaczer, Illes 1887- ConAu P-1

Kadai, Heino Olavi 1931- ConAu 21R

Kaden-Bandrowski, Juliusz 1885-1944
    ClDMEL 80, EncWL 2, ModSL 2

Kadesch, Robert R 1922- ConAu 57,
    SmATA 31

Kadic, Ante 1910- ConAu 107

Kadish, Ferne 1940- ConAu 61

Kadish, Mortimer Raymond 1916- ConAu 106

Kadler, Eric H 1922- ConAu 29R

Kadushin, Alfred 1916- ConAu 25R, WrDr 84

Kadushin, Charles 1932- ConAu 25R

Kae IntAu&W 82X

Kaebitzsch, Reinhold Johannes DrAP&F 83

Kaech, Rene Edgar 1909- IntAu&W 82,
    IntWWP 82

Kaegi, Walter Emil, Jr. 1937- ConAu 10NR,
    –25R

Kael, Pauline 1919- ConAu 6NR, –45,
    IntAu&W 82, WorAu 1970, WrDr 84

Kaelbling, Rudolf 1928- ConAu 17R

Kaelin, Eugene Francis 1926- ConAu 45

Kaellberg, Sture 1928- ConAu 107

Kaempfert, Wade ConAu X

Kaeppler, Adrienne Lois 1935- ConAu 107

Kaese, Harold 1909?-1975 ConAu 57

Kaestle, Carl F 1940- ConAu 85

Kaestner, Dorothy 1920- ConAu 61, WrDr 84

Kaestner, Erich 1899-1974 ConAu 49, –73

Kafe, Joseph Kofi Thompson 1933- ConAu 49

Kaffka, Margit 1880-1918 ClDMEL 80,
    EncWL 2

Kafka, Franz 1883-1924 ClDMEL 80, CnMD,
    CnMWL, ConAu 105, EncWL 2[port],
    LongCTC, ModGL, TwCA, TwCA SUP,

TwCLC 2, –6[port], TwCWr, WhoTwCL

Kafka, Sherry 1937- ConAu 21R

Kafka, Vincent W 1924- ConAu 61

Kafker, Frank A 1931- ConAu 37R

Kagan, Benjamin 1914- ConAu 21R

Kagan, Diane 1940- IntAu&W 82,
    NatPD 81[port]

Kagan, Donald 1932- ConAu 9NR, –21R

Kagan, Jerome 1929- ConAu 2NR, –5R

Kagan, Richard 1943- ConAu 57

Kagan, Richard C 1938- ConAu 53

Kagan-Kans, Eva 1928- ConAu 49

Kaganoff, Nathan M 1926- ConAu 108

Kagawa, Toyohiko 1888-1960 TwCA,
    TwCA SUP

Kageyama, Yuri DrAP&F 83

Kagy, Frederick D 1917- ConAu 13R

Kahan, Gerald 1923- ConAu 33R,
    IntAu&W 82, WrDr 84

Kahan, Stanley 1931- ConAu 5R

Kahan, Stuart 1936- ConAu X 93

Kahane, Anne 1924- CreCan 1

Kahane, Howard 1928- ConAu 1NR, –49

Kahaner, Ellen DrAP&F 83

Kahari, George Payne 1930- IntAu&W 82

Kahl, Ann Hammel 1929- ConAu 17R

Kahl, Joseph A 1923- ConAu 109

Kahl, M P 1934- ConAu 107

Kahl, Virginia 1919- ConAu 2NR, –49,
    TwCCW 83

Kahl, Virginia C 1919- WrDr 84

Kahle, Roger 1943- ConAu 33R

Kahlenberg, Mary Hunt 1940- ConAu 2NR, –45

Kahler, Erich Gabriel 1885-1970 ConAu 5R,
    –7NR, –29R

Kahler, Hugh MacNair 1883-1969 ConAu 102

Kahler, Woodland 1895- ConAu 1R,
    IntAu&W 82

Kahm, H S ConAu 101

Kahn, Albert E 1912?-1979 ConAu 89

Kahn, Alfred E 1917- ConAu 41R

Kahn, Alfred J 1919- ConAu 5R

Kahn, Arnold Dexter 1939- ConAu 101

Kahn, Balthazar 1944- ConAu X

Kahn, Bernard M 1930- NatPD 81[port]

Kahn, David 1930- ConAu 25R, WrDr 84

Kahn, E J, Jr. 1916- ConAu 65

Kahn, Ely Jacques 1884-1972 ConAu 37R

Kahn, Ely Jacques, Jr. 1916- TwCA SUP

Kahn, Frank J 1938- ConAu 33R

Kahn, Gilbert 1912-1971 ConAu 1R, –6NR

Kahn, Grace Leboy 1891-1983 ConAu 109

Kahn, Gustave 1859-1936 ClDMEL 80

Kahn, Hannah DrAP&F 83

Kahn, Hannah 1911- AuNews 2, ConAu 77,
    IntWWP 82

Kahn, Herman 1922- ConAu 65,
    ConIsC 1[port], IntAu&W 82, WrDr 84

Kahn, Herman 1922-1983 ConAu 110

Kahn, Herta Hess 1919- ConAu 25R

Kahn, James 1947- ConAu 109

Kahn, James M 1903?-1978 ConAu 77

Kahn, Joan 1914- ConAu 77

Kahn, Judd 1940- ConAu 101

Kahn, Kathy 1945- ConAu 41R

Kahn, Lawrence E 1937- ConAu 103

Kahn, Lothar 1922- ConAu 25R

Kahn, Louis I 1901-1974 ConAu 49

Kahn, Ludwig W 1910- ConAu 41R

Kahn, Margaret 1949- ConAu 101

Kahn, Michael D 1936- ConAu 109

Kahn, Michele 1940- IntAu&W 82

Kahn, Paul DrAP&F 83

Kahn, Richard 1905- ConAu 97

Kahn, Robert Irving 1910- ConAu 5R

Kahn, Robert L 1918- ConAu 10NR, –17R

Kahn, Roger 1927- ConAu 25R, Conv 3

Kahn, Ronnetta Bisman DrAP&F 83

Kahn, Samuel 1897-1981 ConAu 106

Kahn, Sanders A 1919- ConAu 89

Kahn, Sandra S 1942- ConAu 106

Kahn, Sholom J 1918- ConAu 102

Kahn, Si 1944- ConAu 33R

Kahn, Stephen 1940- ConAu 5R

Kahn, Steve ConAu X

Kahn, Sy M DrAP&F 83

Kahn, Sy M 1924- ConAu 10NR, –25R,
    WrDr 84

Kahn, Theodore C 1912- ConAu 33R

Kahn-Fogel, Daniel 1948- ConAu 97

Kahn-Freund, Otto 1900-1979 ConAu 108

Kahnweiler, Daniel-Henry 1884-1979 ConAu 29R,
    –85

Kahrl, George M 1904- ConAu 105

Kahrl, Stanley J 1931- ConAu 9R

Kahrl, William L 1946- ConAu 109

Kaid, Lynda Lee 1948- ConAu 89

Kaikini, P R 1912- ConAu 61, IntAu&W 82

Kaikkonen, Gus 1951- NatPD 81[port]

Kaiko, Takeshi 1930- ConAu 104

Kail, Owen Cooke 1922- IntAu&W 82

Kaim-Caudle, Peter 1916- WrDr 84

Kaim-Caudle, Peter Robert 1916- ConAu 21R,
    IntAu&W 82

Kain, Gylan DrAP&F 83

Kain, John F 1935- WrDr 84

Kain, John Forrest 1935- ConAu 29R

Kain, Malcolm ConAu X, IntAu&W 82X

Kain, Richard 1936- ConAu 37R, WrDr 84

Kain, Richard Morgan 1908- ConAu 2NR, –5R,
    WrDr 84

Kain, Saul ConAu X

Kains, Josephine ConAu X, WrDr 84

Kaipainen, Anu Helina 1933- IntAu&W 82

Kairys, Anatolijus 1914- ConAu 102

Kaisari, Uri 1899?-1979 ConAu 85

Kaiser, Artur 1943- ConAu 97

Kaiser, Bill ConAu X

Kaiser, Edward J 1935- ConAu 93

Kaiser, Edwin George 1893- ConAu 45

Kaiser, Ernest 1915- ConAu 1NR, –49,
    LivgBAA

Kaiser, Frances E 1922- ConAu 57

Kaiser, Georg 1878-1945 ClDMEL 80, CnMD,
    ConAu 106, EncWL 2[port], LongCTC,
    ModGL, ModWD, TwCA, TwCA SUP,
    TwCLC 9[port], WhoTwCL

Kaiser, Harvey H 1936- ConAu 81

Kaiser, Otto 1924- *ConAu 85*
Kaiser, Robert Blair 1930- *ConAu 9R*
Kaiser, Robert G 1943- *ConAu 65*
Kaiser, Walter 1931- *ConAu 37R*
Kaiser, Ward L 1923- *ConAu 53, WrDr 84*
Kaitz, Edward M 1928- *ConAu 29R*
Kakapo, Leilani 1939- *ConAu 9NR, -17R*
Kakar, Sudhir 1938- *ConAu 33R*
Kaki *ConAu X*
Kakimoto, Kozo 1915- *SmATA 11*
Kakonis, Thomas E 1930- *ConAu 57*
Kakonis, Tom E *ConAu X*
Kakugawa, Frances H 1936- *ConAu 77*
Kal *ConAu X*
Kalamaras, Vasso *IntWWP 82*
Kalamu *IntAu&W 82X*
Kalashnikoff, Nicholas 1888-1961 *ConAu 73, SmATA 16*
Kalb, Bernard 1932- *ASpks, ConAu 109*
Kalb, Jonah 1926- *ConAu 4NR, -53, SmATA 23*
Kalb, Marvin Leonard 1930- *ASpks, ConAu 5R*
Kalb, S William 1897- *ConAu 33R*
Kalberer, Augustine 1917- *ConAu 61*
Kalcheim, Lee 1938- *ConAu 85, ConDr 82, NatPD 81[port]*
Kaldestad, Per Olav 1947- *IntAu&W 82*
Kaldor, Mary 1946- *ConAu 93*
Kaldor, Nicholas 1908- *WrDr 84*
Kale, Arvind And Shanta *ConAu X*
Kaleb, Vjekoslav 1905- *ModSL 2*
Kalechofsky, Roberta *DrAP&F 83*
Kalechofsky, Roberta 1931- *ConAu 2NR, -49*
Kaledin, Eugenia 1929- *ConAu 109*
Kalem, Theodore Eustace 1919- *ConAmTC*
Kalemkerian, Zarouhi 1874?-1971 *ConAu 104*
Kalenik, Sandra 1945- *ConAu 73*
Kaler, James Otis 1848-1912 *SmATA 15*
Kales, Emily Fox 1944- *ConAu 21R*
Kaleta, Roman 1924- *IntAu&W 82*
Kalia, Mamta 1940- *IntWWP 82*
Kalich, Jacob 1891-1975 *ConAu 89*
Kalich, Robert 1947- *ConAu 106*
Kalichmam, Claire 1944- *IntAu&W 82*
Kalicki, Jan H 1948- *ConAu 65*
Kalijarvi, Thorsten V 1897-1980 *ConAu 97, ConAu P-1*
Kalin, Martin 1943- *ConAu 53*
Kalin, Robert 1921- *ConAu 8NR, -61, IntAu&W 82*
Kalin, Rudolf 1938- *ConAu 45*
Kalina, Sigmund 1911-1977 *ConAu 3NR, -49*
Kalins, Dorothy G 1942- *ConAu 25R*
Kalinsky, George 1936- *ConAu 2NR, -49*
Kalish, Betty McKelvey 1913- *ConAu 45*
Kalish, Donald 1919- *ConAu 9R*
Kalish, Richard A 1930- *ConAu 10NR*
Kalish, Richard Allan 1930- *ConAu 5R*
Kalisher, Simpson 1926- *ConAu 17R*
Kallas, Aino Julia Maria 1878-1956 *EncWL 2, TwCA, TwCA SUP*
Kallas, James 1928- *ConAu 10NR, -17R*
Kallaus, Norman F 1924- *ConAu 33R*
Kallberg, Sture *ConAu X*
Kallen, Horace Meyer 1882-1974 *ConAu 49, -93, TwCA SUP*
Kallen, Laurence 1944- *ConAu 41R*
Kallen, Lucille *ConAu 97*
Kallenbach, Joseph E 1903- *ConAu 77*
Kallenbach, W Warren 1926- *ConAu 9R*
Kallesser, Michael 1886?-1975 *ConAu 61*
Kallet, Arthur 1902-1972 *ConAu 33R*
Kallet, Marilyn *DrAP&F 83*
Kallet, Marilyn 1946- *ConAu 104*
Kallich, Martin *WrDr 84*
Kallich, Martin 1918- *ConAu 2NR, -5R, IntAu&W 82*
Kallifatides, Theodor 1938- *ConAu 85*
Kallir, Jane K 1954- *ConAu 109*
Kallir, Otto 1894-1978 *ConAu 49, -81*
Kallman, Chester Simon 1921-1975 *ConAu 3NR, -45, -53, ConLC 2*
Kallmann, Helmut 1922- *CreCan 2*
Kallmann, Helmut Max 1922- *ConAu 108*
Kallsen, T J *DrAP&F 83*
Kallsen, T J 1915- *ConAu 5R*
Kalman, Harold David 1943- *ConAu 103, IntAu&W 82, WrDr 84*
Kalme, Egils 1909- *ConAu 81, IntAu&W 82*
Kalmijn, Jo 1905- *ConAu P-2*
Kalmus, Ain *ConAu X*
Kalnay, Francis 1899- *ConAu 49, SmATA 7*

Kalnoky, Ingeborg L 1909- *ConAu 61*
Kalow, Gert 1921- *ConAu 29R*
Kalow, Gisela 1946- *ConAu 107, SmATA 32[port]*
Kalpakian, Laura *DrAP&F 83*
Kalpakian, Laura Anne 1945- *ConAu 81, IntAu&W 82*
Kals, W S 1910- *ConAu 45*
Kalstone, Shirlee A 1932- *ConAu 8NR, -61*
Kalt, Bryson R 1934- *ConAu 33R*
Kalt, Jeannette Chappell 1898?-1976 *ConAu 69*
Kaltenborn, Hans V 1878-1965 *ConAu 93*
Kalter, Bella Briansky *DrAP&F 83*
Kalter, Joanmarie 1951- *ConAu 102*
Kalu, Ogbu Uke 1944- *ConAu 93*
Kaluger, George 1921- *ConAu 29R*
Kaluger, Meriem Fair 1921- *ConAu 81*
Kalven, Harry, Jr. 1914-1974 *ConAu 53*
Kalyanaraman, Aiyaswamy 1903- *ConAu P-2*
Kamalakanto *IntWWP 82X*
Kamarck, Andrew M 1914- *ConAu 10NR, -21R*
Kamarck, Lawrence 1927- *ConAu 73*
Kamath, Madhav Vithal 1921- *ConAu 69*
Kamban, Guomundur Jonsson 1888-1945 *CIDMEL 80*
Kambanellis, Iakovos 1922- *EncWL 2*
Kambu, Joseph *ConAu X*
Kamen, Gloria 1923- *SmATA 9*
Kamen, Henry Arthur 1936- *ConAu 5R, -7NR, IntAu&W 82, WrDr 84*
Kamenetsky, Ihor 1927- *ConAu 1R, -4NR*
Kamenetz, Rodger *DrAP&F 83*
Kamenka, Eugene 1928- *ConAu 2NR, -5R, IntAu&W 82, WrDr 84*
Kamensky, Vasily Vasilyevich 1884-1961 *CIDMEL 80*
Kamerman, Sheila B 1928- *ConAu 10NR, -65*
Kamerman, Sylvia E *ConAu X*
Kamerschen, David R 1937- *ConAu 53*
Kamien, Marcia 1933- *ConAu 105*
Kamil, Alan C 1941- *ConAu 109*
Kamil, Jill 1930- *ConAu 7NR, -57*
Kamin, Franz *DrAP&F 83*
Kamin, Leon J 1927- *ConAu 103*
Kamin, Nick 1939- *ConAu X*
Kamins, Jeanette *ConAu 5R*
Kamins, Robert Martin 1918- *ConAu 105*
Kaminska, Ida 1899-1980 *ConAu 97*
Kaminski, Margaret 1944- *ConAu 8NR, -61, IntAu&W 82, MichAu 80*
Kaminsky, Alice R *ConAu 33R, IntAu&W 82, WrDr 84*
Kaminsky, Daniel *DrAP&F 83*
Kaminsky, Howard 1940- *ConAu 105*
Kaminsky, Jack 1922- *ConAu 21R, IntAu&W 82, WrDr 84*
Kaminsky, Marc *DrAP&F 83*
Kaminsky, Marc 1943- *ConAu 5NR, -53*
Kaminsky, Melvin *ConAu X*
Kaminsky, Peretz 1916- *ConAu 33R*
Kaminsky, Stuart M 1934- *ConAu 73*
Kaminsky, Susan Stanwood 1937- *ConAu 110*
Kamisar, Yale 1929- *ConAu 69*
Kamm, Dorinda 1952- *ConAu 37R, WrDr 84*
Kamm, Herbert 1917- *ConAu 69*
Kamm, Jacob Oswald 1918- *ConAu 5R, WrDr 84*
Kamm, Josephine 1905- *TwCCW 83*
Kamm, Josephine 1906- *WrDr 84*
Kamm, Josephine Mary 1905- *ConAu 5NR, -9R, SmATA 24[port]*
Kamm, Josephine Mary 1906- *IntAu&W 82*
Kamman, Madeleine M 1930- *ConAu 85*
Kamman, William 1930- *ConAu 25R*
Kammen, Michael 1936- *ConAu 25R, WrDr 84*
Kammerer, Gladys M 1909-1970 *ConAu 1R, -103*
Kammeyer, Kenneth C W 1931- *ConAu 29R*
Kampelman, Max M 1920- *ConAu 41R, IntAu&W 82*
Kampen, Irene Trepel 1922- *ConAu 1R, -1NR, IntAu&W 82*
Kampen, Michael Edwin 1939- *ConAu 110*
Kampf, Abraham 1920- *ConAu 21R*
Kampf, Avram *ConAu X*
Kampf, Louis 1929- *ConAu 33R, IntAu&W 82, WrDr 84*
Kampmann, Christian 1939- *CIDMEL 80, EncWL 2*
Kampov, Boris Nikolayevich 1908-1981 *ConAu 104, -108*
Kamrany, Nake M 1934- *ConAu 37R*
Kamstra, Leslie D 1920- *ConAu 69*

Kanahele, George Sanford 1930- *ConAu 102*
Kanar Al Hagag *IntWWP 82X*
Kanazawa, Masakata 1934- *ConAu 25R*
Kanazawa, Roger *ConAu X*
Kandaouroff, Berice 1912- *ConAu 33R*
Kandel, Denise Bystryn 1933- *ConAu 13R*
Kandel, I L 1881-1965 *ConAu 1R, -3NR*
Kandel, Lenore *WrDr 84*
Kandel, Lenore 1932- *ConP 80, DcLB 16[port]*
Kandell, Alice S 1938- *ConAu 33R, WrDr 84*
Kandinsky, Nina 1896?-1980 *ConAu 101*
Kando, Thomas M 1941- *ConAu 2NR, -49*
Kane, Basil G 1931- *ConAu 69*
Kane, Cheikh Hamidou 1928- *ModBlW, ModFrL*
Kane, Dennis Cornelius 1918- *ConAu 41R*
Kane, E B 1944- *ConAu 57*
Kane, Edward J 1935- *ConAu 41R*
Kane, Frank 1912-1968 *ConAu 5R, -25R, TwCCr&M 80*
Kane, Frank R 1925- *ConAu 77*
Kane, George 1916- *ConAu 103*
Kane, H Victor 1906- *ConAu 29R*
Kane, Hamidou 1928- *CIDMEL 80*
Kane, Harnett Thomas 1910- *TwCA SUP*
Kane, Henry 1918- *TwCCr&M 80, WrDr 84*
Kane, Henry Bugbee 1902-1971 *ConAu 73, SmATA 14*
Kane, J Herbert 1910- *ConAu 97*
Kane, Jack *ConAu X*
Kane, Jim *TwCWW, WrDr 84*
Kane, John Joseph 1909- *ConAu P-2*
Kane, Julia *ConAu X, TwCRGW, WrDr 84*
Kane, Julie *DrAP&F 83*
Kane, Julie 1952- *IntWWP 82*
Kane, Katherine *DrAP&F 83*
Kane, Robert S 1925- *ConAu 7NR, -9R*
Kane, Robert William 1910- *SmATA 18*
Kane, William Everett 1943- *ConAu 49*
Kane, Wilson *ConAu X*
Kaneko, Lonny *DrAP&F 83*
Kaneko, Lonny Minoru 1939- *IntWWP 82*
Kanellopoulos, Panayotis 1902- *IntAu&W 82*
Kanet, Roger E 1936- *ConAu 33R*
Kanfer, Allen 1905?-1983 *ConAu 110*
Kanfer, Frederick H 1925- *ConAu 41R*
Kanfer, Stefan 1933- *ConAu 103*
Kang, Shin T 1935- *ConAu 33R*
Kang, Younghill 1903-1972 *ConAu 37R, TwCA, TwCA SUP*
Kanik, Orhan Veli 1914-1950 *CIDMEL 80*
Kanin, Garson 1912- *AuNews 1, CnMD, ConAu 5R, -7NR, ConDr 82, ConLC 22[port], DcLB 7[port], IntAu&W 82, ModWD, NatPD 81[port], WorAu, WrDr 84*
Kanin, Michael 1910- *ConAu 61*
Kanin, Ruth 1920- *ConAu 107*
Kaniowska-Lewanska, Izabela Maria 1908- *IntAu&W 82*
Kanitz, Walter 1910- *ConAu 97*
Kaniuk, Yoram 1930?- *ConLC 19*
Kann, Robert A 1906-1981 *ConAu 105*
Kannappan, Subbiah 1927- *ConAu 93*
Kanner, Leo 1894-1981 *ConAu 103, -17R*
Kanof, Abram 1903- *ConAu 29R*
Kanovsky, Eliyahu 1922- *ConAu 33R*
Kansil, Joli 1943- *ConAu 81*
Kantakarjuna *IntAu&W 82X*
Kantar, Edwin B 1932- *ConAu 41R*
Kanter, Arnold 1945- *ConAu 89*
Kanter, Hal 1918- *ConAu 81*
Kanter, Rosabeth Moss 1943- *ConAu 77*
Kanto, Peter *WrDr 84*
Kantonen, T A 1900- *ConAu 33R, WrDr 84*
Kantonen, Taito Almar 1900- *IntAu&W 82*
Kantor, Hal 1924- *ConAu 77*
Kantor, Harry 1911- *ConAu 1R, -2NR, WrDr 84*
Kantor, Herman I 1909- *ConAu 57*
Kantor, James 1927-1974 *ConAu P-2*
Kantor, MacKinlay 1904-1977 *ASpks, ConAmA, ConAu 61, -73, ConLC 7, ConSFA, DcLB 9[port], ModAL, TwCA, TwCA SUP, TwCWW, TwCWr*
Kantor, Marvin 1934- *ConAu 2NR, -49*
Kantor, Seth 1926- *ConAu 81*
Kantor-Berg, Friedrich 1908-1979 *ConAu 89*
Kantrowitz, Arnie 1940- *ConAu 77*
Kantrowitz, Joanne Spencer 1931- *ConAu 81*
Kantzer, Kenneth S 1917- *ConAu 106*

Kasper, Sydney H 1911- *ConAu 1R*
Kasperson, Roger E 1938- *ConAu 29R,*
WrDr 84
Kasprowicz, Jan 1860-1926 *CIDMEL 80,*
ModSL 2, ModWD, TwCWr
Kasrils, Ronald 1938- *ConAu 29R*
Kass, Jerome 1923?-1973 *ConAu 104*
Kass, Jerome 1937- *ConAu 57, NatPD 81[port]*
Kass, Norman 1934- *ConAu 29R*
Kassak, Lajos 1887-1967 *CIDMEL 80,*
EncWL 2, WhoTwCL
Kassalow, Everett M 1918- *ConAu 45*
Kassebaum, Gene G 1929- *ConAu 17R*
Kassil, Lev 1905- *TwCWr*
Kassin, Michael 1947- *NatPD 81[port]*
Kassner, Rudolf 1873-1959 *ModGL*
Kassof, Allen 1930- *ConAu 21R*
Kasson, John Franklin 1944- *ConAu 81*
Kassorla, Irene Chamie 1931- *ConAu 110*
Kast, Fremont E 1926- *ConAu 21R*
Kastan, David Scott 1946- *ConAu 109*
Kastein, Shulamith 1903- *ConAu 105*
Kastein, Shulamith 1903-1983 *ConAu 110*
Kastel, Daisylea Carl 1919- *IntWWP 82*
Kastel, Dee *IntWWP 82X*
Kastelan, Jure 1919- *CIDMEL 80, ModSL 2*
Kastenbaum, Robert 1932- *ConAu 9NR, -13R*
Kaster, Joseph 1912- *ConAu P-1*
Kastl, Albert J 1939- *ConAu 57*
Kastl, Lena 1942- *ConAu 61*
Kastle, Herbert D 1924- *ConAu 1R, -1NR,*
ConSFA
Kastner, Erich 1899-1974 *ChlLR 4[port],*
CIDMEL 80, CnMD, EncWL 2, ModGL,
ModWD, SmATA 14, WorAu
Kastner, Jonathan 1937- *ConAu 25R*
Kastner, Joseph 1907- *ConAu 85, WrDr 84*
Kastner, Marianna 1940- *ConAu 25R*
Kasuya, Masahiro 1937- *ConAu 110*
Kaszner, Kurt *ConAu X*
Kaszubski, Marek 1951- *ConAu 105*
Kataev, Valentin Petrovich 1897- *CnMD,*
EncWL 2, ModWD, TwCA, TwCA SUP
Katayev, Valentin Petrovich 1897- *CIDMEL 80,*
ModSL 1, TwCWr
Katcha, Vahe *ConAu X*
Katchadourian, Herant A 1933- *ConAu 103*
Katchadourian, Vahe 1928- *ConAu 29R*
Katchen, Carole 1944- *ConAu 61, SmATA 9*
Katchmer, George Andrew 1916- *ConAu 1R,*
WrDr 84
Kateb, Yacine 1929- *EncWL 2*
Katen, Thomas Ellis 1931- *ConAu 53*
Kates, James *DrAP&F 83*
Kates, Robert W 1929- *ConAu 8NR, -17R*
Kathleen *SmATA X*
Kathman, Michael D 1943- *ConAu 109*
Kathryn *ConAu X, SmATA X*
Kati *ConAu X*
Katicic, Radoslav 1930- *ConAu 37R*
Katkov, Norman 1918- *ConAu 13R*
Kato, Shuichi 1919- *ConAu 37R, IntAu&W 82,*
WrDr 84
Katona, Edita 1913- *ConAu 69*
Katona, George 1901-1981 *ConAu 104*
Katona, Robert 1949- *SmATA 21[port]*
Katope, Christopher G 1918- *ConAu 21R*
Katsarakis, Joan Harries *ConAu X*
Katsaros, Thomas 1926- *ConAu 5R, -8NR*
Katsh, Abraham I 1908- *ConAu 5R, -8NR*
Katsh, Salem M 1948- *ConAu 110*
Kattan, Naim 1928- *ConAu 11NR, -69*
Katterjohn, Arthur D 1930?-1980 *ConAu 93*
Katz, Abraham 1926- *ConAu 49*
Katz, Albert M 1938- *ConAu 93*
Katz, Alfred *ConAu X*
Katz, Alfred 1938- *ConAu 77*
Katz, Basho *ConAu X*
Katz, Bobbi 1933- *ConAu 37R, SmATA 12,*
WrDr 84
Katz, Daniel 1903- *ConAu 41R*
Katz, David M 1948- *IntWWP 82*
Katz, Elia *DrAP&F 83*
Katz, Elias 1912- *ConAu 29R*
Katz, Ellis 1938- *ConAu 29R*
Katz, Ephraim 1932- *WrDr 84*
Katz, Eve 1938- *ConAu 1NR, -45*
Katz, Fred 1938- *ConAu 49, SmATA 6*
Katz, Fred E 1927- *ConAu 77*
Katz, Gloria 1945?- *ConAu 107*
Katz, H W 1906- *TwCA*

Katz, Herbert Melvin 1930- *ConAu 103*
Katz, Irving I 1907- *ConAu 1R*
Katz, Jacob 1904- *ConAu 1R, -4NR*
Katz, Jane 1934- *SmATA 33[port]*
Katz, Jane B 1934- *ConAu 85*
Katz, John Stuart 1938- *ConAu 37R*
Katz, Jonathan *DrAP&F 83*
Katz, Jonathan 1938- *ConAu 85*
Katz, Josef 1918- *ConAu 53*
Katz, Joseph 1910- *ConAu 1R, -2NR*
Katz, Judith Milstein 1943- *ConAu 106*
Katz, Leandro *DrAP&F 83*
Katz, Leon 1919- *ConAu 4NR, -49*
Katz, Leonard 1926- *ConAu 21R*
Katz, Marjorie P *ConAu X, SmATA X*
Katz, Martin 1929- *ConAu 21R, WrDr 84*
Katz, Marvin C 1930- *ConAu 25R*
Katz, Menke *DrAP&F 83*
Katz, Menke 1906- *ConAu 11NR, -13R,*
IntAu&W 82, WrDr 84
Katz, Michael B 1939- *ConAu 33R*
Katz, Michael Ray 1944- *ConAu 102, WrDr 84*
Katz, Mickey *ConAu X*
Katz, Milton 1907- *ConAu P-1*
Katz, Mort 1925- *ConAu 11NR, -61*
Katz, Myron Meyer 1909- *ConAu 81*
Katz, Pierre 1941- *IntAu&W 82*
Katz, Robert 1933- *ConAu 11NR, -25R*
Katz, Robert L 1917- *ConAu 9R*
Katz, Samuel 1914- *ConAu 25R*
Katz, Sanford N 1933- *ConAu 33R, WrDr 84*
Katz, Saul Milton 1915- *IntAu&W 82*
Katz, Stanley Nider 1934- *ConAu 9R*
Katz, Steve *DrAP&F 83*
Katz, Steve 1935- *ConAu 25R,*
DcLB Y83B[port]
Katz, Susan 1944?-1982 *ConAu 107*
Katz, Susan A *DrAP&F 83*
Katz, Susan A 1919- *IntWWP 82*
Katz, William 1940- *ConAu 85*
Katz, William A 1924- *ConAu 10NR, -25R*
Katz, William Loren 1927- *ConAu 9NR, -21R,*
SmATA 13, WrDr 84
Katzander, Howard L 1911?-1983 *ConAu 110*
Katzenbach, Maria 1953- *ConAu 77*
Katzenbach, William E 1904-1975 *ConAu 61*
Katzenstein, Mary Fainsod 1945- *ConAu 93*
Katzenstein, Peter J 1945- *ConAu 93*
Katzin, Olga *LongCTC*
Katzman, Allen *DrAP&F 83*
Katzman, Allen 1937- *ConAu 29R,*
IntWWP 82, WrDr 84
Katzman, Anita 1920- *ConAu 57*
Katzman, David Manners 1941- *ConAu 5NR,*
-53
Katznelson-Shazar, Rachel 1888-1975 *ConAu 61*
Katzner, Kenneth 1930- *ConAu 5R*
Kauder, Emil 1901- *ConAu 17R*
Kaufelt, David A *DrAP&F 83*
Kaufelt, David A 1939- *WrDr 84*
Kaufelt, David Allan 1939- *ConAu 1NR, -45*
Kauffeld, Carl F 1911-1974 *ConAu 49*
Kauffman, Christmas Carol Miller 1902-
ConAu 1R
Kauffman, Christopher J 1936- *ConAu 107*
Kauffman, Donald T 1920- *ConAu 11NR, -25R*
Kauffman, Dorotha S 1925- *ConAu 17R*
Kauffman, Draper L 1946- *ConAu 108*
Kauffman, George B 1930- *ConAu 17R*
Kauffman, Henry J 1908- *ConAu 13R*
Kauffman, James M 1940- *ConAu 7NR, -57*
Kauffman, Janet *DrAP&F 83*
Kauffman, Joseph F 1921- *ConAu 1NR, -45*
Kauffman, Milo 1889- *ConAu 89*
Kauffmann, Georg 1925- *ConAu 49*
Kauffmann, Lane *DrAP&F 83*
Kauffmann, Lane 1921- *ConAu 17R*
Kauffmann, Samuel Hay 1898-1971 *ConAu 89*
Kauffmann, Stanley 1916- *ConAmTC,*
ConAu 5R, -6NR, LongCTC, WorAu,
WrDr 84
Kaufman, Arnold S 1927- *ConAu 25R*
Kaufman, Arthur 1934- *ConAu 107*
Kaufman, Barry Neil 1942- *ConAu 97*
Kaufman, Bel *ConAu 13R, DrAP&F 83,*
IntAu&W 82, WrDr 84
Kaufman, Bob *DrAP&F 83*
Kaufman, Bob 1925- *ConAu 41R,*
DcLB 16[port], LivgBAA
Kaufman, Burton I 1940- *ConAu 33R*
Kaufman, Daniel 1949- *ConAu 85*
Kaufman, Debra Renee 1941- *ConAu 109*

Kaufman, Donald D 1933- *ConAu 29R*
Kaufman, Edmund George 1891- *ConAu 73*
Kaufman, George S 1889-1961 *ConAu 108*
Kaufman, George Simon 1889-1961 *CnMD,*
ConAmA, ConAu 93, DcLB 7[port],
LongCTC, ModWD, TwCA, TwCA SUP,
TwCWr
Kaufman, Gerald 1930- *WrDr 84*
Kaufman, Gerald Bernard 1930- *ConAu 21R,*
IntAu&W 82
Kaufman, Gordon Dester 1925- *ConAu 7NR,*
-13R
Kaufman, H G 1939- *ConAu 69*
Kaufman, I 1892-1978 *ConAu 77*
Kaufman, Irving 1920- *ConAu 21R*
Kaufman, Jacob J 1914- *ConAu 41R*
Kaufman, Joe 1911- *ConAu 107, SmATA 33*
Kaufman, Lenard 1913- *TwCA SUP*
Kaufman, Lloyd 1927- *ConAu 93*
Kaufman, Martin 1940- *ConAu 109*
Kaufman, Max *IntWWP 82X*
Kaufman, Mervyn D 1932- *ConAu 5R,*
SmATA 4
Kaufman, Morris 1919- *IntAu&W 82, WrDr 84*
Kaufman, Paul 1886-1979 *ConAu 89*
Kaufman, Robert 1931- *ConAu 17R*
Kaufman, Roger 1932- *ConAu 9NR, -53*
Kaufman, Rosamond V P 1923- *ConAu 7NR,*
-9R
Kaufman, Sherwin A 1920- *ConAu 10NR, -25R*
Kaufman, Shirley *DrAP&F 83*
Kaufman, Shirley 1923- *ConAu 49,*
IntAu&W 82, IntWWP 82
Kaufman, Sidney 1910-1983 *ConAu 110*
Kaufman, Sue 1926- *ConAu X, ConLC 3, -8*
Kaufman, Wallace 1939- *ConAu 10NR, -25R*
Kaufman, William I 1922- *ConAu 7NR, -13R*
Kaufman, Wolfe 1905?-1970 *ConAu 29R*
Kaufmann, Angelika 1935- *SmATA 15*
Kaufmann, Harry 1927- *ConAu 45*
Kaufmann, Helen L 1887- *ConAu 5R, -7NR*
Kaufmann, Henry William 1913- *ConAu 41R*
Kaufmann, John 1931- *ConAu 81, SmATA 18*
Kaufmann, Juliet Yli-Mattila *DrAP&F 83*
Kaufmann, Myron 1921- *ConAu 25R, WrDr 84*
Kaufmann, R James 1924- *ConAu 13R*
Kaufmann, U Milo 1934- *ConAu 41R*
Kaufmann, Ulrich George 1920- *ConAu 21R*
Kaufmann, Walter 1921-1980 *ConAu 1R, -1NR,*
-101, DcLEL 1940, IntAu&W 82,
IntWWP 82
Kaufmann, Walter 1933- *ConAu 61*
Kaufmann, William J 1942- *WrDr 84*
Kaufmann, William J, III 1942- *ConAu 93*
Kaufmann, William W 1918- *ConAu 13R*
Kaul, Donald 1934- *ConAu 65*
Kaul, Friedrich Karl 1906- *IntAu&W 82*
Kaul, Hari Kirshen 1941- *IntAu&W 82*
Kaula, Edna Mason 1906- *ConAu 5R,*
SmATA 13
Kaumeyer, Dorothy 1914- *ConAu 105*
Kauper, Paul Gerhardt 1907-1974 *ConAu 1R,*
-6NR, -49
Kauppinen, Eino Ilmari 1910- *IntAu&W 82*
Kaur, Sardarni Premka 1943- *ConAu 77*
Kausler, Donald H 1927- *ConAu 17R*
Kauter, Kurt 1913- *IntAu&W 82*
Kauth, Benjamin 1914- *ConAu 5R*
Kauvar, Gerald B 1938- *ConAu 45*
Kavadlo, Edith S 1917- *IntWWP 82*
Kavafis, Konstantinos 1863-1933 *ConAu 104,*
TwCA SUP, WhoTwCL
Kavaler, Lucy 1930- *ConAu 7NR, -57,*
SmATA 23[port]
Kavaler, Rebecca *DrAP&F 83*
Kavaler, Rebecca 1932- *ConAu 89*
Kavan, Anna 1901-1968 *ConAu X, -6NR,*
TwCSFW
Kavan, Anna 1904-1968 *ConLC 5, -13,*
WorAu 1970
Kavanagh, P J 1931- *ConAu 81, ConP 80,*
IntAu&W 82, WrDr 84
Kavanagh, Patrick 1904-1967 *ConP 80A,*
DcLB 15[port], EncWL 2
Kavanagh, Patrick 1905?-1967 *ConLC 22[port],*
LongCTC, ModBrL SUP, RGFMBP,
TwCWr, WhoTwCL, WorAu
Kavanagh, Patrick 1906-1967 *ConAu 25R*
Kavanagh, Patrick Joseph 1931- *DcLEL 1940*
Kavanagh, Paul *TwCCr&M 80, WrDr 84*
Kavanaugh, Cynthia *ConAu X, WrDr 84*
Kavanaugh, James 1932- *WrDr 84*

Kelly, David M 1938- ConAu 29R, MichAu 80
Kelly, Edward H 1930- ConAu 37R
Kelly, Eleanor Mercein 1880-1968 TwCA,
   TwCA SUP
Kelly, Emmett 1898-1979 ConAu 85
Kelly, Eric 1884-1960 TwCCW 83
Kelly, Eric Philbrook 1884-1960 ConAu 93
Kelly, Ernece Beverly LivgBAA
Kelly, Faye L 1914- ConAu 21R
Kelly, Francis R 1927- IntAu&W 82
Kelly, Frank K 1914- ConAu 1R, -1NR
Kelly, Frederic Joseph 1922- ConAu 53
Kelly, Gail P 1940- ConAu 81
Kelly, Gary F 1943- ConAu 89
Kelly, Georga A 1916- ConAu 11NR
Kelly, George Anthony 1916- ConAu 17R
Kelly, George Edward 1887-1974? AuNews 1,
   CnMD, ConAmA, ConAu 49,
   DcLB 7[port], LongCTC, ModAL,
   ModWD, TwCA, TwCA SUP
Kelly, George V 1919- ConAu 93
Kelly, George W 1894- ConAu 9NR, -65
Kelly, Gerald R 1930- ConAu 29R
Kelly, Grace 1929-1982 ConAu 107
Kelly, Guy ConAu X
Kelly, Gwen Nita 1922- IntAu&W 82
Kelly, Henry Ansgar 1934- ConAu 25R,
   IntAu&W 82
Kelly, James B 1905- ConAu 49
Kelly, James Fitzmaurice- TwCA, TwCA SUP
Kelly, James Plunkett 1920- ConAu 53,
   IntAu&W 82
Kelly, Joan 1928?-1982 ConAu 107
Kelly, Joan Berlin 1939- ConAu 107
Kelly, John 1921- ConAu 73
Kelly, John M, Jr. 1919- ConAu 13R
Kelly, John N D 1909- ConAu 5R, -5NR
Kelly, John Rivard 1939- ConAu 103
Kelly, Joyce 1933- ConAu 106
Kelly, Karen 1935- ConAu 101
Kelly, Kathleen Sheridan White 1945- ConAu 49
Kelly, Kevin 1934- ConAmTC
Kelly, L G 1935- ConAu 107
Kelly, Laurence 1933- ConAu 81
Kelly, Lawrence C 1932- ConAu 8NR, -21R
Kelly, Leo J 1925- ConAu 41R
Kelly, Linda 1936- ConAu 103, WrDr 84
Kelly, Louis Gerard 1935- WrDr 84
Kelly, M T 1947- ConAu 97
Kelly, Mahlon 1939- ConAu 53
Kelly, Marguerite 1932- ConAu 65
Kelly, Marie-Noele 1907- WrDr 84
Kelly, Martha Rose 1914- ConAu 69
Kelly, Marty ConAu X
Kelly, Mary 1927- TwCCr&M 80, WrDr 84
Kelly, Mary Theresa Coolican 1927- ConAu 1R,
   -2NR
Kelly, Maurice 1919- WrDr 84
Kelly, Maurice Anthony 1931- ConAu 53
Kelly, Maurice Nugent 1919- ConAu 21R
Kelly, Nora Hickson 1910- ConAu 101,
   WrDr 84
Kelly, Patrick ConAu X
Kelly, Pauline Agnes 1936- ConAu 45
Kelly, Philip John 1896-1972 ConAu 5R, -37R
Kelly, Ralph ConAu X, SmATA X
Kelly, Ray ConAu X
Kelly, Regina Z 1898- ConAu 1R, -2NR,
   SmATA 5
Kelly, Richard DrAP&F 83
Kelly, Richard 1937- ConAu 107, WrDr 84
Kelly, Richard J 1938- ConAu 41R
Kelly, Rita Mae 1939- ConAu 81
Kelly, Robert DrAP&F 83
Kelly, Robert 1935- ConAu 17R, ConP 80,
   ConSFA, CroCAP, DcLB 5[port],
   WrDr 84
Kelly, Robert Glynn 1920- ConAu 1R
Kelly, Ron 1929- CreCan 2
Kelly, Rosalie ConAu 11NR, -61
Kelly, Stan ConAu X
Kelly, Stephen E 1919-1978 ConAu 104, -110
Kelly, Sylvia DrAP&F 83
Kelly, Thomas 1909- ConAu P-1, WrDr 84
Kelly, Thomas 1929- ConAu 109
Kelly, Tim 1935- ConAu 13R
Kelly, Tim 1937- IntAu&W 82,
   NatPD 81[port], WrDr 84
Kelly, Walt 1913-1973 ConAu 45, -73,
   SmATA 18
Kelly, William Leo 1924- ConAu 13R
Kelly, William W 1928- ConAu 9R

Kelly-Bootle, Stan 1929- ConAu 110
Kelly-Gadol, Joan 1928- ConAu 61
Kelman, Charles D 1930- ConAu 110
Kelman, Herbert Chanoch 1927- ConAu 13R,
   WrDr 84
Kelman, Mark 1951- ConAu 93
Kelman, Steven 1948- ConAu 29R
Kelsey, Alice Geer 1896- ConAu 5R, SmATA 1,
   WrDr 84
Kelsey, Joan Marshall 1907- ConAu 5R
Kelsey, Morton T 1917- ConAu 10NR, -21R,
   WrDr 84
Kelsey, Robert J 1927- ConAu 103
Kelso, Louis O 1913- ConAu 25R
Kelson, Allen H 1940- ConAu 77
Keltner, John W 1918- ConAu 29R
Kelton, Elmer 1926- AuNews 1, ConAu 21R,
   FifWWr, TwCWW, WrDr 84
Kelway, Christine WrDr 84
Kemal, Yasar 1922- EncWL 2[port],
   WhoTwCL
Kemal, Yashar 1922- CIDMEL 80, ConLC 14,
   TwCWr, WorAu
Kemal, Yashar 1923- ConAu 89
Kemal Tahir 1910-1973 CIDMEL 80
Kemble, James ConAu P-2
Kemelman, Harry 1908- ASpks, AuNews 1,
   ConAu 6NR, -9R, ConLC 2, DcLEL 1940,
   IntAu&W 82, TwCCr&M 80, WorAu 1970,
   WrDr 84
Kemeny, John G 1926- ConAu 33R,
   IntAu&W 82, WrDr 84
Kemeny, Peter 1938-1975 ConAu 53, -89
Kemerer, Frank R 1940- ConAu 10NR, -65
Kemmerer, Donald Lorenzo 1905- ConAu 1R
Kemmett, William DrAP&F 83
Kemp, Anthony 1939- ConAu 105
Kemp, Arnold LivgBAA
Kemp, Arnold 1938- ConAu 110
Kemp, Bernard Peter 1942- ConAu 107
Kemp, Betty 1916- ConAu 9R, IntAu&W 82,
   WrDr 84
Kemp, Charles F 1912- ConAu 5NR, -9R,
   WrDr 84
Kemp, Diana Moyle 1919- ConAu P-1
Kemp, Edward C 1929- ConAu 81
Kemp, Gene 1926- ConAu 69, IntAu&W 82,
   SmATA 25[port], TwCCW 83, WrDr 84
Kemp, Jack 1935- ConAu 109
Kemp, Jerrold E 1921- ConAu 77
Kemp, John C 1942- ConAu 93
Kemp, Lysander 1920- ConAu 1NR, -45
Kemp, Martin 1942- ConAu 108
Kemp, Patricia Anne 1944- IntWWP 82
Kemp, Patrick S 1932- ConAu 53
Kemp, Penny 1944- IntWWP 82X
Kemp, Peter 1942- WrDr 84
Kemp, Peter Mant Macintyre 1915- ConAu 25R
Kemp, Robert 1908-1967 ConAu P-1
Kemp, Roy Z 1910- ConAu 9R
Kemp, Sarah WrDr 84
Kemp, Tom 1921- ConAu 25R
Kemper, Donald J 1929- ConAu 21R, WrDr 84
Kemper, Inez 1906- ConAu P-1
Kemper, Rachel H 1931- ConAu 102
Kemper, Robert V 1945- ConAu 104
Kemperman, Steve 1955- ConAu 108
Kempf, Josef 1935- IntAu&W 82
Kempfer, Lester Leroy 1932- ConAu 49
Kempher, Ruth Moon 1934- ConAu 25R
Kempner, Mary Jean 1913-1969 ConAu P-2,
   SmATA 10
Kempner, Robert Max Wasilii 1899-
   IntAu&W 82
Kempner, S Marshall 1898- ConAu 85
Kempster, Mary Yates 1911- ConAu P-1
Kempster, Norman 1936- ConAu 77
Kempter, Lothar 1900- IntAu&W 82
Kempton, James Murray, Jr. 1945?-1971
   ConAu 33R
Kempton, Jean Goldschmidt 1946?-1971
   ConAu 33R
Kempton, Jean Welch 1914- ConAu 49,
   SmATA 10
Kempton, Murray 1918- ConAu 97, WorAu
Kempton, Richard 1935- ConAu 106
Kemsley, Viscount ConAu X
Kemsley, William George, Jr. 1928- ConAu 85
Kenan, Amos 1927- CnMD SUP
Kendal, Wallis 1937- ConAu 107
Kendall, Alice B 1919- IntWWP 82
Kendall, Aubyn 1919- ConAu 107, WrDr 84

Kendall, Carol 1917- ConAu 5R, -7NR,
   IntAu&W 82, SmATA 11, TwCCW 83,
   WrDr 84
Kendall, David Evan 1944- ConAu 29R
Kendall, Dorothy Steinbomer 1912- ConAu 57
Kendall, E Lorna 1921- ConAu 5R
Kendall, Elaine 1929- ConAu 17R
Kendall, Elizabeth Ann Fenella 1939-
   IntAu&W 82
Kendall, Elizabeth B 1947- ConAu 81
Kendall, Henry Madison 1901-1966 ConAu 5R
Kendall, Kenneth E 1913- ConAu 45
Kendall, Lace ConAu X, SmATA 3, WrDr 84
Kendall, Lyle H, Jr. 1919- ConAu 17R
Kendall, Maurice 1907-1983 ConAu 109
Kendall, Maurice George 1907- IntAu&W 82
Kendall, Paul Murray 1911-1973 ConAu P-1
Kendall, R T 1935- ConAu 93
Kendall, Robert 1934- ConAu 6NR, -13R
Kendall, T Robert 1935- ConAu 69
Kendall, Willmoore 1909-1967 ConAu 5R, -6NR
Kende, Sandor 1918- IntAu&W 82
Kenderdine, Augustus Frederick Lafosse 1870-1947
   CreCan 2
Kendig, Diane DrAP&F 83
Kendle, John Edward 1937- ConAu 61
Kendler, Helene Phyllis 1950- IntAu&W 82
Kendler, Howard H 1919- ConAu 17R
Kendrake, Carleton ConAu X
Kendrick, Baynard H 1894-1977 ConAu 1R,
   -4NR, -69, TwCCr&M 80, WorAu
Kendrick, David Andrew 1937- ConAu 9NR,
   -21R
Kendrick, Dolores DrAP&F 83
Kendrick, Frank J 1928- ConAu 41R
Kendrick, John W 1917- ConAu 110
Kendrick, Thomas Downing 1895- ConAu 81
Kendricks, James ConAu X, WrDr 84
Kendris, Christopher 1923- ConAu 5R, -7NR
Keneally, Thomas 1935- ASpks, ConAu 10NR,
   -85, ConLC 5, -8, -10, -14, -19, -27[port],
   ConNov 82, DcLEL 1940, ModCmwL,
   WorAu 1970, WrDr 84
Kenealy, James P 1927- ConAu 93, SmATA 29
Kenealy, Jim ConAu X, SmATA X
Kenelly, John W 1935- ConAu 25R
Kenen, Isaiah Leo 1905- ConAu 107
Kenen, Peter B 1932- ConAu 5R, -7NR
Kenez, Peter 1937- ConAu 29R
Kenian, Paul Roger ConAu X
Kenin, Richard M 1947- WrDr 84
Keniston, Kenneth 1930- ConAu 25R
Kenkel, William 1925- ConAu 61, WrDr 84
Kenmuir, Dale 1945- IntAu&W 82
Kenna, Peter 1930- ConAu 61, ConDr 82,
   WrDr 84
Kennamer, Lorrin, Jr. 1924- ConAu 5R, -6NR
Kennan, George 1904- WrDr 84
Kennan, George Frost 1904- ConAu 1R, -2NR,
   DcLEL 1940, WorAu
Kennan, Kent Wheeler 1913- ConAu 1R,
   WrDr 84
Kennard-Davis, Arthur 1910- ConAu P-1
Kennaway, James 1928-1968 ConAu 103, -89,
   ConSFA, WorAu
Kennebeck, Edwin 1924- ConAu 41R
Kennebeck, Paul 1943- ConAu 53
Kennecott, G J ConAu X
Kennedy, Adam AuNews 1, ConAu 107
Kennedy, Adrienne 1931- ConAu 103,
   ConDr 82, CroCD, LivgBAA, WorAu 1970,
   WrDr 84
Kennedy, Andrew 1931- ConAu 61
Kennedy, Bruce M 1929- ConAu 57
Kennedy, Carol 1905- ConAu 105
Kennedy, Charles Rann 1871-1950 LongCTC,
   TwCA, TwCA SUP
Kennedy, Cody, Jr. TwCWW
Kennedy, D James 1930- ConAu 61
Kennedy, David Michael 1941- ConAu 29R,
   IntAu&W 82, WrDr 84
Kennedy, Don H 1911- ConAu 61
Kennedy, Eddie C 1910- ConAu 89
Kennedy, Edward Moore 1932- ConAu 110
Kennedy, Edward R 1923?-1975 ConAu 104
Kennedy, Elliot ConAu X
Kennedy, Eugene C 1928- ConAu 25R
Kennedy, Florynce R 1916- LivgBAA
Kennedy, Gail 1900-1972 ConAu 33R
Kennedy, Gavin 1940- ConAu 9NR, -61,
   IntAu&W 82, WrDr 84
Kennedy, George 1899?-1977 ConAu 73

Kennedy, George 1928- *ConAu 2NR, –5R*
Kennedy, Gerald 1907- *ConAu 5R, –6NR, WrDr 84*
Kennedy, Hubert 1931- *ConAu 93*
Kennedy, J Hardee 1915- *ConAu 13R*
Kennedy, James G 1932- *ConAu 81*
Kennedy, James William 1905- *ConAu 1R, –1NR*
Kennedy, James Y 1916- *ConAu 77*
Kennedy, John Fitzgerald 1917-1963 *ConAu 1R, –1NR, SmATA 11*
Kennedy, John J 1914- *ConAu 57*
Kennedy, John Leo 1907- *CreCan 1*
Kennedy, Joseph 1923- *IntAu&W 82, WrDr 84*
Kennedy, Joseph 1929- *ConAu 1R, –4NR, ConLC 8, DcLEL 1940, IntWWP 82, SmATA 14*
Kennedy, Judith M 1935- *ConAu 41R*
Kennedy, Kathleen 1947?-1975 *ConAu 57*
Kennedy, Kenneth A R 1930- *ConAu 1NR, –45, IntAu&W 82*
Kennedy, Kieran A 1935- *ConAu 37R, IntAu&W 82, WrDr 84*
Kennedy, L D 1924- *ConAu 45*
Kennedy, Lena *ConAu X*
Kennedy, Leo 1907- *CreCan 1*
Kennedy, Leonard Anthony 1922- *ConAu 37R*
Kennedy, Leonard M 1925- *ConAu 73*
Kennedy, Ludovic 1919- *WrDr 84*
Kennedy, Ludovic Henry Coverley 1919- *ConAu 65*
Kennedy, Malcolm Duncan 1895- *ConAu 9R, WrDr 84*
Kennedy, Margaret 1896-1967 *ConAu 25R, LongCTC, ModBrL, ModWD, TwCA, TwCA SUP, TwCRGW, TwCWr*
Kennedy, Marilyn Moats 1943- *ConAu 109*
Kennedy, Mary *ConAu 102*
Kennedy, Michael 1926- *ConAu 5NR, –13R, IntAu&W 82, WrDr 84*
Kennedy, Milward 1894-1968 *TwCCr&M 80*
Kennedy, Paul E 1929- *SmATA 33*
Kennedy, Paul Michael 1945- *ConAu 9NR, –65, WrDr 84*
Kennedy, Peter 1943- *WrDr 84*
Kennedy, Ralph Dale 1897-1965 *ConAu 1R*
Kennedy, Raymond *DrAP&F 83*
Kennedy, Raymond A 1934- *ConAu 5R*
Kennedy, Richard 1910- *ConAu 102*
Kennedy, Richard 1932- *ConAu 7NR, –57, SmATA 22, TwCCW 83*
Kennedy, Richard S 1920- *ConAu 3NR, –5R*
Kennedy, Robert E, Jr. 1937- *ConAu 37R*
Kennedy, Robert F, Jr. 1954- *ConAu 110*
Kennedy, Robert Francis 1925-1968 *ConAu 1R, –1NR*
Kennedy, Robert Lee 1930- *ConAu 57*
Kennedy, Robert Woods 1911- *ConAu 49*
Kennedy, Rose 1890- *ConAu 53*
Kennedy, Sighle Aileen 1919- *ConAu 53*
Kennedy, Stetson *ConAu 5R*
Kennedy, Susan Estabrook 1942- *ConAu 45*
Kennedy, T F 1921- *ConAu 53*
Kennedy, Ted *ConAu X*
Kennedy, Theodore Reginald 1936- *ConAu 105*
Kennedy, William *DrAP&F 83*
Kennedy, William 1928- *ConAu 85, ConLC 6*
Kennedy, X J *DrAP&F 83*
Kennedy, X J 1929- *ConAu X, ConLC 8, ConP 80, DcLB 5, DcLEL 1940, IntAu&W 82, IntWWP 82X, SmATA X, WorAu, WrDr 84*
Kennedy-Martin, Ian 1936- *ConAu 101*
Kenneggy, Richard *ConAu X, WrDr 84*
Kennel, LeRoy E 1930- *ConAu 77*
Kennell, Ruth Epperson 1893-1977 *ConAu P-2, SmATA 25N, –6*
Kennelly, Brendan 1936- *ConAu 5NR, –9R, ConP 80, DcLEL 1940, IntAu&W 82, IntWWP 82, WrDr 84*
Kennelly, Tamara *DrAP&F 83*
Kenner, Charles Leroy 1933- *ConAu 25R*
Kenner, Hugh 1923- *ConAu 21R, ConLCrt 82, WorAu, WrDr 84*
Kenner, William Hugh 1923- *DcLEL 1940*
Kennerly, David Hume 1947- *AuNews 2, ConAu 101*
Kennerly, Karen 1940- *ConAu 33R*
Kennet, Baron Wayland Hilton Young 1923- *IntAu&W 82*
Kenneth, Mister *ConAu X*
Kennett, Jiyu 1924- *ConAu 93*
Kennett, Lee 1931- *ConAu 21R*

Kennett, Peggy Teresa Nancy *ConAu X*
Kenney, Alice P 1937- *ConAu 10NR, –25R, WrDr 84*
Kenney, Douglas C 1947?-1980 *ConAu 101, –107*
Kenney, Edwin James, Jr. 1942- *ConAu 53*
Kenney, George Churchill 1889- *ConAu P-1*
Kenney, John Paul 1920- *ConAu 17R*
Kenney, Sylvia W 1922- *ConAu P-1*
Kennick, W E 1923- *ConAu 13R*
Kenny, Adele *DrAP&F 83*
Kenny, Anthony 1931- *WrDr 84*
Kenny, Anthony James Patrick 1931- *IntAu&W 82*
Kenny, Anthony John Patrick 1931- *ConAu 101*
Kenny, Charles J *ConAu X, LongCTC*
Kenny, Ellsworth Newcomb 1909-1971 *ConAu 5R, –103, SmATA 26N*
Kenny, Herbert A 1912- *ConAu 41R, SmATA 13*
Kenny, James Andrew 1933- *ConAu 107*
Kenny, John P 1909- *ConAu 17R*
Kenny, John Peter 1916- *ConAu 1NR, –45*
Kenny, Kathryn *ConAu X*
Kenny, Kevin *ConAu X*
Kenny, Mary 1936- *ConAu 108*
Kenny, Maurice *DrAP&F 83*
Kenny, Michael 1923- *ConAu 1R, –5NR*
Kenny, Nicholas Napoleon 1895-1975 *ConAu 89*
Kenny, Nick A 1895-1975 *ConAu X*
Kenny, Shirley Strum 1934- *ConAu 45*
Kenny, Vincent 1919- *ConAu 45*
Kenny, W Henry 1918- *ConAu 37R*
Kenofer, C Louis 1923- *ConAu 69*
Kenojuak *CreCan 1*
Kenoyer, Natlee Peoples 1907- *ConAu 5R, –5NR*
Kenrick, Donald Simon 1929- *ConAu 81*
Kenrick, Douglas Moore 1912- *IntAu&W 82*
Kenrick, Tony 1935- *ConAu 104, TwCCr&M 80, WrDr 84*
Kenrick, Vivienne Mary 1920- *IntAu&W 82*
Kenshalo, Daniel R 1922- *ConAu 41R*
Kensinger, George *WrDr 84*
Kent, Alexander *ConAu X, SmATA X, WrDr 84*
Kent, Allegra 1938- *ConAu 105, WrDr 84*
Kent, Allen 1921- *ConAu 3NR, –9R*
Kent, Arden *ConAu X*
Kent, Arthur 1925- *WrDr 84*
Kent, Arthur William Charles 1925- *ConAu 102*
Kent, Deborah Ann 1948- *ConAu 103*
Kent, Donald P 1916- *ConAu 17R*
Kent, Edward Allen 1933- *ConAu 45*
Kent, Ernest W 1940- *ConAu 104*
Kent, Fortune *ConAu X*
Kent, Frank 1907?-1978 *ConAu 81*
Kent, George Edward 1920- *LivgBAA*
Kent, George O 1919- *ConAu 37R*
Kent, George W 1928- *ConAu 25R*
Kent, Harold W 1900- *ConAu 65*
Kent, Helen *WrDr 84*
Kent, Homer Austin, Jr. 1926- *ConAu 3NR, –9R, IntAu&W 82, WrDr 84*
Kent, Jack 1920- *ConAu X, SmATA X*
Kent, John Henry Somerset 1923- *ConAu 9R*
Kent, John Wellington 1920- *ConAu 85, SmATA 24[port]*
Kent, Katherine *ConAu X*
Kent, Kelvin *ConAu X, TwCSFW*
Kent, Larry 1937- *CreCan 1*
Kent, Lawrence L 1937- *CreCan 1*
Kent, Leonard J 1927- *ConAu 77*
Kent, Louise Andrews 1886-1969 *ConAu 1R, –4NR, –25R, TwCA SUP*
Kent, Malcolm 1932- *ConAu 45*
Kent, Mallory *TwCSFW*
Kent, Margaret 1894- *ConAu P-2, SmATA 2*
Kent, Nora 1899- *ConAu P-1*
Kent, Pamela *TwCRGW, WrDr 84*
Kent, Philip *ConAu X, TwCSFW*
Kent, Rockwell 1882-1971 *ConAmA, ConAu 4NR, –5R, –29R, SmATA 6, TwCA, TwCA SUP*
Kent, Rolly *DrAP&F 83*
Kent, Sherman 1903- *ConAu 53, SmATA 20*
Kent, Simon *ConAu X*
Kent, Stella *ConAu X*
Kent, Tony *ConAu X*
Kentfield, Calvin Brice 1924- *ConAu 5R*
Kenton, Maxwell *ConAu X, WrDr 84*
Kenton, Warren 1933- *ConAu 29R, WrDr 84*
Kenward, James Macara 1908- *ConAu 5R*
Kenward, Jean 1920- *ConAu 108,*

IntWWP 82X, WrDr 84
Kenward, Michael 1945- *ConAu 103*
Kenworthy, Brian J 1920- *ConAu 103, WrDr 84*
Kenworthy, Leonard Stout 1912- *ConAu 1R, –1NR, SmATA 6*
Kenyon, Bernice Gilkyson *ConAu X*
Kenyon, Ernest M 1920- *ConAu 85*
Kenyon, F W 1912- *ConAu 1NR*
Kenyon, Frank Wilson 1912- *ConAu 1R, DcLEL 1940*
Kenyon, J P 1927- *ConAu 3NR*
Kenyon, James William 1910- *ConAu P-1*
Kenyon, Jane *DrAP&F 83*
Kenyon, John Philipps 1927- *ConAu 9R, DcLEL 1940*
Kenyon, Karen *DrAP&F 83*
Kenyon, Karen 1938- *ConAu 106*
Kenyon, Kathleen Mary 1906- *ConAu 21R*
Kenyon, Ley 1913- *ConAu 13R, SmATA 6*
Kenyon, Michael 1931- *ConAu 13R, TwCCr&M 80, WrDr 84*
Kenyon, Mildred Adams 1894-1980 *ConAu 105, –108*
Kenyon, Paul *ConAu X*
Kenyon, Robert O *ConAu X*
Keogh, James 1916- *ConAu 45, WrDr 84*
Keogh, James Edward 1948- *ConAmTC*
Keogh, Lilian Gilmore 1927- *ConAu 9R*
Keohane, Nannerl O 1940- *ConAu 106*
Keohane, Robert O 1941- *ConAu 45*
Keown, Eric 1904-1963 *LongCTC*
Kepes, Gyorgy 1906- *ConAu 101*
Kepes, Juliet 1919- *ConAu 69, SmATA 13*
Kephart, Newell C 1911-1973 *ConAu P-2*
Kephart, William M 1921- *ConAu 41R, WrDr 84*
Kepler, Thomas Samuel 1897-1963 *ConAu 1R*
Keppel, Charlotte *TwCRGW, WrDr 84*
Keppel, Sonia 1900- *ConAu 107, WrDr 84*
Keppel-Jones, Arthur 1909- *TwCSFW, WrDr 84*
Kepple, Ella Huff 1902- *ConAu P-2*
Keppler, C F 1909- *ConAu 17R*
Keppler, Herbert 1925- *ConAu 85*
Ker, Neil Ripley 1908-1982 *ConAu 107*
Ker, William Paton 1855-1923 *LongCTC, ModBrL, TwCA, TwCA SUP*
Ker Wilson, Barbara 1929- *ConAu 5R, –7NR, SmATA 20*
Kerber, August Frank 1917- *ConAu 21R*
Kerby, Bill 1937- *ConAu 104*
Kerby, Joe Kent 1933- *ConAu 53*
Kerby, Robert L 1934- *ConAu 41R*
Kerby, Susan *WrDr 84*
Kerby, Susan Alice 1908- *ConAu X*
Kerek, Andrew 1936- *ConAu 102*
Kerekes, Tibor 1893-1969 *ConAu P-2*
Kerensky, Oleg 1930- *ConAu 29R, WrDr 84*
Kerensky, V M 1930- *ConAu 53*
Keres, Paul 1916-1975 *ConAu 57*
Kerestesi, Michael 1929- *ConAu 109*
Kereszty, Roch A 1933- *ConAu 29R, WrDr 84*
Kerewsky-Halpern, Barbara 1931- *ConAu 102*
Kergommeaux, Duncan Robert De *CreCan 1*
Kerigan, Florence 1896- *ConAu 29R, IntWWP 82, SmATA 12, WrDr 84*
Kerin, Roger A 1947- *ConAu 109*
Kerkvliet, Benedict J 1943- *ConAu 93*
Kerlan, Irvin 1912-1963 *ConAu 5R*
Kerley, Gary *DrAP&F 83*
Kerlikowske, Elizabeth *DrAP&F 83*
Kerlinger, Fred N 1910- *ConAu 2NR, –49*
Kerman, Cynthia Earl 1923- *ConAu 57*
Kerman, Gertrude Lerner 1909- *ConAu 5R, SmATA 21[port]*
Kerman, Joseph 1924- *WrDr 84*
Kerman, Joseph Wilfred 1924- *ConAu 65*
Kerman, Judith *DrAP&F 83*
Kerman, Judith 1945- *ConAu 77*
Kerman, Sheppard 1928- *ConAu 85, IntAu&W 82, NatPD 81[port]*
Kermani, Taghi Thomas 1929- *ConAu 25R*
Kermode, Frank 1919- *ConAu 1R, –1NR, ConLCrt 82, IntAu&W 82, WorAu, WrDr 84*
Kermode, John Frank 1919- *DcLEL 1940*
Kern, Alfred 1924- *ConAu 33R*
Kern, Bliem *DrAP&F 83*
Kern, Canyon *ConAu X*
Kern, E R *ConAu X*
Kern, Gary 1938- *ConAu 65*
Kern, Gerhard 1909- *IntAu&W 82*

Kimberly, Gail *ConAu 81*
Kimble, Daniel Porter 1934- *ConAu 41R, IntAu&W 82*
Kimble, David 1921- *ConAu 13R*
Kimble, George 1908- *WrDr 84*
Kimble, George H T 1908- *ConAu 108*
Kimble, Gregory A 1917- *ConAu 21R*
Kimbrell, Grady 1933- *ConAu 33R*
Kimbro, Jean *ConAu X*
Kimbro, John M 1929- *ConAu 2NR, –45*
Kimbrough, Emily 1899- *ConAu 17R, SmATA 2, WorAu, WrDr 84*
Kimbrough, Katheryn *ConAu X, TwCRGW*
Kimbrough, Ralph B 1922- *ConAu 73*
Kimbrough, Richard B 1931- *ConAu 41R*
Kimbrough, Robert 1929- *WrDr 84*
Kimbrough, Robert Alexander, III 1929- *ConAu 6NR, –9R*
Kimbrough, Sara Dodge 1901- *ConAu 93*
Kimche, David *ConAu 103*
Kimenye, Barbara *TwCCW 83, WrDr 84*
Kimenye, Barbara 1940?- *ConAu 101*
Kimes, Beverly Rae 1939- *ConAu 107*
Kimm, Robert Ellis 1941- *IntWWP 82*
Kimmel, Arthur S 1930- *ConAu 41R*
Kimmel, Douglas C 1943- *ConAu 53*
Kimmel, Eric A 1946- *ConAu 3NR, –49, SmATA 13, WrDr 84*
Kimmel, Jo 1931- *ConAu 4NR, –53*
Kimmel, Margaret Mary 1938- *SmATA 33*
Kimmel, Melvin 1930- *ConAu 25R*
Kimmel, Stanley 1894?-1982 *ConAu 109*
Kimmel, William 1908-1982 *ConAu 109*
Kimmelman, Burt *DrAP&F 83*
Kimmey, John Lansing 1922- *ConAu 108*
Kimmich, Christoph M 1939- *ConAu 69*
Kimmich, Flora 1939- *ConAu 106*
Kimmins, Anthony Martin 1901-1964 *LongCTC*
Kimmins, Sybil Jean 1923- *IntWWP 82*
Kimpel, Ben D 1915- *ConAu 57*
Kimpel, Ben F 1905- *ConAu 1R*
Kimpel, Benjamin Franklin 1905- *WrDr 84*
Kimrey, Grace Saunders 1910- *ConAu 45*
Kimura, Jiro 1949- *ConAu 85, IntAu&W 82*
Kimzey, Ardis *DrAP&F 83*
Kincaid, Alan *ConAu X*
Kincaid, James R 1937- *ConAu 65*
Kincaid, Suzanne 1930- *ConAu 9R*
Kinch, Sam E, Jr. 1940- *ConAu 45*
Kincheloe, Raymond McFarland 1909- *ConAu 61*
Kinck, Hans Ernst 1865-1926 *CIDMEL 80*
Kincl, Kay Owens 1955- *ConAu 106*
Kind, Edmund J 1914- *ConAu 5R*
Kindall, Alva Frederick 1906- *ConAu 1R*
Kinder, Faye 1902- *ConAu 5R*
Kinder, Gary 1946- *ConAu 109*
Kinder, James S 1895- *ConAu 13R*
Kinder, Kathleen *ConAu X*
Kinder, Marsha 1940- *ConAu 41R*
Kinderlehrer, Jane 1913- *ConAu 106*
Kinding, Thomas 1939- *IntAu&W 82*
Kindleberger, Charles P, II 1910- *ConAu 73*
Kindley, Jeffrey 1945- *NatPD 81[port]*
Kindred, Alton R 1922- *ConAu 109*
Kindred, Leslie W 1905- *ConAu 41R*
Kindred, Wendy 1937- *ConAu 37R, SmATA 7, WrDr 84*
Kindregan, Charles P 1935- *ConAu 10NR, –21R*
Kindt, Guido J F 1934- *IntAu&W 82*
Kineji, Maborushi *ConAu X, WrDr 84*
Kinert, Reed Charles 1911?- *ConAu 107*
Kines, Pat Decker 1937- *ConAu 65, SmATA 12*
Kines, Thomas Alvin 1922- *ConAu 13R*
Kines, Tom *ConAu X*
King, Adam *ConAu X*
King, Adele Cockshoot 1932- *ConAu 8NR, –13R*
King, Alan 1927- *ConAu 89*
King, Alexander 1909- *ConAu 110*
King, Alfred M 1933- *ConAu 25R*
King, Algin B 1927- *ConAu 41R*
King, Alison *ConAu X*
King, Allan Winton 1930- *CreCan 2*
King, Alvy L 1932- *ConAu 33R*
King, Annette 1941- *ConAu 33R*
King, Anthony 1934- *WrDr 84*
King, Anthony Stephen 1934- *ConAu 17R, IntAu&W 82*
King, Archdale Arthur 1890-1972 *ConAu P-1*
King, Arthur *ConAu X, SmATA X, WrDr 84*
King, Basil 1859-1928 *TwCA, TwCA SUP*
King, Ben F 1937- *ConAu 57*
King, Bert T 1927- *ConAu 45*

King, Betty 1919- *ConAu 103, WrDr 84*
King, Betty Patterson 1925- *ConAu 9R*
King, Billie Jean 1943- *ConAu 10NR, –53, SmATA 12, WrDr 84*
King, Bruce d1976 *ConAu 61*
King, Bruce 1933- *ConAu X*
King, Bruce A 1933- *ConAu 4NR, –53*
King, C Daly 1895-1963 *TwCCr&M 80*
King, C Richard 1924- *ConAu 11NR, –69*
King, Cecil 1901- *WrDr 84*
King, Cecil Harmsworth 1901- *ConAu 110, IntAu&W 82*
King, Charles 1844-1933 *TwCWW*
King, Charles 1922- *ConAu 57*
King, Clarence 1842-1901 *ConAu 110*
King, Clarence 1884?-1974 *ConAu 53*
King, Clive 1924- *ConAu 104, SmATA 28, TwCCW 83, WrDr 84*
King, Clyde Stuart 1919- *ConAu 17R*
King, Coretta Scott 1927- *ConAu 29R, LivgBAA*
King, Cynthia *DrAP&F 83*
King, Cynthia 1925- *ConAu 29R, MichAu 80, SmATA 7, WrDr 84*
King, Daniel Patrick 1942- *ConAu 4NR, –53*
King, Donald B 1913- *ConAu 13R*
King, Dorothy E *DrAP&F 83*
King, Edith W 1930- *ConAu 33R*
King, Edmund J 1914- *ConAu 2NR, –5R*
King, Edmund L 1914- *ConAu 33R*
King, Edward L 1928- *ConAu 81*
King, Florence 1936- *AuNews 1, ConAu 7NR, –57*
King, Francis 1923- *WrDr 84*
King, Francis Edward 1931- *ConAu 61*
King, Francis Henry 1923- *ConAu 1R, –1NR, ConLC 8, ConNov 82, DcLB 15[port], DcLEL 1940, IntAu&W 82, IntWWP 82, TwCWr, WhoTwCL, WorAu*
King, Francis P 1922- *ConAu 13R, WrDr 84*
King, Frank A *ConAu X*
King, Frank O 1883-1969 *ConAu 89, SmATA 22N*
King, Franklin Alexander 1923- *ConAu 45*
King, Frederick Murl 1916- *ConAu 2NR, –5R*
King, Glen D 1925- *ConAu 9R*
King, Harley *DrAP&F 83*
King, Harold 1945- *ConAu 7NR, –57*
King, Harvey Frederick 1947- *IntWWP 82*
King, Helen H 1931- *LivgBAA*
King, Helen H 1937- *ConAu 33R*
King, Homer W 1907- *ConAu P-1*
King, Horace Maybray *ConAu X*
King, Irving H 1935- *ConAu 89*
King, Ivan R 1927- *ConAu 89*
King, Jack *ConAu X*
King, James Cecil 1924- *ConAu 41R*
King, James G 1898?-1979 *ConAu 89*
King, James T 1933- *ConAu 37R*
King, James W 1920- *ConAu 9R*
King, Janet *IntWWP 82*
King, Janet Byers *IntWWP 82X*
King, Janet Kauffman 1935- *ConAu 110*
King, Jere Clemens 1910- *ConAu 5R*
King, Jerome Babcock 1927- *ConAu 103*
King, Jerry 1941- *ConAu 97*
King, Joe 1909?-1979 *ConAu 85*
King, John 1896- *ConAu X*
King, John 1947- *WrDr 84*
King, John Edward 1947- *ConAu 102*
King, John L 1917- *ConAu 41R*
King, John O 1923- *ConAu 108*
King, John Q Taylor 1921- *ConAu 25R*
King, Josie *ConAu X*
King, K DeWayne 1925- *ConAu 13R*
King, Kimball 1934- *ConAu 110*
King, Larry L 1929- *ConAu 13R, ConDr 82D, WrDr 84*
King, Leila Pier 1882-1981 *ConAu 105*
King, Leslie John 1934- *ConAu 106*
King, Lester S 1908- *ConAu 33R*
King, Louise W *ConAu 7NR, –13R*
King, Marcet 1922- *ConAu 25R*
King, Marian *ConAu 2NR, –5R, SmATA 23[port], WrDr 84*
King, Mariann *IntWWP 82X*
King, Marjorie Cameron 1909- *ConAu 33R*
King, Mark 1945- *ConAu 61*
King, Martha *DrAP&F 83*
King, Martha L 1918- *ConAu 109*
King, Martin *ConAu X, SmATA X*
King, Martin Luther, Jr. 1929-1968 *ConAu P-2,*

SmATA 14
King, Mary *IntWWP 82X*
King, Mary Louise 1911- *ConAu 21R*
King, Michael *ConAu X*
King, Morton Brandon 1913- *ConAu 102*
King, N Q 1922- *ConAu 1R, –4NR*
King, Norman A *ConAu X, WrDr 84*
King, O H P 1902- *ConAu 1R*
King, Pat 1932- *IntWWP 82*
King, Patricia 1930- *ConAu 5R*
King, Paul *ConAu X, WrDr 84*
King, Peggy Cameron 1909- *ConAu X, MichAu 80*
King, Philip 1904- *ConAu 103*
King, Phyllis April 1930- *IntWWP 82*
King, Preston 1936- *ConAu 10NR, –21R*
King, Ray A 1933- *ConAu 21R*
King, Reefe *SmATA 8*
King, Richard A 1929- *ConAu 21R*
King, Richard G 1922- *ConAu 37R*
King, Richard H 1942- *ConAu 77*
King, Richard L 1937- *ConAu 1NR, –45*
King, Robert C 1928- *WrDr 84*
King, Robert Charles 1928- *ConAu 17R*
King, Robert G 1929- *ConAu 21R*
King, Robert H 1935- *ConAu 45*
King, Robert L 1950- *ConAu 77*
King, Robert R 1942- *ConAu 8NR, –61, WrDr 84*
King, Robert S *DrAP&F 83*
King, Robert W *DrAP&F 83*
King, Robin 1919- *ConAu 5R*
King, Roma Alvah, Jr. 1914- *ConAu 1R, –1NR*
King, Ron *DrAP&F 83*
King, Ronald 1914- *ConAu 107, WrDr 84*
King, Ruby Thompson *IntWWP 82*
King, Rufus 1893-1966 *TwCCr&M 80*
King, Rufus 1917- *ConAu 25R*
King, Ruth Rodney *ConAu X*
King, Spencer Bidwell, Jr. 1904- *ConAu P-1*
King, Stanley H 1921- *ConAu 110*
King, Stella *ConAu 69*
King, Stephen 1946- *WrDr 84*
King, Stephen 1947- *ConAu 1NR, –61, –61, ConLC 12, –26[port], DcLB Y80B[port], SmATA 9*
King, T J 1925- *ConAu 37R*
King, Tabitha 1949- *ConAu 105*
King, Teri 1940- *ConAu 89, WrDr 84*
King, Terry Johnson 1929-1978 *ConAu 17R, –77*
King, Thomas J 1925- *WrDr 84*
King, Thomas M 1929- *ConAu 57*
King, Tony 1947- *ConAu 109*
King, Veronica *AuNews 1, ConAu X*
King, Vincent 1935- *ConAu X, TwCSFW, WrDr 84*
King, Willard L 1893-1981 *ConAu 1R, –103, IntAu&W 82*
King, William Donald Aelian 1910- *ConAu 89*
King, William Richard 1938- *ConAu 8NR, –21R, IntAu&W 82, WrDr 84*
King, Winston Lee 1907- *ConAu 41R*
King, Woodie, Jr. 1937- *ConAu 103, LivgBAA*
King-Hall, Magdalen 1904-1971 *ConAu 29R, ConAu P-1*
King-Hall, Sir Stephen 1893-1966 *ConAu 5R, LongCTC*
King-Hele, Desmond 1927- *WrDr 84*
King-Hele, Desmond George 1927- *ConAu 1R, –29R, IntAu&W 82*
King-Smith, Dick 1922- *ConAu 105, TwCCW 83*
King-Stoops, Joyce Barlow 1923- *ConAu 81*
Kingdon, Frank 1894-1972 *ConAu 33R*
Kingdon, John W 1940- *ConAu 25R, WrDr 84*
Kingdon, Robert McCune 1927- *ConAu 21R, IntAu&W 82, WrDr 84*
Kingery, Lionel Bruce *DrAP&F 83*
Kingery, Margaret *DrAP&F 83*
Kingery, Robert E 1913-1978 *ConAu 9R, –103*
Kinghorn, A M 1926- *ConAu 93*
Kinghorn, Alexander Manson 1926- *IntAu&W 82*
Kinghorn, Kenneth Cain 1930- *ConAu 41R*
Kingma, Daphne Rose *DrAP&F 83*
Kingman, Lee 1919- *ConAu X, ConLC 17, SmATA 1, TwCCW 83, WrDr 84*
Kingman, Russ 1917- *ConAu 101*
Kingry, Philip L 1942- *ConAu 53*
Kingsbury, Arthur 1939- *ConAu 29R*
Kingsbury, Jack Dean 1934- *ConAu 37R*
Kingsbury, John M 1928- *ConAu 6NR, –13R*

Kingsbury, Robert C 1924- *ConAu 1R, -2NR*

Kingsland, Leslie William 1912- *ConAu 69,*
SmATA 13

Kingsley, Emily Perl 1940- *ConAu 107,*
SmATA 33[port]

Kingsley, Mary St. Leger 1852-1931 *LongCTC*

Kingsley, Michael J 1918?-1972 *ConAu 37R*

Kingsley, Robert *ConAu X*

Kingsley, Sidney 1906- *WrDr 84*

Kingsley, Sidney 1906-1951 *CnMD, ConAmA,*
ConAu 85, CroCD, DcLB 7[port],
LongCTC, ModAL, ModWD, TwCA,
TwCA SUP

Kingsley-Smith, Terence 1940- *ConAu 57*

Kingsmill, Hugh 1889-1949 *LongCTC, TwCA,*
TwCA SUP

Kingsnorth, George William 1924- *ConAu 5R,*
WrDr 84

Kingston, Albert J 1917- *ConAu 21R*

Kingston, Frederick Temple 1925- *WrDr 84*

Kingston, Jeremy Henry Spencer 1931-
ConAu 103

Kingston, Maxine 1940- *WrDr 84*

Kingston, Maxine Hong 1940- *ConAu 69,*
ConLC 12, -19, DcLB Y80B[port]

Kingston, Syd *ConAu X, TwCWW*

Kingston, Temple 1925- *ConAu 33R*

Kington, Miles Beresford 1941- *IntAu&W 82*

Kininmonth, Christopher 1917- *ConAu 53,*
IntAu&W 82, WrDr 84

Kinkade, Richard P 1939- *ConAu 37R*

Kinkaid, Frank Eugene 1922- *ConAmTC*

Kinkaid, Matt *ConAu X, WrDr 84*

Kinkaid, Wyatt E *ConAu X*

Kinkead, Eugene 1906- *ConAu 1R, -1NR*

Kinkead-Weekes, Mark 1931- *WrDr 84*

Kinley, Phyllis Gillespie 1930- *ConAu 1R*

Kinloch, A Murray 1923- *ConAu 103*

Kinmonth, Earl H 1946- *ConAu 107*

Kinnaird, Clark 1901- *ConAu 1NR, -45*

Kinnaird, John William 1924-1980 *ConAu 97*

Kinnaird, William M 1928- *ConAu 101*

Kinnamon, Keneth 1932- *ConAu 37R, WrDr 84*

Kinnamon, Kenneth 1932- *IntAu&W 82*

Kinnard, Douglas 1921- *ConAu 77*

Kinnear, Elizabeth K 1902- *ConAu P-2*

Kinnear, Michael Steward Read 1937-
ConAu 37R, WrDr 84

Kinneavy, James Louis 1920- *ConAu 69*

Kinnell, Galway *DrAP&F 83*

Kinnell, Galway 1927- *ConAu 9R, -10NR,*
ConLC 1, -2, -3, -5, -13, ConP 80, CroCAP,
DcLB 5[port], DcLEL 1940, EncWL 2,
IntAu&W 82, IntWWP 82, ModAL SUP,
WhoTwCL, WorAu, WrDr 84

Kinney, Arthur F 1933- *ConAu 37R,*
IntAu&W 82, WrDr 84

Kinney, C Cle 1915- *ConAu 9R, SmATA 6*

Kinney, Francis S 1915- *ConAu 106*

Kinney, Harrison 1921- *ConAu 1R, SmATA 13*

Kinney, James R 1902?-1978 *ConAu 81*

Kinney, Jean Stout 1912- *ConAu 9R,*
SmATA 12

Kinney, Lucien Blair 1895-1971 *ConAu P-2*

Kinney, Peter 1943- *ConAu 73*

Kinney, Richard 1924?-1979 *ConAu 85*

Kinnick, B Jo *DrAP&F 83*

Kinnict, Kinni *DrAP&F 83*

Kinnicutt, Susan Sibley 1926- *ConAu 77*

Kinnison, William A 1932- *ConAu 21R*

Kinoko *IntWWP 82X*

Kinor, Jehuda *ConAu X*

Kinoshita, Junji 1914- *CnMD, ModWD*

Kinross, Lord 1904- *ConAu X*

Kinross, Lord Patrick 1904-1976 *ConAu 9R, -65*

Kinsbruner, Jay 1939- *ConAu 25R*

Kinsel, Paschal 1895?-1976 *ConAu 69*

Kinsella, Paul L 1923- *ConAu 21R*

Kinsella, Thomas *DrAP&F 83*

Kinsella, Thomas 1927- *TwCWr*

Kinsella, Thomas 1928- *ConAu 17R, ConLC 4,*
-19, ConP 80, DcLEL 1940, IntAu&W 82,
IntWWP 82, ModBrL SUP, WhoTwCL,
WorAu, WrDr 84

Kinsella, W P 1935- *ConAu 97,*
ConLC 27[port], WrDr 84

Kinsey, Barry Allan 1931- *ConAu 17R*

Kinsey, Elizabeth *ConAu X, SmATA X,*
TwCCW 83, WrDr 84

Kinsey-Jones, Brian *ConAu X*

Kinsley, D A 1939- *ConAu 45*

Kinsley, James 1922- *ConAu 1R, -2NR*

Kinsman, Gail *IntWWP 82X*

Kinstler, Everett Raymond 1926- *ConAu 33R*

Kinter, Judith 1928- *ConAu 109*

Kintner, Donald 1922- *IntWWP 82*

Kintner, Earl Wilson 1912- *ConAu 1NR, -45*

Kintner, Robert Edmonds 1909-1980 *ConAu 103*

Kintner, William R 1915- *ConAu 5R, -6NR*

Kinton, Jack F 1939- *ConAu 7NR, -57*

Kintsch, Walter 1932- *ConAu 29R*

Kinzel, Robert K 1904- *WrDr 84*

Kinzer, Betty 1922- *ConAu 21R*

Kinzer, Donald Louis 1914- *ConAu 53*

Kinzer, H M 1923?-1975 *ConAu 57*

Kinzer, Nora Scott 1936- *ConAu 106*

Kiparsky, Valentin Julius Alexander 1904-
ConAu 17R

Kipling, Rudyard 1865-1936 *CnMWL,*
ConAu 105, EncWL 2, LongCTC, ModBrL,
ModBrL SUP, RGFMBP, TwCA,
TwCA SUP, TwCCW 83, TwCLC 8[port],
TwCSFW, TwCWr, WhoTwCL

Kiplinger, Austin Huntington 1918- *ConAu 57*

Kiplinger, Christina *DrAP&F 83*

Kiplinger, David *IntWWP 82X*

Kiplinger, Willard Monroe 1891-1967 *ConAu 89*

Kipnis, Claude 1938-1981 *ConAu 103, -107*

Kipnis, Kenneth 1943- *WrDr 84*

Kippax, Janet 1926- *ConAu 97*

Kippax, John 1915-1974 *ConSFA*

Kipphardt, Heinar 1922- *ClDMEL 80, CnMD,*
ConAu 89, CroCD, ModWD

Kipphardt, Heinar 1922-1982 *ConAu 108*

Kippley, John F 1930- *ConAu 29R*

Kippley, Sheila K 1939- *ConAu 61*

Kiraly, Bela 1912- *ConAu 8NR, -61*

Kirby, Blaik 1928- *ConAu 77*

Kirby, D P 1936- *ConAu 25R*

Kirby, David *DrAP&F 83*

Kirby, David 1944- *ConAu 53, IntWWP 82*

Kirby, David G 1942- *ConAu 101*

Kirby, David Peter 1936- *IntAu&W 82,*
WrDr 84

Kirby, Douglas James 1929- *ConAu 25R*

Kirby, E Stuart 1909- *ConAu 7NR, -13R*

Kirby, F E 1928- *ConAu 65*

Kirby, Gilbert Walter 1914- *ConAu 103,*
IntAu&W 82, WrDr 84

Kirby, Jack Temple 1938- *ConAu 25R*

Kirby, Jean *ConAu X*

Kirby, John B 1936- *ConAu 105*

Kirby, Louise Patricia 1923- *IntWWP 82*

Kirby, M Sheelah Flanagan 1916- *ConAu 5R*

Kirby, Mark *ConAu X*

Kirby, Thomas Austin 1904- *ConAu 5R*

Kirby, William 1817-1906 *CreCan 2*

Kirchheimer, Gloria L *DrAP&F 83*

Kirchner, Audrey Burie 1937- *ConAu 73*

Kirchner, Glenn 1930- *ConAu 29R*

Kirchner, Walther 1905- *ConAu 1R, -1NR*

Kirchwey, Freda 1893-1976 *ConAu 61, -93*

Kirdar, Uner 1933- *ConAu 21R*

Kirk, Clara M 1898-1976 *ConAu 69,*
ConAu P-1

Kirk, David 1935- *ConAu 29R*

Kirk, Donald 1938- *ConAu 37R, IntAu&W 82,*
WrDr 84

Kirk, Donald R 1935- *ConAu 57*

Kirk, Elizabeth D 1937- *ConAu 53*

Kirk, G S 1921- *ConAu 2NR*

Kirk, Geoffrey Stephen 1921- *ConAu 5R,*
WrDr 84

Kirk, George Eden 1911- *ConAu 1R*

Kirk, H David 1918- *ConAu 11NR, -17R*

Kirk, Hans Rudolf 1889-1962 *EncWL 2*

Kirk, Hans Rudolf 1898-1962 *ClDMEL 80*

Kirk, Irene 1926- *ConAu 5R, -6NR*

Kirk, Irina *ConAu X, DrAP&F 83*

Kirk, James A 1929- *ConAu 37R*

Kirk, Jeremy *ConAu X*

Kirk, Jerome 1937- *ConAu 49*

Kirk, John E 1905- *WrDr 84*

Kirk, John Esben 1905-1975 *ConAu 57*

Kirk, John T 1933- *ConAu 49*

Kirk, John W 1932- *NatPD 81[port]*

Kirk, Mary Wallace 1889- *ConAu X*

Kirk, Michael *ConAu X, IntAu&W 82X,*
TwCCr&M 80

Kirk, Norman Andrew *DrAP&F 83*

Kirk, Richard Edmund 1931- *ConAu 13R*

Kirk, Robert Warner 1907-1980 *ConAu 9R, -103*

Kirk, Roger Edward 1930- *ConAu 41R*

Kirk, Russell 1918- *WrDr 84*

Kirk, Russell Amos 1918- *AuNews 1,*
ConAu 1R, -1NR, ConIsC 1[port],
IntAu&W 82, TwCRGW, WorAu

Kirk, Ruth 1925- *ConAu 9NR*

Kirk, Ruth Eleanor 1925- *ConAu 13R,*
SmATA 5

Kirk, Samuel A 1904- *ConAu 1NR, -45*

Kirk, T H 1899- *ConAu P-2*

Kirk, Ted *ConAu X*

Kirk, Thomas Hobson 1899- *WrDr 84*

Kirk, Wayne *ConAu X*

Kirk-Greene, Anthony *WrDr 84*

Kirk-Greene, Anthony 1925- *ConAu 11NR*

Kirk-Greene, Anthony H M *ConAu X*

Kirk-Greene, Anthony Hamilton Millard 1925-
ConAu 61

Kirk-Greene, Christopher 1926- *WrDr 84*

Kirk-Greene, Christopher Walter Edward 1926-
ConAu 13R

Kirkaldy, John Francis 1908- *IntAu&W 82,*
WrDr 84

Kirkbride, Ronald 1912- *ConAu 1R, -2NR*

Kirkconnell, Watson 1895- *CreCan 2*

Kirkconnell, Watson 1895-1977 *ConAu 108*

Kirkendall, Don 1923- *ConAu 49*

Kirkendall, Lester A 1903- *ConAu 1R, -5NR,*
WrDr 84

Kirkendall, Richard Stewart 1928- *ConAu 77*

Kirkham, E Bruce 1938- *ConAu 37R, WrDr 84*

Kirkham, George L 1941- *ConAu 77, WrDr 84*

Kirkham, Michael Campbell 1934- *ConAu 25R,*
WrDr 84

Kirkland, Bryant M 1914- *ConAu 21R*

Kirkland, Caroline Matilda Stansbury 1801-1864
MichAu 80

Kirkland, Edward Chase 1894-1975 *ConAu 1R,*
-6NR, -104

Kirkland, Jack 1901-1969 *CnMD*

Kirkland, Jack 1902-1969 *ModWD*

Kirkland, Wallace W 1891?-1979 *ConAu 89*

Kirkland, Will *ConAu X*

Kirkman, James S 1906- *ConAu 93*

Kirkman, William Patrick 1932- *IntAu&W 82,*
WrDr 84

Kirkpatrick, Arnold 1941- *IntAu&W 82*

Kirkpatrick, Diane 1933- *ConAu 53*

Kirkpatrick, Donald L 1924- *ConAu 41R*

Kirkpatrick, Doris 1902- *ConAu 93*

Kirkpatrick, Dow 1917- *ConAu 21R*

Kirkpatrick, Evron M 1911- *ConAu 57*

Kirkpatrick, Frank 1924- *ConAu 108*

Kirkpatrick, Ivone Augustine 1897-1964
ConAu P-1

Kirkpatrick, Jean 1923- *ConAu 81*

Kirkpatrick, Jeane D J 1926- *ConAu 7NR, -53*

Kirkpatrick, Jeane J 1926- *ConIsC 2[port]*

Kirkpatrick, John 1905- *ConAu 45*

Kirkpatrick, Lyman B, Jr. 1916- *ConAu 33R*

Kirkpatrick, Oliver Austin 1911- *ConAu 49,*
LivgBAA

Kirkpatrick, Ralph 1911- *ConAu 49*

Kirkpatrick, Richard Alan 1947- *IntAu&W 82*

Kirkpatrick, Samuel A, III 1943- *ConAu 41R*

Kirkpatrick, Smith *DrAP&F 83*

Kirkpatrick, Smith 1922- *ConAu 49*

Kirkup, James 1923- *WrDr 84*

Kirkup, James 1928- *IntAu&W 82*

Kirkup, James Falconer 1918- *WorAu*

Kirkup, James Falconer 1923- *ConP 80,*
DcLEL 1940, IntWWP 82, LongCTC

Kirkup, James Falconer 1927- *ConAu 1R, -2NR,*
ConLC 1, SmATA 12

Kirkus, Virginia 1893- *ConAu X, SmATA X*

Kirkwood, Ellen Swan 1904- *ConAu 25R*

Kirkwood, G M 1916- *ConAu 93*

Kirkwood, James 1930- *AuNews 2, ConAu 1R,*
-6NR, ConLC 9, NatPD 81[port],
WrDr 84

Kirkwood, Jim *ConAu X*

Kirkwood, Kenneth P 1899-1968 *ConAu 37R*

Kirn, Ann Minette 1910- *ConAu 93*

Kirp, David L 1944- *ConAu 109*

Kirsanov, Semyon Isaakovich 1906-1972
ClDMEL 80

Kirsch, Anthony Thomas 1930- *ConAu 103*

Kirsch, Arthur C 1932- *ConAu 13R*

Kirsch, Charlotte 1942- *ConAu 109*

Kirsch, Herbert 1924?-1978 *ConAu 104*

Kirsch, Leonard Joel 1934-1977 *ConAu 37R*

Kirsch, Paul John 1914- *ConAu 108*

Kirsch, Robert R 1922-1980 *ConAu 102, -33R*

Kirsch, Walter Paul 1907- *IntAu&W 82*
Kirschen, Leonard 1908-1983 *ConAu 109*
Kirschenbaum, Aaron 1926- *ConAu 33R*
Kirschenbaum, Howard 1944- *ConAu 89*
Kirschner, Allen 1930- *ConAu 29R*
Kirschner, Fritz *ConAu X*
Kirschner, Linda Rae 1939- *ConAu 33R*
Kirschten, Ernest 1902-1974 *ConAu 49,*
ConAu P-1
Kirshenbaum, Jerry 1938- *ConAu 107*
Kirshenblatt-Gimblett, Barbara 1942- *ConAu 81,*
IntAu&W 82
Kirshner, Gloria Ifland *ConAu 41R*
Kirshon, Vladimir Mikhailovich 1902-1938 *CnMD,*
ModWD
Kirshon, Vladimir Mikhaylovich 1902-1938?
CIDMEL 80
Kirsner, Douglas 1947- *ConAu 77*
Kirsner, Robert 1921- *ConAu 21R*
Kirst, Hans Hellmut 1914- *ASpks, ConAu 104,*
ModGL, TwCWr, WorAu
Kirst, Michael W 1939- *ConAu 45*
Kirstein, Lincoln 1907- *WrDr 84*
Kirsten, Grace 1900- *ConAu 104*
Kirstina, Vaino 1936- *IntAu&W 82*
Kirtland, G B *ConAu X, SmATA 2, WrDr 84*
Kirtland, Helen Johns 1890?-1979 *ConAu 89*
Kirtland, Kathleen 1945- *ConAu 65*
Kirvan, John J 1932- *ConAu 10NR, -21R*
Kirwan, Albert D 1904-1971 *ConAu 1R, -4NR*
Kirwan, Laurence Patrick 1907- *ConAu 1R*
Kirwan, Molly 1906- *ConAu P-1*
Kirwin, Harry Wynne 1911-1963 *ConAu 1R*
Kirzner, Israel M 1930- *ConAu 1R, -3NR*
Kis, Danilo 1935- *ConAu 109*
Kisamore, Norman D 1928- *ConAu 5R*
Kiser, Clyde Vernon 1904- *ConAu 25R*
Kiser, Thelma Scott 1916- *IntWWP 82*
Kish, G Hobab *ConAu X*
Kish, George 1914- *ConAu 1R, -1NR*
Kish, Kathleen Vera 1942- *ConAu 69*
Kish, Leslie 1910- *ConAu P-1, WrDr 84*
Kishida, Eriko 1929- *ConAu 7NR, -53,*
SmATA 12
Kishida, Kunio 1890-1954 *EncWL 2*
Kishon, Ephraim 1924- *ConAu 2NR, -49,*
IntAu&W 82
Kisiel, Teodor Klon *IntAu&W 82X*
Kisielewski, Stefan 1911- *IntAu&W 82*
Kisinger, Grace Gelvin 1913-1960? *ConAu P-1,*
SmATA 10
Kisjokai, Erzsebet Maria *IntWWP 82X*
Kisker, George W 1912- *ConAu 21R*
Kisluk, Michael W 1953- *IntWWP 82*
Kismaric, Carole 1942- *ConAu 8NR, -33R*
Kisner, Jack *IntWWP 82X*
Kisner, Jacob 1926- *IntWWP 82*
Kisor, Henry 1940- *ConAu 73*
Kissam, Ed *DrAP&F 83*
Kissam, Edward 1943- *ConAu 61*
Kissane, John M 1928- *ConAu 53*
Kissane, Leedice McAnelly 1905- *ConAu P-2*
Kissel, Howard William 1942- *ConAmTC*
Kissen, Fan 1904- *ConAu P-1*
Kissin, Eva H 1923- *ConAu 29R, SmATA 10*
Kissinger, Henry 1923- *WrDr 84*
Kissinger, Henry Alfred 1923- *ConAu 1R, -2NR,*
DcLEL 1940
Kissling, Dorothy 1904-1969 *ConAu 105*
Kissling, Fred R, Jr. 1930- *ConAu 21R,*
WrDr 84
Kiste, Robert Carl 1936- *ConAu 61*
Kister, Kenneth F 1935- *ConAu 25R*
Kistiakowsky, George B 1900-1982 *ConAu 108*
Kistiakowsky, Vera 1928- *ConAu 21R*
Kistler, Mark O 1918- *ConAu 77*
Kistner, Diane *DrAP&F 83*
Kistner, Robert William 1917- *ConAu 61,*
WrDr 84
Kitagawa, Daisuke 1910- *ConAu P-2*
Kitagawa, Joseph M 1915- *ConAu 1R, -2NR*
Kitano, Harry H L 1926- *ConAu 29R, WrDr 84*
Kitao, T Kaori 1933- *ConAu 106*
Kitchel, Denison 1908- *ConAu 105*
Kitchen, Helen 1920- *ConAu 8NR, -9R*
Kitchen, Herminie B 1901-1973 *ConAu P-1*
Kitchen, Judith *DrAP&F 83*
Kitchen, Martin 1936- *ConAu 10NR, -61,*
WrDr 84
Kitchen, Paddy 1934- *ConAu 25R,*
IntAu&W 82, WrDr 84
Kitchin, C H B 1895-1967 *LongCTC,*

TwCCr&M 80
Kitchin, Laurence 1913- *ConAu 104,*
IntAu&W 82
Kite, Larry *ConAu X*
Kitman, Marvin 1929- *ConAu 101*
Kitson, Jack William 1940- *ConAu 25R*
Kitson Clark, George Sydney Roberts 1900-
ConAu 21R
Kitt, Eartha Mae 1928- *ConAu 77, LivgBAA*
Kitt, Tamara *TwCCW 83, WrDr 84*
Kitterman, Barbara *IntWWP 82X*
Kitto, H D F 1897- *WrDr 84*
Kitto, H D F 1897-1982 *ConAu 105, ConAu P-1,*
ConLCrt 82
Kittredge, George Lyman 1860-1941 *LongCTC,*
TwCA, TwCA SUP
Kittredge, William *DrAP&F 83*
Kittrie, Nicholas N 1928- *ConAu 81*
Kitzinger, Ernst 1912- *ConAu 108*
Kitzinger, Sheila 1929- *ConAu 37R, WrDr 84*
Kitzinger, U W 1928- *ConAu 1NR*
Kitzinger, Uwe 1928- *ConAu 1R, IntAu&W 82,*
WrDr 84
Kivimaa, Arvi 1904- *IntAu&W 82*
Kivy, Peter Nathan 1934- *ConAu 103*
Kiya-Hinidza, Richard 1944- *IntWWP 82*
Kiyana, Richard *IntWWP 82X*
Kiyooka, Harry Mitsuo 1928- *CreCan 2*
Kiyooka, Roy Kenzie 1926- *CreCan 1*
Kizer, Carolyn *DrAP&F 83*
Kizer, Carolyn 1925- *ConAu 65, ConLC 15,*
ConP 80, CroCAP, DcLB 5[port],
DcLEL 1940, WorAu
Kizer, Carolyn 1926- *WrDr 84*
Kizer, Gary Allan *DrAP&F 83*
Kizerman, Rudolph 1934- *DcLEL 1940*
Kjelgaard, James Arthur 1910-1959 *ConAu 109,*
SmATA 17
Kjelgaard, Jim *ConAu X*
Kjelgaard, Jim 1910-1959 *SmATA X,*
TwCCW 83
Kjome, June C 1920- *ConAu 5R*
Kjp *IntAu&W 82X*
Klaas, Joe 1920- *ConAu 29R, WrDr 84*
Klaassen, Leo H 1920- *ConAu 11NR, -21R*
Klabund 1890-1928 *CIDMEL 80, CnMD,*
ModGL, ModWD
Kladstrup, Don 1943- *ConAu 77*
Klafs, Carl E 1911- *ConAu 13R*
Klagsbrun, Francine *ConAu 21R*
Klahr, Myra *DrAP&F 83*
Klahr, Myra 1933- *IntWWP 82*
Klaiber, Jeffrey L 1943- *ConAu 85*
Klaich, Dolores 1936- *ConAu 49*
Klain, Jane 1947- *ConAmTC*
Klainikite, Anne *ConAu X*
Klaits, Barrie 1944- *ConAu 73, MichAu 80*
Klamkin, Charles 1923- *ConAu 61*
Klamkin, Lynn 1950- *ConAu 45*
Klamkin, Marian 1926- *ConAu 1NR, -49,*
IntAu&W 82, WrDr 84
Klampfer, John Walker 1945- *CreCan 2*
Klann, Margaret L 1911- *ConAu 77*
Klaperman, Gilbert 1921- *ConAu 49,*
SmATA 33[port]
Klaperman, Libby Mindlin 1921-1982 *ConAu 9R,*
-107, SmATA 31N, -33
Klapp, Orrin E 1915- *ConAu 9R*
Klapper, Charles F 1905- *WrDr 84*
Klapper, Charles Frederick 1905- *ConAu P-1,*
IntAu&W 82
Klapper, M Roxana 1937- *ConAu 53*
Klapper, Marvin 1922- *ConAu 17R*
Klappert, Peter *DrAP&F 83*
Klappert, Peter 1942- *ConAu 33R,*
DcLB 5[port], IntAu&W 82, IntWWP 82,
WrDr 84
Klappholz, Kurt 1913-1975 *ConAu 61*
Klare, George Roger 1922- *ConAu 5R,*
WrDr 84
Klare, Hugh J 1916- *ConAu 103, IntAu&W 82,*
WrDr 84
Klaren, Peter F 1938- *ConAu 57*
Klarsfeld, Beate 1939- *ConAu 65*
Klass, Allan Arnold 1907- *ConAu 65*
Klass, Morton 1927- *ConAu 1R, -5NR,*
SmATA 11
Klass, Philip *WrDr 84*
Klass, Philip J 1919- *ConAu 25R*
Klass, Sheila Solomon *DrAP&F 83*
Klass, Sheila Solomon 1927- *ConAu 37R,*
WrDr 84

Klass, Sholom 1916- *ConAu 21R*
Klassen, Peter J 1930- *ConAu 1NR, -45*
Klassen, Randolph Jacob 1933- *ConAu 61*
Klassen, William 1930- *ConAu 10NR, -25R*
Klauber, John 1917-1981 *ConAu 104*
Klauber, Laurence M 1883-1968 *ConAu 105*
Klauck, Daniel L *DrAP&F 83*
Klauck, Daniel L 1947- *ConAu 69*
Klauder, Francis John 1918- *ConAu 53*
Klaue, Lola Shelton 1903- *ConAu 5R*
Klausler, Alfred P 1910- *ConAu 21R*
Klausmeier, Herbert John 1915- *ConAu 1R,*
-5NR
Klausner, Abraham J 1915- *ConAu 108*
Klausner, Lawrence D 1939- *ConAu 110*
Klausner, Margot 1905-1976? *ConAu 61*
Klausner, Samuel Z 1923- *ConAu 17R*
Klaw, Spencer 1920- *ConAu 25R*
Klawans, Harold L 1937- *ConAu 106*
Klayman, Maxwell Irving 1917- *ConAu 29R,*
WrDr 84
Klebe, Charles Eugene 1907- *ConAu P-2*
Klebe, Gene *ConAu X*
Kleberger, Ilse 1921- *ConAu 41R, SmATA 5*
Klee, James B 1916- *ConAu 109*
Kleeberg, Irene Cumming 1932- *ConAu 61*
Kleeman, Sydney Loeb 1931- *IntWWP 82*
Kleene, Stephen Cole 1909- *ConAu 41R,*
WrDr 84
Klees, Fredric 1901- *ConAu P-2*
Kleifum, Magnea *IntAu&W 82X*
Kleiler, Frank Munro 1914- *ConAu 89*
Kleiman, Robert 1918- *ConAu 13R*
Klein, A M 1909-1972 *ConAu 101, -37R,*
ConLC 19, EncWL 2
Klein, Aaron E 1930- *ConAu 25R, SmATA 28*
Klein, Abraham Moses 1909-1972 *CreCan 1,*
DcLEL 1940, LongCTC, ModCmwL,
TwCA SUP
Klein, Alan F 1911- *ConAu 57*
Klein, Alexander 1918- *ConAu 5R*
Klein, Alexander 1923- *WrDr 84*
Klein, Arnold William 1945- *ConAu 37R,*
IntAu&W 82
Klein, Bernard 1921- *ConAu 17R*
Klein, Binnie *DrAP&F 83*
Klein, Carol *DrAP&F 83*
Klein, Charlotte 1925- *ConAu 101*
Klein, Daniel Martin 1939- *ConAu 61*
Klein, Dave 1940- *ConAu 89*
Klein, David 1919- *ConAu 1R, -1NR*
Klein, David Ballin 1897- *ConAu 41R*
Klein, Donald C 1923- *ConAu 25R*
Klein, Doris F *ConAu X*
Klein, Edward 1936- *ConAu 69*
Klein, Elizabeth *DrAP&F 83*
Klein, Elizabeth 1939- *ConAu 110*
Klein, Ernest 1899- *ConAu P-2*
Klein, Frederic Shriver 1904- *ConAu 13R,*
WrDr 84
Klein, Gerald Louis 1926- *ConAmTC*
Klein, Gerard 1937- *ConAu 49, TwCSFW A*
Klein, H Arthur *ConAu 13R, SmATA 8*
Klein, Herbert George 1918- *IntAu&W 82*
Klein, Herbert Sanford 1936- *ConAu 93*
Klein, Holger Michael 1938- *ConAu 65*
Klein, Isaac 1905- *ConAu 57*
Klein, Jay Kay 1931- *ConSFA*
Klein, Jeffrey B 1948- *ConAu 77*
Klein, Joe *ConAu X*
Klein, John J 1929- *ConAu 17R*
Klein, Joseph 1946- *ConAu 85*
Klein, Josephine 1926- *ConAu 1R, WrDr 84*
Klein, K K *ConAu X*
Klein, Leonore 1916- *ConAu 1R, -1NR,*
SmATA 6
Klein, Marcus 1928- *ConAu 9R, WrDr 84*
Klein, Martin A 1934- *ConAu 21R*
Klein, Marymae Endsley 1917- *ConAu 97*
Klein, Maury 1939- *ConAu 33R*
Klein, Maxine 1934- *ConAu 10NR, -61*
Klein, Milton M 1917- *ConAu 93*
Klein, Mina Cooper 1906- *ConAu 37R,*
IntAu&W 82, SmATA 8
Klein, Muriel Walzer 1920- *ConAu 29R*
Klein, Norma *DrAP&F 83*
Klein, Norma 1938- *ChlLR 2, ConAu 41R,*
SmATA 7, TwCCW 83, WrDr 84
Klein, Philip Alexander 1927- *ConAu 17R,*
WrDr 84
Klein, Philip S 1909- *ConAu 1R, -1NR,*
IntAu&W 82

Klein, Randolph Shipley 1942- *ConAu 73*
Klein, Richard M 1923- *ConAu 108*
Klein, Rose 1918- *ConAu 21R*
Klein, Stanley 1930- *ConAu 57*
Klein, Stanley D 1936- *ConAu 77*
Klein, Stewart Roy 1933- *ConAmTC*
Klein, Suzanne Marie 1940- *ConAu 57*
Klein, Ted U 1926- *ConAu 25R*
Klein, Thomas D 1941- *ConAu 61*
Klein, Walter J 1923- *ConAu 69*
Klein, William *DrAP&F 83*
Klein, Woody 1929- *ConAu 13R*
Kleinbauer, W Eugene 1937- *ConAu 37R*
Kleinberg, Seymour 1933- *ConAu 105*
Kleinberger, Aharon Fritz 1920- *IntAu&W 82*
Kleine, Glen 1936- *ConAu 73*
Kleine-Ahlbrandt, W Laird 1932- *ConAu 29R,
    IntAu&W 82*
Kleine-Ahlbrandt, William Laird 1932- *WrDr 84*
Kleineidam, Horst 1932- *CroCD*
Kleiner, Dick *IntAu&W 82X*
Kleiner, Henry 1923- *IntWWP 82*
Kleiner, Richard Arthur 1921- *IntAu&W 82*
Kleinfeld, Gerald R 1936- *ConAu 103*
Kleinfeld, Judith S 1944- *ConAu 77*
Kleinfeld, Vincent A 1907- *ConAu 10NR, -17R*
Kleinfield, Sonny 1950- *ConAu 97*
Kleinhans, Theodore 1924- *WrDr 84*
Kleinhans, Theodore John 1924- *ConAu 5R*
Kleinke, Chris 1944- *ConAu 89*
Kleinman, Arthur 1941- *ConAu 105*
Kleinman, Louis 1912- *ConAmTC*
Kleinmann, Jack H 1932- *ConAu 21R*
Kleinmuntz, Benjamin 1930- *ConAu 33R*
Kleinschmidt, Karl 1913- *IntAu&W 82*
Kleinzahler, August *DrAP&F 83*
Klejment, Anne M 1950- *ConAu 101*
Klem, Kaye Wilson 1941- *ConAu 89*
Klement, Frank L 1908- *ConAu 9R,
    IntAu&W 82, WrDr 84*
Klemer, Richard Hudson 1918-1972 *ConAu 4NR,
    -5R, -37R*
Klemesrud, Judy *ConAu 89*
Klemin, Diana *ConAu 49*
Klemke, E D 1926- *ConAu 10NR, -25R*
Klemm, Edward G, Jr. 1910- *ConAu 57,
    SmATA 30*
Klemm, Roberta Kohnhorst 1884-1975 *ConAu 61,
    IntAu&W 82, SmATA 30*
Klemm, W R 1934- *ConAu 93*
Klempner, Irving M 1924- *ConAu 53*
Klempner, John 1898-1972 *ConAu 37R*
Klen, Yuriy 1891-1947 *ModSL 2*
Klenbort, Charlotte *ConAu X*
Klenicki, Leon 1930- *ConAu 106*
Klenk, Robert W 1934- *ConAu 29R*
Klenz, William 1915- *ConAu 5R*
Klepfisz, Irena *DrAP&F 83*
Klerer, Melvin 1926- *ConAu 21R*
Klerman, Lorraine V 1929- *ConAu 81*
Klessmann, Eckart 1933- *IntAu&W 82*
Klett, Guy S 1897- *ConAu P-1*
Kleuser, Louise C 1889?-1976 *ConAu 65*
Klewin, W Thomas 1921- *ConAu 29R*
Kleyman, Paul 1945- *ConAu 57*
Kliban, B 1935- *ConAu 106*
Kliever, Lonnie D 1931- *ConAu 29R*
Kliewer, Evelyn 1933- *ConAu 101*
Kliewer, Warren *DrAP&F 83*
Kliewer, Warren 1931- *ConAu 2NR, -45,
    NatPD 81[port]*
Kligerman, Jack 1938- *ConAu 85*
Kligman, Ruth 1930- *ConAu 101*
Klima, Ivan 1931- *ConAu 25R, ModSL 2*
Klimas, Antanas 1924- *ConAu 41R*
Klimek, David E 1941- *ConAu 89*
Klimenko, Michael 1924- *ConAu 73*
Klimentov, A P *WorAu 1970*
Klimentov, Andrei Platonovich 1899-1951
    ConAu 108
Klimisch, Sister Mary Jane 1920- *ConAu 17R*
Klimo, Jake *ConAu X*
Klimo, Jon *DrAP&F 83*
Klimo, Vernon 1914- *ConAu 101*
Klimowicz, Barbara 1927- *ConAu 21R,
    SmATA 10*
Klin, George 1931- *ConAu 53*
Klinck, Carl Frederick 1908- *ConAu 17R,
    DcLEL 1940*
Klinck, George Alfred 1903-1973 *ConAu 9R,
    -103*
Klindt-Jensen, Ole 1918-1980 *ConAu 10NR, -101,*

    -21R
Kline, George L 1921- *AuNews 1, ConAu 9NR,
    -17R*
Kline, Lloyd W 1931- *ConAu 33R, WrDr 84*
Kline, Morris 1908- *ConAu 2NR, -5R,
    IntAu&W 82, WrDr 84*
Kline, Nancy *DrAP&F 83*
Kline, Nancy Meadors 1946- *ConAu 57*
Kline, Nathan S 1916- *ConAu 81*
Kline, Nathan S 1916-1983 *ConAu 109*
Kline, Norman 1935- *NatPD 81[port]*
Kline, Otis Adelbert 1891-1946 *TwCSFW*
Kline, Peter 1936- *ConAu 25R, WrDr 84*
Kline, Thomas J 1942- *ConAu 85*
Klineberg, Stephen L 1940- *ConAu 77*
Klinefelter, Walter 1899- *ConAu 3NR, -9R*
Klineman, George A 1947- *ConAu 107*
Kling, Robert E, Jr. 1920- *ConAu 29R*
Kling, Simcha 1922- *ConAu 13R*
Klinger, Eric 1933- *ConAu 33R, IntAu&W 82,
    WrDr 84*
Klinger, Henry *TwCCr&M 80, WrDr 84*
Klinger, Kurt 1914- *ConAu 17R*
Klinger, Kurt 1928- *CnMD, CroCD,
    IntAu&W 82*
Klinghoffer, Arthur Jay 1941- *ConAu 65*
Klingler, Maria 1932- *IntAu&W 82*
Klingler, Mary P 1953- *IntWWP 82*
Klingstedt, Joe Lars 1938- *ConAu 53*
Klink, Johanna L 1918- *ConAu 8NR, -61*
Klinkowitz, Jerome 1943- *ConAu 1NR, -45*
Klintberg, Bengt Af 1938- *IntWWP 82*
Klipper, Miriam Z *ConAu 108*
Klise, Eugene Storm 1908- *ConAu 5R*
Klise, Thomas S 1928- *ConAu 57*
Klobuchar, James John 1928- *ConAu 73*
Klobuchar, Jim *ConAu X*
Kloefkorn, William *DrAP&F 83*
Kloepfer, Marguerite 1916- *ConAu 97,
    IntAu&W 82*
Kloetzli, Walter 1921- *ConAu 1R*
Klonglan, Gerald E 1936- *ConAu 41R*
Klonis, N I *ConAu X*
Klonsky, Milton 1921?-1981 *ConAu 105*
Kloor, Mary Conway *ConSFA*
Kloos, Peter 1936- *ConAu 93*
Kloos, Willem Johannes Theodorus 1859-1938
    ClDMEL 80
Klooster, Fred H 1922- *ConAu 1R,
    IntAu&W 82*
Klopf, Donald W 1923- *ConAu 89*
Klopfer, Peter H 1930- *ConAu 85*
Klopfer, Walter G 1923- *ConAu 89*
Kloppenburg, Boaventura 1919- *ConAu 65*
Klos, Frank W, Jr. 1924- *ConAu 13R*
Klose, Kevin 1940- *ConAu 53*
Klose, Norma Cline 1936- *ConAu 17R*
Klosinski, Emil 1922- *ConAu 65*
Kloss, Phillips Wray 1902-1933 *ConAu P-1*
Kloss, Robert J 1935- *ConAu 45*
Kloss, Robert Marsh 1938- *ConAu 65*
Klossowski, Pierre 1903- *ClDMEL 80*
Kloten, Edgar Lawrence 1912- *ConAmTC*
Klotman, Phyllis Rauch *ConAu 93*
Klotman, Robert Howard 1918- *ConAu 53*
Klots, Alexander Barrett 1903- *ConAu 107*
Klotter, James C 1947- *ConAu 77*
Klotter, John C 1918- *ConAu 93*
Klubertanz, George Peter 1912- *ConAu 5R*
Kluckhohn, Clyde Kay Maben 1905-1960
    TwCA SUP
Kluckhohn, Frank L 1907-1970 *ConAu 5R, -29R*
Klug, Eugene F 1917- *ConAu 1NR, -45*
Klug, Ron 1939- *ConAu 107, SmATA 31[port]*
Kluge, Alexander 1932- *ClDMEL 80,
    ConAu 81, ModGL*
Kluge, Eike-Henner W 1942- *ConAu 61*
Kluge, P F 1942- *ConAu 73*
Kluger, James R 1939- *ConAu 29R*
Kluger, Richard 1934- *ConAu 6NR, -9R*
Kluger, Ruth 1914-1980 *ConAu 108*
Klugh, Henry E 1927- *ConAu 53*
Kluwe, Mary Jean 1905-1975 *ConAu P-2*
Klyuev, Nikolay Alexeevich 1887-1937? *EncWL 2*
Klyuyev, Nikolay Alekseyevich 1887-1937
    ClDMEL 80
Klyuyev, Nikolay Alexeyevich 1887-1937 *TwCWr*
Kmoch, Hans 1897?-1973 *ConAu 41R*
Knachel, Philip Atherton 1926- *ConAu 21R*
Knaplund, Paul Alexander 1885-1964 *ConAu P-1*
Knapp, Bettina L 1926- *ConAu 6NR, -13R,
    IntAu&W 82*

Knapp, Budd 1915- *CreCan 2*
Knapp, David A 1938- *ConAu 41R*
Knapp, Herbert W 1931- *ConAu 105*
Knapp, J Merrill 1914- *ConAu 53*
Knapp, James F 1940- *ConAu 107*
Knapp, Jeffrey *DrAP&F 83*
Knapp, Joseph G 1900- *ConAu 37R*
Knapp, Joseph G 1900-1983 *ConAu 110*
Knapp, Joseph G 1924- *ConAu 41R*
Knapp, Lewis M 1894- *ConAu 21R*
Knapp, Mark L 1938- *ConAu 81*
Knapp, Mary L 1931- *ConAu 105*
Knapp, Robert Hampden 1915-1974 *ConAu 53,
    ConAu P-2*
Knapp, Ron 1952- *ConAu 103,
    SmATA 34[port]*
Knapp, Wilfrid Arthur *CreCan 2*
Knapp-Fisher, Edward George 1915- *WrDr 84*
Knapper, Christopher 1940- *ConAu 29R*
Knapton, Ernest John 1902- *ConAu 1R, -1NR,
    IntAu&W 82, WrDr 84*
Knaub, Richard K 1928- *ConAu 41R*
Knauff, Ellen Raphael *WrDr 84*
Knaus, William A 1946- *ConAu 105,
    IntAu&W 82*
Knauth, Joachim 1931- *CnMD*
Knauth, Percy 1914- *ConAu 57*
Knauth, Stephen *DrAP&F 83*
Knauth, Victor W 1895?-1977 *ConAu 73*
Kneale, Nigel 1922- *ConDr 82C, TwCSFW,
    WrDr 84*
Knebel, Fletcher *DrAP&F 83*
Knebel, Fletcher 1911- *AuNews 1, ConAu 1R,
    -1NR, ConLC 14, ConNov 82,
    DcLEL 1940, IntAu&W 82, TwCSFW,
    WrDr 84*
Knecht, Robert Jean 1926- *ConAu 33R,
    IntAu&W 82, WrDr 84*
Knechtges, David R 1942- *ConAu 65*
Kneebone, Geoffrey Thomas 1918- *ConAu 5R*
Kneese, Allen V 1930- *ConAu 8NR, -13R*
Knef, Hildegard 1925- *ASpks, ConAu 4NR, -45*
Kneifel, Christian 1943- *IntAu&W 82*
Knell, William Henry 1927- *IntWWP 82*
Kneller, John W 1916- *ConAu 17R*
Knelman, Fred H 1919- *ConAu 102*
Knelman, Martin 1943- *ConAu 73*
Knepler, Henry 1922- *ConAu 21R,
    IntAu&W 82*
Knezevich, Stephen J 1920- *ConAu 5R, -10NR*
Knibbs, H H 1874-1945 *TwCWW*
Knibbs, Harry Herbert 1874-1945 *TwCA,
    TwCA SUP*
Knickerbocker, Charles Herrick 1922-
    ConAu 13R
Knickerbocker, Kenneth L 1905- *ConAu 5R*
Knickmeyer, Steve 1944- *ConAu 85*
Knies, Elizabeth 1941- *ConAu 109*
Knieza, Emil 1920- *IntAu&W 82*
Knifesmith *ConAu X, SmATA X*
Kniffen, Fred B 1900- *ConAu 1R*
Knight *IntAu&W 82X*
Knight, Adam *ConAu X*
Knight, Alanna *ConAu 81, IntAu&W 82,
    TwCRGW*
Knight, Alice Valle 1922- *ConAu 81*
Knight, Andrew Stephen Bower 1939-
    IntAu&W 82
Knight, Anne 1946- *SmATA 34*
Knight, Anne Katherine 1933- *WrDr 84*
Knight, Arthur 1916- *ConAu 41R*
Knight, Arthur Winfield *DrAP&F 83*
Knight, Arthur Winfield 1937- *ConAu 4NR, -53,
    IntWWP 82*
Knight, Bernard 1931- *ConAu 2NR, -49,
    WrDr 84*
Knight, Bertram 1904- *ConAu 103*
Knight, Bill *IntWWP 82X*
Knight, Charles 1910- *ConAu 109*
Knight, Charles Landon 1867-1933 *AuNews 2*
Knight, Charles W 1891- *ConAu P-1*
Knight, Clayton 1891-1969 *ConAu P-1*
Knight, Damon 1922- *ConAu 3NR, -49,
    ConSFA, DcLB 8[port], DrmM[port],
    SmATA 9, TwCSFW, WorAu*
Knight, David *ConAu X, WrDr 84*
Knight, David C 1925- *ConAu 73, SmATA 14*
Knight, David Marcus 1936- *ConAu 7NR, -57*
Knight, Doug 1925- *ConAu 85*
Knight, Douglas M 1921- *ConAu 2NR, -49*
Knight, Eric 1897-1943 *TwCCW 83*
Knight, Eric Mowbray 1897-1943 *SmATA 18,*

TwCA, TwCA SUP
Knight, Etheridge *DrAP&F 83*
Knight, Etheridge 1931- *ConAu 21R, ConP 80, LivgBAA, WrDr 84*
Knight, Everett Warren 1919- *ConAu 33R*
Knight, Francis Edgar 1905- *ConAu 73, SmATA 14*
Knight, Frank 1905- *ConAu X, SmATA X, TwCCW 83, WrDr 84*
Knight, Frank H 1885-1972 *ConAu 33R*
Knight, Franklin W 1942- *ConAu 101, IntAu&W 82*
Knight, Frida 1910- *ConAu 2NR, -49, IntAu&W 82*
Knight, G Norman 1891- *ConAu 25R*
Knight, G Wilson 1897- *ConAu 10NR, ConLCrt 82*
Knight, Gareth *ConAu X, WrDr 84*
Knight, George A 1909- *WrDr 84*
Knight, George Angus Fulton 1909- *ConAu 1R, IntAu&W 82*
Knight, George Richard Wilson 1897- *IntAu&W 82, WrDr 84*
Knight, George Wilson 1897- *ConAu 13R, TwCA, TwCA SUP*
Knight, Glee 1947- *ConAu 57*
Knight, H Ralph 1895- *ConAu P-2*
Knight, Hardwicke 1911- *IntAu&W 82*
Knight, Harold V 1907- *ConAu 21R*
Knight, Hattie M 1908-1976 *ConAu P-2*
Knight, Hilary 1926- *ConAu 73, SmATA 15*
Knight, Hugh McCown 1905- *ConAu 5R*
Knight, Ione Kemp 1922- *ConAu 37R*
Knight, Isabel F 1930- *ConAu 25R*
Knight, James *ConAu X*
Knight, James Allen 1918- *ConAu 6NR, -13R, IntAu&W 82, WrDr 84*
Knight, Janet M 1940- *ConAu 93*
Knight, John S, III *AuNews 2*
Knight, John Shively 1894-1981 *AuNews 2, ConAu 103, -93*
Knight, K G 1921- *ConAu 25R*
Knight, Karl Frederick 1930- *ConAu 17R, WrDr 84*
Knight, Kathleen M Duell 1952- *IntWWP 82*
Knight, Kit *DrAP&F 83, IntWWP 82X*
Knight, Mallory T *ConAu X, SmATA X*
Knight, Margaret Kennedy 1903- *WrDr 84*
Knight, Margaret Kennedy Horsey 1903- *ConAu P-1, IntAu&W 82*
Knight, Max 1909- *ConAu 93*
Knight, Maxwell 1900- *ConAu P-1*
Knight, Michael E 1935- *ConAu 105*
Knight, Norman L 1895-1970? *ConAu P-2, ConSFA, TwCSFW*
Knight, Oliver 1919- *ConAu 21R*
Knight, Paul Emerson 1925- *ConAu 13R*
Knight, Robin 1943- *ConAu 73*
Knight, Roderic C 1942- *ConAu 61*
Knight, Roy Clement 1907- *ConAu 13R*
Knight, Ruth Adams 1898-1974 *ConAu 5R, -49, SmATA 20N*
Knight, Stephen 1951- *ConAu 69*
Knight, Thomas J 1937- *ConAu 102*
Knight, Thomas S 1921- *ConAu 17R*
Knight, Vick R, Jr. 1928- *ConAu 1NR, -45*
Knight, W Nicholas 1939- *ConAu 37R*
Knight, Walker L 1924- *ConAu 37R*
Knight, Wallace E *DrAP&F 83*
Knight, Wallace E 1926- *ConAu 11NR, -65*
Knight, William Nicholas 1939- *WrDr 84*
Knight, Wilson 1897- *LongCTC*
Knight-Patterson, W M *ConAu X, WrDr 84*
Knightley, Phillip 1929- *ConAu 25R, WrDr 84*
Knights, John Keell 1930?-1981 *ConAu 102*
Knights, L C 1906- *ConAu 3NR, ConLCrt 82, WrDr 84*
Knights, Lionel Charles 1906- *ConAu 5R, IntAu&W 82, TwCA SUP*
Knights, Peter R 1938- *ConAu 37R*
Knights, Ward A, Jr. 1927- *ConAu 97*
Knigin, Michael Jay 1942- *ConAu 85*
Kniker, Charles Robert 1936- *ConAu 77*
Knipe, Humphry 1941- *ConAu 37R*
Knipe, Wayne Bishop, III 1946- *ConAu 53*
Knipschield, Don 1940- *ConAu 5R*
Knist, F Emma 1948- *ConAu 5NR, -53*
Knister, Raymond 1899?-1932 *CreCan 1*
Knittel, John 1891-1970 *ConAu 104, TwCA, TwCA SUP*
Knobel, Betty Wehrli 1904- *IntAu&W 82*

Knobler, Nathan 1926- *ConAu 33R*
Knobler, Peter 1946- *ConAu 97*
Knobloch, Hans Werner 1928- *IntAu&W 82*
Knobloch, Heinz 1926- *IntAu&W 82*
Knoblock, Edward 1874-1945 *ConAu 108, DcLB 10[port], ModWD*
Knock, Warren 1932- *ConAu 65*
Knoebl, Kuno 1936- *ConAu 25R*
Knoepfle, John *DrAP&F 83*
Knoepfle, John 1923- *ConAu 13R, ConP 80, WrDr 84*
Knoepflmacher, U C 1931- *ConAu 10NR, -13R*
Knoerle, Jeanne 1928- *ConAu 45*
Knoke, David 1947- *ConAu 10NR, -65*
Knoles, George Harmon 1907- *ConAu 5R*
Knoll, Erwin 1931- *ConAu 89*
Knoll, Gerald M 1942- *ConAu 29R*
Knoll, Paul W 1937- *ConAu 107, WrDr 84*
Knoll, Robert Edwin 1922- *ConAu 1R, -5NR*
Knollenberg, Bernhard 1892-1973 *ConAu 41R, ConAu P-2*
Knoop, Faith Yingling 1896- *ConAu 97*
Knop, Werner 1912?-1970 *ConAu 29R*
Knopf, Alfred A 1892- *ConAu 106*
Knopf, Edwin H 1899-1982? *ConAu 105*
Knopf, Kenyon A 1921- *ConAu 77*
Knopf, Terry Ann 1940- *ConAu 25R, WrDr 84*
Knopfli, Rui 1932- *CIDMEL 80*
Knopp, Josephine Zadovsky 1941- *ConAu 103*
Knorr, Albert Scofield 1929- *ConAu 25R*
Knorr, Hilde 1919- *IntAu&W 82*
Knorr, Klaus 1911- *WrDr 84*
Knorr, Marian L 1910- *ConAu 102*
Knott, Bill *WrDr 84*
Knott, Bill 1927- *ConAu X, SmATA 3*
Knott, Bill 1940- *ConP 80, WrDr 84*
Knott, John R, Jr. 1937- *ConAu 57*
Knott, Leonard L 1905- *ConAu 107*
Knott, Will C *ConAu X*
Knott, William C 1927- *WrDr 84*
Knott, William Cecil, Jr. 1927- *ConAu 5R, -7NR, SmATA 3*
Knott, William Kilborn 1940- *CroCAP*
Knotts, Howard 1922- *ConAu 11NR, -69, SmATA 25[port]*
Knovitz, Milton Ridcas 1908- *IntAu&W 82*
Knowland, William Fife 1908-1974 *ConAu 89*
Knowler, John 1933?-1979 *ConAu 85*
Knowles, A Sidney, Jr. 1926- *ConAu 101*
Knowles, Alison *DrAP&F 83*
Knowles, Alison 1933- *ConAu 8NR, -17R*
Knowles, Anne 1933- *ConAu 102, WrDr 84*
Knowles, Asa Smallidge 1909- *ConAu 29R*
Knowles, Clayton 1908-1978 *ConAu 73, -81*
Knowles, David 1896-1974 *ConAu 4NR, -5R, -53, WorAu*
Knowles, Dorothy 1906- *ConAu 25R, IntAu&W 82, WrDr 84*
Knowles, Henry P 1912- *ConAu 61*
Knowles, John *DrAP&F 83*
Knowles, John 1926- *ConAu 17R, ConLC 1, -4, -10, -26[port], ConNov 82, DcLB 6, DcLEL 1940, IntAu&W 82, SmATA 8, WorAu, WrDr 84*
Knowles, John H 1926-1979 *ConAu 101, -85*
Knowles, Joseph W 1922- *ConAu 21R*
Knowles, Malcolm Shepherd 1913- *ConAu 5R, -5NR*
Knowles, Michael Clive David 1896-1974 *DcLEL 1940*
Knowles, Susanne 1911- *WrDr 84*
Knowles, Yereth K 1920- *ConAu 93*
Knowlton, Derrick 1921- *ConAu 6NR, -57, WrDr 84*
Knowlton, Edgar Colby, Jr. 1921- *ConAu 41R, IntAu&W 82*
Knowlton, Robert A 1914-1968 *ConAu 1R, -103*
Knowlton, William H 1927- *ConAu 17R, WrDr 84*
Knox, Alexander 1907- *ConAu 81*
Knox, Bill *WrDr 84*
Knox, Bill 1928- *ConAu X, IntAu&W 82X, TwCCr&M 80*
Knox, Calvin *WrDr 84*
Knox, Calvin M *ConAu X, SmATA X, TwCSFW, WorAu 1970*
Knox, Cleone *ConAu X*
Knox, Collie 1897-1977 *ConAu 73, -77*
Knox, David Broughton 1916- *WrDr 84*
Knox, Donald E 1936- *ConAu 45*
Knox, Edmund George Valpy 1881-1971 *ConAu 29R, LongCTC, TwCA,*

TwCA SUP
Knox, Eleanor Jessie 1909- *SmATA 30[port]*
Knox, George Alexander 1919- *WrDr 84*
Knox, Henry Macdonald 1916- *ConAu 13R, WrDr 84*
Knox, Hugh 1942- *ConAu 103*
Knox, James *ConAu X, DrAP&F 83*
Knox, John 1900- *ConAu 13R, WrDr 84*
Knox, John Ballenger 1909- *ConAu P-1*
Knox, Katharine McCook 1890?-1983 *ConAu 110*
Knox, Malcolm 1900-1980 *ConAu 103, -97*
Knox, Raymond Anthony 1926- *IntAu&W 82*
Knox, Robert Buick 1918- *ConAu 25R, IntAu&W 82, WrDr 84*
Knox, Ronald Arbuthnott 1888-1957 *LongCTC, TwCA, TwCA SUP, TwCCr&M 80, TwCWr*
Knox, Samuel James 1918- *WrDr 84*
Knox, Vera Huntingdon *ConAu 9R*
Knox, Warren Barr 1925- *ConAu 49*
Knox, William 1928- *ConAu 1R, -1NR, IntAu&W 82, WrDr 84*
Knox-Johnston, Robin 1939- *ConAu 29R, IntAu&W 82, WrDr 84*
Knox-Mawer, June 1930- *IntAu&W 82*
Knudsen, Erik 1922- *CIDMEL 80*
Knudsen, Hans August Heinrich 1886-1971 *ConAu 29R*
Knudsen, Jakob Christian Lindberg 1858-1917 *CIDMEL 80*
Knudsen, Margrethe June 1934- *WrDr 84*
Knudsen, R R *ConAu X*
Knudson, Danny 1940- *ConAu 11NR*
Knudson, Danny Alan 1940- *ConAu 61, IntAu&W 82, WrDr 84*
Knudson, R R *ConAu X, SmATA 7*
Knudson, Richard L 1930- *ConAu 104, SmATA 34[port]*
Knudson, Rozanne R 1932- *ConAu 33R, SmATA 7, WrDr 84*
Knudtsen, Ingar, Jr. 1944- *IntAu&W 82*
Knuemann, Carl H 1922- *ConAu 77*
Knusel, Jack Leonard 1923- *ConAu 25R, WrDr 84*
Knuth, Helen 1912- *ConAu 53*
Knutson, Jeanne N 1934- *ConAu 41R*
Knutson, Kent S 1924-1973 *ConAu 41R, ConAu P-2*
Knutson, Nancy Roxbury *DrAP&F 83*
Knye, Cassandra *WrDr 84*
Ko, Kanzein *ConAu X*
Ko, Won *DrAP&F 83*
Ko, Won 1925- *ConAu 61*
Kobal, John 1943- *ConAu 11NR, -61*
Kobayashi, Chris *DrAP&F 83, IntWWP 82X*
Kobayashi, Masako Matsuno 1935- *ConAu 5R*
Kobayashi, Noritake 1932- *ConAu 53, IntAu&W 82*
Kobayashi, Tetsuya 1926- *ConAu 69*
Kober, Arthur 1900-1975 *ConAu 57, ConAu P-1, ModWD, TwCA, TwCA SUP*
Kober, Arthur Leon 1920- *ConAu 13R*
Kobler, John 1910- *ConAu 65*
Kobler, Turner S 1930- *ConAu 37R*
Kobrak, Peter 1936- *ConAu 104*
Kobre, Sidney 1907- *ConAu 65*
Kobrin, David 1941- *ConAu 41R*
Kobrin, Janet 1942- *ConAu 57*
Kobryn, A P 1949- *ConAu 93*
Kobs, Jean 1912- *IntAu&W 82*
Koc, Robert Joseph 1914- *IntAu&W 82*
Kocbek, Edvard 1904- *CIDMEL 80*
Koch *IntWWP 82X*
Koch, C J 1932- *ConNov 82*
Koch, Charlotte *ConAu 85*
Koch, Claude 1918- *WrDr 84*
Koch, Claude Francis *DrAP&F 83*
Koch, Claude Francis 1918- *ConAu 9R, IntAu&W 82*
Koch, Dorothy Clarke 1924- *ConAu 5R, SmATA 6*
Koch, Eric 1919- *ConAu 69*
Koch, H W 1933- *ConAu 93*
Koch, Hans-Gerhard 1913- *ConAu 17R*
Koch, Helen L 1895- *ConAu P-2*
Koch, Howard 1902- *ConAu 73, ConDr 82A, DcLB 26[port]*
Koch, James Harold 1926- *ConAu 106, IntWWP 82*
Koch, Joanne 1940- *ConAu 69, NatPD 81[port]*
Koch, Kenneth *DrAP&F 83*

Koch, Kenneth 1925- *ConAu 1R, –6NR,*
ConDr 82, ConLC 5, –8, ConP 80,
CroCAP, DcLB 5[port], DcLEL 1940,
WorAu, WrDr 84
Koch, Kurt E 1913- *ConAu 107*
Koch, Lew Z 1935- *ConAu 69*
Koch, Michael 1916?-1981 *ConAu 103*
Koch, Raymond *ConAu 85*
Koch, Richard 1921- *ConAu 29R*
Koch, Robert 1918- *ConAu 9R*
Koch, Stephen *DrAP&F 83*
Koch, Stephen 1941- *ConAu 77*
Koch, Thilo 1920- *ConAu 11NR, –25R,*
IntAu&W 82
Koch, Thomas J 1947- *ConAu 61, –69*
Koch, Thomas Walter 1933- *ConAu 17R*
Koch, Vivienne 1914-1961 *TwCA SUP*
Koch, Willi August 1903- *IntAu&W 82*
Koch, William H, Jr. 1923- *ConAu 17R*
Kochan, Lionel Edmund 1922- *ConAu 105*
Kochan, Miriam 1929- *ConAu 103, WrDr 84*
Kochan, Paul C 1906- *ConAu 45*
Kochen, Manfred 1928- *ConAu 21R*
Kochenburger, Ralph J 1919- *ConAu 53*
Kocher, Eric 1912- *ConAu 57*
Kocher, Paul H 1907- *ConAu 65*
Kochetov, Vsevolod A 1912-1973 *ConAu 45*
Kochiss, John 1926- *ConAu 97*
Kochman, Thomas 1936- *ConAu 37R*
Kock, Winston E 1909-1982 *ConAu 110*
Kocsis, J C *SmATA X*
Kocsis, Theresa Julia 1907- *IntWWP 82*
Kodanda Rao, Pandurangi 1889- *ConAu 13R*
Koehler, Alan 1928- *ConAu 13R*
Koehler, G Stanley 1915- *ConAu 37R,*
WrDr 84
Koehler, George E 1930- *ConAu 25R*
Koehler, Isabel Winifred 1903- *IntWWP 82*
Koehler, Ludmila 1917- *ConAu 53*
Koehler, Lyle P 1944- *ConAu 109*
Koehler, Margaret Hudson *ConAu 85,*
IntAu&W 82
Koehler, Nikki 1951- *ConAu 25R*
Koehler, Stanley *DrAP&F 83*
Koehler, W R 1914- *ConAu 9R*
Koehn, Ilse *ConAu X, SmATA X*
Koehn-VanZwienen, Ilse Charlotte 1929-
IntAu&W 82
Koelsch, William Alvin 1933- *ConAu 104*
Koen, Ross Y 1918- *ConAu 1R*
Koenig, Allen Edward 1939- *ConAu 21R*
Koenig, C Eldo 1919- *ConAu 21R*
Koenig, Duane 1918- *ConAu 37R*
Koenig, Franz 1905- *ConAu 101*
Koenig, Fritz H 1940- *ConAu 53*
Koenig, Howard D *DrAP&F 83*
Koenig, John 1938- *ConAu 102*
Koenig, Laird *ConAu 29R*
Koenig, Louis William 1916- *ConAu 1R*
Koenig, Rene 1906- *ConAu 81*
Koenig, Samuel 1899-1972 *ConAu 37R,*
ConAu P-2
Koenig, Walter 1936- *ConAu 104*
Koenig, Wolf *CreCan 2*
Koenigsberg, Moses 1879-1945 *DcLB 25[port]*
Koenigsberger, H G 1918- *ConAu 33R*
Koenigsberger, Helmut Georg 1918-
IntAu&W 82, WrDr 84
Koenigswald, Ralph Von *ConAu X*
Koenker, Ernest Benjamin 1920- *ConAu 106*
Koenner, Alfred 1921- *ConAu 101*
Koepf, Michael *DrAP&F 83*
Koepf, Michael 1940- *ConAu 81*
Koepke, Wulf 1928- *ConAu 93*
Koeppel, Gary 1938- *ConAu 49*
Koeppen, Wolfgang 1906- *CIDMEL 80,*
EncWL 2, ModGL
Koerner, James D 1923- *ConAu 9R, WrDr 84*
Koerner, John Michael Anthony *CreCan 2*
Koerner, Stephan 1913- *ConAu 1R*
Koerner, W H D 1878-1938 *SmATA 21[port]*
Koerte, Mary Norbert 1934- *ConAu 103*
Koertge, Noretta 1935- *ConAu 106*
Koertge, Ronald *DrAP&F 83*
Koertge, Ronald 1940- *ConAu 9NR, –65*
Koesis, Robert 1935- *ConAu 29R*
Koestenbaum, Peter 1928- *ConAu 29R*
Koestenbaum, Phyllis *DrAP&F 83*
Koestenbaum, Phyllis 1930- *ConAu 107*
Koester, Helmut 1926- *ConAu 110*
Koestler, Arthur 1905- *ASpks, CnMWL,*
ConAu 1R, –1NR, ConLC 1, –3, –6, –8, –15,

ConNov 82, EncWL 2, IntAu&W 82,
LongCTC, ModBrL, TwCA SUP,
TwCSFW, TwCWr, WhoTwCL, WrDr 84
Koestler, Arthur 1905-1983 *ConAu 109,*
DcLB Y83N[port]
Koethe, John *DrAP&F 83*
Koethe, John 1945- *ConAu 49*
Koff, Richard M 1926- *WrDr 84*
Koff, Richard Myram 1926- *ConAu 89*
Kofoed, Jack *ConAu X*
Kofoed, John C 1894-1979 *ConAu 5R, –93*
Kofoed, Rud 1945- *IntAu&W 82*
Kofsky, Frank 1935- *ConAu 57*
Kogan, Bernard Robert 1920- *ConAu 9R*
Kogan, Herman 1914- *ConAu 5NR, –9R*
Kogan, Leonard S 1919-1976 *ConAu 65*
Kogan, Maurice 1930- *ConAu 107,*
IntAu&W 82
Kogan, Norman 1919- *ConAu 1R, WrDr 84*
Kogan Ray, Deborah 1940- *ConAu 7NR*
Kogawa, Joy Nozomi 1935- *ConAu 101,*
IntWWP 82, WrDr 84
Kogiku, K C 1927- *ConAu 33R*
Kogiku, Kiichiro Chris 1927- *WrDr 84*
Koginos, Manny T 1933- *ConAu 21R*
Kogos, Frederick 1907-1974 *ConAu 53,*
ConAu P-2
Koh, Byung Chul 1936- *ConAu 17R*
Koh, Sung Jae 1917- *ConAu 17R*
Kohak, Erazim V 1933- *ConAu 37R*
Kohan, Rhea *ConAu 89, IntAu&W 82*
Kohanski, Alexander S 1902- *ConAu 108*
Kohavi, Y *ConAu X*
Kohen-Raz, Reuven 1921- *ConAu 37R*
Kohl, Herbert 1937- *ConAu 65*
Kohl, James 1942- *ConAu 57*
Kohl, Marvin 1932- *ConAu 85*
Kohler, Foy David 1908- *ConAu 29R,*
IntAu&W 82, WrDr 84
Kohler, Hans 1921- *IntAu&W 82*
Kohler, Heinz 1934- *ConAu 21R*
Kohler, Julilly H 1908-1976 *ConAu 77,*
SmATA 20N
Kohler, Julilly H 1915-1976 *ConAu 69*
Kohler, Mary Hortense 1892- *ConAu 5R,*
WrDr 84
Kohler, Saul 1928- *ConAu 69*
Kohler, Wolfgang 1887-1967 *TwCA SUP*
Kohlmeier, Louis M, Jr. 1926- *ConAu 49*
Kohls, Richard Louis 1921- *ConAu 106*
Kohlstedt, Sally Gregory 1943- *ConAu 69*
Kohn, Bernice Herstein 1920- *ConAu 9R,*
SmATA 4
Kohn, Clyde F 1911- *ConAu 109*
Kohn, Eugene 1887-1977 *ConAu 69*
Kohn, George C 1940- *ConAu 103*
Kohn, Hans 1891-1971 *ConAu 1R, –4NR, –29R,*
TwCA SUP
Kohn, Jacob 1881-1968 *ConAu 5R, –103*
Kohn, John S 1906-1976 *ConAu 104*
Kohn, Melvin L 1928- *ConAu 41R*
Kohn, Walter S G 1923- *ConAu 107*
Kohner, Frederick 1905- *ConAu 1R, –1NR,*
SmATA 10, TwCWr
Kohout, Pavel 1928- *ConAu 3NR, –45,*
ConLC 13, IntAu&W 82
Kohr, Louise Hannah 1903- *ConAu 41R*
Koht, Halvdan 1873-1965 *ConAu 85*
Kohut, Heinz 1913-1981 *ConAu 1NR, –105, –45*
Kohut, Les *ConAu X*
Kohut, Nester C 1925- *ConAu 45*
Koi Hai *ConAu X*
Koidahl, Ilona 1924- *ConAu 97*
Koilpillai, Charles *ConAu 41R*
Koilpillai, Das *ConAu X*
Koinange, Mbiyu 1907-1981 *ConAu 108*
Koiner, Richard B 1929- *ConAu 17R*
Koivistoinen, Eino Hannes 1907- *IntAu&W 82*
Koizumi, Yakumo 1850-1904 *ConAu X*
Kojecky, Roger 1943- *ConAu 85*
Kojima, Naomi 1950- *ConAu 109*
Kojima, Shozo 1928- *ConAu 69*
Kojima, Takashi 1907- *ConAu P-1*
Kokkonen, Lauri 1918- *CroCD*
Kokoschka, Oskar 1886-1980 *CIDMEL 80,*
CnMD, ConAu 109, –93, ModGL, ModWD
Kokyshev, Lazor 1937-1975 *ConAu 104*
Kolaja, Jiri 1919- *WrDr 84*
Kolaja, Jiri Thomas 1919- *ConAu 9R*
Kolakowski, Leszek 1927- *ConAu 49,*
WorAu 1970
Kolar, Slavko 1891-1963 *CnMD*

Kolars, Frank 1899-1972 *ConAu 5R*
Kolars, Frank 1899-1973 *ConAu 37R*
Kolasky, John 1915- *ConAu 25R*
Kolatch, Alfred Jacob 1916- *ConAu 107*
Kolatch, Jonathan 1943- *ConAu 41R*
Kolatkar, Arun 1932- *ConP 80, WrDr 84*
Kolb, Annette 1870-1967 *EncWL 2*
Kolb, Annette 1875-1967 *ModGL*
Kolb, Carolyn 1942- *ConAu 89*
Kolb, David A 1939- *ConAu 65*
Kolb, Erwin J 1924- *ConAu 37R*
Kolb, Gwin Jackson 1919- *ConAu 1R*
Kolb, Harold H, Jr. 1933- *ConAu 29R*
Kolb, John F 1916?-1974 *ConAu 53*
Kolb, Ken *DrAP&F 83*
Kolb, Ken 1926- *ConAu 21R*
Kolb, Lawrence 1911-1972 *ConAu 37R*
Kolb, Philip 1907- *ConAu 4NR, –53*
Kolba, St. Tamara *ConAu 97*
Kolba, Tamara *SmATA 22[port]*
Kolbas, Grace Holden 1914- *ConAu 93,*
IntAu&W 82
Kolbe, Henry E 1907- *ConAu 5R*
Kolbenheyer, Edwin Guido 1878-1962
CIDMEL 80
Kolbenheyer, Erwin Guido 1878-1962 *ModWD*
Kolbrek, Loyal 1914- *ConAu 29R*
Kolchin, Peter 1943- *ConAu 41R*
Kolde, Endel Jakob 1917- *ConAu 1NR, –45*
Kolenda, Konstantin 1923- *ConAu 13R*
Kolers, Paul A 1926- *ConAu 97*
Kolesar, Paul 1927- *ConAu 105*
Kolesnik, Walter B 1923- *ConAu 2NR, –5R*
Kolevzon, Edward R 1913?-1976 *ConAu 69*
Kolia, John Alexander 1931- *IntAu&W 82*
Kolins, William 1926?-1973 *ConAu 104*
Kolinski, Charles J 1916- *ConAu 17R*
Kolinsky, Martin 1936- *ConAu 8NR, –61,*
WrDr 84
Koljevic, Svetozar 1930- *ConAu 7NR, –17R*
Kolko, Gabriel 1932- *ConAu 4NR, –5R*
Kollar, Sybil *DrAP&F 83*
Kollat, David Truman 1938- *ConAu 41R*
Kollbach, Ingeborg 1946- *IntAu&W 82*
Kollek, Teddy *ConAu X*
Kollek, Theodore 1911- *ConAu P-2*
Koller, Charles W *ConAu 61*
Koller, Charles W 1896?-1983 *ConAu 109*
Koller, James *DrAP&F 83*
Koller, James 1936- *ConAu 2NR, –49, ConP 80,*
IntAu&W 82, IntWWP 82, WrDr 84
Koller, John M 1938- *ConAu 33R*
Koller, Larry *ConAu X*
Koller, Lawrence Robert 1912-1967 *ConAu 1R,*
–6NR
Koller, Marvin Robert 1919- *ConAu 13R,*
IntAu&W 82, WrDr 84
Kollmar, Dick *ConAu X*
Kollmar, Richard Tompkins 1910-1971 *ConAu 89*
Kollock, Will 1940- *ConAu 33R*
Kollock, William 1940- *WrDr 84*
Kolm, Ron *DrAP&F 83*
Kolmar, Gertrud 1894-1943 *CIDMEL 80,*
EncWL 2, ModGL
Kolnai, Aurel 1900-1973 *ConAu 103*
Kolodin, Irving 1908- *ConAu 93*
Kolodny, Annette 1941- *ConAu 8NR, –61*
Kolodziej, Edward Albert 1935- *ConAu 97*
Kolon, Nita *ConAu X*
Kolosimo, Peter 1922- *ConAu 7NR, –53*
Kolozsvari Grandpierre, Emil 1907- *IntAu&W 82*
Kolsen, Helmut Max 1926- *WrDr 84*
Kolson, Clifford J 1920- *ConAu 9R*
Kolstoe, Oliver Paul 1920- *ConAu 17R,*
WrDr 84
Koltun, Frances Lang *ConAu 21R, –69*
Kolumban, Nicholas *DrAP&F 83*
Kolumban, Nicholas 1937- *IntWWP 82*
Kolyer, John 1933- *ConAu 11NR, –69*
Komarnicki, Tytus 1896- *ConAu P-1*
Komarovsky, Mirra 1906- *ConAu P-1,*
IntAu&W 82
Komatsu, Sakyo 1931- *TwCSFW A*
Komer, Robert W 1922- *ConAu 108*
Komisar, Lucy 1942- *ConAu 33R, SmATA 9,*
WrDr 84
Komlos, Aladar 1892- *IntAu&W 82*
Kommerell, Max 1902-1944 *CIDMEL 80,*
CnMD, ModGL
Komoda, Beverly 1939- *ConAu 85,*
SmATA 25[port]
Komoda, Kiyo 1937- *SmATA 9*

Komroff, Manuel 1890-1974 *ConAu 1R, -4NR, -53, DcLB 4, SmATA 2, -20N, TwCA, TwCA SUP*
Komunyakaa, Yusef *DrAP&F 83*
Konadu, Asare 1932- *ConAu X, DcLEL 1940*
Konadu, S A 1932- *ConAu 21R*
Konczacki, Zbigniew Andrzej 1917- *ConAu 10NR, -21R*
Kondrashin, Kiril 1914-1981 *ConAu 108*
Kondrashov, Stanislav 1928- *ConAu 69*
Konecky, Edith *DrAP&F 83*
Konecky, Edith 1922- *ConAu 69*
Konefsky, Samuel J 1915-1970 *ConAu 29R*
Koner, Marvin 1921?-1983 *ConAu 109*
Koner, Richard B 1929- *LivgBAA*
Koneski, Blaze 1921- *ClDMEL 80, ModSL 2*
Konetsky, Viktor Viktorovich 1929- *ClDMEL 80*
Kong, Shiu Loon 1934- *ConAu 108*
Konick, Marcus 1914- *ConAu 37R, IntAu&W 82, IntWWP 82*
Konig, Barbara 1925- *ClDMEL 80*
Konig, David Thomas 1947- *ConAu 97*
Konig, Franz *ConAu X*
Konig, Josef Walter 1923- *IntAu&W 82*
Konig, Rene 1906- *IntAu&W 82*
Konig, Traugott 1934- *IntAu&W 82*
Konigsberg, Conrad Isidore 1916- *ConAu 21R*
Konigsberger, Hans 1912- *WrDr 84*
Konigsburg, E L 1930- *ConAu 21R, TwCCW 83, WrDr 84*
Konigsburg, Elaine L 1930- *ChlLR 1, SmATA 4*
Koning, Hans *ConAu X, DrAP&F 83, SmATA X, WorAu, WrDr 84*
Koningsberger, Hans *DrAP&F 83*
Koningsberger, Hans 1921- *ConAu 1R, -2NR, SmATA 5, WorAu*
Konishi, Masatochi A 1938- *IntAu&W 82*
Konkle, Janet Everest 1917- *ConAu 1R, MichAu 80, SmATA 12, WrDr 84*
Konner, Linda 1951- *ConAu 102*
Konnyu, Leslie 1914- *ConAu 7NR, -13R, IntWWP 82*
Konopka, Gisela 1910- *ConAu 9R, IntAu&W 82*
Konopnicka, Maria 1842-1910 *ClDMEL 80*
Konorski, Boleslav 1892- *IntAu&W 82*
Konovalov, Sergey 1899-1982 *ConAu 106, IntAu&W 82*
Konrad, Evelyn 1930- *ConAu 33R*
Konrad, George *ConAu X*
Konrad, Gyoergy 1933- *ConAu 85*
Konrad, Gyorgy 1933- *ConLC 4, -10*
Konrad, James *ConAu X*
Konstantinovic, Zoran 1920- *IntAu&W 82*
Kontos, Cecille *ConAu X, -69*
Kontos, Peter G 1935- *ConAu 25R*
Konvitz, Jeffrey 1944- *ConAu 7NR, -53, WrDr 84*
Konvitz, Milton R 1908- *WrDr 84*
Konvitz, Milton Ridvas 1908- *ConAu 1R, -4NR*
Konwicki, Tadeusz 1926- *ClDMEL 80, ConAu 101, ConLC 8, EncWL 2*
Koo, Anthony Y C 1918- *ConAu 57*
Koo, Samuel 1941- *ConAu 77*
Koo, V K Wellington 1888- *ConAu 81*
Koob, C Albert 1920- *ConAu 41R*
Koob, Derry D 1933- *ConAu 37R*
Koob, Theodora 1918- *ConAu 5R, SmATA 23[port]*
Kooiker, Leonie *ConAu X*
Kooiman, Gladys 1927- *ConAu 89*
Kooiman, Helen W *ConAu X*
Koolish, Lynda *DrAP&F 83*
Koomoter, Zeno *ConSFA*
Koonce, Ray F 1913- *ConAu 9R*
Koonts, J Calvin *DrAP&F 83*
Koonts, J Calvin 1924- *IntWWP 82*
Koonts, Jones Calvin 1924- *ConAu 49*
Koontz, Dean R 1945- *ConAu 108, ConSFA, TwCSFW, WrDr 84*
Koontz, Harold 1908- *ConAu 41R*
Koop, Katherine C 1923- *ConAu 17R*
Koopman, LeRoy George 1935- *ConAu 101*
Kooser, Ted *DrAP&F 83*
Kooser, Ted 1939- *ConAu X, WrDr 84*
Kooser, Theodore 1939- *ConAu 33R*
Kootz, Samuel Melvin 1898-1982 *ConAu 107*
Kooyker-Romijn, Johanna Maria 1927- *ConAu 107*
Kooyker-Romyn, Johanna Maria 1927- *ConAu X*
Kopal, Zdenek 1914- *ConAu 93, WrDr 84*

Koperwas, Sam *DrAP&F 83*
Koperwas, Sam 1948- *ConAu 105*
Kopf, David 1930- *ConAu 89*
Kopit, Arthur 1937- *AuNews 1, ConAu 81, ConDr 82, ConLC 1, -18, CroCD, DcLB 7[port], DcLEL 1940, NatPD 81[port], WorAu, WrDr 84*
Kopit, Arthur 1938- *CnMD, ModWD*
Kopkind, Andrew 1935- *WrDr 84*
Kopkind, Andrew David 1935- *ConAu 29R, IntAu&W 82*
Koplin, H T 1923- *ConAu 33R, WrDr 84*
Koplinka, Charlotte *ConAu X*
Koplitz, Eugene D 1923- *ConAu 37R*
Kopman, H 1918- *ConAu 89*
Kopp, Anatole 1915- *ConAu 29R*
Kopp, Hans W 1931- *IntAu&W 82*
Kopp, Harriet Green *ConAu 41R*
Kopp, Karl 1934- *IntWWP 82*
Kopp, O W 1918- *ConAu 33R*
Kopp, Richard L 1934- *ConAu 33R, WrDr 84*
Kopp, Sheldon B 1929- *ConAu 37R*
Kopp, William LaMarr 1930- *ConAu 65*
Koppel, Lillian 1926- *ConAu 108*
Koppel, Shelley R 1951- *ConAu 108*
Koppel, Ted 1940?- *ConAu 103*
Kopper, Edward A, Jr. 1937- *ConAu 69*
Kopper, Philip 1937- *ConAu 97*
Kopperman, Paul Edward 1945- *ConAu 69*
Koppett, Leonard 1923- *ConAu 11NR, -25R*
Koppitz, Elizabeth M 1919- *ConAu 13R, WrDr 84*
Koppman, Lionel 1920- *ConAu 6NR, -9R*
Koprowski, Kenneth *DrAP&F 83*
Kops, Bernard 1926- *CnMD, ConAu 5R, ConDr 82, ConLC 4, ConNov 82, ConP 80, DcLB 13[port], DcLEL 1940, IntAu&W 82, ModWD, TwCWr, WorAu, WrDr 84*
Kops, Bernard 1928- *CroCD, ModBrL SUP*
Kopulos, Stella 1906- *ConAu 49*
Kopycinski, Joseph V 1923- *ConAu 33R*
Korach, Mimi 1922- *SmATA 9*
Koran, Dennis *DrAP&F 83*
Koran, Dennis 1947- *IntWWP 82*
Korb, Lawrence J 1939- *ConAu 77*
Korbel, John 1918- *ConAu 9R*
Korbel, Josef 1909-1977 *ConAu 37R, -73*
Korbonski, Andrzej 1927- *ConAu 9R*
Korbonski, Stefan 1903- *ConAu 5R, -5NR*
Korda, Michael 1933- *ConAu 107, WrDr 84*
Kordel, Lelord 1904- *ConAu 106*
Koren, Edward 1935- *ConAu 11NR, -25R, SmATA 5*
Koren, Henry Joseph 1912- *ConAu 9R, IntAu&W 82, WrDr 84*
Korenbaum, Myrtle 1915- *ConAu 57*
Korfker, Dena 1908- *ConAu 1R, MichAu 80, WrDr 84*
Korg, Jacob 1922- *ConAu 2NR, -5R, WrDr 84*
Korges, James 1930-1975 *ConAu P-2*
Korinets, Iurii Iosifovich *ConAu X*
Korinetz, Yuri 1923- *ChlLR 4[port], ConAu 11NR, -61, SmATA 9*
Koriyama, Naoshi 1926- *DcLEL 1940, IntWWP 82*
Korman, A Gerd 1928- *ConAu 53*
Korman, Keith 1956- *ConAu 102*
Kormendi, Ferenc 1900-1972 *ConAu 37R, WorAu*
Kormondy, Edward J 1926- *WrDr 84*
Kormondy, Edward John 1926- *ConAu 33R*
Korn, Alfons L 1906- *ConAu 93*
Korn, Bertram Wallace 1918-1979 *ConAu 1R, -1NR*
Korn, Henry James *DrAP&F 83*
Korn, Henry James 1945- *ConAu 69*
Korn, Noel 1923- *ConAu 73*
Korn, Peggy *ConAu X*
Korn, Walter 1908- *ConAu 73, IntAu&W 82*
Kornblatt, Joyce 1944- *ConAu 106*
Kornblum, Allan *DrAP&F 83*
Kornblum, Allan M 1949- *ConAu 69, IntWWP 82*
Kornblum, Cinda *DrAP&F 83*
Kornblum, Cinda 1950- *ConAu 69*
Kornblum, Sylvan 1927- *ConAu 41R*
Kornbluth, C M 1923-1958 *ConAu 105, DcLB 8[port], DrmM[port], TwCLC 8[port], TwCSFW*
Kornbluth, Cyril M 1922?-1958 *WorAu*

Kornbluth, Jesse 1946- *ConAu 25R*
Korneichuk, Aleksandr Evdokomovich 1905-1972 *CroCD*
Korneichuk, Aleksandr Yevdokimovich 1905-1972 *ConAu 33R, ModWD*
Korneichuk, Alexander Evdokimovich 1905-1972 *CnMD*
Korneichuk, Nikolai Ivanovich *WorAu*
Korner, John 1913- *CreCan 2*
Korner, Stephan 1913- *ConAu X, WrDr 84*
Kornfeld, Anita Clay *DrAP&F 83*
Kornfeld, Anita Clay 1928- *ConAu 97*
Kornfeld, Paul 1889-1942 *CnMD, ModWD*
Kornfeld, Robert J 1919- *ConAu 104, IntAu&W 82, NatPD 81[port]*
Kornhauser, David H 1918- *ConAu 41R*
Kornhauser, William 1925- *ConAu 1R, WrDr 84*
Kornhuber, Hans H 1928- *IntAu&W 82*
Korninger, Siegfried 1925- *IntAu&W 82*
Korniychuk, Oleksandr 1905-1972 *ClDMEL 80*
Kornrich, Milton 1933- *ConAu 17R*
Korol, Alexander G 1900- *ConAu 5R*
Korol, Taras *CreCan 2*
Korol, Ted *CreCan 2*
Korolenko, Vladimir Galaktionovich 1853-1921 *ClDMEL 80, ModSL 1*
Koroleva, Natalena 1888-1966 *ModSL 2*
Korolko, Miroslaw 1935- *IntAu&W 82*
Korotkin, Judith 1931- *ConAu 53*
Kors, Alan Charles 1943- *ConAu 77, IntAu&W 82*
Korschunow, Irina 1925- *IntAu&W 82*
Kort, Carol 1945- *ConAu 106*
Kort, Wesley A 1935- *ConAu 37R, WrDr 84*
Korte, Mary Norbert *ConAu X, DrAP&F 83*
Korten, David Craig 1937- *ConAu 41R*
Kortepeter, Max 1928- *ConAu 41R*
Korth, Francis N 1912- *ConAu 25R*
Kortner, Fritz 1892-1970 *CroCD*
Kortner, Peter 1924- *ConAu 33R, WrDr 84*
Kortooms, Antonius Johannes 1916- *IntAu&W 82*
Kortooms, Toon *IntAu&W 82X*
Korty, Carol 1937- *ConAu 77, SmATA 15*
Korty, John VanCleave 1936- *ConAu 106*
Kory, Robert B 1950- *ConAu 65*
Korzeniowski, Jozef Teodor Konrad *LongCTC*
Korzhavin, Naum Moiseyevich 1925- *ClDMEL 80*
Korzybski, Alfred 1879-1950 *TwCA SUP*
Kos, Erih 1913- *ConAu 106, ModSL 2*
Kosa, John 1914- *ConAu 5R*
Kosch, Erich *ConAu X*
Koschade, Alfred 1928- *ConAu 21R, WrDr 84*
Koselleck, Reinhart 1923- *IntAu&W 82*
Koshetz, Herbert 1907?-1977 *ConAu 73*
Koshi, George M 1911- *ConAu P-2*
Koshland, Ellen 1947- *ConAu 33R*
Kosinski, Jerzy *DrAP&F 83*
Kosinski, Jerzy 1933- *ASpks, ConAu 9NR, -17R, ConLC 1, -2, -3, -6, -10, -15, ConNov 82, DcLB Y82A[port], -2, DcLEL 1940, EncWL 2, ModAL SUP, WorAu, WrDr 84*
Kosinski, Leonard V 1923- *ConAu 25R*
Koskoff, David E 1939- *ConAu 49, WrDr 84*
Koslow, Jules 1916- *ConAu 1R, -6NR*
Kosmac, Ciril 1910- *ModSL 2*
Kosmala, Hans 1904?-1981 *ConAu 104*
Kosmicki, Greg *DrAP&F 83*
Kosof, Anna 1945- *ConAu 85*
Kosoof, Jean Berenece 1909- *IntAu&W 82*
Kosor, Josip 1879-1961 *CnMD*
Kosovel, Srecko 1904-1926 *ClDMEL 80*
Koss, Stephen Edward 1940- *ConAu 25R, WrDr 84*
Kossak, Zofia 1890-1968 *EncWL 2*
Kossak-Szczucka, Zofia 1890-1968 *TwCA SUP*
Kossak-Szczucka-Szatkowska, Zofia 1890-1968 *ClDMEL 80*
Kossin, Sandy 1926- *SmATA 10*
Kossmann, Rudolf Richard 1934- *ConAu 37R, WrDr 84*
Kossoff, David 1919- *ConAu 61, IntAu&W 82, WrDr 84*
Kost, Mary Lu 1924- *ConAu 45*
Kost, Robert John 1913- *ConAu 1R*
Kostash, Myrna 1944- *ConAu 65*
Koste, Robert Francis 1933- *ConAu 81*
Kostelanetz, Andre 1901-1980 *ConAu 107*
Kostelanetz, Richard *DrAP&F 83*

Kostelanetz, Richard 1940- *ConAu 13R,*
  ConP 80, IntAu&W 82, IntWWP 82,
  WrDr 84
Kosten, Andrew 1921- *ConAu 1R*
Kostenko, Lina 1930- *ModSL 2*
Koster, Donald Nelson 1910- *ConAu 53,*
  WrDr 84
Koster, John 1945- *ConAu 5NR, –53*
Koster, R M 1934- *ConAu 37R*
Koster, Simon 1900- *IntAu&W 82*
Koster, Walter 1903- *IntAu&W 82*
Kostich, Dragos D 1921- *ConAu 5R, –10NR*
Kostis, Nicholas *ConAu 103*
Kostiuk, Hryhory 1902- *ConAu 77,*
  IntAu&W 82
Kostka, Edmund Karl 1915- *ConAu 17R*
Kostra, Jan 1910- *ModSL 2*
Kostrowitzki, Wilhelm Apollinaris De 1880-1918
  ConAu 104
Kostrubala, Thaddeus 1930- *ConAu 101*
Kostyu, Frank A 1919- *ConAu 1NR, –49*
Kosygin, Alexei Nikolayevich 1904-1980
  ConAu 102
Kosztolanyi, Dezso 1885-1936 *ClDMEL 80,*
  EncWL 2
Kot, Stanislaw 1886?-1976 *ConAu 65*
Kotarbinski, Tadeusz 1886-1981 *ConAu 105*
Kothari, Hemraj 1933- *IntAu&W 82*
Kothari, Rajni 1928- *ConAu 33R*
Kotikalapudi, K Kurmanadham 1930-
  IntWWP 82
Kotikalapudi, Venkata S M 1925- *IntWWP 82*
Kotker, Mary Zane *DrAP&F 83*
Kotker, Norman *DrAP&F 83*
Kotker, Norman 1931- *ConAu 10NR*
Kotker, Norman R 1931- *ConAu 25R,*
  IntAu&W 82, WrDr 84
Kotker, Zane *DrAP&F 83*
Kotker, Zane 1934- *ConAu 3NR, –49*
Kotker, Zane H 1934- *WrDr 84*
Kotler, Milton 1935- *ConAu 29R, WrDr 84*
Kotler, Philip 1931- *ConAu 33R, IntAu&W 82,*
  WrDr 84
Kotlowitz, Robert *DrAP&F 83*
Kotlowitz, Robert 1924- *ASpks, ConAu 33R,*
  ConLC 4
Kotlum, Johannes Ur *EncWL 2*
Kotowska, Monika 1942- *ConAu 93,*
  IntAu&W 82
Kotowski, Joanne 1930- *ConAu 57*
Kotre, John N 1940- *ConAu 81*
Kotschevar, Lendal H 1908- *ConAu 10NR, –17R*
Kotsilibas-Davis, James 1940- *ConAu 106*
Kotsuji, Abraham S 1899-1973 *ConAu 45,*
  ConAu P-1
Kotsyubinsky, Mykhaylo 1864-1913 *ModSL 2*
Kotsyubynsky, Mykhaylo 1864-1913 *ClDMEL 80*
Kott, Jan 1914- *ConAu 13R, IntAu&W 82,*
  WorAu
Kottler, Dorothy 1918- *ConAu 97*
Kottman, Richard N 1932- *ConAu 25R*
Kotz, David M 1943- *ConAu 81*
Kotz, Mary Lynn 1936- *ConAu 104*
Kotz, Nick 1932- *ConAu 29R*
Kotz, Samuel 1930- *ConAu 7NR, –13R*
Kotzin, Michael C 1941- *ConAu 37R, WrDr 84*
Kotzwinkle, William 1938- *ChlLR 6[port],*
  ConAu 3NR, –45, ConLC 5, –14,
  SmATA 24[port]
Koubourlis, Demetrius J 1938- *ConAu 57*
Koufax, Sandy *ConAu X*
Koufax, Sanford 1935- *ConAu 89*
Koulack, David 1938- *ConAu 102*
Koumjian, Vaughn *DrAP&F 83*
Koumoulides, John 1938- *ConAu 41R*
Koupernik, Cyrille 1917- *ConAu 57*
Kousoulas, D George 1923- *ConAu 17R*
Kousser, J Morgan 1943- *ConAu 57*
Koutoukas, H M *SmATA X*
Koutoukas, H M 1947- *ConAu 69, ConDr 82*
Kouts, Anne 1945- *ConAu 29R, SmATA 8*
Kouts, Hertha Pretorius 1922-1973 *ConAu 1R,*
  –103
Kouwenhoven, John A 1909- *WrDr 84*
Kouwenhoven, John Atlee 1909- *ConAu 1R*
Kouyoumdjian, Dikran *LongCTC*
Kovach, Barbara L Forisha *ConAu X*
Kovach, Bill 1932- *ConAu 11NR, –69*
Kovach, Francis J 1918- *ConAu 61*
Kovacs, Alexander 1930?-1977 *ConAu 73*
Kovacs, E Kalman 1912- *IntAu&W 82*
Kovacs, Gyorgy 1911- *IntAu&W 82*

Kovacs, Imre 1913-1980 *ConAu 102, –21R*
Kovak, Teri *DrAP&F 83*
Kovalev, Mikhail A 1893-1981 *ConAu 108*
Kovalik, Nada 1926- *ConAu 25R*
Kovalik, Vladimir 1928- *ConAu 25R*
Kovarsky, Irving 1918- *ConAu 29R*
Kovel, Joel 1936- *WrDr 84*
Kovel, Joel S 1936- *ConAu 29R*
Kovel, Ralph Mallory *WrDr 84*
Kovel, Ralph Mallory 1920- *ConAu 8NR, –17R*
Kovel, Terry Horvitz 1928- *ConAu 8NR, –17R,*
  WrDr 84
Kovler, Allen *DrAP&F 83*
Kovner, B 1874?-1974 *ConAu X*
Kovrig, Bennett 1940- *ConAu 29R*
Kowalewska, Maria 1901- *IntAu&W 82*
Kowalski, Frank 1907- *ConAu 37R*
Kowalski, John J 1928- *IntWWP 82*
Kowet, Don 1937- *ConAu 10NR, –57*
Kowit, Steve *DrAP&F 83*
Kowit, Steve 1938- *IntWWP 82*
Kowitt, Sylvia *ConAu X*
Kowitz, Gerald T 1928- *ConAu 33R*
Kownslar, Allan Owen 1935- *ConAu 61,*
  IntAu&W 82
Koyama, Kosuke 1929- *ConAu 7NR, –57*
Kozak, Jan B 1889?-1974 *ConAu 45*
Kozar, Andrew Joseph 1930- *ConAu 103*
Kozberg, Donna Walters *DrAP&F 83*
Kozelka, Paul 1909- *ConAu P-2*
Kozer, Jose *DrAP&F 83*
Kozer, Jose 1940- *ConAu 2NR, –49*
Kozicki, Henry 1924- *ConAu 103*
Koziebrodzki, Leopold B 1906- *ConAu 41R*
Kozik, Frantisek 1909- *TwCWr*
Kozintsev, Grigori 1905-1973 *ConAu 53*
Koziol, Urszula 1931- *ClDMEL 80,*
  IntWWP 82
Kozlenko, William 1917- *ConAu 57*
Kozlow, Mark J *ConAu X*
Kozlowski, Theodore T 1917- *ConAu 4NR, –9R*
Kozmoth' Mystic *IntWWP 82X*
Kozol, Jonathan 1936- *ConAu 61, ConLC 17*
Krack, Hans-Gunter 1921- *IntAu&W 82*
Kracmar, John 1916- *WrDr 84*
Kracmar, John Z 1916- *ConAu 37R*
Krader, Lawrence 1919- *ConAu 21R*
Kraditor, Aileen S 1928- *ConAu 13R*
Kraehe, Enno Edward 1921- *ConAu 9R,*
  WrDr 84
Kraemer, Carolyn Terese *DrAP&F 83*
Kraemer, Richard H 1920- *ConAu 4NR, –53*
Kraenzel, Carl F 1906- *ConAu 73*
Kraenzel, Margaret 1899- *ConAu 1R*
Kraf, Elaine *DrAP&F 83*
Kraf, Elaine 1946- *ConAu 11NR, –65,*
  DcLB Y81B[port]
Krafft, Maurice 1946- *ConAu 10NR, –65*
Krafsur, Richard Paul 1940- *ConAu 103*
Kraft *IntAu&W 82X*
Kraft, Barbara 1930- *ConAu 97*
Kraft, Betsy Harvey 1937- *ConAu 89*
Kraft, Charles Howard 1932- *ConAu 1NR, –45*
Kraft, Charlotte 1922- *ConAu 103,*
  NatPD 81[port]
Kraft, Eric 1944- *ConAu 108*
Kraft, Herbert 1938- *IntAu&W 82*
Kraft, Hy S 1899-1975 *ConAu 41R, –57*
Kraft, Joseph *WrDr 84*
Kraft, Joseph 1924- *ConAu 9R*
Kraft, Ken 1907- *ConAu 1R, –1NR*
Kraft, Leo 1922- *ConAu 41R*
Kraft, Leonard E 1923- *ConAu 29R*
Kraft, Robert A 1934- *WrDr 84*
Kraft, Robert Alan 1934- *ConAu 37R*
Kraft, Ruth *IntAu&W 82X*
Kraft, Stephanie 1944- *ConAu 105*
Kraft, Virginia 1932- *ConAu 21R*
Kraft, Walter Andreas *ConAu X*
Kraft, William F 1938- *ConAu 33R, WrDr 84*
Kraft-Christensen, Chris 1945- *IntAu&W 82*
Kragen, Jinx *ConAu 49, IntAu&W 82X*
Krahn, Fernando 1935- *ChlLR 3, ConAu 11NR,*
  –65, SmATA 31
Kraig, Bruce 1939- *ConAu 102*
Krailsheimer, Alban John 1921- *ConAu 2NR,*
  –5R
Kraines, Oscar 1916- *ConAu 97*
Kraines, Samuel H 1906- *ConAu 77*
Krains, Hubert 1862-1934 *ClDMEL 80*
Krajenke, Robert William 1939- *ConAu 29R*
Krajewski, Frank R 1938- *ConAu 10NR, –65*

Krajewski, Robert J 1940- *ConAu 97*
Krakauer, Daniel *DrAP&F 83*
Krakel, Dean Fenton 1923- *ConAu 45*
Krakowski, Lili 1930- *ConAu 85*
Krall, Zena *DrAP&F 83*
Kramarz, Joachim 1931- *ConAu 25R*
Kramer, A T 1892- *ConAu P-1*
Kramer, Aaron *DrAP&F 83*
Kramer, Aaron 1921- *ConAu 21R,*
  IntAu&W 82, IntWWP 82, WrDr 84
Kramer, Bernard M 1923- *ConAu 77*
Kramer, Dale 1936- *ConAu 5NR, –53,*
  WrDr 84
Kramer, Daniel C 1934- *ConAu 53*
Kramer, Edith 1916- *ConAu 33R*
Kramer, Edna Ernestine 1902- *ConAu 107*
Kramer, Eugene F 1921- *ConAu 37R*
Kramer, Frank Raymond 1908- *ConAu P-1*
Kramer, Gene 1927- *ConAu 69*
Kramer, George *ConAu X, SmATA X,*
  WrDr 84
Kramer, Hilton 1928- *ConAu 109*
Kramer, Jack 1923- *ConAu 41R*
Kramer, Jane 1938- *ConAu 102*
Kramer, Joel 1937- *ConAu 97*
Kramer, John Eichholtz, Jr. 1935- *ConAu 108*
Kramer, Judith Rita 1933-1970 *ConAu 1R, –103*
Kramer, Larry *DrAP&F 83*
Kramer, Leonie 1924- *WrDr 84*
Kramer, Leonie Judith 1924- *ConAu 81,*
  IntAu&W 82
Kramer, Mark 1944- *ConAu 97*
Kramer, Milton D 1915-1973 *ConAu 37R*
Kramer, Nancy 1942- *ConAu 101*
Kramer, Nicolaas Jacobus T Antonius 1949-
  IntAu&W 82
Kramer, Nora *ConAu 107, SmATA 26*
Kramer, Paul 1914- *ConAu 21R*
Kramer, Paul J 1904- *WrDr 84*
Kramer, Paul Jackson 1904- *ConAu 1NR, –45*
Kramer, Rita 1929- *ConAu 69*
Kramer, Robert *DrAP&F 83*
Kramer, Roberta 1935- *ConAu 103*
Kramer, Roland Laird 1898- *ConAu 5R*
Kramer, Samuel Noah 1897- *ConAu 9R*
Kramer, Theodor 1897-1958 *EncWL 2*
Kramer, Victor A 1939- *ConAu 85*
Kramer-Badoni, Rudolf 1913- *IntAu&W 82,*
  ModGL
Kramish, Arnold 1923- *ConAu 5R, –7NR*
Kramm, Joseph 1907- *CnMD, DcLEL 1940,*
  ModWD, TwCA SUP
Krammer, Arnold Paul 1941- *ConAu 11NR, –61*
Kramon, Florence 1920- *ConAu 25R*
Kramp, Willy 1909- *IntAu&W 82*
Krampah, Daniel 1935- *IntAu&W 82*
Krampf, Thomas *DrAP&F 83*
Kramrisch, Stella 1898- *ConAu P-2,*
  IntAu&W 82
Kranes, David *DrAP&F 83*
Kranidas, Kathleen Collins *DrAP&F 83*
Kranidas, Kathleen Collins 1931- *ConAu 17R*
Kranidiotis, Nicos 1911- *IntAu&W 82*
Kranjcevic, Silvije Strahimir 1865-1908
  ClDMEL 80, ModSL 2
Krantz, D *IntAu&W 82X*
Krantz, Hazel 1920- *WrDr 84*
Krantz, Hazel Newman 1920- *ConAu 1R, –1NR,*
  SmATA 12
Krantz, Judith *WrDr 84*
Krantz, Judith 1927- *ConAu 11NR*
Krantz, Judith 1932- *ConAu 81*
Kranz, E Kirker 1949- *ConAu 33R*
Kranz, Stewart D 1924- *ConAu 101*
Kranzberg, Melvin 1917- *ConAu 11NR, –21R,*
  IntAu&W 82, WrDr 84
Kranzler, David 1930- *ConAu 93*
Kranzler, George G 1916- *ConAu 57,*
  SmATA 28
Kranzler, Gershon *ConAu X, SmATA X*
Krapf, Norbert *DrAP&F 83*
Krapf, Norbert 1943- *IntWWP 82*
Krapp, Annemarie Maschlanka 1924-
  IntAu&W 82
Krapp, George Philip 1872-1934 *TwCA*
Krapp, R M *ConAu X*
Krar, Stephen Frank 1924- *ConAu 4NR, –53,*
  IntAu&W 82
Kraselchik, R *ConAu X*
Krasilovsky, M William 1926- *ConAu 61*
Krasilovsky, Phyllis 1926- *ConAu 11NR, –29R,*
  SmATA 1, TwCCW 83, WrDr 84

*ConLC 5, –23[port], ConNov 82,
DcLEL 1940, IntAu&W 82, WrDr 84*
Kroetz, Franz Xaver 1946- *ClDMEL 80,
EncWL 2, IntAu&W 82*
Krog, Eustace Walter 1917- *WrDr 84*
Krog, Helge 1889-1962 *ClDMEL 80, CnMD,
ModWD, TwCWr*
Kroger, William S 1906- *ConAu P-1*
Krohn, Ernst C 1888-1975 *AuNews 1,
ConAu 37R*
Krohn, Herbert *DrAP&F 83*
Krohn, Robert 1937- *ConAu 45*
Kroitor, Roman Bogdan 1926- *CreCan 1*
Krokann, Inge 1893-1962 *ClDMEL 80*
Krokvik, Jostein 1927- *IntAu&W 82*
Kroll, Burt *ConAu X, TwCWW*
Kroll, Ernest 1914- *ConAu 97, IntAu&W 82*
Kroll, Francis Lynde 1904-1973 *ConAu P-1,
SmATA 10*
Kroll, Harry Harrison 1888-1967 *TwCA SUP*
Kroll, Jeri *DrAP&F 83*
Kroll, Judith *DrAP&F 83*
Kroll, Judith 1943- *ConAu 65, IntAu&W 82*
Kroll, Morton 1923- *ConAu 49*
Kroll, Steven 1941- *ConAu 9NR, –65,
SmATA 19*
Krolow, Karl 1915- *ClDMEL 80, ConAu 81,
EncWL 2, ModGL*
Kromer, Helen *ConAu 93, IntAu&W 82,
NatPD 81[port]*
Kromminga, John H 1918- *ConAu 77*
Kronegger, Maria Elisabeth 1932- *ConAu 25R,
IntAu&W 82, WrDr 84*
Kronenberg, Henry Harold 1902- *ConAu 1R*
Kronenberg, Maria Elizabeth 1881?-1970
ConAu 104
Kronenberg, Susan *DrAP&F 83*
Kronenberger, Louis 1904-1980 *ConAu 1R, –2NR,
–97, TwCA SUP*
Kroner, Richard 1884- *ConAu 9R*
Kronhausen, Eberhard W 1915- *ConAu 6NR,
–9R*
Kronhausen, Phyllis C 1929- *ConAu 6NR, –9R*
Kronick, David A 1917- *ConAu 9R*
Kroninger, Robert H 1923- *ConAu 13R*
Kronstadt, Henry L 1915- *ConAu 73*
Kronus, Sidney J, Jr. 1937- *ConAu 107*
Kroon, Dirk 1946- *IntAu&W 82*
Krooss, Herman E 1912-1975 *ConAu 57,
ConAu P-2*
Kropf, Linda S 1947- *ConAu 49*
Kropf, Richard W 1932- *ConAu 10NR, –65*
Kropp, Lloyd *WrDr 84*
Kropp, Lloyd 1936?- *ConAu 25R*
Kropp, Paul 1948- *SmATA 34*
Krosby, H Peter 1929- *ConAu 89,
IntAu&W 82*
Krosney, Mary Stewart 1939- *ConAu 17R*
Krosno *IntWWP 82X*
Krotki, Karol J 1922- *ConAu 41R*
Krotkov, Yuri 1917- *ConAu 102, ConLC 19*
Krouse, Charles 1940- *MichAu 80*
Krout, John Allen 1896-1979 *ConAu 85, –97*
Kruchkow, Diane *DrAP&F 83*
Kruchkow, Diane 1947- *ConAu 69*
Kruchonykh, Aleksey Yeliseyevich 1886-1968
ClDMEL 80
Kruczkowski, Leon 1900-1962 *ClDMEL 80,
CnMD, CroCD, EncWL 2, ModWD*
Krudy, Gyula 1878-1933 *ClDMEL 80,
EncWL 2*
Krueger, Anne O 1934- *ConAu 37R*
Krueger, Christoph 1937- *ConAu 33R*
Krueger, Hardy 1928- *ConAu 77*
Krueger, John R 1927- *ConAu 10NR*
Krueger, John Richard 1927- *ConAu 21R*
Krueger, Ralph R 1927- *ConAu 2NR, –49*
Krueger, Robert B 1928- *ConAu 57*
Krueger, Thomas A 1936- *ConAu 21R*
Kruesi, Geraldine Farrar Brady 1918-
IntWWP 82
Kruess, James 1926- *ConAu 5NR, –53*
Krug, Edward August 1911-1980 *ConAu 4NR,
–5R*
Krug, Mark M 1915- *ConAu 109*
Krugar, Paul *DrAP&F 83*
Kruger, Arthur N 1916- *ConAu 1R, –1NR*
Kruger, Daniel H 1922- *ConAu 25R*
Kruger, Hardy *ConAu X*
Kruger, Henrik S 1938- *IntAu&W 82*
Kruger, Michael 1943- *IntAu&W 82*
Kruger, Mollee 1929- *ConAu 69*

Kruger, Paul *ConAu X*
Kruger, Rayne *ConAu 5R*
Kruglak, Haym 1909- *ConAu 53*
Kruglick, Lewis *DrAP&F 83*
Kruif *TwCA, TwCA SUP*
Krulewitch, Melvin Levin 1895-1978 *ConAu 103*
Krulik, Stephen 1933- *ConAu 8NR, –17R*
Krull, Felix *ConAu X*
Krull, Kathleen 1952- *ConAu 106*
Krumb *ConAu X*
Krumboltz, John D 1928- *ConAu 110*
Krumgold, Joseph 1908-1980 *ConAu 7NR, –9R,
–101, ConLC 12, SmATA 1, –23N,
TwCCW 83*
Krumm, John McGill 1913- *ConAu 109*
Krummel, Donald William 1929- *ConAu 106*
Krumpelmann, John T 1892- *ConAu 41R*
Krumwitz *ConAu X*
Krupat, Edward 1945- *ConAu 77*
Krupnik, Baruch *ConAu X*
Krupp, E C 1944- *ConAu 105*
Krupp, Nate 1935- *ConAu 10NR, –21R*
Krupp, Sherman Roy 1926- *ConAu 1R*
Krusch, Werner E 1927- *ConAu 5R*
Kruschke, Earl R 1934- *ConAu 41R*
Kruse, Alexander Z 1888?-1972 *ConAu 33R*
Kruse, Harry D 1900-1977 *ConAu 73*
Kruse, Johann 1889- *IntAu&W 82*
Kruse, Joseph Anton 1944- *IntAu&W 82*
Krush, Beth 1918- *SmATA 18*
Krush, Joe 1918- *SmATA 18*
Krusich, Walter Steve 1922- *ConAu 49*
Kruskal, William 1919- *ConAu 33R*
Krusoe, James *DrAP&F 83*
Kruss, James 1926- *IntAu&W 82, SmATA 8*
Krutch, Joseph Wood 1893-1970 *ConAmA,
ConAu 1R, –4NR, –25R, ConLC 24[port],
TwCA, TwCA SUP*
Krutilla, John Vasil 1922- *ConAu 9NR, –21R*
Krutzch, Gus *ConAu X*
Kruuk, Hans 1937- *ConAu 61*
Kruzas, Anthony Thomas 1914- *ConAu 1R,
–2NR*
Krymov, Vladimir Pimenovich 1878- *TwCWr*
Krymov, Yuri 1908-1941 *TwCWr*
Krymow, Virginia P 1930- *ConAu 69*
Krypton *ConAu X*
Kryptos *IntWWP 82X*
Krysl, Marilyn 1943- *ConAu 105*
Krysl-Thompson, Marilyn *DrAP&F 83*
Kryss, Tom 1948- *IntWWP 82*
Krythe, Maymie Richardson *ConAu 17R*
Krzemien, Pawel *IntWWP 82X*
Krzyszton, Jerzy 1931- *IntAu&W 82*
Krzywan, Jozef *ConAu X*
Krzyzaniak, Marian 1911- *ConAu 9R*
Krzyzanowski, Jerzy R 1922- *ConAu 37R*
Kselman, Thomas A 1948- *ConAu 110*
Kuba 1914-1967 *CroCD*
Kuba, Kurth Barthel 1914-1967 *CnMD*
Kubach, David *DrAP&F 83*
Kubal, David L 1936- *ConAu 45*
Kubeck, James 1920- *ConAu 17R*
Kubek, Anthony 1920- *ConAu 104*
Kubiak, T J 1942- *ConAu 61*
Kubiak, William J 1929- *ConAu 33R,
MichAu 80*
Kubicek, Robert V 1935- *ConAu 29R*
Kubie, Lawrence S 1896?-1973 *ConAu 45*
Kubie, Nora Gottheil Benjamin 1899- *ConAu 5R*
Kubikowski, Zbigniew 1929- *IntAu&W 82*
Kubin, Alfred 1877-1959 *ClDMEL 80, ModGL*
Kubinyi, Laszlo 1937- *ConAu 85, SmATA 17*
Kubis, Pat 1928- *ConAu 25R*
Kubler, George 1912- *ConAu 9R*
Kubler-Ross, Elisabeth 1926- *ConIsC 2[port]*
Kublin, Hyman 1919- *ConAu 9R*
Kubly, Herbert *DrAP&F 83*
Kubly, Herbert 1915- *WrDr 84*
Kubly, Herbert Oswald 1915- *ConAu 4NR, –5R,
IntAu&W 82*
Kubo, Sakae 1926- *ConAu 7NR, –57*
Kubose, Gyomay M 1905- *ConAu 49*
Kubota, Akira 1932- *ConAu 37R, WrDr 84*
Kubrick, Stanley 1928- *ConAu 81, ConDr 82A,
ConLC 16, DcLB 26[port], WrDr 84*
Kuby, Lolette Beth *DrAP&F 83*
Kucera, Henry 1925- *ConAu 21R*
Kucharek, Casimir 1928- *ConAu 57*
Kucharski, Kasimir *ConAu X*
Kucharsky, David 1931- *ConAu 65*

Kucharz, Lawrence *DrAP&F 83*
Kucharz, Lawrence Walter 1946- *IntWWP 82*
Kuczynski, Pedro-Pablo 1938- *ConAu 77,
IntAu&W 82*
Kudaka, Geraldine *DrAP&F 83*
Kudian, Mischa *ConAu 107, IntAu&W 82,
WrDr 84*
Kuebler-Ross, Elisabeth 1926- *ConAu 25R*
Kuehl, John 1928- *ConAu 21R*
Kuehl, Linda 1939?-1978 *ConAu 104*
Kuehl, Warren F 1924- *ConAu 7NR, –17R,
IntAu&W 82, WrDr 84*
Kuehne, Walter 1919- *IntWWP 82*
Kuehnelt-Leddihn, Erik 1909- *WrDr 84*
Kuehnelt-Leddihn, Erik Maria Ritter Von 1909-
ConAu 3NR, –9R, IntAu&W 82
Kuemmerly, Walter 1903- *ConAu 49*
Kuen, Alfred F 1921- *ConAu 107*
Kueng, Hans 1928- *ConAu 53*
Kuenne, Robert Eugene 1924- *ConAu 5R,
IntAu&W 82, WrDr 84*
Kuenzli, Alfred E 1923- *ConAu 17R*
Kuesel, Harry N 1892?-1977 *ConAu 73*
Kuester, David 1938- *ConAu 53*
Kuether, Edith Lyman 1915- *ConAu 49*
Kufeldt, George 1923- *ConAu 37R*
Kuffler, Stephen 1913-1980 *ConAu 105*
Kufner, Herbert L 1927- *ConAu 5R*
Kugel, James 1945- *ConAu 29R*
Kugelman, Richard 1908- *ConAu 41R*
Kugelmass, J Alvin 1910-1972 *ConAu 4NR, –33R*
Kugelmass, Joseph Alvin 1910-1972 *ConAu 5R*
Kuh, Edwin 1925- *ConAu 41R*
Kuh, Frederick Robert 1895-1978 *ConAu 89*
Kuh, Katharine 1904- *ConAu 13R*
Kuh, Richard H 1921- *ConAu 21R, WrDr 84*
Kuhl, Ernest Peter 1881- *ConAu 41R,
IntAu&W 82*
Kuhlenbeck, Hartwig 1897- *WrDr 84*
Kuhlman, James Allen 1941- *ConAu 85,
IntAu&W 82*
Kuhlman, John M 1923- *ConAu 17R*
Kuhlman, Kathryn 1910?-1976 *ConAu 57, –65*
Kuhlmann, Susan 1942- *ConAu 85*
Kuhlmeijer, H J 1916- *IntAu&W 82*
Kuhlwein, Albert Wolfgang 1940- *IntAu&W 82*
Kuhn, Albert J 1926- *WrDr 84*
Kuhn, Alfred 1914- *ConAu 3NR, –9R*
Kuhn, Dieter 1935- *IntAu&W 82*
Kuhn, Edward, Jr. 1924?-1979 *ConAu 102, –93*
Kuhn, Ferdinand 1905-1978 *ConAu 5R, –81*
Kuhn, Fritz 1919- *CnMD*
Kuhn, Harold B 1911- *ConAu 49*
Kuhn, Irene Corbally *ConAu P-1*
Kuhn, Karl F 1939- *ConAu 65*
Kuhn, Maggie *ConAu X*
Kuhn, Margaret E 1905- *ConAu 109*
Kuhn, Martin A 1924- *ConAu 9R*
Kuhn, Reinhard 1930- *ConAu 45*
Kuhn, Thomas S 1922- *ConAu 11NR, –21R,
ConIsC 2[port], WrDr 84*
Kuhn, Tillo E 1919- *ConAu 5R*
Kuhn, William Ernst 1922- *ConAu 37R,
WrDr 84*
Kuhn, Wolfgang Erasmus 1914- *ConAu 5R*
Kuhne, Cecil 1952- *ConAu 93*
Kuhne, Marie 1893-1978 *ConAu 77*
Kuhnelt, Hans Friedrich 1918- *CnMD, CroCD*
Kuhnelt, Wilhelm A 1905- *IntAu&W 82*
Kuhner, Hans 1912- *IntAu&W 82*
Kuhner, Herbert *DrAP&F 83*
Kuhner, Herbert 1935- *ConAu 25R,
IntAu&W 82, IntWWP 82, WrDr 84*
Kuhns, Grant 1929- *ConAu 9R*
Kuhns, Richard 1924- *ConAu 37R*
Kuhns, William *DrAP&F 83*
Kuhns, William 1943- *ConAu 21R*
Kuic, Vukan 1923- *ConAu 37R*
Kuiper, Gerard Peter 1905-1973 *ConAu 45,
ConAu P-2*
Kuisel, Richard F 1935- *ConAu 21R*
Kuitert, H Martinus 1924- *ConAu 25R*
Kujawa, Duane 1938- *ConAu 33R, WrDr 84*
Kujoth, Jean Spealman 1935-1975 *ConAu P-2,
SmATA 30N*
Kuka, King D *DrAP&F 83*
Kukla, Robert J 1932- *ConAu 49*
Kuklick, Bruce 1941- *ConAu 41R*
Kukrit, Pramoj 1911- *EncWL 2*
Kukucin, Martin 1860-1928 *ClDMEL 80,*

Kydd, Sam   *WrDr 84*
Kydd, Sam 1917-1982   *ConAu 106, –109*
Kydd, Thomas   *ConAu X*
Kydd, Tom   *ConAu X*
Kyei, Kojo Gyinaye 1932-   *IntWWP 82*
Kyemba, Henry 1939-   *ConAu 81*
Kyes, Robert L 1933-   *ConAu 49*
Kyger, Joanne   *DrAP&F 83*
Kyger, Joanne 1934-   *ConAu 101,   ConP 80,*
   DcLB 16[port],   WrDr 84
Kyle, Duncan   *WrDr 84*
Kyle, Duncan 1930-   *ConAu X,   IntAu&W 82X*
Kyle, Elisabeth   *ConAu X,   SmATA 3*
Kyle, Elisabeth d1982   *TwCCW 83*
Kyle, Marlaine   *ConAu X*
Kyle, Robert   *ConAu X*
Kyle, Sefton   *TwCCr&M 80*
Kyler, Inge Logenburg 1936-   *IntWWP 82*
Kyllikki, Heino   *IntAu&W 82X*
Kyme, Ernest Hector 1906-   *ConAu 103,*
   WrDr 84
Kyne, Peter Bernard 1880-1957   *TwCA,*
   TwCA SUP,   TwCWW
Kynett, Harold Havelock 1889-1973   *ConAu 106*
Kyper, Frank 1940-   *ConAu 85*
Kyprianos, Iossif   *ConAu X*
Kyre, Joan Randolph 1935-   *ConAu 25R*
Kyre, Martin 1928-   *ConAu 25R*
Kyrklund, Paul Wilhelm 1921-   *CIDMEL 80*
Kyrle, Roger Money   *ConAu X*
Kysar, Robert 1934-   *ConAu 69*
Kyselka, Will 1921-   *ConAu 106*
Kytle, Ray   *DrAP&F 83*
Kytle, Ray 1941-   *ConAu 29R*
Kyvig, David E 1944-   *ConAu 101*

L

La-Anyane, Seth 1922- *ConAu 9R*
Laas, William M 1910?-1975 *ConAu 61*
LaBar, Tom 1937- *ConAu 25R*
Labare, M *DrAP&F 83*
Labaree, Benjamin Woods 1927- *ConAu 6NR,*
 -9R
Labaree, Leonard Woods 1897-1980 *ConAu 73,*
 -97
Labarge, Margaret Wade 1916- *ConAu 11NR,*
 -25R
Labarque, Victor *IntAu&W 82X*
LaBarr, Creighton *ConAu X*
LaBarre, Weston 1911- *ConAu 1R,*
 IntAu&W 82, WrDr 84
LaBastille, Anne 1938- *ConAu 8NR, -57*
Labbe, John T *ConAu 97*
LaBeau, Dennis 1941- *ConAu 97*
Laber, Jeri 1931- *ConAu 9NR, -65*
LaBern, Arthur 1909- *TwCCr&M 80*
Labern, Arthur 1909- *WrDr 84*
Labin, Suzanne 1913- *ConAu 29R*
LaBombard, Joan *DrAP&F 83*
Labor, Earle G 1928- *ConAu 21R*
LaBorde, Rene *ConAu X*
Labovitz, I M 1907- *ConAu 5R*
Labrador, James *ConAu X*
Labrador, Judy *ConAu X*
Labreche, Gaetan 1931- *CreCan 1*
LaBrecque, Claude X *ConAu 85*
LaBrie, Henry George, III 1946- *ConAu 57*
Labroca, Mario 1897?-1973 *ConAu 41R*
Labus, Marta Haake 1943- *ConAu 109*
Labuta, Joseph A 1931- *ConAu 57*
Labys, Walter C 1937- *ConAu 73*
Lacan, Jacques Marie Emile 1901-1981
 CIDMEL 80, ConAu 104
LaCapra, Dominick 1939- *ConAu 109*
LaCapria, Raffaele 1922- *ConAu 4NR, -9R,*
 IntAu&W 82, TwCWr
Lacarta, Manuel *IntAu&W 82X*
Lacarta Salvador, Jose Manuel 1950-
 IntAu&W 82
LaCasce, Steward 1935- *ConAu 37R*
Laccetti, Richard 1941- *ConAu 37R*
Lace, O Jessie 1906- *ConAu 17R*
Lacerda, Alberto De 1928- *TwCWr*
Lacerda, Carlos 1914-1977 *ConAu 69*
Lacey, A R 1926- *WrDr 84*
Lacey, Archie L 1923- *ConAu 9R*
Lacey, Douglas R 1913- *ConAu 29R*
Lacey, Jeannette F *ConAu 77*
Lacey, John *ConAu X*
Lacey, Louise 1940- *ConAu 81, IntAu&W 82*
Lacey, Paul A 1934- *ConAu 41R*
Lacey, Peter 1929- *ConAu 21R*
Lacey, Robert 1944- *ConAu 33R, WrDr 84*
Lacey, W K 1921- *ConAu 11NR, -25R*
Lach, Donald F 1917- *ConAu 102*
Lachance, Sherry *DrAP&F 83*
Lachapelle, Andree *CreCan 1*
LaCharite, Virginia Anding 1937- *ConAu 29R*
Lachenbruch, David 1921- *ConAu 89*
Lachenmeyer, Charles W 1943- *ConAu 105*
Lachmann, Frank M 1929- *ConAu 103*

Lachmann, Vera *DrAP&F 83*
Lachow, Stan 1931- *NatPD 81[port]*
Lachs, John 1934- *ConAu 21R, WrDr 84*
Lachs, Manfred 1914- *IntAu&W 82*
Lack, David Lambert 1910-1973 *ConAu 4NR,*
 -5R, -89
Lackany, Radames Sany 1921- *IntAu&W 82*
Lackey, Douglas Paul 1945- *ConAu 103*
Lackmann, Ron 1934- *ConAu 29R*
Lackner, Stephan 1910- *ConAu 29R*
Lacks, Cecilia 1945- *ConAu 69*
Lacks, Cissy *ConAu X*
Lacks, Roslyn 1933- *ConAu 102*
LaClair, Earl E 1916- *ConAu 21R*
LaClaustra, Vera Berneicia 1903- *ConAu 53*
LaColere, Francois *ConAu X*
Lacolere, Francois *ConAu X*
Lacombe, Gabriel 1905?-1973 *ConAu 37R*
Lacoste, Paul 1923- *ConAu 1NR, -45*
Lacour, Jose Andre 1919- *CnMD*
LaCour, Paul 1902-1956 *CIDMEL 80*
Lacouture, Jean 1921- *ConAu 101*
Lacretelle, Jacques De 1888- *CIDMEL 80,*
 TwCA, TwCA SUP
LaCroix, Mary 1937- *ConAu 106*
Lacroix, Ramon *ConAu X*
Lacroix, Richard 1939- *CreCan 1*
LaCrosse, E Robert 1937- *ConAu 33R*
Lacy, A D 1894-1969 *ConAu P-2*
Lacy, Charles *ConAu X*
Lacy, Creighton Boutelle 1919- *ConAu 13R,*
 WrDr 84
Lacy, Dan 1914- *ConAu 37R*
Lacy, Donald Charles 1933- *ConAu 105*
Lacy, Ed 1911-1968 *TwCCr&M 80*
Lacy, Elsie 1897- *IntWWP 82*
Lacy, Eric Russell 1933- *ConAu 17R*
Lacy, Gene M 1934- *ConAu 53*
Lacy, Gerald M 1940- *ConAu 77*
Lacy, John *IntAu&W 82X*
Lacy, Leslie Alexander 1937- *ConAu 33R,*
 LivgBAA, SmATA 6
Lacy, Mary Lou 1914- *ConAu 17R*
Lacy, Norris J 1940- *ConAu 8NR, -61*
Ladas, Gerasimos 1937- *ConAu 53*
Ladas, Stephen P 1898-1976 *ConAu 102*
Ladd, Bruce 1936- *ConAu 25R*
Ladd, Edward T 1918-1973 *ConAu 4NR, -5R*
Ladd, Everett Carll, Jr. 1937- *ConAu 11NR,*
 -25R
Ladd, George Eldon 1911- *ConAu 5R, -5NR,*
 WrDr 84
Ladd, John 1917- *ConAu 81*
Ladd, Veronica *ConAu X*
Ladenheim, Kala *DrAP&F 83*
Ladenson, Alex 1907- *ConAu 17R*
Lader, Lawrence 1919- *ConAu 1R, -2NR,*
 SmATA 6
Ladipo, Duro 1920- *TwCWr*
Ladner, Joyce A 1943- *ConIsC 1[port],*
 LivgBAA
Ladner, Kurt *ConAu X*
Ladner, Mildred D 1918- *ConAu 97*
Lado, Robert 1915- *ConAu 7NR, -9R*

Lady Gregory *ConAu X*
Lady Mears *ConAu X, SmATA X*
Lady Of Quality, A 1889- *ConAu X, SmATA X,*
 TwCA, TwCA SUP
Ladyman, Phyllis *ConAu 103*
Laemmar, Jack W 1909- *ConAu 1R*
Laemmel, Josef Otto 1891- *IntAu&W 82*
Laertes, Joseph *ConAu X*
Laestadius, Lars-Levi 1909-1982 *ConAu 107*
Laeuchli, Samuel 1924- *ConAu 4NR, -5R*
Laevastu, Taivo 1923- *ConAu 41R*
LaFarge, Christopher Grant 1897-1956 *TwCA,*
 TwCA SUP
LaFarge, Oliver 1901-1963 *ConAmA, ConAu 81,*
 DcLB 9[port], LongCTC, SmATA 19,
 TwCA, TwCA SUP, TwCWW
LaFarge, Phyllis *ConAu 73, SmATA 14*
Lafarge, Rene 1902- *ConAu P-2*
LaFauci, Horatio M 1917- *ConAu 33R*
Lafayette, Carlos *ConAu X*
LaFayette, Rene *WrDr 84*
LaFeber, Walter Frederick 1933- *ConAu 5NR,*
 -9R, IntAu&W 82, WrDr 84
Laffal, Julius 1920- *ConAu 49*
Laffan, Kevin 1922- *WrDr 84*
Laffan, Kevin Barry 1922- *ConAu 37R,*
 ConDr 82, IntAu&W 82
Lafferty, Perry 1917- *ConAu 6NR, -9R*
Lafferty, R A 1914- *ConSFA, DcLB 8[port],*
 TwCSFW, WrDr 84
Lafferty, Raphael Aloysius 1914- *ConAu 57*
Laffin, John 1922- *ConAu 7NR, -53,*
 IntAu&W 82, SmATA 31[port], WrDr 84
LaFitte, Pat Chew 1950- *ConAu 107*
LaFleche, Marie Marguerite L Gisele *CreCan 2*
LaFollette, Suzanne 1894?-1983 *ConAu 109*
Lafont, Robert 1923- *IntAu&W 82*
LaFontaine, Blanche *ConAu X*
LaFontaine, Charles Vivian 1936- *ConAu 57*
LaFontaine, Jean De 1621-1695 *SmATA 18*
LaFore, Laurence *WrDr 84*
Lafore, Laurence Davis 1917- *ConAu 13R*
LaForest, Gerard V 1926- *WrDr 84*
Laforet, Carmen 1921- *CIDMEL 80,*
 WorAu 1970
LaForte, Robert Sherman 1933- *ConAu 57*
LaFortune, Knolly Stephen 1920- *IntAu&W 82,*
 WrDr 84
LaFountaine, George 1934- *ConAu 7NR, -57,*
 WrDr 84
Lafranke, Ronald *DrAP&F 83*
Lagace, Bernard 1930- *CreCan 1*
Lagace, Mireille Begin 1935- *CreCan 1*
Lagencrantz, Olof Gustaf Hugo 1911-
 IntAu&W 82
Lagercrantz, Rose 1947- *ConAu 108*
Lagerkvist, Paer 1891-1974 *ConAu 49, -85*
Lagerkvist, Par 1891-1974 *CIDMEL 80, CnMD,*
 ConAu 49, ConLC 7, -10, -13, ModWD,
 TwCA SUP, TwCWr, WhoTwCL
Lagerloef, Selma 1858-1940 *ConAu 108*
Lagerlof, Selma O Lovisa 1858-1940 *CIDMEL 80,*
 LongCTC, SmATA 15, TwCA,

*TwCA SUP, TwCLC 4[port], TwCWr,
WhoTwCL*

Lagerwall, Edna *ConAu 45*
Lagerwerff, Ellen Best 1919- *ConAu 85*
Lagevi, Bo *ConAu X*
Lagier, Gary G *DrAP&F 83*
Lagneau-Kesteloot, Lilyan *ConAu X*
Lago, Mary M 1919- *ConAu 69*
Lagorio, Gina 1922- *IntAu&W 82*
LaGrand, Louis E 1935- *ConAu 33R, WrDr 84*
Lagrange, Maurice 1900- *IntAu&W 82*
LaGrone, Clarence Oliver 1906- *MichAu 80*
LaGrone, Oliver 1906- *LivgBAA*
Laguerre, Andre 1915?-1979 *ConAu 97*
Laguerre, Andre 1916?-1979 *ConAu 85*
LaGuma, Alex 1923- *DcLEL 1940*
LaGuma, Alex 1925- *ConAu 49, ConLC 19, ConNov 82, ModBlW, ModCmwL, TwCWr, WrDr 84*
LaGumina, Salvatore John 1928- *ConAu 77*
LaHaye, Tim 1926- *ConAu 9NR, –65*
Lahee, Frederic Henry 1884-1968 *ConAu P-2*
Lahey-Dolega, Christine *DrAP&F 83*
Lahey-Dolega, Christine 1949- *IntWWP 82*
LaHood, Marvin J 1933- *ConAu 10NR, –25R, WrDr 84*
Lahr, John *DrAP&F 83*
Lahr, John 1941- *ConAmTC, ConAu 25R, WrDr 84*
Lahr, Raymond Merrill 1914-1973 *ConAu 41R*
Lahue, Kalton C 1934- *ConAu 7NR, –13R*
Lai, T'ien-Ch'ang 1921- *ConAu 11NR, –69*
Laidlaw, A K *ConAu X*
Laidlaw, Harry Hyde, Jr. 1907- *ConAu 5R*
Laidlaw, W A 1898-1983 *ConAu 109*
Laidler, Harry W 1884-1970 *ConAu 5R, –5NR, –29R*
Laidler, Keith James 1916- *WrDr 84*
Laiken, Deirdre S 1948- *ConAu 104*
Laikin, Paul 1927- *ConAu 5R*
Laimgruber, Monika 1946- *SmATA 11*
Lain Entralgo, Pedro 1908- *CIDMEL 80*
Laine, Gloria *ConAu X*
Laing, Alexander Kinnan 1903-1976 *ConAu 4NR, –5R, –65, TwCA, TwCA SUP*
Laing, Anne C *ConAu X*
Laing, Bernard Kojo 1946- *IntWWP 82*
Laing, Frederick *ConAu 105*
Laing, Jennifer 1948- *ConAu 106*
Laing, Lloyd 1944- *ConAu 5NR, –53*
Laing, Martha *ConAu X*
Laing, R D 1927- *ConAu 107, ConISC 1[port], WorAu 1970, WrDr 84*
Laing, Ronald David 1927- *DcLEL 1940, IntAu&W 82*
Laini, Giovanni 1899- *IntAu&W 82*
Lair, Helen Humphrey 1918- *IntWWP 82*
Lair, Jess K 1926- *ConAu 41R*
Lair, Jesse 1926- *IntAu&W 82*
Lair, Robert L 1932- *ConAu 53*
Laird, Betty A 1925- *ConAu 33R*
Laird, Carobeth 1895- *ConAu 8NR, –61, DcLB Y82B[port]*
Laird, Carobeth 1895-1983 *ConAu 110*
Laird, Charlton G 1901- *ConAu 13R*
Laird, Donald A 1897-1969 *ConAu 5R, –25R*
Laird, Dorothy 1912- *ConAu X*
Laird, Dugan 1920- *ConAu 73*
Laird, Eleanor Childs 1908- *ConAu 73*
Laird, J T 1921- *ConAu 69*
Laird, Jean E 1930- *ConAu 6NR, –9R*
Laird, Melvin R 1922- *ConAu 65*
Laird, Roy D 1925- *ConAu 33R*
Lait, Robert 1921- *ConAu 1R, –2NR, IntAu&W 82, WrDr 84*
Laite, Gordon 1925- *SmATA 31*
Laite, William Edward, Jr. 1932- *ConAu 37R*
Laithwaite, Eric Roberts 1921- *ConAu 103, WrDr 84*
Laitin, Ken 1963- *ConAu 102*
Laitin, Lindy 1968- *ConAu 108*
Laitin, Steve 1965- *ConAu 102*
Lajeunesse, Marie-Louise Emma Cecile *CreCan 2*
Lajos, Lajos Dohanyi *CreCan 1*
Lake, Carolyn 1932- *ConAu 25R*
Lake, David 1929- *WrDr 84*
Lake, David J 1929- *ConAu 10NR, –65, TwCSFW*
Lake, Frank 1914- *ConAu 21R*
Lake, Frank 1914-1982 *ConAu 10NR*
Lake, Kenneth Robert 1931- *ConAu 5NR, –53,*

WrDr 84
Lake, Oliver *DrAP&F 83*
Lakeman, Enid 1903- *ConAu 107, WrDr 84*
Laker, Rosalind *TwCRGW*
Lakey, George 1937- *ConAu 7NR, –17R*
Lakin, Martin 1925- *ConAu 73*
Lakin, R D *DrAP&F 83*
Laklan, Carli 1907- *ConAu X, –1NR, SmATA 5*
Lakoff, George 1941- *ConAu 29R*
Lakoff, Robin Tolmach 1942- *ConAu 103*
Lakoff, Sanford A 1931- *ConAu 1R, –1NR*
Lakritz, Esther 1928- *ConAu 1R, WrDr 84*
Laks, S *IntAu&W 82X*
Lal, Gobind Behari 1890?-1982 *ConAu 106*
Lal, Kishori Saran 1920- *ConAu 21R*
Lal, P 1929- *ConAu 9NR, –13R, ConP 80, DcLEL 1940, IntAu&W 82, WrDr 84*
Laliberte, Alfred 1878-1953 *CreCan 2*
Laliberte, Norman 1925- *ConAu 104*
Lalic, Ivan V 1931- *IntWWP 82, ModSL 2*
Lalic, Mihailo 1914- *CIDMEL 80, ModSL 2*
Lalley, Joseph M 1897?-1980 *ConAu 102*
Lalli, Judy 1949- *ConAu 110*
Lallo, M J *DrAP&F 83*
Lally, Michael *DrAP&F 83*
Lally, Michael 1942- *ConAu 77*
LaLonde, Bernard J 1933- *ConAu 33R*
Lalonde, Robert 1947- *ConAu 109*
Lalou, Rene 1889- *TwCA, TwCA SUP*
Lalumia, Joseph 1916- *ConAu 21R*
Lam, Andrzej 1929- *IntAu&W 82*
Lam, Charlotte 1924- *ConAu 37R*
Lam, Philip Y C *IntWWP 82X*
Lam, Truong Buu 1933- *ConAu 25R, WrDr 84*
Lam, Yan-Chiu 1916- *IntWWP 82*
Laman, Russell 1907- *ConAu P-1*
Laman Trip-DeBeaufort, Agathe H Marie 1890- *IntAu&W 82*
LaMancusa, Katherine C *ConAu X*
Lamanna, Dolores B 1930-1980 *ConAu 9R, –97*
Lamantia, Philip *DrAP&F 83*
Lamantia, Philip 1927- *ConP 80, DcLB 16[port], DcLEL 1940, WorAu 1970, WrDr 84*
Lamar, Howard Roberts 1923- *ConAu 17R, WrDr 84*
Lamar, Lavoisier 1907- *ConAu 5R*
Lamar, Nedra Newkirk *ConAu 69*
LaMare, Walter De *TwCA, TwCA SUP*
LaMarsh, Judy *ConAu X*
LaMarsh, Julia Verlyn 1924-1980 *ConAu 105, –29R*
Lamb, Antonia 1943- *ConAu 21R, WrDr 84*
Lamb, Beatrice Pitney 1904- *ConAu 5R, SmATA 21[port]*
Lamb, Charles 1775-1834 *SmATA 17*
Lamb, Charles 1914- *WrDr 84*
Lamb, Charles Bentall 1914-1981 *ConAu 102, –105*
Lamb, Charlotte *ConAu X, IntAu&W 82X, TwCRGW*
Lamb, David 1940- *ConAu 110*
Lamb, Edward 1902- *ConAu 108*
Lamb, Eleanor 1917- *ConAu 69*
Lamb, Elizabeth Searle *DrAP&F 83*
Lamb, Elizabeth Searle 1917- *ConAu 33R, IntAu&W 82, SmATA 31[port], WrDr 84*
Lamb, F Bruce 1913- *ConAu 33R, WrDr 84*
Lamb, G F *ConAu 4NR*
Lamb, Geoffrey Frederick *ConAu 53, IntAu&W 82, SmATA 10, WrDr 84*
Lamb, H H 1913- *ConAu 21R*
Lamb, Harold Albert 1892-1962 *ConAu 101, –89, TwCA, TwCA SUP*
Lamb, Helen B *ConAu X*
Lamb, Helen Keithley *DrAP&F 83*
Lamb, Hubert Horace 1913- *IntAu&W 82, WrDr 84*
Lamb, Hugh 1946- *ConAu 1NR, –49*
Lamb, Karl A 1933- *ConAu 3NR, –5R, WrDr 84*
Lamb, Lawrence E 1926- *ConAu 97*
Lamb, Lynton Harold 1907-1977 *ConAu 1R, –4NR, SmATA 10*
Lamb, Marion M 1905- *ConAu 5R*
Lamb, Mary Ann 1764-1847 *SmATA 17*
Lamb, Molly *CreCan 2*
Lamb, Myrna *NatPD 81[port]*
Lamb, Robert 1941- *ConAu 29R, SmATA 13*
Lamb, Ruth S *ConAu 45*
Lamb, Sydney M 1929- *ConAu 33R, WrDr 84*

Lamb, William *ConAu X, WrDr 84*
Lamb, William Kaye 1904- *ConAu 81*
Lambdin, William 1936- *ConAu 102*
Lambec, Zoltan *ConAu X*
Lamberg, Robert F 1929- *ConAu 65*
Lamberg-Karlovsky, Clifford Charles 1937- *ConAu 85*
Lambert, B Geraldine 1922- *ConAu 41R*
Lambert, Betty 1933- *ConAu X*
Lambert, Byron Cecil 1923- *ConAu 97*
Lambert, Christine *ConAu X, WrDr 84*
Lambert, Darwin 1916- *ConAu 2NR, –5R, WrDr 84*
Lambert, Derek 1929- *WrDr 84*
Lambert, Derek William 1929- *ConAu 25R*
Lambert, Eleanor *ConAu 102, WrDr 84*
Lambert, Elisabeth *ConAu X*
Lambert, Elizabeth 1933- *ConAu 102*
Lambert, Eric 1918-1966 *ConAu P-1*
Lambert, Eric 1921-1966 *DcLEL 1940*
Lambert, Gavin 1924- *ConAu 1R, –1NR, DcLEL 1940, IntAu&W 82, TwCWr, WrDr 84*
Lambert, Hazel Margaret *ConAu 1R*
Lambert, Herbert H 1929- *ConAu 69*
Lambert, J W 1917- *ConAu 108, WrDr 84*
Lambert, Jacques Edward 1901- *ConAu P-2*
Lambert, Janet Snyder 1894-1973 *ConAu 41R, SmATA 25[port]*
Lambert, John 1936- *ConAu 5R, –8NR*
Lambert, Leslie Harrison *LongCTC*
Lambert, Margery 1939- *CreCan 2*
Lambert, Mark 1942- *ConAu 73*
Lambert, Ronald Dick 1936- *ConAu 108*
Lambert, Roy Eugene 1918- *ConAu 37R*
Lambert, Royston James 1932- *IntAu&W 82*
Lambert, Royston James 1932-1982 *ConAu 108*
Lambert, Saul 1928- *ConAu 106, SmATA 23*
Lambert, Sheila 1926- *ConAu 85*
Lambert, Virginia VanHouten 1938- *ConAmTC*
Lambert, William Wilson 1919- *ConAu 9R*
Lamberti, Marjorie 1937- *ConAu 103*
Lamberton, Donald McLean 1927- *ConAu 103, IntAu&W 82, WrDr 84*
Lamberts, J J 1910- *ConAu 37R*
Lambertus *IntWWP 82X*
Lambie, Nat 1929- *LivgBAA*
Lambley, Peter 1946- *ConAu 109*
Lambo, Thomas Adeoye 1923- *ConAu 29R*
Lamborn, LeRoy L 1937- *ConAu 21R*
Lambot, Isobel Mary 1926- *ConAu 73, IntAu&W 82, WrDr 84*
Lambourne, John 1893- *ConAu X*
Lambrecht, Jan Arthur Medard Jozef 1926- *IntAu&W 82*
Lambrick, Hugh Trevor 1904- *ConAu 6NR, –9R*
Lambright, William Henry 1939- *ConAu 103*
Lambro, Donald 1940- *ConAu 7NR, –57*
Lambton, Anne *DrAP&F 83*
Lambton, Anne 1918- *ConAu 85*
Lamburn, John Battersby Crompton 1893- *ConAu P-1*
Lamburn, Richmal Crompton 1890-1969 *ConAu 25R, ConAu P-1, LongCTC, SmATA 5*
Lame Deer 1895?-1976 *ConAu 69*
Lamensdorf, Leonard 1930- *ConAu 29R*
L'Ami, Charles Ernest 1896- *ConAu 102*
Lamirande, Emilien 1926- *ConAu 8NR, –17R, IntAu&W 82, WrDr 84*
Lamm, Joyce 1933- *ConAu 57*
Lamm, Maurice 1930- *ConAu 17R*
Lamm, Norman 1927- *ConAu 49, IntAu&W 82*
Lamme, Linda Leonard 1942- *ConAu 102*
Lammers, Monica 1916- *IntWWP 82*
Lamming, George *DrAP&F 83*
Lamming, George 1927- *ConAu 85, ConLC 2, –4, ConNov 82, DcLEL 1940, LongCTC, ModBlW, ModCmwL, WorAu, WrDr 84*
Lamming, George 1932- *TwCWr*
Lamon, Lester C 1942- *ConAu 89*
Lamond, Henry George 1885-1969 *ConAu 25R*
Lamont, Corliss 1892- *WrDr 84*
Lamont, Corliss 1902- *ConAu 11NR, –13R, IntAu&W 82, TwCA, TwCA SUP*
Lamont, Douglas Felix 1937- *ConAu 41R*
Lamont, Helen Lamb 1906?-1975 *ConAu 61*
Lamont, Lansing 1930- *ConAu 11NR, –17R*
Lamont, Marianne *ConAu X, TwCRGW, WrDr 84*
Lamont, Marrianne *IntAu&W 82X*
Lamont, N B *ConAu X*

Lamont, Nedda *ConAu X*
Lamont, Rosette C *ConAu 33R*
Lamont, William D 1901-1982 *ConAu 108*
Lamont, William Dawson 1901- *ConAu P-1, IntAu&W 82*
Lamont-Brown, Raymond 1939- *WrDr 84*
Lamorisse, Albert 1922-1970 *ConAu 101, SmATA 23[port]*
Lamothe, Arthur 1928- *CreCan 2*
Lamott, Kenneth 1923- *WrDr 84*
Lamott, Kenneth 1923-1979 *ConAu 25R, –89*
Lamotte, Angela 1908- *IntAu&W 82*
Lamotte, Etienne 1904?-1983 *ConAu 109*
Lamour, Dorothy *ConAu X*
L'Amour, Louis 1908- *AuNews 1, –2, ConAu 1R, –3NR, ConLC 25[port], DcLB Y80B[port], FifWWr, TwCWW, WrDr 84*
Lamparski, Richard *ConAu 21R*
Lampe, Bernd 1939- *IntAu&W 82*
Lampe, David 1923- *ConAu 1R, –1NR*
Lampedusa, Prince Giuseppe Tomasi Di 1896-1957 *ModRL, TwCWr, WhoTwCL, WorAu*
Lampel, Peter Martin 1894-1962 *CnMD*
Lampell, Millard 1919- *ConAu 9R*
Lampert, Diane Charlotte 1924- *NatPD 81[port]*
Lamphere, Louise 1940- *ConAu 89*
Lampkin, William R 1932- *ConAu 106*
Lampl, Paul 1915- *ConAu 104*
Lamplugh, Lois 1921- *ConAu 9NR, IntAu&W 82, SmATA 17, TwCCW 83*
Lampman, Evelyn Sibley 1907-1980 *ConAu 101, –11NR, –13R, SmATA 23N, –4, TwCCW 83*
Lampman, Robert James 1920- *ConAu 103*
Lampo, Hubert 1920- *CIDMEL 80, ConAu 105*
Lamport, Felicia 1916- *ConAu 1R*
Lamppa, William R 1928- *ConAu 53, WrDr 84*
Lamprecht, Sterling Power 1890-1973 *ConAu P-1*
Lampson, Robin 1900-1978 *ConAu 77*
Lamptey, Jonathan Kwesi 1909- *IntAu&W 82*
Lamsa, George M 1892-1975 *ConAu 9NR*
Lamsa, George M 1893- *ConAu P-2*
Lamson, Peggy Friedlander 1912- *ConAu 25R*
LaMure, Pierre 1909-1976 *ConAu 104*
Lan, David 1952- *ConAu 97, ConDr 82, WrDr 84*
Lan-Chan *IntWWP 82X*
Lana, Robert E 1932- *ConAu 33R*
Lancaster, Bruce 1896-1963 *ConAu P-1, SmATA 9, TwCA, TwCA SUP*
Lancaster, Clay 1917- *ConAu 5R, –8NR*
Lancaster, Evelyn *ConAu X*
Lancaster, F Donald *ConAu X*
Lancaster, F Wilfrid 1933- *ConAu 4NR, –53*
Lancaster, Henry Oliver 1913- *WrDr 84*
Lancaster, Kelvin 1924- *ConAu 33R*
Lancaster, Lydia *ConAu X*
Lancaster, Marie-Jaqueline 1922- *ConAu 25R*
Lancaster, Osbert 1908- *ConAu 105, LongCTC, TwCA SUP, WrDr 84*
Lancaster, Otis Ewing 1909- *ConAu 103*
Lancaster, Richard *ConAu 21R*
Lancaster, Sheila *ConAu X, IntAu&W 82X, TwCRGW*
Lancaster, Vicky *TwCRGW, WrDr 84*
Lancaster Brown, Peter 1927- *WrDr 84*
Lance, Betty R G *DrAP&F 83*
Lance, Derek 1932- *ConAu 9NR, –13R*
Lance, Dorothea *IntWWP 82X*
Lance, James Waldo 1926- *ConAu 65, WrDr 84*
Lance, Jeanne *DrAP&F 83*
Lance, Jeanne Louise 1945- *IntWWP 82*
Lance, LaBelle D 1931- *ConAu 81*
Lance, Leslie *ConAu X, –13R, TwCRGW, WrDr 84*
Lanciano, Claude O, Jr. 1922- *ConAu 1NR, –45*
Lancour, Gene *ConAu X*
Lancour, Harold 1908-1981 *ConAu 105, –21R*
Lancret, Charles *CreCan 1*
Lancy, David F 1945- *ConAu 110*
Land *ConAu X*
Land, Aubrey Christian 1912- *ConAu 41R*
Land, Barbara Neblett 1923- *ConAu 81, IntAu&W 82, SmATA 16*
Land, Brian 1927- *ConAu 101*
Land, Dave *IntAu&W 82X*
Land, George Thomas Lock 1933- *ConAu 53*
Land, Jane *ConAu X, MichAu 80, SmATA X, WrDr 84*
Land, Jane And Ross *ConAu X*

Land, Myrick 1922- *ConAu 11NR, –13R, SmATA 15*
Land, Rosina *ConAu X*
Land, Ross *ConAu X, SmATA X, WrDr 84*
Landar, Herbert 1927- *ConAu 33R*
Landau, Annette Henkin *DrAP&F 83*
Landau, Edwin Maria 1904- *IntAu&W 82*
Landau, Elaine 1948- *ConAu 5NR, –53, SmATA 10*
Landau, Genevieve Millet 1927- *ConAu 107*
Landau, Jacob M 1924- *ConAu 8NR, –17R, IntAu&W 82*
Landau, Mark Aleksandrovich 1886- *TwCA, TwCA SUP*
Landau, Martin 1921- *ConAu 45*
Landau, Rom 1899-1974 *ConAu 1R, –4NR, –49*
Landau, Sidney I 1933- *ConAu 7NR, –57*
Landau, Sol 1920- *ConAu 49*
Landauer, Carl 1891- *ConAu 1R, IntAu&W 82*
Landauer, Jerry Gerd 1932-1981 *ConAu 103, –109*
Lande, Henry F 1920- *ConAu 29R*
Lande, Lawrence Montague 1906- *ConAu 105, IntWWP 82, WrDr 84*
Lande, Nathaniel 1939- *ConAu 104*
Lande, Trygve 1935- *IntAu&W 82*
Landeck, Beatrice 1904- *ConAu 73, SmATA 15*
Landecker, Lewis *IntAu&W 82X*
Landecker, Manfred 1929- *ConAu 29R, WrDr 84*
Landeen, William M 1891-1982 *ConAu 109*
Landeira, Ricardo L 1917- *ConAu 81*
Landell, F E Nils-Erik 1935- *IntAu&W 82*
Landen, Robert Geran 1930- *ConAu 21R*
Lander, Ernest McPherson, Jr. 1915- *ConAu 1R, –4NR, IntAu&W 82, WrDr 84*
Lander, Jack Robert 1921- *ConAu 101, WrDr 84*
Lander, Jeannette 1931- *ConAu 33R*
Lander, Louise 1938- *ConAu 85*
Lander, Mamie Stubbs 1891?-1975 *ConAu 53*
Landers, Ann 1918- *ConAu X*
Landers, Gunnard W 1944- *ConAu 93*
Landers, Vernette Trosper 1912- *IntWWP 82*
Landert, Walter 1929- *IntAu&W 82*
Landes, David Saul 1924- *ConAu 103*
Landes, Ruth 1908- *ConAu P-2, WrDr 84*
Landes, Sonia 1925- *ConAu 104*
Landesman, Charles 1932- *ConAu 85*
Landesman, Fran 1927- *DcLB 16[port]*
Landesman, Jay 1919- *DcLB 16[port]*
Landgraf, Susan *DrAP&F 83*
Landgren, Marchal E 1907?-1983 *ConAu 109*
Landin, Les 1923- *ConAu 5R, SmATA 2*
Landis, Benson Y 1897-1966 *ConAu P-1*
Landis, Dennis Channing 1947- *ConAu 110*
Landis, Fred S 1943- *ConAu 107*
Landis, Jessie Royce 1904-1972 *ConAu 33R*
Landis, John 1950- *ConLC 26[port]*
Landis, Judson R 1935- *ConAu 33R*
Landis, Lincoln 1922- *ConAu 45*
Landis, Paul H 1901- *ConAu 5R, –5NR*
Landman, David 1917- *ConAu 11NR, –69*
Lando, Barry Mitchell 1939- *ConAu 77*
Landolfi, Tommaso 1908-1979 *CIDMEL 80, ConLC 11, ModRL*
Landon, Donald D 1930- *ConAu 25R*
Landon, H C Robbins 1926- *ConAu 77, WrDr 84*
Landon, Howard Chandler Robbins 1926- *IntAu&W 82*
Landon, Margaret Dorothea 1903- *ConAu P-1, TwCA SUP*
Landon, Michael DeL 1935- *ConAu 29R*
Landorf, Joyce *AuNews 1*
Landori, Edith 1940- *CreCan 1*
Landory, Veronique 1940- *CreCan 1*
Landow, George P 1940- *ConAu 4NR, –53*
Landreth, Catherine 1899- *ConAu 77*
Landrith, Harold Fochone 1919- *ConAu 103*
Landrum, Phil 1939- *ConAu 81*
Landry, Hilton 1924- *ConAu 13R*
Landry, Robert John 1903- *ConAu 69*
Landsberg, Hans H 1913- *ConAu 10NR, –17R*
Landsberg, Helmut Erich 1906- *ConAu 107*
Landsbergis, Algirdas J 1924- *ConAu 33R*
Landsbergis, Algiroas 1924- *IntAu&W 82*
Landsburg, Alan William 1933- *ConAu 103*
Landsburg, Sally 1933- *ConAu 57*
Landshoff, Ursula 1908- *ConAu 29R, SmATA 13*
Landsley, Patrick Alfred 1926- *CreCan 2*

Landstrom, Bjorn Olof August 1917- *ConAu 13R*
Landsverk, O G 1901- *ConAu 61*
Landvater, Dorothy 1927- *ConAu 103, WrDr 84*
Landwehr, Arthur J, II 1934- *ConAu 37R*
Landwirth, Heinz 1927- *ConAu 7NR, WorAu*
Landy, David 1917- *ConAu 77*
Landy, Eugene E 1934- *ConAu 41R*
Landynski, Jacob W 1930- *ConAu 21R*
Lane, Allen 1902-1970 *ConAu 29R, LongCTC*
Lane, Ann J 1931- *ConAu 110*
Lane, Anthony 1916- *ConAu 13R*
Lane, Arthur 1937- *ConAu 41R*
Lane, Carl Daniel 1899- *ConAu 105*
Lane, Carolyn 1926- *ConAu 29R, SmATA 10, WrDr 84*
Lane, Charles *ConAu X*
Lane, David Stuart 1933- *ConAu 29R, IntAu&W 82, WrDr 84*
Lane, E 1936- *ConAu 37R*
Lane, Ferdinand Cole 1885- *TwCA SUP*
Lane, Frank W 1908- *WrDr 84*
Lane, Frank Walter 1908- *ConAu 9R*
Lane, Frederic Chapin 1900- *ConAu 105*
Lane, Gary 1943- *WrDr 84*
Lane, Gary Martin 1943- *ConAu 37R, IntWWP 82*
Lane, Helen R 1921- *ConAu 2NR, –45, IntAu&W 82*
Lane, Irving M 1944- *ConAu 53*
Lane, Jack C 1932- *ConAu 4NR, –53*
Lane, James B 1942- *ConAu 93*
Lane, Jane 1905- *ConAu X, LongCTC, TwCWr*
Lane, Jerry *ConAu X*
Lane, John *ConAu X, DrAP&F 83*
Lane, John 1854-1925 *LongCTC*
Lane, John 1910- *IntWWP 82*
Lane, John 1932- *ConAu 106, SmATA 15*
Lane, Laura Gordon 1913- *ConAu 102*
Lane, Marc J 1946- *ConAu 105*
Lane, Margaret 1907- *ConAu 25R, LongCTC, WorAu*
Lane, Mark 1927- *ConAu 61*
Lane, Mary *DrAP&F 83*
Lane, Mary B 1911- *ConAu 9NR*
Lane, Mary Beauchamp 1911- *ConAu 13R*
Lane, Mary D *ConAu X, WrDr 84*
Lane, Mervin *DrAP&F 83*
Lane, Michael 1941- *ConAu 85*
Lane, Patrick 1939- *ConAu 97, ConLC 25[port], ConP 80, WrDr 84*
Lane, Pinkie Gordon *DrAP&F 83*
Lane, Pinkie Gordon 1923- *ConAu 41R*
Lane, Ralph Norman Angell 1874-1967 *LongCTC*
Lane, Raymond A 1894?-1974 *ConAu 53*
Lane, Richard 1926- *ConAu 10NR, –21R, IntAu&W 82, WrDr 84*
Lane, Robert E 1917- *ConAu 1R, –6NR*
Lane, Roger 1934- *ConAu 105*
Lane, Ronald 1931- *WrDr 84*
Lane, Ronnie M 1949- *ConAu 41R, MichAu 80*
Lane, Rose Wilder 1886-1968 *SmATA 29[port]*
Lane, Rose Wilder 1887-1968 *ConAu 102, SmATA 28, TwCA, TwCA SUP*
Lane, Roumelia *TwCRGW*
Lane, Sherry *ConAu X*
Lane, Sylvia 1916- *ConAu 5R, –8NR*
Lane, Thomas A 1906- *ConAu 13R*
Lane, William G 1919- *ConAu 25R*
Lane, William L 1931- *WrDr 84*
Lane, William Lister 1931- *ConAu 29R*
Lane, Yoti *ConAu 1R*
Lanegran, David A 1941- *ConAu 89*
Lanes, Selma Gordon 1929- *ConAu 25R, SmATA 3*
Laney, Al 1896- *ConAu 108, DcLB 4*
Laney, James Thomas 1927- *ConAu 103*
Laney, Ruth *DrAP&F 83*
Lanford, H W 1919- *ConAu 41R*
Lanfranco, Guido Gaetan 1930- *WrDr 84*
Lang, Allen Kim 1928- *ConAu 17R, ConSFA*
Lang, Andre 1893- *IntAu&W 82*
Lang, Andrew 1844-1912 *LongCTC, ModBrL, SmATA 16*
Lang, Barbara 1935- *ConAu 9R*
Lang, Berel 1933- *ConAu 41R*
Lang, Daniel 1915-1981 *ConAu 4NR, –5R, –105*
Lang, David 1913- *ConAu 106*
Lang, David Marshall 1924- *ConAu 2NR, –5R, WrDr 84*
Lang, Derek 1913- *ConAu 102, WrDr 84*

Lang, Elmy *IntAu&W 82X*
Lang, Frances *ConAu X*, *IntAu&W 82X*, *WrDr 84*
Lang, Fritz 1890-1976 *ConAu 69, –77*, *ConLC 20*
Lang, George 1924- *ConAu 101*
Lang, Gottfried O 1919- *ConAu 45*
Lang, Grace *ConAu X*
Lang, Gregor 1900- *ConAu X*
Lang, Helmer 1924- *IntAu&W 82*, *IntWWP 82*
Lang, Isaac *WorAu*
Lang, Jack 1921- *ConAu 5R*
Lang, Jon *DrAP&F 83*
Lang, Jovian Peter 1919- *ConAu 41R*, *IntAu&W 82*
Lang, King *ConAu X*, *WrDr 84*
Lang, Kurt 1924- *ConAu 33R*, *WrDr 84*
Lang, Mabel Louise 1917- *ConAu 106*
Lang, Martin *ConAu X*
Lang, Maud *ConAu X*
Lang, Miriam 1915- *ConAu 5R*
Lang, Ned *ConAu X*
Lang, Paul Henry 1901- *ConAu 103*
Lang, Rex *ConAu X*
Lang, Robert 1912- *ConAu 41R*
Lang, Ronald William 1933- *ConAu 103*
Lang, T T *ConAu X*
Lang, William Rawson 1909- *ConAu 103*, *WrDr 84*
Lang-Dillenburger, Elmy 1921- *IntAu&W 82*
Lang-Sims, Lois 1917- *WrDr 84*
Lang-Sims, Lois Dorothy 1917- *ConAu 106*
Langacker, Ronald W 1942- *ConAu 21R*
Langan, Ruth Ryan 1937- *ConAu 107*
Langan, Thomas 1929- *ConAu 1R*
Langart, Darrel T *WrDr 84*
Langbaum, Robert 1924- *ConAu 1NR, –45*, *ConLCrt 82*, *WrDr 84*
Langbein, John Harriss 1941- *IntAu&W 82*, *WrDr 84*
Langdale, Eve *ConAu X*
Langdon, Charles 1934- *ConAu 77*
Langdon, Frank C 1919- *ConAu 21R*
Langdon, George D, Jr. 1933- *ConAu 21R*
Langdon, Grace 1889- *ConAu 1R*
Langdon, James *DrAP&F 83*
Langdon, John 1913- *ConAu 5R, IntAu&W 82*
Langdon, Margaret Hoffmann 1926- *ConAu 107*
Langdon, Philip 1937- *ConAu 109*
Langdon, Robert Adrian 1924- *ConAu 104*, *IntAu&W 82*, *WrDr 84*
Langdon-Davies, John 1897- *TwCA*, *TwCA SUP*
Lange, Antoni 1861-1929 *ClDMEL 80*
Lange, Art *DrAP&F 83*
Lange, Dorothea 1895-1965 *ConAu 107*
Lange, Gerald *DrAP&F 83*
Lange, Gerald Williams 1946- *ConAu 69*
Lange, Hartmut 1937- *CroCD*
Lange, John *ConAu X*, *IntAu&W 82X*, *SmATA X*, *TwCCr&M 80*, *WorAu 1970*, *WrDr 84*
Lange, John Frederick, Jr. 1931- *ConAu 8NR, –97*
Lange, Joseph 1932- *ConAu 8NR, –17R*
Lange, Joseph 1933- *WrDr 84*
Lange, Kelly *ConAu 89*
Lange, Oda 1900- *IntWWP 82*
Lange, Oliver 1927- *ConAu 103*
Lange, Per 1901- *IntAu&W 82*
Lange, Suzanne 1945- *ConAu 29R, SmATA 5*
Lange, Victor 1908- *ConAu 9R, WrDr 84*
Langelaan, George *ConSFA*
Langenbeck, Curt 1906-1953 *CnMD*
Langendoen, D Terence 1939- *ConAu 33R*, *WrDr 84*
Langer, Ellen J 1947- *ConAu 49*
Langer, Frantisek 1888-1965 *ClDMEL 80*, *CnMD, ModWD*
Langer, Jonas 1936- *ConAu 33R*
Langer, Lawrence L 1929- *ConAu 11NR, –65*
Langer, Marshall J 1928- *ConAu 105*
Langer, Rudolf 1923- *IntAu&W 82*
Langer, Susanne Katherina 1895- *ConAu 41R*, *TwCA SUP*
Langer, Sydney 1914- *ConAu 109*
Langer, Thomas Edward 1929- *ConAu 5R*
Langer, Walter Charles 1899-1981 *ConAu 102*, *–104*
Langer, William Leonard 1896-1977 *ConAu 29R*, *–73, TwCA SUP*
Langevin, Andre 1927- *CreCan 2*, *ModFrL*

Langevin, Sister Jean Marie 1917- *ConAu 53*
Langford, Alec J 1926- *ConAu 97*
Langford, Gary R 1947- *ConAu 103*, *WrDr 84*
Langford, George 1939- *ConAu 53*
Langford, Gerald 1911- *ConAu 1R*, *WrDr 84*
Langford, James Rouleau 1937- *ConAu 53*
Langford, Jane *ConAu X*, *WrDr 84*
Langford, Jerome 1937- *WrDr 84*
Langford, Jerome J 1937- *ConAu X*
Langford, Thomas Anderson 1929- *ConAu 9R*
Langford, Walter McCarty 1908- *ConAu 33R*
Langfus, Anna *TwCWr*
Langgasser, Elisabeth 1899-1950 *ClDMEL 80*, *ModGL*
Langguth, A J *DrAP&F 83*
Langguth, A J 1933- *ConAu 61*
Langham, Barbara *DrAP&F 83*
Langham, Michael Seymour 1919- *CreCan 1*
Langholm, Neil *ConAu X*
Langhorne, Elizabeth *WrDr 84*
Langhorne, Elizabeth 1909- *ConAu 49*
Langiulli, Nino 1932- *ConAu 53*
Langland, Joseph *DrAP&F 83*
Langland, Joseph 1917- *WrDr 84*
Langland, Joseph Thomas 1917- *ConAu 5R*, *–8NR, ConP 80, IntWWP 82*
Langland, William *IntAu&W 82X*
Langley, Adria 1899?-1983 *ConAu 110*
Langley, Bob 1936- *ConAu 85*
Langley, Bob 1938- *WrDr 84*
Langley, Dorothy 1904- *ConAu X*
Langley, Harold D 1925- *ConAu 21R*
Langley, Helen *ConAu X*
Langley, James Maydon 1916- *ConAu 102*, *IntAu&W 82, WrDr 84*
Langley, James Maydon 1916-1983 *ConAu 109*
Langley, John *TwCWW*
Langley, Lester Danny 1940- *ConAu 102*
Langley, Louise *IntWWP 82X*
Langley, Michael John 1933- *ConAu 97*, *IntAu&W 82*
Langley, Noel Aubrey 1911-1980 *ConAu 102*, *–13R, IntAu&W 82, SmATA 25N*
Langley, Noel Aubrey 1916- *TwCWr*
Langley, Raymond J 1935- *ConAu 108*
Langley, Roger 1930- *ConAu 73*
Langley, Stephen Gould 1938- *ConAu 41R*
Langley, Tania *ConAu X*
Langley, Wright 1935- *ConAu 57*
Langlois, Walter G 1925- *ConAu 9NR, –21R*
Langman, Ida Kaplan 1904- *ConAu P-1*
Langman, Larry 1930- *ConAu 109*
Langner, Ilse 1899- *CnMD*
Langner, Lawrence 1890-1962 *ModWD, TwCA*, *TwCA SUP*
Langner, Nola 1930- *ConAu 37R, SmATA 8*
Langone, John 1929- *ConAu 1NR, –49*
Langsam, Walter Consuelo 1906- *ConAu 1R*, *–2NR, IntAu&W 82, WrDr 84*
Langslet, Lars Roar 1936- *IntAu&W 82*
Langsley, Donald G 1925- *ConAu 4NR, –53*
Langstadt, Anne Kahane *CreCan 1*
Langstaff, John Brett 1889- *ConAu 1R*
Langstaff, John Meredith 1920- *ChlLR 3*, *ConAu 1R, –4NR, SmATA 6*
Langstaff, Josephine *ConAu X*
Langstaff, Nancy 1925- *ConAu 73*
Langton, Clair V 1895- *ConAu 5R*
Langton, Daniel J *DrAP&F 83*
Langton, Daniel J 1927- *ConAu 93*
Langton, Jane 1922- *ConAu 1R, –1NR*, *SmATA 3, TwCCW 83, WrDr 84*
Langton, Kenneth P 1933- *ConAu 25R*
Langton, Roger W *DrAP&F 83*
Languirand, Jacques 1931- *CreCan 1*
Langwill, Lyndesay Graham 1897- *ConAu 13R*, *WrDr 84*
Langworth, Richard M 1941- *ConAu 73*
Langworthy, Harry W 1939- *ConAu 57*
Lanham, Charles Trueman 1902-1978 *ConAu 81*
Lanham, Edwin 1904-1979 *ConAu 9R, –89*, *DcLB 4, WorAu*
Lanham, Frank W 1914- *ConAu 1R, –6NR*
Lanham, Richard Alan 1936- *ConAu 10NR*, *–25R, WrDr 84*
Lanham, Url 1918- *ConAu 25R*
Lanier, Alison Raymond 1917- *ConAu 17R*
Lanier, Robert S *IntWWP 82X*
Lanier, Sidney 1842-1881 *SmATA 18*
Lanier, Sterling E 1927- *TwCSFW, WrDr 84*
Lanigan, Catherine 1947- *ConAu 108*
Laning, Edward 1906- *ConAu 53*

Lank, Edith H 1926- *ConAu 109*
Lankevich, George J 1939- *ConAu 77*
Lankford, John 1934- *ConAu 17R*
Lankford, Philip Marlin 1945- *ConAu 7NR, –57*
Lankford, T Randall 1942- *ConAu 65*
Lankin, Dorothy *MichAu 80*
Lanne, William F *ConAu X*
Lanner, Ronald Martin 1930- *ConAu 107*
Lanning, Edward P 1930- *ConAu 17R*
Lanning, George *DrAP&F 83*
Lanning, George William 1925- *WrDr 84*
Lanning, George William, Jr. 1925- *ConAu 9R*, *DcLEL 1940*
Lanning, John Tate 1902-1976 *ConAu 108*
Lannoy, Christiane 1916- *IntAu&W 82*
Lannuier, Dorothy *ConAu X*
Lanoue, Fred Richard 1908-1965 *ConAu P-1*
LaNoue, George Richard 1937- *ConAu 73*
Lanoux, Armand 1913- *IntWWP 82*
Lanoux, Armand 1913-1983 *ConAu 109*
Lansbury, Angela 1946- *ConAu 81*
Lansdale, Robert Tucker 1900-1980 *ConAu 103*
Lansdowne, J F 1937- *ConAu 49*
Lanser, Susan Sniader *ConAu 107*
Lansing, Alfred 1921-1975 *ConAu 13R, –61*
Lansing, Elisabeth Hubbard 1911- *ConAu 5R*
Lansing, Gerrit Yates 1928- *ConAu 73*
Lansing, Henry *ConAu X*
Lansing, John B 1919-1970 *ConAu 108*
Lansky, Bruce 1941- *ConAu 109*
Lansky, Vicki 1942- *ConAu 81*
Lanson, Lucienne 1930- *ConAu 108*
Lant, Harvey *ConAu X, TwCWW*
Lant, Jeffrey Ladd 1947- *ConAu 109*
Lantay, Patricia Joan Marx 1946- *IntWWP 82*
Lanterman, Ray 1916- *ConAu 106*
Lantier, Nadine Jez 1922- *IntAu&W 82*
Lantis, David W 1917- *ConAu 13R*
Lantis, Margaret 1906- *ConAu P-2*
Lantry, Mike *ConAu X, WrDr 84*
Lantz, Herman R 1919- *ConAu 37R*
Lantz, J Edward 1911- *WrDr 84*
Lantz, Louise K 1930- *ConAu 45*
Lantz, Robert 1914- *IntAu&W 82*
Lantz, Ruth Cox 1914- *IntWWP 82*
Lantz, Thelma *DrAP&F 83*
Lantz, Walter 1900- *ConAu 108*
Lanyon, Carla 1906- *ConAu P-1*
Lanzillotti, Robert F 1921- *ConAu 77*
Lao, Kan 1907- *ConAu 41R*
Lao, She *ConAu X*
Lapage, Geoffrey 1888- *ConAu P-1*
Lapalma *IntWWP 82X*
LaPalma, Marina *DrAP&F 83*
LaPalma, Marina 1949- *IntAu&W 82*
LaPalombara, Joseph 1925- *ConAu 1R, –6NR*, *IntAu&W 82*
Lapaquellerie, Yvon *ConAu X*
Lapati, Americo D 1924- *ConAu 1R, –1NR*
LaPatra, Jack W 1927- *ConAu 93*
Lape, Esther Everett 1881-1981 *ConAu 108*
Lape, Fred 1900- *ConAu 102*
Lapedes, Daniel N 1913?-1979 *ConAu 93*
LaPenta, Anthony V, Jr. 1943- *ConAu 69*
Lapesa, Rafael 1908- *IntAu&W 82*
Lapeza, David 1950- *ConAu 73*
Lapham, Arthur L 1922- *ConAu 49*
Lapham, Lewis H 1935- *ConAu 77*
Lapham, Maxwell E 1900?-1983 *ConAu 110*
Lapham, Samuel, Jr. 1892-1972 *ConAu 106*
Lapide, Phinn E *ConAu X*
Lapide, Pinchas E 1922- *ConAu 21R*
Lapidus, Elaine 1939- *ConAu 21R*
Lapidus, Jacqueline *DrAP&F 83*
Lapidus, Jacqueline 1941- *ConAu 97*, *IntWWP 82*
Lapidus, Morris 1902- *ConAu 77*
Lapierre, Dominique 1931- *ConAu 69*
Lapierre, Eugene 1899- *CreCan 2*
Lapierre, Joseph Eugene *CreCan 2*
LaPierre, Laurier L 1929- *ConAu 107*
LaPietra, Mary 1929- *ConAu 61*
Lapin, Howard S 1922- *ConAu 17R*
Lapin, Jackie 1951- *ConAu 85*
Lapine, Andre 1868-1952 *CreCan 1*
Lapine, Andreas Christian Gottfried 1868-1952 *CreCan 1*
Lapine, James 1949- *NatPD 81[port]*
Lapinski, Zdzislaw 1930- *IntAu&W 82*
LaPlace, John 1922- *ConAu 103*
LaPointe, Frank 1936- *ConAu 93*
Lapointe, Gatien 1931- *CreCan 2*

Lapointe, Paul-Marie 1929- *ConAu 109,*
CreCan 2
Laponce, Jean Antoine 1925- *ConAu 53,*
IntAu&W 82, WrDr 84
Laporte, Jean 1924- *ConAu 41R*
LaPorte, Robert, Jr. 1940- *ConAu 41R*
Lapp, Charles 1914- *ConAu 1NR, -45*
Lapp, Chuck *ConAu X*
Lapp, Eleanor J 1936- *ConAu 69*
Lapp, Horace 1904- *CreCan 1*
Lapp, John Allen 1933- *ConAu 41R*
Lapp, John Clarke 1917-1977 *ConAu 85*
Lapp, Ralph Eugene 1917- *ConAu 81*
Lappalainen, Kalevi *IntWWP 82X*
Lappalainen, Kauko Kalevi 1940- *IntWWP 82*
Lappe, Frances Moore 1944- *ConAu 37R,*
IntAu&W 82, WrDr 84
Lappin, Ben *ConAu X*
Lappin, Bernard William 1916- *ConAu 9R*
Lappin, Peter 1911- *ConAu 7NR, -57,*
SmATA 32[port]
Lapping, Brian 1937- *ConAu 25R, WrDr 84*
Laprade, William Thomas 1883-1975 *ConAu 89*
LaPray, Helen 1916- *ConAu 7NR*
LaPray, Helen 1919- *ConAu 53*
Lapsley, James N 1930- *ConAu 25R*
Lapuente Benavente, Pablo Antonio 1921-
IntAu&W 82
Laqueur, Walter 1921- *ConAu 5R, WrDr 84*
Laquian, Aprodicio A 1935- *ConAu 29R*
Lara, Agustin 1900-1970 *ConAu 104*
Laramore, Darryl 1928- *ConAu 101*
Larangeira, Crispin 1940- *NatPD 81[port]*
Larbaud, Valery 1881-1957 *CIDMEL 80,*
ConAu 106, ModFrL, TwCA, TwCA SUP,
TwCLC 9[port], TwCWr
Larco, Isabel Granda 1911?-1983 *ConAu 109*
Lardas, Konstantines 1927- *IntWWP 82*
Lardas, Konstantinos *DrAP&F 83*
Lardas, Konstantinos 1927- *ConAu 13R*
Lardner, George, Jr. 1934- *ConAu 73*
Lardner, John 1912-1960 *ConAu 93*
Lardner, Ring 1885-1933 *CnMWL, ConAmA,*
ConAu 104, DcLB 25[port], LongCTC,
ModAL, ModAL SUP, TwCA,
TwCA SUP, TwCLC 2, TwCWr,
WhoTwCL
Lardner, Ring, Jr. *DrAP&F 83*
Lardner, Ring, Jr. 1915- *ConAu 25R, Conv 1,*
DcLB 26[port]
Lardner, Wilmer Ringold 1885-1933 *MichAu 80*
Laredo, Betty *ConAu X*
Laredo, Johnny *ConAu X, MichAu 80*
LaReyniere *ConAu X*
Large, Peter Somerville *ConAu X*
Large, R Geddes 1901- *ConAu 102, WrDr 84*
Largo, Michael 1950- *ConAu 73*
Lariar, Lawrence 1908- *ConAu P-1*
Larimore, Bertha B 1915- *ConAu 61*
Larista, Pepe *IntAu&W 82X*
LaRivers, Ira, II 1915-1977 *ConAu 41R*
Lark, Raymond 1939- *IntAu&W 82*
Larkey, Patrick Darrel 1943- *ConAu 85*
Larkin, Emmet 1927- *ConAu 9NR*
Larkin, Emmet J 1927- *ConAu 13R*
Larkin, Joan *DrAP&F 83*
Larkin, John Alan 1936- *ConAu 41R*
Larkin, Maia *ConAu X*
Larkin, Mary Ann *DrAP&F 83*
Larkin, Maurice 1932- *ConAu 102, WrDr 84*
Larkin, Miriam Therese 1930- *ConAu 108*
Larkin, Oliver Aterman 1896-1970 *DcLEL 1940*
Larkin, Oliver Waterman 1896-1970 *ConAu 1R,*
-29R, TwCA SUP
Larkin, Philip 1922- *CnMWL, ConAu 5R,*
ConLC 3, -5, -8, -9, -13, -18, ConP 80,
DcLEL 1940, IntAu&W 82, LongCTC,
ModBrL, ModBrL SUP, RGFMBP,
TwCWr, WhoTwCL, WorAu, WrDr 84
Larkin, R T *ConAu X*
Larkin, Rochelle 1935- *ConAu 33R, WrDr 84*
Larkin, Sarah *ConAu X*
Larmon 1910- *IntWWP 82*
Larmore, Lewis 1915- *ConAu 45*
Larn, Richard James Vincent 1930- *ConAu 103,*
WrDr 84
Larner, Jeremy *DrAP&F 83*
Larner, Jeremy 1937- *ConAu 9R, WrDr 84*
Larner, John 1930- *ConAu 81*
Larneuil, Michel *ConAu X*
Larney, Judith 1942- *WrDr 84*
LaRoche *TwCA, TwCA SUP*

Laroche, Rene *ConAu X*
Laroche, Roland 1927- *CreCan 2*
Larock, Bruce Edward 1940- *ConAu 53*
Larom, Henry V 1903?-1975 *ConAu 61,*
SmATA 30N
Larose, Ludger 1868-1915 *CreCan 2*
Larouche, Jean-Claude 1944- *IntAu&W 82*
Larrabee, Carroll Burton 1896-1983 *ConAu 110*
Larrabee, Eric 1922- *ConAu 1R, -1NR,*
DcLEL 1940
Larrabee, Harold A 1894-1979 *ConAu 85,*
ConAu P-1
Larranaga, Robert O 1940- *ConAu 49*
Larrea, Jean-Jacques 1960- *ConAu 45*
Larrea, Juan 1895- *CIDMEL 80*
Larrecq, John M 1926-1980 *SmATA 25N*
Larrick, Nancy 1910- *WrDr 84*
Larrick, Nancy G 1910- *ConAu 1R, -1NR,*
SmATA 4
Larrie, Reginald R 1928- *MichAu 80*
Larrison, Earl J 1919- *ConAu 9NR, -57*
Larrowe, Charles P 1916- *ConAu 41R,*
IntAu&W 82
Larrowe, Lash *IntAu&W 82X*
Larry *ConAu X*
Larsen, Beverly 1929- *ConAu 17R*
Larsen, Carl *DrAP&F 83*
Larsen, Carl 1934- *ConAu 77, NatPD 81[port]*
Larsen, Charles E 1923- *ConAu 33R*
Larsen, David C 1944- *ConAu 73*
Larsen, E John 1926- *ConAu 25R*
Larsen, Egon 1904- *ConAu 3NR, -9R,*
IntAu&W 82, SmATA 14, WrDr 84
Larsen, Elyse 1957- *ConAu 41R*
Larsen, Eric *DrAP&F 83*
Larsen, Erik 1911- *ConAu 41R, IntAu&W 82*
Larsen, Erling 1909- *ConAu 13R*
Larsen, Ernest *DrAP&F 83*
Larsen, Ernest 1946- *ConAu 106*
Larsen, Jeanne *DrAP&F 83*
Larsen, Johannes Anker *TwCA, TwCA SUP*
Larsen, Kalee 1952- *ConAu 41R*
Larsen, Knud S 1938- *ConAu 53*
Larsen, Lawrence H 1931- *ConAu 21R*
Larsen, Otto N 1922- *ConAu 1R, -2NR,*
IntAu&W 82X
Larsen, Paul E 1933- *ConAu 93*
Larsen, Peter 1933- *ConAu 29R, WrDr 84*
Larsen, Ronald J 1948- *ConAu 41R*
Larsen, Roy E 1899-1979 *ConAu 89*
Larsen, Stephen 1941- *ConAu 69*
Larsen, Tony 1949- *ConAu 107*
Larsen, William Edward 1936- *ConAu 17R,*
WrDr 84
Larson, Alf 1885-1967 *CIDMEL 80*
Larson, Amada Wiljanen 1910- *MichAu 80*
Larson, Andrew Karl 1899- *ConAu P-2*
Larson, Arthur 1910- *ConAu 1R, -1NR,*
IntAu&W 82, WrDr 84
Larson, Bob 1944- *ConAu 5NR, -53*
Larson, Bruce 1925- *ConAu 57*
Larson, Bruce L 1936- *ConAu 85*
Larson, Calvin J 1933- *ConAu 49*
Larson, Carl M 1916- *ConAu 41R*
Larson, Cedric Arthur 1908- *ConAu 65*
Larson, Charles 1922- *ConAu 25R, WrDr 84*
Larson, Charles R *DrAP&F 83*
Larson, Charles R 1938- *ConAu 4NR, -53*
Larson, Charles U 1940- *ConAu 97*
Larson, Clinton F 1919- *ConAu 57*
Larson, Donald 1925- *ConAu 57*
Larson, E Richard 1944- *ConAu 105*
Larson, Esther Elisabeth *ConAu 17R*
Larson, Eve *ConAu X, SmATA X*
Larson, George C 1942- *ConAu 9NR, -65*
Larson, Gerald James 1938- *ConAu 93*
Larson, Gustive O 1897- *ConAu 29R*
Larson, Harold J 1934- *ConAu 53*
Larson, Henrietta M 1894- *ConAu P-2*
Larson, Henrietta M 1894-1983 *ConAu 110*
Larson, Jack *NatPD 81[port]*
Larson, Janet Karsten 1945- *ConAu 104*
Larson, Jean Russell 1930- *ConAu 21R*
Larson, Jeanne 1920- *ConAu 57*
Larson, Knute 1919- *ConAu 9R*
Larson, Kris *DrAP&F 83*
Larson, Kris 1953- *ConAu 77*
Larson, Magali Sarfatti 1936- *ConAu 97*
Larson, Martin Alfred 1897- *ConAu 2NR, -5R*
Larson, Mel 1916- *ConAu 5R*
Larson, Muriel 1924- *ConAu 9NR*
Larson, Muriel Koller 1924- *ConAu 21R,*

WrDr 84
Larson, Norita D 1944- *ConAu 105,*
SmATA 29[port]
Larson, Orvin Prentiss 1910- *ConAu 77*
Larson, P Merville 1903- *ConAu 41R*
Larson, Peggy 1931- *ConAu 81*
Larson, R A *DrAP&F 83*
Larson, Richard Francis 1931- *ConAu 41R*
Larson, Robert W 1927- *ConAu 85*
Larson, Simeon 1925- *ConAu 61*
Larson, T A 1910- *ConAu 33R*
Larson, Thomas B 1914- *ConAu 25R*
Larson, Victor Emanuel 1898- *ConAu 25R*
Larson, William H 1938- *ConAu 21R,*
SmATA 10
Larsson, Flora 1904- *ConAu 93*
Larsson, Martha 1908- *IntAu&W 82*
Larsson, Zenia 1922- *IntAu&W 82*
Larteguy, Jean 1920- *TwCWr*
Lartigue, Jacques-Henri 1894- *ConAu 33R,*
-33R
Larue, Gerald A 1916- *ConAu 21R*
LaRusso, Dominic A 1924- *ConAu 33R*
LaRusso, Louis, II 1935- *NatPD 81[port]*
Lary, N M 1940- *ConAu 61*
Lasagna, Louis 1923- *ConAu 106*
LaSalle, Donald P 1933- *ConAu 29R, WrDr 84*
LaSalle, Dorothy 1895- *ConAu 5R,*
IntAu&W 82
LaSalle, Peter 1947- *ConAu 103*
LaSalle, Victor *ConAu X*
Lasana, Oronde *DrAP&F 83*
Lasater, Alice E 1936- *ConAu 57*
Lasby, Clarence G 1933- *ConAu 105*
Lasch, Christopher 1932- *ConAu 73,*
ConIsC 1[port], WrDr 84
Lasch, Robert 1907- *ConAu 102*
Laschever, Barnett D 1924- *ConAu 1R, -6NR*
LaScola, Ray L 1915- *ConAu 1R*
Lasell, Elinor H 1929- *ConAu 7NR,*
SmATA 19
Lasell, Fen H 1929- *ConAu X, SmATA X*
Laser, Marvin 1914- *ConAu 9R*
LaSerna, Ramon Gomez De *ModRL, TwCA,*
TwCA SUP
Lash, Jennifer 1938- *WrDr 84*
Lash, Joseph P 1909- *ConAu 17R,*
WorAu 1970, WrDr 84
Lash, Kenneth *DrAP&F 83*
Lasher, Albert C 1928- *ConAu 25R*
Lasher, Faith Betty 1921- *ConAu 37R,*
SmATA 12
Laska *IntWWP 82X*
Laska, P J *DrAP&F 83*
Laska, P J 1938- *ConAu 65*
Laska, Peter Jerome 1938- *IntWWP 82*
Lasker, Edward 1885-1981 *ConAu 5R, -103*
Lasker, Gabriel Ward 1912- *ConAu 1R*
Lasker, Joe 1919- *ConAu 1NR, -49, SmATA 9*
Lasker-Schuler, Else 1876?-1945 *CIDMEL 80,*
CnMD, ModGL
Laski, Audrey 1931- *WrDr 84*
Laski, Harold Joseph 1893-1950 *LongCTC,*
TwCA, TwCA SUP
Laski, Marghanita 1915- *ConAu 105, LongCTC,*
ModBrL, TwCA SUP, WrDr 84
Laski, Marghanita 1917- *DcLEL 1940*
Laskin, Pam *DrAP&F 83*
Laskowski, Jerzy 1919- *ConAu 77*
Lasky, Jesse Louis, Jr. 1910- *AuNews 1,*
ConAu 1R, -4NR, WrDr 84
Lasky, Kathryn 1944- *ConAu 11NR, -69,*
SmATA 13
Lasky, Melvin Jonah 1920- *ConAu 53*
Lasky, Victor 1918- *AuNews 1, ConAu 5R,*
-10NR, WrDr 84
Lasky, William R 1921- *ConAu 97*
Laslett, John H M 1933- *ConAu 29R*
Laslett, Peter 1915- *ConAu 73*
Lasley, Jack *ConAu X*
Lasley, John Wayne, III 1925- *ConAu 17R*
Lasnier, Rina 1915- *CreCan 1*
LaSor, William Sanford 1911- *ConAu 1R, -2NR,*
IntAu&W 82
LaSorte, A Michael 1931- *ConAu 13R*
LaSpina, Greye 1880-1969 *ConAu P-1*
Lass, Abraham H 1907- *ConAu 9R*
Lass, Betty 1908?-1976 *ConAu 69*
Lass, William E 1928- *ConAu 1R, -2NR*
Lass, William H 1910?-1975 *ConAu 104*
Lassalle, Caroline *WrDr 84*
Lassang, Iwan *WorAu*

Lea, David A M 1934- *ConAu 10NR, –21R*
Lea, F A 1915-1977 *ConAu 1R, –3NR*
Lea, Fanny Heaslip 1884-1955 *TwCA, TwCA SUP*
Lea, Frederick 1900- *WrDr 84*
Lea, Joan *ConAu X*
Lea, Richard *SmATA X*
Lea, Sydney *DrAP&F 83*
Lea, Sydney Wright 1942- *ConAu 106*
Lea, Timmy *ConAu X*
Lea, Timothy *ConAu X*
Lea, Tom 1907- *DcLB 6, TwCA SUP, TwCWW, WrDr 84*
Leab, Daniel Josef 1936- *ConAu 11NR, –29R, WrDr 84*
Leabo, Dick A 1921- *ConAu 9R, WrDr 84*
Leacacos, John P 1908- *ConAu 25R*
Leach, Aroline Beecher 1899- *ConAu 61*
Leach, Barry Arthur 1930- *ConAu 102*
Leach, Bernard Howell 1887-1979 *ConAu 85, –97*
Leach, Decima *ConSFA*
Leach, Douglas Edward 1920- *ConAu 17R, WrDr 84*
Leach, Eleanor Winsor 1937- *ConAu 103*
Leach, Gerald Adrian 1933- *ConAu 5R*
Leach, John Robert 1922- *ConAu 21R*
Leach, Joseph 1921- *ConAu 29R*
Leach, Maria 1892-1977 *ConAu 53, –69, SmATA 28*
Leach, Max 1909- *ConAu 41R*
Leach, Michael 1940- *ConAu 73*
Leach, Paul Roscoe 1890-1977 *ConAu 73*
Leach, Penelope 1937- *ConAu 97, WrDr 84*
Leach, Robert J 1916- *ConAu 29R*
Leach, Wilford 1932- *ConAu 2NR*
Leach, Wilford 1934- *ConAu 45*
Leachman, Robert Briggs 1921- *ConAu 104*
Leacock, Eleanor Burke 1922- *ConAu 37R*
Leacock, Ruth 1926- *ConAu 37R*
Leacock, Stephen Butler 1869-1944 *ConAu 104, CreCan 2, LongCTC, ModCmwL, TwCA, TwCA SUP, TwCLC 2, TwCWr*
Leacroft, Helen Mabel 1919- *ConAu 2NR, –5R, SmATA 6*
Leacroft, Richard V B 1914- *ConAu 2NR, –5R, SmATA 6*
Leadbeater, William Douglas 1931- *IntAu&W 82, IntWWP 82*
Leadbetter, Eric 1892?-1971 *ConAu 104*
Leadbitter, Mike 1942- *ConAu 41R*
Leader, Barbara 1898- *ConAu 61*
Leader, Charles *ConAu X*
Leader, Evelyn Barbara 1898- *IntAu&W 82*
Leader, Mary *ConAu 85*
Leader, Ninon 1933- *ConAu 21R*
Leader, Shelah Gilbert 1943- *ConAu 110*
Leaf, Munro 1905-1976 *ConAu 69, –73, LongCTC, SmATA 20, TwCA, TwCA SUP, TwCCW 83*
Leaf, Murray J 1939- *ConAu 1NR, –45*
Leaf, Russell C 1935- *ConAu 21R*
Leaf, VaDonna Jean 1929- *ConAu 57, SmATA 26[port]*
Leaf, Walter 1852-1927 *LongCTC, TwCA*
Leagans, John Paul 1911- *ConAu 103*
Leahy, James D 1938- *WrDr 84*
Leahy, Patrick *DrAP&F 83*
Leahy, Syrell Rogovin 1935- *ConAu 57*
Leake, Chauncey D 1896-1978 *ConAu 3NR, –49, –73*
Leake, Jane Acomb 1928- *ConAu 21R*
Leakey, Louis Seymour Bazett 1903-1972 *ConAu 37R, –97*
Leakey, Mary Douglas Nicol 1913- *ConAu 97*
Leakey, Richard E 1944- *ConAu 93*
Leale, B C 1930- *IntWWP 82*
Leamer, Edward E 1944- *ConAu 29R*
Leamer, Laurence Allen 1941- *ConAu 65*
Leaming, Barbara *ConAu 107*
Lean, Arthur Edward 1909- *ConAu 73*
Lean, E Tangye 1911-1974 *ConAu 53*
Lean, Garth Dickinson 1912- *ConAu 29R*
Leander *IntWWP 82X*
Leander, Ed *ConAu X, SmATA X*
Leaney, Alfred Robert Clare 1909- *ConAu 2NR, –5R, IntAu&W 82, WrDr 84*
Leap, Harry P 1908-1976 *ConAu 1R, –103*
Leapman, Michael 1938- *ConAu 109*
Lear, Edward 1812-1888 *ChlLR 1, SmATA 18*
Lear, Floyd Seyward 1895- *ConAu P-1*
Lear, John 1909- *ConAu 37R, WrDr 84*
Lear, Martha Weinman 1930- *ConAu 9R, –9NR*

Lear, Martha Weinman 1932- *WrDr 84*
Lear, Melva Gwendoline Bartlett 1917- *ConAu 5R*
Lear, Norman 1922- *ConAu 73, ConLC 12*
Lear, Peter *ConAu X*
Leard, G Earl 1918- *ConAu 9R*
Leard, John E 1916- *ConAu 9R*
Learmonth, Andrew 1916- *WrDr 84*
Learmonth, Andrew Thomas Amos 1916- *ConAu 13R*
Learned, Edmund Philip 1900- *ConAu 104*
Leary, Edward A 1913- *ConAu 29R, WrDr 84*
Leary, John P 1919- *ConAu 9R*
Leary, Lewis 1906- *WrDr 84*
Leary, Lewis Gaston 1906- *ConAu 1R, –4NR, DcLEL 1940*
Leary, Paris 1931- *ConAu 17R, DcLEL 1940*
Leary, Timothy 1920- *ConAu 107, DcLB 16[port]*
Leary, William G 1915- *ConAu 49*
Leary, William M, Jr. 1934- *ConAu 93*
Leas, Speed 1937- *ConAu 49*
Lease, Gary 1940- *ConAu 45*
Lease, Joseph *DrAP&F 83*
Leaska, Mitchell A 1934- *ConAu 77*
Leasor, James 1923- *ConAu 1R, –2NR, IntAu&W 82, TwCCr&M 80, WrDr 84*
Leasor, Thomas James 1923- *DcLEL 1940*
Leataud, Paul 1872-1956 *WorAu*
Leath, I B 1893- *IntWWP 82*
Leath, Mrs. John R *IntWWP 82X*
Leather, Edwin 1919- *ConAu 97*
Leather, George *ConAu X, WrDr 84*
Leatherman, LeRoy 1922- *ConAu 21R*
Leaton, Anne *ConDr 82B*
Leautaud, Paul 1872-1956 *ClDMEL 80*
Leavell, Landrum P, II 1926- *ConAu 89*
Leavenworth, Carol 1940- *ConAu 81*
Leavenworth, James Lynn 1915- *ConAu 21R*
Leaver, Robin Alan 1939- *ConAu 9NR, –61*
Leaver, Ruth *WrDr 84*
Leavis, F R 1895-1978 *ConAu 21R, –77, ConLC 24[port], ConLCrt 82*
Leavis, Frank Raymond 1895- *LongCTC, ModBrL, ModBrL SUP, TwCA SUP, TwCW, WhoTwCL*
Leavis, Q D 1906-1981 *ConAu 108, –97, ConLCrt 82*
Leavis, Queenie Dorothy *LongCTC*
Leavitt, Hart Day 1909- *ConAu 13R*
Leavitt, Harvey R 1934- *ConAu 65*
Leavitt, Jack 1931- *ConAu 97*
Leavitt, Jerome Edward 1916- *ConAu 1R, –1NR, SmATA 23[port]*
Leavitt, Judith A 1947- *ConAu 110*
Leavitt, Richard Freeman 1929- *ConAu 89*
Leavitt, Ruby Rohrlich *ConAu X, –53*
Leax, John *DrAP&F 83*
Leb, Edith *CreCan 1*
LeBar, Lois E 1907- *ConAu 21R*
LeBar, Mary E 1910- *ConAu 107*
LeBaron, Charles W 1943- *ConAu 9NR, –61*
Lebe, Reinhard 1935- *IntAu&W 82*
LeBeaux, Richard 1946- *ConAu 73*
Lebegue, Raymond 1895- *IntAu&W 82*
Lebel, Robert 1904- *IntAu&W 82*
Lebentritt, Julia *DrAP&F 83*
Leber, George L 1917?-1976 *ConAu 61*
Lebergott, Stanley 1918- *ConAu 103*
Lebert, Randy *ConAu X*
Lebeson, Anita Libman 1896- *ConAu 29R*
Lebherz, Richard 1921- *ConAmTC*
Leblanc, Maurice 1864-1941 *ConAu 110, LongCTC, TwCA*
LeBlanc, Rena Dictor 1938- *ConAu 104*
Leblon, Jean 1928- *ConAu 41R*
Lebo, Dell 1922- *ConAu 57, WrDr 84*
LeBoeuf, Michael 1942- *ConAu 93, WrDr 84*
LeBoutillier, Cornelia Geer 1973- *ConAu 45*
Lebovitz, Harold Paul 1916- *ConAu 77*
Lebow, Victor 1902- *ConAu 37R*
Lebowitz, Alan 1934- *ConAu 25R*
Lebowitz, Albert 1922- *ConAu 73, WrDr 84*
Lebowitz, Fran 1951?- *ConAu 81, ConLC 11*
Lebowitz, Naomi 1932- *ConAu 37R*
Leboyer, Frederick 1918- *ConAu 106*
Lebra, Joyce C *ConAu 1NR, –45*
Lebra, Takie Sugiyama 1930- *ConAu 77*
Lebra, William P 1922- *ConAu 33R*
Lebreo, Steward *ConAu X*
Lebreo, Stewart *ConAu X*
LeBreton, Auguste *ConAu X*

LeBrun, Gautier *ConAu X*
LeBrun, George P 1862-1966 *ConAu 5R*
Lebrun, Richard Allen 1931- *ConAu 41R*
Lec, Stanislaw Jerzy 1909-1966 *ClDMEL 80*
LeCain, Errol John 1941- *ConAu 33R, SmATA 6*
Lecale, Errol *ConAu X*
Lecar, Helene Lerner 1938- *ConAu 25R*
LeCarre, John 1931- *ConAu X, ConLC 3, –5, –9, –15, ConNov 82, DcLEL 1940, TwCCr&M 80, TwCWr, WorAu, WrDr 84*
Lechlitner, Ruth *DrAP&F 83*
Lechlitner, Ruth N 1901- *ConAu 105*
Lechner, Robert 1918- *WrDr 84*
Lechner, Robert F 1918- *ConAu 33R*
Lechon, Jan 1899-1955? *ModSL 2*
Lechon, Jan 1899-1956 *ClDMEL 80*
Lecht, Charles Philip 1933- *ConAu 21R*
Lecht, Leonard A 1920- *ConAu 11NR, –25R, WrDr 84*
Leckey, Dolores 1933- *ConAu 109*
Leckie, Robert 1920- *ConAu 13R*
Leckie, William H 1915- *ConAu 21R*
LeClaire, Gordon 1905- *ConAu 69, IntAu&W 82*
Leclavele, Roland 1886-1973 *ConAu 41R*
Leclerc, Felix 1914- *CreCan 1*
Leclerc, Ivor 1915- *ConAu 33R, WrDr 84*
Leclerc, Thomas *IntAu&W 82X*
Leclerc, Victor *ConAu X*
LeClercq, Jacques Georges Clemenceau 1898-1972 *ConAu 37R*
LeClere, Rene 1940- *IntAu&W 82*
LeClezio, J M G 1940- *ModFrL*
LeClezio, Jean Marie Gustave 1931- *TwCWr*
LeClezio, Jean Marie Gustave 1940- *ClDMEL 80, WorAu*
LeCocq, Rhoda P 1921- *ConAu 73*
Lecoin, Louis 1888?-1971 *ConAu 33R*
Lecomber, Brian 1945- *ConAu 73*
LeComte, Edward 1916- *ConAu 1R, –5NR, IntAu&W 82*
LeCorbusier 1887-1965 *TwCA SUP*
LeCroy, Anne K 1930- *ConAu 41R*
LeCroy, Ruth Brooks *ConAu 45*
Ledbetter, J T *DrAP&F 83*
Ledbetter, J T 1934- *ConAu 73*
Ledbetter, Jack Tracy 1934- *IntWWP 82*
Ledbetter, Jack Wallace 1930- *ConAu 5R*
Ledbetter, Joe O 1927- *ConAu 45*
Ledbetter, Virgil C 1918- *ConAu P-1*
Ledderose, Lothar 1942- *ConAu 85*
Leder, Lawrence H 1927- *ConAu 25R, WrDr 84*
Lederer, Charles 1910-1976 *ConAu 65, DcLB 26*
Lederer, Chloe 1915- *ConAu 77*
Lederer, Edith Madelon 1943- *ConAu 97*
Lederer, Esther Pauline 1918- *ConAu 89*
Lederer, Ivo John 1929- *ConAu 9R, IntAu&W 82*
Lederer, Joseph 1927- *ConAu 73*
Lederer, Muriel 1929- *ConAu 77*
Lederer, Rhoda Catharine 1910- *ConAu 6NR*
Lederer, William Julius 1912- *ConAu 1R, –5NR, WorAu*
Ledergerber, Karl 1914- *IntAu&W 82*
Lederman, Leonard L 1931- *ConAu 61*
Ledermann, Erich 1908- *WrDr 84*
Ledermann, Erich Kurt 1908- *ConAu 107*
Ledermann, Walter 1911- *ConAu 49, IntAu&W 82*
Ledesert, Margaret 1916- *ConAu 45*
Ledesert, R P L 1913- *ConAu 45*
LeDuc, Don R 1933- *ConAu 49*
Leduc, Fernand 1916- *CreCan 2*
Leduc, Jean 1910- *CreCan 1*
Leduc, Ozias 1864-1955 *CreCan 1*
Leduc, Roland 1907- *CreCan 2*
Leduc, Violette 1907-1972 *ConAu 33R, ConAu P-1, ConLC 22[port], ModFrL, WorAu*
Leduc, Violette 1913-1972 *ClDMEL 80*
Ledwidge, Francis 1891-1917 *LongCTC, TwCA, TwCA SUP*
Ledwidge, William John 1915- *ConAu 103*
Ledwith, Frank 1907- *ConAu 103, WrDr 84*
Ledyard, Gleason H 1919- *ConAu 5R*
Lee, A R *ConAu X*
Lee, Addison E 1914- *ConAu 9R*
Lee, Adrian Iselin, Jr. 1920- *ConAu 89*
Lee, Al *DrAP&F 83*

Lee, Al 1938- *ConAu 45*
Lee, Alfred McClung 1906- *ConAu 1R, -3NR, IntAu&W 82, WrDr 84*
Lee, Alvin A 1930- *ConAu 33R*
Lee, Amber *ConAu X*
Lee, Amy Freeman 1914- *IntWWP 82*
Lee, Andrew *ConAu X, WrDr 84*
Lee, Arthur M 1918- *ConAu 41R*
Lee, Asher 1909- *ConAu 73*
Lee, Audrey *ConAu 25R, DrAP&F 83*
Lee, Austin 1904- *ConAu P-1, TwCCr&M 80*
Lee, Barbara 1932- *ConAu 109*
Lee, Barbara 1934- *ConAu 9NR*
Lee, Brother Basil Leo 1909-1974 *ConAu 53*
Lee, Benjamin 1921- *ConAu 104, SmATA 27, WrDr 84*
Lee, Betsy 1949- *ConAu 106*
Lee, Betty *ConAu X*
Lee, Betty 1921- *ConAu 103*
Lee, Bill *ConAu X*
Lee, Bob *ConAu X*
Lee, Brad *IntWWP 82X*
Lee, C Nicholas 1933- *ConAu 45*
Lee, C P 1913- *ConAu 49*
Lee, C Y 1917- *ConAu 9R, WorAu*
Lee, Calvin B T 1934- *ConAu 33R, WrDr 84*
Lee, Carol *ConAu X, SmATA X*
Lee, Carolina *ConAu X*
Lee, Carvel 1910- *ConAu P-1*
Lee, Charles 1913- *ConAu 33R*
Lee, Charles Robert, Jr. 1929- *ConAu 5R*
Lee, Charlotte I 1909- *ConAu 21R*
Lee, Chong-Sik 1931- *ConAu 41R*
Lee, Christine Eckstrom 1952- *ConAu 110*
Lee, Christopher Frank Carandini 1922- *ConAu 73*
Lee, David *DrAP&F 83*
Lee, David 1944- *IntWWP 82*
Lee, Dennis 1939- *ConAu 11NR, TwCCW 83, WrDr 84*
Lee, Dennis Beynon 1939- *ChlLR 3, ConAu 25R, ConP 80, IntAu&W 82, IntWWP 82, SmATA 14*
Lee, Derek 1937- *ConAu 107, WrDr 84*
Lee, Desmond 1908- *ConAu 102, WrDr 84*
Lee, Devon *ConAu X, IntAu&W 82X*
Lee, Don *DrAP&F 83*
Lee, Don L 1942- *ConAu 73, ConLC 2, ConP 80, CroCAP, LivgBAA, WrDr 84*
Lee, Donald 1931- *WrDr 84*
Lee, Doris Emrick 1905-1983 *ConAu 110*
Lee, Dorris M 1905- *ConAu 13R*
Lee, Douglas A 1932- *ConAu 53*
Lee, Dwight Erwin 1898- *ConAu 5R*
Lee, Eddie H 1917- *ConAu 69*
Lee, Edward Edson *AuNews 1*
Lee, Edward N 1935- *ConAu 29R*
Lee, Elizabeth Riley Briant 1908- *ConAu 37R*
Lee, Elsie 1912- *ConAu 85, TwCRGW*
Lee, Eric *ConAu X*
Lee, Essie E 1920- *ConAu 4NR, -49*
Lee, Eugene 1941- *ConAu 49*
Lee, Fleming 1933- *ConAu 7NR*
Lee, Florence Henry 1910- *ConAu P-1*
Lee, Francis Nigel 1934- *ConAu 8NR, -57*
Lee, Frank F 1920- *ConAu 1R*
Lee, Fred 1927- *ConAu 109*
Lee, G Avery 1916- *ConAu 104*
Lee, George J 1920?-1976 *ConAu 65*
Lee, George Leslie 1909-1974 *ConAu X*
Lee, Gerard 1951- *ConAu 93*
Lee, Ginffa 1900?-1976 *ConAu 69*
Lee, Gordon C 1916- *ConAu 13R*
Lee, H Alton 1942- *ConAu 81*
Lee, Hahn-Been 1921- *ConAu 11NR, -25R, IntAu&W 82*
Lee, Harold Newton 1899- *ConAu 37R, IntAu&W 82, WrDr 84*
Lee, Harper *DrAP&F 83*
Lee, Harper 1926- *ConAu 13R, ConLC 12, DcLB 6, SmATA 11, TwCWr, WorAu*
Lee, Hector 1908- *ConAu 97*
Lee, Helen Clara 1919- *ConAu 49*
Lee, Helen Jackson 1908- *ConAu 81*
Lee, Henry 1911- *ConAu 5R*
Lee, Henry Desmond Pritchard 1908- *IntAu&W 82*
Lee, Henry F 1913- *ConAu 89*
Lee, Herbert D'H *ConAu X*
Lee, Hermione 1948- *ConAu 73*
Lee, Howard *ConAu X, WrDr 84*
Lee, Hun 1917- *IntWWP 82*

Lee, Irvin H 1932- *ConAu 21R, LivgBAA*
Lee, J W 1932- *ConAu 93*
Lee, James F 1905?-1975 *ConAu 61*
Lee, James Michael 1931- *ConAu 17R*
Lee, James W 1931- *ConAu 25R*
Lee, Janice 1944- *ConAu 33R*
Lee, Jeanne *DrAP&F 83*
Lee, Joe Won 1921- *ConAu 41R*
Lee, John 1931- *ConAu 9NR, -25R, IntAu&W 82, WrDr 84*
Lee, John Alexander 1891- *ConAu 7NR, -53, ConNov 82, LongCTC*
Lee, John Eric 1919- *ConAu 33R*
Lee, John Michael 1932- *ConAu 6NR, -13R*
Lee, John Robert 1923-1976 *ConAu 57, MichAu 80, SmATA 27*
Lee, Joyce Isabel 1913- *IntWWP 82*
Lee, Judy *ConAu X*
Lee, Julian *ConAu X, TwCCW 83, WrDr 84*
Lee, June *IntWWP 82X*
Lee, Jung Young 1935- *ConAu 33R*
Lee, Kay *ConAu X*
Lee, Kuei-Shien 1937- *IntWWP 82*
Lee, L L 1924- *ConAu 73*
Lee, Lamar, Jr. 1911- *ConAu 17R*
Lee, Lance 1942- *ConAu 77, NatPD 81[port]*
Lee, Laurie 1914- *ConAu 77, ConP 80, DcLEL 1940, IntAu&W 82, LongCTC, ModBrL, TwCWr, WorAu, WrDr 84*
Lee, Lawrence 1903- *ConAu 25R*
Lee, Lawrence 1912- *ConAu 13R*
Lee, Leo Ou-Fan 1939- *ConAu 102*
Lee, Leslie *NatPD 81[port]*
Lee, Lincoln 1922- *ConAu 9R*
Lee, Linda 1947- *ConAu 77*
Lee, Loyd Ervin 1939- *ConAu 102*
Lee, Lucy *ConAu X*
Lee, M Owen 1930- *ConAu 33R, WrDr 84*
Lee, Mabel Barbee 1886?-1978 *ConAu 85*
Lee, Malka 1905?-1976 *ConAu 65*
Lee, Manfred B 1905-1971 *ASpks, ConAu 1R, -2NR, -29R, ConLC 11, LongCTC, TwCA, TwCA SUP, TwCCr&M 80*
Lee, Manning DeVilleneuve 1894-1980 *ConAu 104, SmATA 22N*
Lee, Maria Berl *DrAP&F 83*
Lee, Maria Berl 1924- *ConAu 9NR, -61, IntAu&W 82, IntWWP 82*
Lee, Marjorie Lederer 1921- *ConAu 1R, -4NR*
Lee, Mark W 1923- *ConAu 3NR, -9R*
Lee, Mary 1949- *ConAu 29R*
Lee, Mary Price 1934- *ConAu 9NR, -57, SmATA 8*
Lee, Maryat *ConAu 25R, WrDr 84*
Lee, Matt *TwCSFW*
Lee, Maurice, Jr. 1925- *ConAu 45*
Lee, Meredith 1945- *ConAu 93*
Lee, Mildred 1908- *ConAu X, SmATA 6, TwCCW 83, WrDr 84*
Lee, Molly K S C 1934- *ConAu 53*
Lee, Muna 1895-1965 *ConAu 25R*
Lee, Nata *ConAu X*
Lee, Nelle Harper 1926- *WorAu*
Lee, Nellie Harper 1926- *DcLEL 1940*
Lee, Norma E 1924- *ConAu 65*
Lee, Oliver M 1927- *ConAu 41R*
Lee, Parker *ConAu X*
Lee, Patrick C 1936- *ConAu 65*
Lee, Peter H 1929- *ConAu 3NR, -9R, IntAu&W 82, WrDr 84*
Lee, Polly Jae 1929- *ConAu 29R*
Lee, R Alton 1931- *ConAu 21R*
Lee, Ranger *TwCWW*
Lee, Raymond 1910?-1974 *ConAu 49*
Lee, Raymond L 1911- *ConAu 41R*
Lee, Rebecca Smith 1894- *ConAu 5R*
Lee, Rena *DrAP&F 83*
Lee, Richard Borshay 1937- *ConAu 45*
Lee, Robert 1929- *ConAu 3NR, -5R*
Lee, Robert C 1931- *ConAu 10NR, -25R, SmATA 20*
Lee, Robert E 1918- *WrDr 84*
Lee, Robert E A 1921- *ConAu 9R*
Lee, Robert Earl 1906- *AuNews 1, ConAu 53*
Lee, Robert Edson 1921- *ConAu 25R*
Lee, Robert Edwin 1918- *ConAu 2NR, -45, ConDr, ModWD, NatPD 81[port]*
Lee, Robert Greene 1886- *ConAu 1R, -3NR*
Lee, Robert J 1921- *SmATA 10*
Lee, Roberta *ConAu X*
Lee, Ronald 1934- *ConAu 37R*
Lee, Rowena 1918- *ConAu X*

Lee, Roy *ConAu X, SmATA X*
Lee, Roy Stuart 1899- *ConAu P-1*
Lee, Russel V 1895-1982 *ConAu 110*
Lee, Ruth 1892- *ConAu P-2*
Lee, S *DrAP&F 83*
Lee, S E 1894- *ConAu 73*
Lee, S G M 1920-1973 *ConAu P-2*
Lee, Samuel J 1906- *ConAu P-2*
Lee, Sheldon *IntAu&W 82X*
Lee, Sherman Emery 1918- *ConAu 1R, -1NR, WrDr 84*
Lee, Sir Sidney 1859-1926 *LongCTC, TwCA*
Lee, Stan 1922- *ConAu 108, ConLC 17*
Lee, Stewart M 1925- *ConAu 57*
Lee, Susan 1944- *ConAu 110*
Lee, Susan Dye 1939- *ConAu 85*
Lee, Tanith 1947- *ConAu 37R, IntAu&W 82, SmATA 8, TwCSFW, WrDr 84*
Lee, Terence *IntWWP 82X*
Lee, Terence R 1938- *ConAu 29R*
Lee, Tom L 1950- *ConAu 65, MichAu 80*
Lee, Vernon 1856-1935 *ConAu X, LongCTC, ModBrL, TwCA, TwCA SUP, TwCLC 5[port]*
Lee, Veronica *IntAu&W 82X, WrDr 84*
Lee, Virginia 1905?-1981 *ConAu 105*
Lee, Virginia 1927- *ConAu 9R*
Lee, W Storrs *ConAu X*
Lee, Walt 1931- *ConAu 61*
Lee, Warren M 1908- *ConAu 77*
Lee, Wayne C 1917- *ConAu 1R, -2NR, IntAu&W 82, TwCWW, WrDr 84*
Lee, William *ConAu X, WrDr 84*
Lee, William David 1944- *IntWWP 82*
Lee, William Rowland *WrDr 84*
Lee, William Rowland 1911- *ConAu 4NR, -9R*
Lee, William Saul 1938- *ConAu 104*
Lee, William Storrs, III 1906- *ConAu 1R, -1NR, IntAu&W 82, WrDr 84*
Lee, Willy *ConAu X*
Lee, Yur Bok 1934- *ConAu 29R*
Lee, Yur-Bok 1934- *WrDr 84*
Lee Howard, Leon Alexander 1914-1979? *ConAu 104*
Leech, Alfred B 1918?-1974 *ConAu 49*
Leech, Bryan Jeffery 1931- *ConAu 93*
Leech, Clifford 1909-1977 *ConAu 1R, -4NR, DcLEL 1940*
Leech, Geoffrey Neil 1936- *ConAu 29R, WrDr 84*
Leech, Kenneth 1939- *ConAu 103, WrDr 84*
Leech, Margaret Kernochan 1893-1974 *ConAu 49, -93, TwCA SUP*
Leechak, Joseph N 1911- *IntAu&W 82*
Leecing, Walden A 1932- *ConAu 33R*
Leed, Eric J 1942- *ConAu 89*
Leed, Jacob *DrAP&F 83*
Leed, Jacob 1924- *WrDr 84*
Leed, Jacob R 1924- *ConAu 7NR, -17R*
Leed, Richard L 1929- *ConAu 13R*
Leed, Theodore William 1927- *ConAu 106*
Leedham, Charles 1926- *ConAu 13R*
Leedham, John 1912- *ConAu 21R*
Leeds, Anthony 1925- *ConAu 17R*
Leeds, Barry H 1940- *ConAu 29R, WrDr 84*
Leeds, Dixie 1934- *ConAmTC*
Leeds, Morton Harold 1921- *ConAu 13R, IntWWP 82, WrDr 84*
Leedy, Jack J 1921- *ConAu 21R*
Leedy, Paul D 1908- *ConAu 1R, -1NR, WrDr 84*
Leefeldt, Christine 1941- *ConAu 93*
Leek, Sybil 1923- *ConAu 102*
Leek, Sybil 1923-1982 *ConAu 108*
Leekley, Richard N 1912-1976 *ConAu 69*
Leekley, Thomas Briggs 1910- *ConAu 5R, SmATA 23[port]*
Leeman, Wayne A 1924- *ConAu 13R*
Leeming, David Adams 1937- *ConAu 49*
Leeming, Glenda 1943- *ConAu 4NR, -53, IntAu&W 82*
Leeming, Jill *WrDr 84*
Leeming, Jo Ann *ConAu X, SmATA X*
Leeming, John F 1900- *ConAu P-1*
Leeming, Joseph 1897-1968 *ConAu 73, SmATA 26[port]*
Leeming, Owen 1930- *WrDr 84*
Leeming, Owen Alfred 1930- *ConAu 65, ConP 80, DcLEL 1940*
Leenhouts, Keith J 1925- *ConAu 61*
Leepa, Allen 1919- *ConAu 45*
Leeper, Geoffrey Winthrop 1903- *WrDr 84*

Leeper, Sarah H 1912- *ConAu 57*
Leer, Norman Robert 1937- *ConAu 17R*
Leerburger, Benedict A 1932- *WrDr 84*
Leerburger, Benedict A, Jr. 1932- *ConAu 9R*
Lees, Carlton Brown 1924- *ConAu 103*
Lees, Charles J 1919- *ConAu 25R*
Lees, Dan 1927- *ConAu 33R*
Lees, Francis A 1931- *ConAu 9NR, -65*
Lees, Gene 1928- *ConAu 9NR, -21R*
Lees, Hannah *ConAu X*
Lees, John David 1936- *ConAu 53,*
 IntAu&W 82, WrDr 84
Lees, John G 1931- *ConAu 57*
Lees, Ray 1931- *ConAu 8NR, -61, WrDr 84*
Lees, Richard 1948- *ConAu 108,*
 NatPD 81[port]
Lees-Milne, James 1908- *ConAu 9R,*
 IntAu&W 82, WrDr 84
Leese, Elizabeth d1962 *CreCan 2*
Leese, Elizabeth 1937- *ConAu 85*
Leeson, C Roland 1926- *ConAu 93*
Leeson, R A *ConAu X*
Leeson, Robert 1928- *ConAu 105, TwCCW 83,*
 WrDr 84
Leet, Judith *DrAP&F 83*
Leet, Judith 1935- *ConLC 11*
Lefco, Helene 1922- *ConAu 53*
Lefcoe, George 1938- *ConAu 21R*
Lefcowitz, Barbara F *DrAP&F 83*
Lefcowitz, Barbara F 1935- *ConAu 104*
Lefebure, Molly *ConAu 57, WrDr 84*
Lefebvre, Henri 1901- *ConAu 11NR, -25R*
Lefebvre, Jean-Pierre 1941- *CreCan 1*
Lefebvre D'Argence, Rene-Yvon 1928-
 ConAu 11NR
Lefebvre D'Argence, Rene-Yvon Marie Marc 1928-
 ConAu 21R, IntAu&W 82
Lefer, Diane *DrAP&F 83*
LeFeuvre, Amy d1929 *TwCCW 83*
Lefever, D Welty 1901- *ConAu 49*
Lefever, Ernest W 1919- *ConAu 1R, -1NR*
Lefevre, Adam *DrAP&F 83*
LeFevre, Adam 1950- *ConAu 81*
Lefevre, Carl A 1913- *ConAu 7NR, -9R*
Lefevre, Gui *ConAu X*
Lefevre, Helen *ConAu 17R*
LeFevre, Perry D 1921- *ConAu 10NR*
Lefevre, Perry Deyo 1921- *ConAu 21R*
LeFevre, Robert 1911- *ConAu 9NR, -57,*
 WrDr 84
Leff, Arthur A 1935-1981 *ConAu 105*
Leff, Gordon 1926- *ConAu 3NR, -9R,*
 IntAu&W 82, WrDr 84
Leff, Nathaniel H 1938- *ConAu 25R*
Leffelaar, Hendrik Louis 1929- *ConAu 5R*
Lefferts, George 1921- *ConAu 69*
Leffland, Ella 1931- *ConAu 29R, ConLC 19*
Leffler, Melvyn Paul 1945- *ConAu 89*
Lefkoe, Morty R 1937- *ConAu 29R*
Lefkowitz, Annette S 1922- *ConAu 17R*
Lefkowitz, Bernard 1937- *ConAu 29R*
Lefkowitz, Joel M 1940- *ConAu 45*
Lefkowitz, Mary Rosenthal 1935- *ConAu 103*
Lefkowitz, R J 1942- *ConAu 45*
Leflar, Robert A 1901- *ConAu 29R,*
 IntAu&W 82
Lefler, Hugh Talmage 1901- *ConAu 5R*
Lefler, Irene 1917- *ConAu 1NR, -45,*
 MichAu 80, SmATA 12
LeFontaine, Joseph 1927- *ConAu 106*
LeForge, P V *DrAP&F 83*
LeFort, Gertrud, Freiin Von 1876-1971
 CIDMEL 80, ModGL, WorAu
LeFort, Gertrud Von 1876-1971 *ConAu 33R*
Lefranc, Pierre 1927- *ConAu 41R*
Lefrancois, Guy R 1940- *ConAu 2NR, -45*
Lefton, Robert Eugene 1931- *ConAu 49*
Leftwich, James 1902- *ConAu 41R*
Leftwich, Joseph 1892- *ConAu 5R*
Leftwich, Joseph 1892-1983 *ConAu 109*
Leftwich, Richard Henry 1920- *ConAu 5NR,*
 -13R
LeGalley, Donald P 1901- *ConAu P-2*
LeGallienne, Eva 1899- *ConAu 45, SmATA 9*
LeGallienne, Richard 1866-1947 *ConAu 107,*
 DcLB 4, LongCTC, TwCA, TwCA SUP
Legany, Dezso 1916- *IntAu&W 82*
Legaret, Jean 1913-1976 *ConAu P-2*
Legault, Albert 1938- *ConAu 53*
Leger, Alexis Saint-Leger 1887-1975 *ConAu 13R,*
 -61, ConLC 11, TwCA, TwCA SUP
Leger, Saintleger *ConAu X*

Legeza, Laszlo 1934- *ConAu 65*
Leggatt, Alexander 1940- *ConAu 97,*
 IntAu&W 82, WrDr 84
Legge, J D 1921- *ConAu 2NR*
Legge, John David 1921- *ConAu 1R,*
 IntAu&W 82, WrDr 84
Legge-Bourke, Sir Henry 1914- *ConAu 33R*
Legget, John *DrAP&F 83*
Leggett, B J 1938- *ConAu 53*
Leggett, Eric *ConAu X*
Leggett, Glenn 1918- *ConAu 5NR, -13R*
Leggett, John 1917- *ConAu 1R, -2NR*
Leggett, John C 1930- *ConAu 25R*
Leggett, Linda 1941- *ConAu 108*
Leggett, Stephen 1949- *ConAu 77*
Leggitt, Hunter 1935- *ConAu 65*
Legler, Henry M 1897- *ConAu 97*
Legler, Philip *DrAP&F 83*
Legler, Philip 1928- *ConAu 9R, MichAu 80,*
 WrDr 84
Legman, G 1917- *ConAu 21R*
Legouis, Emile Hyacinthe 1861-1937 *LongCTC,*
 TwCA
LeGouriadec, Yvette Brind'Amour *CreCan 1*
LeGrand 1901-1964 *ConAu X, SmATA X*
Legrand, Lucien 1926- *ConAu 5R*
Legters, Lyman H 1928- *ConAu 33R*
Leguin, Ursula K *DrAP&F 83*
LeGuin, Ursula K 1929- *AuNews 1, ChlLR 3,*
 ConAu 9NR, -21R, ConLC 8, -13, -22[port],
 ConNov 82, ConSFA, DcLB 8[port],
 SmATA 4, TwCCW 83, TwCSFW,
 WorAu 1970, WrDr 84
Legum, Colin 1919- *ConAu 1R, -4NR,*
 IntAu&W 82, SmATA 10, WrDr 84
Legvold, Robert 1940- *ConAu 85*
Lehan, Richard 1930- *ConAu 21R*
Lehane, Brendan 1936- *ConAu 10NR, -21R*
Lehiste, Ilse 1922- *ConAu 37R*
Lehman, Anita Jacobs 1920- *ConAu 21R*
Lehman, Celia 1928- *ConAu 1NR, -49*
Lehman, Chester K 1895-1980 *ConAu 1R, -1NR*
Lehman, Dale 1920- *ConAu 9R*
Lehman, David *DrAP&F 83*
Lehman, David 1948- *ConAu 8NR, -57,*
 IntWWP 82
Lehman, Ernest Paul 1915- *ConAu 85*
Lehman, F K 1924- *ConAu 9R*
Lehman, Godfrey *ConAu 25R*
Lehman, Harold D 1921- *ConAu 81*
Lehman, John F, Jr. 1942- *ConAu 13R*
Lehman, Jon Leonard 1940- *ConAmTC*
Lehman, Milton 1917-1966 *ConAu P-1*
Lehman, Paul Evan *TwCWW*
Lehman, Sam 1899- *ConAu 49*
Lehman, Warren 1930- *ConAu 21R*
Lehman, Yvonne 1936- *ConAu 29R,*
 IntAu&W 82, WrDr 84
Lehmann, A George 1922- *ConAu 1R, -4NR*
Lehmann, Arno 1901- *ConAu P-2*
Lehmann, Erich Arno 1901- *IntAu&W 82*
Lehmann, Geoffrey 1940- *ConAu 107, ConP 80,*
 WrDr 84
Lehmann, Irvin J 1927- *ConAu 53*
Lehmann, Johannes 1929- *ConAu 37R*
Lehmann, John 1907- *WrDr 84*
Lehmann, John Frederick 1907- *ConAu 8NR,*
 -9R, ConP 80, IntAu&W 82, LongCTC,
 ModBrL, TwCA, TwCA SUP, TwCWr
Lehmann, Linda 1906- *ConAu 85*
Lehmann, Lotte 1888-1976 *ConAu 69, -73*
Lehmann, Martin Ernest 1915- *ConAu 5R*
Lehmann, Paul Louis 1906- *ConAu 85*
Lehmann, Peter 1938- *ConAu 57*
Lehmann, R C 1856-1929 *LongCTC*
Lehmann, Robert A 1932- *ConAu 57*
Lehmann, Rosamond 1901- *ConAu 8NR, -77,*
 ConNov 82, DcLB 15[port]
Lehmann, Rosamond 1905- *WrDr 84*
Lehmann, Rosamond Nina 1903- *LongCTC,*
 ModBrL, TwCA, TwCA SUP, WhoTwCL
Lehmann, Rosamond Nina 1905- *ConLC 5*
Lehmann, Rosamund Nina 1903- *TwCWr*
Lehmann, Rudolph C 1856-1929 *TwCA,*
 TwCA SUP
Lehmann, Theo 1934- *ConAu 41R*
Lehmann, Wilhelm 1882-1968 *ModGL, WorAu*
Lehmann, Winfred P 1916- *ConAu 33R*
Lehmann-Haupt, Christopher 1934- *ConAu 109*
Lehmann-Haupt, Hellmut E 1903- *ConAu 9R*
Lehmberg, Paul 1946- *ConAu 102*
Lehmberg, Stanford Eugene 1931- *ConAu 1R,*

 -2NR, IntAu&W 82, WrDr 84
Lehn, Cornelia 1920- *ConAu 29R*
Lehner, Christine 1952- *ConAu 109*
Lehnert, Herbert 1925- *ConAu 41R*
Lehning, James R 1947- *ConAu 105*
Lehnus, Donald James 1934- *ConAu 9NR, -57*
Lehnus, Opal Hull 1920- *ConAu 9R, WrDr 84*
Lehovich, Eugenie Ouroussow 1908-1975
 ConAu X
Lehr, Delores 1920- *ConAu 17R, SmATA 10*
Lehr, Paul E 1918- *ConAu 65*
Lehrer, Adrienne 1937- *ConAu 29R*
Lehrer, James 1934- *ConAu 109*
Lehrer, Keith 1936- *ConAu 17R*
Lehrer, Robert N 1922- *ConAu 61*
Lehrer, Stanley 1929- *ConAu 2NR, -5R,*
 IntAu&W 82, WrDr 84
Lehrman, Liza *ConAu X*
Lehrman, Nat 1929- *ConAu 93*
Lehrman, Robert L 1921- *ConAu 5R, -7NR*
Lehrman, Simon Maurice 1900- *ConAu P-1*
Lehrmann, Chanan *ConAu X*
Lehrmann, Charles F 1905-1977 *ConAu 33R*
Lehrmann, Cuno Chanan *ConAu X*
Leib, Amos Patten 1917- *ConAu 45*
Leib, Mark 1954- *NatPD 81[port]*
Leibbrand, Kurt 1914- *ConAu 45*
Leibel, Charlotte P 1899- *ConAu 33R*
Leibenguth, Charla Ann *ConAu X*
Leibenstein, Harvey 1922- *ConAu 103*
Leiber, Fritz *DrAP&F 83*
Leiber, Fritz 1910- *ConAu 2NR, -45,*
 ConLC 25[port], ConNov 82, ConSFA,
 DcLB 8[port], TwCSFW, WrDr 84
Leiber, Justin Fritz 1938- *ConAu 97*
Leibert, Julius A 1888- *ConAu P-2*
Leibold, John 1926- *ConAu 37R, WrDr 84*
Leibowitz, Herbert A 1935- *ConAu 25R*
Leibowitz, Herschel W 1925- *ConAu 8NR, -17R*
Leibowitz, Irving 1922-1979 *ConAu 9R, -85*
Leibowitz, Rene 1913-1972 *ConAu 37R*
Leibson, Jacob J 1883?-1971 *ConAu 33R*
Leiby, Adrian C 1904-1976 *ConAu 65,*
 ConAu P-1
Leiby, James 1924- *ConAu 33R*
Leichman, Seymour 1933- *ConAu 25R,*
 SmATA 5
Leichter, Otto 1898?-1973 *ConAu 41R*
Leiden, Carl 1922- *ConAu 5R*
Leider, Emily Wortis *DrAP&F 83*
Leider, Emily Wortis 1937- *ConAu 81*
Leider, Frida 1888-1975 *ConAu 57*
Leigh, Angela 1927- *CreCan 2*
Leigh, Egbert Giles, Jr. 1940- *ConAu 57*
Leigh, Eugene *ConAu X*
Leigh, James L 1930- *ConAu 9R*
Leigh, Johanna *ConAu X*
Leigh, Kathy *ConAu X*
Leigh, Michael 1914- *ConAu 13R*
Leigh, Mike 1943- *ConAu 109, ConDr 82*
Leigh, Palmer *ConAu X, IntWWP 82X*
Leigh, Roberta *TwCRGW, WrDr 84*
Leigh, Spencer 1945- *ConAu 102, WrDr 84*
Leigh, Susannah 1938- *ConAu 81*
Leigh Fermor, Patrick *WrDr 84*
Leigh Fermor, Patrick Michael 1915-
 IntAu&W 82
Leigh-Pemberton, John 1911- *ConAu 108*
Leighin, Sean O *IntWWP 82X*
Leight, Robert L 1932- *ConAu 110*
Leighton, A C 1901-1965 *CreCan 2*
Leighton, Albert C 1919- *ConAu 37R,*
 WrDr 84
Leighton, Alexander 1908- *ConAu 41R,*
 WrDr 84
Leighton, Ann *ConAu X*
Leighton, Clare 1899- *ConAu 108*
Leighton, Clare Veronica Hope 1899- *LongCTC*
Leighton, Clare Veronica Hope 1900- *TwCA,*
 TwCA SUP
Leighton, David S R 1928- *ConAu 2NR, -5R*
Leighton, Frances Spatz *ConAu 81*
Leighton, Jack Richard 1918- *ConAu 1R*
Leighton, Lee *ConAu X, TwCWW, WrDr 84*
Leighton, Margaret Carver 1896- *ConAu 9R,*
 SmATA 1, WrDr 84
Leighton, Marie Connor d1941 *LongCTC*
Leighton, Robert 1859-1934 *LongCTC*
Leijonhufvud, Sigfrid C E 1939- *IntAu&W 82*
Leikind, Morris C 1906?-1976 *ConAu 65*
Leimbach, Patricia Penton 1927- *ConAu 57*
Leimert, Lucille 1895?-1983 *ConAu 110*

Leinbach, Esther V 1924- *ConAu 61*
Leinfellner, Werner 1921- *ConAu 5NR, –53*
Leininger, Madeleine M 1925- *ConAu 33R*
Leino, Eino 1878-1926 *CIDMEL 80*
Leinster, Murray 1896-1975 *ConAu X,*
DcLB 8[port], TwCSFW
Leinwand, Gerald 1921- *ConAu 5R, –9NR*
Leip, Hans 1893-1983 *ConAu 110*
Leipart, Charles 1944- *ConAu 108,*
NatPD 81[port]
Leiper, Esther M *DrAP&F 83*
Leiper, Esther Mather 1946- *IntWWP 82*
Leiper, Henry Smith 1891-1975 *ConAu 53*
Leipold, L Edmond 1902- *ConAu 69,*
SmATA 16
Leiris, Michel 1901- *CIDMEL 80, ModFrL,*
WorAu
Leiser, Burton M 1930- *ConAu 29R*
Leiser, Erwin 1923- *ConAu 29R*
Leiserson, Michael 1939- *ConAu 37R*
Leishman, J Blair 1902-1963 *ConAu 5R, –6NR,*
LongCTC
Leishman, Thomas L 1900-1978 *ConAu 81*
Leisk, David Johnson 1906-1975 *ConAu 9R, –57,*
SmATA 1, –26N, –30[port]
Leisner, Dorothy Mary Gostwick Roberts
CreCan 1
Leiss, William 1939- *ConAu 41R*
Leister, Mary 1917- *ConAu 11NR, –65,*
SmATA 29[port]
Leistritz, F Larry 1945- *ConAu 104*
Leisy, James Franklin 1927- *ConAu 4NR, –9R,*
WrDr 84
Leitch, Adelaide 1921- *ConAu 101, WrDr 84*
Leitch, David Bruce 1940- *ConAu 57, WrDr 84*
Leitch, Maurice *WrDr 84*
Leitch, Maurice 1933- *ConAu 102,*
DcLB 14[port], IntAu&W 82
Leitch, Patricia 1933- *ConAu 9NR, –61,*
SmATA 11
Leitenberg, Milton 1933- *ConAu 101*
Leiter, Louis 1921- *ConAu 37R*
Leiter, Robert D 1922- *WrDr 84*
Leiter, Robert D 1922-1976 *ConAu 4NR, –5R,*
–69
Leiter, Samuel Louis 1940- *ConAu 93*
Leiter, Sharon 1942- *ConAu 57*
Leith, Andrew 1931- *ConAu 45*
Leith, J Clark 1937- *ConAu 57*
Leith, John H 1919- *ConAu 3NR, –5R*
Leith, Prue 1940- *WrDr 84*
Leithauser, Brad 1953- *ConAu 107,*
ConLC 27[port]
Leithauser, Gladys Garner 1925- *ConAu 13R,*
MichAu 80
Leitmann, George 1925- *ConAu 53*
Leitner, Moses J 1908- *ConAu P-1*
Leivick, H 1888-1962 *ModWD*
Lejeune, Anthony 1928- *TwCCr&M 80,*
WrDr 84
Lejeune, Caroline Alice d1973 *DcLEL 1940*
Lekachman, Robert 1920- *ConAu 106*
Lekai, J Louis 1916- *ConAu 33R*
Lekai, Louis J 1916- *WrDr 84*
Lekis, Lisa Crichton 1917- *ConAu 9R*
Leland, Christopher Towne *DrAP&F 83*
Leland, Christopher Towne 1951- *ConAu 108*
Leland, Henry 1923- *ConAu 89*
Leland, Jeremy Francis David 1932- *ConAu 33R*
Leland, Jeremy Francis Davis 1932- *WrDr 84*
Leland, Timothy 1937- *ConAu 102*
Lelchuk, Alan *DrAP&F 83*
Lelchuk, Alan 1938- *ConAu 1NR, –45,*
ConLC 5, ConNov 82, WrDr 84
Lele, Uma 1941- *ConAu 73*
Leleux, S A 1939- *WrDr 84*
Leliaert, Richard Maurice 1940- *ConAu 101*
LeLoup, Lance T 1949- *ConAu 110*
Lelyveld, Arthur J 1913- *ConAu 25R*
Lem, Stanislaw 1921- *CIDMEL 80, ConAu 105,*
ConLC 8, –15, IntAu&W 82, TwCSFW A,
WorAu 1970
LeMahieu, D L 1945- *ConAu 69*
LeMair, H Willebeek 1889-1966 *SmATA 29*
Lemaitre, Georges E 1898-1973 *ConAu P-2*
Lemaitre, Georges Edouard 1898-1972
ConAu 37R
Lemaitre, Jules 1853-1914 *CIDMEL 80,*
ModWD, TwCA, TwCA SUP
Lemann, Bernard 1905- *ConAu 41R*
Lemarchal, Robert 1908- *IntWWP 82*
Lemarchand, Elizabeth 1906- *ConAu 10NR,*

WrDr 84
Lemarchand, Elizabeth Wharton 1906-
ConAu 25R, IntAu&W 82, TwCCr&M 80
Lemarchand, Jacques 1908- *TwCA SUP*
Lemarchand, Rene 1932- *ConAu 13R*
LeMaster, J R *DrAP&F 83*
LeMaster, J R 1934- *ConAu 33R, WrDr 84*
LeMay, Alan 1899-1964 *TwCWW*
LeMay, G H L 1920- *WrDr 84*
Lemay, Harding 1922- *ConAu 1NR, –45,*
NatPD 81[port]
Lemay, J A Leo 1935- *ConAu 9NR, –17R*
LeMay, Reginald Stuart 1885- *ConAu 5R*
Lembeck, Ruth 1919- *ConAu 105*
Lembke, Janet *DrAP&F 83*
Lembke, Janet 1933- *ConAu 45*
Lembo, John M 1937- *ConAu 29R*
Lembourn, Hans Joergen 1923- *ConAu 105*
Lemelin, Roger 1919- *CreCan 2, TwCWr*
LeMelle, Tilden J 1929- *LivgBAA*
Lemelle, Wilbert J 1931- *ConAu 45*
Lemert, Edwin M 1912- *ConAu 93*
Lemert, James B 1935- *ConAu 73*
Lemert, Jim *ConAu X*
Lemesurier, Peter *ConAu X*
Lemieux, Jean-Paul 1904- *CreCan 1*
Lemieux, Lucien 1934- *ConAu 41R*
Lemieux, Marc 1948- *ConAu 102*
Lemir, Andre *ConAu X*
LeMire, Eugene D 1929- *ConAu 41R*
Lemire, Robert A 1933- *ConAu 101*
Lemish, John 1921- *ConAu 5R*
Lemke, Horst 1922- *ConAu 107*
Lemme, Janet E 1941- *ConAu 29R*
Lemmon, Kenneth 1911- *ConAu 65*
Lemmon, Sarah McCulloh 1914- *ConAu 21R*
Lemoine, Ernest *ConAu X*
LeMon, Cal 1945- *ConAu 53*
Lemon, James Thomas 1929- *ConAu 37R*
Lemon, Lee Thomas 1931- *ConAu 17R,*
WrDr 84
LeMon, Lynn *ConAu X*
LeMond, Alan 1938- *ConAu 9NR, –61,*
WrDr 84
Lemonnier, Camille 1844-1913 *CIDMEL 80*
Lemons, J Stanley 1938- *ConAu 37R*
Lemons, James Stanley 1938- *WrDr 84*
Lemont, George 1927- *ConAu 65*
Lemos, Ramon Marcelino 1927- *ConAu 37R,*
IntAu&W 82, WrDr 84
Lemp, Liselotte 1916- *IntAu&W 82*
Lenanton, C *ConAu X*
Lenanton, Carola Mary Anima Oman 1897-1978
ConAu X
Lenarcic, R J 1942- *ConAu 49*
Lenard, Alexander 1910-1972 *ConAu 4NR, –5R,*
–89, SmATA 21N
Lenard, Yvone 1921- *ConAu 7NR, –53*
Lenardon, Robert J 1928- *ConAu 33R*
Lenburg, Greg 1956- *ConAu 105*
Lenburg, Jeff 1956- *ConAu 104*
Lenczowski, George 1915- *ConAu 1R, –4NR,*
IntAu&W 82
Lendon, Kenneth Harry 1928- *ConAu 9R*
Lendvai, Paul 1929- *ConAu 85, WrDr 84*
Lenehan, William T 1930- *ConAu 21R*
Lenero, Vicente 1933- *ModLAL*
L'Enfant, Julie 1944- *ConAu 109*
Lengel, Frances *ConAu X*
Lengle, James I 1949- *ConAu 106*
L'Engle, Madeleine 1918- *AuNews 2, ChlLR 1,*
ConAu 1R, –3NR, ConLC 12, SmATA 1,
–27[port], TwCCW 83, TwCSFW,
WrDr 84
Lengyel, Balazs 1918- *IntAu&W 82*
Lengyel, Cornel 1915- *WrDr 84*
Lengyel, Cornel Adam *DrAP&F 83*
Lengyel, Cornel Adam 1915- *ConAu 1R, –1NR,*
IntWWP 82, SmATA 27
Lengyel, Emil 1895- *ConAu 3NR, –9R,*
SmATA 3, TwCA, TwCA SUP
Lengyel, Jozsef 1896-1975 *CIDMEL 80,*
ConAu 57, –85, ConLC 7
Lengyel, Melchior 1880-1974 *CnMD, ConAu 53*
Lengyel, Menyhert 1880-1957 *ModWD*
Lenhart, Gary *DrAP&F 83*
Lenhart, Gary 1947- *IntWWP 82*
Lenhoff, Alan 1951- *ConAu 73*
Lenihan, John 1941- *ConAu 105*
Lenihan, Kenneth J 1928- *ConAu 97*
Lenk, Kurt Heinz 1929- *IntAu&W 82*
Lenke, Hal *DrAP&F 83*

Lenman, Bruce Philip 1938- *IntAu&W 82*
Lenn, Theodore I 1914- *ConAu 45*
Lennart, Isobel 1915-1971 *ConAu 29R*
Lennartz, Franz 1910- *IntAu&W 82*
Lenneberg, Eric H 1921-1975 *ConAu 7NR, –53*
Lennenberg, Eric H 1921-1975 *ConAu 53, –57*
Lennig, Arthur 1933- *ConAu 57*
Lennon, Florence Becker *DrAP&F 83*
Lennon, Florence Becker 1895- *ConAu 13R*
Lennon, Helen M *ConAu X*
Lennon, John 1940-1980 *ConAu 102, ConLC 12,*
DcLEL 1940
Lennon, Joseph Luke 1919- *ConAu 33R*
Lennon, Sister M Isidore 1901- *ConAu 41R*
Lennon, Nigey 1954- *ConAu 109*
Lennon And McCartney *ConLC 12*
Lennox-Short, Alan 1913- *ConAu 102,*
IntAu&W 82, WrDr 84
Lenormand, Henri-Rene 1882-1951 *CIDMEL 80,*
CnMD, LongCTC, ModFrL, ModWD,
TwCA, TwCA SUP
Lenowitz, Harris *DrAP&F 83*
Lens, Sidney 1912- *ConAu 1R, –1NR,*
SmATA 13
Lense, Edward *DrAP&F 83*
Lensen, George Alexander 1923-1980 *ConAu 1R,*
–2NR
Lenski, Gerhard Emmanuel, Jr. 1924- *ConAu 1R*
Lenski, Lois 1893-1974 *ConAu 53, ConAu P-1,*
DcLB 22[port], SmATA 1, –26[port],
TwCCW 83
Lenson, David 1945- *ConAu 73*
Lent, Blair *ConAu 11NR*
Lent, Blair 1930- *ConAu 21R, SmATA 2,*
WrDr 84
Lent, D Geneva 1904- *ConAu 5R*
Lent, Henry Bolles 1901-1973 *ConAu 73,*
SmATA 17
Lent, John A 1936- *ConAu 29R, IntAu&W 82,*
WrDr 84
Lentfoehr, Therese 1902- *ConAu 97*
Lentilhon, Robert Ward 1925- *ConAu 9R*
Lentin, Antony 1941- *ConAu 103*
Lentner, Howard H 1931- *ConAu 106*
Lenton, Henry Trevor 1924- *ConAu 103*
Lentricchia, Frank 1940- *ConAu 25R*
Lentz, Donald Anthony 1908- *WrDr 84*
Lentz, Donald Anthony 1910- *ConAu 17R*
Lentz, Harold H 1910- *ConAu 57*
Lentz, Perry 1943- *ConAu 21R*
Lenz, Carolyn Ruth Swift *ConAu X*
Lenz, Frederick 1950- *ConAu 97*
Lenz, Hermann 1913- *CIDMEL 80,*
IntAu&W 82, ModGL
Lenz, Siegfried 1926- *CIDMEL 80,*
CnMD SUP, ConAu 89, ConLC 27[port],
CroCD, ModGL
Leo *IntAu&W 82X*
Leo, Kathleen Ripley *DrAP&F 83*
Leodhas, Sorche Nic *ConAu X, SmATA X*
Leogrande, Ernest *ConAmTC*
Leon, Henry Cecil 1902- *LongCTC,*
WorAu[port]
Leon, Pauline Lightstone *CreCan 1*
Leon, Pierre R 1926- *ConAu 1NR, –45*
Leon-Portilla, Miguel 1926- *ConAu 11NR, –21R*
Leon Tello, Pilar 1917- *IntAu&W 82*
Leon Y Roman, Ricardo 1877-1943 *CIDMEL 80*
Leonard, Calista V 1919- *ConAu 21R*
Leonard, Charlene M 1928- *ConAu 33R*
Leonard, Constance 1923- *ConAu 49, WrDr 84*
Leonard, Dick 1930- *IntAu&W 82*
Leonard, Edith Marian 1896- *ConAu P-1*
Leonard, Elmore 1925- *AuNews 1, ConAu 81,*
MichAu 80, TwCWW, WrDr 84
Leonard, Eugenie Andruss 1888-1980 *ConAu 97,*
ConAu P-2
Leonard, Frank G 1935?-1974 *ConAu 49*
Leonard, Frederick 1881-1954 *LongCTC*
Leonard, George B 1923- *ConAu 3NR, –9R*
Leonard, George E 1931- *ConAu 21R*
Leonard, George H 1921- *ConAu 65*
Leonard, George K, Jr. 1915- *ConAu 17R*
Leonard, Graham Douglas 1921- *ConAu 103*
Leonard, Hugh *ConAu X, IntAu&W 82X,*
WrDr 84
Leonard, Hugh 1926- *ConDr 82, ConLC 19,*
CroCD, DcLB 13[port], WorAu 1970
Leonard, Irving A 1896- *WrDr 84*
Leonard, Irving Albert 1896- *ConAu 5R, –5NR*
Leonard, Jane 1951- *IntAu&W 82*
Leonard, John *DrAP&F 83*

Lindars, Frederick C 1923- *WrDr 84*
Lindauer, John Howard 1937- *ConAu 21R*
Lindauer, Lois Lyons 1933- *ConAu 49*
Lindauer, Martin 1918- *ConAu 5R*
Linday, Ryllis Elizabeth Paine 1919- *ConAu 13R*
Lindbeck, Assar 1930- *ConAu 37R,*
IntAu&W 82, WrDr 84
Lindberg, David C 1935- *ConAu 11NR, -69*
Lindberg, Gary H 1941- *ConAu 65*
Lindberg, Karl Sivert 1933- *IntAu&W 82*
Lindberg, Lars *IntAu&W 82X*
Lindberg, Leon N 1932- *ConAu 33R*
Lindberg, Lucile 1913- *ConAu 37R*
Lindberg, Paul M 1905- *ConAu 5R*
Lindberg, Richard 1953- *ConAu 110*
Lindbergh, Anne Morrow 1906- *ConAu 17R,*
IntAu&W 82, LongCTC, SmATA 33[port],
TwCA, TwCA SUP, WrDr 84
Lindbergh, Charles A 1902-1974 *ConAu 53, -93,*
SmATA 33[port]
Lindblom, Charles E 1917- *ConAu 1R, -1NR*
Lindblom, Johannes 1882-1974 *ConAu 53*
Lindblom, Steven 1946- *ConAu 106*
Linde, Einar Olof Verner 1922- *IntAu&W 82*
Linde, Freda *IntAu&W 82*
Linde, Gunnel 1924- *ConAu 11NR, -21R,*
IntAu&W 82, SmATA 5
Linde, Nancy *DrAP&F 83*
Linde, Nancy 1949- *IntWWP 82*
Linde, Shirley Motter *WrDr 84*
Linde, Shirley Motter 1929- *ConAu 1NR, -45,*
LivgBAA
Lindeburg, Franklin Alfred 1918- *ConAu 5R*
Lindegren, Erik 1910-1968 *ClDMEL 80,*
WhoTwCL, WorAu 1970
Lindeman, Jack *DrAP&F 83*
Lindeman, Jack 1924- *ConAu 21R,*
IntWWP 82, WrDr 84
Lindemann, Albert S 1938- *ConAu 49*
Lindemann, Constance 1923- *ConAu 61,*
WrDr 84
Lindemann, Herbert Fred 1909- *ConAu 29R*
Linden, Catherine 1939- *ConAu 110*
Linden, Eddie Sean 1935- *IntAu&W 82,*
IntWWP 82
Linden, George W 1928- *IntWWP 82*
Linden, George William 1938- *ConAu 65*
Linden, Kathryn Evans 1925- *ConAu 37R*
Linden, Sara *ConAu X*
Lindenau, Judith Wood *DrAP&F 83*
Lindenau, Judith Wood 1941- *ConAu 77*
Lindenberg, Vladimir Tchelistcheff 1905-
IntAu&W 82
Lindenberger, Herbert 1929- *ConAu 3NR, -5R*
Lindenfeld, David Frank 1944- *ConAu 106*
Lindenfeld, Frank 1934- *ConAu 33R*
Lindenmeyer, Otto J 1936- *ConAu 77*
Linder, Bertram L 1931- *ConAu 2NR, -49*
Linder, Darwyn E 1939- *ConAu 57*
Linder, Erich 1925?-1983 *ConAu 109*
Linder, Ivan H 1894- *ConAu P-1*
Linder, Leslie d1973 *ConAu 41R*
Linder, Norma West 1928- *ConAu 97*
Linder, Robert D 1933- *ConAu 41R*
Linder, Robert D 1934- *WrDr 84*
Linder, Staffan B 1931- *ConAu 105*
Linderman, Earl W 1931- *ConAu 33R*
Linderman, Gerald F 1934- *ConAu 85*
Linderman, Winifred B *ConAu P-2*
Lindesmith, Alfred Ray 1905- *ConAu P-1*
Lindgren, Alvin J 1917- *ConAu 8NR, -17R*
Lindgren, Astrid 1907- *ChlLR 1, ConAu 13R,*
SmATA 2
Lindgren, Eric 1934- *IntAu&W 82*
Lindgren, Ernest Henry 1910-1973 *ConAu P-1*
Lindgren, Henry Clay 1914- *ConAu 1R, -1NR,*
WrDr 84
Lindheim, Irma Levy 1886-1978 *ConAu 5R, -77*
Lindholm, Richard W 1914- *ConAu 1R, -5NR,*
WrDr 84
Lindley, Betty G 1900?-1976 *ConAu 65*
Lindley, Denver 1904-1982 *ConAu 106*
Lindley, Erica *ConAu X*
Lindley, Ernest Kidder 1899-1979 *ConAu 89*
Lindley, Hilda 1919?-1980 *ConAu 102*
Lindley, Kenneth 1928- *ConAu 10NR*
Lindley, Kenneth Arthur 1928- *ConAu 5R,*
IntAu&W 82, WrDr 84
Lindman-Strafford, Kerstin 1939- *IntAu&W 82*
Lindner, Carl *DrAP&F 83*
Lindner, D Berry *ConAu X*

Lindner, Edgar T 1911- *ConAu 57*
Lindner, Ernest 1897- *CreCan 1*
Lindner, Vicki *DrAP&F 83*
Lindop, Edmund 1925- *ConAu 2NR, -5R,*
SmATA 5
Lindop, Grevel 1948- *ConAu 61*
Lindow, Wesley 1910- *ConAu 45*
Lindquist, Donald 1930- *ConAu 65*
Lindquist, E F 1901-1978 *ConAu 77*
Lindquist, Emory Kempton 1908- *ConAu 49*
Lindquist, Jennie Dorothea 1899-1977 *ConAu 69,*
-73, SmATA 13
Lindquist, John H 1931- *ConAu 41R*
Lindquist, Ray *DrAP&F 83*
Lindquist, Ray 1941- *ConAu 45*
Lindquist, Willis 1908- *ConAu 73, SmATA 20*
Lindsay, Bryan *DrAP&F 83*
Lindsay, Catherine Brown 1928- *ConAu 21R*
Lindsay, Cressida 1934- *ConAu 21R*
Lindsay, Cressida Anne 1930- *IntAu&W 82,*
WrDr 84
Lindsay, David 1878-1945 *TwCSFW*
Lindsay, Dorothy 1902?-1983 *ConAu 110*
Lindsay, Frank Whiteman 1909- *ConAu 104*
Lindsay, Harold Arthur 1900- *ConAu 5R*
Lindsay, Howard 1889-1968 *ConAu 25R,*
ModWD, TwCA SUP
Lindsay, Howard And Russel Crouse *CnMD*
Lindsay, Ian G 1906-1966 *ConAu P-1*
Lindsay, Inabel B 1900-1983 *ConAu 110*
Lindsay, J Robert 1925- *ConAu 13R*
Lindsay, Jack 1900- *ConAu 9R, -11NR,*
ConNov 82, IntAu&W 82, IntWWP 82,
LongCTC, TwCA, TwCA SUP, TwCWr,
WrDr 84
Lindsay, James Martin 1924- *ConAu 29R*
Lindsay, Jean 1926- *ConAu 11NR, -25R,*
IntAu&W 82
Lindsay, Jeanne Warren 1929- *ConAu 106*
Lindsay, John 1921- *WrDr 84*
Lindsay, John Maurice 1918- *IntAu&W 82*
Lindsay, John Vliet 1921- *ConAu 101*
Lindsay, Martin Alexander 1905-1981
ConAu 103
Lindsay, Maurice 1918- *ConAu 6NR, -9R,*
ConP 80, WrDr 84
Lindsay, Merrill K 1915- *ConAu 73*
Lindsay, Michael Francis Morris 1909-
ConAu 1NR, -45
Lindsay, Norman 1879-1969 *TwCCW 83*
Lindsay, Norman Alfred William 1879-1969
ConAu 102, LongCTC, ModCmwL, TwCA,
TwCA SUP, TwCWr
Lindsay, Perry *ConAu X*
Lindsay, Philip 1906-1958 *LongCTC*
Lindsay, R Bruce 1900- *ConAu 8NR, -13R*
Lindsay, Rachel *TwCRGW, WrDr 84*
Lindsay, Rae *ConAu 109*
Lindsay, Robert 1924- *ConAu 77*
Lindsay, Thomas Fanshawe 1910- *ConAu 21R*
Lindsay, Thomas Martin 1843-1914 *TwCA*
Lindsay, Vachel 1879-1931 *CnMWL, ConAmA,*
LongCTC, ModAL, TwCA, TwCA SUP,
TwCWr, WhoTwCL
Lindsay, Zaidee 1923- *ConAu 29R*
Lindsell, Harold 1913- *ConAu 5NR, -13R*
Lindsey, Alfred J 1931- *ConAu 41R*
Lindsey, Almont 1906- *ConAu 1R*
Lindsey, Benjamin Barr 1869-1943 *LongCTC*
Lindsey, David 1914- *ConAu 9R*
Lindsey, George R 1920- *ConAu 65*
Lindsey, Hal *ConAu 104, WrDr 84*
Lindsey, Jim *DrAP&F 83*
Lindsey, Jim 1957- *ConAu 65*
Lindsey, Johanna 1952- *ConAu 73*
Lindsey, Karen *DrAP&F 83*
Lindsey, Karen 1944- *ConAu 73*
Lindsey, Robert 1935- *ConAu 97*
Lindskoog, Kathryn 1934- *ConAu 10NR, -65*
Lindsley, Mary F *ConAu 9NR*
Lindsley, Mary Frances *ConAu 61*
Lindstrom, Carl E 1896-1969 *ConAu 1R, -103*
Lindstrom, Goran 1927- *IntAu&W 82*
Lindstrom, Pia *ConAmTC*
Lindstrom, Thais 1917- *ConAu 21R*
Lindt, Gillian 1932- *ConAu 107*
Line, Les 1935- *ConAu 73, SmATA 27[port]*
Line, Maurice Bernard 1928- *ConAu 107,*
IntAu&W 82, WrDr 84
Lineaweaver, Thomas H, III 1926- *ConAu 73*
Lineback, Richard H 1936- *ConAu 29R*
Linebarger, J M *DrAP&F 83*

Linebarger, J M 1934- *ConAu 2NR, -49*
Linebarger, James M 1934- *IntAu&W 82,*
IntWWP 82
Linebarger, Paul Myron Anthony 1913-1966
ConAu 5R, -6NR
Lineberry, John H 1926- *ConAu 1R*
Lineberry, Robert L 1942- *ConAu 73*
Linecar, Howard 1912- *ConAu 110, WrDr 84*
Linecar, Howard Walter Arthur 1912-
IntAu&W 82
Linedecker, Clifford L 1931- *ConAu 73*
Linenthal, Frances Jaffer 1921- *IntWWP 82*
Linenthal, Mark *DrAP&F 83*
Linet, Beverly 1929- *ConAu 89*
Linett, Deena *DrAP&F 83*
Ling, Arthur William 1901- *ConAu 5R*
Ling, Cyril Curtis 1936- *ConAu 17R*
Ling, Dwight L 1923- *ConAu 11NR, -21R*
Ling, Edgar Roberts 1900- *WrDr 84*
Ling, H C 1910- *ConAu 57*
Ling, Hung-Hsun 1894?-1981 *ConAu 105*
Ling, Jack 1930- *ConAu 25R*
Ling, Mona *ConAu 9R*
Ling, Roger 1942- *ConAu 103, WrDr 84*
Ling, Trevor 1920- *ConAu 11NR*
Ling, Trevor Oswald 1920- *ConAu 21R*
Lingard, Joan *TwCCW 83, WrDr 84*
Lingard, Joan 1932- *ConAu 41R, IntAu&W 82,*
SmATA 8
Lingeman, Richard R 1931- *ConAu 11NR*
Lingeman, Richard Roberts 1931- *ConAu 17R*
Lingenfelter, Richard Emery 1934- *ConAu 5NR,*
-13R, WrDr 84
Lingenfelter, Sherwood Galen 1941- *ConAu 53*
Lingis, Alphonso Frank 1933- *ConAu 37R*
Lings, Martin 1909- *ConAu 17R, IntAu&W 82*
Linhartova, Vera 1938- *ModSL 2*
Linington, Elizabeth 1921- *ConAu 1R, -1NR,*
TwCCr&M 80, WrDr 84
Link, Arthur Stanley 1920- *ConAu 1R, -3NR,*
DcLB 17[port], IntAu&W 82, WorAu,
WrDr 84
Link, Edwin A 1904-1981 *ConAu 108*
Link, Eugene P 1907- *ConAu 37R*
Link, Frederick M 1930- *ConAu 4NR, -53,*
WrDr 84
Link, John R 1907- *ConAu 17R*
Link, Mark J 1924- *ConAu 5NR, -13R*
Link, Martin 1934- *ConAu 106, SmATA 28*
Link, Perry 1944- *ConAu 105*
Link, Ruth 1923- *ConAu 29R*
Link, Theodore Carl 1905?-1974 *ConAu 104*
Link, William 1933- *ConAu 73*
Linke, Maria 1908- *ConAu 65*
Linke-Poot *ConAu X*
Linker, Robert White 1905- *ConAu 104*
Linklater, Eric 1899-1974 *CnMD, ConAu 53,*
ConAu P-2, LongCTC, ModBrL, ModWD,
TwCA, TwCA SUP, TwCCW 83, TwCWr
Linkletter, Art 1912- *ConAu 4NR, -9R,*
WrDr 84
Linkletter, John A 1923- *ConAu 69*
Links, J G 1904- *ConAu 81*
Linkugel, Wilmer A 1929- *ConAu 17R*
Linley, John 1916- *ConAu 41R*
Linn, Charles F 1930- *ConAu 85*
Linn, Edward Allen 1922- *ConAu 97*
Linn, John Gaywood 1917- *ConAu 25R*
Linnell, Charles Lawrence Scruton 1915-
ConAu 5R
Linnell, Robert H 1922- *ConAu 53*
Linneman, Robert E 1928- *ConAu 29R*
Linnemann, Willy-August 1914- *ClDMEL 80*
Linner, Birgitta 1920- *ConAu 10NR, -21R*
Linner, Birgtta 1920- *IntAu&W 82*
Linney, Romulus *DrAP&F 83*
Linney, Romulus 1930- *ConAu 1R, ConDr 82,*
IntAu&W 82, NatPD 81[port], WrDr 84
Linowes, David Francis 1917- *ConAu 49,*
WrDr 84
Lins, Osman 1924- *ConAu 105, IntAu&W 82*
Lins DoRego, Jose 1901-1957 *TwCWr,*
WhoTwCL, WorAu
Linsenmeyer, Helen Walker 1906- *ConAu 1NR,*
-45
Linsley, William A 1933- *ConAu 25R*
Linssen, Robert 1911- *IntAu&W 82*
Linstrum, Derek 1925- *ConAu 107, WrDr 84*
Linthicum, Robert Charles 1936- *ConAu 65*
Lintner, John 1916- *ConAu 104*
Lintner, John 1916-1983 *ConAu 110*
Linton, Barbara Leslie 1945- *ConAu 33R*

Linton, Calvin D 1914- *ConAu 5NR, -13R*
Linton, David 1923- *ConAu 9R*
Linton, Ralph 1893-1953 *TwCA SUP*
Linton, Robert R 1909?-1979 *ConAu 89*
Linton, Ron M 1929- *ConAu 33R, -41R,*
WrDr 84
Linton, Virginia *DrAP&F 83*
Lintz, Harry McCormick *ConAu 1R*
Linwood, Lucy-Anne *ConAu X*
Linze, Georges 1900- *CIDMEL 80, IntWWP 82*
Linze, Jacques-Gerard 1925- *CIDMEL 80*
Linzee, David 1952- *ConAu 73*
Linzey, Donald Wayne 1939- *ConAu 61*
Lionberger, Herbert F 1912- *ConAu 73*
Lionel, Robert *ConAu X*
Lionni, Leo 1910- *ConAu 53, SmATA 8,*
TwCCW 83, WrDr 84
Lipe, Dewey 1933- *ConAu 85*
Lipetz, Ben-Ami 1927- *ConAu 33R*
Lipez, Richard 1938- *ConAu 101*
Lipham, James Maurice 1927- *ConAu 81*
Lipinsky DeOrlov, Lino Sigismondo 1908-
SmATA 22[port]
Lipkin, Gladys B 1925- *ConAu 2NR, -49*
Lipkin, Mack, Jr. 1943- *ConAu 101*
Lipkind, William 1904-1974 *ConAu 101, -53,*
SmATA 15, TwCCW 83
Lipking, Lawrence 1934- *ConAu 41R*
Lipman, Aaron 1925- *ConAu 21R*
Lipman, Burton E 1931- *ConAu 109*
Lipman, Daniel *NatPD 81[port]*
Lipman, David 1931- *ConAu 21R,*
SmATA 21[port], WrDr 84
Lipman, Eugene Jay 1919- *ConAu 9R*
Lipman, Ira A 1940- *ConAu 65*
Lipman, Jean *ConAu 10NR*
Lipman, Jean 1909- *ConAu 21R*
Lipman, Joel *DrAP&F 83*
Lipman, Joel 1942- *IntWWP 82*
Lipman, Marilyn 1938- *ConAu 69*
Lipman, Matthew 1923- *ConAu 33R,*
SmATA 14, WrDr 84
Lipman, Samuel 1934- *ConAu 77*
Lipman, Vivian David 1921- *ConAu 9R,*
IntAu&W 82, WrDr 84
Lipok, Erich 1909- *IntAu&W 82*
Lipp, Frederick 1916- *ConAu 106*
Lipp, Martin R 1940- *ConAu 106*
Lippard, Lucy R *DrAP&F 83*
Lippard, Lucy Rowland 1937- *ConAu 25R,*
IntAu&W 82
Lippe, Jane *DrAP&F 83*
Lippe, Jane 1943- *IntWWP 82*
Lippert, Clarissa Start 1917- *ConAu 77*
Lipphard, William Benjamin 1886-1971
ConAu P-2
Lippincott, David 1925- *ConAu 9NR, -61*
Lippincott, Joseph Wharton 1887-1976 *ConAu 69,*
-73, SmATA 17, TwCCW 83
Lippincott, Sarah Lee 1920- *ConAu 17R,*
SmATA 22[port]
Lippitt, Gordon L 1920- *ConAu 29R*
Lippitt, Ronald O 1914- *ConAu 37R*
Lippman, Leopold 1919- *ConAu 49*
Lippman, Peter J 1936- *ConAu 108,*
SmATA 31
Lippman, Theo, Jr. 1929- *ConAu 33R*
Lippmann, Walter 1889-1974 *AuNews 1,*
ConAmA, ConAu 6NR, -9R, -53, LongCTC,
TwCA, TwCA SUP
Lipschutz, Ilse Hempel 1923- *ConAu 41R*
Lipscomb, Commander F W *ConAu X*
Lipscomb, David M 1935- *ConAu 1NR, -49*
Lipscomb, F W 1903- *ConAu 29R*
Lipscomb, James 1926- *ConAu 85*
Lipscomb, William Nunn 1919- *WrDr 84*
Lipsen, Charles B 1925- *ConAu 73*
Lipset, Seymour Martin 1922- *ConAu 1R, -1NR,*
ConIsC 1[port], WrDr 84
Lipsett, Arthur *CreCan 2*
Lipsett, Laurence Cline 1915- *ConAu 9R*
Lipsey, Richard A 1930- *ConAu 107*
Lipsey, Richard G 1928- *ConAu 97*
Lipsey, Robert E 1926- *ConAu 2NR, -5R*
Lipsitz, Lou *DrAP&F 83*
Lipsitz, Lou 1938- *ConAu 101, ConP 80,*
WrDr 84
Lipski, Alexander 1919- *ConAu 49*
Lipsky, David Bruce 1939- *ConAu 103*
Lipsky, Michael 1940- *ConAu 61*
Lipsky, Mortimer 1915- *ConAu 73*
Lipson, Goldie 1905- *ConAu 33R*

Lipson, Harry A 1919- *ConAu 61*
Lipson, Leon Samuel 1921- *ConAu 104*
Lipson, Leslie 1912- *ConAu 106*
Lipson, Milton 1913- *ConAu 65*
Lipstein, Kurt 1909- *WrDr 84*
Lipstreu, Otis 1919-1970 *ConAu P-1*
Lipsyte, Marjorie 1932- *ConAu 105*
Lipsyte, Robert 1938- *ConAu 8NR, -17R,*
ConLC 21[port], SmATA 5
Lipton, David R 1947- *ConAu 97*
Lipton, Dean 1919- *ConAu 29R, WrDr 84*
Lipton, Lawrence 1898-1975 *ConAu 57, -93,*
DcLB 16[port]
Lipton, Lenny 1940- *ConAu 101, WrDr 84*
Lipton, Leonard 1940- *IntAu&W 82*
Liptzin, Sol 1901- *ConAu 9R, IntAu&W 82,*
WrDr 84
Liroff, Richard A 1948- *ConAu 11NR, -69*
Lisagor, Peter 1915-1976 *ConAu 69*
Lisboa, Irene 1892-1958 *CIDMEL 80*
Lisca, Peter 1925- *ConAu 37R, IntAu&W 82*
Lischer, Richard 1943- *ConAu 101*
Lischke, Barbara 1924- *IntAu&W 82*
Lishka, Gerald R 1949- *ConAu 89*
Lisi, Albert 1929- *ConAu X*
Lisk, Jill 1938- *ConAu 25R, WrDr 84*
Liska, George 1922- *ConAu 104*
Lisker, Sonia O 1933- *ConAu 2NR, -49*
Lismer, Arthur 1885-1969 *CreCan 2*
Lison-Tolosana, Carmelo 1929- *ConAu 21R*
Lisowski, Gabriel 1946- *ConAu 97, SmATA 31*
Lispector, Clarice 1924- *ModLAL*
Liss, Howard 1922- *ConAu 25R, SmATA 4*
Liss, Jerome 1938- *ConAu 53*
Liss, Peggy K 1927- *ConAu 41R*
Liss, Sheldon B 1936- *ConAu 21R,*
IntAu&W 82, WrDr 84
Lissak, Moshe 1928- *ConAu 97*
Lissim, Simon 1900-1981 *ConAu 109,*
SmATA 28
Lissitzyn, Oliver J 1912- *ConAu 45*
Lissner, Will 1908- *ConAu 101*
List, Ilka 1935- *WrDr 84*
List, Ilka Katherine 1935- *ConAu 37R,*
SmATA 6
List, Jacob Samuel 1896-1967 *ConAu P-1*
List, Robert Stuart 1903-1983 *ConAu 109*
List, Shelley *DrAP&F 83*
List, Shelley 1930- *IntAu&W 82*
Lister, Hal *ConAu X*
Lister, Harold 1922- *ConAu 73*
Lister, Moira 1923- *WrDr 84*
Lister, R P 1914- *ConAu 5NR*
Lister, Raymond George 1919- *ConAu 8NR,*
-13R, IntAu&W 82, WrDr 84
Lister, Richard Percival 1914- *ConAu 9R,*
IntAu&W 82, WrDr 84
Liston, Jack *ConAu X*
Liston, Mary Dawn 1936- *ConAu 53*
Liston, Robert A 1927- *ConAu 17R, SmATA 5*
Listowel, Judith 1904- *ConAu 13R*
Litchfield, Ada B 1916- *ConAu 10NR, -25R,*
SmATA 5
Litchfield, Harry R 1898-1973 *ConAu 41R*
Litchfield, Robert O d1977 *ConAu 73*
Lite, James *ConAu X*
Lite, Jams *ConAu X*
Lithwick, Norman Harvey 1938- *ConAu 61*
Litoff, Judy Barrett 1944- *ConAu 85*
Litowinsky, Olga *DrAP&F 83*
Litowinsky, Olga 1936- *ConAu 81,*
SmATA 26[port]
Litsey, Sarah *ConAu 5R, IntWWP 82X*
Litt, Iris *DrAP&F 83*
Litt, Iris 1928- *IntWWP 82X*
Littauer, Raphael 1925- *ConAu 109*
Littell, Robert 1896-1963 *ConAu 93*
Littell, Robert 1935?- *ConAu 109*
Litterer, Joseph A 1926- *ConAu 3NR, -9R*
Littke, Lael J 1929- *ConAu 85*
Little, A Edward *SmATA X*
Little, Alan Macnaughton Gordon 1901-
IntAu&W 82
Little, Bryan 1913- *WrDr 84*
Little, Bryan Desmond Greenway 1913-
ConAu 104, IntAu&W 82
Little, Carl *DrAP&F 83*
Little, Constance *TwCCr&M 80*
Little, David 1933- *ConAu 29R*
Little, Elbert L, Jr. 1907- *ConAu 57*
Little, Elbert Payson 1912?-1983 *ConAu 110*
Little, Geraldine C *ConAu 109, DrAP&F 83*

Little, Gwyneth *TwCCr&M 80*
Little, Ian 1918- *ConAu 21R, WrDr 84*
Little, Jack *ConAu X*
Little, Jean 1932- *ChlLR 4[port], ConAu 21R,*
SmATA 2, TwCCW 83, WrDr 84
Little, John D 1894- *ConAu 65*
Little, Kenneth *ConAu X*
Little, Kenneth Lindsay 1908- *ConAu 17R*
Little, Larry Douglas 1948- *IntWWP 82*
Little, Lawrence Calvin 1897-1976 *ConAu 1R,*
-3NR
Little, Lessie Jones 1906- *ConAu 101*
Little, Lester Knox 1935- *ConAu 103*
Little, Loyd, Jr. 1940- *ConAu 81*
Little, Loyd Harry 1940- *IntAu&W 82*
Little, Mary E 1912- *ConAu 105,*
SmATA 28[port]
Little, Nina Fletcher 1903- *ConAu 106*
Little, Paul E 1928-1975 *ConAu P-2*
Little, Paul H 1915- *ConAu 17R*
Little, Paula *ConAu X*
Little, Ray 1918?-1980 *ConAu 102*
Little, Roger W 1922- *ConAu 29R*
Little, Royal 1896- *ConAu 106*
Little, S George 1903-1974 *ConAu 49*
Little, Stuart W 1921- *ConAu 1NR, -45,*
WrDr 84
Little, Thomas Russell 1911- *ConAu 13R*
Little, William Alfred *ConAu X*
Little, Wm A 1929- *ConAu 57*
Littleboy, Sheila M *ConAu X*
Littledale, Freya *ConAu 10NR, WrDr 84*
Littledale, Freya 1929- *ConAu 21R,*
IntAu&W 82, SmATA 2
Littledale, Harold 1927- *ConAu 5R*
Littlefair, Duncan 1912- *ConAu 45*
Littlefield, David Joseph 1928- *ConAu 41R*
Littlefield, James Edward 1932- *ConAu 53*
Littlejohn, Bruce 1913- *ConAu 61*
Littlejohn, David 1937- *ConAmTC, ConAu 41R*
Littleton, C Scott 1933- *ConAu 21R*
Littleton, Harvey K 1922- *ConAu 53*
Littlewit, Humphrey *ConAu X*
Littlewood, Joan 1914- *CroCD, DcLB 13[port],*
LongCTC
Littlewood, Robert Percy 1910- *ConAu 5R,*
WrDr 84
Littlewood, S R 1875-1963 *LongCTC*
Littlewood, Thomas B 1928- *ConAu 29R*
Littman, Robert J 1943- *ConAu 81, WrDr 84*
Litto, Fredric M 1939- *ConAu 25R*
Litto, Gertrude 1929- *ConAu 69*
Litvag, Irving 1928- *ConAu 57*
Litvak, Isaiah A 1936- *ConAu 13R*
Litvinoff, Barnet 1917- *ConAu 17R*
Litvinoff, Emanuel 1915- *ConNov 82,*
DcLEL 1940, WrDr 84
Litvinoff, Saul 1925- *ConAu 41R*
Litvinov, Ivy 1890?-1977 *ConAu 69,*
TwCCr&M 80
Litvinov, Pavel 1940- *ConAu 89*
Litwack, Leon 1929- *WrDr 84*
Litwack, Leon F 1929- *ConAu 1R, -1NR*
Litwak, Leo *DrAP&F 83*
Litwak, Leo E 1924- *ConAu 5R, MichAu 80,*
WrDr 84
Litwos *ConAu X*
Litz, A Walton 1929- *ConAu 33R*
Litzel, Otto 1901- *ConAu 57*
Litzinger, Boyd 1929- *ConAu 5NR, -13R*
Liu, Aimee 1953- *ConAu 89*
Liu, Alan P L 1937- *ConAu 61*
Liu, Da 1910- *ConAu 85*
Liu, James J Y 1926- *ConAu 5R, -7NR*
Liu, James T C 1919- *ConAu 21R*
Liu, Jung-Chao 1929- *ConAu 29R*
Liu, Leo 1940- *WrDr 84*
Liu, Leo Yueh-Yun 1940- *ConAu 41R*
Liu, Stephen Shu Ning *DrAP&F 83*
Liu, Stephen Shu-Ning 1930- *IntWWP 82*
Liu, Sydney 1920- *ConAu 103*
Liu, Tsu-Chien *ConAu X*
Liu, William T 1930- *ConAu 21R*
Liu, Wu-Chi 1907- *ConAu 10NR, -13R,*
IntAu&W 82, WrDr 84
Lively, Penelope 1933- *ConAu 41R,*
DcLB 14[port], IntAu&W 82, SmATA 7,
TwCCW 83, WrDr 84
Lively, Walter *ConAu X*
Liverani, Giuseppe 1903- *ConAu 5R, -6NR*
Liverani, Mary Rose 1939- *ConAu 104,*
WrDr 84

ConAu 25R

Lockridge, Frances Louise 1896-1963 *ConAu 93, TwCA, TwCA SUP, TwCCr&M 80*
Lockridge, Hildegarde 1908-1981 *ConAu 3NR, –102*
Lockridge, Kenneth A 1940- *ConAu 107*
Lockridge, Norman *ConAu 49*
Lockridge, Richard 1898-1982 *ConAu 107, –85, TwCA, TwCA SUP, TwCCr&M 80*
Lockridge, Ross, Jr. 1914-1948 *ConAu 108, DcLB Y80B[port]*
Lockridge, Ross Franklin, Jr. 1914-1948 *ModAL, TwCA SUP*
Lockspeiser, Edward 1905-1973 *ConAu 5R, –6NR*
Lockwood, Barbara 1907- *WrDr 84*
Lockwood, Charles Andrews 1890-1968 *ConAu 1R*
Lockwood, David 1929- *WrDr 84*
Lockwood, Douglas 1918- *ConAu 21R*
Lockwood, Guy C 1943- *ConAu 65*
Lockwood, Lee 1932- *ASpks, ConAu 37R*
Lockwood, Mary *ConAu X, SmATA X*
Lockwood, Theodore Davidge 1924- *ConAu 1R, –1NR*
Lockwood, W B 1917- *ConAu 29R*
Lockwood, William Burley 1917- *WrDr 84*
Lockwood, William Wirt 1906- *ConAu P-2*
Lockyer, Roger Walter 1927- *ConAu 17R, WrDr 84*
Lode, Rex *ConAu X*
Loden, Barbara 1937-1980 *ConAu 101*
Lodge, Bernard 1933- *ConAu 107, SmATA 33[port]*
Lodge, David 1935- *ConAu 17R, ConLCrt 82, ConNov 82, DcLB 14[port], IntAu&W 82, WrDr 84*
Lodge, Edith Bennett 1908- *IntWWP 82*
Lodge, George Cabot 1927- *ConAu 17R*
Lodge, Henry Cabot, Jr. 1902- *ConAu 53, IntAu&W 82*
Lodge, John Christian 1862-1950 *MichAu 80*
Lodge, Maureen Roffey *SmATA X*
Lodge, Sir Oliver Joseph 1851-1940 *LongCTC, TwCA, TwCA SUP*
Lodge, Orlan Robert 1917-1975 *ConAu 57*
Lodge, Thomas 1909- *WrDr 84*
Lodger, The *ConAu X*
Lodrick, Deryck O 1942- *ConAu 106*
Loeb, Catherine 1949- *ConAu 89*
Loeb, Gerald M 1899-1974 *ConAu 49, ConAu P-1*
Loeb, Harold A 1891-1974 *ConAu 106, –45, DcLB 4*
Loeb, Karen *DrAP&F 83*
Loeb, Madeleine H 1905?-1974 *ConAu 45*
Loeb, Marshall Robert 1929- *ConAu 21R*
Loeb, Paul Rogat 1952- *ConAu 109*
Loeb, Robert F 1895-1973 *ConAu 45*
Loeb, Robert H, Jr. 1917- *ConAu 29R, SmATA 21[port]*
Loeb, William 1905-1981 *ConAu 104, –93*
Loebl, Suzanne *ConAu 69*
Loefgren, Ulf 1931- *ConAu 25R, SmATA 3*
Loefstedt, Bengt 1931- *ConAu 1NR, –45*
Loehlin, John C 1926- *ConAu 21R*
Loemker, Leroy E 1900- *ConAu 41R*
Loening, Grover C 1889?-1976 *ConAu 65*
Loening, Sarah Larkin 1896- *ConAu 45, IntAu&W 82*
Loeoef, Jan 1940- *ConAu 81*
Loeper, John J 1929- *WrDr 84*
Loeper, John Joseph 1929- *ConAu 29R, IntAu&W 82, SmATA 10*
Loerges, Margrethe 1926- *IntWWP 82*
Loerke, Oskar 1884-1941 *ModGL*
Loesch, Juli 1951- *ConAu 89*
Loescher, Ann Dull 1942- *ConAu 9NR, –61, SmATA 20*
Loescher, Gil 1945- *ConAu 9NR, –61, SmATA 20*
Loeser, Herta 1921- *ConAu 57*
Loeser, Katinka *DrAP&F 83*
Loeser, Katinka 1913- *ConAu 17R*
Loether, Herman John 1930- *ConAu 21R, WrDr 84*
Loetscher, Lefferts A 1904- *ConAu 5R, IntAu&W 82*
Loevetand, Hans Thorup 1951- *IntAu&W 82*
Loevinger, Jane 1918- *ConAu 41R*
Loevinger, Lee 1913- *ConAu 81*

Loew, Ralph William 1907- *ConAu P-1, WrDr 84*
Loew, Sebastian 1939- *ConAu 103*
Loewald, Hans W 1906- *ConAu 101*
Loewe, Ralph E 1923- *ConAu 21R, WrDr 84*
Loewen, James W 1942- *ConAu 37R*
Loewenberg, Bert James 1905-1974 *ConAu 5NR, –9R*
Loewenberg, Frank M 1925- *ConAu 2NR, –45*
Loewenberg, Gerhard 1928- *ConAu 9NR, –21R*
Loewenberg, J Joseph 1933- *ConAu 33R*
Loewenberg, Peter J 1933- *ConAu 109*
Loewenfeld, Claire 1899-1974 *ConAu P-2*
Loewenstein, Hubertus Prinz Zu *ConAu X*
Loewenstein, Prince Hubertus Zu 1906- *ConAu 4NR, –5R*
Loewenstein, Karl 1891-1973 *ConAu 41R*
Loewenstein, Louis Klee 1927- *ConAu 37R, WrDr 84*
Loewenstein, Rudolph M 1898-1976 *ConAu 65, ConAu P-2*
Loewenstein-Scharffenick, Hubertus Von *ConAu X*
Loewenstein-Wertheim-Freudenberg, H 1906- *ConAu X*
Loewenthal, L J A *ConAu 61*
Loewinsohn, Ron *DrAP&F 83*
Loewinsohn, Ron 1937- *ConAu 25R, ConP 80, WrDr 84*
Loewinsohn, Ronald William 1937- *DcLEL 1940*
Loewy, Ariel G 1925- *ConAu 89*
Loewy, Raymond Fernand 1893- *ConAu 104*
Lofaro, Michael Anthony 1948- *ConAu 89*
Lofland, John 1936- *ConAu 33R*
Lofland, Lyn 1937- *ConAu 61*
Lofstedt, Benat *ConAu X*
Loftas, Tony 1940- *ConAu 21R*
Lofthouse, Jessica 1916- *ConAu 29R*
Loftin, Eloise *DrAP&F 83*
Lofting, Hugh 1886-1947 *ConAu 109, LongCTC, SmATA 15, TwCA, TwCA SUP, TwCCW 83*
Loftis, Anne 1922- *ConAu 45*
Loftis, John 1919- *ConAu 1R, –3NR*
Loftis, N J *DrAP&F 83*
Lofton, C A *DrAP&F 83*
Lofton, John M 1919- *ConAu 6NR, –9R, WrDr 84*
Lofts, Norah 1904- *AuNews 2, ConAu 5R, –6NR, IntAu&W 82, LongCTC, SmATA 8, TwCA, TwCA SUP, TwCCr&M 80, TwCRGW, WrDr 84*
Lofts, Norah 1904-1983 *ConAu 110*
Loftus, Elizabeth F 1944- *ConAu 105*
Loftus, Richard J 1929- *ConAu 13R*
Logan, Albert Boyd 1909- *ConAu 53*
Logan, Daniel 1936- *ConAu 25R*
Logan, Dixie Leah 1907- *IntWWP 82*
Logan, Don *ConAu X*
Logan, Elizabeth D 1914- *ConAu 61*
Logan, F Donald 1930- *ConAu 45*
Logan, Ford *ConAu X, WrDr 84*
Logan, Frank A 1924- *ConAu 41R*
Logan, Gene A 1922- *ConAu 7NR, –9R*
Logan, Gerald E 1924- *ConAu 73*
Logan, Jake *ConAu X, WrDr 84*
Logan, James Phillips 1921- *ConAu 37R*
Logan, John *DrAP&F 83*
Logan, John 1923- *ConAu 1R, –77, ConLC 5, ConP 80, CroCAP, DcLB 5[port], WorAu, WrDr 84*
Logan, Joshua Lockwood 1908- *AuNews 1, ConAu 89, ConDr 82D, ModWD*
Logan, Lillian 1909- *WrDr 84*
Logan, Lillian Stern 1909- *ConAu 1R, –1NR*
Logan, Mark *ConNov 82, TwCRGW, WrDr 84*
Logan, Sister Mary Francis Louise 1928- *ConAu 5R*
Logan, Rayford Whittingham 1897- *ConAu 1R, –1NR*
Logan, Rayford Whittingham 1897-1982 *ConAu 108*
Logan, Sara *ConAu X*
Logan, Spencer 1912?-1980 *ConAu 93*
Logan, Terence P 1936- *ConAu 57*
Logan, Virgil G 1904- *ConAu 21R, WrDr 84*
Logan, William *DrAP&F 83*
Loganbill, G Bruce 1938- *ConAu 37R*
Loggins, Vernon 1893-1968 *ConAu 5R*
Loggins, William Kirk 1946- *ConAu 77*

Logsdon, Joseph 1938- *ConAu 25R*
Logsdon, Richard Henry 1912- *ConAu 2NR, –5R*
Logsdon, Thomas S 1937- *ConAu 6NR, –57*
Logsdon, Tom *ConAu X*
Logue, Cal 1935- *ConAu 105*
Logue, Christopher 1926- *CnMD, ConAu 3NR, –9R, ConP 80, DcLEL 1940, IntWWP 82, IntWWP 82, ModBrL, ModWD, SmATA 23, WorAu, WrDr 84*
Logue, Jeanne 1921- *ConAu 89*
Logue, William Herbert 1934- *ConAu 45*
Loh, Jules 1931- *ConAu 33R*
Loh, Pichon P Y 1928- *ConAu 17R, WrDr 84*
Loh, Robert 1924- *ConAu 17R*
Lohf, Kenneth A 1925- *ConAu 3NR, –9R*
Lohitaksha *IntAu&W 82X*
Lohman, Joseph D 1910-1968 *ConAu P-2*
Lohmann, Jeanne Ruth Ackley 1923- *IntWWP 82*
Lohnes, Walter F W 1925- *ConAu 49*
Lohr, Thomas F 1926- *ConAu 77*
Lohrer, Frieda 1906- *IntAu&W 82*
Lohrer, M Alice 1907- *ConAu 17R*
Lohrke, Eugene William 1897-1953 *TwCA, TwCA SUP*
Lohse, Eduard 1924- *ConAu 107*
Loiselle, Helene 1928- *CreCan 2*
Lojek, Jerzy 1932- *IntAu&W 82*
Loken, Newton Clayton 1919- *ConAu 1R, SmATA 26[port]*
Lokken, Bjorg Egeland 1943- *IntAu&W 82*
Lokken, Roy N 1917- *ConAu 53*
Lokos, Lionel 1928- *ConAu 25R*
Loland, Rasmus 1861-1907 *ClDMEL 80*
Loll, Leo M, Jr. 1923-1968 *ConAu P-2*
Lollar, Coleman Aubrey 1946- *ConAu 49*
Lolli, Giorgio 1905-1979 *ConAu 1R, –2NR, –85*
Lollis, Lorraine 1911- *ConAu P-2, WrDr 84*
Lolos, Kimon 1917- *ConAu 1R*
Lom, Josephine *WrDr 84*
Loman, Judy 1936- *CreCan 1*
Lomas, Charles W 1907- *ConAu P-1*
Lomas, Derek 1933- *ConAu 29R*
Lomas, Geoffrey 1950- *ConAu 93*
Lomas, Peter 1923- *ConAu 21R, WrDr 84*
Lomas, Steve *ConAu X, SmATA 6*
Lomask, Milton 1909- *ConAu 1R, –1NR, SmATA 20*
Lomax, Alan 1915- *ConAu 1R, –1NR, TwCA SUP*
Lomax, Bliss *ConAu X, TwCWW*
Lomax, Eric Sutherland 1919- *WrDr 84*
Lomax, John A 1930- *ConAu 61*
Lomax, John Avery 1872?-1948 *TwCA SUP*
Lomax, Louis E 1922-1970 *ConAu P-2*
Lomax, Pearl Cleage 1948- *ConAu 41R*
Lombard, Alf 1902- *IntAu&W 82*
Lombard, C M 1920- *ConAu 1NR, –49*
Lombard, Nap *ConAu X*
Lombardi, John V 1942- *ConAu 5NR, –53*
Lombardi, Mary 1940- *ConAu 61*
Lombardo, Gaetano Albert 1902- *CreCan 1*
Lombardo, Guy 1902- *CreCan 1*
Lombardo, Josef Vincent 1908- *ConAu 5R*
Lombroso, Cesare 1836-1909 *LongCTC*
Lommasson, Robert C 1917- *ConAu 41R*
Lomnicka, Josephine *WrDr 84*
Lomupo, Brother Robert 1939- *ConAu 13R*
London, Artur 1915- *ConAu 65*
London, Carolyn 1918- *ConAu 57*
London, George 1920- *CreCan 1*
London, H H 1900- *ConAu 49*
London, Hannah R 1894- *ConAu 29R*
London, Herbert I 1939- *ConAu 33R, IntAu&W 82, WrDr 84*
London, Jack *ConAu X*
London, Jack 1876-1916 *AuNews 2, DcLB 8[port], FifWWr, LongCTC, ModAL, ModAL SUP, SmATA 18, TwCA, TwCA SUP, TwCLC 9[port], TwCSFW, TwCWW, TwCWr, WhoTwCL*
London, Jack 1915- *ConAu 89*
London, Jane *ConAu X, SmATA X*
London, Joan 1901-1971 *ConAu P-2*
London, John Griffith 1876-1916 *ConAu 110, SmATA 3*
London, Jonathan *DrAP&F 83*
London, Kurt L *WrDr 84*
London, Kurt L 1900- *ConAu 1R, –6NR*
London, Laura *WrDr 84*
London, Laura 1952- *TwCRGW*

Lord, Athena V 1932- *ConAu 109*
Lord, Beman 1924- *ConAu 33R, SmATA 5*
Lord, Bette Bao 1938- *ConAu 107,*
ConLC 23[port]
Lord, Clifford L 1912-1980 *ConAu 8NR, -102,*
-13R
Lord, Donald Charles 1930- *ConAu 37R*
Lord, Doreen Mildred Douglas 1904-
IntAu&W 82
Lord, Douglas 1904- *ConAu P-1, SmATA 12,*
WrDr 84
Lord, Eda 1907-1976 *ConAu 104*
Lord, Edith Elizabeth 1907- *ConAu 41R*
Lord, Eric Meredith 1923- *NatPD 81[port]*
Lord, Eugene Hodgdon 1894- *ConAu 1R*
Lord, Francis A 1911- *ConAu 17R*
Lord, Frederic Mather 1912- *ConAu 37R*
Lord, Gabrielle 1946- *ConAu 106*
Lord, George DeF 1919- *ConAu 10NR, -65*
Lord, Gigi *DrAP&F 83, IntWWP 82*
Lord, Graham John 1943- *ConAu 4NR, -53,*
WrDr 84
Lord, H Beman, Jr. 1924- *ConAu 1R*
Lord, Howard Blaine 1926- *ConAmTC*
Lord, Jeffrey *WrDr 84*
Lord, Jeremy *ConAu X*
Lord, Jess R 1911- *ConAu 65*
Lord, John Vernon 1939- *ConAu 53,*
SmATA 21[port], WrDr 84
Lord, Mary Stinson Pillsbury 1904-1978
ConAu 81, -85
Lord, Nancy *ConAu X, SmATA 2, WrDr 84*
Lord, Phillips H *ConAu X*
Lord, Priscilla Sawyer 1908- *ConAu 9R*
Lord, Robert 1945- *ConAu 61, ConDr 82,*
NatPD 81[port], WrDr 84
Lord, Shirley *ConAu X*
Lord, Vivian *ConAu X*
Lord, Walter 1917- *ConAu 1R, -5NR,*
IntAu&W 82, SmATA 3, WorAu,
WrDr 84
Lord, William Jackson, Jr. 1926- *ConAu 5R*
Lord Auch *ConAu X*
Lord Boyle Of Handsworth *ConAu X*
Lord Butler Of Saffron Walden *ConAu X*
Lord Evans Of Hungershall *ConAu X*
Lord Francis Williams *ConAu X*
Lord Hailsham Of St. Marylebone *ConAu X*
Lord Home *ConAu X*
Lord Killanin *ConAu X*
Lord Rhyll *ConAu X*
Lord Strange *ConAu X*
Lord Thomas *ConAu X*
Lord Windlesham *ConAu X*
Lorde, Audre *DrAP&F 83*
Lorde, Audre 1934- *ConAu 25R, ConLC 18,*
ConP 80, LivgBAA, WrDr 84
Lordi, Robert J 1923- *ConAu 89*
Loreau, Max 1928- *CIDMEL 80*
Loree, Kate 1920- *ConAu X*
Lorek, Daniel N 1958?-1983 *ConAu 110*
Lorel, Phil *IntAu&W 82X, IntWWP 82X*
Loren, Santiago 1918- *IntAu&W 82*
Lorenz, Alfred Lawrence 1937- *ConAu 45*
Lorenz, Gunter W 1932- *IntAu&W 82*
Lorenz, J D 1938- *ConAu 102*
Lorenz, Konrad Zacharias 1903- *ConAu 61,*
WorAu 1970
Lorenz, Lincoln 1895- *IntAu&W 82,*
IntWWP 82
Lorenz, Sarah *WrDr 84*
Lorenz, Sarah E *ConAu X, IntAu&W 82X*
Lorenzen, David N 1940- *ConAu 33R*
Lorenzini, Carlo 1826-1890 *SmATA 29[port]*
Lorenzo, Carol Lee 1939- *ConAu 53*
Lorenzo, Pedro De 1917- *CIDMEL 80*
Loria, Jeffrey H 1940- *ConAu 17R*
Lorie, James Hirsch 1922- *ConAu 103*
Lorimer, Lawrence T 1941- *ConAu 6NR, -57*
Lorimer, Scat *ConAu X, IntAu&W 82X*
Loring, Ann 1915- *ConAu 97*
Loring, Emilie d1951 *TwCRGW*
Loring, Frances Norma 1887-1968 *CreCan 2*
Loring, J M *ConAu X, IntAu&W 82X*
Loring, Murray 1917- *ConAu 45*
Lorion, R P 1946- *ConAu 85*
Loris *ConAu X*
L'Ormeau, F W *IntAu&W 82X*
Lorning, Ray *ConAu X*
Lornquest, Olaf *ConAu X*
Lorr, Kathy Auchincloss *DrAP&F 83*
Lorrah, Jean *ConAu 103*

Lorraine, Walter Henry 1929- *SmATA 16*
Lorrance, Arleen 1939- *ConAu 85*
Lorrimer, Claire *ConAu 89, TwCRGW*
Lorsch, Jay William 1932- *ConAu 97*
Lorts, Jack E *DrAP&F 83*
Lortz, Richard 1917-1980 *ConAu 11NR*
Lortz, Richard 1930-1980 *ConAu 102, -57*
Lory, Robert 1936- *ConAu 10NR, -53*
Los, George *ConAu X*
Losang, Rato Khyongla Ngawang 1923-
ConAu 81
Losche, Peter 1939- *IntAu&W 82*
Lose, M Phyllis 1925- *ConAu 101*
Loshak, David 1933- *ConAu 41R*
Losoncy, Lawrence J 1941- *ConAu 37R*
Losoncy, Mary Jan 1942- *ConAu 37R*
Loss, Joan 1933- *SmATA 11*
Loss, Louis 1914- *ConAu 2NR, -5R, WrDr 84*
Loss, Richard 1938- *ConAu 65*
Losse, Arlyle Mansfield 1917- *IntWWP 82*
Lossky, Andrew 1917- *ConAu 93*
Lossy, Rella *DrAP&F 83*
Lossy, Rella 1934- *ConAu 81*
Losty, Patrick Alfred 1924- *WrDr 84*
Loth, Calder 1943- *ConAu 73*
Loth, David G 1899- *WrDr 84*
Loth, David Goldsmith 1899- *ConAu 1R, -1NR*
Loth, Roman 1931- *IntAu&W 82*
Lothar, Ernst 1890- *TwCA SUP*
Lotherington, Tom 1950- *IntAu&W 82*
Lothian, John Maule 1896-1970 *ConAu P-1*
Lothian, Thomas 1915- *WrDr 84*
Lothian, Thomas Robert Noel 1915-
IntAu&W 82
Lothrop, Harriet Mulford Stone 1844-1924
SmATA 20
Loti, Pierre 1850-1923 *CIDMEL 80, ConAu X,*
LongCTC, ModFrL, TwCA, TwCA SUP,
TwCLC 11[port]
Lott, Arnold 1912- *ConAu 13R, WrDr 84*
Lott, Clarinda Harriss *DrAP&F 83*
Lott, Davis Newton 1913- *ConAu 10NR, -21R*
Lott, Milton 1919- *WrDr 84*
Lott, Milton James 1919- *ConAu 17R,*
TwCWW
Lott, Monroe *ConAu X*
Lott, Robert E 1926- *ConAu 4NR, -5R*
Lottich, Kenneth 1904- *WrDr 84*
Lottich, Kenneth Verne 1904- *ConAu 17R,*
IntAu&W 82
Lottinville, Savoie 1906- *ConAu 105*
Lottman, Eileen 1927- *ConAu 57*
Lottman, Herbert 1927- *WrDr 84*
Lottman, Herbert R 1927- *ConAu 105*
Lotz, James Robert 1929- *ConAu 37R*
Lotz, John 1913-1973 *ConAu 45*
Lotz, Wolfgang 1912- *ConAu 81*
Louch, A R 1927- *ConAu 17R*
Louch, Elizabeth Irene Quekett *IntWWP 82*
Louchheim, Kathleen 1903- *ConAu 21R*
Louchheim, Katie *ConAu X*
Loucks, William Negele 1899- *ConAu 1R*
Louden, Robert Stuart 1912- *ConAu 5R*
Lougee, Robert W 1919- *ConAu 5R, WrDr 84*
Loughary, John William 1930- *ConAu 41R,*
IntAu&W 82
Loughead, LaRue A 1927- *ConAu 61*
Loughlin, Richard L *DrAP&F 83*
Loughlin, Richard L 1907- *ConAu 45, ConSFA*
Loughmiller, Campbell 1906- *ConAu 77*
Loughran, Bernice B 1919- *ConAu 5R*
Loughran, Peter 1938- *ConAu 25R*
Louie, Ai-Ling 1949- *SmATA 34*
Louis, Arthur M 1938- *ConAu 106*
Louis, Debbie 1945- *ConAu 29R*
Louis, Dr. Paul *IntAu&W 82X*
Louis, J C, Jr. 1949- *ConAu 105*
Louis, Jean-Victor 1938- *IntAu&W 82*
Louis, Joe *ConAu X*
Louis, Father M *ConAu X*
Louis, Paul P 1918- *ConAu 61*
Louis, Pierre 1870-1925 *ConAu 105*
Louis, Ray Baldwin 1949- *ConAu 65*
Louis, Tobi 1940- *ConAu 57, IntAu&W 82,*
NatPD 81[port]
Louise, Ann *DrAP&F 83*
Louise, Esther *DrAP&F 83*
Louise Linton, Stella *IntWWP 82X*
Louisell, David William 1913-1977 *ConAu 1R,*
-4NR, -73
Loukes, Harold 1912- *ConAu 17R*
Lounela, Pekka 1932- *IntAu&W 82*

Lounsbury, Myron 1940- *ConAu 37R, WrDr 84*
Louria, Donald B 1928- *ConAu 107*
Lourie, Dick *DrAP&F 83*
Lourie, Dick 1937- *ConAu 33R*
Lourie, Helen *ConAu X, SmATA X*
Lourie, Iven *DrAP&F 83*
Lourie, Iven B 1946- *IntWWP 82*
Lousley, J E 1907-1976 *ConAu 104*
Louthan, Robert *DrAP&F 83*
Louthan, Robert 1951- *ConAu 109*
Louverne, Jean *IntAu&W 82X*
Louviere, Vernon Ray 1920- *ConAu 108*
Louvish, Misha 1909- *ConAu 1NR, -45*
Louw, Nicholaas Petrus VanWyk 1906-1970
ConAu 89
Louw, Nicolaas Petrus VanSyk 1906-1970
WhoTwCL
Loux, Michael Joseph 1942- *ConAu 103*
Louys, Pierre 1870-1925 *CIDMEL 80,*
ConAu X, LongCTC, TwCA, TwCA SUP,
WhoTwCL
Louzeiro, Josee 1932- *IntAu&W 82*
Lovaas, Ivar O 1927- *ConAu 45*
Lovasik, Lawrence George 1913- *ConAu 1R,*
-1NR
Lovay, Jean-Marc 1948- *IntAu&W 82*
Love, Alan C 1937- *ConAu 53*
Love, Barbara J 1937- *ConAu 37R*
Love, Charles 1932- *ConAu 25R*
Love, Edmund G 1912- *ConAu 1R, -4NR*
Love, Glen A 1932- *ConAu 29R*
Love, Iris Cornelia 1933- *ConAu 29R*
Love, Janet *ConAu X*
Love, Jean O 1920- *ConAu 29R*
Love, John *DrAP&F 83*
Love, Joseph L 1938- *ConAu 29R*
Love, Katherine Isabel 1907- *SmATA 3*
Love, Kennett 1924- *ConAu 77*
Love, Philip H 1905-1977 *ConAu 73, -77*
Love, Richard S 1923- *ConAu 81*
Love, Sandra 1940- *ConAu 11NR, -69,*
SmATA 26[port]
Love, Sydney F 1923- *ConAu 81*
Love, Thomas Teel 1931- *ConAu 13R*
Lovecraft, H P 1890-1937 *ConAu 104,*
TwCLC 4[port], TwCSFW
Lovecraft, Howard Phillips 1890-1937
TwCA SUP
Lovegrove, Philip *ConAu X*
Lovehill, C B *ConAu X*
Lovejoy, Arthur Oncken 1873-1962 *TwCA SUP*
Lovejoy, Bahija F 1914- *ConAu 5R*
Lovejoy, Clarence Earle 1894-1974 *ConAu 5R,*
-45
Lovejoy, David Sherman 1919- *ConAu 103*
Lovejoy, Elijah P 1940- *ConAu 45*
Lovejoy, L C 1893- *ConAu 1R*
Lovel, Isabel Evelyn 1902- *IntWWP 82*
Lovelace, Delos Wheeler 1894-1967 *ConAu 5R,*
-25R, SmATA 7, TwCA, TwCA SUP
Lovelace, Earl 1935- *ConAu 77, ConNov 82,*
WrDr 84
Lovelace, Marc Hoyle 1920- *ConAu 37R*
Lovelace, Maud Hart 1892-1980 *ConAu 5R, -104,*
SmATA 2, -23N, TwCA, TwCA SUP,
TwCCW 83
Lovelace, Richard Franz 1930- *ConAu 101*
Loveless, E E 1919- *ConAu 57*
Lovell, Sir Alfred Charles Bernard 1913-
DcLEL 1940
Lovell, Ann 1933- *ConAu 97*
Lovell, Bernard 1913- *ConAu 6NR, -13R,*
IntAu&W 82, WrDr 84
Lovell, Colin Rhys 1917- *ConAu 5R*
Lovell, Ernest J, Jr. 1918-1975 *ConAu 1R, -103*
Lovell, Ingraham *ConAu X*
Lovell, John, Jr. 1907-1974 *ConAu 49,*
ConAu P-2, LivgBAA
Lovell, John P 1932- *ConAu 29R*
Lovell, Marc *WrDr 84*
Lovell, Marc 1930- *ConAu X, TwCCr&M 80*
Lovell, Mark 1934- *ConAu 8NR, -61*
Lovell, Michael Christopher 1930- *ConAu 33R*
Lovell, Ronald P 1937- *ConAu 73*
Lovell, Stanley P 1890- *ConAu 5R*
Loveman, Brian E 1944- *ConAu 89*
Loveman, Samuel 1885?-1976 *ConAu 65*
Lovenstein, Meno 1909- *ConAu 3NR, -5R*
Lovequist, Gwendlelynn *ConAu X*
Loverde, James M *DrAP&F 83*
Loverde, Lorin 1943- *ConAu 45*
Loveridge, Ronald O 1938- *ConAu 33R*

Lucas, Jim Griffing 1914-1970 *ConAu 104*
Lucas, John 1937- *ConAu 37R, IntAu&W 82, WrDr 84*
Lucas, John Randolph 1929- *WrDr 84*
Lucas, Joseph 1928- *ConAu 69*
Lucas, Joyce 1927- *ConAu 57*
Lucas, Lawrence Edward 1933- *ConAu 65, LivgBAA*
Lucas, Marion B 1935- *ConAu 81*
Lucas, N B C 1901- *ConAu 81*
Lucas, Noah 1927- *ConAu 57, WrDr 84*
Lucas, Robert 1904- *ConAu 101*
Lucas, Robert Emerson, Jr. 1937- *ConAu 107*
Lucas, Robert Harold 1933- *ConAu 37R*
Lucas, Ruth 1909- *ConAu P-2*
Lucas, Scott 1937- *ConAu 93*
Lucas, T E 1919- *ConAu 77*
Lucas, Victoria *ConAu X, LongCTC, WorAu*
Lucas, W F *DrAP&F 83*
Lucas, W F 1927- *ConAu 77*
Lucas Phillips, C E 1897- *ConAu 3NR*
Lucas Phillips, Cecil Ernest 1897- *ConAu 1R*
Lucca, Juan Senta *IntAu&W 82X*
Lucchesi, Aldo *ConAu X*
Luce, Celia 1914- *ConAu 61*
Luce, Clare Boothe 1903- *ConAu 45, TwCA SUP, WrDr 84*
Luce, Don 1934- *ConAu 29R*
Luce, Gay 1930- *WrDr 84*
Luce, Gay Gaer 1930- *ConAu 103*
Luce, Gregory *DrAP&F 83*
Luce, Henry Robinson 1898-1967 *ConAu 104, -89*
Luce, J V 1920- *ConAu 61*
Luce, John Victor 1920- *IntAu&W 82*
Luce, Willard 1914- *ConAu 61*
Luce, William 1931- *ConAu 11NR, -65*
Lucebert 1924- *ClDMEL 80*
Lucentini, Mauro 1924- *ConAu 69*
Lucerno, Marcela *DrAP&F 83*
Lucero, Roberto *ConAu X*
Lucey, James D 1923- *ConAu 25R, WrDr 84*
Luchins, Abraham S 1914- *ConAu 11NR, -69*
Luchins, Edith H 1921- *ConAu 11NR*
Luchins, Edith Hirsch 1921- *ConAu 17R*
Luchins, Edith Hirsh 1921- *WrDr 84*
Luchsinger, Elaine King 1902- *ConAu P-2*
Luchsinger, Fred W 1921- *IntAu&W 82*
Lucia, Ellis 1922- *WrDr 84*
Lucia, Ellis Joel 1922- *ConAu 1R, -4NR, IntAu&W 82*
Lucia, Salvatore Pablo 1901- *ConAu 13R*
Luciani, Vincent 1906- *ConAu 61*
Luciano, Felipe *DrAP&F 83*
Lucid, Robert F 1930- *ConAu 25R*
Lucie-Smith, Edward 1933- *ConAu 7NR, -13R, ConP 80, IntAu&W 82, WorAu, WrDr 84*
Lucie-Smith, John Edward McKenzie 1933- *DcLEL 1940*
Lucina, Sister Mary *DrAP&F 83*
Luciolli, Mario 1910- *IntAu&W 82*
Luck, David Johnston 1912- *ConAu 4NR, -53*
Luck, G Coleman 1913- *ConAu 13R*
Luck, Georg Hans Bhavani 1926- *ConAu 5R*
Luck, Thomas Jefferson 1922- *ConAu 5R*
Lucke, Hans 1927- *CnMD*
Luckert, Karl W 1934- *ConAu 81*
Luckett, Hubert Pearson 1916- *ConAu 77*
Luckett, Karen Beth 1944- *ConAu 77*
Luckey, Eleanore Braun 1915- *ConAu 33R*
Luckey, T D 1919- *WrDr 84*
Luckhardt, C Grant 1943- *ConAu 93*
Luckhardt, Mildred Corell 1898- *ConAu 13R, IntAu&W 82, SmATA 5*
Luckless, John *ConAu X*
Luckmann, Thomas 1927- *ConAu 101, IntAu&W 82*
Luckock, Elizabeth 1914- *ConAu 21R*
Luckyj, George S N 1919- *ConAu 45*
Lucy, Sean 1931- *IntWWP 82*
Ludbrook, John 1929- *WrDr 84*
Ludden, Allen 1918?-1981 *ConAu 104, SmATA 27N*
Luder, William Fay 1910- *ConAu 29R*
Ludington, Townsend 1936- *ConAu 9NR, -45*
Ludium, Mabel Cleland *ConAu X*
Ludlam, Charles 1943- *ConAu 85, ConDr 82, NatPD 81*
Ludlow, Edmund 1898- *ConSFA*
Ludlow, Geoffrey *ConAu X, WrDr 84*
Ludlow, George *ConAu X*
Ludlow, Howard Thomas 1921- *ConAu 21R,*

WrDr 84*
Ludlow, James Minor 1917-1974 *ConAu 53*
Ludlum, Mabel Cleland *SmATA 5*
Ludlum, Robert 1927- *ConAu 33R, ConLC 22[port], DcLB Y82B[port], TwCCr&M 80, WrDr 84*
Ludlum, Robert P 1909- *ConAu P-1*
Ludmerer, Kenneth M 1947- *ConAu 45*
Ludovici, Anthony M 1882- *ConAu P-1*
Ludovici, L J *ConAu X*
Ludovici, Laurence J 1910- *ConAu 21R*
Ludovici, Laurence James *ConAu X*
Ludovici, Lorenz James 1910- *ConAu X, -10NR, WrDr 84*
Ludowyk, Evelyn Frederick Charles 1906- *ConAu P-1*
Ludtke, James Buren 1924- *ConAu 1R*
Ludvigsen, Karl 1934- *ConAu 73*
Ludvigson, Susan *DrAP&F 83*
Ludvigson, Susan 1942- *ConAu 7NR*
Ludwig, Charles Shelton 1918- *ConAu 5NR, -9R*
Ludwig, Ed 1920- *ConAu 97*
Ludwig, Emil 1881-1948 *LongCTC, TwCA, TwCA SUP*
Ludwig, Eric *ConAu X*
Ludwig, Frederic *ConAu X*
Ludwig, Helen *SmATA 33[port]*
Ludwig, Jack *DrAP&F 83*
Ludwig, Jack 1922- *ConAu 1R, -1NR, ConNov 82, DcLEL 1940, WrDr 84*
Ludwig, Jerry 1934- *ConAu 81*
Ludwig, Myles Eric 1942- *ConAu 25R*
Ludwig, Richard Milton 1920- *ConAu 17R*
Ludwigson, Kathryn Romaine 1921- *ConAu 6NR, -53*
Luebke, Frederick Carl 1927- *ConAu 33R, IntAu&W 82, WrDr 84*
Luecke, Jane-Marie 1924- *IntWWP 82*
Luecke, Janemarie *DrAP&F 83*
Luecke, Janemarie 1924- *ConAu 104*
Lueders, Edward *DrAP&F 83*
Lueders, Edward 1923- *ConAu 5NR, -13R, SmATA 14*
Luedtke, Kurt 1939- *ConAu 109*
Lueker, Erwin L 1914- *ConAu 8NR, -17R*
Luellen, Valentina *WrDr 84*
Lueloff, Jorie *ConAmTC*
Luening, Otto 1900- *ConAu 102*
Lueschen, Guenther R 1930- *ConAu 4NR, -53*
Luescher, Max 1923- *ConAu 101*
Luesma Castan, Miguel 1929- *IntAu&W 82*
Luetgen, Kurt 1911- *ConAu 108*
Luethi, Max 1909- *ConAu 29R*
Luff, S G A 1921- *ConAu 9R*
Luft, David Sheers 1944- *ConAu 106*
Luft, Ludmilla Gorny-Otzoup *CreCan 1*
Luft, Uriel 1933- *CreCan 1*
Lugard, Flora Louisa Shaw 1852-1929 *SmATA 21[port]*
Luger, Harriett Mandelay 1914- *ConAu 1NR, -45, SmATA 23[port]*
Lugg, George Wilson 1902- *ConAu 105*
Lugne-Poe, Aurelien 1869-1940 *ClDMEL 80*
Lugo, Ariel E 1943- *ConAu 41R*
Lugo, James O 1928- *ConAu 29R*
Lugones, Leopoldo 1874-1938 *ModLAL*
Lugt, Herbert Vander *ConAu X*
Luh, Bor Shium 1916- *IntAu&W 82*
Luhan, Mabel Dodge 1879-1962 *ConAmA, LongCTC, TwCA, TwCA SUP*
Luhar, Tribhuvandas Purushottandas 1908- *IntAu&W 82*
Luhr, William 1946- *ConAu 106*
Luhrmann, Tom *DrAP&F 83*
Luhrmann, Winifred B 1934- *ConAu 61, SmATA 11*
Luick, John F 1920- *ConAu 25R*
Luis, Earlene W 1929- *ConAu 61, SmATA 11*
Luisi, Billie M 1940- *ConAu 73*
Luk, Charles 1898- *ConAu 9R*
Luka, Ronald 1937- *ConAu 61*
Lukac, Emil Boleslav 1900- *ClDMEL 80*
Lukacs, George 1885-1971 *ConAu X, ConLC 24[port]*
Lukacs, George *ConAu X*
Lukacs, Gyorgy 1885-1971 *ClDMEL 80, ConAu 101, -29R, WorAu*
Lukacs, John 1923- *ConAu 1R, -1NR*
Lukas, Charlotte Koplinka 1954- *ConAu 93*
Lukas, Ellen *ConAu 97*
Lukas, J Anthony 1933- *ConAu 2NR, -49*
Lukas, Mary *ConAu 101, -103*

Lukas, Richard Conrad 1937- *ConAu 33R, WrDr 84*
Lukas, Susan *DrAP&F 83*
Lukas, Susan 1940- *ConAu 53*
Lukashevich, Stephen 1931- *ConAu 33R*
Luke, Hugh J 1932- *ConAu 89*
Luke, Mary M 1919- *ConAu 21R*
Luke, Peter 1919- *ConAu 81, ConDr 82, DcLB 13[port], IntAu&W 82, WrDr 84*
Luke, Thomas *ConAu X, WrDr 84*
Lukenbill, Willis B 1939- *ConAu 103*
Luker, Kristin Carol 1946- *ConAu 61*
Lukes, Steven M 1941- *ConAu 93, IntAu&W 82, WrDr 84*
Lukodianov, Isai 1913- *ConAu 101*
Lukonin, Mikhail K 1920?-1977 *ConAu 69*
Lum, Peter *ConAu X, IntAu&W 82X, SmATA X, WrDr 84*
Lum, Vernette Trosper *IntWWP 82X*
Lumian, Norman C 1928- *ConAu 29R*
Lummis, Keith 1904- *ConAu 104*
Lumpkin, Grace *ConAmA, ConAu 69, TwCA, TwCA SUP*
Lumpkin, William Latane 1916- *ConAu 1R, -4NR*
Lumsden, Barry 1939- *ConAu 45*
Luna, Felix Cesar 1925- *IntAu&W 82*
Lunacharski, Anatoli Vasilyevich 1875-1933 *CnMD*
Lunacharsky, Anatoli Vasilevich 1875-1933 *ModWD*
Lunacharsky, Anatoly Vasilyevich 1875-1933 *ClDMEL 80*
Lunan, Duncan 1945- *ConAu 107, WrDr 84*
Lunar, Dennis *ConAu X*
Lund, A Morten 1926- *ConAu 13R*
Lund, Alan *CreCan 2*
Lund, Blanche Harris *CreCan 1*
Lund, Doris Herold 1919- *ConAu 17R, SmATA 12*
Lund, Gerald N 1939- *ConAu 33R, WrDr 84*
Lund, Gilda Edith 1909- *ConAu 5R*
Lund, Herb 1926- *ConAu 45*
Lund, Jorgen-Richard 1923- *IntAu&W 82*
Lund, Philip R 1938- *ConAu 57*
Lund, Robert Perry 1915- *ConAu 1R*
Lund, Roslyn Rosen *DrAP&F 83*
Lund, Thomas A 1922- *ConAu 33R, WrDr 84*
Lundahl, Gene 1933- *ConAu 21R*
Lundberg, Donald E 1916- *ConAu 33R, WrDr 84*
Lundberg, Erik F 1907- *ConAu 25R*
Lundberg, Ferdinand 1905- *ConAu P-1*
Lundberg, Margaret 1919- *ConAu 61*
Lundberg, Ulla-Lena 1947- *IntAu&W 82*
Lundborg, Louis B 1906- *ConAu 81*
Lunde, David E *DrAP&F 83*
Lunde, Donald T 1937- *ConAu 101*
Lundeberg, Philip 1923- *WrDr 84*
Lundell, Ulf Gerhard 1949- *IntAu&W 82*
Lunden, Walter A 1899- *ConAu 21R*
Lundgren, Paul Arthur 1925-1981 *ConAu 103*
Lundgren, William R 1918- *ConAu 13R*
Lundholm, Anja 1928- *IntAu&W 82*
Lundin, Judith *DrAP&F 83*
Lundin, Robert W 1920- *ConAu 1R*
Lundkvist, Artur 1906- *ClDMEL 80, IntAu&W 82, WorAu*
Lundmark, Helge Birger 1933- *IntAu&W 82*
Lundquist, James 1941- *ConAu 65*
Lundsgaarde, Henry P 1938- *ConAu 73*
Lundsteen, Sara W *ConAu 109*
Lundwall, Sam J 1941- *ConAu 1NR, -49*
Lundy, Robert F 1937- *ConAu 5R*
Lunenfeld, Marvin C 1934- *ConAu 61*
Lunin, Lois F *ConAu 102*
Lunn, Sir Arnold 1888-1974 *ConAu 49, -81*
Lunn, Eugene 1941- *ConAu 45*
Lunn, Hugh Kingsmill 1889-1949 *LongCTC, TwCA, TwCA SUP*
Lunn, Janet 1928- *ConAu 33R, SmATA 4*
Lunn, Jean *DrAP&F 83*
Lunn, John Edward 1930- *ConAu 41R*
Lunsford, M Rosser *DrAP&F 83*
Lunt, Elizabeth Graves 1922- *ConAu 33R*
Lunt, George 1943- *WrDr 84*
Lunt, Horace Gray 1918- *ConAu 107*
Lunt, James Doiran 1917- *ConAu 1R, -3NR, IntAu&W 82, WrDr 84*
Lunt, Lois *ConAu X*
Lunt, Richard D 1933- *ConAu 13R*

Lyon, E Wilson 1904- *ConAu 97*
Lyon, Elinor 1921- *ConAu 25R, SmATA 6, WrDr 84*
Lyon, Eugene 1929- *ConAu 106*
Lyon, George Ella *DrAP&F 83*
Lyon, Harold C, Jr. 1935- *ConAu 41R*
Lyon, James K 1934- *ConAu 1NR, -45*
Lyon, Jessica *ConAu X*
Lyon, John 1932- *ConAu 41R*
Lyon, Katherine *ConAu X*
Lyon, Lilian Bowes *ModBrL*
Lyon, Lyman R *ConAu X, SmATA X*
Lyon, Mabelle A 1904- *IntWWP 82*
Lyon, Melvin 1927- *ConAu 33R*
Lyon, Peter 1915- *ConAu 5R, -5NR*
Lyon, Peyton V 1921- *ConAu 3NR, -9R*
Lyon, Quinter M 1898- *ConAu P-1*
Lyon, Thomas Edgar, Jr. 1939- *ConAu 37R*
Lyon, William Henry 1926- *ConAu 13R*
Lyon Herald, Blanch *IntAu&W 82X*
Lyons, Arthur 1946- *ConAu 29R*
Lyons, Augusta Wallace *ConAu 85*
Lyons, Barbara 1912- *ConAu 93*
Lyons, Catherine 1944- *ConAu 85*
Lyons, Daniel 1920- *ConAu 41R*
Lyons, David 1935- *ConAu 33R, IntAu&W 82, WrDr 84*
Lyons, Delphine C *WrDr 84*
Lyons, Dorothy Marawee 1907- *ConAu 1R, IntAu&W 82, SmATA 3, WrDr 84*
Lyons, Elena *ConAu X, WrDr 84*
Lyons, Enid 1897- *ConAu 21R*
Lyons, Enid 1897-1981 *ConAu 108*
Lyons, Eugene 1898- *ConAu 9R, TwCA, TwCA SUP*
Lyons, F S L 1923- *ConAu 29R*
Lyons, F S L 1923-1983 *ConAu 110*
Lyons, Francis 1923- *WrDr 84*
Lyons, Grant *DrAP&F 83*
Lyons, Grant 1941- *ConAu 41R, SmATA 30[port]*
Lyons, Ivan 1934- *ConAu 101*
Lyons, J B 1922- *ConAu 97*
Lyons, Sister Jeanne Marie 1904- *ConAu 13R, ConAu P-1*
Lyons, Jerry L 1939- *IntAu&W 82*
Lyons, John O 1927- *ConAu 1R*
Lyons, John T 1926- *ConAu 29R*
Lyons, Joseph 1918- *ConAu 13R*
Lyons, Len 1942- *ConAu 93*
Lyons, Leonard 1906-1976 *ConAu 69*
Lyons, Louis M 1897-1982 *ConAu 106*
Lyons, Mark Joseph 1910- *ConAu 5R*
Lyons, Nan 1935- *ConAu 101*
Lyons, Nick 1932- *ConAu 4NR, -53, IntAu&W 82, WrDr 84*
Lyons, Richard *DrAP&F 83*
Lyons, Richard D 1928- *ConAu 69*
Lyons, Richard E 1920- *ConAu 45*
Lyons, Thomas Tolman 1934- *ConAu 3NR, -9R, WrDr 84*
Lyons, Timothy J 1944- *ConAu 73*
Lyons, W T 1919- *IntAu&W 82, LivgBAA, WrDr 84*
Lyre, Pinchbeck *ConAu X*
Lys, Daniel 1924- *ConAu 21R*
Lysaght, Averil M *ConAu 85*
Lysaught, Jerome P 1930- *WrDr 84*
Lysaught, Jerome Paul 1930- *ConAu 5R, -6NR*
Lysenko, T D 1898-1976 *ConAu 69*
Lysholm, Gustaf Adolf 1909- *IntAu&W 82*
Lysohorsky, Ondra 1905- *IntWWP 82X*
Lysons, Dennis 1944- *IntWWP 82*
Lysons, Kenneth 1923- *ConAu 85*
Lystad, Mary 1928- *ConAu 10NR, -65, SmATA 11*
Lystad, Robert A 1920- *ConAu 13R*
Lyte, Charles 1935- *ConAu 104*
Lyte, Richard *ConAu X*
Lytle, Andrew *DrAP&F 83*
Lytle, Andrew 1902- *WrDr 84*
Lytle, Andrew Nelson 1902- *ConAu 9R, ConLC 22[port], ConNov 82, DcLB 6[port], IntAu&W 82, WorAu*
Lytle, Clifford M 1932- *ConAu 93*
Lytle, Ruby 1917- *ConAu P-1*
Lyttkens, Alice 1897- *IntAu&W 82*
Lyttle, Charles Harold 1885?-1980 *ConAu 109, -97*
Lyttle, Gerald Roland 1908- *ConAu P-1*
Lyttle, Jean *ConAu X*
Lyttle, Richard B 1927- *ConAu 33R,*

SmATA 23[port]
Lyttleton, Raymond Arthur *WrDr 84*
Lytton, David 1927- *ConNov 82, TwCWr, WrDr 84*
Lytton, Baron Edward G E Lytton Bulwer- 1803-1873 *SmATA 23[port]*
Lytton, Hugh 1921- *ConAu 45*
Lytton, Noel Anthony Scawen, Earl Of 1900- *ConAu P-1*
Lytton-Sells, Iris 1903- *ConAu 29R*
Lytton Strachey *TwCA, TwCA SUP*
Lyudvinskaya, Tatyana 1885?-1976 *ConAu 65*

M

M, E *DrAP&F 83*
M *ConAu X*
M G *ConAu X*
M H *IntWWP 82X*
M T *IntWWP 82X*
Ma, John Ta-Jen 1920- *ConAu 49*
Ma, Nancy Chih 1919- *ConAu 10NR, –65*
Ma, Yinchu 1882-1982 *ConAu 110*
Maar, Leonard 1927- *ConAu 106, SmATA 30*
Maartens, Maarten 1858-1915 *LongCTC, TwCA, TwCA SUP*
Maas, Audrey Gellen 1936-1975 *ConAu 57, ConAu P-2*
Maas, Henry 1929- *ConAu 25R*
Maas, Jeremy Stephen 1928- *ConAu 29R, IntAu&W 82*
Maas, Peter 1929- *ConAu 93, WrDr 84*
Maas, Selve *ConAu 69, SmATA 14*
Maas, Virginia H 1913- *ConAu 105*
Maas, Willard 1911-1971 *ConAu 29R, ConAu P-1*
Maasarani, Aly Mohamed 1927- *ConAu 49*
Maass, Arthur 1917- *ConAu 105*
Maass, Edgar 1896- *TwCA SUP*
Maass, Joachim 1901-1972 *ConAu 37R, WorAu*
Maass, John 1918- *ConAu 108*
Maattanen, Sakari 1938- *IntAu&W 82*
Mabbett, I W 1939- *ConAu 29R*
Mabbett, Ian William 1939- *WrDr 84*
Mabbott, John David 1898- *ConAu 13R, IntAu&W 82, WrDr 84*
Mabbott, Thomas Ollive 1898-1968 *TwCA, TwCA SUP*
Mabee, Carleton 1914- *ConAu 1R, TwCA SUP, WrDr 84*
Mabee, Carlton 1914- *IntAu&W 82*
Mabee, Fred Carleton 1914- *TwCA SUP*
Maberly, Allan 1922-1977 *ConAu 103*
Maberly, Norman C 1926- *ConAu 33R*
Mabey, Richard 1941- *ConAu 9NR*
Mabey, Richard Thomas 1941- *ConAu 21R, IntAu&W 82, WrDr 84*
Mabie, Hamilton Wright 1845?-1916 *TwCA, TwCA SUP*
Mabley, Edward H 1906- *ConAu 29R, NatPD 81[port]*
Mabley, Jack 1915- *ConAu 105*
Mabogunje, Akin L 1931- *ConAu 77*
Mabon, John Scott 1910?-1980 *ConAu 104*
Mabry, Bevars Dupre 1928- *ConAu 45*
Mabry, Donald J 1941- *ConAu 49*
Mac *ConAu X, IntAu&W 82X, SmATA X*
Mac, Carm *ConAu X*
MacAdam, Eve *ConAu X*
Macadam, Ian *IntAu&W 82X*
Macadams, Lewis *DrAP&F 83*
MacAdams, Lewis 1944- *WrDr 84*
MacAdams, Lewis Perry, Jr. 1944- *ConAu 97, ConP 80*
Macadams, Tobi *ConAu X*
MacAedhagan, Eamon *ConAu X*
MacA'Ghobhainn, Iain *WorAu 1970*
MacAgy, Douglas G 1913-1973 *ConAu 102*
Macainsh, Noel Leslie 1926- *ConAu 103,*

IntAu&W 82, IntWWP 82, WrDr 84
MacAlpin, Rory *ConAu X*
MacAlpine, Margaret Hesketh 1907- *ConAu P-1*
Macan, T T 1910- *ConAu 107*
Macan, Thomas Townley 1910- *WrDr 84*
Macao, Marshall *ConAu X*
MacAodhagain, Eamon *ConAu X*
MacApp, C C 1917?-1971 *ConSFA*
Macardle, Dorothy 1899-1958 *TwCRGW*
Macarov, David 1918- *ConAu 29R*
MacArthur, Charles 1895-1956 *ConAu 108, DcLB 7[port], –25[port], ModWD*
MacArthur, D Wilson 1903- *ConAu 5NR*
MacArthur, David Wilson 1903- *ConAu 9R*
MacArthur, John F, Jr. 1939- *ConAu 81*
MacArthur, Robert H 1930-1972 *ConAu 37R*
MacArthur-Onslow, Annette 1933- *ConAu 102, SmATA 26*
Macartney, Aylmer 1895- *ConAu 17R*
Macartney, Frederick Thomas Bennett 1887- *IntAu&W 82, TwCWr*
Macaulay, David A 1946- *ChlLR 3, ConAu 5NR, –53, SmATA 27, WrDr 84*
Macaulay, John Ure 1925- *ConAu 107, WrDr 84*
Macaulay, Neill 1935- *ConAu 21R*
Macaulay, Rose 1881-1958 *CnMWL, ConAu 104, LongCTC, ModBrL, TwCA, TwCA SUP, TwCLC 7[port], TwCWr*
Macaulay, Stewart 1931- *ConAu 77*
Macauley, Robie *DrAP&F 83*
Macauley, Robie 1919- *WrDr 84*
Macauley, Robie Mayhew 1919- *ConAu 1R, –3NR, ConNov 82, DcLEL 1940, WorAu*
MacAusland, Earle R 1893-1980 *ConAu 101*
MacAvoy, Paul W 1934- *ConAu 105*
MacBean, Dilla Whittemore 1895- *ConAu 5R*
Macbeath, Innis 1928- *IntAu&W 82, WrDr 84*
Macbeth, George *DrAP&F 83*
MacBeth, George 1932- *ConAu 25R, ConLC 2, –5, –9, ConP 80, DcLEL 1940, IntAu&W 82, ModBrL SUP, SmATA 4, WorAu, WrDr 84*
Macbeth, Norman 1910- *ConAu P-2*
MacBride, Robert O 1926- *ConAu 17R*
MacBride, Roger Lea 1929- *ConAu 81*
Maccabeus, Iain *IntWWP 82X*
MacCaffrey, Isabel Gamble 1924-1978 *ConAu 77, –81*
MacCaig, Norman 1910- *ConAu 3NR, –9R, ConP 80, DcLEL 1940, IntAu&W 82, IntWWP 82, ModBrL, ModBrL SUP, WorAu, WrDr 84*
MacCall, Libby *ConAu X*
MacCallum Scott, John H 1911- *ConAu 25R*
MacCampbell, James C 1916- *ConAu 9R*
MacCann, Donnarae 1931- *ConAu 1NR, –45*
MacCann, Richard Dyer 1920- *ConAu 5NR, –9R*
MacCarthy, Aidan 1913- *WrDr 84*
MacCarthy, Sir Desmond 1878?-1952 *LongCTC, ModBrL, TwCA, TwCA SUP*
MacCarthy, Fiona 1940- *ConAu 105*
MacCarthy, J A 1913- *ConAu 107*
MacCauley, Rose Agnes 1911- *WrDr 84*

MacCauley, Sister Rose Agnes 1911- *ConAu 37R*
MacCecht *IntAu&W 82X*
Macciocchi, Maria Antoinetta 1922- *ConAu 73*
MacClintock, Dorcas 1932- *ConAu 6NR, –57, SmATA 8*
MacCloskey, Monro 1902- *ConAu 5NR, –9R*
Maccoby, Michael 1933- *ConAu 33R, WrDr 84*
MacCollam, Joel A 1946- *ConAu 105*
MacCombie, John 1932- *ConAu 37R*
MacCorkle, Stuart A 1903- *ConAu 17R, IntAu&W 82, WrDr 84*
MacCormac, Earl Ronald 1935- *ConAu 85*
MacCormack, Sabine G 1941- *ConAu 106*
MacCormick, Austin H 1893-1979 *ConAu 93*
MacCorquodale, Patricia 1950- *ConAu 101*
MacCracken, Henry Noble 1880-1970 *ConAu 29R, ConAu P-1*
MacCracken, Mary 1926- *ConAu 49, WrDr 84*
MacCraig, Hugh *ConAu X*
MacCreigh, James *WorAu*
Maccullagh, Richard John 1913- *WrDr 84*
MacCurdy, Raymond R 1916- *ConAu 41R*
Macdermott, Mercia *WrDr 84*
Macdermott, Mercia 1927- *ConAu 106, IntAu&W 82*
MacDiarmid, Hugh 1892-1978 *CnMWL, ConAu X, ConLC 2, –4, –11, –19, ModBrL, ModBrL SUP, RGFMBP, WhoTwCL*
MacDonagh, Donagh 1912-1968 *ConAu 93, LongCTC, TwCWr*
MacDonagh, Thomas 1878-1916 *LongCTC, TwCA, TwCWr*
MacDonald, Aeneas *ConAu X*
MacDonald, Anson *ConAu X, SmATA X*
MacDonald, Betty Heskett 1908-1958 *LongCTC, TwCA SUP*
Macdonald, Blackie *ConAu X,   SmATA X*
Macdonald, Brian 1928- *CreCan 2*
MacDonald, Charles B 1922- *ConAu 6NR, –9R*
Macdonald, Coll 1924- *ConAu 17R*
MacDonald, Craig 1949- *ConAu 9NR, –57*
Macdonald, Cynthia *DrAP&F 83*
Macdonald, Cynthia 1928- *ConAu 4NR, –49, ConLC 13, –19*
Macdonald, David W 1951- *ConAu 106*
MacDonald, Dwight 1906- *ConAu 29R, DcLEL 1940, ModAL, SmATA 29[port], WhoTwCL, WorAu*
Macdonald, Dwight 1906- *WrDr 84*
Macdonald, Dwight 1906-1982 *ConAu 108, SmATA 33N*
MacDonald, Edwin A 1907- *ConAu 41R*
Macdonald, Eleanor 1910- *ConAu P-1*
Macdonald, Elisabeth 1926- *ConAu 65*
MacDonald, George 1824-1905 *ConAu 106, LongCTC, SmATA 33[port], TwCLC 9[port]*
MacDonald, Golden *ConAu X, TwCCW 83*
Macdonald, Gordon A 1911- *ConAu 65*
Macdonald, Grant Kenneth 1909- *CreCan 1*
MacDonald, H Malcolm 1914- *ConAu 17R*
Macdonald, Ian David 1932- *WrDr 84*
Macdonald, James Alexander Stirling 1921- *CreCan 1*

MacDonald, James Edward Hervey 1873-1932
  CreCan 2
Macdonald, James Williamson Galloway
  1897-1960 *CreCan 2*
MacDonald, Jock 1897-1960 *CreCan 2*
MacDonald, John *ConAu X*
Macdonald, John *ConAu X*
MacDonald, John 1918- *ConAu 1NR, -49*
MacDonald, John D 1916- *ASpks, ConAu 1R,
  -1NR, ConLC 3, -27[port], DcLB 8[port],
  IntAu&W 82, TwCCr&M 80, TwCSFW,
  WorAu, WrDr 84*
Macdonald, John M 1920- *ConAu 1R, -2NR,
  WrDr 84*
Macdonald, John Ross *ConAu X,
  TwCCr&M 80*
Macdonald, Julie 1926- *ConAu 17R*
Macdonald, Kenneth 1905- *ConAu 73*
MacDonald, Lucy Maud Montgomery 1874-1942
  CreCan 2
Macdonald, Malcolm *WrDr 84*
MacDonald, Malcolm 1901- *WrDr 84*
Macdonald, Malcolm 1932- *IntAu&W 82X*
Macdonald, Malcolm John 1901-1981 *ConAu 9R,
  -102, IntAu&W 82*
Macdonald, Malcolm John Ross 1932- *ConAu X*
MacDonald, Malcolm M 1935- *ConAu 41R*
MacDonald, Manly Edward 1889- *CreCan 2*
MacDonald, Marcia *TwCRGW*
MacDonald, Margaret Read 1940- *ConAu 110*
MacDonald, Mary *ConAu X, IntAu&W 82X*
Macdonald, Nancy May 1921- *DcLEL 1940*
MacDonald, Neil 1936- *ConAu 89*
Macdonnell, Nina Hansell *ConAu X*
MacDonald, Philip 1890?- *LongCTC, TwCA,
  TwCA SUP*
MacDonald, Philip 1896?- *ConAu 81*
MacDonald, Philip 1899- *TwCCr&M 80*
Macdonald, R Ross 1923?-1983 *ConAu 110*
Macdonald, Robert M 1923- *ConAu 9R*
Macdonald, Robert S 1925- *ConAu 13R*
Macdonald, Robert William 1922- *ConAu 17R,
  WrDr 84*
Macdonald, Ronald St. John 1928- *ConAu 103*
Macdonald, Ross *ConAu X, DrAP&F 83,
  WrDr 84*
Macdonald, Ross 1915- *ASpks,
  ConLC 1, -2, -3, -14, ConNov 82, ModAL,
  ModAL SUP, TwCCr&M 80, WorAu*
MacDonald, Sandy 1949- *ConAu 103*
Macdonald, Shelagh 1937- *ConAu 97,
  SmATA 25[port], WrDr 84*
Macdonald, Simon Gavin George 1923-
  ConAu 53, WrDr 84
MacDonald, Susan *DrAP&F 83*
MacDonald, Thoreau 1901- *CreCan 1*
MacDonald, William Colt 1891- *TwCWW*
MacDonald, William L 1921- *ConAu 21R,
  WrDr 84*
MacDonald, Wilson 1880-1967 *CreCan 1*
MacDonald, Zillah Katherine 1885- *ConAu P-1,
  SmATA 11*
MacDonald Douglas, Ronald Angus
  IntAu&W 82
MacDonald-Miller, Mary 1940- *IntAu&W 82*
MacDonell, Archibald Gordon 1895-1941
  LongCTC, TwCA, TwCA SUP, TwCWr
MacDonnell, James Edmond 1917- *ConAu 5R*
Macdonnell, James Edmund 1917- *ConAu 8NR*
MacDonnell, Kevin 1919- *ConAu 45*
MacDouall, Robertson *ConAu X*
Macdouall, Robertson *WrDr 84*
MacDougall, A Kent 1931- *ConAu 45*
Macdougall, Curtis Daniel 1903- *ConAu 53*
MacDougall, Donald 1912- *ConAu 106*
MacDougall, Fiona *ConAu X*
MacDougall, Malcolm D 1928- *ConAu 110*
MacDougall, Mary Katherine *ConAu 29R*
Macdougall, Mary Katherine *WrDr 84*
MacDougall, Roger 1910- *ConDr 82, ModBrL,
  WrDr 84*
MacDougall, Ruth Doan *DrAP&F 83*
MacDougall, Ruth Doan 1939- *ConAu 8NR,
  -17R*
MacDowell, Douglas Maurice 1931- *ConAu 5R,
  -6NR, WrDr 84*
Mace, Carroll Edward 1926- *ConAu 41R*
Mace, Cecil Alec 1894- *ConAu P-1*
Mace, David 1907- *WrDr 84*
Mace, David Robert 1907- *ConAu 7NR, -57*
Mace, Don 1899?-1983 *ConAu 109*
Mace, Elisabeth 1933- *ConAu 77,*

SmATA 27[port], *WrDr 84*
Mace, Myles L 1911- *ConAu 110*
Macedonski, Alexandru 1854-1920 *CIDMEL 80*
MacEoin, Gary 1909- *ConAu 1R, -2NR,
  WrDr 84*
Macer-Story, E 1945- *ConAu 107,
  NatPD 81[port]*
Macesich, George 1927- *ConAu 13R, WrDr 84*
Macewan, Gwendolyn Margaret 1941-
  DcLEL 1940
MacEwan, J W G 1902- *WrDr 84*
MacEwan, J W Grant 1902- *ConAu 41R*
MacEwan, Paul W 1943- *ConAu 7NR, -61*
MacEwen, Gwendolyn 1941- *ConAu 7NR, -9R,
  ConDr 82B, ConLC 13, ConP 80,
  CreCan 1, ModCmwL, WrDr 84*
MacEwen, Malcolm 1911- *ConAu 110*
Macey, John 1906- *WrDr 84*
Macey, Samuel L 1922- *ConAu 102*
Macfadden, Bernarr 1868-1955 *DcLB 25[port]*
Macfadyen, Amyan 1920- *IntAu&W 82,
  WrDr 84*
Macfadyen, Kenneth Alexander 1908- *WrDr 84*
MacFall, Haldane 1860-1928 *LongCTC, TwCA*
MacFall, Russell P 1903-1983 *ConAu 110*
MacFall, Russell Patterson 1903- *ConAu P-1*
Macfarlan, Allan A *ConAu 107*
MacFarlane, Iris 1922- *ConAu 89, SmATA 11*
MacFarlane, Kenneth *ConAu X*
Macfarlane, Leslie John 1924- *ConAu 21R,
  IntAu&W 82, WrDr 84*
MacFarlane, Louise 1917?-1979 *ConAu 89*
MacFarlane, Stephen *ConAu X*
MacFarquhar, Roderick 1930- *ConAu 21R*
MacFee, Maxwell *ConAu X*
MacGaffey, Wyatt 1932- *ConAu 73*
MacGaig, Norman 1910- *TwCWr*
MacGibbon, Jean 1913- *ConAu 97, TwCCW 83,
  WrDr 84*
MacGill, Mrs. Patrick *TwCRGW*
MacGillivray, John H 1899- *ConAu P-2*
MacGorman, J W 1920- *ConAu 102*
Macgowan, Kenneth 1888-1963 *ConAu 93*
MacGrath, Harold 1871?-1932 *TwCA*
MacGregor, Alasdair Alpin 1899-1970
  ConAu 29R, ConAu P-1
MacGregor, Bruce 1945- *ConAu 77*
MacGregor, David Roy 1925- *ConAu 93,
  IntAu&W 82*
MacGregor, Ellen 1906-1954 *SmATA 27,
  TwCCW 83*
Macgregor, Frances Cooke *ConAu 1R, -1NR*
MacGregor, Franklyn *NatPD 81[port]*
MacGregor, Geddes 1909- *ConAu 1R, -2NR,
  IntAu&W 82, WrDr 84*
Macgregor, James 1925- *ConAu 5NR, -13R*
MacGregor, James G 1905- *ConAu 10NR*
MacGregor, James Grierson 1905- *ConAu 25R,
  WrDr 84*
Macgregor, James Murdoch 1925- *IntAu&W 82,
  WrDr 84*
MacGregor, Malcolm D 1945- *ConAu 102*
MacGregor, Mary Esther 1876-1961 *CreCan 1*
MacGregor, Richard *ConSFA*
MacGregor, Robert Mercer 1911-1974
  ConAu 104
MacGregor-Hastie, Roy *WrDr 84*
MacGregor-Hastie, Roy 1929- *ConAu 1R, -2NR,
  SmATA 3*
Macgregor-Morris, Pamela 1925- *ConAu 29R*
MacGuigan, Mark R 1931- *ConAu 21R,
  WrDr 84*
Mach, Wilhelm 1917-1965 *CIDMEL 80*
Machado, Antonio 1875-1939 *CnMWL,
  ConAu 104, ModRL, TwCLC 3, TwCWr,
  WhoTwCL, WorAu*
Machado, Manuel Anthony, Jr. 1939-
  ConAu 29R
Machado DeAssis 1839-1908 *TwCLC 10[port]*
Machado DeAssis, Joaquim Maria 1839-1908
  ConAu 107, ModLAL, WhoTwCL
Machado Y Ruiz, Antonio 1875-1939
  CIDMEL 80
Machado Y Ruiz, Manuel 1874-1947 *CIDMEL 80*
Machan, Tibor R 1939- *ConAu 1NR, -45*
Machar, Josef Svatopluk 1864-1942 *CIDMEL 80,
  ModSL 2*
MacHardy, Charles 1926- *ConAu 104*
Macharg, William Briggs 1872-1951
  TwCCr&M 80
Machen, Arthur 1863-1947 *ConAu X, LongCTC,
  ModBrL, TwCA, TwCA SUP,*

TwCLC 4[port], *TwCWr*
Machetanz, Frederick 1908- *SmATA 34[port]*
Machetanz, Sara Burleson 1918- *ConAu 1R*
Machiavelli *ConAu X*
Machin, George Ian Thom 1937- *ConAu 13R,
  IntAu&W 82, WrDr 84*
Machin Goodall, Daphne Edith 1915- *ConAu 5R,
  -7NR, IntAu&W 82*
Machlin, Milton Robert 1924- *ConAu 1R, -2NR*
Machlis, Joseph 1906- *ConAu 1R, -2NR*
Machlowitz, Marilyn M 1952- *ConAu 101*
Machlup, Fritz 1902- *ConAu 1R, -6NR,
  WrDr 84*
Machlup, Fritz 1902-1983 *ConAu 109*
Machol, Libby 1916- *ConAu 21R*
Machol, Robert E 1917- *ConAu 37R*
Macholtz, James Donald 1926- *ConAu 53*
Machon, V A 1920- *IntAu&W 82*
MacHorton, Ian *ConAu X*
Machorton, Ian Duncan 1923- *ConAu 8NR,
  -17R, IntAu&W 82*
Machotka, Otakar 1899-1970 *ConAu 29R,
  ConAu P-1*
Macht, Joel 1938- *ConAu 57*
Macia, Rafael 1946- *ConAu 97*
Maciejewski, Jaroslaw 1924- *IntAu&W 82*
Maciejewski, Marian 1937- *IntAu&W 82*
Maciel, Judi 1942- *ConAu 33R*
MacInnes, Colin 1914-1976 *ConAu 65, -69,
  ConLC 4, -23[port], DcLB 14[port],
  DcLEL 1940, LongCTC, ModBrL,
  ModBrL SUP, WorAu*
MacInnes, Helen 1907- *ASpks, ConAu 1R,
  -1NR, ConLC 27[port], IntAu&W 82,
  SmATA 22[port], TwCA SUP,
  TwCCr&M 80, WrDr 84*
MacInnes, Mairi *DrAP&F 83*
MacInnis, Donald E 1920- *ConAu 41R*
MacIntosh, J J 1934- *ConAu 37R*
Macintosh, Joan 1924- *ConAu 107,
  IntAu&W 82X, WrDr 84*
MacIntosh, Phoebe-Joan 1924- *IntAu&W 82*
Macintyre, Alasdair 1929- *WrDr 84*
MacIntyre, Carlyle Ferren 1890-1967 *TwCA,
  TwCA SUP*
Macintyre, Donald 1904- *ConAu 5R, WrDr 84*
MacIntyre, Elisabeth 1916- *ConAu 5NR, -9R,
  SmATA 17, TwCCW 83, WrDr 84*
MacIre, Esor B *ConAu X*
MacIsaac, David 1935- *ConAu 77*
MacIsaac, Sharon *ConAu 57*
Maciuszko, Jerzy J 1913- *ConAu 25R*
MacIver, Pegge Farmer *WrDr 84*
MacIver, Robert Morrison 1882-1970 *ConAu 25R,
  ConAu P-1, TwCA SUP*
Mack *IntAu&W 82X*
Mack, C K 1941- *NatPD 81[port]*
Mack, Donna *DrAP&F 83*
Mack, Edward C 1905?-1973 *ConAu 45*
Mack, Evalina *ConAu X*
Mack, Gerstle 1894-1983 *ConAu 109*
Mack, J A 1906- *ConAu 65*
Mack, James D 1916- *ConAu 21R*
Mack, Jerry *ConAu X*
Mack, John E 1929- *ConAu 106*
Mack, Karin E 1946- *ConAu 97*
Mack, Kirby *ConAu X*
Mack, Marjorie *ConAu X*
Mack, Mary Peter 1927-1973 *ConAu 1R, -103*
Mack, Max Noble 1916- *ConAu 61*
Mack, Maynard 1909- *ConAu 9R, WrDr 84*
Mack, Raymond 1927- *ConAu 13R*
Mack, Stan *ConAu 85, SmATA 17*
Mack, Walter Staunton 1895- *ConAu 109*
Mack Smith, Denis 1920- *ConAu 21R,
  WrDr 84*
Mackail, Denis George 1892-1971 *LongCTC,
  TwCA, TwCA SUP*
Mackail, John William 1859-1945 *LongCTC,
  ModBrL, TwCA, TwCA SUP*
Mackal, Roy P 1925- *ConAu 73*
Mackarness, Richard 1916- *ConAu 103*
MacKay, Alfred F 1938- *ConAu 104*
MacKay, Alistair McColl 1931- *ConAu 81*
Mackay, Barbara Edith 1944- *ConAmTC,
  ConAu 77*
Mackay, Claire 1930- *ConAu 105*
Mackay, Constance D'Arcy d1966 *ConAu 102,
  TwCCW 83*
MacKay, D I 1937- *ConAu 29R*
MacKay, Donald 1937- *WrDr 84*
MacKay, Donald M 1922- *ConAu 29R*

Mackay, Ian Keith 1909- *IntAu&W 82,*
WrDr 84
Mackay, James Alexander 1936- *ConAu 7NR,*
-53, IntAu&W 82, WrDr 84
Mackay, Jean Grace 1916- *WrDr 84*
Mackay, John Alexander 1889-1983 *ConAu 110*
MacKay, Joy 1918- *ConAu 65*
Mackay, Louis Alexander 1901- *CreCan 2*
Mackay, Malcolm George 1919- *ConAu 108*
Mackay, Mary 1855-1924 *LongCTC*
Mackay, Mercedes 1906- *ConAu P-1*
MacKay, Robert A 1894- *ConAu 9R*
Mackay, Ruddock Finlay 1922- *ConAu 102,*
IntAu&W 82, WrDr 84
Mackay, Shena 1944- *ConAu 104,*
DcLEL 1940
MacKay, William 1943?- *ConAu 110*
MacKaye, Benton 1879-1975 *ConAu 61*
MacKaye, Milton 1901-1979 *ConAu 85, -93*
MacKaye, Percy 1875-1956 *SmATA 32[port]*
MacKaye, Percy Wallace 1875-1956 *CnMD,*
ConAmA, ModAL, ModWD, TwCA,
TwCA SUP
MacKaye, William Ross 1934- *ConAu 109*
MacKeever, Maggie *ConAu X*
MacKeith, Ronald Charles 1908-1977 *ConAu 77*
MacKellar, William 1914- *ConAu 33R,*
SmATA 4
Mackelworth, R W 1930- *ConAu 29R, ConSFA,*
TwCSFW, WrDr 84
Macken, Walter 1915-1967 *CnMD, ConAu 25R,*
ConAu P-1, DcLB 13[port], TwCCW 83,
WorAu
Mackendrick, John 1946- *ConAu 81*
MacKendrick, Paul Lachlan 1914- *ConAu 1R,*
-1NR
Mackensen, Heinz Friedrich 1921- *ConAu 107*
MacKenzie, Andrew Carr 1911- *ConAu 49*
Mackenzie, Andrew Carr 1911- *WrDr 84*
MacKenzie, Christine Butchart 1917-
ConAu 13R
Mackenzie, Sir Compton 1883-1972 *ConAu 37R,*
ConAu P-2, ConLC 18, LongCTC,
ModBrL, TwCA, TwCA SUP, TwCWr,
WhoTwCL
MacKenzie, David 1927- *ConAu 21R, WrDr 84*
MacKenzie, Donald 1918- *ConAu 25R,*
IntAu&W 82, TwCCr&M 80, WrDr 84
Mackenzie, Faith Compton d1960 *LongCTC*
MacKenzie, Fred 1905- *ConAu P-2*
MacKenzie, Garry 1921- *SmATA 31*
MacKenzie, Ginny *DrAP&F 83*
MacKenzie, Gisele 1927- *CreCan 2*
MacKenzie, Jean 1928- *ConAu 103, -93,*
WrDr 84
MacKenzie, Jean West *DrAP&F 83*
MacKenzie, John P 1930- *ConAu 65*
Mackenzie, Kathleen 1907- *WrDr 84*
Mackenzie, Kathleen Guy 1907- *ConAu 5R*
Mackenzie, Kenneth 1928- *TwCWr*
Mackenzie, Kenneth Donald 1937- *ConAu 37R*
Mackenzie, Kenneth Ivo 1913-1955 *TwCWr*
Mackenzie, Locke L 1900?-1977 *ConAu 69*
MacKenzie, Louise 1920- *ConAu 29R*
Mackenzie, Manfred 1934- *ConAu 65*
MacKenzie, Norman H 1915- *ConAu 21R,*
IntAu&W 82
Mackenzie, Norman H 1915- *WrDr 84*
MacKenzie, Ossian 1907- *ConAu 25R*
MacKenzie, R A F 1911- *ConAu 5R*
Mackenzie, R Alec *ConAu X*
MacKenzie, Rachel 1909-1980 *ConAu 102, -97*
Mackenzie, Richard Alexander 1923- *ConAu 109*
Mackenzie, Seaforth 1913-1955 *WhoTwCL*
Mackenzie, W J M 1909- *ConAu 104*
MacKenzie, Willard *ConAu X*
Mackenzie-Grieve, Averil Salmond 1903-
ConAu 9R
Mackerras, Colin Patrick 1939- *ConAu 85,*
IntAu&W 82, WrDr 84
Mackerras, Malcolm Hugh 1939- *IntAu&W 82*
Mackesy, Piers Gerald *WrDr 84*
Mackesy, Piers Gerald 1924- *ConAu 3NR, -9R,*
IntAu&W 82
MacKethan, Lucinda Hardwick 1945-
ConAu 102
Mackey, Ernan *ConAu X*
Mackey, Helen T 1918- *ConAu 5R*
Mackey, J P 1934- *ConAu 9NR, -65*
Mackey, Louis H 1926- *ConAu 33R*
Mackey, Mary *DrAP&F 83*
Mackey, Mary 1945- *ConAu 77*

Mackey, William Francis 1918- *ConAu 37R*
Mackey, William J, Jr. 1902?-1972 *ConAu 37R*
Mackie, Alastair 1925- *ConAu 17R, ConP 80,*
WrDr 84
Mackie, Albert David 1904- *ConAu P-1,*
WrDr 84
Mackie, J L 1917- *ConAu 7NR, -57*
Mackie, James 1932- *ConAu 41R*
Mackie, Margaret Davidson 1914- *ConAu 102,*
WrDr 84
Mackie, Maron *ConAu X, SmATA X*
Mackie, Philip 1918- *ConAu 103, ConDr 82C,*
IntAu&W 82, WrDr 84
Mackin, Anita *ConAu X*
Mackin, Catherine 1939-1982 *ConAu 108, -109*
Mackin, Cooper R 1933- *ConAu 41R*
Mackin, Dorothy 1917- *ConAu 107*
Mackin, John H 1921- *ConAu 33R*
Mackinlay, Leila 1910- *WrDr 84*
Mackinlay, Leila Antoinette Sterling 1910-
ConAu P-1, IntAu&W 82, TwCRGW
Mackinlock, Duncan *ConAu X, WrDr 84*
Mackinnon, Charles Roy 1924- *ConAu 7NR,*
-9R
Mackinnon, Donald Mackenzie 1913-
DcLEL 1940
MacKinnon, Edward Michael 1928- *ConAu 61*
Mackinnon, Eric Francis Rayne 1937-
IntWWP 82
MacKinnon, Frank 1919- *ConAu 49*
MacKinnon, John 1947- *WrDr 84*
MacKinnon, John Ramsay 1947- *ConAu 103*
MacKinnon, Sheila 1937- *CreCan 2*
MacKinnon, Stephen Robert 1940- *ConAu 107*
Mackintosh, Athole S 1926- *ConAu 5R*
Mackintosh, Elizabeth 1896?-1952 *ConAu 110*
Mackintosh, Elizabeth 1897-1952 *LongCTC,*
TwCA SUP
MacKintosh, Ian 1940- *ConAu 73*
Mackintosh, John 1929-1978 *ConAu 103*
Mackintosh, Malcolm 1921- *ConAu 5R*
Mackle, Jeff *ConAu X*
Mackler, Bernard 1934- *ConAu 21R*
Mackley, George 1900-1983 *ConAu 109*
Mackowski, Richard M 1929- *ConAu 106*
Macksey, Joan 1925- *ConAu 65*
Macksey, K J 1923- *WrDr 84*
Macksey, Kenneth 1923- *ConAu 25R,*
IntAu&W 82
Macksey, Kenneth J 1923- *ConAu 11NR*
Macksey, Major K J *ConAu X*
Macksey, Richard 1930- *ConAu 101*
Mackworth, Cecily *WrDr 84*
Mackworth, Cecily 1911- *ConAu 57,*
IntAu&W 82
Mackworth, Jane F 1917- *ConAu 37R,*
WrDr 84
Macky, Peter W 1937- *ConAu 53*
Macky, Willow 1921- *IntWWP 82*
MacLachlan, James Angell 1891-1967 *ConAu P-2*
Maclachlan, Lewis 1894-1980 *ConAu 5R, -6NR*
Maclagan, Bridget *ConAu X, LongCTC*
Maclagan, Michael 1914- *ConAu 5R,*
IntAu&W 82, WrDr 84
MacLaine, Allan H 1924- *ConAu 13R,*
WrDr 84
Maclaine, Ross *IntAu&W 82X*
MacLaine, Shirley 1934- *ConAu X, WrDr 84*
MacLaren, A Allan 1938- *ConAu 106,*
WrDr 84
Maclaren, Ian 1850-1907 *LongCTC*
Maclaren, James *ConAu X*
Maclaren-Ross, Julian 1913-1964 *LongCTC*
MacLaughlin, Wendy 1931- *NatPD 81[port]*
Maclay, George 1943- *ConAu 45*
Maclean, Alasdair 1926- *ConP 80, WrDr 84*
MacLean, Alistair 1922- *ConAu 57, ConLC 3,*
-13, DcLEL 1940, TwCCr&M 80, WorAu,
WrDr 84
MacLean, Alistair 1923- *SmATA 23[port]*
MacLean, Art *WrDr 84*
Maclean, Arthur *ConAu X, WrDr 84*
Maclean, Catherine MacDonald *TwCA SUP*
Maclean, Charles 1946- *ConAu 109*
Maclean, Donald Duart 1913-1983 *ConAu 109*
Maclean, Enid Alicia Joy 1925- *IntAu&W 82*
Maclean, Fitzroy 1911- *ConAu 29R, -29R,*
IntAu&W 82, WrDr 84
MacLean, Jane 1935- *ConAu 101*
Maclean, Janet Rockwood 1917- *ConAu 33R*
MacLean, Katherine 1925- *ConAu 33R,*
ConSFA, DcLB 8, TwCSFW, WrDr 84

Maclean, Kenneth *DrAP&F 83*
Maclean, Norman 1902- *ConAu 102*
MacLean, Quentin Stuart Morvaren 1896-1962
CreCan 2
MacLean, Ross 1954- *NatPD 81[port]*
Maclean, Una 1925- *ConAu 69*
MacLeish, Andrew 1923- *ConAu 17R*
MacLeish, Archibald 1892-1982 *CnMD,*
CnMWL, ConAmA, ConAu 9R, -106,
ConDr 82, ConLC 3, -8, -14, ConP 80,
CroCD, DcLB Y82A[port], -4, -7[port],
IntAu&W 82, IntWWP 82, LongCTC,
ModAL, ModAL SUP, ModWD, TwCA,
TwCA SUP, TwCWr
MacLeish, Kenneth 1917-1977 *ConAu 73, -81*
MacLeish, Rod 1926- *ConAu 41R*
MacLennan, David Alexander 1903-1978
ConAu 2NR
MacLennan, David Alexander 1908- *ConAu 1R*
MacLennan, Hugh 1907- *ConAu 5R, ConLC 2,*
-14, ConNov 82, CreCan 2, IntAu&W 82,
LongCTC, ModCmwL, TwCA SUP,
TwCWr, WrDr 84
MacLennan, John Hugh 1907- *CreCan 2,*
DcLEL 1940
Macleod, Alison 1920- *ConAu 53, WrDr 84*
MacLeod, Angus 1906- *ConSFA*
MacLeod, Beatrice 1910- *ConAmTC,*
ConAu P-1, SmATA 10
MacLeod, Celeste 1931- *ConAu 105*
MacLeod, Charlotte 1922- *ConAu 21R,*
SmATA 28[port], TwCRGW, WrDr 84
MacLeod, Donald 1914- *ConAu 17R*
MacLeod, Duncan J 1939- *ConAu 61*
MacLeod, Earle Henry 1907- *ConAu P-1*
MacLeod, Ellen Jane *WrDr 84*
MacLeod, Ellen Jane 1916- *ConAu 3NR, -5R,*
SmATA 14
MacLeod, Ellen Jane 1918- *IntAu&W 82*
Macleod, Fiona 1855-1905 *LongCTC*
MacLeod, Jean S 1908- *WrDr 84*
MacLeod, Jean Sutherland 1908- *ConAu 3NR,*
-9R, IntAu&W 82, TwCRGW
Macleod, Jennifer Selfridge 1929- *ConAu 102*
MacLeod, Joseph 1903- *WrDr 84*
MacLeod, Joseph Todd Gordon 1903- *ConAu 65,*
ConP 80, IntAu&W 82
MacLeod, Margaret Kathleen Nichol 1904-1949
CreCan 1
Macleod, Norman *DrAP&F 83*
Macleod, Norman Wicklund 1906- *ConAu 73,*
DcLB 4
MacLeod, Pegi Nicol 1904-1949 *CreCan 1*
MacLeod, Robert *ConAu X, IntAu&W 82X,*
TwCCr&M 80, TwCWW
Macleod, Robert *WrDr 84*
MacLeod, Robert 1906- *WrDr 84*
MacLeod, Robert F 1917- *ConAu 77*
MacLeod, Ruth 1903- *ConAu 93*
MacLiaimmhoir, Micheal *ConAu X*
MacLiammhoir, Micheal *ConAu X*
MacLiammoir, Micheal 1899-1978 *ConAu 3NR,*
-45, -77, ModWD
MacLow, Jackson *DrAP&F 83*
MacLow, Jackson 1922- *ConAu 81, ConDr 82,*
ConP 80, DcLEL 1940, WrDr 84
Maclure, Stuart 1926- *ConAu 61*
MacLysaght, Edward Anthony 1887-
ConAu 1NR, WrDr 84
Macmahon, Arthur W 1890- *ConAu 17R*
MacMahon, Bryan Michael 1909- *ConAu 41R,*
IntAu&W 82, WrDr 84
Macmann, Elaine *ConAu X*
MacManus, James *ConAu X, SmATA X*
MacManus, Seumas 1869-1960 *ConAu 102, -93,*
SmATA 25, TwCA, TwCA SUP
MacManus, Yvonne 1931- *ConAu 11NR*
MacManus, Yvonne Cristina 1931- *ConAu 25R,*
IntAu&W 82
MacMaster, Robert Ellsworth 1919- *ConAu 33R*
Macmaster, Robert Ellsworth 1919- *WrDr 84*
MacMillan, Andrew 1914-1967 *CreCan 2*
Macmillan, Annabelle 1922- *SmATA 2*
Macmillan, C J B 1935- *ConAu 21R*
Macmillan, David Stirling 1925- *WrDr 84*
MacMillan, Donald L 1940- *ConAu 57*
MacMillan, Sir Ernest Campbell 1893- *CreCan 1*
MacMillan, Gail 1944- *ConAu 97*
Macmillan, Harold 1894- *WrDr 84*
MacMillan, John A 1934- *WrDr 84*
MacMillan, Keith 1920- *CreCan 1*
Macmillan, Mona 1908- *ConAu 33R*

Macmillan, Norman 1892-1976 *ConAu 69,*
  ConAu P-1
Macmillan, William Miller 1885-1974
  ConAu 9NR, -53, ConAu P-1
Macmullan, Charles Walden Kirkpatrick
  1889-1973 *ConAu 89, LongCTC*
MacMullen, Ramsay 1928- *ConAu 21R*
Macnab, Francis Auchline 1931- *ConAu 25R*
Macnab, P A 1903- *ConAu 33R, WrDr 84*
Macnab, Roy 1923- *ConAu 65, ConP 80,*
  DcLEL 1940, IntAu&W 82, WrDr 84
Macnair, Dorothy *CreCan 2*
MacNalty, Arthur 1880-1969 *ConAu 5R, -5NR*
Macnamara, Brinsley 1890-1963 *CnMD,*
  DcLB 10, LongCTC, ModWD
MacNamara, Donal E J 1916- *ConAu 33R*
Macnamara, Ellen 1924- *ConAu 103, WrDr 84*
Macnamara, John 1929- *ConAu 21R*
Macnamara, Michael Raymond Harley 1925-
  IntWWP 82
MacNeice, Louis 1907-1963 *CnMD, CnMWL,*
  ConAu 85, ConLC 1, -4, -10,
  DcLB 10[port], LongCTC, ModBrL,
  ModBrL SUP, RGFMBP, TwCA,
  TwCA SUP, TwCWr, WhoTwCL
MacNeil, Duncan *ConAu X, TwCCr&M 80,*
  WrDr 84
Macneil, Ian Roderick 1929- *ConAu 33R,*
  WrDr 84
MacNeil, Neil *ConAu X, TwCCr&M 80*
Macneil, Neil *WrDr 84*
MacNeil, Neil 1891-1969 *ConAu 29R,*
  ConAu P-1
MacNeil, Robert 1931- *ConAu 108*
MacNeill, Dand *ConAu X*
Macneill, Earl S 1893-1972 *ConAu 37R*
Macneill, Janet *ConAu X*
MacNeish, Richard S 1918- *ConAu 37R*
MacNell, James *ConAu X*
MacNelly, Jeff 1947- *ConAu 102*
MacNib *ConAu X, WrDr 84*
Macnicol, Eona Kathleen 1910- *ConAu 9R*
MacNutt, Francis S 1925- *ConAu 73*
Macomber, Daria *ConAu X*
Macomber, William 1921- *ConAu 61*
MacOrlan, Pierre 1882?-1970 *ConAu X, TwCA,*
  TwCA SUP
MacOrlan, Pierre 1883-1970 *ClDMEL 80*
Macovescu, George 1913- *IntAu&W 82*
MacPeek, Walter G 1902-1973 *ConAu 41R,*
  ConAu P-2, SmATA 25N, -4
MacPherson, A D L *WrDr 84*
Macpherson, C Brough 1911- *ConAu 2NR, -5R*
Macpherson, Jay 1931- *ConAu 5R, ConLC 14,*
  ConP 80, CreCan 1, WorAu 1970,
  WrDr 84
Macpherson, Jean Jay 1931- *CreCan 1,*
  DcLEL 1940
Macpherson, Kenneth 1903?-1971 *ConAu 29R*
MacPherson, Malcolm Cook 1943- *ConAu 102*
MacPherson, Margaret 1908- *ConAu 49,*
  SmATA 9, TwCCW 83, WrDr 84
MacPherson, Thomas George 1915-1976
  ConAu 1R, -4NR, SmATA 30N
Macquarrie, Heath Nelson 1919- *ConAu 41R*
Macquarrie, John 1919- *ConAu 1R, -1NR,*
  WrDr 84
Macqueen, Donald Richard 1925- *IntWWP 82*
Macqueen, James G 1932- *ConAu 17R*
MacQueen, John 1929- *WrDr 84*
MacQuitty, William *ConAu 7NR, -17R*
MacRae, C Fred 1909- *ConAu 45*
MacRae, Donald E 1907- *ConAu 93*
MacRae, Donald G 1921- *ConAu 13R*
MacRae, Duncan 1921- *ConAu 21R*
Macrae, Hawk *SmATA 8*
Macrae, Marjorie Knight d1973 *ConAu 41R*
Macrae, Mason 1894- *TwCWW*
Macrae, Norman 1923- *ConAu 106*
MacRae, Travis *ConAu X, SmATA X*
Macro, Eric 1920- *ConAu 29R*
Macrorie, Ken 1918- *ConAu 65*
Macrow, Brenda G Barton 1916- *ConAu 9R*
MacShane, Denis 1948- *ConAu 109*
MacShane, Frank 1927- *ConAu 3NR, -9R,*
  IntAu&W 82, WrDr 84
MacSweeney, Barry 1948- *ConAu 25R,*
  ConP 80, WrDr 84
MacTaggart, Morna Doris 1907- *ConAu X*
MacThomais, Ruaraidh *ConAu X, WrDr 84*
MacTyre, Paul 1924- *ConSFA*
Macumber, Mari *ConAu X, SmATA 5*

Macura, Paul 1924- *ConAu 8NR, -17R*
MacVane, John 1912- *ConAu 65*
MacVeagh, Lincoln 1890-1972 *ConAu 33R*
Macvean, Jean *WrDr 84*
Macvey, John Wishart 1923- *ConAu 7NR, -17R,*
  IntAu&W 82, WrDr 84
MacVicar, Angus 1908- *ConAu 10NR, -13R,*
  TwCCW 83
Macvicar, Angus 1908- *WrDr 84*
Macy, Helen 1904?-1978 *ConAu 81*
Macy, John Albert 1877-1932 *TwCA*
Macy, John W, Jr. 1917- *ConAu 33R, WrDr 84*
Madachy, Joseph S 1927- *ConAu 33R*
Madan, T N 1931- *ConAu 7NR, -17R*
Madaras, Lynda 1947- *ConAu 107*
Madariaga, Isabel De *ConAu X*
Madariaga, Salvador De 1886-1978 *ClDMEL 80,*
  ConAu 6NR, -9R, -81, LongCTC, TwCA,
  TwCA SUP, TwCWr
Maday, Bela Charles 1912- *ConAu 41R,*
  IntAu&W 82
Madden, Arthur Gerard 1911- *ConAu 1R*
Madden, Betty I Carroll 1915- *ConAu 57,*
  WrDr 84
Madden, Carl H 1920-1978 *ConAu 41R, -81*
Madden, Charles F 1921- *ConAu 25R*
Madden, Daniel Michael 1916- *ConAu 65*
Madden, David *DrAP&F 83*
Madden, David 1933- *ConAu 1R, -4NR,*
  ConLC 5, -15, ConNov 82, DcLB 6[port],
  IntAu&W 82, IntWWP 82, WrDr 84
Madden, Don 1927- *ConAu 25R, SmATA 3*
Madden, Donald L 1937- *ConAu 4NR, -53*
Madden, E S 1919- *ConAu 9R*
Madden, Edward H 1925- *ConAu 1R, -1NR*
Madden, Henry Miller 1912-1982 *ConAu 108*
Madden, Richard Raymond 1924- *ConAu 5R*
Madden, Warren *ConAu X*
Madden, William A 1923- *ConAu 21R*
Maddern, Al *ConAu X*
Maddern, Pip 1952- *TwCSFW*
Madderom, Gary 1937- *ConAu 45*
Maddi, Salvatore R 1933- *ConAu 13R*
Maddison, Angela Mary *WrDr 84*
Maddison, Angela Mary 1923- *ConAu 53,*
  SmATA 10
Maddison, Angus 1926- *ConAu 10NR, -13R,*
  IntAu&W 82, WrDr 84
Maddison, Carol 1923- *WrDr 84*
Maddison, Carol Evelyn Beryl Hopkins 1923-
  ConAu 17R
Maddock, Brent 1950- *ConAu 81*
Maddock, Kenneth d1971 *ConAu 104*
Maddock, Larry 1931- *ConAu X, ConSFA*
Maddock, R B 1912- *WrDr 84*
Maddock, Reginald 1912- *ConAu 81,*
  SmATA 15
Maddocks, Margaret 1906- *TwCRGW,*
  WrDr 84
Maddox, Brenda 1932- *ConAu 97*
Maddox, Carl *ConAu X, WrDr 84*
Maddox, Conroy 1912- *ConAu 101*
Maddox, Everette *DrAP&F 83*
Maddox, Gaynor *ConAu 9R*
Maddox, George Lamar, Jr. 1925- *ConAu 17R*
Maddox, James G 1907-1973 *ConAu 45,*
  ConAu P-2
Maddox, Jerrold 1932- *ConAu 17R*
Maddox, Marion Errol 1910- *ConAu 21R*
Maddox, Robert James 1931- *ConAu 33R,*
  WrDr 84
Maddox, Russell Webber 1921- *ConAu 1R,*
  WrDr 84
Maddux, Rachel *DrAP&F 83*
Maddux, Rachel 1912- *ConAu 1R, -5NR*
Madeleva, Sister Mary 1887-1964 *TwCA,*
  TwCA SUP
Madelung, A Margaret 1926- *ConAu 13R*
Mader, Chris 1943?-1980 *ConAu 103*
Madge, Charles 1912- *WrDr 84*
Madge, Charles Henry 1912- *ConAu 97,*
  ConP 80, LongCTC, ModBrL, TwCA
Madge, John 1914-1968 *ConAu P-1*
Madge, Violet 1916- *ConAu P-2*
Madgett, Naomi Long *DrAP&F 83*
Madgett, Naomi Long 1923- *ConAu 33R,*
  IntWWP 82, LivgBAA, MichAu 80,
  WrDr 84
Madgwick, P J 1925- *ConAu 29R*
Madgwick, Peter James 1925- *IntAu&W 82*
Madhauikutty *DcLEL 1940*
Madhavikutty *WrDr 84*

Madhubuti, Haki R *DrAP&F 83*
Madhubuti, Haki R 1942- *ConAu X, ConLC 6,*
  DcLB 5
Madian, Jon 1941- *ConAu 61, SmATA 9*
Madigan, Marian East 1898- *ConAu P-2*
Madigan, Mary Jean Smith 1941- *ConAu 110*
Madison, Arnold 1937- *ConAu 9NR, -21R,*
  SmATA 6
Madison, Charles A 1895- *WrDr 84*
Madison, Charles Allan 1895- *ConAu 1R, -1NR,*
  IntAu&W 82
Madison, Frank *ConAu X, IntAu&W 82X,*
  WrDr 84
Madison, Hank *ConAu X, TwCWW*
Madison, Jane *ConAu X*
Madison, Joyce *ConAu X*
Madison, Peter 1918- *ConAu 9R*
Madison, Russ 1929- *ConAu 25R*
Madison, Thomas A 1926- *ConAu 57*
Madison, Tom *ConAu X*
Madison, Winifred *ConAu 37R, SmATA 5*
Madle, Dorothy *ConAu X*
Madlee, Dorothy 1917- *ConAu 17R*
Madlee, Dorothy 1917-1980 *ConAu 10NR*
Madow, Leo 1915- *ConAu 33R*
Madow, Pauline *ConAu 9R*
Madrid, Michael Joseph 1953- *IntWWP 82*
Madrigal, Margarita 1912?-1983 *ConAu 110*
Madruga, Lenor 1942- *ConAu 102*
Madsen, Axel 1930- *ConAu 25R*
Madsen, Borge Gedso 1920- *ConAu 1R*
Madsen, Brigham Dwaine 1914- *ConAu 103*
Madsen, Christian 1927- *IntAu&W 82*
Madsen, David Lawrence 1929- *ConAu 21R*
Madsen, Roy Paul 1928- *ConAu 89,*
  IntAu&W 82
Madsen, Svend Age 1939- *ClDMEL 80*
Madsen, Truman Grant 1926- *ConAu 106*
Maduell, Charles Rene, Jr. 1918- *ConAu 73*
Mae, Eydie *ConAu X*
Maedke, Wilmer O 1922- *ConAu 57*
Maehl, William Harvey 1915- *ConAu 89,*
  IntAu&W 82
Maehl, William Henry, Jr. 1930- *ConAu 21R*
Maelandsmo, Ingebjorg 1898- *IntAu&W 82*
Maenchen, Otto John 1894-1969 *ConAu 109*
Maenchen-Helfer, Otto J *ConAu X*
Maend, Evald *ConAu X*
Maepenn, Hugh *ConAu X*
Maepenn, K H *ConAu X*
Maerker, Friedrich 1893- *IntAu&W 82*
Maeroff, Gene I 1939- *ConAu 61*
Maertz, Richard Charles 1935- *ConAu 73*
Maes, Jeanette C *DrAP&F 83*
Maes-Jelinek, Hena *WrDr 84*
Maes-Jelinek, Hena 1929- *ConAu 107*
Maestro, Betsy 1944- *ConAu 8NR, -61,*
  SmATA 30
Maestro, Giulio 1942- *ConAu 8NR, -57,*
  SmATA 8, WrDr 84
Maeterlinck, Maurice 1862-1949 *ClDMEL 80,*
  CnMD, ConAu 104, LongCTC, ModFrL,
  ModRL, ModWD, TwCA, TwCA SUP,
  TwCLC 3, TwCWr, WhoTwCL
Maeztu, Ramiro De 1876-1936 *ClDMEL 80*
Maffei, Paolo 1926- *ConAu 108*
Maffi, Mario 1947- *IntAu&W 82*
Mag *IntWWP 82X*
Magalaner, Marvin 1920- *ConAu 1R, -1NR*
Magaret, Helene 1906- *ConAu 1R*
Magarshack, David 1899- *ConAu 5R, WorAu*
Magary, Alan 1944- *ConAu 8NR, -61*
Magary, James F 1933- *ConAu 25R*
Magary, Kerstin Fraser 1947- *ConAu 61*
Magdol, Edward 1918- *ConAu 9NR, -21R*
Magee, Bryan 1930- *ConAu 2NR, -5R,*
  DcLEL 1940, IntAu&W 82, WrDr 84
Magee, David 1905-1977 *ConAu 73, -81*
Magee, John 1914- *WrDr 84*
Magee, Wes 1939- *ConAu 107, ConP 80,*
  WrDr 84
Magee, William Kirkpatrick *LongCTC*
Magelund, Johannes 1909- *IntAu&W 82*
Mager, Don *DrAP&F 83*
Mager, George C 1937- *ConAu 49*
Mager, Nathan H 1912- *ConAu 2NR, -45*
Maggal, Moshe Morris 1908- *ConAu P-2,*
  WrDr 84
Maggin, Elliot S 1950- *ConAu 102*
Maggio, Joe 1938- *ConAu 1NR, -45*
Maggio, Michael 1949- *IntAu&W 82*
Maggiolo, Walter A 1908- *ConAu 85*

Makinson, Randell L 1932- *WrDr 84*
Makkai, Adam 1935- *ConAu 10NR, -57*
Makow, Henry 1949- *ConAu 5R*
Makower, Addie 1906- *ConAu 65*
Maksimov, Vladimir Yemelyanovich 1932- *ClDMEL 80*
Maktari, Abdulla M A 1936- *ConAu 37R*
Maktos, John 1902-1977 *ConAu 69*
Mal *ConAu X*
Malabre, Alfred L 1931- *ConAu 65*
Malamud, Bernard *DrAP&F 83*
Malamud, Bernard 1914- *CnMWL, ConAu 5R,
ConLC 1, -2, -3, -5, -8, -9, -11, -18,
-27[port], ConNov 82, DcLB Y80A[port],
-2, DcLEL 1940, IntAu&W 82, ModAL,
ModAL SUP, TwCWr, WhoTwCL, WorAu,
WrDr 84*
Malan, Roy Mark 1911- *ConAu 41R*
Maland, David 1929- *ConAu 103, WrDr 84*
Malanga, Gerard *DrAP&F 83*
Malanga, Gerard 1943- *DcLEL 1940,
IntWWP 82*
Malanos, George J 1919-1962 *ConAu 1R, -103*
Malanyuk, Yevhen 1897-1968 *ClDMEL 80,
ModSL 2*
Malaparte, Curzio 1898-1957 *ClDMEL 80,
CnMD, ModRL, TwCA SUP, TwCWr*
Malaquais, Jean Paul 1908- *TwCA SUP*
Malaschak, Dolores Boyer 1923- *IntWWP 82*
Malavie, M J 1920- *ConAu 29R*
Malbin, Michael J 1943- *ConAu 73*
Malcolm, Andrew 1927- *ConAu 97*
Malcolm, Andrew H 1943- *ConAu 53*
Malcolm, Diana *IntAu&W 82X*
Malcolm, Donald 1932?-1975 *ConAu 104*
Malcolm, Ian *ConAu X*
Malcolm, Margaret *ConAu 49*
Malcolm, Norman 1911- *ConAu 37R*
Malcolm, River *DrAP&F 83*
Malcolmson, Anne Elizabeth 1910- *ConAu X,
SmATA 1*
Malcolmson, David 1899- *ConAu 5R,
SmATA 6*
Malcolmson, Robert W 1943- *ConAu 103*
Malcom, Robert E 1933- *ConAu 17R*
Malcomson, William L 1932- *ConAu 25R*
Malcoskey, Edna Walker *ConAu 17R*
Malcuzynski, Karol 1922- *IntAu&W 82*
Malde, Gualtiero *WrDr 84*
Maldonado, Jesus Maria *DrAP&F 83*
Male, David Arthur 1928- *ConAu 57*
Male, Roy R 1919- *ConAu 104*
Malec, Alexander 1929- *ConSFA*
Malec, Emily Keller *DrAP&F 83*
Malecki, Edward Stanley 1938- *ConAu 41R*
Malefakis, Edward 1932- *WrDr 84*
Malefakis, Edward E 1932- *ConAu 29R*
Malek, Frederic Vincent 1937- *ConAu 81*
Malek, James S 1941- *ConAu 57, WrDr 84*
Malek, John *DrAP&F 83, IntWWP 82X*
Malek, John Francis, II 1950- *IntWWP 82*
Malenbaum, Wilfred 1913- *ConAu 1R, -1NR*
Malenfant, Lloyd *CreCan 1*
Malerba, Luigi 1927- *ClDMEL 80,
IntAu&W 82*
Malerich, Edward P *WrDr 84*
Malerich, Edward P 1940- *ConAu 33R*
Maleska, Eugene Thomas 1916- *ConAu 1R,
-1NR*
Malet, Baldwin Hugh Grenville 1928-
ConAu 17R
Malet, Baldwyn Hugh Grenville 1928-
IntAu&W 82
Malet, Hugh 1928- *WrDr 84*
Malet, Lucas 1852-1931 *LongCTC, TwCA,
TwCA SUP*
Malewska, Hanna 1911- *ClDMEL 80*
Malgonkar, Manohar 1913- *ConAu 1R, -1NR,
ConNov 82, WorAu, WrDr 84*
Malgonkar, Manohar 1914- *ModCmwL*
Malgonkar, Monohar 1913- *DcLEL 1940*
Malherbe, Abraham J 1930- *ConAu 1NR, -49*
Malherbe, Ernst Gideon 1895- *ConAu P-1,
IntAu&W 82*
Malherbe, Janie Antonia 1897- *ConAu P-1*
Malhotra, Ashok Kumar 1940- *ConAu 110*
Mali, Paul 1926- *ConAu 8NR, -57*
Malick, Terrence 1943- *ConAu 101*
Malick, Terry *ConAu X*
Malickson, David L 1928- *ConAu 110*
Malik, Charles Habib 1906- *ConAu 7NR, -45*
Malik, Hafeez 1930- *ConAu 77, IntAu&W 82*

Malik, Yogendra K 1929- *ConAu 81*
Malikin, David 1913- *ConAu 77*
Malin, Irving 1934- *ConAu 6NR, -13R,
IntAu&W 82, WrDr 84*
Malin, Peter *ConAu X, LongCTC, WrDr 84*
Malina, Frank J 1912- *ConAu 93*
Malina, Frank J 1912-1981 *ConAu 108*
Malina, Judith 1926- *ConAu 102*
Maling, Arthur 1923- *ConAu 3NR, -49,
TwCCr&M 80, WrDr 84*
Malinin, Theodore I 1933- *ConAu 93,
IntAu&W 82*
Malinovski, Ivan 1926- *ClDMEL 80,
IntAu&W 82*
Malinowitz, Michael *DrAP&F 83*
Malinowski, Bronislaw 1884-1942 *LongCTC,
TwCA, TwCA SUP*
Malins, Edward 1910- *ConAu 103*
Malipiero, Gian Francesco 1882-1973 *ConAu 45*
Malk, August 1900- *IntAu&W 82*
Malkiel, Burton Gordon 1932- *ConAu 49*
Malkiel, Yakov 1914- *ConAu 25R, WrDr 84*
Malkiewicz, J Kris 1931- *ConAu 57*
Malkin, Maurice L 1900- *ConAu 49*
Malkoff, Karl 1938- *ConAu 17R*
Malko, George *DrAP&F 83*
Malkus, Alida Wright Sims 1895- *MichAu 80*
Malkus, Alida Wright Sims 1899- *ConAu 5R*
Mall, E Jane 1920- *ConAu 21R*
Mall, Viktor *ConAu X, IntAu&W 82X*
Mallaby, George 1902-1978 *ConAu 108*
Mallalieu, John Percival William 1908-1980
ConAu 97
Mallan, Lloyd 1914- *ConAu 5R*
Mallarme, Stephane 1842-1898 *ClDMEL 80,
ModRL*
Mallart, Jose 1897- *IntAu&W 82*
Malle, Louis 1932- *ConAu 101*
Mallea, Eduardo 1903- *ModLAL, TwCWr,
WorAu*
Mallen, Bruce E 1937- *ConAu 21R*
Mallery, David 1923- *ConAu 5R*
Malleson, Lucy Beatrice 1899-1973 *ConAu 49,
-97, LongCTC, WorAu*
Mallet, Francoise 1930- *TwCWr*
Mallet-Joris, Francoise 1930- *ClDMEL 80,
ConAu 65, ConLC 11, ModFrL, ModRL,
WorAu*
Mallett, Anne 1913- *ConAu 49*
Mallett, Jane Keenleyside *CreCan 1*
Malley, Ern *ConAu X, WorAu 1970*
Mallik, Umesh 1916- *WrDr 84*
Mallin, Jay 1927- *ConAu 17R, IntAu&W 82,
WrDr 84*
Mallin, Tom 1927?-1978 *ConAu 89*
Mallinson, George Greisen 1918- *ConAu 1R,
-1NR*
Mallinson, Jeremy *WrDr 84*
Mallinson, Jeremy John Crosby 1937-
ConAu 6NR, -57
Mallinson, Vernon 1910- *ConAu 5R,
IntAu&W 82, WrDr 84*
Malloch, Douglas 1877-1938 *MichAu 80*
Malloch, Peter *ConAu X, TwCCr&M 80*
Mallock, William Hurrell 1849-1923 *LongCTC*
Mallon, Thomas 1951- *ConAu 110*
Mallone, Ronald Stephen 1916- *ConAu P-1*
Mallonee, Richard C, II 1923- *ConAu 109*
Mallory, Bob F 1932- *ConAu 89*
Mallory, Drew *WrDr 84*
Mallory, Ella Phillips *IntWWP 82X*
Mallory, Ella Sereta Phillips 1898- *IntWWP 82*
Mallory, Enid Lorraine 1938- *ConAu 105*
Mallory, Lee *DrAP&F 83*
Mallory, Lee W, III 1946- *IntWWP 82*
Mallory, Mark *ConAu X*
Mallory, Walter Hampton 1892-1980 *ConAu 9R,
-101*
Mallough, Don 1914- *ConAu 21R*
Mallowan, Agatha Christie *ConAu X*
Mallowan, Max 1904-1978 *ConAu 69, -81*
Malloy, Ruth Lor 1932- *ConAu 69*
Malloy, Terry 1950- *ConAu 69*
Mally, E Louise 1908- *ConAu 33R*
Mally, Leo Hans 1901- *IntAu&W 82*
Malm, F T 1919- *ConAu 17R*
Malm, Johan Einar Fredrik 1900- *IntAu&W 82*
Malm, Margaretha *IntAu&W 82X*
Malm, William Paul 1928- *ConAu 9R,
IntAu&W 82*
Malmberg, Bertil 1889-1958 *ClDMEL 80*
Malmberg, Carl 1904- *ConAu 33R, SmATA 9*

Malmgren, Harald B 1935- *ConAu 45,
WrDr 84*
Malmo, Robert Beverley 1912- *ConAu 61*
Malmstrom, Jean 1908- *ConAu 53*
Malo, John W 1911- *ConAu 33R, SmATA 4*
Malocsay, Zoltan 1946- *ConAu 81*
Malof, Joseph F 1934- *ConAu 29R*
Maloff, Saul *DrAP&F 83*
Maloff, Saul 1922- *ConAu 33R, ConLC 5*
Malone, Bill C 1934- *ConAu 65*
Malone, Dick *ConAu X*
Malone, Dumas 1892- *ConAu 1R, -2NR,
DcLB 17[port], IntAu&W 82, TwCA SUP,
WrDr 84*
Malone, E T, Jr. *DrAP&F 83*
Malone, Elmer Taylor, Jr. 1943- *ConAu 1NR,
-49*
Malone, John *DrAP&F 83*
Malone, Kemp 1889-1971 *ConAu 89*
Malone, Louis *ConAu X, LongCTC*
Malone, Marvin *DrAP&F 83*
Malone, Mary *ConAu 1R, -2NR*
Malone, Michael 1942- *ConAu 77*
Malone, Michael P 1940- *ConAu 29R*
Malone, Michael Patrick *DrAP&F 83*
Malone, Pamela Altfeld *DrAP&F 83*
Malone, Richard Sankey 1909- *ConAu 107*
Malone, Ruth 1918- *ConAu 93*
Malone, Ted *ConAu X*
Malone, Wex S 1906- *ConAu 9R*
Maloney, Dennis *DrAP&F 83*
Maloney, Dennis M 1951- *IntWWP 82*
Maloney, Frank E 1918-1980 *ConAu 73, -97*
Maloney, George A 1924- *ConAu 8NR, -21R*
Maloney, J J 1940- *ConAu 109*
Maloney, Joan M 1931- *ConAu 37R*
Maloney, John *DrAP&F 83*
Maloney, Pat *ConAu X*
Maloney, Ralph Liston 1927-1973 *ConAu 1R,
-3NR, -45*
Maloney, Tighe *IntAu&W 82X*
Malony, H Newton 1931- *ConAu 104*
Malory, Thomas 1410?-1471? *SmATA 33*
Malouf, David 1934- *ConNov 82, ConP 80,
IntWWP 82X, WrDr 84*
Malouf, George Joseph David 1934- *IntWWP 82*
Maloy, Miriam Craig 1908- *IntWWP 82*
Malpass, E L 1910- *ConAu 3NR*
Malpass, Eric 1910- *WrDr 84*
Malpass, Eric Lawson 1910- *ConAu 9R,
IntAu&W 82*
Malpass, Leslie F 1922- *ConAu 8NR, -17R*
Malpede, Karen *ConAu X*
Malraux, Andre 1901-1976 *ClDMEL 80, CnMD,
CnMWL, ConAu 21R, -69, ConAu P-2,
ConLC 1, -4, -9, -13, -15, LongCTC,
ModFrL, ModRL, TwCA, TwCA SUP,
TwCWr, WhoTwCL*
Malraux, Clara 1897?-1982 *ConAu 108*
Malraux-Goldschmidt, Clara *ConAu X*
Malster, Robert William 1932- *IntAu&W 82*
Maltby, Arthur 1935- *ConAu 10NR, -25R*
Maltby, Henry Francis 1880-1963 *LongCTC*
Malten, William 1902- *ConAu P-2*
Maltese, Michael 1908?-1981 *SmATA 24N*
Maltese, Michael 1909?-1981 *ConAu 103*
Maltin, Leonard 1950- *ConAu 29R*
Maltz, Albert 1908- *CnMD, ConAu 41R,
ConDr 82, ConNov 82, IntAu&W 82,
ModAL, ModWD, TwCA, TwCA SUP,
WrDr 84*
Maltz, Maxwell 1899-1975 *ConAu 57, -65*
Maltz, Stephen 1932- *ConAu 57*
Maluf, Chafic 1905?-1976 *ConAu 69*
Malveaux, Julianne M 1953- *ConAu 105*
Malvern, Corinne 1905-1956 *SmATA 34[port]*
Malvern, Gladys d1962 *ConAu 73,
SmATA 23[port]*
Maly, Eugene H 1920- *ConAu 21R,
IntAu&W 82, WrDr 84*
Malzberg, Barry N 1939- *ConAu 61, ConLC 7,
DcLB 8[port], DrmM[port], TwCSFW*
Malzberg, Barry Norman 1939- *WrDr 84*
Malzberg, Benjamin 1893-1975 *ConAu 57,
ConAu P-1*
Mama G *ConAu X*
Mamalakis, Markos J 1932- *ConAu 45,
IntAu&W 82*
Maman, Andre 1927- *ConAu 73*
Mamatey, Victor S 1917- *ConAu 9R*
Mamet, David *NatPD 81[port]*

Mamet, David 1947- *ConAu 81, ConDr 82, DcLB 7[port], WrDr 84*
Mamet, David 1948- *ConLC 9, -15*
Mamis, Justin E 1929- *ConAu 9R*
Mamleyev, Yuri *DrAP&F 83*
Mamleyev, Yuri 1931- *ConAu 85, IntAu&W 82*
Mammatt, Doreen Rosalie 1947- *IntWWP 82*
Mammeri, Mouloud 1917- *ClDMEL 80, ModFrL*
Mamoulian, Rouben 1897- *ConAu 25R*
Mamoulian, Rouben 1898- *ConLC 16*
Man, John 1941- *ConAu 93*
Man Without A Spleen, A *ConAu X*
Mana-Zucca *ConAu X*
Manaf, Mohammed Zaini 1941- *IntAu&W 82*
Manarin, Louis H 1932- *ConAu 21R*
Mancewicz, Bernice Winslow 1917- *ConAu 37R*
Manch, Joseph 1910- *ConAu 53*
Mancha, Donald L *IntAu&W 82X*
Manchee, Fred B 1903?-1981 *ConAu 105*
Manchel, Frank 1935- *ConAu 37R, IntAu&W 82, SmATA 10, WrDr 84*
Manchester, Harland 1898-1977 *ConAu 1R, -73*
Manchester, Joe 1932- *NatPD 81[port]*
Manchester, Paul Thomas 1893- *ConAu 61*
Manchester, William 1922- *WrDr 84*
Manchester, William Raymond 1922- *ASpks, AuNews 1, ConAu 1R, -3NR, DcLEL 1940, IntAu&W 82, WorAu*
Mancini, Anthony 1939- *ConAu 73*
Mancini, Joseph *ConAmTC*
Mancini, Pat McNees *ConAu X*
Mancke, Richard B 1943- *ConAu 81*
Mancroft, Baron 1914- *WrDr 84*
Mancroft, Lord 1872-1942 *LongCTC*
Mancroft, Stormont Mancroft Samuel 1914- *ConAu 49*
Mancusi-Ungaro, Harold R, Jr. 1947- *ConAu 97*
Mancuso, Joe *ConAu X*
Mancuso, Joseph R 1941- *ConAu 93*
Mand, Ewald 1906- *ConAu 17R*
Mandel, Adrienne Schizzano 1934- *ConAu 37R*
Mandel, Benjamin 1891?-1973 *ConAu 45*
Mandel, Bernard 1920- *ConAu 1R, LivgBAA*
Mandel, Charlotte *DrAP&F 83*
Mandel, Eli 1922- *ConAu 73, ConP 80, CreCan 2, IntAu&W 82, ModCmwL, WrDr 84*
Mandel, Elias Wolf 1922- *DcLEL 1940*
Mandel, Ernest 1923- *ConAu 37R, IntAu&W 82, WrDr 84*
Mandel, George 1920- *ConAu 1R*
Mandel, Jerome Herbert 1937- *ConAu 37R*
Mandel, Leon 1928- *ConAu 77*
Mandel, Loring 1928- *ConAu 73*
Mandel, Morris 1911- *ConAu 5R, -6NR*
Mandel, Oscar *DrAP&F 83*
Mandel, Oscar 1926- *ConAu 1R, -2NR, WrDr 84*
Mandel, Ruth Blumenstock 1938- *ConAu 105*
Mandel, Sally Elizabeth 1944- *ConAu 102*
Mandel, Sidney Albert 1923- *ConAu 93*
Mandel, Siegfried 1922- *ConAu 1R, -5NR, IntAu&W 82*
Mandel, William M 1917- *ConAu 9R*
Mandelbaum, Allen *DrAP&F 83*
Mandelbaum, David G 1911- *ConAu 41R*
Mandelbaum, Michael 1946- *ConAu 101*
Mandelbaum, Seymour J 1936- *ConAu 17R*
Mandelker, Daniel Robert 1926- *ConAu 1R, -5NR*
Mandelkorn, Eugenia Miller 1916- *ConAu 9R*
Mandell, Arnold Joseph 1934- *ConAu 101*
Mandell, Betty Reid 1924- *ConAu 8NR, -61*
Mandell, Marvin *DrAP&F 83*
Mandell, Maurice I 1925- *ConAu 11NR, -25R*
Mandell, Mel 1926- *ConAu 41R*
Mandell, Muriel Levin 1921- *ConAu 9R*
Mandell, Richard Donald 1929- *ConAu 10NR, -25R*
Mandelshtam, Nadezhda *ConAu X*
Mandelshtam, Osip Emilyevich 1891?-1938? *ClDMEL 80, CnMWL, ModSL 1*
Mandelstam, Nadezhda 1899-1980 *ConAu 110*
Mandelstam, Nadezhda Yakovlevha 1899-1980 *ConAu 102, WorAu 1970*
Tmandelstam, Osip Emilyevich 1891?-1938? *ConAu 104, TwCLC 2, -6[port], TwCWr, WhoTwCL, WorAu*
Mandelstamm, Allan B 1928- *ConAu 41R*
Mander, A E 1894- *ConAu P-1*

Mander, Anica Vesel 1934- *ConAu 8NR, -61*
Mander, Gertrud 1927- *ConAu 93*
Mander, Jane 1877-1949 *LongCTC, TwCWr*
Mander, Jerry 1936- *ConAu 81*
Mander, Raymond *ConAu 101*
Mander, Rosalie Grylls *ConAu 5R*
Mandino, Og 1923- *ConAu 103*
Mandler, George 1924- *ConAu 1R, -4NR*
Mandler, Jean Matter 1929- *ConAu 13R*
Mandrake, Ethel Belle *ConAu X*
Mandrepelias, Loizos *ConAu X*
Mane, Robert 1926- *ConAu 37R*
Manella, Raymond L 1917- *ConAu 17R*
Manes, Stephen *DrAP&F 83*
Manes, Stephen 1949- *ConAu 97*
Manfred, Frederick *DrAP&F 83*
Manfred, Frederick Feikema 1912- *ConAu 5NR, -9R, ConNov 82, DcLB 6, FifWWr, IntAu&W 82, SmATA 30[port], TwCA SUP, TwCWW, WrDr 84*
Manfred, Freya *DrAP&F 83*
Manfred, Freya 1944- *ConAu 69*
Manfred, Robert *ConAu X*
Manfredi, John Francis 1920- *ConAu 109*
Mang, Karl 1922- *ConAu 101*
Mangalam, J J 1924- *ConAu 37R*
Mangan, James Thomas 1896- *ConAu P-2*
Mangan, Kathy *DrAP&F 83*
Mangan, Sherry 1904-1961 *DcLB 4*
Mangat, J S 1937- *ConAu 73*
Mangione, Jerre *DrAP&F 83*
Mangione, Jerre 1909- *ConAu 13R, ConNov 82, IntAu&W 82, SmATA 6, WrDr 84*
Mango, Cyril 1928- *ConAu 109*
Mangold, Elva 1919- *ConAmTC*
Mangold, Tom 1934- *ConAu 69*
Mangum, Garth L 1926- *ConAu 81, IntAu&W 82*
Mangurian, David 1938- *ConAu 10NR, -57, SmATA 14*
Manhattan, Avro 1914- *ConAu 5NR, -9R, IntAu&W 82*
Manheim, Jarol B 1946- *ConAu 6NR, -57, WrDr 84*
Manheim, Leonard 1902- *ConAu P-2*
Manheim, Michael 1928- *ConAu 81*
Manheim, Sylvan D 1897-1977 *ConAu 73*
Manheim, Theodore 1921- *ConAu 108*
Manheim, Werner 1915- *ConAu 53*
Manhire, Bill 1946- *ConAu 103, ConP 80, WrDr 84*
Manhoff, Bill *ConAu 49*
Manhoff, Wilton 1919-1974 *ConAu 49*
Manicas, Peter T 1934- *ConAu 53*
Maniere, J-E *ConAu X*
Manifold, John 1915- *WrDr 84*
Manifold, John Streeter 1915- *ConAu 69, ConP 80, DcLEL 1940, LongCTC, TwCA SUP*
Manigault, Edward 1897?-1983 *ConAu 109*
Manilla, James *ConAu 97*
Manis, Jerome G 1917- *ConAu 25R*
Manis, Melvin 1931- *ConAu 21R*
Maniscalco, Joseph 1926- *ConAu 5R, -8NR, SmATA 10*
Manjula *IntWWP 82X*
Mank, Gregory William 1950- *ConAu 89, IntAu&W 82*
Mankekar, D R 1910- *ConAu 21R*
Mankiewicz, Don 1922- *WrDr 84*
Mankiewicz, Don Martin 1922- *ConAu 13R*
Mankiewicz, Frank 1924- *ConAu 89*
Mankiewicz, Herman 1897-1953 *DcLB 26[port]*
Mankiewicz, Joseph Leo 1909- *ConAu 73, ConDr 82A*
Mankin, Paul A 1924- *ConAu 37R*
Mankoff, Allan H 1935- *ConAu 45*
Mankowitz, Wolf 1924- *ConAu 5R, -5NR, ConDr 82, ConNov 82, DcLB 15[port], DcLEL 1940, IntAu&W 82, LongCTC, TwCWr, WorAu, WrDr 84*
Mankowska, Joyce Kells Batten 1919- *ConAu P-1*
Manley, Deborah 1932- *ConAu 105, SmATA 28[port]*
Manley, Frank 1930- *ConAu 5R*
Manley, John F 1939- *ConAu 77*
Manley, Lawrence 1949- *ConAu 109*
Manley, Michael Norman 1923- *ConAu 85*
Manley, Ruth Rodney King 1907?-1973 *ConAu 41R*
Manley, Seon *ChlLR 3, ConAu 85,*

SmATA 15
Manley-Tucker, Audrie *TwCRGW, WrDr 84*
Manley-Tucker, Audrie 1924?-1983? *ConAu 108*
Manlove, Colin 1942- *WrDr 84*
Manly, Charles Macdonald 1855-1924 *CreCan 2*
Mann, Abby 1927- *ConAu 109*
Mann, Abel *ConAu X*
Mann, Anthony 1914- *ConAu P-1, IntAu&W 82, WrDr 84*
Mann, Arthur 1922- *ConAu 109*
Mann, Avery *ConAu X*
Mann, Bob 1948- *ConAu 61*
Mann, Carol 1950- *WrDr 84*
Mann, Charles William 1929- *ConAu 41R*
Mann, Christopher Stephen 1917- *ConAu 89*
Mann, Christopher Zithulele 1948- *IntWWP 82*
Mann, D J *ConAu X*
Mann, Dale 1938- *ConAu 61*
Mann, David Douglas 1934- *ConAu 49*
Mann, Dean Edson 1927- *ConAu 5NR, -9R*
Mann, Deborah *ConAu X, TwCRGW, WrDr 84*
Mann, E B 1902- *TwCWW, WrDr 84*
Mann, Edward *ConAu X*
Mann, Edward Andrew 1932- *ConAu 103*
Mann, Erika 1905-1969 *ConAu 25R, LongCTC, TwCA, TwCA SUP*
Mann, Ethel *IntAu&W 82X*
Mann, Ethel E *MichAu 80*
Mann, Floyd C 1917- *ConAu 1R*
Mann, Georg K F 1913- *ConAu 1R*
Mann, Golo 1909- *ConAu 97, IntAu&W 82*
Mann, Harold W 1925- *ConAu 17R*
Mann, Heinrich 1871-1950 *ClDMEL 80, ConAu 106, LongCTC, ModGL, ModWD, TwCA, TwCA SUP, TwCLC 9[port], TwCWr, WhoTwCL*
Mann, Ida 1893- *WrDr 84*
Mann, James *WrDr 84*
Mann, Jan *IntWWP 82X*
Mann, Jessica *WrDr 84*
Mann, Jessica 1937- *ConAu 2NR, -49, IntAu&W 82, TwCCr&M 80*
Mann, John H 1928- *ConAu 85*
Mann, Katharina 1883?-1980 *ConAu 97*
Mann, Kenneth Walker 1914- *ConAu 29R*
Mann, Klaus 1906-1949 *LongCTC, ModGL, TwCA, TwCA SUP*
Mann, Klaus 1908-1949 *ClDMEL 80*
Mann, Leonard 1895- *ConNov 82, WhoTwCL, WorAu*
Mann, Marty 1904-1980 *ConAu 101, -103*
Mann, Mary E d1929 *LongCTC*
Mann, Michael 1919-1977 *ConAu 3NR, -49, -69*
Mann, Milton B 1937- *ConAu 45*
Mann, Patrick *ConAu X*
Mann, Peggy *ConAu 10NR, -25R, DrAP&F 83, IntAu&W 82, SmATA 6, WrDr 84*
Mann, Peter 1948- *ConAu 93*
Mann, Peter H 1926- *ConAu 25R, WrDr 84*
Mann, Philip A 1934- *ConAu 73*
Mann, Thaddeus Robert Rudolph 1908- *IntAu&W 82*
Mann, Thomas 1875-1955 *ClDMEL 80, CnMWL, ConAu 104, LongCTC, ModGL, TwCA[port], TwCA SUP, TwCLC 2, -8[port], TwCWr, WhoTwCL*
Mann, W Edward 1918- *ConAu 49*
Mann, William S 1924- *ConAu 109*
Mann, Zane B 1924- *ConAu 101*
Manne, Henry G 1928- *ConAu 33R, WrDr 84*
Manne, Macho *IntAu&W 82X*
Mannello, George, Jr. 1913- *ConAu 33R*
Manner, Eeva-Liisa 1921- *CroCD*
Mannering, Julia *ConAu X*
Manners, Alexandra *ConAu X, IntAu&W 82X, TwCRGW, WrDr 84*
Manners, Ande Miller 1923?-1975 *ConAu 57*
Manners, David X 1912- *ConAu 106*
Manners, Lady Diana *LongCTC*
Manners, Elizabeth 1917- *ConAu 49*
Manners, Gerald 1932- *ConAu 37R, WrDr 84*
Manners, John 1914- *ConAu 106, WrDr 84*
Manners, John Hartley 1870-1928 *LongCTC, ModWD*
Manners, Julia *ConAu X*
Manners, Robert Alan 1913- *ConAu 33R, IntAu&W 82, WrDr 84*
Manners, William 1907- *ConAu 65*
Mannes, Marya *DrAP&F 83, IntAu&W 82*
Mannes, Marya 1904- *ConAu 1R, -3NR,*

ConSFA, DcLEL 1940, WorAu, WrDr 84
Manney, Bridget *DrAP&F 83*
Manngian, Peter *ConAu X*
Mannheim, Grete 1909- *ConAu 9R, SmATA 10*
Mannheim, Karl 1893-1947 *TwCA SUP*
Mannheimer, Henry 1944- *IntWWP 82*
Manniche, Lise 1943- *ConAu 107, SmATA 31[port]*
Mannin, Ethel 1900- *WrDr 84*
Mannin, Ethel Edith 1900- *ConAu 8NR, –53, ConNov 82, IntAu&W 82, LongCTC, TwCA, TwCA SUP*
Manning, Adelaide Frances Oke d1959 *LongCTC, TwCA SUP*
Manning, Bayless Andrew 1923- *ConAu 9NR, –13R*
Manning, Beverley J 1942- *ConAu 109*
Manning, Clarence A 1893-1972 *ConAu 37R*
Manning, David *ConAu X, TwCWW*
Manning, David 1938- *ConAu 103, WrDr 84*
Manning, Frank E 1944- *ConAu 7NR, –53*
Manning, Frederic 1887?-1935 *CnMWL, LongCTC, TwCA, TwCA SUP, TwCWr*
Manning, Jack 1920- *ConAu 69*
Manning, Laurence 1899-1972 *TwCSFW*
Manning, Lynn *DrAP&F 83*
Manning, Marsha *TwCRGW, WrDr 84*
Manning, Mary Louise *ConAu X*
Manning, Michael 1940- *ConAu 65*
Manning, Olivia 1911-1980 *ConAu 5R, ConLC 5, –19, ModBrL, ModBrL SUP, TwCWr, WorAu*
Manning, Olivia 1915-1980 *ConAu 101, ConNov 82A*
Manning, Paul 1912- *ConAu 107*
Manning, Peter K 1940- *ConAu 37R*
Manning, Philip 1930?-1983 *ConAu 110*
Manning, Phyllis A Sergeant 1903- *ConAu 5R*
Manning, Robert Joseph 1919- *ConAu 69*
Manning, Rosemary *WrDr 84*
Manning, Rosemary 1911- *ConAu X, –1R, –1NR, DcLEL 1940, IntAu&W 82, SmATA 10, TwCCW 83, WorAu*
Manning, Roy *TwCWW*
Manning, S A 1921- *WrDr 84*
Manning, Stanley Arthur 1921- *ConAu 110, IntAu&W 82*
Manning, Sylvia 1943- *ConAu 81*
Manning, Thomas Davys 1898-1972 *ConAu P-1*
Manning-Sanders, Ruth 1895- *ConAu 73, SmATA 15, TwCCW 83, WrDr 84*
Mannion, John J 1941- *ConAu 73*
Mannix, Edward 1928- *ConAu 13R*
Mannon, James M 1942- *ConAu 110*
Mannon, Warwick 1914- *ConAu X*
Mannoni, Octave 1899- *ConAu 102*
Mano, D Keith *DrAP&F 83*
Mano, D Keith 1942- *ConAu 25R, ConLC 2, –10, DcLB 6[port]*
Mano, M Morris 1927- *ConAu 103*
Manocchia, Benito 1934- *ConAu 69*
Manolson, Frank 1925- *ConAu 17R*
Manoni, Mary H 1924- *ConAu 4NR, –49*
Manoogian, Haig P 1916?-1980 *ConAu 97*
Manor, Jason *ConAu X, WrDr 84*
Manos, Charley 1923- *ConAu 29R*
Manosevitz, Martin 1938- *ConAu 29R*
Manross, William Wilson 1905- *ConAu 57, IntAu&W 82, WrDr 84*
Manry, Robert 1918-1971 *ConAu 29R, ConAu P-2*
Mansbach, Richard W 1943- *ConAu 53*
Mansbridge, John 1901?-1981 *ConAu 105*
Manschreck, Clyde Leonard 1917- *ConAu 5NR, –9R*
Mansell, Darrel 1934- *ConAu 57, WrDr 84*
Mansera Conde, Emilio 1929- *IntAu&W 82*
Mansergh, Nicholas 1910- *ConAu 105, IntAu&W 82, WrDr 84*
Mansergh, Philip Nicholas Seton 1910- *IntAu&W 82*
Mansfield, Bruce Edgar 1926- *ConAu 103, WrDr 84*
Mansfield, Edwin 1930- *ConAu 3NR, –9R, IntAu&W 82*
Mansfield, Elizabeth *ConAu X*
Mansfield, Harold Hamilton 1912- *ConAu 17R*
Mansfield, Harvey C 1905- *ConAu 1R*
Mansfield, John *IntAu&W 82X*
Mansfield, John M 1936- *ConAu 29R*
Mansfield, Katherine 1888-1923 *CnMWL, ConAu X, LongCTC, ModBrL,*

ModBrL SUP, ModCmwL, TwCA, TwCA SUP, TwCLC 2, –8[port], TwCWr, WhoTwCL
Mansfield, Libby *ConAu X*
Mansfield, N *WrDr 84*
Mansfield, Norman *ConAu X*
Mansfield, Peter 1928- *ConAu 65*
Mansfield, Roger 1939- *ConAu 11NR, –25R, ConSFA*
Mansfield, Walter Kenneth 1921- *WrDr 84*
Manship, David 1927- *ConAu 25R*
Manso, Peter 1940- *ConAu 29R*
Manson, Cecil Murray 1896- *IntAu&W 82*
Manson, Harley A W *TwCWr*
Manson, Richard 1939- *ConAu 29R*
Mansoor, Menahem 1911- *ConAu 41R, IntAu&W 82, WrDr 84*
Mantel, Feliz *IntAu&W 82X*
Mantel, Samuel J, Jr. 1921- *WrDr 84*
Mantel, Samuel Joseph, Jr. 1921- *ConAu 13R*
Mantell, Leroy Harris 1919- *ConAu 37R*
Mantell, Martin E 1936- *ConAu 45*
Mantey, Julius Robert 1890- *ConAu P-1*
Mantle, Burns 1873-1948 *TwCA, TwCA SUP*
Mantle, Mickey 1931- *ConAu 89*
Mantle, Winifred Langford 1911- *ConAu 6NR, –13R, IntAu&W 82, WrDr 84*
Manton, Jo 1919- *ConAu X, SmATA 3*
Manton, Peter *ConAu X, LongCTC, TwCCr&M 80*
Manuel, Frank Edward 1910- *ConAu 6NR, –9R*
Manuel, George 1921- *ConAu 107*
Manus, Willard 1930- *ConAu 108, NatPD 81[port]*
Manushkin, Fran 1942- *ConAu 1NR*
Manushkin, Frances 1942- *ConAu 49, SmATA 7*
Manvell, Arnold Roger 1909- *DcLEL 1940*
Manvell, Roger 1909- *ConAu 1R, –6NR, IntAu&W 82, WrDr 84*
Manville, W H 1930- *ConAu 93*
Manwell, Reginald D 1897- *WrDr 84*
Manwell, Reginald Dickinson 1897- *ConAu 37R*
Many, Seth E 1939- *ConAu 97*
Manyan, Gladys 1911- *ConAu 57*
Manzalaoui, Mahmoud 1924- *ConAu 29R*
Manzella, David 1924- *ConAu 5R*
Manzini, Gianna 1896?-1974 *CIDMEL 80, ConAu 53, WorAu*
Manzoni, Pablo Michelangelo 1939- *ConAu 106*
Mao, James C T 1925- *ConAu 37R*
Mao, Tse-Tung 1893-1976 *ConAu 69, –73*
Mapelli, Erique 1921- *IntAu&W 82*
Mapes, Mary A *ConAu X, SmATA 4, WrDr 84*
Maple, Eric William 1915- *ConAu 6NR, –53, IntAu&W 82, WrDr 84*
Maple, Terry 1946- *ConAu 1NR, –49*
Maples, Evelyn Palmer 1919- *ConAu 2NR, –5R, WrDr 84*
Maples, Phyllis L Buehrens 1918- *IntWWP 82*
Mapp, Alf Johnson, Jr. 1925- *ConAu 1R, –1NR, WrDr 84*
Mapp, Edward *WrDr 84*
Mapp, Edward Charles *ConAu 33R, LivgBAA*
Mappes, Carl Richard 1935- *IntAu&W 82*
Maquet, Jacques Jerome Pierre 1919- *ConAu 8NR, –61*
Mar, Elias 1924- *IntAu&W 82*
Mar, Laureen D *DrAP&F 83*
Mara, Barney *ConAu X, SmATA X*
Mara, Jeanette *SmATA X*
Mara, Thalia 1911- *ConAu 9R*
Marable, Manning 1950- *ConAu 110*
Maragall I Gorina, Joan 1860-1911 *CIDMEL 80*
Marai, Sandor 1900- *CIDMEL 80*
Maraini, Dacia 1936- *ConAu 5R, –11NR, ModRL*
Maraini, Dacia 1937- *TwCWr*
Maraini, Fosco 1912- *IntAu&W 82, WorAu*
Marais, Josef 1905-1978 *ConAu 77, SmATA 24N*
Maramzin, Vladimir Rafailovich 1934- *CIDMEL 80*
Maran, Rene 1887-1960 *ConAu 107, ModBlW, ModFrL*
Maran, Stephen P 1938- *ConAu 57*
Maranda, Elli Kongas 1932- *ConAu 107*
Maranda, Pierre 1930- *ConAu 37R, WrDr 84*
Maranell, Gary M 1932- *ConAu 37R*
Marangell, Virginia Johnson 1924- *ConAu 93, IntAu&W 82*

Marano, Russell *DrAP&F 83*
Marano, Russell 1931- *IntWWP 82*
Maranon, Gregorio 1887-1960 *CIDMEL 80*
Maras, Karl *ConAu X*
Marasmus, Seymour *SmATA X*
Marath, Laurie *ConAu X*
Marath, Sparrow *ConAu X*
Marazzi, Rich 1943- *ConAu 102*
Marberry, M M 1905-1968 *ConAu P-2*
Marble, Harriet Clement 1903-1975 *ConAu 73*
Marble, Samuel D 1915- *ConAu 106*
Marbrook, Del *ConAu X*
Marbrook, Djelloul 1934- *ConAu 73*
Marbut, F B 1905- *ConAu 33R*
Marbut, Frederick B 1905- *WrDr 84*
Marcatante, John 1930- *ConAu 10NR, –25R*
Marceau, Felicien 1913- *CnMD, ConAu X, IntAu&W 82, ModWD, WorAu*
Marceau, LeRoy 1907- *ConAu P-1*
Marceau, Marcel 1923- *ConAu 85*
Marcel, Gabriel Honore 1889-1973 *CIDMEL 80, CnMD, ConAu 102, –45, ConLC 15, ModFrL, ModWD, TwCWr, WorAu*
Marcelin, Pierre 1908- *ConAu 106, ModBlW, ModFrL, TwCA SUP*
Marcelino *ConAu X, SmATA X*
Marcell, David Wyburn 1937- *ConAu 41R*
Marcello, Leo Luke *DrAP&F 83*
Marcellus, Antonius *IntAu&W 82X*
March, Andrew Lee 1932- *ConAu 110*
March, Anthony 1912-1973 *ConAu 45*
March, Hilary *ConAu X, WrDr 84*
March, James Gardner 1928- *ConAu 13R*
March, Joseph Moncure 1899?-1977 *ConAu 69*
March, Katherine B 1910- *IntWWP 82*
March, Maria Teresa 1928- *IntAu&W 82*
March, N H 1927- *WrDr 84*
March, Robert H 1934- *ConAu 61*
March, William *ConAu X*
March, William 1893-1954 *ConAmA, DcLB 9[port], LongCTC, ModAL, TwCA SUP*
March, William J 1915- *ConAu 13R*
Marchaj, C A 1918- *ConAu 5NR, –9R*
Marcham, Frederick George 1898- *ConAu 13R*
Marchand, C Roland 1933- *ConAu 110*
Marchand, Clement 1912- *CreCan 1*
Marchand, Leslie A 1900- *ConAu 65, WrDr 84*
Marchand, Olivier 1928- *CreCan 1*
Marchant, Anyda 1911- *ConAu 13R*
Marchant, Bessie 1862-1941 *TwCCW 83*
Marchant, Catherine *ConAu X, SmATA X, TwCRGW, WrDr 84*
Marchant, Herbert S *ConAu 106*
Marchant, Leslie R 1924- *ConAu 110*
Marchant, Maurice P 1927- *ConAu 110*
Marchant, Rex Alan 1933- *ConAu 13R, WrDr 84*
Marchant, William 1923- *ConAu 69*
Marchenko, Anatoly 1938- *ConAu 25R*
Marcher, Marion Walden 1890- *ConAu 1R, SmATA 10*
Marchese Lander, Peter *IntAu&W 82X*
Marchetti, Albert 1947- *ConAu 89*
Marchetti, Victor *ConAu 108*
Marchi, Giacomo *ConAu X*
Marchione, Margherita Frances 1922- *ConAu 37R, IntAu&W 82*
Marchman, Fred A *DrAP&F 83*
Marchman, Frederick Alan 1941- *IntWWP 82*
Marciniak, Ed 1917- *ConAu 29R*
Marckwardt, Albert H 1903-1975 *ConAu 1R, –4NR, –61*
Marco, Anton N 1943- *ConAu 110*
Marco, Barbara 1934- *ConAu 9R*
Marco, Lou *ConAu X*
Marcombe, Edith Marion *ConAu X, IntAu&W 82X*
Marcosson, Isaac Frederick 1877-1961 *ConAu 89*
Marcoux-Boivin, Cosette 1916- *IntAu&W 82*
Marcson, Simon 1910- *ConAu 49*
Marcum, John A 1927- *ConAu 25R*
Marcus, Aaron 1943- *ConAu 53, IntAu&W 82*
Marcus, Adrianne *DrAP&F 83*
Marcus, Adrianne 1935- *ConAu 1NR, –45, IntAu&W 82*
Marcus, Anne M 1927- *ConAu 73*
Marcus, David 1926- *ConAu 110*
Marcus, Edward 1918- *ConAu 21R*
Marcus, Frank 1928- *ConAu 2NR, –45, ConDr 82, CroCD, DcLB 13[port], DcLEL 1940, IntAu&W 82, WrDr 84*

Marcus, Fred H 1921- *ConAu 104*
Marcus, Harold G 1936- *ConAu 37R, WrDr 84*
Marcus, Howard 1950?- *CreCan 1*
Marcus, Irwin M 1919- *ConAu 45*
Marcus, Jacob Rader 1896- *ConAu 21R*
Marcus, Jerry 1924- *ConAu 97*
Marcus, Joanna *WrDr 84*
Marcus, Joe 1933- *ConAu 65*
Marcus, Maeva 1941- *ConAu 108*
Marcus, Martin 1933- *ConAu 25R*
Marcus, Mildred Rendl 1928- *ConAu 1R, -2NR*
Marcus, Mordecai *DrAP&F 83*
Marcus, Mordecai 1925- *ConAu 77*
Marcus, Morton *DrAP&F 83*
Marcus, Morton 1936- *ConAu 105*
Marcus, Rebecca B 1907- *WrDr 84*
Marcus, Rebecca Brian 1907- *ConAu 1R, -1NR, -5R, SmATA 9*
Marcus, Robert B, Jr. 1947- *IntAu&W 82*
Marcus, Robert D 1936- *ConAu 110*
Marcus, Ruth Barcan 1921- *ConAu 41R*
Marcus, Sheldon 1937- *ConAu 106*
Marcus, Stanley 1905- *ConAu 53, WrDr 84*
Marcus, Steven 1928- *ConAu 41R, IntAu&W 82, WorAu 1970, WrDr 84*
Marcuse, Frederick Lawrence 1916- *ConAu 9R, WrDr 84*
Marcuse, Herbert 1898-1979 *ConAu 89, WorAu*
Marcuse, Ludwig 1894-1971 *ConAu 33R*
Marczewski, Jan 1908- *IntAu&W 82*
Marden, Charles Frederick 1902- *ConAu 37R, WrDr 84*
Marden, William Edward 1947- *ConAu 61, WrDr 84*
Marder, Arthur Jacob 1910-1980 *ConAu 102, -105*
Marder, Daniel 1923- *ConAu 21R*
Marder, Herbert 1934- *ConAu 69*
Marder, Louis 1915- *ConAu 5R*
Mardock, Robert W 1921- *ConAu 17R*
Mardon, Michael 1919- *ConAu 13R*
Mardor, Munya Meir 1913- *ConAu 17R*
Mardus, Elaine Bassler 1914- *ConAu 9R*
Mare, W Harold 1918- *ConAu 61*
Mare, Walter DeLa *TwCA, TwCA SUP*
Marechal, Leopoldo 1900-1970 *ModLAL*
Marei, Sayed Ahmed 1913- *ConAu 73*
Marein, Shirley 1926- *ConAu 1NR, -45*
Marek, George R 1902- *ASpks, ConAu 1NR, -49*
Marek, Hannelore M C 1926- *ConAu 13R*
Marek, Kurt W 1915-1972 *ConAu 33R, ConAu P-2, WorAu*
Marelli, Leonard R 1933-1973 *ConAu P-1*
Marelsson, Thorsteinn 1941- *IntAu&W 82*
Maremaa, Thomas 1945- *ConAu 85, IntAu&W 82*
Marenco, Ethne K 1925- *ConAu 103*
Marer, Paul 1936- *ConAu 105*
Mares, Ernest Anthony *DrAP&F 83*
Mares, F H 1925- *ConAu 25R*
Maresca, Thomas Edward 1938- *ConAu 85*
Mareth, Glenville *ConAu X, IntAu&W 82X*
Marett, Robert Hugh Kirk 1907- *ConAu 25R, IntAu&W 82*
Margadant, Ted W 1941- *ConAu 93*
Margalith, Pinhas Z 1926- *ConAu 110*
Margaret, Karla *ConAu X, SmATA X*
Margenau, Henry 1901- *ConAu 37R, WrDr 84*
Marger, Mary Ann 1934- *ConAu 93*
Margerson, David *ConAu X, IntAu&W 82X*
Margetson, Stella 1912- *ConAu 33R*
Marghieri, Clotilde 1901?-1981 *ConAu 105*
Margold, Stella K *ConAu 81*
Margolies, Edward 1925- *ConAu 11NR, -65*
Margolies, Joseph A 1889-1982 *ConAu 108*
Margolies, Luise 1945- *ConAu 102*
Margolies, Marjorie 1942- *ConAu 65*
Margolin, Edythe *ConAu 69*
Margolin, Malcolm 1940- *ConAu 57*
Margolin, Michael *DrAP&F 83*
Margolin, Victor 1941- *ConAu 65*
Margolis, Diane Rothbard 1933- *ConAu 97, WrDr 84*
Margolis, Ellen 1934- *ConAu 1R*
Margolis, Gary *DrAP&F 83*
Margolis, Gary 1945- *ConAu 73*
Margolis, Jack S 1934- *ConAu 69*
Margolis, Joseph 1924- *ConAu 37R, WrDr 84*
Margolis, Julius 1920- *ConAu 109*
Margolis, Maxine L 1942- *ConAu 53*
Margolis, Michael 1940- *ConAu 93*

Margolis, Richard J 1929- *ConAu 29R, SmATA 4*
Margolis, Susan Spector 1941- *ConAu 81*
Margolis, Susanna 1944- *ConAu 107*
Margolis, William J *DrAP&F 83*
Margolis, William Julius 1927- *IntWWP 82*
Margolius, Sidney 1911-1980 *ConAu 11NR, -21R, -93*
Margon, Lester 1892- *ConAu P-1*
Margroff, Robert E 1930- *ConSFA*
Margulies, Harry D 1907?-1980 *ConAu 97*
Margulies, Herbert F 1928- *ConAu 77*
Margulies, Leo 1900-1975 *ConAu 61, ConSFA*
Margulies, Newton 1932- *ConAu 61*
Margulis, Lynn 1938- *ConAu 4NR, -53*
Margull, Hans Jochen 1925- *ConAu 9R*
Marhoefer, Barbara 1936- *ConAu 61*
Maria DelRey, Sister 1908- *ConAu 5R*
Mariah, Paul *DrAP&F 83*
Mariah, Paul 1937- *ConAu 4NR, -53, WrDr 84*
Mariana *ConAu X, SmATA X*
Mariani, Paul *DrAP&F 83*
Mariani, Paul L 1940- *ConAu 29R*
Mariano, Frank 1931?-1976 *ConAu 69*
Marias, Julian 1914- *ConAu 5NR, -9R, WrDr 84*
Marias Aguilera, Julian 1914- *CIDMEL 80*
Marie Andre DuSacre-Coeur, Sister 1899- *ConAu 5R, IntAu&W 82*
Marie DeLaSagesse, Soeur *CreCan 1*
Marie Therese, Mother 1891- *ConAu P-1*
Marie, Beverly Sainte *ConAu X*
Marie, Buffy Sainte *ConAu X*
Marie, Charles P 1939- *IntAu&W 82*
Marie, Geraldine 1949- *ConAu 108*
Marie, Janet *DrAP&F 83*
Marie, Jeanne 1922- *ConAu X*
Marien, Michael 1938- *ConAu 1NR, -49*
Maril, Nadja 1954- *ConAu 85*
Marill, Alvin H 1934- *ConAu 73*
Marilla *IntAu&W 82X*
Marilla, E L 1900- *ConAu P-2*
Marilue *ConAu X*
Marimow, William K 1947- *ConAu 93*
Marin, A C *ConAu X, WrDr 84*
Marin, Diego 1914- *ConAu 17R*
Marin, Luis Munoz *ConAu X*
Marina, Jeanne *DrAP&F 83*
Marinacci, Barbara 1933- *ConAu 9NR, -21R*
Marinaccio, Anthony 1912- *ConAu 53*
Marine, David 1880?-1976 *ConAu 69*
Marine, Gene 1926- *ConAu 65*
Marine, Nick *ConAu X*
Marinelli, Peter V 1933- *ConAu 41R*
Mariner, David 1920- *ConAu X, IntAu&W 82*
Mariner, Scott *ConAu X*
Marinetti, F T 1876-1944 *TwCLC 10[port]*
Marinetti, Filippo Tommaso 1876-1944 *CIDMEL 80, CnMD, ConAu 107, LongCTC, ModWD, WhoTwCL*
Maring, Joel M 1935- *ConAu 49*
Maring, Norman H 1914- *ConAu 17R*
Marini, Frank N 1935- *ConAu 45*
Marinkovic, Ranko 1913- *CIDMEL 80, ModSL 2*
Marino, Carolyn Fitch 1942- *ConAu 110*
Marino, Dorothy Bronson 1912- *ConAu 73, SmATA 14*
Marino, John J 1948- *ConAu 106*
Marino, Joseph D 1912?-1983 *ConAu 109*
Marino, Trentino J 1917- *ConAu 65*
Marinoni, Rosa Zagnoni 1888?-1970 *ConAu P-1*
Marion, Frances 1886-1973 *ConAu 41R*
Marion, Frieda 1912- *ConAu 8NR, -61*
Marion, Henry *ConAu X*
Marion, John Francis 1922- *ConAu 3NR, -5R*
Marion, Paul *DrAP&F 83*
Mariotti, Marcello 1938- *ConAu 29R*
Marique, Joseph M F 1899- *ConAu 33R*
Marisa *ConAu X*
Mariscal, Richard N 1935- *ConAu 53*
Maritain, Jacques 1882-1973 *CIDMEL 80, ConAu 41R, -85, LongCTC, TwCA, TwCA SUP*
Maritano, Nino 1919- *ConAu 13R*
Maritz, Empie *IntAu&W 82X*
Maritz, Magdalena Petronella 1922- *IntAu&W 82*
Marius, Richard 1933- *ConAu 25R*
Marjoram, J *ConAu X, LongCTC*
Mark, Charles Christopher 1927- *ConAu 1R, -1NR*

Mark, David 1922- *ConAu 1R*
Mark, Edwina *ConAu X*
Mark, Irving 1908- *ConAu P-1, WrDr 84*
Mark, Jan 1943- *ConAu 93, IntAu&W 82, SmATA 22[port], TwCCW 83, WrDr 84*
Mark, John *IntAu&W 82X*
Mark, Jon *ConAu X*
Mark, Julius 1898-1977 *ConAu 73, -81*
Mark, Matthew *ConAu X*
Mark, Max 1910- *ConAu 73*
Mark, Michael L 1936- *ConAu 93*
Mark, Paul J 1931- *IntWWP 82*
Mark, Pauline 1913- *ConAu 7NR, -17R, SmATA 14*
Mark, Polly *ConAu X, SmATA X*
Mark, Robert 1930- *ConAu 110*
Mark, Shelley M 1922- *ConAu 1R, -1NR*
Mark, Steven J *WrDr 84*
Mark, Steven J 1913- *ConAu 17R*
Mark, Ted *ConAu X*
Mark, Theonie Diakidis 1938- *ConAu 69*
Mark, Wendy *DrAP&F 83*
Mark, Yudel 1897-1975 *ConAu 61*
Mark-Alan, Roy *ConAu X*
Markandandaya, Kamala Purnalya 1924- *DcLEL 1940*
Markandaya, Kamala 1924- *ConAu X, ConLC 8, ConNov 82, ModCmwL, WorAu, WrDr 84*
Markandaya, Kamela *IntAu&W 82*
Markbreit, Jerry 1935- *ConAu 49*
Marke, Julius J 1913- *ConAu 17R*
Markel, Geraldine 1939- *ConAu 108*
Markel, Lester 1894-1977 *ConAu 37R, -73*
Markels, Julian 1925- *ConAu 25R*
Marken, Jack W 1922- *ConAu 45, -49*
Marker, Frederick J, Jr. 1936- *ConAu 41R, IntAu&W 82*
Marker, Lise-Lone 1934- *ConAu 8NR, -61, IntAu&W 82*
Markert, Lawrence *DrAP&F 83*
Market Man *ConAu X, WrDr 84*
Markevitch, Igor 1912-1983 *ConAu 109*
Markey, Gene 1895-1980 *ConAu 97, ConAu P-1*
Markfield, Wallace *DrAP&F 83*
Markfield, Wallace 1926- *ConAu 69, ConLC 8, ConNov 82, Conv 1, DcLB 2, DcLEL 1940, WorAu, WrDr 84*
Markgraf, Carl 1928- *ConAu 49*
Markham, Clarence M, Jr. 1911- *ConAu 69*
Markham, Dewey 1904-1981 *ConAu 108*
Markham, Edwin 1852-1940 *LongCTC, ModAL, TwCA, TwCA SUP*
Markham, Felix 1908- *ConAu P-1, DcLEL 1940*
Markham, James M 1943- *ConAu 93*
Markham, James W 1910-1972 *ConAu P-2*
Markham, Jesse William 1916- *ConAu 9R*
Markham, Julie *IntWWP 82X*
Markham, Marion M *DrAP&F 83*
Markham, Marion M 1929- *IntAu&W 82*
Markham, Meeler 1914- *ConAu 25R*
Markham, Pigmeat *ConAu X*
Markham, Reed 1957- *ConAu 110*
Markham, Robert *ConAu X, ConLC 8, WorAu, WrDr 84*
Marki, Ivan 1934- *ConAu 97*
Markides, Kyriacos 1942- *ConAu 81*
Markievicz, Countess 1868-1927 *LongCTC*
Markiewicz, Henryk 1922- *IntAu&W 82*
Markiewicz, Wladyslaw 1920- *IntAu&W 82*
Markins, W S *ConAu X, SmATA 7*
Markish, David 1938- *ConAu 69*
Markle, Fletcher 1921- *CreCan 1*
Markle, Joyce B 1942- *ConAu 69*
Markle, Robert 1936- *CreCan 1*
Markle, William Fletcher 1921- *CreCan 1*
Markley, Kenneth A 1933- *ConAu 61*
Markman, Howard 1950- *ConAu 69*
Markman, Sherwin J 1929- *ConAu 104*
Markman, Sidney David 1911- *ConAu P-2*
Markmann, Charles Lam 1913- *ConAu 13R*
Marko, Katherine D 1913- *ConAu 29R, SmATA 28[port], WrDr 84*
Marko, Kurt 1928- *IntAu&W 82*
Markoe, Karen 1942- *ConAu 81*
Markoff, Hildy 1929- *ConAmTC*
Markoff, Sol *DrAP&F 83*
Markoosie 1942- *ConAu X, TwCCW 83, WrDr 84*

Markov, Georgi 1929?-1978 *ConAu 104*
Markov, Vladimir 1920- *ConAu 17R*
Markova, Alicia 1910- *ConAu P-2*
Markovic, Vida E 1916- *ConAu 33R, WrDr 84*
Markovitz, Irving Leonard 1934- *ConAu 33R*
Markowitz, Norman Daniel 1943- *ConAu 45*
Marks, Ada Greiner 1896- *IntWWP 82*
Marks, Alfred H 1920- *ConAu 45*
Marks, Aline Musyl 1920- *IntWWP 82*
Marks, Arnold 1912- *ConAmTC*
Marks, Barry A 1926- *ConAu 17R*
Marks, Burton 1930- *ConAu 107*
Marks, Charles 1922- *ConAu 5NR, -53*
Marks, Claude 1915- *ConAu 61*
Marks, Edith Bobroff 1924- *ConAu 17R*
Marks, Edward S 1936- *ConAu 45*
Marks, Elaine 1930- *ConAu 7NR, -17R*
Marks, Eli S 1911- *ConAu 85*
Marks, Frederick 1940- *ConAu 97*
Marks, Geoffrey 1906- *ConAu 33R*
Marks, Henry S 1933- *ConAu 73*
Marks, J *ConAu X, DrAP&F 83, SmATA X*
Marks, J M 1921- *SmATA 13*
Marks, James Macdonald 1921- *ConAu 61, IntAu&W 82, WrDr 84*
Marks, James R 1932- *ConAu 17R*
Marks, Jeannette 1875-1964 *TwCA, TwCA SUP*
Marks, John 1943- *ConAu 110*
Marks, John H 1923- *ConAu 17R*
Marks, Laurence 1948- *IntAu&W 82*
Marks, Margaret L 1911?-1980 *ConAu 101, SmATA 23N*
Marks, Mickey Klar 1914- *ConAu 1R, -6NR, SmATA 12*
Marks, Norton E 1932- *ConAu 21R*
Marks, Pat R *ConAu X*
Marks, Percy 1891-1956 *TwCA, TwCA SUP*
Marks, Peter *ConAu X, SmATA X*
Marks, Rita 1938- *ConAu 106*
Marks, Sally 1931- *ConAu 102*
Marks, Sema 1942- *ConAu 29R*
Marks, Stan 1929- *ConAu 29R, SmATA 14, WrDr 84*
Marks, Stuart A 1939- *ConAu 69*
Marks-Highwater, J *SmATA X*
Marksberry, Mary Lee *ConAu 13R, WrDr 84*
Markson, David *DrAP&F 83*
Markson, David M 1927- *ConAu 1NR, -49, WrDr 84*
Markstein, David L 1920- *ConAu 29R*
Markun, Alan Fletcher 1925- *ConAu 45*
Markun, Patricia Maloney 1924- *ConAu 4NR, -5R, SmATA 15*
Markus, Julia *DrAP&F 83*
Markus, Julia 1939- *ConAu 105, WrDr 84*
Markus, R A 1924- *ConAu 65*
Marland, Edward Allen 1912- *ConAu 17R*
Marland, Michael 1934- *ConAu 103, WrDr 84*
Marland, Sidney P 1914- *ConAu 53*
Marlatt, Daphne *DrAP&F 83*
Marlatt, Daphne 1942- *ConAu 25R, IntWWP 82*
Marlborough *ConAu X*
Marleau, Louise *CreCan 1*
Marley, Augusta Anne d1973 *ConAu 41R*
Marley, Bob 1945- *ConAu X, ConLC 17*
Marley, Robert Nesta 1945-1981 *ConAu 103, -107*
Marlin, Henry *ConAu X, IntAu&W 82X*
Marlin, Hilda *ConAu X*
Marlin, Jeffrey 1940- *ConAu 45*
Marling, Yvonne Rodd *ConAu X*
Marlis, Stefanie *DrAP&F 83*
Marlo, John A 1934- *ConAu 29R*
Marlor, Clark Strang 1922- *ConAu 37R, WrDr 84*
Marlot, Raymond *ConAu X*
Marlow, David 1943- *ConAu 107, WrDr 84*
Marlow, Edwina *ConAu X*
Marlow, Joyce *ConAu X*
Marlow, Joyce 1929- *WrDr 84*
Marlow, Joyce Mary 1929- *ConAu 65, IntAu&W 82*
Marlow, Louis 1881- *LongCTC*
Marlowe, Alan Stephen 1937- *ConAu 21R*
Marlowe, Amy Bell *ConAu P-2, SmATA 1*
Marlowe, Dan J 1914- *ConAu 1R, -1NR, TwCCr&M 80, WrDr 84*
Marlowe, Derek 1938- *ConAu 11NR, -17R, TwCCr&M 80, WrDr 84*

Marlowe, Don *ConAu 61*
Marlowe, Hugh *WrDr 84*
Marlowe, Hugh 1929- *ConAu X, TwCCr&M 80*
Marlowe, Kenneth 1926- *ConAu 13R*
Marlowe, Stephen *WrDr 84*
Marlowe, Stephen 1928- *ConAu 6NR, TwCCr&M 80*
Marlowe, Webb *ConAu X*
Marlyn, John 1912- *ConAu 9R, DcLEL 1940*
Marmion, Harry A 1931- *ConAu 25R*
Marmon, William F, Jr. 1942- *ConAu 77*
Marmor, J 1910- *ConAu 25R*
Marmor, T R 1939- *ConAu 29R*
Marmur, Jacland 1901- *ConAu 9R*
Marmur, Mildred 1930- *ConAu 5R*
Marne, Patricia 1928- *IntAu&W 82*
Marnell, William H 1907- *ConAu 21R*
Marney, Carlyle 1916- *ConAu 57*
Marney, Dean 1952- *ConAu 110*
Marney, John 1933- *ConAu 69*
Marnham, Patrick 1943- *ConAu 102*
Marokvia, Artur 1909- *SmATA 31*
Marokvia, Mireille 1918- *ConAu 29R, SmATA 5*
Marossi, Ruth *ConAu X*
Marot, Marc *ConAu X*
Marothy, Janos 1925- *IntAu&W 82*
Marovic, Tonci Petrasov 1934- *IntWWP 82*
Marowitz, Charles 1934- *IntAu&W 82, WrDr 84*
Marowitz, Charles 1935- *DcLEL 1940*
Marple, Allen Clark 1901?-1968 *ConAu 106*
Marple, Hugo D 1920- *ConAu 53*
Marples, William F 1907- *ConAu P-1*
Marquand, John P, Jr. *DrAP&F 83*
Marquand, John Phillips 1893-1960 *ConAu 85, ConLC 2, -10, DcLB 9[port], LongCTC, ModAL, TwCA, TwCA SUP, TwCCr&M 80, TwCWr*
Marquard, Leopold 1897- *ConAu 5R*
Marquardt, Dorothy Ann 1921- *ConAu 13R*
Marquardt, Hedi *IntAu&W 82X*
Marques, Rene 1919-1979 *ConAu 85, -97, CroCD, ModLAL, ModWD*
Marquess, Harlan E 1931- *ConAu 49*
Marquez, Gabriel Garcia *ConLC 2, WorAu*
Marquez, Robert 1942- *ConAu 53*
Marquina, Eduardo 1879-1946 *ClDMEL 80*
Marquis, Arnold *ConAu 57*
Marquis, Don 1878-1937 *DcLB 25[port]*
Marquis, Don Robert Perry 1878-1937 *ConAmA, ConAu 104, LongCTC, ModAL, TwCA, TwCA SUP, TwCLC 7[port], TwCWr*
Marquis, Donald G 1908-1973 *ConAu 45*
Marquis, G Welton 1916- *ConAu 17R, WrDr 84*
Marr, David G 1937- *WrDr 84*
Marr, David George 1937- *ConAu 33R*
Marr, John S 1940- *ConAu 81*
Marr, Lem *IntWWP 82X*
Marr, William Wei-Yi 1936- *IntWWP 82*
Marr-Johnson, Diana 1908- *WrDr 84*
Marr-Johnson, Diana Julia 1908- *ConAu 13R*
Marrafino, Elizabeth *DrAP&F 83*
Marranca, Bonnie 1947- *ConAmTC, ConAu 9NR, -65*
Marreco, Anne *WrDr 84*
Marreco, Anne 1912- *ConAu X*
Marric, J J *ConAu X, LongCTC, TwCCr&M 80, WorAu*
Marrin, Albert 1936- *ConAu 49*
Marriner, Ernest 1891-1983 *ConAu 109*
Marriner, Ernest Cummings 1891- *ConAu 37R, WrDr 84*
Marrington, Pauline 1921- *ConAu 10NR, -65*
Marriott, Alice Lee 1910- *ConAu 57, SmATA 31[port]*
Marriott, Anne 1913- *ConAu 102, CreCan 1*
Marriott, Charles 1869-1957 *LongCTC, ModBrL, TwCA, TwCA SUP*
Marriott Watson *LongCTC*
Marriott-Watson, Nan 1899-1982 *ConAu 107*
Marris, Robin Lapthorn 1924- *ConAu 5R, -8NR*
Marris, Ruth 1948- *ConAu 106*
Marrison, L W 1901- *ConAu 29R*
Marrocco, W Thomas 1909- *ConAu 9R*
Marrodan, Mario Angel 1932- *IntAu&W 82*
Marrone, Robert 1941- *ConAu 77*
Marroquin, Patricio *ConAu X*
Marrow, Alfred J 1905-1978 *ConAu 77, -81*
Marrow, Stanley B 1931- *ConAu 10NR, -25R*

Marrs, Edwin W, Jr. 1928- *ConAu 25R*
Marrus, Michael Robert 1941- *ConAu 33R*
Mars, Florence L 1923- *ConAu 101*
Mars, Witold Tadeusz 1912- *ConAu 25R, SmATA 3*
Mars-Jones, Adam 1954- *ConAu 109*
Marsano, Ramon *ConAu X*
Marsch, Lucy-Leone 1912- *IntWWP 82*
Marsden, George 1939- *ConAu 73*
Marsden, James *ConAu X*
Marsden, Lorna R 1942- *ConAu 85*
Marsden, Malcolm Morse 1922- *ConAu 5R*
Marsden, Peter Richard Valentine 1940- *ConAu 77, WrDr 84*
Marsden, Philip Kitson 1916- *WrDr 84*
Marsden-Smedley, Hester 1901-1982 *ConAu 107*
Marse, Juan 1933- *ClDMEL 80*
Marsh, Analyticus *ConAu X*
Marsh, Andrew *ConAu X*
Marsh, Clifton E *DrAP&F 83*
Marsh, Clifton E 1946- *ConAu 77*
Marsh, Dave 1950- *ConAu 97*
Marsh, David Charles 1917- *ConAu 103*
Marsh, Derick Rupert Clement 1928- *WrDr 84*
Marsh, Edith Ngaio 1899- *IntAu&W 82*
Marsh, Sir Edward Howard 1872-1953 *LongCTC, ModBrL*
Marsh, Edwin *ConAu X*
Marsh, Henry 1911-1976 *ConAu X*
Marsh, Irving T 1907-1982 *ConAu 9R, -107*
Marsh, J E *ConAu X, SmATA X*
Marsh, Jean 1897- *ConAu X, SmATA X, TwCRGW, WrDr 84*
Marsh, Jeri 1940- *ConAu 85*
Marsh, John 1904- *ConAu P-1, WrDr 84*
Marsh, John 1907- *ConAu P-1, IntAu&W 82*
Marsh, John Leslie 1927- *ConAu 1NR, -45*
Marsh, Leonard 1906- *ConAu 37R, IntAu&W 82, WrDr 84*
Marsh, Leonard 1930- *ConAu 73*
Marsh, Margaret Sammartino 1945- *ConAu 106*
Marsh, Mary Val 1925- *ConAu 11NR, -69*
Marsh, Meredith 1946- *ConAu 77*
Marsh, Ngaio 1899-1982 *ConAu 6NR, -9R, ConLC 7, ConNov 82, LongCTC, TwCA[port], TwCA SUP, TwCCr&M 80, TwCWr*
Marsh, Norman Stayner 1913- *IntAu&W 82, WrDr 84*
Marsh, Patrick O 1928- *ConAu 25R*
Marsh, Paul *ConAu X*
Marsh, Peter T 1935- *ConAu 33R, IntAu&W 82, WrDr 84*
Marsh, Philip M 1893- *ConAu 9R*
Marsh, Rebecca *ConAu X*
Marsh, Robert 1926- *ConAu 17R*
Marsh, Robert C 1924- *ConAu 13R*
Marsh, Robert Mortimer 1931- *ConAu 1R, -2NR, IntAu&W 82, WrDr 84*
Marsh, Ronald 1914- *ConAu 13R, WrDr 84*
Marsh, Spencer 1931- *ConAu 61*
Marsh, Susan 1914- *ConAu 9R*
Marsh, U Grant 1911- *ConAu 57*
Marsh, Willard 1922-1970 *ConAu P-2*
Marshak, Robert Eugene 1916- *ConAu 107, WrDr 84*
Marshak, Samuil Yakovlevich 1887-1964 *ClDMEL 80, ModWD*
Marshall *IntWWP 82X*
Marshall, Alan 1902- *ConAu 85*
Marshall, Alfred 1884-1965 *ConAu 5R*
Marshall, Annie Jessie 1922- *ConAu P-1*
Marshall, Anthony D 1924- *ConAu 29R, SmATA 18*
Marshall, Archibald 1866-1934 *LongCTC, TwCA*
Marshall, Arthur 1910- *IntAu&W 82*
Marshall, Bill 1937- *ConAu 65*
Marshall, Bruce 1899- *ConAu 5R, ConNov 82, LongCTC, TwCA, TwCA SUP, WrDr 84*
Marshall, Burke 1922- *ConAu 13R*
Marshall, Byron K 1936- *ConAu 33R*
Marshall, Catherine 1914- *ConAu 8NR, -17R, SmATA 2, WrDr 84*
Marshall, Catherine 1914-1983 *ConAu 109, SmATA 34N*
Marshall, Charles Burton 1908- *ConAu 37R*
Marshall, Charles Wheeler 1906- *ConAu 110*
Marshall, Christabel *LongCTC*
Marshall, D Bruce 1931- *ConAu 65*
Marshall, David F 1938- *ConAu 25R*

Masefield, Geoffrey Bussell 1911- *ConAu 5R*
Masefield, John 1878-1967 *CnMD, CnMWL, ConAu 25R, ConAu P-2, ConLC 11, DcLB 10[port], LongCTC, ModBrL, ModBrL SUP, ModWD, SmATA 19, TwCA, TwCA SUP, TwCCW 83, TwCWr, WhoTwCL*
Maser, Edward A 1923- *ConAu 45*
Maser, Jack D 1937- *ConAu 57*
Masey, Mary Lou 1932- *ConAu 21R*
Masha *ConAu X*
Masheck, Joseph 1942- *ConAu 105*
Masia, Seth 1948- *ConAu 110*
Masiello, Thomas *DrAP&F 83*
Masinton, Charles G 1938- *ConAu 77*
Maskell, David 1940- *WrDr 84*
Maslin, Alice 1914?-1981 *ConAu 104*
Maslin, Bonnie L 1947- *ConAu 107*
Maslow, Abraham H 1908-1970 *ConAu 1R, -4NR, -29R*
Maslowski, Peter 1944- *ConAu 97*
Maslowski, Raymond M 1931- *ConAu 93*
Maslowski, Stanley 1937- *ConAu 21R*
Masnata, Albert 1900- *ConAu 93*
Maso, Salustiano 1923- *IntAu&W 82*
Mason, A E W 1865-1948 *TwCCr&M 80*
Mason, Alfred Edward Woodley 1865-1948 *LongCTC, ModBrL, TwCA, TwCA SUP, TwCWr*
Mason, Alpheus Thomas 1899- *ConAu 1R, IntAu&W 82*
Mason, Arthur Telford *LongCTC*
Mason, B J 1944- *LivgBAA*
Mason, Betty Oxford 1930- *ConAu 37R, IntAu&W 82*
Mason, Bobbie Ann *DrAP&F 83*
Mason, Bobbie Ann 1940- *ConAu 11NR, -53*
Mason, Bruce 1921- *ConDr 82, WrDr 84*
Mason, Bruce 1923- *ConAu 9R*
Mason, Bruce Edward George 1921-1982 *ConAu 110*
Mason, Carola *ConAu X*
Mason, Chuck *ConAu X, TwCWW*
Mason, Clarence, Jr. 1904- *ConAu 57*
Mason, David E 1928- *ConAu 21R*
Mason, Douglas Rankine 1918- *ConAu 1NR, -49, ConSFA, IntAu&W 82, TwCSFW, WrDr 84*
Mason, Edmund 1911- *ConAu 103, IntAu&W 82, WrDr 84*
Mason, Edward S 1899- *ConAu 73*
Mason, Edwin A 1905-1979 *ConAu 89, ConAu P-2, SmATA 32N*
Mason, Ernst *ConAu X*
Mason, Eudo C 1901-1969 *ConAu P-1*
Mason, F VanWyck 1901-1978 *ConAu 5R, -8NR, -81, SmATA 26N, -3, TwCCr&M 80*
Mason, Francis Kenneth 1928- *ConAu 103, WrDr 84*
Mason, Frank Earl 1893-1979 *ConAu 89*
Mason, Frank W 1901- *ConAu X, SmATA X*
Mason, Gabriel Richard 1884-1979 *ConAu 85*
Mason, Gene 1928- *ConAu 89*
Mason, George E 1932- *ConAu 29R*
Mason, George Frederick 1904- *ConAu 73, SmATA 14*
Mason, Haydn Trevor 1929- *ConAu 3NR, -9R, IntAu&W 82, WrDr 84*
Mason, Herbert 1927- *WrDr 84*
Mason, Herbert Molloy, Jr. 1927- *ConAu 6NR, -13R*
Mason, Herbert Warren, Jr. 1932- *ConAu 85, IntAu&W 82*
Mason, John Brown 1904- *ConAu 49*
Mason, John-Frederick 1940- *IntWWP 82*
Mason, Julian D, Jr. 1931- *ConAu 37R*
Mason, Lee W *WrDr 84*
Mason, Lowell Blake 1893-1983 *ConAu 110*
Mason, Madeline 1913- *ConAu 9R*
Mason, Malcolm John 1912- *WrDr 84*
Mason, Michael Henry 1900-1982 *ConAu 108*
Mason, Miriam Evangeline 1900-1973 *ConAu 1R, -103, SmATA 2, -26N*
Mason, Nicholas 1938- *ConAu 104, WrDr 84*
Mason, Pamela 1918- *ConAu 105*
Mason, Paul T 1937- *ConAu 33R*
Mason, Philip *WrDr 84*
Mason, Philip 1906- *ConAu 3NR, -9R, IntAu&W 82*
Mason, Philip 1927- *ConAu 17R, MichAu 80*
Mason, R A K 1905-1971 *ConAu 89*
Mason, Raymond 1926- *ConAu 9R*

Mason, Richard 1919- *ConAu 9R, DcLEL 1940*
Mason, Robert E 1914- *ConAu 1R*
Mason, Ronald Alison Kells 1905-1971 *LongCTC, TwCWr, WorAu*
Mason, Ronald Charles 1912- *ConAu 13R, IntAu&W 82, WrDr 84*
Mason, Ruth Fitch 1890-1974 *ConAu 53*
Mason, Stanley 1917- *IntWWP 82*
Mason, Stuart *LongCTC*
Mason, Tally *ConAu X, SmATA 5*
Mason, Ted *ConAu X*
Mason, Theodore C 1921- *ConAu 109*
Mason, Tyler *ConAu X*
Mason, VanWyck 1897- *TwCA, TwCA SUP*
Mason, VanWyck 1901-1978 *ConAu X*
Mason, Walt 1862-1939 *LongCTC, TwCA*
Mason, Will Edwin 1912- *ConAu 5R*
Masotti, Louis Henry 1934- *ConAu 41R, IntAu&W 82*
Maspero, Sir Gaston Camille Charles 1846-1916 *TwCA, TwCA SUP*
Mass, William *ConAu X*
Massa, Ann 1940- *ConAu 29R*
Massa, Richard W 1932- *ConAu 57*
Massanari, Jared 1943- *ConAu 65*
Massaquoi, Hans J 1926- *ConAu 69*
Massari, Roberto 1946- *IntAu&W 82*
Massarik, Fred 1926- *ConAu 1R*
Massel, Mark S 1910- *ConAu P-1*
Masselink, Ben 1919- *ConAu 17R*
Masselman, George 1897-1971 *ConAu 9R, SmATA 19*
Masserman, Jules H 1905- *ConAu 69*
Massey, Erika 1900- *ConAu 61*
Massey, Floyd, Jr. 1915- *ConAu 65*
Massey, Gerald J 1934- *ConAu 89*
Massey, Harrie Stewart Wilson 1908- *WrDr 84*
Massey, Irving 1924- *ConAu 77*
Massey, James Earl 1930- *ConAu 29R, WrDr 84*
Massey, Joseph Earl 1897- *ConAu 29R, IntAu&W 82, WrDr 84*
Massey, Mary Elizabeth 1915- *ConAu P-2*
Massey, Raymond 1896- *ConAu 104*
Massey, Raymond 1896-1983 *ConAu 110*
Massey, Reginald 1932- *ConAu 21R, DcLEL 1940*
Massialas, Byron G 1929- *ConAu 8NR, -21R, WrDr 84*
Massie, Diane Redfield 1930- *ConAu 81, SmATA 16*
Massie, Joseph Logan 1921- *ConAu 1R, -2NR, WrDr 84*
Massie, Robert K 1929- *ASpks, ConAu 77*
Massine, Leonide *ConAu X*
Massing, Hede 1899-1981 *ConAu 108*
Massingham, Harold 1932- *WrDr 84*
Massingham, Harold John 1888-1952 *LongCTC, TwCA, TwCA SUP*
Massingham, Harold William 1932- *ConAu 65, ConP 80, DcLEL 1940*
Massingham, Henry William 1860-1924 *LongCTC*
Massis, Henri 1886-1970 *CIDMEL 80, ConAu 29R*
Massman, Virgil Frank 1929- *ConAu 37R*
Masson, David 1822-1907 *LongCTC*
Masson, David I 1915- *ConAu 25R, ConSFA, TwCSFW, WrDr 84*
Masson, Georgina 1912- *ConAu X*
Masson, Henri Leopold 1907- *CreCan 2*
Masson, Jean-Pierre *CreCan 1*
Masson, Loyes 1915-1969 *ConAu P-1*
Massow, Rosalind *ConAu 89*
Massy, William F 1934- *ConAu 41R*
Mast, Gerald 1940- *ConAu 69*
Mast, Russell L 1915- *ConAu 13R*
Masterman, C F G 1874-1927 *LongCTC*
Masterman, John Cecil 1891-1977 *ConAu 6NR, -9R, -69*
Masterman-Smith, Virginia 1937- *ConAu 110*
Masteroff, Joe 1919- *ConDr 82D*
Masters, Anthony *ConAu 25R, DcLEL 1940*
Masters, Edgar Lee 1868?-1950 *TwCLC 2*
Masters, Edgar Lee 1869?-1950 *CnMWL, ConAmA, ConAu 104, LongCTC, ModAL, TwCA, TwCA SUP, TwCWr, WhoTwCL*
Masters, Elaine 1932- *ConAu 57*
Masters, G Mallary 1936- *ConAu 25R*
Masters, Greg *DrAP&F 83*
Masters, Greg 1952- *IntWWP 82*

Masters, Hardin 1899?-1979 *ConAu 89*
Masters, Hilary *DrAP&F 83*
Masters, Hilary 1928- *ConAu 25R, WrDr 84*
Masters, John 1914- *ConAu 108, ConNov 82, DcLEL 1940, LongCTC, ModBrL, TwCA SUP, TwCWr, WrDr 84*
Masters, John 1914-1983 *ConAu 110*
Masters, Kelly Ray 1897- *ConAu 1R, SmATA 3*
Masters, Les *ConAmTC*
Masters, Mildred 1932- *ConAu 110*
Masters, Nicholas A 1929- *ConAu 13R*
Masters, Roger D 1933- *ConAu 21R, IntAu&W 82, WrDr 84*
Masters, William *ConAu X, SmATA 2*
Masters, William H 1915- *AuNews 1, ConAu 21R, IntAu&W 82, WrDr 84*
Masters, Zeke *ConAu X*
Masterson, Dan *DrAP&F 83*
Masterson, Dan 1934- *ConAu 81, IntWWP 82*
Masterson, J B *ConAu X*
Masterson, James F 1925- *ConAu 69*
Masterson, Patrick 1936- *ConAu 73*
Masterson, Peter *ConDr 82D*
Masterson, Thomas R 1915- *ConAu 25R, WrDr 84*
Masterson, Whit *ConAu X, TwCCr&M 80, WrDr 84*
Masterton, Elsie 1914-1966 *ConAu 5R*
Masterton, Graham 1946- *ConAu 105, WrDr 84*
Mastny, Vojtech 1936- *ConAu 33R, WrDr 84*
Maston, T B 1897- *ConAu 2NR, -5R*
Maston, Thomas B 1897- *WrDr 84*
Maston, Thomas Bufford 1897- *IntAu&W 82*
Mastro, Susan 1945- *ConAu 69*
Mastroianni, Tony *ConAmTC*
Mastronardi, Lucio 1930-1979 *CIDMEL 80*
Masuda, Yoneji 1909- *ConAu 109*
Masur, Gerhard Strassman 1901-1975 *ConAu 1R, -4NR*
Masur, Harold Q 1909- *ConAu 77, TwCCr&M 80, WrDr 84*
Masur, Jenny 1948- *ConAu 65*
Mata, Daya 1914- *ConAu 77*
Mata Hari 1876-1917 *LongCTC*
Matanzo, Jane Brady 1940- *ConAu 103*
Matarazzo, James Michael 1941- *ConAu 37R*
Matarazzo, Joseph D 1925- *ConAu 57*
Matcha, Jack *DrAP&F 83*
Matcha, Jack 1919- *ConAu 1R, -2NR, IntAu&W 82*
Matchett, William H *DrAP&F 83*
Matchett, William H 1923- *ConAu 13R, ConP 80, IntWWP 82, WrDr 84*
Matchette, Katharine E 1941- *ConAu 53*
Matczak, Sebastian A 1914- *ConAu 9R*
Matejka, Ladislav 1919- *ConAu 73*
Matejko, Alexander J 1924- *ConAu 6NR, -57*
Matek, Ord 1922- *ConAu 89*
Matenko, Percy 1901- *ConAu 1NR, -45*
Materer, Timothy 1940- *ConAu 89*
Mates, Julian 1927- *ConAu 1R*
Matesky, Ralph 1913-1979 *ConAu 5R*
Mathai, M O 1909-1981 *ConAu 108*
Mathay, Francis 1925- *ConAu 57*
Mathe, Albert *ConAu X*
Mather, Anne *TwCRGW, WrDr 84*
Mather, Berkely *TwCCr&M 80, WrDr 84*
Mather, Bertrand 1914- *ConAu P-1*
Mather, Frank Jewett, Jr. 1868-1953 *TwCA, TwCA SUP*
Mather, June 1924- *ConAu 107*
Mather, Kirtley Fletcher 1888- *ConAu 17R*
Mather, Leonard 1909- *WrDr 84*
Mather, Richard B 1913- *ConAu 73*
Mathers, Michael 1945- *ConAu 65*
Mathers, Peter 1931- *ConNov 82, WrDr 84*
Mathes, J C 1931- *ConAu 49*
Mathes, W Michael 1936- *ConAu 8NR, -61*
Matheson, Joan 1924- *ConAu 97*
Matheson, John Ross 1917- *ConAu 106*
Matheson, Richard 1926- *ConAu 97, ConSFA, DcLB 8[port], TwCSFW, WrDr 84*
Matheson, Sylvia A *ConAu X, WrDr 84*
Matheson, William H 1929- *ConAu 21R*
Mathew, David 1902-1975 *ConAu P-2*
Mathew, Gervase 1905- *ConAu 9R*
Mathew, Ray 1929- *ConAu 17R, ConDr 82,*

TwCWr, WrDr 84
Mathew, Raymond Frank 1929- DcLEL 1940
Mathews, Anthony Stuart 1930- ConAu 93
Mathews, Arthur 1903?-1980 ConAu 102
Mathews, Denise ConAu X
Mathews, Donald G 1932- ConAu 17R
Mathews, Donald K 1923- ConAu 57
Mathews, Eleanor Muth 1923- ConAu 13R
Mathews, Evelyn Craw 1906- ConAu P-2
Mathews, F X DrAP&F 83
Mathews, F X 1935- ConAu 25R
Mathews, H Lee 1939- ConAu 37R
Mathews, Harry DrAP&F 83
Mathews, Harry 1930- ConAu 21R, ConLC 6
Mathews, J Howard 1881-1970 ConAu 9R, -103
Mathews, Jackson 1907?-1978 ConAu 104
Mathews, Jane DeHart 1936- ConAu 21R,
    WrDr 84
Mathews, John Joseph 1895- ConAu P-2,
    TwCWW, WrDr 84
Mathews, Lorraine IntWWP 82X
Mathews, Louise ConAu X
Mathews, Marcia M ConAu 9R, WrDr 84
Mathews, Patricia J 1929?-1983 ConAu 109
Mathews, Richard DrAP&F 83
Mathews, Richard B 1944- ConAu 1NR, -45,
    IntAu&W 82, IntWWP 82
Mathews, Russell Lloyd 1921- ConAu 109,
    WrDr 84
Mathews, Thomas George 1925- ConAu 49
Mathews, Walter M 1942- ConAu 110
Mathewson, Rufus Wellington, Jr. 1919?-1978
    ConAu 81
Mathewson, William 1940- ConAu 106
Mathias, Frank Furlong 1925- ConAu 61
Mathias, Peter 1928- ConAu 17R
Mathias, Peter 1929- WrDr 84
Mathias, Roland 1915- ConAu 97, ConP 80,
    IntAu&W 82, IntWWP 82, WrDr 84
Mathiesen, Egon 1907-1976 ConAu 109,
    SmATA 28N
Mathieson, Donald Lindsay 1936- WrDr 84
Mathieson, Theodore 1913- ConAu 9R
Mathieu, Beatrice 1904-1976 ConAu 65
Mathieu, Bertrand DrAP&F 83
Mathieu, Bertrand 1936- ConAu 73
Mathieu, Rodolphe 1894-1962 CreCan 2
Mathis, Claude 1927- ConAu 45
Mathis, Cleopatra DrAP&F 83
Mathis, Cleopatra 1947- ConAu 104
Mathis, Doyle 1936- ConAu 45
Mathis, F John 1941- ConAu 37R
Mathis, G Ray 1937- WrDr 84
Mathis, James L 1925- ConAu 105
Mathis, Ray 1937- ConAu 37R
Mathis, Sharon Bell DrAP&F 83
Mathis, Sharon Bell 1937- ChlLR 3,
    ConAu 41R, LivgBAA, SmATA 7,
    TwCCW 83, WrDr 84
Mathison, Richard Randolph 1919-1980
    ConAu 1R, -3NR
Mathison, Stuart L 1942- ConAu 29R
Mathur, Dinesh C 1918- ConAu 41R
Mathur, Y B 1930- ConAu 49
Mati IntWWP 82X
Matias, Waldemar 1934- ConAu 5R
Matiason, K G IntAu&W 82X
Matiges, Mark IntAu&W 82X
Matilal, Bimal Krishna 1935- ConAu 21R
Matisoff, James A 1937- ConAu 103
Matisoff, Susan 1940- ConAu 104
Matkovic-Vlasic, Ljiljana 1938- IntAu&W 82
Matlaw, Myron 1924- ConAu 33R
Matloff, Maurice 1915- ConAu 6NR, -13R,
    IntAu&W 82
Matney, Bill ConAu X
Matney, William C, Jr. 1924- ConAu 69
Maton, Jean 1926- IntWWP 82X
Matos, Antun Gustav 1873-1914 ClDMEL 80
Matrat, Jean 1915- ConAu 61
Matschat, Cecile H 1895?-1976 ConAu 65
Matsen, Herbert Stanley 1926- ConAu 57
Matsikiti, Claudius Murau 1951- IntAu&W 82
Matson, Clive DrAP&F 83
Matson, Emerson N 1926- ConAu 45,
    SmATA 12, WrDr 84
Matson, Floyd W 1921- ConAu 13R
Matson, Norman Haghejm 1893-1965 LongCTC,
    TwCA, TwCA SUP
Matson, Theodore E 1906- ConAu 1R
Matson, Virginia Freeberg 1914- ConAu 33R
Matson, Wallace I 1921- ConAu 13R, WrDr 84

Matson, Weli Nickolaus 1905- IntWWP 82
Matsuba, Moshe 1917- ConAu 37R, WrDr 84
Matsubara, Hisako 1935- IntAu&W 82
Matsuda, Michael IntWWP 82X
Matsui, Tadashi 1926- ConAu 41R, SmATA 8
Matsumoto, Shigeharu 1899- IntAu&W 82
Matsumoto, Toru 1914?-1979 ConAu 89
Matsunaga, Alicia 1936- ConAu 29R, WrDr 84
Matsunaga, Alicia Orloff 1937- IntAu&W 82
Matsunaga, Daigan Lee 1941- ConAu 41R
Matsunaga, Suimusanjin IntAu&W 82X
Matsuno, Masako 1935- ConAu X, SmATA 6
Matsushita, Konosuke 1894- IntAu&W 82
Matsutani, Miyoko 1925- ConAu 69
Matt, Paul R 1926- ConAu 33R
Mattam, Donald 1909- ConAu 45
Matte, L'Enc 1936- SmATA 22[port]
Matte, Robert, Jr. DrAP&F 83
Matte, Robert G, Jr. 1948- ConAu 65,
    IntWWP 82
Matteo, P B, Jr. ConAu X
Matter, Joseph Allen 1901- ConAu 29R
Mattes, Arthur S 1901- ConSFA
Mattes, Jack Royston 1920- WrDr 84
Mattes, Merrill J 1910- ConAu 41R
Matteson, Michael T 1943- ConAu 89
Mattessich, Richard V 1922- ConAu 9NR, -13R
Matthaei, Julie Ann 1951- ConAu 110
Mattheson, Rodney ConAu X
Matthews, Christopher C F 1939- IntAu&W 82,
    WrDr 84
Matthew, Donald J A 1930- ConAu 5R
Matthew, Henry Colin Gray 1941- ConAu 53,
    IntAu&W 82
Matthews, Anthony ConAu X
Matthews, Brad ConAu X
Matthews, C M 1908- ConAu 25R
Matthews, Carola 1937- ConAu 25R
Matthews, Clayton 1918- ConAu 9NR, -53
Matthews, Clyde 1917- ConAu 103
Matthews, Curt 1934- ConAu 73
Matthews, Denis 1919- ConAu 103, WrDr 84
Matthews, Desmond S 1922- ConAu 21R
Matthews, Donald Rowe 1925- ConAu 1R, -2NR
Matthews, Ellen 1950- ConAu 89,
    SmATA 28[port]
Matthews, Elmora Messer 1925- ConAu 21R
Matthews, Harry S 1939- ConAu 73
Matthews, Herbert L 1900- WrDr 84
Matthews, Herbert Lionel 1900-1977 ConAu 1R,
    -2NR, -73
Matthews, Honor 1901- ConAu P-2
Matthews, J H 1930- ConAu 5NR, -13R,
    IntAu&W 82, IntWWP 82
Matthews, Jack DrAP&F 83
Matthews, Jack 1917- ConAu 9R
Matthews, Jack 1925- ConAu X, ConNov 82,
    DcLB 6[port], WrDr 84
Matthews, Jacklyn Meek ConAu X, SmATA X
Matthews, James David 1929- IntAu&W 82
Matthews, Jessie 1907-1981 ConAu 108
Matthews, Joan E 1914- ConAu 21R
Matthews, John H 1930- WrDr 84
Matthews, John Harold 1925- ConAu 33R
Matthews, John L 1899- LivgBAA
Matthews, Kathy 1949- ConAu 110
Matthews, Kevin 1942- ConAu X, WrDr 84
Matthews, L Harrison 1901- ConAu 4NR, -53,
    WrDr 84
Matthews, Lena Dale DrAP&F 83
Matthews, Luri Ann IntWWP 82X
Matthews, Marmaduke Matthews 1837-1913
    CreCan 1
Matthews, Patricia 1927- ConAu 9NR, -29R,
    -69, SmATA 28[port], TwCRGW,
    WrDr 84
Matthews, Ralph 1904?-1978 ConAu 81, -85
Matthews, Robert J 1926- ConAu 65
Matthews, Roy 1927- WrDr 84
Matthews, Roy Anthony 1927- ConAu 33R
Matthews, Roy T 1932- ConAu 109
Matthews, Stanley G 1924- ConAu 21R
Matthews, Thomas Stanley 1901- ConAu P-1,
    IntAu&W 82, WrDr 84
Matthews, Tom ConAu X
Matthews, Victor Monroe 1921- ConAu 93
Matthews, Walter Robert 1881-1973 ConAu P-1
Matthews, William DrAP&F 83
Matthews, William 1942- ConAu 29R, ConP 80,
    DcLB 5[port], IntAu&W 82, IntWWP 82,
    WrDr 84
Matthews, William Henry, III 1919- ConAu 9R,

SmATA 28
Matthews, William Richard 1905-1975 ConAu 57,
    -61
Matthias, Catherine 1945- ConAu 110
Matthias, John DrAP&F 83
Matthias, John 1941- ConAu 33R, ConLC 9,
    IntAu&W 82, IntWWP 82, WrDr 84
Matthias, Klaus 1929- IntAu&W 82
Matthiesen, Hinrich 1928- IntAu&W 82
Matthiessen, F O 1902-1950 ConLCrt 82
Matthiessen, Francis Otto 1902-1950 LongCTC,
    ModAL, TwCA, TwCA SUP
Matthiessen, Peter DrAP&F 83
Matthiessen, Peter 1927- ConAu 9R, ConLC 5,
    -7, -11, ConNov 82, DcLB 6[port],
    DcLEL 1940, SmATA 27[port], WorAu,
    WrDr 84
Matthijs, Georges-Marie 1916- IntAu&W 82
Matthis, Raimund Eugen 1928- ConAu 37R
Matthofer, Hans 1925- IntAu&W 82
Matthyssen, Joannes Michael 1902-
    IntAu&W 82
Mattice, Hortense Crompton CreCan 2
Mattil, Edward LaMarr 1918- ConAu 106
Mattill, A J, Jr. 1924- ConAu 37R
Mattingley, Christobel 1931- ConAu 97,
    IntAu&W 82, TwCCW 83, WrDr 84
Mattingly, Garrett 1900-1962 LongCTC, WorAu
Mattingly, George DrAP&F 83
Mattingly, George E 1950- ConAu 105
Mattioli, Raffaele 1895-1973 ConAu 45
Mattis, George 1905- ConAu P-2
Mattison, Alice DrAP&F 83
Mattison, Alice 1942- ConAu 110, IntWWP 82
Mattison, Judith 1939- ConAu 8NR, -61
Mattlage, Louise AuNews 1
Mattlin, Paula Plotnick 1934?-1981 ConAu 104
Mattlin, Sharon DrAP&F 83
Matton, Roger 1929- CreCan 1
Mattson, George E 1937- ConAu 5R
Mattson, Lloyd 1923- ConAu 93
Matulka, Jan 1890-1972 SmATA 28
Matura, Mustapha 1939- ConAu 65, ConDr 82,
    WrDr 84
Matus, Greta 1938- ConAu 93, SmATA 12
Matusche, Alfred 1909- CroCD
Matute, Ana Maria 1925- ConAu 89
Matute, Ana Maria 1926- ClDMEL 80,
    ConLC 11, IntAu&W 82, ModRL,
    TwCWr
Matveyeva, Novella Nikolayevna 1934-
    ClDMEL 80
Mau, James A 1935- ConAu 25R
Mauchline, Mary 1915- ConAu 53
Maude, Angus Edmund Upton 1912-
    DcLEL 1940, IntAu&W 82
Maude, Aylmer 1858-1938 LongCTC, TwCA,
    TwCA SUP
Maude, H E 1906- ConAu 103, WrDr 84
Maududi, Maulana Abdul Ala 1903?-1979
    ConAu 89
Maue, Kenneth 1947- ConAu 97
Mauermann, Mary Anne 1927- ConAu 33R
Maugham, Diana ConAu X
Maugham, Francs IntAu&W 82X
Maugham, Robert Cecil Romer 1916-1981
    ConAu 9R, -103, DcLEL 1940,
    TwCA SUP
Maugham, Robin 1916- ConAu X,
    DcLEL 1940, IntAu&W 82, LongCTC,
    TwCCr&M 80, WorAu 1970
Maugham, W Somerset 1874-1965 ConAu 25R,
    ConLC 11, -15, DcLB 10[port],
    TwCCr&M 80
Maugham, William Somerset 1874-1965 CnMD,
    CnMWL, ConAu 5R, ConLC 1, LongCTC,
    ModBrL, ModBrL SUP, ModWD, TwCA,
    TwCA SUP, TwCWr, WhoTwCL
Maughan, Anne Margery ConAu 53, WrDr 84
Maughan, Joyce Bowen 1928- WrDr 84
Mauldin, William Henry 1921- TwCA SUP
Maule, Christopher J 1934- ConAu 37R
Maule, Hamilton Bee 1915- ConAu 1R, -3NR
Maule, Harry E 1886-1971 ConAu 104
Maule, Tex ConAu X
Maulnier, Thierry 1909- ClDMEL 80
Maultsby, Maxie C, Jr. 1932- ConAu 81
Maumela, Titus Nisieni 1924- IntAu&W 82
Maund, Alfred 1923- ConAu 1R
Maunder, Elwood R 1917- ConAu 85
Maunder, W J 1932- ConAu 33R
Maung, Mya 1933- ConAu 37R

Maunula, Allan Arthur 1924- *IntWWP 82*
Maura, Sister *ConAu X*
Maurano, Peter J, Jr. 1945- *IntWWP 82*
Maureen, Sister Mary 1924- *ConAu 21R*
Maurer, Armand A 1915- *ConAu 21R*
Maurer, Charles Benes 1933- *ConAu 33R*
Maurer, David J 1935- *ConAu 102*
Maurer, David W 1906-1981 *ConAu 104, –17R*
Maurer, John G 1937- *ConAu 37R*
Maurer, Otto *ConAu X*
Maurer, Rachel Elizabeth Huddle 1894-
    IntWWP 82
Maurer, Rose *ConAu X*
Maurhut, Richard *ConAu X*
Mauriac, Claude 1910- *ModRL*
Mauriac, Claude 1914- *ClDMEL 80, ConAu 89,*
    ConLC 9, ModFrL, TwCWr, WorAu
Mauriac, Francois 1885-1970 *ClDMEL 80,*
    CnMD, CnMWL, ConAu P-2, ConLC 4,
    –9, LongCTC, ModFrL, ModRL, ModWD,
    TwCA, TwCA SUP, TwCWr, WhoTwCL
Maurice, David John Kerr 1899- *ConAu P-1*
Maurice, Eoger *IntAu&W 82X*
Maurice, Roger *ConAu X*
Mauricio, Victoria Courtney 1928- *ConAu 106*
Maurier, Daphne Du 1907- *LongCTC, TwCA,*
    TwCA SUP
Maurina, Zenta 1897-1978 *ConAu 85*

Maurois, Andre 1885-1967 *ClDMEL 80,*
    ConAu 25R, ConAu P-2, LongCTC,
    ModFrL, TwCA, TwCA SUP,
    TwCSFW A, TwCWr, WhoTwCL
Mauron, Charles 1899-1966 *ClDMEL 80,*
    ConAu P-1
Maurras, Charles 1868-1952 *ClDMEL 80,*
    WorAu
Maury, Inez 1909- *ConAu 61*
Maury, Reuben 1899-1981 *ConAu 103*
Mauser, Ferdinand F 1914- *ConAu 1R, –2NR*
Mauser, Patricia Rhoads 1943- *ConAu 106*
Mauser, Wolfram 1928- *IntAu&W 82*
Mauskopf, Seymour Harold 1938- *ConAu 104*
Mautner, Franz H 1902- *ConAu 61*
Mauzey, Merritt 1897-1975 *ConAu 102*
Maves, Carl 1940- *ConAu 69*
Maves, Karl *ConAu X*
Maves, Mary Carolyn 1916- *ConAu 49,*
    SmATA 10
Maves, Paul B 1913- *ConAu 1NR, –45,*
    SmATA 10
Mavin, John *ConAu X*
Mavis, Walter Curry 1905- *ConAu 5R*
Mavor, Elizabeth 1927- *ConAu 107,*
    ConNov 82, DcLB 14[port], WrDr 84
Mavor, Osborne Henry 1888-1951 *ConAu 104,*
    LongCTC, WorAu
Mavrodes, George I 1926- *ConAu 21R*
Mawdsley, Norman 1921- *ConAu X*
Mawer, Betty Oliphant *CreCan 1*
Mawicke, Tran 1911- *SmATA 15*
Mawson, Christopher Orlando Sylvester 1870-1938
    TwCA
Max, Lucy *ConAu X, IntWWP 82X*
Max, Nicholas 1923- *ConAu X*
Maxa, Rudolph Joseph, Jr. 1949- *ConAu 65*
Maxa, Rudy *ConAu X*
Maxcy, Spencer J 1939- *ConAu 110*
Maxey, Chester Collins 1890- *ConAu P-1*
Maxey, David R 1936- *ConAu 73*
Maxfield, Elizabeth *ConAu X*
Maxfield-Miller, Elizabeth 1910- *IntAu&W 82*
Maxhim, Tristan *ConAu X*
Maximov, Vladimir 1930- *ConAu 104*
Maxmen, Jerrold S 1942- *ConAu 106*
Maxon, Anne *ConAu X, SmATA X*
Maxon, John 1916-1977 *ConAu 69*
Maxson, Harry A *DrAP&F 83*
Maxtone Graham, James Anstruther 1924-
    ConAu 69
Maxtone-Graham, John 1929- *ConAu 69*
Maxtone Graham, Joyce 1901-1953 *TwCA,*
    TwCA SUP
Maxwell, A E *ConAu X*
Maxwell, Albert Ernest 1916- *ConAu 5R*
Maxwell, Ann 1944- *ConAu 105*
Maxwell, Arthur S 1896-1970 *ConAu P-1,*
    SmATA 11
Maxwell, D E S 1925- *ConAu 33R, WrDr 84*
Maxwell, Edith 1923- *ConAu 49, SmATA 7*
Maxwell, Edward *ConAu X*
Maxwell, Elsa 1883-1963 *ConAu 89*

Maxwell, Gavin 1914-1969 *ConAu 5R, –25R,*
    LongCTC, TwCWr, WorAu
Maxwell, Gavin 1914-1970 *DcLEL 1940*
Maxwell, Gilbert 1910-1979 *ConAu 93,*
    ConAu P-1
Maxwell, Grover 1918- *ConAu 5R*
Maxwell, Grover 1918-1981 *ConAu 9NR*
Maxwell, Ian Robert 1923- *IntAu&W 82*
Maxwell, Sister Immaculata 1913- *ConAu 13R*
Maxwell, Jack *ConAu X*
Maxwell, James A 1912- *ConAu 13R*
Maxwell, John *WrDr 84*
Maxwell, Kenneth E 1908- *ConAu 73*
Maxwell, Kenneth Robert 1941- *ConAu 85,*
    WrDr 84
Maxwell, Margaret F 1927- *ConAu 109*
Maxwell, Sister Mary 1913- *ConAu 37R*
Maxwell, Mary Elizabeth Braddon 1837-1915
    LongCTC
Maxwell, Maurice 1910-1982 *ConAu 107*
Maxwell, Neville 1926- *ConAu 4NR, –49*
Maxwell, Nicole *ConAu 1R*
Maxwell, Patricia Anne 1942- *ConAu 29R,*
    IntAu&W 82, WrDr 84
Maxwell, Richard C 1919- *ConAu 41R*
Maxwell, Robert 1923- *ConAu 9R*
Maxwell, Robert S 1911- *ConAu 57*
Maxwell, Ronald *ConAu X*
Maxwell, Vicky *ConAu X,   IntAu&W 82X,*
    TwCRGW, WrDr 84
Maxwell, Victor *CreCan 2*
Maxwell, W David 1926- *ConAu 61*
Maxwell, William *DrAP&F 83, WrDr 84*
Maxwell, William 1908- *ConAu 93, ConLC 19,*
    ConNov 82, DcLB Y80B, TwCA SUP,
    WrDr 84
Maxwell, William Babington 1866-1938
    LongCTC, TwCA
Maxwell-Hudson, Clare 1946- *ConAu 69*
Maxwell-Lefroy, Cecil Anthony 1907-
    ConAu P-1
May, Allan 1923- *ConAu 85*
May, Arthur James 1899-1968 *ConAu P-1*
May, Charles Paul 1920- *ConAu 1R, –5NR,*
    IntAu&W 82, SmATA 4
May, Dean Edward 1944- *ConAu 57*
May, Derwent 1930- *ConAu 11NR, –25R,*
    WrDr 84
May, Derwent James 1930- *IntAu&W 82,*
    IntWWP 82
May, Derwent Janus 1930- *DcLEL 1940*
May, Edgar 1929- *ConAu 9R*
May, Elaine 1932- *ConDr 82A, ConLC 16,*
    WrDr 84
May, Elizabeth 1907- *ConAu P-2*
May, Ernest Richard 1928- *ConAu 1R, –6NR*
May, Eugene 1906- *ConAu 1R*
May, Francis Barns 1915- *ConAu 9R*
May, George S 1924- *ConAu 65, MichAu 80*
May, Georges Claude 1920- *ConAu 6NR, –13R*
May, Gita 1929- *ConAu 29R, IntAu&W 82,*
    WrDr 84
May, Henrietta Mabel 1884- *CreCan 1*
May, Henry F 1915- *ConAu 9R, WrDr 84*
May, Henry John 1903- *ConAu 13R*
May, Herbert Gordon 1904-1977 *ConAu 5R,*
    –6NR, –89
May, J C *ConAu X*
May, Jacques M 1896-1975 *ConAu 57*
May, James Boyer 1904- *ConAu P-1*
May, John D 1932- *ConAu 45*
May, John R 1931- *ConAu 2NR, –45,*
    IntAu&W 82
May, Judy Gail 1943- *ConAu 57*
May, Julian 1931- *ConAu 1R, –6NR,*
    SmATA 11
May, Karl Friedrich 1842-1912 *ClDMEL 80*
May, Kenneth Ownsworth 1915-1977 *ConAu 73*
May, Lawrence Alan 1948- *ConAu 106*
May, Muriel Wallace 1897- *IntAu&W 82*
May, Philip Radford 1928- *ConAu 45*
May, Robert E 1943- *ConAu 57*
May, Robert Lewis 1905-1976 *ConAu 104,*
    SmATA 27N
May, Robert M 1936- *ConAu 69*
May, Robert Stephen 1929- *ConAu 29R*
May, Robin 1929- *ConAu X, IntAu&W 82,*
    WrDr 84
May, Timothy C 1940- *ConAu 73*
May, William E 1928- *ConAu 41R*
May, Winifred Jean 1921- *IntAu&W 82*
May, Wynne *IntAu&W 82X, TwCRGW,*

WrDr 84
Maya, Tristan 1926- *IntWWP 82X*
Mayakovski, Vladimir 1893-1930 *CnMD,*
    ConAu 104, ModSL 1
Mayakovsky, Vladimir 1893-1930 *ClDMEL 80,*
    CnMWL, LongCTC, ModWD,
    TwCLC 4[port], TwCSFW A, TwCWr,
    WhoTwCL, WorAu
Mayall, R Newton 1904- *ConAu P-1*
Maybaum, Ignaz 1897- *ConAu P-1*
Mayberry, Florence V Wilson *ConAu 9R,*
    SmATA 10
Mayberry, Genevieve 1900- *ConAu P-1*
Maybray-King, Horace 1901- *ConAu 29R, –29R,*
    WrDr 84
Maybury, Anne *TwCRGW, WrDr 84*
Maybury-Lewis, David H P 1929- *ConAu 17R*
Maye, Patricia 1940- *ConAu 53*
Mayer, Adrian C 1922- *ConAu 1R, WrDr 84*
Mayer, Agatha *ConAu X*
Mayer, Albert 1897-1981 *ConAu 105, –73,*
    IntAu&W 82
Mayer, Albert Ignatius, Jr. 1906-1960 *ConAu 109,*
    SmATA 29N
Mayer, Andre 1946- *ConAu 110*
Mayer, Ann M 1938- *ConAu 57, SmATA 14*
Mayer, Arno J 1926- *ConAu 85*
Mayer, Arthur L 1886-1981 *ConAu 108*
Mayer, Bernadette *DrAP&F 83*
Mayer, Bernadette 1945- *ConAu 33R,*
    WrDr 84
Mayer, Charles Leopold 1881- *ConAu 1R, –6NR*
Mayer, Christa Charlotte *ConAu X*
Mayer, Clara Woollie 1895- *ConAu P-2*
Mayer, Debby *ConAu X, DrAP&F 83*
Mayer, Deborah Anne 1946- *ConAu 109*
Mayer, Edwin Justus 1896?-1960 *ModWD*
Mayer, Edwin Justus 1897-1960 *CnMD*
Mayer, Ellen Moers *ConAu X*
Mayer, Frederick Joseph 1950- *IntWWP 82*
Mayer, Gary 1945- *ConAu 53*
Mayer, Gerda 1927- *ConAu 106, ConP 80,*
    IntWWP 82, WrDr 84
Mayer, Hannelore 1929- *IntAu&W 82*
Mayer, Harold M 1916- *ConAu 41R,*
    IntAu&W 82
Mayer, Harry F 1912- *ConAu 101*
Mayer, Herbert Carleton 1893-1978 *ConAu 41R*
Mayer, Herbert T 1922- *ConAu 33R, WrDr 84*
Mayer, Ira 1952- *ConAmTC*
Mayer, Jane Rothschild 1903- *ConAu 9R*
Mayer, Joseph E 1904- *WrDr 84*
Mayer, Lawrence C 1936- *ConAu 97*
Mayer, Leo V 1936- *ConAu 73*
Mayer, Lynne Rhodes 1926- *ConAu 73*
Mayer, Marianna 1945- *ConAu 93,*
    SmATA 32[port]
Mayer, Martin Prager 1928- *ConAu 5R,*
    WorAu
Mayer, Mercer 1943- *ConAu 85, SmATA 16,*
    –32[port]
Mayer, Michael F 1917- *ConAu 13R*
Mayer, Milton 1908- *ConAu 37R*
Mayer, Philip 1910- *ConAu 49, IntAu&W 82*
Mayer, Ralph 1895-1979 *ConAu 29R, –89*
Mayer, Raymond 1924- *WrDr 84*
Mayer, Raymond Richard 1922- *ConAu 1R*
Mayer, Renate 1944- *IntAu&W 82*
Mayer, S L 1937- *ConAu 103*
Mayer, Thomas 1927- *ConAu 9NR, –21R*
Mayer, Tom 1943- *ConAu 9R*
Mayer-Koenig, Wolfgang 1946- *IntAu&W 82,*
    IntWWP 82
Mayer-Thurman, Christa Charlotte 1934-
    ConAu 49
Mayers, Lewis 1890-1975 *ConAu 61*
Mayers, Marvin K 1927- *ConAu 41R*
Mayerson, Charlotte Leon *ConAu 13R*
Mayerson, Evelyn Wilde 1935- *ConAu 101*
Mayerson, Philip 1918- *ConAu 41R*
Mayes, Edythe Beam 1902- *ConAu 7NR, –53,*
    WrDr 84
Mayes, Frances *ConAu 81, DrAP&F 83*
Mayes, Herbert Raymond 1900- *ConAu 105*
Mayes, Stanley Herbert 1911- *ConAu 1R*
Mayes, Wendell 1919- *ConAu 103,*
    DcLB 26[port]
Mayfair, Bertha *ConAu X*
Mayfair, Franklin *ConAu X*
Mayfield, Chris 1951- *ConAu 107*
Mayfield, Guy 1905- *ConAu 5R*
Mayfield, Jack *ConAu X*

Mayfield, James Bruce 1934- *ConAu 69*
Mayfield, John S 1904-1983 *ConAu 109*
Mayfield, Julia *ConAu X, WrDr 84*
Mayfield, Julian 1928- *ConAu 13R, ConNov 82, DcLEL 1940, LivgBAA, WrDr 84*
Mayfield, L H, II 1910- *ConAu P-2*
Mayfield, Marlys *ConAu X*
Mayfield, Robert C 1928- *ConAu 37R*
Mayfield, Sara 1905-1979 *ConAu 25R, -85*
Mayhall, Jane *DrAP&F 83*
Mayhall, Jane 1921- *ConAu 8NR*
Mayhall, Mary Mildred 1902- *WrDr 84*
Mayhall, Mildred P 1902- *ConAu 1R, -1NR*
Mayhar, Ardath Frances 1930- *ConAu 103*
Mayhew, Christopher 1915- *WrDr 84*
Mayhew, Christopher Paget 1915- *ConAu 106, IntAu&W 82*
Mayhew, David Raymond 1937- *ConAu 17R, WrDr 84*
Mayhew, Edgar DeNoailles 1913- *ConAu 37R, IntAu&W 82*
Mayhew, Elizabeth *ConAu X*
Mayhew, Lenore 1924- *ConAu 49, IntAu&W 82*
Mayhew, Lewis B 1917- *ConAu 1R, -4NR*
Mayman, Martin 1924- *ConAu 9R*
Maynard, Alan 1944- *ConAu 7NR, -57*
Maynard, Christopher 1949- *WrDr 84*
Maynard, Fredelle 1922- *ConAu 85*
Maynard, Geoffrey 1921- *WrDr 84*
Maynard, Geoffrey Walter 1921- *ConAu 5R*
Maynard, Harold Bright 1902-1975 *ConAu 9R, -103*
Maynard, John 1941- *ConAu 65*
Maynard, Joyce 1953- *ConLC 23[port]*
Maynard, Merrill Alfred 1918- *IntWWP 82*
Maynard, Nan 1910- *IntAu&W 82X, WrDr 84*
Maynard, Nancy Kathleen Brazier 1910- *IntAu&W 82*
Maynard, Richard Allen 1942- *ConAu 33R*
Maynard, Robert C 1937- *ConAu 110*
Maynard, Theodore 1890-1956 *LongCTC, TwCA SUP*
Mayne, Ethel Colburn 1870?-1941 *LongCTC, TwCA*
Mayne, Richard 1926- *ConAu 5R, -6NR, -13R, DcLEL 1940, IntAu&W 82, WrDr 84*
Mayne, Rutherford 1878-1967 *LongCTC*
Mayne, Seymour 1944- *ConAu 101, ConP 80, IntWWP 82, WrDr 84*
Mayne, William 1928- *ConAu 9R, ConLC 12, DcLEL 1940, IntAu&W 82, SmATA 6, TwCCW 83, WrDr 84*
Maynes, E Scott 1922- *ConAu 45*
Mayo, Bernard 1902-1979 *ConAu 89*
Mayo, Bernard 1920- *WrDr 84*
Mayo, E L 1904- *ConAu 97, ConP 80, WrDr 84*
Mayo, James *ConAu X, TwCCr&M 80, WrDr 84*
Mayo, Katherine 1867-1940 *LongCTC, TwCA*
Mayo, Lucy Graves 1909-1963 *ConAu 5R*
Mayo, Margaret 1935- *ConAu 107*
Mayo, Margot 1910- *ConAu P-1*
Mayo, Mark *ConAu X*
Mayo, Nick 1922- *ConAu 103*
Mayo, Nick 1922-1983 *ConAu 110*
Mayo, Patricia Elton 1915- *ConAu 103, IntAu&W 82, WrDr 84*
Mayo, William L 1931- *ConAu 17R*
Mayor, A Hyatt 1901-1980 *ConAu 1NR, -97*
Mayor, Alfred Hyatt 1934- *ConAu 65*
Mayor, Alpheus Hyatt 1901- *ConAu 45*
Mayor, Beatrice d1971 *ConAu P-1*
Mayor, Stephen 1927- *ConAu 21R*
Mayr, Ernst 1904- *ConAu 2NR, -5R*
Mayrant, Drayton *ConAu X*
Mayrocker, Friederike 1924- *ClDMEL 80, IntWWP 82*
Mays, Benjamin Elijah *IntAu&W 82*
Mays, Benjamin Elijah 1895- *ConAu 45, LivgBAA*
Mays, Buddy 1943- *ConAu 73*
Mays, Cedric Wesley 1907- *ConAu 29R*
Mays, James A 1939- *ConAu 57*
Mays, John Barron 1914- *WrDr 84*
Mays, Lee 1898- *IntWWP 82*
Mays, Lucinda L 1924- *ConAu 101*
Mays, Spike *ConAu X*
Mays, Victor 1927- *ConAu 25R, SmATA 5*
Mays, Willie 1931- *ConAu 105*
Mayshark, Cyrus 1926- *ConAu 17R*

Maysi, Kadra *ConAu X*
Maysles, Albert 1926- *ConAu 29R, ConLC 16*
Maysles, David 1932- *ConLC 16*
Mayson, Marina *AuNews 1, ConAu 49, WrDr 84*
Maytham, Thomas N 1931- *ConAu 103*
Mazani, Eric C F Nhando 1948- *DcLEL 1940*
Maze, Edward 1925- *ConAu 5R*
Mazer, Harry 1925- *ConAu 97, SmATA 31[port]*
Mazer, Milton 1911- *ConAu 85*
Mazer, Norma Fox *DrAP&F 83*
Mazer, Norma Fox 1931- *ConAu 69, ConLC 26[port], SmATA 24[port]*
Maziarz, Edward A 1915- *ConAu 37R*
Mazlish, Bruce 1923- *ConAu 1R, -2NR, -5R, IntAu&W 82*
Mazmanian, Arthur B 1931- *ConAu 77*
Mazmanian, Daniel 1945- *ConAu 5NR, -53*
Mazo, Earl 1919- *ConAu 37R*
Mazo, Joseph H 1938- *ConAu 69*
Mazonowicz, Douglas 1920- *ConAu 57*
Mazor, Julian *DrAP&F 83*
Mazour, Anatole Gregory 1900- *ConAu 13R*
Mazow, Julia Wolf 1937- *ConAu 103*
Mazrui, Ali Al'Amin 1933- *ConAu 21R*
Mazur, Allan Carl 1939- *ConAu 105*
Mazur, Gail *DrAP&F 83*
Mazur, Gail 1937- *ConAu 77, IntWWP 82*
Mazur, John Mark *DrAP&F 83*
Mazur, Paul M 1892-1979 *ConAu 102, -89*
Mazur, Rita Z *DrAP&F 83*
Mazur, Ronald Michael 1934- *ConAu 25R*
Mazurkiewicz, Albert J 1926- *ConAu 3NR, -9R*
Mazursky, Paul 1930- *ConAu 77*
Mazza, Adriana 1928- *ConAu 4NR, SmATA 19*
Mazzaro, Jerome *DrAP&F 83*
Mazzaro, Jerome 1934- *ConAu 33R, WrDr 84*
Mazzarolo, Evo Andrea 1953- *IntWWP 82*
Mazze, Edward M 1941- *ConAu 5NR, -13R*
Mazzei, Angel 1920- *IntWWP 82*
Mazzeo, Guido E 1914- *ConAu 45*
Mazzeo, Joseph Anthony 1923- *ConAu 17R*
Mazzetti, Lorenza 1933- *ConAu 9R*
Mazzoleni, Ettore 1905-1968 *CreCan 2*
Mazzotta, Giuseppe 1942- *ConAu 93*
Mazzulla, Fred 1903- *ConAu P-2*
Mbali, Ona *IntAu&W 82X*
Mbembe *DrAP&F 83*
Mberi, Antar Sudan Katara 1949- *ConAu 81*
Mbita, Hashim Iddi 1933- *IntAu&W 82*
Mbiti, John S 1931- *ConAu 11NR*
Mbiti, John Samuel 1931- *ConAu 21R, IntAu&W 82*
McAdam, Robert E 1920- *ConAu 81*
McAdams, Benny Frank 1941- *IntWWP 82*
McAdoo, Henry Robert 1916- *ConAu 107*
McAfee, James Thomas 1928- *IntAu&W 82, IntWWP 82*
McAfee, Thomas 1928- *ConAu 1NR, -45, IntAu&W 82X, WrDr 84*
McAfee, Ward M 1939- *ConAu 57*
McAleavey, David *DrAP&F 83*
McAleavey, David 1946- *ConAu 65, IntWWP 82*
McAleavy, Henry 1912-1968 *ConAu P-2*
McAleer, John J 1923- *ConAu 21R*
McAlindon, Thomas 1932- *ConAu 97, WrDr 84*
McAlister, Neil Harding 1952- *ConAu 110*
McAlister, W Robert 1930- *ConAu 69*
McAllaster, Elva 1922- *ConAu 33R*
McAllister, Amanda *ConAu X*
McAllister, Bruce 1946- *ConAu 33R*
McAllister, Bruce H *DrAP&F 83*
McAllister, Claire *DrAP&F 83*
McAllister, Harry E *ConAu 5R*
McAllister, Lester Grover 1919- *ConAu 41R*
McAlmon, Robert 1895-1956 *ConAu 107*
McAlmon, Robert 1896-1956 *DcLB 4*
McAlpin, Heller 1955- *ConAu 109*
McAnally, Mary *DrAP&F 83*
McAnally, Mary E 1939- *ConAu 105*
McAnally, Mary Ellen 1940- *IntWWP 82*
McAnally-Knight, Mary *DrAP&F 83*
McAndrew, John 1904-1978 *ConAu 77*
McAnelly, James R 1932- *ConAu 57*
McArdle, Hugh McLure 1905- *ConAu 107*
McArdle, William D 1939- *ConAu 110*
McArthur, Charles S 1909- *ConAu 41R*
McArthur, Edwin Douglas 1907- *ConAu 17R*
McArthur, Harvey King 1912- *ConAu 25R,*

McArthur, John *ConAu X*
McArthur, Norma 1921- *WrDr 84*
McArthur, Peter 1866-1924 *CreCan 2*
McAulay, John D 1912- *ConAu 13R*
McAulay, Sara *DrAP&F 83*
McAuley, Almut Renate 1942- *IntWWP 82*
McAuley, Jacquelin Rollit 1925- *ConSFA*
McAuley, James 1917-1976 *ConAu 97, DcLEL 1940, ModCmwL, TwCWr, WhoTwCL, WorAu 1970*
McAuley, James J *DrAP&F 83*
McAuley, James J 1936- *ConAu 21R, -77, ConP 80, IntWWP 82, WrDr 84*
McAuliffe, Clarence 1903- *ConAu P-2*
McAuliffe, Kevin Michael 1949- *ConAu 81*
McAuliffe, Mary Sperling 1943- *ConAu 81*
McAvoy, Thomas Timothy 1903-1969 *ConAu 1R*
McBain, Donald J 1945- *ConAu 45*
McBain, Ed *DrAP&F 83, WrDr 84*
McBain, Ed 1926- *ConAu X, ConLC 11, ConNov 82, SmATA X, TwCCr&M 80, TwCWr, WorAu*
McBain, Gordon D, III 1946- *ConAu 106*
McBain, John M 1921- *ConAu 41R*
McBain, Laurie 1949- *WrDr 84*
McBain, Laurie Lee 1949- *ConAu 97, IntAu&W 82, TwCRGW*
McBath, James Harvey 1922- *ConAu 17R*
McBeath, Lida W 1913- *IntWWP 82*
McBee, Mary Louise 1924- *ConAu 103*
McBie, Julie *MichAu 80*
McBirney, Mara 1905- *CreCan 1*
McBirney, Mona 1905- *CreCan 1*
McBriar, Alan M 1918- *ConAu 5R*
McBride, Alfred 1928- *ConAu 6NR, -13R*
McBride, Angela Barron 1941- *ConAu 1NR, -49*
McBride, Chris 1941- *ConAu 81*
McBride, Donald O 1903-1978 *ConAu 77*
McBride, Earl Duwain 1891- *ConAu P-1*
McBride, Jack *WrDr 84*
McBride, James H 1924- *ConAu 25R*
McBride, John Cosgrove 1911-1983 *ConAu 110*
McBride, John G 1919- *ConAu 9R*
McBride, John Joseph 1898- *WrDr 84*
McBride, Joseph 1947- *ConAu 41R*
McBride, Katharine 1904-1976 *ConAu 65*
McBride, Mary Margaret 1899-1976 *ConAu 65, -69*
McBride, Mekeel *DrAP&F 83*
McBride, Patricia *ConAu X*
McBride, Richard William 1928- *ConAu 17R*
McBride, Robert 1941- *IntAu&W 82, WrDr 84*
McBride, Robert H 1918- *ConAu 107*
McBride, William Leon 1938- *ConAu 6NR, -57*
McBrien, Richard P 1936- *ConAu 10NR*
McBrien, Richard Peter 1936- *ConAu 17R, IntAu&W 82, WrDr 84*
McBrien, William Augustine 1930- *ConAu 107*
McBroom, R Curtis 1910- *ConAu P-2*
McBurney, James H 1905- *ConAu 17R*
McCabe, Angela *WrDr 84*
McCabe, Bernard P, Jr. 1933- *ConAu 53*
McCabe, Cameron *ConAu X, WrDr 84*
McCabe, Charles B 1899-1970 *ConAu 89*
McCabe, Charles Raymond 1915-1983 *ConAu 109*
McCabe, David Aloysius 1884?-1974 *ConAu 45*
McCabe, Donald Lee 1925- *IntAu&W 82*
McCabe, Herbert 1926- *ConAu 13R*
McCabe, James P 1937- *ConAu 101*
McCabe, John C, III 1920- *ConAu 1R, -1NR, IntAu&W 82, WrDr 84*
McCabe, Joseph E 1912- *ConAu 17R*
McCabe, Joseph Martin 1867-1955 *LongCTC*
McCabe, Sybil Anderson 1902- *ConAu P-1*
McCabe, Victoria 1948- *ConAu 29R*
McCafferty, Lawrence *ConAu 25R*
McCaffery, Margo 1938- *ConAu 37R, WrDr 84*
McCaffrey, Anne 1926- *AuNews 2, ConAu 25R, ConLC 17, ConSFA, DcLB 8[port], IntAu&W 82, SmATA 8, TwCSFW, WrDr 84*
McCaffrey, Joseph A 1940- *ConAu 37R*
McCaffrey, Lawrence John 1925- *ConAu 25R*
McCaffrey, Phillip *DrAP&F 83*
McCaffrey, Phillip 1945- *ConAu 77*
McCagg, William O, Jr. 1930- *ConAu 93*
McCaghy, Charles H 1934- *ConAu 25R*
McCague, James 1909-1977 *ConAu 1R, -2NR*
McCahill, Thomas 1907?-1975 *ConAu 104*

McCaig, Donald *ConAu 104*
McCaig, Robert Jesse 1907-1982 *ConAu 1R, −1NR, TwCWW*
McCain, Murray 1926-1981 *ConAu 1R, −105, SmATA 29N, −7*
McCaleb, Walter Flavius 1873-1967 *ConAu P-1*
McCall, Anthony *WrDr 84*
McCall, Dan *DrAP&F 83*
McCall, Daniel F 1918- *ConAu 17R*
McCall, Dorothy Lawson 1889?-1982 *ConAu 106, −109*
McCall, Edith 1911- *ConAu 1R, −4NR, −5R, SmATA 6, WrDr 84*
McCall, George J 1939- *ConAu 9NR, −21R*
McCall, Grant 1943- *ConAu 107*
McCall, John R 1920- *ConAu 1NR, −45*
McCall, Marsh H, Jr. 1939- *ConAu 29R*
McCall, Marsh Howard, Jr. 1939- *WrDr 84*
McCall, Robert B 1940- *ConAu 33R, WrDr 84*
McCall, Storrs 1930- *ConAu 9R*
McCall, Thomas 1913-1983 *ConAu 108*
McCall, Thomas S 1936- *ConAu 1NR, −49*
McCall, Tom *ConAu X*
McCall, Vincent *WrDr 84*
McCall, Virginia Nielsen 1909- *ConAu 1R, −1NR, SmATA 13*
McCall, William A 1891- *ConAu P-1*
McCalley, John W 1916-1983 *ConAu 110*
McCallum, George Edward 1931- *ConAu 37R, WrDr 84*
McCallum, Ian Robert More 1919- *ConAu 13R*
McCallum, James Dow 1893-1971 *ConAu 104*
McCallum, John D 1924- *ConAu 4NR, −53*
McCallum, Neil 1916- *ConAu 13R*
McCallum, Phyllis 1911- *ConAu 4NR, −53, IntAu&W 82, SmATA 10, WrDr 84*
McCallum, Ronald Buchanan 1898-1973 *ConAu 5R, −89*
McCamant, John F 1933- *ConAu 25R*
McCammon, Robert R 1952- *ConAu 81*
McCampbell, James M 1924- *ConAu 49*
McCamy, James L 1906- *WrDr 84*
McCamy, James Lucian 1906- *ConAu 5R*
McCamy, Jean *DrAP&F 83*
McCance, Larry 1917-1970 *CreCan 2*
McCandless, Hugh 1907- *ConAu 5R*
McCandless, Perry 1917- *ConAu 1NR, −49*
McCandlish, George E 1914-1975 *ConAu 61, −65*
McCanles, Michael 1936- *ConAu 69*
McCann, Arthur *ConAu X*
McCann, Coolidge *ConAu X*
McCann, David R *DrAP&F 83*
McCann, David Richard 1944- *IntAu&W 82, IntWWP 82*
McCann, Eamonn *WrDr 84*
McCann, Edson *ConAu X, WorAu, WrDr 84*
McCann, Kevin 1904-1981 *ConAu 103*
McCann, Philip *IntAu&W 82X*
McCann, Richard *DrAP&F 83*
McCann, Thomas 1934- *ConAu 73*
McCants, Dorothea Olga 1901- *ConAu 73*
McCardell, John 1949- *ConAu 101*
McCardle, Carl W 1904?-1972 *ConAu 37R*
McCardle, Dorothy Bartlett 1904-1978 *ConAu 81, −85*
McCarr, Ken 1903-1977 *ConAu 106, −109*
McCarrick, Earlean M 1930- *ConAu 103*
McCarriston, Linda *DrAP&F 83*
McCarroll, Marion C 1893?-1977 *ConAu 73*
McCarroll, Tolbert 1931- *ConAu 110*
McCarry, Charles *DrAP&F 83*
McCarry, Charles 1929- *TwCCr&M 80*
McCarry, Charles 1930- *ConAu 103, WrDr 84*
McCarter, Alan 1943- *ConAu 107*
McCarter, Neely Dixon 1929- *ConAu 109*
McCarter, P Kyle 1945- *ConAu 105*
McCarthy, Agnes 1933- *ConAu 17R, SmATA 4*
McCarthy, Cavan 1943- *ConAu 61*
McCarthy, Charlene B 1929- *ConAu 41R*
McCarthy, Clarence F 1909- *ConAu 29R*
McCarthy, Cormac *DrAP&F 83*
McCarthy, Cormac 1933- *ConAu 10NR, −13R, ConLC 4, DcLB 6[port], WrDr 84*
McCarthy, Darry 1930- *ConAu 5R*
McCarthy, David Edgar 1925- *ConAu 1R*
McCarthy, Dennis John 1924- *ConAu 21R*
McCarthy, Sir Desmond 1877-1952 *TwCWr*
McCarthy, Edward V, Jr. 1924- *ConAu 93*
McCarthy, Eugene 1916- *WrDr 84*
McCarthy, Eugene Joseph 1916- *ConAu 1R,*

−2NR
McCarthy, Gary 1943- *ConAu 69, TwCWW, WrDr 84*
McCarthy, Gerald A *DrAP&F 83*
McCarthy, James Jerome 1927- *ConAu 41R*
McCarthy, Joanne *DrAP&F 83*
McCarthy, Joe *ConAu X*
McCarthy, John 1898- *ConAu 45*
McCarthy, John P 1938- *ConAu 97*
McCarthy, Joseph M 1940- *ConAu 97*
McCarthy, Joseph Weston 1915-1980 *ConAu 1NR, −97*
McCarthy, Justin 1830-1912 *LongCTC, TwCA*
McCarthy, Justin Huntly 1860-1936 *LongCTC, ModWD*
McCarthy, Marvin 1902-1983 *ConAu 110*
McCarthy, Mary *DrAP&F 83*
McCarthy, Mary 1912- *ASpks, ConAu 5R, ConLC 1, −3, −5, −14, −24[port], ConLCrt 82, ConNov 82, DcLB Y81A[port], −2, DcLEL 1940, IntAu&W 82, LongCTC, ModAL, ModAL SUP, TwCA SUP, TwCWr, WhoTwCL, WrDr 84*
McCarthy, Max *ConAu X*
McCarthy, Patrick Joseph 1922- *ConAu 9R*
McCarthy, Paul Eugene 1921- *ConAu 103*
McCarthy, R Delphina 1894- *ConAu P-1*
McCarthy, Richard D 1927- *ConAu 41R*
McCarthy, Shaun 1928- *ConAu 6NR, −9R, WrDr 84*
McCarthy, Teresa *ConAu X*
McCarthy, Thomas N 1927- *ConAu 37R*
McCarthy, Thomas P 1920- *ConAu 13R*
McCarthy, Tim *DrAP&F 83*
McCarthy, Todd 1950- *ConAu 105*
McCarthy, William E J 1925- *ConAu 6NR, −9R, WrDr 84*
McCartin, James T *DrAP&F 83*
McCartney, Dorothy *DrAP&F 83*
McCartney, Dorothy Wilson *IntWWP 82*
McCartney, James H 1925- *ConAu 73*
McCartney, Mike *ConAu X*
McCartney, Peter Michael 1944- *ConAu 109*
McCarty, Clifford 1929- *ConAu 17R, WrDr 84*
McCarty, Doran Chester 1931- *ConAu 10NR, −65*
McCarty, Jesse *DrAP&F 83*
McCarty, Norma *ConAu X, IntWWP 82X*
McCarty, Raymond M 1908- *IntWWP 82*
McCarty, Rega Kramer 1904- *ConAu 5R, SmATA 10*
McCary, James Leslie 1919-1978 *ConAu 85*
McCash, June Hall 1938- *ConAu 37R*
McCasland, S Vernon 1896- *ConAu 5R*
McCaslin, Nellie 1914- *ConAu 33R, IntAu&W 82, SmATA 12, WrDr 84*
McCaslin, Walter *ConAmTC*
McCaughey, Robert A 1939- *ConAu 77*
McCauley, Carole Spearin *DrAP&F 83*
McCauley, Carole Spearin 1939- *ConAu 8NR, −57, IntWWP 82*
McCauley, Elfrieda B 1915- *ConAu 9R*
McCauley, Martin 1934- *ConAu 107, WrDr 84*
McCauley, Michael F 1947- *ConAu 9NR, −61*
McCaull, M E *ConAu X*
McCaw, Kenneth Malcolm 1907- *ConAu 109*
McCaw, Mabel Niedermeyer 1899- *ConAu P-2*
McCay, Winsor 1871-1934 *DcLB 22[port]*
McClain, Alva J 1888- *ConAu 65*
McClain, Carl S 1899- *ConAu 37R*
McClain, John O 1942- *ConAu 110*
McClain, Russell H 1910- *ConAu P-2*
McClane, Albert Jules 1922- *ConAu 106*
McClane, Kenneth Anderson *DrAP&F 83*
McClane, Kenneth Anderson, Jr. 1951- *ConAu 6NR, −57*
McClary, Andrew 1927- *ConAu 61*
McClary, Ben Harris 1931- *ConAu 3NR, −9R*
McClary, Jane Stevenson 1919- *ConAu 1R, −1NR*
McClary, Thomas Calvert *TwCSFW*
McClatchy, C K 1858-1936 *DcLB 25*
McClatchy, Eleanor Grace 1895?-1980 *ConAu 102*
McClatchy, J D *DrAP&F 83*
McClatchy, J D 1945- *ConAu 105, WrDr 84*
McClaurin, Irma *DrAP&F 83*
McClaurin, Irma Pearl 1952- *ConAu 57, IntWWP 82*
McClean, Father Joseph Lucius 1919- *ConAu P-1*
McCleary, Eliott H 1927- *ConAu 57*
McCleary, Robert A 1923- *ConAu 17R*

McCleery, Edna 1925- *IntWWP 82*
McCleery, Nancy *DrAP&F 83*
McCleery, William 1911- *ConAu 1R, −5NR*
McClellan, A W 1908- *ConAu 77*
McClellan, James 1937- *ConAu 21R*
McClellan, James Edward, Jr. 1922- *ConAu 25R*
McClellan, Robert F, Jr. 1934- *ConAu 33R*
McClelland, Bruce *DrAP&F 83*
McClelland, Charles A 1917- *ConAu 85*
McClelland, Charles Edgar 1940- *ConAu 33R, WrDr 84*
McClelland, David C 1917- *ConAu 25R*
McClelland, Diane Margaret 1931- *ConAu 105*
McClelland, Doug 1934- *ConAu 41R*
McClelland, Ivy Lilian 1908- *ConAu 29R*
McClelland, Ivy Lillian 1908- *WrDr 84*
McClelland, Lucille Hudlin 1920- *ConAu 21R*
McClelland, Vincent Alan 1933- *ConAu 103, WrDr 84*
McClendon, James William, Jr. 1924- *ConAu 5NR, −9R*
McClendon, Sarah 1910- *ConAu 73*
McClennen, Sandra Elaine 1942- *ConAu 103*
McClintock, Marshall 1906-1967 *ConAu P-1, SmATA 3*
McClintock, Michael *DrAP&F 83*
McClintock, Mike *ConAu X, SmATA 3*
McClintock, Robert 1909- *ConAu P-2*
McClintock, Theodore 1902-1971 *ConAu 33R, −73, SmATA 14*
McClinton, Katharine Morrison 1899- *ConAu 1R, −5NR*
McClinton, Leon 1933- *ConAu 65, SmATA 11*
McClory, Robert J 1932- *ConAu 77*
McCloskey, Donald N 1942- *ConAu 8NR, −57*
McCloskey, Eunice 1906- *ConAu 9R*
McCloskey, H J 1925- *ConAu 110*
McCloskey, Mark *DrAP&F 83*
McCloskey, Mark 1938- *ConAu 1NR, −45, WrDr 84*
McCloskey, Maxine E 1927- *ConAu 33R*
McCloskey, Paul N, Jr. 1927- *ConAu 37R*
McCloskey, Robert 1914- *ConAu 9R, DcLB 22[port], SmATA 2[port], TwCCW 83, WrDr 84*
McCloskey, William B, Jr. 1928- *ConAu 101*
McCloud, Susan Evans 1945- *IntWWP 82*
McCloy, Helen 1904- *ConAu 25R, TwCCr&M 80, WorAu, WrDr 84*
McCloy, James F 1941- *ConAu 103*
McCloy, Shelby Thomas 1898- *ConAu P-2*
McClung, Floyd, Jr. 1945- *ConAu 61*
McClung, Nellie Letitia Mooney 1873-1951 *CreCan 1*
McClung, Robert Marshall 1916- *AuNews 2, ConAu 6NR, −13R, SmATA 2, WrDr 84*
McClure, Arthur F, II 1936- *ConAu 10NR, −65*
McClure, Gillian Mary 1948- *ConAu 103, SmATA 31[port], WrDr 84*
McClure, Hal 1921- *ConAu 81*
McClure, James *DrAP&F 83*
McClure, James 1939- *ConAu 69, TwCCr&M 80, WrDr 84*
McClure, Joanna 1930- *DcLB 16[port]*
McClure, Larry 1941- *ConAu 69*
McClure, Michael *DrAP&F 83*
McClure, Michael 1932- *ConAu 21R, ConP 82, ConLC 6, −10, ConP 80, CroCAP, DcLB 16[port], WorAu 1970, WrDr 84*
McClure, Ron 1941- *ConAu 37R*
McClure, Ruth Koonz *ConAu 107*
McCluskey, John 1944- *ConAu 7NR, −57*
McCluskey, John A, Jr. *DrAP&F 83*
McCluskey, Neil Gerard 1921- *ConAu 25R*
McCollam, James Graham 1913- *ConAu 4NR*
McCollam, Jim *ConAu X*
McColley, Robert 1933- *ConAu 13R*
McCollin, Russ *DrAP&F 83*
McCollough, Albert W 1917- *ConAu 102*
McCollough, Celeste 1926- *ConAu 13R*
McCollum, Audrey T 1924- *ConAu 107*
McCollum, Elmer Verner 1879-1967 *ConAu P-1*
McComas, Annette Peltz 1911- *ConAu 109*
McComas, J Francis 1911-1978 *ConAu 104, TwCSFW*
McComb, David Glendinning 1934- *ConAu 29R*
McComb, K 1895- *ConAu 13R*
McCombie, John Alexander Somerville 1925- *IntAu&W 82*
McCombs, Judith *DrAP&F 83*
McCombs, Judith 1939- *ConAu 102,*

McGann, Jerome J 1937- *ConAu 1NR, –45*
McGann, Thomas F 1920- *ConAu 13R*
McGannon, J Barry 1924- *ConAu 13R*
McGarey, Gladys T 1920- *ConAu 57*
McGarey, William A 1919- *ConAu 57*
McGarrigle, Francis Joseph 1888- *ConAu 5R*
McGarrity, Mark 1943- *ConAu 1NR, –45*
McGarry, Daniel D 1907- *ConAu P-1*
McGarry, Jean *DrAP&F 83*
McGarry, Kevin J 1935- *ConAu 102*
McGarry, Mark J *DrAP&F 83*
McGarry, Michael B 1948- *ConAu 102*
McGaugh, James L 1931- *ConAu 7NR, –57*
McGaughy, Florence Helen 1904- *IntAu&W 82,
    IntWWP 82, WrDr 84*
McGaughey, Helen 1904- *ConAu 37R*
McGaughy, Mary Stallard 1910- *IntWWP 82*
McGavin, E Cecil 1900- *ConAu P-1*
McGavran, Donald 1897- *ConAu 13R*
McGaw, Charles James 1910-1978 *ConAu 106*
McGaw, Jessie Brewer 1913- *ConAu 1R,
    SmATA 10, WrDr 84*
McGaw, Naomi Blanche Thoburn 1920-
    ConAu 9R
McGaw, William C 1914- *ConAu 101*
McGeachy, D P, III 1929- *ConAu 8NR, –61*
McGear, Mike *ConAu X*
McGee, Barbara J 1943- *ConAu 25R,
    SmATA 6*
McGee, Frank 1921-1974 *ConAu 105, –89*
McGee, Reece 1929- *ConAu 2NR, –5R*
McGee, T G 1936- *ConAu 10NR, –21R*
McGee, Terence Gary 1936- *WrDr 84*
McGee, Victor 1935- *ConAu 41R*
McGeehan, Robert 1933- *ConAu 33R*
McGeehan, W O 1879-1933 *DcLB 25*
McGeeney, Patrick John 1918- *ConAu 5R*
McGeown, Patrick 1897- *ConAu P-2*
McGerr, Patricia 1917- *AuNews 1, ConAu 1R,
    –1NR, TwCCr&M 80, WrDr 84*
McGhan, Barry 1939- *ConAu 69*
McGhie, Andrew 1926- *ConAu 97*
McGiffert, Michael 1928- *ConAu 13R*
McGiffert, Robert C 1922- *ConAu 49*
McGiffin, Lee 1908- *ConAu P-1, SmATA 1*
McGill, Angus *WrDr 84*
McGill, Dan M 1919- *ConAu 107*
McGill, Ian Earl *ConAu X, WrDr 84*
McGill, Ormond 1913- *ConAu 2NR, –49*
McGill, Ralph E 1898-1969 *ConAu 5R, –25R,
    DcLEL 1940*
McGill, Thomas E 1930- *ConAu 17R*
McGilligan, Patrick 1951- *ConAu 10NR, –65*
McGilvery, Laurence 1932- *ConAu 33R*
McGimsey, Charles Robert, III 1925-
    ConAu 37R
McGinley, Phyllis 1905-1978 *CnMWL,
    ConAu 9R, –77, ConLC 14, LongCTC,
    ModAL, SmATA 2, –24N, TwCSA SUP,
    TwCCW 83, TwCWr, WhoTwCL*
McGinn, Donald Joseph 1905- *ConAu P-2*
McGinn, John T 1900?-1972 *ConAu 33R*
McGinn, Matt 1928-1977 *ConAu 106*
McGinn, Maureen Ann *ConAu 61*
McGinn, Noel F 1934- *ConAu 73*
McGinnies, Elliott M 1921- *ConAu 77*
McGinnies, W G 1899- *ConAu 7NR, –57*
McGinnis, Bruce 1941- *ConAu 97*
McGinnis, Dorothy Jean 1920- *ConAu 29R*
McGinnis, Duane *ConAu X*
McGinnis, Lila S 1924- *ConAu 93*
McGinnis, Marilyn 1939- *ConAu 57*
McGinnis, Robert 1927- *ConAu 45*
McGinnis, Thomas C 1925- *ConAu 65*
McGinniss, Joe 1942- *AuNews 2, ConAu 25R,
    WrDr 84*
McGirr, Edmund 1922-1972 *TwCCr&M 80*
McGivering, John H 1923- *ConAu 25R*
McGivern, James Sabine 1908- *WrDr 84*
McGivern, Maureen Daly *ConAu 9R*
McGivern, William P 1922-1982 *ConAu 108*
McGivern, William P 1927- *ConAu 7NR, –49,
    TwCCr&M 80*
McGivern, William Peter 1920- *WorAu*
McGlade, Francis S 1930- *ConAu 41R*
McGlashan, Alan Fleming 1898- *ConAu 41R,
    IntAu&W 82*
McGlashan, M L 1924- *WrDr 84*
McGlinchee, Claire *ConAu P-2, WrDr 84*
McGlinchee, Constance 1897- *IntWWP 82*
McGlinn, Dwight *ConAu X*
McGloin, John Bernard 1912- *ConAu 33R,*

WrDr 84
McGloin, Joseph Thaddeus 1917- *ConAu 1R,
    –1NR*
McGlone, Edward Leon 1941- *ConAu 108*
McGlothlin, William J 1908- *ConAu P-2*
McGluphy *ConAu X*
McGlynn, Christopher *ConAu X*
McGlynn, James V 1919-1973 *ConAu 1R, –103*
McGoey, John Heck 1915- *ConAu 6NR, –9R*
McGoldrick, Desmond Francis 1919- *ConAu 17R*
McGoldrick, Edward J, Jr. 1909-1967 *ConAu P-1*
McGoldrick, Joseph D 1901-1978 *ConAu 97*
McGough, Elizabeth 1934- *ConAu 107,
    SmATA 33[port]*
McGough, Roger 1937- *ConAu 105, ConP 80,
    DcLEL 1940, WrDr 84*
McGovern, Ann *ConAu 2NR, –49,
    IntAu&W 82, SmATA 8*
McGovern, Bernard Francis 1940- *ConAmTC*
McGovern, George S 1922- *ConAu 8NR, –45*
McGovern, James 1923- *ConAu 7NR, –17R*
McGovern, James R 1928- *ConAu 108*
McGovern, John Phillip 1921- *ConAu 21R,
    WrDr 84*
McGovern, Robert *DrAP&F 83*
McGovern, Robert 1927- *ConAu 49*
McGowan, Jack 1896?-1977 *ConAu 69*
McGowan, James *DrAP&F 83*
McGowan, James A 1932- *ConAu 97*
McGowan, John J 1936?-1982 *ConAu 106*
McGowan, Jouvette *IntWWP 82X*
McGowan, Mabel 1921- *IntWWP 82*
McGowan, Margaret M *ConAu 69*
McGowen, Charles H 1936- *ConAu 69*
McGowen, Thomas 1927- *ConAu 8NR, –21R,
    SmATA 2*
McGowen, Tom 1927- *ConAu X, SmATA X*
McGrade, Arthur Stephen 1934- *ConAu 25R*
McGrady, Donald Lee 1935- *ConAu 25R*
McGrady, Mike 1933- *ConAu 2NR, –49,
    SmATA 6*
McGrady, Patrick M, Jr. 1932- *ConAu 29R,
    IntAu&W 82*
McGrady, Patrick Michael, Sr. 1908-1980
    ConAu 103, –97
McGrail, Joie 1922?-1977 *ConAu 69*
McGrath, Doyle *ConAu X*
McGrath, Earl James 1902- *ConAu P-1*
McGrath, Edward G 1917- *ConAu 25R*
McGrath, Francis E 1903?-1976 *ConAu 61*
McGrath, J H 1923- *ConAu 29R*
McGrath, James Bernard, Jr. 1917- *ConAu 5R*
McGrath, Jim *DrAP&F 83*
McGrath, John 1935- *ConDr 82, IntAu&W 82,
    WrDr 84*
McGrath, Juliet Kaufmann *DrAP&F 83*
McGrath, Kristina *DrAP&F 83*
McGrath, Lee Parr 1933- *ConAu 29R*
McGrath, Mary *WrDr 84*
McGrath, Morgan *WrDr 84*
McGrath, Robert L 1920- *ConAu 97*
McGrath, Sylvia Wallace 1937- *ConAu 61*
McGrath, Thomas *DrAP&F 83*
McGrath, Thomas M 1916- *ConAu 6NR, –9R,
    ConP 80, WrDr 84*
McGrath, Tom *ConDr 82, WrDr 84*
McGrath, William J 1937- *ConAu 85*
McGrath, William Thomas 1917- *ConAu 103,
    WrDr 84*
McGratty, Arthur Raymond 1909-1975
    ConAu 53
McGraw, Eloise Jarvis 1915- *ConAu 4NR, –5R,
    IntAu&W 82, SmATA 1, TwCCW 83,
    WrDr 84*
McGraw, Harold Whittlesey, Sr. 1890?-1970
    ConAu 29R
McGraw, James 1913- *ConAu 1R*
McGraw, James R 1935- *ConAu 93*
McGraw, Walter John, Jr. 1919?-1978 *ConAu 81*
McGraw, William Corbin 1916- *ConAu 29R,
    SmATA 3*
McGreal, Ian Philip 1919- *ConAu 77*
McGreevey, William Paul 1938- *ConAu 11NR,
    –69*
McGregor *ConAu X*
McGregor, Craig 1933- *ConAu 21R, SmATA 8*
McGregor, Iona 1929- *ConAu 105, SmATA 25,
    TwCCW 83, WrDr 84*
McGregor, John C 1905- *ConAu P-1*
McGregor, Malcolm Francis 1910- *ConAu 45,
    WrDr 84*
McGregor, Rob Roy, Jr. 1929- *ConAu 108*

McGrew, Jan *IntAu&W 82X, IntWWP 82X*
McGrew, Janice Waggener *IntAu&W 82,
    IntWWP 82*
McGrory, Mary 1918- *AuNews 2, ConAu 106*
McGuane, Thomas *DrAP&F 83*
McGuane, Thomas 1939- *AuNews 2,
    ConAu 5NR, –49, ConLC 3, –7, –18,
    ConNov 82, DcLB Y80A[port], –2,
    TwCWW, WorAu 1970, WrDr 84*
McGuane, Thomas 1940- *ModAL SUP*
McGuffie, Tom H 1902- *ConAu P-2*
McGuigan, Dorothy Gies 1914- *ConAu 21R,
    MichAu 80*
McGuigan, Dorothy Gies 1914-1982
    ConAu 11NR
McGuigan, F J 1924- *WrDr 84*
McGuigan, F Joseph 1924- *ConAu 5R, –8NR*
McGuinness, Arthur E 1936- *ConAu 25R*
McGuire, E Patrick 1932- *ConAu 25R*
McGuire, Edna 1899- *ConAu 2NR, –5R,
    SmATA 13*
McGuire, Frances Margaret 1900- *ConAu P-1,
    WrDr 84*
McGuire, James Dean 1936- *ConAu 21R*
McGuire, Jerry 1934- *ConAu 93*
McGuire, Joseph William 1925- *ConAu 9R,
    WrDr 84*
McGuire, Leslie Sarah 1945- *ConAu 107*
McGuire, Martin C 1933- *ConAu 37R*
McGuire, Michael Terrance 1929- *ConAu 41R*
McGuire, Paul 1903- *TwCCr&M 80, WrDr 84*
McGuire, Richard L 1940- *ConAu 57*
McGuire, Robert G 1938?-1975 *ConAu 61*
McGuire, Thomas 1945- *ConAu 73*
McGurk, Slater *ConAu X, SmATA X*
McGurn, Barrett 1914- *ConAu 1R, –1NR,
    IntAu&W 82, WrDr 84*
McHale, John *ConAu 61*
McHale, Philip John 1928- *ConAu 103,
    WrDr 84*
McHale, Tom 1942?-1982 *AuNews 1,
    ConAu 106, –77, ConLC 3, –5, ConNov 82*
McHam, David 1933- *ConAu 73*
McHaney, Thomas L 1936- *ConAu 9NR, –65*
McHarg, Ian L 1920- *ConAu 29R*
McHargue, Georgess 1941- *ChlLR 2,
    ConAu 25R, SmATA 4*
McHenry, Dean E 1910- *ConAu 109*
McHenry, Paul G, Jr. 1924- *ConAu 61*
McHugh, Arona *DrAP&F 83*
McHugh, Arona 1924- *ConAu 5R, WrDr 84*
McHugh, Edna *ConAu 69*
McHugh, Heather *DrAP&F 83*
McHugh, Heather 1948- *ConAu 11NR, –69,
    IntWWP 82*
McHugh, John 1927- *ConAu 103,
    IntAu&W 82, WrDr 84*
McHugh, Leroy 1891?-1975 *ConAu 104*
McHugh, Mary 1928- *ConAu 85*
McHugh, Maxine Davis 1899?-1978 *ConAu 77*
McHugh, P J 1922- *ConAu 21R*
McHugh, Roger Joseph 1908- *ConAu 5R*
McHugh, Roland 1945- *ConAu 10NR, –65*
McHugh, Ruth Nelson *ConAu X*
McHugh, Stuart *ConAu X, TwCWW*
McHugh, Thomas Cannell 1926- *ConAu 103*
McHugh, Tom *ConAu X*
McHugh, Vincent 1904- *TwCA, TwCA SUP,
    TwCSFW*
McHugh, Vincent 1904-1983 *ConAu 109*
McIlhenny, William H, II 1951- *ConAu 6NR, –57*
McIlvaine, Jane 1919- *ConAu X*
McIlvanney, William 1936- *ConAu 25R,
    DcLB 14[port]*
McIlwain, Charles Howard 1871-1968
    ConAu 102, TwCA, TwCA SUP
McIlwain, David *WrDr 84*
McIlwain, David 1921- *ConAu 104, –109*
McIlwain, Henry 1912- *WrDr 84*
McIlwain, William Franklin, Jr. 1925- *ConAu 1R,
    –1NR*
McIlwham, Ebenezer *IntAu&W 82X*
McIlwraith, Maureen Mollie Hunter 1922-
    ConAu 29R, SmATA 2
McInerney, Brian *DrAP&F 83*
McInerney, Brian 1948- *IntWWP 82*
McInerny, Dennis Q 1936- *ConAu 97*
McInerny, Ralph Matthew 1929- *ConAu 21R,
    WrDr 84*
McInnes, Colin 1914- *TwCWr*
McInnes, Edward 1935- *ConAu 109*
McInnes, Graham 1912-1970 *ConAu P-2*

McLaughlin, Mignon *ConAu 9R*
McLaughlin, Sister Raymond 1897- *ConAu 25R*
McLaughlin, Robert 1908-1973 *ConAu 1R, -45*
McLaughlin, Robert T *DrAP&F 83*
McLaughlin, Robert W 1900- *ConAu 1R*
McLaughlin, Ruth *DrAP&F 83*
McLaughlin, Samuel Clarke 1924- *ConAu 89*
McLaughlin, Ted John 1921- *ConAu 13R*
McLaughlin, Terence Patrick 1928- *ConAu 33R,
IntAu&W 82, WrDr 84*
McLaughlin, Virginia Yans *ConAu X*
McLaughlin, William 1918- *ConAu 107,
IntWWP 82X*
McLaughlin, William DeWitt 1918- *IntWWP 82*
McLaughlin, William Raffan Davidson 1908-
ConAu P-1
McLaurin, Anne 1953- *ConAu 106,
SmATA 27[port]*
McLaurin, Melton Alonza 1941- *ConAu 81*
McLaurin, R D 1944- *ConAu 65*
McLaverty, Michael 1904- *ConAu P-1*
McLaverty, Michael 1907- *DcLB 15[port],
LongCTC, TwCA SUP*
McLean, Albert F, Jr. 1928- *ConAu 17R*
McLean, Allan Campbell 1922- *ConAu 1R,
-4NR, TwCCW 83, WrDr 84*
McLean, Beth Bailey 1892- *ConAu P-2*
McLean, Donald 1905-1975 *ConAu 1R, -4NR*
McLean, Sir Fitzroy Hew 1911- *DcLEL 1940*
McLean, George 1905?-1983 *ConAu 109*
McLean, George F 1929- *ConAu 6NR, -13R*
McLean, Gordon R 1934- *ConAu 2NR, -49*
McLean, Hugh 1925- *ConAu 65*
McLean, Hugh John 1930- *CreCan 1*
McLean, J Sloan *ConAu X, MichAu 80,
WrDr 84*
McLean, John David Ruari 1917- *IntAu&W 82*
McLean, Kathryn 1909-1966 *ConAu 25R,
ConAu P-2, SmATA 9*
McLean, Malcolm Dallas 1913- *ConAu 93,
IntAu&W 82*
McLean, Robert 1891-1980 *ConAu 103*
McLean, Robert Colin 1927- *ConAu 17R*
McLean, Ruari 1917- *ConAu 10NR, -21R,
WrDr 84*
McLean, Sammy 1929- *ConAu 37R, WrDr 84*
McLean, Susan 1937- *ConAu 106*
McLean, William L 1852-1931 *DcLB 25*
McLeave, Hugh George 1923- *ConAu 5R, -6NR*
McLeavy, Gus 1951- *ConAu 105*
McLeish, Garen *AuNews 1, ConAu X*
McLeish, John 1917- *ConAu 7NR, -57*
McLeish, Kenneth 1940- *ConAu 29R,
IntAu&W 82, WrDr 84*
McLellan, David 1940- *ConAu 33R,
IntAu&W 82, WrDr 84*
McLellan, David S 1924- *ConAu 103, WrDr 84*
McLellan, Joyce Anne *CreCan 1*
McLellan, Robert 1907- *ConAu 41R,
IntAu&W 82, WrDr 84*
McLemore, Richard Aubrey 1903-1976
ConAu 103, -53
McLemore, S Dale 1928- *ConAu 9R*
McLemore, William P 1931- *LivgBAA*
McLendon, James 1942-1982 *ConAu 106, -41R,
IntAu&W 82*
McLendon, Jonathon C 1919- *ConAu 17R*
McLendon, Will L 1925- *ConAu 9R*
McLendon, Winzola Poole *ConAu 93*
McLenighan, Valjean 1947- *ConAu 108*
McLennan, Barbara N 1940- *ConAu 85*
McLeod, Alan L 1928- *ConAu 9R*
McLeod, Emilie Warren 1926-1982 *ConAu 108,
-33R, -69, SmATA 23[port], -31N*
McLeod, James Richard 1942- *ConAu 41R*
McLeod, Janet *DrAP&F 83*
McLeod, John F 1917- *ConAu 69*
McLeod, Kirsty *ConAu X, SmATA X*
McLeod, Malcolm Donald 1941- *ConAu 110*
McLeod, Margaret Vail *ConAu X, SmATA X*
McLeod, Raymond, Jr. 1932- *ConAu 3NR, -49*
McLeod, Ross *ConAu X*
McLeod, Wallace 1931- *ConAu 37R,
IntAu&W 82, WrDr 84*
McLiam, John 1918- *NatPD 81[port]*
McLin, Jon 1938- *ConAu 102*
McLin, Ruth 1924- *ConAu 61*
McLoughlin, John C 1949- *ConAu 108*
McLoughlin, William G 1922- *ConAu 6NR,
-13R*
McLowery, Frank *ConAu X, TwCWW*
McLuhan, Herbert Marshall 1911- *DcLEL 1940*

McLuhan, Marshall 1911-1980 *ConAu 9R, -102,
IntAu&W 82, WhoTwCL, WorAu*
McLure, Charles E, Jr. 1940- *ConAu 8NR, -57*
McLysaght, Edward Anthony 1887-
IntAu&W 82
McLysaght, Edward Anthony 1889- *ConAu 1R*
McMahon, Bryan T *DrAP&F 83*
McMahon, Bryan T 1950- *ConAu 45*
McMahon, Charles P 1916?-1983 *ConAu 109*
McMahon, Ed 1923- *ConAu 89*
McMahon, Edwin M 1930- *ConAu 21R*
McMahon, Jeremiah 1919- *ConAu 109*
McMahon, Joseph H 1930- *ConAu 9R,
IntAu&W 82, WrDr 84*
McMahon, Michael 1943- *ConAu 69*
McMahon, Pat *ConAu X, IntAu&W 82X,
TwCCr&M 80*
McMahon, Robert *ConAu X*
McMahon, Robert J 1949- *ConAu 109*
McMahon, Thomas 1923?-1972 *ConAu 37R*
McMahon, Thomas 1943- *ConAu 33R*
McManis, Douglas R *ConAu 69*
McManners, John 1916- *ConAu 37R,
IntAu&W 82*
McManus, Edgar J 1924- *ConAu 97*
McManus, Frederick R 1923- *ConAu 1R*
McManus, James *DrAP&F 83*
McManus, James 1951- *IntAu&W 82*
McManus, James Kenneth 1921- *ConAu 85*
McManus, Kay 1922- *WrDr 84*
McManus, Marjorie 1950- *ConAu 73*
McManus, Patrick 1933- *ConAu 105*
McManus, Seumas 1869-1960 *LongCTC*
McMaster, Juliet 1937- *ConAu 37R,
IntAu&W 82, WrDr 84*
McMeekin, Clark *ConAu X, SmATA 3*
McMeekin, Isabel McLennan 1895- *ConAu 5R,
SmATA 3*
McMenemey, William Henry 1905- *ConAu P-1*
McMenemy, Nickie 1925- *ConAu 97*
McMichael, George 1927- *ConAu 103*
McMichael, James 1939- *ConAu 69*
McMichael, Joan K 1906- *ConAu 107*
McMillan, Bruce 1947- *ConAu 73,
SmATA 22[port]*
McMillan, Colin 1923- *ConAu 29R*
McMillan, Constance 1949- *ConAu 85*
McMillan, Florri *DrAP&F 83*
McMillan, George 1913- *ConAu 102*
McMillan, James *WrDr 84*
McMillan, James 1925- *IntAu&W 82*
McMillan, James B 1907- *ConAu 85*
McMillan, Polly Miller 1920- *ConAu 1R*
McMillan, Priscilla Johnson 1928- *ConAu 41R*
McMillan, Roddy 1923-1979 *ConAu 109*
McMillen, Barbara *DrAP&F 83*
McMillen, Howard 1938- *ConAu 57*
McMillen, Neil Raymond 1939- *ConAu 33R,
WrDr 84*
McMillen, S I 1898- *ConAu 5R*
McMillen, Wheeler 1893- *ConAu 33R*
McMillen, William *DrAP&F 83*
McMillin, Laurence 1923- *ConAu 33R*
McMillion, Bonner 1921- *ConAu 13R*
McMorrow, Fred 1925- *ConAu 57*
McMullan, Frank 1907- *ConAu 5R*
McMullen, Catherine *ConAu X, SmATA X*
McMullen, Jeremy 1948- *ConAu 103, WrDr 84*
McMullen, Mary 1920- *TwCCr&M 80,
WrDr 84*
McMullen, Richard E *DrAP&F 83*
McMullen, Roy 1911- *ConAu 25R*
McMullin, Ernan 1924- *ConAu 6NR, -13R*
McMullin, Ruth R 1942- *ConAu 61*
McMurray, George R 1925- *ConAu 103*
McMurray, Nancy A 1936- *ConAu 41R*
McMurrin, Sterling M 1914- *ConAu 29R*
McMurry, James Burton 1941- *ConAu 69*
McMurry, Linda O 1945- *ConAu 106*
McMurry, Robert N 1901- *ConAu 17R*
McMurtrey, Martin A 1921- *ConAu 69,
SmATA 21*
McMurtry, Jo 1929- *ConAu 89*
McMurtry, Larry *DrAP&F 83*
McMurtry, Larry 1936- *AuNews 2, ConAu 5R,
ConLC 2, -3, -7, -11, -27[port], ConNov 82,
DcLB 2, FifWWr, TwCWW, WrDr 84*
McMurtry, Robert Gerald 1906- *ConAu P-1,
IntAu&W 82, WrDr 84*
McMurty, Larry 1936- *DcLB Y80A[port]*
McNab, Thomas 1933- *ConAu 108*
McNab, Tom *ConAu X*

McNail, Eddie Gathings 1905- *ConAu 6NR, -57*
McNair, Kate 1911- *ConAu 17R, SmATA 3,
WrDr 84*
McNair, Malcolm P 1894- *ConAu P-1*
McNair, Philip Murray Jourdan 1924-
ConAu 21R
McNair, Wesley *DrAP&F 83*
McNairy, Philip F 1911- *ConAu 17R*
McNall, P E 1888- *ConAu 29R*
McNall, Scott G 1941- *ConAu 11NR, -25R*
McNally, Curtis *ConAu X*
McNally, Dennis 1949- *ConAu 103*
McNally, John *DrAP&F 83*
McNally, John 1914- *ConAu 17R*
McNally, Raymond T 1931- *ConAu 37R*
McNally, Robert 1946- *ConAu 107*
McNally, Robert E 1917- *ConAu 21R*
McNally, Robert E 1917-1978 *ConAu 11NR*
McNally, Terence 1939- *DcLEL 1940*
McNally, Terrence 1939- *ConAu 2NR, -45,
ConDr 82, ConLC 4, -7, CroCD,
DcLB 7[port], NatPD 81[port],
WorAu 1970, WrDr 84*
McNally, Tom 1923- *ConAu 85*
McNamara, Brooks 1937- *ConAu 25R*
McNamara, Eugene *DrAP&F 83*
McNamara, Eugene 1930- *ConAu 10NR*
McNamara, Eugene Joseph 1930- *ConAu 21R,
WrDr 84*
McNamara, Jo Ann 1931- *ConAu 85*
McNamara, John J, Jr. 1932- *ConAu 41R*
McNamara, John S 1908?-1977 *ConAu 69*
McNamara, Kevin 1926- *ConAu 25R*
McNamara, Lena Brooke 1891- *ConAu P-1*
McNamara, Margaret C 1915-1981 *SmATA 24N*
McNamara, Michael M 1940-1979 *ConAu 89*
McNamara, Robert 1916- *WrDr 84*
McNamara, William E 1926- *ConAu 1R, -4NR*
McNamee, James Owen 1904- *ConAu 5R*
McNamee, Lawrence F 1917- *ConAu 25R*
McNamee, Maurice Basil 1909- *ConAu 5R,
WrDr 84*
McNamee, Thomas *DrAP&F 83*
McNaspy, Clement James 1915- *ConAu 2NR,
-5R*
McNaught, Brian Robert 1948- *ConAu 105*
McNaught, Harry *ConAu 106, SmATA 32*
McNaught, John Charles Kirkpatrick *CreCan 1*
McNaught, Kenneth 1918- *ConAu 29R*
McNaughton, Arnold 1930- *ConAu 57*
McNaughton, Frank 1906?-1978 *ConAu 81*
McNaughton, H D 1945- *WrDr 84*
McNaughton, Howard Douglas 1945- *ConAu 57,
IntAu&W 82*
McNaughton, Wayne L 1902- *ConAu 1R*
McNaughton, William Frank 1933- *ConAu 41R,
IntAu&W 82*
McNeal, Robert H 1930- *ConAu 9R, WrDr 84*
McNeely, Jeannette 1918- *ConAu 41R,
SmATA 25[port]*
McNeer, May Yonge 1902- *ConAu 2NR, -5R,
SmATA 1*
McNees, Pat 1940- *ConAu 7NR*
McNeil, Barbara L 1951- *ConAu 97*
McNeil, Dee Dee 1943- *IntWWP 82X*
McNeil, Doris 1943- *IntWWP 82*
McNeil, Elton B 1924-1974 *ConAu P-2*
McNeil, Neil 1940- *IntWWP 82*
McNeile, H C 1888-1937 *TwCCr&M 80*
McNeile, Herman Cyril 1888-1937 *LongCTC,
TwCA, TwCA SUP*
McNeill, Anthony *DrAP&F 83*
McNeill, Anthony 1941- *ConAu 97, ConP 80,
WrDr 84*
McNeill, Donald P 1936- *ConAu 107*
McNeill, Janet 1907- *ConAu X, -9R,
IntAu&W 82X, SmATA 1, TwCCW 83,
WrDr 84*
McNeill, John J 1925- *ConAu 65*
McNeill, John Thomas 1885-1975 *ConAu 10NR,
-57, ConAu P-1*
McNeill, Robert B 1915- *ConAu 17R*
McNeill, Stuart 1942- *ConAu 65*
McNeill, William Hardy 1917- *ConAu 2NR,
-5R, WrDr 84*
McNeilly, Wilfred Glassford 1921- *ConAu 29R*
McNeir, Waldo F 1908- *ConAu 17R*
McNeish, James 1931- *ConAu 69, ConNov 82,
WrDr 84*
McNelly, Theodore Hart 1919- *ConAu 5R,
IntAu&W 82, WrDr 84*
McNelly, Willis E 1920- *ConAu 107*

McNerney, Joan *DrAP&F 83*
McNerney, Joan 1945- *IntWWP 82*
McNew, Ben B 1931- *ConAu 3NR, –9R*
McNichols, Charles L 1887- *TwCWW*
McNickle, D'Arcy 1904-1977 *ConAu 5NR, –9R, –85, ConIsC 1[port], SmATA 22N, TwCWW*
McNicoll, Helen Galloway 1879-1915 *CreCan 1*
McNicoll, Robert E 1907- *ConAu 37R*
McNiece, Harold Francis 1923-1972 *ConAu 37R*
McNierney, Mary Alice *ConAu 9R*
McNitt, Gale 1921- *ConAu 57*
McNiven, Malcolm A 1929- *ConAu 29R*
McNown, John S 1916- *ConAu 57*
McNulty, Edward N 1936- *ConAu 10NR, –65*
McNulty, Faith 1918- *ConAu 1NR, –49, SmATA 12, WrDr 84*
McNulty, James Edmund, Jr. 1924-1965 *ConAu 1R, –103*
McNutt, Dan James 1938- *ConAu 61*
McNutt, James 1944- *ConAu 49*
McPhail, David 1940- *ConAu 85*
McPhail, David M 1940- *SmATA 32*
McPharlin, Paul 1903-1948 *ConAu 110, SmATA 31*
McPhaul, Jack *ConAu X*
McPhaul, John J 1904- *ConAu 9R*
McPhaul, John J 1904-1983 *ConAu 110*
McPhee, John 1931- *ConAu 65, WorAu 1970*
McPhee, William N 1921- *ConAu 17R*
McPherson, Anna Talbott 1904- *ConAu 1R, –4NR*
McPherson, Gertrude H 1923- *ConAu 45*
McPherson, Harry Cummings, Jr. 1929- *ConAu 104*
McPherson, Holt 1907?-1979 *ConAu 89*
McPherson, Hugo 1921- *ConAu 29R*
McPherson, James A *DrAP&F 83*
McPherson, James A 1943- *WrDr 84*
McPherson, James Alan 1943- *ConAu 25R, ConLC 19, ConNov 82, LivgBAA*
McPherson, James Lowell 1921- *ConAu 13R*
McPherson, James Munro 1936- *ConAu 9R, IntAu&W 82, SmATA 16[port], WrDr 84*
McPherson, Sandra *DrAP&F 83*
McPherson, Sandra 1943- *ConAu 29R, ConP 80, WrDr 84*
McPherson, Thomas Herdman 1925- *ConAu 17R*
McPherson, William 1933- *ConAu 69*
McPherson, William 1939- *ConAu 57*
McPhie, Walter E 1926- *ConAu 29R*
McPolk, Andre 1935- *ConAu 93*
McQuade, Ann Aikman 1928- *ConAu 1R*
McQuade, DeRosset Morrissey 1934?-1978 *ConAu 81*
McQuade, Donald A 1941- *ConAu 65*
McQuade, Walter 1922- *ConAu 103*
McQuaid, Kim 1947- *ConAu 107*
McQuaig, Jack Hunter *ConAu 9R*
McQueen, Ian 1930- *ConAu 104*
McQueen, Mildred Hark 1908- *ConAu P-1, SmATA 12*
McQueen, William A 1926- *ConAu 21R*
McQuigg, R Bruce 1927- *ConAu 17R*
McQuilkin, Frank *DrAP&F 83*
McQuilkin, Frank 1936- *ConAu 33R*
McQuilkin, Rennie *DrAP&F 83*
McQuown, F R 1907- *WrDr 84*
McQuown, Frederic Richard 1907- *ConAu 9R*
McQuown, Judith H 1941- *ConAu 107, WrDr 84*
McQuown, Norman Anthony 1914- *ConAu 106*
McRae, Hamish 1943- *ConAu 57*
McRae, Kenneth Douglas 1925- *ConAu 1R, IntAu&W 82, WrDr 84*
McRae, Lindsay *ConAu X*
McRae, Robert 1914- *ConAu 77*
McRae, William John 1933- *ConAu 106*
McReynolds, David 1929- *ConAu 29R*
McReynolds, Edwin C 1890-1967 *ConAu P-1*
McReynolds, Janet 1933- *ConAmTC, NatPD 81[port]*
McReynolds, Ronald W *DrAP&F 83*
McReynolds, Ronald W 1934- *ConAu 49*
McRobbie, Kenneth Alan 1929- *DcLEL 1940*
McRoberts, Agnesann *ConAu X*
McRoberts, R Lewis 1944- *ConAu 33R*
McRoberts, Robert *DrAP&F 83*
McShan, James 1937- *ConAu 69*
McShane, Mark 1929- *TwCCr&M 80, WrDr 84*
McShane, Mark 1930- *ConAu 7NR, –17R*

McShane, Philip 1932- *ConAu 69*
McShean, Gordon 1936- *ConAu 108*
McSherry, Frank D, Jr. 1927- *ConAu 107*
McSherry, James E 1920- *ConAu 49*
McSorley, Joseph 1874-1963 *ConAu P-1*
McSweeny, Maxine 1905- *ConAu 61*
McSwigan, Marie 1907-1962 *ConAu 73, SmATA 24[port]*
McTaggart, Fred 1939- *ConAu 65*
McTeer, Wilson 1905- *ConAu 41R*
McVay, Gordon 1941- *ConAu 73*
McVean, James *ConAu X*
McVeigh, Malcolm J 1931- *ConAu 61*
McVey, Ruth T 1930- *ConAu 109*
McVickar, Elinor Guthrie 1902?-1982 *ConAu 106*
McVicker, Daphne Alloway 1895-1979 *ConAu 85*
McWaters, Barry 1937- *ConAu 108*
McWhiney, Grady 1928- *ConAu 5R, –6NR*
McWhinney, Edward 1926- *ConAu 29R*
McWhirter, A Ross 1925-1975 *ConAu 17R, –61, SmATA 31N*
McWhirter, George 1939- *ConAu 77, ConP 80, IntAu&W 82, WrDr 84*
McWhirter, Glenna S 1929- *ConAu 89*
McWhirter, Nickie *ConAu X*
McWhirter, Norris Dewar 1925- *ConAu 13R*
McWhorter, Charles Coker 1904- *IntWWP 82*
McWhorter C C *IntWWP 82X*
McWilliams, Carey 1905-1980 *ConAu 2NR, –101, –45, TwCA SUP*
McWilliams, John P, Jr. 1940- *ConAu 49*
McWilliams, Margaret 1929- *WrDr 84*
McWilliams, Margaret Ann Edgar 1929- *ConAu 8NR, –17R*
McWilliams, Peter 1949- *ConAu 41R*
McWilliams, Wilson Carey 1933- *ConAu 103*
Mdledle, Gertrude Jumartha 1896- *IntAu&W 82*
Meacham, Ellis K *DrAP&F 83*
Meacham, Ellis K 1913- *ConAu 25R, WrDr 84*
Meacham, Harry M 1901-1975 *ConAu P-2*
Meacham, Standish 1932- *ConAu 110*
Meacher, Michael Hugh 1939- *ConAu 109*
Mead, D Eugene 1934- *ConAu 65*
Mead, Edward Shepherd 1914- *IntAu&W 82*
Mead, Frank Spencer 1898-1982 *ConAu 9NR, –107, ConAu P-1*
Mead, Harold 1910- *ConAu P-1*
Mead, Jude 1919- *ConAu 25R*
Mead, Margaret 1901-1978 *AuNews 1, ConAu 1R, –4NR, –81, ConIsC 1[port], LongCTC, SmATA 20N, TwCA, TwCA SUP*
Mead, Matthew 1924- *ConAu 101, ConP 80, WrDr 84*
Mead, Robert Douglas 1928- *ConAu 41R, IntAu&W 82*
Mead, Robert Douglas 1928-1983 *ConAu 110*
Mead, Russell *ConAu X, IntAu&W 82X*
Mead, Russell 1935- *ConAu 9R, SmATA 10, WrDr 84*
Mead, Shepherd 1914- *ConAu 9R, ConSFA, IntAu&W 82X, TwCSFW, WrDr 84*
Mead, Sidney E 1904- *ConAu P-1*
Mead, Sidney Moko 1927- *ConAu 106, WrDr 84*
Mead, Stella d1981 *ConAu 103, SmATA 27N*
Mead, Taylor *DcLB 16[port]*
Mead, Walter B 1934- *ConAu 37R*
Mead, William B 1934- *ConAu 85*
Mead, William Richard 1915- *ConAu 103*
Meade, Dorothy Joan 1923- *ConAu 9R, WrDr 84*
Meade, Ellen 1936- *ConAu X, SmATA 5*
Meade, Everard 1914- *ConAu 25R*
Meade, James 1907- *WrDr 84*
Meade, James Edward 1907- *ConAu 1R, –2NR*

Meade, L T 1854-1914 *TwCCr&M 80*
Meade, Marion 1934- *ConAu 1NR, –49, SmATA 23[port]*
Meade, Mary *ConAu X*
Meade, Richard 1926-1977 *ConAu X, TwCWW*
Meade, Richard A 1911- *ConAu 45*
Meade, Robert Douthat 1903- *ConAu P-2*
Meader, Stephen W 1892-1977 *TwCCW 83*
Meader, Stephen Warren 1892- *ConAu 5R, SmATA 1*
Meador, Roy 1929- *ConAu 11NR, –69*
Meadow, Charles T 1929- *ConAu 29R, SmATA 23[port], WrDr 84*
Meadow, Kathryn Pendleton 1929- *ConAu 7NR,*

–57
Meadowcroft, Enid LaMonte 1898- *ConAu X, SmATA 3*
Meadowcroft, Ernest 1914- *WrDr 84*
Meadows, Eddie S 1939- *ConAu 109*
Meadows, Edward 1944- *ConAu 101*
Meadows, Paul 1913- *ConAu 41R*
Meadows, Peter *ConAu X, –X*
Meadows, Stephen *IntWWP 82X*
Meads, Kathy *DrAP&F 83*
Meagher, Aileen Alethea 1910- *CreCan 2*
Meagher, John C 1935- *ConAu 11NR, –17R*
Meagher, Paul Kevin 1907-1976 *ConAu 69*
Meagher, Robert E 1943- *ConAu 10NR, –25R*
Meagher, Robert F 1927- *ConAu 41R*
Meaker, Eloise 1915- *ConAu 105*
Meaker, M J *ConAu X, SmATA X*
Meaker, Marijane *WrDr 84*
Meaker, Marijane 1927- *ConAu 107, SmATA 20*
Meakin, David 1943- *ConAu 69*
Mealy, Rosemari 1941- *IntWWP 82*
Meano, Cesare 1906-1958 *CnMD*
Means, Florence Crannell 1891-1980 *ConAu 1R, –103, IntAu&W 82, SmATA 1, –25N, TwCCW 83*
Means, Gordon Paul 1927- *ConAu 33R, IntAu&W 82, WrDr 84*
Means, John Barkley 1939- *ConAu 33R*
Means, Louis Edgar 1902- *ConAu 2NR, –5R*
Means, Marianne Hansen 1934- *ConAu 9R*
Means, Richard Keith 1929- *ConAu 2NR, –5R*
Meany, George 1894-1980 *ConAu 97*
Meares, Ainslie 1910- *WrDr 84*
Meares, Ainslie Dixon 1910- *ConAu 11NR, –25R*
Mearian, Judy Frank 1936- *ConAu 101*
Mearns, David Chambers 1899-1981 *ConAu 1R, –104*
Mears, Brainerd, Jr. 1921- *ConAu 53*
Mears, Richard Chase 1935- *ConAu 101*
Measday, George *ConAu X*
Measham, D C 1932- *ConAu 21R*
Measham, Donald Charles 1932- *WrDr 84*
Measures, Howard 1894- *ConAu P-1*
Mebane, John Harrison 1909- *ConAu 13R, WrDr 84*
Mebane, Mary E *DrAP&F 83*
Mebane, Mary E 1933- *ConAu 73*
Mech, Dave *ConAu X*
Mech, L David 1937- *ConAu 33R, IntAu&W 82, WrDr 84*
Mecham, John Lloyd 1893- *ConAu 1R*
Mechanic, David 1936- *ConAu 3NR, –5R*
Mechanic, Sylvia 1920- *ConAu 69*
Mechtel, Angelika 1943- *CIDMEL 80, IntAu&W 82X*
Meckel, Christoph 1935- *CIDMEL 80*
Meckier, Jerome T 1941- *ConAu 33R, WrDr 84*
Meckler, Alan Marshall 1945- *ConAu 57*
Meckley, Richard F 1928- *ConAu 37R*
Mecklin, John Martin 1918-1971 *ConAu 33R*
Medalia, Leon S 1881- *ConAu 85*
Medary, Marjorie 1890- *ConAu 73, SmATA 14*
Medawar, Peter 1915- *WrDr 84*
Medawar, Sir Peter Brian 1915- *ConAu 97, DcLEL 1940, WorAu 1970*
Medd, Patrick 1919- *ConAu 25R*
Meddaugh, Susan 1944- *ConAu 106, SmATA 29*
Meddis, Ray 1944- *ConAu 77*
Medea, Andra 1953- *ConAu 57*
Medearis, Mary 1915- *ConAu 69, SmATA 5*
Medeiros, Earl Caton 1933- *ConAu 89*
Medhin, Tsegaye Gabre *ConAu X*
Medhurst, Joan *ConAu X*
Medicus II *ConAu X*
Medina, Jeremy T 1942- *ConAu 11NR, –69*
Medina, Jose Ramon 1921- *IntWWP 82*
Medina, Pablo *DrAP&F 83*
Medina, Pablo 1948- *IntWWP 82*
Medina, Vicente 1866-1937 *CIDMEL 80*
Medio, Dolores 1914- *CIDMEL 80*
Medley, Anne *ConAu X*
Medley, Margaret 1918- *ConAu 13R*
Medley, Morris L 1942- *ConAu 57*
Medlicott, Alexander G, Jr. 1927- *ConAu 37R*
Medlicott, Margaret P 1913- *ConAu 29R*
Medlicott, William Norton 1900- *ConAu 9R, IntAu&W 82, WrDr 84*
Medlin, Virgil D 1943- *ConAu 57*

Mednick, Murray *DrAP&F 83*
Mednick, Murray 1939- *ConAu 21R, ConDr 82, WrDr 84*
Medoff, Mark 1940- *AuNews 1, ConAu 5NR, -53, ConDr 82, ConLC 6, -23[port], DcLB 7[port], IntAu&W 82, NatPD 81[port], WrDr 84*
Medsker, Leland L 1905- *ConAu 1R, -2NR*
Medved, Harry 1961?- *ConAu 93*
Medved, Michael 1948- *ConAu 11NR, -65*
Medvedb, Andrei Pisatel *IntWWP 82X*
Medvedev, Roy 1925- *ConAu 81, WrDr 84*
Medvedev, Zhores 1925- *ConAu 69, IntAu&W 82, WrDr 84*
Medvei, Victor Cornelius 1905- *WrDr 84*
Mee, Arthur Henry 1875-1943 *LongCTC*
Mee, Charles L, Jr. 1938- *ConAu 3NR, -45, SmATA 8*
Mee, Fiona 1946?-1978 *ConAu 104*
Mee, John Franklin 1908- *ConAu P-1*
Mee, Susie *DrAP&F 83*
Meechan, Hugh L 1933- *ConAu 17R*
Meehan, Daniel Joseph 1930-1978 *ConAu 77*
Meehan, Danny *ConAu X*
Meehan, Eugene J 1923- *ConAu 37R, IntAu&W 82*
Meehan, Richard Lawrence 1939- *ConAu 107*
Meehan, Thomas Edward 1932- *ConAu 29R, ConDr 82D*
Meehl, Paul E 1920- *ConAu 93*
Meek, Forrest B 1928- *ConAu 110, MichAu 80*
Meek, Jacklyn O'Hanlon 1933- *ConAu 77, SmATA 34*
Meek, Jay *DrAP&F 83*
Meek, Jay 1937- *ConAu 107*
Meek, Lois Hayden *ConAu X*
Meek, Loyal George 1918- *ConAu 73*
Meek, Margaret *ConAu X*
Meek, Pauline Palmer 1917- *ConAu 106*
Meek, Ronald Lindley 1917-1978 *ConAu 6NR, -9R*
Meek, S P 1894-1972 *ConAu 1R, -103, ConSFA, SmATA 28N, TwCSFW*
Meeker, Alice 1904- *ConAu P-2*
Meeker, Joseph W 1932- *ConAu 49*
Meeker, Mary Nacol 1928- *ConAu 53*
Meeker, Oden 1918?-1976 *SmATA 14*
Meeker, Oden 1919?-1976 *ConAu 65, -73*
Meeker, Richard Kilburn 1925- *ConAu P-2*
Meeks, Esther MacBain 1921- *ConAu 1R, SmATA 1, WrDr 84*
Meeks, John E *ConAu 33R, WrDr 84*
Meeks, Linda A *ConAu X*
Meeks, M Douglas 1941- *ConAu 93*
Meeks, Wayne A 1932- *ConAu 5NR, -13R, WrDr 84*
Meen, Victor Ben 1910-1971 *ConAu 106*
Meer, Fatima 1929- *ConAu 73*
Meerhaeghe, M A G Van *ConAu X*
Meerloo, Joost Abraham Maurits 1903-1976 *ConAu 1R, -4NR, -69*
Meersch, Maxence VanDer 1907-1951 *TwCA, TwCA SUP*
Mees, Steve *ConAu X*
Meeter, Glenn 1934- *ConAu 33R*
Meeth, Louis Richard 1934- *ConAu 17R*
Meeuwesse, Antonius Catharina Maria 1914- *IntAu&W 82*
Megargee, Edwin I 1937- *ConAu 7NR, -17R*
Meged, Aharon 1920- *ConAu X*
Meged, Aron *ConAu X*
Megged, Aharon 1920- *ConAu 1NR, -49, ConLC 9, IntAu&W 82, WorAu, WrDr 84*
Meggers, Betty J 1921- *ConAu 17R, WrDr 84*
Meggitt, Mervyn John 1924- *ConAu 13R, WrDr 84*
Meggs, Brown 1930- *ConAu 7NR, -61, TwCCr&M 80, WrDr 84*
Meggyesy, Dave *ConAu X*
Meggyesy, David M 1941- *ConAu 33R*
Megill, Kenneth Alden 1939- *ConAu 106*
Meglin, Nick 1935- *ConAu 69*
Meglitsch, Paul A 1914- *ConAu 53*
Megson, Barbara 1930- *ConAu 29R*
Mehan, Joseph Albert 1929- *ConAu 101*
Mehdevi, Alexander Sinclair 1947- *ConAu 49, SmATA 7*
Mehdevi, Anne Sinclair 1922- *ConAu 5R, SmATA 8, WorAu*
Mehdi, M T 1928- *ConAu 8NR, -17R*
Mehegan, John 1920- *ConAu 5R*
Mehl, Roger 1912- *ConAu 6NR, -9R,*

IntAu&W 82
Mehlinger, Howard D 1931- *ConAu 6NR, -9R*
Mehlinger, Kermit 1918- *WrDr 84*
Mehnert, Klaus 1906- *ConAu 1R, -2NR, IntAu&W 82, WrDr 84*
Mehrabian, Albert 1939- *ConAu 33R, WrDr 84*
Mehren, Stein 1935- *ClDMEL 80*
Mehrens, William A 1937- *ConAu 37R*
Mehring, Walter 1896-1981 *CnMD, ConAu 105, WorAu*
Mehrotra, Arvind Krishna 1947- *ConP 80, DcLEL 1940, WrDr 84*
Mehrotra, Ram 1931- *ConAu 8NR, -13R, IntAu&W 82*
Mehrotra, Sriram 1931- *WrDr 84*
Mehrtens, Susan E 1945- *ConAu 53*
Mehta, Gaganvihari L 1900-1974 *ConAu 49*
Mehta, Purnima 1947- *IntWWP 82*
Mehta, Rustam Jehangir 1912- *ConAu 9R*
Mehta, Shahnaz *ConAu 106*
Mehta, Ved 1934- *WrDr 84*
Mehta, Ved Parkash 1934- *ConAu 1R, -2NR, DcLEL 1940, IntAu&W 82, WorAu*
Mehta, Vrajendra Raj 1944- *IntAu&W 82*
Mei, Ko-Wang 1918- *ConAu 2NR, -45*
Meiden, Walter 1907- *ConAu 8NR, -13R*
Meidinger, Ingeborg Lucie 1923- *IntAu&W 82*
Meidinger-Geise, Inge *IntAu&W 82X*
Meier, August 1923- *ConAu 3NR, -9R*
Meier, Gerhard 1917- *IntAu&W 82*
Meier, Heinz K 1929- *ConAu 61*
Meier, Herbert 1928- *CnMD, IntAu&W 82*
Meier, Joel F 1940- *ConAu 109*
Meier, Matt S 1917- *ConAu 41R*
Meier, Richard Louis 1920- *ConAu 17R*
Meier-Graefe, Julius A 1867-1935 *TwCA*
Meier-Haas, Yvonne 1928- *IntAu&W 82*
Meierhenry, Wesley Carl 1915- *ConAu 41R*
Meiggs, Russell 1902- *ConAu 103*
Meighan, Donald Charles 1929- *ConAu 107, SmATA 30[port]*
Meigs, Alexander James 1921- *ConAu 104*
Meigs, Cornelia 1884-1973 *TwCCW 83*
Meigs, Cornelia Lynde 1884-1973 *ConAu 9R, -45, SmATA 6*
Meigs, Peveril 1903- *ConAu 37R*
Meigs, Walter B 1912- *ConAu 21R*
Meij, Jacob L 1900- *ConAu 5R*
Meijer, M J 1912- *ConAu 69*
Meikle, Clive *ConAu X*
Meikle, Jeffrey L 1949- *ConAu 101*
Meiklejohn, John Miller Dow 1836?-1902 *LongCTC*
Meilach, Dona Z 1926- *SmATA 34[port]*
Meilach, Dona Zweigoron 1926- *ConAu 5NR, -9R*
Meilach, Michael D 1932- *ConAu 2NR, -5R*
Meilaender, Gilbert 1946- *ConAu 109*
Meilen, Bill 1932- *ConAu 69*
Meillassoux, Claude Albert 1925- *ConAu 25R, IntAu&W 82*
Meilleur, Jacques *CreCan 1*
Meimaippithan *IntWWP 82X*
Mein, Margaret 1924- *ConAu 61, IntAu&W 82*
Meinardus, Otto F A 1925- *IntAu&W 82*
Meinel, Peter Ole 1943- *IntAu&W 82*
Meiners, R K *DrAP&F 83*
Meiners, R K 1932- *ConAu 3NR, -5R*
Meiners, Roger Evert 1948- *ConAu 110*
Meinhardt, Ernst August 1924- *IntAu&W 82*
Meinhardt, Gunther 1925- *IntAu&W 82*
Meinhardt, Peter 1903- *WrDr 84*
Meinke, Peter *DrAP&F 83*
Meinke, Peter 1932- *ConAu 25R, DcLB 5[port], IntAu&W 82, IntWWP 82, WrDr 84*
Meintjes, Johannes 1923-1980 *ConAu 8NR, -17R*
Meir, Golda 1898-1978 *ConAu 81, -89*
Meireles, Cecilia 1901-1964 *ModLAL, TwCWr, WorAu 1970*
Meiring, Desmond *ConAu X*
Meiring, Jane M 1920- *ConAu 103, IntAu&W 82, WrDr 84*
Meisch, Lynn A 1945- *ConAu 105*
Meisch, Richard A 1943- *ConAu 33R*
Meisel, Anthony C 1943- *ConAu 105*
Meisel, Gerald Stanley 1937- *ConAu 9R*
Meisel, John 1923- *ConAu 17R*
Meisel, Martin 1931- *ConAu 5R*
Meisel, Perry 1949- *ConAu 102*
Meisel, Tony *ConAu X*
Meiselas, Susan 1948- *ConAu 106*

Meiselman, David I 1924- *ConAu 13R*
Meisenholder, Robert 1915- *ConAu 37R, IntAu&W 82*
Meisler, Stanley 1931- *ConAu 73*
Meisner, Maurice 1931- *ConAu 21R*
Meiss, Millard 1904-1975 *ConAu 57, -61*
Meissner, Bill *DrAP&F 83*
Meissner, Hans-Otto 1909- *ConAu 2NR, -49*
Meissner, Kurt 1885-1976 *ConAu P-2*
Meissner, W W 1931- *ConAu 33R*
Meissner, William 1948- *IntWWP 82*
Meister, Barbara 1932- *ConAu 102*
Meister, Ernst 1911-1979 *ClDMEL 80*
Meister, Peter William 1948- *IntAu&W 82*
Meister, Richard J 1938- *ConAu 57*
Meister, Robert 1926- *ConAu 5R, -9NR*
Meixner, John A 1925- *ConAu 5R*
Mejia, Arthur, Jr. 1934- *ConAu 81*
Melady, Thomas 1927- *WrDr 84*
Melady, Thomas Patrick 1927- *ConAu 5NR, -9R*
Melahn, Martha 1924- *ConAu 107*
Melamid, Alexander 1914- *ConAu 45*
Meland, Bernard Eugene 1899- *ConAu 17R*
Melaro, Constance L 1929- *ConAu 17R*
Melas, Evi 1930- *ConAu 65*
Melas, Spyros 1883- *CnMD*
Melba, Nellie 1861-1931 *LongCTC*
Melber, Jehuda 1916- *ConAu 29R, WrDr 84*
Melbin, Murray 1927- *ConAu 45*
Melbo, Irving Robert 1908- *ConAu 49*
Melby, John Fremont 1913- *ConAu 106*
Melcher, Daniel 1912- *ConAu 33R*
Melcher, Frederic Gershom 1879-1963 *ConAu 89, SmATA 22N*
Melcher, Marguerite Fellows 1879-1969 *ConAu 5R, SmATA 10*
Melcher, Robert Augustus 1910- *ConAu 17R*
Melchert, Norman Paul 1933- *ConAu 25R*
Melchinger, Siegfried 1906- *ConAu 81*
Melchior, Ib *DrAP&F 83*
Melchior, Ib 1917- *ConAu 2NR, -45, WrDr 84*
Melchior-Bonnet, Christian 1904- *IntAu&W 82*
Meldal-Johnsen, Trevor Bernard 1944- *ConAu 101*
Melden, A I 1910- *ConAu 17R*
Melder, Keith E 1932- *ConAu 81*
Meldrum, James *WrDr 84*
Mele, Frank Michael 1935- *ConAu 53*
Melendez, Jesus Papoleto *DrAP&F 83*
Melendy, H Brett 1924- *ConAu 8NR, -17R*
Meleski, Patricia F 1935- *ConAu 61*
Melezh, Ivan 1921?-1976 *ConAu 69*
Melfi, Leonard 1935- *ConAu 73, ConDr 82, NatPD 81[port], WrDr 84*
Melhem, D H *ConAu 2NR, -49, DrAP&F 83, IntAu&W 82, IntWWP 82*
Melhorn, Charles M 1918- *ConAu 57*
Melick, Arden Davis 1940- *ConAu 106*
Melikow, Loris *ConAu X*
Melin, Grace Hathaway 1892-1973 *ConAu 45, ConAu P-2, SmATA 10*
Mell *ConAu X*
Mell, Max 1882-1971 *ClDMEL 80, CnMD, CroCD, ModGL, ModWD*
Mellaart, Helen 1929- *IntAu&W 82*
Mellan, Eleanor 1905- *ConAu 5R*
Mellan, Ibert 1901- *ConAu 5R*
Mellanby, Kenneth 1908- *ConAu 85, IntAu&W 82, WrDr 84*
Mellander, G A 1935- *WrDr 84*
Mellander, Gustavo 1935- *ConAu 33R*
Mellard, James Milton 1938- *ConAu 105*
Mellen, Ida M 1877- *ConAu 5R*
Mellen, Joan 1941- *ConAu 11NR, -65, WrDr 84*
Mellencamp, Virginia Lynn 1917- *ConAu 9R*
Meller, Norman 1913- *ConAu 25R, WrDr 84*
Mellers, Wilfrid 1914- *WrDr 84*
Mellers, Wilfrid Howard 1914- *ConAu 4NR, -5R, IntAu&W 82*
Mellersh, H E L 1897- *ConAu 9NR*
Mellersh, Harold Edward Leslie 1897- *ConAu 53, SmATA 10*
Mellert, Robert B 1937- *ConAu 61*
Mellichamp, Josephine 1923- *ConAu 93, IntAu&W 82*
Mellin, Jeanne 1929- *ConAu 49*
Mellini, Peter 1935- *ConAu 93*
Mellinkoff, David 1914- *ConAu 13R*
Mellinkoff, Ruth 1924- *ConAu 37R*
Mellon, James R 1942- *ConAu 69*
Mellon, John C 1933- *ConAu 107*

Mellon, Knox *ConAu X*
Mellon, Matthew T 1897- *ConAu 29R*
Mellon, Melvin Guy *WrDr 84*
Mellon, Stanley 1927- *ConAu 108*
Mellon, William Knox, Jr. 1925- *ConAu 37R*
Mellor, Anne Kostelanetz 1941- *ConAu 45*
Mellor, David 1903- *WrDr 84*
Mellor, David P 1903- *IntAu&W 82*
Mellor, J Leigh 1928- *WrDr 84*
Mellor, John Leigh 1928- *ConAu 17R*
Mellor, John W 1928- *WrDr 84*
Mellor, John Williams 1928- *ConAu 33R*
Mellor, William Bancroft 1906- *ConAu 61*
Mellors, John 1920- *ConAu 65*
Mellott, Leland *DrAP&F 83*
Mellow, James R 1926- *ConAu 105*
Mellown, Elgin W 1931- *ConAu 17R, WrDr 84*
Mellows, Anthony 1936- *WrDr 84*
Mellows, Joan *ConAu 77, IntAu&W 82*
Melly, Alan George Heywood 1926-
  IntAu&W 82
Melly, George 1926- *ConAu 81, WrDr 84*
Melman, Seymour 1917- *ConAu 1R, -4NR*
Melmoth, Sebastian *LongCTC*
Melnick, David *DrAP&F 83*
Melnick, David John 1938- *IntWWP 82*
Melnick, Donald 1926-1977 *ConAu 69*
Melnick, Jack 1929- *ConAu 89*
Melnyk, Z Lew 1928- *ConAu 41R*
Melo Neto, Joao Cabral De 1920- *WorAu 1970*
Meloan, Taylor Wells 1919- *ConAu 45*
Melody, Rose 1922- *IntWWP 82*
Melograni, Piero 1930- *IntAu&W 82*
Melone, Albert P 1942- *ConAu 109*
Melone, Joseph J 1931- *ConAu 13R*
Meloney, Franken *TwCRGW, WrDr 84*
Meloney, William Brown 1905?-1971 *ConAu 104*
Meloon, Marion 1921- *ConAu 65*
Melosi, Martin Victor 1947- *ConAu 77, IntAu&W 82*
Melsa, James L 1938- *ConAu 104*
Melson, Robert 1937- *ConAu 85*
Melton, David 1934- *ConAu 69, WrDr 84*
Melton, J Gordon 1942- *ConAu 110*
Melton, John L 1920- *ConAu 9R*
Melton, Julius Wemyss, Jr. 1933- *ConAu 21R*
Melton, William 1920- *ConAu 37R, WrDr 84*
Meltsner, Arnold J 1931- *ConAu 57*
Meltsner, Michael 1937- *ConAu 108*
Meltzer, Allan H 1928- *ConAu 3NR, -5R*
Meltzer, Bernard N 1916- *ConAu 21R*
Meltzer, David *DrAP&F 83*
Meltzer, David 1937- *ConAu 6NR, -9R, ConP 80, ConSFA, DcLB 16[port], DcLEL 1940, TwCSFW, WrDr 84*
Meltzer, Milton 1915- *ConAu 13R, ConLC 26[port], SmATA 1*
Meltzer, Morton Franklin 1930- *ConAu 21R, WrDr 84*
Meltzoff, Julian 1921- *ConAu 21R*
Meltzoff, Nancy 1952- *ConAu 93*
Meluch, R M 1956- *ConAu 109*
Melvill, Harald 1895- *ConAu 5R*
Melville, Alan 1910- *IntAu&W 82, WrDr 84*
Melville, Annabelle McConnell 1910- *ConAu 5R*
Melville, Anne *ConAu X, IntAu&W 82X, SmATA X, TwCRGW, WrDr 84*
Melville, Frederick 1876-1938 *LongCTC*
Melville, J Keith 1921- *ConAu 53*
Melville, Jennie *ConAu X, TwCCr&M 80, TwCRGW, WrDr 84*
Melville, Joy 1932- *ConAu 85*
Melville, Keith 1945- *ConAu 41R*
Melville, Walter 1875-1937 *LongCTC*
Melvin, A Gordon 1894- *WrDr 84*
Melvin, Arthur Gordon 1894- *ConAu 9R*
Melwani, Murli Das 1939- *ConAu 61*
Melwood, Mary *ConAu X, SmATA X, TwCCW 83, WrDr 84*
Melzack, Ronald 1929- *ConAu 41R, SmATA 5, WrDr 84*
Melzer, John Henry 1908-1967 *ConAu P-1*
Melzi, Robert C 1915- *ConAu 37R*
Memling, Carl 1918-1969 *ConAu 1R, -4NR, SmATA 6*
Memmi, Albert 1920- *CIDMEL 80, ConAu 81, IntAu&W 82, ModFrL, TwCWr, WorAu*
Memmott, Roger Ladd *DrAP&F 83*
Memory *ConAu X*
Menacker, Julius 1933- *ConAu 41R*
Menaker, Daniel 1941- *ConAu 65*
Menander *LongCTC*

Menard, H William 1920- *ConAu 37R*
Menard, Henry William 1920- *WrDr 84*
Menard, Jean 1930?-1977 *ConAu 69*
Menard, Orville D 1933- *ConAu 21R, WrDr 84*
Menasco, Norman *ConAu X*
Menashe, Louis 1935- *ConAu 21R*
Menashe, Samuel *DrAP&F 83*
Menchan, W McKinley 1898- *LivgBAA*
Mencher, Melvin 1927- *ConAu 73*
Menchin, Robert S 1923- *ConAu 21R*
Mencken, H L 1880-1956 *CnMWL, ConAmA, ConAu 105, LongCTC, ModAL, ModAL SUP, TwCWr, WhoTwCL*
Mencken, Henry Louis 1880-1956 *TwCA, TwCA SUP*
Menczer, Bela 1902-1983 *ConAu 110*
Mendel, Arthur 1905-1979 *ConAu 41R, -89*
Mendel, Arthur P 1927- *ConAu 13R*
Mendel, Douglas H, Jr. 1921- *ConAu 17R*
Mendel, Jo *ConAu X, IntAu&W 82X, SmATA X, WrDr 84*
Mendel, Mark *DrAP&F 83*
Mendel, Mark 1947- *IntWWP 82*
Mendel, Roberta *DrAP&F 83*
Mendel, Sydney 1925- *ConAu 109*
Mendel, Werner M 1927- *ConAu 11NR, -21R*
Mendele Mocher Sforim 1836-1917 *CIDMEL 80*
Mendell, Clarence W 1883-1970 *ConAu P-1*
Mendelowitz, Daniel M 1905- *ConAu 9R*
Mendels, Joseph 1937- *ConAu 29R*
Mendelsohn, Allan R 1928- *ConAu 45*
Mendelsohn, Everett 1931- *ConAu 11NR, -17R*
Mendelsohn, Felix, Jr. 1906- *ConAu 29R*
Mendelsohn, Harold 1923- *ConAu 49*
Mendelsohn, Jack 1918- *ConAu 1R, -1NR*
Mendelsohn, Martin 1935- *ConAu 33R, WrDr 84*
Mendelsohn, Michael John 1931- *ConAu 85*
Mendelsohn, Oscar 1896- *ConAu 9R*
Mendelsohn, Pamela 1944- *ConAu 101*
Mendelson, Edward 1946- *ConAu 11NR, -65*
Mendelson, Lee 1933- *ConAu 33R, WrDr 84*
Mendelson, Mary Adelaide 1917- *ConAu 85, IntAu&W 82*
Mendelson, Morris 1922- *ConAu 2NR, -5R, WrDr 84*
Mendelson, Wallace 1911- *ConAu 1R*
Mendelssohn, Kurt Alfred Georg 1906-1980 *ConAu 7NR, -105, -53*
Mendelssohn, Oscar Adolf 1896- *DcLEL 1940*
Mendenhall, George Emery 1916- *ConAu 33R, WrDr 84*
Mendenhall, James Edgar 1903-1971 *ConAu 33R*
Mendenhall, John D 1911?-1983 *ConAu 110*
Mendenhall, Ruth Dyar 1912- *ConAu 65*
Mendes, Catulle 1841?-1909 *LongCTC*
Mendes, Murilo 1901- *ModLAL*
Mendes-France, Pierre 1907- *ConAu 81*
Mendes-France, Pierre 1907-1982 *ConAu 108*
Mendez, Angel Luis *DrAP&F 83*
Mendez, Charlotte Walker *DrAP&F 83*
Mendez Herrera, Jose 1904- *IntAu&W 82*
Mendini, Douglas A *DrAP&F 83*
Mendizabal Y Garcia Lavin, Federico 1901- *IntAu&W 82*
Mendlovitz, Saul H 1925- *ConAu 21R*
Mendonca, Susan 1950- *ConAu 102*
Mendonsa, Eugene L 1942- *ConAu 109*
Mendoza, George 1934- *ConAu 73*
Mendoza, Manuel G 1936- *ConAu 53*
Mendras, Henri 1927- *ConAu 73*
Menebroker, Ann *DrAP&F 83*
Menebroker, Ann 1936- *IntWWP 82*
Menen, Aubrey 1912- *ConAu 1R, -2NR, ConNov 82, LongCTC, ModBrL, ModCmwL, TwCA SUP, WrDr 84*
Menen, Salvator Aubrey Clarence 1912- *DcLEL 1940*
Menendez, Albert J 1942- *ConAu 7NR, -53, WrDr 84*
Menendez Pelayo, Marcelino 1856-1912 *CIDMEL 80*
Menendez Pidal, Ramon 1869-1968 *CIDMEL 80*
Meneses, Carlos 1929- *IntAu&W 82*
Meneses, Enrique 1929- *ConAu 11NR, -25R*
Meng, Brigitte 1932- *IntAu&W 82*
Meng, Heinz 1924- *ConAu 69, SmATA 13*
Menges, Karl Heinrich 1908- *ConAu 37R, WrDr 84*
Menhennet, Alan 1933- *ConAu 97*
Menikoff, Barry 1939- *ConAu 37R*
Menkiti, Ifeanyi *DrAP&F 83*

Menkiti, Ifeanyi 1940- *ConAu 65, IntWWP 82*
Menkus, Belden 1931- *ConAu 17R*
Mennel, Robert McKisson 1938- *ConAu 109*
Mennell, Stephen 1944- *ConAu 107*
Mennier-Bourg DeLaRouche, A *IntAu&W 82X*
Menning, J H 1915- *ConAu 21R*
Menninger, Edwin A 1896- *ConAu 9R*
Menninger, Karl Augustus 1893- *ConAu 17R, TwCA, TwCA SUP*
Menninger, William Claire 1899-1966 *ConAu 25R*
Mennis, Bernard 1938- *ConAu 41R*
Menolascino, Frank J 1930- *ConAu 73*
Menon, K P S 1898- *ConAu 5R, -5NR, DcLEL 1940*
Menon, K P S 1898-1982 *ConAu 108*
Menon, R R *IntWWP 82X*
Menon, R Rabindranath 1927- *ConAu 11NR, -65, IntWWP 82*
Menon, Rabindranath *IntWWP 82X*
Menotti, Gian Carlo 1911- *ConAu 104, SmATA 29[port]*
Menshikov, Marina 1928?-1979 *ConAu 93*
Mensoian, Michael George 1927- *ConAu 85, IntAu&W 82*
Menton, Seymour 1927- *ConAu 45*
Mentor *ConAu X, WrDr 84*
Menuhin, Hephzibah 1920-1981 *ConAu 108*
Menuhin, Yehudi 1916- *ConAu 2NR, -45, WrDr 84*
Menut, Albert D 1894- *ConAu 25R*
Menville, Douglas 1935- *ConAu 57*
Menyuk, Paula 1929- *ConAu 37R*
Menze, Clemens 1928- *IntAu&W 82*
Menzel, Donald H 1901-1976 *ConAu 69, ConAu P-2*
Menzel, Gerhard 1894- *ModWD*
Menzel, Gerhard W 1922- *IntAu&W 82*
Menzel, Johanna *ConAu X*
Menzel, Paul T 1942- *ConAu 53*
Menzel, Roderich 1907- *ConAu 93, IntWWP 82*
Menzies, Archibald Norman 1904- *IntAu&W 82*
Menzies, Elizabeth 1915- *WrDr 84*
Menzies, Elizabeth Grant Cranbrook 1915- *ConAu 17R*
Menzies, Robert Gordon 1894-1978 *ConAu 77, -81*
Menzies, William W 1931- *ConAu 110*
Meo, Lucy Dorothy 1920- *ConAu 25R*
Merak, A J *ConSFA*
Meras, Phyllis 1931- *ConAu 41R*
Merbaum, Michael 1933- *ConAu 65*
Mercatante, Anthony Stephen 1940- *ConAu 41R, IntAu&W 82*
Mercer, Betty Deborah 1926- *IntWWP 82*
Mercer, Blaine E 1921- *ConAu 1R, -2NR*
Mercer, Cecil William 1885-1960 *LongCTC, TwCA, TwCA SUP*
Mercer, Charles E 1917- *ConAu 1R, -2NR, SmATA 16*
Mercer, David 1928-1980 *ConAu 9R, -102, ConDr 82E, ConLC 5, CroCD, DcLB 13[port], DcLEL 1940*
Mercer, Frances 1934- *WrDr 84*
Mercer, Jane Ross 1924- *ConAu 45*
Mercer, Jean *ConAu X*
Mercer, Jessie *ConAu 1R, -2NR*
Mercer, Joan Bodger 1923- *ConAu 101*
Mercer, Johnny 1906-1976 *ConAu 65*
Mercer, Marilyn 1923- *ConAu 107*
Mercer, Virginia Fletcher 1916- *ConAu 5R*
Mercey, Arch Andrew 1906-1980 *ConAu 102*
Merchant, Jane 1919-1972 *ConAu 1R, -4NR, -33R*
Merchant, Larry 1931- *ConAu 102, WrDr 84*
Merchant, Paul *ConAu X*
Mercie, Jean-Luc Henri 1939- *ConAu 49*
Mercier, Jean Doyle 1916- *ConAu 1R*
Mercier, Margaret *CreCan 1*
Mercier, Vivian 1919- *ConAu 81*
Mercouri, Melina 1925- *ConAu 106*
Mercure, Pierre 1927-1966 *CreCan 2*
Mercury *ConAu X*
Merdinger, Charles 1918- *WrDr 84*
Meredith, Anne *ConAu X, LongCTC, WorAu*
Meredith, Arnold *ConAu X*
Meredith, Char 1921- *ConAu 106*
Meredith, David William *ConAu X, SmATA X,*

Meredith, Don *DrAP&F 83*
Meredith, Don 1938- *ConAu 102*

Meredith, George 1828-1909 *LongCTC*
Meredith, George 1923- *ConAu 4NR, –9R*
Meredith, George Patrick 1904-1978 *ConAu 108*
Meredith, James *LivgBAA*
Meredith, James Howard 1933- *ConAu 77*
Meredith, Jeff *ConAu X*
Meredith, John 1933- *CreCan 2*
Meredith, Joseph C 1914- *ConAu 53*
Meredith, Nicolete 1896- *ConAu X*
Meredith, Richard C 1937-1979 *ConAu 85,*
   TwCSFW
Meredith, Robert 1923- *ConAu 5R*
Meredith, Robert C 1921- *ConAu 5R*
Meredith, Scott 1923- *ConAu 3NR, –9R,*
   WrDr 84
Meredith, William *DrAP&F 83, IntWWP 82X*
Meredith, William 1919- *ConAu 6NR, –9R,*
   ConLC 4, –13, –22[port], ConP 80,
   DcLB 5[port], DcLEL 1940, IntAu&W 82,
   IntWWP 82, ModAL SUP, WorAu,
   WrDr 84
Merewitz, Leonard 1943- *ConAu 69*
Merezhkovski, Dmitri Sergeyevich 1865-1941
   ModSL 1
Merezhkovsky, Dmitry Sergeyevich 1865-1941
   CIDMEL 80, LongCTC, TwCA,
   TwCA SUP
Merezhkovsky, Zinaida *ConAu X*
Meri, Veijo 1928- *CroCD*
Merideth, Robert 1935- *ConAu 49*
Merillat, Herbert C L 1915- *ConAu 29R*
Merin, Jennifer *ConAmTC*
Merin, Peter *ConAu X, IntAu&W 82X*
Merino, Joaquin 1927- *IntAu&W 82*
Meritt, Lucy Shoe 1906- *ConAu 37R*
Merivale, Patricia 1934- *ConAu 29R*
Meriwether, James B 1928- *ConAu 13R*
Meriwether, Louise *DrAP&F 83*
Meriwether, Louise M 1923- *ConAu 77,*
   LivgBAA, SmATA 31
Merk, Frederick 1887-1977 *ConAu 41R, –73*
Merkel, Miles Adair 1929- *ConAu 53*
Merkin, Daphne *DrAP&F 83*
Merkin, Donald H 1945- *ConAu 69*
Merkin, Robert 1947- *ConAu 109*
Merkl, Peter H 1932- *ConAu 5R, –7NR*
Merkle, Judith A 1942- *ConAu 105*
Merl, Dorothea 1920- *IntAu&W 82*
Merlak, Milena 1935- *IntWWP 82*
Merle, Robert 1908- *ConAu 93*
Merleau-Ponty, Maurice 1908-1961 *CIDMEL 80,*
   ConAu 89, WorAu
Merlin, Christina *TwCRGW, WrDr 84*
Merlin, David *ConAu X, IntAu&W 82X,*
   WrDr 84
Merlin, Jan 1925- *ConAu 108*
Merlis, George 1940- *ConAu 33R*
Merliss, Reuben 1915- *ConAu 17R*
Mermin, Samuel 1912- *ConAu 53*
Merne, Oscar James 1943- *ConAu 102,*
   WrDr 84
Mernit, Susan *DrAP&F 83*
Mernit, Susan 1953- *ConAu 69*
Meroff, Deborah 1948- *ConAu 89*
Merola, Mario Virgilio 1931- *CreCan 1*
Merrell, James Lee 1930- *ConAu 17R*
Merrell, Karen Dixon 1936- *ConAu 6NR, –13R*
Merrell, V Dallas 1936- *ConAu 9R*
Merrens, H Roy 1931- *ConAu 9R*
Merrett, Cyril Vincent 1902- *IntWWP 82*
Merriam, Alan F 1923-1980 *ConAu 1R, –1NR*
Merriam, Charles Edward 1874-1953 *TwCA SUP*
Merriam, Eve *DrAP&F 83*
Merriam, Eve 1916- *ConAu 5R, SmATA 3,*
   TwCCW 83, WrDr 84
Merriam, Harold G 1883-1981 *ConAu 10NR*
Merriam, Harold Guy 1883- *ConAu 61*
Merriam, Kendall Arthur 1942- *IntWWP 82*
Merriam, Robert E 1918- *ConAu 5R*
Merrick, Gordon 1916- *ConAu 11NR, –13R,*
   IntAu&W 82, WrDr 84
Merrick, Hugh 1898- *ConAu X, IntAu&W 82*
Merrick, Leonard 1864-1939 *LongCTC, TwCA,*
   TwCA SUP
Merrick, William 1916-1969 *ConAu P-1*
Merrifield, Gladys 1907- *IntAu&W 82*
Merril, Judith 1923- *ConAu 13R, ConSFA,*
   TwCSFW, WorAu, WrDr 84
Merrill, Antoinette June 1912- *ConAu 45*
Merrill, Arch 1895?-1974 *ConAu 49*
Merrill, Boynton, Jr. 1925- *ConAu 69*
Merrill, David W 1928- *ConAu 108*

Merrill, Dean 1943- *ConAu 8NR, –61*
Merrill, Dick *ConAu X*
Merrill, Edward C, Jr. 1920- *ConAu 21R*
Merrill, Edward H 1903- *ConAu P-1*
Merrill, Francis Ellsworth 1904-1969 *ConAu P-1*
Merrill, Frederick Thayer 1905-1974 *ConAu 53*
Merrill, Henry Tindall 1897-1982 *ConAu 108*
Merrill, James *DrAP&F 83*
Merrill, James 1926- *ConAu 10NR, –13R,*
   ConLC 2, –3, –6, –8, –13, –18, ConP 80,
   CroCAP, DcLB 5[port], DcLEL 1940,
   ModAL, ModAL SUP, WorAu, WrDr 84
Merrill, James M 1920- *ConAu 9R*
Merrill, Jean 1923- *TwCCW 83, WrDr 84*
Merrill, Jean Fairbanks 1923- *ConAu 1R, –4NR,*
   IntAu&W 82, SmATA 1
Merrill, John Calhoun 1924- *ConAu 73*
Merrill, John Nigel 1943- *ConAu 103,*
   IntAu&W 82
Merrill, M David 1937- *ConAu 41R*
Merrill, P J *ConAu X*
Merrill, Phil *ConAu X*
Merrill, Robert 1919- *ConAu 81*
Merrill, Robert 1944- *ConAu 89*
Merrill, Stuart Fitzrandolph 1863-1915
   CIDMEL 80, TwCA, TwCA SUP
Merrill, Thomas F 1932- *ConAu 29R, WrDr 84*
Merrill, Toni *ConAu X*
Merrill, Walter M 1915- *ConAu 21R*
Merrill, Wilfred K 1903- *ConAu 9R*
Merrill, William 1934- *ConAu 29R, WrDr 84*
Merriman, Ann Lloyd 1934- *ConAu 77*
Merriman, Beth *ConAu X*
Merriman, Henry Seton 1862-1903 *LongCTC*
Merriman, Jerry Johnson 1939- *ConAu 25R*
Merriman, John 1924-1974 *ConAu 104*
Merriman, Pat *WrDr 84*
Merritt, A 1884-1943 *TwCSFW*
Merritt, Abraham 1884-1943 *WorAu*
Merritt, Dixon 1879-1972 *ConAu 33R*
Merritt, Don 1945- *ConAu 106*
Merritt, E B *ConAu X*
Merritt, Helen Henry 1920- *ConAu 17R*
Merritt, James D 1934- *ConAu 33R*
Merritt, LeRoy Charles 1912-1970 *ConAu P-2*
Merritt, Miriam 1925- *ConAu 17R*
Merritt, Muriel 1905- *ConAu 69*
Merritt, Ray E, Jr. 1948- *ConAu 73*
Merritt, Raymond H 1936- *ConAu 85*
Merritt, Richard L 1933- *ConAu 41R*
Merritt, Si *IntAu&W 82X*
Merritt, T E *IntAu&W 82X*
Merry, Henry J 1908- *ConAu 37R*
Mersand, Joseph 1907- *ConAu 1R, –1NR*
Mersereau, John, Jr. 1925- *ConAu 1R, –2NR*
Mersky, Roy M 1925- *ConAu 37R*
Mersmann, James Frederick 1938- *ConAu 61*
Mertens, Lawrence E 1929- *ConAu 85*
Mertens, Thomas Robert 1930- *ConAu 6NR, –57*
Mertins, Christa 1936- *CreCan 2*
Mertins, Herman, Jr. 1931- *ConAu 41R*
Mertins, Louis 1885-1973 *ConAu 41R*
Merton, Andrew H 1944- *ConAu 107*
Merton, Giles *ConAu X*
Merton, Robert King 1910- *ConAu 41R,*
   IntAu&W 82
Merton, Stephen 1912- *ConAu 21R*
Merton, Thomas 1915-1968 *ConAu 5R, –25R,*
   ConLC 1, –3, –11, DcLB Y81B[port],
   LongCTC, ModAL, TwCA SUP
Mertz, Barbara 1927- *ConAu 11NR*
Mertz, Barbara G *WrDr 84*
Mertz, Barbara G 1927- *ConAu 21R,*
   TwCCr&M 80
Mertz, Richard Rolland 1927- *ConAu 21R*
Merved, Hervard H 1944- *IntAu&W 82*
Merwe, A V D *ConAu X*
Merwin, Decie 1894-1961 *SmATA 32*
Merwin, Sam, Jr. 1910- *TwCSFW, WrDr 84*
Merwin, Samuel 1874-1936 *LongCTC, TwCA*
Merwin, W S *DrAP&F 83*
Merwin, W S 1927- *ConLC 8, –13, –18,*
   ConP 80, DcLB 5[port], WrDr 84
Merwin, William Stanley 1927- *ConAu 13R,*
   ConLC 1, –2, –3, –5, CroCAP, DcLEL 1940,
   ModAL, ModAL SUP, WhoTwCL, WorAu
Mery, Fernand 1897- *ConAu 105*
Meryon, Penelope Jane 1942- *IntWWP 82*
Merz, Charles 1893-1977 *ConAu 73, TwCA,*
   TwCA SUP
Merzer, Meridee 1947- *ConAu 102*
Mesa-Lago, Carmelo 1934- *ConAu 10NR, –25R,*

Mesa Y Rosales, Enrique De 1878?-1929
   IntAu&W 82, WrDr 84
Mesa Y Rosales, Enrique De 1878?-1929
   CIDMEL 80
Meserve, Walter Joseph, Jr. 1923- *ConAu 1R,*
   –1NR, IntAu&W 82, WrDr 84
Meshack, B A 1922- *ConAu 93*
Meshenberg, Michael J 1942- *ConAu 93*
Meske, Eunice Boardman 1926- *ConAu 4NR*
Meskill, Johanna Menzel 1930- *ConAu 17R*
Meskill, Robert 1918?-1970 *ConAu 104*
Mesler, Corey J *DrAP&F 83*
Mess, Suzanne *CreCan 2*
Messager, Charles 1882-1971 *ConAu 93*
Messegue, Maurice 1921- *ConAu 103*
Messel, Harry 1922- *ConAu 103, IntAu&W 82,*
   WrDr 84
Messenger, Charles 1941- *ConAu 73*
Messenger, Elizabeth Margery 1908- *ConAu P-1*
Messent, Peter Ronald 1949- *ConAu 106*
Messer, Alfred A 1922- *ConAu 29R*
Messer, Ronald Keith 1942- *ConAu 57*
Messer, Thomas M 1920- *ConAu 106, WrDr 84*
Messerer, Asaf Mikhailovich 1903- *ConAu 104*
Messerli, Douglas *DrAP&F 83*
Messerli, Douglas 1947- *IntWWP 82*
Messerli, Jonathan C 1926- *ConAu 41R*
Messick, Hank *ConAu X*
Messick, Henry H 1922- *ConAu 2NR, –45*
Messieres, Nicole De *ConAu X*
Messing, Robin *DrAP&F 83*
Messing, Robin 1952- *IntWWP 82*
Messing, Shelley *DrAP&F 83*
Messing, Simon D 1922- *ConAu 57*
Messinger, C F 1913- *ConAu 21R*
Messinger, Sheldon L 1925- *ConAu 25R*
Messner, Fred R 1926- *ConAu 13R*
Messner, Gerald 1935- *ConAu 29R*
Messner, Reinhold 1944- *ConAu 81,*
   IntAu&W 82
Messner, Stephen Dale 1936- *ConAu 21R*
Mesta, Perle 1893?-1975 *ConAu 57*
Mesthene, Emmanuel George 1920- *ConAu 77*
Meston, John 1915?-1979 *ConAu 85*
Meszaros, Istvan 1930- *ConAu 9NR, –57*
Meta *ConAu X*
Metalious, Grace 1924-1964 *ConAu P-2,*
   LongCTC, TwCWr
Metaxas, B N 1925- *ConAu 37R*
Metaxas, Basil N 1925- *WrDr 84*
Meta'yel *IntWWP 82X*
Metcalf, Donald 1929- *WrDr 84*
Metcalf, E W 1945- *ConAu 65*
Metcalf, George R 1914- *ConAu 25R*
Metcalf, Kenneth N 1923-1965 *ConAu 5R*
Metcalf, Keyes DeWitt 1889- *ConAu 17R*
Metcalf, Lawrence E 1915- *ConAu 21R*
Metcalf, Lee 1911- *ASpks*
Metcalf, Norm 1937- *ConSFA*
Metcalf, Paul *DrAP&F 83*
Metcalf, Paul 1917- *ConAu 1NR, –45*
Metcalf, Suzanne *ConAu X, SmATA X*
Metcalf, Thomas R 1934- *ConAu 13R*
Metcalf, Vicky 1901- *ConAu 89*
Metcalfe, John 1891-1965 *TwCA, TwCA SUP*
Metcalfe, John Wallace 1901-1982 *ConAu 107*
Metcalfe, Steve 1953- *ConAu 108, NatPD 81*
Metchnikoff, Elie 1845-1916 *LongCTC*
Metesky, George *ConAu X*
Metge, Alice Joan 1930- *WrDr 84*
Meth, David L *DrAP&F 83*
Method, Kenneth Walter 1931- *ConAu 13R*
Methvin, Eugene H 1934- *ConAu 29R*
Metos, Thomas H 1932- *ConAu 93*
Metras, Gary *DrAP&F 83*
Metraux, Guy S 1917- *ConAu 9R*
Metraux, Rhoda 1914- *ConAu 57*
Metress, James F *ConAu X*
Metress, Seamus P 1933- *ConAu 6NR*
Metropolis, Nicholas Constantine 1915-
   ConAu 110
Mettler, George B 1934- *ConAu 93*
Metwally, M M 1939- *ConAu 65*
Metz, Donald L 1935- *ConAu 21R*
Metz, Donald S 1916- *ConAu 45*
Metz, Herbert Edward *ConAmTC*
Metz, Jerred *DrAP&F 83*
Metz, Jerred 1943- *ConAu 104, IntWWP 82*
Metz, Leon C 1930- *ConAu 1NR, –45*
Metz, Lois Lunt 1906- *ConAu P-1*
Metz, Mary 1937- *ConAu 53*
Metz, Mary Haywood 1939- *ConAu 85*
Metz, Mike *DrAP&F 83*

Metz, Robert 1928- *ConAu 61*
Metz, Roberta *DrAP&F 83*
Metz, William 1918- *ConAu 77*
Metzdorf, Robert Frederic 1912-1975 *ConAu 57*
Metzger, Barbara 1944- *ConAu 110*
Metzger, Bruce M 1914- *WrDr 84*
Metzger, Bruce Manning 1914- *ConAu 4NR,*
  -9R, IntAu&W 82
Metzger, Charles R 1921- *ConAu 25R*
Metzger, Deena *DrAP&F 83*
Metzger, Diane Hamill *DrAP&F 83*
Metzger, Erika A 1933- *ConAu 33R*
Metzger, H Peter 1931- *ConAu 107*
Metzger, Michael M 1935- *ConAu 21R,*
  WrDr 84
Metzger, Norman 1924- *ConAu 9NR, -53*
Metzger, Philip W 1931- *ConAu 45*
Metzger, Stanley D 1916- *ConAu 9R, WrDr 84*
Metzger, Thomas A 1933- *ConAu 97*
Metzger, Walter P 1922- *ConAu 61*
Metzker, Isaac 1901- *ConAu 45*
Metzler, Ken 1929- *ConAu 4NR, -53*
Metzler, Lloyd A 1913- *ConAu 104*
Metzler, Paul 1914- *ConAu 6NR, -57*
Metzner, Ralph 1936- *ConAu 69*
Metzner, Seymour 1924- *ConAu 21R*
Meudt, Edna 1906- *WrDr 84*
Meudt, Edna Kritz 1906- *ConAu 9NR, -13R,*
  IntWWP 82
Meuller, Melinda *DrAP&F 83*
Meurice, Blanca *ConAu X*
Meux, Milton O 1930- *ConAu 45*
Meves, Christa 1925- *ConAu 93*
Mew, Charlotte 1869-1927 *RGFMBP*
Mew, Charlotte 1870-1928 *ConAu 105,*
  TwCLC 8[port]
Mew, Charlotte Mary 1869?-1928 *LongCTC,*
  ModBrL, TwCA, TwCA SUP
Mewburn, Martin *ConAu X*
Mews, Hazel 1909-1975 *ConAu P-2*
Mews, Siegfried 1933- *ConAu 7NR, -57*
Mewshaw, Michael 1943- *ConAu 7NR, -53,*
  ConLC 9, DcLB Y80B[port], IntAu&W 82,
  WrDr 84
Mey, Jacob Lovis *ConAu X*
Meyen, Edward L 1937- *ConAu 33R*
Meyendorff, John 1926- *ConAu 9NR, -21R,*
  IntAu&W 82, WrDr 84
Meyer, Agnes E 1887-1970 *ConAu 29R*
Meyer, Alfred George 1920- *ConAu 17R*
Meyer, Alfred Herman 1893- *ConAu P-1*
Meyer, Armin Henry 1914- *ConAu 85*
Meyer, Ben Franklin 1927- *ConAu 37R,*
  WrDr 84
Meyer, Bernard C 1910- *ConAu 73*
Meyer, Bernard F 1891?-1975 *ConAu 57*
Meyer, Carl S 1907-1972 *ConAu P-1*
Meyer, Carol H 1924- *ConAu 73*
Meyer, Carolyn 1935- *ConAu 2NR, -49,*
  SmATA 9
Meyer, Charles R 1926- *ConAu 69*
Meyer, Charles Robert 1920- *ConAu 33R,*
  IntAu&W 82, WrDr 84
Meyer, Clarence 1903- *ConAu 97*
Meyer, D Swing 1938- *ConAu 17R*
Meyer, David R 1943- *ConAu 65*
Meyer, Donald 1923- *ConAu 21R*
Meyer, Doris 1942- *ConAu 89*
Meyer, Duane Gilbert 1926- *ConAu 5R*
Meyer, Edith Patterson 1895- *ConAu 1R, -1NR,*
  SmATA 5
Meyer, Elizabeth C 1958- *ConAu 69*
Meyer, Erika 1904- *ConAu 73*
Meyer, Frank Straus 1909-1972 *ConAu 33R,*
  ConAu P-1
Meyer, Franklyn Edward 1932- *ConAu 1R,*
  SmATA 9, WrDr 84
Meyer, Fred 1922- *ConAu 57*
Meyer, H A 1898-1980 *ConAu 4NR, -5R, -102*
Meyer, H K Houston *ConAu 49*
Meyer, Harold Diedrich 1892-1974? *ConAu P-2*
Meyer, Heinrich 1904-1977 *ConAu 49, -85*
Meyer, Herbert W 1892- *ConAu P-2,*
  IntAu&W 82
Meyer, Herman 1911- *ConAu 21R,*
  IntAu&W 82
Meyer, Howard N 1914- *ConAu 13R*
Meyer, Jean Shepherd 1929- *SmATA 11*
Meyer, Jerome Sydney 1895-1975 *ConAu 1R,*
  -4NR, -57, SmATA 25N, -3
Meyer, Joachim-Ernst 1917- *ConAu 57*
Meyer, John R 1927- *WrDr 84*

Meyer, John Robert 1927- *ConAu 9NR, -13R*
Meyer, June *ConAu X, SmATA 4, WrDr 84*
Meyer, Karl Ernest 1928- *ConAu 1R, -1NR*
Meyer, Kuno 1858-1919 *LongCTC*
Meyer, Lawrence 1941- *ConAu 73, WrDr 84*
Meyer, Leonard B 1918- *ConAu 13R, WrDr 84*
Meyer, Lillian Nicholson 1917?-1983 *ConAu 109*
Meyer, Linda D 1948- *ConAu 93*
Meyer, Louis A 1942- *ConAu 37R, SmATA 12*
Meyer, Mabel H 1890?-1976 *ConAu 61*
Meyer, Marie-Louise 1936- *ConAu 97*
Meyer, Mary Keysor 1919- *ConAu 102*
Meyer, Michael A 1937- *ConAu 21R,*
  IntAu&W 82
Meyer, Michael C 1935- *ConAu 10NR, -21R*
Meyer, Michael Leverson 1921- *ConAu 25R,*
  IntAu&W 82, WrDr 84
Meyer, Nicholas 1945- *ConAu 7NR, -49,*
  TwCCr&M 80, WrDr 84
Meyer, Philip 1930- *ConAu 10NR, -65*
Meyer, Renate 1930- *ConAu 53, SmATA 6*
Meyer, Robert H 1934- *ConAu 37R*
Meyer, Roy W 1925- *ConAu 17R*
Meyer, Ruth F 1910- *ConAu P-2*
Meyer, Susan E 1940- *ConAu 2NR, -45*
Meyer, Thomas *DrAP&F 83*
Meyer, Thomas 1947- *ConAu 1NR, -49*
Meyer, William Eugene 1923- *ConAu 45*
Meyer, William R 1949- *ConAu 77*
Meyerhoff, Howard A 1899- *ConAu P-2*
Meyering, Ralph A 1930- *ConAu 29R,*
  WrDr 84
Meyerowitz, Eva L R 1899- *ConAu 9R,*
  IntAu&W 82
Meyerowitz, Patricia 1933- *ConAu 21R,*
  WrDr 84
Meyers, Albert L 1904?-1981 *ConAu 102*
Meyers, Bert *WrDr 84*
Meyers, Bert 1928-1979 *ConAu 101, ConP 80*
Meyers, Carlton R 1922- *ConAu 57*
Meyers, Carole Terwilliger 1945- *ConAu 69*
Meyers, Cecil H 1920- *ConAu 29R*
Meyers, David W 1942- *ConAu 29R*
Meyers, Denise *CreCan 1*
Meyers, Edward 1934- *ConAu 101*
Meyers, Eric M 1940- *ConAu 110*
Meyers, Gertrude Barlow 1902- *ConAu 1R*
Meyers, Jeffrey 1939- *ConAu 73, WrDr 84*
Meyers, Joan Simpson 1927- *ConAu 17R*
Meyers, Lawrence Stanley 1943- *ConAu 57*
Meyers, Marvin 1921- *ConAu 108*
Meyers, Michael Jay 1946- *ConAu 65*
Meyers, Patricia *CreCan 1*
Meyers, Robert Rex 1923- *ConAu 17R*
Meyers, Roy 1910-1974 *ConAu P-2, ConSFA,*
  TwCSFW
Meyers, Susan 1942- *ConAu 21R, SmATA 19,*
  WrDr 84
Meyers, Walter E 1939- *ConAu 6NR, -53*
Meyerson, Edward L 1904- *ConAu 61,*
  IntWWP 82
Meyerson, Tuvia *IntAu&W 82X*
Meyerstein, Edward Harry William 1889-1952
  ModBrL, WorAu
Meylan, Elisabeth 1937- *IntAu&W 82*
Meynell, Alice Christiana 1847-1922 *ConAu 104,*
  LongCTC, ModBrL, TwCA, TwCA SUP,
  TwCLC 6[port]
Meynell, Everard 1882-1926 *LongCTC*
Meynell, Sir Francis Meredith Wilfrid 1891-1975
  ConAu 57, ConAu P-2, LongCTC
Meynell, Laurence 1899- *ConAu 81,*
  IntAu&W 82, TwCCW 83, TwCCr&M 80,
  WrDr 84
Meynell, Viola 1886-1956 *LongCTC, ModBrL,*
  TwCA, TwCA SUP
Meynell, Wilfrid 1852-1948 *LongCTC*
Meyners, J Robert 1922- *ConAu 104*
Meynier, Yvonne 1908- *ConAu 73, SmATA 14*
Meyrink, Gustav 1868-1932 *ModGL*
Meza, Pedro Thomas 1941- *ConAu 37R*
Mezei, Andras 1930- *IntWWP 82*
Mezey, Robert *DrAP&F 83*
Mezey, Robert 1935- *ConAu 7NR, -57,*
  ConP 80, CroCAP, IntWWP 82,
  SmATA 33, WorAu 1970, WrDr 84
Mezvinsky, Edward M 1937- *ConAu 103*
Mezvinsky, Shirley Shapiro 1936- *ConAu 13R*
Mezzrow, Mezz *ConAu X*
Mezzrow, Milton 1890?-1972 *ConAu 37R*
Miall, Robert *ConAu X, IntAu&W 82X*
Micale, Albert 1913- *SmATA 22[port]*

Micallef, Benjamin A 1925-1980 *ConAu 103, -53*
Micallef, John 1923- *ConAu 25R*
Micaud, Charles Antoine 1910- *ConAu 5R*
Miceli, Frank 1932- *ConAu 57*
Michael, David J 1944- *ConAu 29R*
Michael, Franz H 1907- *ConAu 4NR, -5R*
Michael, Friedrich 1892- *CnMD, ModWD*
Michael, George Edward 1919- *ConAu 41R*
Michael, Henry N 1913- *ConAu 33R*
Michael, Ian 1915- *ConAu 104*
Michael, James *ConAu X*
Michael, Manfred *ConAu X*
Michael, Paul 1934- *ConAu 17R, WrDr 84*
Michael, Paul Martin 1934- *ConAu 10NR*
Michael, Phyllis C 1908- *ConAu 2NR, -5R*
Michael, S T 1912- *ConAu 13R*
Michael, Thomas A 1933- *ConAu 33R*
Michael, Tom *ConAu X*
Michael, William B 1922- *ConAu 45*
Michael, Wolfgang F 1909- *ConAu 41R,*
  IntAu&W 82
Michael Bee *IntWWP 82X*
Michael Jesse *IntWWP 82X*
Michael-Titus, Constantin 1925- *IntWWP 82*
Michaeles, M M *ConAu X*
Michaelides, Constantine E 1930- *ConAu 25R*
Michaelidou-Nicolaou, Ino 1929- *IntAu&W 82*
Michaelis, John U 1912- *ConAu 41R*
Michaelis, Karin Marie Bech 1872-1950
  LongCTC, TwCA, TwCA SUP, TwCWr
Michaels, Barbara 1927- *ConAu X,*
  TwCCr&M 80, TwCRGW, WrDr 84
Michaels, Carolyn Leopold *ConAu X*
Michaels, Dale *ConAu X, WrDr 84*
Michaels, Joanne 1950- *ConAu 107*
Michaels, Joe *ConAu X*
Michaels, Kasey *ConAu X*
Michaels, Kristin *TwCWW, WrDr 84*
Michaels, Leonard *DrAP&F 83*
Michaels, Leonard 1933- *ConAu 61, ConLC 6,*
  -25[port], ConNov 82, WrDr 84
Michaels, Lynn *ConAu X*
Michaels, Norman *ConAu 97*
Michaels, Pearl Dorothy Blissak 1936-
  IntWWP 82
Michaels, Ralph *ConAu X*
Michaels, Ruth Gruber *ConAu X*
Michaels, Sidney Ramon 1927- *CnMD SUP,*
  ConAu 17R, ModWD
Michaels, Ski *ConAu X*
Michaels, Steve *ConAu X, WrDr 84*
Michaelsen, Frank Stubb 1947- *IntAu&W 82*
Michaelson, L W *DrAP&F 83*
Michaelson, L W 1920- *ConAu 77*
Michaelson, Michael *DrAP&F 83*
Michaely, Michael 1928- *ConAu 103*
Michalczyk, John Joseph 1941- *ConAu 104*
Michalkov, Sergei 1913- *CnMD*
Michalopoulos, Andre 1897- *ConAu P-2*
Michalos, Alex C 1935- *ConAu 37R*
Michalowski, Kazimierz 1901-1981 *ConAu 108*
Michalski, John 1934- *ConAu 25R*
Michalson, Carl 1915-1965 *ConAu 1R*
Michanek, C Germund I 1926- *IntAu&W 82*
Michaud, Charles Regis 1910- *ConAu P-2*
Michaud, Stephen G 1948- *ConAu 109*
Michaux, Henri 1899- *CIDMEL 80, CnMWL,*
  ConAu 85, ConLC 8, -19, ModFrL,
  ModRL, TwCA SUP, TwCWr, WhoTwCL
Michaux, William W 1919- *ConAu 41R*
Miche, Giuseppe *ConAu X*
Michel, Anna 1943- *ConAu 85*
Michel, Beth *ConAu X*
Michel, Georges 1926- *ConAu 25R, CroCD*
Michel, Henri 1907- *ConAu 4NR, -53,*
  IntAu&W 82
Michel, Joseph 1922- *ConAu 25R*
Michel, Milton Scott 1916- *ConAu 1R,*
  WrDr 84
Michel, Pierre 1934- *ConAu 57*
Michel, Sandra Seaton 1935- *ConAu 77*
Michel, Sandy *ConAu X*
Michel, Walter 1922- *ConAu 81*
Michelet, Jon 1944- *IntAu&W 82*
Micheli, Lyle Joseph 1940- *ConAu 97*
Micheline, Jack *DrAP&F 83*
Micheline, Jack 1929- *DcLB 16[port]*
Michell, John 1933- *ConAu 107*
Michelman, Herbert 1913-1980 *ConAu 102*
Michelman, Irving S 1917- *ConAu 69*
Michelmore, Peter 1930- *ConAu 5R, -7NR*

Miller, Marshall Lee 1942- *ConAu 9NR, -57*
Miller, Martha *ConAu X*
Miller, Martha Porter 1897?-1983 *ConAu 109*
Miller, Martin A 1938- *ConAu 65*
Miller, Mary *ConAu X, WrDr 84*
Miller, Mary Agnes 1888?-1973 *ConAu 45*
Miller, Mary Beth 1942- *ConAu 61, SmATA 9*
Miller, Mary Britton 1883-1975 *ASpks,*
    ConAu 1R, -57, LongCTC, TwCA SUP
Miller, Max 1899?-1967 *ConAu 1R, -25R,*
    TwCA, TwCA SUP
Miller, Max Cameron 1908- *IntAu&W 82*
Miller, May *DrAP&F 83*
Miller, Melvin H 1920- *ConAu 13R*
Miller, Merle 1919- *ASpks, AuNews 1,*
    ConAu 4NR, -9R, WorAu, WrDr 84
Miller, Merton Howard 1923- *ConAu 109*
Miller, Michael M 1910?-1977 *ConAu 73*
Miller, Minnie M 1899- *ConAu P-2*
Miller, Minnie M 1899-1983 *ConAu 110*
Miller, Mona *IntWWP 82*
Miller, Monique *CreCan 2*
Miller, Morris 1914- *ConAu 17R*
Miller, N Edd 1920- *ConAu 25R*
Miller, Nathan 1927- *ConAu 4NR, -53*
Miller, Neal E 1909- *ConAu 81*
Miller, Nicole Puleo 1944- *ConAu 49*
Miller, Nina Hull 1894- *ConAu P-1*
Miller, Nolan 1912- *ConAu 9R*
Miller, Norman 1933- *ConAu 37R*
Miller, Norman C 1934- *ConAu 37R*
Miller, Nyle H 1907- *ConAu P-2*
Miller, Olga K 1908- *ConAu 107*
Miller, Orlo 1911- *WrDr 84*
Miller, Orson K, Jr. 1930- *ConAu 110*
Miller, Osborn 1896?-1979 *ConAu 89*
Miller, Oscar J 1913- *ConAu 37R*
Miller, P Schuyler 1912-1974 *TwCSFW*
Miller, Paul Martin 1914- *ConAu 10NR, -17R*
Miller, Paul Richard 1929- *ConAu 21R*
Miller, Paul William 1926- *ConAu 41R*
Miller, Perry 1905-1963 *ConAu 93,*
    DcLB 17[port], TwCA SUP
Miller, Peter 1920- *DcLEL 1940*
Miller, Peter 1934- *ConAu 37R*
Miller, Peter M 1942- *ConAu 69*
Miller, Philip L 1906- *ConAu P-1*
Miller, R June 1923- *ConAu 65*
Miller, R S 1936- *ConAu 45*
Miller, Raeburn *DrAP&F 83*
Miller, Randall Martin 1945- *ConAu 81,*
    IntAu&W 82
Miller, Randolph Crump 1910- *ConAu 1R,*
    -1NR, WrDr 84
Miller, Rene Fueloep *ConAu X*
Miller, Rene Fulop *ConAu X, TwCA,*
    TwCA SUP
Miller, Rex 1929- *ConAu 110*
Miller, Richard *ConAu X*
Miller, Richard 1925- *ConAu 17R*
Miller, Richard I 1924- *ConAu 41R*
Miller, Richard S 1930- *ConAu 21R*
Miller, Richard Ulric 1932- *ConAu 41R*
Miller, Rita A 1930- *MichAu 80*
Miller, Rob Hollis *DrAP&F 83*
Miller, Rob Hollis 1944- *ConAu 37R*
Miller, Robert A 1932- *ConAu 33R*
Miller, Robert Henry 1889- *ConAu 33R*
Miller, Robert Henry 1938- *ConAu 110*
Miller, Robert L 1928- *ConAu 25R*
Miller, Robert Moats 1924- *ConAu 105*
Miller, Robert Ryal 1923- *ConAu 41R*
Miller, Robinder Rahoula 1961- *IntWWP 82*
Miller, Roger LeRoy 1943- *ConAu 107*
Miller, Ronald 1910- *IntAu&W 82*
Miller, Ronald Dean 1928- *IntAu&W 82*
Miller, Ronald E 1933- *ConAu 5R*
Miller, Roy Andrew 1924- *ConAu 2NR, -5R*
Miller, Ruby 1890?-1976 *ConAu 65*
Miller, Russell Elliott 1916- *ConAu 110*
Miller, Ruth *ConAu X*
Miller, Ruth 1921- *ConAu 106*
Miller, S M 1922- *ConAu 17R*
Miller, Sally M 1937- *ConAu 45, IntAu&W 82*
Miller, Samuel Jefferson 1919- *ConAu 53*
Miller, Shane 1907- *ConAu P-2*
Miller, Shirley 1920- *ConAu 93*
Miller, Sigmund Stephen 1917- *ConAu 1R,*
    -4NR
Miller, Stanley 1916?-1977 *ConAu 69*
Miller, Stanley L 1930- *ConAu 45*
Miller, Stanley S 1924- *ConAu 13R*

Miller, Stephen J 1936- *ConAu 33R, WrDr 84*
Miller, Stephen M *DrAP&F 83*
Miller, Stephen Paul *DrAP&F 83*
Miller, Stephen Paul 1951- *IntWWP 82*
Miller, Steve *DrAP&F 83*
Miller, Stuart 1937- *ConAu 41R, IntAu&W 82*
Miller, Stuart C 1927- *WrDr 84*
Miller, Stuart Creighton 1927- *ConAu 33R*
Miller, Susan 1944- *ConAu 107, ConDr 82,*
    NatPD 81[port]
Miller, T C 1944- *NatPD 81[port]*
Miller, Teresa 1952- *ConAu 105*
Miller, Thomas Lloyd 1913- *ConAu 25R*
Miller, Tom 1947- *ConAu 73*
Miller, Vassar *DrAP&F 83*
Miller, Vassar 1924- *ConAu 4NR, -9R,*
    ConP 80, WorAu, WrDr 84
Miller, Victor 1940- *ConAu 107*
Miller, Wade *ConAu X, TwCCr&M 80,*
    WrDr 84
Miller, Walter James *DrAP&F 83*
Miller, Walter James 1918- *ConAu 81*
Miller, Walter M, Jr. 1922- *TwCSFW,*
    WrDr 84
Miller, Walter M, Jr. 1923- *ConAu 85,*
    ConLC 4, ConSFA, DcLB 8[port]
Miller, Warren 1921-1966 *ConAu 25R, WorAu*
Miller, Warren C *DrAP&F 83*
Miller, Warren E 1924- *ConAu 11NR, -13R,*
    WrDr 84
Miller, Wayne *DrAP&F 83*
Miller, Wayne Charles 1939- *ConAu 1NR, -45*
Miller, William 1909- *ConAu 81*
Miller, William Alvin 1931- *ConAu 1NR, -49*
Miller, William D 1916- *ConAu 13R*
Miller, William Hugh 1905- *ConAu 1R*
Miller, William McElwee 1892- *ConAu 6NR,*
    -57
Miller, William Robert 1927-1970 *ConAu 29R,*
    ConAu P-1
Miller, Wilma Hildruth 1936- *ConAu 33R,*
    WrDr 84
Miller, Wright W 1903- *ConAu 17R*
Miller, Zane L 1934- *ConAu 25R*
Miller-Duggan, Devon *DrAP&F 83*
Millerson, Geoffrey L 1931- *ConAu 17R*
Millerson, Gerald 1923- *WrDr 84*
Millet, Stanton 1931- *ConAu 25R*
Millett, Allan R 1937- *ConAu 21R*
Millett, Fred B 1890-1976 *ConAu 61*
Millett, John *WrDr 84*
Millett, John 1922- *ConAu 103*
Millett, John 1928- *IntWWP 82*
Millett, John David 1912- *ConAu 104*
Millett, Kate 1934- *AuNews 1, ConAu 73,*
    WrDr 84
Millett, Mervyn 1910- *WrDr 84*
Millette, Jean-Louis *CreCan 1*
Millgate, Jane 1937- *ConAu 57*
Millgate, Michael 1929- *ConAu 29R*
Millgram, Abraham E 1901- *ConAu 33R,*
    IntAu&W 82, WrDr 84
Millham, C B 1936- *ConAu 37R*
Millhauser, Milton 1910- *ConAu P-1*
Millhauser, Steven 1943- *ConAu 108, -110,*
    ConLC 21, DcLB 2
Millhiser, Marlys 1938- *ConAu 53, TwCRGW,*
    WrDr 84
Millican, Arthenia Jackson Bates 1920-
    ConAu 105, LivgBAA
Millicent *ConAu X, MichAu 80*
Millies, Suzanne 1940- *ConAu 49*
Milligan, Alfred L 1893- *ConSFA*
Milligan, Edward Archibald 1903-1977
    ConAu 41R
Milligan, James 1928-1961 *CreCan 2*
Milligan, Spike 1918- *ConAu X, SmATA X,*
    WrDr 84
Milligan, Terence Alan 1918- *ConAu 4NR, -9R,*
    SmATA 29[port]
Milligan, Thomas *DrAP&F 83*
Milliken, Ernest Kenneth 1899- *ConAu 5R*
Milliken, Stephen F 1928- *ConAu 93,*
    IntAu&W 82
Milliken, William Mathewson 1889- *ConAu P-2*
Millimaki, Robert H 1931- *ConAu 57*
Millin, Sarah Gertrude 1889-1968 *ConAu 102,*
    -93, LongCTC, ModCmwL, TwCA,
    TwCA SUP, TwCWr
Millington, Alaric 1922- *WrDr 84*
Millington, Frances Ryan 1899-1977 *ConAu 69*
Millington, Patrick 1910-1982 *ConAu 107*

Millington, Roger 1939- *ConAu 65, WrDr 84*
Million, Elmer M 1912- *ConAu 41R*
Millis, Christopher *DrAP&F 83*
Millis, Walter 1899-1968 *ConAu 37R,*
    ConAu P-1, TwCA, TwCA SUP
Millman, Joan *DrAP&F 83*
Millman, Lawrence 1946- *ConAu 93*
Millon, Henry 1927- *ConAu 97*
Millon, Robert Paul 1932- *ConAu 21R*
Millon, Theodore 1929- *ConAu 57*
Millotat, Paula 1913- *IntAu&W 82*
Mills, A R *WrDr 84*
Mills, Alan 1914- *CreCan 2*
Mills, Alison 1951- *ConAu 53*
Mills, Anthony R 1930- *IntAu&W 82*
Mills, Barriss *DrAP&F 83*
Mills, Barriss 1912- *ConAu 25R, WrDr 84*
Mills, Belen Collantes 1930- *ConAu 37R*
Mills, Betty 1926- *ConAu 9R*
Mills, C Wright 1916-1962 *ConAu 107,*
    ConIsC 1[port]
Mills, Carley 1897-1962 *ConAu 1R, -103*
Mills, Charles Wright 1916- *TwCA SUP*
Mills, Clarence Alonzo 1891-1974 *ConAu 53,*
    ConAu P-1
Mills, Claudia 1954- *ConAu 109*
Mills, David Harlow 1932- *ConAu 104*
Mills, Dorothy *ConAu X*
Mills, Edward D 1915- *WrDr 84*
Mills, Edward David 1915- *ConAu 4NR, -5R*
Mills, Enos Abijah 1870-1922 *TwCA*
Mills, G E 1908- *ConAu P-1*
Mills, Gary B 1944- *ConAu 81*
Mills, George S 1906- *ConAu 97*
Mills, Helen 1923- *ConAu 97, IntAu&W 82*
Mills, J M A 1894- *ConAu 69*
Mills, James 1932- *ASpks, WrDr 84*
Mills, James R 1927- *ConAu 85*
Mills, Jeannie 1939- *ConAu 93*
Mills, John 1908- *ConAu 108*
Mills, John 1930- *ConAu 81, IntAu&W 82*
Mills, John FitzMaurice 1917- *ConAu 103*
Mills, John W 1933- *ConAu 69*
Mills, Leonard Russell 1917- *ConAu 45*
Mills, Liston O 1928- *ConAu 107*
Mills, Lloyd L *DrAP&F 83*
Mills, Mervyn 1906- *ConAu P-1, IntAu&W 82,*
    WrDr 84
Mills, Paul 1948- *WrDr 84*
Mills, Ralph J, Jr. 1931- *ConAu 3NR, -9R,*
    WrDr 84
Mills, Richard 1945- *WrDr 84*
Mills, Robert P 1920- *ConAu 97, ConSFA*
Mills, Terry Kenneth 1949- *ConAu 107,*
    WrDr 84
Mills, Theodore Mason 1920- *ConAu 21R*
Mills, Watson Early 1939- *ConAu 57*
Mills, William *DrAP&F 83*
Mills, William Donald 1925- *ConAu 33R*
Millsaps, Daniel 1919- *WrDr 84*
Millstead, Thomas E *ConAu 106, SmATA 30*
Millstein, Rose Silverman 1903?-1975 *ConAu 61*
Millum, Trevor *WrDr 84*
Millum, Trevor 1945- *ConAu 104*
Millward, Celia M 1935- *ConAu 53*
Millward, Eric 1935- *ConAu 65, ConP 80,*
    WrDr 84
Millward, John Scandrett 1924- *ConAu 13R*
Miln, Louise 1864-1933 *TwCA*
Milne, A A 1882-1956 *ConAu 104,*
    DcLB 10[port], TwCCW 83,
    TwCCr&M 80, TwCLC 6[port]
Milne, Alan Alexander 1882-1956 *ChlLR 1,*
    CnMD, LongCTC, ModBrL, ModWD,
    TwCA, TwCA SUP, TwCWr
Milne, Alexander Taylor 1906- *IntAu&W 82*
Milne, Antony 1942- *ConAu 101*
Milne, Christopher 1920- *ConAu 11NR*
Milne, Christopher Robin 1920- *AuNews 2,*
    ConAu 61, IntAu&W 82, WrDr 84
Milne, David Brown 1882-1953 *CreCan 1*
Milne, Edward James 1915- *IntAu&W 82*
Milne, Edward James 1915-1983 *ConAu 109*
Milne, Evander Mackay 1920- *ConAu 5R*
Milne, Ewart 1903- *ConAu 97, ConP 80,*
    WrDr 84
Milne, Gordon 1921- *ConAu 21R*
Milne, Jean 1920- *ConAu 17R*
Milne, Lorus J *ConAu 33R, IntAu&W 82,*
    SmATA 5, WrDr 84
Milne, Margery *WrDr 84*
Milne, Margery Joan Greene 1915- *ConAu 33R,*

SmATA 5
Milne, Robert Scott 1917- IntAu&W 82
Milne, Roseleen 1945- ConAu 73
Milne, W Gordon 1921- WrDr 84
Milne, William Gordon 1921- IntAu&W 82
Milner, Alfred 1854-1925 LongCTC
Milner, Christina 1942- ConAu 49
Milner, Clyde A, II 1948- ConAu 108
Milner, Esther 1918- ConAu 21R, WrDr 84
Milner, George 1921- LongCTC
Milner, Ian Frank George 1911- ConAu 104,
  WrDr 84
Milner, Jay 1926- ConAu 1R
Milner, Lucille Bernheimer 1888?-1975
  ConAu 61
Milner, Marion 1900- ConAu 9R, WrDr 84
Milner, Murray, Jr. 1935- ConAu 41R
Milner, Nina Marion 1900- IntAu&W 82
Milner, Richard B 1941- ConAu 49
Milner, Ron 1938- ConAu 73, ConDr 82,
  WrDr 84
Milner, Ronald DrAP&F 83
Milner, Ronald 1938- AuNews 1, LivgBAA
Milnes, Eric Charles 1912- WrDr 84
Milns, R D 1938- ConAu 33R
Milo, Ronald D 1935- ConAu 25R
Milonas, Rolf ConAu X, SmATA X
Miloradovich, Milo 1901?-1972 ConAu 37R
Milos, Jon 1930- IntAu&W 82
Milosh, Joseph Edmund 1936- ConAu 21R,
  WrDr 84
Milosz, Czeslaw 1911- ClDMEL 80, ConAu 81,
  ConLC 5, -11, -22[port], ModSL 2,
  WhoTwCL, WorAu
Milosz, Oscar-Vladislas DeLubisez 1877-1939
  ClDMEL 80
Milotte, Alfred George 1904- ConAu P-1,
  SmATA 11, WrDr 84
Milroy, Vivian 1917- WrDr 84
Milsen, Oscar ConAu X
Milsom, Charles Henry 1926- WrDr 84
Milsom, Stroud Francis Charles 1923- WrDr 84
Milson, Fred 1912- ConAu 73
Milstead, John 1924- ConAu 49
Milstein, Mike M 1937- ConAu 81
Milton, Arthur 1922- ConAu 109
Milton, Charles R 1925- ConAu 53
Milton, David Scott DrAP&F 83
Milton, David Scott 1934- ConAu 73,
  NatPD 81[port]
Milton, Edith DrAP&F 83
Milton, Hilary 1920- ConAu 6NR, -57,
  SmATA 23[port]
Milton, Jack ConAu X
Milton, John R DrAP&F 83
Milton, John R 1924- ConAu 33R,
  IntAu&W 82, IntWWP 82,
  SmATA 24[port], WrDr 84
Milton, Joyce DrAP&F 83
Milton, Joyce 1946- ConAu 106
Milton, Mark ConAu X
Milton, Oliver ConAu X
Milunsky, Aubrey 1936- ConAu 103
Milverton, Charles A ConAu X
Milward, Alan S 1935- ConAu 45, WrDr 84
Milward, Peter 1925- ConAu 101
Mims, Forrest M, III 1944- ConAu 97
Mims, Frances Larkin Flynn 1922- IntWWP 82
Mims, Lambert C 1930- ConAu 29R
Mims, Roddey Earl 1936?-1982 ConAu 108
Minac, Vladimir 1922- ModSL 2
Minadeo, Richard 1929- ConAu 25R
Minahan, John 1933- ConAu 2NR, -45
Minale, Marcello 1938- ConAu 108
Minarik, Else 1920- TwCCW 83
Minarik, Else H WrDr 84
Minarik, Else Holmelund 1920- ConAu 73,
  SmATA 15
Minarik, John Paul DrAP&F 83
Minarik, John Paul 1947- ConAu 73
Minassian, Michael G DrAP&F 83
Minchinton, W E 1921- ConAu 29R
Minchinton, Walter Edward 1921- IntAu&W 82,
  WrDr 84
Mincieli, Rose Laura 1912- ConAu 4NR, -5R
Minckler, Leon 1906- ConAu 57
Minczeski, John DrAP&F 83
Mindel, Eugene D 1934- ConAu 41R
Mindell, Earl L 1940- ConAu 105
Mindszenty, Cardinal Jozsef 1892-1975
  ConAu 57, -65
Minear, Paul Sevier 1906- ConAu 1R, -3NR,

IntAu&W 82, WrDr 84
Minear, Richard Hoffman 1938- ConAu 33R,
  IntAu&W 82, WrDr 84
Minehaha, Cornelius ConAu X
Mineka, Francis Edward 1907- ConAu 106
Miner, Caroline Eyring 1907- ConAu 11NR,
  -25R, IntAu&W 82
Miner, Charles S 1906- ConAu P-1
Miner, Dwight Carroll 1904-1978 ConAu 81
Miner, Earl 1927- ConAu 1R, -1NR, WrDr 84
Miner, H Craig 1944- ConAu 1NR, -45
Miner, Irene Sevrey 1906- ConAu 5R
Miner, Jane Claypool 1933- ConAu 106
Miner, John B 1926- ConAu 5NR, -9R
Miner, Joshua L 1920- ConAu 106
Miner, Lewis S 1909- ConAu P-1, SmATA 11
Miner, Mary Green 1928- ConAu 69
Miner, Matthew ConAu X
Miner, O Irene 1906- MichAu 80
Miner, Scott IntWWP 82X
Miner, Valerie DrAP&F 83
Miner, Valerie Jane 1947- ConAu 97,
  IntAu&W 82
Miner, Virginia Scott 1901- IntWWP 82
Miner, Ward L 1916- ConAu 9R, WrDr 84
Mines, Samuel 1909- ConAu 1NR, -45,
  WrDr 84
Mines, Stephanie DrAP&F 83
Mines, Stephanie 1944- ConAu 77
Minetree, Harry 1935- ConAu 93
Mingay, G E 1923- ConAu 11NR, WrDr 84
Mingay, Gordon Edmund 1923- ConAu 17R,
  IntAu&W 82
Minge, Ward Alan 1924- ConAu 97
Minghi, Julian Vincent 1933- ConAu 29R
Mingus, Charles 1922-1979 ConAu 85, -93
Minick, Michael 1945- ConAu 65
Minier, Nelson ConAu X, SmATA 3
Minifie, James MacDonald 1900-1974 ConAu 49
Minimo, Duca ConAu X
Minium, Edward W 1917- ConAu 29R,
  WrDr 84
Mink, Louis Otto, Jr. 1921- ConAu 104
Mink, Louis Otto, Jr. 1921-1983 ConAu 109
Minkin, Stephen DrAP&F 83
Minkovitz, Moshe ConAu X
Minnaar-Vos, Anna IntAu&W 82X
Minney, R J 1895- ConAu 5NR
Minney, Rubeigh James 1895- ConAu 5R
Minnich, Helen Benton 1892- ConAu P-1
Minnick, Wayne C 1915- ConAu 25R
Minnigerode, Meade 1887-1967 TwCA,
  TwCA SUP
Minogue, Kenneth Robert 1930- ConAu 5R,
  WrDr 84
Minor, Andrew Collier 1918- ConAu 13R,
  IntAu&W 82
Minor, Anthropopagus ConAu X
Minor, Audax ConAu X
Minor, Edward Orville 1920- ConAu 9R
Minor, James DrAP&F 83
Minor, Marz 1928- ConAu 103
Minor, Nono 1932- ConAu 103
Minor, Pearl 1903- IntWWP 82
Minot, Stephen DrAP&F 83
Minot, Stephen 1927- ConAu 13R, WrDr 84
Minott, Rodney G 1928- ConAu 9R
Minow, Newton N 1926- ConAu 13R, -69,
  WrDr 84
Minrath, William R 1900-1971 ConAu 89,
  ConAu P-1
Minshall, Vera 1924- ConAu 13R, WrDr 84
Minshull, Evelyn 1929- ConAu 37R
Minshull, Roger 1935- ConAu 21R, WrDr 84
Minsky, Betty Jane 1932- ConAu 5R, WrDr 84
Minsky, Hyman P 1919- ConAu 85
Minsky, Marvin 1927- ConAu 21R
Minter, David Lee 1935- ConAu 25R, WrDr 84
Minters, Arthur Herman 1932- ConAu 102
Minto-Cowen, Frances ConAu X
Minton, Helena DrAP&F 83
Minton, Lynn ConAu 107
Minton, Madge Rutherford 1920- ConAu 45
Minton, Paula ConAu X
Minton, Robert 1918- ConAu 57
Minton, Sherman Anthony 1919- ConAu 45
Mintonye, Grace 1928- ConAu 25R, SmATA 4
Minturn, Leigh 1928- ConAu 21R
Minty, Judith DrAP&F 83
Minty, Judith 1937- ConAu 2NR, -49,
  IntWWP 82, MichAu 80
Mintz, Barbara 1931- ConAu 110

Mintz, Donald E 1932- ConAu 17R
Mintz, Elizabeth E 1913- ConAu 73
Mintz, Joyce Lois 1933- ConAu 65
Mintz, Leigh W 1939- ConAu 57
Mintz, Max M 1919- ConAu 33R
Mintz, Morton A 1922- ConAu 13R
Mintz, Norman N 1934- ConAu 41R
Mintz, Phil DrAP&F 83
Mintz, Ruth Finer DrAP&F 83
Mintz, Ruth Finer 1919- ConAu 13R,
  IntAu&W 82, WrDr 84
Mintz, Samuel I 1923- ConAu 5R, WrDr 84
Mintz, Sidney Wilfred 1922- ConAu 1R, -5NR
Mintz, Thomas 1931- ConAu 108
Mintzberg, Henry 1939- ConAu 1NR, -45
Mintzer, Yvette DrAP&F 83
Mintzer, Yvette 1947- ConAu 77
Mioto, Eusi IntWWP 82X
Mirabelli, Eugene DrAP&F 83
Mirabelli, Eugene 1931- ConAu 25R
Mirabelli, Eugene, Jr. 1931- WrDr 84
Miracle, Gordon E 1930- ConAu 33R
Miracle, Marvin Preston 1933- ConAu 17R,
  WrDr 84
Miranda, Gary DrAP&F 83
Miranda, Javier ConAu X
Miravalies Rodriguez, Luis 1934- IntAu&W 82
Mirbeau, Octave 1848-1917 CnMD
Mirbeau, Octave 1850-1917 ClDMEL 80,
  ModWD
Mireaux, Emile 1885?-1969 ConAu 104
Mirenberg, Anita DrAP&F 83
Mirenburg, Barry L 1952- ConAu 101,
  WrDr 84
Mirepoix, Camille 1926- ConAu 105
Mirikitani, Janice DrAP&F 83
Miro, Gabriel 1879-1930 CnMWL, ConAu 104,
  ModRL, TwCLC 5[port]
Miro Ferrer, Gabriel 1879-1930 ClDMEL 80,
  TwCWr
Miron, Dan 1934- ConAu 77
Miron, Gaston 1928- WorAu 1970
Miron, Murray S 1932- ConAu 81
Mirsky, Dmitry Svyatopolk 1890- LongCTC,
  TwCA, TwCA SUP
Mirsky, Jeannette 1903- ConAu P-2, SmATA 8
Mirsky, Mark DrAP&F 83
Mirsky, Mark 1939- WrDr 84
Mirsky, Mark Jay 1939- ConAu 25R,
  ConNov 82, IntAu&W 82
Mirsky, Reba Paeff 1902-1966 ConAu 1R,
  SmATA 1
Mirsky, Stanley 1929- ConAu 110
Mirus, Ludmilla 1905- IntAu&W 82
Mirus-Kauba, Ludmilla IntAu&W 82X
Mirvish, Robert F 1921- WrDr 84
Mirvish, Robert Franklin 1921- ConAu 1R
Misch, Robert J 1905- ConAu 21R
Mische, Gerald F 1926- ConAu 97
Mische, Patricia M 1939- ConAu 93
Mischke, Bernard Cyril 1926- ConAu 13R
Mises, Ludwig Von 1881-1973 ConAu 5R, -45
Mish DrAP&F 83
Mish, Charles C 1913- ConAu 33R
Mish, Joseph Walter Bernard 1950- IntWWP 82
Mishan, E J 1917- ConAu 73, WrDr 84
Mishan, Ezra 1917- IntAu&W 82
Misheiker, Betty Fairly 1919- ConAu 9R
Mishima, Yukio 1925-1970 CnMD, ConAu X,
  ConLC 2, -4, -6, -9, -27[port], ModWD,
  WhoTwCL, WorAu
Mishkin, Julie DrAP&F 83
Mishkin, Paul J 1927- ConAu 17R
Mishra, Vishwa Mohan 1937- ConAu 61
Misiak, Henryk 1911- ConAu 1R, -5NR
Misiunas, Romuald John 1945- ConAu 109
Miska, Leonard F 1921- WrDr 84
Miskimin, Harry A 1932- ConAu 109
Miskovits, Christine 1939- ConAu 53,
  SmATA 10
Misner, Arthur J 1921- ConAu 21R
Misra, Bankey Bihari 1909- ConAu 104
Misra, Ramdeo 1908- IntAu&W 82
Miss Frances ConAu X
Miss Lou ConAu X
Miss Manners ConAu X
Miss Read ConAu X
Missen, Leslie R 1897-1983 ConAu 110
Missildine, Hugh 1915- ConAu 77
Missiroli, Mario 1886-1974 ConAu 53
Mister Rogers ConAu X, SmATA X
Mister X ConAu X

Mistral, Frederic 1830-1914 *ClDMEL 80,*
ModRL, TwCWr
Mistral, Gabriela 1889-1957 *ConAu X,*
ModLAL, TwCA SUP, TwCLC 2, TwCWr,
WhoTwCL
Mitcalfe, Barry 1930- *ConAu 110, IntWWP 82*
Mitcham, Carl 1941- *ConAu 85*
Mitcham, Gilroy 1923- *ConAu X, -1R*
Mitcham, Samuel W, Jr. 1949- *ConAu 106*
Mitchel, Jackson *ConAu X*

Mitchell, Adam *ConAu X*
Mitchell, Adrian 1932- *ConAu 33R, ConDr 82,*
ConNov 82, ConP 80, DcLEL 1940,
IntAu&W 82, IntWWP 82, WrDr 84
Mitchell, Alan 1922- *ConAu 8NR, -57*
Mitchell, Alexander Ross Kerr 1934- *ConAu 73*
Mitchell, Allan 1933- *ConAu 102*
Mitchell, Arthur A 1926- *ConAu 9R*
Mitchell, Austin 1934- *ConAu 25R*
Mitchell, B R 1929- *ConAu 49*
Mitchell, Barbara A 1939- *ConAu 25R*
Mitchell, Basil George 1917- *ConAu 104*
Mitchell, Betty 1896- *CreCan 1*
Mitchell, Betty L 1947- *ConAu 107*
Mitchell, Bonner 1929- *ConAu 25R*
Mitchell, Broadus 1892- *ConAu 1R, -5NR,*
IntAu&W 82, WrDr 84
Mitchell, Burroughs 1914?-1979 *ConAu 89*
Mitchell, Charles 1912- *ConAu 9R*
Mitchell, Charles Julian 1935- *DcLEL 1940*
Mitchell, Clyde *ConAu X*
Mitchell, Colin W 1927- *ConAu 73*
Mitchell, Curtis Cornelius, Jr. 1927- *ConAu 105*
Mitchell, Cynthia 1922- *ConAu 106,*
SmATA 29[port]
Mitchell, David 1924- *WrDr 84*
Mitchell, David 1940- *ConP 80, WrDr 84*
Mitchell, David John 1924- *ConAu 53,*
IntAu&W 82
Mitchell, Diana Mary 1932- *IntAu&W 82*
Mitchell, Don *DrAP&F 83*
Mitchell, Don 1947- *ConAu 33R*
Mitchell, Donald 1925- *ConAu 103*
Mitchell, Donald William 1911- *WrDr 84*
Mitchell, Edgar D 1930- *ConAu 53*
Mitchell, Edward B 1937- *ConAu 21R*
Mitchell, Elizabeth *CreCan 1*
Mitchell, Elizabeth P 1946- *ConAu 101*
Mitchell, Elyne 1913- *TwCCW 83, WrDr 84*
Mitchell, Elyne Keith 1913- *ConAu 5NR, -53,*
SmATA 10
Mitchell, Emerson Blackhorse *DrAP&F 83*
Mitchell, Emerson Blackhorse Barney 1945-
ConAu 45
Mitchell, Ewan *ConAu X, IntAu&W 82X*
Mitchell, Fay Langellier 1884-1964 *ConAu 5R*
Mitchell, Frank *ConAu X*
Mitchell, Frank Vincent 1919- *ConAu 9R*
Mitchell, G Duncan 1921- *ConAu 11NR, -29R*
Mitchell, Geoffrey Duncan *WrDr 84*
Mitchell, Geoffrey Duncan 1921- *IntAu&W 82*
Mitchell, George Archibald Grant 1906-
WrDr 84
Mitchell, George Francis 1912- *ConAu 77*
Mitchell, Giles 1928- *ConAu 93*
Mitchell, Gladys 1901- *ConAu 9R, -9NR,*
IntAu&W 82, LongCTC, TwCCr&M 80,
WrDr 84
Mitchell, Gladys 1901-1983 *ConAu 110*
Mitchell, Greg 1947- *ConAu 73*
Mitchell, Harold 1900- *WrDr 84*
Mitchell, Harold P 1900-1983 *ConAu 109*
Mitchell, Harold Paton 1900- *ConAu 9R*
Mitchell, Helen S 1895- *ConAu 25R*
Mitchell, Henry H 1919- *ConAu 10NR, -57*
Mitchell, Homer *DrAP&F 83*
Mitchell, Howard E 1921- *ConAu 108*
Mitchell, J Clyde 1918- *ConAu 9NR, -13R*
Mitchell, Jack 1925- *ConAu 9R*
Mitchell, Jackson *ConAu X*
Mitchell, James 1926- *ConAu 13R*
Mitchell, James Leslie 1901-1935 *ConAu 104,*
DcLB 15[port], LongCTC, TwCA,
TwCA SUP
Mitchell, Janet 1915- *CreCan 2*
Mitchell, Jeremy 1929- *ConAu 41R*
Mitchell, Jerome 1935- *ConAu 25R,*
IntAu&W 82, WrDr 84
Mitchell, Jerry 1905?-1972 *ConAu 33R*
Mitchell, Joan Cattermole 1920- *ConAu P-1*
Mitchell, Joan E *WrDr 84*

Mitchell, Joe H *DrAP&F 83*
Mitchell, John D 1917- *ConAu 49*
Mitchell, John D B 1917-1980 *ConAu 105*
Mitchell, John Howard 1921- *ConAu 9R,*
WrDr 84
Mitchell, John J 1941- *ConAu 1NR, -45*
Mitchell, John Phillimore 1918- *WrDr 84*
Mitchell, Joni 1943- *ConLC 12*
Mitchell, Joseph 1908- *ConAu 77, ConNov 82,*
WrDr 84
Mitchell, Joseph Brady 1915- *ConAu 9R,*
DcLEL 1940
Mitchell, Joseph Stanley 1909- *WrDr 84*
Mitchell, Joyce Slayton 1933- *ConAu 65*
Mitchell, Julian 1935- *ConAu 5R, -5NR,*
ConNov 82, DcLB 14[port], WorAu 1970,
WrDr 84
Mitchell, Juliet 1940- *ConAu 45,*
ConIsC 1[port], WrDr 84
Mitchell, K L *ConAu X, IntAu&W 82X*
Mitchell, Ken 1940- *ConAu 93*
Mitchell, Kenneth R 1930- *ConAu 17R*
Mitchell, Kerry *ConAu X*
Mitchell, Lane 1907- *ConAu P-1*
Mitchell, Langdon Elwyn 1862-1935 *CnMD,*
DcLB 7[port], ModWD
Mitchell, Lee M 1943- *ConAu 1NR, -49*
Mitchell, Leeds 1912- *ConAu 89*
Mitchell, Leonel Lake 1930- *ConAu 89*
Mitchell, Lionel H 1942- *ConAu 106*
Mitchell, Loften 1919- *ConAu 81, ConDr 82,*
LivgBAA, WrDr 84
Mitchell, Margaret 1900-1949 *ConAu 109,*
DcLB 9[port], LongCTC, ModAL, TwCA,
TwCA SUP, TwCLC 11[port], TwCRGW,
TwCWr
Mitchell, Margaretta 1935- *ConAu 29R,*
WrDr 84
Mitchell, Marianne Helen 1937- *ConAu 85*
Mitchell, Memory F 1924- *ConAu 37R,*
WrDr 84
Mitchell, Nora *DrAP&F 83*
Mitchell, Otis C 1935- *ConAu 37R*
Mitchell, P M 1916- *ConAu 104*
Mitchell, Paige 1932- *ConAu X*
Mitchell, Pamela Holsclaw 1940- *ConAu 6NR,*
-57
Mitchell, Patricia E 1943- *ConAmTC*
Mitchell, Peggy *ConAu X*
Mitchell, Peter M 1934- *ConAu 85*
Mitchell, Richard H 1931- *ConAu 21R*
Mitchell, Robby K 1916- *WrDr 84*
Mitchell, Roger *DrAP&F 83*
Mitchell, Roger 1935- *ConAu 25R, WrDr 84*
Mitchell, Ruth K *ConAu 33R*
Mitchell, S Valentine *ConAu X*
Mitchell, Sally 1937- *ConAu 110*
Mitchell, Scott *ConAu X*
Mitchell, Sibyl Elyne Keith 1913- *IntAu&W 82*
Mitchell, Sidney Alexander 1895- *ConAu 5R*
Mitchell, Stephen Arnold 1903-1974 *ConAu 49*
Mitchell, Stephen O 1930- *ConAu 13R*
Mitchell, Susan *DrAP&F 83*
Mitchell, Susan Valerie 1963- *IntWWP 82*
Mitchell, Thomas N 1939- *ConAu 103*
Mitchell, W J T 1942- *ConAu 81*
Mitchell, W O 1914- *ConAu 77,*
ConLC 25[port], ConNov 82, WrDr 84
Mitchell, William E 1927- *ConAu 81*
Mitchell, William E 1936- *ConAu 93*
Mitchell, William Hamilton 1907?-1982
ConAu 107
Mitchell, William Ormond 1914- *CreCan 1,*
DcLEL 1940, TwCWr
Mitchell, Yvonne 1925-1979 *ConAu 10NR, -17R,*
-85, DcLEL 1940, SmATA 24N
Mitchelson, Marvin M 1928- *ConAu 104*
Mitchelson, Tom *DrAP&F 83*
Mitchenson, Francis Joseph Blackett *ConAu 101*
Mitchenson, Joe *ConAu X*
Mitchison, Lois *ConAu 1R*
Mitchison, Naomi 1897- *TwCCW 83, WrDr 84*
Mitchison, Naomi Margaret 1897- *ConAu 77,*
ConNov 82, ConSFA, IntAu&W 82,
LongCTC, ModBrL, SmATA 24[port],
TwCA, TwCA SUP, TwCSFW
Mitchison, Rosalind 1919- *ConAu 33R,*
WrDr 84
Mitchison, Sonja Lois 1928- *DcLEL 1940*
Mitchner, Stuart 1938- *ConAu 61*
Mitchum, Hank *ConAu X, TwCWW,*
WrDr 84

Mitford, Jessica 1917- *ASpks, ConAu 1R,*
-1NR, WorAu, WrDr 84
Mitford, Nancy Freeman 1904-1973 *ConAu 9R,*
LongCTC, ModBrL, TwCA SUP, TwCWr
Mitgang, Herbert 1920- *ConAu 4NR, -9R,*
WrDr 84
Mitgang, Lee D 1949- *ConAu 77*
Mitra, Gajendrakumar 1908- *IntAu&W 82*
Mitra, Premendra 1904- *ModCmwL*
Mitrany, David 1888-1975 *ConAu 61, -65*
Mitru, Alexandru 1914- *IntAu&W 82*
Mitscherlich, Alexander Joseph 1909-1982
ConAu 107
Mitson, Eileen N 1930- *ConAu 25R, WrDr 84*
Mitsuhashi, Yoko *SmATA 33*
Mitsui, James Masao *DrAP&F 83*
Mittelholzer, Edgar Austin 1909-1965 *ConAu P-1,*
DcLEL 1940, LongCTC, ModBlW,
ModCmwL, TwCWr, WorAu
Mittelman, James H 1944- *ConAu 73*
Mittelmann, Norman 1932- *CreCan 1*
Mitterer, Erika 1906- *IntAu&W 82*
Mitterling, Philip Ira 1926- *ConAu 102*
Mittlebeeler, Emmet V 1915- *ConAu 57*
Mittleman, Norman 1932- *CreCan 1*
Mitton, Bruce H 1950- *ConAu 108*
Mitton, Charles Leslie 1907- *ConAu 1R, -4NR*
Mitton, Jacqueline 1948- *ConAu 97*
Mitton, Simon 1946- *ConAu 97*
Mittra, S 1930- *ConAu 41R*
Mitzman, Arthur Benjamin 1931- *ConAu 104*
Mitzman, Max E 1908- *ConAu 97*
Miura, Ayako 1922- *ConAu 73*
Mix, Amelia Evans 1912- *IntWWP 82*
Mix, C Rex 1935- *ConAu 29R*
Mix, Katherine Lyon *ConAu 53*
Mix, Paul E 1934- *ConAu 45*
Mix, Susan Shank 1943- *ConAu 29R*
Mixter, Elisabeth W *ConAu X*
Mixter, Keith Eugene 1922- *ConAu 41R*
Mixter, Russell Lowell 1906- *ConAu P-1*
Miyakawa, T Scott 1906- *ConAu 17R*
Miyamoto, Kazuo 1900- *ConAu P-1*
Miyamoto, Kenji 1908- *IntAu&W 82*
Miyoshi, Masao 1928- *ConAu 29R*
Mizener, Arthur 1907- *ConAu 5R, -5NR,*
IntAu&W 82, TwCA SUP, WrDr 84
Mizner, Elizabeth Howard 1907- *ConAu 13R,*
IntAu&W 82, MichAu 80,
SmATA 27[port]
Mizra, Baldev *IntWWP 82X*
Mizruchi, Ephraim H 1926- *ConAu 41R*
Mizruchi, Mark S 1953- *ConAu 110*
Mizumura, Kazue *ConAu 85, SmATA 18*
Mjelde, Michael Jay 1938- *ConAu 69*
Mladenovic, Ranko 1893-1947 *CnMD*
Mlynar, Linda Herren *DrAP&F 83*
Mnacko, Ladislav 1919- *ClDMEL 80,*
ConAu 29R, ModSL 2, TwCWr
Mnguni *IntAu&W 82X*
Mo Jen *IntWWP 82X*
Moak, Lennox L 1912- *ConAu 21R*
Moak, Samuel K 1929- *ConAu 37R*
Moamrath, M M *TwCSFW*
Moan, Terrence 1947- *ConAu 97*
Moat, John 1936- *ConAu 33R, ConP 80,*
IntAu&W 82, IntWWP 82, WrDr 84
Moats, Alice-Leone *ConAu P-1*
Moberg, David O 1922- *ConAu 1R, -2NR,*
WrDr 84
Moberg, Vilhelm 1898-1973 *ClDMEL 80,*
CnMD, ConAu 45, -97, ModWD, WorAu
Moberg-Gidlund, Aili *IntAu&W 82X*
Moberley, Anne *LongCTC*
Moberly, Elizabeth Rosamund 1949-
IntAu&W 82
Moberly, R B 1920- *ConAu 29R*
Moberly, Robert Basil 1920- *WrDr 84*
Moberly, Walter 1881-1974 *ConAu P-2*
Moberly-Bell, Enid 1881- *ConAu 5R*
Mobley, Harris W 1929- *ConAu 37R*
Mobley, Tony Allen 1938- *ConAu 102*
Mobley, Walt *ConAu X*
Moche, Dinah L 1936- *ConAu 89*
Mock, Edward J 1934- *ConAu 21R*
Mockel, Albert 1866-1945 *ClDMEL 80*
Mocker, Donald W 1935- *ConAu 102*
Mockler, Anthony 1937- *ConAu 69*
Mockler, Mike 1945- *ConAu 109*
Mockler, Robert J 1932- *ConAu 33R*
Mockridge, Norton 1915- *ConAu 110*
Mocsy, Andras 1929- *ConAu 65*

Modak, Manorama Ramkrishna 1895- *ConAu 97*
Model, Lisette 1906-1983 *ConAu 109*
Modell, John 1941- *ConAu 93*
Modell, Merriam 1908- *WrDr 84*
Modelski, George 1926- *ConAu 2NR, –49*
Modesitt, L E, Jr. 1943- *ConAu 109*
Modiano, Patrick Jean 1945- *ConAu 85,
ConLC 18, IntAu&W 82*
Modigliani, Andre 1940- *ConAu 53*
Modisane, Bloke 1923- *TwCWr*
Modisane, William Bloke 1923- *DcLEL 1940*
Modley, Rudolph 1906-1976 *ConAu 69*
Modlmayr, Hans-Jorg 1940- *IntWWP 82*
Modras, Ronald E 1937- *ConAu 9NR, –21R*
Moe, Barbara 1937- *ConAu 69, SmATA 20*
Moe, Christian H 1929- *WrDr 84*
Moe, Christian Hollis 1929- *ConAu 41R,
IntAu&W 82*
Moehlman, Arthur H 1907- *ConAu 9R*
Moehlmann, F Herbert 1893- *ConAu 93*
Moelleken, Wolfgang W 1934- *ConAu 33R*
Moeller, Charles 1912- *ConAu 73*
Moeller, Dorothy Wilson 1902- *ConAu 45*
Moeller, Helen 1921- *ConAu 21R*
Moeller, Philip 1880-1958 *ModWD*
Moellering, Ralph Luther 1923- *ConAu 13R,
WrDr 84*
Moenkemeyer, Heinz 1914- *ConAu 102*
Moens, Wies 1898- *CIDMEL 80*
Moenssens, Andre A 1930- *ConAu 29R,
WrDr 84*
Moeri, Louise 1924- *ConAu 9NR, –65,
SmATA 24[port]*
Moerman, Daniel E 1941- *ConAu 105*
Moerman, Michael 1934- *ConAu 25R*
Moers, Ellen 1928-1979 *ConAu 9R, –89*
Moers, Hermann 1930- *CnMD, ModWD*
Moersch, Karl 1926- *IntAu&W 82*
Moes, John E 1926- *ConAu 1R*
Moffat, Abbot Low 1901- *ConAu 1R*
Moffat, Alexander W 1891- *ConAu 69*
Moffat, Anne Simon 1947- *ConAu 107*
Moffat, Frances 1912- *ConAu 97*
Moffat, Gwen 1924- *ConAu 10NR, –13R,
TwCCr&M 80, WrDr 84*
Moffat, John Lawrence 1916- *ConAu 103,
WrDr 84*
Moffat, Mary Jane 1933- *ConAu 97*
Moffatt, Doris 1919- *ConAu 105*
Moffatt, Michael 1944- *ConAu 85*
Moffeit, Tony *DrAP&F 83*
Moffett, Hugh 1910- *ConAu 73*
Moffett, Judith *DrAP&F 83*
Moffett, Judith 1942- *ConAu 69, ConP 80,
WrDr 84*
Moffett, Martha 1934- *ConAu 37R, SmATA 8*
Moffett, Samuel Hugh 1916- *ConAu 5NR, –9R,
IntAu&W 82, WrDr 84*
Moffett, Toby 1944- *ConAu 85*
Moffitt, John 1908- *ConAu 10NR, –25R,
WrDr 84*
Moffitt, Phillip *ConAu 110*
Moffitt, William J 1930- *ConAu 57*
Mofolo, Thomas 1877-1948 *ModBlW*
Mofolo, Thomas Mokopu 1875-1948 *ModCmwL,
TwCWr*
Mofsie, Louis B 1936- *SmATA 33*
Mogal, Doris P 1918- *ConAu 69*
Mogan, Joseph J, Jr. 1924- *ConAu 49*
Mogel, Leonard Henry 1922- *ConAu 104*
Mogens, Nina Arkina 1891- *IntAu&W 82*
Moger, Allen Wesley 1905- *ConAu P-2,
WrDr 84*
Moger, Joe *IntAu&W 82X*
Moggach, Deborah 1948- *ConAu 89, WrDr 84*
Moggridge, D E 1943- *ConAu 29R*
Mogin, Jean 1921- *CIDMEL 80, ModWD*
Moglen, Helene 1936- *ConAu 65*
Mogulof, Melvin B 1926- *ConAu 105*
Mohan, Beverly Moffett 1918- *ConAu 5R*
Mohan, Brij 1939- *ConAu 110*
Mohan, Peter John 1930- *ConAu 10NR, –61*
Mohan, Robert Paul 1920- *ConAu 41R*
Mohl, Raymond A 1939- *ConAu 33R*
Mohl, Ruth 1891- *ConAu P-1, IntAu&W 82,
WrDr 84*
Mohlenbrock, Robert H 1931- *ConAu 5NR, –53*
Mohler, Charles 1913- *ConAu 29R*
Mohler, James A 1923- *WrDr 84*
Mohler, James Aylward 1923- *ConAu 8NR,
–21R*
Mohn, Peter B 1934- *ConAu 106, SmATA 28*

Mohn, Viola Kohl 1914- *SmATA 8*
Mohr, Gordon 1916- *ConAu 25R*
Mohr, Jack *ConAu X*
Mohr, James C 1943- *ConAu 73*
Mohr, Nicholasa 1935- *ConAu 1NR, –49,
SmATA 8*
Mohr, Nicholasa 1935- *ConLC 12*
Mohr, William J *DrAP&F 83*
Mohrhardt, Foster E 1907- *ConAu P-1*
Mohrmann, Christine A E M 1903- *ConAu P-1,
IntAu&W 82*
Mohrt, Michel 1914- *ConAu 13R,
IntAu&W 82*
Mohsin *IntWWP 82X*
Moir, Alfred 1924- *ConAu 9NR, –21R*
Moir, Duncan Wilson 1930-1983 *ConAu 110*
Moir, James 1908- *IntAu&W 82, WrDr 84*
Moir, John S 1926- *ConAu 41R*
Moir, Ronald Eugene 1928- *ConAu 29R*
Moise, Lotte E 1917- *ConAu 103*
Moiseiwitsch, Tanya 1914- *CreCan 2*
Mojica, Jose 1896-1974 *ConAu 93*
Mojtabai, A G 1938- *ConAu 85, ConLC 5, –9,
–15*
Mojtabai, Ann Grace *DrAP&F 83*
Mok, Albert Louis 1930- *IntAu&W 82*
Mok, Paul P 1934- *ConAu 9R*
Mokashi-Punekar, Shankar 1925- *ConAu 97*
Mokashi-Punekar, Shankar 1928- *ConP 80,
WrDr 84*
Mokgatle, Nyadioe Naboth 1911- *ConAu P-2*
Mokres, James A 1945- *ConAu 49*
Mol, Johannis J 1922- *ConAu 2NR, –49,
WrDr 84*
Molan, Dorothy L 1911- *ConAu 9R*
Moland, Ruby Louise 1918- *IntWWP 82*
Molarsky, Osmond 1909- *ConAu 25R,
SmATA 16*
Molbjerg, Hans 1915- *IntWWP 82*
Moldafsky, Annie 1930- *ConAu 61*
Moldenhaar, Hans 1906- *ConAu 1R, –3NR,
WrDr 84*
Moldenhauer, Joseph J 1934- *ConAu 33R*
Moldenhauer, Rosaleen 1926- *ConAu 97*
Moldovsky, Joel S 1939- *ConAu 97*
Mole, John 1941- *ConAu 101, ConP 80,
IntAu&W 82, IntWWP 82, WrDr 84*
Mole, Robert L 1923- *ConAu 29R*
Molen, Ronald Lowry 1929- *ConAu 65*
Molenaar, Dee 1918- *ConAu 37R*
Moler, Kenneth Lloyd 1938- *ConAu 89*
Moleski, Terese Maria 1954- *IntWWP 82*
Molesworth, Mrs. 1839-1921 *LongCTC*
Molesworth, Charles *DrAP&F 83*
Molesworth, Charles 1941- *ConAu 77,
IntWWP 82*

Molette, Barbara Jean 1940- *ConAu 45,
NatPD 81[port]*
Molette, Carlton W, II 1939- *ConAu 1NR, –45,
NatPD 81[port]*
Moley, Raymond 1886-1975 *ConAu 61*
Molho, Anthony 1939- *ConAu 106*
Molin, Sven Eric 1929- *ConAu 17R*
Molina Prieto, Andres 1925- *IntAu&W 82*
Molina Santaolalla, Luis 1922- *IntAu&W 82*
Molinari, Guido 1933- *CreCan 2*
Molinari, Ricardo E 1898- *ModLAL, WorAu*
Molinaro, Julius A 1918- *ConAu 41R*
Molinaro, Ursule *ConAu 69, DrAP&F 83*
Moline, Mary 1932- *ConAu 7NR, –57*
Moll, Elick 1907- *ConAu 1R, –2NR*
Moll I Casanovas, Francesc DeBorja 1903-
CIDMEL 80
Molland, Einar 1908- *ConAu 53*
Mollegen, Anne Rush *ConAu X*
Mollenhoff, Clark 1921- *WrDr 84*
Mollenhoff, Clark Raymond 1921- *ConAu 17R,
IntAu&W 82*
Mollenkott, Virginia Ramey 1932- *ConAu 33R,
WrDr 84*
Moller, Eberhard Wolfgang 1906- *ModWD*
Moller, Richard Jay 1952- *ConAu 106*
Mollinger, Robert N 1945- *ConAu 106*
Mollo, Andrew 1940- *ConAu 65*
Mollo, Terry 1949- *ConAu 102*
Mollo, Victor 1909- *ConAu 5NR, –9R,
IntAu&W 82, WrDr 84*
Molloy, Anne Baker 1907- *SmATA 32[port]*
Molloy, Anne Stearns Baker 1907- *ConAu 13R*
Molloy, John T 1937?- *ConAu 81*
Molloy, Julia Sale 1905- *ConAu 1R, –1NR*

Molloy, Julia Sale 1905-1983 *ConAu 110*
Molloy, M J 1917- *ConAu 103*
Molloy, Martha Bankhead 1916- *IntWWP 82*
Molloy, Michael 1917- *ConDr 82,
IntAu&W 82, WrDr 84*
Molloy, Paul 1920- *ConAu 1R, SmATA 5*
Molloy, Robert 1906-1977 *ConAu 69,
ConAu P-2, TwCA SUP*
Molloy, Tom 1948- *ConAu 107*
Molnar, Ferenc 1878-1952 *CIDMEL 80, CnMD,
ConAu 109, LongCTC, ModWD, TwCA,
TwCA SUP*
Molnar, George 1910- *IntAu&W 82*
Molnar, Thomas 1921- *ConAu 1R, –3NR*
Molody, Konan Trofimovich *ConAu X*
Molofsky, Merle *DrAP&F 83*
Molotch, Harvey L 1940- *ConAu 41R*
Moltmann, Juergen 1926- *ConAu 93*
Molumby, Lawrence E 1932- *ConAu 21R*
Molz, Kathleen 1928- *ConAu 49*
Momaday, N Scott *DrAP&F 83*
Momaday, N Scott 1934- *ConAu 25R,
ConLC 2, –19, ConNov 82, FifWWr,
SmATA 30, TwCWW, WrDr 84*
Momaday, Natachee Scott 1934- *DcLEL 1940*
Mombert, Alfred 1872-1942 *CIDMEL 80,
ModGL*
Momboisse, Raymond M 1927- *ConAu 29R*
Moment, David 1925- *ConAu 9R*
Mommsen, Katharina 1925- *ConAu 69*
Mommsen, Theodor 1817-1903 *LongCTC*
Mommsen, Wolfgang J 1930- *ConAu 101*
Mon, Franz 1926- *CIDMEL 80*
Monaco, James 1942- *ConAu 69*
Monaco, Richard *DrAP&F 83*
Monaco, Richard 1940- *ConAu 65*
Monad, Jacques 1910-1976 *ConAu 65*
Monagan, Charles A 1950- *ConAu 109*
Monaghan, Jay 1891-1981 *ConAu 103, –41R*
Monaghan, M Patricia 1946- *IntWWP 82*
Monaghan, Patricia *DrAP&F 83*
Monaghan, Patricia 1946- *ConAu 107*
Monaghan, Patrick C 1903?-1972 *ConAu 37R*
Monahan, Arthur P 1928- *ConAu 57*
Monahan, Brent J 1948- *ConAu 93*
Monahan, Kaspar *AuNews 1*
Monas, Sidney 1924- *ConAu 13R*
Monath, Elizabeth 1907- *ConAu 5R*
Monbeck, Michael E 1942- *ConAu 2NR, –49*
Moncrieff *TwCA, TwCA SUP*
Moncrieff, Charles K Scott *LongCTC*
Moncrieff, Earnest *ConAu X*
Moncure, Jane Belk 1926- *ConAu 6NR, –9R,
IntAu&W 82, SmATA 23[port]*
Mondada, Giuseppe 1907- *IntAu&W 82*
Mondadori, Alberto 1914?-1976 *ConAu 65*
Mondadori, Arnoldo 1889-1971 *ConAu 29R*
Mondale, Joan Adams 1930- *ConAu 41R*
Mondale, Walter F 1928- *ConAu 65*
Monday, James 1951- *ConAu 61*
Monday, Michael *ConAu X*
Mondey, David 1917- *ConAu 93*
Monet, Dorothy 1927- *ConAu 81*
Monet, Jacques 1930- *ConAu 11NR, –65,
WrDr 84*
Money, David Charles 1918- *ConAu 107,
IntAu&W 82, WrDr 84*
Money, John 1921- *ConAu 1NR, –45*
Money, Keith 1935- *ConAu 107, IntAu&W 82,
WrDr 84*
Money-Kyrle, Roger 1898-1980 *ConAu 101*
Monfalcone, Wesley R 1942- *ConAu 109*
Monfolo, Rodolpho 1899?-1976 *ConAu 69*
Mongeau, Jean-Guy 1931- *CreCan 1*
Monger, Ifor David 1908- *ConAu 5R*
Mongo, Beti *IntAu&W 82X*
Monguio, Luis 1908- *ConAu 5R, IntAu&W 82*
Monheim, Leonard M 1911-1971 *ConAu 33R*
Monig, Christopher *ConAu X, TwCCr&M 80,
WrDr 84*
Monjo, F N 1924-1978 *ChlLR 2, ConAu 81,
SmATA 16, TwCCW 83*
Monk, Alan *ConAu X*
Monk, Galdo *ConAu X*
Monk, Hilton *ConAu X*
Monk, Janice J 1937- *ConAu 93*
Monk, Lorraine *ConAu X*
Monk, Robert C 1930- *ConAu 21R, WrDr 84*
Monka, Paul 1935- *ConAu 29R*
Monkhouse, Allan Noble 1858-1936 *DcLB 10,
LongCTC, ModBrL, ModWD, TwCA*

Monkhouse, Francis John 1914-1975
ConAu 10NR, -13R, -57
Monkkonen, Eric H 1942- *ConAu 61*
Monkland, George *IntAu&W 82X*
Monmonier, Mark Stephen 1943- *ConAu 109*
Monnet, Jean 1888-1979 *ConAu 102, -85*
Monnich, Horst 1918- *IntAu&W 82*
Monnin-Hornung, Juliette *IntAu&W 82*
Monnow, Peter *ConAu X*
Monod, Jacques 1910-1976 *ConAu 69*
Monod, Rene *ConAu X*
Monod, Sylvere 1921- *ConAu 21R*
Monod, Theodore 1902- *ConAu 65*
Monongo *ConAu X*
Monro, Gavin 1905- *ConAu X, WrDr 84*
Monro, Harold Edward 1879-1932 *LongCTC,*
ModBrL, TwCA, TwCA SUP, WhoTwCL
Monro, Isabel S 1884- *ConAu P-2*
Monro, Kate M 1883- *ConAu P-2*
Monro-Higgs, Gertrude *WrDr 84*
Monro-Higgs, Gertrude 1905- *ConAu 105*
Monroe, Alan D 1944- *ConAu 57*
Monroe, Alan Houston 1903- *ConAu 5R*
Monroe, Bill *ConAu X*
Monroe, Carole 1944- *ConAu 105*
Monroe, Charles R 1905- *ConAu 73*
Monroe, Elizabeth 1905- *ConAu 13R*
Monroe, Harriet 1860-1936 *ConAu 109,*
LongCTC, TwCA, TwCA SUP,
TwCLC 12[port]
Monroe, Jonathan Beck 1954- *IntWWP 82*
Monroe, Keith 1917- *ConAu 2NR, -5R*
Monroe, Lyle *ConAu X, SmATA X*
Monroe, Lynn Lee 1935- *ConAu 53*
Monroe, Margaret Ellen 1914- *ConAu 5R*
Monroe, Marion *ConAu X*
Monroe, Marion 1898-1983 *SmATA 34N*
Monroe, Reginald 1938- *LivgBAA*
Monroe, William Blanc, Jr. 1920- *ConAu 108*
Monsarrat, Ann Whitelaw 1937- *ConAu 73,*
WrDr 84
Monsarrat, Nicholas John Turney 1910-1979
ConAu 1R, -3NR, ConSFA, DcLB 15[port],
LongCTC, ModBrL, TwCA SUP, TwCWr
Monsell, Helen 1895-1971 *ConAu P-1,*
SmATA 24
Monsen, R Joseph, Jr. 1931- *ConAu 9R*
Monsey, Derek 1921-1979 *ConAu 1R, -2NR, -85*
Monsky, Mark 1941- *ConAu 65*
Monsma, James E 1929- *ConAu 29R*
Monsma, Stephen V 1936- *ConAu 33R*
Monsman, Gerald Cornelius 1940- *ConAu 8NR,*
-21R
Monson, Charles H, Jr. 1924- *ConAu 5R*
Monson, Karen Ann 1945- *ConAmTC,*
ConAu 97
Monsour, Sally A 1929- *ConAu 21R*
Mont, Paul De 1895-1950 *ModWD*
Montag, Thomas 1947- *ConAu 103*
Montag, Tom 1947- *ConAu X, WrDr 84*
Montagnes, E Ian 1932- *IntAu&W 82*
Montagnes, Ian 1932- *ConAu 45*
Montagu, Ashley 1905- *ConAu 5R, -5NR,*
TwCA SUP, WrDr 84
Montagu, Lady Elizabeth 1917- *ConAu 9R,*
WorAu
Montagu, Ewen 1901- *WrDr 84*
Montagu, Ewen Edward Samuel 1901- *ConAu 77,*
IntAu&W 82
Montagu, Ivor 1904- *ConAu 13R,*
IntAu&W 82, WrDr 84
Montagu, Jeremy 1927- *ConAu 93*
Montagu Of Beaulieu, Lord 1926- *ConAu X,*
IntAu&W 82, WrDr 84
Montagu Of Beaulieu, Edward J Barrington 1926-
ConAu 6NR
Montague, Bruce Alexander 1939- *IntAu&W 82*
Montague, Charles Edward 1867-1928 *LongCTC,*
TwCA, TwCWr
Montague, Elizabeth 1917- *DcLEL 1940*
Montague, Gene Bryan 1928- *ConAu 93*
Montague, Jeanne *ConAu X*
Montague, Joel B, Jr. 1912- *ConAu 5R*
Montague, John 1929- *ConAu 9NR, WrDr 84*
Montague, John Patrick 1929- *ConAu 9R,*
ConLC 13, ConP 80, WorAu
Montague, Lisa *ConAu X*
Montague, Peter Gunn 1938- *ConAu 85*
Montague-Smith, Patrick Wykeham 1920-
ConAu 107, IntAu&W 82
Montaigne, Sanford H 1935- *ConAu 65*
Montal, Robert 1927- *CIDMEL 80*

Montalbano, William Daniel 1940- *ConAu 105*
Montale, Eugenio 1896-1981 *CIDMEL 80,*
CnMWL, ConAu 104, -17R, ConLC 7, -9,
-18, ModRL, TwCWr, WhoTwCL, WorAu
Montana, Bob 1920-1975 *ConAu 89,*
SmATA 21N
Montana, Patrick J 1937- *ConAu 10NR, -25R*
Montanari, A J 1917- *ConAu 104*
Montandon, Pat *ConAu 57*
Montaner, Carlos Alberto 1943- *IntAu&W 82*
Montapert, Alfred Armand 1906- *ConAu 108*
Montapert, William D 1930- *ConAu 107*
Montardit, Teresa Grifoll *IntAu&W 82*
Montardit, Th G *IntAu&W 82X*
Montardit, Dennis *ConAu X*
Monteiro, Adolfo Casais 1908-1972 *CIDMEL 80*
Monteiro, Domingos 1903- *CIDMEL 80*
Monteiro, George 1932- *ConAu 7NR, -17R*
Monteiro, Luis DeSttau 1926- *ConAu 10NR,*
-13R
Monteith, Lionel 1921- *IntWWP 82*
Monteleone, Thomas F 1946- *ConAu 109,*
IntAu&W 82, TwCSFW, WrDr 84
Montell, William Lynwood 1931- *ConAu 11NR,*
-29R
Monter, E William 1936- *ConAu 21R*
Montero, Darrel Martin 1946- *ConAu 101*
Monterosso, Carlo 1921- *ConAu 29R*
Montes, Antonio Llano 1924- *ConAu 69*
Montes DeOca, Marco Antonio 1932-
WorAu 1970
Montesi, Albert Joseph 1921- *ConAu 37R*
Montesquiou-Fezensac, Count Robert De
1855-1921 *CIDMEL 80*
Montessori, Maria 1870-1952 *LongCTC*
Monteux, Doris 1894- *ConAu P-2*
Montey, Vivian M 1956- *ConAu 105*
Montfort, Auguste 1913- *ConAu 101*
Montgomerie, Norah Mary 1913- *ConAu 105,*
SmATA 26
Montgomerie, William 1904- *IntAu&W 82*
Montgomery, Albert A 1929- *ConAu 13R*
Montgomery, Bernard Law 1887-1976 *ConAu 65,*
-69
Montgomery, Brian 1903- *ConAu 53,*
IntAu&W 82
Montgomery, Bruce 1921-1978 *ConAu 104*
Montgomery, Charles F 1910-1978 *ConAu 77,*
-81
Montgomery, Charlotte Baker 1910-
IntAu&W 82
Montgomery, Constance *ConAu X*
Montgomery, Constance Cappel 1936-
ConAu 21R, SmATA X
Montgomery, David 1927- *ConAu 81*
Montgomery, David Bruce 1938- *ConAu 29R,*
WrDr 84
Montgomery, Edward F 1918- *ConAu 9R*
Montgomery, Elizabeth Rider 1902- *ConAu 1R,*
-3NR, IntAu&W 82, SmATA 3, -34[port]
Montgomery, Elizabeth Wakefield 1891-
ConAu 41R
Montgomery, George *DrAP&F 83*
Montgomery, Herbert J 1933- *ConAu 3NR, -49*
Montgomery, Horace 1906- *ConAu 9R*
Montgomery, John 1916- *IntAu&W 82*
Montgomery, John 1919- *ConAu 25R,*
DcLB 16[port]
Montgomery, John D 1920- *ConAu 3NR, -5R,*
WrDr 84
Montgomery, John Warwick 1931- *ConAu 10NR,*
-21R
Montgomery, L M 1874-1942 *ConAu 108,*
TwCCW 83, TwCRGW
Montgomery, Leslie Alexander 1873-1961
LongCTC
Montgomery, Lucy Maud 1874-1942 *CreCan 2,*
LongCTC, TwCA, TwCWr
Montgomery, Marge 1922- *IntWWP 82*
Montgomery, Marion *DrAP&F 83*
Montgomery, Marion 1925- *AuNews 1,*
ConAu 1R, -3NR, ConLC 7, DcLB 6[port],
IntAu&W 82, WrDr 84
Montgomery, Max *ConAu X*
Montgomery, Nancy S *ConAu 93*
Montgomery, Raymond A, Jr. 1936- *ConAu 97*
Montgomery, Robert 1904-1981 *ConAu 108*
Montgomery, Robert 1946- *NatPD 81*
Montgomery, Robert Bruce *WorAu*
Montgomery, Robert L, Jr. 1927- *ConAu 5R*
Montgomery, Ruth *WrDr 84*
Montgomery, Ruth Shick 1912- *AuNews 1,*

ConAu 1R, -2NR, IntAu&W 82
Montgomery, Rutherford 1894- *TwCCW 83*
Montgomery, Rutherford George *WrDr 84*
Montgomery, Rutherford George 1894-
ConAu 9R, SmATA 3, TwCWW
Montgomery, Stuart 1940- *DcLEL 1940*
Montgomery, Thomas Andrew 1925- *ConAu 49*
Montgomery, Vivian *ConAu 102*
Montherlant, Henri De 1896-1972 *ConLC 8, -19*
Montherlant, Henry De 1896-1971 *CIDMEL 80*
Montherlant, Henry De, Comte 1896-1972 *CnMD,*
CnMWL, ConAu 37R, -85, CroCD,
LongCTC, ModFrL, ModRL, ModWD,
TwCA, TwCA SUP, TwCWr, WhoTwCL
Montias, John Michael 1928- *ConAu 1R, -2NR*
Monticone, Ronald Charles 1937- *ConAu 73*
Montini, Giovanni Battista *ConAu X*
Monton Puerto, Pedro 1925- *IntAu&W 82*
Montoya, Jose *DrAP&F 83*
Montresor, Beni 1926- *ConAu 29R, SmATA 3*
Montrose, Graham *ConAu X*
Montrose, James St. David *ConAu X*
Montross, David *ConAu X*
Monty, Jeanne R 1935- *ConAu 49*
Monty Python *ConAu X, ConLC 21[port]*
Monypenny, William Flavelle 1866-1912 *TwCA*
Mood, Alexander M 1913- *ConAu 53*
Mood, John J L 1932- *ConAu 57*
Moodie, Graeme Cochrane 1924- *ConAu 1R,*
-2NR, IntAu&W 82, WrDr 84
Moodie, T Dunbar 1940- *ConAu 77*
Moody, Anne 1940- *ConAu 65, LivgBAA*
Moody, Dale 1915- *ConAu 17R*
Moody, Dwight Lyman 1837-1899 *LongCTC*
Moody, Ernest A 1903-1975 *ConAu 13R, -61*
Moody, G F *ConAu X*
Moody, Henry Laurence 1907- *IntAu&W 82*
Moody, J Carroll 1934- *ConAu 33R*
Moody, Jess C 1925- *ConAu 21R*
Moody, Joseph Nestor 1904- *ConAu 1NR, -49*

Moody, Paul Amos 1903- *ConAu 53*
Moody, Peter R 1943- *ConAu 107*
Moody, R Bruce *DrAP&F 83*
Moody, R Bruce 1933- *ConAu 17R*
Moody, Ralph Owen 1898- *ConAu P-1,*
SmATA 1
Moody, Raymond Avery, Jr. 1944- *ConAu 93*
Moody, Richard Anselm 1911- *ConAu 33R*
Moody, Ron 1924- *ConAu 108*
Moody, Shirley *DrAP&F 83*
Moody, Theodore William 1907- *ConAu 13R,*
IntAu&W 82
Moody, William Vaughn 1869-1910 *ConAu 110,*
DcLB 7[port], LongCTC, ModAL,
ModWD, TwCA, TwCA SUP
Mookerjea, Sobhanlal 1929- *IntAu&W 82*
Moolson, Melusa *ConAu X, IntAu&W 82X,*
WrDr 84
Moomaw, Ira W 1894- *ConAu P-1*
Moon, Carl 1879-1948 *SmATA 25[port]*
Moon, Douglas Mark 1937- *ConAu 17R*
Moon, G J H 1915- *ConAu 105*
Moon, Grace Purdie 1877-1947 *SmATA 25[port]*
Moon, Harold K 1932- *ConAu 53*
Moon, Michael E 1948- *ConAu 85*
Moon, Rexford G, Jr. 1922- *ConAu 41R*
Moon, Robert 1925- *ConAu 73*
Moon, Sheila 1910- *ConAu 25R, SmATA 5*
Moonblood, Q *ConAu X*
Mooney, Booth 1912-1977 *ConAu 3NR, -49, -69*
Mooney, Canice 1911-1963 *ConAu 5R*
Mooney, Chase Curran 1913-1972 *ConAu P-2*
Mooney, Christopher Francis 1925- *ConAu 37R,*
IntAu&W 82, WrDr 84
Mooney, Elizabeth C 1918- *ConAu 9NR, -61*
Mooney, Eugene French 1930- *ConAu 17R*
Mooney, George A 1911-1979 *ConAu 89*
Mooney, Harry J, Jr. 1927- *ConAu 5R*
Mooney, Michael Macdonald *DrAP&F 83*
Mooney, Michael Macdonald 1930- *ConAu 65,*
WrDr 84
Mooney, Ted 1951- *ConLC 25[port]*
Mooneyham, W Stanley 1926- *ConAu 6NR,*
-13R
Moonitz, Maurice 1910- *ConAu 2NR, -5R*
Moonman, Eric 1929- *ConAu 103,*
IntAu&W 82, WrDr 84
Moor, Emily *SmATA X, WrDr 84*
Mooradian, Karlen 1935- *ConAu 97*
Moorbauer, Peter *IntAu&W 82X*
Moorcock, Michael 1939- *ConAu 2NR, -45,*

Moore, *ConLC 5, –27[port], ConSFA, DcLB 14[port], DrmM[port], TwCSFW, WrDr 84*

Moore, Acel 1940- *ConAu 69*

Moore, Alma Chesnut 1901- *ConAu P-1*

Moore, Amos 1884-1958 *TwCWW*

Moore, Andrew *ConAu X*

Moore, Anne Carroll 1871-1961 *ConAu 73, SmATA 13*

Moore, Archie Lee 1916- *ConAu 33R*

Moore, Arthur 1906?-1977 *ConAu 69*

Moore, Arthur James 1888-1974 *ConAu 5R, –49*

Moore, Austin *ConAu X, WrDr 84*

Moore, Barbara *ConAu X, DrAP&F 83*

Moore, Barbara 1934- *ConAu 53, WrDr 84*

Moore, Bernard 1904- *ConAu 69*

Moore, Bidwell 1917- *ConAu 33R*

Moore, Bob 1948- *ConAu 61*

Moore, Brian *DrAP&F 83*

Moore, Brian 1921- *ASpks, ConAu 1R, –1NR, ConLC 1, –3, –5, –7, –8, –19, ConNov 82, CreCan 2, DcLEL 1940, IntAu&W 82, ModBrL SUP, TwCSFW, TwCWr, WorAu, WrDr 84*

Moore, Briscoe 1891- *WrDr 84*

Moore, C L 1911- *ConAu 104, ConSFA, TwCSFW*

Moore, Carey Armstrong 1930- *ConAu 37R, IntAu&W 82, WrDr 84*

Moore, Carl Leland 1921- *ConAu 5R, WrDr 84*

Moore, Carman 1936- *WrDr 84*

Moore, Carman Leroy 1936- *ConAu 61, IntAu&W 82, LivgBAA*

Moore, Catherine L 1911- *WrDr 84*

Moore, Catherine Lucille 1911- *DcLB 8[port]*

Moore, Charles *ConAu X*

Moore, Charles A 1901-1967 *ConAu 1R, –3NR*

Moore, Charles Garrett Ponsonby 1910- *ConAu 108*

Moore, Charles W 1925- *WrDr 84*

Moore, Chauncey O 1895-1965 *ConAu P-1*

Moore, Clayton *ConAu X*

Moore, Clement Clarke 1779-1863 *SmATA 18*

Moore, Clyde B 1886-1973 *ConAu 1R, –4NR*

Moore, Cora R 1902- *ConAu P-2*

Moore, Cory *ConAu X*

Moore, Dan Tyler 1908- *ConAu 5R*

Moore, Daniel G 1899- *ConAu 57*

Moore, David G 1918- *ConAu 1R, –2NR*

Moore, Deborah Dash 1946- *ConAu 108*

Moore, Dick 1925- *ConAu X*

Moore, Donald Joseph 1929- *ConAu 57*

Moore, Dora Mavor 1888- *CreCan 2*

Moore, Doris Langley *WrDr 84*

Moore, Doris Langley 1903- *ConAu 1R, –1NR, IntAu&W 82, TwCRGW, WorAu*

Moore, Dorothea d1933 *TwCCW 83*

Moore, Dorothy N 1915- *ConAu 89*

Moore, Douglas Stuart 1893-1969 *ConAu P-1*

Moore, Edmund A 1903- *ConAu 5R*

Moore, Edward *ConAu X*

Moore, Edward Carter 1917- *ConAu 1R, –5NR, IntAu&W 82*

Moore, Edward J 1935- *ConAu 65, NatPD 81[port]*

Moore, Edward M 1940- *ConAu 57*

Moore, Elizabeth *ConAu X, WrDr 84*

Moore, Ethel Pauline Perry 1902- *ConAu P-1*

Moore, Eva 1942- *ConAu 45, SmATA 20*

Moore, Evelyn Garth *WrDr 84*

Moore, Evelyn Garth 1906- *ConAu P-1, IntAu&W 82*

Moore, Everett T 1909- *ConAu P-1*

Moore, Fenworth *ConAu P-2*

Moore, Francis Edward 1898- *ConAu P-1*

Moore, Frank Frankfort 1855-1931 *LongCTC, TwCA*

Moore, Frank Harper 1920- *ConAu 5R*

Moore, Frank Ledlie 1923- *ConAu 5R*

Moore, Franklin G 1905- *ConAu 1R*

Moore, G Alexander, Jr. 1937- *ConAu 21R*

Moore, Gary T 1945- *ConAu 85*

Moore, Gene D 1919- *ConAu 21R*

Moore, Geoffrey H 1914- *ConAu 81*

Moore, Geoffrey Herbert 1920- *ConAu 109*

Moore, George Augustus 1852-1933 *ConAu 104, DcLB 10[port], LongCTC, ModBrL, ModWD, TwCA, TwCA SUP, TwCLC 7[port], TwCWr, WhoTwCL*

Moore, George Edward 1873-1958 *LongCTC, TwCA SUP*

Moore, George Ellis 1916- *ConAu 5R*

Moore, Gerald 1899- *ConAu 1R, –5NR, IntAu&W 82, WrDr 84*

Moore, Glover 1911- *ConAu 107*

Moore, Hal G 1929- *WrDr 84*

Moore, Harmon 1911- *ConAu 13R*

Moore, Harold A 1913- *ConAu 33R*

Moore, Harris *ConAu X*

Moore, Harry Estill 1897- *ConAu P-1*

Moore, Harry T 1908-1981 *ConAu 3NR, –5R, –103, WorAu*

Moore, Honor *DrAP&F 83*

Moore, Honor 1945- *ConAu 85, NatPD 81[port]*

Moore, J Preston 1906- *ConAu 65*

Moore, J William 1928- *ConAu 5R*

Moore, Jack 1941- *SmATA 32*

Moore, Jack B 1933- *ConAu 33R*

Moore, Jack L 1920- *ConAu 89*

Moore, James 1928- *ConAu 97*

Moore, James Mavor 1919- *CreCan 1*

Moore, James R 1947- *ConAu 105*

Moore, James T, III 1939- *ConAu 29R*

Moore, James Tice 1945- *ConAu 73*

Moore, Jane Ann 1931- *ConAu 37R*

Moore, Janet Gaylord 1905- *ConAu 77, SmATA 18*

Moore, Janice Townley *DrAP&F 83*

Moore, Janice Townley 1939- *IntWWP 82*

Moore, Jenny 1923-1973 *ConAu 45*

Moore, Jerome 1903- *ConAu 81*

Moore, Jerrold Northrup 1934- *ConAu 104*

Moore, Jessie Eleanor 1886- *ConAu P-1*

Moore, Jimmy *ConAu X*

Moore, John A 1915- *IntAu&W 82, WrDr 84*

Moore, John A 1918-1972 *ConAu 37R*

Moore, John Alexander 1915- *ConAu 45*

Moore, John C 1933- *ConAu 49*

Moore, John Cecil 1907-1967 *ConAu 5R, LongCTC, WorAu*

Moore, John Eugene 1913- *IntWWP 82*

Moore, John Hammond 1924- *ConAu 57*

Moore, John Hebron 1920- *ConAu 21R*

Moore, John Michael 1935- *ConAu 104, IntAu&W 82, WrDr 84*

Moore, John N 1937- *WrDr 84*

Moore, John Norton 1937- *ConAu 37R*

Moore, John R 1928- *ConAu 1R, –3NR*

Moore, John Rees 1918- *ConAu 33R*

Moore, John Richard, Jr. 1925- *ConAu 17R*

Moore, John Robert 1890-1973 *ConAu P-1*

Moore, John Travers 1908- *ConAu 3NR, –5R, SmATA 12*

Moore, Joyce 1927- *IntWWP 82*

Moore, Katharine 1898- *ConAu 89*

Moore, Katherine Davis 1915- *ConAu 13R*

Moore, Keith L 1925- *ConAu 69, IntAu&W 82*

Moore, Kenneth Clark 1943- *ConAu 102*

Moore, Kenneth E 1930- *ConAu 73*

Moore, Kenny *ConAu X*

Moore, L Hugh 1935- *ConAu 49*

Moore, L Silas 1936- *ConAu 41R*

Moore, Lamont 1909- *SmATA 29*

Moore, Lander *ConAu X*

Moore, Lester L 1924- *ConAu 33R*

Moore, Lilian *ConAu 103*

Moore, Lillian 1917-1967 *ConAu 1R, –2NR*

Moore, Linda Perigo 1946- *ConAu 107*

Moore, Marcia 1928- *ConAu 61*

Moore, Margaret R 1903- *ConAu 9R, SmATA 12*

Moore, Marianne Craig 1887-1972 *CnMWL, ConAmA, ConAu 1R, –3NR, –33R, ConLC 1, –2, –4, –8, –10, –13, –19, LongCTC, ModAL, ModAL SUP, SmATA 20, TwCA, TwCA SUP, TwCWr, WhoTwCL*

Moore, Marie Drury 1926- *ConAu 33R*

Moore, Marna *ConAu X*

Moore, Mavor 1919- *ConDr 82, CreCan 1, WrDr 84*

Moore, Maxine 1927- *ConAu 73*

Moore, Merrill 1903-1957 *ConAmA, ModAL, TwCA SUP*

Moore, Michael *ConAu X, IntAu&W 82X*

Moore, N L *IntAu&W 82X*

Moore, Nicholas 1918- *ConAu 69, ConP 80, DcLEL 1940, IntAu&W 82, ModBrL, WrDr 84*

Moore, Olive *TwCA*

Moore, Pamela 1937-1964 *ConAu 1R*

Moore, Pamela Robinson 1903- *IntAu&W 82*

Moore, Patrick 1923- *ConAu 8NR, –13R,*

Moore, *DcLEL 1940, IntAu&W 82, TwCSFW, WrDr 84*

Moore, Paul, Jr. 1919- *ConAu 89*

Moore, Paul L 1917-1976 *ConAu 1R, –103*

Moore, Peter Gerald 1928- *ConAu 45*

Moore, R Laurence 1940- *ConAu 29R*

Moore, Rayburn Sabatzky 1920- *ConAu 1R, –2NR, IntAu&W 82, WrDr 84*

Moore, Raylyn *DrAP&F 83*

Moore, Raylyn 1928- *ConAu 29R, WrDr 84*

Moore, Raymond Arthur, Jr. 1925- *ConAu 5R*

Moore, Raymond S 1915- *ConAu 29R, WrDr 84*

Moore, Reg 1930- *ConAu 104*

Moore, Regina *ConAu X, SmATA X*

Moore, Richard *DrAP&F 83*

Moore, Richard 1927- *ConAu 33R, IntWWP 82, WrDr 84*

Moore, Richard B 1893?-1978 *ConAu 81*

Moore, Richard R 1934- *ConAu 105*

Moore, Robert *ConAu X*

Moore, Robert 1936- *ConAu 11NR*

Moore, Robert E 1914- *ConAu 57*

Moore, Robert Etheridge 1919- *ConAu 61*

Moore, Robert Lowell, Jr. 1925- *AuNews 1, ConAu 13R*

Moore, Robert Samuel 1936- *ConAu 25R, IntAu&W 82*

Moore, Robin *AuNews 1, ConAu X*

Moore, Roger George 1927- *ConAu 109*

Moore, Rosalie *DrAP&F 83*

Moore, Rosalie 1910- *ConAu X, –3NR, IntAu&W 82, IntWWP 82, SmATA X, WrDr 84*

Moore, Russell Franklin 1920- *ConAu 6NR, –9R*

Moore, Ruth 1908- *ConAu 1R, –6NR, SmATA 23*

Moore, Ruth Nulton 1923- *ConAu 81, IntAu&W 82*

Moore, S E *ConAu 2NR, –49, SmATA 23*

Moore, Sally Falk 1924- *ConAu 6NR, –57*

Moore, Samuel Taylor 1893-1974 *ConAu 53*

Moore, Sebastian 1917- *ConAu 21R*

Moore, Sonia 1902- *ConAu 2NR, –45*

Moore, Susanna 1948- *ConAu 109*

Moore, T Inglis 1901- *ConAu 21R*

Moore, Thomas Gale 1930- *ConAu 29R*

Moore, Thomas Sturge 1870-1944 *LongCTC, ModBrL, TwCA, TwCA SUP, TwCWr*

Moore, Todd Allen 1937- *IntWWP 82*

Moore, Tom 1950- *ConAu 101*

Moore, Trevor Wyatt 1924- *ConAu 29R, WrDr 84*

Moore, Tui DeRoy 1953- *ConAu 107*

Moore, Vardine Russell 1906- *ConAu 41R*

Moore, Virginia Dryden 1911- *ConAu 17R*

Moore, W Glenn 1925- *ConAu 49*

Moore, Walter Lane 1905- *ConAu P-1*

Moore, Wanda Allen 1909- *IntWWP 82, WrDr 84*

Moore, Ward 1903-1978 *ConAu P-2, ConSFA, DcLB 8[port], TwCSFW, WorAu*

Moore, Warren 1923- *ConAu 25R*

Moore, Wilbert E 1914- *ConAu 1R, –5NR, IntAu&W 82, WrDr 84*

Moore, Wilfred G 1907- *WrDr 84*

Moore, Wilfred George 1907- *ConAu 4NR, –9R*

Moore, William Howard 1942- *ConAu 73*

Moore, William L 1943- *ConAu 93*

Moore-Rinvolucri, Mina 1902- *WrDr 84*

Moore-Rinvolucri, Mina Josephine 1902- *ConAu 107, IntAu&W 82*

Moorehead, Agnes 1906-1974 *ConAu 49*

Moorehead, Alan 1910- *ConAu 5R, –6NR, DcLEL 1940, IntAu&W 82, LongCTC, TwCA SUP, WrDr 84*

Moorehead, Alan 1910-1983 *ConAu 110*

Moorehead, Caroline 1944- *ConAu 101, WrDr 84*

Moores, Dick *ConAu X*

Moores, Richard 1909- *ConAu 69*

Moorey, Peter Roger Stuart 1937- *IntAu&W 82, WrDr 84*

Moorhead, Andrea *DrAP&F 83*

Moorhead, Diana 1940- *ConAu 105, TwCCW 83, WrDr 84*

Moorhead, Max L 1914- *ConAu 21R*

Moorhouse, Charles Edmund 1911- *ConAu 108*

Moorhouse, Frank Thomas 1938- *ConNov 82*

Moorhouse, Geoffrey 1931- *ConAu 25R, IntAu&W 82, WrDr 84*

Moorhouse, Hilda Vansittart *ConAu P-1*

Moorman, John Richard Humpidge 1905-
　　ConAu 1R, –2NR, IntAu&W 82
Moorshead, Henry *ConAu X, IntAu&W 82X*
Moorsom, Sasha 1931- *ConAu 69*
Moorsteen, Richard H 1926?-1975 *ConAu 57*
Moos, Malcolm C 1916-1982 *ConAu 105, –37R*
Moos, Michael *DrAP&F 83*
Moos, Rudolf H 1934- *ConAu 1NR, –49*
Moose, Ruth *DrAP&F 83*
Moose, Ruth 1938- *ConAu 101*
Mooser, Stephen 1941- *ConAu 89,*
　　SmATA 28[port]
Moote, A Lloyd 1931- *ConAu 33R, WrDr 84*
Mootz, William Hoyt 1924- *ConAmTC*
Mopeli-Paulus, Attwell Sidwell 1913- *ModCmwL*
Moquin, Wayne F 1930- *ConAu 33R*
Mora, Carl J 1936- *ConAu 109*
Mora, George 1923- *ConAu 1NR, –45*
Moraes, Dom 1938- *ConAu 25R, ConP 80,*
　　LongCTC, ModCmwL, TwCWr, WorAu,
　　WrDr 84
Moraes, Dominic F 1938- *DcLEL 1940*
Moraes, Frank Robert 1907-1974 *ConAu 49,*
　　ConAu P-1
Moraes, Vinicius De 1913-1980 *ConAu 101,*
　　ModLAL, WorAu 1970
Moraff, Barbara *DrAP&F 83*
Moraff, Barbara 1939- *IntWWP 82*
Moraga, Cherrie *DrAP&F 83*
Morain, Lloyd L 1917- *ConAu 69*
Morais, Michael *DrAP&F 83*
Morais, Vamberto 1921- *ConAu 69*
Morales, Angel Luis 1919- *ConAu 49*
Morales, Goldie Pearl Laden 1909- *IntWWP 82*
Morales, Tomas 1884-1921 *CIDMEL 80*
Morales Y Marin, Jose Luis 1946- *IntAu&W 82*
Moramarco, Fred Stephen 1938- *ConAu 57*
Moran, Lord 1882-1977 *DcLEL 1940*
Moran, Charles McMoran Wilson 1882-
　　ConAu X
Moran, Christopher *IntWWP 82X*
Moran, Gabriel 1935- *ConAu 4NR, –53*
Moran, Hugh Anderson 1881-1977 *ConAu 73*
Moran, James Sterling 1909- *ConAu 9R*
Moran, Jim *ConAu X*
Moran, John 1930- *ConAu 45*
Moran, John C 1942- *ConAu 110*
Moran, Mike *ConAu X*
Moran, Patrick Alfred Pierce 1917- *ConAu 9R,*
　　WrDr 84
Moran, Ronald 1936- *ConAu 37R*
Moran, William E, Jr. 1916- *ConAu 13R*
Morand, Paul 1888-1976 *CIDMEL 80,*
　　ConAu 65, –69, ModFrL, TwCA,
　　TwCA SUP
Morand, Paul 1889- *LongCTC*
Morano, Donald V 1934- *ConAu 45*
Morante, Elsa 1915- *TwCWr*
Morante, Elsa 1916- *CnMWL, ModRL*
Morante, Elsa 1918- *CIDMEL 80, ConAu 85,*
　　ConLC 8, WhoTwCL, WorAu
Morasky, Robert Louis 1940- *ConAu 105*
Moratinos Iglesias, Jose-F 1944- *IntAu&W 82*
Moraud, Marcel I 1917- *ConAu 53*
Moravia, Alberto 1907- *CIDMEL 80, CnMD,*
　　CnMWL, ConAu X, ConLC 2, –7, –11, –18,
　　–27[port], LongCTC, ModRL, TwCA SUP,
　　TwCWr, WhoTwCL
Morawa, Michael *IntWWP 82X*
Morawetz, Oskar 1917- *CreCan 1*
Morawetz, Thomas H 1942- *ConAu 101*
Morawski, Stefan T 1921- *ConAu 81*
Morax, Rene 1873-1963 *ModWD*
Moray, Helga *ConAu 89*
Moray, Neville 1935- *ConAu 29R*
Moray Williams, Ursula 1911- *TwCCW 83,*
　　WrDr 84
Morck, Paal *ConAmA*
Morcom, John Brian 1925- *ConAu 5R*
Mordaunt, Elinor 1877?-1942 *LongCTC*
Mordaunt, Evelyn May 1877?-1942 *TwCA,*
　　TwCA SUP
Mordden, Ethan 1947- *ConAu 73*
Mordechai, Ben *ConAu X*
Mordock, John B 1938- *ConAu 61*
Mordvinoff, Nicolas 1911-1973 *ConAu 41R, –73,*
　　SmATA 17
More, Caroline *ConAu X, SmATA X,*
　　WrDr 84
More, Daphne 1929- *ConAu 65*
More, Dennis *IntAu&W 82X*
More, Harry W, Jr. 1929- *ConAu 4NR, –53*

More, Jasper 1907- *ConAu P-1*
More, Kenneth 1914-1982 *ConAu 107*
More, Paul Elmer 1864-1937 *ConAmA,*
　　LongCTC, ModAL, TwCA, TwCA SUP
Moreas, Jean 1856-1910 *CIDMEL 80*
Moreau, David Merlin 1927- *ConAu 93,*
　　IntAu&W 82, WrDr 84
Moreau, John Adam 1938- *ConAu 37R*
Moreau, Jules Laurence 1917-1971 *ConAu 1R,*
　　–103
Moreau, Marcel 1933- *CIDMEL 80*
Moreau, Reginald E 1897-1970 *ConAu 104*
Morehead, Albert Hodges 1909-1966 *ConAu P-1*
Morehead, Joe 1931- *ConAu X, –57*
Morehead, Joseph H, Jr. 1931- *ConAu 6NR*
Morehouse, Clifford Phelps 1904- *ConAu 9R*
Morehouse, Laurence E 1913- *ConAu 4NR, –9R*
Morehouse, Ward 1899?-1966 *ConAu 25R*
Moreiro, Jose Maria 1941- *IntAu&W 82*
Morel, Dighton 1915- *ConAu X*
Morel, Francois 1926- *CreCan 2*
Moreland, Jane P *DrAP&F 83*
Moreland, Lois B *ConAu 45*
Morell, David 1939- *ConAu 110*
Morella, Joseph 1949- *ConAu 104*
Moremen, Grace E 1930- *ConAu 1NR, –45*
Moren, Sally M 1947- *ConAu 97*
Moreno, Antonio 1918- *WrDr 84*
Moreno, Antonio Elosegui 1918- *ConAu 33R*
Moreno, Dorinda *DrAP&F 83*
Moreno, Francisco Jose 1934- *ConAu 29R*
Moreno, Jacob L 1892-1974 *ConAu 49,*
　　ConAu P-2
Moreno, Jose A 1928- *ConAu 25R*
Moreno, Martin *ConAu X*
Moreno, Pedro R 1947- *ConAu 69*
Moreno, Virginia R 1925- *DcLEL 1940*
Moreno Garcia, Jose M 1922- *IntAu&W 82*
Moreno Villa, Jose 1887-1955 *CIDMEL 80*
Morentz, Ethel Irene Klimeck 1925- *ConAu 29R*
Morentz, Pat *ConAu X*
Moresby, Louis *LongCTC, TwCA,*
　　TwCA SUP, TwCRGW
Moreton, Douglas Arthur *WrDr 84*
Moreton, John *ConAu X, WrDr 84*
Moretti, Marino 1885-1979 *CIDMEL 80,*
　　ConAu 89
Morewedge, Parviz 1934- *ConAu 93*
Morey, Charles *ConAu X, SmATA X*
Morey, Phyllis Alice 1907- *IntAu&W 82*
Morey, Roy D 1937- *ConAu 17R*
Morey, Walt 1907- *ConAu 29R, SmATA 3,*
　　TwCCW 83, WrDr 84
Morgan, Al 1920- *ConAu 1NR*
Morgan, Albert 1920- *ConAu 45*
Morgan, Alfred P 1889-1972 *SmATA 33[port]*
Morgan, Alfred Powell 1889-1972 *ConAu 107*
Morgan, Alison 1930- *TwCCW 83*
Morgan, Alison M 1930- *WrDr 84*
Morgan, Alison Mary 1930- *ConAu 1NR, –49,*
　　SmATA 30[port]
Morgan, Angela *ConAu X*
Morgan, Arlene *ConAu X*
Morgan, Arthur Ernest 1878-1975 *ConAu 3NR,*
　　–5R, –61
Morgan, Barton 1889- *ConAu P-1*
Morgan, Bayard Quincy 1883-1967 *ConAu P-1*
Morgan, Berry 1919- *ConAu 49, ConLC 6,*
　　DcLB 6
Morgan, Bill 1949- *ConAu 110*
Morgan, Brian 1919- *ConAu 5R*
Morgan, Brian S 1924?-1976 *ConAu 69*
Morgan, Bryan S 1923-1976 *ConAu 9NR*
Morgan, Bryan Stanford 1923-1978 *ConAu 5R,*
　　–8NR
Morgan, Carole *DrAP&F 83*
Morgan, Charles, Jr. 1930- *ConAu 17R*
Morgan, Charles H 1902- *ConAu 37R*
Morgan, Charles Langbridge 1894-1958 *CnMD,*
　　CroCD, LongCTC, ModBrL, ModWD,
　　TwCA, TwCA SUP, TwCWr
Morgan, Chester Alan 1914- *ConAu 17R,*
　　WrDr 84
Morgan, Christopher 1952- *ConAu 105*
Morgan, Claire *ConAu X, WorAu*
Morgan, Clifford T 1915-1976 *ConAu 1R, –4NR,*
　　–65
Morgan, Dale L 1914-1971 *ConAu 104*
Morgan, Dan 1925- *ConAu 37R, ConSFA,*
　　TwCSFW, WrDr 84
Morgan, Daniel C, Jr. 1931- *ConAu 17R*
Morgan, Darold H 1924- *ConAu 21R*

Morgan, Davd 1937- *ConAu 45*
Morgan, David Rhys 1937- *IntAu&W 82*
Morgan, David T 1937- *ConAu 69*
Morgan, Denise 1947- *IntAu&W 82*
Morgan, Dewi 1916- *ConAu 1R, –1NR,*
　　IntAu&W 82, WrDr 84
Morgan, DeWolfe *ConAmA*
Morgan, Diana 1910- *IntAu&W 82*
Morgan, Donald G 1911- *WrDr 84*
Morgan, Donald Grant 1911- *ConAu 17R,*
　　IntAu&W 82
Morgan, Edmund Sears 1916- *ConAu 4NR, –9R,*
　　DcLB 17[port]
Morgan, Edward James Ranembe 1900-1978
　　ConAu 108
Morgan, Edward P 1910- *ConAu P-1*
Morgan, Edwin 1920- *ConAu 3NR, –5R,*
　　ConP 80, DcLEL 1940, IntAu&W 82,
　　IntWWP 82, RGFMBP, WorAu 1970,
　　WrDr 84
Morgan, Elaine Neville 1920- *ConAu 41R,*
　　IntAu&W 82, WrDr 84
Morgan, Elizabeth 1947- *ConAu 108*
Morgan, Emanuel *ConAmA, ConAu X*
Morgan, Frank *ConAu X*
Morgan, Fred Bruce, Jr. 1919-1975 *ConAu 61,*
　　–65
Morgan, Fred Troy 1926- *ConAu 89*
Morgan, Frederick *DrAP&F 83*
Morgan, Frederick 1922- *ConAu 17R,*
　　ConLC 23[port], ConP 80, IntWWP 82,
　　WrDr 84
Morgan, G J *TwCWW*
Morgan, Geoffrey 1916- *ConAu 21R*
Morgan, Gerald 1925- *ConAu 41R*
Morgan, Glenn G 1926- *ConAu 9R*
Morgan, Gwen *ConAu 101*
Morgan, Gwyneth *ConAu X*
Morgan, H Wayne 1934- *ConAu 2NR, –5R*
Morgan, Helen 1921- *TwCCW 83, WrDr 84*
Morgan, Helen G 1921- *ConAu 57, SmATA 29*
Morgan, Henry *ConAu X*
Morgan, Howard G 1934- *WrDr 84*
Morgan, Irvonwy 1907-1982 *ConAu 107*
Morgan, J Elizabeth 1947- *ConAu 73*
Morgan, James Newton 1918- *ConAu 21R*
Morgan, Jane *ConAu X, SmATA X*
Morgan, Janet 1945- *ConAu 65*
Morgan, Jean 1922- *ConAu 102*
Morgan, Jefferson 1940- *ConAu 73*
Morgan, Jim 1950- *ConAu 45*
Morgan, Jinx *IntAu&W 82X*
Morgan, Joan 1905- *ConAu 5R, IntAu&W 82*
Morgan, Joe Warner 1912- *ConAu 9R*
Morgan, John *ConAu X, DrAP&F 83*
Morgan, John A, Jr. 1935- *ConAu 49*
Morgan, John S 1911- *WrDr 84*
Morgan, John S 1921- *ConAu 13R*
Morgan, John Stewart 1911- *IntAu&W 82*
Morgan, Judith 1939- *ConAu 49, IntAu&W 82*
Morgan, Kay Summersby 1909-1975 *ConAu 53*
Morgan, Kenneth Owen 1934- *ConAu 7NR,*
　　–13R
Morgan, Kenneth R 1916- *ConAu 13R*
Morgan, Lael 1936- *ConAu 5NR, –53,*
　　WrDr 84
Morgan, Len 1922- *IntAu&W 82*
Morgan, Lenore H 1907- *WrDr 84*
Morgan, Lenore H 1908-1976 *ConAu P-2,*
　　SmATA 8
Morgan, Louise *ConAu 9R, SmATA X*
Morgan, Lucy 1940- *ConAu 108*
Morgan, M Ruth 1942?-1983 *ConAu 109*
Morgan, Mal 1935- *IntWWP 82*
Morgan, Marabel *WrDr 84*
Morgan, Marabel 1937- *AuNews 1,*
　　ConAu 2NR, –49
Morgan, Marjorie *WrDr 84*
Morgan, Marjorie 1915- *ConAu X*
Morgan, Mark *WrDr 84*
Morgan, McKayla *ConAu X*
Morgan, Memo *ConAu X*
Morgan, Michael Croke 1911- *ConAu 93*
Morgan, Michaela *ConAu X*
Morgan, Murray Cromwell 1916- *ConAmTC,*
　　ConAu 107
Morgan, Neil 1924- *ConAu 2NR, –5R,*
　　WrDr 84
Morgan, Nicholas *ConAu X*
Morgan, Patricia 1944- *ConAu 89, WrDr 84*
Morgan, Patrick M 1940- *ConAu 37R*
Morgan, Paul 1928- *ConAu 61*

SmATA 24[port]
Mousseau, Jean Paul 1927- *CreCan 2*
Mousso, Dyne 1930- *CreCan 1*
Moustiers, Pierre Jean 1924- *IntAu&W 82*
Moutoux, John T 1901?-1979 *ConAu 89*
Mouzelis, Nicos P 1939- *ConAu 33R*
Mouzon, Olin T 1912- *ConAu 5R*
Movius, Geoffrey *DrAP&F 83*
Mow, Anna Beahm 1893- *ConAu 3NR, -9R,*
WrDr 84
Mowat, C L 1911-1970 *ConAu P-1*
Mowat, David 1943- *ConAu 77, ConDr 82,*
IntAu&W 82, WrDr 84
Mowat, Farley 1921- *ConLC 26[port],*
TwCCW 83, WrDr 84
Mowat, Farley McGill 1921- *ConAu 1R, -4NR,*
CreCan 2, DcLEL 1940, IntAu&W 82,
SmATA 3, WorAu
Mowat, R C 1913- *ConAu 29R*
Mowatt, Ian 1948- *ConAu 41R*
Mowery, Dee Dunsing *WrDr 84*
Mowery, William Byron 1899-1957 *TwCWW*
Mowitz, Robert J 1920- *ConAu 3NR, -5R*
Mowrer, Edgar Ansel 1892-1977 *ConAu 69,*
ConAu P-1, TwCA, TwCA SUP
Mowrer, Lilian T *ConAu 65, IntAu&W 82,*
WrDr 84
Mowrer, O Hobart 1907- *ConAu 1R, -1NR*
Mowrer, Paul Scott 1887-1971 *ConAu 4NR, -5R,*
-29R
Mowry, George E 1909- *ConAu 1R*
Mowshowitz, Abbe 1939- *ConAu 109*
Moxham, Robert Morgan 1919-1978 *ConAu 77*
Moxon, Roland James 1920- *WrDr 84*
Moyano, Daniel 1928- *ModLAL*
Moyer, Claire B 1905- *ConAu P-2*
Moyer, Elgin Sylvester 1890- *ConAu 5R*
Moyer, Jennifer *DrAP&F 83*
Moyer, K E 1919- *WrDr 84*
Moyer, Kenneth E 1919- *ConAu 33R*
Moyers, Bill 1934- *AuNews 1, ConAu 61*
Moyers, William Don 1934- *AuNews 1*
Moyes, Gertrude Patricia 1923- *IntAu&W 82*
Moyes, John Stoward 1884- *ConAu P-1*
Moyes, Norman Barr 1931- *ConAu 37R*
Moyes, Patricia 1923- *ConAu 17R,*
TwCCr&M 80, WrDr 84
Moyles, Lois *DrAP&F 83*
Moyles, R Gordon 1939- *ConAu 65*
Moynahan, Julian 1925- *ConAu 1R, -1NR,*
WrDr 84
Moyne, Baron 1905- *IntWWP 82*
Moyne, Bryan Walter Guinness 1905-
IntAu&W 82
Moyne, Ernest J 1916-1976 *ConAu P-2*
Moynihan, Daniel Patrick 1927- *ConAu 5R,*
DcLEL 1940, WrDr 84
Moynihan, John Dominic 1932- *ConAu 103,*
IntAu&W 82, WrDr 84
Moynihan, Maurice 1902- *ConAu 107,*
WrDr 84
Moynihan, William T 1927- *ConAu 21R*
Moyse-Bartlett, Hubert 1902?-1973? *ConAu 104*
Mozeson, Isaac Elchanan *DrAP&F 83*
Mozhayev, Boris Andreyevich 1923- *CIDMEL 80*
Mozley, Charles 1915- *SmATA 32*
Mphahlele, Ezekiel *DrAP&F 83*
Mphahlele, Ezekiel 1919- *ConAu 81,*
ConLC 25[port], ConNov 82, DcLEL 1940,
LongCTC, ModBlW, ModCmwL, TwCWr,
WhoTwCL, WorAu 1970, WrDr 84
Mphande, Lupenga 1947- *IntWWP 82*
Mpp *IntAu&W 82X*
Mqhayi, S E K 1875-1945 *ModBlW*
Mqhayi, Samuel Edward Krune Loliwe 1875-1945
ModCmwL
Mr. Cleveland *ConAu X*
Mr. Dooley 1867-1936 *LongCTC*
Mr. McGillicuddy *ConAu X*
Mr. Metropolitan Opera *ConAu X*
Mr. Sniff *ConAu X*
Mr. Wizard *ConAu X*
Mrabet, Mohammed 1940- *ConAu 97*
Mratos *IntAu&W 82X*
Mrazek, James E 1914- *ConAu 33R, WrDr 84*
Mrkonjic, Zvonimir 1938- *IntWWP 82*
Mroczka, Paul 1954- *NatPD 81*
Mrowczynski, Boleslaw 1910- *IntAu&W 82*
Mrozek, Donald J 1945- *ConAu 107*
Mrozek, Slavomir 1930- *CnMD SUP, WorAu*
Mrozek, Slawomir 1930- *CIDMEL 80,*
ConAu 13R, ConLC 3, -13, CroCD,

ModSL 2, ModWD
Mrs. Belloc-Lowndes *ConAu X*
Mrs. Fairstar *SmATA X*
Mrs. G *ConAu X*
Mrs. R F D *ConAu X*
M'Taggart, J M 1866-1925 *LongCTC*
M'Timkulu, Donald 1910- *ConAu 97*
Mtshali, Oswald 1940- *ConP 80, WrDr 84*
Mu, Yang *ConAu X*
Mucha, Jiri 1915- *ConAu 11NR, -21R,*
IntAu&W 82, ModSL 2, TwCWr,
WrDr 84
Muche, Georg 1895- *IntAu&W 82*
Muchnic, Helen 1903- *ConAu 1R, -5NR*
Mudd, Emily H 1898- *WrDr 84*
Mudd, Emily Hartshorne 1898- *ConAu 13R*
Mudd, Harvey *DrAP&F 83*
Mudd, Roger H 1928- *ConAu 105*
Mudd, Stuart 1893-1975 *ConAu 9R, -57*
Mude, O *ConAu X*
Mudge, Jean McClure 1933- *ConAu 5R, -6NR*
Mudge, Lewis Seymour 1929- *ConAu 89*
Mudgeon, Apeman *ConAu X*
Mudgett, Herman W *ConAu X*
Mudiarasan *IntWWP 82X*
Mudie, Charles Edward 1818-1890 *LongCTC*
Mudie, Ian 1911- *ConAu 25R, ConP 80,*
DcLEL 1940, WrDr 84
Mudrick, Marvin 1921- *ConAu 25R, WrDr 84*
Muecke, D C 1919- *ConAu 53*
Muehl, Lois Baker 1920- *ConAu 1R, WrDr 84*
Muehl, William 1919- *ConAu 45*
Muehlen, Norbert 1909-1981 *ConAu 104, -69*
Muehsam, Gerd 1913?-1979 *ConAu 93*
Muelder, Walter George 1907- *ConAu P-1*
Mueller, Amelia 1911- *ConAu 57*
Mueller, Barbara R 1925- *ConAu 9R*
Mueller, Charles S 1929- *ConAu 5NR, -13R*
Mueller, Claus 1941- *ConAu 65*
Mueller, David L 1929- *ConAu 29R, WrDr 84*
Mueller, Dorothy 1901- *ConAu 102*
Mueller, Erwin W 1911-1977 *ConAu 69*
Mueller, Gerald F 1927- *ConAu 13R*
Mueller, Gerhard G 1930- *ConAu 25R*
Mueller, Gerhard O W 1926- *ConAu 1R, -5NR,*
IntAu&W 82
Mueller, Gerhardt *ConAu X*
Mueller, Gustav Emil 1898- *ConAu 7NR, -17R,*
IntAu&W 82
Mueller, James W 1941- *ConAu 57*
Mueller, John E 1937- *ConAu 37R, -61*
Mueller, Kate Hevner 1898- *ConAu 41R,*
IntAu&W 82
Mueller, Klaus Andrew 1921- *ConAu 4NR, -49*
Mueller, Lisel *DrAP&F 83*
Mueller, Lisel 1924- *ConAu 93, ConLC 13*
Mueller, M G 1925- *ConAu 17R*
Mueller, Melinda 1953- *IntWWP 82*
Mueller, Merrill 1916-1980 *ConAu 103*
Mueller, Red *ConAu X*
Mueller, Reuben Herbert 1897-1982 *ConAu 107*
Mueller, Robert Emmett 1925- *ConAu 1R,*
WrDr 84
Mueller, Robert Kirk 1913- *ConAu 73*
Mueller, Virginia 1924- *ConAu 10NR, -65,*
SmATA 28[port]
Mueller, Willard Fritz 1925- *ConAu 17R*
Mueller, William R 1916- *ConAu 1R, -2NR,*
WrDr 84
Muenchen, Al 1917- *ConAu 49*
Muffett, D J M 1919- *ConAu 45*
Mufti, Masud 1934- *IntAu&W 82*
Muganwa-Nsiku-Jensi *IntAu&W 82X*
Muggeridge, Malcolm 1903- *AuNews 1,*
ConAu 101, WorAu, WrDr 84
Muggeson, Margaret Elizabeth 1942- *ConAu 103,*
IntAu&W 82, WrDr 84
Mugler, James Kerr *DrAP&F 83*
Muhajir, El 1944- *ConAu X*
Muhajir, El *DrAP&F 83*
Muheim, Harry Miles 1920- *ConAu 85*
Muhlenfeld, Elisabeth 1944- *ConAu 108*
Muhlhausen, John Prague 1940- *ConAu 61*
Muhlstock, Louis 1904- *CreCan 1*
Muhringer, Doris 1920- *IntWWP 82*
Mui, Hoh-Cheung 1916- *ConAu 45*
Muileman, Kathryn Saltzman 1946- *ConAu 85*
Muilenburg, Grace 1913- *ConAu 61*
Muir, Alan *IntAu&W 82X*
Muir, Augustus *WrDr 84*
Muir, Augustus 1892- *ConAu 13R,*
IntAu&W 82

Muir, Barbara Kenrick 1908- *ConAu 9R*
Muir, Dexter *ConAu X, TwCCr&M 80,*
WrDr 84
Muir, Edwin 1887-1959 *CnMWL, ConAu 104,*
ConLCrt 82, LongCTC, ModBrL,
ModBrL SUP, RGFMBP, TwCA,
TwCA SUP, TwCLC 2, TwCWr,
WhoTwCL
Muir, Frank 1920- *ConAu 81,*
SmATA 30[port], WrDr 84
Muir, Helen 1937- *AuNews 2, DcLB 14[port]*
Muir, Jane *ConAu X*
Muir, Jean 1906-1973 *ConAu 41R, ConAu P-2*
Muir, John 1838-1914 *TwCA, TwCA SUP*
Muir, Kenneth 1907- *ConAu 1R, -4NR,*
IntAu&W 82, WrDr 84
Muir, Malcolm 1885-1979 *ConAu 85, -93*
Muir, Marie Agnes 1904- *ConAu 1R, -5NR,*
IntAu&W 82
Muir, Percival Horace 1894-1979 *ConAu 5NR,*
-9R, -97, IntAu&W 82
Muir, Percy H 1894-1979 *ConAu X*
Muir, Ramsay 1872-1941 *LongCTC*
Muir, Richard 1943- *ConAu 106, WrDr 84*
Muir, William Ker, Jr. 1931- *ConAu 53*
Muirden, Bruce Wallace 1928- *WrDr 84*
Muirhead, Ian Adair 1913- *ConAu 13R,*
WrDr 84
Muirhead, Thorburn 1899- *ConAu 5R*
Muizniece, Lalita *IntWWP 82X*
Muizniece, Lalita Ruta 1935- *IntWWP 82*
Muiznieks, Sarma Gundega 1960- *IntWWP 82*
Mujica Lainez, Manuel 1910- *ConAu 81,*
IntAu&W 82, ModLAL
Mukerji, Dhan Gopal 1890-1936 *LongCTC,*
TwCA, TwCCW 83
Mukerji, Kshitimohon 1920- *ConAu 17R*
Mukherjee, Bharati 1940- *ConAu 107,*
WrDr 84
Mukherjee, Kamalakanto 1913- *IntWWP 82*
Mukherjee, Meenakshi 1937- *ConAu 65*
Mukherjee, Ramkrishna 1919- *ConAu 7NR, -57*
Mukherji, Brittendu Kumar 1951- *IntWWP 82*
Mukhopadhyaya, Uma Prasad 1902-
IntAu&W 82
Mulac, Margaret E 1912- *ConAu 2NR, -5R*
Mulaisho, Dominic 1933- *ConAu 97*
Mularchyk, Sylva *ConAu 93*
Mulcahy, Lucille Burnett *ConAu 5R,*
SmATA 12
Mulchrone, Vincent 1919?-1977 *ConAu 73*
Mulder, Arnold 1885-1959 *MichAu 80*
Mulder, Robert Glenn 1936- *IntWWP 82*
Mulder, Tiny 1921- *IntWWP 82*
Muldoon, Paul 1951- *ConP 80, WrDr 84*
Muldoon, Roland W 1941- *ConAu 105*
Mule, Marty 1944- *ConAu 108*
Mulesko, Angelo *ConAu X, IntAu&W 82X*
Mulford, Clarence Edward 1883-1956 *LongCTC,*
TwCA, TwCA SUP, TwCWW
Mulford, David Campbell 1937- *ConAu 9R*
Mulford, Maxene Fabe *DrAP&F 83*
Mulgan, Catherine *SmATA X*
Mulgan, Catherine 1931- *ConAu 11NR*
Mulgan, John Alan Edward 1911-1945 *LongCTC*
Mulgrew, Peter David 1927- *ConAu 13R*
Mulgrue, George Edward 1911- *IntAu&W 82*
Mulhauser, Ruth 1913- *WrDr 84*
Mulhauser, Ruth 1913-1980 *ConAu 5R, -7NR*
Mulhearn, John 1932- *ConAu 65*
Mulholland, Jim 1949- *ConAu 61*
Mulholland, John 1898-1970 *ConAu 5R, -89*
Mulholland, John F 1903- *ConAu 41R*
Mulikita, Fwanyanga Matale 1928- *DcLEL 1940*
Mulisch, Harry Kurt Victor 1927- *CIDMEL 80,*
ConAu 6NR, -9R
Mulkeen, Anne 1927- *ConAu X, WrDr 84*
Mulkeen, Thomas P 1923- *ConAu 85*
Mulkerne, Donald James Dennis 1921-
ConAu 9R
Mulkerns, Val 1925- *IntAu&W 82*
Mull, Martin 1943- *ConAu 105, ConLC 17*
Mullally, Frederic 1920- *ConAu 1R, -1NR*
Mullaly, Edward 1941- *ConAu 41R*
Mullan, Fitzhugh 1942- *ConAu 69*
Mullaney, Thomas E 1922?-1978 *ConAu 81, -93*
Mullard, Chris 1944- *WrDr 84*
Mullarky, Taylor 1922- *ConAu 103*
Mullen, Barbara 1914-1979 *ConAu 85*
Mullen, C J J *ConAu X*
Mullen, Cyril J 1908- *ConAu 61*
Mullen, Dore *ConAu X*

Mullen, Dorothy 1933- *ConAu 104*
Mullen, Edward John, Jr. 1942- *ConAu 2NR,* *−49*
Mullen, Harris H 1924- *ConAu 69*
Mullen, James H 1924- *ConAu 1R*
Mullen, Robert R 1908- *ConAu P-1*
Mullen, Thomas James 1934- *ConAu 5NR, −9R*
Mullen, William Charles 1944- *ConAu 73*
Mullenix, Dennis 1941- *WrDr 84*
Muller, Alexander V 1932- *ConAu 45*
Muller, Andre 1926- *CreCan 1*
Muller, Armin 1928- *IntAu&W 82*
Muller, Artur 1909- *CnMD, IntAu&W 82*
Muller, Charles G 1897- *ConAu 1R, −2NR,* *IntAu&W 82, WrDr 84*
Muller, Charles Geoffrey *ConAu X*
Muller, Edward John 1916- *ConAu 57*
Muller, Gilbert H 1941- *ConAu 41R*
Muller, H J 1890-1967 *ConAu 106*
Muller, Heiner 1928- *CnMD*
Muller, Heiner 1929- *CIDMEL 80, CroCD*
Muller, Herbert J 1905- *WrDr 84*
Muller, Herbert Joseph 1905-1967 *ConAu 1R,* *−1NR, TwCA SUP*
Muller, Herman J 1909- *ConAu 73*
Muller, John E *ConAu X, ConSFA*
Muller, John P 1940- *ConAu 103*
Muller, Leo C, Jr. 1924- *ConAu 5R*
Muller, Marcia 1944- *ConAu 81*
Muller, Peter O 1942- *ConAu 110*
Muller, Priscilla E 1930- *ConAu 61*
Muller, Robert 1923- *ConAu 103*
Muller, Robert 1925- *WrDr 84*
Muller, Ronald E 1939- *ConAu 107*
Muller, Siegfried H 1902-1965 *ConAu P-1*
Muller-Bergh, Klaus 1936- *IntAu&W 82*
Muller-Felsenburg, Alfred 1926- *IntAu&W 82*
Mullern, Harryette *DrAP&F 83*
Mullett, John St. Hilary 1925- *WrDr 84*
Mulligan, Hugh A 1925- *ConAu 11NR, −21R*
Mulligan, James J 1936- *ConAu 45*
Mulligan, John Joseph 1918- *ConAu 33R*
Mulligan, Raymond A 1914- *ConAu 37R,* *WrDr 84*
Mulligan, Robert Smith 1941- *ConAu 65*
Mulliken, Robert Sanderson 1896- *ConAu 109*
Mullin, Michael 1944- *ConAu 103*
Mullin, Robert N 1893- *ConAu 89*
Mullin, Willard 1902-1978 *ConAu 89*
Mullings, Llewellyn M 1932- *ConAu 37R*
Mullings, Peter Coningsby 1928- *IntAu&W 82*
Mullins, Aloysius 1910- *ConAu P-1*
Mullins, Ann *ConAu X*
Mullins, Carolyn J 1940- *ConAu 10NR, −65*
Mullins, Claud 1887-1968 *ConAu P-1*
Mullins, Edward S 1922- *ConAu 17R,* *SmATA 10*
Mullins, Edwin 1933- *ConAu 4NR, −53,* *IntAu&W 82, WrDr 84*
Mullins, Helen 1899- *IntWWP 82*
Mullins, Helene *DrAP&F 83*
Mullins, Helene 1899- *ConAu 77, WrDr 84*
Mullins, Nicholas C 1939- *ConAu 33R*
Mullins, Vera Cooper 1903- *ConAu 61*
Mulloy, Elizabeth D 1945- *ConAu 93*
Mulock, Dinah Maria *SmATA X*
Multhauf, Robert P 1919- *ConAu 93*
Mulvaney, Johannes 1912- *IntAu&W 82*
Mulvanity, George 1903?-1976 *ConAu 69*
Mulvey, Ruth Watt *ConAu X*
Mulvihill, Edward Robert 1917- *ConAu 9R*
Mulvihill, William *DrAP&F 83*
Mulvihill, William Patrick 1923- *ConAu 1R,* *SmATA 8*
Mulville, Frank 1924- *ConAu 107*
Mumey, Glen A 1933- *ConAu 73*
Mumford, Bob 1930- *ConAu 103*
Mumford, Emily 1920- *ConAu 57*
Mumford, Erika *DrAP&F 83*
Mumford, Lewis 1895- *ConAmA, ConAu 1R,* *−5NR, LongCTC, ModAL, ModAL SUP,* *TwCA, TwCA SUP*
Mumford, Ruth *WrDr 84*
Mumford, Samuel T 1906- *LivgBAA*
Mummery, David Rest *WrDr 84*
Mummery, David Rest 1932- *ConAu 29R*
Mun *SmATA X*
Munari, Bruno 1907- *ConAu 73, SmATA 15*
Munby, Alan Noel Latimer 1913-1974 *ConAu 53*
Munby, D L 1919-1976 *ConAu 1R, −2NR*
Munby, Lionel Maxwell 1918- *IntAu&W 82*

Munce, Ruth Hill 1898- *ConAu P-1,* *SmATA 12*
Munch, Peter A 1908- *ConAu 29R*
Munch, Theodore W 1919- *ConAu 57*
Munch-Petersen, Gustaf 1912-1938 *CIDMEL 80*
Munchhausen, Baron Borries Von 1874-1945 *CIDMEL 80*
Muncy, Raymond Lee 1928- *ConAu 49*
Mund, Vernon A 1906- *ConAu 1R*
Mundel, Marvin Everett 1916- *ConAu 21R,* *WrDr 84*
Mundell, Robert A 1932- *ConAu 2NR, −45*
Mundell, William Daniel 1913- *ConAu 73*
Mundis, Hester *DrAP&F 83*
Mundis, Hester 1938- *ConAu 69, WrDr 84*
Mundis, Jerrold *DrAP&F 83*
Mundis, Jerrold 1941- *ConAu 11NR, −69,* *WrDr 84*
Mundlak, Max 1899- *ConAu P-1*
Mundy, John Hine 1917- *ConAu 45*
Mundy, Max *ConAu X, WrDr 84*
Mundy, Talbot Chetwynd 1879-1940 *TwCA,* *TwCA SUP*
Munford, William Arthur 1911- *IntAu&W 82,* *WrDr 84*
Mungello, David Emil 1943- *ConAu 110*
Munger, Al *ConAu X*
Munger, Frank James 1929- *ConAu 1R, −1NR*
Munger, Hortense Roberta *ConAu X*
Munger, Robert Boyd 1910- *ConAu 77*
Mungo, Raymond 1946- *ConAu 2NR, −49*
Mungoshi, Charles 1947- *IntAu&W 82*
Munholland, J Kim 1934- *ConAu 29R*
Muni, Moodgal *IntWWP 82X*
Munir, Muhammad 1895-1981 *ConAu 108*
Munitz, Milton K 1913- *ConAu 93*
Muniz, Carlos 1927- *CIDMEL 80, CroCD*
Munk, Arthur W 1909- *ConAu 7NR, −13R*
Munk, Erika 1939- *ConAu 17R*
Munk, Kai 1898-1944 *CnMD*
Munk, Kaj Harald Leininger 1898-1944 *CIDMEL 80, ModWD, TwCWr, WorAu*
Munn, Glenn 1890?-1977 *ConAu 73*
Munn, H Warner 1903- *ConAu 21R, ConSFA*
Munn, H Warner 1903-1981 *ConAu 11NR*
Munn, Harry Victor 1910- *IntWWP 82*
Munn, Hart *ConAu X*
Munnell, Alicia H 1942- *ConAu 73*
Muno, Jean 1924- *CIDMEL 80*
Munonye, John 1929- *ConAu 103, ConNov 82,* *DcLEL 1940, IntAu&W 82, WrDr 84*
Munowitz, Ken 1935-1977 *SmATA 14*
Munoz, Braulio 1946- *ConAu 110*
Munoz-Marin, Luis 1898-1980 *ConAu 97*
Munoz Ortiz, Sofia 1938- *IntAu&W 82*
Munoz Seca, Pedro 1881-1936 *CIDMEL 80*
Munro, Alice 1931- *AuNews 2, ConAu 33R,* *ConLC 6, −10, −19, ConNov 82, CreCan 1,* *DcLEL 1940, SmATA 29[port], WrDr 84*
Munro, Bertha 1887- *ConAu 45*
Munro, C K 1889- *ConAu X*
Munro, Charles Kirkpatrick 1889- *CnMD,* *LongCTC, ModBrL*
Munro, Christy *ConAu X*
Munro, Dana Gardner 1892- *ConAu 1R*
Munro, David *ConAu X*
Munro, Duncan H *ConAu X*
Munro, Eleanor C 1928- *ConAu 1R*
Munro, Grant 1923- *CreCan 1*
Munro, Hector Hugh 1870-1916 *ConAu 104,* *LongCTC, ModBrL, TwCA, TwCA SUP,* *TwCLC 3*
Munro, Hugh Macfarlane *WrDr 84*
Munro, Ian S 1914- *ConAu 29R, WrDr 84*
Munro, James *ConAu X*
Munro, John 1938- *ConAu 41R*
Munro, John M 1932- *ConAu 11NR, −69,* *WrDr 84*
Munro, Leslie Knox 1901-1974 *ConAu 49*
Munro, Mary *ConAu 49, WrDr 84*
Munro, Neil 1864-1930 *LongCTC, TwCA*
Munro, Ronald Eadie *IntAu&W 82X,* *IntWWP 82X, WrDr 84*
Munro, Thomas 1897-1974 *ConAu 3NR, −5R*
Munroe, Elizabeth L 1900- *ConAu 2NR, −17R*
Munroe, Elizabeth Lee 1900- *IntWWP 82*
Munroe, Hugh *ConAu 9R*
Munroe, John A 1914- *ConAu 49*
Munroe, Kirk 1850-1930 *TwCA*
Munrow, David John 1942-1976 *ConAu 103, −106*
Munsch, Robert 1945- *TwCCW 83*
Munsey, Cecil Richard, Jr. 1935- *ConAu 41R*

Munsey, Frank A 1854-1925 *DcLB 25[port]*
Munshi, Shehnaaz *ConAu X*
Munshower, Susan Scott 1942- *IntWWP 82*
Munshower, Suzanne 1945- *ConAu 97*
Munsinger, Harry 1935- *ConAu 45*
Munsinger, Lynn 1951- *SmATA 33[port]*
Munson, Amelia H d1972 *ConAu 33R*
Munson, Byron Edwin 1921- *ConAu 41R*
Munson, Charlie E 1877- *ConAu 57*
Munson, Don 1908- *ConAu 73*
Munson, Fred C 1928- *ConAu 33R*
Munson, Gorham Bert 1896-1969 *ConAu P-1,* *TwCA, TwCA SUP*
Munson, Harold L 1923- *ConAu 29R*
Munson, Kenneth George 1929- *IntAu&W 82*
Munson, Lou *ConAu X*
Munson, Mary Lou 1935- *ConAu 9R*
Munson, Thomas Nolan 1924- *ConAu 1R,* *IntAu&W 82, WrDr 84*
Munson, Thurman 1947-1979 *ConAu 108, −89*
Munson, Tunie 1946- *SmATA 15*
Munson-Benson, Tunie 1946- *ConAu 77*
Munsterberg, Hugo 1916- *ConAu 2NR, −5R*
Munsterhjelm, Erik 1905- *ConAu 49*
Munter, Robert 1926- *ConAu 21R*
Munthe, Adam John 1946- *ConAu 107*
Munthe, Axel Martin Fredrik 1857-1949 *LongCTC, TwCA, TwCA SUP, TwCWr*
Munthe, Frances 1915- *ConAu 9R*
Munthe, Malcolm Grane 1920- *ConAu 5R*
Munton, Alan 1945- *ConAu 107*
Muntz, Hope 1907- *IntAu&W 82*
Muntz, Isabelle Hope 1907- *ConAu 13R*
Muntz, James *ConAu X*
Muntz, Laura *CreCan 1*
Munves, James 1922- *ConAu 3NR, −5R,* *SmATA 30*
Munz, Peter 1921- *ConAu 13R, IntAu&W 82,* *WrDr 84*
Munz, Philip Alexander 1892- *ConAu 5R*
Munzer, Martha E 1899- *ConAu 1R, −4NR,* *IntAu&W 82, SmATA 4, WrDr 84*
Mur *IntAu&W 82X*
Murad, Anatol 1904- *ConAu 73, IntAu&W 82*
Muraji Uchiki, Tamotsu Uchiki 1904- *IntAu&W 82*
Murajiuchiki *IntAu&W 82X*
Muralt, Inka Von 1919- *IntAu&W 82*
Murari, Timeri N 1941- *ConAu 102*
Muratori, Fred *DrAP&F 83*
Muratori, Fred 1951- *IntWWP 82*
Muravin, Victor R 1929- *ConAu 85,* *IntAu&W 82*
Murawski, Benjamin J 1926- *ConAu 45*
Murawski, Elisabeth *DrAP&F 83*
Murbarger, Nell Lounsberry 1909- *ConAu P-1*
Murch, Edward William Lionel 1920- *ConAu 61,* *IntAu&W 82*
Murch, James DeForest 1892-1973 *ConAu 4NR,* *−5R*
Murchie, Guy 1907- *ConAu 1R, WrDr 84*
Murden, Forrest D, Jr. 1921-1977 *ConAu 73*
Murdick, Robert Gordon 1920- *ConAu 5R,* *−6NR*
Murdin, Paul 1942- *ConAu 106*
Murdoch, Derrick 1909- *ConAu 89*
Murdoch, Iris 1919- *ConAu 8NR, −13R,* *ConDr 82, ConLC 1, −2, −3, −4, −6, −8, −11,* *−15, −22[port], ConNov 82, DcLB 14[port],* *LongCTC, ModBrL, ModBrL SUP,* *TwCWr, WhoTwCL, WorAu, WrDr 84*
Murdoch, Jean Iris 1919- *DcLEL 1940*
Murdoch, Joseph S F 1919- *ConAu 102*
Murdock, Eugene C 1921- *ConAu 33R,* *WrDr 84*
Murdock, George Peter 1897- *ConAu P-1*
Murdock, Kenneth Ballard 1895-1975 *ConAu 61,* *−65*
Murdock, Laurette P 1900- *ConAu 101*
Murdock, Myrtle Cheney 1886?-1980 *ConAu 97*
Murdy, Louise Baughan 1935- *ConAu 33R,* *WrDr 84*
Mure, G R G 1893-1979 *ConAu 107*
Murena, H A 1923- *ModLAL*
Murguia, Alejandro *DrAP&F 83*
Murie, Margaret E 1902- *WrDr 84*
Murie, Margaret Elizabeth 1902- *ConAu 110*
Muro, Diane Patricia 1940- *ConAu 65*
Muro, James J 1934- *ConAu 33R*
Murphet, Howard 1906- *ConAu 61*
Murphey, Murray Griffin 1928- *ConAu 5R,* *−6NR*

Murphey, Rhoads 1919- *ConAu 33R*, *WrDr 84*
Murphey, Robert W 1916- *ConAu 13R*
Murphy, Agnes Keating 1912- *ConAu 1R*,
 WrDr 84
Murphy, Arthur Lister 1906- *ConAu 77*,
 ConDr 82, *IntAu&W 82*, *WrDr 84*
Murphy, Barbara Beasley *DrAP&F 83*
Murphy, Barbara Beasley 1933- *ConAu 41R*,
 SmATA 5
Murphy, Beatrice M 1908- *ConAu 9NR*, *-53*,
 LivgBAA
Murphy, Brian 1931- *ConAu 21R*
Murphy, Brian 1939- *ConAu 108*
Murphy, Buck *ConAu X*
Murphy, C L *ConAu X*, *WrDr 84*
Murphy, Charlotte A 1924- *ConAu 105*
Murphy, Cornelius Francis, Jr. 1933- *ConAu 89*
Murphy, Dervla Mary 1931- *ConAu 103*,
 IntAu&W 82, *WrDr 84*
Murphy, Dorothy Dey 1911?-1983 *ConAu 110*
Murphy, E Jefferson 1926- *ConAu 25R*,
 SmATA 4, *WrDr 84*
Murphy, Earl Finbar 1928- *ConAu 13R*
Murphy, Ed *ConAu X*
Murphy, Edward Francis 1914- *ConAu 102*
Murphy, Edward J 1927- *ConAu 37R*
Murphy, Elaine *DrAP&F 83*
Murphy, Emmy Lou Osborne 1910- *ConAu 5R*
Murphy, Francis 1932- *ConAu 7NR*, *-13R*
Murphy, Frank *DrAP&F 83*
Murphy, Frank Hughes 1940- *ConAu 61*
Murphy, Fred P 1889-1979 *ConAu 89*
Murphy, Gardner 1895-1979 *ConAu 85*, *-93*,
 TwCA SUP
Murphy, George E 1948- *ConAu 77*
Murphy, George E, Jr. *DrAP&F 83*
Murphy, George G S 1924- *ConAu 21R*
Murphy, George Lloyd 1902- *ConAu 45*
Murphy, Gordon J *WrDr 84*
Murphy, Grace E Barstow 1888-1975 *ConAu 57*
Murphy, Hazel *ConAu X*
Murphy, Herta A 1908- *ConAu 49*
Murphy, Irene L 1920- *ConAu 53*
Murphy, J Carter 1921- *ConAu 13R*
Murphy, James F 1943- *ConAu 8NR*, *-61*
Murphy, James J 1923- *ConAu 33R*
Murphy, James M 1917- *ConAu 29R*
Murphy, James R 1932-1966? *ConAu P-1*
Murphy, Jane Brevoort Walden 1902?-1980
 ConAu 97
Murphy, Jill 1949- *ConAu 105*, *TwCCW 83*
Murphy, Jim 1947- *SmATA 32*
Murphy, John *ConAu X*
Murphy, John L 1924- *ConAu 1R*
Murphy, Joseph Francis 1917- *IntWWP 82*
Murphy, Kay A *DrAP&F 83*
Murphy, Larry *ConAu X*
Murphy, Lawrence A 1924- *ConAu 104*
Murphy, Lawrence R 1942- *ConAu 105*
Murphy, Lois Barclay 1902- *ConAu 1R*, *-4NR*
Murphy, Louis J *ConAu X*
Murphy, Mario *ConAu X*
Murphy, Marion Fisher 1902- *ConAu 53*
Murphy, Michael *DrAP&F 83*
Murphy, Michael 1930- *ConAu 73*
Murphy, Nonie Carol *ConAu X*
Murphy, Pat *ConAu X*, *SmATA 4*
Murphy, Patrick T 1939- *ConAu 108*
Murphy, Patrick V 1920- *ConAu 105*
Murphy, Paul L 1923- *ConAu 7NR*, *-17R*
Murphy, Peter Anthony 1945- *IntAu&W 82*,
 IntWWP 82
Murphy, Peter E *DrAP&F 83*
Murphy, Raymond E 1898- *ConAu 41R*
Murphy, Reg 1934- *ConAu 33R*
Murphy, Rich *DrAP&F 83*
Murphy, Richard 1927- *ConAu 29R*, *ConP 80*,
 DcLEL 1940, *ModBrL SUP*, *WorAu*,
 WrDr 84
Murphy, Richard Thomas 1908- *ConAu 1R*,
 -1NR, *WrDr 84*
Murphy, Robert Cushman 1887-1973 *ConAu 41R*,
 ConAu P-2
Murphy, Robert D 1894-1978 *ConAu 73*,
 ConAu P-1
Murphy, Robert William 1902-1971 *ConAu 29R*,
 ConAu P-1, *SmATA 10*
Murphy, Roland Edmund 1917- *ConAu 5R*,
 -6NR, *WrDr 84*
Murphy, Romaine 1941- *ConAu 77*
Murphy, Sharon M 1940- *ConAu 77*
Murphy, Sheila Ellen 1951- *IntWWP 82*

Murphy, Shirley R 1928- *WrDr 84*
Murphy, Shirley Rousseau 1928- *ConAu 21R*
Murphy, Terrence J 1921- *ConAu 5R*
Murphy, Thelma 1907- *IntWWP 82*
Murphy, Thomas 1935- *ConAu 101*, *ConDr 82*,
 IntAu&W 82, *WrDr 84*
Murphy, Thomas Basil, Jr. 1935- *ConAu 11NR*,
 -69
Murphy, Thomas P 1931- *ConAu 41R*
Murphy, Tom *ConAu X*
Murphy, Walter Francis 1929- *ConAu 1R*, *-2NR*,
 IntAu&W 82, *WrDr 84*
Murphy, Warren B 1933- *ConAu 33R*
Murphy, William Francis 1906- *ConAu 17R*,
 WrDr 84
Murphy, William M 1916- *ConAu 85*,
 IntAu&W 82
Murphy-O'Connor, Jerome James 1935-
 ConAu 5NR, *-13R*
Murra, John V 1916- *ConAu 1NR*, *-45*
Murrah, David Joe 1941- *ConAu 106*
Murranka, Mary 1944- *WrDr 84*
Murray, Adrian *ConAu X*
Murray, Albert 1916- *ConAu 49*, *LivgBAA*,
 WrDr 84
Murray, Andrew Evans 1917- *ConAu 25R*
Murray, Beatrice *ConAu X*, *WrDr 84*
Murray, Bruce C 1931- *ConAu 103*
Murray, Carole *DrAP&F 83*
Murray, Catherine *DrAP&F 83*
Murray, Clara Elizabeth 1894- *ConAu P-1*
Murray, Cromwell *ConAu X*
Murray, Dan *DrAP&F 83*
Murray, Daniel E 1925- *ConAu 45*
Murray, David Leslie 1888-1962 *LongCTC*
Murray, Dick 1924- *ConAu 106*
Murray, Donald M 1924- *ConAu 1R*
Murray, Dorothy Garst 1915- *ConAu 21R*
Murray, Earl P 1950- *IntAu&W 82*
Murray, Edmund P 1930- *ConAu 81*
Murray, Edna *ConAu X*
Murray, Edward 1928- *ConAu 1NR*, *-49*
Murray, Edward J 1928- *ConAu 13R*
Murray, Elwood 1897- *ConAu 73*
Murray, Eugene Bernard 1927- *ConAu 104*
Murray, Eva VonGencsy *CreCan 2*
Murray, Frances 1928- *ConAu X*, *TwCRGW*
Murray, G E *DrAP&F 83*
Murray, G E 1945- *ConAu 5NR*, *-53*
Murray, George 1909- *ConAu 17R*
Murray, George McIntosh 1900-1970 *ConAu P-1*
Murray, Gilbert *LongCTC*
Murray, Gilbert 1866-1957 *ConAu 110*,
 DcLB 10[port], *LongCTC*, *ModBrL*,
 TwCA, *TwCA SUP*
Murray, Hallard T, Jr. 1937- *ConAu 17R*
Murray, Irene 1913- *ConAu X*, *-1R*
Murray, J Alex *ConAu 41R*
Murray, J Harley 1910?-1977 *ConAu 73*
Murray, J Joseph 1915- *ConAu 4NR*
Murray, James 1946- *ConAu 1NR*
Murray, James Patrick 1946- *ConAu 49*,
 LivgBAA
Murray, Jerome 1928- *ConAu 33R*, *WrDr 84*
Murray, Jesse George 1909- *IntAu&W 82*
Murray, Jill *WrDr 84*
Murray, Jim 1919- *ConAu 65*
Murray, Joan *DrAP&F 83*
Murray, Joan 1945- *ConAu 77*
Murray, Joan E 1941- *ConAu 81*, *LivgBAA*
Murray, John 1898- *WrDr 84*
Murray, John 1923- *ConAu 4NR*, *-5R*
Murray, John Bernard 1915- *ConAu 41R*
Murray, John Courtney 1904-1967 *ConAu 106*
Murray, John E, Jr. 1932- *ConAu 45*
Murray, John F 1923-1977 *ConAu 69*,
 ConAu P-2
Murray, John Joseph 1915- *ConAu 5R*,
 WrDr 84
Murray, John L 1937- *ConAu 108*
Murray, John MacDougall 1910- *ConAu 33R*
Murray, K F *ConAu X*
Murray, K M Elisabeth 1909- *ConAu 77*
Murray, Katherine Maud Elisabeth 1909-
 IntAu&W 82
Murray, Keith Alexander 1910- *ConAu P-2*
Murray, Ken *ConAu X*
Murray, Les A 1938- *ConAu 11NR*, *-21R*,
 ConP 80, *IntWWP 82X*, *WrDr 84*
Murray, Leslie Allan 1938- *DcLEL 1940*,
 IntWWP 82
Murray, Lois Smith 1906- *ConAu 37R*

Murray, Margaret *IntAu&W 82X*
Murray, Margaret Alice 1863-1963 *ConAu 5R*
Murray, Marian *ConAu 41R*, *SmATA 5*
Murray, Mary 1925- *ConAu 25R*
Murray, Sister Mary Verona 1909- *ConAu 17R*
Murray, Max 1901-1956 *TwCCr&M 80*
Murray, Maynard 1911?-1983 *ConAu 110*
Murray, Merrill G 1900?-1976 *ConAu 69*
Murray, Michael *ConAu X*
Murray, Michael V 1906- *ConAu 5R*
Murray, Michele 1933-1974 *ConAu 49*,
 SmATA 7
Murray, Neil *IntWWP 82X*
Murray, Neil James 1956- *IntWWP 82*
Murray, Patrick 1908- *IntAu&W 82*
Murray, Peter 1920- *ConAu 10NR*, *-13R*
Murray, Philip 1924- *ConAu 65*
Murray, R H 1933- *ConAu 25R*
Murray, Ralph L 1921- *ConAu 13R*
Murray, Rebecca 1936- *ConAu 57*
Murray, Robert Allen 1929- *ConAu 29R*,
 WrDr 84
Murray, Robert Gray 1936- *CreCan 1*
Murray, Robert Keith 1922- *ConAu 53*
Murray, Robert Patrick Ruthven 1925-
 IntAu&W 82
Murray, Roger N 1932- *ConAu 21R*
Murray, Ruth Lovell 1900- *ConAu 103*
Murray, Sonia Bennett 1936- *ConAu 65*
Murray, Thomas C 1873-1959 *CnMD*, *LongCTC*,
 ModWD, *TwCA SUP*
Murray, Thomas J 1943- *ConAu 77*
Murray, Walter I 1910-1978 *ConAu 73*, *-85*,
 LivgBAA
Murray, William *DrAP&F 83*
Murray, William Cotter 1929- *ConAu 53*
Murray, William Hutchison 1913- *ConAu 4NR*,
 -9R, *IntAu&W 82*, *WrDr 84*
Murray, William J, III 1946- *ConAu 110*
Murray-Brown, Jeremy 1932- *ConAu 77*
Murray Hill *TwCA*, *TwCA SUP*
Murray-Oliver, Anthony A St. C Murray 1915-
 IntAu&W 82
Murray-Smith, Stephen 1922- *ConAu 103*,
 WrDr 84
Murrell, Elsie Kathleen Seth-Smith 1883-
 ConAu P-1
Murrett, John Charles 1892- *ConAu 1R*
Murros, Helena 1914- *IntAu&W 82*
Murrow, Casey 1945- *ConAu 97*
Murrow, Edward R 1908-1965 *ConAu 103*, *-89*
Murry, Colin Middleton 1926- *IntAu&W 82X*,
 TwCSFW, *WrDr 84*
Murry, John Middleton 1889-1957 *LongCTC*,
 ModBrL, *TwCA*, *TwCA SUP*, *TwCWr*,
 WhoTwCL
Murry, Mary Middleton 1897-1983 *ConAu 110*
Murschetz, Luis Marian 1936- *IntAu&W 82*
Murstein, Bernard I 1929- *ConAu 3NR*, *-9R*
Murtagh, John Martin 1911-1976 *ConAu 17R*,
 -61
Murtagh, William J 1923- *ConAu 25R*
Murti, Kotikalapudi V Suryanarayana 1925-
 IntAu&W 82
Murton, Jessie Wilmore *ConAu 5R*, *MichAu 80*
Musa, Mark 1934- *ConAu 13R*
Musafir *ConAu X*
Musaphia, Joseph 1935- *ConAu 97*, *ConDr 82*,
 WrDr 84
Muscat, Robert J 1931- *ConAu 17R*
Muscatine, Charles 1920- *ConAu 21R*
Muscatine, Doris 1926- *ConAu 9R*
Muschamp, Thomas *ConAu X*
Muschenheim, Carl 1905-1977 *ConAu 69*
Muschenheim, William 1902- *ConAu P-1*
Muschg, Adolf 1934- *CIDMEL 80*
Muse, Beatriz DeRegil 1901?-1983 *ConAu 109*
Muse, Benjamin 1898- *ConAu 1R*, *-1NR*,
 IntAu&W 82, *WrDr 84*
Muse, Clarence 1889-1979 *ConAu 104*
Muse, Ellen 1941- *IntWWP 82*
Muse, Patricia *DrAP&F 83*
Muse, Patricia 1923- *ConAu 69*
Musgrave, Barbara S 1913- *ConAu 5R*
Musgrave, Clifford 1904-1982 *ConAu 107*
Musgrave, Florence 1902- *ConAu P-1*,
 SmATA 3
Musgrave, Susan 1951- *ConAu 69*, *ConLC 13*,
 ConP 80, *WrDr 84*
Musgraves, Don 1935- *ConAu 65*
Musgrove, Alexander Johnston 1882-1952
 CreCan 2

N

Na GCopaleen, Myles *ConAu X*
Na Gopaleen, Myles *ConAu X*
Na'aman, Shlomo 1912- *IntAu&W 82*
Naamani, Israel Tarkow 1913?- *ConAu 106*
Naar, Jon 1920- *ConAu 102*
Nabert, Jean 1881-1960 *ClDMEL 80*
Nabholtz, John R 1931- *ConAu 65*
Nabokov, Nicolas 1903-1978 *ConAu 77, -85*
Nabokov, Peter 1940- *ConAu 9NR, -21R*
Nabokov, Vladimir 1899-1977 *ClDMEL 80, CnMWL, ConAu 5R, -69, ConLC 1, -2, -3, -6, -8, -11, -15, -23[port], DcLB DS3[port], -Y80A[port], -2, IntWWP 82, LongCTC, ModAL, ModAL SUP, ModSL 1, TwCA SUP, TwCWr, WhoTwCL*
Nacci, Chris 1909- *ConAu 41R*
Nachbar, Herbert 1930?-1980 *ConAu 97*
Nachbar, Jack 1941- *ConAu 53*
Nachman, Gerald 1938- *ConAu 65*
Nachtigall, Lila Ehrenstein 1934- *ConAu 105*
Nachtmann, Francis Weldon 1913- *ConAu 37R*
Nadan, Paul 1933?-1978 *ConAu 104*
Naddor, Eliezer 1920- *ConAu 21R*
Nadeau, Maurice 1911- *ConAu 49*
Nadeau, R E 1913- *ConAu 107*
Nadeau, Ray E *ConAu X*
Nadeau, Remi A 1920- *ConAu 1R, -2NR*
Nadeau, Roland 1928- *ConAu 4NR, -53*
Nadel, Frances 1905?-1977 *ConAu 69*
Nadel, Gerald H 1944-1977 *ConAu 73, -81*
Nadel, Ira Bruce 1943- *ConAu 102*
Nadel, Mark V 1943- *ConAu 33R, WrDr 84*
Nadel, Norman Sanford 1915- *ConAmTC, ConAu 106*
Nader, G A 1940- *WrDr 84*
Nader, George 1921- *ConAu 109*
Nader, Laura 1930- *ConAu 7NR, -17R*
Nader, Ralph 1934- *ConAu 77, WrDr 84*
Nadir, Rikki *IntWWP 82X*
Nadir, Zakee *DrAP&F 83*
Nadler, Harvey 1933- *ConAu 13R*
Nadler, Leonard 1922- *ConAu 5NR, -53*
Nadler, Paul S 1930- *ConAu 25R*
Nadler, Susan *ConAu X*
Nadolski, Bronislaw Emilian 1903- *IntAu&W 82*
Naeslund, Erik 1948- *ConAu 103*
Naess, Harald Sigurd 1925- *ConAu 41R*
Naether, Carl Albert 1892- *ConAu 25R*
Nafziger, E Wayne 1938- *ConAu 85*
Nafziger, Estel Wayne 1938- *IntAu&W 82*
Nag, Moni 1925- *ConAu 41R, IntAu&W 82*
Nagai, Kafu 1879-1959 *CnMWL, WorAu*
Nagamatsu, Sadamu 1904- *IntAu&W 82*
Naganowska, Irena 1914- *IntAu&W 82*
Naganowski, Egon 1913- *IntAu&W 82*
Nagara, Susumu 1932- *ConAu 3NR, -45*
Nagatsu, Toshiharu 1930- *ConAu 107*
Nagayama, Mokuo 1929- *IntWWP 82*
Nagel, Ernest 1901- *ConAu 93*
Nagel, James 1940- *ConAu 29R*
Nagel, Otto 1894-1967 *ConAu 106*
Nagel, Paul C 1926- *ConAu 5NR, -9R, WrDr 84*
Nagel, Shirley 1922- *ConAu 93*

Nagel, Stuart 1934- *WrDr 84*
Nagel, Stuart S 1934- *ConAu 33R*
Nagel, Thomas 1937- *ConAu 4NR, -53*
Nagel, William G 1916- *ConAu 49*
Nagenda, Musa *ConAu X*
Nagera, Humberto 1927- *ConAu 57*
Nagi, Mostafa H 1934- *ConAu 33R*
Nagi, Saad Z 1925- *ConAu 29R*
Nagibin, Yuri Markovich 1920- *ModSL 1, TwCWr*
Nagibin, Yury Markovich 1920- *ClDMEL 80*
Nagle, James J 1909-1978 *ConAu 81, -85*
Naglee, David Ingersoll 1930- *ConAu 53*
Nagler, Alois Maria 1907- *ConAu 103, IntAu&W 82*
Nagler, Barney 1912- *ConAu 17R*
Nagler, Michael N 1937- *ConAu 73*
Naglerowa, Herminia 1890-1957 *ClDMEL 80*
Nagorski, Andrew 1947- *ConAu 93*
Nagorski, Zygmunt 1885?-1973 *ConAu 41R*
Nagorski, Zygmunt, Jr. 1912- *ConAu 73*
Nagourney, Peter 1940- *ConAu 37R*
Nagy, Ferenc 1903-1979 *ConAu 89*
Nagy, Gil D 1933- *ConAu 25R*
Nagy, Gregory 1942- *ConAu 102*
Nagy, Lajos 1883-1954 *ClDMEL 80*
Nagy, Laszlo 1925-1978 *ClDMEL 80, ConLC 7*
Nagy, Peter 1920- *IntAu&W 82*
Nagy-Talavera, Nicholas Manuel 1929- *ConAu 33R, WrDr 84*
Naha, Ed 1950- *ConAu 109*
Nahal, Chaman 1927- *ConAu 37R, WrDr 84*
Nahas, Gabriel G 1920- *ConAu 1NR, -49, WrDr 84*
Nahas, Rebecca 1946- *ConAu 69*
Nahm, Milton C 1903- *ConAu 13R, WrDr 84*
Naiden, James *DrAP&F 83*
Naiden, James 1943- *IntWWP 82, WrDr 84*
Naidis, Mark 1918- *ConAu 33R, WrDr 84*
Naidu, Sarojini 1879-1949 *LongCTC, TwCWr*
Naifeh, Steven Woodward 1952- *ConAu 102*
Naik, Balwant 1920- *IntWWP 82*
Naik, J A 1933- *IntAu&W 82*
Naik, Madhukar Krishna 1926- *ConAu 10NR, -21R*
Naiman, Arthur 1941- *ConAu 108*
Naipaul, Shiva 1945- *ConAu 110, ConNov 82, WrDr 84*
Naipaul, V S 1932- *ConAu 1NR, ConLC 7, -9, -13, -18, ConNov 82, IntAu&W 82, ModCmwL, WrDr 84*
Naipaul, Vidiadhar Surajprasad 1932- *ConAu 1R, ConLC 4, DcLEL 1940, LongCTC, TwCWr, WhoTwCL, WorAu*
Nair, Krishnapillai, Krishnan 1918- *IntAu&W 82*
Nairn, Ian 1930-1983 *ConAu 110*
Nairn, Ian Douglas 1930- *WorAu*
Nairn, Ronald C 1922- *ConAu 21R*
Naisawald, L VanLoan 1920- *ConAu 5R, -6NR*
Naismith, Grace 1904- *ConAu 65*
Naismith, Helen 1929- *ConAu 69*
Naismith, Horace *ConAu X*
Naismith, Marion 1922- *ConAu 29R*

Najafi, Najmeh *ConAu 25R*
Najder, Zdzislaw 1930- *ConAu 17R*
Nakae, Noriko 1940- *ConAu 49*
Nakagawa, Atsuo 1927- *IntWWP 82*
Nakagawa, Ichiro 1939- *IntAu&W 82*
Nakagawa, Onsey *IntWWP 82X*
Nakamura, Hajime 1912- *ConAu 10NR, -53*
Nakamura, James I 1919- *ConAu 21R*
Nakamura, Kazuo 1926- *CreCan 2*
Nakamura, Kichizo 1877-1941 *ModWD*
Nakamura, Yasuo 1919- *ConAu 45*
Nakano, Hirotaka 1942- *ConAu 33R*
Nakarai, Toyozo W 1898- *ConAu 41R, IntAu&W 82, WrDr 84*
Nakashima, George Katsutoshi 1905- *ConAu 106, TwCCW 83*
Nakatani, Chiyoko 1930- *ConAu 77, IntAu&W 82*
Nakayama, Shigeru 1928- *ConAu 29R, WrDr 84*
Nakell, Mark *DrAP&F 83*
Nakhleh, Emile A 1938- *ConAu 77, IntAu&W 82*
Nakhnikian, George 1920- *ConAu 1R, -2NR, WrDr 84*
Nalder, Eric C 1946- *ConAu 89*
Nale, Sharon Anne 1944- *ConAu 108*
Nale Roxlo, Conrado 1898-1970 *ModLAL*
Nalkowska, Zofia 1884-1954 *ClDMEL 80*
Nalkowska, Zofia 1885?-1954 *CnMD, ModSL 2, ModWD*
Nall, Hiram Abiff 1950- *ConAu 57*
Nall, Torney Otto 1900- *ConAu 17R*
Nalle *IntAu&W 82X*
Nallin, Walter E 1917?-1978 *ConAu 77*
Nalty, Bernard Charles 1931- *ConAu 102*
Nam, Charles B 1926- *ConAu 10NR, -65*
Nam, Koon Woo 1928- *ConAu 61*
Namath, Joe *ConAu X*
Namath, Joseph William 1943- *ConAu 89*
Nambiar, O K 1910- *ConAu 13R*
Nameroff, Rochelle *DrAP&F 83*
Nameroff, Rochelle 1943- *ConAu 41R*
Namias, Jerome 1910- *WrDr 84*
Namias, June 1941- *ConAu 81*
Namier, Julia 1893- *ConAu 61*
Namier, Sir Lewis Bernstein 1888-1960 *LongCTC, TwCA SUP*
Namik, Mustafa *IntAu&W 82X*
Namikawa, Banri 1931- *ConAu 8NR, -53*
Namikawa, Ryo 1905- *ConAu 93, IntAu&W 82*
Namioka, Lensey 1929- *ConAu 11NR, -69, SmATA 27[port]*
Namir, Mordecai 1897-1975 *ConAu 57*
Namjoshi, Siniti 1941- *DcLEL 1940*
Namora, Fernando 1919- *ClDMEL 80*
Namovicz, Gene Inyart 1927- *ConAu 17R*
Nan Kivell, Joice M *ConAu X*
Nanassy, Louis C 1913- *ConAu 4NR, -53*
Nance, Guinevera Ann 1939- *ConAu 106*
Nance, Joseph Milton 1913- *ConAu 1R, -1NR*
Nanda, B R 1917- *ConAu 7NR*
Nanda, Bal Ram 1917- *ConAu 13R, WrDr 84*

Nandakumar, Prema 1939- *ConAu 9R*
Nandan, Kanhaiyalal 1933- *IntAu&W 82*
Nandan, Satendra Pratap 1939- *IntWWP 82*
Nandy, Pritish 1947- *ConAu 65, ConP 80, DcLEL 1940, WrDr 84*
Nangia, Sudesh 1942- *ConAu 4NR, -53*
Nangle, Julian Gostelow 1947- *IntWWP 82*
Nanji, Salim 1951- *IntWWP 82*
NanKivell, Joice M *ConAu R*
Nannes, Caspar Harold 1906-1978 *ConAu 9R, -81*
Nanry, Charles 1938- *ConAu 73*
Nansen, Fridtjof 1861-1930 *LongCTC*
Nanushka *IntAu&W 82X*
Napier, B Davie 1915- *ConAu 1R, -4NR*
Napier, John Russell 1917- *WrDr 84*
Napier, Mark *ConAu X, SmATA X, WrDr 84*
Napier, Mary *ConAu X, WrDr 84*
Napier, Priscilla 1908- *ConAu 21R*
Napier, William *ConAu X*
Napjus, Alice James 1913- *ConAu 21R*
Napjus, James *ConAu X*
Napoleon, Art *ConAu X*
Napolitan, Joseph 1929- *ConAu 37R*
Napolitane, Catherine A Durrum 1936- *ConAu 85*
Napora, Joseph *DrAP&F 83*
Napora, Paul Edward 1939- *WrDr 84*
Narain, Jai Prakash *ConAu X*
Narain, Laxmi 1930- *IntAu&W 82*
Narang, Gopi Chand 1931- *ConAu 29R, WrDr 84*
Narasimha Char, K T 1903- *ConAu 5NR, -53*
Narasimhan, Chakravarthi V 1915- *ConAu 17R*
Narayan, Jayaprakash 1902-1979 *ConAu 89, -97*
Narayan, Ongkar 1926- *ConAu 103*
Narayan, R K 1906- *ConAu 81, ConNov 82, ModCmwL*
Narayan, R K 1907- *ConLC 7, WrDr 84*
Narayan, Rasipuram Krishnaswami 1906- *LongCTC, TwCA SUP*
Narayn, Deane 1929- *ConAu 1R*
Narcejac, Thomas 1908- *WorAu*
Nardin, Terry 1942- *ConAu 41R*
Narell, Irena 1923- *ConAu 1NR*
Naremore, James 1941- *ConAu 11NR, -69*
Narenderpal, Singh 1924- *IntWWP 82*
Naroll, Raoul 1920- *ConAu 33R, WrDr 84*
Narrache, Jean *CreCan 2*
Narramore, Stanley Bruce 1941- *ConAu 57*
Nartsissov, Boris 1906- *IntWWP 82*
Narveson, Jan F 1936- *ConAu 9NR, -21R*
Narvion Royo, Pilar 1927- *IntAu&W 82*
Nasatir, A P 1904- *ConAu 5NR, WrDr 84*
Nasatir, Abraham Phineas 1904- *ConAu 9R, IntAu&W 82*
Nasatir, David 1934- *ConAu 41R*
Nasaw, Jonathan Lewis 1947- *ConAu 61*
Nasby, A 1909-1983 *ConAu 109*
Nash, Allan N 1932- *ConAu 41R*
Nash, Bruce M 1947- *SmATA 34[port]*
Nash, Bruce Mitchell 1947- *ConAu 85, IntAu&W 82*
Nash, David T 1929- *ConAu 93*
Nash, Eno *ConAu X*
Nash, Ethel Miller 1909- *ConAu P-1*
Nash, Gary B 1933- *ConAu 37R, WrDr 84*
Nash, Gerald D 1928- *ConAu 8NR, -21R, WrDr 84*
Nash, Grinley *IntWWP 82X*
Nash, Howard P, Jr. 1900- *ConAu 73*
Nash, J Madeleine 1943- *ConAu 69*
Nash, James E 1933- *ConAu 29R*
Nash, Jay Robert 1937- *ConAu 21R*
Nash, June 1927- *ConAu 29R*
Nash, Lee 1927- *ConAu 41R*
Nash, Linell *SmATA 2*
Nash, Manning 1924- *ConAu 17R*
Nash, Mary 1925- *ConAu 5R*
Nash, Mildred J *DrAP&F 83*
Nash, N Richard 1913- *ConAu 85, NatPD 81[port]*
Nash, N Richard 1916- *CnMD, ModWD*
Nash, Nancy 1943- *ConAu 21R*
Nash, Newlyn *ConAu 49, WrDr 84*
Nash, Ogden 1902-1971 *CnMWL, ConAmA, ConAu 29R, ConAu P-1, ConLC 23[port], LongCTC, ModAL, SmATA 2, TwCA, TwCA SUP, TwCWr, WhoTwCL*
Nash, Padder *ConAu X*
Nash, Patrick Gerard 1933- *WrDr 84*

Nash, Paul 1924- *ConAu 17R, IntAu&W 82, WrDr 84*
Nash, Ralph 1925- *ConAu 17R, -61*
Nash, Ray 1905-1982 *ConAu 106*
Nash, Robert 1902- *ConAu P-1*
Nash, Roderick 1939- *ConAu 17R, WrDr 84*
Nash, Ronald H 1936- *ConAu 5R, -8NR*
Nash, Simon *ConAu X, IntAu&W 82X*
Nash, Valery *DrAP&F 83*
Nash, Valery 1930- *IntWWP 82*
Nash, William, Jr. 1928- *ConAu 85*
Nash, William George 1920- *WrDr 84*
Naske, Claus-M 1935- *ConAu 77*
Naslund, Erik *ConAu X*
Naslund, Sena Jeter *DrAP&F 83*
Nason, Alvin 1919-1978 *ConAu 77*
Nason, Donna 1944- *ConAu 97*
Nason, Leonard Hastings 1895- *TwCA, TwCA SUP*
Nason, Leslie J *ConAu 5R*
Nason, Thelma *DrAP&F 83*
Nasr, Seyyed Hossein 1933- *ConAu 10NR, -21R, WrDr 84*
Nass, Elyse 1947- *IntAu&W 82, NatPD 81[port]*
Nassaar, Christopher S 1944- *ConAu 97*
Nassar, Eugene Paul 1935- *ConAu 33R, WrDr 84*
Nassau, Richard *IntWWP 82X*
Nassauer, Rudolf 1924- *ConAu 105, WrDr 84*
Nassivera, John 1950- *ConAu 109, NatPD 81[port]*
Nast, Elsa Ruth *ConAu X, SmATA 3*
Nast, Thomas 1840-1902 *SmATA 33*
Nastasijevic, Momcilo 1894-1938 *ClDMEL 80, ModSL 2*
Nasty, Uncle *IntWWP 82X*
Natali, Alfred Maxim 1915- *ConAu 57*
Natanson, George 1928- *ConAu 73*
Natanson, Maurice 1924- *WrDr 84*
Natanson, Maurice Alexander 1924- *ConAu 17R*
Natchez, Gladys 1915- *ConAu 4NR, -9R, IntAu&W 82, WrDr 84*
Natella, Arthur A, Jr. 1941- *ConAu 89*
Nath, Dwijendra Lal 1915- *IntAu&W 82*
Nath, Shiv Kumar 1936- *WrDr 84*
Nathan, Adele *ConAu 73*
Nathan, Andrew J 1943- *ConAu 65*
Nathan, Daniel *ConAu X, LongCTC*
Nathan, David 1926- *ConAu 29R, WrDr 84*
Nathan, Dorothy d1966 *ConAu 81, SmATA 15*
Nathan, Edward Leonard 1924- *IntWWP 82*
Nathan, George *IntWWP 82X*
Nathan, George Jean 1882-1958 *ConAmA, LongCTC, ModAL, TwCA, TwCA SUP*
Nathan, Hans 1910- *ConAu 1R, -1NR, WrDr 84*
Nathan, James A 1942- *ConAu 85*
Nathan, Jo *IntWWP 82X*
Nathan, Joan 1943- *ConAu 61*
Nathan, Leonard *DrAP&F 83*
Nathan, Leonard 1924- *WrDr 84*
Nathan, Leonard E 1924- *ConAu 5R, -7NR, ConP 80, IntAu&W 82*
Nathan, Norman *DrAP&F 83*
Nathan, Norman 1915- *ConAu 1R, -1NR, IntAu&W 82, IntWWP 82, WrDr 84*
Nathan, Otto 1893- *IntAu&W 82*
Nathan, Peter 1914- *WrDr 84*
Nathan, Peter E 1935- *ConAu 73*
Nathan, Richard P 1935- *ConAu 7NR, -57*
Nathan, Robert 1894- *ConAmA, ConAu 6NR, -13R, ConNov 82, DcLB 9[port], IntAu&W 82, LongCTC, SmATA 6, TwCA, TwCA SUP, WrDr 84*
Nathan, Robert Stuart *DrAP&F 83*
Nathan, Robert Stuart 1948- *ConAu 81, IntAu&W 82*
Nathaniel, Isabel *DrAP&F 83*
Nathanson, Jerome 1908-1975 *ConAu 57*
Nathanson, Leonard 1933- *ConAu 21R*
Nathanson, Nathaniel L 1908- *ConAu 89*
Nathanson, Tenney *DrAP&F 83*
Nathanson, Yale S 1895- *ConAu 77*
Nathusius, Marie-Sophie 1906- *IntAu&W 82*
Nation, Carry Amelia 1846-1911 *LongCTC*
Nations, Opal Louis *DrAP&F 83*
Nations, Opal Louis 1941- *IntWWP 82*
Natkie, John L *DrAP&F 83*
Natkiewicz, Jan *DrAP&F 83*
Natsume, Kinnosuke 1867-1916 *ConAu 104*
Natsume, Soseki 1867-1916 *CnMWL, ConAu X,*

TwCLC 2, -10[port], WorAu
Natti, Lee 1919- *ConAu 2NR*
Natti, Susanna 1948- *SmATA 32[port]*
Natusch, Sheila 1926- *WrDr 84*
Natusch, Sheila Ellen 1926- *ConAu 103, IntAu&W 82*
Natwar-Singh, K 1931- *ConAu 13R, IntAu&W 82, WrDr 84*
Nau, Erika S 1918- *ConAu 65*
Naude, Adele 1910- *WrDr 84*
Naude, Adele DaFonseca-Wollheim 1910- *ConAu 9R, ConP 80, IntWWP 82*
Nauen, Elinor *DrAP&F 83, IntWWP 82*
Nauer, Barbara Joan 1932- *ConAu 105*
Naughton, Bill 1910- *ConAu 105, ConDr 82, ConNov 82, CroCD, DcLB 13[port], DcLEL 1940, TwCCW 83, WrDr 84*
Naughton, John 1933- *ConAu 57*
Naugle, Helen Harrold 1920- *ConAu 53*
Naugle, John E 1923- *ConAu 65*
Nauheim, Ferd 1909- *ConAu 1NR, -49*
Nault, Fernand 1921- *CreCan 1*
Nauman, St. Elmo, Jr. 1935- *ConAu 53*
Naumann, Anthony Frank 1921-1971 *ConAu 21R, -89*
Naumann, Marina 1938- *ConAu 93*
Naumann, Oscar E 1912- *ConAu 77*
Naumann, Rose 1919- *ConAu 65*
Naumburg, Margaret 1890-1983 *ConAu 109*
Nauticus *ConAu X*
Nava, Julian 1927- *ConAu 61*
Naval, Frederik *IntAu&W 82X*
Navarra, Fernand Jean 1915- *ConAu 108*
Navarra, John Gabriel 1927- *ConAu 41R, SmATA 8*
Navarre, Jane *DrAP&F 83*
Navarro, Antonio 1922- *ConAu 107*
Navarro, Marysa 1934- *ConAu 106*
Navarro Hernan, Manuel 1924- *IntAu&W 82*
Navas-Ruiz, Ricardo 1932- *ConAu 107*
Navasky, Victor S 1932- *ConAu 10NR, -21R*
Navaz Sanz, Karmele 1896- *IntAu&W 82*
Navero, William *DrAP&F 83*
Navone, John J 1930- *ConAu 10NR, -21R*
Navrozov, Lev 1928- *ConAu 61, IntAu&W 82*
Nayar, Kuldip 1923- *DcLEL 1940*
Naydler, Merton 1920- *ConAu 45*
Nayer, Louise *DrAP&F 83*
Nayler, Joseph Lawrence 1891- *WrDr 84*
Naylor, Eliot *LongCTC, TwCA SUP*
Naylor, Eric W 1936- *ConAu 45*
Naylor, Gloria *DrAP&F 83*
Naylor, Gloria 1950- *ConAu 107*
Naylor, Harriet H 1915- *ConAu 9NR, -21R*
Naylor, James C 1932- *ConAu 1NR, -45*
Naylor, John 1920- *ConAu 93*
Naylor, Margot Ailsa 1907- *ConAu 9R*
Naylor, Penelope 1941- *ConAu 37R, SmATA 10*
Naylor, Phyllis Reynolds *DrAP&F 83*
Naylor, Phyllis Reynolds 1933- *ConAu 8NR, -21R, IntAu&W 82, SmATA 12, WrDr 84*
Nazareth, Peter 1940- *ConAu 101*
Nazarian, Nikki *ConAu X*
Nazaroff, Alexander I 1898- *ConAu 33R, SmATA 4*
Nazhivin, Ivan Fyodorovich 1874-1940 *TwCA*
Nazor, Vladimir 1876-1949 *ClDMEL 80, ModSL 2*
Nazrul Islam, Kazi 1899- *ModCmwL*
Nazzaro, Anthony M 1927- *ConAu 106*
Ndebele, James Pambano 1940- *IntAu&W 82*
Neagley, Ross 1907- *ConAu 106, WrDr 84*
Neagoe, Peter 1881-1960 *ConAu 105, DcLB 4*
Neal, Arminta Pearl 1921- *ConAu 85*
Neal, Bruce W 1931- *ConAu 21R*
Neal, Charles Dempsey 1908- *ConAu 5R, -5NR*
Neal, Emily Gardiner *ConAu 3NR, -5R*
Neal, Eric Victor 1913- *IntAu&W 82*
Neal, Ernest Gordon 1911- *ConAu 13R, WrDr 84*
Neal, Frank 1932- *WrDr 84*
Neal, Fred Warner 1915- *ConAu 2NR, -5R, WrDr 84*
Neal, Harry *ConAu X*
Neal, Harry Edward 1906- *ConAu 2NR, -5R, IntAu&W 82, SmATA 5, WrDr 84*
Neal, Hilary *ConAu X, TwCRGW, WrDr 84*
Neal, James M 1925- *ConAu 73*
Neal, James T 1936- *ConAu 57*
Neal, Julia 1905- *ConAu 69*

Nevins, Edward M 1938- *ConAu 29R*

Nevins, Francis M, Jr. 1943- *ConAu 41R, TwCCr&M 80, WrDr 84*

Nevinson, Henry Woodd 1856-1941 *LongCTC, TwCA, TwCA SUP*

Nevitt, H J Barrington 1908- *ConAu 37R*

Nevius, Blake 1916- *ConAu 17R*

Nevo, Ruth 1924- *ConAu 61*

New, Anthony 1924- *ConAu 107, WrDr 84*

New York, Michael *IntWWP 82X*

Newall, Venetia June 1935- *ConAu 37R, IntAu&W 82, WrDr 84*

Newberry, Clare Turlay 1903-1970 *ConAu P-2, SmATA 1, -26N*

Newberry, E G *IntAu&W 82X*

Newberry, Lida 1909- *ConAu 97*

Newberry, Wilma 1927- *ConAu 73*

Newbery, John 1713-1767 *SmATA 20*

Newbigin, Lesslie 1909- *ConAu 10NR, -13R*

Newbill, James Guy 1931- *ConAu 61*

Newbold, H L 1921- *ConAu 1R, -5NR*

Newbold, Robert Thomas, Jr. 1920- *ConAu 89, IntAu&W 82*

Newbold, Stokes *ConAu X*

Newbolt, Sir Henry John 1862-1938 *LongCTC, ModBrL, TwCA, TwCA SUP*

Newbound, Bernard Slade 1930- *ConAu 81*

Newbury, Colin 1929- *ConAu 5R, -8NR*

Newbury, Will 1912- *ConAu 45*

Newby, Eric 1919- *ConAu 5R, IntAu&W 82, WrDr 84*

Newby, George Eric 1919- *DcLEL 1940*

Newby, I A 1931- *ConAu 17R*

Newby, P H 1918- *ConLC 13, ConNov 82, DcLB 15[port], WrDr 84*

Newby, Percy Howard 1918- *ConAu 5R, ConLC 2, DcLEL 1940, IntAu&W 82, LongCTC, ModBrL, ModBrL SUP, TwCA SUP, TwCWr*

Newby, Richard L *DrAP&F 83*

Newcomb, Benjamin H 1938- *ConAu 45*

Newcomb, Covelle 1908- *ConAu P-2*

Newcomb, Duane G 1929- *ConAu 5NR, -53*

Newcomb, Ellsworth *ConAu X, SmATA X*

Newcomb, Franc Johnson 1887-1970 *ConAu 17R*

Newcomb, Kerry *ConAu X*

Newcomb, Kerry 1946- *ConAu 10NR*

Newcomb, Norma *ConAu X*

Newcomb, Richard Fairchild 1913- *ConAu 1R*

Newcomb, Robert N 1925- *ConAu 21R*

Newcomb, Simon 1835-1909 *ConAu 108, TwCSFW*

Newcomb, Theodore Mead 1903- *ConAu 33R*

Newcomb, Wilburn Wendell 1935- *ConAu 17R*

Newcomb, William W, Jr. 1921- *ConAu 102*

Newcombe, Jack *SmATA 33*

Newcombe, John 1944- *ConAu 69*

Newcombe, Park Judson 1930- *ConAu 106*

Newcomer, James W 1912- *WrDr 84*

Newcomer, James William 1912- *ConAu 41R, IntAu&W 82*

Newell, Allen 1927- *ConAu 104*

Newell, Barbara Warne 1929- *ConAu 1R*

Newell, Crosby *ConAu X, SmATA X, TwCCW 83, WrDr 84*

Newell, Edythe W 1910- *ConAu 65, SmATA 11*

Newell, Fred D 1912- *ConAu 97*

Newell, Gordon R 1913- *ConAu 4NR, -9R*

Newell, Helen M 1909- *ConAu 93*

Newell, Homer E 1915-1983 *ConAu 110*

Newell, Homer Edward 1915- *ConAu 97*

Newell, Hope 1896-1965 *ConAu 73, SmATA 24[port]*

Newell, Kenneth Bernard 1930- *ConAu 41R, IntAu&W 82*

Newell, Norman Dennis 1909- *ConAu 104*

Newell, Peter 1916- *WrDr 84*

Newell, Peter Francis 1915- *ConAu 13R*

Newell, Rosemary 1922- *ConAu 49*

Newell, William H 1922- *ConAu 103, WrDr 84*

Newell, William T 1929- *ConAu 37R, WrDr 84*

Newfeld, Frank 1928- *ConAu 105, SmATA 26[port]*

Newfield, Jack 1939- *ConAu 21R*

Newhafer, Richard L 1922- *ConAu 13R*

Newhall, Beaumont 1908- *ConAu 9R*

Newhall, Nancy 1908-1974 *ConAu 49*

Newhall, Richard A 1888-1973 *ConAu 41R*

Newhouse, Edward 1911- *ConAu 97, ConNov 82, IntAu&W 82, TwCA SUP, WrDr 84*

Newhouse, Neville H 1919- *ConAu 21R*

Newhouse, Samuel I 1895-1979 *ConAu 89*

Newick, John 1919- *ConAu P-1*

Newill, Robert 1921- *WrDr 84*

Newkirk, Glen A 1931- *ConAu 37R*

Newland, Kathleen 1951- *ConAu 97*

Newland, T Ernest 1903- *ConAu 105*

Newley, Anthony 1931- *ConAu 105, ConDr 82D, IntAu&W 82*

Newlin, Dika 1923- *ConAu 107*

Newlin, Margaret Rudd 1925- *ConAu 1NR, -49, IntAu&W 82, IntWWP 82, WrDr 84*

Newlon, Clarke *ConAu 49, SmATA 6*

Newlon, Clarke 1905?-1982 *ConAu 10NR, -108, SmATA 33N*

Newlove, Donald 1928- *ConAu 29R, ConLC 6*

Newlove, John 1938- *ConAu 9NR, -21R, ConLC 14, ConP 80, CreCan 1, DcLEL 1940, IntWWP 82, WrDr 84*

Newlyn, Walter T 1915- *ConAu 21R*

Newman, Adrien Ann 1941- *ConAu 102*

Newman, Alyse 1953- *ConAu 107*

Newman, Andrea 1938- *ConAu 73, IntAu&W 82, WrDr 84*

Newman, Aubrey N 1927- *ConAu 29R, IntAu&W 82, WrDr 84*

Newman, Barbara *ConAu X, WrDr 84*

Newman, Barclay M, Jr. 1931- *ConAu 9NR, -17R*

Newman, Bernard 1897-1968 *ConAu 25R, -97, ConSFA, LongCTC, TwCCr&M 80*

Newman, C J 1935- *ConNov 82*

Newman, Charles 1938- *ConAu 21R, ConLC 2, -8, ConNov 82, WrDr 84*

Newman, Charles L 1923- *ConAu 6NR, -13R*

Newman, Coleman J 1935- *ConAu 77, WrDr 84*

Newman, Daisy *WrDr 84*

Newman, Daisy 1904- *ConAu 37R, SmATA 27[port]*

Newman, David 1937- *ConAu 102, ConDr 82A*

Newman, E J 1943- *ConAu 61*

Newman, Edwin 1919- *AuNews 1, ConAu 5NR, -69, ConLC 14, IntAu&W 82*

Newman, Edwin S 1922- *WrDr 84*

Newman, Elmer S 1919- *ConAu 106*

Newman, Eric P 1911- *ConAu 5R*

Newman, Ernest 1868-1959 *LongCTC, TwCA, TwCA SUP*

Newman, Felice *DrAP&F 83*

Newman, Frances 1883?-1928 *ConAu 110, DcLB Y80B[port], TwCA*

Newman, G F 1942- *ConAu 104*

Newman, George 1936- *ConAu 106*

Newman, Gerald 1939- *ConAu 101*

Newman, Gerald Miller 1926- *CreCan 2*

Newman, Gordon F *WrDr 84*

Newman, Harold 1899- *ConAu 10NR, -65*

Newman, Harold 1927- *ConAu 53*

Newman, Herbert Ellis 1914- *ConAu 25R*

Newman, Howard 1911- *ConAu 57*

Newman, Howard R 1913?-1977 *ConAu 73*

Newman, Jacob 1914- *ConAu 9R*

Newman, Jay Hartley 1951- *ConAu 9NR, -65*

Newman, Jeremiah Joseph 1926- *ConAu 5R, -8NR*

Newman, Joel *DrAP&F 83*

Newman, Jon O 1932- *ConAu 21R*

Newman, Joseph 1892- *ConAu 89*

Newman, Joseph W 1918- *ConAu 37R*

Newman, Katharine D 1911- *ConAu 37R*

Newman, Lee Scott 1953- *ConAu 65*

Newman, Leonard Hugh 1909- *ConAu 9R*

Newman, Leslea *DrAP&F 83*

Newman, Leslie *DrAP&F 83*

Newman, Loretta Marie 1911- *ConAu 45*

Newman, Louis Israel 1893-1972 *ConAu 33R, ConAu P-1*

Newman, Margaret *IntAu&W 82X, WrDr 84*

Newman, Mildred 1920- *AuNews 1*

Newman, Mona Alice Jean 1910- *ConAu 102, IntAu&W 82, WrDr 84*

Newman, Oscar 1935- *ConAu 102, WrDr 84*

Newman, P B *DrAP&F 83*

Newman, P B 1919- *ConAu 33R, WrDr 84*

Newman, Parley Wright 1923- *ConAu 106*

Newman, Paul Baker 1919- *IntAu&W 82*

Newman, Peter 1928- *ConAu 17R*

Newman, Peter 1929- *WrDr 84*

Newman, Peter C 1929- *ConAu 3NR, -9R, IntAu&W 82*

Newman, Philip L 1931- *ConAu 17R*

Newman, Ralph Abraham 1892- *ConAu 1R,*

–6NR

Newman, Ralph Geoffrey 1911- *ConAu 45*

Newman, Randolph H 1904-1975 *ConAu 61*

Newman, Richard 1930- *ConAu 110*

Newman, Robert 1909- *ConAu 1R, -4NR, SmATA 4, TwCCW 83*

Newman, Robert P 1922- *ConAu 1R*

Newman, Robert S 1935- *ConAu 65*

Newman, Ruth G 1914- *ConAu 105*

Newman, Sharan 1949- *ConAu 106*

Newman, Shirlee Petkin 1924- *ConAu 5R, SmATA 10*

Newman, Sidney 1917- *CreCan 2*

Newman, Sol *DrAP&F 83*

Newman, Stephen A 1946- *ConAu 97*

Newman, Stewart A 1907- *ConAu P-2*

Newman, Sydney 1917- *CreCan 2*

Newman, Terence 1927- *ConAu 5R*

Newman, Terry *ConAu X*

Newman, Thelma R 1925-1978 *ConAu 7NR, -13R, -81*

Newman, Walter 1920- *ConAu 110*

Newman, William H 1909- *ConAu 3NR, -5R*

Newman, William Mark 1943- *ConAu 57*

Newman, William S 1912- *ConAu 1R, -3NR, WrDr 84*

Newman Turner, Roger 1940- *IntAu&W 82*

Newmar, Rima *ConAu X*

Newmark, Hans 1904- *CreCan 1*

Newmark, John 1904- *CreCan 1*

Newmark, Joseph 1943- *ConAu 53*

Newmark, Leonard 1929- *ConAu 17R, WrDr 84*

Newmyer, R Kent 1930- *ConAu 77*

Newnes, Sir George 1851-1910 *LongCTC*

Newport, John P 1917- *ConAu 33R*

Newquist, Jerreld L 1919- *ConAu 17R*

Newquist, Roy Arvid 1925- *ConAu 13R*

Newsom, Carroll Vincent 1904- *ConAu P-2*

Newsom, Doug 1934- *ConAu 73*

Newsome, Arden J 1932- *ConAu 29R*

Newsome, David Hay 1929- *ConAu 89, IntAu&W 82, WrDr 84*

Newsome, George Lane 1923- *ConAu 29R, WrDr 84*

Newsome, Walter L 1941- *ConAu 105*

Newson, Elizabeth 1929- *ConAu 5NR, -9R*

Newson, John 1925- *ConAu 9R*

Newth, Rebecca *DrAP&F 83*

Newth, Rebecca 1940- *ConAu 33R, MichAu 80*

Newton, Alfred Edward 1863-1940 *LongCTC, TwCA, TwCA SUP*

Newton, Brian 1928- *ConAu 49*

Newton, Byron Louis 1913- *ConAu 53*

Newton, D B 1916- *ConAu 2NR, TwCWW*

Newton, David C *ConAu X, WrDr 84*

Newton, Douglas 1920- *ConAu 104*

Newton, Dwight B 1916- *WrDr 84*

Newton, Dwight Bennett 1916- *ConAu 5R*

Newton, Earle Williams 1917- *ConAu 41R*

Newton, Edmund *ConAmTC*

Newton, Eric 1893-1965 *ConAu P-1, LongCTC*

Newton, Ethel 1921- *ConAu 101*

Newton, Frances *CreCan 1*

Newton, Francis *ConAu X, WorAu 1970*

Newton, Mrs. Frank 1896- *CreCan 1*

Newton, Huey P *LivgBAA*

Newton, Ivor 1892-1981 *ConAu 108*

Newton, James R 1935- *ConAu 101, SmATA 23[port]*

Newton, Julius P *ConSFA*

Newton, Kenneth 1940- *ConAu 29R, WrDr 84*

Newton, Lilias Torrance 1896- *CreCan 1*

Newton, Macdonald *ConAu X*

Newton, Michael 1951- *ConAu 108*

Newton, Norman Lewis 1929- *ConAu 9R, IntAu&W 82, WrDr 84*

Newton, Norman Thomas 1898- *ConAu 104*

Newton, Peter 1906- *ConAu P-1*

Newton, Ray C 1935- *ConAu 77*

Newton, Robert Henry Gerald 1903- *ConAu P-1*

Newton, Robert R 1918- *WrDr 84*

Newton, Roy 1904?-1974 *ConAu 104*

Newton, Stanley 1874-1950 *MichAu 80*

Newton, Stu *ConAu X*

Newton, Suzanne *DrAP&F 83*

Newton, Suzanne 1936- *ConAu 41R, SmATA 5, WrDr 84*

Newton, Violette *IntWWP 82*

Newton, Virgil Miller, Jr. 1904-1977 *ConAu 1R, -103*

Newton, William Simpson 1923- *ConAu 7NR,*

–53

Nexo, Martin Andersen 1869-1954 *ClDMEL 80,*
   TwCA, TwCA SUP, TwCWr
Ney, James W 1932- *ConAu 41R*
Ney, John 1923- *SmATA 33*
Ney, Patrick *ConAu X*
Ney, Remigius *IntAu&W 82X*
Ney, Richard 1917?- *AuNews 1*
Ney, Virgil 1905-1979 *ConAu 85*
Neyland, James 1939- *ConAu 103*
Neylon, James M *DrAP&F 83*
Neyman, Jerzy 1899-1981 *ConAu 108*
Nezval, Vitezslav 1900-1958 *ClDMEL 80,*
   ModSL 2, WorAu 1970
Ng, Larry K Y 1940- *ConAu 9NR, –17R*
Ngagoyeanes, Nicholas 1939- *ConAu 49*
Ngara, Emmanuel 1947- *ConAu 109*
Ngiam, Tong Fatt 1917- *IntWWP 82*
Ngugi, J T 1938- *WrDr 84*
Ngugi, James Thiong'o 1938- *ConAu 81,*
   ConLC 3, –7, –13, DcLEL 1940, TwCWr
Ngugi Wa Thiong'o 1938- *ConDr 82,*
   ConNov 82, ModBlW, ModCmwL,
   WorAu 1970
Nguyen, Dinh Hoa 1924- *ConAu 10NR*
Nguyen, Ngoc Bich 1937- *IntAu&W 82*
Nguyen-Dinh-Hoa 1924- *ConAu 21R*
Nguyen Ngoc Bich 1937- *ConAu 81*
Niall, Ian *DcLEL 1940*
Nias, D K B 1940- *ConAu 105*
Niatum, Duane *DrAP&F 83*
Niatum, Duane 1938- *ConAu 41R*
Niazi, Munir 1928- *IntWWP 82*
Nibbelink, Cynthia *DrAP&F 83*
Nibbelink, Cynthia 1948- *MichAu 80*
Niblett, W R 1906- *ConAu 3NR*
Niblett, William Roy *WrDr 84*
Niblett, William Roy 1906- *ConAu 1R,*
   IntAu&W 82
Nibor, Kay 1950- *ConAu X*
Nic Leodhas, Sorche 1898-1969 *ConAu X*
Niccodemi, Dario 1874-1934 *ClDMEL 80*
Nicely, Thomas S, Jr. 1939- *ConAu 93*
Nicely, Tom *ConAu X*
Nichelson, F Patrick 1942- *ConAu 33R*
Nichol, B P 1944- *ConLC 18, WrDr 84*
Nichol, Barrie Phillip 1944- *ConAu 53,*
   ConP 80, DcLEL 1940
Nichol, John Thomas 1928- *ConAu 17R*
Nichol, Margaret Kathleen *CreCan 1*
Nichol, Pegi *CreCan 1*
Nicholas *IntWWP 82X*
Nicholas, Anna Katherine 1917- *ConAu 93*
Nicholas, Barry 1919- *ConAu 5R*
Nicholas, David M 1939- *ConAu 49*
Nicholas, Donald 1909- *ConAu 5R*
Nicholas, F R E *WrDr 84*
Nicholas, Herbert George 1911- *ConAu 1R,*
   IntAu&W 82, WrDr 84
Nicholas, Leslie 1913- *ConAu 81*
Nicholas, Robert L 1937- *ConAu 53*
Nicholds, Elizabeth *ConAu P-1*
Nicholl, Louise Townsend 1890?-1981 *ConAu 105,*
   –97
Nicholls, David 1948- *ConAu 97*
Nicholls, Frederick Francis 1926- *ConAu 5R,*
   WrDr 84
Nicholls, Mark *ConAu X*
Nicholls, Peter 1939- *ConAu 105*
Nicholls, Robert Horace 1917- *WrDr 84*
Nicholls, William 1921- *ConAu 17R*
Nichols, Anne 1891-1966 *LongCTC, ModWD,*
   TwCWr
Nichols, Beverley 1898- *TwCCr&M 80,*
   WrDr 84
Nichols, Beverley 1898-1983 *ConAu 110*
Nichols, Beverley 1899- *ConAu 93, LongCTC,*
   ModBrL, TwCA, TwCA SUP, TwCWr
Nichols, Bill *ConAu X*
Nichols, Cecilia Fawn 1906- *ConAu P-1,*
   SmATA 12
Nichols, Charles Harold 1919- *ConAu 6NR, –53,*
   LivgBAA
Nichols, Dale 1904- *ConAu P-2*
Nichols, Dave *ConAu X*
Nichols, David A 1939- *ConAu 104*
Nichols, Dudley 1895-1960 *ConAu 89,*
   DcLB 26[port]
Nichols, Edward Jay 1900- *ConAu 5R*
Nichols, Harold 1903- *ConAu P-1*
Nichols, Harold 1921- *WrDr 84*
Nichols, Irby Coghill, Jr. 1926- *ConAu 41R*

Nichols, Jack 1921- *CreCan 2*
Nichols, Jack 1938- *ConAu 41R, WrDr 84*
Nichols, James R *DrAP&F 83*
Nichols, James R 1938- *ConAu 105*
Nichols, Jeannette 1931- *ConAu 77*
Nichols, Jeannette Paddock 1890-1982 *ConAu 9R,*
   –107
Nichols, John 1940- *ConAu 6NR, –9R,*
   DcLB Y82B[port], TwCWW, WrDr 84
Nichols, John Gordon 1930- *ConAu 33R,*
   WrDr 84
Nichols, Leigh *ConAu 102*
Nichols, Lewis 1903-1982 *ConAu 106*
Nichols, Maggie *ConAu X*
Nichols, Margaret 1931- *ConAu 81*
Nichols, Marie Hochmuth 1908-1978 *ConAu 103*
Nichols, Marion 1921- *ConAu 102*
Nichols, Nina DaVinci *DrAP&F 83*
Nichols, Nina DaVinci 1932- *ConAu 73*
Nichols, Paul D 1938- *ConAu 109*
Nichols, Peter *ConAu X, SmATA X*
Nichols, Peter 1927- *ConAu 104, ConDr 82,*
   ConLC 5, DcLB 13[port], DcLEL 1940,
   IntAu&W 82, ModBrL SUP, WorAu,
   –1970, WrDr 84
Nichols, Peter 1928- *IntAu&W 82*
Nichols, R Eugene 1914- *ConAu 29R, WrDr 84*
Nichols, Robert *DrAP&F 83*
Nichols, Robert 1919- *ConAu 93*
Nichols, Robert Malise Bowyer 1893-1944
   LongCTC, ModBrL, ModWD, TwCA,
   TwCA SUP
Nichols, Roger 1939- *ConAu 108, WrDr 84*
Nichols, Roger L 1933- *ConAu 5NR, –13R*
Nichols, Roy Franklin 1896-1973 *ConAu 3NR,*
   –5R, –37R, DcLB 17[port], TwCA SUP
Nichols, Ruth 1948- *ConAu 25R, SmATA 15,*
   TwCCW 83, WrDr 84
Nichols, Scott *ConAu X*
Nichols, Stephen G 1936- *ConAu 45*
Nichols, Sue *ConAu 9R*
Nichols, William James 1942- *ConAu 93*
Nichols, William Thomas 1927- *ConAu 41R*
Nicholsen, Margaret E 1904- *ConAu 29R*
Nicholson, Arnold 1902- *ConAu P-2*
Nicholson, Ben 1894-1982 *ConAu 110*
Nicholson, C A, III 1922- *ConAu 41R*
Nicholson, Christina *ConNov 82,*
   IntAu&W 82X, TwCRGW, WrDr 84
Nicholson, Dorothy Nelis 1923- *ConAu 109*
Nicholson, Frederick James 1903- *IntWWP 82*
Nicholson, Geoffrey 1929- *ConAu 5R, –8NR,*
   WrDr 84
Nicholson, Gerald William Lingen 1902-1980
   ConAu 101, IntAu&W 82
Nicholson, Hubert 1908- *ConAu 13R, WrDr 84*
Nicholson, James 1946- *IntAu&W 82,*
   NatPD 81[port]
Nicholson, Jane *ConAu X*
Nicholson, Joe *ConAu X*
Nicholson, John Greer 1929- *ConAu 45*
Nicholson, Joseph *DrAP&F 83*
Nicholson, Joseph Hugh, Jr. 1943- *ConAu 81*
Nicholson, Joyce Thorpe 1919- *ConAu 5NR, –9R*
Nicholson, Kenyon 1894- *TwCA, TwCA SUP*
Nicholson, Margaret Beda *WrDr 84*
Nicholson, Margaret Beda 1924- *ConAu 5R*
Nicholson, Max 1904- *ConAu 106*
Nicholson, Meredith 1866-1947 *LongCTC,*
   TwCA, TwCA SUP
Nicholson, Norman 1914- *WrDr 84*
Nicholson, Norman Cornthwaite 1914-
   ConAu 3NR, –9R, ConP 80, CroCD,
   DcLEL 1940, IntAu&W 82, IntWWP 82,
   LongCTC, ModBrL, TwCA SUP
Nicholson, Norman Leon 1919- *ConAu 3NR,*
   –9R, WrDr 84
Nicholson, Paul, Jr. 1937- *ConAu 73*
Nicholson, Ranald 1931- *ConAu 37R, WrDr 84*
Nicholson, Robert 1920- *IntAu&W 82*
Nicholson, Robert Lawrence 1908- *ConAu 53*
Nicholson, Shirley J 1925- *ConAu 29R*
Nicholson, W G 1935- *ConAu 93*
Nicholson, William 1872-1949 *TwCCW 83*
Nichter, Rhoda 1926- *ConAu 81*
Nichtern, Sol 1920- *ConAu 17R*
Nick, Dagmar 1926- *IntAu&W 82*
Nickel, Herman 1928- *ConAu 73*
Nickel, Mildred L 1912- *ConAu 108*
Nickell, Joe 1944- *ConAu 110*
Nickell, Lesley J 1944- *ConAu 103*
Nickels, Sylvie 1930- *IntAu&W 82*

Nickels, William G 1939- *ConAu 108*
Nickelsburg, George W E, Jr. 1934- *ConAu 5NR,*
   –53
Nickelsburg, Janet 1893- *ConAu 65,*
   SmATA 11
Nickerson, Betty 1922- *ConAu 77, SmATA X*
Nickerson, Clarence B 1906- *ConAu 5R*
Nickerson, Elizabeth 1922- *SmATA 14*
Nickerson, Jan *ConAu 1R*
Nickerson, Jane Soames *ConAu 77*
Nickerson, John Mitchell 1937- *ConAu 53*
Nickerson, Sheila *DrAP&F 83*
Nickerson, Sheila 1942- *IntWWP 82*
Nickerson, William 1908- *ConAu 1R*
Nicklanovich, Michael David 1941- *ConAu 107*
Nicklaus, Carol *SmATA 33*
Nicklaus, Frederick *DrAP&F 83*
Nicklaus, Frederick 1936- *ConAu 37R*
Nicklaus, Jack 1940- *ConAu 89*
Nickless, Will 1902- *ConAu 81*
Nickolay, Michael *DrAP&F 83*
Nickson, Arthur *TwCWW*
Niclas, Yolla 1900- *ConAu 25R*
Nicol, Abioseh 1920- *TwCWr*
Nicol, Abioseh 1924- *ConAu X, ConNov 82,*
   DcLEL 1940, IntAu&W 82X,
   IntWWP 82X, WrDr 84
Nicol, Ann *ConAu X, SmATA X*
Nicol, D M 1923- *ConAu 4NR*
Nicol, Davidson Sylvester H Willoughby 1924-
   ConAu 61, IntAu&W 82, IntWWP 82
Nicol, Donald MacGillivray 1923- *ConAu 53,*
   WrDr 84
Nicol, Eric Patrick 1919- *ConAu 1NR, –49,*
   CreCan 2, DcLEL 1940, IntAu&W 82
Nicol, Jean 1919- *ConAu 21R*
Nicol, Pegi *CreCan 1*
Nicolaeff, Ariadne 1915- *ConAu 57,*
   IntAu&W 82, WrDr 84
Nicolai, Aldo 1920- *CnMD*
Nicolaisen, Thormod James 1920- *IntWWP 82*
Nicolaou, Kyriakos 1918- *IntAu&W 82*
Nicolas 1911-1973 *ConAu X, SmATA X*
Nicolas, Claire *ConAu X*
Nicolas, F R E *ConAu X, WorAu*
Nicolau D'Olwer, Lluis 1888-1961 *ClDMEL 80*
Nicolaysen, Bruce 1934- *ConAu 105, WrDr 84*
Nicole, Christopher 1930- *WrDr 84*
Nicole, Christopher Robin 1930- *ConAu 13R,*
   ConNov 82, DcLEL 1940, IntAu&W 82,
   SmATA 5, TwCCr&M 80, TwCRGW
Nicoll, Allardyce 1894-1976 *ConAu 5NR, –9R,*
   –65, LongCTC, TwCA, TwCA SUP
Nicoll, Helen *TwCCW 83*
Nicoll, Marion 1909- *CreCan 1*
Nicoll, Ronald Ewart 1921- *IntAu&W 82*
Nicoll, Sir William Robertson 1851-1923
   LongCTC, TwCA
Nicolle, Jacques Maurice Raoul 1901- *ConAu 9R*
Nicoloff, Philip Loveless 1926- *ConAu 1R*
Nicolson, Adela Florence 1865-1904 *TwCA,*
   TwCA SUP
Nicolson, Benedict 1914-1978 *ConAu 6NR, –13R*
Nicolson, Sir Harold George 1886-1968
   ConAu P-1, LongCTC, ModBrL, TwCA,
   TwCA SUP, TwCWr
Nicolson, I F 1921- *ConAu 29R*
Nicolson, Ian 1928- *WrDr 84*
Nicolson, Ian Ferguson 1921- *IntAu&W 82*
Nicolson, James R 1934- *ConAu 9NR, –65*
Nicolson, Marjorie Hope 1894-1981 *ConAu 9R,*
   –103
Nicolson, Nigel 1917- *ConAu 101, WrDr 84*
Nicolson, Victoria Mary *ConAu X*
Nicorovici, Vasile 1924- *IntAu&W 82*
Nicosia, Francesco M 1933- *ConAu 81*
Nicosia, Franco M *ConAu X*
Nida, Eugene A 1914- *ConAu 1R, –1NR,*
   IntAu&W 82
Nidditch, Peter 1928- *WrDr 84*
Nidditch, Peter 1928-1983 *ConAu 109*
Niddrie, David Lawrence 1917- *ConAu 25R*
Nideffer, Robert M 1942- *ConAu 9NR, –65*
Nidetch, Jean 1923- *ConAu 89*
Nie, Norman H 1943- *ConAu 65*
Niebuhr, Reinhold 1892-1971 *ConAu 29R, –41R,*
   DcLB 17[port], LongCTC, ModAL, TwCA,
   TwCA SUP
Niebuhr, Richard R 1926- *ConAu 77*
Niebuhr, Ursula 1907- *ConAu 89*
Nieburg, H L 1927- *ConAu 9R, WrDr 84*
Nieburg, Harold L 1927- *IntAu&W 82*

Niedecker, Lorine 1903-1970 *ConAu P-2,*
ConLC 10
Niederauer, David J 1924- *ConAu 45*
Niedergesass, Siegfried 1945- *IntAu&W 82*
Niederhoffer, Arthur 1917-1981 *ConAu 103*
Niederland, William G 1904- *ConAu 81,*
IntAu&W 82
Niedzielski, Henri 1931- *ConAu 49*
Nieh, Hualing 1925- *ConAu 81*
Niehoff, Arthur H 1921- *ConAu 21R*
Nieland, Christine *ConAmTC*
Nielander, William Ahlers 1901- *ConAu 5R*
Nielsen, Aage Rosendal 1921- *ConAu 25R*
Nielsen, Dulcimer 1943- *ConAu 93*
Nielsen, Eduard 1923- *ConAu 29R*
Nielsen, Gary 1939- *ConAu 97*
Nielsen, Helen 1918- *ConAu 1R, -1NR,*
TwCCr&M 80, WrDr 84
Nielsen, Herluf 1922- *IntAu&W 82*
Nielsen, Jean Sarver 1922- *ConAu 5R*
Nielsen, Jorgen 1902-1945 *ClDMEL 80*
Nielsen, Kay 1886-1957 *SmATA 16*
Nielsen, Margaret A *ConAu 105*
Nielsen, Niels Christian, Jr. 1921- *ConAu 3NR,*
-9R, WrDr 84
Nielsen, Oswald 1904- *ConAu P-2*
Nielsen, Sven Sigurd 1901-1976 *ConAu 104*
Nielsen, Veneta Leatham 1909- *ConAu 89*
Nielsen, Virginia *ConAu X, SmATA X*
Nielsen, Waldemar August 1917- *ConAu 103*
Nielson, Ingrid *ConAu X*
Nielson, Roger Charles 1952- *IntWWP 82*
Nielssen, Eric *ConAu X*
Nieman, Egbert William 1909- *ConAu P-1*
Nieman, Lucius W 1857-1935 *DcLB 25[port]*
Niemann, Roelof Johannes 1935- *IntAu&W 82*
Niemann, Roy *IntAu&W 82X*
Niemeier, Jean 1912- *ConAu 25R*
Niemeyer, Eberhardt Victor, Jr. 1919-
ConAu 102
Niemeyer, Gerhart 1907- *ConAu 1R,*
IntAu&W 82
Niemeyer, Roy K 1922- *ConAu 1R*
Niemi, Albert, Jr. 1942- *ConAu 73*
Niemi, John A 1932- *ConAu 77*
Niemi, Richard G 1941- *ConAu 41R*
Nieminen, Hannu Pertti 1929- *IntWWP 82*
Niemojowski, Jerzy Klosowski 1918- *IntWWP 82*
Niemoller, Ara *ConAu X*
Niemoller, Martin 1892- *LongCTC*
Niepold, Mary Martin *ConAmTC*
Nierenberg, Gerard I 1923- *ConAu 25R, -61,*
WrDr 84
Nierman, M Murray 1918- *ConAu 1R*
Nies, Judith 1941- *ConAu 77*
Niesewand, Peter 1944- *ConAu 101,*
IntAu&W 82, WrDr 84
Niesewand, Peter 1944-1983 *ConAu 109*
Niess, Robert Judson 1911- *ConAu P-2*
Niethammer, Carolyn 1944- *ConAu 85*
Nietz, John Alfred 1888- *ConAu 1R*
Nietzke, Ann 1945- *ConAu 105*
Nietzsche, Friedrich 1844-1900 *TwCLC 10[port]*
Nietzsche, Friedrich Wilhelm 1844-1900
ClDMEL 80, ConAu 107
Nievergelt, Jurg 1938- *ConAu 29R*
Niewyk, Donald L 1940- *ConAu 33R*
Niflis, Michael *DrAP&F 83*
Niggli, Josefina 1910- *ConAu P-2,*
DcLB Y80B[port]
Nightingale, Anne Redmon 1943- *ConAu 103*
Nightingale, Barbra *DrAP&F 83*
Nightingale, Florence 1820-1910 *LongCTC*
Nightingale, Sir Geoffrey 1904- *ConAu P-1*
Nightrate, Emil *ConAu X*
Nigro, Felix A 1914- *ConAu 37R, WrDr 84*
Nihal Singh, Surendra 1929- *ConAu 93,*
IntAu&W 82
Nihilo, Arthur X 1938- *ConAu 105*
Niininen, Margit *IntAu&W 82X*
Niisaka, Kazuo 1943- *IntAu&W 82*
Niizaka, Kazuo 1943- *ConAu 77*
Nijhoff, Martinus 1894-1953 *ClDMEL 80,*
CnMD
Nijinsky, Romola Flavia 1891-1978 *ConAu 81*
Nijinsky, Vaslav 1890-1950 *LongCTC*
Nik *ConAu X*
Nik T O *ConAu X*
Nikelly, Arthur G 1927- *ConAu 17R*
Nikhileswar, K Yadav Reddy 1938- *IntWWP 82*
Nikitin, Nikolay Nikolayevich 1895-1963
ClDMEL 80

Nikitin, Nikolay Nikolayevich 1897- *TwCWr*
Niklander, Hannu Kustaa 1951- *IntWWP 82*
Niklaus, Robert 1910- *ConAu 9R,*
IntAu&W 82, WrDr 84
Niklaus, Thelma 1912- *ConAu 9R*
Nikolaievic, Dusan 1885-1961 *CnMD*
Nikolajsen, Ejgil 1924- *IntAu&W 82*
Nikolas, T A *IntAu&W 82X*
Nikolay, Michael 1941- *ConAu 97*
Nikula, Karl Oscar 1907- *IntAu&W 82*
Nilak, Robert *IntAu&W 82X*
Nilak, Trebor *IntAu&W 82X*
Niland, D'Arcy Francis 1920-1967 *ConAu 1R,*
-3NR, TwCWr
Niland, Deborah 1951- *ConAu 106, SmATA 27*
Niland, Powell 1919- *ConAu 21R*
Nile, Dorothea *ConAu X, TwCCr&M 80,*
WrDr 84
Niles, Blair 1880?-1959 *TwCA, TwCA SUP*
Niles, D T 1908-1970 *ConAu 29R*
Niles, Gwendolyn 1914- *ConAu 9R, MichAu 80*
Niles, John Jacob 1892-1980 *ConAu 41R, -97*
Nilin, Pavel Filippovich 1908- *TwCWr*
Nilles, Jack M 1932- *ConAu 108*
Nilsen, Don L F 1934- *ConAu 41R*
Nilsen, Rudolf 1901-1929 *ClDMEL 80*
Nilson, Bee 1908- *WrDr 84*
Nilsskog, Audun 1930- *IntAu&W 82*
Nilsson, Nic 1933- *IntAu&W 82*
Nilsson, Usha Saksena 1930- *ConAu 41R*
Nilsson Piraten, Fritiof 1895-1972 *ClDMEL 80*
Nimavat, Batukdas Sunderdas 1947- *IntWWP 82*
Nimble, Jack B *ConAu X*
Nimeth, Albert J 1918- *ConAu 25R*
Nimier, Roger 1925-1962 *ClDMEL 80*
Nimmer, Melville B 1923- *ConAu 49*
Nimmo, Dan D 1933- *ConAu 7NR, -13R*
Nimmo, Derek 1933- *ConAu 109*
Nimmo, Jenny 1942- *ConAu 108, WrDr 84*
Nimmons, Phil 1923- *CreCan 2*
Nimnicht, Nona *DrAP&F 83*
Nimnicht, Nona 1930- *ConAu 73, IntWWP 82*
Nimocks, Walter Buford 1930- *ConAu 41R,*
WrDr 84
Nimoy, Leonard 1931- *ConAu 57*
Nims, Charles F 1906- *ConAu 17R*
Nims, John Frederick *DrAP&F 83*
Nims, John Frederick 1913- *ConAu 6NR, -13R,*
ConP 80, DcLB 5[port], IntWWP 82,
TwCA SUP, WrDr 84
Nin, Anais 1903-1977 *AuNews 2, ConAu 13R,*
-69, ConLC 1, -4, -8, -11, -14, DcLB 2, -4,
ModAL, ModAL SUP, TwCA SUP
Nin, Anais 1914- *WhoTwCL*
Nineham, Dennis Eric 1921- *ConAu 85,*
IntAu&W 82, WrDr 84
Nininger, H H 1887- *ConAu 21R*
Nioche, Brigitte *ConAu 109*
Nips, Nick L *IntAu&W 82X, IntWWP 82X*
Nir, Yehuda 1930- *ConAu 107*
Nirenberg, Jesse S 1921- *ConAu 69*
Nirmala-Kumara, V *ConAu X*
Nirodi, Hira 1930- *ConAu 5R*
Nisbet, Ada Blanche 1907- *ConAu 41R*
Nisbet, Joanne 1931- *CreCan 2*
Nisbet, Robert A 1913- *ConAu 25R,*
ConIsC 1[port]
Nisbet, Stanley Donald 1912- *ConAu P-1,*
WrDr 84
Nisbett, Alec 1930- *ConAu 81*
Nisbett, Richard E 1941- *ConAu 37R*
Nisetich, Frank Joseph 1942- *ConAu 97*
Nish, Ian Hill 1926- *ConAu 21R, WrDr 84*
Nishihara, Masashi 1937- *ConAu 69*
Nishio, Suehiro 1891-1981 *ConAu 108*
Nishiwaki, Junzaburo 1894-1982 *ConAu 107*
Nishiyama, Chiaki 1924- *ConAu 110*
Niskanen, William Arthur, Jr. 1933- *ConAu 41R*
Nissen, Lowell A 1932- *ConAu 33R*
Nissenbaum, Stephen 1941- *ConAu 77*
Nissenson, Hugh *DrAP&F 83*
Nissenson, Hugh 1933- *ConAu 17R, ConLC 4,*
-9, WrDr 84
Nissman, Albert 1930- *ConAu 37R, WrDr 84*
Nissman, Blossom S 1928- *ConAu 37R,*
WrDr 84
Nist, John 1925- *ConAu 21R, WrDr 84*
Nist, John 1925-1981 *ConAu 11NR*
Nitchie, George Wilson 1921- *ConAu 9R,*
WrDr 84
Nitram *IntAu&W 82X*
Nitske, W Robert 1909- *ConAu 5NR, -13R,*

Nittler, Alan Hopkins 1918- *ConAu 61*
Nityanandan, Perumpilavil Madhava Menon 1926-
ConAu 9R
Nitzsche, Jane Chance 1945- *ConAu 8NR, -57,*
IntWWP 82
Niven, Alastair 1944- *ConAu 81, IntAu&W 82,*
WrDr 84
Niven, Alexander Curt 1920- *ConAu 2NR, -5R*
Niven, David 1910- *ASpks, ConAu 77,*
WrDr 84
Niven, David 1910-1983 *ConAu 110*
Niven, Frederick John 1878-1944 *CreCan 1,*
LongCTC, TwCA, TwCA SUP, TwCWW
Niven, John 1921- *ConAu 65*
Niven, Larry *DrAP&F 83*
Niven, Larry 1938- *ConAu X, ConLC 8,*
ConSFA, DcLB 8[port], IntAu&W 82,
TwCSFW, WrDr 84
Niven, Laurence VanCott 1938- *ConAu 21R*
Niven, Marian *ConAu X*
Niven, Rex 1898- *WrDr 84*
Niven, Sir Rex 1898- *IntAu&W 82*
Niven, Vern *ConAu X*
Niverville, Louis De 1933- *CreCan 1*
Nivison, David Shepherd 1923- *ConAu 103*
Niwa, Tamako 1922- *ConAu 106*
Nixon, Agnes Eckhardt 1927- *ConAu 110,*
ConLC 21[port]
Nixon, Allan 1918- *ConAu 17R*
Nixon, Colin Harry 1939- *IntWWP 82*
Nixon, David Michael *DrAP&F 83*
Nixon, Edna Mary 1892- *ConAu 5R*
Nixon, George 1924- *ConAu 49*
Nixon, Hershell Howard 1923- *ConAu 89*
Nixon, Howard Millar 1909-1983 *ConAu 109*
Nixon, Ivor Gray 1905- *ConAu P-2*
Nixon, Joan Lowery 1927- *ConAu 7NR, -9R,*
SmATA 8
Nixon, John Erskine 1917- *ConAu 101*
Nixon, K *ConAu X, SmATA X*
Nixon, Kathleen Irene *ConAu 73, SmATA 14*
Nixon, Lucille M 1908-1963 *ConAu 5R*
Nixon, Marion 1930- *ConAu 49*
Nixon, Richard 1913- *WrDr 84*
Nixon, Richard M 1913- *ConAu 73*
Nixon, Robert E 1918- *ConAu 5R*
Nixon, Sallie *DrAP&F 83*
Nixon, St. John Cousins 1885- *ConAu 5R*
Nixon, William R 1918- *ConAu 29R*
Nixson, Frederick Ian 1943- *ConAu 104,*
WrDr 84
Nizan, Paul 1905-1940 *ClDMEL 80, ModFrL*
Nizer, Louis 1902- *ConAu 53, WrDr 84*
Nizzi, Guido 1900- *ConSFA*
Njururi, Ngumbu 1930- *ConAu 17R*
Nkabinde, Thulani *DrAP&F 83*
Nketia, J H Kwabena 1921- *ConAu 7NR*
Nketia, John Hanson Kwabena 1921- *ConAu 9R*
Nkosi, Lewis 1935- *TwCWr*
Nkosi, Lewis 1936- *ConAu 65, ConDr 82,*
DcLEL 1940, WrDr 84
Nkrumah, Bahala *LivgBAA*
Nkrumah, Kwame 1909-1972 *DcLEL 1940*
Noad, Frederick 1929- *ConAu 4NR, -9R*
Noah, Harold J 1925- *ConAu 33R, WrDr 84*
Noah, Joseph W 1928- *ConAu 61*
Noailles, Anna, Comtesse De 1876-1933
ClDMEL 80
Noak, Christian 1927- *CnMD*
Noakes, Jeremy 1941- *ConAu 101*
Noakes, Michael 1933- *IntAu&W 82, WrDr 84*
Noakes, Vivien 1937- *ConAu 65, WrDr 84*
Noall, Roger 1935- *ConAu 9R*
Nobile, Umberto 1885-1978 *ConAu 81*
Noble, Charles *ConAu X, WrDr 84*
Noble, David Watson 1925- *ConAu 1NR, -49*
Noble, Dudley 1893?-1970 *ConAu 104*
Noble, Elizabeth Marian 1945- *ConAu 9NR, -65*
Noble, G Bernard 1892-1972 *ConAu 37R,*
ConAu P-2
Noble, Iris 1922- *ConAu 1R, -2NR, SmATA 5*
Noble, J Kendrick 1896?-1978 *ConAu 104*
Noble, J Kendrick, Jr. 1928- *ConAu 17R*
Noble, James *IntWWP 82X*
Noble, James William 1941- *IntWWP 82*
Noble, Jeanne 1926- *LivgBAA*
Noble, John 1923- *ConAu 45*
Noble, John Appelbe 1914- *ConAu 1NR, -45,*
WrDr 84
Noble, John Wesley 1913- *ConAu 9R*
Noble, Joseph Veach 1920- *ConAu 61*

Noble, June 1924- *ConAu 97*
Noble, Marguerite 1910- *ConAu 105*
Noble, Stanley R 1904?-1977 *ConAu 104*
Noble, William Charles 1935- *ConAu 107,*
WrDr 84
Noble, William P 1932- *ConAu 101*
Noboa, Julio, Jr. *DrAP&F 83*
Nocerino, Kathryn *DrAP&F 83*
Nochlin, Linda Weinberg 1931- *ConAu 6NR,*
-9R
Nock, Albert Jay 1873-1945 *TwCA, TwCA SUP*
Nock, Francis J 1905-1969 *ConAu P-1*
Nock, O S 1905- *ConAu 85, WrDr 84*
Nockolds, Harold 1907-1982 *ConAu 108*
Noda, Barbara Ruth 1953- *IntWWP 82*
Noddings, Thomas C 1933- *ConAu 2NR, -49*
Nodel, Sol 1912-1976 *ConAu 107*
Nodset, Joan *ConAu X, SmATA 1*
Nodset, Joan L *ConAu X, TwCCW 83,*
WrDr 84
Noel, Daniel C 1936- *ConAu 101*
Noel, Eugenio 1885-1936 *CIDMEL 80*
Noel, Gerard Eyre 1926- *IntAu&W 82*
Noel, Hilda Bloxton, Jr. *ConAu X*
Noel, John *WrDr 84*
Noel, John V, Jr. 1912- *ConAu 21R*
Noel, Marie 1883-1967 *CIDMEL 80*
Noel, Ruth 1947- *ConAu 69*
Noel, Thomas Jacob 1945- *ConAu 107*
Noel-Baker, Philip John 1889-1982 *ConAu 108*
Noel Hume, Ivor 1927- *ConAu 13R*
Noel-Hume, Ivor 1927- *WrDr 84*
Noel-Paton, Margaret Hamilton 1896- *WrDr 84*
Noelle-Neumann, Elisabeth 1916- *IntAu&W 82*
Noer, Thomas John 1944- *ConAu 102*
Noether, Emiliana P *ConAu 101*
Noff *IntAu&W 82X*
Nofziger, Margaret 1946- *ConAu 110*
Nogee, Joseph L 1929- *ConAu 17R, WrDr 84*
Noggle, Burl L 1924- *ConAu 107*
Noguera, Magdalena *IntAu&W 82X*
Noguere, Suzanne 1947- *ConAu 107,*
SmATA 34[port]
Nohl, Frederick 1927- *ConAu 3NR, -5R,*
WrDr 84
Nohrnberg, James 1941- *ConAu 69*
Nojiri, Kiyohiko 1897-1973 *ConAu 41R, -93,*
WorAu
Nokes, Gerald Dacre 1899-1971 *ConAu 104*
Nolamo, Stanley *IntAu&W 82X*
Nolan, Alan T 1923- *ConAu 1R*
Nolan, Bob 1908?-1980 *ConAu 101*
Nolan, Brian *ConAu X*
Nolan, Carroll A 1906- *ConAu 17R*
Nolan, Chuck *ConAu X*
Nolan, Dennis 1945- *SmATA 34*
Nolan, Edward Francis 1915- *ConAu 108*
Nolan, Frederick *WrDr 84*
Nolan, James *DrAP&F 83*
Nolan, James 1947- *ConAu 5NR, -53,*
IntWWP 82
Nolan, Jeannette Covert 1897?-1974 *ConAu 4NR,*
-5R, -53, SmATA 2, -27N
Nolan, Madeena Spray 1943- *ConAu 89*
Nolan, Paul T 1919- *ConAu 2NR, -5R,*
WrDr 84
Nolan, Richard Thomas 1937- *ConAu 10NR,*
-25R
Nolan, Robert Leon 1912- *IntAu&W 82*
Nolan, Tom 1948- *ConAu 77*
Nolan, William F 1928- *ConAu 1R, -1NR,*
ConSFA, DcLB 8[port], SmATA 28,
TwCCr&M 80, TwCSFW, WrDr 84
Nolan, Winefride 1913- *ConAu 13R*
Noland, Patricia Hampton *IntWWP 82*
Noland, Ronald G 1936- *ConAu 41R*
Nolde, O Frederick 1899-1972 *ConAu 37R,*
ConAu P-2
Nolen, Barbara 1902- *ConAu 104*
Nolen, Claude 1921- *ConAu 21R, WrDr 84*
Nolen, William A 1928- *ASpks, ConAu 77*
Nolin, Bertil 1926- *ConAu 65*
Noling, A W 1899- *ConAu P-2*
Noll, Bink *DrAP&F 83*
Noll, Bink 1927- *ConAu X, WrDr 84*
Noll, Lou Barker 1924- *ConAu 5R*
Noll, Martin *ConAu X*
Noll, Roger G 1940- *ConAu 8NR, -53*
Nollau, Gunther 1911- *ConAu 5R*
Nollen, Stanley D 1940- *ConAu 110*
Nolte, Carl William 1933- *ConAu 77*
Nolte, Elleta 1919- *ConAu 61*

Nolte, M Chester 1911- *ConAu 9R*
Nolte, William H 1928- *ConAu 33R*
Nolting, Orin F 1903- *ConAu 29R*
Noltingk, Bernard Edward 1918- *ConAu 17R,*
IntAu&W 82, WrDr 84
Nomad, Max 1880?-1973 *ConAu 41R*
Nomar, Benjamin Ono *IntAu&W 82X*
Nonet, Philippe 1939- *ConAu 57*
Nonzame *IntAu&W 82X*
Noon, Brian 1919- *ConAu 49*
Noon, William T 1912-1975 *ConAu 53, -65*
Noonan, John Ford 1943- *ConAu 85, ConDr 82,*
WrDr 84
Noonan, John T, Jr. 1926- *ConAu 13R*
Noonan, Julia 1946- *ConAu 33R, SmATA 4*
Noonan, Lowell G 1922- *ConAu 29R, WrDr 84*
Noonan, Michael 1921- *WrDr 84*
Noonan, Michael John 1921- *ConAu 21R*
Noone, Edwina *ConAu X, TwCCr&M 80,*
WrDr 84
Noone, John 1936- *ConAu 109, DcLB 14[port],*
WrDr 84
Noone, Richard 1918?-1973 *ConAu 104*
Noorbergen, Rene B 1928- *ConAu 77,*
IntAu&W 82
Nora, James Jackson 1928- *ConAu 104*
Noras, Thor Gunnar 1935- *IntAu&W 82*
Norbeck, Edward 1915- *ConAu 1R, -1NR,*
IntAu&W 82, WrDr 84
Norberg-Schulz, Christian 1926- *ConAu 81,*
IntAu&W 82
Norbert, Henri 1904- *CreCan 1*
Norbu, Thubten Jigme *ConAu X*
Norby, Irene Jellinek De *CreCan 1*
Norcott, Ronald *IntAu&W 82X*
Norcross, John *ConAu X, IntAu&W 82X,*
SmATA X
Norcross, Lisabet *ConAu X*
Nord, Carol Ann *DrAP&F 83*
Nord, Ole C 1935- *ConAu 13R*
Nord, Paul 1900?-1981 *ConAu 103*
Nord, Walter R 1939- *ConAu 37R*
Nordal, Sigurdur Johannesson 1886-1974
CIDMEL 80
Nordau, Max Simon 1849-1923 *LongCTC,*
TwCA SUP
Nordberg, H Orville 1916- *ConAu 1R*
Nordberg, Robert B 1921- *ConAu 13R*
Nordbrandt, Henrik 1945- *IntWWP 82*
Nordby, Vernon James 1945- *ConAu 57*
Nordell, Roderick 1925- *ConAu 104*
Norden, Albert 1904-1982 *ConAu 107*
Norden, Charles *ConAu X, LongCTC,*
TwCA SUP, WrDr 84
Norden, Denis 1922- *ConAu 104*
Norden, Heinz 1905- *ConAu 53*
Norden, Helen Brown *ConAu X*
Nordham, George Washington 1929- *ConAu 106*
Nordhaus, William D 1941- *ConAu 97*
Nordhoff, Charles 1887-1947 *ConAu 108*
Nordhoff, Charles Bernard 1887-1947
DcLB 9[port], LongCTC, SmATA 23[port],
TwCA, TwCA SUP
Nordholm, Harriet 1912- *ConAu 29R*
Nordicus *ConAu X*
Nordin, D Sven 1942- *ConAu 61*
Nordland, Gerald John 1927- *ConAu 104*
Nordlicht, Lillian *ConAu 105,*
SmATA 29[port]
Nordlinger, Eric A 1939- *ConAu 77*
Nordmann, Joseph Behrens 1922- *ConAu 25R,*
WrDr 84
Nordness, Lee 1924- *ConAu 9R*
Nordoff, Paul 1909-1977 *ConAu 102*
Nordquist, Barbara K 1940- *ConAu 77*
Nordra, Olav 1911- *IntAu&W 82*
Nordskog, John Eric 1893- *ConAu 1R*
Nordstrom, Ursula 1910- *ConAu 13R, SmATA 3*
Nordwall, Ove Bjornson 1938- *IntAu&W 82*
Nordyke, Eleanor C 1927- *ConAu 107*
Nordyke, James W 1930- *ConAu 49*
Noreen, Robert Gerald 1938- *ConAu 77*
Norelli, Martina R 1942- *ConAu 73*
Noren, Catherine 1938- *ConAu 65*
Noren, Kjerstin Margareta 1945- *IntAu&W 82*
Noren, Paul Harold Andreas 1910- *ConAu P-1*
Noreng, Harald 1913- *IntAu&W 82*
Norfleet, Barbara P 1926- *ConAu 107*
Norfleet, Mary Crockett 1919- *ConAu 1R*
Norgate, Matthew 1901- *ConAu 103*
Norge, Geo 1898- *CIDMEL 80*
Nori, Claude 1949- *ConAu 101*

Norkin, Samuel N 1920- *ConAmTC*
Norland, Howard Bernett 1932- *ConAu 49*
Norling, Bernard 1924- *ConAu 29R, WrDr 84*
Norling, Josephine Stearns 1895- *ConAu 1R*
Norling, Rita *ConAu 61*
Norman, Adrian R D 1938- *ConAu 29R*
Norman, Alexander Vesey Bethune 1930-
ConAu 9NR, -21R
Norman, Ames *ConAu X*
Norman, Barbara 1927- *ConAu 33R,*
IntAu&W 82, WrDr 84
Norman, Bruce 1936- *WrDr 84*
Norman, Bruce Anthony John 1936- *ConAu 61,*
IntAu&W 82
Norman, Cecilia 1927- *ConAu 7NR, -57*
Norman, Charles 1904- *ConAu 107,*
TwCA SUP
Norman, Don Cleveland 1909?-1979 *ConAu 89*
Norman, Donald A 1935- *ConAu 1NR, -49*
Norman, Dorothy 1905- *ConAu 25R*
Norman, Edward 1938- *ConAu 10NR*
Norman, Edward Robert 1938- *ConAu 17R*
Norman, Frank 1930-1980 *ConAu 1R, -6NR,*
-102, IntAu&W 82
Norman, Frank 1931- *CroCD, ModWD*
Norman, Frank 1939- *DcLEL 1940*
Norman, Geraldine 1940- *ConAu 93*
Norman, Gurney *DrAP&F 83*
Norman, James *DrAP&F 83*
Norman, James 1912- *ConAu X, SmATA X,*
TwCCr&M 80, WrDr 84
Norman, Jillian 1940- *ConAu 25R*
Norman, Joe *ConAu X*
Norman, John 1912- *ConAu 17R, WrDr 84*
Norman, John 1931- *ConAu X, ConSFA,*
TwCSFW, WrDr 84
Norman, Joyce Ann 1937- *ConAu 65*
Norman, Kerry *ConAu X*
Norman, Lilith 1927- *ConAu 1NR, -45,*
TwCCW 83, WrDr 84
Norman, Lloyd H 1913- *ConAu 102*
Norman, Louis *ConAu X, CreCan 1*
Norman, Marc *DrAP&F 83*
Norman, Marc 1941- *ConAu 49*
Norman, Marsha 1947- *ConAu 105*
Norman, Maxwell H 1917- *ConAu 29R,*
WrDr 84
Norman, Ruth 1903?-1977 *ConAu 73*
Norman, Steve *ConAu X, SmATA X*
Norman, Sylva 1901- *ConAu P-1*
Norman, Vesey *ConAu X*
Norman, W S *ConAu X*
Normyx *LongCTC*
Norodom Sihanouk, Samdech Preah 1922-
ConAu 106
Norquest, Carrol 1901- *ConAu 41R*
Norrie, Ian 1927- *ConAu 106*
Norris, Benjamin Franklin, Jr. 1870-1902
ConAu 110
Norris, Charles Gilman 1881-1945 *DcLB 9[port],*
LongCTC, TwCA, TwCA SUP
Norris, Donald F 1942- *ConAu 2NR, -49*
Norris, Dorothy E Koch 1907- *ConAu P-2*
Norris, Edgar Poe *ConAu X*
Norris, Francis Hubert 1909- *ConAu 5R*
Norris, Frank *ConAu X*
Norris, Frank 1870-1902 *FifWWr, LongCTC,*
ModAL, TwCA, TwCA SUP, TwCWW,
TwCWr
Norris, Frank Callan 1907-1967 *ConAu 25R*
Norris, Geoffrey 1947- *WrDr 84*
Norris, Gunilla Brodde *DrAP&F 83*
Norris, Gunilla Brodde 1939- *ConAu 93,*
SmATA 20
Norris, Harold 1918- *ConAu 108*
Norris, Hoke 1913-1977 *ConAu 9R, -73*
Norris, J A 1929- *ConAu 25R*
Norris, James Alfred 1929- *IntAu&W 82*
Norris, James Donald 1930- *ConAu 17R*
Norris, Joan *DrAP&F 83*
Norris, Joan 1943- *ConAu 73*
Norris, John 1925- *ConAu 9R*
Norris, Kathleen *DrAP&F 83*
Norris, Kathleen 1947- *ConAu 33R*
Norris, Kathleen Thompson 1880-1966
ConAu 25R, LongCTC, TwCA,
TwCA SUP, TwCRGW, TwCWr
Norris, Kenneth S 1924- *ConAu 77*
Norris, Leslie 1921- *ConAu P-1, ConLC 14,*
ConP 80, IntAu&W 82, WrDr 84
Norris, Louanne 1930- *ConAu 53*
Norris, Louis William 1906- *ConAu P-1*

Norris, Nigel 1943- *ConAu 65*
Norris, Phyllis Irene 1909- *WrDr 84*
Norris, Richard A, Jr. 1930- *ConAu 17R*
Norris, Ruby Turner 1908- *ConAu X, –1R*
Norris, Russell Bradner 1942- *ConAu 53*
Norris, Theo L 1926- *ConAu 21R*
Norris, Toni *IntAu&W 82X*
Norse, Harold *DrAP&F 83*
Norse, Harold 1916- *ConAu 4NR, –53,*
ConP 80, DcLB 16[port], DcLEL 1940,
WrDr 84
Norstrom, Goran 1928- *IntAu&W 82*
North, Alvin J 1917- *ConAu X*
North, Andrew *ConAu X, SmATA 1,*
TwCCW 83, TwCSFW, WorAu, WrDr 84
North, Charles *DrAP&F 83*
North, Charles 1941- *IntWWP 82*
North, Charles W *ConAu X*
North, Christopher R 1888-1975 *ConAu 61*
North, Colin *ConAu X, TwCWW*
North, Eleanor Beryl 1898- *ConAu 49,*
IntWWP 82
North, Elizabeth 1932- *ConAu 81,*
IntAu&W 82, WrDr 84
North, Gary 1942- *ConAu 65*
North, Gil *WrDr 84*
North, Gil 1916- *ConAu X, IntAu&W 82X,*
TwCCr&M 80
North, Helen Florence 1921- *ConAu 104*
North, Jessica Nelson 1894- *TwCA, TwCA SUP*
North, Joan Marian 1920- *ConAu 13R,*
SmATA 16, WrDr 84
North, John 1894-1973 *ConAu 104, –107*
North, Joseph 1904-1976 *ConAu 1R, –4NR, –69*
North, M H *IntWWP 82X*
North, Mary Hayne *DrAP&F 83*
North, Mary Hayne Baldwin 1945- *IntWWP 82*
North, Morgan 1915?-1978 *ConAu 104*
North, Robert *ConAu X, SmATA X*
North, Robert 1916- *ConAu 17R, IntAu&W 82,*
WrDr 84
North, Robert Carver 1914- *ConAu·4NR, –5R*
North, Sara *ConAu X*
North, Sterling 1906-1974 *ConAu 5R, –53,*
SmATA 1, –26N, TwCA, TwCA SUP,
TwCCW 83
North, Wheeler James 1922- *ConAu 101*
Northam, Ray M 1929- *ConAu 73*
Northart, Leo J 1929- *ConAu 69*
Northcliffe, Alfred Harmsworth, Viscount
1865-1922 *LongCTC*
Northcote *ConAu X*
Northcote, Boulting *ConAu X*
Northcote, Peter *IntAu&W 82X*
Northcott, Cecil 1902- *ConAu 9R, WrDr 84*
Northcott, Douglas 1916- *WrDr 84*
Northcott, Kenneth J 1922- *ConAu 45*
Northedge, Frederick 1918- *WrDr 84*
Northedge, Frederick Samuel 1918- *ConAu 104,*
IntAu&W 82
Northen, Helen 1914- *ConAu 33R*
Northen, Henry T 1908-1979 *ConAu 97*
Northen, Rebecca Tyson 1910- *ConAu 105,*
IntAu&W 82
Northey, John Frederick 1920- *WrDr 84*
Northgrave, Anne *ConAu X*
Northmore, Elizabeth Florence 1906-1974
ConAu P-2
Northnagel, E W *DrAP&F 83*
Northouse, Cameron 1948- *ConAu 81*
Northrop, Filmer Stuart Cuckow 1893-
ConAu 1R, TwCA SUP
Northrup, Herbert Roof 1918- *ConAu 9R*
Northumbrian Gentleman, The *ConAu X*
Northway, Mary L 1909- *ConAu 45*
Northwood, Lawrence K 1917- *ConAu 13R*
Norton, Alan 1926- *ConAu 81*
Norton, Alden H 1903- *ConAu 101, ConSFA*
Norton, Alice 1926- *ConAu 33R*
Norton, Alice Mary 1912- *ConAu 1R, –2NR,*
SmATA 1
Norton, Andre 1912- *ConAu X, ConLC 12,*
ConSFA, DcLB 8, SmATA 1, TwCCW 83,
TwCSFW, WorAu
Norton, Andre Alice 1912- *WrDr 84*
Norton, Bess *ConAu X, TwCRGW, WrDr 84*
Norton, Bettina A 1936- *ConAu 93*
Norton, Boyd 1936- *ConAu 37R*
Norton, Bram *ConAu X*
Norton, Browning *ConAu X, SmATA X*
Norton, Charles A 1920- *ConAu 109*
Norton, Charles Eliot 1827-1908 *LongCTC*

Norton, David Fate 1937- *ConAu 107*
Norton, David L 1930- *ConAu 37R*
Norton, Elliot 1903- *ConAmTC, ConAu 109*
Norton, Frank R B 1909- *ConAu 61,*
SmATA 10
Norton, Frederick H 1896- *ConAu 61*
Norton, Graham Peter George 1935-
IntAu&W 82
Norton, Herman A 1921- *ConAu 5R, –7NR*
Norton, Howard Melvin 1911- *ConAu 1R, –3NR*
Norton, Hugh S 1921- *ConAu 9R*
Norton, Joseph L 1918- *ConAu 29R*
Norton, Joshua *DrAP&F 83*
Norton, Lucy 1902- *IntAu&W 82*
Norton, Mary *DcLEL 1940*
Norton, Mary 1903- *ChlLR 6[port], ConAu 97,*
SmATA 18, TwCCW 83, WrDr 84
Norton, Mary Beth 1943- *ConAu 5NR, –49,*
MichAu 80
Norton, Mary E 1913- *ConAu 41R*
Norton, Olive *WrDr 84*
Norton, Olive Marion 1913- *ConAu 9R*
Norton, Paul Foote 1917- *ConAu 41R*
Norton, Perry L 1920- *ConAu 13R*
Norton, Peter John 1913- *ConAu 13R*
Norton, Philip 1951- *WrDr 84*
Norton, Thomas Elliot 1942- *ConAu 61*
Norton, Victor 1906-1983 *ConAu 109*
Norton-Smith, John 1931- *ConAu 107,*
WrDr 84
Norton-Taylor, Duncan 1904-1982 *ConAu 102,*
–107
Norvil, Manning *ConAu X, TwCSFW*
Norville, Warren 1923- *ConAu 73*
Norwak, Mary 1929- *ConAu 109, IntAu&W 82*
Norway, Kate 1913- *ConAu X, TwCRGW,*
WrDr 84
Norway, Nevil Shute 1899-1960 *ConAu 102, –93,*
LongCTC, TwCA, TwCA SUP
Norwich, Viscount *LongCTC*
Norwich, Viscountess *LongCTC*
Norwich, John Julius 1929- *ConAu 5NR, –49,*
IntAu&W 82, WrDr 84
Norwid, Cyprian Kamil 1821-1883 *CIDMEL 80*
Norwoo, Victor George Charles 1920-
IntAu&W 82
Norwood, Frederick Abbott 1914- *ConAu 1R,*
–5NR
Norwood, Hayden Eugene 1907- *IntAu&W 82*
Norwood, John *ConAu X*
Norwood, Paul *ConAu X*
Norwood, Victor G C 1920- *ConAu 10NR*
Norwood, Victor George Charles 1920-
ConAu 21R, ConSFA, WrDr 84
Norwood, Warren *DrAP&F 83*
Nosco, Peter 1950- *ConAu 93*
Nosille, Nabrah *ConAu X*
Noss, John Boyer 1896- *ConAu 85*
Noss, Luther 1907- *ConAu 5R*
Nossack, Hans Erich 1901- *CnMD, ConLC 6,*
ModGL, TwCWr, WhoTwCL, WorAu
Nossack, Hans Erich 1901-1977 *CIDMEL 80*
Nossack, Hans Erich 1901-1978 *ConAu 85, –93*
Nossal, Frederick Christian 1927-1979 *ConAu 5R,*
–89
Nossal, Gustav 1931- *WrDr 84*
Nossal, Gustav Joseph Victor 1931- *ConAu 109*
Nossiter, Bernard D 1926- *ConAu 41R*

Nostrand, Howard Lee 1910- *ConAu 9R,*
WrDr 84
Nostrand, Jennifer *DrAP&F 83*
Nostrand, S *DrAP&F 83*
Notehelfer, F G 1939- *ConAu 81*
Notestein, Frank Wallace 1902-1983 *ConAu 109*
Notestein, Wallace 1878-1969 *ConAu P-1*
Noth, Dominique Paul 1944- *ConAmTC*
Noth, Martin D 1902-1968 *ConAu P-2*
Nothing Venture *ConAu X*
Notlep, Robert *ConAu X*
Notley, Alice *DrAP&F 83*
Notman, Edith 1937- *ConAmTC*
Nott, Barry *IntAu&W 82X*
Nott, David 1928- *ConAu 45*
Nott, Kathleen *WrDr 84*
Nott, Kathleen Cecilia *ConAu 1R, –3NR,*
ConP 80, TwCWr, WorAu
Notterman, Joseph M 1923- *ConAu 17R*
Nottingham, Elizabeth K 1900- *ConAu 93*
Nottingham, William Jesse 1927- *ConAu 25R*
Notz, Rebecca Love 1888-1974 *ConAu 104*

Nou, Helga 1934- *IntAu&W 82*
Nourissier, Francois 1927- *CIDMEL 80,*
ConAu 81
Nourse, Alan E 1928- *ConAu 1R, –3NR,*
ConSFA, DcLB 8[port], TwCSFW,
WrDr 84
Nourse, Edwin G 1883-1974 *ConAu 49*
Nourse, Hugh O 1933- *ConAu 107*
Nourse, James G 1947- *ConAu 105*
Nourse, Joan Thellusson 1921- *ConAmTC,*
ConAu 9R
Nourse, Mary Augusta 1880?-1971 *ConAu 33R*
Nourse, Robert Eric Martin 1938- *ConAu 21R*
Nouveau, Arthur *ConAu X*
Nouveau, Germain 1851-1920 *CIDMEL 80*
Nouwen, Henri J 1932- *ConAu 73*
Nova, Craig *DrAP&F 83*
Nova, Craig 1945- *ConAu 2NR, –45, ConLC 7*
Novack, Evelyn Reed 1906?-1979 *ConAu 85*
Novack, George 1905- *ConAu 49, WrDr 84*
Novak, Arne 1880-1939 *CIDMEL 80*
Novak, Barbara *ConAu 97*
Novak, Bogdan C 1919- *ConAu 33R*
Novak, David 1941- *ConAu 93*
Novak, Estelle Gershgoren *DrAP&F 83*
Novak, Helga 1935- *CIDMEL 80*
Novak, Jane Dailey 1917- *ConAu 105,*
WrDr 84
Novak, Jane Daily 1917- *IntAu&W 82*
Novak, Joe *ConAu X*
Novak, Joseph *ConAu X, WorAu,*
WrDr 84
Novak, Joseph 1898- *ConAu P-1*
Novak, Lela *IntAu&W 82X*
Novak, Lorna 1927- *ConAu 17R*
Novak, Maximillian Erwin 1930- *ConAu 33R,*
IntAu&W 82, WrDr 84
Novak, Michael *DrAP&F 83*
Novak, Michael 1933- *ConAu 1R, –1NR,*
ConIsC 1[port], WrDr 84
Novak, Michael Paul *DrAP&F 83*
Novak, Michael Paul 1935- *ConAu 49*
Novak, Robert D 1931- *ConAu 13R*
Novak, Robert Lee 1933- *IntWWP 82*
Novak, Rose 1940- *ConAu 105*
Novak, Slobodan 1924- *ModSL 2*
Novak, Stephen R 1922- *ConAu 85*
Novak, William 1948- *ConAu 93*
Novakova, Tereza 1853-1912 *CIDMEL 80*
Novakovic, Mileva 1938- *IntAu&W 82*
Novarr, David 1917- *ConAu 17R*
Nove, Alec 1915- *ConAu 3NR, WrDr 84*
Nove, Alexander 1915- *ConAu 1R*
Novello, Don 1943- *ConAu 107*
Novello, Ivor 1893-1951 *LongCTC, ModWD,*
TwCA SUP, TwCWr
November, Sharyn *DrAP&F 83*
Noventa, Giacomo 1898-1960 *CIDMEL 80*
Nover, Barnet 1899-1973 *ConAu 41R*
Noverr, Douglas A 1942- *ConAu 102*
Novick, David 1906- *ConAu 33R, WrDr 84*
Novick, Julius Lerner 1939- *ConAmTC,*
ConAu 103
Novick, Marian *DrAP&F 83*
Novik, Mary 1945- *ConAu 61*
Novitz, Charles R 1934- *ConAu 69*
Novo, Salvador 1904-1974 *ConAu 110,*
ModLAL
Novogrod, R Joseph 1916- *ConAu 29R*
Novomesky, Ladislav 1904-1976 *CIDMEL 80,*
ConAu 69, ModSL 2
Novoneyra, Uxio 1930- *IntAu&W 82*
Novotny, Ann M 1936- *ConAu 25R, WrDr 84*
Novotny, Ann M 1936-1982 *ConAu 108*
Novotny, Fritz 1903- *ConAu 65*
Novotny, Louise Miller 1889- *ConAu P-2*
Nowacki, Walenty 1906- *ConAu 37R*
Nowaczynski, Adolf 1876-1944 *CIDMEL 80,*
CnMD, ModWD
Nowak, Kurt 1942- *IntAu&W 82*
Nowak, Mariette 1941- *ConAu 102*
Nowak, Tadeusz 1930- *CIDMEL 80*
Nowakowski, Tadeusz 1918- *CIDMEL 80*
Nowakowski, Zygmunt 1891-1963 *CIDMEL 80*
Nowell, Elizabeth Cameron *ConAu 1NR,*
SmATA 12
Nowicka *IntAu&W 82X*
Nowlan, Alden 1933- *WrDr 84*
Nowlan, Alden A 1933- *ConAu 5NR, –9R,*
ConLC 15, ConP 80, CreCan 2,
DcLEL 1940, ModCmwL
Nowlan, James Dunlap 1941- *ConAu 105*

Nowlan, Philip Francis 1888-1940 *ConAu 108,*
TwCSFW
Nowottny, Winifred May Tilley 1917-
IntAu&W 82
Nowra, Louis 1950- *ConDr 82, WrDr 84*
Noxon, James Herbert 1924- *ConAu 85*
Noyce, Gaylord B 1926- *ConAu 37R*
Noyes, Alfred 1880-1958 *ConAu 104, LongCTC,*
ModBrL, TwCA, TwCA SUP,
TwCLC 7[port], TwCWr
Noyes, Charles Edmund 1904-1972 *ConAu 37R*
Noyes, David 1898?-1981 *ConAu 104*
Noyes, Jeanice W 1914- *ConAu 25R*
Noyes, Kathryn Johnston 1930- *ConAu 17R*
Noyes, Morgan Phelps 1891-1972 *ConAu 37R,*
ConAu P-1
Noyes, Nell Braly 1921- *ConAu 37R*
Noyes, Peter R 1930- *ConAu 49*
Noyes, Russell 1901- *ConAu 25R*
Noyes, Stanley *DrAP&F 83*
Noyes, Stanley 1924- *ConAu 1NR, -45,*
IntWWP 82, WrDr 84
Noyes-Kane, Dorothy 1906- *ConAu P-1*
Noyle, Ken 1922- *ConAu 85*
Nozick, Martin 1917- *ConAu 37R*
Nozick, Robert 1938- *ConAu 61*
Nsarkoh, J K 1931- *ConAu 13R*
Nucera, Marisa Lonette 1959- *ConAu 17R*
Nuchtern, Jean 1939- *ConAu 25R,*
NatPD 81[port]
Nudelman, Jerrold 1942- *ConAu 33R*
Nudleman, Nordyk *CreCan 2*
Nuechterlein, Donald Edwin 1925- *ConAu 1R,*
-1NR
Nuelle, Helen S 1923- *ConAu 61*
Nuetzel, Charles 1934- *ConAu 105, ConSFA*
Nugent, Donald G 1930- *ConAu 45*
Nugent, Elliott 1899-1980 *ConAu 5R, -101, -103*
Nugent, Elliott 1900- *CnMD, ModWD*
Nugent, Frances Roberts 1904-1964? *ConAu 5R*
Nugent, Jeffrey B 1936- *ConAu 93*
Nugent, John Peer 1930- *ConAu 13R*
Nugent, Nancy 1938- *ConAu 65*
Nugent, Robert 1920- *ConAu 61*
Nugent, Tom 1943- *ConAu 49*
Nugent, Vincent Joseph 1913- *ConAu 41R*
Nugent, Walter T K 1935- *ConAu 5R, -5NR,*
WrDr 84
Null, Gary 1945- *ConAu 65*
Nulman, Macy 1923- *ConAu 57*
Numano, Allen Stanislaus Motoyuki 1908-
IntAu&W 82
Numbers, Ronald L 1942- *ConAu 101*
Numeroff, Laura Joffe 1953- *ConAu 106,*
SmATA 28[port]
Numers, Lorenz Von 1913- *IntAu&W 82*
Nummi, Seppo 1932-1981 *ConAu 108*
Nunan, Desmond J 1927- *ConAu 17R*
Nunes, Armando DaSilva *CreCan 1*
Nunes, Claude 1924- *ConSFA*
Nunes, Margery Lambert *CreCan 2*
Nunez, Ana Rosa 1926- *ConAu 69*
Nunis, Doyce B, Jr. 1924- *ConAu 3NR, -5R,*
WrDr 84
Nunley, Maggie Rennert *ConAu X*
Nunn, Frederick McKinley 1937- *ConAu 33R,*
WrDr 84
Nunn, G Raymond 1918- *ConAu 33R,*
IntAu&W 82, WrDr 84
Nunn, Henry L 1878-1972 *ConAu 37R*
Nunn, John 1955- *WrDr 84*
Nunn, Walter 1942- *ConAu 45*
Nunn, William Curtis 1908- *ConAu 1R, -1NR,*
IntAu&W 82, WrDr 84
Nunnerley, David 1947- *ConAu 45*
Nuquist, Andrew E 1905-1975 *ConAu 61*
Nuraini *ConAu X*
Nurcombe, Barry 1933- *ConAu 65*
Nurenberg, Thelma 1903- *ConAu 69*
Nurge, Ethel 1920- *ConAu 33R, WrDr 84*
Nurmi, Martin Karl 1920- *ConAu 1R*
Nurnberg, Maxwell 1897- *ConAu 2NR, -5R,*
SmATA 27
Nurnberg, Walter 1907- *ConAu 13R, WrDr 84*
Nurse, Peter H 1926- *ConAu 9R*
Nursten, Jean Patricia *WrDr 84*
Nusbaum, N Richard *ConAu X*
Nusic, Branislav 1864-1938 *ClDMEL 80,*
ModSL 2
Nussbaum, Aaron 1910-1981 *ConAu 104, -49*
Nussbaum, Al 1934- *ConAu 85*

Nussbaumer, Paul Edmund 1934- *ConAu 93,*
SmATA 16
Nusser, J L 1925- *ConAu 1R*
Nutini, Hugo G 1928- *ConAu 109*
Nutt, Grady 1934- *ConAu 97*
Nuttal, Geoffrey Fillingham 1911- *ConAu 10NR*
Nuttall, A D 1937- *ConAu 11NR, -21R*
Nuttall, Geoffrey Fillingham 1911- *ConAu 13R,*
IntAu&W 82
Nuttall, Jeff 1933- *ConAu 29R, ConP 80,*
DcLEL 1940, WrDr 84
Nuttall, Kenneth 1907- *ConAu 17R*
Nuttall-Smith, Margaret Emily Noel 1919-
ConAu 104
Nutter, G Warren 1923-1979 *ConAu 1R, -2NR,*
-85
Nutting, Anthony 1920- *ConAu 5R, -7NR,*
WrDr 84
Nutting, Harold Anthony 1920- *DcLEL 1940*
Nutting, Willis Dwight 1900-1975 *ConAu P-2*
Nwankwo, Nkem 1936- *ConAu 65*
Nwapa, Flora 1931- *DcLEL 1940, TwCCW 83*
Nwogugu, Edwin Ifeanyichukwu 1933-
ConAu 17R
Nyabongo, Prince Akiki K 1905?-1975 *ConAu 61*
Nyanaponika 1901- *ConAu P-1, IntAu&W 82,*
WrDr 84
Nybakken, Oscar Edward 1904- *ConAu 93*
Nyberg, David 1943- *ConAu 107*
Nyberg, Kathleen Neill 1919- *ConAu 21R*
Nyce, Helene VonStrecker 1885-1969 *SmATA 19*
Nyce, Vera 1862-1925 *SmATA 19*
Nye, F Ivan 1918- *ConAu 6NR, -9R*
Nye, Harold G *SmATA X, WrDr 84*
Nye, Hermes 1908- *ConAu P-2*
Nye, Joseph Samuel 1939- *IntAu&W 82*
Nye, Joseph Samuel, Jr. 1937- *ConAu 25R,*
WrDr 84
Nye, Loyal 1921- *ConAu 106*
Nye, Miriam Baker 1918- *ConAu 85*
Nye, Naomi Shihab *DrAP&F 83*
Nye, Nelson 1907- *WrDr 84*
Nye, Nelson Coral 1907- *ConAu 4NR, -5R,*
IntAu&W 82, TwCWW
Nye, Robert 1939- *ConAu 33R, ConLC 13,*
ConNov 82, ConP 80, DcLB 14[port],
IntAu&W 82, IntWWP 82, SmATA 6,
TwCCW 83, WorAu 1970, WrDr 84
Nye, Robert D 1934- *ConAu 73*
Nye, Robert Evans 1911- *ConAu 1R, -1NR*
Nye, Russel 1913- *WrDr 84*
Nye, Russel Blaine 1913- *ConAu 1R, -4NR,*
MichAu 80, TwCA SUP
Nye, Russell Blaine 1913- *DcLEL 1940*
Nye, Sarah Litsey 1901- *IntWWP 82*
Nye, Vernice Trousdale 1913- *ConAu 1R, -1NR*
Nye, Wilbur S 1898-1970 *ConAu 1R, -103*
Nyerere, Julius Kambarage 1922- *ConAu 105*
Nygaard, Anita 1934- *ConAu 65*
Nygaard, Norman Eugene 1897-1971 *ConAu 1R,*
-2NR
Nygard, Olav 1884-1924 *ClDMEL 80*
Nygard, Roald 1935- *ConAu 103*
Nygren, Anders T S 1890- *ConAu 9R*
Nyhart, Nina *DrAP&F 83*
Nylander, Carl 1932- *ConAu 33R*
Nyquist, Thomas E 1931- *ConAu 41R*
Nyren, Dorothy Elizabeth 1927- *ConAu X, -5NR*
Nyro, Laura 1947- *ConLC 17*
Nystedt, Bob *DrAP&F 83*
Nzekwu, Onuora 1928- *DcLEL 1940, LongCTC,*
ModBlW, ModCmwL, TwCWr
Nzimiro, Ikenna 1927- *ConAu 2NR, -45*

O

O, Jaime E Rodriguez *ConAu X*
O Broin, Leon 1902- *WrDr 84*
O Ceirin, Cyril 1934- *IntAu&W 82*
O Danachair, Caoimhin *ConAu X*
O Fiaich, Tomas 1923- *ConAu 103*
O Hearn, Peter J T 1917- *WrDr 84*
O Hehir, Diana *ConAu 93*
O Henry *TwCA, TwCA SUP*
O Mude *SmATA X*
O Nuallain, Brian 1911-1966 *ConAu 25R*
Oak, Liston M 1895-1970 *ConAu 104*
Oakes, James 1953- *ConAu 107, WrDr 84*
Oakes, John Bertram 1913- *ConAu 13R*
Oakes, Philip 1928- *ConAu 4NR, -53, ConP 80, DcLEL 1940, IntWWP 82, WrDr 84*
Oakes, Vanya 1909- *ConAu 33R, SmATA 6*
Oakeshott, Michael 1901- *ConAu 1R*
Oakeshott, Walter Fraser 1903- *ConAu 13R, IntAu&W 82*
Oakland, Thomas David 1939- *ConAu 53*
Oakley, Ann 1944- *ConAu 6NR, -57, WrDr 84*
Oakley, Barry *WrDr 84*
Oakley, Barry Kingham 1931- *ConAu 104, ConNov 82, DcLEL 1940*
Oakley, Charles Allen 1900- *ConAu 108, WrDr 84*
Oakley, Don 1927- *ConAu 29R, SmATA 8*
Oakley, Eric Gilbert 1916- *ConAu 9R*
Oakley, Francis 1931- *ConAu 13R*
Oakley, Giles 1946- *ConAu 103*
Oakley, Graham 1929- *ConAu 106, SmATA 30[port], TwCCW 83, WrDr 84*
Oakley, Helen 1906- *ConAu 17R, SmATA 10*
Oakley, Josephine 1903?-1978 *ConAu 81*
Oakley, Kenneth 1911-1981 *ConAu 108*
Oakley, Kenneth Page 1911- *IntAu&W 82*
Oakley, Mary Ann B 1940- *ConAu 45*
Oakley, Stewart Philip 1931- *ConAu 21R, WrDr 84*
Oakman, Barbara F 1931- *ConAu 57*
Oakman, Henry Octave 1906- *IntAu&W 82*
Oaks, Dallin H 1932- *ConAu 25R, WrDr 84*
Oaksey, Baron 1929- *WrDr 84*
Oaksey, John 1929- *ConAu 105*
Oana, Katherine 1929- *ConAu 108*
Oates, John 1944- *ConAu 69*
Oates, John F 1934- *ConAu 17R*
Oates, Joyce Carol *DrAP&F 83*
Oates, Joyce Carol 1938- *AuNews 1, ConAu 5R, ConLC 1, -2, -3, -6, -9, -11, -15, -19, ConNov 82, DcLB Y81A[port], -2, -5[port], DcLEL 1940, ModAL SUP, WorAu 1970, WrDr 84*
Oates, Stephen Baery 1936- *ConAu 4NR, -9R, IntAu&W 82, WrDr 84*
Oates, Titus *DcLEL 1940*
Oates, Wallace Eugene 1937- *ConAu 37R, WrDr 84*
Oates, Wayne Edward 1917- *ConAu 85*
Oates, Whitney Jennings 1904-1973 *ConAu 3NR, -5R, -45*
Oatley, Keith 1939- *ConAu 45*
Oatman, Eric F 1939- *ConAu 103*

Oatts, Balfour *ConAu X*
Oatts, Henry Augustus 1898-1980 *ConAu 5R, -103*
Oatts, Lewis Balfour 1902- *ConAu 110, WrDr 84*
Obach, Robert 1939- *ConAu 106*
Obaldia, Rene De 1918- *ClDMEL 80, CnMD SUP, CroCD, ModWD*
O'Ballance, Edgar 1918- *ConAu 5R, -7NR, IntAu&W 82, WrDr 84*
O'Banion, Terry 1936- *ConAu 33R*
O'Barr, William M 1942- *ConAu 49*
O'Beirne, Thomas Hay 1915- *ConAu 17R, IntAu&W 82*
Obele, Norma Taylor 1933- *ConAu 104*
Obenhaus, Victor 1903- *ConAu P-1*
Ober, Stuart Alan 1946- *ConAu 103*
Ober, Warren U 1925- *ConAu 13R*
Oberg, James Edward 1944- *ConAu 108*
Oberhelman, Harley D 1928- *ConAu 53*
Oberholtzer, Peter *ConAu X*
Oberholtzer, W Dwight 1939- *ConAu 101*
Oberholzer, Emil, Jr. 1926?-1981 *ConAu 102*
Oberman, Heiko Augustinus 1930- *ConAu 5R, -7NR*
Obermann, C Esco 1904- *ConAu 53*
Obermayer, Herman J 1924- *ConAu 65*
Obermeyer, Barrett John 1937- *ConAu 5R*
Obermeyer, Henry 1899- *ConAu P-2*
Obermeyer, Marion Barrett *ConAu 5R*
Oberschall, Antony R 1936- *ConAu 97*
Obets, Bob *TwCWW*
Obey, Andre 1892-1975 *ClDMEL 80, CnMD, ConAu 57, -97, LongCTC, ModWD*
Obichere, Boniface Ihewunwa 1932- *ConAu 41R*
Obiechina, Emmanuel Nwanonye 1933- *ConAu 41R, IntAu&W 82*
Oboe, Peter *ConAu X*
Obojski, Robert 1929- *ConAu 108*
Obolensky, Dimitri 1918- *ConAu 45, IntAu&W 82*
Oboler, Arch 1907- *CnMD, ModWD, TwCA SUP*
Oboler, Arch 1909- *ConAu 105*
Oboler, Eli M 1915- *ConAu 6NR, -57*
Oboler, Eli M 1915-1983 *ConAu 110*
Obourn, Ellsworth Scott 1897- *ConAu P-2*
O'Brady, Frederic Michael Maurice 1903- *ConAu 9R*
O'Brady, Frederic Michel 1903- *ConAu 3NR, WrDr 84*
Obrant, Susan 1946- *SmATA 11*
Obregon, Mauricio 1921- *ConAu 1NR, -106, -45*
O'Brian, Frank *ConAu X, IntAu&W 82X, TwCWW, WrDr 84*
O'Brian, Jack 1921- *ConAu 103*
O'Brian, John Lord 1874-1973 *ConAu 41R*
O'Briant, Walter H 1937- *ConAu 25R, WrDr 84*
O'Brien, Andrew William 1910- *ConAu 25R*
O'Brien, Andy 1910- *ConAu X, WrDr 84*
O'Brien, Beatrice *DrAP&F 83*
O'Brien, Conor Cruise 1917- *ConAu 65, DcLEL 1940, WorAu, WrDr 84*

O'Brien, Cyril Cornelius 1906- *ConAu 53*
O'Brien, Darcy 1939- *ConAu 8NR, -21R, ConLC 11*
O'Brien, David J 1938- *ConAu 25R*
O'Brien, Dean D *ConAu X*
O'Brien, Dee *ConAu X*
O'Brien, E G *ConAu X*
O'Brien, Edna *ASpks*
O'Brien, Edna 1932- *ConAu 1R, ConLC 3, -5, -8, -13, ConNov 82, DcLB 14[port], DcLEL 1940, ModBrL SUP, TwCWr, WorAu*
O'Brien, Edna 1936- *ConAu 6NR, IntAu&W 82, WrDr 84*
O'Brien, Edward Joseph Harrington 1890-1941 *LongCTC, TwCA, TwCA SUP*
O'Brien, Elmer 1911- *ConAu 17R, WrDr 84*
O'Brien, Esse Forrester 1895?-1975 *ConAu 61, SmATA 30N*
O'Brien, Flann 1911-1966 *ConAu X, ConLC 1, -4, -5, -7, -10, LongCTC, ModBrL SUP, TwCWr, WorAu*
O'Brien, Frances 1906- *ConAu P-2*
O'Brien, Francis J 1903- *ConAu 81*
O'Brien, Frederick 1869-1932 *TwCA*
O'Brien, Geoffrey 1948- *ConAu 106*
O'Brien, George Dennis 1931- *ConAu 103*
O'Brien, J W 1931- *ConAu 13R*
O'Brien, Jacqueline Robin 1949- *ConAu 105*
O'Brien, James A 1936- *ConAu 110*
O'Brien, James J 1929- *ConAu 9NR*
O'Brien, James Jerome 1929- *ConAu 17R*
O'Brien, John *DrAP&F 83*
O'Brien, John Anthony 1893-1980 *ConAu 1R, -1NR, -97*
O'Brien, Justin 1906-1968 *ConAu 5R, -5NR*
O'Brien, Kate 1897-1974 *ConAu 53, -93, DcLB 15[port], LongCTC, TwCA, TwCA SUP*
O'Brien, Katharine *DrAP&F 83*
O'Brien, Katharine E 1901- *IntWWP 82, WrDr 84*
O'Brien, Kevin P 1922- *ConAu 53*
O'Brien, Lawrence F 1917- *WrDr 84*
O'Brien, Lawrence Francis 1917- *ConAu 57*
O'Brien, Lee 1948- *ConAu 61*
O'Brien, Marian P 1915- *ConAu 53*
O'Brien, Sister Mary Celine 1922- *ConAu 21R*
O'Brien, Michael *DrAP&F 83*
O'Brien, Michael J 1920- *ConAu 25R*
O'Brien, Patrick 1932- *ConAu 21R*
O'Brien, Richard *ConDr 82D, ConLC 17*
O'Brien, Richard 1934- *ConAu 73*
O'Brien, Robert C 1918-1973 *ChlLR 2, ConAu X, SmATA X, TwCCW 83*
O'Brien, Robert W 1907- *ConAu 45*
O'Brien, Saliee *ConAu X*
O'Brien, Terence Henry 1904- *IntAu&W 82*
O'Brien, Thomas C 1938- *ConAu 106, SmATA 29[port]*
O'Brien, Tim 1946- *ConAu 85, ConLC 7, -19, DcLB Y80B[port]*
O'Brien, Vincent 1916- *ConAu 9R*
O'Brien, William V 1923- *ConAu 13R*

O'Broin, Leon 1902- *ConAu 8NR, –61, IntAu&W 82*
O'Brynt, Jon *ConAu X*
Obst, Frances Melanie *ConAu 17R*
Obstfeld, Raymond *DrAP&F 83*
Obstfelder, Sigbjorn 1866-1900 *ClDMEL 80*
O'Byrne, Dermot *LongCTC*
Oca, Jorge Montes DeOca *WorAu 1970*
O'Callaghan, Denis F 1931- *ConAu 17R*
O'Callaghan, Joseph Francis 1928- *ConAu 81, IntAu&W 82*
Ocampo, Victoria 1891-1979 *ConAu 105, –85*
O'Carroll, Ryan *ConAu X, SmATA X*
O'Casey, Eileen 1924- *ASpks*
O'Casey, Sean 1880?-1964 *CnMWL, ConAu 89, ConLC 1, –5, –9, –11, –15, CroCD, DcLB 10[port], LongCTC, ModBrL, ModBrL SUP, ModWD, TwCA, TwCA SUP, TwCWr, WhoTwCL*
O'Casey, Sean 1884-1964 *CnMD*
O'Cathasaigh, Donal *ConAu X*
O'Cathasaigh, Sean *ConAu X*
O'Cathasaigh, Shaun *LongCTC*
Ocean, Julian *ConAu X, IntAu&W 82X, IntWWP 82X*
OCeithearnaigh, Seumas *ConAu X*
Ochester, Ed *DrAP&F 83*
Ochester, Ed 1939- *ConAu 45, IntAu&W 82X*
Ochester, Edwin Frank 1939- *IntAu&W 82, IntWWP 82*
Ochiltree, Thomas H 1912- *ConAu 77*
Ochojski, Paul M 1916- *ConAu 25R*
Ochs, Adolph S 1858-1935 *DcLB 25[port]*
Ochs, Donovan Joseph 1938- *ConAu 45*
Ochs, Phil 1940-1976 *ConAu 65, ConLC 17*
Ochs, Robert J 1930- *ConAu 29R*
Ochse, Orpha Caroline 1925- *ConAu 93*
Ochsenschlager, Edward L 1932- *ConAu 17R*
Ochsner, Alton 1896-1981 *ConAu 105, –17R*
Ockenga, Harold John 1905- *ConAu 1R, –1NR*
Ockerse, Tom *DrAP&F 83*
O'Clair, Robert M 1923- *ConAu 77*
O'Clery, Helen 1910- *ConAu 9R*
O'Collins, Gerald Glynn 1931- *ConAu 85, IntAu&W 82, WrDr 84*
O'Connell, Brian 1923- *WrDr 84*
O'Connell, Daniel Patrick 1924-1979 *ConAu 29R, –89*
O'Connell, David 1940- *ConAu 102, IntAu&W 82*
O'Connell, Donat *DcLEL 1940*
O'Connell, Frank B 1892- *ConAu 5R*
O'Connell, Jeffrey 1928- *ConAu 11NR, –25R*
O'Connell, Jeremiah J 1932- *WrDr 84*
O'Connell, Jeremiah Joseph 1932- *ConAu 7NR, –13R*
O'Connell, John James, III 1921-1982 *ConAu 107*
O'Connell, Margaret F 1935-1977 *ConAu 73, SmATA 30N*
O'Connell, Maurice R 1922- *ConAu 17R*
O'Connell, Michael 1943- *ConAu 101, IntWWP 82X*
O'Connell, Peg *ConAu X, SmATA X*
O'Connell, Richard *DrAP&F 83*
O'Connell, Richard L, Jr. 1912-1975 *ConAu 41R*
O'Connell, Timothy E 1943- *ConAu 73*
O'Connell, Walter E 1925- *ConAu 41R*
O'Conner, L R *ConAu X*
O'Conner, R L 1928- *ConAu 17R*
O'Connor, A M 1939- *ConAu 11NR, –21R*
O'Connor, Anthony d1983? *ConAu 109*
O'Connor, Anthony Michael 1939- *WrDr 84*
O'Connor, Clint *ConAu X*
O'Connor, Daniel John 1914- *IntAu&W 82*
O'Connor, Daniel William 1925- *ConAu 33R*
O'Connor, David 1949- *ConAu 110*
O'Connor, Dick 1930- *ConAu 97*
O'Connor, Edward Dennis Joseph 1922- *ConAu 41R, IntAu&W 82*
O'Connor, Edwin 1918-1968 *ConAu 25R, –93, ConLC 14, DcLEL 1940, ModAL, WorAu*
O'Connor, Elizabeth Anita 1921- *ConAu 25R*
O'Connor, Flannery 1925-1964 *ConAu 1R, –3NR, ConLC 1, –2, –3, –6, –10, –13, –15, –21[port], ConNov 82A, DcLB Y80A[port], –2, DcLEL 1940, ModAL, ModAL SUP, TwCWr, WhoTwCL, WorAu*
O'Connor, Francis Valentine 1937- *ConAu 21R, WrDr 84*
O'Connor, Frank 1903-1966 *CnMD, ConAu X, –25R, ConLC 14, –23[port], LongCTC, ModBrL, ModBrL SUP, TwCA SUP*

O'Connor, Garry Peter 1938- *ConAu 89, IntAu&W 82*
O'Connor, Harvey 1897- *ConAu 5R*
O'Connor, Jack 1902-1978 *ConAu X, TwCWW*
O'Connor, James Ignatius 1910- *ConAu P-1, WrDr 84*
O'Connor, John 1937- *ConAu 29R*
O'Connor, John E 1943- *ConAu 109*
O'Connor, John J 1918- *ConAu 73*
O'Connor, John Joseph 1904-1978 *ConAu 77*
O'Connor, John Woolf 1902-1978 *ConAu 3NR, –5R, –77*
O'Connor, Karen 1938- *SmATA 34[port]*
O'Connor, L L *ConAu X*
O'Connor, Liam *ConAu X*
O'Connor, Mark 1945- *ConAu 11NR, –65*
O'Connor, Martin T 1925- *IntWWP 82*
O'Connor, Sister Mary Catharine *ConAu P-2*
O'Connor, Michael Patrick *DrAP&F 83*
O'Connor, Patricia W 1931- *ConAu 37R, IntAu&W 82, WrDr 84*
O'Connor, Patrick *ChlLR 3, ConAu X, –77, IntAu&W 82X, SmATA 2, TwCCW 83, WrDr 84*
O'Connor, Patrick Joseph *WrDr 84*
O'Connor, Patrick Joseph 1924- *ConAu 53*
O'Connor, Philip F *DrAP&F 83*
O'Connor, Philip Francis 1932- *ConAu 33R*
O'Connor, Philip Marie Constant B 1916- *ConAu 9R, DcLEL 1940, WorAu*
O'Connor, Raymond G 1915- *ConAu 4NR, –5R, IntAu&W 82, WrDr 84*
O'Connor, Richard 1915-1975 *ConAu 57, –61, SmATA 21N, TwCCr&M 80*
O'Connor, Rory 1951- *ConAu 109*
O'Connor, Thomas Henry 1922- *ConAu 33R*
O'Connor, Thomas Power 1848-1929 *LongCTC*
O'Connor, Ulick 1928- *ConAu 4NR, –9R*
O'Connor, William E 1922- *ConAu 37R, IntAu&W 82, WrDr 84*
O'Connor, William P, Jr. 1916- *ConAu 9R*
O'Connor, William Van 1915-1966 *ConAu 1R, –1NR, –25R, TwCA SUP*
O'Conor, John F 1918- *ConAu 33R*
October, John *ConAu X, IntAu&W 82X*
Octopus *ConAu X*
Ocvirk, Otto G 1922- *ConAu 61*
Odaga, Asenath 1938- *TwCCW 83*
Odahl, Charles Matson 1944- *ConAu 37R*
Odajnyk, Walter 1938- *ConAu 13R*
Odam, Joyce *DrAP&F 83*
ODanachair, Caoimhin *ConAu X*
O'Daniel, Janet *WrDr 84*
O'Daniel, Janet 1921- *ConAu 29R, SmATA 24[port]*
O'Daniel, Therman Benjamin 1908- *ConAu 45, LivgBAA*
O'Day, Cathy *ConAu X*
O'Day, Edward Francis 1925- *ConAu 29R*
O'Day, Rey 1947- *ConAu 105*
Odd, Gilbert 1902- *WrDr 84*
Odd, Gilbert E 1902- *ConAu 110*
Oddo, Gilbert L 1922- *ConAu 1R, –1NR*
Oddo, Sandra 1937- *ConAu 65*
O'Dea, Marjory Rachel 1928- *WrDr 84*
O'Dea, Thomas F 1915-1974 *ConAu 53, ConAu P-2*
Odegaard, Charles Edwin 1911- *ConAu 106*
Odegard, Douglas Andrew 1935- *ConAu 108*
Odegard, Holtan Peter 1923- *ConAu 61*
Odegard, Knut 1945- *IntAu&W 82*
Odell, Albert Charles 1922- *LivgBAA*
O'Dell, Andrew C 1909-1966 *ConAu P-1*
O'Dell, David *DrAP&F 83*
Odell, Gill *ConAu X*
Odell, Ling Chung 1945- *ConAu 45*
Odell, M E *ConAu 9R*
Odell, Peter R 1930- *ConAu 97, WrDr 84*
Odell, Rice 1928- *ConAu 77*
Odell, Robin Ian 1935- *ConAu 73, IntAu&W 82, WrDr 84*
O'Dell, Scott 1903- *ChlLR 1, ConAu 61, SmATA 12, TwCCW 83, WrDr 84*
O'Dell, William F 1909- *ConAu 25R*
Odem, J *ConAu X*
Oden, Clifford 1916- *ConAu 65*
Oden, Gloria *DrAP&F 83*
Oden, Gloria C 1923- *IntWWP 82, LivgBAA*
Oden, Gloria Catherine 1923- *ConAu 108*
Oden, Marilyn Brown 1937- *ConAu 33R*
Oden, Thomas C 1931- *ConAu 5NR, –9R*
Oden, William E 1923- *ConAu 37R*

Odendaal, Louwrens Badenhorst 1941- *IntAu&W 82*
Odenwald, Robert Paul 1899-1965 *ConAu 1R, SmATA 11*
Odescalchi, Esther Kando 1938- *ConAu 69*
Odets, Clifford 1906-1963 *CnMD, CnMWL, ConAmA, ConAu 85, ConLC 2, CroCD, DcLB 7[port], –26[port], LongCTC, ModAL, ModWD, TwCA, TwCA SUP, TwCWr, WhoTwCL*
Odgers, Annette 1931- *IntWWP 82*
Odgers, Merle Middleton 1900-1983 *ConAu 110*
Odier, Daniel 1945- *ConAu 29R*
Odiorne, George Stanley 1920- *ConAu 1R, –1NR*
Odiorne, Maggie Jean *IntWWP 82*
Odireain, Martin 1910- *IntAu&W 82*
Odle, E V *TwCSFW*
Odle, Joe T 1908-1980 *ConAu 33R, –97*
Odlum, Doris Maude 1890- *ConAu P-1, IntAu&W 82, WrDr 84*
O'Doherty, Brian 1934- *ConAu 105*
O'Doherty, E F 1918- *ConAu 37R*
O'Doherty, Eamonn 1918- *WrDr 84*
O'Doire, Annraoi *ConAu X*
Odojewski, Wlodzimierz 1930- *ClDMEL 80*
Odom, William E 1932- *ConAu 73*
O'Donnell, Bernard 1929- *ConAu 41R*
O'Donnell, Cyril 1900- *ConAu P-1*
O'Donnell, Dick *ConAu X*
O'Donnell, Donat *ConAu X, WorAu*
O'Donnell, Elliott 1872-1965 *ConAu P-1*
O'Donnell, James H, III 1937- *ConAu 45*
O'Donnell, James J 1950- *ConAu 89*
O'Donnell, James Kevin 1951- *ConAu 6NR, –57*
O'Donnell, Jim *ConAu X*
O'Donnell, John A 1916- *ConAu 17R*
O'Donnell, John P 1923- *ConAu 17R*
O'Donnell, K M *ConAu X, TwCSFW, WrDr 84*
O'Donnell, Kenneth 1924-1977 *ConAu 73, –81*
O'Donnell, Kenneth P *ConAu X*
O'Donnell, Kevin, Jr. 1950- *ConAu 106*
O'Donnell, Lawrence *ConAu X*
O'Donnell, Lillian 1926- *ConAu 3NR, –5R, TwCCr&M 80, WrDr 84*
O'Donnell, Lorena 1929- *LivgBAA*
O'Donnell, Margaret Jane 1899- *ConAu 5R*
O'Donnell, Mark 1954- *ConAu 104*
O'Donnell, Peadar 1893- *TwCA, TwCA SUP*
O'Donnell, Peter 1920- *TwCCr&M 80, WrDr 84*
O'Donnell, Thomas Francis 1915- *ConAu 1R, –1NR*
O'Donnell, Thomas J 1918- *ConAu 65*
O'Donnevan, Finn *ConAu X*
O'Donoghue, Bryan 1921- *ConAu 77*
O'Donoghue, Gregory 1951- *ConAu 109, WrDr 84*
O'Donoghue, Joseph 1931- *ConAu 21R*
O'Donohue, Ciaran *IntAu&W 82X*
O'Donovan, Joan Mary 1914- *DcLEL 1940, WrDr 84*
O'Donovan, John 1921- *ConAu 11NR, –25R, IntAu&W 82, WrDr 84*
O'Donovan, Michael 1903-1966 *ConAu 93, LongCTC*
O'Dowd, Bernard Patrick 1866-1953 *ModCmwL, TwCWr*
Odoyevtseva, Irina Vladimirovna 1901- *ClDMEL 80*
O'Driscoll, Robert 1938- *ConAu 53, IntAu&W 82*
Odrowaz-Pieniazek, Janusz 1931- *IntAu&W 82*
Odum, Howard Washington 1884-1954 *TwCA SUP*
O'Dwyer, James Francis 1939- *ConAu 33R, WrDr 84*
O'Dwyer, Joseph Louis 1912- *IntWWP 82*
O'Dwyer, Paul 1907- *ConAu 97*
Odysseus *ConAu X*
Oe, Kenzaburo 1935- *ASpks, ConAu 97, ConLC 10*
Oechsli, Kelly 1918- *ConAu 97, SmATA 5*
Oehmke, T H 1947- *ConAu 11NR, –65*
Oehser, Paul H 1904- *ConAu 29R*
Oeksenholt, Svein 1925- *ConAu 106*
Oelschlegel, Gerd *CnMD, ModWD*
Oemler, Marie Conway 1879-1932 *TwCA*
Oenslager, Donald 1902-1975 *ConAu 57, –61*
Oerke, Andrew *DrAP&F 83*
Oerkeny, Istvan *ConAu X*
Oerlemans, Jacques Willem 1926- *IntAu&W 82*

Olson, Sigurd F 1899-1982 *ConAu 1R, -1NR, -105*
Olson, Stanley 1948- *ConAu 89*
Olson, Ted 1899- *ConAu 49*
Olson, Theodore B 1899- *ConAu 49*
Olson, Toby *DrAP&F 83*
Olson, Toby 1937- *ConAu 9NR, -65, ConP 80, WrDr 84*
Olssen, Erik Newland 1941- *IntAu&W 82*
Olsson, Axel Adolf 1889-1977 *ConAu 73*
Olsson, Hagar 1893- *CroCD*
Olsson, Karl A 1913- *ConAu 4NR, -5R*
Olsson, Nils 1909- *ConAu 73*
Olstad, Charles 1932- *ConAu 17R*
Olszak, Waclaw 1902- *IntAu&W 82*
Olthuis, James H 1938- *ConAu 61*
Oltmans, Willem Leonard 1925- *ConAu 57*
Olton, Charles S 1938- *ConAu 108*
Olton, Roy 1922- *ConAu 103*
Oltra, Benjamin 1945- *IntAu&W 82*
Olugebefola, Ademole 1941- *SmATA 15*
Olvera, Joe *DrAP&F 83*
Olvera, Joe 1944- *IntWWP 82*
Olyesha, Yuri Karlovich 1899-1960 *CnMWL, TwCWr*
O'Mahoney, Rich *ConAu X, IntAu&W 82X*
O'Mahony, Patrick 1911- *ConAu 13R*
O'Malley, Brian 1918?-1980 *ConAu 101*
O'Malley, Charles Donald 1907-1970 *ConAu 109*
O'Malley, Dianemarie *DrAP&F 83*
O'Malley, Emanuela *DrAP&F 83*
O'Malley, Frank *WrDr 84*
O'Malley, J Steven 1942- *ConAu 53*
O'Malley, Joseph James 1930- *ConAu 37R*
O'Malley, Kevin *ConAu X*
O'Malley, Mary *ConAu 110*
O'Malley, Mary 1941- *ConDr 82, WrDr 84*
O'Malley, Mary Dolling 1889-1974 *ConAu 65, LongCTC, TwCA SUP*
O'Malley, Michael *ConAu 1R*
O'Malley, Patrick *WrDr 84*
O'Malley, Richard K 1911- *ConAu 97*
O'Malley, Suzanne 1951- *ConAu 110*
O'Malley, William J 1931- *ConAu 73*
Oman, Carola Mary Anima 1897-1978 *ConAu 4NR, -5R, LongCTC, WorAu*
Oman, Charles Chichele 1901-1982 *ConAu 103, -105*
Oman, Sir Charles William Chadwick 1860-1946 *LongCTC*
Omansky, Dorothy Linder 1905?-1977 *ConAu 73*
O'Maonaigh, Cainneach *ConAu X*
Omari, Cuthbert Kashingo 1936- *IntAu&W 82*
Omari, T Peter 1930- *ConAu 29R, WrDr 84*
Omeara, Anick *DrAP&F 83*
O'Meara, John Joseph 1915- *ConAu 1R, -3NR, IntAu&W 82, WrDr 84*
O'Meara, Thomas A 1935- *ConAu 17R*
O'Meara, Thomas F 1935- *ConAu 9NR, -110*
O'Meara, Thomas Franklin *WrDr 84*
O'Meara, Walter Andrew 1897- *ConAu 13R*
Omer, Garth St. *ConAu X*
Omer, Seyfettin 1884-1920 *CIDMEL 80*
Ommanney, F D 1903-1980 *ConAu 7NR, -101, SmATA 23*
Ommanney, Francis Downes 1903- *ConAu 13R, LongCTC, WrDr 84*
O'More, Peggy *ConAu X*
O'Morrison, Kevin *ConAu 9NR*
O'Morrison, Kevin 1916- *ConAu 53, IntAu&W 82, NatPD 81[port]*
Omotoso, Kole 1943- *DcLEL 1940*
Onadipe, Kola *WrDr 84*
Onadipe, Kola 1922- *ConAu 101*
O'Nair, Mairi *ConAu X, IntAu&W 82X*
Ondaatje, Christopher 1933- *ConAu 49, WrDr 84*
Ondaatje, Michael 1943- *ConAu 77, ConLC 14, ConP 80, IntAu&W 82, WrDr 84*
Ondaatje, Philip Michael 1943- *DcLEL 1940*
O'Neal, Bill *ConAu X*
O'Neal, Charles E 1904- *ConAu P-2*
O'Neal, Cothburn M 1907- *ConAu 1R*
Oneal, Elizabeth 1934- *ConAu 106, SmATA 30[port]*
O'Neal, Forest Hodge 1917- *ConAu 5R*
O'Neal, Glenn 1919- *ConAu 49*
O'Neal, John W 1942- *ConAu 89*
O'Neal, Opal Jean Langston 1919- *IntWWP 82*
O'Neal, William B 1907- *ConAu 5R*
Oneal, Zibby *ConAu X, SmATA X*
O'Neil, Daniel J 1936- *ConAu 89*

O'Neil, Dennis 1939- *ConAu 97*
O'Neil, Eric *ConAu X*
O'Neil, George 1898-1940 *CnMD*
O'Neil, Isabel MacDonald 1908?-1981 *ConAu 105*
O'Neil, Robert M 1934- *ConAu 106*
O'Neil, Terrence 1928- *IntWWP 82*
O'Neil, Terry 1949- *ConAu 61*
O'Neil, Will 1938- *ConAu 101*
O'Neil, William 1912- *WrDr 84*
O'Neill, Alexandre 1924- *CIDMEL 80*
O'Neill, Archie *ConAu X*
O'Neill, Barbara Powell 1929- *ConAu 17R*
O'Neill, Carlota 1918- *ConAu 101, IntAu&W 82*
O'Neill, Carlotta Monterey 1888-1970 *ConAu 29R*
O'Neill, Charles 1882-1964 *CreCan 2*
O'Neill, Charles Edwards 1927- *ConAu 9NR, -21R*
O'Neill, Daniel Joseph 1905- *ConAu 106*
O'Neill, David P 1918- *ConAu 17R*
O'Neill, E Bard 1941- *ConAu 85*
O'Neill, Egan *ConAu X, WrDr 84*
O'Neill, Eugene 1888-1953 *ConAu 110*
O'Neill, Eugene 1922- *ConAu 77*
O'Neill, Eugene Gladstone 1888-1953 *AuNews 1, CnMD, CnMWL, ConAmA, CroCD, DcLB 7[port], LongCTC, ModAL, ModAL SUP, ModWD, TwCA, TwCA SUP, TwCLC 1, -6[port], TwCWr, WhoTwCL*
O'Neill, Frank F 1926?-1983 *ConAu 109*
O'Neill, George 1921?-1980 *AuNews 1, ConAu 102*
O'Neill, Gerard 1942- *ConAu 69*
O'Neill, Gerard Kitchen 1927- *ConAu 93, IntAu&W 82*
O'Neill, John 1933- *ConAu 53*
O'Neill, John Joseph 1920- *ConAu 21R*
O'Neill, Joseph Harry 1915- *ConAu 13R*
O'Neill, Judith 1930- *ConAu 109, SmATA 34[port]*
O'Neill, Kevin 1934- *IntAu&W 82, WrDr 84*
O'Neill, Lawrence T *DrAP&F 83*
O'Neill, Mary LeDuc 1908- *ConAu 4NR, -5R, SmATA 2*
O'Neill, Michael *ConAu 104, ConDr 82*
O'Neill, Michael J 1913- *ConAu 13R*
O'Neill, Michael J 1922- *ConAu 108*
O'Neill, Nena *AuNews 1*
O'Neill, Patrick Geoffrey 1924- *ConAu 21R, IntAu&W 82, WrDr 84*
O'Neill, Paul 1928- *ConAu 107*
O'Neill, Reginald F 1915- *ConAu 1R*
O'Neill, Richard Michael 1923- *IntAu&W 82*
O'Neill, Richard W 1925- *ConAu 107*
O'Neill, Robert John 1936- *ConAu 25R, WrDr 84*
O'Neill, Rose Cecil 1874-1944 *TwCA, TwCA SUP*
O'Neill, S M *IntWWP 82X*
O'Neill, Seamus 1910- *IntWWP 82*
O'Neill, Shane *ConAu X*
O'Neill, Shirley Marelle 1932- *IntWWP 82*
O'Neill, Terence Marne 1914- *ConAu 108*
O'Neill, Tim 1918- *ConAu 1R*
O'Neill, Timothy P 1941- *ConAu 85*
O'Neill, William 1927- *ConAu 37R*
O'Neill, William F 1931- *ConAu 29R*
O'Neill, William L 1935- *ConAu 21R, DcLEL 1940, IntAu&W 82, WrDr 84*
O'Neill Of The Maine, Baron Of Ahoghill *ConAu X*
O'Nell, Carl William 1925- *ConAu 73*
Onetti, Juan Carlos 1909- *ConAu 85, ConLC 7, -10, ModLAL, WhoTwCL, WorAu 1970*
Ong, Walter Jackson 1912- *ConAu 1R, -4NR, IntAu&W 82, WrDr 84*
Ongaro, Alberto 1925- *ConAu 25R*
Onians, Richard Broxton 1899- *IntAu&W 82*
O'Niell, C M *ConAu X*
Onions, Charles Talbut 1873-1965 *ConAu 107, LongCTC*
Onions, Oliver 1873-1961 *LongCTC, ModBrL, TwCA, TwCA SUP, TwCWr*
Onley, Toni 1928- *CreCan 1*
Onlooker *ConAu X, IntAu&W 82X*
Ono, Chiyo 1941- *ConAu 29R*
Onoda, Hiroo 1922?- *ConAu 108*
O'Nolan, Brian 1911-1966 *ConAu X*
O'Nolan, Brian 1912-1966 *LongCTC, WorAu*

Onorato, Richard James 1933- *ConAu 108*
Onstott, Kyle 1887-1978? *ConAu 5R, TwCRGW*
ONuallain, Brian 1911-1966 *ConAu 25R, ConAu P-2*
Onyeama, Dillibe 1951- *WrDr 84*
Oogam, LeRoi *ConAu X*
Ooi, Jin-Bee 1931- *ConAu 73*
Ooka, Shohei 1909- *CnMWL, WorAu*
Oost, Stewart Irvin 1921- *ConAu 29R*
Oosterman, Gordon 1927- *ConAu 49*
Oosterwal, Gottfried 1930- *ConAu 93*
Oosthuizen, Gerhardus C 1922- *ConAu 29R*
Opacki, Ireneusz 1933- *IntAu&W 82*
Opalov, Leonard *IntWWP 82X*
Oparin, Aleksandr 1894-1980 *ConAu 108*
Opdahl, Keith Michael 1934- *ConAu 61*
Opdahl, Richard D 1924- *ConAu 21R*
Opfermann, H C 1907- *IntAu&W 82*
Opie, Iona 1923- *ConAu 61, IntAu&W 82, SmATA 3, WrDr 84*
Opie, John 1934- *ConAu 29R*
Opie, June 1926- *WrDr 84*
Opie, Peter 1918-1982 *ConAu 2NR, -5R, -106, IntAu&W 82, SmATA 28N, -3*
Opitz, Edmund A 1914- *ConAu 29R*
Opland, Jeff 1943- *ConAu 106*
Opler, Marvin K 1914- *ConAu 21R*
Opler, Morris E 1907- *ConAu 45*
Opotowsky, Stan 1923- *ConAu 1R, -1NR*
Oppen, George *DrAP&F 83*
Oppen, George 1908- *ConAu 8NR, -13R, ConLC 7, -13, ConP 80, DcLB 5, WorAu 1970, WrDr 84*
Oppenheim, A Leo 1904-1974 *ConAu 49*
Oppenheim, E Phillips 1866-1946 *TwCCr&M 80*
Oppenheim, Edward Phillips 1866-1946 *LongCTC, TwCA, TwCA SUP, TwCWr*
Oppenheim, Felix E 1913- *ConAu 1R, WrDr 84*
Oppenheim, Irene 1928- *ConAu 77*
Oppenheim, James 1882-1932 *TwCA, TwCA SUP*
Oppenheim, Joanne 1934- *ConAu 9NR, -21R, SmATA 5*
Oppenheim, Joel Lester 1930- *DcLEL 1940*
Oppenheim, Paul 1885?-1977 *ConAu 69*
Oppenheim, Shulamith 1930- *ConAu 73*
Oppenheimer, Evelyn 1907- *ConAu 1R, -3NR*
Oppenheimer, George 1900-1977 *ConAmTC, ConAu 13R, -73*
Oppenheimer, Harold L 1919- *ConAu 17R*
Oppenheimer, J Robert 1904-1967 *ConAu 103*
Oppenheimer, Joan L 1925- *ConAu 37R, IntAu&W 82, SmATA 28[port]*
Oppenheimer, Joel 1930- *ConAu 4NR, -9R, ConP 80, CroCAP, DcLB 5[port], IntAu&W 82, IntWWP 82, WrDr 84*
Oppenheimer, Joel L *DrAP&F 83*
Oppenheimer, Martin 1930- *ConAu 29R*
Oppenheimer, Max, Jr. 1917- *ConAu 17R*
Oppenheimer, Paul 1939- *ConAu 21R, WrDr 84*
Oppenheimer, Samuel P 1903- *ConAu 33R*
Opper, Frederick Burr 1857-1937 *AuNews 1*
Opper, Jacob 1935- *ConAu 49*
Opperby, Preben 1924- *ConAu 110*
Opperman, David Michael Henry 1929- *IntWWP 82*
Oppitz, Rene 1905?-1976 *ConAu 65*
Oppong, Christine 1940- *ConAu 7NR, -57*
Opthof, Cornelis 1930- *CreCan 2*
Optic, Oliver *ConAu X*
Optic, Oliver 1822-1897 *SmATA X*
Opton, Edward M, Jr. 1936- *ConAu 11NR, -21R*
O'Quill, Scarlett *ConAu X*
O'Quinn, Garland 1935- *ConAu 21R*
O'Quinn, Hazel Hedick *ConAu 37R*
Orage, Alfred Richard 1873-1934 *LongCTC, TwCA, TwCA SUP*
Oraison, Marc 1914- *ConAu 85*
Oram, Clifton 1917- *WrDr 84*
Oram, Hiawyn 1946- *ConAu 106*
Oram, Malcolm 1944?-1976 *ConAu 104*
O'Ramus, Seamus *ConAu X*
O'Rand, Angela M 1945- *ConAu 104*
O'Randa, Jack *IntAu&W 82X*
Oras, Ants 1900- *ConAu P-1*
Orbaan, Albert F 1913- *ConAu 5R, -8NR*
Orbach, Ruth Gary 1941- *ConAu 65, SmATA 21[port]*
Orbach, Susie 1946- *ConAu 85*
Orbach, William W 1946- *ConAu 73*
Orban, Otto 1936- *IntWWP 82*

Orben, Robert 1927- *ConAu 81*
Orbis, Victor *ConAu X*
Orchard, Dennis Frank 1912- *WrDr 84*
Orczy, Baroness 1865-1947 *TwCCr&M 80,*
TwCRGW
Orczy, Emma Magdalena R M Josefa Barbara
1865-1947 *ConAu 104*
Orczy, Baroness Emmuska 1865-1947 *ConAu X,*
LongCTC, TwCA, TwCA SUP, TwCWr
Ord, John E 1917- *ConAu 81*
Ord-Hume, Arthur W J G *ConAu 101,*
IntAu&W 82, WrDr 84
Orde, Lewis 1943- *ConAu 109*
Ordish, George 1906- *WrDr 84*
Ordish, George 1908- *ConAu 9NR, –61*
Ordnung, Carl 1927- *IntAu&W 82*
Ordway, Frederick I, III 1927- *ConAu 5R, –5NR,*
WrDr 84
Ordway, Roger *ConAu X*
Ordway, Sally 1939- *ConAu 57,*
NatPD 81[port]
O'Regan, Richard Arthur 1919- *ConAu 73*
O'Reilly, Jane 1936- *ConAu 73*
O'Reilly, John 1945- *ConAu 29R*
O'Reilly, Montagu *ConAu X*
O'Reilly, Robert P 1936- *ConAu 29R*
O'Reilly, Timothy 1954- *ConAu 106*
Orel, Harold 1926- *ConAu 3NR, –5R,*
IntAu&W 82, WrDr 84
O'Rell, Max 1848-1903 *LongCTC*
Orem, Reginald 1931- *WrDr 84*
Orem, Reginald Calvert 1931- *ConAu 17R*
Oren, Uri 1931- *ConAu 65*
Orenburgsky, Sergey Gusev 1867- *TwCA,*
TwCA SUP
Orengo, Charles 1913?-1974 *ConAu 104*
Orenstein, Denise Gosliner 1950- *ConAu 110*
Orenstein, Gloria Feman 1938- *ConAu 65*
Orenstein, Henry 1924- *ConAu 13R*
Orent, Norman B 1920- *ConAu 17R*
Oreshnik, A F *ConAu X*
Oresick, Peter *DrAP&F 83*
Oresick, Peter 1955- *ConAu 73*
Orewa, George Oka 1928- *ConAu 5R*
Orfalea, Greg *DrAP&F 83*
Orff, Carl 1895-1982 *ConAu 106*
Orfield, Olivia 1922- *ConAu 103*
Orga, Ates 1944- *WrDr 84*
Orga, Ates D'Arcy 1944- *ConAu 93,*
IntAu&W 82
Organ, John 1925- *ConAu 5R, –7NR*
Organ, Troy Wilson 1912- *ConAu 37R,*
WrDr 84
Organski, A F K 1923- *ConAu 103,*
IntAu&W 82, WrDr 84
Orgel, Doris 1929- *AuNews 1, ConAu 2NR,*
–45, SmATA 7, TwCCW 83, WrDr 84
Orgel, Irene *DrAP&F 83*
Orgel, Joseph Randolph 1902- *ConAu P-1*
Orgel, Stephen K 1933- *ConAu 73*
Orgill, Douglas 1922- *ConAu 81, IntAu&W 82*
Orgill, Michael 1946- *ConAu 61*
Orhan Kemal 1914-1970 *CIDMEL 80*
Orians, George Harrison 1900- *ConAu 49*
Orians, Gordon H 1932- *ConAu 45*
Oriard, Michael 1948- *ConAu 110*
Origo, Iris 1902- *ConAu 105, WorAu*
Orion *ConAu X*
O'Riordan, Conal Holmes O'Connell 1874-1948
LongCTC, TwCA, TwCA SUP, TwCWr
Orjasaeter, Tore 1886-1968 *CIDMEL 80*
Orjuela, Hector H 1930- *ConAu 2NR, –45*
Orkan, Wladyslaw 1875-1930 *CIDMEL 80*
Orkan, Wladyslaw 1876?-1930 *ModSL 2*
Orkeny, Istvan 1912-1979 *ConAu 103, –89,*
CroCD
Orkin, Harvey 1918?-1975 *ConAu 61*
Orkow, Ben 1896- *ConSFA*
Orland, Henry 1918- *IntAu&W 82*
Orlandis, Jose 1918- *IntAu&W 82*
Orlans, Harold 1921- *ConAu 33R, WrDr 84*
Orleans, Ilo 1897-1962 *ConAu 1R, SmATA 10*
Orleans, Leo A 1924- *ConAu 41R*
Orlen, Steve *DrAP&F 83*
Orlen, Steve 1942- *ConAu 101*
Orlev, Uri 1931- *ConAu 101*
Orlich, Donald C 1931- *ConAu 7NR, –13R*
Orlick, Terrance D 1945- *ConAu 6NR, –57*
Orlicky, Joseph A 1922- *ConAu 25R*
Orlier, Blaise *ConAu X*
Orlinsky, Harry M 1908- *ConAu 85*
Orlob, Helen Seaburg 1908- *ConAu 5R*

Orloff, Ed 1923- *ConAu 69*
Orloff, Ed 1923-1983 *ConAu 110*
Orloff, Max *ConAu X*
Orlofsky, Myron 1928?-1976 *ConAu 69*
Orlos, Kazimierz Henryk 1935- *IntAu&W 82*
Orloski, Richard J 1947- *ConAu 97*
Orlovitz, Gil 1918-1973 *ConAu 45, –77,*
ConLC 22[port], DcLB 2, –5[port],
DcLEL 1940
Orlovsky, Peter *DrAP&F 83*
Orlovsky, Peter 1933- *ConAu 9NR, –13R,*
DcLB 16[port]
Orlow, Dietrich 1937- *ConAu 65*
Orlowitz, Hubert *IntAu&W 82X*
Orlt, Rudolf 1928- *IntAu&W 82*
Orme, Antony R 1936- *ConAu 73*
Ormerod, Roger *WrDr 84*
Ormerod, Roger 1920- *ConAu 77,*
TwCCr&M 80
Ormes, Robert M 1904- *ConAu P-1*
Ormesson, Jean, Comte D' 1925- *IntAu&W 82*
Ormesson, Wladimir 1888-1973 *ConAu 45*
Ormiston, Roberta *ConAu X*
Ormond, Clyde 1906- *ConAu 9R*
Ormond, John 1923- *ConAu 65, ConP 80,*
WrDr 84
Ormond, Leonee 1940- *ConAu 85*
Ormond, Richard Louis 1939- *ConAu 41R,*
IntAu&W 82
Ormond, Willard Clyde 1906- *WrDr 84*
Ormondroyd, Edward 1925- *ConAu 73,*
SmATA 14, TwCCW 83, WrDr 84
Ormont, Louis Robert 1918- *ConAu 13R*
Ormsbee, David *ConAu X, TwCA SUP,*
WrDr 84
Ormsby, Frank 1947- *ConAu 107, ConP 80,*
IntWWP 82, WrDr 84
Ormsby, Virginia H *ConAu 9R, SmATA 11*
Ormsby, William 1921- *ConAu 73*
Ormsson, Olafur 1943- *IntAu&W 82*
Orna, Mary Virginia 1934- *ConAu 29R*
Ornati, Oscar A 1922- *ConAu 37R*
Ornis *ConAu X*
Ornkloo, Ulf 1934- *IntAu&W 82*
Ornsbo, Jess 1932- *CIDMEL 80*
Ornstein, Allan C 1941- *ConAu 4NR, –53*
Ornstein, Dolph 1947- *ConAu 77*
Ornstein, J L *ConAu X*
Ornstein, Jack H 1938- *ConAu 103*
Ornstein, Norman J 1948- *ConAu 93*
Ornstein, Robert 1925- *ConAu 1R, WrDr 84*
Ornstein, Robert E 1942- *ConAu 53*
Ornstein-Galicia, J L 1915- *ConAu 93*
O'Rourke, Frank 1916- *TwCWW, WrDr 84*
O'Rourke, John James Joseph 1926- *ConAu 33R*
O'Rourke, Lawrence Michael 1938- *ConAu 69*
O'Rourke, P J 1947- *ConAu 77*
O'Rourke, Terrence James 1932- *ConAu 41R*
O'Rourke, William *DrAP&F 83*
O'Rourke, William 1945- *ConAu 1NR, –45,*
WrDr 84
Orpaz, Yitzhak 1923- *ConAu 101*
Orpen, Eve 1926?-1978 *ConAu 104*
Orr, Christine Grant Millar 1899-1963 *LongCTC*
Orr, Clyde 1921- *WrDr 84*
Orr, Daniel 1933- *ConAu 29R*
Orr, David 1929- *ConAu 33R*
Orr, Gregory *DrAP&F 83*
Orr, Gregory 1947- *ConAu 105*
Orr, J Edwin 1912- *ConAu 4NR*
Orr, James Edwin 1912- *ConAu 9R*
Orr, Linda 1943- *ConAu 97*
Orr, Mary *ConAu X*
Orr, Mary E E McCombe 1917- *ConAu 5R*
Orr, Myron David *MichAu 80*
Orr, Oliver H, Jr. 1921- *ConAu 1R*
Orr, Robert Richmond 1930- *ConAu 25R,*
WrDr 84
Orr, Robert T 1908- *ConAu 33R*
Orr, William F 1907- *ConAu 108*
Orrell, John 1934- *ConAu 37R*
Orris *SmATA X*
Orrmont, Arthur 1922- *ConAu 1R, –4NR*
Orsini, Gian Napoleone Giordano 1903-
ConAu 5R
Orsini, Joseph Emmanuel 1937- *ConAu 37R*
Orso, Kathryn Wickey 1921-1979 *ConAu 57, –85*
Orsy, Ladislas M 1921- *ConAu 25R*
Ort, Ana *ConAu X*
Ortega, Jose 1883-1955 *WhoTwCL*
Ortega Y Gasset, Jose 1883-1955 *CIDMEL 80,*
CnMWL, ConAu 106, LongCTC, ModRL,

TwCA, TwCA SUP, TwCLC 9[port],
TwCWr
Ortego, Philip D *DrAP&F 83*
Ortelli, Siro 1937- *IntAu&W 82*
Orten, Jiri 1919-1941 *ModSL 2*
Orth, Charles D, III 1921- *ConAu 5R*
Orth, Penelope 1938- *ConAu 45*
Orth, Ralph H 1930- *ConAu 21R*
Orth, Richard *ConAu X, SmATA X*
Orthwine, Rudolf 1900?-1970 *ConAu 104*
Ortiz, Adalberto 1914- *ModLAL*
Ortiz, Alfonso A 1939- *ConAu 29R, WrDr 84*
Ortiz, Antonio G *DrAP&F 83*
Ortiz, Antonio Gilberto 1946- *IntWWP 82*
Ortiz, Elisabeth Lambert 1928- *ConAu 97*
Ortiz, Miguel A *DrAP&F 83*
Ortiz, Simon J *DrAP&F 83*
Ortiz, Simon J 1941- *ConP 80, WrDr 84*
Ortiz, Victoria 1942- *ConAu 107*
Ortleb, Chuck *DrAP&F 83*
Ortlund, Anne 1923- *ConAu 106*
Ortman, E Jan 1884- *ConAu P-2*
Ortman, Elmer John *ConAu X*
Ortmann, Edwin 1941- *IntAu&W 82*
Ortner-Zimmerman, Toni *DrAP&F 83*
Ortner-Zimmerman, Toni 1941- *ConAu 5NR,*
IntWWP 82
Orton, Harold 1898-1975 *ConAu 57*
Orton, Joe 1933-1967 *ConAu X, –25R,*
ConDr 82E, ConLC 4, –13, CroCD,
DcLB 13[port], DcLEL 1940, LongCTC,
ModBrL SUP, ModWD, WorAu 1970
Orton, John Kingsley 1933-1967 *ConAu 85*
Orton, Vrest 1897- *ConAu 33R, WrDr 84*
Orton, William Aylott 1889-1952 *TwCA SUP*
Orum, Anthony M 1939- *ConAu 41R*
O'Russell *IntWWP 82X*
Orvell, Miles 1944- *ConAu 41R*
Orvil, Ernst 1898- *IntAu&W 82, IntWWP 82*
Orwell, George 1903-1950 *CnMWL, ConAu X,*
DcLB 15[port], LongCTC, ModBrL,
ModBrL SUP, SmATA X, TwCA,
TwCA SUP, TwCLC 2, –6[port], TwCSFW,
TwCWr, WhoTwCL
Orwell, Sonia 1919?-1980 *ConAu 102*
Orwell, Virginia Wakelyn *CreCan 1*
Orwen, Gifford *ConAu 37R*
Ory, Carlos Edmundo De 1923- *CIDMEL 80*
Ory, Edward 1886-1973 *ConAu 41R*
Ory, Kid *ConAu X*
Orzeck, Arthur Z 1921- *ConAu 1NR, –45*
Orzeszkowa, Eliza 1841-1910 *CIDMEL 80*
Osaki, Mark *DrAP&F 83*
Osanka, Franklin Mark 1936- *ConAu 5R*
Osaragi, Jiro 1897-1973 *ConAu X, WorAu*
Osbeck, Kenneth W 1924- *ConAu 1R, –3NR*
Osborn, Albert D 1896?-1972 *ConAu 104*
Osborn, Alex F 1888-1966 *ConAu 106*
Osborn, Arthur Walter 1891- *ConAu 21R*
Osborn, Barbara M *ConAu X*
Osborn, Carolyn *DrAP&F 83*
Osborn, Carolyn 1934- *ConAu 93*
Osborn, Catherine B 1914- *ConAu 29R*
Osborn, Chase Salmon 1860-1949 *MichAu 80*
Osborn, David 1923- *ConAu 109*
Osborn, Eric Francis 1922- *ConAu 65,*
IntAu&W 82, WrDr 84
Osborn, Sir Frederic James 1885-1978 *ConAu 5R,*
–5NR
Osborn, Frederick 1889-1981 *ConAu 102, –25R*
Osborn, George Coleman 1904- *ConAu 25R*
Osborn, James M 1906-1976 *ConAu 69,*
ConAu P-2
Osborn, John Jay, Jr. *DrAP&F 83*
Osborn, John Jay, Jr. 1945- *ConAu 6NR, –57*
Osborn, Mary Elizabeth 1898- *ConAu 5R*
Osborn, Merton B 1908- *ConAu 25R*
Osborn, Paul 1901- *CnMD, ConAu 108,*
ModWD
Osborn, Percy George 1899?-1972 *ConAu 104*
Osborn, Robert Chesley 1904- *ConAu 13R*
Osborn, Robert T 1926- *ConAu 21R*
Osborn, Ronald Edwin 1917- *ConAu 13R,*
IntAu&W 82, WrDr 84
Osborn, Stellanova 1894- *MichAu 80*
Osborne, Adam 1939- *ConAu 109*
Osborne, Arthur 1906- *ConAu 17R*
Osborne, C H C 1891- *ConAu 5R*
Osborne, Cecil G 1904- *ConAu 1NR, –45*
Osborne, Charles 1927- *ConAu 13R,*
DcLEL 1940, IntAu&W 82, IntWWP 82,
WrDr 84

Osborne, Chester G 1915- *ConAu 9NR, –21R, IntAu&W 82, SmATA 11, WrDr 84*
Osborne, Dan 1948?-1983 *ConAu 110*
Osborne, David *ConAu X, SmATA X, WorAu 1970, WrDr 84*
Osborne, Dorothy Gladys Yeo 1917- *ConAu 9R*
Osborne, Ernest 1903-1963 *ConAu 5R*
Osborne, G S 1926- *ConAu 21R*
Osborne, Geoffrey 1930- *ConAu 110, WrDr 84*
Osborne, George E 1893- *ConAu P-2*
Osborne, Gwendolyn *CreCan 2*
Osborne, Harold 1905- *ConAu 6NR, –13R, IntAu&W 82, WrDr 84*
Osborne, Harold W 1930- *ConAu 57*
Osborne, J K 1941- *ConAu 33R*
Osborne, John 1907- *ConAu 61*
Osborne, John 1907-1981 *ConAu 10NR, –108*
Osborne, John 1911- *WrDr 84*
Osborne, John 1929- *CnMD, CnMWL, ConAu 13R, ConDr 82, ConLC 1, –2, –5, –11, CroCD, DcLB 13[port], DcLEL 1940, IntAu&W 82, LongCTC, ModBrL, ModBrL SUP, ModWD, TwCWr, WhoTwCL, WorAu, WrDr 84*
Osborne, John 1938- *IntAu&W 82*
Osborne, John W 1927- *ConAu 33R*
Osborne, Juanita Tyree 1916- *ConAu 8NR, –61*
Osborne, Leone Neal 1914- *ConAu 21R, SmATA 2*
Osborne, Linda Barrett 1949- *ConAu 65*
Osborne, Maggie *ConAu X*
Osborne, Margaret 1909- *ConAu 13R*
Osborne, Margaret Ellen 1941- *ConAu 102*
Osborne, Maureen 1924- *ConAu 109*
Osborne, Milton 1936- *ConAu 13R, WrDr 84*
Osborne, Milton Edgeworth 1936- *ConAu 9NR*
Osborne, Richard Horsley 1925- *ConAu 21R*
Osborne, Richard L *DrAP&F 83*
Osborne, William 1934- *ConAu 25R*
Osborne, William A 1919- *ConAu 61*
Osborne, William S 1923- *ConAu 53*
Osbourne, Ivor 1951- *WrDr 84*
Osbourne, Ivor Livingstone 1951- *ConAu 108*
Osburn, Charles B 1939- *ConAu 33R*
Osceola *ConAu X*
Oschilewski, Walther G 1904- *IntAu&W 82*
Osen, Lynn M 1920- *ConAu 65*
Osenenko, John 1918-1983 *ConAu 109*
Oser, Jacob 1915- *ConAu 2NR, –5R, WrDr 84*
Osers, Ewald 1917- *IntAu&W 82, IntWWP 82*
Osgood, Charles *ConAu X*
Osgood, Charles E 1916- *ConAu 17R*
Osgood, Charles Grosvenor 1871-1964 *ConAu 4NR, –5R*
Osgood, David William 1940- *ConAu 89*
Osgood, Don 1930- *ConAu 11NR, –61*
Osgood, Ernest S 1888- *ConAu P-1*
Osgood, Lawrence 1929- *ConAu 85, ConDr 82*
Osgood, Richard E 1901- *ConAmTC*
Osgood, Robert Endicott 1921- *ConAu 1R, –3NR*
Osgood, Samuel M 1920-1975 *ConAu 33R*
Osgood, William E 1926- *ConAu 33R*
O'Shaughnessy, John 1927- *IntAu&W 82*
O'Shea, Katherine *LongCTC*
O'Shea, Lester 1938- *ConAu 108*
O'Shea, Sean *ConAu X, WrDr 84*
Oshima, Nagisa 1932- *ConLC 20*
Osiek, Betty Tyree 1931- *ConAu 45*
OSiochain, P A 1905- *ConAu P-2*
Osipow, Samuel H 1934- *ConAu 1NR, –49*
Osiris, Jean *IntAu&W 82X*
Osis, Karlis 1917- *ConAu 85*
Oskam, Bob *ConAu X*
Oskam, Robert T 1945- *ConAu 108*
Oskamp, Stuart 1930- *ConAu 29R*
Oskarsdottir, Valdis 1949- *IntAu&W 82*
Oskarsson, Baldur 1932- *IntAu&W 82*
Osler, Robert Willard 1911- *ConAu 1R, WrDr 84*
Os'machka, Todos' 1895-1962 *ModSL 2*
Osman, Betty B 1929- *ConAu 93*
Osman, Jack D 1943- *ConAu 11NR, –61*
Osman, John 1907?-1978 *ConAu 77*
Osmanczyk, Edmund Jan 1913- *IntAu&W 82*
Osmer, Margaret *ConAu 93*
Osmond, Andrew 1938- *ConAu 25R*
Osmond, Edward 1900- *ConAu P-1, SmATA 10, –7*
Osmond, Humphrey 1917- *ConAu 21R*
Osmond, Laurie *WrDr 84*
Osmun, Mark 1952- *ConAu 93*

Osmunson, Robert Lee 1924- *ConAu 9R*
Osner, Dorothy Faye 1913- *IntWWP 82*
Osofsky, Gilbert 1935-1974 *ConAu 53, –65*
Osolinski, Stan, Jr. 1942- *MichAu 80*
Osorgin, Mikhail Andreyevich 1878-1942 *ClDMEL 80, TwCWr*
Ossendowski, Ferdynand Antoni 1878-1945 *ClDMEL 80*
Osserman, Richard A 1930- *ConAu 29R*
Ossman, David 1936- *ConAu 9R*
Ossoli, Sarah Margaret Fuller 1810-1850 *SmATA 25[port]*
Ossowska, Maria 1896- *ConAu 29R*
Ossowski, Leonie 1925- *IntAu&W 82*
Ossowski, Stanislaw 1897-1963 *ConAu P-1*
Ost, David H 1940- *ConAu 6NR, –53*
Ost, John William Philip 1931- *ConAu 37R*
Ostaijen, Paul Van 1896-1928 *ClDMEL 80, WhoTwCL*
Osten, Gar 1923- *ConAu 65*
Ostendorf, Lloyd 1921- *ConAu 1R, –6NR*
Ostenso, Martha 1900-1963 *ConAu P-1, CreCan 1, TwCA, TwCA SUP, TwCWW*
Oster, Jerry 1943- *ConAu 77*
Oster, Ludwig 1931- *ConAu 53*
Osterbrock, Donald E 1924- *WrDr 84*
Osterburg, James W 1917- *ConAu 45*
Ostergaard, G N 1926- *ConAu 25R*
Osterhaven, M Eugene 1915- *ConAu 49*
Osterhoudt, Robert Gerald 1942- *ConAu 53*
Osterling, Anders Johan 1884- *IntAu&W 82*
Osterlund, Steven 1943- *ConAu 77, IntWWP 82*
Osterman, Susan *DrAP&F 83*
Osterman, Susan 1949- *IntWWP 82*
Osterritter, John F 1923- *ConAu 45*
Osterweis, Rollin G 1907-1982? *ConAu 106, –41R*
Ostheimer, John 1938- *ConAu 41R*
Ostle, Bernard 1921- *ConAu 5R*
Ostlere, Gordon 1921- *ConAu 107*
Ostling, Richard N 1940- *ConAu 53*
Ostow, Mortimer 1918- *ConAu 49*
Ostrander, Fred 1926- *IntWWP 82*
Ostrander, Gilman Marston 1923- *ConAu 65*
Ostriker, Alicia *DrAP&F 83*
Ostriker, Alicia 1937- *ConAu 10NR, –25R, IntWWP 82*
Ostrinsky, Meir Simha 1906- *ConAu P-2*
O'Strit, Henning 1918- *IntAu&W 82*
Ostroff, Anthony J 1923-1978 *ConAu 3NR, –5R, –77, WorAu*
Ostrom, Alan 1925- *ConAu 21R*
Ostrom, John Ward 1903- *ConAu 1R*
Ostrom, Thomas M 1936- *ConAu 37R*
Ostrovski, Nikolai Alexeyevich 1904-1936 *ModSL 1*
Ostrovsky, Nikolai Alexeyevich 1904-1936 *TwCWr*
Ostrovsky, Nikolay Alekseyevich 1904-1936 *ClDMEL 80*
Ostrow, Joanna *DrAP&F 83*
Ostrow, Joanna 1938- *ConAu 29R*
Ostrower, Alexander 1901- *ConAu 17R*
Ostrowsky *ConAu X*
Ostry, Sylvia 1927- *ConAu 41R*
Ostwald, Martin 1922- *ConAu 33R*
Ostwald, Peter F 1928- *ConAu 17R*
OSuilleabhain, Sean 1903- *ConAu 25R*
O'Sullivan, Joan *ConAu 77*
O'Sullivan, Maurice 1904-1950 *CnMWL*
O'Sullivan, P Michael 1940- *ConAu 93*
O'Sullivan, Sean 1905- *ConAu X*
O'Sullivan, Seumas 1879-1958 *LongCTC, TwCA, TwCA SUP*
O'Sullivan, Timothy 1945- *WrDr 84*
O'Sullivan, Vincent 1872-1940 *TwCA*
O'Sullivan, Vincent 1937- *WrDr 84*
O'Sullivan, Vincent Gerard 1937- *ConAu 97, ConP 80, DcLEL 1940*
Osusky, Stefan 1889-1973 *ConAu 45*
Oswald, Ernest John *DrAP&F 83*
Oswald, Ernest John 1943- *IntWWP 82*
Oswald, Ian 1929- *ConAu 17R, WrDr 84*
Oswald, J Gregory 1922- *ConAu 104*
Oswald, Lori Jo *DrAP&F 83*
Oswald, Roy *DrAP&F 83*
Oswald, Roy Lee 1944- *IntWWP 82*
Oswald, Russell G 1908- *ConAu 45*
Oswalt, Sabine *ConAu X*
Oswalt, Wendell H 1927- *ConAu 17R*

Otake, Sadao 1913?-1983 *ConAu 109*
Otambo, Mary Emily Inda 1941- *IntWWP 82*
Otcenasek, Jan 1924- *TwCWr*
Otchis, Ethel 1920- *ConAu 13R*
Otcuoglu *IntWWP 82X*
Otero, Blas De 1916-1979 *ClDMEL 80, CnMWL, ConAu 89, ConLC 11, ModRL, TwCWr, WorAu*
Otero, Manuel Ramos *DrAP&F 83*
Otero Pedrayo, Ramon 1888-1975 *ClDMEL 80*
Otis, Charles Herbert 1886- *MichAu 80*
Otis, George *ConAu X*
Otis, Jack 1923- *ConAu 1R*
Otis, James 1848-1912 *SmATA X*
O'Toole, Kate *IntAu&W 82X*
O'Toole, Rex *ConAu X, WrDr 84*
O'Trigger, Sir Lucius *SmATA X*
Ott, Attiat F 1935- *ConAu 10NR, –21R*
Ott, David Jackson 1934-1975 *ConAu 5R, –8NR*
Ott, Maggie Glen *ConAu X*
Ott, Peter *ConAu X*
Ott, Thomas O, III 1938- *ConAu 49*
Ott, Virginia 1917- *ConAu 77*
Ott, William Griffith 1909- *ConAu 1R, –1NR*
Ottemiller, John H 1916-1968 *ConAu P-2*
Otten, Anna *ConAu 21R*
Otten, C Michael 1934- *ConAu 33R*
Otten, Charlotte M 1915- *ConAu 29R*
Otten, Terry 1938- *ConAu 37R, IntAu&W 82, WrDr 84*
Ottenberg, Miriam 1914- *ConAu 5R*
Ottenberg, Miriam 1914-1982 *ConAu 10NR, –108*
Ottenberg, Simon 1923- *ConAu 33R, WrDr 84*
Otter, Florence Wahl 1918- *IntAu&W 82, IntWWP 82*
Otterbein, Keith Frederick 1936- *ConAu 21R*
Ottersen, Ottar 1918- *ConAu 33R*
Ottesen, Thea Tauber 1913- *ConAu 5R*
Otteson, Schuyler Franklin 1917- *ConAu 106*
Ottley, Carlton Robert 1914- *WrDr 84*
Ottley, Reginald *ConAu 93, SmATA 26[port], WrDr 84*
Ottley, Roi 1906-1960 *ConAu 89*
Ottlik, Geza 1912- *ConAu 17R*
Ottman, Robert W 1914- *ConAu 1R, –3NR*
Otto, Calvin P 1930- *ConAu 29R*
Otto, Georg 1920- *IntAu&W 82*
Otto, Henry J 1901- *ConAu P-2*
Otto, Herbert 1925- *IntAu&W 82*
Otto, Herbert Arthur 1922- *ConAu 1NR, –45*
Otto, Lon *DrAP&F 83*
Otto, Margaret Glover 1909-1976 *ConAu 61, SmATA 30N*
Otto, Wayne 1931- *ConAu 11NR, –29R*
Otwell, John H 1915- *ConAu 73*
Ouchi, William G 1943- *ConIsC 2[port]*
Ouellet DuHaut-Pas, Alphonse 1925- *IntAu&W 82*
Ouellette, Fernand 1930- *ConAu 2NR, –49, CreCan 1*
Oughton, Frederick 1923- *ConAu 1R*
Ouida *SmATA X*
Ouida 1839?-1908 *LongCTC*
Ouimette, Victor 1944- *ConAu 73*
Oulahan, Richard 1918- *ConAu 33R*
Oulanoff, Hongor 1929- *ConAu 25R*
Ould, Herman 1886-1951 *CnMD*
Ould, Hermon 1886-1951 *ModWD*
Ouroussow, Eugenie 1908-1975 *ConAu 53*
Oursler, Fulton 1893-1952 *ConAu 108, TwCA SUP, TwCCr&M 80*
Oursler, Will 1913- *ConAu 2NR, –5R*
Ousby, Ian 1947- *ConAu 89*
Ousley, Odille 1896- *ConAu P-1, SmATA 10*
Ousmane, Sembene 1923- *WorAu 1970*
Ouspensky, P D *LongCTC, TwCA SUP*
Outerbridge, David E 1933- *ConAu 93*
Outhwaite, Leonard 1892- *ConAu 53*
Outka, Gene 1937- *ConAu 41R*
Outland, Charles 1910- *ConAu 9R*
Outler, Albert C 1908- *ConAu 1R, –1NR*
Ovard, Glen F 1928- *ConAu 33R, WrDr 84*
Ovechkin, Valentin Vladimirovich 1904-1968 *ClDMEL 80, TwCWr*
Overacker, Louise 1891- *ConAu P-2*
Overbeck, Pauletta 1915- *ConAu 97*
Overbeek, J 1932- *ConAu 73*
Overend, William George 1921- *WrDr 84*
Overfield, Mary Garner 1923- *IntWWP 82*
Overholser, Stephen 1944- *ConAu 97*
Overholser, Wayne D 1906- *ConAu 2NR, –5R,*

TwCWW, WrDr 84
Overland, Arnulf 1889-1968 *CIDMEL 80,*
WorAu 1970
Overman, Michael 1920- *ConAu 108, WrDr 84*
Overstreet, Harry Allen 1875-1970 *ConAu 29R,*
ConAu P-1, TwCA, TwCA SUP
Overton, Grant Martin 1887-1930 *TwCA*
Overton, Jenny 1942- *TwCCW 83, WrDr 84*
Overton, Jenny Margaret Mary 1942- *ConAu 57*
Overton, Richard Cleghorn 1907- *ConAu 108*
Overton, Ron *DrAP&F 83*
Overy, Claire May *IntAu&W 82X,*
IntWWP 82X, WrDr 84
Overy, Paul 1940- *ConAu 29R, IntAu&W 82,*
WrDr 84
Ovesen, Ellis *ConAu X, IntWWP 82X*
Ovstedal, Barbara *TwCRGW*
Owa 1944- *NatPD 81[port]*
Owen, Alan Robert George 1919- *ConAu 9R*
Owen, Alun 1925- *ConDr 82*
Owen, Alun 1926- *WrDr 84*
Owen, Alun Davies 1924- *DcLEL 1940*
Owen, Alun Davies 1926- *ConAu 5R, CroCD,*
TwCWr, WorAu
Owen, Benjamin Evan 1918- *WrDr 84*
Owen, Bob *ConAu X*
Owen, Bruce M 1943- *ConAu 57*
Owen, Charles 1915- *IntAu&W 82, WrDr 84*
Owen, Charles A, Jr. 1914- *ConAu 53*
Owen, Clifford *ConAu X, SmATA X*
Owen, D F 1931- *ConAu 4NR, -53*
Owen, David 1898-1968 *ConAu P-1*
Owen, David 1938- *WrDr 84*
Owen, David Elystan 1912- *WrDr 84*
Owen, Dean *ConSFA, TwCWW*
Owen, Derwyn 1914- *WrDr 84*
Owen, Dolores B *ConAu 53*
Owen, Don *CreCan 1*
Owen, Douglas David Roy 1922- *ConAu 89,*
IntAu&W 82, WrDr 84
Owen, Edmund *ConAu X, WrDr 84*
Owen, Eileen *DrAP&F 83*
Owen, Evan 1918- *ConAu 109*
Owen, Frank 1907?-1979 *ConAu 85*
Owen, G L 1937- *ConAu 45*
Owen, Garnet *IntWWP 82*
Owen, George Earle 1908- *ConAu 77*
Owen, Guy *DrAP&F 83*
Owen, Guy 1925- *WrDr 84*
Owen, Guy 1925-1981 *ConAu 1R, -3NR, -104,*
ConNov 82, DcLB 5[port], IntAu&W 82
Owen, Gwilym Ellis Lane 1922-1982 *ConAu 107*
Owen, Harold 1897-1971 *ConAu 13R, -89*
Owen, Hugh *ConAu X, TwCWW*
Owen, Irvin 1910- *ConAu 97*
Owen, Jack *WrDr 84*
Owen, Jack 1929- *ConAu 33R*
Owen, John Elias 1919- *ConAu 4NR, -9R*
Owen, John Gareth 1936- *IntWWP 82*
Owen, John Pickard *LongCTC*
Owen, Lewis 1915- *ConAu 29R*
Owen, Mably 1912-1969 *ConSFA*
Owen, Marsha *ConAu X*
Owen, Maude Lurline 1956- *IntWWP 82*
Owen, Maureen A *DrAP&F 83*
Owen, Oliver S 1920- *ConAu 104*
Owen, Reginald 1887-1972 *ConAu 37R*
Owen, Robert N *ConAu X*
Owen, Roderic 1921- *IntAu&W 82X, WrDr 84*
Owen, Roger C 1928- *ConAu 77*
Owen, Sue *DrAP&F 83*
Owen, Thomas 1910- *IntWWP 82*
Owen, Thomas Richard 1918- *ConAu 10NR,*
-21R
Owen, Tom *ConAu X, IntAu&W 82X,*
WrDr 84
Owen, Warwick 1916- *WrDr 84*
Owen, Wilfred 1893-1918 *CnMWL, ConAu 104,*
LongCTC, ModBrL, ModBrL SUP,
RGFMBP, TwCA, TwCA SUP,
TwCLC 5[port], TwCWr, WhoTwCL
Owen, Wilfred 1912- *ConAu 37R*
Owen, William Vern 1894- *ConAu P-2*
Owendoff, Robert Scott 1945- *ConAu 17R*
Owens, Bill 1938- *ConAu 73*
Owens, Carolyn 1946- *ConAu 109*
Owens, Daniel Walter 1948- *NatPD 81[port]*
Owens, Gary 1936- *ConAu 97*
Owens, Iris *DrAP&F 83*
Owens, James Cleveland 1913-1980 *ConAu 97*
Owens, Jesse 1913-1980 *ConAu 110*
Owens, Jessie *ConAu X*

Owens, Joan Llewelyn 1919- *ConAu 13R*
Owens, John R 1926- *ConAu 77*
Owens, Joseph 1908- *ConAu 5R, -5NR,*
IntAu&W 82, WrDr 84
Owens, Pat J 1929- *ConAu 73*
Owens, Richard Meredith 1944- *ConAu 61*
Owens, Robert Goronwy 1923- *ConAu 29R*
Owens, Rochelle *DrAP&F 83*
Owens, Rochelle 1936- *ConAu 17R, ConDr 82,*
ConLC 8, ConP 80, CroCD, IntAu&W 82,
IntWWP 82, NatPD 81[port], WorAu 1970,
WrDr 84
Owens, Thelma 1905- *ConAu 69*
Owens, Virginia Stem 1941- *ConAu 81*
Owens, William A 1905- *ConAu 9R*
Ower, John 1942- *ConAu 77*
Owings, Loren C 1928- *ConAu 37R*
Owings, Mark 1945- *ConSFA*
Owings, Nathaniel 1903- *WrDr 84*
Owings, Nathaniel Alexander 1903- *ConAu 61*
Owiredu, Peter Augustus 1926- *IntAu&W 82*
Owl, Sebastian *ConAu X*
Owsley, Frank Lawrence 1890-1956
DcLB 17[port]
Owsley, Harriet Chappell 1901- *ConAu 81*
Oxenbury, Helen 1938- *ConAu 25R, SmATA 3*
Oxenham, Andrew William 1945- *CreCan 2*
Oxenham, Elsie J d1960 *TwCCW 83*
Oxenham, John 1852-1941 *LongCTC, TwCA,*
TwCA SUP
Oxenhandler, Neal 1926- *ConAu 6NR, -13R*
Oxholm, Jose M 1927- *MichAu 80*
Oxholm, Jose M, Jr. 1967- *MichAu 80*
Oxley, William 1939- *ConAu 73, ConP 80,*
IntWWP 82, WrDr 84
Oxnam, Robert B 1942- *ConAu 5NR, -53*
Oxnard, Charles Ernest 1933- *ConAu 1NR, -45,*
IntAu&W 82
Oxtoby, Willard Gurdon 1933- *ConAu 49*
Oy-Vik *ConAu X*
Oyama, Richard *DrAP&F 83*
Oyamo *DrAP&F 83*
Oyamo 1943- *NatPD 81[port]*
Oyle, Irving 1925- *ConAu 6NR, -57*
Oyler, Philip 1879- *ConAu P-1*
Oyono, Ferdinand Leopold 1929- *ModBlW,*
ModFrL
Oz, Amos 1939- *ASpks, ConAu 53, ConLC 5,*
-8, -11, -27[port], IntAu&W 82,
WorAu 1970, WrDr 84
Ozaki, Robert S 1934- *ConAu 49*
Ozawa, Terutomo 1935- *ConAu 85*
Ozdogru, Nuvit 1925- *IntAu&W 82*
Ozer, Jerome S 1927- *ConAu 107*
Ozick, Cynthia *DrAP&F 83*
Ozick, Cynthia 1928- *ConAu 17R, ConLC 3,*
-7, ConNov 82, DcLB Y82B[port],
ModAL SUP, WorAu 1970, WrDr 84
Ozinga, James Richard 1932- *ConAu 97*
Ozment, Robert V 1927- *ConAu 17R*
Ozment, Steven E 1939- *ConAu 108*
Ozmon, Howard 1935- *ConAu 25R, WrDr 84*
Ozu, Yasujiro 1903-1963 *ConLC 16*
Ozy *ConAu X*

P

P, E *ConAmA*
P A S *IntWWP 82X*
P B *IntAu&W 82X*
P L K *ConAu X*
Pa, Chin 1904- *ConAu X, ConLC 18*
Paak, Carl Erich 1922- *ConAu 106*
Paananen, Victor Niles 1938- *ConAu 73*
Paarlberg, Don 1911- *ConAu 21R*
Paasche, Carol L 1937- *ConAu 5R*
Paassen *TwCA, TwCA SUP*
Paauw, Douglas Seymour 1921- *ConAu 103*
Pab *ConAu X*
Pablos Y Viejo, Eliseo De 1950- *IntAu&W 82*
Paca, Lillian Grace 1883- *ConAu P-1*
Pacaut, Marcel 1920- *ConAu 29R*
Pace, C Robert 1912- *ConAu 81*
Pace, Denny F 1925- *ConAu 49*
Pace, Donald Metcalf 1906-1982 *ConAu 108*
Pace, Eric 1936- *ConAu 45, WrDr 84*
Pace, J Blair 1916- *ConAu 69*
Pace, Mildred Mastin 1907- *ConAu 5R, –5NR, SmATA 29*
Pace, Nathaniel 1925- *ConAu 110*
Pace, Peter *ConAu X*
Pace, R Wayne 1931- *ConAu 1NR, –45*
Pace, Robert Lee 1924- *ConAu 1R*
Pace, Rosella *DrAP&F 83*
Pacernick, Gary 1941- *ConAu 73*
Pacernick, Gary Bernard *DrAP&F 83*
Pacey, Desmond 1917-1975 *ConAu 4NR, –5R*
Pacey, Philip Kay Rutherford 1946- *IntWWP 82*
Pacey, William Cyril Desmond 1917- *DcLEL 1940*
Pach, Walter 1883-1958 *TwCA, TwCA SUP*
Pachai, Bridglal 1927- *ConAu 93*
Pache, Jean 1933- *IntWWP 82*
Pacheco, Ferdie 1927- *ConAu 81*
Pacheco, Henry L 1947- *ConAu 49*
Pacheco, Javier *DrAP&F 83*
Pacheco, Javier 1949- *IntWWP 82*
Pachmuss, Temira 1927- *ConAu 4NR, –9R*
Pachter, Henry M 1907- *ConAu 9R*
Pacifici, Sergio 1925- *ConAu 1R, –3NR*
Pacifico, Carl 1921- *ConAu 21R, WrDr 84*
Pack, Lola Catherine Lee 1924- *IntWWP 82*
Pack, Robert *DrAP&F 83*
Pack, Robert 1929- *ConAu 1R, –3NR, ConLC 13, ConP 80, DcLB 5[port], WorAu, WrDr 84*
Pack, Roger A 1907- *ConAu P-1, WrDr 84*
Pack, Stanley Walter Croucher 1904- *ConAu 13R*
Packard, Andrew 1929- *ConAu 1R*
Packard, Frank Lucius 1877-1942 *CreCan 2, TwCA, TwCA SUP, TwCCr&M 80*
Packard, Jerrold M 1943- *ConAu 106*
Packard, Karl 1911?-1977 *ConAu 69*
Packard, Reynolds 1903-1976 *ConAu 69, –73*
Packard, Robert G 1933- *ConAu 97*
Packard, Rosa Covington 1935- *ConAu 97*
Packard, Rosalie *ConAu 1R, MichAu 80*
Packard, Sidney R 1893- *ConAu 61*
Packard, Vance 1914- *ASpks, AuNews 1, ConAu 7NR, –9R, DcLEL 1940,*

IntAu&W 82, LongCTC, WorAu, WrDr 84
Packard, William *DrAP&F 83*
Packard, William 1933- *ConAu 7NR, –13R, NatPD 81[port]*
Packenham, Robert Allen 1937- *ConAu 73*
Packer, Arnold H 1935- *ConAu 37R*
Packer, Bernard J 1934- *ConAu 65*
Packer, David W 1937- *ConAu 9R*
Packer, Herbert L 1925-1972 *ConAu 37R*
Packer, J I 1926- *ConAu 1NR*
Packer, James Innell 1926- *ConAu 49, WrDr 84*
Packer, Joy 1905-1977 *ConAu 1R, –3NR, DcLEL 1940, TwCWr*
Packer, Nancy Huddleston 1925- *ConAu 65*
Packer, Rod Earle 1931- *ConAu 109*
Packer, Vin *ConAu X, SmATA X*
Packett, Charles Neville 1922- *IntAu&W 82, WrDr 84*
Paco D'Arcos, Joaquim 1908-1979 *CIDMEL 80, TwCWr*
Pacosz, Christina V *DrAP&F 83*
Pacosz, Christina V 1946- *ConAu 77*
Padberg, Daniel Ivan 1931- *ConAu 33R, WrDr 84*
Padberg, John W 1926- *ConAu 25R*
Padden, R C 1922- *ConAu 21R*
Paddleford, Clementine Haskin 1900-1967 *ConAu 89*
Paddock, John 1918- *ConAu 17R*
Paddock, Paul 1907-1975 *ConAu 61, ConAu P-2*
Paddock, William 1921- *ConAu 21R*
Padfield, Peter 1932- *ConAu 101, IntAu&W 82, WrDr 84*
Padgett, Desmond *ConAu X*
Padgett, Dora 1893?-1976 *ConAu 61*
Padgett, Lewis *ConAu X, TwCSFW, WrDr 84*
Padgett, Ron *DrAP&F 83*
Padgett, Ron 1942- *ConAu 25R, ConP 80, DcLB 5[port], DcLEL 1940, WrDr 84*
Padilla, Heberto 1932- *AuNews 1*
Padilla, Victoria 1907- *ConAu 103*
Padmanabhan, Neela 1938- *IntWWP 82*
Padovano, Anthony T 1934- *ConAu 7NR, –17R, WrDr 84*
Padover, Saul K 1905-1981 *ConAu 2NR, –103, –49*
Padros DePalacios, Esteban 1925- *IntAu&W 82*
Paech, Neil John 1949- *IntWWP 82*
Paemel, Monika Van 1945- *CIDMEL 80*
Paetow, Karl 1903- *IntAu&W 82*
Paffard, Michael 1928- *WrDr 84*
Paffard, Michael Kenneth 1928- *ConAu 103*
Pafford, John Henry Pyle 1900- *ConAu 104, WrDr 84*
Pagaczewski, Stanislaw 1916- *IntAu&W 82*
Pagden, Anthony 1945- *ConAu 101*
Page, Andre *CreCan 1*
Page, B Sanford *IntWWP 82X*
Page, Bonnie Sanford 1939- *IntWWP 82*
Page, Charles 1909- *WrDr 84*

Page, Charles H 1909- *ConAu 4NR, –5R*
Page, Curtis C 1914- *ConAu 21R*
Page, Drew 1905- *ConAu 105*
Page, Eileen *ConAu X, SmATA 7*
Page, Eleanor *ConAu X, SmATA 1*
Page, Elizabeth 1889- *TwCA, TwCA SUP*
Page, Ellis Batten 1924- *ConAu 13R*
Page, Emma *ConAu X, TwCCr&M 80, WrDr 84*
Page, Evelyn 1902- *ConAu 5R*
Page, Frederick 1879-1962 *LongCTC*
Page, G S *ConAu X*
Page, Geneva *IntWWP 82X*
Page, Gerald W 1939- *ConAu 93*
Page, Grover, Jr. 1918- *ConAu 17R*
Page, Harry Robert 1915- *ConAu 9R*
Page, Jake *ConAu X*
Page, James A 1918- *ConAu 107*
Page, James D 1910- *ConAu 73*
Page, James K, Jr. 1936- *ConAu 97*
Page, Jimmy 1944- *ConLC 12*
Page, Jimmy And Plant, Robert *ConLC 12*
Page, Joseph A 1934- *ConAu 81*
Page, Lorna *ConAu X*
Page, Lou Williams 1912- *ConAu 5R, –5NR*
Page, Malcolm 1935- *ConAu 45*
Page, Marco 1909-1968 *TwCCr&M 80*
Page, Marian *ConAu 69*
Page, Martin 1938- *ConAu 17R*
Page, Mary *ConAu X*
Page, Norman 1930- *ConAu 8NR, –61*
Page, P K 1916- *ConAu 4NR, ConLC 7, –18, ConP 80, WrDr 84*
Page, Patricia Kathleen 1916- *ConAu 53, CreCan 1, DcLEL 1940, IntAu&W 82*
Page, Robert Anthony 1949- *IntAu&W 82*
Page, Robert Collier 1908-1977 *ConAu 73*
Page, Robert Jeffress 1922- *ConAu 17R*
Page, Robert Morris 1903- *ConAu P-2*
Page, Robin 1943- *ConAu 103, WrDr 84*
Page, Roch 1939- *ConAu 33R*
Page, S Geneva *IntWWP 82X*
Page, Sarah Geneva 1913- *IntWWP 82*
Page, Stanton *ConAu X*
Page, Thomas 1942- *ConAu 81*
Page, Thornton 1913- *ConAu 2NR, –5R*
Page, Tom *DrAP&F 83*
Page, Vicki *ConAu X, IntAu&W 82X*
Page, William *DrAP&F 83*
Page, William Howard 1929- *IntWWP 82*
Page, William Roberts 1904- *ConAu 21R*
Pagel, Walter T U 1898-1983 *ConAu 109*
Pagels, Elaine *WrDr 84*
Pagels, Elaine Hiesey 1943- *ConAu 2NR, –45*
Pagels, Heinz Rudolf 1939- *ConAu 107*
Pages, Pedro *ConAu X*
Paget, George Charles Henry Victor 1922- *ConAu 17R*
Paget, John *ConAu X*
Paget, Julian 1921- *ConAu 21R, IntAu&W 82, WrDr 84*
Paget, Margaret *ConAu X*
Paget, Violet 1856?-1935 *ConAu 104, LongCTC, TwCA, TwCA SUP*

Paget-Fredericks, Joseph E P Rous-Marten
1903-1963 *SmATA 30*
Paget-Lowe, Henry *ConAu X*
Paglin, Morton 1922- *ConAu 97*
Pagnol, Marcel 1895-1974 *ClDMEL 80, CnMD,
ConAu 49, ModFrL, ModWD, TwCWr,
WorAu*
Pagnucci, Gianfranco 1940- *IntWWP 82*
Paher, Stanley W 1940- *ConAu 29R*
Pahl, R E 1935- *ConAu 25R*
Pahlen, Kurt 1907- *ConAu 7NR, –13R,
IntAu&W 82*
Pahlevi, Mohammed Riza 1919-1980 *ConAu 106*
Pahlow, Mannfried Otto Siegfried 1926-
IntAu&W 82
Pahz, Cheryl Suzanne 1949- *ConAu 8NR,
MichAu 80, SmATA 11*
Pahz, James Alon 1943- *ConAu 8NR,
SmATA 11*
Pai, Anna C 1935- *ConAu 89*
Pai, Young 1929- *ConAu 33R*
Paice, Margaret 1920- *ConAu 29R,
IntAu&W 82, SmATA 10*
Paidagogos, Petros *IntAu&W 82X*
Paier, Robert 1943- *ConAu 89*
Paiewonsky-Conde, Edgar *DrAP&F 83*
Paige, Brydon *CreCan 1*
Paige, Glenn D 1929- *ConAu 25R*
Paige, Leo *ConAu X*
Paige, Leroy Robert 1907?-1982 *ConAu 107*
Paige, Satchel *ConAu X*
Pain, Barry 1864-1928 *ConAu 109*
Pain, Barry Eric Odell 1864-1928 *LongCTC,
TwCA*
Pain, Margaret 1922- *IntWWP 82*
Paine, Albert Bigelow 1861-1937 *ConAu 108,
TwCA, TwCSFW*
Paine, Canio Francis 1920- *ConAmTC*
Paine, J Lincoln *ConAu X*
Paine, Lauran 1916- *ConAu 7NR, –45*
Paine, Philbrook 1910- *ConAu P-1*
Paine, R Howard 1922- *ConAu 5R*
Paine, Ralph Delahaye 1871-1925 *TwCA*
Paine, Roberta M 1925- *ConAu 33R,
SmATA 13*
Paine, Roger W, III 1942- *ConAu 65*
Paine, Stephen William 1908- *ConAu 1R*
Painter, Charlotte *DrAP&F 83, WrDr 84*
Painter, Charlotte 1926- *ConAu 1R, –3NR*
Painter, Daniel *ConAu X*
Painter, George Duncan 1914- *ConAu 101,
DcLEL 1940, WorAu*
Painter, Helen 1913- *WrDr 84*
Painter, Helen Welch 1913- *ConAu 33R*
Painter, Nell Irvin 1942- *ConAu 65*
Painter, Pamela *DrAP&F 83*
Painter, Raymond 1934- *WrDr 84*
Painton, Ivan Emory 1909- *IntWWP 82*
Pairault, Pierre 1922- *ConAu 53*
Pais, Abraham 1918- *ConAu 109*
Paish, F W 1898- *WrDr 84*
Paish, Frank Walter 1898- *ConAu 17R*
Paisley, Miriam Rose *IntWWP 82X*
Paisley, Miriam Rose Jungblut 1920-
IntWWP 82
Paisley, Tom 1932- *ChlLR 3, ConAu 61,
SmATA X*
Pak, Chan-Ki *IntAu&W 82X*
Pak, Chong-Hui *ConAu X*
Pakenham, Francis Aungier *WrDr 84*
Pakenham, Francis Aungier 1905- *ConAu 109*
Pakenham, Frank, Earl Of Longford *ConAu X*
Pakenham, Simona Vere 1916- *ConAu 1R, –3NR*
Pakenham, Thomas 1933- *ConAu 109,
WrDr 84*
Pakington, Humphrey 1888- *LongCTC, TwCA,
TwCA SUP*
Pakolitz, Istvan 1919- *IntAu&W 82*
Pakula, Marion Broome 1926- *ConAu 7NR, –57*
Pal, Pratapaditya 1935- *ConAu 37R,
IntAu&W 82, WrDr 84*
Palabe *IntAu&W 82X*
Palacio Valdes, Armando 1853-1938 *ClDMEL 80,
ModRL*
Palamas, Kostes 1859-1943 *ConAu 105,
TwCLC 5[port], WorAu*
Palamas, Kostis 1859-1943 *ClDMEL 80*
Palamountain, Joseph Cornwall, Jr. 1920-
ConAu 45
Palandri, Angela Jung 1926- *ConAu 37R*
Palange, Anthony, Jr. 1942- *ConAu 37R,*

WrDr 84
Palangyo, Peter K 1939- *DcLEL 1940*
Palau, Joseph M 1914- *IntAu&W 82*
Palazzeschi, Aldo Giurlani 1885-1974
*ClDMEL 80, ConAu 53, –89, ConLC 11,
ModRL, WhoTwCL, WorAu 1970*
Palazzo, Anthony D 1905-1970 *ConAu 29R,
SmATA 3*
Palazzo, Tony 1905-1970 *ConAu 4NR, –5R*
Palder, Edward L 1922- *SmATA 5*
Paleckis, Justas 1899-1980 *ConAu 105*
Palen, J John 1939- *ConAu 41R*
Palen, Jennie M *ConAu 5R, DrAP&F 83,
IntAu&W 82*
Palermo, David Stuart 1929- *ConAu 17R*
Pales Matos, Luis 1898-1959 *ModLAL*
Palestrant, Simon S 1907- *ConAu P-1*
Paley, Alan L 1943- *ConAu 69*
Paley, Grace *DrAP&F 83*
Paley, Grace 1922- *AuNews 1, ConAu 25R,
ConLC 4, –6, ConNov 82, DcLEL 1940,
WorAu 1970, WrDr 84*
Paley, Morton D 1935- *ConAu 33R*
Paley, Nicholas Miroslav 1911- *ConAu 41R,
IntAu&W 82*
Paley, Vivian Gussin 1929- *ConAu 93*
Paley, William S 1901- *ConAu 110*
Palffy-Alpar, Julius 1908- *ConAu P-2*
Palfrey, Colin 1939- *IntAu&W 82*
Palfrey, Thomas Rossman 1895- *ConAu 61*
Palin, Michael 1943- *ConAu 107,
ConLC 21[port]*
Palinchak, Robert S 1942- *ConAu 49*
Palinurus *ConAu X, LongCTC*
Palisca, Claude V 1921- *ConAu 17R*
Pall, Ellen Jane 1952- *ConAu 93*
Palladini, David 1946- *SmATA 32*
Pallas, Dorothy Constance 1933-1971
ConAu 33R
Pallas, Norvin 1918- *ConAu 1R, –3NR,
SmATA 23[port], WrDr 84*
Pallavera, Franco *ConAu X*
Palle, Albert Jacques 1916- *ConAu 13R,
TwCWr*
Pallenberg, Corrado 1912- *ConAu 13R*
Palley, Julian I 1925- *ConAu 73*
Palley, Marian Lief 1939- *ConAu 8NR, –61*
Palli, Pitsa *ConAu X*
Pallidini, Jodi *ConAu X*
Pallis, Alexander 1883-1975 *ConAu 61*
Pallister, Jan *DrAP&F 83, IntAu&W 82X,
IntWWP 82X*
Pallister, Janis L 1926- *ConAu 41R,
IntAu&W 82, IntWWP 82*
Pallister, John C 1891-1980 *ConAu 5R, –103,
SmATA 26N*
Pallone, Nathaniel John 1935- *ConAu 10NR,
–21R*
Palm, Anders L 1940- *IntAu&W 82*
Palm, Goeran 1931- *ConAu 29R*
Palm, Goran 1931- *ClDMEL 80, ConAu X,
IntAu&W 82*
Palm, John Daniel 1924- *ConAu 106*
Palmanteer, Ted *DrAP&F 83*
Palmason, Baldur 1919- *IntAu&W 82*
Palmatier, Robert Allen 1926- *ConAu 37R*
Palmedo, Roland 1895-1977 *ConAu 53, –69*
Palmer, Alan Warwick 1926- *ConAu 6NR, –13R,
IntAu&W 82, WrDr 84*
Palmer, Archie M 1896- *ConAu 13R*
Palmer, Arnold 1929- *ConAu 85*
Palmer, B C *ConAu X*
Palmer, Bernard 1914- *ConAu 7NR, –57,
SmATA 26[port]*
Palmer, Brooks 1900?-1974 *ConAu 45*
Palmer, Bruce Hamilton 1932- *ConAu 1R, –3NR*
Palmer, C Everard 1930- *ConAu 41R,
DcLEL 1940, SmATA 14, TwCCW 83*
Palmer, Candida 1926- *ConAu 61, SmATA 11*
Palmer, Carey 1943- *ConAu 103, WrDr 84*
Palmer, Cedric King 1913- *ConAu 13R,
WrDr 84*
Palmer, Charles Earl 1919- *ConAu 13R*
Palmer, Cruise 1917- *ConAu 69*
Palmer, Cyril Everard 1930- *WrDr 84*
Palmer, Dave Richard 1934- *ConAu 1NR, –45*
Palmer, David 1921- *ConAu 21R*
Palmer, David 1935- *IntWWP 82*
Palmer, Donald C 1934- *ConAu 53*
Palmer, Dorothy Ann 1935- *ConAu 57*
Palmer, Edgar Z 1898- *ConAu 21R*
Palmer, Edward L 1938- *ConAu 101*

Palmer, Elsie Pavitt 1922- *ConAu 5R*
Palmer, Eve 1916- *ConAu 21R*
Palmer, Everett W 1906-1970 *ConAu P-2*
Palmer, Frank 1921- *CreCan 2*
Palmer, Frank Robert 1922- *ConAu 17R,
WrDr 84*
Palmer, Frederick 1873-1958 *TwCA,
TwCA SUP*
Palmer, G, Jr. *DrAP&F 83*
Palmer, George E 1908- *ConAu 1R*
Palmer, George Herbert 1842-1933 *TwCA,
TwCA SUP*
Palmer, Heidi 1948- *SmATA 15*
Palmer, Helen H 1911- *ConAu 21R*
Palmer, Helen Marion 1898-1967 *ConAu X,
SmATA X*
Palmer, Henrietta Eliza Vaughan *LongCTC*
Palmer, Henry R, Jr. 1911- *ConAu 21R*
Palmer, Herbert Edward 1880-1961 *LongCTC*
Palmer, Herbert Franklin *CreCan 2*
Palmer, Herbert Sydney 1881- *CreCan 2*
Palmer, Humphrey 1930- *ConAu 29R*
Palmer, Jack Horace 1939- *IntWWP 82*
Palmer, James B 1929- *ConAu 25R*
Palmer, Jerome Robert 1904- *ConAu 45*
Palmer, Jim *ConAu X*
Palmer, John Alfred 1926- *ConAu 29R,
WrDr 84*
Palmer, John L 1943- *ConAu 73*
Palmer, John Leslie 1885-1944 *LongCTC, TwCA,
TwCA SUP, TwCCr&M 80*
Palmer, Joseph Mansergh 1912- *ConAu 5R*
Palmer, Juliette 1930- *ConAu 81, SmATA 15,
WrDr 84*
Palmer, Kenneth T 1937- *ConAu 77*
Palmer, L R 1906- *ConAu 25R*
Palmer, Larry Garland 1938- *ConAu 17R*
Palmer, Laura *ConAu X*
Palmer, Leslie *DrAP&F 83*
Palmer, Lilli *ConAu X*
Palmer, Lynn *ConAu X, IntWWP 82X*
Palmer, Madelyn 1910- *ConAu 103, WrDr 84*
Palmer, Marian 1930- *ConAu 53, WrDr 84*
Palmer, Marjorie 1919- *ConAu 57*
Palmer, Michael *DrAP&F 83*
Palmer, Michael 1943- *ConP 80, WrDr 84*
Palmer, Michael Denison 1933- *ConAu 37R,
WrDr 84*
Palmer, Miriam *DrAP&F 83*
Palmer, Nicholas 1950- *ConAu 89*
Palmer, Norman D 1909- *ConAu 1R, –3NR,
IntAu&W 82, WrDr 84*
Palmer, Pamela Lynn 1951- *ConAu 4NR, –53,
IntWWP 82*
Palmer, Penelope 1943- *WrDr 84*
Palmer, Peter *ConAu X*
Palmer, Peter John 1932- *ConAu 103, WrDr 84*
Palmer, Ralph Simon 1914- *ConAu 73*
Palmer, Raymond A 1910-1977 *TwCSFW*
Palmer, Raymond Edward 1927- *ConAu 77*
Palmer, Richard 1904- *ConAu 97*
Palmer, Richard Edward 1933- *ConAu 1NR, –45*
Palmer, Richard Phillips 1921- *ConAu 57*
Palmer, Robert Roswell 1909- *ConAu 13R*
Palmer, Robin 1911- *ConAu 109*
Palmer, Roy 1932- *ConAu 8NR, –61*
Palmer, Spencer J 1927- *ConAu 10NR, –61*
Palmer, Stuart 1905-1968 *TwCCr&M 80*
Palmer, Stuart 1924- *ConAu 1R, –3NR*
Palmer, Thomas 1955- *ConAu 109*
Palmer, Tobias *ConAu X*
Palmer, Vance Edward 1885-1959 *LongCTC,
ModCmwL, TwCWr*
Palmer, William J 1890- *ConSFA, WrDr 84*
Palmer, Winthrop B *DrAP&F 83*
Palmer, Winthrop B 1899- *ConAu 65,
IntWWP 82*
Palmore, Erdman B 1930- *ConAu 37R*
Palms, Roger C 1936- *ConAu 93*
Paloczi-Horvath, George 1908-1973 *ConAu 5R,
–37R*
Palomino, Angel 1929- *IntAu&W 82*
Palomo, G J 1952- *ConAu 61*
Palotai, Boris 1904- *IntAu&W 82*
Palovic, Clara Lora 1918- *ConAu 25R*
Palsson, Hermann 1921- *WrDr 84*
Palsson, Sigurdur 1948- *IntAu&W 82*
Paltenghi, Madeleine *ConAu X*
Paludan, Jacob 1896-1975 *ClDMEL 80*
Paludan, Phillip S 1938- *ConAu 73*
Palumbo, Dennis 1929- *ConAu 29R, WrDr 84*
Palusci, Larry 1916- *ConAu 29R*

Paluszny, Maria Janina 1939- *ConAu 103*
Palyi, Melchior 1892?-1970 *ConAu 104*
Pama, Cornelis 1916- *IntAu&W 82*, *WrDr 84*
Pampel, Martha 1913- *IntAu&W 82*
Pan, Peter *ConAu X*
Pan, Stephen C Y 1915- *ConAu 45*
Panagopoulos, Epaminondas Peter 1915-
ConAu 13R
Panama, Norman 1920- *ConAu 104*
Panama, Norman And Melvin Frank
DcLB 26[port]
Panassie, Hugues 1912-1974 *ConAu 53*, *-97*
Panati, Charles 1943- *ConAu 81*
Panavision Kid, The *ConAu X*
Pancake, Breece D'J 1952?-1979 *ConAu 109*
Pancake, John S 1920- *ConAu 53*
Pandey, B N 1929- *ConAu 25R*, *WrDr 84*
Pandey, B N 1929-1982 *ConAu 108*
Pandi, Marianne 1924- *IntAu&W 82*
Pandit, Vijaya Lakshmi 1900- *ConAu 104*
Panduro, Leif 1923-1977 *ClDMEL 80*
Panella, Vincent 1939- *ConAu 97*
Panero Torbado, Leopoldo 1909-1962
ClDMEL 80
Panetta, George 1915-1969 *ConAu 81*,
SmATA 15[port]
Panetta, Leon Edward 1938- *ConAu 101*
Panfyorov, Fyodor Ivanovich 1896-1960 *TwCWr*
Pangborn, Edgar 1909-1976 *ConAu 1R*, *-4NR*,
ConSFA, *DcLB 8[port]*, *TwCSFW*
Panger, Daniel 1926- *ConAu 93*
Panglaykim, J 1922- *ConAu 21R*
Pangle, Thomas L 1944- *ConAu 1NR*, *-49*
Pangratz, Paul *IntAu&W 82X*
Paniagua Bermudez, Domingo 1880?-1973
ConAu 41R
Panichas, George A 1930- *ConAu 10NR*
Panichas, George Andrew 1930- *ConAu 25R*,
IntAu&W 82, *WrDr 84*
Panickavede, Paul Louis 1918- *IntAu&W 82*
Paniker, K Ayyappa *IntWWP 82*
Paniker, Salvador 1927- *IntAu&W 82*
Panikkar, Kavalam Madhava 1895-1963
ConAu P-1
Panikkar, Raimundo 1918- *ConAu 81*
Panitch, Leo 1945- *WrDr 84*
Panitt, Merrill 1917- *ConAu 106*
Pank, John 1939- *WrDr 84*
Pankhurst, Christabel 1880-1958 *LongCTC*
Pankhurst, Emmeline 1857-1928 *LongCTC*
Pankhurst, Richard 1927- *WrDr 84*
Pankhurst, Richard Keir Pethick 1927-
ConAu 6NR, *-9R*
Pankhurst, Sylvia 1882-1960 *LongCTC*
Panko, William 1894-1948 *CreCan 1*
Pannabecker, Samuel Floyd 1896- *ConAu 65*
Pannell, Anne Gary 1910- *ConAu P-2*
Pannenberg, Wolfhart 1928- *ConAu 11NR*, *-25R*
Panneton, Philippe 1895-1960 *CreCan 2*
Pannor, Reuben 1922- *ConAu 61*
Pannwitz, Rudolf 1881-1969 *ConAu 89*, *ModGL*
Pano, Nicholas C 1934- *ConAu 37R*
Panofsky, Erwin 1892-1968 *WorAu 1970*
Panos, Chris 1935- *ConAu 65*
Panov, Valery 1938- *ConAu 102*
Panova, Vera Fyodorovna 1905-1973 *ClDMEL 80*,
ConAu 102, *-89*, *ModSL 1*, *ModWD*,
TwCWr, *WorAu*
Panowski, Eileen Janet Thompson 1920-
ConAu 5R
Panshin, Alexei 1940- *ConAu 57*, *ConSFA*,
DcLB 8[port], *TwCSFW*, *WrDr 84*
Pansing, Nancy Pelletier *DrAP&F 83*
Panter, Carol 1936- *ConAu 49*, *SmATA 9*
Panter, Gideon G 1935- *ConAu 77*
Panter-Downes, Mollie Patricia 1906-
ConAu 101, *LongCTC*, *TwCA*,
TwCA SUP
Panton, Lawrence Arthur Colley 1894-1954
CreCan 2
Panurge *IntAu&W 82X*
Panzarella, Andrew 1940- *ConAu 25R*
Panzarella, Joseph John, Jr. 1919- *ConAu 85*
Panzer, Pauline 1911?-1972 *ConAu 37R*
Panzini, Alfredo 1863-1939 *ClDMEL 80*, *TwCA*,
TwCA SUP
Pao, Ping-Nie 1922- *ConAu 103*
Paoli, Pia 1930- *ConAu 25R*
Paolini, Gilberto 1928- *ConAu 45*
Paolotti, John *WrDr 84*
Paolucci, Anne *ConAu 73*, *DrAP&F 83*
Paolucci, Henry 1921- *ConAu 102*

Paone, Anthony J 1913- *ConAu 5R*
Papachristou, Judy 1930- *ConAu 93*
Papakongos, Kostis 1936- *IntAu&W 82*
Papaleo, Joseph *DrAP&F 83*
Papaleo, Joseph 1925- *ConAu 25R*
Papandreou, Andreas G 1919- *ConAu 37R*
Papandreou, Margaret C 1923- *ConAu 29R*
Papanek, Ernst 1900-1973 *ConAu 1R*, *-4NR*
Papanek, Gustav F 1926- *ConAu 1NR*, *-45*
Papas, William *WrDr 84*
Papas, William 1927- *ConAu 25R*,
IntAu&W 82
Papashvily, George 1898-1978 *ConAu 77*, *-81*,
SmATA 17, *TwCA SUP*
Papashvily, Helen 1906- *ConAu 81*, *SmATA 17*,
TwCA SUP
Papazian, Dennis Richard 1931- *ConAu 45*
Pape, D L *ConAu X*
Pape, D L 1930- *ConAu X*, *SmATA 2*
Pape, Donna 1930- *ConAu 9NR*, *-21R*
Pape, Gordon 1936- *ConAu 105*
Pape, Greg *DrAP&F 83*
Papenfuse, Edward C, Jr. 1943- *ConAu 8NR*,
-57
Paper, Herbert H 1925- *ConAu 1NR*, *-45*
Paperny, Myra 1932- *ConAu 69*, *SmATA 33*
Papert, Emma N 1926- *ConAu 101*
Papi, G Ugo 1893- *ConAu 25R*
Papich, Stephen 1925- *ConAu 69*
Papier, Judith Barnard 1932- *ConAu 21R*
Papin, Joseph 1914- *ConAu 65*
Papineau-Couture, Jean 1916- *CreCan 1*
Papini, Giovanni 1881-1956 *ClDMEL 80*,
CnMWL, *LongCTC*, *TwCA*, *TwCA SUP*,
TwCWr
Papp, Charles Steven 1917- *ConAu 41R*
Pappageotes, George C 1926-1963 *ConAu 1R*,
-2NR
Pappas, George 1929- *ConAu 29R*
Pappas, George S 1930- *WrDr 84*
Pappas, Lou Seibert 1930- *ConAu 8NR*, *-61*
Pappas, Neva J 1917- *IntWWP 82*
Pappworth, M H 1910- *ConAu 21R*
Paprika *ConAu X*
Paquet, Alfons 1881-1944 *CnMD*, *ModWD*
Paradis, Adrian Alexis 1912- *ConAu 1R*, *-3NR*,
SmATA 1, *WrDr 84*
Paradis, James G 1942- *ConAu 93*
Paradis, Marjorie Bartholomew 1886-1970
ConAu 29R, *-73*, *SmATA 17*
Paradis, Philip *DrAP&F 83*
Paradis, Suzanne 1936- *CreCan 1*
Parakh, Jal Sohrab 1932- *ConAu 105*
Paral, Vladimir 1932- *ModSL 2*
Parandowski, Jan 1895-1978 *ClDMEL 80*,
ConAu P-1, *ModSL 2*
Paransky, Leah 1925- *IntWWP 82*
Parasuram, T V 1923- *ConAu 106*
Paratore, Angela 1912- *ConAu 13R*
Paratte, Henri D 1950- *IntAu&W 82*
Parchman, William E 1936- *ConAu 93*,
NatPD 81[port]
Pardee, Alice DeWolf 1897- *IntAu&W 82*
Pardey, Larry *ConAu X*
Pardey, Lawrence Fred 1939- *ConAu 93*
Pardey, Lin 1944- *ConAu 93*
Pardis, Marjorie B 1886?-1970 *ConAu 104*
Pardo Bazan, Emilia 1851-1921 *ClDMEL 80*
Pardo Bazan, Emilia, Condesa De 1852?-1921
ModRL
Pardoe, M 1902- *TwCCW 83*
Paredes, Americo 1915- *ConAu 37R*,
IntAu&W 82
Pareek, Udai 1925- *ConAu 11NR*, *-21R*
Parelius, Ann Parker 1943- *ConAu 81*
Parelius, Robert J 1941- *ConAu 81*
Parens, Henri 1928- *ConAu 89*
Parent, David J 1931- *ConAu 9NR*, *-57*
Parent, Gail 1940- *ConAu 101*
Parent, Ronald 1937-1982 *ConAu 107*
Parente, Pascal P 1890-1971 *ConAu 33R*,
ConAu P-1
Parente, Sarah Eleanor 1913- *ConAu 41R*
Parenteau, Shirley Laurolyn 1935- *ConAu 85*
Parenti, Michael 1933- *ConAu 73*
Pares, Sir Bernard 1867-1949 *LongCTC*,
TwCA SUP
Pares, Marion Stapylton 1914- *ConAu 17R*,
IntAu&W 82
Pares, Richard 1902-1958 *LongCTC*
Pareto, Vilfredo 1848-1923 *TwCA*, *TwCA SUP*
Paretti, Sandra *ConAu 7NR*, *-53*

Pareyson, Luigi 1918- *IntAu&W 82*
Parfitt, George 1939- *ConAu 109*
Pargeter, Edith 1913- *WrDr 84*
Pargeter, Edith Mary 1913- *ConAu 1R*, *-4NR*,
IntAu&W 82, *LongCTC*, *TwCCr&M 80*,
TwCRGW
Pargeter, Margaret *TwCRGW*
Parham, Joseph Byars 1919- *ConAu 65*
Parham, Robert *DrAP&F 83*
Parham, Robert Randall 1943- *ConAu 57*
Parham, William 1914- *ConAu 103*
Parham, William Thomas 1913- *ConAu 103*,
WrDr 84
Parikh, Dhiru 1933- *IntWWP 82*
Parikh, Pravin A 1948- *IntWWP 82*
Parini, Jay 1948- *ConAu 97*, *IntWWP 82*
Parins, James William 1939- *ConAu 109*
Paris, Bernard Jay 1931- *ConAu 7NR*, *-17R*,
WrDr 84
Paris, Erna 1938- *ConAu 105*
Paris, Jeanne 1918- *ConAu 1R*
Paris, Matthew *DrAP&F 83*
Parise, Goffredo 1929- *ClDMEL 80*
Pariseau, Earl J 1928- *ConAu 9R*
Parish, Barbara Shirk *DrAP&F 83*
Parish, Charles 1927- *ConAu 25R*
Parish, David 1932- *ConAu 73*
Parish, James 1944- *WrDr 84*
Parish, James Robert 1944- *ConAu 33R*
Parish, James Robert 1946- *IntAu&W 82*
Parish, Peggy *WrDr 84*
Parish, Peggy 1927- *ConAu 73*, *SmATA 17*,
TwCCW 83
Parish, Peter Anthony 1930- *IntAu&W 82*
Parish, Peter J 1929- *ConAu 57*, *WrDr 84*
Parish, Townsend *ConAu X*
Parisi, Joseph 1944- *ConAu 93*
Park, Bill *SmATA X*
Park, Chan-Ki 1928- *IntAu&W 82*
Park, Charles F, Jr. 1903- *ConAu 57*
Park, Chung Hee 1917-1979 *ConAu 10NR*, *-61*,
-97
Park, Clara Claiborne 1923- *ConAu 21R*
Park, D U *ConAu X*
Park, David 1919- *ConAu 105*
Park, Ed 1930- *ConAu 73*
Park, Elm *ConAu X*
Park, George 1925- *ConAu 77*
Park, Joe 1913- *ConAu 21R*
Park, Jordan *ConAu X*
Park, Joseph H 1890?-1979 *ConAu 89*
Park, Maeva *ConAu X*
Park, Michael 1941- *IntWWP 82*
Park, O'Hyun 1940- *ConAu 53*
Park, Peter 1929- *ConAu 29R*
Park, Richard L 1920- *ConAu 77*
Park, Robert L 1932- *ConAu 89*
Park, Ruth *ConAu 105*, *SmATA 25*,
TwCCW 83, *TwCWr*, *WrDr 84*
Park, W B 1936- *ConAu 97*, *SmATA 22[port]*
Park, William John 1930- *ConAu 49*
Parke, Herbert William 1903- *ConAu 105*
Parke, Margaret Bittner 1901- *ConAu 89*
Parke, Ross D 1938- *ConAu 1NR*, *-45*
Parker, Adrian 1947- *WrDr 84*
Parker, Adrian David 1947- *ConAu 103*
Parker, Alexander A 1908- *ConAu 21R*
Parker, Alfred Browning 1916- *ConAu 17R*
Parker, Barrett 1908- *WrDr 84*
Parker, Beatrice *ConAu X*
Parker, Bert *ConAu X*
Parker, Bertha Morris 1890-1980 *ConAu 5R*,
-5NR, *-102*
Parker, Betty June 1929- *ConAu 7NR*, *-57*
Parker, Beulah 1912- *ConAu 81*
Parker, Bonnie Elizabeth 1929- *MichAu 80*
Parker, Catherine E 1912- *IntWWP 82*
Parker, Clifford S 1891- *ConAu 5R*
Parker, Clyde A 1927- *ConAu 41R*
Parker, David L 1935- *ConAu 108*
Parker, David Marshall 1929- *ConAu 77*
Parker, Dee *ConAu X*
Parker, Derek 1932- *ConAu 29R*, *IntAu&W 82*,
IntWWP 82, *WrDr 84*
Parker, Don H 1912- *ConAu 5R*, *-6NR*
Parker, Donald Dean 1899- *ConAu 37R*
Parker, Donn B 1929- *ConAu 9NR*, *-65*
Parker, Dorothy 1893-1967 *ConAmA*,
ConAu 25R, *ConAu P-2*, *ConLC 15*,
LongCTC, *ModAL*, *TwCA*, *TwCA SUP*,
TwCWr
Parker, Dorothy 1922- *ConAu 93*

Parker, Dorothy Mills *ConAu 11NR, –21R*
Parker, Douglas Hugh 1926- *ConAu 1R*
Parker, Edna Jean 1935- *ConAu 101*
Parker, Edwin B 1932- *ConAu 13R*
Parker, Elinor Milnor 1906- *ConAu 1R, –3NR,*
SmATA 3
Parker, Elliott S 1939- *ConAu 103*
Parker, Francis H 1920- *ConAu 21R*
Parker, Frank J 1940- *ConAu 49*
Parker, Franklin 1921- *ConAu 7NR, –33R,*
IntAu&W 82, WrDr 84
Parker, Franklin D 1918- *ConAu 13R*
Parker, Gail Thain 1943- *ConAu 104*
Parker, Geoffrey 1933- *ConAu 49*
Parker, Sir Gilbert 1862-1932 *LongCTC, TwCA,*
TwCA SUP
Parker, Gordon 1940- *ConAu 103, WrDr 84*
Parker, H M D 1896?-1971 *ConAu 104*
Parker, Harold T 1907- *ConAu 9NR, –21R*
Parker, Hershel 1935- *ConAu 33R*
Parker, Howard J 1948- *ConAu 57*
Parker, J Carlyle 1931- *ConAu 7NR, –57*
Parker, James *ConAu X*
Parker, Jean 1938- *ConAu X*
Parker, Joan H 1932- *ConAu 85*
Parker, John *ConAu X*
Parker, John 1906- *ConAu 5R, IntAu&W 82*
Parker, John 1923- *ConAu 5R, –5NR*
Parker, Julia 1932- *ConAu 101*
Parker, Kay Grayman 1912- *IntWWP 82*
Parker, Lois M 1912- *ConAu 11NR, –69,*
SmATA 30[port]
Parker, Louis Napoleon 1852-1944 *LongCTC,*
ModWD, TwCA, TwCA SUP
Parker, Marion Dominica Hope 1914-
IntAu&W 82, WrDr 84
Parker, Marsha Zurich 1952- *ConAu 107*
Parker, Nancy Winslow 1930- *ConAu 1NR, –49,*
SmATA 10, WrDr 84
Parker, Nathan Carlyle 1960- *ConAu 102*
Parker, Pat *DrAP&F 83*
Parker, Pat 1944- *ConAu 57*
Parker, Percy Spurlark 1940- *ConAu 53*
Parker, Richard 1915- *ConAu 73, SmATA 14,*
TwCCW 83, WrDr 84
Parker, Robert *ConAu X, SmATA X*
Parker, Robert 1920- *ConAu 77*
Parker, Robert Allerton 1889?-1970 *ConAu 29R*
Parker, Robert B 1932- *ConAu 1NR, –49,*
ConLC 27[port], TwCCr&M 80, WrDr 84
Parker, Robert Stewart 1915- *ConAu 103,*
WrDr 84
Parker, Rolland 1928- *ConAu 2NR, –45*
Parker, Ronald K 1939- *ConAu 108*
Parker, Rowland 1912- *ConAu 10NR, –65*
Parker, Sanford S 1919?-1980 *ConAu 97*
Parker, Stanley R 1927- *ConAu 103, WrDr 84*
Parker, Stewart 1941- *ConAu 103, ConDr 82,*
WrDr 84
Parker, T H L 1916- *ConAu 6NR*
Parker, Thomas 1916- *WrDr 84*
Parker, Thomas F 1932- *ConAu 73*
Parker, Thomas Henry Louis 1916- *ConAu 5R,*
IntAu&W 82
Parker, Thomas Maynard 1906- *ConAu P-2,*
IntAu&W 82
Parker, W Dale 1925- *WrDr 84*
Parker, W H 1912- *ConAu 33R, WrDr 84*
Parker, W Oren 1911- *ConAu 41R*
Parker, Watson 1924- *ConAu 106*
Parker, William Riley 1906-1968 *ConAu P-2*
Parker, Willie J 1924- *ConAu 77*
Parker, Wyman W 1912- *ConAu 13R*
Parker-Rich, J *ConSFA*
Parkerson, John 1885?-1978 *ConAu 77*
Parkes, Colin Murray 1928- *ConAu 81*
Parkes, Frank Kobina 1932- *DcLEL 1940*
Parkes, Henry Bamford 1904-1972 *ConAu 33R*
Parkes, James William 1896-1981 *ConAu 104*
Parkes, Lucas *ConAu X, WorAu*
Parkes, Roger Graham 1933- *ConAu 53,*
IntAu&W 82, WrDr 84
Parkes, Terence 1927- *ConAu 104*
Parkhill, Forbes 1892- *ConAu 1R*
Parkhill, Wilson 1901- *ConAu 5R*
Parkhurst, Helen 1887-1973 *ConAu 41R*
Parkhurst, Winthrop 1892?-1983 *ConAu 110*
Parkin, Alan 1934- *ConAu 29R*
Parkin, David 1940- *ConAu 25R*
Parkin, G Raleigh 1896-1977? *ConAu 106*
Parkin, Molly 1932- *ConAu 104, WrDr 84*
Parkinson, C Northcote 1909- *ConAu 5NR*

Parkinson, Charles Douglas 1916- *ConAu P-1*
Parkinson, Cornelia M 1925- *ConAu 81*
Parkinson, Cyril Northcote 1909- *ConAu 5R,*
IntAu&W 82, LongCTC, WorAu,
WrDr 84
Parkinson, Ethelyn M 1906- *ConAu 1NR, –49,*
SmATA 11
Parkinson, J R 1922- *ConAu 102*
Parkinson, Michael *WrDr 84*
Parkinson, Michael 1944- *ConAu 29R*
Parkinson, Roger 1939-1978 *ConAu 106*
Parkinson, Thomas *DrAP&F 83*
Parkinson, Thomas 1920- *ConAu 3NR, –5R,*
ConP 80, IntAu&W 82, IntWWP 82,
WrDr 84
Parkinson, Thomas P *ConAu 102*
Parkinson, Tom *ConAu X*
Parks, Aileen Wells 1916- *ConAu 5R*
Parks, Arva Moore 1939- *ConAu 103*
Parks, David 1944- *ConAu 25R*
Parks, Edd Winfield 1906-1968 *ConAu 5R,*
SmATA 10
Parks, Edmund 1911- *ConAu 69*
Parks, Edna Dorintha 1910- *ConAu 13R,*
WrDr 84
Parks, Gerald B *DrAP&F 83*
Parks, Gerald Bartlett 1945- *IntWWP 82*
Parks, Gordon 1912- *AuNews 2, ConAu 41R,*
ConLC 1, –16, LivgBAA, SmATA 8,
WrDr 84
Parks, Joseph Howard 1903- *ConAu 1R*
Parks, Lloyd Clifford 1922- *ConAu 57*
Parks, Pat 1924- *ConAu 61*
Parks, Robert James 1940- *ConAu 65*
Parks, Stephen Davis 1949- *NatPD 81[port]*
Parks, Stephen Robert 1940- *ConAu 65*
Parksmith, George *ConAu X*
Parlato, Salvatore J, Jr. 1936- *ConAu 73*
Parlett, David 1939- *ConAu 103*
Parlett, James *DrAP&F 83*
Parley, Peter 1793-1860 *SmATA X*
Parlin, Bradley W 1938- *ConAu 69*
Parlin, John *ConAu X, SmATA 4*
Parlow, Kathleen 1890-1963 *CreCan 2*
Parma, Clemens *ConAu X, IntWWP 82X*
Parman, Donald L 1932- *ConAu 65*
Parmelee, Alice 1903- *ConAu P-2*
Parmenter, Ross 1912- *ConAu 17R*
Parmer, Jess Norman 1925- *ConAu 5R*
Parmet, Herbert S 1929- *ConAu 11NR, –21R,*
WrDr 84
Parmet, Robert D 1938- *ConAu 77*
Parmet, Simon 1897- *ConAu P-1*
Parnaby, Owen Wilfred 1921- *ConAu 9R*
Parnall, Peter 1936- *ConAu 81, SmATA 16*
Parnas, Raymond I 1937- *ConAu 33R*
Parnell, Charles Stewart 1846-1891 *LongCTC*
Parnell, Peter 1953- *NatPD 81[port]*
Parnes, Herbert S 1919- *ConAu 41R*
Parnes, Sidney J 1922- *ConAu 10NR, –21R*
Parnicki, Teodor 1908- *CIDMEL 80, ModSL 2*
Parr, Charles McKew 1884- *ConAu P-1*
Parr, James A 1936- *ConAu 49*
Parr, John 1928- *ConAu 102*
Parr, Letitia Evelyn 1906- *ConAu 103,*
WrDr 84
Parr, Lucy 1924- *ConAu 29R, SmATA 10*
Parr, Michael 1927- *ConAu 17R*
Parra, Gregory 1929- *IntAu&W 82*
Parra, Nicanor 1914- *ConAu 85, ConLC 2,*
ModLAL, WorAu 1970
Parratt, Anne Chapman 1926- *IntAu&W 82*
Parrinder, E Geoffrey 1910- *ConAu 10NR, –21R*
Parrington, Vernon L 1871-1929 *DcLB 17[port],*
LongCTC, ModAL, TwCA, TwCA SUP
Parrini, Carl P 1933- *ConAu 107*
Parrino, John J 1942- *ConAu 101*
Parrino, Michael 1915?-1976 *ConAu 65*
Parriott, Sara 1953- *ConAu 107*
Parris, Addison W 1923-1975 *ConAu P-2*
Parris, Guichard 1903- *ConAu 81*
Parris, Judith H 1939- *ConAu 57*
Parrish, Anne 1888-1957 *LongCTC,*
SmATA 27[port], TwCA, TwCA SUP,
TwCCW 83, TwCWr
Parrish, Bernard P 1936- *ConAu 103*
Parrish, Bernie *ConAu X*
Parrish, Carl 1904-1965 *ConAu 5R*
Parrish, Eugene *ConAu X, IntWWP 82X*
Parrish, John A 1939- *ConAu 37R*
Parrish, Louis 1927- *ConAu 107*
Parrish, Mary *ConAu X, SmATA 2*

Parrish, Mary Frances *ConAu X*
Parrish, Maxfield 1870-1966 *SmATA 14*
Parrish, Michael E 1942- *ConAu 29R*
Parrish, Robert 1916- *ConAu 81*
Parrish, Stephen Maxfield 1921- *ConAu 104*
Parrish, Thomas 1927- *ConAu 93*
Parrish, Wayland Maxfield 1887- *ConAu P-2*
Parrish, Wendy 1950- *ConAu 73*
Parrish, William E 1931- *ConAu 1R, –3NR,*
IntAu&W 82, WrDr 84
Parronchi, Alessandro 1914- *CIDMEL 80*
Parrott, Cecil 1909- *ConAu 103, IntAu&W 82,*
WrDr 84
Parrott, Fred J 1913- *ConAu 41R*
Parrott, Ian 1916- *ConAu 2NR, –5R,*
IntAu&W 82, WrDr 84
Parrott, Leslie 1922- *ConAu 97*
Parrott, Lora Lee 1923- *ConAu 25R*
Parry, Albert 1901- *ConAu 1R, –6NR,*
WrDr 84
Parry, Anne *IntWWP 82X*
Parry, Sir Charles Hubert Hastings 1848-1918
LongCTC, TwCA
Parry, Clive 1917-1982 *ConAu 107*
Parry, Ellwood C, III 1941- *ConAu 93,*
WrDr 84
Parry, Hugh J *DrAP&F 83*
Parry, Hugh Jones 1916- *ConAu 13R,*
WrDr 84
Parry, J H 1914- *ConAu 6NR*
Parry, John *ConAu X*
Parry, John Horace 1914- *ConAu 5R*
Parry, Marian 1924- *ConAu 41R,*
IntAu&W 82, SmATA 13
Parry, Michael Patrick 1947- *ConAu 101*
Parry, S Chalmers 1900- *WrDr 84*
Parry, Shedden Chalmers Cole 1900-
IntAu&W 82
Parry, Thomas 1904- *IntAu&W 82*
Parry, Wilfrid Hocking 1924- *WrDr 84*
Parry-Jones, Daniel 1891- *ConAu 13R,*
IntAu&W 82, WrDr 84
Parseghian, Ara 1923- *ConAu 105*
Parsegian, V Lawrence 1908- *ConAu 57*
Parshley, Howard Madison 1884-1953 *TwCA,*
TwCA SUP
Parsifal *ConAu X*
Parsloe, Guy 1900- *ConAu P-1*
Parson, Ruben L 1907- *ConAu 13R*
Parson, Tom *DrAP&F 83*
Parsons, C J 1941- *ConAu 103, WrDr 84*
Parsons, Charles 1933- *ConAu 45*
Parsons, Clere Trevor James Herbert 1908-1931
CnMWL
Parsons, Coleman O 1905- *ConAu P-1,*
WrDr 84
Parsons, Cynthia 1926- *ConAu 45*
Parsons, Denys 1914- *ConAu 13R*
Parsons, Edward 1900- *IntAu&W 82*
Parsons, Elmer E 1919- *ConAu 25R*
Parsons, Geoffrey 1879-1956 *TwCA,*
TwCA SUP
Parsons, Geoffrey 1908-1981 *ConAu 105*
Parsons, Harriet Oettinger 1906?-1983?
ConAu 108
Parsons, Howard L 1918- *ConAu 1NR, –49*
Parsons, Ian 1906-1980 *ConAu 102, –97*
Parsons, Jack 1920- *ConAu 104, IntAu&W 82,*
WrDr 84
Parsons, James Bunyan 1921- *ConAu 29R*
Parsons, Kermit Carlyle 1927- *ConAu 29R*
Parsons, Kitty *ConAu 13R*
Parsons, Louella 1881-1972 *ConAu 37R, –93*
Parsons, Malcolm Barningham 1919- *ConAu 108*
Parsons, Martin 1907- *ConAu 53, WrDr 84*
Parsons, Peter Angas 1933- *WrDr 84*
Parsons, Priscilla *IntWWP 82X*
Parsons, R A *ConAu 101*
Parsons, Richard Augustus *WrDr 84*
Parsons, Stanley B, Jr. 1927- *ConAu 45*
Parsons, Talcott 1902-1979 *ConAu 4NR, –5R,*
–85
Parsons, Thornton H 1921- *ConAu 73*
Parsons, Tom *ConAu X, SmATA X*
Parsons, Wilfrid 1887-1958 *TwCA, TwCA SUP*
Parsons, William Edward, Jr. 1936- *ConAu 21R*
Parsons, William T 1923- *ConAu 65*
Partch, Virgil Franklin, II 1916- *ConAu 108*
Parthasarathy, R 1934- *ConP 80, WrDr 84*
Partington, F H *ConAu X*
Partington, Susan Trowbridge 1924- *ConAu 9R*
Partner, Peter 1924- *ConAu 85*

Parton, Ian 1908- *WrDr 84*
Parton, Margaret 1915- *ConAu 97*
Partridge, Anthony *TwCCr&M 80*
Partridge, Astley Cooper 1901- *ConAu 103,
    IntAu&W 82, WrDr 84*
Partridge, Bellamy 1878-1960 *TwCA,
    TwCA SUP*
Partridge, Benjamin W, Jr. 1915- *ConAu 25R,
    SmATA 28*
Partridge, Sir Bernard 1861-1945 *LongCTC*
Partridge, David 1919- *CreCan 1*
Partridge, Edward B 1916- *ConAu 65*
Partridge, Eric Honeywood 1894-1979 *ConAu 1R,
    -3NR, -85, LongCTC, TwCA SUP*
Partridge, Frances Catherine 1900- *ConAu 29R*
Partridge, James W 1936- *WrDr 84*
Partridge, Jenny 1947- *ConAu 109*
Partridge, William L 1944- *ConAu 1NR, -45*
Parulski, George R, Jr. 1954- *ConAu 97*
Parun, Vesna 1922- *CIDMEL 80, ModSL 2*
Parvin, Betty 1916- *ConAu 97, ConP 80,
    IntAu&W 82, IntWWP 82*
Parvin, Betty 1917- *WrDr 84*
Pary, C C *ConAu X*
Parzen, Herbert 1896- *ConAu 25R*
Pasamanik, Luisa 1930- *ConAu 101,
    IntAu&W 82*
Pascal, Anthony H 1933- *ConAu 29R*
Pascal, David 1918- *ConAu 9R, SmATA 14*
Pascal, Gerald Ross 1907- *ConAu 37R*
Pascal, John Robert 1932?-1981 *ConAu 102*
Pascal, Paul 1925- *ConAu 21R*
Pascal, Roy 1904-1980 *ConAu 5R, -6NR*
Pascale, Richard Tanner 1938- *WrDr 84*
Pascarella, Perry 1934- *ConAu 93, WrDr 84*
Paschal, Andrew G 1907- *LivgBAA*
Paschal, George H, Jr. 1925- *ConAu 29R*
Paschal, Nancy *ConAu X, SmATA X*
Paschall, H Franklin 1922- *ConAu 25R*
Pascoaes, Joaquim Teixeira De 1877-1952
    CIDMEL 80
Pascoe, Elizabeth Jean *ConAu 69*
Pascoe, John Dobree 1908-1972 *ConAu P-1*
Pascoli, Giovanni 1855-1912 *CIDMEL 80,
    TwCWr, WhoTwCL*
Pascudniak, Pascal *ConAu X*
Pasdeloup, Jean-Marie *IntAu&W 82X,
    IntWWP 82X*
Pasek, Catherine Louise Kern 1910- *IntWWP 82*
Pasek, Mya Kern *IntWWP 82X*
Pasewark, William Robert 1924- *ConAu 33R,
    WrDr 84*
Pashko, Stanley 1913- *ConAu 97, SmATA 29*
Pasinetti, P M 1913- *ConAu 73*
Pasinetti, Pier-Maria 1913- *CIDMEL 80,
    ModRL, TwCWr*
Pask, Raymond Frank 1944- *ConAu 105,
    WrDr 84*
Pasmanik, Wolf *DrAP&F 83*
Pasmanik, Wolf 1924- *ConAu 101*
Paso, Alfonso 1925-1978 *CIDMEL 80*
Paso, Alfonso 1926- *CnMD, CroCD, ModWD*
Pasolini, Pier Paolo 1922-1975 *CIDMEL 80,
    ConAu 61, -93, ConLC 20, TwCWr,
    WorAu*
Pasquier, Marie-Claire 1933- *ConAu 29R*
Pass, Gail 1940- *ConAu 65*
Passage, Charles Edward 1913- *ConAu 33R*
Passage, Charles Edward 1913-1983 *ConAu 110*
Passante, Dom *TwCSFW*
Passantino, Gretchen 1953- *ConAu 110*
Passantino, Robert Louis 1951- *ConAu 108*
Passel, Anne W 1918- *ConAu 11NR, -29R,
    IntWWP 82*
Passell, Peter 1944- *ConAu 2NR, -45*
Passerin D'Entreves, Alessandro 1902- *ConAu 69*
Passeron, Rene 1920- *ConAu 97, IntAu&W 82*
Passes, Alan 1943- *ConAu 85*
Passeur, Steve 1899-1966 *CIDMEL 80, CnMD,
    ModWD*
Passfield, Lord *LongCTC*
Passin, Herbert 1916- *ConAu 1NR, -45,
    IntAu&W 82*
Passion, Robert *DrAP&F 83*
Passman, Brian 1934- *ConAu 25R*
Passmore, John Arthur 1914- *ConAu 6NR, -13R*
Passmore, Richard E d1982 *ConAu 107*
Passonneau, Joseph Russell 1921- *ConAu 17R*
Passos, John Dos 1896- *TwCA, TwCA SUP*
Passow, A Harry 1920- *ConAu 1R, -3NR,
    WrDr 84*
Passwater, Richard 1937- *ConAu 97*

Past, Ray 1918- *ConAu 29R*
Pastan, Linda *DrAP&F 83*
Pastan, Linda 1932- *ConAu 61,
    ConLC 27[port], ConP 80, DcLB 5[port],
    WrDr 84*
Pasternack, Stefan Alan 1939- *ConAu 108*
Pasternak, Boris Leonidovich 1890-1960
    *CIDMEL 80, CnMWL, ConLC 7, -10, -18,
    LongCTC, ModSL 1, TwCA SUP, TwCWr,
    WhoTwCL*
Pasternak, Burton 1933- *ConAu 109*
Pasternak, Velvel 1933- *ConAu 73*
Pastine, Maureen 1944- *ConAu 8NR, -57*
Paston, George d1936 *LongCTC*
Paston, Herbert S 1928- *ConAu 49*
Pastor, Lucille E 1920- *IntWWP 82*
Pastor, Robert 1947- *ConAu 105*
Pastor X *ConAu X*
Pastore, Arthur R, Jr. 1922- *ConAu 17R*
Pastore, Nicholas 1916- *ConAu 29R*
Patai, Raphael 1910- *ConAu 29R, WrDr 84*
Pataki, Heidi 1940-. *IntAu&W 82*
Pataky, Denes 1921- *ConAu 13R*
Patanne, Maria *ConAu X*
Patapoff, Elizabeth 1917- *ConAu 29R*
Patch, Blanche 1879-1966 *LongCTC*
Patchen, Kenneth 1911-1972 *ConAu 1R, -3NR,
    -33R, ConLC 1, -2, -18, ConP 80A,
    DcLB 16[port], ModAL, TwCA,
    TwCA SUP, WhoTwCL*
Patchen, Martin 1932- *ConAu 57*
Patchett, Mary Elwyn 1897- *TwCCW 83,
    WrDr 84*
Patchett, Mary Osborne Elwyn 1897-
    ConAu 3NR, -5R, IntAu&W 82
Pate, Billie 1932- *ConAu 61*
Pate, Bob *ConAmTC*
Pate, Martha B Lucas 1912-1983 *ConAu 110*
Patel, Harshad C 1934- *ConAu 53*
Patel, Yogesh 1952- *IntWWP 82*
Pateman, Carole 1940- *ConAu 85*
Pateman, Kim *ConAu X*
Pateman, Trevor John 1947- *ConAu 49,
    WrDr 84*
Patent, Dorothy Hinshaw 1940- *ConAu 9NR,
    -61, SmATA 22[port]*
Pater, Elias *IntAu&W 82X, IntWWP 82X,
    WrDr 84*
Paterson, Adolphus Anang 1927- *IntAu&W 82*
Paterson, Alasdair 1947- *IntWWP 82*
Paterson, Alistair 1929- *ConAu 107, ConP 80,
    WrDr 84*
Paterson, Allen P 1933- *ConAu 93*
Paterson, Andrew Barton 1864-1941 *LongCTC*
Paterson, Ann 1916- *ConAu 33R*
Paterson, Banjo 1864-1941 *TwCWr*
Paterson, Diane 1946- *ConAu 101, SmATA 33*
Paterson, Evangeline 1928- *IntWWP 82*
Paterson, George W 1931- *ConAu 103*
Paterson, Huntley *ConAu X*
Paterson, Isabel M Bowler 1885-1961 *TwCA,
    TwCA SUP*
Paterson, James Bland Sutherland 1925-
    IntWWP 82
Paterson, John 1887- *ConAu P-1*
Paterson, John Harris 1923- *ConAu 5R, -6NR*
Paterson, Judith *ConAu X*
Paterson, Katherine 1932- *ConAu 21R,
    ConLC 12, SmATA 13, TwCCW 83,
    WrDr 84*
Paterson, Neil 1916- *ConAu 13R, WrDr 84*
Paterson, R W K 1933- *ConAu 33R*
Paterson, Ronald 1933- *WrDr 84*
Paterson, Thomas G 1941- *ConAu 1NR, -45*
Paterson, Thomas Thomson 1909- *IntAu&W 82*
Paterson, William E 1941- *ConAu 61*
Paterson-Jones, Judith *ConAu X*
Pathak, Jayant H 1920- *IntWWP 82*
Patient Observer, The *TwCA, TwCA SUP*
Patinkin, Don 1922- *ConAu 10NR, -17R,
    IntAu&W 82*
Patitz, D R *IntWWP 82X*
Patitz, Dolores R 1931- *IntWWP 82*
Patka, Frederick 1922- *ConAu 9R*
Patler, Louis *DrAP&F 83*
Patman, Wright 1893-1976 *ConAu 107, -109*
Patmore, Derek Coventry 1908-1972 *ConAu 5R,
    -103*
Patmore, John Allan 1931- *ConAu 104*
Paton, Alan 1903- *ConLC 25[port], WrDr 84*
Paton, Alan Stewart 1903- *ConAu P-1,*

ConLC 4, -10, ConNov 82, DcLEL 1940,
    IntAu&W 82, LongCTC, ModCmwL,
    SmATA 11, TwCA SUP, TwCWr,
    WhoTwCL*
Paton, David Macdonald *WrDr 84*
Paton, George 1902- *ConAu P-1*
Paton, Herbert James 1887-1969 *ConAu P-1*
Paton, Steven C 1928?-1980 *ConAu 97*
Paton Walsh, Gillian 1939- *SmATA 4*
Paton Walsh, Jill 1937- *TwCCW 83, WrDr 84*
Paton Walsh, Jill 1939- *SmATA X*
Patoski, Margaret 1930- *ConAu 69*
Patra, Atul Chandra 1915- *ConAu 57*
Patrice, Ann *ConAu X*
Patricio, Antonio 1878-1930 *CIDMEL 80*
Patrick, Alison 1921- *ConAu 49*
Patrick, Clarence H 1907- *ConAu 33R*
Patrick, Claudia *ConAu X*
Patrick, Connie *IntWWP 82X*
Patrick, Corbin 1905- *ConAmTC*
Patrick, Douglas Arthur 1905- *ConAu 17R*
Patrick, Hugh 1930- *ConAu 41R*
Patrick, J Max 1911- *ConAu 5R, -5NR*
Patrick, James 1933- *ConAu 104*
Patrick, John 1902- *CnMD*
Patrick, John 1905- *ConAu X*
Patrick, John 1906- *DcLB 7[port], TwCA SUP*
Patrick, John 1907- *ConDr 82, DcLEL 1940,
    WrDr 84*
Patrick, John 1910- *ModWD*
Patrick, Johnstone G 1918- *ConAu 2NR, -5R*
Patrick, Leal *ConAu X*
Patrick, Lilian *ConAu X*
Patrick, Martha 1956- *ConAu 109*
Patrick, Maxine *IntAu&W 82X, WrDr 84*
Patrick, Q *ConAu X, TwCCr&M 80, WorAu,
    WrDr 84*
Patrick, Rembert Wallace 1909- *ConAu 5R*
Patrick, Robert 1937- *AuNews 2, ConAu 1NR,
    -45, ConDr 82, IntAu&W 82,
    NatPD 81[port], WrDr 84*
Patrick, Vincent 1935- *ConAu 104*
Patrick, Walton Richard 1909- *ConAu 37R*
Patrick, William *DrAP&F 83*
Patrides, C A 1930- *ConAu 5NR, WrDr 84*
Patrides, Constantinos Apostolos 1930-
    ConAu 13R, DcLEL 1940, IntAu&W 82
Patris, Louis 1931- *ConAu 85*
Patrouch, Joseph F, Jr. 1935- *ConAu 49*
Patry, Pierre 1933- *CreCan 2*
Patsauq, Markoosie 1942- *ConAu 101*
Patsouras, Louis *ConAu X*
Pattee, Fred Lewis 1863-1950 *TwCA,
    TwCA SUP*
Pattee, Howard Hunt, Jr. 1926- *ConAu 109*
Pattemore, Arnel Wilfred 1934- *ConAu 53,
    WrDr 84*
Patten, Bebe Harrison 1913- *ConAu 61,
    IntAu&W 82*
Patten, Brian 1946- *ConAu 25R, ConP 80,
    IntAu&W 82, IntWWP 82, SmATA 29,
    TwCCW 83, WrDr 84*
Patten, Gilbert 1866-1945 *TwCA, TwCA SUP*
Patten, Karl *DrAP&F 83*
Patten, Lewis B 1915-1981 *ConAu 103, -25R,
    TwCWW*
Patten, Nigel 1940- *ConAu 25R*
Patten, Robert L 1939- *ConAu 109*
Patten, Thomas H 1929- *WrDr 84*
Patten, Thomas H, Jr. 1929- *ConAu 21R*
Patterson, A Temple 1902- *ConAu 103*
Patterson, Alfred Temple 1902- *WrDr 84*
Patterson, Alicia Brooks 1906-1963 *ConAu 89*
Patterson, Barbara 1944- *ConAu 110*
Patterson, C H 1912- *ConAu 21R*
Patterson, Carolyn Bennett 1921- *ConAu 106*
Patterson, Charles E, Jr. 1934- *ConAu 41R*
Patterson, Charles H 1896- *ConAu 37R*
Patterson, Charlotte 1942- *ConAu 29R*
Patterson, Craig E 1945- *ConAu 93*
Patterson, David S 1937- *ConAu 65*
Patterson, Edwin W 1889-1965 *ConAu 1R*
Patterson, Elizabeth Chambers *ConAu 29R,
    WrDr 84*
Patterson, Emma L 1904- *ConAu P-2*
Patterson, Eric James 1891-1972 *ConAu P-1*
Patterson, Evelyn Roelofs 1917- *ConAu 5R*
Patterson, Frank Harmon 1912- *ConAu 109*
Patterson, Frank M 1931- *ConAu 45*
Patterson, Franklin 1916- *ConAu 45*
Patterson, Gardner 1916- *ConAu 106*
Patterson, Geoffrey 1943- *ConAu 103*

Patterson, Gerald R 1926- *ConAu 41R*
Patterson, Harriet-Louise Holland 1903-
   ConAu P-1
Patterson, Harry *ConAu X, WrDr 84*
Patterson, Harry Thomas *CreCan 2*
Patterson, Helen Temple 1904- *IntAu&W 82*
Patterson, Henry 1929- *ConAu 13R,*
   TwCCr&M 80, WrDr 84
Patterson, Horace Orlando 1940- *DcLEL 1940*
Patterson, James 1935- *ConAu 21R*
Patterson, Jane *ConAu X*
Patterson, Janet McFadden 1915- *ConAu 89*
Patterson, Janice Louise Capps 1938-
   IntWWP 82
Patterson, Jerry E 1931- *ConAu 107*
Patterson, John McCready 1913-1983 *ConAu 109*
Patterson, K David 1941- *ConAu 65*
Patterson, L G, Jr. 1929- *ConAu 41R*
Patterson, L Ray 1929- *ConAu 33R*
Patterson, Lawrence Thomas, II 1937-
   ConAu 104
Patterson, Letha L 1913- *ConAu 5R*
Patterson, Lillie G *ConAu 73, SmATA 14*
Patterson, Lindsay 1942- *ConAu 77, LivgBAA*
Patterson, Margaret C 1923- *ConAu 7NR, -57*
Patterson, Mary H 1928-1973 *ConAu 37R*
Patterson, Milton 1927- *ConAu 53*
Patterson, Oliver *ConAu X*
Patterson, Orlando 1940- *ConAu 65,*
   ConNov 82, WrDr 84
Patterson, Paige 1942- *ConAu 10NR, -25R*
Patterson, Paul 1909- *ConAu 85*
Patterson, Peter *WrDr 84*
Patterson, Peter 1932- *ConAu X*
Patterson, Raymond Murray 1898- *IntAu&W 82*
Patterson, Raymond R *DrAP&F 83*
Patterson, Raymond R 1929- *WrDr 84*
Patterson, Raymond Richard 1929- *ConAu 29R,*
   ConP 80, IntWWP 82, LivgBAA
Patterson, Rebecca Elizabeth Coy 1911-1975
   ConAu 103
Patterson, Richard 1908?-1976 *ConAu 69*
Patterson, Richard North 1947- *ConAu 85,*
   IntAu&W 82
Patterson, Robert B 1934- *ConAu 73*
Patterson, Robert Leet 1893- *ConAu 17R*
Patterson, Samuel C 1931- *ConAu 7NR, -17R*
Patterson, Samuel White 1883-1975 *ConAu 61,*
   ConAu P-2
Patterson, Sheila Caffyn 1918- *ConAu 9R*
Patterson, Sylvia Wiese 1940- *ConAu 61*
Patterson, Tom 1920- *CreCan 2*
Patterson, Veronica *DrAP&F 83*
Patterson, Veronica Shantz 1945- *IntWWP 82*
Patterson, Virginia 1931- *ConAu 102*
Patterson, W M 1912?-1976 *ConAu 69*
Patterson, W Morgan 1925- *ConAu 65*
Patterson, Walter C 1936- *ConAu 103*
Patterson, Ward L 1933- *ConAu 8NR, -57*
Patterson, Wayne 1946- *ConAu 85*
Patterson, Webster T 1920- *ConAu 25R*
Patterson, William L 1890-1980 *ConAu 41R, -97*
Patteson, Carter *DrAP&F 83*
Patti, Archimedes L A 1913- *ConAu 106*
Patti, Ercole 1904?-1976 *CIDMEL 80,*
   ConAu 69
Pattie, Alice 1906- *ConAu P-2*
Pattillo, James W 1937- *ConAu 11NR, -17R*
Pattillo, Manning M, Jr. 1919- *ConAu 21R*
Pattinson, Nancy Evelyn *WrDr 84*
Pattison, O R B 1916- *ConAu 29R*
Pattison, Walter T 1903- *ConAu 81,*
   IntAu&W 82
Patton, Alva Rae 1908- *ConAu 5R*
Patton, Arch 1908- *ConAu P-1*
Patton, Bobby R 1935- *ConAu 1NR, -45*
Patton, Elizabeth *DrAP&F 83*
Patton, Frances Gray 1906- *ConAu 101,*
   DcLEL 1940, WrDr 84
Patton, James Welch 1900- *ConAu P-1*
Patton, Kenneth L 1911- *ConAu 7NR, -17R*
Patton, Oliver B 1920- *ConAu 81,*
   IntAu&W 82
Patton, Rob *DrAP&F 83*
Patton, Rob 1943- *ConAu 37R, WrDr 84*
Pattullo, George 1879-1967 *TwCWW*
Patty, C Robert 1925- *ConAu 10NR, -25R*
Patty, Ernest N 1894-1976 *ConAu P-2*
Patty, James S 1925- *ConAu 53*
Patyn, Ann *MichAu 80*
Pau-Llosa, Ricardo *DrAP&F 83*
Pauck, Marion Katherine 1928- *IntAu&W 82*

Pauck, Wilhelm 1901-1981 *ConAu 104, -81*
Pauk, Walter 1914- *ConAu 2NR, -5R,*
   WrDr 84
Pauker, Guy J 1916- *ConAu 1NR, -45*
Pauker, John *DrAP&F 83*
Pauker, John 1920- *ConAu 25R*
Pauker, Ted *ConAu X*
Paul VI, Pope 1897-1978 *ConAu 77, -81*
Paul, Aileen 1917- *ConAu 41R, SmATA 12*
Paul, Anthony 1937- *ConAu 77, IntAu&W 82*
Paul, Anthony 1941- *ConAu 77*
Paul, Auren 1913- *ConAu X*
Paul, Barbara *TwCRGW*
Paul, Cedar *LongCTC*
Paul, Charles B 1931- *ConAu 105*
Paul, Charlotte 1916- *ConAu 5R, -7NR*
Paul, Daniel *ConAu X*
Paul, David W 1944- *ConAu 107*
Paul, Eden 1865-1944 *LongCTC*
Paul, Elizabeth *ConAu X*
Paul, Elliot Harold 1891-1958 *ConAu 107,*
   DcLB 4, LongCTC, TwCA, TwCA SUP,
   TwCCr&M 80
Paul, Emily *ConAu X*
Paul, Florrie 1928- *ConAu 61*
Paul, Geoffrey John 1921-1983 *ConAu 110*
Paul, Gordon L 1935- *ConAu 7NR, -17R*
Paul, Grace 1908- *ConAu 17R, WrDr 84*
Paul, Hugo 1915- *ConAu X*
Paul, I H 1928- *ConAu 103*
Paul, James 1936- *SmATA 23*
Paul, Jan S 1929- *IntAu&W 82*
Paul, Jordan 1936- *ConAu 97*
Paul, Judith Edison 1939- *ConAu 29R*
Paul, Kegan 1828-1902 *LongCTC*
Paul, Leslie Allen 1905- *ConAu 1R, -3NR,*
   IntAu&W 82, LongCTC, WrDr 84
Paul, Louis 1901-1970 *ConAu X, TwCA,*
   TwCA SUP
Paul, Margaret 1939- *ConAu 97*
Paul, Norman L 1926- *ConAu 61*
Paul, Raymond 1940- *ConAu 106*
Paul, Robert *ConAu X, SmATA X*
Paul, Robert S 1918- *ConAu 1R, -3NR*
Paul, Rodman Wilson 1912- *ConAu 1R, -3NR*
Paul, Roland A 1937- *ConAu 41R*
Paul, Sheri *ConAu X*
Paul, Sherman 1920- *ConAu 3NR, -5R*
Paul, Thomas Francis 1924- *WrDr 84*
Paul, William *ConAu X*
Paulden, Sydney 1932- *ConAu 29R, WrDr 84*
Pauley, Barbara Anne 1925- *ConAu 89,*
   TwCRGW, WrDr 84
Pauley, Bruce Frederick 1937- *ConAu 41R,*
   IntAu&W 82
Pauley, Jane 1950- *ConAu 106*
Paulhan, Jean 1884-1968 *CIDMEL 80,*
   ConAu 25R, ModFrL, WorAu
Pauli, Hertha Ernestine 1909-1973 *ConAu 1R,*
   -2NR, -41R, SmATA 26N, -3
Paulin, Tom 1949- *ConP 80, WrDr 84*
Pauling, Linus 1901- *ConAu 110, WrDr 84*
Pauling, Linus Carl 1901- *IntAu&W 82*
Paull, Grace A 1898- *SmATA 24[port]*
Paull, Raymond Allan 1906-1972 *ConAu P-1*
Pauls, John P 1916- *ConAu 45*
Paulsen, F Robert 1922- *ConAu 21R*
Paulsen, Gary 1939- *ConAu 73,*
   SmATA 22[port]
Paulsen, Gary James *DrAP&F 83*
Paulsen, Lois 1905- *ConAu P-2*
Paulsen, Wolfgang 1910- *ConAu 11NR, -17R*
Paulson, A B *DrAP&F 83*
Paulson, Belden 1927- *ConAu 21R*
Paulson, Jack *ConAu X, MichAu 80,*
   SmATA 6
Paulson, Ronald 1930- *ConAu 17R, WrDr 84*
Paulsson, Bjoern 1932- *ConAu 61*
Paulsson, Thomas A 1923- *ConAu 9R*
Paulston, Christina Bratt *ConAu 10NR, -65*
Paulston, Rolland G 1929- *ConAu 33R,*
   WrDr 84
Paulu, Burton 1910- *ConAu 13R, WrDr 84*
Paulus, John Douglas 1917- *ConAu 69*
Paun, Maggie *ConAu X*
Paust, Marian 1908- *IntWWP 82, WrDr 84*
Paustovski, Konstantin Georgievich 1892-1968
   ModSL 1
Paustovsky, Konstantin Georgievich 1892-1968
   ConAu 25R, -93, TwCWr, WorAu
Paustovsky, Konstantin Georgiyevich 1892-1968
   CIDMEL 80

Pautler, Albert J, Jr. 1935- *ConAu 33R*
Pauw, Berthold Adolf 1924- *ConAu 9R*
Pavalko, Ronald M 1934- *ConAu 57*
Pavel, Frances 1907- *ConAu 21R, SmATA 10*
Pavenstedt, Eleanor 1903- *ConAu 21R*
Pavese, Cesare 1908-1950 *CIDMEL 80,*
   CnMWL, ConAu 104, ModRL,
   TwCA SUP, TwCLC 3, TwCWr,
   WhoTwCL
Pavey, Don 1922- *ConAu 107, WrDr 84*
Pavitranda, Swami 1896?-1977 *ConAu 73*
Pavlakis, Christopher 1928- *ConAu 73*
Pavlenko, Pyotr Andreyevich 1899-1951 *TwCWr*
Pavletich, Aida *ConAu 101*
Pavlik, Evelyn Marie 1954- *ConAu 97*
Pavlov, Ivan Petrovich 1849-1936 *LongCTC*
Pavlovic, Miodrag 1928- *CIDMEL 80,*
   IntAu&W 82, ModSL 2
Pavlowitch, Stevan K 1933- *ConAu 33R,*
   WrDr 84
Pawelczynska, Anna 1922- *ConAu 101*
Pawlak, Mark *DrAP&F 83*
Pawle, Gerald 1913- *ConAu 5R*
Pawley, Bernard Clinton 1911- *WrDr 84*
Pawley, Bernard Clinton 1911-1981 *ConAu 105,*
   -25R
Pawley, Martin 1938- *WrDr 84*
Pawley, Martin Edward 1938- *ConAu 101*
Pawley, Thomas Desire, III 1917- *ConAu 29R,*
   LivgBAA
Pawlicki, T B 1930- *ConAu 109*
Pawlikowska-Jasnorzewska, Maria 1891-1945
   CIDMEL 80
Pawlikowska-Jasnorzewska, Maria 1894-1945
   ModSL 2
Pawlikowski, John T 1940- *ConAu 9NR*
Pawlikowski, John Thaddeus 1940- *ConAu 21R,*
   IntAu&W 82, WrDr 84
Pawlowicz, Sala Kaminska 1925- *ConAu 5R*
Pawlowski, Gareth L 1939- *ConAu 29R*
Pawson, Geoffrey Philip Henry 1904- *ConAu 5R*
Pawson, Henry Anthony 1921- *IntAu&W 82*
Pawson, Tony *IntAu&W 82X*
Pax, Clyde 1928- *ConAu 49*
Paxman, Jeremy Dickson 1950- *ConAu 108*
Paxson, Ethel 1885- *ConAu 25R*
Paxson, Frederick Logan 1877-1948 *TwCA,*
   TwCA SUP
Paxton, Jack *ConAu X*
Paxton, John *ConAu X*
Paxton, John 1923- *IntAu&W 82, WrDr 84*
Paxton, Lois *ConAu X, IntAu&W 82X,*
   WrDr 84
Paxton, Mary Jean Wallace 1930- *ConAu 109*
Paxton, Robert O 1932- *ConAu 73*
Paxton, Thomas R 1937- *ConAu 105*
Paxton, Tom *ConAu X*
Payack, Paul J *DrAP&F 83*
Payack, Paul J J 1950- *ConAu 69,*
   IntAu&W 82
Payack, Peter *DrAP&F 83*
Paye, Robert *LongCTC*
Payelle, Raymond-Gerard 1898-1971 *ConAu 33R*
Payer, Cheryl 1940- *ConAu 61, WrDr 84*
Payes, Rachel Cosgrove 1922- *ConAu 1NR, -49,*
   IntAu&W 82
Payne, Alan *ConAu X, WrDr 84*
Payne, Alma Smith *ConAu X*
Payne, B Iden 1888-1976 *ConAu 73*
Payne, Basil *DrAP&F 83*
Payne, Basil 1928- *ConAu 81, ConP 80,*
   WrDr 84
Payne, Ben Iden 1881-1976 *ConAu 65*
Payne, Bruce 1911- *ConAu 9R, WrDr 84*
Payne, Charles 1909- *ConAu 103*
Payne, David Allen 1935- *ConAu 25R*
Payne, Donald Gordon 1924- *ConAu 9NR, -13R,*
   IntAu&W 82, WrDr 84
Payne, Emmy *ConAu X*
Payne, Eric Francis Jules 1895- *ConAu 57*
Payne, Ernest A 1902-1980 *ConAu 9NR*
Payne, Ernest Alexander 1902-1980 *ConAu 9R,*
   -105
Payne, F Anne 1932- *ConAu 73*
Payne, J Barton 1922- *ConAu 1R, -3NR*
Payne, Jack 1926- *ConAu 33R*
Payne, James L 1939- *ConAu 33R*
Payne, James Richmond 1921- *WrDr 84*
Payne, Joan Balfour 1923-1973 *ConAu 41R*
Payne, John Burnett *DrAP&F 83*
Payne, Laurence 1919- *ConAu 5R*
Payne, LaVeta Maxine 1916- *ConAu 37R*

Payne, Michael 1941- *ConAu 29R*
Payne, Mildred Y 1906- *ConAu 41R*
Payne, Pierre Stephen Robert 1911- *TwCA SUP*
Payne, Richard A 1934- *ConAu 97*
Payne, Robert 1911-1983 *ConAu 109*
  ConAu 25R
Payne, Robert O 1924- *ConAu 97*
Payne, Ronald 1926- *ConAu 97*
Payne, Sam *CreCan 1*
Payne, Stanley G 1934- *ConAu 1R, –3NR*
Payne-Townshend, Charlotte Frances *LongCTC*
Paynter, William Henry 1901- *ConAu 13R*
Paynton, Clifford T 1929- *ConAu 37R*
Payro, Roberto Jorge 1867-1928 *ModLAL*
Payson, Dale 1943- *ConAu 3NR, –49,*
  SmATA 9
Payzant, Charles *SmATA 18*
Payzant, Jessie Mercer Knechtel *SmATA X*
Paz, A *ConAu X, SmATA X*
Paz, Carlos F 1937- *ConAu 109*
Paz, Octavio 1914- *CnMWL, ConAu 73,*
  ConLC 3, –4, –6, –10, –19, ModLAL,
  TwCWr, WhoTwCL, WorAu
Paz, Zan *ConAu X, SmATA X*
Pazder, Lawrence Henry 1936- *ConAu 107*
P'Bitek, Okot 1931-1982 *ConAu 107, ConP 80,*
  DcLEL 1940, ModBlW
PBP *IntAu&W 82X*
PE *IntAu&W 82X*
Peabody, Josephine Preston 1874-1922 *LongCTC,*
  ModWD, TwCA
Peabody, Richard, Jr. *DrAP&F 83*
Peabody, Richard Myers, Jr. 1951- *IntWWP 82*
Peabody, Robert Lee 1931- *ConAu 9R,*
  WrDr 84
Peabody, Velton 1936- *ConAu 53*
Peace, Dick *ConAu 25R*
Peace, Richard 1938- *ConAu 25R*
Peace, Roger Craft 1899-1968 *ConAu 89*
Peach, Lawrence DuGarde 1890-1974 *ConAu 101,*
  LongCTC
Peach, William Nelson 1912- *ConAu 21R*
Peacher, Georgiana M 1919- *ConAu 25R*
Peachey, Laban 1927- *ConAu 17R*
Peacock, Alan 1922- *WrDr 84*
Peacock, Alan Turner 1922- *ConAu 1R, –3NR*
Peacock, Basil 1898- *ConAu 103, WrDr 84*
Peacock, David 1924- *CreCan 1*
Peacock, Dick *ConAu X*
Peacock, James Craig 1888?-1977 *ConAu 73*
Peacock, Kenneth 1922- *CreCan 1*
Peacock, L J 1928- *ConAu 21R*
Peacock, Mary 1942- *ConAu 69*
Peacock, Mary Reynolds 1916- *ConAu 57*
Peacock, Molly *DrAP&F 83*
Peacock, Molly 1947- *ConAu 103*
Peacock, Richard 1933- *ConAu 107*
Peacock, Ronald 1907- *ConAu 5NR, –53,*
  IntAu&W 82, WrDr 84
Peacock, Tom *DrAP&F 83*
Peacock, Wilbur Scott 1915?-1979 *ConAu 89*
Peacocke, A R 1924- *ConAu 41R*
Peacocke, Arthur Robert 1924- *IntAu&W 82*
Peacocke, Isabel Maud 1881-1973 *TwCCW 83*
Peairs, Lillian Gehrke 1925- *ConAu 103*
Peairs, Richard Hope 1929- *ConAu 105*
Peake, Lilian *WrDr 84*
Peake, Lilian 1924- *IntAu&W 82X, TwCRGW*
Peake, Margaret Lilian 1924- *IntAu&W 82*
Peake, Mervyn 1911-1968 *ConAu 3NR, –5R,*
  –25R, ConLC 7, DcLB 15[port],
  DcLEL 1940, SmATA 23[port],
  TwCSFW B
Peake, Mervyn Lawrence 1911-1968 *LongCTC,*
  WorAu
Peake, Miriam Morrison 1901- *ConAu 57*
Peake, Pamela Joyce 1940- *WrDr 84*
Peaker, G F 1903?-1983? *ConAu 109*
Peale, Norman Vincent 1898- *AuNews 1,*
  ConAu 81, SmATA 20, WrDr 84
Peale, Ruth Stafford 1906- *ConAu 73*
Pear, Lillian Myers *ConAu 73*
Pearce, A H *IntAu&W 82X, WrDr 84*
Pearce, A Philippa *IntAu&W 82X, WrDr 84*
Pearce, Ann Philippa *ConAu X, IntAu&W 82*
Pearce, Ann Philippa 1921- *DcLEL 1940*
Pearce, Brian Leonard 1915- *IntAu&W 82*
Pearce, Brian Louis 1933- *ConAu 103,*
  IntAu&W 82, IntWWP 82, WrDr 84
Pearce, Carol Ann 1947- *IntWWP 82*
Pearce, Charles A 1906-1970 *ConAu 104*
Pearce, Dick *ConAu X*

Pearce, Donn 1928- *ConAu 13R*
Pearce, Frank 1909- *ConAu 109*
Pearce, J Kenneth 1898- *ConAu 45*
Pearce, J Winston 1907- *ConAu 106*
Pearce, Jack Kingston 1925- *IntAu&W 82*
Pearce, Janice 1931- *ConAu 61*
Pearce, John Kingston *IntAu&W 82X,*
  WrDr 84
Pearce, Mary E 1932- *ConAu 69, WrDr 84*
Pearce, Moira *ConAu 103*
Pearce, Philippa *TwCCW 83*
Pearce, Philippa 1920- *ConAu X, –5R,*
  ConLC 21[port], SmATA 1
Pearce, Richard 1932- *ConAu 41R*
Pearce, Richard Elmo 1909- *ConAu 1R*
Pearce, Roy Harvey 1919- *ConAu 1R, –3NR,*
  ConLCrt 82, WrDr 84
Pearce, Thomas Matthews 1902- *ConAu 7NR,*
  –17R, WrDr 84
Pearce, William M 1913- *ConAu 9R*
Pearcy, G Etzel 1905-1980 *ConAu 3NR*
Pearcy, George Etzel 1905- *ConAu 1R*
Peare, Catherine Owens 1911- *ConAu 5R,*
  SmATA 9
Pearl, Arthur 1922- *ConAu 13R*
Pearl, Chaim 1919- *ConAu 49*
Pearl, Eric *ConAu X*
Pearl, Esther Elizabeth *ConAu X*
Pearl, Hal 1914?-1975 *ConAu 61*
Pearl, Jack 1923- *ConAu X*
Pearl, Jacques Bain 1923- *ConAu 5R*
Pearl, Joseph L 1886?-1974 *ConAu 53*
Pearl, Leon 1922- *ConAu 5R*
Pearl, Leonard 1911- *ConAu P-2*
Pearl, Ralph 1910- *ConAu 73*
Pearl, Richard Maxwell 1913- *ConAu 3NR, –9R*
Pearl, Virginia L 1930- *ConAu 61*
Pearlman, Daniel 1935- *ConAu 9NR, –61*
Pearlman, Maurice 1911- *ConAu 6NR*
Pearlman, Moshe 1911- *ConAu X, –5R,*
  WrDr 84
Pearlstein, Howard J 1942- *ConAu 57*
Pearman, Jean R 1915- *ConAu 49*
Pears, Charles 1873-1958 *SmATA 30*
Pears, David Francis 1921- *ConAu 65*
Pearsall, Derek 1931- *ConAu 107, WrDr 84*
Pearsall, Robert Brainard 1920- *ConAu 2NR,*
  –45
Pearsall, Ronald 1927- *ConAu 21R, WrDr 84*
Pearsall, Thomas E 1925- *ConAu 25R*
Pearsall, William Harold 1891-1964 *ConAu 106*
Pearse, Padraic Henry 1879-1916 *LongCTC,*
  TwCA, TwCA SUP
Pearse, Richard *DrAP&F 83*
Pearson, Alan 1930- *IntWWP 82*
Pearson, Andrew Russell 1897-1969 *ConAu 6NR*
Pearson, Sir Arthur 1866-1921 *LongCTC*
Pearson, B H 1893- *ConAu 65*
Pearson, Bill 1922- *ConAu X, ConNov 82,*
  IntAu&W 82, WrDr 84
Pearson, Bruce L 1932- *ConAu 73*
Pearson, Carol 1944- *ConAu 57*
Pearson, Diane 1931- *ConAu X, –105,*
  WrDr 84
Pearson, Drew 1897-1969 *ConAu X, –5R, –25R,*
  TwCA SUP
Pearson, Edmund Lester 1880-1937 *LongCTC,*
  TwCA
Pearson, Hesketh 1887-1964 *ConAu 5R,*
  LongCTC, TwCA SUP
Pearson, J Michael *AuNews 1*
Pearson, James Larkin 1879-1981 *ConAu 104*
Pearson, Jim Berry 1924- *ConAu 17R*
Pearson, John 1930- *WrDr 84*
Pearson, John 1934- *ConAu 4NR, –49,*
  WrDr 84
Pearson, Karl 1857-1936 *LongCTC, TwCA,*
  TwCA SUP
Pearson, Katharine *WrDr 84*
Pearson, Keith David *WrDr 84*
Pearson, Keith David 1925- *IntAu&W 82*
Pearson, Lester B 1897-1972 *ConAu 37R*
Pearson, Linnea 1942- *ConAu 65*
Pearson, Lionel 1908- *ConAu 1R,*
  IntAu&W 82, WrDr 84
Pearson, Lon *ConAu X*
Pearson, Michael *ConAu 102*
Pearson, Milo Lorentz 1939- *ConAu 73*
Pearson, Neville P 1917- *ConAu 45*
Pearson, Norman Holmes 1909-1975 *ConAu 61,*
  ConAu P-1
Pearson, Richard Joseph 1938- *ConAu 65*

Pearson, Robert Paul 1938- *ConAu 65*
Pearson, Ronald Hooke 1915- *ConAu 13R*
Pearson, Roy 1914- *ConAu 1R, WrDr 84*
Pearson, Scott Roberts 1938- *ConAu 11NR,*
  –29R, IntAu&W 82, WrDr 84
Pearson, Susan 1946- *ConAu 65, SmATA 27*
Pearson, Sybille 1937- *NatPD 81[port]*
Pearson, W H 1922- *DcLEL 1940*
Pearson, William Harrison *WrDr 84*
Pearson, William Harrison 1922- *ConAu 57,*
  IntAu&W 82
Peary, Dannis 1949- *ConAu 109*
Peary, Danny *ConAu X*
Peary, Marie Ahnighito 1893- *ConAu X*
Peary, Robert Edwin 1856-1920 *LongCTC*
Pease, Deborah *DrAP&F 83*
Pease, Dorothy Wells 1896- *ConAu 5R*
Pease, Howard 1894-1974 *ConAu 5R, –106,*
  SmATA 2, –25N, TwCCW 83
Pease, Jane H 1929- *ConAu 4NR, –9R*
Pease, Robert *DrAP&F 83*
Pease, Roland *DrAP&F 83*
Pease, Victor Philip 1938- *ConAu 107*
Pease, William H 1924- *ConAu 3NR, –4NR,*
  –9R, IntAu&W 82
Peaston, Monroe 1914- *ConAu 49*
Peate, Iorwerth C 1901-1982 *ConAu 108*
Peate, Iorwerth Cyfeiliog 1901- *IntAu&W 82*
Peatman, John Gray 1904- *ConAu 5R*
Peattie, Donald Culross 1898-1964 *ConAmA,*
  ConAu 102, TwCA, TwCA SUP
Peattie, Lisa Redfield 1924- *ConAu 10NR, –25R*
Peattie, Louise Redfield 1900-1965 *TwCA,*
  TwCA SUP
Peattie, Mark R 1930- *ConAu 8NR, –61*
Peattie, Roderick 1891-1955 *TwCA SUP*
Peavy, Charles D 1931- *ConAu 25R*
Peavy, Linda *DrAP&F 83*
Peavy, Linda 1943- *ConAu 109*
Peccorini, Francisco L 1915- *ConAu 45*
Pech, Stanley Z 1924- *ConAu 33R, WrDr 84*
Pechman, Joseph 1918- *ConAu 85, WrDr 84*
Pechter, Edward 1941- *ConAu 85*
Peck, Abe 1945- *ConAu 73*
Peck, Anne Merriman 1884- *ConAu 77,*
  SmATA 18
Peck, David Warner 1902- *ConAu 1R*
Peck, Frederic Taylor 1920?-1983 *ConAu 110*
Peck, Gail J *DrAP&F 83*
Peck, Helen E 1910- *ConAu 5R*
Peck, Ira 1922- *ConAu 77*
Peck, John *DrAP&F 83*
Peck, John 1941- *ConAu 3NR, –49, ConLC 3,*
  IntWWP 82
Peck, John B 1918?-1973 *ConAu 104*
Peck, Kathryn Blackburn 1904-1975 *ConAu P-2*
Peck, Leonard *ConAu X*
Peck, M Scott 1936- *ConAu 89*
Peck, Merton Joseph 1925- *ConAu 13R,*
  WrDr 84
Peck, Paula 1927?-1972 *ConAu 104*
Peck, Ralph H *ConAu 69*
Peck, Richard *DrAP&F 83*
Peck, Richard 1934- *ConAu 85,*
  ConLC 21[port], IntAu&W 82, SmATA 18,
  TwCCW 83, WrDr 84
Peck, Richard E 1936- *ConAu 81*
Peck, Robert F 1919- *ConAu 13R*
Peck, Robert Newton *WrDr 84*
Peck, Robert Newton 1928- *ConAu 1R, –81,*
  ConLC 17, SmATA 21[port], TwCCW 83
Peck, Russell A 1933- *ConAu 108*
Peck, Ruth L 1915- *ConAu 29R, WrDr 84*
Peck, Sidney M 1926- *ConAu 5R*
Peck, Theodore P 1924- *ConAu 103*
Peck, Winifred 1882-1962 *LongCTC*
Peckenpaugh, Angela *DrAP&F 83*
Peckenpaugh, Angela J 1942- *ConAu 104*
Peckham, Howard Henry 1910- *ConAu 9R,*
  MichAu 80
Peckham, Lawton 1904-1979 *ConAu 89*
Peckham, Morse 1914- *ConAu 1R, –1NR,*
  ConLCrt 82, WrDr 84
Peckham, Richard *ConAu X*
Peckinpah, Sam 1925- *ConAu 109, ConLC 20*
Pecsok, Mary Bodell 1919- *ConAu 5R*
Peddie, Francis Grove *CreCan 2*
Peddie, Frank 1897-1959 *CreCan 2*
Peden, David Stanton 1892- *IntWWP 82*
Peden, Margaret Sayers 1927- *ConAu 37R*
Peden, Rachel 1901- *ConAu 110*
Peden, William *DrAP&F 83*

Peden, William 1913- *ConAu 21R, WrDr 84*
Pederek, Simon *IntWWP 82X*
Pedersen, Elsa Kienitz 1915- *ConAu 1R, -2NR*
Pedersen, Gert K 1940- *WrDr 84*
Pedersen, Jean J 1934- *ConAu 6NR, -57*
Pedersen, Jorgen Flindt 1940- *IntAu&W 82*
Pedersen, Knut 1859-1952 *ConAu 104*
Pedersen, Maia *IntWWP 82X*
Pedersen, Paul B 1936- *ConAu 41R*
Pederson, Kern O 1910- *ConAu 102*
Pederson, Miriam *DrAP&F 83*
Pedery-Hunt, Dora De *CreCan 1*
Pedicord, Harry William 1912- *ConAu 33R, WrDr 84*
Pedler, Christopher Magnus Howard 1927- *ConAu 97*
Pedler, Frederick 1908- *ConAu 107, IntAu&W 82, WrDr 84*
Pedler, Kit 1927- *ConAu X, TwCSFW, WrDr 84*
Pedler, Margaret *TwCRGW*
Pedley, Robin 1914- *ConAu 9R, IntAu&W 82, WrDr 84*
Pedoe, Daniel 1910- *ConAu 65, WrDr 84*
Pedretti, Erica 1930- *IntAu&W 82*
Pedrick, Jean *DrAP&F 83*
Pedrick, Jean 1922- *ConAu 6NR, -57*
Pedro, Antonio 1909-1966 *ClDMEL 80*
Peebles, Dick 1918-1980 *ConAu 77, -97*
Peek, Merle 1938- *ConAu 105*
Peek, Walter W 1922- *ConAu 45*
Peekner, Ray *DrAP&F 83, WrDr 84*
Peeks, Edward *LivgBAA*
Peel, Bruce Braden 1916- *ConAu 17R, IntAu&W 82, WrDr 84*
Peel, Doris Nannette 1909- *TwCA, TwCA SUP*
Peel, Edwin 1911- *WrDr 84*
Peel, Edwin Arthur 1911- *ConAu 13R*
Peel, H M 1930- *ConAu 4NR, WrDr 84*
Peel, Hazel Mary 1930- *ConAu 9R*
Peel, Hugh B 1913- *WrDr 84*
Peel, J D Y 1941- *ConAu 33R*
Peel, John Donald 1908- *ConAu 33R*
Peel, Malcolm L 1936- *WrDr 84*
Peel, Malcolm Lee 1936- *ConAu 29R*
Peel, Marie Eugene 1922- *IntAu&W 82*
Peel, Norman Lemon *ConAu X*
Peel, Robert 1909- *ConAu 77*
Peel, Wallis *ConAu X*
Peele, David A 1929- *ConAu 102*
Peele, Stanton 1946- *ConAu 57*
Peelor, Harry N 1922- *ConAu 17R*
Peeples, Edwin 1915- *WrDr 84*
Peeples, Edwin A 1915- *ConAu 9R, SmATA 6*
Peer, Lyndon A 1899?-1977 *ConAu 73*
Peeradina, Saleem 1944- *IntWWP 82*
Peerce, Jan 1904- *ConAu 101*
Peerman, Dean G 1931- *ConAu 13R*
Peers, William R 1914- *ConAu 13R*
Peery, Paul D 1906- *ConAu P-2*
Peeslake, Gaffer *ConAu X*
Peet, Bill 1915- *SmATA 2, TwCCW 83, WrDr 84*
Peet, C Donald, Jr. 1927- *ConAu 13R*
Peet, Creighton 1903- *ConAmTC*
Peet, Creighton B 1899-1977 *ConAu 106, -69, SmATA 30*
Peet, Louise Jenison 1885- *ConAu 1R, -5R, WrDr 84*
Peet, William Bartlett 1915- *ConAu 17R, SmATA 2*
Peeters, Gerardus Henricus 1928- *IntAu&W 82*
Peffer, Nathaniel 1890-1964 *TwCA, TwCA SUP*
Peffer, Randall S 1948- *ConAu 101*
Pegada *IntWWP 82X*
Pegasus *CreCan 2*
Pegge, Cecil Denis 1902- *ConAu P-1, IntWWP 82, WrDr 84*
Pegis, Anton Charles 1905- *ConAu 106*
Pegis, Jessie Corrigan 1907- *ConAu P-1*
Pegler, Westbrook 1894-1969 *ConAu 103, -89*
Pegram, Marjorie Anne 1925- *ConAu 9R*
Pegrum, Dudley F 1898- *ConAu 33R*
Pegues, Franklin J 1924- *ConAu 5R*
Peguy, Charles 1873-1914 *TwCLC 10[port]*
Peguy, Charles Pierre 1873-1914 *ClDMEL 80, CnMWL, ConAu 107, LongCTC, ModFrL, ModRL, TwCA SUP, WhoTwCL*
Pehnt, Wolfgang 1931- *ConAu 107, WrDr 84*
Pei, Mario A 1901-1978 *ConAu 5R, -5NR, -77, TwCA SUP*

Peifer, Claude J 1927- *ConAu 17R*
Peikoff, Leonard 1933- *ConAu 108*
Peil, Margaret 1929- *ConAu 8NR, -61, IntAu&W 82*
Peillard, Leonce Sylvain 1898- *IntAu&W 82*
Peirce, Charles Sanders 1839-1914 *LongCTC*
Peirce, J F 1918- *ConAu 41R*
Peirce, Neal R 1932- *ConAu 25R, WrDr 84*
Peirce, Waldo 1884-1970 *SmATA 28*
Peiser, Maria Lilli 1914- *ConAu 110*
Peissel, Michel 1937- *ConAu 25R*
Peitchinis, Stephen G 1925- *ConAu 45*
Pejovich, Svetozar 1931- *ConAu 17R*
Pekic, Borislav 1930- *ConAu 69*
Peladeau, Marius B 1935- *ConAu 73*
Pelaez, Jill Fletcher 1924- *ConAu 33R, SmATA 12, WrDr 84*
Pelavin, Cheryl 1946- *ConAu 106*
Pelc, Janusz Stefan 1930- *IntAu&W 82*
Pelegri Alegret, Sebastian 1916- *IntAu&W 82*
Pelfrey, William 1947- *ConAu 33R*
Pelger, Lucy J 1913-1971 *ConAu P-2*
Pelikan, Jaroslav 1923- *WrDr 84*
Pelikan, Jaroslav Jan, Jr. 1923- *ConAu 1R, -1NR*
Pelissier, Roger 1924-1972 *ConAu 37R, ConAu P-2*
Pell, Arthur R 1920- *ConAu 11NR, -29R*
Pell, Claiborne 1918- *ConAu 49*
Pell, Derek *DrAP&F 83*
Pell, Derek 1947- *ConAu 77, IntAu&W 82, IntWWP 82*
Pell, Eve 1937- *ConAu 33R*
Pell, Olive Bigelow 1886-1980 *ConAu 103*
Pell, Robert *ConAu X*
Pell, Walden, II 1902-1983 *ConAu 109*
Pella, Milton O 1914- *ConAu 17R*
Pellan, Alfred 1906- *CreCan 2*
Pelland, Alfred *CreCan 2*
Pellaton, Jean-Paul 1920- *IntAu&W 82*
Pelle *IntAu&W 82X*
Pellegreno, Ann Holtgren *ConAu 33R*
Pellegrini, Angelo M 1904- *ConAu 17R*
Pellegrino, Victoria Y 1944- *ConAu 107*
Pellerin, Jean Victor 1889-1970 *ClDMEL 80*
Pelletier, Denise 1928- *CreCan 2*
Pelletier, Gilles *CreCan 2*
Pelletier, Ingrid 1912- *ConAu 29R*
Pelletier, Kenneth R 1946- *ConAu 11NR, -69*
Pelletier, Wilfrid 1896- *CreCan 2*
Pellew, Jill 1942- *ConAu 109*
Pellicer, Carlos 1899- *ModLAL*
Pellicer, Carlos 1900?-1977 *ConAu 69*
Pelling, Henry Mathison 1920- *ConAu 61, WrDr 84*
Pellow, Deborah 1945- *ConAu 73*
Pellowski, Anne 1933- *ConAu 9NR, -21R, SmATA 20*
Pellowski, Michael 1949- *ConAu 110*
Pells, Richard Henry 1941- *ConAu 53*
Pelshe, Arvid Yanovich 1899-1983 *ConAu 109*
Pelta, Kathy 1928- *ConAu 85, SmATA 18*
Peltason, J W 1923- *ConAu 1R, -4NR*
Peltier, Leslie C 1900- *ConAu 17R, SmATA 13*
Pelto, Bert *ConAu X*
Pelto, Pertti J 1927- *ConAu 97*
Pelton, Barry C 1935- *ConAu 61*
Pelton, Beverly Jo 1939- *ConAu 49*
Pelton, Joseph N 1943- *ConAu 107*
Pelton, Robert D 1935- *ConAu 103*
Pelton, Robert Stuart 1921- *ConAu 5R*
Pelton, Robert W 1934- *ConAu 29R*
Peltz, Mary Ellis 1896-1981 *ConAu 105, -85*
Peluso, Joseph L 1929- *ConAu 97*
Pelz, Lotte Auguste 1924- *ConAu 9R*
Pelz, Stephen E 1942- *ConAu 110*
Pelz, Werner 1921- *ConAu 9R*
Peman, Jose Maria 1897-1981 *ClDMEL 80, ConAu 104, CroCD, ModWD*
Pemba, Tsewang Yishey 1932- *WrDr 84*
Pemberton, John Alexander 1926- *WrDr 84*
Pemberton, John E 1930- *ConAu 33R*
Pemberton, Madge 188-?-1970 *ConAu 29R*
Pemberton, Margaret 1943- *ConAu 93, WrDr 84*
Pemberton, Sir Max 1863-1950 *LongCTC, TwCCr&M 80*
Pemberton, Sophie 1869-1959 *CreCan 1*
Pemberton, William Baring 1897- *ConAu 5R*
Pemberton, William E 1940- *ConAu 97*
Pemberton Billing *LongCTC*
Pembroke, Herbert *LongCTC*

Pembroke, Thomas *WrDr 84*
Pembrook, Linda 1942- *ConAu 61*
Pembrooke, Kenneth *ConAu X*
Pembury, Bill *ConAu X, SmATA X*
Pen, Jan 1921- *ConAu 1R, WrDr 84*
Pena, Humberto J 1928- *ConAu 73*
Pena, Ramon DelValle Y *ConAu X*
Penaranda, Oscar Florentino *DrAP&F 83*
Penarth, Wyn *ConAu X*
Pendar, Kenneth 1906-1972 *ConAu 37R*
Pendarvis, China Clark *NatPD 81[port]*
Pendell, Elmer 1894- *ConAu P-1, IntAu&W 82*
Pendennis, Arthur *SmATA X*
Pender, Lex *ConAu X*
Pender, Lydia 1907- *WrDr 84*
Pender, Lydia Podger 1907- *ConAu 2NR, -5R, IntAu&W 82, SmATA 3*
Pender, Marilyn *ConAu X*
Pender, Norman *IntAu&W 82X*
Pendergast, Charles 1950- *ConAu 65*
Pendergast, Chuck *ConAu X*
Pendergast, James *DrAP&F 83*
Pendergast, Richard J 1927- *ConAu 93*
Penderwhistle, Judith Blair 1952- *ConAu 81*
Pendery, Rosemary Schmitz *ConAu 53, SmATA 7*
Pendle, Alexy 1943- *SmATA 29[port]*
Pendle, George 1906-1977 *ConAu 5R, -103, SmATA 28N*
Pendlebury, B J 1898- *ConAu P-2*
Pendlebury, Bevis John 1898- *WrDr 84*
Pendleton, Conrad *ConAu X, IntWWP 82X*
Pendleton, Don 1927- *ConAu 33R, TwCCr&M 80, WrDr 84*
Pendleton, James D 1930- *ConAu 107, NatPD 81[port]*
Pendleton, Mary *ConAu 65*
Pendleton, Winston K 1910- *ConAu P-1*
Pendo, Stephen 1947- *ConAu 65*
Pendower, Jacques 1899-1976 *ConAu 9R, -89, TwCCr&M 80*
Penfield, Thomas 1903- *ConAu 5R*
Penfield, Wilder 1891-1976 *ConAu 3NR, -5R, -65*
Pengelley, Eric T 1919- *ConAu 89*
Penha, James W *DrAP&F 83*
Penick, James Lal, Jr. 1932- *ConAu 33R, WrDr 84*
Penn, Anne *ConAu X*
Penn, Asher 1908?-1979 *ConAu 93*
Penn, Christopher *ConAu X*
Penn, Dell *IntWWP 82X*
Penn, Emily Josephine *IntWWP 82*
Penn, Margaret d1981 *ConAu 105*
Penn, Ruth Bonn *ConAu X, SmATA 3*
Penn, William S *DrAP&F 83*
Penn Warren, Robert 1905- *TwCWr*
Penna, Sandro 1906-1977 *ClDMEL 80*
Pennage, E M *ConAu X, SmATA 8*
Pennanen, Lea Airi Sirkka 1929- *IntAu&W 82*
Pennant, Edmund *DrAP&F 83*
Pennant, Edmund 1917- *IntAu&W 82, IntWWP 82X*
Pennekamp, John 1897-1978 *AuNews 2, ConAu 89*
Pennell, Joseph 1857?-1926 *LongCTC*
Pennell, Joseph Stanley 1908-1963 *TwCA SUP*
Penner, Jonathan *DrAP&F 83*
Penner, Jonathan 1940- *ConAu 97, DcLB Y83B[port]*
Penney, Annette Culler 1916- *ConAu 45*
Penney, Grace Jackson 1904- *ConAu 5R*
Penney, J C 1875-1971 *ConAu 29R*
Pennick, Nigel Campbell 1946- *ConAu 110*
Penniman, Howard R 1916- *ConAu 13R*
Penniman, Thomas Kenneth 1896?-1977 *ConAu 69*
Penninger, F Elaine 1927- *ConAu 57*
Penningroth, Paul W 1901-1974 *ConAu 103, -49*
Pennington, Albert Joe 1950- *ConAu 57*
Pennington, Alberta Lawson 1914- *IntAu&W 82*
Pennington, Chester Arthur 1916- *ConAu 104*
Pennington, Donald Henshaw 1919- *ConAu 5R, WrDr 84*
Pennington, Eunice 1923- *ConAu 57, SmATA 27[port]*
Pennington, Howard 1923- *ConAu 49*
Pennington, John Selman 1924?-1980 *ConAu 102*
Pennington, Lee *DrAP&F 83*
Pennington, Lee 1939- *ConAu 69, DcLB Y82B[port], IntWWP 82*

Pennington, M Basil 1931- *ConAu 93*
Pennington, Penny *ConAu X*
Pennington, Robert 1927- *ConAu 73*
Pennington, Ron *ConAmTC*
Pennington, Stuart *ConAu X*
Pennink, Frank 1913- *ConAu 5R*
Pennock, J Roland 1906- *ConAu 33R*
Penny, Prudence *ConAu X*
Penny, Ruthanna 1914- *ConAu 17R*
Pennycuick, John 1943- *ConAu 97*
Penoyre, Mary 1940- *WrDr 84*
Penrod, James 1934- *ConAu 77*
Penrose, Boies 1902-1976 *ConAu 65*
Penrose, Edith Tilton 1914- *ConAu 25R*
Penrose, Harald 1904- *ConAu 13R*
Penrose, Harold 1904- *ConAu 6NR*
Penrose, Margaret *ConAu P-2*
Penrose, Roland 1900- *ConAu 85, WrDr 84*
Pentecost, Edward C 1917- *ConAu 57*
Pentecost, Hugh *WrDr 84*
Pentecost, Hugh 1903- *AuNews 1, ConAu X, TwCCr&M 80*
Pentecost, J Dwight 1915- *ConAu 2NR, -5R*
Pentecost, Martin *ConAu X*
Pentland, Barbara 1912- *CreCan 1*
Penton, Brian Con 1904-1951 *TwCWr*
Pentony, DeVere Edwin 1924- *ConAu 5R, -8NR*
Pentreath, Arthur Godolphin Guy Carleton 1902- *ConAu P-1*
Pentreath, Guy 1902- *WrDr 84*
Pentz, Croft Miner *ConAu 5R, -9NR*
Penuel, Arnold M 1936- *ConAu 57*
Penuelas, Marcelino C 1916- *ConAu 25R*
Penzavecchia, James *DrAP&F 83*
Penzel, Frederick 1948- *ConAu 85*
Penzi, James *DrAP&F 83*
Penzi, James 1952- *IntWWP 82*
Penzik, Irena *ConAu X*
Penzl, Herbert 1910- *ConAu 45*
Penzler, Otto M 1942- *ConAu 81*
Penzoldt, Ernst 1892-1955 *CnMD, ModWD*
Pepe, John Frank 1920- *ConAu 9R*
Pepe, Phil 1935- *ConAu 25R, SmATA 20*
Pepelasis, Adam A 1923- *ConAu 1R, -2NR*
Peper, George Frederick 1950- *ConAu 108*
Pepin, Clermont 1926- *CreCan 2*
Pepin, Jacques Georges 1935- *ConAu 103*
Pepin, Jean Joseph Clermont *CreCan 2*
Pepitone, Albert 1923- *ConAu 9R*
Pepitone, Joe 1940- *ConAu 109*
Pepitone, Joseph Anthony *ConAu X*
Peppard, Murray B 1917-1974 *ConAu 53, ConAu P-2*
Peppe, Rodney 1934- *WrDr 84*
Peppe, Rodney Darrell 1934- *ConAu 33R, SmATA 4*
Pepper, Adeline *ConAu 41R*
Pepper, Art 1925-1982 *ConAu 107*
Pepper, Choral 1918- *ConAu 25R*
Pepper, Curtis Bill *ConAu X*
Pepper, Curtis G 1920- *ConAu 10NR, -21R*
Pepper, George Douglas 1903-1962 *CreCan 1*
Pepper, Joan 1920- *ConAu X*
Pepper, Martin *ConAu X*
Pepper, Stephen Coburn 1891-1972 *ConAu 1R, -103*
Pepper, Thomas 1939- *ConAu 97*
Pepper, William M, Jr. 1903-1975 *ConAu 57, -97*
Peppin, Brigid 1941- *ConAu 65*
Peppler, Alice Stolper 1934- *ConAu 53, IntAu&W 82X*
Pepys, Samuel 1632?-1703 *LongCTC*
Peradotto, John Joseph 1933- *ConAu 41R*
Peraile Redondo, Meliano 1921- *IntAu&W 82*
Perceval-Maxwell, Michael 1933- *ConAu 53*
Perchik, Simon *DrAP&F 83*
Percival *IntWWP 82*
Percival, Alicia C 1903- *WrDr 84*
Percival, Alicia Constance 1903- *ConAu 9R, IntAu&W 82*
Percival, John 1927- *ConAu 33R*
Percival, Robert C 1908- *WrDr 84*
Percival, Walter 1896- *ConAu P-1*
Percy, Charles Harting 1919- *ConAu 65*
Percy, Charles Henry *ConAu X, SmATA 4*
Percy, Douglas C 1914- *ConAu 3NR, -5R, IntAu&W 82, WrDr 84*
Percy, Edward 1891-1968 *LongCTC*
Percy, Herbert Roland 1920- *ConAu 5R*
Percy, Walker *DrAP&F 83*
Percy, Walker 1916- *ConAu 1R, -1NR, ConLC 2, -3, -6, -8, -14, -18, ConNov 82,*

DcLB 2, DcLEL 1940, ModAL, ModAL SUP, TwCSFW, WorAu, WrDr 84 DcLB Y80A[port]
Percy, William A, Jr. 1933- *ConAu 29R*
Percy, William Alexander 1885-1942 *TwCA SUP*
Perdiguero Perez, Fernando 1929- *IntAu&W 82*
Perdue, Theda 1949- *ConAu 93*
Perdurabo, Frater *ConAu X*
Perearnau Torras, Maria Angeles 1946- *IntAu&W 82*
Pereda, Jose Maria De 1833-1906 *CIDMEL 80*
Peregoy, Calvin *TwCSFW*
Peregrine *ConAu X*
Pereira, Antonio 1923- *IntAu&W 82*
Pereira, Harold Bertram 1890- *ConAu 9R*
Pereira, Michael Nicholas O'Donnell 1928- *IntAu&W 82*
Pereira, Teresinha 1934- *IntWWP 82*
Pereira, Teresinha Alves 1944- *IntAu&W 82*
Pereira, Teresinka *DrAP&F 83, IntAu&W 82X, IntWWP 82X*
Pereira, W D 1921- *ConAu 104*
Perel, Jane Lunin *DrAP&F 83*
Perel, William M 1927- *ConAu 33R*
Pereleshin, Valery 1913- *CIDMEL 80*
Perella, Nicholas James 1927- *ConAu 73*
Perelman, Chaim 1912- *ConAu 103*
Perelman, Lewis J 1946- *ConAu 73, WrDr 84*
Perelman, S J 1904-1979 *AuNews 1, -2, ConAu 73, -89, ConLC 3, -5, -9, -15, -23[port], LongCTC, TwCA, TwCA SUP, TwCWr*
Pereny, George *DrAP&F 83*
Perera, Gretchen G 1940- *ConAu 93*
Perera, Padma *DrAP&F 83*
Perera, Thomas Biddle 1938- *ConAu 37R, SmATA 13*
Perera, Victor *DrAP&F 83*
Perera, Victor 1934- *ConAu 29R*
Perera Molina, Ramos 1939- *IntAu&W 82*
Peres, Richard 1947- *ConAu 93*
Peres, Shimon 1923- *ConAu 85*
Peret, Benjamin 1899-1959 *CIDMEL 80, ModFrL*
Peretz, Don 1922- *ConAu 4NR, -9R, IntAu&W 82*
Peretz, Isaac Loeb 1851?-1915 *ConAu 109*
Peretz, Isaac Loeb 1852-1915 *CnMD*
Peretz, Yitskhok Leybush 1852-1915 *ModWD*
Peretz, Yitzhok Leibush *ConAu X*
Peretz, Yitzkhok Leibush 1852-1915 *CIDMEL 80*
Pereverzev, Valerian Fydorovich 1882-1968 *CIDMEL 80*
Pereyra, Lillian A 1920- *ConAu 21R*
Perez, Guillermo C *DrAP&F 83*
Perez, Joseph F 1930- *ConAu 29R*
Perez, Louis C 1923- *ConAu 77*
Perez, Reimundo *DrAP&F 83*
Perez DeAyala, Ramon 1880?-1962 *CIDMEL 80, CnMWL, ModRL, TwCA, TwCA SUP, TwCWr*
Perez DeAyala, Ramon 1881-1962 *ConAu 93*
Perez-Diotima, Leigh *DrAP&F 83*
Perez Galdos, Benito 1843-1920 *CIDMEL 80, CnMD, ModRL, ModWD, TwCA, TwCA SUP*
Perez Lopez, Francisco 1916- *ConAu 49*
Pergola, Edith Della *CreCan 1*
Pergola, Luciano Della *CreCan 1*
Perham, Margery Freda 1895-1982 *ConAu 1R, -1NR, -106, IntAu&W 82*
Pericoli, Ugo 1923- *ConAu 97*
Perier, Odilon Jean 1900-1928 *CIDMEL 80*
Perigoe, J Rae 1910- *ConAu 61*
Perillo, Joseph M 1933- *ConAu 17R*
Perin, Constance *ConAu 29R*
Perinbanayagam, Robert S 1934- *ConAu 109*
Perino, Joseph 1946- *ConAu 106*
Perino, Sheila C 1948- *ConAu 106*
Peripatus *ConAu X*
Perish, Melanie *DrAP&F 83*
Peristiany, John G 1911- *ConAu 17R*
Peritz, Rene 1933- *ConAu 45*
Perkel *IntAu&W 82X*
Perkes, Dan 1931- *ConAu 69*
Perkin, Harold James 1926- *ConAu 77, IntAu&W 82*
Perkin, Robert L 1914-1978 *ConAu 77*
Perkins, Agnes 1926- *ConAu 10NR, -57*
Perkins, Al 1904-1975 *ConAu 107, -57, SmATA 30[port]*

Perkins, Bradford 1925- *ConAu 1R*
Perkins, Carl 1932- *ConAu 102*
Perkins, David *DrAP&F 83*
Perkins, David 1928- *ConAu 77, IntAu&W 82*
Perkins, David 1939- *ConAu 73*
Perkins, Dexter 1889- *ConAu 5R*
Perkins, Doug 1952- *IntAu&W 82*
Perkins, Dwight Heald 1934- *ConAu 7NR, -17R, WrDr 84*
Perkins, Edward A, Jr. 1928- *ConAu 21R*
Perkins, Edwin Judson 1939- *ConAu 106*
Perkins, Ernest Benson 1881- *ConAu 5R*
Perkins, Faith *ConAu X*
Perkins, George 1930- *ConAu 13R, WrDr 84*
Perkins, Hugh V 1918- *WrDr 84*
Perkins, James 1911- *WrDr 84*
Perkins, James Alfred 1911- *ConAu 108*
Perkins, James Ashbrook *DrAP&F 83*
Perkins, James Ashbrook 1941- *ConAu 73*
Perkins, James Oliver Newton 1924- *ConAu 9R*
Perkins, James S 1899- *ConAu 89*
Perkins, John 1935- *ConAu 73*
Perkins, John Bryan Ward *ConAu X*
Perkins, Lawrence A 1917?-1979 *ConAu 89*
Perkins, Lucy Fitch 1865-1937 *TwCCW 83*
Perkins, Marlin 1905- *ConAu 103, SmATA 21[port]*
Perkins, Merle Lester 1919- *ConAu 45, IntAu&W 82*
Perkins, Michael *DrAP&F 83*
Perkins, Michael 1942- *ConAu 8NR, -17R, WrDr 84*
Perkins, Newton Stephens 1925- *ConAu 49*
Perkins, Owen Adelbert 1930- *MichAu 80*
Perkins, R Marlin 1905- *ConAu 77*
Perkins, Ralph 1913- *ConAu 13R*
Perkins, Robert L 1930- *ConAu 25R*
Perkins, Rollin M 1889- *ConAu 53*
Perkins, Steve *ConAu 49*
Perkins, Van L 1930- *ConAu 106*
Perkins, Virginia Chase *WrDr 84*
Perkins, Virginia Chase 1902- *ConAu P-2*
Perkins, Whitney Trow 1921- *ConAu 106*
Perkins, William H 1923- *ConAu 53*
Perkins, Wilma Lord 1897-1976 *ConAu 104*
Perkinson, Henry J 1930- *ConAu 17R*
Perkoff, Stuart Z 1930-1974 *DcLB 16*
Perkowski, Jan Louis 1936- *ConAu 2NR, -45*
Perl, Arnold 1914-1971 *ConAu 33R*
Perl, Lila *ConAu 33R, SmATA 6*
Perl, Ruth June 1929- *ConAu 25R, WrDr 84*
Perl, Susan 1922- *ConAu 17R, SmATA 22[port]*
Perl, Susan 1922-1983 *ConAu 11NR, -110, SmATA 34N*
Perl, Teri 1926- *ConAu 93*
Perl, William R 1906- *WrDr 84*
Perlberg, Mark *DrAP&F 83*
Perlberg, Mark 1929- *ConAu 37R*
Perle, George 1915- *ConAu 1R, -3NR*
Perles, Benjamin Max 1922- *ConAu 45*
Perlis, Vivian 1928- *ConAu 85*
Perlman, Anne S *DrAP&F 83*
Perlman, Bennard B 1920- *ConAu 89*
Perlman, Helen Harris 1905- *ConAu 1R, -3NR*
Perlman, Janice E 1943- *ConAu 61*
Perlman, Jess 1891- *ConAu 89, IntWWP 82*
Perlman, John Niels 1946- *ConAu 33R, IntWWP 82*
Perlman, Mark 1923- *ConAu 1R, -3NR*
Perlman, Niels John *DrAP&F 83*
Perlman, Samuel 1905-1975 *ConAu P-2*
Perlmutter, Jerome H 1924- *ConAu 17R*
Perlmutter, Leonard L *NatPD 81[port]*
Perlmutter, Nathan 1923- *ConAu 13R*
Perlmutter, O William 1920-1975 *ConAu 57, SmATA 8*
Perlmutter, Ruth Ann 1924- *ConAu 109*
Perlo, Victor 1912- *ConAu 2NR, -5R*
Perloff, Harvey S 1915-1983 *ConAu 110*
Perloff, Marjorie 1931- *WrDr 84*
Perloff, Marjorie G 1931- *ConAu 7NR, -57*
Perls, Eugenia Soderberg 1904?-1973 *ConAu 37R*
Perls, Frederick S 1893-1970 *ConAu 101, -29R*
Perls, Fritz *ConAu X*
Perls, Hugo 1886?-1977 *ConAu 73*
Perlstein, Gary R 1940- *ConAu 57*
Perman, Dagmar Horna 1926?-1978 *ConAu 77*
Pernath, Hugues C 1931-1975 *CIDMEL 80*
Pernet, A 1940- *ConAu 107*
Perniciaro, Tony *DrAP&F 83*

ConLC 7, IntAu&W 82, IntWWP 82
Peters, Ronald M, Jr. 1947- ConAu 85
Peters, Roy TwCWW
Peters, Ruth Marie 1913?-1978 ConAu 104
Peters, S H ConAu X
Peters, S T ConAu X
Peters, Steven ConAu X
Peters, T R, Sr. 1929- MichAu 80
Peters, Ted ConAu X
Peters, Theodore F 1941- ConAu 81
Peters, Victor 1915- ConAu 17R
Peters, Virginia Bergman 1918- ConAu 93
Peters, William 1921- ConAu 3NR, -9R,
    IntAu&W 82
Peters, William C 1920- WrDr 84
Petersen, A M IntWWP 82X
Petersen, Arne Herlov 1943- IntWWP 82
Petersen, Arnold 1885-1976 ConAu 65
Petersen, Art IntWWP 82X
Petersen, Arthur Meredith 1942- IntWWP 82
Petersen, Carol Otto 1914- ConAu 57
Petersen, Clarence G 1933- ConAu 77
Petersen, David M 1939- ConAu 41R
Petersen, Donald DrAP&F 83
Petersen, Donald 1928- ConAu 13R, ConP 80,
    WrDr 84
Petersen, Gwenn Boardman 1924- ConAu 2NR
Petersen, Karen Daniels 1910- ConAu 73
Petersen, Melba F Runtz 1919- ConAu 5R
Petersen, Nis 1897-1943 CIDMEL 80, TwCWr
Petersen, Peter 1932- ConAu 57
Petersen, Sigurd Damskov 1904- ConAu 9R
Petersen, Simone IntAu&W 82X
Petersen, Soren Arne 1946- IntAu&W 82
Petersen, Sydney Vernon 1914- IntAu&W 82
Petersen, William 1912- ConAu 1R, -3NR
Petersen, William J 1929- ConAu 9NR, -21R
Petersen, William John Henry 1901- ConAu 5R
Petersham, Maud 1889-1971 ConAu 33R,
    DcLB 22[port], TwCCW 83
Petersham, Maud 1890-1971 ConAu 73,
    SmATA 17
Petersham, Miska 1888-1960 ConAu 73,
    DcLB 22[port], SmATA 17, TwCCW 83
Peterson, A D C 1908- ConAu 108
Peterson, Agnes F 1923- ConAu 29R
Peterson, Arthur L 1926- ConAu 9R
Peterson, Bruce Henry 1918- IntAu&W 82,
    WrDr 84
Peterson, Carl 1896?-1983 ConAu 110
Peterson, Carolyn Sue 1938- ConAu 73
Peterson, Carroll V 1929- ConAu 45
Peterson, Charles 1900?-1976 ConAu 69
Peterson, Mrs. Charles MichAu 80
Peterson, Charles S 1927- ConAu 49
Peterson, Dale 1944- ConAu 109
Peterson, Donald 1923- ConAu 25R
Peterson, Douglas L 1924- ConAu 41R
Peterson, Edward N 1925- ConAu 29R,
    WrDr 84
Peterson, Edwin 1904-1972 ConAu 37R
Peterson, Edwin Loose 1915- ConAu 5R,
    WrDr 84
Peterson, Eldridge 1905?-1977 ConAu 73
Peterson, Eleanor M 1912- ConAu 25R
Peterson, Elmer 1930- ConAu 37R,
    IntAu&W 82, WrDr 84
Peterson, Esther 1934- ConAu 89
Peterson, Evan T 1925- ConAu 45
Peterson, F Ross 1941- ConAu 97
Peterson, Forrest H 1912- ConAu 45
Peterson, Franklynn 1938- ConAu 110
Peterson, Frederick Alvin 1920- ConAu 49,
    IntAu&W 82
Peterson, Hans 1922- ConAu 1NR, -49,
    IntAu&W 82, SmATA 8
Peterson, Harold Bruce 1939- ConAu 29R,
    WrDr 84
Peterson, Harold F 1900- ConAu 5R, WrDr 84
Peterson, Harold Leslie 1922-1978 ConAu 1R,
    -4NR, -73, SmATA 8
Peterson, Helen Stone 1910- ConAu 37R,
    SmATA 8, WrDr 84
Peterson, Houston 1897-1981 ConAu 103, -107,
    TwCA, TwCA SUP
Peterson, James ConAu X
Peterson, James Alfred 1913- ConAu 104
Peterson, James Allan 1932- ConAu 29R
Peterson, Jeanne Whitehouse ConAu X,
    SmATA X
Peterson, Jeannie 1940- IntAu&W 82
Peterson, Jim ConAu X

Peterson, John Eric 1933- ConAu 53, WrDr 84
Peterson, John J 1918- ConAu 53
Peterson, John W 1921- ConAu 97
Peterson, Kenneth G 1927- ConAu 33R
Peterson, Len 1917- CreCan 1
Peterson, Leonard Byron 1917- CreCan 1,
    DcLEL 1940
Peterson, Levi S 1933- ConAu 109
Peterson, Lloyd R 1922- ConAu 107
Peterson, M Jeanne 1937- ConAu 103
Peterson, Margaret 1902- CreCan 2
Peterson, Marilyn Ann 1933- ConAu 57
Peterson, Marsha DrAP&F 83
Peterson, Martin Severin 1897- ConAu 1R,
    -3NR, IntAu&W 82, WrDr 84
Peterson, Mary DrAP&F 83
Peterson, Mary Ellis DrAP&F 83
Peterson, Maurice 1952- ConAmTC
Peterson, Mendel 1918- ConAu 73
Peterson, Merrill D 1921- ConAu 1R, -3NR,
    WrDr 84
Peterson, Nancy L 1939- ConAu 105
Peterson, Norma Lois 1922- ConAu 13R
Peterson, Oscar Emmanuel 1925- CreCan 1
Peterson, Ottis 1907- ConAu 21R
Peterson, Owen M 1924- ConAu 108
Peterson, Paul E 1940- ConAu 45
Peterson, R D 1932- ConAu 41R
Peterson, Randolph Lee 1920- WrDr 84
Peterson, Reona 1941- ConAu 73
Peterson, Richard Austin 1932- ConAu 25R,
    WrDr 84
Peterson, Robert DrAP&F 83
Peterson, Robert 1924- ConAu 25R,
    IntWWP 82
Peterson, Robert E 1928- ConAu 13R
Peterson, Robert W 1925- ConAu 33R
Peterson, Roger Tory 1908- ConAu 1R, -1NR,
    IntAu&W 82, TwCA SUP
Peterson, Russell Arthur 1922- ConAu 33R
Peterson, Susan H 1925- ConAu 57
Peterson, Theodore 1918- ConAu 9R
Peterson, Virgilia 1904-1966 ConAu 25R,
    WorAu
Peterson, Wallace C WrDr 84
Peterson, Wallace Carroll 1921- ConAu 5R
Peterson, Walter Scott 1944- ConAu 21R
Peterson, Wilferd Arlan 1900- ConAu 6NR, -9R,
    MichAu 80
Peterson, Willard James 1938- ConAu 103
Peterson, William S 1939- ConAu 11NR, -29R
Petersson, Robert Torsten 1918- ConAu 45
Petesch, Natalie L M ConAu 6NR, -57,
    DrAP&F 83
Pethybridge, Roger William 1934- ConAu 5R,
    WrDr 84
Petie, Haris ConAu X
Petie, Haris 1915- ConAu X, SmATA 10
Petievich, Gerald 1944- ConAu 105
Petit, Gaston 1930- ConAu 73, IntAu&W 82
Petit, Jean-Marie 1941- IntWWP 82
Petitclerc, Denne Bart 1929- ConAu 93,
    IntAu&W 82
Petitpierre, Jacques 1890- IntAu&W 82
Petkas, Peter 1945- ConAu 37R
Petmecky, Ben 1922- ConAu 1R
Peto ConAu X
Peto, James ConAu X
Petrakis, Harry Mark DrAP&F 83
Petrakis, Harry Mark 1923- ConAu 4NR, -9R,
    ConLC 3, ConNov 82, IntAu&W 82,
    WrDr 84
Petras, James Frank 1937- ConAu 7NR, -61
Petras, John W 1940- ConAu 29R, WrDr 84
Petrement, Simone 1907- ConAu 77
Petres, Robert E 1939- ConAu 104
Petrescu, Camil 1894-1957 CIDMEL 80
Petrich, Patricia Barrett 1942- ConAu 61
Petrides, Avra NatPD 81[port]
Petrides, George Athan 1916- ConAu 106
Petrides, Heidrun 1944- SmATA 19
Petrie, Alexander 1881- ConAu P-1
Petrie, Asenath 1914- ConAu 21R
Petrie, Catherine 1947- ConAu 109
Petrie, Sir Charles Alexander 1895-1977
    ConAu 8NR, -17R, -89, TwCA SUP
Petrie, Sir Flinders 1853-1942 LongCTC
Petrie, Mildred McClary 1912- ConAu 21R
Petrie, Paul DrAP&F 83
Petrie, Paul 1928- WrDr 84
Petrie, Paul James 1928- ConAu 3NR, -9R,
    ConP 80, IntAu&W 82, IntWWP 82

Petrie, Rhona ConAu X, WrDr 84
Petrie, Rhona 1922- ConAu X, TwCCr&M 80
Petrie, Sidney 1923- ConAu 21R
Petrie, Sir William Matthew Flinders 1853-1942
    TwCA, TwCA SUP
Petrikovits, Harald Friedrich A Von 1911-
    IntAu&W 82
Petrinovich, Lewis 1930- ConAu 41R
Petro, Sylvester 1917- ConAu 1R
Petrocelli, Orlando R 1930- ConAu 1NR, -45
Petrone, Jane Muir 1929- ConAu 5R
Petroni, Frank A 1936- ConAu 85
Petroni, Guglielmo 1911- WorAu
Petropulos, John A 1929- ConAu 25R
Petroski, Catherine DrAP&F 83
Petroski, Catherine 1939- ConAu 106
Petroski, Henry DrAP&F 83
Petrosky, Anthony DrAP&F 83
Petrou, David Michael 1949- ConAu 73
Petrouske, Rosalie Sanara 1952- IntWWP 82
Petrov, Eugene 1903-1942 TwCA, TwCA SUP
Petrov, Evgeny Petrovich 1903-1942 CnMWL
Petrov, Fyodor 1877?-1973 ConAu 41R
Petrov, Victor P 1907- ConAu 10NR, -21R
Petrov, Vladimir 1915- ConAu 21R
Petrov, Yevgeni 1903-1942 ModSL 1, TwCWr
Petrova, Olga 1884?-1977 ConAu 73
Petrovic, Gajo 1927- IntAu&W 82
Petrovic, Rastko 1898-1949 CIDMEL 80
Petrovich, Michael B 1922- ConAu 108
Petrovska, Marija 1926- ConAu 107
Petrovskaya, Kyra 1918- ConAu X, -1R,
    SmATA 8
Petrovsky, N ConAu X
Petrucci, Kenneth R 1947- ConAu 57
Petry, Ann DrAP&F 83, IntAu&W 82
Petry, Ann 1908- TwCCW 83, WrDr 84
Petry, Ann Lane 1908- ConNov 82
Petry, Ann Lane 1911- ConAu 5R, ConLC 1,
    -7, -18, SmATA 5, TwCA SUP
Petry, Ann Lane 1912- ConAu 4NR,
    DcLEL 1940, LivgBAA
Petry, Carl Forbes 1943- ConAu 106
Petry, Ray C 1903- ConAu 5R, IntAu&W 82,
    WrDr 84
Petryni, Michael ConAmTC
Pettas, Mary 1918- ConAu 25R
Petterson, Henry William 1922- ConAu 9R
Pettersen, Sverre 1898-1974 ConAu 53
Pettersson, H Bertil N 1932- IntAu&W 82
Pettersson, Karl-Henrik 1937- ConAu 65
Pettersson, Sven-Ingmar 1949- IntAu&W 82
Pettes, Dorothy E ConAu 25R
Petteys, D F DrAP&F 83
Pettigrew, Thomas Fraser 1931- ConAu 33R,
    IntAu&W 82, WrDr 84
Pettinella, D M DrAP&F 83
Pettingill, Amos ConAu X
Pettingill, Olin Sewall, Jr. 1907- ConAu 1NR,
    -45
Pettit, Arthur Gordon 1938- ConAu 53
Pettit, Clyde Edwin 1932- ConAu 65
Pettit, Henry 1906- ConAu 1R
Pettit, Lawrence K 1937- ConAu 33R
Pettit, Michael DrAP&F 83
Pettit, Norman 1929- ConAu 17R
Pettit, Pascal 1932- IntAu&W 82
Pettit, Philip Noel 1945- ConAu 97
Pettit, Stephen Lewis Ingham 1921- IntWWP 82
Pettitt, George A 1901- WrDr 84
Pettitt, George A 1901-1976 ConAu P-2
Pettiward, Daniel 1913- IntWWP 82, WrDr 84
Petty, Mary 1899-1976 ConAu 65
Petty, Roberta 1915- ConAu 10NR, -61
Petty, W H 1921- ConP 80, WrDr 84
Petty, Walter T 1918- ConAu 9NR, -21R
Petty, William Henry 1921- ConAu 65,
    IntAu&W 82, IntWWP 82
Petuchowski, Jakob Josef 1925- ConAu 1R,
    -3NR, WrDr 84
Petulla, Joseph M 1932- ConAu 9NR, -21R
Petursson, Hannes Palmi 1931- CIDMEL 80
Petzold, Paul 1940- ConAu 9NR
Petzold, Paul Marcus 1940- ConAu 61,
    IntAu&W 82
Petzoldt, Paul Kiesow 1908- ConAu 57
Pevear, Richard DrAP&F 83
Pevsner, Nikolaus 1902- WrDr 84
Pevsner, Nikolaus 1902-1983 ConAu 110
Pevsner, Sir Nikolaus 1902- ConAu 7NR, -9R,
    IntAu&W 82, LongCTC, WorAu
Pevsner, Stella ConAu 57, SmATA 8

Peyre, Henri 1901- *ConAu 3NR, –5R*
Peyrefitte, Alain Antoine 1925- *ConAu 85*
Peyrefitte, Pierre Roger 1907- *IntAu&W 82*
Peyrefitte, Roger 1907- *ClDMEL 80,*
  ConAu 65, TwCWr, WorAu
Peyster, Steven *DrAP&F 83*
Peyton, K M 1929- *ChlLR 3, ConAu X,*
  IntAu&W 82X, SmATA X, TwCCW 83,
  WrDr 84
Peyton, Karen 1897-1960? *ConAu P-1*
Peyton, Kathleen Wendy 1929- *ChlLR 3,*
  ConAu 69, IntAu&W 82, SmATA 15
Peyton, Patrick J 1909- *ConAu P-2*
Pezhuk-Romanoff, Ivan *CreCan 1*
Pezzetti, Emilia Cundari *CreCan 2*
Pezzulo, Ted 1936?-1979 *ConAu 89*
Pezzuti, Thomas Alexander 1936- *ConAu 61*
Pfadt, Robert Edward 1915- *ConAu 73*
Pfaff, William 1928- *ConAu 5R*
Pfaffenberger, Clarence J 1889-1967 *ConAu P-1*
Pfaffenroth, Sara Beekey 1941- *IntWWP 82*
Pfahl, John K 1927- *ConAu 1R, –1NR*
Pfaltz, Marilyn 1933- *ConAu 103*
Pfaltzgraff, Robert L, Jr. 1934- *ConAu 9NR,*
  –21R
Pfanner, Helmut Franz 1933- *ConAu 57*
Pfau, Hugo 1908- *ConAu 29R*
Pfeffer, J Alan 1907- *ConAu 1R, –3NR*
Pfeffer, Jeffrey 1946- *ConAu 109*
Pfeffer, Leo 1910- *ConAu 7NR, –13R*
Pfeffer, Susan Beth 1948- *ConAu 29R,*
  SmATA 4, WrDr 84
Pfeffermann, Guy 1941- *ConAu 25R*
Pfeifer, Carl J 1929- *ConAu 49*
Pfeifer, Luanne 1932- *ConAu 89*
Pfeiffer, C Boyd 1937- *ConAu 57*
Pfeiffer, Carl Curt 1908- *ConAu 101*
Pfeiffer, Charles F 1919-1976 *ConAu 1R, –4NR,*
  –65
Pfeiffer, Eric 1935- *ConAu 10NR, –13R*
Pfeiffer, Hans 1925- *IntAu&W 82*
Pfeiffer, John E 1914- *ConAu 101*
Pfeiffer, Karl G *ConAu 1R*
Pfeil, Fred *DrAP&F 83*
Pfeilschifter, Boniface 1900- *ConAu P-2*
Pfiffner, John M 1893- *ConAu 5R*
Pfingston, Roger *DrAP&F 83*
Pfingston, Roger Carl 1940- *ConAu 104,*
  IntWWP 82
Pfister, Arthur *DrAP&F 83*
Pfister, Arthur 1949- *ConAu 45*
Pflanze, Otto 1918- *ConAu 5R*
Pflanzer, Howard 1944- *NatPD 81[port]*
Pflaum, Irving Peter 1906- *ConAu 13R*
Pflaum, Melanie L 1909- *ConAu 6NR, –13R*
Pflaum, Susanna Whitney *ConAu X*
Pflaum, Susanna Whitney 1937- *ConAu 110*
Pflaum-Connor, Susanna *ConAu X*
Pflaum-Connor, Susanna 1937- *ConAu 106*
Pflieger, Elmer F 1908- *ConAu 17R*
Pflum, John 1934- *ConAu 107*
Pfordresher, John 1943- *ConAu 65*
Pfouts, Ralph W 1920- *ConAu 41R*
Pfoutz, Shirley Eclov 1922- *ConAu 1R*
Pfriem, John E 1923?-1983 *ConAu 110*
Pfuetze, Paul E 1904- *ConAu 1R*
Phadnis, Urmila 1931- *IntAu&W 82*
Phair, Judith Turner 1946- *ConAu 61*
Phantom *IntWWP 82X*
Phares, Donald 1942- *ConAu 81*
Phares, Ross 1908- *ConAu P-1*
Phares, Timothy B 1954- *ConAu 97*
Pharis, Gwen *CreCan 2*
Pharr, Emory Charles 1896?-1981 *ConAu 104*
Pharr, Robert D 1916- *ConAu 49, LivgBAA*
Pharr, Susan J 1944- *ConAu 105*
Pheasant, Dr. Lundy *IntAu&W 82X*
Phelan, Francis Joseph 1925- *ConAu 5R*
Phelan, John Leddy 1924- *ConAu 21R,*
  WrDr 84
Phelan, John Martin 1932- *ConAu 73*
Phelan, Josephine 1905- *SmATA 30, WrDr 84*
Phelan, Mary Kay 1914- *ConAu 1R, –4NR,*
  IntAu&W 82, SmATA 3, WrDr 84
Phelan, Mary Michenfelder 1936- *ConAu 97*
Phelan, Nancy Eleanor 1913- *ConAu 101*
Phelan, Terry Wolfe 1941- *ConAu 97*
Phelge, Nanker *ConAu X*
Phelps, Arthur Warren 1909- *ConAu 49*
Phelps, Ashton 1913-1983 *ConAu 109*
Phelps, D Maynard 1897- *ConAu P-2*
Phelps, Dean *DrAP&F 83*

Phelps, Digger *ConAu X*
Phelps, Donald 1929- *ConAu 45*
Phelps, Ethel Johnston 1914- *ConAu 106*
Phelps, Gilbert 1915- *ConAu 5R, –7NR,*
  ConNov 82, IntAu&W 82, WrDr 84
Phelps, Humphrey 1927- *WrDr 84*
Phelps, Jack 1926- *ConAu 29R*
Phelps, O Wheelock 1906- *ConAu 1R*
Phelps, Phelps 1897-1981 *ConAu 104*
Phelps, Richard *ConAu 103*
Phelps, Robert 1922- *ConAu 17R*
Phelps, Roger P 1920- *ConAu 49*
Phelps, Thomas Ross 1929- *ConAu 61*
Phelps, William Lyon 1865-1943 *LongCTC,*
  TwCA
Phenix, Philip Henry 1915- *WrDr 84*
Phibbs, Brendan 1916- *ConAu 33R*
Phifer, Kenneth G 1915- *ConAu 17R*
Philbrick, Charles, II 1922-1971 *ConAu 1R,*
  –4NR
Philbrick, Helen L 1910- *ConAu 103*
Philbrick, Joseph Lawrence 1927- *ConAu 45*
Philbrick, Stephen *DrAP&F 83*
Philbrook, Clem 1917- *ConAu 104,*
  SmATA 24[port]
Philby, Eleanor *ASpks*
Philip, Cynthia Owen 1928- *ConAu 49*
Philip, J A 1901- *ConAu P-2*
Philip, John Robert 1927- *ConAu 108*
Philip, Lotte Brand *ConAu X*
Philipp, Elliot Elias 1915- *ConAu 3NR, –9R,*
  WrDr 84
Philippatos, George Crito 1938- *ConAu 106*
Philippe, Charles-Louis 1874-1909 *ClDMEL 80*
Philippi, Donald L 1930- *ConAu 108*
Philips, Cyril 1912- *ConAu 103, WrDr 84*
Philips, Frank *ConAu X*
Philips, G Edward 1926- *ConAu 41R*
Philips, Judson 1903- *WrDr 84*
Philips, Judson Pentecost 1903- *AuNews 1,*
  ConAu 89, TwCCr&M 80
Philips, Thomas *ConAu X*
Philipson, Morris H 1926- *ConAu 1R, –4NR*
Philipson, Susan Sacher 1934- *ConAu 9R*
Phillifent, John Thomas 1916-1976 *ConAu 102,*
  TwCSFW
Phillippi, Wendell Crane 1918- *ConAu 77*
Phillips, Alan *ConAu X*
Phillips, Alan Meyrick Kerr 1916- *ConAu 5R*
Phillips, Almarin 1925- *ConAu 1R, –1NR*
Phillips, Anne G 1924- *ConAu 73*
Phillips, Arthur 1907- *IntAu&W 82*
Phillips, Barty 1933- *ConAu 8NR, –61*
Phillips, Bernard S 1931- *ConAu 25R*
Phillips, Bernice Maxine 1925- *ConAu 45*
Phillips, Betty *DrAP&F 83*
Phillips, Billie Ann 1925- *LivgBAA*
Phillips, Billie M 1925- *ConAu 102*
Phillips, Bob 1940- *ConAu 69*
Phillips, C E Lucas *ConAu X*
Phillips, Cabell 1904-1975 *ConAu 61, –97*
Phillips, Carole 1938- *ConAu 108*
Phillips, Cecil R 1933- *ConAu 13R*
Phillips, Celeste R 1933- *ConAu 110*
Phillips, Charles F 1910- *ConAu 85*
Phillips, Charles F, Jr. 1934- *ConAu 2NR, –5R*
Phillips, Claude S, Jr. 1923- *ConAu 9R*
Phillips, Clifton J 1919- *ConAu 37R,*
  IntAu&W 82, WrDr 84
Phillips, Craig 1922- *ConAu 9R*
Phillips, D J 1924- *ConAu 10NR, –13R*
Phillips, David Atlee 1922- *ConAu 69*
Phillips, David Graham 1867-1911 *ConAu 108,*
  DcLB 9[port], LongCTC, TwCA,
  TwCA SUP
Phillips, David Lindsay 1914- *IntAu&W 82*
Phillips, Debora R 1939- *ConAu 93*
Phillips, Derek L 1934- *ConAu 33R, WrDr 84*
Phillips, Dewi Zephaniah 1934- *ConAu 9NR,*
  –17R, IntAu&W 82, WrDr 84
Phillips, Dorothy S 1893-1972 *ConAu 37R*
Phillips, Dorothy W 1906-1977 *ConAu 73*
Phillips, Douglas 1929- *IntWWP 82*
Phillips, E Bryant 1905-1975 *ConAu 5R, –6NR*
Phillips, E Lakin 1915- *ConAu 37R*
Phillips, Edwin A 1915- *ConAu 53*
Phillips, Elizabeth C 1906- *ConAu 41R*
Phillips, Emma Julia 1900- *ConAu P-1*
Phillips, Frances *DrAP&F 83*
Phillips, Gene D 1935- *ConAu 1NR, –45,*
  IntAu&W 82
Phillips, Gerald Marvin 1928- *ConAu 33R,*

  WrDr 84
Phillips, Glenly Roy Elliott *IntWWP 82*
Phillips, Gordon Lewis 1911-1982 *ConAu 108*
Phillips, Henry Wallace 1869-1930 *TwCA*
Phillips, Herbert P 1929- *ConAu 13R*
Phillips, Hiram Stone 1912?-1979 *ConAu 85*
Phillips, Hubert 1891-1964 *LongCTC*
Phillips, Irv 1908- *ConAu 65, SmATA X*
Phillips, Irving W 1908- *SmATA 11*
Phillips, J B 1906-1982 *ConAu 108*
Phillips, Jack *ConAu X, SmATA 8*
Phillips, James Atlee 1915- *TwCCr&M 80,*
  WrDr 84
Phillips, James Emerson, Jr. 1912-1979
  ConAu 101, –89
Phillips, James M 1929- *ConAu 106*
Phillips, James W 1922- *ConAu 33R, WrDr 84*
Phillips, Jane 1944- *LivgBAA*
Phillips, Jayne Anne *DrAP&F 83*
Phillips, Jayne Anne 1952- *ConAu 101,*
  ConLC 15, DcLB Y80B[port]
Phillips, Jennifer *ConDr 82B*
Phillips, Jerome C *ConAu X*
Phillips, Jewell Cass 1900- *ConAu P-2*
Phillips, Jill 1952- *ConAu 65*
Phillips, John Bertram 1906- *ConAu 106,*
  LongCTC
Phillips, John Lawrence, Jr. 1923- *ConAu 33R,*
  WrDr 84
Phillips, Josephine E 1896-1975 *ConAu 5R, –61*
Phillips, Julien L 1945- *ConAu 77*
Phillips, Keith W 1946- *ConAu 102*
Phillips, Kevin Price 1940- *ConAu 65*
Phillips, Laughlin 1924- *ConAu 102*
Phillips, Leon *ConAu X, SmATA X*
Phillips, Leona Rasmussen 1925- *ConAu 65*
Phillips, Loretta 1893- *ConAu P-1, SmATA 10*
Phillips, Louis *DrAP&F 83*
Phillips, Louis 1942- *ConAu 3NR, –49,*
  IntAu&W 82, NatPD 81[port], SmATA 8
Phillips, Louis Christopher 1939- *ConAu 57,*
  WrDr 84
Phillips, Mac *ConAu X*
Phillips, Margaret Mann 1906- *ConAu 13R,*
  IntAu&W 82, WrDr 84
Phillips, Margaret McDonald 1910?-1978
  ConAu 77
Phillips, Marjorie *ConAu 5R*
Phillips, Mark *ConAu X, TwCSFW, WrDr 84*
Phillips, Mary Geisler 1881-1964 *ConAu 5R,*
  SmATA 10
Phillips, Maurice J 1914-1976 *ConAu 5R, –103*
Phillips, Michael *ConAu X*
Phillips, Michael 1938- *ConAu 108*
Phillips, Michael Joseph *DrAP&F 83*
Phillips, Michael Joseph 1937- *ConAu 3NR, –49,*
  IntWWP 82, WrDr 84
Phillips, Mickey 1916- *ConAu X*
Phillips, O Hood 1907- *ConAu 2NR*
Phillips, O M 1930- *ConAu 89*
Phillips, Osborne *ConAu X*
Phillips, Owen Hood 1907- *ConAu 5R*
Phillips, Patricia 1935- *ConAu 103*
Phillips, Paul 1938- *ConAu 73*
Phillips, Pauline Esther Friedman 1918-
  ConAu 1R
Phillips, Peggy *NatPD 81[port]*
Phillips, Prentice 1894- *ConAu P-1, SmATA 10*
Phillips, Rachel 1934- *ConAu 49*
Phillips, Ray C 1922- *ConAu 10NR, –25R*
Phillips, Richard *ConAu X*
Phillips, Richard C 1934- *ConAu 65*
Phillips, Robert *DrAP&F 83*
Phillips, Robert 1922- *WrDr 84*
Phillips, Robert 1938- *ConAu 8NR, –17R,*
  IntWWP 82, WrDr 84
Phillips, Robert L, Jr. 1940- *ConAu 77*
Phillips, Rog 1909-1965 *TwCSFW*
Phillips, Stella 1927- *ConAu 11NR, –21R*
Phillips, Stephen 1864?-1915 *DcLB 10[port],*
  LongCTC, ModBrL, ModWD, TwCA
Phillips, Steve *ConAu X*
Phillips, Steven 1947- *ConAu 103*
Phillips, Tom *ConAu X*
Phillips, Ulrich Bonnell 1877-1934 *DcLB 17[port]*
Phillips, Velma 1894- *ConAu P-2*
Phillips, Walter Joseph 1884-1963 *CreCan 1*
Phillips, Ward *ConAu X*
Phillips, Warren 1926- *ConAu 107*
Phillips, Wendell 1921-1975 *ConAu 61,*
  ConAu P-2
Phillips, William *ConAu 29R*

Pilarski, Laura P 1926- *ConAu 29R, SmATA 13, WrDr 84*
Pilat, Oliver Ramsay 1903- *ConAu 5R*
Pilbrow, Richard 1933- *ConAu 29R*
Pilcer, Sonia *DrAP&F 83*
Pilcer, Sonia 1949- *ConAu 89*
Pilch, John J 1936- *ConAu 108*
Pilch, Judah 1902- *ConAu 5R, –6NR*
Pilcher, George William 1935- *ConAu 105*
Pilcher, Rosamunde 1924- *ConAu 57, IntAu&W 82, TwCRGW, WrDr 84*
Pilcher, William W 1930- *ConAu 45*
Pilditch, James 1929- *ConAu 9R*
Pile, John F 1924- *ConAu 93*
Pile, Stephen 1949- *WrDr 84*
Pilgrim *IntWWP 82X*
Pilgrim, Anne *ConAu X, IntAu&W 82X, SmATA X, –5, TwCCW 83, WrDr 84*
Pilgrim, David *LongCTC, TwCCr&M 80*
Pilgrim, Derral *ConAu X, WrDr 84*
Pilgrim, Geneva Hanna 1914- *ConAu 25R*
Pilinszky, Janos 1921-1981 *CIDMEL 80, ConAu 104*
Pilio, Gerone *ConAu X*
Pilisuk, Marc 1934- *ConAu 29R, IntAu&W 82*
Pilk, Henry *ConAu X*
Pilkey, Orrin H 1934- *ConAu 97*
Pilkington, Betty 1912- *ConAu 69*
Pilkington, Cynthia *ConAu X*
Pilkington, E C A 1907- *ConAu P-2*
Pilkington, Francis Meredyth 1907- *ConAu P-2, SmATA 4, WrDr 84*
Pilkington, John, Jr. 1918- *ConAu 17R*
Pilkington, Kevin *DrAP&F 83*
Pilkington, Roger Windle 1915- *ConAu 1R, –5NR, IntAu&W 82, SmATA 10, WrDr 84*
Pilkington, Walter d1983 *ConAu 109*
Pilkington, William T 1939- *ConAu 8NR, –61*
Pill, Virginia 1922- *ConAu 61*
Pillai, Karnam Chengalvaroya 1901- *ConAu 5R*
Pillar, James Jerome 1928- *ConAu 13R*
Pillecijn, Filip De 1891-1962 *CIDMEL 80*
Pillin, William *DrAP&F 83*
Pillin, William 1910- *ConAu 9R, ConP 80, IntWWP 82, WrDr 84*
Pilling, Arnold R 1926- *ConAu 1R, –3NR*
Pilling, Christopher 1936- *ConAu 101, ConP 80, WrDr 84*
Pillon, Nancy Bach 1917- *ConAu 110*
Pilniak, Boris 1894-1938? *CnMWL, ModSL 1, TwCA, TwCA SUP, TwCWr*
Pilnyak, Boris 1894-1941 *CIDMEL 80*
Pilo, Giuseppe Maria 1929- *ConAu 5NR, –9R*
Pilon, Jean-Guy 1930- *CreCan 2*
Pilon, Juliana Geran 1947- *ConAu 97*
Pilot, Robert W 1898-1967 *CreCan 1*
Pilou *ConAu X*
Pilpel, Harriet Fleischl 1911- *ConAu P-2*
Pilpel, Robert H *DrAP&F 83*
Pilpel, Robert H 1943- *ConAu 9NR, –65*
Piltch, Bernie *CreCan 2*
Pimentel, George C 1922- *WrDr 84*
Pimsleur, Meira Goldwater 1905?-1979 *ConAu 13R, –89*
Pimsleur, Paul 1927- *WrDr 84*
Pimsleur, Paul 1927-1976 *ConAu 65, ConAu P-2*
Pin, Oscar *IntAu&W 82X*
Pinar, William 1947- *ConAu 57*
Pinard, Maurice 1929- *ConAu 41R*
Pincher, Chapman 1914- *ConSFA, IntAu&W 82, WrDr 84*
Pincher, Henry Chapman 1914- *ConAu 13R*
Pincherle, Alberto 1907- *ConAu 25R, ConLC 11, –18, LongCTC, TwCA SUP*
Pincherle, Marc 1888-1974 *ConAu 49*
Pinchin, Jane Lagoudis 1942- *ConAu 69*
Pinchot, Ann *ConAu 1R, –4NR, WrDr 84*
Pinchot, David 1914?-1983 *ConAu 109, SmATA 34N*
Pinckard, Terri Ellen 1930- *IntAu&W 82*
Pinckney, Catherine L *ConAu 17R*
Pinckney, Cathey *ConAu X*
Pinckney, Edward R 1924- *ConAu 17R*
Pinckney, Josephine 1895-1957 *ConAu 107, DcLB 6[port], TwCA SUP*
Pincus, Edward R 1938- *ConAu 33R, WrDr 84*
Pincus, Harriet 1938- *ConAu 102, SmATA 27*
Pincus, Joseph 1919- *ConAu 25R*
Pincus, Lily 1898-1981 *ConAu 5NR, –105, –53*
Pinder, John H M *ConAu 3NR, –9R*

Pindyck, Robert 1945- *ConAu 89*
Pine, L G 1907- *WrDr 84*
Pine, Leslie Gilbert 1907- *ConAu 13R, IntAu&W 82*
Pine, Robert 1928- *NatPD 81[port]*
Pine, Theodore *ConAu X*
Pine, Tillie S 1896- *ConAu 69*
Pine, Tillie S 1897- *SmATA 13*
Pine, William *ConAu X, WrDr 84*
Pineau, Roger 1916- *ConAu 25R, IntAu&W 82*
Pinero, Arthur Wing 1855-1934 *ConAu 110*
Pinero, Sir Arthur Wing 1855-1934 *DcLB 10[port], LongCTC, ModBrL, ModWD*
Pinero, Miguel 1946- *ConAu 61, ConDr 82, WrDr 84*
Pinero, Miguel 1947?- *ConLC 4*
Pines, Maya *ConAu 13R, WrDr 84*
Pines, Paul *DrAP&F 83*
Ping, Charles J 1930- *ConAu 17R*
Pinget, Robert 1919- *CIDMEL 80, ConAu 85, ConLC 7, –13, ModFrL, TwCWr, WorAu*
Pinget, Robert 1920- *CnMD, CroCD, ModWD*
Pinion, F B 1908- *ConAu 25R, WrDr 84*
Pinion, Francis Bertram 1908- *IntAu&W 82*
Pinkerton, Edward C 1911- *ConAu 108*
Pinkerton, James R 1932- *ConAu 45*
Pinkerton, Joan Trego 1928- *ConAu 107*
Pinkerton, Kathrene Sutherland 1887-1967 *ConAu 1R, –103, SmATA 26N*
Pinkerton, Marjorie Jean 1934- *ConAu 45*
Pinkerton, Robert E 1882-1970 *ConAu 29R*
Pinkerton, Todd 1929- *ConAu 69*
Pinkerton, Virginia Brown 1926- *IntAu&W 82*
Pinkerton, W Anson *ConAu X*
Pinkett, Harold Thomas 1914- *ConAu 29R, WrDr 84*
Pinkham, Mary Ellen *ConAu 101*
Pinkney, Alphonso 1929- *ConAu 25R, LivgBAA*
Pinkney, David H 1914- *ConAu 9R*
Pinkney, Jerry 1939- *SmATA 32*
Pinkowski, Edward 1916- *ConAu 9R*
Pinkpank, Peter *IntAu&W 82X*
Pinkston, Joe M 1931- *ConAu 5R*
Pinkus, Oscar 1927- *ConAu 5R*
Pinkwater, D Manus 1941- *ChlLR 4[port]*
Pinkwater, Daniel Manus 1941- *ConAu 29R*
Pinkwater, Manus 1941- *SmATA 8*
Pinna, Giovanni 1939- *ConAu 4NR, –49*
Pinner, David 1940- *ConAu 25R, ConDr 82, DcLEL 1940, WrDr 84*
Pinner, Erna 1896- *ConAu P-1*
Pinner, Joma *ConAu X*
Pinney, Peter Patrick 1922- *ConAu 25R*
Pinney, Roy 1911- *ConAu 5R, –6NR*
Pinney, Thomas 1932- *ConAu 85*
Pinney, Wilson G 1929- *ConAu 45*
Pino, E *ConAu X*
Pinsent, Arthur 1888- *ConAu P-2*
Pinsent, Gordon 1930- *ConAu 106*
Pinsker, Sanford *DrAP&F 83*
Pinsker, Sanford 1941- *ConAu 33R, –73, IntAu&W 82*
Pinsker, Sanford S 1941- *WrDr 84*
Pinski, David 1872-1959 *CnMD, ModWD, TwCA, TwCA SUP*
Pinsky, Robert *DrAP&F 83*
Pinsky, Robert 1940- *ConAu 29R, ConLC 9, –19, ConP 80, DcLB Y82B[port], WrDr 84*
Pinson, Ira David 1922- *LivgBAA*
Pinson, William M, Jr. 1934- *ConAu 9NR, –17R, WrDr 84*
Pintauro, Joseph *DrAP&F 83*
Pintauro, Joseph 1930- *ConAu 81, NatPD 81[port]*
Pintel, Gerald 1922- *ConAu 4NR, –49*
Pinter, Harold 1930- *ConAu 5R, ConDr 82, ConLC 1, –3, –6, –9, –11, –15, –27[port], CroCD, DcLB 13[port], DcLEL 1940, LongCTC, ModBrL, ModBrL SUP, ModWD, TwCWr, WhoTwCL, WorAu, WrDr 84*
Pinter, Harold 1932- *CnMD*
Pinter, Walter S 1928- *ConAu 102*
Pintner, Walter McKenzie 1931- *ConAu 21R*
Pinto, David 1937- *ConAu 61*
Pinto, Edward Henry 1901-1972 *ConAu P-1*
Pinto, Jacqueline 1927- *WrDr 84*
Pinto, Peter *ConAu X*
Pinto, Vivian DeSola 1895- *ConAu 5R*
Pinto, Vivian DeSola 1895-1969 *ConAu 10NR*

Pintoff, Ernest 1931- *ConAu 17R*
Pintoro, John 1947- *ConAu 103*
Pintye, Carolyn Ann 1936- *IntWWP 82*
Pioneer *ConAu X, SmATA X*
Piontek, Heinz 1925- *CIDMEL 80, ConAu 25R, ModGL, TwCWr, WorAu 1970*
Piotrowski, Andrzej 1931- *IntAu&W 82*
Piovene, Count Guido 1907-1974 *CIDMEL 80, ConAu 53, –97, WorAu*
Pipa, Arshi 1920- *ConAu 10NR, –25R*
Piper, Anson C 1918- *ConAu 41R*
Piper, Don Courtney 1932- *ConAu 41R*
Piper, Evelyn 1908- *TwCCr&M 80*
Piper, H Beam 1904-1964 *ConAu 110, DcLB 8[port], TwCSFW*
Piper, Henry Dan 1918- *ConAu 17R*
Piper, Herbert Walter 1915- *ConAu 5R, WrDr 84*
Piper, Jim 1937- *ConAu 97*
Piper, John Egerton Christmas 1903- *IntAu&W 82, LongCTC*
Piper, Otto A 1891- *ConAu 5R*
Piper, Philippa *IntWWP 82X*
Piper, Roger *ConAu X, SmATA X*
Piper, Watty *DcLB 22, SmATA X*
Piper, William Bowman 1927- *ConAu 61*
Pipes, Richard 1923- *ConAu 21R, WrDr 84*
Pippert, Wesley Gerald 1934- *ConAu 53*
Pippett, Aileen 1895- *ConAu P-1*
Pippin, Frank Johnson 1906-1968 *ConAu P-2*
Pipping, Ella 1897- *ConAu 61*
Piquet, Howard S 1903- *ConAu P-2*
Piquet-Wicks, Eric 1915- *ConAu 5R*
Piraianu, Alexandru *IntAu&W 82X*
Pirandello, Luigi 1867-1936 *CIDMEL 80, CnMD, CnMWL, ConAu 104, LongCTC, ModRL, ModWD, TwCA, TwCA SUP, TwCLC 4[port], TwCWr, WhoTwCL*
Pires, Joe *ConAu X*
Pires, Jose Cardoso 1925- *CIDMEL 80*
Pirie, David 1946- *ConAu 97, IntAu&W 82, WrDr 84*
Pirie, Henry Ward 1922- *IntAu&W 82*
Pirie, N W 1907- *ConAu 29R*
Pirie-Gordon, Harry 1883?-1969 *ConAu 104*
Pirmantgen, Patricia H 1933- *ConAu 45*
Piro, Richard 1934- *ConAu 49, SmATA 7*
Pirone, Pascal Pompey 1907- *ConAu 9R*
Pirro, Ugo 1920- *TwCWr*
Pirsig, Robert M 1928- *ConAu 53, ConLC 4, –6*
Pirson, Sylvain J 1905- *ConAu 5R*
Pirtle, Caleb, III 1941- *ConAu 11NR, –69*
Pisano, Ronald George 1948- *ConAu 102*
Pisar, Samuel 1929- *DcLB Y83B[port]*
Piscator, Erwin 1893-1966 *CroCD*
Piserchia, Doris 1928- *ConAu 107, TwCSFW, WrDr 84*
Pishkin, Vladimir 1931- *ConAu 45*
Pisk, Paul A 1893- *ConAu P-1*
Pismire, Osbert *ConAu X*
Pisor, Robert 1939- *ConAu 109*
Pistole, Elizabeth 1920- *ConAu 8NR, –17R*
Piston, Walter 1894-1976 *ConAu 69*
Pistorius, Pieter 1920- *IntAu&W 82*
Pitarra, Serafi 1839-1895 *CIDMEL 80*
Pitavy, Francois L 1934- *ConAu 73*
Pitcairn, Frank *ConAu X, WorAu*
Pitcairn, Leonora 1912- *ConAu 21R*
Pitcher, Evelyn G 1915- *ConAu 17R*
Pitcher, George 1925- *ConAu 21R, IntAu&W 82, WrDr 84*
Pitcher, Gladys 1890- *ConAu P-1*
Pitcher, Harvey John 1936- *ConAu 3NR, –45, IntAu&W 82, WrDr 84*
Pitcher, Oliver *DrAP&F 83*
Pitcher, Robert W 1918- *ConAu 29R*
Pitches, Douglas Owen 1930- *IntWWP 82*
Pitchford, Kenneth S 1931- *ConAu 104, ConP 80, WrDr 84*
Pitfield, Thomas Baron 1903- *WrDr 84*
Pithan, Pulamai *IntWWP 82X*
Pithan, Pulavar Pulamai 1935- *IntWWP 82*
Pitkin, Anne *DrAP&F 83*
Pitkin, Anne Wilson 1940- *IntWWP 82*
Pitkin, Dorothy 1899?-1972 *ConAu 37R*
Pitkin, Thomas M 1901- *ConAu 17R*
Pitkin, Walter, Jr. 1913- *ConAu 13R*
Pitkin, Walter Boughton 1878-1953 *TwCA, TwCA SUP*
Pitman, Sir Isaac 1813-1897 *LongCTC*
Pitman, James 1901- *ConAu P-2, WrDr 84*

Pitoeff, Georges 1886-1939 *CIDMEL 80*
Pitrone, Anne *DrAP&F 83*
Pitrone, Jean Maddern 1920- *ConAu 8NR, -17R, SmATA 4, WrDr 84*
Pitseolak, Peter 1902-1973 *ConAu 93*
Pitt, Barrie 1918- *ConAu 5R, IntAu&W 82, WrDr 84*
Pitt, David Charles 1938- *ConAu 29R, WrDr 84*
Pitt, Frances 1888-1964 *LongCTC*
Pitt, Jeremy *ConAu X*
Pitt, Peter 1933- *ConAu 33R*
Pitt, Valerie 1939- *IntAu&W 82*
Pitt, Valerie Joan 1925- *ConAu 5R*
Pitt-Rivers, Julian Alfred 1919- *ConAu 101*
Pittenger, Norman 1905- *WrDr 84*
Pittenger, W Norman 1905- *ConAu 1R, -5NR*
Pittenger, William Norman 1905- *IntAu&W 82*
Pitter, Ruth 1897- *ConAu P-1, LongCTC, ModBrL, TwCA, TwCA SUP, TwCWr, WrDr 84*
Pittman, David J 1927- *ConAu 5R, -6NR*
Pittman, Sample N 1925- *WrDr 84*
Pittman, Sample Noel 1925- *LivgBAA*
Pittock, Joan 1930- *ConAu 107, WrDr 84*
Pitts, Denis 1930- *ConAu 65, WrDr 84*
Pitts, Robert F 1908-1977 *ConAu 69*
Pitz, Henry C 1895-1976 *ConAu 9NR*
Pitz, Henry Clarence 1895-1976 *ConAu 9R, -69, SmATA 24N, -4*
Pitzer, Sara 1938- *ConAu 107*
Pivar, David J 1933- *ConAu 45*
Piven, Frances Fox 1932- *ConAu 49*
Pixie *IntWWP 82X*
Pixley, Jorge V 1937- *ConAu 1NR, -45*
Pizer, Donald 1929- *ConAu 9R*
Pizer, Harry F 1947- *ConAu 101*
Pizer, Marjorie 1920- *IntWWP 82*
Pizer, Vernon 1918- *ConAu 1R, -4NR, SmATA 21[port], WrDr 84*
Pizzat, Frank J 1924- *ConAu 49*
Pizzey, Erin 1939- *ConAu 81*
Pla, Josep 1897-1981 *ConAu 103*
Pla I Casadevall, Josep 1897- *CIDMEL 80*
Plaatje, Sol T 1877-1932 *ModBlW*
Plaatje, Solomon T 1877?-1932 *ModCmwL, TwCWr*
Place, Irene Magdaline 1912- *ConAu 1R, -1NR*
Place, Janey Ann 1946- *ConAu 73*
Place, Marian Templeton 1910- *ConAu 1R, -5NR, SmATA 3*
Placere, Morris N *ConAu X*
Placet, Leroi 1901-1970 *ConAu 29R*
Plagemann, Bentz 1913- *ConAu 1R, -4NR, TwCRGW, WrDr 84*
Plagens, Peter 1941- *ConAu 107*
Plager, Sheldon J 1931- *ConAu 25R*
Plaidy, Jean *ConAu X, WrDr 84*
Plaidy, Jean 1906- *ConAu X, ConLC 7, SmATA 2, TwCRGW, TwCWr, WorAu*
Plain, Belva *DrAP&F 83*
Plain, Belva 1918- *WrDr 84*
Plain, Belva 1919?- *ConAu 81*
Plain, Warren *ConAu X*
Plaine, Alfred R 1898?-1981 *ConAu 105, SmATA 29N*
Plamenatz, John Petrov 1912-1975 *ConAu 5NR, -13R*
Planchon, Roger 1931- *CIDMEL 80, CnMD SUP*
Planck, Carolyn H 1910- *ConAu 73*
Planck, Charles Evans 1896- *ConAu 73*
Plank, Emma N 1905- *ConAu P-2*
Plank, Robert 1907- *ConAu 25R*
Plano, Jack Charles 1921- *ConAu 2NR, -5R, WrDr 84*
Plant, Marcus L 1911- *ConAu 1R*
Plant, Raymond 1945- *ConAu 29R*
Plante, David *DrAP&F 83*
Plante, David 1940- *ConAu 37R, ConLC 7, -23[port], ConNov 82, DcLB Y83B[port], IntAu&W 82, WrDr 84*
Plante, Jacques 1929- *ConAu 108*
Plante, Julian G *ConAu 41R*
Plantinga, Alvin *WrDr 84*
Plantinga, Alvin C 1932- *ConAu 11NR, -21R, IntAu&W 82*
Plantinga, Leon B 1935- *ConAu 21R*
Planz, Allen *DrAP&F 83*
Planz, Allen 1937- *ConAu 53, ConP 80, WrDr 84*
Plaskett, Joseph Francis 1918- *CreCan 2*

Plaskow, Judith Ellen 1947- *ConAu 108*
Plastaras, James C 1931- *ConAu 21R*
Plat, Wolfgang 1923- *IntAu&W 82*
Plate, Robert 1918- *ConAu 17R, WrDr 84*
Plate, Thomas 1944- *ConAu 69*
Plater, Alan 1935- *ConAu 85, ConDr 82, IntAu&W 82, WrDr 84*
Plater, William M 1945- *ConAu 85*
Plath, David W 1930- *ConAu 3NR, -9R*
Plath, Sylvia 1932-1963 *ConAu P-2, ConLC 1, -2, -3, -5, -9, -11, -14, -17, ConP 80A, CroCAP, DcLB 5, -6[port], DcLEL 1940, LongCTC, ModAL SUP, WhoTwCL, WorAu*
Plath, Sylvia 1932-1964 *TwCWr*
Platig, E Raymond 1924- *ConAu 37R*
Platonov, Andrei *ConAu X*
Platonov, Andrei 1899-1951 *ModSL 1, WorAu 1970*
Platonov, Andrey Platonovich 1899-1951 *CIDMEL 80*
Platov, Mariquita *DrAP&F 83*
Platov, Mariquita 1905- *ConAu 5R*
Platt, Anthony M 1942- *ConAu 25R*
Platt, Charles *DrmM[port]*
Platt, Charles 1944- *ConAu 21R, ConSFA, TwCSFW, WrDr 84*
Platt, Colin 1934- *WrDr 84*
Platt, D C M 1934- *ConAu 109*
Platt, Eugene *DrAP&F 83*
Platt, Eugene 1939- *WrDr 84*
Platt, Eugene Robert 1939- *ConAu 3NR, -49*
Platt, Frederick 1946- *ConAu 61*
Platt, Gerald M 1933- *ConAu 97*
Platt, Harrison Gray 1902- *ConAu 41R*
Platt, Jennifer 1937- *ConAu 29R*
Platt, John 1918- *ConAu 17R*
Platt, Kathleen *DrAP&F 83*
Platt, Kin 1911- *ConAu 11NR, -17R, ConLC 26[port], SmATA 21[port]*
Platt, Lyman De 1943- *ConAu 102*
Platt, Raymond *NatPD 81[port]*
Platt, Rutherford Hayes 1894-1975 *ConAu 61*
Platt, Washington 1890- *ConAu 1R*
Platten, Thomas George 1899- *ConAu P-1*
Platthy, Jeno 1920- *IntWWP 82*
Platts, Beryl 1918- *ConAu 61, IntAu&W 82*
Platz, Judith *DrAP&F 83*
Plauger, P J 1944- *ConAu 57*
Plaut, Jonathan 1936- *ConAmTC*
Plaut, Thomas F A 1925- *ConAu 25R*
Plaut, W Gunther 1912- *ConAu 2NR, -5R, IntAu&W 82, WrDr 84*
Plawin, Paul 1938- *ConAu 89*
Player, Gary 1935- *ConAu 101*
Player, Ian 1927- *ConAu 49*
Player, Robert 1905-1978 *TwCCr&M 80*
Playfair, Giles William 1910- *IntAu&W 82*
Playfair, Guy Lyon 1935- *ConAu 106*
Playfair, Sir Nigel 1874-1934 *LongCTC*
Pleasants, Ben 1940- *WrDr 84*
Pleasants, Henry 1910- *ConAu 107, IntAu&W 82, WrDr 84*
Pleasants, Henry, Jr. 1884-1963 *ConAu 1R*
Pleasants, Samuel A 1918- *ConAu 77*
Pleck, Joseph H 1946- *ConAu 7NR, -57*
Plekhanov, Georgy Valentinovich 1857-1918 *CIDMEL 80*
Plekker, Robert J 1929- *ConAu 69*
Plendello, Leo *ConAu X*
Plender, Richard O 1945- *ConAu 101*
Plenzdorf, Ulrich 1934- *CIDMEL 80*
Plesset, Isabel R 1912- *ConAu 103*
Plessner, Helmuth 1892- *IntAu&W 82*
Plesur, Milton 1927- *ConAu 45, IntAu&W 82*
Pletcher, David M 1920- *ConAu 1R*
Plevin, Miriam 1957- *IntWWP 82*
Pleydell, Susan *ConAu X*
Plezia, Marian 1917- *IntAu&W 82*
Plick Et Plock *ConAu X*
Plievier, Theodor 1892-1955 *CnMD, ModGL, ModWD, TwCA SUP*
Plimmer, Charlotte 1916- *ConAu 104*
Plimmer, Denis 1914- *ConAu 104*
Plimpton, George 1927- *AuNews 1, ConAu 21R, SmATA 10, WrDr 84*
Plimpton, Ruth Talbot 1916- *ConAu 13R*
Plischke, Elmer 1914- *ConAu 1R, -2NR, WrDr 84*
Plisnier, Charles 1896-1952 *CIDMEL 80*
Plochmann, George Kimball 1914- *ConAu 5R*
Plog, Fred 1944- *ConAu 25R*

Plog, Stanley C 1930- *ConAu 41R*
Ploghoft, Milton E 1923- *ConAu 104*
Plomer, William 1903-1973 *ConLC 8, IntAu&W 82, ModCmwL, SmATA 24[port]*
Plomer, William Charles Franklin 1903-1973 *ConAu P-2*
Plomer, William Charles Franklyn 1903-1973 *ConLC 4, LongCTC, ModBrL, ModBrL SUP, TwCA, TwCA SUP, TwCWr, WhoTwCL*
Plomley, Roy *WrDr 84*
Plomley, Roy 1914- *ConAu 107, IntAu&W 82*
Plommer, Hugh d1983 *ConAu 109*
Plopper, Julie Jynelle 1916- *ConAu 69*
Ploscowe, Morris 1904-1975 *ConAu 2NR, -45, -61*
Ploss, Sidney I 1932- *ConAu 13R*
Plossl, George W 1918- *ConAu 21R*
Plotnick, Alan R 1926- *ConAu 17R*
Plotnicov, Leonard 1930- *ConAu 21R*
Plotnik, Arthur 1937- *ConAu 69*
Plotz, Helen Ratnoff 1913- *ConAu 8NR, -9R*
Plowden, Alison 1931- *ConAu 33R, WrDr 84*
Plowden, David 1932- *ConAu 33R*
Plowden, Gene 1906- *ConAu 21R*
Plowman, E Grosvenor 1899- *ConAu 13R*
Plowman, Edward E 1931- *ConAu 37R, WrDr 84*
Plowman, Stephanie 1922- *ConAu 5NR, -53, SmATA 6, TwCCW 83, WrDr 84*
Pluck, Derek John 1951- *IntWWP 82*
Pluckrose, Henry 1931- *ConAu 33R, IntAu&W 82, SmATA 13, WrDr 84*
Pluff, Barbara 1926- *ConAu 5R*
Plum, J *ConAu X, SmATA X*
Plum, Jennifer *ConAu X, WrDr 84*
Plum, Lester Virgil 1906-1972 *ConAu 1R, -37R*
Plumb, Barbara Louise Brown 1934- *ConAu 89*
Plumb, Beatrice Anne 1886- *ConAu X*
Plumb, Charles P 1900?-1982 *ConAu 105, SmATA 29N*
Plumb, Charlie *ConAu 49*
Plumb, J H 1911- *ConAu 3NR*
Plumb, John Harold 1911- *ConAu 5R, DcLEL 1940, IntAu&W 82, LongCTC, WorAu, WrDr 84*
Plumb, Joseph Charles, Jr. 1942- *ConAu 3NR, -49*
Plumly, Stanley *DrAP&F 83*
Plumly, Stanley 1939- *ConAu 108, -110, ConP 80, DcLB 5[port], WrDr 84*
Plumm, Norman D *ConAu X*
Plummer, Alfred 1896- *ConAu 29R*
Plummer, Arthur Christopher Orme 1929- *CreCan 2*
Plummer, Ben *ConAu X, TwCWW*
Plummer, Beverly J 1918- *ConAu 29R, WrDr 84*
Plummer, Catharine 1922- *ConAu 21R, WrDr 84*
Plummer, Christopher 1929- *CreCan 2*
Plummer, Clare 1912- *WrDr 84*
Plummer, Clare Emsley 1912- *ConAu 25R, TwCRGW*
Plummer, Desmond 1914- *WrDr 84*
Plummer, Kenneth 1946- *ConAu 73*
Plummer, L Gordon 1904- *ConAu P-2*
Plummer, Margaret 1911- *ConAu P-2, SmATA 2*
Plummer, Mark A 1929- *ConAu 37R*
Plummer, William 1945- *ConAu 102*
Plummer, William J 1927- *ConAu 53, WrDr 84*
Plump, Sterling Dominc 1940- *LivgBAA*
Plumpp, Sterling *DrAP&F 83*
Plumpp, Sterling Dominic 1940- *ConAu 45*
Plumptre, Arthur Fitzwalter Wynne 1907-1977 *ConAu 106, -109*
Plumstead, A William 1933- *ConAu 11NR, -25R*
Plunkett, Edward John Morton Drax *LongCTC, TwCA, TwCA SUP*
Plunkett, James 1920- *ConAu X, DcLB 14[port], IntAu&W 82X, WrDr 84*
Plunkett, Joseph Mary 1887-1916 *LongCTC, TwCA*
Plunkett, Thomas J 1921- *ConAu 33R*
Plutchik, Robert 1927- *ConAu 11NR, -21R*
Pluto, Terry 1955- *ConAu 107*
Plutonius *ConAu X*
Plutschow, Herbert Eugen 1939- *ConAu 102*
Plutzik, Roberta 1948- *ConAmTC*
Plutzik, Roberta Ann 1948- *ConAu 110*

Plyer, Cranford O, Jr. 1927- *IntAu&W 82*
Plymell, Charles *DrAP&F 83*
Plymell, Charles 1935- *ConAu 11NR, -21R, DcLB 16[port]*
Plympton, Bill *ConAu X*
Plympton, William M 1946- *ConAu 110*
Pneemi, A *IntWWP 82X*
Pniel, Noah 1905- *IntWWP 82*
Poag, James F 1934- *ConAu 107*
Poage, Godfrey Robert 1920- *ConAu 5R*
Poage, Scott T 1931- *ConAu 53*
Poague, Leland A 1948- *ConAu 6NR, -57*
Pobo, Kenneth *DrAP&F 83*
Pobo, Kenneth 1954- *ConAu 104*
Pochmann, Henry A 1901-1973 *ConAu 37R*
Pochmann, Ruth Fouts 1903- *ConAu P-2*
Pockley, Peter 1935- *IntAu&W 82*
Pocock, H R S 1904- *ConAu 25R*
Pocock, Hugh 1904- *WrDr 84*
Pocock, Nick 1934- *ConAu 53*
Pocock, Roger 1865-1941 *TwCWW*
Pocock, Thomas Allcot Guy 1925- *ConAu 103*
Pocock, Tom *WrDr 84*
Pocock, Tom 1925- *ConAu X*
Podbielski, Gisele 1918- *ConAu 53*
Podendorf, Illa E *ConAu 81, SmATA 18*
Podendorf, Illa E 1903?-1983 *ConAu 110*
Podeschi, John B 1942- *ConAu 110*
Podgorecki, Adam 1925- *WrDr 84*
Podhajsky, Alois 1898-1973 *ConAu 69*
Podheretz, Norman 1930- *DcLEL 1940*
Podhoretz, Norman 1930- *ConAu 7NR, -9R, WorAu, WrDr 84*
Podhradsky, Gerhard 1929- *ConAu 21R*
Podlecki, Anthony Joseph 1936- *ConAu 3NR, -49, IntAu&W 82*
Podmarsh, Rollo *ConAu X*
Podmore, Frank 1856?-1910 *TwCA*
Podoksik, David 1904- *IntWWP 82*
Podoliak, Boris *ConAu X, IntAu&W 82X*
Podraza-Kwiatkowska, Maria 1926- *IntAu&W 82*
Podulka, Fran 1933- *ConAu 49*
Poduschka, Walter 1922- *ConAu 107*
Poe, Charlsie 1909- *ConAu P-2*
Poe, Edgar Allan 1809-1849 *SmATA 23[port]*
Poe, James 1921-1980 *ConAu 93*
Poel, William 1852-1934 *LongCTC*
Poen, Monte Mac 1930- *ConAu 107*
Poern, Ingmar 1935- *ConAu 33R*
Poetker, Frances Jones 1912- *ConAu 85*
Poetry Lady, The *MichAu 80*
Poez *DrAP&F 83*
Poganski, Donald John 1928- *ConAu 25R, WrDr 84*
Pogany, Andras H 1919- *ConAu 21R*
Pogany, Hortenzia Lers *ConAu 21R*
Pogany, Willy 1882-1955 *SmATA 30*
Poggi, Emil J 1928- *ConAu 29R*
Poggi, Gianfranco 1934- *ConAu 85*
Poggi, Jack *ConAu X*
Poggie, John J, Jr. 1937- *ConAu 107*
Poggioli, Renato 1907-1963 *ConAu 1R, -2NR, WorAu*
Pogodin, Nikolai F 1900-1962 *CnMD, ModWD*
Pogodin, Nikolai Fyodorovich 1900-1962 *ModSL 1*
Pogodin, Nikolay Fyodorovich 1900-1962 *CIDMEL 80*
Pogrebin, Letty Cottin 1939- *ConAu 29R, WrDr 84*
Pogue, Forrest Carlisle 1912- *ConAu 3NR, -5R, WrDr 84*
Poh, Caroline 1938- *ConAu 61*
Pohl, Frederick 1919- *ConAu 61*
Pohl, Frederick Julius 1889- *ConAu 1R, -5NR*
Pohl, Frederik *DrAP&F 83*
Pohl, Frederik 1919- *ConAu 11NR, ConLC 18, ConNov 82, ConSFA, DcLB 8[port], DrmM[port], IntAu&W 82, SmATA 24, TwCSFW, WorAu, WrDr 84*
Pohle, Linda C 1947- *ConAu 45*
Pohle, Robert W, Jr. 1949- *ConAu 81, IntAu&W 82*
Pohlman, Edward 1933- *ConAu 33R*
Pohlmann, Lillian 1902- *ConAu 9R, SmATA 11, -8, WrDr 84*
Pohndorf, Richard Henry 1916-1977 *ConAu 73*
Poignant, Raymond 1917- *ConAu 29R*
Poincare, Raymond 1860-1934 *LongCTC*
Poindexter, David 1929- *ConAu 29R*
Poindexter, Hally Beth Walker 1927- *ConAu 110*

Poindexter, Marian J 1929- *ConAu 29R*
Poinsett, Alex Ceasar 1926- *ConAu 29R, LivgBAA*
Pointer, Larry 1940- *ConAu 101*
Pointer, Michael 1927- *ConAu 57*
Pointon, Marcia R 1943- *ConAu 33R*
Pointon, Robert *ConAu X, IntAu&W 82X, SmATA X*
Poirier, Frank E 1940- *ConAu 3NR, -49*
Poirier, Gerard 1930- *CreCan 2*
Poirier, Leonie M *IntAu&W 82*
Poirier, Louis *ConLC 11, TwCA SUP*
Poirier, Normand 1928?-1981 *ConAu 102*
Poirier, Richard 1925- *ConAu 1R, -3NR, ConLCrt 82, DcLEL 1940, WorAu 1970, WrDr 84*
Pois, Joseph 1905- *ConAu P-1*
Poitier, Sidney 1924?- *ConLC 26[port]*
Poitiers, Angele *MichAu 80*
Pokrovsky, Boris Aleksandrovich 1912- *ConAu 109*
Pola *ConAu X* *SmATA X*
Polach, Jaroslav G 1914- *ConAu 9R, WrDr 84*
Polack, Albert Isaac 1892- *ConAu P-1*
Polak, Jacques Jacobus 1914- *ConAu 104*
Polakoff, Keith 1941- *ConAu 49, WrDr 84*
Poland, Dorothy 1937- *WrDr 84*
Poland, Dorothy Elizabeth Hayward 1937- *ConAu 103, IntAu&W 82*
Poland, Larry 1939- *ConAu 101*
Polanowski, Tadeusz 1922- *IntAu&W 82*
Polanski, Roman 1933- *ConAu 77, ConLC 16*
Polansky, Norman A 1918- *ConAu 85*
Polanyi, Michael 1891-1976 *ConAu 65, -81, DcLEL 1940, WorAu*
Polatnick, Florence T 1923- *ConAu 29R, SmATA 5*
Polcher, Egon 1907- *ConAu X*
Polcovar, Carol *DrAP&F 83*
Polder, Markus *ConAu X, IntAu&W 82X, SmATA X*
Poldervaart, Arie 1909-1969 *ConAu 1R, -103*
Poldino *IntAu&W 82X*
Pole, J R 1922- *ConAu 8NR*
Pole, Jack Richon 1922- *ConAu 17R, IntAu&W 82, WrDr 84*
Polebaum, Elliot E 1950- *ConAu 107*
Poleman, Thomas T 1928- *ConAu 13R*
Polenberg, Richard 1937- *ConAu 21R, WrDr 84*
Polese, Marcia Ann 1949- *ConAu 65*
Polette, Nancy 1930- *ConAu 6NR, -57*
Polevoi, Boris *ConAu X*
Polgar, Alfred 1873-1955 *ModGL*
Polgar, D Katherine 1924- *IntAu&W 82*
Polhamus, Jean Burt 1928- *ConAu 103, SmATA 21[port]*
Poli, Bernard 1929- *ConAu 21R*
Poli, Umberto *WorAu*
Poliakoff, Stephen 1952- *ConAu 106, DcLB 13[port]*
Poliakoff, Stephen 1953- *WrDr 84*
Poliakoff, Steven 1952- *ConDr 82*
Poliakov, Leon 1910- *ConAu 104, IntAu&W 82*
Police, The *ConLC 26[port]*
Polier, Justine Wise 1903- *ConAu 104*
Polin, Raymond 1918- *ConAu 37R, IntAu&W 82*
Poling, Daniel Alfred 1884-1968 *ConAu 93*
Poling, David 1928- *ConAu 85*
Polinger, Elliot Hirsch 1898-1970 *ConAu 104*
Polis, A Richard 1937- *ConAu 6NR, -57*
Polisensky, Josef V 1915- *ConAu 107*
Polish, David 1910- *ConAu 13R*
Polishook, Irwin H 1935- *ConAu 21R*
Polite, Carlene Hatcher *DrAP&F 83*
Polite, Carlene Hatcher 1932- *ASpks, ConAu 21R, LivgBAA*
Polite, Frank *DrAP&F 83*
Politella, Dario 1921- *ConAu 13R, WrDr 84*
Politella, Joseph 1910- *ConAu P-2*
Politi, Leo 1908- *ConAu 17R, SmATA 1, WrDr 84*
Politicus *ConAu X*
Politzer, Heinrich 1910-1978 *ConAu 3NR*
Politzer, Heinz 1910-1978 *ConAu X, -5R, -81*
Politzer, Robert L 1921- *ConAu 5R*
Poljanski, Hristo Andonov *ConAu X*
Polk, Dora 1923- *ConAu 49*
Polk, Edwin Weiss 1916- *ConAu 37R*
Polk, James 1939- *ConAu 105*

Polk, James R 1937- *ConAu 69*
Polk, Judd 1913?-1975 *ConAu 57*
Polk, Kenneth 1935- *ConAu 1R, -1NR*
Polk, Mary 1898- *ConAu P-1*
Polk, Ralph Weiss 1890-1978 *ConAu 37R, -77*
Polk, Stella Gipson 1901- *ConAu 93*
Polk, William Roe 1929- *ConAu 25R*
Polking, Kirk 1925- *ConAu 29R, SmATA 5, WrDr 84*
Polkingharn, Anne T 1937- *ConAu 109*
Poll, Richard Douglas 1918- *ConAu 101*
Pollack, Cecelia 1909- *ConAu 29R*
Pollack, Ervin H 1913-1972 *ConAu P-1*
Pollack, Erwin 1935- *ConAu 49*
Pollack, Harvey 1913- *ConAu 5R*
Pollack, Herman 1907- *ConAu 69*
Pollack, Joe 1931- *ConAmTC*
Pollack, Merrill S 1924- *ConAu 5R*
Pollack, Norman 1933- *ConAu 13R*
Pollack, Peter 1911-1978 *ConAu 77, -81*
Pollack, Reginald 1924- *ConAu 37R, WrDr 84*
Pollack, Robert H 1927- *ConAu 49*
Pollack, Seymour V 1933- *ConAu 25R*
Pollak, Felix *DrAP&F 83*
Pollak, Felix 1909- *ConAu 10NR, -25R, WrDr 84*
Pollak, Kurt 1919- *ConAu 29R*
Pollak, Louis Heilprin 1922- *ConAu 17R*
Pollan Cohen, Shirley *DrAP&F 83*
Polland, Barbara K 1939- *ConAu 73*
Polland, Madeleine A 1918- *TwCCW 83, WrDr 84*
Polland, Madeleine Angela Cahill 1918- *ConAu 3NR, -5R, SmATA 6*
Pollard, Albert Frederick 1869-1948 *LongCTC, TwCA, TwCA SUP*
Pollard, Alfred William 1859-1944 *LongCTC*
Pollard, Arthur 1922- *WrDr 84*
Pollard, Eve 1944- *WrDr 84*
Pollard, Graham 1903-1976 *ConAu 69, LongCTC*
Pollard, Jack 1926- *ConAu 29R*
Pollard, James Edward 1894-1979 *ConAu 89, ConAu P-1*
Pollard, John 1914- *WrDr 84*
Pollard, John Richard Thornhill 1914- *ConAu 5R, IntAu&W 82*
Pollard, Sidney 1925- *ConAu 17R, WrDr 84*
Pollard, T E 1921- *ConAu 29R*
Pollard, Thomas Evan 1921- *WrDr 84*
Pollard, William G 1911- *ConAu 6NR, -13R*
Pollens, David *DrAP&F 83*
Pollet, Elizabeth *DrAP&F 83*
Pollet, Sylvester *DrAP&F 83*
Polley, Judith Anne 1938- *WrDr 84*
Polley, Robert Lutz 1933- *ConAu 17R*
Pollinger, Kenneth Joseph 1933- *ConAu 57*
Pollini, Francis 1930- *ConAu 1R, -1NR, DcLEL 1940, IntAu&W 82, WrDr 84*
Pollio, Howard R 1937- *ConAu 37R, IntAu&W 82*
Pollitt, Jerome J 1934- *ConAu 21R*
Pollitt, Katha *DrAP&F 83*
Pollock, Bruce 1945- *ConAu 7NR, -57*
Pollock, Channing 1880-1946 *ModWD, TwCA, TwCA SUP*
Pollock, David H 1922- *ConAu 49*
Pollock, Sir Frederick 1845-1937 *TwCA, TwCA SUP*
Pollock, George 1938- *ConAu 61*
Pollock, Harry 1920- *ConAu 89*
Pollock, James K 1898-1968 *ConAu 29R, ConAu P-2*
Pollock, John 1923- *ConAu 2NR*
Pollock, Sir John 1878-1963 *LongCTC*
Pollock, John Charles *WrDr 84*
Pollock, John Charles 1923- *ConAu 5R, IntAu&W 82*
Pollock, John L 1940- *ConAu 37R*
Pollock, Mary *ConAu X, SmATA X, TwCCW 83*
Pollock, Norman H, Jr. 1909- *ConAu P-2*
Pollock, Penny 1935- *ConAu 101*
Pollock, Robert 1930- *ConAu 45*
Pollock, Seton 1910- *ConAu 5R, WrDr 84*
Pollock, Sharon *WrDr 84*
Pollock, Sharon 1936- *ConDr 82*
Pollock, Ted 1929- *ConAu 85*
Pollock, Thomas Clark 1902- *ConAu P-2*
Pollock, Walter Herries 1850-1926 *TwCA*
Pollock, William 1899-1982 *ConAu 110*
Pollowitz, Melinda Kilborn 1944- *ConAu 77,*

SmATA 26[port]
Polly, Natale Safir *DrAP&F 83*
Polmar, Norman 1938- *ConAu 49*
Polnaszek, Frank P 1947- *ConAu 107*
Polnay, Peter De *LongCTC, TwCA SUP*
Polner, Murray 1928- *ConAu 5NR, -13R*
Polner, Zoltan 1933- *IntAu&W 82*
Polome, Edgar C 1920- *ConAu 29R*
Polon, Linda Beth 1943- *ConAu 103*
Polonsky, Abraham 1910- *ConAu 104, ConDr 82A, DcLB 26[port]*
Polonsky, Antony 1940- *ConAu 73, WrDr 84*
Polonsky, Arthur 1925- *SmATA 34[port]*
Polony, Raymond *ConAu X*
Polos, Nicholas Christopher 1917- *ConAu 17R, WrDr 84*
Pols, Edward 1919- *ConAu 9R*
Polsby, Nelson W 1934- *ConAu 5NR, -53*
Polseno, Jo *ConAu 81, SmATA 17*
Polsky, Abe 1935- *ConAu 109, NatPD 81[port]*
Polsky, Howard W 1928- *ConAu 25R*
Polsky, Ned 1928- *ConAu 25R*
Polson, A Irene 1925- *IntWWP 82*
Polson, Cyril John *WrDr 84*
Poltoratzky, N P 1921- *ConAu 73*
Poltroon, Milford *ConAu X*
Polunin, Nicholas 1909- *ConAu 65, WrDr 84*
Polunin, Oleg 1914- *ConAu 85*
Polva, Anni *IntAu&W 82X*
Polvay, Marina 1928- *IntAu&W 82*
Polviander, Anni Kyllikki 1915- *IntAu&W 82*
Polya, John Bela 1914- *WrDr 84*
Pomada, Elizabeth 1940- *ConAu 8NR, -61*
Pomerance, Bernard 1940- *ConAu 101, ConDr 82, ConLC 13, WrDr 84*
Pomerans, Arnold Julius 1920- *IntAu&W 82*
Pomerantz, Charlotte 1930- *ConAu 85, SmATA 20*
Pomerantz, Edward *DrAP&F 83*
Pomerantz, Edward 1934- *ConAu 65*
Pomerantz, Joel 1930- *ConAu 29R*
Pomerantz, Sidney I 1909-1975 *ConAu 61*
Pomerleau, Cynthia S 1943- *ConAu 73*
Pomerleau, Gervais 1952- *IntAu&W 82*
Pomerleau, Ovide F 1940- *ConAu 73*
Pomeroy, Charles A 1930- *ConAu 25R*
Pomeroy, Earl Spencer 1915- *ConAu 17R*
Pomeroy, Florence Mary 1892- *ConAu X*
Pomeroy, Hub *ConAu X*
Pomeroy, Kenneth B 1907-1975 *ConAu 61*
Pomeroy, Pete *ConAu X, SmATA X*
Pomeroy, Ralph *DrAP&F 83*
Pomeroy, Ralph 1926- *ConP 80, WrDr 84*
Pomeroy, Sarah B 1938- *ConAu 65*
Pomeroy, Wardell Baxter 1913- *ConAu 1R, -1NR*
Pomeroy, William J 1916- *ConAu 85, IntAu&W 82*
Pomfred, Joan *IntWWP 82X*
Pomfret, Baron *ConAu X*
Pomfret, Joan *IntAu&W 82X*
Pomfret, John Edwin 1898-1981 *ConAu 1R, -3NR, -105*
Pommer, Henry F 1918- *ConAu 1R*
Pommery, Jean 1932- *ConAu 101*
Pomorska, Krystyna 1928- *ConAu 41R*
Pompa, Leon 1933- *ConAu 7NR, -57*
Pomper, Gerald M 1935- *ConAu 5NR, -9R*
Pomper, Philip 1936- *ConAu 77*
Pompian, Richard 1935- *WrDr 84*
Pompian, Richard O 1935- *ConAu 11NR, -29R*
Pompidou, Georges 1911-1974 *ConAu 49*
Pomrenke, Norman E 1930- *ConAu 21R*
Pomroy, Martha 1943- *ConAu 101*
Ponce DeLeon, Jose Luis S 1931- *ConAu 49*
Poncin, Jacques 1948- *IntAu&W 82*
Pond, Alonzo W 1894- *ConAu 1R, -1NR, SmATA 5*
Pond, Grace 1910- *WrDr 84*
Pond, Grace Isabelle 1910- *ConAu 5NR, -13R, IntAu&W 82*
Pond, L W *ConAu X*
Pondal, Eduardo 1835-1917 *CIDMEL 80*
Ponder, Catherine 1927- *ConAu 1R, -1NR*
Ponder, James A 1933- *ConAu 69*
Ponder, Patricia *WrDr 84*
Ponge, Francis Jean Gaston Alfred 1899- *CIDMEL 80, CnMWL, ConAu 85, ConLC 6, -18, ModFrL, ModRL, WorAu*
Poniatowska, Elena 1933- *ConAu 101*
Ponicsan, Darryl *DrAP&F 83*
Ponicsan, Darryl 1938- *ConAu 29R*

Poniewaz, Jeff 1946- *IntWWP 82*
Ponnamperuma, Cyril A 1923- *ConAu 101*
Pons, Maurice 1927- *ConAu 5NR, -53*
Ponsonby, Arthur A W H 1871-1946 *LongCTC*
Ponsonby, D A 1907- *ConAu 2NR, -5R, IntAu&W 82, TwCRGW, WrDr 84*
Ponsonby, Frederick Edward Neuflize 1913- *ConAu 13R*
Ponsot, Marie *DrAP&F 83*
Ponsot, Marie Birmingham *ConAu 9R*
Pont, Clarice Holt 1907- *ConAu 5R*
Ponte, Lowell 1946- *ConAu 57*
Ponte, Pierre Viansson *ConAu X*
Ponten, Josef 1883-1940 *CIDMEL 80*
Pontes, Paulo 1941?-1976 *ConAu 69*
Pontiero, Giovanni 1932- *ConAu 29R*
Pontiflet, Ted 1932- *ConAu 105, SmATA 32*
Pontney, Jack A 1931- *ConAu 21R*
Pontoppidan, Henrik 1857-1943 *CIDMEL 80, TwCA, TwCA SUP, WhoTwCL*
Pool, David DeSola 1885-1970 *ConAu 29R*
Pool, Eugene 1943- *ConAu 85*
Pool, Ithiel DeSola 1917- *ConAu 17R*
Pool, Phoebe Dorothy 1913- *ConAu 5R*
Pool, Tamar DeSola 1891?-1981 *ConAu 104*
Poole, Ernest 1880-1950 *ConAmA, ConAu 109, DcLB 9, TwCA, TwCA SUP*
Poole, Francis *DrAP&F 83*
Poole, Frederick King 1934- *ConAu 25R*
Poole, Gary Thomas 1931- *ConAu 107*
Poole, Gray Johnson 1906- *ConAu 5R, -6NR, SmATA 1*
Poole, Herbert *ConAu 103*
Poole, Josephine 1933- *ConAu 10NR, -21R, ConLC 17, SmATA 5, TwCCW 83, WrDr 84*
Poole, Lynn 1910-1969 *ConAu 5R, SmATA 1*
Poole, Margaret Barbara 1925- *IntWWP 82*
Poole, Peggy 1925- *ConAu 107*
Poole, Roger 1939- *ConAu 102*
Poole, Seth *ConAu X*
Poole, Victoria 1927- *ConAu 102*
Poole, Vivian *ConAu X*
Pooler, Victor H, Jr. 1924- *ConAu 13R*
Pooley, Beverley J 1934- *ConAu 45*
Pooley, Robert C 1898-1978 *ConAu 5R, -7NR*
Poolla, Tirupati Raju 1904- *ConAu X, IntAu&W 82*
Poor, Harold Lloyd 1935- *ConAu 45*
Poor, Henry Varnum 1914?-1972 *ConAu 37R*
Poore, Charles 1902-1971 *ConAu 29R*
Poorman, Paul Arthur 1930- *ConAu 106*
Poorten-Schwartz, J M W VanDer *LongCTC, TwCA, TwCA SUP*
Poots-Booby, Edna *ConAu X*
Poovey, W A 1913- *ConAu 10NR, -21R*
Poovey, William Arthur 1913- *WrDr 84*
Pop, Simion 1930- *IntAu&W 82*
Popa, Vasko 1922- *CIDMEL 80, ConLC 19, ModSL 2, TwCWr, WhoTwCL, WorAu 1970*
Pope, Arthur Upham 1881-1969 *ConAu 25R*
Pope, Clifford Hillhouse 1899-1974 *ConAu 1R, -103*
Pope, Deborah *DrAP&F 83*
Pope, Dudley 1925- *WrDr 84*
Pope, Dudley Bernard Egerton 1925- *ConAu 2NR, -5R, DcLEL 1940, IntAu&W 82, WorAu*
Pope, Edwin 1928- *ConAu 73*
Pope, Elizabeth Marie 1917- *ConAu 49*
Pope, Harrison, Jr. 1947- *ConAu 41R*
Pope, John Alexander 1906-1982 *ConAu 107*
Pope, Maurice 1926- *ConAu 69*
Pope, Michael James 1940- *ConAu 101*
Pope, Phyllis Ackerman 1894?-1977 *ConAu 69*
Pope, Ray 1924- *ConAu 29R, WrDr 84*
Pope, Richard Martin 1916- *ConAu 17R, WrDr 84*
Pope, Robert G 1936- *ConAu 29R*
Pope, Robert H 1925- *ConAu 33R*
Pope, Susan L *DrAP&F 83*
Pope, Thomas Harrington 1913- *ConAu 73*
Pope, Whitney 1935- *ConAu 69*
Pope-Hennessey, Una Constance 1876-1949 *TwCA SUP*
Pope-Hennessy, James 1916-1974 *ConAu 45, -97, DcLEL 1940, LongCTC, WorAu*
Pope-Hennessy, John 1913- *WrDr 84*
Pope-Hennessy, John Wyndham 1913- *ConAu 1R, -1NR, LongCTC, WorAu 1970*

Popenoe, David 1932- *ConAu 29R*
Popenoe, Paul 1888- *ConAu 1R*
Popescu, Christine 1930- *ConAu 7NR, -13R, IntAu&W 82*
Popescu, Julian John Hunter 1928- *ConAu 1R, -1NR*
Popham, Estelle I 1906- *ConAu 1R, -5NR*
Popham, Hugh 1920- *ConAu 5R, -6NR, DcLEL 1940, IntWWP 82, WrDr 84*
Popham, Margaret Evelyn 1895?-1982 *ConAu 106*
Popham, Melinda *DrAP&F 83*
Popham, Melinda 1944- *ConAu 49*
Popiel, Elda S 1915- *ConAu 57*
Popkin, Jeremy D 1948- *ConAu 102*
Popkin, John William 1909- *ConAu P-1*
Popkin, Richard H 1923- *ConAu 77*
Popkin, Roy 1921- *ConAu 25R*
Popkin, Zelda 1898- *ConAu 25R, TwCCr&M 80, WrDr 84*
Popkin, Zelda F 1898-1983 *ConAu 109*
Poplavsky, Boris Yulianovich 1903-1935 *CIDMEL 80*
Popov, Dusko 1912?-1981 *ASpks, ConAu 105*
Popov, Haralan Ivanov 1907- *ConAu 21R*
Popovic, Nenad D 1909- *ConAu P-2, WrDr 84*
Popovsky, Mark 1922- *ConAu 102, WrDr 84*
Popowski, Bert 1904- *ConAu 1R*
Popp, Lilian M *ConSFA*
Poppe, Nicholas N 1897- *ConAu 73, WrDr 84*
Popper, Frank James 1944- *ConAu 29R, WrDr 84*
Popper, Karl 1902- *WrDr 84*
Popper, Karl Raimund 1902- *ConAu 3NR, -5R, IntAu&W 82, TwCA SUP*
Poppino, Kathryn *DrAP&F 83*
Poppino, Rollie E 1922- *ConAu 13R, WrDr 84*
Popple, James 1927- *ConAu 107, WrDr 84*
Poppleton, Marjorie 1895- *ConAu P-1*
Popplewell, Jack 1911- *ConAu 9R*
Porada, Edith 1912- *ConAu 103*
Poray, J B *IntAu&W 82X*
Poray-Biernacki, Janusz 1907- *IntAu&W 82*
Porcari, Constance Kwolek 1933- *ConAu 33R*
Porch, Douglas 1944- *ConAu 107, WrDr 84*
Porche, Verandah *DrAP&F 83*
Porcher, Mary F Wickham 1898- *ConAu X*
Porell, Bruce 1947- *ConAu 102*
Porges, Arthur 1915- *TwCSFW*
Porges, Michael *DrAP&F 83*
Porges, Michel 1924- *IntWWP 82*
Poriss, Martin 1948- *ConAu 81*
Porlock, Martin *ConAu X, LongCTC, TwCA, TwCA SUP, TwCCr&M 80*
Porn, Gustav Ingmar 1935- *IntAu&W 82*
Porn, Ingmar 1935- *WrDr 84*
Porosky, P H *ConAu 45*
Porqueras-Mayo, Alberto 1930- *ConAu 45*
Porsche, Ferdinand 1909- *ConAu 89*
Porsche, Ferry *ConAu X*
Port, M H 1930- *ConAu 69*
Port, Wymar *ConAu X*
Portal, Colette 1936- *ConAu 53, SmATA 6*
Portal, Ellis *WrDr 84*
Portal, Ellis 1925- *ConAu X*
Portchmouth, Jon *IntWWP 82X*
Portchmouth, Roland John 1923- *IntWWP 82*
Porte, Joel 1933- *ConAu 8NR, -17R*
Porten, Bezalel 1931- *ConAu 11NR, -25R, WrDr 84*
Porteous, Ian Robertson 1930- *WrDr 84*
Porteous, Leslie 1901- *WrDr 84*
Porteous, Leslie Crichton 1901- *ConAu 5R*
Porter, Alan *ConAu X*
Porter, Albert Wright 1923- *ConAu 107*
Porter, Alvin *ConAu X, TwCWW*
Porter, Andrew 1928- *ConAu 5NR, -53, IntAu&W 82, WrDr 84*
Porter, Arthur T 1924- *ConAu 5R*
Porter, Bern *DrAP&F 83*
Porter, Bern 1911- *ConAu 9NR, -21R, IntAu&W 82, IntWWP 82X, WrDr 84*
Porter, Bernard 1941- *ConAu 107, WrDr 84*
Porter, Bernard Harden 1911- *IntWWP 82*
Porter, Brian 1928- *ConAu 25R, IntAu&W 82, WrDr 84*
Porter, Burton F 1936- *ConAu 106, WrDr 84*
Porter, C L 1905- *ConAu P-2*
Porter, Charles A 1932- *ConAu 21R*
Porter, Cole 1893-1964 *ConAu 93, LongCTC*
Porter, Darwin 1937- *ConAu 69*
Porter, David John 1948- *IntAu&W 82*

Porter, David L 1941- *ConAu 107*
Porter, David T 1928- *ConAu 17R*
Porter, Donald 1939- *ConAu 103*
Porter, Dorothy Burnett 1905- *LivgBAA*
Porter, Dorothy Featherstone 1954- *IntWWP 82*
Porter, Edward A 1936- *ConAu 21R*
Porter, Eleanor H 1868-1920 *ConAu 108,*
TwCCW 83
Porter, Eleanor Hodgman 1868-1920 *DcLB 9,*
LongCTC, TwCA, TwCA SUP, TwCRGW,
TwCWr
Porter, Elias H 1914- *ConAu 9R*
Porter, Eliot 1901- *ConAu 5R*
Porter, Enid 1910- *IntAu&W 82*
Porter, Ernest Graham 1889- *ConAu 1R*
Porter, Ethel K 1901- *ConAu P-2*
Porter, Farifield 1907-1975 *ConAu 61*
Porter, Frank W, III 1947- *ConAu 97*
Porter, Gene L 1935- *ConAu 25R*
Porter, Gene Stratton 1863-1924 *TwCCW 83,*
TwCRGW
Porter, Gene Stratton 1868-1924 *LongCTC,*
TwCA, TwCA SUP, TwCWr
Porter, George 1920- *ConAu 107,*
IntAu&W 82, WrDr 84
Porter, Glenn 1944- *ConAu 73*
Porter, H Boone 1923- *ConAu 5R, –8NR*
Porter, H C 1927- *ConAu 33R*
Porter, Hal 1911- *ConAu 3NR, –9R, ConDr 82,*
ConNov 82, ConP 80, DcLEL 1940,
IntAu&W 82, IntWWP 82, ModCmwL,
WrDr 84
Porter, Hal 1917- *TwCWr*
Porter, Harold Everett 1887-1936 *TwCA*
Porter, J M 1937- *ConAu 103*
Porter, J R 1921- *ConAu 5NR*
Porter, Jack Nusan 1944- *ConAu 41R,*
IntAu&W 82
Porter, Jeannette Stratton *TwCA, TwCA SUP*
Porter, Joe Ashby *DrAP&F 83*
Porter, Joe Ashby 1942- *ConAu 73*
Porter, John 1919- *ConAu 21R*
Porter, Jonathan 1938- *ConAu 77*
Porter, Joshua Roy 1921- *ConAu 53,*
IntAu&W 82, WrDr 84
Porter, Joyce 1924- *ConAu 8NR, –17R,*
TwCCr&M 80, WrDr 84
Porter, Judith D R 1940- *ConAu 81*
Porter, Katherine Anne 1890-1980 *AuNews 2,*
ConAu 1R, –1NR, –101, ConLC 1, –3, –7,
–10, –13, –15, –27[port], DcLB 4, –9[port],
LongCTC, SmATA 23N, WhoTwCL
DcLB Y80A[port]
Porter, Katherine Anne 1894- *CnMWL,*
ConAmA, ModAL, ModAL SUP, TwCA,
TwCA SUP, TwCWr
Porter, Kathryn *ConAu X*
Porter, Kenneth Wiggins 1905- *ConAu 2NR,*
–5R, IntAu&W 82, WrDr 84
Porter, Laurence M 1936- *ConAu 107*
Porter, Lyman William 1930- *ConAu 21R*
Porter, Margaret Eudine 1905-1975 *ConAu 8NR,*
–57
Porter, Mark *ConAu X*
Porter, McKenzie 1911- *ConAu 69*
Porter, Michael E 1947- *ConAu 105*
Porter, Michael Leroy 1947- *IntAu&W 82*
Porter, Monica 1952- *ConAu 107*
Porter, Peter 1929- *ConAu 85, ConLC 5, –13,*
ConP 80, DcLEL 1940, IntAu&W 82,
ModBrL SUP, WorAu 1970, WrDr 84
Porter, Philip W 1900- *ConAu 69*
Porter, Raymond J 1935- *ConAu 85*
Porter, Richard C 1931- *ConAu 9R*
Porter, Sheena 1935- *ConAu 81, IntAu&W 82,*
SmATA 24[port], TwCCW 83, WrDr 84
Porter, Sylvia 1913- *WrDr 84*
Porter, Sylvia F 1913- *ConAu 81*
Porter, T E *DrAP&F 83*
Porter, Thomas E 1928- *ConAu 29R*
Porter, Timothy L *DrAP&F 83*
Porter, W Thomas, Jr. 1934- *ConAu 29R*
Porter, Willard H 1920- *ConAu 57*
Porter, William E 1918- *ConAu 69*
Porter, William Sydney 1862-1910 *ConAu 104,*
LongCTC, TwCA, TwCA SUP
Porterfield, Bruce 1925- *ConAu 21R*
Porterfield, Nolan *DrAP&F 83*
Porterfield, Nolan 1936- *ConAu 33R*
Portes, Alejandro 1944- *ConAu 93*
Porteus, Stanley D 1883- *ConAu 1R*

Portillo, Estela *DrAP&F 83*
Portis, Charles 1933- *ConAu 1NR, –45,*
DcLB 6, TwCWW, WrDr 84
Portisch, Hugo 1927- *ConAu 21R*
Portman, David N 1937- *ConAu 45*
Portman, James Bickle 1935- *ConAmTC*
Portner, Paul 1925- *CroCD, IntAu&W 82*
Portnoy, Howard N 1946- *ConAu 81*
Porto-Riche, Georges De 1849-1930 *CIDMEL 80,*
CnMD, ModFrL, ModWD
Portobello, Petronella *WrDr 84*
Portoghesi, Paolo 1931- *ConAu 108*
Portugal, Jose Blanc De 1914- *CIDMEL 80*
Portuges, Paul *DrAP&F 83*
Portuges, Paul 1945- *ConAu 77, IntAu&W 82*
Portway, Christopher 1923- *ConAu 57,*
IntAu&W 82
Porush, David H 1952- *ConAu 93*
Porzelt, Paul 1902- *ConAu 108*
Posell, Elsa Z *ConAu 1R, –4NR, SmATA 3*
Posey, Sam 1944- *ConAu 93*
Posey, Walter B 1900- *ConAu P-1*
Posin, Daniel Q 1909- *ConAu P-1*
Posin, Jack A 1900- *ConAu 13R*
Posner, Alice *ConAu X*
Posner, David *DrAP&F 83*
Posner, David 1938- *ConAu 106*
Posner, Ernst 1892-1980 *ConAu 41R, –97*
Posner, Michael Vivian 1931- *WrDr 84*
Posner, Mitchell Jay 1949- *ConAu 110*
Posner, Richard 1944- *ConAu 5NR, –53,*
WrDr 84
Pospelov, Pyotr Nikolayevich 1898-1979
ConAu 85
Pospesel, Howard Andrew 1937- *ConAu 73*
Pospielovsky, Dimitry V 1935- *ConAu 29R*
Pospisil, J Leopold 1923- *ConAu 13R*
Pospisil, Leopold Jaroslav 1923- *IntAu&W 82,*
WrDr 84
Post, Alpha Lucille 1911- *IntWWP 82*
Post, Austin 1922- *ConAu 85*
Post, C Gordon 1903- *ConAu P-1*
Post, Elizabeth L 1920- *ConAu 49*
Post, Emily 1873-1960 *ConAu 103, –89*
Post, Felix 1913- *ConAu 21R*
Post, Gaines 1902- *ConAu P-1*
Post, Gaines, Jr. 1937- *ConAu 73*
Post, Henry 1948- *ConAu 61*
Post, Homer A 1888- *ConAu P-2*
Post, J B 1937- *ConAu 97*
Post, Jonathan V *DrAP&F 83*
Post, Joyce 1939- *ConAu 8NR, –61*
Post, Marie J 1919- *MichAu 80*
Post, Melville Davisson 1869-1930 *ConAu 110,*
TwCCr&M 80
Post, Melville Davisson 1871-1930 *TwCA*
Post, Mortimer *WrDr 84*
Post, Steve 1944- *ConAu 103, WrDr 84*
Postal, Bernard 1905-1981 *ConAu 2NR, –5R,*
–103
Postan, Michael Moissey 1899-1981 *ConAu 105*
Posten, Margaret L 1915- *ConAu 29R,*
SmATA 10
Poster, Carol *DrAP&F 83*
Poster, Cyril Dennis 1924- *ConAu 7NR, –13R,*
WrDr 84
Poster, John B 1939- *ConAu 29R*
Poster, Mark 1941- *ConAu 33R, WrDr 84*
Posteuca, Vasile 1912-1972 *ConAu 37R*
Postgate, Raymond William 1896-1971
ConAu 3NR, –5R, –89, LongCTC, TwCA,
TwCA SUP, TwCCr&M 80, TwCWr
Posthumus, Cyril 1918- *ConAu 104*
Postlethwait, S N 1918- *ConAu 8NR, –17R*
Postma, Lidia 1952- *ConAu 101*
Postma, Magdalena Jacomina 1908- *ConAu 65*
Postma, Minnie *ConAu X*
Postman, Neil *ConAu 102*
Poston, Richard W 1914- *ConAu 65*
Poston, Theodore Roosevelt Augustus M
1906-1974 *ConAu 104*
Posvar, Wesley W 1925- *ConAu 17R*
Posy, Arnold 1894- *ConAu 9R*
Potash, Robert A 1921- *ConAu 102*
Poteet, G Howard 1935- *ConAu 33R*
Pothan, Kap 1929- *ConAu 29R*
Potholm, Christian Peter, II 1940- *ConAu 29R*
Potichnyj, Peter J 1930- *ConAu 41R*
Potiphar *ConAu X*
Potok, Chaim *DrAP&F 83*
Potok, Chaim 1929- *ASpks, AuNews 1, –2,*
ConAu 17R, ConLC 2, –7, –14, –26[port],

SmATA 33[port], WrDr 84
Potoker, Edward Martin 1931- *ConAu 33R,*
WrDr 84
Pottebaum, Gerald A 1934- *ConAu 5NR, –9R*
Potter, A Neal 1915- *ConAu 13R*
Potter, Beatrix 1866-1943 *ChlLR 1, ConAu 108,*
LongCTC, TwCCW 83
Potter, Charles E 1916- *ConAu 61*
Potter, Dan *DrAP&F 83*
Potter, Dan 1932- *ConAu 33R*
Potter, David 1915- *ConAu 29R*
Potter, David M 1910-1971 *DcLB 17[port],*
WorAu 1970[port]
Potter, David Morris 1910-1971 *ConAu 108*
Potter, Dennis 1935- *ConAu 107, ConDr 82,*
DcLEL 1940, WrDr 84
Potter, E B 1908- *ConAu 37R*
Potter, Eloise Fretz 1931- *ConAu 105*
Potter, Faith *ConAu X*
Potter, Gail M 1914- *ConAu 25R*
Potter, George Richard 1900- *ConAu 5R*
Potter, George William 1930- *ConAu 1R*
Potter, J 1922- *ConAu 21R*
Potter, Jack M 1936- *ConAu 41R*
Potter, James Gerrard 1944- *ConAu 97*
Potter, James H 1912-1978 *ConAu 77*
Potter, James L 1922- *ConAu 107*
Potter, Jeremy 1922- *ConAu 53, IntAu&W 82,*
WrDr 84
Potter, Joanna *WrDr 84*
Potter, John Mason 1907- *ConAu P-1*
Potter, Karl Harrington 1927- *ConAu 5R*
Potter, Kathleen Jill 1932- *ConAu 104*
Potter, Lois 1941- *ConAu 41R*
Potter, M David 1900- *ConAu P-2*
Potter, Margaret 1926- *ConAu 6NR, –13R,*
IntAu&W 82, SmATA 21, WrDr 84
Potter, Marian 1915- *ConAu 1NR, –49,*
SmATA 9
Potter, Miriam Clark 1886-1965 *ConAu 5R,*
SmATA 3
Potter, Robert Alonzo 1934- *ConAu 1NR, –45*
Potter, Robert Ducharme 1905-1978 *ConAu 77*
Potter, Simeon 1898-1976 *ConAu 4NR, –5R*
Potter, Stephen 1900-1969 *ConAu 101, –25R,*
LongCTC, ModBrL, TwCA SUP, TwCWr
Potter, Sulamith Heins 1944- *ConAu 81*
Potter, Van Rensselaer 1911- *ConAu 37R*
Potter, Vincent G 1928- *ConAu 25R, WrDr 84*
Potter, William Hotchkiss 1914- *ConAu 1R*
Potterton, Gerald 1931- *ConAu 49*
Potterton, Homan 1946- *ConAu 108*
Pottle, Frederick Albert 1897- *ConAu 3NR, –5R,*
IntAu&W 82, LongCTC, TwCA SUP
Pottle, Patricia *IntWWP 82X*
Potts, Charles *DrAP&F 83*
Potts, Charles 1943- *ConAu 105*
Potts, E Daniel 1930- *ConAu 25R*
Potts, Eve 1929- *ConAu 103*
Potts, George Chapman 1898- *ConAu P-1*
Potts, Jean 1910- *ConAu 2NR, –5R,*
TwCCr&M 80, WrDr 84
Potts, Paul Hugh Patrick Howard 1911-
DcLEL 1940
Potts, Ralph Bushnell 1901- *ConAu 57*
Potts, Richard 1938- *ConAu 103, WrDr 84*
Potvin, Georges C 1928- *ConAu 45*
Potvin, Raymond H 1924- *ConAu 21R*
Poucher, William Arthur 1891- *ConAu P-1*
Pough, Frederick Harvey 1906- *ConAu 81*
Pouillon, Fernand 1912- *ConAu 29R*
Poulakidas, Andreas K 1934- *ConAu 45*
Poulet, Georges 1902- *CIDMEL 80,*
ConAu 13R, IntAu&W 82
Poulin, A, Jr. *DrAP&F 83*
Poulin, A, Jr. 1938- *ConAu 21R, ConP 80,*
WrDr 84
Poulin, Gabrielle 1929- *IntAu&W 82*
Poulos, Clara Jean 1941- *IntAu&W 82*
Poulter, S L 1943- *ConAu 49*
Poulton, Edith Eleanor Chloe 1903- *ConAu 85*
Poulton, Helen Jean 1920-1971 *ConAu P-2*
Poulton, Richard 1938- *ConAu 107*
Pound, Arthur 1884-1966 *ConAu 89*
Pound, Ezra 1885-1972 *CnMD, CnMWL,*
ConAmA, ConAu 5R, –37R, ConLC 1, –2,
–3, –4, –5, –7, –10, –13, –18, ConLCrt 82,
DcLB 4, LongCTC, ModAL, ModAL SUP,
TwCA, TwCA SUP, TwCWr, WhoTwCL
Pound, Merritt B 1898-1970 *ConAu P-2*
Pound, Omar S 1926- *ConAu 1NR, –49*
Pounds, Norman John Greville 1912- *ConAu 1R,*

Pratt, Keith L 1938- *ConAu 29R*
Pratt, Mildred Claire 1921- *WrDr 84*
Pratt, Minnie Bruce *DrAP&F 83*
Pratt, Ned *CreCan 2*
Pratt, Rhona Olive 1903- *IntAu&W 82*
Pratt, Robert Cranford 1926- *ConAu 101*
Pratt, Theodore 1901-1969 *ConAu 1R, –4NR, TwCA SUP*
Pratt, Viola Leone 1892- *WrDr 84*
Pratt, William Crouch, Jr. 1927- *ConAu 6NR, –13R, IntWWP 82*
Pratt, Willis Winslow 1908- *ConAu 105*
Pratt-Butler, Grace Kipp 1916- *ConAu 103*
Pratte, Richard 1929- *ConAu 93*
Prattis, Percival L 1895-1980 *ConAu 97*
Prawer, Joshua 1917- *ConAu 41R*
Prawer, S S 1925- *ConAu 103*
Prawer, Siegbert Salomon 1925- *IntAu&W 82*
Praz, Mario 1896-1982 *CIDMEL 80, ConAu 101, –106, IntAu&W 82, LongCTC, TwCA SUP*
Prchal, Mildred 1895-1983 *ConAu 109*
Prebble, John 1915- *WrDr 84*
Prebble, John Edward Curtis 1915- *ConAu 3NR, –5R, DcLEL 1940, IntAu&W 82, TwCWW*
Prebble, Marjorie Mary Curtis 1912- *ConAu 17R*
Prebish, Charles S 1944- *ConAu 57*
Preble, Duane 1936- *ConAu 61*
Preda, Marin 1922- *CIDMEL 80*
Predmore, Michael 1938- *ConAu 45*
Predmore, Richard L 1911- *ConAu 17R*
Preece, Harold 1906- *ConAu 5R*
Preedy, George *TwCCr&M 80, TwCRGW*
Preedy, George Runnell 1886-1952 *LongCTC, TwCA, TwCA SUP, TwCWr*
Preeg, Ernest Henry 1934- *ConAu 33R, WrDr 84*
Prefontaine, Claude *CreCan 2*
Pregel, Boris 1893-1976 *ConAu 106*
Pregelj, Ivan 1883-1960 *CIDMEL 80*
Preger, Paul D, Jr. 1926- *ConAu 49*
Preheim, Marion Keeney 1934- *ConAu 25R*
Preil, Gabriel 1911- *ConAu 1NR, –49*
Preiser, Wolfgang F E 1941- *ConAu 7NR, –57*
Preiss, Byron *ConAu 69*
Preiss, David 1935- *ConAu 69*
Prelinger, Ernst 1926- *ConAu 9R*
Prelutsky, Jack *ConAu 93, SmATA 22[port]*
Prelutsky, Jack 1940- *TwCCW 83*
Prem, Dhani 1904?-1979 *ConAu 93*
Prem Chand 1880-1936 *ModCmwL*
Premack, Ann J 1929- *ConAu 57*
Preminger, Alex 1915- *ConAu 13R*
Preminger, Erik Lee 1944- *IntAu&W 82*
Preminger, Marion Mill 1913-1972 *ConAu 33R*
Preminger, Otto 1906- *ConAu 110*
Premont, Henri 1933- *IntWWP 82*
Premont, Brother Jeremy *ConAu X*
Prentice, Ann E 1933- *ConAu 6NR, –57*
Prentice, Penelope *DrAP&F 83*
Prenting, Theodore O 1933- *ConAu 57*
Prentiss, Augustin M 1890-1977 *ConAu 69*
Presberg, Miriam *WrDr 84*
Presberg, Miriam Goldstein 1919-1978 *ConAu 1R, –3NR*
Prescott, Allen 1904?-1978 *ConAu 73*
Prescott, Caleb *ConAu X, TwCWW*
Prescott, Dorothea Mildred 1904- *IntAu&W 82*
Prescott, Frederick 1904- *WrDr 84*
Prescott, G W 1899- *WrDr 84*
Prescott, Hilda Frances Margaret 1896- *LongCTC, TwCA SUP*
Prescott, J R V 1931- *ConAu 107, WrDr 84*
Prescott, John Brewster 1919- *ConAu 5R, TwCWW*
Prescott, Kenneth W 1920- *ConAu 8NR, –57*
Prescott, Orville 1906- *ASpks, ConAu 41R*
Prescott, Peter S 1935- *ConAu 37R*
Preshing, W A 1929- *ConAu 85*
Preslan, Kristina 1945- *ConAu 106*
Presland, John 1889-1975 *ConAu X*
Presley, James 1930- *ConAu 10NR, –21R*
Press, Charles 1922- *ConAu 6NR, –13R*
Press, John 1920- *WrDr 84*
Press, John Bryant 1920- *ConAu 3NR, –9R, DcLEL 1940, IntAu&W 82, IntWWP 82, WorAu*
Press, O Charles 1922- *IntAu&W 82, WrDr 84*
Press, Simone Juda *DrAP&F 83*
Press, Simone Juda 1943- *IntWWP 82X, MichAu 80*

Press, Simone Naomi 1943- *IntWWP 82*
Press, Toni 1949- *ConAu 108, NatPD 81[port]*
Pressau, Jack Renard 1933- *ConAu 77*
Pressburger, Emeric 1902- *ConAu 104*
Presseisen, Ernst L 1928- *ConAu 13R*
Presser, Helmut 1914- *IntAu&W 82*
Presser, Jacob 1899-1970 *ConAu P-2*
Presser, Janice 1946- *ConAu 107*
Pressly, Thomas J 1919- *ConAu 17R*
Pressman, David 1937- *ConAu 89*
Pressman, Jeffrey L 1943- *ConAu 3NR, –45*
Pressnell, Constance Elizabeth *CreCan 2*
Prest, Alan Richmond 1919- *ConAu 93, IntAu&W 82, WrDr 84*
Prestbo, John A 1941- *ConAu 2NR, –49*
Prester John *LongCTC*
Prestera, Hector A 1932- *ConAu 65*
Presthus, Robert 1917- *ConAu 1R, –5NR*
Prestia, Phyllis S 1948- *IntWWP 82*
Prestidge, Pauline 1922- *ConAu 103*
Preston, Dickson J 1914- *ConAu 8NR, –61*
Preston, Edward *ConAu X*
Preston, Florence Margaret 1905- *ConAu 103, WrDr 84*
Preston, Frances I 1898- *ConAu 61*
Preston, Harry 1923- *ConAu 57*
Preston, Ivan L 1931- *ConAu 57*
Preston, Ivy 1913- *TwCRGW, WrDr 84*
Preston, Ivy Alice 1914- *ConAu P-1*
Preston, James *ConAu X*
Preston, James 1913- *ConAu P-1*
Preston, James J 1941- *ConAu 109*
Preston, James Ralph 1947- *IntAu&W 82*
Preston, John Hyde 1906-1980 *ConAu 102*
Preston, Lee E 1930- *ConAu 11NR, –21R*
Preston, Lillian Elvira 1918- *ConAu 108*
Preston, Nathaniel Stone 1928- *ConAu 29R*
Preston, Ralph C 1908- *ConAu 6NR, –13R*
Preston, Reginald Dawson 1908- *WrDr 84*
Preston, Richard *ConAu X, WrDr 84*
Preston, Richard 1910- *WrDr 84*
Preston, Richard Arthur 1910- *ConAu 3NR, –5R, IntAu&W 82*
Preston, Thomas R 1936- *ConAu 109*
Preston, William L 1949- *ConAu 105*
Prestwich, Menna 1917- *ConAu 21R*
Prestwidge, Kathleen J 1927- *LivgBAA*
Preto-Rodas, Richard 1936- *ConAu 49*
Pretorius, Hertha *ConAu X*
Pretre *IntAu&W 82X*
Pretre-DeLuigi, Anne Catherine 1948- *IntAu&W 82*
Prettyman, E Barrett, Jr. 1925- *ConAu 9R*
Preus, Anthony 1936- *ConAu 49*
Preus, Herman Amberg 1896- *ConAu 85*
Preus, Jacob A O 1920- *ConAu 33R*
Preus, Robert 1924- *ConAu 33R*
Preuss, Helmut *IntAu&W 82X*
Preussler, Otfried 1923- *ConAu 77, ConLC 17, SmATA 24[port]*
Prevelakis, Pandelis G 1909- *WorAu*
Prevert, Jacques 1900-1977 *CIDMEL 80, CnMWL, ConAu 69, –77, ConLC 15, ModFrL, SmATA 30N, TwCWr, WorAu*
Prevost, Alain 1930?-1971 *ConAu 33R*
Prevost, Andre 1934- *CreCan 2*
Prevost, Jean 1901-1944 *CIDMEL 80*
Prevost, Marcel 1862-1941 *TwCA, TwCA SUP*
Prevost, Robert *CreCan 1*
Prewitt, Kenneth 1936- *ConAu 29R, WrDr 84*
Prezihov, Voranc 1893-1950 *CIDMEL 80, ModSL 1*
Preziosi, Donald 1941- *ConAu 93*
Prezzolini, Giuseppe 1882- *CIDMEL 80*
Prezzolini, Giuseppi 1882-1982 *ConAu 107*
Pribam, Kar 1878?-1973 *ConAu 41R*
Pribichevich, Stoyan 1905?-1976 *ConAu 65*
Pribram, Karl Harry *WrDr 84*
Price, Alfred 1936- *ConAu 9NR*
Price, Alfred Walter 1936- *ConAu 21R, IntAu&W 82*
Price, Alice *DrAP&F 83*
Price, Alice 1910?- *IntWWP 82*
Price, Anthony 1928- *ConAu 77, IntAu&W 82, TwCCr&M 80, WrDr 84*
Price, Archibald Grenfell 1892- *ConAu 9R*
Price, Arnold H 1912- *ConAu 45*
Price, Barbara Pradal *ConAu 103*
Price, Beverley *WrDr 84*
Price, Beverley Joan 1931- *ConAu 106*
Price, Bruce D 1941- *ConAu 25R*

Price, Byron 1891-1981 *ConAu 104*
Price, Cecil 1915- *ConAu 21R, IntAu&W 82, WrDr 84*
Price, Charles 1925- *ConAu 9R*
Price, Charles C 1913- *ConAu 107*
Price, Christine Hilda 1928-1980 *ConAu 4NR, –5R, –93, SmATA 23N, –3*
Price, Daniel O 1918- *ConAu 21R*
Price, David Deakins 1902-1983 *ConAu 110*
Price, Derek DeSolla 1922- *ConAu 1R, –3NR, WrDr 84*
Price, Derek DeSolla 1922-1983 *ConAu 110*
Price, Don C 1937- *ConAu 81*
Price, Don K 1910- *ConAu 73*
Price, E Hoffman 1898- *ConAu 10NR*
Price, E Hoffmann 1898- *ConAu 61*
Price, Edward Reynolds 1933- *DcLEL 1940*
Price, Edwin Currmie *DrAP&F 83*
Price, Emerson 1902?-1977 *ConAu 104*
Price, Eugenia 1916- *ConAu 2NR, –5R*
Price, Evadne 1896- *TwCCW 83, TwCRGW*
Price, Frances Brown 1895- *ConAu 49, IntWWP 82*
Price, Francis Wilson 1895-1974 *ConAu P-1*
Price, Frank James 1917- *ConAu 104*
Price, Frank W *ConAu X*
Price, Garrett 1896-1979 *ConAu 85, SmATA 22N*
Price, George 1901- *ConAu 103*
Price, George 1910- *ConAu P-1*
Price, George R 1909- *ConAu 1R, –4NR*
Price, Glenn W 1918- *ConAu 21R*
Price, J H 1924- *ConAu 25R*
Price, Jacob M 1925- *ConAu 1NR, –45*
Price, James Ligon, Jr. 1915- *ConAu 1R, WrDr 84*
Price, Jennifer *ConAu X, SmATA X, WrDr 84*
Price, Jimmie *ConAu X*
Price, John A 1933- *ConAu 7NR, –57*
Price, John Leslie 1942- *WrDr 84*
Price, John Valdimir 1937- *ConAu 17R*
Price, Jonathan *DrAP&F 83*
Price, Jonathan Reeve 1941- *ConAu 3NR, –45*
Price, Joseph Henry 1924- *WrDr 84*
Price, Ken 1924- *IntWWP 82*
Price, Kingsley Blake 1917- *ConAu 21R, WrDr 84*
Price, Leo 1941- *ConAu 77*
Price, Lucie Locke 1904- *ConAu X, IntWWP 82, SmATA X*
Price, Margaret 1888-1973 *ConAu 109*
Price, Margaret Evans 1888-1973 *SmATA 28*
Price, Marjorie 1929- *ConAu 53*
Price, Martin 1920- *ConAu 17R*
Price, Miles Oscar 1890-1968 *ConAu P-1*
Price, Morgan Philips 1885-1973 *ConAu P-1*
Price, Nancy *DrAP&F 83*
Price, Nelson Lynn 1931- *ConAu 8NR, –61*
Price, Olive M 1903- *ConAu 41R, SmATA 8*
Price, R F 1926- *ConAu 29R*
Price, Ray 1931- *ConAu 25R*
Price, Ray Glenn 1903- *ConAu 2NR, –5R*
Price, Raymond 1930- *ConAu 105*
Price, Reynolds *DrAP&F 83*
Price, Reynolds 1933- *ConAu 1R, –1NR, ConLC 3, –6, –13, ConNov 82, DcLB 2, WorAu, WrDr 84*
Price, Rhys *ConAu X*
Price, Richard *DrAP&F 83*
Price, Richard 1941- *ConAu 105*
Price, Richard 1949- *ConAu 3NR, –49, ConLC 6, –12, DcLB Y81B[port]*
Price, Richard G 1910- *WrDr 84*
Price, Richard Geoffrey George 1910- *ConAu P-1, IntAu&W 82*
Price, Robert 1900- *ConAu 33R*
Price, Robert W 1925?-1979 *ConAu 89*
Price, Roger 1921- *ConAu 9R*
Price, Roger 1944- *ConAu 107, IntAu&W 82, WrDr 84*
Price, Ronald Francis 1926- *WrDr 84*
Price, Ruth A 1903- *IntWWP 82*
Price, S David *DrAP&F 83*
Price, S Stephen 1919- *ConAu 25R*
Price, Sally 1943- *ConAu 106*
Price, Stanley 1931- *ConAu 13R, WrDr 84*
Price, Steven D 1940- *ConAu 1NR, –49*
Price, Susan 1955- *ConAu 105, SmATA 25, TwCCW 83, WrDr 84*
Price, V B 1940- *ConAu 69*
Price, Victor 1930- *ConAu 9R, IntAu&W 82,*

WrDr 84
Price, Vincent 1911- ConAu 89
Price, Vincent Barrett DrAP&F 83
Price, Walter K 1924- ConAu 7NR, -17R,
   WrDr 84
Price, Willadene Anton 1914- ConAu 5R
Price, Willard 1887- TwCCW 83, WrDr 84
Price, Willard DeMille 1887- ConAu 1R, -1NR
Price, William DrAP&F 83
Price, William 1938- ConAu 37R
Price, Wilson T 1931- ConAu 37R
Prichard, Caradog 1904-1980 ConAu 103, -97
Prichard, Hesketh Vernon Hesketh- 1876-1922
   TwCA
Prichard, James W 1925- ConAu 13R
Prichard, Katharine Susannah 1884?-1969
   ConAu P-1, TwCWr, WorAu
Prichard, Katherine Susannah 1883-1969
   ModCmwL
Prichard, Nancy S 1924- ConAu 29R
Prichard, Robert Williams 1923- ConAu 89
Prichard, Susan Perez 1953- ConAu 108
Prickett, Alexander Thomas Stephen 1939-
   IntAu&W 82
Prickett, Stephen 1939- ConAu 29R, WrDr 84
Priddy, Frances Rosaleen 1931- ConAu 1R
Pride, Cletis 1925- ConAu 41R
Pride, J B 1929- ConAu 110
Pride, John Bernard 1929- WrDr 84
Prideaux, James 1935- NatPD 81[port]
Prideaux, Tom 1908- ConAu 108
Pridham, Geoffrey 1942- ConAu 97
Pridham, Radost 1922- ConAu 21R
Pries, Johannes Heinrich 1920- IntAu&W 82
Priesand, Sally J 1946- ConAu 65
Priest, Alice L 1931- ConAu 102
Priest, Christopher 1943- ConAu 33R,
   DcLB 14[port], IntAu&W 82, TwCSFW,
   WrDr 84
Priest, Harold Martin 1902- ConAu 73
Priest, Joan Frances 1920- IntAu&W 82
Priestley, Barbara 1937- ConAu 33R
Priestley, F E L 1905- ConAu 21R
Priestley, Harold Edford 1901- ConAu 73,
   IntAu&W 82
Priestley, J B 1894- ConAu 9R, ConDr 82,
   ConLC 2, -5, -9, CroCD,
   DcLB 10[port], LongCTC, ModBrL,
   ModBrL SUP, ModWD, TwCCr&M 80,
   TwCSFW, TwCWr, WhoTwCL, WrDr 84
Priestley, John Boynton 1894- CnMD,
   IntAu&W 82, TwCA, TwCA SUP
Priestley, Lee 1904- ConAu 2NR, -5R,
   SmATA 27[port]
Priestley, Mary 1925- ConAu 61
Prieto, Antonio 1930- CIDMEL 80
Prieto, Mariana Beeching 1912- ConAu 5R,
   -5NR, SmATA 8, WrDr 84
Prigmore, Charles S 1919- ConAu 45
Prigogine, Helene 1921- IntWWP 82X
Priley, Margaret Hubbard 1909- ConAu 1R
Prill, Felician 1904- ConAu 103, IntAu&W 82
Primack, Joel 1945- ConAu 61
Prime, C T 1909-1979 ConAu 3NR, -49
Prime, Derek 1931- ConAu 108,
   SmATA 34[port]
Prime, Derek James 1931- WrDr 84
Primeau, Ronald 1946- ConAu 108
Primeaux, Walter J, Jr. 1928- ConAu 41R
Primm, James Neal 1918- ConAu 45
Primm, Brother Orrin ConAu X
Primmer, Phyllis 1926- WrDr 84
Primmer, Phyllis Griesbach 1926- ConAu 5R
Primo, Albert T 1935- ConAu 73
Primrose, William 1904-1982 ConAu 106
Prince, Alison 1931- ConAu 29R,
   SmATA 28[port]
Prince, Carl E 1934- ConAu 21R
Prince, Don 1905?-1983 ConAu 110
Prince, F T 1912- ConAu 101, ConLC 22[port],
   ConP 80, WrDr 84
Prince, Frank Templeton 1912- DcLEL 1940,
   IntAu&W 82, IntWWP 82, ModBrL,
   TwCWr, WorAu
Prince, Gary Michael 1948- ConAu 89
Prince, Gerald 1942- ConAu 57
Prince, J H 1908- ConAu 81, SmATA 17
Prince, Peter 1942- WrDr 84
Prince, Thomas Richard 1934- ConAu 13R
Princess Grace ConAu X
Principe, Quirino 1935- IntAu&W 82

Prindl, A R 1939- ConAu 69
Pring, Julian Talbot 1913- ConAu 5R
Pring-Mill, Robert D F 1924- ConAu 9R
Pringle, Henry Fowles 1897-1958 TwCA,
   TwCA SUP
Pringle, John 1912- WrDr 84
Pringle, John Martin Douglas 1912- ConAu 13R
Pringle, Laurence P 1935- ChlLR 4[port],
   ConAu 29R, SmATA 4
Pringle, Mia Kellmer ConAu 65, IntAu&W 82,
   WrDr 84
Pringle, Mia Kellmer 1920?-1983 ConAu 109
Pringle, Peter 1940- ConAu 69
Printz, Peggy 1945- ConAu 73
Prinz, Joachim 1902- ConAu P-1
Priolo, Pauline Pizzo 1907- ConAu 1R
Prior, A N 1914-1969 ConAu 1R, -3NR
Prior, Allan 1922- ConAu 10NR, -65,
   IntAu&W 82, TwCCr&M 80, WrDr 84
Prior, Ann 1949- ConAu 25R
Prior, James 1851-1922 TwCA
Prior, Kenneth Francis William 1926-
   ConAu 17R, WrDr 84
Prisco, Michele 1920- CIDMEL 80, ConAu 53
Prisco, Salvatore, III 1943- ConAu 61
Prishvin, Mikhail Mikhailovich 1873-1954
   CnMWL, ModSL 1, TwCWr
Prishvin, Mikhail Mikhaylovich 1873-1954
   CIDMEL 80
Prising, Robin 1933- ConAu 57
Prisman, Jessie WrDr 84
Pritchard, Arnold 1949- ConAu 97
Pritchard, J Harris 1923- ConAu 21R
Pritchard, James Bennett 1909- ConAu 5R
Pritchard, John Paul 1902- ConAu 9R
Pritchard, John Wallace WrDr 84
Pritchard, John Wallace 1912- ConAu 81,
   IntAu&W 82
Pritchard, Katharine Susannah LongCTC
Pritchard, Leland J 1908- ConAu P-1
Pritchard, Norman Henry, II DrAP&F 83
Pritchard, Norman Henry, II 1939- ConAu 77,
   LivgBAA
Pritchard, R E 1936- ConAu 37R
Pritchard, R John 1945- WrDr 84
Pritchard, Ronald Edward 1936- WrDr 84
Pritchard, Sheila 1909- ConAu P-1
Pritchard, William H 1932- ConAu 65
Pritchard Jones, Harri Elwyn 1933-
   IntAu&W 82
Pritchett, C Herman 1907- ConAu 1R, -3NR
Pritchett, Elaine H 1920- ConAu 108
Pritchett, John Perry 1902- ConAu 1R
Pritchett, V S 1900- ASpks, ConLC 13, -15,
   ConLCrt 82, ConNov 82, DcLB 15[port],
   WrDr 84
Pritchett, Victor Sawdon 1900- ConAu 61,
   ConLC 5, IntAu&W 82, LongCTC,
   ModBrL, ModBrL SUP, TwCA SUP,
   TwCWr, WhoTwCL
Pritchett, W Kendrick 1909- ConAu 97
Pritikin, Nathan 1915- ConAu 89, WrDr 84
Pritikin, Robert C 1929- ConAu 104
Pritikin, Roland I 1906- WrDr 84
Prittie, Terence 1913- WrDr 84
Prittie, Terence Cornelius Farmer 1913-
   ConAu 1R, -4NR, IntAu&W 82
Priyamvada, Usha ConAu X
Probert, Walter 1925- ConAu 77
Probst, Jacques 1951- IntAu&W 82
Probst, Leonard 1921-1982 ConAmTC,
   ConAu 106, -65
Procassion, Michael WrDr 84
Prochaska, Robert DrAP&F 83
Prochnau, William W 1937- ConAu 33R
Prochnow, Herbert V, Jr. 1931- ConAu 110
Prochnow, Herbert Victor 1897- ConAu 1R,
   -4NR, IntAu&W 82, WrDr 84
Prockter, Noel James 1910- WrDr 84
Procktor, Richard 1933- ConAu 53
Procopio, Mariellen ConAu X
Procter, Ben H 1927- ConAu 5R, -9NR
Procter, E E S 1897-1980 ConAu 97
Procter, Maurice 1906-1973 TwCCr&M 80
Proctor, Charles S 1925- ConAu 29R
Proctor, Dennis 1905-1983 ConAu 110
Proctor, Dorothea Hardy 1910- ConAu 61
Proctor, E E S 1897-1980 ConAu 103
Proctor, Elsie 1902- ConAu 29R
Proctor, Everett ConAu X, SmATA 3,
   TwCCW 83, WrDr 84

Proctor, Lillian Cummins 1900- ConAu P-2
Proctor, Priscilla 1945- ConAu 65
Proctor, Raymond Lambert 1920- ConAu 45
Proctor, Roy ConAmTC
Proctor, Samuel 1919- ConAu 3NR, -9R
Proctor, Samuel Dewitt 1921- LivgBAA
Proctor, Thelwall 1912- ConAu 29R, WrDr 84
Proctor, William Gilbert, Jr. 1941- ConAu 37R,
   WrDr 84
Prodan, Mario 1911- ConAu 9R
Professor Zingara SmATA X
Proffer, Carl R 1938- ConAu 41R
Proffer, Ellendea C 1944- ConAu 1NR, -45,
   IntAu&W 82
Proffitt, Charles G 1896-1982 ConAu 108
Profile IntWWP 82X
Proger, Samuel 1906- ConAu 106
Prohias, Antonio 1921- ConAu 104
Prokasy, William F 1930- ConAu 49
Prokhovnik, Simon Jacques 1920- ConAu 107,
   WrDr 84
Prokofiev, Aleksandr Andreyevich 1900-1971
   ConAu 33R
Prokofiev, Camilla Gray 1938?-1971 ConAu 33R
Prokop, Phyllis Stillwell 1922- ConAu 9NR,
   -21R
Prokopczyk, Czeslaw 1935- ConAu 108
Prokosch, Frederic DrAP&F 83
Prokosch, Frederic 1908- ConAu 73, ConLC 4,
   ConNov 82, ConP 80, LongCTC, TwCA,
   TwCA SUP, WrDr 84
Prokosch, Frederic 1909- ConAmA
Prole, Lozania ConAu X, IntAu&W 82X,
   TwCRGW, WrDr 84
Pronin, Alexander 1927- ConAu 49
Pronko, Leonard Cabell 1927- ConAu 1R, -1NR
Pronko, N Henry 1908- ConAu 9R
Pronzini, Bill 1943- ConAu 1NR, -49,
   TwCCr&M 80, WrDr 84
Proops, Marjorie WrDr 84
Propes, Stephen Charles 1942- ConAu 1NR
Propes, Steve ConAu X
Propper, Dan DrAP&F 83
Propper, Dan 1937- ConAu 104,
   DcLB 16[port], IntWWP 82X
Propper, Daniel Thomas 1937- IntWWP 82
Propper, Milton 1906-1962 TwCCr&M 80
Prorok, Leszek 1919- IntAu&W 82
Prosch, Harry 1917- ConAu 13R, WrDr 84
Prose, Francine 1947- ConAu 109
Prosen, Rose Mary DrAP&F 83
Proske, Beatrice Gilman 1899- ConAu P-1
Prosper, John ConAu X
Prosper, Lincoln ConAu X
Pross, Harry 1923- IntAu&W 82
Pross, Helge 1927- IntAu&W 82
Prosser, Eleanor 1922- ConAu 1R
Prosser, H L DrAP&F 83
Prosser, H L 1944- ConAu 77, IntAu&W 82,
   WrDr 84
Prosser, Michael H 1936- ConAu 25R
Prostano, Emanuel Theodore, Jr. 1931-
   ConAu 29R
Prosterman, Roy L 1935- ConAu 57
Prothero, Sir George Walter 1848-1922 TwCA
Prothero, R Mansell 1924- ConAu 41R
Prothero, Rowland Edmund 1852?-1937 TwCA,
   TwCA SUP
Prothro, Edwin Terry 1919- ConAu 53
Prothro, James W 1922- WrDr 84
Prothro, James Warren 1922- ConAu 5R, -8NR
Protopapas, George 1917- ConAu 57
Prou, Suzanne 1920- ConAu 33R
Proudfoot, J J 1918- ConAu 21R
Proujan, Carl 1929- ConAu 81
Proussis, Costas M 1911- ConAu 41R,
   IntAu&W 82
Proust, Marcel 1871-1922 CIDMEL 80,
   CnMWL, ConAu 104, LongCTC, ModFrL,
   ModRL, TwCA, TwCA SUP,
   TwCLC 7[port], TwCWr, WhoTwCL
Prout, William Leslie 1922- ConAu 9R
Prouty, L Fletcher 1917- ConAu 45
Prouty, Morton D, Jr. 1918- ConAu 1R
Prouty, Olive Higgins 1882-1974 ConAu 9R, -49,
   TwCA, TwCA SUP
Prouvost, Jean 1885-1978 ConAu 89
Provensen, Alice 1918- ConAu 5NR, -53,
   SmATA 9
Provensen, Martin 1916- ConAu 5NR, -53,
   SmATA 9
Providence, Wayne DrAP&F 83

Putter, Irving 1917- *ConAu 65*
Putterman, Ron 1946- *ConAu 108*
Puttner, Mario 1916- *IntWWP 82*
Putz, Louis J 1909- *ConAu P-1*
Putzar, Edward 1930- *ConAu 41R*
Putzel, Max 1910- *ConAu 9R*
Putzel, Michael 1942- *ConAu 73*
Puxon, Grattan 1939- *ConAu 81*
Puzdrowski, Edmund Franciszek 1942-
    IntAu&W 82
Puzo, Mario *DrAP&F 83*
Puzo, Mario 1920- *ConAu 4NR, –65, ConLC 1,*
    –2, –6, ConNov 82, DcLB 6, DcLEL 1940,
    WorAu 1970, WrDr 84
Pyatt, Edward Charles 1916- *IntAu&W 82,*
    WrDr 84
Pybus, Rodney 1938- *ConAu 107, ConP 80,*
    WrDr 84
Pye, David 1932- *ConAu 25R*
Pye, Lloyd 1946- *ConAu 77*
Pye, Lucian Wilmot 1921- *ConAu 21R*
Pye, Michael 1946- *WrDr 84*
Pye, Norman 1913- *ConAu 109*
Pye, Virginia 1901- *TwCCW 83, WrDr 84*
Pyk, Ann Phillips 1937- *ConAu 77*
Pyke, Helen Godfrey 1941- *ConAu 29R*
Pyke, Magnus 1908- *ConAu 6NR, –13R,*
    WrDr 84
Pyle, Ernest Taylor 1900-1945 *TwCA SUP*
Pyle, Fitzroy 1907- *ConAu P-2, IntAu&W 82*
Pyle, Hilary 1936- *ConAu 77*
Pyle, Howard 1853-1911 *ConAu 109,*
    SmATA 16
Pyle, William Fitzroy 1907- *WrDr 84*
Pyles, Aitken *ConAu X*
Pyles, Thomas 1905- *ConAu 13R*
Pylyshyn, Zenon W 1937- *ConAu 29R*
Pym, Barbara 1913-1980 *ConAu 97, ConAu P-1,*
    ConLC 13, –19, DcLB 14[port],
    WorAu 1970
Pym, Christopher 1929- *ConAu 13R, WrDr 84*
Pym, Denis 1936- *ConAu 25R*
Pym, Dora Olive 1890- *ConAu P-1*
Pym, Michael 1890?-1983 *ConAu 109*
Pynchon, Thomas *DrAP&F 83*
Pynchon, Thomas 1936- *ModAL, ModAL SUP*
Pynchon, Thomas 1937- *ConAu 13R, ConLC 2,*
    –3, –6, –9, –11, –18, ConNov 82, DcLB 2,
    DcLEL 1940, TwCSFW, WorAu, WrDr 84
Pyne, Mable Mandeville 1903-1969 *ConAu 1R,*
    –103, SmATA 9
Pyne, Stephen J 1949- *ConAu 106*
Pynn, Ronald 1942- *ConAu 85*
Pyper, Nancy Phillips 1893- *CreCan 1*
Pyros, John 1931- *ConAu 77, NatPD 81[port]*

Q

Q *LongCTC*
Qadar, Basheer *ConAu X*
Quackenbush, Margery 1943- *ConAu 73*
Quackenbush, Robert Mead 1929- *ConAu 2NR,*
  −45, SmATA 7
Quade, Quentin Lon 1933- *ConAu 106*
Quagliano, Anthony 1941- *IntWWP 82*
Quagliano, Tony *DrAP&F 83*
Quaife, Milo Milton 1880-1959 *MichAu 80*
Quain, Edwin A 1906?-1975 *ConAu 61*
Quale, G Robina 1931- *ConAu 21R, WrDr 84*
Qualey, Carlton C 1904- *ConAu 77*
Qualter, Terence H 1925- *ConAu 37R,*
  WrDr 84
Quammen, David 1948- *ConAu 29R, SmATA 7*
Quanbeck, Philip A 1927- *ConAu 25R*
Quandt, B Jean 1932- *ConAu 33R*
Quandt, Richard 1930- *WrDr 84*
Quandt, Richard E 1930- *ConAu 45,*
  IntAu&W 82
Quandt, William Bauer 1931- *WrDr 84*
Quandt, William Bauer 1941- *ConAu 29R*
Quantrill, Malcolm 1931- *ConAu 13R*
Quaritch, Bernard 1819-1899 *LongCTC*
Quarles, Benjamin Arthur 1904- *ConAu 1R,*
  −1NR, LivgBAA, SmATA 12
Quarles, John R, Jr. 1935- *ConAu 65*
Quarm, Joan Helana Phelan *ConAmTC*
Quarmby, Arthur 1934- *ConAu 45*
Quarrie, Bruce 1947- *ConAu 103, WrDr 84*
Quarry, Nick *WrDr 84*
Quart, Pere 1899- *ClDMEL 80*
Quartermain, James *ConAu X, WrDr 84*
Quartey, Fred Rex 1944- *IntWWP 82*
Quartey, Leonard Michael 1921- *IntAu&W 82*
Quartey, Rex *IntWWP 82X*
Quasha, George *DrAP&F 83*
Quasimodo, Salvatore 1901-1968 *ClDMEL 80,*
  CnMWL, ConAu 25R, ConAu P-1,
  ConLC 10, LongCTC, ModRL, TwCWr,
  WhoTwCL, WorAu
Quasten, Johannes 1900- *ConAu 9R*
Quatrone, Rich *DrAP&F 83*
Quay, Herbert C 1927- *ConAu 13R*
Quayle, Eric 1921- *ConAu 21R, IntAu&W 82,*
  WrDr 84
Qubain, Fahim I 1924- *ConAu 1R*
Quebedeaux, Richard 1944- *ConAu 73*
Queen, Ellery *ASpks, ConAu X, ConLC 3, −11,*
  LongCTC, TwCA, TwCA SUP,
  TwCCr&M 80, TwCWr, WrDr 84
Queen, Ellery, Jr. *ConAu X, SmATA 3*
Queen, Stuart Alfred 1890- *ConAu 21R*
Queiroz, Rachel De 1910- *ModLAL, TwCWr*
Queller, Donald E 1925- *ConAu 4NR, −53,*
  IntAu&W 82
Queneau, Raymond 1903-1976 *ClDMEL 80,*
  CnMWL, ConAu 69, −77, ConLC 2, −5, −10,
  ModFrL, ModRL, TwCA SUP, TwCWr,
  WhoTwCL
Quenelle, Gilbert 1914- *ConAu 25R*
Quennell, Charles Henry Bourne 1872-1935
  LongCTC, TwCA, TwCA SUP
Quennell, Marjorie 1884-1972 *ConAu 73,*

LongCTC, SmATA 29[port], TwCA,
TwCA SUP
Quennell, Peter 1905- *WrDr 84*
Quennell, Peter Courtney 1905- *LongCTC,*
  ModBrL, TwCA, TwCA SUP, TwCWr
Quentin, Patrick *WrDr 84*
Quentin, Patrick 1912- *ConAu X,*
  TwCCr&M 80, WorAu
Quenzer, Gerlinde 1924- *IntAu&W 82*
Querol Rosso, Leopoldo 1899- *IntAu&W 82*
Query, William T, Jr. 1929- *ConAu 41R*
Quesnell, John G 1936- *ConAu 1NR, −45*
Quest, Erica *TwCRGW, WrDr 84*
Quest, Linda 1935- *ConAu 77*
Quest, Rodney *ConAu P-2*
Quester, George 1936- *ConAu 25R,*
  IntAu&W 82, WrDr 84
Quester, George H 1936- *ConAu 10NR*
Quezada, Abel 1920- *ConAu 5R*
Quibell, Agatha Hunt 1921- *IntAu&W 82,*
  WrDr 84
Quichot, Dona *ConAu X*
Quick, Annabelle 1922- *ConAu 21R, SmATA 2*
Quick, Armand James 1894-1978 *ConAu 73*
Quick, Herbert 1861-1925 *TwCA*
Quick, Orville *IntAu&W 82X*
Quick, Philip *ConAu X*
Quick, Thomas Lee 1929- *ConAu 41R*
Quickel, Stephen 1936- *ConAu 73*
Quiery, William H 1926- *ConAu 21R*
Quigg, Philip W 1920- *ConAu 9R*
Quigless, Helen Gordon 1944- *ConAu 105,*
  LivgBAA
Quigley, Aileen 1930- *ConAu 104*
Quigley, Austin E 1942- *ConAu 101*
Quigley, Carroll 1910-1977 *ConAu 37R, −69*
Quigley, Eileen Elliott *ConAu X*
Quigley, Harold Scott 1889-1968 *ConAu 1R,*
  −103
Quigley, Joan *ConAu 29R*
Quigley, John *WrDr 84*
Quigley, John 1927- *ConAu 17R*
Quigley, John M 1942- *ConAu 107, −110*
Quigley, Martin *DrAP&F 83*
Quigley, Martin 1913- *ConAu 17R*
Quigley, Martin, Jr. 1917- *ConAu 1R*
Quijote, Don *IntAu&W 82X*
Quilici, Folco 1930- *ConAu 105*
Quilico, Louis 1926- *CreCan 2*
Quill *ConAu X*
Quill, Barnaby *ConAu X*
Quill, Gynter Clifford 1915- *ConAmTC*
Quiller, Andrew *ConAu X*
Quiller-Couch, Sir Arthur Thomas 1863-1944
  LongCTC, ModBrL, TwCA, TwCA SUP,
  TwCWr
Quilligan, Maureen 1944- *ConAu 89*
Quimber, Mario *ConAu X*
Quimby, George 1913- *WrDr 84*
Quimby, George Irving 1913- *ConAu 57,*
  MichAu 80
Quimby, Myron J *ConAu 25R*
Quimby, Myrtle 1891- *ConAu P-2*
Quin, Ann 1936-1973 *ConAu 9R, −45, ConLC 6,*

DcLB 14
Quin-Harkin, Janet 1941- *ConAu 81,*
  IntAu&W 82, SmATA 18
Quinan, George *DrAP&F 83*
Quince, Peter *ConAu X*
Quince, Peter Lum *ConAu X*
Quinderpunte, Raoul 1907- *ConAu 85*
Quine, Willard V 1908- *WrDr 84*
Quine, Willard VanOrman 1908- *ConAu 1R,*
  −1NR, WorAu
Quinlan, Red *ConAu X*
Quinlan, Sterling C 1916- *ConAu 5R, −8NR*
Quinley, Harold E 1942- *ConAu 61*
Quinn, A James 1932- *ConAu 29R, WrDr 84*
Quinn, Arthur 1942- *ConAu 110*
Quinn, Arthur Hobson 1875-1960 *TwCA,*
  TwCA SUP
Quinn, Bernetta 1915- *ConAu 105,*
  IntAu&W 82
Quinn, Sister Bernetta *ConAu X, DrAP&F 83*
Quinn, Charles Nicholas 1930- *ConAu 110*
Quinn, David 1909- *WrDr 84*
Quinn, David Beers 1909- *ConAu 77,*
  IntAu&W 82
Quinn, Derry 1918- *WrDr 84*
Quinn, Edward 1932- *ConAu 77*
Quinn, Elisabeth 1881-1962 *SmATA 22[port]*
Quinn, Esther Casier 1922- *ConAu 5R*
Quinn, Francis X 1932- *ConAu 4NR, −9R*
Quinn, Herbert Furlong *WrDr 84*
Quinn, Herbert Furlong 1910- *ConAu P-1*
Quinn, James 1919- *ConAu 13R*
Quinn, James Brian 1928- *ConAu 13R*
Quinn, Jane Bryant 1939- *ConAu 93*
Quinn, John *DrAP&F 83*
Quinn, John Michael 1922- *ConAu 45,*
  IntAu&W 82
Quinn, John Paul 1943- *ConAu 33R*
Quinn, John R 1938- *ConAu 97*
Quinn, Kenneth 1920- *ConAu 25R, WrDr 84*
Quinn, Sister M Bernetta 1915- *ConAu 2NR,*
  −5R
Quinn, Martin *ConAu X*
Quinn, Michael A 1945- *ConAu 45*
Quinn, Niall 1943- *ConAu 108*
Quinn, Peter 1941- *CreCan 1, WrDr 84*
Quinn, R M 1920- *ConAu 21R*
Quinn, Sally 1941- *AuNews 2[port], ConAu 65*
Quinn, Seabury 1889-1969 *ConAu 104, −108*
Quinn, Simon *ConAu X*
Quinn, Susan 1940- *ConAu 103, SmATA X*
Quinn, Terry 1945- *ConAu 101*
Quinn, Vernon 1881-1962 *SmATA X*
Quinn, Vincent 1926- *ConAu 21R*
Quinn, William Arthur 1920- *ConAu 5R*
Quinn, Zdenka 1942- *ConAu 33R*
Quinney, Richard 1934- *ConAu 9NR, −57,*
  WrDr 84
Quinones, Magaly *DrAP&F 83*
Quint, Barbara Gilder 1928- *ConAu 103*
Quint, Bert 1930- *ConAu 69*
Quint, Howard H 1917- *ConAu 97*
Quint, Jeanne *ConAu 49*
Quintal, Claire 1930- *ConAu 13R*

Quintana, Jose 1922- *IntWWP 82*
Quintana, Leroy V *DrAP&F 83*
Quintana, Ricardo 1898- *ConAu 25R*
Quintanilla, Maria Aline Griffith Y D 1921-
  ConAu 9R
Quintero *TwCA, TwCA SUP*
Quintero, Joaquin Alvarez 1873-1944 *LongCTC,*
  ModRL
Quintero, Serafin Alvarez 1871-1938 *CnMD,*
  LongCTC, ModRL
Quinto, Leon 1926- *ConAu 37R*
Quinton, Anthony Meredith 1925- *ConAu 10NR,*
  –21R, WrDr 84
Quirarte, Jacinto 1931- *ConAu 45*
Quirin, G David 1931- *ConAu 9NR, –21R*
Quirin, William L 1942- *ConAu 93*
Quirk, Cathleen *DrAP&F 83*
Quirk, James P 1926- *ConAu 7NR, –57*
Quirk, John Edward 1920- *ConAu 5R,*
  MichAu 80
Quirk, Lawrence Joseph 1923- *ConAu 25R*
Quirk, Paul J 1949- *ConAu 108*
Quirk, Randolph 1920- *ConAu 2NR, –5R,*
  IntAu&W 82, WrDr 84
Quirk, Robert E 1918- *ConAu 1R*
Quiroga, Elena 1919- *CIDMEL 80*
Quiroga, Horacio 1878-1937 *ModLAL*
Quiroga, Malvina Rosa 1900- *IntWWP 82*
Quiroga Clerigo, Manuel 1945- *IntAu&W 82*
Quisling, Vidkun 1887-1945 *LongCTC*
Quispel, Gilles 1916- *ConAu 89*
Quist, Felicia *ConAu X*
Quist, Susan *DrAP&F 83*
Quist, Susan 1944- *AuNews 1, ConAu 57*
Quitslund, Sonya A 1935- *ConAu 1NR, –49*
Quoirez, Francoise 1935- *ConAu 6NR, –49,*
  ConLC 9, WorAu
Quoist, Michel 1921- *ConAu 65*
Quong, Rose Lanu 1879?-1972 *ConAu 37R*
Qureshi, Ishtiaq Husain 1903- *ConAu P-1,*
  WrDr 84

R

R K *ConAmA*

Ra, Jong Oh 1945- *ConAu 85*

Raab, Lawrence *DrAP&F 83*

Raab, Lawrence 1946- *ConAu 65*

Raab, Robert Allen 1924- *ConAu 29R*

Raab, Selwyn 1934- *ConAu 73*

Raack, R C 1928- *ConAu 41R*

Raad, Virginia 1925- *IntAu&W 82*

Ra'anan, Gavriel D 1954?-1983 *ConAu 110*

Ra'anan, Uri 1926- *ConAu 108*

Raat, W Dirk 1939- *ConAu 106*

Rabalais, Maria 1921- *ConAu 61*

Raban, Jonathan 1942- *ConAu 61, ConDr 82B, WrDr 84*

Rabassa, Gregory 1922- *ConAu 2NR, –45*

Rabasseire, Henry *ConAu X*

Rabb, Theodore K 1937- *ConAu 10NR, –21R, WrDr 84*

Rabbie *ConAu X*

Rabbitt, Thomas *DrAP&F 83*

Rabbitt, Thomas 1943- *ConAu 57*

Rabby, Pat *DrAP&F 83*

Rabdau, Marianne *ConAu X*

Rabe, Berniece 1928- *WrDr 84*

Rabe, Berniece Louise 1928- *ConAu 1NR, –49, IntAu&W 82, SmATA 7*

Rabe, David 1940- *ConAu 85, ConDr 82, ConLC 4, –8, DcLB 7[port], DcLEL 1940, ModAL SUP, NatPD 81, WorAu 1970, WrDr 84*

Rabe, Olive H 1887-1968 *ConAu P-2, SmATA 13*

Rabe, Stephen G 1948- *ConAu 108*

Rabearivelo, Jean-Joseph 1901-1937 *TwCWr*

Raben, Joseph 1924- *ConAu 69*

Rabie, Jan Sebastiaan 1920- *ConAu 29R*

Rabikovitz, Dalia 1936- *ConAu 108*

Rabikowitz, Dalyah *ConAu X*

Rabil, Albert, Jr. 1934- *ConAu 10NR, –25R*

Rabin, A I 1912- *ConAu 4NR, –53*

Rabin, Chaim 1915- *ConAu 105, WrDr 84*

Rabin, Edward H 1937- *ConAu 49*

Rabin, Ozer 1921- *IntWWP 82*

Rabindranath Tagore *TwCA, TwCA SUP*

Rabindranath, R *IntWWP 82X*

Rabinovich, Abraham 1933- *ConAu 61*

Rabinovich, Isaiah 1904-1972 *ConAu P-2*

Rabinovitch, Sholem 1859-1916 *ConAu 104*

Rabinovitz, Rubin 1938- *ConAu 21R, WrDr 84*

Rabinow, Paul 1944- *ConAu 61*

Rabinowich, Ellen 1946- *ConAu 106, SmATA 29[port]*

Rabinowicz, Mordka Harry 1919- *ConAu 5R, IntAu&W 82, WrDr 84*

Rabinowitch, Alexander 1934- *ConAu 21R*

Rabinowitch, Eugene 1901-1973 *ConAu 41R, –77*

Rabinowitz, Alan 1927- *ConAu 29R*

Rabinowitz, Ezekiel 1892- *ConAu 25R*

Rabinowitz, Howard Neil 1942- *ConAu 105*

Rabinowitz, Peter MacGarr 1956- *ConAu 104*

Rabinowitz, Sandy 1954- *ConAu 103*

Rabinowitz, Solomon J 1859-1916 *ConAu X, LongCTC, TwCA, TwCA SUP*

Rabins, Peter V 1947- *ConAu 109*

Rabkin, Brenda 1945- *ConAu 101*

Rabkin, Eric S 1946- *ConAu 4NR, –49*

Rabkin, Gerald Edward 1930- *ConAu 105*

Rabkin, Norman C 1930- *ConAu 1R, –4NR*

Rabkin, Richard 1932- *ConAu 33R, WrDr 84*

Raborg, Frederick A, Jr. *DrAP&F 83*

Raborg, Frederick A, Jr. 1934- *ConAu 103, NatPD 81[port]*

Rabow, Gerald 1928- *ConAu 25R, WrDr 84*

Rabowicz, Edmund 1928- *IntAu&W 82*

Raby, Derek 1927- *ConAu 103, ConDr 82B, WrDr 84*

Raby, William L 1927- *ConAu 8NR, –17R*

Race, Jeffrey 1943- *ConAu 37R*

Rachal, Patricia *DrAP&F 83*

Rachel, Naomi *DrAP&F 83*

Rachford, Fred *DrAP&F 83*

Rachleff, Owen S 1934- *ConAu 21R*

Rachlin, Carol K 1919- *ConAu 57*

Rachlin, Harvey 1951- *ConAu 107*

Rachlin, Nahid *ConAu 81, DrAP&F 83*

Rachlis, Eugene 1920- *ConAu 5R*

Rachman, David Jay 1928- *ConAu 57*

Rachman, Stanley Jack 1934- *ConAu 89, WrDr 84*

Rachow, Louis A 1927- *ConAu 57*

Rachwalski, Jerzy 1915- *IntAu&W 82*

Racina, Thom 1946- *ConAu 73*

Rack, Henry Denman 1931- *ConAu 13R, WrDr 84*

Racker, Efraim 1913- *ConAu 89*

Rackham, Arthur 1867-1939 *LongCTC, SmATA 15*

Rackham, George 1914- *WrDr 84*

Rackham, John 1916-1976 *ConAu X, ConSFA, TwCSFW*

Rackham, Thomas W 1919- *ConAu 25R*

Rackin, Phyllis 1933- *ConAu 85*

Rackman, Emanuel 1910- *ConAu 29R*

Rackowe, Alec 1897- *ConAu 25R*

Ractliffe, John Fuller 1910- *WrDr 84*

Radauskas, Henrikas 1910-1970 *CIDMEL 80*

Radavich, David Allen 1949- *IntWWP 82*

Radbill, Samuel X 1901- *ConAu 49*

Radcliff, Alan L 1920- *ConAu 49*

Radcliff, Peter 1932- *ConAu 21R*

Radcliff-Umstead, Douglas 1944- *ConAu 33R, WrDr 84*

Radcliffe, George L 1878?-1974 *ConAu 53*

Radcliffe, Janette *ConAu X, IntAu&W 82X, TwCRGW, WrDr 84*

Radcliffe, Lynn James 1896- *ConAu 1R, IntAu&W 82*

Radcliffe, Virginia *ConAu X*

Raddall, Thomas Head 1903- *ConAu 1R, CreCan 1, IntAu&W 82, TwCWr, WrDr 84*

Raddall, Thomas Head 1913- *ConNov 82*

Radel, John J 1934- *ConAu 29R*

Radelet, Louis A 1917- *ConAu 89*

Rader, Benjamin G 1935- *ConAu 21R*

Rader, Dotson *DrAP&F 83*

Rader, Dotson 1942- *ConAu 11NR, –61*

Rader, John Trout, III 1938- *WrDr 84*

Rader, Melvin Miller 1903-1981 *ConAu 5NR, –13R*

Rader, Ralph Wilson 1930- *ConAu 13R*

Rader, Trout 1938- *ConAu 37R*

Radest, Howard B 1928- *ConAu 41R*

Radford, E 1891- *TwCCr&M 80*

Radford, Edwin Isaac 1891- *ConAu 104*

Radford, John 1901-1967 *ConAu P-2*

Radford, Mona Augusta *TwCCr&M 80*

Radford, Richard F, Jr. *DrAP&F 83*

Radford, Richard F, Jr. 1939- *ConAu 104*

Radford, Ruby Lorraine 1891-1971 *ConAu 1R, –4NR, SmATA 6*

Radhakrishnan, C 1939- *ConAu 57*

Radhakrishnan, Sarvepalli 1888-1975 *ConAu 57, ConAu P-1*

Radice, Betty 1912- *ConAu 25R, IntAu&W 82, WrDr 84*

Radice, Giles 1936- *ConAu 25R*

Radiguet, Raymond 1903-1923 *CIDMEL 80, CnMWL, ModFrL, ModRL, TwCA, TwCA SUP*

Radimsky, Ladislaw 1898-1970 *ConAu 29R*

Radin, Doris *DrAP&F 83*

Radin, Edward D 1909-1966 *WorAu*

Radin, George 1896-1981 *ConAu 102*

Radke, Don 1940- *ConAu 57*

Radl, Shirley L 1935- *ConAu 69*

Radlauer, David 1952- *ConAu 106, SmATA 28[port]*

Radlauer, Edward 1921- *ConAu 69, SmATA 15*

Radlauer, Ruth 1926- *ConAu 81, SmATA 15*

Radler, D H 1926- *ConAu 13R*

Radley, Eric John 1917- *ConAu 109, WrDr 84*

Radley, Gail 1951- *ConAu 89, SmATA 25[port]*

Radley, Sheila *WrDr 84*

Radley, Virginia L 1927- *ConAu 25R*

Radner, Rebecca *DrAP&F 83*

Radner, Roy 1927- *ConAu 49*

Radnoti, Miklos 1909-1944 *CIDMEL 80, WorAu 1970*

Rado, Alexander *ConAu X*

Rado, James *ConDr 82D*

Rado, James 1932- *ConLC 17*

Rado, James 1905- *ConAu 105*

Rado, Sandar 1900-1981 *ConAu 105*

Rado, Sandor 1900-1981 *ConAu 109*

Radoff, Morris Leon 1905-1978 *ConAu 81, –85*

Radom, Matthew 1905- *ConAu 57*

Radosh, Ronald 1937- *ConAu 101*

Radowitz, Stuart P *DrAP&F 83*

Radtke, Guenter 1920- *ConAu 110*

Radtke, Gunter *ConAu X*

Radtke, Gunter 1925- *IntAu&W 82*

Radvanyi, Janos 1922- *ConAu 41R*

Radvanyi, Netty 1900- *ConAu 85*

Radvanyi, Netty 1900-1983 *ConAu 110*

Radwanski, Pierre Arthur 1903- *ConAu P-2*

Radwanski-Szinagel, Pierre A *ConAu X*

Radway, Ann *ConAu X*

Radyr, Tomos *ConAu X*

Radzinowicz, Leon 1906- *ConAu 106, IntAu&W 82, WrDr 84*

Rae, Daphne 1933- *ConAu 109*
Rae, Doris *ConAu P-1, IntAu&W 82X*
Rae, Doris 1907- *WrDr 84*
Rae, Douglas Whiting 1939- *ConAu 77*
Rae, Evonne 1928-1974 *ConAu 104*
Rae, Gwynedd 1892- *ConAu 65*
Rae, Gwynedd 1892-1977 *TwCCW 83*
Rae, Hugh C 1935- *WrDr 84*
Rae, Hugh Crauford 1935- *ConAu 8NR, –17R,
    TwCCr&M 80, TwCRGW*
Rae, John Bell 1911- *ConAu 13R, WrDr 84*
Rae, John Malcolm 1931- *ConAu 1R, –4NR,
    IntAu&W 82, WrDr 84*
Rae, Margaret Doris 1907- *IntAu&W 82*
Rae, Milford Andersen 1946- *ConAu 8NR, –61*
Rae, Rusty *ConAu X*
Rae, Walter 1916- *ConAu 57*
Rae, Wesley D 1932- *ConAu 21R*
Raebeck, Lois 1921- *ConAu 13R, SmATA 5*
Raeburn, Antonia 1934- *ConAu 101,
    IntAu&W 82, WrDr 84*
Raeburn, John 1941- *ConAu 57*
Raeburn, Michael 1940- *ConAu 107*
Raeburn, Michael 1943- *ConAu 103*
Raef, Laura C *ConAu 11NR, –29R*
Raeff, Marc 1923- *ConAu 61*
Rael, Leyla 1948- *ConAu 106*
Raes, Hugo 1929- *IntAu&W 82*
Raeschild, Sheila *DrAP&F 83*
Raeschild, Sheila 1936- *ConAu 105,
    IntWWP 82*
Rafael, Gideon 1913- *ConAu 106*
Rafat, Taufiq 1927- *IntWWP 82*
Raffa, Frederick Anthony 1944- *ConAu 53*
Raffa, Joseph L *DrAP&F 83*
Raffaele, Joseph A 1916- *ConAu 5R, –8NR*
Raffel, Burton *DrAP&F 83*
Raffel, Burton Nathan 1928- *ConAu 7NR, –9R,
    IntAu&W 82, IntWWP 82*
Raffelock, David 1897- *AuNews 1, ConAu P-2*
Rafferty, Kathleen Kelly 1915-1981 *ConAu 103*
Rafferty, Max L 1917-1982 *ConAu 1R, –1NR,
    –107*
Rafferty, Milton 1932- *ConAu 101*
Rafferty, S S 1930- *ConAu X, TwCCr&M 80,
    WrDr 84*
Raftery, Gerald 1905- *ConAu P-1, SmATA 11*
Ragan, David 1925- *ConAu 65*
Ragan, James *DrAP&F 83*
Ragan, Samuel Talmadge 1915- *ConAu 13R*
Ragan, William Burk 1896-1973 *ConAu 1R,
    –2NR*
Ragaway, Martin A 1928- *ConAu 61*
Ragen, Joseph E 1897-1971 *ConAu 33R,
    ConAu P-2*
Ragged Staff *IntAu&W 82X*
Raghavan, Manayath D 1892- *ConAu P-2*
Raghubir Sinh 1908- *IntAu&W 82*
Raglan, Baron 1885-1964 *ConAu X*
Raglan, Lord 1885-1964 *LongCTC*
Raglan, Baron FitzRoy Richard Somerset
    1885-1964 *ConAu 5R, TwCA SUP*
Ragnerstam, Bunny 1944- *IntAu&W 82*
Ragni, Gerome 1942- *ConAu 105, ConDr 82D,
    ConLC 17*
Rago, Henry Anthony 1915-1969 *ConAu P-2,
    WorAu*
Rago, Louis J 1924- *ConAu 9R*
Rago, Louis Von *ConAu X*
Ragosta, Millie J 1931- *ConAu 73*
Ragsdale, Ray Waldo 1909- *ConAu 45*
Ragsdale, W B 1898- *ConAu 73*
Raguin, Yves Emile 1912- *ConAu 81,
    IntAu&W 82*
Rahikainen, Kalevi Ferdinand 1927-
    IntAu&W 82
Rahill, Peter J 1910- *ConAu 5R*
Rahim, Enayetur 1938- *ConAu 107*
Rahl, James A 1917- *ConAu 77*
Rahm, David A 1931- *ConAu 57*
Rahman, Abdul *ConAu X*
Rahmmings, Keith *DrAP&F 83*
Rahn, Joan Elma 1929- *ConAu 37R,
    SmATA 27[port]*
Rahner, Karl 1904- *ConAu 109*
Rahner, Raymond M *ConAu 101*
Rahsepar *ConAu X, IntAu&W 82X*
Rahtjen, Bruce Donald 1933- *ConAu 21R,
    WrDr 84*
Rahv, Betty T 1931- *ConAu 105*
Rahv, Philip 1908-1973 *ConAu X,
    ConLC 24[port], ConLCrt 82, DcLEL 1940,*

ModAL, ModAL SUP, TwCA SUP
Rai, Kul B 1937- *ConAu 105*
Raia, Anthony P 1928- *ConAu 61*
Raickovic, Stevan 1928- *ModSL 2*
Raidy, William Anthony 1925- *ConAmTC*
Raiff, Stan 1930- *ConAu 61, SmATA 11*
Railton, Esther P 1929- *ConAu 101*
Raimond, C E 1862-1952 *LongCTC*
Raimy, Eric 1942- *ConAu 93*
Raimy, Victor 1913- *ConAu 81*
Rain, Douglas *CreCan 1*
Rain, Martha Buhs *CreCan 1*
Raina, Peter 1935- *IntAu&W 82*
Raine, Craig 1944- *ConAu 108, ConP 80,
    WrDr 84*
Raine, Kathleen 1908- *WrDr 84*
Raine, Kathleen Jessie 1908- *ConAu 85,
    ConLC 7, ConP 80, DcLEL 1940,
    LongCTC, ModBrL, ModBrL SUP,
    TwCA SUP, TwCWr, WhoTwCL*
Raine, Norman Reilly 1895-1971 *ConAu 33R*
Raine, Richard *ConAu X*
Raine, William MacLeod 1871-1954 *TwCA,
    TwCA SUP, TwCWW*
Rainer, Dachine 1921- *IntWWP 82*
Rainer, George *ConAu X*
Rainer, Julia *ConAu X*
Raines, Helon *DrAP&F 83*
Raines, Howell 1943- *ConAu 73*
Raines, John C 1933- *ConAu 73*
Raines, Robert A 1926- *ConAu 7NR, –13R*
Rainey, Bill G 1926- *ConAu 89*
Rainey, Buck *ConAu X*
Rainey, Gene Edward 1934- *ConAu 25R,
    WrDr 84*
Rainey, Patricia Ann 1937- *ConAu 49*
Rainham, Thomas *ConAu X*
Rainis, Janis 1865-1929 *CIDMEL 80*
Rainsberger, Todd J 1951- *ConAu 106*
Rainsford, George Nichols 1928- *ConAu 49*
Raintree, Diane *DrAP&F 83*
Raintree, Lee *ConAu X*
Rainwater, Dorothy Thornton 1918- *ConAu 1NR,
    –45, IntAu&W 82*
Rainwater, Lee 1928- *ConAu 53*
Raistrick, Arthur 1896- *ConAu 3NR, –9R*
Raisz, Erwin J 1893-1968 *ConAu 1R, –103*
Raitt, A W 1930- *ConAu 29R*
Raitt, Alan William 1930- *WrDr 84*
Raizis, M Byron 1931- *ConAu 41R*
Raiziss, Sonia *DrAP&F 83*
Raja Rao 1909- *WorAu*
Rajan, Balachandra 1920- *ConAu 69,
    DcLEL 1940, WorAu*
Rajan, M S 1920- *ConAu 13R, WrDr 84*
Rajan, Mannaraswamighala Sreeranga 1920-
    IntAu&W 82
Rajan, Tilottama 1951- *ConAu 107,
    IntAu&W 82, IntWWP 82, WrDr 84*
Rajanen, Aini *ConAu 109*
Rajani, Mom Chao Chand 1910- *IntWWP 82*
Rajaram *IntWWP 82X*
Rajaram, R R *ConAu X*
Rajasekharaiah, T R 1926- *ConAu 33R*
Rajasekharaiah, Tumkur 1926- *WrDr 84*
Rajec, Elizabeth M 1931- *ConAu 109*
Rajneesh, Acharya 1931- *ConAu 93*
Rajneesh, Bhagwan Shree 1931- *ConAu X,
    IntAu&W 82*
Rajput, A B *IntAu&W 82*
Rajski, Raymond B 1917- *ConAu 21R*
Raju, Poolla Tirupati 1904- *ConAu 33R,
    WrDr 84*
Rakel, Robert E 1932- *ConAu 107*
Rakette, Egon 1909- *IntAu&W 82*
Rakic, Milan 1876-1938 *CIDMEL 80, ModSL 2*
Rakine, Marthe *CreCan 2*
Raknes, Ola 1887-1975 *ConAu P-2*
Rakoff, Alvin 1927- *ConAu 102, IntAu&W 82,
    WrDr 84*
Rakosi, Carl *DrAP&F 83*
Rakosi, Carl 1903- *ConAu 21R, ConP 80,
    WrDr 84*
Rakosi, Matyas 1892-1971 *ConAu 29R*
Rakove, Jack N 1947- *ConAu 93*
Rakove, Milton L 1918- *ConAu 65*
Rakowski, James Peter 1945- *ConAu 105*
Rakowski, John 1922- *ConAu 106*
Rakowski, Mieczyslaw F 1926- *IntAu&W 82*
Raksha, Dabe *IntWWP 82X*
Rakshaben Prahladrai, Dave 1946- *IntWWP 82*
Rakstis, Ted J 1932- *ConAu 101*

Ralbovsky, Martin Paul 1942- *ConAu 49*
Rale, Nero *ConAu X*
Raleigh, John Henry 1920- *ConAu 1R, –3NR*
Raleigh, Richard *ConAu X*
Raleigh, Sir Walter Alexander 1861-1922
    LongCTC, TwCA, TwCA SUP
Raley, Harold 1934- *ConAu 41R*
Raley, Patricia E 1940- *ConAu 73*
Ralph, David Clinton 1922- *ConAu 2NR, –5R*
Ralph, Elizabeth K 1921- *ConAu 33R*
Ralph, Wayne Douglas 1946- *IntAu&W 82*
Ralphs, Sheila 1923- *ConAu 106, IntAu&W 82,
    WrDr 84*
Ralston, Alma *ConAu 11NR, –17R*
Ralston, Gilbert A 1912- *ConAu 2NR, –45*
Ralston, James Kenneth 1896- *ConAu 49*
Ralston, Jan *ConAu X,   SmATA 3*
Ralston, Leonard F 1925- *ConAu 45*
Ralston, Melvin B 1937- *ConAu 49*
Ram, Immanuel *ConAu X*
Rama *ConAu X*
Rama Rau, Dhanvanthi 1893- *ConAu 106*
Rama Rau, Santha 1923- *ConAu X, WorAu*
Ramage, Edwin S 1929- *ConAu 65*
Ramage, James A 1940- *ConAu 61*
Ramal, Walter *ConAu X, LongCTC,
    SmATA X*
Ramamurty, K Bhaskara 1924- *ConAu 53*
Ramanujan, A K *DrAP&F 83*
Ramanujan, A K 1929- *ConAu 8NR, –17R,
    ConP 80, IntAu&W 82, WrDr 84*
Ramanujan, Attipat Krishnaswami 1929-
    DcLEL 1940, IntWWP 82
Ramanujan, Molly 1932- *ConAu 29R*
Ramanujan, Shouri *ConAu X*
Ramaswamy, Mysore 1902- *ConAu P-1*
Ramati, Alexander 1921- *ConAu 7NR, –13R*
Ramazani, Rouhollah K 1928- *ConAu 10NR,
    –13R*
Rambam, Cyvia *ConAu X*
Rambam, Myriam *ConAu X*
Rambert, Marie 1888-1982 *ConAu 103, –107*
Rambo, Lewis Ray 1943- *ConAu 109*
Rame, David *ConAu X, IntAu&W 82X*
Ramee, Marie Louise DeLa 1839-1908 *LongCTC*
Rameh, Clea 1927- *ConAu 53*
Ramge, Sebastian Victor 1930- *ConAu 9R,
    WrDr 84*
Ramirez, Alice *DrAP&F 83*
Ramirez, Carolyn H 1933- *ConAu 2NR, –5R*
Ramirez-De-Arellano, Diana *DrAP&F 83*
Ramirez DeArellano, Diana 1919- *ConAu 45*
Ramirez-DeArellano, Diana 1919- *IntWWP 82*
Ramke, Bin *DrAP&F 83*
Ramke, Bin 1947- *ConAu 81*
Ramm, Eva Alfarnaes 1925- *IntAu&W 82*
Rammelkamp, Julian S 1917- *ConAu 17R*
Ramo, Simon 1913- *WrDr 84*
Ramon *TwCA, TwCA SUP*
Ramond, Charles Knight 1930- *ConAu 101*
Ramos, Graciliano 1892-1953 *ModLAL, TwCWr,
    WhoTwCL, WorAu 1970*
Ramos, Suzanne 1942- *ConAu 101*
Ramos-Oliveira, Antonio 1907-1973 *ConAu 104*
Ramp, Eugene A 1942- *ConAu 49*
Rampa, Tuesday Lobsang *ConAu X*
Rampal, Satendra Nath 1928- *IntAu&W 82*
Ramquist, Grace Chapman 1907- *ConAu 3NR,
    –9R*
Ramrus, Al 1930- *ConAu 105*
Rams, Edwin M 1922- *ConAu 17R*
Ramsaur, Ernest Edmondson, Jr. 1915-
    ConAu 41R
Ramsay, Lisa *CreCan 1*
Ramsay, Raymond 1927- *ConAu 77,
    IntAu&W 82*
Ramsay, William M 1922- *ConAu 109*
Ramsbottom, John 1885-1974 *ConAu 53*
Ramsden, E H *ConAu 102, IntAu&W 82,
    WrDr 84*
Ramsden, Herbert 1927- *ConAu 108,
    IntAu&W 82, WrDr 84*
Ramsden, John Andrew 1947- *ConAu 108,
    WrDr 84*
Ramsell, Donald 1926?-1983 *ConAu 110*
Ramsett, David E 1942- *ConAu 29R, WrDr 84*
Ramsey, Arthur Michael 1904- *ConAu 77,
    IntAu&W 82, WrDr 84*
Ramsey, Charles Eugene 1923- *ConAu 13R*
Ramsey, Dan 1945- *ConAu 101*
Ramsey, Eric *ConAu X*
Ramsey, Frederic, Jr. 1915- *ConAu 5R*

Ramsey, G C 1941- ConAu 9NR, –21R
Ramsey, Gordon Clark 1941- WrDr 84
Ramsey, Ian T 1915-1972 ConAu 4NR, –5R
Ramsey, Jarold DrAP&F 83
Ramsey, Jarold 1937- ConAu 33R, IntWWP 82, WrDr 84
Ramsey, John F 1907- ConAu 49
Ramsey, Norman F 1915- WrDr 84
Ramsey, Norman Foster 1915- IntAu&W 82
Ramsey, Paul DrAP&F 83
Ramsey, Paul 1913- ConAu 1NR
Ramsey, Paul 1924- ConAu 41R, ConP 80, IntAu&W 82, IntWWP 82, WrDr 84
Ramsey, Paul W 1905-1976 ConAu 69
Ramsey, Peter 1921- NatPD 81[port]
Ramsey, R Paul 1913- ConAu 1R
Ramsey, Robert D 1934- ConAu 25R
Ramsey, Roy S 1920?-1976 ConAu 65
Ramseyer, John A 1908-1968 ConAu 4NR, –5R
Ramseyer, Lloyd L 1899- ConAu P-2
Ramskill, Valerie Patricia ConAu P-1
Ramson, W S 1933- ConAu 45
Ramundo, Bernard A 1925- ConAu 21R
Ramuz, Charles Ferdinand 1878-1947 CIdMEL 80, ModFrL, ModRL, TwCA SUP, TwCWr, WhoTwCL
Rana, Christina IntAu&W 82X
Rana, J ConAu X, IntAu&W 82X, WrDr 84
Rana Bengtsson, Christina IntAu&W 82
Ranadive, Gail 1944- ConAu 53, SmATA 10
Rand, Ann ConAu 106, SmATA 30[port]
Rand, Austin Loomer 1905- ConAu 89
Rand, Ayn 1905-1982 ConAu 105, –13R, ConLC 3, ConNov 82, TwCA SUP, TwCSFW, WhoTwCL
Rand, Brett ConAu X, WrDr 84
Rand, Christopher 1912-1968 ConAu 77
Rand, Clayton 1891-1971 ConAu 5R, –29R
Rand, Earl 1933- ConAu 21R
Rand, Frank Prentice 1889- ConAu P-1
Rand, J H ConAu X, IntAu&W 82X, WrDr 84
Rand, James S ConAu X
Rand, Paul 1914- ConAu 21R, SmATA 6
Rand, Peter DrAP&F 83
Rand, Peter 1942- ConAu 77
Rand, Sumner G, Jr. 1923- ConAmTC
Rand, Willard J, Jr. 1913- ConAu 9R
Randal, Beatrice 1916- ConAu 61
Randal, Vera 1922- ConAu 9R
Randall, Belle DrAP&F 83
Randall, Belle 1940- IntWWP 82
Randall, Bob 1937- ConAu 106, ConDr 82D, IntAu&W 82, NatPD 81[port]
Randall, Charles Edgar 1897- ConAu 41R
Randall, Clarence Belden 1891-1967 ConAu P-1
Randall, Clay ConAu X, TwCWW, WrDr 84
Randall, Dale B J 1929- WrDr 84
Randall, Dale Bertrand Jonas 1929- ConAu 2NR, –5R, IntAu&W 82
Randall, David Anton 1905-1975 ConAu 57
Randall, Donald A 1933- ConAu 61
Randall, Dudley DrAP&F 83
Randall, Dudley 1914- ConAu 25R, ConLC 1, ConP 80, DcLEL 1940, IntAu&W 82, IntWWP 82, LivgBAA, MichAu 80, WrDr 84
Randall, Florence Engel 1917- ConAu 41R, SmATA 5, TwCRGW, WrDr 84
Randall, Francis Ballard 1931- ConAu 9R, WrDr 84
Randall, James Garfield 1881-1953 DcLB 17[port], TwCA SUP
Randall, Janet WrDr 84
Randall, Janet 1919- ConAu X, IntAu&W 82X
Randall, John E 1924- ConAu 65
Randall, John Herman, Jr. 1899-1980 ConAu 1R, –1NR, –102
Randall, John L 1933- ConAu 107, WrDr 84
Randall, Joseph Hungerford 1897- ConAu 1R
Randall, Julia DrAP&F 83
Randall, Julia 1923- ConAu 33R, ConP 80, WrDr 84
Randall, Laura 1935- ConAu 37R
Randall, Lilian M C 1931- ConAu 21R
Randall, Margaret DrAP&F 83
Randall, Margaret 1936- ConAu 41R, ConP 80, DcLEL 1940, WrDr 84
Randall, Marta 1948- ConAu 107, TwCSFW, WrDr 84
Randall, Mary ConAu X
Randall, Mercedes M 1895-1977 ConAu 13R, –69

Randall, Michael Bennett 1919- IntAu&W 82
Randall, Monica 1944- ConAu 97
Randall, Paula DrAP&F 83
Randall, Randolph C 1900- ConAu 17R
Randall, Robert ConAu X, SmATA X, WorAu 1970, WrDr 84
Randall, Rona TwCRGW, WrDr 84
Randall, Ruth Elaine Painter 1892-1971 ConAu 1R, –103, SmATA 3
Randall, Steven ConAu X
Randall, Willard Sterne 1942- ConAu 69
Randall-Mills, Elizabeth West 1906- ConAu 13R
Randel, William Peirce 1909- ConAu 13R
Randell, Beverley 1931- ConAu X, WrDr 84
Randell, John Bulmer 1918-1982 ConAu 106, –109
Randenborgh, Elisabeth Van 1893- IntAu&W 82
Randhawa, Mohinder Singh 1909- ConAu 29R, DcLEL 1940, IntAu&W 82, WrDr 84
Randles, Anthony V, Jr. 1942- ConAu 65
Randles, Slim ConAu X
Randlev, Karen DrAP&F 83
Randolph, A Philip 1889-1979 ConAu 85
Randolph, Arthur C ConAu X
Randolph, David James 1934- ConAu 3NR, –49
Randolph, Ellen ConAu X
Randolph, Gordon ConAu X
Randolph, John 1915- ConAu 45
Randolph, Marion 1912-1975 ConAu X, TwCCr&M 80
Randolph, Nancy ConAu X
Randolph, Vance 1892- ConAu 105, TwCA SUP
Random, Alan ConAu X
Rands, William Brighty 1823-1882 SmATA 17
Raney, Carolyn IntAu&W 82
Ranga, N G 1900- ConAu 29R
Ranganathan, S R 1892-1972 ConAu 5NR
Ranganathan, Shiyali Ramamrita 1892- ConAu 5R
Range, Willard Edgar Allen 1910- ConAu 1R
Rangel, Carlos 1929- ConAu 104
Rangell, Leo 1913- ConAu 105
Rangely, E R ConAu X
Rangely, Olivia ConAu X, WrDr 84
Ranger, Ken ConAu X
Ranger, Paul 1933- ConAu 37R, WrDr 84
Ranger, T O 1929- ConAu 25R
Rangoonwalla, Firoze J 1933- IntAu&W 82
Ranis, Gustav 1929- ConAu 3NR, –9R, WrDr 84
Ranis, Peter 1935- ConAu 41R
Ranjee ConAu X
Rank, Benjamin 1911- ConAu 109
Rank, Hugh 1932- ConAu 73
Rankin, Caroline 1864-1945 MichAu 80
Rankin, Carroll Watson 1864-1945 MichAu 80
Rankin, Daniel S 1895-1972 ConAu P-1
Rankin, David J 1945- ConAu 108
Rankin, Ernest Harvey, Sr. 1888- MichAu 80
Rankin, Herbert David 1931- ConAu 103, IntAu&W 82, WrDr 84
Rankin, Hugh Franklin 1913- ConAu 1R, –1NR
Rankin, Jeannette 1880-1973 ConAu 41R
Rankin, Judith Torluemke 1945- ConAu 107
Rankin, Judy ConAu X
Rankin, Karl Lott 1898- ConAu P-1
Rankin, Paula DrAP&F 83
Rankin, Paula C 1945- ConAu 104
Rankin, Robert 1915- ConAu 108
Rankin, Robert P 1912- ConAu 77
Rankin, Ruth I 1924- ConAu 61
Rankine, John WrDr 84
Rankine, John 1918- ConAu X, IntAu&W 82X, TwCSFW
Rankine, Paul Scott 1909?-1983 ConAu 109
Ranly, Ernest W 1930- ConAu 37R
Ranney, Agnes V 1916- ConAu 5R, SmATA 6
Ranney, Austin 1920- ConAu 77
Rannit, Aleksis 1914- ConAu 109
Ranous, Charles A 1912- ConAu 13R
Ransel, David Lorimer 1939- ConAu 73
Ransemar, Erik 1926- IntWWP 82
Ransford, Oliver 1914- ConAu 10NR, –21R, WrDr 84
Ransley, Peter 1931- ConAu 69, ConDr 82
Ransohoff, Paul M 1948- ConAu 103
Ransom, Bill DrAP&F 83
Ransom, Bill 1945- ConAu 101
Ransom, Harry Howe 1922- ConAu 9R, IntAu&W 82, WrDr 84
Ransom, Jay Ellis 1914- ConAu 3NR, –9R,

IntAu&W 82, WrDr 84
Ransom, John Crowe 1888-1974 CnMWL, ConAmA, ConAu 5R, –6NR, –49, ConLC 2, –4, –5, –11, –24[port], ConLCrt 82, LongCTC, ModAL, ModAL SUP, TwCA, TwCA SUP, TwCWr, WhoTwCL
Ransom, William Michael 1945- ConAu 108
Ransom, William R 1876-1973 ConAu 37R
Ransome, Arthur 1884-1967 TwCCW 83
Ransome, Arthur Michell 1884-1967 ConAu 73, LongCTC, SmATA 22[port], TwCA, TwCA SUP
Ransome, Eleanor 1915- ConAu 93
Ransome, Stephen TwCCr&M 80
Ransome-Davies, Basil ConAu X
Ranson, Nicholas DrAP&F 83
Ransone, Coleman B, Jr. 1920- ConAu 45
Rant, Tol E ConAu X
Ranum, Orest Allen 1933- ConAu 8NR, –9R
Ranum, Patricia M 1932- ConAu 45
Ranz, James 1921- ConAu 9R
Ranz, Jim ConAu X
Ranzetta, Luan ConSFA
Ranzini, Addis Durning 1909-1983 ConAu 110
Rao, B Shiva 1900?-1975 ConAu 61
Rao, C H Hanumantha 1929- ConAu 7NR
Rao, Hanumantha 1929- ConAu 17R
Rao, R P 1924- ConAu 13R
Rao, Raja 1908- ConNov 82
Rao, Raja 1909- ConAu 73, ConLC 25[port], ModCmwL, WorAu, WrDr 84
Raoul, Anthony ConAu X
Rapaport, Ionel F 1909?-1972 ConAu 37R
Rapaport, Stella F ConAu 1R, SmATA 10
Raper, Arthur Franklin 1899-1979 ConAu 61, –89
Raper, J R 1938- ConAu 33R
Raper, Jack ConAu X
Raphael, Bertram 1936- ConAu 97
Raphael, Chaim 1908- ConAu 85
Raphael, Dan DrAP&F 83
Raphael, Dan 1952- ConAu 104
Raphael, Dana ConAu 61
Raphael, David Daiches 1916- ConAu 2NR, –5R, WrDr 84
Raphael, Elaine 1933- ConAu X, SmATA 23
Raphael, Ellen IntAu&W 82X
Raphael, Frederic 1931- WrDr 84
Raphael, Frederic Michael 1931- ConAu 1R, –1NR, ConDr 82A, ConLC 2, ConNov 82, DcLB 14[port], DcLEL 1940, IntAu&W 82, ModBrL SUP, WorAu
Raphael, Frederick 1931- ConLC 14
Raphael, Frederick Michael DrAP&F 83
Raphael, Jay ConAu X
Raphael, Lennox DrAP&F 83
Raphael, Phyllis DrAP&F 83
Raphael, Phyllis 1938- ConAu 49
Raphael, Phyllis 1940- ConAu 45
Raphael, Rick 1919- ConAu 10NR, –21R, ConSFA, TwCSFW, WrDr 84
Raphael, Robert 1927- ConAu 45
Raphael, Sandra 1939- ConAu 104
Raphaelson, Samson 1896- ConAu 65, TwCA SUP
Raphaelson, Samson 1896-1983 ConAu 110
Rapin, Simone 1901- IntAu&W 82, IntWWP 82
Rapkin, Chester 1918- ConAu 17R
Rapoport, Amos 1929- ConAu 65
Rapoport, Anatol 1911- ConAu 41R, IntAu&W 82
Rapoport, Janis Beth 1946- ConAu 101, IntAu&W 82, IntWWP 82
Rapoport, Rhona 1927- ConAu 8NR, –61
Rapoport, Robert Norman 1924- ConAu 2NR, –5R, WrDr 84
Rapoport, Roger 1946- ConAu 33R, WrDr 84
Rapoport, Ron 1940- ConAu 89
Rapp, Doris Jean 1929- ConAu 37R
Rapp, Joel AuNews 1
Rapp, Lynn AuNews 1
Rapp, Ruth Jensen 1923- IntWWP 82
Rapp, Susan 1944- IntWWP 82
Rappaport, Alfred 1932- ConAu 110
Rappaport, David 1907- ConAu P-2
Rappaport, Eva 1924- ConAu 29R, SmATA 6
Rappaport, Roy A 1926- ConAu 41R
Rappaport, Sheldon R 1926- ConAu 29R
Rappoport, Ken 1935- ConAu 4NR, –53
Rappoport, Leon 1932- ConAu 41R
Rapson, Richard L 1937- ConAu 10NR, –21R, IntAu&W 82, WrDr 84

Redfield, Alden 1941- *ConAu 77*
Redfield, Alfred Clarence 1890-1983 *ConAu 109*
Redfield, Clark *ConAu X*
Redfield, Jennifer *ConAu X*
Redfield, Malissa *ConAu X*
Redfield, Margaret Park 1899?-1977 *ConAu 69*
Redfield, William 1927-1976 *ConAu 69*
Redford, Polly 1925-1972 *ConAu P-2*
Redford, Robert 1937- *ConAu 107*
Redgate, John *ConAu X*
Redgrave, Paul 1920- *ConAu 5R*
Redgrove, Peter 1932- *ConAu 1R, –3NR,*
  ConDr 82B, ConLC 6, ConP 80,
  DcLEL 1940, IntAu&W 82, IntWWP 82,
  WorAu, WrDr 84
Redher, Jessie Clifford 1908-1967 *ConAu P-1*
Reding, Josef 1929- *IntAu&W 82*
Redinger, Ruby V 1915- *ConAu 65*
Redish, Bessie Braid 1905-1974 *ConAu P-2*
Redkey, Edwin S 1931- *ConAu 29R*
Redlich, Frederick Carl 1910- *ConAu 106*
Redman, Ben Ray 1896-1961 *ConAu 93*
Redman, Eric 1948- *ConAu 49*
Redman, Joseph *IntAu&W 82X*
Redman, L A 1933- *ConAu 108*
Redman, Lister Appleton 1933- *WrDr 84*
Redman, Theodore Francis 1916- *WrDr 84*
Redmayne, Barbara *ConAu X, IntAu&W 82X,*
  WrDr 84
Redmayne, John *ConAu X*
Redmayne, Paul Brewis 1900- *ConAu 5R*
Redmon, Anne 1943- *ConAu X,*
  ConLC 22[port]
Redmond, Eugene B *DrAP&F 83*
Redmond, Eugene B 1937- *ConAu 25R,*
  WrDr 84
Redmond, Eugene B 1938- *LivgBAA*
Redmond, Gerald 1934- *ConAu 37R,*
  IntAu&W 82, WrDr 84
Redmond, Howard Alexander *WrDr 84*
Redmond, Howard Alexander 1925- *ConAu 13R*
Redmond, Juanita *ConAu X*
Redmont, Bernard Sidney 1918- *ConAu 73*
Redmont, Dennis Foster 1942- *ConAu 77*
Redner, Harry 1937- *ConAu 110*
Redol, Alves 1911-1969 *CIDMEL 80*
Redpath, Theodore 1913- *ConAu 104*
Redshaw, Thomas Dillon *DrAP&F 83*
Redstone, Louis G 1903- *ConAu 2NR, –49*
Redway, Ralph *ConAu X, LongCTC,*
  SmATA X
Redway, Ridley *ConAu X, SmATA X*
Redwood, Alec *ConAu X*
Redwood, John 1951- *ConAu 102, WrDr 84*
Ree, Jonathan 1948- *ConAu 57*
Reece, Alys 1912- *WrDr 84*
Reece, Benny Ramon 1930- *ConAu 41R,*
  IntAu&W 82
Reece, Jack Eugene 1941- *ConAu 101*
Reeck, Darrell 1939- *ConAu 104*
Reed, A H 1875-1975 *ConAu 4NR*
Reed, A W 1908-1979 *ConAu 4NR*
Reed, Alexander Wyclif 1908- *ConAu 9R,*
  IntAu&W 82
Reed, Alfred Hamish 1875-1975 *ConAu 9R, –57*
Reed, Alison Touster 1952- *ConAu 105*
Reed, Barry Clement 1927- *ConAu 29R*
Reed, Betty Jane 1921- *ConAu 29R, SmATA 4*
Reed, Bobbie Lynn 1944- *ConAu 77,*
  IntAu&W 82
Reed, Carroll E 1914- *ConAu 103*
Reed, Clifford C 1911- *ConSFA*
Reed, Daniel 1892?-1978 *ConAu 77*
Reed, Dennis *DrAP&F 83*
Reed, Don C 1945- *ConAu 106*
Reed, Donald A 1935- *ConAu 103*
Reed, Douglas 1895-1976 *ConAu 103, –89,*
  TwCA, TwCA SUP
Reed, Edward W 1913- *ConAu 29R*
Reed, Eliot *ConAu X, TwCCr&M 80,*
  WrDr 84
Reed, Elizabeth Liggett 1895- *ConAu 77*
Reed, Elizabeth Stewart 1914- *ConAu 1R*
Reed, Emmett X *AuNews 1, ConAu X*
Reed, Evelyn 1905-1979 *ConAu 102,*
  ConIsC 1[port]
Reed, Graham 1923- *ConAu 45*
Reed, Gwendolyn E 1932- *ConAu 25R,*
  SmATA 21, –7
Reed, Harrison Merrick, Jr. 1898- *ConAu 1R*
Reed, Henry 1914- *ConAu 104, ConDr 82B,*
  ConP 80, DcLEL 1940, LongCTC, WorAu,

WrDr 84
Reed, Herbert Owen 1910- *ConAu 53, WrDr 84*
Reed, Howard Alexander 1920- *ConAu 13R*
Reed, Ishmael *DrAP&F 83*
Reed, Ishmael 1938- *ConAu 21R, ConLC 2, –3,*
  –5, –6, –13, ConNov 82, ConP 80, Conv 3,
  DcLB 2, –5[port], DcLEL 1940, LivgBAA,
  ModAL SUP, ModBlW, TwCCr&M 80,
  WorAu 1970, WrDr 84
Reed, J D 1940- *ConAu 33R*
Reed, James 1922- *ConAu 102, WrDr 84*
Reed, James D 1940- *MichAu 80*
Reed, James F 1909- *ConAu P-1*
Reed, John 1887-1920 *ConAu 106, LongCTC,*
  ModAL, TwCA, TwCA SUP,
  TwCLC 9[port]
Reed, John F 1911- *ConAu 13R*
Reed, John L 1938- *ConAu 57*
Reed, John P 1921- *ConAu 65*
Reed, John Q 1918-1978 *ConAu 103, –45*
Reed, John R *DrAP&F 83*
Reed, John R 1938- *ConAu 8NR, –17R*
Reed, John Shelton 1942- *ConAu 5NR, –53*
Reed, Joseph Verner 1902-1973 *ConAu 45*
Reed, Joseph W, Jr. 1932- *ConAu 37R,*
  WrDr 84
Reed, Kenneth 1944- *ConAu 57*
Reed, Kenneth T 1937- *ConAu 73*
Reed, Kit *DrAP&F 83*
Reed, Kit 1932- *ConAu X, SmATA 34[port],*
  TwCSFW, WrDr 84
Reed, Langford 1889-1954 *LongCTC*
Reed, Lillian Craig 1932- *ConAu 1R, –1NR*
Reed, Lou 1944- *ConLC 21[port]*
Reed, Louis S 1902-1975 *ConAu 61*
Reed, Luther Dotterer 1873- *ConAu 5R*
Reed, M N 1905- *ConAu 1R*
Reed, Mark L, III 1935- *ConAu 93*
Reed, Mary Jane 1920- *ConAu 25R*
Reed, Mort 1912- *ConAu 61*
Reed, Nelson A 1926- *ConAu 9R*
Reed, Peter *ConAu X*
Reed, Peter J 1935- *ConAu 53*
Reed, Philip G 1908- *SmATA 29*
Reed, Rex 1938- *ConAmTC, ConAu 9NR, –53,*
  WrDr 84
Reed, Rex 1940- *AuNews 1*
Reed, Robert C 1937- *ConAu 10NR, –65*
Reed, Robert Rentoul, Jr. 1911- *ConAu 33R,*
  IntAu&W 82, WrDr 84
Reed, S Kyle 1922- *ConAu 41R*
Reed, Stanley 1911- *WrDr 84*
Reed, T J 1937- *WrDr 84*
Reed, Talbot Baines 1852-1893 *LongCTC*
Reed, Thomas 1947- *ConAu 103,*
  SmATA 34[port]
Reed, Thomas Harrison 1881-1971 *ConAu 110*
Reed, Thomas Thornton 1902- *ConAu 107,*
  WrDr 84
Reed, Victor 1926- *ConAu 33R*
Reed, Walter Logan 1943- *ConAu 102*
Reed, William Maxwell 1871-1962 *SmATA 15*
Reed, Willis 1942- *ConAu 104*
Reeder, Colonel Red *ConAu X, SmATA X*
Reeder, John P, Jr. 1937- *ConAu 101*
Reeder, Russell Potter, Jr. 1902- *ConAu 1R,*
  –5NR, SmATA 4
Reedstrom, Ernest Lisle 1928- *ConAu 89*
Reedy, George Edward 1917- *ConAu 29R*
Reedy, William A 1916?-1975 *ConAu 61*
Reedy, William James 1921- *ConAu 13R*
Reedy, William Marion 1862-1920 *TwCA*
Reel, A Frank 1907- *ConAu 93*
Reeman, Douglas 1924- *WrDr 84*
Reeman, Douglas Edward 1924- *ConAu 1R,*
  –3NR, DcLEL 1940, SmATA 28
Reems, Harry 1947- *ConAu 61*
Reens, Mary *ConAu X*
Reep, Edward 1918- *ConAu 33R*
Rees, Alan M 1929- *ConAu 106*
Rees, Albert 1921- *ConAu 29R*
Rees, Albert Lloyd George 1916- *WrDr 84*
Rees, Barbara 1934- *ConAu 9NR, –53,*
  IntAu&W 82, WrDr 84
Rees, Brinley Roderick 1919- *IntAu&W 82*
Rees, David 1928- *ConAu 9R, –11NR*
Rees, David 1936- *TwCCW 83*
Rees, David Alway 1932- *WrDr 84*
Rees, David Bartlett 1936- *ConAu 105,*
  IntAu&W 82, WrDr 84
Rees, David Morgan 1904- *ConAu 104*
Rees, Dilwyn *ConAu X, WrDr 84*

Rees, Ennis *DrAP&F 83*
Rees, Ennis 1925- *ConAu 1R, –2NR,*
  IntAu&W 82, IntWWP 82, SmATA 3
Rees, Gomer *DrAP&F 83*
Rees, Goronwy 1909- *ConAu 3NR, –45*
Rees, Helen Christina Easson 1903-1970*
  ConAu 5R, –89
Rees, Henry 1916- *ConAu 107, WrDr 84*
Rees, Ioan Bowen 1929- *ConAu 29R,*
  IntAu&W 82, WrDr 84
Rees, Jean Anglin Sinclair 1912- *ConAu 1R,*
  –1NR
Rees, Joan 1927- *ConAu 25R, WrDr 84*
Rees, Leslie 1905- *ConAu 104, IntAu&W 82,*
  TwCCW 83, WrDr 84
Rees, Lucy 1943- *ConAu 107*
Rees, Margaret A 1933- *ConAu 101*
Rees, Meriel *ConAu X*
Rees, Paul Stromberg 1900- *ConAu 5R,*
  WrDr 84
Rees, Richard 1900-1970 *ConAu 4NR, –5R, –89*
Rees, Robert A 1935- *ConAu 81*
Rees, William 1887-1978? *ConAu 5R, –104*
Rees, William Linford 1914- *IntAu&W 82,*
  WrDr 84
Reese, Alexander 1881-1969 *ConAu 97*
Reese, Algernon B 1896-1981 *ConAu 105*
Reese, Carolyn *LivgBAA*
Reese, Curtis W 1887-1961 *ConAu 110*
Reese, Francesca Gardner 1940- *ConAu 65*
Reese, Gustave 1899-1977 *ConAu 73*
Reese, Heloise 1919-1977 *ConAu 9R, –73*
Reese, Jim E 1912- *ConAu 13R*
Reese, John 1910-1981 *ConAu 102, TwCWW*
Reese, Lizette Woodworth 1856-1935 *ConAmA,*
  LongCTC, TwCA, TwCA SUP
Reese, M M 1910- *ConAu 3NR, –9R, WrDr 84*
Reese, Mason 1966- *ConAu 97*
Reese, Sammy *ConAu 49*
Reese, Samuel Pharr 1930- *ConAu 49*
Reese, Sullivan *WrDr 84*
Reese, Terence 1913- *ConAu 109*
Reese, Thomas J 1945- *ConAu 106*
Reese, Thomas R 1890?-1974 *ConAu 53*
Reese, Trevor Richard 1929- *ConAu 9R*
Reese, William Lewis 1921- *ConAu 8NR, –17R*
Reese, Willis L M 1913- *ConAu 57*
Reeser, Cecilia M 1910- *MichAu 80*
Reesink, Maryke 1919- *ConAu 25R*
Reeve, Arthur Benjamin 1880-1936 *TwCA,*
  TwCA SUP, TwCCr&M 80
Reeve, F D *DrAP&F 83*
Reeve, F D 1928- *ConAu 77, ConP 80,*
  IntWWP 82, WrDr 84
Reeve, Frank D 1899-1967 *ConAu P-1*
Reeve, Franklin Dolier 1928- *ConAu 1R,*
  DcLEL 1940
Reeve, G Joan 1901- *ConAu 13R*
Reeve, Joel *ConAu X, SmATA X, WrDr 84*
Reeve, Richard M 1935- *ConAu 37R*
Reeve, Wilfred Douglas 1895- *ConAu P-1*
Reeve, William Charles 1943- *ConAu 93*
Reeves, Amber *ConAu X*
Reeves, Ambrose 1899-1980 *ConAu 105*
Reeves, Bruce Douglas 1940- *ConAu 11NR*
Reeves, Bruce Douglas 1941- *ConAu 21R*
Reeves, C Thomas 1936- *ConAu 29R*
Reeves, Campbell *DrAP&F 83*
Reeves, Charles Everand 1889- *ConAu 5R*
Reeves, Donald St. George 1952- *ConAu 37R,*
  LivgBAA
Reeves, Dorothea D 1901- *ConAu P-1*
Reeves, Earl J 1933- *ConAu 61*
Reeves, Elton T 1912- *ConAu 29R, WrDr 84*
Reeves, Floyd 1890-1979 *ConAu 89*
Reeves, Gene 1933- *ConAu 61*
Reeves, Gregory Shaw 1950- *ConAu 77*
Reeves, James 1909- *ConAu 5R, DcLEL 1940,*
  SmATA 15, WhoTwCL, WorAu
Reeves, James 1909-1978 *TwCCW 83*
Reeves, Joan Wynn 1910-1972 *ConAu P-2*
Reeves, John *ConDr 82B*
Reeves, John K 1907- *ConAu P-2*
Reeves, Joyce 1911- *ConAu X, IntAu&W 82X,*
  SmATA 17
Reeves, Lawrence F 1926- *ConAu 105,*
  SmATA 29[port]
Reeves, Marjorie E 1905- *WrDr 84*
Reeves, Marjorie Ethel 1905- *ConAu 5NR, –13R,*
  IntAu&W 82
Reeves, Martha Emilie 1941- *ConAu 65*
Reeves, Mavis Mann 1921- *ConAu 45*

Reeves, Nancy 1913- *ConAu 33R*
Reeves, Paschal 1917-1976 *ConAu 81*
Reeves, Richard 1936- *ConAu 69*
Reeves, Richard Ambrose 1899- *IntAu&W 82*,
    WrDr 84
Reeves, Rosser 1910- *ConAu 89*
Reeves, Ruth Ellen *SmATA 6*
Reeves, Thomas C 1936- *ConAu 9NR*,
    WrDr 84
Reeves, Thomas Carl 1939- *ConAu 33R*
Reeves, Thomas Charles 1936- *ConAu 57*
Reeves, William Pember 1857-1932 *TwCWr*
Reff, Theodore Franklin 1930- *ConAu 89*
Refregier, Anton 1905- *ConAu 5R*
Regalado, Nancy Freeman 1935- *ConAu 17R*
Regan, Brad *ConAu X, WrDr 84*
Regan, Cronan 1925- *ConAu 45*
Regan, Donald Thomas 1918- *ConAu 106*
Regan, Jennifer *DrAP&F 83*
Regan, Lewis Michael 1949- *IntWWP 82*
Regan, Richard Joseph 1930- *ConAu 5R*
Regan, Robert 1930- *ConAu 17R*
Regan, Sylvia 1908- *NatPD 81[port]*
Regan, Thomas Howard 1938- *ConAu 104*
Regan, Tom *ConAu X*
Regardie, Israel 1907- *ConAu 85*
Regehr, Lydia 1903- *ConAu 45*
Regelski, Thomas A 1941- *ConAu 57*
Regelson, Abraham 1896- *IntWWP 82*
Regenstein, Lewis 1943- *ConAu 57*
Regenstreif, S Peter 1936- *WrDr 84*
Reger, Roger 1933- *ConAu 21R, WrDr 84*
Reggiani, Renee 1925- *ConAu 85, SmATA 18*
Reghaby, Heydar 1932- *ConAu 29R, WrDr 84*
Regin, Deric Wagenvoort 1915- *ConAu 37R*,
    IntAu&W 82
Reginald *ConAu X*
Reginald, R 1948- *ConAu X*
Reginald, Robert 1948- *IntAu&W 82*
Regio, Jose 1901-1969 *CIDMEL 80*
Regis, Sister Mary 1908- *ConAu P-1*
Register, Willie Raymond 1937- *ConAu 45*
Regler, Gustav 1898- *TwCA, TwCA SUP*
Regnery, Henry 1912- *ConAu 101*
Regnier, Henri Francois Joseph De 1864-1936
    CIDMEL 80, LongCTC, ModFrL
Rego, Jose Lins Do 1901-1957 *ModLAL*
Regosin, Richard L 1937- *ConAu 109*
Regueiro, Helen 1943- *ConAu 104*
Rehak, Peter 1936- *ConAu 77*
Rehberg, Hans 1901-1963 *CnMD, ModWD*
Rehder, Helmut 1905-1977 *ConAu 4NR, -5R*
Rehfisch, Hans Jose 1891-1960 *CnMD, ModWD*
Rehfuss, John Alfred 1934- *ConAu 85*
Rehrauer, George 1923- *ConAu 53*
Reibstein, Regina *DrAP&F 83*
Reich, Bernard 1941- *ConAu 81*
Reich, Charles Alan 1928- *ConAu 108*
Reich, Edward 1903?-1983 *ConAu 109*
Reich, Ilse Ollendorff 1909- *ConAu 49*
Reich, Kenneth 1938- *ConAu 69*
Reich, Peter M 1929- *ConAu 85*
Reich, Richard *NatPD 81[port]*
Reich, Steve 1936- *ConAu 8NR, -61*
Reich, Tova Rachel 1942- *ConAu 103*
Reich, Wilhelm 1897-1957 *TwCA SUP*,
    WhoTwCL
Reichard, Gary Warren 1943- *ConAu 10NR, -61*
Reichard, Robert S 1923- *ConAu 21R*
Reichardt, Jasia 1933- *ConAu 2NR, -5R*
Reichart, Walter A 1903- *ConAu 5R, WrDr 84*
Reiche, Dietlof 1941- *IntAu&W 82*
Reiche, Reimut 1941- *ConAu 41R*
Reichek, Morton A 1924- *ConAu 85*
Reichel, O Asher 1921- *ConAu 45*
Reichenbach, Bruce 1943- *WrDr 84*
Reichenbach, Bruce R 1943- *ConAu 33R*,
    IntAu&W 82
Reichenberger, Arnold G 1903- *ConAu 17R*
Reichert, Herbert W 1917- *ConAu 45*
Reichert, Victor Emanuel 1897- *ConAu 13R*
Reichl, Ernst 1900-1980 *ConAu 102*
Reichl, Ruth 1948- *ConAu 61*
Reichler, Joseph Lawrence 1918- *ConAu 103*
Reichley, A James 1929- *ConAu 1R*
Reichmann, Felix 1899- *ConAu 104*
Reicke, Bo I 1914- *ConAu 13R*
Reid, Alastair 1926- *ConAu 3NR, -5R*,
    ConP 80, WorAu, WrDr 84
Reid, Albert Clayton 1894- *ConAu 53*
Reid, Alfred S 1924-1976 *ConAu 2NR, -45*
Reid, Anthony 1916- *ConAu 29R*

Reid, Barbara *DrAP&F 83*
Reid, Barbara 1922- *ConAu 25R*,
    SmATA 21[port]
Reid, Benjamin Lawrence 1918- *ConAu 17R*
Reid, Charles 1900- *ConAu 101*
Reid, Charles K, II 1912- *ConAu P-1*
Reid, Charles L 1927- *ConAu 37R, WrDr 84*
Reid, Clyde Henderson 1928- *ConAu 25R*,
    IntAu&W 82
Reid, Clyde Henderson, Jr. 1928- *WrDr 84*
Reid, Daphne Kate *CreCan 2*
Reid, Desmond *ConAu X*
Reid, Dorothy M d1974 *ConAu 109*,
    SmATA 29
Reid, E Emmet 1872-1973 *ConAu 45*
Reid, Ela 1907-1982 *ConAu 107*
Reid, Escott 1905- *ConAu 101*
Reid, Eugenie Chazal 1924- *ConAu 13R*,
    SmATA 12
Reid, Forrest 1875?-1947 *LongCTC, ModBrL*,
    TwCA, TwCA SUP
Reid, Frances P 1910- *ConAu 2NR, -5R*,
    WrDr 84
Reid, George Agnew 1860-1947 *CreCan 2*
Reid, H 1925- *ConAu 17R*
Reid, Helen Evans 1911- *WrDr 84*
Reid, Henrietta *TwCRGW, WrDr 84*
Reid, Hilary Fay 1928- *IntAu&W 82*
Reid, Hilda 1898-1982 *ConAu 106*
Reid, Inez Smith *ConAu 49, LivgBAA*
Reid, J C 1916-1972 *ConAu 103*
Reid, James Macarthur 1900-1970 *ConAu P-1*
Reid, James Malcolm 1902-1982 *ConAu 5R, -107*
Reid, James W 1912- *ConAu P-2*
Reid, Jan 1945- *ConAu 61*
Reid, Jim 1929- *ConAu 61*
Reid, John 1910- *WrDr 84*
Reid, John Calvin *ConAu 11NR, -25R*,
    SmATA 21
Reid, John Cowie 1916- *ConAu 9R*,
    DcLEL 1940
Reid, John Kelman Sutherland 1910- *ConAu 1R*,
    -3NR, IntAu&W 82
Reid, John P 1930- *WrDr 84*
Reid, John Phillip 1930- *ConAu 25R*
Reid, John T 1908-1978 *ConAu 81*
Reid, Kate 1930- *CreCan 2*
Reid, Leslie Hartley 1895- *ConAu P-1*
Reid, Loren 1905- *ConAu 1R, -1NR*,
    IntAu&W 82, WrDr 84
Reid, Louis Arnaud 1895- *ConAu P-1*,
    IntAu&W 82
Reid, Malcolm 1941- *ConAu 53*
Reid, Mary Hiester 1854-1921 *CreCan 2*
Reid, Mayne 1818-1883 *SmATA 24[port]*
Reid, Meta Mayne *WrDr 84*
Reid, Meta Mayne 1905- *ConAu 13R*,
    IntAu&W 82, TwCCW 83
Reid, Mildred I 1908- *ConAu 21R*
Reid, Patrick Robert 1910- *IntAu&W 82*
Reid, Philip *ConAu X*
Reid, R W 1933- *ConAu 29R*
Reid, Randall *DrAP&F 83*
Reid, Randall 1931- *ConAu 25R*
Reid, Robert 1933- *WrDr 84*
Reid, Seerley 1909?-1972 *ConAu 37R*
Reid, Sue Titus 1939- *ConAu 37R*
Reid, Timothy E H 1936- *ConAu 17R*
Reid, Vic 1913- *ConNov 82, WrDr 84*
Reid, Victor Stafford 1913- *ConAu 65*,
    DcLEL 1940, LongCTC
Reid, W Stanford 1913- *ConAu 1NR, -49*
Reid, William 1926- *ConAu 85*
Reid, William H 1945- *ConAu 93*
Reid, William J 1908- *ConAu 77*
Reid, William Stanford 1913- *IntAu&W 82*
Reid Banks, Lynne 1929- *ConAu 1R, -6NR*,
    ConNov 82, SmATA 22[port], TwCCW 83,
    WrDr 84
Reida, Bernice 1915- *ConAu 93*
Reidel, Carl Hubert 1937- *ConAu 107*
Reidy, John Patrick 1930- *ConAu 17R*
Reidy, Joseph 1920- *ConAu 63*
Reidy, Maurice 1922- *IntWWP 82*
Reif, Rita 1929- *ConAu 41R*
Reifen, David 1911- *ConAu 93*
Reiff, Henry 1899-1983 *ConAu 110*
Reiff, Robert 1918- *ConAu 17R*
Reiff, Stephanie Ann 1948- *ConAu 93*,
    SmATA 28
Reiffel, Leonard 1927- *ConAu 101*
Reifler, Samuel *DrAP&F 83*

Reifler, Samuel 1939- *ConAu 93*
Reifsnyder, William E 1924- *ConAu 65*
Reig, June 1933- *ConAu 105, SmATA 30[port]*
Reigelman, Milton Monroe 1942- *ConAu 65*
Reiger, George Wesley 1939- *ConAu 101*
Reiger, John F 1943- *ConAu 57*
Reigstad, Paul 1921- *ConAu 81*
Reik, Theodor 1888-1969 *ConAu 5R, -5NR*,
    -25R, TwCA SUP
Reile, Louis 1925- *ConAu 29R, WrDr 84*
Reill, Peter Hanns 1938- *ConAu 101*
Reilly, Christopher T 1924- *ConAu 101*
Reilly, D Robin 1928- *ConAu 8NR*
Reilly, David Robin 1928- *ConAu 5R*,
    IntAu&W 82
Reilly, Edward Jad *DrAP&F 83*
Reilly, Edward Jad 1938- *IntWWP 82*
Reilly, Edward R 1929- *ConAu 93*
Reilly, Esther H 1917- *ConAu 33R*
Reilly, Francis E 1922- *ConAu 29R*
Reilly, Helen 1891-1962 *TwCCr&M 80*
Reilly, Jacquelyn Ivings *CreCan 1*
Reilly, John H 1934- *ConAu 77*
Reilly, John M 1933- *ConAu 104*
Reilly, Judith G 1935- *ConAu 61*
Reilly, Mary Lonan 1926- *ConAu 33R*
Reilly, Michael 1910?-1973 *ConAu 41R*
Reilly, Nancy Olivia *DrAP&F 83*
Reilly, Noel Marcus Prowse 1902- *WrDr 84*
Reilly, Robert Thomas 1922- *ConAu 2NR, -5R*,
    IntAu&W 82, WrDr 84
Reilly, Robin 1928- *ConAu 5NR, -53, WrDr 84*
Reilly, William John 1899-1958 *ConAu P-2*
Reilly, William K *ConAu X*
Reiman, Donald H 1934- *ConAu 33R*
Reiman, Jeffrey H 1942- *ConAu 93*
Reimann, Arnold Luehrs 1898- *WrDr 84*
Reimann, Guenter Hans 1904- *ConAu 25R*
Reimann, Lewis C 1890-1961 *MichAu 80*
Reimann, Viktor 1915- *ConAu 69*
Reimer, Bennett 1932- *ConAu 3NR, -45*
Reimers, Emil 1912- *IntAu&W 82*
Rein, Irving J 1937- *ConAu 25R*
Rein, Karl 1935- *IntWWP 82*
Rein, Martin 1928- *ConAu 93*
Rein, Richard *ConAu X*
Reina, Ruben E 1924- *ConAu 49*
Reinach, Jacquelyn 1930- *ConAu 105*,
    SmATA 28[port]
Reinblatt, Moe 1917- *CreCan 1*
Reinblatt, Moses *CreCan 1*
Reinbold, James S *DrAP&F 83*
Reincheld, Bill 1946- *ConAu 57*
Reindorf, George Edmund 1911- *WrDr 84*
Reindorp, George Edmund 1911- *ConAu 5R*,
    -5NR, IntAu&W 82
Reindorp, Reginald C 1907- *ConAu 25R*
Reineck, Gay Beste *DrAP&F 83*
Reinemer, Vic 1923- *ASpks, ConAu 21R*
Reiner, Laurence E *ConAu 102*
Reiner, Max *ConAu X, WrDr 84*
Reiner, William B 1910-1976 *ConAu 3NR, -45*,
    -61, SmATA 30N
Reinert, Paul C 1910- *ConAu 85*
Reines, Alvin J 1926- *ConAu 53*
Reinfeld, Fred 1910-1964 *ConAu P-1*,
    SmATA 3
Reinfrank, Arno 1934- *IntWWP 82*
Reinhardt, Gottfried 1913- *ConAu 93*
Reinhardt, Heinz Rainer 1913- *IntAu&W 82*
Reinhardt, James Melvin 1894-1974 *ConAu 1R*,
    -4NR, -49
Reinhardt, Jon M 1936- *ConAu 41R*
Reinhardt, Kurt Frank 1896- *ConAu 1R, -1NR*
Reinhardt, Madge *DrAP&F 83*
Reinhardt, Max 1873-1943 *LongCTC*
Reinhardt, Richard 1927- *ConAu 25R*
Reinhart, Bruce Aaron 1926- *ConAu 5R*
Reinhart, Charles 1946- *ConAu 104*
Reinharz, Jehuda 1944- *ConAu 9NR, -65*
Reinhold, Meyer 1909- *ConAu 5R, -5NR*
Reinig, Christa 1926- *CIDMEL 80, ModGL*
Reiniger, Lotte 1899-1981 *ConAu 108*,
    SmATA 33N
Reining, Conrad C 1918- *ConAu 21R*
Reinitz, Richard 1934- *ConAu 89*
Reinke, Klaus Ulrich 1936- *IntAu&W 82*
Reinke, William A 1928- *ConAu 45*
Reinmuth, O W 1900- *WrDr 84*
Reinmuth, Oscar William 1900- *ConAu 37R*,
    IntAu&W 82
Reinowski, Werner 1908- *IntAu&W 82*

Ricci, Larry J 1948- *ConAu 109*
Ricci, Roy *DrAP&F 83*
Ricciardi, Lorenzo 1930- *ConAu 109*
Ricciuti, Edward R 1938- *ConAu 41R,*
SmATA 10
Rice, A Kenneth 1908- *ConAu 5R*
Rice, Albert *ConAu X*
Rice, Alice Caldwell Hegan 1870-1942 *LongCTC,*
TwCA, TwCA SUP, TwCWr
Rice, Alice Hegan 1870-1942 *TwCCW 83*
Rice, Allan Lake 1905- *ConAu 37R*
Rice, Anne 1941- *ConAu 65, WrDr 84*
Rice, Berkeley 1937- *ConAu 21R*
Rice, Brian Keith 1932- *IntAu&W 82,*
WrDr 84
Rice, C Duncan 1942- *ConAu 10NR, −57,*
WrDr 84
Rice, Cale Young 1872-1943 *LongCTC, TwCA,*
TwCA SUP
Rice, Charles D 1910-1971 *ConAu 104,*
SmATA 27N
Rice, Charles E 1931- *ConAu 1R, −1NR*
Rice, Charles L 1936- *ConAu 65*
Rice, Craig 1908-1957 *TwCCr&M 80*
Rice, Cy 1905-1971 *ConAu 33R, ConAu P-1*
Rice, David G 1938- *ConAu 101*
Rice, David L *DrAP&F 83*
Rice, David L 1947- *IntWWP 82*
Rice, David Talbot 1903-1972 *ConAu 5NR, −9R,*
LongCTC
Rice, Desmond Charles 1924- *ConAu 5NR, −9R*
Rice, Don *DrAP&F 83*
Rice, Donald L 1938- *ConAu 37R, WrDr 84*
Rice, Dorothy Mary 1913- *ConAu 9R*
Rice, Edmund C 1910?-1982 *ConAu 106*
Rice, Edward E 1909- *ConAu 41R*
Rice, Edward E 1918- *ConAu 1NR, −49*
Rice, Elinor *ConAu X*
Rice, Elizabeth 1913- *ConAu 21R, SmATA 2*
Rice, Elmer 1892-1967 *CnMD, ConAmA,*
ConAu 25R, ConAu P-2, ConLC 7,
DcLB 4, −7[port], LongCTC, ModAL,
ModWD, TwCA, TwCA SUP, TwCWr,
WhoTwCL
Rice, Eugene F, Jr. 1924- *ConAu 29R*
Rice, Eve 1951- *ConAu 4NR, −53,*
SmATA 34[port]
Rice, Frank M 1908- *ConAu 45*
Rice, George H, Jr. 1923- *ConAu 53*
Rice, Homer C 1927- *ConAu 73*
Rice, Inez 1907- *ConAu 29R, SmATA 13*
Rice, James 1934- *ConAu 8NR, −61,*
SmATA 22[port]
Rice, John R 1895-1980 *ConAu 5R, −5NR*
Rice, Joseph Peter 1930- *ConAu 29R*
Rice, Julius 1923- *ConAu 41R*
Rice, Keith A 1954- *ConAu 109*
Rice, Lawrence D 1929- *ConAu 33R, WrDr 84*
Rice, Martin P 1938- *ConAu 57*
Rice, Max M 1928- *ConAu 93*
Rice, Otis K 1919- *ConAu 29R, WrDr 84*
Rice, Paul *DrAP&F 83*
Rice, Ross Richard 1922- *ConAu 45,*
IntAu&W 82
Rice, Stan *DrAP&F 83*
Rice, Stan 1942- *ConAu 77, IntWWP 82*
Rice, Thomas Jackson 1945- *ConAu 101*
Rice, Tim 1944- *ConAu 103, ConDr 82D,*
ConLC 21[port]
Rice, Wayne 1945- *ConAu 89*
Rice, William C 1911- *ConAu 9R*
Rich, Adrienne *DrAP&F 83*
Rich, Adrienne 1929- *ConAu 9R, ConLC 3, −6,*
−7, −11, −18, ConP 80, CroCAP,
DcLB 5[port], DcLEL 1940, ModAL,
ModAL SUP, WorAu, WrDr 84
Rich, Alan 1924- *ConAmTC, ConAu 9R*
Rich, Barbara *ConAmA, ConAu X*
Rich, Daniel Catton 1904-1976 *ConAu 69, −73*
Rich, Edwin Ernest 1904-1979 *ConAu 89*
Rich, Elaine Sommers 1926- *ConAu 9NR, −17R,*
SmATA 6, WrDr 84
Rich, Elizabeth 1935- *ConAu 29R*
Rich, Everett 1900- *ConAu P-1*
Rich, Frank 1949- *ConAu 73*
Rich, Gerry *ConAu X*
Rich, Gibson 1936- *ConAu 57*
Rich, Joe 1935- *ConAu 57*
Rich, John H, Jr. 1917- *ConAu 81*
Rich, John Martin 1931- *ConAu 21R*
Rich, Josephine Bouchard 1912- *ConAu 5R,*
SmATA 10

Rich, Louise Dickinson 1903- *ConAu 73,*
TwCA SUP
Rich, Michael B 1935- *ConAu 29R*
Rich, Norman 1921- *ConAu 45*
Rich, Robert *ConAu X*
Rich, Russell R 1912- *ConAu 101*
Rich-McCoy, Lois 1941- *ConAu 101*
Richard, Adrienne 1921- *ConAu 29R,*
SmATA 5, WrDr 84
Richard, Betty Byrd 1922- *ConAu 106*
Richard, Etienne *IntWWP 82X*
Richard, Hughes 1934- *IntWWP 82*
Richard, James Robert *ConAu X*
Richard, Jean-Pierre 1922- *ClDMEL 80*
Richard, John 1954- *ConAu 106*
Richard, Keith 1943- *ConAu X, ConLC 17*
Richard, Lee *ConAu X*
Richard, Lionel 1938- *ConAu 93*
Richard, Lucien J 1931- *ConAu 105*
Richard, Marthe 1889-1982 *ConAu 110*
Richard, Michel Paul 1933- *ConAu 45*
Richard, Olga 1914- *ConAu 103*
Richards, Alfred Luther 1939- *ConAu 45*
Richards, Allen *ConAu X*
Richards, Alun 1929- *ConAu 65, WrDr 84*
Richards, Arlene Kramer 1935- *ConAu 11NR,*
−65
Richards, Audrey Isabel 1899- *ConAu 21R*
Richards, Blair P 1940- *ConAu 69*
Richards, Cara E 1927- *ConAu 1NR, −49*
Richards, Carl Edward, Jr. 1933- *ConAu 45*
Richards, Caroline 1939- *ConAu 77*
Richards, Charles *ConAu X*
Richards, Christine-Louise 1910- *WrDr 84*
Richards, Clay *ConAu X, TwCCr&M 80,*
WrDr 84
Richards, Curtis *SmATA X*
Richards, David *ConAu X*
Richards, David Adams 1950- *ConAu 93*
Richards, David Bryant 1942- *ConAmTC*
Richards, Denis George 1910- *ConAu 9R,*
IntAu&W 82, WrDr 84
Richards, Dennis L 1938- *ConAu 102*
Richards, Dorothy B 1894- *ConAu 85*
Richards, Duane *ConAu X*
Richards, E B *ConAu X*
Richards, Frank 1875-1961 *ConAu X, LongCTC,*
SmATA X
Richards, Frank 1876-1961 *TwCCW 83*
Richards, Fred *ConAu X*
Richards, Grant 1872-1948 *LongCTC*
Richards, Guy 1905-1979 *ConAu 11NR, −61, −81*
Richards, H M S 1894- *ConAu P-2*
Richards, Harold Marshall Sylvester 1894-
WrDr 84
Richards, Henry *WrDr 84*
Richards, Hilda *ConAu X, LongCTC,*
SmATA X, TwCCW 83
Richards, Horace Gardiner 1906- *ConAu 5R,*
IntAu&W 82, WrDr 84
Richards, I A 1893-1979 *ConAu 41R, −89,*
ConLC 14, −24[port], ConLCrt 82
Richards, Ivor Armstrong 1893-1979 *LongCTC,*
ModBrL, ModBrL SUP, TwCA,
TwCA SUP, TwCWr
Richards, J Howard 1916- *ConAu 2NR, −45*
Richards, J M 1907- *ConAu 5NR*
Richards, Jack W 1933- *ConAu 33R*
Richards, James 1907- *IntAu&W 82*
Richards, James Maude 1907- *ConAu 5R,*
WrDr 84
Richards, James O 1936- *ConAu 37R*
Richards, Jane 1934- *ConAu 33R*
Richards, Jason *ConAu X*
Richards, Jeffrey 1945- *ConAu 73*
Richards, Jock 1918- *ConAu 107*
Richards, Joe 1909- *ConAu P-1*
Richards, John 1939- *ConAu 57*
Richards, John Marvin 1929- *ConAu 13R*
Richards, Kay *ConAu X, SmATA X*
Richards, Keith 1943- *ConAu 107*
Richards, Kenny *ConAu X*
Richards, Kent David 1938- *ConAu 104*
Richards, Larry *ConAu X*
Richards, Laura E 1850-1943 *TwCCW 83*
Richards, Laura Elizabeth 1850-1943 *TwCA,*
TwCA SUP
Richards, Lawrence O 1931- *ConAu 29R*
Richards, Leslie *AuNews 1*
Richards, Lewis A 1925- *ConAu 45*
Richards, M C 1916- *ConAu 108*
Richards, Mark *ConAu X*

Richards, Mark 1922- *WrDr 84*
Richards, Martin P M 1940- *ConAu 8NR, −61*
Richards, Max D 1923- *ConAu 21R*
Richards, Melanie *DrAP&F 83*
Richards, Michael Edward 1932- *WrDr 84*
Richards, Nat 1942- *ConAu X*
Richards, Peter *ConAu X*
Richards, Peter Godfrey 1923- *ConAu 108,*
IntAu&W 82, WrDr 84
Richards, Phyllis *ConAu X*
Richards, R C W 1923- *ConAu 10NR, −21R*
Richards, Ray 1921- *IntAu&W 82*
Richards, Ronald Charles *WrDr 84*
Richards, Ronald Charles William 1923-
ConAu 1R, IntAu&W 82
Richards, Stanley 1918-1980 *ConAu 101, −25R,*
IntAu&W 82
Richards, Todd *ConAu X*
Richards, Victor 1918- *ConAu 57*
Richards, William Leslie 1916- *IntAu&W 82*
Richardson, Baron 1910- *WrDr 84*
Richardson, Alan 1923- *ConAu 29R, WrDr 84*
Richardson, Anne *ConAu X*
Richardson, Arleta 1923- *ConAu 93*
Richardson, Beth *ConAu X*
Richardson, Betty 1935- *ConAu 53*
Richardson, Bradley M 1928- *ConAu 49*
Richardson, C *ConAu X*
Richardson, Charles E 1928- *ConAu 57*
Richardson, Cyril Charles 1909-1976 *ConAu 37R,*
−69
Richardson, David 1942- *WrDr 84*
Richardson, Deborah *DrAP&F 83*
Richardson, Don 1935- *ConAu 9NR, −65*
Richardson, Dorothy 1922- *WrDr 84*
Richardson, Dorothy Lee *DrAP&F 83*
Richardson, Dorothy Lee 1900- *ConAu 106,*
IntAu&W 82
Richardson, Dorothy Miller 1873-1957
ConAu 104, LongCTC, ModBrL,
ModBrL SUP, TwCA, TwCA SUP,
TwCLC 3, TwCWr
Richardson, Dorsey 1896-1981 *ConAu 105*
Richardson, Edgar Preston 1902- *ConAu 110*
Richardson, Elmo 1930- *ConAu 11NR, −13R*
Richardson, Ethel Florence Lindesay 1870-1946
ConAu 105
Richardson, Evelyn May 1902- *ConAu P-1,*
CreCan 2
Richardson, Frank Howard 1882-1970
ConAu 104, SmATA 27N
Richardson, Frank McLean 1904- *ConAu 103,*
IntAu&W 82, WrDr 84
Richardson, Gayle Elwin 1911- *ConAu 9R*
Richardson, Geoffrey Alan 1936- *WrDr 84*
Richardson, George Barclay 1924- *ConAu 1R,*
WrDr 84
Richardson, Grace Lee *ConAu X, SmATA 8*
Richardson, H Edward 1929- *ConAu 29R*
Richardson, Harry V 1901- *ConAu 69*
Richardson, Harry W 1938- *ConAu 29R,*
WrDr 84
Richardson, Henrietta *ConAu X*
Richardson, Henry Handel 1870-1946 *ConAu X,*
LongCTC, ModCmwL, TwCA, TwCA SUP,
TwCLC 4[port], TwCWr, WhoTwCL
Richardson, Henry V M 1923- *ConAu 25R,*
WrDr 84
Richardson, Howard 1917- *ConAu 41R,*
IntAu&W 82, NatPD 81[port]
Richardson, Isla Paschal 1886-1971 *ConAu P-1*
Richardson, Ivan L 1920- *ConAu 101*
Richardson, Ivor Lloyd Morgan 1930- *ConAu 9R*
Richardson, Jack 1935- *CnMD, ConAu 5R,*
ConDr 82, CroCD, DcLB 7[port],
DcLEL 1940, ModWD, WorAu, WrDr 84
Richardson, James *DrAP&F 83*
Richardson, James 1950- *ConAu 77*
Richardson, James F 1931- *ConAu 29R*
Richardson, James L 1933- *ConAu 21R*
Richardson, James Nathaniel 1942- *ConAu 53*
Richardson, James R 1911- *ConAu 1R*
Richardson, Jeremy John 1942- *ConAu 29R*
Richardson, Joanna *ConAu 10NR, −13R,*
IntAu&W 82, WrDr 84
Richardson, Joe Martin 1934- *ConAu 45*
Richardson, John 1910- *IntAu&W 82*
Richardson, John Adkins 1929- *ConAu 57*
Richardson, John Martin, Jr. 1938- *ConAu 33R*
Richardson, Justin 1900?-1975 *ConAu 61*
Richardson, Kenneth Ridley 1934- *ConAu 29R*
Richardson, Laurence E 1893- *ConAu P-1*

Richardson, Lee 1940- *ConAu 9NR, -21R*
Richardson, Leopold John Dixon 1893-1979? *ConAu 104*
Richardson, Margaret Onrust 1923- *IntWWP 82*
Richardson, Marion Jane *IntWWP 82*
Richardson, Midge Turk 1930- *ConAu 33R, -65, IntAu&W 82, WrDr 84*
Richardson, Miles 1932- *ConAu 33R, WrDr 84*
Richardson, Mozelle Groner 1914- *ConAu 33R*
Richardson, Neil R 1944- *ConAu 103*
Richardson, Nelson *DrAP&F 83*
Richardson, Nola 1936- *ConAu 57*
Richardson, R Daniel 1931- *ConAu 109*
Richardson, Ralph C H 1902- *WrDr 84*
Richardson, Richard C, Jr. 1933- *ConAu 77*
Richardson, Richard Judson 1935- *ConAu 29R, WrDr 84*
Richardson, Robert Dale, Jr. 1934- *ConAu 29R*
Richardson, Robert Dale, Jr. 1943- *IntAu&W 82*
Richardson, Robert Galloway 1926- *ConAu 7NR, -13R, IntAu&W 82, WrDr 84*
Richardson, Robert S 1902- *ConAu 49, IntAu&W 82, SmATA 8, WrDr 84*
Richardson, Rupert Norval 1891- *ConAu 17R*
Richardson, S D 1925- *ConAu 10NR, -21R*
Richardson, Stephen A 1920- *ConAu 61*
Richardson, Thomas Dow 1887- *ConAu 5R*
Richardson, W C 1902- *ConAu 1NR*
Richardson, Walter 1902- *WrDr 84*
Richardson, Walter Cecil 1902- *ConAu 1R*
Richardson, William John 1920- *ConAu 21R*
Richardson, Winona Belle 1914- *IntWWP 82*
Richardson Paddington Lynch *IntAu&W 82X*
Richason, Benjamin Franklin 1922- *ConAu 41R*
Riche, Robert *NatPD 81[port]*
Riche, Robert 1925- *ConAu 108*
Riche, William Harding Le *ConAu X*
Richelieu, Peter *ConAu X*
Richelson, Geraldine 1922- *ConAu 106, SmATA 29*
Richen, Byambyn 1905?-1977 *ConAu 69*
Richepin, Jean 1849-1926 *ModWD*
Richepin, Jean 1849-1930 *CIDMEL 80*
Richeson, Cena Golder *DrAP&F 83*
Richeson, Cyndi *DrAP&F 83*
Richette, Lisa Aversa 1928- *ConAu 25R*
Richetti, John J 1938- *ConAu 110, WrDr 84*
Richey, David 1939- *ConAu 10NR*
Richey, David John 1939- *ConAu 57, MichAu 80*
Richey, Dorothy Hilliard *ConAu 6NR, -9R*
Richey, Elinor 1920- *ConAu 45*
Richey, Margaret Fitzgerald 1883?-1974 *ConAu 53*
Richey, Robert William 1912-1978 *ConAu 25R*
Richey, Russell Earle 1941- *ConAu 69*
Richie, Donald 1924- *ConAu 8NR, -17R*
Richland, W Bernard 1909- *ConAu 102*
Richler, Mordecai 1931- *AuNews 1, ConAu 65, ConLC 3, -5, -9, -13, -18, ConNov 82, CreCan 1, DcLEL 1940, ModCmwL, SmATA 27, TwCWr, WhoTwCL, WorAu, WrDr 84*
Richman, Barry M 1936- *ConAu 21R*
Richman, Milton 1922- *ConAu 69*
Richman, Phyllis C 1939- *ConAu 89*
Richman, Saul 1917?-1979 *ConAu 85*
Richmond, Al 1913- *ConAu 41R*
Richmond, Anthony Henry 1925- *ConAu 21R, WrDr 84*
Richmond, Sir Bruce 1871-1964 *LongCTC*
Richmond, Dick 1933- *ConAu 61*
Richmond, Grace *ConAu X, IntAu&W 82X*
Richmond, Grace 1866-1959 *TwCA*
Richmond, H M 1932- *ConAu 3NR*
Richmond, Hugh Macrae 1932- *ConAu 9R, WrDr 84*
Richmond, John C B 1909- *ConAu 106*
Richmond, Julius B 1916- *ConAu 29R*
Richmond, Lee 1943- *ConAu 49*
Richmond, Leigh *WrDr 84*
Richmond, Leigh 1911- *ConAu 21R, ConSFA, TwCSFW*
Richmond, Robert P 1914- *ConAu 21R, WrDr 84*
Richmond, Robert W 1927- *ConAu 53*
Richmond, Rod *ConAu X*
Richmond, Roe 1910- *TwCWW, WrDr 84*
Richmond, Samuel B 1919- *ConAu 41R*
Richmond, Stanley 1906- *ConAu 45*
Richmond, Steve *DrAP&F 83*
Richmond, Velma E B 1931- *ConAu 61*

Richmond, W Kenneth 1910- *ConAu 10NR, -25R*
Richmond, Walt 1922-1977 *ConAu 21R, ConSFA, TwCSFW*
Richmond, William *WrDr 84*
Richoux, Pat 1927- *ConAu 25R*
Richoux, Patricia 1927- *SmATA 7*
Richter, Alice 1941- *ConAu 105, SmATA 30[port]*
Richter, Conrad Michael 1890-1968 *ConAu 5R, -25R, DcLB 9[port], FifWWr, ModAL, SmATA 3, TwCA, TwCA SUP, TwCWW*
Richter, David H 1945- *ConAu 101*
Richter, Derek 1907- *ConAu 101, IntAu&W 82*
Richter, Dorothy 1906- *ConAu 29R*
Richter, Gerard R 1905- *ConAu 5R*
Richter, Gisela M A 1882-1972 *ConAu 4NR, -5R*
Richter, Hans 1888-1976 *ConAu 65, -73*
Richter, Hans Peter 1925- *ConAu 2NR, -45, IntAu&W 82, SmATA 6*
Richter, Hans Werner 1908- *CIDMEL 80, ConAu 97*
Richter, Harvena 1919- *ConAu 3NR, -5R, IntAu&W 82, WrDr 84*
Richter, Horst-Eberhard 1923- *ConAu 5NR, -53*
Richter, Irving 1911- *ConAu 57*
Richter, J H 1901- *ConAu P-1*
Richter, Joan 1930- *ConAu 101*
Richter, Lin 1936- *ConAu 73*
Richter, Maurice N, Jr. 1930- *ConAu 49*
Richter, Melvin 1921- *ConAu 110*
Richter, Valentin *ConAu X*
Richter, Vernon *ConAu X*
Richthofen, Frieda Von 1879-1956 *LongCTC*
Rickard, Bob *ConAu X*
Rickard, Robert J M 1945- *ConAu 106*
Rickards, Colin William 1937- *ConAu 25R, IntAu&W 82*
Rickards, Maurice 1919- *ConAu 103, IntAu&W 82*
Rickels, Karl 1924- *ConAu 1NR, -45*
Rickels, Milton H 1920- *ConAu 5R*
Rickenbacker, Eddie *ConAu X*
Rickenbacker, Edward Vernon 1890-1973 *ConAu 101, -41R*
Ricker, George Marvin 1922- *ConAu 89*
Rickert, Corinne Holt *ConAu X*
Rickert, John E 1923- *ConAu 45*
Rickett, Frances 1921- *ConAu 107*
Rickett, Harold William 1896- *ConAu 17R, WrDr 84*
Ricketts, C E 1906- *ConAu 57*
Ricketts, Charles 1866-1931 *LongCTC*
Ricketts, Ralph Robert 1902- *WrDr 84*
Ricketts, Viva Leone 1900- *ConAu P-1*
Rickey, Don, Jr. 1925- *ConAu 5R, -9NR*
Rickey, George Warren 1907- *ConAu 65*
Rickey, Mary Ellen 1929- *ConAu 21R*
Rickey, Sara Patterson Brandon 1902- *IntWWP 82*
Rickman, Geoffrey 1932- *ConAu 29R*
Rickman, Hans Peter 1918- *ConAu 17R, WrDr 84*
Ricks, Christopher 1933- *ConAu 7NR, -9R, ConLCrt 82, DcLEL 1940, WorAu 1970, WrDr 84*
Ricks, David F 1927- *ConAu 10NR, -21R*
Ricks, David Trulock 1936- *ConAu 25R*
Ricks, Don M 1936- *ConAu 25R*
Ricks, Nadine 1925- *ConAu 77*
Rickword, Edgell 1898-1982 *ConAu 101, -106, ConLCrt 82, ConP 80, ModBrL, RGFMBP, WorAu*
Rickword, J Edgell 1898- *IntWWP 82*
Rico, Don 1917- *ConAu 81*
Rico, Gabriele Lusser 1937- *ConAu 110*
Rico, Noel *DrAP&F 83*
Rico, Noel 1953- *IntWWP 82*
Ricoeur, Paul 1913- *ConAu 10NR, -61*
Ricou, Laurence 1944- *ConAu 8NR, -61*
Riday, George E 1912- *ConAu 13R*
Riddel, Frank S 1940- *ConAu 85*
Riddel, Joseph Neill 1931- *ConAu 5NR, -9R, WrDr 84*
Riddell, Alan 1927- *ConAu 104*
Ridder, Bernard J 1913-1983 *ConAu 110*
Ridder, Marie 1925- *ConAu X*
Ridderbos, Herman Nicolaas 1909- *ConAu 57*
Riddle, Donald Husted 1921- *ConAu 9R*
Riddle, John M 1937- *ConAu 45*
Riddle, Kenneth Wilkinson 1920- *ConAu 1R*

Riddle, Maxwell 1907- *ConAu 3NR, -5R*
Riddle, Thomas Wilkinson 1886-1983 *ConAu 110*
Riddleberger, Patrick Williams 1915- *ConAu 21R*
Riddolls, Brenda Harks *IntAu&W 82*
Ride, W D L 1926- *WrDr 84*
Ride, William David Lindsay 1926- *IntAu&W 82*
Ridenour, Fritz 1932- *ConAu 108*
Ridenour, George M 1928- *ConAu 93*
Ridenour, Ron 1939- *ConAu 69*
Rideout, Darryl *DrAP&F 83*
Rideout, Patricia 1931- *CreCan 2*
Rider, Alice Damon 1895- *ConAu 69*
Rider, Brett *TwCWW*
Rider, Fremont 1885-1962 *ConAu 89*
Rider, John R 1923- *ConAu 25R*
Ridge, Antonia d1981 *ConAu 9R, -104, IntAu&W 82, SmATA 27N, -7*
Ridge, Antonia 1895-1981 *TwCCW 83*
Ridge, George Ross 1931- *ConAu 1R*
Ridge, Lola 1883?-1941 *ConAmA, TwCA, TwCA SUP*
Ridge, William Pett 1860?-1930 *LongCTC*
Ridgely, Beverly S 1920- *ConAu 25R*
Ridgely, Joseph Vincent 1921- *ConAu 5R*
Ridgeway, James Fowler 1936- *ConAu 106*
Ridgeway, Jason *ConAu X, WrDr 84*
Ridgeway, Marian E 1913- *ConAu 33R*
Ridgeway, Rick 1949- *ConAu 93*
Ridgway, Brunilde Sismondo 1929- *ConAu 1NR, -45*
Ridgway, Jason *ConAu X, TwCCr&M 80*
Ridgway, John 1938- *ConAu 25R, IntAu&W 82, WrDr 84*
Ridgway, Judith 1939- *ConAu 109*
Ridgway, Judy *ConAu X*
Ridgway, Matthew B 1895- *WrDr 84*
Ridgway, Ronald Sidney 1923- *ConAu 45, IntAu&W 82*
Ridgway, Whitman H 1941- *ConAu 101*
Riding, Laura 1901- *ConAmA, ConAu X, ConLC 3, -7, ConP 80, LongCTC, TwCA, TwCA SUP, WhoTwCL, WrDr 84*
Ridland, John M *DrAP&F 83*
Ridle, Julia Brown 1923- *ConAu 1R*
Ridler, Anne 1912- *WrDr 84*
Ridler, Anne Barbara 1912- *ConAu 3NR, -5R, ConDr 82, ConP 80, DcLEL 1940, IntWWP 82, LongCTC, ModBrL, WorAu*
Ridley, Anthony 1933- *ConAu 107, IntAu&W 82, WrDr 84*
Ridley, B K 1931- *ConAu 104*
Ridley, Charles P 1933- *ConAu 73*
Ridley, Clifford Anthony 1935- *ConAmTC*
Ridley, Florence H 1922- *IntAu&W 82*
Ridley, Jasper 1920- *WrDr 84*
Ridley, Jasper Godwin 1920- *ConAu 6NR, -13R, IntAu&W 82*
Ridley, Maurice Roy 1890-1969 *LongCTC*
Ridley, Nancy 1911- *IntAu&W 82*
Ridley, Nat, Jr. *ConAu P-2*
Ridlon, Marci 1942- *ConAu X, SmATA 22*
Ridout, Albert K 1905- *ConAu P-2*
Ridout, Godfrey 1918- *CreCan 2*
Ridout, Ronald 1916- *ConAu 103, WrDr 84*
Ridpath, Ian 1947- *ConAu 77, IntAu&W 82*
Ridruejo, Dionisio 1912-1975 *CIDMEL 80, ConAu 57*
Rieber, Alfred J 1931- *ConAu 9R*
Rieber, R W 1932- *ConAu 3NR, -45*
Riedel, Gerhard 1932- *IntAu&W 82*
Riedel, Richard Langham 1908- *ConAu P-2*
Riedel, Walter E 1936- *ConAu 45*
Rieder, Heinz 1911- *IntAu&W 82*
Riedesel, C Alan 1930- *ConAu 25R*
Riedl, John O 1905- *ConAu P-2*
Riedman, Sarah Regal 1902- *ConAu 1R, -1NR, SmATA 1*
Riefe, Alan 1925- *ConAu 9NR, -61, WrDr 84*
Riefe, Barbara *ConAu X, WrDr 84*
Riefe, Barbara 1925- *ConAu X, TwCRGW*
Riefenstahl, Berta Helene Amalia 1902- *ConAu 108*
Riefenstahl, Leni *ConAu X*
Riefenstahl, Leni 1902- *ConLC 16*
Rieff, Philip 1922- *ConAu 49, WrDr 84*
Riegel, Robert Edgar 1897- *ConAu 5R*
Rieger, James H 1936- *ConAu 93*
Rieger, Shay 1929- *ConAu 29R*
Riegert, Eduard Richard 1932- *ConAu 69*
Riegert, Ray 1947- *ConAu 105*
Riegle, Donald W, Jr. 1938- *ConAu 61*
Riehl, Herbert 1915- *WrDr 84*

Riemer, George 1920-1973 *ConAu 41R,*
ConAu P-2
Riemer, Neal 1922- *ConAu 21R*
Riemer, Ruby *DrAP&F 83*
Rienits, Rex 1909-1971 *ConAu 29R, ConAu P-1*
Rienow, Robert 1909- *ConAu 21R*
Riepe, Dale 1918- *ConAu 37R*
Ries, Estelle H 1896- *ConAu 25R*
Ries, John C 1930- *ConAu 13R*
Ries, Lawrence R 1940- *ConAu 65*
Riese, Walther 1890- *ConAu 49*
Rieseberg, Harry E 1892- *ConAu 5R*
Riesel, Victor 1915- *ConAmTC*
Rieselbach, Leroy N 1934- *ConAu 9NR, –21R*
Riesenberg, Felix 1879-1939 *TwCA*
Riesenberg, Felix, Jr. 1913-1962 *ConAu 101,*
SmATA 23
Riesenberg, Saul H 1911- *ConAu 49*
Rieser, Dolf 1898-1983 *ConAu 109*
Rieser, Henry *ConAu X*
Riesman, David 1909- *ConAu 5R, DcLEL 1940,*
TwCA SUP, WrDr 84
Riesman, Evelyn Thompson 1912- *ConAu 21R*
Riess, Claudia 1937- *ConAu 110*
Riess, Oswald George Lorenz 1896- *ConAu 5R*
Riess, Walter 1925- *ConAu 17R*
Riessen, Martin Clare 1941- *ConAu 41R*
Riessman, Frank 1924- *ConAu 1R, –6NR*
Riesterer, Berthold P 1935- *ConAu 41R*
Riesterer, Peter P 1919- *IntAu&W 82*
Rietdijk, Cornelis Willem 1927- *IntAu&W 82*
Rieu, E V 1887-1972 *ConAu 103, SmATA 26N,*
TwCCW 83, WorAu 1970
Rieu, Emile Victor 1887-1972 *ConAu 1R*
Riewald, J G 1910- *ConAu 6NR, –57*
Riewald, Jacobus Gerhardus 1910- *IntAu&W 82*
Rif *IntWWP 82X*
Rifbjerg, Klaus 1931- *ClDMEL 80, CroCD,*
IntAu&W 82, IntWWP 82, WorAu 1970
Rife, J Merle 1895- *ConAu 61*
Rife, Joanne 1932- *ConAu 110*
Riffe, Ernest *ConAu X*
Rifkin, Arthur *DrAP&F 83*
Rifkin, Shepard *DrAP&F 83*
Rifkin, Shepard 1918- *ConAu 1R, –1NR,*
WrDr 84
Rifkind, Carole 1935- *ConAu 85*
Rifkind, Simon H 1901- *ConAu 109*
Rift, Valerie *ConAu X*
Riga, Frank P 1936- *ConAu 89*
Riga, Peter J 1933- *ConAu 5R*
Rigault, Andre Albert Louis 1922- *ConAu 45*
Rigby, Andrew 1944- *ConAu 61*
Rigby, Ida Katherine 1944- *ConAu 10NR, –65*
Rigby, Paul H 1924- *ConAu 17R*
Rigby, Ray 1916- *WrDr 84*
Rigby, T H 1925- *ConAu 10NR, –17R*
Rigdon, Raymond M 1919- *ConAu 29R*
Rigdon, Walter 1930- *ConAu 13R*
Rigg, A G 1937- *ConAu 37R*
Rigg, H K 1911-1980 *ConAu 29R, –93*
Rigg, John Linton 1894- *ConAu 5R*
Rigg, Robinson Peter 1918- *ConAu 33R*
Riggan, William 1946- *ConAu 103*
Riggio, Thomas P 1943- *ConAu 109*
Riggs, Dionis Coffin 1898- *ConAu P-2,*
IntAu&W 82, IntWWP 82, WrDr 84
Riggs, Fred W 1917- *ConAu 25R*
Riggs, James L 1929- *ConAu 33R, WrDr 84*
Riggs, Lynn 1899-1954 *CnMD, ConAmA,*
ModWD, TwCA, TwCA SUP
Riggs, Robert E 1927- *WrDr 84*
Riggs, Robert Edwon 1927- *ConAu 8NR, –13R*
Riggs, Sidney Noyes 1892-1975 *ConAu 1R, –103,*
SmATA 28N
Riggs, William 1938- *ConAu 61*
Righter, Carroll 1900- *ConAu 93*
Righter, Robert Willms 1933- *ConAu 108*
Rigisepp *IntAu&W 82X*
Rigoni, Omando Joseph 1917- *IntAu&W 82*
Rigoni, Orlando 1897- *ConAu 11NR, –13R*
Rigoni, Orlando 1917- *WrDr 84*
Rigsbee, David *DrAP&F 83*
Rigsby, Howard 1909-1975 *ConAu 9R,*
TwCWW
Riha, Thomas 1929- *ConAu 9R*
Rihner, Fred 1917- *IntAu&W 82*
Riker, Tom L 1936- *ConAu 104*
Riker, William H 1920- *ConAu 1R*
Rikhoff, James C 1931- *ConAu 13R*
Rikhoff, Jean *DrAP&F 83*
Rikhoff, Jean 1928- *ConAu 61, IntAu&W 82,*

SmATA 9
Rikhye, Indar Jit 1920- *ConAu 93*
Rikki *ConAu X, DrAP&F 83,*
IntAu&W 82X
Rikon, Irving 1931- *ConAu 29R*
Riley, Carroll L 1923- *ConAu 10NR, –25R,*
IntAu&W 82, WrDr 84
Riley, Clara Deatherage 1931- *ConAu 25R*
Riley, Cyril Leslie 1922- *IntAu&W 82,*
IntWWP 82
Riley, Dick 1946- *ConAu 101, WrDr 84*
Riley, Edward Calverley 1923- *ConAu 9R,*
IntAu&W 82, WrDr 84
Riley, G Micheal 1940- *ConAu 45*
Riley, Glenda 1938- *ConAu 106*
Riley, James Frederic 1912- *ConAu 29R,*
WrDr 84
Riley, James Whitcomb 1849-1916 *LongCTC,*
SmATA 17
Riley, Jean 1916- *NatPD 81[port]*
Riley, Jocelyn *DrAP&F 83*
Riley, Lawrence 1897?-1975 *ConAu 61*
Riley, Madeleine 1933- *WrDr 84*
Riley, Madeleine Veronica 1933- *ConAu 25R*
Riley, Miles O'Brien 1937- *ConAu 104*
Riley, Nord 1914- *ConAu 13R*
Riley, Ridge 1907-1976 *ConAu 101*
Riley, Roy, Jr. 1943?-1977 *ConAu 73*
Riley, Sandra 1938- *ConAu 104*
Riley, Tex *ConAu X*
Riley, Thomas J 1901?-1977 *ConAu 73*
Riley-Smith, Jonathan 1938- *ConAu 21R*
Riling, Raymond L J 1896?-1974 *ConAu 53*
Rilke, Rainer Maria 1875-1926 *ClDMEL 80,*
CnMWL, ConAu 104, LongCTC, ModGL,
TwCA, TwCA SUP, TwCLC 1, –6[port],
TwCWr, WhoTwCL
Rilla, Wolf Peter 1925- *ConAu 49*
Rils *ConAu X*
Rima, I H 1925- *ConAu 21R*
Rima, Ingrid H *WrDr 84*
Rimanelli, Giose 1926- *ClDMEL 80*
Rimanoczy, Richard Stanton 1902- *ConAu 73*
Rimbaud, Arthur 1854-1891 *ClDMEL 80,*
LongCTC, ModRL
Rimberg, John 1929- *ConAu 57*
Rimel, Duane 1915- *ConAu 29R*
Rimington, Critchell 1907-1976 *ConAu 61*
Rimland, Bernard 1928- *ConAu 6NR, –13R*
Rimland, Ingrid 1936- *ConAu 61*
Rimlinger, Gaston V 1926- *ConAu 37R,*
WrDr 84
Rimmer, C Brandon 1918- *ConAu 61*
Rimmer, Robert H 1917- *ConAu 4NR, –9R*
Rimmer, W J *ConAu X*
Rimmington, Gerald Thorneycroft 1930-
ConAu 17R, WrDr 84
Rimus *IntWWP 82X*
Rinaldi, Nicholas M *DrAP&F 83*
Rinaldi, Nicholas Michael 1934- *ConAu 104,*
IntWWP 82
Rinaldini, Angiolo *ConAu X*
Rinard, Judith Ellen 1947- *ConAu 97,*
IntAu&W 82
Rind, Sherry *DrAP&F 83*
Rinder, Walter 1934- *ConAu 11NR*
Rinder, Walter Murray 1934- *ConAu 69*
Rindfleisch, Norval *DrAP&F 83*
Rindfleisch, Norval 1930- *ConAu 65*
Rinehart, Frederick Roberts 1903?-1981
ConAu 104
Rinehart, Mary Roberts 1876-1958 *ConAu 108,*
LongCTC, ModWD, TwCA, TwCA SUP,
TwCCr&M 80, TwCRGW, TwCWr
Rinehart, Stanley Marshall, Jr. 1897-1969
ConAu 29R
Rinfret, Jean-Claude 1929- *CreCan 2*
Ring, Alfred A 1905- *ConAu 29R*
Ring, Douglas *ConAu X, WrDr 84*
Ring, Elizabeth 1912- *ConAu 103, WrDr 84*
Ringdahl, Mark *ConAu X*
Ringe, Donald A 1923- *ConAu 1R*
Ringelnatz, Joachim 1883-1934 *ModGL*
Ringenbach, Paul T 1936- *ConAu 45*
Ringenberg, Lawrence Albert 1915- *WrDr 84*
Ringer, Alexander L 1921- *ConAu 45*
Ringer, Barbara Alice 1925- *ConAu 9R,*
WrDr 84
Ringer, Fritz K 1934- *ConAu 73*
Ringer, Robert J 1938- *ConAu 81, WrDr 84*
Ringgold, Gene 1918- *ConAu 25R*
Ringgren, Helmer 1917- *ConAu 3NR, –5R*

Ringi, Kjell 1939- *ConAu 1NR, –45,*
SmATA 12
Ringkamp, Jonathan 1929- *NatPD 81[port]*
Ringler, William A 1912- *ConAu 5R, WrDr 84*
Ringo, Johnny *ConAu X, TwCWW*
Ringold, Clay *ConAu X, TwCWW, WrDr 84*
Ringold, Francine *DrAP&F 83*
Ringold, May Spencer 1914- *ConAu 21R*
Ringrose, David R 1938- *ConAu 53*
Ringuet 1895-1960 *CreCan 2, ModFrL*
Ringwald, Donald C 1917- *ConAu 21R,*
WrDr 84
Ringwood, Gwen Pharis 1910- *CreCan 2*
Rinhart, Floyd 1915- *ConAu 10NR*
Rinhart, Floyd Lincoln 1915- *ConAu 25R,*
WrDr 84
Rinhart, Marion 1916- *ConAu 10NR*
Rinhart, Marion Hutchinson 1916- *ConAu 25R,*
WrDr 84
Rinker, Rosalind Beatrice 1906- *ConAu 5R,*
–5NR
Rinkoff, Barbara Jean 1923-1975 *ConAu 57,*
ConAu P-2, SmATA 27N, –4
Rinser, Luise 1911- *IntAu&W 82, ModGL,*
TwCWr
Rintels, David 1939- *ConAu 73*
Rinvolucri, Mario 1940- *ConAu 10NR, –21R*
Rinvolucri, Mina Josephine Moore *ConAu X*
Rinzema, Jakob 1931- *ConAu 102*
Rinzler, Alan 1938- *ConAu 21R*
Rinzler, Carol Eisen 1941- *ConAu 49*
Riopelle, Arthur J 1920- *ConAu 37R*
Riopelle, Jean-Paul 1923- *CreCan 1*
Riordan, James 1936- *ConAu 11NR, –69,*
SmATA 28[port], WrDr 84
Riordan, Mary Marguerite 1931- *ConAu 106*
Riordan, Michael 1946- *ConAu 106*
Rios, Alberto Alvaro *DrAP&F 83*
Rios, Juan 1914- *IntAu&W 82*
Rios, Tere 1917- *ConAu X, SmATA 2*
Riotte, Louise 1909- *ConAu 57*
Riotto, Guy Michael 1943- *ConAu 73*
Riou, Roger 1909- *ConAu 61*
Ripa, Karol 1895-1983 *ConAu 109*
Ripley, Dillon 1913- *ConAu 57*
Ripley, Elizabeth Blake 1906-1969 *ConAu 1R,*
–3NR, SmATA 5
Ripley, Francis Joseph 1912- *ConAu 1R, –3NR*
Ripley, Jack *ConAu X, TwCCr&M 80,*
WrDr 84
Ripley, Randall Butler 1938- *ConAu 5NR, –53,*
IntAu&W 82, WrDr 84
Ripley, S Dillon 1913- *IntAu&W 82*
Ripley, Sheldon N 1925- *ConAu 5R*
Ripley, Theresa M 1944- *ConAu 85*
Ripley, Warren 1921- *ConAu 33R*
Riposte, A *LongCTC*
Rippa, S Alexander 1925- *ConAu 53*
Ripper, Charles L 1929- *ConAu 1R, –1NR,*
SmATA 3
Ripper, Chuck *ConAu X*
Ripperger, Helmut Lothar 1897-1974 *ConAu 53*
Ripperger, Henrietta 1889- *ConAu 49*
Rippey, Robert Max 1926- *ConAu 45*
Rippier, Joseph Storey 1935- *IntAu&W 82*
Ripple, Richard E 1931- *ConAu 33R*
Rippley, LaVern J 1935- *ConAu 33R, WrDr 84*
Rippon, Geoffrey 1924- *IntAu&W 82*
Rippon, Marion E 1921- *ConAu 1NR, –49*
Rippy, Frances Mayhew 1929- *ConAu 89*
Rips, Ervine M 1921- *ConAu 101*
Rips, Geoffrey 1950- *ConAu 108*
Rips, Rae Elizabeth 1914-1970 *ConAu 104*
Risatti, Howard A 1943- *ConAu 49*
Rischin, Moses 1925- *ConAu 3NR, –9R,*
WrDr 84
Riseley, Jerry B 1920- *ConAu 21R*
Riseling, John J W 1888?-1977 *ConAu 73*
Risenhoover, Morris 1940- *ConAu 65*
Riser, Wayne H 1909- *ConAu P-1*
Rishel, Mary Ann Malinchak *DrAP&F 83*
Risjord, Norman K 1931- *ConAu 7NR, –17R*
Riskin, Robert 1897-1955 *DcLB 26[port]*
Riskind, Mary 1944- *ConAu 108*
Rislakki, Ensio 1896- *CroCD*
Riss, Richard 1952- *ConAu 81*
Risse, Heinz 1898- *IntAu&W 82*
Rissi, Mathias 1920- *ConAu 45*
Rissover, Fredric 1940- *ConAu 33R*
Rist, John M 1936- *ConAu 101*
Rist, Ray C 1944- *ConAu 3NR, –49*
Rist Arnold, Elisabeth 1950- *ConAu 65*

Riste, Olav 1933- *ConAu 29R, WrDr 84*
Ristic, Dragisha N 1909- *ConAu P-2*
Ristow, Walter W 1908- *ConAu 17R, WrDr 84*
Rita d1938 *LongCTC*
Ritchey, John Arthur 1919- *ConAu 21R*
Ritchie, Andrew 1943- *ConAu 85*
Ritchie, Andrew Carnduff 1907-1978 *ConAu 81*
Ritchie, Lady Anne Isabella Thackeray 1837-1919 *LongCTC*
Ritchie, Barbara Gibbons *ConAu 73, SmATA 14*
Ritchie, Bill *ConAu X*
Ritchie, C T 1914- *WrDr 84*
Ritchie, Cicero Theodore 1914- *ConAu 9R, IntAu&W 82*
Ritchie, Claire *TwCRGW, WrDr 84*
Ritchie, Donald Arthur 1945- *ConAu 106*
Ritchie, Edwin *WrDr 84*
Ritchie, Edwin 1931- *ConAu 29R*
Ritchie, Elisavietta *ConAu 2NR, –49, DrAP&F 83, IntAu&W 82, IntWWP 82*
Ritchie, Elisavietta Artamonoff *WrDr 84*
Ritchie, Evelyn *IntWWP 82X*
Ritchie, George Stephen 1914- *ConAu 13R, IntAu&W 82, WrDr 84*
Ritchie, Jack *ConAu X*
Ritchie, Jack 1922- *TwCCr&M 80, WrDr 84*
Ritchie, James McPherson 1927- *ConAu 25R*
Ritchie, James T R 1908- *ConAu P-2*
Ritchie, John C 1927- *ConAu 49*
Ritchie, Sir Lewis Anselmo 1886-1967 *LongCTC*
Ritchie, M A F 1909- *ConAu P-2*
Ritchie, Paul 1923- *ConAu 21R*
Ritchie, Rita 1930- *ConAu X*
Ritchie, Ruth 1900- *ConAu 2NR*
Ritchie, Ward 1905- *ConAu 7NR, –57*
Ritchie, William A 1903- *ConAu 45*
Ritchie-Calder, Baron 1906- *WorAu*
Ritchie-Calder, Peter Ritchie 1906-1982 *ConAu 4NR, –105*
Ritner, Peter Vaughn 1927?-1976 *ConAu 69, –77*
Ritschel, Karl Heinz 1930- *IntAu&W 82*
Ritschl, Dietrich 1929- *ConAu 9NR, –21R*
Ritsos, Giannes *ConAu X*
Ritsos, Yannis 1909- *ClDMEL 80, ConAu 77, ConLC 6, –13, WorAu 1970*
Rittenhouse, Jessie Belle 1869-1948 *TwCA, TwCA SUP*
Rittenhouse, Mignon 1904- *ConAu 41R*
Ritter, Ed 1917- *ConAu 17R*
Ritter, Felix *ConAu X*
Ritter, Henry, Jr. 1920- *ConAu 93*
Ritter, Jess 1930- *ConAu 37R*
Ritter, Julian *IntAu&W 82X*
Ritter, Lawrence S 1922- *ConAu 21R*
Ritterbush, Philip C 1936- *ConAu 6NR, –9R*
Rittner, Tadeusz 1873-1921 *CnMD, ModWD*
Ritts, Paul 1920?-1980 *ConAu 102, SmATA 25N*
Ritvala, M *ConAu X*
Ritz, Charles 1891-1976 *ConAu 65*
Ritz, David 1943- *ConAu 85*
Ritz, Jean-Georges 1906- *ConAu 5R*
Ritz, Joseph P 1929- *ConAu 21R*
Ritzenthaler, Pat 1914- *ConAu 25R*
Ritzer, George 1940- *ConAu 5NR, –53*
Rivas, Gilberto Lopez Y *ConAu X*
Rivaz, Alice 1901- *IntAu&W 82*
Rive, Richard 1931- *ConAu 13R, DcLEL 1940, ModCmwL, TwCWr*
Rivel, Isa De *ConAu X*
Rivemale, Alexandre 1918- *CnMD*
Rivenburgh, Viola K 1897- *ConAu 17R, WrDr 84*
Rivera, Edward *DrAP&F 83*
Rivera, Etnairis *DrAP&F 83*
Rivera, Feliciano 1932- *ConAu 45*
Rivera, Geraldo 1943- *ConAu 108, SmATA 28*
Rivera, Jose Eustacio 1889-1928 *ModLAL*
Rivera, Louis Reyes *DrAP&F 83*
Rivera, Louis Reyes 1945- *IntWWP 82*
Rivera, Tomas *DrAP&F 83*
Rivera, Tomas 1935- *ConAu 49*
Rivere, Alec *ConAu X*
Rivero, Andres *DrAP&F 83*
Rivero, Eliana Suarez 1942- *ConAu 41R*
Rivero DeMeneses San Jose, Jorge Ma 1945- *IntAu&W 82*
Rivers, Ann *DrAP&F 83*
Rivers, Ann 1939- *IntWWP 82*
Rivers, Caryl 1937- *ConAu 4NR, –49*
Rivers, Clarence Joseph 1931- *ConAu 77,*

Rivers, Conrad Kent 1933-1968 *ConAu 85, ConLC 1*
LivgBAA
Rivers, Elfrida *ConAu X*
Rivers, Elias L 1924- *ConAu 17R*
Rivers, J W *DrAP&F 83*
Rivers, Julian Alfred Pitt *ConAu X*
Rivers, Louis 1922- *NatPD 81[port]*
Rivers, Susan 1954- *NatPD 81[port]*
Rivers, William L 1925- *ConAu 7NR, –17R*
Rivers-Coffey, Rachel 1943- *ConAu 73*
Riverside, John *ConAu X, SmATA X*
Rives, Amelie 1863-1945 *LongCTC, TwCA, TwCA SUP*
Rives, Leigh *ConAu X*
Rives, Stanley G 1930- *ConAu 11NR, –21R*
Rivet, A L F 1915- *ConAu 9NR, –21R*
Rivet, Albert Lionel Frederick 1915- *IntAu&W 82, WrDr 84*
Rivett, Carol *ConAu X*
Rivett, Edith Caroline *LongCTC*
Rivett, Edith Caroline 1894-1958 *ConAu 110*
Rivett, Rohan Deakin 1917- *ConAu 25R*
Rivett-Carnac, Charles Edward 1901- *ConAu P-2*
Rivette, Marc 1916- *ConAu 5R*
Riviere, Bill *ConAu X*
Riviere, Claude 1932- *ConAu 102*
Riviere, Jacques 1886-1925 *ClDMEL 80, WorAu*
Riviere, Peter Gerard 1934- *ConAu 103*
Riviere, William Alexander 1916- *ConAu 5R, –8NR*
Rivkin, Allen 1903- *ConAu 11NR, –65, DcLB 26[port]*
Rivkin, Arnold 1919-1968 *ConAu 1R, –3NR*
Rivkin, Ellis 1918- *ConAu 33R, WrDr 84*
Rivlin, Alice M 1931- *ConAu 33R*
Rivlin, Harry N 1904- *ConAu 17R*
Rivoire, Jean 1929- *ConAu 5NR, –9R*
Rivoli, Mario 1943- *SmATA 10*
Rizzo, Horacio Fausto Emilio 1932- *IntAu&W 82*
Rizzoli, Andrea 1914-1983 *ConAu 109*
Rizzoli, Angelo 1889-1970 *ConAu 104*
Rizzuto, Anthony 1937- *ConAu 106*
Rizzuto, James J 1939- *ConAu 107*
Rizzuto, Jim *ConAu X*
Ro, Tae-Yong *ConAu X*
Roa, Raul 1908-1982 *ConAu 107*
Roa Bastos, Augusto 1917- *ModLAL*
Roach, Helen P 1903- *ConAu P-1*
Roach, Hildred 1937- *ConAu 57*
Roach, Jack L 1925- *ConAu 109*
Roach, James P 1907-1978 *ConAu 77*
Roach, Joyce Gibson 1935- *ConAu 101*
Roach, Marilynne K 1946- *ConAu 57, SmATA 9*
Roach, Mary Ellen 1921- *ConAu 17R*
Roach, Portia *SmATA X*
Roadarmel, Gordon 1932-1972 *ConAu 104*
Roadarmel, Paul 1942- *ConAu 93*
Roaden, Arliss L 1930- *ConAu 37R*
Roadstrum, William H 1915- *ConAu 25R*
Roalfe, William R 1896- *ConAu 93*
Roam, Pearl Louise Sovern 1920- *ConAu 1R*
Roan, Tom *TwCWW*
Roark, Albert E 1933- *ConAu 85*
Roark, Dallas M 1931- *ConAu 37R, WrDr 84*
Roark, Garland 1904- *ConAu 1R, –1NR, TwCWW, WrDr 84*
Roark, James L 1941- *ConAu 85*
Roazen, Paul 1936- *ConAu 25R, IntAu&W 82, WrDr 84*
Roback, Abraham Aaron 1890-1965 *ConAu 5R*
Robacker, Earl Francis 1904- *ConAu 53*
Robana, Abderrahman 1938- *ConAu 65*
Robard, Jackson *ConAu X*
Robards, Sherman M 1939- *ConAu 61*
Robards, Terry *ConAu X*
Robathan, Dorothy M 1898- *ConAu 41R*
Robb, David Metheny 1903- *AuNews 1*
Robb, Frank Thomson 1908- *ConAu 57*
Robb, Inez 1901?-1979 *ConAu 85, –97*
Robb, J Wesley 1919- *ConAu 5R*
Robb, James Harding 1920- *ConAu 9R, WrDr 84*
Robb, James Willis 1918- *ConAu 41R*
Robb, Mary K 1908- *ConAu P-2*
Robb, Nesca Adeline 1905- *ConAu 9R*
Robbe-Grillet, Alain 1922- *ASpks, ClDMEL 80, CnMWL, ConAu 9R, ConLC 1, –2, –4, –6, –8, –10, –14, IntAu&W 82, ModFrL,*

ModRL, TwCWr, WhoTwCL, WorAu
Robben, John 1930- *ConAu 93*
Robbert, Louise Buenger 1925- *ConAu 41R*
Robbin, Luna 1936- *ConAu 103*
Robbins, Baron 1898- *WrDr 84*
Robbins, Caroline 1903- *ConAu 107*
Robbins, Daniel 1933- *ConAu 3NR, –45*
Robbins, Doren Richard 1949- *IntWWP 82*
Robbins, Frank 1917- *ConAu 109*
Robbins, Brother Gerald 1940- *ConAu 13R*
Robbins, Glaydon Donaldson 1908- *ConAu 5R*
Robbins, Harold 1912- *ConLC 5, TwCWr, WrDr 84*
Robbins, Harold 1916- *ConAu 73*
Robbins, Henry 1928?-1979 *ConAu 89*
Robbins, Horace 1909-1982 *ConAu 107*
Robbins, Jerry Leo 1940- *IntWWP 82*
Robbins, John Albert 1914- *ConAu 17R, WrDr 84*
Robbins, June *ConAu 61*
Robbins, Keith 1940- *ConAu 11NR*
Robbins, Keith Gilbert 1940- *ConAu 25R, IntAu&W 82*
Robbins, Martin *DrAP&F 83*
Robbins, Martin 1931- *ConAu 29R*
Robbins, Marty *ConAu X*
Robbins, Matthew *ConAu 110*
Robbins, Mildred Brown *ConAu P-2*
Robbins, Millie *ConAu X*
Robbins, Raleigh *ConAu X, SmATA X*
Robbins, Richard *DrAP&F 83*
Robbins, Richard G, Jr. 1939- *ConAu 53*
Robbins, Richard Leroy 1953- *IntWWP 82*
Robbins, Rossell Hope 1912- *ConAu 2NR, –45*
Robbins, Roy Marvin 1904- *ConAu 65*
Robbins, Ruth 1917?- *ConAu 73, SmATA 14*
Robbins, S A 1940- *ConAu 21R*
Robbins, Sheryl *DrAP&F 83*
Robbins, Thomas Eugene 1936- *ConAu 81*
Robbins, Tom 1936- *ConAu X, ConLC 9, ConNov 82, DcLB Y80B[port], WrDr 84*
Robbins, Tony *ConAu X, SmATA X*
Robbins, Trina 1938- *ConLC 21[port]*
Robbins, Vesta Ordelia 1891- *ConAu 53*
Robe, Stanley L 1915- *ConAu 5R, –6NR*
Robeck, Mildred C 1915- *ConAu 57*
Robens, Alfred 1910- *IntAu&W 82*
Robens Of Woldingham, Baron 1910- *WrDr 84*
Roberge, Earl 1918- *ConAu 85*
Roberson, Charles Ed *DrAP&F 83*
Roberson, Ed 1939- *ConAu 77, LivgBAA*
Roberson, Marie *ConAu X*
Roberson, Ricky James 1956- *ConAu 101*
Roberson, William H 1952- *ConAu 110*
Robert, Jacques 1928- *IntAu&W 82*
Robert, Marika Barna *ConAu 9R, CreCan 1*
Robert, Michael 1908- *WrDr 84*
Robert, Paul 1911?-1980 *ConAu 101*
Robert The Rhymer *IntWWP 82X*
Robert The Rymer *IntAu&W 82X*
Robertiello, Richard C 1923- *ConAu 3NR, –9R, WrDr 84*
Roberts, Adam 1940- *ConAu 9NR, –21R, WrDr 84*
Roberts, Allen 1914- *ConAu 29R*
Roberts, Anthony *ConAu X*
Roberts, Archibald Edward 1915- *ConAu 6NR, –57*
Roberts, Arthur Owen 1923- *ConAu 25R*
Roberts, Arthur Sydney 1905?-1978 *ConAu 81, –85*
Roberts, Barney 1920- *IntWWP 82*
Roberts, Benjamin Charles 1917- *ConAu 102, WrDr 84*
Roberts, Bill 1914?-1978 *ConAu 81*
Roberts, Bleddyn Jones 1906- *ConAu P-1*
Roberts, Brian 1930- *ConAu 29R, WrDr 84*
Roberts, Bruce 1930- *ConAu 6NR, –9R*
Roberts, C 1917- *ConAu 21R*
Roberts, Carey 1935- *ConAu 106*
Roberts, Carl Eric Bechhofer 1894- *LongCTC*
Roberts, Carol A 1933- *ConAu 37R*
Roberts, Catherine 1917- *WrDr 84*
Roberts, Cecil E Mornington 1892-1976 *ConAu 69, ConAu P-2, LongCTC, TwCA, TwCA SUP*
Roberts, Chalmers 1910- *WrDr 84*
Roberts, Chalmers McGeagh 1910- *ConAu 41R, IntAu&W 82*
Roberts, Charles G D 1860-1943 *TwCCW 83*
Roberts, Sir Charles George Douglas 1860-1943 *ConAu 105, CreCan 2, LongCTC,*

SmATA 29, TwCA, TwCA SUP,
TwCLC 8[port]
Roberts, Charles Wesley 1916- ConAu 17R
Roberts, Clayton 1923- ConAu 21R
Roberts, Dan ConAu X
Roberts, Daniel 1922- ConAu 6NR, –9R
Roberts, David ConAu X, SmATA X
Roberts, David D 1943- ConAu 101
Roberts, David S 1943- ASpks, ConAu 33R
Roberts, Dell ConAu X
Roberts, Dennis W 1947- ConAu 109
Roberts, Denys 1923- WrDr 84
Roberts, Denys Kilham 1904?-1976 ConAu 65
Roberts, Denys Tudor Emil 1923- ConAu P-1,
IntAu&W 82
Roberts, Derek Harry 1931- WrDr 84
Roberts, Derrell C 1927- ConAu 29R
Roberts, Donald Alfred 1897-1978 ConAu 77
Roberts, Donald Frank, Jr. 1939- ConAu 107
Roberts, Doreen 1922- ConAu 108
Roberts, Dorothy IntWWP 82X
Roberts, Dorothy 1906- CreCan 1,
DcLEL 1940, IntWWP 82, WrDr 84
Roberts, Dorothy James 1903- ConAu P-1
Roberts, E A Kevin 1940- IntWWP 82
Roberts, Edgar V 1928- ConAu 21R
Roberts, Edward B 1935- ConAu 9NR, –21R
Roberts, Edward Barry 1900-1972 ConAu P-2
Roberts, Edwin A, Jr. 1932- ConAu 21R
Roberts, Eigra Lewis 1939- IntAu&W 82
Roberts, Eirlys R C 1911- IntAu&W 82,
WrDr 84
Roberts, Elizabeth H 1913- ConAu 61
Roberts, Elizabeth Madox 1881-1941
DcLB 9[port]
Roberts, Elizabeth Madox 1886-1941 ConAmA,
LongCTC, ModAL, SmATA 27, –33[port],
TwCA, TwCA SUP, TwCCW 83
Roberts, Elizabeth Mauchline 1936-
IntAu&W 82
Roberts, Ellen Elizabeth Mayhew 1946-
ConAu 108
Roberts, Elliott B 1899- ConAu 1R, WrDr 84
Roberts, Emrys 1929- IntAu&W 82
Roberts, Eric 1914- ConAu 5R, WrDr 84
Roberts, Eugene 1932- ConAu 97
Roberts, Evelyn Lutman 1917- ConAu 65
Roberts, F David 1923- ConAu 5R
Roberts, Florence Bright 1941- ConAu 65
Roberts, Frances C 1916- ConAu 9R
Roberts, Francis Warren 1916- ConAu 13R,
IntAu&W 82
Roberts, Geoffrey R 1924- ConAu 101
Roberts, George DrAP&F 83
Roberts, George E Theodore Goodridge 1877-1953
CreCan 1
Roberts, Goodridge 1904- CreCan 2
Roberts, Grant ConAu X
Roberts, Harold 1896?-1982 ConAu 108
Roberts, Harold S 1911-1970 ConAu P-2
Roberts, Henry L 1916-1972 ConAu 37R
Roberts, Homer 1912- MichAu 80
Roberts, Hortense Roberta ConAu 89
Roberts, Howard R 1906- ConAu 109
Roberts, I ConAu X
Roberts, I F 1925- ConAu 29R
Roberts, I M ConAu X, WrDr 84
Roberts, Iolo Francis 1925- WrDr 84
Roberts, Irene 1925- TwCRGW, WrDr 84
Roberts, Irene 1926- ConAu 6NR, –13R
Roberts, Ivor ConAu X, WrDr 84
Roberts, James D 1927- WrDr 84
Roberts, James Deotis, Sr. 1927- ConAu 33R,
LivgBAA
Roberts, James Hall WrDr 84
Roberts, James Hall 1927- ConAu X,
TwCCr&M 80
Roberts, Jane 1929- ConAu 41R, ConSFA,
WrDr 84
Roberts, Janet Louise 1925- ConAu 61,
IntAu&W 82, TwCRGW, WrDr 84
Roberts, Jason ConAu X
Roberts, Jean 1926- CreCan 1
Roberts, Jeanne Addison ConAu 89
Roberts, Jim ConAu X, SmATA X
Roberts, Joan Ila 1935- ConAu 29R,
IntAu&W 82, WrDr 84
Roberts, Joe ConAu X, IntAu&W 82X
Roberts, John ConAmTC, ConAu X, TwCWW
Roberts, John G 1913- ConAu 49,
SmATA 27[port]
Roberts, John M 1916- ConAu 37R

Roberts, John Morris 1928- ConAu 85,
IntAu&W 82, WrDr 84
Roberts, John Richard 1934- ConAu 33R
Roberts, John Storm 1936- ConAu 25R
Roberts, Joseph B, Jr. 1918- ConAu 41R
Roberts, Julian ConAu X
Roberts, K ConAu X
Roberts, Kate 1891- ConAu 107, ConLC 15
Roberts, Keith 1935- ConAu 25R, ConLC 14,
ConSFA, TwCSFW, WrDr 84
Roberts, Keith 1937?-1979 ConAu 85
Roberts, Ken ConAu X, WrDr 84
Roberts, Kenneth 1885-1957 ConAu 109
Roberts, Kenneth H 1930- ConAu 33R
Roberts, Kenneth Lewis 1885-1957 ConAmA,
DcLB 9[port], LongCTC, ModAL, TwCA,
TwCA SUP, TwCWr
Roberts, Lawrence WrDr 84
Roberts, Lee ConAu X
Roberts, Len DrAP&F 83
Roberts, Leonard W 1912- ConAu 33R
Roberts, Leslie 1896-1980 ConAu 103
Roberts, Lionel ConAu X, ConSFA,
IntAu&W 82X
Roberts, Lisa ConAu X
Roberts, Lloyd 1884-1966 CreCan 2
Roberts, MacLennan ConAu X
Roberts, Mary Duffy 1925- ConAu 1R
Roberts, Mervin F 1922- ConAu 9NR, –65
Roberts, Michael 1902-1948 LongCTC, ModBrL
Roberts, Michael 1945- ConAu 69
Roberts, Morley 1857-1942 LongCTC
Roberts, Myron 1923- ConAu 29R
Roberts, Nancy Correll 1924- ConAu 6NR, –9R,
SmATA 28
Roberts, Oral 1918- ConAu 41R
Roberts, Patrick 1920- ConAu 61
Roberts, Paul Craig 1939- ConAu 33R,
WrDr 84
Roberts, Paul McHenry 1917-1967 ConAu 1R,
–103
Roberts, Percival R, III DrAP&F 83
Roberts, Percival Rudolph, III 1935- ConAu 41R,
IntAu&W 82, IntWWP 82
Roberts, Philip 1938- ConP 80, WrDr 84
Roberts, Philip Davies 1938- ConAu 109
Roberts, Phyllis Barzollay 1932- ConAu 41R
Roberts, Rand ConAu X
Roberts, Richard J 1928- ConAu 5R
Roberts, Richard W 1935-1978 ConAu 73
Roberts, Rinalda ConAu X
Roberts, Robert C 1942- ConAu 69
Roberts, Ron E 1939- ConAu 33R
Roberts, Roy Allison 1887-1967 ConAu 89
Roberts, Rufus Putnam 1926- ConAu 1R
Roberts, Sally 1935- ConAu X, WrDr 84
Roberts, Selyf 1912- IntAu&W 82
Roberts, Sheila 1942- ConAu 102
Roberts, Spencer Eugene 1920- ConAu 89
Roberts, Steven V 1943- ConAu 61
Roberts, Susan F 1919- ConAu 104
Roberts, Suzanne 1931- ConAu 106
Roberts, Sydney Castle 1887-1966 ConAu P-1,
LongCTC
Roberts, Terence 1911-1973 ConAu X,
SmATA 6
Roberts, Theodore Goodridge 1877-1953
CreCan 1
Roberts, Thom 1940- ConAu 81
Roberts, Thomas J 1925- ConAu 41R
Roberts, Tom ConAu X
Roberts, Trev ConAu X
Roberts, Vera Mowry 1918- ConAu 17R
Roberts, Virginia ConAu X
Roberts, Wagner WrDr 84
Roberts, Walter R 1916- ConAu 1NR, –49
Roberts, Warren 1933- ConAu 73
Roberts, Warren Aldrich 1901- ConAu P-1
Roberts, Wayne ConAu X
Roberts, William Goodridge CreCan 2
Roberts, William Harris Lloyd CreCan 2
Roberts, Willo Davis 1928- ConAu 3NR, –49,
MichAu 80, SmATA 21[port], TwCRGW,
WrDr 84
Roberts-Jones, Phillipe John A G 1924-
IntAu&W 82
Roberts-Wray, Kenneth Owen 1899- ConAu P-2,
IntAu&W 82, WrDr 84
Robertshaw, Denis 1911- ConAu 65
Robertson, Agnes DrAP&F 83
Robertson, Alec ConAu X

Robertson, Alexander Thomas Parke A C
1892-1982 ConAu 104, –105
Robertson, Arnot 1903-1961 TwCA, TwCA SUP
Robertson, Arthur Henry 1913- ConAu 9R,
IntAu&W 82, WrDr 84
Robertson, Barbara Anne 1931- ConAu 25R,
SmATA 12, WrDr 84
Robertson, Brian 1951- ConAu 101
Robertson, Brian Paul DrAP&F 83
Robertson, Charles L 1927- ConAu 21R
Robertson, Charles Martin 1911- ConAu 104
Robertson, Colin 1906- ConAu 9R
Robertson, Constance Noyes 1897- ConAu 29R,
WrDr 84
Robertson, D J 1926-1970 ConAu 10NR
Robertson, D W, Jr. 1914- ConAu 9NR, –61
Robertson, Dale 1923- ConAu 107
Robertson, David 1915- ConAu 81
Robertson, Don 1929- ConAu 7NR, –9R,
SmATA 8
Robertson, Donald James 1926- ConAu 5R
Robertson, Dorothy Lewis 1912- ConAu 25R,
SmATA 12
Robertson, Dougal 1924- ConAu 61
Robertson, Durant Waite, Jr. 1914- ConAu 109
Robertson, E Arnot 1903-1961 LongCTC
Robertson, Edith Anne 1883- ConAu P-1
Robertson, Eileen Arbuthnot 1903-1961 TwCA,
TwCA SUP
Robertson, Elizabeth Chant 1899- ConAu 49,
WrDr 84
Robertson, Ellis ConAu X
Robertson, Elspeth IntAu&W 82X, WrDr 84
Robertson, Esmonde Manning 1923- ConAu 9R,
–29R, WrDr 84
Robertson, Forbes 1853-1937 LongCTC
Robertson, Foster DrAP&F 83
Robertson, Frank Chester 1890-1969 ConAu 1R,
–4NR, TwCWW
Robertson, George 1929- CreCan 1
Robertson, Heather Margaret 1942- ConAu 93
Robertson, Howard Stephen 1931- ConAu 41R
Robertson, James 1911- ConAu 5R
Robertson, James Douglas 1904- ConAu 5R
Robertson, James I, Jr. 1930- ConAu 6NR, –9R,
IntAu&W 82, WrDr 84
Robertson, James Louis 1907- ConAu P-2
Robertson, James Oliver 1932- ConAu 106
Robertson, James Wilson 1899- ConAu 109
Robertson, James Wilson 1899-1983 ConAu 110
Robertson, Jennifer Sinclair 1942- ConAu 5NR,
–53, SmATA 12
Robertson, Jenny ConAu X
Robertson, John George 1867-1933 LongCTC
Robertson, John Mackinnon 1856-1933 LongCTC
Robertson, John Monteath 1900- WrDr 84
Robertson, Kathaleen Ann Powell 1948-
IntWWP 82
Robertson, Keith 1914- TwCCW 83, WrDr 84
Robertson, Keith Charlton 1914- ConAu 9R,
SmATA 1
Robertson, Kirk DrAP&F 83
Robertson, Lanie 1941- NatPD 81[port]
Robertson, Leon S 1936- ConAu 41R
Robertson, Marian 1921- WrDr 84
Robertson, Martin ConAu X
Robertson, Mary D 1927- ConAu 102
Robertson, Mary Elsie DrAP&F 83
Robertson, Mary Elsie 1937- ConAu 81
Robertson, Morgan Andrew 1861-1915 TwCA
Robertson, Olivia Melian 1917- ConAu 9R
Robertson, Patrick 1940- ConAu 61
Robertson, Priscilla 1910- ConAu P-2
Robertson, Roland 1938- ConAu 29R
Robertson, Sarah Margaret 1891-1948 CreCan 1
Robertson, Thomas Anthony 1897- ConAu P-1
Robertson, Walford Graham 1867-1948 LongCTC
Robertson, Wally ConAu X
Robertson, Walter 1892-1983 ConAu 109
Robertson, Wilfrid 1892- ConAu 5R
Robertson, William P DrAP&F 83
Robertson-Glasgow, R C 1901-1965 LongCTC
Robertson Scott, J W 1866- LongCTC
Robertston, Howard W DrAP&F 83
Robeson, Gerald B 1938- ConAu 65
Robeson, Kenneth ConAu X, TwCCr&M 80,
TwCSFW, WrDr 84
Robeson, Paul 1898-1976 ConAu 109
Robey, Edward George 1900-1983 ConAu 109
Robey, Harriet 1900- ConAu 107
Robey, Ralph W 1899-1972 ConAu 37R
Robhs, Dwight ConAu X

Robichaud, Gerald A 1912-1979 *ConAu 85*
Robichaud, Gerard 1908- *ConAu P-2*
Robichon, Jacques 1920- *ConAu 101*
Robida, Albert 1848-1926 *TwCSFW A*
Robie, Edward H 1886- *ConAu P-2*
Robilliard, Eileen Dorothy 1921- *ConAu 21R*
Robin *ConAu X*
Robin, Arthur DeQuetteville 1929- *ConAu 104,*
WrDr 84
Robin, Ralph *DrAP&F 83*
Robin, Ralph 1914- *ConAu 65, IntWWP 82*
Robin, Richard S 1926- *ConAu 21R*
Robinet, Harriette Gillem 1931- *ConAu 69,*
SmATA 27[port]
Robinett, Betty Wallace 1919- *ConAu 41R*
Robinett, Stephen 1941- *ConAu 101, TwCSFW,*
WrDr 84
Robins, Corinne *DrAP&F 83*
Robins, Denise 1897- *ConAu 10NR, -65,*
IntAu&W 82, TwCRGW, TwCWr,
WrDr 84
Robins, Eli 1921- *ConAu 109*
Robins, Elizabeth 1855-1936 *LongCTC*
Robins, Elizabeth 1865?-1952 *LongCTC, TwCA,*
TwCA SUP
Robins, Harry Franklin 1915- *ConAu 5R*
Robins, John D 1884-1952 *CreCan 2*
Robins, Lee N 1922- *ConAu 21R*
Robins, Natalie *DrAP&F 83*
Robins, Natalie 1938- *ConAu 17R, IntWWP 82*
Robins, Patricia 1921- *WrDr 84*
Robins, Patricia Denise 1921- *TwCRGW*
Robins, Robert Henry 1921- *ConAu 5R,*
IntAu&W 82, WrDr 84
Robins-Mowry, Dorothy B 1921- *ConAu 25R*
Robinson, A M Lewin 1916- *ConAu 1R, -9NR,*
-21R, WrDr 84
Robinson, A N R 1926- *ConAu 33R*
Robinson, Adjai 1932- *ConAu 45, SmATA 8*
Robinson, Alan R 1920- *ConAu P-1*
Robinson, Albert Henry 1881-1956 *CreCan 1*
Robinson, Albert J 1926- *ConAu 53*
Robinson, Alice M 1920- *ConAu 108*
Robinson, Alice M 1920-1983 *ConAu 109*
Robinson, Anthony *DrAP&F 83*
Robinson, Anthony 1931- *ConAu 1R, -1NR*
Robinson, Antony Meredith Lewin 1916-
IntAu&W 82
Robinson, Armstead *LivgBAA*
Robinson, B W 1912- *ConAu 3NR*
Robinson, Barbara Webb 1927- *ConAu 1R,*
SmATA 8
Robinson, Barry 1938- *ConAu 25R*
Robinson, Basil William 1912- *ConAu 5R,*
IntAu&W 82, WrDr 84
Robinson, Betsy Julia 1951- *ConAu 109,*
NatPD 81[port]
Robinson, Bill *ConAu X*
Robinson, Blackwell P 1916- *ConAu 45*
Robinson, Budd *ConAu X*
Robinson, C A, Jr. 1900-1965 *ConAu 4NR*
Robinson, Cecil 1921- *ConAu 13R*
Robinson, Cervin 1928- *ConAu 61*
Robinson, Chaille Howard *ConAu 13R*
Robinson, Charles 1870-1937 *SmATA 17*
Robinson, Charles 1931- *ConAu 2NR, -49,*
SmATA 6
Robinson, Charles Alexander, Jr. 1900-
ConAu 1R
Robinson, Charles E 1941- *ConAu 77*
Robinson, Charles Knox 1909-1980 *ConAu 103,*
-97
Robinson, Corinne H 1909- *ConAu 93*
Robinson, Daniel N 1937- *ConAu 33R*
Robinson, Daniel Sommer 1888- *ConAu 29R*
Robinson, David 1915- *ConAu 81*
Robinson, David A 1925- *ConAu 17R*
Robinson, Derek 1932- *ConAu 77,*
IntAu&W 82, WrDr 84
Robinson, Donald 1913- *ConAu 25R*
Robinson, Donald H 1910- *ConAu P-2*
Robinson, Donald L 1936- *ConAu 41R*
Robinson, Donald W 1911- *ConAu 21R*
Robinson, Dorothy Anderson 1924- *IntWWP 82*
Robinson, Douglas Hill 1918- *ConAu 5R, -8NR*
Robinson, Earl 1910- *ConAu 2NR, -45*
Robinson, Edgar Eugene 1887-1977 *ConAu 73*
Robinson, Edward G 1893-1973 *ConAu 45*
Robinson, Edward L 1921- *ConAu 41R*
Robinson, Edwin Arlington 1869-1935 *CnMWL,*
ConAmA, ConAu 104, LongCTC, ModAL,
ModAL SUP, TwCA, TwCA SUP,

TwCLC 5[port], TwCWr, WhoTwCL
Robinson, Elizabeth Cameron *ConAu 1R*
Robinson, Elwyn B 1905- *ConAu P-2*
Robinson, Eric Henry 1924- *ConAu 49*
Robinson, Florine 1920- *LivgBAA, WrDr 84*
Robinson, Forrest G 1940- *ConAu 41R*
Robinson, Francis 1910-1980 *ConAu 97*
Robinson, Frank M 1926- *ConAu 3NR, -49,*
TwCSFW, WrDr 84
Robinson, Frank M, Jr. 1928- *ConAu 57*
Robinson, Frank S 1947- *ConAu 97*
Robinson, Fred Colson 1930- *ConAu 37R,*
WrDr 84
Robinson, Fred Miller 1942- *ConAu 107*
Robinson, G Melville 1909- *WrDr 84*
Robinson, Gilbert DeBeauregard 1906- *WrDr 84*
Robinson, Godfrey Clive 1913- *ConAu 13R*
Robinson, Gustavus H 1881-1972 *ConAu 37R*
Robinson, Haddon W 1931- *ConAu 73*
Robinson, Halbert B 1925- *ConAu 17R*
Robinson, Halbert B 1925-1981 *ConAu 9NR*
Robinson, Helen Caister 1899- *ConAu 93*
Robinson, Helen Mansfield 1906- *ConAu 13R*
Robinson, Helene M *ConAu 13R*
Robinson, Henry Morton 1898-1961 *TwCA SUP*
Robinson, Herbert Spencer *ConAu 93*
Robinson, Horace W 1909- *ConAu 93*
Robinson, Howard 1885- *ConAu P-1*
Robinson, Hubbell 1905-1974 *ConAu 53*
Robinson, Ian 1938- *IntAu&W 82*
Robinson, Ira E 1927- *ConAu 81*
Robinson, J Lewis 1918- *ConAu 107*
Robinson, J W 1934- *ConAu 17R*
Robinson, James A 1932- *ConAu 17R*
Robinson, James Harvey 1863-1936 *TwCA,*
TwCA SUP
Robinson, James K 1916- *ConAu 17R*
Robinson, James M 1924- *ConAu 13R*
Robinson, Jan M 1933- *ConAu 61, SmATA 6*
Robinson, Janet O 1939- *ConAu 33R*
Robinson, Jay 1932- *ConAu 41R*
Robinson, Jean O 1934- *ConAu 29R, SmATA 7*
Robinson, Jeremy *DrAP&F 83*
Robinson, Jerry 1922- *SmATA 34*
Robinson, Jill *DrAP&F 83*
Robinson, Jill 1936- *ConAu 102, ConLC 10*
Robinson, Joan G *WrDr 84*
Robinson, Joan G 1910- *TwCCW 83*
Robinson, Joan Mary Gale Thomas 1910-
ConAu 5R, -5NR, IntAu&W 82,
SmATA 7
Robinson, Joan Violet 1903- *ConAu 6NR, -9R*
Robinson, Joan Violet 1903-1983 *ConAu 110*
Robinson, John Arthur Thomas 1919- *ConAu 5R,*
-6NR, DcLEL 1940, IntAu&W 82,
WrDr 84
Robinson, John Lewis 1918- *WrDr 84*
Robinson, John W 1929- *ConAu 2NR, -49*
Robinson, Joseph 1927- *ConAu 45*
Robinson, Joseph Frederick 1912- *ConAu 13R*
Robinson, Joseph William 1908- *ConAu P-2*
Robinson, Karl Frederic 1904-1967 *ConAu 5R,*
-5NR
Robinson, Kathleen *ConAu X*
Robinson, Keith 1933- *WrDr 84*
Robinson, Kenneth Ernest 1914- *ConAu 5R,*
IntAu&W 82
Robinson, L W 1912- *ConAu 69*
Robinson, Lennox 1886-1958 *CnMD,*
DcLB 10[port], LongCTC, ModBrL,
ModWD, TwCA, TwCA SUP
Robinson, Leonard A 1904?-1980 *ConAu 97*
Robinson, Leonard Wallace *DrAP&F 83*
Robinson, Lewis Green 1929- *LivgBAA*
Robinson, Lillian S *DrAP&F 83*
Robinson, Linda Jane Rookwood 1914-
IntWWP 82
Robinson, Lisa 1936- *ConAu 93*
Robinson, Logan Gilmore 1949- *ConAu 108*
Robinson, Louie, Jr. 1926- *ConAu 107,*
LivgBAA
Robinson, Lytle W 1913- *ConAu 61*
Robinson, Mabel Louise 1874-1962
DcLB 22[port]
Robinson, Margaret A *DrAP&F 83*
Robinson, Margaret A 1937- *ConAu 107*
Robinson, Marguerite S 1935- *ConAu 49,*
WrDr 84
Robinson, Sister Marian Dolores 1916-
ConAu 9R
Robinson, Marileta 1942- *ConAu 101,*
SmATA 32[port]

Robinson, Marilynne 1944- *ConLC 25[port]*
Robinson, Martin David 1925-1982 *ConAu 108*
Robinson, Matt 1937- *ConAu 45*
Robinson, Maudie Millian Oller 1914-
ConAu 8NR, -61, SmATA 11
Robinson, Maurice R 1895-1982 *ConAu 106,*
SmATA 29N
Robinson, Max 1939- *ConAu 110*
Robinson, Nancy K 1942- *ConAu 106,*
SmATA 31, -32[port]
Robinson, Nancy M 1930- *ConAu 61*
Robinson, Norman Hamilton Galloway 1912-
ConAu 13R
Robinson, O Preston 1903- *ConAu 13R*
Robinson, Olvis 1923- *ConAu 53*
Robinson, P W 1893- *ConAu 103*
Robinson, Patricia *ConAu X*
Robinson, Patricia Colbert 1923- *ConAu 77*
Robinson, Paul 1940- *ConAu 81*
Robinson, Philip 1926- *ConAu 21R, WrDr 84*
Robinson, Ras 1935- *ConAu 105*
Robinson, Ray 1920- *ConAu 77, SmATA 23*
Robinson, Raymond Henry 1927- *ConAu 41R*
Robinson, Richard 1945- *ConAu 57*
Robinson, Richard Dunlop 1921- *ConAu 5R*
Robinson, Robert 1922- *ConAu 41R*
Robinson, Robert 1927- *ConAu 9R, WrDr 84*
Robinson, Robert H 1936- *ConAu 5R, -6NR*
Robinson, Roland 1912- *WrDr 84*
Robinson, Roland Edward 1912- *ConP 80,*
DcLEL 1940, IntAu&W 82, IntWWP 82
Robinson, Roland Inwood 1907- *ConAu 1R,*
-1NR
Robinson, Rollo S 1915- *ConAu 41R*
Robinson, Rose *ConAu 77, LivgBAA*
Robinson, S Garrett 1939- *NatPD 81[port]*
Robinson, Selma 1899?-1977 *ConAu 73*
Robinson, Shari *ConAu X*
Robinson, Sheila 1928- *WrDr 84*
Robinson, Smokey 1940- *ConLC 21[port]*
Robinson, Sondra Till 1931- *ConAu 7NR, -53*
Robinson, Spider 1948- *ConAu 11NR, -65,*
IntAu&W 82, TwCSFW, WrDr 84
Robinson, T H 1869-1950 *SmATA 17*
Robinson, T M 1936- *ConAu 29R*
Robinson, Terry 1916- *ConAu 108*
Robinson, Theodore Henry 1881-1964 *LongCTC*
Robinson, Thomas Rufer Barnard 1905-
IntAu&W 82
Robinson, Thomas W 1935- *ConAu 33R*
Robinson, Trevor 1929- *ConAu 53*
Robinson, Veronica 1926- *ConAu 105,*
SmATA 30[port]
Robinson, Vince *ConAu X*
Robinson, Virgil E 1908- *ConAu 21R*
Robinson, W Gordon 1903-1977 *ConAu 5R,*
-5NR
Robinson, W Heath 1872-1944 *SmATA 17*
Robinson, W R 1927- *ConAu 21R, WrDr 84*
Robinson, W Stitt 1917- *ConAu 105*
Robinson, Wayne 1916- *ConAu 1R*
Robinson, Wayne A 1937- *ConAu 73*
Robinson, Wilhelmena S 1912- *ConAu 25R*
Robinson, Willard B 1935- *ConAu 57*
Robinson, William Childs 1897- *ConAu 1R*
Robinson, William Henry 1922- *ConAu 37R,*
LivgBAA
Robinson, William P 1910- *ConAu 5R*
Robinson, William Wheeler 1918- *ConAu 3NR,*
-5R
Robison, Bonnie 1924- *ConAu 57, SmATA 12*
Robison, David V 1911?-1978 *ConAu 81, -93*
Robison, Mabel Otis 1891- *ConAu P-1*
Robison, Margaret *DrAP&F 83*
Robison, Nancy L 1934- *ConAu 93,*
SmATA 32[port]
Robison, Sophia Moses 1888-1969 *ConAu 5R,*
-103
Robitscher, Jonas B 1920-1981 *ConAu 103, -21R*
Robles, Alfred A *DrAP&F 83*
Robles, Emmanuel Francois 1913- *CnMD*
Robles, Emmanuel Francois 1914- *CIDMEL 80,*
ConAu 81, IntAu&W 82, ModFrL
Robles, Mireya *DrAP&F 83*
Robles, Mireya 1934- *ConAu 81, IntAu&W 82,*
IntWWP 82
Robley, Grace 1918- *ConAu 61*
Robley, Rob *ConAu X*
Robley, Wendell 1916- *ConAu 61*
Robo, Etienne 1879- *ConAu P-1*
Robock, Stefan H 1915- *ConAu 17R*
Robottom, John *WrDr 84*

Robottom, John Carlisle 1934- *ConAu 29R,*
SmATA 7
Robsjohn-Gibbings, Terence Harold 1905-1976
ConAu 69
Robson, B T 1939- *ConAu 29R*
Robson, Brian Turnbull 1939- *IntAu&W 82,*
WrDr 84
Robson, D I 1935- *ConAu 25R*
Robson, Deborah *DrAP&F 83*
Robson, Derek Ian 1935- *WrDr 84*
Robson, Dirk *ConAu X, WrDr 84*
Robson, E W 1897- *ConAu 65*
Robson, Elizabeth 1942- *ConAu 101*
Robson, Ernest *DrAP&F 83*
Robson, Ernest M 1902- *ConAu 45*
Robson, James 1890- *ConAu 5R*
Robson, Jeremy 1939- *WrDr 84*
Robson, Jeremy Michael 1939- *ConAu 4NR, –5R,*
ConP 80, IntWWP 82
Robson, John Mercel 1927- *ConAu 29R,*
IntAu&W 82
Robson, Lucia St. Clair 1942- *ConAu 108*
Robson, Marion M 1908- *ConAu 89*
Robson, William Alexander 1895-1980
ConAu 103, –97, IntAu&W 82
Robson, William N *AuNews 1*
Roby, Kinley E 1929- *ConAu 77*
Roby, Mary Linn 1930- *ConAu 7NR, –13R,*
TwCRGW, WrDr 84
Roby, Pamela Ann 1942- *ConAu 29R, WrDr 84*
Roby, Robert C 1922- *ConAu 5R*
Robyns, Gwen 1917- *ConAu 93*
Roca-Pons, Josep 1914- *ConAu 49*
Rocafuerte, Jose Maria *IntAu&W 82X*
Roch, Dalby *IntAu&W 82X*
Roch, John H 1916- *ConAu 102*
Rocha, Adolfo *WorAu 1970*
Rocha, Rina Garcia 1954- *IntWWP 82*
Rochard, Henri *ConAu X, IntAu&W 82X,*
WrDr 84
Roche, A K *ConAu X, SmATA X*
Roche, Alphonse Victor 1895- *ConAu 104*
Roche, Arthur Somers 1883-1935 *TwCA*
Roche, Denis 1937- *CIDMEL 80, WorAu 1970*
Roche, Douglas J 1929- *ConAu 101*
Roche, George Charles, III 1935- *ConAu 29R*
Roche, J Jeffrey 1916?-1975 *ConAu 61*
Roche, John *ConAu X*
Roche, John P 1923- *ConAu 69, WrDr 84*
Roche, Kennedy Francis 1911- *ConAu 61*
Roche, Maurice 1925- *CIDMEL 80*
Roche, Mazo DeLa *TwCA, TwCA SUP*
Roche, Orion 1948- *ConAu 61*
Roche, Owen I A 1911?-1973 *ConAu 41R*
Roche, P K *SmATA 34*
Roche, Paul 1928- *ConAu 4NR, –5R, ConP 80,*
DcLEL 1940, WrDr 84
Roche, T W E 1919- *ConAu P-2*
Roche, Terry *ConAu X, IntWWP 82X*
Roche, Thomas P, Jr. 1931- *ConAu 106*
Rochefort, Christiane 1917- *CIDMEL 80,*
TwCWr, WorAu
Rochelle, Barbara *IntAu&W 82X*
Rochelle, Jay C 1938- *ConAu 53*
Rochelle, Pierre Eugene Drieu La *WorAu 1970*
Rocher, Guy 1924- *ConAu 45*
Rocher, Ludo 1926- *ConAu 106*
Rochers, Joseph Alfred Houle Des *CreCan 1*
Rochester, Devereaux 1917- *ConAu 105*
Rochester, Harry A 1897?-1983 *ConAu 109*
Rochester, J Martin 1945- *ConAu 37R*
Rochlin, Gregory 1912- *ConAu 49*
Rochmis, Lyda N 1912- *ConAu 29R*
Rocholl, Rudolf 1925- *IntAu&W 82*
Rock, David 1945- *ConAu 101*
Rock, Gail *SmATA 32*
Rock, Irvin 1922- *ConAu 10NR, –21R*
Rock, James M 1935- *ConAu 102*
Rock, Milton L 1921- *ConAu 49*
Rock, Phillip 1927- *ConAu 101*
Rock, Richard *ConAu X, IntWWP 82X,*
MichAu 80
Rock, Stanley A 1937- *ConAu 101*
Rock, William R 1930- *ConAu 41R*
Rockas, Leo 1924- *ConAu 13R*
Rockcastle, Verne N 1920- *ConAu 73*
Rocke, Russell 1945- *ConAu 33R, WrDr 84*
Rockefeller, John Davison, III 1906-1978
ConAu 77, –81
Rockingham, Montague *ConAu X*
Rockland, Mae Shafter 1937- *ConAu 65*
Rockland, Michael Aaron 1935- *ConAu 37R,*

WrDr 84
Rockley, L E 1916- *ConAu 29R, WrDr 84*
Rocklin, Ross Louis 1913- *ConAu 61*
Rocklynne, Ross 1913- *ConAu X, TwCSFW,*
WrDr 84
Rockne, Dick 1939- *ConAu 61*
Rockowitz, Murray 1920- *ConAu 25R*
Rocks, Lawrence 1933- *ConAu 85*
Rockwell, Anne 1934- *ConAu 21R*
Rockwell, Anne F 1934- *SmATA 33[port]*
Rockwell, F F 1884-1976 *ConAu 103, –49*
Rockwell, Harlow *ConAu 109,*
SmATA 33[port]
Rockwell, Jane 1929- *ConAu 65*
Rockwell, Kiffin Ayres 1917- *ConAu 37R*
Rockwell, Matt *ConAu X*
Rockwell, Norman 1894-1978 *ConAu 81, –89,*
SmATA 23[port]
Rockwell, Thomas 1933- *ChlLR 6[port],*
ConAu 29R, SmATA 7, WrDr 84
Rockwell, Wilson 1909- *ConAu P-2*
Rockwood, Joyce 1947- *ConAu 6NR, –57*
Rockwood, Louis G 1925- *ConAu 45*
Rockwood, Roy *ConAu P-2, SmATA X, –1*
Rodahl, Kaare 1917- *ConAu 9R, WrDr 84*
Rodale, J I 1898-1971 *ConAu 29R*
Rodale, Robert 1930- *ConAu 53*
Rodan, Paul N Rosenstein *ConAu X*
Rodas, Virginia 1932- *IntWWP 82*
Rodberg, Leonard S 1932- *ConAu 45*
Rodberg, Lillian 1936- *ConAu 29R*
Rodd, Sir James Rennell 1858-1941 *LongCTC*
Rodd, John 1905- *WrDr 84*
Rodd, Kylie Tennant 1912- *ConAu 5R, –5NR*
Rodd, Mitford *ConAu X*
Rodd, Nancy Freeman-Mitford *ConAu X*
Rodd-Marling, Yvonne 1912-1982 *ConAu 107*
Rodda, Charles 1891- *ConAu 5R*
Rodda, Peter 1937- *ConAu 81*
Roddenberry, Eugene Wesley 1921- *ConAu 110*
Roddenberry, Gene *ConAu X*
Roddenberry, Gene 1921- *ConLC 17, ConSFA*
Roddick, Alan 1937- *ConAu 77, ConP 80,*
WrDr 84
Roddick, Ellen 1936- *ConAu 41R*
Roddis, Louis Harry 1886- *ConAu 5R*
Roddis, Roland J 1908- *ConAu 5R*
Rode, Helge 1870-1937 *CIDMEL 80*
Rodefer, Stephen 1940- *ConAu 107, ConP 80,*
IntWWP 82, WrDr 84
Rodell, Fred 1907-1980 *ConAu 97*
Rodell, Marie F 1912-1975 *ConAu 61,*
TwCCr&M 80
Rodenbach, Georges-Raymond-Constantin
1855-1898 *CIDMEL 80*
Rodenberg, Julius 1884-1970 *ConAu 104*
Rodenbough, Jean *DrAP&F 83*
Roder, Wolf 1932- *ConAu 17R*
Roderus, Frank 1942- *ConAu 89, TwCWW*
Rodes, John Edward 1923- *ConAu 13R,*
WrDr 84
Rodewyk, Adolf 1894- *ConAu 65*
Rodger, Alec *ConAu X*
Rodger, Ian 1926- *WrDr 84*
Rodger, Ian Graham 1926- *ConAu 4NR, –5R,*
IntAu&W 82
Rodger, Thomas Alexander 1907-1982
ConAu 106
Rodgers, Betsy 1907- *ConAu P-1*
Rodgers, Betty June 1921- *ConAu 9R*
Rodgers, Brian 1910- *ConAu 29R*
Rodgers, Carolyn M *ConAu 2NR, –45,*
ConP 80, WrDr 84
Rodgers, Dorothy F 1909- *ConAu 89*
Rodgers, Frank *ConAu X*
Rodgers, Frank P 1924- *ConAu 9R*
Rodgers, Harrell R, Jr. 1939- *ConAu 7NR, –53*
Rodgers, Joann Ellison 1941- *ConAu 77*
Rodgers, John 1906- *ConAu P-1, IntAu&W 82,*
WrDr 84
Rodgers, Mary 1931- *ConAu 8NR, –49,*
ConLC 12, SmATA 8, TwCCW 83,
WrDr 84
Rodgers, Richard 1902-1979 *ConAu 89*
Rodgers, Sarah *DrAP&F 83*
Rodgers, Stanley 1928-1977 *ConAu 106*
Rodgers, W R 1909-1969 *ConAu 85, ConLC 7,*
LongCTC, ModBrL
Rodgers, William H 1918- *ConAu 17R*
Rodgers, William Henry 1947- *ConAu 101*
Rodgers, William Robert 1909-1969 *DcLEL 1940,*

TwCA SUP
Rodick, Burleigh Cushing 1889- *ConAu 5R*
Rodimer, Eva 1895- *ConAu P-2*
Rodimstev, Aleksandr 1905?-1977 *ConAu 69*
Rodin, Arnold W 1917- *ConAu 89*
Rodini, Robert J 1936- *ConAu 29R*
Rodinson, Maxime 1915- *ConAu 4NR, –53*
Roditi, Edouard 1910- *WrDr 84*
Roditi, Edouard Herbert 1910- *ConAu 101,*
ConP 80, WorAu 1970
Rodli, Agnes Sylvia 1921- *ConAu 9R*
Rodman, Bella 1903- *ConAu P-2*
Rodman, Hyman 1931- *ConAu 8NR, –17R*
Rodman, Maia *ConAu X, DrAP&F 83,*
SmATA X, TwCCW 83
Rodman, Selden 1909- *ConAu 5R, –5NR,*
SmATA 9, TwCA SUP
Rodney, Bob *ConAu X*
Rodney, Janet *DrAP&F 83*
Rodney, Robert M 1911- *ConAu 77*
Rodney, Walter 1942-1980 *ConIsC 2[port]*
Rodney, William 1923- *ConAu 25R, WrDr 84*
Rodnick, David 1908- *ConAu 33R,*
IntAu&W 82
Rodnitzky, Jerome Leon 1936- *ConAu 41R*
Rodo, Jose Enrique 1871-1917 *ModLAL*
Rodo, Jose Enrique 1872?-1917 *TwCA,*
TwCA SUP, TwCWr
Rodowsky, Colby 1932- *ConAu 69, SmATA 21*
Rodrigo, Robert 1928- *ConAu 13R*
Rodrigues, Jose Honorio 1913- *ConAu 29R*
Rodrigues, Louis Jerome 1938- *IntWWP 82*
Rodrigues, Santan Rosario 1948- *IntWWP 82*
Rodrigues, Urbano Tavares 1923- *CIDMEL 80*
Rodriguez, Aleida *DrAP&F 83*
Rodriguez, Claudio 1934- *CIDMEL 80,*
ConLC 10
Rodriguez, Judith 1936- *ConAu 107, ConP 80,*
IntWWP 82, WrDr 84
Rodriguez, Mario 1922- *ConAu 17R*
Rodriguez, Richard 1944- *ConAu 110*
Rodriguez, William Robert *DrAP&F 83*
Rodriguez-Alcala, Hugo 1917- *ConAu 21R*
Rodriguez-Alcala, Sally 1938- *ConAu 21R*
Rodriguez Batllori, Francisco 1908- *IntAu&W 82*
Rodriguez Buded, Ricardo *CroCD*
Rodriguez Cepeda, Enrique 1939- *ConAu 45*
Rodriguez Delgado, Jose M *ConAu X*
Rodriguez Mendez, Jose Maria 1926-
CIDMEL 80
Rodriguez O, Jaime E 1940- *ConAu 110, –73*
Rodriguez Solis, Eduardo 1938- *IntAu&W 82*
Rodway, Allan Edwin 1919- *ConAu 13R,*
IntAu&W 82, WrDr 84
Rodwin, Lloyd 1919- *ConAu 4NR, –5R,*
IntAu&W 82, WrDr 84
Rodzinski, Halina 1904- *ConAu 69*
Roe, Anne 1904- *ConAu 17R*
Roe, Daphne A 1923- *ConAu 93*
Roe, Derek Arthur 1937- *ConAu 107, WrDr 84*
Roe, Ernest 1920- *WrDr 84*
Roe, F Gordon 1894- *WrDr 84*
Roe, Frederic Gordon 1894- *ConAu 9R,*
IntAu&W 82
Roe, Harry Mason *ConAu P-2*
Roe, Ivan 1917- *WrDr 84*
Roe, Kathleen Robson 1910- *ConAu 93*
Roe, Richard Lionel 1936- *ConAu 65*
Roe, W G 1932- *ConAu 21R*
Roe, William Henry 1918- *ConAu 5R*
Roeber, Edward C 1913-1969 *ConAu 5R, –5NR*
Roebuck, Carl Angus 1914- *ConAu 105*
Roebuck, Derek 1935- *WrDr 84*
Roebuck, Janet 1943- *ConAu 49*
Roebuck, Julian B 1920- *ConAu 101*
Roeburt, John 1909?-1972 *ConAu 33R*
Roecker, W A 1942- *ConAu 61*
Roeder, Bill 1922-1982 *ConAu 107*
Roeder, Ralph Leclerq 1890-1969 *ConAu 104*
Roehr, George L 1931?-1983 *ConAu 110*
Roehrs, Walter R 1901- *ConAu 103*
Roelants, Maurits 1895-1966 *CIDMEL 80*
Roelker, Nancy Lyman 1915- *ConAu 9R*
Roemer, Milton I 1916- *ConAu 6NR, –57*
Roemer, Norma H 1905-1973 *ConAu P-2*
Roeming, Robert Frederick 1911- *ConAu 29R*
Roepke, Wilhelm 1899-1966 *ConAu P-1*
Roer, Berniece Marie *ConAu 9R*
Roes, Nicholas 1926- *ConAu 29R*
Roesch, Roberta F 1919- *ConAu 2NR, –5R,*
IntAu&W 82
Roesch, Ronald 1947- *ConAu 106*

Rollins, Alfred Brooks, Jr. 1921- *ConAu 5R*
Rollins, Bryant 1937- *ConAu 49, LivgBAA*
Rollins, C D 1918- *ConAu 41R*
Rollins, Charlemae Hill 1897-1979 *ConAu 9R, –104, LivgBAA, SmATA 26N, –3*
Rollins, Kelly 1924- *ConAu 106*
Rollins, Leighton 1900- *IntAu&W 82, IntWWP 82*
Rollins, Peter C 1942- *ConAu 108*
Rollins, Royce *ConAu X*
Rollins, Wayne Gilbert 1929- *ConAu 3NR, –9R, WrDr 84*
Rollison, William D 1897-1971 *ConAu P-2*
Rollo, Vera Foster 1924- *ConAu 81, WrDr 84*
Rollo, Charles J 1887- *ConAu 107*
Rolls, Anthony *ConAu X, TwCCr&M 80*
Rolls, Charles J 1887- *ConAu 107*
Rolls, Eric Charles 1923- *ConAu 33R, IntAu&W 82, IntWWP 82, WrDr 84*
Rolo, Charles J 1916- *ConAu 101, WorAu*
Rolo, Charles J 1916-1982 *ConAu 108*
Rolo, Paul Jacques Victor 1917- *ConAu 21R, WrDr 84*
Roloff, Leland Harold 1927- *ConAu 49*
Rolph, C H 1901- *ConAu X, WrDr 84*
Rolph, Earl R 1910- *ConAu P-2*
Rolston, Holmes 1900-1977 *ConAu 1R, –3NR*
Rolt, L T C 1910-1974 *ConAu 1NR*
Rolt, Lionel Thomas Caswall 1910- *ConAu 1R*
Rolt-Wheeler, Francis William 1876-1960 *ConAu 89*
Rolvaag, O E 1876-1931 *DcLB 9[port], FifWWr, TwCWW*
Rolvaag, Ole Edvart 1876-1931 *CIDMEL 80, ConAmA, LongCTC, ModAL, TwCA, TwCA SUP, TwCWr*
Rom, M Martin 1946- *ConAu 81*
Romagnoli, G Franco 1926- *ConAu 73*
Romagnoli, Margaret O'Neill 1922- *ConAu 73*
Romaine, Elaine *DrAP&F 83*
Romaine, Lawrence B 1900- *ConAu P-1*
Romains, Jules 1885-1972 *CIDMEL 80, CnMD, CnMWL, ConAu 85, ConLC 7, LongCTC, ModFrL, ModRL, ModWD, TwCA, TwCA SUP, TwCWr, WhoTwCL*
Romaiz *IntAu&W 82X*
Roman, Amanda *IntAu&W 82X*
Roman, Daniel 1921- *ConAu 41R*
Roman, Eric 1926- *ConAu 1R, –1NR*
Roman, Jerome *IntAu&W 82X*
Romanell, Patrick 1912- *ConAu 21R*
Romanelli, Charles S 1930- *ConAu 13R*
Romaniello, Charlotte *DrAP&F 83*
Romano, Clare *ConAu 41R*
Romano, Deane Louis 1927- *ConAu 25R, IntAu&W 82*
Romano, Don *ConAu X*
Romano, Liboria Elizabeth 1899- *IntWWP 82*
Romano, Louis 1921- *ConAu 8NR, –17R, WrDr 84*
Romano, Paol *IntAu&W 82X*
Romanoff, Alexis Lawrence 1892-1980 *ConAu 5NR, –9R*
Romanoff, Harry 1892?-1970 *ConAu 104*
Romanoff, Ivan 1915- *CreCan 1*
Romanones, Countess Of *ConAu X*
Romanov, Panteleymon Sergeyevich 1884-1936 *CIDMEL 80, TwCA, TwCA SUP*
Romanowiczowa, Zofia 1922- *CIDMEL 80*
Romans, J Thomas 1933- *ConAu 13R*
Romanucci-Ross, Lola 1928- *ConAu 101*
Romanus, Charles Franklin 1915- *ConAu 21R*
Romanyshyn, Robert Donald 1942- *ConAu 108*
Romasco, Albert U 1930- *ConAu 110*
Romberger, Judy 1940- *ConAu 106*
Rombouts, Tony 1941- *IntWWP 82*
Rome, Anthony *ConAu X, WrDr 84*
Rome, Beatrice K 1913- *ConAu 13R*
Rome, Florence 1910- *ConAu 33R*
Rome, Margaret *TwCRGW, WrDr 84*
Romeo, Rosario 1924- *IntAu&W 82*
Romer, Alfred 1906- *ConAu 37R*
Romer, John 1941- *ConAu 110*
Romero, Dorothy Lankin *MichAu 80*
Romero, Gerry *ConAu X*
Romero, Jose Ruben 1890-1952 *ModLAL*
Romero, Leo *DrAP&F 83*
Romero, Luis 1916- *CIDMEL 80, IntAu&W 82*
Romero, Orlando 1945- *ConAu 69*
Romero, Patricia W 1935- *ConAu 37R*
Romerstein, Herbert 1931- *ConAu 9R*
Romeu, Jorge Luis *DrAP&F 83*
Romey, Bill *ConAu X*

Romey, William Dowden 1930- *ConAu 57*
Romig, Edna Davis 1889-1978 *ConAu 103, –45*
Romig, Walter 1903-1977 *ConAu 110*
Romig, Walter 1905-1977 *MichAu 80*
Romijn, Johanna Maria Kooyker *ConAu X*
Romm, Ethel Grodzins 1925- *ConAu 33R*
Rommel, Dayton *ConAu 5R, WrDr 84*
Rommetveit, Ragnar 1924- *ConAu 57*
Romney, George W 1907- *ConAu 106*
Romney, Rodney Ross 1931- *ConAu 102*
Romney, Steve *ConAu X*
Romo, Rolando *DrAP&F 83*
Romoser, George K 1929- *ConAu 41R*
Romtvedt, David *DrAP&F 83*
Romulo, Carlos P 1899- *ConAu 10NR*
Romulo, Carlos Pena 1899- *ConAu 13R, IntAu&W 82*
Romun, Isak *DrAP&F 83*
Romyn, Johanna Maria Kooyker *ConAu X*
Rona, Peter A 1934- *ConAu 108*
Ronald, Bruce W 1931- *ConSFA*
Ronald, David William 1937- *ConAu 65*
Ronald, Hugh 1912?-1983 *ConAu 109*
Ronald, William 1926- *CreCan 1*
Ronalds, Mary Teresa 1946- *ConAu 25R, WrDr 84*
Ronaldson, Agnes S 1916- *ConAu 17R*
Ronaldson, James 1930- *CreCan 1*
Ronan, Colin Alistair 1920- *ConAu 5R, –6NR, IntAu&W 82, WrDr 84*
Ronan, Georgia *ConAu X*
Ronan, John J *DrAP&F 83*
Ronan, Margaret 1918- *ConAu 102*
Ronan, Richard *DrAP&F 83*
Ronan, Thomas Matthew 1907- *ConAu P-1*
Ronan, Tom 1907- *ConAu X, WrDr 84*
Ronan, William W 1917- *ConAu 33R*
Ronay, Gabriel Ernest 1930- *ConAu 85*
Rondell, Florence 1907- *ConAu 57*
Ronder, Paul 1940?-1977 *ConAu 73*
Rondthaler, Edward 1905- *ConAu 13R*
Ronen, Dov 1933- *ConAu 10NR, –57*
Roney, Alice Lorraine 1926- *IntWWP 82*
Roney, Irene Salemka *CreCan 2*
Roney, Ruth Anne *ConAu X*
Rongen, Bjoern 1906- *ConAu P-2, SmATA 10*
Rongione, Louis Anthony 1912- *ConAu 57*
Ronken, Harriet *ConAu X, –73*
Ronne, Finn 1899-1980 *ConAu 1R, –1NR, –97*
Ronnie, Art 1931- *ConAu 41R*
Ronning, C Neale 1927- *ConAu 5R*
Ronns, Edward *ConAu X, TwCCr&M 80*
Ronsheim, Sally B *ConAu 57*
Ronsin, Jean *ConAu X*
Ronsley, Joseph 1931- *ConAu 10NR, –25R, IntAu&W 82, WrDr 84*
Ronsman, M M *ConAu X*
Rontgen, Wilhelm Konrad Von 1845-1923 *LongCTC*
Rood, Allan 1894- *ConAu P-1*
Rood, John 1902- *ConAu 5R*
Rood, Karen Lane 1946- *ConAu 102*
Rood, Robert Thomas 1942- *ConAu 107*
Rood, Ronald 1920- *ConAu 9NR, –21R, SmATA 12*
Roodenburg, Nancy McKee 1909-1972 *ConAu 104*
Rook, Alan 1909- *ConAu 97, ConP 80, IntWWP 82, WrDr 84*
Rook, Earnest Robert 1917- *ConAu 104*
Rook, Gerrit Jan De 1943- *IntAu&W 82*
Rook, Pearl Lucille Newton 1923- *IntWWP 82*
Rook, Tony 1932- *ConAu 69, IntAu&W 82, WrDr 84*
Rook, William Alan 1909- *IntAu&W 82*
Rooke, Daphne 1914- *WrDr 84*
Rooke, Daphne Marie 1914- *ConAu 53, ConNov 82, IntAu&W 82, SmATA 12, TwCW, WorAu*
Rooke, Leon *DrAP&F 83*
Rooke, Leon 1934- *ConAu 25R, ConLC 25[port]*
Rookmaaker, Hendrik Roelof 1922- *ConAu 57*
Rooks, George 1951- *ConAu 105*
Room, Adrian 1933- *ConAu 97, IntAu&W 82*
Roome, Katherine Ann Davis 1952- *ConAu 85*
Rooney, Andrew A 1919- *ConAu 5R, –9NR*
Rooney, Andy *ConAu X*
Rooney, David Douglas 1924- *ConAu 11NR, –21R*
Rooney, James 1938- *ConAu 101*
Rooney, James R 1927- *ConAu 61*

Rooney, Jim *ConAu X*
Rooney, John F, Jr. 1939- *ConAu 101*
Rooney, Miriam Theresa *ConAu 81*
Rooney, Patrick C 1937- *ConAu 29R*
Rooney, William Richard 1938- *ConAu 102*
Roos, Audrey 1912- *WrDr 84*
Roos, Audrey Kelley 1912-1982 *ConAu 108*
Roos, Charles A 1914?-1974 *ConAu 53*
Roos, Hans *ConAu X*
Roos, Hans Dietrich 1919- *ConAu 17R*
Roos, Kelley *ConAu X, TwCCr&M 80, WrDr 84*
Roos, Leslie L, Jr. 1940- *ConAu 33R*
Roos, Noralou P 1942- *ConAu 33R, IntAu&W 82, WrDr 84*
Roos, William 1911- *WrDr 84*
Roosa, Robert 1918- *ConAu 25R, WrDr 84*
Roose, Ronald 1945- *ConAu 81*
Roose-Evans, James 1927- *ConAu 29R, IntAu&W 82, TwCCW 83, WrDr 84*
Roosenburg, Henriette 1920-1972 *ConAu 37R*
Roosevelt, Edith Kermit 1926- *ConAu 69*
Roosevelt, Eleanor 1884-1962 *ConAu 89, LongCTC*
Roosevelt, Elliott 1910- *AuNews 1, ConAu 105*
Roosevelt, Felicia Warburg 1927- *ConAu 57*
Roosevelt, Franklin Delano 1882-1945 *LongCTC*
Roosevelt, James 1907- *ConAu 69*
Roosevelt, Nicholas 1893-1982 *ConAu 106*
Roosevelt, Theodore 1858-1919 *LongCTC*
Root, Albert 1891- *ConSFA*
Root, Deane L 1947- *ConAu 107*
Root, Edward Merrill 1895-1973 *ConAu P-1*
Root, Franklin Russell 1923- *ConAu 5R*
Root, Judith C *ConAu 65, DrAP&F 83*
Root, Lin *ConAu 69*
Root, Oren 1911- *ConAu 85*
Root, Waverley 1903- *WrDr 84*
Root, Waverley 1903-1982 *ConAu 108*
Root, Waverley Lewis 1903- *ConAu 25R, DcLB 4, IntAu&W 82*
Root, William Pitt *DrAP&F 83*
Root, William Pitt 1941- *ConAu 25R, ConP 80, WrDr 84*
Rooth, Gerhard Theodore 1898?-1983 *ConAu 110*
Rootham, Jasper St. John 1910- *ConAu 4NR, –5R, IntAu&W 82, WrDr 84*
Roots, Ivan Alan 1921- *ConAu 9R, IntAu&W 82*
Rope, Henry Edward George 1880-1978 *ConAu 5R, –103*
Roper, Gayle G 1940- *ConAu 97*
Roper, H R Trevor *ConAu X*
Roper, John Stephen 1924?-1980 *ConAu 102*
Roper, June *CreCan 1*
Roper, Lanning 1912-1983 *ConAu 109*
Roper, Laura Wood 1911- *ConAu 57, SmATA 34[port], WrDr 84*
Roper, Neil 1941- *WrDr 84*
Roper, Neil Campbell Ommanney 1941- *IntAu&W 82, IntWWP 82*
Roper, Renee *DrAP&F 83*
Roper, Robert 1946- *ConAu 73*
Roper, Ronnalie J 1936- *ConAu 41R*
Roper, Steve 1941- *ConAu 103*
Roper, Susan Bonthron 1948- *ConAu 81*
Roper, William L 1897- *ConAu 33R*
Ropp, Theodore 1911- *ConAu 69*
Roppolo, Joseph Patrick 1913- *ConAu 13R, WrDr 84*
Roquemore, Kathleen 1941- *ConAu 61*
Rorabaugh, William Joseph 1945- *ConAu 101*
Rorem, Ned 1923- *ConAu 17R*
Roripaugh, A Robert 1930- *ConAu 13R*
Rorke, Margaret 1915- *ConAu 110, MichAu 80*
Rorty, Amelie Oksenberg 1932- *ConAu 107*
Rorty, James 1891?-1973 *ConAu 41R*
Rorty, Richard M 1931- *ConAu 9NR, –21R*
Rorty, Winifred Raushenbush 1894?-1979 *ConAu 93*
Rorvik, David Michael 1946- *ConAu 85, IntAu&W 82*
Ros, Amanda McKittrick 1860?-1939 *LongCTC*
Ros, Eva Voncile Livandais 1932- *IntWWP 82*
Rosa, Alfred F 1942- *ConAu 41R*
Rosa, Antonio Ramos 1924- *CIDMEL 80*
Rosa, Joao Guimaraes 1908-1967 *ConAu 89, ConLC 23[port], ModLAL, WorAu*
Rosa, Joseph George 1932- *ConAu 13R*
Rosa, Nicholas 1926- *ConAu 110*
Rosa-Nieves, Cesareo 1901-1974 *ConAu 57*
Rosage, David E 1913- *ConAu 6NR, –13R*

Rosaldo, Michelle Z 1944-1981 *ConAu 108*
Rosaldo, Michelle Zimbalist 1944- *ConAu 101*
Rosaldo, Renato I, Jr. 1941- *ConAu 89*
Rosales, Luis 1910- *CIDMEL 80*
Rosalie *IntWWP 82X*
Rosberg, Rose *DrAP&F 83*
Rosberg, Rose 1916- *WrDr 84*
Rosbottom, Ronald C 1942- *ConAu 61*
Roscoe, A A 1939- *ConAu 49*
Roscoe, Charles *ConAu X, TwCWW*
Roscoe, Edwin Scott 1896-1978 *ConAu 5R, –103*
Roscoe, George B 1907- *ConAu 65*
Rosdail, Jesse Hart 1914?-1977 *ConAu 73*
Rose, A James 1927- *ConAu 17R*
Rose, Ada Campbell 1902?-1976 *ConAu 65*
Rose, Al 1916- *ConAu 97, IntAu&W 82, WrDr 84*
Rose, Alan Henry 1938- *ConAu 93*
Rose, Albert H 1903- *ConAu 41R*
Rose, Alvin E 1903-1983 *ConAu 109*
Rose, Anna Perrott *ConAu X*
Rose, Anne *ConAu 2NR, –49, SmATA 8*
Rose, Anthony Lewis 1939- *ConAu 101*
Rose, Arnold 1916-1983 *ConAu 109*
Rose, Arnold M 1918-1968 *ConAu 5R*
Rose, Betsy *ConAu X*
Rose, Brian Waldron 1915- *ConAu 97*
Rose, Camille Davied 1893- *ConAu P-2*
Rose, Carl 1903-1971 *ConAu 29R, SmATA 31*
Rose, Clarkson 1890-1968 *ConAu 5R*
Rose, Constance Hubbard 1934- *ConAu 29R*
Rose, Daniel Asa *DrAP&F 83*
Rose, Daniel M 1940- *ConAu 33R*
Rose, Elinor K *MichAu 80*
Rose, Elinor K 1920- *ConAu 29R, IntAu&W 82, WrDr 84*
Rose, Elinor K 1925- *IntWWP 82*
Rose, Eliot Joseph Benn 1909- *IntAu&W 82, WrDr 84*
Rose, Elizabeth 1915- *ConAu 73*
Rose, Elizabeth 1933- *ConAu 9NR*
Rose, Elizabeth Jane 1933- *ConAu 5R, SmATA 28*
Rose, Elliot 1928- *ConAu 65, WrDr 84*
Rose, Ernst 1899- *WrDr 84*
Rose, Ernst A G 1899- *ConAu 4NR, –5R, IntAu&W 82*
Rose, Evelyn Gita 1925- *WrDr 84*
Rose, Florella *ConAu X, SmATA X*
Rose, Frank 1949- *ConAu 103*
Rose, Gerald 1935- *ConAu 9NR, –65, SmATA 30*
Rose, Gilbert J 1923- *ConAu 103*
Rose, Gordon 1920-1975 *ConAu 1R, –4NR*
Rose, Grace B 1914- *ConAu 108*
Rose, Grace B 1920- *WrDr 84*
Rose, Hannah T 1909?-1976 *ConAu 69*
Rose, Harold 1921-1967 *ConAu 5R, –103*
Rose, Harold Wickliffe 1896- *ConAu P-1*
Rose, Harriet Ellen *IntWWP 82*
Rose, Hilary *ConAu X*
Rose, Horace Edgar 1913- *WrDr 84*
Rose, Ian 1920- *WrDr 84*
Rose, Ida Marguerite 1910- *IntWWP 82*
Rose, James M 1941- *ConAu 102*
Rose, Jeanne 1940- *ConAu 93, IntAu&W 82*
Rose, Jennifer *ConAu X, WrDr 84*
Rose, Jerome G 1926- *ConAu 8NR, –13R*
Rose, Jerry D 1933- *ConAu 33R*
Rose, John Holland 1855-1942 *LongCTC*
Rose, Leo E 1926- *ConAu 85*
Rose, Lisle A 1936- *ConAu 10NR, –65*
Rose, Lynn Edmondson 1934- *ConAu 105*
Rose, Lynne Carol *DrAP&F 83*
Rose, Marcia *ConAu X*
Rose, Marilyn Gaddis 1930- *ConAu 33R, IntAu&W 82, WrDr 84*
Rose, Mark 1939- *ConAu 10NR, –25R*
Rose, Nancy A 1934- *ConAu 37R, IntAu&W 82X*
Rose, Norman Anthony 1934- *ConAu 104, IntAu&W 82, WrDr 84*
Rose, Paul 1935- *ConAu 103, IntAu&W 82, WrDr 84*
Rose, Peter Isaac 1933- *ConAu 5NR, –13R, IntAu&W 82, WrDr 84*
Rose, Philip *ConDr 82D*
Rose, Phyllis *ConAu X*
Rose, R B 1929- *ConAu 61*
Rose, Reginald 1920- *ConAu 73, DcLB 26[port]*
Rose, Reuben 1921- *IntWWP 82*

Rose, Richard 1933- *ConAu 10NR, –21R, IntAu&W 82, WrDr 84*
Rose, Robert *WrDr 84*
Rose, Robert Barrie 1929- *IntAu&W 82*
Rose, Stuart 1899?-1975 *ConAu 61*
Rose, Thomas 1938- *ConAu 33R*
Rose, Wendy *DrAP&F 83*
Rose, Wendy 1948- *ConAu 5NR, –53, IntWWP 82, SmATA 12*
Rose, Will 1889- *ConAu 57*
Rose, Willie Lee 1927- *ConAu 13R*
Roseberry, Cecil R 1902- *ConAu 21R*
Rosebery, Archibald P Primrose, Earl Of 1847-1929 *LongCTC*
Roseboom, Eugene Holloway 1892- *ConAu 5R*
Roseboro, John 1933- *ConAu 102*
Rosebrock, Ellen Fletcher 1947- *ConAu 10NR, –57*
Rosebury, Theodor 1904-1976 *ConAu 69, ConAu P-2*
Rosecrance, Francis Chase 1897- *ConAu 5R*
Rosedale, Valerie *ConAu X*
Rosefielde, Steven 1942- *ConAu 45*
Roseliep, Raymond *DrAP&F 83*
Roseliep, Raymond 1917- *ConAu 6NR, –9R, ConP 80, IntAu&W 82, IntWWP 82, WrDr 84*
Roselle, Daniel 1920- *ConAu 13R, IntAu&W 82*
Roseman, Kenneth David 1939- *ConAu 110*
Rosemond, John K 1947- *ConAu 110*
Rosemont, Henry, Jr. 1934- *ConAu 41R*
Rosen, Barbara 1929- *ConAu 37R*
Rosen, Dan 1935- *IntAu&W 82*
Rosen, Edward 1906- *ConAu 21R, WrDr 84*
Rosen, Elliot A 1928- *ConAu 93*
Rosen, George 1910-1977 *ConAu 73, –81*
Rosen, George 1920- *ConAu 57*
Rosen, Gerald *DrAP&F 83*
Rosen, Gerald 1938- *ConAu 33R, WrDr 84*
Rosen, Haiim B 1922- *ConAu 1R*
Rosen, Hjalmar 1922- *ConAu 17R*
Rosen, James Alan 1908?-1972 *ConAu 37R*
Rosen, Joe *ConAu X*
Rosen, Joe 1937- *ConAu 65*
Rosen, Joseph 1937- *ConAu 9NR*
Rosen, Kenneth *DrAP&F 83*
Rosen, Lawrence R 1938- *ConAu 57*
Rosen, Lillian 1928- *ConAu 108*
Rosen, Martin Meyer *ConAu X*
Rosen, Marvin J 1929- *ConAu 69*
Rosen, Michael 1946- *ConAu 25R, DcLEL 1940, TwCCW 83*
Rosen, Moishe 1932- *ConAu 4NR, –49*
Rosen, Mortimer 1931- *ConAu 101*
Rosen, Norma *DrAP&F 83*
Rosen, Norma 1925- *ConAu 33R*
Rosen, Paul L 1939- *ConAu 61*
Rosen, R D 1949- *ConAu 77*
Rosen, Robert C 1947- *ConAu 106*
Rosen, S McKee 1902?-1978 *ConAu 77*
Rosen, Sam 1920- *ConAu 5R, WrDr 84*
Rosen, Samuel 1897-1981 *ConAu 108*
Rosen, Seymour Michael 1924- *ConAu 33R, WrDr 84*
Rosen, Sheldon 1943- *ConAu 109, NatPD 81[port]*
Rosen, Shirley 1933- *ConAu 105*
Rosen, Sidney 1916- *ConAu 9R, IntAu&W 82, SmATA 1, WrDr 84*
Rosen, Stanley Howard 1929- *ConAu 25R, WrDr 84*
Rosen, Stephen 1934- *ConAu 65*
Rosen, Winifred 1943- *ConAu 29R, SmATA 8*
Rosenast, Eleanor S 1929- *ConAu 97*
Rosenau, Helen *ConAu 101, WrDr 84*
Rosenau, James N 1924- *ConAu 1R, –2NR*
Rosenauer, Johnnie L 1951- *ConAu 110*
Rosenbach, Abraham Simon Wolf 1876-1952 *LongCTC*
Rosenbaum, Alan Shelby 1941- *ConAu 106*
Rosenbaum, Bernard L 1937- *ConAu 107*
Rosenbaum, Eileen 1936- *ConAu 21R*
Rosenbaum, Ernest H 1929- *ConAu 97*
Rosenbaum, H Jon 1941- *ConAu 41R*
Rosenbaum, Jean 1927- *ConAu 17R*
Rosenbaum, Kurt 1926- *ConAu 13R*
Rosenbaum, Maurice 1907- *ConAu 17R, SmATA 6*
Rosenbaum, Max 1923- *ConAu 41R*
Rosenbaum, Nathan 1897- *ConAu P-2*
Rosenbaum, Patricia L 1932- *ConAu 105*

Rosenbaum, Peter S 1940- *ConAu 21R*
Rosenbaum, S P 1929- *ConAu 13R*
Rosenbaum, Samuel R 1888-1972 *ConAu 37R*
Rosenbaum, Sylvia 1928- *IntWWP 82*
Rosenbaum, Veryl 1936- *ConAu 1NR, –49*
Rosenbaum, Walter A 1937- *ConAu 21R*
Rosenberg, Alfred 1893-1946 *LongCTC*
Rosenberg, Arthur D 1939- *ConAu 61*
Rosenberg, Bruce Alan 1934- *ConAu 29R, WrDr 84*
Rosenberg, Charles E 1936- *ConAu 97*
Rosenberg, Claude N, Jr. 1928- *ConAu 1R, –5NR, WrDr 84*
Rosenberg, David *DrAP&F 83*
Rosenberg, David A 1940- *ConAu 93*
Rosenberg, Dorothy 1906- *ConAu 2NR*
Rosenberg, Edgar 1925- *ConAu 13R*
Rosenberg, Emily S 1944- *ConAu 108*
Rosenberg, Ethel 1915- *ConAu 29R, SmATA 3*
Rosenberg, George Stanley 1930- *ConAu 29R, IntAu&W 82, WrDr 84*
Rosenberg, Harold 1906-1978 *ConAu 21R, –77, DcLEL 1940, WorAu*
Rosenberg, Harry E 1932- *ConAu 57*
Rosenberg, Isaac 1890-1918 *ConAu 107, LongCTC, ModBrL, RGFMBP, TwCA, TwCA SUP, TwCLC 12[port], TwCWr, WhoTwCL*
Rosenberg, Israel 1909- *ConAu 49*
Rosenberg, J Mitchell 1906- *ConAu 37R, WrDr 84*
Rosenberg, Jakob 1893-1980 *ConAu 97*
Rosenberg, James Leroy *DrAP&F 83*
Rosenberg, James LeRoy 1921- *ConAu 13R, IntAu&W 82, NatPD 81[port], WrDr 84*
Rosenberg, Jerome Roy 1926- *ConAu 104*
Rosenberg, Jerry M 1935- *ConAu 9NR, –21R*
Rosenberg, Jessie 1941- *ConAu 21R*
Rosenberg, John D 1929- *ConAu 1R, –5NR, IntAu&W 82, WrDr 84*
Rosenberg, Judith K 1945- *ConAu 57*
Rosenberg, Kenyon Charles 1933- *ConAu 57*
Rosenberg, Marvin *WrDr 84*
Rosenberg, Marvin 1912- *ConAu 1R*
Rosenberg, Maurice 1919- *ConAu 81*
Rosenberg, Morris 1922- *ConAu 2NR, –5R, IntAu&W 82, WrDr 84*
Rosenberg, Nancy Sherman 1931- *ConAu 1R, –5NR, SmATA 4*
Rosenberg, Norman J 1930- *ConAu 57*
Rosenberg, Philip 1942- *ConAu 103*
Rosenberg, Rosalind 1946- *ConAu 108*
Rosenberg, Samuel 1912- *ConAu 53*
Rosenberg, Sharon 1942- *ConAu 10NR, –57, SmATA 8*
Rosenberg, Shirley Sirota 1925- *ConAu 21R*
Rosenberg, Stuart E 1922- *ConAu 5R, –9NR*
Rosenberg, Sydell Lorraine 1935- *IntWWP 82*
Rosenberg, William Gordon 1938- *ConAu 61*
Rosenberg, Wolfgang 1915- *ConAu 9NR, –65, WrDr 84*
Rosenberger, Francis Coleman *DrAP&F 83*
Rosenberger, Francis Coleman 1915- *ConAu 41R, IntAu&W 82, IntWWP 82*
Rosenberger, Harleigh M 1913- *ConAu 21R*
Rosenberger, Homer T 1908- *WrDr 84*
Rosenberger, Homer Tope 1908- *ConAu 8NR, –17R, IntAu&W 82*
Rosenblatt, Bernard A 1886- *ConAu P-1*
Rosenblatt, Fred 1914- *ConAu 41R*
Rosenblatt, Gary 1947- *ConAu 77*
Rosenblatt, Joe 1933- *ConAu X, ConLC 15, ConP 80*
Rosenblatt, Jon M 1947- *ConAu 89*
Rosenblatt, Joseph 1933- *ConAu 89, WrDr 84*
Rosenblatt, Louise M 1904- *ConAu 49*
Rosenblatt, Milton B 1908?-1975 *ConAu 53*
Rosenblatt, Roger 1940- *ConAu 85*
Rosenblatt, Samuel 1902- *ConAu 53*
Rosenblatt, Stanley M 1936- *ConAu 29R*
Rosenblatt, Suzanne Maris 1937- *ConAu 69*
Rosenblith, Judy Francis 1921- *ConAu 25R*
Rosenbloom, Bert 1944- *ConAu 109*
Rosenbloom, David H 1943- *ConAu 73*
Rosenbloom, David L 1944- *ConAu 45*
Rosenbloom, Jerry S 1939- *ConAu 110*
Rosenbloom, Joseph R 1928- *ConAu 6NR, –29R, –57, SmATA 21[port], WrDr 84*
Rosenbloom, Noah H 1915- *ConAu 37R, WrDr 84*
Rosenblum, Art 1927- *ConAu 57*
Rosenblum, Davida 1927- *ConAu 93*

Rosenblum, Gershen 1924- *ConAu 41R*
Rosenblum, Leonard A 1936- *ConAu 11NR, -57*
Rosenblum, Marc J 1936- *ConAu 29R*
Rosenblum, Martin J *DrAP&F 83*
Rosenblum, Martin Jack 1946- *ConAu 2NR, -45, IntAu&W 82, IntWWP 82*
Rosenblum, Mort 1943- *ConAu 73*
Rosenblum, Richard 1928- *ConAu 9NR, -65, SmATA 11*
Rosenblum, Robert H 1927- *ConAu 1R, -5NR, IntAu&W 82*
Rosenbluth, Gideon 1921- *ConAu 61*
Rosenburg, John M 1918- *ConAu 21R, SmATA 6*
Rosenburg, Robert K 1920- *ConAu 4NR, -5R*
Rosenburg, Stuart E 1922- *ConAu 5R*
Rosendall, Betty 1916- *ConAu 49*
Rosenfarb, Chawa 1923- *ConAu 53*
Rosenfeld, Albert 1920- *ConAu 11NR, -65*
Rosenfeld, Alvin 1919- *ConAu 73*
Rosenfeld, Alvin H 1938- *ConAu 4NR, -49*
Rosenfeld, Arnold 1933- *ConAu 65*
Rosenfeld, Edward J 1943- *ConAu 41R*
Rosenfeld, Harry M 1929- *ConAu 69*
Rosenfeld, Harvey 1939- *ConAu 110*
Rosenfeld, Isaac 1918-1956 *WorAu*
Rosenfeld, Isadore 1926- *ConAu 81*
Rosenfeld, Lulla 1914- *ConAu 85*
Rosenfeld, Marthe 1928- *ConAu 45*
Rosenfeld, Morris 1862-1923 *TwCA*
Rosenfeld, Paul 1890-1946 *TwCA, TwCA SUP*
Rosenfeld, Sam 1920- *ConAu 9R*
Rosenfeld, Samuel 1896-1963 *ConAu 89, WorAu[port]*
Rosenfeld, Sybil Marion 1903- *IntAu&W 82*
Rosenfeld, William *DrAP&F 83*
Rosenfield, Isadore 1893-1980 *ConAu 97*
Rosenfield, James A 1943- *ConAu 49*
Rosenfield, John M 1924- *ConAu 21R*
Rosenfield, Leonora Cohen 1909-1982 *ConAu 105, -41R, IntAu&W 82*
Rosenfield, Patricia Alanah 1925- *IntWWP 82X*
Rosenfield, Patricia Byrne 1925- *IntWWP 82*
Rosenfield, Rita Leah 1936- *IntWWP 82*
Rosengart, Oliver A 1941- *ConAu 49*
Rosengarten, Frank 1927- *ConAu 73*
Rosengarten, Theodore 1944- *ConAu 103*
Rosenhaupt, Hans 1911- *WrDr 84*
Rosenheim, Edward Weil, Jr. 1918- *ConAu 25R*
Rosenhouse, Archie 1878- *ConAu P-2*
Rosenkrantz, Linda *DrAP&F 83*
Rosenkrantz, Linda 1934- *ConAu 11NR, -25R*
Rosenkranz, Richard S 1942- *ConAu 37R*
Rosenman, John B *DrAP&F 83*
Rosenman, John B 1941- *ConAu 106*
Rosenman, Ray H 1920- *ConAu 97*
Rosenman, Samuel I 1896-1973 *ConAu 41R*
Rosenof, Theodore 1943- *ConAu 10NR, -65*
Rosenow, John E 1949- *ConAu 97*
Rosenquist, Carl M 1895-1973 *ConAu P-2*
Rosensaft, Menachem Z 1948- *ConAu 21R, WrDr 84*
Rosenstein-Rodan, Paul N 1902- *ConAu 107, WrDr 84*
Rosenstiel, Leonie 1947- *ConAu 85, IntAu&W 82*
Rosenstock, Janet 1933- *ConAu 108*
Rosenstock-Huessy, Eugen 1888-1973 *ConAu 41R, ConAu P-1*
Rosenstone, Robert Allan 1936- *ConAu 29R, IntAu&W 82*
Rosenstone, Steven J 1952- *ConAu 104*
Rosenthal, A M 1922- *ConAu 21R*
Rosenthal, Abby Jane *DrAP&F 83*
Rosenthal, Alan 1936- *ConAu 105*
Rosenthal, Albert H 1914- *ConAu 21R*
Rosenthal, Andrew 1918?-1979 *ConAu 89*
Rosenthal, Bernard G 1922- *ConAu 11NR, -29R, WrDr 84*
Rosenthal, Bob *DrAP&F 83*
Rosenthal, Carole *DrAP&F 83*
Rosenthal, David 1916- *ConAu 41R*
Rosenthal, David H *DrAP&F 83*
Rosenthal, Donald B 1937- *ConAu 37R, IntAu&W 82, WrDr 84*
Rosenthal, Douglas E 1940- *ConAu 57*
Rosenthal, Earl E 1921- *ConAu 41R*
Rosenthal, Edwin Stanley 1914- *ConAu 77, IntAu&W 82*
Rosenthal, Eric 1905- *ConAu 6NR, -9R, IntAu&W 82*
Rosenthal, Erwin 1904- *WrDr 84*

Rosenthal, Erwin Isak Jacob 1904- *ConAu 102*
Rosenthal, F F 1911?-1979 *ConAu 89*
Rosenthal, Harold David 1917- *ConAu 5R, DcLEL 1940, IntAu&W 82, WrDr 84*
Rosenthal, Harry F 1927- *ConAu 65*
Rosenthal, Harry Kenneth 1941- *ConAu 57*
Rosenthal, Henry Moses 1906-1977 *ConAu 73*
Rosenthal, Jack 1931- *ConDr 82C, IntAu&W 82*
Rosenthal, Joe *ConAu X*
Rosenthal, Joel T 1934- *ConAu 57*
Rosenthal, Joseph J 1911- *ConAu 69*
Rosenthal, Jules M 1924- *ConAu 17R*
Rosenthal, M L *DrAP&F 83*
Rosenthal, M L 1917- *ConAu 1R, -4NR, ConP 80, DcLB 5[port], WorAu, WrDr 84*
Rosenthal, Macha Louis 1917- *IntWWP 82*
Rosenthal, Mitchell S 1935- *ConAu 104*
Rosenthal, Renee d1975 *ConAu 57*
Rosenthal, Richard A 1925- *ConAu 1R*
Rosenthal, Robert 1933- *ConAu 41R*
Rosenthal, Sylvia 1911- *ConAu 109*
Rosenus, Alan 1940- *ConAu 73*
Rosenwald, Henry M 1905- *ConAu 33R*
Rosenwasser, Dorothy Eckmann 1917- *ConAu 1R*
Rosenzweig, Michael L 1941- *ConAu 101*
Rosenzweig, Norman 1924- *ConAu 6NR, -57*
Rosenzweig, Phyllis *DrAP&F 83*
Roser, Homer C 1909-1967 *ConAu P-1*
Rosett, Arthur 1934- *ConAu 69*
Rosevear, John 1936- *ConAu 21R*
Roseveare, Helen Margaret 1925- *ConAu 73*
Rosewell, Paul Truman 1926- *ConAu 17R*
Rosewood, James Alfred *IntWWP 82X*
Roshco, Bernard 1929- *ConAu 5R*
Roshwald, Irving 1924- *ConAu 45*
Roshwald, Mordecai 1921- *ConAu 1R, ConSFA, IntAu&W 82, TwCSFW, WrDr 84*
Roshwald, Mordecai M *DrAP&F 83*
Rosi, Eugene J 1931- *ConAu 61*
Rosichan, Richard H 1941- *ConAu 45*
Rosidi, Ajip 1938- *IntWWP 82*
Rosier, Bernard 1931- *ConAu 29R*
Rosier, James L 1932- *ConAu 1R, IntAu&W 82*
Rosioru, Ion *IntAu&W 82X*
Rositzke, Harry 1911- *ConAu 45*
Roskam, Karel Lodewijk 1931- *IntAu&W 82*
Roskamp, Karl Wilhelm 1923- *ConAu 13R, WrDr 84*
Roskies, Ethel 1933- *ConAu 45*
Roskill, Mark Wentworth 1933- *ConAu 5R, -6NR, IntAu&W 82, WrDr 84*
Roskill, Stephen W 1903-1982 *ConAu 108*
Roskill, Stephen Wentworth 1903- *ConAu 6NR, -13R, IntAu&W 82*
Rosko, Milt 1930- *ConAu 41R*
Roskolenko, Harry 1907- *WrDr 84*
Roskolenko, Harry 1907-1980 *ConAu 101, -13R*
Roslavleva, Natalia *ConAu X*
Rosler, Martha *DrAP&F 83*
Rosman, Abraham 1930- *ConAu 89*
Rosman, Alice Grant 1887- *TwCA, TwCA SUP*
Rosmond, Babette 1921- *ConAu 5R, -6NR*
Rosner, David *DrAP&F 83*
Rosner, Joseph 1914- *ConAu 57*
Rosner, Lynn 1944- *ConAu 61*
Rosner, Stanley 1928- *ConAu 41R*
Rosnow, Ralph 1936- *ConAu 21R, IntAu&W 82*
Rosnow, Ralph L 1936- *ConAu 10NR*
Rosny, J H, Aine 1856-1940 *CIDMEL 80*
Rosochacki, Daniel *DrAP&F 83*
Rosochacki, Daniel 1942- *ConAu 45*
Rosoff, Sidney D 1924- *ConAu 1R*
Rosovsky, Henry 1927- *ConAu 105*
Rosow, Irving 1921- *ConAu 85*
Rosow, Jerome M 1919- *ConAu 81*
Ross, Alan 1922- *ConAu 6NR, -9R, ConP 80, DcLEL 1940, IntAu&W 82, LongCTC, ModBrL, TwCA SUP, WrDr 84*
Ross, Alan O 1921- *ConAu 41R*
Ross, Alan Strode Campbell 1907-1980 *ConAu 9R, -102, IntAu&W 82*
Ross, Albert *WrDr 84*
Ross, Alec 1926- *ConAu 29R*
Ross, Alex 1909- *SmATA 29*
Ross, Alf Niels Christian 1899- *ConAu 53*
Ross, Angus *WrDr 84*
Ross, Angus 1911- *ConAu 21R, IntAu&W 82, WrDr 84*

Ross, Angus 1927- *ConAu X, IntAu&W 82X, TwCCr&M 80*
Ross, Barnaby *ConAu X, LongCTC, TwCA, TwCA SUP, TwCCr&M 80*
Ross, Bernard H 1934- *ConAu 102*
Ross, Bette M 1932- *ConAu 106*
Ross, Betty *ConAu 69*
Ross, Billy I 1925- *ConAu 57*
Ross, Catherine *ConAu X, TwCRGW, WrDr 84*
Ross, Clarissa *ConAu X, WrDr 84*
Ross, Colin *ConAu X*
Ross, Corinne Madden 1931- *ConAu 106*
Ross, Dallas *ConAu X*
Ross, Dan *ConAu X*
Ross, Dana *ConAu X, WrDr 84*
Ross, Dave 1949- *SmATA 32[port]*
Ross, David *DrAP&F 83*
Ross, David 1896-1975 *ConAu 61, -65, SmATA 20N*
Ross, David 1929- *IntWWP 82*
Ross, Davis R B 1934- *ConAu 33R, WrDr 84*
Ross, Dennis H 1943- *IntWWP 82*
Ross, Diana 1910- *ConAu X, SmATA X, TwCCW 83, WrDr 84*
Ross, Donald K 1943- *ConAu 49*
Ross, Emory Warren 1887-1973 *ConAu 41R*
Ross, Eric 1929- *ConAu 29R*
Ross, Eulalie Steinmetz 1910- *ConAu 17R*
Ross, Eva Jeany 1903-1969 *ConAu P-2*
Ross, Floyd Hiatt 1910- *ConAu 73*
Ross, Frances Aileen 1909- *ConAu P-1*
Ross, Frank, Jr. 1914- *ConAu 93, SmATA 28[port]*
Ross, Frank E 1925- *ConAu 17R*
Ross, Fred *DrAP&F 83*
Ross, George *ConAu X*
Ross, Glenn *IntWWP 82X*
Ross, H Laurence 1934- *ConAu 77*
Ross, Hal 1941- *ConAu 65*
Ross, Harold Raymond 1904- *ConAu P-2*
Ross, Harold Wallace 1892-1951 *LongCTC*
Ross, Helaine *ConAu X, WrDr 84*
Ross, Helen 1890?-1978 *ConAu 81, -85*
Ross, Ian *ConAu X*
Ross, Ian Simpson 1930- *ConAu 3NR, -45*
Ross, Irwin 1919- *ConAu 97*
Ross, Ishbel 1897-1975 *ASpks, ConAu 61, -93*
Ross, Ivan Terence 1932- *ConAu X*
Ross, J H *TwCA, TwCA SUP*
Ross, James Davidson 1942- *ConAu 49*
Ross, James F 1931- *ConAu 11NR, -21R*
Ross, James Frederick Stanley 1886- *ConAu 9R*
Ross, James Sinclair *CreCan 2*
Ross, James Stiven 1892-1975 *ConAu 57*
Ross, Janet 1914- *ConAu 37R*
Ross, Joel E 1922- *ConAu 29R*
Ross, John 1921- *ConAu 108*
Ross, John Addison 1919- *ConAu 17R*
Ross, John O'C 1916- *ConAu 25R*
Ross, Jonathan *ConAu X, TwCCr&M 80, WrDr 84*
Ross, Joseph 1929- *ConAu 49, ConSFA*
Ross, Katherine *ConAu X*
Ross, Kenneth 1941- *WrDr 84*
Ross, Kenneth G 1941- *IntAu&W 82*
Ross, Kenneth Michael Andrew 1941- *ConAu 107*
Ross, Kenneth N 1908-1970 *ConAu 5R, -5NR*
Ross, Laura *ConAu X*
Ross, Laurence *WrDr 84*
Ross, Leah 1938- *ConAu 61*
Ross, Leonard *ConAu X*
Ross, Leonard M 1945- *ConAu 29R*
Ross, Leonard Q *WrDr 84*
Ross, Leo 1908- *ConAu X, IntAu&W 82X, LongCTC, TwCA, TwCA SUP*
Ross, Lillian 1927- *ConAu 9R, WorAu*
Ross, Lola Romanucci *ConAu X*
Ross, Lynne Nannen *ConAu 107*
Ross, Mabel H 1909- *ConAu 81*
Ross, Maggie *DcLEL 1940*
Ross, Malcolm *WrDr 84*
Ross, Malcolm 1911- *DcLEL 1940*
Ross, Marilyn *ConAu X, WrDr 84*
Ross, Marilyn A 1939- *WrDr 84*
Ross, Marilyn Heimberg 1939- *ConAu 81*
Ross, Marjorie Drake Rhoades 1901- *ConAu 1R*
Ross, Martha 1951- *ConAu 103*
Ross, Martin 1865?-1915 *LongCTC, TwCA, TwCA SUP*

Ross, Martin J 1912- *ConAu 53*
Ross, Marvin C 1904-1977 *ConAu 69, ConAu P-2*
Ross, Michael 1905- *ConAu 85*
Ross, Mitchell S 1953- *ConAu 81*
Ross, Murray George 1910- *WrDr 84*
Ross, Murray George 1912- *ConAu 17R*
Ross, Nancy *ConAu X*
Ross, Nancy Wilson *DrAP&F 83*
Ross, Nancy Wilson 1907- *TwCA SUP*
Ross, Nancy Wilson 1910- *ConAu 97*
Ross, Nathaniel 1904- *ConAu 21R*
Ross, Patricia *ConAu X, IntAu&W 82X*
Ross, Paul *ConAu X*
Ross, Philip 1939- *ConAu 69*
Ross, Phyllis 1926-1970 *ConAu P-2*
Ross, Ralph Gilbert 1911- *ConAu 13R, IntAu&W 82, WrDr 84*
Ross, Raymond George *ConSFA*
Ross, Raymond S 1925- *ConAu 8NR, -21R*
Ross, Robert Baldwin 1869-1918 *LongCTC*
Ross, Robert H, Jr. 1916- *ConAu 13R*
Ross, Robert Horace *ConAu 106*
Ross, Robert S 1938- *NatPD 81[port]*
Ross, Robert S 1940- *ConAu 57*
Ross, Robert W *ConAu X*
Ross, Ronald 1857-1932 *LongCTC*
Ross, Russell M 1921- *ConAu 21R*
Ross, Sam 1912- *ConAu 13R, WrDr 84*
Ross, Sheila 1925- *WrDr 84*
Ross, Sheila Muriel 1925- *ConAu 106*
Ross, Sinclair 1908- *ConAu 73, ConLC 13, ConNov 82, CreCan 2, DcLEL 1940, TwCWW, TwCWr, WrDr 84*
Ross, Stanley R 1921- *ConAu 7NR, -17R*
Ross, Stanley Ralph 1940- *ConAu 97*
Ross, Stephen David 1935- *ConAu 41R*
Ross, Steven Thomas 1937- *ConAu 41R*
Ross, Sutherland *ConAu X*
Ross, T E *LongCTC*
Ross, T J 1924- *ConAu 57*
Ross, Terrence *DrAP&F 83*
Ross, Terrence 1947- *ConAu 103*
Ross, Thomas B 1929- *ConAu 29R*
Ross, Thomas Wynne 1923- *ConAu 41R*
Ross, Timothy A 1936- *ConAu 57*
Ross, Tony 1938- *ConAu 77, IntAu&W 82, SmATA 17*
Ross, W E D 1912- *ConAu 81*
Ross, W Gordon 1900- *ConAu 45*
Ross, Wilda 1915- *ConAu 85, WrDr 84*
Ross, William *ConAu X*
Ross, William 1912- *WrDr 84*
Ross, William B 1915- *ConAu 25R*
Ross, William Wrightson Eustace 1894-1966 *CreCan 1*
Ross, Zola 1912- *WrDr 84*
Ross, Zola Helen 1912- *ConAu 53, TwCWW*
Ross-Macdonald, Malcolm 1932- *WrDr 84*
Ross-Macdonald, Malcolm John 1932- *ConAu 65, IntAu&W 82*
Ross Williamson, Hugh 1901-1978 *ConAu 8NR, -17R, LongCTC*
Rossabi, Morris 1941- *ConAu 102, WrDr 84*
Rossberg, Robert H 1926- *ConAu 45*
Rosse, Ian *ConAu X, IntAu&W 82X, WrDr 84*
Rosse, Susanna *ConAu X*
Rossel, Seymour 1945- *ConAu 5NR, -53, SmATA 28, WrDr 84*
Rossel, Sven H 1943- *ConAu 105*
Rossel-Waugh, C C *ConAu X*
Rossellini, Roberto 1906-1977 *ConAu 69*
Rossen, Robert 1908-1966 *DcLB 26[port]*
Rosser, Neill A 1916-1973 *ConAu P-1*
Rosset, B C 1910-1974 *ConAu 9R, -103*
Rosset, Barnet Lee, Jr. 1922- *ConAu 97*
Rosset, Barney *ConAu X*
Rossetti, Christina Georgina 1830-1894 *SmATA 20*
Rossi, Aga *ConAu X*
Rossi, Alfred 1935- *ConAu 29R*
Rossi, Alice S 1922- *ConAu 1NR, -45*
Rossi, Antonio 1952- *IntAu&W 82*
Rossi, Ernest Lawrence 1933- *ConAu 37R*
Rossi, Ino *ConAu 89*
Rossi, Lino 1923- *ConAu 104*
Rossi, Mario 1916- *ConAu 5R, -8NR*
Rossi, Nicholas Louis, Jr. 1924- *ConAu 6NR, -13R*
Rossi, Nick *ConAu X*
Rossi, Paul A 1929- *ConAu 110*

Rossi, Peter Henry 1921- *ConAu 1R, -4NR*
Rossi, Sanna Morrison Barlow 1917- *ConAu 93*
Rossi, William A 1916- *ConAu 65*
Rossie, Jonathan Gregory 1935- *ConAu 106*
Rossini, Frederick A 1939- *ConAu 73*
Rossini, Frederick D 1899- *WrDr 84*
Rossit, Edward A 1921- *ConAu 17R*
Rossiter, Charles *DrAP&F 83*
Rossiter, Clinton 1917-1970 *ConAu 25R*
Rossiter, Frank R 1937- *ConAu 61*
Rossiter, Ian *ConAu X*
Rossiter, Jane *ConAu X*
Rossiter, John 1916- *ConAu 33R, TwCCr&M 80, WrDr 84*
Rossiter, Margaret W 1944- *ConAu 77*
Rossiter, Percival Stuart Bryce 1923- *IntAu&W 82*
Rossiter, Stuart 1923- *ConAu 85, WrDr 84*
Rosskopf, Myron Frederick 1907-1973 *ConAu 5R, -5NR, -41R*
Rossman, Evelyn *ConAu X*
Rossman, Michael Dale 1939- *ConAu 101*
Rossman, Parker 1919- *ConAu 69*
Rossmann, Hermann 1902- *CnMD*
Rossmann, Jack E 1936- *ConAu 49*
Rossmann, John F 1942- *ConAu 101*
Rossner, Judith *DrAP&F 83*
Rossner, Judith 1935- *AuNews 2, ConAu 17R, ConLC 6, -9, DcLB 6, WrDr 84*
Rossner, Robert 1932- *ConAu 1R, -1NR*
Rosso DiSan Secondo, Pier Luigi Maria 1887-1956 *CIDMEL 80, ModWD*
Rossoff, Martin 1910- *ConAu 9R*
Rossomando, Frederic William 1924- *ConAu 49*
Rostand, Edmond Eugene Alexis 1868-1918 *CIDMEL 80, CnMD, ConAu 104, LongCTC, ModFrL, ModRL, ModWD, TwCA, TwCA SUP, TwCLC 6[port]*
Rostand, Jean 1894- *CIDMEL 80*
Rostand, Maurice 1891-1968 *CnMD, ModWD*
Rosten, Leo 1908- *WrDr 84*
Rosten, Leo Calvin 1908- *ConAu 5R, -6NR, ConNov 82, IntAu&W 82, TwCA, TwCA SUP*
Rosten, Norman *DrAP&F 83*
Rosten, Norman 1914- *ConAu 77, TwCA SUP*
Rostenberg, Leona 1908- *ConAu 5R, -5NR*
Roston, Murray 1928- *ConAu 5NR, -53, IntAu&W 82, WrDr 84*
Roston, Ruth *DrAP&F 83*
Rostovtzeff, Michael I 1870-1952 *LongCTC*
Rostow, Eugene V 1913- *ConAu 5R, WrDr 84*
Rostow, Walt W 1916- *WrDr 84*
Rostow, Walt Whitman 1916- *ConAu 8NR, -13R*
Rostvald, Gerhard 1919- *WrDr 84*
Rostvold, Gerhard N 1919- *ConAu 10NR, -21R*
Rostworowski, Karol Hubert 1877-1938 *CIDMEL 80, CnMD, ModWD*
Roszak, Betty 1933- *ConAu 29R*
Roszak, Theodore 1933- *ConAu 77*
Rotarius *ConAu X*
Rotberg, Robert I 1935- *ConAu 6NR, -13R*
Rotblat, Joseph 1908- *ConAu 109, WrDr 84*
Rotchstein, Janice 1944- *ConAu 106*
Rote, Kyle 1928- *ConAu 21R*
Rotella, Alexis Kaye 1947- *IntWWP 82*
Rotenstreich, Nathan 1914- *ConAu 8NR, -61, IntAu&W 82*
Roth, Alexander *ConAu X*
Roth, Andrew 1919- *ConAu 53, IntAu&W 82, WrDr 84*
Roth, Arlen 1952- *ConAu 103*
Roth, Arnold 1929- *ConAu 21R, SmATA 21[port]*
Roth, Arthur 1920- *ConAu 1R*
Roth, Arthur J *DrAP&F 83*
Roth, Arthur J 1925- *ConAu 7NR, -53, SmATA 28*
Roth, Audrey J 1927- *ConAu 21R, WrDr 84*
Roth, Cecil 1899-1970 *ConAu 9R, -25R, LongCTC, TwCA SUP*
Roth, Claire Jarett 1923- *ConAu 5R*
Roth, David 1940- *ConAu 106*
Roth, David F 1939- *ConAu 41R, IntAu&W 82*
Roth, David M 1874?-1971 *ConAu 104*
Roth, David M 1935- *ConAu 57*
Roth, Dewey *DrAP&F 83*
Roth, Don A 1927- *ConAu 25R*
Roth, Ernst 1896-1971 *ConAu P-2*
Roth, Eugen 1895-1976 *ConAu 65*
Roth, Ghitta Caiserman *CreCan 1*

Roth, Hal 1927- *ConAu 37R*
Roth, Harold L 1919-1982 *ConAu 108*
Roth, Harry 1903?-1976 *ConAu 65*
Roth, Henry 1906- *ConAu P-1, ConLC 2, -6, -11, ConNov 82, ModAL, WhoTwCL, WorAu, WrDr 84*
Roth, Henry H *DrAP&F 83*
Roth, Herbert Otto 1917- *ConAu 61, IntAu&W 82*
Roth, Herrick S 1916- *ConAu 77*
Roth, Holly 1916-1964 *ConAu 1R, -6NR, TwCCr&M 80*
Roth, Jack J 1920- *ConAu 21R*
Roth, John K 1940- *ConAu 10NR, -25R*
Roth, Jordan T 1920- *WrDr 84*
Roth, Joseph 1894-1939 *CIDMEL 80, ModGL, TwCA, TwCA SUP, WhoTwCL*
Roth, Julius A 1924- *ConAu 21R*
Roth, June 1926- *ConAu 5NR, -9R, IntAu&W 82, WrDr 84*
Roth, Leland M 1943- *ConAu 93*
Roth, Leon 1896-1963 *ConAu 106*
Roth, Lillian 1910-1980 *ConAu 97*
Roth, Mark J 1941- *ConAu 77*
Roth, Sister Mary Augustine 1926- *ConAu 3NR, -9R*
Roth, Mary Jane *ConAu 21R*
Roth, Molke *IntWWP 82X*
Roth, Peggy d1973 *ConAu 104*
Roth, Philip *DrAP&F 83*
Roth, Philip 1933- *ConAu 1R, -1NR, ConLC 1, -2, -3, -4, -6, -9, -15, -22[port], ConNov 82, DcLB Y82A[port], -2, DcLEL 1940, IntAu&W 82, ModAL, ModAL SUP, TwCWr, WhoTwCL, WorAu, WrDr 84*
Roth, Richard H 1949- *ConAu 77*
Roth, Robert Howard 1933- *ConAu 41R*
Roth, Robert Joseph 1920- *ConAu 17R, IntAu&W 82, WrDr 84*
Roth, Robert Paul 1919- *ConAu 61*
Roth, Samuel 1894-1974 *ConAu 49*
Roth, Sol 1927- *ConAu 65*
Roth, Theodore W 1916- *ConAu 57*
Roth, William 1942- *ConAu 101*
Roth, Wolfgang M W 1930- *ConAu 41R*
Rotha, Paul 1907- *ConAu 9R, WrDr 84*
Rothbard, Murray Newton 1926- *ConAu 5R, -6NR*
Rothbaum, Melvin 1926- *ConAu 5R*
Rothberg, Abraham 1922- *ConAu 33R*
Rothblatt, Ben 1924- *ConAu 25R*
Rothblatt, Donald N 1935- *ConAu 8NR, -61*
Rothblatt, Henry B 1916- *ConAu 25R*
Rothchild, Donald 1928- *ConAu 41R*
Rothchild, Sylvia 1923- *ConAu 77*
Rothebert, Winterset *MichAu 80*
Rothel, David 1936- *ConAu 10NR, -65*
Rothenberg, Alan B 1907-1977 *ConAu 73*
Rothenberg, Albert 1930- *ConAu 8NR, -57*
Rothenberg, B Annye 1940- *ConAu 107*
Rothenberg, Gunther Eric 1923- *ConAu 8NR, -21R*
Rothenberg, Jerome *DrAP&F 83*
Rothenberg, Jerome 1924- *ConAu 29R*
Rothenberg, Jerome 1931- *ConAu 1NR, -45, ConLC 6, ConP 80, CroCAP, DcLB 5[port], DcLEL 1940, IntAu&W 82, WorAu 1970, WrDr 84*
Rothenberg, Joshua 1911- *ConAu 37R, IntAu&W 82, WrDr 84*
Rothenberg, Lillian 1922- *ConAu 9R*
Rothenberg, Polly 1916- *ConAu 85*
Rothenberg, Robert Edward 1908- *ConAu 37R, -61, IntAu&W 82, WrDr 84*
Rothenstein, John 1901- *WrDr 84*
Rothenstein, Sir John K M 1901- *ConAu 1R, -1NR, IntAu&W 82, LongCTC*
Rothenstein, Sir William 1872-1945 *LongCTC, TwCA, TwCA SUP*
Rothermere, Viscount *ConAu X*
Rothermere, Viscount 1868-1940 *LongCTC*
Rothery, Brian 1934- *ConAu 1NR, -49, IntAu&W 82, WrDr 84*
Rothfork, John 1946- *ConAu 110*
Rothkopf, Carol Z 1929- *ConAu 25R, SmATA 4*
Rothman, David J *WrDr 84*
Rothman, David J 1937- *ConAu 33R*
Rothman, Esther P 1919- *ConAu 37R*
Rothman, Joel 1938- *ConAu 37R, SmATA 7, WrDr 84*
Rothman, Judith *ConAu X, WrDr 84*

Rothman, Milton A 1919- *ConAu 41R*
Rothman, Stanley 1927- *ConAu 93*
Rothman, Theodore 1907- *ConAu P-2*
Rothman, Tony 1953- *ConAu 85*
Rothmuller, Aron Marko 1908- *ConAu 73*
Rothrock, George Abel 1932- *ConAu 61,*
 IntAu&W 82
Rothschild, Alfred 1894?-1972 *ConAu 37R*
Rothschild, Emma 1948- *ConIsC 1[port]*
Rothschild, Fritz A 1919- *ConAu 106*
Rothschild, J H 1907- *ConAu P-2*
Rothschild, Joseph 1931- *ConAu 3NR, –9R,*
 IntAu&W 82, WrDr 84
Rothschild, Kurt Wilhelm 1914- *IntAu&W 82*
Rothschild, Kurt William 1914- *ConAu 102,*
 WrDr 84
Rothschild, Lincoln 1902- *ConAu 45*
Rothschild, Lincoln 1902-1983 *ConAu 109*
Rothschild, Norman 1913- *ConAu 103*
Rothschild, Richard Charles 1895- *IntAu&W 82*
Rothstein, Arthur 1915- *ConAu 6NR, –57*
Rothstein, Eric 1936- *ConAu 73*
Rothstein, Samuel 1902?-1978 *ConAu 77*
Rothstein, Samuel 1921- *ConAu 61, WrDr 84*
Rothstein, William G 1937- *ConAu 73*
Rothweiler, Paul R 1931- *ConAu 65,*
 IntAu&W 82, WrDr 84
Rothweiler, Paul Roger 1931- *ConAu 10NR*
Rothwell, Kenneth J 1925- *ConAu 21R*
Rothwell, Kenneth Sprague 1921- *ConAu 33R,*
 WrDr 84
Rothwell, Talbot 1916- *WrDr 84*
Rothwell, Talbot 1916-1981 *ConAu 103*
Rothwell, V H 1945- *ConAu 37R*
Rothwell, Victor Howard 1945- *WrDr 84*
Rotkin, Charles E 1916- *ConAu 5R*
Rotmans, Elmer A 1896- *ConAu 5R*
Rotondi, Cesar 1926- *ConAu 97*
Rotsler, William 1926- *ConAu 4NR, –53,*
 IntAu&W 82, TwCSFW, WrDr 84
Rotstein, Abraham 1929- *ConAu 104*
Rottenberg, Daniel 1942- *ConAu 102*
Rottenberg, Isaac C 1925- *ConAu 13R*
Rottensteiner, Franz 1942- *ConAu 81*
Rotter, Julian B 1916- *ConAu 33R*
Rotter, Marion 1940?-1973 *ConAu 104*
Rottiers, Arthur-Kamiel 1920- *IntWWP 82*
Rotwein, Eugene 1918- *IntAu&W 82*
Roubakine, Boris 1908- *CreCan 1*
Roubinek, Darrell L 1935- *ConAu 57*
Roucek, Joseph S 1902- *ConAu 9R*
Roudiez, Leon S 1917- *ConAu 37R*
Roudin, Pierre *IntWWP 82X*
Roudybush, Alexandra 1911- *ConAu 65*
Roueche, Berton *DrAP&F 83*
Roueche, Berton 1911- *ConAu 1R, –1NR,*
 SmATA 28[port]
Roueche, John E 1938- *ConAu 49,*
 IntAu&W 82
Rougemont, Denis Louis De 1906- *TwCA SUP*
Roughead, William 1870-1952 *LongCTC, TwCA,*
 TwCA SUP
Roughsey, Dick 1921?- *ConAu 109,*
 TwCCW 83
Rougier, Louis 1889- *ConAu 29R*
Rougier, Nicole 1929- *ConAu 29R*
Rougier, Paul Auguste Louis 1889- *IntAu&W 82*
Rouhani, Fuad 1907- *ConAu 37R*
Roukes, Nicholas 1925- *ConAu 25R*
Roulac, Stephen E 1945- *ConAu 104*
Rouleau, Raymond 1904-1981 *ConAu 108*
Roulston, Marjorie Hillis 1890-1971 *ConAu 104*
Roumain, Jacques 1907-1944 *ModBlW, ModFrL*
Roumanille, Joseph 1818-1891 *CIDMEL 80*
Rounds, Glen 1906- *TwCCW 83, WrDr 84*
Rounds, Glen H 1906- *ConAu 7NR, –53,*
 SmATA 8
Rouner, Arthur A, Jr. 1929- *ConAu 5NR, –9R*
Rouner, Leroy S 1930- *ConAu 73*
Rountree, Owen *ConAu X*
Rountree, Thomas J 1927- *ConAu 25R,*
 IntAu&W 82, IntWWP 82, WrDr 84
Rouquette, Pierre Antoine 1898- *IntWWP 82*
Rourke, Constance 1885-1941 *TwCLC 12[port]*
Rourke, Constance Mayfield 1885-1941 *ConAmA,*
 ConAu 107, ModAL, TwCA, TwCA SUP
Rourke, Elizabeth Massie 1908- *IntWWP 82*
Rourke, Francis Edward 1922- *ConAu 1R, –6NR*
Rous, Stanley 1895- *ConAu 108*
Rousculp, Charles G 1923- *ConAu 29R*
Rouse, Blair 1912- *ConAu 1R*
Rouse, Irene *DrAP&F 83*

Rouse, Irving 1913- *ConAu 9R, WrDr 84*
Rouse, John E 1892- *ConAu 73*
Rouse, John E, Jr. 1942- *ConAu 89*
Rouse, Parke Shepherd, Jr. 1915- *ConAu 17R,*
 IntAu&W 82, WrDr 84
Rouse, Richard H 1933- *ConAu 29R*
Rouse Jones, Lewis 1907- *ConAu P-1*
Roush, Barbara 1940- *ConAu 109*
Roush, John Huston, Jr. 1923- *ConAu 37R,*
 IntAu&W 82
Rousmaniere, John 1944- *ConAu 93*
Rousseau, George S 1941- *WrDr 84*
Rousseau, George Sebastian 1941- *ConAu 11NR,*
 –29R, IntAu&W 82
Rousseau, Richard W 1924- *ConAu 110*
Rousseau, Victor 1879-1960 *TwCSFW*
Roussel, Raymond 1877-1933 *CIDMEL 80,*
 ModFrL, WhoTwCL, WorAu
Rousset, David 1912- *TwCA SUP*
Roussin, Andre 1911- *CnMD, ModWD,*
 WorAu
Rout, Leslie B, Jr. 1936- *ConAu 57*
Routh, C R N 1896- *ConAu P-1*
Routh, Donald K 1937- *ConAu 57*
Routh, Francis John 1927- *ConAu 13R,*
 IntAu&W 82, WrDr 84
Routh, Jonathan *ConAu 110, WrDr 84*
Routh, Porter W 1911- *ConAu 77*
Routier, Simone 1901- *CreCan 1*
Routledge, George 1822-1888 *LongCTC*
Routley, Erik 1917-1982 *ConAu 108*
Routley, Erik Reginald 1917- *ConAu 1R, –5NR,*
 IntAu&W 82
Routsong, Alma 1924- *ConAu 49, MichAu 80*
Routtenberg, Max Jonah 1909- *ConAu 77*
Rouverol, Jean *ConAu X*
Roux, Edward R 1903- *ConAu 13R*
Roux, Georges 1914- *ConAu 17R*
Roux, Jean-Louis 1923- *CreCan 2*
Roux, Willan Charles 1902- *ConAu P-2*
Rover, Constance Mary 1910- *ConAu 21R,*
 WrDr 84
Rovere, Richard H 1915-1979 *ConAu 3NR, –49,*
 –89, –97, DcLEL 1940
Rovin, Alex *IntAu&W 82X, IntWWP 82X*
Rovin, Ben *ConAu X*
Rovin, Jeff 1951- *ConAu 77*
Rovinaru, Traian *IntAu&W 82X*
Rovit, Earl *DrAP&F 83*
Rovit, Earl 1927- *ConAu 5R, ConLC 7,*
 WrDr 84
Rovner, Arkady *DrAP&F 83*
Rowan, Carl T 1925- *ConAu 89,*
 ConIsC 1[port], LivgBAA
Rowan, Deirdre *ConAu X, WrDr 84*
Rowan, Ford 1943- *ConAu 69*
Rowan, Helen 1927?-1972 *ConAu 37R*
Rowan, Hester *WrDr 84*
Rowan, Richard Lamar 1931- *ConAu 9R*
Rowan, Stephen A 1928- *ConAu 45*
Rowans, Virginia *ConAu X, WorAu*
Rowat, Donald C 1921- *ConAu 5NR, –9R,*
 IntAu&W 82, WrDr 84
Rowbotham, David 1924- *WrDr 84*
Rowbotham, David Harold 1924- *ConP 80,*
 DcLEL 1940
Rowbotham, Sheila 1943- *ConAu 101, WrDr 84*
Rowdon, Larry 1923- *IntWWP 82*
Rowdon, Maurice 1922- *ConAu 110*
Rowe, A W 1915- *ConAu 21R*
Rowe, Alick Edward 1938- *IntAu&W 82*
Rowe, Clarence J, Jr. 1916- *ConAu 104*
Rowe, D Trevor 1929- *WrDr 84*
Rowe, David Knox *ConAu 77*
Rowe, David Nelson 1905- *ConAu 2NR, –5R*
Rowe, Erna 1926- *ConAu X*
Rowe, Frederick William 1912- *ConAu 101*
Rowe, George E, Jr. 1947- *ConAu 93*
Rowe, H Edward 1927- *ConAu 69*
Rowe, James L, Jr. 1948- *ConAu 69*
Rowe, James N 1938- *ConAu 37R*
Rowe, Jeanne A 1938- *ConAu 29R*
Rowe, John L 1914- *ConAu 17R*
Rowe, John Seymour 1936- *ConAu 109,*
 WrDr 84
Rowe, Margaret 1920- *ConAu 13R*
Rowe, Robert 1920- *ConAu 17R*
Rowe, Stephen *IntAu&W 82X*
Rowe, Terry *AuNews 2*
Rowe, Viola Carson 1903-1969 *ConAu 1R, –103,*
 SmATA 26N
Rowe, Vivian C 1902-1978 *ConAu 1R, –2NR*

Rowe, William L 1931- *ConAu 108*
Rowell, Charles H *DrAP&F 83*
Rowell, Douglas Geoffrey 1943- *IntAu&W 82,*
 WrDr 84
Rowell, Galen 1940- *ConAu 65*
Rowell, George 1923- *ConAu 2NR, –5R,*
 IntAu&W 82, WrDr 84
Rowell, Henry T 1904- *ConAu P-1*
Rowell, John William 1914- *ConAu 33R*
Rowen, Betty Jane Rose 1920- *ConAu 109*
Rowen, Herbert H 1916- *ConAu 3NR, –9R,*
 IntAu&W 82, WrDr 84
Rowen, Hobart 1918- *ConAu 9R*
Rowen, Lilian 1925- *ConAu 108*
Rowen, Ruth Halle 1918- *ConAu 33R,*
 IntAu&W 82
Rowes, Barbara Gail *ConAu 101*
Rowett, Helen 1915- *WrDr 84*
Rowland, Arthur Ray 1930- *ConAu 6NR, –13R,*
 WrDr 84
Rowland, Benjamin, Jr. 1904-1972 *ConAu 37R*
Rowland, Beryl *ConAu 89*
Rowland, D S 1928- *ConAu 21R*
Rowland, Donald S 1928- *TwCWW*
Rowland, Florence Wightman 1900- *ConAu 5R,*
 –5NR, SmATA 8
Rowland, Iris *ConAu X, TwCRGW, WrDr 84*
Rowland, J R 1925- *ConAu 101, ConP 80,*
 WrDr 84
Rowland, Peter Kenneth 1938- *ConAu 25R,*
 IntAu&W 82, WrDr 84
Rowland, Sidney 1922- *IntWWP 82*
Rowland, Stanley J, Jr. 1928- *ConAu 13R*
Rowland, Virgil K 1909- *ConAu 5R*
Rowland-Entwhistle, Theodore 1925-
 IntAu&W 82
Rowland-Entwistle, Theodore 1925- *ConAu 107,*
 SmATA 31[port]
Rowlands, Effie Adelaide *LongCTC, TwCRGW*
Rowlands, John *IntAu&W 82*
Rowlands, John Robert 1947- *ConAu 109*
Rowlands, Peter *ConAu X*
Rowlatt, Mary 1908- *ConAu 5R*
Rowley, Ames Dorrance *ConAu X*
Rowley, Anthony 1939- *ConAu 61*
Rowley, Brian Alan 1923- *ConAu 5R*
Rowley, Charles 1906- *ConAu 103, WrDr 84*
Rowley, Gordon Douglas 1921- *IntAu&W 82*
Rowley, Peter 1934- *ConAu 65*
Rowley, Thomas *ConAu X*
Rowling, Marjorie A 1900- *WrDr 84*
Rowling, Marjorie Alice 1900- *ConAu 5R*
Rowlingson, Donald T 1907- *ConAu 1R, –6NR*
Rowney, Don Karl 1936- *ConAu 108*
Rowntree, Derek G F 1936- *WrDr 84*
Rowse, A L 1903- *ConAu 1NR, ConP 80,*
 WrDr 84
Rowse, Alfred Leslie 1903- *ConAu 1R,*
 IntAu&W 82, IntWWP 82, LongCTC,
 ModBrL, TwCA SUP
Roxas, Savina A *ConAu 37R*
Roxborough, Henry Hall 1891- *ConAu 5R*
Roy, Archibald Edmiston 1924- *ConAu 102*
Roy, Archie E 1924- *ConAu X, WrDr 84*
Roy, Claude 1915- *IntAu&W 82*
Roy, David Tod 1933- *ConAu 41R*
Roy, Emil L 1933- *ConAu 25R*
Roy, Ewell Paul 1929- *ConAu 9R*
Roy, G Ross 1924- *ConAu 77*
Roy, Gabrielle 1909- *ConAu 5NR, –53,*
 ConLC 10, –14, CreCan 2, ModCmwL,
 ModFrL, TwCA SUP, TwCWr
Roy, Gabrielle 1909-1983 *ConAu 110*
Roy, Gregor Andrew 1929- *ConAu 21R,*
 IntAu&W 82
Roy, Jack *ConAu X*
Roy, James 1922- *WrDr 84*
Roy, James Alexander 1884- *ConAu P-1*
Roy, Joaquin 1943- *ConAu 77*
Roy, John 1913- *ConAu 93*
Roy, Jules 1907- *WorAu*
Roy, Katherine 1907- *ConAu 1R*
Roy, Liam *ConAu X, SmATA 2*
Roy, Michael 1913-1976 *ConAu 10NR, –61, –65*
Roy, Mike *ConAu X*
Roy, Percy Gordon *IntAu&W 82X*
Roy, Reginald H 1922- *ConAu 49*
Roy, Robert L 1947- *ConAu 106*
Royal, Claudia Smith 1904- *ConAu 5R*
Royal, D *ConAu X*
Royal, Denise 1935- *ConAu 25R*

Royal, Richard Everett DrAP&F 83
Royal, Tom IntAu&W 82X
Royal, William Robert 1905- ConAu 101
Royall, Vanessa ConAu X
Royce, Anya Peterson 1940- ConAu 101,
  IntAu&W 82
Royce, James E 1914- ConAu 1R, WrDr 84
Royce, Joseph Russell WrDr 84
Royce, Josiah 1855-1916 TwCA, TwCA SUP
Royce, Kenneth 1920- ConAu 13R,
  IntAu&W 82X, TwCCr&M 80, WrDr 84
Royce, Patrick M 1922- ConAu 13R
Royce, R Joseph 1921- ConAu 9NR, –21R
Royde-Smith, Naomi Gwladys 1875?-1964
  LongCTC, ModBrL, TwCA, TwCA SUP
Royer, Fanchon 1902- ConAu 5R
Royko, Mike 1922- WrDr 84
Royko, Mike 1932- ConAu 89
Roylance, William H 1927- ConAu 61
Royle, Edward 1944- ConAu 61
Royle, Selena 1904-1983 ConAu 109
Royle, Stanley 1888-1962 CreCan 1
Royster, Charles 1944- ConAu 101
Royster, Philip M 1943- ConAu 65, LivgBAA
Royster, Salibelle 1895-1975 ConAu P-2
Royster, Sandra Howe 1942- LivgBAA
Royster, Vermont 1914- WrDr 84
Royster, Vermont Connecticut 1914- ConAu 21R
Royston, Olive 1904- ConAu 102, WrDr 84
Rozanov, Vasili Vasilyevich 1856-1919 ModSL 1
Rozanov, Vasily Vasilyevich 1856-1919
  CIDMEL 80
Rozeboom, William W 1928- ConAu 17R
Rozek, Evalyn Robillard 1941- ConAu 61
Rozental, Alek A 1920- ConAu 33R
Rozet, Francois CreCan 2
Rozewicz, Tadeusz 1921- CIDMEL 80,
  ConAu 108, ConLC 9, –23[port], CroCD,
  ModSL 2, ModWD, WorAu 1970
Rozhdestvensky, Robert Ivanovich 1932-
  CIDMEL 80
Rozhdestvensky, Vsevolod A 1895?-1977
  ConAu 73
Rozier, John W 1918- ConAu 107
Rozin, Skip 1941- ConAu 89
Rozman, Gilbert Friedell 1943- ConAu 109
Rozmiarek, Joseph ConAmTC
Rozov, Victor Sergeevich 1913- CnMD, ModWD
Rozov, Victor Sergeyevich 1916- TwCWr
Rozov, Viktor Sergeyevich 1913- CIDMEL 80
Rozovsky, Lorne Elkin 1942- ConAu 108
Rozwenc, Edwin C 1915-1974 ConAu P-1
Ruan, Peter 1939- SmATA 15
Ruane, Gerald P 1934- ConAu 69
Ruano, Argimiro 1924- ConAu 33R
Ruano, Nazario ConAu X
Ruark, Gibbons DrAP&F 83
Ruark, Gibbons 1941- ConAu 33R, ConLC 3
Ruark, Robert 1915-1965 ConAu 25R,
  ConAu P-2, LongCTC
Rubadeau, Duane O 1927- ConAu 29R
Rubadir, David 1930- IntWWP 82
Rubadiri, David 1930- DcLEL 1940
Rubashov, Schneor Zalman ConAu X
Rubashov, Zalman ConAu X
Rubbra, Edmund 1901- WrDr 84
Rubel, Arthur J 1924- ConAu 41R
Rubel, James L TwCWW
Rubel, Maximilien 1905- ConAu P-1
Rubel, Nicole 1953- SmATA 18
Rubel, Paula G 1933- ConAu 89
Ruben, Brent David 1944- ConAu 41R
Rubens, Bernice 1923- ConAu 25R
Rubens, Bernice 1927- ConLC 19, ConNov 82,
  WrDr 84
Rubens, Bernice 1928- DcLB 14[port],
  DcLEL 1940
Rubens, Jeff 1941- ConAu 25R
Rubenstein, Boris B 1907?-1974 ConAu 53
Rubenstein, Carol DrAP&F 83
Rubenstein, Carol 1934- IntWWP 82
Rubenstein, Joshua 1949- ConAu 103
Rubenstein, Nancy 1929- ConAmTC
Rubenstein, Richard E 1938- ConAu 29R,
  WrDr 84
Rubenstein, Richard Lowell 1924- ConAu 21R,
  WrDr 84
Rubenstein, Robert 1926- ConAu 21R
Rubenstein, Roberta 1944- ConAu 89
Rubenstone, Jessie 1912- ConAu 69
Rubert Y Candau, Jose Maria 1901-
  IntAu&W 82

Rubes, Jan 1920- CreCan 1
Rubia Barcia, Jose 1914- ConAu 103
Rubicam, Harry Cogswell, Jr. 1902- ConAu P-2
Rubicon ConAu X
Rubin, Amy Kateman 1945- ConAu 106
Rubin, Arnold P 1946- ConAu 69
Rubin, Barry 1950- ConAu 108
Rubin, Charles J 1950- ConAu 101
Rubin, Cynthia Elyce 1944- ConAu 97
Rubin, David Lee 1939- ConAu 41R
Rubin, David M 1945- ConAu 77
Rubin, Dorothy 1932- ConAu 101
Rubin, Duane R 1931- ConAu 57
Rubin, Eli Z 1922- ConAu 17R
Rubin, Ernest 1915-1978 ConAu 81
Rubin, Frederick 1926- ConAu 33R
Rubin, Ida Ely 1923- ConAu 107
Rubin, Isadore 1912-1970 ConAu 29R,
  ConAu P-1
Rubin, Israel 1923- ConAu 37R
Rubin, Jacob A 1910-1972 ConAu 37R,
  ConAu P-1
Rubin, James Henry 1944- ConAu 106
Rubin, Jean DrAP&F 83
Rubin, Jean 1928- IntWWP 82
Rubin, Jerry 1938- ConAu 69
Rubin, Joan 1932- ConAu 102
Rubin, Joan Alleman 1931- ConAmTC
Rubin, Larry DrAP&F 83
Rubin, Larry 1930- WrDr 84
Rubin, Larry Jerome 1930- ConAu 5R,
  ConP 80, IntAu&W 82, IntWWP 82
Rubin, Leona G 1920- ConAu 49
Rubin, Lillian B 1924- ConIsC 2[port]
Rubin, Lillian Breslow 1924- ConAu 65
Rubin, Louis D, Jr. 1923- ConAu 1R, –6NR
Rubin, Mark DrAP&F 83
Rubin, Mark 1946- ConAu 9NR, –53
Rubin, Michael DrAP&F 83
Rubin, Michael 1935- ConAu 1R, –1NR
Rubin, Morris H 1911-1980 ConAu 101
Rubin, Morton 1923- ConAu 41R
Rubin, Riva Regina 1932- IntWWP 82
Rubin, Stan Sanvel DrAP&F 83
Rubin, Stanley 1928- ConAu 107, WrDr 84
Rubin, Steven Jay 1951- ConAu 110
Rubin, Steven Joel 1943- ConAu 107
Rubin, Theodore I 1923- WrDr 84
Rubin, Theodore Isaac 1923- AuNews 1,
  ConAu 108, –110
Rubin, Vitalii 1923-1981 ConAu 105, –69
Rubin, William 1927- ConAu 77
Rubin, Zick 1944- ConAu 1NR, –49
Rubington, Earl 1923- ConAu 73
Rubinoff, Lionel 1930- ConAu 25R, WrDr 84
Rubinow, Sol 1923-1981 ConAu 103
Rubins, Jack L 1916-1982 ConAu 107, –85
Rubinstein, Alvin Zachary 1927- ConAu 3NR,
  –9R, IntAu&W 82
Rubinstein, Amnon 1931- ConAu 7NR, –13R
Rubinstein, Arthur 1887-1982 ConAu 108
Rubinstein, Artur ConAu X
Rubinstein, Daryl Reich 1938?-1981 ConAu 102
Rubinstein, David H 1915- ConAu 109
Rubinstein, David M 1942- ConAu 93
Rubinstein, E 1936- ConAu 41R
Rubinstein, Hilary 1926- WrDr 84
Rubinstein, Hilary Harold 1926- ConAu 57,
  IntAu&W 82
Rubinstein, Moshe F 1930- ConAu 57
Rubinstein, Paul 7NR, –61
Rubinstein, Robert E 1943- ConAu 106
Rubinstein, S Leonard 1922- ConAu 45
Rubinstein, Stanley 1890-1975 ConAu P-2
Rubio I Ors, Joaquim 1818-1899 CIDMEL 80
Rublowsky, John M 1928- ConAu 17R
Rubsamen, Walter H 1911- ConAu 13R
Rubulis, Aleksis 1922- ConAu 37R, WrDr 84
Ruby, Kathryn DrAP&F 83
Ruby, Kathryn 1947- ConAu 65, IntWWP 82
Ruby, Lois 1942- ConAu 97, SmATA 34
Ruby, Robert H WrDr 84
Ruby, Robert Holmes 1921- ConAu 7NR, –17R
Ruchames, Louis 1917-1976 ConAu 1R, –2NR,
  –65
Ruchelman, Leonard I 1933- ConAu 29R,
  WrDr 84
Ruchlis, Hy 1913- ConAu 1R, –2NR,
  SmATA 3
Ruck, Amy Roberta 1878-1978 ConAu 5R, –5NR
Ruck, Berta 1878-1978 ConAu X, LongCTC,
  TwCA, TwCA SUP, TwCRGW, TwCWr

Ruck, Carl A P 1935- ConAu 25R
Ruck, Peter F Carter ConAu X
Rucker, Bryce W 1921- ConAu 9R
Rucker, Darnell 1921- ConAu 41R
Rucker, Frank Warren 1886-1975 ConAu 1R,
  –103
Rucker, Helen Bornstein ConAu 1R
Rucker, W Ray 1920- ConAu 13R
Rud IntAu&W 82X
Rud, Nils Johan 1908- CIDMEL 80
Rudberg, Gertrude J 1907- IntWWP 82
Rudd, Enid ConAu 108, NatPD 81[port]
Rudd, Hughes 1921- ConAu 73
Rudd, Margaret ConAu X, WrDr 84
Rudd, Margaret Thomas 1907- ConAu 17R,
  WrDr 84
Rudd, Robert Dean 1924- ConAu 93
Rudd, Steele 1868-1935 TwCWr
Ruddell, Robert B 1937- ConAu 93
Rudder, Robert S 1937- ConAu 5NR, –53
Rudder, Virginia L 1941- ConAu 65
Ruddick, Sara 1935- ConAu 77
Ruddock, Ralph 1913- ConAu 53
Rude, George F E 1910- ConAu 5R, –5NR
Rudel, Hans-Ulrich 1916-1982 ConAu 110
Rudelius, William 1931- ConAu 45
Rudenstine, Neil Leon 1935- ConAu 105
Ruder, William 1921- ConAu 17R
Rudhart, Alexander 1930- ConAu 61
Rudhyar, Dane 1895- ConAu 29R, WrDr 84
Rudin, Jacob Philip 1902-1982 ConAu 107
Rudin, Marcia Ruth 1940- ConAu 102
Rudinger, Joel DrAP&F 83
Rudinsky, Joseph F 1891- ConAu 5R
Rudis, Al 1943- ConAu 77
Rudisill, D P 1902- ConAu 45
Rudkin, David 1936- ConAu 89, ConDr 82,
  ConLC 14, CroCD, DcLB 13[port],
  WrDr 84
Rudkin, James David 1936- DcLEL 1940,
  IntAu&W 82
Rudley, Stephen 1946- ConAu 106, SmATA 30
Rudloe, Jack 1943- ConAu 97
Rudman, Mark DrAP&F 83
Rudman, Mark 1948- IntWWP 82
Rudman, Masha Kabakow 1933- ConAu 110
Rudnick, Hans H 1935- ConAu 41R
Rudnick, Milton Leroy 1927- ConAu 1R, –3NR
Rudnicki, Adolf 1912- CIDMEL 80
Rudnik, Raphael DrAP&F 83
Rudnik, Raphael 1933- ConAu 29R, ConLC 7
Rudofsky, Bernard 1905- ConAu 17R
Rudol, Anthony 1942- ConAu 9NR, –61,
  ConP 80, IntWWP 82, WrDr 84
Rudolph, Donna Keyse 1934- ConAu 33R
Rudolph, Erwin Paul 1916- ConAu 33R
Rudolph, Frederick 1920- ConAu 9R
Rudolph, L C 1921- ConAu 2NR
Rudolph, Lavere Christian 1921- ConAu 5R
Rudolph, Lee DrAP&F 83
Rudolph, Lee 1948- ConAu 7NR, –57,
  IntWWP 82
Rudolph, Lloyd I 1927- ConAu 57
Rudolph, Marguerita 1908- ConAu 33R,
  SmATA 21[port]
Rudolph, Nancy 1923- ConAu 57
Rudolph, Robert S 1937- ConAu 41R
Rudolph, Susanne Hoeber 1930- ConAu 25R
Rudomin, Esther ConAu X, SmATA 4,
  WrDr 84
Rudorf, Gunther 1921- CnMD
Rudrum, Alan William 1932- ConAu 25R,
  IntAu&W 82, WrDr 84
Rudwick, Elliot M 1927- ConAu 104
Rudy, Ann 1927- ConAu 101
Rudy, D L DrAP&F 83, IntWWP 82X
Rudy, Dorothy L 1924- IntWWP 82
Rudy, Peter 1922- ConAu 53
Rudy, Willis 1920- ConAu 37R, IntAu&W 82,
  WrDr 84
Rue, John E 1924- ConAu 21R
Rue, Leonard Lee, III 1926- ConAu 1R, –1NR,
  IntAu&W 82, WrDr 84
Rue, Leslie W 1944- ConAu 110
Rueber, Johannes 1928- IntAu&W 82
Ruebner, Towia 1924- IntAu&W 82
Ruebner, Tuvia 1924- IntAu&W 82
Ruebsaat, Helmut J 1920- ConAu 61
Ruechelle, Randall C 1920- ConAu 41R
Rueckert, William H 1926- ConAu 21R
Rueda, Salvador 1857-1933 CIDMEL 80
Ruederer, Josef 1861-1915 ModWD

Ruedi, Norma Paul *ConAu X, SmATA X*
Ruef, John Samuel 1927- *ConAu 37R,*
  WrDr 84
Rueff, Jacques 1896-1978 *ConAu 65, –77*
Ruefle, Mary *DrAP&F 83*
Ruege, Klaus 1934- *ConAu 11NR, –65*
Ruehle, Juergen 1924- *ConAu 25R*
Ruehlmann, William 1946- *ConAu 105*
Ruell, Patrick *ConAu X, TwCCr&M 80,*
  WrDr 84
Ruesch, Hans 1913- *ConAu 13R*
Ruesch, Jurgen 1909- *ConAu 73*
Rueschhoff, Phil H 1924- *ConAu 29R*
Ruether, Rosemary Radford 1936- *ConAu 97,*
  WrDr 84
Rueveni, Uri 1933- *ConAu 102*
Ruff, Howard J *ConAu 93*
Ruffell, Ann 1941- *ConAu 107,*
  SmATA 30[port]
Ruffian, M *ConAu X*
Ruffin, C Bernard, III 1947- *ConAu 109*
Ruffin, Paul *DrAP&F 83*
Ruffin, Paul D 1941- *IntWWP 82*
Ruffini, Renno 1942- *ConAu 57*
Ruffle, The *ConAu X*
Ruffner, Budge *ConAu X*
Ruffner, Lester Ward 1918- *ConAu 89*
Ruffo, Vinnie *ConAu 25R*
Ruffridge, Frank 1931- *ConAu 25R*
Rugel, Miriam 1911- *ConAu 101*
Rugg, Dean S 1923- *ConAu 41R*
Rugg, Harold Ordway 1886-1960 *TwCA SUP*
Ruggier, Joseph Mary 1956- *IntWWP 82*
Ruggieri, Helen *DrAP&F 83*
Ruggiers, Paul G 1918- *ConAu 25R*
Ruggles, Eleanor 1916- *ConAu 5R, TwCA SUP*
Ruggles, Eugene *DrAP&F 83*
Ruggles, Glenn I 1930- *MichAu 80*
Ruggles, Joanne Beaule 1946- *ConAu 73*
Ruggles, Philip 1944- *ConAu 73*
Rugh, Belle Dorman 1908- *ConAu P-1*
Rugh, Roberts 1903-1978 *ConAu 81, –93*
Rugo, Marieve *DrAP&F 83*
Rugoff, Milton 1913- *ConAu 21R,*
  SmATA 30[port]
Ruhen, Olaf 1911- *ConAu 1R, –5NR,*
  IntAu&W 82, SmATA 17, WrDr 84
Ruhle, Jurgen 1924- *IntAu&W 82*
Ruhm, Gerhard 1930- *CIDMEL 80*
Ruhmkorf, Peter 1929- *CIDMEL 80*
Ruhumbika, Gabriel 1938- *DcLEL 1940*
Ruibal, Jose 1925- *CIDMEL 80*
Ruihley, Glenn Richard *ConAu 107*
Ruitenbeek, Hendrik M 1928- *ConAu 5R, –8NR*
Ruitenbeek, Hendrik M 1928-1983 *ConAu 109*
Ruiz, Jose Martinez G 1873-1967 *ConAu X, –25R,*
  ConLC 11, TwCA, TwCA SUP
Ruiz, Ramon Eduardo 1921- *ConAu 11NR,*
  –25R
Ruiz, Ricardo Navas *ConAu X*
Ruiz, Roberto 1925- *ConAu 41R*
Ruiz-De-Conde, Justina 1909- *ConAu 73*
Ruiz-Fornells, Enrique 1925- *ConAu 33R*
Ruiz Iriarte, Victor 1912- *CIDMEL 80, CroCD*
Ruja, Harry 1912- *ConAu 41R*
Rukeyser, Louis 1933- *ConAu 65*
Rukeyser, Merryle Stanley 1897-1974 *ConAu P-2*
Rukeyser, Muriel 1913-1980 *ConAu 5R, –93,*
  ConLC 6, –10, –15, –27[port], ConP 80,
  IntWWP 82, ModAL, ModAL SUP,
  SmATA 22N, TwCA, TwCA SUP,
  TwCWr
Rukeyser, William Simon 1939- *ConAu 69*
Ruksenas, Algis 1942- *ConAu 49*
Ruland, Richard 1932- *ConAu 21R*
Ruland, Vernon Joseph 1931- *ConAu 17R*
Rule, Gordon Wade 1906-1982 *ConAu 107*
Rule, James B 1943- *ConAu 73*
Rule, Jane 1931- *ConAu 25R, ConLC 27[port],*
  IntAu&W 82, WrDr 84
Rulfo, Juan 1918- *ConAu 85, ConLC 8,*
  ModLAL, TwCWr, WorAu 1970
Rulon, Philip Reed 1934- *ConAu 37R, WrDr 84*
Rumaker, Michael *DrAP&F 83*
Rumaker, Michael 1932- *ConAu 1R, –2NR,*
  ConNov 82, DcLB 16[port], WrDr 84
Rumanes, George N 1925- *ConAu 45*
Rumbelow, Donald 1940- *ConAu 49, WrDr 84*
Rumberger, Russell W 1949- *ConAu 109*
Rumble, Thomas C 1919- *ConAu 13R*
Rumble, Wilfrid E, Jr. 1931- *ConAu 25R*

Rumbold-Gibbs, Henry St. John Clair 1913-
  ConAu 3NR
Rummel, J Francis 1911- *ConAu 17R*
Rummel, R J 1932- *ConAu 65*
Rumpleforeskin *ConAu X*
Rumscheidt, H Martin 1935- *ConAu 57*
Rumsey, Marian 1928- *ConAu 21R,*
  SmATA 16
Runcie, Robert Alexander Kennedy 1921-
  ConAu 108
Runciman, Alexander, Jr. 1951- *IntWWP 82*
Runciman, Lex *DrAP&F 83, IntWWP 82X*
Runciman, Steven 1903- *ConAu 1R, –3NR,*
  IntAu&W 82, LongCTC, WorAu,
  WrDr 84
Rundell, Walter, Jr. 1928- *ConAu 3NR, –9R*
Rundle, Anne *ConAu 57, IntAu&W 82,*
  TwCRGW, WrDr 84
Runes, Dagobert D 1902-1982 *ConAu 108*
Runes, Dagobert David 1902- *ConAu 25R*
Runge, William H 1927- *ConAu 1R*
Runia, Klaas 1926- *ConAu 5R, –5NR*
Runkel, Philip J 1917- *ConAu 11NR, –29R*
Runkle, Gerald 1924- *ConAu 37R*
Running, Leona Glidden 1916- *ConAu 89*
Runte, Alfred 1947- *ConAu 102*
Runyan, Harry 1913- *ConAu P-2*
Runyan, John *ConAu X, SmATA X*
Runyan, Thora J 1931- *ConAu 69*
Runyon, A Milton 1905-1983 *ConAu 109*
Runyon, Catherine 1947- *ConAu 61*
Runyon, Charles W 1928- *ConAu 17R*
Runyon, Damon 1880-1946 *TwCLC 10[port]*
Runyon, Damon 1884?-1946 *CnMWL,*
  ConAu 107, LongCTC, ModAL, ModWD,
  TwCA, TwCA SUP, TwCWr
Runyon, John H 1945- *ConAu 33R*
Runyon, Richard P 1925- *ConAu 3NR, –45*
Ruoff, James E 1925- *ConAu 41R, WrDr 84*
Ruotolo, Andrew K 1926?-1979 *ConAu 103, –89*
Ruotolo, Lucio P 1927- *ConAu 41R,*
  IntAu&W 82
Rupert, Hoover 1917- *ConAu 1R, –3NR,*
  IntAu&W 82, WrDr 84
Rupert, Raphael Rudolph 1910- *ConAu P-2*
Ruple, Wayne Douglas 1950- *ConAu 53,*
  WrDr 84
Rupp, Leila J 1950- *ConAu 81*
Rupp, Richard H 1934- *ConAu 29R, WrDr 84*
Ruppenthal, Karl M 1917- *ConAu 17R,*
  WrDr 84
Ruppert, James *DrAP&F 83*
Ruppli, Michel 1934- *ConAu 101*
Rus, Vladimir 1931- *ConAu 17R*
Rusalem, Herbert 1918- *ConAu 41R*
Rusch, Hermann G 1907- *ConAu 61*
Rusch, John J 1942- *ConAu 106*
Rusco, Elmer R 1928- *ConAu 65*
Ruse, Gary Alan 1946- *ConAu 61*
Ruse, Michael E 1940- *ConAu 107*
Ruse-Gason, Kate *IntWWP 82X*
Rush, Anne Kent 1945- *ConAu 8NR, –61*
Rush, Joseph H 1911- *WrDr 84*
Rush, Joseph Harold 1911- *ConAu 5R*
Rush, Joshua *ConAu X*
Rush, Michael David 1937- *ConAu 61,*
  IntAu&W 82
Rush, Myron 1922- *ConAu 45*
Rush, N Orwin 1907- *ConAu 45*
Rush, Peter 1937- *SmATA 32[port]*
Rush, Philip 1908- *ConAu 104, IntAu&W 82,*
  TwCCW 83, WrDr 84
Rush, Ralph E 1903-1965 *ConAu 5R*
Rush, Richard Henry 1915- *ConAu 5R, –6NR*
Rush, Theressa Gunnels 1945- *ConAu 104*
Rushbrook Williams, L F 1890-1978 *ConAu 97*
Rushdie, Salman 1947- *ConAu 108,*
  ConLC 23[port], WrDr 84
Rushdoony, R J 1916- *ConAu 93*
Rusher, William Allen 1923- *ConAu 103,*
  WrDr 84
Rushforth, Peter 1945- *ConAu 101, ConLC 19*
Rushing, Jane Gilmore 1925- *ConAu 49,*
  TwCWW, WrDr 84
Rushing, William A 1930- *ConAu 81*
Rushmore, Helen 1898- *ConAu 25R, SmATA 3*
Rushmore, Robert *DrAP&F 83*
Rushmore, Robert 1926- *ConAu 25R,*
  SmATA 8
Rusholm, Peter *ConAu X, WrDr 84*
Rushton, William *WrDr 84*
Rushton, William Faulkner 1947- *ConAu 101*

Rusinek, Alla 1949- *ConAu 45*
Rusinek, Michal 1904- *IntAu&W 82*
Rusinol, Santiago 1861-1931 *CIDMEL 80,*
  ModWD
Rusinow, Dennison I 1930- *ConAu 85*
Rusk, Howard A 1901- *ConAu 103*
Rusk, Ralph Leslie 1888-1962 *ConAu 5R*
Ruskay, Joseph A 1910- *ConAu P-2*
Ruskay, Sophie 1887-1980 *ConAu 69, –97*
Ruskin, Ariane 1935- *ConAu 13R, SmATA 7*
Ruskin, John 1819-1900 *SmATA 24[port]*
Russ, Joanna 1937- *ConAu 11NR, –25R,*
  ConLC 15, ConSFA, DcLB 8[port],
  TwCSFW, WrDr 84
Russ, Lavinia 1904- *ConAu 25R*
Russ, Lawrence *DrAP&F 83*
Russ, Lawrence 1950- *IntWWP 82*
Russ, Martin 1931- *ConAu 106*
Russ, William Adam, Jr. 1903- *ConAu 1R*
Russel, Robert R 1890- *ConAu 13R*
Russel, Timothy William *DrAP&F 83*
Russell, Countess *LongCTC*
Russell, Albert *ConAu X*
Russell, Amanda *ConAu X*
Russell, Andy 1915- *ConAu 10NR, –21R*
Russell, Anne Dora 1931- *MichAu 80*
Russell, Annie V 1880?-1974 *ConAu 49*
Russell, Arthur 1908- *ConAu P-1*
Russell, Bertrand Arthur William, Earl 1872-1970
  ConAu 25R, ConAu P-1, LongCTC,
  ModBrL, TwCA[port], TwCA SUP,
  TwCSFW, TwCWr
Russell, Bill *ConAu X*
Russell, Brian Fitzgerald 1904- *WrDr 84*
Russell, C Allyn 1920- *ConAu 65*
Russell, Carol Ann *DrAP&F 83*
Russell, Carol Ann Marie 1951- *IntWWP 82*
Russell, Charles Edward 1860-1941
  DcLB 25[port], TwCA, TwCA SUP
Russell, Charles Marion 1864?-1926? *TwCWW*
Russell, Charlie L 1932- *LivgBAA*
Russell, Charlotte *ConAu X, IntAu&W 82X,*
  SmATA X
Russell, Claude Vivian 1919- *ConAu 17R*
Russell, Clifford S 1938- *ConAu 73*
Russell, Clinton *IntAu&W 82X*
Russell, Colin Archibald 1928- *ConAu 45*
Russell, Conrad 1937- *ConAu 33R, WrDr 84*
Russell, D E H 1938- *ConAu 8NR, –61*
Russell, D S 1916- *ConAu 13R*
Russell, Daniel 1937- *ConAu 41R*
Russell, David Seager 1940- *IntWWP 82*
Russell, David Syme 1916- *IntAu&W 82,*
  WrDr 84
Russell, Diana Elizabeth Hamilton 1938-
  IntAu&W 82
Russell, Diarmuid 1902?-1973 *ConAu 45*
Russell, Don 1899- *ConAu 1NR, WrDr 84*
Russell, Donald Andrew 1920- *ConAu 110*
Russell, Donald Bert 1899- *ConAu 1R*
Russell, Douglas Andrew 1927- *ConAu 41R,*
  IntAu&W 82
Russell, Edward Frederick Langley 1895-1981
  ConAu 103, –107
Russell, Countess Elizabeth Mary 1866-1941
  TwCWr
Russell, Eric Frank 1905-1978 *ConAu 102,*
  ConSFA, TwCSFW
Russell, Francis 1910- *ConAu 25R, WrDr 84*
Russell, Franklin 1926- *ConAu 11NR, –17R,*
  SmATA 11, WrDr 84
Russell, Frederick 1897- *WrDr 84*
Russell, George Horne 1861-1933 *CreCan 2*
Russell, George William 1867-1935 *ConAu 104,*
  LongCTC, ModBrL, ModWD, TwCA,
  TwCA SUP
Russell, George William Erskine 1853-1919
  LongCTC
Russell, Gordon 1892- *ConAu P-2*
Russell, Gordon 1930?-1981 *ConAu 102*
Russell, H Diane 1936- *ConAu 110*
Russell, Helen Ross 1915- *ConAu 33R,*
  SmATA 8, WrDr 84
Russell, Howard S 1887-1980 *ConAu 105*
Russell, Ivy Ethel 1909- *ConAu 5R*
Russell, J *ConAu X*
Russell, James *ConAu X, WrDr 84*
Russell, James E 1916-1975 *ConAu 57*
Russell, James Ward 1919- *IntWWP 82*
Russell, Jeffrey Burton 1934- *ConAu 11NR,*
  –25R
Russell, Jeremy 1935- *WrDr 84*

SmATA X, WrDr 84
Rydell, Wendy 1927- *ConAu 33R,*
IntAu&W 82, SmATA 4, WrDr 84
Ryden, Ernest Edwin 1886-1981 *ConAu 102*
Ryden, Hope *ConAu 33R, SmATA 8*
Rydenfelt, Sven 1911- *IntAu&W 82*
Ryder, A J 1913- *ConAu 21R*
Ryder, Arthur John 1913- *IntAu&W 82,*
WrDr 84
Ryder, Ellen 1913- *ConAu 29R*
Ryder, Frank G 1916- *ConAu 5R*
Ryder, G H 1920- *WrDr 84*
Ryder, Joanne *SmATA 34*
Ryder, John 1917- *ConAu 5R, –5NR,*
IntAu&W 82
Ryder, Jonathan *ConAu X, WrDr 84*
Ryder, M L 1927- *ConAu 102, WrDr 84*
Ryder, Meyer S 1909- *ConAu 21R*
Ryder, Michael Lawson 1927- *IntAu&W 82*
Ryder, Norman B 1923- *ConAu 37R*
Ryder, Ron 1904- *ConAu 61*
Ryder, Rowland Vint 1914- *ConAu 85*
Ryder, Sarah *DrAP&F 83*
Ryder, Thom *WrDr 84*
Ryder, Thomas Arthur 1902- *ConAu 5R*
Ryding, William W 1924- *ConAu 77*
Rye, Anthony *ConAu X, SmATA X, WorAu*
Rye, Bjoern Robinson 1942- *ConAu 61*
Ryecroft, Henry *LongCTC*
Ryerson, Alice *DrAP&F 83*
Ryerson, Lowell *ConAu X*
Ryerson, Martin 1907- *ConAu 8NR, –13R*
Ryf, Robert Stanley 1918- *ConAu 17R*
Ryga, George 1932- *ConAu 101, ConDr 82,*
ConLC 14, WrDr 84
Ryken, Leland 1942- *ConAu 29R, WrDr 84*
Rykwert, Joseph 1926- *ConAu 11NR, –69,*
WrDr 84
Ryland, Lee *ConAu X*
Ryle, Anthony 1927- *ConAu 107, WrDr 84*
Ryle, Gilbert 1900-1976 *ConAu 69, –73,*
DcLEL 1940, LongCTC, WorAu
Rylsky, Maksym 1895-1964 *ClDMEL 80*
Ryl's'kyy, Maksym 1895-1964 *ModSL 2*
Rymer, Alta May 1925- *ConAu 1NR, –49,*
SmATA 34[port]
Rymes, Thomas K 1932- *ConAu 37R, WrDr 84*
Rymkiewicz, Aleksander 1913- *IntWWP 82*
Rynew, Arden N 1943- *ConAu 37R*
Ryrie, Charles C 1925- *ConAu 3NR, –9R*
Ryskamp, Charles 1928- *ConAu 104*
Ryskind, Morrie 1895- *ConAu 109, ConDr 82D,*
DcLB 26[port], ModWD
Rystrom, Kenneth 1932- *ConAu 110*
Rytten, Jack Edward 1914- *IntAu&W 82*
Ryum, Ulla 1937- *ClDMEL 80*
Ryweck, Charles *ConAmTC*
Rywell, Martin 1905-1971 *ConAu P-2*
Rywkin, Michael 1925- *ConAu 13R*
Ryzl, Milan 1928- *ConAu 29R*
Rzhevsky, Leonid 1905- *ConAu 41R*

S

S, I *ConAmA*

S F-R *IntAu&W 82X*

S-Ringi, Kjell *ConAu X, SmATA X*

S S E *ConAu X*

Sa-Carneiro, Mario De 1890-1916 *CIDMEL 80*

Saab, E Ann Pottinger 1934- *ConAu 107*

Saab, Edouard 1929-1976 *ConAu 65*

Saalman, Howard 1928- *ConAu 1R, -1NR, IntAu&W 82*

Saarikoski, Pentti Ilmari 1937- *IntWWP 82*

Saarinen, Aline B 1914-1972 *ConAu 37R*

Saarsen-Karlstedt, Karin Marie 1926- *IntWWP 82*

Saaty, Thomas L 1926- *ConAu 8NR, -57*

Saba *IntWWP 82X*

Saba, Umberto 1883-1957 *CIDMEL 80, ModRL, WhoTwCL, WorAu*

Sabaliunas, Leonas 1934- *ConAu 61*

Sabaroff, Rose Epstein 1918- *ConAu 85*

Sabath, Bernard *NatPD 81[port]*

Sabatier, Robert 1928- *ConAu 102*

Sabatini, Rafael 1875-1950 *LongCTC, TwCA, TwCA SUP, TwCRGW, TwCWr*

Sabato, Ernesto 1911- *ConAu 97, ConLC 10, -23[port], IntAu&W 82, ModLAL*

Sabato, Larry 1952- *ConAu 108*

Sabbag, Robert 1946- *ConAu 101*

Sabbah, Hassan I *ConAu X*

Saberhagen, Fred 1930- *ConAu 7NR, -57, ConSFA, DcLB 8[port], TwCSFW, WrDr 84*

Sabiad *ConAu X*

Sabin, Arthur Knowles 1879-1959 *LongCTC*

Sabin, Francene *ConAu 11NR, -69, SmATA 27*

Sabin, Katharine Cover 1910- *ConAu 57*

Sabin, Lou *ConAu X*

Sabin, Louis 1930- *ConAu 11NR, -69, SmATA 27*

Sabine, B E V 1914- *ConAu 97*

Sabine, Ellen S 1908- *ConAu P-1, IntAu&W 82, WrDr 84*

Sabine, Waldo *ConAu X*

Sabine, William Henry Waldo 1903- *ConAu 4NR, -53, WrDr 84*

Sabini, John Anthony 1921- *ConAu 9R*

Sabki, Hisham M 1934- *ConAu 106*

Sable, Martin Howard 1924- *ConAu 33R, WrDr 84*

Sabloff, Jeremy A 1944- *ConAu 8NR, -61*

Sabom, Michael Bruce 1944- *ConAu 109*

Sabourin, Anne Winifred 1910- *ConAu 101*

Sabourin, Justine *ConAu X*

Sabourin, Leopold 1919- *ConAu 11NR, -65*

Sabourin, Marcel 1935- *CreCan 1*

Sabre, Dirk *ConAu X, SmATA X, WrDr 84*

Sabre, Mark *IntAu&W 82X*

Sabri-Tabrizi, Gholam-Reza 1934- *ConAu 61*

Sabuso *SmATA X*

Sacastru, Martin *ConAu X*

Saccio, Peter 1941- *ConAu 61*

Sachar, Abram Leon 1899- *ConAu 97*

Sachar, Howard Morley 1928- *ConAu 5R, -6NR*

Sachar, Louis 1954- *ConAu 81*

Sacharoff, Shanta Nimbark 1945- *ConAu 61*

Sachem, E B *ConAu X*

Sacher, Jack, Jr. 1931- *ConAu 57*

Sacher-Masoch, Alexander 1902?-1972 *ConAu 37R*

Sachs, Albert Louis 1935- *ConAu 21R*

Sachs, Albie *ConAu X*

Sachs, Alexander 1893-1973 *ConAu 41R*

Sachs, Andrew *ConDr 82B*

Sachs, Arieh 1932- *IntWWP 82*

Sachs, Curt 1881-1959 *TwCA SUP*

Sachs, Elizabeth-Ann *DrAP&F 83*

Sachs, Georgia *ConAu X*

Sachs, Harvey 1946- *ConAu 85*

Sachs, Herbert L 1929- *ConAu 25R*

Sachs, Lewis Benjamen 1938- *ConAu 61*

Sachs, Marilyn 1927- *TwCCW 83*

Sachs, Marilyn Stickle 1927- *ChlLR 2, ConAu 17R, IntAu&W 82, SmATA 3, WrDr 84*

Sachs, Mary P K 1882?-1973 *ConAu 45*

Sachs, Mendel 1927- *ConAu 29R, IntAu&W 82, WrDr 84*

Sachs, Murray 1924- *ConAu 37R, IntAu&W 82, WrDr 84*

Sachs, Nelly 1891-1970 *CIDMEL 80, ConAu 25R, ConAu P-2, ConLC 14, ModGL, TwCWr, WorAu*

Sachse, William L 1912- *ConAu 25R*

Sack, James J 1944- *ConAu 101*

Sack, John 1930- *ConAu 21R*

Sack, Saul 1912- *ConAu 53*

Sackerman, Henry *ConAu X*

Sackett, S J 1928- *ConAu 6NR, SmATA 12*

Sackett, Samuel John 1928- *ConAu 1R, WrDr 84*

Sackett, Susan 1943- *ConAu 106*

Sackett, Theodore Alan 1940- *ConAu 89*

Sackett, Walter W, Jr. 1905- *ConAu 5R*

Sackheim, Maxwell 1890-1982 *ConAu 108*

Sackler, Howard 1929- *ConAu 61, ConDr 82, ConLC 14, DcLB 7[port], NatPD 81*

Sackler, Howard 1929-1982 *ConAu 108*

Sackman, Harold 1927- *ConAu 21R*

Sackrey, Charles 1936- *ConAu 77*

Sacks, Benjamin 1903- *ConAu P-2*

Sacks, Karen 1941- *ConAu 109*

Sacks, Norman P 1914- *ConAu 45*

Sacks, Oliver 1933- *ConAu 53, WrDr 84*

Sacks, Sheldon 1930- *ConAu 17R*

Sackson, Sid 1920- *ConAu 69, SmATA 16*

Sackton, Alexander H 1911- *ConAu 37R*

Sackville, Lady Margaret 1881-1963 *LongCTC*

Sackville-West, Edward Charles 1901-1965 *LongCTC, ModBrL, TwCA, TwCA SUP, TwCWr*

Sackville-West, V 1892-1962 *ConAu 104, -93*

Sackville-West, Victoria Mary 1892-1962 *LongCTC, ModBrL, TwCA, TwCA SUP, TwCWr*

Sadat, Anwar 1918-1981 *ConAu 101, -104*

Sadd, Susan 1951- *ConAu 103*

Saddhatissa, Hammalawa 1914- *ConAu 97*

Saddlemyer, Ann 1932- *IntAu&W 82, WrDr 84*

Saddlemyer, E Ann 1932- *ConAu 17R*

Saddler, Allen *ConAu X, IntAu&W 82X*

Saddler, Allen 1923- *WrDr 84*

Saddler, K Allen *ConAu X*

Sadecky, Petr Milos 1943- *ConAu 41R*

Sadeh, Pinhas 1929- *ConAu 25R, IntAu&W 82*

Sadgrove, Sidney Henry *WrDr 84*

Sadie, Stanley 1930- *ConAu 9NR, WrDr 84*

Sadie, Stanley John 1930- *ConAu 17R, IntAu&W 82, SmATA 14*

Sadiq, Muhammad 1898- *ConAu 17R*

Sadker, Myra Pollack 1943- *ConAu 5NR, -53*

Sadleir, Michael Thomas Harvey 1888-1957 *LongCTC, TwCA, TwCA SUP, TwCWr*

Sadler, Arthur Lindsay 1882- *ConAu 5R*

Sadler, Christine 1908- *ConAu P-1*

Sadler, Christine 1908-1983 *ConAu 110*

Sadler, Ella Jo 1942- *ConAu 57*

Sadler, Glenn Edward 1935- *ConAu 97*

Sadler, Jerry *DrAP&F 83*

Sadler, Julius Trousdale, Jr. 1923- *ConAu 65*

Sadler, Mark *ConAu X, TwCCr&M 80, WrDr 84*

Sadler, Michael *ConDr 82B*

Sadler, Sir Michael Ernest 1861-1943 *LongCTC*

Sadler, William A, Jr. 1931- *ConAu 25R*

Sadock, Benjamin James 1933- *ConAu 105*

Sadoff, Ira *DrAP&F 83*

Sadoff, Ira 1945- *ConAu 5NR, -53, ConLC 9, IntWWP 82*

Sadoveanu, Mihail 1880-1961 *CIDMEL 80, TwCWr*

Sadun, Elvio H 1918?-1974 *ConAu 49*

Saenz, Dalmiro 1926- *ModLAL*

Saerchinger, Cesar 1884-1971 *ConAu 33R*

Saeter, Alf A 1935- *IntAu&W 82*

Saetone *ConAu X*

Safa, Helen Icken 1930- *ConAu 1NR, -45*

Safarian, Albert Edward 1924- *ConAu 105*

Safdie, Moshe 1938- *ConAu 69, WrDr 84*

Safer, Daniel J 1934- *ConAu 11NR, -69*

Safer, Elaine Berkman 1937- *ConAu 41R*

Safer, Morley 1931- *AuNews 2, ConAu 93*

Saffell, David C 1941- *ConAu 11NR, -61*

Safford, Edwin Ruthven, III 1924- *ConAmTC*

Saffron, Morris Harold 1905- *ConAu 45*

Safian, Jill *ConAu X*

Safilios-Rothschild, Constantina 1936- *ConAu 45*

Safir, Leonard 1921- *ConAu 109*

Safire, William 1929- *ConAu 17R, ConLC 10*

Safran, Claire 1930- *ConAu 101*

Safran, Nadav 1925- *ConAu 5R*

Sagall, Elliot L 1918- *ConAu 29R, WrDr 84*

Sagan, Carl 1934- *ConAu 11NR, -25R, ConIsC 2[port], WrDr 84*

Sagan, Francoise 1935- *CIDMEL 80, ConAu X, ConLC 3, -6, -9, -17, LongCTC, ModFrL, ModRL, WhoTwCL, WorAu*

Sagan, Francoise 1936- *TwCWr*

Sagan, Leonard A 1928- *ConAu 49*

Sagan, Miriam *DrAP&F 83*

Sagan, Miriam 1954- *ConAu 77*

Sagar, Keith 1934- *ConAu 21R*

Sagarin, Edward 1913- *ConAu 4NR, –5R*
Sagarin, Mary 1903- *ConAu 81*
Sagarra, Eda 1933- *ConAu 11NR, –65*
Sagarra I Castellarnau, Josep Maria De 1894-1961? *ClDMEL 80*
Sage, George Harvey 1929- *ConAu 61*
Sage, Howard *DrAP&F 83*
Sage, Juniper *ConAu X, SmATA X*
Sage, Leland L 1899- *ConAu 61*
Sage, Robert 1899-1962 *ConAu 106, DcLB 4*
Sagel, Jim *DrAP&F 83*
Sagen, Rolf 1940- *IntWWP 82*
Sagendorph, Kent 1902-1958 *MichAu 80*
Sagendorph, Robb Hansell 1900-1970 *ConAu 5R, –7NR, –29R*
Sager, Clifford J 1916- *ConAu 29R*
Sageser, A Bower 1902- *ConAu 29R*
Saggs, Henry 1920- *WrDr 84*
Saggs, Henry William Frederick 1920- *ConAu 5R, IntAu&W 82*
Saghir, Marcel T 1937- *ConAu 49*
Sagnier, Thierry 1946- *ConAu 53*
Sagredo Fernandez, Felix 1937- *IntAu&W 82*
Sagrera, Martin 1935- *IntAu&W 82*
Sagsoorian, Paul 1923- *SmATA 12*
Sagstetter, Karen *DrAP&F 83*
Sagstetter, Karen 1941- *ConAu 105*
Sagstetter, Karen R 1947- *IntWWP 82*
Saha, Subhas 1946- *IntAu&W 82, IntWWP 82*
Sahakian, Lucille 1894- *ConAu 53*
Sahakian, Mabel Lewis 1921- *ConAu 21R, WrDr 84*
Sahakian, William S 1921- *ConAu 8NR, –17R, IntAu&W 82, WrDr 84*
Sahgal, Nayantara 1927- *ConAu 9R, –11NR, ConNov 82, DcLEL 1940, IntAu&W 82, WrDr 84*
Sahni, Balbir S 1934- *ConAu 3NR, –45*
Said, Abdul Aziz 1930- *ConAu 81, IntAu&W 82*
Said, Edward W 1935- *ConAu 21R, ConIsC 2[port]*
Saida *SmATA X*
Saidy, Anthony Fred 1937- *ConAu 89*
Saidy, Fareed Milhem 1907-1982 *ConAu 106*
Saidy, Fred 1907-1982 *ConAu X, ConDr 82D, NatPD 81[port]*
Saihoku *IntAu&W 82X*
Saiko, George Emmanuel 1892-1962 *ModGL*
Sailor, Charles 1947- *ConAu 97*
Sailor, Merlin F 1906- *ConAu P-1*
Saine, Thomas P 1941- *ConAu 41R*
Sainer, Arthur 1924- *ConAmTC, GonAu 3NR, –49, ConDr 82, NatPD 81[port], ·WrDr 84*
Saini, B S 1930- *ConAu 107, WrDr 84*
Sainsbury, Eric 1925- *ConAu 33R*
Sainsbury, Maurice Joseph 1927- *ConAu 108, WrDr 84*
Saint, Andrew 1946- *ConAu 65, WrDr 84*
Saint, Dora Jessie *WrDr 84*
Saint, Dora Jessie 1913- *ConAu 7NR, –13R, IntAu&W 82, SmATA 10, WorAu*
Saint, Phil 1912- *ConAu 61*
St. Andre, Lucien *ConAu X*
St. Angelo, Douglas 1931- *ConAu 45*
St. Antoine, Theodore J 1929- *ConAu 41R*
St. Aubyn, F C 1921- *ConAu 25R*
St. Aubyn, Fiona 1952- *ConAu 106*
St. Aubyn, Giles 1925- *WrDr 84*
St. Aubyn, Giles Rowan 1925- *ConAu 4NR, –5R, IntAu&W 82*
St. Briavels, James *SmATA 1*
St. Bruno, Albert Francis 1909- *ConAu P-1*
Saint-Charles, Joseph 1868-1956 *CreCan 2*
St. Clair, Byrd Hooper 1905-1976 *ConAu 1R, –103, SmATA 28N*
St. Clair, Clovis *ConAu X*
St. Clair, David 1932- *ConAu 33R*
St. Clair, Elizabeth *ConAu X*
St. Clair, Katherine *ConAu X*
St. Clair, Leonard 1916- *ConAu 101*
St. Clair, Margaret 1911- *ConAu 49, ConSFA, IntAu&W 82, TwCSFW, WrDr 84*
St. Clair, Philip *ConAu X, DrAP&F 83*
St. Clair, Robert James 1925- *ConAu 9R*
St. Clair, William 1937- *ConAu 77, IntAu&W 82*
St. Cyr, Cyprian *ConAu X*
St. Cyr, Margaret 1920- *ConAu 29R*
St. Cyr, Napoleon J 1924- *IntWWP 82*
St. Denis, Michael George *IntWWP 82X*

Saint-Denis, Michel 1897-1971 *ConAu 33R, ConAu P-2*
Saint-Denys-Garneau, Hector De 1912-1943 *CreCan 1, WorAu 1970*
Saint-Denys Garneau, Henri De *CreCan 1*
Saint-Eden, Dennis *ConAu X, WrDr 84*
Saint-Exupery, Antoine De 1900-1944 *ClDMEL 80, CnMWL, ConAu 108, LongCTC, ModFrL, ModRL, SmATA 20, TwCA, TwCA SUP, TwCLC 2, TwCWr, WhoTwCL*
Saint-Gall, Auguste Amedee De *ConAu X*
St. George, Arthur *ConAu X*
St. George, David *ConAu X*
St. George, George 1904- *ConAu 25R*
St. George, Judith 1931- *ConAu 69, SmATA 13*
Saint-Gil, Philippe *IntWWP 82X*
St. Hereticus *ConAu X*
Saint-Hilaire, Paul-A-F De 1926- *IntAu&W 82*
Saint-J Perse *TwCA, TwCA SUP*
Saint-Jacques, Bernard 1928- *ConAu 41R*
St. Jacques, Elizabeth 1939- *IntWWP 82*
Saint James, Andrew *WorAu, WrDr 84*
St. James, Bernard *ConAu X, –85*
St. John, Beth *ConAu X, IntAu&W 82X*
St. John, Bruce 1923- *WrDr 84*
St. John, Bruce Carlisle 1923- *ConAu 107, ConP 80, IntWWP 82*
St. John, Christopher Marie d1960 *LongCTC*
St. John, David *ConAu X, DrAP&F 83*
St. John, Elizabeth *ConAu X*
St. John, John 1917- *ConAu 5R, –5NR, IntAu&W 82, WrDr 84*
St. John, Leonie *ConAu X*
St. John, Mabel *TwCRGW*
St. John, Nicole *ConAu X, SmATA X, TwCRGW, WrDr 84*
St. John, Patricia Mary 1919- *ConAu 3NR, –5R, WrDr 84*
St. John, Philip *ConAu X, SmATA X, WrDr 84*
St. John, Primus *DrAP&F 83*
St. John, Robert 1902- *ConAu 1R, –5NR, IntAu&W 82, WrDr 84*
St. John, Wylly Folk 1908- *ConAu 21R, IntAu&W 82, SmATA 10, WrDr 84*
St. John Ervine *TwCA, TwCA SUP*
St. John Gogarty *TwCA, TwCA SUP*
Saint-John Perse 1887-1975 *ClDMEL 80, ConAu X, ModFrL*
St. John-Stevas, Norman 1929- *ConAu 4NR, –49, WrDr 84*
St. Johns, Adela Rogers 1894- *AuNews 1, ConAu 108, WrDr 84*
Saint-Laurent, Cecil *IntAu&W 82X*
St. Leger-Leger *TwCA, TwCA SUP*
Saint-Luc, Jean De *CreCan 2*
Saint Martin, Karmele *IntAu&W 82X*
St. Mawr, Erin *DrAP&F 83*
St. Myer, Ned *ConAu X*
St. Omer, Garth *WrDr 84*
St. Omer, Garth 1938?- *ConAu 73, ConNov 82, DcLEL 1940*
St. Phalle, Thibaut De *ConAu X*
Saint-Pierre, Denyse *CreCan 2*
St. Pierre, Dorothy *ConAu X*
Saint-Pol-Roux 1861-1940 *ClDMEL 80*
St. Tamara *ConAu X, SmATA X*
St. Vivant, M *ConAu X*
Sainte-Croix, A *CreCan 1*
Sainte-Marie, Beverly 1941- *ConAu 107*
Sainte-Marie, Buffy 1941- *ConAu X, ConLC 17*
Saintsbury, George Edward Bateman 1845-1933 *LongCTC, ModBrL, TwCA, TwCA SUP*
Sainty, John Christopher 1934- *ConAu 93*
Sainz, Gustavo 1940- *ModLAL*
Sainz DeLaMaza, Regino 1896-1981 *ConAu 108*
Sainz Rodriguez, Pedro 1898- *IntAu&W 82*
Saisselin, Remy G 1925- *ConAu 9R*
Sait Faik 1906-1954 *ClDMEL 80*
Saito, Fred *ConAu X*
Saito, Hiroyuki 1917- *ConAu 61*
Saito, Michiko 1946- *ConAu X, SmATA X*
Sakamaki, Shunzo 1906-1973 *ConAu 1R, –103*
Sakamoto, Edward 1940- *NatPD 81[port]*
Sakell, Achilles Nicholas 1906- *ConAu 1R*
Sakers, George *DrAP&F 83*
Sakers, George 1950- *ConAu 108*
Sakharov, Andrei Dimitrievich 1921- *ConAu 105*
Saki 1870-1916 *CnMWL, ConAu X, LongCTC,*

ModBrL, TwCA, TwCA SUP, TwCWr, WhoTwCL
Saklatvala, Beram 1911-1976 *ConAu 89*
Sakoian, Frances 1912- *ConAu 65*
Sakol, Jeanne 1928- *ConAu 5R*
Sakol, Jeannie 1928- *ConAu 11NR, WrDr 84*
Sakowski, Helmut 1924- *CroCD*
Saks, Elmer Eliot *ConAu X*
Saks, Katia 1939- *ConAu 29R*
Salaam, Kalamu Ya *DrAP&F 83*
Salacrou, Armand 1899- *CnMD, CroCD, IntAu&W 82, ModFrL, ModWD, WorAu*
Salacrou, Armand 1900- *ClDMEL 80*
Saladino, Salvatore 1922- *ConAu 33R, WrDr 84*
Salama, Hannu 1936- *ConLC 18*
Salaman, Esther 1900- *ConAu 61, IntAu&W 82*
Salaman, Raphael A 1906- *WrDr 84*
Salamanca, J R 1922- *ConAu 25R*
Salamanca, J R 1924?- *ConLC 4, –15*
Salamanca, Lucy *ConAu X*
Salamatullah *ConAu X*
Salamatullah, Doctor 1913- *WrDr 84*
Salamon, Lester M 1943- *ConAu 89*
Salant, Nathan N 1955- *ConAu 106*
Salant, Walter S 1911- *ConAu 2NR, –5R*
Salas, Floyd *DrAP&F 83*
Salasin, Robert A *DrAP&F 83*
Salassi, Otto R 1939- *ConAu 106*
Salaverria E Ipinza, Jose Maria 1873-1940 *ClDMEL 80*
Salazar, Fred A 1942- *ConAu 21R*
Salazar Bondy, Sebastian 1924-1965 *ModLAL*
Salcedo-Bastardo, Jose Luis 1926- *IntAu&W 82*
Salchert, Brian *DrAP&F 83*
Salda, Frantisek Xaver 1867-1937 *ClDMEL 80*
Sale, J Kirkpatrick *ConAu X*
Sale, Kirkpatrick 1937- *ConAu 10NR, –13R, IntAu&W 82*
Sale, Richard 1911- *ConAu 9R, TwCCr&M 80, WrDr 84*
Sale, Roger 1932- *ConAu 21R*
Sale, William 1929- *ConAu 45*
Saleh, Dennis *DrAP&F 83*
Saleh, Dennis 1942- *ConAu 33R, IntWWP 82*
Salem, Elie Adib 1930- *ConAu 49*
Salem, James M 1937- *ConAu 21R*
Salemka, Irene 1931- *CreCan 2*
Salemme, Lucia *ConAu 89*
Salemson, Harold J 1910- *ConAu 108, –110, DcLB 4*
Salerno, Salvatore *DrAP&F 83*
Sales, Grover 1919- *ConAmTC, ConAu 65*
Sales, Jane M 1931- *ConAu 49*
Sales, M E 1936- *ConAu 29R*
Sales, M Vance 1929- *ConAu 53*
Saletan, Alberta L 1917- *WrDr 84*
Saletore, Bhasker Anand 1900- *ConAu 5R*
Salfi, Angelo *IntWWP 82X*
Salgado, Gamini 1929- *ConAu 102, WrDr 84*
Salgado, Maria Antonia 1933- *ConAu 41R*
Salih, H Ibrahim 1939- *ConAu 93*
Salinas, Louis Omar *DrAP&F 83*
Salinas, Pedro 1891?-1951 *ClDMEL 80, CnMWL, ModRL, TwCA SUP, TwCWr*
Salinger, Herman 1905- *ConAu P-1, IntAu&W 82, IntWWP 82, WrDr 84*
Salinger, J D *DrAP&F 83*
Salinger, J D 1919- *CnMWL, ConAu 5R, ConLC 1, –3, –8, –12, ConNov 82, DcLB 2, LongCTC, ModAL, ModAL SUP, TwCA SUP, TwCWr, WhoTwCL, WrDr 84*
Salinger, Jerome David 1919- *DcLEL 1940*
Salinger, Pierre 1925- *ConAu 17R, DcLEL 1940, WrDr 84*
Salinger, Wendy *DrAP&F 83*
Salis, Jean Rodolphe De 1901- *IntAu&W 82*
Salisachs Rovilralta, Mercedes 1916- *IntAu&W 82*
Salisbury, Carola *WrDr 84*
Salisbury, Carola 1924- *TwCRGW*
Salisbury, Carola 1943- *ConAu 89*
Salisbury, Dorothy 1891?-1976 *ConAu 69*
Salisbury, Sir Edward James 1886- *ConAu P-1*
Salisbury, Frank 1930- *ConAu 108, NatPD 81[port]*
Salisbury, Frank B 1926- *ConAu 8NR, –17R, IntAu&W 82, WrDr 84*
Salisbury, Harrison E 1908- *WrDr 84*
Salisbury, Harrison Evans 1908- *ConAu 1R,*

-3NR, IntAu&W 82, WorAu
Salisbury, John WrDr 84
Salisbury, Ralph DrAP&F 83
Salisbury, Ralph 1926- ConAu 41R
Salisbury, Richard Frank 1926- ConAu 5R,
  -9NR
Salisbury, Robert H 1930- ConAu 9R,
  WrDr 84
Salisbury, Ruth 1921- ConAu 73
Salivarova, Zdena ConAu X
Salk, Erwin Arthur 1918- ConAu 81
Salk, Jonas Edward 1914- ConAu 49, LongCTC
Salk, Lee 1926- AuNews 1, ConAu 104
Salkeld, Robert J 1932- ConAu 29R
Salkever, Louis R 1914- ConAu 17R
Salkey, Andrew 1928- ConAu 5R, ConNov 82,
  LongCTC, TwCCW 83, WorAu 1970,
  WrDr 84
Salkey, Felix Andrew Alexander 1928-
  DcLEL 1940
Sallah, Tijan M 1958- IntWWP 82
Sallaska, Georgia 1933- ConAu 25R
Sallaska, Georgia M WrDr 84
Sallaway, George H 1930- ConAu 21R
Sallis, James 1944- ConAu 33R, TwCSFW,
  WrDr 84
Sallis, John C 1938- ConAu 41R
Salls, Betty Ruth 1926- ConAu 69
Salm, Peter 1919- ConAu 41R, IntAu&W 82
Salma, Abu ConAu X
Salminen, Sally 1906- TwCA, TwCA SUP
Salmon, Andre 1881-1969 CIDMEL 80
Salmon, Annie Elizabeth 1899- ConAu 69,
  SmATA 13, WrDr 84
Salmon, Charles Gerald 1930- ConAu 49
Salmon, Edward Togo 1905- ConAu 2NR, -5R,
  IntAu&W 82, WrDr 84
Salmon, J H M 1925- ConAu 25R
Salmon, John 1925- WrDr 84
Salmon, John Hearsey McMillan 1925-
  IntAu&W 82
Salmon, John Tenison 1910- ConAu 13R,
  IntAu&W 82, WrDr 84
Salmon, Margaret Belais 1921- ConAu 8NR,
  -17R
Salmon, Nathan Ucuzoglu 1951- ConAu 109
Salmon, Wesley C 1925- ConAu 8NR, -17R
Salmonson, R F 1922- ConAu 25R
Salo, Arvo Jaako Henrik 1932- IntAu&W 82
Salola, Eero 1902- IntAu&W 82
Salom, Jaime 1925- CIDMEL 80, CroCD
Saloma, John S, III 1935?-1983 ConAu 110
Salomon, Albert 1891-1966 ConAu 5R
Salomon, Ernst Von 1902-1972 ModGL
Salomon, Herman Prins 1930- ConAu 41R
Salomon, Horst 1929- CroCD
Salomon, I L 1899- ConAu 73, WrDr 84
Salomon, Irving 1897-1979 ConAu 85
Salomon, Janet Lynn 1953- ConAu 61
Salomon, Roger Blaine 1928- ConAu 1R
Salomone, A William 1915- ConAu 13R,
  WrDr 84
Salomonson, Kurt 1929- IntAu&W 82
Salop, Lynne ConAu X
Salot, Lorraine 1914- ConAu 17R
Saloutos, Theodore 1910- ConAu 9R
Salper, Roberta Linda 1940- ConAu 105
Salpeter, Eliahu 1927- ConAu 93
Salpeter, Wolfgang 1920- IntAu&W 82
Salsbury, Edith Colgate 1907-1971 ConAu P-2
Salsbury, Kathryn H 1924- ConAu 107
Salsbury, Stephen 1931- ConAu 11NR, -21R,
  WrDr 84
Salsini, Paul E 1935- ConAu 77
Salsman, Lillian Viola 1899- IntWWP 82
Salt, Beryl 1931- ConAu 110, WrDr 84
Salt, Henry Stephens 1851-1939 LongCTC
Saltboy, Razor ConAu X
Salten, Felix ConAu X
Salten, Felix 1869-1945 LongCTC, SmATA X,
  TwCA, TwCA SUP
Salter, Cedric ConAu X, SmATA X,
  WrDr 84
Salter, Donald P M 1942- ConAu 93
Salter, Elizabeth 1918-1981 ConAu 9NR
Salter, Elizabeth 1925-1980 ConAu 105, -97
Salter, Elizabeth Fulton 1918-1981 ConAu 103,
  -53, IntAu&W 82
Salter, James DrAP&F 83
Salter, James 1925- ConAu 73, ConLC 7
Salter, Sir James Arthur 1881- LongCTC,
  TwCA, TwCA SUP

Salter, Lionel 1914- ConAu 3NR, -5R,
  WrDr 84
Salter, Margaret Lennox ConAu X
Salter, Mary D ConAu X, WrDr 84
Salter, Paul Sanford 1926- ConAu 45, -61
Salter-Mathieson, Nigel Cedric Stephen 1932-
  ConAu 1R
Salthe, Stanley N 1930- ConAu 53
Saltman, Juliet 1923- ConAu 101
Saltonstall, Richard, Jr. 1937-1981 ConAu 103,
  -33R
Saltus, Edgar E 1855-1921 ConAu 105, TwCA,
  TwCLC 8[port]
Saltz, Donald 1933- ConAu 102
Saltz, Eli 1926- ConAu 108
Saltzman, Joe 1939- ConAu X, IntAu&W 82
Saltzman, Joseph 1939- ConAu 81
Saltzman, Marvin L 1922- ConAu 85
Salu, Mary 1919- ConAu 93
Salvadori, Joyce ConAu X
Salvadori, Mario 1907- ConAu 108
Salvadori, Massimo 1908- ConAu X
Salvadori, Max William 1908- ConAu X,
  IntAu&W 82, WrDr 84
Salvadori-Paleotti, Massimo 1908- ConAu 7NR,
  -9R
Salvan, Jacques Leon 1898- ConAu 1R,
  WrDr 84
Salvato, Sharon 1938- ConAu 65
Salvatore, Nicholas 1943- ConAu 109
Salvatore, Nick ConAu X
Salvendy, Gavriel 1938- ConAu 49
Salverson, Laura Goodman 1890- CreCan 1
Salzano, Angelo 1938- IntWWP 82
Salzano, F M 1928- ConAu 29R
Salzer, Felix 1904- ConAu 109
Salzer, L E ConAu X, SmATA X
Salzinger, Kurt 1929- ConAu 107
Salzman, Eric 1933- ConAu 25R
Salzman, Jack 1937- ConAu 11NR, -25R
Salzmann, Siegmund 1869-1945 ConAu 108,
  SmATA 25
Salzmann, Zdenek 1925- ConAu 97
Samachson, Dorothy 1914- ConAu 9R,
  SmATA 3
Samachson, Joseph 1906- ConAu 17R,
  SmATA 3
Samad Said, A 1935- IntAu&W 82
Samarakis, Antonis 1919- ConAu 25R,
  ConLC 5
Samarin, William J 1926- ConAu 93
Samartha, S J 1920- ConAu P-1
Samay, Sebastian 1926- ConAu 37R
Sambrook, A J 1931- WrDr 84
Sambrook, Arthur James 1931- ConAu 13R,
  IntAu&W 82
Sambrot, William Anthony 1920- ConAu 25R,
  ConSFA, IntAu&W 82, WrDr 84
Samchuk, Ulas 1905- ModSL 2
Samelson, William 1928- ConAu 25R, WrDr 84
Sametz, Arnold W 1919- ConAu 1R, -1NR
Samford, Clarence D 1905- ConAu P-2
Samford, Doris E 1923- ConAu 21R
Samhaber, Ernst Marzell 1901- ConAu 9R
Samkange, Stanlake J T 1922- ConAu 29R
Samli, A Coskun 1931- ConAu 105
Sammartino, Peter 1904- ConAu 7NR, -57
Sammis, John 1942- ConAu 29R, SmATA 4
Sammons, David 1938- ConAu 73
Sammons, Jeffrey L 1936- ConAu 21R
Samoff, Joel 1943- IntAu&W 82
Samoiloff, Louise Cripps ConAu X
Samolin, William 1911- ConAu 61
Samora, Julian 1920- ConAu 37R
Samore, Theodore 1924- ConAu 108
Samoylov, David Samuilovich 1920- CIDMEL 80
Sampedro, Jose Luis 1917- ConAu 11NR, -21R,
  IntAu&W 82
Samperi, Frank DrAP&F 83
Sampford, Michael 1924?-1983 ConAu 109
Sampley, Arthur M 1903-1975 ConAu 41R
Sampley, J Paul 1935- ConAu 105
Sampson, Anthony 1926- WrDr 84
Sampson, Anthony Terrell Seward 1926-
  ConAu 1R, -3NR, DcLEL 1940,
  IntAu&W 82, WorAu
Sampson, Edward C 1920- ConAu 57
Sampson, Edward E 1934- ConAu 37R,
  WrDr 84
Sampson, Fay 1935- ConAu 101
Sampson, Geoffrey 1944- ConAu 97, WrDr 84
Sampson, George 1873-1950 LongCTC,

TwCA SUP
Sampson, H Grant 1932- ConAu 45
Sampson, John 1862-1931 LongCTC
Sampson, R Neil 1938- ConAu 106
Sampson, R V 1918- ConAu 5NR
Sampson, Richard Henry 1896- LongCTC,
  TwCA, TwCA SUP
Sampson, Robert C 1909- ConAu 21R
Sampson, Ronald Victor 1918- ConAu 9R,
  IntAu&W 82, WrDr 84
Sampson, Roy J 1919- ConAu 1R, -1NR
Samra, Cal 1931- ConAu 37R
Sams, Eric 1926- IntAu&W 82, WrDr 84
Sams, Jonathan Carter 1942- ConAu 110
Sams, Larry Marshall DrAP&F 83
Samsell, R L 1925- ConAu 69
Samson, Anne S 1933- ConAu 25R, SmATA 2
Samson, Horst 1954- IntWWP 82
Samson, Jack ConAu X
Samson, Joan 1937-1976 ConAu 73, SmATA 13
Samson, John Gadsden 1936- ConAu 109
Samstag, Nicholas 1903-1968 ConAu 5R, -25R
Samtur, Susan J 1944- ConAu 97
Samuel, Viscount 1870-1963 LongCTC
Samuel, A M LongCTC
Samuel, Alan E 1932- ConAu 73
Samuel, Archbishop Athanasius Y 1907-
  ConAu X
Samuel, Dorothy T 1918- ConAu 45
Samuel, Edwin Herbert 1898-1978 ConAu 1R,
  -2NR
Samuel, Irene 1915- ConAu 17R
Samuel, Maurice 1895-1972 ConAu 102, -33R,
  TwCA SUP
Samuel, Yeshue 1907- ConAu P-2
Samuels, Charles 1902-1982 ConAu 1R, -5NR,
  -106, SmATA 12
Samuels, Charles Thomas 1936-1974 ConAu 41R,
  -49
Samuels, E A ConAu X
Samuels, Ernest 1903- ConAu P-1,
  IntAu&W 82, WorAu, WrDr 84
Samuels, Gertrude ConAu 6NR, -9R,
  NatPD 81[port], SmATA 17
Samuels, Harold 1917- ConAu 93
Samuels, Harry 1893- ConAu 13R
Samuels, Lesser 1894?-1980 ConAu 102
Samuels, M L 1920- ConAu 41R
Samuels, Peggy 1922- ConAu 97
Samuels, Warren Joseph 1933- ConAu 21R,
  WrDr 84
Samuelson, Janet DrAP&F 83
Samuelson, Paul Anthony 1915- ConAu 5R,
  IntAu&W 82, WrDr 84
Samway, Patrick H 1939- ConAu 105
San Agustin, Gloria 1929- IntWWP 82
San-Giorgiu, Ion 1893-1950 CnMD
San Juan, Epifanio, Jr. 1938- ConAu 10NR,
  -25R
San Martin, Marta 1942- ConAu 102
San Secondo, Rosso Di 1887-1956 CnMD
San Souci, Robert D 1946- ConAu 108
Sanborn, B X ConAu X
Sanborn, Duane 1914- ConAu 1R, -1NR
Sanborn, Margaret 1915- ConAu 4NR, -53,
  WrDr 84
Sanborn, Patricia F 1937- ConAu 25R
Sanborn, Pitts 1879?-1941 TwCA
Sanborn, Ruth Cummings 1917- ConAu 29R
Sancha, Sheila 1924- ConAu 11NR, -69
Sanchez, Florencio 1875-1910 ModLAL,
  ModWD
Sanchez, Jose M 1932- ConAu 9R, WrDr 84
Sanchez, Luis Rafael 1936- ConLC 23[port]
Sanchez, Ramon Diaz 1903- CnMD
Sanchez, Ricardo DrAP&F 83
Sanchez, Ricardo 1941- ConAu 73
Sanchez, Sonia DrAP&F 83
Sanchez, Sonia 1934- ConAu 33R, ConLC 5,
  ConP 80, LivgBAA, SmATA 22[port],
  WrDr 84
Sanchez, Sonia 1935- CroCAP
Sanchez, Thomas DrAP&F 83
Sanchez, Thomas Robert 1944- ConAu 2NR, -45
Sanchez Drago, Fernando 1936- IntAu&W 82
Sanchez Faba, Francisco 1899- IntAu&W 82
Sanchez Ferlosio, Rafael 1927- CIDMEL 80,
  TwCWr
Sanchez-Hidalgo, Efrain Sigisfredo 1918-1974
  ConAu 57
Sanchez-Puig, Maria 1940- IntAu&W 82

Sanchez-Silva, Jose Maria 1911- *ConAu 73,*
SmATA 16
Sanctuary, Brenda 1934- *WrDr 84*
Sanctuary, Gerald 1930- *ConAu 29R*
Sand, George X *ConAu 13R*
Sand, Margaret 1932- *ConAu 85*
Sand, Richard E 1924- *ConAu 33R*
Sandak, Cass R 1950- *ConAu 108*
Sandars, N K 1914- *ConAu 61*
Sandauer, Arthur 1913- *IntAu&W 82*
Sandbach, Francis Henry 1903- *ConAu 93*
Sandbach, Mary Warburton 1901- *ConAu 25R*
Sandberg, Henri Willem 1898- *IntAu&W 82*
Sandberg, Inger 1930- *ConAu 11NR, –65,*
SmATA 15
Sandberg, John H 1930- *ConAu 49*
Sandberg, Karl C 1931- *ConAu 49*
Sandberg, Larry 1944- *ConAu 77*
Sandberg, Lars G 1939- *ConAu 53*
Sandberg, Lasse E M 1924- *SmATA 15*
Sandberg, Margaret M 1919- *ConAu 61*
Sandberg, Peter Lars 1934- *ConAu 9NR, –61*
Sandbrook, K R J 1943- *ConAu 97*
Sandburg, Carl 1878-1967 *CnMWL, ConAmA,*
ConAu 5R, –25R, ConLC 1, –4, –10, –15,
DcLB 17[port], LongCTC, ModAL,
ModAL SUP, SmATA 8, TwCA,
TwCA SUP, TwCWr, WhoTwCL
Sandburg, Charles August *ConAmA, ConAu X,*
SmATA X
Sandburg, Helga 1918- *ConAu 1R, –5NR,*
IntAu&W 82, IntWWP 82, MichAu 80,
SmATA 3, WrDr 84
Sande, Theodore Anton 1933- *ConAu 65*
Sandeen, Ernest *DrAP&F 83*
Sandeen, Ernest 1908- *ConAu 13R*
Sandeen, Ernest Robert 1931- *ConAu 1NR, –45*
Sandel, Cora 1880-1974 *CIDMEL 80,*
WhoTwCL
Sandell, Tom Johan Ludwig 1936- *IntAu&W 82*
Sandemose, Aksel 1899-1965 *CIDMEL 80*
Sander, Ellen 1944- *ConAu 41R*
Sander, Joseph Lincoln 1926- *ConAu 108*
Sanderlin, George 1915- *ConAu 13R,*
IntAu&W 82, SmATA 4, WrDr 84
Sanderlin, Owenita 1916- *ConAu 7NR, –17R,*
SmATA 11, WrDr 84
Sanderlin, Reed 1937- *IntWWP 82*
Sanders, Colonel *ConAu X*
Sanders, Ann 1935- *ConAu 5R*
Sanders, Buck *ConAu X*
Sanders, Byrne Hope *ConAu X*
Sanders, Charles 1935- *ConAu 25R*
Sanders, D G 1899- *ConAu 85*
Sanders, David 1926- *ConAu 25R, WrDr 84*
Sanders, David 1934- *ConAu 41R*
Sanders, Dennis 1949- *ConAu 108*
Sanders, Donald 1915?-1979 *ConAu 89*
Sanders, Donald H 1932- *ConAu 10NR, –25R*
Sanders, Dorothy Lucie *WrDr 84*
Sanders, Dorothy Lucie 1917- *ConAu 33R,*
TwCRGW
Sanders, Ed *DrAP&F 83*
Sanders, Ed 1939- *ConAu 13R, ConP 80,*
DcLB 16[port], WrDr 84
Sanders, Ed Parish 1937- *ConAu 105*
Sanders, Frederick K 1936- *ConAu 65*
Sanders, Gerald D 1895- *ConAu P-1*
Sanders, Harland 1890-1980 *ConAu 102*
Sanders, Henry Lewis 1945- *IntWWP 82*
Sanders, Herbert H 1909- *ConAu 13R*
Sanders, J Oswald 1902- *ConAu 6NR*
Sanders, Jack T 1935- *ConAu 37R*
Sanders, Jacquin 1922- *ConAu 1R*
Sanders, James Alvin 1927- *ConAu 21R*
Sanders, James Bernard 1924- *ConAu 41R*
Sanders, James Edward 1911- *ConAu 103,*
IntAu&W 82, WrDr 84
Sanders, Jeanne *ConAu X, WrDr 84*
Sanders, Jennings Bryan 1901- *ConAu P-2*
Sanders, Joan Allred 1924- *ConAu 9R*
Sanders, John Oswald 1902- *ConAu 13R*
Sanders, Joseph Lee 1940- *ConAu 105*
Sanders, Kent *ConAu X*
Sanders, Lawrence 1920- *ASpks, ConAu 81,*
TwCCr&M 80, WrDr 84
Sanders, Leonard 1929- *ConAu 3NR, –9R*
Sanders, Margaret *ConAu 5R*
Sanders, Marion K 1905-1977 *ConAu 33R, –73*
Sanders, Marlene 1931- *ConAu 65*
Sanders, Mary Dolling *ConAu 49*
Sanders, Noah *ConAu X*

Sanders, Noah 1941- *ConAu X*
Sanders, Norman Joseph 1929- *ConAu 9R*
Sanders, Peter 1938- *ConAu 105, WrDr 84*
Sanders, Pieter 1912- *ConAu 29R*
Sanders, Richard 1904- *ConAu 53*
Sanders, Ronald 1932- *ConAu 21R,*
IntAu&W 82, WrDr 84
Sanders, Scott Patrick *DrAP&F 83*
Sanders, Scott Russell 1945- *ConAu 85*
Sanders, Sol 1926- *ConAu 2NR, –49*
Sanders, Stephen 1919- *ConAu 29R*
Sanders, Thomas E 1926- *ConAu 21R*
Sanders, Thomas Griffin 1932- *ConAu 9R*
Sanders, William B 1944- *ConAu 10NR, –65*
Sanders, William T 1926- *ConAu 3NR, –45*
Sanders, Winston P *ConAu X, IntAu&W 82X*
Sanderson, Frederick William 1857-1922
LongCTC
Sanderson, Ivan T 1911-1973 *ConAu 37R, –41R,*
SmATA 6, TwCA, TwCA SUP
Sanderson, Jayne 1943- *ConAu 21R*
Sanderson, Milton W 1910- *ConAu 9R, –9NR*
Sanderson, Peter 1929- *ConAu 33R*
Sanderson, Sabina W 1931- *ConAu 3NR, –9R*
Sanderson, Stewart 1924- *ConAu 108*
Sanderson, Stewart F 1924- *WrDr 84*
Sanderson, Warren 1931- *ConAu 105*
Sandford, Christopher 1902-1983 *ConAu 109*
Sandford, Jeremy 1930- *DcLEL 1940*
Sandford, Jeremy 1934- *IntAu&W 82,*
WrDr 84
Sandford, John 1929- *ConAu 101*
Sandford, Nell Mary 1936- *ConAu 81*
Sandford, Paula 1931- *ConAu 101*
Sandford, William P 1896-1975 *ConAu P-2*
Sandhaus, Paula 1923- *ConAu 25R*
Sandifer, Durward Valdamir 1900-1981
ConAu 108
Sandin, Joan 1942- *SmATA 12*
Sandison, Alan George 1932- *ConAu 21R,*
WrDr 84
Sandison, Janet *ConAu X, SmATA X*
Sandle, Floyd Leslie 1913- *ConAu 106*
Sandler, Benjamin P 1902?-1979 *ConAu 85*
Sandler, Irving 1925- *ConAu 29R*
Sandlin, Joann S DeLora 1935- *ConAu 4NR*
Sandlin, John L 1908- *ConAu 1R, –4NR*
Sandman, Peter 1945- *WrDr 84*
Sandman, Peter Mark 1945- *ConAu 25R*
TwCCW 83
Sandmel, Samuel 1911-1979 *ConAu 1R, –2NR*
Sandon, Henry 1928- *ConAu 81, IntAu&W 82*
Sandon, J D *TwCWW, WrDr 84*
Sandor, Bela I 1935- *ConAu 102*
Sandor, Gyorgy *ConAu 108*
Sandor, Laszlo 1909- *IntAu&W 82*
Sandoval, Jorge *IntAu&W 82X*
Sandoval, Roberto *DrAP&F 83*
Sandown, Margaret *IntAu&W 82X*
Sandoz, Ellis 1931- *ConAu 37R*
Sandoz, G Ellis 1931- *WrDr 84*
Sandoz, Mari 1896-1966 *DcLB 9[port], FifWWr*
Sandoz, Mari 1901-1966 *ConAu 1R, –25R,*
SmATA 5, TwCA, TwCA SUP, TwCWW
Sandrof, Ivan 1912?-1979 *ConAu 85, –93*
Sandroff, Ronni *DrAP&F 83*
Sandroff, Ronni 1943- *ConAu 102*
Sandrow, Edward T 1906-1975 *ConAu 61*
Sands, Donald B 1920- *ConAu 13R*
Sands, Dorothy 1893-1980 *ConAu 102*
Sands, Edith Sylvia 1912- *ConAu 21R*
Sands, John Edward 1930- *ConAu 13R*
Sands, Leo G 1912- *ConAu 17R*
Sands, Martin *ConAu X, IntAu&W 82X,*
WrDr 84
Sands, Melissa 1949- *ConAu 109*
Sandsdalen, Oddjan 1944- *IntAu&W 82*
Sandusky, Annie Lee 1900?-1976 *ConAu 69*
Sandved, Arthur O 1931- *ConAu 33R*
Sandy *IntAu&W 82X*
Sandy, Max *ConAu X*
Sandy, Stephen *DrAP&F 83*
Sandy, Stephen 1934- *ConAu 5NR, –49,*
ConP 80, IntAu&W 82, IntWWP 82,
WrDr 84
Sandys, Elspeth *ConAu X*
Sandys, Stephen 1935- *ConAu 49*
Sanecki, Kay Naylor *WrDr 84*
Saner, Hans 1934- *IntAu&W 82*
Saner, Reg *DrAP&F 83*
Saner, Reg 1931- *ConAu 65, ConLC 9,*

ConP 80, WrDr 84
Sanfield, Steve *DrAP&F 83*
Sanfilip, Thomas 1952- *ConAu 57*
Sanford, Agnes 1897- *ConAu 17R*
Sanford, Charles LeRoy 1920- *ConAu 5R*
Sanford, Fillmore H 1914-1967 *ConAu 1R, –103*
Sanford, Geraldine A J *DrAP&F 83*
Sanford, Harry Allen 1929- *ConAu 1R*
Sanford, Jack D 1925- *ConAu 5R*
Sanford, John A 1929- *ConAu 10NR, –25R*
Sanford, Leda 1934- *ConAu 65*
Sanford, Terry 1917- *ConAu 17R*
Sanford, Thomas K, Jr. 1921-1977 *ConAu 73*
Sanger, Charles Percy 1871-1930 *LongCTC*
Sanger, Fritz Paul 1901- *IntAu&W 82*
Sanger, Margaret 1883-1966 *ConAu 89,*
LongCTC
Sanger, Marjory Bartlett 1920- *ConAu 37R,*
SmATA 8, WrDr 84
Sanger, Richard H 1905?-1979 *ConAu 85*
Sangrey, Dawn 1942- *ConAu 85*
Sangster, Ian 1934- *ConAu 61*
Sangster, Jimmy 1927- *ConAu 21R, WrDr 84*
Sangster, Margaret Elizabeth 1894-1981
ConAu 105
Sanguineti, Edoardo 1930- *CIDMEL 80,*
IntAu&W 82
Sanguinetti, Elise Ayers 1926- *ConAu 1R, –1NR*
Sani *IntWWP 82X*
Saniel, Josefa M 1925- *ConAu 13R*
Sanin, Roberto Escobar 1929- *IntAu&W 82*
Sanin Cano, Baldomero 1861-1957 *ModLAL*
Sanjian, Avedis K 1921- *ConAu 33R, WrDr 84*
Sankar, D V Siva 1927- *ConAu 53*
Sankey, Alice 1910- *ConAu 61,*
SmATA 27[port]
Sankey, Ira David 1840-1908 *LongCTC*
Sankhala, Kailash S 1925- *ConAu 101*
Sankhasubra *IntAu&W 82X*
Sanminiatelli, Bino 1896- *IntAu&W 82*
Sann, Paul 1914- *ConAu 5NR, –13R, WrDr 84*
Sannebeck, Norvelle 1909- *ConAu 97*
Sanowar, Marjorie Enid Wilmot 1922-
IntWWP 82
Sanowar, Wilmot *IntWWP 82X*
Sansom, Clive 1910- *ConAu 104, WrDr 84*
Sansom, William 1912-1976 *CnMWL,*
ConAu 5R, –65, ConLC 2, –6, DcLEL 1940,
LongCTC, ModBrL, ModBrL SUP,
TwCA SUP, TwCWr
Sansweet, Stephen Jay 1945- *ConAu 61*
Sant Marc, Llorenc *IntAu&W 82X*
Sant-VanBommel, Aartje Wilhelmina 1901-
IntAu&W 82
Santa Maria *ConAu X, WrDr 84*
Santaliz, Pedro *DrAP&F 83*
Santareno, Bernardo 1924- *CIDMEL 80*
Santas, Joan Foster 1930- *ConAu 17R*
Santayana, George 1863-1952 *ConAmA,*
LongCTC, ModAL, ModAL SUP, TwCA,
TwCA SUP, TwCWr, WhoTwCL
Santee, Collier *ConAu X*
Santee, Ross 1888-1965 *TwCA SUP, TwCWW*
Santee, Ross 1889?-1965 *ConAu 108*
Santen, Sal 1915- *IntAu&W 82*
Santesson, Hans Stefan 1914-1975 *ConAu 57,*
–93, ConSFA, SmATA 30N
Santhi, S 1934- *DcLEL 1940*
Santini, Rosemarie *ConAu 81, DrAP&F 83*
Santmire, H Paul 1935- *ConAu 53*
Santmyer, Helen H *DrAP&F 83*
Santmyer, Helen Hooven 1895- *ConAu 1R,*
WrDr 84
Santoli, Al 1949- *ConAu 105*
Santoni, Georges V 1938- *ConAu 103*
Santoni, Ronald Ernest 1931- *ConAu 5R*
Santos, Bienvenido N *DrAP&F 83*
Santos, Bienvenido N 1911- *ConAu 101,*
ConLC 22[port]
Santos, Eduardo 1888-1974 *ConAu 89*
Santos, Helen 1939- *IntAu&W 82X*
Santos, Jose Abel Royo Dos 1938- *IntAu&W 82*
Santostefano, Sebastiano 1929- *ConAu 41R*
Santrey, Louis *ConAu X*
Sanville, Jean 1918- *ConAu 89*
Sanwal, B D 1917- *ConAu 17R*
Sanyal, Ashis 1938- *IntWWP 82*
Sanz Y Diaz, Jose 1907- *IntAu&W 82*
Saperstein, Alan *ConAu 103*
Saphier, Michael 1911- *ConAu 25R*
Saphire, Saul 1896?-1974 *ConAu 53*
Sapiets, Janis 1921-1983? *ConAu 109*

Sapinsley, Alvin 1921- *ConAu 104*
Sapir, Richard 1936- *ConAu 69*
Sapori, Armando 1892- *ConAu 33R*
Saporta, Marc 1923- *CIDMEL 80, ConAu 21R, IntAu&W 82*
Saporta, Sol 1925- *ConAu 17R*
Saposnik, Irving Seymour 1936- *ConAu 97*
Saposs, David Joseph 1886-1968 *ConAu 1R, –103*
Sapp, Phyllis Woodruff 1908- *ConAu 1R, –1NR*
Sapper 1888-1937 *LongCTC, TwCA, TwCA SUP, TwCCr&M 80, TwCWr*
Sappington, Roger E 1929- *ConAu 13R*
Saqorewec, E 1939- *ConAu X*
Sara *ConAu X, DrAP&F 83, IntAu&W 82X, WrDr 84*
Sara, Dorothy 1897?-1976 *ConAu 69*
Sarabhai, Bharatidevi 1912- *IntAu&W 82*
Sarac, Roger 1928- *ConAu X, ConSFA, SmATA X*
Saracevic, Tefko 1930- *ConAu 37R*
Saral, Manmohan 1934- *IntAu&W 82*
Sarano, Jacques 1920- *ConAu 29R*
Sarant, P C 1933?-1979 *ConAu 89*
Sarasy, Phyllis Powell 1930- *ConAu 13R*
Sarat, Austin Dean 1947- *ConAu 106*
Sarauw, Paul 1883- *CnMD*
Sarban *WrDr 84*
Sarban 1910- *TwCSFW*
SarDesai, D R 1931- *ConAu 11NR, –25R*
Sardeson, Charles T 1921- *ConAu 5R*
Sardou, Victorien 1831-1908 *LongCTC, ModWD*
Sarducci, Father Guido *ConAu X*
Sarduy, Severo 1937- *ConAu 89, ConLC 6, ModLAL*
Sarett, Alma 1908- *ConAu P-2*
Sarett, Lew R 1888-1954 *ConAmA, MichAu 80, TwCA, TwCA SUP*
Sarett, Morton R 1916- *ConAu 93*
Sargant, Norman 1909-1982 *ConAu 107*
Sargant, William 1907- *ConAu 65*
Sargeant, Winthrop 1903- *ConAu 29R, WrDr 84*
Sargent, Alice G 1939- *ConAu 110*
Sargent, Brian 1927- *ConAu 97*
Sargent, David R 1920- *ConAu 93*
Sargent, E N *DrAP&F 83*
Sargent, Frederic O 1919- *ConAu 41R*
Sargent, Jean Vieth 1918- *ConAu 106*
Sargent, John Richard 1925- *ConAu 13R*
Sargent, John Singer 1856-1925 *LongCTC*
Sargent, Lois B 1934- *IntWWP 82*
Sargent, Lyman Tower 1940- *ConAu 29R, WrDr 84*
Sargent, Pamela *DrAP&F 83*
Sargent, Pamela 1948- *ConAu 8NR, –61, DcLB 8, SmATA 29, TwCSFW, WrDr 84*
Sargent, Ralph Millard 1904- *ConAu 37R*
Sargent, Robert *DrAP&F 83*
Sargent, Robert Edward 1933- *ConAu 21R, SmATA 2*
Sargent, Robert Strong 1912- *IntWWP 82*
Sargent, Sarah 1937- *ConAu 106*
Sargent, Shirley 1927- *ConAu 1R, –2NR, SmATA 11*
Sargent, William 1946- *ConAu 106*
Sargent, Wyn *ConAu 49, WrDr 84*
Sargeson, Frank 1903-1982 *ConAu 106, –25R, ConNov 82, IntAu&W 82, LongCTC, ModCmwL, TwCWr, WhoTwCL, WorAu*
Sarhan, Samir 1941- *ConAu 103*
Sari *SmATA X*
Saricks, Ambrose 1915- *ConAu 17R, WrDr 84*
Sariego, Patricia Treece *ConAu X*
Sariola, Sakari 1919- *ConAu 41R*
Sarjeant, William A S 1935- *ConAu 105*
Sarkadi, Imre 1921-1961 *CroCD*
Sarkar, Anil Kumar 1912- *WrDr 84*
Sarkar, Asoke 1911?-1983 *ConAu 109*
Sarkar, Kumar 1912- *ConAu 37R*
Sarkesian, Sam C 1927- *ConAu 57*
Sarlos, Robert Karoly 1931- *ConAu 109*
Sarma, G V L N 1925- *ConAu 17R*
Sarment, Jean 1897-1976 *CIDMEL 80, CnMD, ModFrL, ModWD*
Sarmento, William Edward 1946- *ConAmTC*
Sarmiento, Felix Ruben Garcia 1867-1916 *ConAu 104*
Sarna, Jonathan D 1955- *ConAu 109*
Sarna, Nahum M 1923- *ConAu 17R, WrDr 84*
Sarnat, Marshall 1929- *ConAu 10NR, –21R, WrDr 84*
Sarndal, Carl Erik 1937- *ConAu 105*

Sarner, Harvey 1934- *ConAu 17R*
Sarno, Arthur D 1921?-1982 *ConAu 106*
Sarno, Ronald Anthony 1941- *ConAu 29R, WrDr 84*
Sarnoff, Dorothy *WrDr 84*
Sarnoff, Dorothy 1917- *ConAu 33R*
Sarnoff, Irving 1922- *ConAu 8NR, –17R, WrDr 84*
Sarnoff, Jane 1937- *ConAu 9NR, –53, SmATA 10*
Sarnoff, Paul 1918- *ConAu 2NR, –5R*
Sarnoff, Suzanne 1928- *ConAu 97*
Saroyan, Aram 1943- *ConAu 21R, ConP 80, DcLEL 1940, WrDr 84*
Saroyan, Arshalyus 1923-1974 *ConAu 53*
Saroyan, William 1908-1981 *CnMD, CnMWL, ConAmA, ConAu 5R, –103, ConLC 1, –8, –10, DcLB Y81A[port], –7[port], –9[port], LongCTC, ModAL, ModAL SUP, ModWD, SmATA 23[port], –24N, TwCA, TwCA SUP, TwCWr, WhoTwCL*
Sarraute, Nathalie 1900- *IntAu&W 82, ModFrL*
Sarraute, Nathalie 1902- *ConAu 9R, ConLC 1, –2, –4, –8, –10, ModRL, TwCWr, WhoTwCL, WorAu*
Sarraute, Nathalie 1905- *CIDMEL 80*
Sarrazin, Albertine 1937-1967 *CIDMEL 80*
Sarre, Winifred Turner 1931- *ConAu 29R*
Sarri, I Margareta 1944- *IntAu&W 82*
Sarris, Andrew 1928- *ConAu 21R*
Sarruf, Fuad 1900- *IntAu&W 82*
Sarsfield, C P *ConAu X*
Sartain, Aaron Quinn 1905- *ConAu 1R*
Sarti, Roland 1937- *ConAu 37R*
Sarto, Ben *ConAu X*
Sarton, George Alfred Leon 1884-1956 *TwCA SUP*
Sarton, May *DrAP&F 83*
Sarton, May 1912- *ConAu 1R, –1NR, ConLC 4, –14, ConNov 82, ConP 80, DcLB Y81B[port], ModAL, ModAL SUP, TwCA SUP, WrDr 84*
Sartori, Eva Maria *IntAu&W 82*
Sartori, Franco 1922- *IntAu&W 82*
Sartori, Giovanni 1924- *ConAu 2NR, –5R*
Sartre, Jean-Paul 1905-1980 *CIDMEL 80, CnMD, CnMWL, ConAu 9R, –97, ConLC 1, –4, –7, –9, –13, –18, –24[port], CroCD, LongCTC, ModFrL, ModRL, ModWD, TwCA SUP, TwCWr, WhoTwCL*
Sarvepalli, Gopal 1923- *ConAu 81*
Sarver, Hannah *ConAu X*
Sarvig, Ole 1921- *CIDMEL 80, IntAu&W 82, IntWWP 82*
Sasaki, Tazu 1932- *ConAu 10NR, –25R*
Sasdi, Sandor 1898- *IntAu&W 82*
Sasek, Lawrence A 1923- *ConAu 1R, –1NR*
Sasek, M 1916-1980 *ChlLR 4[port]*
Sasek, Miroslav 1916-1980 *ConAu 101, –73, SmATA 16, –23N*
Saslow, Helen *DrAP&F 83*
Saslow, Helen 1926- *ConAu 105*
Sasnett, Martena T 1908- *ConAu 53*
Sass, Lorna Janet 1945- *ConAu 102*
Sasso, Laurence J, Jr. *DrAP&F 83*
Sassoon, Beverly Adams *ConAu 65*
Sassoon, Siegfried 1886-1967 *ConAu 104, –25R*
Sassoon, Siegfried Lorraine 1886-1967 *CnMWL, LongCTC, ModBrL, ModBrL SUP, TwCA, TwCA SUP, TwCWr, WhoTwCL*
Sassoon, Vidal 1928- *ConAu 65*
Sasthi, Brata 1939- *DcLEL 1940*
Sastre, Alfonso 1926- *CIDMEL 80, CnMD, CroCD, ModWD*
Sasuly, Richard 1913- *ConAu 109*
Satchell, William 1860-1942 *LongCTC, TwCWr*
Satchidananda, Swami 1914- *ConAu 101*
Sather, Julia Coley Duncan 1940- *ConAu 103*
Satin, Joseph 1922- *ConAu 9R*
Satin, Mark 1946- *ConAu 41R*
Satiricus *ConAu X*
Sato, Esther Masako Tateishi 1915- *ConAu 108*
Satprem 1923- *ConAu 85*
Satran, Pamela Redmond 1953- *ConAu 110*
Satterfield, Archie 1933- *ConAu 57*
Satterfield, Charles *ConAu X*
Satterlund, Donald R 1928- *ConAu 53*
Satterly, Weston *ConAu X*
Sattler, Helen Roney 1921- *ConAu 33R, SmATA 4*
Sattler, Henry V 1917- *ConAu 5R, –7NR*

Sattler, Jerome M 1931- *ConAu 49*
Sattler, Warren 1934- *ConAu 65*
Sattley, Helen R *ConAu 1R*
Satz, Paul 1932- *ConAu 61*
Satz, Ronald Norman 1944- *ConAu 8NR, –61*
Sau Sanchez, Victoria 1930- *IntAu&W 82*
Saue, Gronvold Gerd 1930- *IntAu&W 82*
Sauer, Carl Ortwin 1889-1975 *ConAu 9NR, –57, –61*
Sauer, Gordon C 1921- *IntAu&W 82, WrDr 84*
Sauer, Julia 1891- *SmATA 32[port], TwCCW 83*
Sauer, Julia L 1891- *ConAu 81*
Sauer, Muriel Stafford *ConAu 13R*
Sauer, Val John, Jr. 1938- *ConAu 107*
Sauerhaft, Stan 1926- *ConAu 85*
Sauers, Richard James 1930- *ConAu 53*
Saul, George Brandon *DrAP&F 83*
Saul, George Brandon 1901- *ConAu 6NR, –13R, IntAu&W 82, IntWWP 82, WrDr 84*
Saul, John 1942- *ConAu 81*
Saul, Leon J 1901- *ConAu 10NR*
Saul, Leon Joseph 1901- *ConAu 21R, IntAu&W 82, WrDr 84*
Saul, Mary *ConAu 105*
Saul, Norman Eugene 1932- *ConAu 53*
Saul, Oscar *ConAu X*
Saulnier, Raymond Joseph 1908- *ConAu 5R*
Sauls, Roger *DrAP&F 83*
Sauls, Roger 1944- *ConAu 33R, WrDr 84*
Saunders, Alexander Carr *ConAu X*
Saunders, Allen 1899- *ConAu 69*
Saunders, Ann Loreille 1930- *ConAu 103, IntAu&W 82, WrDr 84*
Saunders, Aretas 1884- *ConAu P-1*
Saunders, Beatrice *ConAu 49*
Saunders, Blanche 1906-1964 *ConAu P-1*
Saunders, C M 1918- *WrDr 84*
Saunders, Caleb *ConAu X, SmATA X*
Saunders, Carl Maxon 1890-1974 *ConAu 89*
Saunders, Charles B, Jr. 1928- *ConAu 61*
Saunders, David *ConAu X*
Saunders, Doris E 1921- *ConAu 77*
Saunders, Dudley *ConAmTC*
Saunders, E Dale 1919- *ConAu 5R*
Saunders, Ernest 1901?-1983 *ConAu 109*
Saunders, Geraldine *DrAP&F 83*
Saunders, Helen E 1912- *ConAu 25R*
Saunders, Hilary Aidan St. George 1898-1951 *LongCTC, TwCA, TwCA SUP, TwCCr&M 80*
Saunders, Ione *ConAu X*
Saunders, Jack *DrAP&F 83*
Saunders, James A 1925- *ConDr 82, CroCD, DcLB 13[port], DcLEL 1940, WrDr 84*
Saunders, Jason Lewis 1922- *ConAu 106*
Saunders, Jean 1932- *ConAu 102, IntAu&W 82, WrDr 84*
Saunders, John *TwCWW*
Saunders, John Monk 1897-1940 *DcLB 26[port]*
Saunders, John Turk 1929-1974 *ConAu P-2*
Saunders, Keith 1910- *ConAu 57, SmATA 12*
Saunders, Lorna D *DrAP&F 83*
Saunders, Marshall 1861-1947 *TwCA, TwCA SUP*
Saunders, Owen 1904- *WrDr 84*
Saunders, Patricia Anne 1931- *IntWWP 82*
Saunders, Richard 1947- *ConAu 105*
Saunders, Roy 1911- *ConAu P-1*
Saunders, Rubie 1929- *ConAu 49, SmATA 21*
Saunders, Sally Love 1940- *IntWWP 82*
Saunders, Susan 1945- *ConAu 106*
Saunders, Thomas 1909- *ConAu 73, DcLEL 1940*
Saunders, Walter Gerard 1930- *IntWWP 82*
Saunders, Wes *WrDr 84*
Saura, Carlos 1932- *ConLC 20*
Saurat, Denis 1890-1958 *LongCTC, TwCA, TwCA SUP*
Sauro, Joan *DrAP&F 83*
Sauro, Regina Calderone 1924- *ConAu 9R*
Saus, Anders 1919- *IntAu&W 82*
Sause, George G 1919- *ConAu 41R*
Sauser, Frederic *TwCA SUP*
Sauser-Hall, Frederic 1887-1961 *ConAu 102, –93, ConLC 18, LongCTC*
Sautel, Maureen Ann 1951- *ConAu 61*
Sauter, Edwin Charles Scott, Jr. 1930- *ConAu 13R*
Sauter, Leilani *DrAP&F 83*
Sauter, Van Gordon 1935- *ConAu 73*
Sautter, R Craig *DrAP&F 83*

Sautter, Richard Craig 1947- *IntWWP 82*
Sauvage, Franck *ConAu X*
Sauvage, Roger 1917-1977 *ConAu 73*
Sauvageau, Juan 1917- *ConAu 11NR, –65*
Sauvin, Philip Arthur 1933- *ConAu 104,*
WrDr 84
Sauvajon, Marc Gilbert 1909- *CnMD*
Sauvant, Karl P 1944- *ConAu 77*
Sauvy, Jean 1916- *ConAu 65*
Sauvy, Simonne 1922- *ConAu 65*
Sava, George 1903- *ConAu X, LongCTC,*
WrDr 84
Savacool, John K 1917- *ConAu 45*
Savage, Anne 1896- *CreCan 1*
Savage, Annie Douglas *CreCan 1*
Savage, Blake *ConAu X, SmATA X*
Savage, Brian 1933- *ConAu 41R*
Savage, Catharine *IntWWP 82X*
Savage, Charles 1918- *ConAu 53*
Savage, Christina *ConAu X*
Savage, Christopher I 1924-1969 *ConAu 5R,*
–6NR
Savage, D S 1917- *ConAu 104*
Savage, David *WrDr 84*
Savage, Derek Stanley 1917- *ModBrL,*
TwCA SUP
Savage, Elizabeth Fitzgerald 1918- *ConAu 1R,*
–1NR
Savage, Frances Higginson 1898- *ConAu P-1*
Savage, George 1909- *ConAu 5NR, –9R,*
IntAu&W 82
Savage, Helen 1915- *ConAu 97*
Savage, Henry, Jr. 1903- *ConAu P-2*
Savage, Ian *IntAu&W 82X*
Savage, James F 1939- *ConAu 73*
Savage, Joan *MichAu 80*
Savage, Joseph P 1895?-1977 *ConAu 69*
Savage, Katharine James Sanford 1905-
ConAu 13R
Savage, Lee 1928- *ConAu 101*
Savage, Leonard J 1917-1971 *ConAu 33R,*
ConAu P-2
Savage, Marc 1945- *ConAu 65*
Savage, Michael 1946- *WrDr 84*
Savage, Michael D 1946- *ConAu 101*
Savage, Mildred *WrDr 84*
Savage, Mildred 1919- *ConAu 9R*
Savage, Oscar *IntAu&W 82X*
Savage, Richard *WrDr 84*
Savage, Robert L 1939- *ConAu 109*
Savage, Thomas Gerard 1926- *ConAu 49*
Savage, Tom *DrAP&F 83*
Savage, W Sherman 1890- *ConAu 69*
Savage, William W 1914- *ConAu 37R*
Savage, William W, Jr. 1943- *ConAu 57*
Savain, Petion 1906-1973 *ConAu 41R*
Savan, Bruce 1927- *ConAu 5R, WrDr 84*
Savarese, Julia *WrDr 84*
Savarese, Julia 1935- *ConAu 37R*
Savarin *ConAu X*
Savary, Louis M 1936- *ConAu 9NR, –21R*
Savas, E S 1931- *ConAu 17R*
Saveland, Robert N 1921- *ConAu 41R*
Savelle, Max 1896- *ConAu 21R*
Savery, Constance Winifred 1897- *ConAu 7NR,*
–9R, SmATA 1, WrDr 84
Savery, Ranald 1903?-1974 *ConAu 104*
Saveson, John E 1923- *ConAu 41R*
Saveth, Edward N 1915- *ConAu 21R*
Savi, Ethel Winifred 1865-1954 *LongCTC*
Saviane, Giorgio 1916- *IntAu&W 82*
Saville, Eugenia Curtis 1913- *ConAu 41R*
Saville, Ken *DrAP&F 83*
Saville, Ken 1949- *IntWWP 82*
Saville, Lloyd 1913- *ConAu 21R*
Saville, Malcolm 1901-1982 *ConAu 101, –107,*
IntAu&W 82, SmATA 23[port], –31N,
TwCCW 83
Savin, Marc 1948- *ConAu 106*
Saviozzi, Adriana 1928- *ConAu X, SmATA X*
Saviozzi, Andriana Mazza 1918- *ConAu 1R*
Savitch, Jessica 1948- *ConAu 108*
Savitch, Jessica 1948-1983 *ConAu 110*
Savitri *IntAu&W 82X*
Savitt, Lynne *DrAP&F 83*
Savitt, Ronald 1939- *ConAu 33R*
Savitt, Sam *WrDr 84*
Savitt, Sam 1917- *ConAu 1R, –1NR,*
SmATA 8
Savitt, Todd Lee 1943- *ConAu 102*
Savitz, Harriet May 1933- *ConAu 41R,*
SmATA 5

Savitz, Leonard D 1926- *ConAu 8NR, –21R*
Savnoam *IntWWP 82X*
Savory, Alan Forsyth 1905- *ConAu 9R*
Savory, Gerald 1909- *CnMD*
Savory, Hubert Newman 1911- *ConAu 10NR,*
–25R
Savory, Jerold 1933- *ConAu 10NR, –25R*
Savory, Teo *ConAu 29R, ConP 80, WrDr 84*
Savory, Theodore Horace 1896- *WrDr 84*
Savory, Theodore Horace 1896-1980 *ConAu 5R,*
–6NR
Savours, Ann 1927- *ConAu 57*
Savoy, Mark *ConAu X*
Savvas, Minas *DrAP&F 83*
Savvas, Minas 1939- *IntWWP 82*
Sawa, Yuki 1945- *IntWWP 82*
Sawa Y Martinez, Alejandro 1862-1909
CIDMEL 80
Saward, Michael 1932- *ConAu 97*
Sawatsky, Harry Leonard 1931- *ConAu 89*
Sawer, Geoffrey 1910- *ConAu 17R*
Sawey, Orlan 1920- *ConAu 29R*
Sawkins, Raymond H 1923- *ConAu 103*
Sawley, Petra *TwCRGW, WrDr 84*
Sawyer, Albert E 1898- *ConAu 5R*
Sawyer, Charles 1887-1979 *ConAu 85,*
ConAu P-2
Sawyer, Corinne Holt 1924- *ConAu 17R,*
WrDr 84
Sawyer, Diane 1946?- *ConAu 109*
Sawyer, Jack 1931- *ConAu 61*
Sawyer, Jesse O 1918- *ConAu 17R*
Sawyer, John *ConAu X*
Sawyer, John 1919- *WrDr 84*
Sawyer, Lynwood *DrAP&F 83*
Sawyer, Mark *ConAu X*
Sawyer, Nancy 1924- *WrDr 84*
Sawyer, P H 1928- *ConAu 6NR, –9R*
Sawyer, R McLaran 1929- *ConAu 45*
Sawyer, Ralph Alanson 1895-1978 *ConAu 81*
Sawyer, Ruth 1880-1970 *ConAu 73,*
DcLB 22[port], SmATA 17, TwCA,
TwCA SUP, TwCCW 83
Sawyer, W W 1911- *ConAu 53*
Sawyerr, Harry Alphonso Ebun 1909-
ConAu 37R, IntAu&W 82
Sax, Boria *DrAP&F 83*
Sax, Boria 1949- *IntWWP 82*
Sax, Gilbert 1930- *ConAu 21R*
Sax, Joseph L 1936- *ConAu 33R, WrDr 84*
Sax, Karl 1892-1973 *ConAu 45*
Sax, Saville 1924- *ConAu 97*
Saxberg, Borje O 1928- *ConAu 41R*
Saxe, Isobel *ConAu X*
Saxe, Richard W 1923- *ConAu 49*
Saxe, Thomas E, Jr. 1903-1975 *ConAu 61*
Saxon, A H 1935- *ConAu 25R*
Saxon, Alex *ConAu X, WrDr 84*
Saxon, Bill *ConAu X*
Saxon, Gladys Relyea *ConAu 5R*
Saxon, Lyle 1891-1946 *TwCA, TwCA SUP*
Saxon, Richard *WrDr 84*
Saxon, Richard 1905- *ConSFA, TwCSFW*
Saxon, Van *ConAu X*
Saxton, Alexander P 1919- *ConAu 105*
Saxton, Josephine 1935- *ConAu 29R, TwCSFW,*
WrDr 84
Saxton, Judith *WrDr 84*
Saxton, Judith 1936- *ConAu 105*
Saxton, Lloyd 1919- *ConAu 29R*
Saxton, Mark 1914- *ConAu 93*
Saxton, Martha 1945- *ConAu 81*
Say, Allen 1937- *ConAu 29R,*
SmATA 28[port]
Saya, Peter *ConAu X*
Sayce, Richard Anthony 1917- *ConAu 61*
Saydah, J Roger 1939- *ConAu 25R*
Saye, Albert B 1912- *ConAu 5R, –5NR*
Sayeed, Bano Tahira 1922- *IntWWP 82*
Sayeed, Khalid B 1926- *ConAu 25R*
Sayegh, Fayez A 1922-1980 *ConAu 9R, –102*
Sayer, Angela 1935- *ConAu 89*
Sayer, Nancy Margetts *WrDr 84*
Sayers, Dorothy Leigh 1893-1957 *CnMD,*
ConAu 104, DcLB 10[port], LongCTC,
ModBrL, ModBrL SUP, ModWD, TwCA,
TwCA SUP, TwCCr&M 80, TwCLC 2,
TwCWr
Sayers, Frances Clarke 1897- *ConAu 17R,*
SmATA 3
Sayers, Gale 1943- *ConAu 73*
Sayers, Raymond S 1912- *ConAu 10NR, –25R*

Sayles, E B 1892- *ConAu P-2*
Sayles, George Osborne 1901- *ConAu 4NR, –53*
Sayles, John 1950- *ConAu 57, ConLC 7, –10,*
–14
Sayles, Leonard Robert 1926- *ConAu 1R, –1NR*
Sayles, Ted *ConAu X*
Saylor, David J 1945- *ConAu 89*
Saylor, Irene 1932- *ConAu 33R*
Saylor, J Galen 1902- *ConAu 9NR*
Saylor, John Galen 1902- *ConAu 17R,*
WrDr 84
Saylor, Neville 1922- *ConAu 61*
Sayn-Wittgenstein, Franz 1910- *IntAu&W 82*
Sayre, Anne 1923- *ConAu 61*
Sayre, Eleanor Axson 1916- *ConAu 25R*
Sayre, J Woodrow 1913- *ConAu 5NR, –9R*
Sayre, Joel 1900-1979 *ConAu 89*
Sayre, John L 1924- *ConAu 53*
Sayre, Kenneth Malcolm 1928- *ConAu 3NR,*
–9R
Sayre, Leslie C 1907- *ConAu P-1*
Sayre, Robert F 1933- *ConAu 9R*
Sayre, Wallace Stanley 1905-1972 *ConAu 33R*
Sayres, Alfred Nevin 1893- *ConAu P-1*
Sayres, William C 1927- *ConAu 17R*
Sayrs, Henry John 1904- *ConAu 5R*
Saywell, John T 1929- *ConAu 13R*
Sazer, Nina 1949- *ConAu 69, SmATA 13*
Sbarbaro, Camillo 1888-1967 *CIDMEL 80*
Scabrini, Janet 1953- *SmATA 13*
Scacco, Anthony M, Jr. 1939- *ConAu 109*
Scaduto, Anthony *ConAu 104*
Scaduto, Tony *ConAu X, WrDr 84*
Scaer, David P 1936- *ConAu 33R*
Scaglione, Aldo 1925- *WrDr 84*
Scaglione, Aldo D 1925- *ConAu 6NR, –13R*
Scaglione, Ann *DrAP&F 83*
Scaglione, Cecil F 1934- *ConAu 81*
Scagnetti, Jack 1924- *ConAu 4NR, –49,*
MichAu 80, SmATA 7
Scalapino, Leslie *DrAP&F 83*
Scalapino, Leslie 1948- *IntWWP 82*
Scalapino, Robert Anthony 1919- *ConAu 1R,*
–2NR, IntAu&W 82, WrDr 84
Scali, John 1918- *ConAu 65*
Scally, Sister Anthony 1905- *ConAu 110*
Scally, M A *ConAu X*
Scally, Sister Mary Anthony *ConAu X*
Scally, Robert James 1937- *ConAu 61*
Scalzo, Joe 1941- *ConAu 49*
Scamehorn, H Lee 1926- *ConAu 69*
Scammell, William McConnell 1920- *ConAu 5R,*
–6NR
Scammon, John H 1905- *ConAu 53*
Scammon, Richard M 1915- *ConAu 61,*
WrDr 84
Scandura, Joseph M 1931- *ConAu 5NR, –53*
Scanlan, Arthur Brian 1907- *WrDr 84*
Scanlan, James P 1927- *ConAu 9R*
Scanlan, Michael 1931- *ConAu 7NR, –57*
Scanlan, Patrick F 1895?-1983 *ConAu 109*
Scanlon, David G 1921- *ConAu 13R*
Scanlon, Kathryn I 1909- *ConAu P-1*
Scanlon, Marion Stephany d1977 *ConAu 5R,*
MichAu 80, SmATA 11
Scannell, Vernon 1922- *ConAu 5R, –8NR,*
ConP 80, DcLEL 1940, IntAu&W 82,
WorAu 1970, WrDr 84
Scantlan, Samuel William 1901- *IntWWP 82*
Scanziani, Piero 1908- *IntAu&W 82*
Scanzoni, John H 1935- *ConAu 9NR, –21R*
Scanzoni, Letha 1935- *ConAu 57*
Scarborough, Alma May C 1913- *ConAu 5R*
Scarborough, Dorothy 1877-1935 *TwCA,*
TwCWW
Scarborough, John 1940- *ConAu 41R*
Scarborough, William Kauffman 1933-
ConAu 17R, WrDr 84
Scarbrough, George Addison *DrAP&F 83*
Scarbrough, George Addison 1915- *ConAu 77*
Scaretti, Marjorie d1982 *ConAu 107*
Scarf, Maggi *ConAu X, SmATA X*
Scarf, Maggie 1932- *ConAu 29R, SmATA 5,*
WrDr 84
Scarfe, Allan John 1931- *ConAu 25R*
Scarfe, Francis Harold 1911- *DcLEL 1940,*
ModBrL, TwCA SUP
Scarfe, Wendy Elizabeth 1933- *ConAu 25R,*
WrDr 84
Scargall, Jeanne Anna 1928- *ConAu 93*
Scargill, David Ian 1935- *ConAu 61,*
IntAu&W 82, WrDr 84

Schon, Isabel 1940- *ConAu 110*
Schonbeck, Marianne Kleiner- 1925-
  IntAu&W 82
Schonberg, Harold C 1915- *WrDr 84*
Schonberg, Rosalyn Krokover 1913?-1973
  ConAu 41R
Schonberger, Richard J 1937- *ConAu 110*
Schonborg, Virginia 1913- *ConAu 77*
Schondorff, Joachim 1912- *IntAu&W 82*
Schone, Virginia *ConAu 97, SmATA 22[port]*
Schonell, Fred Joyce 1900-1969 *ConAu 1R,*
  -2NR
Schonfeld, William R 1942- *ConAu 37R,*
  IntAu&W 82
Schonfield, Hugh Joseph 1901- *ConAu 9R,*
  IntAu&W 82, WrDr 84
Schonherr, Karl 1867-1943 *CnMD, ModGL,*
  ModWD
Schoolcraft, Henry Rowe 1793-1864 *MichAu 80*
Schooler, Dean, Jr. 1941- *ConAu 73*
Schoolfield, George C 1925- *ConAu 1R, -6NR*
Schoolland, Marian M 1902- *ConAu 2NR, -5R,*
  WrDr 84
Schoonhoven, Calvin R 1931- *ConAu 21R*
Schoonmaker, Alan N 1936- *ConAu 25R*
Schoonmaker, Ann 1928- *ConAu 73*
Schoonmaker, Frank Musselman 1905-1976
  ConAu 61
Schoonover, Amy Jo *DrAP&F 83*
Schoonover, Frank 1877-1972 *ConAu 106,*
  SmATA 24[port]
Schoonover, Lawrence Lovell 1906-1980
  ConAu 1R, -4NR, -97, ConSFA
Schoonover, Shirley 1936- *ConAu 77*
Schoonover, Shirley W *DrAP&F 83*
Schoonover, Thelma I 1907- *ConAu 41R*
Schoor, Gene 1921- *ConAu 29R, SmATA 3*
Schopfer, Jean 1868-1931 *TwCA*
Schopflin, George A *ConAu X*
Schor, Amy 1954- *ConAu 105*
Schor, Lynda *DrAP&F 83*
Schor, Lynda 1938- *ConAu 73*
Schor, Naomi 1943- *ConAu 89*
Schor, Sandra *DrAP&F 83*
Schorb, E M *DrAP&F 83*
Schorb, E M 1940- *ConAu 61*
Schorer, Mark 1908-1977 *ConAu 5R, -7NR, -73,*
  ConLC 9, ConLCrt 82, TwCA SUP
Schorr, Alan Edward 1945- *ConAu 85*
Schorr, Alvin L 1921- *ConAu 29R*
Schorr, Daniel 1916- *ConAu 65*
Schorr, Daniel Louis 1913- *AuNews 2*
Schorr, Jerry 1934- *ConAu 29R*
Schorske, Carl E 1915- *ConAu 85*
Schosberg, Paul A 1938- *ConAu 13R*
Schossberger, Emily Maria 1905-1979
  ConAu 104
Schott, Carol *DrAP&F 83*
Schott, John R 1936- *ConAu 7NR, -57*
Schott, Penelope Scambly *DrAP&F 83*
Schott, Penelope Scambly 1942- *ConAu 77,*
  IntWWP 82
Schott, Webster 1927- *ConAu 49*
Schotte, Paulus *IntAu&W 82X*
Schotter, Richard 1944- *NatPD 81[port]*
Schotter, Roni *DrAP&F 83*
Schottland, Charles Irwin 1906- *ConAu 13R*
Schowalter, John E 1936- *ConAu 109*
Schoyer, B Preston 1912?-1978 *ConAu 77*
Schrader, Constance 1933- *ConAu 101*
Schrader, Dorothy Cole 1905- *IntWWP 82*
Schrader, George Alfred 1917- *ConAu 21R*
Schrader, Ludwig 1932- *IntAu&W 82*
Schrader, Margarete Maria Elisabeth 1915-
  IntWWP 82
Schrader, Paul 1946- *ConAu 37R, ConDr 82A,*
  ConLC 26[port], MichAu 80
Schrader, Richard James 1941- *ConAu 85*
Schraff, Anne E 1939- *ConAu 1NR, -49,*
  SmATA 27[port]
Schraff, Francis Nicholas 1937- *ConAu 101*
Schraffenberger, Nancy 1933- *ConAu 93*
Schrag, Adele Frisbie 1921- *ConAu 105*
Schrag, Calvin Orville 1928- *ConAu 1R, -1NR*
Schrag, Oswald 1916- *ConAu 49*
Schrag, Peter 1931- *ConAu 8NR, -13R,*
  WrDr 84
Schrag, Philip G 1943- *ConAu 102*
Schram, Martin 1942- *ConAu 69*
Schram, Stuart Reynolds 1924- *ConAu 97*
Schramm, Darrell G H *DrAP&F 83*
Schramm, Percy Ernst 1894-1970 *ConAu 104*

Schramm, Richard *DrAP&F 83*
Schramm, Richard 1934- *ConAu 41R*
Schramm, Sarah Slavin 1942- *ConAu 93*
Schramm, Wilbur 1907- *ConAu 105, WrDr 84*
Schrank, Jeffrey 1944- *ConAu 29R, WrDr 84*
Schrank, Joseph 1900- *ConAu 5R,*
  NatPD 81[port]
Schreck, Everett M 1897- *ConAu P-2*
Schreiber, Daniel 1909-1981 *ConAu 103,*
  ConAu P-1
Schreiber, Elizabeth Anne 1947- *ConAu 69,*
  SmATA 13
Schreiber, Flora Rheta 1918- *AuNews 1,*
  ConAu 11NR, -53
Schreiber, Georg 1922- *IntAu&W 82*
Schreiber, Georges 1904-1977 *ConAu 109,*
  SmATA 29
Schreiber, Hermann O L 1920- *ConAu 25R,*
  WrDr 84
Schreiber, Jan *DrAP&F 83*
Schreiber, Jan 1941- *ConAu 65, IntWWP 82*
Schreiber, Ralph W 1942- *ConAu 69,*
  SmATA 13
Schreiber, Ron *DrAP&F 83*
Schreiber, Ron 1934- *ConAu 41R, IntWWP 82*
Schreiber, Vernon R 1925- *ConAu 61*
Schreider, Frank 1924- *ConAu 5R*
Schreier, Josef 1943- *IntWWP 82*
Schreiner, Ludwig 1928- *IntAu&W 82*
Schreiner, Olive Emilie Albertina 1855?-1920
  ConAu 105, LongCTC, ModCmwL, TwCA,
  TwCA SUP, TwCLC 9[port], TwCWr
Schreiner, Samuel 1921- *ConAu 65, WrDr 84*
Schreiner, Samuel A, Jr. 1921- *ConAu 9NR*
Schreiner-Mann, Joan 1939- *ConAu 45*
Schreiter, Rick 1936- *ConAu 21R*
Schreivogel, Paul A 1930- *ConAu 25R*
Schreyer, George M 1913- *ConAu 5R*
Schreyer, Wolfgang 1927- *IntAu&W 82*
Schreyvogl, Friedrich 1899- *CnMD, CroCD,*
  ModWD
Schrier, Arnold 1925- *ConAu 49*
Schrier, William 1900-1973 *ConAu 41R*
Schrift, Shirley 1922- *ConAu 110*
Schriftgiesser, Karl 1903- *ConAu P-1,*
  TwCA SUP
Schrire, Theodore 1906- *ConAu 21R*
Schroder, Amund A Schulze 1925- *ConAu 5NR,*
  -13R
Schroder, John Henry Erle 1895- *ConAu P-1*
Schroder, Rudolf Alexander 1878-1962
  CIDMEL 80, ModGL, TwCWr
Schroeder, Albert H 1914- *ConAu 41R*
Schroeder, Andreas 1946- *ConAu 93, ConP 80,*
  IntAu&W 82, WrDr 84
Schroeder, David 1924- *ConAu 21R*
Schroeder, Eric 1904- *ConAu P-1*
Schroeder, Fred E H 1932- *ConAu 41R*
Schroeder, Frederick William 1896- *ConAu 1R*
Schroeder, Gary *DrAP&F 83*
Schroeder, Henry A 1906-1975 *ConAu P-2*
Schroeder, John H 1943- *ConAu 49*
Schroeder, Mary 1903- *ConAu 73*
Schroeder, Oliver Charles, Jr. 1916- *ConAu 110*
Schroeder, Paul Walter 1927- *ConAu 5R*
Schroeder, Sandra *DrAP&F 83*
Schroeder, Ted 1931?-1973 *SmATA 20N*
Schroeter, James 1927- *ConAu 21R*
Schroeter, Louis C 1929- *ConAu 29R, WrDr 84*
Schroetter, Hilda Noel 1917- *ConAu 29R*
Schroll, Herman T 1946- *ConAu 33R*
Schruben, Francis W 1918- *ConAu 45*
Schruth, Peter Elliott 1917-1979 *ConAu 89*
Schubart, Mark Allen 1918- *ConAu 105*
Schubert, Delwyn George 1919- *ConAu 9R*
Schubert, Glendon 1918- *ConAu 5R, -6NR*
Schubert, Kurt 1923- *ConAu 5R*
Schuberth, Christopher J 1933- *ConAu 25R*
Schuchat, Simon *DrAP&F 83*
Schuchman, Joan 1934- *ConAu 101,*
  IntAu&W 82
Schuck, F H P 1916- *ConSFA*
Schudson, Michael 1946- *ConAu 101*
Schuebel, Theodor 1925- *IntAu&W 82*
Schueler, Donald G 1929- *ConAu 106*
Schuerer, Ernst 1933- *ConAu 1NR, -45*
Schuessler, Hermann E 1929?-1975 *ConAu 61*
Schuessler, Karl Frederick 1915- *ConAu 105*
Schuettinger, Robert Lindsay 1936- *ConAu 33R*
Schuetz, John Howard 1933- *ConAu 97*
Schuetze, Armin William 1917- *ConAu 57*

Schuff, Karen Elizabeth 1937- *IntWWP 82*
Schug, Willis E 1924- *ConAu 49*
Schuh, Dwight R 1945- *ConAu 101*
Schuh, G Edward 1930- *ConAu 29R, WrDr 84*
Schuker, Stephen Alan 1939- *ConAu 69*
Schul, Bill D 1928- *ConAu 8NR, -61*
Schulberg, Budd *DrAP&F 83*
Schulberg, Budd 1914- *ConAu 25R,*
  ConDr 82D, ConLC 7, ConNov 82,
  DcLB 6[port], -26[port], DcLEL 1940,
  LongCTC, ModAL, TwCA SUP, WrDr 84
Schulberg, Herbert C 1934- *ConAu 8NR, -61*
Schulberg, Stuart 1922-1979 *ConAu 89*
Schulder, Diane Blossom 1937- *ConAu 37R*
Schuler, Carol Ann 1946- *ConAu 106*
Schuler, Edgar A 1905- *ConAu P-2*
Schuler, Ruth May Wildes 1933- *IntWWP 82*
Schuler, Ruth Wildes *DrAP&F 83*
Schuler, Stanley Carter 1915- *ConAu 5R, -5NR*
Schulke, Flip Phelps Graeme 1930- *ConAu 105*
Schulkind, Eugene 1923- *ConAu 97*
Schull, John Joseph *CreCan 2*
Schull, Joseph 1910- *CreCan 2*
Schull, Joseph 1916-1980 *ConAu 8NR, -53*
Schuller, Gunther 1925- *ConAu 69, WrDr 84*
Schuller, Robert H 1926- *WrDr 84*
Schuller, Robert Harold 1926- *ConAu 9R*
Schulman, Arnold 1925- *ConAu 103*
Schulman, Bob *ConAu X*
Schulman, Grace *ConAu 65, DrAP&F 83,*
  IntAu&W 82, IntWWP 82
Schulman, J Neil 1953- *ConAu 89*
Schulman, Janet 1933- *ConAu 101, SmATA 22*
Schulman, L M 1934- *ConAu 33R, SmATA 13*
Schulman, Robert 1916- *ConAu 77*
Schulman, Rosalind 1914- *ConAu 41R*
Schulman, Sam 1924- *ConAu 45*
Schulte, Elaine L 1934- *ConAu 73*
Schulte, Henry F 1924- *ConAu 25R, WrDr 84*
Schulte, Rainer *DrAP&F 83*
Schulte, Rainer 1937- *ConAu 21R, IntWWP 82*
Schultes, Richard Evans 1915- *ConAu 108*
Schulthess, Emil 1913- *ConAu 65*
Schults, Raymond L 1926- *ConAu 105*
Schultz, Barbara 1923- *ConAu 21R*
Schultz, Dodi 1930- *ConAu 1NR, -45,*
  IntAu&W 82
Schultz, Donald O 1939- *ConAu 25R*
Schultz, Duane P 1934- *ConAu 29R*
Schultz, Ed 1933- *ConAu 45*
Schultz, Edna Moore 1912- *ConAu 13R*
Schultz, Edward W 1936- *ConAu 1NR, -45*
Schultz, George Franklin 1908- *ConAu P-2*
Schultz, George J 1932- *ConAu 109*
Schultz, Gerard 1902-1974 *ConAu 110,*
  MichAu 80
Schultz, Gwendolyn *ConAu 65,*
  SmATA 21[port]
Schultz, Harold John 1932- *ConAu 103*
Schultz, Harry D 1923- *ConAu 21R*
Schultz, John *DrAP&F 83*
Schultz, John 1943- *ConAu 41R*
Schultz, Morton J 1930- *ConAu 73*
Schultz, Ole Sofus 1944- *IntAu&W 82*
Schultz, Pearle Henriksen 1918- *ConAu 1NR,*
  -49, SmATA 21[port]
Schultz, Philip *DrAP&F 83*
Schultz, Philip 1945- *ConAu 104, IntWWP 82*
Schultz, Samuel J 1914- *ConAu 25R, WrDr 84*
Schultz, Sigrid 1893-1980 *ConAu 97*
Schultz, Terri 1946- *ConAu 10NR, -65*
Schultz, Theodore William 1902- *ConAu 85*
Schultz, Vernon B 1924- *ConAu 9R*
Schultze, William Andrew 1937- *ConAu 37R*
Schulz, Bruno 1892-1942 *CIDMEL 80,*
  ModSL 2, TwCLC 5[port], WorAu 1970
Schulz, Charles 1922- *WrDr 84*
Schulz, Charles Monroe 1922- *ConAu 6NR, -9R,*
  ConLC 12, SmATA 10
Schulz, Clare Elmore 1924- *ConAu 13R*
Schulz, David A 1933- *ConAu 29R*
Schulz, Ernst B 1896- *ConAu 73*
Schulz, Florence 1908- *ConAu P-2*
Schulz, Gerhard 1924- *IntAu&W 82*
Schulz, Hans 1912- *IntAu&W 82*
Schulz, James Henry 1936- *ConAu 89*
Schulz, John E 1939- *ConAu 29R*
Schulz, Juergen 1927- *ConAu 41R, -81*
Schulz, Max Frederick 1923- *ConAu 5R,*
  WrDr 84
Schulz-Behrend, George 1913- *ConAu 45*
Schulz-Fielbrandt, Hans *IntAu&W 82X*

Schulze, Franz 1927- *ConAu 41R*, *WrDr 84*
Schulze, Gene 1912- *ConAu 85*
Schulzinger, Robert D 1945- *ConAu 61*
Schumacher, Alvin J 1928- *ConAu 13R*
Schumacher, E F 1911?-1977 *ConIsC 1[port]*
Schumacher, Ernest Friedrich 1911?-1977
  ConAu 73
Schumacher, Ernst Friedrich 1911?-1977
  ConAu 81
Schuman, Beatrice C *DrAP&F 83*
Schuman, Ben N 1923- *ConAu 17R*
Schuman, David Feller 1942- *ConAu 97*
Schuman, Frederick Lewis 1904- *ConAu 45*,
  TwCA, *TwCA SUP*, *WrDr 84*
Schuman, Patricia Glass 1943- *ConAu 33R*
Schumann, Elizabeth Creighton 1907- *ConAu P-1*
Schumann, Maurice 1911- *IntAu&W 82*
Schuon, Frithjof 1907- *ConAu 73*
Schuon, Karl Albert 1913- *ConAu 13R*
Schur, Edwin M 1930- *ConAu 7NR, -13R*
Schur, Norman W 1907- *ConAu 41R*
Schurch, Gertrud 1916- *IntAu&W 82*
Schurer, Ernst *ConAu X*
Schurer, Leopold Launitz, Jr. *ConAu X*
Schurfranz, Vivian 1925- *ConAu 61*,
  SmATA 13
Schurmacher, Emile C 1903?-1976 *ConAu 69*
Schurman, D M 1924- *ConAu 37R*
Schurr, Cathleen *ConAu 9R*
Schuschnigg, Kurt Von 1897- *ConAu X*
Schusky, Ernest L 1931- *ConAu 8NR, -17R*,
  WrDr 84
Schuster, George 1873-1972 *ConAu 37R*
Schuster, George 1881-1982 *ConAu 107*
Schuster, Louis A 1916- *ConAu 13R*
Schuster, Max Lincoln 1897-1970 *ConAu 29R*
Schutte, William Metcalf 1919- *ConAu 5R*
Schutz, Anton Friedrich Joseph 1894-1977
  ConAu 73, -81
Schutz, Benjamin Merrill 1949- *ConAu 107*
Schutz, John Adolph 1919- *ConAu 5R*
Schutz, John Howard *ConAu X*
Schutz, Susan Polis 1944- *ConAu 105*
Schutz, Wilhelm Wolfgang 1911- *ConAu 25R*
Schutz, Will 1925- *WrDr 84*
Schutz, William C 1925- *ConAu 10NR, -25R*
Schutze, Gertrude 1917- *ConAu X*
Schutze, Gladys Henrietta 1881-1946 *TwCA*
Schutzer, A I 1922- *ConAu 25R*, *SmATA 13*
Schutzman, Steven *DrAP&F 83*
Schuuring, Casper 1927- *IntAu&W 82*
Schuyler, George Samuel 1895-1977 *ConAu 73,
  -81*
Schuyler, James *DrAP&F 83*
Schuyler, James 1923- *WrDr 84*
Schuyler, James Marcus 1923- *ConAu 101*,
  ConLC 5, -23[port], *ConP 80*, *CroCAP*,
  DcLB 5[port], *DcLEL 1940*, *IntWWP 82*
Schuyler, Jane 1943- *ConAu 65*
Schuyler, Joseph Bernard 1921- *ConAu 1R*
Schuyler, Keith C 1919- *ConAu 29R*, *WrDr 84*
Schuyler, Pamela R 1948- *ConAu 106*,
  SmATA 30[port]
Schuyler, Philippa Duke 1934-1967 *ConAu 5R*
Schuyler, Robert Livingston 1883-1966
  ConAu P-1
Schvaneveldt, Jay D 1937- *ConAu 103*
Schwab, Arnold T 1922- *ConAu 9R*
Schwab, George 1931- *ConAu 1NR, -45*
Schwab, Gunther 1904- *IntAu&W 82*
Schwab, John J 1923- *ConAu 85*
Schwab, Joseph J 1909- *ConAu 5R, -5NR*
Schwab, Paul Josiah 1894-1966 *ConAu 5R, -103*
Schwab, Peter 1940- *ConAu 41R*, *IntAu&W 82*
Schwabe, William *ConAu X*
Schwaber, Paul 1936- *ConAu 13R*
Schwalberg, Carol 1930- *ConAu 69*
Schwalm, Jurgen 1932- *IntAu&W 82*
Schwartz, Alan *ConSFA*
Schwartz, Alfred 1922- *ConAu 17R*
Schwartz, Alvin 1927- *ChlLR 3*, *ConAu 7NR,
  -13R*, *SmATA 4*
Schwartz, Amy 1954- *ConAu 110*
Schwartz, Anne Powers 1913- *ConAu 1R, -1NR*,
  SmATA 10
Schwartz, Arthur Nathaniel 1922- *ConAu 8NR,
  -61*
Schwartz, Audrey James 1928- *ConAu 89*
Schwartz, Barry 1938- *ConAu 77*
Schwartz, Barry 1942- *WrDr 84*
Schwartz, Barry N 1942- *ConAu 33R*
Schwartz, Benjamin I 1916- *ConAu 13R*

Schwartz, Bernard 1945- *ConAu 106*
Schwartz, Bertie G 1901?-1976 *ConAu 69*
Schwartz, Betty 1927- *ConAu 93*
Schwartz, Charles *ConAu 73*
Schwartz, Charles Walsh 1914- *ConAu 13R*,
  SmATA 8
Schwartz, Daniel 1929- *SmATA 29*
Schwartz, David C 1939- *ConAu 37R*
Schwartz, David Joseph, Jr. 1927- *ConAu 17R*
Schwartz, Delmore 1913-1966 *CnMWL*,
  ConAu 25R, *ConAu P-2*, *ConLC 2, -4, -10*,
  ConLCrt 82, *ConP 80A*, *ModAL*,
  ModAL SUP, *TwCA*, *TwCA SUP*,
  TwCWr, *WhoTwCL*
Schwartz, Donald Ray 1943- *IntAu&W 82*
Schwartz, Douglas W 1929- *ConAu 25R*
Schwartz, Eleanor Brantley 1937- *ConAu 57*
Schwartz, Eli 1921- *ConAu 1R*, *IntAu&W 82*,
  WrDr 84
Schwartz, Elias 1923- *ConAu 41R*
Schwartz, Elizabeth Reeder 1912- *ConAu 13R*,
  SmATA 8
Schwartz, Elkanah 1937- *ConAu 21R*
Schwartz, Elliott S 1936- *ConAu 13R*,
  IntAu&W 82, *WrDr 84*
Schwartz, Emanual K 1912-1973 *ConAu 37R*,
  -41R
Schwartz, Eugene M 1927- *ConAu 13R*
Schwartz, George 1908-1974 *ConAu 104*
Schwartz, George Leopold 1891-1983 *ConAu 109*
Schwartz, George R 1942- *ConAu 97*
Schwartz, Helene E 1941- *ConAu 65*
Schwartz, Hillel 1948- *ConAu 102*
Schwartz, Howard *DrAP&F 83*
Schwartz, Howard 1945- *ConAu 5NR, -49*
Schwartz, Israel J 1885-1971 *ConAu 33R*
Schwartz, Jeffrey *DrAP&F 83*
Schwartz, Jerome *ConAu X*
Schwartz, Jonathan 1938- *ConAu 97*,
  DcLB Y82B[port]
Schwartz, Joseph 1925- *ConAu 33R*,
  IntAu&W 82, *WrDr 84*
Schwartz, Jozua M W VanDerPoorten 1858-1915
  TwCA
Schwartz, Julius 1907- *ConAu 109*
Schwartz, K V 1936- *ConAu 104*
Schwartz, Kessel 1920- *ConAu 1R, -6NR*,
  IntAu&W 82, *WrDr 84*
Schwartz, Larry 1922- *ConAu 53*
Schwartz, Lewis M 1935- *ConAu 45*
Schwartz, Lita Linzer 1930- *ConAu 29R*
Schwartz, Lloyd *DrAP&F 83*
Schwartz, Lloyd 1941- *IntWWP 82*
Schwartz, Lois C 1935- *ConAu 33R*
Schwartz, Loretta 1943- *ConAu 97*
Schwartz, Louis Brown 1913- *ConAu 21R*,
  WrDr 84
Schwartz, Lynne Sharon *DrAP&F 83*
Schwartz, Lynne Sharon 1939- *ConAu 103*
Schwartz, Marian *DrAP&F 83*
Schwartz, Mildred A 1932- *ConAu 9NR*
Schwartz, Mildred Anne 1932- *ConAu 21R*,
  WrDr 84
Schwartz, Morris S 1916- *ConAu 17R*
Schwartz, Muriel A *ConAu X*
Schwartz, Nancy Lynn 1952-1978 *ConAu 107*
Schwartz, Ned 1948- *ConAu 107*
Schwartz, Paula 1925- *ConAu 85*
Schwartz, Pedro 1935- *ConAu 107*
Schwartz, Pepper 1945- *ConAu 33R*
Schwartz, Poorten- *LongCTC*
Schwartz, Rhoda *DrAP&F 83*
Schwartz, Richard B 1941- *ConAu 85*
Schwartz, Richard D 1925- *ConAu 1R, -6NR*
Schwartz, Ronald 1937- *ConAu 65*
Schwartz, Sheila *DrAP&F 83*
Schwartz, Sheila 1929- *ConAu 11NR, -25R*,
  SmATA 27[port]
Schwartz, Sheila R *WrDr 84*
Schwartz, Stephen 1948- *ConAu 85*,
  SmATA 19
Schwartz, Stuart B 1940- *ConAu 108*
Schwartz, William 1916-1982 *ConAu 107*
Schwartzberg, Julie 1943- *ConAu 29R*
Schwartzman, Aaron 1900?-1981 *ConAu 102*
Schwartzman, David 1924- *ConAu 41R*
Schwartzman, Edward 1927- *ConAu 73*
Schwartzman, Sylvan David 1913- *ConAu 41R*
Schwartzmann, Mischa 1919- *ConAu 29R*
Schwarz, Alice *IntAu&W 82X*
Schwarz, Boris 1906- *ConAu 37R*,
  IntAu&W 82, *WrDr 84*

Schwarz, Egon 1922- *ConAu 57*
Schwarz, Fred Charles 1913- *ConAu 1R*
Schwarz, Hans 1939- *ConAu 41R*
Schwarz, Helmut G 1928- *CroCD*
Schwarz, Henry G 1928- *ConAu 37R*,
  IntAu&W 82, *WrDr 84*
Schwarz, Jack *ConAu X*
Schwarz, Jacob 1924- *ConAu 103*
Schwarz, Jordan A 1937- *ConAu 105*
Schwarz, Leo W 1906-1967 *ConAu 5R*
Schwarz, Richard W 1925- *ConAu 29R*
Schwarz, Robert 1921- *ConAu 77*
Schwarz, Solomon M 1882?-1973 *ConAu 45*
Schwarz, Ted *ConAu X*
Schwarz, Theodore R, Jr. 1945- *ConAu 10NR,
  -65*
Schwarz, Walter 1930- *ConAu 13R*
Schwarz, Wilhelm Johannes 1929- *ConAu 65*
Schwarz, Yevgeni 1896-1958 *CnMD*
Schwarz-Bart, Andre 1928- *ConAu 89*,
  ConLC 2, -4, *TwCWr*, *WorAu*
Schwarz-Bart, Simone 1938- *ConAu 97*,
  ConLC 7
Schwarz-Gardos, Alice 1916- *IntAu&W 82*
Schwarzenberger, Georg 1908- *ConAu 13R*,
  IntAu&W 82, *WrDr 84*
Schwarzenegger, Arnold 1947- *ConAu 81*
Schwarzkopf-Legge, Elisabeth 1915- *ConAu 109*
Schwarzschild, Bettina 1925- *ConAu 29R*
Schwarzschild, Stuart 1918- *ConAu 5R*
Schwarzweller, Harry K 1929- *ConAu 37R*
Schwebel, Milton 1914- *ConAu 17R*
Schwebel, Stephen M 1929- *ConAu 77*
Schwebell, Gertrude C *ConAu 9R*
Schwed, Peter 1911- *ConAu 57*
Schweid, Eliezer 1929- *ConAu 1NR, -45*
Schweid, Richard M 1946- *ConAu 106*
Schweik, Robert C 1927- *ConAu 45*
Schweikart, Hans 1895-1975 *CnMD*
Schweitzer, Albert 1875-1965 *ConAu 93*,
  LongCTC, *TwCA SUP*, *TwCWr*
Schweitzer, Arthur 1905- *ConAu 9R*,
  IntAu&W 82, *WrDr 84*
Schweitzer, Byrd Baylor *ChlLR 3*, *ConAu X*
Schweitzer, Christoph E 1922- *ConAu 107*
Schweitzer, George K 1924- *ConAu 17R*
Schweitzer, Gertrude 1909- *ConAu 85*
Schweitzer, Jerome William 1908- *ConAu 41R*
Schweitzer, John C 1934- *ConAu 17R*
Schweizer, Eduard 1913- *ConAu 5NR, -13R*
Schweizer, Marc 1931- *IntAu&W 82*
Schwemer, Erna Anne Helene 1915-
  IntAu&W 82
Schwemer-Uhlhorn, Erna *IntAu&W 82X*
Schwendeman, J R 1897- *ConAu 81*
Schwendeman, Joseph Raymond 1897-
  IntAu&W 82
Schwengeler, Arnold H 1906- *IntAu&W 82*
Schwenger, Hannes 1941- *IntAu&W 82*
Schweninger, Ann 1951- *ConAu 107*,
  SmATA 29[port]
Schweninger, Loren 1941- *ConAu 101*
Schwenn, Gunther 1903- *IntAu&W 82*
Schwerin, Doris *DrAP&F 83*
Schwerin, Doris H 1922- *ConAu 9NR, -65*
Schwerin, Kurt 1902- *ConAu 45*
Schwerner, Armand *DrAP&F 83*
Schwerner, Armand 1927- *ConAu 9R*, *ConP 80*,
  IntAu&W 82, *IntWWP 82*, *WrDr 84*
Schwiebert, Ernest George 1895- *ConAu P-1*
Schwieder, Dorothy 1933- *ConAu 89*
Schwiefert, Fritz 1890- *CnMD*
Schwitzgebel, Robert L 1934- *ConAu 41R*
Schwob, Marcel 1867-1905 *CIDMEL 80*
Schwoerer, Lois G *ConAu 77*
Schydlowsky, Daniel M 1940- *ConAu 45*
Sciascia, Leonardo 1921- *CIDMEL 80*,
  ConAu 85, *ConLC 8, -9*, *WorAu 1970*
Scibor-Rylski, Aleksander 1927?-1983
  ConAu 109
Scicluna, Hannibal Publius 1880-1981?
  ConAu 106
Scifres, Bill 1925- *ConAu 103*
Scigliano, Robert 1925- *ConAu 9R*
Scipio *ConAu X*
Scirlea *IntWWP 82X*
Scism, Carol K 1931- *ConAu 41R*
Scithers, George H 1929- *ConAu 57*
Scitovsky, Tibor 1910- *ConAu 104*
Scoales, William 1933- *ConAu 33R*
Scobey, Joan 1927- *ConAu 7NR, -57*
Scobey, Mary-Margaret 1915- *ConAu 1R, -1NR*

Scobie, Edward 1918- *LivgBAA*
Scobie, Ilka 1950- *IntWWP 82*
Scobie, James Ralston 1929- *WrDr 84*
Scobie, James Ralston 1929-1981 *ConAu 6NR, -9R, -104*
Scobie, Llka *DrAP&F 83*
Scoby, Donald R 1931- *ConAu 33R*
Scofield, Arthur Gilbert 1900- *IntAu&W 82*
Scofield, Jonathan *ConAu X, WrDr 84*
Scofield, Norma Margaret Cartwright 1924- *ConAu 103*
Scofield, William H 1915- *ConAu 17R*
Scoggin, Margaret C 1905-1968 *SmATA 28*
Scoggins, James 1934- *ConAu 21R*
Scoles, Eugene F 1921- *ConAu 37R*
Scollan, E A *ConAu X*
Scollard, Clinton 1860-1932 *TwCA*
Scolnick, Sylvan 1930?-1976 *ConAu 69*
Scopes, John T 1900-1970 *ConAu 29R*
Scoppettone, Sandra 1936- *ConAu 5R, ConLC 26[port], NatPD 81[port], SmATA 9*
Scorer, Richard 1919- *ConAu 77*
Scorsese, Martin 1942- *ConAu 110, ConLC 20*
Scortia, Thomas N 1926- *ConAu 1R, -6NR, TwCSFW, WrDr 84*
Scot, Chesman *ConAu X*
Scotford, John Ryland 1888-1976 *ConAu 5R, -103*
Scotland, Andrew 1905- *ConAu 5R*
Scotland, James 1917- *ConAu 33R, IntAu&W 82, WrDr 84*
Scotland, James 1917-1983 *ConAu 110*
Scotland, Jay *ConAu X, IntAu&W 82X, WrDr 84*
Scotson, John L 1928- *ConAu 21R*
Scott, Captain 1868-1912 *LongCTC*
Scott, A C 1909- *ConAu 2NR, -5R, WrDr 84*
Scott, Alexander 1920- *ConAu 105, ConP 80, WrDr 84*
Scott, Allen John 1938- *ConAu 97*
Scott, Amoret 1930- *ConAu 10NR, -21R, IntAu&W 82, WrDr 84*
Scott, Andrew M 1922- *ConAu 17R*
Scott, Ann Herbert 1926- *ConAu 21R, SmATA 29*
Scott, Anne Firor 1921- *ConAu 33R*
Scott, Anthony *ConAu X*
Scott, Anthony Dalton 1923- *ConAu 11NR, -65*
Scott, Arthur Finley 1907- *ConAu 2NR, -5R, IntAu&W 82, WrDr 84*
Scott, Arthur L 1914- *ConAu 21R*
Scott, Austin 1885?-1981 *ConAu 103*
Scott, Beth *IntAu&W 82X*
Scott, Bill 1923- *TwCCW 83*
Scott, C P 1846-1932 *LongCTC*
Scott, C Winfield 1905- *ConAu 5R*
Scott, Carolyn Susan 1941- *IntAu&W 82*
Scott, Carolynne *DrAP&F 83*
Scott, Casey *ConAu X*
Scott, Cecil Alexander 1902?-1981 *ConAu 104*
Scott, Charles Hepburn 1886-1964 *CreCan 1*
Scott, Charles R, Jr. 1914- *ConAu 89*
Scott, Charles T 1932- *ConAu 21R*
Scott, Christopher 1930- *ConAu 21R, WrDr 84*
Scott, Clement William 1841-1904 *LongCTC*
Scott, Clinton Lee 1890- *ConAu P-2*
Scott, Cora Annett 1931- *ConAu 17R, SmATA 11*
Scott, Dan *ConAu P-2, SmATA X*
Scott, Dana *ConAu X, WrDr 84*
Scott, David 1919- *ConAu 109*
Scott, David L 1920- *WrDr 84*
Scott, David Robert 1928- *CreCan 2*
Scott, David W 1916- *ConAu 109*
Scott, Donald Fletcher 1930- *ConAu 89, WrDr 84*
Scott, Donald Malcolm 1931- *IntAu&W 82*
Scott, Dorothea Hayward *ConAu 93*
Scott, Duncan Campbell 1862-1947 *ConAu 104, CreCan 2, LongCTC, TwCA, TwCA SUP, TwCLC 6[port]*
Scott, Edward M 1919- *ConAu 33R, WrDr 84*
Scott, Elaine 1940- *ConAu 105*
Scott, Eleanor 1921- *ConAu 61*
Scott, Elizabeth Austin *IntWWP 82X*
Scott, Elizabeth Patricia 1938- *IntWWP 82*
Scott, Ellis L 1915- *ConAu 49*
Scott, Eve *ConAu X*
Scott, Evelyn 1893-1963 *ConAmA, ConAu 104, DcLB 9[port], TwCA, TwCA SUP*
Scott, F R 1899- *ConAu 101, ConLC 22[port],*

ConP 80, ModCmwL, WorAu 1970, WrDr 84
Scott, Frances V *ConAu X*
Scott, Francis Reginald 1899- *CreCan 1, DcLEL 1940, IntWWP 82*
Scott, Frank 1899- *ConAu X, CreCan 1*
Scott, Franklin D 1901- *ConAu 5R, -5NR, IntAu&W 82, WrDr 84*
Scott, Frederick George 1861-1944 *CreCan 2*
Scott, G Michael 1907- *IntAu&W 82*
Scott, Gavin 1936- *ConAu 77*
Scott, Gavin 1950- *WrDr 84*
Scott, Geoffrey 1885?-1929 *LongCTC, WorAu*
Scott, Geoffrey 1952- *ConAu 106*
Scott, George 1925- *WrDr 84*
Scott, George Edwin 1925- *ConAu 29R*
Scott, George Walton 1921- *ConAu 21R, WrDr 84*
Scott, Glori Van *LivgBAA*
Scott, Harold George 1925- *ConAu 61*
Scott, Harold Richard 1887- *ConAu 5R*
Scott, Herbert *DrAP&F 83*
Scott, Herbert 1931- *ConAu 6NR, -53, MichAu 80*
Scott, Ira O, Jr. 1918- *ConAu 17R*
Scott, J D 1917-1980 *ConAu 77, -97*
Scott, J Irving E *ConAu 73*
Scott, J M 1906- *ConAu 105*
Scott, J W Robertson 1866-1962 *LongCTC*
Scott, Jack B 1928- *ConAu 77*
Scott, Jack Denton 1915- *ConAu 108, SmATA 31*
Scott, Jack S *ConAu X*
Scott, James B 1926- *ConAu 85*
Scott, James Campbell 1936- *ConAu 29R, IntAu&W 82*
Scott, James Frazier 1934- *ConAu 77*
Scott, Jane *ConAu X, TwCRGW, WrDr 84*
Scott, Janey *TwCRGW, WrDr 84*
Scott, Jean *ConAu X*
Scott, Jeffrey *ConAu X*
Scott, Joanne Nisbet *CreCan 2*
Scott, Jody *ConAu 81*
Scott, John 1912-1976 *ConAu 5R, -6NR, -69, SmATA 14*
Scott, John 1937- *NatPD 81[port]*
Scott, John Anthony 1916- *ConAu 6NR, -9R, SmATA 23[port], WrDr 84*
Scott, John M 1913- *ConAu 10NR, -65, SmATA 12*
Scott, Johnie Harold 1946- *ConAu 33R*
Scott, Joseph 1917- *ConAu 57*
Scott, Joseph Reid 1926- *ConAu 41R*
Scott, Joseph Walter 1935- *LivgBAA*
Scott, Judith Unger 1916- *ConAu 5R*
Scott, Justin *ConAu 104*
Scott, Kenneth 1900- *ConAu 11NR, -69*
Scott, Lalla 1893- *ConAu P-2*
Scott, Latayne Colvett 1952- *ConAu 97*
Scott, Lauren *ConAu X*
Scott, Laurence Prestwich 1909-1983 *ConAu 110*
Scott, Lloyd *ConAu X*
Scott, Lloyd F 1926- *ConAu 21R*
Scott, Louise Binder 1908- *ConAu 1R*
Scott, Louise Binder 1910- *ConAu 4NR*
Scott, Marcia 1943- *ConAu 97*
Scott, Marco *IntAu&W 82X*
Scott, Margaret B d1976 *ConAu 61*
Scott, Margaret Daphne 1934- *IntWWP 82*
Scott, Martin *ConAu X*
Scott, Mel 1906- *ConAu 29R*
Scott, Michael 1907-1983 *ConAu 110*
Scott, Milward *WrDr 84*
Scott, Nancy *DrAP&F 83*
Scott, Natalie Anderson 1906- *ConAu P-2*
Scott, Nathan A, Jr. 1925- *ConAu 5NR, -9R, IntAu&W 82, LivgBAA, WrDr 84*
Scott, Nerissa *ConAu X*
Scott, Norford *ConAu X, TwCWW*
Scott, Otto J 1918- *ConAu 85*
Scott, P T *ConAu X*
Scott, Paul 1920-1978 *ConAu 77, -81, ConLC 9, ConNov 82A, DcLB 14[port], DcLEL 1940, WorAu*
Scott, Peter Dale 1929- *ConAu 9NR, -21R, DcLEL 1940*
Scott, Peter Markham 1909- *ConAu 101, IntAu&W 82, LongCTC*
Scott, R T M 1882- *TwCCr&M 80*
Scott, Rachel 1947- *ConAu 103*
Scott, Ralph S 1927- *ConAu 41R*
Scott, Richard A 1931- *ConAu 25R*

Scott, Robert A 1936- *ConAu 89*
Scott, Robert Adrian 1901?-1972 *ConAu 37R*
Scott, Robert E 1923- *ConAu 1R, -1NR*
Scott, Robert Haney 1927- *ConAu 17R*
Scott, Robert Ian 1931- *ConAu 106*
Scott, Robert Lee 1928- *ConAu 3NR, -5R*
Scott, Robert Lee, Jr. 1908- *ConAu P-1*
Scott, Robin *ConAu X*
Scott, Roger 1939- *ConAu 97*
Scott, Ronald Bodley 1906-1982 *ConAu 106, -109*
Scott, Roney *ConAu X*
Scott, Roy Vernon 1927- *ConAu 1R, -1NR, IntAu&W 82, WrDr 84*
Scott, Sheila 1927- *ConAu 53, WrDr 84*
Scott, Stanley *ConAu X*
Scott, Steve *ConAu X*
Scott, Stuart *ConAu X*
Scott, Tirsa Saavedra 1920- *ConAu 13R*
Scott, Titus *IntAu&W 82X*
Scott, Tom 1918- *ConAu 9R, ConP 80, WrDr 84*
Scott, Tony *SmATA X*
Scott, Vera E Austen 1908- *IntWWP 82*
Scott, Virgil Joseph 1914- *ConAu 2NR, -5R, IntAu&W 82, MichAu 80*
Scott, Virginia *DrAP&F 83*
Scott, W E, Jr. 1929- *ConAu 49*
Scott, W Richard 1932- *ConAu 17R*
Scott, Walter Sidney 1900- *IntAu&W 82*
Scott, Warwick *ConAu X, SmATA X, TwCCr&M 80, WrDr 84*
Scott, Willard H, Jr. 1934- *ConAu 109*
Scott, William Abbott 1926- *ConAu 5R, -9NR*
Scott, William G 1926- *ConAu 11NR, -21R*
Scott, William R 1907- *ConAu 77*
Scott, William R 1918- *ConAu 101*
Scott, Wilson L 1909- *ConAu 45*
Scott, Winfield H 1932- *ConAu 21R*
Scott, Winfield Townley 1910-1968 *ConAu 5R, -7NR, -25R, ModAL, ModAL SUP, TwCA SUP*
Scott-Giles, C W 1893-1982? *ConAu 106*
Scott-Heron, Gil 1949- *ConAu 45, LivgBAA*
Scott-James, Anne Eleanor 1913- *ConAu 105*
Scott-James, R A 1878-1959 *LongCTC*
Scott-Moncreiff, George 1910- *ConAu P-1*
Scott-Moncrieff, Charles Kenneth 1889-1930 *LongCTC, TwCA*
Scott Moncrieff, Martha Christian 1897- *ConAu 61, IntAu&W 82*
Scott Stokes, Henry J M 1918- *WrDr 84*
Scott-Taggart, John 1897-1979 *ConAu 104*
Scott Thomson, Gladys d1966 *LongCTC*
Scott Thorn, Ronald *ConAu X*
Scotto, Robert M 1942- *ConAu 57*
Scottsdale, Jone *IntAu&W 82X*
Scouten, Arthur H 1910- *WrDr 84*
Scouten, Arthur Hawley 1910- *ConAu 11NR, ConAu P-1*
Scovel, Myra *DrAP&F 83*
Scovel, Myra 1905- *ConAu 2NR, -5R, IntAu&W 82, IntWWP 82, WrDr 84*
Scovell, E J 1907- *ConP 80*
Scovell, E J 1915- *WrDr 84*
Scovell, Edith Joy 1907- *CnMWL, DcLEL 1940*
Scoville, Herbert, Jr. 1915- *ConAu 29R, IntAu&W 82, WrDr 84*
Scoville, James Griffin 1940- *ConAu 29R, WrDr 84*
Scoville, Warren Candler 1913-1969 *ConAu 1R, -2NR*
Scowcroft, Richard P 1916- *ConAu 9R*
Screech, M A 1926- *WrDr 84*
Scriabine, Helen 1906- *ConAu 21R*
Scribner, Charles, Jr. 1921- *ConAu 69, IntAu&W 82, SmATA 13*
Scribner, Joanne L 1949- *SmATA 33[port]*
Scribner, Lucille *IntWWP 82X*
Scribo *IntWWP 82X*
Scrimgeour, Gary J 1934- *ConAu 108*
Scrimgeour, James R *DrAP&F 83*
Scrimshaw, Nevin Stewart 1918- *ConAu 89*
Scrimsher, Lila Gravatt 1897-1974 *ConAu 1R, -103, SmATA 28N*
Scripps, E W 1854-1926 *DcLB 25[port]*
Scriven, Michael 1928- *ConAu 21R*
Scriven, R C *ConDr 82B*
Scrivner, Wilma Possien 1915- *ConAu 107*
Scroggie, Marcus Graham 1901- *WrDr 84*
Scroggins, Daniel C 1937- *ConAu 33R*
Scroggins, Daryl *DrAP&F 83*

Scrum, R ConAu X
Scrutator LongCTC
Scruton, Roger 1944- ConAu 89, IntAu&W 82,
    WrDr 84
Scudder, C W 1915- ConAu 1R, –3NR
Scudder, Kenyon J 1890-1977 ConAu 73
Scudder, Mildred Lee 1908- ConAu 9R
Scudder, Rogers V 1912- ConAu 17R
Scudder, Thayer 1930- ConAu 106
Scudder, Virgil Elmer 1936- ConAmTC
Sculatti, Gene 1947- ConAu 110
Scull, Andrew 1947- ConAu 81
Scull, Florence Doughty 1905- ConAu P-1,
    WrDr 84
Scullard, Howard Hayes 1903- ConAu 3NR, –9R,
    IntAu&W 82, WrDr 84
Scullard, Howard Hayes 1903-1983 ConAu 109
Scully, Anthony 1942- NatPD 81[port]
Scully, Frank 1892-1964 ConAu 5R
Scully, Gerald William 1941- ConAu 65
Scully, James DrAP&F 83
Scully, James 1937- ConAu 11NR, –25R,
    ConP 80, DcLEL 1940, WrDr 84
Scully, Julia S 1929- ConAu 103
Scum ConAu X
Scumbag, Little Bobby ConAu X
Scuorzo, Herbert E 1928- ConAu 21R
Scupham, John Peter 1933- ConAu 9NR, –65,
    IntAu&W 82
Scupham, Peter 1933- ConP 80, WrDr 84
Scuro, Vincent 1951- ConAu 5NR, –53,
    SmATA 21
Scutt, Ronald 1916- ConAu 97, IntAu&W 82
Sea-Lion ConAu X, WrDr 84
Sea-Lion 1909- ConAu X, IntAu&W 82X
Seaberg, Stanley 1929- ConAu 21R
Seaberg, Glenn Theodore 1912- ConAu 2NR,
    –49
Seabough, Ed 1932- ConAu 29R
Seabright, Idris IntAu&W 82X
Seabrook, Jeremy 1939- ConAu 108, ConDr 82,
    WrDr 84
Seabrook, William Buehler 1886-1945
    ConAu 107, DcLB 4, TwCA, TwCA SUP
Seabrooke, Brenda 1941- ConAu 107,
    SmATA 30[port]
Seabury, Paul 1923- WrDr 84
Seagears, Clayton B 1902?-1983 ConAu 110
Seager, Allan 1906-1968 ConAu 5R, –25R,
    MichAu 80, TwCA SUP
Seager, Ralph W DrAP&F 83
Seager, Ralph William 1911- ConAu 6NR, –9R,
    IntAu&W 82, IntWWP 82, WrDr 84
Seager, Robert, II 1924- ConAu 5R, –6NR
Seagle, Janet 1924- ConAu 102
Seagle, William 1898-1977 ConAu 5R, –73, –77
Seagoe, May V 1906- ConAu 13R
Seagoe, May V 1906-1980 ConAu 10NR
Seagrave, Barbara Ann Garvey WrDr 84
Seagroatt, Margaret 1920- ConAu 73
Seal, Anil 1938- ConAu 25R
Seale, Bobby ConAu X, LivgBAA
Seale, Jan Epton DrAP&F 83
Seale, Patrick 1930- ConAu 97
Seale, Robert George 1936- ConAu 110
Seale, Sara TwCRGW, WrDr 84
Seale, William 1939- ConAu 7NR, –17R,
    WrDr 84
Sealey, Danguole 1931- ConAu 33R
Sealey, Leonard 1923- WrDr 84
Sealey, Leonard George William 1923-
    ConAu 103
Sealey, Raphael 1927- ConAu 65
Sealock, Richard Burl 1907- ConAu P-2
Sealts, Merton M, Jr. 1915- ConAu 13R,
    WrDr 84
Sealts, Morton M, Jr. 1915- IntAu&W 82
Seaman, Augusta Huiell 1879-1950 ConAu 110,
    SmATA 31[port]
Seaman, Barbara Ann 1935- ConAu 29R
Seaman, Barrett 1945- ConAu 73
Seaman, Don F 1935- ConAu 77
Seaman, Gerald Roberts 1934- ConAu 25R,
    IntAu&W 82, WrDr 84
Seaman, John E 1932- ConAu 89
Seaman, L C B 1911- ConAu 57
Seaman, Lewis Charles Bernard 1911-
    IntAu&W 82
Seaman, Sir Owen 1861-1936 LongCTC, TwCA,
    TwCA SUP
Seaman, Sylvia Sybil 1910- ConAu P-2,
    WrDr 84

Seaman, William M 1907- ConAu 41R
Seamands, John Thompson 1916- ConAu 9R
Seamands, Ruth 1916- ConAu 45, SmATA 9
Seamonds, Gainal Tucker 1912- IntWWP 82
Seara Vazquez, M 1931- ConAu 17R
Search, Alexander WorAu 1970
Search-Light ConAmA, ConAu X
Searcy, Margaret Zehmer 1926- ConAu 81
Seare, Nicholas ConAu X, WrDr 84
Searight, Mary W 1918- ConAu 29R,
    SmATA 17
Searle, Graham William 1937- WrDr 84
Searle, Humphrey 1915-1982 ConAu 9R, –106,
    IntAu&W 82
Searle, John Rogers 1932- ConAu 25R,
    IntAu&W 82
Searle, Kathryn Adrienne 1942- ConAu 29R,
    SmATA 10
Searle, Leroy F 1942- ConAu 73
Searle, Ronald 1920- ConAu 9R, DcLEL 1940,
    WrDr 84
Searles, Herbert L 1891- ConAu 45
Searls, Hank 1922- ConAu X, TwCSFW,
    WrDr 84
Searls, Henry Hunt, Jr. 1922- ConAu 13R
Sears, David O 1935- WrDr 84
Sears, David O'Keefe 1935- ConAu 29R,
    IntAu&W 82
Sears, Deane ConAu X
Sears, Donald A DrAP&F 83
Sears, Donald A 1923- ConAu 5R, –6NR
Sears, Francis W 1898-1975 ConAu 61
Sears, Paul Bigelow 1891- ConAu 17R
Sears, Paul M 1920- ConAu 1R
Sears, Pauline Snedden 1908- ConAu 29R
Sears, Peter DrAP&F 83
Sears, Peter 1937- ConAu 110
Sears, Robert Richardson 1908- ConAu 17R
Sears, Sallie 1932- ConAu 41R
Sears, Stephen W 1932- ConAu 33R,
    SmATA 4
Sears, Val 1927- ConAu 73
Sears, William P, Jr. 1902-1976 ConAu 61
Seary, E R 1908- ConAu 41R
Seary, Edgar Ronald 1908- WrDr 84
Seashore, Stanley E 1915- ConAu 33R
Seasoltz, R Kevin 1930- ConAu 9R
Seasongood, Murray 1878-1983 ConAu 109
Seat, William Robert 1920- ConAu 13R
Seaton, Beryl ConAu X, IntAu&W 82X
Seaton, Don Cash 1902- ConAu P-1
Seaton, Douglas P 1947- ConAu 107
Seaton, Esta DrAP&F 83
Seaton, Frederick Andrew 1909-1974 ConAu 89
Seaton, George 1911-1979 ConAu 105, –89
Seaton, Mary Ethel d1974 ConAu 53
Seaton, Peter DrAP&F 83
Seator, Lynette Hubbard DrAP&F 83
Seaver, Edwin 1900- TwCA, TwCA SUP
Seaver, George 1890- ConAu P-1
Seaver, Paul Siddall 1932- ConAu 29R
Seawell, Molly Elliot 1860-1916 TwCA
Seay, James DrAP&F 83
Seay, James 1939- ConAu 29R
Seay, Thomas A 1942- ConAu 97
Sebald, Hans 1929- ConAu 73
Sebald, William J 1901-1980 ConAu 101,
    ConAu P-1
Sebastian, Jeanne ConAu X
Sebastian, Lee ConAu X, SmATA X,
    WorAu 1970, WrDr 84
Sebastian, Margaret ConAu X
Sebenthall, R E 1917- ConAu 33R
Sebeok, Thomas A 1920- ConAu 9R,
    IntAu&W 82, WrDr 84
Seberg, Jean 1938-1979 ConAu 89
Sebesta, Sam L 1930- ConAu 85
Sebestyen, Gyorgy 1930- ConAu 6NR, –9R
Sebestyen, Ouida 1924- ConAu 107, WrDr 84
Sebley, Frances Rae WrDr 84
Seboldt, Roland H A 1924- ConAu 5R
Sec WorAu
Seccombe, Thomas 1866-1923 LongCTC
Secher, Bjorn 1929- ConAu 33R
Sechrest, Lee 1929- ConAu 17R
Sechrist, Elizabeth Hough 1903- ConAu 5R,
    SmATA 2
Secombe, Harry Donald 1921- ConAu 57,
    IntAu&W 82
Secondari, John Hermes 1919-1975 ConAu 57,
    –61
Secor, Robert 1939- ConAu 89

Secrest, Meryle ConAu X
Secrist, Margaret C 1905- MichAu 80
Secter, David 1943- CreCan 2
Secunda, Sholom 1894-1974 ConAu 49
Sedaka, Neil 1939- ConAu 103
Seddon, Alexandra Mary 1944- IntWWP 82
Seddon, Richard Harding 1915- IntAu&W 82
Sederberg, Arelo 1931- WrDr 84
Sederberg, Arelo Charles 1930- ConAu 37R
Sederberg, Peter C 1943- ConAu 65
Sedges, John ConAu X, SmATA X
Sedgewick, Ellery 1872-1960 ConAu 89
Sedgwick, Alexander 1930- ConAu 17R
Sedgwick, Anne Douglas 1873-1935 ConAmA,
    LongCTC, TwCA, TwCA SUP
Sedgwick, Michael 1926- ConAu 89, WrDr 84
Sedgwick, Peter 1934-1983 ConAu 110
Sedgwick, Walter 1885- ConAu P-1
Sedlacek, William E 1939- ConAu 69
Sedlak, John 1942- NatPD 81[port]
Sedler, Robert Allen 1935- ConAu 41R
Seduro, Vladimir Ilyich 1910- ConAu 41R,
    IntAu&W 82
Sedwick, B Frank 1924- ConAu 9R
Sedwick, Frank 1924- WrDr 84
Sedych, Andrei ConAu X
See, Carolyn DrAP&F 83
See, Carolyn 1934- ConAu 29R, IntAu&W 82,
    WrDr 84
See, Ruth Douglas 1910- ConAu 1R, –1NR
Seeber, Edward Derbyshire 1904- ConAu 13R
Seeberg, Peter 1925- CIDMEL 80,
    IntAu&W 82
Seebohm, Caroline 1940- ConAu 102
Seebord, G R ConAu X
Seed, Cecile Eugenie 1930- ConAu 10NR
Seed, Jenny ConAu X
Seed, Jenny 1930- ConAu 21R, SmATA 8,
    TwCCW 83, WrDr 84
Seed, Sheila Turner 1937?-1979 ConAu 89,
    SmATA 23N
Seeger, Alan 1888-1916 LongCTC, TwCA,
    TwCWr
Seeger, Charles Louis 1886-1979 ConAu 101, –85
Seeger, Elizabeth 1889-1973 ConAu 45,
    SmATA 20N
Seeger, Pete 1919- ConAu 69, SmATA 13
Seeger, Robert S 1941- IntAu&W 82
Seegers, Kathleen Walker 1915- ConAu 21R
Seeley, Ivor Hugh 1924- IntAu&W 82,
    WrDr 84
Seeley, John R 1913- ConAu 25R
Seeley, Mabel 1903- TwCA SUP,
    TwCCr&M 80
Seelhammer, Ruth 1917- ConAu 41R
Seely, Gordon M 1930- ConAu 37R
Seely, Rebecca Z 1935- ConAu 104
Seelye, H Ned 1934- ConAu 102
Seelye, John 1931- ConAu 97, ConLC 7,
    TwCWW, WrDr 84
Seeman, Bernard 1911- ConAu 21R
Seeman, Elizabeth 1904- ConAu P-1
Seeman, Ernest Albright 1887- ConAu 85
Seers, Dudley 1920- WrDr 84
Seers, Dudley 1920-1983 ConAu 109
Seerval, Hormasji Maneckji 1906- IntAu&W 82
Seery, Janet DrAP&F 83
Seese, Ethel Gray 1903- ConAu 89,
    IntWWP 82, MichAu 80
Seever, R ConAu X, SmATA X
Seferiades, Giorgos Stylianou 1900-1971
    ConAu 5R, –5NR, –33R, ConLC 11
Seferis, George 1900-1971 CIDMEL 80,
    CnMWL, ConAu X, ConLC 5, –11,
    WhoTwCL, WorAu
Seferis, Giorgos 1900-1971 TwCWr
Seff, Richard 1927- NatPD 81[port]
Sefler, George Francis 1945- ConAu 81
Sefton, Catherine 1941- TwCCW 83
Sefton, James E 1939- ConAu 21R
Segal, Abraham 1911?-1977 ConAu 69
Segal, Charles Paul 1936- ConAu 41R
Segal, David I 1928?-1970 ConAu 104
Segal, Edith DrAP&F 83
Segal, Elliot A 1938- ConAu 93
Segal, Erich 1937- ASpks, ConAu 25R,
    ConLC 3, –10, IntAu&W 82, WrDr 84
Segal, Fred 1924?-1976 ConAu 65, –69
Segal, Hanna M 1918- ConAu 101
Segal, Harold S 1903- ConAu 29R, WrDr 84
Segal, Harvey H 1922- ConAu 1R
Segal, Helen Gertrude 1929- WrDr 84

Sen Gupta, Rajeswar 1908- *ConAu P-1, WrDr 84*
Sen Gupta, Subodh Chandra 1903- *IntAu&W 82*
Sena, John F 1940- *ConAu 110*
Sena, Jorge De 1919-1978 *CIDMEL 80*
Sena Medina, Guillermo 1944- *IntAu&W 82*
Senarens, Luis P 1865-1939 *TwCSFW*
Sencourt, Robert Esmonde 1890-1969 *ConAu X*
Sendak, Jack *ConAu 77, SmATA 28[port]*
Sendak, Maurice 1928- *ChlLR 1, ConAu 5R, -11NR, SmATA 1, -27[port], TwCCW 83, WrDr 84*
Sender, Ramon Jose 1901- *ModRL*
Sender, Ramon Jose 1902-1982 *CIDMEL 80, ConAu 5R, -8NR, -105, ConLC 8, TwCA, TwCA SUP, TwCWr*
Sendler, David A 1938- *ConAu 65*
Sendrey, A Alfred 1884- *ConAu 13R*
Sendy, Jean 1910- *ConAu 53*
Senekal, Johannes Hendrik 1929- *IntAu&W 82*
Senelick, Laurence P 1942- *ConAu 106*
Senesi, Mauro 1931- *ConAu 17R*
Seng, Peter J 1922- *ConAu 17R*
Senghor, Leopold Sedar 1906- *CIDMEL 80, IntWWP 82, ModBlW, ModFrL, TwCWr, WhoTwCL, WorAu*
Sengler, Johanna 1924- *SmATA 18*
Sengstacke, John Herman Henry 1912- *ConAu 101*
Senick, Gerard J 1953- *ConAu 97*
Senior, Clarence 1903-1974 *ConAu 53, -65*
Senior, Donald 1940- *ConAu 77*
Senior, Isabel J *ConAu 9NR*
Senior, Isabel J C Syme *ConAu 5R*
Senior, Michael 1940- *ConAu 103, WrDr 84*
Senkevitch, Anatole, Jr. 1942- *ConAu 101*
Senn, Fritz 1928- *ConAu 41R*
Senn, Milton J E 1902- *ConAu 81*
Senn, Peter R 1923- *ConAu 33R*
Senn, Steve 1950- *ConAu 105*
Senna, Carl *DrAP&F 83*
Senna, Carl 1944- *ConAu 4NR, -49*
Senna, Carl Francois Jose 1944- *IntWWP 82*
Sennachie *IntAu&W 82X*
Sennett, John *DrAP&F 83*
Sennett, John Patrick Joseph 1952- *IntWWP 82*
Sennett, Richard 1943- *ConAu 73, IntAu&W 82, WrDr 84*
Sennett, Ted 1928- *ConAu 33R*
Sens, Al 1933- *CreCan 1*
Sensabaugh, George Frank 1906- *ConAu P-1*
Senser, Robert A 1921- *ConAu 5R*
Senter, Florence H *ConAu X*
Sentner, David P 1898-1975 *ConAu 57*
Sentner, Mary Steele 1900?-1983 *ConAu 110*
Seoane, Rhoda 1905- *ConAu P-2*
Sepetys, Jonas 1901- *ConAu 57*
Sepheriades, Georgios Stylianou *ConAu X, WorAu*
Sepia *ConAu X*
Sequoia, Anna *ConAu 109*
Serafian, Michael *ConAu X*
Serafimovich, Aleksandr 1863-1949 *CIDMEL 80, ModSL 1, TwCWr*
Serage, Nancy 1924- *ConAu 65, SmATA 10*
Seraillier, Ian Lucien 1912- *DcLEL 1940*
Serao, Matilde 1856-1927 *CIDMEL 80*
Serb, Ann Toland 1937- *ConAu 81*
Serban, William M 1949- *ConAu 102*
Serchuk, Peter *DrAP&F 83*
Serebryakova, Galina Iosifovna 1905-1980 *ConAu 102*
Seredy, Kate 1899?-1975 *ConAu 5R, -57, DcLB 22[port], SmATA 1, -24N, TwCCW 83*
Sereni, Vittorio 1913- *CIDMEL 80, WorAu 1970*
Sereni, Vittorio 1913-1983 *ConAu 109*
Sereny, Marika Robert *CreCan 1*
Serenyi, Peter 1931- *ConAu 61, IntAu&W 82*
Serfaty, Simon 1940- *ConAu 10NR, -25R*
Serge, Victor 1890-1947 *TwCA SUP*
Sergeant, Howard 1914- *ConAu 5R, -5NR, ConP 80, IntAu&W 82, WrDr 84*
Sergeyev-Tsensky, Sergey Nikolayevich 1875-1958 *CIDMEL 80*
Serghi, Cella *IntAu&W 82X*
Serghi Bogdan, Cella 1907- *IntAu&W 82*
Sergio, Antonio 1883-1969 *CIDMEL 80*
Sergio, Lisa 1905- *ConAu 61*
Seriel, Jerome *ConAu X*
Serif, Med 1924- *ConAu 17R*

Serig, Beverly J 1934- *ConAu 101*
Serin, Judith *DrAP&F 83*
Sering, Paul *IntAu&W 82X*
Serjeant, Richard *IntAu&W 82X, WrDr 84*
Serle, Alan Geoffrey 1922- *IntAu&W 82, WrDr 84*
Serle, Geoffrey 1922- *ConAu 13R*
Serlen, Bruce 1947- *NatPD 81[port]*
Serling, Robert 1918- *ConAu 1NR, -45, WrDr 84*
Serling, Rod 1924-1975 *AuNews 1, ConAu 57, -65, DcLB 26[port], TwCSFW*
Serna, Concha Espina De *ModRL*
Serna, Espina De *TwCA, TwCA SUP*
Serna, Ramon Gomez DeLa 1888- *ModRL, TwCA, TwCA SUP*
Serna-Maytorena, M A 1932- *ConAu 45*
Serna-Maytorena, Manuel Antonio 1932- *ConAu 3NR*
Sernett, Milton C 1942- *ConAu 61*
Seroff, Victor I 1902-1979 *ConAu 25R, -85, SmATA 12, -26N*
Serpieres *ConAu X*
Serra, Diana *ConAu X*
Serra, Renato 1884-1915 *CIDMEL 80*
Serrahima I Bofill, Maurici 1902- *CIDMEL 80*
Serraillier, Ian 1912- *TwCCW 83, WrDr 84*
Serraillier, Ian Lucien 1912- *ChlLR 2, ConAu 1R, -1NR, SmATA 1*
Serrano, Napoleon Diestro Valeriano *ConAu X*
Serrano, Nina *DrAP&F 83*
Serrano, Pio E 1941- *IntAu&W 82*
Serrano Plaja, Arturo 1909- *ConAu 29R*
Serrano Poncela, Segundo 1912-1976 *CIDMEL 80*
Serrano Suner, Ramon 1901- *IntAu&W 82*
Serres, Marthe Des *CreCan 2*
Serrifile, F O O *ConAu X*
Serron, Luis A 1930- *ConAu 102*
Sert, Josep Lluis 1902-1983 *ConAu 109*
Serumaga, Robert 1939- *DcLEL 1940*
Servadio, Gaia 1938- *ConAu 11NR, -25R, WrDr 84*
Servadio, Gaia Cecilia *IntAu&W 82*
Servadio, Gaio *ConAu X*
Servais, Jean M A E A 1902- *IntAu&W 82*
Servan-Schreiber, Jean-Jacques 1924- *ConAu 102*
Servello, Joe 1932- *SmATA 10*
Serventy, Vincent *ConAu 10NR*
Serventy, Vincent Noel *ConAu 65, IntAu&W 82, WrDr 84*
Service, Robert William 1874?-1958 *CreCan 1, LongCTC, SmATA 20, TwCA, TwCA SUP, TwCWr*
Servien, Louis-Marc 1934- *IntAu&W 82*
Servin, Manuel Patricio 1920- *ConAu 37R*
Serviss, Garrett Putnam 1851-1929 *TwCSFW*
Servolini, Luigi 1906- *IntAu&W 82*
Serwadda, W Moses 1931- *ConAu 107*
Serwadda, William Moses 1931- *SmATA 27[port]*
Serwer, Blanche L 1910- *ConAu 65, SmATA 10*
Serwicher, Kurt 1912-1979 *ConAu 89*
Serwicher, Kurt 1912-1979 *ConAu 89*
Sesha Charlu, Sreenivasapuram 1921- *IntAu&W 82*
Seshadri, Krishna *IntWWP 82X*
Seskin, Eugene P 1948- *ConAu 89*
Sesonske, Alexander 1917- *ConAu 13R*
Sessions, Kyle Cutler 1934- *ConAu 106*
Sessions, Roger Huntington 1896- *ConAu 93*
Sessions, Will 1905- *ConAu 1R*
Sessoms, H Douglas 1931- *ConAu 41R*
Seth, Ronald 1911- *ConAu 106*
Seth-Smith, Elsie K *ConAu X*
Seth-Smith, Leslie James *WrDr 84*
Seth-Smith, Leslie James 1923- *ConAu 104*
Seth-Smith, Michael 1928- *ConAu 29R, IntAu&W 82, WrDr 84*
Sethi, Narendra Kumar 1935- *ConAu 37R, WrDr 84*
Sethi, S Prakash 1934- *ConAu 41R*
Sethna, Jehangir Minocher 1941- *ConAu 37R*
Sethna, M J 1911- *WrDr 84*
Sethna, Minocher Jehangirji 1911- *ConAu 9R, IntAu&W 82*
Sethuraman, Vaal Muthu 1935- *IntWWP 82*
Seton, Anya *WrDr 84*
Seton, Anya 1916- *ConAu 17R, IntAu&W 82, LongCTC, SmATA 3, TwCA SUP, TwCRGW*
Seton, Cynthia Propper 1926- *ConAu 5R, -7NR*

Seton, Cynthia Propper 1926-1982 *ConAu 108, ConLC 27[port]*
Seton, Ernest Thompson 1860-1946 *ConAu 109, CreCan 2, LongCTC, SmATA 18, TwCA, TwCA SUP, TwCCW 83, TwCWr*
Seton, Julia *IntAu&W 82*
Seton, Marie 1910- *ConAu 105*
Seton-Thompson, Ernest *ConAu X*
Seton-Thompson, Ernest 1860-1946 *CreCan 2*
Seton-Watson, Christopher 1918- *ConAu 11NR, -21R*
Seton-Watson, George Hugh Nicholas 1916- *WorAu*
Settel, Gertrude S 1919- *ConAu 17R*
Settel, Irving 1916- *ConAu 17R*
Settel, Trudy *ConAu X*
Setterberg, Ruth Elizabeth *IntWWP 82*
Settle, Alison 1891- *IntAu&W 82*
Settle, Edith *ConAu X*
Settle, Mary Lee *DrAP&F 83*
Settle, Mary Lee 1918- *ConAu 89, ConLC 19, DcLB 6[port], WorAu*
Setton, Kenneth M 1914- *ConAu 3NR, -9R*
Setzekorn, William David 1935- *ConAu 65*
Setzler, Frank M 1902-1975 *ConAu 57*
Seufert, Karl Rolf 1923- *ConAu 9R*
Seuling, Barbara 1937- *ConAu 8NR, -61, SmATA 10*
Seung, Thomas Kaehao 1930- *ConAu 108*
Seuphor, Michel *ConAu X*
Seuren, Pieter A M 1934- *ConAu 49*
Seuss, Dr. 1904- *SmATA X, TwCA, TwCA SUP, TwCCW 83, WrDr 84*
Sevareid, Eric 1912- *AuNews 1, ConAu 69*
Seveilhac, Pauline Lightstone *CreCan 1*
Sevela, Efraim 1928- *ConAu 69*
Severin, Mark 1906- *ConAu 107*
Severin, Tim 1940- *IntAu&W 82*
Severin, Timothy 1940- *ConAu 10NR, -21R, WrDr 84*
Severino, Alexandrino E 1931- *ConAu 41R*
Severn, Bill 1914- *ConAu X, SmATA 1*
Severn, David *WrDr 84*
Severn, David 1918- *ConAu X, IntAu&W 82X, SmATA X, TwCCW 83*
Severn, Sue 1918- *ConAu 5R*
Severn, William Irving 1914- *ConAu 1R, -1NR, SmATA 1*
Severo, Richard 1932- *ConAu 73*
Severs, Jerome *ConAu X*
Severs, Vesta-Nadine 1935- *ConAu 89*
Severson, John H 1933- *ConAu 13R*
Severy, Bruce W *DrAP&F 83*
Severyanin, Igor 1887-1941 *CIDMEL 80*
Sewalk, Kathleen M *DrAP&F 83*
Sewall, Marcia 1935- *ConAu 1NR, -45*
Sewall, Mary Franklin 1884- *ConAu P-2*
Sewall, Richard B 1908- *ConAu 93*
Seward, Jack *ConAu X*
Seward, James H 1928- *ConAu 65*
Seward, John Neil 1924- *ConAu 8NR, -21R*
Seward, Prudence 1926- *SmATA 16*
Seward, William W, Jr. 1913- *ConAu 9R, IntAu&W 82, WrDr 84*
Sewart, Alan 1928- *ConAu 108*
Sewel, John 1946- *ConAu 103*
Sewell, Anna 1820-1878 *SmATA 24[port]*
Sewell, Brocard 1912- *ConAu 107, WrDr 84*
Sewell, Elizabeth *DrAP&F 83*
Sewell, Elizabeth 1919- *ConAu 49, IntWWP 82, WorAu*
Sewell, Helen 1896-1957 *TwCCW 83*
Sewell, J Leslie 1923- *ConAu 21R*
Sewell, James Patrick 1930- *ConAu 73*
Sewell, W R Derrick 1931- *ConAu 9NR, -21R*
Sewell, William 1909- *WrDr 84*
Sewell, William H 1909- *ConAu 45*
Sewell, Winifred 1917- *ConAu 102*
Sewny, Kathryn Wiehe 1909- *ConAu P-1*
Sewter, Albert Charles 1912- *ConAu 89*
Sexauer, Arwin F B Garellick 1921- *IntWWP 82*
Sexton, A Jeanette 1924- *ConAu 65*
Sexton, Anne Harvey 1928-1974 *ConAu 1R, -3NR, -53, ConLC 2, -4, -6, -8, -10, -15, ConP 80A, CroCAP, DcLB 5[port], DcLEL 1940, ModAL, ModAL SUP, SmATA 10, WhoTwCL, WorAu*
Sexton, Linda Gray 1953- *ConAu 101, WrDr 84*
Sexton, Michael J 1939- *ConAu 45*

Sexton, Richard J 1912- *ConAu 45*, *WrDr 84*
Sexton, Thomas F *DrAP&F 83*
Sexton, Virgil Wesley 1918- *ConAu 33R*, *WrDr 84*
Sexton, Virginia Staudt 1916- *ConAu 29R*, *IntAu&W 82*, *WrDr 84*
Sexton, Wendell P *DrAP&F 83*
Seybolt, Peter J 1934- *ConAu 53*
Seydel, Mildred *ConAu 37R*
Seydell, Mildred *ConAu X*
Seydor, Paul 1947- *ConAu 97*
Seyersted, Per *ConAu 29R*, *WrDr 84*
Seyfert, Carl K 1938- *ConAu 57*
Seyfullina, Lidiya Nikolayevna 1889-1954 *CIDMEL 80*
Seyler, Dorothy U 1938- *ConAu 109*
Seymour *IntAu&W 82X*
Seymour, A J 1914- *ConAu 97*, *ConP 80*
Seymour, Alan 1927- *ConAu 53*, *ConDr 82*, *TwCSFW*, *TwCWr*, *WrDr 84*
Seymour, Alta Halverson *ConAu P-1*, *SmATA 10*
Seymour, Arthur J 1914- *WrDr 84*
Seymour, Beatrice Kean d1955 *LongCTC*, *TwCA*, *TwCA SUP*
Seymour, Charles, Jr. 1912-1977 *ConAu 9R*, *-69*
Seymour, Digby G 1923- *ConAu 17R*
Seymour, Dorothy Jane Z 1928- *ConAu 89*
Seymour, Edward *IntAu&W 82X*
Seymour, Emery W 1921- *ConAu 13R*
Seymour, Gerald 1941- *ConAu 101*, *WrDr 84*
Seymour, Henry 1931- *ConAu X*, *IntAu&W 82*, *WrDr 84*
Seymour, John 1914- *ConAu 9NR*, *-13R*
Seymour, Kayla *IntAu&W 82X*, *IntWWP 82X*
Seymour, Lynn 1939- *CreCan 2*
Seymour, Miranda Jane 1948- *ConAu X*, *WrDr 84*
Seymour, Raymond B 1912- *ConAu 73*
Seymour, Rogers James 1942- *ConAu 110*
Seymour, Stephan A 1920- *ConAu 21R*
Seymour, W Douglas 1910- *ConAu 49*
Seymour, Whitney North, Jr. 1923- *ConAu 81*
Seymour, William Kean 1887- *ConAu 9R*, *LongCTC*
Seymour, William Napier 1914- *ConAu 77*
Seymour-Smith, Martin 1928- *ConAu 5R*, *ConP 80*, *DcLEL 1940*, *IntAu&W 82*, *WorAu 1970*, *WrDr 84*
Seymour-Ure, Colin K 1938- *ConAu 25R*
Seyton, Marion *ConAu X*
Seznec, Jean J 1905- *IntAu&W 82*
Sgarlato, Nico 1944- *IntAu&W 82*
Sgroi, Peter Philip 1936- *ConAu 57*
Sgroi, Suzanne M 1943- *ConAu 108*
Sh, Shoshana *IntWWP 82X*
Sh Sh Sh *IntWWP 82X*
Shaara, Michael *AuNews 1*
Shaara, Michael 1928- *ConLC 15*
Shaara, Michael 1929- *ConAu 102*, *DcLB Y83B[port]*, *WrDr 84*
Shabad, Theodore 1922- *ConAu 10NR*, *-25R*
Shachtman, Tom 1942- *ConAu 89*
Shackelford, Jean 1946- *ConAu 105*
Shacket, Sheldon R 1941- *ConAu 102*
Shackford, Martha Hale 1875-1963 *ConAu 1R*
Shackford, R H 1908- *ConAu 1R*
Shackle, G L S 1903- *ConAu 2NR*
Shackle, George Lennox Sharman 1903- *ConAu 5R*, *WrDr 84*
Shackleford, Bernard L 1889-1975 *ConAu P-2*
Shackleford, Ruby Paschall 1913- *ConAu 57*, *IntWWP 82*
Shackleton, Baron 1911- *WrDr 84*
Shackleton, Bert *IntWWP 82X*
Shackleton, C C *ConAu X*, *SmATA X*
Shackleton, Doris 1918- *ConAu 93*
Shackleton, Edward Arthur Alexander 1911- *ConAu 13R*, *IntAu&W 82*
Shackleton, Sir Ernest Henry 1874-1922 *LongCTC*
Shackleton, Herbert 1916- *IntWWP 82*
Shackleton, Keith 1923- *WrDr 84*
Shackleton, Keith Hope 1923- *ConAu 5R*
Shackleton, Philip 1923- *ConAu 101*
Shackleton, Robert 1919- *ConAu 1R*, *IntAu&W 82*, *WrDr 84*
Shackleton Bailey, D R *ConAu X*
Shacochis, Bob *DrAP&F 83*
Shadbolt, Jack Leonard 1909- *CreCan 2*
Shadbolt, Maurice 1932- *WrDr 84*

Shadbolt, Maurice Francis Richard 1932- *ConAu 5NR*, *-13R*, *ConNov 82*, *DcLEL 1940*, *IntAu&W 82*, *ModCmwL*, *TwCWr*, *WorAu*
Shade, Rose 1927- *ConAu 57*
Shade, William G 1939- *ConAu 41R*
Shadegg, Stephen C 1909- *ConAu 13R*
Shadi, Dorothy Clotelle Clarke 1908- *ConAu 13R*
Shadick, Harold 1902- *ConAu 41R*
Shadily, Hassan 1920- *ConAu 105*
Shadoian, Jack 1940- *ConAu 105*
Shadow, Slim *ConAu X*
Shadowitz, Albert 1915- *ConAu 69*
Shaevitz, Marjorie Hansen 1943- *ConAu 101*
Shaevitz, Morton H 1935- *ConAu 102*
Shafarevich, Igor Rostislavovich 1923- *ConAu 105*
Shafer, Boyd Carlisle 1907- *ConAu 17R*
Shafer, Elizabeth Jane 1924- *IntWWP 82*
Shafer, Neil 1933- *ConAu 33R*, *WrDr 84*
Shafer, Robert 1925- *WrDr 84*
Shafer, Robert E 1925- *ConAu 10NR*, *-57*, *SmATA 9*
Shafer, Robert Jones 1915- *IntAu&W 82*
Shafer, Robert Jones 1920- *ConAu 37R*
Shafer, Ronald G 1939- *ConAu 10NR*, *-65*
Shaff, Albert L 1937- *ConAu 29R*
Shaffer, Anthony 1926- *ConAu 110*, *ConDr 82*, *ConLC 19*, *DcLB 13[port]*, *DcLEL 1940*, *TwCCr&M 80*, *WrDr 84*
Shaffer, Dale Eugene 1929- *ConAu 37R*, *IntAu&W 82*, *WrDr 84*
Shaffer, Harry G 1919- *WrDr 84*
Shaffer, Harry George 1919- *ConAu 5R*, *-6NR*
Shaffer, Helen B 1909?-1978 *ConAu 81*, *-85*
Shaffer, Jerome Arthur 1929- *ConAu 37R*, *WrDr 84*
Shaffer, K Stevenson 1902- *ConAu P-2*
Shaffer, Kenneth R 1914- *WrDr 84*
Shaffer, Kenneth Raymond 1914- *ConAu 5R*
Shaffer, Laurance Frederic 1903-1976 *ConAu 65*
Shaffer, Olive Charlotte 1896- *IntWWP 82*
Shaffer, Peter 1926- *CnMD*, *ConAu 25R*, *ConDr 82*, *ConLC 5*, *-14*, *-18*, *CroCD*, *DcLB 13[port]*, *DcLEL 1940*, *ModBrL SUP*, *ModWD*, *TwCCr&M 80*, *TwCWr*, *WorAu*, *WrDr 84*
Shaffer, Samuel 1910- *ConAu 104*
Shaffer, Thomas Lindsay 1934- *ConAu 37R*, *IntAu&W 82*
Shaffer, Wilma L 1916- *ConAu 17R*
Shaftel, Oscar 1912- *ConAu 57*
Shaftner, Dorothy 1918- *ConAu 25R*
Shagan, Steve 1927- *ConAu 6NR*, *-53*, *WrDr 84*
Shaginyan, Marietta Sergeyevna 1888-1982 *CIDMEL 80*, *ConAu 106*
Shah, A M 1931- *ConAu 73*
Shah, Amina 1918- *ConAu 49*
Shah, Diane K 1945- *ConAu 73*
Shah, Idries 1924- *ConAu 7NR*, *-17R*, *IntAu&W 82*, *IntWWP 82*, *WrDr 84*
Shah, Krishna B 1938- *ConAu 17R*
Shah, Rajendra Keshavlal 1913- *IntWWP 82*
Shah Of Iran *ConAu X*
Shaha, Akshaya Kumar 1900- *IntAu&W 82*
Shaha, Rishikesh 1925- *ConAu 69*
Shahabuddin, Fazal 1936- *IntWWP 82*
Shahan, Lynn 1941- *ConAu 106*
Shahane, Vasant A 1923- *WrDr 84*
Shahane, Vasant Anant 1923- *ConAu 25R*, *DcLEL 1940*, *IntAu&W 82*
Shahani, Ranjee 1904-1968 *ConAu 1R*, *-2NR*
Shahar, David 1926- *ConAu 65*
Shaheen, Naseeb 1931- *ConAu 65*
Shahn, Ben 1898-1969 *ConAu 89*, *SmATA 21N*
Shahn, Bernarda Bryson *ConAu X*, *SmATA X*
Shain, Henry 1941- *ConAu 57*
Shain, Merle 1935- *AuNews 1*, *ConAu 61*
Shain, Richard 1948- *WrDr 84*
Shainmark, Eliezer L 1900-1976 *ConAu 104*
Shainmark, Lou *ConAu X*
Shairp, Mordaunt 1887-1939 *ConAu 110*, *DcLB 10*, *ModWD*
Shakabpa, Tsepon W D 1907- *ConAu P-2*
Shakdany, Yehuda 1904- *IntAu&W 82*
Sha'Ked, Ami 1945- *ConAu 101*
Shakely, Lauren *DrAP&F 83*
Shakesby, Paul S 1946- *ConAu 57*
Shakespeare, Geoffrey 1893-1980 *ConAu 105*
Shakey, Bernard *ConAu X*
Shakow, David 1901-1981 *ConAu 108*

Shalamov, Varlam 1907-1982 *CIDMEL 80*, *ConAu 105*, *ConLC 18*
Shale, Richard 1947- *ConAu 89*
Shales, Thomas William 1948- *ConAu 110*
Shales, Tom *ConAu X*
Shalev-Toren, Puah 1930- *IntWWP 82*
Shalhope, Robert E 1941- *ConAu 85*
Shallcross, John James 1922- *ConAu 103*, *IntAu&W 82*, *WrDr 84*
Shallow, Robert *ConAu X*
Shaloff, Stanley 1939- *ConAu 29R*
Shalom Aleichem *TwCA*, *TwCA SUP*
Shalvey, Thomas 1937- *ConAu 105*
Shamah, Sydelle 1940- *IntAu&W 82*
Shambaugh, Joan *DrAP&F 83*
Shambaugh, Joan Dibble 1928- *IntWWP 82*
Shamburger, Page *ConAu 9R*, *WrDr 84*
Shamlu, Ahmad 1925- *ConLC 10*
Shamon, Albert Joseph 1915- *ConAu 13R*
Shan, Yeh *ConAu X*
Shanahan, Eileen 1924- *ConAu 102*
Shanahan, William J 1935- *ConAu 29R*
Shands, Harley C 1916-1981 *ConAu 105*
Shands, Harley Cecil 1916-1981 *ConAu 109*
Shane, Alex M 1933- *ConAu 45*
Shane, Bart *TwCWW*
Shane, C Donald 1895-1983 *ConAu 109*
Shane, Don G 1933- *ConAu 53*
Shane, Harold Gray 1914- *ConAu 3NR*, *-9R*
Shane, John *ConAu X*, *IntAu&W 82X*, *TwCWW*, *WrDr 84*
Shane, Mark *ConAu X*, *WrDr 84*
Shane, Rhondo *ConAu X*, *WrDr 84*
Shane, S *IntWWP 82X*
Shane, Victor *WrDr 84*
Shaner, Madeleine 1932- *ConAu 73*
Shaner, Richard C *DrAP&F 83*
Shaner, Richard Clark 1948- *IntWWP 82*
Shange, Ntozake *DrAP&F 83*, *WrDr 84*
Shange, Ntozake 1948- *ConAu 85*, *ConDr 82*, *ConLC 8*, *-25[port]*, *NatPD 81[port]*
Shango, Skaka Aku *DrAP&F 83*
Shank, Adele Edling 1940- *NatPD 81[port]*
Shank, Alan 1936- *ConAu 53*
Shank, David Arthur 1924- *ConAu 29R*
Shank, Joseph E 1892- *ConAu P-2*
Shank, Margarethe Erdahl 1910- *ConAu P-2*, *WrDr 84*
Shank, Theodore 1929- *WrDr 84*
Shankel, George Edgar 1894- *ConAu P-2*
Shankland, Peter Macfarlane 1901- *ConAu P-1*, *IntAu&W 82*, *WrDr 84*
Shankle, Ralph O 1933- *ConAu 9R*
Shankman, Florence V 1912- *ConAu 41R*
Shankman, Paul 1943- *ConAu 93*
Shanks, Ann Zane *ConAu 53*, *SmATA 10*
Shanks, Bob 1932- *ConAu 101*
Shanks, Bruce *AuNews 1*
Shanks, Edward Buxton 1892-1953 *LongCTC*, *ModBrL*
Shanks, Hershel 1930- *ConAu 106*
Shanks, Michael James 1927- *ConAu 5R*, *-8NR*, *WrDr 84*
Shanley, Helen *DrAP&F 83*
Shann, Renee 1907?-1979 *ConAu 89*
Shannon, David Allen 1920- *ConAu 1R*
Shannon, Dell *ConAu X*, *TwCCr&M 80*, *WrDr 84*
Shannon, Doris 1924- *ConAu 8NR*, *-61*, *WrDr 84*
Shannon, Edgar Finley, Jr. 1918- *ConAu 9R*
Shannon, Ellen 1927- *ConAu 77*
Shannon, Foster 1930- *ConAu 106*
Shannon, Fred Albert 1893-1963 *TwCA*, *TwCA SUP*
Shannon, George 1952- *ConAu 106*
Shannon, Jasper Berry 1903- *ConAu 1R*
Shannon, Jeanne *DrAP&F 83*
Shannon, John 1943- *ConAu 57*
Shannon, John Kingsley *DrAP&F 83*
Shannon, Lyle William 1920- *ConAu 61*
Shannon, M *ConAu X*
Shannon, Monica d1965 *TwCCW 83*
Shannon, Monica 1905?-1965 *ConAu 109*, *SmATA 28[port]*
Shannon, Richard 1945- *ConAu 73*
Shannon, Robert *ConAu X*
Shannon, Robert C 1930- *ConAu 13R*
Shannon, Robert Leroy 1926- *ConAu 93*
Shannon, Steve *WrDr 84*
Shannon, Terry *ConAu X*, *SmATA 21[port]*
Shannon, Thomas A 1940- *ConAu 5NR*, *-53*

Shields, Charles 1944- *SmATA 10*
Shields, Currin Vance 1918- *ConAu 1R*
Shields, David 1935- *CreCan 1*
Shields, Donald J 1937- *ConAu 53*
Shields, Gerald R 1925- *ConAu 110*
Shields, Joyce Farley 1930- *ConAu 109*
Shields, Michael Joseph 1938- *IntWWP 82*
Shields, Mike *IntWWP 82X*
Shiels, George 1886-1949 *DcLB 10, ModWD, TwCA SUP*
Shiels, William Eugene 1897- *ConAu P-1*
Shiers, George 1908- *ConAu 73*
Shiff, Nathan A 1914- *ConAu 25R*
Shiffert, Edith *DrAP&F 83*
Shiffert, Edith 1916- *ConAu 6NR, -13R, IntAu&W 82, IntWWP 82*
Shiffrin, Nancy 1944- *ConAu 81*
Shiflet, Kenneth E 1918-1978 *ConAu 1R, -2NR, -81*
Shiga, Naoya 1883-1971 *ConAu 101, -33R, WorAu*
Shigley, Forrest Dwight 1930- *ConAu 1R*
Shih, Chung-Wen *ConAu 81*
Shih, Vincent Y C 1903- *ConAu 77*
Shihab, Naomi *DrAP&F 83*
Shikes, Ralph Edmund 1912- *ConAu 29R, IntAu&W 82, WrDr 84*
Shiller, Jack G 1928- *ConAu 73*
Shilling, Dana 1953- *ConAu 109*
Shilling, N 1924- *ConAu 29R*
Shillinglaw, Gordon 1925- *ConAu 7NR, -17R, WrDr 84*
Shillony, Ben-Ami 1937- *ConAu 73*
Shiloh, Ailon 1924- *ConAu 33R, IntAu&W 82, WrDr 84*
Shils, Edward B 1915- *ConAu 5R, -6NR*
Shilton, Lance R 1921- *ConAu 5R*
Shimazaki, Haruki 1872-1943 *ConAu 105, WorAu 1970*
Shimazaki, Toson 1872-1943 *ConAu X, TwCLC 5[port], WorAu 1970[port]*
Shimberg, Benjamin 1918- *ConAu 45*
Shimer, Dorothy Blair 1911- *ConAu 45*
Shimin, Symeon 1902- *ConAu 81, SmATA 13*
Shimoniak, Wasyl 1923- *ConAu 108*
Shimpu, Yanagimura *ConAu X*
Shinagel, Michael 1934- *ConAu 25R, WrDr 84*
Shindell, Sidney 1923- *ConAu 13R*
Shine, Deborah 1932- *ConAu 110*
Shine, Frances L 1927- *ConAu 25R, WrDr 84*
Shine, Ted 1931- *ConAu 77*
Shiner, Larry 1934- *ConAu 21R*
Shiner, Roger A 1940- *ConAu 109*
Shingleton, Royce 1935- *ConAu 29R*
Shinkle, James D 1897?-1973 *ConAu 104*
Shinkle, Tex *ConAu X*
Shinn, Everett 1876-1953 *SmATA 21[port]*
Shinn, Larry Dwight 1942- *ConAu 107*
Shinn, Roger Lincoln 1917- *ConAu 1R*
Shinnie, Peter Lewis 1915- *ConAu 103*
Shinoda, Minoru 1915- *ConAu 5R*
Shipler, David Karr 1942- *ConAu 103*
Shiplett, June Lund 1930- *ConAu 81*
Shipley, David *ConAu X*
Shipley, David O 1925- *ConAu 37R*
Shipley, Joseph T 1893- *ConAu 9NR*
Shipley, Joseph Twaddell 1893- *ConAu 13R*
Shipley, Joseph Twadell 1893- *ConAmTC, IntAu&W 82, WrDr 84*
Shipley, Nan *ConAu 9R*
Shipley, Peter 1946- *ConAu 103*
Shipley, Thorne 1927- *ConAu 5R*
Shipley, Vivian *DrAP&F 83*
Shipman, David 1932- *ConAu 29R, WrDr 84*
Shipman, Harry L 1948- *ConAu 10NR, -65*
Shipman, Henry Longfellow 1948- *WrDr 84*
Shipp, Nelson 1892- *ConAu 57*
Shipp, Thomas J 1918- *ConAu 13R*
Shippen, Katherine Binney 1892-1980 *ConAu 5R, -93, SmATA 1, -23N*
Shippen, Zoe 1902- *WrDr 84*
Shippey, Frederick Alexander 1908- *ConAu P-1*
Shippey, Lee 1884-1969 *ConAu 89*
Shippey, T A 1943- *WrDr 84*
Shippey, Thomas Alan 1943- *ConAu 108*
Shippy, Richard W 1927- *ConAmTC, ConAu 81*
Shipton, Clifford K 1902-1973 *ConAu P-2*
Shipton, Eric Earle 1907-1977 *ConAu 65, -69, SmATA 10*
Shipway, George 1908- *ConAu 25R*
Shirakawa, Yoshikazu 1935- *ConAu 73*

Shiras, Wilmar H 1908- *TwCSFW, WrDr 84*
Shire, Helena Mennie 1912- *ConAu 29R*
Shirer, William L 1904- *WrDr 84*
Shirer, William Lawrence 1904- *ConAu 7NR, -9R, DcLB 4, IntAu&W 82, TwCA SUP*
Shires, Henry Millis 1913- *ConAu 17R, WrDr 84*
Shirk, Evelyn Urban 1918- *ConAu 17R*
Shirk, George H 1913- *ConAu 17R*
Shirk, Susan L 1945- *ConAu 108*
Shirkey, Albert P 1904- *ConAu P-2*
Shirley, Frances Ann 1931- *ConAu 2NR, -5R, WrDr 84*
Shirley, George E 1898- *ConSFA*
Shirley, Glenn D 1916- *ConAu 89, IntAu&W 82*
Shirley, Hardy Lomax 1900- *ConAu 37R*
Shiro *IntAu&W 82X*
Shirreffs, Gordon Donald 1914- *ConAu 6NR, -13R, SmATA 11, WrDr 84*
Shirts, Morris A 1922- *ConAu 73*
Shishkov, Vasiliy *IntWWP 82X*
Shishkov, Vyacheslav Yakovlevich 1873-1945 *CIDMEL 80*
Shissler, Barbara J 1931- *ConAu 29R*
Shivanandan, Mary 1932- *ConAu 73*
Shively, George Jenks 1893?-1980 *ConAu 97*
Shivers, Alfred Samuel 1929- *ConAu 41R*
Shivers, Jay Sanford 1930- *ConAu 33R, WrDr 84*
Shivers, Samuel A *ConAu X*
Shklovsky, Victor Borisovich 1893- *TwCWr*
Shklovsky, Viktor Borisovich 1893- *CIDMEL 80, ModSL 1*
Shkvarkin, Vasili Vasilevich 1893- *ModWD*
Shlonsky, Abraham 1898?-1973 *ConAu 41R*
Shlonsky, Abraham 1900-1973 *WorAu 1970*
Shmelyov, Ivan Sergeyevich 1873-1950 *CIDMEL 80*
Shmueli, Adi 1941- *ConAu 1NR, -45*
Shneerson, Grigory Mikhailovich 1901-1982 *ConAu 106*
Shneiderman, Samuel L 1906- *ConAu 97*
Shneidman, Edwin S 1918- *ConAu 29R*
Shneidman, J Lee 1929- *ConAu 37R, WrDr 84*
Shneour, Elie Alexis 1925- *ConAu 37R, WrDr 84*
Shneour, Zalman 1887-1959 *WorAu*
Shoben, Edward Joseph, Jr. 1918- *ConAu 21R*
Shober, Joyce Lee 1932- *ConAu 1R*
Shoberg, Lore 1949- *ConAu 33R*
Shobin, David 1945- *ConAu 104, WrDr 84*
Shoblad, Richard H 1937- *ConAu 41R*
Shock, Nathan W 1906- *ConAu 5R, WrDr 84*
Shockley, Ann Allen *DrAP&F 83*
Shockley, Ann Allen 1927- *ConAu 1NR, -49, LivgBAA, WrDr 84*
Shockley, Donald G 1937- *ConAu 103*
Shoe, Lucy T *ConAu X*
Shoemaker, Brant 1924- *WrDr 84*
Shoemaker, Don C 1912- *ConAu 97*
Shoemaker, Donald J 1927- *ConAu 37R*
Shoemaker, Jack *DrAP&F 83*
Shoemaker, Leonard Calvin 1881- *ConAu P-1*
Shoemaker, Lynn *DrAP&F 83*
Shoemaker, Lynn Henry 1939- *ConAu 9NR, -65, IntWWP 82*
Shoemaker, Richard H 1907-1970 *ConAu P-1*
Shoemaker, Robert John 1919- *ConAu 13R*
Shoemaker, Robin 1949- *ConAu 108*
Shoemaker, William H 1902- *ConAu 13R*
Shoenight, Aloise 1914- *ConAu 77*
Shoesmith, Kathleen A 1938- *ConAu 1NR, -49, WrDr 84*
Shoesmith, Kathleen Anne *IntAu&W 82*
Shofner, Jerrell H 1929- *ConAu 57*
Shofner, Robert D 1933- *ConAu 57*
Shokeid, Moshe 1936- *ConAu 41R*
Sholem Aleichem 1859-1916 *CnMD, ModWD*
Sholinsky, Jane 1943- *ConAu 89*
Sholl, Betsy *DrAP&F 83*
Sholl, Betsy 1945- *IntWWP 82*
Sholokhov, Mikhail Aleksandrovich 1905- *CIDMEL 80, CnMWL, ConAu 101, ConLC 7, -15, LongCTC, ModSL 1, TwCA, TwCA SUP, TwCWr, WhoTwCL*
Sholom Aleichem 1859-1916 *CIDMEL 80*
Shomaker, Dianna 1934- *ConAu 109*
Shomon, Joseph James 1914- *ConAu 73*
Shomroni, Reuven *ConAu X*
Shone, Patric *ConAu X, WrDr 84*
Shone, Robert 1906- *ConAu 109*

Shone, Ronald 1946- *ConAu 103, WrDr 84*
Shonfield, Andrew Akiba 1917-1981 *ConAu 102, -105*
Shontz, Franklin C 1926- *ConAu 17R, WrDr 84*
Shook, Laurence K 1909- *ConAu 73*
Shook, Robert L 1938- *ConAu 8NR, -61*
Shoolbred, C F 1901- *ConAu P-2*
Shor, Elizabeth N 1930- *ConAu 110*
Shor, Joel 1919- *ConAu 89*
Shor, Pekay 1923- *ConAu 45*
Shor, Ronald 1930- *ConAu 61*
Shorb, Wil 1938- *ConAu 45*
Shore, Jane *DrAP&F 83*
Shore, Jane 1947- *ConAu 77*
Shore, June Lewis *AuNews 1, ConAu 105, SmATA 30[port]*
Shore, Norman *ConAu X, WrDr 84*
Shore, Philippa *ConAu X*
Shore, Sidney 1921-1981 *ConAu 103*
Shore, William B 1925- *ConAu 53*
Shore, Wilma 1913- *ConAu 13R*
Shores, Louis 1904-1981 *ConAu 8NR, -104, -13R*
Shorey, Kenneth Paul 1937- *ConAmTC*
Shorris, Earl 1936- *ConAu 10NR, -65*
Shorrock, William Irwin 1941- *ConAu 65*
Short, Alison 1920- *ConAu 61*
Short, Bobby *ConAu X*
Short, C Christopher D *WrDr 84*
Short, Carroll Dale *DrAP&F 83*
Short, Christopher d1978 *ConAu 1R, -2NR*
Short, Clarice 1910-1977 *ConAu 103, -45*
Short, Edmund C 1931- *ConAu 25R*
Short, Frank *DrAP&F 83*
Short, Howard E 1907- *ConAu 61*
Short, Jackson 1939- *ConAu 53*
Short, James F 1924- *ConAu 5R, -8NR*
Short, James R 1922?-1980 *ConAu 103*
Short, John 1924- *WrDr 84*
Short, Lucille Doughton 1903- *IntWWP 82*
Short, Luke 1908-1975 *ConAu X, FifWWr, TwCWW*
Short, Philip 1945- *ConAu 105, WrDr 84*
Short, Robert L 1932- *ConAu 77*
Short, Robert Stuart 1938- *ConAu 29R, WrDr 84*
Short, Robert Waltrip 1924?- *ConAu 107*
Short, Roger *ConAu X*
Short, Ruth Gordon *ConAu 1R, -6NR*
Short, Thayne R 1929- *ConAu 108*
Short, Wayne 1926- *ConAu 9R*
Shortall, Leonard W *ConAu 81, SmATA 19*
Shorter, Aylward 1932- *ConAu 81, IntAu&W 82*
Shorter, Carl *ConAu X*
Shorter, Clement King 1857?-1926 *LongCTC, TwCA*
Shorter, Edward 1941- *ConAu 73, WrDr 84*
Shorto, Harry L 1919- *ConAu 5R*
Shortt, Terence Michael 1911- *ConAu 77*
Shostak, Arthur B 1937- *ConAu 108*
Shostak, Jerome 1913- *ConAu 7NR, -17R*
Shosteck, Robert 1910-1979 *ConAu 11NR, -61, -85*
Shotwell, James Thomson 1874-1965 *TwCA, TwCA SUP*
Shotwell, Louisa R 1902- *TwCCW 83, WrDr 84*
Shotwell, Louisa Rossiter 1902- *ConAu 1R, -4NR, SmATA 3*
Shouksmith, George A 1931- *ConAu 49*
Shoumatoff, Alex 1946- *ConAu 9NR, -53*
Shoup, Carl Sumner 1902- *ConAu 49*
Shoup, Laurence H 1943- *ConAu 102*
Shoup, Paul Snedden 1929- *ConAu 106*
Shover, John L 1927- *ConAu 21R*
Showalter, Dennis 1942- *ConAu 89*
Showalter, Elaine 1941- *ConAu 57*
Showalter, English, Jr. 1935- *ConAu 53*
Showalter, Jean B *ConAu 21R, SmATA 12*
Showalter, Ronda Kerr 1942- *ConAu 37R*
Showell, Ellen Harvey 1934- *ConAu 85, SmATA 33[port]*
Showers, Paul 1910- *ChlLR 6[port]*
Showers, Paul C 1910- *ConAu 1R, -4NR, MichAu 80, SmATA 21[port]*
Showers, Renald E 1935- *ConAu 77*
Showers, Victor 1910- *ConAu 53*
Shown, Suzan *DrAP&F 83*
Shoy, Lee Ang *ConAu X*
Shrade *IntAu&W 82X*

Shrader, Stephen *DrAP&F 83*
Shrader, Welman Austin 1906- *IntAu&W 82*
Shrady, Maria 1924- *ConAu 49*
Shragin, Boris 1926- *ConAu 102*
Shrake, Edwin 1931- *TwCWW, WrDr 84*
Shramek, Dennis *DrAP&F 83*
Shrand, David 1913- *WrDr 84*
Shrapnel, Norman 1912- *IntAu&W 82, WrDr 84*
Shreve, L G 1910- *ConAu 101*
Shreve, Susan Richards *DrAP&F 83*
Shreve, Susan Richards 1939- *ConAu 5NR, –49, ConLC 23[port], WrDr 84*
Shridharani, Krishnalal Jethalal 1911-1960 *TwCA SUP*
Shrimsley, Bernard 1931- *ConAu 103, WrDr 84*
Shrira, Shoshana 1917- *IntWWP 82*
Shriver, Donald W, Jr. 1927- *ConAu 1NR, –45*
Shriver, George H, Jr. 1931- *ConAu 21R*
Shriver, Harry C 1904- *ConAu 10NR, –65*
Shriver, Peggy L 1931- *ConAu 107*
Shriver, Phillip Raymond 1922- *ConAu 13R*
Shroder, Maurice Z 1933- *ConAu 1R*
Shrodes, Caroline 1908- *ConAu 1R, –4NR*
Shrout, Thomas R 1919- *ConAu 41R*
Shroyer, Frederick Benjamin 1916- *ConAu 13R*
Shryock, Harold 1906- *ConAu 8NR, –21R*
Shryock, Richard Harrison 1893-1972 *ConAu 33R, ConAu P-2*
Shtainmets, Leon *ConAu 105, SmATA 32*
Shtein, Aleksandr Petrovich 1906- *ModWD*
Shtemenko, Sergei Matveyevich 1907-1976 *ConAu 103*
Shtern, Dr. Israel H *IntWWP 82X*
Shtern, Israel Hersh 1913- *IntWWP 82*
Shternfeld, Ari A 1905-1980 *ConAu 105*
Shu, Austin Chi-Wei 1915- *ConAu 29R*
Shu, Ch'ing-Ch'un 1899-1966 *ConAu 109*
Shu-Jen, Chou 1881-1936 *ConAu 104*
Shub, Beth *ConAu X*
Shub, David 1887-1973 *ConAu 41R*
Shub, Elizabeth *ConAu 41R, SmATA 5*
Shubik, Martin 1926- *ConAu 2NR, –5R*
Shubin, Seymour *WrDr 84*
Shubin, Seymour 1921- *ConAu 1R*
Shucard, Alan *DrAP&F 83*
Shucard, Alan R 1935- *ConAu 61*
Shuchman, Abraham 1919-1978 *ConAu 77*
Shue, Larry 1946- *NatPD 81[port]*
Shuford, Cecil Eugene 1907- *AuNews 1, ConAu 13R*
Shuford, Gene *AuNews 1, ConAu X*
Shugrue, Michael Francis 1934- *ConAu 21R, WrDr 84*
Shukla, Krishna Chandra 1937- *IntWWP 82*
Shukman, Harold 1931- *ConAu 53, WrDr 84*
Shukshin, Vasily Makarovich 1929-1974 *ClDMEL 80*
Shula, Don 1930- *ConAu 106*
Shulberg, Alan *ConAu X*
Shulberg, Budd 1914- *DcLB Y81A[port]*
Shulevitz, Uri 1935- *ChlLR 5[port], ConAu 3NR, –9R, IntAu&W 82, SmATA 3*
Shull, Fremont A, Jr. 1924- *ConAu 1R, –1NR, WrDr 84*
Shull, Leo 1913- *ConAmTC, IntAu&W 82*
Shull, Margaret Anne Wyse 1940- *ConAu 77*
Shull, Peg *ConAu X*
Shulman, Albert M 1902- *ConAu 49*
Shulman, Alix Kates *DrAP&F 83*
Shulman, Alix Kates 1932- *ConAu 29R, ConLC 2, –10, SmATA 7*
Shulman, Arnold 1914- *ConAu 29R*
Shulman, Bernard H 1922- *ConAu 108*
Shulman, Charles E 1900?-1968 *ConAu P-1*
Shulman, David Dean 1949- *ConAu 102*
Shulman, Frank Joseph 1943- *ConAu 29R*
Shulman, Harry Manuel 1899- *ConAu 1R, WrDr 84*
Shulman, Irving 1913- *ConAu 1R, –6NR, SmATA 13, WrDr 84*
Shulman, Marshall Darrow 1916- *ConAu 1R, WrDr 84*
Shulman, Max *DrAP&F 83*
Shulman, Max 1919- *ConAu 89*
Shulman, Milton 1913- *ConAu 103, WrDr 84*
Shulman, Morton 1925- *AuNews 1, ConAu 21R*
Shulman, Neil B 1945- *ConAu 9NR, –65*
Shulman, Sandra 1944- *ConAu 9NR, –21R*
Shulman, Sondra *DrAP&F 83*

Shultz, George P 1920- *ConAu 104, WrDr 84*
Shultz, Gladys Denny 1895- *ConAu 49*
Shultz, William J 1902-1970 *ConAu 1R, –103*
Shulvass, Moses A 1909- *ConAu 13R, IntAu&W 82, WrDr 84*
Shumaker, Peggy *DrAP&F 83*
Shumaker, Wayne 1910- *ConAu 5R, IntAu&W 82, WrDr 84*
Shuman, Bruce A 1941- *ConAu 110*
Shuman, James B 1932- *ConAu 61*
Shuman, Nicholas R 1921- *ConAu 109*
Shuman, R Baird 1929- *ConAu 4NR*
Shuman, R Baird 1932- *ConAu 1R*
Shuman, Samuel I 1925- *ConAu 3NR, –9R, WrDr 84*
Shumsky, Oscar *CreCan 2*
Shumsky, Zena *WrDr 84*
Shumsky, Zena 1926- *ConAu 1R, SmATA X*
Shumway, Floyd M 1917- *ConAu 29R, WrDr 84*
Shumway, George 1928- *ConAu 9R*
Shumway, Mary *DrAP&F 83*
Shumway, Mary L 1926- *ConAu 7NR, –17R*
Shuptrine, Hubert 1936?- *AuNews 1*
Shura, Mary *WrDr 84*
Shura, Mary Francis *ConAu X, IntAu&W 82X, SmATA 6*
Shurden, Walter B 1937- *ConAu 69*
Shurin, Aaron *DrAP&F 83*
Shurkin, Joel N 1938- *ConAu 69*
Shurr, William H 1932- *ConAu 41R*
Shurter, Robert L 1907-1974 *ConAu 1R, –2NR*
Shurtleff, Malcolm C, Jr. 1922- *ConAu 5R*
Shurtleff, Michael 1930- *ConAu 41R, NatPD 81[port]*
Shurtleff, William 1941- *ConAu 93*
Shuster, Albert H, Jr. 1917- *ConAu 17R*
Shuster, Frank 1916- *CreCan 2*
Shuster, George Nauman 1894-1977 *ConAu 69, –77, TwCA, TwCA SUP*
Shuster, Joe 1914- *ConLC 21[port]*
Shuster, Ronald Lowell 1927- *ConAu 45*
Shusterman, David 1912- *ConAu 25R*
Shute, Alberta V 1906- *ConAu 7NR, –57*
Shute, Henry Augustus 1856-1943 *DcLB 9[port]*
Shute, Nerina 1908- *ConAu 101*
Shute, Nevil 1899-1960 *ConAu X, LongCTC, ModBrL, TwCA, TwCA SUP, TwCCr&M 80, TwCSFW, TwCWr, WhoTwCL*
Shute, R Wayne 1933- *ConAu 29R*
Shute, Wallace B 1911- *ConAu 29R*
Shute, Wilfred Eugene 1907- *ConAu 105*
Shuttle, Penelope 1947- *ConAu 93, ConLC 7, ConP 80, DcLB 14[port], WrDr 84*
Shuttlesworth, Dorothy Edwards 1907- *ConAu 1R, –4NR, SmATA 3*
Shuttleworth, Gisele *CreCan 2*
Shuttleworth, Jane *AuNews 1*
Shuttleworth, John 1937- *AuNews 1*
Shuttleworth, Paul *DrAP&F 83*
Shuval, Judith T 1925- *ConAu 45*
Shuy, Roger W 1931- *ConAu 61*
Shvarts, Yevgeni Lvovich 1896?-1958 *ModWD*
Shvarts, Yevgeny Lvovich 1896-1958 *ClDMEL 80*
Shwadran, Benjamin 1907- *ConAu 5NR, –13R*
Shwartz, Susan Martha 1949- *ConAu 109*
Shwayder, David S 1926- *ConAu 106*
Shy, John W 1931- *ConAu 3NR, –5R*
Shy, Timothy *LongCTC*
Shyer, Marlene Fanta *ConAu 11NR, –69, SmATA 13*
Shyre, Paul 1926- *IntAu&W 82*
Shyre, Paul 1929- *ConAu 103*
Si Merritt *IntWWP 82X*
Siano, Mary Martha 1924- *ConAu 77*
Siberell, Anne *ConAu 104, SmATA 29[port]*
Sibley, Agnes M 1914- *ConAu 61*
Sibley, Celestine 1917- *ConAu 85*
Sibley, Don 1922- *SmATA 12*
Sibley, Elbridge 1903- *ConAu P-1*
Sibley, Marilyn McAdams 1923- *ConAu 21R*
Sibley, Mulford Quickert 1912- *ConAu 5R, –6NR*
Sibley, Patricia 1928- *ConAu 97*
Sibley, Susan *ConAu X*
Sibly, John 1920- *ConAu 1R*
Sices, David 1933- *ConAu 25R*
Sichel, Peter M F 1922- *ConAu 65*
Sichel, Pierre 1915- *ConAu 1R*
Sichel, Walter 1855-1933 *LongCTC*
Sichel, Werner 1934- *ConAu 8NR, –21R*

Sichov, Vladimir 1945- *ConAu 108*
Siciliano, Vincent Paul 1911- *ConAu P-2*
Sickels, Robert J 1931- *ConAu 41R*
Sicker, Philip 1951- *ConAu 103*
Sickert, Walter Richard 1860-1942 *CnMWL, LongCTC*
Sickles, William Russell 1913- *ConAu 57*
Sickman, Laurence C S 1906- *ConAu P-1*
Sicoli, Dan *DrAP&F 83*
Sicotte, Sylvie 1936- *IntAu&W 82*
Siculan, Daniel 1922- *SmATA 12*
Sid *IntWWP 82X*
Siddall, William R 1928- *ConAu 41R*
Siddiqi, Akhtar Husain 1925- *ConAu 61*
Siddiqui, Ashraf 1927- *ConAu 2NR, –5R*
Siddons, Anne Rivers *ConAu 101*
Sidel, Victor W 1931- *ConAu 9NR, –65*
Sider, Don 1933- *ConAu 77*
Sider, Robert Dick 1932- *ConAu 37R*
Sider, Ronald J 1939- *ConAu 93*
Siders, Ellis L 1920- *ConAu 17R, WrDr 84*
Sidetracked Home Executives *ConAu X*
Sidgwick, Ethel 1877-1970 *LongCTC, ModBrL, TwCA, TwCA SUP*
Sidgwick, John Robert Lindsay 1923- *CreCan 2*
Sidhwa, Bapsy N 1938- *ConAu 108*
Sidhwa, Keki R 1926- *ConAu 69*
Sidimus, Joysanne 1938- *CreCan 2*
Sidjakov, Nicolas 1924- *SmATA 18*
Sidney, Jonathan *ConAu 49*
Sidney, Kathleen M 1944- *ConAu 103*
Sidney, Margaret 1844-1924 *SmATA X*
Sidney, Neilma 1922- *ConAu X, WrDr 84*
Sidney-Fryer, Donald 1934- *ConAu 45*
Sidobre, Andre *IntAu&W 82X*
Sidowski, Joseph B 1925- *ConAu 21R*
Sidran, Ben H 1943- *ConAu 102*
Siebeck, Fred C 1925- *IntAu&W 82*
Siebel, Julia *DrAP&F 83*
Siebenheller, Norma 1937- *ConAu 107*
Siebenschuh, William R 1942- *ConAu 89*
Sieber, Roy 1923- *ConAu 102*
Sieber, Sam Dixon 1931- *ConAu 13R*
Siebert, Fred Seaton 1901- *ConAu 21R*
Siebner, Herbert Johannes Josef 1925- *CreCan 1*
Siebrasse, Glen 1939- *ConP 80, WrDr 84*
Sieburg, Friedrich 1893-1964 *ModGL*
Siedel, Frank 1914- *ConAu 25R*
Siedel, James M 1937- *ConAu 25R*
Siegal, Mordecai 1934- *ConAu 102*
Siegal, Sanford 1928- *ConAu 105*
Siegan, Bernard H 1924- *ConAu 65*
Siegel, Adrienne 1936- *ConAu 61*
Siegel, Beatrice *ConAu 101*
Siegel, Ben 1925- *ConAu 77*
Siegel, Benjamin 1914- *ConAu 1R, –4NR, WrDr 84*
Siegel, Bertram M 1936- *ConAu 25R*
Siegel, Dorothy 1932- *ConAu 9R*
Siegel, Eli 1902-1978 *ConAu 9NR, –17R, –81*
Siegel, Ernest 1922- *ConAu 73*
Siegel, Esther 1949- *ConAu 102*
Siegel, Gonnie McClung 1928- *ConAu 110*
Siegel, Helen *SmATA X*
Siegel, Irving H 1914- *ConAu 9NR, –21R, WrDr 84*
Siegel, Jack *ConAu X*
Siegel, Jacob 1913- *ConAu 17R*
Siegel, Jerome 1914- *ConLC 21[port]*
Siegel, June 1929- *ConAu 77*
Siegel, Julie *DrAP&F 83*
Siegel, Marcia B 1932- *ConAu 69*
Siegel, Mark Richard 1949- *ConAu 110*
Siegel, Martin 1933- *ConAu 33R*
Siegel, Max 1904-1972 *ConAu 104*
Siegel, Maxwell E 1933- *ConAu 101*
Siegel, Paul N 1916- *ConAu 37R, IntAu&W 82, WrDr 84*
Siegel, Richard L 1940- *ConAu 73*
Siegel, Robert *DrAP&F 83*
Siegel, Robert 1939- *ConAu 5NR*
Siegel, Stanley E 1928- *ConAu 41R*
Siegelman, James Howard 1951- *ConAu 81*
Siegelman, Jim *ConAu X*
Siegfried, Andre 1875-1959 *LongCTC, TwCA, TwCA SUP*
Siegfried, K E *IntAu&W 82X*
Siegl, Helen 1924- *SmATA 34[port]*
Siegle, Bernard Andrew 1914- *ConAu 89, IntAu&W 82*
Siegler, Alan *DrAP&F 83*
Siegler, Frederick Adrian 1932- *ConAu 49*

Siegmeister, Elie 1909- *ConAu 1R, –1NR, WrDr 84*
Siegner, C Vernon, Jr. 1920- *ConAu 1R*
Sielaff, Theodore J 1920- *ConAu 13R*
Sieller, William Vincent 1917- *ConAu 29R*
Siemanowski, Richard F 1922?-1981 *ConAu 104*
Siemens, Reynold Gerrard 1932- *ConAu 41R*
Siemon, Jeff 1950- *ConAu 103*
Sienkiewicz, Henryk 1846-1916 *ClDMEL 80, ConAu 104, LongCTC, ModSL 2*
Sienkiewitz, Henryk 1846-1916 *TwCLC 3*
Siepmann, Charles Arhtur 1899- *ConAu 1R*
Sieroszewska, Barbara-Zofia 1904- *IntAu&W 82*
Sieroszewski, Waclaw 1858-1945 *ClDMEL 80*
Sierp, Allan 1905- *WrDr 84*
Sierra, Gregorio Martinez *LongCTC, ModRL, TwCA, TwCA SUP*
Sierra Bravo, Restituto 1923- *IntAu&W 82*
Siev, Asher 1913- *ConAu 57*
Sieveking, Lancelot DeGiberne 1896- *LongCTC*
Sievers, Allen M 1918- *ConAu 89*
Sievers, Harry J 1920-1977 *ConAu 25R, –73*
Sievers, Leopold 1917- *IntAu&W 82*
Sievers, W David 1919-1966 *ConAu 1R, –103*
Siewert, Frances E 1881- *ConAu P-1*
Sifakis, G M 1935- *ConAu 25R*
Siffert, Robert S 1918- *ConAu 109*
Sifford, Darrell 1931- *ConAu 77*
Sifton, Claire 1897?-1980 *ConAu 93*
Sifton, Paul 1898-1972 *CnMD, ModWD*
Sifton, Paul F 1893?-1972 *ConAu 33R*
Sigal, Clancy *DrAP&F 83*
Sigal, Clancy 1926- *ConAu 1R, ConLC 7, ConNov 82, DcLEL 1940, WorAu, WrDr 84*
Sigband, Norman Bruce 1920- *ConAu 2NR, –5R, WrDr 84*
Sigelschiffer, Saul 1902- *ConAu 81, IntAu&W 82*
Sigerson, Dora 1866-1918 *LongCTC, TwCA, TwCA SUP, TwCWr*
Sigfusdottir, Greta 1910- *IntAu&W 82*
Sigfusson, Hannes 1922- *ClDMEL 80*
Sigler, Jay A 1933- *ConAu 25R*
Sigmon, Betty Richards 1940- *IntWWP 82*
Sigmund, Paul E 1929- *ConAu 2NR, –5R*
Signor, Randy Michael *DrAP&F 83*
Sigurdardottir, Steinunn 1950- *IntAu&W 82*
Sigurdsson, Olafur Johann 1918- *IntAu&W 82*
Sigurdsson, Sigurjon B 1962- *IntAu&W 82*
Sigurjonsson, Johann 1880-1919 *ClDMEL 80*
Sigurodsson, Olafur Johann 1913- *ClDMEL 80*
Sigworth, Oliver F 1921- *ConAu 13R, IntAu&W 82, WrDr 84*
Sihanouk, Norodom *ConAu X*
Siirala, Aarne Johannes 1919- *ConAu 13R, IntAu&W 82, WrDr 84*
Sik, Endre 1891-1978 *ConAu 77*
Sikelianos, Angelos 1884-1951 *ClDMEL 80, WorAu*
Sikes, Herschel Moreland 1928- *ConAu 17R*
Sikes, Shirley *DrAP&F 83*
Sikes, Walter W 1925- *ConAu 57*
Sikora, Joseph 1932-1967 *ConAu P-2*
Siks, Geraldine Brain 1912- *ConAu 25R, IntAu&W 82*
Sikula, Andrew F 1944- *ConAu 2NR, –49*
Silangan, Manuel *ConAu X*
Silbajoris, Frank *ConAu X*
Silbajoris, Rimvydas 1926- *ConAu 25R*
Silber, Irwin 1925- *ConAu 9R*
Silber, Joan *DrAP&F 83*
Silber, Joan 1945- *ConAu 104*
Silber, Kate 1902- *ConAu 77*
Silber, Mark 1946- *ConAu 45*
Silber, Sherman J 1941- *WrDr 84*
Silber, William L 1942- *ConAu 29R, WrDr 84*
Silberg, Moshe 1900-1975 *ConAu 61*
Silberg, Richard 1942- *ConAu 21R*
Silberger, Julius, Jr. 1929- *ConAu 105*
Silberman, Charles Eliot 1925- *ConAu 7NR, –9R, WrDr 84*
Silberman, Neil Asher 1950- *ConAu 108*
Silberrad, Una Lucy 1872-1955 *LongCTC*
Silbersack, John 1954- *ConAu 107*
Silberschlag, Eisig 1903- *ConAu 1R, –1NR, IntAu&W 82*
Silberschmidt, Max 1899- *ConAu 65*
Silberstang, Edwin 1930- *ConAu 3NR, –49*
Silberstein, Gerard Edward 1926- *ConAu 37R*
Silberstein, Warren P 1948- *ConAu 110*
Silbert, Layle *DrAP&F 83*

Silbey, Joel H 1933- *ConAu 21R*
Silcock, Sara Lesley 1947- *SmATA 12*
Silcock, Thomas H 1910- *ConAu 9R*
Silcox, David Phillips 1937- *ConAu 109*
Silen, Juan Angel 1938- *ConAu 33R*
Siler, Lari Field *DrAP&F 83*
Silet, Charles L P 1942- *ConAu 93*
Silje, Tone *IntAu&W 82X*
Silk, Andrew 1953?-1981 *ConAu 106*
Silk, Joseph 1942- *WrDr 84*
Silk, Leonard S 1918- *ConAu 1R, –4NR, WrDr 84*
Silkin, Jon 1930- *ConAu 5R, ConLC 2, –6, ConP 80, DcLEL 1940, ModBrL, ModBrL SUP, RGFMBP, WorAu, WrDr 84*
Silko, Leslie 1948- *WrDr 84*
Silko, Leslie Marmon *DrAP&F 83*
Silko, Leslie Marmon 1948- *ConLC 23[port], TwCWW*
Sill, Gertrude Grace *ConAu 69*
Sill, Sterling Welling 1903- *ConAu 6NR, –57*
Sillanpaa, Frans Eemil 1888-1964 *ConAu 93, ConLC 19, TwCA, TwCA SUP, TwCWr*
Sillanpaa, Frans Emil 1888-1964 *ClDMEL 80*
Sillem, Edward 1916-1964 *ConAu 5R*
Sillen, Samuel 1911?-1973 *ConAu 41R*
Siller, Van *TwCCr&M 80, WrDr 84*
Sillery, Anthony 1903-1976 *ConAu 5R, –5NR, –65*
Silliman, Ron *DrAP&F 83*
Silliman, Ron 1946- *ConAu 45*
Silliphant, Stirling 1918- *ConAu 73, DcLB 26[port]*
Sillitoe, Alan 1928- *AuNews 1, ConAu 8NR, –9R, ConLC 1, –3, –6, –10, –19, ConNov 82, ConP 80, DcLB 14[port], DcLEL 1940, IntAu&W 82, LongCTC, ModBrL, ModBrL SUP, TwCSFW, TwCWr, WhoTwCL, WorAu, WrDr 84*
Sillman, Leonard 1908-1982 *ConAu 105*
Sillo-Seidl, Georg 1925- *IntAu&W 82*
Sills, Beverly 1929- *ConAu 89*
Sills, David Lawrence 1920- *ConAu 33R*
Sills, Frank D 1914- *ConAu 1R*
Sills, Jennifer *AuNews 1, ConAu X*
Sills, Ruth C *ConAu 29R*
Sills-Docherty, Jonathon *IntWWP 82X*
Silman, Roberta *DrAP&F 83*
Silman, Roberta 1934- *ConAu 101, IntAu&W 82*
Silmon, Delphine *IntAu&W 82X*
Silone, Ignazio 1900-1978 *ClDMEL 80, CnMD, CnMWL, ConAu 81, ConAu P-2, ConLC 4, LongCTC, ModRL, TwCA, TwCA SUP, TwCWr, WhoTwCL*
Siluriensis, Leolinus *ConAu X*
Silva, Beverly *DrAP&F 83*
Silva, Joseph *ConAu X*
Silva, Julio A 1933- *ConAu 17R*
Silva, Ruth C *ConAu 13R, WrDr 84*
Silva Nunes, Armando Da *CreCan 1*
Silvanus *IntAu&W 82X*
Silvanus, P W *ConAu X*
Silvaroli, Nicholas J 1930- *ConAu 29R*
Silver, Abba Hillel 1893-1963 *ConAu 1R*
Silver, Alain 1947- *ConAu 10NR, –57*
Silver, Alfred 1951- *ConAu 85*
Silver, Christopher *DrAP&F 83*
Silver, Daniel J 1928- *WrDr 84*
Silver, Daniel Jeremy 1928- *ConAu 3NR, –5R*
Silver, Gary 1944- *ConAu 89*
Silver, Gerald A 1932- *ConAu 33R*
Silver, Harold 1928- *ConAu 10NR, –21R, WrDr 84*
Silver, Howard *DrAP&F 83*
Silver, Isidore 1934- *ConAu 53*
Silver, James W 1907- *ConAu 9R*
Silver, Joan B 1932- *IntAu&W 82*
Silver, Joan Micklin 1935- *ConLC 20*
Silver, Jody 1942- *ConAu 109*
Silver, Marjorie A 1948- *ConAu 93*
Silver, Nathan 1936- *ConAu 11NR, –21R, WrDr 84*
Silver, Nicholas *ConAu X*
Silver, Philip Warnock 1932- *ConAu 106*
Silver, Richard *ConAu X*
Silver, Rollo G 1909- *ConAu P-1*
Silver, Roy R 1918-1979 *ConAu 89*
Silver, Ruth *ConAu X, SmATA 7*
Silver, Samuel 1915?-1976 *ConAu 69*
Silver, Samuel M 1912- *ConAu 11NR, –21R*

Silver, Warren A 1914- *ConAu 65*
Silvera, Alain 1930- *ConAu 21R*
Silverberg, Robert *ConAu 1R, ConLC 7, ConSFA, DcLEL 1940, DrmM[port], SmATA 13*
Silverberg, Robert 1935- *ConAu 1NR, DcLB 8[port], IntAu&W 82, TwCSFW, WrDr 84*
Silverberg, Robert 1936?- *WorAu 1970*
Silverman, Al 1926- *ASpks, ConAu 9R*
Silverman, Alvin Michaels 1912- *ConAu 9R*
Silverman, Burt 1928- *ConAu 103*
Silverman, Corinne 1930- *ConAu 5R*
Silverman, David 1907- *ConAu P-2*
Silverman, Herschel *DrAP&F 83*
Silverman, Herschel 1926- *IntWWP 82*
Silverman, Hillel E 1924- *ConAu 11NR, –21R, WrDr 84*
Silverman, Hirsch Lazaar 1915- *ConAu 45*
Silverman, Jason H 1952- *ConAu 110*
Silverman, Jerry 1931- *ConAu 7NR, –13R, IntAu&W 82, WrDr 84*
Silverman, Joseph H 1924- *ConAu 104*
Silverman, Judith 1933- *ConAu 103*
Silverman, Kenneth 1936- *ConAu 57*
Silverman, Maxine *DrAP&F 83*
Silverman, Melvin Frank 1931-1966 *ConAu 5R, SmATA 9*
Silverman, Milton J 1944- *ConAu 108*
Silverman, Morris 1894-1972 *ConAu 33R*
Silverman, Oscar Ansell 1903-1977 *ConAu 69*
Silverman, Robert A 1943- *ConAu 57*
Silverman, Robert E 1924- *ConAu 41R*
Silverman, Robert J 1940- *ConAu 101*
Silverman, Rose *ConAu X*
Silverman, S Richard 1911- *ConAu 107*
Silverman, Samuel *AuNews 1*
Silverman, Sherri Lynn *DrAP&F 83*
Silverman, Sydel 1933- *ConAu 77*
Silverman, William B 1913- *ConAu 49*
Silvern, Leonard C 1919- *ConAu 7NR, –17R, WrDr 84*
Silvers, Vicki 1941- *ConAu 93*
Silverstein, Alvin 1933- *ConAu 2NR, –49, ConLC 17, IntAu&W 82, SmATA 8*
Silverstein, Charles 1935- *ConAu 73*
Silverstein, Josef 1922- *ConAu 37R, IntAu&W 82*
Silverstein, Mel 1940- *ConAu 101*
Silverstein, Norman 1922-1974 *ConAu 37R, –49*
Silverstein, Shel 1932- *ChlLR 5, ConAu 107, SmATA 27, –33[port], TwCCW 83*
Silverstein, Theodore 1904- *ConAu 106, WrDr 84*
Silverstein, Virginia B 1937- *ConAu 2NR, –49, ConLC 17, IntAu&W 82, SmATA 8*
Silverstone, Lou 1928- *ConAu 108*
Silverstone, Paul H 1931- *ConAu 21R*
Silvert, Kalman H 1921- *WrDr 84*
Silvert, Kalman H 1921-1976 *ConAu 6NR, –13R, –65*
Silverthorn, J E 1906- *ConAu P-1*
Silverthorne, Elizabeth 1930- *ConAu 89*
Silverton, Michael *DrAP&F 83*
Silverton, Michael 1935- *ConAu 65*
Silvester, Frank *ConAu X, TwCWW*
Silvester, Frederick Caton 1901-1966 *CreCan 1*
Silvester, Victor 1900- *ConAu P-1*
Silvestri, Richard 1944- *ConAu 81, IntAu&W 82*
Silving, Helen 1906- *ConAu 41R*
Silvis, Randall *DrAP&F 83*
Silvius, Behram Cheir *IntAu&W 82X*
Silvius, G Harold 1908-1981 *ConAu 3NR, –5R, –104*
Sim, Georges *ConAu X*
Sim, John Cameron 1911- *ConAu 25R, WrDr 84*
Sim, Katharine 1913- *ConAu 13R*
Sim, Katharine Phyllis 1913- *WrDr 84*
Sim, Myre 1915- *ConAu 61*
Sim, Yawsoon 1937- *ConAu 108*
Simak, Clifford D 1904- *ConAu 1R, –1NR, ConLC 1, ConSFA, DcLB 8[port], DcLEL 1940, TwCSFW, WorAu, WrDr 84*
Simard, Francois-Xavier 1945- *IntAu&W 82*
Simard, Jean 1916- *CreCan 1*
Simbari, Nicola 1927- *ConAu 1R, –1NR*
Simckes, L S 1937- *ConAu 9R*
Simckes, Lazare Seymore *DrAP&F 83*
Simckes, Seymour *NatPD 81[port]*
Sime, Mary 1911- *ConAu 53, IntAu&W 82,*

WrDr 84

Simenon, Georges 1903- *CIDMEL 80, CnMWL,*
ConAu 85, ConLC 1, –2, –3, –8, –18,
IntAu&W 82, LongCTC, ModFrL, ModRL,
TwCA, TwCA SUP, TwCWr, WhoTwCL
Simeon, Mother Mary 1888- *ConAu P-1*
Simeon, Richard 1943- *ConAu 9NR, –61*
Simeone, Diane A 1953?-1983 *ConAu 109*
Simic, Andrei 1930- *ConAu 93*
Simic, Antun Branko 1898-1925 *ModSL 2*
Simic, Charles *DrAP&F 83*
Simic, Charles 1938- *ConAu 29R, ConLC 6, –9,*
–22[port], ConP 80, WorAu 1970,
WrDr 84
Simini, Joseph Peter 1921- *ConAu 8NR, –17R*
Simion, Eugen 1933- *IntAu&W 82*
Simionescu, Mircea Horia 1928- *IntAu&W 82*
Simirenko, Alex 1931- *ConAu 13R*
Simister, Florence Parker 1913- *ConAu 2NR,*
–5R
Simkin, C G F 1915- *ConAu 29R*
Simkin, Colin George Frederick 1915- *WrDr 84*
Simkin, William E 1907- *ConAu 45*
Simkins, Lawrence D 1933- *ConAu 41R*
Simley, Anne 1891- *ConAu 5R*
Simmel, Edward C 1932- *ConAu 45*
Simmel, Georg 1858-1918 *TwCA SUP*
Simmel, Johannes Mario 1924- *ConAu 81,*
IntAu&W 82
Simmel, Marianne L 1923- *ConAu 21R*
Simmie, James 1941- *WrDr 84*
Simmonds, A J 1943- *ConAu 81*
Simmonds, George W 1929- *ConAu 21R*
Simmonds, James D 1933- *ConAu 104*
Simmons, A John 1950- *ConAu 106*
Simmons, Alan Frank 1916- *WrDr 84*
Simmons, Anthony *WrDr 84*
Simmons, Anthony 1922- *ConAu 103*
Simmons, Billy 1931- *ConAu 21R*
Simmons, Billy E 1931- *ConAu 10NR*
Simmons, Blake *ConAu X*
Simmons, Charles *DrAP&F 83*
Simmons, Charles 1924- *ConAu 89*
Simmons, D R 1930- *ConAu 110*
Simmons, David *ConAu X*
Simmons, David Roy 1930- *WrDr 84*
Simmons, Dawn Langley *ConAu 29R*
Simmons, Edwin Howard 1921- *ConAu 89*
Simmons, Ernest Joseph 1903-1972 *ConAu 1R,*
–3NR, TwCA SUP
Simmons, Geoffrey 1943- *ConAu 104*
Simmons, Gloria Mitchell 1932- *ConAu 37R,*
LivgBAA
Simmons, Henry Eugene 1929- *LivgBAA*
Simmons, Herbert Alfred 1930- *ConAu 1R*
Simmons, Ian 1937- *ConAu 106*
Simmons, J Edgar 1921- *ConAu 21R*
Simmons, J L 1933- *ConAu 29R*
Simmons, Jack 1915- *ConAu 2NR, –5R*
Simmons, James 1933- *ConAu 105, ConP 80,*
WrDr 84
Simmons, James E 1923- *ConAu 41R*
Simmons, James William 1936- *ConAu 17R*
Simmons, Joseph Larry 1935- *ConAu 65*
Simmons, Judy Dothard *DrAP&F 83*
Simmons, Judy Dothard 1944- *ConAu 77*
Simmons, Lydia 1933- *NatPD 81[port]*
Simmons, Marc 1937- *ConAu 10NR*
Simmons, Marc Steven 1937- *ConAu 25R,*
WrDr 84
Simmons, Mary Kay 1933- *ConAu 81*
Simmons, Matty 1926- *ConAu 29R*
Simmons, Merle Edwin 1918- *ConAu 2NR, –5R*
Simmons, Otis D 1928- *ConAu 57*
Simmons, Ozzie Gordon 1919- *ConAu 9R*
Simmons, Patricia A 1930- *ConAu 93*
Simmons, Paul D 1936- *ConAu 45*
Simmons, Robert R 1940- *ConAu 97*
Simmons, S H *ConAu 49*
Simmons, Shirley *DrAP&F 83*
Simmons, Sylvia *ConAu 49*
Simms, D Harper 1912- *ConAu 29R*
Simms, Eric 1921- *WrDr 84*
Simms, Eric Arthur 1921- *ConAu 101*
Simms, George 1910- *ConAu 108*
Simms, Laura *DrAP&F 83*
Simms, Peter Francis Jordan 1925- *ConAu 21R*
Simms, Ruth P 1937- *ConAu 17R*
Simms, Willard S 1943- *ConAu 29R*
Simon, Alfred 1907- *ConAu 41R, IntAu&W 82*
Simon, Andre Louis 1877-1970 *ConAu 29R,*
LongCTC

Simon, Anne W 1914- *ConAu 105*
Simon, Arthur 1930- *ConAu 33R, WrDr 84*
Simon, Bennett 1933- *ConAu 101*
Simon, Boris-Jean 1913?-1972 *ConAu 33R*
Simon, Carl P 1945- *ConAu 107*
Simon, Carly 1945- *ConAu 105,*
ConLC 26[port]
Simon, Charlie May 1897- *ConAu X,*
SmATA 3
Simon, Claude 1913- *CIDMEL 80, ConAu 89,*
ConLC 4, –9, –15, IntAu&W 82, ModFrL,
ModRL, TwCWr, WhoTwCL, WorAu
Simon, Eckehard 1939- *ConAu 61*
Simon, Edith 1917- *ConAu 13R, WorAu,*
WrDr 84
Simon, George Thomas 1912- *ConAu 25R,*
IntAu&W 82
Simon, Gregory 1948- *IntWWP 82*
Simon, Henry W 1901-1970 *ConAu 4NR, –5R,*
–29R
Simon, Herbert 1898?-1974 *ConAu 53*
Simon, Herbert A 1916- *ConAu 9NR, –13R*
Simon, Hilda Rita 1921- *ConAu 77,*
SmATA 28
Simon, Howard 1903-1979 *ConAu 33R, –89,*
SmATA 21N, –32[port]
Simon, Hubert K 1917- *ConAu 13R*
Simon, Jo Ann 1946- *ConAu 106*
Simon, Joan L 1921- *ConAu 13R*
Simon, Joe *ConAu X, SmATA 7*
Simon, John G 1928- *ConAu 37R*
Simon, John Ivan 1925- *ConAmTC, ConAu 21R,*
WorAu
Simon, John Oliver *DrAP&F 83*
Simon, John Y 1933- *ConAu 25R*
Simon, Joseph H 1913- *ConAu 29R, SmATA 7*
Simon, Julian Lincoln 1932- *ConAu 33R,*
WrDr 84
Simon, Karl Gunter 1933- *IntAu&W 82*
Simon, Leonard 1922- *ConAu 9R*
Simon, Linda 1946- *ConAu 73*
Simon, Lorena 1897- *ConAu 5R*
Simon, Louis M 1906- *ConAu 77*
Simon, Marcia L 1939- *ConAu 93*
Simon, Martin P 1903-1969 *ConAu P-1,*
SmATA 12
Simon, Marvin Neil 1927- *DcLEL 1940*
Simon, Matila 1908- *ConAu 17R*
Simon, Michael A 1936- *ConAu 33R, WrDr 84*
Simon, Mina Lewiton *ConAu X, SmATA 2*
Simon, Morton J 1913- *ConAu 17R*
Simon, Neil 1927- *AuNews 1, ConAu 21R,*
ConDr 82, ConLC 6, –11, CroCD,
DcLB 7[port], ModAL, ModWD,
NatPD 81[port], WorAu, WrDr 84
Simon, Norma 1927- *ConAu 5R, –6NR,*
SmATA 3
Simon, Paul 1928- *ConAu 81*
Simon, Paul 1941- *ConLC 17*
Simon, Pierre-Henri 1903-1972 *ConAu 37R*
Simon, Pierre-Henri 1903-1975 *CIDMEL 80*
Simon, Richard Dages 1922- *ConAmTC*
Simon, Rita James 1931- *ConAu 8NR, –21R,*
WrDr 84
Simon, Robert *ConAu X, WrDr 84*
Simon, Robert A 1897?-1981 *ConAu 103*
Simon, Roger David 1943- *ConAu 109*
Simon, Roger L 1943- *TwCCr&M 80, WrDr 84*
Simon, S J *TwCCr&M 80*
Simon, Seymour 1931- *ConAu 11NR, –25R,*
SmATA 4, WrDr 84
Simon, Sheldon W 1937- *ConAu 10NR*
Simon, Sheldon Weiss 1937- *ConAu 25R,*
IntAu&W 82, WrDr 84
Simon, Shirley 1921- *ConAu 1R, –1NR, –5R,*
SmATA 11
Simon, Sidney B 1927- *ConAu 101, –21R*
Simon, Solomon 1895-1970 *ConAu 104*
Simon, Ted 1931- *ConAu 105*
Simon, Tony 1921- *ConAu 5R*
Simon, Ulrich E 1913- *ConAu 29R*
Simon, Walter G 1924- *ConAu 17R*
Simon, William E 1927- *ConAu 9R, –81*
Simonds, Frank Herbert 1878-1936 *TwCA*
Simonds, John Ormsbee 1913- *ConAu 77*
Simonds, Roger 1929- *ConAu 93*
Simonds, Rollin Head 1910- *ConAu 1R*
Simonds, William Adams 1887-1963 *ConAu P-1*
Simone, Albert Joseph 1935- *ConAu 17R*
Simone, Jacqueline *IntAu&W 82X*
Simoneau, Leopold 1918- *CreCan 1*
Simoneau, Pierrette Alarie *CreCan 1*

Simonelli, Maria Picchio 1921- *ConAu 49*
Simonetta, Linda 1948- *ConAu 77, SmATA 14*
Simonetta, Sam 1936- *ConAu 77, SmATA 14*
Simonhoff, Harry 1891- *ConAu 5R*
Simoni, John Peter 1911- *ConAu 106*
Simonin, Albert 1905-1980 *ConAu 104*
Simonini, R C, Jr. 1922-1967 *ConAu P-1*
Simonov, Konstantin Mikhailovich 1915-1979
CnMD, ConAu 89, CroCD, ModSL 1,
ModWD, TwCA SUP, TwCWr,
WorAu 1970
Simonov, Konstantin Mikhaylovich 1915-1979
CIDMEL 80
Simons, Barbara B 1934- *ConAu 108*
Simons, Beverley 1938- *ConAu 104, ConDr 82,*
WrDr 84
Simons, David G 1922- *ConAu 17R*
Simons, Elwyn LaVerne 1930- *ConAu 105*
Simons, Eric Norman 1896- *ConAu 13R,*
IntAu&W 82, WrDr 84
Simons, Hans 1893-1972 *ConAu 33R*
Simons, Harry 1912- *ConAu 1R*
Simons, Howard 1929- *ConAu 65*
Simons, James Marcus 1939- *ConAu 106*
Simons, Jim *ConAu X*
Simons, John Donald 1935- *ConAu 41R*
Simons, Joseph 1933- *ConAu 81*
Simons, Katherine Drayton Mayrant 1890-1969
DcLB Y83B[port]
Simons, Katherine Drayton Mayrant 1892-
ConAu 9R
Simons, Louise *DrAP&F 83*
Simons, Robin 1951- *ConAu 65*
Simons, William Edward 1927- *ConAu 17R*
Simonson, Conrad 1931- *ConAu 49*
Simonson, Harold P 1926- *ConAu 33R,*
WrDr 84
Simonson, Lee 1888-1967 *ConAu 9R*
Simonson, Mary Jane *ConAu X*
Simonson, Solomon S 1914- *ConAu 21R*
Simont, Marc 1915- *ConAu 61, SmATA 9*
Simoons, Frederick J 1922- *ConAu 1R*
Simos, Miriam 1951- *ConAu 104*
Simper, Robert 1937- *ConAu 8NR, –61*
Simpich, Frederick, Jr. 1911-1975 *ConAu 57, –61*
Simpson, A W Brian 1931- *ConAu 5R,*
WrDr 84
Simpson, Alan 1912- *ConAu 1R*
Simpson, Alan Francis 1929- *IntAu&W 82*
Simpson, Barbara Flanagan 1920- *IntWWP 82*
Simpson, Charles Walter 1878-1942 *CreCan 2*
Simpson, Claude M, Jr. 1910-1976 *ConAu 5R,*
–65
Simpson, Colin 1908- *ConAu 5NR, –53,*
IntAu&W 82, SmATA 14, WrDr 84
Simpson, Daisy *IntWWP 82X*
Simpson, David Penistan 1917- *ConAu 9R,*
WrDr 84
Simpson, Dick 1940- *ConAu 33R,*
IntAu&W 82, WrDr 84
Simpson, Dorothy 1933- *ConAu 107*
Simpson, Elizabeth Leonie *ConAu 33R*
Simpson, Ervin 1911- *WrDr 84*
Simpson, Ervin Peter Young 1911- *ConAu 17R,*
IntAu&W 82
Simpson, Evan 1940- *ConAu 97*
Simpson, George E 1944- *ConAu 101*
Simpson, George Eaton 1904- *ConAu 77*
Simpson, George Gaylord 1902- *ConAu P-1,*
TwCA SUP
Simpson, Harold Brown 1917- *ConAu 4NR, –9R*
Simpson, Hassell A 1930- *ConAu 41R*
Simpson, Helen 1897-1940 *ConAu 109*
Simpson, Helen DeGuerry 1897-1940 *LongCTC,*
TwCA, TwCA SUP, TwCCr&M 80,
TwCWr
Simpson, Howard *ConSFA*
Simpson, Howard Russell 1925- *ConAu 1R,*
–1NR
Simpson, Ian James 1895- *ConAu P-1*
Simpson, Ida Harper 1928- *ConAu 17R*
Simpson, Jacqueline 1930- *WrDr 84*
Simpson, Jacqueline Mary 1930- *ConAu 5NR,*
–13R, IntAu&W 82
Simpson, James B 1926- *ConAu 5R, –9NR*
Simpson, Jean B 1925- *WrDr 84*
Simpson, Jean I 1896- *ConAu 5R*
Simpson, Joan Murray 1918-1977 *ConAu 89*
Simpson, John Liddle 1912- *ConAu 9R*
Simpson, Judith H 1941- *ConAu 110*
Simpson, Kemper 1893- *ConAu P-1*
Simpson, Kenneth W *DrAP&F 83*

Slack, Robert C 1914- ConAu 81
Slack, Walter H 1932- ConAu 21R
Slackman, Charles B 1934- SmATA 12
Slade, Afton 1919- ConAu 89
Slade, Bernard 1930- ConAu X, ConLC 11,
   NatPD 81[port]
Slade, Caroline 1886-1975 ConAu 61,
   TwCA SUP
Slade, Joseph W 1941- ConAu 89
Slade, Peter 1912- ConAu 13R, WrDr 84
Slade, Richard 1910-1971 ConAu 21R,
   ConAu P-2, SmATA 9
Slade, Tony 1936- ConAu 33R, WrDr 84
Sladek, John 1937- ConAu 25R, ConSFA,
   TwCSFW, WrDr 84
Sladen, Douglas Brooke Wheelton 1856-1947
   LongCTC
Sladen, Kathleen 1904- ConAu 69
Sladen, Norman St. Barbe d1969 ConAu P-1
Slaght, Lawrence T 1912- ConAu 73
Slakter, Malcolm J 1929- ConAu 41R
Slamecka, Vladimir 1928- ConAu 5R
Slaney, George Wilson 1884- ConAu P-1
Slappey, Mary McGowan 1914- IntAu&W 82,
   IntWWP 82
Slappey, Sterling G 1917- ConAu 65
Slate, Joseph 1927- ConAu 45
Slate, Joseph 1928- ConAu 110
Slate, Sam J 1909- ConAu 49
Slaten, Yeffe Kimball 1914?-1978 ConAu 77
Slater, Charlotte 1944- ConAu 65
Slater, Eliot 1904- ConAu 53, WrDr 84
Slater, Francis Carey 1876-1958 LongCTC,
   TwCWr
Slater, Humphrey 1906- LongCTC, TwCA SUP
Slater, Ian 1941- ConAu 85
Slater, Jerome N 1935- ConAu 17R
Slater, Jim 1929- SmATA 34
Slater, Leonard 1920- ConAu 13R
Slater, Lydia Elizabeth 1902- IntWWP 82
Slater, Mary 1909- WrDr 84
Slater, Mary Louise 1923- ConAu 29R
Slater, Nigel 1944- ConAu 102
Slater, Peter Gregg 1940- ConAu 81
Slater, Philip E 1927- ConAu 21R
Slater, Ralph P 1915- ConAu 21R
Slater, Robert A DrAP&F 83
Slater, Robert Henry Lawson 1896- ConAu P-1
Slater, Veronica ConAu X
Slatkin, Charles Eli 1907-1977 ConAu 73
Slatkin, Marcia DrAP&F 83
Slatoff, Walter J 1922- ConAu 9R
Slattery, Bradley IntWWP 82
Slattery, Timothy Patrick 1911- ConAu 25R,
   WrDr 84
Slattery, William J 1930- ConAu 101
Slatzer, Robert 1927- WrDr 84
Slauerhoff, Jan Jacob 1898-1936 CIDMEL 80
Slaughter, Carolyn 1946- ConAu 85, WrDr 84
Slaughter, Eugene Edward 1909- ConAu 37R,
   WrDr 84
Slaughter, Frank G 1908- WrDr 84
Slaughter, Frank Gill 1908- AuNews 2,
   ConAu 5R, -5NR, IntAu&W 82, LongCTC,
   TwCA SUP, TwCRGW
Slaughter, Howard K 1927- ConAu 45
Slaughter, Jane M 1908- ConAu 73
Slaughter, Jean ConAu X, SmATA X
Slaughter, Jim ConAu X
Slavens, Thomas Paul 1928- ConAu 104
Slavet, Joseph S 1920- ConAu 61
Slaveykov, Pencho 1866-1912 ModSL 2
Slavic, Rosalind Welcher 1922- ConAu X
Slavick, William H 1927- ConAu 104
Slavin, Arthur Joseph 1933- ConAu 3NR, -9R
Slavitt, David 1935- WrDr 84
Slavitt, David R DrAP&F 83
Slavitt, David Rytman 1935- ConAu 21R,
   ConLC 5, -14, ConP 80, DcLB 5[port],
   -6[port], DcLEL 1940, IntAu&W 82,
   IntWWP 82
Slavov, George 1932- IntAu&W 82
Slavson, Samuel Richard 1891- ConAu 17R
Slavutych, Yar 1918- ConAu 2NR, -45,
   WrDr 84
Slawson, William David 1931- ConAu 110
Slaymaker, R Samuel, II 1923- ConAu 65
Slayton, Mariette Paine 1908- ConAu 65
Sleator, William 1945- ConAu 29R, SmATA 3
Sledd, James Hinton 1914- ConAu 17R
Sledge, Linda Ching 1944- ConAu 108
Sleigh, Barbara 1906-1982 ConAu 6NR, -106,

-13R, SmATA 3, -30N, TwCCW 83
Sleigh, Daniel 1938- IntAu&W 82
Sleigh, Linwood 1902- ConAu 5R
Sleigh, Robert Collins, Jr. 1932- ConAu 37R
Sleight, Roberrt B 1922- ConAu 41R
Slemon, Gordon Richard 1924- WrDr 84
Sles, Steven Lawrence 1940- IntWWP 82
Slesar, Henry 1927- ConAu 1R, -1NR,
   TwCCr&M 80, TwCSFW, WrDr 84
Slesinger, Reuben E 1916- ConAu 5R
Slesinger, Tess 1905-1945 ConAmA, ConAu 107,
   TwCA, TwCA SUP, TwCLC 10[port]
Slesinger, Warren DrAP&F 83
Slesinger, Warren 1933- ConAu 33R, WrDr 84
Slesser, Malcolm 1926- ConAu 17R
Slessor, Kenneth 1901-1971 ConAu 102, -89,
   ConLC 14, LongCTC, ModCmwL, TwCWr,
   WorAu
Sletholt, Erik 1919- ConAu 77
Sletto, Olav 1886-1963 CIDMEL 80
Slezak, Walter 1902-1983 ConAu 109
Slicer, Margaret O 1920- ConAu 25R,
   SmATA 4
Slichter, Sumner Huber 1892-1959 TwCA SUP
Slide, Anthony 1944- ConAu 33R
Slim, William Joseph 1891-1970 ConAu 107
Slimming, John 1927-1979 ConAu 25R, -89
Slitor, Richard Eaton 1911- ConAu 45
Slive, Seymour 1920- ConAu 103
Sliwinski, Wincenty Piotr 1915- IntWWP 82
Sljivic-Simsic, Biljana 1933- ConAu 41R
Sloan, Benjamin DrAP&F 83
Sloan, Clara Helen 1916- IntWWP 82
Sloan, Edward William, III 1931- ConAu 37R
Sloan, Harold Stephenson 1887- ConAu P-1
Sloan, Irving J 1924- ConAu 7NR, -17R
Sloan, James Park DrAP&F 83
Sloan, James Park 1944- ConAu 29R
Sloan, Kay 1951- ConAu 108
Sloan, Pat 1908- ConAu 65
Sloan, Phillip R 1938- ConAu 109
Sloan, Raymond Paton 1893- ConAu P-1
Sloan, Raymond Paton 1893-1983 ConAu 109
Sloan, Ruth Catherine 1898?-1976 ConAu 65
Sloan, Stephen 1936- ConAu 33R
Sloan, Thomas 1928- ConAu 93
Sloan, William Wilson 1901- ConAu 1R
Sloane, Arthur A 1931- ConAu 33R
Sloane, Beverly LeBov 1936- IntAu&W 82
Sloane, Eric 1910- ConAu 108
Sloane, Eugene A 1926- ConAu 65
Sloane, Howard N 1932- ConAu 81
Sloane, Joseph C 1909- ConAu P-1
Sloane, Leonard 1932- ConAu 21R
Sloane, Peter J 1942- ConAu 108, WrDr 84
Sloane, R Bruce 1923- ConAu 53
Sloane, Sara ConAu X, WrDr 84
Sloane, Thomas O 1929- ConAu 37R
Sloane, William Milligan, III 1906-1974
   ConAu 53
Sloane, William Mulligan, III 1906-1974
   TwCSFW
Slobin, Dan Isaac 1939- ConAu 11NR, -65
Slobin, Mark 1943- ConAu 93
Slobodin, Richard 1915- ConAu 102
Slobodkin, Florence Gersh 1905- ConAu 1R,
   SmATA 5
Slobodkin, Louis 1903-1975 ConAu 13R, -57,
   SmATA 1, -26[port], TwCCW 83
Slobodkina, Esphyr 1908- ConAu 1NR,
   TwCCW 83, WrDr 84
Slobodkina, Esphyr 1909- ConAu 1R,
   SmATA 1
Slobodnik, Wlodzimierz 1900- IntAu&W 82,
   IntWWP 82
Slochower, Harry 1900- ConAu 2NR, -49
Slocombe, George Edward 1894-1963 LongCTC
Slocum, Bill ConAu X
Slocum, Donald Barclay 1911-1983 ConAu 110
Slocum, Joshua 1844-1910? LongCTC
Slocum, Michael ConAu X
Slocum, Robert Bigney 1922- ConAu 9R
Slocum, Walter L 1910- ConAu 21R
Slocum, William J, Jr. 1912?-1974 ConAu 53
Sloggatt, Arthur H 1917?-1975 ConAu 61
Sloma, Richard Stanley 1929- ConAu 103
Sloman, Albert Edward 1921- ConAu 5R,
   IntAu&W 82, WrDr 84
Sloman, Joel DrAP&F 83
Sloman, Larry 1948- ConAu 81
Slome, Jesse R 1952- IntAu&W 82
Slomovitz, Philip 1896- ConAu 81

Slone, Dennis 1930-1982 ConAu 106
Slone, Verna Mae 1914- ConAu 89
Slonim, Marc 1894-1976 ConAu 65, WorAu
Slonim, Morris J 1909- ConAu 1R
Slonim, Reuben 1914- ConAu 97, WrDr 84
Slonim, Ruth 1918- ConAu 17R
Slonimski, Antoni 1895-1976 CIDMEL 80,
   ConAu 65, ModSL 2, WorAu 1970
Slonimsky, Mikhail Leonidovich 1897-1972
   CIDMEL 80
Slonimsky, Nicolas 1894- ConAu 17R,
   IntAu&W 82, WrDr 84
Slonimsky, Yuri 1902-1978 ConAu 77
Slosberg, Mike 1934- ConAu 69, WrDr 84
Slosser, Bob G 1929- ConAu 10NR, -65
Slosson, Preston William 1892- ConAu 8NR, -61
Slote, Alfred 1926- ChlLR 4[port], SmATA 8
Slote, Bernice D 1915?-1983 ConAu 109
Slote, Michael A 1941- ConAu 61
Slote, Stanley J 1917- ConAu 61
Slotkin, Richard S 1942- ConAu 102
Slovenko, Ralph 1926- ConAu 17R
Slovenko, Ralph 1927- WrDr 84
Slowinski, Lech 1922- IntAu&W 82
Sloyan, Gerard Stephen 1919- ConAu 2NR, -5R
Sluckin, W 1919- ConAu 21R
Sluckin, Wladyslaw 1919- IntAu&W 82,
   WrDr 84
Slung, Louis Sheaffer 1912- ConAu 53
Slung, Michele 1947- ConAu 102
Slusher, Howard S 1937- ConAu 25R, WrDr 84
Slusser, Dorothy M 1922- ConAu 33R,
   WrDr 84
Slusser, George Edgar 1939- ConAu 69,
   IntAu&W 82
Slusser, Gerald H 1920- ConAu 13R
Slusser, Robert M 1916- ConAu 1R, -3NR
Slutsky, Boris 1919- CIDMEL 80, WorAu 1970
Smailes, Arthur Eltringham 1911- WrDr 84
Smalacombe, John CreCan 2
Small, Bertrice 1937- ConAu 77
Small, David DrAP&F 83
Small, David 1937- ConAu 108
Small, Dwight Hervey 1919- ConAu 8NR, -61
Small, Ernest ConAu X, SmATA 2,
   WrDr 84
Small, George L 1924- ConAu 85
Small, George Raphael 1918- ConAu 57
Small, Mary Vivian IntWWP 82X
Small, Melvin 1939- ConAu 29R
Small, Miriam Rossiter 1899- ConAu 1R,
   WrDr 84
Small, Norman M 1944- ConAu 41R
Small, Robert VanDyke 1924- LivgBAA,
   WrDr 84
Small, William ConAu X
Smallenburg, Harry W 1907- ConAu P-1
Smalley, Barbara Martin 1926- ConAu 105
Smalley, Beryl 1905- ConAu 103
Smalley, Donald Arthur 1907- ConAu 17R
Smalley, Ruth E 1903- ConAu P-2
Smalley, Stephen S 1931- WrDr 84
Smalley, Stephen Stewart 1931- ConAu 103
Smalley, William A 1923- ConAu 1NR, -45
Smallwood, Jason IntWWP 82X
Smallwood, Joseph Roberts 1900- ConAu 105
Smaridge, Norah 1903- ConAu 37R, SmATA 6
Smario, Tom DrAP&F 83
Smart, Alastair 1922- ConAu 37R, WrDr 84
Smart, Carol 1948- ConAu 73
Smart, Charles Allen 1904-1967 ConAu P-1,
   TwCA, TwCA SUP
Smart, Elizabeth 1913- ConAu 81,
   IntAu&W 82
Smart, Harold R 1892- ConAu P-1
Smart, J J C 1920- ConAu 7NR
Smart, James Dick 1906-1982 ConAu 8NR, -105,
   -57
Smart, John Jamieson Carswell 1920-
   ConAu 13R, WrDr 84
Smart, Mollie S 1916- ConAu 61
Smart, Ninian 1927- ConAu 29R, WrDr 84
Smart, Peter Alastair 1922- IntAu&W 82
Smart, Roderick Ninian 1927- IntAu&W 82
Smart, William 1933- ConAu 7NR, -13R
Smeaton, Kenneth Graham 1951- IntWWP 82
Smedes, Lewis B 1921- ConAu 11NR, -69
Smedley, Agnes 1894?-1950 TwCA, TwCA SUP
Smedley, Hester Marsden ConAu X
Smedley, John C DrAP&F 83
Smeeton, Miles 1906- ConAu 13R

Smellie, Kingsley Bryce Speakman 1897- *ConAu 5R*
Smelser, Marshall 1912- *ConAu 17R*
Smelser, Neil Joseph 1930- *ConAu 8NR, -17R, IntAu&W 82, WrDr 84*
Smelser, William T 1924- *ConAu 29R*
Smeltzer, Clarence Harry 1900- *ConAu 1R*
Smelyakov, Yaroslav 1913?-1972 *ConAu 37R*
Smerk, George M 1933- *ConAu 107, WrDr 84*
Smertenko, Johan J 1897?-1983 *ConAu 109*
Smerud, Warren D 1928- *ConAu 49*
Smetana, Josette 1928- *ConAu 93*
Smetzer, Michael *DrAP&F 83*
Smidt, Kristian 1916- *ConAu 17R, IntAu&W 82*
Smigel, Erwin O 1917-1973 *ConAu 41R, -45*
Smiley, David Leslie 1921- *ConAu 5R*
Smiley, Jane 1949- *ConAu 104*
Smiley, Sam Max 1931- *ConAu 105*
Smiley, Virginia Kester 1923- *ConAu 29R, SmATA 2*
Smiljanich, Dorothy Weik 1947- *ConAmTC*
Smirnov, Sergei Sergeevich 1915-1976 *ConAu 65*
Smit, Bartho 1924- *IntAu&W 82*
Smit, Philippus 1936- *IntAu&W 82*
Smith *IntAu&W 82X*
Smith, A C H *IntAu&W 82X*
Smith, A H 1903- *ConAu 5R*
Smith, A J 1924- *ConAu 65*
Smith, A J M 1902-1980 *ConAu 1R, -4NR, -102, ConLC 15, ConP 80, LongCTC, ModCmwL*
Smith, A Robert 1925- *ConAu 73*
Smith, A Weston 1900?-1975 *ConAu 57*
Smith, Abbie Whitney 1919- *MichAu 80*
Smith, Abbot E 1906-1983 *ConAu 109*
Smith, Adam *ConAu X*
Smith, Alan M 1937- *ConAu 41R*
Smith, Alfred Aloysius *LongCTC, TwCA, TwCA SUP*
Smith, Alfred Edward 1895-1969 *ConAu P-1*
Smith, Alfred G 1921- *ConAu 4NR, -9R, WrDr 84*
Smith, Alice Upham 1908- *ConAu 45*
Smith, Allen William 1938- *ConAu 61*
Smith, Alson Jesse 1908-1965 *ConAu 1R, -103*
Smith, Alton E 1917- *ConAu 17R*
Smith, Anna Hester 1912- *ConAu 6NR, -57, WrDr 84*
Smith, Anna Piszczan-Czaja 1920- *ConAu 110*
Smith, Anne Mollegen 1940- *ConAu 81*
Smith, Anne Warren 1938- *SmATA 34*
Smith, Anthony 1926- *WrDr 84*
Smith, Anthony 1938- *ConAu 10NR, -53*
Smith, Anthony Charles 1935- *IntAu&W 82*
Smith, Anthony D 1939- *ConAu 101*
Smith, Anthony John Francis 1926- *ConAu 3NR, -9R, IntAu&W 82*
Smith, Anthony Peter 1912-1980 *ConAu 105*
Smith, Arnold Cantwell 1915- *ConAu 109*
Smith, Arthur *DrAP&F 83*
Smith, Arthur C 1916- *ConAu 21R*
Smith, Arthur Cosslett 1852-1926 *TwCA, TwCA SUP*
Smith, Arthur James Marshall 1902- *CreCan 2, TwCA SUP*
Smith, Arthur L *WrDr 84*
Smith, Arthur L, Jr. 1927- *ConAu 37R, WrDr 84*
Smith, Arthur Lee 1942- *ConAu X, LivgBAA*
Smith, Arthur Mumford 1903- *ConAu P-2*
Smith, Barbara *DrAP&F 83*
Smith, Barbara A 1932- *IntAu&W 82, IntWWP 82*
Smith, Barbara Herrnstein 1932- *ConAu 13R, ConLCrt 82, WrDr 84*
Smith, Bardwell L 1925- *ConAu 41R*
Smith, Barry D 1940- *ConAu 29R*
Smith, Beatrice S *ConAu 10NR, -57, SmATA 12*
Smith, Ben A 1916- *ConAu 1R*
Smith, Benjamin Franklin 1902- *ConAu 41R*
Smith, Bernard 1916- *ConAu 1R, -1NR, WrDr 84*
Smith, Bert Kruger 1915- *ConAu 11NR, -13R, WrDr 84*
Smith, Bertie Reece 1913- *IntWWP 82*
Smith, Betty 1896-1972 *ConAu 33R, ConLC 19, DcLB Y82B[port], DcLEL 1940, SmATA 6*
Smith, Betty 1904-1972 *ConAu 5R, LongCTC, TwCA SUP*
Smith, Beulah Fenderson 1915- *ConAu 13R*

Smith, Bonnie Gene 1940- *ConAu 108*
Smith, Boyd M 1888?-1973 *ConAu 41R*
Smith, Bradford 1909-1964 *ConAu 1R, SmATA 5*
Smith, Bradley 1910- *ConAu 2NR, -5R*
Smith, Bradley F 1931- *ConAu 108, IntAu&W 82, WrDr 84*
Smith, Brian 1938- *ConAu 110, WrDr 84*
Smith, Bruce 1949- *ConAu 108*
Smith, C A *DrAP&F 83*
Smith, C Busby *ConAu X, WrDr 84*
Smith, C Fox 1882-1954 *TwCCW 83*
Smith, C Pritchard *ConAu X*
Smith, C Ray 1929- *ConAu 109*
Smith, C T 1924- *ConAu 21R*
Smith, C U 1901- *ConAu 41R*
Smith, C U M 1930- *ConAu 33R*
Smith, C W *DrAP&F 83*
Smith, C W 1940- *ConAu 61*
Smith, C Willard 1899?-1979 *ConAu 89*
Smith, Caesar *ConAu X, SmATA X, WrDr 84*
Smith, Calvin Ray 1929- *WrDr 84*
Smith, Carlton *ConAu X*
Smith, Carmichael *ConAu X*
Smith, Carol H 1929- *ConAu 5R*
Smith, Carol Sturm *DrAP&F 83*
Smith, Carol Sturm 1938- *ConAu 25R, DcLB Y81B[port]*
Smith, Carole 1935- *ConAu 101*
Smith, Carter 1930- *ConAu 107*
Smith, Catherine C 1929- *ConAu 29R*
Smith, Cecil 1917- *ConAu 69*
Smith, Chard Powers 1894-1977 *ConAu 5R, -73, TwCA, TwCA SUP*
Smith, Charles E 1904-1970 *ConAu 29R*
Smith, Charles Harvard Gibbs- *ConAu X*
Smith, Charles W 1905- *ConAu 13R*
Smith, Christopher Martin *ConAu X*
Smith, Christopher U M 1930- *WrDr 84*
Smith, Christopher Upham Murray 1930- *IntAu&W 82*
Smith, Clagett G 1930- *ConAu 37R*
Smith, Clark Ashton 1893-1961 *TwCSFW*
Smith, Clifford Neal 1923- *ConAu 41R*
Smith, Clifford Thorpe 1924- *IntAu&W 82, WrDr 84*
Smith, Clodus R 1928- *ConAu 8NR, -21R*
Smith, Colin 1927- *ConAu 102*
Smith, Cordelia Titcomb 1902- *ConAu P-1, ConSFA*
Smith, Cordwainer 1913-1966 *ConAu X, DcLB 8, TwCSFW*
Smith, Cornelius C 1913- *ConAu 21R*
Smith, Courtland L 1939- *ConAu 81*
Smith, Craig R 1944- *ConAu 81*
Smith, Curt 1951- *ConAu 81*
Smith, Cynthia S 1924- *ConAu 106*
Smith, Cyril 1928- *ConAu 109*
Smith, Cyril James 1909-1974 *ConAu 53*
Smith, D Howard 1900- *ConAu 25R*
Smith, D MacLeod *ConAu X*
Smith, D Moody, Jr. 1931- *ConAu 41R*
Smith, D V 1933- *ConAu 25R*
Smith, Dale O 1911- *ConAu 73*
Smith, Dan Throop 1908-1982 *ConAu 106*
Smith, Dana Prom 1927- *ConAu 49*
Smith, Daniel M 1922- *WrDr 84*
Smith, Daniel M 1922-1976 *ConAu 8NR, -17R*
Smith, Datus C, Jr. 1907- *ConAu 11NR, ConAu P-1, SmATA 13*
Smith, Dave *DrAP&F 83*
Smith, Dave 1942- *ConAu X, ConLC 22[port], ConP 80, DcLB 5[port], WrDr 84*
Smith, David 1942- *ConAu 1NR, -49*
Smith, David C 1929- *ConAu 49*
Smith, David C 1931- *ConAu 69*
Smith, David E 1939- *WrDr 84*
Smith, David Elvin 1939- *ConAu 29R*
Smith, David Horton 1939- *ConAu 7NR, -57, -93*
Smith, David Howard 1900- *WrDr 84*
Smith, David MacLeod 1920- *ConAu 5NR, -53*
Smith, David Marshall 1936- *ConAu 29R, WrDr 84*
Smith, David Shiverick 1918- *ConAu 108*
Smith, David T 1935- *ConAu 53*
Smith, David W 1921-1981 *ConAu 108, -110*
Smith, David Warner 1932- *ConAu 17R, WrDr 84*
Smith, Dean E 1923- *ConAu 4NR, -9R*
Smith, Delos Owen 1905-1973 *ConAu 41R*

Smith, Denison Langley 1924- *ConAu 13R*
Smith, Dennis *DrAP&F 83*
Smith, Dennis 1940- *ConAu 10NR, -61, WrDr 84*
Smith, Desmond 1927- *ConAu 103*
Smith, Dick 1908-1974 *ConAu P-1*
Smith, Dinitia *DrAP&F 83*
Smith, Dodie *WrDr 84*
Smith, Dodie 1896- *ConAu 33R, ConDr 82, DcLB 10[port], IntAu&W 82, LongCTC, SmATA 4, TwCCW 83, WorAu*
Smith, Dolletta Jean 1931- *IntWWP 82*
Smith, Don 1909- *ConAu 49*
Smith, Don Ian 1918- *ConAu 45*
Smith, Donal Ian Bryce 1934- *ConAu 41R*
Smith, Donald Eugene 1927- *ConAu 9R*
Smith, Donald G 1927- *ConAu 13R*
Smith, Doris Buchanan 1934- *ConAu 11NR, -69, SmATA 28[port]*
Smith, Doris E 1919- *ConAu 25R, TwCRGW, WrDr 84*
Smith, Dorothy Anita 1927- *IntWWP 82*
Smith, Dorothy Dumbrille *CreCan 2*
Smith, Dorothy Gladys 1896- *LongCTC*
Smith, Dorothy Stafford 1905- *ConAu 21R, SmATA 6*
Smith, Dorothy Valentine 1908- *ConAu 29R*
Smith, Doug 1935- *ConAmTC*
Smith, Douglas 1918- *ConAu 73*
Smith, Duane Allan 1937- *ConAu 8NR, -21R, IntAu&W 82, WrDr 84*
Smith, Dudley 1926- *IntAu&W 82, WrDr 84*
Smith, Dwight C, Jr. 1930- *ConAu 77*
Smith, Dwight L 1918- *ConAu 33R, IntAu&W 82, WrDr 84*
Smith, Dwight R 1921- *ConAu 106*
Smith, E Brooks 1917- *ConAu 5R*
Smith, E E 1890-1965 *DcLB 8[port], TwCSFW*
Smith, Earl Hobson 1898- *IntAu&W 82, NatPD 81[port]*
Smith, Edgar H 1934- *ConAu 25R*
Smith, Edna Hopkins 1932?-1979 *ConAu 89*
Smith, Edward Conrad 1891- *ConAu 45*
Smith, Edward Ellis 1921- *ConAu 25R*
Smith, Edward Elmer 1890-1965 *ConAu 102*
Smith, Edward W 1920-1975 *ConAu 57*
Smith, Edwin H 1919- *WrDr 84*
Smith, Edwin H 1920- *ConAu 13R*
Smith, Elbert B 1920- *ConAu 21R*
Smith, Lady Eleanor Furneaux 1902-1945 *LongCTC, TwCA, TwCA SUP, TwCRGW*
Smith, Eleanor Touhey 1910- *ConAu 25R*
Smith, Elinor Goulding 1917- *ConAu 1R, -3NR*
Smith, Ella 1933- *WrDr 84*
Smith, Elliott Dunlap 1890?-1976 *ConAu 61*
Smith, Elsdon Coles 1903- *ConAu 1R, -6NR, IntAu&W 82, WrDr 84*
Smith, Elske V P 1929- *ConAu 77*
Smith, Elton Edward 1915- *ConAu 13R, IntAu&W 82, WrDr 84*
Smith, Elva Sophronia 1871-1965 *ConAu 107, SmATA 31*
Smith, Elwyn Allen 1919- *ConAu 5R, -9NR*
Smith, Emma 1923- *ConAu 73, ConNov 82, DcLEL 1940, IntAu&W 82, LongCTC, TwCCW 83, WrDr 84*
Smith, Ernest A 1911-1977 *ConAu 1R, -103*
Smith, Ernest Bramah 1869?-1942 *LongCTC, TwCA*
Smith, Ethel Sabin 1887- *ConAu P-1, WrDr 84*
Smith, Eugene L 1912- *ConAu 21R*
Smith, Eugene Waldo 1905- *ConAu P-1*
Smith, Eunice Young 1902- *ConAu 2NR, ConAu P-1, SmATA 5*
Smith, Evelyn E 1927- *ConSFA, TwCSFW, WrDr 84*
Smith, F G Walton 1909- *ConAu 45*
Smith, F Joseph 1925- *ConAu 2NR, -45*
Smith, Fay Jackson 1912- *ConAu 25R*
Smith, Florence Margaret 1902-1971 *ConAu 29R, ConAu P-2, ConLC 8, WorAu*
Smith, Frances C 1904- *ConAu 1R, -1NR, SmATA 3*
Smith, Frances Scott Fitzgerald 1921- *AuNews 1*
Smith, Francis J *DrAP&F 83*
Smith, Frank 1917- *ConAu 69*
Smith, Frank Ellis 1918- *ConAu 17R, WrDr 84*
Smith, Frank Kingston 1919- *ConAu 102*
Smith, Frank O M d1983 *ConAu 109*
Smith, Frank Seymour 1898-1972 *ConAu 9R, -89*
Smith, Fred 1898?-1976 *ConAu 69*
Smith, Frederick E 1922- *ConAu 3NR, -5R,*

IntAu&W 82, WrDr 84
Smith, Frederick W 1920- *ConAu 73*
Smith, Frederick Winston Furneaux 1907-1975
  ConAu 57, –65
Smith, Fredrika Shumway 1877-1968 *ConAu 109,*
  SmATA 30
Smith, G E Kidder 1913- *ConAu 9R*
Smith, Gaddis 1932- *ConAu 21R*
Smith, Garry 1933- *ConAu 5R*
Smith, Gary 1943- *ConAu 97*
Smith, Gary R 1932- *ConAu 69, SmATA 14*
Smith, Gary V 1943- *ConAu 101*
Smith, Gene 1924- *ConAu 77*
Smith, Gene 1929- *ConAu 81*
Smith, Genevieve Love 1917- *ConAu 21R*
Smith, Geoffrey Sutton 1941- *ConAu 49*
Smith, George 1922- *ConAu 103*
Smith, George E 1938- *ConAu 37R*
Smith, George H 1922- *ConSFA, TwCSFW,*
  WrDr 84
Smith, George Harmon 1920- *ConAu 49,*
  SmATA 5
Smith, George O 1911- *WrDr 84*
Smith, George O 1911-1981 *ConAu 103, –97,*
  DcLB 8[port], TwCSFW
Smith, Gerald A 1921- *ConAu 37R*
Smith, Gerald B 1909- *ConAu P-2*
Smith, Gerald L K 1898-1976 *ConAu 65*
Smith, Glenn Allen 1935- *NatPD 81[port]*
Smith, Godfrey 1926- *ConAu 9R*
Smith, Goldwin 1823-1910 *LongCTC*
Smith, Goldwin 1912- *ConAu 41R*
Smith, Gord 1937- *CreCan 2*
Smith, Gordon Appelbe 1919- *CreCan 1*
Smith, Gordon Ross 1917- *ConAu 5R*
Smith, Grahame 1933- *ConAu 25R*
Smith, Gretchen L d1972 *ConAu 104*
Smith, Grover Cleveland 1923- *ConAu 33R,*
  WrDr 84
Smith, Gudmund J W 1920- *ConAu 102*
Smith, Guy-Harold 1895- *ConAu P-2*
Smith, H Allen 1907-1976 *AuNews 2,*
  ConAu 5R, –5NR, –65, LongCTC,
  SmATA 20N
Smith, Hale G 1918- *ConAu 61*
Smith, Hallett 1907- *ConAu 21R*
Smith, Harmon L 1930- *ConAu 29R*
Smith, Harris 1921- *ConAu 49*
Smith, Harrison 1888-1971 *ConAu 29R*
Smith, Harry *DrAP&F 83*
Smith, Harry 1936- *ConAu 77, IntWWP 82*
Smith, Harry Allen 1907- *TwCA SUP*
Smith, Harry C *DrAP&F 83*
Smith, Harry E 1928- *ConAu 25R*
Smith, Harvey K 1904-1968 *ConAu P-1*
Smith, Hedrick 1933- *ConAu 11NR, –65,*
  IntAu&W 82, WrDr 84
Smith, Helen C 1903- *WrDr 84*
Smith, Helen Creeger 1924- *ConAmTC*
Smith, Helen Zenna *TwCRGW*
Smith, Henry Clay 1913- *ConAu 1R*
Smith, Henry Lee, Jr. 1913-1972 *ConAu 37R*
Smith, Henry Nash 1906- *ConAu 1R, –2NR,*
  IntAu&W 82
Smith, Henry Peter 1910-1968 *ConAu 1R, –103*
Smith, Herbert F 1922- *ConAu 77*
Smith, Herbert F A 1915-1969 *ConAu P-1*
Smith, Hermon Dunlap 1900-1983 *ConAu 109*
Smith, Hobart M 1912- *ConAu 9NR*
Smith, Hobart Muir 1912- *ConAu 65,*
  IntAu&W 82, WrDr 84
Smith, Hope M 1916- *ConAu 1R*
Smith, Howard E, Jr. 1927- *ConAu 25R,*
  SmATA 12, WrDr 84
Smith, Howard K 1914- *WrDr 84*
Smith, Howard Kingsbury 1914- *ConAu 2NR,*
  –45, IntAu&W 82
Smith, Howard Ross 1917- *ConAu 1R,*
  WrDr 84
Smith, Howard Van 1910- *ConAu 5R*
Smith, Hugh L 1921-1968 *ConAu P-2,*
  SmATA 5
Smith, Huston 1919- *ConAu 61*
Smith, I Norman 1909- *ConAu 107*
Smith, Iain Crichton 1928- *ConAu 21R,*
  ConNov 82, ConP 80, DcLEL 1940,
  WhoTwCL, WorAu 1970, WrDr 84
Smith, Imogene Henderson 1922- *ConAu 5R,*
  SmATA 12
Smith, Irene 1903- *ConAu 73*
Smith, Irving H 1932- *ConAu 49*
Smith, Irwin 1892-1977 *ConAu 5R, –73*

Smith, Isadore Leighton Luce 1901- *ConAu 101*
Smith, Ivan Harford 1931- *IntAu&W 82*
Smith, J Holland 1932- *ConAu 17R*
Smith, J L B 1897-1968 *ConAu P-1*
Smith, J Malcolm 1921- *ConAu 49*
Smith, Jack 1916- *ConAu 69*
Smith, Jackie M 1930- *ConAu 93*
Smith, Jackson Algernon 1917- *ConAu 105*
Smith, James 1904-1972 *ConAu 85,*
  ConLCrt 82
Smith, James A 1914- *ConAu 21R, WrDr 84*
Smith, James L 1936- *ConAu 25R, WrDr 84*
Smith, James Morton 1919- *ConAu 103*
Smith, James R 1941- *ConAu 101*
Smith, James Roy 1920- *ConAu 21R*
Smith, Jane I 1937- *ConAu 107*
Smith, Janet Buchanan Adam 1905- *LongCTC*
Smith, Jared *DrAP&F 83*
Smith, Jared 1950- *IntWWP 82*
Smith, Jean *ConAu X, SmATA X*
Smith, Jean DeMouthe 1949- *ConAu 65*
Smith, Jean Edward 1932- *ConAu 37R*
Smith, Jean Moore 1905- *IntWWP 82*
Smith, Jean Pajot 1945- *ConAu 53, SmATA 10*
Smith, Jerome F 1928- *ConAu 107*
Smith, Jessica 1895- *ConAu 2NR, –49,*
  IntAu&W 82
Smith, Jessie Carney 1930- *ConAu 89,*
  LivgBAA
Smith, Jessie Willcox 1863-1935
  SmATA 21[port]
Smith, Joan 1935- *ConAu 61*
Smith, Joan 1938- *TwCRGW, WrDr 84*
Smith, Joan K 1939- *ConAu 93*
Smith, Joanmarie 1932- *ConAu 85*
Smith, Joe William Ashley 1914- *ConAu 5R*
Smith, John *ConAu X, WrDr 84*
Smith, John 1924- *ConAu 103, ConP 80*
Smith, John Chabot 1915- *ConAu 69*
Smith, John Edwin 1921- *ConAu 103*
Smith, John F 1934- *ConAu 81*
Smith, John H 1928- *ConAu 9R*
Smith, John Ivor 1927- *CreCan 2*
Smith, John Meredith *CreCan 2*
Smith, John Norton *ConAu X*
Smith, Johnston *ConAu X*
Smith, Jon R 1946- *ConAu 77*
Smith, Jordan *DrAP&F 83*
Smith, Jordan 1954- *ConAu 110*
Smith, Joseph B 1921- *ConAu 65*
Smith, Joseph Fielding 1876-1972 *ConAu 37R*
Smith, Joseph H 1913-1981 *ConAu 105*
Smith, Joseph Russell 1874-1966 *ConAu P-1*
Smith, Josephine Jones 1907- *IntWWP 82*
Smith, Julia Floyd 1914- *ConAu 85*
Smith, Julian 1937- *ConAu 61*
Smith, Julian W 1901- *ConAu 13R*
Smith, Justin Harvey 1857-1930 *TwCA*
Smith, K Wayne 1938- *ConAu 29R*
Smith, Karl U 1907- *ConAu 9NR, –61*
Smith, Kathleen J 1929- *WrDr 84*
Smith, Kathleen Joan 1929- *ConAu 103*
Smith, Kay *ConAu X*
Smith, Kay 1911- *CreCan 1*
Smith, Kay 1925- *MichAu 80*
Smith, Kay Nolte 1932- *ConAu 101*
Smith, Ken *DrAP&F 83*
Smith, Ken 1902- *ConAu 1NR, –45*
Smith, Ken 1938- *ConAu 33R, ConP 80,*
  WrDr 84
Smith, Kenneth Edward 1944- *IntWWP 82*
Smith, Kenneth Lee 1925- *ConAu 77*
Smith, Kenneth M 1892-1981 *ConAu 108*
Smith, L Glenn 1939- *ConAu 93*
Smith, L Shelbert 1922- *LivgBAA*
Smith, Lacey Baldwin 1922- *ConAu 5R, –6NR,*
  WrDr 84
Smith, Lafayette *SmATA 4*
Smith, Larry *DrAP&F 83*
Smith, Larry 1940- *ConAu 49*
Smith, Larry 1950- *IntWWP 82*
Smith, Laura I 1902- *ConAu 17R*
Smith, Lavon B 1921- *ConAu 21R*
Smith, Lawrence Berk 1939- *ConAu 73*
Smith, Lee *DrAP&F 83, SmATA X*
Smith, Lee 1937- *ConAu 73*
Smith, Lee 1944- *ConLC 25[port],*
  DcLB Y83B[port]
Smith, Lee L 1930- *ConAu 29R*

Smith, Lena 1914- *ConAu 93*
Smith, Lendon H 1921- *ConAu 81*
Smith, LeRoi 1934- *ConAu 29R*
Smith, Leslie F 1901- *ConAu P-1*
Smith, Leslie R 1904- *ConAu 1R*
Smith, Lew *ConAu X, WrDr 84*
Smith, Lillian Eugenia 1897-1966 *ConAu 25R,*
  ConAu P-2, LongCTC, TwCA SUP
Smith, Lillian H 1887-1983 *SmATA 32N*
Smith, Linell Nash 1932- *ConAu 5R,*
  SmATA 2
Smith, Liz 1923- *ConAu 65*
Smith, Logan Pearsall 1865-1946 *CnMWL,*
  ConAmA, LongCTC, ModBrL, TwCA,
  TwCA SUP, TwCWr
Smith, Lois Irene 1929- *CreCan 1*
Smith, Lou 1918- *ConAu 73*
Smith, Louis M 1929- *ConAu 17R*
Smith, Lucia B 1943- *ConAu 108,*
  SmATA 30[port]
Smith, M Brewster 1919- *ConAu 61*
Smith, M Estellie 1935- *ConAu 8NR, –61*
Smith, M Weston *ConAu X*
Smith, Malcolm 1938- *ConAu 97*
Smith, Manuel 1934- *ConAu 105*
Smith, Marc P 1934- *NatPD 81[port]*
Smith, Marcus J 1918- *ConAu 73*
Smith, Margaret Chase 1897- *ConAu 73*
Smith, Margaret F 1915- *ConAu 102*
Smith, Margaret Mary 1916- *ConAu 108,*
  WrDr 84
Smith, Margaret Ruth 1902- *ConAu P-1,*
  IntAu&W 82, WrDr 84
Smith, Margarita G 1923?-1983 *ConAu 109*
Smith, Margery 1916- *IntAu&W 82,*
  IntWWP 82
Smith, Marie D *ConAu 13R*
Smith, Marion Hagens 1913- *ConAu 17R,*
  SmATA 12
Smith, Marion Jaques 1899- *ConAu 11NR, –69,*
  SmATA 13
Smith, Mark *DrAP&F 83*
Smith, Mark 1915- *DcLB Y82B[port]*
Smith, Mark 1935- *ConAu 10NR*
Smith, Mark Richard 1935- *ConAu 13R,*
  WrDr 84
Smith, Marny 1932- *ConAu 108*
Smith, Martha Ann 1949- *ConAmTC*
Smith, Martin 1942- *ConAu 6NR, –85*
Smith, Martin Cruz 1942- *ConLC 25[port]*
Smith, Martin William *ConAu X*
Smith, Mary 1918- *IntAu&W 82*
Smith, Mary Benton 1903- *ConAu P-2*
Smith, Mary Elizabeth 1932- *ConAu 41R*
Smith, Mary Ellen *ConAu 69, SmATA 10*
Smith, Mary Prudence Wells 1840-1930 *TwCA*
Smith, Mason *DrAP&F 83*
Smith, Mason McCann 1952- *ConAu 108*
Smith, Maxwell A 1894- *WrDr 84*
Smith, Maxwell Austin 1894- *ConAu 37R,*
  IntAu&W 82
Smith, Mbembe Milton *DrAP&F 83*
Smith, Merriman 1913-1970 *ConAu 1R, –2NR,*
  –29R
Smith, Merritt Roe 1940- *ConAu 77*
Smith, Michael 1935- *ConAu 11NR, –21R,*
  ConDr 82, WrDr 84
Smith, Michael 1942- *ConP 80, WrDr 84*
Smith, Michael A 1942- *ConAu 102*
Smith, Michael P 1942- *ConAu 65*
Smith, Michael Stephen 1944- *ConAu 103*
Smith, Mike *ConAu X, SmATA X*
Smith, Mike 1951- *IntWWP 82*
Smith, Mildred C 1891-1973 *ConAu 101, –45*
Smith, Mildred Nelson 1918- *ConAu 69*
Smith, Mortimer B 1906-1981 *ConAu 104, –107*
Smith, Morton 1915- *ConAu 5R, –6NR,*
  WrDr 84
Smith, Morton Howison 1923- *ConAu 45*
Smith, Murphy D 1920- *ConAu 37R*
Smith, Myron J, Jr. 1944- *ConAu 1NR, –45,*
  IntAu&W 82
Smith, N J 1930- *ConAu 103*
Smith, Nancy Covert 1935- *ConAu 10NR, –57,*
  SmATA 12
Smith, Nancy Taylor *ConAu 57*
Smith, Naomi Royde 1891- *TwCA, TwCA SUP*
Smith, Neil Homer 1909?-1972 *ConAu 37R*
Smith, Nigel J H 1949- *ConAu 109*
Smith, Nila Banton *ConAu 21R, WrDr 84*
Smith, Norman David 1923- *IntAu&W 82,*
  WrDr 84

Smith, Norman Edward Mace 1914- *ConAu 103,*
WrDr 84
Smith, Norman F 1920- *ConAu 29R,*
SmATA 5
Smith, Norman Lewis 1941- *ConAu 77*
Smith, Norris Kelly 1917- *ConAu 21R*
Smith, Ophia Delilah 1891- *ConAu 5R,*
IntAu&W 82
Smith, P J 1931- *ConAu 41R*
Smith, Page 1917- *ConAu 1R, -2NR, WrDr 84*
Smith, Pater H 1940- *ConAu 41R*
Smith, Patrick 1936- *ConAu 77, IntAu&W 82*
Smith, Patrick D *DrAP&F 83*
Smith, Patrick David 1927- *ConAu 77*
Smith, Patrick J 1932- *ConAu 41R*
Smith, Patrick Wykeham Montague *ConAu X*
Smith, Patti *DrAP&F 83*
Smith, Patti 1946- *ConAu 93, ConLC 12*
Smith, Pattie Sherwood 1909?-1974 *ConAu 53*
Smith, Paul 1920?- *ConAu 1R, -2NR*
Smith, Paul B 1921- *ConAu 10NR*
Smith, Paul Brainerd 1921- *ConAu 13R*
Smith, Paul C 1908-1976 *ConAu 65*
Smith, Paul F 1919- *ConAu 57*
Smith, Paul H 1931- *ConAu 89*
Smith, Pauline 1882?-1959? *TwCWr*
Smith, Pauline C 1908- *ConAu 29R,*
SmATA 27[port]
Smith, Perry McCoy 1934- *ConAu 29R*
Smith, Peter 1897-1982 *ConAu 107*
Smith, Peter Charles Horstead 1940-
ConAu 7NR, -57, WrDr 84
Smith, Peter J 1931- *WrDr 84*
Smith, Peter John 1931- *ConAu 1R*
Smith, Phil *DrAP&F 83*
Smith, Philip Chadwick Foster 1939- *ConAu 77*
Smith, Philip Edward, II 1943- *ConAu 25R*
Smith, Philip L 1943- *ConAu 108*
Smith, Philip Raymond 1947- *IntWWP 82*
Smith, Quinn 1943- *IntWWP 82*
Smith, R C 1907- *ConAu 65*
Smith, R E *DrAP&F 83*
Smith, R Philip 1907- *ConAu 81*
Smith, R Selby 1914- *ConAu 108*
Smith, R T *DrAP&F 83*
Smith, Ralph Alexander 1929- *ConAu 77*
Smith, Ralph Bernard 1939- *ConAu 33R,*
WrDr 84
Smith, Ralph Lee 1927- *ConAu 1R, -1NR,*
WrDr 84
Smith, Ray *DrAP&F 83*
Smith, Ray 1915- *ConAu 11NR, -13R,*
IntWWP 82
Smith, Ray 1941- *ConAu 101*
Smith, Ray Winfield 1897-1982 *ConAu 110*
Smith, Raymond Harley 1945- *IntAu&W 82,*
WrDr 84
Smith, Raymond T 1925- *ConAu 5R*
Smith, Red 1905-1982 *ConAu X*
Smith, Reginald Arthur 1904- *WrDr 84*
Smith, Rex Alan 1921- *ConAu 61*
Smith, Rhea Marsh 1907- *ConAu P-1*
Smith, Rhoten A 1921- *ConAu 13R*
Smith, Richard 1941- *ConAu 81*
Smith, Richard Albert Newton 1908- *ConAu 9R*
Smith, Richard Austin 1911- *ConAu 17R*
Smith, Richard C 1948- *ConAu 81*
Smith, Richard Harris 1946- *ConAu 41R*
Smith, Richard Joseph 1944- *ConAu 97*
Smith, Richard K 1936- *ConAu 41R*
Smith, Richard M 1946- *ConAu 73*
Smith, Richard N 1937- *ConAu 21R*
Smith, Richard Rein 1930- *ConAu 97*
Smith, Rick *DrAP&F 83*
Smith, Robert A 1944- *ConAu 69*
Smith, Robert Allan 1909-1980 *ConAu 105*
Smith, Robert Charles 1938- *ConAu 65*
Smith, Robert D 1937- *ConAu 37R*
Smith, Robert Dickie 1928- *ConAu 9R,*
IntAu&W 82
Smith, Robert Eliot 1899- *ConAu 37R*
Smith, Robert Ellis 1940- *ConAu 89, WrDr 84*
Smith, Robert Freeman 1930- *ConAu 1R, -1NR*
Smith, Robert G 1913- *ConAu 45*
Smith, Robert G 1947- *ConAu 102*
Smith, Robert Griffin, Jr. 1920- *ConAu 41R*
Smith, Robert Houston 1931- *ConAu 105*
Smith, Robert J 1927- *ConAu 53*
Smith, Robert Kimmel 1930- *ConAu 8NR, -61,*
NatPD 81[port], SmATA 12
Smith, Robert L *DrAP&F 83*
Smith, Robert Nelson 1916- *WrDr 84*

Smith, Robert Paul 1915-1977 *ConAu 69, -73,*
SmATA 30N, WorAu
Smith, Robert S 1904-1969 *ConAu P-1*
Smith, Robert Wayne 1926- *ConAu 45,*
IntAu&W 82
Smith, Robert William 1926- *ConAu 13R*
Smith, Rockwell Carter 1908- *ConAu 53*
Smith, Rodney P, Jr. 1930- *ConAu 29R*
Smith, Roger H 1932-1980 *ConAu 101, -69*
Smith, Roger Montgomery 1915-1975 *ConAu 57*
Smith, Roland B 1909- *ConAu 1R*
Smith, Ronald Gregor 1913-1968 *ConAu P-1*
Smith, Ronald L 1952- *ConAu 110*
Smith, Rowland 1938- *ConAu 45, WrDr 84*
Smith, Roy H, III 1936- *ConAu 25R*
Smith, Russell E 1932- *ConAu 77*
Smith, Russell F W 1915?-1975 *ConAu 61*
Smith, Ruth Leslie 1902- *ConAu P-2,*
SmATA 2
Smith, Ruth Schluchter 1917- *ConAu 11NR, -69*
Smith, S G Denis 1932- *ConAu 103*
Smith, S S *ConAmA, TwCA, TwCA SUP*
Smith, Sally Liberman 1929- *ConAu 11NR,*
-21R
Smith, Sam 1937- *ConAu 73*
Smith, Samuel 1904- *ConAu 11NR, -29R*
Smith, Sarah Stafford *ConAu X, SmATA 6*
Smith, Scottie Fitzgerald *AuNews 1*
Smith, Sharon 1947- *ConAu 77*
Smith, Sheila Kaye *LongCTC, TwCA,*
TwCA SUP
Smith, Shelley 1912- *IntAu&W 82X,*
TwCCr&M 80, WrDr 84
Smith, Shelly *ConAu X*
Smith, Shirley M 1923- *ConAu 4NR, -53,*
IntWWP 82
Smith, Stan 1946- *ConAu 85*
Smith, Stephen Murray *ConAu X*
Smith, Steven A 1939- *ConAu 57*
Smith, Steven Phillip *DrAP&F 83*
Smith, Steven Phillip 1943- *ConAu 10NR, -57*
Smith, Stevie 1902-1971 *ConAu X, ConLC 3,*
-8, -25[port], ConP 80A, LongCTC,
ModBrL, ModBrL SUP, WorAu
Smith, Stevie 1903-1971 *RGFMBP*
Smith, Susan Carlton 1923- *SmATA 12*
Smith, Susy 1911- *ConAu 5R, -6NR*
Smith, Sydney Bernard 1936- *IntAu&W 82,*
IntWWP 82
Smith, Sydney Goodsir 1915- *DcLEL 1940*
Smith, Sydney Goodsir 1915-1975? *ConAu 101,*
-57, ConP 80A, ModBrL, WorAu
Smith, T C 1915- *ConAu 49*
Smith, T E 1916- *ConAu 13R*
Smith, T Lynn 1903- *ConAu 5R*
Smith, Talbot 1899- *ConAu P-1*
Smith, Terence 1938- *ConAu 73*
Smith, Thomas B 1915- *WrDr 84*
Smith, Thomas Broun 1915- *IntAu&W 82*
Smith, Thomas Lynn 1903- *WrDr 84*
Smith, Thomas Malcolm 1921- *ConAu 106*
Smith, Thorne 1892?-1934 *LongCTC, TwCA*
Smith, Timothy Dudley *ConAu X*
Smith, Tom *DrAP&F 83*
Smith, Tony *ConAu X, -93*
Smith, Varrel Lavere 1925- *ConAu 29R*
Smith, Verla Lee 1927?-1982 *ConAu 106*
Smith, Vernon Lomax 1927- *ConAu 1R, -6NR*
Smith, Vesta 1933- *ConAu 5R*
Smith, Vian 1919-1969 *SmATA 11*
Smith, Vian 1920-1969 *ConAu 1R, -3NR,*
TwCCW 83
Smith, Victor C 1902- *ConAu 5R*
Smith, Vincent Edward 1915-1972 *ConAu 33R*
Smith, Virginia Carlson 1904- *ConAu 49*
Smith, Virginia E *DrAP&F 83*
Smith, Virginia Masterman *ConAu X*
Smith, Vivian 1933- *WrDr 84*
Smith, Vivian Brian 1933- *ConAu 8NR, -61,*
ConP 80, IntAu&W 82, IntWWP 82
Smith, W David 1928- *ConAu 77*
Smith, W Eugene 1918?-1978 *ConAu 81*
Smith, Wade *TwCWW*
Smith, Wallace 1888?-1937 *TwCA*
Smith, Walter W 1905-1982 *ConAu 105, -77*
Smith, Ward *ConAu X, SmATA X*
Smith, Warren L 1914-1972 *ConAu P-2*
Smith, Warren Sylvester 1912- *ConAu 21R*
Smith, Webster *ConAu X*
Smith, Wendell 1914-1972 *ConAu 104*
Smith, Wendell I 1921- *ConAu 13R*
Smith, Wesley E 1938- *ConAu 29R*

Smith, Whitney, Jr. 1940- *ConAu 97*
Smith, Wilbur 1933- *WrDr 84*
Smith, Wilbur Addison 1933- *ConAu 7NR, -13R*
Smith, Wilbur Moorehead 1894- *ConAu 17R*
Smith, Wilford E 1916- *ConAu 49*
Smith, Wilfred Cantwell 1916- *ConAu 7NR,*
-13R, WrDr 84
Smith, Wilfred R 1915- *ConAu 13R*
Smith, Willard L 1927- *ConAu 5R*
Smith, William A 1929- *ConAu 45*
Smith, William Allen 1904- *ConAu 45*
Smith, William Arthur 1918- *SmATA 10*
Smith, William Dale 1929- *ConAu 49*
Smith, William Ernest 1892- *ConAu 5R*
Smith, William Frank 1925- *ConAu 103*
Smith, William Gardner 1926-1974 *ConAu 53,*
-65, LivgBAA
Smith, William I 1932- *ConAu 29R*
Smith, William Jay *DrAP&F 83*
Smith, William Jay 1918- *ConAu 5R, ConLC 6,*
ConP 80, DcLB 5[port], DcLEL 1940,
SmATA 2, TwCCW 83, WorAu, WrDr 84
Smith, William Martin 1911- *ConAu 105*
Smith, William Ronald *CreCan 1*
Smith, William S 1917- *ConAu 13R*
Smith, William Stevenson 1907-1969 *ConAu P-2*
Smith, Wilson 1922- *ConAu 81*
Smith, Winchell 1871-1933 *CnMD, ModWD*
Smith, Woodrow Wilson *ConAu X*
Smith, Woodruff D 1946- *ConAu 85*
Smith, Z Z *ConAu X, IntAu&W 82X,*
SmATA X
Smith Brindle, Reginald 1917- *ConAu 89*
Smith Holley, Barbara *IntWWP 82X*
Smithdas, Robert Joseph 1925- *ConAu 17R,*
IntWWP 82
Smithells, Roger 1905- *ConAu P-1*
Smither, Elizabeth 1941- *ConAu 107, ConP 80,*
WrDr 84
Smitherman, P H 1910- *ConAu 21R*
Smithers, Don LeRoy 1933- *ConAu 45*
Smithers, Peter 1913- *WrDr 84*
Smithers, Peter Henry Berry Otway 1913-
ConAu 29R, -29R
Smithgall, Elizabeth *ConAu X*
Smithies, Arthur 1907-1981 *ConAu 104*
Smithies, Muriel *IntAu&W 82*
Smithies, Richard H R 1936- *ConAu 21R*
Smithson, Alison 1928- *ConAu 5NR, -25R,*
WrDr 84
Smithson, Norman 1931- *ConAu 33R*
Smithson, Peter 1923- *WrDr 84*
Smithson, Peter Denham 1923- *ConAu 5NR, -53*
Smithson, Rulon N 1927- *ConAu 45*
Smithyman, Kendrick 1922- *ConAu 101,*
ConP 80, IntWWP 82, WrDr 84
Smithyman, William Kendrick 1922-
DcLEL 1940
Smits, Teo *ConAu X, SmATA X*
Smits, Theodore R 1905- *ConAu 77,*
SmATA 28
Smitten, Jeffrey Roger 1941- *ConAu 105*
Smitter, Wessel 1894-1951 *TwCA, TwCA SUP*
Smoke, Jim *ConAu 109*
Smoke, Richard 1944- *ConAu 10NR, -65*
Smolansky, Oles M 1930- *ConAu 1NR, -45*
Smolar, Boris 1897- *ConAu 41R*
Smolich, Yurik K 1899?-1976 *ConAu 69*
Smolin, C Roger 1948- *ConAu 110*
Smolinski, Madeleine Joyce 1948- *IntWWP 82*
Smolka Harry *IntAu&W 82X*
Smoller, Sanford Jerome 1937- *ConAu 57*
Smollett, Harry Peter 1912- *IntAu&W 82*
Smooha, Sammy 1941- *ConAu 101*
Smoot, Dan 1913- *ConAu 1NR*
Smoot, H D 1913- *ConAu 1R*
Smothers, Frank A 1901-1981 *ConAu 104*
Smout, T C 1933- *ConAu 9NR, -21R*
Smrek, Jan 1898- *CIDMEL 80, ModSL 2*
Smucker, Barbara 1915- *ConAu 106,*
SmATA 29[port]
Smucker, Barbara Claassen 1915- *TwCCW 83*
Smucker, Leonard 1928- *ConAu 21R*
Smullyan, Arthur Francis 1912- *ConAu 1R*
Smurl, James F 1934- *ConAu 45*
Smurr, John Welling 1922- *ConAu 1R*
Smurthwaite, Ronald 1918-1975 *ConAu P-2*
Smuts, Jan Christian 1870-1950 *LongCTC*
Smyer, Richard 1935- *ConAu 102*
Smykay, Edward Walter 1924- *ConAu 17R*
Smylie, James H 1925- *ConAu 37R*
Smyser, Adam A 1920- *ConAu 77*

Smyser, H M 1901- *ConAu P-1*
Smyser, Jane Worthington 1914-1975 *ConAu 61, -65*
Smyth, Alice M *ConAu X*
Smyth, David 1929- *ConAu 61*
Smyth, Ethel 1858-1944 *LongCTC*
Smyth, Harriet Rucker 1926- *ConAu 1R, WrDr 84*
Smyth, Howard McGaw 1901-1971 *ConAu 61*
Smyth, James Desmond 1917- *WrDr 84*
Smyth, John 1893- *WrDr 84*
Smyth, John 1893-1983 *ConAu 109, -11NR*
Smyth, Sir John 1893- *ConAu 61*
Smyth, Paul *DrAP&F 83*
Smyth, Paul 1944- *ConAu 8NR, -61*
Smyth, R L 1922- *ConAu 9R, -10NR*
Smythe, Colin Peter 1942- *ConAu 97, IntAu&W 82*
Smythe, Daniel Webster 1908- *ConAu 13R*
Smythe, David Mynders 1915- *ConAu 1R*
Smythe, Donald 1927- *ConAu 41R*
Smythe, Hugh H 1913-1977 *ConAu 9R, -69, LivgBAA*
Smythe, Mabel M 1918- *ConAu 37R, LivgBAA*
Smythe, Reginald 1918?- *AuNews 1*
Smythe, Ted Curtis 1932- *ConAu 101*
Smythies, J R 1922- *ConAu 37R*
Smythies, John Raymond 1922- *WrDr 84*
Snadowsky, Alvin M 1938- *ConAu 61*
Snailham, Richard 1930- *ConAu 37R*
Snaith, John Collis 1876-1936 *LongCTC, TwCA*
Snaith, Norman Henry 1898-1982 *ConAu 106*
Snaith, William Theodore 1908-1974 *ConAu 106, -110*
Snap *IntAu&W 82X*
Snape, Henry Currie 1902- *ConAu 9R*
Snape, R H 1936- *ConAu 29R*
Snapes, Joan 1925- *ConAu 107*
Snavely, Adam A 1930- *ConAu 25R*
Snavely, Ellen Bartow 1910- *ConAu P-2*
Snavely, Guy Everett 1881-1974 *ConAu 5R, -49*
Snavely, Tipton Ray 1890- *ConAu 17R, WrDr 84*
Snavely, William P 1920- *ConAu 17R*
Snead, Rodman Eldredge 1931- *ConAu 73*
Sneddon, Ian Naismith 1919- *WrDr 84*
Snedeker, Caroline Dale 1871-1956 *TwCCW 83*
Sneed, Joseph Donald 1938- *ConAu 49*
Sneed, Joseph Tyree 1920- *ConAu 21R*
Sneider, Vern 1916-1981 *ConAu 5R, -103, MichAu 80*
Snell, Bruno 1896- *ConAu P-1*
Snell, David 1936- *ConAu 77*
Snell, David 1942- *IntAu&W 82*
Snell, Foster Dee 1898- *WrDr 84*
Snell, Foster Dee 1898-1980 *ConAu 108*
Snell, Frank 1920- *ConAu 1R*
Snell, George Davis 1903- *ConAu 106*
Snell, John Leslie, Jr. 1923-1972 *ConAu 3NR, -5R, -33R*
Snell, Tee Loftin 1922- *ConAu 105*
Sneller, Delwyn Lee 1945- *MichAu 80*
Snellgrove, L E 1928- *ConAu 3NR*
Snellgrove, Laurence Ernest 1928- *ConAu 9R, WrDr 84*
Snellgrove, Louis 1928- *ConAu 45*
Snelling, Lois *ConAu 5R*
Snelling, O F 1916- *ConAu 17R*
Snelling, W Rodman 1931- *ConAu 93*
Snepp, Frank 1943- *ConAu 105*
Snetsinger, John 1941- *ConAu 73*
Snetsinger, Robert 1928- *ConAu 107*
Sneve, Virginia Driving Hawk 1933- *ChlLR 2, ConAu 3NR, -49, SmATA 8*
Sneyd, Steve 1941- *IntWWP 82*
Snider, Clifton *DrAP&F 83*
Snider, Delbert Arthur 1914- *ConAu 1R, WrDr 84*
Sniderman, Florence 1915- *ConAu 33R*
Sniff, Mr. *SmATA X*
Snipes, Wilson Currin 1924- *ConAu 29R*
Snively, W D, Jr. 1911- *ConAu 29R*
Snodgrass, A M 1934- *ConAu 10NR, -21R*
Snodgrass, Anthony McElrea 1934- *WrDr 84*
Snodgrass, Joan Gay 1934- *ConAu 77*
Snodgrass, Milton M 1931- *ConAu 29R*
Snodgrass, Thomas Jefferson *ConAu X*
Snodgrass, W D *DrAP&F 83*
Snodgrass, W D 1926- *ConAu 1R, -6NR, ConLC 2, -6, -10, -18, ConP 80, CroCAP, DcLB 5[port], ModAL, ModAL SUP, WhoTwCL, WorAu, WrDr 84*

Snodgrass, William DeWitt 1926- *DcLEL 1940, IntAu&W 82, IntWWP 82, MichAu 80*
Snoek, J Diedrick 1931- *ConAu 49*
Snoek, Paul 1933- *CIDMEL 80*
Snook, Barbara 1913- *ConAu 109*
Snook, Barbara 1913-1976 *SmATA 34*
Snook, Barbara L 1913- *WrDr 84*
Snook, I A 1933- *ConAu 77*
Snook, John B 1927- *ConAu 106*
Snortum, Niel K 1928- *ConAu 21R*
Snow, Bonnie *DrAP&F 83*
Snow, Bonnie 1952- *IntAu&W 82*
Snow, Sir C P 1905-1980 *ASpks, ConAu 5R, -101, ConLC 1, -4, -6, -9, -13, -19, DcLB 15[port], ModBrL, ModBrL SUP, TwCWr, WhoTwCL*
Snow, Charles Horace 1877- *TwCWW*
Snow, Sir Charles Percy 1905- *LongCTC, TwCA SUP*
Snow, D W 1924- *ConAu 65*
Snow, Davis W 1913?-1975 *ConAu 61*
Snow, Don 1943- *ConAu 106*
Snow, Donald Clifford 1917- *ConAu 85, SmATA 16*
Snow, Dorothea J 1909- *ConAu 1R, -3NR, SmATA 9*
Snow, Dorothy Mary Barter 1897- *ConAu P-1*
Snow, Edgar Parks 1905-1972 *ConAu 33R, -81, TwCA, TwCA SUP*
Snow, Edith 1909- *IntWWP 82*
Snow, Edward Rowe 1902-1982 *ConAu 6NR, -9R, -106*
Snow, Frances Compton *ConAu X*
Snow, George D'Oyly 1903- *ConAu 5R*
Snow, Helen Foster 1907- *ConAu 57, IntAu&W 82, WrDr 84*
Snow, John Hall 1924- *ConAu 37R*
Snow, John Harold Thomas 1911- *CreCan 2*
Snow, Joyce Wieland *CreCan 1*
Snow, Kathleen 1944- *ConAu 81*
Snow, Keith Ronald 1943- *ConAu 110, WrDr 84*
Snow, Lois Wheeler 1920- *ConAu 57*
Snow, Lyndon *TwCRGW, WrDr 84*
Snow, Michael James Aleck 1929- *CreCan 1*
Snow, Peter G 1933- *ConAu 21R*
Snow, Philip 1915- *WrDr 84*
Snow, Philip Albert 1915- *ConAu 9R, IntAu&W 82*
Snow, Richard F 1947- *ConAu 106*
Snow, Roslyn 1936- *ConAu 9NR, -21R*
Snow, Russell E 1938- *ConAu 65*
Snow, Sinclair 1909-1972 *ConAu P-2*
Snow, Vernon F 1924- *ConAu 37R*
Snow, Wilbert 1884-1977 *ConAmA, ConAu 9R, -73, WorAu*
Snow, William George Sinclair 1908- *ConAu 5R*
Snowden, Frank M, Jr. 1911- *ConAu 41R, LivgBAA*
Snowdon *IntWWP 82X*
Snowman, Daniel 1938- *ConAu 4NR, -53, IntAu&W 82, WrDr 84*
Snukal, Robert 1942- *ConAu 45*
Snyder, Anne 1922- *ConAu 37R, SmATA 4, WrDr 84*
Snyder, Carol 1941- *ConAu 85*
Snyder, Cecil 1927- *WrDr 84*
Snyder, Cecil K, Jr. 1927- *ConAu 29R*
Snyder, Charles M 1909- *ConAu 49*
Snyder, Charles Royce 1924- *ConAu 105*
Snyder, D Paul 1933- *ConAu 45*
Snyder, E V 1943- *ConAu 41R*
Snyder, Eldon E 1930- *ConAu 49*
Snyder, Eloise C 1928- *ConAu 29R*
Snyder, Francis Gregory 1942- *ConAu 7NR, WrDr 84*
Snyder, Frank Gregory 1942- *ConAu 17R*
Snyder, Fred A 1931- *ConAu 37R*
Snyder, Gary *DrAP&F 83*
Snyder, Gary 1930- *WrDr 84*
Snyder, Gary Sherman 1930- *ConAu 17R, ConLC 1, -2, -5, -9, ConP 80, CroCAP, DcLB 5[port], -16[port], DcLEL 1940, FifWWr, ModAL SUP, WorAu*
Snyder, Gerald S 1933- *ConAu 61, SmATA 34*
Snyder, Glenn Herald 1924- *ConAu 1R*
Snyder, Graydon 1930- *ConAu 13R, IntAu&W 82, WrDr 84*
Snyder, Guy 1951- *ConAu 57*
Snyder, Henry Leonard 1929- *ConAu 41R*
Snyder, Jerome 1916-1976 *ConAu 65, SmATA 20N*

Snyder, Joan 1943- *ConAu 41R*
Snyder, John Parr 1926- *ConAu 41R, IntAu&W 82*
Snyder, John William 1924- *ConAu 1R*
Snyder, Louis L 1907- *ConAu 1R, -2NR, WrDr 84*
Snyder, Maryhelen *DrAP&F 83*
Snyder, Paul 1933- *ConAu 1NR*
Snyder, Rachel 1924- *ConAu 9R*
Snyder, Richard *DrAP&F 83*
Snyder, Richard C 1916- *ConAu 61*
Snyder, Richard Laurence 1925- *IntWWP 82*
Snyder, Robert L 1928- *ConAu 25R*
Snyder, Solomon H 1938- *ConAu 37R*
Snyder, Susan 1934- *ConAu 93*
Snyder, Tom 1936- *ConAu 109*
Snyder, Wendy Katherine 1961- *IntWWP 82*
Snyder, William 1929- *WrDr 84*
Snyder, William 1951- *ConAu 104*
Snyder, William P 1928- *ConAu 13R*
Snyder, Zilpha Keatley 1927- *ConAu 9R, ConLC 17, SmATA 1, -28[port], TwCCW 83, WrDr 84*
Snyderman, Reuven K 1922- *ConAu 29R, SmATA 5*
Soares, Anthony T 1923- *ConAu 45*
Sobel, B Z 1933- *ConAu 77*
Sobel, Bernard 1887-1964 *ConAu 5R*
Sobel, Brian M 1954- *ConAu 107*
Sobel, Harold W 1933- *ConAu 61*
Sobel, Irwin Philip 1901- *ConAu 45*
Sobel, Lester A 1919- *ConAu 9NR, -21R*
Sobel, Robert 1931- *ConAu 5R, -8NR*
Sobel, Robert Murray 1925- *ConAmTC*
Sobell, Morton 1917- *ConAu 53, WrDr 84*
Soberman, Richard M 1937- *ConAu 10NR, -25R*
Sobi *IntAu&W 82X*
Sobieski Stuart, Charles Edward 1935- *IntWWP 82*
Sobiloff, Hy 1912-1970 *ConAu 29R*
Sobin, A G *DrAP&F 83*
Sobin, Anthony 1944- *IntWWP 82*
Sobinova, Natasha *CreCan 2*
Soble, Jennie *ConAu X*
Sobol, Donald J 1924- *ChlLR 4[port], ConAu 1R, -1NR, SmATA 1, -31[port], TwCCW 83, WrDr 84*
Sobol, Harriet Langsam 1936- *ConAu 8NR, -61, SmATA 34*
Sobol, Ken 1938- *WrDr 84*
Sobol, Louis 1896- *ConAu P-2*
Sobol, Rose 1931- *ConAu 101*
Sobolev, Leonid Sergeyevich 1898?-1971 *ConAu 29R*
Soboul, Albert Marius 1914-1982 *ConAu 107*
Sobrino, Josephine 1915- *ConAu 45*
Soby, James Thrall 1906-1979 *ConAu 103, TwCA SUP*
Sochen, June 1937- *ConAu 41R*
Sockman, Ralph Washington 1889-1970 *ConAu 5R, -89*
Socolofsky, Homer Edward 1922- *ConAu 1R, -1NR, WrDr 84*
Socolow, Elizabeth Anne *DrAP&F 83*
Socolow, Elizabeth Anne 1940- *IntWWP 82*
Socolow, Robert H 1937- *ConAu 37R*
Sodaro, Craig 1948- *ConAu 101*
Soddy, Frederick 1877-1956 *LongCTC*
Soddy, Kenneth 1911- *WrDr 84*
Sodenkamp, Andree 1906- *CIDMEL 80*
Soder, Coralie Ruth 1949- *IntWWP 82*
Soderberg, Hjalmar 1869-1941 *CIDMEL 80, CnMD, WhoTwCL, WorAu 1970*
Soderberg, Paul Stephen 1949- *ConAu 103*
Soderberg, Percy Measday 1901-1969 *ConAu P-1*
Sodergran, Edith Irene 1892-1923 *CIDMEL 80*
Soderholm, Marjorie Elaine 1923- *ConAu 13R*
Soderlind, Arthur E 1920- *ConAu 69, SmATA 14*
Sodums, Dzintars 1922- *IntWWP 82*
Soelle, Dorothee 1929- *ConAu 11NR, -69*
Soerheim, Thor 1949- *IntAu&W 82*
Sofen, Edward 1919- *ConAu 9R, WrDr 84*
Sofer, Cyril 1921- *ConAu 5R*
Soffer, Reba N 1934- *ConAu 85*
Sofronov, Anatol Vladimirovich 1911- *CnMD*
Sofronov, Anatoli Vladimirovich 1911- *ModWD*
Softly, Barbara 1924- *ConAu 2NR, -5R, SmATA 12, TwCCW 83, WrDr 84*
Softly, Edgar *ConAu X*
Softly, Edward *ConAu X*
Soglow, Otto 1900-1975 *ConAu 57, -93,*

Sopov, Aco 1923- *ModSL 2*
Sor, Daniel 1923- *IntWWP 82*
Sorauf, Francis Joseph 1928- *ConAu 9R*
Sorauf, Frank J *ConAu X*
Sorcerer Of The Realm *IntWWP 82X*
Sorden, L G 1898- *ConAu 1R, –1NR*
Soreil, Arsene 1893- *IntAu&W 82,*
  IntWWP 82
Sorel, Byron *ConAu X*
Sorel, Edward 1929- *ConAu 9R*
Sorel, Georges 1847-1922 *ClDMEL 80,*
  LongCTC, WorAu
Sorel, Julia *ConAu X*
Sorel, Nancy Caldwell 1934- *ConAu 37R,*
  WrDr 84
Sorel, Ruth *CreCan 2*
Sorell, Walter 1905- *ConAu 21R*
Sorensen, Andrew Aaron 1938- *ConAu 65*
Sorensen, Chris 1942- *ConAu 107*
Sorensen, Jacki 1942- *ConAu 110*
Sorensen, Knud 1928- *IntWWP 82*
Sorensen, Robert C 1923- *ConAu 45*
Sorensen, Theodore Chaikin 1928- *ConAu 2NR,*
  –45
Sorensen, Thomas Chaikin 1926- *ConAu 21R,*
  WrDr 84
Sorensen, Villy 1929- *ClDMEL 80*
Sorensen, Virginia 1912- *ConAu 13R,*
  SmATA 2, TwCA SUP, TwCCW 83,
  TwCWW, WrDr 84
Sorensen Waugh, Virginia 1912- *IntAu&W 82*
Sorenson, Herbert 1898- *ConAu 21R*
Sorenson, Marian 1925-1968 *ConAu P-1*
Sorenson, Theodore 1926- *WrDr 84*
Sorge, Reinhard Johannes 1892-1916 *CnMD,*
  ModGL, ModWD
Sorgman, Mayo 1912- *ConAu 13R*
Sorin, Gerald 1940- *ConAu 77*
Sorine, Stephanie Riva 1954- *ConAu 105*
Sorkin, Alan Lowell 1941- *ConAu 41R*
Sorley, Charles Hamilton 1895-1915 *LongCTC,*
  ModBrL, TwCA, WhoTwCL
Sorley Walker, Kathrine *ConAu 5R, –6NR,*
  IntAu&W 82, WrDr 84
Sorokin, Elena 1894?-1975 *ConAu 61*
Sorokin, Pitirim A 1889-1968 *ConAu 5R, –5NR,*
  –25R, TwCA SUP
Soromenho, Castro 1910-1968 *ClDMEL 80*
Sorrell, Alan 1904-1974 *ConAu 93*
Sorrells, Dorothy C *ConAu 9R*
Sorrells, Helen *DrAP&F 83*
Sorrells, Helen 1908- *ConAu 37R*
Sorrells, Robert T *DrAP&F 83*
Sorrenson, Maurice Peter Keith 1932- *WrDr 84*
Sorrentino, Gilbert *DrAP&F 83*
Sorrentino, Gilbert 1918- *ConLC 7*
Sorrentino, Gilbert 1929- *ConAu 77, ConLC 3,*
  –14, –22[port], ConNov 82, ConP 80,
  DcLB Y80B[port], –5[port], WrDr 84
Sorrentino, Joseph N 1930?- *ConAu 49,*
  SmATA 6
Sorrentino, Joseph N 1937- *ConAu 3NR*
Sorsby, Arnold 1900- *ConAu 85*
Sortor, June Elizabeth 1939- *ConAu 61,*
  SmATA 12
Sortor, Toni *ConAu X, SmATA X*
Sorum, Paul Clay 1943- *ConAu 103*
Sosa, Ernest 1940- *ConAu 53*
Sosa DeQuesada, Aristides V 1908- *ConAu 53*
Soseki, Natsume 1867-1916 *WhoTwCL, WorAu*
Soskin, V H *ConAu X, SmATA 4, WrDr 84*
Sosna, Morton 1945- *ConAu 102*
Sosnick, Stephen H 1930- *ConAu 45*
Sosnora, Viktor 1936- *ClDMEL 80,*
  WorAu 1970
Sossaman, Stephen *DrAP&F 83*
Sossaman, Stephen 1944- *ConAu 77*
Sosyura, Volodymyr 1898-1965 *ModSL 2*
Sotelo, Joaquin Calvo 1905- *CnMD*
Soter, Istvan 1913- *IntAu&W 82*
Soth, Lauren 1910- *ConAu P-1*
Soto, Gary *DrAP&F 83*
Soto, Pedro Juan 1928- *ModLAL*
Soto, Vicente 1919- *ClDMEL 80*
Soto-Ramos, Julio 1903- *IntWWP 82*
Sotomayor, Antonio 1902- *ConAu 73,*
  SmATA 11
Soucy, Jean-Baptiste 1915- *CreCan 2*
Soucy, Robert Joseph 1933- *ConAu 45,*
  IntAu&W 82
Souders, Bruce 1920- *IntWWP 82*
Soudley, Henry *SmATA 1*

Souerwine, Andrew H 1924- *ConAu 81*
Soukup, James R 1928- *ConAu 79*
Soule, Gardner 1913- *ConAu 2NR, –5R,*
  SmATA 14
Soule, George 1930- *ConAu 57*
Soule, George Henry, Jr. 1887-1970 *ConAu 29R,*
  ConAu P-2, TwCA, TwCA SUP
Soule, Isabel Walker 1898?-1972 *ConAu 37R*
Soule, Jean Conder 1919- *ConAu 5R,*
  SmATA 10
Soules, Terrill Shepard *DrAP&F 83*
Soumagne, Henri 1891-1951 *ModWD*
Soupault, Philippe 1897- *ClDMEL 80, ModFrL,*
  ModRL, ModWD, WorAu
Soupcoff, Murray 1943- *ConAu 101*
Souper, Patrick C 1928- *WrDr 84*
Souper, Patrick Charles 1928- *ConAu 110*
Sourian, Peter *DrAP&F 83*
Sourian, Peter 1933- *ConAu 1R, WrDr 84*
Sourkes, Theodore L 1919- *ConAu 17R*
Sourry, Lois Cathleen 1914- *WrDr 84*
Sours, John Appling *DrAP&F 83*
Sours, John Appling 1931- *ConAu 9NR, –21R*
Sours, John Appling 1931-1983 *ConAu 110*
Sousa, Marion 1941- *ConAu 65*
Souster, Raymond 1921- *ConAu 13R, ConLC 5,*
  –14, ConP 80, CreCan 1, DcLEL 1940,
  IntAu&W 82, IntWWP 82, ModCmwL,
  WrDr 84
Soutar, William 1898-1943 *TwCWr*
South, Clark *ConAu X*
South, Grace *ConAu X*
South, Malcolm Hudson 1937- *ConAu 107*
Southall, Aidan 1920- *ConAu 77*
Southall, Ivan 1921- *TwCCW 83, WrDr 84*
Southall, Ivan Francis 1921- *ChlLR 2,*
  ConAu 7NR, –9R, SmATA 3
Southam, B C 1931- *ConAu 10NR, WrDr 84*
Southam, Brian Charles 1931- *ConAu 13R*
Southard, Frank Allan, Jr. 1907- *ConAu 107*
Southard, Helen Fairbairn 1906- *ConAu 5R*
Southard, Samuel 1925- *ConAu 1R, –3NR*
Southerington, F R 1938- *ConAu 57*
Southerland, Ellease 1943- *ConAu 107*
Southern, David W 1938- *ConAu 25R*
Southern, Eileen Jackson 1920- *ConAu 37R,*
  LivgBAA
Southern, Richard 1903- *IntAu&W 82*
Southern, Richard William 1912- *ConAu 9R*
Southern, Robert *ConAu X*
Southern, Terry *ConDr 82A, DrAP&F 83*
Southern, Terry 1924- *ConNov 82, DcLB 2,*
  WhoTwCL, WorAu, WrDr 84
Southern, Terry 1926- *ConAu 1R, –1NR,*
  ConLC 7
Southgate, Vera *ConAu 109, WrDr 84*
Southgate, W M 1910- *ConAu P-2*
Southouse-Cheney, Reginald Evelyn Peter
  1896-1951 *LongCTC*
Southwell, Eugene A 1928- *ConAu 17R*
Southwell, Samuel B *DrAP&F 83*
Southwell, Samuel B 1922- *ConAu 17R*
Southwick, Charles H 1928- *ConAu 65*
Southwick, Marcia *DrAP&F 83*
Southwold, Stephen 1887-1964 *LongCTC, TwCA,*
  TwCA SUP
Southwood, Thomas Richard Edmund 1931-
  WrDr 84
Southworth, Herbert Rutledge 1908- *ConAu 85*
Southworth, Horton C 1926- *ConAu 17R*
Southworth, James Granville 1896- *ConAu P-2*
Southworth, John 1904- *WrDr 84*
Southworth, John VanDuyn 1904- *ConAu 5R,*
  –6NR
Southworth, Louis *ConAu X*
Southworth, Warren H 1912- *ConAu 37R,*
  WrDr 84
Souto, Claudio Fernando DaSilva 1931-
  IntAu&W 82
Soutter, Fred *ConAu X, WrDr 84*
Souza, Ernest *ConAmA, ConAu X, TwCA,*
  TwCA SUP
Souza, Raymond D 1936- *ConAu 69*
Souza, Steven M 1953- *ConAu 49*
Souza Bandeira, Manuel Carneiro De *WorAu*
Sova, Antonin 1864-1928 *ClDMEL 80,*
  ModSL 2
Sowards, J K 1924- *ConAu 73*
Sowden, Lewis 1905- *ConAu P-1*
Sowell, Thomas 1930- *ConAu 41R,*
  ConIsC 2[port]

Sowerby, Arthur Lindsay McRae 1899-
  ConAu P-1
Sowerby, E Millicent 1883-1977 *ConAu 73,*
  ConAu P-2
Sowers, Miriam 1922- *ConAu 89, IntAu&W 82*
Sowers, Robert 1923- *ConAu 17R*
Sowers, Sidney Gerald, Jr. 1935- *ConAu 17R*
Soya, Carl Erik Martin 1896- *ClDMEL 80,*
  CnMD, ModWD, TwCWr
Soyer, Raphael 1899- *ConAu 81*
Soyinka, Wole 1934- *ConAu 13R, ConDr 82,*
  ConLC 3, –5, –14, ConP 80, LongCTC,
  ModBlW, ModCmwL, ModWD, WorAu,
  WrDr 84
Soyinka, Wole 1935- *TwCWr, WhoTwCL*
Spaak, Paul-Henri 1899-1972 *ConAu 37R*
Spaans VanDerBijl, Tineke 1929- *IntAu&W 82*
Spaatz, Carl A 1891-1974 *ConAu 49*
Space, Ace *DrAP&F 83*
Spach, John Thom *DrAP&F 83*
Spach, John Thom 1928- *ConAu 29R*
Spache, Evelyn B 1929- *ConAu 29R*
Spache, George D 1909- *WrDr 84*
Spache, George Daniel 1909- *ConAu 1R, –5R,*
  –6NR
Spackman, Robert R, Jr. 1917- *ConAu 13R,*
  WrDr 84
Spackman, W M 1905- *ConAu 81*
Spacks, Barry *DrAP&F 83*
Spacks, Barry 1931- *ConAu 29R, ConLC 14,*
  ConP 80, IntWWP 82, WrDr 84
Spacks, Patricia Meyer 1929- *ConAu 1R, –1NR,*
  WrDr 84
Spada, James 1950- *ConAu 7NR, –57*
Spade, Mark *ConAu X, LongCTC*
Spade, Rupert *ConAu X, WrDr 84*
Spaeth, Eloise O'Mara 1904- *ConAu 104*
Spaeth, Gerold 1939- *ConAu 9NR, –65*
Spaeth, Harold J 1930- *ConAu 45*
Spaeth, Sigmund Gottfried 1885-1965 *ConAu 5R,*
  TwCA, TwCA SUP
Spafford, Ronald Norman 1928- *IntAu&W 82*
Spafford, Roswell *DrAP&F 83*
Spahn, Mary Attea 1929- *ConAu 7NR*
Spain, David H 1939- *ConAu 57*
Spain, James William 1926- *ConAu 5R*
Spain, Jane Spalding 1901- *IntWWP 82*
Spain, John *TwCCr&M 80*
Spain, Mary *IntWWP 82*
Spain, Nancy 1917-1964 *LongCTC*
Spain, Rufus B 1923- *ConAu 21R*
Spake, Amanda 1947- *ConAu 77*
Spalatin, Christopher 1909- *ConAu 49*
Spalding, Billups Phinizy 1930- *ConAu 41R*
Spalding, Frances 1950- *ConAu 104*
Spalding, Graydon 1911- *ConAu 89*
Spalding, Henry D 1915- *ConAu 11NR*
Spalding, Henry Daniel 1915- *ConAu 25R*
Spalding, Jack 1913- *ConAu 69*
Spalding, Keith 1913- *WrDr 84*
Spalding, Lucile *ConAu X, WrDr 84*
Spalding, Philip Anthony 1911- *ConAu 5R*
Spalding, R W 1904- *ConAu 81*
Spalding, Ruth *ConAu 104, WrDr 84*
Spalek, John M 1928- *ConAu 104*
Spalten, Rona *DrAP&F 83*
Spalter, Max 1929- *ConAu 21R*
Span *IntWWP 82X*
Spandl, Oskar Peter 1939- *IntAu&W 82*
Spanfeller, James John 1930- *SmATA 19*
Spangenberg, Judith Dunn 1942- *ConAu 29R,*
  SmATA 8
Spangler, Earl 1920- *ConAu 5R, –5NR*
Spanier, David 1932- *ConAu 101*
Spanier, John 1930- *ConAu 1R, –2NR*
Spanier, Muriel *DrAP&F 83*
Spann, Edward K 1931- *ConAu 45*
Spann, Gloria Carter 1926- *ConAu 77*
Spann, Meno 1903- *ConAu 1R*
Spann, Weldon Oma 1924- *ConAu 17R,*
  WrDr 84
Spanner, Valerie *WrDr 84*
Spano, Charles 1948- *ConAu 93*
Spanos, William V 1925- *ConAu 11NR, –21R*
Spar, Jerome 1918- *ConAu 25R, SmATA 10*
Sparano, Vin T 1934- *ConAu 45*
Spargo, John 1876-1966 *ConAu 89*
Spark, Muriel *WrDr 84*
Spark, Muriel Sarah 1918- *ConAu 5R,*
  ConLC 2, –3, –5, –8, –13, –18, ConNov 82,
  ConP 80, DcLB 15[port], DcLEL 1940,
  IntAu&W 82, IntWWP 82, LongCTC,

ModBrL, ModBrL SUP, TwCWr, WhoTwCL, WorAu
Sparke, Archibald 1871-1970 *ConAu P-2*
Sparkes, Ivan George *IntAu&W 82*
Sparkia, Roy 1924- *ConAu 77*
Sparkman, Brandon B 1929- *ConAu 61*
Sparkman, G Temp 1932- *ConAu 89*
Sparkman, William *ConAu X*
Sparks, Asa H 1937- *ConAu 97*
Sparks, Beatrice Mathews 1918- *ConAu 97, SmATA 28*
Sparks, Bertel M 1918- *ConAu 21R*
Sparks, Edgar H 1908- *ConAu 13R*
Sparks, Fred 1916?-1981 *ConAu 103*
Sparks, Hypatia Katharine *IntWWP 82*
Sparks, Jack Norman 1928- *ConAu 102*
Sparks, James Allen 1933- *ConAu 109*
Sparks, John 1939- *ConAu 103*
Sparks, Judith Rosemary *CreCan 2*
Sparks, Katharine *IntWWP 82X*
Sparks, Mary W 1920- *SmATA 15*
Sparks, Merla Jean *ConAu X*
Sparks, Merrill 1922- *ConAu 21R*
Sparks, Will 1924- *ConAu 37R*
Sparnon, Norman 1913- *WrDr 84*
Sparrow, Dominic *IntWWP 82X*
Sparrow, Gerald 1903- *ConAu 49*
Sparrow, John H Angus 1906- *ConAu 103*
Sparshott, F E *ConAu X*
Sparshott, F E 1926- *ConAu 25R*
Sparshott, Francis *ConAu X*
Sparshott, Francis 1926- *ConP 80, WrDr 84*
Sparshott, Francis Edward 1926- *ConAu 10NR*
Spartacus, Deutero *ConAu X*
Spartacus, Tertius *ConAu X*
Spate, O H K 1911- *ConAu 10NR, -25R*
Spath, Gerold *ConAu X*
Spatz, Chris 1940- *ConAu 37R*
Spatz, Christa Mertins *CreCan 2*
Spatz, Jonas 1935- *ConAu 29R*
Spatz, Kenneth Christopher, Jr. 1940- *WrDr 84*
Spatz, Ronald *DrAP&F 83*
Spaulding, Dayton M 1922- *ConAu 61*
Spaulding, Douglas *ConAu X*
Spaulding, John *DrAP&F 83*
Spaulding, Leonard *ConAu X*
Spaulding, Robert Kilburn 1898- *ConAu 5R*
Spaulding, William E 1898-1979 *ConAu 93*
Spaull, Hebe 1893- *ConAu 9R*
Spavieri Subhas, Jeannette 1937- *IntWWP 82*
Speaight, George 1914- *ConAu 29R, IntAu&W 82, WrDr 84*
Speaight, Robert William 1904-1976 *ConAu 13R, LongCTC*
Speaker, William *IntWWP 82X*
Spear, Allan Henry 1937- *ConAu 21R, WrDr 84*
Spear, Benjamin *ConAu X*
Spear, Charles 1910- *ConP 80, DcLEL 1940, WrDr 84*
Spear, George E 1925- *ConAu 102*
Spear, Hilda D 1926- *ConAu 107, WrDr 84*
Spear, Jean *DrAP&F 83*
Spear, Percival 1901- *ConAu 106*
Spear, Percival 1901-1982 *ConAu 108*
Spear, Richard Edmund 1940- *ConAu 45*
Spear, Roberta *DrAP&F 83*
Spear, T G Percival 1901- *WrDr 84*
Speare, Elizabeth George 1908- *ConAu 1R, IntAu&W 82, SmATA 5, TwCCW 83, WrDr 84*
Spearing, Judith 1922- *ConAu 3NR, -49, SmATA 9*
Spearman, Arthur Dunning 1899- *ConAu P-2*
Spearman, Frank Hamilton 1859-1937 *TwCA, TwCWW*
Spearman, Walter 1908- *ConAu P-2*
Spears, Betty Mary 1918- *ConAu 1R, -6NR*
Spears, Dorothea 1901- *ConAu P-1*
Spears, Sir Edward 1886-1974 *ConAu 45, ConAu P-2*
Spears, Heather 1934- *DcLEL 1940, IntWWP 82X, WrDr 84*
Spears, Jack 1919- *ConAu 29R*
Spears, Monroe K 1916- *ConAu 2NR, -5R, WrDr 84*
Spears, Richard A 1939- *ConAu 104*
Spears, Woodridge 1913- *ConAu 13R, IntAu&W 82, IntWWP 82, WrDr 84*
Specht, Ernst Konrad 1926- *ConAu 29R*
Specht, Harry 1929- *ConAu 8NR, -53*
Specht, Robert 1928- *ConAu 103*

Specht, Walter F 1912- *ConAu 97*
Speck, Bette *IntWWP 82X*
Speck, Gordon 1898- *ConAu P-2, WrDr 84*
Speck, Ross V 1927- *ConAu 107*
Specking, Inez 1890-196-? *SmATA 11*
Specking, Inez 1895- *ConAu 5R*
Spectator *ConAu X*
Spector, Debra 1953- *ConAu 109*
Spector, Irwin 1916- *ConAu 45*
Spector, Ivar 1898- *ConAu 1R, WrDr 84*
Spector, Jack Jerome 1925- *ConAu 29R, WrDr 84*
Spector, Marshall 1936- *ConAu 45*
Spector, Robert D 1922- *WrDr 84*
Spector, Robert Donald 1922- *ConAu 13R*
Spector, Ronald 1943- *ConAu 57*
Spector, Samuel I 1924- *ConAu 77*
Spector, Sherman David 1927- *ConAu 1R, WrDr 84*
Spector, Shushannah 1903- *ConAu 9R*
Spector, Stanley 1924- *ConAu 9R*
Spectorsky, A C 1910-1972 *ConAu 33R, ConAu P-2*
Spedding, C R W 1925- *ConAu 53*
Speed, F Maurice 1911- *ConAu 107*
Speed, Frank Warren 1911- *ConAu 104, IntAu&W 82, WrDr 84*
Speed, Frederick Maurice 1912- *WrDr 84*
Speelman, Arlene 1916- *ConAu 41R*
Speer, Albert 1905-1981 *ConAu 104, -65*
Speer, David G 1913- *ConAu 45*
Speer, Laurel *DrAP&F 83*
Speer, Michael L 1934- *ConAu 93*
Speeth, Kathleen Riordan 1937- *ConAu 89*
Spehar, Betty M 1924- *ConAu 45*
Speicher, Helen Ross 1915- *WrDr 84*
Speicher, Helen Ross Smith 1915- *ConAu 4NR, -5R, SmATA 8*
Speidel, Michael P 1937- *ConAu 108*
Speier, Hans 1905- *ConAu 9NR, -21R*
Speight, Harold *WrDr 84*
Speight, Harold 1916- *ConAu 5R*
Speight, Johnny 1920- *ConDr 82*
Speight, Johnny 1921- *DcLEL 1940, WrDr 84*
Speight, Kathleen 1903- *WrDr 84*
Speirs, John 1906- *ConAu 61*
Speirs, Logan 1938- *ConAu 37R*
Speirs, Russell 1901-1975 *ConAu 4NR, -45, -61*
Speiser, Jean *ConAu 69*
Speiser, Stuart Marshall 1923- *ConAu 106*
Speizer, Judy *DrAP&F 83*
Speizman, Morris 1905- *ConAu 77*
Spekke, Arnolds 1887-1972 *ConAu 37R*
Spektor, Dr. *ConAu X*
Spelios, Thomas John 1930- *ConAu 25R*
Spellman, Alfred B 1934- *LivgBAA*
Spellman, Alfred B 1935- *ConAu 97*
Spellman, John W 1934- *ConAu 13R, SmATA 14*
Spellman, Roger G *WrDr 84*
Spelman, Mary 1934- *ConAu 77, SmATA 28[port]*
Spelvin, George *ConAu X*
Spence, Bill *ConAu X*
Spence, Clark C 1923- *ConAu 6NR*
Spence, Donald P 1926- *ConAu 109*
Spence, Duncan *ConAu X, WrDr 84*
Spence, Eleanor 1927- *SmATA 21[port]*
Spence, Eleanor 1928- *ConAu 3NR, -49, DcLEL 1940, IntAu&W 82, TwCCW 83, WrDr 84*
Spence, Gordon William 1936- *ConAu 25R*
Spence, Hartzell 1908- *ConAu 5R*
Spence, J A D *ConAu X*
Spence, J E 1931- *ConAu 25R*
Spence, James R 1927- *ConAu 25R*
Spence, Jonathan D 1936- *ConAu 21R*
Spence, Lewis 1874-1955 *TwCA SUP*
Spence, Mary Lee 1927- *ConAu 45*
Spence, Michael *DrAP&F 83*
Spence, Vernon Gladden 1924- *ConAu 37R*
Spence, William John Duncan 1923- *ConAu 103, WrDr 84*
Spencer *ConAu X*
Spencer, Ann 1918- *ConAu 29R, SmATA 10*
Spencer, Bernard 1909-1963 *DcLEL 1940, ModBrL, TwCWr, WorAu*
Spencer, Bonnell 1909- *ConAu 106*
Spencer, Charles 1920- *ConAu 49, IntAu&W 82, WrDr 84*
Spencer, Christopher 1930- *ConAu 13R, WrDr 84*

Spencer, Claire 1899- *TwCA*
Spencer, Clark C 1923- *ConAu 1R*
Spencer, Colin 1933- *ConAu 21R, ConDr 82, ConNov 82, IntAu&W 82, WrDr 84*
Spencer, Cornelia 1899- *ConAu X, SmATA 5*
Spencer, Dale R 1925- *ConAu 57*
Spencer, Donald D 1931- *ConAu 108*
Spencer, Dora 1916- *WrDr 84*
Spencer, Edgar Winston 1931- *ConAu 41R*
Spencer, Edward *IntAu&W 82X*
Spencer, Elizabeth *DrAP&F 83*
Spencer, Elizabeth 1921- *ConAu 13R, ConLC 22[port], ConNov 82, DcLB 6[port], DcLEL 1940, IntAu&W 82, SmATA 14, TwCA SUP, WrDr 84*
Spencer, Harold 1920- *ConAu 45*
Spencer, Hertha A 1910- *IntWWP 82*
Spencer, James 1932- *ConAu 109*
Spencer, Jean E 1933- *ConAu 17R*
Spencer, Jeffry Withers Burress 1927- *ConAu 45*
Spencer, John 1922- *WrDr 84*
Spencer, John Hall 1928- *ConAu 5R*
Spencer, John Walter 1922- *ConAu 9R*
Spencer, Joseph E 1907- *ConAu 45*
Spencer, LaVyrle 1943- *ConAu 102*
Spencer, Margaret 1916- *ConAu 21R*
Spencer, Metta Wells 1931- *ConAu 69*
Spencer, Michael 1936- *ConAu 57*
Spencer, Milton Harry 1926- *ConAu 1R, -6NR*
Spencer, Paul 1932- *WrDr 84*
Spencer, Philip *IntAu&W 82X*
Spencer, Robert Allan 1920- *ConAu 5R*
Spencer, Robert F 1917- *ConAu 108*
Spencer, Ross 1921- *ConAu 101*
Spencer, Scott *DrAP&F 83, WrDr 84*
Spencer, Sharon *DrAP&F 83*
Spencer, Sharon Doughterty 1933- *ConAu 5R*
Spencer, Sidney 1888- *ConAu 5R*
Spencer, Steven M 1905- *ConAu P-1*
Spencer, Terence John Bew 1915-1978 *ConAu 77*
Spencer, Theodore 1902-1949 *TwCA SUP*
Spencer, Warren F 1923- *ConAu 29R*
Spencer, William 1922- *ConAu 8NR, -17R, IntAu&W 82, SmATA 9, WrDr 84*
Spencer, Zane A 1935- *ConAu 89, MichAu 80*
Spencer Meek, Margaret 1925- *ConAu 105*
Spender, Harold 1864-1926 *LongCTC*
Spender, John Alfred 1862-1942 *LongCTC*
Spender, Stephen 1909- *CnMD, CnMWL, ConAu 9R, ConLC 1, -2, -5, -10, ConLCrt 82, ConP 80, LongCTC, ModBrL, ModBrL SUP, ModWD, TwCA, TwCA SUP, TwCWr, WhoTwCL, WrDr 84*
Spengemann, William Charles 1932- *ConAu 102*
Spengler, Edwin H 1906-1981 *ConAu 104*
Spengler, Oswald 1880-1936 *LongCTC, TwCA, TwCA SUP, TwCWr*
Speranza *LongCTC*
Sperber, Al E 1916- *ConAu 65*
Sperber, Manes 1905- *IntAu&W 82, WorAu*
Sperber, Murray A 1940- *ConAu 61*
Sperber, Perry Arthur 1907- *ConAu 37R*
Sperber, Philip 1944- *ConAu 109*
Spergel, Irving A 1924- *ConAu 11NR, -21R*
Sperka, Joshua S 1905- *ConAu 49*
Sperlich, Peter Werner 1934- *ConAu 37R, WrDr 84*
Sperling, John G 1921- *ConAu 49*
Spero, Bette 1944- *ConAmTC*
Spero, Sterling D 1896-1976 *ConAu 61, -65*
Speroni, Charles 1911- *ConAu 93*
Sperr, Martin 1944- *CroCD, ModGL*
Sperry, Armstrong 1897-1976 *TwCCW 83*
Sperry, Armstrong W 1897-1976 *ConAu 107, ConAu P-1, SmATA 1, -27N*
Sperry, Baxter 1914- *ConAu 1NR, -49, IntAu&W 82X*
Sperry, Byrne Hope 1902- *ConAu 69*
Sperry, J E 1920- *ConAu X*
Sperry, Kip 1940- *ConAu 101*
Sperry, Len 1943- *ConAu 61*
Sperry, Margaret 1900- *ConAu 37R*
Sperry, Margaret 1908- *IntAu&W 82, WrDr 84*
Sperry, Ralph A 1944- *ConAu 106*
Sperry, Raymond, Jr. *ConAu P-2, SmATA 1*
Sperry, Sally Baxter 1914- *IntAu&W 82*
Sperry, Stuart M 1929- *ConAu 49*
Speshock, Phyllis 1925- *ConAu 17R*
Spewack, Bella Cohen 1899- *ConDr 82D, ModWD, TwCA, TwCA SUP*

Spewack, Samuel 1899-1971 *CnMD, ConAu 33R, ModWD, TwCA, TwCA SUP*
Speyer, Leonora 1872-1956 *TwCA, TwCA SUP*
Spice, Marjorie Davis 1924- *ConAu 9R*
Spicehandler, Daniel 1923- *ConAu 1R*
Spicer, Bart 1918- *ConAu 103, TwCCr&M 80, WorAu, WrDr 84*
Spicer, David *DrAP&F 83*
Spicer, Dorothy d1975 *SmATA 32*
Spicer, Dorothy Gladys *ConAu 1R, –4NR*
Spicer, Jack 1925-1965 *ConAu 85, ConLC 8, –18, ConP 80A, DcLB 5[port], –16[port]*
Spicer, James 1928?-1979 *ConAu 85*
Spicer, Marcella 1920- *IntWWP 82*
Spicer, Marcy *IntWWP 82X*
Spicker, Stuart Francis 1937- *ConAu 65*
Spickett, Ronald J 1926- *CreCan 1*
Spiegel, Clara *ConAu X*
Spiegel, Don 1926- *ConAu 41R*
Spiegel, Henry William 1911- *ConAu 1R, WrDr 84*
Spiegel, John P 1911- *ConAu 103*
Spiegel, Joseph 1928- *ConAu 9R*
Spiegel, Richard Alan 1947- *ConAu 104*
Spiegel, Robert H 1922- *ConAu 81*
Spiegel, Steven L 1941- *ConAu 77*
Spiegel, Ted 1934- *ConAu 105*
Spiegelberg, Herbert 1904- *ConAu 9R*
Spiegelman, J Marvin 1926- *ConAu 57*
Spiegelman, Judith 1942- *ConAu 101*
Spiegelman, Judith M *ConAu 21R, SmATA 5*
Spiegler, Charles G 1911- *ConAu 3NR, –9R*
Spiegler, Michael D 1943- *ConAu 61*
Spiel, Hilde 1911- *ConAu P-1, IntAu&W 82*
Spielberg, Edith D *DrAP&F 83*
Spielberg, Peter *DrAP&F 83*
Spielberg, Peter 1929- *ConAu 4NR, –5R, ConLC 6, DcLB Y81[port], WrDr 84*
Spielberg, Steven 1947- *ConAu 77, ConLC 20, SmATA 32[port]*
Spielberger, Charles D 1927- *ConAu 102*
Spielberger, Walter Jakob 1925- *ConAu 21R*
Spielman, Patrick E 1936- *ConAu 7NR, –13R*
Spielmann, Marion Harry 1858-1948 *LongCTC*
Spielmann, Peter James 1952- *ConAu 97*
Spier, Peter 1927- *ChlLR 5[port], ConAu 5R, SmATA 4*
Spier, Robert F G 1922- *ConAu 41R*
Spier, William H 1907?-1973 *ConAu 41R*
Spiering, Frank 1938- *ConAu 10NR, –25R*
Spies, Werner 1937- *ConAu 37R*
Spigel, Irwin M 1926- *ConAu 17R*
Spigelgass, Leonard 1908- *ConAu 103*
Spike, Paul *DrAP&F 83*
Spike, Paul 1947- *ConAu 101*
Spikes, Brian S J *ConAu 101*
Spilhaus, Athelstan 1911- *ConAu 17R, SmATA 13, WrDr 84*
Spilka, Arnold 1917- *ConAu 49, SmATA 6*
Spilka, Mark 1925- *ConAu 81*
Spilke, Francine S *ConAu 101*
Spillane, Frank Morrison 1918- *ConAu 25R*
Spillane, Mickey 1918- *ConAu X, ConLC 3, –13, DcLEL 1940, LongCTC, TwCCr&M 80, TwCWr, WrDr 84*
Spillebeen, Willy 1932- *IntWWP 82*
Spiller, Burton L 1886- *ConAu 5R*
Spiller, Earl A, Jr. 1934- *ConAu 21R*
Spiller, Robert Ernest 1896- *ConAu 4NR, –5R*
Spillmann, Betty Evelyn 1920- *ConAu 53*
Spilsbury, Sir Bernard 1877-1947 *LongCTC*
Spilsbury, Richard 1919- *ConAu 104, WrDr 84*
Spin *IntAu&W 82X*
Spina, Tony 1914- *ConAu 69*
Spinage, Clive A 1933- *ConAu 13R*
Spindel, Jerry 1944- *NatPD 81[port]*
Spindler, Arthur 1918- *ConAu 104*
Spindler, George Dearborn 1920- *ConAu 21R, WrDr 84*
Spindler, Louise Schaubel 1917- *ConAu 49*
Spinelli, Altiero 1907- *ConAu 21R*
Spinelli, Eileen 1942- *ConAu 107*
Spinelli, Marcos 1904-1970 *ConAu 29R*
Sping, Dan *ConAu X*
Spingarn, Joel Elias 1875-1939 *TwCA*
Spingarn, Lawrence *DrAP&F 83*
Spingarn, Lawrence 1917- *IntWWP 82*
Spingarn, Lawrence P 1917- *ConAu 1R*
Spingarn, Lawrence Perreira 1917- *ConAu 6NR, IntAu&W 82*
Spingarn, Lawrence Perry 1917- *IntWWP 82*
Spingarn, Natalie Davis 1922- *ConAu 85*

Spinifex *ConAu X*
Spink, Ian 1932- *WrDr 84*
Spink, John Stephenson 1909- *WrDr 84*
Spink, Reginald 1905- *ConAu 4NR, –53, IntAu&W 82, SmATA 11, WrDr 84*
Spink, Walter M 1928- *ConAu 61*
Spinka, Matthew 1890-1972 *ConAu 1R, –2NR, –37R*
Spinks, G Stephens 1903- *ConAu P-2*
Spinks, John William Tranter 1908- *ConAu 109*
Spinnelli, Eileen *DrAP&F 83*
Spinner, Stephanie 1943- *ConAu 45*
Spinner, Thomas J, Jr. 1929- *ConAu 45*
Spinney, David *ConAu X*
Spinney, J D 1912- *ConAu 29R*
Spinosissimus *IntAu&W 82X*
Spinossimus *ConAu X, SmATA X*
Spinrad, Norman *DrAP&F 83*
Spinrad, Norman 1940- *ConAu 37R, ConSFA, DcLB 8[port], DrmM[port], TwCSFW, WrDr 84*
Spinrad, William 1917- *ConAu 29R*
Spira, Ruth Rodale 1928- *ConAu 61*
Spire, Andre 1868-1966 *CIDMEL 80*
Spirer, Herbert F 1925- *ConAu 93*
Spires, Elizabeth *DrAP&F 83*
Spires, Elizabeth 1952- *ConAu 106*
Spirit, Diana L 1925- *ConAu 17R*
Spiro, Edward 1908- *ConAu 25R*
Spiro, Herbert 1924- *WrDr 84*
Spiro, Herbert J 1924- *ConAu 1R, –6NR*
Spiro, Herzl Robert 1935- *ConAu 104*
Spiro, Jack D 1933- *ConAu 6NR, –9R*
Spiro, Melford E 1920- *ConAu 1NR, –45*
Spit, Sam *ConAu X*
Spittel, Richard Lionel 1881-1969 *ConAu P-1*
Spitteler, Carl 1845-1924 *ConAu 109, TwCLC 12[port]*
Spitteler, Carl Friedrich Georg 1845-1924 *CIDMEL 80, TwCA, TwCA SUP*
Spitz, A Edward 1923- *ConAu 73*
Spitz, Allan A 1928- *ConAu 13R*
Spitz, David 1916-1979 *ConAu 41R, –85*
Spitz, Lewis William 1922- *ConAu 1R, –6NR, IntAu&W 82, WrDr 84*
Spitzer, E E 1910- *ConAu P-2*
Spitzer, Herbert Frederick 1906- *ConAu P-1*
Spitzer, John 1956- *ConAu 102*
Spitzer, Leo 1939- *ConAu 61*
Spitzer, Lyman 1914- *WrDr 84*
Spitzer, Morton Edward *ConAu 41R*
Spitzer, Robert S 1926- *ConAu 61*
Spitzing, Gunter 1931- *IntAu&W 82*
Spivack, Charlotte 1926- *ConAu 21R, IntAu&W 82, WrDr 84*
Spivack, Ellen Sue 1937- *ConAu 106*
Spivack, George 1927- *ConAu 109*
Spivack, Kathleen *DrAP&F 83*
Spivack, Kathleen 1938- *ConAu 49, ConLC 6, WrDr 84*
Spivack, Kathleen Romda Drucker 1938- *IntWWP 82*
Spivack, Robert 1915-1970 *ConAu 104*
Spivack, Susan Fantl *DrAP&F 83*
Spivak, Gayatri Chakravorty 1942- *ConAu 110*
Spivak, John L 1897-1981 *ConAu 105*
Spivak, Mel 1937- *ConAu 57*
Spivak, Talbot 1937- *ConAu 77*
Spivakovsky, Erika 1909- *ConAu 49*
Spivey, Robert Atwood 1931- *ConAu 106*
Spivey, Ted R 1927- *ConAu 105*
Splake, T Kilgore *DrAP&F 83*
Splane, Richard B 1916- *ConAu 17R*
Splaver, Sarah 1921- *ConAu 85, SmATA 28*
Spock, Benjamin 1903- *WrDr 84*
Spock, Benjamin McLane 1903- *AuNews 1, ConAu 21R*
Spodek, Bernard 1931- *ConAu 7NR, –17R*
Spoehr, Alexander 1913- *ConAu 109*
Spoelstra, Nyle 1939- *ConAu 29R*
Spofford, Walter O, Jr. 1936- *ConAu 107*
Spohr, Arnold *CreCan 2*
Spollen, Christopher 1952- *SmATA 12*
Spolsky, Bernard 1932- *ConAu 1NR, –45*
Spong, John Shelby 1931- *ConAu 104*
Spooner, Ella Brown Jackson 1880-1963 *MichAu 80*
Spooner, Frank 1924- *ConAu 85*
Spooner, Frederick Percy 1898- *ConAu P-1*
Spooner, Glenda Victoria Maude Graham 1897- *ConAu P-1*
Spooner, Jane R 1922- *ConAu 5R*

Spooner, John D 1937- *ConAu 21R*
Spooner, William Archibald 1844-1930 *LongCTC*
Spores, Ronald 1931- *ConAu 21R*
Spot, Ryhen *ConAu X*
Spota, Luis 1925- *ModLAL, WorAu*
Spotnitz, Hyman 1908- *ConAu 1R, –6NR*
Spoto, Donald 1941- *ConAu 11NR, –65*
Spotte, Stephen 1942- *ConAu 1NR, –45*
Spottiswoode, Raymond J 1913-1970 *ConAu 104*
Spotts, Charles D 1899-1974? *ConAu P-2*
Spotts, Frederic 1930- *ConAu 101*
Spracklen, Myrtle Lily 1926- *IntWWP 82*
Sprackling, Michael Thomas 1934- *WrDr 84*
Spradley, James P 1933- *ConAu 29R*
Spradling, Mary Elizabeth Mace 1911- *ConAu 104*
Spragens, Thomas A, Jr. 1942- *ConAu 85*
Spragens, William Clark 1925- *ConAu 41R, IntAu&W 82*
Spraggett, Allen 1932- *ConAu 25R*
Sprague, Arthur Colby 1895- *ConAu 89*
Sprague, Carter *TwCSFW*
Sprague, Charles Arthur 1887-1969 *ConAu 89*
Sprague, Claire S 1926- *ConAu 25R*
Sprague, Gretchen 1926- *ConAu 13R, SmATA 27[port]*
Sprague, Howard B 1898- *ConAu 41R*
Sprague, Ken 1945- *ConAu 108*
Sprague, Marshall 1909- *ConAu 1R, –1NR*
Sprague, Richard E 1921- *ConAu 5R, –29R*
Sprague, Rosamond Kent 1922- *ConAu 2NR, –5R*
Sprague, Rosemary 1922- *ConAu 17R*
Sprague, W D *ConAu X*
Sprague DeCamp, L *DrAP&F 83*
Spraos, John 1926- *ConAu 5R*
Spratling, Neil Robert 1945- *IntWWP 82*
Spratt, Hereward Philip 1902- *ConAu 5R*
Spray, Pauline 1920- *ConAu 10NR, –25R*
Spray, Sherrad L 1935- *ConAu 104*
Spreadbury, F G 1908- *WrDr 84*
Spreiregen, Paul 1931- *WrDr 84*
Spreiregen, Paul David 1931- *ConAu 21R*
Sprengel, Donald P 1938- *ConAu 53*
Sprengel, William R 1893- *ConAu 5R*
Sprigel, Olivier *ConAu X*
Sprigg, Christopher St. John 1907-1937 *LongCTC, TwCA, TwCA SUP, TwCCr&M 80*
Sprigg, June 1953- *ConAu 65*
Sprigge, Elizabeth Miriam Squire 1900-1974 *ConAu 13R, SmATA 10, TwCA, TwCA SUP*
Sprigge, Timothy 1932- *WrDr 84*
Sprigge, Timothy Lauro Squire 1932- *ConAu 57*
Sprinchorn, Evert Manfred 1923- *ConAu 107*
Spring, Bob *ConAu X*
Spring, David 1918- *ConAu 81*
Spring, Gerald M 1897- *ConAu 61*
Spring, Howard 1889-1965 *ConAu P-1, LongCTC, SmATA 28[port], TwCA, TwCA SUP, TwCWr*
Spring, Ira L 1918- *ConAu 7NR, –57*
Spring, Joel Henry 1940- *ConAu 3NR, –49*
Spring, Norma 1917- *ConAu 61*
Spring, Philip *ConAu X*
Spring, Robert W 1918- *ConAu 7NR, –57*
Springbett, Lynn Berta *CreCan 2*
Springer, Bernhard J 1907?-1970 *ConAu 29R*
Springer, E Laurence 1903- *ConAu 21R*
Springer, John 1916- *ConAu 53*
Springer, John L 1915- *ConAu 1R*
Springer, L Elsinore 1911- *ConAu 69*
Springer, Marilyn Harris 1931- *ConAu 9NR, –21R*
Springer, Marlene Ann 1937- *ConAu 107*
Springer, Nancy *DrAP&F 83*
Springer, Nancy 1948- *ConAu 101*
Springer, Nesha Bass 1930- *ConAu 81*
Springer, Otto 1905- *ConAu P-1, IntAu&W 82*
Springer, Sally P 1947- *ConAu 108*
Springfield 1931- *ConAu X*
Springfield, David *ConAu X, IntAu&W 82X*
Springford, Norma Linton *CreCan 1*
Springford, Ruth *CreCan 1*
Springsteen, Bruce 1949- *ConLC 17*
Springstubb, Tricia *DrAP&F 83*
Springstubb, Tricia 1950- *ConAu 105*
Sprinkel, Beryl Wayne 1923- *ConAu 9R, WrDr 84*
Sprinthall, Richard C 1930- *ConAu 45*
Sproat, John G 1921- *ConAu 25R*
Sproston, John *ConAu X*

Stas *IntAu&W 82X*
Stasch, Stanley F 1931- *ConAu 41R*
Stasheff, Christopher 1944- *ConAu 10NR, -65, TwCSFW*
Stasheff, Edward 1909- *ConAu 5R*
Stasio, Marilyn L 1940- *ConAmTC, ConAu 33R*
Stassinopoulos, Arianna 1950- *WrDr 84*
Stasz, Clarice *ConAu 7NR, -61*
Staten, Patricia S 1945- *ConAu 53*
Staten, Vince *ConAmTC*
Statera, Gianni 1943- *ConAu 8NR, -57*
States, Bert O 1929- *ConAu 73*
Statham, Frances P 1931- *ConAu 101*
Statham, Jane 1917- *ConAu 13R*
Statler, Oliver 1915- *WrDr 84*
Statler, Oliver Hadley 1915- *ConAu 5R*
Staton, Thomas Felix 1917- *ConAu 5R*
Statten, Vargo *TwCSFW*
Staub, August W 1931- *ConAu 2NR, -45*
Staubach, Charles N 1906- *ConAu 4NR, -5R*
Staubach, Roger 1942- *ConAu 104*
Staudacher, Joseph M 1914- *ConAu 25R*
Staudacher, Rosemarian V 1918- *ConAu 5R, IntAu&W 82, WrDr 84*
Staudacher, Wilhelm 1928- *IntAu&W 82*
Staudenraus, P J 1928-1971 *ConAu 1R, -103*
Stauder, Jack 1939- *ConAu 37R*
Stauderman, Albert P 1910- *ConAu 77*
Staudt, Virginia *ConAu X*
Stauffer, D *ConAu X*
Stauffer, Don *ConAu X, SmATA X*
Stauffer, Donald Alfred 1902-1952 *TwCA SUP*
Stauffer, Donald Barlow 1930- *ConAu 57*
Stauffer, Helen Winter 1922- *ConAu 109*
Staum, Martin Sheldon 1943- *ConAu 103*
Staunton, Schuyler *SmATA X*
Stavaux, Michel 1948- *IntAu&W 82*
Stave, Bruce M 1937- *ConAu 29R, IntAu&W 82, WrDr 84*
Staveley, Gaylord L 1931- *ConAu 37R*
Stavely, Margaret *DrAP&F 83*
Stavenhagen, Lee 1933- *ConAu 104*
Stavenhagen, Rodolfo 1932- *ConAu 29R, IntAu&W 82*
Stavis, Barrie 1906- *ConAu 49, ConDr 82, NatPD 81[port], WrDr 84*
Stavis, Ben 1941- *ConAu 29R*
Stavrianos, Leften S 1913- *WrDr 84*
Stavrianos, Leften Stavros 1913- *ConAu 5R, -6NR*
Stavros, Niko *AuNews 1, ConAu X*
Stavrou, Theofanis G 1934- *ConAu 45*
Stayer, James M 1935- *ConAu 45*
Stead, C K 1932- *ConP 80, WorAu 1970, WrDr 84*
Stead, Christian Karlson 1932- *ConAu 6NR, -57, DcLEL 1940*
Stead, Christina 1902- *WrDr 84*
Stead, Christina 1902-1983 *ConAu 109*
Stead, Christina Ellen 1902- *ConAu 13R, ConLC 2, -5, -8, ConNov 82, LongCTC, ModCmwL, TwCA, TwCA SUP, TwCWr, WhoTwCL*
Stead, Chuck *DrAP&F 83*
Stead, Philip John 1916- *ConAu 108, IntAu&W 82, WrDr 84*
Stead, Robert James Campbell 1880-1959 *CreCan 2, TwCWW*
Stead, Thistle Y 1902- *ConAu 107, WrDr 84*
Stead, William Force 1884-1967 *LongCTC*
Stead, William Thomas 1849-1912 *LongCTC*
Steadman, David 1936- *ConAu 107*
Steadman, John Marcellus, III 1918- *ConAu 25R, IntAu&W 82*
Steadman, Mark *DrAP&F 83*
Steadman, Mark 1930- *ConAu 37R, DcLB 6[port]*
Steadman, Ralph 1936- *ConAu 107, SmATA 32[port]*
Steahly, Vivian Eugenia Emrick 1915- *ConAu 61, IntAu&W 82*
Stealingworth, Slim *ConAu X*
Steamer, Robert J 1920- *ConAu 41R*
Steane, John Barry 1928- *ConAu 9R, WrDr 84*
Stearn, Gerald E 1934?-1982 *ConAu 108*
Stearn, Jess *ConAu 97, WrDr 84*
Stearn, William Thomas 1911- *WrDr 84*
Stearns, Harold Edmund 1891-1943 *ConAu 107, DcLB 4, TwCA, TwCA SUP*
Stearns, Linda *CreCan 1*
Stearns, Marshall Winslow 1908-1966 *ConAu 110*

Stearns, Martha Genung 1886- *ConAu 9R*
Stearns, Monroe 1913- *ConAu 2NR, -5R, SmATA 5, WrDr 84*
Stearns, Pamela Fujimoto 1935- *ConAu 65*
Stearns, Peter N 1936- *ConAu 10NR, -21R, IntAu&W 82*
Stearns, Raymond Phineas 1904-1970 *ConAu P-1*
Stebbins, George Ledyard, Jr. 1906- *ConAu 45*
Stebbins, Richard P 1913- *ConAu 2NR, -5R*
Stebbins, Robert A 1938- *ConAu 29R, WrDr 84*
Stebbins, Robert Cyril 1915- *ConAu 49, WrDr 84*
Stebbins, Theodore Ellis, Jr. 1938- *ConAu 89*
Stebel, S L 1924- *ConAu 29R*
Stebelski, Julian *IntAu&W 82X*
Stebner, Gerhard Audy Siegfried 1928- *IntWWP 82*
Stecher, Miriam B 1917- *ConAu 106*
Stechow, Wolfgang 1896-1974 *ConAu 9NR, -53, -53, -65*
Steck, James S 1911- *ConAu 41R*
Steckel, William Reed 1915- *ConAu 17R*
Steckler, Arthur 1921- *ConAu 108*
Steckler, Doug 1948- *ConAu 107*
Steckler, Phyllis B 1933- *ConAu 9R*
Stedman, James Murphy 1938- *ConAu 77*
Stedman, Jane W 1920- *ConAu 37R*
Stedman, Murray S, Jr. 1917- *ConAu 17R*
Stedman, R William 1930- *ConAu 29R*
Stedman, Ray C 1917- *ConAu 104*
Stedman Jones, Gareth 1942- *ConAu 45*
Stedmond, John Mitchell 1916- *ConAu 103*
Stedwell, Paki 1945- *ConAu 103*
Steed, Gitel P 1914-1977 *ConAu 41R*
Steed, Henry Wickham 1871-1956 *TwCA, TwCA SUP*
Steed, Thomas Jefferson 1904-1983 *ConAu 110*
Steed, Tom *ConAu X*
Steed, Wickham 1871-1956 *LongCTC*
Steedman, Marguerite Couturier 1908- *ConAu 1R, -1NR*
Steefel, Lawrence D 1894- *ConAu P-2*
Steeger, Henry 1903- *ConAu 41R*
Steeger, Henry 1929?-1978 *ConAu 77*
Steegmuller, Francis *DrAP&F 83*
Steegmuller, Francis 1906- *ConAu 2NR, -49, IntAu&W 82, TwCA SUP, WrDr 84*
Steel, Anthony Bedford 1900-1973 *ConAu 5R, -89*
Steel, Byron *DrAP&F 83, WrDr 84*
Steel, Byron 1906- *ConAu X, IntAu&W 82X*
Steel, Danielle *WrDr 84*
Steel, Danielle F 1947- *ConAu 81, IntAu&W 82, TwCRGW*
Steel, David R 1948- *WrDr 84*
Steel, Edward M, Jr. 1918- *ConAu 9R*
Steel, Eric M 1904- *ConAu 89*
Steel, Flora Annie 1847-1929 *LongCTC, TwCA*
Steel, Ronald 1931- *ConAu 7NR, -9R, WrDr 84*
Steel, Tex *ConAu X*
Steele, A T 1903- *ConAu P-2*
Steele, Addison, II *ConAu X*
Steele, Arthur R 1916- *ConAu 9R*
Steele, Chester K *ConAu X*
Steele, Colin Robert 1944- *ConAu 104*
Steele, Curtis *TwCCr&M 80*
Steele, Dale *ConAu X*
Steele, Dirk *ConAu X*
Steele, Elizabeth 1921- *ConAu 45*
Steele, Erskine *ConAu X*
Steele, Fletcher 1885-1971 *ConAu P-1*
Steele, Frank 1935- *ConAu 37R*
Steele, Fred I 1938- *ConAu 2NR, -45*
Steele, Fritz *ConAu X*
Steele, George 1924- *ConAu 1R, WrDr 84*
Steele, Gordon 1892-1981 *ConAu 102, -105*
Steele, Harwood 1897- *ConAu P-1, TwCWW*
Steele, Harwood E 1897- *WrDr 84*
Steele, Henry 1931- *ConAu 41R*
Steele, Howard *WrDr 84*
Steele, I E *DrAP&F 83*
Steele, I K 1937- *ConAu 45*
Steele, Jack 1914-1980 *ConAu 102, -109*
Steele, James B 1943- *ConAu 110*
Steele, John Gladstone 1935- *IntAu&W 82*
Steele, Mary Q 1922- *TwCCW 83, WrDr 84*
Steele, Mary Quintard 1922- *ConAu 1R, -6NR, SmATA 3*
Steele, Max *DrAP&F 83*
Steele, Max 1922- *ConAu 25R,*

Steele, Patricia Joudry *CreCan 2*
Steele, Paul Curry *DrAP&F 83*
Steele, Peter 1935- *ConAu 108, WrDr 84*
Steele, Phillip W 1934- *ConAu 61*
Steele, Richard W 1934- *ConAu 107*
Steele, Robert 1917- *ConAu 49*
Steele, Robert Michael 1942- *ConAmTC*
Steele, Thomas J 1933- *ConAu 61*
Steele, Timothy 1948- *ConAu 93*
Steele, Wilbur Daniel 1886-1970 *ConAmA, ConAu 109, -29R, ModAL, TwCA, TwCA SUP*
Steele, William O 1917-1979 *TwCCW 83*
Steele, William Owen 1917-1979 *ConAu 1R, -2NR, -5R, SmATA 1, -27N*
Steelman, Robert J 1914- *ConAu 11NR, -69, TwCWW, WrDr 84*
Steely, John E 1922- *ConAu 37R*
Steen *IntAu&W 82X*
Steen, Alex 1929- *IntAu&W 82*
Steen, Edwin Benzel 1901- *ConAu 101*
Steen, Frank *ConAu X, IntAu&W 82X*
Steen, John Warren, Jr. 1925- *ConAu 13R*
Steen, Malcolm Harold 1928- *ConAu 29R*
Steen, Marguerite 1894-1975 *ConAu 61, -97, LongCTC, TwCA, TwCA SUP, TwCRGW*
Steen, Mike 1928- *ConAu X, WrDr 84*
Steen, Sara Jayne 1949- *ConAu 106*
Steenberg, Sven 1905- *ConAu 37R*
Steene, Birgitta 1928- *ConAu 85, IntAu&W 82*
Steensma, Robert Charles 1930- *ConAu 41R*
Steenson, Gary P 1944- *ConAu 107*
Steer, Alfred G, Jr. 1913- *ConAu 45*
Steere, Daniel C 1938- *ConAu 93*
Steere, Douglas V 1901- *ConAu 13R*
Steese, Edward 1902-1981 *ConAu 105, IntWWP 82*
Steese, Peter B 1933- *ConAu 17R*
Steevens, George Warrington 1869-1900 *LongCTC*
Steeves, Frank Leslie 1921- *ConAu 13R*
Steeves, Harrison Ross 1881-1981 *ConAu 104*
Stefan, Ion M 1922- *IntAu&W 82*
Stefanile, Felix *DrAP&F 83*
Stefanile, Felix 1920- *ConAu 1NR, -45*
Stefanile, Felix Neil 1920- *IntWWP 82*
Stefansson, David 1895-1954 *ClDMEL 80*
Stefansson, Evelyn Baird 1913- *ConAu 49*
Stefansson, Thorsteinn 1912- *ConAu 77, IntAu&W 82*
Stefansson, Vilhjalmur 1879-1962 *TwCA, TwCA SUP*
Stefanyk, Vasyl 1871-1936 *ClDMEL 80, ModSL 2*
Steffan, Alice Kennedy 1907- *ConAu 5R*
Steffan, Jack *ConAu X*
Steffan, Ruth *IntAu&W 82X*
Steffan, Siobhan R *ConAu X*
Steffan, Truman Guy 1910- *ConAu 29R, IntAu&W 82*
Steffanson, Con *ConAu X, TwCSFW, WrDr 84*
Steffek, Edwin F 1912- *ConAu 89*
Steffen, Albert 1884-1963 *CnMD, ConAu 93, ModWD*
Steffens, Lincoln 1866-1936 *LongCTC, ModAL, TwCA, TwCA SUP*
Stefferud, Alfred Daniel 1903- *ConAu P-1*
Steffler, John 1947- *ConAu 110*
Stefflre, Buford 1916- *ConAu 5R*
Stegall, Carrie Coffey 1908- *ConAu P-2*
Stegeman, John Foster 1918- *ConAu 17R*
Stegenga, James A 1937- *ConAu 25R, WrDr 84*
Steger, Shelby 1906- *ConAu 49*
Steglich, W G 1921- *ConAu 45*
Stegman, Michael A 1940- *ConAu 41R*
Stegner, Page *DrAP&F 83*
Stegner, Page 1937- *ConAu 10NR, -21R*
Stegner, Wallace *DrAP&F 83*
Stegner, Wallace 1909- *WrDr 84*
Stegner, Wallace Earle 1909- *AuNews 1, ConAu 1R, -1NR, ConLC 9, ConNov 82, DcLB 9[port], FifWWr, ModAL, TwCA, TwCA SUP, TwCWW*
Stehlik, Miroslav 1916- *CnMD*
Stehling, Kurt R 1919- *ConAu 110*
Stehman, John *DrAP&F 83*
Stehman, John Anthony 1942- *IntWWP 82*

Stevens, Lucile Vernon 1899- *ConAu 61*
Stevens, Martin 1927- *ConAu 13R*
Stevens, Michael 1919- *ConAu 53, WrDr 84*
Stevens, Norma Young 1927- *ConAu 21R*
Stevens, Pam *ConAu X*
Stevens, Patricia Bunning 1931- *ConAu 53, SmATA 27*
Stevens, Peter *ConAu X, SmATA X*
Stevens, Peter 1927- *ConAu 93, ConP 80*
Stevens, Peter John 1926- *WrDr 84*
Stevens, Peter Smith 1936- *ConAu 53*
Stevens, Peter Stanley 1927- *WrDr 84*
Stevens, R 1933- *ConAu 21R*
Stevens, R B 1933- *ConAu 9NR*
Stevens, R L *ConAu X, IntAu&W 82X, TwCCr&M 80*
Stevens, Richard P 1931- *ConAu 10NR, –21R, WrDr 84*
Stevens, Robert 1933- *ConAu 102*
Stevens, Robert Tyler *ConAu X, WrDr 84*
Stevens, Robert Warren 1918- *ConAu 1NR, –45*
Stevens, Roger 1906-1980 *ConAu 105*
Stevens, Rolland E 1915- *ConAu 81*
Stevens, Rosemary 1935- *ConAu 85*
Stevens, S P *ConAu X*
Stevens, Shane *DrAP&F 83*
Stevens, Shane 1941- *ConAu 21R*
Stevens, Sharon 1949- *ConAu 77*
Stevens, Steve *IntAu&W 82X*
Stevens, Sylvester K 1904-1974 *ConAu 45, ConAu P-1*
Stevens, Wallace 1879-1955 *CnMWL, ConAmA, ConAu 104, LongCTC, ModAL, ModAL SUP, TwCA, TwCA SUP, TwCLC 3, –12[port], TwCWr, WhoTwCL*
Stevens, Wendy *DrAP&F 83*
Stevens, William 1925- *ConAu 21R*
Stevens, William Christopher *WrDr 84*
Stevens, William W 1914- *WrDr 84*
Stevens, William Wilson 1914-1978 *ConAu 37R*
Stevenson, Adlai Ewing 1900-1965 *ConAu P-1*
Stevenson, Anna P 1905- *SmATA 12*
Stevenson, Anne *DrAP&F 83, TwCRGW, WrDr 84*
Stevenson, Anne 1933- *ConAu X, –9NR, ConLC 7, ConP 80, IntAu&W 82, WrDr 84*
Stevenson, Augusta 1869?-1976 *ConAu 1R, –65, SmATA 2, –26N*
Stevenson, Bruce 1906- *ConAu 49*
Stevenson, Burton Egbert 1872-1962 *ConAu 102, –89, SmATA 25, TwCA, TwCA SUP*
Stevenson, Carol Dornfeld 1931- *ConAu 5R*
Stevenson, Charles 1908?-1979 *ConAu 85*
Stevenson, D E 1892-1973 *TwCRGW*
Stevenson, David 1942- *ConAu 109, IntAu&W 82, WrDr 84*
Stevenson, David Lloyd 1910-1975 *ConAu 57, ConAu P-2*
Stevenson, Dorothy Emily 1892-1973 *ConAu 49, ConAu P-1, LongCTC, TwCA, TwCA SUP*
Stevenson, Dwight Eshelman 1906- *ConAu 1R, –1NR, WrDr 84*
Stevenson, Elizabeth 1919- *ConAu 1R, IntAu&W 82, WrDr 84*
Stevenson, Florence *ConAu 97, TwCRGW, WrDr 84*
Stevenson, George James 1924- *ConAu 9R, WrDr 84*
Stevenson, Gloria 1945- *ConAu 61*
Stevenson, Grace Thomas 1900- *ConAu 37R*
Stevenson, Harold W 1921- *ConAu 25R*
Stevenson, Henry M 1914- *ConAu 77*
Stevenson, Herbert Frederick 1906- *ConAu 2NR, –5R*
Stevenson, Ian 1918- *WrDr 84*
Stevenson, Ian Ralph 1943- *ConAu 102, WrDr 84*
Stevenson, J P *ConAu X*
Stevenson, J P 1910- *WrDr 84*
Stevenson, James 1929- *SmATA 34*
Stevenson, James Perry 1942- *IntAu&W 82*
Stevenson, Janet 1913- *ConAu 13R, SmATA 8*
Stevenson, John Albert 1890?-1979 *ConAu 89*
Stevenson, John P *ConAu X, WrDr 84*
Stevenson, L W 1916- *ConAu 107*
Stevenson, Leslie 1943- *ConAu 65*
Stevenson, Lionel 1902-1973 *ConAu 103, –45*
Stevenson, Mary Blanche 1889- *IntWWP 82*
Stevenson, Michael Ian 1953- *ConAu 103*
Stevenson, Robert 1916- *ConAu 1R, –1NR*

Stevenson, Robert Murrell 1916- *IntAu&W 82*
Stevenson, Suzanne Silvercruys 1898?-1973 *ConAu 41R*
Stevenson, T H 1919- *ConAu 61*
Stevenson, Tom 1899?-1982 *ConAu 106*
Stevenson, Vera Kemp 1920- *ConAu 57*
Stevenson, Victoria F 1878?-1973 *ConAu 41R*
Stevenson, W Taylor 1928- *ConAu 25R*
Stevenson, Warren 1933- *ConAu 41R*
Stevenson, William 1924- *WrDr 84*
Stevenson, William 1925- *ConAu 13R*
Stevenson, William Taylor 1928- *WrDr 84*
Stever, Margo Taft *DrAP&F 83*
Stevo, Jean 1914-1974 *ClDMEL 80*
Steward, D E *DrAP&F 83*
Steward, F C 1904- *ConAu 41R*
Steward, Hal D 1922- *ConAu 69*
Steward, Julian H 1902-1972 *ConAu 33R*
Stewart, A C *ConAu 77, SmATA 15, TwCCW 83, WrDr 84*
Stewart, A T Q 1929- *ConAu 25R*
Stewart, Alfred Walter 1880-1947 *LongCTC, TwCA, TwCA SUP*
Stewart, Allan 1939- *ConAu 1R*
Stewart, Allegra 1899- *ConAu 45*
Stewart, Angus 1936- *ConAu 106, IntAu&W 82, WrDr 84*
Stewart, Bertie Ann Gardner 1912- *ConAu 5R*
Stewart, Bill 1942?-1979 *ConAu 89*
Stewart, Charles *ConAu X, SmATA X*
Stewart, Charles J 1936- *ConAu 41R*
Stewart, Charles T, Jr. 1922- *ConAu 101*
Stewart, Christina Duff 1926- *ConAu 65*
Stewart, D H 1926- *ConAu 21R*
Stewart, Daniel Kenneth 1925- *ConAu 29R, IntAu&W 82, WrDr 84*
Stewart, David *ConAu X, WrDr 84*
Stewart, Desmond 1924-1981 *ConAu 104, –37R, DcLEL 1940, IntAu&W 82*
Stewart, Donald Charles 1930- *ConAu 37R, WrDr 84*
Stewart, Donald H 1911- *ConAu 29R, WrDr 84*
Stewart, Donald Ogden 1894-1980 *ConAu 101, –81, Conv 1, DcLB 4, –26[port], TwCA, TwCA SUP*
Stewart, Dorothy Mary 1917-1965 *ConAu 104*
Stewart, Douglas 1913- *WrDr 84*
Stewart, Douglas Alexander 1913- *ConAu 81, ConDr 82, ConP 80, ModCmwL, TwCWr, WorAu*
Stewart, Edgar I 1900- *ConAu 5R*
Stewart, Edith Hamilton 1883- *ConAu P-1*
Stewart, Elbert Wilton 1916- *ConAu 37R*
Stewart, Eleanor *ConAu X*
Stewart, Elizabeth Grey *ConAu X*
Stewart, Elizabeth Laing 1907- *ConAu 49, SmATA 6*
Stewart, Ella Winter 1898-1980 *ConAu 101*
Stewart, Eve *ConAu X*
Stewart, Frank *DrAP&F 83*
Stewart, Frank 1946- *ConAu 104*
Stewart, Fred Mustard 1936- *ConAu 37R, WrDr 84*
Stewart, Garrett 1945- *ConAu 93*
Stewart, George 1892-1972 *ConAu 33R*
Stewart, George Rippey 1895-1980 *ConAu 1R, –3NR, –101, DcLB 8[port], FifWWr, SmATA 23N, –3, TwCA SUP, TwCSFW*
Stewart, Hal D 1899- *ConAu P-1, IntAu&W 82*
Stewart, Harold C 1891?-1976 *ConAu 69*
Stewart, Harold Frederick 1916- *ConAu 69, ConP 80, DcLEL 1940, IntAu&W 82, IntWWP 82, TwCWr, WrDr 84*
Stewart, Harris B, Jr. 1922- *ConAu 45*
Stewart, Hilary 1924- *ConAu 93*
Stewart, Horace Floyd, Jr. 1928- *ConAu 49*
Stewart, J I M 1906- *ConAu 85, ConLC 7, –14, ConNov 82, TwCCr&M 80, WrDr 84*
Stewart, James Brewer 1940- *ConAu 29R*
Stewart, James Stuart 1896- *ConAu 9R, WrDr 84*
Stewart, Jean *ConAu X, WrDr 84*
Stewart, John *DrAP&F 83*
Stewart, John 1920- *ConAu 33R, SmATA 14*
Stewart, John 1933- *ConAu 97*
Stewart, John 1941- *ConAu 97*
Stewart, John B 1924- *ConAu 9R*
Stewart, John Innes Mackintosh 1906- *LongCTC, TwCA, TwCA SUP, TwCWr*

Stewart, Joy 1931- *WrDr 84*
Stewart, Judith Anne *ConAu X*
Stewart, Katharine Jeanne 1914- *ConAu 9R*
Stewart, Kaye *ConAu 49*
Stewart, Kenneth N 1901-1978 *ConAu 77*
Stewart, Kerry *ConAu X*
Stewart, Lawrence D 1926- *ConAu 89*
Stewart, Lawrence H 1922- *ConAu 17R*
Stewart, Linda *ConAu 101*
Stewart, Margaret 1912- *ConAu 25R*
Stewart, Marie M 1899- *ConAu 5R*
Stewart, Marie Vogl *DrAP&F 83*
Stewart, Mark Armstrong 1929- *ConAu 89*
Stewart, Mary 1916- *ConAu 1R, –1NR, ConLC 7, DcLEL 1940, IntAu&W 82, LongCTC, SmATA 12, TwCCr&M 80, TwCRGW, TwCWr, WorAu, WrDr 84*
Stewart, Mary Rainbow 1916- *ConAu X*
Stewart, Michael *ConDr 82D, DrAP&F 83, WrDr 84*
Stewart, Michael 1906- *ConAu 106*
Stewart, Michael 1933- *WrDr 84*
Stewart, Oliver 1895-1980 *ConAu 5R, –5NR*
Stewart, Ora Pate 1910- *IntAu&W 82, IntWWP 82*
Stewart, Pamela *DrAP&F 83*
Stewart, Pat 1944- *ConAu 97*
Stewart, Paul D 1918- *ConAu 1R*
Stewart, Perry 1942- *ConAmTC*
Stewart, Philip Robert 1940- *ConAu 29R*
Stewart, Phyllis Langton 1933- *ConAu 106*
Stewart, Porter *DrAP&F 83*
Stewart, Porter Ellis 1944- *LivgBAA*
Stewart, Ramona 1922- *ASpks, ConAu 1R, –6NR*
Stewart, Randall 1896-1964 *ConAu 1R, –1NR*
Stewart, Rattray *IntAu&W 82X*
Stewart, Reginald 1900- *CreCan 1*
Stewart, Rex William 1907-1967 *ConAu 110*
Stewart, Rhea Talley 1915- *ConAu 41R*
Stewart, Robert *DrAP&F 83*
Stewart, Robert G 1931- *ConAu 65*
Stewart, Robert Michael Maitland 1906- *IntAu&W 82*
Stewart, Robert Neil 1891-1972 *ConAu 9R, SmATA 7*
Stewart, Robert T 1920?-1977 *ConAu 73*
Stewart, Robert Wilson 1935- *ConAu 49*
Stewart, Rosemary *ConAu 37R, WrDr 84*
Stewart, Sam *ConAu X*
Stewart, Seumas 1919- *ConAu 61*
Stewart, Sheila 1928- *ConAu 21R*
Stewart, Stanley N 1931- *ConAu 17R*
Stewart, Suzanne *ConAu 61*
Stewart, Vincent 1939- *ConAu 29R*
Stewart, Walter Bingham 1913- *ConAu 85*
Stewart, Will *ConAu X*
Stewart, William Alexander Campbell 1915- *ConAu 13R, IntAu&W 82, WrDr 84*
Stewart, William Stanley 1938- *ConAu 89*
Stewart, Zeph 1921- *ConAu 41R*
Stewart Of Fulham, Baron 1906- *IntAu&W 82, WrDr 84*
Stewig, John Warren 1937- *ConAu 81, SmATA 26[port]*
Steyaert, Thomas A 1930- *ConAu 37R*
Steyer, Wesley W 1923- *ConAu 29R*
Steyermark, Julian Alfred 1909- *ConAu P-1*
Stibbs, Alan Marshall 1901- *ConAu 1R, –2NR*
Stiber, Alex *DrAP&F 83*
Stich, Stephen P 1943- *ConAu 41R*
Stick, David 1919- *ConAu 97*
Stickells, Austin T 1914- *ConAu 41R*
Stickgold, Bob 1945- *ConAu 104*
Stickney, Joseph Trumbull 1874-1904 *ModAL, ModAL SUP, TwCA, TwCA SUP*
Stieber, Carolyn 1923- *MichAu 80*
Stieber, Jack 1919- *ConAu 1R, –6NR*
Stiehm, Judith 1935- *ConAu 61*
Stierlin, Helm 1926- *ConAu 29R, WrDr 84*
Stierwell, Jay 1930- *ConAu X*
Stigall, John Clement 1951- *IntWWP 82*
Stigen, Terje 1922- *ClDMEL 80*
Stigler, George J 1911- *WrDr 84*
Stigler, George Joseph 1911- *ConAu 41R*
Stigum, Marcia 1934- *ConAu 8NR, –61*
Stigwood, Robert C 1934- *ConAu 102*
Stiles, John R 1916?-1976 *ConAu 65*
Stiles, Joseph 1903- *ConAu P-2*
Stiles, Lindley 1913- *WrDr 84*
Stiles, Lindley Joseph 1913- *ConAu 3NR, –5R*
Stiles, Martha Bennett *ConAu 37R,*

DrAP&F 83, IntAu&W 82, MichAu 80,
SmATA 6
Stiles, Merritt N 1899-1975 ConAu 57
Stiles, Ned B 1932- ConAu 17R
Stilgoe, John R ConAu 109
Still, C Henry 1920- ConAu 9R
Still, Gloria DrAP&F 83
Still, James DrAP&F 83
Still, James 1906- ConAu 10NR, –65,
DcLB 9[port], IntAu&W 82,
SmATA 29[port], TwCA, TwCA SUP
Still, Richard 1921- ConAu 1R, –1NR,
WrDr 84
Still, William N 1932- ConAu 25R, WrDr 84
Stiller, Klaus George 1941- IntAu&W 82
Stillerman, Robbie 1947- SmATA 12
Stilley, Frank 1918- ConAu 61,
SmATA 29[port]
Stillinger, Jack 1931- ConAu 1R, –1NR,
IntAu&W 82, WrDr 84
Stillman, Damie 1933- ConAu 45
Stillman, Frances 1910-1975 ConAu 57,
ConAu P-1
Stillman, Irwin M 1895-1975 ConAu 49, –61
Stillman, Myra Stephens 1915- ConAu 5R,
–6NR
Stillman, Nathan 1914- ConAu 5R
Stillman, Richard Joseph 1917- ConAu 37R,
IntAu&W 82, WrDr 84
Stillwell, Margaret Bingham 1887- ConAu 41R,
WrDr 84
Stillwell, Mary Kathryn DrAP&F 83
Stillwell, Mary Kathryn 1944- IntWWP 82
Stillwell, Norma Jamieson 1894- ConAu P-1
Stilson, Max 1919- ConAu 9R
Stilwell, Hart 1902- TwCWW
Stilwell, William E, III 1936- ConAu 107
Stimmel, Barry 1939- ConAu 11NR, –69
Stimpson, Catherine R 1936- ConAu 41R
Stinchcombe, Arthur L 1933- ConAu 8NR, –13R
Stinchcombe, William 1937- ConAu 105
Stine, G Harry 1928- ConAu 9NR, –65,
WrDr 84
Stine, George Harry 1928- SmATA 10
Stine, Hank 1945- ConSFA, DrmM[port],
TwCSFW, WrDr 84
Stine, Jovial Bob ConAu X, SmATA X
Stine, Robert Lawrence 1943- ConAu 105,
SmATA 31[port]
Stine, Whitney Ward 1930- AuNews 1,
ConAu 7NR, –57
Stineman, Esther F 1947- ConAu 97
Stinetorf, Louise 1900- ConAu 9R, SmATA 10
Stingelin-Venturini, Attilia Fiorenza
IntAu&W 82X
Stinger, Charles L 1944- ConAu 77
Stini, William A 1930- ConAu 107
Stinnett, Caskie 1911- ConAu 5R
Stinnett, Nick 1942- ConAu 110
Stinnett, Ronald F 1929- ConAu 21R
Stinnett, Tim Moore 1901- ConAu 17R
Stinnette, Charles R, Jr. 1914- ConAu 77
Stinus, Erik 1934- IntWWP 82
Stipcevic, Augustin 1912- IntWWP 82
Stipe, Robert Edwin 1928- ConAu 49
Stirling, Alfred 1902- WrDr 84
Stirling, Alfred 1902-1981 ConAu 108, –110
Stirling, Anna Maria Diana Wilhelmina 1865-1965
ConAu P-1, LongCTC
Stirling, Anthony MichAu 80
Stirling, Arthur ConAmA, ConAu X,
SmATA X
Stirling, Betty Rutledge 1923- ConAu 9R
Stirling, Brents 1904- ConAu P-2
Stirling, Jessica WrDr 84
Stirling, Jessica 1920- ConAu X, TwCRGW
Stirling, Lilla 1902- ConAu 107
Stirling, Matthew Williams 1896-1975 ConAu 53
Stirling, Monica 1916- ConAu 81, ConNov 82,
DcLEL 1940, IntAu&W 82, WrDr 84
Stirling, Nora B WrDr 84
Stirling, Nora Bromley 1900- ConAu 3NR, –5R,
SmATA 3
Stirling, Thomas Brents 1904- WrDr 84
Stirn-Faschon, Susanne IntAu&W 82X
Stirnweis, Shannon 1931- SmATA 10
Stitch, Wilhelmina 1889- LongCTC
Stitelman, Leonard 1932- ConAu 41R
Stites, Francis Noel 1938- ConAu 41R
Stites, Raymond S 1899-1974 ConAu 53, –65
Stitskin, Leon D 1910-1978 ConAu 1R, –1NR
Stitt, Milan 1941- ConAu 69, NatPD 81[port]

Stitzel, Thomas E 1936- ConAu 93
Stivens, Dal 1911- ConAu 69, ConNov 82,
WrDr 84
Stivens, Dallas George 1911- TwCWr
Stiver, Mary Dorothy Weeden 1909- ConAu P-1,
IntWWP 82
Stivers, Robert L 1940- ConAu 69
Stjernberg, Lloyd A 1937- ConAu 25R
Stob, Ralph 1894-1965 ConAu 1R, –103
Stobart, Thomas Ralph 1914- ConAu 13R
Stobaugh, Robert B 1927- ConAu 101
Stobbs, John Louis Newcombe 1921- ConAu 13R
Stobbs, William 1914- ConAu 81, SmATA 17
Stoberski, Zygmunt Julian 1916- IntAu&W 82
Stock, B E DrAP&F 83
Stock, Brian 1939- ConAu 41R
Stock, Claudette 1934- ConAu 65
Stock, Ernest 1924- ConAu 21R
Stock, Irvin 1920- ConAu 25R
Stock, Phyllis H 1930- ConAu 85
Stock, R D 1941- ConAu 41R
Stockanes, Anthony E DrAP&F 83
Stockanes, Anthony E 1935- ConAu 109
Stockard, James Wright, Jr. 1935- ConAu 13R
Stockard, Jimmy ConAu X
Stockdale, Eric 1929- ConAu 25R
Stockham, Peter Alan 1928- IntAu&W 82
Stockhammer, Morris 1904- ConAu 13R
Stocking, David M 1919- ConAu 25R
Stocking, George W, Jr. 1928- ConAu 73
Stocking, George Ward 1892-1975 ConAu 61
Stocking, Hobart E 1906- ConAu 101
Stocking, Marion Kingston 1922- ConAu 25R
Stocks, Bryan IntAu&W 82X
Stocks, John Bryan 1917- IntAu&W 82
Stocks, Lady Mary Danvers 1891- ConAu 13R
Stockton, Adrian James 1935- ConAu 29R
Stockton, Francis Richard 1834-1902 ConAu 108,
LongCTC
Stockton, Frank R ConAu X
Stockton, Frank R 1834-1902 SmATA 32
Stockton, Frank Richard 1834-1902 TwCSFW
Stockton, J Roy 1893?-1972 ConAu 37R
Stockton, Jim ConAu X
Stockton, John R 1903- ConAu 13R
Stockton, Richard 1932- NatPD 81[port]
Stockwell, Edward G 1933- ConAu 21R
Stockwell, John R 1937- ConAu 104
Stockwell, Nancy DrAP&F 83
Stockwell, Robert P 1925- ConAu 17R
Stockwin, Arthur 1935- ConAu 103
Stockwin, James 1935- WrDr 84
Stockwood, Arthur Mervyn 1913- WrDr 84
Stoddard, Alan 1915- WrDr 84
Stoddard, Charles ConAu X
Stoddard, Edward G 1923- ConAu 9R,
SmATA 10
Stoddard, Ellwyn R 1927- ConAu 1NR, –45,
IntAu&W 82
Stoddard, George Dinsmore 1897-1981
ConAu 106
Stoddard, Hope 1900- ConAu 49, SmATA 6
Stoddard, Richard 1942- ConAu 102
Stoddard, Sandol 1927- ConAu 8NR,
SmATA X
Stoddard, Tom 1933- ConAu 37R
Stoddard, Whitney Snow 1913- ConAu 109
Stodghill, Pat 1935- IntWWP 82
Stoehr, C Eric 1945- ConAu 65
Stoessinger, John G 1927- ASpks, ConAu 9NR,
–13R, IntAu&W 82, WrDr 84
Stoessl, Franz 1910- IntAu&W 82
Stoessl, Otto 1875-1936 ModGL
Stoetzer, O Carlos 1921- ConAu 109
Stof IntAu&W 82X
Stoff, Sheldon 1930- ConAu 21R
Stoffel, Albert Law 1909- ConAu 65
Stoffel, Betty W 1922- ConAu 17R
Stoffel, Lester L 1920- ConAu 45
Stoffle, Carla J 1943- ConAu 7NR, –61
Stogdill, Ralph M 1904- ConAu 1R, –1NR,
WrDr 84
Stohl, Michael 1947- ConAu 107
Stohlman, Martha Lou Lemmon 1913- ConAu 65
Stoianovich, Traian 1921- ConAu 21R
Stoiber, Rudolph M 1925- ConAu 1R
Stoiko, Michael 1919- ConAu 9R, SmATA 14
Stoil, Michael Jon 1950- ConAu 53
Stokely, James R, Jr. 1913-1977 ConAu 9R, –69
Stokely, Wilma Dykeman 1920- ConAu 1R
Stoker, Abraham 1847-1912 ConAu 105,

SmATA 29[port]
Stoker, Alan WrDr 84
Stoker, Alan 1930- ConAu 9NR, –21R
Stoker, Bram 1847-1912 ConAu X, LongCTC,
SmATA X, TwCA, TwCA SUP,
TwCCr&M 80, TwCLC 8[port]
Stoker, H Stephen 1939- ConAu 8NR, –61
Stokes, Adrian Durham 1902-1972 ConAu 5NR,
–13R, –89, WorAu 1970
Stokes, Bob ConAu X
Stokes, Carl B 1927- ConAu 69
Stokes, Cedric ConAu X, SmATA X
Stokes, Charles 1932- ConAu 103
Stokes, Charles J 1922- ConAu 10NR, –25R
Stokes, Daniel M DrAP&F 83
Stokes, Daniel M J 1950- ConAu 57,
IntWWP 82
Stokes, Donald Elkinton 1927- ConAu 1R, –1NR
Stokes, Eric Thomas 1924-1981 ConAu 103, –107
Stokes, Geoffrey 1940- ConAu 69
Stokes, Jack 1923- ConAu 29R, SmATA 13
Stokes, John DrAP&F 83
Stokes, Olivia Pearl 1916- ConAu 37R,
SmATA 32[port]
Stokes, Peg Ewing ConAu 1R
Stokes, Robert ConAu X, DrAP&F 83
Stokes, Roy 1915- ConAu 17R
Stokes, Simpson ConAu X
Stokes, Terry DrAP&F 83
Stokes, William Lee 1915- ConAu 41R
Stokesbury, James L 1934- ConAu 93
Stokesbury, Leon 1945- ConAu 69
Stokke, Baard Richard 1937- ConAu 25R
Stokoe, William C, Jr. 1919- ConAu 41R
Stokstad, Marilyn 1929- ConAu 37R
Stoler, Peter 1935- ConAu 97
Stoll, Clarice Stasz ConAu X
Stoll, Dennis G 1912- ConAu 13R
Stoll, John E 1933- ConAu 49
Stoller, Alan 1911- WrDr 84
Stollnitz, Fred 1939- ConAu 45
Stoloff, Carolyn DrAP&F 83
Stoloff, Carolyn 1927- ConAu 9NR, –65
Stolorow, Robert D 1942- ConAu 102
Stolpacker, Pete DrAP&F 83
Stolper, Alice 1934- IntAu&W 82
Stolper, Wolfgang F 1912- ConAu 21R,
WrDr 84
Stolten, Jane ConAu 97
Stoltenberg, Donald Hugo 1927- ConAu 89
Stoltzfus, Ben DrAP&F 83
Stoltzfus, Ben Franklin 1927- ConAu 103, –13R,
IntAu&W 82, WrDr 84
Stolz, Lois Meek 1891- ConAu P-2
Stolz, Mary 1920- TwCCW 83, WrDr 84
Stolz, Mary Slattery 1920- AuNews 1,
ConAu 5R, ConLC 12, SmATA 10
Stolzenbach, Norma Frizzell 1904- ConAu 41R
Stolzenberg, Mark 1950- ConAu 102
Stonberg, Selma F ConAu 69
Stone IntAu&W 82X
Stone, Alan ConAu P-2, SmATA X
Stone, Alan A 1929- ConAu 17R, WrDr 84
Stone, Albert E, Jr. ConAu X
Stone, Albert Edward 1924- ConAu 8NR, –17R
Stone, Alfred R 1926- ConAu 17R
Stone, Alma DrAP&F 83
Stone, Alma 1908- ConAu 77
Stone, Arlene DrAP&F 83
Stone, Barbara Haskins 1924?-1979 ConAu 89
Stone, Betty E 1926- ConAu 9R
Stone, Brian Ernest 1919- ConAu 13R,
WrDr 84
Stone, Carole DrAP&F 83
Stone, Charles Sumner, Jr. 1924- ConAu 77
Stone, Christopher D 1937- ConAu 53
Stone, Christopher Reynolds 1882-1965 LongCTC
Stone, Chuck 1924- ConAu X, LivgBAA
Stone, David 1929- ConAu 5R
Stone, David K 1922- ConAu 85, SmATA 9
Stone, David U 1927- ConAu 7NR, –17R
Stone, Donald Adelbert, Jr. 1937- ConAu 29R
Stone, Donald D 1942- ConAu 81,
IntAu&W 82
Stone, Doris 1909- ConAu 105
Stone, Edward 1913- ConAu 37R
Stone, Elaine Murray WrDr 84
Stone, Elaine Murray 1922- ConAu 89,
IntAu&W 82
Stone, Elizabeth W 1918- ConAu 107
Stone, Ellery W 1894-1981 ConAu 105
Stone, Elna ConAu 5NR, –13R

Stone, Ena Margaret 1911- *IntAu&W 82*
Stone, Eugenia 1879-1971 *ConAu 9R, SmATA 7*
Stone, Frank A 1929- *ConAu 8NR, -61*
Stone, Gene *ConAu X, SmATA 7*
Stone, George Winchester, Jr. 1907- *ConAu 5R, -6NR*
Stone, Gerald 1932- *ConAu 104, WrDr 84*
Stone, Gillian Emily Custance 1930- *IntWWP 82*
Stone, Grace Zaring 1891- *ConAu P-2*
Stone, Grace Zaring 1896- *ConAmA, LongCTC, TwCA, TwCA SUP*
Stone, Graham Brice 1926- *ConSFA*
Stone, Gregory P 1921- *ConAu 1NR, -49*
Stone, Hampton *ConAu X, IntAu&W 82X, TwCCr&M 80, WrDr 84*
Stone, Harris B 1934- *ConAu 57*
Stone, Harry Edward Markham 1928- *ConAu 13R*
Stone, Helen 1904- *ConAu 25R, SmATA 6*
Stone, Henry *DrAP&F 83*
Stone, Hoyt E 1935- *ConAu 101*
Stone, I F 1907- *WorAu 1970*
Stone, Idella Purnell 1901- *ConAu X*
Stone, Ikey *ConAu X*
Stone, Irving 1903- *AuNews 1, ConAu 1R, -1NR, ConLC 7, ConNov 82, LongCTC, SmATA 3, TwCA, TwCA SUP, TwCWr, WrDr 84*
Stone, Isidor F 1907- *ConAu 61, WrDr 84*
Stone, James Champion 1916- *ConAu 17R*
Stone, James H 1918- *ConAu 41R*
Stone, Jennifer *DrAP&F 83*
Stone, Joan *DrAP&F 83*
Stone, Joan 1930- *ConAu 77, IntWWP 82*
Stone, John *DrAP&F 83*
Stone, John 1933- *ConAu 102*
Stone, John H 1936- *ConAu 89*
Stone, Jon 1931- *ConAu 107*
Stone, Josephine Rector *ConAu X, SmATA X*
Stone, Julie *DrAP&F 83*
Stone, Julius 1907- *ConAu 5NR, -53, IntAu&W 82, WrDr 84*
Stone, Ken *DrAP&F 83*
Stone, L Joseph 1912-1975 *ConAu 61*
Stone, Lawrence 1919- *ConAu 13R, WrDr 84*
Stone, Leslie F 1905- *ConSFA*
Stone, Louis 1871-1935 *TwCWr*
Stone, Marvin Lawrence 1924- *ConAu 69*
Stone, Melville 1848-1929 *DcLB 25[port]*
Stone, Merlin 1931- *ConAu 101*
Stone, Merlin 1948- *WrDr 84*
Stone, Mildred Fairbanks 1902- *ConAu P-1*
Stone, Nancy Young 1925- *ConAu 49, MichAu 80*
Stone, Oliver 1946- *ConAu 110*
Stone, Patti 1926- *ConAu 5R*
Stone, Peter 1930- *ConAu 7NR, -9R, ConDr 82D, IntAu&W 82*
Stone, Peter A 1919- *WrDr 84*
Stone, Philip James, III 1936- *ConAu 21R*
Stone, Ralph 1934- *ConAu 37R, WrDr 84*
Stone, Raymond *ConAu P-2, SmATA 1*
Stone, Reynolds 1909-1979 *ConAu 89*
Stone, Richard 1913- *WrDr 84*
Stone, Richard A *ConAu X*
Stone, Robert *DrAP&F 83*
Stone, Robert 1937?- *ConAu 85, ConLC 5, -23[port]*
Stone, Robert B 1916- *ConAu 29R*
Stone, Ronald H 1939- *ConAu 77*
Stone, Ruth *DrAP&F 83*
Stone, Ruth 1915- *ConAu 2NR, -45*
Stone, Scott C S 1932- *ConAu 25R*
Stone, Shelley C 1928- *ConAu 61*
Stone, Susan Berch 1944- *ConAu 61*
Stone, Thomas H *ConAu X, WrDr 84*
Stone, Vernon A 1929- *ConAu 65*
Stone, Wilfred 1917- *ConAu 21R*
Stone, William F 1931- *ConAu 41R*
Stone, William S 1928- *ConAu 13R, WrDr 84*
Stoneburner, Charles Joseph 1926- *IntAu&W 82, IntWWP 82*
Stoneburner, Tony 1926- *ConAu 41R*
Stonehouse, Bernard 1926- *ConAu 2NR, -49, IntAu&W 82, SmATA 13, WrDr 84*
Stonehouse, Frederick 1948- *MichAu 80*
Stonehouse, Merlin 1911- *ConAu 13R*
Stoneman, Elvyn Arthur 1919- *ConAu 17R*
Stoneman, Paul 1947- *WrDr 84*
Stonequist, Everett Verner 1901-1979 *ConAu 85*

Stoner, Carol Hupping 1949- *ConAu 53*
Stoner, Oliver *WrDr 84*
Stoner, Oliver 1903- *IntAu&W 82*
Stones, E 1922- *ConAu 37R*
Stonesifer, Richard James 1922- *ConAu 13R*
Stong, Clair L 1902?-1975 *ConAu 61*
Stong, Phil 1899-1957 *SmATA 32[port], TwCCW 83*
Stong, Philip Duffield 1899-1957 *ConAmA, TwCA, TwCA SUP*
Stonier, George Walter 1903- *IntAu&W 82*
Stonier, Tom 1927- *ConAu 5R*
Stonor, Oliver 1903- *ConAu P-1*
Stonum, Gary Lee 1947- *ConAu 89*
Stoodley, Bartlett Hicks 1907-1978 *ConAu 1R, -103*
Stookey, Richard 1938- *ConAu 93*
Stookey, Robert W 1917- *ConAu 81*
Stoop, Norma McLain 1920- *ConAu 65, IntAu&W 82*
Stoops, Emery 1902- *ConAu 1R, -1NR*
Stoops, John A 1926- *ConAu 29R*
Stopelman, Francis *ConAu X*
Stopes, Marie Charlotte Carmichael 1880-1958 *LongCTC*
Stopford, Robert Wright 1901- *ConAu P-1*
Stopp, Elisabeth Charlotte 1911- *ConAu 5R*
Stoppard, Tom 1937- *ConAu 81, ConDr 82, ConLC 1, -3, -4, -5, -8, -15, CroCD, DcLB 13[port], DcLEL 1940, ModBrL SUP, ModWD, WhoTwCL, WorAu 1970, WrDr 84*
Stoppelman, Francis *ConAu X*
Stoppelman, Frans 1921- *ConAu P-1*
Storer, Doug 1899- *ConAu 57*
Storer, J D 1928- *ConAu 107*
Storer, James Donald 1928- *WrDr 84*
Storer, Norman W 1930- *ConAu 41R*
Storer, Tracy I 1889- *ConAu 13R*
Storey, Anthony 1928- *ConAu 2NR, -49, ConNov 82, DcLB 14[port], WrDr 84*
Storey, Arthur 1915- *ConAu 45*
Storey, David 1923- *CroCD*
Storey, David 1933- *ConAu 81, ConDr 82, ConLC 2, -4, -5, -8, ConNov 82, DcLB 13[port], -14[port], DcLEL 1940, LongCTC, ModBrL SUP, TwCWr, WorAu, WrDr 84*
Storey, Edward 1930- *ConAu 97, WrDr 84*
Storey, Edward J 1901- *ConAu 89*
Storey, Margaret 1926- *ConAu 1NR, -49, SmATA 9, TwCCW 83, WrDr 84*
Storey, R L 1927- *ConAu 11NR, -21R*
Storey, Robert F 1945- *ConAu 85*
Storey, Robin Lindsay 1927- *WrDr 84*
Storey, Robin Londsay 1927- *IntAu&W 82*
Storey, Victoria Carolyn 1945- *ConAu 33R, SmATA 16*
Storey, W George 1923- *ConAu 5R, -6NR*
Storing, Herbert James 1928-1977 *ConAu 73*
Storke, Thomas More 1876-1971 *ConAu 89*
Storm, Anthony *ConAu X*
Storm, Christopher *ConAu X, WrDr 84*
Storm, Hans Otto 1895-1941 *TwCA, TwCA SUP*
Storm, Hester G 1903- *ConAu 9R*
Storm, Hyemeyohsts 1935- *ConAu 81, ConLC 3*
Storm, Lesley *ConAu X*
Storm, Marian 1892?-1975 *ConAu 61*
Storm, Russell *ConAu X*
Storm, Virginia *ConAu X, WrDr 84*
Storme, Peter *ConAu X, SmATA X*
Stormer, John A 1928- *ConAu 25R*
Storni, Alfonsina 1892-1938 *ConAu 104, ModLAL, TwCLC 5[port]*
Storr, Anthony 1920- *ConAu 97*
Storr, Catherine 1913- *ConAu 13R, SmATA 9, TwCCW 83, WrDr 84*
Storrow, H A 1926- *ConAu 21R*
Storry, Richard 1914?-1982 *ConAu 106*
Storsve, LaVaughn 1921- *ConAu 1R*
Story, E Macer *ConAu X*
Story, Edith 1920- *IntWWP 82*
Story, Edward M 1921- *ConAu 29R*
Story, G M 1927- *ConAu 9NR, -21R*
Story, Jack Trevor 1917- *ConAu 29R, DcLEL 1940, WrDr 84*
Story, Ralph D *DrAP&F 83*
Story, Richard *IntAu&W 82X*
Story, Ronald 1946- *ConAu 11NR, -65*
Stotland, Ezra 1924- *ConAu 17R, WrDr 84*

Stott, D H 1909- *ConAu 8NR, -13R*
Stott, Douglas W 1948- *ConAu 109*
Stott, Jane 1940- *ConAu 85*
Stott, John Robert Walmsley 1921- *ConAu 2NR, -5R, WrDr 84*
Stott, Leland H 1897- *ConAu 25R*
Stott, Mary *WrDr 84*
Stott, Mary 1907- *ConAu 104*
Stott, Mike 1944- *ConAu 104, ConDr 82, WrDr 84*
Stott, William 1940- *ConAu 61*
Stotts, Herbert Edward 1916- *ConAu 1R, -1NR*
Stotts, Jack L 1932- *ConAu 49*
Stouck, David 1940- *ConAu 61*
Stoudemire, Sterling A 1902- *ConAu 37R*
Stoudt, John Joseph 1911- *ConAu 49*
Stough, Furman C 1928- *ConAu 107*
Stoughton, Clarence Charles 1895-1975 *ConAu 61*
Stoughton, Gertrude K 1901- *ConAu P-2*
Stout, Alan Ker 1900-1983 *ConAu 110*
Stout, George L 1897-1978 *ConAu 77, -81*
Stout, Irving Wright 1903-1972 *ConAu 1R, -3NR*
Stout, Jeffrey Lee 1950- *ConAu 106*
Stout, Joseph A, Jr. 1939- *ConAu 2NR, -45, IntAu&W 82, WrDr 84*
Stout, Neil Ralph 1932- *ConAu 97*
Stout, Rex Todhunter 1886-1975 *AuNews 2, ConAu 61, ConLC 3, LongCTC, TwCA, TwCA SUP, TwCCr&M 80, TwCWr*
Stout, Robert Joe *DrAP&F 83*
Stout, Robert Joe 1936- *ConAu 65*
Stout, Russell, Jr. 1932- *ConAu 101*
Stout, Ruth 1884- *ConAu 33R*
Stout, Wesley Winans 1889-1971 *ConAu 89*
Stoutamire, Albert 1921- *ConAu 41R*
Stoutenburg, Adrien 1916- *ConAu 5R, ConP 80, SmATA 3, WrDr 84*
Stovall, Floyd 1896- *ConAu 9R*
Stover, Allan C 1938- *ConAu 69, SmATA 14*
Stover, Bill *ConAu X*
Stover, Iva Clemmons Childers 1896- *IntWWP 82*
Stover, Jo Ann 1931- *ConAu 37R*
Stover, John Ford 1912- *ConAu 1R, -1NR, WrDr 84*
Stover, Leon E 1929- *ConAu 2NR, -49, ConSFA, TwCSFW, WrDr 84*
Stover, Marjorie Filley 1914- *ConAu 45, SmATA 9*
Stover, W H M 1898-1980 *ConAu 103, -97*
Stover, Webster 1902- *ConAu 53*
Stow, Julian Randolph 1935- *DcLEL 1940*
Stow, Randolph 1935- *ConAu 13R, ConLC 23[port], ConNov 82, ConP 80, IntAu&W 82, ModCmwL, TwCWr, WorAu, WrDr 84*
Stowe, David Metz 1919- *ConAu 9R, IntAu&W 82, WrDr 84*
Stowe, James L *DrAP&F 83*
Stowe, James L 1950- *ConAu 89, IntAu&W 82*
Stowe, Leland 1899- *ConAu 77, TwCA SUP*
Stowe, Noel James 1942- *ConAu 106*
Stowe, Richard S 1925- *ConAu 73*
Stowe, Rosetta *ConAu X*
Stowe, William McFerrin 1913- *ConAu 5R*
Stowers, Carlton 1942- *ConAu 81*
Stoy, R H 1910- *ConAu 57*
Strabolgi, Bartolomeo *ConAu X*
Strachan, Hew 1949- *ConAu 61*
Strachan, J George 1910- *ConAu 107, WrDr 84*
Strachan, Margaret Pitcairn 1908- *ConAu 5R, SmATA 14, WrDr 84*
Strachan, Tony Simpson 1920- *ConAu 13R*
Strachan, Winona Peacock 1918- *ConAu 5R*
Strachey, Barbara *ConAu X*
Strachey, Evelyn John St. Loe 1901-1963 *TwCA, TwCA SUP*
Strachey, Giles Lytton 1880-1932 *TwCA, TwCA SUP*
Strachey, Lady Jane d1928 *LongCTC*
Strachey, John 1901-1963 *ConAu 93, LongCTC, TwCA, TwCA SUP*
Strachey, Lytton 1880-1932 *CnMWL, ConAu 110, LongCTC, ModBrL, TwCA, TwCA SUP, TwCLC 12[port], TwCWr, WhoTwCL*
Strachey, Marjorie 1882-1963 *LongCTC*
Strachey, St. Loe 1860-1927 *LongCTC*
Strackbein, O R 1900- *ConAu 21R*

Straczynski, J Michael 1954- *ConAu 109*
Strader, June 1925- *ConAu 97*
Stradley, Mark *ConAu X*
Stradling, Leslie Edward 1908- *ConAu 104, WrDr 84*
Strage, Mark 1927- *ConAu 81*
Strahan, Bradley R *DrAP&F 83*
Strahl, Leonard E 1926- *ConAu 29R*
Strahl, Rudi 1931- *IntAu&W 82*
Strahlem, Richard Earl 1909- *ConAu 37R*
Straight, Michael 1916- *WrDr 84*
Straight, Michael Whitney 1916- *ConAu 5R, -7NR, TwCWW*
Strain, Dudley 1909- *ConAu P-1*
Strain, Frances Bruce 1892-1975 *ConAu P-2*
Strain, Lucille Brewton *ConAu 69*
Strainchamps, Ethel 1912- *ConAu 53*
Strait, Raymond E 1924- *ConAu 4NR, -53, IntAu&W 82*
Strait, Treva Adams 1909- *ConAu 97, IntAu&W 82*
Straiton, E C 1917- *ConAu 3NR, -45*
Straka, Gerald Milton 1931- *ConAu 2NR, -5R*
Straker, J F 1904- *ConAu 11NR, TwCCr&M 80, WrDr 84*
Straker, John Foster 1904- *ConAu 13R, IntAu&W 82*
Strakosch, Avery *ConAu X*
Straley, John A 1894-1966 *ConAu 1R, -103*
Stramm, August 1874-1915 *ClDMEL 80, ModGL, ModWD*
Strand, Betsy Denker 1940- *IntWWP 82*
Strand, Kenneth A 1927- *ConAu 3NR, -9R, WrDr 84*
Strand, Mark *DrAP&F 83*
Strand, Mark 1934- *ConAu 21R, ConLC 6, -18, ConP 80, CroCAP, DcLB 5[port], DcLEL 1940, WorAu 1970, WrDr 84*
Strand, Paul 1890-1976 *ConAu 65*
Strand, Paul E *ConAu X*
Strand, Thomas *DrAP&F 83*
Strand, Thomas 1944- *ConAu 65*
Strand, William K 1931- *ConAu 29R*
Strandberg, Victor H 1935- *ConAu 89*
Strang, Barbara M H 1925-1982 *ConAu 106, -37R*
Strang, Gerald 1908- *ConAu P-2*
Strang, Herbert *LongCTC, TwCCW 83*
Strang, Ruth May 1895-1971 *ConAu 1R, -2NR*
Strange, Dillon *ConAu X*
Strange, Jack Roy 1921- *ConAu 17R*
Strange, John Stephen 1896- *TwCCr&M 80*
Strange, Maureen 1948- *ConAu 89*
Strange, N Blair *ConAu X*
Strange, Nora K *ConAu X*
Strange, Philippa *ConAu X, SmATA X*
Strange, Susan 1923- *ConAu 49*
Stranger, Joyce *ConAu X, SmATA X, TwCCW 83, WrDr 84*
Strankay, Sam J 1905- *ConAu 57*
Strasberg, Lee 1901-1982 *ConAu 106, -13R*
Strasburger, Victor C 1949- *WrDr 84*
Strassels, Paul N *ConAu 109*
Strasser, Bernard Paul 1895- *ConAu P-1*
Strasser, Marland K 1915- *ConAu 5R, -6NR*
Strasser, Otto 1897-1974 *ConAu 53*
Strasser, Susan 1948- *ConAu 107*
Strassfeld, Sharon M 1950- *ConAu 107*
Strassmann, W Paul 1926- *ConAu 41R*
Strassova, Helena 1924- *ConAu 49*
Stratakis, Anastasia *CreCan 2*
Stratas, Teresa 1938- *CreCan 2*
Strate, Grant Elroy 1927- *CreCan 2*
Stratemeyer, Edward L 1862-1930 *ConAu P-2, SmATA 1*
Stratford, H Philip *ConAu X*
Stratford, Philip 1927- *ConAu 5NR, -9R*
Strathern, Andrew Jamieson 1939- *ConAu 2NR, -49, IntAu&W 82*
Strathern, Ann Marilyn 1941- *ConAu 3NR, -49*
Strati, Saverio 1924- *ConAu 7NR, -17R*
Stratidakis, Eileen 1945- *IntWWP 82*
Stratidakis, Eileen H *DrAP&F 83*
Stratman, Carl J 1917-1972 *ConAu P-2*
Straton, Hillyer H 1905- *ConAu P-1*
Stratton, Arthur M 1910?-1975 *ConAu 61*
Stratton, Henry *ConAu X, IntAu&W 82X*
Stratton, J T 1902- *ConAu 61*
Stratton, John R 1935- *ConAu 45*
Stratton, Porter Andrew 1918- *ConAu 37R*
Stratton, Rebecca *TwCRGW, WrDr 84*
Stratton, Roy Olin 1909?- *ConAu P-2*

Stratton, Ted *ConAu X*
Stratton, Thomas *ConAu X, IntAu&W 82X, WrDr 84*
Stratton, William David 1896- *ConAu P-1*
Stratton-Porter, Gene 1863-1924 *SmATA 15*
Straub, Peter 1943- *ConAu 85, WrDr 84*
Strauch, Carl F 1908- *ConAu 41R*
Strauch, Judith V 1942- *ConAu 107*
Strauch, Katina 1946- *ConAu 105*
Straughan, Robert P L 1924- *ConAu 49*
Straumann, Heinrich 1902- *ConAu 13R, WrDr 84*
Straus *IntAu&W 82X*
Straus, Austin *DrAP&F 83*
Straus, Dennis *ConAu 105, DrAP&F 83*
Straus, Dorothea 1916- *ConAu 37R, WrDr 84*
Straus, Murray A 1926- *ConAu 10NR, -21R, WrDr 84*
Straus, Nathan 1889-1961 *ConAu 89*
Straus, Richard 1925- *ConAu 1R*
Straus, Robert 1923- *ConAu 6NR, -57*
Straus, Roger A 1948- *ConAu 109*
Strauss, Albrecht B 1921- *ConAu 37R*
Strauss, Bert Wiley 1901- *ConAu 13R*
Strauss, Botho 1944- *ConLC 22[port]*
Strauss, David 1937- *ConAu 89*
Strauss, Elaine Mandle 1916?-1982 *ConAu 107*
Strauss, Erich 1911- *ConAu 13R, WrDr 84*
Strauss, Frances 1904- *ConAu P-2*
Strauss, Gerald 1922- *ConAu 9R*
Strauss, Hans 1898?-1977 *ConAu 69*
Strauss, Harold 1907-1975 *ConAu 104*
Strauss, Jennifer 1933- *IntWWP 82*
Strauss, Joyce 1936- *ConAu 93*
Strauss, Leo 1899-1973 *ConAu 101, -45*
Strauss, Lewis Lichtenstein 1896-1974 *ConAu 45*
Strauss, Lucille Jackson 1908- *ConAu P-1*
Strauss, Marjorie *DrAP&F 83*
Strauss, Maurice B 1904-1974 *ConAu P-2*
Strauss, Ralph 1882-1950 *LongCTC*
Strauss, Richard L 1933- *ConAu 1NR, -49*
Strauss, Victor 1907?-1979 *ConAu 89*
Strauss, W Patrick 1923- *ConAu 41R*
Strauss, Walter A 1923- *ConAu 81*
Strauss, Walter L 1928- *ConAu 81*
Strauss, Walter L 1932- *IntAu&W 82*
Strauss, Werner 1930- *ConAu 29R*
Strauss, William Louis 1914- *ConAu 61*
Strauss Und Torney, Lulu Von 1873-1956 *ClDMEL 80*
Straussler, Thomas *WorAu 1970*
Strausz-Hupe, Robert 1903- *ConAu 9R*
Stravinski, Igor Fedorovich *ConAu X*
Stravinsky, Igor Fedorovich 1882-1971 *ConAu 107, -29R*
Stravinsky, Vera 1888-1982 *ConAu 106, -107*
Strawinsky, Igor Fedorovich *ConAu X*
Strawson, John 1921- *ConAu 29R*
Strawson, Sir P F 1919- *ConAu 25R, WorAu 1970*
Strawson, Peter Frederick 1919- *IntAu&W 82, LongCTC, WrDr 84*
Strax, Philip 1909- *ConAu 61*
Strayer, Barry L 1932- *ConAu 29R*
Strayer, E Ward *ConAu X*
Strayer, Joseph Reese 1904- *ConAu 103*
Strean, Herbert S 1931- *ConAu 103*
Streano, Vince 1945- *ConAu 53, SmATA 20*
Streatfeild, Noel 1895- *TwCCW 83, WrDr 84*
Streatfeild, Noel 1897- *ConAu 81, ConLC 21[port], LongCTC, SmATA 20*
Streblow, Lothar 1929- *IntAu&W 82*
Streek, Stanley James 1911- *IntWWP 82*
Street, Alicia 1911- *ConAu 5R*
Street, Arthur George 1892-1966 *ConAu P-1, LongCTC, TwCWr*
Street, Cecil John Charles 1884- *LongCTC, TwCA, TwCA SUP*
Street, G S 1867-1936 *LongCTC*
Street, James 1903-1954 *TwCA SUP*
Street, James H 1915- *ConAu 4NR, -53*
Street, Jay *ConAu X*
Street, Jonathan *ConAu X*
Street, Julia Montgomery 1898- *ConAu 2NR, -5R, SmATA 11, WrDr 84*
Street, Julian Leonard 1879-1947 *TwCA, TwCA SUP*
Street, Lee *ConAu X*
Street, Lucie *ConAu 13R, IntAu&W 82, WrDr 84*
Street, Margaret M 1907- *ConAu 65*
Street, Mattie 1896- *ConAu P-1*

Street, Pamela 1921- *ConAu 45*
Street, Robert *ConAu X*
Streeten, Paul Patrick 1917- *ConAu 11NR, -25R, WrDr 84*
Streeter, Edward 1891-1976 *ConAu 1R, -2NR, -65, WorAu*
Streeter, Herbert Andrus 1918- *ConAu 5R*
Streeter, Herbert Andrus 1919- *WrDr 84*
Streeter, James *ConAu 61*
Strehlow, Theodor 1908- *WrDr 84*
Strehlow, Theodor George Henry 1908- *ConAu 106*
Streib, Dan 1928- *ConAu 106*
Streiker, Lowell D 1939- *ConAu 49*
Streit, Clarence Kirshman 1896- *ConAu 1R, IntAu&W 82, TwCA, TwCA SUP*
Streithorst, Tom 1932?-1981 *ConAu 103*
Streitwieser, Andrew, Jr. 1927- *WrDr 84*
Strelka, Joseph P 1927- *ConAu 8NR, -61, IntAu&W 82*
Strelsky, Katharine *ConAu 108*
Strempek, Carol Campbell *ConAu 37R*
Stren, Patti 1949- *ChlLR 5[port]*
Streng, Frederick John 1933- *ConAu 21R, IntAu&W 82, WrDr 84*
Streng, William D 1909- *ConAu 1R, -1NR*
Streng, William Paul 1937- *ConAu 108*
Streshinsky, Shirley G 1934- *ConAu 85*
Strete, Craig *TwCSFW, WrDr 84*
Stretton, Charles *ConAu X*
Stretton, Hesba 1832-1911 *LongCTC*
Stretton, Hugh 1924- *ConAu 104, WrDr 84*
Stretton, Renshaw *ConAu X*
Streuvels, Stijn 1871-1969 *ClDMEL 80*
Stribling, T S 1881-1965 *ConAu 107, ConLC 23[port], DcLB 9[port], TwCCr&M 80*
Stribling, Thomas Sigismund 1881-1965 *ConAmA, LongCTC, TwCA*
Strich, Christian 1930- *ConAu 109*
Strick, Ivy *DrAP&F 83*
Strick, Ivy 1952- *ConAu 85*
Strick, Philip 1939- *ConAu 109*
Stricker, George 1936- *ConAu 37R*
Strickland, Arvarh E 1930- *ConAu 21R, LivgBAA*
Strickland, Charles E 1930- *ConAu 77*
Strickland, Cowles 1903?-1971 *ConAu 33R*
Strickland, D A *ConAu X*
Strickland, Dorothy S 1933- *ConAu 108*
Strickland, Glenn G 1917- *ConAu 97*
Strickland, Joshua 1896- *ConAu 81*
Strickland, Margot 1927- *ConAu 10NR, -65*
Strickland, Margot 1937- *WrDr 84*
Strickland, Phil D 1941- *ConAu 29R*
Strickland, Rennard 1940- *ConAu 21R*
Strickland, Rex W 1897- *ConAu 45*
Strickland, Ruth Gertrude 1898- *ConAu 5R, -5NR*
Strickland, Stephanie *DrAP&F 83*
Strickland, Stephen P 1933- *ConAu 3NR, -45*
Stricklin, Robert *DrAP&F 83*
Strickon, Arnold 1930- *ConAu 108*
Strieber, Whitley 1945- *ConAu 81*
Strieby, Irene Macy 1894- *ConAu P-1*
Strietelmeier, John 1920- *ConAu 25R*
Stright, Hayden Leroy 1898-1975 *ConAu 37R*
Strike, Jeremy 1939- *ConAu X*
Strike, Maurice 1945- *CreCan 2*
Striker, Cecil Leopold 1932- *ConAu 109*
Strimple, Earl O 1938- *ConAu 97*
Strindberg, August 1849-1912 *ClDMEL 80, CnMD, ConAu 104, LongCTC, ModWD, TwCA, TwCA SUP, TwCLC 1, -8[port], WhoTwCL*
Strindberg, Axel 1910- *CnMD*
Stringer, Arthur John Arbuthnott 1874-1950 *CreCan 2, TwCA, TwCA SUP*
Stringer, David *ConAu X*
Stringer, Lorene Adair 1908- *ConAu 37R, WrDr 84*
Stringer, Ruth M Pearson 1905- *ConAu 5R*
Stringer, William Henry 1908-1976 *ConAu 65*
Stringfellow, William 1928- *ConAu 5R, -9NR, WrDr 84*
Stringfield, Leonard H 1920- *ConAu 85*
Stringhalt, J Sweeney *IntAu&W 82X*
Strittmatter, Erwin 1912- *CnMD, CroCD, ModGL*
Strobel, Fredric 1936- *CreCan 1*
Strober, Gerald S 1935- *ConAu 85*
Stroblas, Laurie *DrAP&F 83*

Stroblas, Laurie Anne 1948- *IntWWP 82*
Strobos, Robert Julius 1921- *ConAu 102*
Strobridge, Truman Russell 1927- *ConAu 41R*
Strodach, George Kleppinger 1905- *ConAu 5R*
Strode, Hudson 1892-1976 *ConAu 8NR, –13R, –69*
Strode, Hudson 1893- *TwCA, TwCA SUP*
Strodtbeck, Fred L 1919- *ConAu 5R*
Stroeyer, Poul 1923- *ConAu 77*
Stroh, Guy W 1931- *ConAu 49*
Stroh, Thomas F 1924- *ConAu 11NR, –21R*
Strom, Ingrid Mathilda 1912- *ConAu 13R*
Strom, Leslie Winter 1932- *ConAu X, –1R*
Strom, Robert 1935- *WrDr 84*
Strom, Robert D 1935- *ConAu 10NR, –25R*
Stroman, Duane F 1934- *ConAu 104*
Stromberg, Ragnar Olof 1950- *IntAu&W 82*
Stromberg, Roland N 1916- *ConAu 5R, –6NR*
Strome, Celia Watson *DrAP&F 83*
Stromholm, Stig Fredrik 1931- *IntAu&W 82*
Strommen, Merton P 1919- *ConAu 5NR, –9R*
Strong, Anna Louise 1885-1970 *ConAu 29R, TwCA, TwCA SUP*
Strong, Austin 1881-1952 *LongCTC, ModWD*
Strong, Charles *ConAu X, SmATA X*
Strong, Charles Olen 1925- *ConAu 5R*
Strong, David *ConAu X*
Strong, Donald Stuart 1912- *ConAu 41R*
Strong, Eithne 1923- *ConAu 97, IntAu&W 82, IntWWP 82, WrDr 84*
Strong, Eric *IntAu&W 82X*
Strong, J J *ConAu X*
Strong, Jeremy 1949- *ConAu 108*
Strong, John Wentworth 1930- *ConAu 37R, IntAu&W 82*
Strong, John William 1935- *ConAu 37R*
Strong, Jonathan *DrAP&F 83*
Strong, Jonathan 1944- *ConAu 37R*
Strong, Kenneth William Dobson 1900-1982 *ConAu 104, –105*
Strong, L A G 1896-1958 *TwCCW 83*
Strong, Leah Audrey 1922- *ConAu 21R, WrDr 84*
Strong, Lennox *ConAu X*
Strong, Leonard Alfred George 1896-1958 *LongCTC, ModBrL, TwCA, TwCA SUP, TwCWr*
Strong, Pat *WrDr 84*
Strong, Philip Nigel Warrington 1899- *ConAu 109*
Strong, Philip Nigel Warrington 1899-1983 *ConAu 110*
Strong, Roy Colin 1935- *ConAu 1NR, –49, IntAu&W 82, WrDr 84*
Strong, Rupert 1911- *ConAu 13R*
Strong, Solange *ConAu X*
Strong, Susan *WrDr 84*
Strong, Tracy B 1943- *ConAu 93*
Strongblood, Casper *ConAu X*
Strongin, Lynn *DrAP&F 83*
Strongin, Lynn 1939- *ConAu 1NR, –49, IntWWP 82*
Strongman, K T 1940- *ConAu 10NR, WrDr 84*
Strongman, Kenneth Thomas 1940- *ConAu 61*
Stroop, Helen E *ConAu X*
Strother, David B 1928- *ConAu 25R*
Strother, Elsie 1912- *ConAu 11NR, –65*
Strother, Horatio Theodore 1930- *ConAu 5R*
Strother, Pat Wallace 1929- *ConAu 9NR*
Stroube, Hal 1921?-1983 *ConAu 110*
Stroud, Joe H 1936- *ConAu 103*
Stroud, Kandy 1942- *ConAu 108*
Stroup, Herbert 1916- *WrDr 84*
Stroup, Herbert Hewitt 1916- *ConAu 13R*
Stroup, Thomas B 1903- *ConAu 25R*
Strouse, Jean 1945- *ConAu 103*
Strousse, Flora G 1897?-1974 *ConAu 49*
Strout, Cushing 1923- *ConAu 13R*
Strout, Richard Lee 1898- *ConAu 69*
Strover, Dorothea *ConAu 9R, WrDr 84*
Stroyen, William Basil 1925- *ConAu 25R*
Stroyer, Poul 1923- *ConAu X, IntAu&W 82, SmATA 13*
Stroynowski, Julius 1919- *IntAu&W 82*
Strozier, Charles B 1944- *ConAu 107*
Strube, Wilhelm Hermann Ludwig 1925- *IntAu&W 82*
Struble, Mitch 1945- *ConAu 93*
Struble, Virginia *ConAu X*
Struever, Stuart McKee 1931- *ConAu 104*
Strug, Andrzej 1871?-1937 *CIDMEL 80*
Strugatskii, Arkadii 1925- *ConAu 106,*

Strugatskii, Boris 1933- *ConAu 106, ConLC 27[port]*
Strugatsky, Arkady 1925- *CIDMEL 80, TwCSFW A*
Strugatsky, Boris 1933- *TwCSFW A*
Struglia, Erasmus Joseph 1915- *ConAu 13R*
Struik, Dirk Jan 1894- *ConAu 5R, –6NR*
Struk, Danylo 1940- *ConAu 57*
Strum, Philippa 1938- *ConAu 61*
Strumpen-Darrie, Robert L 1912- *ConAu 13R*
Strung, Norman M 1941- *ConAu 41R*
Strunk, Oliver 1901-1980 *ConAu 105, –97*
Strunk, Orlo, Jr. 1925- *ConAu 1R, –1NR*
Strunsky, Simeon 1879-1948 *TwCA, TwCA SUP*
Strunz, Hugo 1910- *IntAu&W 82*
Strunz, Wolfgang 1936- *IntAu&W 82*
Strupp, Hans H 1921- *ConAu 1R, –2NR*
Struther, Jan 1901-1953 *LongCTC, TwCA, TwCA SUP*
Struthers, Dorothy M 1900- *IntWWP 82*
Strutton, Bill 1918- *WrDr 84*
Strutton, William Harold 1918- *ConAu 77*
Strutz, Henry 1932- *ConAu 5R, –7NR*
Struve, Walter 1935- *ConAu 49*
Struyk, Raymond J 1944- *ConAu 107*
Stryk, Lucien *DrAP&F 83*
Stryk, Lucien 1924- *ConAu 10NR, –13R, ConP 80, WrDr 84*
Stryker, David 1916- *ConAu 45*
Stryker, Perrin 1908- *ConAu 5R, WrDr 84*
Stryker, Sheldon 1924- *ConAu 9R*
Stryker-Rodda, Harriet 1905- *ConAu 81*
Stryker-Rodda, Kenn 1903- *ConAu 73*
Stuart, Aimee 1886?-1981 *ConAu 103*
Stuart, Alex *ConAu X, WrDr 84*
Stuart, Alex R *WrDr 84*
Stuart, Alice Vandockum 1899- *ConAu 13R, IntAu&W 82, IntWWP 82*
Stuart, Anthony *ConAu X*
Stuart, Charles *ConAu X*
Stuart, Clay *ConAu X*
Stuart, Colin 1910- *ConAu 104*
Stuart, D M 1889-1963 *LongCTC*
Stuart, Dabney *DrAP&F 83*
Stuart, Dabney 1937- *ConAu 8NR, –17R, ConP 80, DcLEL 1940, WrDr 84*
Stuart, David *ConAu X, SmATA X*
Stuart, Don A *ConAu X, WorAu*
Stuart, Donald Robert 1913- *WrDr 84*
Stuart, Eleanor *CreCan 2*
Stuart, Floyd C *DrAP&F 83*
Stuart, Forbes *WrDr 84*
Stuart, Forbes 1924- *ConAu 69, IntAu&W 82, SmATA 13*
Stuart, Francis 1902- *ConAu 13R, ConNov 82, LongCTC, ModBrL, TwCA, TwCA SUP, WrDr 84*
Stuart, Frederick *IntAu&W 82X*
Stuart, George 1863-1927 *WorAu*
Stuart, Graham Henry 1887- *ConAu P-1, WrDr 84*
Stuart, Henry Longan 1875?-1928 *TwCA*
Stuart, Ian *ConAu X, DcLEL 1940, SmATA X, TwCCr&M 80, WorAu, WrDr 84*
Stuart, Ian 1927- *ConAu 73*
Stuart, Irving R 1916- *ConAu 41R*
Stuart, Jane 1942- *ConAu 41R*
Stuart, Jay Allison *ConAu X*
Stuart, Jesse 1906- *WrDr 84*
Stuart, Jesse 1907- *ConAu 5R, ConLC 1, –8, –11, –14, ConNov 82, DcLB 9[port], SmATA 2, TwCA SUP, TwCWr*
Stuart, Kenneth *ConAu X, IntWWP 82X*
Stuart, Leslie *ConAu X*
Stuart, Lyle 1922- *ConAu 81*
Stuart, Margaret *ConAu X*
Stuart, Mary *IntWWP 82X*
Stuart, Matt *WrDr 84*
Stuart, Monroe *ConAu X*
Stuart, Richard Bernard 1933- *ConAu 41R, IntAu&W 82*
Stuart, Sheila *ConAu X, SmATA X*
Stuart, Sidney *ConAu X, TwCCr&M 80, WrDr 84*
Stuart, Simon 1930- *ConAu 29R, WrDr 84*
Stuart, V A *IntAu&W 82X*
Stuart, Vivian 1914- *ConAu 13R, IntAu&W 82,*

WrDr 84
Stuart, W J *ConAu X*
Stuart, Warren *ConAu X*
Stuart, William *IntAu&W 82X*
Stuart-Clark, Christopher 1940- *ConAu 107, SmATA 32[port]*
Stuart-Jones, Edwyn Henry 1895- *ConAu P-1*
Stub, Holger R 1922- *ConAu 41R*
Stubbings, Hilda Uren *ConAu X*
Stubblebine, James H 1920- *ConAu 97*
Stubblefield, Harold W 1934- *ConAu 17R*
Stubbs, Harry C 1922- *ConAu 7NR, –13R*
Stubbs, Harry Clement *WrDr 84*
Stubbs, Jean 1926- *ConAu 5R, IntAu&W 82, TwCCr&M 80, TwCRGW, WrDr 84*
Stubbs, John C 1936- *ConAu 29R*
Stubbs, Peter Charles 1937- *WrDr 84*
Stuber, Florian 1947- *ConAu 106*
Stuber, Stanley Irving 1903- *ConAu P-1*
Stubhaug, Arild 1948- *IntAu&W 82*
Stubis, Talivaldis 1926- *SmATA 5*
Stubley, Trevor Hugh 1932- *SmATA 22[port]*
Stuckenberg, Viggo Henrik Fog 1863-1905 *CIDMEL 80*
Stuckenschmidt, H H 1901- *ConAu 25R*
Stuckenschmidt, Hans H 1901- *IntAu&W 82*
Stuckey, Gilbert B 1912- *ConAu 65*
Stuckey, Sterling 1932- *ConAu 101*
Stuckey, William Joseph 1923- *ConAu 41R*
Stucki, Curtis W 1928- *ConAu 13R*
Stucki, Lorenz P 1922- *IntAu&W 82*
Stucki, Margaret Elizabeth 1928- *IntAu&W 82*
Stucky, Steven 1949- *ConAu 109*
Stucley, Elizabeth 1906-1974 *ConAu X, TwCCW 83*
Studebaker, William *DrAP&F 83*
Studer, Gerald C 1927- *ConAu 65*
Stueart, Robert D 1935- *ConAu 105*
Stuebing, Douglas 1913- *ConAu 25R*
Stueck, William Whitney, Jr. 1945- *ConAu 105*
Stuempke, Harald *ConAu X*
Stuermann, Walter E 1919-1965 *ConAu 5R*
Stuermer, Nina Roberta 1933- *ConAu 104*
Stuerup, Georg Kristoffer 1905- *ConAu 25R*
Stuhlmann, Gunther 1927- *ConAu 25R, IntAu&W 82*
Stuhlmueller, Carroll 1923- *ConAu 9NR, –13R, WrDr 84*
Stull, Richard *DrAP&F 83*
Stultifer, Morton *ConAu X, SmATA X*
Stultz, Newell M 1933- *ConAu 29R*
Stummvoll, Josef 1902- *IntAu&W 82*
Stump, Doris Joyce 1928- *IntWWP 82*
Stumpf, Samuel 1918- *ConAu 41R, WrDr 84*
Stumpke, Harald 1908- *ConAu X*
Stuntz, Albert Edward 1902-1976 *ConAu 65*
Stuntz, Laurance F 1908- *ConAu 61*
Stupak, Ronald Joseph 1934- *ConAu 29R, IntAu&W 82, WrDr 84*
Sturdivant, Frederick D 1937- *ConAu 41R*
Sture-Vasa, Mary *SmATA X*
Sture-Vasa, Mary Alsop 1885-1980 *SmATA 2, TwCA SUP*
Sturgeon, Foolbert *ConAu X,*
Sturgeon, Theodore *DrAP&F 83*
Sturgeon, Theodore 1918- *ConAu 81, ConLC 22[port], ConSFA, DcLB 8[port], TwCSFW, WorAu, WrDr 84*
Sturgeon, Wina *ConAu 85*
Sturges, Patricia P 1930- *ConAu 69*
Sturges, Preston 1898-1959 *DcLB 26[port], ModWD*
Sturgill, Claude C 1933- *ConAu 9NR, –13R*
Sturgis, Howard Overing 1855-1920 *LongCTC*
Sturgis, James L 1936- *ConAu 37R*
Sturhahn, Joan 1930- *IntAu&W 82*
Sturhahn, Lawrence *DrAP&F 83*
Sturm, Ernest 1932- *ConAu 65*
Sturm, John E 1927- *ConAu 37R*
Sturm, Rudolf 1912- *ConAu 109*
Sturm, Sara *ConAu X*
Sturm-Maddox, Sara Higgins 1938- *ConAu 108*
Sturmer, Michael 1938- *IntAu&W 82*
Sturmey, S G 1924- *ConAu 9R*
Sturmthal, Adolf F 1903- *ConAu 9R, WrDr 84*
Sturrock, Jeremy *WrDr 84*
Sturrock, Jeremy 1908- *IntAu&W 82X, TwCCr&M 80*
Stursberg, Peter 1913- *ConAu 101*
Sturt, George 1863-1927 *LongCTC*
Sturt, Mary 1896- *ConAu P-2, WrDr 84*
Sturtevant, Catherine d1970 *ConAu 104*

Summers, Robert E 1918- ConAu 25R
Summers, Robert S 1933- ConAu 11NR, –69
Summers, Rowena ConAu X, IntAu&W 82X,
    WrDr 84
Summerscales, William 1921- ConAu 29R
Summerskill, Charles Grayson 1908- ConAu 1R,
    –3NR
Summerskill, Edith 1901-1980 ConAu 93
Summerson, Sir John 1904- WrDr 84
Summerson, Rachel 1944- ConAu 107
Summerton, Margaret TwCCr&M 80
Sumner, Aurea 1913- WrDr 84
Sumner, Cid Ricketts 1890-1970 ConAu 5R,
    –29R
Sumner, David 1937- ConAu 57
Sumner, Eldon ConAu X
Sumner, Lloyd Quinton 1943- ConAu 103
Sumner, Richard 1949- ConAu 69
Sumwalt, Martha Murray 1924- ConAu 69
Sun, Hugo Sui-Hwan 1940- IntWWP 82
Sun, Ruth Q 1907- ConAu 57
Sun, Yat-Sen, Madame ConAu X
Sun, Yefang 1908-1983 ConAu 109
Sun, Yi 1927- IntAu&W 82
Sunagel, Lois A 1926- ConAu 93
Sunandana IntWWP 82X
Sund, Robert DrAP&F 83
Sund, Robert B 1926- ConAu 29R
Sundaram IntAu&W 82X
Sundaram, Gowri Shankar 1947- IntAu&W 82
Sundarananda ConAu X
Sunday, Billy 1862-1935 LongCTC
Sundberg, Kjell 1934-1978 CIDMEL 80
Sundberg, Trudy James 1925- ConAu 17R
Sundell, Roger H 1936- ConAu 21R
Sunderland, Eric 1930- ConAu 103, WrDr 84
Sunderland, Glenn W 1925- ConAu 25R
Sunderland, Lane V 1945- ConAu 97
Sunderland, Sydney 1910- WrDr 84
Sunderlin, Sylvia 1911- ConAu 73, SmATA 28
Sunderman, James F 1919- ConAu 17R
Sunderman, Lloyd Frederick 1905-1983
    ConAu 109
Sundgaard, Arnold 1909- ConAu 2NR, –45
Sundiata, Sekou DrAP&F 83
Sundiata, Sekou 1948- IntWWP 82
Sundiata, Shaka A DrAP&F 83
Sundman, Per Olof 1922- CIDMEL 80,
    IntAu&W 82
Sundquist, James 1915- WrDr 84
Sundquist, James Lloyd 1915- ConAu 29R,
    IntAu&W 82
Sundquist, Ralph Roger, Jr. 1922- ConAu 106
Sung, Betty Lee ConAu 10NR, –25R,
    SmATA 26[port]
Sung, Chiao IntAu&W 82X
Sung, P M ConAu 49
Sungolowsky, Joseph 1931- ConAu 41R
Suni Paz IntWWP 82X
Sunners, William 1903- ConAu P-1
Sunoo, Harold Hak-Won 1918- ConAu 41R
Sunseri, Alvin R 1925- ConAu 93
Sunstein, Emily W 1924- ConAu 53
Super, Donald E 1910- ConAu 1R, –3NR
Super, Robert Henry 1914- ConAu 13R,
    IntAu&W 82, WrDr 84
Super Santa ConAu X
Supervielle, Jules 1884-1960 CIDMEL 80,
    CnMD, CnMWL, ModFrL, ModWD,
    TwCWr, WhoTwCL, WorAu
Suponev, Michael 1923- ConAu 65
Suppe, Frederick 1940- ConAu 41R,
    IntAu&W 82
Suppes, Patrick 1922- ConAu 1R, –4NR,
    IntAu&W 82
Supraner, Robyn 1930- ConAu 69, SmATA 20
Supree, Burt 1941- ConAu 65
Sur Bourbon Of Honk IntWWP 82X
Surace, Samuel J 1919- ConAu 21R
Suran, Bernard G 1939- ConAu 81
Surdin, Morris CreCan 2
Suret-Canale, Jean 1921- ConAu 1NR, –49,
    IntAu&W 82
Surette, Leon 1938- ConAu 110
Surface, Bill ConAu X
Surface, William E 1935- ConAu 5R
Surfaceman LongCTC
Surge, Frank 1931- ConAu 69, SmATA 13
Surkin, Marvin 1938- ConAu 61
Surkov, Alexei Aleksandrovich 1899-1983
    ConAu 110
Surles, Lynn 1917- ConAu 13R

Surman, Charles Edward 1901- ConAu 5R
Surmejan, Hazaros 1943- CreCan 2
Surmelian, Leon 1907- ConAu P-2
Surov, Anatol CnMD
Surov, Anatoli Alekseevich 1910- ModWD
Surovell, Hariette DrAP&F 83
Surplus, Jean Craig 1936- WrDr 84
Surplus, Robert W 1923- ConAu 5R, WrDr 84
Surrey, Peter J 1928- ConAu 106
Surrey, Philip Henry 1910- CreCan 2
Surrey, Richard CreCan 1
Surtees, Virginia WrDr 84
Surti, Abid 1935- IntAu&W 82
Surtz, Edward 1910?-1973 ConAu 41R
Susac, Andrew 1929- ConAu 49, SmATA 5
Susan ConAu X
Susann, Jacqueline 1921-1974 ASpks, AuNews 1,
    ConAu 53, –65, ConLC 3
Suskind, Richard 1925- ConAu 9NR, –13R
Suslov, Alexander 1950- ConAu 105
Suslov, Mikhail Andreyevich 1902-1982
    ConAu 105
Suss, Elaine ConAu 102
Susser, Mervyn 1921- ConAu 1NR, –45
Susser, Samuel S 1910- ConAu 97
Sussie IntAu&W 82X
Susskind, Charles 1921- ConAu 85
Susskind, Harriet DrAP&F 83
Susskind, Walter 1913- CreCan 2
Sussman, Barry 1934- ConAu 53, WrDr 84
Sussman, Cornelia Silver 1914- ConAu 5R
Sussman, Herbert L 1937- ConAu 25R
Sussman, Irving M 1908- IntAu&W 82
Sussman, Leonard R 1920- ConAu 4NR, –53
Sussman, M L DrAP&F 83
Sussman, Marvin B 1918- ConAu 4NR, –9R
Sussman, Samuel 1913- NatPD 81[port]
Sussman, Sharron 1943- ConAmTC
Sutch, Richard C 1942- ConAu 107
Sutch, William Ball 1907- DcLEL 1940
Sutcliff, Rosemary 1920- ChlLR 1, ConAu 5R,
    ConLC 26[port], DcLEL 1940,
    IntAu&W 82, SmATA 6, TwCCW 83,
    WrDr 84
Sutcliffe, Anthony 1942- ConAu 106
Sutcliffe, Reginald Cockcroft 1904- WrDr 84
Suter, Ronald 1930- ConAu 41R
Sutermeister, Robert Arnold 1913- ConAu 5R
Suther, Marshall E, Jr. 1918- ConAu 1R
Sutherland, Arthur Eugene, Jr. 1902-1973
    ConAu 41R, ConAu P-1
Sutherland, Carol Humphrey Vivian 1908-
    ConAu 13R
Sutherland, Daniel E 1946- ConAu 109
Sutherland, Donald 1915- ConAu 37R
Sutherland, Donald W 1931- ConAu 9R
Sutherland, Douglas 1919- ConAu 21R
Sutherland, Earl Wilbur 1915-1974 ConAu 49
Sutherland, Efua 1924- ConAu 105, ConDr 82,
    DcLEL 1940, SmATA 25, TwCCW 83,
    WrDr 84
Sutherland, Elizabeth WrDr 84
Sutherland, Elizabeth 1926- ConAu 85,
    IntAu&W 82X
Sutherland, Fraser 1946- ConAu 102
Sutherland, Gordon 1907-1980 ConAu 108
Sutherland, Herbert Warren 1917- ConAu 13R,
    IntAu&W 82
Sutherland, James 1900- WrDr 84
Sutherland, James 1948- ConAu 2NR, –49
Sutherland, James Alan 1912- WrDr 84
Sutherland, James Runcieman 1900-
    IntAu&W 82
Sutherland, John 1933- ConAu 93
Sutherland, John P 1920- ConAu 21R
Sutherland, Jon Nicholas 1941- ConAu 41R
Sutherland, Lucy Stuart 1903-1980 ConAu 105,
    ConAu P-1
Sutherland, Margaret 1941- ConAu 77,
    SmATA 15, WrDr 84
Sutherland, Monica LaFontaine 1897-
    IntAu&W 82
Sutherland, N M 1925- ConAu 49,
    IntAu&W 82
Sutherland, Norman Stuart 1927- WrDr 84
Sutherland, R Galbraith 1924- ConAu P-1
Sutherland, Robert D 1937- ConAu 37R
Sutherland, Ronald 1933- ConAu 25R
Sutherland, Stuart 1927- ConAu 65
Sutherland, William Temple Gairdner 1906-
    ConAu P-1
Sutherland, Zena Bailey 1915- ConAu 102

Suthinee ConAu X
Suthren, Victor 1942- ConAu 107
Sutnar, Ladislav 1897-1976 ConAu 104
Sutphen, Dick ConAu X
Sutphen, Richard Charles 1937- ConAu 11NR,
    –25R, WrDr 84
Sutro, Alfred 1863-1933 ConAu 105,
    DcLB 10[port], LongCTC, ModBrL,
    ModWD, TwCA, TwCA SUP,
    TwCLC 6[port]
Sutter, Barton DrAP&F 83
Sutter, Franz ConAu X
Sutter, Frederic Koehler 1938- ConAu 107
Sutter, Ruth E 1935- ConAu 45
Suttles, Gerald 1932- ConAu 85
Suttles, Shirley 1922- ConAu 13R,
    SmATA 21[port]
Suttmeier, Richard Peter 1942- ConAu 6NR, –57
Sutto, Jeanine CreCan 2
Sutton, Ann 1923- ConAu 5R, –10NR,
    SmATA 31
Sutton, Antony C 1925- ConAu 97
Sutton, Bridie 1928- IntAu&W 82
Sutton, Caroline 1953- ConAu 106
Sutton, Clive 1937- WrDr 84
Sutton, David 1947- ConAu 101
Sutton, David John 1944- WrDr 84
Sutton, Denys 1917- ConAu 5NR, –53,
    DcLEL 1940, IntAu&W 82, WrDr 84
Sutton, Eve 1906- ConAu 10NR, –65,
    IntAu&W 82X, SmATA 26[port],
    TwCCW 83, WrDr 84
Sutton, Evelyn Mary 1906- IntAu&W 82
Sutton, Felix 1910?- ConAu 77,
    SmATA 31[port]
Sutton, George Miksch 1898- ConAu 107
Sutton, George Miksch 1898-1982 ConAu 109
Sutton, Gordon 1910- ConAu 21R
Sutton, Henry ConAu X, DrAP&F 83,
    IntAu&W 82X, IntWWP 82X, WrDr 84
Sutton, Horace 1919- ConAu 10NR, –13R
Sutton, Howard 1930- ConAu 65
Sutton, Jane 1950- ConAu 89
Sutton, Jean 1916- TwCSFW, WrDr 84
Sutton, Jean 1917- ConSFA
Sutton, Jeff 1913-1979 ConAu X, ConSFA,
    TwCSFW
Sutton, Jefferson 1913-1979 ConAu 10NR, –21R
Sutton, John L 1917- ConAu 105
Sutton, Larry M 1931- ConAu 37R,
    SmATA 29[port]
Sutton, Lorraine J DrAP&F 83
Sutton, Louise Weibert WrDr 84
Sutton, Louise Weibert 1920- IntAu&W 82,
    IntWWP 82
Sutton, Margaret Beebe 1903- ConAu 1R,
    IntAu&W 82, SmATA 1
Sutton, Maurice Lewis 1927- ConAu 13R
Sutton, Max Keith 1937- ConAu 93
Sutton, Myron Daniel 1925- ConAu 107,
    SmATA 31[port]
Sutton, Penny ConAu X
Sutton, Rachel Beeb IntAu&W 82X
Sutton, Robert M 1915- ConAu 77
Sutton, Roberta Briggs 1899- ConAu 5R
Sutton, S B 1940- ConAu 29R, WrDr 84
Sutton, Stack ConAu X
Sutton, Tony C ConAu X
Sutton, Walter 1916- ConAu 85, IntAu&W 82
Sutton, William Alfred 1915- ConAu 61
Sutton-Smith, Brian 1924- ConAu 29R
Sutton-Vane, V H 1888-1963 LongCTC
Suttor, T L 1926- ConAu 21R
Suvin, Darko 1930- ConAu 89
Suvishree IntWWP 82X
Suyin, Han ConAu X
Suzor-Cote, Aurele DeFoy 1869-1937 CreCan 1
Suzor-Cote, Marcus Aurele DeFoy CreCan 1
Suzuki, Chizu Shindo 1941- IntWWP 82
Svagelj, Dionizije 1923- IntWWP 82
Svajian, Stephen G 1906?-1977 ConAu 73
Svareff, Count Vladimir ConAu X
Svarlien, Oscar 1906- ConAu P-1
Svartvik, Jan 1931- WrDr 84
Svartvik, Jan Lars 1931- ConAu 21R
Svejda, George J 1927- ConAu 41R
Svendsen, Kari Anne 1928- IntAu&W 82
Svenningsen, Paul Floe 1919- IntAu&W 82X
Svenningsen, Poul Floe 1919- IntAu&W 82
Svenson, Andrew E 1910-1975 ConAu 5R, –61,
    SmATA 2, –26N

Svensson, Arne 1929- *ConAu 49*
Svensson, Jon Stefan 1857-1944 *ClDMEL 80*
Svensson, Sven *IntAu&W 82X, IntWWP 82X*
Sverdrup, Harald Ulrik 1923- *IntWWP 82*
Sverkers, Stig *IntAu&W 82X*
Svestka, Oldrich 1922-1983 *ConAu 110*
Svetlov, Mikhail Arkadyevich 1903-1964 *ClDMEL 80*
Svevo, Italo 1861-1928 *ClDMEL 80, CnMWL, ConAu X, LongCTC, ModRL, TwCA, TwCA SUP, TwCLC 2, TwCWr, WhoTwCL*
Svinsaas, Ingvald 1912- *IntAu&W 82*
Svirsky, Grigori 1921- *ConAu 69*
Svoboda, Terese *DrAP&F 83*
Svoboda, Oldrich *DrAP&F 83*
Svobodova, Ruzena 1868-1920 *ClDMEL 80*
Swaan, Wim 1927- *ConAu 25R*
Swabey, Marie Collins 1890-1966 *ConAu 1R*
Swadley, Elizabeth 1929- *ConAu 21R*
Swados, Elizabeth 1951- *ConAu 97, ConLC 12*
Swados, Harvey 1920-1972 *ConAu 5R, -6NR, -37R, ConLC 5, DcLB 2, DcLEL 1940, ModAL, WorAu*
Swaim, Alice Mackenzie 1911- *ConAu 6NR, -9R, IntAu&W 82, IntWWP 82, WrDr 84*
Swaim, Lawrence 1942- *ConAu 69*
Swain, Bruce M 1943- *ConAu 101*
Swain, Donald Christie 1931- *ConAu 29R, WrDr 84*
Swain, Dwight V 1915- *ConAu 7NR, -17R*
Swain, Frank G 1893?-1975 *ConAu 53*
Swain, James E 1897-1975 *ConAu P-2*
Swain, Joseph Ward 1891-1971 *ConAu P-2*
Swain, Margaret 1909- *ConAu 53*
Swain, Martha H 1929- *ConAu 85*
Swain, Olive 1896- *ConAu 5R*
Swain, Raymond Charles 1912- *ConAu 9R*
Swain, Roger 1949- *ConAu 102*
Swain, Su Zan 1916- *ConAu 5R, -6NR, SmATA 21[port]*
Swainson, Donald 1938- *ConAu 109*
Swales, Martin 1940- *ConAu 81, IntAu&W 82*
Swallow, Alan 1915-1966 *ConAu 1R, -25R*
Swallow, Norman 1921- *ConAu 21R, WrDr 84*
Swamy, Subramanian 1939- *ConAu 49*
Swan, Annie S 1859?-1943 *LongCTC, TwCRGW*
Swan, Berta W 1928- *ConAu 29R*
Swan, Bradford Fuller 1908?-1976 *ConAu 65*
Swan, Christopher C 1946- *ConAu 103*
Swan, Gladys *DrAP&F 83*
Swan, Gladys 1934- *ConAu 101*
Swan, Jon 1929- *ConAu 89*
Swan, Marie *ConAu X*
Swan, Susan 1944- *SmATA 22*
Swanberg, Ingrid *DrAP&F 83*
Swanberg, W A 1907- *ConAu 8NR, WrDr 84*
Swanberg, William Andrew 1907- *ConAu 5R, DcLEL 1940, WorAu*
Swander, Mary *DrAP&F 83*
Swanger, David 1940- *ConAu 49*
Swank, Patsy 1919- *ConAmTC*
Swann, Brian *DrAP&F 83*
Swann, Brian 1940- *ConAu 37R*
Swann, Donald 1923- *ConAu 21R, IntAu&W 82, WrDr 84*
Swann, Francis 1913- *ConAu 4NR, -9R*
Swann, Ingo 1933- *ConAu 57*
Swann, Lois 1944- *ConAu 65*
Swann, Peggy *ConAu X*
Swann, Peter Charles 1921- *ConAu 5R, IntAu&W 82*
Swann, Roberta Metz *DrAP&F 83*
Swann, Thomas Burnett 1928-1976 *ConAu 4NR, -5R, ConSFA*
Swansea, Charleen 1932- *ConAu 103*
Swansea, Charleen Whisnant *DrAP&F 83*
Swansen, Vern 1916- *ConAu 49*
Swanson, Arlene Collyer 1913- *ConAu 5R*
Swanson, Austin D 1930- *ConAu 25R*
Swanson, Beda Elisabeth 1897- *IntWWP 82*
Swanson, Bert E 1924- *ConAu 29R*
Swanson, Carl P 1911- *ConAu 45*
Swanson, Don R 1924- *ConAu 13R*
Swanson, Donald Roland 1927- *ConAu 41R*
Swanson, Edward I 1923- *ConAu 29R*
Swanson, Gloria 1899?-1983 *ConAu 109*
Swanson, Gloria Borseth 1927- *ConAu 77*
Swanson, Gustav A 1910- *ConAu 77*
Swanson, Harold B 1917- *ConAu 37R*
Swanson, Neil H 1896-1983 *ConAu 109*
Swanson, Neil Harmon 1896- *TwCA,*

TwCA SUP
Swanson, R A *DrAP&F 83*
Swanson, Roy Arthur 1925- *ConAu 17R*
Swanson, Thor 1922- *ConAu 45*
Swanson, Walter S J 1917- *ConAu 29R*
Swanton, Ernest William 1907- *ConAu 2NR, -5R, IntAu&W 82*
Sward, Jeffrey Edwin 1953- *IntWWP 82*
Sward, Robert *DrAP&F 83*
Sward, Robert S 1933- *ConAu 5R, -5NR, ConP 80, IntAu&W 82, IntWWP 82, WrDr 84*
Swardson, Harold Roland, Jr. 1925- *ConAu 1R*
Swarthout, Doris L 1931- *ConAu 77*
Swarthout, Glendon *DrAP&F 83*
Swarthout, Glendon 1918- *ConAu 1R, -1NR, ConNov 82, DcLEL 1940, MichAu 80, SmATA 26[port], TwCWW, WrDr 84*
Swarthout, Kathryn 1919- *ConAu 41R, MichAu 80, SmATA 7*
Swartley, David Warren 1950- *ConAu 102*
Swartz, Harry 1911- *ConAu 6NR, -57, MichAu 80*
Swartz, Herbert *DrAP&F 83*
Swartz, Jon David 1934- *ConAu 69, WrDr 84*
Swartz, Marc J 1931- *ConAu 21R*
Swartz, Marvin 1941- *ConAu 101*
Swartz, Mary I 1942- *ConAu 97*
Swartz, Melvin Jay 1930- *ConAu 97*
Swartz, Paul 1927- *ConAu 5R*
Swartz, Robert D 1937- *ConAu 41R*
Swartz, Robert J 1936- *ConAu 17R*
Swartz, William *DrAP&F 83*
Swartz, Willis George 1902-1965 *ConAu 1R*
Swartzlow, Ruby Johnson 1903- *ConAu P-1, WrDr 84*
Swatridge, Charles *ConAu 7NR, -13R*
Swatridge, Irene Maude *WrDr 84*
Swatridge, Irene Maude Mossop *ConAu 7NR, -29R*
Swaybill, Roger E 1943- *ConAu 105*
Swayne, Geoffrey *ConAu X*
Swayze, Beulah G 1907- *ConAu 5R*
Swayze, E Harold 1930- *ConAu 1R*
Swayze, John Cameron 1906- *ConAu 102*
Swearengen, Thomas F 1924- *ConAu 17R*
Swearer, Donald K 1934- *ConAu 37R, IntAu&W 82, WrDr 84*
Swearingen, Arthur Rodger 1923- *ConAu 10NR*
Swearingen, Rodger 1923- *ConAu 5R*
Sweazey, George E 1905- *ConAu 1R, -4NR*
Swedberg, Charles Robert 1954- *IntWWP 82*
Swedberg, Chuck *IntWWP 82X*
Swedburg, Wilma Adeline *ConAu 5R*
Swede, George 1940- *IntAu&W 82*
Sweeney, Amin 1938- *ConAu 105*
Sweeney, Barry *ConAu X*
Sweeney, Charles 1922- *ConAu 21R*
Sweeney, Francis 1916- *ConAu 5R*
Sweeney, Henry Whitcomb 1898-1967 *ConAu P-2*
Sweeney, James B 1910- *ConAu 29R, SmATA 21[port]*
Sweeney, James Johnson 1900- *ConAu 5R, -6NR, TwCA SUP, WrDr 84*
Sweeney, Karen O'Connor *SmATA X*
Sweeney, Karen O'Connor 1938- *ConAu 89*
Sweeney, Leo 1918- *ConAu 37R, WrDr 84*
Sweeney, Matthew Gerard 1952- *IntWWP 82*
Sweeney, R C H 1922- *ConAu X*
Sweeney, Robert Dale 1939- *ConAu 45*
Sweeney, Thomas J 1936- *ConAu 41R*
Sweeney, William J, III 1922- *ConAu 45*
Sweet, Franklyn Haley 1916- *ConAu 9R*
Sweet, Frederick A 1903- *ConAu P-2*
Sweet, George Elliott 1904- *ConAu 45, IntAu&W 82*
Sweet, Henry 1845-1912 *LongCTC*
Sweet, James Stouder 1918- *ConAu 41R*
Sweet, Jeffrey 1950- *ConAu 81, NatPD 81[port]*
Sweet, Leonard Ira 1947- *ConAu 97*
Sweet, Muriel W 1888-1977 *ConAu 106*
Sweet, Paul R 1907- *ConAu 77*
Sweet, Robert Burdette *DrAP&F 83*
Sweet, Robert Burdette 1930- *ConAu 85, IntAu&W 82*
Sweet, Waldo Earle 1912- *ConAu 1R*
Sweeting, George 1924- *ConAu 11NR, -65, WrDr 84*
Sweetkind, Morris 1898- *ConAu 13R*
Sweetland, Nancy Rose 1934- *WrDr 84*
Sweetman, Jack 1940- *ConAu 10NR, -25R*

Sweetman, Rosita 1948- *WrDr 84*
Sweets, John Frank 1945- *ConAu 89*
Sweetser, Mary 1894- *ConAu 41R*
Sweetser, Ted *ConAu X*
Sweetser, Wesley 1919- *WrDr 84*
Sweetser, Wesley Duaine 1919- *ConAu 37R, IntAu&W 82*
Sweezy, Alan Richardson 1907- *ConAu 41R*
Sweezy, Paul Marlor 1910- *ConAu 1R, -5NR*
Sweigard, Lulu E d1974 *ConAu 53*
Swell, Lila *ConAu 97*
Sweney, Fredric 1912- *ConAu 1R*
Swensen, Clifford H, Jr. 1926- *ConAu 45*
Swenson, Allan A 1933- *ConAu 77, SmATA 21*
Swenson, Karen *DrAP&F 83*
Swenson, Karen 1936- *ConAu 53, IntWWP 82*
Swenson, Loyd S, Jr. 1932- *ConAu 41R*
Swenson, May *DrAP&F 83*
Swenson, May 1919- *ConAu 5R, ConLC 4, -14, ConP 80, CroCAP, DcLB 5[port], DcLEL 1940, IntWWP 82, SmATA 15, WorAu, WrDr 84*
Swenson, Peggy *ConAu X*
Swenson, Peggye 1933- *ConAu 73*
Swensson, Paul S 1907- *ConAu 77*
Swerdloff, Arthur Leroy 1921- *IntAu&W 82*
Swerdlow, Amy G 1923- *ConAu 105*
Swet, Peter 1942- *NatPD 81[port]*
Swetman, Glenn Robert *DrAP&F 83*
Swetman, Glenn Robert 1936- *ConAu 4NR, -53, IntWWP 82, WrDr 84*
Swetnam, Evelyn 1919- *ConAu 93*
Swets, John A 1928- *ConAu 9NR, -21R*
Swezey, Kenneth M 1905?-1972 *ConAu 33R*
Swicegood, Thomas L P 1930- *ConAu 53*
Swick, Clarence 1883?-1979 *ConAu 89*
Swidler, Arlene 1929- *ConAu 61*
Swidler, Leonard 1929- *ConAu 7NR, -17R*
Swierenga, Robert P 1935- *ConAu 25R, IntAu&W 82, WrDr 84*
Swift, Anthony *TwCA SUP*
Swift, Augustus *ConAu X*
Swift, Benjamin *ConAu X*
Swift, Bryan *ConAu X, WrDr 84*
Swift, Carolyn 1923- *IntAu&W 82*
Swift, Carolyn Ruth 1928- *ConAu 107*
Swift, David *ConAu X, SmATA X*
Swift, E M 1951- *ConAu 107*
Swift, Edd *ConAu X*
Swift, Edward 1943- *ConAu 37R*
Swift, George B 1902?-1983 *ConAu 110*
Swift, Helen Miller 1914- *ConAu 1R*
Swift, Hildegarde Hoyt 1890?-1977 *ConAu 69, SmATA 20N*
Swift, Howard W 1908- *ConAu P-1*
Swift, Joan *DrAP&F 83*
Swift, Joan 1926- *IntWWP 82*
Swift, Jonathan 1667-1745 *SmATA 19*
Swift, Kate 1923- *ConAu 69*
Swift, Marshall S 1936- *ConAu 53*
Swift, Mary Grace 1927- *ConAu 29R, WrDr 84*
Swift, Merlin *ConAu X, SmATA X*
Swift, Patrick 1927-1983 *ConAu 110*
Swift, Richard Newton 1924- *ConAu 1R, WrDr 84*
Swift, W Porter 1914- *ConAu 29R, WrDr 84*
Swigart, Rob *DrAP&F 83*
Swigart, Rob 1941- *ConAu 11NR, -69, IntAu&W 82*
Swiger, Elinor Porter 1927- *ConAu 37R, SmATA 8*
Swigg, Richard 1938- *ConAu 103*
Swihart, Altman K 1903- *ConAu 1R*
Swihart, Thomas L 1929- *ConAu 107, WrDr 84*
Swilky, Jody *DrAP&F 83*
Swinburne, Algernon Charles 1837-1909 *ConAu 105, TwCLC 8[port]*
Swinburne, Laurence 1924- *ConAu 61, SmATA 9*
Swinburne, Richard 1934- *ConAu 10NR, -25R, WrDr 84*
Swindell, Larry 1929- *ConAu 25R*
Swindells, Robert E 1939- *ConAu 97, SmATA 34*
Swinden, Patrick 1941- *ConAu 49*
Swindler, William F 1913- *WrDr 84*
Swindler, William Finley 1913- *ConAu 13R*
Swineford, Ada 1917- *ConAu 61*
Swinfen, D B 1936- *ConAu 37R*
Swinford, Betty June Wells 1927- *ConAu 5R, -7NR*
Swinford, Bob *ConAu X*

Swing, Raymond Gram 1887-1968 *ConAu 89,*
LongCTC, TwCA SUP
Swing, Thomas Kaehao 1930- *ConAu 9R*
Swingle, Paul G 1937- *ConAu 41R*
Swinglehurst, Edmund 1917- *ConAu 8NR, -57*
Swinnerton, A R 1912- *ConAu 106*
Swinnerton, Frank Arthur 1884- *ConNov 82,*
LongCTC, ModBrL, TwCA, TwCA SUP,
TwCWr
Swinnerton, Frank Arthur 1884-1982 *ConAu 108*
Swinnerton, James Guilford 1875-1974 *ConAu 93*
Swinson, Arthur 1915-1970 *ConAu P-2*
Swint, Henry L 1909- *ConAu 37R*
Swinton, E D 1868-1951 *LongCTC*
Swinton, George 1917- *ConAu 85, CreCan 1*
Swinton, Stanley M 1919-1982 *ConAu 107*
Swinton, William Elgin 1900- *ConAu 13R*
Swinyard, Alfred W 1915- *ConAu 9R*
Swire, Otto F 1898-1973 *ConAu P-1*
Swirko, Stanislaw 1911- *IntAu&W 82*
Swisher, Carl Brent 1897-1968 *ConAu 1R, -103*
Swisher, Earl 1902- *ConAu P-2*
Swisher, Robert K, Jr. 1947- *ConAu 61*
Swiss, Thomas *DrAP&F 83*
Swist, Wally *DrAP&F 83*
Switzer, David Karl 1925- *ConAu 57*
Switzer, Ellen 1923- *ConAu 2NR, -45*
Switzer, Richard 1925- *ConAu 25R*
Swivett, R G O *ConAu X*
Swoboda, Helmut 1924- *IntAu&W 82*
Swomley, John M, Jr. 1915- *ConAu 9R*
Swoope, Ded *IntWWP 82X*
Swoope, Dorothy Etta Dowdall 1948-
IntWWP 82
Swope, George S 1915- *ConAu 29R*
Swope, Herbert Bayard 1882-1958 *DcLB 25[port]*
Swope, Mary *DrAP&F 83*
Swor, Chester Eugene 1907- *ConAu 9R*
Sword, Wiley 1937- *ConAu 85, WrDr 84*
Swortzell, Lowell 1930- *ConAu 1NR, -49*
Swyhart, Barbara Ann DeMartino 1942-
ConAu 61
Syberberg, Hans-Juergen 1935- *ConAu 93*
Syburg, Jane 1927- *ConAu 29R*
Sydenham, Michael John 1923- *ConAu 17R,*
WrDr 84
Sydney, Carol *IntAu&W 82X*
Sydney, Cynthia *ConAu X, WrDr 84*
Sydney, Gale *IntWWP 82X*
Sydnor, Charles W, Jr. 1943- *ConAu 77*
Sydnor, James Rawlings 1911- *ConAu 5R*
Syed, Anwar H 1926- *ConAu 102*
Syers, Ed 1914- *ConAu X, WrDr 84*
Syers, William Edward 1914- *ConAu 1R, -4NR*
Sykee, Gloria *DrAP&F 83*
Sykes, Adam 1940- *ConAu 29R*
Sykes, Alrene *ConAu 77, IntAu&W 82,*
WrDr 84
Sykes, Christopher Hugh 1907- *ConAu 29R,*
LongCTC, TwCA SUP, WorAu
Sykes, Gerald 1903- *TwCA SUP*
Sykes, Graham 1948- *IntWWP 82*
Sykes, Jay G 1922- *ConAu 45*
Sykes, John 1918- *ConAu 17R*
Sykes, Roosevelt 1906-1983 *ConAu 110*
Sylva, Carmen 1843-1916 *LongCTC*
Sylvan, Urbanus *LongCTC*
Sylvanus, Erwin 1917- *CnMD, IntAu&W 82,*
ModWD
Sylvester, A J 1889- *ConAu 101*
Sylvester, Arline 1914- *ConAu 65*
Sylvester, Bill *DrAP&F 83*
Sylvester, Dorothy 1906- *ConAu 29R*
Sylvester, Harry 1908- *TwCA SUP*
Sylvester, Natalie G 1922- *ConAu 97,*
SmATA 22[port]
Sylvester, Philip *IntWWP 82X, WrDr 84*
Sylvester, Richard Standish 1926-1978 *ConAu 1R,*
-2NR, -77
Sylvester, Robert M 1907-1975 *ConAu 57, -61*
Sylvester, William 1918- *ConAu 45*
Sylvestre, Guy Jean 1918- *ConAu 61*
Sylvestre, Jean Guy 1918- *IntAu&W 82*
Sylvestre, Paul-Francois 1947- *IntAu&W 82*
Sylvia *ConAu X*
Sylvia, James *DrAP&F 83*
Sylvin, Francis *ConAu X, WrDr 84*
Syme, Ronald 1903- *WrDr 84*
Syme, Ronald 1910- *TwCCW 83, WrDr 84*
Syme, Ronald 1913- *ConAu 6NR, -9R,*
SmATA 2
Symington, David 1904- *ConAu P-2*

Symmons-Symonolewicz, Konstantin 1909-
ConAu 37R, IntAu&W 82, WrDr 84
Symonds, Emily Morse d1936 *LongCTC*
Symonds, Helen Sanford 1899- *ConAu 5R*
Symonds, John *ConAu 105, TwCCW 83,*
WrDr 84
Symonds, Norm 1920- *CreCan 2*
Symonds, Pamela 1916- *WrDr 84*
Symonds, Richard 1918- *ConAu 21R, WrDr 84*
Symonenko, Vasyl 1935-1963 *CIDMEL 80,*
ModSL 2
Symons, Esquire *IntWWP 82X*
Symons, Allene 1944- *ConAu 110*
Symons, Alphonse James Albert 1900-1941
LongCTC, TwCA SUP
Symons, Arthur 1865-1945 *ConAu 107,*
LongCTC, ModBrL, TwCA, TwCA SUP,
TwCLC 11[port], TwCWr
Symons, Geraldine 1909- *ConAu 85,*
SmATA 33[port], TwCCW 83, WrDr 84
Symons, Julian 1912- *WrDr 84*
Symons, Julian Gustave 1912- *ConAu 3NR, -49,*
ConLC 2, -14, ConNov 82, ConP 80,
DcLEL 1940, LongCTC, ModBrL,
TwCA SUP, TwCCr&M 80
Symons, Kevin John Casmir Jacob Donovan 1954-
IntWWP 82
Symons, Leslie John 1926- *ConAu 109,*
WrDr 84
Symons, R D 1898-1973 *ConAu 41R*
Symons, Scott 1933- *ConAu 77, ConNov 82,*
WrDr 84
Syna, Seymour Meyer 1928- *ConAmTC*
Synan, Edward A 1918- *ConAu 17R, WrDr 84*
Synan, Vinson 1934- *ConAu 37R, WrDr 84*
Synge, J M 1871-1909 *ConAu 104*
Synge, John Millington 1871-1909 *CnMD,*
CnMWL, DcLB 10[port], LongCTC,
ModBrL, ModBrL SUP, ModWD, TwCA,
TwCLC 6[port], TwCWr, WhoTwCL
Synge, Ursula 1930- *ConAu 1NR, -49,*
SmATA 9, WrDr 84
Synnestvedt, Sig 1924-1977 *ConAu 37R*
Syntax, John *ConAu X*
Sypher, Francis Jacques 1941- *ConAu 57*
Sypher, Francis Jacques, Jr. 1941- *ConAu 10NR*
Sypher, Lucy Johnston 1907- *ConAu 2NR, -45,*
SmATA 7, WrDr 84
Sypher, Wylie 1905- *ConAu 1R, -3NR,*
IntAu&W 82, WorAu, WrDr 84
Syquia, Luis Salvador, Jr. *DrAP&F 83*
Syracuse, Marcella Pfeiffer 1930- *ConAu 21R*
Syrdal, Rolf A 1902- *ConAu 25R*
Syred, Celia 1911- *ConAu 29R*
Syrett, David 1939- *ConAu 106*
Syrkin, Marie 1899- *ConAu 6NR, -9R*
Syrop, Konrad 1914- *ConAu 5NR, -9R,*
WrDr 84
Syruc, J *ConAu X*
Sysak, Juliette Augustina *CreCan 2*
Syse, Glenna *ConAmTC*
Syvertsen, Edythe 1921- *ConAu 73*
Syverud, Genevieve Wold 1914- *ConAu 21R*
Szabo, Denis 1929- *ConAu 89*
Szabo, Dezso 1879-1945 *CIDMEL 80*
Szabo, Gyorgy 1932- *IntAu&W 82*
Szabo, Lorinc 1900-1957 *CIDMEL 80*
Szabo, Magda 1917- *CroCD, IntAu&W 82*
Szabo, Wilhelm 1901- *IntAu&W 82*
Szabolcsi, Miklos 1921- *IntAu&W 82*
Szacsvay-Feher, Tibor 1907- *IntAu&W 82*
Szajkowski, Zosa 1911- *ConAu X*
Szakonyi, Karoly 1931- *IntAu&W 82*
Szancer, Henryk 1904-1976 *ConAu 61*
Szaniawski, Jerzy 1886-1970 *CIDMEL 80,*
CnMD, ConAu 29R, CroCD, ModWD
Szanto, George H 1940- *ConAu 41R,*
IntAu&W 82
Szanton, Peter L 1930- *ConAu 69*
Szaraz, Gyorgy 1930- *IntAu&W 82*
Szarota, Elida Maria 1904- *IntAu&W 82*
Szasz, Kathleen 1912- *ConAu 25R*
Szasz, Margaret Connell 1935- *ConAu 97*
Szasz, Suzanne Shorr 1919- *ConAu 3NR, -5R,*
SmATA 13
Szasz, Thomas 1920- *ConAu 9NR*
Szasz, Thomas Stephen 1920- *ConAu 17R,*
IntAu&W 82, WrDr 84
Szathmary, Louis, II 1919- *ConAu 81*
Szaz, Zoltan Michael 1930- *ConAu 1R, -3NR*
Szczepanski, Jan Jozef 1919- *IntAu&W 82*
Szczesniak, Boleslaw B 1908- *ConAu 9R,*

IntAu&W 82
Szczygiel, Jerzy 1932- *IntAu&W 82*
Sze, Arthur *DrAP&F 83*
Szechter, Szymon 1920?-1983 *ConAu 110*
Szekely, Endre 1922- *ConAu 17R, WrDr 84*
Szekeres, Cyndy 1933- *SmATA 5*
Szelburg-Zarembina, Ewa 1899- *CIDMEL 80*
Szep, Paul Michael 1941- *ConAu 110*
Szeplaki, Joseph 1932- *ConAu 73*
Szerb, Antal 1901-1945 *CIDMEL 80*
Szerlip, Barbara *DrAP&F 83*
Szerlip, Barbara 1949- *ConAu 3NR, -49*
Szigeti, Joseph 1892-1973 *ConAu P-1*
Szilard, Leo 1898-1964 *ConSFA, TwCSFW*
Szirtes, George 1948- *ConAu 109*
Szobotka, Tibor 1913- *IntAu&W 82*
Szogyi, Alex 1929- *ConAu 45*
Szoverffy, Joseph 1920- *ConAu 65*
Szpilman, Boruch *IntAu&W 82X*
Szporluk, Roman 1933- *ConAu 1NR, -45*
Szulc, Tad 1926- *ConAu 4NR, -9R,*
SmATA 26[port], WrDr 84
Szumigalski, Anne *DrAP&F 83*
Szumigalski, Anne 1926- *ConAu 1NR, -49*
Szydlow, Jarl *ConAu X*
Szydlowski, Mary Vigliante *DrAP&F 83*
Szydlowski, Mary Vigliante 1946- *ConAu 104*
Szydlowski, Roman 1918- *IntAu&W 82*
Szyliowicz, Joseph S 1931- *ConAu 41R,*
IntAu&W 82
Szymborska, Wislawa 1923- *CIDMEL 80*
Szyszkowitz, Gerald 1938- *IntAu&W 82*

T

T, Pat *IntWWP 82X*
T *IntWWP 82X, LongCTC*
T B D *ConAu X*
T N T *ConAu X*
T R B *ConAu X*
T V Vet *ConAu X*
Taaffe, Edward James 1921- *ConAu 85*
Taaffe, James G 1932- *ConAu 17R*
Taaffe, Michael *ConAu X*
Taagepera, Rein 1933- *ConAu 109*
Tabachnik, Abraham B 1902-1970 *ConAu 29R*
Tabak, Israel 1904- *ConAu 105*
Tabard, Geoffrey *ConAu X*
Tabard, Peter *ConAu X, IntAu&W 82X*
Tabas, Shirlee 1929- *IntAu&W 82*
Tabb, Jay Yanai 1907- *ConAu P-2*
Tabelak, John-Michael *ConDr 82D*
Taber, Anthony Scott 1944- *ConAu 105*
Taber, George M 1942- *ConAu 65*
Taber, Gladys Bagg 1899-1980 *ConAu 4NR, –5R, –97, SmATA 22N*
Taber, Julian Ingersoll 1929- *ConAu 106*
Taber, Robert *ConAu 17R*
Taber, Robert W 1921- *ConAu 73*
Tabler, Edward C 1916- *ConAu 5R*
Tablet, Hilda *ConAu X*
Tabor, Paul *ConAu X*
Tabori, George 1914- *ConAu 4NR, –49, ConDr 82, ConLC 19, TwCA SUP, WrDr 84*
Tabori, Paul 1908-1974 *ConAu 5R, –5NR, –53, ConSFA*
Taborsky, Edward J 1910- *WrDr 84*
Taborsky, Edward Joseph 1910- *ConAu 1R, –3NR, IntAu&W 82*
Tabrah, Ruth M 1921- *ConAu 13R, IntAu&W 82, SmATA 14*
Tabrah, Ruth Milander 1921- *ConAu 10NR*
Tacey, William S 1904- *ConAu 37R*
Tachau, Mary K Bonsteel 1926- *ConAu 85*
Tacheron, Donald Glen 1928- *ConAu 21R*
Tack, Alfred 1906- *ConAu 104*
Tada, Yukei 1912- *IntAu&W 82*
Tadijanovic, Dragutin 1905- *CIDMEL 80*
Tadlock, Max R 1919- *ConAu 17R*
Tadrack, Moss *ConAu X*
Tae-Yong, Ro *ConAu X*
Taegel, William S 1940- *ConAu 45*
Taetzsch, Lyn 1941- *ConAu 8NR, –57*
Taeuber, Alma Ficks 1933- *ConAu 17R*
Taeuber, Conrad 1906- *ConAu 45*
Taeuber, Irene Barnes 1906-1974 *ConAu 106*
Taeuber, Karl E 1936- *ConAu 17R*
Tafel, Edgar 1912- *WrDr 84*
Tafel, Edgar Allen 1912- *ConAu 89*
Taffrail 1883-1968 *LongCTC, TwCWr*
Taffy *ConAu X*
Taft, Charles P 1897-1983 *ConAu 110*
Taft, Charles Phelps 1897- *ConAu 105*
Taft, Pauline Dakin 1891- *ConAu P-1*
Taft, Philip 1902-1976 *ConAu 69*
Taft, Ronald 1920- *ConAu 21R*
Taft, William H 1915- *ConAu 13R*
Tafuri, Manfredo 1935- *ConAu 69*

Tagami, Marshal L 1949- *IntWWP 82*
Tager, Marcia *DrAP&F 83*
Tageson, Carroll W 1925- *ConAu 53*
Tagett, Richard *DrAP&F 83*
Taggard, Genevieve 1894-1948 *ConAmA, TwCA, TwCA SUP*
Taggart, Dorothy T 1917- *ConAu 102*
Taggart, John *DrAP&F 83*
Taggart, John 1942- *ConAu 1NR, –45*
Taggart, Patrick Ewing 1949- *ConAmTC*
Taggert, Brian *NatPD 81[port]*
Tagiuri, Renato 1919- *ConAu 77*
Tagliabue, John *DrAP&F 83*
Tagliabue, John 1923- *ConAu 21R, ConP 80, IntAu&W 82, IntWWP 82, WrDr 84*
Tagliacozzo, Rhoda S *DrAP&F 83*
Tagliaferri, Aldo 1931- *ConAu 77*
Tagliavia, Sheila 1936- *ConAu 104*
Tagore, Amitendranath 1922- *ConAu 61*
Tagore, Sir Rabindranath 1861-1941 *CnMD, ConAu X, LongCTC, ModCmwL, ModWD, TwCA, TwCA SUP, TwCWr, WhoTwCL*
Taha, Hamdy A 1937- *ConAu 37R*
Tahara, Mildred Machiko 1941- *ConAu 104*
Tahir, Abe M, Jr. 1931- *ConAu 69*
Tahir, Kemal 1910?-1973 *ConAu 45*
Tahlaquah, David *ConAu X*
Tahtinen, Dale R 1945- *ConAu 65*
Tai, Hung-Chao 1929- *ConAu 73*
Taichert, Louise C 1925- *ConAu 89*
Taikeff, Stanley 1940- *ConAu 109, NatPD 81[port]*
Taine, John 1883-1960 *TwCA SUP, TwCSFW*
Taines, Beatrice 1923- *ConAu 73*
Taira, Koji 1926- *ConAu 41R*
Taishoff, Sol J 1904-1982 *ConAu 107, –73*
Tait, Alan A 1934- *ConAu 10NR, –21R*
Tait, Dorothy 1902?-1972 *ConAu 33R*
Tait, Douglas William Campbell 1944- *SmATA 12[port]*
Tait, Elizabeth Leeds 1906- *IntWWP 82*
Tait, George Edward 1910- *ConAu 5R, WrDr 84*
Tait, Katharine 1923- *ConAu 65*
Tait, L Gordon 1926- *ConAu 45*
Taitz, Emily 1937- *ConAu 85*
Takagi, Akimitsu 1920- *ConAu 108*
Takahashi, Akira 1932- *ConAu 29R*
Takahashi, Yasundo 1912- *ConAu 41R*
Takaki, Ronald T 1939- *ConAu 37R*
Takakjian, Portia 1930- *SmATA 15*
Takashima, Shizuye 1928- *ConAu 45, CreCan 2, SmATA 13*
Takats, Gyula 1911- *IntWWP 82*
Takayama, Akira 1932- *ConAu 2NR, –49*
Takeshita, Thomas Kohachiro 1891?-1973 *ConAu 45*
Takiff, Jonathan Henry 1946- *ConAmTC*
Takman, John 1912- *IntAu&W 82*
Taktsis, Costas 1927- *ConAu 21R*
Talamantes, Florence Williams 1931- *ConAu 6NR, –57*
Talarico, Ross *DrAP&F 83*
Talarico, Ross 1945- *ConAu 73*

Talarzyk, W Wayne 1940- *WrDr 84*
Talbert, Charles Gano 1912- *ConAu 5R*
Talbert, Charles Harold 1934- *ConAu 41R, IntAu&W 82*
Talbot, Allan R 1934- *ConAu 10NR, –21R*
Talbot, Carol Terry 1913- *ConAu 13R*
Talbot, Charlene Joy 1924- *WrDr 84*
Talbot, Charlene Joy 1928- *ConAu 8NR, –17R, SmATA 10*
Talbot, Ethel *TwCCW 83*
Talbot, Fannie Sprague 1873-1957 *MichAu 80*
Talbot, Godfrey 1908- *ConAu 107*
Talbot, Godfrey Walker 1908- *WrDr 84*
Talbot, Gordon 1928- *ConAu 69*
Talbot, Kay *ConAu X*
Talbot, Lawrence *ConAu X*
Talbot, Nathan B 1909- *ConAu 104*
Talbot, Norman 1936- *ConAu 9NR*
Talbot, Norman Clare 1936- *ConAu 21R, IntAu&W 82, IntWWP 82, WrDr 84*
Talbot, Ross B 1919- *ConAu 17R*
Talbot, Toby 1928- *ConAu 21R, SmATA 14*
Talbot Rice, Tamara 1904- *IntAu&W 82*
Talbott, John E 1940- *ConAu 25R*
Talbott, Robert D 1928- *ConAu 57*
Talbott, Strobe 1946- *AuNews 1, ConAu 93*
Talcott, William *DrAP&F 83*
Talcove, Rick 1948- *ConAmTC*
Talese, Gay *WrDr 84*
Talese, Gay 1932- *AuNews 1, ConAu 1R, –9NR, ConIsC 1[port]*
Talev, Dimitur 1898-1966 *ModSL 2*
Talker, T *SmATA X*
Talkin, Gil *ConAu X*
Tall, Deborah *DrAP&F 83*
Tall, Deborah 1951- *ConAu 105*
Tall, Stephen 1908- *TwCSFW, WrDr 84*
Tall Mountain, Mary *DrAP&F 83*
Tallafierro, Gabriel *MichAu 80*
Talland, George A 1917- *ConAu P-2*
Tallant, Robert 1909-1957 *TwCA SUP*
Tallcott, Emogene *ConAu 29R, SmATA 10*
Tallent, Elizabeth Ann *DrAP&F 83*
Tallent, Norman 1921- *ConAu 17R, WrDr 84*
Talleur, Richard W 1931- *ConAu 97*
Talley-Morris, Neva B 1909- *ConAu 57*
Tallman, Albert 1902- *ConAu 53*
Tallon, Robert 1935- *ConAu 8NR*
Tallon, Robert 1940- *ConAu 9R, SmATA 28*
Tally, Ted 1952- *ConDr 82, NatPD 81[port], WrDr 84*
Talmadge, Jeffrey D 1953- *IntWWP 82*
Talmadge, Marian *SmATA 14*
Talmage, Anne *ConAu X*
Talmage, Frank 1938- *ConAu 97*
Talmon, Jacob L 1916-1980 *ConAu 101, –13R*
Talmon, Shemaryahu 1920- *ConAu 29R, IntAu&W 82*
Talpalar, Morris 1900- *ConAu 73*
Talwalkar, Govind S 1925- *IntAu&W 82*
Tamar, I *IntWWP 82X*
Tamari, Moshe 1910- *IntWWP 82*
Tamarin, Alfred 1913- *WrDr 84*
Tamarin, Alfred H 1913-1980 *ConAu 4NR, –102,*

–29R, SmATA 13

Tamas, Attila 1930- *IntAu&W 82*
Tamasi, Aron 1877-1966 *ClDMEL 80*
Tamasi, Aron 1897-1966 *CnMD, WorAu*
Tambi *ConAu X*
Tambimuttu, Thurairajah 1915?-1983 *ConAu 110*
Tambs, Lewis Arthur 1927- *ConAu 4NR, –53*
Tamburine, Jean 1930- *ConAu 9R, SmATA 12*
Tambuzi, Jitu *DrAP&F 83, IntWWP 82X*
Tamedly, Elisabeth L 1931- *ConAu 29R*
Tamen, Pedro Mario Alles 1934- *IntWWP 82*
Tames, Richard Lawrence 1946- *ConAu 103, WrDr 84*
Tamir, Max Mordecai 1912- *ConAu 29R*
Tamir, Vicki 1924- *ConAu 29R*
Tammaro, Thom 1951- *ConAu 109*
Tammsaare, Anton Hansen 1878-1940 *ClDMEL 80*
Tammuz, Benjamin 1919- *ConAu 85, IntAu&W 82*
Tamny, Martin 1941- *ConAu 37R*
Tampion, John 1937- *ConAu 73*
Tamulaitis, Vytas 1913- *ConAu 17R*
Tamuno, Tekena N 1932- *ConAu 21R*
Tan, S H 1920- *IntAu&W 82*
Tan Pai, Joshua 1914- *IntWWP 82*
Tana, Tomoe 1913- *ConAu 21R*
Tanabe, Takao 1926- *CreCan 2*
Tanaka, Michitaro 1902- *IntAu&W 82*
Tanaquil, Paul *ConAu X*
Tanay, Emanuel 1928- *ConAu 93*
Tanchuck, Nathaniel 1912- *ConAu 13R*
Tancock, John 1942- *ConAu 105, WrDr 84*
Tandem, Felix *ConAu X*
Tandon, Prakash 1911- *ConAu 93*
Tandori, Dezso 1938- *IntAu&W 82*
Tandy, Clifford Ronald Vivien 1919?-1981 *ConAu 104*
Tanenbaum, Jan Karl 1936- *ConAu 61*
Tanenhaus, Beverly *DrAP&F 83*
Tang, Peter Sheng-Hao 1919- *ConAu 1R*
Tangerman, Elmer John 1907- *ConAu 106*
Tangri, Shanti S 1928- *ConAu 25R*
Tangye, Nigel 1909- *WrDr 84*
Tanham, George Kilpatrick 1922- *ConAu 1R, –1NR, WrDr 84*
Tania B *ConAu X*
Taniguchi, Kazuko 1946- *ConAu 93*
Tanis, Norman Earl 1929- *ConAu 110*
Tanizaki, Jun'ichiro 1886-1965 *CnMWL, ConAu 25R, –93, ConLC 8, –14, WhoTwCL, WorAu*
Tank, Herbert 1922?-1982 *ConAu 108*
Tank, Ronald W 1929- *ConAu 49*
Tankard, James William, Jr. 1941- *ConAu 73*
Tanksley, Perry 1928- *ConAu 37R*
Tann, Jennifer 1939- *ConAu 103, WrDr 84*
Tannahill, John Allan 1918- *WrDr 84*
Tannahill, Reay *WrDr 84*
Tannahill, Reay 1929- *ConAu 2NR, –49*
Tannehill, Robert C 1934- *ConAu 45*
Tannen, Mary 1943- *ConAu 105*
Tannenbaum, Arnold S 1925- *ConAu 17R*
Tannenbaum, Beulah Goldstein 1916- *ConAu 5R, –7NR, SmATA 3*
Tannenbaum, Edward R 1921- *ConAu 17R*
Tannenbaum, Frank 1893-1968? *ConAu 9R*
Tannenbaum, Harold E 1914- *ConAu 5R*
Tannenbaum, Judith *DrAP&F 83*
Tannenbaum, Percy Hyman 1927- *ConAu 106*
Tannenbaum, Robert 1915- *ConAu 21R*
Tanner, C Kenneth 1938- *ConAu 53*
Tanner, Clara L 1905- *ConAu 41R*
Tanner, Daniel 1926- *ConAu 17R*
Tanner, Edward Everett, III 1921-1976 *ConAu 69, –73, WorAu*
Tanner, Helen Hornbeck 1916- *ConAu 61*
Tanner, Henry 1918- *ConAu 73*
Tanner, James Mourilyan 1920- *ConAu 5NR, –13R*
Tanner, James T F 1937- *ConAu 41R*
Tanner, John *ConAu X, DrAP&F 83*
Tanner, John 1927- *ConAu 103, IntAu&W 82, WrDr 84*
Tanner, Louise S 1922- *ConAu 69, SmATA 9*
Tanner, Paul O W 1917- *ConAu 61*
Tanner, Tony 1935- *ConAu 85, ConLCrt 82, WrDr 84*
Tanner-Rutherford, C *ConAu X*
Tanobe, Miyuki 1937- *ConAu 69, SmATA 23[port]*
Tanous, Peter 1938- *ConAu 7NR, –61*

Tanselle, G Thomas 1934- *ConAu 11NR, –21R, WrDr 84*
Tanselle, George Thomas 1934- *IntAu&W 82*
Tansill, Charles Callan 1890-1964 *ConAu 1R*
Tante, Dilly *WrDr 84*
Tanter, Raymond 1938- *ConAu 45*
Tantrist *ConAu X*
Tanveer *IntWWP 82X*
Tanyzer, Harold Joseph 1929- *ConAu 9R*
Tanzer, Lester 1929- *ConAu 17R*
Tanzer, Michael David 1935- *ConAu 57*
Tanzi, Diane *DrAP&F 83*
Tanzi, Vito 1935- *ConAu 5NR, –53*
Tao-Li *IntWWP 82X*
Taphorn, Phyllis Ann 1919- *IntWWP 82*
Tapia, John Reyna 1922- *IntWWP 82*
Tapia, Ralph J 1925- *ConAu 41R*
Tapio, Pat Decker *ConAu X, SmATA X*
Tapley, Caroline 1934- *ConAu 97*
Taplin, Glen W 1917- *ConAu 107*
Taplin, Oliver 1943- *ConAu 102*
Taplin, Walter 1910- *ConAu P-1, IntAu&W 82*
Taplinger, Cecily Lent 1943-1983 *ConAu 110*
Taplinger, Richard Jacques 1911-1973 *ConAu 41R*
Taplinger, Terry *ConAu X*
Tapp, Jack Thomas 1934- *ConAu 49*
Tapp, June Louin 1929- *ConAu 41R*
Tapp, Nicholas Charles Theodore 1952- *IntWWP 82*
Tapp, Robert B 1925- *ConAu 41R*
Tappan, Eva March 1854-1930 *TwCA*
Tappan, Paul Wilbur 1911-1964 *ConAu 5R*
Tappe, Eric Ditmar 1910- *IntAu&W 82*
Tappert, Theodore G 1904-1973 *ConAu 1R, –2NR*
Tapply, H G 1910- *ConAu 13R*
Tapscott, Stephen 1948- *ConAu 89*
Tapscott, Stephen J *DrAP&F 83*
Tapsell, R F 1936- *ConAu 21R*
Tar, Jack *IntAu&W 82X*
Tarachow, Michael *DrAP&F 83*
Tarachow, Michael 1954- *IntWWP 82*
Taradash, Daniel 1913- *ConAu 101*
Taranow, Gerda *ConAu 37R*
Tarascio, Vincent J 1930- *ConAu 45*
Tarasov-Rodionov, Aleksandr Ignatiyevich 1885-1938 *ClDMEL 80*
Tarasov-Rodionov, Alexander Ignatyevich 1888-1937? *TwCWr*
Tarassoff, Lev *ConAu X, WorAu*
Tarazaga, Santiago Genoves *ConAu X*
Tarbell, Ida Minerva 1857-1944 *TwCA, TwCA SUP*
Tarbert, Gary C 1937- *ConAu 101*
Tarcher, Martin 1921- *ConAu 17R*
Tarchila, Dan 1923- *IntAu&W 82*
Tardieu, Jean 1903- *ClDMEL 80, CnMD, ModFrL, ModWD, WorAu*
Tardiff, Olive 1916- *ConAu 73*
Tardineau, Rene Marie Auguste *TwCA, TwCA SUP*
Tardy, Gaye 1929?-1982 *ConAu 108*
Targ, Russell 1934- *ConAu 104*
Targ, William 1907- *ConAu 61*
Targan, Barry *DrAP&F 83*
Targan, Barry 1932- *ConAu 73*
Target, G W 1924- *ConAu 7NR*
Target, George William 1924- *ConAu 5R, DcLEL 1940, WrDr 84*
Tarkenton, Fran 1940- *ConAu 103*
Tarkington, Booth 1869-1946 *ConAmA, ConAu 110, DcLB 9[port], LongCTC, ModAL, ModWD, SmATA 17, TwCA, TwCA SUP, TwCLC 9[port], TwCWr*
Tarkka, Pekka 1934- *IntAu&W 82*
Tarkovsky, Arseny Aleksandrovich 1907- *ClDMEL 80*
Tarling, Nicholas 1931- *ConAu 21R, WrDr 84*
Tarling, Peter Nicholas 1931- *IntAu&W 82*
Tarlock, A Dan 1940- *ConAu 97*
Tarlov, I M 1905?-1977 *ConAu 69*
Tarn, John Nelson 1934- *ConAu 41R*
Tarn, Nathaniel *DrAP&F 83*
Tarn, Nathaniel 1928- *ConAu 5NR, –9R, ConP 80, DcLEL 1940, IntAu&W 82, IntWWP 82, WrDr 84*
Tarn, Stanley *IntWWP 82X*
Tarnawsky, Ostap 1917- *ConAu 73, IntAu&W 82*
Tarnawsky, Patricia W 1936- *ConAu 45*
Tarnawsky, Yuriy *DrAP&F 83*

Tarnoky, Andras Laszlo 1920- *WrDr 84*
Tarnopol, Lester 1913- *ConAu 77*
Tarnower, Herman 1910-1980 *ConAu 89, –97*
Tarpey, Elizabeth 1880-1979 *ConAu 4NR, –5R*
Tarpey, Lawrence Xavier 1928- *ConAu 21R*
Tarpley, Fred 1932- *ConAu 41R*
Tarpy, Roger M 1941- *ConAu 93*
Tarr, Fred *DrAP&F 83*
Tarr, Herbert *DrAP&F 83*
Tarr, Herbert 1929- *ConAu 13R*
Tarr, Joel Arthur 1934- *ConAu 37R, IntAu&W 82, WrDr 84*
Tarr, Rodger L 1941- *ConAu 110*
Tarr, Yvonne Young 1929- *ConAu 8NR, –61*
Tarrab, Gilbert 1940- *IntAu&W 82*
Tarrance, V Lance, Jr. 1940- *ConAu 37R*
Tarrant, Desmond 1924- *ConAu 21R*
Tarrant, John *ConAu X, WrDr 84*
Tarrant, John J 1924- *ConAu 4NR, –53*
Tarrant, John Rex 1941- *WrDr 84*
Tarrant, Wilma *ConAu X*
Tarrok, Peer *ConAu X*
Tarry, Ellen 1906- *ConAu 73, LivgBAA, SmATA 16*
Tarsaidze, Alexandre 1901-1978 *ConAu 37R, –77*
Tarshis, Jerome 1936- *ConAu 61, SmATA 9*
Tarsicio *IntWWP 82X*
Tarsis, Valeriy 1906- *TwCWr*
Tarsis, Valery 1906- *WorAu*
Tarsis, Valery Yakovlevich 1906-1983 *ConAu 109*
Tart, Charles T 1937- *ConAu 29R, WrDr 84*
Tartre, Raymond S 1901-1975 *ConAu P-2*
Tasca, Henry J 1912-1979 *ConAu 89*
Tasca, Jules 1938- *AuNews 1, ConAu 109, NatPD 81[port]*
Tasch, Peter A 1933- *ConAu 73*
Taschdjian, Claire L 1914- *ConAu 73*
Tashjian, Dickran 1940- *ConAu 61*
Tashjian, Virginia A 1921- *ConAu 29R, SmATA 3*
Tashlin, Frank 1913-1972 *ConAu 110*
Tasis I Marca, Rafael 1906-1967 *ClDMEL 80*
Tasker, James 1908- *ConAu 49, SmATA 9*
Tasker, Joe 1948-1982 *ConAu 108*
Tassin, Myron Jude 1933- *ConAu 61*
Tassin, Ray 1926- *ConAu 53*
Tatar, Maria M 1945- *ConAu 85*
Tatarka, Dominik 1913- *ClDMEL 80, ModSL 2*
Tatarkiewicz, Wladyslaw 1886-1980 *ConAu 103, –97*
Tate, Allen 1899-1979 *ConAmA, ConAu 5R, –85, ConLC 2, –4, –6, –9, –11, –14, –24[port], ConLCrt 82, DcLB 4, LongCTC, ModAL, ModAL SUP, TwCA, TwCA SUP, TwCWr, WhoTwCL*
Tate, B H *ConAu X*
Tate, Edward *ConAu X*
Tate, Eleanora E 1948- *ConAu 105*
Tate, Ellalice *ConAu X, SmATA 2, TwCRGW, WorAu, WrDr 84*
Tate, Gary 1930- *ConAu 21R*
Tate, George T 1931- *ConAu 21R*
Tate, Jackson R 1899?-1978 *ConAu 81*
Tate, James *DrAP&F 83*
Tate, James 1943- *ConLC 25[port], WrDr 84*
Tate, James Edward 1920- *IntAu&W 82*
Tate, James Vincent 1943- *ConAu 21R, ConLC 2, –6, ConP 80, DcLB 5, DcLEL 1940, WorAu 1970*
Tate, Joan 1922- *ConAu 1NR, –49, SmATA 9, TwCCW 83, WrDr 84*
Tate, Marilyn Freeman 1921- *ConAu 13R*
Tate, Mary Anne *ConAu X*
Tate, Merle W 1903- *ConAu P-1*
Tate, Merze 1905- *ConAu 17R, LivgBAA, WrDr 84*
Tate, Peter *TwCSFW, WrDr 84*
Tate, Richard *ConAu X*
Tate, Robin *ConAu X*
Tate, Velma 1913- *ConAu 21R*
Tatelbaum, Judith Ann 1938- *ConAu 104*
Tatelbaum, Judy *ConAu X*
Tatford, Brian Frederick Barrington 1927- *ConAu P-1*
Tatford, Frederick Albert 1901- *ConAu 10NR, –13R*
Tatgenhorst, John J 1938- *ConAu 65*
Tatham, C Ernest 1905- *ConAu P-1*
Tatham, Campbell *ConAu X, SmATA 2*
Tatham, Laura 1919- *ConAu 13R, WrDr 84*
Tati, Jacques *ConAu X*

Tatischeff, Jacques 1908-1982 *ConAu 108*
Tatlow, Josephine Barrington *CreCan 2*
Taton, Rene 1915- *ConAu 9R*
Tatray, Istvan *ConAu X*
Tattersall, Jill 1931- *ConAu 10NR, -25R, TwCRGW, WrDr 84*
Tattersall, Lawrence H 1933- *ConAu 29R*
Tattersall, Muriel Joyce *WrDr 84*
Tattersall, Muriel Joyce 1931- *ConAu P-1*
Tatu, Michel 1933- *ConAu 25R*
Tatum, Arlo 1923- *ConAu 25R*
Tatum, Billy Joe 1933- *ConAu 61*
Tatum, Jack *ConAu X*
Tatum, John David 1948- *ConAu 104*
Taub, Harald 1918- *ConAu 110*
Taube, Evert 1890-1976 *ConAu 61*
Taube, Lester S 1920- *ConAu 69*
Taube, Myron *DrAP&F 83*
Taubenfield, Howard J 1924- *ConAu 13R*
Tauber, Abraham 1915?-1977 *ConAu 69*
Tauber, Gerald E 1922- *ConAu 89*
Tauber, Gilbert 1935- *ConAu 9NR, -21R*
Tauber, Kurt P 1922- *ConAu 21R*
Tauber, Maurice F 1908-1980 *ConAu 102, -105*
Tauber, Peter 1947- *ConAu 37R*
Taubert, William H 1934- *ConAu 103*
Taubes, Frederic 1900-1981 *ConAu 9NR, -104, -17R*
Taubes, Susan *ConAu X*
Taubman, William 1941- *ConAu 21R*
Taubr, Paul Raymond 1937- *ConAu 29R*
Taunton, Eric *ConAu X*
Taus, Roger *DrAP&F 83*
Tavard, George Henry 1922- *ConAu 1R, -1NR*
Tave, Stuart M 1923- *ConAu 104*
Tavel, Ronald *DrAP&F 83, IntAu&W 82, IntWWP 82, NatPD 81[port]*
Tavel, Ronald 1940- *ConAu 21R, ConLC 6*
Tavel, Ronald 1941- *ConDr 82, WrDr 84*
Taverne, Dick 1928- *ConAu 85, WrDr 84*
Taverner, Sonia 1936- *CreCan 2*
Taves, Ernest H 1916- *ConAu 93*
Taves, Isabella 1915- *ConAu 8NR, -21R, SmATA 27[port]*
Tavis, Alec *IntAu&W 82X*
Taviss, Irene *ConAu X*
Tavo, Gus *ConAu X*
Tavuchis, Nicholas 1934- *ConAu 57*
Tawney, R H 1880-1962 *ConAu 93*
Tawney, Richard Henry 1880-1962 *LongCTC, TwCA, TwCA SUP*
Tawny *IntWWP 82X*
Tax, Sol 1907- *ConAu 5R*
Taydo *ConAu X*
Taylor, A J P 1906- *WrDr 84*
Taylor, Alan John Percivale 1906- *ConAu 5R, LongCTC, WorAu*
Taylor, Alan R 1926- *ConAu 109*
Taylor, Alastair M 1915- *ConAu 17R*
Taylor, Albert E 1908- *ConAu 89*
Taylor, Alexander *DrAP&F 83*
Taylor, Alfred 1896-1973 *ConAu 105*
Taylor, Alice J 1909-1969 *ConAu P-2*
Taylor, Alice Louise 1911- *ConAu 61, IntAu&W 82, WrDr 84*
Taylor, Alison 1927- *ConAu 21R*
Taylor, Alix 1921- *ConAu 5R*
Taylor, Andrew 1940- *ConAu 11NR, -69, ConP 80, WrDr 84*
Taylor, Andrew 1951- *ConAu 110*
Taylor, Anique 1946- *ConAu 109*
Taylor, Ann *ConAu X*
Taylor, Anna 1944- *ConAu 25R*
Taylor, Archer 1890-1973 *ConAu 107*
Taylor, Arnold H 1929- *ConAu 33R*
Taylor, Arthur Samuel 1894-1963 *ConAu 1R, -103*
Taylor, Barbara G 1942- *ConAu 25R*
Taylor, Barbara J 1927- *ConAu 53, SmATA 10*
Taylor, Benjamin J 1934- *ConAu 21R*
Taylor, Bernard 1937- *ConAu 69*
Taylor, Bert Leston 1866-1921 *DcLB 25[port], TwCA, TwCA SUP*
Taylor, Betty Jo 1933- *ConAu 13R*
Taylor, Bob L 1923- *ConAu 33R*
Taylor, Brad *ConAu X*
Taylor, Brian Dormer 1946- *IntWWP 82*
Taylor, Bruce *DrAP&F 83*
Taylor, C P 1929-1981 *ConLC 27[port]*
Taylor, Carl 1937- *ConAu 69, SmATA 14*
Taylor, Cecil Philip 1929-1981 *ConAu 105, -25R*
Taylor, Cecily 1930- *IntWWP 82*

Taylor, Charlene M 1938- *ConAu 33R*
Taylor, Charles 1922- *WrDr 84*
Taylor, Charles 1931- *ConAu 11NR, -13R*
Taylor, Charles Alfred 1922- *ConAu 109*
Taylor, Charles D 1938- *ConAu 101*
Taylor, Charles H 1846-1921 *DcLB 25[port]*
Taylor, Charles Lewis 1935- *ConAu 77*
Taylor, Clyde R 1931- *ConAu 45*
Taylor, Conciere *DrAP&F 83*
Taylor, Conciere Marlana 1950- *IntWWP 82*
Taylor, Constance Lindsay *WrDr 84*
Taylor, Constance Lindsay 1907- *ConAu 106*
Taylor, Dalmas A 1933- *ConAu 57*
Taylor, David 1900-1965 *ConAu 1R, SmATA 10*
Taylor, David 1934- *ConAu 105*
Taylor, David Alan 1943- *ConAu 108*
Taylor, David Bruce 1938- *WrDr 84*
Taylor, David Conrad 1934- *WrDr 84*
Taylor, Dawson 1916- *ConAu 13R, MichAu 80*
Taylor, Day *ConAu X*
Taylor, Deems 1885-1966 *ConAu 89, TwCA, TwCA SUP*
Taylor, Demetria 1903-1977 *ConAu 73*
Taylor, Desmond 1930- *ConAu 37R*
Taylor, Don 1910- *ConAu 13R*
Taylor, Donald L 1916- *ConAu 17R*
Taylor, Donald Stewart 1924- *ConAu 106*
Taylor, Donna June 1949- *ConAu 37R*
Taylor, Dorothy A 1938- *WrDr 84*
Taylor, Duncan 1912- *ConAu 25R*
Taylor, Duncan Norton *ConAu X*
Taylor, Earl Aulick 1904-1965 *ConAu P-1*
Taylor, Edith 1913- *ConAu 45*
Taylor, Edward C 1923- *WrDr 84*
Taylor, Eleanor Ross *DrAP&F 83*
Taylor, Eleanor Ross 1920- *ConAu 81, ConLC 5*
Taylor, Elizabeth 1912-1975 *ConAu 9NR, -13R, ConLC 2, -4, DcLEL 1940, LongCTC, SmATA 13, TwCA SUP, TwCWr*
Taylor, Elizabeth Tebbetts *ConAu 101*
Taylor, Eric Openshaw 1902- *WrDr 84*
Taylor, Eric Scollick 1918- *IntAu&W 82*
Taylor, Estelle Davis *IntWWP 82X*
Taylor, Ethel Stoddard 1895?-1975 *ConAu 57*
Taylor, Eugene Jackson 1913-1978 *ConAu 81*
Taylor, Florance Walton *ConAu 37R, SmATA 9*
Taylor, Florence M 1892- *ConAu 13R, SmATA 9*
Taylor, Frank J 1894-1972 *ConAu 37R, ConAu P-1*
Taylor, Fred James 1919- *ConAu 107, WrDr 84*
Taylor, Frederick 1928- *ConAu 77*
Taylor, George *ConAu X*
Taylor, George A 1942- *ConAu 102*
Taylor, George Edward 1905- *ConAu 1R*
Taylor, Gordon *DrAP&F 83*
Taylor, Gordon O 1938- *ConAu 25R*
Taylor, Gordon Rattray 1911-1981 *ConAu 105, -85*
Taylor, Griffin 1917- *ConAu 65*
Taylor, H Baldwin *ConAu X, TwCCr&M 80, WrDr 84*
Taylor, H Kerr 1891?-1977 *ConAu 73*
Taylor, Harold 1914- *ConAu 25R*
Taylor, Harold L 1934- *ConAu 110*
Taylor, Harold McCarter 1907- *ConAu 109*
Taylor, Harry *ConAu X*
Taylor, Harry H 1926- *ConAu 57*
Taylor, Henry *DrAP&F 83*
Taylor, Henry 1942- *DcLB 5[port], WrDr 84*
Taylor, Henry 1943- *ConAu 33R*
Taylor, Henry J 1902- *ConAu P-2*
Taylor, Herb 1942- *ConAu 97, SmATA 22*
Taylor, Hiram 1952- *NatPD 81[port]*
Taylor, Howard F 1939- *ConAu 110*
Taylor, Ian 1944- *ConAu 77*
Taylor, Irving A 1925- *ConAu 61*
Taylor, J Thomas 1930- *ConAu 107*
Taylor, Jack W 1915- *ConAu 9R*
Taylor, James B 1930- *ConAu 37R*
Taylor, James C 1937- *ConAu 77*
Taylor, James R 1907- *ConAu P-2*
Taylor, James Spear 1897?-1979 *ConAu 85*
Taylor, Jed H 1902- *ConAu P-1*
Taylor, Jennifer *WrDr 84*
Taylor, Jenny 1910- *ConAu 105*
Taylor, Jerome 1918- *ConAu 1R, -1NR*

Taylor, Jesse *ConAu X*
Taylor, Joan DuPlat d1983 *ConAu 109*
Taylor, Joe Gray 1920- *ConAu 6NR, -57*
Taylor, John 1916- *ConAu 93*
Taylor, John 1921- *ConAu 21R*
Taylor, John 1925- *ConAu 81*
Taylor, John 1931- *WrDr 84*
Taylor, John 1937- *WrDr 84*
Taylor, John 1938- *IntWWP 82*
Taylor, John Alfred *DrAP&F 83*
Taylor, John Alfred 1931- *ConAu 61*
Taylor, John F A 1915- *ConAu 17R*
Taylor, John Gerald 1931- *ConAu 29R*
Taylor, John Laverack 1937- *ConAu 1NR, -45*
Taylor, John M 1930- *ConAu 25R*
Taylor, John Randolph 1929- *ConAu 1R*
Taylor, John Russell 1935- *ConAu 5R, DcLEL 1940, WrDr 84*
Taylor, John Stephen 1916- *IntAu&W 82, WrDr 84*
Taylor, John Vernon 1914- *ConAu 5NR, -9R, WrDr 84*
Taylor, John William Ransom 1922- *ConAu 49, IntAu&W 82, WrDr 84*
Taylor, Joshua Charles 1917-1981 *ConAu 104*
Taylor, Kamala 1924- *ConAu 77, WorAu*
Taylor, Karen Malpede 1945- *ConAu 45*
Taylor, Karl K 1938- *ConAu 41R*
Taylor, Katharine Whiteside 1897- *ConAu P-2*
Taylor, Ken 1922- *ConAu 108*
Taylor, Kenneth N 1917- *AuNews 2, ConAu 8NR, -17R, SmATA 26[port]*
Taylor, Kent *DrAP&F 83*
Taylor, Kent 1940- *ConAu 9NR, -17R, IntWWP 82*
Taylor, L A *DrAP&F 83*
Taylor, L B, Jr. 1932- *ConAu 11NR, -57, SmATA 27[port]*
Taylor, Larry 1932- *ConAmTC*
Taylor, Laurie *DrAP&F 83*
Taylor, Lawrence 1942- *ConAu 105*
Taylor, Lee 1930- *ConAu 41R*
Taylor, Lester D 1938- *ConAu 17R, WrDr 84*
Taylor, Lloyd A 1921- *ConAu 41R*
Taylor, Lloyd C, Jr. 1923- *ConAu 57*
Taylor, Lois Dwight Cole *ConAu X*
Taylor, Louis 1900- *ConAu 2NR, -5R*
Taylor, Malcolm Gordon 1915- *ConAu 109*
Taylor, Marcella B *DrAP&F 83*
Taylor, Margaret 1917- *ConAu X*
Taylor, Margaret Stewart *WrDr 84*
Taylor, Margaret Stewart 1902- *ConAu 89, IntAu&W 82*
Taylor, Marion Ansel 1904- *ConAu 13R*
Taylor, Mark *SmATA 28*
Taylor, Mark 1927- *ConAu 108, SmATA 32*
Taylor, Markland James 1936- *ConAmTC*
Taylor, Mary Ann 1912- *ConAu 97*
Taylor, Michael J 1924- *ConAu 7NR, -17R, WrDr 84*
Taylor, Michael John 1949- *ConAu 77, IntAu&W 82*
Taylor, Michael M 1944- *ConAu 97*
Taylor, Mildred D *ConAu 85, ConLC 21[port], SmATA 15, TwCCW 83*
Taylor, Morris F 1915- *ConAu 37R*
Taylor, Nellie 1901- *IntAu&W 82*
Taylor, Norman 1883-1967 *ConAu P-2*
Taylor, Paul B 1930- *ConAu 81*
Taylor, Paul Schuster 1895- *ConAu 81, WrDr 84*
Taylor, Paul W 1923- *ConAu 1R*
Taylor, Paula 1942- *SmATA 33*
Taylor, Peter *DrAP&F 83*
Taylor, Peter 1917- *ConAu 9NR, DcLB Y81B[port]*
Taylor, Peter 1919- *WrDr 84*
Taylor, Peter Hillsman 1917- *ConNov 82, DcLEL 1940, ModAL, ModAL SUP, TwCA SUP*
Taylor, Peter Hillsman 1919- *ConAu 13R, ConLC 1, -4, -18*
Taylor, Philip Elbert 1908-1975 *ConAu 61*
Taylor, Phoebe Atwood 1909-1976 *ConAu 61, TwCA, TwCA SUP, TwCCr&M 80*
Taylor, Phoebe Jean 1921?-1979 *ConAu 89*
Taylor, R D *DrAP&F 83*
Taylor, Rachel Annand 1876-1960 *LongCTC, TwCA, TwCA SUP*
Taylor, Ransom Theodore 1913- *ConAu 45*
Taylor, Ray J 1918?-1977 *ConAu 69*

Taylor, Ray Ward 1908- *ConAu P-2*
Taylor, Rebe Prestwich 1911- *ConAu 13R*
Taylor, Rex 1921- *ConAu 13R*
Taylor, Richard *DrAP&F 83*
Taylor, Richard 1919- *ConAu 17R*
Taylor, Richard K 1933- *ConAu 101*
Taylor, Richard W 1924- *ConAu 3NR, -5R, IntAu&W 82, WrDr 84*
Taylor, Robert 1925- *ConAu 81*
Taylor, Robert 1940- *ConAmTC*
Taylor, Robert, Jr. *DrAP&F 83*
Taylor, Robert B 1926- *ConAu 81*
Taylor, Robert Brown 1936- *ConAu 61*
Taylor, Robert Lewis 1912- *ConAu 1R, -3NR, ConLC 14, SmATA 10, TwCWW, WorAu, WrDr 84*
Taylor, Robert Martin 1909- *ConAu P-2*
Taylor, Robert R 1939- *ConAu 53*
Taylor, Rod *DrAP&F 83*
Taylor, Roland Vincent 1907- *ConAu P-1*
Taylor, Ron W 1922- *ConAu P-1*
Taylor, Ronald 1924- *ConAu 93, IntAu&W 82*
Taylor, Ronald J 1926- *ConAu 41R*
Taylor, Ronald L 1938- *ConAu 77*
Taylor, Ross McLaury 1909?-1977 *ConAu 69*
Taylor, Rupert 1946- *ConAu 45*
Taylor, Ruth Mattson 1922- *ConAu 101*
Taylor, Sam A 1918- *ConAmTC*
Taylor, Samuel 1907- *ConAu 73*
Taylor, Samuel 1912- *ConAu 25R, ConDr 82D, IntAu&W 82, WrDr 84*
Taylor, Sydney 1904-1978 *TwCCW 83*
Taylor, Sydney Brenner 1904-1978 *ConAu 4NR, -5R, -77, SmATA 1, -26N, -28[port]*
Taylor, Telford 1908- *ConAu 25R, WrDr 84*
Taylor, Theodore *DrAP&F 83*
Taylor, Theodore 1921- *ConAu 9NR, -21R, TwCCW 83, WrDr 84*
Taylor, Theodore 1924- *SmATA 5*
Taylor, Theodore Brewster 1925- *ConAu 102*
Taylor, Thomas 1934- *ConAu 21R*
Taylor, Tim 1920-1974 *ConAu 45, -53*
Taylor, Tom *ConAu X*
Taylor, Valerie *ConAu X*
Taylor, Vernon L 1922- *ConAu 33R*
Taylor, Walter Fuller 1900-1966 *ConAu 1R*
Taylor, Walter Harold 1905- *WrDr 84*
Taylor, Walter W 1913- *ConAu 61*
Taylor, Warren 1903- *ConAu 21R*
Taylor, Weldon J 1908- *ConAu 1R*
Taylor, Welford Dunaway 1938- *ConAu 37R, WrDr 84*
Taylor, Wendell Hertig 1905- *ConAu 102*
Taylor, William 1930- *ConAu 81*
Taylor, William David, Jr. 1902-1975 *ConAu 107*
Taylor, William E *DrAP&F 83*
Taylor, William E 1920- *ConAu 10NR, -25R*
Taylor, William L 1937- *ConAu 29R*
Taylor, Zack 1927- *ConAu 65*
Tazewell, Charles 1900-1972 *ConAu 37R*
Tazky, Ladislav 1921- *ModSL 2*
Tchaadaieff *ConAu X*
Tchekhov, Anton Pavlovich 1860-1904 *LongCTC*
Tchernichovski, Saul 1875-1943 *WorAu*
Tchicaya, Gerald-Felix 1931- *WorAu 1970*
Tchividjian, Gigi Graham 1945- *ConAu 108*
Tchobanoglous, George 1935- *ConAu 102*
Tead, Ordway 1891-1973 *ConAu 45*
Teaford, Jon C 1946- *ConAu 10NR, -65*
Teague, Bob *SmATA X*
Teague, Bob 1929- *ConAu X, LivgBAA, SmATA X*
Teague, Kathleen 1931- *IntAu&W 82*
Teague, Kathleen 1937- *ConAu 97*
Teague, Michael 1932- *ConAu 109*
Teague, Robert 1929- *ConAu 106, SmATA 31, -32[port]*
Teal, G Donn 1932- *ConAu 33R, WrDr 84*
Teal, John J, Jr. 1921-1982 *ConAu 110*
Teal, Val 1903- *ConAu 61, SmATA 10*
Teale, Edwin Way 1899- *WrDr 84*
Teale, Edwin Way 1899-1980 *ConAu 1R, -2NR, -102, SmATA 25N, -7, TwCA SUP*
Teasdale, Sara 1884-1933 *ConAmA, ConAu 104, LongCTC, SmATA 32[port], TwCA, TwCA SUP, TwCLC 4[port], TwCWr*
Tebbel, John 1912- *ConAu 85, SmATA 26[port]*
Tebbel, Robert E 1924- *ConAu 5R*
Tebbetts-Taylor, Elizabeth *ConAu X*
Tebeau, Charlton Watson 1904- *ConAu 110*
Tec, Leon 1919- *ConAu 97*

Tec, Nechama 1931- *ConAu 9R*
Teck, Alan 1934- *ConAu 25R*
Tedder, Lord *ConAu X*
Tedder, Arthur William 1890-1967 *ConAu P-2*
Tedder, John M 1926- *IntAu&W 82, WrDr 84*
Tedeschi, James, Jr. 1928- *ConAu 41R*
Tedlock, E W, Jr. 1910- *ConAu P-2*
Tee-Van, Helen Damrosch 1893-1976 *ConAu 49, -65, SmATA 10, -27N*
Teegen, Otto John 1899-1983 *ConAu 109*
Teer, Frank 1934- *ConAu 53*
Teeter, Don E 1934- *ConAu 73*
Teeter, Karl V 1929- *ConAu 17R*
Teeters, Negley K 1896-1971 *ConAu 33R, ConAu P-2*
Teets, Bruce Earle 1914- *ConAu 37R*
Teevan, Richard C 1919- *ConAu 1R, -4NR*
Teffi, N A 1875-1952 *CIDMEL 80*
Tefft, Bess H 1913?-1977 *MichAu 80*
Tefft, Bess H 1915?-1977 *ConAu 110*
Tega, Vasile 1921- *ConAu 102*
Tegenfeldt, Herman G 1913- *ConAu 73*
Tegner, Bruce 1928- *ConAu 8NR, -61*
Tegner, Henry Stuart 1901- *ConAu 13R*
Teich, Albert H 1942- *ConAu 45*
Teicher, Morton I 1920- *ConAu 11NR, -69*
Teichmann, Howard 1916- *ConAu 69, NatPD 81[port]*
Teikmanis, Arthur L 1914- *ConAu 13R*
Teilhard DeChardin, Pierre 1881-1955 *CIDMEL 80, ConAu 105, LongCTC, TwCLC 9[port], WorAu*
Teirlinck, Herman Louis Cesar 1879-1967 *CIDMEL 80, CnMD, ModWD*
Teiser, Ruth 1915- *ConAu 109*
Teissier DuCros, Janet 1906- *ConAu P-2*
Teitelbaum, Harry 1930- *ConAu 21R*
Teitelbaum, Mashel 1921- *CreCan 1*
Teitelbaum, Myron 1929- *ConAu 13R*
Teitelman, Jill *DrAP&F 83*
Teixeira, Bernardo 1926- *ConAu 108*
Teixeira DaMota, Avelino d1982 *ConAu 106*
Teixeira DeMattos, Alexander Louis 1865-1921 *LongCTC*
Teixeira DePascoaes, Joaquim *CIDMEL 80*
Teja, Edward Ray 1948- *IntAu&W 82*
Tejo *IntAu&W 82X*
Tekahionwake *CreCan 2*
Tekeyan, Charles 1927- *ConAu 29R, WrDr 84*
Teknos, Peter 1920- *IntAu&W 82*
Telander, Richard F 1948- *ConAu 65*
Teleki, Geza 1943- *ConAu 3NR, -49*
Telemaque, Eleanor Wong *DrAP&F 83*
Telemaque, Eleanor Wong 1934- *ConAu 104*
Telemaque, Harold Milton 1910- *IntWWP 82*
Telenga, Suzette 1915- *ConAu 1R*
Telescope, Tom *SmATA X*
Telfair, Nancy *ConAu X*
Telfair, Richard *TwCWW*
Telfer, Dariel 1905- *ConAu P-2*
Telfer, R 1937- *ConAu 106*
Telfer, William 1886-1968 *ConAu P-1*
Telford, Charles W 1903- *ConAu 65*
Teliha, Olena 1907-1942 *ModSL 2*
Tell, Jack 1909?-1979 *ConAu 89*
Tellechea Idigoras, Jose Ignacio 1928- *IntAu&W 82*
Teller, Edward 1908- *ConAu P-1, ConIsC 2[port]*
Teller, James D 1906- *ConAu 41R*
Teller, Judd L 1912-1972 *ConAu 33R*
Teller, Neville 1931- *ConAu 103, WrDr 84*
Teller, Raphael 1938- *WrDr 84*
Teller, Walter Magnes 1910- *ConAu 2NR, -5R, WrDr 84*
Telser, Lester G 1931- *ConAu 33R, WrDr 84*
Tem, Steve Rasnic *DrAP&F 83*
Tem, Steve Rasnic 1950- *IntWWP 82*
Temianka, Henri 1906- *ConAu 45*
Temin, Peter 1937- *ConAu 13R, WrDr 84*
Temkin, Pauline B 1919- *ConAu 25R*
Temkin, Sara Anne Schlossberg 1913- *ConAu 1R, SmATA 26[port]*
Temko, Florence 1927- *ConAu 1NR, -49, IntAu&W 82, SmATA 13*
Temmer, Mark J 1922- *ConAu 107*
Temp, George 1929- *ConAu 45*
Temperley, Alan 1936- *IntAu&W 82*
Temperley, Howard 1932- *ConAu 85*
Temperley, Neville 1915- *WrDr 84*
Temperley, Nicholas 1932- *ConAu 107, WrDr 84*

Tempest, Jan *ConAu X, TwCRGW, WrDr 84*
Tempest, Margaret Mary 1892-1982 *ConAu 108, SmATA 33N*
Tempest, Sarah *ConAu X, IntAu&W 82X, WrDr 84*
Tempest, Theresa *ConAu X*
Tempest, Victor *ConAu X, WrDr 84*
Templar, Maurice *ConAu X, SmATA X*
Temple, Ann *ConAu X*
Temple, Arthur *ConAu X*
Temple, Dan *ConAu X, TwCWW, WrDr 84*
Temple, Joe 1917- *ConAu 97*
Temple, Nigel 1926- *WrDr 84*
Temple, Nigel Hal Longdale 1926- *ConAu 29R, IntAu&W 82*
Temple, Paul *ConAu X*
Temple, Philip 1939- *ConAu 104, IntAu&W 82, WrDr 84*
Temple, Robert 1945- *WrDr 84*
Temple, Robert Kyle Grenville 1945- *ConAu 89*
Temple, Robert M, Jr. 1935- *ConAu 107*
Temple, Ruth Z 1908- *ConAu 61*
Temple, Wayne C 1924- *ConAu 1R, -1NR, IntAu&W 82, WrDr 84*
Temple, Willard H 1912- *ConAu 1R*
Temple, William F 1914- *ConSFA, TwCSFW, WrDr 84*
Templeton, Charles 1915- *ConAu 101*
Templeton, Edith 1916- *ConAu 53, WrDr 84*
Templeton, Fiona *DrAP&F 83*
Templeton, Janet *ConAu X*
Templeton, John J, Jr. 1928- *ConAu 25R*
Tenax *ConAu X*
TenBerge, Hans C 1938- *IntAu&W 82*
TenBoom, Corrie 1892-1983 *ConAu 109*
Tendryakov, Vladimir 1923- *TwCSFW A*
Tendryakov, Vladimir Fyodorovich 1923- *CIDMEL 80, ConAu 104, ModSL 1, TwCWr*
Tene, Benjamin 1914- *IntWWP 82*
Tenenbaum, Frances 1919- *ConAu 73*
Tenenbaum, Shea 1910- *ConAu 1NR, -49, IntAu&W 82*
Tener, Robert L *DrAP&F 83*
Tener, Robert L 1924- *ConAu 110*
Teng, S-Y 1906- *ConAu 13R*
Tengbom, Mildred 1921- *ConAu 97*
Tenggren, Gustaf 1896-1970 *SmATA 18, -26N*
TenHarmsel, Henrietta 1921- *ConAu 106*
TenHoor, Elvie Marie 1900- *ConAu 9R*
TenHouten, Warren David 1939- *ConAu 108*
Tenison, Robin Hanbury *ConAu X*
Tenn, Ada N 1915- *ConAu 11NR, -25R*
Tenn, William 1919- *DcLB 8[port]*
Tenn, William 1920- *ConSFA, TwCSFW, WrDr 84*
Tennant, Alan 1943- *ConAu 108*
Tennant, Emma 1937- *ConAu 10NR, -65, ConLC 13, ConNov 82, DcLB 14[port], TwCSFW, WhoTwCL, WrDr 84*
Tennant, Kylie 1912- *ConAu X, ConNov 82, IntAu&W 82, SmATA 6, TwCWr, WorAu, WrDr 84*
Tennant, Nora Jackson 1915- *ConAu 4NR, -9R*
Tennant, Peter 1910- *WrDr 84*
Tennant, Roger 1919- *ConAu 106*
Tennant, Veronica 1946- *CreCan 1*
Tennant, Veronica 1947- *ConAu 103*
Tennenbaum, Silvia *DrAP&F 83*
Tennenbaum, Silvia 1928- *ConAu 77*
Tennes, George *ConAu X*
Tenneshaw, S M *ConAu X, TwCSFW*
Tenney, H Kent 1892-1982 *ConAu 107*
Tenney, Merrill Chapin 1904- *ConAu 1R, -4NR, WrDr 84*
Tenniel, Sir John 1820-1914 *LongCTC, SmATA 27*
Tennien, Mark A 1900?-1983 *ConAu 108*
Tennies, Arthur C 1931- *ConAu 53*
Tennison, Patrick Joseph 1928- *ConAu 106, IntAu&W 82, WrDr 84*
Tennov, Dorothy 1928- *ConAu 41R*
Tennyson, Charles Bruce Locker 1879-1977 *ConAu 73, -81*
Tennyson, G B 1930- *ConAu 9NR, -21R, WrDr 84*
Tenpas, Margaret 1923- *ConAu 85*
Tenreiro, Francisco Jose DeVasques 1921-1963 *CIDMEL 80*
Tensen, Ruth Marjorie *ConAu 5R, WrDr 84*
Tent, Ned *ConAu X*
Teofil *IntWWP 82X*

Tepaleatero *DrAP&F 83*
Tepper, Albert 1928- *ConAu 25R*
Tepper, Michael 1941- *ConAu 73*
Tepper, Terri P 1942- *ConAu 107*
Ter Haar, Jaap 1922- *ConAu 37R, SmATA 6*
Ter Horst, J F 1922- *ConAu 107*
Ter Horst, Jerald Franklin 1922- *AuNews 1*
Terahata, Jun *IntAu&W 82X*
Teran, Heriberto *DrAP&F 83*
Terayama, Shuji 1936-1983 *ConAu 109*
Terborgh, George 1897- *ConAu P-2*
Terbovich, John B 1933-1969 *ConAu P-2*
Terchek, Ronald John 1936- *ConAu 49*
Terdiman, Richard 1941- *ConAu 73*
Teresa, Sister Margaret *ConAu X*
Terhune, Albert Payson 1872-1942 *DcLB 9[port], SmATA 15, TwCA, TwCA SUP, TwCCW 83*
Terhune, William Barclay 1893- *ConAu 61*
Terkel, Studs *WrDr 84*
Terkel, Studs 1912- *AuNews 1, ConAu 57*
Terlecki, Wladyslaw 1933- *IntAu&W 82*
Terlouw, Jan 1931- *ConAu 108, SmATA 30[port]*
Terman, Sibyl 1902?-1975 *ConAu 57*
Terme, Hilary *ConAu X*
Terner, Janet 1938- *ConAu 102*
Terni, Fausta Cialente 1900- *ConAu 5R*
Terni-Cialente, Fausta 1900- *ConAu 5NR*
Terpstra, Vern 1927- *ConAu 11NR, -21R, IntAu&W 82, WrDr 84*
Terr, Leonard *DrAP&F 83*
Terr, Leonard B 1946- *ConAu 73*
Terra, F *IntAu&W 82X*
Terrace, Edward L B 1936?-1973 *ConAu 45*
Terrace, Herbert S 1936- *ConAu 102, WrDr 84*
Terrace, Vincent 1948- *ConAu 9NR, -65*
Terraine, John Alfred 1921- *ConAu 5R, WrDr 84*
Terrall, Robert 1914- *ConAu 102*
Terranova, Elaine *DrAP&F 83*
Terrell, Carroll Franklin 1917- *ConAu 102*
Terrell, Donna McManus 1908- *ConAu 57*
Terrell, John Upton 1900- *ConAu 29R*
Terrell, Robert L 1943- *ConAu 41R*
Terrence, Frederick J *ConAu X*
Terres, John Kenneth 1905- *ConAu 5R, -5NR*
Terrien, Samuel Lucien 1911- *ConAu 81*
Terrill, Kathryn *DrAP&F 83*
Terrill, Richard *DrAP&F 83*
Terrill, Ross Gladwin 1938- *ConAu 25R, IntAu&W 82*
Terrill, Tom E 1935- *ConAu 41R*
Terris, Susan *DrAP&F 83*
Terris, Susan 1937- *ConAu 29R, IntAu&W 82, SmATA 3, WrDr 84*
Terris, Virginia Rinaldy *DrAP&F 83*
Terris, Virginia Rinaldy 1917- *ConAu 65, IntWWP 82*
Terry, Arthur 1927- *ConAu 85*
Terry, C V *ConAu X, LongCTC, TwCRGW, WrDr 84*
Terry, Charles S 1926?-1982 *ConAu 107*
Terry, Edward D 1927- *ConAu 29R*
Terry, Ellen 1848?-1928 *LongCTC*
Terry, Luther L 1911- *ConAu P-2, SmATA 11*
Terry, Mark 1947- *ConAu 37R*
Terry, Marshall, Jr. 1931- *ConAu 1R*
Terry, Megan *DrAP&F 83*
Terry, Megan 1932- *ConAu 77, ConDr 82, ConLC 19, CroCD, DcLB 7[port], NatPD 81[port], WorAu 1970, WrDr 84*
Terry, Michael 1899- *WrDr 84*
Terry, Michael 1899-1981 *ConAu 104, IntAu&W 82*
Terry, Robert H 1935- *ConAu 29R*
Terry, Robert Meredith 1939- *ConAu 41R*
Terry, Robert William 1937- *ConAu 37R, MichAu 80*
Terry, Saralee *ConAu X*
Terry, Walter 1913-1982 *ConAu 10NR, -107, -21R, SmATA 14*
Terry, William *ConAu X, TwCWW, WrDr 84*
Terson, Peter 1932- *ConAu 104, ConDr 82, CroCD, DcLB 13, DcLEL 1940, WrDr 84*
Terstegge, Mabel Alice 1905- *ConAu 93*
Tertis, Lionel 1876-1975 *ConAu 57, -93*
Tertz, Abram 1925- *CIDMEL 80, ConAu X, ConLC 8, TwCSFW A, TwCWr, WorAu*
Tertz, Avram 1925- *ModSL 1*
Tervapaa, Juhani *CroCD*
Terwilliger, Robert E 1917- *ConAu 65*

Terzani, Tiziano 1938- *ConAu 77*
Terzi, Niyazi 1958- *IntAu&W 82*
Terzian, James P 1915- *ConAu 13R, SmATA 14*
TeSelle, Eugene 1931- *ConAu 37R*
TeSelle, Eugene 1931- *WrDr 84*
TeSelle, Sallie McFague *ConAu X*
TeSelle, Sallie McFague 1933- *ConAu 21R*
Tesich, Steve *NatPD 81*
Tesich, Steve 1942- *ConDr 82, WrDr 84*
Tesich, Steve 1943?- *ConAu 105, DcLB Y83B[port]*
Tesmer, Louise M 1942- *IntWWP 82*
Tessier, Ernest Maurice *LongCTC*
Tessier, Ernst-Maurice *ConAu X*
Tessier, M 1885-1973 *ConAu 3NR*
Tessimond, A S J d1962 *LongCTC*
Tessler, Mark A 1941- *ConAu 1NR, -45, IntAu&W 82*
Tessler, Yvonne Fair 1934- *IntWWP 82*
Tester, Sylvia Root 1939- *ConAu 8NR, -9R*
Testori, Giovanni 1923- *CIDMEL 80*
Teta, Jon 1933- *ConAu 25R*
Tetel, Marcel 1932- *ConAu 21R*
Tetens, Tete Harens 1899?-1976 *ConAu 65*
Teternikov, Feodor Kuzmich 1863-1927 *TwCA, TwCA SUP*
Teternikov, Fyodor Kuzmich 1863-1927 *ConAu 104*
Tether, Graham 1950- *ConAu 6NR, -57*
Tetlow, Edwin 1905- *ConAu 17R*
Tetmajer Przerwa, Kazimierz 1865-1940 *CIDMEL 80*
Tetreault, Wilfred F 1927- *ConAu 106*
Teufel, Dolores Enid Arlene 1921- *IntWWP 82*
Teune, Henry 1936- *ConAu 3NR, -49*
Teuscher, Robert H 1934- *ConAu 77*
Tevfik Fikret 1867-1915 *CIDMEL 80*
Tevis, Walter *DrAP&F 83*
Tevis, Walter 1928- *ConSFA, TwCSFW, WrDr 84*
Tewkesbury, Joan 1936- *ConAu 101*
Tey, Josephine *ConAu X*
Tey, Josephine 1897?-1952 *LongCTC, TwCA SUP, TwCCr&M 80, TwCWr*
Teychenne, G Maree 1949- *IntAu&W 82*
Teye, Nicholas 1939- *IntAu&W 82*
Teyte, Maggie 1888-1976 *ConAu 65*
Tezla, Albert 1915- *ConAu 37R*
Thacher, Alida McKay 1951- *ConAu 11NR, -69*
Thacher, Mary McGrath 1933- *SmATA 9*
Thacker, Eric 1923- *ConAu 107, ConSFA*
Thacker, Ernest W 1914- *ConAu 13R*
Thackeray, Milton G 1914- *ConAu 13R*
Thackeray, William Makepeace 1811-1863 *SmATA 23[port]*
Thackray, Arnold 1939- *ConAu 49*
Thackray, Arnold Wilfrid 1939- *IntAu&W 82*
Thackray, Derek Vincent 1926- *ConAu 103, WrDr 84*
Thackray, Rupert Manfred 1921- *WrDr 84*
Thackray, Russell I 1904- *ConAu 37R*
Thaddeus, Janice *DrAP&F 83*
Thaddeus, Janice 1933- *ConAu 13R, IntWWP 82*
Thaden, Edward Carl 1922- *ConAu 17R, IntAu&W 82, WrDr 84*
Thain, Donald H 1928- *ConAu 1R*
Thakur, Shivesh Chandra 1936- *ConAu 29R*
Thakur, Tanraj *IntWWP 82X*
Thakur, Upendra 1929- *IntAu&W 82*
Thakura, Ravindranatha 1861-1941 *ConAu 104*
Thalacker, Donald William 1939- *ConAu 108*
Thalberg, Irving 1930- *ConAu 41R*
Thale, Jerome 1927- *ConAu 13R*
Thaler, Alwin 1891- *ConAu P-1*
Thaler, M N *ConAu X, WrDr 84*
Thaler, Susan 1939- *ConAu 21R*
Thalheimer, Ross 1905-1977 *ConAu 41R*
Thalman, Mark *DrAP&F 83*
Thalman, Mark 1953- *IntWWP 82*
Thalmann, Rita Renee Line 1926- *ConAu 4NR, -53*
Thames, C H *ConAu X, WrDr 84*
Thames, Jack *ConAu X*
Thamm, Robert 1933- *ConAu 89*
Thampi, Parvathi 1925- *ConAu 5R*
Thane, Adele 1904- *ConAu 25R*
Thane, Elswyth 1900- *ConAu 5R, SmATA 32[port], TwCRGW, WrDr 84*
Thanet, Neil *ConAu X*
Thanet, Octave 1850-1934 *LongCTC*

Thangappa, Lenin 1934- *IntWWP 82*
Thangappa, M L *IntWWP 82X*
Thant, U 1909-1974 *ConAu 108*
Thapar, Romila 1931- *DcLEL 1940*
Tharaud, Jean Charles 1877-1952 *CIDMEL 80, TwCA, TwCA SUP*
Tharaud, Jerome Ernest 1874-1953 *CIDMEL 80, TwCA, TwCA SUP*
Tharaud, Lucien Rostaing, Jr. 1953- *ConAu 69*
Tharaud, Ross *ConAu X*
Tharp, Louise Hall 1898- *ConAu 1R, SmATA 3, WorAu*
Tharp, Roland *DrAP&F 83*
Tharpe, Jac Lyndon 1928- *ConAu 7NR, -57*
Thass-Thienemann, Theodore 1900- *ConAu 25R*
Thatcher, Alice Dora 1912- *WrDr 84*
Thatcher, Amelia *IntWWP 82X*
Thatcher, David 1922- *ConAu 77*
Thatcher, Dora 1912- *ConAu 13R*
Thatcher, Dorothy Southwell 1903- *ConAu P-1*
Thatcher, Floyd W 1917- *ConAu 102*
Thatcher, Joan 1934- *ConAu 106*
Thatcher, Julia *ConAu X*
Thayer, Charles Wheeler 1910-1969 *ConAu 1R, -103*
Thayer, Emma Redington Lee 1874-1973 *ConAu 45, ConAu P-1*
Thayer, Frederick C, Jr. 1924- *ConAu 73*
Thayer, George 1933-1973 *ConAu 45, ConAu P-2*
Thayer, Geraldine *ConAu X, WrDr 84*
Thayer, H S 1923- *ConAu 45*
Thayer, James Stewart 1949- *ConAu 73*
Thayer, Jane *ConAu X, SmATA 3*
Thayer, Lee 1874-1973 *ConAu X, TwCCr&M 80*
Thayer, Lee 1927- *ConAu 3NR, -49*
Thayer, Mary VanRensselaer *ConAu 97*
Thayer, Nathaniel B 1929- *ConAu 45*
Thayer, Peter *ConAu X, SmATA X*
Thayer, Theodore 1904-1981 *ConAu 103*
Thayer, Tiffany Ellsworth 1902-1959 *TwCA, TwCA SUP*
Thayer, V T 1886-1979 *ConAu 89, ConAu P-2*
Thayer, William Roscoe 1859-1923 *TwCA*
Thayler, Carl *DrAP&F 83*
Thayler, Carl 1933- *ConAu 37R*
Thayne, Emma Lou *DrAP&F 83*
Thayne, Emma Lou 1924- *ConAu 65*
Thayne, Mirla Greenwood 1907- *ConAu 21R*
The Captain *IntAu&W 82X*
The Countryman *ConAu X*
The Gallerite *ConAu X*
The Gordons *ConAu X*
The Great Comte *ConAu X*
The Great Merlini *ConAu X*
The Phantom *IntWWP 82X*
The Smith *IntWWP 82X*
Theall, Donald Francis 1928- *ConAu 105*
Thebaud, Jo 1914- *ConAu 49*
Theberge, James 1930- *WrDr 84*
Theberge, James Daniel 1930- *ConAu 25R*
Thede, Marion 1903- *ConAu P-2, WrDr 84*
Thee, Marek 1918- *ConAu 101*
Theen, Rolf H W 1937- *ConAu 41R*
Theer, Otakar 1880-1917 *CIDMEL 80*
Theil, Henri 1924- *ConAu 7NR, -17R, WrDr 84*
Theiner, George 1927- *ConAu 29R*
Theis, John William 1911- *ConAu 109*
Theis, Paul A 1923- *ConAu 41R*
Thekaekara, Matthew P 1914-1976 *ConAu 69, -77*
Thelen, David Paul 1939- *ConAu 110*
Thelen, Gil 1938- *ConAu 73*
Thelen, Herbert Arnold 1913- *ConAu 108*
Thelin, John R 1947- *ConAu 11NR, -69*
Thelwell, Michael 1939- *ConAu 101, ConLC 22[port]*
Thelwell, Norman 1923- *ConAu 4NR, -5R, DcLEL 1940, SmATA 14*
Themerson, Stefan 1910- *ConAu 9NR, -65, WrDr 84*
Theobald, Lewis, Jr. *ConAu X*
Theobald, Robert 1929- *ConAu 37R, WrDr 84*
Theocharis, Reghinos D 1929- *ConAu 11NR, -13R*
Theodorakis, Michalis 1925- *ConAu 105*
Theodorakis, Mikis *ConAu X*
Theodorakopoulos, Ioannis 1900-1981 *ConAu 108*
Theodoratus, Robert J 1928- *ConAu 41R*
Theodore, Athena 1919- *ConAu 41R*

Theodore, Chris A 1920- *ConAu 13R*
Theodore, David *IntWWP 82X*
Theodore, Sister Mary 1907- *ConAu 5R*
Theodorescu, Ion *WorAu 1970*
Theodorson, George A 1924- *ConAu 29R*
Theoharis, Athan George 1936- *ConAu 29R*
Theriault, Albert A, Jr. 1928- *ConAu 53*
Theriault, Yves 1915- *ConAu 102*
Theriault, Yves 1916- *CreCan 1*
Thernstrom, Stephan 1834- *ConAu 13R*
Theron, Hilary *MichAu 80*
Theroux, Alexander 1939- *ConLC 25[port]*
Theroux, Alexander Louis *DrAP&F 83*
Theroux, Alexander Louis 1939- *ConAu 85,*
ConLC 2
Theroux, Paul *DrAP&F 83*
Theroux, Paul 1941- *ConAu 33R, ConLC 5, –8,*
–11, –15, ConNov 82, DcLB 2,
IntAu&W 82, WorAu 1970, WrDr 84
Theroux, Phyllis 1939- *ConAu 110*
Therson-Cofie, Larweh 1943- *IntWWP 82*
Thesen, Hjalmar Peter 1925- *ConAu 107,*
WrDr 84
Thesiger, Wilfred 1910- *WrDr 84*
Thesiger, Wilfred Patrick 1910- *ConAu P-2,*
IntAu&W 82, LongCTC
Thevenin, Denis *ConAu X*
Thevoz, Jacqueline 1926- *IntAu&W 82,*
IntWWP 82
Thibaudeau, Jean 1935- *CIDMEL 80*
Thibaudet, Albert 1874-1936 *CIDMEL 80*
Thibault, Jacques Anatole Francois 1844-1924
ConAu 106
Thibault, John C 1922- *ConAu 77*
Thibeau, Jack *DrAP&F 83*
Thibodeaux, Mary Rodgers *LivgBAA*
Thiebaud, Wayne 1920- *ConAu 45*
Thiebaux, Marcelle 1931- *ConAu 110*
Thieda, Shirley Ann 1943- *ConAu 69,*
SmATA 13
Thiele, Colin 1920- *ConAu 29R, ConLC 17,*
DcLEL 1940, SmATA 14, TwCCW 83,
WrDr 84
Thiele, Edwin Richard 1895- *ConAu P-1,*
WrDr 84
Thiele, Margaret R 1901- *ConAu 21R,*
WrDr 84
Thielen, Thoralf Theodore 1921- *ConAu 5R*
Thielens, Wagner P, Jr. 1925- *ConAu 1R*
Thielicke, Helmut 1908- *ConAu 11NR, –69,*
IntAu&W 82
Thien-An, Thich 1926- *ConAu 57*
Thier, Herbert D 1932- *ConAu 29R*
Thierauf, Robert James 1933- *ConAu 29R,*
WrDr 84
Thierrin, Paul 1923- *IntAu&W 82*
Thiesenhusen, William C 1936- *ConAu 21R*
Thiess, Frank 1890- *CnMD, TwCA,*
TwCA SUP
Thiessen, John 1931- *ConAu 41R*
Thiessen, John C 1890- *ConAu 5R*
Thiher, Allen 1941- *ConAu 41R*
Thilakam, Neela *IntWWP 82X*
Thiman, Eric Harding 1900- *ConAu P-1*
Thimann, Kenneth Vivian 1904- *WrDr 84*
Thimblethorpe, June Sylvia *WrDr 84*
Thimm, Alfred L 1923- *ConAu 8NR, –61*
Thimmesch, Nicholas 1927- *WrDr 84*
Thimmesch, Nick 1927- *ConAu 13R*
Thines, Georges Louis Jean Hubert 1923-
IntAu&W 82
Thiong'o, Ngugi Wa *ConAu X*
Thirion, Andre 1907- *ConAu 101*
Thirkell, Angela Margaret 1890-1961 *ConAu 93,*
LongCTC, ModBrL, TwCA, TwCA SUP,
TwCWr
Thirkell, John *WrDr 84*
Thirkell, John Henry 1913- *ConAu 10NR, –13R*
Thirkell, Lance 1921- *WrDr 84*
Thirleby, Ashley *IntAu&W 82X*
Thirlwall, John C 1904- *ConAu 69*
Thirsk, Irene Joan 1922- *IntAu&W 82,*
WrDr 84
Thirsk, Joan 1922- *ConAu 25R*
Thiry, Marcel 1897-1977 *CIDMEL 80*
Thisby *ConAu X*
Thistle, Mel 1914- *ConAu 53, WrDr 84*
Thistlethwaite, Miles 1945- *SmATA 12*
Thoby-Marcelin, Philippe 1904-1975 *ConAu 61,*
ModBlW, ModFrL, TwCA SUP
Thody, Philip 1928- *ConAu 1R, –5R, –9NR,*
IntAu&W 82, WrDr 84

Thoene, Alma E 1903- *ConAu 49*
Thoene, Peter *ConAu X, IntAu&W 82X*
Thoger, Marie 1923- *ConAu 11NR, –25R*
Tholfsen, Trygve R 1924- *ConAu 108*
Thollander, Earl 1922- *ConAu 101,*
SmATA 22[port]
Thom, Hendrik Bernardus 1905- *IntAu&W 82*
Thom, James Alexander *DrAP&F 83*
Thom, James Alexander 1933- *ConAu 77*
Thom, Robert 1929-1979 *ConAu 21R, –85*
Thom, Robert Anderson 1915- *ConAu 61*
Thoma, Henry F 1909?-1983 *ConAu 110*
Thoma, Ludwig 1867-1921 *CnMD, ModWD*
Thoma, Richard 1902- *DcLB 4*
Thomae, Betty Kennedy 1920- *ConAu 61,*
IntAu&W 82, IntWWP 82, WrDr 84
Thoman, Richard S 1919- *ConAu 65*
Thomas *IntWWP 82X*
Thomas, A J, Jr. 1918- *ConAu 5R*
Thomas, A J, Jr. 1918-1982 *ConAu 10NR*
Thomas, A R B 1904- *ConAu 65*
Thomas, Abraham V 1934- *ConAu 61*
Thomas, Alan 1933- *ConAu 81*
Thomas, Alan Gradon 1911- *ConAu 25R,*
IntAu&W 82, WrDr 84
Thomas, Alexander 1914- *ConAu 103*
Thomas, Alfred Strickland 1900- *IntAu&W 82,*
WrDr 84
Thomas, Andrea *ConAu X*
Thomas, Ann VanWynen 1919- *ConAu 5R,*
–10NR
Thomas, Anna 1948- *ConAu 41R*
Thomas, Annabel 1929- *ConAu 106*
Thomas, Arline 1913- *ConAu 49*
Thomas, Armstrong 1909?-1975 *ConAu 57*
Thomas, Art 1952- *ConAu 105*
Thomas, Audrey *DrAP&F 83*
Thomas, Audrey 1935- *WrDr 84*
Thomas, Audrey Grace 1935- *AuNews 2,*
ConAu 21R, ConLC 7, –13, ConNov 82,
DcLEL 1940, IntAu&W 82
Thomas, Augustus 1857?-1934 *ModAL,*
ModWD, TwCA
Thomas, Barbara 1945- *ConAmTC*
Thomas, Ben Bowen 1899-1977 *ConAu 108*
Thomas, Bill 1934- *ConAu 8NR, –61,*
IntAu&W 82
Thomas, Bob *ConAu X*
Thomas, Brandon 1856-1914 *LongCTC,*
ModWD
Thomas, Brinley 1906- *IntAu&W 82*
Thomas, Carl H *ConAu X*
Thomas, Charles 1929- *WrDr 84*
Thomas, Charles Columbus *DrAP&F 83*
Thomas, Charles W 1903-1973 *ConAu 41R*
Thomas, Charles W 1943- *ConAu 65*
Thomas, Claire Sherman 1923- *ConAu 108*
Thomas, Clara McCandless 1919- *ConAu 25R,*
IntAu&W 82, WrDr 84
Thomas, Conrad Ward 1914- *ConAu 37R*
Thomas, Conrelius Dickinson 1920-1972
ConAu P-1
Thomas, Craig 1942- *ConAu 108, WrDr 84*
Thomas, D M 1935- *ConLC 13, –22[port],*
ConP 80, TwCSFW
Thomas, Dan 1929- *ConAu X, ConSFA*
Thomas, Daniel B *ConAu X*
Thomas, Daniel H 1904- *ConAu 13R*
Thomas, Dante 1922- *ConAu 53*
Thomas, David 1931- *ConAu 103, WrDr 84*
Thomas, David Arthur 1925- *ConAu 13R,*
WrDr 84
Thomas, David H 1945- *ConAu 108, WrDr 84*
Thomas, David St. John 1929- *IntAu&W 82,*
WrDr 84
Thomas, David Winton 1901-1970 *ConAu P-1*
Thomas, Denis 1922- *ConAu 77, IntAu&W 82,*
WrDr 84
Thomas, Dian 1945- *ConAu 10NR, –65*
Thomas, Donald 1926- *ConAu 49*
Thomas, Donald F 1913- *ConAu 29R*
Thomas, Donald M 1935- *WrDr 84*
Thomas, Donald Michael 1935- *ConAu 61,*
DcLEL 1940, IntAu&W 82
Thomas, Dorothy Swaine 1899-1977 *ConAu 69,*
ConAu P-2
Thomas, Dylan 1914-1953 *CnMD, CnMWL,*
ConAu 104, DcLB 13[port], LongCTC,
ModBrL, ModBrL SUP, ModWD,
RGFMBP, TwCA, TwCA SUP, TwCLC 1,
–8[port], TwCWr, WhoTwCL
Thomas, Earl W 1915- *ConAu 53*

Thomas, Edison H 1912- *ConAu 85*
Thomas, Edmund Barrington 1929- *WrDr 84*
Thomas, Edward 1878-1917 *CnMWL,*
ConAu 106, LongCTC, ModBrL,
ModBrL SUP, RGFMBP, TwCA,
TwCA SUP, TwCLC 10[port], TwCWr,
WhoTwCL
Thomas, Edward Boaden 1901- *IntWWP 82*
Thomas, Edwin J 1927- *ConAu 21R*
Thomas, Elizabeth Ann 1952- *ConAu 85*
Thomas, Elizabeth Marshall 1931- *ConAu 17R,*
IntAu&W 82
Thomas, Emory M 1939- *ConAu 97*
Thomas, Ernest Lewis *WorAu*
Thomas, Ernest Lewys 1904- *ConAu 1NR*
Thomas, Estelle Webb 1899- *ConAu 21R,*
SmATA 26, WrDr 84
Thomas, F Richard *DrAP&F 83*
Thomas, F Richard 1940- *ConAu 77*
Thomas, Franklin Richard 1940- *IntWWP 82*
Thomas, G K *ConAu X*
Thomas, George Finger 1899-1977 *ConAu 73*
Thomas, George I 1915- *ConAu 25R*
Thomas, George Leicester, Jr. 1907- *ConAu P-1*
Thomas, Gilbert Oliver 1891- *ConAu 5R*
Thomas, Gordon 1933- *ConAu 9R,*
IntAu&W 82, WrDr 84
Thomas, Gordon L 1914- *ConAu 37R*
Thomas, Graham Charles Gordon 1942-
IntAu&W 82
Thomas, Graham Stuart 1909- *ConAu 4NR, –9R,*
IntAu&W 82, WrDr 84
Thomas, Gwyn 1913-1981 *ConAu 103, –65,*
CroCD, DcLB 15[port], DcLEL 1940,
LongCTC, TwCWr, WorAu
Thomas, Gwyn 1931-1981 *ConAu 9NR*
Thomas, H C *ConAu X, SmATA X*
Thomas, Harold Becken 1888-1971 *ConAu 104*
Thomas, Heather Smith 1944- *ConAu 6NR, –57*
Thomas, Helen 1877-1967 *CnMWL*
Thomas, Helen A 1920- *ConAu 101*
Thomas, Helen Douglass *IntWWP 82X*
Thomas, Helen Shirley 1931-1968 *ConAu 5R,*
–103
Thomas, Henri 1912- *CIDMEL 80, ConAu P-1*
Thomas, Henry 1886-1970 *ConAu 29R*
Thomas, Hugh 1931- *WrDr 84*
Thomas, Hugh Swynnerton 1931- *ConAu 5NR,*
–9R, DcLEL 1940, IntAu&W 82, WorAu
Thomas, I D E 1921- *ConAu 65*
Thomas, Ivo Herbert Christopher 1912-
ConAu 5R
Thomas, Ivor *WrDr 84*
Thomas, J C *ConAu 57*
Thomas, J D 1910- *ConAu 6NR, –57*
Thomas, J F *ConAu X, SmATA 8*
Thomas, J James 1933- *ConAu 53*
Thomas, J W 1917- *ConAu 101*
Thomas, Jack Ray 1931- *ConAu 41R*
Thomas, Jack W 1930- *ConAu 1NR, –49*
Thomas, James *DrAP&F 83*
Thomas, Jane Resh 1936- *ConAu 106*
Thomas, Jeannette Grise 1935- *ConAu 101*
Thomas, Jessie O *LivgBAA*
Thomas, Jim *ConAu X*
Thomas, Jim 1930- *IntWWP 82*
Thomas, Joan Gale *ConAu X, IntAu&W 82X,*
SmATA 4, –7, TwCCW 83, WrDr 84
Thomas, John 1890- *ConAu 49*
Thomas, John 1900-1932 *DcLB 4*
Thomas, John Allen Miner 1900-1932 *ConAu 107*
Thomas, John Hunter 1928- *ConAu 57*
Thomas, John Lawrence 1910- *ConAu 5R*
Thomas, Joyce Carol *DrAP&F 83*
Thomas, K H *ConAu X*
Thomas, Keith 1933- *ConAu 37R*
Thomas, Kenneth Bryn 1915-1978 *ConAu 81*
Thomas, Latta R 1927- *ConAu 65*
Thomas, Lawrence L 1924- *ConAu 45*
Thomas, Lee *ConAu X, WrDr 84*
Thomas, Lee 1918- *ConAu 1R, –1NR*
Thomas, Leslie 1931- *WrDr 84*
Thomas, Leslie John 1931- *ConAu 13R*
Thomas, Lewis 1913- *ConAu 85, WrDr 84*
Thomas, Lewis H 1917- *ConAu 73*
Thomas, Lionel Arthur John 1915- *CreCan 2*
Thomas, Lionel H C 1922?-1978 *ConAu 104*
Thomas, Liz *ConAu X*
Thomas, Lorenzo *DrAP&F 83*
Thomas, Lorenzo 1944- *ConAu 73, LivgBAA*
Thomas, Lowell Jackson 1892-1981 *AuNews 1, –2,*
ConAu 3NR, –104, –45, TwCA,

TwCA SUP
Thomas, Lowell Jackson, Jr. 1923- *ConAu 85, SmATA 15*
Thomas, M Halsey 1903-1977 *ConAu 25R, -73*
Thomas, Mack 1928- *ConAu 9R*
Thomas, Martin 1913- *ConSFA*
Thomas, Mary Martha Hosford 1927- *ConAu 53*
Thomas, Mason Page, Jr. 1928- *ConAu 25R*
Thomas, Mervyn *ConAu X*
Thomas, Michael *ConAu X*
Thomas, Michael Wolf 1945- *IntAu&W 82*
Thomas, Miles 1897-1980 *ConAu 105*
Thomas, Neal *ConAu X*
Thomas, Norman 1884-1968 *ConAu 101, -25R*
Thomas, Norman C 1932- *ConAu 17R*
Thomas, Norman L 1925- *ConAu 41R*
Thomas, Owen Clark 1922- *ConAu 9R*
Thomas, Patricia J 1934- *ConAu 37R*
Thomas, Paul 1908- *ConAu P-1, IntAu&W 82, WrDr 84*
Thomas, Peter *DrAP&F 83*
Thomas, Peter 1928- *ConAu 37R, IntWWP 82, MichAu 80*
Thomas, Piri *DrAP&F 83, WrDr 84*
Thomas, Piri 1928- *ConAu 73, ConLC 17*
Thomas, Powys 1925- *CreCan 2*
Thomas, R Hinton 1912- *ConAu 5R, -5NR*
Thomas, R Hinton 1912-1983 *ConAu 110*
Thomas, R Murray 1921- *ConAu 7NR, -17R*
Thomas, R S 1913- *ConAu 89, ConLC 13, ConP 80, RGFMBP, WrDr 84*
Thomas, Richard 1951- *ConAu 107*
Thomas, Robert 1930- *ConAu 25R*
Thomas, Robert C 1925- *ConAu 101*
Thomas, Robert Joseph 1922- *ConAu 77*
Thomas, Rollin George 1896- *ConAu P-1*
Thomas, Ronald Stuart 1913- *ConLC 6, DcLEL 1940, LongCTC, ModBrL, ModBrL SUP, TwCWr, WhoTwCL, WorAu*
Thomas, Roscoe A 1928- *LivgBAA*
Thomas, Ross 1926- *ConAu 33R, TwCCr&M 80, WrDr 84*
Thomas, S Claudewell 1932- *ConAu 17R*
Thomas, Sara 1911?-1982 *ConAu 106*
Thomas, Scott 1959- *IntWWP 82*
Thomas, Sewell 1884- *ConAu P-1*
Thomas, Sherilyn 1948- *ConAu 73*
Thomas, Sherry *ConAu X*
Thomas, Shirley *ConAu 5R, IntWWP 82*
Thomas, Stanley 1933- *ConAu 21R*
Thomas, Stelleta Marie Angel 1910- *IntWWP 82*
Thomas, Stephen N 1942- *ConAu 89*
Thomas, T M 1933- *ConAu 53*
Thomas, Ted *ConAu X*
Thomas, Theodore L 1920- *ConAu 29R, ConSFA*
Thomas, Thom 1940- *ConAu 108, NatPD 81[port]*
Thomas, Tony 1947- *ConAu 61*
Thomas, Trevor 1907- *IntAu&W 82*
Thomas, Vaughan 1934- *ConAu 81, WrDr 84*
Thomas, Virginia Castleton *ConAu 49*
Thomas, Vonnie *DrAP&F 83*
Thomas, W Ian 1914- *ConAu 17R*
Thomas, William 1906- *ConAu 73*
Thomas, William F 1924- *ConAu 69*
Thomas, William G 1931- *ConAu 93*
Thomas, William LeRoy 1920- *ConAu 41R, IntAu&W 82*
Thomasma, David Charles 1939- *ConAu 104*
Thomason, John William, Jr. 1893-1944 *TwCA, TwCA SUP, TwCWW*
Thomason, Tommy 1949- *ConAu 73*
Thometz, Carol Estes 1938- *ConAu 9R*
Thomey, Tedd 1920- *ConAu 2NR, -5R, WrDr 84*
Thomison, Dennis 1937- *ConAu 53*
Thomlinson, Ralph 1925- *ConAu 41R*
Thommem, George S 1896- *ConAu P-1*
Thompson, A Gray 1928- *ConAu 41R*
Thompson, A L B 1917-1975 *ConAu 5NR, -53, -61*
Thompson, Alan Eric 1924- *ConAu 109*
Thompson, Anne Armstrong 1939- *ConAu 85*
Thompson, Arthur A, Jr. 1940- *ConAu 85*
Thompson, Arthur Bell *WorAu 1970*
Thompson, Arthur W 1920-1966 *ConAu 1R*
Thompson, Baird M 1950- *ConAmTC*
Thompson, Bard 1925- *ConAu 1R, -1NR*
Thompson, Blanche Jennings 1887- *ConAu 5R*
Thompson, Brenda 1935- *ConAu 106,*

SmATA 34[port], WrDr 84
Thompson, Brian 1935- *ConAu 109*
Thompson, Buck *ConAu X*
Thompson, C Mildred 1881-1975 *ConAu 57*
Thompson, Caroline 1956- *ConAu 110*
Thompson, Charles Lowell 1937- *ConAu 3NR, -49*
Thompson, Charles Waters, Jr. *ConAu X*
Thompson, China *ConAu X, WrDr 84*
Thompson, Christine Pullein *SmATA 3*
Thompson, Claude Holmes 1908- *ConAu P-1*
Thompson, Corrie 1887- *ConAu 61*
Thompson, Daniel 1916- *ConAu 13R*
Thompson, David 1938- *ConAu 57*
Thompson, David E *DrAP&F 83*
Thompson, David H 1941- *ConAu 81, SmATA 17*
Thompson, Denman 1833-1911 *ModWD*
Thompson, Dennis F 1940- *ConAu 53*
Thompson, Dennis L 1935- *ConAu 41R*
Thompson, Denys 1907- *ConAu 4NR, -9R*
Thompson, Diana Pullein *SmATA X*
Thompson, Don 1935- *ConAu 53*
Thompson, Donald Eugene 1913- *ConAu 109*
Thompson, Donald L 1930- *ConAu 49*
Thompson, Donald Neil 1939- *ConAu 37R, WrDr 84*
Thompson, Donnis H 1937- *LivgBAA*
Thompson, Donnis Stark 1928- *ConAu 21R*
Thompson, Dorothy 1894-1961 *ConAu 89, TwCA, TwCA SUP*
Thompson, Duane G 1933- *ConAu 73*
Thompson, Earl 1931?-1978 *ConAu 81, -85*
Thompson, Edgar Tristram 1900- *ConAu 17R, IntAu&W 82*
Thompson, Edward Anthony *WrDr 84*
Thompson, Edward John 1886-1946 *LongCTC, TwCA, TwCA SUP*
Thompson, Edward Thorwald 1928- *ConAu 105*
Thompson, Eileen 1920- *ConAu X, WrDr 84*
Thompson, Elizabeth Allen *MichAu 80*
Thompson, Era Bell 1905- *ConAu 89, LivgBAA*
Thompson, Eric 1912- *ConAu 5R*
Thompson, Ernest Seton 1860-1946 *CreCan 2*
Thompson, Ernest Trice 1894- *ConAu 1R*
Thompson, Esther Lee 1919- *IntWWP 82*
Thompson, Evelyn Wingo 1921- *ConAu 21R*
Thompson, Ewa M 1937- *ConAu 49*
Thompson, Flora 1877?-1947 *LongCTC*
Thompson, Frances C 1906- *ConAu P-1*
Thompson, Francis 1859-1907 *ConAu 104, LongCTC, TwCLC 4[port]*
Thompson, Francis George 1931- *ConAu 106, WrDr 84*
Thompson, Frank Hugh, Jr. 1926- *ConAu 25R*
Thompson, Fred Dalton 1942- *ConAu 69*
Thompson, Fred P, Jr. 1917- *ConAu 89*
Thompson, G R 1937- *ConAu 2NR, -45*
Thompson, Gary *DrAP&F 83*
Thompson, Gene *TwCWW, WrDr 84*
Thompson, Gene 1924- *ConAu 103, -104*
Thompson, George Clifford 1920- *ConAu 104*
Thompson, George G 1914- *ConAu 21R*
Thompson, George Selden *WrDr 84*
Thompson, George Selden 1929- *ConAu 5R, SmATA 4*
Thompson, Gerald E 1924- *ConAu 53*
Thompson, Harlan H 1894- *ConAu P-1, SmATA 10*
Thompson, Harry C 1921?-1980 *ConAu 97*
Thompson, Harwood 1894- *ConAu 65*
Thompson, Helen M 1903- *ConAu P-1*
Thompson, Henry O 1931- *ConAu 45*
Thompson, Hildegard 1901- *ConAu 17R, IntAu&W 82, WrDr 84*
Thompson, Hunter S 1939- *ConAu 17R, ConLC 9, -17, IntAu&W 82*
Thompson, Ian Bentley 1936- *ConAu 37R, IntAu&W 82, WrDr 84*
Thompson, Irene 1919- *ConAu 110*
Thompson, J Eric S 1898-1975 *ConAu 61, -65*
Thompson, Jack Maynard 1924- *ConAu 41R*
Thompson, Jacqueline 1945- *ConAu 97*
Thompson, James 1902-1983 *ConAu 109*
Thompson, James 1932- *ConAu 73, WrDr 84*
Thompson, James D 1920-1973 *ConAu P-2*
Thompson, James H *ConAu X*
Thompson, James Matthew 1878- *TwCA SUP*
Thompson, James W *DrAP&F 83*
Thompson, James W 1935- *ConAu 105, LivgBAA, MichAu 80*
Thompson, Jean *DrAP&F 83*

Thompson, Jeanie *DrAP&F 83*
Thompson, Jesse J 1919- *WrDr 84*
Thompson, Jesse Jackson 1919- *ConAu 5R*
Thompson, Joan 1943- *ConAu 97*
Thompson, Joan Berengild 1915- *ConAu 17R*
Thompson, Joanna *DrAP&F 83*
Thompson, Joe Allen 1936- *ConAu 37R*
Thompson, John 1918- *ConAu 5R*
Thompson, John A *DrAP&F 83*
Thompson, John Leslie 1917- *ConAu 5R*
Thompson, Josephine Pullein *SmATA X*
Thompson, Josiah 1935- *ConAu 41R, -77*
Thompson, Joyce *DrAP&F 83*
Thompson, Julius Eric 1946- *ConAu 49, LivgBAA, WrDr 84*
Thompson, Karl F 1917- *ConAu 37R*
Thompson, Kay 1912- *ConAu 85, SmATA 16*
Thompson, Ken D 1926- *ConAu 65*
Thompson, Kenneth W 1921- *ConAu 1R, -5NR, -9R, IntAu&W 82, WrDr 84*
Thompson, Kent Elgin 1936- *ConAu 49, WrDr 84*
Thompson, Kristin 1950- *ConAu 108*
Thompson, Larry E *DrAP&F 83*
Thompson, Laura 1905- *ConAu 53*
Thompson, Laurence C 1926- *ConAu 5R, -7NR*
Thompson, Laurence Graham 1920- *ConAu 37R, IntAu&W 82, WrDr 84*
Thompson, Lawrance 1906-1973 *ConAu 10NR*
Thompson, Lawrance Roger 1906-1973 *ConAu 5R, -41R*
Thompson, Lawrence Sidney 1916- *ConAu 5NR, -9R, WrDr 84*
Thompson, Leonard Monteath 1916- *ConAu 1R, -1NR*
Thompson, Lewis 1915?-1972 *ConAu 37R*
Thompson, Loring M 1918- *ConAu 45*
Thompson, Luther Joe 1918- *ConAu 21R*
Thompson, Marian Spitzer 1899?-1983 *ConAu 110*
Thompson, Marilyn *DrAP&F 83*
Thompson, Mary Wolfe 1886- *ConAu X*
Thompson, Mel 1929- *ConAu 73*
Thompson, Morris Mordecai 1912- *ConAu 109*
Thompson, Neil 1929- *ConAu 108, IntAu&W 82, WrDr 84*
Thompson, Neville 1938- *ConAu 37R, WrDr 84*
Thompson, Nola D 1927- *WrDr 84*
Thompson, Paul 1935- *ConAu 21R*
Thompson, Paul 1943- *ConAu 77, IntAu&W 82*
Thompson, Phyllis 1926- *ConAu X, IntWWP 82*
Thompson, Phyllis Hoge *DrAP&F 83*
Thompson, Ralph 1904-1979 *ConAu 89*
Thompson, Ralph 1910- *ConAu 53*
Thompson, Richard 1924- *ConAu 9R*
Thompson, Richard Arlen 1930- *ConAu 61*
Thompson, Robert 1916- *ConAu 49, IntAu&W 82, WrDr 84*
Thompson, Robert Bruce 1920- *IntWWP 82, WrDr 84*
Thompson, Robert Elliott 1921- *AuNews 2, ConAu 77*
Thompson, Robert Farris 1932- *ConAu 103*
Thompson, Robert Norman 1914- *ConAu 106, WrDr 84*
Thompson, Robert S *DrAP&F 83*
Thompson, Roger Francis 1933- *ConAu 73, WrDr 84*
Thompson, Roy Anton 1897- *ConAu P-2*
Thompson, Russ *ConAu X*
Thompson, Ruth Plumly 1891-1976 *DcLB 22[port]*
Thompson, Samuel M 1902-1983 *ConAu 110*
Thompson, Sandra *DrAP&F 83*
Thompson, Sandra S *DrAP&F 83*
Thompson, Sharon *DrAP&F 83*
Thompson, Stanbury Dugard 1905- *ConAu P-1*
Thompson, Stith 1885-1976 *ConAu 5R, -5NR, -61, SmATA 20N*
Thompson, Susan O 1931- *ConAu 85*
Thompson, Sylvia Elizabeth 1902-1968 *LongCTC, ModBrL, TwCA, TwCA SUP*
Thompson, Sylvia Vaughn *WrDr 84*
Thompson, Sylvia Vaughn 1935- *ConAu 5R*
Thompson, Thomas 1913- *TwCWW, WrDr 84*
Thompson, Thomas 1933- *ConAu 65*
Thompson, Thomas 1933-1982 *ConAu 108*
Thompson, Thomas 1935- *IntAu&W 82*
Thompson, Thomas Kirkland 1914- *ConAu 13R*
Thompson, Toby 1944- *ConAu 65*
Thompson, Tom 1953- *IntWWP 82*

Thompson, Travis I 1937- *ConAu 37R*
Thompson, Victor A 1912- *ConAu 25R*
Thompson, Virginia 1937- *ConAu 108*
Thompson, Vivian L 1911- *ConAu 1R, -1NR,*
    IntAu&W 82, SmATA 3, WrDr 84
Thompson, W Scott 1942- *ConAu 25R,*
    IntAu&W 82
Thompson, Wayne C 1943- *ConAu 109*
Thompson, Wayne N 1914- *ConAu 21R*
Thompson, Wilbur R 1923- *ConAu 13R*
Thompson, Willa 1916- *ConAu 9R*
Thompson, Willard Mead 1913- *ConAu 5R*
Thompson, William A 1931- *ConAu 77*
Thompson, William B 1914- *WrDr 84*
Thompson, William Bernard 1914- *ConAu P-1*
Thompson, William C L *ConAu X*
Thompson, William David 1929- *ConAu 17R,*
    WrDr 84
Thompson, William E, Jr. 1923- *ConAu 13R*
Thompson, William Fletcher, Jr. 1929-
    ConAu 1R
Thompson, William Irwin 1938- *ConAu 9NR,*
    -21R, WrDr 84
Thompson, Wolfe *ConAu X*
Thoms, Herbert 1885-1972 *ConAu 110*
Thomsen, Harry 1928- *ConAu 5R*
Thomsen, Moritz 1915- *ConAu 29R*
Thomsen, Otto Asmus 1907- *IntAu&W 82*
Thomsen, Russel J 1941- *ConAu 37R*
Thomson, Sir Arthur 1861-1933 *LongCTC*
Thomson, Arthur Alexander Malcolm 1894-1968
    ConAu P-1, LongCTC
Thomson, Basil 1861-1939 *ConAu 110,*
    TwCCr&M 80
Thomson, Betty Flanders 1913- *ConAu 9R*
Thomson, Charles Leslie 1914- *ConAu 9R*
Thomson, D H 1918- *IntAu&W 82X, WrDr 84*
Thomson, Daisy Hicks 1918- *ConAu 103,*
    IntAu&W 82
Thomson, Dale C 1923- *ConAu 25R*
Thomson, David 1912-1970 *ConAu 1R, -2NR,*
    -29R
Thomson, David 1914- *ConAu 107, WrDr 84*
Thomson, David Landsborough 1901-1964
    LongCTC
Thomson, Derick S 1921- *ConAu 25R, ConP 80,*
    WrDr 84
Thomson, Don W *IntAu&W 82X*
Thomson, Donald Walter 1906- *IntAu&W 82*
Thomson, Douglas Ferguson Scott 1919-
    ConAu 41R
Thomson, Edward *ConAu X, TwCSFW,*
    WrDr 84
Thomson, Edward William 1849-1924 *CreCan 2,*
    TwCA
Thomson, F P 1914- *ConAu 21R*
Thomson, Francis Paul 1914- *IntAu&W 82,*
    WrDr 84
Thomson, Frank S 1881-1975 *ConAu 57*
Thomson, Garry 1925- *ConAu 109*
Thomson, George Derwent 1903- *TwCA SUP*
Thomson, George Henry 1924- *ConAu 21R,*
    IntAu&W 82, WrDr 84
Thomson, George Ian Falconer 1912-
    IntAu&W 82, WrDr 84
Thomson, George Malcolm 1899- *ConAu 9R,*
    IntAu&W 82, WrDr 84
Thomson, Sir George Paget 1892-1975
    ConAu 4NR, -5R, -61, LongCTC
Thomson, Gladys Scott *LongCTC*
Thomson, Ian F 1912- *ConAu 9R*
Thomson, Irene Taviss 1941- *ConAu 29R*
Thomson, J A K 1879-1959 *LongCTC*
Thomson, James C 1909- *ConAu 61*
Thomson, James C, Jr. 1931- *ConAu 29R*
Thomson, James Miln 1921- *ConAu 109,*
    WrDr 84
Thomson, Joan *ConAu X*
Thomson, John 1936- *ConAu 109*
Thomson, Sir John Arthur 1861-1933 *TwCA,*
    TwCA SUP
Thomson, John H *IntAu&W 82X*
Thomson, Jonathan H *ConAu X, WrDr 84*
Thomson, June 1930- *ConAu 81, IntAu&W 82,*
    TwCCr&M 80, WrDr 84
Thomson, Keith 1912- *ConAu 29R*
Thomson, Peggy 1922- *ConAu 85,*
    SmATA 31[port]
Thomson, Peter 1913- *ConAu 5R*
Thomson, Peter 1938- *ConAu 108, WrDr 84*
Thomson, Randall J 1946- *ConAu 109*
Thomson, Robert 1921- *ConAu 25R,*

IntAu&W 82, WrDr 84
Thomson, Robert William 1934- *ConAu 104*
Thomson, Ronald William 1908- *ConAu 25R*
Thomson, Roy Herbert 1894-1976 *ConAu 69*
Thomson, S Harrison 1895-1975 *ConAu 41R*
Thomson, Samuel Harrison 1895-1972 *ConAu 61*
Thomson, Sharon *DrAP&F 83*
Thomson, Thomas John 1877-1917 *CreCan 1*
Thomson, Tom 1877-1917 *CreCan 1*
Thomson, Virgil 1896- *ConAu 41R,*
    IntAu&W 82, TwCA, TwCA SUP
Thomson, William 1906- *WrDr 84*
Thomson, William A 1879-1971 *ConAu 33R*
Thomson, William Archibald Robson 1906-
    ConAu 103, IntAu&W 82
Thomssen, Wolfdietrich *IntWWP 82X*
Thomy, Al *ConAu 69*
Thonssen, Lester 1904- *ConAu 5R*
Thor, Johannes *WorAu*
Thor, Tristan *WorAu*
Thorat, Sudhakar S 1935- *ConAu 45*
Thorburn, David 1940- *ConAu 7NR, -53*
Thorburn, Hugh G 1924- *ConAu 13R*
Thorburn, James Alexander 1923- *IntWWP 82*
Thorelli, Hans B 1921- *ConAu 6NR, -13R,*
    IntAu&W 82, WrDr 84
Thoren, Arne 1927- *ConAu 69*
Thorer, Konrad *ConAu X*
Thoresen, Carl E 1933- *ConAu 57*
Thorgeirsson, Thorgeir 1933- *IntAu&W 82*
Thorlby, Anthony K 1928- *ConAu 25R*
Thorman, Donald J 1924-1977 *ConAu 17R, -73*
Thorman, Richard 1924- *ConAu 105*
Thormodsson, Ulfar 1944- *IntAu&W 82*
Thorn, Barbara *ConAu X*
Thorn, John 1947- *ConAu 97*
Thorn, Richard S 1929- *ConAu 17R*
Thorn, Ronald Scott *ConAu X*
Thorn, William E 1923- *ConAu 9R*
Thornber, Jean H 1919- *ConAu 61*
Thornbrough, Emma Lou 1913- *ConAu 25R*
Thornburg, Hershel D 1936- *ConAu 37R*
Thornburg, Newton *DrAP&F 83*
Thornburg, Newton K 1930- *ConAu 9NR, -21R*
Thorndike, Ashley Horace 1871-1933 *TwCA*
Thorndike, Joseph J 1913- *WrDr 84*
Thorndike, Lynn 1882-1965 *TwCA SUP*
Thorndike, Robert Ladd 1910- *ConAu 1R, -1NR*
Thorndike, Russell 1885-1972 *ConAu 37R,*
    LongCTC
Thorndike, Susan 1944- *ConAu 41R*
Thorndyke, Helen Louise *ConAu P-2,*
    SmATA 1
Thorne, Anthony Charles 1926- *IntWWP 82*
Thorne, Bliss K 1916- *ConAu 17R*
Thorne, Bradley D *ConAu X*
Thorne, Christopher 1934- *ConAu 11NR, -21R,*
    WrDr 84
Thorne, Edouard *ConAu X*
Thorne, Florence Calvert 1878?-1973 *ConAu 41R*
Thorne, Hart *ConAu X*
Thorne, Ian *ConAu X, SmATA X*
Thorne, Jean Wright *ConAu X*
Thorne, Jim 1922- *ConAu 1R, -1NR*
Thorne, Joy Coghill *CreCan 2*
Thorne, Kirby *ConAu X*
Thorne, Nicola *ConAu X, TwCRGW,*
    WrDr 84
Thorne, Ramsay *ConAu X*
Thorne, Sabina 1927- *ConAu 106*
Thorne, Sterling *ConAu X*
Thorne, Ted *ConAu X*
Thorne, Tony *IntWWP 82X*
Thorne, William James 1898- *ConAu 5R*
Thorner, Horace Edward 1909- *IntAu&W 82*
Thornhill, Lionel 1897- *LivgBAA*
Thorning, Joseph Francis 1896- *ConAu P-1*
Thornton, Donald 1936- *IntWWP 82*
Thornton, Francis John 1938- *ConAu 85*
Thornton, Gene *ConAu 93*
Thornton, J Mills, III 1943- *ConAu 77*
Thornton, James W, Jr. 1908- *ConAu 1R, -1NR*
Thornton, Jean Francis 1926- *IntAu&W 82*
Thornton, John Leonard 1913- *ConAu 4NR, -9R,*
    WrDr 84
Thornton, John W 1922- *ConAu 106*
Thornton, John W, Jr. 1948- *ConAu 106*
Thornton, Lee 1944- *ConAu 73*
Thornton, Margaret *IntWWP 82X*
Thornton, Martin 1915- *WrDr 84*
Thornton, Martin Stuart Farrin 1915- *ConAu 9R*
Thornton, Michael 1941- *ConAu 105, WrDr 84*

Thornton, Peter Kai 1925- *ConAu 102*
Thornton, Richard C 1936- *ConAu 81*
Thornton, Thomas Perry 1931- *ConAu 9R*
Thornton, W B *ConAu X, SmATA X*
Thornton, Weldon 1934- *ConAu 25R*
Thornton, Willis 1900- *ConAu P-1*
Thoroarson, Thorbergur 1889-1975 *ClDMEL 80*
Thorp, Duncan Roy 1914- *ConAu 13R*
Thorp, Edward Oakley 1932- *ConAu 21R,*
    IntAu&W 82, WrDr 84
Thorp, Joseph Peter 1873-1962 *LongCTC*
Thorp, Margaret Farrand 1891-1970 *ConAu 104*
Thorp, Roderick 1936- *WrDr 84*
Thorp, Roderick Mayne, Jr. 1936- *ConAu 1R,*
    -6NR
Thorp, Willard 1899- *ConAu 1R, -3NR, -5R,*
    WorAu
Thorpe, Dobbin *ConAu X*
Thorpe, Donald W 1928- *ConAu 29R*
Thorpe, E G 1916- *SmATA 21[port], WrDr 84*
Thorpe, Earl E 1924- *ConAu 61, LivgBAA*
Thorpe, Elliott R 1897- *ConAu 65*
Thorpe, Eustace George 1916- *ConAu 9R*
Thorpe, George P 1913?-1983 *ConAu 110*
Thorpe, James 1876-1949 *LongCTC*
Thorpe, James 1915- *ConAu 2NR, -5R,*
    WrDr 84
Thorpe, Kay *TwCRGW, WrDr 84*
Thorpe, Lewis 1913- *ConAu 9R*
Thorpe, Lewis 1913-1977 *ConAu 10NR*
Thorpe, Louis Peter 1893- *ConAu 1R*
Thorpe, Michael 1932- *ConAu 8NR, -21R*
Thorpe, Peter 1932- *ConAu 57*
Thorpe, Russell T *IntWWP 82X*
Thorpe, Stephen J *DrAP&F 83*
Thorpe, Sylvia 1926- *TwCRGW, WrDr 84*
Thorpe, Trebor *ConAu X, ConSFA*
Thorpe, Trevor *ConAu X*
Thorpe, William 1902- *WrDr 84*
Thorpe, William Homan 1902- *ConAu 2NR, -5R,*
    IntAu&W 82
Thorsell, Richard Lawrence 1938- *ConAu 89*
Thorsen, Effi *IntAu&W 82X*
Thorsen, Erik 1930- *IntAu&W 82*
Thorsen, Harry D, Jr. 1913- *WrDr 84*
Thorslev, Peter L, Jr. 1929- *ConAu 5R*
Thorson, Thomas Landon 1934- *ConAu 17R*
Thorstad, David 1941- *ConAu 57*
Thorstein, Eric *ConAu X, WorAu*
Thorstein Fra Hamri 1938- *CIDMEL 80*
Thorsteinsson, Indridi G 1926- *IntAu&W 82*
Thorsteinsson, Ragnar 1908- *IntAu&W 82*
Thorton, Don Ray *DrAP&F 83*
Thorvall, Kerstin 1925- *ConAu 17R,*
    SmATA 13
Thorwald, Juergen 1916- *ConAu 1NR, -49*
Thouless, Robert Henry 1894- *ConAu 5R, -77,*
    IntAu&W 82, WrDr 84
Thrapp, Dan Lincoln 1913- *ConAu 4NR, -9R*
Thrasher, Crystal 1921- *ConAu 8NR, -61,*
    SmATA 27[port]
Thrasher, Peter Adam 1923- *WrDr 84*
Threlkeld, Richard 1937- *ConAu 65*
Thribb, E J *WrDr 84*
Throckmorton, Burton Hamilton, Jr. 1921-
    ConAu 5R
Throckmorton, Peter 1928- *ConAu 17R*
Throne, Alice Dunn 1910-1973 *ConAu 45*
Throneberry, Jimmy B 1933- *ConAu 89*
Throneburg, James *ConAu 5R*
Thrower, Norman J W 1919- *ConAu 41R*
Thrower, Percy 1913- *WrDr 84*
Thrower, Percy John 1913- *ConAu 4NR, -9R,*
    IntAu&W 82
Thubron, Colin Gerald Dryden 1939- *ConAu 25R,*
    IntAu&W 82, WrDr 84
Thubten, Sigme Norbu 1922- *ConAu 109*
Thuesen, Gerald J 1938- *ConAu 37R*
Thuillier, Jacques 1928- *ConAu 7NR, -9R*
Thulstrup, Ake 1904- *IntAu&W 82*
Thulstrup, Niels 1924- *ConAu 10NR, -21R*
Thum, Gladys 1920- *ConAu 41R,*
    SmATA 26[port]
Thum, Marcella *ConAu 6NR, -9R,*
    SmATA 28[port], -3, WrDr 84
Thumboo, Edwin Nadason 1933- *IntWWP 82*
Thumm, Garold W 1915- *ConAu 13R*
Thuna, Lee *ConAu X*
Thuna, Leonora 1929- *ConAu 21R*
Thunberg, Lars Anders 1928- *IntAu&W 82*
Thundercloud, Katherine *ConAu X, SmATA X*
Thundy, Zacharias Pontian 1936- *ConAu 102*

Tipton, David 1934- *WrDr 84*
Tipton, Ian Charles 1937- *WrDr 84*
Tipton, James 1942- *ConAu 8NR, –57,*
IntWWP 82, MichAu 80
Tiptree, James, Jr. *ConAu X*
Tiptree, James, Jr. 1915- *DcLB 8*
Tiptree, James, Jr. 1916- *TwCSFW, WrDr 84*
Tira, J *IntWWP 82X*
Tirbutt, Honoria *ConAu 106, WrDr 84*
Tironi, Carla 1926- *IntAu&W 82*
Tirro, Frank 1935- *ConAu 81*
Tiryakian, Edward A 1929- *ConAu 2NR, –5R*
Tischler, Hans 1915- *ConAu 1R, –6NR,*
IntAu&W 82, WrDr 84
Tischler, Nancy Marie 1931- *ConAu 5R*
Tisdale, Celes 1941- *ConAu 57*
Tisdell, Clement Allan 1939- *ConAu 25R,*
IntAu&W 82, WrDr 84
Tise, Larry Edward 1942- *ConAu 102*
Tissant-Bernac, Mathieu *IntAu&W 82X*
Tisserand, Jacques *ConAu X, IntAu&W 82X*
Titchener, James Lampton 1922- *ConAu 45*
Titcomb, Caldwell 1926- *ConAmTC*
Titcomb, Margaret 1891- *ConAu 5R, –5NR*
Titleman, M *IntWWP 82X*
Titler, Dale Milton 1926- *ConAu 81,*
SmATA 28
Titley, David Paul 1929- *ConAu 110, WrDr 84*
Titmarsh, Michael Angelo *SmATA X*
Titmuss, Richard M 1907-1973 *ConAu 109*
Titmuss, Richard Morris 1907-1973 *ConAu 107,*
DcLEL 1940
Titterton, Ernest 1916- *WrDr 84*
Titterton, Ernest William 1916- *ConAu 109,*
IntAu&W 82
Titterton, William Richard 1876-1963 *LongCTC*
Tittle, Charles R 1939- *ConAu 41R*
Tittler, Robert 1942- *ConAu 81*
Tittmann, George Fabian 1915-1978 *ConAu 5R,*
–81
Titus, Barry J 1938- *ConAu 1R*
Titus, Charles 1942- *ConAu 45*
Titus, David Anson 1934- *ConAu 97*
Titus, Edward William 1870-1952 *DcLB 4*
Titus, Eve 1922- *ConAu 29R, SmATA 2,*
TwCCW 83, WrDr 84
Titus, Harold H 1896- *ConAu 5R*
Titus, Tom Warren 1938- *ConAmTC*
Titus, Warren Irving 1921- *ConAu 17R*
Tiusanen, Timo 1936- *ConAu 85, IntAu&W 82*
Tiwana, Dalip Kaur 1935- *IntAu&W 82*
Tjader, Marguerite 1901- *ConAu 17R*
Tjepkes, Michael *DrAP&F 83*
Tjernagel, Neelak S 1906- *ConAu 17R*
Tkacik, Arnold J 1919- *ConAu 81*
Toan, Arthur B, Jr. 1915- *ConAu 25R*
Tobach, Ethel 1921- *ConAu 81*
Toback, James 1944- *ConAu 41R*
Tobe, John Harold 1907-1979 *ConAu 1R, –1NR*
Tobey, George B, Jr. 1917- *ConAu 49*
Tobey, Kathrene McLandress 1908- *ConAu P-2*
Tobey, Mark 1890-1976 *ConAu 65*
Tobey, Ronald C 1942- *ConAu 73*
Tobias, Andrew P 1947- *ConAu 37R, WrDr 84*
Tobias, Arthur *DrAP&F 83*
Tobias, Henry J 1925- *ConAu 41R*
Tobias, John Jacob 1925- *ConAu 53, WrDr 84*
Tobias, Katherine *ConAu X*
Tobias, Philip Vallentine 1925- *IntAu&W 82*
Tobias, Phillip Vallentine 1925- *ConAu 37R*
Tobias, Richard C 1925- *ConAu 29R, WrDr 84*
Tobias, Russell L 1948- *IntWWP 82*
Tobias, Sally Brayley *CreCan 2*
Tobias, Sheila 1935- *ConAu 93*
Tobias, Tobi 1938- *ChlLR 4, ConAu 29R,*
SmATA 5
Tobias-Turner, Bessye *IntWWP 82*
Tobin, James 1918- *ConAu 5NR, –53,*
WrDr 84
Tobin, James Edward 1905-1968 *ConAu P-2*
Tobin, Kay 1930- *ConAu 37R*
Tobin, Richard Lardner 1910- *ConAu 1R, –1NR*
Tobin, Richard Lawrence 1932- *ConAmTC*
Tobin, Sheldon S 1931- *ConAu 110*
Tobin, Terence 1938- *ConAu 53*
Tobino, Mario 1910- *ClDMEL 80, TwCWr*
Toby, Liz *ConAu X*
Toby, Mark 1913?-1972 *ConAu 37R*

Toch, Hans 1930- *ConAu 7NR, –17R*
Toch, Henry *ConAu X*
Toch, Henry 1923- *ConAu 6NR, –9R*
Toczek, Nick 1950- *ConAu 106, WrDr 84*
Tod, Ian J 1945- *ConAu 103*
Tod, Osma Gallinger 1898- *ConAu P-1*
Tod, Osma Gallinger 1898-1982? *ConAu 108*
Todd, Alden 1918- *ConAu 1R, –6NR*
Todd, Anne Ophelia *ConAu X, SmATA 7*
Todd, Barbara Euphan 1890?-1976 *ConAu 104,*
TwCCW 83
Todd, Barbara K 1917- *ConAu 61, SmATA 10*
Todd, Clark 1945?-1983 *ConAu 110*
Todd, Edgeley W 1914- *ConAu 109*
Todd, Edward N 1931- *ConAu 53*
Todd, Frances 1910- *ConAu 13R*
Todd, Frederick Porter 1903-1977 *ConAu 73*
Todd, Galbraith Hall 1914- *ConAu 1R*
Todd, H E 1908- *SmATA 11, TwCCW 83,*
WrDr 84
Todd, Herbert Eatton 1908- *ConAu P-1*
Todd, Hollis N 1914- *ConAu 57*
Todd, Ian Menzies 1923- *ConAu 69*
Todd, James Maclean 1907- *WrDr 84*
Todd, Janet M 1942- *ConAu 1NR, –49,*
IntAu&W 82
Todd, Jerry D 1941- *ConAu 53*
Todd, John M 1918- *WrDr 84*
Todd, John Murray 1918- *ConAu 9R,*
IntAu&W 82
Todd, Leonard 1940- *ConAu 65*
Todd, Loreto 1942- *ConAu 107, SmATA 30*
Todd, Mabel Loomis 1856?-1932 *TwCA,*
TwCA SUP
Todd, Malcolm 1939- *ConAu 101*
Todd, Margaret G 1859- *LongCTC*
Todd, Paul *ConAu X, WrDr 84*
Todd, Ruth VanDorn 1889?-1976 *ConAu 65*
Todd, Ruthven 1914- *ConAu 81, LongCTC,*
ModBrL, TwCA SUP
Todd, Theodora *DrAP&F 83*
Todd, Virgil H 1921- *ConAu 106*
Todd, Vivian Edmiston 1912- *ConAu 17R*
Todd, William Burton 1919- *ConAu 41R*
Todd, William Mills, III 1944- *ConAu 65*
Todhunter, John 1839-1916 *LongCTC*
Todman, Bill *ConAu X*
Todman, William S 1916-1979 *ConAu 89*
Todorov, Tzvetan 1939- *ConAu 73*
Todrank, Gustave Herman 1924- *ConAu 41R*
Todrin, Boris 1915- *ConAu 61, IntAu&W 82*
Todsicher, J Edgar 1926- *ConAu 29R*
Toekes, Rudolf L 1935- *ConAu 21R*
Toepfer, Ray Grant 1923- *ConAu 21R*
Toeplitz, Jerzy 1909- *ConAu 65, IntAu&W 82*
Toernqvist, Egil 1932- *ConAu 29R*
Toffler, Alvin 1928- *ConAu 13R,*
ConIsC 1[port], DcLEL 1940, WrDr 84
Toft, John 1933- *ConAu 103, WrDr 84*
Tofte, Arthur 1902-1980 *ConAu 103, –73*
Tohata, Seiichi 1899-1983 *ConAu 110*
Toka, Salchak Kalbakkhoreviich 1901-1973
ConAu 41R
Tokayer, Marvin 1936- *ConAu 102*
Toker, Franklin K B S 1944- *ConAu 81*
Toklas, Alice B 1877-1967 *ConAu 25R, –81,*
DcLB 4, LongCTC
Tolan, Stephanie S *DrAP&F 83*
Tolan, Stephanie S 1942- *ConAu 77*
Toland, John 1912- *WrDr 84*
Toland, John Willard 1912- *ConAu 1R, –6NR,*
WorAu
Tolbert, E L 1915- *ConAu 1R, –3NR*
Tolbert, Frances Xavier 1912- *ConAu 1R*
Tolbert, Frank X 1912- *ConAu X, TwCWW*
Tolbert, Malcolm O 1924- *ConAu 65*
Tolby, Arthur *ConAu X*
Toledano, Ralph De 1916- *AuNews 1,*
ConAu 9R, WrDr 84
Toledano, Roulhac 1938- *ConAu 101*
Tolegian, Aram 1909- *ConAu 1R, –6NR*
Tolf, Robert W 1929- *ConAu 73*
Tolgesy, Victor 1928- *CreCan 1*
Tolgyesy, Victor 1928- *CreCan 1*
Tolischus, Otto David 1890-1967 *ConAu 93*
Toliver, Harold E 1932- *ConAu 21R*
Toliver, Raymond Frederick 1914- *ConAu 17R,*
WrDr 84
Tolkien, J R R 1892-1973 *ConAu P-2, ConLC 8,*
–12, DcLB 15[port], SmATA 24N,
–32[port], TwCCW 83, TwCSFW B
Tolkien, John Ronald Reuel 1892-1973 *AuNews 1,*

CnMWL, ConAu 45, ConLC 1, –2, –3,
LongCTC, ModBrL, ModBrL SUP,
SmATA 2, TwCWr, WhoTwCL, WorAu
Toll, Robert Charles 1938- *ConAu 53, WrDr 84*
Toll, Seymour I 1925- *ConAu 29R*
Tollas, Tibor *IntWWP 82X*
Toller, Ernst 1893-1939 *ClDMEL 80, CnMD,*
CnMWL, ConAu 107, LongCTC, ModGL,
ModWD, TwCA, TwCA SUP,
TwCLC 10[port], WhoTwCL
Toller, Kate Caffrey *ConAu X*
Tollers, Vincent L 1939- *ConAu 57*
Tollerud, Jim *DrAP&F 83*
Tolles, Frederick B 1915-1975 *ConAu 5R, –103*
Tolles, Martha 1921- *ConAu 49, SmATA 8*
Tolley, Howard B, Jr. 1943- *ConAu 53*
Tolley, Kemp 1908- *ConAu 45*
Tolley, William Pearson 1900- *ConAu 93*
Tolman, Newton F 1908- *ConAu 1R*
Tolmie, Ken 1941- *SmATA 15*
Tolmie, Kenneth Donald 1941- *ConAu 69*
Tolnai, Karoly *ConAu X*
Tolnai, Vagujhelyi Karoly *ConAu X*
Tolson, M B 1898?-1966 *WorAu*
Tolson, M B 1900-1966 *ConAu 89*
Tolson, Melvin Beaunorus 1900-1966 *ModBlW*
Tolstoi, Aleksei 1882-1945 *ConAu X, ModSL 1*
Tolstoi, Aleksei 1883-1945 *ModWD*
Tolstoi, Leo 1828-1910 *ModWD,*
SmATA 26[port]
Tolstoi, Lev 1828-1910 *ModSL 1*
Tolstoy, Aleksey Nikolayevich 1883-1945
ClDMEL 80
Tolstoy, Alexandra L 1884-1979 *ConAu 65, –89,*
LongCTC
Tolstoy, Alexei 1883-1945 *CnMD*
Tolstoy, Alexey 1882-1945 *TwCSFW A*
Tolstoy, Alexey Nikolaevich 1882-1945
ConAu 107
Tolstoy, Alexey Nikolayevich 1882?-1945
LongCTC, TwCA, TwCA SUP, TwCWr
Tolstoy, Dimitry 1912- *ConAu 29R*
Tolstoy, Leo 1828-1910 *ConAu 104,*
TwCLC 4[port], –11[port]
Tolstoy, Leo Nikolayevich 1828-1910 *LongCTC*
Tolstoy, Leo Nikolayevitch 1828-1910 *CnMD*
Tolstoy, Lev Nikolayevich 1828-1910
ClDMEL 80
Tolstoy, Mary Koutouzov 1884?-1976 *ConAu 69*
Tolstoy, Nikolai 1935- *ConAu 81,*
IntAu&W 82
Tolzmann, Don Heinrich 1945- *ConAu 2NR, –49*
Tomadakis, Nicholas 1907- *IntAu&W 82*
Tomalin, Claire 1933- *ConAu 89, WrDr 84*
Tomalin, Miles *WrDr 84*
Tomalin, Nicholas 1931-1973 *ConAu 45*
Tomalin, Ruth *ConAu 13R, DcLEL 1940,*
IntAu&W 82, SmATA 29[port],
TwCCW 83, WrDr 84
Toman, Josef 1899- *TwCWr*
Toman, Walter 1920- *ConAu 5R, WrDr 84*
Tomas, Andrew Paul *ConAu 73*
Tomas, Boris *IntAu&W 82X*
Tomas-Cabot, Jose 1930- *IntAu&W 82*
Tomasek, Robert D 1928- *ConAu 17R*
Tomasevic, Nebojsa 1929- *ConAu 81,*
IntAu&W 82
Tomasi, Giuseppe, Principe DiLampedusa
1896-1957 *CnMWL*
Tomasi DiLampedusa, Giuseppe 1896-1957
ClDMEL 80
Tomasic, D A 1902- *ConAu P-1*
Tomasson, Katherine 1895- *ConAu P-1*
Tomasson, Richard F 1928- *ConAu 1NR, –45*
Tombo, Dolores Mundi *IntWWP 82X*
Tomelty, Joseph 1911- *DcLEL 1940*
Tomes, Margot Ladd 1917- *SmATA 27*
Tomeski, Edward A 1930- *WrDr 84*
Tomeski, Edward Alexander 1930- *ConAu 37R*
Tomfool *ConAu X, SmATA 2*
Tomikel, John 1928- *ConAu 4NR, –53*
Tomizza, Fulvio 1935- *ClDMEL 80*
Tomkiewicz, Mina 1917-1975 *ConAu P-2*
Tomkins, Calvin 1925- *ConAu 8NR, –13R,*
WrDr 84
Tomkins, Jasper *ConAu X*
Tomkins, Mary E 1914- *ConAu 61*
Tomkins, Oliver Stratford 1908- *WrDr 84*
Tomkins, Walker A 1909- *WrDr 84*
Tomkinson, Constance 1915- *ConAu X,*
IntAu&W 82X, WrDr 84
Tomkinson, Michael 1940- *ConAu 93*

Tripp, Wallace 1940- *ConAu 106, SmATA 31*
Trippett, Frank 1926- *ConAu 21R*
Trisco, Robert Frederick 1929- *ConAu 41R*
Triska, Jan Francis 1922- *ConAu 5R, -7NR*
Triton, A N *ConAu X*
Tritt, Robert E 1921- *ConAu 21R*
Trittschuh, Travis Edward 1920- *ConAu 5R*
Trivas, A Victor 1894-1970? *ConAu 29R,
  ConAu P-1*
Trivelpiece, Laurel *DrAP&F 83*
Trivers, Howard 1909- *ConAu 73*
Trivett, Daphne 1940- *ConAu 97, SmATA 22*
Trnka, Jiri 1912-1969 *SmATA 32*
Trobian, Helen R 1918- *ConAu 5R*
Trobisch, Ingrid 1926- *ConAu 97*
Trocchi, Alexander 1925- *ConAu 9R,
  ConNov 82, DcLB 15[port], WrDr 84*
Trocme, Etienne 1924- *ConAu 49*
Troeger, Thomas H 1945- *ConAu 89*
Troelstrup, Arch William 1901- *ConAu 17R*
Troen, Selwyn K 1940- *ConAu 104*
Trofimenkoff, Susan Mann 1941- *ConAu 73*
Trohan, Walter 1903- *ConAu 81*
Troiden, Richard 1946- *ConAu 89,
  IntAu&W 82*
Troise, Joe 1942- *ConAu 103*
Troisgros, Jean 1926-1983 *ConAu 110*
Trojanowicz, John M *ConAu 49*
Trojanowicz, Robert 1941- *ConAu 45,
  MichAu 80*
Trojanski, John 1943- *ConAu 45*
Trolander, Judith Ann 1942- *ConAu 61*
Trolliet, Gilbert 1910- *IntAu&W 82*
Trollope, Anthony 1815-1882 *SmATA 22[port]*
Trollope, Joanna 1943- *ConAu 101, TwCRGW,
  WrDr 84*
Troman, Morley 1918- *ConAu 13R*
Tromanhauser, Edward 1932- *ConAu 41R*
Trombley, Charles C 1928- *ConAu 65*
Tronchin-James, Robert Nevil 1916- *ConAu P-1*
Trooboff, Peter D 1942- *ConAu 65*
Troop, Elizabeth 1931- *ConDr 82B,
  DcLB 14[port]*
Troop, Miriam 1917- *ConAu 13R*
Tropp, Martin 1945- *ConAu 65*
Trosper, Vernette *IntWWP 82X*
Trossau, Burkhard Astl *IntAu&W 82X*
Trost, Lucille W 1938- *ConAu 9NR*
Trost, Lucille Wood 1938- *ConAu 61,
  SmATA 12*
Trotman-Dickenson, Aubrey Fiennes 1926-
  WrDr 84
Trotsky, Leon 1879-1940 *LongCTC*
Trott, Rosemary 1914- *WrDr 84*
Trott, Susan 1937- *ConAu 97*
Trotta, John 1936- *ConAu 45*
Trotter, Grace Violet 1900- *ConAu 1R, -1NR,
  SmATA 10*
Trotter, Jesse McLane d1983 *ConAu 110*
Trotter, Sallie 1915- *ConAu 29R*
Trottier, Gerald 1925- *CreCan 1*
Trottier, Pierre 1925- *CreCan 2*
Trotzig, Birgitta 1929- *ClDMEL 80*
Troubetzkoy, Princess Amelie Rives 1863-1945
  LongCTC, TwCA, TwCA SUP
Troubetzkoy, Dorothy Livingston Ulrich
  IntAu&W 82, IntWWP 82
Troubetzkoy, Ulrich *IntAu&W 82X,
  IntWWP 82X*
Troubridge, Sir St. Vincent 1895-1963 *LongCTC*
Troughton, Joanna 1947- *ConAu 109*
Trouncer, Margaret 1903-1982 *ConAu 10NR*
Trouncer, Margaret Lahey 1903- *IntAu&W 82*
Trouncer, Margaret Lahey 1903-1982 *ConAu 108*
Trouncer, Margaret Lahey 1906- *ConAu 5R*
Troup, Cornelius V 1902- *ConAu P-1*
Troupe, Quincy *DrAP&F 83*
Trout, Kilgore *ConAu X, DrAP&F 83,
  WorAu 1970, WrDr 84*
Troutman, Charles 1914- *ConAu 69*
Trow, W Clark 1894- *ConAu 6NR*
Trow, William Clark 1894- *ConAu 5R*
Trowbridge, Clinton 1928- *ConAu 10NR, -65*
Trowbridge, Keith W 1937- *ConAu 108*
Trowbridge, Leslie Walter 1920- *ConAu 77*
Trowbridge, William *DrAP&F 83*
Trowell, Kathleen Margaret 1904- *ConAu 65*
Troxell, Eugene A 1937- *ConAu 73*
Troxell, Mary D 1907- *ConAu 37R*
Troy, George F, Jr. 1909-1969 *ConAu 1R, -103*
Troy, Katherine *TwCRGW, WrDr 84*
Troy, Lawrence M 1928- *ConAu 21R*

Troy, Leonie Fuller Adams 1899- *IntWWP 82*
Troy, Simon *TwCCr&M 80*
Troy, Una *WrDr 84*
Troy, Una 1913- *ConAu 1R, -3NR*
Troy, William 1903-1961 *ConAu 89, WorAu*
Troyanovich, John M 1936- *ConAu 49*
Troyanovich, Steve *DrAP&F 83*
Troyat, Henri 1911- *ClDMEL 80, ConAu 2NR,
  -45, ConLC 23[port], IntAu&W 82,
  TwCWr, WorAu*
Troyer, Byron Leroy 1909-1980 *ConAu 65*
Troyer, Warner 1932- *ConAu 101*
Troyka, Lynn Quitman 1938- *ConAu 37R*
Truax, Carol 1900- *ConAu 5R, -5NR*
Truax, Charles B 1933- *ConAu P-2*
Truax, R Hawley 1889?-1978 *ConAu 81*
Trubitt, Allen R 1931- *ConAu 77*
Trubo, Richard 1946- *ConAu 11NR, -61*
Trubowitz, Sidney 1926- *ConAu 21R*
Truby, J David 1938- *ConAu 4NR, -53*
Truck, Fred *DrAP&F 83*
Trudeau, G B 1948- *ConAu 81*
Trudeau, Garry *WrDr 84*
Trudeau, Garry 1948- *AuNews 2, ConAu X,
  ConLC 12*
Trudeau, Margaret 1948- *ConAu 93*
Trudeau, Pierre Elliott 1919- *ConAu 3NR, -45*
Trudeau, Yves 1930- *CreCan 2*
Trudel, Jean-Paul 1915- *IntAu&W 82*
Trudel, Marcel 1917- *ConAu 104*
Trudell, Dennis *DrAP&F 83*
Trudix, Marty 1931- *ConAu X*
True, Michael 1933- *ConAu 41R*
Trueblood, Alan Stubbs 1917- *ConAu 103*
Trueblood, D Elton 1900- *ConAu 41R*
Trueblood, John E 1954- *IntWWP 82*
Trueblood, Paul G 1905- *WrDr 84*
Trueblood, Paul Graham 1905- *ConAu P-1,
  IntAu&W 82*
Trueheart, Charles 1951- *ConAu 45*
Truesdale, C W *DrAP&F 83*
Truesdale, C W 1929- *ConAu 29R*
Truesdale, C William 1929- *WrDr 84*
Truesdell, Leon Edgar 1881?-1979 *ConAu 85*
Truett, Fred M 1899- *ConAu P-2*
Truffaut, Francois 1932- *ConAu 81, ConLC 20*
Truitt, Deborah H 1945- *ConAu 45*
Truitt, Evelyn Mack 1931- *ConAu 57*
Truitt, Willis H 1936- *ConAu 57*
Trujillo, Paul Edward 1952- *IntWWP 82*
Trujilo, Paul Edward *DrAP&F 83*
Trull *IntAu&W 82X*
Truman, Harry S 1884-1972 *ConAu 106, -37R*
Truman, Margaret 1924- *ConAu 105*
Truman, Ruth 1931- *ConAu 53, WrDr 84*
Trumbo, Dalton 1905-1976 *ASpks,
  ConAu 10NR, -21R, -69, ConLC 19,
  DcLB 26[port], TwCA, TwCA SUP*
Trumbull, Robert 1912- *ConAu 5NR, -9R*
Trump *CreCan 1*
Trump, Fred 1924- *ConAu 13R*
Trumpener, Ulrich 1930- *ConAu 25R, WrDr 84*
Trumper, Hubert Bagster 1902- *ConAu P-1*
Trundlett, Helen B *ConAu X*
Trungpa, Chogyam 1939- *ConAu 25R,
  IntAu&W 82*
Trunk, Isaiah 1905- *ConAu 89, WrDr 84*
Trunk, Isaiah Elezer 1905-1981 *ConAu 108*
Trupin, James E 1940- *ConAu 37R*
Trupp, Beverly Ann 1937- *ConAu 105*
Truscott, Alan 1925- *ConAu 25R*
Truscott, Lucian K, IV 1947- *ConAu 89,
  WrDr 84*
Truscott, Robert Blake *DrAP&F 83*
Truscott, Robert Blake 1944- *ConAu 77*
Truse, Kenneth 1946- *ConAu 105*
Truss, Jan 1925- *ConAu 102, TwCCW 83*
Truss, Seldon *ConAu X*
Trussell, C P 1892-1968 *ConAu 89*
Trussler, Simon 1942- *ConAu 25R,
  IntAu&W 82, WrDr 84*
Truumaa, Aare 1926- *ConAu 49*
Truzzi, Marcello 1935- *ConAu 41R*
Trylinski, Wladyslaw 1907- *IntAu&W 82*
Tryon, Darrell Trevor 1942- *WrDr 84*
Tryon, Thomas 1926- *ASpks, AuNews 1,
  ConAu 29R, ConLC 3, -11, Conv 1,
  WrDr 84*
Tryon, Tom *ConAu X*
Tryon, Warren S 1901- *ConAu P-1*
Trypanis, C A 1909- *ConAu 7NR*
Trypanis, Constantine 1909- *WrDr 84*

Trypanis, Constantine Athanasius 1909-
  *ConAu 5R, ConP 80, DcLEL 1940,
  IntAu&W 82, IntWWP 82*
Trythall, Anthony John 1927- *ConAu 77*
Trythall, J W D 1944- *ConAu 29R*
Trythall, John 1944- *WrDr 84*
Tsambassis, Alexander N 1919- *ConAu 21R*
Ts'ao, Yu 1905- *ModWD*
Tsatsos, Jeanne 1909- *ConAu 29R*
Tschebotarioff, Gregory P 1899- *ConAu 13R*
Tschichold, Jan 1902?-1974 *ConAu 53*
Tschiffely, A F 1895-1954 *LongCTC*
Tschudy, James Jay 1925- *ConAu 13R*
Tschumi, Raymond 1924- *WrDr 84*
Tschumi, Raymond Robert 1924- *ConAu 3NR,
  -5R, IntAu&W 82, IntWWP 82*
Tschumperlin, Marie Dolores 1945- *IntWWP 82*
Tsegaye, Gabre-Medhin 1936- *ConAu X*
Tsegaye Gabre-Medhin 1936- *ConDr 82*
Tseng, Yu-Ho *ConAu X*
Tshiamala, Kabasele d1983? *ConAu 109*
Tsien, Tsuen-Hsuin 1909- *ConAu 7NR, -17R*
Tsiolkovsky, Konstantin 1857-1935 *TwCSFW A*
Tsipis, Kosta 1934- *ConAu 110*
Tso, Yiu-Kam 1918?-1983 *ConAu 110*
Tsodzo, Thompson Kumbirai 1947- *IntAu&W 82*
Tsongas, George *DrAP&F 83*
Tsongas, Paul Efthemios 1941- *ConAu 108*
Tsou, Tang 1918- *ConAu 5R, -8NR*
Tsuda, Margaret 1921- *IntWWP 82*
Tsui, Kitty *DrAP&F 83*
Tsukahira, Toshio George 1915- *ConAu 21R*
Tsukinabe, Isao *ConAu X*
Tsuneishi, Warren M 1921- *ConAu 17R*
Tsung Su *IntAu&W 82X*
Tsurutani, Taketsugu 1935- *ConAu 104*
Tsushima, Shuji 1909-1948 *ConAu 107, WorAu*
Tsutsui, Minoru 1918- *IntAu&W 82, WrDr 84*
Tsuyuki, Shigeru *IntAu&W 82X*
Tsuzuki, Chushichi 1926- *ConAu 1R, -3NR,
  IntAu&W 82*
Tsvetaeva, Marina Ivanovna 1892-1941
  ConAu 104, TwCLC 7[port]
Tsvetayeva, Marina Ivanovna 1892-1941
  ClDMEL 80, ModSL 1, WorAu
Tu, Wei-Ming 1940- *ConAu 65*
Tuan, Yi-Fu 1930- *ConAu 93*
Tuann, Lucy H C 1938- *ConAu 85*
Tubb, E C 1919- *ConAu 101, ConSFA,
  DrmM[port], TwCSFW, WrDr 84*
Tubbs, Douglas Burnell 1913- *IntAu&W 82*
Tubbs, Stewart L 1943- *ConAu 6NR, -57*
Tucci, Niccolo *DrAP&F 83*
Tucci, Niccolo 1908- *ConAu 81, ConNov 82,
  DcLEL 1940, IntAu&W 82, WorAu,
  WrDr 84*
Tuccille, Jerome 1937- *ConAu 29R, WrDr 84*
Tuchinsky, Joseph S 1937- *ConAu 10NR, -25R*
Tuchman, Barbara 1912- *WrDr 84*
Tuchman, Barbara Wertheim 1912- *ConAu 1R,
  -3NR, ConIsC 1[port], WorAu*
Tuchman, Gaye 1943- *ConAu 85*
Tuchman, Maurice 1936- *ConAu 4NR, -49*
Tucholsky, Kurt 1890-1935 *ModGL*
Tucic, Srdan 1873-1940 *CnMD*
Tuck, Dorothy *ConAu X*
Tuck, James A 1940- *ConAu 37R*
Tucker, Ann *ConAu X*
Tucker, Anne 1945- *ConAu 102*
Tucker, Anthony 1924- *ConAu 104, WrDr 84*
Tucker, Archibald Norman 1904-1980
  ConAu 101
Tucker, Benjamin Ricketson 1854-1939 *TwCA,
  TwCA SUP*
Tucker, Caroline *ConAu X, SmATA X*
Tucker, David M 1937- *ConAu 101*
Tucker, Edward L 1921- *ConAu 17R*
Tucker, Elizabeth A 1957- *IntWWP 82*
Tucker, Ernest Edward 1916-1969 *ConAu 61*
Tucker, Eva 1929- *ConAu 17R*
Tucker, Frank H 1923- *ConAu 10NR, -25R*
Tucker, Gabe *ConAu X*
Tucker, Gaylord B 1915- *ConAu 110*
Tucker, Gene M 1935- *ConAu 37R*
Tucker, Georgina P 1911- *ConAu 97*
Tucker, Gina *ConAu X*
Tucker, Glenn *ConAmTC*
Tucker, Glenn Irving 1892-1976 *ConAu 5R, -69*
Tucker, Harry, Jr. 1921- *ConAu 41R*
Tucker, Helen 1926- *ConAu 11NR, -29R,
  WrDr 84*
Tucker, Irwin St. John 1886-1982 *ConAu 105*

Tucker, James 1929- *ConAu 9NR, –21R, –29R, WrDr 84*
Tucker, Jonathan B 1954- *ConAu 109*
Tucker, Lael *ConAu X*
Tucker, Link *ConAu X, TwCWW*
Tucker, Liza *IntWWP 82X*
Tucker, Marcia 1940- *ConAu 65*
Tucker, Martin *DrAP&F 83*
Tucker, Martin 1928- *ConAu 17R, IntAu&W 82, WrDr 84*
Tucker, Maurice Graham 1912- *WrDr 84*
Tucker, Michael R 1941- *ConAu 61*
Tucker, Nicholas 1936- *ConAu 11NR, –65*
Tucker, Patricia 1912- *ConAu 65*
Tucker, Paul Hayes 1950- *ConAu 110*
Tucker, Robert C 1918- *ConAu 1R, –3NR, IntAu&W 82, WrDr 84*
Tucker, Robin 1950- *ConAu 53*
Tucker, Sterling *LivgBAA*
Tucker, William Edward 1932- *ConAu 3NR, –9R, IntAu&W 82, WrDr 84*
Tucker, William Rayburn 1923- *ConAu 61, IntAu&W 82*
Tucker, Wilson 1914- *ConAu 17R, ConSFA, TwCSFW, WrDr 84*
Tucker-Fettner, Ann *ConAu X*
Tuckey, John S 1921- *ConAu 5R, –7NR*
Tuckman, Bruce W 1938- *ConAu 11NR*
Tuckman, Bruce Wayne 1938- *ConAu 25R, WrDr 84*
Tuckman, Howard P 1941- *ConAu 10NR, –57*
Tuckner, Howard 1932?-1980 *ConAu 101*
Tudhope, Richard *ConAu X*
Tudor, Andrew Frank 1942- *ConAu 107, IntAu&W 82, WrDr 84*
Tudor, Dean 1943- *ConAu 8NR, –61*
Tudor, Nancy 1943- *ConAu 109*
Tudor, Stephen H *DrAP&F 83*
Tudor, Tasha *WrDr 84*
Tudor, Tasha 1915- *ConAu 81, SmATA 20*
Tudyman, Al 1914- *ConAu 21R*
Tuell, Jack Marvin 1923- *ConAu 29R*
Tueni, Nadia 1935-1983 *ConAu 110*
Tuerck, David G 1941- *ConAu 21R*
Tuffnell, Everett S 1917- *ConAu 5R, –7NR*
Tuffs, Jack Elsden 1922- *ConAu 5R*
Tufte, Edward R 1942- *ConAu 1NR, –49*
Tufte, Virginia J 1918- *ConAu 106*
Tufts, Eleanor *ConAu 77*
Tufty, Barbara 1923- *ConAu 37R, IntAu&W 82, WrDr 84*
Tugay, Emine Foat *ConAu X*
Tugendhat, Christopher 1937- *ConAu 89, IntAu&W 82, WrDr 84*
Tugendhat, Julia 1941- *WrDr 84*
Tuggle, A M *DrAP&F 83*
Tuggy, Joy Turner 1922- *ConAu 21R*
Tugwell, Franklin 1942- *ConAu 57*
Tugwell, Rexford Guy 1891-1979 *ConAu 85, –89*
Tulasiewicz, J B 1913- *ConAu 41R*
Tulchin, Joseph S 1939- *ConAu 37R, IntAu&W 82, WrDr 84*
Tulchin, Lewis 1905-1971 *ConAu P-1*
Tuleja, Tad *ConAu X*
Tuleja, Thaddeus F 1944- *ConAu 108*
Tull, Charles Joseph 1931- *ConAu 17R*
Tull, Donald S 1924- *ConAu 81*
Tull, James E 1913- *ConAu 77*
Tullett, James Stuart 1912- *ConAu 106, WrDr 84*
Tullis, F LaMond 1935- *ConAu 81*
Tulloch, G Janet 1924- *ConAu 65*
Tullock, Gordon 1922- *ConAu 1R, –3NR*
Tulloss, Rod *DrAP&F 83*
Tully, Andrew Frederick, Jr. 1914- *ConAu 17R, WrDr 84*
Tully, Gordon F 1935- *ConAu 106*
Tully, Jim 1891?-1947 *TwCA, TwCA SUP*
Tully, John 1923- *ConAu 69, SmATA 14*
Tully, Mary Jo 1937- *ConAu 105*
Tully, Sydney Strickland 1860-1911 *CreCan 1*
Tuma, Mirko 1921- *ConAmTC*
Tumelty, James J 1921?-1979? *ConAu 104*
Tumin, Melvin M 1919- *ConAu 45, WrDr 84*
Tumler, Franz Ernest Aubert 1912- *IntAu&W 82*
Tumpson, Helen *AuNews 1*
Tung, Ling *ConAu X*
Tung, Shih-Tsin 1900- *ConAu 5R*
Tung, William L 1907- *ConAu 85*
Tunick, Stanley B 1900- *ConAu P-1*
Tunink, Wilfrid Bernard 1920- *ConAu 5R*
Tunis, Edwin Burdett 1897-1973 *ChlLR 2,*

ConAu 5R, –7NR, –45, SmATA 1, –24N, –28[port]
Tunis, John R 1889-1975 *DcLB 22[port], TwCCW 83*
Tunis, John Roberts 1889-1975 *ConAu 57, –61, ConLC 12, SmATA 30, TwCA, TwCA SUP*
Tunley, Roul 1912- *ConAu 13R, WrDr 84*
Tunnard, Christopher 1910-1979 *ConAu 5R, –6NR, –85*
Tunnell, Doug 1949- *ConAu 97*
Tunner, William H 1906- *ConAu P-1*
Tunner, William H 1906-1983 *ConAu 109*
Tunney, John V 1934- *ConAu 61*
Tunnicliffe, C F 1901- *ConAu 104*
Tunstall, C Jeremy 1934- *IntAu&W 82, WrDr 84*
Tunstall, Cuthbert Jeremy 1934- *ConAu 5R*
Tunstall, Jeremy 1934- *ConAu 4NR*
Tunstall, Shana Barrett *ConAu X*
Tunstall, Velma Barrett 1914- *ConAu 53*
Tunyogi, Andrew C 1907- *ConAu P-2*
Tuohy, Frank 1925- *ConAu X, ConNov 82, DcLB 14[port], DcLEL 1940, IntAu&W 82, LongCTC, TwCWr, WorAu, WrDr 84*
Tuohy, John Francis 1925- *ConAu X*
Tuohy, William Joseph 1941- *ConAu 37R, WrDr 84*
Tuohy, William Klaus 1926- *ConAu 104*
Tuohy, William S 1938- *ConAu 41R*
Tupper, Margo 1919- *ConAu 17R*
Tur, Leonid Davidovich 1905-1961 *ModWD*
Tur, Pyotr Davidovich 1907- *ModWD*
Tur-Malka *WorAu 1970*
Turbayne, Colin Murray 1916- *ConAu 1R*
Turberville, Ruby W 1922- *IntAu&W 82*
Turbott, Evan Graham 1914- *IntAu&W 82, WrDr 84*
Turbyfill, Mark 1896- *ConAu 108*
Turchin, Valentin F 1931- *ConAu 101*
Turco, Lewis *DrAP&F 83*
Turco, Lewis 1934- *WrDr 84*
Turco, Lewis Putnam 1934- *ConAu 13R, ConLC 11, ConP 80, IntWWP 82, MichAu 80*
Tureck, Rosalyn 1914- *IntAu&W 82, WrDr 84*
Turetzky, Bertram Jay 1933- *ConAu 57*
Turgeon, Bernard *CreCan 2*
Turgeon, Charlotte Snyder 1912- *ConAu 3NR, –5R*
Turgeon, Gregoire *DrAP&F 83*
Turgeon, Lynn 1920- *ConAu 5R*
Turing, John 1908- *ConAu P-2*
Turing, Penelope 1925- *IntAu&W 82*
Turja, Ilmari 1901- *CroCD*
Turk, Frances 1915- *WrDr 84*
Turk, Frances Mary 1915- *ConAu P-1, IntAu&W 82*
Turk, Herman 1929- *ConAu 45*
Turk, Laurel Herbert 1903- *ConAu 21R*
Turk, Midge *WrDr 84*
Turk, Midge 1930- *ConAu X*
Turk, Rudy H 1927- *ConAu 97*
Turkay, Osman 1927- *IntWWP 82*
Turkel, Christopher 1955?-1983 *ConAu 110*
Turkel, Pauline *ConAu X*
Turkevich, Ludmilla Buketoff 1909- *ConAu 5R*
Turki, Fawaz 1940- *ConAu 41R*
Turkle, Brinton 1915- *TwCCW 83, WrDr 84*
Turkle, Brinton Cassaday 1915- *ConAu 25R, SmATA 2*
Turkle, Sherry 1948- *ConAu 102*
Turknett, Clifford 1946- *NatPD 81[port]*
Turkus, Burton B 1902-1982 *ConAu 108*
Turley, William S 1943- *ConAu 105*
Turlington, Bayly 1919- *ConAu 29R, SmATA 5*
Turlington, Catherine Hackett 1900?-1978 *ConAu 77*
Turlington, Henry E 1918- *ConAu 21R*
Turmeau, Constance Evelyn 1906- *IntWWP 82*
Turmer, Tobias *IntAu&W 82X*
Turnage, Anne Shaw 1927- *ConAu 77*
Turnage, Mac N 1927- *ConAu 77*
Turnbull, Agnes Sligh 1888-1982 *ConAu 1R, –2NR, –105, SmATA 14, TwCA, TwCA SUP*
Turnbull, Andrew Winchester 1921-1970 *ConAu 1R, –3NR, –25R, DcLEL 1940*
Turnbull, Ann 1943- *ConAu 65, SmATA 18*
Turnbull, Bob 1900- *ConAu 37R*
Turnbull, Colin M 1924- *ASpks, AuNews 1, ConAu 1R, –3NR, WorAu 1970*

Turnbull, Gael 1928- *WrDr 84*
Turnbull, Gael Lundin 1928- *ConAu 10NR, –65, ConP 80, DcLEL 1940*
Turnbull, John G 1913- *ConAu 1R*
Turnbull, Patrick Edward Xenophon 1908- *ConAu 5R, –6NR, IntAu&W 82*
Turnbull, Stephen 1948- *ConAu 104, IntAu&W 82, WrDr 84*
Turnell, Martin 1908- *WrDr 84*
Turnell, Martin 1908-1979 *ConAu 103, –45, WorAu*
Turner, A Richard 1932- *ConAu 17R*
Turner, Alberta T *DrAP&F 83*
Turner, Alberta Tucker 1919- *ConAu 1NR, –49, IntWWP 82*
Turner, Alexander 1901- *WrDr 84*
Turner, Alice K 1940- *ConAu 53, SmATA 10*
Turner, Amedee 1929- *WrDr 84*
Turner, Amedee Edward 1929- *ConAu 9R, IntAu&W 82*
Turner, Ann W 1945- *ConAu 69, SmATA 14*
Turner, Arlin 1909-1980 *ConAu 5R, –6NR, –97*
Turner, Arthur C 1918- *ConAu 17R*
Turner, Bessye Tobias 1917- *ConAu 53, IntAu&W 82*
Turner, Bill *ConAu X, WrDr 84*
Turner, Bryan S 1945- *WrDr 84*
Turner, Charles W 1916- *ConAu 37R*
Turner, Clair Elsmere 1890- *ConAu P-1*
Turner, Daniel F 1947- *ConAu 97*
Turner, Darwin T 1931- *ConAu 11NR, –21R, LivgBAA, WrDr 84*
Turner, David 1927- *ConDr 82, CroCD, DcLEL 1940, WrDr 84*
Turner, David R 1915- *ConAu 57*
Turner, Dean 1927- *ConAu 29R*
Turner, Dennis C 1948- *ConAu 61*
Turner, Dona M 1951- *ConAu 103*
Turner, E S 1909- *WrDr 84*
Turner, Edward R A 1924- *ConAu 81*
Turner, Eloise Fain 1906- *ConAu 5R*
Turner, Eric Gardner 1911- *IntAu&W 82*
Turner, Eric Gardner 1911-1983 *ConAu 109*
Turner, Ernest Sackville 1909- *IntAu&W 82, WorAu*
Turner, Ethel 1872-1958 *TwCCW 83*
Turner, Francis Joseph 1929- *ConAu 69*
Turner, Frederick *DrAP&F 83*
Turner, Frederick 1943- *ConAu 73, IntWWP 82*
Turner, Frederick C 1938- *ConAu 25R, WrDr 84*
Turner, Frederick Jackson 1861-1932 *DcLB 17[port], TwCA, TwCA SUP*
Turner, Frederick W, III 1937- *ConAu 37R*
Turner, George 1916- *ConAu 103, ConNov 82, DcLEL 1940, TwCSFW, WrDr 84*
Turner, George Allen 1908- *ConAu 10NR, –13R*
Turner, George E 1925- *ConAu 5NR, –53*
Turner, George William 1921- *ConAu 104, WrDr 84*
Turner, Gladys T 1935- *ConAu 77*
Turner, Graham 1932- *ConAu 21R*
Turner, H W 1911- *ConAu 10NR, –21R*
Turner, Harold Walter 1911- *IntAu&W 82, WrDr 84*
Turner, Henry 1919- *WrDr 84*
Turner, Henry Andrew 1919- *ConAu 9R, IntAu&W 82*
Turner, Henry Ashby, Jr. 1932- *ConAu 49*
Turner, Henry Dicken 1919- *ConAu 61*
Turner, Henry Ernest William 1907- *ConAu P-1*
Turner, Herbert Snipes 1891-1976 *ConAu 41R*
Turner, Hetty *IntAu&W 82X*
Turner, Howard M, Jr. 1918- *ConAu 13R*
Turner, James 1909- *ModBrL*
Turner, John Christopher 1928- *WrDr 84*
Turner, John Elliot 1917- *ConAu 3NR, –5R*
Turner, John F 1942- *ConAu 97*
Turner, John Frayn 1923- *ConAu 3NR, –9R, IntAu&W 82, WrDr 84*
Turner, John H 1938- *ConAu 77*
Turner, Jonathan H 1942- *ConAu 37R*
Turner, Josie *SmATA 3*
Turner, Judy 1936- *ConAu X, WrDr 84*
Turner, Justin George 1898-1976 *ConAu 41R*
Turner, Katharine Charlotte 1910- *ConAu P-2, WrDr 84*
Turner, Kay 1932- *ConAu 69*
Turner, Kermit *DrAP&F 83*

Turner, Kermit 1936- *ConAu 104*
Turner, Knox 1949- *NatPD 81[port]*
Turner, L C F 1914- *ConAu 29R*
Turner, Len *WrDr 84*
Turner, Leonard C F 1914- *WrDr 84*
Turner, Leonard Charles Frederick 1914-
    IntAu&W 82
Turner, Lloyd 1924- *ConAu 103*
Turner, Louis Mark 1942- *ConAu 37R,*
    WrDr 84
Turner, Lynn Warren 1906- *ConAu 5R,*
    WrDr 84
Turner, Mae Caesar 1889- *LivgBAA*
Turner, Mary *ConAu X, IntAu&W 82X*
Turner, Mary Ann 1922- *IntWWP 82*
Turner, Mary G 1917- *LivgBAA*
Turner, Merfyn 1915- *ConAu 104, WrDr 84*
Turner, Morrie 1923- *ConAu 29R*
Turner, Paul 1917- *WrDr 84*
Turner, Paul Digby Lowry 1917- *ConAu 105*
Turner, Paul R 1929- *ConAu 45*
Turner, Philip 1925- *ConAu 11NR, –25R,*
    IntAu&W 82, SmATA 11, TwCCW 83,
    WrDr 84
Turner, Ralph 1919- *ConAu 37R, WrDr 84*
Turner, Ralph 1936- *ConAu 107, WrDr 84*
Turner, Ralph Lilley 1888-1983 *ConAu 109*
Turner, Sir Ralph Lilley 1888- *ConAu 5R*
Turner, Ralph V 1939- *ConAu 77*
Turner, Richard E 1920- *ConAu 29R*
Turner, Richard Julian 1936- *CreCan 1*
Turner, Robert 1915- *ConAu 1NR, –45*
Turner, Robert 1920- *CreCan 1*
Turner, Robert Clemens 1908-1978 *ConAu 77*
Turner, Robert F 1944- *ConAu 77*
Turner, Robert Kean, Jr. 1926- *ConAu 17R*
Turner, Robert Y 1927- *ConAu 110*
Turner, Roland 1943- *ConAu 106*
Turner, Ronald Cordell 1939- *ConAu 41R*
Turner, Sheila *ConAu X*
Turner, Sheila 1906- *ConAu P-1*
Turner, Sheila R *ConAu X, SmATA X*
Turner, Steven 1923- *ConAu 29R*
Turner, Susan 1952- *ConAu 106*
Turner, Thomas Bourne 1902- *ConAu 41R*
Turner, Thomas Coleman 1927- *ConAu 5R,*
    WrDr 84
Turner, Victor 1920- *WrDr 84*
Turner, Victor Witter 1920- *ConAu 3NR, –5R*
Turner, W J 1889-1946 *CnMD*
Turner, W Price 1927- *ConAu 21R, ConP 80,*
    WrDr 84
Turner, Wallace 1921- *ConAu 17R*
Turner, Walter James Redfern 1889-1946
    LongCTC, ModBrL, TwCA, TwCA SUP,
    TwCWr
Turner, William Oliver *IntAu&W 82*
Turner, William Oliver 1914- *AuNews 1,*
    ConAu 1R, –3NR
Turner, William Raymond 1928- *IntAu&W 82*
Turner, William Weyand 1927- *ConAu 25R,*
    IntAu&W 82, WrDr 84
Turney, Alfred W 1916- *ConAu 29R, –73*
Turney, Catherine 1906- *ConAu 101*
Turngren, Annette 1902-1980 *ConAu 9R, –101,*
    SmATA 23N
Turngren, Ellen d1964 *ConAu 5R, SmATA 3*
Turnill, Reginald 1915- *ConAu 37R,*
    IntAu&W 82, WrDr 84
Turnock, David 1938- *ConAu 109, WrDr 84*
Turock, Betty J *ConAu 110*
Turow, Rita P 1919- *ConAu 101*
Turow, Scott 1949- *ConAu 73*
Turp, Andre 1925- *CreCan 2*
Turpin, James W 1927- *ConAu 21R*
Turpin, Lorna 1950- *ConAu 107*
Turska, Krystyna Zofia 1933- *ConAu 106,*
    SmATA 27, –31
Tursun-Zade, Mirzo 1911-1977 *ConAu 104*
Turton, Godfrey Edmund 1901- *ConAu 21R,*
    WrDr 84
Turton-Jones, Edith Constance 1904-1968
    ConAu P-1
Turvey, Ralph 1927- *WrDr 84*
Turville-Petre, Edward Oswald Gabriel 1908-1978
    ConAu 9R, –77
Turyn, Alexander 1900-1981 *ConAu 104*
Tusan, Stan 1936- *ConAu 105, SmATA 22*
Tushingham, A Douglas 1914- *ConAu 41R,*
    IntAu&W 82, WrDr 84
Tushnet, Leonard 1908-1973 *ConAu 45,*
    ConAu P-1

Tusiani, Joseph 1924- *ConAu 5NR, –9R,*
    IntAu&W 82
Tuska, Jon 1942- *ConAu 73*
Tuson, Sheila Irene Mary 1911- *IntWWP 82*
Tussing, Aubrey Dale 1935- *ConAu 17R,*
    WrDr 84
Tutaev, David 1916- *ConAu 21R*
Tute, Warren 1914- *ConAu 1R, –1NR,*
    IntAu&W 82, WrDr 84
Tuten, Frederic *DrAP&F 83*
Tuten, Frederic 1936- *ConAu 37R*
Tuthill, John Wills 1910- *ConAu 108*
Tutko, Thomas A 1931- *ConAu 69*
Tutorow, Norman E 1934- *ConAu 25R*
Tutte, William Thomas 1917- *WrDr 84*
Tuttle, Alva Maurice 1900- *ConAu 5R*
Tuttle, Frank W 1896- *ConAu 61*
Tuttle, Howard Nelson 1935- *ConAu 41R*
Tuttle, Lisa 1952- *TwCSFW, WrDr 84*
Tuttle, Russell 1939- *ConAu 77*
Tuttle, W C 1883- *ConAu P-2, TwCWW*
Tuttle, William M, Jr. 1937- *ConAu 11NR*
Tuttle, William McCullough, Jr. 1937-
    ConAu 29R, WrDr 84
Tuttleton, James Welsey 1934- *ConAu 41R*
Tutton, Barbara 1914- *WrDr 84*
Tutuola, Amos 1920- *CnMWL, ConAu 9R,*
    ConLC 5, –14, ConNov 82, DcLEL 1940,
    IntAu&W 82, LongCTC, ModBlW,
    ModCmwL, TwCWr, WorAu, WrDr 84
Tuve, Merle Antony 1901-1982 *ConAu 106*
Tuve, Rosemond 1903-1964 *ConAu P-1,*
    TwCA SUP
Tuveson, Ernest 1915- *ConAu 17R*
Tuwhare, Hone 1922- *ConAu 103, ConP 80,*
    LongCTC, WrDr 84
Tuwim, Julian 1894-1953 *CIDMEL 80,*
    ModSL 2
Tuzin, Donald F 1945- *ConAu 106*
Tvardovski, Aleksandr Trifonovich 1910-1971
    ModSL 1
Tvardovsky, Aleksandr Trifonovich 1910-1971
    CIDMEL 80, TwCWr, WorAu
Tvardovsky, Alexandr Trifonovich 1910-1971
    ConAu 102, –33R
Tvedt, Jens 1857-1935 *CIDMEL 80*
Tveteraas, Harald Ludvig 1904- *IntAu&W 82*
Twaddell, W F 1906- *ConAu X*
Twain, Mark 1835-1910 *ConAu X, ModAL,*
    ModAL SUP, TwCLC 6[port], –12[port],
    TwCSFW, WhoTwCL
Twark, Allan J 1931- *ConAu 49*
Twedt, Dik Warren 1920- *ConAu 37R*
Tweed, J H *ConAu X*
Tweed, Thomas William 1908-1971 *CreCan 1*
Tweed, Tommy 1908-1971 *CreCan 1*
Tweedale, Duncan William 1943- *WrDr 84*
Tweedale, J *ConAu X*
Tweedie, Donald F, Jr. 1926- *ConAu 13R*
Tweedsmuir, Baron *TwCA, TwCA SUP*
Tweedsmuir, Lord *LongCTC*
Tweedsmuir, Lady Susan *LongCTC*
Tweeten, Luther 1931- *ConAu 89*
Tweleponies, Mary *ConAu X*
Twersky, Jacob 1920- *ConAu 49*
Twichell, Chase *DrAP&F 83*
Twiggy *ConAu X*
Twin, Stephanie L 1948- *ConAu 101*
Twiname, Eric 1942?-1980 *ConAu 102*
Twining, Nathan F 1897-1982 *ConAu 106*
Twisleton-Wykeham-Fiennes, Richard N 1909-
    ConAu 11NR
Twiss, Dorothy *DrAP&F 83*
Twist, Ananias *ConAu X, IntAu&W 82X,*
    WrDr 84
Twitchett, Denis Crispin 1925- *ConAu 106*
Twitchett, John Anthony Murray 1932-
    IntAu&W 82
Twombly, Robert C 1940- *ConAu 85*
Twombly, Wells A 1935-1977 *ConAu 41R, –69*
Tworkov, Jack 1900-1982 *ConAu 107,*
    SmATA 31N
Twum, Kyei Michael 1954- *IntWWP 82*
Twyman, Gib *ConAu X*
Twyman, Gilbert Oscar, III 1943- *ConAu 109*
Ty-Casper, Linda 1931- *ConAu 107*
Tyack, Jim *DrAP&F 83*
Tyarks, Frederic E 1908- *WrDr 84*
Tyarks, Fredric Ewald 1908- *IntAu&W 82*
Tychyna, Pavlo 1891-1967 *CIDMEL 80,*
    ModSL 2
Tydeman, William 1935- *WrDr 84*

Tydings, Joseph D 1928- *ConAu 29R*
Tyerman, Donald 1908- *IntAu&W 82*
Tyerman, Hugo 1880-1977 *ConAu 77*
Tyl, Noel 1936- *ConAu 93*
Tylden-Wright, David 1923- *ConAu 25R*
Tylecote, Mabel 1896- *ConAu P-1*
Tyler, A E *ConAu X*
Tyler, Ann 1941- *ConAu 11NR*
Tyler, Anne *DrAP&F 83*
Tyler, Anne 1941- *ConAu 9R, ConLC 7, –11,*
    –18, ConNov 82, DcLB Y82A[port], –6,
    DcLEL 1940, SmATA 7, WorAu 1970,
    WrDr 84
Tyler, Converse 1903?-1978 *ConAu 81*
Tyler, Cyril 1911- *WrDr 84*
Tyler, David B 1899- *ConAu 77*
Tyler, Elias S 1904?-1977 *ConAu 73*
Tyler, Hamilton A 1917- *ConAu 5NR, –9R*
Tyler, J Allen 1924- *ConAu 101*
Tyler, John Ecclesfield d1966 *ConAu P-1*
Tyler, Leona E 1906- *ConAu 17R*
Tyler, Lillian *IntWWP 82X*
Tyler, Parker 1907-1974 *ConAu 5R, –5NR, –49,*
    TwCA SUP
Tyler, Paul Archer 1941- *IntAu&W 82*
Tyler, Poyntz 1907-1971 *ConAu 1R, –103*
Tyler, Ralph Winfred 1902- *ConAu 109*
Tyler, Richard W 1917- *ConAu 41R*
Tyler, Robert L *DrAP&F 83*
Tyler, Robert L 1922- *ConAu 13R*
Tyler, Ronnie C 1941- *ConAu 29R*
Tyler, S Lyman 1920- *ConAu 77*
Tyler, Stephen Albert 1932- *ConAu 29R,*
    WrDr 84
Tyler, Theodore 1932- *ConSFA*
Tyler, Varro Eugene 1926- *ConAu 110*
Tyler, William Royall 1910- *ConAu 37R,*
    WrDr 84
Tyler-Whittle, Michael 1927- *WrDr 84*
Tyler-Whittle, Michael Sidney 1927-
    ConAu 4NR, –5R
Tymchuk, Alexander J 1942- *ConAu 57*
Tymieniecka, Anna-Teresa *ConAu 9NR, –61*
Tymms, Ralph Vincent 1913- *WrDr 84*
Tymn, Marshall 1937- *ConAu 107*
Tymon, Dorothy 1928- *ConAu 85,*
    IntAu&W 82
Tyms, James D 1905- *LivgBAA*
Tynan, Katharine 1861-1931 *ConAu 104, TwCA,*
    TwCA SUP
Tynan, Katherine 1861-1931 *LongCTC,*
    TwCLC 3, TwCWr
Tynan, Kathleen 1940- *ConAu 97,*
    IntAu&W 82
Tynan, Kenneth 1927-1980 *ConAu 101, –13R,*
    CroCD, DcLEL 1940, LongCTC, ModBrL,
    WorAu
Tynyanov, Yury Nikolayevich 1894-1943
    CIDMEL 80
Tyre, Nedra *WrDr 84*
Tyre, Nedra 1921- *ConAu 104, TwCCr&M 80*
Tyrell, Donald J 1929- *ConAu 110*
Tyrmand, Leopold 1920- *ConAu 5NR, –49*
Tyrone, Paul *ConAu X*
Tyrrell, Bernard 1933- *ConAu 57*
Tyrrell, David Arthur John 1925- *WrDr 84*
Tyrrell, Francis M 1916- *ConAu 107*
Tyrrell, George 1861-1909 *TwCA*
Tyrrell, Joseph M 1927- *ConAu 41R*
Tyrrell, R Emmett, Jr. 1943- *ConAu 85,*
    IntAu&W 82
Tyrrell, Robert 1929- *ConAu 41R*
Tyrwhitt, Jacqueline 1905-1983? *ConAu 109*
Tyrwhitt, Janice 1928- *ConAu 97*
Tysdahl, B J 1933- *ConAu 25R*
Tysdahl, Bjorn Johan 1933- *WrDr 84*
Tyson, Joseph B 1928- *ConAu 37R, WrDr 84*
Tyson, Richard 1944- *ConAu 69*
Tysse, Agnes N 1904- *ConAu 101*
Tytell, John 1939- *ConAu 29R*
Tzannes, Nicolaos S 1937- *ConAu 57*
Tzara, Tristan 1896-1963 *CIDMEL 80,*
    ConAu X, ModFrL, ModWD, TwCWr,
    WhoTwCL, WorAu
Tzitsikas, Helene 1926- *ConAu 45*
Tzonis, Alexander 1937- *ConAu 101*

U

U Tam'si, Gerald Felix Tchicaya 1931-
WorAu 1970
U Tam'si, Tchicaya 1931- ModBlW
Ubbelohde, Alfred R 1907- IntAu&W 82,
WrDr 84
Ubbelohde, Carl 1924- ConAu 1R, -6NR
Ubell, Earl 1926- ConAu 37R, SmATA 4
Uble, T R O 1931- ConAu 29R
Ucelay, Margarita 1916- ConAu 21R
Uchida, Tadao 1939- ConAu 65
Uchida, Yoshiko DrAP&F 83
Uchida, Yoshiko 1921- ChlLR 6[port],
ConAu 6NR, -13R, SmATA 1, TwCCW 83,
WrDr 84
Udall, Jan Beaney 1938- ConAu 65,
SmATA 10
Udall, Morris 1922- WrDr 84
Udall, Morris K 1922- ConAu 1NR, -45
Udall, Stewart 1920- WrDr 84
Udall, Stewart Lee 1920- ConAu 69
Ude, Wayne DrAP&F 83
Ude, Wayne 1946- ConAu 77, TwCWW,
WrDr 84
Udell, Jon G 1935- ConAu 1NR, -45
Udell, Leah AuNews 1
Udell, Peter 1934- ConDr 82D
Uden, Grant 1910- ConAu 102, SmATA 26
Udo, Reuben Kenrick 1935- ConAu 77
Udoff, Yale M 1935- ConAu 57,
NatPD 81[port]
Udolf, Roy 1926- ConAu 4NR, -53
Udovitch, Abraham Labe 1933- ConAu 105
Udry, J Richard 1928- ConAu 33R, WrDr 84
Udry, Janice 1928- WrDr 84
Udry, Janice May 1928- ConAu 5R, -6NR,
SmATA 4
Udy, Stanley Hart, Jr. 1928- ConAu 106
Ueda, Makoto 1931- ConAu 21R,
IntAu&W 82, WrDr 84
Uehling, Carl Theodore 1927- ConAu 29R
Uehling, Theodore Edward, Jr. 1935- ConAu 104
Ueno, Noriko ConAu 49
Uffenbeck, Lorin A 1924- ConAu 61
Ugama, LeRoi ConAu X
Ugarte, Francisco 1910-1969 ConAu P-1
Ugboajah, Francis Okwuadigbo 1945-
IntAu&W 82
Ugboajah, Okwu 1945- ConAu 93
Uhalley, Stephen, Jr. 1930- ConAu 106
Uhl, Alexander H 1899?-1976 ConAu 69
Uhl, Melvin John 1915- ConAu 5R
Uhlfelder, Myra L 1923- ConAu 109
Uhlin, Donald M 1930- ConAu 49
Uhlinger, Susan J 1942- ConAu 57
Uhlman, Fred 1901- ConAu 105
Uhnak, Dorothy 1933- AuNews 1, ConAu 81,
TwCCr&M 80, WrDr 84
Uhr, Carl George 1911- ConAu 81
Uhr, Elizabeth 1929- ConAu 25R
Uhr, Leonard 1927- ConAu 5R, -7NR
Uhrman, Celia 1927- IntAu&W 82,
IntWWP 82
Uhrman, Esther 1921- IntWWP 82
Uirsche, C S IntWWP 82X

Uitti, Karl David 1933- ConAu 10NR, -17R
Ujevic, Augustin 1891-1953? ModSL 2
Ujevic, Tin 1891-1955 CIDMEL 80
Ujfalussy, Jozsef 1920- IntAu&W 82
Ukrainow, Fjodor IntAu&W 82X
Ukrayinka, Lesya 1871-1913 CIDMEL 80,
ModSL 2
Ulam, Adam Bruno 1922- ConAu 7NR, -13R,
WrDr 84
Ulam, S M 1909- ConAu 61
Ulanoff, Stanley M 1922- ConAu 7NR, -17R,
IntAu&W 82
Ulanov, Ann Belford 1938- ConAu 49
Ulanov, Barry 1918- ConAu 1R
Ulasi, Adaora Lily DcLEL 1940
Ulc, Otto 1930- ConAu 77, IntAu&W 82
Ulen, Pietter IntAu&W 82X
Ulene, Art 1936- ConAu 103
Ulett, George A 1918- ConAu 21R
Ulevich, Neal Hirsch 1946- ConAu 108
Ulewicz, Laura Louise DrAP&F 83
Ulewicz, Laura Louise 1930- IntWWP 82
Ulibarri, Sabine R 1919- ConAu 105
Ulich, Robert 1890?-1977 ConAu 69
Ulisse, Peter J DrAP&F 83
Ullah, Najib 1914- ConAu 13R
Ullah, Salamat 1913- ConAu 13R
Ullendorff, Edward 1920- ConAu 1R, -2NR,
WrDr 84
Ullian, Joseph S 1930- ConAu 41R
Ullian, Robert DrAP&F 83
Ullman, Allan 1909?-1982 ConAu 106
Ullman, Barbara ConAu X
Ullman, Edward L 1912- ConAu 45
Ullman, James Ramsey 1907-1971 ConAu 1R,
-3NR, -29R, LongCTC, SmATA 7,
TwCA SUP
Ullman, Leslie DrAP&F 83
Ullman, Leslie 1947- ConAu 104
Ullman, Michael 1945- ConAu 103
Ullman, Montague 1916- ConAu 41R
Ullman, Pierre Lioni 1929- ConAu 33R,
IntAu&W 82
Ullman, Richard Henry 1933- ConAu 3NR
Ullmann, John E 1923- ConAu 17R, WrDr 84
Ullmann, Leonard P 1930- ConAu 17R
Ullmann, Liv 1939- ConAu 102
Ullmann, Stephen 1914-1976 ConAu 4NR, -5R,
-65
Ullmann, Walter 1910- ConAu 21R
Ullmann, Walter 1910-1983 ConAu 10NR, -108
Ullrich, Helen D 1922- ConAu 109
Ullyot, Joan 1940- ConAu 73
Ulm, Robert 1934-1977 SmATA 17
Ulman, William A 1908?-1979 ConAu 103, -89
Ulmer, Curtis 1923- ConAu 103
Ulmer, Karl 1915- IntAu&W 82
Ulmer, Melville J 1911- ConAu 21R
Ulmer, S Sidney 1923- ConAu 41R
Ulrich, Betty Garton 1919- ConAu 29R,
WrDr 84
Ulrich, Carolyn F 1881?-1970 ConAu 104
Ulrich, Heinz 1927?-1980 ConAu 97
Ulrich, Homer 1906- ConAu 2NR, -5R

Ulrich, Louis E, Jr. 1918- ConAu 13R
Ulrich, Roger E 1931- ConAu 41R
Ulshofer, Robert 1910- IntAu&W 82
Ultee, Maarten 1949- ConAu 109
Ulyatt, Kenneth 1920- ConAu 8NR, -61,
SmATA 14
Umbral, Francisco 1935- CIDMEL 80,
IntAu&W 82
Umbrico, Judy Loman CreCan 1
Umland, Craig 1947- ConAu 61
Umphlett, Wiley Lee 1931- ConAu 1NR, -49
Umscheid, Christina-Ma DrAP&F 83
Umscheid, Christina-Marie 1946- MichAu 80
Umscheid, Christine Marie 1946- IntWWP 82
Umstead, William Lee 1921- ConAu 81
Unada ConAu X, SmATA 3, WrDr 84
Unamuno, Miguel De 1864-1936 CnMD,
CnMWL, ConAu 104, ModRL, ModWD,
TwCLC 2, -9[port], TwCWr, WhoTwCL
Unamuno Y Jugo, Miguel De 1864-1936
CIDMEL 80, LongCTC, TwCA,
TwCA SUP
Unbegaun, Boris Ottokar 1898-1973 ConAu 41R
Uncle Gordon ConAu X, WrDr 84
Uncle Gus ConAu X, SmATA X
Uncle Kwesi IntAu&W 82X
Uncle Mac ConAu X, SmATA X
Uncle Ray ConAu X, SmATA X
Uncle Shelby ConAu X, SmATA X
Uncle Treacle IntAu&W 82X
Under, Marie 1883- CIDMEL 80
Undercliffe, Errol ConAu X, IntAu&W 82X
Underdown, David 1925- ConAu 5R, -11NR
Underhill, Alice Mertie 1900-1971 ConAu 1R,
-103, SmATA 10
Underhill, Charles ConAu X, WrDr 84
Underhill, Evelyn 1875-1941 LongCTC, TwCA,
TwCA SUP, TwCWr
Underhill, Hal ConAu X
Underhill, Harold 1926-1972 ConAu P-2
Underhill, Miriam E 1898?-1976 ConAu 61
Underhill, Peter ConAu X
Underhill, Ruth Murray 1884- ConAu 1R, -3NR
Underwood, Barbara 1952- ConAu 101
Underwood, Benton J 1915- ConAu 101
Underwood, Betty 1921- ConAu 37R
Underwood, Jane H 1931- ConAu 61
Underwood, John Weeden 1932- ConAu 17R
Underwood, Lewis Graham ConAu X
Underwood, Mavis Eileen 1916- ConAu 108
Underwood, Michael 1916- ConAu X,
IntAu&W 82, TwCCr&M 80, WrDr 84
Underwood, Miles ConAu X, CreCan 2
Underwood, Norman 1878?-1974 ConAu 53
Underwood, Paul S 1915- ConAu 77
Underwood, Peter 1923- ConAu 104,
IntAu&W 82, WrDr 84
Underwood, Sam J 1922- ConAu 2NR, -45
Underwood, Tim 1948- ConAu 105
Undine, P F ConAu X
Undset, Sigrid 1882-1949 CIDMEL 80,
ConAu 104, LongCTC, TwCA,
TwCA SUP, TwCLC 3, TwCWr
Unett, John ConAu 13R

Ungar, Sanford J 1945- *ConAu 37R*, *WrDr 84*
Ungaretti, Giuseppe 1888-1970 *CIDMEL 80*, *CnMWL*, *ConAu 25R*, *ConAu P-2*, *ConLC 7*, *-11*, *-15*, *ModRL*, *TwCWr*, *WhoTwCL*, *WorAu*
Ungaro, Harold R Mancusi, Jr. *ConAu X*
Ungaro, Susan Kelliher 1953- *ConAu 103*
Unger, Alfred Herman 1902- *IntAu&W 82*
Unger, Arthur 1924- *ConAu 1R*
Unger, Barbara *DrAP&F 83*
Unger, Barbara 1932- *ConAu 77*, *IntWWP 82*
Unger, David *DrAP&F 83*
Unger, Gladys Buchanan 1885-1940 *LongCTC*
Unger, Hans 1915- *ConAu 17R*
Unger, Henry F 1912- *ConAu 13R*
Unger, Irwin 1927- *ConAu 7NR*, *-9R*
Unger, Jim 1937- *ConAu 61*
Unger, Joan 1931- *MichAu 80*
Unger, Len *ConAu X*
Unger, Leonard 1916- *ConAu 5R*
Unger, Leonard 1934- *ConAu 69*
Unger, Marion *ConAu X*
Unger, Marvin H 1936- *ConAu 29R*
Unger, Maurice Albert 1917- *ConAu 3NR*, *-9R*
Unger, Merrill F 1909- *ConAu 1R*, *-6NR*, *IntAu&W 82*
Unger, Peter K 1942- *ConAu 109*
Unger, Richard 1939- *ConAu 65*
Unger, Robert 1925- *IntAu&W 82*, *NatPD 81[port]*
Unger-Hamilton, Clive 1942- *ConAu 101*
Ungerer, Jean Thomas 1931- *ConAu 41R*, *SmATA 5*
Ungerer, Kathryn *DrAP&F 83*
Ungerer, Thomas 1931- *SmATA 33[port]*
Ungerer, Tomi *SmATA X*
Ungerer, Tomi 1931- *ChlLR 3*, *ConAu X*, *SmATA 5*, *TwCCW 83*
Ungermann, Kenneth Armistead 1916- *ConAu 9R*
Ungs, Thomas D 1928- *ConAu 81*
Unilowski, Zbigniew 1909-1937 *CIDMEL 80*
Unkelbach, Kurt 1913- *ConAu 8NR*, *-21R*, *SmATA 4*
Unkovic, Charles M 1922- *ConAu 45*
Unnerstad, Edith Totterman 1900- *ConAu 5R*, *-6NR*, *SmATA 3*
Unrau, Ruth 1922- *ConAu 61*, *SmATA 9*
Unrau, William E 1929- *ConAu 37R*
Unruh, Adolph 1908- *ConAu 53*
Unruh, Fritz Von 1885-1970 *CIDMEL 80*, *CnMD*, *ConAu X*, *ModGL*, *ModWD*, *TwCA*, *TwCA SUP*
Unruh, Glenys Grace 1910- *ConAu 29R*
Unruh, John D, Jr. 1938?-1976 *ConAu 105*
Unser, Bobby *ConAu X*
Unser, Robert William 1934- *ConAu 97*
Unstead, R J 1915- *ConAu 7NR*, *SmATA 12*
Unstead, Robert John 1915- *ConAu 9R*, *DcLEL 1940*, *IntAu&W 82*, *WrDr 84*
Unsworth, Barry 1930- *ConAu 25R*, *WrDr 84*
Unsworth, Mair 1909- *ConAu 10NR*, *-25R*
Unsworth, Walt 1928- *ConAu X*, *SmATA 4*
Unsworth, Walter 1928- *ConAu 29R*
Unterberger, Betty Miller *WrDr 84*
Unterberger, Betty Miller 1923- *ConAu 25R*, *IntAu&W 82*
Unterecker, John *DrAP&F 83*
Unterecker, John 1922- *ConAu 17R*, *IntAu&W 82*, *IntWWP 82*
Unterecker, John E 1922- *WrDr 84*
Untereiner, Raymond Edward 1898-1983 *ConAu 110*
Unterman, Alan 1942- *ConAu 97*
Unterman, Issar Y 1886-1976 *ConAu 61*
Untermeyer, Bryna Ivens 1909- *ConAu 3NR*, *-5R*, *-77*
Untermeyer, Jean Starr 1886-1970 *ConAu 29R*, *TwCA SUP*
Untermeyer, Louis 1885-1977 *ConAmA*, *ConAu 5R*, *-73*, *IntWWP 82*, *LongCTC*, *SmATA 2*, *-26N*, *TwCA*, *TwCA SUP*, *TwCWr*
Unthank, Luisa-Teresa 1924- *ConAu 33R*
Unthank, Tessa Brown *ConAu X*
Unthank, Tessa Nelson *WrDr 84*
Unwalla, Darab B 1928- *ConAu 25R*
Unwin, David 1918- *WrDr 84*
Unwin, David Storr 1918- *ConAu 6NR*, *-9R*, *IntAu&W 82*, *SmATA 14*
Unwin, Derick 1931- *ConAu 21R*

Unwin, Nora Spicer 1907- *ConAu 21R*, *SmATA 3*
Unwin, Rayner Stephens 1925- *ConAu 1R*, *WrDr 84*
Unwin, Sir Stanley 1884-1968 *ConAu 5R*, *LongCTC*
Upchurch, Boyd Bradfield *WrDr 84*
Upchurch, Boyd Bradfield 1919- *ConAu 25R*
Upchurch, Deb'y Soper 1951- *IntAu&W 82*
Upchurch, Michael Vincent *DrAP&F 83*
Updike, John *DrAP&F 83*
Updike, John 1932- *ConAu 1R*, *-4NR*, *ConLC 1*, *-2*, *-3*, *-5*, *-7*, *-9*, *-13*, *-15*, *-23[port]*, *ConNov 82*, *ConP 80*, *DcLB DS3[port]*, *-Y80A[port]*, *-Y82A[port]*, *-2*, *-5[port]*, *DcLEL 1940*, *ModAL*, *ModAL SUP*, *TwCWr*, *WhoTwCL*, *WorAu*, *WrDr 84*
Updike, L Wayne 1916- *ConAu 49*
Updyke, James *ConAu X*
Upfield, Arthur William 1888-1964 *LongCTC*, *TwCA SUP*, *TwCCr&M 80*
Uphaus, Robert W 1942- *ConAu 57*
Uphaus, Willard Edwin 1890- *ConAu P-1*
Uphoff, Norman T 1940- *ConAu 11NR*
Uphoff, Norman Thomas 1940- *ConAu 29R*
Uphoff, Walter H 1913- *ConAu 25R*
Upits, Andrejs 1877-1970 *ConAu 104*
Upjohn, Everard M 1903-1978 *ConAu 81*, *ConAu P-1*
Uppal, Jogindar S 1927- *ConAu 1NR*, *-45*
Uppdal, Kristofer 1878-1961 *CIDMEL 80*
Upson, Norma 1919- *ConAu 8NR*, *-61*
Upson, William Hazlett 1891-1975 *ConAu 5R*, *-57*
Upton, Albert 1897- *ConAu P-2*
Upton, Anthony F 1929- *ConAu 17R*
Upton, Arvin 1914- *ConAu 81*
Upton, Bertha 1849-1912 *TwCCW 83*
Upton, Charles *DrAP&F 83*
Upton, Charles 1948- *DcLB 16[port]*
Upton, Florence K 1873-1922 *LongCTC*
Upton, Joseph C N 1946- *ConAu 81*
Upton, L F S 1931- *ConAu 61*
Upton, Lawrence John 1949- *IntWWP 82*
Upton, Lee *DrAP&F 83*
Upton, Martin 1933- *WrDr 84*
Upton, Monroe 1898- *ConAu P-2*
Upton, Robert *ConAu 73*
Upward, Edward 1903- *ConAu 77*, *ConNov 82*, *IntAu&W 82*, *WrDr 84*
Urbach, Reinhard 1939- *IntAu&W 82*
Urbach, Susan 1933- *IntAu&W 82*
Urbain, Jacques 1924- *IntAu&W 82*
Urban, Milo 1904- *CIDMEL 80*
Urban, William L 1939- *ConAu 2NR*, *-45*
Urbanek, Mae 1903- *ConAu 9R*, *-77*
Urbano, Victoria 1926- *ConAu 2NR*, *-45*, *IntAu&W 82*
Urbanski, Edmund Stephen 1909- *ConAu 45*
Urbanski, Marie M Olesen 1922- *ConAu 102*
Urch, Elizabeth 1921- *ConAu 103*, *IntAu&W 82*, *WrDr 84*
Urda, Nicholas 1922- *ConAu 21R*
Urdang, Constance *DrAP&F 83*
Urdang, Constance 1922- *ConAu 9NR*, *-21R*, *ConP 82*, *IntWWP 82*, *WrDr 84*
Urdang, Laurence 1927- *ConAu 89*
Ure, Peter 1919-1969 *ConAu P-1*, *DcLEL 1940*
U'Ren, Hilda *ConAu X*
Uren, Hilda *ConAu X*
Uren, Rhona *IntAu&W 82*
U'Ren-Stubbings, Hilda 1914- *ConAu 29R*, *IntAu&W 82*
Uretsky, Myron 1940- *ConAu 53*
Urey, Harold C 1893-1981 *ConAu 102*
Uri, Pierre Emmanuel 1911- *ConAu 97*
Urick, Kevin *DrAP&F 83*
Uriel, Henry *ConAu X*
Uris, Auren 1913- *ConAu 17R*
Uris, Dorothy *ConAu 9NR*
Uris, Dorothy 1910- *ConAu 61*, *WrDr 84*
Uris, Leon 1924- *ASpks*, *AuNews 1*, *-2*, *ConAu 1R*, *-1NR*, *ConLC 7*, *ConNov 82*, *DcLEL 1940*, *TwCWr*, *WorAu*, *WrDr 84*
Urista, Alberto H 1947- *ConAu 2NR*, *IntWWP 82*
Urmson, J O 1915- *ConAu 25R*
Urmuz *ConAu X*
Uroff, Margaret Dickie 1935- *ConAu 93*
Urofsky, Melvin I 1939- *ConAu 37R*
Urooj, Kazi Tabbasum 1959- *IntAu&W 82*

Urquhart, Alvin W 1931- *ConAu 13R*
Urquhart, Anthony Morse 1934- *CreCan 1*
Urquhart, Brian Edward 1919- *ConAu 105*, *WrDr 84*
Urquhart, Fred 1912- *ConAu 6NR*, *-9R*, *ConNov 82*, *WrDr 84*
Urquhart, Frederick Burrows 1912- *IntAu&W 82*
Urquhart, Guy *ConAu X*
Urquhart, Tony 1934- *CreCan 1*
Urrutia Lleo, Manuel 1901-1981 *ConAu 104*
Urry, David 1931- *ConAu 85*
Urry, W G 1913-1981 *ConAu 103*
Ursini, James 1947- *ConAu 61*
Urvater, Michele 1946- *ConAu 102*
Urwick, Lyndall Fownes 1891- *ConAu P-1*
Ury, William Langer 1953- *ConAu 109*
Ury, Zalman F 1924- *ConAu 65*
Urzidil, Johannes 1896-1970 *CIDMEL 80*, *ConAu 29R*, *ModGL*
Usborne, Richard A 1910- *WrDr 84*
Usborne, Richard Alexander 1910- *ConAu 104*, *IntAu&W 82*
Uscatescu, George 1919- *IntAu&W 82*
Usco *ConAu X*
Usdin, Gene 1922- *ConAu 37R*
Useem, Michael 1942- *ConAu 61*
Usher, Dan 1934- *ConAu 29R*
Usher, Frank 1909-1976 *ConAu 5R*, *-5NR*
Usher, George 1930- *ConAu 109*, *WrDr 84*
Usher, Margo Scegge *ConAu X*, *SmATA 4*
Usher, Shaun 1937- *ConAu 77*
Usher, Stephen 1931- *ConAu 29R*, *WrDr 84*
Usher-Wilson, Rodney N 1908?-1983 *ConAu 109*
Usherwood, Stephen 1907- *ConAu 3NR*, *-5R*, *IntAu&W 82*, *WrDr 84*
Usigli, Rodolfo 1903- *CroCD*
Usigli, Rodolfo 1905- *ModLAL*, *ModWD*
Usikota *ConAu X*
Uslar Pietri, Arturo 1905- *ModLAL*
Uspensky, Petr Dem'yanovich 1878-1947 *LongCTC*, *TwCA SUP*
Usry, Milton F 1931- *ConAu 17R*
Ussher, Arland 1899-1980 *ConAu 10NR*, *-102*, *ConAu P-1*, *TwCA SUP*
Ussher, Percy Arland *ConAu X*
Ustinov, Peter 1921- *ASpks*, *AuNews 1*, *CnMD*, *ConAu 13R*, *ConDr 82*, *ConLC 1*, *CroCD*, *DcLB 13[port]*, *DcLEL 1940*, *LongCTC*, *ModBrL*, *ModWD*, *TwCWr*, *WorAu*, *WrDr 84*
Uston, Ken 1935- *ConAu 108*
Utechin, S V 1921- *ConAu 9R*
Utgard, Russell O 1933- *ConAu 49*
Utke, Allen R 1936- *ConAu 81*
Utley, Francis Lee 1907-1974 *ConAu 1R*, *-2NR*, *-49*
Utley, Freda 1898-1978 *ConAu 77*, *-81*
Utley, Garrick 1939- *ConAu 69*
Utley, Ralph *ConAu X*
Utley, Robert M 1929- *ConAu 2NR*, *-5R*, *WrDr 84*
Utley, Steven 1948- *TwCSFW*
Utt, Richard H 1923- *ConAu 7NR*, *-9R*
Utt, Walter C 1921- *ConAu 21R*
Uttley, Alice Jane 1884-1976 *ConAu 7NR*, *-53*, *-65*, *SmATA 26N*, *-3*
Uttley, Alison 1884-1976 *ConAu X*, *LongCTC*, *SmATA X*, *TwCCW 83*
Uttley, John 1914- *ConAu 21R*
Utton, Albert Edgar 1931- *ConAu 1NR*, *-45*
Utz, Lois 1932- *ConAu 25R*, *SmATA 5*
Utz, Robert T 1934- *ConAu 53*
Uu, David 1948- *ConAu X*
Uveges, Joseph A, Jr. 1938- *ConAu 41R*
Uvezian, Sonia *ConAu 9NR*, *-57*
Uzair, Salem Ben *SmATA X*
Uzgiris, Ina Cepenas 1937- *ConAu 108*
Uzodinma, Edmund Chukuemeka Chieke 1936- *DcLEL 1940*
Uzzell, J Douglas 1937- *ConAu 93*

V

V, Nina *ConAu X*
V Nogradi, Guy *IntAu&W 82X*
Vaa, Aslaug 1889-1967 *ClDMEL 80*
Vaca Cangas, Cesar 1908- *IntAu&W 82*
Vacca, Roberto 1927- *ConAu 1NR, –49*
Vaccaro, Ernest B 1905?-1979 *ConAu 89*
Vaccaro, Joseph P 1935- *ConAu 104*
Vaccaro, Louis C 1930- *ConAu 1NR, –45*
Vaccaro, Tony *ConAu X*
Vachell, Horace Annesley 1861-1955 *LongCTC,*
  ModBrL, TwCA, TwCA SUP, TwCWr
Vachon, Brian 1941- *ConAu 41R*
Vachon, Jingo Viitala 1918- *MichAu 80*
Vaculik, Ludvik 1926- *ClDMEL 80, ConAu 53,*
  ConLC 7, ModSL 2
Vaczek, Louis Charles 1913- *ConAu 9R*
Vadakin, James C 1924- *ConAu 29R*
Vada'sz, Ferenc 1916- *IntAu&W 82*
Vadeboncoeur, Joan E *ConAmTC*
Vadney, Thomas E 1939- *ConAu 45*
Vaeth, J Gordon 1921- *ConAu 5R, SmATA 17*
Vaginov, Konstantin Konstantinovich 1899-1934
  ClDMEL 80
Vago, Bela Adalbert 1922- *ConAu 93*
Vagts, Alfred Herman Friedrich 1892- *ConAu 5R*
Vagts, Detlev F 1929- *ConAu 25R*
Vagts, Miriam Beard 1901-1983 *ConAu 110*
Vahanian, Gabriel 1927- *ConAu 6NR,*
  WrDr 84
Vahlefeld, Hans Wilhelm 1928- *IntAu&W 82*
Vaid, Krishna Baldev 1927- *ConAu 8NR, –61,*
  IntAu&W 82
Vaidon, Lawdom *ConAu X*
Vail, Amanda *WorAu*
Vail, Elaine 1948- *ConAu 109*
Vail, Laurence 1891-1968 *DcLB 4*
Vail, Priscilla L 1931- *ConAu 101*
Vail, Robert William 1921- *ConAu 17R*
Vaillancourt, Armand 1931- *CreCan 2*
Vaillancourt, Jean-Guy 1937- *ConAu 105*
Vaillancourt, Pauline M *ConAu 104*
Vailland, Roger 1907-1965 *ClDMEL 80, CnMD,*
  ConAu 103, –89, ModFrL, TwCWr,
  WorAu
Vaillant, George E 1934- *ConAu 77*
Vairo, Philip Dominic 1933- *ConAu 102*
Vaish, Yogi Nandan 1932- *IntWWP 82*
Vaizey, Mrs. George DeHorne 1857- *TwCRGW*
Vaizey, John 1929- *ConAu 4NR, –5R,*
  DcLEL 1940, IntAu&W 82, WrDr 84
Vaizey, Marina 1938- *IntAu&W 82*
Vajda, Gyorg M 1914- *IntAu&W 82*
Vajda, Stephan 1926- *ConAu 29R*
Vakar, N P 1897-1970 *ConAu 103*
Vakar, Nicholas P 1897- *ConAu 1R*
Valaskakis, Kimon Plato 1941- *ConAu 89*
Valbonne, Jean *ConAu X*
Valbuena-Briones, A Julian 1928- *ConAu 45*
Valbuena-Briones, Angel 1928- *ConAu 3NR*
Valcoe, H Felix *ConAu X*
Valcourt, Jean *CreCan 2*
Valdes, Armando Palacio 1853-1938 *ModRL*
Valdes, Donald M 1922- *ConAu 21R*
Valdes, Ivy 1921- *ConAu 105*

Valdes, Joan 1931- *ConAu 49*
Valdes, Mario J 1934- *ConAu 6NR, –13R,*
  WrDr 84
Valdes, Nelson P 1945- *ConAu 33R*
Valdez, Luis 1940- *ConAu 101, ConDr 82,*
  WrDr 84
Valdivia, Omara 1947- *IntAu&W 82X,*
  IntWWP 82
Valdman, Albert 1931- *ConAu 103*
Valdombre *CreCan 2*
Vale, C P 1921- *ConAu 49*
Vale, Edmund 1888-1969 *ConAu P-1*
Vale, Eugene 1916- *ConAu 57*
Vale, Lewis *ConAu X*
Vale, Malcolm Graham Allan 1942- *ConAu 109,*
  WrDr 84
Vale, Rena 1898- *ConSFA*
Valek, Miroslav 1927- *ModSL 2*
Valen, Nanine 1950- *ConAu 65, SmATA 21*
Valencak, Hannelore *IntAu&W 82X*
Valency, Maurice 1903- *ConAu 10NR, –25R,*
  IntAu&W 82, WrDr 84
Valens, E G, Jr. 1920- *ConAu 3NR*
Valens, Evans G, Jr. 1920- *ConAu 81,*
  SmATA 1
Valenstein, Suzanne G 1928- *ConAu 77*
Valente, Jose Angel 1929- *ClDMEL 80*
Valente, Michael F *ConAu 57*
Valenti, Jack 1921- *ConAu 73*
Valentin *CroCD*
Valentin, Thomas 1922-1981 *ConAu 103,*
  IntAu&W 82
Valentine, Alan 1901- *WrDr 84*
Valentine, Alan 1901-1980 *ConAu 2NR, –5R,*
  –101, IntAu&W 82
Valentine, Alec *IntAu&W 82X, WrDr 84*
Valentine, Charles A 1929- *ConAu 25R*
Valentine, Charles Wilfrid 1879-1964 *ConAu 107*
Valentine, David *ConAu X*
Valentine, Donald Graham 1929- *ConAu 5R*
Valentine, Foy 1923- *ConAu 10NR, –17R*
Valentine, Helen *ConAu X*
Valentine, James C 1935- *ConAu 45*
Valentine, Jean *DrAP&F 83*
Valentine, Jean 1934- *ConAu 65, ConP 80,*
  WrDr 84
Valentine, Jo *ConAu X*
Valentine, Lloyd Magnus 1922- *ConAu 110*
Valentine, Sister Mary Hester 1909- *ConAu P-2*
Valentine, Roger *ConAu X, IntAu&W 82X*
Valentine, Tom *ConAu X*
Valentine, William Alexander 1905- *ConAu 57*
Valenzuela, Arturo A 1944- *ConAu 101*
Valenzuela, Luisa 1938- *ConAu 101*
Valeo, Francis Ralph 1916- *ConAu 108*
Valera, Juan 1824-1905 *ClDMEL 80,*
  TwCLC 10[port]
Valera Y Alcala Galiano, Juan 1824-1905
  ConAu 106
Valeri, Diego 1887-1976 *ClDMEL 80*
Valeriani, Richard 1932- *ConAu 65*
Valeriano, Napoleon D 1917?-1975 *ConAu 53*
Valeriy, Ivan *WorAu*
Valero, Eduardo 1925- *IntAu&W 82*

Valery, Paul Ambroise 1871-1945 *ClDMEL 80,*
  CnMD, CnMWL, ConAu 104, LongCTC,
  ModFrL, ModRL, TwCA, TwCA SUP,
  TwCLC 4[port], TwCWr, WhoTwCL
Vales, Robert L 1933- *ConAu 53*
Valett, Robert E 1927- *ConAu 7NR, –17R*
Valette, Rebecca M 1938- *ConAu 8NR, –21R*
Valgardson, W D *DrAP&F 83*
Valgardson, W D 1939- *ConAu 41R*
Valgardson, William Dempsey 1939-
  IntAu&W 82
Valgemae, Mardi 1935- *ConAu 41R*
Vali, Ferenc Albert 1905- *ConAu 1R, –3NR,*
  IntAu&W 82, WrDr 84
Valiani, Leo 1909- *ConAu 101*
Valin, Jonathan Louis 1948- *ConAu 101*
Valin, Martial 1898-1980 *ConAu 105*
Valis, Noel M 1945- *ConAu 110*
Vallance, Elizabeth 1945- *ConAu 102*
Valldaura, Juan De *IntAu&W 82X*
Valle, Carmen *DrAP&F 83*
Valle, Cyro Eyer Do 1937- *IntAu&W 82*
Valle-Inclan, Ramon Maria Del 1866?-1936
  ClDMEL 80, CnMD SUP, CnMWL,
  ConAu 106, ModRL, ModWD, TwCA,
  TwCA SUP, TwCLC 5[port], TwCWr,
  WhoTwCL
Vallee, Hubert P 1901- *ConAu 1R, –2NR*
Vallee, Jacques F 1939- *ConAu 10NR, –17R*
Vallee, Rudy *ConAu X*
Vallejo, Cesar 1892-1938 *CnMWL, ConAu 105,*
  ModLAL, TwCLC 3, TwCWr, WhoTwCL,
  WorAu
Vallen, Jerome J 1928- *ConAu 93*
Vallentin, Antonina 1893- *TwCA, TwCA SUP*
Vallentine, John F 1931- *ConAu 4NR, –53*
Vallerand, Jean 1915- *CreCan 2*
Vallis, Val 1916- *IntWWP 82X, WrDr 84*
Vallis, Valentine Thomas 1916- *IntWWP 82*
Valmaggia, Juan S 1895-1980 *ConAu 97*
Valois, Lucile 1918- *IntWWP 82*
Valsan, E H 1933- *ConAu 29R*
Valtiala, Kaarle-Juhani Bertel 1938-
  IntAu&W 82
Valtin, Jan 1905-1951 *TwCA SUP*
Valtz, Lynn Berta Springbett *CreCan 2*
Valtz, Robert C K 1936- *ConAu 13R*
Valverde, Jose Maria 1926- *ClDMEL 80*
Vambe, Lawrence 1917- *ConAu 110, WrDr 84*
Vamplew, Wray 1943- *ConAu 103, WrDr 84*
VanAbbe, Derek Maurice 1916- *ConAu 57*
VanAbbe, Salaman 1883?-1955 *SmATA 18*
VanAllsburg, Chris 1949- *ChlLR 5[port]*
VanAlstyne, Richard W 1900- *ConAu 9R,*
  IntAu&W 82, WrDr 84
VanAmmers-Kuller *TwCA, TwCA SUP*
VanAnda, Carr 1864-1945 *DcLB 25[port]*
VanAnrooy, Francine 1924- *ConAu 21R,*
  SmATA 2
VanAnrooy, Frans *ConAu X, SmATA X*
VanAppledorn, Mary Jeanne 1927- *ConAu 10NR,*
  –25R
Vanardy, Varick *TwCCr&M 80*
VanArnam, Dave *ConSFA*

VanArsdel, Rosemary T 1926- *ConAu 108*
VanAssendorp, Erzsebet *IntWWP 82*
VanAtta, Chester 1906- *WrDr 84*
VanAtta, Winfred 1910- *ConAu 1R, -1NR*
Vanauken, Sheldon 1914- *ConAu 85*
VanAvond, Jan *LongCTC*
VanBibber, Max A 1913?-1981 *ConAu 103*
VanBriggle, Margaret Frances Jessup 1917-
  ConAu 9R
VanBrocklin, Norm 1926-1983 *ConAu 109*
VanBrunt, H L *DrAP&F 83*
VanBrunt, H L 1936- *ConAu 49*
VanBuitenen, J A B 1928?-1979 *ConAu 103*
VanBuitenen, Johannes Adrian Bernard
  1928?-1979 *ConAu 89*
VanBuren, Abigail *ConAu X*
VanBuren, David *DrAP&F 83*
VanBuren, James G 1914- *ConAu 57*
VanBuren, Paul 1924- *ConAu 11NR, -61*
VanBuren, Raeburn 1891- *ConAu 103*
VanCaenegem, R C 1927- *ConAu 45*
VanCampen, Karl *ConAu X*
VanCaspel, Venita 1922- *ConAu 104*
Vance, Adrian 1936- *ConAu 77*
Vance, Barbara Jane 1934- *ConAu 57*
Vance, Bruce 1931- *ConAu 33R*
Vance, Edgar *ConAu X*
Vance, Eleanor Graham 1908- *ConAu 9R,
  SmATA 11, WrDr 84*
Vance, Ethel 1896- *ConAu X, LongCTC,
  TwCA, TwCA SUP*
Vance, Jack *TwCSFW*
Vance, Jack 1916- *DcLB 8, WrDr 84*
Vance, Jack 1920?- *ConAu X, ConSFA*
Vance, John Holbrook *TwCCr&M 80,
  WrDr 84*
Vance, John Holbrook 1920- *ConAu 29R*
Vance, Lawrence L 1911- *ConAu 49*
Vance, Louis Joseph 1879-1933 *LongCTC,
  TwCA, TwCCr&M 80*
Vance, Marguerite 1889-1965 *ConAu 109,
  SmATA 29[port]*
Vance, Ronald *DrAP&F 83*
Vance, Rupert Bayless 1899-1975 *ConAu 61*
Vance, Samuel 1939- *ConAu 29R*
Vance, Stanley 1915- *ConAu 1R, -3NR*
Vance, William E *WrDr 84*
Vance, William E 1911- *ConAu 105, TwCWW*
Vancil, Richard F 1931- *ConAu 5R, -8NR*
VanCleef, Eugene 1887-1973 *ConAu 107*
VanCleve, Thomas Curtis 1888-1976 *ConAu 41R,
  -65*
VanCoevering, Jack 1900- *ConAu X*
VanCoevering, Jan Adrian 1900- *ConAu P-1*
VanColler, Hendrik Petrus 1949- *IntAu&W 82*
VanCorstanje, Auspicius *ConAu X*
VanCorstanje, Charles 1913- *ConAu 107*
VanCroonenburg, Bert 1909- *WrDr 84*
VanCroonenburg, Engelbert J 1909- *ConAu 37R*
Vancura, Vladislav 1891-1942 *ClDMEL 80,
  ModSL 2, TwCWr*
VanDahm, Thomas E 1924- *ConAu 65*
Vandal, Cameron *ConAu X*
VanDalen, Deobold B 1911- *ConAu 1R*
VanDam, Ine 1947- *ConAu 109*
VanDam, J *ConAu X*
VanDeKamp, Peter 1901- *IntAu&W 82,
  WrDr 84*
VandeKieft, Ruth M 1925- *ConAu 17R,
  WrDr 84*
VanD'Elden, Karl H 1923- *ConAu 45*
Vandeloo, Jos 1925- *ClDMEL 80*
Vandenberg, Donald 1931- *ConAu 29R*
Vandenberg, Philipp 1941- *ConAu 8NR*
Vandenberg, T F 1941- *ConAu 25R*
VanDenBerghe, Pierre L 1933- *ConAu 5NR, -9R*
VanDenBogaerde, Dirk Niven 1921-
  IntAu&W 82
VanDenBogaerdes, Derek Niven *ConLC 19*
VanDenBogarde, Derek Jules G U Niven 1921-
  ConAu 77
Vandenbosch, Amry 1894- *ConAu 61*
Vandenbosch, Robert 1922-1978 *ConAu 107*
Vandenburg, Mary Lou 1943- *ConAu 73,
  SmATA 17*
Vandenburg, Philipp 1941- *ConAu 61*
Vandenburgh, Mildred 1898- *ConAu 97*
Vandenbusche, Duane 1937- *ConAu 45*
VanDenBussche, Henri O A *ConAu X*
VanDenHaag, Ernest 1914- *ConAu 5R, -6NR*
VanDenHeuvel, Albert H 1932- *ConAu 17R*
VanDenHeuvel, Cornelisz A 1931- *ConAu 13R*

VanDePerre, Hugo A J 1914- *IntAu&W 82*
VanDePitte, Frederick P 1932- *ConAu 45*
Vander, Harry Joseph, III 1913-1969 *ConAu P-2*
VanDerBeets, Richard 1932- *ConAu 29R*
Vanderbilt, Amy 1908-1974 *ConAu 1R, -3NR,
  -53*
Vanderbilt, Cornelius, Jr. 1898-1974 *AuNews 1,
  ConAu 49, ConAu P-1*
Vanderbilt, Gloria 1924- *ConAu 89*
VanderBoom, Mae M *SmATA 14*
Vanderburgh, R M 1926- *ConAu 105*
Vandergriff, Aola 1920- *ConAu 89*
VanDerHeyden, A A M 1922- *ConAu 7NR, -57*
VanderHill, C Warren 1937- *ConAu 33R*
VanderHill, Charles Warren 1937- *MichAu 80*
Vanderhoof, Jack W 1921- *ConAu 53*
VanDerHorst, Brian 1944- *ConAu 41R*
VanderKooi, Ronald C *ConAu 2NR, -45*
VanDerKroef, Justus M 1925- *ConAu 41R*
Vanderlip, D George 1926- *ConAu 77*
VanDerLip, Dodava George 1926- *IntAu&W 82*
VanderLugt, Herbert 1920- *ConAu 101*
VanDerMeersch, Maxence 1907-1951 *TwCA,
  TwCA SUP*
VanDerMerwe, Nikolaas J 1940- *ConAu 41R*
Vandermolen, Robert *DrAP&F 83*
VanderMolen, Robert 1947- *IntWWP 82,
  MichAu 80*
VanDerPloeg, Johannes Petrus Maria 1909-
  ConAu P-1
VanDerPoel, Cornelius J 1921- *ConAu 4NR, -53*
Vanderpool, Harold Y 1936- *ConAu 53*
Vanderpool, James A 1916-1983 *ConAu 109*
VanDerPost, Laurens 1906- *WrDr 84*
VanDerPost, Laurens Jan 1906- *ConAu 5R,
  ConLC 5, ConNov 82, IntAu&W 82,
  LongCTC, ModCmwL, TwCWr, WorAu*
VanDersal, William R 1907- *ConAu 77,
  IntAu&W 82*
Vandersee, Charles *DrAP&F 83*
Vandersee, Charles 1938- *ConAu 41R*
VanDerSlik, Jack R 1936- *ConAu 29R*
VanDerSmissen, Betty *ConAu X*
VanDerSmissen, Margaret Elisabeth 1927-
  ConAu 9NR, -17R
VanDerSpiel, Luigi 1920- *ConAu 102*
VanDerSpuy, Una 1912- *WrDr 84*
VanDerTrim, Beverley Eanne 1942-
  IntAu&W 82
VanDerVat, Dan 1939- *ConAu 109*
Vanderveen, Bareld Harmannus 1932-
  ConAu 103
Vanderveen, Bart H *ConAu X*
VanDerVeer, Judy 1912- *ConAu 33R,
  SmATA 4*
VanDerVeer, Judy 1912-1982 *ConAu 108,
  SmATA 33N*
Vandervelde, Marjorie 1908- *ConAu 10NR, -21R*
VanDerVeldt, James A 1893?-1977 *ConAu 73*
VanDerVennet, Hugo 1944- *IntAu&W 82*
VanDerVeur, Paul W 1921- *ConAu 21R*
VanDerVoort, Richard Lee 1936- *ConAu 37R*
Vanderwall, Francis W 1946- *ConAu 108*
VanDerWee, Herman 1928- *IntAu&W 82*
Vanderwerth, W C 1904- *ConAu 73*
Vanderwood, Paul J *ConAu 29R*
VanderZanden, James Wilfrid 1930- *ConAu 5NR,
  -13R*
VanDerZee, James 1886- *ConAu 104*
VanDerZee, James 1886-1983 *ConAu 109*
VanDerZee, John 1936- *ConAu 21R*
Vanderzell, John H 1924- *ConAu 45*
VanderZwaag, Harold J 1929- *ConAu 45*
VanDeurs, George 1901- *ConAu 25R, WrDr 84*
VanDeusen, Dayton G 1914- *ConAu 9R*
VanDeusen, Glyndon Garlock 1897- *ConAu 1R,
  -1NR*
VanDeusen, L Marshall 1922- *ConAu 61*
VanDeusen, Ruth B 1907- *ConAu 5R*
VanDeVall, Mark 1923- *ConAu 29R,
  IntAu&W 82, WrDr 84*
VanDeVate, Dwight, Jr. 1928- *ConAu 61*
VanDeVelde, Anton 1895- *ModWD*
VanDeventer, Fred L 1903-1971 *ConAu P-1*
VanDeventer, Robert *ConAu 105*
VanDeWater, Frederic F 1890-1968 *ConAu 110*
VanDeWater, Frederic Franklyn 1890-1968
  TwCA SUP
VanDeWetering, Janwillem 1931- *ConAu 4NR,
  -49*
VanDine, S S 1888-1939 *LongCTC, TwCA,
  TwCA SUP, TwCCr&M 80, TwCWr*

Vandiver, Edward P, Jr. 1902- *ConAu P-1*
Vandiver, Frank Everson 1925- *ConAu 5R, -7NR,
  WrDr 84*
Vandivert, Rita 1905- *ConAu 5R, -6NR,
  SmATA 21[port]*
VanDommelen, David B 1929- *ConAu 5R,
  MichAu 80*
VanDooren, Leonard Alfred Theophile 1912-
  ConAu 3NR, -5R
VanDoornik, Piet *IntAu&W 82X*
VanDoren, Carl Clinton 1885-1950 *ConAmA,
  LongCTC, TwCA, TwCA SUP, TwCWr*
VanDoren, Charles L 1926- *ConAu 4NR, -5R*
VanDoren, Dorothy Graffe 1896- *ConAu 1R*
VanDoren, Irita 1891-1966 *ConAu 89,
  LongCTC*
VanDoren, Mark 1894-1972 *ConAmA,
  ConAu 1R, -3NR, -37R, ConLC 6, -10,
  LongCTC, ModAL, ModAL SUP, TwCA,
  TwCA SUP, TwCWr*
VanDorne, R *ConAu X*
Vandour, Cyril *ConAu X*
VanDruten, John William 1901-1957 *CnMD,
  ConAu 104, DcLB 10[port], LongCTC,
  ModAL, ModBrL, ModWD, TwCA,
  TwCA SUP, TwCLC 2, TwCWr*
VanDusen, Albert 1916- *WrDr 84*
VanDusen, Albert E 1916- *ConAu 3NR, -5R,
  IntAu&W 82*
VanDusen, C Raymond 1907- *WrDr 84*
VanDusen, Clarence Raymond 1907- *ConAu 5R*
VanDusen, Henry Pitney 1897-1975 *ConAu 1R,
  -3NR, -57*
VanDusen, Robert LaBranche 1929- *ConAu 41R*
VanDuyn, Janet 1910- *ConAu 69, SmATA 18*
VanDuyn, Mona *DrAP&F 83*
VanDuyn, Mona 1921- *ConAu 7NR, -9R,
  ConLC 3, -7, ConP 80, DcLB 5[port],
  WorAu 1970, WrDr 84*
VanDuzee, Mabel 1895- *ConAu 5R*
VanDyke, Henry *DrAP&F 83*
VanDyke, Henry 1928- *ConAu 49, LivgBAA*
Vandyke, Henry 1928- *WrDr 84*
VanDyke, Henry Jackson, Jr. 1852-1933
  LongCTC, TwCA, TwCA SUP
VanDyke, Jon M 1943- *ConAu 29R*
VanDyke, Lauren A 1906- *ConAu 29R*
VanDyke, Richard L *LivgBAA*
VanDyke, Vernon B 1912- *ConAu 1R,
  WrDr 84*
VanDyke, Vonda *WrDr 84*
VanDyne, Edith *ConAu X, SmATA X,
  TwCCW 83*
Vane, Bret *WrDr 84*
Vane, Brett *ConAu X*
Vane, Michael *ConAu X, WrDr 84*
Vane, Roland *ConAu X*
Vane, Sutton 1888-1963 *DcLB 10[port],
  LongCTC, ModWD, TwCA, TwCWr*
VanEerde, Katherine S 1920- *ConAu 61*
VanEgmond, Peter 1937- *ConAu 61*
Vanek, Jaroslav 1930- *ConAu 103*
VanErmengem, Frederic 1881-1972 *ConAu 33R*
VanEss, Dorothy 1885?-1975 *ConAu 61*
VanEssen, W 1910- *WrDr 84*
VanEssen, William 1910- *IntAu&W 82*
VanEttinger, Jan 1902- *ConAu 1R*
VanEvery, Dale 1896-1976 *ConAu 1R, -3NR*
VanFossen, Richard W 1927- *ConAu 5R, -6NR*
VanFraassen, Bas C 1941- *WrDr 84*
VanFraassen, Bastiaan Cornelis *ConAu 37R*
VanGeil, Mercury E C L *ConAu X*
VanGelder, Lindsy 1944- *ConAu 97*
VanGelder, Richard George 1928- *ConAu 73*
Vangelisti, Paul *DrAP&F 83*
Vangelisti, Paul 1945- *ConAu 77, IntWWP 82*
Vangen, Roland Dean 1935- *ConAu 105*
Vanger, Milton Isadore 1925- *ConAu 13R*
VanGlahn, Gerhard Ernst 1911- *WrDr 84*
VanGoethem, Larry 1934- *ConAu 101,
  WrDr 84*
VanGogh, Lucy *CreCan 1*
VanGroningen, Bernhard A 1894- *IntAu&W 82*
VanGulik, Robert H 1910-1967 *ConAu 1R, -3NR,
  -25R*
VanGundy, Arthur B, Jr. 1946- *ConAu 110*
VanHaaften, Julia 1946- *ConAu 109*
VanHamel, Martine 1945- *CreCan 2*
VanHassen, Amy *ConAu X*
VanHattum, Rolland J 1924- *ConAu 105*
VanHecke, B C 1926- *ConAu 29R*
VanHeerden, Ernst 1916- *IntWWP 82*

VanHelder, Vincent *IntWWP 82X*
VanHeller, Marcus *WrDr 84*
VanHerik, Judith 1947- *ConAu 108*
VanHerk, Aritha 1954- *ConAu 101*
VanHet Reve, Gerard Kornelis Franciscus
  WorAu 1970
VanHet Reve, Karel 1921- *ConAu 49*
VanHeyningen, Christina 1900- *ConAu 17R*
VanHoesel, Aloysius Franciscus Gerardus 1920-
  IntAu&W 82
VanHoesen, Walter H 1898?-1977 *ConAu 69*
VanHook, Roger Eugene 1943- *ConAu 29R*
VanHoose, William H 1927- *ConAu 89*
VanHorn, Richard L 1932- *ConAu 53*
VanHouten, Lois *DrAP&F 83*
VanHouten, Lois 1918- *ConAu 77, IntWWP 82*
VanHuss, Wayne D 1917- *ConAu 61*
VanItallie, Jean-Claude 1936- *ConAu 1NR, –45,
  ConDr 82, ConLC 3, CroCD,
  DcLB 7[port], IntAu&W 82, IntWWP 82,
  ModWD, NatPD 81[port], WorAu 1970,
  WrDr 84*
VanItallie, Philip H 1899- *ConAu P-1*
VanIterson, S R *ConAu 102, SmATA 26[port]*
VanJaarsveld, Floris Albertus 1922- *ConAu 5R,
  –7NR*
VanKaam, Adrian 1920- *ConAu 10NR, –17R,
  IntAu&W 82*
VanKampen, Anthony 1911- *IntAu&W 82*
VanKleek, Peter Eric 1929- *ConAu 53*
VanKrevelen, Alice 1914- *ConAu 45*
VanLawick, Hugo 1937- *ConAu 85, WrDr 84*
VanLawick-Goodall, Jane 1934- *ASpks,
  ConAu X*
VanLeeuwen, Jean 1937- *ConAu 11NR, –25R,
  SmATA 6*
VanLente, Charles R 1941- *ConAu 65*
VanLerberghe, Charles 1861-1907 *CIDMEL 80*
VanLhin, Erik *ConAu X, SmATA X*
VanLierde, John 1907- *ConAu P-1*
VanLierde, Peter Canisius *ConAu X*
VanLinh, Erik *WrDr 84*
VanLint, June 1928- *ConAu 65*
VanLoan, Charles E 1876?-1919 *TwCA*
VanLoenen, Gabrielle *IntAu&W 82X*
VanLoggem, Manuel 1916- *IntAu&W 82*
VanLoon, Gerard Willem 1911- *ConAu 45*
VanLoon, Hendrik Willem 1882-1944 *ConAmA,
  LongCTC, SmATA 18, TwCA,
  TwCA SUP*
VanLoot, Cornelius Obenchain *ConAmA*
VanLooy, Herman 1922- *IntAu&W 82*
VanMeerhaeghe, M A G *ConAu 73*
VanMeerhaeghe, Marcel Alfons Gilbert 1921-
  ConAu 77, IntAu&W 82
VanMelsen, Andreas Gerardus Maria 1912-
  ConAu 1R, –4NR, IntAu&W 82
Vann, J Don 1938- *ConAu 29R*
Vann, James Allen 1939- *ConAu 110*
Vann, Richard T 1931- *ConAu 21R*
VanNess, Peter 1933- *ConAu 29R*
Vannier, Maryhelen 1915- *ConAu 1R, –6NR*
VanNieuwenhuijze, C A O 1920- *ConAu 25R*
VanNooten, Barend A 1932- *ConAu 45*
VanNoppen, Ina W 1906-1980 *ConAu 5R, –103*
VanNostrand, A D 1922- *ConAu 41R*
Vannoy, Cheryl 1953- *ConAmTC*
Vanocur, Edith C 1924?-1975 *ConAu 57*
Vanocur, Sander 1928- *ConAu 109*
VanOort, Jan 1921- *ConAu 29R*
VanOrden, M D 1921- *ConAu 37R, SmATA 4*
VanOrman, Richard Albert 1936- *ConAu 21R*
VanOsdol, William R 1927- *ConAu 53*
VanOver, Raymond 1934- *IntAu&W 82*
VanOverbeek, Johannes 1908- *ConAu P-1*
VanPaassen, Pierre 1895-1968 *TwCA,
  TwCA SUP*
VanPeebles, Melvin 1932- *ConAu 85,
  ConDr 82D, ConLC 2, –20, LivgBAA*
VanPeursen, Cornelis A 1920- *WrDr 84*
VanPeursen, Cornelius Anthonie 1920- *ConAu 53*
VanPraag, Siegfried-Emanuel 1899-
  IntAu&W 82
VanPraagh, Margaret 1910- *ConAu P-2*
VanPraagh, Peggy *ConAu X*
VanProosdy, Cornelis 1919- *ConAu 5NR, –9R*
VanRensburg, Francois Izak Janse 1922-
  IntAu&W 82
VanRensburg, Jaco *IntAu&W 82X*
VanRensburg, Roelf *IntAu&W 82X*
VanRensburg, Roelog Jacobus Jansen 1935-
  IntAu&W 82

VanRensselaer, Alexander 1892-1962 *ConAu 73,
  SmATA 14*
VanRheenen, Gailyn 1946- *ConAu 69*
VanRijn, Ignatius 1938- *ConAu X*
VanRijsewijk, Adrianus 1948- *IntWWP 82*
VanRiper, Francis A 1946- *ConAu 11NR*
VanRiper, Frank *ConAu X*
VanRiper, Frank A 1946- *ConAu 69*
VanRiper, Guernsey, Jr. 1909- *ConAu 5R, –6NR,
  SmATA 3, WrDr 84*
VanRiper, Paul Pritchard 1916- *ConAu 1R*
VanRiper, Robert 1921- *ConAu 37R*
VanRjndt, Philippe 1950- *ConAu 65, WrDr 84*
VanRooy, C A 1923- *ConAu 17R*
VanSaanen, Christine Dumitriu 1932-
  IntAu&W 82
VanSaher, Lilla 1912-1968 *ConAu P-1*
Vansant, Carl 1938- *ConAu 37R*
VanSanten, Louise 1924- *IntAu&W 82*
VanSchaick, Frances L 1912?-1979 *ConAu 89*
VanSchaik-Willing, Jeanne Gabrielle 1895-
  IntAu&W 82
VanScyoc, Sydney 1939- *ConAu 89, TwCSFW,
  WrDr 84*
VanSertima, Ivan Gladstone 1935- *ConAu 104*
VanSickle, John V 1892- *ConAu 5R*
VanSickle, Neil D 1915- *ConAu 41R*
VanSickle, V A *ConAu X*
VanSiller, Hilda *WrDr 84*
Vansina, Jan 1929- *ConAu 10NR, –65*
VanSittart, Jane 1908- *ConAu X*
Vansittart, Peter 1920- *ConAu 1R, –3NR,
  DcLEL 1940, IntAu&W 82, WorAu,
  WrDr 84*
VanSlingerland, Peter 1929- *ConAu 21R*
VanSlooten, Henry 1916- *ConAu 1R*
VanSlyck, Philip 1920- *ConAu 13R*
VanSlyke, Donald Dexter 1883-1971 *ConAu 104*
VanSlyke, Helen 1919-1979 *ConAu 37R, –89,
  TwCRGW*
VanSlyke, Lyman P 1929- *ConAu 21R*
VanSomeren, Liesje *ConAu X*
VanSomeren, Liesji *WrDr 84*
Vanson, Frederic 1919- *IntWWP 82*
VanSpanckeren, Kathryn *DrAP&F 83*
VanSteenwyk, Elizabeth Ann 1928- *ConAu 101,
  SmATA 34[port]*
VanStockum, Hilda 1908- *ConAu 5NR, –9R,
  SmATA 5, TwCCW 83, WrDr 84*
VanStraten, Florence W 1913- *ConAu 17R*
Van't Sant, Mien *IntAu&W 82X*
VanTassel, Alfred James 1910- *ConAu 41R*
VanTassel, David Dirck 1928- *ConAu 103*
VanTassel, Dennie L *WrDr 84*
VanTassel, Dennie L 1939- *ConAu 8NR, –57*
VanTassel, Katrina *DrAP&F 83*
VanTassel, Roger 1924- *ConAu 45*
VanThal, Herbert 1904- *ConAu 65, WrDr 84*
VanTil, Cornelius 1895- *ConAu 1R, –3NR*
VanTil, William 1911- *ConAu 10NR, –25R,
  WrDr 84*
VanTine, Warren R 1942- *ConAu 53*
VanTrump, James D 1908- *ConAu 41R*
VanTuyl, Barbara 1940- *ConAu 53, SmATA 11*
VanTuyl, Zaara 1901- *ConSFA*
VanTuyll VanSerooskereken, Agnes Renee 1905-
  IntAu&W 82
VanTyne, Claude Halstead 1869-1930 *TwCA*
VanValkenburg, Samuel 1891-1976 *ConAu 5R,
  –103*
VanValkenburgh, Paul 1941- *ConAu 89*
VanVechten, Benjamin D 1935- *ConAu 110*
VanVechten, Carl 1880-1964 *ConAmA,
  ConAu 89, DcLB 4, –9[port], LongCTC,
  TwCA, TwCA SUP*
VanVleck, David B 1929- *ConAu 101*
VanVleck, John Hasbrouck 1899-1980
  ConAu 102
VanVleck, L Dale 1933- *ConAu 53*
VanVleck, Sarita 1933- *ConAu 13R*
VanVogt, A E 1912- *ConAu 21R, ConSFA,
  DcLB 8[port], DrmM[port], SmATA 14,
  TwCSFW, WrDr 84*
VanVogt, Alfred Elton 1912- *ConLC 1,
  IntAu&W 82, TwCA SUP*
VanVogt, Alfred Elton 1914- *CnMWL*
VanVooren, Monique 1933- *ConAu 107*
VanVoorhis, Linda Lyon 1902- *IntWWP 82*
VanVoris, Jacqueline 1922- *ConAu 57*
VanVuuren, Nancy 1938- *ConAu 49*
VanWagenen, Gertrude 1893-1978 *ConAu 77*
VanWageningen, J *ConAu X*

VanWagenvoorde, H *IntAu&W 82X*
VanWallegehen, Michael 1938- *IntWWP 82*
VanWaters, Miriam 1887-1974 *ConAu 45*
VanWeddingen, Marthe 1924- *ConAu 81*
Vanwert, William F *DrAP&F 83*
VanWert, William F 1945- *ConAu 105,
  IntWWP 82*
Vanwinckel, Nance Lee *DrAP&F 83*
VanWitsen, Leo 1912- *ConAu 106*
VanWoeart, Alpheus *ConAu X*
VanWoerkom, Dorothy 1924- *ConAu 11NR, –57,
  IntAu&W 82, SmATA 21[port]*
VanWormer, Joe *ConAu X*
VanWormer, Joseph Edward 1913- *ConAu 5NR,
  –9R*
VanWyck Mason *SmATA X*
VanWyck Mason, F *SmATA X*
VanWylen, Gordon J 1920- *WrDr 84*
VanZandt, E F *ConAu X*
VanZandt, Roland 1918- *ConAu 17R*
VanZante, Helen Johnson 1906- *ConAu 13R*
VanZanten, John W 1913- *ConAu 101*
VanZeller, Claud 1905- *ConAu 6NR*
VanZeller, Hubert 1905- *ConAu X, –1R*
VanZwienen, Ilse 1929- *SmATA 34[port]*
VanZwienen, Ilse Charlotte Koehn 1929-
  ConAu 85
VanZwienin, Ilse Charlotte Koehn 1929-
  SmATA 28
VanZwoll, James A 1909- *ConAu P-1*
Vaqar, Nasrollah 1920- *ConAu 41R*
Vara, Albert C 1931- *ConAu 33R*
Varah, Chad 1911- *ConAu 57, IntAu&W 82*
Varandyan, Emmanuel P 1904- *ConAu 65*
Varas, Florencia *ConAu X*
Varda, Agnes 1928- *ConLC 16, IntAu&W 82*
Vardaman, E Jerry 1927- *ConAu 17R*
Vardaman, George T 1920- *ConAu 1R, –4NR*
Vardaman, James Money 1921- *ConAu 104*
Vardaman, Patricia Black 1931- *ConAu 37R,
  WrDr 84*
Vardamis, Alex A 1934- *ConAu 77*
Vardre, Leslie *ConAu X, WrDr 84*
Vardy, Steven Bela 1936- *ConAu 4NR, –53*
Vardys, V Stanley 1924- *ConAu 5NR, –13R*
Vare, Robert 1945- *ConAu 103, WrDr 84*
Varelaibarra, Jose L *DrAP&F 83*
Varese, Louise 1890- *ConAu 41R*
Varga, Judy *ConAu X, SmATA X*
Vargas, Herminio *DrAP&F 83*
Vargas, Julie S 1938- *ConAu 57*
Vargas, Lopez Modesto 1938- *IntAu&W 82*
Vargas, Robert *DrAP&F 83*
Vargas Llosa, Mario 1936- *ConAu 73,
  ConLC 3, –6, –9, –10, –15, ModLAL,
  TwCWr, WhoTwCL, WorAu 1970*
Vargas-Machuca, Antonio 1933- *IntAu&W 82*
Vargish, Thomas 1939- *ConAu 37R, WrDr 84*
Vargyas, Lajos 1914- *IntAu&W 82*
Varick, Rose *MichAu 80*
Varkonyi, Mihaly 1931- *IntAu&W 82*
Varlay, Rene G 1927- *ConAu 1R*
Varley, Dimitry V 1906- *ConAu P-1,
  SmATA 10, WrDr 84*
Varley, Frederick Horsman 1881-1969 *CreCan 1*
Varley, Gloria 1932- *ConAu 101*
Varley, H Paul 1931- *ConAu 77*
Varley, John 1947- *ConAu 69,
  DcLB Y81B[port], TwCSFW, WrDr 84*
Varley, M E *ConAu X*
Varlund, Rudolf 1900-1945 *ModWD*
Varma, Baidya Nath 1921- *ConAu 41R*
Varma, Monika 1916- *ConAu 77, ConP 80,
  IntAu&W 82, WrDr 84*
Varnac, D'Hugues *ConAu X*
Varnado, Jewel Goodgame 1915- *ConAu 9R*
Varnalis, Costas 1884-1974 *ConAu 53*
Varnalis, Kostas 1883-1974 *CIDMEL 80*
Varner, John Grier 1905- *ConAu 25R*
Varner, Velma V 1916-1972 *ConAu 37R*
Varney, Carleton B 1937- *ConAu 89*
Varnlund, Rudolf 1900-1945 *CnMD*
Vars, Gordon F 1923- *ConAu 21R*
Varshavsky, Ilya 1909- *TwCSFW A*
Vartan, Vartanig Garabed 1923- *ConAu 61*
Vartanian, Aram 1922- *ConAu 1R, –3NR*
Varvarande, Robert Emile 1922- *CreCan 1*
Vas, Istvan 1910- *CIDMEL 80, IntAu&W 82,
  IntWWP 82*
Vas Dias, Robert *DrAP&F 83*
Vas Dias, Robert 1931- *ConAu 7NR, –17R,
  ConP 80, WrDr 84*

Vasconcelos, Mario Cesariny De 1923-
    ClDMEL 80
Vasil, R K 1931- ConAu 37R
Vasil, Raj Kumar 1931- WrDr 84
Vasiliu, Mircea 1920- ConAu 21R, SmATA 2
Vaske, Martin O 1915- ConAu 2NR, –5R
Vasovec, Ernst 1917- IntAu&W 82
Vasquez, John A 1945- ConAu 108
Vasquez, Pura 1918- IntAu&W 82
Vasquez, Richard DrAP&F 83
Vasquez Iglesias, Dora 1913- IntAu&W 82
Vass, George 1927- ConAu 37R, SmATA 31
Vass, Winifred Kellersberger 1917- ConAu 57
Vassall, John 1924- WrDr 84
Vassi, Marco 1937- ConAu 61
Vassiliadis, Martha-Ariadne Catherine 1933-
    IntAu&W 82
Vassilikos, Vassilis 1933- ConAu 81, ConLC 4,
    –8, WorAu
Vasta, Edward 1928- ConAu 17R,
    IntAu&W 82, WrDr 84
Vasu, Nirmala-Kumara ConAu X
Vasudeva DrAP&F 83
Vasudeva, Vishnudayal WrDr 84
Vasvary, Edmund 1888-1977 ConAu 73
Vatikiotis, P J 1928- ConAu 6NR, –13R,
    WrDr 84
Vatikiotis, Panayiotis J 1928- IntAu&W 82
Vatsend, Helge A 1928- IntWWP 82
Vatter, Harold Goodhue 1910- ConAu 5R
Vaudreuil, Guy De CreCan 1
Vaudrin, Bill ConAu X
Vaudrin, William 1943-1976 ConAu P-2
Vaughan, Agnes Carr 1887- ConAu P-1
Vaughan, Alan 1936- ConAu 81
Vaughan, Alden True 1929- ConAu 7NR, –17R,
    WrDr 84
Vaughan, Beatrice 1909?-1972 ConAu 37R
Vaughan, Bill ConAu X
Vaughan, Carter A ConAu X, SmATA X
Vaughan, Clark 1924- ConAu 108
Vaughan, David 1924- ConAu 77, IntAu&W 82
Vaughan, Denis 1920- ConAu 61
Vaughan, Donald S 1921- ConAu 10NR, –17R
Vaughan, Frances E 1935- ConAu 107
Vaughan, Harold Cecil 1923- ConAu 29R,
    SmATA 14
Vaughan, Hilda WrDr 84
Vaughan, Hilda 1892- IntAu&W 82, LongCTC,
    TwCA, TwCA SUP
Vaughan, James A 1936- ConAu 49
Vaughan, John Edmund 1935- ConAu 61
Vaughan, Leo ConAu X
Vaughan, Paul William 1925- ConAu 29R,
    WrDr 84
Vaughan, Peter ConAmTC
Vaughan, Richard 1904- ConAu X, WorAu
Vaughan, Richard Patrick 1919- ConAu 13R,
    WrDr 84
Vaughan, Robert 1937- ConAu 103
Vaughan, Roger 1937- ConAu 85
Vaughan, Sam S 1928- ConAu 13R,
    SmATA 14
Vaughan, Sheila Marie 1930- ConAu 21R
Vaughan, Virginia M 1947- ConAu 110
Vaughan, William E 1915-1977 ConAu 5R, –69
Vaughan-Thomas, Wynford 1908- IntAu&W 82,
    WrDr 84
Vaughan Williams, Ursula 1911- ConAu 6NR,
    –9R, IntAu&W 82, WrDr 84
Vaughn, Sister Ann Carol 1922- ConAu 9R
Vaughn, Charles L 1911- ConAu 41R
Vaughn, Donald E 1932- ConAu 21R
Vaughn, Jack A 1935- ConAu 85
Vaughn, Jesse Wendell 1903-1968 ConAu 1R,
    –103
Vaughn, Michael J 1943- ConAu 37R
Vaughn, Richard 1904- DcLEL 1940
Vaughn, Richard C 1925- ConAu 9NR, –21R
Vaughn, Robert 1932- ConAu 61
Vaughn, Ruth Wood 1935- ConAu 41R,
    SmATA 14
Vaughn, Stephen L 1947- ConAu 101
Vaughn, Toni ConAu X
Vaughn, William Preston 1933- ConAu 73
Vaughn-Brown, Patricia 1933- IntAu&W 82
Vaurie, Charles 1906-1975 ConAu 4NR, –5R
Vaussard, Maurice 1888- ConAu 9R
Vauthier, Jean 1910- ClDMEL 80, CnMD,
    CroCD, ModFrL, ModWD
Vavra, Robert James 1935- ConAu 25R,
    SmATA 8

Vawter, Francis Bruce 1921- ConAu 1R, –4NR
Vayda, Andrew P 1931- ConAu 17R,
    IntAu&W 82, WrDr 84
Vayhinger, John Monroe 1916- ConAu 73
Vayle, Valerie ConAu X
Vaz, Edmund 1924- ConAu 108
Vaz DeSoto, Jose Maria 1938- ClDMEL 80,
    IntAu&W 82
Vazakas, Byron DrAP&F 83
Vazakas, Byron 1905- ConAu P-2,
    IntAu&W 82, IntWWP 82, WrDr 84
Vazov, Ivan 1850-1921 ClDMEL 80, ModSL 2
Vazquez Azpiri, Hector 1931- ClDMEL 80
Vazquez DePrada, Andres 1924- IntAu&W 82
Veach, William B Templeton 1896- ConAu P-1
Veaner, Allen B 1929- ConAu 41R
Veasey, Jack DrAP&F 83
Veatch, Henry Babcock 1911- ConAu 5R, –6NR
Veatch, Robert M 1939- ConAu 11NR, –69,
    IntAu&W 82
Veblen, Peter DrAP&F 83
Veblen, Thorstein Bunde 1857-1929 LongCTC,
    ModAL, TwCA, TwCA SUP, TwCWr,
    WhoTwCL
Vechten, TwCA, TwCA SUP
Vecoli, Rudolph J 1927- ConAu 10NR, –17R
Vecsey, George 1939- ConAu 61, SmATA 9
Vecsey, George Spencer 1939- ConAu 10NR
Vedder, John K ConAu X
Veder, Bob 1940- ConAu 104
Veedam, Voldemar 1912-1983 ConAu 109
Veenboer, Paul Ernst Nico 1945- IntAu&W 82
Veenendaal, Cornelia DrAP&F 83
Veenendaal, Cornelia 1924- IntWWP 82
Vega, Ed DrAP&F 83
Vega, J IntWWP 82X
Vega, Janine Pommy DrAP&F 83
Vega, Janine Pommy 1942- ConAu 2NR, –49,
    DcLB 16[port], IntWWP 82
Vege, Nageswara Rao 1932- IntAu&W 82
Veglahn, Nancy Crary 1937- ConAu 7NR, –17R,
    SmATA 5
Veiga, Jose Jacinto 1915- ConAu 37R,
    IntAu&W 82
Veiller, Bayard 1869-1943 TwCA, TwCA SUP
Veillon, Lee 1942- ConAu 49
Veit, Stan 1929- ConAu 110
Veitch, Thomas 1912- WrDr 84
Veitch, Tom DrAP&F 83
Veits, Ulf IntAu&W 82X
Vekemans, Roger 1921- ConAu 37R
Velardo, Joseph Thomas 1923- WrDr 84
Veler, Richard P 1936- ConAu 49
Velie, Alan R 1937- ConAu 1NR, –45
Velie, Lester 1908- ConAu P-2
Velikovsky, Immanuel 1895-1979 ConAu 69, –89
Veliz, Claudio 1930- ConAu 25R
Vella, Walter F 1924- ConAu 45
Vella, Tony 1945- ConAu 65
Velleman, Ruth A 1921- ConAu 110
Velthuijs, Max 1923- ConAu 89
Veltman, Vera ConAu X
Velvel, Lawrence R 1939- ConAu 29R
Ven, Ton WorAu 1970
Venable, Alan 1944- ConAu 45, SmATA 8
Venable, Tom C 1921- ConAu 29R
Venable, Vernon 1906- ConAu P-2
Venables, Roger Evelyn Cavendish 1911-
    IntAu&W 82, IntWWP 82
Venables, Terry WrDr 84
Venafro, Mark ConAu 49
Vendler, Helen 1933- WrDr 84
Vendler, Helen Hennessy 1933- ConAu 41R
Vendler, Zeno 1921- ConAu 105
Vendrovskii, David Efimovich 1879-1971
    ConAu 33R
Vendrovsky, David ConAu X
Veness, Thelma 1919- ConAu 5R
Vengroff, Richard 1945- ConAu 10NR, –65
Venison, Alfred ConAu X
Venn, George DrAP&F 83
Venn, Grant 1919- ConAu 13R
Vennard, Edwin 1902- ConAu P-2
Vennberg, Karl 1910- ClDMEL 80,
    WorAu 1970
Vennema, Alje 1932- ConAu 101
Venner, J G ConAu X, IntAu&W 82X
Venning, Corey 1924- ConAu 49
Venning, Hugh 1905- ConAu X
Venning, Michael TwCCr&M 80
Ventadour, Fanny DrAP&F 83
Venter, Albertus Johannes 1938- IntAu&W 82

Venton, W B 1898-1976 ConAu P-2
Ventura, Adao IntWWP 82X
Ventura, Jeffrey ConAu X
Ventura, Joan IntAu&W 82X
Ventura, Piero Luigi 1937- ConAu 103
Ventura Ferreira Reis, Adao 1946- IntWWP 82
Venturi, Denise Scott Brown ConAu X
Venturi, Franco 1914- IntAu&W 82
Venturi, Lionello 1885- TwCA SUP
Venturi, Marcello 1925- ConAu 29R
Venturi, Robert 1925- ConAu 61, WrDr 84
Venturini, Fiorenza 1919- IntAu&W 82
Venturo, Betty Lou Baker 1928- ConAu 1R
Vequin, Capini SmATA X
Verba, Sidney 1932- ConAu 1R, –3NR
VerBecke, W Edwin 1912- NatPD 81[port]
Verbitsky, Bernardo 1907- ModLAL
Vercammen, Jan 1906- IntWWP 82
Vercel, Roger 1894-1957 TwCA, TwCA SUP
Vercors 1902- ClDMEL 80, ConAu X,
    IntAu&W 82, LongCTC, ModFrL, ModRL,
    TwCA SUP, TwCSFW A, TwCWr
Verdaguer I Santalo, Jacint 1845-1902
    ClDMEL 80
Verdenius, W J 1913- ConAu 25R
Verdenius, Willem Jacob 1913- IntAu&W 82
Verdery, John D 1917- ConAu 9R
Verdick, Mary 1923- ConAu 1R, –4NR
Verdon, Dorothy WrDr 84
Verdross, Alfred 1890- IntAu&W 82
Verdu, Matilde ConAu X
Verduin, John R, Jr. 1931- ConAu 9NR
Verduin, John Richard, Jr. 1931- ConAu 21R,
    WrDr 84
Verduin, Leonard 1897- ConAu 61
Verene, Donald Phillip 1937- ConAu 41R
Veresayev, Vikenti Vikentievich 1867-1946
    TwCWr
Verey, David 1913- ConAu 65
Verga, Giovanni 1840-1922 ClDMEL 80,
    ConAu 104, LongCTC, ModRL, ModWD,
    TwCA SUP, TwCLC 3, WhoTwCL
Vergani, Luisa 1931- ConAu 21R
Vergara, Jose Manuel 1929- ConAu 97
Vergara, Joseph R 1915- ConAu 29R
Vergara, William C 1923- ConAu 1R
Verghese, Paul IntAu&W 82X
Verghese, T Paul ConAu X
Verghese, T Paul 1922- ConAu 25R
Verhaeren, Emile 1855-1916 ConAu 109,
    TwCLC 12[port]
Verhaeren, Emile Adolphe Gustave 1855-1916
    ClDMEL 80, LongCTC, ModFrL, ModRL,
    ModWD, TwCA, TwCA SUP, WhoTwCL
Verhalen, Philip A 1934- ConAu 69
Verhavert, Roland 1927- IntAu&W 82
Verheghe, Willie 1947- IntWWP 82
Verheyen, Piet A 1931- IntAu&W 82
Verhoeven, Corn 1928- ConAu 61
Verhoeven, Cornelis 1928- ConAu 8NR
Verhonick, Phillis J 1922?-1977 ConAu 73
Verhoogen, John 1912- ConAu 109
Verin, Velko ConAu X
Verissimo, Erico 1905- ModLAL, TwCWr,
    WorAu
Verkade-Cartier VanDissel, Eline F 1906-
    IntAu&W 82
Verkennes, Geneva Alice 1914- IntWWP 82
Verlaine, Paul 1844-1896 ClDMEL 80, ModRL
Verma, Ravivermajwala 1933- IntWWP 82
Vermes, Geza 1924- ConAu 57, IntAu&W 82,
    WrDr 84
Vermes, Jean C 1907- ConAu 106
Vermeule, Cornelius Clarkson, III 1925-
    ConAu 41R
Vermeule, E D T 1928- ConAu 17R
Vermeylen, August 1872-1945 ClDMEL 80
Vermont, Charles 1945- IntWWP 82
Vermont, Charlie IntWWP 82X
Vernadsky, George 1887-1973 ConAu 41R
Vernam, Glenn R 1896- ConAu 17R
Vernam, Glenn R 1896-1980 ConAu 10NR
Vernant, Jean-Pierre 1914- ConAu 109
Vernazza, Marcelle Wynn 1909- ConAu 17R
Verne, Jules 1828-1905 ClDMEL 80,
    ConAu 110, LongCTC, SmATA 21[port],
    TwCLC 6[port], TwCSFW A
Verner, Coolie 1917- WrDr 84
Verner, Coolie 1917-1979 ConAu 7NR, –53
Verner, Gerald 1897?-1980 ConAu 102,
    SmATA 25N
Vernet, Gwynne DrAP&F 83

W

Wa-Sha-Quon-Asin *CreCan 1, SmATA X*
Wa Thiong'o, Ngugi 1938- *ConLC 13*
Waage, Frederick 1943- *ConAu 104*
Waage, Frederick O *DrAP&F 83*
Waagenaar, Sam 1908- *ConAu 57, WrDr 84*
Waber, Bernard 1924- *ConAu 1R, −2NR, TwCCW 83, WrDr 84*
Wabun *ConAu X*
Wacher, John Stewart 1927- *ConAu 105*
Wachhorst, Wyn 1938- *ConAu 106*
Wachs, Mark Marshall 1933- *ConAu 25R*
Wachsmann, Klaus Philipp 1907- *ConAu 106*
Wachtel, Chuck *DrAP&F 83*
Wachtel, Howard M 1938- *ConAu 49*
Wachtel, Isidore H 1909?-1979 *ConAu 89*
Waciuma, Wanjohi 1938- *ConAu 77*
Wacken, Francoise *IntWWP 82X*
Wacker, Charles H, Jr. 1925- *ConAu 73*
Wackerbarth, Marjorie *ConAu P-1*
Wadbrook, William P 1933- *ConAu 45*
Waddams, Herbert Montague 1911-1972 *ConAu 107*
Waddell, D A G 1927- *ConAu 1R*
Waddell, Eric 1939- *ConAu 45*
Waddell, Evelyn Margaret 1918- *ConAu 53, IntAu&W 82, SmATA 10, WrDr 84*
Waddell, Heather 1950- *IntAu&W 82*
Waddell, Helen Jane 1889-1965 *ConAu 102, LongCTC, TwCA, TwCA SUP, TwCWr*
Waddell, Jack O 1933- *ConAu 33R*
Waddell, Martin *TwCCW 83*
Waddell, Samuel J *LongCTC*
Waddington, C H 1905-1975 *ConAu 6NR*
Waddington, Conrad Hal 1905-1975 *ConAu 13R, −61*
Waddington, Geoffrey 1904-1966 *CreCan 2*
Waddington, Miriam 1917- *ConAu 21R, ConP 80, CreCan 1, DcLEL 1940, ModCmwL, WrDr 84*
Waddington, Raymond B 1935- *ConAu 53, WrDr 84*
Waddington-Feather, John Joseph 1933- *IntAu&W 82, IntWWP 82, WrDr 84*
Waddy, Charis 1909- *ConAu 69, WrDr 84*
Waddy, Lawrence Heber 1914- *ConAu 7NR, −13R, IntAu&W 82, WrDr 84*
Wade, Alan *WrDr 84*
Wade, Arthur Sarsfield *TwCA, TwCA SUP*
Wade, Bob *ConAu X*
Wade, Bob 1920- *ConAu X*
Wade, Carlson 1928- *ConAu 29R*
Wade, David 1929- *ConAu 103, WrDr 84*
Wade, David Lawson 1934- *IntWWP 82*
Wade, Francis Clarence 1907- *ConAu P-1*
Wade, Graham 1940- *ConAu 107*
Wade, Gwen *IntWWP 82X*
Wade, Gwendolen 1904- *IntWWP 82*
Wade, Harry Vincent 1894-1973 *ConAu 89*
Wade, Henry 1887-1969 *TwCCr&M 80*
Wade, Henry 1918- *WrDr 84*
Wade, Henry William Rawson 1918- *ConAu 109*
Wade, Herbert *ConAu X*
Wade, Ira Owen 1896- *ConAu 73*
Wade, Ira Owen 1896-1983 *ConAu 109*

Wade, Jennifer *WrDr 84*
Wade, Jennifer 1936- *ConAu X, TwCRGW*
Wade, Jerry L 1941- *ConAu 53*
Wade, Jewel Millsap 1937- *ConAu 107*
Wade, Joanna *ConAu X*
Wade, John Stevens *DrAP&F 83*
Wade, John Stevens 1927- *ConAu 6NR, −13R*
Wade, Kit *ConAu X*
Wade, L L 1935- *ConAu 33R*
Wade, Mason 1913- *ConAu 9R, WrDr 84*
Wade, Nicholas 1942- *ConAu 77*
Wade, Rex A 1936- *ConAu 61*
Wade, Richard Clement 1922- *ConAu 17R*
Wade, Robert *ConAu X, WrDr 84*
Wade, Robert 1920- *ConAu 108, TwCCr&M 80, WrDr 84*
Wade, Rosalind 1909- *WrDr 84*
Wade, Rosalind Herschel 1909- *ConAu P-1*
Wade, Stephen 1948- *IntWWP 82*
Wade, Tom *ConSFA*
Wade, William 1918- *ConAu 1R, −4NR*
Wade, Wyn Craig 1944- *ConAu 103*
Wadekin, Karl-Eugen *ConAu X*
Wadepuhl, Walter 1895- *ConAu 61*
Wadey, Victor *ConSFA*
Wadia, Maneck S 1931- *ConAu 17R, WrDr 84*
Wadinasi, Sedeka *ConAu X*
Wadley, Susan Snow 1943- *ConAu 77, IntAu&W 82*
Wadlington, Walter 1931- *ConAu 33R*
Wadlington, Warwick 1938- *ConAu 73*
Wadman, Anne 1919- *IntAu&W 82*
Wadsworth, Barry James 1935- *ConAu 37R*
Wadsworth, Frank Whittemore 1919- *ConAu 9R*
Wadsworth, James J 1905- *ConAu P-2*
Wadsworth, M D 1936- *ConAu 45*
Wadsworth, Michael E J 1942- *ConAu 93*
Wadsworth, Nelson B 1930- *ConAu 65*
Waedekin, Karl-Eugen 1921- *ConAu 73*
Waehrer, Helen 1938- *ConAu 53*
Waelder, Robert 1900-1967 *ConAu P-1*
Waengler, Hans-Heinrich B 1921- *ConAu 41R*
Waffle, Harvey W 1904- *ConAu 5R*
Wagar, W Warren 1932- *ConAu 3NR*
Wagar, Warren 1932- *ConAu 5R*
Wagatsuma, Hiroshi 1927- *ConAu 21R*
Wagemaker, Herbert, Jr. 1929- *ConAu 93*
Wagener, Hans 1940- *ConAu 1NR, −45*
Wagenheim, Kal 1935- *ConAu 29R, SmATA 21*
Wagenknecht, Edward 1900- *ConAu 1R, −6NR, IntAu&W 82, TwCA SUP, WrDr 84*
Wagenvoord, James 1937- *ConAu 41R*
Wager, Walter H 1924- *ConAu 5R, −8NR, IntAu&W 82*
Wager, Willis Joseph 1911- *ConAu 37R*
Waggaman, William Henry 1884?-1978 *ConAu 77*
Waggerl, Karl Heinrich 1897-1973 *ClDMEL 80, ModGL*
Waggoner, Hyatt H 1913- *ConAu 9NR, −21R*
Wagley, Charles 1913- *ConAu 10NR, −13R*
Waglow, Irving Frederick 1915- *ConAu 1R*
Wagman, Fredrica 1937- *ConAu 97, ConLC 7*

Wagman, Naomi 1937- *ConAu 57*
Wagman, Robert John 1942- *ConAu 93, IntAu&W 82*
Wagner, Anneliese *DrAP&F 83*
Wagner, Anthony 1908- *WrDr 84*
Wagner, Anthony Richard 1908- *ConAu 1R, −5NR*
Wagner, C Peter 1930- *ConAu 9NR, −21R*
Wagner, Charles A *DrAP&F 83*
Wagner, Charles Abraham 1901- *ConAu 5R, IntAu&W 82, IntWWP 82*
Wagner, Edwin E 1930- *ConAu 45*
Wagner, Elaine 1939- *ConAu 45*
Wagner, Eliot 1917- *ConAu 105*
Wagner, Francis S 1911- *ConAu 8NR, −61*
Wagner, Frederick 1928- *ConAu 5R*
Wagner, Geoffrey 1922- *WorAu*
Wagner, Geoffrey Atheling 1927- *ConAu 1R, −2NR*
Wagner, Georg Michael 1924- *IntWWP 82*
Wagner, Harvey M 1931- *ConAu 6NR, −13R*
Wagner, Helmut R 1904- *ConAu 4NR, −53*
Wagner, Jack Russell 1916- *ConAu 49*
Wagner, Jane *ConAu 109, SmATA 33*
Wagner, Jean Pierre 1919- *ConAu 21R*
Wagner, Jon G 1944- *ConAu 109*
Wagner, Joseph Frederick 1900?-1974 *ConAu 53*
Wagner, Karl Edward 1945- *ConAu 3NR, −49, IntAu&W 82*
Wagner, Ken 1911- *ConAu 37R*
Wagner, Kenneth Allan 1919- *ConAu 53*
Wagner, Linda 1936- *WrDr 84*
Wagner, Linda W *DrAP&F 83*
Wagner, Linda Welshimer 1936- *ConAu 3NR, −9R, MichAu 80*
Wagner, Margaret D 1949- *ConAu 5R*
Wagner, Marsden 1930- *ConAu 69*
Wagner, Maryfrances *DrAP&F 83*
Wagner, Nathaniel N 1930- *ConAu 57*
Wagner, Peggy *ConAu X*
Wagner, Philip L 1921- *ConAu 41R*
Wagner, Philip Marshall 1904- *ConAu 102*
Wagner, Ray David 1924- *ConAu 3NR, −5R*
Wagner, Ray Jay 1931- *ConAu 77*
Wagner, Richard 1813-1883 *ClDMEL 80*
Wagner, Richard Vansant 1935- *ConAu 105*
Wagner, Roy 1938- *ConAu 41R*
Wagner, Rudolph Fred 1921- *ConAu 37R, WrDr 84*
Wagner, Ruth H 1909- *ConAu 29R*
Wagner, Sharon B 1936- *ConAu 10NR*
Wagner, Sharon Blythe 1936- *ConAu 25R, SmATA 4, WrDr 84*
Wagner, Stanley P 1923- *ConAu 29R*
Wagner, Walter 1927?-1983? *ConAu 109*
Wagner, Walter F, Jr. 1926- *ConAu 69*
Wagner, Wenceslas J 1917- *WrDr 84*
Wagner, Wenceslas Joseph 1917- *ConAu 37R*
Wagner, Wolfgang 1912- *IntAu&W 82*
Wagoner, David *DrAP&F 83*
Wagoner, David 1926- *ConAu 1R, −2NR, ConLC 3, −5, −15, ConNov 82, ConP 80, CroCAP, DcLB 5, DcLEL 1940, SmATA 14, TwCWW, WorAu, WrDr 84*

Walker, Ira *ConAu X*
Walker, Irma Ruth 1921- *ConAu 5R, –6NR*
Walker, J *ConAu X, WrDr 84*
Walker, Jack *ConAu X*
Walker, James Lynwood 1940- *ConAu 37R*
Walker, Janet 1941- *IntWWP 82*
Walker, Jauvanta Maurine 1926- *IntWWP 82*
Walker, Jav *IntWWP 82X*
Walker, Jean Trafford 1922- *WrDr 84*
Walker, Jeanne 1924- *ConAu 61*
Walker, Jeanne Murray *DrAP&F 83*
Walker, Jeanne Murray 1944- *IntWWP 82*
Walker, Jeremy D B 1936- *ConAu 21R*
Walker, Joan *ConAu 5R*
Walker, John 1906- *ConAu 5R, –6NR,
  WrDr 84*
Walker, Joseph A 1935- *ConAu 89, ConDr 82,
  ConLC 19, WrDr 84*
Walker, Joseph E 1911- *ConAu 37R, WrDr 84*
Walker, Kenneth Francis 1924- *ConAu 33R*
Walker, Kenneth Macfarlane 1882?-1966
  ConAu 5R, LongCTC
Walker, Kenneth Richard 1931- *ConAu 17R,
  IntAu&W 82, WrDr 84*
Walker, Kenneth Roland 1928- *ConAu 37R,
  IntAu&W 82, WrDr 84*
Walker, Laurence C 1924- *ConAu 53*
Walker, Lawrence David 1931- *ConAu 53*
Walker, Lenore E 1942- *ConAu 97,
  IntAu&W 82*
Walker, Leo *ConAu 13R*
Walker, Lois V *DrAP&F 83*
Walker, Louise Jean 1891-1976 *ConAu 110,
  MichAu 80*
Walker, Lucy *ConAu X*
Walker, Lucy 1907- *TwCRGW, WrDr 84*
Walker, Mack 1929- *ConAu 9R*
Walker, Margaret *DrAP&F 83*
Walker, Margaret 1915- *ConAu 73, ConLC 1,
  –6, ConNov 82, ConP 80, CroCAP,
  LivgBAA, ModBlW, WrDr 84*
Walker, Margaret Pope 1901?-1980 *ConAu 101*
Walker, Marshall John 1912- *ConAu 17R*
Walker, Martin 1947- *ConAu 101*
Walker, Mary Alexander *DrAP&F 83*
Walker, Mary Alexander 1927- *ConAu 104*
Walker, Mickey 1901-1981 *ConAu 108*
Walker, Mildred 1905- *ConAu X, MichAu 80,
  SmATA X, TwCA SUP, WrDr 84*
Walker, Mort 1923- *ConAu 3NR, –49,
  SmATA 8*
Walker, Morton 1929- *ConAu 85*
Walker, Nicolette Milnes 1943- *ConAu 41R*
Walker, Nigel David 1917- *ConAu 61,
  IntAu&W 82*
Walker, Pamela *DrAP&F 83*
Walker, Pamela 1948- *ConAu 69,
  SmATA 24[port]*
Walker, Peter Benson 1922- *WrDr 84*
Walker, Peter F 1931- *ConAu 13R*
Walker, Peter Norman 1936- *ConAu 77*
Walker, Philip Mitchell 1943- *ConAu 29R*
Walker, Ralph Spence 1904- *IntAu&W 82*
Walker, Richard Louis 1922- *ConAu 7NR, –9R,
  IntAu&W 82*
Walker, Robert H 1924- *ConAu 7NR, –13R*
Walker, Robert Newton 1911- *ConAu 53*
Walker, Robert Wayne 1948- *ConAu 93,
  IntAu&W 82*
Walker, Roger W 1931- *ConAu 45*
Walker, Ronald G 1945- *ConAu 93*
Walker, Samuel 1942- *ConAu 85, WrDr 84*
Walker, Shel *ConAu X*
Walker, Stanley 1898-1962 *ConAu 93*
Walker, Stella Archer *WrDr 84*
Walker, Stella Archer 1907- *ConAu 61,
  IntAu&W 82*
Walker, Stephen J 1951- *SmATA 12*
Walker, Stuart 1880-1941 *TwCCW 83*
Walker, Stuart H 1923- *ConAu 45*
Walker, Sue *DrAP&F 83*
Walker, Sydney, III 1931- *ConAu 21R*
Walker, T Michael 1937- *ConAu 77*
Walker, Ted *DrAP&F 83*
Walker, Ted 1934- *ConAu 21R, ConLC 13,
  ConP 80, DcLEL 1940, WrDr 84*
Walker, Theodore J 1922- *ConAu 102*
Walker, Warren S 1921- *ConAu 3NR, –9R*
Walker, Willard 1926- *ConAu 45*
Walker, William Edward 1925- *ConAu 9R*
Walker, William George 1928- *ConAu 77,
  WrDr 84*

Walker, William H 1913- *ConAu 17R*
Walker, William Otis 1896-1981 *ConAu 105*
Walker-Little, Eunice Arnaud *IntAu&W 82*
Walkerley, Rodney Lewis 1905- *ConAu P-1*
Walkinshaw, Colin *ConAu X*
Walkinshaw, Lawrence H 1904- *ConAu 45,
  MichAu 80*
Walkley, Arthur Bingham 1855-1926 *LongCTC,
  ModBrL, TwCA*
Walko, Gyorgy 1920- *IntAu&W 82*
Walkowitz, Daniel J 1942- *ConAu 81*
Wall, Barbara 1911- *ConAu 97*
Wall, Bennett H 1914- *ConAu 77*
Wall, C Edward 1942- *ConAu 37R*
Wall, Dorothy 1894-1942 *TwCCW 83*
Wall, Elizabeth S 1924- *ConAu 93*
Wall, Isabelle Louise 1909- *IntAu&W 82*
Wall, John W *WrDr 84*
Wall, Joseph Frazier 1920- *ConAu 29R,
  WrDr 84*
Wall, Maggie 1937- *ConAu 65*
Wall, Margaret *ConAu X*
Wall, Martha 1910- *ConAu P-2*
Wall, Mervyn 1908- *IntAu&W 82*
Wall, Michael Morris 1942- *ConAu 53*
Wall, Mike 1942- *ConAu X*
Wall, Patrick 1916- *ConAu 104, IntAu&W 82,
  WrDr 84*
Wall, Patrick D 1925- *ConAu 17R*
Wall, Richard 1944- *ConAu 41R*
Wall, Robert Emmet, Jr. 1937- *ConAu 45*
Wall, Wendy Somerville 1942- *ConAu 49*
Wallace, Alexander Fielding 1918- *ConAu 33R*
Wallace, Alexander Ross 1891-1982 *ConAu 107*
Wallace, Amy 1955- *ConAu 81*
Wallace, Andrew 1930- *ConAu 37R*
Wallace, Anthony F C 1923- *ConAu 61*
Wallace, Barbara Brooks *ConAu 11NR, –29R,
  SmATA 4, WrDr 84*
Wallace, Ben J 1937- *ConAu 45*
Wallace, Beverly Dobrin 1921- *ConAu 101,
  SmATA 19*
Wallace, Bill *ConAu X*
Wallace, Bruce 1920- *ConAu 85, WrDr 84*
Wallace, David H 1926- *ConAu 25R*
Wallace, David Rains 1945- *ConAu 81*
Wallace, DeWitt 1889-1981 *ConAu 103*
Wallace, Dexter *ConAmA, ConAu X*
Wallace, Doreen 1897- *ConAu X, LongCTC,
  WrDr 84*
Wallace, Ed 1906-1976 *ConAu 69*
Wallace, Edgar 1875-1932 *LongCTC, ModBrL,
  TwCA, TwCA SUP, TwCCr&M 80,
  TwCSFW, TwCWr, WhoTwCL*
Wallace, Ernest 1906- *ConAu 13R*
Wallace, F L *TwCSFW, WrDr 84*
Wallace, Francis 1894?-1977 *ConAu 73*
Wallace, G L 1938- *ConAu 97*
Wallace, Helen Kingsbury 1897- *ConAu P-2*
Wallace, Helen M 1913- *ConAu 61*
Wallace, Henry Agard 1888-1965 *ConAu 105,
  –89*
Wallace, Ian 1912- *ConAu X, ConSFA,
  IntAu&W 82X, TwCSFW, WrDr 84*
Wallace, Ian 1950- *ConAu 107*
Wallace, Irving 1916- *ASpks, AuNews 1,
  ConAu 1R, –1NR, ConLC 5, –13,
  DcLEL 1940, TwCWr, WrDr 84*
Wallace, James Donald 1937- *ConAu 108*
Wallace, John Adam 1915- *ConAu 5R,
  SmATA 3*
Wallace, John Malcolm 1928- *ConAu 25R,
  WrDr 84*
Wallace, Karl R 1906-1973 *ConAu 101*
Wallace, Lewis Grant 1910- *ConAu P-2*
Wallace, Lila Bell Acheson 1889- *ConAu 105*
Wallace, Lillian Parker 1890-1971 *ConAu 1R,
  –103*
Wallace, Luther T 1928- *ConAu 13R*
Wallace, Sister M Jean *ConAu X*
Wallace, Marjorie *ConAu 101*
Wallace, Michael David 1943- *ConAu 77*
Wallace, Michele Faith 1952- *ConAu 108*
Wallace, Mike 1918- *ConAu 65*
Wallace, Myron Leon *ConAu X*
Wallace, Nigel *ConAu X, SmATA X*
Wallace, Pamela 1949- *ConAu 105*
Wallace, Pat *ConAu X*
Wallace, Pat 1929- *ConAu 65*
Wallace, Paul 1931- *ConAu 61*
Wallace, Paul A W 1891- *ConAu P-1*
Wallace, Philip Hope *ConAu X*

Wallace, Phyllis Ann *ConAu 105*
Wallace, Richard *ConAu X*
Wallace, Robert *DrAP&F 83*
Wallace, Robert 1932- *ConAu 10NR, –13R*
Wallace, Robert Ash 1921- *ConAu 1R*
Wallace, Robert Kimball 1944- *ConAu 69*
Wallace, Roger *IntAu&W 82X*
Wallace, Ronald *DrAP&F 83*
Wallace, Ronald 1945- *ConAu 6NR, –57,
  IntWWP 82*
Wallace, Ronald S 1911- *ConAu 5NR, –9R*
Wallace, Samuel E 1935- *ConAu 41R*
Wallace, Sarah Leslie 1914- *ConAu 9R*
Wallace, Sylvia *ConAu 73, WrDr 84*
Wallace, Terry H Smith *DrAP&F 83*
Wallace, Tom 1874-1961 *ConAu 93*
Wallace, Walter L 1927- *ConAu 81*
Wallace, Willard Mosher 1911- *ConAu 13R*
Wallace, William A 1918- *ConAu 41R*
Wallace, William A 1935- *ConAu 49*
Wallace, William N 1924- *ConAu 13R*
Wallace-Brodeur, Ruth 1941- *ConAu 107*
Wallace-Clarke, George *WrDr 84*
Wallace-Clarke, George 1916- *IntAu&W 82*
Wallace-Crabbe, Chris 1934- *ConAu 77,
  ConP 80, IntWWP 82*
Wallace-Crabbe, Christopher 1934- *WrDr 84*
Wallace-Hadrill, D S 1920- *ConAu 29R*
Wallace-Hadrill, John Michael 1916- *ConAu 5R*
Wallach, Allan Henry 1927- *ConAmTC*
Wallach, Erica 1922- *ConAu 21R, WrDr 84*
Wallach, Ira 1913- *WrDr 84*
Wallach, Ira Jan 1913- *ConAu 9R*
Wallach, Janet 1942- *ConAu 106*
Wallach, Mark I 1949- *ConAu 69*
Wallach, Michael A 1933- *ConAu 11NR, –13R*
Wallach, Paul I 1927- *ConAu 8NR, –17R*
Wallach, Robert Charles 1935- *ConAu 107*
Wallach, Sidney 1905-1979 *ConAu 103, –89*
Wallance, Gregory Joseph 1948- *ConAu 109*
Wallant, Edward Lewis 1926-1962 *ConAu 1R,
  ConLC 5, –10, DcLB 2, DcLEL 1940,
  ModAL, WhoTwCL, WorAu*
Wallas, Graham 1858-1932 *LongCTC, TwCA,
  TwCA SUP*
Wallechinsky, David 1948- *ConAu 61*
Wallek, Lee *ConAu X, DrAP&F 83*
Wallen, Carl J 1931- *ConAu 93*
Wallenquist, Ake 1904- *IntAu&W 82*
Wallenstein, Barry *DrAP&F 83*
Wallenstein, Barry J 1940- *ConAu 11NR, –45*
Wallenstein, Meir 1903- *ConAu P-1*
Waller, Brown *ConAu X*
Waller, Charles T 1934- *ConAu 61*
Waller, George Macgregor *WrDr 84*
Waller, George Macgregor 1919- *ConAu 9R,
  IntAu&W 82*
Waller, Irene Ellen 1928- *ConAu 109,
  IntAu&W 82, WrDr 84*
Waller, J Irvin 1944- *ConAu 61*
Waller, J Pembroke *IntWWP 82X*
Waller, Sir John Stanier 1917- *ConAu 45,
  DcLEL 1940*
Waller, Joseph Pembroke 1890- *IntWWP 82*
Waller, Leslie 1923- *ConAu 1R, –2NR,
  SmATA 20, WrDr 84*
Waller, Mary Ella 1855-1938 *LongCTC, TwCA*
Waller, Peter Louis 1935- *ConAu 106*
Waller, Rhoda *DrAP&F 83*
Waller, Ross Douglas 1899- *IntAu&W 82*
Waller, Theresa Annette Horton 1952-
  IntWWP 82
Wallerstein, Immanuel 1930- *ConAu 9NR, –21R*
Wallerstein, Judith Hannah Saretsky 1921-
  ConAu 105
Wallerstein, Mitchel B 1949- *ConAu 105*
Wallerstein, Robert Solomon 1921- *ConAu 33R*
Walley, David Gordon 1945- *ConAu 41R*
Wallhauser, Henry T 1930- *ConAu 29R*
Wallich, Henry C 1914- *ConAu 1R, –6NR,
  WrDr 84*
Wallich-Clifford, Anton 1923- *ConAu 61*
Wallig, Gaird 1942- *ConAu 106*
Wallin, Amos *IntAu&W 82X*
Walling, R A J 1869-1949 *TwCCr&M 80*
Walling, Robert Alfred John 1869-1949 *LongCTC,
  TwCA, TwCA SUP*
Walling, William 1926- *ConAu 103*
Wallis, Charles L *ConAu 5R, –8NR*
Wallis, Dave 1917- *ConSFA*
Wallis, G C *TwCSFW*
Wallis, G McDonald *ConAu X*

Wallis, G McDonald 1925- *ConAu X, ConSFA, SmATA X*
Wallis, George A 1892- *ConAu 17R*
Wallis, Jim 1948- *ConAu 102*
Wallis, Keith 1930- *ConAu 25R*
Wallis, Kenneth F 1938- *ConAu 45*
Wallis, R T 1941- *ConAu 45*
Wallis, Redmond Frankton 1933- *ConAu 5R*
Wallis, Robert 1900- *ConAu P-2*
Wallis, Roy 1945- *ConAu 97*
Wallis, Ruth O S 1895-1978 *ConAu 73*
Wallis, W Allen 1912- *ConAu 41R*
Wallis, William *DrAP&F 83*
Wallmann, Jeffrey M 1941- *ConAu 77, IntAu&W 82*
Wallner, Alexandra 1946- *ConAu 73*
Wallner, John C 1945- *SmATA 10*
Wallop, Douglass *DrAP&F 83*
Wallop, Douglass, III 1920- *ConAu 73*
Wallower, Lucille *ConAu 9NR*
Wallower, Lucille 1910- *ConAu 21R, IntAu&W 82, SmATA 11, WrDr 84*
Wallraff, Charles F 1909- *WrDr 84*
Wallraff, Charles Frederic 1909- *ConAu 1R*
Walls, David Stuart 1941- *ConAu 37R*
Walls, Dwayne E 1932- *ConAu 41R*
Walls, Henry James 1907- *ConAu 9R*
Walls, Ian G 1922- *WrDr 84*
Walls, Ian Gascoigne 1922- *ConAu 104*
Walls, Ronald 1920- *ConAu 103*
Walls, William J 1885-1975 *ConAu 81*
Wallsten, Robert 1912- *ConAu 101*
Wallwork, Ernest 1937- *ConAu 41R*
Walmsley, Arnold Robert 1912- *ConAu 41R*
Walmsley, Charles 1910-1983 *ConAu 110*
Walmsley, Leo 1892-1966 *ConAu P-1, LongCTC, TwCA, TwCA SUP, TwCWr*
Walmsley, Lewis C 1897- *ConAu 61*
Walmsley, Robert 1905-1976 *ConAu P-2*
Waln, Nora 1895-1964 *ConAu 89, LongCTC, TwCA, TwCA SUP*
Walpole, Sir Hugh Seymour 1884-1941 *ConAu 104, LongCTC, ModBrL, TwCA, TwCA SUP, TwCLC 5[port], TwCWr, WhoTwCL*
Walpole, Ronald Noel 1903- *ConAu 106*
Walrath, Jane Dwyer 1939- *ConAu 97*
Walravens, Jan 1920-1965 *ClDMEL 80*
Walschap, Gerard 1898- *ClDMEL 80, ConAu 103*
Walser, Martin 1927- *ClDMEL 80, CnMD, ConAu 8NR, -57, ConLC 27[port], CroCD, IntAu&W 82, ModGL, ModWD, WorAu*
Walser, Martin 1928- *TwCWr*
Walser, Richard Gaither 1908- *ConAu 2NR, -5R*
Walser, Robert 1878-1956 *ClDMEL 80, ModGL, WhoTwCL*
Walsh, Annmarie Hauck 1938- *ConAu 25R*
Walsh, Chad *DrAP&F 83*
Walsh, Chad 1914- *ConAu 1R, -6NR, ConP 80, WorAu, WrDr 84*
Walsh, Charlie *DrAP&F 83*
Walsh, Donald Devenish 1903-1980 *ConAu 3NR, -49, -97*
Walsh, Edward J 1937- *ConAu 37R*
Walsh, Ellen Stoll 1942- *ConAu 104*
Walsh, Ernest 1895-1926 *ConAu 109, DcLB 4[port]*
Walsh, George 1923- *ConAu 109*
Walsh, Gillian Paton 1937- *ConAu 37R*
Walsh, J M 1897-1952 *TwCSFW*
Walsh, James *ConAu X*
Walsh, James 1924- *ConAu 9R*
Walsh, James Edward 1891-1981 *ConAu 104*
Walsh, Jill Paton *TwCCW 83*
Walsh, Jill Paton 1939- *ChlLR 2, ConAu X, SmATA 4*
Walsh, John *WrDr 84*
Walsh, John 1927- *ConAu 17R*
Walsh, John Evangelist 1927- *ConAu 85, IntAu&W 82*
Walsh, Joy *DrAP&F 83*
Walsh, Joy 1935- *IntWWP 82*
Walsh, Justin E 1933- *ConAu 10NR*
Walsh, Justin Earl 1933- *ConAu 25R*
Walsh, Lewis 1944- *ConAu 9NR*
Walsh, M M B *ConAu 101*
Walsh, Marnie *ConAu X*
Walsh, Maurice 1879-1964 *LongCTC, TwCA, TwCA SUP*

Walsh, Michael J 1937- *ConAu 106*
Walsh, Myles E 1937- *ConAu 109*
Walsh, P G 1923- *ConAu 25R, WrDr 84*
Walsh, Patricia L 1942- *ConAu 109*
Walsh, Patrick Gerard 1923- *IntAu&W 82*
Walsh, Paul 1951- *ConAmTC*
Walsh, Raoul 1887-1980 *ConAu 102*
Walsh, Richard 1923- *ConAu 25R*
Walsh, Sheila 1928- *TwCRGW, WrDr 84*
Walsh, Stephen 1942- *ConAu 37R, WrDr 84*
Walsh, Taylor 1947- *ConAu 73*
Walsh, Thomas 1908- *TwCCr&M 80, WrDr 84*
Walsh, Thomas Joseph 1911- *IntAu&W 82*
Walsh, Timothy J 1927- *ConAu 41R*
Walsh, W Bruce 1936- *ConAu 93*
Walsh, Warren Bartlett 1909- *ConAu P-2*
Walsh, William 1916- *ConAu 11NR, -65, WrDr 84*
Walsh, William B 1920- *ConAu 4NR, -49*
Walshe, Maurice O'Connell 1911- *ConAu 5R*
Walshe, R D 1923- *ConAu 104, WrDr 84*
Walster, Elaine Hatfield *ConAu X*
Walster, Elaine Hatfield 1937- *ConAu 25R*
Walster, G William 1941- *ConAu 85*
Walston, Joseph *ConAu X*
Walston, Marie 1925- *ConAu 41R*
Walt, Lewis W 1913- *ConAu 33R*
Waltari, Mika 1908-1979 *ConAu 9R, -89, DcLEL 1940, TwCA SUP*
Walter, Arnold Maria 1902- *CreCan 1*
Walter, Claire 1943- *ConAu 81*
Walter, Daniel *DrAP&F 83, IntWWP 82X*
Walter, Dorothy Blake 1908- *ConAu P-1, WrDr 84*
Walter, Elizabeth *WrDr 84*
Walter, Eugene 1910-1943 *ModWD*
Walter, Eugene Ferdinand Francis 1927- *ConAu 9R*
Walter, Eugene Victor 1925- *ConAu 25R*
Walter, Gladys Mae 1901-1973 *ConAu 41R*
Walter, Hartmut 1940- *ConAu 89*
Walter, Heinrich 1898- *IntAu&W 82*
Walter, Ingo 1940- *ConAu 7NR, -17R*
Walter, Joseph Daniel 1948- *IntWWP 82*
Walter, Nancy 1939- *ConAu X, WrDr 84*
Walter, Nicolas *IntAu&W 82*
Walter, Nina Willis *WrDr 84*
Walter, Nina Willis 1900- *ConAu 5R*
Walter, Otis M 1921- *ConAu 5R*
Walter, Otto F 1928- *ClDMEL 80*
Walter, Robert H K 1922- *ConAu 5R*
Walter, Samuel 1916- *ConAu 5R*
Walter, William Grey 1910-1977 *ConAu 103*
Walters, A A 1926- *ConAu 29R*
Walters, Alan Arthur 1926- *WrDr 84*
Walters, Anna Lee *DrAP&F 83*
Walters, Anna Lee 1946- *ConAu 73*
Walters, Sister Annette 1910- *ConAu 37R*
Walters, Audrey 1929- *SmATA 18*
Walters, Barbara 1931- *AuNews 2, ConAu 65*
Walters, Basil L 1896-1975 *ConAu 89*
Walters, C Glenn 1929- *ConAu 81*
Walters, Chad *ConAu X*
Walters, Dirk R 1942- *WrDr 84*
Walters, Dorothy 1928- *ConAu 65*
Walters, Dorothy Mae Wells 1924- *ConAu 2NR, -5R*
Walters, Dottie *ConAu X*
Walters, Eleanor 1955- *ConAu 108*
Walters, Elizabeth *ConAu 97*
Walters, Hugh 1910- *ConAu X, ConSFA, SmATA X, TwCSFW, WrDr 84*
Walters, Jack Edward 1896- *ConAu 5R*
Walters, Janet Lane 1936- *ConAu 49*
Walters, John Beauchamp 1906- *ConAu 5R, -6NR, WrDr 84*
Walters, John Bennett, Jr. 1912- *ConAu 105*
Walters, LeRoy 1940- *ConAu 108*
Walters, Nell *ConAu X*
Walters, Ralph M *IntAu&W 82X*
Walters, Richard P 1935- *ConAu 107*
Walters, Rick *ConAu X*
Walters, Robert Mark 1938- *ConAu 69*
Walters, Robert S 1941- *ConAu 29R*
Walters, Ronald G 1942- *ConAu 85*
Walters, Roy 1918- *ConAu 93*
Walters, Shelly *AuNews 1, ConAu X*
Walters, Stanley D 1931- *ConAu 53*
Walters, Thomas N *DrAP&F 83*
Walters, Thomas N 1935- *ConAu 65*
Walthall, Hugh *DrAP&F 83*
Waltham, Antony Clive 1942- *ConAu 10NR, -65,*

IntAu&W 82
Waltham, Tony 1942- *WrDr 84*
Walther, R E 1921- *ConAu 41R*
Walther, Regis 1917- *ConAu 8NR, -17R*
Walther, Thomas A 1950- *ConAu 107, SmATA 31*
Walther, Tom *ConAu X, SmATA X*
Waltner, Elma 1912- *ConAu 17R*
Walton, Alfred Grant 1887-1970 *ConAu P-1*
Walton, Bryce 1918- *ConAu 21R*
Walton, Clarence C 1915- *ConAu 1R, -3NR*
Walton, Clyde C 1925- *ConAu 29R*
Walton, Craig 1934- *ConAu 41R*
Walton, Ed 1931- *ConAu 105*
Waloord, Elizabeth Cheatham *ConAu 5R, WrDr 84*
Walton, George 1904- *ConAu 17R*
Walton, Hanes, Jr. 1942- *ConAu 41R, LivgBAA*
Walton, Henry John 1924- *ConAu 53, WrDr 84*
Walton, James 1911- *IntAu&W 82, WrDr 84*
Walton, John 1910- *ConAu 1R, -5NR, WrDr 84*
Walton, John 1937- *ConAu 89*
Walton, Luke 1941- *ConAu X*
Walton, Ortiz *WrDr 84*
Walton, Ortiz Montaigne 1933- *ConAu 45, LivgBAA*
Walton, Paul *IntAu&W 82X*
Walton, Peter 1936- *IntWWP 82*
Walton, Richard Eugene 1931- *ConAu 81*
Walton, Richard J 1928- *ConAu 25R, SmATA 4, WrDr 84*
Walton, Robert Cutler 1932- *ConAu 73*
Walton, Ronald 1936- *ConAu 65*
Walton, Su 1944- *ConAu 25R*
Walton, Vicki 1949- *ConAu 65*
Walton, W Robert 1902- *ConAu 69*
Waltrip, Lela 1904- *ConAu 5R, IntAu&W 82, SmATA 9*
Waltrip, R C 1898- *IntAu&W 82*
Waltrip, Robert *ConAu X*
Waltrip, Rufus 1898- *ConAu 5R, SmATA 9*
Waltz, Jon R 1929- *ConAu 17R*
Waltz, Kenneth N 1924- *ConAu 37R, WrDr 84*
Waltzer, Herbert 1930- *ConAu 41R, IntAu&W 82*
Walvin, James 1942- *ConAu 1NR, -49*
Walvoord, John Flipse 1910- *ConAu 6NR, -9R*
Walwik, Theodore J 1937- *ConAu 25R*
Walworth, Alice 1905- *ConAu X*
Walworth, Arthur 1903- *ConAu 21R, IntAu&W 82, WrDr 84*
Walworth, Nancy Zinsser 1917- *ConAu 3NR, -5R, SmATA 14*
Walz, Audrey Boyers 1907?-1983 *ConAu 109*
Walz, Edgar 1914- *ConAu 29R*
Walz, Jay 1907- *ConAu 49*
Walzer, Michael 1935- *ConAu 37R, WrDr 84*
Wambaugh, Joseph 1937- *ASpks, AuNews 1, ConAu 33R, ConLC 3, -18, DcLB Y83A[port], -6[port], TwCCr&M 80, WorAu 1970, WrDr 84*
Wamble, Gaston Hugh 1923- *ConAu 5R*
Wamble, Thelma 1916- *ConAu 106, LivgBAA*
Wamsley, Gary L 1935- *ConAu 3NR, -49*
Wan Hsi, Chang 1920- *IntWWP 82*
Wanamaker, A Temple 1918- *ConAu 17R*
Wand, William 1885- *ConAu 103*
Wandel, Joseph 1918- *ConAu 93*
Wanderer, Zev W 1932- *ConAu 105*
Wandesforde-Smith, Geoffrey Albert 1943- *ConAu 29R*
Wandrei, Donald 1908- *TwCSFW, WrDr 84*
Wandro, Mark 1948- *ConAu 106*
Wandycz, Piotr Stefan 1923- *ConAu 1R, -2NR*
Wang, C H 1940- *ConAu 8NR, -61*
Wang, Chung-Shu 1925- *ConAu 109*
Wang, Fang Yu 1913- *ConAu 37R*
Wang, Gungwu 1930- *ConAu 65*
Wang, Hao 1921- *ConAu 65*
Wang, Hui-Ming 1922- *ConAu 33R, IntAu&W 82, WrDr 84*
Wang, J Y 1918- *ConAu 45*
Wang, John Ching-Yu 1934- *ConAu 41R*
Wang, Jung-Chih 1928- *IntWWP 82*
Wang, Karl *DrAP&F 83*
Wang, Leonard J 1926- *ConAu 33R*
Wang, Sabine E 1925- *ConAu 37R*
Wang, Yi Chu 1916- *ConAu 61*
Wang Gungwu 1930- *ConAu 10NR*

Wangberg, Mark Thomas *DrAP&F 83*
Wangchuk, Anangavajra Khamsum
  IntAu&W 82X
Wangenheim, Chris Von *ConAu X*
Wangenheim, Gustav Von 1895- *CnMD*
Wangensteen, Owen Harding 1898-1981
  ConAu 103
Wangerin, Theodora Scharffenberg 1888-
  ConAu 5R
Wangerin, Walter, Jr. 1944- *ConAu 108*
Wangermann, Ernst 1925- *ConAu 103*
Wangyal, Geshe 1901?-1983 *ConAu 108*
Waniek, Marilyn Nelson 1946- *ConAu 89*
Wankowicz, Melchior 1892?-1974 *CIDMEL 80,*
  ConAu 53
Wanlass, Stanley G 1941- *ConAu 61*
Wann, Kenneth D 1915- *ConAu 5R*
Wannamaker, Bruce *ConAu X, SmATA X*
Wannan, Bill *ConAu X*
Wannan, William Fielding 1915- *ConAu 10NR,*
  –21R
Wanner, Irene *DrAP&F 83*
Wanner, Paul 1896- *CnMD*
Wanshel, Jeff 1947- *ConAu 57,*
  NatPD 81[port]
Wantling, William 1933-1974 *ConAu 105, –89*
Waples, Douglas 1893-1978 *ConAu 77*
Warbler, J M *ConAu X, SmATA 7*
Warbridge, C W *ConAu X*
Warburg, Fredric 1898-1981 *ConAu 105*
Warburg, James Paul 1896-1969 *ConAu 25R,*
  ConAu P-2, TwCA SUP
Warburg, Sandol Stoddard 1927- *ConAu X, –5R,*
  SmATA 14
Warburton, Amber Arthun 1898?-1976 *ConAu 61*
Warburton, Clark 1896-1979 *ConAu 73, –89*
Warburton, Minnie *DrAP&F 83*
Warburton, Minnie 1949- *ConAu 101*
Warch, Richard 1939- *ConAu 105*
Ward, Aileen 1919- *ConAu 5R, IntAu&W 82*
Ward, Alan J 1937- *WrDr 84*
Ward, Alan Joseph 1936- *ConAu 73*
Ward, Allen M 1942- *ConAu 89*
Ward, Andrew 1946- *ConAu 81*
Ward, Anne G 1932- *ConAu 77*
Ward, Arthur Henry Sarsfield 1883-1959
  ConAu 108
Ward, Arthur Sarsfield 1883?-1959 *LongCTC*
Ward, Barbara 1914- *ConAu X, IntAu&W 82,*
  TwCA SUP
Ward, Benedicta 1933- *ConAu 65*
Ward, Brendan Noel 1947- *NatPD 81[port]*
Ward, Charles Dexter *ConAu X*
Ward, Charles Duane 1935- *ConAu 33R*
Ward, Chester 1907-1977 *ConAu 69*
Ward, Christopher *WrDr 84*
Ward, Colin 1924- *ConAu 57*
Ward, Craig 1892-1979 *ConAu 85*
Ward, David 1938- *ConAu 29R, IntAu&W 82,*
  WrDr 84
Ward, Dennis 1924- *ConAu 13R*
Ward, Diane *DrAP&F 83*
Ward, Don 1911- *ConAu 17R*
Ward, Donald 1909- *ConAu 109, WrDr 84*
Ward, Donald 1930- *ConAu 37R*
Ward, Donald Edward 1909- *IntAu&W 82,*
  IntWWP 82
Ward, Douglas Turner 1930- *ConAu 81,*
  ConDr 82, ConLC 19, DcLB 7[port],
  LivgBAA, WorAu 1970, WrDr 84
Ward, Elizabeth 1952- *ConAu 110*
Ward, Elizabeth Campbell 1936- *ConAu 45*
Ward, Elizabeth Honor 1926- *ConAu 9R,*
  WrDr 84
Ward, Elizabeth Rebecca *LongCTC*
Ward, Eric *ConAu X*
Ward, Fred 1935- *ConAu 85*
Ward, Harry Merrill 1929- *ConAu 1R, –2NR,*
  WrDr 84
Ward, Herman Matthew 1914- *ConAu 2NR,*
  –5R, –9R
Ward, Hiley Henry 1929- *ConAu 1R, –2NR*
Ward, Mrs. Humphry 1851-1920 *LongCTC*
Ward, J Neville 1915- *ConAu 77*
Ward, J P 1937- *ConAu 109*
Ward, J T 1930- *ConAu 7NR, IntAu&W 82*
Ward, James A 1941- *ConAu 49*
Ward, Jerry W, Jr. *DrAP&F 83*
Ward, Jerry Washington, Jr. 1943- *IntWWP 82*
Ward, John *IntAu&W 82X*
Ward, John Manning 1919- *ConAu 21R,*
  IntAu&W 82, WrDr 84

Ward, John Owen 1919- *ConAu 13R*
Ward, John Powell 1937- *WrDr 84*
Ward, John Stephen Keith 1938- *ConAu 109,*
  WrDr 84
Ward, John Towers 1930- *ConAu 5R, –109,*
  WrDr 84
Ward, John William 1922- *ConAu 5R,*
  WrDr 84
Ward, Jonas *ConAu X, IntAu&W 82X,*
  WrDr 84
Ward, Jonas 1922-1960 *TwCWW*
Ward, Jonathan *AuNews 1*
Ward, Jonathon *ConAu X*
Ward, Joseph A 1931- *ConAu 1R*
Ward, Justine Bayard Cutting 1879-1975
  ConAu 61
Ward, Keith 1938- *ConAu 29R*
Ward, Sir Leslie Matthew 1851-1922 *LongCTC*
Ward, Lynd 1905- *DcLB 22[port]*
Ward, Lynd Kendall 1905- *ConAu 17R,*
  SmATA 2, WrDr 84
Ward, Maisie 1889-1975 *ConAu 53, –69*
Ward, Martha 1921- *ConAu 17R, SmATA 5*
Ward, Mary Augusta 1851-1920 *TwCA,*
  TwCA SUP
Ward, Mary Jane 1905- *LongCTC, TwCA SUP*
Ward, Mary Josephine *ConAu 77*
Ward, Melanie *ConAu X, SmATA X*
Ward, Michael 1939- *ConAu 37R*
Ward, Norman 1918- *ConAu 41R,*
  IntAu&W 82, WrDr 84
Ward, Olivia Tucker 1927- *ConAu 57*
Ward, Patricia A 1940- *ConAu 57*
Ward, Paul W 1905-1976 *ConAu 69*
Ward, Pearl L 1920- *ConAu 107*
Ward, Peter *ConAu X*
Ward, Philip 1938- *ConAu 25R, IntAu&W 82,*
  WrDr 84
Ward, Philip C 1932- *ConAu 21R*
Ward, R H 1910-1969 *ConAu P-1, LongCTC*
Ward, R Patrick *ConAu X*
Ward, Ralph Gerard 1933- *ConAu 107,*
  WrDr 84
Ward, Ralph T 1927- *ConAu 49*
Ward, Richard J 1921- *ConAu 41R*
Ward, Ritchie R 1906- *ConAu 29R, WrDr 84*
Ward, Robert 1943- *ConAu 104*
Ward, Robert E 1927- *ConAu 49*
Ward, Robert Elmer 1937- *ConAu 49*
Ward, Robert M *DrAP&F 83*
Ward, Robert R *DrAP&F 83*
Ward, Ronald Arthur 1908- *ConAu 53,*
  IntAu&W 82, WrDr 84
Ward, Russel Braddock 1914- *ConAu 103,*
  WrDr 84
Ward, Russell A 1947- *ConAu 110*
Ward, Stephen R 1938- *ConAu 65*
Ward, Ted 1930- *ConAu 97*
Ward, Theodora 1890-1974 *ConAu 53,*
  ConAu P-2
Ward, Theodore 1902-1983 *ConAu 109*
Ward, Virgil S 1916- *ConAu 1R*
Ward, Wilfrid Philip 1856-1916 *TwCA,*
  TwCA SUP
Ward, William Arthur 1921- *ConAu 29R*
Ward, William B 1912- *ConAu 5R*
Ward, William Ernest Frank 1900- *ConAu 4NR,*
  –9R, IntAu&W 82
Ward, William G 1929- *ConAu 21R*
Ward, William R 1918- *ConAu 61*
Ward, Winfred O 1933- *ConAu 106*
Ward-Perkins, John Bryan 1912- *ConAu 93*
Ward-Perkins, John Bryan 1912-1981 *ConAu 108*
Ward Thomas, Evelyn Bridget Patricia *WrDr 84*
Ward-Thomas, Evelyn Bridget Patricia 1928-
  ConAu 5NR, –9R
Warde, William F *ConAu 49*
Wardell, Dean *ConAu X, SmATA X*
Wardell, Phyllis 1909- *ConAu P-1*
Warden, Bette Ruth Coker 1925- *IntWWP 82*
Warden, G B 1939- *ConAu 29R*
Warden, John 1936- *ConAu 41R*
Warden, Lewis Christopher 1913- *ConAu 13R,*
  IntAu&W 82, WrDr 84
Wardhaugh, Ronald 1932- *ConAu 37R,*
  WrDr 84
Wardlaw, Catherine 1902- *IntWWP 82*
Wardle, Dan *TwCWW*
Wardle, David 1930- *ConAu 69, WrDr 84*
Wardle, Irving 1929- *ConAu 77, WrDr 84*
Wardle, John Irving 1929- *IntAu&W 82*

Wardle, Lynn D 1947- *ConAu 109*
Wardle, Ralph Martin 1909- *ConAu 1R, –5NR*
Wardman, Alan 1926- *ConAu 77*
Wardroper, John Edmund 1923- *ConAu 29R,*
  WrDr 84
Wardropper, Bruce W 1919- *ConAu 13R*
Ware, Ciji 1942- *ConAu 103*
Ware, Clyde 1932- *ConAu 33R, IntAu&W 82*
Ware, Emma 1896?-1975 *ConAu 57*
Ware, George Whitaker 1902- *ConAu 13R*
Ware, Gilbert 1933- *ConAu 65*
Ware, Jean 1914- *ConAu P-1, WrDr 84*
Ware, John *ConAu X*
Ware, Kallistos 1934- *ConAu 7NR,*
  IntAu&W 82, WrDr 84
Ware, Leon 1909-1976 *ConAu 1R, –2NR,*
  SmATA 4
Ware, Leonard 1900?-1976 *ConAu 69*
Ware, Patricia J *DrAP&F 83*
Ware, Runa Erwin *ConAu P-2*
Ware, Timothy 1932- *ConAu X, –9R*
Ware, W Porter 1904- *ConAu 105*
Ware, Wallace *ConAu X, IntAu&W 82X,*
  WrDr 84
Wareham, John 1940- *ConAu 101*
Warfel, Harry R 1899-1971 *ConAu P-1*
Warford, Jeremy J 1938- *ConAu 37R*
Wargo, Dan M 1920- *ConAu 21R*
Warhaft, Sidney 1921- *ConAu 61*
Warham, John 1919- *WrDr 84*
Warhol, Andy 1928- *ConAu 89, ConLC 20*
Wark, David M 1934- *ConAu 33R*
Wark, Ian W 1899- *ConAu P-2*
Wark, Robert R 1924- *ConAu 8NR, –61*
Warkentin, Germaine 1933- *ConAu 109*
Warkentin, John 1928- *ConAu 9R*
Warland, John *ConAu X*
Warlimont, Walter 1894- *ConAu P-1*
Warlum, Michael Frank *DrAP&F 83*
Warlum, Michael Frank 1940- *ConAu 37R,*
  WrDr 84
Warman, Eric 1904- *ConAu P-1, WrDr 84*
Warman, Henry J 1907- *ConAu 41R*
Warmbrand, Max 1896?-1976 *ConAu 65*
Warmbrunn, Werner 1920- *ConAu 21R*
Warmington, Eric Herbert 1898- *WrDr 84*
Warmington, William Allan 1922- *ConAu 5R,*
  WrDr 84
Warmke, Roman F 1929- *ConAu 9NR, –17R*
Warnath, Charles F 1925- *ConAu 37R*
Warne, Clinton L 1921- *ConAu 13R*
Warne, William Elmo 1905- *ConAu 41R*
Warner, Alan 1912- *ConAu 104, WrDr 84*
Warner, B F *ConAu X*
Warner, Bob *ConAu X*
Warner, David S 1907- *ConAu 1R*
Warner, Deborah Jean 1941- *ConAu 108*
Warner, Denis Ashton 1917- *ConAu 3NR, –5R*
Warner, Edythe Records 1916- *ConAu 5R*
Warner, Emily S 1902?-1980 *ConAu 97*
Warner, Esther S *ConAu X*
Warner, Francis 1937- *ConAu 11NR, –53,*
  ConLC 14, ConP 80, DcLEL 1940,
  WrDr 84
Warner, Frank A *ConAu P-2, SmATA 1*
Warner, Gary 1936- *ConAu 21R*
Warner, Geoffrey John *WrDr 84*
Warner, Geoffrey John 1923- *ConAu 1R*
Warner, Gertrude Chandler 1890-1979
  ConAu 1R, –3NR, SmATA 9
Warner, H Landon 1911- *ConAu 13R*
Warner, Harry, Jr. 1922- *ConAu 29R*
Warner, Jack 1896-1981 *ConAu 108*
Warner, Jack L 1892-1978 *ConAu 108*
Warner, James A 1918- *ConAu 45*
Warner, Ken 1928- *ConAu 10NR*
Warner, Kenneth 1915- *ConAu P-1*
Warner, Kenneth Wilson, Jr. 1928- *ConAu 65*
Warner, Lucille Schulberg *ConAu 11NR, –69,*
  SmATA 30[port]
Warner, Marina 1946- *ConAu 65,*
  IntAu&W 82, WrDr 84
Warner, Matt *WrDr 84*
Warner, Mmax 1922- *ConAu X*
Warner, Oliver 1903-1976 *ConAu 1R, –3NR, –69,*
  DcLEL 1940, LongCTC, SmATA 29
Warner, Philip 1914- *ConAu 101, IntAu&W 82,*
  WrDr 84
Warner, Rex 1905- *ConAu 89, ConNov 82,*
  ConP 80, DcLB 15[port], LongCTC,
  ModBrL, TwCA, TwCA SUP, TwCWr,
  WrDr 84

Warner, Robert 1905- *ConAu 53*
Warner, Robert M 1927- *ConAu 7NR, –9R, MichAu 80*
Warner, Sam Bass, Jr. 1928- *ConAu 2NR, –5R*
Warner, Seth 1927- *ConAu 53*
Warner, Sylvia Townsend 1893-1978 *ConAu 61, –77, ConLC 7, –19, LongCTC, ModBrL, ModBrL SUP, TwCA, TwCA SUP, TwCWr, WhoTwCL*
Warner, Val 1946- *ConAu 49, WrDr 84*
Warner, Virginia *ConAu X*
Warner, W Lloyd 1898-1970 *ConAu 1R, –2NR, –29R*
Warner, Wayne E 1933- *ConAu 3NR, –49*
Warner-Crozetti, R 1913- *ConAu 101, IntAu&W 82X*
Warnock, Amelia B *CreCan 1*
Warnock, G J 1923- *ConAu 21R, WrDr 84*
Warnock, Mary 1924- *ConAu 5R, –8NR, WrDr 84*
Warr, Peter Bryan 1937- *ConAu 25R, IntAu&W 82*
Warrack, John 1928- *ConAu 5NR, –13R, WrDr 84*
Warren, Alyce 1940- *LivgBAA*
Warren, Andrew *ConAu X, WrDr 84*
Warren, Austin 1899- *ConAu 17R, ConLCrt 82, TwCA SUP, WrDr 84*
Warren, Betsy *ConAu X*
Warren, Billy *ConAu X, SmATA X*
Warren, C Henry 1895-1966 *LongCTC*
Warren, Charles 1868-1954 *TwCA, TwCA SUP*
Warren, Charles Marquis 1912- *TwCWW, WrDr 84*
Warren, Dave *ConAu X*
Warren, David 1943- *ConAu 77*
Warren, David S *DrAP&F 83*
Warren, Donald Irwin 1935- *ConAu 1NR, –45*
Warren, Doug 1935- *ConAu 61*
Warren, Earl 1891-1974 *ConAu 49*
Warren, Eileen 1921- *IntWWP 82*
Warren, Elizabeth *ConAu X, SmATA X*
Warren, Elizabeth Avery 1916- *ConAu 5R, –8NR*
Warren, Eugene *DrAP&F 83*
Warren, Eugene 1941- *ConAu 1NR, –49*
Warren, Harris Gaylord 1906- *ConAu 1R, –5NR, WrDr 84*
Warren, Harry *ConAu X*
Warren, James E, Jr. *DrAP&F 83*
Warren, James E, Jr. 1908- *ConAu 21R, IntAu&W 82, IntWWP 82, WrDr 84*
Warren, James Hugo, Jr. 1928?-1983 *ConAu 110*
Warren, Jefferson T 1912- *ConAu 41R*
Warren, Joyce *DrAP&F 83*
Warren, Joyce W 1935- *ConAu 77, SmATA 18*
Warren, Kenneth 1931- *ConAu 109, WrDr 84*
Warren, Larkin *DrAP&F 83*
Warren, Lella 1899-1982 *DcLB Y83B[port]*
Warren, Louis Austin 1885- *ConAu 5R*
Warren, Louis Austin 1885-1983 *ConAu 110*
Warren, Louise 1909?-1981 *ConAu 104*
Warren, Lucian 1913- *ConAu 101*
Warren, Mary Bondurant 1930- *ConAu 73*
Warren, Mary Douglas *ConAu X, TwCRGW*
Warren, Mary Phraner 1929- *ConAu 5NR, –53, SmATA 10*
Warren, Patricia Nell 1936- *ConAu 1NR*
Warren, Peter Whitson 1941- *ConAu 5NR, –53*
Warren, Robert Penn *DrAP&F 83*
Warren, Robert Penn 1905- *AuNews 1, CnMD, ConAmA, ConAu 10NR, –13R, ConLC 1, –4, –6, –8, –10, –13, –18, ConLCrt 82, ConNov 82, ConP 80, Conv 1, DcLB Y80A[port], –2, IntAu&W 82, IntWWP 82, LongCTC, ModAL, ModAL SUP, ModWD, TwCA, TwCA SUP, WhoTwCL, WrDr 84*
Warren, Roland L 1915- *ConAu 10NR, –57*
Warren, Sidney 1916- *ConAu 25R, IntAu&W 82, WrDr 84*
Warren, Thomas 1920- *ConAu 103*
Warren, Vernon *ConAu X*
Warren, Vincent *CreCan 2*
Warren, Virginia Burgess 1913- *ConAu 13R*
Warren, W Preston 1901- *ConAu 37R*
Warren, Wilfred Lewis 1929- *ConAu 1R, WrDr 84*
Warren, William Stephen 1882-1968 *ConAu P-2, SmATA 9*
Warrick, Patricia Scott 1925- *ConAu 8NR, –61*
Warriner, Charles K 1920- *ConAu 41R*

Warriner, Thurman *TwCCr&M 80*
Warry, J G 1916- *ConAu 5R*
Warsaw, Irene 1908- *ConAu P-1, MichAu 80*
Warsh, Lewis *DrAP&F 83*
Warsh, Lewis 1944- *ConAu 61, ConP 80, WrDr 84*
Warshaw, Jerry 1929- *ConAu 37R, SmATA 30[port]*
Warshaw, Leon J 1917- *ConAu 107*
Warshawski, Morrie *DrAP&F 83*
Warshawski, Morrie 1947- *IntWWP 82*
Warshofsky, Fred 1931- *ConAu 9R, SmATA 24[port]*
Warshofsky, Isaac *ConAu X, SmATA X*
Warter, Louis 1900- *IntWWP 82*
Warth, Robert Douglas 1921- *ConAu 9R*
Wartofsky, Marx W 1928- *ConAu 41R*
Wartofsky, Victor 1931- *ConAu 29R*
Wartofsky, William Victor 1931- *WrDr 84*
Wartski, Maureen 1940- *ConAu 89*
Warwick, Christopher 1949- *ConAu 110*
Warwick, Dennis 1930- *ConAu 73*
Warwick, Dolores *ConAu X*
Warwick, Jack 1930- *ConAu 29R*
Warwick, James 1894?-1983 *ConAu 110*
Warwick, Jarvis *ConAu X, CreCan 1*
Warwick, Ray 1911?-1983 *ConAu 109*
Warwick, Roger *WrDr 84*
Warwick, Roger 1912- *ConAu 109*
Warzeski, Walter C 1929- *ConAu 37R*
Washburn, Bradford 1910- *ConAu 3NR, –49*
Washburn, Charles 1890?-1972 *ConAu 104*
Washburn, Dorothy K 1945- *ConAu 106*
Washburn, Jan 1926- *ConAu 93*
Washburn, Mark 1948- *ConAu 77*
Washburn, O A 1914- *ConAu 57*
Washburn, Sherwood L 1911- *ConAu 105*
Washburn, Wilcomb Edward 1925- *ConAu 41R*
Washburne, Carleton Wolsey 1889-1968 *ConAu P-1*
Washburne, Heluiz Chandler 1892-1970 *ConAu 104, ConAu P-1, MichAu 80, SmATA 10, –26N*
Washington, Alex *ConAu X*
Washington, Booker T 1856-1915 *TwCLC 10[port]*
Washington, Booker T 1858?-1915 *SmATA 28[port]*
Washington, Booker Taliaferro 1856-1915 *LongCTC*
Washington, C *ConAu 49*
Washington, Chester Lloyd 1902-1983 *ConAu 110*
Washington, Gil *IntAu&W 82X*
Washington, Gladys J 1931- *ConAu 29R*
Washington, Ida Harrison 1924- *ConAu 107*
Washington, Joseph R, Jr. 1930- *WrDr 84*
Washington, Joseph Reed, Jr. 1930- *ConAu 9R, IntAu&W 82, LivgBAA*
Washington, Marguerite Beauchamp 1892?-1972 *ConAu P-1*
Washington, Mary Helen 1941- *ConAu 65*
Washington, Pat Beauchamp *ConAu X*
Washington, Raymond 1942- *LivgBAA, WrDr 84*
Washton, Nathan S 1916- *ConAu 53*
Wasiolek, Edward 1924- *ConAu 1R, –6NR, IntAu&W 82, WrDr 84*
Waskin, Yvonne 1923- *ConAu 21R*
Waskow, Arthur I 1933- *ConAu 4NR, –5R*
Wasley, Robert S 1918- *ConAu 17R*
Wasmuth, William J 1925- *ConAu 45*
Wason, Betty *ConAu X*
Wason, Elizabeth 1912- *ConAu 2NR*
Wason, P C 1924- *ConAu 45*
Wasow, Mona 1933- *ConAu 110*
Wassenbergh, Henri Abraham 1924- *ConAu 21R*
Wasser, Henry H 1919- *ConAu 8NR, –21R*
Wasserfall, Adel 1918- *ConAu 6NR*
Wasserman, Aaron O 1927- *ConAu 53*
Wasserman, Burton 1929- *ConAu 53*
Wasserman, Dale 1917- *ConAu 49, ConDr 82D, NatPD 81[port], WrDr 84*
Wasserman, Earl Reeves 1913-1973 *ConAu P-2*
Wasserman, Gary 1944- *ConAu 69*
Wasserman, Harvey 1945- *ConAu 45*
Wasserman, Jack 1921- *ConAu 61*
Wasserman, John L 1938- *ConAu 77*
Wasserman, Max Judd 1895-1977 *ConAu 4NR, –5R*
Wasserman, Paul 1924- *ConAu 1R, –1NR,*

Wr*Dr 84*
Wasserman, Pauline 1943- *ConAu 110*
Wasserman, Selma 1929- *ConAu 5R*
Wasserman, Sheldon 1940- *ConAu 9NR, –65*
Wassermann, Jakob 1873-1934 *CIDMEL 80, ConAu 104, ModGL, TwCA, TwCA SUP, TwCLC 6[port]*
Wassermann, Selma 1929- *ConAu 9R*
Wasserstein, Abraham 1921- *ConAu 109*
Wasserstein, Bruce 1947- *ConAu 37R*
Wasserstein, Susan 1952- *ConAu 107*
Wasserstein, Wendy 1950- *NatPD 81[port]*
Wasserstrom, Richard Alan 1936- *ConAu 1R, –6NR*
Wasserstrom, William 1922- *ConAu 9R*
Wassersug, Joseph David 1912- *ConAu 17R*
Wassil, Aly 1930- *ConAu 17R*
Wassmer, Arthur C 1947- *ConAu 103*
Wassmo, Herbjorg 1942- *IntAu&W 82*
Wassner, Selig O 1923- *ConAu 25R*
Wasson, Chester R 1906- *ConAu 10NR, –13R*
Wasson, Donald 1914?-1976 *ConAu 69*
Wasson, John M 1928- *ConAu 45*
Wast, Hugo 1883-1962 *TwCA, TwCA SUP*
Wastberg, Per 1933- *CIDMEL 80, IntAu&W 82*
Wasti, Syed R 1929- *ConAu 7NR, –13R*
Waswo, Richard 1939- *ConAu 53*
Wat, Aleksander 1900-1967 *CIDMEL 80, ModSL 2, WorAu 1970*
Watanabe, Hitoshi 1919- *ConAu 73*
Watanabe, Ruth T 1916- *ConAu 37R*
Watanabe, Shigeo 1928- *SmATA 32*
Waten, Judah 1911- *WrDr 84*
Waten, Judah Leon 1911- *ConAu 101, ConNov 82, DcLEL 1940, IntAu&W 82*
Water, Silas *ConAu X*
Water Rat *ConAu X*
Waterfield, Gordon 1903- *ConAu 61, IntAu&W 82, WrDr 84*
Waterfield, Robin 1914- *ConAu 49*
Waterhouse, Charles 1924- *ConAu 29R*
Waterhouse, Ellis Kirkham 1905- *ConAu 65*
Waterhouse, Keith 1929- *ConAu 5R, ConDr 82, ConNov 82, CroCD, DcLB 13[port], –15[port], DcLEL 1940, LongCTC, ModBrL SUP, TwCWr, WorAu, WrDr 84*
Waterhouse, Larry G 1944- *ConAu 37R*
Waterloo, Stanley 1846-1913 *TwCSFW*
Waterlow, Charlotte 1915- *ConAu 25R*
Waterman, Andrew 1940- *ConAu 109, WrDr 84*
Waterman, Arthur E 1926- *ConAu 17R*
Waterman, Bic *ConAu X*
Waterman, Cary *DrAP&F 83*
Waterman, Cary 1942- *ConAu 103*
Waterman, Charles F 1913- *ConAu 49*
Waterman, Charles K *DrAP&F 83*
Waterman, Guy 1932- *ConAu 97*
Waterman, John Thomas 1918- *ConAu 5R, –8NR*
Waterman, Laura 1939- *ConAu 97*
Waterman, Leroy 1875-1972 *ConAu 33R, ConAu P-1*
Waterman, Margaret 1909- *ConAu 37R*
Watermeier, Daniel J 1940- *ConAu 73*
Waters, Brian Power *ConAu X*
Waters, Chocolate *DrAP&F 83*
Waters, Chocolate 1949- *ConAu 77, IntWWP 82*
Waters, Chris *ConAu X*
Waters, D W 1911- *ConAu 25R*
Waters, David Watkin 1911- *IntAu&W 82, WrDr 84*
Waters, Ethel 1896-1977 *ConAu 73, –81*
Waters, Frank *DrAP&F 83*
Waters, Frank 1902- *ConAu 3NR, –5R, FifWWr, IntAu&W 82, TwCWW, WrDr 84*
Waters, Harold A 1926- *ConAu 53*
Waters, John Frederick 1930- *ConAu 37R, IntAu&W 82, SmATA 4, WrDr 84*
Waters, Marianne *ConAu X*
Waters, Mary-Alice 1942- *ConAu 9NR, –61*
Waters, Michael *DrAP&F 83*
Waters, Michael 1949- *ConAu 10NR, –65*
Waters, Thomas F 1926- *ConAu 81*
Waters, William Alexander 1903- *WrDr 84*
Waters, William R 1920- *ConAu 49*
Waterston, Albert 1907- *ConAu P-1, WrDr 84*
Waterston, Barbara Johns 1940- *ConAu 25R*

Weinberg, Florence May 1933- *ConAu 37R,*
  WrDr 84
Weinberg, Gerald M 1933- *ConAu 89*
Weinberg, Gerhard L 1928- *ConAu 3NR, –9R*
Weinberg, Helen A 1927- *ConAu 73*
Weinberg, Herman G 1908- *ConAu 45,*
  IntAu&W 82
Weinberg, Ian 1938-1969 *ConAu P-2*
Weinberg, Janet Hopson *ConAu X*
Weinberg, Julius 1922- *ConAu 37R*
Weinberg, Julius R 1908-1971 *ConAu P-1*
Weinberg, Kenneth G 1920- *ConAu 41R*
Weinberg, Kerry *ConAu 29R, WrDr 84*
Weinberg, Kurt 1912- *ConAu 41R*
Weinberg, Lila *ConAu 25R*
Weinberg, Martin S 1939- *ConAu 41R*
Weinberg, Meyer 1920- *ConAu 1R, –4NR,*
  WrDr 84
Weinberg, Nathan Gerald 1945- *ConAu 104*
Weinberg, Robert 1946- *ConAu 97*
Weinberg, Robert Charles 1901-1974 *ConAu 45*
Weinberg, Samuel Kirson 1912- *ConAu 1R,*
  –1NR
Weinberg, Sanford Bruce 1950- *ConAu 109*
Weinberg, Steven 1933- *ConAu 5NR, –53*
Weinberg, Werner 1915- *ConAu 41R*
Weinberger, Betty Kiralfy 1932- *ConAu 65*
Weinberger, Leon J 1926- *ConAu 77,*
  IntAu&W 82
Weinberger, Paul E 1931- *ConAu 29R*
Weinbrot, Howard D 1936- *ConAu 107*
Weiner, Annette B 1933- *ConAu 93*
Weiner, Bernard 1935- *ConAu 57*
Weiner, Bernard 1940- *ConAmTC*
Weiner, Charles 1931- *ConAu 109*
Weiner, Dora B 1924- *ConAu 25R*
Weiner, Egon 1906- *ConAu 97*
Weiner, Florence 1931- *ConAu 25R*
Weiner, Hannah *DrAP&F 83*
Weiner, Henri *ConAu X, WrDr 84*
Weiner, Herbert *ConAu 5R*
Weiner, Howard L *DrAP&F 83*
Weiner, Hyman J 1926- *ConAu 49*
Weiner, Irving B 1933- *ConAu 29R*
Weiner, Leonard 1927- *ConAu 21R*
Weiner, Leslie *NatPD 81[port]*
Weiner, Marcella Bakur 1925- *ConAu 105*
Weiner, Myron 1931- *ConAu 1R, –4NR*
Weiner, Richard 1884-1937 *CIDMEL 80*
Weiner, Richard 1927- *ConAu 89*
Weiner, Sandra 1922- *ConAu 49, SmATA 14*
Weiner, Skip *ConAu X*
Weiner, Stewart 1945- *ConAu 89*
Weinfeld, Marsha E *DrAP&F 83*
Weinfield, Henry *DrAP&F 83*
Weinfield, Henry 1949- *ConAu 37R*
Weingart, L O 1931- *ConAu 17R*
Weingarten, Henry *ConAu 57*
Weingarten, Roger *DrAP&F 83*
Weingarten, Roger 1945- *ConAu 10NR, –61*
Weingarten, Romain 1926- *CIDMEL 80,*
  CroCD
Weingarten, Violet 1915-1976 *ConAu 7NR, –9R,*
  –65, SmATA 27N, –3
Weingartner, Charles 1922- *ConAu 49,*
  SmATA 5
Weingartner, James J 1940- *ConAu 93*
Weingartner, Rudolph H 1927- *ConAu 13R*
Weingast, David E 1912- *ConAu 5R*
Weinheber, Josef 1892-1945 *CIDMEL 80,*
  ModGL
Weinig, Jean Maria 1920- *ConAu 29R,*
  IntWWP 82
Weinig, Sister Mary Anthony *ConAu X*
Weininger, Richard 1887?-1979 *ConAu 89*
Weinland, James D 1894- *ConAu 57*
Weinlein, Gregg Thomas *DrAP&F 83*
Weinman, Paul *DrAP&F 83*
Weinman, Paul 1940- *ConAu 77*
Weinrauch, Herschel 1905- *ConAu P-1*
Weinreb, Lloyd L 1936- *ConAu 69*
Weinrich, A K H 1933- *ConAu 37R, WrDr 84*
Weinryb, Bernard D 1905- *ConAu 45*
Weinstein, Allen 1937- *ConAu 41R*
Weinstein, Arnold 1927- *ConAu 9R, ConDr 82,*
  WrDr 84
Weinstein, Brian 1937- *ConAu 21R*
Weinstein, Donald 1926- *ConAu 13R*
Weinstein, Fred 1931- *ConAu 65*
Weinstein, Gerald 1930- *ConAu 25R*
Weinstein, Grace W 1935- *ConAu 10NR, –61*
Weinstein, Howard 1954- *ConAu 107*

Weinstein, Jacob Joseph 1902-1974 *ConAu 108,*
  –110
Weinstein, James 1926- *ConAu 21R*
Weinstein, Jeff *DrAP&F 83*
Weinstein, Leo 1921- *ConAu 110*
Weinstein, Mark Allen 1937- *ConAu 25R,*
  WrDr 84
Weinstein, Marlene 1946- *ConAu 45*
Weinstein, Martin E 1934- *ConAu 85*
Weinstein, Michael 1898- *ConAu P-1*
Weinstein, Nathan Wallenstein 1903?-1940
  ConAu 104, LongCTC, TwCA,
  TwCA SUP
Weinstein, Norman *DrAP&F 83*
Weinstein, Norman Charles 1948- *ConAu 37R*
Weinstein, Robert A 1914- *ConAu 29R*
Weinstein, Sol 1928- *ConAu 13R*
Weinstein, Warren 1941- *ConAu 93*
Weinstock, Herbert 1905-1971 *ConAu 1R, –2NR,*
  –33R
Weinstock, John M 1936- *ConAu 81*
Weinswig, Melvin H 1935- *ConAu 107*
Weintal, Edward 1901-1973 *ConAu 41R*
Weintraub, Dov 1926- *ConAu 109, WrDr 84*
Weintraub, Karl Joachim 1924- *ConAu 25R*
Weintraub, Robert E 1925?-1983 *ConAu 110*
Weintraub, Rodelle 1933- *ConAu 97*
Weintraub, Sidney 1914- *ConAu 1R, –6NR,*
  IntAu&W 82, WrDr 84
Weintraub, Sidney 1914-1983 *ConAu 110*
Weintraub, Sidney 1922- *ConAu 108*
Weintraub, Stanley 1929- *ASpks, ConAu 1R,*
  –2NR, WrDr 84
Weintraub, Wiktor 1908- *ConAu 3NR, –5R,*
  WrDr 84
Weintraub, William 1926- *ConAu 1R*
Weinwurm, George F 1935- *ConAu 33R*
Weinzweig, Helen 1915- *ConAu 106*
Weinzweig, John Jacob 1913- *CreCan 2*
Weir, Alice M *ConAu X*
Weir, J E 1935- *DcLEL 1940*
Weir, John *ConAu X*
Weir, John Edward 1935- *IntAu&W 82,*
  IntWWP 82
Weir, LaVada *ConAu 9NR, –21R, SmATA 2,*
  WrDr 84
Weir, Molly 1920- *ConAu 29R, WrDr 84*
Weir, Nancie MacCullough 1933- *ConAu 65*
Weir, Peter 1944- *ConLC 20*
Weir, Robert M 1933- *ConAu 93*
Weir, Ronald Blackwood 1944- *WrDr 84*
Weir, Rosemary 1905- *ConAu 10NR, –13R,*
  SmATA 21[port], TwCCW 83, WrDr 84
Weir, Thomas R 1912- *ConAu 41R*
Weir, Walter 1909- *ConAu 5R*
Weirich, Frank *ConAmTC*
Weis, Jack 1932- *ConAu 105*
Weis, Norman D 1923- *ConAu 61*
Weisberg, Barry *ConAu 33R*
Weisberg, Gabriel P 1942- *ConAu 73*
Weisberg, Harold 1913- *ConAu 41R,*
  IntAu&W 82
Weisberg, Joseph 1937- *WrDr 84*
Weisberg, Joseph S 1937- *ConAu 107*
Weisberger, Bernard A 1922- *ConAu 5R, –7NR,*
  SmATA 21[port]
Weisberger, Eleanor 1920- *ConAu 97*
Weisberger, L Arnold 1907-1981 *ConAu 103*
Weisbord, Albert 1900?-1977 *ConAu 69*
Weisbord, Marvin R 1931- *ConAu 9NR, –65*
Weisbord, Robert G 1933- *ConAu 109*
Weisbord, Vera Buch 1895- *ConAu 73*
Weisbrod, Burton Allen 1931- *ConAu 1NR, –45*
Weisbuch, Robert 1946- *ConAu 104*
Weisburd, Martin Harold 1940?-1978 *ConAu 77*
Weise, R Eric 1933- *ConAu 41R*
Weisenborn, Gunther 1902-1969 *CnMD, CroCD,*
  ModWD
Weisenburger, Francis Phelps 1900- *ConAu P-1*
Weisenfeld, Murray 1923- *ConAu 104*
Weiser, Eric 1907- *ConAu 17R*
Weiser, Marjorie P K 1934- *ConAu 103,*
  SmATA 33
Weisgal, Meyer W 1894-1977 *ConAu 89*
Weisgard, Leonard 1916- *ConAu 9R,*
  SmATA 2, –30[port]
Weisgerber, Charles A 1912-1977 *ConAu 41R*
Weisgerber, Jean 1924- *ConAu 65,*
  IntAu&W 82
Weisgerber, Robert A 1929- *ConAu 49*
Weishaus, Joel *DrAP&F 83*
Weisheipl, James Athanasius 1923- *ConAu 41R*

Weisheit, Eldon 1933- *ConAu 29R*
Weisinger, Mort 1915-1978 *ConAu 9R*
Weiskopf, Franz 1900- *TwCA SUP*
Weisman, Ann Elisabeth *DrAP&F 83*
Weisman, Ann Elisabeth 1948- *IntWWP 82*
Weisman, Herman M 1916- *ConAu 9R*
Weisman, Joan 1921- *MichAu 80*
Weisman, John 1942- *ConAu 1NR, –45*
Weisman, Marilee 1939- *ConAu 65*
Weisman, Mary-Lou 1937- *ConAu 109*
Weismann, Donald L 1914- *ConAu 33R,*
  IntAu&W 82, WrDr 84
Weismiller, Edward Ronald 1915- *ConAu 1R,*
  –1NR
Weiss, Abraham 1895-1971 *ConAu 104*
Weiss, Adelle 1920- *ConAu 81, SmATA 18*
Weiss, Allen 1918- *ConAu 109*
Weiss, Ann E 1943- *ConAu 1NR, –11NR, –45,*
  SmATA 30
Weiss, Arthur 1912- *ConAu 25R*
Weiss, Bennet A, Jr. 1926?-1983 *ConAu 109*
Weiss, Bernard J 1936- *ConAu 109*
Weiss, David *WrDr 84*
Weiss, David 1909- *ConAu 13R*
Weiss, David W 1927- *IntAu&W 82*
Weiss, Edna *ConAu X*
Weiss, Edna Smith 1916- *ConAu 5R*
Weiss, Elizabeth S 1944- *ConAu 11NR, –61*
Weiss, Francis Joseph 1899?-1975 *ConAu 53*
Weiss, G A M 1922- *ConAu 41R*
Weiss, Harry Bischoff 1883-1972 *ConAu 45*
Weiss, Harvey 1922- *ChlLR 4[port],*
  ConAu 5R, –6NR, SmATA 1, –27[port]
Weiss, Herbert F 1930- *ConAu 21R*
Weiss, Irving J *DrAP&F 83*
Weiss, Irving J 1921- *ConAu 10NR, –17R*
Weiss, Jason Lee *DrAP&F 83*
Weiss, Jess E 1926- *ConAu 49*
Weiss, Joan Talmage 1928- *ConAu 2NR, –5R*
Weiss, John 1927- *ConAu 17R, WrDr 84*
Weiss, Jonathan A 1939- *ConAu 93*
Weiss, Kenneth M 1941- *ConAu 101*
Weiss, Konrad 1880-1940 *ModGL*
Weiss, Leatie 1928- *ConAu 65*
Weiss, Leonard W 1925- *ConAu 5R, –6NR*
Weiss, Lillian d1972 *ConAu 104*
Weiss, Louise 1893-1983 *ConAu 109*
Weiss, M Jerome 1926- *ConAu 9NR, –17R*
Weiss, M Jerry *ConAu X*
Weiss, Malcolm E 1928- *ConAu 11NR, –25R,*
  SmATA 3
Weiss, Margaret R *ConAu 57*
Weiss, Mark 1943- *IntWWP 82*
Weiss, Mark E *DrAP&F 83*
Weiss, Melford Stephen 1937- *ConAu 53*
Weiss, Miriam *ConAu X, SmATA 2*
Weiss, Miriam 1905- *ConAu P-2*
Weiss, Morris S 1915- *ConAu 89*
Weiss, Nancy J 1944- *ConAu 77*
Weiss, Nicki 1954- *ConAu 108,*
  SmATA 33[port]
Weiss, Paul 1901- *ConAu 3NR, –5R, WrDr 84*
Weiss, Peter 1916-1982 *CIDMEL 80,*
  ConAu 3NR, –106, –45, ConLC 3, –15,
  CroCD, ModGL, ModWD, TwCWr,
  WorAu
Weiss, Renee Karol 1923- *ConAu 41R,*
  SmATA 5
Weiss, Robert M 1929- *ConAu 37R*
Weiss, Robert S 1925- *ConAu 25R*
Weiss, Roger W 1930- *ConAu 45*
Weiss, Ruth *DrAP&F 83*
Weiss, Ruth 1928- *IntWWP 82*
Weiss, Samuel A 1922- *ConAu 41R*
Weiss, Sanford *DrAP&F 83*
Weiss, Sanford 1927- *ConAu 25R*
Weiss, Sigmund *DrAP&F 83*
Weiss, Theodore *DrAP&F 83*
Weiss, Theodore 1916- *ConAu 9R, ConLC 3,*
  –8, –14, ConP 80, CroCAP, DcLB 5[port],
  DcLEL 1940, IntAu&W 82, IntWWP 82,
  WorAu, WrDr 84
Weiss, Thomas J 1942- *ConAu 105*
Weissbort, Daniel 1935- *ConAu 2NR, –45,*
  ConP 80, WrDr 84
Weissenborn, Hellmuth 1898-1982 *ConAu 107,*
  SmATA 31N
Weisskopf, Kurt 1907- *ConAu 25R*
Weisskopf, Victor Frederick 1908- *ConAu 107*
Weisskopf, Walter A 1904- *ConAu 37R*
Weissman, Benjamin M 1917- *ConAu 73*
Weissman, Dick *ConAu X*

Weissman, Dorothea Y T 1939- *IntAu&W 82*
Weissman, Jack 1921- *ConAu 13R*
Weissman, Paul 1932- *ConAu 45*
Weissman, Philip 1911?-1972 *ConAu 33R*
Weissman, Richard 1935- *ConAu 81*
Weissman, Rozanne 1942- *ConAu 101*
Weissman, Stephen R 1941- *ConAu 11NR, -57*
Weissman, Steve *ConAu X*
Weissmann, David *DrAP&F 83*
Weisstein, Ulrich W 1925- *ConAu 21R, IntAu&W 82, WrDr 84*
Weisstub, D N 1944- *ConAu 29R*
Weisstub, David N 1944- *IntWWP 82, WrDr 84*
Weithorn, Stanley S 1924- *ConAu 13R*
Weitling, Gunter 1935- *IntAu&W 82*
Weitz, Hans Joachim Nikolaus 1904- *IntAu&W 82*
Weitz, Henry 1911- *ConAu 41R*
Weitz, John 1923- *ConAu 29R*
Weitz, Martin Mishli 1909- *ConAu P-2*
Weitz, Morris 1916-1981 *ConAu 5R, -7NR, -102*
Weitz, Raanan 1913- *ConAu 1NR, -45*
Weitzel, Eugene Joseph 1927- *ConAu 5R*
Weitzenhoffer, Andre M 1921- *ConAu 5R*
Weitzman, Alan 1933- *ConAu 29R*
Weitzman, Arthur J 1933- *ConAu 53*
Weitzman, Elliot D 1929-1983 *ConAu 110*
Weitzman, Sarah Brown *DrAP&F 83*
Weitzman, Sarah Brown 1935- *IntWWP 82*
Weitzmann, Kurt 1904- *ConAu 41R*
Weixlman, Joe *ConAu X*
Weixlmann, Joseph Norman 1946- *ConAu 109*
Wekwerth, Manfred 1929- *CroCD*
Welber, Robert *ConAu 104, SmATA 26*
Welblund, Erling 1906- *IntAu&W 82*
Welbourn, F B 1912- *ConAu 21R*
Welburn, Ron *DrAP&F 83*
Welburn, Ron 1944- *ConAu 1NR, -45, IntAu&W 82, IntWWP 82*
Welburn, Vivienne C *WrDr 84*
Welburn, Vivienne C 1941- *IntAu&W 82*
Welby, T Earle 1881-1933 *LongCTC*
Welch, Ann Courtenay 1917- *ConAu 3NR, -9R, IntAu&W 82, WrDr 84*
Welch, Charles Scott *ConAu X*
Welch, Claude Emerson, Jr. 1939- *ConAu 41R, IntAu&W 82*
Welch, D'Alte Aldridge 1907-1970 *ConAu 104, SmATA 27N*
Welch, Denton 1915-1948 *CnMWL, LongCTC, ModBrL, TwCWr, WorAu*
Welch, Don *DrAP&F 83*
Welch, Don 1932- *ConAu 104, IntWWP 82*
Welch, George Patrick 1901-1976 *ConAu 65, ConAu P-1*
Welch, Herbert 1862-1969 *ConAu P-1*
Welch, Holmes Hinkley 1921- *ConAu 21R, IntAu&W 82*
Welch, J Edmund 1922- *ConAu 57*
Welch, James *DrAP&F 83*
Welch, James 1940- *ConAu 85, ConLC 6, -14, ConP 80, TwCWW, WrDr 84*
Welch, Jean-Louise *ConAu 49, SmATA X*
Welch, Jennifer Groce *DrAP&F 83*
Welch, Jerome Anthony 1933- *ConAu 65*
Welch, June Rayfield 1927- *ConAu 41R*
Welch, Kenneth Frederick 1917- *ConAu 105, WrDr 84*
Welch, Lew 1926-1971? *DcLB 16[port]*
Welch, Liliane 1937- *ConAu 110*
Welch, Mary Ross 1918- *ConAu 53*
Welch, Mary Scott *IntAu&W 82*
Welch, Mary-Scott 1914- *ConAu 104*
Welch, Michael Irene 1940- *ConAu 97*
Welch, Patrick *ConAu X*
Welch, Pauline *ConAu X, SmATA X*
Welch, Richard Edwin, Jr. 1924- *ConAu 85*
Welch, Robert 1947- *WrDr 84*
Welch, Ronald 1909- *ConAu X, SmATA 3*
Welch, Ronald 1909-1982 *TwCCW 83*
Welch, Rowland *ConAu X*
Welch, Stuart Cary 1928- *ConAu 103*
Welch, Timothy L 1935- *ConAu 85*
Welch, William A 1915?-1976 *ConAu 65*
Welcher, Rosalind 1922- *ConAu 45, WrDr 84*
Welcome, John *WrDr 84*
Welcome, John 1914- *ConAu X, TwCCr&M 80*
Welding, Patsy Ruth 1924- *ConAu 61*
Weldon, Fay *ConDr 82C, WrDr 84*
Weldon, Fay 1931- *DcLB 14[port]*
Weldon, Fay 1933- *ConAu 21R, ConLC 6, -9, -11, -19, ConNov 82*

Weldon, John 1890-1963 *LongCTC*
Weldon, Lynn Leroy 1930- *ConAu 97*
Weldon, N Warren, Jr. 1919- *WrDr 84*
Weldon, Rex 1915- *ConAu X*
Weldon, Warren 1919- *ConAu 29R*
Welfle, Richard A 1901- *ConAu P-1*
Welford, A T 1914- *ConAu 5NR, -13R*
Welish, Marjorie *DrAP&F 83*
Welk, Ehm 1884-1966 *CnMD*
Welk, Lawrence 1903- *ConAu 105, WrDr 84*
Welke, Elton 1941- *ConAu 65, IntAu&W 82*
Welker, David 1917- *ConAu 57*
Welker, Robert Henry 1917- *ConAu 89*
Welker, Robert Louis 1924- *ConAu 9R, IntWWP 82*
Welkowitz, Joan 1929- *ConAu 53*
Well, Alan Stewart *ConAu X*
Welland, Colin *ConAu X, ConDr 82C*
Welland, Dennis 1919- *ConAu 2NR, -5R*
Wellard, James Howard 1909- *ConAu 3NR, -5R, IntAu&W 82, WrDr 84*
Wellborn, Charles 1924- *ConAu 29R*
Wellborn, Fred W 1894- *ConAu 9R*
Wellborn, Grace Pleasant 1906- *ConAu P-2*
Wellek, Rene 1903- *ConAu 5R, -8NR, ConLCrt 82, IntAu&W 82, WorAu, WrDr 84*
Wellen, Edward 1919- *ConAu 85*
Weller, Allen Stuart 1907- *ConAu 1R*
Weller, Charles 1911- *ConAu 21R*
Weller, George Anthony 1907- *ConAu 65, SmATA 31[port], WrDr 84*
Weller, Michael 1942- *ConAu 85, ConDr 82, ConLC 10, NatPD 81, WrDr 84*
Weller, Paul 1958- *ConLC 26[port]*
Weller, Sheila *DrAP&F 83*
Weller, Sheila 1945- *ConAu 77*
Wellershoff, Dieter 1925- *ClDMEL 80, ConAu 89*
Welles, Elizabeth *WrDr 84*
Welles, Orson 1915- *ConAu 93, ConDr 82A, ConLC 20, WrDr 84*
Welles, Samuel Gardner 1913?-1981 *ConAu 105*
Welles, Samuel Paul 1907- *WrDr 84*
Welles, Sumner 1892-1961 *TwCA SUP*
Welles, Winifred 1893-1939 *ConAmA, SmATA 27*
Wellesley, Dorothy Violet 1889-1956 *ModBrL*
Wellesley, Gerald 1885-1972 *ConAu 104*
Wellesley, Kenneth 1911- *ConAu 106, WrDr 84*
Wellesz, Egon Joseph 1885-1974 *ConAu 53*
Welling, William 1924- *ConAu 81*
Wellington, C Burleigh 1920- *ConAu 1R*
Wellington, Harry 1926- *ConAu 25R, WrDr 84*
Wellington, Jean Willett 1922- *ConAu 1R*
Wellington, John *WrDr 84*
Wellington, John H 1892- *ConAu P-2*
Wellington, Richard Anthony 1919- *ConAu 61, WrDr 84*
Wellisch, Hans H 1920- *ConAu 102*
Wellisz, Leopold T 1882-1972 *ConAu 37R*
Wellman, Alice 1900- *ConAu 89*
Wellman, Carl Pierce 1926- *ConAu 37R, IntAu&W 82, WrDr 84*
Wellman, Donald *DrAP&F 83*
Wellman, Frederick L 1897- *ConAu 77*
Wellman, Henry Q 1945- *ConAu 37R*
Wellman, Manly Wade 1903- *ConAu 1R, -6NR, ConSFA, SmATA 6, TwCSFW, WrDr 84*
Wellman, Paul Iselin 1898-1966 *ConAu 1R, -25R, SmATA 3, TwCA SUP, TwCWW*
Wellman, William A 1896-1975 *ConAu 61*
Wellmann, Manly Wade 1903- *IntAu&W 82*
Wells, A F 1912- *WrDr 84*
Wells, Anna Mary 1906- *ConAu 2NR, -5R*
Wells, Annie Elizabeth 1906- *IntAu&W 82*
Wells, Arvin Robert 1927- *ConAu 1R*
Wells, Barry *ConSFA*
Wells, Bella Fromm 1901?-1972 *ConAu 104*
Wells, C M 1933- *ConAu 41R*
Wells, Carolyn 1869?-1942 *TwCA, TwCCr&M 80, TwCWr*
Wells, Charles 1898- *WrDr 84*
Wells, David Franklin 1928- *ConAu 108*
Wells, Dee 1925- *AuNews 1, ConAu 85*
Wells, Dicky 1910- *ConAu 61*
Wells, Donald A 1917- *ConAu 21R*
Wells, Ellen B 1934- *ConAu 103*
Wells, Evelyn *ConAu 53*
Wells, George Albert 1926- *ConAu 81, IntAu&W 82*

Wells, H G 1866-1946 *CnMWL, ConAu 110, LongCTC, ModBrL, ModBrL SUP, SmATA 20, TwCLC 6[port], -12[port], TwCSFW, TwCWr, WhoTwCL*
Wells, Harold P 1925- *ConAu 10NR, -65*
Wells, Harry Kohlsaat 1911-1976 *ConAu 5R, -65*
Wells, Helen *ConAu X*
Wells, Helen 1915- *IntAu&W 82, WrDr 84*
Wells, Helen Frances 1910- *ConAu 29R, SmATA 2*
Wells, Henry W 1895-1978 *ConAu 77, -81*
Wells, Herbert George 1866-1946 *TwCA, TwCA SUP*
Wells, Hondo *ConAu X*
Wells, J Wellington *ConAu X. SmATA X*
Wells, James B 1909- *ConAu 45*
Wells, James M 1917- *ConAu 17R, WrDr 84*
Wells, Jerome C 1936- *ConAu 41R*
Wells, Jessica *ConAu X*
Wells, Joel Freeman 1930- *ConAu 13R, WrDr 84*
Wells, John 1936- *ConAu 104, WrDr 84*
Wells, John Jay *ConAu X*
Wells, John Warren 1938- *ConAu 4NR, -49*
Wells, June *ConAu X*
Wells, Kenneth McNeill 1905- *ConAu P-1*
Wells, Leon W 1925- *ConAu 17R*
Wells, Linton 1893-1976 *ConAu 61, -97*
Wells, Louis T, Jr. 1937- *ConAu 65*
Wells, M Gawain 1942- *ConAu 101*
Wells, Martin John 1928- *WrDr 84*
Wells, Merle William 1918- *ConAu 85*
Wells, Peter D 1936- *ConAu 25R*
Wells, Peter Frederick 1918- *WrDr 84*
Wells, Robert *ConAu X*
Wells, Robert 1929- *ConAu 97*
Wells, Robert Vale 1943- *ConAu 73*
Wells, Robert W 1918- *ConAu 2NR, -49*
Wells, Ronald Vale 1913- *ConAu 37R, WrDr 84*
Wells, Rosemary 1943- *ConAu 85, ConLC 12, SmATA 18, TwCCW 83*
Wells, Samuel F 1935- *ConAu 104*
Wells, Stanley 1930- *WrDr 84*
Wells, Stanley W 1930- *ConAu 10NR, -21R*
Wells, Susan Jocelyn 1920- *WrDr 84*
Wells, Tobias *ConAu X, TwCCr&M 80, WrDr 84*
Wells, Tom H 1917- *ConAu 21R*
Wells, Walter 1937- *ConAu 25R, WrDr 84*
Wells, William *DrAP&F 83*
Wells, William D 1926- *ConAu 61*
Wellstone, Paul David 1944- *ConAu 107*
Wellwarth, George E 1932- *ConAu 3NR, -9R, IntAu&W 82, WrDr 84*
Welmers, William Evert 1916- *ConAu 104*
Wels, Byron G 1924- *ConAu 8NR, -61, SmATA 9*
Welsch, Erwin Kurt 1935- *ConAu 17R*
Welsch, Glenn Albert 1915- *ConAu 10NR, -13R*
Welsch, Roger L 1936- *ConAu 9NR, -21R*
Welsh, Alexander 1933- *ConAu 5R, -6NR, WrDr 84*
Welsh, Andrew 1937- *ConAu 110*
Welsh, Anne 1922- *ConAu 101, ConP 80, DcLEL 1940, WrDr 84*
Welsh, David J 1920- *ConAu 17R, WrDr 84*
Welsh, George Schlager 1918- *ConAu 17R*
Welsh, James Michael 1938- *ConAu 4NR, -53*
Welsh, John R 1916-1974 *ConAu 37R*
Welsh, Ken 1941- *ConAu 77*
Welsh, Paul 1911- *ConAu 104*
Welsh, Peter C 1926- *ConAu 25R*
Welsh, Stanley L 1928- *ConAu 103*
Welsh, Susan *ConAu X*
Welsh, William *DrAP&F 83*
Welsh, William Allen 1940- *ConAu 45*
Welsh, William Francis 1950- *IntWWP 82*
Welsman, Ernest Maxwell 1912- *ConAu 5R*
Welt, Bernard *DrAP&F 83*
Welt, Louis G 1913-1974 *ConAu 45*
Welter, Erich 1900-1982 *ConAu 107*
Welter, Rush 1923- *ConAu 2NR, -5R, WrDr 84*
Weltge, Ralph 1930- *ConAu 21R*
Welthy, Soni Halstead 1933- *ConAu 13R*
Welti, Albert Jakob 1894-1965 *CnMD*
Weltmann, Lutz 1901- *ConAu P-1*
Weltner, Linda R 1938- *ConAu 105*
Weltsch, Robert 1891-1982 *ConAu 108*
Welty, Carl 1901- *WrDr 84*
Welty, Eudora *DrAP&F 83*

Wharton, George Frederick, III 1916-
  ConAu 109
Wharton, John Franklin 1894-1977 ConAu 73,
  –81
Wharton, William DcLB Y80B
Wharton, William 1925- ConAu 93, ConLC 18,
  WrDr 84
Whatmore, Leonard Elliott 1912- ConAu 13R
Whatmough, Joshua 1897-1964 ConAu 5R
Wheat, Cathleen Hayhurst 1904- ConAu P-1
Wheat, Gilbert Collins, Jr. 1927- ConAu 1R
Wheat, Joe Ben 1916- ConAu 41R
Wheat, Leonard F 1931- ConAu 29R
Wheat, Patte 1935- ConAu 101
Wheat, Peter Isaac 1939- IntAu&W 82
Wheatcroft, Andrew 1944- ConAu 110
Wheatcroft, John DrAP&F 83
Wheatcroft, John Stewart 1925- ConAu 37R,
  WrDr 84
Wheatcroft, Stephen Frederick 1921- ConAu 5R
Wheatley, Agnes ConAu X
Wheatley, Arabelle 1921- SmATA 16
Wheatley, Dennis 1897-1977 ConAu 5R, –9NR,
  –73, TwCCr&M 80, TwCSFW, TwCWr
Wheatley, Henry Benjamin 1838-1917 LongCTC
Wheatley, Jon 1931- ConAu 29R
Wheatley, Richard Charles 1904- ConAu P-1
Wheatley, Vera ConAu P-1
Wheaton, Anne 1892-1977 ConAu 69
Wheaton, Bruce R 1944- ConAu 104
Wheaton, Philip D 1916- ConAu 104
Wheaton, William L C 1913-1978 ConAu 1R,
  –3NR
Whedon, Julia AuNews 1, ConAu 49
Whedon, Margaret B 1926- ConAu 105
Whedon, Peggy ConAu X
Wheeler, Bayard O 1905- ConAu 41R
Wheeler, Bonnie G 1943- ConAu 109
Wheeler, Burton K 1882-1975 ConAu 53
Wheeler, Charles 1892-1974 ConAu 53,
  ConAu P-2
Wheeler, Cindy 1955- ConAu 110
Wheeler, Colin Vernon 1919- WrDr 84
Wheeler, David L 1934- ConAu 37R
Wheeler, David Raymond 1942- ConAu 73
Wheeler, Douglas L 1937- ConAu 29R
Wheeler, Gidley 1938- ConAu 107
Wheeler, Harvey 1918- ConAu 1NR, –45
Wheeler, Helen Rippier 1926- ConAu 17R,
  WrDr 84
Wheeler, Hugh 1912- ConAu 89, ConDr 82,
  TwCCr&M 80, WorAu
Wheeler, Hugh 1913- WrDr 84
Wheeler, Hugh 1916- NatPD 81[port]
Wheeler, J Clyde 1910- ConAu 1R
Wheeler, Janet D ConAu P-2, SmATA 1
Wheeler, Jesse H, Jr. 1918- ConAu 45
Wheeler, John Archibald 1911- ConAu 57,
  WrDr 84
Wheeler, Keith 1911- ConAu 5R, –7NR
Wheeler, Leslie A 1945- ConAu 11NR, –65
Wheeler, Lora Jeanne 1923- ConAu 33R
Wheeler, Margaret 1916- ConAu P-2
Wheeler, Mary Jane ConAu 29R
Wheeler, Michael 1943- ConAu 9NR, –65
Wheeler, Molly 1920- ConAu 29R, WrDr 84
Wheeler, Monroe 1900- DcLB 4
Wheeler, Sir Mortimer 1890-1976 ConAu 65, –77,
  –77, LongCTC
Wheeler, Opal 1898- SmATA 23[port]
Wheeler, Paul 1934- ConAu 25R
Wheeler, Penny Estes 1943- ConAu 33R,
  WrDr 84
Wheeler, R E Mortimer 1890-1976 ConAu 69
Wheeler, Raymond Milner 1919-1982 ConAu 106
Wheeler, Richard 1922- ConAu 8NR, –17R
Wheeler, Richard Paul 1943- ConAu 108
Wheeler, Richard S 1928- ConAu 45
Wheeler, Robert C 1913- ConAu 61
Wheeler, Ruth Lellah Carr 1899- ConAu 5R
Wheeler, Sessions S 1911- ConAu 17R
Wheeler, Sylvia DrAP&F 83
Wheeler, Thomas C 1927- ConAu 104
Wheeler, Thomas H 1947- ConAu 93
Wheeler, Tom ConAu X
Wheeler, W Lawrence 1925- ConAu 13R
Wheeler, William Morton 1865-1937 TwCA
Wheeler-Bennett, Sir John Wheeler 1902-1975
  ConAu 61, –65, LongCTC
Wheelis, Allen B 1915- ConAu 17R

Wheelock, Arthur Kingsland, Jr. 1943-
  ConAu 107
Wheelock, Carter 1924- ConAu 61
Wheelock, Frederic M 1902- ConAu 97
Wheelock, John Hall 1886-1978 ConAmA,
  ConAu 13R, –77, ConLC 14, ModAL,
  TwCA, TwCA SUP
Wheelock, Martha E 1941- ConAu 25R
Wheelwright, Edward Lawrence 1921-
  ConAu 103, WrDr 84
Wheelwright, John Brooks 1897-1940 ModAL,
  ModAL SUP, WorAu
Wheelwright, Philip 1901-1970 ConAu P-2
Wheelwright, Richard Palmer 1936- ConAu 33R,
  WrDr 84
Whelan, Elizabeth M 1943- ConAu 8NR, –57,
  SmATA 14
Whelan, Gloria 1923- ConAu 101
Whelan, James Robert 1933- ConAu 102
Whelan, Joseph P 1932- ConAu 41R
Wheldon, Huw Pyrs 1916- ConAu 107
Whelpton, Eric 1894-1981 ConAu 5NR, –9R,
  –103
Whelpton, Pascal K 1893-1964 ConAu 1R
Whelton, Clark DrAP&F 83
Whelton, Clark 1937- ConAu 69
Whetham, W C D TwCA SUP
Whetten, Lawrence L 1932- ConAu 11NR, –61
Whetten, Nathan Laselle 1900- ConAu 1R
Whibley, Charles 1859-1930 LongCTC, TwCA
Whicher, John F 1919- ConAu 17R
Whicker, Alan Donald 1925- IntAu&W 82
Whiffen, Marcus 1916- ConAu 61,
  IntAu&W 82
Whigham, Peter 1925- ConAu 25R, ConP 80,
  WrDr 84
Whincup, Brenda Rose IntWWP 82
Whinney, Margaret Dickens 1897-1975 ConAu 61
Whipkey, Kenneth Lee 1932- ConAu 4NR, –53
Whipple, Beverly 1941- ConAu 109
Whipple, Chandler 1905- ConAu 25R
Whipple, Dorothy 1893-1966 ConAu P-1,
  LongCTC
Whipple, Fred Lawrence 1906- ConAu P-1
Whipple, James B 1913- ConAu 29R
Whipple, Maurine 1909- WrDr 84
Whipple, Maurine 1910- ConAu 5R
Whisenand, Paul M 1935- ConAu 69
Whisenhunt, Donald W 1938- ConAu 9NR, –57
Whisler, John A 1951- ConAu 109
Whisler, Robert F 1940- IntWWP 82
Whisnant, Charleen DrAP&F 83
Whisnant, Charleen 1933- ConAu 21R
Whisnant, David E 1938- ConAu 41R
Whistler, Laurence 1912- ConAu 3NR, –9R,
  ConP 80, IntAu&W 82, IntWWP 82,
  WrDr 84
Whistler, Reginald John 1905-1944
  SmATA 30[port]
Whistler, Rex 1905-1944 SmATA X
Whiston, Lionel 1895- ConAu 69
Whitacre, Agnes Lucile Finch 1911- IntWWP 82
Whitacre, Donald 1920- ConAu 69
Whitaker, Ben 1934- ConAu 53, IntAu&W 82,
  WrDr 84
Whitaker, Beryl 1916- ConSFA
Whitaker, C S, Jr. 1935- ConAu 29R
Whitaker, David 1930- ConAu 21R, ConSFA
Whitaker, Dorothy Stock 1925- ConAu 13R
Whitaker, Frederic 1891-1980 ConAu 4NR, –5R,
  –97
Whitaker, Gilbert R, Jr. 1931- ConAu 9R,
  WrDr 84
Whitaker, Haddon 1908?-1982 ConAu 105
Whitaker, Henry Ewart 1925- WrDr 84
Whitaker, James W 1936- ConAu 102
Whitaker, John O, Jr. 1935- ConAu 105
Whitaker, Malachi Taylor 1895-1976 ConAu 104
Whitaker, Mary 1896?-1976 ConAu 65
Whitaker, Rod 1925- WrDr 84
Whitaker, Rod 1931- ConAu 29R
Whitaker, Rogers E M 1899-1981 ConAu 103
Whitaker, T J 1949- ConAu 53
Whitaker, Thomas R 1925- ConAu 25R
Whitaker, Urban George, Jr. 1924- ConAu 9R
Whitbeck, George W 1932- ConAu 73
Whitbread, Jane ConAu X
Whitbread, Leslie George 1917- ConAu 37R,
  WrDr 84
Whitbread, Thomas DrAP&F 83

Whitbread, Thomas 1931- WrDr 84
Whitbread, Thomas Bacon 1931- ConAu 13R,
  ConP 80, DcLEL 1940
Whitburn, Joel Carver 1939- ConAu 33R
Whitby, Henry Augustus Morton 1898-1969
  ConAu P-1
Whitby, Julie Louise 1944- IntWWP 82
Whitby, Sharon ConAu X, TwCRGW,
  WrDr 84
Whitcher, Alice DrAP&F 83
Whitcomb, Edgar D 1918- ConAu 21R
Whitcomb, Hale C 1907- ConAu P-2
Whitcomb, Helen Hafemann ConAu 6NR, –13R
Whitcomb, Ian 1941- ConAu 8NR, –57
Whitcomb, John Clement 1924- WrDr 84
Whitcomb, John Clement, Jr. 1924- ConAu 1R,
  –4NR, IntAu&W 82
Whitcomb, Jon 1906- ConAu P-1, SmATA 10
Whitcomb, Philip W 1891- ConAu 73
Whitcomb, Pineapple DrAP&F 83
White, Alan ConAu 3NR, –45, DcLEL 1940,
  WrDr 84
White, Alan Richard 1922- ConAu 25R,
  WrDr 84
White, Alex Sandri 1916?-1983? ConAu 108
White, Alice Violet 1922- ConAu 61
White, Alicen ConAu 77
White, Anne Hitchcock 1902-1970 ConAu 108,
  SmATA 33
White, Anne S ConAu 93
White, Anne Shanklin 1916- IntAu&W 82
White, Anne Terry 1896- ConAu 9R,
  SmATA 2
White, Anthony Gene 1946- ConAu 73
White, Antonia 1899-1980 ConAu 104, –97,
  LongCTC, WorAu
White, Babington ConAu X
White, Barbara A 1942- ConAu 109
White, Benjamin V 1908- ConAu 101
White, Betty 1917- ConAu 5R
White, Brian Terence 1927- ConAu 105
White, Burton L 1929- ConAu 4NR, –45
White, Carl M 1903- ConAu 13R
White, Carol Hellings 1939- ConAu 81
White, Chappell 1920- ConAu 25R
White, Claire Nicolas DrAP&F 83
White, Claire Nicolas 1925- ConAu 108
White, Curtis 1951- ConAu 110
White, Cynthia L 1940- ConAu 37R
White, Dale ConAu X, SmATA 3
White, Dan S 1939- ConAu 97
White, David Manning 1917- ConAu 1R, –4NR
White, David Omar 1927- ConAu 17R
White, Dori 1919- ConAu 37R, SmATA 10
White, Dorothy Shipley 1896- ConAu P-1
White, Douglas M 1909- ConAu 1R, –4NR
White, E B 1899- ChlLR 1, ConAu 13R,
  ConLC 10, DcLB 22[port], LongCTC,
  ModAL, SmATA 2, –29[port], TwCCW 83,
  TwCWr, WrDr 84
White, Edgar B 1947- ConAu 61, LivgBAA
White, Edmund DrAP&F 83
White, Edmund 1940- WrDr 84
White, Edmund, III 1940- ConAu 3NR, –45,
  ConLC 27[port]
White, Edward Lucas 1866-1934 TwCA
White, Edward M 1933- ConAu 37R,
  IntAu&W 82, WrDr 84
White, Elijah 1938- ConAu 69
White, Eliza Orne 1856-1947 TwCCW 83
White, Elizabeth H 1901?-1972 ConAu 37R
White, Elizabeth Wade 1906- ConAu 97
White, Elmer G 1926- ConAu 21R
White, Elwyn Brooks 1899- AuNews 2, TwCA,
  TwCA SUP
White, Emmons E 1891- ConAu 73
White, Eric Walter 1905- ConAu P-1, WrDr 84
White, Ethel Lina 1887-1944 ConAu 108,
  TwCCr&M 80
White, Eugene E 1919- ConAu 13R
White, Florence M 1910- ConAu 41R,
  SmATA 14
White, G A IntAu&W 82X
White, G Edward 1941- ConAu 69
White, Gail DrAP&F 83
White, Gerald Taylor 1913- ConAu 2NR, –5R
White, Gertrude Mason 1915- ConAu 81,
  IntAu&W 82
White, Gillian Mary 1936- ConAu 17R,
  WrDr 84
White, Glenn M 1918?-1978 ConAu 81, –93

White, Gordon Eliot 1933- *ConAu 101*
White, H T *ConAu X*
White, Harrison C 1930- *ConAu 45*
White, Harry *ConAu X*
White, Helen Constance 1896-1967 *ConAmA,
    ConAu 5R, TwCA, TwCA SUP*
White, Hilda Crystal 1917- *ConAu 5R*
White, Howard Ashley 1913- *ConAu 29R*
White, Howard B 1912?-1974 *ConAu 53*
White, Hugh Clayton 1936- *ConAu 45*
White, Hugh Vernon 1889- *ConAu 5R*
White, Irvin L 1932- *ConAu 8NR, -57*
White, Ivan 1929- *ConP 80, WrDr 84*
White, J P *DrAP&F 83*
White, James 1913- *ConAu 109, -85*
White, James 1928- *ConAu 4NR, -53, ConSFA,
    IntAu&W 82, TwCSFW, WrDr 84*
White, James Dillon 1913- *ConAu X*
White, James Floyd 1932- *ConAu 5R, -6NR,
    -107, WrDr 84*
White, James P *DrAP&F 83*
White, James P 1940- *ConAu 11NR, -69*
White, James W 1941- *ConAu 29R*
White, Jan Viktor 1928- *ConAu 73*
White, Jane Neal 1918- *ConAu 110*
White, Jay C 1925- *ConSFA*
White, Jo Ann 1941- *ConAu 53*
White, John 1919- *ConDr 82, WrDr 84*
White, John 1924- *ConAu 69*
White, John Albert 1910- *ConAu P-2*
White, John Baker *ConAu X*
White, John Hoxland, Jr. 1933- *ConAu 25R*
White, John I 1902- *ConAu 57*
White, John W 1939- *ConAu 37R*
White, John Wesley 1928- *ConAu 29R*
White, Jon Manchip *DrAP&F 83*
White, Jon Manchip 1924- *ConAu 13R,
    ConNov 82, DcLEL 1940, IntAu&W 82,
    IntWWP 82, TwCCr&M 80, WrDr 84*
White, Jonathan *WrDr 84*
White, Joseph 1933- *LivgBAA*
White, Jude Gilliam 1947- *ConAu 106*
White, June 1930- *IntWWP 82*
White, K D 1908- *ConAu 69*
White, K Owen 1902- *ConAu P-2*
White, Karol Koenigsberg 1938- *ConAu 5R*
White, Katherine Sergeant 1892-1977 *ConAu 104*
White, Kenneth 1936- *ConAu 25R, ConP 80,
    WrDr 84*
White, Kenneth Steele 1922- *ConAu 93*
White, Laurence B, Jr. 1935- *ConAu 9NR, -65,
    SmATA 10*
White, Lawrence J 1943- *ConAu 37R, WrDr 84*
White, Leslie A 1900-1975 *ConAu 1R, -3NR,
    -57*
White, Leslie Turner 1903- *ConAu P-1*
White, Lionel 1905- *ConAu 103,
    TwCCr&M 80, WrDr 84*
White, Lola *DrAP&F 83*
White, Lonnie J 1931- *ConAu 13R*
White, Lynn R *IntAu&W 82X*
White, Lynn Townsend, Jr. 1907- *ConAu 2NR,
    -5R*
White, M E 1938- *ConAu 21R*
White, M J D 1910- *WrDr 84*
White, Mary 1904- *IntWWP 82*
White, Mary Alice 1920- *ConAu 9R*
White, Mary Jane *DrAP&F 83*
White, Maury 1919- *ConAu 77*
White, Melvin R 1911- *ConAu 21R*
White, Milton *DrAP&F 83*
White, Minor 1908-1976 *ConAu 10NR, -17R,
    -65*
White, Morton 1917- *WrDr 84*
White, Morton Gabriel 1917- *ConAu 5R, -7NR*
White, Nancy Bean 1922- *ConAu 13R*
White, Nelia Gardner 1894-1957 *TwCA SUP*
White, Nicholas P 1942- *ConAu 73*
White, Norval 1926- *ConAu 77*
White, Orion F, Jr. 1938- *ConAu 53*
White, Osmar Egmont Dorkin 1909- *ConAu 105*
White, Owen Roberts 1945- *ConAu 41R*
White, Patrick 1912- *ConAu 81, ConDr 82,
    ConLC 3, -4, -5, -7, -9, -18, ConNov 82,
    LongCTC, ModCmwL, TwCA, TwCA SUP,
    WhoTwCL, WrDr 84*
White, Patrick 1915- *TwCWr*
White, Patrick C T 1924- *ConAu 85,
    IntAu&W 82*
White, Paul Dudley 1886-1973 *ConAu 45*
White, Paul Hamilton Hume 1910- *ConAu 5R,
    -7NR*

White, Paulette Childress 1928- *MichAu 80*
White, Percival 1887-1970 *ConAu 1R, -2NR*
White, Philip L 1923- *ConAu 81*
White, Phyllis Dorothy *WrDr 84*
White, Poppy Cannon 1906?-1975 *ConAu 57, -65*
White, Ramy Allison *ConAu P-2, SmATA 1*
White, Ray Lewis 1941- *ConAu 9NR, -21R,
    WrDr 84*
White, Reginald 1914- *WrDr 84*
White, Reginald Ernest Oscar 1914- *ConAu 5R,
    -5NR*
White, Reginald James 1905-1971 *ConAu 104,
    -108*
White, Rhea A 1931- *ConAu 77*
White, Richard 1931- *ConAu 110*
White, Richard Alan 1944- *ConAu 97*
White, Richard Clark 1926- *ConAu 45*
White, Robb 1909- *ChlLR 3, ConAu 1R, -1NR,
    SmATA 1*
White, Robert I 1908- *ConAu 1R*
White, Robert Lee 1928- *ConAu 17R, WrDr 84*
White, Robert M, II 1915- *ConAu 73,
    IntAu&W 82*
White, Robin *DrAP&F 83, IntAu&W 82X*
White, Robin 1928- *ConAu 4NR, -9R,
    IntAu&W 82, WrDr 84*
White, Roger 1929- *IntWWP 82*
White, Ron 1944- *ConAmTC*
White, Ronald C, Jr. 1939- *ConAu 93*
White, Ruth M 1914- *ConAu 17R*
White, Ruth Morris 1902?-1978 *ConAu 81*
White, Sarah Harriman 1929- *ConAu 9R*
White, Sheldon Harold 1928- *ConAu 105*
White, Stanford 1853-1906 *LongCTC*
White, Stanhope 1913- *ConAu 21R, WrDr 84*
White, Stanley 1913- *ConAu 6NR, -9R*
White, Stephanie F T 1942- *ConAu 17R*
White, Stephen D 1945- *ConAu 93*
White, Stephen Leonard 1945- *IntAu&W 82*
White, Stewart Edward 1873-1946 *ConAmA,
    LongCTC, TwCA, TwCA SUP, TwCWW*
White, Suzanne 1938- *ConAu 77*
White, T H 1906-1964 *CnMWL, ConAu 73,
    LongCTC, ModBrL, SmATA 12,
    TwCCW 83, TwCWr*
White, Ted 1938- *ConAu X, ConSFA,
    TwCSFW, WrDr 84*
White, Terence DeVere 1912- *ConAu 3NR, -49,
    DcLEL 1940, WrDr 84*
White, Terence Hanbury 1906-1964 *TwCA,
    TwCA SUP*
White, Theodore Edwin 1938- *ConAu 21R*
White, Theodore H 1915- *ASpks, ConAu 1R,
    -3NR, DcLEL 1940, IntAu&W 82,
    WorAu, WrDr 84*
White, Vann *IntWWP 82X*
White, Vona Ann 1916- *IntWWP 82*
White, W D 1926- *ConAu 37R*
White, W J 1920-1980 *ConAu 97*
White, Walter Francis 1893-1955 *TwCA,
    TwCA SUP*
White, William 1910- *ConAu 21R,
    IntAu&W 82, MichAu 80, WrDr 84*
White, William, Jr. 1934- *ConAu 37R,
    IntAu&W 82, SmATA 16, WrDr 84*
White, William Allen 1868-1944 *ConAu 108,
    DcLB 9[port], -25[port], LongCTC, TwCA,
    TwCA SUP*
White, William Anthony Parker 1911-1968
    ConAu 25R, ConAu P-1, TwCA SUP
White, William F 1928- *ConAu 1NR, -45*
White, William Hale 1831-1913 *LongCTC*
White, William J 1926- *ConAu 97*
White, William John 1920- *ConAu 13R*
White, William Lindsay 1900-1973 *ConAu 101,
    -41R, TwCA SUP*
White, William Luther 1931- *ConAu 29R,
    WrDr 84*
White, William M *DrAP&F 83*
White, William S 1907- *ConAu 5R*
White, Zita *ConAu X*
White Elk, Michael *ConAu X*
Whitebird, J 1951- *ConAu 69*
Whitechurch, Victor Lorenzo 1868-1933
    TwCCr&M 80
Whitefield, Ann *ConAu X*
Whiteford, Andrew Hunter 1913- *ConAu 45*
Whitefriar *ConAu X*
Whitehall, Harold 1905- *ConAu P-2*
Whitehead, Alfred 1887- *CreCan 1*
Whitehead, Alfred North 1861-1947 *LongCTC,
    TwCA, TwCA SUP*

Whitehead, Barbara 1930- *ConAu 97*
Whitehead, Don F 1908-1981 *ConAu 9R, -102,
    SmATA 4*
Whitehead, E A 1933- *ConAu 65, ConLC 5*
Whitehead, Edward 1908-1978 *ConAu 77, -81*
Whitehead, Evelyn Annette Eaton 1938-
    ConAu 104
Whitehead, Frank 1916- *ConAu 37R, WrDr 84*
Whitehead, G Kenneth 1913- *ConAu 8NR, -61*
Whitehead, Geoffrey Michael 1921- *WrDr 84*
Whitehead, James *DrAP&F 83*
Whitehead, James 1936- *ConAu 77, ConP 80,
    DcLB Y81B[port], WrDr 84*
Whitehead, James D 1939- *ConAu 105*
Whitehead, Raymond Leslie 1933- *ConAu 77*
Whitehead, Robert John 1928- *ConAu 37R*
Whitehead, Ted 1933- *ConDr 82, WrDr 84*
Whitehill, Arthur M 1919- *ConAu 77*
Whitehill, Walter Muir 1905-1978 *ConAu 6NR,
    -13R, -77*
Whitehorn, Katharine *WrDr 84*
Whitehorn, Katharine Elizabeth 1928- *ConAu X,
    DcLEL 1940, IntAu&W 82*
Whitehouse, Arch 1895- *ConAu X, SmATA X*
Whitehouse, Arthur George Joseph 1895-1979
    ConAu 4NR, -5R, -89, SmATA 14, -23N
Whitehouse, Elizabeth S 1893-1968 *ConAu P-1*
Whitehouse, Jeanne 1939- *ConAu 103,
    SmATA 29[port]*
Whitehouse, Roger 1939- *ConAu 57*
Whitehouse, W A 1915- *ConAu 3NR*
Whitehouse, Walter Alexander 1915- *ConAu 1R,
    WrDr 84*
Whiteing, Eileen Maude Emily 1912-
    IntWWP 82
Whiteing, Richard 1840-1928 *LongCTC, TwCA*
Whitelaw, William Menzies 1890?-1974
    ConAu 45
Whitelock, Dorothy 1901-1982 *ConAu 107*
Whitely, Oliver R 1918- *ConAu 13R*
Whiteman, Maxwell 1914- *ConAu 10NR, -21R*
Whiteman, Michael 1906- *WrDr 84*
Whitemeyer, Hugh Hazen 1939- *IntAu&W 82*
Whitemore, George *DrAP&F 83*
Whitesell, Edwin 1909- *ConAu 41R*
Whitesell, Faris Daniel 1895- *ConAu 5R*
Whiteside, Lynn W 1908- *ConAu 25R*
Whiteside, Robert L 1907- *ConAu 53*
Whiteside, Thomas 1918?- *ConAu 109*
Whiteside, Thomas C 1901- *IntWWP 82*
Whiteside, Tom *IntWWP 82X*
Whiteson, Leon 1930- *ConAu 21R*
Whitewood, Simone *IntWWP 82X*
Whitfield, George 1891- *IntAu&W 82,
    IntWWP 82*
Whitfield, George 1909- *WrDr 84*
Whitfield, George Joshua Newbold 1909-
    ConAu P-1, IntAu&W 82
Whitfield, John Humphreys *WrDr 84*
Whitfield, John Humphreys 1906- *ConAu 9R*
Whitfield, Phil 1944- *ConAu 97*
Whitfield, Raoul 1897-1945 *TwCCr&M 80*
Whitfield, Raoul M 1897?-1945 *ConAu 109*
Whitfield, Shelby 1935- *ConAu 49*
Whitfield, Stephen E *ConSFA*
Whitfield, Stephen J 1942- *ConAu 61*
Whitford, Bessie 1885?-1977 *ConAu 69*
Whitford, Frank 1941- *ConAu 97*
Whitin, Thomson McLintock 1923- *ConAu 1R,
    -3NR*
Whiting, Allen S 1926- *ConAu 105*
Whiting, Beatrice Blyth 1914- *ConAu 5R*
Whiting, Charles E 1914?-1980 *ConAu 97*
Whiting, Frank M 1907- *ConAu 101*
Whiting, John 1915-1963 *DcLEL 1940*
Whiting, John 1917-1963 *CnMD, ConAu 102,
    -89, ConDr 82E, CroCD, DcLB 13[port],
    LongCTC, ModBrL SUP, ModWD,
    TwCWr, WorAu*
Whiting, John Roger Scott 1933- *IntAu&W 82*
Whiting, Kenneth R 1913- *ConAu 5R, -5NR*
Whiting, Nathan *DrAP&F 83*
Whiting, Nathan 1946- *ConAu 41R,
    IntWWP 82*
Whiting, Percy H 1880- *ConAu P-1*
Whiting, Robert 1942- *ConAu 102*
Whiting, Robert L 1918- *ConAu 17R*
Whiting, Thomas A 1917- *ConAu 1R, -3NR*
Whitinger, R D *ConAu X, SmATA 3*
Whitington, R S 1912- *ConAu 77*
Whitington, Richard 1912- *WrDr 84*

Whitlam, Gough 1916- *ConAu 109, WrDr 84*
Whitley, Elizabeth Young 1915- *IntAu&W 82*
Whitley, George *ConAu X, IntAu&W 82X*
Whitley, Oliver R 1918- *ConAu 77*
Whitlock, Brand 1869-1934 *ConAu 110, TwCA*
Whitlock, Glenn E 1917- *ConAu 21R*
Whitlock, Pamela 1921?-1982 *ConAu 107, SmATA 31N*
Whitlock, Quentin A 1937- *ConAu 109*
Whitlock, Ralph 1914- *ConAu 101, IntAu&W 82, WrDr 84*
Whitlock, Virginia Bennett d1972 *ConAu 37R*
Whitlow, Roger 1940- *ConAu 41R*
Whitman, Alden 1913- *ConAu 17R*
Whitman, Ardis *ConAu 9R*
Whitman, Cedric H 1916- *ConAu 17R*
Whitman, Edmund Spurr 1900- *ConAu 17R*
Whitman, Howard 1914?-1975 *ConAu 53*
Whitman, John 1944- *ConAu 11NR, -61*
Whitman, Marina 1935- *WrDr 84*
Whitman, Marina VonNeumann 1935- *ConAu 17R*
Whitman, Martin J 1924- *ConAu 104*
Whitman, Robert Freeman 1925- *ConAu 81*
Whitman, Ruth *DrAP&F 83*
Whitman, Ruth 1922- *ConAu 21R, ConP 80, IntAu&W 82, IntWWP 82, WrDr 84*
Whitman, Virginia Bruner 1901- *ConAu 4NR, -5R*
Whitman, W Tate 1909- *ConAu P-1*
Whitman, Walt 1819-1892 *SmATA 20*
Whitman, Wanda d1976 *ConAu 65*
Whitman, William *DrAP&F 83*
Whitmarsh, Anne 1933- *ConAu 106*
Whitmore, Cilla *ConAu X*
Whitmore, Eugene 1895- *ConAu 5R*
Whitmore, George 1945- *ConAu 102*
Whitmore, Raymond Leslie 1920- *WrDr 84*
Whitnah, Donald Robert 1925- *ConAu 9R, WrDr 84*
Whitnah, Dorothy L 1926- *ConAu 93*
Whitnell, Barbara *ConAu X*
Whitney, Abbie *MichAu 80*
Whitney, Alec *ConAu X*
Whitney, Alex 1922- *ConAu 53, SmATA 14*
Whitney, Bryl A 1901- *ConAu P-1*
Whitney, Charles Allen 1929- *ConAu 81*
Whitney, Cornelius Vanderbilt 1899- *ConAu 85*
Whitney, David *ConAu X*
Whitney, David C 1921- *ConAu 5NR, -9R, SmATA 29*
Whitney, Eleanor Noss 1938- *ConAu 6NR, -13R*
Whitney, Elizabeth Dalton 1906- *ConAu 21R*
Whitney, George D 1918- *ConAu 93*
Whitney, Hallam *ConAu X*
Whitney, J D *DrAP&F 83*
Whitney, J D 1940- *ConAu 3NR, -49*
Whitney, J L H *ConAu X*
Whitney, John Hay 1904-1982 *ConAu 106*
Whitney, John Raymond 1920- *ConAu 105*
Whitney, Leon Fradley 1894-1973 *ConAu 5R, -5NR*
Whitney, Peter Dwight 1915- *ConAu 9R*
Whitney, Phyllis A 1903- *TwCCW 83, WrDr 84*
Whitney, Phyllis Ayame 1903- *AuNews 2, ConAu 1R, -3NR, SmATA 1, -30[port], TwCCr&M 80, TwCRGW*
Whitney, Steve 1946- *ConAu 81*
Whitney, Thomas P 1917- *ConAu 104, SmATA 25[port]*
Whiton, James Nelson 1932- *ConAu 13R*
Whitridge, Arnold 1891- *ConAu 9R*
Whitrow, Gerald James 1912- *ConAu 3NR, -5R*
Whitson, Cis *ConAu X*
Whitson, John Harvey 1854-1936 *TwCWW*
Whitt, Richard 1944- *ConAu 81, IntAu&W 82*
Whittaker, Herbert William 1911- *CreCan 1*
Whittaker, Kathryn Putnam 1931- *ConAu 13R*
Whittaker, Otto 1916- *ConAu 25R*
Whittaker, Robert Harding 1920- *ConAu 105*
Whittemore, Charles P 1921- *ConAu 9R*
Whittemore, Don *ConAu 69*
Whittemore, Edward Reed, Jr. 1919- *DcLEL 1940*
Whittemore, L H 1941- *ConAu 45*
Whittemore, Mildred 1946- *ConAu 9R*
Whittemore, Reed *DrAP&F 83*
Whittemore, Reed 1919- *ConAu 4NR, -9R, ConLC 4, ConP 80, CroCAP, DcLB 5[port], ModAL, WorAu, WrDr 84*
Whittemore, Robert Clifton 1921- *ConAu 9R*

Whitten, Jamie L 1910- *ConAu P-2*
Whitten, Les *IntAu&W 82X*
Whitten, Leslie Hunter 1928- *ConAu 17R, IntAu&W 82, WrDr 84*
Whitten, Mary Evelyn 1922- *ConAu 17R, WrDr 84*
Whitten, Norman E, Jr. 1937- *ConAu 17R, IntAu&W 82, WrDr 84*
Whitten, Wilfred d1942 *LongCTC*
Whittet, G S 1918- *ConAu 21R*
Whittet, George Sorley *IntAu&W 82*
Whittet, George Sorley 1918- *WrDr 84*
Whittick, Arnold 1898- *ConAu P-1, IntAu&W 82, WrDr 84*
Whitting, Philip David 1903- *ConAu 97, WrDr 84*
Whittingham, Charles Percival 1922- *WrDr 84*
Whittingham, Harry E, Jr. 1918- *ConAu 5R*
Whittingham, Jack 1910-1972 *ConAu 37R*
Whittingham, Richard 1939- *ConAu 37R*
Whittington, Geoffrey 1938- *ConAu 104, WrDr 84*
Whittington, H G 1929- *ConAu 21R*
Whittington, Harry 1915- *ConAu 5NR, -21R, TwCCr&M 80, TwCWW, WrDr 84*
Whittington, Peter *ConAu X, IntAu&W 82X, WrDr 84*
Whittington-Egan, Richard 1924- *ConAu 5NR, -9R, IntAu&W 82*
Whittle, Amberys R 1935- *ConAu 45*
Whittle, Peter 1927- *WrDr 84*
Whittle, Tyler *ConAu X, WrDr 84*
Whittlebot, Hernia *ConAu X*
Whittlesey, E S 1907- *ConAu 93*
Whittlesey, Susan 1938- *ConAu 29R*
Whitton, Charlotte 1896-1975 *ConAu 89*
Whitton, John Boardman 1892- *ConAu P-2*
Whitworth, John McKelvie 1942- *ConAu 77, WrDr 84*
Whitworth, Reginald Henry 1910- *ConAu 109*
Whitworth, Rex 1916- *WrDr 84*
Whitworth, William 1937- *ConAu 37R, WrDr 84*
Whiz, Walter *ConAu X*
Whone, George Herbert 1925- *IntAu&W 82*
Whone, Herbert 1925- *ConAu 108, WrDr 84*
Whorton, James C 1942- *ConAu 77*
Whritner, John Alden 1935- *ConAu 45*
Why Are *IntAu&W 82X*
Whyatt, Frances *ConAu X, DrAP&F 83*
Whybray, Roger Norman 1923- *ConAu 89*
Whybrew, William E 1920- *WrDr 84*
Whyte, Barbara Birkbeck 1913- *IntWWP 82*
Whyte, Beverley Sheena Ferguson 1942- *IntAu&W 82*
Whyte, Donald 1926- *IntAu&W 82*
Whyte, Fredrica 1905- *ConAu P-1*
Whyte, Henry Malcolm 1920- *ConAu 3NR, -5R*
Whyte, James Huntington 1909- *ConAu 5R*
Whyte, Johnny 1935- *IntAu&W 82*
Whyte, Lancelot Law 1896-1972 *ConAu P-1, WorAu*
Whyte, Mal 1933- *ConAu 106*
Whyte, Martin King 1942- *ConAu 81*
Whyte, Maxwell 1908- *ConAu 105*
Whyte, Robert Orr 1903- *ConAu 106*
Whyte, Ron *NatPD 81*
Whyte, William Foote 1914- *ConAu 1R, -3NR*
Whyte, William Hollingsworth 1917- *ConAu 9R, DcLEL 1940, IntAu&W 82*
Wiarda, Howard J 1939- *ConAu 4NR, -53*
Wiat, Philippa 1933- *ConAu 102*
Wibberley, Gerald Percy 1915- *IntAu&W 82*
Wibberley, Leonard 1915- *TwCCW 83, WrDr 84*
Wibberley, Leonard Patrick O'Connor 1915- *ChlLR 3, ConAu 3NR, -5R, IntAu&W 82, SmATA 2, TwCCr&M 80, TwCSFW, WorAu*
Wice, Paul B 1942- *ConAu 57*
Wick, Carter *WrDr 84*
Wick, John W 1935- *ConAu 41R*
Wickberg, Nils Erik 1909- *IntAu&W 82*
Wicke, Charles Robinson 1928- *ConAu 37R, WrDr 84*
Wickenden, Dan 1913- *TwCA SUP*
Wickenden, Elizabeth 1909- *ConAu 1R*
Wickens, Delos D 1909- *ConAu P-1*
Wickens, James F 1933- *ConAu 57*
Wickens, Peter Charles 1912- *WrDr 84*
Wicker, Brian John 1929- *ConAu 17R, IntAu&W 82, WrDr 84*

Wicker, Ireene 1905- *ConAu 69*
Wicker, Nina A *DrAP&F 83*
Wicker, Randolfe Hayden 1938- *ConAu 45*
Wicker, Thomas Grey 1926- *ASpks, ConAu 65*
Wicker, Tom 1926- *ConAu X, ConLC 7, WrDr 84*
Wickers, David 1944- *ConAu 77*
Wickersham, Edward Dean 1927-1966 *ConAu 5R*
Wickersham, Joan Barrett 1957- *ConAu 105*
Wickert, Frederic R 1912- *ConAu 21R*
Wickert, Max A *DrAP&F 83*
Wickes, George 1923- *ConAu 9R*
Wickes, Kim 1947- *ConAu 109*
Wickett, William Harold, Jr. 1919- *ConAu 108*
Wickey, Gould 1891- *ConAu 25R*
Wickham, Anna 1884-1947 *LongCTC, TwCA, TwCWr*
Wickham, Edward Ralph *WrDr 84*
Wickham, Edward Ralph 1911- *ConAu 5R, IntAu&W 82*
Wickham, Glynne 1922- *WrDr 84*
Wickham, Glynne William Gladstone 1922- *ConAu 5R, -7NR*
Wickham, Jean 1903- *ConAu 69*
Wickham, Mary Fanning 1898- *ConAu X*
Wickham, Thomas Frederick 1926- *ConAu 13R*
Wicklein, John 1924- *ConAu 106*
Wickramasinghe, Nalin Chandra 1939- *DcLEL 1940, WrDr 84*
Wickremasinghe, S A 1901-1981 *ConAu 108*
Wicks, Ben 1926- *ConAu 73*
Wicks, Harold Vernon, Jr. 1931- *ConAu 102*
Wicks, Harry *ConAu X*
Wicks, Jared 1929- *ConAu 25R*
Wicks, John H 1936- *ConAu 17R*
Wicks, Robert Stewart 1923- *ConAu 17R*
Wickstrom, Gordon M 1926- *ConAmTC*
Wickstrom, Lois *DrAP&F 83*
Wickstrom, Lois 1948- *ConAu 106*
Wickwar, Hardy 1903- *ConAu 57*
Wickwire, Franklin B 1931- *ConAu 21R*
Wickwire, Mary Botts 1935- *ConAu 104*
Widdemer, Mabel Cleland 1902-1964 *ConAu 5R, SmATA 5*
Widdemer, Margaret d1978 *ConAu 4NR*
Widdemer, Margaret 1884-1978 *ConAu 77*
Widder, Keith R 1943- *MichAu 80*
Widder, Robert B 1923- *WrDr 84*
Widell, Helene 1912- *WrDr 84*
Wideman, John E 1941- *ConAu 85, ConLC 5, LivgBAA*
Widener, Don 1930- *ConAu 37R*
Widenor, William C 1937- *ConAu 102*
Widerberg, Siv 1931- *ConAu 53, SmATA 10*
Widgery, Alban Gregory 1887- *ConAu 5R*
Widgery, David 1947- *ConAu 69*
Widgery, Jan *DrAP&F 83*
Widgery, Jan 1920- *ConAu 17R, WrDr 84*
Widick, B J 1910- *ConAu 9R, MichAu 80*
Widicus, Wilbur W, Jr. 1932- *ConAu 53*
Widmer, Eleanor Rackow 1925- *ConAu 17R, WrDr 84*
Widmer, Emmy Louise 1925- *ConAu 29R*
Widmer, Kingsley 1925- *ConAu 1R, -3NR*
Wiebe, Dallas *DrAP&F 83*
Wiebe, Robert H 1930- *ConAu 5R*
Wiebe, Rudy 1934- *ConAu 37R, ConLC 6, -11, -14, ConNov 82, WrDr 84*
Wiebenson, Dora 1926- *ConAu 37R, IntAu&W 82*
Wiecek, William Michael 1938- *ConAu 37R*
Wiechert, Ernst Emil 1887-1950 *CIDMEL 80, ModGL, TwCA SUP, TwCWr*
Wieck, Fred D 1910-1973 *ConAu 104*
Wieckert, Jeanne E 1939- *ConAu 89*
Wiecking, Anna M 1887-1973 *ConAu P-1*
Wieczynski, Joseph L 1934- *ConAu 37R*
Wied, Gustav Johannes 1858-1914 *CIDMEL 80, CnMD*
Wieder, Laurance *DrAP&F 83*
Wieder, Laurance 1946- *ConAu 8NR, -57*
Wieder, Robert S 1944- *ConAu 85*
Wiederumb, Trotzhard *ConAu X*
Wiedner, Donald L 1930- *ConAu 13R*
Wiegand, Charmion Von *ConAu X*
Wiegand, G Carl 1906- *ConAu 21R*
Wiegand, Ursula 1930- *IntAu&W 82*
Wiegand, William *DrAP&F 83*
Wiegand, William 1928- *ConAu 9R, MichAu 80, TwCCr&M 80, WrDr 84*
Wieghart, James G 1933- *ConAu 77*
Wiegner, Kathleen K 1938- *ConAu 93*

Wiley, Bell Irvin 1906-1980 *ConAu 4NR, –5R, –97, DcLB 17[port], IntAu&W 82*
Wiley, David Sherman 1935- *ConAu 61*
Wiley, Jack 1936- *ConAu 8NR, –61*
Wiley, Jay Wilson 1913- *ConAu 5R*
Wiley, John P, Jr. 1936- *ConAu 89*
Wiley, Karla H 1918- *ConAu 61*
Wiley, Margaret L *ConAu X, WrDr 84*
Wiley, Paul L 1914- *ConAu 5R*
Wiley, Paul L 1914-1979 *ConAu 10NR*
Wiley, Raymond A 1923- *ConAu 37R, IntAu&W 82*
Wiley, Stan *ConAu X*
Wiley, Tom 1906- *ConAu 25R*
Wiley, Vivian 1896- *IntWWP 82*
Wilf, Alexander 1905?-1981 *ConAu 103*
Wilford, John Noble 1933- *ConAu 29R, IntAu&W 82*
Wilford, Walton T 1937- *ConAu 49*
Wilgus, A Curtis 1897- *ConAu 3NR, –5R, WrDr 84*
Wilgus, D K 1918- *ConAu 37R, IntAu&W 82, WrDr 84*
Wilhelm, Hellmut 1905- *ConAu 5R*
Wilhelm, James Jerome 1932- *ConAu 17R, IntAu&W 82*
Wilhelm, John R 1916- *ConAu 5R, WrDr 84*
Wilhelm, Kate 1928- *ConAu 37R, ConLC 7, ConSFA, DcLB 8[port], DrmM[port], TwCSFW, WrDr 84*
Wilhelm, Kathryn Stephenson 1915- *ConAu 13R*
Wilhelm, Paul A 1916- *ConAu 61*
Wilhelm, Walt 1893- *ConAu 29R*
Wilhelmina *ConAu X*
Wilhelmsen, Frederick D 1923- *ConAu 1R, –3NR*
Wilhoit, Francis M 1920- *ConAu 109*
Wilk, David *DrAP&F 83*
Wilk, David 1951- *ConAu 4NR, –53*
Wilk, Gerard H 1902- *ConAmTC, ConAu 69*
Wilk, Max *DrAP&F 83*
Wilk, Max 1920- *ConAu 1R, –1NR*
Wilk, Melvin *DrAP&F 83*
Wilke, Ekkehard-Teja 1941- *ConAu 65*
Wilke, Ulfert 1907- *ConAu P-1*
Wilken, Robert L 1936- *ConAu 29R*
Wilkening, Howard 1909- *ConAu 89*
Wilkens, Emily 1917- *ConAu 103*
Wilkerson, David R 1931- *ConAu 41R*
Wilkerson, Hugh 1939- *ConAu 104*
Wilkerson, Loree A R 1923- *ConAu 17R*
Wilkes, Glenn Newton 1928- *ConAu 1R*
Wilkes, Ian 1932- *ConAu 41R*
Wilkes, John W 1924- *ConAu 25R*
Wilkes, Paul 1938- *ConAu 81, IntAu&W 82*
Wilkes, William Alfred 1910- *ConAu 45*
Wilkes-Hunter, Richard 1906- *ConAu 13R*
Wilkie, Brian 1929- *ConAu 13R*
Wilkie, James W 1936- *ConAu 21R*
Wilkie, Jane 1917- *ConAu 102*
Wilkie, Katharine E 1904-1980 *SmATA 31[port]*
Wilkie, Katharine Elliott 1904- *ConAu 21R*
Wilkie, Kenneth Bruce 1942- *ConAu 85, IntAu&W 82*
Wilkins, Beatrice 1928- *ConAu 61*
Wilkins, Burleigh Taylor 1932- *ConAu 105*
Wilkins, Ernest J 1918- *ConAu 53*
Wilkins, Frances 1923- *ConAu 73, SmATA 14*
Wilkins, Kathleen Sonia 1941- *ConAu 104*
Wilkins, Kay S *ConAu X*
Wilkins, Leslie T 1915- *ConAu 7NR, –17R*
Wilkins, Marilyn 1926- *ConAu 105, SmATA 30[port]*
Wilkins, Marne *ConAu X, SmATA X*
Wilkins, Mary Eleanor 1852-1930 *ConAu X, TwCA, TwCA SUP*
Wilkins, Mary Huiskamp 1926- *ConAu 2NR*
Wilkins, Mesannie 1891- *ConAu P-2*
Wilkins, Roger 1932- *ConAu 109*
Wilkins, Ronald J 1916- *ConAu 93*
Wilkins, Roy 1901-1981 *ConAu 104*
Wilkins, Susan *DrAP&F 83*
Wilkins, Thurman 1915- *ConAu 5R, IntAu&W 82*
Wilkins, Vaughan 1890-1959 *LongCTC*
Wilkins, William R 1933- *ConAu 61*
Wilkins, William Vaughan 1890-1959 *TwCA SUP*
Wilkinson, Alec 1952- *ConAu 109*
Wilkinson, Anne 1910-1961 *CreCan 2, DcLEL 1940*
Wilkinson, Barry 1923- *SmATA 32*

Wilkinson, Bertie 1898- *ConAu 9R*
Wilkinson, Brenda 1946- *ConAu 69, SmATA 14*
Wilkinson, Bud *ConAu X*
Wilkinson, Burke 1913- *ConAu 9R, SmATA 4, WrDr 84*
Wilkinson, C E *DrAP&F 83*
Wilkinson, C E 1948- *ConAu 109, NatPD 81[port]*
Wilkinson, Carol Lynn *DrAP&F 83*
Wilkinson, Charles B 1916- *ConAu 105*
Wilkinson, Charlotte Jefferson *ConAu 69*
Wilkinson, Christopher 1941- *ConDr 82*
Wilkinson, Clyde Winfield 1910- *ConAu 1R*
Wilkinson, David *ConAu 93*
Wilkinson, Denys 1922- *WrDr 84*
Wilkinson, Denys Haigh 1922- *IntAu&W 82*
Wilkinson, Doris Yvonne 1936- *ConAu 29R*
Wilkinson, Doris Yvonne 1938- *LivgBAA*
Wilkinson, Ernest Leroy 1899-1978 *ConAu 3NR, –49*
Wilkinson, Geoffrey Kedlington 1907- *ConAu 1R*
Wilkinson, Iris Guiver d1939 *LongCTC*
Wilkinson, J F 1925- *ConAu 105*
Wilkinson, James Harvie, III 1944- *ConAu 101*
Wilkinson, John 1929- *WrDr 84*
Wilkinson, John Burke 1913- *IntAu&W 82*
Wilkinson, John Donald 1929- *ConAu 9R*
Wilkinson, John Thomas 1893-1980 *ConAu 104, –107, IntAu&W 82*
Wilkinson, Lancelot Patrick 1907- *ConAu 3NR, –5R*
Wilkinson, Lorna Hilda Kathleen 1909- *ConAu P-1*
Wilkinson, Louis 1881-1966 *LongCTC*
Wilkinson, Marguerite Ogden 1883-1928 *TwCA*
Wilkinson, Norman Beaumont 1910- *ConAu 37R*
Wilkinson, Paul 1937- *ConAu 77, IntAu&W 82, WrDr 84*
Wilkinson, Richard Gerald 1943- *ConAu 45*
Wilkinson, Roderick 1917- *ConAu 13R*
Wilkinson, Ronald 1920- *ConAu 5R*
Wilkinson, Rosemary C *DrAP&F 83*
Wilkinson, Rosemary C 1924- *ConAu 1NR, –49, IntWWP 82*
Wilkinson, Rupert Hugh 1936- *ConAu 9R*
Wilkinson, Sylvia *DrAP&F 83*
Wilkinson, Sylvia J 1940- *AuNews 1, ConAu 17R, WrDr 84*
Wilkinson, Tim 1912- *WrDr 84*
Wilkinson, Walter 1888-1970 *ConAu 104*
Wilkinson, Winifred *ConAu X*
Wilkinson, Winifred 1922- *ConAu 21R*
Wilkinson, Winnifred *WrDr 84*
Wilkinson-Latham, Robert John 1943- *WrDr 84*
Wilkon, Jozef 1930- *ConAu 107, SmATA 31[port]*
Wilks, Brian 1933- *ConAu 69*
Wilks, John 1922- *ConAu 73*
Wilks, Michael Thomas 1947- *ConAu 110*
Wilks, Mike *ConAu X*
Wilks, Yorick 1939- *ConAu 73*
Will *ConAu X, SmATA X, TwCCW 83*
Will, Frederic *DrAP&F 83*
Will, Frederic 1928- *ConAu 1NR, –49*
Will, Frederick L 1909- *ConAu 13R*
Will, George F 1941- *ConAu 77*
Will, John N *ConSFA*
Will, Lawrence Elmer 1893- *ConAu P-2*
Will, Robert E 1928- *ConAu 17R*
Willan, Anne 1938- *ConAu 6NR, –57*
Willan, Healey 1880-1968 *CreCan 2*
Willan, James Healey *CreCan 2*
Willan, Thomas Stuart 1910- *ConAu 9R*
Willans, Jean Stone 1924- *ConAu 65*
Willard, Barbara 1909- *ChlLR 2, ConAu 81, SmATA 17, TwCCW 83, WrDr 84*
Willard, Beatrice E 1925- *ConAu 41R*
Willard, Charles *ConAu X*
Willard, Charlotte 1906?-1977 *ConAu 73*
Willard, Charlotte 1914-1977 *ConAu 81*
Willard, Contant *IntWWP 82X*
Willard, Josiah F 1869-1907 *TwCA, TwCA SUP*
Willard, Lee *IntWWP 82X*
Willard, Mildred Wilds 1911- *ConAu 21R, SmATA 14*
Willard, Nancy *DrAP&F 83*
Willard, Nancy 1936- *ChlLR 5[port], ConAu 10NR, –89, ConLC 7, ConP 80, DcLB 5, SmATA 30, TwCCW 83, WrDr 84*
Willard, Portman *ConAu X*

Willcock, M M 1925- *ConAu 65*
Willcox, Donald J 1933- *ConAu 49*
Willcox, Jean 1945- *IntWWP 82*
Willcox, Sheila 1936- *ConAu 73*
Willcox, William Bradford 1907- *ConAu 3NR, –5R*
Wille, Janet Neipris 1936- *ConAu 109*
Willee, Albert William 1916- *WrDr 84*
Willee, Albert William 1916-1982 *ConAu 109*
Willeford, Charles 1919- *ConAu 33R, ConSFA, WrDr 84*
Willeford, William 1929- *ConAu 25R*
Willem, John M 1909-1979 *ConAu 93, ConAu P-1*
Willems, Emilio 1905- *ConAu 105*
Willems, J Rutherford 1944- *ConAu 45*
Willems, Paul 1912- *CIDMEL 80, CnMD*
Willensky, Elliot 1933- *ConAu 29R, WrDr 84*
Willenson, Kim Jeremy 1937- *ConAu 103*
Willerding, Margaret F 1919- *ConAu 57*
Willets, F W 1930- *ConAu 21R*
Willets, Walter E 1924- *ConAu 25R*
Willett, Edward R 1923- *ConAu 2NR, –5R*
Willett, Brother Franciscus 1922- *ConAu 13R*
Willett, Frank 1925- *ConAu 25R, IntAu&W 82, WrDr 84*
Willett, John 1917- *ConAu 4NR, –9R, WrDr 84*
Willett, T C 1918- *ConAu 37R*
Willett, Thomas D 1942- *ConAu 108*
Willetts, R F 1915- *ConAu 2NR*
Willetts, Ronald Frederick 1915- *ConAu 5R, IntAu&W 82, IntWWP 82, WrDr 84*
Willey, Basil 1897- *ConAu 9R, LongCTC, TwCA SUP*
Willey, Darrell S 1925- *ConAu 41R*
Willey, Gordon R 1913- *ConAu 2NR, –5R*
Willey, Keith 1930- *ConAu 9NR, –21R*
Willey, Margaret *DrAP&F 83*
Willey, Mary Louise *DrAP&F 83*
Willey, Peter Robert Everard 1922- *ConAu 13R, WrDr 84*
Willey, R DeVerl 1910- *ConAu P-2*
Willey, Richard J 1934- *ConAu 41R*
Willey, Robert *ConAu X, SmATA 2*
Willey, Ron *IntAu&W 82X*
Willey, Ronald 1930- *IntAu&W 82*
Willgoose, Carl E 1916- *ConAu 6NR, –13R*
Willhelm, Sidney McLarty 1934- *ConAu 9R, IntAu&W 82, WrDr 84*
William, Arnold *WrDr 84*
William, Maurice 1882?-1973 *ConAu 45*
Williams, Alan 1935- *WrDr 84*
Williams, Alan F 1933- *ConAu 49*
Williams, Alan Lee 1930- *IntAu&W 82, WrDr 84*
Williams, Alan Moray 1915- *IntAu&W 82, IntWWP 82*
Williams, Alden 1932- *ConAu 41R*
Williams, Alice Cary 1892- *ConAu 65*
Williams, Arthur E *DrAP&F 83*
Williams, Aston R 1912- *ConAu 21R*
Williams, Aubrey L 1922- *ConAu 1R, –6NR*
Williams, Barbara 1925- *ConAu 1NR, –49, SmATA 11*
Williams, Barry 1932- *ConAu 29R, WrDr 84*
Williams, Ben Ames 1889-1953 *TwCA, TwCA SUP*
Williams, Benjamin Harrison 1889-1974 *ConAu 37R*
Williams, Benjamin J *DrAP&F 83*
Williams, Bernard 1929- *WrDr 84*
Williams, Bert 1930- *WrDr 84*
Williams, Bert Nolan 1930- *ConAu 103*
Williams, Beryl 1910- *ConAu X, SmATA X*
Williams, Bill *ConAu X*
Williams, Brad 1918- *ConAu 1R, –1NR*
Williams, Bruce Rodda 1919- *ConAu 13R, IntAu&W 82, WrDr 84*
Williams, Burton John 1927- *ConAu 41R*
Williams, Byron 1934- *ConAu 29R*
Williams, C Arthur, Jr. 1924- *ConAu 1R, –2NR, WrDr 84*
Williams, C Glyn 1928- *ConAu 29R*
Williams, C J F 1930- *ConAu 103, –108*
Williams, C K *DrAP&F 83*
Williams, C K 1936- *ConAu 37R, ConP 80, DcLB 5[port], IntAu&W 82, IntWWP 82X*
Williams, Carl C 1903- *ConAu 45*
Williams, Carol *WrDr 84*
Williams, Carol M 1917- *ConAu 65*

Williams, Philip W 1941- *ConAu 11NR, -69*
Williams, Phyllis S 1931- *ConAu 65*
Williams, Pieter Daniel DeWet 1929-
    DcLEL 1940
Williams, Ralph Mehlin 1911- *ConAu 5R*
Williams, Raymond 1921- *ConAu 21R,
    ConLCrt 82, ConNov 82, DcLB 14[port],
    DcLEL 1940, IntAu&W 82, ModBrL,
    TwCWr, WorAu, WrDr 84*
Williams, Rebecca 1899-1976 *ConAu 65*
Williams, Regina E *DrAP&F 83*
Williams, Richard Hays 1912- *ConAu 1R, -2NR*
Williams, Richard Lippincott 1910- *ConAu 101*
Williams, Robert Chadwell 1938- *ConAu 37R*
Williams, Robert Coleman 1940- *ConAu 21R*
Williams, Robert Deryck 1917- *ConAu 1R, -103,
    IntAu&W 82, WrDr 84*
Williams, Robert Hugh 1907?-1983 *ConAu 109*
Williams, Robert L 1903- *ConAu 10NR, -13R*
Williams, Robert Moore 1907- *ConSFA*
Williams, Robert Moore 1907-1977 *ConAu 102,
    TwCSFW*
Williams, Robert P 1906?-1977 *ConAu 69*
Williams, Robin M, Jr. 1914- *ConAu 13R*
Williams, Roger, Jr. 1920- *WrDr 84*
Williams, Roger John 1893- *ConAu 7NR, -17R,
    IntAu&W 82, WrDr 84*
Williams, Roger M 1934- *ConAu 37R*
Williams, Roger Neville 1943- *ConAu 37R,
    WrDr 84*
Williams, Roland 1910- *WrDr 84*
Williams, Ronald Ralph 1906-1979 *ConAu 7NR,
    -13R*
Williams, Rosalind H 1944- *ConAu 109*
Williams, Rose *ConAu X*
Williams, Russ *DrAP&F 83*
Williams, Russell J 1944- *ConAu 104*
Williams, Samm-Art 1946- *NatPD 81*
Williams, Selma R 1925- *ConAu 1NR, -49,
    SmATA 14*
Williams, Sherley Anne 1944- *ConAu 73,
    LivgBAA*
Williams, Shirley *ConAu X*
Williams, Shirley Anne *DrAP&F 83*
Williams, Shirley Vivien Teresa Brittain 1930-
    IntAu&W 82
Williams, Slim *ConAu X, SmATA X*
Williams, Stanley W 1917- *ConAu 17R*
Williams, Stirling B, Jr. 1943- *ConAu 29R*
Williams, Strephon Kaplan 1934- *ConAu 102*
Williams, T C 1925- *ConAu 29R*
Williams, T Harry 1909-1979 *ConAu 3NR,
    DcLB 17[port]*
Williams, Tennessee 1911- *AuNews 2,
    ConDr 82, ConLC 5, ConNov 82, CroCD,
    DcLB 7[port], IntAu&W 82, LongCTC,
    ModWD, NatPD 81[port], WhoTwCL*
Williams, Tennessee 1911?-1983 *ConAu 108,
    DcLB DS4[port], -Y83N[port]*
Williams, Tennessee 1914- *AuNews 1, CnMD,
    CnMWL, ConAu 5R, ConLC 1, -2, -7, -8,
    -11, -15, -19, DcLEL 1940, ModAL,
    ModAL SUP, TwCA SUP, TwCWr*
Williams, Theodore C 1930- *ConAu 69*
Williams, Thomas *DrAP&F 83*
Williams, Thomas 1926- *ConAu 1R, -2NR,
    ConLC 14, IntAu&W 82, WrDr 84*
Williams, Thomas 1931- *ConAu 49*
Williams, Thomas Harry 1909- *ConAu 1R*
Williams, Thomas Howard 1935- *ConAu 13R*
Williams, Tina *ConAu X*
Williams, Tom *IntAu&W 82X*
Williams, Trevor Illtyd 1921- *ConAu 109,
    IntAu&W 82, WrDr 84*
Williams, Ursula Moray *TwCCW 83, WrDr 84*
Williams, Ursula Moray 1911- *ConAu 10NR,
    -13R, IntAu&W 82, SmATA 3*
Williams, Valentine 1883-1946 *LongCTC, TwCA,
    TwCA SUP, TwCCr&M 80*
Williams, Vera B *SmATA 33*
Williams, Vergil L 1935- *ConAu 9NR, -57*
Williams, Wallace Edward 1926- *ConAu 105*
Williams, Walter G 1903- *ConAu P-1*
Williams, Wetherby *ConAu 3NR*
Williams, Willard F 1921- *ConAu 13R*
Williams, William 1921- *WrDr 84*
Williams, William Appleman 1921- *ConAu 1R,
    -3NR, ConIsC 2[port], DcLB 17[port]*
Williams, William Carlos 1883-1963 *CnMD,
    CnMWL, ConAmA, ConAu 89, ConLC 1,
    -2, -5, -9, -13, -22[port], DcLB 4, -16[port],*

*LongCTC, ModAL, ModAL SUP, ModWD,
    TwCA, TwCA SUP, TwCWr, WhoTwCL*
Williams, William David 1917- *ConAu 5R*
Williams, William H 1936- *ConAu 69*
Williams, William P 1939- *ConAu 45*
Williams, Willie J *DrAP&F 83*
Williams, Wilma Dean 1929- *IntWWP 82*
Williams, Wirt 1921- *WrDr 84*
Williams, Wirt Alfred, Jr. 1921- *ConAu 9R,
    ConNov 82, DcLB 6[port]*
Williams-Ellis, A S 1894- *ConSFA*
Williams-Ellis, Amabel 1894- *ConAu 105,
    IntAu&W 82, LongCTC, SmATA 29,
    TwCA, TwCA SUP, TwCWr*
Williams-Ellis, Sir Clough 1883- *ConAu 13R,
    LongCTC*
Williamson, A M 1869-1933 *LongCTC,
    TwCRGW*
Williamson, Alan *DrAP&F 83*
Williamson, Alan 1944- *ConAu 57*
Williamson, Albert Curtis 1867-1944 *CreCan 1*
Williamson, Alice Muriel 1869-1933 *TwCA*
Williamson, Anthony 1932- *ConAu 101*
Williamson, Audrey 1913- *ConAu 3NR, -49,
    WrDr 84*
Williamson, Bruce 1930- *ConAu 101*
Williamson, C N 1859-1920 *TwCRGW*
Williamson, Charles Norris 1859-1920 *LongCTC,
    TwCA, TwCA SUP*
Williamson, Chilton 1916- *ConAu 13R*
Williamson, Chilton, Jr. 1947- *ConAu 102*
Williamson, Claude C H 1891- *ConAu P-1*
Williamson, Craig *DrAP&F 83*
Williamson, Craig 1943- *ConAu 29R,
    IntWWP 82*
Williamson, Curtis 1867-1944 *CreCan 1*
Williamson, David 1942- *WrDr 84*
Williamson, David Keith 1942- *ConAu 103,
    ConDr 82, IntAu&W 82*
Williamson, Ellen Douglas *ConAu 17R*
Williamson, Eugene L 1930- *ConAu 9R*
Williamson, Geoffrey 1897- *ConAu 9R*
Williamson, Glen 1909- *ConAu 9NR, -57*
Williamson, H D 1907- *ConAu 65*
Williamson, Harold Francis 1901- *ConAu 5R*
Williamson, Henry 1895-1977 *ConAu 73, -81,
    LongCTC, SmATA 30N, TwCCW 83*
Williamson, Henry 1897- *ModBrL, TwCA,
    TwCA SUP, TwCWr*
Williamson, Hugh Ross 1901- *LongCTC,
    ModBrL*
Williamson, J A 1886-1964 *LongCTC*
Williamson, J N *DrAP&F 83*
Williamson, J N 1932- *IntAu&W 82*
Williamson, J Peter 1929- *ConAu 1R, -6NR*
Williamson, Jack 1908- *ConAu X, ConSFA,
    DcLB 8[port], TwCSFW, WrDr 84*
Williamson, Jeffrey G 1935- *ConAu 85*
Williamson, Joanne Small 1926- *ConAu 13R,
    SmATA 3*
Williamson, John Butler 1943- *ConAu 89*
Williamson, John G 1933- *ConAu 45*
Williamson, John Stewart 1908- *ConAu 17R*
Williamson, Joseph 1895- *ConAu P-1*
Williamson, Juanita V 1917- *ConAu 37R*
Williamson, Lamar, Jr. 1926- *ConAu 89*
Williamson, Moncrieff 1915- *ConAu 102*
Williamson, Norma 1934- *ConAu 65*
Williamson, Oliver E 1932- *ConAu 81*
Williamson, Porter B 1916- *ConAu 110*
Williamson, Rene DeVisme 1908- *ConAu P-1*
Williamson, Richard 1930- *ConAu 37R*
Williamson, Richard 1935- *ConAu 109,
    WrDr 84*
Williamson, Robert C 1916- *ConAu 21R,
    IntAu&W 82, WrDr 84*
Williamson, Robin 1938- *ConAu 29R*
Williamson, Robin 1943- *ConAu 102,
    IntWWP 82*
Williamson, Rosemarie Gay 1925- *IntWWP 82*
Williamson, Stanford Winfield 1916- *ConAu 5R*
Williamson, Thames Ross 1894- *ConAmA,
    TwCA, TwCA SUP*
Williamson, Tony *ConAu X*
Williamson, Tony 1932- *WrDr 84*
Williamson, William Bedford 1918- *ConAu 1R,
    -6NR*
Williamson, William Landram 1920- *ConAu 9R,
    IntAu&W 82*
Wilibald, Graf *IntAu&W 82X*
Willie, Charles V 1927- *ConAu 41R,
    IntAu&W 82, LivgBAA*

Willie, Frederick *ConAu X*
Willig, George 1949- *ConAu 102*
Willig, John M 1913-1982 *ConAu 107*
Willimon, William H 1946- *ConAu 106*
Willing, Jules Z 1914-1981 *ConAu 108*
Willing, Martha Kent 1920- *ConAu 37R,
    WrDr 84*
Willingham, Calder *DrAP&F 83*
Willingham, Calder 1922- *CnMD, ConAu 3NR,
    -5R, ConLC 5, ConNov 82, DcLB 2,
    DcLEL 1940, TwCA SUP, TwCWr,
    WrDr 84*
Willingham, John J 1935- *ConAu 37R*
Willingham, John R 1919- *ConAu 37R*
Willis, Anthony Armstrong 1897-1976 *ConAu 69*
Willis, Arthur James 1895- *ConAu 5R, -5NR*
Willis, C M *IntWWP 82X*
Willis, Charles *ConAu X*
Willis, Corinne Denneny *ConAu 21R*
Willis, Donald C 1947- *ConAu 41R*
Willis, Donna Brown *IntWWP 82X*
Willis, E David 1932- *ConAu 37R*
Willis, Edgar E *WrDr 84*
Willis, Edgar Ernest 1913- *ConAu 5R*
Willis, Edward Henry 1918- *DcLEL 1940*
Willis, Ellen 1941- *ConIsC 2[port]*
Willis, Ellen Jane 1941- *ConAu 106*
Willis, F Roy 1930- *ConAu 13R*
Willis, George Anthony Armstrong 1897-
    LongCTC
Willis, Irene 1929- *ConAu 10NR, -65*
Willis, James 1928- *ConAu 109, WrDr 84*
Willis, James Frank 1909-1969 *CreCan 2*
Willis, Jerry W 1943- *ConAu 85*
Willis, John A 1916- *WrDr 84*
Willis, John Alvin 1916- *ConAmTC,
    ConAu 17R*
Willis, John H, Jr. 1929- *ConAu 37R*
Willis, John Ralph 1938- *LivgBAA*
Willis, Lowell E *ConAu X*
Willis, Margaret 1899- *ConAu 3NR, -5R*
Willis, Maud *ConAu X*
Willis, Meredith Sue *DrAP&F 83*
Willis, Meredith Sue 1946- *ConAu 85*
Willis, Roy 1927- *ConAu 77*
Willis, Samuel *ConAu X*
Willis, Sharon O 1938- *ConAu 37R*
Willis, Stanley E, II 1923- *ConAu 21R*
Willis, Ted 1914- *TwCWr*
Willis, Ted 1918- *ConAu 7NR, -9R, ConDr 82,
    IntAu&W 82, TwCCr&M 80, WrDr 84*
Willis, Wayne 1942- *ConAu 29R*
Willison, George Findlay 1896-1972 *ConAu 37R,
    ConAu P-1, TwCA SUP*
Willison, Marilyn Murray 1948- *ConAu 105*
Willitts, Martin, Jr. *DrAP&F 83*
Willke, John Charles 1925- *ConAu 9NR, -65*
Willkens, William Henry Robert 1919-
    ConAu 21R, IntAu&W 82
Willmer, Edward Nevill 1902- *WrDr 84*
Willmington, Harold L 1932- *ConAu 49*
Willmott, Peter 1923- *ConAu 21R, WrDr 84*
Willner, Ann Ruth 1924- *ConAu 21R*
Willner, Dorothy 1927- *ConAu 53*
Willner, Sven Evert 1918- *IntAu&W 82*
Willnow, Ronald D 1933- *ConAu 77*
Willock, Colin 1919- *ConAu 10NR, -13R,
    IntAu&W 82, WrDr 84*
Willock, Ruth *ConAu 13R*
Willott, Robert Graham 1942- *IntAu&W 82*
Willoughby, Cass *WrDr 84*
Willoughby, Charles Andrew 1892-1972
    ConAu 104
Willoughby, David P 1901- *ConAu 37R*
Willoughby, Elaine Macmann 1926- *ConAu 101*
Willoughby, Hugh *ConAu X, WrDr 84*
Willoughby, Lee Davis *ConAu X, WrDr 84*
Willoughby, Robin Kay *DrAP&F 83*
Willoughby, Robin Kay 1946- *IntWWP 82*
Willoughby, William Reid 1910- *ConAu 1R*
Willoughby-Higson, Philip *WrDr 84*
Willoughby-Higson, Philip John 1933-
    IntAu&W 82
Willrich, Mason 1933- *ConAu 77,
    IntAu&W 82, WrDr 84*
Willrich, Ted L 1924- *ConAu 29R*
Wills, A J 1927- *ConAu 21R*
Wills, Alfred J 1927- *WrDr 84*
Wills, Cecil M 1891- *TwCCr&M 80*
Wills, Chester *TwCWW*
Wills, Garry 1934- *ConAu 1R, -1NR, WrDr 84*
Wills, Jean 1929- *ConAu 105*

Wilson, Michael 1914-1978 *ConAu 77, -85*
Wilson, Mitchell 1913-1973 *ConAu 1R, -3NR, -41R, DcLEL 1940*
Wilson, Monica Hunter 1908- *ConAu 1R, -6NR*
Wilson, Monica Hunter 1908-1982 *ConAu 108*
Wilson, Morris Emett 1894- *ConAu 5R, WrDr 84*
Wilson, N Scarlyn 1901- *ConAu 5R, -5NR*
Wilson, Neill C 1889- *ConAu 5R*
Wilson, Nelly 1930- *ConAu 106*
Wilson, Noel Avon 1914- *ConAu 73*
Wilson, Norma Jean Clark 1946- *IntWWP 82*
Wilson, Pat *IntAu&W 82X*
Wilson, Pat 1910- *ConAu 29R, WrDr 84*
Wilson, Patrick Seymour 1926- *DcLEL 1940*
Wilson, Paul C 1944- *ConAu 77*
Wilson, Paul Hastings *DrAP&F 83*
Wilson, Paul R 1942- *ConAu 109*
Wilson, Peter N 1928- *ConAu 25R*
Wilson, Philip Whitwell 1875-1956 *LongCTC, TwCA SUP*
Wilson, Phillip 1922- *ConAu 57, IntAu&W 82, WrDr 84*
Wilson, Phoebe Rous 1924?-1980 *ConAu 101*
Wilson, Phyllis Starr 1928- *ConAu 69*
Wilson, Quentin *IntWWP 82X*
Wilson, R H L 1920- *ConAu 13R*
Wilson, Ramona C *DrAP&F 83*
Wilson, Raymond 1925- *ConAu 97, ConSFA, IntWWP 82*
Wilson, Richard 1920- *ConSFA, TwCSFW, WrDr 84*
Wilson, Richard Garratt 1928- *ConAu 106*
Wilson, Richard Guy 1940- *ConAu 93*
Wilson, Richard Lawson 1905-1981 *ConAu 102*
Wilson, Richard W 1933- *ConAu 73*
Wilson, Robert 1941- *IntAu&W 82*
Wilson, Robert Anton 1932- *ConAu 65, TwCSFW, WrDr 84*
Wilson, Robert L 1925- *ConAu 9NR, -57*
Wilson, Robert M 1929- *ConAu 9NR, -21R*
Wilson, Robert M 1944- *ConAu 2NR, -49, ConDr 82, ConLC 7, -9*
Wilson, Robert McLachlan 1916- *ConAu 109, WrDr 84*
Wilson, Robert Neal 1924- *ConAu 17R, IntAu&W 82, WrDr 84*
Wilson, Robert Renbert 1898- *ConAu 45*
Wilson, Robin Scott 1928- *ConAu 101*
Wilson, Robley, Jr. *DrAP&F 83*
Wilson, Robley, Jr. 1930- *ConAu 77*
Wilson, Roger Burdett 1919- *ConAu 45, WrDr 84*
Wilson, Romer 1891-1930 *LongCTC, TwCA*
Wilson, Ronald E 1932- *ConAu 105*
Wilson, Ronald York 1907- *CreCan 1*
Wilson, Ross 1914- *ConAu 5R, WrDr 84*
Wilson, Samuel, Jr. 1911- *ConAu 6NR, -53*
Wilson, Sandra 1944- *ConAu 102, WrDr 84*
Wilson, Sandy 1924- *ConDr 82D, DcLEL 1940, WrDr 84*
Wilson, Sarah Elizabeth Turpin 1934- *IntWWP 82*
Wilson, Sloan 1920- *ConAu 1R, -1NR, ConNov 82, DcLEL 1940, WorAu, WrDr 84*
Wilson, Snoo 1948- *ConAu 69, ConDr 82, IntAu&W 82, WrDr 84*
Wilson, Steve 1943- *ConAu 73*
Wilson, Sue *IntWWP 82X*
Wilson, Ted *DrAP&F 83*
Wilson, Theodore A 1940- *ConAu 37R*
Wilson, Thomas 1916- *WrDr 84*
Wilson, Thomas Williams, Jr. 1912- *ConAu 3NR, -5R*
Wilson, Tom 1931- *ConAu 106, SmATA 30, -33[port]*
Wilson, Trevor Frederick *WrDr 84*
Wilson, Trevor Gordon 1928- *ConAu 53, WrDr 84*
Wilson, W Harmon 1905- *ConAu 37R*
Wilson, Walt 1939- *ConAu 69, SmATA 14*
Wilson, Wesley M *WrDr 84*
Wilson, Wesley M 1927- *ConAu 9R*
Wilson, Wilfrid George 1910- *ConAu P-2*
Wilson, William A 1933- *ConAu 105*
Wilson, William E 1906- *WrDr 84*
Wilson, William Edward 1906- *ConAu 2NR, -5R, IntAu&W 82*
Wilson, William H 1935- *ConAu 13R*
Wilson, William J 1935- *ConAu 1NR, -45*
Wilson, William Ritchie 1911- *ConAu 41R*

Wilson, William S *DrAP&F 83*
Wilson, William S 1932- *ConAu 81*
Wilson, Woodrow 1856-1924 *LongCTC*
Wilson, York 1907- *CreCan 1*
Wilson-Barry, Alma Louise 1913- *IntWWP 82*
Wilt, Fred 1920- *ConAu 9NR, -57*
Wilt, Judith 1941- *ConAu 57*
Wiltgen, Ralph 1921- *WrDr 84*
Wiltgen, Ralph M 1921- *ConAu 11NR*
Wiltgen, Ralph Michael 1921- *ConAu 25R, IntAu&W 82*
Wilthorn, John Knut 1926- *IntAu&W 82*
Wilton, Andrew 1942- *ConAu 97*
Wilton, Elizabeth 1937- *ConAu 69, SmATA 14*
Wiltse, Charles M 1907- *ConAu 1R, -3NR*
Wiltse, David 1940- *ConAu 105*
Wiltsee, Joseph L 1920- *ConAu 110*
Wiltz, Chris 1948- *ConAu 106*
Wiltz, John Edward 1930- *ConAu 9R*
Wilwerding, Walter Joseph 1891-1966 *ConAu P-1, SmATA 9*
Wimmer, Larry T 1935- *ConAu 101*
Wimp, Jet *DrAP&F 83*
Wimsatt, James I 1927- *ConAu 61*
Wimsatt, W K, Jr. 1907-1975 *ConAu 3NR, ConLCrt 82*
Wimsatt, William Kurtz, Jr. 1907-1975 *ConAu 1R, -61, WhoTwCL, WorAu*
Winans, A D *DrAP&F 83*
Winans, A D 1936- *ConAu 57*
Winans, Allan Davis 1936- *IntWWP 82*
Winans, Edgar Vincent 1930- *ConAu 5R*
Winant, Fran *DrAP&F 83*
Winant, Fran 1943- *ConAu 53*
Winant, Francine 1943- *IntWWP 82*
Winawer, Bonnie P 1938- *ConAu 17R*
Wincelberg, Shimon 1924- *ConAu 45, NatPD 81[port]*
Winch, D M 1933- *ConAu 45*
Winch, Harriet Gragg 1908- *IntWWP 82*
Winch, John *LongCTC, TwCA, TwCA SUP*
Winch, Michael Bluett 1907- *ConAu P-1, WrDr 84*
Winch, Peter 1926- *ConAu 29R, WrDr 84*
Winch, Robert F 1911- *ConAu 25R*
Winch, Sally G *IntWWP 82X*
Winch, Terence *DrAP&F 83*
Winch, Terence 1945- *ConAu 93*
Winchell, Carol Ann 1936- *ConAu 7NR, -61*
Winchell, Constance M 1896- *ConAu P-1*
Winchell, Constance M 1896-1983 *ConAu 109*
Winchell, Wallace 1914- *ConAu 53, IntWWP 82*
Winchell, Walter 1897-1972 *ConAu 101, -33R*
Winchester, A M 1908- *ConAu 41R*
Winchester, Clarence 1895-1981 *ConAu 104*
Winchester, James Hugh 1917- *ConAu 17R, SmATA 30[port]*
Winchester, Kay *WrDr 84*
Winchester, Olive May 1919- *IntWWP 82*
Winchester, Otis 1933- *ConAu 21R*
Winchester, Simon 1944- *ConAu 107, WrDr 84*
Winckler, Paul A 1926- *ConAu 102*
Wind, Edgar 1900-1971 *ConAu 104*
Wind, Herbert Warren 1916- *ConAu 1R, -6NR*
Windal, Floyd W 1930- *ConAu 9R*
Windchy, Eugene G 1930- *ConAu 41R*
Windeler, Robert 1944- *ConAu 102*
Winder, Alvin E 1923- *ConAu 93*
Winder, Barbara *DrAP&F 83*
Winder, George Herbert 1895- *ConAu P-1*
Winder, Mavis Areta 1907- *ConAu 21R, IntAu&W 82, WrDr 84*
Winder, Richard Bayly 1920- *ConAu 17R, WrDr 84*
Winders, Gertrude Hecker 1897- *ConAu 1R, -6NR, SmATA 3*
Windhager, Juliane 1912- *IntWWP 82*
Windham, Basil *ConAu X, SmATA X*
Windham, Donald 1920- *ConAu 1R, -6NR, ConNov 82, DcLB 6[port], WorAu, WrDr 84*
Windham, Douglas M 1943- *ConAu 29R*
Windham, Joan 1904- *ConAu 21R*
Windham, Kathryn T 1918- *ConAu 11NR, -69, SmATA 14*
Windle, William Frederick 1898- *ConAu 108*
Windley, Charles Ellis 1942- *ConAu 65*
Windmiller, Marshall 1924- *ConAu 21R*
Windmuller, John P 1923- *ConAu 10NR, -25R*
Windolph, F Lyman 1889-1978 *ConAu 41R*
Windrow, Martin 1944- *ConAu 110*

Windrow, Martin Clive 1944- *IntAu&W 82*
Windsor, Duke Of 1894-1972 *ConAu X*
Windsor, Annie *ConAu X*
Windsor, Betty *IntWWP 82X*
Windsor, Claire *ConAu X, SmATA X*
Windsor, Patricia 1938- *ConAu 4NR, -49, SmATA 30[port], WrDr 84*
Windsor, Philip 1935- *ConAu 5R, -8NR*
Windsor, Rex *ConAu X, IntAu&W 82X*
Windsor, Rudolph R 1935- *ConAu 107, LivgBAA*
Windsor-Richards, Arthur Bedlington 1904- *ConAu P-1*
Wine, Dick *ConAu X, WrDr 84*
Wine, Sherwin T 1928- *ConAu 93*
Winearls, Jane 1908- *ConAu 103*
Wineberg, Henry J 1905?-1983 *ConAu 109*
Winebrenner, D Kenneth 1908- *ConAu P-1*
Winegarten, Renee 1922- *ConAu 65, WrDr 84*
Winehouse, Irwin 1922- *ConAu 9R*
Winek, Charles L 1936- *ConAu 65*
Winer, Linda *ConAmTC*
Winer, Richard 1929- *ConAu 73*
Wines, Roger 1933- *ConAu 21R*
Winetrout, Kenneth 1912- *ConAu 21R, WrDr 84*
Winfield, Arthur M *ConAu X*
Winfield, Edna *ConAu X*
Winfield, Leigh *ConAu X*
Winfrey, Dorman H 1924- *ConAu 17R, IntAu&W 82*
Winfrey, John Crawford 1935- *ConAu 57*
Winfrey, Lee 1932- *ConAu 69*
Winful, Emmanuel Archibald 1922- *IntWWP 82*
Wing, Cliff W, Jr. 1922- *ConAu 49*
Wing, Donald G 1904-1972 *ConAu 37R*
Wing, Frances 1907- *ConAu P-1*
Wing, George 1921- *ConAu 17R, WrDr 84*
Wing, J K 1923- *ConAu 29R*
Wing, Jennifer Patai 1942- *ConAu 57*
Wing, John K 1923- *WrDr 84*
Wingate, Gifford W 1925- *ConAu 65*
Wingate, Isabel 1901- *WrDr 84*
Wingate, Isabel Barnum 1901- *ConAu 21R, IntAu&W 82*
Wingate, John 1920- *ConAu 77, IntAu&W 82, WrDr 84*
Wingate, John Williams 1899- *ConAu 9R*
Wingate, Peter *CreCan 1*
Wingenbach, Father Gregory C 1938- *ConAu 13R*
Winger, Fred E 1912- *ConAu 13R*
Winger, Howard W 1914- *ConAu 7NR, -17R*
Wingert, Paul S 1900?-1974 *ConAu 53*
Wingfield, Sheila 1906- *ConP 80, WrDr 84*
Wingfield, Sheila Claude 1906- *ConAu 108*
Wingfield, Susan *WrDr 84*
Wingfield Digby, George 1911- *ConAu P-1, IntAu&W 82, WrDr 84*
Wingler, Hans M 1920- *ConAu 29R*
Wingo, E Otha 1934- *ConAu 37R, WrDr 84*
Wingo, Glenn Max 1913- *ConAu 5R, WrDr 84*
Wingo, T Lowdon, Jr. 1923- *ConAu 21R*
Wingo, Walter Scott 1931- *ConAu 81, IntAu&W 82*
Wingren, Gustaf Fredrik 1910- *ConAu 13R, WrDr 84*
Winick, Charles 1922- *ConAu 109*
Winick, Myron 1929- *ConAu 107*
Winick, Steven 1944- *ConAu 61*
Winik, Marion *DrAP&F 83*
Winiki, Ephriam *TwCSFW*
Wink, Richard L 1930- *ConAu 93*
Wink, Walter Philip 1935- *ConAu 37R*
Winkelman, Donald M 1934- *ConAu 41R*
Winkler, Allan M 1945- *ConAu 81*
Winkler, Bee 1919- *ConAu 13R*
Winkler, Cornelis 1927- *IntAu&W 82, IntWWP 82*
Winkler, Erhard M 1921- *ConAu 89*
Winkler, Franz E 1907- *ConAu 5R*
Winkler, Henry R 1916- *ConAu 10NR*
Winkler, Henry Ralph 1916- *ConAu 17R, IntAu&W 82, WrDr 84*
Winkler, John 1935- *WrDr 84*
Winkler, Kees *IntWWP 82X*
Winkler, Manfred 1922- *IntWWP 82*
Winkler, Paul 1898-1982 *ConAu 107*
Winkler, Win Ann 1935- *ConAu 73*
Winkless, Nels, III 1934- *ConAu 57*
Winks, Donald 1928- *ConAu 25R*
Winks, Robin William 1930- *ConAu 3NR, -5R*

Witcover, Jules 1927- *ConAu 25R*
Witcutt, William Purcell 1907- *ConAu P-1*
Witemeyer, Hugh Hazen 1939- *ConAu 25R,*
 WrDr 84
Witham, James *DrAP&F 83*
Witham, Ross 1917- *ConAu 105*
Witham, W Tasker 1914- *ConAu 13R*
Witheford, Hubert 1921- *ConAu 102, ConP 80,*
 WrDr 84
Witheridge, Elizabeth Plumb 1907- *ConAu 97,*
 IntAu&W 82
Withers, Carl A 1900-1970 *ConAu 73,*
 SmATA 14
Withers, E L *ConAu X*
Withers, John Herbert 1911- *WrDr 84*
Withers, Josephine 1938- *ConAu 101*
Withers, Percy 1867-1945 *LongCTC*
Withers, Sara Cook 1924- *ConAu 17R*
Withers, William 1905- *ConAu 13R, WrDr 84*
Witherspoon, Frances 1887?-1973 *ConAu 45*
Witherspoon, Ina McAuley 1920- *IntWWP 82*
Witherspoon, Irene Murray 1913- *ConAu 1NR*
Witherspoon, Mary Elizabeth *DrAP&F 83*
Witherspoon, Mary Elizabeth 1919- *ConAu 77*
Witherspoon, Naomi Long *ConAu X,*
 MichAu 80
Witherspoon, Thomas E 1934- *ConAu 81*
Witherup, William *DrAP&F 83*
Withey, J A 1918- *ConAu 25R*
Withington, William Adriance 1924- *ConAu 41R*
Withrow, Dorothy E 1910- *ConAu 21R*
Witkacy *ConAu X, WorAu 1970*
Witke, Roxane 1938- *ConAu 69, WrDr 84*
Witker, Kristi *ConAu 77*
Witker, Kristi 1943- *WrDr 84*
Witkiewicz, Stanislaw Ignacy 1885-1939
 ClDMEL 80, CnMD, ConAu 105, CroCD,
 ModSL 2, ModWD, TwCLC 8[port],
 WorAu 1970
Witkin, Erwin 1926- *ConAu 37R*
Witkin, Herman A 1916-1979 *ConAu 1R, -1NR*
Witman, Walt *IntWWP 82X*
Witmer, Helen L 1898-1979 *ConAu 89,*
 ConAu P-2
Witschel, John *DrAP&F 83*
Witt, Harold *DrAP&F 83*
Witt, Harold Vernon 1923- *ConAu 1R, -1NR,*
 IntAu&W 82, IntWWP 82, WrDr 84
Witt, Howell Arthur John 1920- *ConAu 109*
Witt, Hubert 1935- *ConAu 65*
Witt, James F 1937- *ConAu 89*
Witt, John 1907-1982 *ConAu 106*
Witt, Reginald Eldred 1907-1980 *ConAu 37R,*
 -97
Witt, Shirley Hill 1934- *ConAu 5NR, -53,*
 SmATA 17
Witte, Ann Dryden 1942- *ConAu 107*
Witte, Glenna Finley 1925- *AuNews 1,*
 ConAu 10NR, -13R
Witte, John *DrAP&F 83*
Witte, John 1948- *ConAu 93*
Wittels, Anne F *DrAP&F 83*
Wittels, Harriet Joan 1938- *ConAu 107,*
 SmATA 31
Witten, Anne R *DrAP&F 83*
Witten, Herbert F 1920- *ConAu 5R*
Wittenbach, Henry August 1900- *WrDr 84*
Wittenberg, Judith Bryant 1938- *ConAu 102*
Wittenberg, Philip 1895- *ConAu P-2*
Wittenberg, Rudolph *DrAP&F 83*
Wittenberg, Rudolph M 1906- *ConAu 69*
Wittermans, Elizabeth *ConAu 17R*
Witters, Weldon L 1929- *ConAu 93*
Wittgenstein, Herta *DrAP&F 83*
Wittgenstein, Ludwig Josef Johann 1889-1951
 LongCTC, WorAu
Wittich, Walter A 1910- *ConAu 49*
Wittig, Alice J 1929- *ConAu 101*
Wittig, Judith *DrAP&F 83*
Wittig, Monique 1935- *ConLC 22[port],*
 WorAu 1970
Witting, Clifford 1907-1947 *ConAu 1R,*
 TwCCr&M 80
Wittke, Carl Frederick 1892-1971 *ConAu 29R*
Wittkofski, Joseph Nicholas 1912- *ConAu 9R,*
 WrDr 84
Wittkop, Justus Franz 1899- *IntAu&W 82*
Wittkop-Menardeau, Gabrielle 1920-
 IntAu&W 82
Wittkower, Rudolf 1901-1971 *ConAu 33R*
Wittkowski, Wolfgang 1925- *ConAu 8NR, -61*
Wittler, Janet Marie *DrAP&F 83*

Wittlin, Alma S *ConAu 45*
Wittlin, Joseph 1896-1976 *ConLC 25[port]*
Wittlin, Jozef 1896-1976 *ClDMEL 80,*
 ConAu 3NR, -49, -65, ModSL 2
Wittlin, Thaddeus 1909- *ConAu 2NR, -45,*
 IntAu&W 82, WrDr 84
Wittlinger, Ellen *DrAP&F 83*
Wittlinger, Karl 1922- *CnMD, CroCD,*
 ModWD
Wittman, Sally 1941- *ConAu 107,*
 SmATA 30[port]
Wittmer, Joe 1937- *ConAu 45*
Wittner, Lawrence Stephen 1941- *ConAu 25R,*
 WrDr 84
Wittner, Mary Margaret 1920- *IntWWP 82*
Witton, Dorothy *ConAu 73, MichAu 80*
Witton-Davies, Carlyle 1913- *ConAu 9R,*
 WrDr 84
Wittreich, Joseph Anthony, Jr. 1939- *ConAu 29R*
Wittrock, M C 1931- *ConAu 2NR, -49*
Witty, Helen E S 1921- *ConAu 105*
Witty, Paul 1898-1976 *ConAu 65, -73,*
 SmATA 30N
Witty, Robert Gee 1906- *ConAu P-2, WrDr 84*
Witucke, Virginia 1937- *ConAu 37R*
Witze, Claude 1909?-1977 *ConAu 73*
Wivel, Ole 1921- *ClDMEL 80*
Wizard, Mariann G 1946- *ConAu 37R*
Wizard, Mr. *ConAu X, SmATA X*
Wizard Of Dreams *IntWWP 82X*
Wobbe, R A 1938- *ConAu 102*
Wobig, Ellen 1911- *ConSFA*
Wodehouse, Lawrence 1934- *ConAu 4NR, -53*
Wodehouse, P G 1881-1975 *ConAu 3NR, -45,*
 -57, ConLC 2, -5, -10, -22[port], LongCTC,
 ModBrL, ModBrL SUP, SmATA 22[port],
 TwCWr, WhoTwCL
Wodehouse, Pelham Grenville 1881-1975
 AuNews 2, TwCA, TwCA SUP
Woden, George *ConAu X*
Wodge, Dreary *ConAu X, SmATA X*
Wodhams, Jack 1931- *TwCSFW, WrDr 84*
Woebcke, Mary-Jane 1933- *ConAu 25R*
Woehr, Richard 1942- *ConAu 57*
Woehrlin, William F 1928- *ConAu 45*
Woelfel, James W 1937- *ConAu 41R,*
 IntAu&W 82
Woelfl, Paul A 1913- *ConAu 17R*
Woerner, Karl Heinrich 1910-1969 *ConAu 110*
Woessner, Nina C 1933- *ConAu 29R*
Woessner, Warren *DrAP&F 83*
Woessner, Warren 1944- *ConAu 37R*
Woestemeyer, Ina Faye *ConAu X*
Woestijne, Karel VanDe 1879-1929 *ClDMEL 80*
Woetzel, Robert Kurt 1930- *ConAu 5R, -6NR*
Wofford, Azile 1896- *ConAu 5R*
Wofford, Chloe Anthony *LivgBAA*
Wofsey, Marvin M 1913- *ConAu 105*
Wogaman, J Philip 1932- *WrDr 84*
Wogaman, Philip 1932- *ConAu 25R*
Wohl, Gerald 1934- *ConAu 17R*
Wohl, James P 1937- *ConAu 77*
Wohl, Robert 1936- *ConAu 104*
Wohlgelernter, Maurice 1921- *ConAu 6NR,*
 -13R, WrDr 84
Wohlrabe, Raymond A 1900- *WrDr 84*
Wohlrabe, Raymond A 1900-1977 *ConAu 1R,*
 -3NR, SmATA 4
Wohmann, Gabriele 1932- *ClDMEL 80,*
 IntAu&W 82, ModGL
Woititz, Janet G *ConAu 101*
Woiwode, Larry *DrAP&F 83*
Woiwode, Larry 1941- *ConAu 73, ConLC 6,*
 -10, ConNov 82, DcLB 6[port], WrDr 84
Wojciechowska, Maia *DrAP&F 83*
Wojciechowska, Maia 1927- *ChlLR 1,*
 ConAu 4NR, -9R, ConLC 26[port],
 SmATA 1, -28[port], TwCCW 83,
 WrDr 84
Wojciechowski, Cecile Cloutier *CreCan 1*
Wojna, Ryszard 1920- *IntAu&W 82*
Wojtasiewicz, Olgierd Adrian 1916-
 IntAu&W 82
Wojtyla, Karol *ConAu X*
Wolberg, Lewis Robert 1905- *ConAu 2NR, -45*
Wolcott, Harry F 1929- *ConAu 65*
Wolcott, Leonard Thompson *ConAu 11NR,*
 -13R, WrDr 84
Wolcott, Patty 1929- *ConAu 57, IntAu&W 82,*
 SmATA 14, WrDr 84
Wold, Allen L 1943- *ConAu 105*

Wold, Jo Anne 1938- *ConAu 61,*
 SmATA 30[port]
Wold, Ruth 1923- *ConAu 37R*
Woldendorp, R 1927- *ConAu 29R*
Woldin, Beth Weiner 1955- *ConAu 102,*
 SmATA 34[port]
Wolf, Arnold Jacob 1924- *ConAu 29R*
Wolf, Arnold Veryl 1916-1975 *ConAu 104*
Wolf, Barbara H 1932- *ConAu 57*
Wolf, Charlotte Elizabeth 1926- *ConAu 29R,*
 WrDr 84
Wolf, Christa 1929- *ClDMEL 80, ConAu 85,*
 ConLC 14, WorAu 1970
Wolf, Deborah Goleman 1938- *ConAu 97*
Wolf, Donald J 1929- *ConAu 13R*
Wolf, Edwin, II 1911- *ConAu 1R, -4NR*
Wolf, Eric R 1923- *ConAu 17R*
Wolf, Frank 1940- *ConAu 57*
Wolf, Frank L 1924- *ConAu 57*
Wolf, Frederick *ConAu X*
Wolf, Friedrich 1888-1953 *CnMD, CroCD,*
 ModWD, TwCA, TwCA SUP
Wolf, Gary K *TwCSFW, WrDr 84*
Wolf, George 1890?-1980 *ConAu 97*
Wolf, George D 1923- *ConAu 29R*
Wolf, Harold A 1923- *ConAu 13R*
Wolf, Harvey 1935- *ConAu 57*
Wolf, Hazel Catherine 1907- *ConAu 5R*
Wolf, Herbert C 1923- *ConAu 13R*
Wolf, Jack C 1922- *ConAu 57*
Wolf, Jacqueline 1928- *ConAu 109*
Wolf, Joan *DrAP&F 83*
Wolf, John B 1907- *ConAu 9R*
Wolf, Karl E 1921- *ConAu 17R*
Wolf, Leonard 1923- *ConAu 3NR, -49*
Wolf, Margaret Mercier *CreCan 1*
Wolf, Marguerite Hurrey 1914- *ConAu 53*
Wolf, Miriam Bredow 1895- *ConAu P-1*
Wolf, Peter 1935- *ConAu 53*
Wolf, Ray 1948- *ConAu 107*
Wolf, Robert Charles 1955- *ConAu 109*
Wolf, Stephen *DrAP&F 83*
Wolf, Thomas H 1916- *ConAu 69*
Wolf, William *ConAu 103*
Wolf, William B 1920- *ConAu 10NR, -17R*
Wolf, William C, Jr. 1933- *ConAu 41R*
Wolf-Catz, Loeka 1930- *IntAu&W 82*
Wolf-Phillips, Leslie 1929- *ConAu 21R*
Wolfbein, Seymour L 1915- *ConAu 6NR, -13R,*
 WrDr 84
Wolfe, Alan 1942- *ConAu 108*
Wolfe, Alvin William 1928- *ConAu 1R*
Wolfe, Bernard 1915- *ConAu 1R, -3NR,*
 ConNov 82, TwCSFW, WrDr 84
Wolfe, Bertram David 1896-1977 *ConAu 5R, -69,*
 WorAu
Wolfe, Burton H 1932- *ConAu 25R,*
 IntAu&W 82, SmATA 5, WrDr 84
Wolfe, Charles Keith 1943- *ConAu 77*
Wolfe, Don Marion 1902-1976 *ConAu 65*
Wolfe, Edgar 1906- *ConAu P-2*
Wolfe, Gene *DrAP&F 83*
Wolfe, Gene 1931- *ConAu 6NR, -57,*
 ConLC 25[port], DcLB 8, TwCSFW,
 WrDr 84
Wolfe, Gerard R 1926- *ConAu 11NR, -69*
Wolfe, Harry Deane 1901-1975 *ConAu 41R*
Wolfe, Harvey 1938- *ConAu 45*
Wolfe, Henry Cutler 1898-1976 *ConAu 69*
Wolfe, Humbert 1885-1940 *LongCTC, ModBrL,*
 TwCA, TwCA SUP, TwCWr
Wolfe, James H 1934- *ConAu 93*
Wolfe, John N 1910?-1974 *ConAu 53*
Wolfe, Josephine Brace 1917- *ConAu 5R*
Wolfe, Kurt H 1912- *WrDr 84*
Wolfe, Linda *DrAP&F 83*
Wolfe, Linnie Marsh 1881-1945 *TwCA SUP*
Wolfe, Louis 1905- *ConAu 3NR, -5R,*
 SmATA 8
Wolfe, Martin 1920- *ConAu 37R*
Wolfe, Michael 1917- *ConAu X, WrDr 84*
Wolfe, Peter 1933- *ConAu 8NR, -21R,*
 WrDr 84
Wolfe, Randolph 1946- *ConAu 104*
Wolfe, Richard J 1928- *ConAu 110*
Wolfe, Rinna 1925- *ConAu 109*
Wolfe, Ron 1945- *ConAu 109*
Wolfe, Roy I 1917- *ConAu 13R*
Wolfe, Thomas 1900-1938 *CnMD, CnMWL,*
 ConAmA, ConAu 104, DcLB DS2[port],
 -9[port], LongCTC, ModAL, ModWD,
 TwCA, TwCA SUP, TwCLC 4[port],

Wood, Peggy 1892-1978 *ConAu 77*
Wood, Peter 1930- *ConAu 93*
Wood, Phyllis Anderson 1923- *ConAu 37R, SmATA 30, -33[port], WrDr 84*
Wood, Playsted *ConAu X*
Wood, R Coke 1905-1979 *ConAu 7NR, -53*
Wood, Ramsay 1943- *ConAu 103*
Wood, Raymund F 1911- *ConAu 61*
Wood, Robert 1923- *WrDr 84*
Wood, Robert Coldwell 1923- *ConAu 1R*
Wood, Robert Henry 1923- *WrDr 84*
Wood, Robert Lee 1925- *ConAu 21R*
Wood, Robert Paul 1931- *ConAu 5NR*
Wood, Robert S 1938- *ConAu 7NR, -57*
Wood, Robin 1931- *ConAu X, -53, WrDr 84*
Wood, Ruth C *ConAu 37R*
Wood, Serry *ConAu X*
Wood, Susan 1946- *ConAu 108*
Wood, Thomas 1919- *IntAu&W 82, WrDr 84*
Wood, Thomas Wesley, Jr. 1920- *ConAu 81, IntAu&W 82*
Wood, Tom J 1930- *IntAu&W 82*
Wood, Ursula *ConAu X, WrDr 84*
Wood, Wallace 1927-1981 *ConAu 108, SmATA 33N*
Wood, Wendy *DrAP&F 83*
Wood, William John 1877-1954 *CreCan 2*
Wood-Legh, Kathleen Louise 1901-1981 *ConAu 105*
Wood-Thompson, Susan *DrAP&F 83*
Woodall, Corbet 1929?-1982 *ConAu 106*
Woodall, Ronald 1935- *ConAu 73*
Woodall, Stella 1899- *IntWWP 82*
Woodard, Bronte 1941?-1980 *ConAu 101*
Woodard, Carol 1929- *ConAu 73, SmATA 14*
Woodard, Christopher Roy 1913- *ConAu 13R, WrDr 84*
Woodard, Gloria H 1937- *ConAu 45*
Woodberry, George Edward 1855-1930 *TwCA, TwCA SUP*
Woodberry, Joan Merle 1921- *ConAu 6NR, -9R, WrDr 84*
Woodbridge, Hensley Charles 1923- *ConAu 3NR, -9R*
Woodburn, Arthur 1890-1978 *ConAu 108*
Woodburn, John Henry 1914- *ConAu 1R, -4NR, SmATA 11*
Woodbury, Lael Jay 1927- *ConAu 81, IntAu&W 82*
Woodbury, Marda 1925- *ConAu 97*
Woodbury, Mildred Fairchild 1894-1975 *ConAu 57*
Woodbury, Richard B 1917- *ConAu 109*
Woodcock, George 1912- *ConAu 1R, -1NR, ConDr 82B, ConP 80, DcLEL 1940, IntAu&W 82, ModBrL, WorAu 1970, WrDr 84*
Woodcock, Percy Franklin 1855-1936 *CreCan 1*
Woodcott, Keith *ConAu X, TwCSFW, WrDr 84*
Wooden, Kenneth 1935- *ConAu 81*
Wooden, Wayne S 1943- *ConAu 109*
Woodfield, William Read 1928- *ConAu 9R*
Woodford, Arthur M 1940- *ConAu 7NR, -53, MichAu 80*
Woodford, Bruce P *DrAP&F 83*
Woodford, Bruce P 1919- *ConAu 57*
Woodford, Cecile *WrDr 84*
Woodford, Frank Bury 1903-1967 *ConAu P-1, MichAu 80*
Woodford, Irene Cecile 1913- *IntAu&W 82*
Woodford, Jack 1894- *ConAu X*
Woodford, Peggy 1937- *ConAu 104, SmATA 25[port], WrDr 84*
Woodforde, John 1925- *ConAu 10NR*
Woodforde, John Ffooks 1925- *ConAu 25R, WrDr 84*
Woodgate, Mildred Violet *ConAu 9R*
Woodham-Smith, Cecil Blanche 1896-1977 *ConAu 69, -77, LongCTC, TwCA SUP*
Woodhouse, Barbara 1910- *ConAu 5R*
Woodhouse, C M 1917- *ConAu 108*
Woodhouse, Charles Platten 1915- *ConAu 105, WrDr 84*
Woodhouse, Christopher Montague 1917- *DcLEL 1940, ModBrL*
Woodhouse, Martin 1932- *ASpks, ConAu 21R, WrDr 84*

Woodhouse, Montague 1917- *WrDr 84*
Woodin, Ann Snow 1926- *ConAu 13R*
Woodin, Noel 1929- *ConAu 1R*
Wooding, Dan 1940- *ConAu 102*
Woodiwiss, Kathleen E *ConAu 89, TwCRGW, WrDr 84*
Woodley, Winifred *ConAu X*
Woodman, Allen *DrAP&F 83*
Woodman, Anthony John 1945- *ConAu 8NR, -61*
Woodman, Harold D 1928- *ConAu 9NR*
Woodman, Harold David 1928- *ConAu 21R, WrDr 84*
Woodman, James Monroe 1931- *ConAu 17R*
Woodman, Jim *ConAu X*
Woodman, John E 1932?-1983 *ConAu 109*
Woodman, Loring 1942- *ConAu 45*
Woodress, James 1916- *ConAu 3NR, -5R, WrDr 84*
Woodrew, Greta 1930- *ConAu 106*
Woodrich, Mary Neville 1915- *ConAu 25R, SmATA 2*
Woodring, Carl 1919- *ConAu 5R, WrDr 84*
Woodring, Paul 1907- *ConAu 17R, WrDr 84*
Woodrock, R A *ConAu X*
Woodroff, Horace M 1906- *WrDr 84*
Woodroof, Horace Malcolm 1906- *ConAu P-2*
Woodruff, Archibald Mulford, Jr. 1912- *ConAu 105*
Woodruff, Asahel D 1904- *ConAu 1R*
Woodruff, J Douglas 1897-1978 *ConAu 107*
Woodruff, John Douglas 1897-1978 *ConAu 104*
Woodruff, Judy 1946- *ConAu 73*
Woodruff, Michael 1911- *WrDr 84*
Woodruff, Philip *WrDr 84*
Woodruff, Philip 1906- *ConAu X, IntAu&W 82X*
Woodruff, William 1916- *ConAu 101*
Woodrum, Lon 1901- *ConAu 104*
Woods, Aubrey *ConDr 82D*
Woods, B W 1930- *ConAu 25R*
Woods, Barbara Gullo 1939- *IntWWP 82*
Woods, Clee 1893- *ConAu 108*
Woods, Donald H 1933- *ConAu 25R*
Woods, Elizabeth 1940- *ConAu 101*
Woods, Frances Jerome 1913- *WrDr 84*
Woods, Sister Frances Jerome 1913- *ConAu 21R*
Woods, Frederick 1932- *ConAu 7NR, -17R, IntAu&W 82, WrDr 84*
Woods, George A 1926- *ConAu 29R, SmATA 30[port]*
Woods, Geraldine 1948- *ConAu 97*
Woods, Grace L 1919- *IntWWP 82*
Woods, Harold 1945- *ConAu 97*
Woods, Helen Ferguson *ConLC 13*
Woods, Isa Lou *IntAu&W 82X*
Woods, Joan 1932- *ConAu 9R*
Woods, John *DrAP&F 83*
Woods, John 1926- *ConAu 13R, ConP 80, MichAu 80, WorAu 1970, WrDr 84*
Woods, John 1937- *ConAu 11NR, -57*
Woods, John A 1927- *ConAu 13R*
Woods, John B 1933- *ConAu 107*
Woods, John David 1939- *ConAu 37R*
Woods, John E 1938- *ConAu 104*
Woods, Kenneth F 1930- *ConAu 13R*
Woods, Margaret 1921- *ConAu 21R, SmATA 2*
Woods, Margaret Louisa 1856?-1945 *LongCTC*
Woods, Margaret S 1911- *ConAu 81*
Woods, Nat *ConAu X*
Woods, P F *ConAu X*
Woods, Pamela 1938- *ConAu 106*
Woods, Peter Flaxman 1958- *IntWWP 82*
Woods, Ralph L 1904- *ConAu 2NR, -5R*
Woods, Randall Bennett 1944- *ConAu 106*
Woods, Richard 1941- *ConAu 4NR, -53, WrDr 84*
Woods, Richard G 1933- *ConAu 109*
Woods, Samuel H, Jr. 1926- *ConAu 25R*
Woods, Sara 1922- *ConAu X, IntAu&W 82, TwCCr&M 80, WrDr 84*
Woods, Shadrach 1923-1973 *ConAu 45*
Woods, Stockton *ConAu X*
Woods, Stuart 1938- *ConAu 93, IntAu&W 82*
Woods, William 1916- *ConAu 77, WrDr 84*
Woods, William Crawford 1944- *ConAu 29R*
Woodson, Carter Godwin 1875-1950 *DcLB 17[port]*
Woodson, Jack *SmATA X*
Woodson, Jeff *ConAu X, IntAu&W 82X*
Woodson, John Waddie, Jr. 1913- *SmATA 10*

Woodson, Leslie H 1929- *ConAu 41R*
Woodson, Meg *ConAu X*
Woodson, Thomas 1931- *ConAu 104*
Woodson, Wesley E 1918- *ConAu 37R*
Woodstone, Arthur *ConAu 69*
Woodward, Bob 1943- *AuNews 1, ConAu X, WrDr 84*
Woodward, C Vann 1908- *ConAu 2NR, DcLB 17[port], IntAu&W 82, WorAu 1970, WrDr 84*
Woodward, Carl Raymond 1890-1974 *ConAu 41R*
Woodward, Cleveland 1900- *SmATA 10*
Woodward, Comer Vann 1908- *ConAu 5R*
Woodward, Daniel Holt 1931- *ConAu 37R*
Woodward, David B 1918- *ConAu 65*
Woodward, G W O 1924- *ConAu 3NR*
Woodward, George William Otway 1924- *ConAu 5R, WrDr 84*
Woodward, Grace Steele 1899- *ConAu P-1*
Woodward, Helen Beal 1914?-1982 *ConAu 108*
Woodward, Helen Rosen 1882- *ConAu 5R*
Woodward, Herbert N 1911- *ConAu 65*
Woodward, Hildegard 1898- *ConAu 5R*
Woodward, Ian 1941- *IntAu&W 82*
Woodward, James B 1935- *ConAu 2NR, -49*
Woodward, John 1920- *ConAu 21R*
Woodward, John 1945- *WrDr 84*
Woodward, Lilian *ConAu X, IntAu&W 82X*
Woodward, Ralph Lee, Jr. 1934- *ConAu 21R, IntAu&W 82, WrDr 84*
Woodward, Robert H 1925- *WrDr 84*
Woodward, Robert Hanson 1925- *ConAu 17R, IntAu&W 82*
Woodward, Robert Upshur 1943- *AuNews 1, ConAu 69*
Woodward, Stanley 1890- *ConAu 5R*
Woodward, W Mary 1921- *ConAu 45*
Woodward, William E 1874-1950 *TwCA, TwCA SUP*
Woodworth, Constance 1911-1983 *ConAu 109*
Woodworth, David 1932- *ConAu 37R*
Woodworth, G Wallace 1902-1969 *ConAu P-1*
Woodworth, G Walter 1903- *ConAu P-1*
Woodworth, Hugh 1906-1978 *ConAu 107*
Woody, Regina J 1894- *WrDr 84*
Woody, Regina Llewellyn Jones 1894- *ConAu 3NR, -5R, SmATA 3*
Woody, Robert H 1936- *ConAu 93*
Woody, Russell O, Jr. 1934- *ConAu 17R*
Woodyard, David O 1932- *ConAu 21R*
Woodyard, George 1934- *ConAu 81*
Woofe, Herbert S 1908- *ConAu P-1*
Woolard, Edgar 1899?-1978 *ConAu 77*
Wooldridge, Rhoda 1906- *ConAu 77, SmATA 22[port]*
Wooldridge, William C 1943- *ConAu 45*
Wooley, John 1949- *ConAu 109*
Woolf, Daniel J 1916- *ConAu 5R*
Woolf, Dennis 1934- *IntAu&W 82*
Woolf, Douglas *DrAP&F 83*
Woolf, Douglas 1922- *ConAu 1R, -2NR, ConNov 82, TwCWW, WrDr 84*
Woolf, Harry 1923- *ConAu 1R, -1NR, WrDr 84*
Woolf, James Dudley 1914- *ConAu 37R*
Woolf, Leonard Sidney 1880-1969 *ConAu 5R, -25R, LongCTC, ModBrL, ModBrL SUP, TwCA, TwCA SUP, TwCWr*
Woolf, Robert G 1928- *ConAu 73*
Woolf, Stuart Joseph 1936- *WrDr 84*
Woolf, Virginia 1882-1941 *CnMWL, ConAu 104, ConLCrt 82, LongCTC, ModBrL, ModBrL SUP, TwCA, TwCA SUP, TwCLC 1, -5[port], TwCWr, WhoTwCL*
Woolfe, Harold Geoffrey 1902- *ConAu P-1, WrDr 84*
Woolfolk, Joanna Martine 1940- *ConAu 110*
Woolfolk, Josiah Pitts 1894-1971 *ConAu 29R*
Woolgar, Jack 1894- *ConAu 17R*
Woollam, William Gifford 1921- *ConAu 9R*
Woollcombe, Robert 1922- *WrDr 84*
Woollcott, Alexander Humphreys 1887-1943 *ConAmA, ConAu 105, LongCTC, ModWD, TwCA, TwCA SUP, TwCLC 5[port]*
Woolley, A E 1926- *ConAu 41R*
Woolley, Alfred Russell 1899- *ConAu 5R*
Woolley, Bryan *DrAP&F 83*
Woolley, Bryan 1937- *ConAu 4NR, -49*
Woolley, Catherine 1904- *ConAu 1R, -6NR, SmATA 3*

Woolley, Geoffrey Harold 1892-1968 *ConAu P-1*
Woolley, Herbert B 1917-1978 *ConAu 81*
Woolley, Sir Leonard 1880-1960 *LongCTC*
Woolley, Russell 1899- *WrDr 84*
Woolman, David S 1916- *ConAu 29R, IntAu&W 82*
Woolner, Frank 1916- *ConAu 53*
Woolrich, Cornell 1903?-1968 *ConAu X, TwCA SUP, TwCCr&M 80*
Woolrych, Austin Herbert 1918- *ConAu 1R, WrDr 84*
Woolsey, Arthur 1906- *ConAu 45*
Woolsey, Janette 1904- *ConAu 1R, -2NR, SmATA 3*
Woolson, Roland S, Jr. 1930?-1977 *ConAu 104*
Woon, Basil 1894?-1974 *ConAu 49*
Wooster, Claire 1942- *ConAu 101*
Wooster, Ralph A 1928- *ConAu 2NR, -5R*
Wooton, Anthony 1935- *IntAu&W 82*
Wootten, Dick *ConAmTC*
Wootten, Morgan 1931- *ConAu 101*
Wootton, Barbara 1897- *WrDr 84*
Wootton, Graham 1917- *ConAu 5R, -10NR, IntAu&W 82, WrDr 84*
Wootton Of Abinger, Barbara Frances 1897- *IntAu&W 82*
Worblefister, Petunia *ConAu X*
Worboys, Anne *WrDr 84*
Worboys, Anne Eyre *ConAu 9NR*
Worboys, Anne Isobel *ConAu 65, TwCRGW*
Worboys, Annette Isobel *IntAu&W 82*
Worcester, Dean A, Jr. 1918- *ConAu 21R*
Worcester, Donald E 1915- *WrDr 84*
Worcester, Donald Emmet 1915- *ConAu 1R, -4NR, IntAu&W 82, SmATA 18*
Worcester, Gurdon Saltonstall 1897- *ConAu P-1*
Worcester, Roland *WrDr 84*
Worchel, Stephen 1946- *ConAu 89*
Word, Ola Mae 1918- *IntAu&W 82*
Worden, Alfred M 1932- *ConAu 101*
Worden, Mark *DrAP&F 83*
Worden, William L 1910- *ConAu P-1*
Wordsmith, James Alfred *IntWWP 82X*
Wordsworth, Jane 1909- *IntAu&W 82*
Wordsworth, Jonathan 1932- *ConAu 29R*
Worell, Judith 1928- *ConAu 7NR, -57*
Workman, Samuel K 1907- *ConAu P-2*
Workman, William D, Jr. 1914- *ConAu 5R, IntAu&W 82, WrDr 84*
Works, John *DrAP&F 83*
Worland, Stephen T 1923- *ConAu 21R*
Worley, Robert Cromwell 1929- *ConAu 108*
Worley, Stella *DrAP&F 83, IntWWP 82X*
Worline, Bonnie Bess 1914- *ConAu 69, SmATA 14*
Worlock, Derek 1920- *WrDr 84*
Worlock, Derek John Harford 1920- *ConAu 103, IntAu&W 82*
Worm, Piet 1909- *ConAu 81*
Wormald, Francis 1904?-1972 *ConAu 104*
Worman, Eli *ConAu X*
Wormington, H M 1914- *ConAu 3NR, -45*
Wormley, Cinda *ConAu X*
Wormley, Stanton Lawrence 1909- *ConAu 73*
Wormser, Baron Chesley 1948- *ConAu 110*
Wormser, Rene A 1896-1981 *ConAu 104, -11NR, -13R*
Wormser, Richard 1908-1977 *ConSFA, TwCWW*
Wormser, Sophie 1897- *ConAu 65, SmATA 22*
Worner, Karl Heinrich *ConAu X*
Worner, Philip 1910- *WrDr 84*
Worner, Philip Arthur Incledon 1910- *IntWWP 82*
Woroniak, Alexander 1920- *ConAu 41R*
Woronoff, Jon 1938- *ConAu 11NR, -29R*
Woroszylski, Wiktor 1927- *IntAu&W 82, IntWWP 82*
Worrall, Ambrose A 1899-1972 *ConAu P-2*
Worrall, Olga 1906- *ConAu 29R*
Worrall, Ralph Lyndal 1903- *WrDr 84*
Worrell, Albert C 1913- *ConAu 37R*
Worrell, Eric 1924- *WrDr 84*
Worsham, Fabian *DrAP&F 83*
Worsley, Alice F *DrAP&F 83*
Worsley, Dale *DrAP&F 83*
Worsley, Dale 1948- *ConAu 104*
Worster, Donald E 1941- *ConAu 57*
Worsthorne, Peregrine 1923- *ConAu 45*
Worswick, Clark 1940- *ConAu 104*
Worth, C Brooke 1908- *ConAu 101*
Worth, Douglas *DrAP&F 83*

Worth, Douglas 1940- *ConAu 9NR, -65, IntWWP 82*
Worth, Fred L 1943- *ConAu 97*
Worth, Helen 1913- *ConAu 13R, IntAu&W 82, WrDr 84*
Worth, Margaret *ConAu X*
Worth, Martin 1926- *WrDr 84*
Worth, Peter *TwCSFW*
Worth, Sol 1922?-1977 *ConAu 73, -81*
Worth, Valerie 1933- *ConAu X, SmATA 8*
Wortham, John David 1941- *ConAu 37R*
Worthen, Blaine Richard 1936- *ConAu 85*
Worthington, Edgar Barton 1905- *ConAu 109, WrDr 84*
Worthington, Marjorie 1898?-1976 *ConAu 1R, -2NR, -65*
Worthington Ball, John *IntAu&W 82X*
Worthley, Jean Reese 1925- *ConAu 77*
Worthy, Morgan 1936- *ConAu 65*
Worthy, William *LivgBAA*
Worthylake, Mary Moore 1904- *ConAu 1R, -4NR*
Wortis, Avi 1937- *ConAu 69, SmATA 14*
Wortley, Ben Atkinson 1907- *ConAu 57, IntAu&W 82, WrDr 84*
Wortman, Max S, Jr. 1932- *ConAu 21R*
Wortman, Richard 1938- *ConAu 9NR, -21R*
Wortman, Sterling 1923-1981 *ConAu 108*
Worton, Stanley N 1923- *ConAu 57*
Woshinsky, Oliver Hanson 1939- *ConAu 109*
Wosmek, Frances 1917- *ConAu 11NR*
Wosmek, Frances E 1917- *ConAu 29R, SmATA 29[port], WrDr 84*
Woudenberg, Paul Richard 1927- *ConAu 69*
Woudhuysen, Jan Frank 1942- *ConAu 107*
Woudstra, Marten H 1922- *ConAu 25R*
Wouil, George *ConAu X*
Wouk, Herman 1915- *CnMD, ConAu 5R, -6NR, ConLC 1, -9, ConNov 82, CroCD, DcLB Y82B[port], DcLEL 1940, IntAu&W 82, LongCTC, ModAL, ModWD, NatPD 81[port], TwCA SUP, TwCWr, WrDr 84*
Woy, James Bayly 1927- *ConAu 13R*
Woychuk, N A 1915- *ConAu 13R*
Woytinsky, Emma S 1893-1969 *ConAu P-1*
Wozniakowski, Jacek 1920- *IntAu&W 82*
Woznicki, Andrew Nicholas 1931- *ConAu 45*
Wrage, Ernest J 1911-1965 *ConAu 1R*
Wragg, David William 1946- *ConAu 4NR, -53, IntAu&W 82, WrDr 84*
Wragg, E C 1938- *ConAu 8NR, -57*
Wraight, A Joseph 1913- *ConAu 21R*
Wray, Elizabeth *DrAP&F 83*
Wray, Elizabeth 1950- *NatPD 81[port]*
Wray, Ron *DrAP&F 83*
Wreford, James *WrDr 84*
Wreford, James 1915- *ConAu X, DcLEL 1940*
Wren, Chris -1982 *ConAu 108*
Wren, Christopher S 1936- *ConAu 21R*
Wren, Daniel Alan 1932- *ConAu 41R*
Wren, Ellaruth *ConAu X*
Wren, M K *ConAu X*
Wren, Melvin C 1910- *ConAu 37R*
Wren, P C 1885-1941 *TwCRGW*
Wren, Percival Christopher 1885-1941 *LongCTC, TwCA, TwCWr*
Wren, Robert Meriwether 1928- *ConAu 106*
Wren, Thomas Edward 1938- *ConAu 77*
Wren, Wilfrid John 1930- *ConAu 109, WrDr 84*
Wrench, David F 1932- *ConAu 41R*
Wrench, Sir Evelyn 1882-1966 *ConAu 5R, LongCTC*
Wrenn, John H 1920- *ConAu 1R*
Wrenn, Robert L 1933- *ConAu 29R*
Wrenn, Tony P 1938- *ConAu 89*
Wrenn, Winnie Holden 1886?-1979 *ConAu 89*
Wriggins, Sally Hovey 1922- *ConAu 97, SmATA 17*
Wriggins, W Howard 1918- *ConAu 61, WrDr 84*
Wright, A J *DrAP&F 83*
Wright, A J 1952- *ConAu 93, IntAu&W 82, IntWWP 82X, WrDr 84*
Wright, Alice E 1905-1980 *ConAu 104*
Wright, Amos Jasper 1952- *IntWWP 82*
Wright, Andrew 1923- *ConAu 17R*
Wright, Anna Rose 1890-1968 *ConAu 109*
Wright, Arthur Frederick 1913-1976 *ConAu 77*
Wright, Arthur Frederick 1913-1977 *ConAu 69*
Wright, Austin *DrAP&F 83*

Wright, Austin 1904- *ConAu 61*
Wright, Austin M 1922- *WrDr 84*
Wright, Austin McGiffert 1922- *ConAu 1R, -4NR*
Wright, Austin Tappan 1883-1931 *TwCSFW*
Wright, Barton A 1920- *ConAu 8NR, -61*
Wright, Basil Charles 1907- *ConAu 105*
Wright, Beatrice A 1917- *ConAu 21R*
Wright, Benjamin Fletcher 1900-1976 *ConAu 69, -77*
Wright, Brooks 1922- *ConAu 25R*
Wright, Bruce Stanley 1912-1975 *ConAu P-2*
Wright, Burton 1917- *ConAu 81, IntAu&W 82*
Wright, C D *DrAP&F 83*
Wright, Carolyne *DrAP&F 83*
Wright, Carolyne Lee 1949- *IntWWP 82*
Wright, Celeste Turner 1906- *ConAu P-1, IntAu&W 82, IntWWP 82, WrDr 84*
Wright, Charles *DrAP&F 83*
Wright, Charles 1932- *ConNov 82, WorAu 1970, WrDr 84*
Wright, Charles 1935- *ConAu 29R, ConLC 6, -13, ConP 80, DcLB Y82B[port], WrDr 84*
Wright, Charles Alan 1927- *ConAu 1NR, -45*
Wright, Charles David 1932-1978 *ConAu 104*
Wright, Charles H 1918- *ConAu 61*
Wright, Charles R 1927- *ConAu 1NR, -45*
Wright, Charles S *DrAP&F 83*
Wright, Charles Stevenson 1932- *ConAu 9R, LivgBAA*
Wright, Christopher 1924- *WrDr 84*
Wright, Christopher 1926- *ConAu 9R*
Wright, Conrad 1917- *ConAu 21R, WrDr 84*
Wright, Constance 1897- *WrDr 84*
Wright, Constance Choate 1897- *ConAu 13R*
Wright, Cynthia Challed 1953- *ConAu 77, IntAu&W 82*
Wright, D G 1937- *ConAu 65*
Wright, D I 1934- *ConAu 3NR, -49*
Wright, Dale, Sr. 1925- *LivgBAA*
Wright, Dare 1926?- *ConAu 93, SmATA 21[port]*
Wright, David 1920- *ConAu 3NR, -9R, ConP 80, IntAu&W 82, WorAu, WrDr 84*
Wright, David McCord 1909-1968 *ConAu P-2*
Wright, Deil S 1930- *ConAu 13R*
Wright, Denis 1911- *ConAu 81*
Wright, Don 1934- *ConAu 104*
Wright, Dorothy 1910- *ConAu 13R, IntAu&W 82, WrDr 84*
Wright, E Whitman 1921- *WrDr 84*
Wright, Edward A 1906- *ConAu 29R*
Wright, Elizabeth Atwell 1919-1976 *ConAu 65*
Wright, Elizabeth Prince 1905- *IntWWP 82, MichAu 80*
Wright, Enid Meadowcroft 1898-1966 *ConAu P-2, SmATA 3*
Wright, Esmond 1915- *ConAu 1R, -6NR, IntAu&W 82, SmATA 10, WrDr 84*
Wright, Esther Clark 1895- *IntAu&W 82, WrDr 84*
Wright, Frances Fitzpatrick 1897- *ConAu P-1, SmATA 10*
Wright, Frances J *ConAu X*
Wright, Francesca *ConAu X, WrDr 84*
Wright, Frank Cookman, Jr. 1904-1982 *ConAu 107*
Wright, Frank Joseph 1905- *ConAu 9R*
Wright, Frank Lloyd 1869-1959 *LongCTC, TwCA SUP*
Wright, Fred W, Jr. *DrAP&F 83*
Wright, Frederick William, Jr. 1940- *ConAmTC*
Wright, G Ernest 1909-1974 *ConAu 2NR*
Wright, Gavin Peter 1943- *ConAu 89*
Wright, George B 1912- *ConAu 21R*
Wright, George Ernest 1909-1974 *ConAu 1R, -53*
Wright, George Nelson 1921- *ConAu 1NR, -45*
Wright, George T *DrAP&F 83*
Wright, George Thaddeus 1925- *ConAu 5R, IntWWP 82, WrDr 84*
Wright, Gordon 1912- *ConAu 9R*
Wright, Grahame 1947-1977 *ConAu 103*
Wright, H Bunker 1907- *ConAu 5R*
Wright, H Elliott 1937- *ConAu 37R*
Wright, H Norman 1937- *ConAu 8NR, -57*
Wright, Harold Bell 1872-1944 *ConAu 110, DcLB 9[port], LongCTC, TwCA, TwCA SUP, TwCSFW*
Wright, Harrison M 1928- *ConAu 41R*
Wright, Helen 1914- *ConAu 9R*
Wright, Helen L 1932- *WrDr 84*

Wright, Helena 1887-1982 *ConAu 110*
Wright, Herbert Curtis 1928- *ConAu 105*
Wright, Howard Wilson 1915- *ConAu 3NR, –5R*
Wright, Ione Stuessy 1905- *ConAu P-1*
Wright, Irene Aloha 1879-1972 *ConAu 33R*
Wright, J Leitch, Jr. 1929- *ConAu 21R*
Wright, J Patrick 1941- *ConAu 103*
Wright, J Stafford 1905- *ConAu 11NR*
Wright, Jack R *ConAu X*
Wright, James 1927-1980 *ConAu 4NR, –97, ConLC 10, ConP 80, DcLB 5[port]*
Wright, James Arlington 1927- *AuNews 2, ConAu 49, ConLC 3, –5, CroCAP, DcLEL 1940, ModAL, ModAL SUP, WhoTwCL, WorAu*
Wright, James C, Jr. 1922- *ConAu 49*
Wright, James Leitch, Jr. 1929- *WrDr 84*
Wright, Jay 1935- *ConAu 73, IntWWP 82, LivgBAA*
Wright, Jeffrey Cyphers *DrAP&F 83*
Wright, Jeffrey Cyphers 1951- *IntWWP 82*
Wright, Jim 1922- *ConAu 49*
Wright, John *IntWWP 82X*
Wright, John J 1909-1979 *ConAu 1R, –2NR*
Wright, John Marriott 1950- *IntWWP 82*
Wright, John S 1910- *ConAu 37R*
Wright, John S 1920- *ConAu 5R, –6NR*
Wright, John Stafford 1905- *ConAu 57, WrDr 84*
Wright, Judith Arundell 1915- *CnMWL, ConAu 13R, ConLC 11, ConP 80, DcLEL 1940, IntAu&W 82, LongCTC, ModCmwL, SmATA 14, TwCWr, WhoTwCL, WorAu, WrDr 84*
Wright, K C *DrAP&F 83*
Wright, Kenneth *ConAu X, SmATA X, WrDr 84*
Wright, Kit 1944- *ConP 80, WrDr 84*
Wright, Lafayette Hart 1917- *ConAu 41R*
Wright, Lafayette Hart 1917-1983 *ConAu 109*
Wright, Lan 1923- *ConSFA*
Wright, Lawrence 1947- *ConAu 93*
Wright, Leigh Richard 1925- *ConAu 93*
Wright, Leonard M, Jr. 1923- *ConAu 61*
Wright, Linda Raney 1945- *ConAu 11NR, –69*
Wright, Louis Booker 1899- *ConAu 1R, –1NR, DcLB 17[port], IntAu&W 82, WrDr 84*
Wright, Mary Clabaugh 1917-1970 *ConAu 109*
Wright, Mary Pamela Godwin 1917- *ConAu P-1*
Wright, Mary Patricia 1932- *IntAu&W 82*
Wright, Sir Michael R 1901- *ConAu P-1*
Wright, Monte Duane 1930- *ConAu 41R*
Wright, Muriel Hazel 1889-1975 *ConAu 57*
Wright, Nancy Means *ConAu 104, DrAP&F 83, IntAu&W 82*
Wright, Nathan, Jr. 1923- *ConAu 37R, LivgBAA*
Wright, Nathaniel, Jr. *ConAu X*
Wright, Norman Edgar 1927- *ConAu 101*
Wright, Patricia 1932- *ConAu 10NR, –65, WrDr 84*
Wright, Philip Arthur 1908- *ConAu P-1, WrDr 84*
Wright, Quincy 1890-1970 *ConAu 5R, –5NR, –29R*
Wright, R H 1906- *ConAu 7NR, –17R, SmATA 6*
Wright, Rebecca *DrAP&F 83*
Wright, Rebecca 1942- *ConAu 105*
Wright, Richard 1908-1960 *ConAu 108, ConLC 1, –3, –4, –9, –14, –21[port], DcLB DS2[port], LongCTC, ModAL, ModAL SUP, ModBlW, TwCA, TwCA SUP, TwCWr, WhoTwCL*
Wright, Richard B 1937- *ConAu 85, ConLC 6, IntAu&W 82*
Wright, Richard J 1935- *ConAu 89*
Wright, Richardson Little 1886-1961 *TwCA, TwCA SUP*
Wright, Robert Lee 1920- *ConAu 17R, WrDr 84*
Wright, Robert Roy 1917- *ConAu 9R*
Wright, Ronald Selby 1908- *ConAu 1R, –6NR, IntAu&W 82*
Wright, Ronald W V Selby 1908- *WrDr 84*
Wright, Rosalie Muller 1942- *ConAu 77*
Wright, Rosalind *DrAP&F 83*
Wright, Rosalind 1952- *ConAu 61*
Wright, Russel 1904-1976 *ConAu 69*
Wright, S Fowler 1874-1965 *TwCCr&M 80, TwCSFW*
Wright, Sarah E *ConAu 37R, LivgBAA*

Wright, Sarah Elizabeth *DrAP&F 83*
Wright, Stephen 1922- *ConAu 1NR, –49, IntAu&W 82, WrDr 84*
Wright, Sydney Fowler 1874- *LongCTC*
Wright, Sylvia 1917-1981 *ConAu 104, –29R*
Wright, Theodore P, Jr. 1926- *ConAu 9NR*
Wright, Theodore Paul, Jr. 1926- *ConAu 13R, IntAu&W 82, WrDr 84*
Wright, Theon 1904- *ConAu 109*
Wright, Walter F 1912- *WrDr 84*
Wright, Walter Francis 1912- *ConAu 5R*
Wright, Willard Hull 1894-1982 *ConAu 107*
Wright, Willard Huntington 1888-1939 *LongCTC, TwCA, TwCA SUP, TwCCr&M 80*
Wright, William 1930- *ConAu 7NR, –53*
Wright, William C 1939- *ConAu 41R*
Wright, William David 1906- *WrDr 84*
Wright, William Edward 1926- *ConAu 21R, IntAu&W 82, WrDr 84*
Wrightsman, Lawrence S 1931- *WrDr 84*
Wrightsman, Lawrence S, Jr. 1931- *ConAu 11NR*
Wrightsman, Lawrence Samuel, Jr. 1931- *ConAu 21R*
Wrightson, Patricia 1921- *ChlLR 4[port], ConAu 3NR, –45, SmATA 8, TwCCW 83, WrDr 84*
Wrigley, Christopher John 1947- *IntAu&W 82*
Wrigley, Elizabeth S 1915- *ConAu 41R*
Wrigley, Gordon 1923- *WrDr 84*
Wrigley, Robert *DrAP&F 83*
Wriston, Henry Merritt 1889-1978 *ConAu 77, ConAu P-1*
Wrobel, Sylvia 1941- *ConAu 65*
Wroblewski, Sergius C 1918- *ConAu 5R, –8NR*
Wrocka, Maria *IntAu&W 82X*
Wrone, David R 1933- *ConAu 6NR, –57*
Wrong, Dennis Hume 1923- *ConAu 81*
Wronker, Lili Cassel 1924- *SmATA 10*
Wronski, Stanley P 1919- *ConAu 13R*
Wroth, Lawrence Counselman 1884-1970 *ConAu 29R*
Wrottesley, Arthur John Francis 1908- *ConAu 45, IntAu&W 82*
Wrottesley, John Francis 1908- *WrDr 84*
Wroughton, John Presbury 1934- *WrDr 84*
Wryde, Dogear *ConAu X*
Wrzos, Joseph Henry 1929- *ConAu 49*
Wu, Hsiu-Kwang 1935- *ConAu 17R*
Wu, John Chin Hsung 1899- *ConAu 104*
Wu, Joseph S 1934- *ConAu 97*
Wu, K C 1903- *ConAu 1R*
Wu, Nelson I 1919- *ConAu 9R*
Wu, Silas H L 1929- *ConAu 37R, IntAu&W 82*
Wu, William F 1951- *ConAu 109*
Wu, Yuan-Li *ConAu 17R*
Wubben, Hubert H 1928- *ConAu 102*
Wubben, John 1938- *ConAu 65*
Wucherer, Ruth Marie 1948- *ConAu 8NR, –61*
Wuellner, Flora Slosson 1928- *ConAu 53, WrDr 84*
Wuerpel, Charles Edward 1906- *ConAu 105, WrDr 84*
Wul, Stefan 1922- *ConAu X*
Wulf, Helen Harlan 1913- *ConAu 53*
Wulfekoetter, Gertrude 1895- *ConAu 1R*
Wulff, Lee 1905- *ConAu 61*
Wulff, Robert M 1926- *ConAu 49*
Wulff, Tabita 1932- *IntAu&W 82*
Wulff, Thomas Fredrik 1953- *IntAu&W 82*
Wulffson, Don L 1943- *ConAu 102, SmATA 32[port]*
Wuliger, Betty 1921- *ConAu 65*
Wullstein, L H 1931- *ConAu 29R*
Wunder, John Remley 1945- *ConAu 107*
Wunderlich, Ray Charles, Jr. 1929- *ConAu 37R, IntAu&W 82, WrDr 84*
Wunsch, Josephine M 1914- *ConAu 1R, MichAu 80, WrDr 84*
Wunsch, Karen Jackel *DrAP&F 83*
Wunsche, Konrad 1920- *CroCD*
Wuolijoki, Hella 1886-1954 *CroCD*
Wuorio, Eva-Lis 1918- *ConAu 77, CreCan 1, SmATA 28, –34[port]*
Wurdemann, Audrey May 1911-1960 *ConAmA, TwCA, TwCA SUP*
Wurfel, Seymour W 1907- *ConAu 73*
Wurlitzer, Rudolph *DrAP&F 83*
Wurlitzer, Rudolph 1938- *ConAu 85, ConLC 2, –4, –15*
Wurmbrand, Richard 1909- *ConAu 61*

Wurmser, Leon 1931- *ConAu 106*
Wurster, Michael *DrAP&F 83*
Wurster, Michael 1940- *IntWWP 82*
Wuthnow, Robert 1946- *ConAu 65*
Wyandotte, Steve *ConAu X*
Wyant, William K 1913- *ConAu 108*
Wyatt, Arthur Ramer 1927- *ConAu 1R*
Wyatt, B D *ConAu X*
Wyatt, David K 1937- *ConAu 29R*
Wyatt, Dorothea E 1909- *ConAu P-2*
Wyatt, Elizabeth 1944- *NatPD 81[port]*
Wyatt, James *ConAu X*
Wyatt, Joan 1934- *ConAu 97*
Wyatt, John 1925- *ConAu 105*
Wyatt, Rachel 1929- *ConAu 101*
Wyatt, Robert John 1931- *ConAu 73*
Wyatt, Stanley P 1921- *ConAu 9R*
Wyatt, Stephen John 1948- *ConAu 81, IntAu&W 82*
Wyatt, Will 1942- *ConAu 101*
Wyatt, William F, Jr. 1932- *ConAu 37R*
Wyatt, Woodrow 1918- *ConAu 103, WrDr 84*
Wyatt, Wyatt *DrAP&F 83*
Wyatt-Brown, Bertram 1932- *ConAu 25R*
Wybourne, Brian Garner 1935- *WrDr 84*
Wycherley, R E 1909- *ConAu 77*
Wycherley, Richard Newman *LongCTC*
Wyckoff, Charlotte Chandler 1893-1966 *ConAu P-2*
Wyckoff, D Daryl 1936- *ConAu 7NR, –57*
Wyckoff, Edith Hay 1916- *ConAu 107*
Wyckoff, James M 1918- *ConAu 17R*
Wyckoff, Jerome 1911- *ConAu 9R*
Wyckoff, Peter 1914- *ConAu 41R*
Wyckoff, Ralph W G 1897- *ConAu 73*
Wycoff, Mary Elizabeth Jordan 1932- *ConAu 13R*
Wyden, Peter H 1923- *ASpks, ConAu 105*
Wyers, Jan G 1888- *CreCan 2*
Wyeth, Betsy James 1921- *ConAu 89*
Wyeth, N C 1882-1945 *SmATA 17*
Wyeth, Paul James Logan 1920-1982 *ConAu 107*
Wykeham, Peter 1915- *WrDr 84*
Wykes, Alan 1914- *ConAu 1R, –2NR, IntAu&W 82, WrDr 84*
Wykstra, Ronald A 1935- *ConAu 106*
Wyland, Johanna Elsbeth *IntWWP 82*
Wylcotes, John *ConAu X*
Wyld, Lionel D 1925- *ConAu 1R, –4NR*
Wylder, Delbert E 1923- *ConAu 29R*
Wylder, Edith Perry 1925- *ConAu 29R, WrDr 84*
Wylder, Robert C 1921- *ConAmTC, ConAu 9R*
Wyle, Florence 1881-1968 *CreCan 2*
Wyler, Brenda 1951- *ConAu 89*
Wyler, Rose 1909- *ConAu 93, SmATA 18*
Wyler, William 1902-1981 *ConAu 108*
Wylie, Betty Jane 1931- *ConAu 105*
Wylie, C R, Jr. 1911- *ConAu 45*
Wylie, Craig 1908-1976 *ConAu 69*
Wylie, Elinor Hoyt 1885-1928 *ConAmA, ConAu 105, DcLB 9[port], LongCTC, ModAL, ModAL SUP, TwCA, TwCA SUP, TwCLC 8[port], TwCWr*
Wylie, Francis Ernest 1905- *ConAu 73*
Wylie, Ida Alexa Ross 1885-1959 *LongCTC, TwCA, TwCA SUP*
Wylie, Jeff *ConAu X*
Wylie, Laura *SmATA X, WrDr 84*
Wylie, Laurence 1909- *WrDr 84*
Wylie, Laurence William 1909- *ConAu 21R, IntAu&W 82*
Wylie, Laurie *ConAu X*
Wylie, Max 1904-1975 *ConAu 61, –97*
Wylie, Philip Gordon 1902-1971 *ConAu 33R, ConAu P-2, DcLB 9[port], TwCA, TwCA SUP, TwCCr&M 80, TwCSFW, TwCWr*
Wylie, Ruth C 1920- *ConAu 89*
Wylie, Turrell V 1927- *ConAu 41R*
Wylie, William Percy 1898- *ConAu 5R*
Wylie, Woodroe Wilson 1918- *IntWWP 82*
Wyllie, John 1914- *ConAu 5NR, –9R*
Wyllie, Peter J 1930- *ConAu 5NR, –53, WrDr 84*
Wyly, Rachel Lumpkin 1892- *ConAu P-2*
Wyman, David S 1929- *ConAu 25R*
Wyman, Donald 1903- *ConAu 2NR, –5R*
Wyman, Marc *ConAu X*
Wyman, Mark 1938- *ConAu 101*
Wyman, Mary Alice 1889?-1976 *ConAu 61*
Wyman, Walker DeMarquis 1907- *ConAu 17R,*

IntAu&W 82
Wymark, Olwen *WrDr 84*
Wymark, Olwen 1932- *ConAu 104, ConDr 82, DcLEL 1940, TwCCW 83*
Wymer, Norman 1911- *ConAu 104, SmATA 25, WrDr 84*
Wymer, Thomas L 1938- *ConAu 105*
Wynand, Derk 1944- *ConAu 77, IntAu&W 82, IntWWP 82*
Wynants, Miche 1934- *SmATA 31*
Wynar, Bohdan S 1926- *ConAu 10NR, –17R*
Wynar, Christine L 1933- *ConAu 73*
Wynar, Lubomyr R 1932- *ConAu 73*
Wynd, Oswald 1913- *ConAu 1NR, IntAu&W 82, TwCCr&M 80, WrDr 84*
Wynder, Mavis Areta *ConAu X, IntAu&W 82X, WrDr 84*
Wyndham, Esther *ConAu X, TwCRGW, WrDr 84*
Wyndham, Everard Humphrey 1888- *ConAu P-1*
Wyndham, George 1863-1913 *TwCA, TwCA SUP*
Wyndham, Harald *DrAP&F 83*
Wyndham, John 1903-1969 *ConAu X, ConLC 19, DcLEL 1940, LongCTC, TwCSFW, TwCWr, WorAu*
Wyndham, Lee 1912-1978 *ConAu X, –5R, IntAu&W 82, SmATA X*
Wyndham, Robert 1906-1973 *ConAu X, –41R, SmATA X*
Wyner White, Lynn 1952- *IntAu&W 82*
Wynes, Charles E 1929- *ConAu 9R, WrDr 84*
Wyness, Fenton 1903- *ConAu P-1*
Wynkoop, Mildred Bangs 1905- *ConAu 57*
Wynkoop, Sally 1944- *ConAu 41R*
Wynkoop, William M 1916- *ConAu 21R*
Wynn, Alfred *ConAu X*
Wynn, D Richard 1918- *ConAu 4NR*
Wynn, Dale Richard 1918- *ConAu 1R, WrDr 84*
Wynn, Daniel Webster 1919- *ConAu 25R, WrDr 84*
Wynn, J C 1920- *WrDr 84*
Wynn, John Charles 1920- *ConAu 1R, –2NR*
Wynn-Jones, Michael 1941- *ConAu 69*
Wynne, Brian *ConAu X, IntAu&W 82X, TwCWW, WrDr 84*
Wynne, Frank *ConAu X, IntAu&W 82X, TwCWW, WrDr 84*
Wynne, May 1875- *TwCCW 83, TwCRGW*
Wynne, Nancy Blue 1931- *ConAu 85*
Wynne, Ronald D 1934- *ConAu 102*
Wynne, Thorne D 1908- *ConAu 5R*
Wynne-Jones, Tim 1948- *ConAu 105*
Wynne-Parker, Michael 1945- *IntWWP 82*
Wynne-Tyson, Esme 1898- *ConAu 21R*
Wynne-Tyson, Timothy Jon Lynden 1924- *ConAu 17R*
Wynot, Edward D, Jr. 1943- *ConAu 105*
Wynter, Edward 1914- *ConAu 69, SmATA 14*
Wynter, Sylvia Rufinia 1927?- *TwCWr*
Wynyard, Talbot *ConAu X, SmATA X*
Wyon, Olive 1890- *ConAu P-1*
Wyrick, V Neil, Jr. 1928- *ConAu 13R*
Wyschogrod, Michael 1928- *ConAu 89*
Wyse, Lois 1926- *ConAu 108*
Wysor, Bettie *DrAP&F 83*
Wysor, Bettie 1928- *ConAu 77, IntAu&W 82, WrDr 84*
Wyspianski, Stanislav 1869-1907 *CnMD, ModSL 2*
Wyspianski, Stanislaw 1869-1907 *CIDMEL 80, ModWD*
Wyss, Johann David Von 1743-1818 *SmATA 27, –29*
Wyss, Max Albert 1908-1977 *ConAu 106*
Wyss, Thelma Hatch 1934- *ConAu 29R, SmATA 10*
Wyss, Wallace A 1944- *ConAu 107*
Wyszynski, Stefan 1901-1981 *ConAu 108*
Wytrwal, Joseph A 1924- *WrDr 84*
Wyvis, Ben *ConAu X*
Wyzanski, Charles E, Jr. 1906- *ConAu P-1*
Wyzewa, Teodor De 1862-1917 *CIDMEL 80*

X

X, Frank *DrAP&F 83*
X, Malcolm 1925-1965 *ConIsC 2[port]*
X, Marvin *DrAP&F 83*
X, Mr. *TwCCr&M 80*
Xeno *ConAu X, WrDr 84*
Ximenes, Ben Cuellar, Jr. 1911- *ConAu 5R*
Xuriguera Parramona, Joan Baptiste 1908-
   IntAu&W 82
X27Z *IntAu&W 82X*

Y

Yaari, Ehud 1945- *ConAu 37R*
Yabes, Leopoldo Y 1912- *ConAu 101*
Yablokoff, Herman 1903-1981 *ConAu 108*
Yablonsky, Lewis 1924- *ConAu 21R*
Yacine, Kateb 1929- *ConAu 9R, ModFrL*
Yacorzynski, George Kassimer 1907- *ConAu 1R*
Yacowar, Maurice 1942- *ConAu 41R*
Yadin, Yigael 1917- *ConAu 6NR, -9R, IntAu&W 82*
Yaeger, Bart *ConAu X*
Yafa, Stephen H 1941- *ConAu 21R*
Yaffe, Alan *ConAu X, SmATA X*
Yaffe, Barbara 1953- *ConAu 85*
Yaffe, James *DrAP&F 83*
Yaffe, James 1927- *ConAu 5R, ConNov 82, DcLEL 1940, IntAu&W 82, WrDr 84*
Yaffe, Richard 1903- *ConAu 69*
Yager, Rosemary 1909- *ConAu 1R*
Yaggy, Elinor 1907- *ConAu 89*
Yahil, Leni *ConAu 29R*
Yahraes, Herbert 1905- *ConAu 81*
Yahuda, Joseph 1900- *ConAu P-1*
Yair, Ish *IntWWP 82X*
Yajnavalkya *IntWWP 82X*
Yakanes, Ya-Ka-Nes *DrAP&F 83*
Yaker, Henri 1922- *ConAu 109*
Yakobson, Helen B 1913- *ConAu 17R*
Yakobson, Sergius O 1901-1979 *ConAu 89*
Yalden, Derek William 1940- *ConAu 69*
Yale, Wesley W 1900- *ConAu P-2*
Yale, William 1888?-1975 *ConAu 57*
Yalem, Ronald J 1926- *ConAu 17R*
Yalman, Ahmet Emin 1888-1972 *ConAu 37R*
Yamada, Mitsuye *DrAP&F 83*
Yamada, Mitsuye 1923- *ConAu 77*
Yamaguchi, John Tohr 1932- *ConAu 17R*
Yamaguchi, Marianne Illenberger 1936- *ConAu 29R, SmATA 7*
Yamamoto, Hisaye *DrAP&F 83*
Yamamoto, J Isamu 1947- *ConAu 77*
Yamamoto, Kaoru 1932- *ConAu 25R*
Yamanouchi, Hisaaki 1934- *ConAu 93*
Yamasaki, Takeo 1905- *IntAu&W 82*
Yamauchi, Edwin Masao 1937- *ConAu 3NR, -45, IntAu&W 82*
Yamauchi, Wakako 1942- *NatPD 81[port]*
Yan, Chiou-Shuang Jou 1934- *ConAu 105*
Yanaga, Chitoshi 1903- *ConAu P-2, WrDr 84*
Yancey, Philip D 1949- *ConAu 101*
Yancey, William L 1938- *ConAu 21R*
Yancy, Robert J 1944- *ConAu 57*
Yandell, Keith Edward 1938- *ConAu 37R, IntAu&W 82, WrDr 84*
Yanev, Peter 1946- *ConAu 77*
Yaney, George L 1930- *ConAu 104*
Yaney, Joseph P 1939- *ConAu 9NR, -65*
Yanez, Agustin 1904- *ModLAL*
Yang, C K 1911- *ConAu 5R, WrDr 84*
Yang, Ching-Kun 1911- *IntAu&W 82*
Yang, Jay 1941- *SmATA 12*
Yang, Linda 1937- *ConAu 57*
Yang, Mu *ConAu X*
Yang, Richard F S 1918- *ConAu 10NR, -25R*
Yang-Jen *ConAu X*

Yankelovich, Daniel 1924- *ConAu 105*
Yanker, Gary 1947- *ConAu 37R*
Yankowitz, Susan *DrAP&F 83*
Yankowitz, Susan 1941- *ConAu 1NR, -45, ConDr 82, NatPD 81[port], WrDr 84*
Yannarella, Philip A 1942- *ConAu 73*
Yannatos, James 1929- *ConAu 102*
Yannella, Donald 1934- *ConAu 8NR, -57*
Yanoff, Morris 1907- *ConAu 108*
Yanouzas, John N 1928- *ConAu 41R*
Yanovsky, Basile S *ConAu X*
Yanovsky, V S 1906- *ConAu 97*
Yanovsky, Vassily S 1906- *ConLC 2, -18*
Yanovsky, Yuriy 1902-1954 *CIDMEL 80*
Yans-McLaughlin, Virginia 1943- *ConAu 89*
Yap, Arthur Chioh Hiong 1943- *IntWWP 82*
Yapp, W B 1909- *WrDr 84*
Yar-Shater, Ehsan O 1920- *ConAu 37R*
Yarber, Robert Earl 1929- *ConAu 49*
Yarborough, Betty Hathaway 1927- *ConAu 45*
Yarborough, Camille *DrAP&F 83*
Yarbro, Chelsea Quinn 1942- *ConAu 9NR, -65, TwCRGW, TwCSFW, WrDr 84*
Yarbrough, Anna Nash 1897- *IntWWP 82*
Yarbrough, Camille *ConAu 105*
Yarbrough, Ira 1910?-1983 *ConAu 110*
Yarbrough, Tinsley E 1941- *ConAu 109*
Yarde, Jeanne Betty Frances Treasure 1925- *ConAu 105*
Yardley, Alice 1913- *ConAu 106*
Yardley, Jonathan 1939- *ConAu 73*
Yardley, Richard Q 1903-1979 *ConAu 89*
Yaremko, Michael 1914-1970 *ConAu P-2*
Yarmey, A Daniel 1938- *ConAu 101*
Yarmolinsky, Adam 1922- *ConAu 37R, WrDr 84*
Yarmolinsky, Avrahm 1890-1975 *ConAu 5R, -7NR, -61, TwCA, TwCA SUP*
Yarmon, Morton 1916- *ConAu 9R*
Yarn, David H, Jr. 1920- *ConAu 17R*
Yarnall, Sophia *ConAu X*
Yarnell, Allen 1942- *ConAu 101*
Yarrow, Arnold 1920- *ConAu 106, WrDr 84*
Yarrow, Marian J 1918- *ConAu 105*
Yarrow, Philip John 1917- *ConAu 13R, WrDr 84*
Yarry, Mark Robert 1940- *ConAu 110*
Yarshater, Ehsan 1920- *WrDr 84*
Yarshater, Ehsan Ollah 1920- *IntAu&W 82*
Yartz, Frank Joseph *ConAu 65*
Yarwood, A Walter Hawley *CreCan 2*
Yarwood, Doreen 1918- *ConAu 101, IntAu&W 82, WrDr 84*
Yarwood, Walter 1917- *CreCan 2*
Yashaschandra, Sitanshu 1941- *IntWWP 82*
Yashima, Taro 1908- *ChlLR 4[port], ConAu X, SmATA X, TwCCW 83*
Yashin, Aleksandr Yakovlevich 1913-1968 *CIDMEL 80*
Yastrzemski, Carl 1939- *ConAu 104*
Yates, A G 1923- *ConAu 3NR*
Yates, Alan Geoffrey *WrDr 84*
Yates, Alan Geoffrey 1923- *ConAu 1R*
Yates, Alayne 1929- *ConAu 81*

Yates, Alfred 1917- *ConAu 21R, WrDr 84*
Yates, Aubrey James 1925- *ConAu 9R, WrDr 84*
Yates, Brock Wendel 1933- *ConAu 9R*
Yates, David C *DrAP&F 83*
Yates, David O *ConAu X*
Yates, Donald A 1930- *ConAu 41R*
Yates, Dornford 1885-1960 *LongCTC, TwCA, TwCA SUP, TwCRGW, TwCWr*
Yates, Elizabeth 1905- *ConAu 1R, -6NR, -13R, SmATA 4, TwCA SUP, TwCCW 83, WrDr 84*
Yates, Frances Amelia 1899-1981 *ConAu 105, -57, IntAu&W 82*
Yates, Frank 1902- *WrDr 84*
Yates, Gerard Francis 1907-1979 *ConAu 89*
Yates, J Michael 1938- *ConAu 21R, ConDr 82B, ConP 80, WrDr 84*
Yates, Madeleine 1937- *ConAu 109*
Yates, Norris W 1923- *ConAu 9R*
Yates, Paul 1954- *IntWWP 82*
Yates, Peter Bertram 1909-1976 *ConAu 65*
Yates, Raymond F 1895-1966 *ConAu 110*
Yates, Raymond Francis 1895-1966 *SmATA 31[port]*
Yates, Richard *DrAP&F 83*
Yates, Richard 1926- *ConAu 5R, -10NR, ConLC 7, -8, -23[port], ConNov 82, DcLB Y81A[port], -2, DcLEL 1940, WorAu, WrDr 84*
Yates, W E 1938- *ConAu 49*
Yates, William Edgar 1938- *IntAu&W 82*
Yatron, Michael 1921- *ConAu 37R*
Yau, John *DrAP&F 83*
Yauch, Wilbur Alden 1904-1982 *ConAu 106*
Yaukey, David 1927- *ConAu 61*
Yaukey, Grace Sydenstricker 1899- *ConAu 1R, -1NR, SmATA 5*
Yavetz, Zvi 1925- *ConAu 29R, IntAu&W 82*
Yavorov, Peyo 1878-1914 *CIDMEL 80, ModSL 2*
Yaw, Yvonne 1936- *ConAu 65*
Yawetz, Zwy *ConAu X*
Yazijian, Harvey Z 1948- *ConAu 107*
Ybarra, Thomas Russell 1880- *TwCA SUP*
Ydigoras, Carlos Maria 1924- *IntAu&W 82*
Yeadon, David 1942- *ConAu 104*
Yeager, Allan Edward 1943- *ConAu 101*
Yeager, Robert Cushing 1942- *ConAu 102*
Yeager, W Hayes 1897- *ConAu P-2*
Yeagley, Joan *DrAP&F 83*
Yeakley, Marjory Hall 1908- *ConAu 1R, -2NR, IntAu&W 82, SmATA 21[port]*
Yearley, Clifton K, Jr. 1925- *ConAu 13R*
Yearwood, Richard M 1934- *ConAu 37R*
Yeates, Mabel *ConAu X*
Yeates, Maurice Henry 1938- *ConAu 41R, IntAu&W 82*
Yeatman, R J 1898-1968 *LongCTC*
Yeats, Jack Butler 1871-1957 *CnMD*
Yeats, W B 1865-1939 *RGFMBP*
Yeats, William Butler 1865-1939 *CnMD, CnMWL, ConAu 104, DcLB 10[port], LongCTC, ModBrL, ModBrL SUP,*

Z

Z IntAu&W 82X

Zabaneh, Natalia Shefka 1946- ConAu 105

Zabeeh, Farhang 1919- ConAu 41R

Zabel, Morton Dauwen 1901-1964 TwCA SUP

Zabih, Sepehr 1925- ConAu 9NR, –21R

Zabilka, Gladys M 1917- ConAu 5R

Zablocki, Benjamin 1941- ConAu 37R

Zabolotski, Nikolai 1903-1958 ModSL 1

Zabolotsky, Nikolay 1903-1958 ClDMEL 80, WorAu

Zacek, Jane Shapiro 1938- ConAu 109

Zacek, Joseph Frederick 1930- ConAu 37R, WrDr 84

Zach, Nathan 1930- ConAu 105

Zacharias, Lee ConAu X, DrAP&F 83

Zacharias, Lela Ann 1944- ConAu 85

Zacharis, John C 1936- ConAu 73

Zachary, Elizabeth 1928- ConAu 109, WrDr 84

Zachary, Hugh 1928- ConAu 21R, WrDr 84

Zachary, Saul 1934- NatPD 81[port]

Zacher, Christian Keeler 1941- ConAu 105

Zacher, Mark W 1938- ConAu 85

Zacher, Robert Vincent 1917- ConAu 1R, WrDr 84

Zaciu, Mircea 1928- IntAu&W 82

Zack, Arnold M 1931- ConAu 3NR, –9R

Zade, Hans Peter 1907- WrDr 84

Zadeh, Norman 1950- ConAu 61

Zadravec, Katherine DrAP&F 83

Zaehner, Robert Charles 1913-1974 ConAu 109

Zaffuto, Anthony A 1926- ConAu 101

Zafren, Herbert C 1925- ConAu 45

Zagat, Arthur Leo 1895?-1949 ConAu 110, TwCSFW

Zagona, Salvatore Vincent 1920- ConAu 108

Zagoren, Marc Alan 1940- NatPD 81[port]

Zagoren, Ruby 1922-1974 ConAu P-1

Zagoria, Donald S 1928- ConAu 21R

Zagorin, Perez 1920- ConAu 53

Zaharopoulos, George K 1933- ConAu 41R

Zahava, Irene 1951- ConAu 57

Zahler, Helene S 1911-1981 ConAu 104

Zahler, Leah DrAP&F 83

Zahn, Curtis DrAP&F 83

Zahn, Curtis 1912- ConAu 5R, –5NR, NatPD 81[port]

Zahn, Frank 1936- ConAu 97

Zahn, Gordon C 1918- ConAu 9R, WrDr 84

Zahn, Muriel 1894- ConAu 5R

Zahniser, Marvin R 1934- ConAu 21R

Zahorchak, Michael G 1929- ConAu 41R

Zahrnt, Heinz Freidrich Bernhard 1915- IntAu&W 82

Zaida, Syed Mohammad Hafeez 1929- IntAu&W 82

Zaidenberg, Arthur 1908?- ConAu 108, SmATA 34[port]

Zaidi, S M Hafeez 1929- ConAu 45

Zaidys, Pranas IntAu&W 82X

Zaimof, Gueni 1922- IntAu&W 82

Zainu'ddin, Ailsa Gwennyth 1927- ConAu 29R

Zaitsev, Boris Konstantinovich 1881-1972 ClDMEL 80

Zajonc, Robert Boleslaw 1923- ConAu 106

Zakaria, Rafiq 1920- DcLEL 1940

Zakarian, Richard H 1925- ConAu 41R

Zakia, Richard D 1925- ConAu 9NR, –65

Zakon, Alan J 1935- ConAu 17R

Zakuta, Leo 1925- ConAu 17R

Zalamea, Luis 1921- ConAu 17R

Zalben, Jane Breskin DrAP&F 83, WrDr 84

Zalben, Jane Breskin 1950- ConAu 4NR, –49, SmATA 7

Zald, Mayer Nathan 1931- ConAu 8NR, –17R, WrDr 84

Zaleski, Eugene 1918- ConAu 77

Zaleznik, Abraham 1924- ConAu 73

Zali, Paul M 1922- ConAu 108

Zalka, Miklos 1928- IntAu&W 82

Zalkind, Sheldon S 1922- ConAu 65

Zall, Paul M 1922- ConAu 1R, –6NR, WrDr 84

Zaller, Angeliki Bita IntWWP 82

Zaller, Robert DrAP&F 83

Zaller, Robert Michael 1940- ConAu 77, IntAu&W 82, IntWWP 82

Zallinger, Jean Day 1918- SmATA 14

Zallinger, Peter Franz 1943- ConAu 108

Zalon, Jean E 1919- ConAu 102

Zaltman, Gerald 1938- ConAu 7NR, –17R

Zaltzberg, Charlotte ConDr 82D

Zalygin, Sergey Pavlovich 1913- ClDMEL 80

Zalzanick, Sheldon 1928- ConAu 77

Zamacois, Eduardo 1873- TwCA, TwCA SUP

Zamacois, Eduardo 1873-1971 ClDMEL 80

Zambaras, Vassilis DrAP&F 83

Zamble, Edward 1942- ConAu 108

Zameliphron IntWWP 82X

Zamfirescu, Duiliu 1858-1922 ClDMEL 80

Zamiatin, Yevgueny Ivanovich 1884-1937 CnMWL

Zamonski, Stanley W 1919- ConAu 9R

Zamora, Marlene IntAu&W 82X

Zamoyski, Adam 1949- ConAu 103

Zamoyta, Vincent C 1921- ConAu 21R

Zampaglione, Gerardo 1917- ConAu 77

Zamvil, Stella DrAP&F 83

Zamyatin, Eugene Ivanovich 1884-1937 TwCA, TwCA SUP

Zamyatin, Evgeny Ivanovich 1884-1937 ConAu 105

Zamyatin, Yevgeni Ivanovich 1884-1937 CnMD, ModSL 1, ModWD, TwCWr

Zamyatin, Yevgeny Ivanovich 1884-1937 ClDMEL 80, TwCLC 8[port], TwCSFW A, WhoTwCL

Zander, Alvin Frederick 1913- ConAu 1R

Zanderbergen, George ConAu X

Zaner, Richard M 1933- ConAu 29R

Zanetti, J Enrique 1885-1974 ConAu 45

Zangrando, Robert L 1932- ConAu 25R

Zangwill, Israel 1864-1926 ConAu 109, DcLB 10[port], LongCTC, ModWD, TwCA, TwCCr&M 80, TwCWr

Zangwill, Oliver Louis 1913- ConAu 109, WrDr 84

Zants, Emily 1937- ConAu 37R, IntAu&W 82, WrDr 84

Zanuck, Daryl F 1902-1979 ConAu 93

Zanussi, Krzysztof 1939- IntAu&W 82

Zanzotto, Andrea 1921- ClDMEL 80

Zapoleon, Marguerite Wykoff 1907- WrDr 84

Zapolska, Gabriela 1857-1921 ClDMEL 80

Zapolska, Gabriela 1860-1921 CnMD, ModWD

Zapor, John Randolph 1944- NatPD 81[port]

Zappa, Francis Vincent, Jr. 1940- ConAu 108

Zappa, Frank ConAu X

Zappa, Frank 1940- ConLC 17

Zappler, Lisbeth 1930- ConAu 4NR, –49, SmATA 10

Zara, Louis 1910- ConAu P-2, TwCA, TwCA SUP

Zaranka, William DrAP&F 83

Zarchy, Harry 1912- ConAu 1R, –2NR, SmATA 34[port]

Zarcone, Vincent P, Jr. 1937- ConAu 61

Zardi, Federicao 1912- CnMD

Zardoya, Concha 1914- ClDMEL 80

Zarefsky, David 1946- ConAu 109

Zarellio, Florian IntWWP 82X

Zaretsky, Eli 1940- ConAu 85

Zarif, Margaret Min'imah MichAu 80

Zarif, Margaret Min'imah d1983 SmATA 33[port]

Zaring, Jane 1936- ConAu 108

Zariski, Oscar 1899- WrDr 84

Zariski, Raphael 1925- ConAu 49

Zarnecki, George 1915- ConAu 10NR, –57

Zarnecki, Jerzy ConAu X

Zarnowitz, Victor 1919- ConAu 21R, WrDr 84

Zarou, Jeannette 1936- CreCan 1

Zarro, Richard A 1946- ConAu 33R

Zartman, I William 1932- ConAu 5NR, –9R

Zary, Stefan 1918- ModSL 2

Zaslavsky, Claudia 1917- ConAu 1NR, –49

Zaslow, Edmund M 1917- IntWWP 82

Zaslow, Morris 1918- ConAu 45

Zassenhaus, Hiltgunt 1916- AuNews 1, ConAu 49

Zastrow, Erika ConAu X

Zatuchni, Gerald I 1935- ConAu 37R

Zaturenska, Marya 1902-1982 ConAu 105, –13R, ConLC 6, –11, ConP 80, TwCA, TwCA SUP

Zavala, Iris M DrAP&F 83

Zavala, Iris M 1936- ConAu 1NR, –45

Zavarzadeh, Mas'ud 1938- ConAu 106

Zavatsky, Bill ConAu X, DrAP&F 83

Zavatsky, William Alexander 1943- ConAu 1NR, –49

Zavattini, Cesare 1903- CnMD

Zavin, Benjamin B 1920?-1981 ConAu 103

Zavin, Theodora 1922- ConAu 53

Zavrian, Ostro Suzanne DrAP&F 83

Zawacki, Franklin DrAP&F 83

Zawadiwsky, Christine DrAP&F 83

Zawadsky, Patience 1927- ConAu 9NR, –21R

Zawadzki, Edward S 1914-1967 ConAu P-2

Zawieyski, Jerzy 1902-1968 ClDMEL 80

Zawieyski, Jerzy 1902-1969 CroCD

Zawodny, J K 1921- ConAu 11NR

Zawodny, Janusa K 1921- ConAu 13R